Badger
STATE ANIMAL

Muskellunge
STATE FISH

Sugar Maple
STATE TREE

Wood Violet
STATE FLOWER

STATE REPRESENTATIVE
ANDY JORGENSEN

State Capitol: PO Box 8952
Madison, WI 53708
(608) 266-3790
FAX: (608) 282-3643
Toll-free: (888) 534-0043
E-mail: rep.jorgensen@legis.wi.gov

43rd ASSEMBLY DISTRICT • ASSEMBLY DEMOCRATIC CAUCUS CHAIR

Dear Ms.
Follstad -
Please accept, with
my best wishes. And.
remember - I'm here to help!

Andy

State of Wisconsin
2013 - 2014
Blue Book

Compiled by the
Wisconsin Legislative Reference Bureau

LRB
Wisconsin Legislative
Reference Bureau

Published Biennially
In Odd-Numbered Years

The following LRB staff members produced the
2013-2014 Wisconsin Blue Book:

Julie Pohlman, editor
Lynn Lemanski, lead publications editor and co-editor

Jason Anderson, legislative analyst
Kinnic Eagan, legislative analyst
Lauren Jackson, legislative analyst
Michael J. Keane, senior legislative analyst
Jenni Le, legislative analyst
Kristina Martinez, reference and instruction librarian
Ryan Miller, legislative analyst
Robert A. Paolino, senior legislative analyst
Daniel F. Ritsche, senior legislative analyst

Wisconsin Legislative Reference Bureau, Madison 53703
http://legis.wisconsin.gov/lrb
©2013 by the Joint Committee on Legislative Organization,
Wisconsin Legislature
All Rights Reserved, Published 2013.
Printed in the United States of America

ISBN-13: 978-0-9752820-6-9

Sold and Distributed By:
Document Sales Unit
Department of Administration
4622 University Avenue
Madison, WI 53705-2156
Telephone: (608) 266-3358
DOADocumentSalesInformation@wisconsin.gov

Front cover photograph by Greg Anderson, Legislative Photographer
Back cover image provided by Dane County Land Information Office

Scott Walker

Office of the Governor
State of Wisconsin

P.O. Box 7863
Madison, WI 53707

July 2013

Fellow Wisconsinites,

Over the past two years, we have worked together to move Wisconsin forward. We turned a $3.6 billion dollar deficit into a surplus of more than a half billion dollars. The improved business climate is getting people back to work by giving job creators the confidence and optimism they need to grow and expand in Wisconsin. Four years ago, the statewide chamber did a survey of employers and found that just 4 percent said we were heading in the right direction. Today, 94 percent say Wisconsin is heading in the right direction.

Our tough, but prudent, decisions are allowing us to invest in our priorities – growing our economy, developing our workforce, transforming education, reforming government, and investing in infrastructure.

Our current budget includes more than $1 billion in tax relief for the hard-working people of Wisconsin, a $322 million investment in our public schools, and a 2-year tuition freeze at all of our UW campuses.

We're not going back to the days of overspending. For the first time in state history, we are making the third consecutive deposit into the Rainy Day Fund. Our pension system is fully funded and our bond rating is solid. We are putting our state on sound fiscal footing, so future generations can enjoy prosperity here in Wisconsin.

Our priorities pave the way for more prosperity, better performance, and true independence for all. By working together, we have achieved success. Our goal is to continue the important work of ensuring every citizen of Wisconsin has the best opportunities available to them.

This year, the *2013-2014 Wisconsin Blue Book* focuses on our state's history with a featured article titled, "The Wisconsin Historical Society: Collecting, Preserving, and Sharing Stories Since 1846." Wisconsin has a rich history, which continuously influences the way we live, work, and play. As you delve into the *2013-2014 Blue Book,* I hope you take the opportunity to also explore something new in our great state.

It is my honor to serve as Governor of Wisconsin. I hope the *Blue Book* is a useful tool for each of you as you learn more about our state government, both past and present.

Together, we are moving Wisconsin forward.

Scott Walker
Governor

State of Wisconsin
LEGISLATIVE REFERENCE BUREAU

LRB
Wisconsin Legislative
Reference Bureau

INTRODUCTION

There is a tremendous amount of information available today across mediums and on every manner of topics. For those who are doing the looking, the difficultly lies in identifying a source that is both accurate as well as comprehensive. The *Wisconsin Blue Book* is such a source for information on the state and people of Wisconsin and has been for over 150 years. Its pages detail names and biographies of officials and agencies; statutory references and the complete state constitution; assembly and senate district maps; election information; municipal contacts; population, economical and commercial data, and more. Each biennium, the release of a new *Blue Book* provides the most current intelligence on the state, its people, and those who represent it. It is documentation of where the state is situated at the time of publication and provides the background on how it got there by including relevant historical details. This amalgamation of currency and history documented in the *Blue Book* reflects a parallel in the works of the Wisconsin State Historical Society.

The feature article for this, the 91st edition of the *Wisconsin Blue Book*, is entitled *The Wisconsin Historical Society: Collecting, Preserving, and Sharing Stories Since 1846.* Written by John Zimm at the Wisconsin Historical Society Press, with contributions from other staff and society departments, the article provides a singular, comprehensive look at the history, innovations, and contributions the society has made to Wisconsin.

It was in 1846 that territorial residents first conceived of a historical society and the actual formation occurred a full two years before statehood. In 1853, the same year the first *Blue Book* was published, the Wisconsin State Historical Society began receiving state funding – the first such institution in the country to do so. The society became an example to others across the nation for its inclusionary nature: its membership open to anyone who wanted to join, the partnerships it formed with schools, as well as its broad and varied collections and services.

Today the Wisconsin Historical Society is more than just a library or a museum. It is a press, producing textbooks, magazines, and books; it is a partner in public television and radio; it is the manager of national registers and archaeological programs; and it is an administrator of historical and recreational sites. The society still provides high quality research services and archiving of Wisconsin's rich history, however its recognition should not only be for preserving the past, but encompass its provision for the needs of the present and future.

This edition of the *Blue Book* continues the tradition of providing up-to-date information and historical perspective on Wisconsin government. In particular, there are a few notable updates to watch for in this edition. All the maps found in the legislative biography section are new, reflecting the 2010 redistricting, and includes the adjustments to Assembly Districts 8 and 9 as a result of subsequent judicial action. Agency changes that occurred during the 2011-2012 biennium are more fully detailed as their organization and structure were completed. There is also expanded coverage of elections to accommodate both the 2012 recalls as well as the presidential election. Finally, in June of this year, the state gained a new state symbol in the kringle as state pastry; the endpaper at the back of the book has been updated to include an image of this latest addition.

For this, my first edition as editor of the *Blue Book*, I'm grateful to have had the expertise and professionalism of the entire research staff at the Legislative Reference Bureau. With over 120 combined years of experience, the legislative analysts and publications editor have a keen commitment and skill creating and compiling the information found throughout the book. Their knowledge and dedication are invaluable. I would also like to thank the director of the Wisconsin Historical Society Press, Kathy Borkowski, and editor Barbara Walsh for coordinating the feature article and arranging the amazing images and maps found in both the article and on the divider pages. To successfully summarize such a vast amount of information is not a simple undertaking, and the resulting article is an excellent addition to *2013-2014 Wisconsin Blue Book*.

We hope readers enjoy this latest inclusion to the *Blue Book* series, and that the information within continues to impart knowledge and appreciation for the people and operations of the state.

Julie Pohlman
Blue Book Editor
July 2013

TABLE OF CONTENTS

Biographies

Biographies and photos: Wisconsin constitutional executive officers, Supreme Court justices, members of the U.S. Congress from Wisconsin, and legislators (also includes congressional and legislative district maps)

View of a Newly Refurbished Column in the Wisconsin Historical Society Reading Room

(Wisconsin Historical Society, 94.1.70)

ALPHABETICAL INDEX TO BIOGRAPHIES

GOVERNOR

Scott Walker (Rep.): Born Colorado Springs, CO, November 2, 1967; married; 2 children. Graduate Delavan-Darien H.S. 1986; attended Marquette U. 1986-90. Former salesman, IBM Corporation; financial developer, American Red Cross. State representative 1993-2002; Milwaukee County Executive 2002-10.

Elected to Assembly in June 1993 special election; reelected 1994-2000; resigned 5/9/2002.

Elected governor 2010.

Telephone: Office: (608) 266-1212; Fax: (608) 267-8983.

E-mail: governor@wisconsin.gov

Mailing address: Office: P.O. Box 7863, Madison 53707-7863.

LIEUTENANT GOVERNOR

Rebecca Kleefisch (Rep.): Born Pontiac, MI, August 7, 1975; married; 2 children. Graduate Anthony Wayne H.S. (Whitehouse, OH) 1993; B.A. journalism UW-Madison 1997. Former news reporter, media and marketing consultant. Member: National Lieutenant Governors Association; National Rifle Association; Aerospace States Association (manufacturing chair); Executive Committee of Republican Lieutenant Governors Association.

Elected lieutenant governor 2010.

Telephone: Office: (608) 266-3516; Fax: (608) 267-3571.

E-mail: ltgov@wisconsin.gov

Mailing address: Office: P.O. Box 2043, Madison 53702-2043.

Governor
SCOTT WALKER

SECRETARY OF STATE

Douglas J. La Follette (Dem.): Single. B.S. in chemistry Marietta College 1963; M.S. in chemistry Stanford U. 1964; Ph.D. in organic chemistry Columbia U. 1967. Former director of training and development with an energy marketing company; assistant professor, UW-Parkside; public affairs director, Union of Concerned Scientists; owner and operator of a small business; research associate, UW-Madison. Member: Amer. Solar Energy Society; Audubon Society; Friends of the Earth; Phi Beta Kappa. Former member: Council of Economic Priorities; Amer. Federation of Teachers; Federation of American Scientists; Lake Michigan Federation; Southeastern Wis. Coalition for Clean Air; Clean Wisconsin (formerly Wis. Environmental Decade, founder).

Elected secretary of state 1974 and 1982; reelected since 1986. Member: State Board of Commissioners of Public Lands (chp.).

Elected to Senate 1972.

Telephone: Office: (608) 266-8888 press 3; Fax: (608) 266-3159.

Mailing address: Office: 30 West Mifflin Street, 10th Floor, P.O. Box 7848, Madison 53707-7848.

STATE TREASURER

Kurt W. Schuller (Rep.): Born Milwaukee, June 21, 1955; married. Graduate Milwaukee James Madison H.S. 1973; associate degree in management and communication, Concordia U. 1998. Former small business owner and restaurant manager.

Elected state treasurer 2010. Member: Board of Commissioners of Public Lands; Wis. College Savings Program Board; Treasurer's Advisory Committee; Wis. Insurance Securities Fund (bd. of dir.).

Telephone: Office: (608) 266-1714.

Mailing address: Office: 1 South Pinckney Street, 3rd Floor, Suite 360, P.O. Box 7871, Madison 53707-7871.

ATTORNEY GENERAL

J.B. Van Hollen (Rep.): Born Rice Lake, February 19, 1966; married; 2 children. Graduate Ondossagon H.S. 1984; B.A. political science and economics, St. Olaf College (Northfield, MN) 1988; J.D. UW-Madison 1990. Attorney. Former U.S. Attorney, Western District of Wis. (2002-05); Bayfield County District Attorney (1999-2002); Ashland County District Attorney (1993-99). Former assistant U.S. attorney and former state public defender. Member: State Bar of Wis.; National Association of Attorneys General (vice pres./pres-elect; pres. 6/2013); Republican Attorneys General Association; Republican Party of Wisconsin; Republican Party of Dane County; National Rifle Association; Living Water Lutheran Church; Free and Accepted Masons; George Washington Masonic National Memorial Assn. (bd. of dir.). Former member: Iron River Fire Department; Iron River EMS.

Elected attorney general 2006; reelected 2010. Member: State Board of Commissioners of Public Lands.

Telephone: Office: (608) 266-1221; Fax: (608) 267-2779.

Mailing address: Office: Room 114 East, State Capitol, Madison 53702.

STATE SUPERINTENDENT OF PUBLIC INSTRUCTION

Tony Evers (nonpartisan office): Born Plymouth, November 5, 1951; married; 3 children, 5 grandchildren. Graduate Plymouth H.S. 1969; B.S. UW-Madison 1973; M.S. UW-Madison 1976; Ph.D. UW-Madison 1986. Former teacher, technology coordinator, principal, Tomah; superintendent of schools, Oakfield, Verona; CESA 6 administrator, Oshkosh; deputy state superintendent of public instruction. Member: Council of Chief State School Officers (past pres., Deputies Leadership Comn.); Next Generation Learners (NxGL) Com. (co-chp.). Former member: Wis. Association of CESA Administrators; Wis. Association of School District Administrators.

Elected state superintendent 2009; reelected 2013. Member: UW Board of Regents; Wisconsin Technical College System Bd.

Telephone: Office: (608) 266-1771.

E-mail: dpistatesuperintendent@dpi.wi.gov

Mailing address: Office: 125 South Webster Street, P.O. Box 7841, Madison 53707-7841.

**Lieutenant Governor
KLEEFISCH**

**Secretary of State
La FOLLETTE**

**State Treasurer
SCHULLER**

**Attorney General
VAN HOLLEN**

**State Superintendent of
Public Instruction
EVERS**

SUPREME COURT JUSTICES

Mailing address: Supreme Court, P.O. Box 1688, Madison 53701-1688. Telephone: (608) 266-1298.

CHIEF JUSTICE

Shirley S. Abrahamson: Born New York City, December 17, 1933; married; 1 child. Graduate Hunter College H.S. 1950; B.A. N.Y.U. 1953; J.D. Indiana U. Law Sch. 1956; S.J.D. UW Law Sch. 1962; D.L. (honorary) Willamette U. 1978, Ripon College 1981, Beloit College 1982, Capital U. 1983, John Marshall Law Sch. 1984, Northeastern U. 1985, Indiana U. 1986, Northland College 1988, Hamline U. 1988, Notre Dame U. 1993, Suffolk U. 1994, DePaul U. 1996, Lawrence U. 1998, Marian College 1998, Roger Williams U. School of Law 2007. Member: American Philosophical Society (elected 1998); American Academy of Arts and Sciences (fellow 1997). Recipient: ABA *John Marshall Award* 2010; Wisconsin Counties Association *Friend of County Government Award* 2007; American Judicature Society *Dwight D. Opperman Award* 2004 and *Herbert Harley Award* 1999; ABA Commission on Women in the Profession *Margaret Brent Women Lawyers of Achievement Award* 1995; UW-Madison *Distinguished Alumni Award* 1994. Featured in *Great American Judges: An Encyclopedia* 2003.

Appointed to Supreme Court August 1976 to fill vacancy created by death of Chief Justice Horace W. Wilkie; elected to full term 1979; reelected 1989, 1999, and 2009. Became chief justice August 1, 1996, upon the retirement of Chief Justice Roland B. Day.

JUSTICES

(In Order of Seniority)

Ann Walsh Bradley: Born Richland Center, July 5, 1950; married; 4 children. Graduate Richland Center H.S.; B.A. Webster College (St. Louis, MO) 1972; J.D. UW-Madison (Knapp Scholar) 1976. Former high school teacher, practicing attorney, and Marathon Co. circuit court judge. Member: Elected member of the American Law Institute; Bd. of Directors, International Judicial Academy; North American Director, International Assn. of Women Judges; Bd. of Directors, National Assn. of Women Judges; state coordinator for iCivics; Wisconsin Bench Bar Committee; UW Law School Board of Visitors; Amer. Judicature Soc.; American Bar Assn.; State Bar of Wis.; Federal-State Judicial Council; Rotary International; lecturer for the ABA's Asian Law Initiative. Former member: National Conference on Uniform State Laws; Wis. Judicial College (associate dean and faculty); Wis. Rhodes Scholarship Com. (chp.); Wis. Judicial Council; Wis. Equal Justice Task Force; Wis. Jud. Conference (chp. and legis. com.); Civil Law Com. (exec. com.); Task Force on Children and Families; Wis. State Public Defender Board (bd. of dir.); Com. on the Admin. of Courts. Recipient: American Judicature Society's *Herbert Harley Award; Business and Professional Woman of the Year; Business Woman of the Year Athena Award.*

Elected to Supreme Court 1995; reelected 2005.

N. Patrick Crooks: Born Green Bay, May 16, 1938; married; 6 children. Graduate Green Bay Premontre H.S. 1956; B.A. (*magna cum laude*) St. Norbert Coll. 1960; J.D. U. of Notre Dame Law Sch. 1963; Army Judge Advocate General's School at U. of VA 1963-64; Natl. Jud. Coll. at U. of Nevada-Reno May 1984; Inst. of Jud. Admin. at N.Y.U. Law Sch. 1996. Former practicing attorney (1966-77); business law instructor, UW-Green Bay (1970-72); faculty, Wis. Jud. Coll.; attorney, Military Affairs Div., Army Judge Advocate General Office, Pentagon (1964-66); legal intern, Internal Security Div., U.S. Dept. of Justice (1962). Vietnam Era vet.; served in Army (capt.) 1963-66. Member: Federal-State Judicial Council; Amer. Bar Assn. and law school evaluator in its judicial division; Fellow of the American Bar Foundation; State Bar of Wis. and its Media and Law Relations Com.; Dane Co. Bar Assn.; Brown Co. Bar Assn. (pres. 1977); Assn. for Women Lawyers of Brown Co.; Notre Dame Law Assn. (bd. of dir.); Wis. Law Foundation (exec. com.). Former member: Wis. Judicial Council (1998-2002); Juvenile Justice Study Task Force (1994-95); United Way of Brown Co. (pres. 1976-78); East Central Criminal Justice Planning Coun. (1973-85); Brown Co. Legal Aid (chp. 1971-73); Fed. Bar Assn. (1964-65). Participant, Fifth Sir Richard May Seminar on International Law and International Courts, The Hague (2009). Recipient: Notre Dame *Academy Distinguished Alumnus of the Year Award* 2002; Amer. Bd. of Trial Advocates *Trial Judge of the Year* 1994; St. Norbert Coll. *Alma Mater Award* 1992 and *Distinguished Achievement Award in Social Science* 1977; U. of Notre Dame *Award of the Year* 1978; Army Judge Advocate General *Commendation Medal* 1966. Author of works in *Notre Dame Lawyer* 1961-63; *Judges Bench Book-Juvenile.* Brown Co. Ct. judge 1977-78; Brown Co. Circuit Ct. judge 1978-96.

Elected to Supreme Court 1996; reelected 2006.

**Justice
BRADLEY**

**Justice
CROOKS**

**Justice
PROSSER**

**Chief Justice
ABRAHAMSON**

**Justice
ROGGENSACK**

**Justice
ZIEGLER**

**Justice
GABLEMAN**

David T. Prosser, Jr.: Born Chicago, IL, December 24, 1942; single. Graduate Appleton H.S.; B.A. DePauw Univ. 1965; J.D. UW-Madison Law School 1968. Former practicing attorney; admin. asst. to U.S. Congressman Harold V. Froehlich 1973-74; attorney-advisor, U.S. Dept. of Justice 1969-72; lecturer, Indiana U.-Indianapolis Law School 1968-69. Member: State Bar of Wis.; Dane Co., Milwaukee Co., and Outagamie Co. Bar Assns.; James E. Doyle American Inn of Court; Friends of the Fox; James Watrous Gallery Advisory Committee. Former member: Wis. Coun. on Criminal Justice 1980-83 (exec. com.); Judicial Coun. Com. on Prelim. Examinations 1981; Wis. Sentencing Comn. 1984-88 and 1994-95; Wis. Sesquicentennial Comn. 1993-99; National Conference of Commissioners on Uniform State Laws 1983-96, 2005-07, 2012-present. Outagamie Co. District Attorney 1977-78. Commissioner, Wis. Tax Appeals Comn. 1997-98.

Elected to Wisconsin Assembly 1978 and served nine terms through 1996. Speaker of the Assembly 1995-96; Minority Leader 1989-94.

Appointed to Supreme Court September 1998 to fill vacancy created by resignation of Justice Janine P. Geske; elected to full term 2001; reelected 2011. Supreme Court Planning and Policy Advisory Committee's Court Financing Subcommittee 2002-04; Judicial Council of Wis. 2002-06; Citation of Unpublished Opinions Committee (2009); Rules Procedures Committee (2010-11).

Patience Drake Roggensack: Born Joliet, IL, July 7; married; 3 children. Graduate Lockport Township H.S.; B.A. Drake University; J.D. UW-Madison Law School (*cum laude*). Former practicing attorney. Member: Commissioner, Uniform Laws Commission; Fellow, American Bar Foundation; Wisconsin Judicial Council, 2011-present; Supreme Court Rules Procedure Committee; Supreme Court Finance Committee; Committee for Public Trust and Confidence in the Courts; American Bar Association; State Bar Association of Wisconsin; Western District of Wisconsin Bar Association (past pres.); Dane County Bar Association, served on Personnel Review Board (supreme court delegate); 2005 Judicial Conference (co-chair); 2005 Statewide Bench Bar Conference (co-chair). Board service on: YMCA; YWCA; Wisconsin Center for Academically Talented Youth; Olbrich Botanical Society; International Women's Forum (past president); A Fund For Women; Friends of the Arboretum.

Court of Appeals Judge, District IV (1996-2003). Served on Judicial Conference (legislative liaison); Publication Committee for the Court of Appeals; State Court/Tribal Court Planning Committee (co-chair); Personnel Review Board (appeals court delegate).

Elected to Supreme Court 2003; reelected 2013.

Annette K. Ziegler: Born Grand Rapids, MI, March 6, 1964; married; 3 children. Graduate Forest Hills Central H.S.; B.A. in Business Administration and Psychology Hope College (Holland, MI) 1986; J.D. Marquette University Law School 1989. Former practicing attorney (civil litigation) 1989-1995; Pro bono Special Asst. D.A. Milwaukee County 1992, 1996; Asst. U.S. Atty. Eastern Dist. of Wis. 1995-1997; Washington County Circuit Court Judge 1997-2007; Ct. of Appeals Dist. II (Judicial Exchange Program 1999); Deputy Chief Judge – Third Judicial District; Judicial faculty at various seminars. Member: State Bar of Wis.; American Bar Assn.; American Law Institute (elected member); American Bar Foundation (fellow); Washington County Bar Assn.; Milwaukee County Bar Assn.; Eastern Dist. of Wis. Bar Assn.; Boys & Girls Club of Washington County (trustee bd. pres.); Marquette U. Law Sch. Advisory Bd.; Rotary Club West Bend-Noon. Former member: Criminal Benchbook Com.; Criminal Jury Instruction Com.; Legal Assn. for Women; James E. Doyle American Inn of Court.

Elected to Supreme Court 2007.

Michael J. Gableman: Born West Allis, September 18, 1966. Graduate New Berlin West H.S.; A.B. in History/Education Ripon College 1988; J.D. Hamline U. Law School 1993. Former practicing attorney; Deputy corporation counsel, Forest County 1997-99; Assistant District Attorney, Langlade County 1996-99; Assistant District Attorney, Marathon County 1998-99; District Attorney, Ashland County, appointed 1999, elected 2002; Administrative Law Judge, Department of Workforce Development 2002; Burnett County Circuit Court Judge, appointed 2002, elected 2003. Member: State Bar of Wis.; Grantsburg Rotary International; Siren Fraternal Order of Moose. Past member: Burnett County Republican Party (chairman); Ashland Knights of Columbus (Grand Knight); Ashland Masons; Milwaukee Teachers Assoc.; Burnett County Restorative Justice (chairman of the board); Burnett County Drug and Alcohol Court (founding and first presiding judge); Siren Rotary International.

Elected to Supreme Court 2008.

WISCONSIN MEMBERS OF THE 113th CONGRESS
2013-2014
MEMBERS OF THE U.S. SENATE

U.S. Senator
BALDWIN

Tammy Baldwin (Dem.)

Born Madison, February 11, 1962. Graduate Madison West H.S.; A.B. in mathematics and government, Smith College (MA) 1984; J.D. UW-Madison 1989. Former practicing attorney, 1989-92. Madison City Council 1986; Dane Co. Board 1986-94.

State legislative service: Elected to Assembly, 78th District, 1992-96 (served until January 4, 1999).

Elected to U.S. House of Representatives 1998; reelected 2000-2010. Elected to U.S. Senate 2012. Committee assignments: **113th Congress** — Budget Committee; Health, Education, Labor, and Pensions Committee and its Subcommittees on Employment and Workplace Safety, on Primary Health and Aging; Homeland Security and Governmental Affairs Committee and its Subcommittees on Financial and Contracting Oversight, on the Efficiency and Effectiveness of Federal Programs and the Federal Workforce, and Permanent Subcommittee on Investigations; Special Committee on Aging.

Telephones: Washington office: (202) 224-5653; District offices: La Crosse: (608) 796-0045; Madison: (608) 264-5338; Milwaukee: (414) 297-4451 or (800) 247-5645.

Internet address: http://www.baldwin.senate.gov/

Voting address: Madison 53703.

Mailing addresses: Washington office: 717 Hart Senate Office Building, Washington, D.C. 20510; District offices: 205 5th Avenue South, Room 216, La Crosse 54601; 14 West Mifflin Street, Suite 207, Madison 53703; 310 West Wisconsin Avenue, Suite 950, Milwaukee 53203.

U.S. Senator
JOHNSON

Ron Johnson (Rep.)

Born Mankato, MN, April 8, 1955; 3 children. Graduate Edina H.S. 1973; B.S.B. U. of Minnesota 1977. Former CEO Pacur LLC. Former member: Partners in Education Council, Oshkosh Chamber of Commerce (business co-chair); Oshkosh Opera House Foundation (treas.); Lourdes Foundation (bd. pres.); Diocese of Green Bay Finance Council; Oshkosh Chamber of Commerce Board of Directors (chairman-elect); Oshkosh Area Community Foundation Investment Council.

Elected to U.S. Senate 2010. Committee assignments: **113th Congress** — Budget Committee (since 112th Congress); Commerce, Science and Transportation Committee and its Subcommittees on Aviation Operations, Safety, and Security, on Communications, Technology, and the Internet, on Competitiveness, Innovation, and Export Promotion, on Science and Space, on Surface Transportation and Merchant Marine Infrastructure, Safety, and Security; Foreign Relations Committee and its Subcommittees on European Affairs (ranking min. mbr.), on Near Eastern and South and Central Asian Affairs, on East Asian and Pacific Affairs, on International Operations and Organizations, Human Rights, Democracy, and Global Women's Issues; Homeland Security and Governmental Affairs Committee (since 112th Congress) and its Subcommittees on Financial and Contracting Oversight (ranking min. mbr.), on the Efficiency and Effectiveness of Federal Programs and the Federal Workforce, and Permanent Subcommittee on Investigations; Small Business and Entrepreneurship Committee.

Telephones: Washington office: (202) 224-5323; District offices: Milwaukee: (414) 276-7282; Oshkosh: (920) 230-7250.

Internet address: http://ronjohnson.senate.gov

Voting address: Oshkosh 54901.

Mailing addresses: Washington office: 328 Hart Senate Office Building, Washington, D.C. 20510; District offices: 517 East Wisconsin Avenue, Suite 408, Milwaukee 53202; 219 Washington Avenue, Suite 100, Oshkosh 54901.

U.S. Representative
RYAN

U.S. Representative
POCAN

MEMBERS OF THE U.S. HOUSE OF REPRESENTATIVES

Paul Ryan (Rep.), 1st Congressional District

Born Janesville, 1970; married; 3 children. Graduate Janesville Craig H.S.; B.A. in economics and political science Miami U. of Ohio 1992. Former aide to U.S. Senator Robert Kasten and employed at family construction business. Member: Janesville Bowmen, Inc.; St. John Vianney's Parish.

Elected to U.S. House of Representatives 1998; reelected since 2000. Committee assignments: **113th Congress** — Budget Committee (chp., ranking member since 110th Congress, mbr. since 108th Congress, also 106th Congress); Ways and Means Committee (since 107th Congress) and its Subcommittee on Health. **109th Congress** — Joint Economic Committee (also 108th and 106th Congresses). **106th Congress** — Banking Committee; Government Reform Committee.

Telephones: Washington office: (202) 225-3031; District offices: Janesville: (608) 752-4050; Kenosha: (262) 654-1901; Racine: (262) 637-0510; Toll free: (888) 909-7926.

Internet address: http://paulryan.house.gov

Voting address: Janesville 53545.

Mailing addresses: Washington office: 1233 Longworth House Office Building, Washington, D.C. 20515; District offices: 20 South Main Street, Suite 10, Janesville 53545; 5455 Sheridan Road, Suite 125, Kenosha 53140; 216 6th Street, Racine 53403.

1st Congressional District: Kenosha, Milwaukee (part), Racine, Rock (part), Walworth (part), and Waukesha (part) Counties. (For detailed description, see Section 3.11, Wisconsin Statutes.)

Mark Pocan (Dem.), 2nd Congressional District

Born Kenosha, August 14, 1964; married. Graduate Mary D. Bradford H.S. (Kenosha); B.A. UW-Madison 1986. Small businessperson. Member: American Civil Liberties Union; Colombia Support Network/Apartadó Sister City Organization; Clean Wisconsin; Painters and Allied Trades Union (AFL-CIO); Sierra Club; Fair Wisconsin; Southern Poverty Law Center. Former member: Big Brothers-Big Sisters. Recipient: SEIU *Legislator of the Year* 2009; Planned Parenthood Advocates of Wis. *Rebecca C. Young Leadership Award* 2009; Fair Wis. *Statewide Leader* 2009; Wis. Library Assn. *Public Policy Award* 2008; Wis. Coalition Against Sexual Assault *Voices of Courage Public Policy Award* 2008; Professional Fire Fighters of Wis. *Legislator of the Year* 2008; Wis. League of Conservation Voters *Conservation Honor Roll* 2008; Wis. AIDS Fund *Educate, Prevent, Protect* 2007; Wis. League of Conservation Voters *Conservation Champion* 2006; Wis. Counties Assn. *Outstanding Legislator Award* 2008, 2006; Clean Wisconsin *Clean 16 Award* 2004, 2002, 2000; ACLU *Special Recognition Award* 2001; Wis. Federation of Teachers State Employees Council *Representative of the Year* 2003, 2002. Dane Co. Board 1991-96.

State legislative service: Elected to Assembly, 78th District, 1998-2010 (served until January 3, 2013).

Elected to U.S. House of Representatives 2012. Committee assignments: **113th Congress** — Budget Committee; Oversight and Government Reform Committee.

Telephones: Washington office: (202) 225-2906; District office: Madison: (608) 258-9800.

Internet address: http://pocan.house.gov/

Voting address: 309 North Baldwin Street, Madison 53703.

Mailing addresses: Washington office: 313 Cannon House Office Building, Washington, D.C. 20515; District office: 10 East Doty Street, Suite 405, Madison 53703.

2nd Congressional District: Dane, Green, Iowa, Lafayette, Richland (part), Rock (part), Sauk Counties. (For detailed description, see Section 3.12, Wisconsin Statutes.)

**U.S. Representative
KIND**

**U.S. Representative
MOORE**

Ron Kind (Dem.), **3rd Congressional District**
Born La Crosse, March 16, 1963; married; 2 children. Graduate Logan H.S.; B.A. Harvard U. 1985; M.A. London School of Economics (England); J.D. U. of Minnesota Law School 1990. Attorney. Former La Crosse County assistant district attorney and State of Wisconsin special prosecutor. Member: U.S. Supreme Court Bar; State Bar of Wis. and La Crosse Co. Bar Assn.; Assn. of State Prosecutors; Democratic Party; Wis. Harvard Club (bd. of dir.); Boys and Girls Club of La Crosse (bd. of dir.); Coulee Council on Alcohol and Other Drug Abuse (bd. of dir.); Moose Club; Optimist Club.

Elected to U.S. House of Representatives 1996; reelected since 1998. Committee assignments: **113th Congress** — Ways and Means Committee (since 110th Congress) and its Subcommittees on Health, on Trade. **111th Congress** — Natural Resources Committee (since 105th Congress) and its Subcommittees on Insular Affairs, Oceans and Wildlife, on National Parks, Forests and Public Lands. Congressional memberships: New Democrat Coalition (chair); Upper Mississippi River Task Force (founder and co-chair); Congressional Wildlife Refuge Caucus (founder); Rural Health Care Coalition; Congressional Sportsmen's Caucus (former co-chair); Human Rights Caucus; Native American Caucus (vice chair); Renewable Energy and Energy Efficiency Caucus (vice chair); National Parks Caucus (co-chair); Congressional Caucus of the EU (co-chair); Congressional Organic Caucus (co-chair); Congressional Fitness Caucus (co-chair). House Leadership: Regional Whip.

Telephones: Washington office: (202) 225-5506; District offices: Eau Claire: (715) 831-9214; La Crosse: (608) 782-2558; Toll free: (888) 442-8040; TTY: (888) 880-9180.

Internet address: http://kind.house.gov/

Voting address: La Crosse 54603.

Mailing addresses: Washington office: 1502 Longworth House Office Building, Washington, D.C. 20515-4906; District offices: 131 S. Barstow Street, Suite 301, Eau Claire 54701; 205 5th Avenue South, Suite 400, La Crosse 54601.

3rd Congressional District: Adams, Buffalo, Chippewa (part), Crawford, Dunn, Eau Claire, Grant, Jackson (part), Juneau (part), La Crosse, Monroe (part), Pepin, Pierce, Portage, Richland (part), Trempealeau, Vernon, and Wood (part) Counties. (For detailed description, see Section 3.13, Wisconsin Statutes.)

Gwendolynne S. Moore (Dem.), **4th Congressional District**
Born Racine, April 18, 1951; 3 children. Graduate North Division H.S. (Milwaukee); B.A. in political science, Marquette U. 1978; certification in credit union management, Milwaukee Area Technical College 1983. Former housing officer with Wisconsin Housing and Economic Development Authority; development specialist Milwaukee City Development; program and planning analyst with Wisconsin Departments of Employment Relations and Health and Social Services. Member: National Black Caucus of State Legislators; National Conference of State Legislators' Host Committee, Milwaukee 1995; National Black Caucus of State Legislators – Host Committee (chair) 1997; Wisconsin Legislative Black and Hispanic Caucus (chair since 1997).

State legislative service: Elected to Assembly 1988 and 1990; elected to Senate 1992, 1996, and 2000. Senate President Pro Tempore 1997, 1995 (eff. 7/15/96).

Elected to U.S. House of Representatives 2004; reelected since 2006. Committee assignments: **113th Congress** — Budget Committee (since 110th Congress); Financial Services Committee (since 109th Congress) and its Subcommittees on Capital Markets, Insurance, and Government Sponsored Enterprises, on International Monetary Policy. **110th Congress** — Small Business Committee and its Subcommittees on Contracting and Technology, on Regulations, Healthcare and Trade, on Rural and Urban Entrepreneurship.

Telephones: Washington office: (202) 225-4572; District office: Milwaukee: (414) 297-1140.

Internet address: http://gwenmoore.house.gov

Voting address: 4043 North 19th Place, Milwaukee 53209.

Mailing addresses: Washington office: 2245 Rayburn House Office Building, Washington, D.C. 20515; District office: 219 N. Milwaukee Street, Suite 3A, Milwaukee 53202-5818.

4th Congressional District: Milwaukee County (part): consisting of the Villages of Bayside (part), Brown Deer, Fox Point, Shorewood, West Milwaukee, and Whitefish Bay; the Cities of Cudahy, Glendale, Milwaukee (part), St. Francis, and South Milwaukee; Waukesha County (part). (For detailed description, see Section 3.14, Wisconsin Statutes.)

U.S. Representative
SENSENBRENNER

U.S. Representative
PETRI

F. James Sensenbrenner, Jr. (Rep.), 5th Congressional District

Born Chicago, June 14, 1943; married; 2 children. Graduate Milwaukee Country Day School 1961; A.B. Stanford U. 1965; J.D. UW-Madison Law School 1968. Attorney. Former assistant to State Senate Majority Leader Jerris Leonard and to U.S. Congressman Arthur Younger. Member: State Bar of Wis.; Friends of the Museum, Milwaukee County; Riveredge Nature Center; American Philatelic Society; Waukesha Co. Republican Party. Former member: Whitefish Bay Jaycees; Shorewood Men's Club.

State legislative service: Elected to Assembly 1968-74; elected to Senate in April 1975 special election and reelected 1976. Assistant Minority Leader 1977.

Elected to U.S. House of Representatives 1978; reelected since 1980. Committee assignments: **113th Congress** — Judiciary Committee (chp. 107th-109th Congress, mbr. since 97th Congress) and its Subcommittees on Crime, Terrorism, and Homeland Security (chp.), on Courts, Intellectual Property, and the Internet; Science, Space, and Technology Committee (vice chp. 112th Congress, mbr. since 110th Congress) and its Subcommittees on Environment, on Oversight. **106th Congress** — Science Committee (chp., also mbr. since 97th Congress). **103rd Congress** — House Select Committee on Narcotics Abuse and Control (since 100th Congress). **96th Congress** — Standards of Official Conduct Committee.

Telephones: Washington office: (202) 225-5101; District office: (262) 784-1111; Toll free: (800) 242-1119.

Internet address: http://sensenbrenner.house.gov

Voting address: N76 W14726 North Point Drive, P.O. Box 186, Menomonee Falls 53052-0186.

Mailing addresses: Washington office: 2449 Rayburn House Office Building, Washington, D.C. 20515-4905; District office: 120 Bishops Way, Room 154, Brookfield 53005-6294.

5th Congressional District: Dodge (part), Jefferson, Milwaukee (part), Walworth (part), Washington, Waukesha (part) Counties. (For detailed description, see Section 3.15, Wisconsin Statutes.)

Thomas E. Petri (Rep.), 6th Congressional District

Born Marinette, May 28, 1940; married; 1 child. Graduate Goodrich H.S.; B.A. Harvard College 1962; J.D. Harvard Law School 1965. Attorney. Former Peace Corps volunteer; White House aide.

State legislative service: Elected to Senate 1972 and 1976.

Elected to U.S. House of Representatives in April 1979 special election; reelected since 1980. Committee assignments: **113th Congress** — Education and the Workforce (mbr. since 96th Congress) and its Subcommittees on Early Childhood, Elementary, and Secondary Education, on Higher Education and Workforce Training; Transportation and Infrastructure Committee (mbr. since 98th Congress) and its Subcommittees on Aviation, on Economic Development, Public Buildings, and Emergency Management, on Highways and Transit (chp.).

Telephones: Washington office: (202) 225-2476; District offices: Fond du Lac: (920) 922-1180; Oshkosh: (920) 231-6333; Toll free: (800) 242-4883.

Internet address: http://petri.house.gov

Voting address: (Town of Empire) N5329 DeNeveu Lane, Fond du Lac 54937.

Mailing addresses: Washington office: 2462 Rayburn House Office Building, Washington, D.C. 20515-4906; District offices: 490 West Rolling Meadows Drive, Suite B, Fond du Lac 54937; 2390 State Road 44, Suite B, Oshkosh 54904.

6th Congressional District: Columbia, Dodge (part), Fond du Lac, Green Lake, Manitowoc, Marquette, Milwaukee (part), Ozaukee, Sheboygan, Waushara, Winnebago (part) Counties. (For detailed description, see Section 3.16, Wisconsin Statutes.)

U.S. Representative
DUFFY

U.S. Representative
RIBBLE

Sean P. Duffy (Rep.), 7th Congressional District

Born October 3, 1971; married; 6 children. Graduate Hayward H.S.; B.A. in business marketing St. Mary's (Winona, MN) 1994; J.D. William Mitchell College of Law 1999. Attorney. Former special prosecutor and district attorney, Ashland County.

Elected to U.S. House of Representatives 2010; reelected 2012. Committee assignments: **113th Congress** — Budget Committee; Financial Services Committee and its Subcommittees on Financial Institutions and Consumer Credit, on Insurance, Housing, and Community Opportunity, on Oversight and Investigations; Joint Economic Committee.

Telephones: Washington office: (202) 225-3365; District offices: Superior: (715) 392-3984; Wausau: (715) 298-9344.

Voting address: 5805 Pine Terrace, Weston 54476.

Mailing addresses: Washington office: 1208 Longworth House Office Building, Washington, D.C. 20515; District offices: 823 Belknap Street, Suite 225, Superior 54880; 208 Grand Avenue, Wausau 54403.

7th Congressional District: Ashland, Barron, Bayfield, Burnett, Chippewa (part), Clark, Douglas, Florence, Forest, Iron, Jackson (part), Juneau (part), Langlade, Lincoln, Marathon, Monroe (part), Oneida, Polk, Price, Rusk, St. Croix, Sawyer, Taylor, Vilas, Washburn, and Wood (part) Counties. (For detailed description, see Section 3.17, Wisconsin Statutes.)

Reid J. Ribble (Rep.), 8th Congressional District

Born Neenah, April 5, 1956; married; 2 children. Graduate Appleton East H.S. 1974; attended Grand Rapids School of Bible and Music 1975. Former president, Ribble Group, Inc., Reid Ribble Properties LLC, Reel Loud Records. Member: YMCA of the Fox Valley (fmr. bd. mbr.); National Roofing Contractors Assn. (fmr. pres.); Brown County Home Builders Assn.; Fox Valley Chamber of Commerce; National Association of Home Builders; United States Chamber of Commerce; Wisconsin Roofing Contractors Assn.

Elected to U.S. House of Representatives 2010; reelected 2012. Committee assignments: **113th Congress** — Agriculture Committee (mbr. since 112th Congress) and its Subcommittees on Conservation, Energy and Forestry, on Livestock, Rural Development, and Credit; Budget Committee (since 112th Congress); Transportation and Infrastructure Committee and its Subcommittees on Aviation, on Highways and Transit (vice chp.), on Water Resources and Environment.

Telephones: Washington office: (202) 225-5665; District offices: Appleton: (920) 380-0061; Green Bay: (920) 471-1950.

Voting address: Sherwood 54169.

Mailing addresses: Washington office: 1513 Longworth House Office Building, Washington, D.C. 20515; District offices: 333 West College Avenue, Appleton 54911; 550 North Military Avenue, Suite 4B, Green Bay 54303.

8th Congressional District: Brown, Calumet, Door, Kewaunee, Marinette, Menominee, Oconto, Outagamie, Shawano, Waupaca, Winnebago (part) Counties. (For detailed description, see Section 3.18, Wisconsin Statutes.)

CONGRESSIONAL DISTRICTS
Enacted by 2011 Wisconsin Act 44

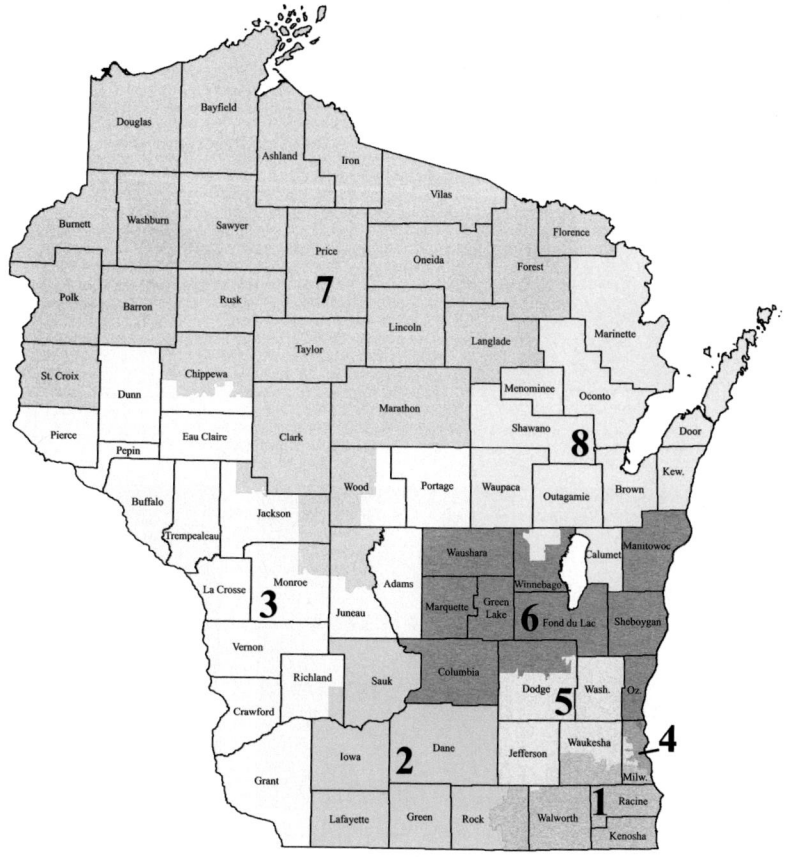

2010 POPULATION OF CONGRESSIONAL DISTRICTS

District	Population*	Deviation from Equal Population Number	Percent	Minority Population Hispanic	Other
Cong. Dist. 1	710,874	+1	+0.00	63,235	61,428
Cong. Dist. 2	710,874	+1	+0.00	41,423	71,683
Cong. Dist. 3	710,873	0	0.00	14,983	33,270
Cong. Dist. 4	710,873	0	0.00	110,488	285,413
Cong. Dist. 5	710,873	0	0.00	35,606	38,816
Cong. Dist. 6	710,873	0	0.00	27,087	36,154
Cong. Dist. 7	710,873	0	0.00	12,537	37,728
Cong. Dist. 8	710,873	0	0.00	30,697	48,027
TOTAL	5,686,986			336,056	612,519

*Wisconsin's 8 congressional districts were established by 2011 Wisconsin Act 44, based on the 2010 U.S. Census of Population. The ideal size of each district is 710,873.

Source: U.S. Department of Commerce, Census Bureau, P.L. 94-171 Redistricting File, March 2011.

2013 STATE SENATE OFFICERS

President
ELLIS

President Pro Tempore
LEIBHAM

Majority Leader
FITZGERALD

Assistant Majority Leader
GROTHMAN

Minority Leader
LARSON

Assistant Minority Leader
HANSEN

Chief Clerk
RENK

Sergeant at Arms
BLAZEL

2013 STATE ASSEMBLY OFFICERS

Speaker
VOS

Speaker Pro Tempore
KRAMER

Majority Leader
SUDER

Assistant Majority Leader
STEINEKE

Minority Leader
BARCA

Assistant Minority Leader
PASCH

Chief Clerk
FULLER

Sergeant at Arms
TONNON BYERS

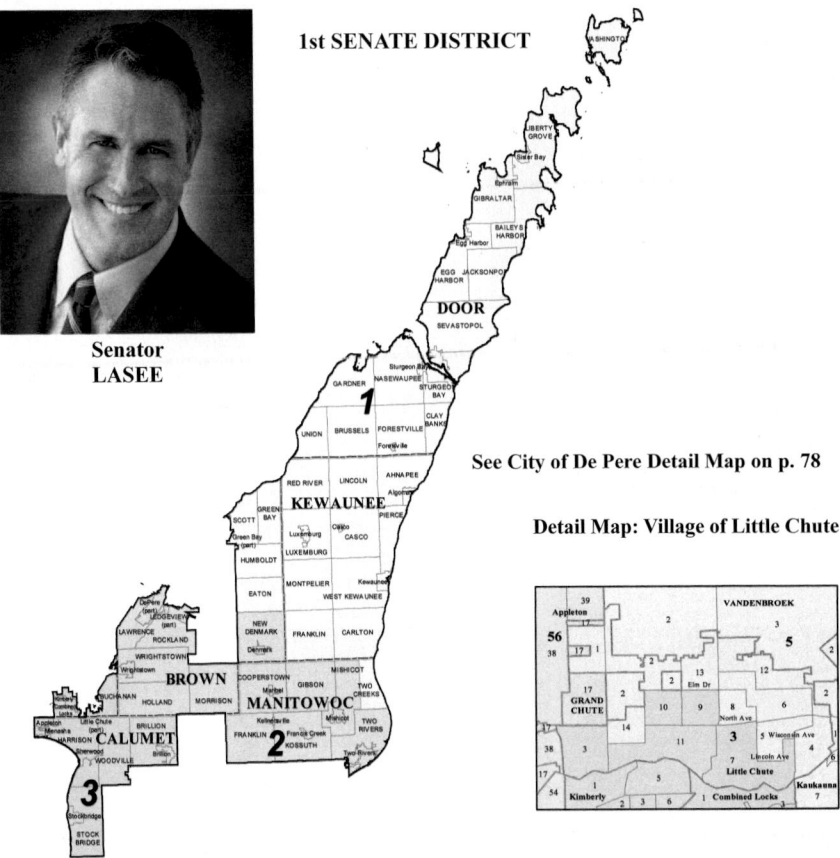

1st SENATE DISTRICT

Senator
LASEE

See City of De Pere Detail Map on p. 78

Detail Map: Village of Little Chute

Frank Lasee (Rep.), 1st Senate District

Born Oceanside, CA, December 11, 1961; married; 6 children. B.A. UW-Green Bay 1986. Full-time legislator. Former manufacturing computer hardware and software salesman, business long-distance salesman. Former real estate salesman. Former member: Optimists; Rotary; Telecommunications Specialists of Wisconsin. Town of Ledgeview chairman 1993-97.

Elected to Assembly 1994-2006; elected to Senate 2010. Majority Caucus Chairperson 2013. Biennial committee assignments: **2013** — Insurance and Housing (chp., also 2011); Jt. Survey Com. on Tax Exemptions (co-chp.); Financial Institutions and Rural Issues (vice chp., also 2011); Elections and Urban Affairs; Government Operations, Public Works, and Telecommunications. **2011** —State and Federal Relations and Information Technology (vice chp.); Transportation and Elections.

Telephone: Office: (608) 266-3512.

E-mail: Sen.Lasee@legis.wisconsin.gov

Voting address: De Pere 54115.

Mailing address: Office: Room 316 South, State Capitol, P.O. Box 7882, Madison 53707-7882.

**Representative
BIES**

**Representative
JACQUE**

**Representative
A. OTT**

Garey Bies (Rep.), 1st Assembly District

Born Manitowoc; married; 4 children, 5 grandchildren. Graduate Lincoln H.S., Manitowoc; Associate Degree Northeastern Technical College 1982. Full-time legislator. Former chief deputy sheriff, deputy sheriff, Door County Sheriff's Dept. 30 years, and project director for Door/Kewaunee Drug Task Force, 1990-2000. Navy veteran, 1964-69. Member: American Legion Post 527, 1970-present; Knights of Columbus, 1970-present; Northern Door Child Care (bd. dir.); St. Rosalia Catholic Church (former trustee and council member); Sturgeon Bay Rotary; volunteer guardian for disabled adults. Former member: Boy Scouts of America (cubmaster, scout master); Door/Kewaunee Selective Service Bd. (chp., vice chp.); Door Co. Highway Safety Com.; Door Co. Local Emergency Planning Com.; Help of Door County (bd. dir.).

Elected to Assembly since 2000. Biennial committee assignments: **2013** — Corrections (chp.); Tourism (vice chp.); Criminal Justice; Natural Resources and Sporting Heritage; Veterans. **2011** — Criminal Justice and Corrections (chp.); Public Health and Public Safety (chp.); Tourism, Recreation and State Properties (since 2007); Veterans and Military Affairs (also 2007, 2003). **2009** — Public Safety; Transportation (vice chp. 2007). **2007** — Corrections and the Courts (chp. since 2003); Natural Resources (since 2003); Legis. Coun. Spec. Com. on Placement of Sex Offenders (co-chp.); Gov.'s Comn. on Reducing Racial Disparities. **2005** — Highway Safety (vice chp. since 2001); Veterans Affairs; Gov.'s Coun. on Highway Safety (since 2001); Wis. Sentencing Comn. (since 2003); Legis. Coun. Com. on State and Tribal Relations. **2003** — Speaker's Task Force on Technical College System (co-chp.).

Telephone: Office: (608) 266-5350; (888) 482-0001 (toll free); District: (920) 854-2811.
E-mail: Rep.Bies@legis.wisconsin.gov
Voting address: 2520 Settlement Road, Sister Bay 54234.
Mailing address: Office: Room 216 North, State Capitol, P.O. Box 8952, Madison 53708.

André Jacque (Rep.), 2nd Assembly District

Born Beaver Dam, October 13, 1980; married; 3 children. Graduate Green Bay Southwest 1999; B.S. UW-Madison 2003; legislative capstone graduate certificate from UW-Madison La Follette Inst. of Public Affairs. Full-time legislator. Former transit planning coordinator, communications dir., grant-writing consultant. Member: Green Bay Area Crimestoppers (bd. mbr.); Brown Co. Taxpayers Assn; Knights of Columbus; NRA. Former member: Brown Co. Teen Leadership (bd. mbr.); Brown Co. United Way (marketing and communications com.); Higher Educ. Aids Bd. 2001-03. Recipient: Wis. Coalition Against Domestic Violence *Legislative Champion Award;* Wis. Counties Assn. *Outstanding Legislator Award;* Pro-Life Wis. *Legislator of the Year* 2012; American Wis. Coalition of Virtual Schools Families *Shining Star of Education Reform;* Dairy Business Assn. *Legislative Excellence Award;* Phillips Foundation *Distinguished Young Conservative Leader of the Year* 2012; Green Bay Area Chamber of Commerce Henry S. Baird *Legislator of the Year Award* 2012.

Elected to Assembly 2010; reelected 2012. Biennial committee assignments: **2013** — Public Safety and Homeland Security (chp.); Jt. Review Com. on Criminal Penalties (co-chp.); Jt. Legis. State Supported Programs Study and Adv. Com. (co-chp.); Judiciary (vice chp.); Criminal Justice; Energy and Utilities; Jobs, Economy and Mining; Urban and Local Affairs (also 2011). **2011** — Criminal Justice and Corrections (vice chp.); Judiciary and Ethics.

Telephone: Office: (608) 266-9870; (888) 534-0002 (toll free); District: (920) 336-4727.
E-mail: Rep.Jacque@legis.wisconsin.gov
Voting address: 1615 Lost Dauphin Road, De Pere 54115.
Mailing address: Office: Room 123 West, State Capitol, P.O. Box 8952, Madison 53708.

Al Ott (Alvin R. Ott) (Rep.), 3rd Assembly District

Born Green Bay, June 19, 1949; married; 4 children, 8 grandchildren. Graduate Brillion H.S.; UW-Madison Farm and Industry Short Course 1968; 1st Class of Participants in WI Rural Leadership Program 1986. Former agri-business salesman, owner/operator of independent agri-business, tenant dairy farmer, and cash crop farmer. Member: Republican Party of Wis.; Calumet Co. Agricultural Assn.; Calumet Co. Farm Progress 1993 Exec. Com. (chm.). Calumet Co. Board 1973-92 (vice chp.), chp. of its Ag/Extension Educ. Com. and vice chp. of its Land Conservation and Planning/Zoning Coms.; Wis. Land Conservation Bd. 1984-88 (secy.).

Elected to Assembly since 1986. Biennial committee assignments: **2013** — Natural Resources and Sporting Heritage (chp.); Agriculture (since 1995, also 1989, 1987, chp. 1995-2007); Consumer Protection; Tourism; Transportation (since 2003). **2011** — Rural Economic Development and Rural Affairs (chp.). **2009** — Public Safety. **2007** — Rural Economic Development (vice chp.); Forestry. **2005** — Natural Resources (mbr. since 1995); Rural Development (mbr. since 2003). **2001** — Energy and Utilities; Environment.

Telephone: Office: (608) 266-5831; (888) 534-0003 (toll free); District: (920) 989-1240.
E-mail: Rep.Ott@legis.wisconsin.gov
Voting address: (Town of Brillion) W2168 Campground Road, Forest Junction 54123-0112.
Mailing address: Office: Room 323 North, State Capitol, P.O. Box 8953, Madison 53708; District: P.O. Box 112, Forest Junction 54123-0112.

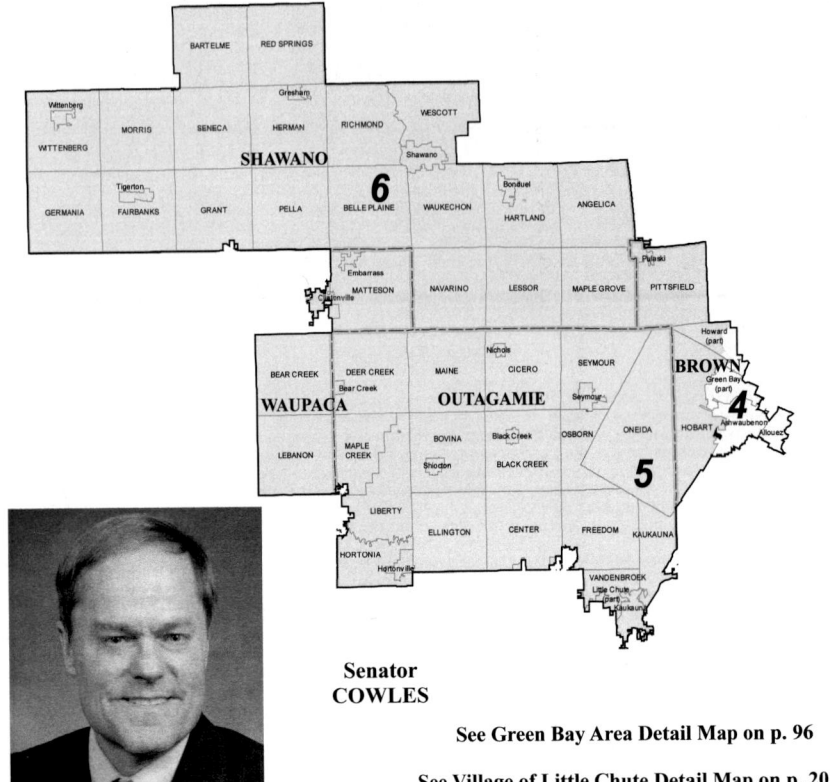

Senator
COWLES

See Green Bay Area Detail Map on p. 96

See Village of Little Chute Detail Map on p. 20

2nd SENATE DISTRICT

Robert L. Cowles (Rep.), 2nd Senate District

Born Green Bay, July 31, 1950. B.S. UW-Green Bay 1975; graduate work UW-Green Bay. Full-time legislator. Former director of an alternative energy division for a communications construction company. Member: Allouez Kiwanis; Friends of the Fox River Trail; Salvation Army Volunteer.

Elected to Assembly 1982-86 (resigned 4/21/87); elected to Senate in April 1987 special election; reelected since 1988. Biennial Senate committee assignments: **2013** — Energy, Consumer Protection, and Governmental Reform (chp.); Jt. Legis. Audit Com. (co-chp. since 2011, mbr. since 1993); Jt. Com. on Information Policy and Technology (vice chp. since 2011, mbr. 2009); State and Federal Relations (vice chp.); Transportation, Public Safety, and Veterans and Military Affairs. **2011** — Energy, Biotechnology, and Consumer Protection (chp.); Workforce Development, Small Business and Tourism. **2009** — Commerce, Utilities, Energy, and Rail; Joint Com. for Review of Administrative Rules (also 2001, 1987 to 4/20/93). **2007** — Commerce, Utilities and Rail; Public Health, Senior Issues, Long-Term Care and Privacy. **2005** — Energy, Utilities and Information Technology (chp.); Jt. Com. on Finance (also 1993-99). **2003** — Energy and Utilities (chp.); Higher Education and Tourism; Building Comn. **2001** — Environmental Resources; Health, Utilities, Veterans and Military Affairs. **1999** — Jt. Survey Com. on Tax Exemptions; Joint Legislative Council (also 1997). **1997** — Environmental Education Bd. (since 1991). **1995** — Environment and Energy (chp.). **1993** — Urban Affairs, Financial Institutions and Environmental Resources (mbr. and vice chp. to 4/20/93); Judiciary and Consumer Affairs (mbr. to 4/20/93); Legis. Coun. Com. on State Fire Programs (co-chp.). **1991** — Urban Affairs, Environmental Resources and Elections; Legis. Coun. Com. on Energy Resources; Gov.'s Council on Recycling. **1989** — Educational Financing, Higher Education and Tourism; Science, Technology, Communications and Energy; Legis. Coun. Com. on Nonpoint Source Pollution; Low-Level Radioactive Waste Council. **1987** — Economic Development, Financial Institutions and Fiscal Policies; Housing, Government Operations and Cultural Affairs. Assembly committee assignments: **1987** — Jt. Com. for Review of Administrative Rules (since 1983); Trade, Industry and Small Business. **1985** — Jt. Com. on Debt Management; Energy; Legis. Coun. Com. on Environmental Resource Management. **1983** — Energy and Utilities; Economic Development (eff. 10/25/83); Family and Economic Assistance; Revenue.

Telephone: Office: (608) 266-0484; (800) 334-1465 (toll free); District: (920) 448-5092; Fax: (920) 448-5093.

E-mail: Sen.Cowles@legis.wisconsin.gov

Voting address: 300 West St. Joseph Street, Green Bay 54301.

Mailing address: Office: Room 118 South, State Capitol, P.O. Box 7882, Madison 53707-7882.

Representative
WEININGER

Representative
STEINEKE

Representative
TAUCHEN

Chad Weininger (Rep.), 4th Assembly District

Born Green Bay; married, twin daughters. Graduate Ashwaubenon H.S. 1991; BBA St. Norbert College 1995; MBA Cardinal Stritch University 2004. Former city clerk of Green Bay; foreign service, U.S. State Department; international election observer; chief of staff for mayor of Green Bay; deputy chief of staff to Cong. Mark Green; staff assistant to state senator Robert Cowles; former small business owner. Member: Brown Co. Taxpayers Assn.; Whitetails Unlimited; Ruffed Grouse; Ducks Unlimited. Former member: Wis. Municipal Clerks Assn.; Project Vote; On Broadway. Recipient: *Legislator of the Year Award; Freshman Legislator Leadership Award; Working Wisconsin Award; Defender of Liberty Award;* Named as *Future 15.*

Elected to Assembly 2010; reelected 2012. Biennial committee assignments: **2013** — International Trade and Commerce (chp.); Insurance (vice chp.); Campaigns and Elections; Energy and Utilities (also 2011); Financial Institutions; Urban Education; Jt. Com. on Information Policy and Technology.

Telephone: Office: (608) 266-5840; District: (920) 632-7998; E-mail: Rep.Weininger@legis.wisconsin.gov

Voting address: 163 Hilltop, Green Bay 54301.

Mailing address: Office: Room 125 West, State Capitol, P.O. Box 8953, Madison 53708.

Jim Steineke (Rep.), 5th Assembly District

Born Milwaukee, November 23, 1970; married, 3 children. Graduate Wauwatosa West H.S. 1989; attended UW-Milwaukee and UW-Oshkosh. Regional manager. Former realtor, salesman. Former member: Realtors Assn. of Northeast Wis.; Wis. Realtors Assn. Town supervisor, Town of Vandenbroeck 2005-07; town chp. 2007-11. Outagamie Co. supervisor 2006-11.

Elected to Assembly 2010; reelected 2012. Assistant Majority Leader 2013. Biennial committee assignments: **2013** — Assembly Organization; Natural Resources and Sporting Heritage; Rules; Jt. Com. on Legislative Organization. **2011** — Rural Economic Development (vice chp.); Housing; Natural Resources.

Telephone: Office: (608) 266-2418; (888) 534-0005 (toll free).

E-mail: Rep.Steineke@legis.wisconsin.gov

Voting address: Kaukauna 54130.

Mailing address: Office: Room 204 North, State Capitol, P.O. Box 8953, Madison 53708.

Gary Tauchen (Rep.), 6th Assembly District

Born Rice Lake, November 23, 1953; single. Graduate Bonduel H.S. 1971; attended UW-Madison 1971-72; B.S. in Animal Science, UW-River Falls 1976. Dairy farmer. Member: Wis. Farm Bureau; Badger AgVest, LLC (dir.); Professional Dairy Producers of Wis. (fmr. dir.); Dairy Business Assn.; Wis. Livestock Identification Consortium (fmr. dir., fmr. chm.); Brown, Shawano, Outagamie, Waupaca Co. Republican Party; Shawano Area Chamber of Commerce; Shawano Co. Dairy Promotions (fmr. dir.); Cooperative Resources International (fmr. vice chm.); AgSource Cooperative Services (fmr. chm.); National Dairy Herd Improvement Assn. (fmr. dir.); UW Center for Dairy Profitability (fmr. chm.); Shawano Rotary.

Elected to Assembly 2006; reelected since 2008. Minority Caucus Sergeant at Arms 2009. Biennial committee assignments: **2013** — Rural Affairs (chp., vice chp. 2007); Agriculture (vice chp., mbr. since 2007); Constitution and Ethics; International Trade and Commerce; State and Local Finance. **2011** — Elections and Campaign Reform (chp.); Energy and Utilities; Rural Economic Development and Rural Affairs. **2009** — Renewable Energy and Rural Affairs; Workforce Development. **2007** — Biofuels and Sustainable Energy; State Affairs.

Telephone: Office: (608) 266-3097; (888) 529-0006 (toll free); District: (715) 758-6181.

E-mail: Rep.Tauchen@legis.wisconsin.gov

Voting address: Bonduel 54107.

Mailing address: Office: Room 13 West, State Capitol, P.O. Box 8953, Madison 53708.

3rd SENATE DISTRICT

See Milwaukee County Detail Map on pp. 92 & 93

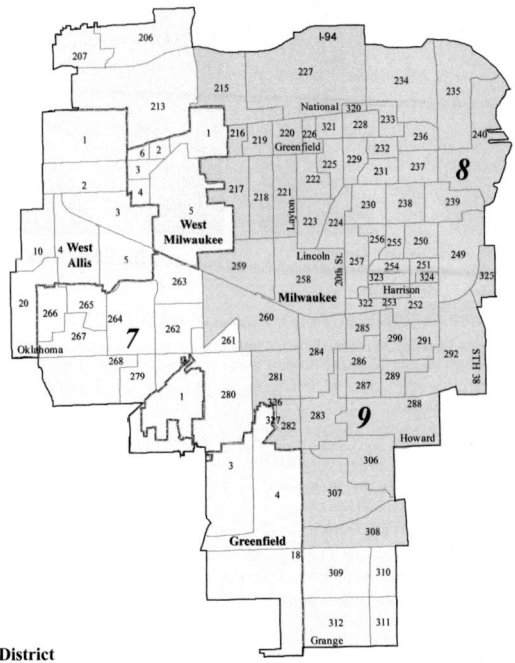

**Senator
CARPENTER**

Tim Carpenter (Dem.), 3rd Senate District

Born Milwaukee. Graduate Pulaski H.S.; B.A. UW-Milwaukee; M.A. UW-Madison La Follette Institute. Member: Sierra Club; Jackson Park Neighborhood Assn.; Story Hill Neighborhood Assn.; Milw. VA Soldiers Home Advisory Council. Recipient: Wisconsin Public Health Association's *Champion of Public Health* 2008; Coalition of Wisconsin Aging Groups *Russ Feingold Award for Service to Seniors* 2007; Shepherd Express *Best State Legislator* 2008; Wisconsin League of Conservation Voters *Conservation Champion* 2008; Shepherd Express *Legislator of the Year* 2003; Wis. Professional Fire Fighters *Legislator of the Year* 2002; Environmental Decade *Clean 16 Awards*.

Elected to Assembly 1984-2000; elected to Senate 2002; reelected since 2006. President Pro Tempore 2011 (eff. 7/17/12), 2007; Speaker Pro Tempore 1993. Biennial Senate committee assignments: **2013** — Health and Human Services; State and Federal Relations (also 2005); Transportation, Public Safety, and Veterans and Military Affairs; Jt. Com. on Information Policy and Technology; Coun. on Alcohol and Other Drug Abuse (also 2003-07); State Fair Park Bd.; Transportation Projects Comn. **2011** — Health; Insurance and Housing; Public Health, Human Services, and Revenue; Jt. Survey Com. on Tax Exemptions; Leg. Council Study Com. on Strategic Job Creation. **2009** — Public Health, Senior Issues, Long-Term Care and Job Creation (chp.); Health, Health Insurance, Privacy, Property Tax Relief, and Revenue (vice chp.); Veterans and Military Affairs, Biotechnology and Financial Institutions (also 2007); Jt. Survey Com. on Retirement Systems. **2007** — Public Health, Senior Issues, Long-Term Care and Privacy (chp.); Small Business, Emergency Preparedness, Workforce Development, Technical Colleges and Consumer Protection (vice chp.); Health and Human Services (Health, Human Services, Insurance and Job Creation eff. 11/6/07); Jt. Legislative Council. **2005** — Health, Children, Families, Aging and Long-Term Care (also 2003); Labor and Election Process Reform. **2003** — Jt. Com. for Review of Administrative Rules (through 5/23/03); Administrative Rules (through 5/23/03); Judiciary, Corrections and Privacy; Council on Migrant Labor. Assembly committee assignments: **2001** — Aging and Long-Term Care (also 1997, 1995); Health (chp. 1991, mbr. since 1987); Public Health (also 1999); State and Local Finance. **1999** — Census and Redistricting; Urban and Local Affairs (also 1985). **1997** — Managed Care. **1995** — Legis. Coun. Com. to Review the Election Process. **1993** — Financial Institutions and Housing; Insurance, Securities and Corporate Policy; Joint Legislative Council and co-chp. of its Com. on Communication of Governmental Proceedings; Rules. **1991** — Elections and Constitutional Law (chp. 1989); Financial Institutions and Insurance (mbr. 1989, 1987, vice chp. 1985); Judiciary; Labor (since 1985); Public Health and Regulation; Special Com. on Reapportionment (vice chp.); Special Com. on Reform of Health Insurance; Legis. Coun. Com. on Campaign Financing. **1989** — Select Com. on the Census (co-chp.); Environmental Resources and Utilities; Legis. Coun. Coms. on Prenatal Care, on Privacy and Information Technology. **1987** — Elections (vice chp., also 1985); Housing and Securities; Legis. Coun. Com. on Solid Waste Management. **1985** — Economic Development; Transportation.

Telephone: Office: (608) 266-8535; (800) 249-8173 (toll free); Fax: (608) 282-3543.

E-mail: Sen.Carpenter@legis.wisconsin.gov

Voting address: 2957 South 38th Street, Milwaukee 53215.

Mailing address: Office: Room 109 South, State Capitol, P.O. Box 7882, Madison 53707-7882.

| Representative | Representative | Representative |
| RIEMER | ZAMARRIPA | ZEPNICK |

Daniel Riemer (Dem.), 7th Assembly District

Born Milwaukee, December 10, 1986; single. Graduate Rufus King H.S. (Milwaukee) 2005; B.A. U. of Chicago 2009. Full-time legislator.

Elected to Assembly 2012. Biennial committee assignments: **2013** — Health; International Trade and Commerce; Transportation; Ways and Means.

Telephone: Office: (608) 266-1733; District: (414) 543-0017; E-mail: Rep.Riemer@legis.wisconsin.gov

Voting address: 3721 West Oklahoma Avenue, #7, Milwaukee 53215.

Mailing address: Office: Room 409 North, State Capitol, P.O. Box 8953, Madison 53708.

JoCasta Zamarripa (Dem.), 8th Assembly District

Born Milwaukee, March 8, 1976; single. Graduate St. Joan Antida H.S. (Milwaukee) 1994; BFA UW-Milwaukee 2005. Full-time legislator. Former nonprofit professional. Member: Wisconsin Minority Health Leadership Council.

Elected to Assembly 2010; reelected 2012. Minority Caucus Vice Chairperson 2013. Biennial committee assignments: **2013** — Campaigns and Elections; Corrections; Jobs, Economy and Mining; Public Safety and Homeland Security; Rules; State Affairs; Gov.'s Council on Migrant Labor. **2011** — Homeland Security and State Affairs; Public Health and Public Safety; Ways and Means.

Telephone: Office: (608) 267-7669; (888) 534-0008 (toll free); District: (414) 384-2786.

E-mail: Rep.Zamarripa@legis.wisconsin.gov; Internet address: www.legis.wisconsin.gov/assembly/zamarripa

Voting address: Milwaukee 53204.

Mailing address: Office: Room 320 West, State Capitol, P.O. Box 8953, Madison 53708.

Josh Zepnick (Dem.), 9th Assembly District

Born Milwaukee, March 21, 1968; married. Graduate Rufus King H.S. (Milwaukee); B.A. UW-Madison 1990; M.A. Univ. of Minnesota 1998. Full-time legislator. Former project consultant, Milwaukee Jobs Initiative, Milwaukee Community Service Corps, and Urban Economic Development Association of Wisconsin; research associate, Center for Democracy and Citizenship; aide to State Senator Bob Jauch and Congressman David R. Obey. Member: Jackson Park Neighborhood Assn.; Jackson Park Business Assn.; South Side Business Club. Former member: UFCW Local 1444.

Elected to Assembly since 2002. Minority Caucus Sergeant at Arms 2013, 2011. Biennial committee assignments: **2013** — Energy and Utilities (since 2005, vice chp. 2009); Financial Institutions (since 2003); State and Federal Relations; State and Local Finance. **2011** —Tourism, Recreation and State Properties; Leg. Coun. Spec. Com. on Local Service Consolidation (chp.). **2009** — Jt. Com. for Review of Administrative Rules (co-chp.); Ways and Means; Workforce Development (also 2007, 2003). **2007** — Gov.'s Council on Workforce Investment (also 2005). **2005** — Government Operations and Spending Limitations (also 2003); Southeast Wisconsin Freeways; State-Federal Relations; Jt. Select Com. on Road to the Future. **2003** — Transportation.

Telephone: Office: (608) 266-1707; (888) 534-0009 (toll free).

E-mail: Rep.Zepnick@legis.wisconsin.gov

Voting address: 3145 West Drury Lane, Milwaukee 53215.

Mailing address: Office: Room 7 North, State Capitol, P.O. Box 8953, Madison 53708.

4th SENATE DISTRICT

Senator
TAYLOR

See Milwaukee County Detail Map on pp. 92 & 93

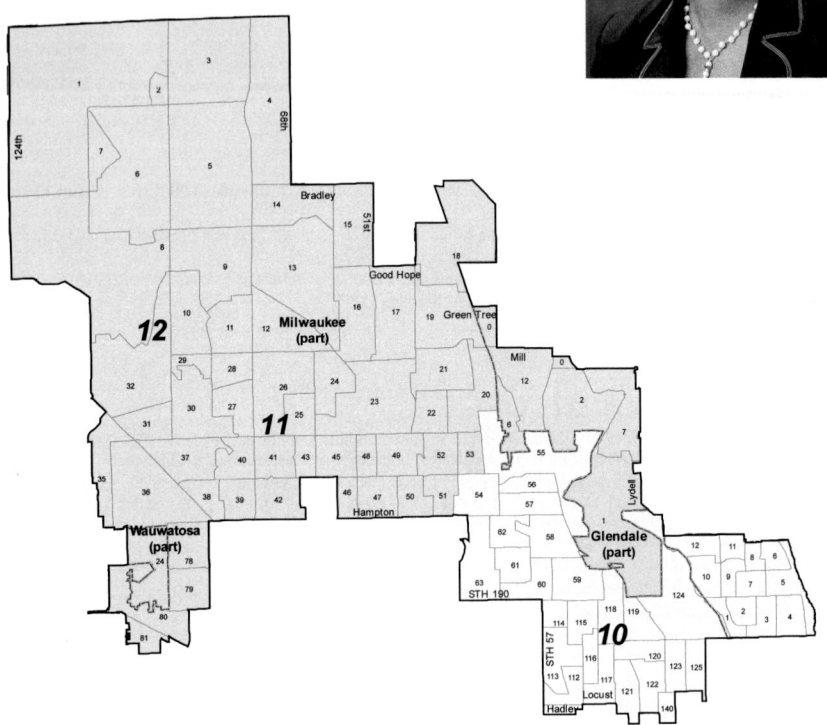

Lena C. Taylor (Dem.), 4th Senate District

Born Milwaukee, July 25, 1966; 1 child. Graduate Rufus King H.S. (Milwaukee) 1984; B.A. in English UW-Milwaukee 1990; J.D. SIU-Carbondale 1993. Attorney. Member: Democratic Party of Wisconsin (former 1st vice chr.); Milwaukee Boy Scouts (advisory bd.); NAACP; Urban League of Milwaukee; Girl Scouts of Milwaukee Area; Unity Caucus; Milwaukee Community Justice Council.

Elected to Assembly in April 2003 special election; elected to Senate 2004; reelected since 2008. Biennial Senate committee assignments: **2013** — Agriculture, Small Business and Tourism; Economic Development and Local Government; Elections and Urban Affairs; Jt. Review Com. on Criminal Penalties (since 2007, co-chp. 2009); **2011** — Jt. Com. on Finance (since 2005, co-chp., eff. 7/24/12); Economic Development, Veterans and Military Affairs; Health, Revenue, Tax Fairness and Insurance; Judiciary and Government Operations (vice chp.); Jt. Legis. Audit Com; Jt. Com. on Employment Relations; Jt. Com. for Review of Admin. Rules; Jt. Legislative Council; Wis. Center Dist. Bd.; Claims Bd. **2009** — Judiciary, Corrections, Insurance, Campaign Finance Reform, and Housing (chp.); Judicial Council (also 2007); Wisconsin Housing and Economic Development Authority (since 2005). **2007** — Judiciary and Corrections (chp., Judiciary, Corrections and Housing eff. 11/6/07); Health, Human Services, Insurance and Job Creation (eff. 11/6/07); Jt. Survey Com. on Retirement Systems; Sentencing Commission. **2005** — Judiciary, Corrections and Privacy. Assembly committee assignments: **2003** — Criminal Justice; Economic Development; Financial Institutions; Tourism; Urban and Local Affairs.

Telephone: Office: (608) 266-5810; District: (414) 342-7176.

E-mail: Sen.Taylor@legis.wisconsin.gov; Internet address: www.senatortaylor.com

Facebook: facebook.com/SenLenaTaylor; Twitter: @sentaylor

Voting address: Ward 59, City of Milwaukee.

Mailing address: Office: Room 19 South, State Capitol, P.O. Box 7882, Madison 53707-7882.

Representative
PASCH

Representative
BARNES

Representative
KESSLER

Sandy Pasch (Dem.), 10th Assembly District

Born Milwaukee, May 19, 1954; married; 3 children. Graduate Bay View H.S. 1972; B.S. Nursing UW-Madison 1976; M.S. Psychiatric nursing U. of Rochester (NY) 1981; M.A. Bioethics Medical Coll. of Wisconsin 1999. Full-time legislator. Former assistant professor Columbia College of Nursing; clinical nurse specialist; community health nurse. Member: American Public Health Assn.; Wis. Nurses Assn.; National Alliance on Mental Illness (fmr. pres.); American Society for Bioethics and Humanities; NCSL Health Com.; Midwest CSG Health and Human Services Com.; Wis. Women's Council; UW Population Health Institute Advisory Bd.; City of Milw. Flooding Study Task Force; Milwaukee Legislative Caucus (chp.). Former member: Hope House (bd. mbr., secy.); American Red Cross – Southeastern Wis. Recipient: Milwaukee Shepard Express *Best State Legislator* 2011; Wis. Psychiatric Assn. *Friend of the WPA Award* 2011; HealthWatch Wis. *Elected Official of the Year* 2010; Wis. Public Health Assn. *Legislator of the Year* 2010; Nat'l. Alliance on Mental Illness – Greater Milw. *Legislator of the Year* 2010; Nat'l. Assn. of Social Workers – Wis. Chapter *Public Service Award* 2010; Wis. Nurses Assn. *Service to the WNA Award* 2010; Wis. Dietetic Assn. *Leadership in Nutrition Awareness Award* 2010; Wis. Academy of Family Physicians *Friend of Family Physicians* 2010; Wis. League of Conservation Voters *Conservation Champion* 2010; Wis. Soc. of Anesthesiologists *Excellence in Government Award* 2010; Equality Wis. *Equal Rights Champion* 2009.

Elected to Assembly 2008; reelected since 2010. Assistant Minority Leader 2013, 2011 (eff. 2/15/12). Biennial committee assignments: **2013** — Assembly Organization; Corrections; Family Law; Health (also 2011); Rules; Urban Education; Joint Legislative Council (ranking min. mbr., also 2011).

Telephone: Office: (608) 266-7671; (888) 534-0010 (toll free).

Voting address: 1717 East Kensington Boulevard, Apt. 404, Shorewood 53211.

Mailing address: Office: Room 119 North, State Capitol, P.O. Box 8953, Madison 53708.

Mandela Barnes (Dem.), 11th Assembly District

Born Milwaukee, December 1, 1986; single. Graduate John Marshall H.S. (Milwaukee) 2003; attended Alabama A&M U. 2003-08. Full-time legislator. Former community organizer; lead organizer and Exec. Dir. of MICAH (Milwaukee Inner City Congregations Allied for Hope). Member: ACLU of Wisconsin (bd. mbr.); NAACP Milwaukee Branch; Kappa Alpha Psi Fraternity, Inc.; Peace Action of Wisconsin; Democratic Party of Wisconsin.

Elected to Assembly 2012. Biennial committee assignments: **2013** — State and Federal Relations; Urban and Local Affairs; Urban Education; Ways and Means; Workforce Development.

Telephone: Office: (608) 266-3756; (888) 534-0011 (toll free); District: (414) 466-1660.

E-mail: Rep.Barnes@legis.wisconsin.gov

Voting address: Milwaukee 53223.

Mailing address: Office: Room 9 West, State Capitol, P.O. Box 8952, Madison 53708.

Frederick P. Kessler (Dem.), 12th Assembly District

Born Milwaukee, January 11, 1940; married; 2 children. Graduate Milw. Luth. H.S. and Capitol Page School 1957; B.A. U. of Wisconsin-Madison 1962; L.L.B. U. of Wisconsin 1966. Labor arbitrator. Member: Goethe House (vice pres., former pres.); Milwaukee Chap. ACLU (bd. mbr., former pres.); World Affairs Council of Milw. (bd. mbr.); Wis. Bar Assn.; Labor/Employment Relations Assn. (advisory com. mbr.); Democratic Party; DANK (German-American National Congress); Milwaukee chap. (former vice pres.); Milwaukee Donauschwaben; Amnesty International Group 107 (former chairman); Milw. Turners; NAACP. Former member: City of Milwaukee Harbor Comn. Recipient: Wisconsin ACLU *Eunice Edgar Lifetime Service Award* 2008; State Bar of Wis. *Scales of Justice Award* 2010. Presidential Elector for President Barack Obama 2012. County court judge (Milw. Co.) 1972-78; Circuit court judge (Milw. Co.) 1978-81, 1986-88. On January 11, 1961, his 21st birthday, he became the youngest person, up to that time, ever to serve in the legislature.

Elected to Assembly 1960, 1964-70; reelected since 2004. Biennial committee assignments: **2013** — Campaigns and Elections (also 2005); Criminal Justice (vice chp. 2009, mbr. 2007); Govt. Operations and State Licensing (eff. 4/29/13); Public Safety and Homeland Security. **2011** — Criminal Justice and Corrections; Election and Campaign Reform (also 2009); Jt. Com. for Review of Admin. Rules. **2009** — State Affairs and Homeland Security (chp.); Corrections and the Courts; Judiciary and Ethics (also 2007). **2007** — Elections and Constitutional Law. **2005** — Criminal Justice and Homeland Security; Judiciary (also 1965-71). **1971** — Elections (chp., mbr. 1969, 1965); Rules. **1961** — Education.

Telephone: Office: (608) 266-5813; (888) 534-0012 (toll free); District: (414) 368-3015.

E-mail: Rep.Kessler@legis.wisconsin.gov

Voting address: 9312 West Clovernook Street, Milwaukee 53224.

Mailing address: Office: Room 128 North, State Capitol, P.O. Box 8952, Madison 53708.

5th SENATE DISTRICT

Senator
VUKMIR

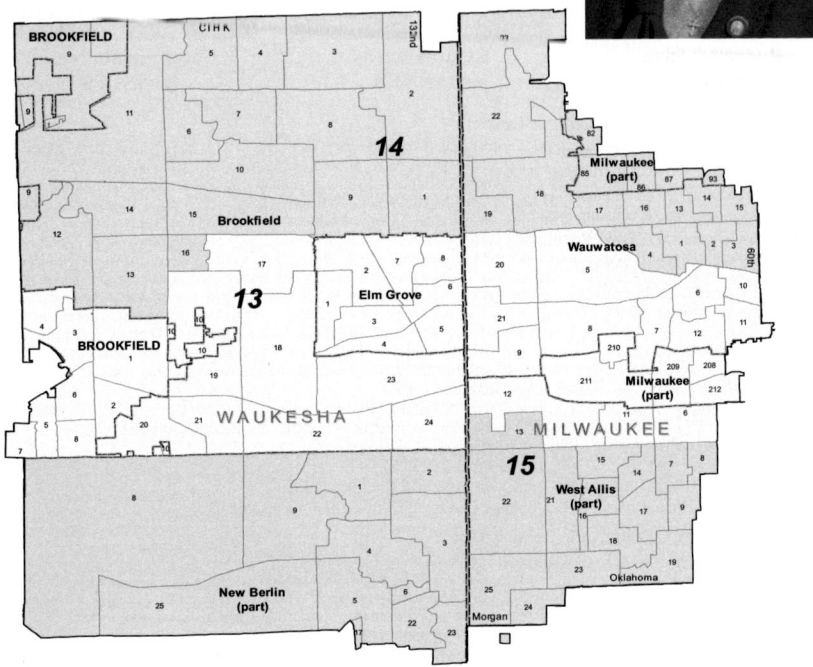

See Milwaukee County Detail Map on pp. 92 & 93

See Waukesha County Detail Map on pp. 94 & 95

Leah Vukmir (Rep.), 5th Senate District

Born Milwaukee, April 26, 1958; 2 children. Graduate Brookfield East H.S. 1976; B.S. in nursing Marquette U. 1980; M.S. in nursing UW-Madison 1983. Registered nurse; nationally certified pediatric nurse practitioner. Former research fellow, Wisconsin Policy Research Institute; Past Pres. and Co-founder of Parents Raising Educational Standards in Schools (PRESS). Member: Republican Party of Milwaukee Co., Republican Party of Waukesha Co., Wauwatosa Republican Club; West Allis Speedskating Club (former ASU Speedskating Referee). Former member: Standards and Assessments Subcommittee of Gov. Thompson's Task Force on Education and Learning; English/Language Arts Task Force of Gov. Thompson's Council on Model Academic Standards. Nationally recognized authority and speaker on education issues and educational standards. Recipient: Center for Education Reform's *Unsung Hero Award* 1998; Brookfield East High School *Alumni Achievement Award* 2002; American Legislative Exchange Council *Legislator of the Year* 2009.

Elected to Assembly 2002-08; elected to Senate 2010. Biennial Senate committee assignments: **2013** — Health and Human Services (chp.); Jt. Com. for Review of Admin. Rules (co-chp., also 2011); Judiciary and Labor (vice chp.); Education (vice chp. 2011). **2011** — Health (chp.); Public Health, Human Services, and Revenue. Assembly committee assignments: **2009** — Education (also 2007); Education Reform (chp. 2005, 2003, eff. 8/17/04, vice chp. 2003); Health and Health Care Reform (chp. 2007); Public Health (vice chp. 2007). **2007** — Criminal Justice (also 2003). **2005** — Health (vice chp., mbr. 2003); Children and Families (since 2003); Criminal Justice and Homeland Security; Medicaid Reform. **2003** — Economic Development.

Telephone: Office: (608) 266-2512.

E-mail: Sen.Vukmir@legis.wisconsin.gov

Voting address: Wauwatosa 53226.

Mailing address: Office: Room 131 South, State Capitol, P.O. Box 7882, Madison 53707-7882.

| Representative | Representative | Representative |
| HUTTON | KOOYENGA | SANFELIPPO |

Rob Hutton (Rep.), 13th Assembly District

Born Milwaukee, April 7, 1967; married; 4 children. Graduate Brookfield East H.S. 1985; B.A. history UW-Whitewater 1990. Executive/owner in trucking industry. Waukesha County Supervisor 2005-12.

Elected to Assembly 2012. Biennial committee assignments: **2013** — Urban and Local Affairs (vice chp.); Government Operations and State Licensing; Small Business Development; Urban Education.

Telephone: Office: (608) 267-9836; (888) 534-0013 (toll free); District: (414) 380-9665.

E-mail: Rep.Hutton@legis.wisconsin.gov

Voting address: Brookfield 53045.

Mailing address: Office: Room 3 North, State Capitol, P.O. Box 8952, Madison 53708.

Dale Kooyenga (Rep.), 14th Assembly District

Born Oak Lawn, IL, February 12, 1979; married; 3 children. Graduate Chicago Christian H.S. 1997; A.A. Moraine Valley Comm. College 2000; B.A. Lakeland College 2000; M.B.A. Marquette U. 2007. Certified public accountant. Member U.S. Army Reserve, 2005-present. Iraq War veteran. Member: American Legion; American Institute of Certified Public Accountants; Wis. Institute of Certified Public Accountants.

Elected to Assembly 2010; reelected 2012. Biennial committee assignments: **2013** — Government Operations and State Licensing; Jt. Com. on Finance. **2011** — Financial Institutions (vice chp.); Consumer Protection and Personal Privacy; Homeland Security and State Affairs.

Telephone: Office: (608) 266-9180; District: (414) 678-1586

E-mail: Rep.Kooyenga@legis.wisconsin.gov

Voting address: Brookfield 53005.

Mailing address: Office: Room 321 East, State Capitol, P.O. Box 8952, Madison 53708.

Joe Sanfelippo (Rep.), 15th Assembly District

Born Milwaukee February 26, 1964; married; 3 children. Graduate Thomas More H.S. 1982; attended Marquette U. 1982-84. Small businessman. Owned and operated a landscaping business for 20 years. Member: Mary Queen of Heaven Catholic Church, West Allis and St. John the Evangelist Parish, Greenfield. Milwaukee County Bd. of Supervisors 2008-12.

Elected to Assembly 2012. Biennial committee assignments: **2013** — Housing and Real Estate (vice chp.); Financial Institutions; Health; Jobs, Economy and Mining; Transportation; Urban Education; Speaker's Task Force on Mental Health.

Telephone: Office: (608) 266-0620; (888) 534-0015 (toll free).

E-mail: Rep.Sanfelippo@legis.wisconsin.gov

Voting address: West Allis 53227.

Mailing address: Room 21 North, State Capitol, P.O. Box 8953, Madison 53708.

6th SENATE DISTRICT

See Milwaukee County Detail Map on pp. 92 & 93

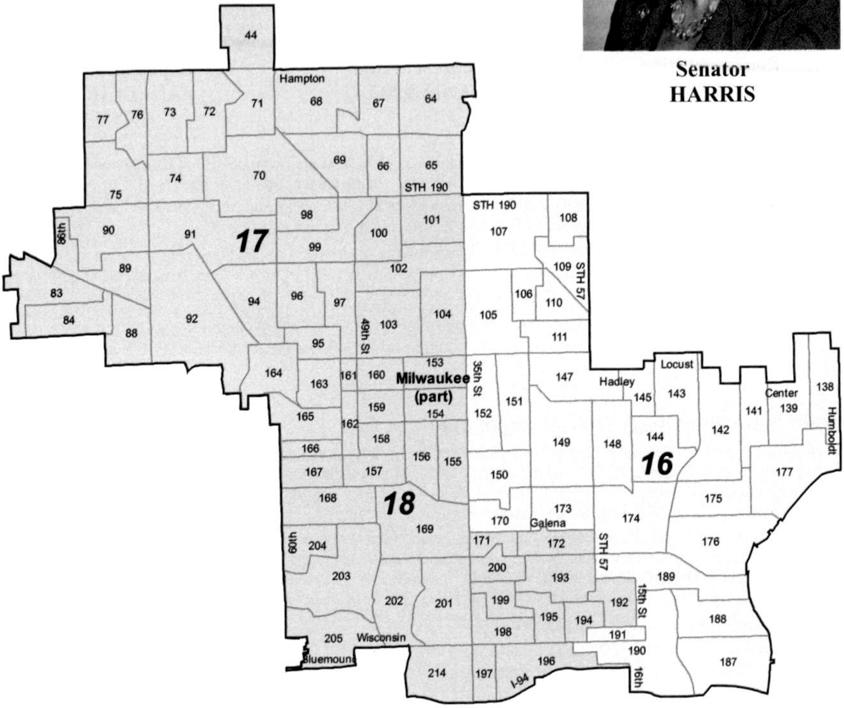

**Senator
HARRIS**

[District map showing numbered wards including 44, Hampton, 76, 73, 72, 71, 68, 67, 64, 77, 69, 66, 65, 74, 70, STH 190, 75, 98, 101, 107, 108, 90, 91, 17, 100, 99, STH 190, 89, 102, 109, 83, 94, 96, 97, 104, 105, 106, 110, 84, 92, 88, 103, 111, 95, 164, 153, Locust, 163, 161, 160, Milwaukee (part), 147, Hadley, 145, 143, 138, 165, 159, 151, 152, 149, 148, 144, 142, Center, 141, 139, 162, 158, 155, 16, 177, 166, 156, 150, 167, 157, 168, 18, 175, 169, 170, 173, Galena, 174, 176, 204, 171, 172, 200, 203, 193, 189, 202, 201, 199, 192, 205, Wisconsin, 195, 194, 188, 198, 191, 190, Bluemound, 214, 197, I-94, 196, 187]

Nikiya Harris (Dem.), 6th Senate District

Born Milwaukee, February 22, 1975; single. Graduate Washington H.S. 1994; B.S. education and community studies UW-Milwaukee 2001; M.S. administrative leadership UW-Milwaukee 2007. Full-time legislator. Former nonprofit fundraising professional, precollege coordinator, preschool teacher. Member: Nia Imani Family (bd. mbr.); League of Conservation Voters. Former member: Kids Matter, Inc. (bd. mbr.); Milw. Urban League Young Professionals; Assn. of Fundraising Professionals. Milwaukee County Bd. of Supervisors 2010-12.

Elected to Senate 2012. Minority Caucus Sergeant at Arms 2013. Biennial committee assignments: **2013** — Education; Government Operations, Public Works and Telecommunications; Judiciary and Labor; Jt. Com. for Review of Administrative Rules.

Telephone: Office: (608) 266-2500.

E-mail: Sen.Harris@legis.wisconsin.gov

Voting address: Milwaukee 53218.

Mailing address: Office: Room 3 South, State Capitol, P.O. Box 7882, Madison 53707-7882.

| Representative | Representative | Representative |
| YOUNG | JOHNSON | GOYKE |

Leon D. Young (Dem.), 16th Assembly District

Born Los Angeles, July 4, 1967; single. Graduate Rufus King H.S.; attended UW-Milwaukee. Full-time legislator. Former police aide and police officer. Member: Democratic Party; Harambee Ombudsman Project; Milwaukee Police Association; League of Martin; House of Peace (Love Committee); NAACP; Urban League; Social Development Commission Minority Male Forum on Corrections; National Black Caucus of State Legislators' Task Force on African American Males; 100 Black Men; Milwaukee Metropolitan Fair Housing; Boy Scouts of America (Urban Emphasis Com.); Martin Luther King Community Center (Revitalization Com.).

Elected to Assembly since 1992. Biennial committee assignments: **2013** — Financial Institutions (also 2011); Housing and Real Estate; Insurance (also 2011); State and Federal Relations. **2011** — Housing (since 2005, chp. 2009); Tourism, Recreation and State Properties (also 2007). **2009** — State Affairs and Homeland Security (vice chp.); Education Reform. **2007** — State Affairs (since 1993, vice chp. 1993). **2005** — Highway Safety (since 1999); Tourism (also 2003 eff. 2/14/03). **2003** — Criminal Justice (since 1999); Ways and Means (eff. 5/13/03). **2001** — Council on Alcohol and Other Drug Abuse (also 1999). **1999** — Transportation. **1997** — Government Operations; Highways and Transportation (also 1995). **1995** — Urban Education (also 1993) **1993** — Children and Human Services; Small Business and Economic Development; Urban and Local Affairs; Speaker's Task Force on African American Males; Legis. Coun. Com. on Educational Communications Technology.

Telephone: Office: (608) 266-3786; (888) 534-0016 (toll free); District: (414) 374-7414.

E-mail: Rep.Young@legis.wisconsin.gov

Voting address: 2224 North 17th Street, Milwaukee 53205.

Mailing address: Office: Room 11 North, State Capitol, P.O. Box 8953, Madison 53708.

La Tonya Johnson (Dem.), 17th Assembly District

Born Somerville, Tenn., June 22, 1972; 1 child. Graduate Bay View H.S. 1990; B.S. criminal justice Tennessee State U. 1997; attended UW-Milwaukee 1990-92. Full-time legislator. Former family child care provider/owner 2002-12; insurance agent 2000-02; financial employment planner 1997-2000. Member: AFSCME Wisconsin Child Care Providers Together Local 502 (pres.) AFSCME District Council 48 (vice pres.); African American Chamber of Commerce; Emerge Wisconsin Class 2012; CBTU-Coalition of Black Trade Unionists.

Elected to Assembly 2012. Biennial committee assignments: **2013** — Children and Families; Consumer Protection; Criminal Justice; Urban Education.

Telephone: Office: (608) 266-5580; (888) 534-0017 (toll free); District: (414) 871-8306.

E-mail: Rep.Johnson@legis.wisconsin.gov

Voting address: Milwaukee 53210.

Mailing address: Office: Room 303 West, State Capitol, P.O. Box 8952, Madison 53708.

Evan Goyke (Dem.), 18th Assembly District

Born Neenah, November 24, 1982; single. Graduate Edgewood H.S. (Madison) 2001; B.A. political science St. John's U. (Minnesota) 2005; J.D. Marquette U. Law School 2009. Attorney. Former state public defender. Member: St. Michael's/St. Rose of Lima Catholic Church; American Federation of Teachers Local 4822; ACLU; NAACP; State Bar of Wisconsin; Milwaukee Young Lawyers Assn. (fmr. bd. mbr.); Historic Concordia Neighborhood Assn.; Eagle Scout, Boy Scouts of America.

Elected to Assembly 2012. Biennial committee assignments: **2013** — Agriculture; Criminal Justice; Judiciary; Veterans; Jt. Review Com. on Criminal Penalties.

Telephone: Office: (608) 266-0645; (888) 534-0018 (toll free).

E-mail: Rep.Goyke@legis.wisconsin.gov

Voting address: Milwaukee 53208.

Mailing address: Office: Room 412 North, State Capitol, P.O. Box 8952, Madison 53708.

7th SENATE DISTRICT

**Senator
LARSON**

See Milwaukee County Detail Map on
pp. 92 & 93

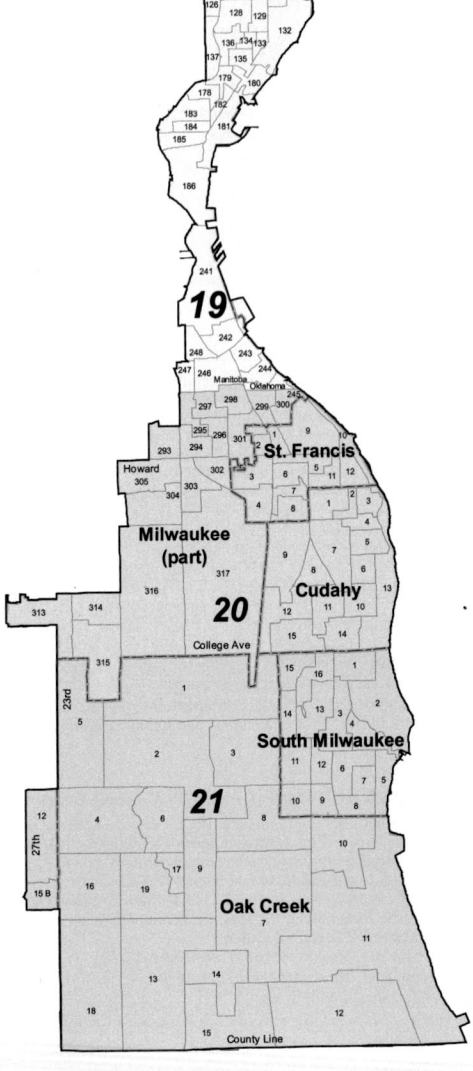

Chris Larson (Dem.), **7th Senate District**

Born Milwaukee County, November 12, 1980; married; 1 child. Graduate Thomas More H.S. 1999; degree in finance, UW-Milwaukee 2007. Full-time legislator. Former business manager. Member: Coalition to Save the Hoan Bridge (co-founder); League of Conservation Voters; Airport Area Economic Development Group; Bay View Neighborhood Assn.; Coalition for Advancing Transit (steering com.); Planned Parenthood Advocates of Wis.; Sierra Club; Humboldt Park Watch; South Side Business Club of Milw.; Bay View Historical Soc.; Arbor Day Foundation; Tri-Wisconsin; Badgerland Striders; Young Elected Officials; South Shore Park Watch; Bay View Lions Club; Lake Park Friends; Thomas More Alumni Club; MPTV Friends. Former member: WISPIRG (campus intern). Milwaukee Co. Bd. supervisor 2008-10.

Elected to Senate in 2010. Minority Leader 2013. Biennial committee assignments: **2013** — Senate Organization; Jt. Com. on Employment Relations; Jt. Com. on Legislative Organization. **2011** — Jt. Com. on Review of Admin. Rules (co-chp., eff. 7/24/12); Education; Education and Corrections; Environment, Natural Resources and Tourism; Insurance and Housing; Natural Resources and Environment; Jt. Com. on Audit (eff. 7/24/12); Jt. Com. on Finance (eff. 7/24/12); Jt. Com. on Information Policy and Technology; Gov.'s Comn. on Waste, Fraud and Abuse; Spec. Task Force on UW Restructuring and Operational Flexibilities.

Telephone: Office: (608) 266-7505; (800) 361-5487 (toll free).

E-mail: Sen.Larson@legis.wisconsin.gov

Voting address: 3261 South Herman Street, Milwaukee 53207.

Mailing address: Office: Room 206 South, State Capitol, P.O. Box 7882, Madison 53707-7882.

| Representative | Representative | Representative |
| RICHARDS | SINICKI | HONADEL |

Jon Richards (Dem.), 19th Assembly District

Born Waukesha, September 5, 1963; married; 1 child. Graduate Waukesha North H.S.; B.A. Lawrence U. 1986; J.D. UW-Madison (Law Review) 1994; attended Keio University (Tokyo). Attorney. Former English teacher in Japan and former volunteer with Mother Teresa, Calcutta, India. Former Community Special Prosecutor Kenosha Co. District Attorney's Office. Volunteer Big Brothers/Big Sisters. Member: New Brady Street Area Assn. (bd. mbr.); Bay View Historical Soc.; Amer. Coun. of Young Political Leaders; Natl. Caucus of Environmental Legislators; Bay View Lions Club; Historic Third Ward Assn.; Clean Wisconsin; League of Conservation Voters. Recipient: ABC for Health *Legislator of the Year*; St. Bar of Wis. *Scales of Justice Award*; Wis. Freedom of Information Council *Political Openness Advocate of the Year*; Environmental Decade *Clean 16 Award Winner and Conservation Honor Roll;* Planned Parenthood of Wis. *Voice for Choice Award Winner;* Wis. Family Planning and Reproductive Health Assn. *Legislator of the Year;* Wis. Farm Bureau *Friend of Agriculture*; Wis. Cancer Coun. *Cancer Control Champion;* AIDS Resource Center of Wis. *Leadership Award;* MTEA *Don Feilbach Friend of Public Education in Milwaukee Award;* Equality Wis. *Equal Rights Champion;* Shepherd Express's *Milwaukee's Best Legislator* 2010, 2007, 2006, 2005, 2001.

Elected to Assembly since 1998. Assistant Minority Leader 2003-2007, Biennial committee assignments: **2013** — Financial Institutions (also 2011, 2001-07, ranking min. mbr. 2003-07); Jt. Com. on Audit (also 2011); Jt. Com. on Finance (also 2011, eff. 2/13/12). **2011** — Health. **2009** — Health and Health Care Reform (chp.).

Telephone: Office: (608) 266-0650; (888) 534-0019 (toll free).
E-mail: Rep.Richards@legis.wisconsin.gov; Internet address: www.jonrichards.org
Voting address: Milwaukee 53202.
Mailing address: Office: Room 118 North, State Capitol, P.O. Box 8953, Madison 53708.

Christine Sinicki (Dem.), 20th Assembly District

Born Milwaukee, March 28, 1960; married; 2 children. Graduate Bay View H.S. Former small business manager. Member: Delegate-U.S. Pres. Electoral College, 2000; Amer. Coun. of Young Political Leaders, Delegate to Israel and Palestine, 2001; Milw. Com. on Domestic Violence and Sexual Assault; Wis. Civil Air Patrol, Major; Milw. City Coun. Parents and Teachers Assn.; Bay View Historical Soc.; Bay View Neighborhood Assn.; Fellow, Bowhay Institute, La Follette School, UW-Madison 2001; Founder, Conservatory of Lifelong Learning, Innovative School, Milw. Public School District; Flemming Fellow, Center for Policy Alternatives 2003. Awards: Wis. Environmental Decade *Clean 16 2000;* Wis. Ob/Gyn Physicians' *Legislator of the Year* 2000; Wis. Coalition Against Domestic Violence *DV Diva* 2003; Wis. Dept. of Veterans Affairs *Certificates of Commendation* 2006, 2005; Wis. League of Conservation Voters *Conservation Champion* 2011, 2009, 2007; Professional Firefighters of Wis. *Legislator of the Year* 2010; Wis. Grocers Assn. *Friend of Grocers* 2010; Cudahy Veterans' *Service Award* 2010; AMVETS *State Legislative Advocacy Award* 2011. Assembly Democratic Task Force on Working Families (chp.) 2003. State Assembly Milw. Caucus (chp. 2005, 2003). Dept. of Workforce Development State Minimum Wage Council (gov. appointee) 2005. Milw. School Board 1991-98.

Elected to Assembly 1998; reelected since 2000. Minority Caucus Secretary 2001. Biennial committee assignments: **2013** — Government Operations and State Licensing; Labor (chp. 2009, mbr. 2005, 2003); Urban Education; Veterans.

Telephone: Office: (608) 266-8588; (888) 534-0020 (toll free); District: (414) 481-7667.
E-mail: Rep.Sinicki@legis.wisconsin.gov
Voting address: Milwaukee 53207.
Mailing address: Office: Room 114 North, State Capitol, P.O. Box 8953, Madison 53708.

Mark R. Honadel (Rep.), 21st Assembly District

Born Milwaukee, March 29, 1956; married; 3 children. Graduate Oak Creek H.S. 1974; attended Milwaukee Area Technical College and Marquette U. Independent businessman. Former professional metal fabricator, welding instructor, industrial manager. Member: South Milwaukee Street Scaping; Grant Park Garden Club; South Milwaukee Chamber of Commerce; South Milwaukee Lions. Former member: American Welding Society, V.I.C.A. welding judge.

Elected to Assembly in July 2003 special election; reelected since 2004. Majority Caucus Chairperson 2007. Biennial committee assignments: **2013** — Energy and Utilities (chp. since 2011, mbr. since 2003 eff. 8/23/03); Insurance (also 2003 eff. 9/18/03); Urban and Local Affairs; Ways and Means; Workforce Development (also 2009); Jt. Survey Com. on Tax Exemptions. **2011** —Labor and Workforce Development; Transportation (also 2003 eff. 9/8/03). **2009** — Labor. **2007** — Labor and Industry (chp.); Jobs and the Economy (vice chp.); Assembly Organization; Housing; Rules. **2005** — Southeast Wisconsin Freeways (chp.); Small Business (vice chp.); Economic Development (also 2003 eff. 8/23/03). **2003** — Corrections and the Courts (eff. 8/28/03, res. 9/18/03).

Telephone: Office: (608) 266-0610; (888) 534-0021 (toll free); District: (414) 764-9921.
E-mail: Rep.Honadel@legis.wisconsin.gov
Voting address: South Milwaukee 53172.
Mailing address: Office: Room 113 West, State Capitol, P.O. Box 8952, Madison 53708.

8th SENATE DISTRICT

See Waukesha County Detail Map on pp. 94 & 95

See Milwaukee County Detail Map on pp. 92 & 93

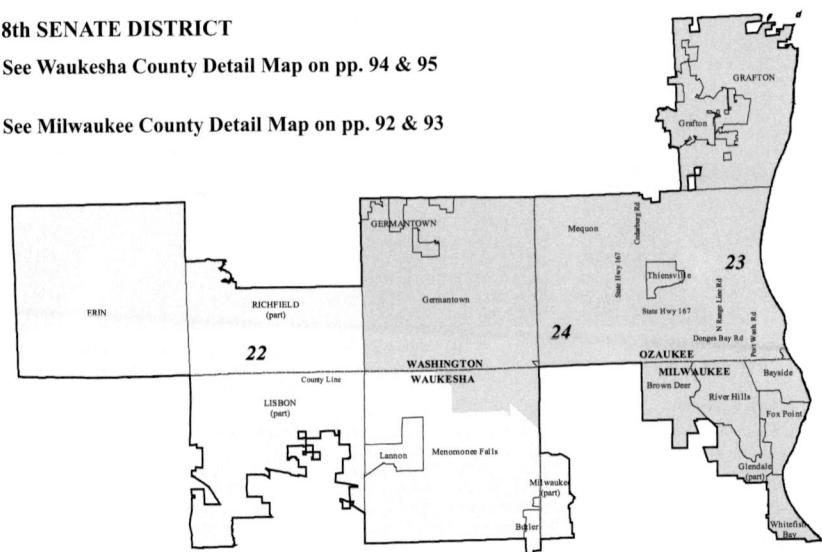

Senator
DARLING

Alberta Darling (Rep.), 8th Senate District

Born Hammond, IN, April 28, 1944; married; 2 children, 3 grandchildren. Graduate UW-Madison 1966; grad. work UW-Milwaukee 1972-74. Former teacher and marketing director. Member: North Shore Rotary; College Savings Program Bd. (EdVest); Junior League of Milwaukee (former pres.); Tempo Professional Women's Organization; Blood Center of Wis. Bd. Former member: Next Door Foundation; Public Policy Forum; Wis. Strategic Planning Council for Economic Development; Greater Milwaukee Com.; Goals for Greater Milwaukee 2000 Project (exec. com.); United Way Bd. (chp., allocations com.); Future Milwaukee (pres.); Milwaukee Forum; Children's Service Soc. of Wis. (bd. of dir.); American Red Cross of Wis. (exec. com., bd. of dir.); League of Women Voters; Today's Girls/Tomorrow's Women/Boys Girls Club (founder); NCSL Education Com. (chp.); YMCA (bd. mbr.). Recipient: *Shining Star of Education Reform* 2011; Hispanic Chamber of Commerce *Government Advocates Award;* Greater Milwaukee Committee *Leadership Award* 2011; Leukemia and Lymphoma Society *Legislative Leadership Award* 2011, Friend of Housing *Legislator of the Year* 2012, 2006-2011, 2002, Wisconsin Manufacturers and Commerce *Working for Wisconsin* 2012, 2002; American Conservative Union Foundation *Defender of Liberty Award* 2012; *Friend of Grocers* 2012, 2000; 2011 Coalition of Wisconsin Aging Groups *Tommy G. Thompson Award for Service;* Wis. Stem Cell Now *Courage Award;* Wis. Multiple Sclerosis (MS) *Advocate of the Year* 2006; 2006 Inductee into the National MS Hall of Fame; Wisconsin Manufacturers and Commerce *100% Pro-Business Legislator* 2006; Wis. Builders Assn. *Friend of Housing* 2008; Amer. Cancer Soc. *Legislative Champion* 2006; Fair Air Coalition *Friend of Education;* Metropolitan Milwaukee Assn. of Commerce *Champion of Commerce;* Wis. Head Start Directors Assn. *Award of Excellence;* National Assn. of Community Leadership *Leadership Award;* United Way *Gwen Jackson Leadership Award;* William Steiger *Award for Human Service;* St. Francis Children's Center *Children Service Award.*

Elected to Assembly in May 1990 special election; reelected November 1990; elected to Senate 1992; reelected since 1996. Biennial committee assignments: **2013** — Jt. Com. on Finance (co-chp., also 2011, 2003, mbr. since 1999, eff. 2/7/00); Workforce Development, Forestry, Mining and Revenue (vice chp.); Education (also 2011, 2005, 2001, 1999, 1997, 1993); Jt. Legis. Audit (also 2011, 2003); Jt. Com. on Employment Relations (also 2011, 2003); Jt. Legislative Council (since 2001); Milwaukee Child Welfare Partnership Council (since 1995); Wis. Center District Board of Dir. (also 2011, 2005, 2003); UW Hospitals and Clinics Authority Bd. (also 2003). **2011** —Economic Development, Veterans and Military Affairs. **2009** — Economic Development; Health, Health Insurance, Privacy, Property Tax Relief, and Revenue. **2007** — Economic Development, Job Creation, Family Prosperity and Housing. **2005** — Health, Children, Families, Aging and Long-Term Care. **1999** — Jt. Com. for Review of Administrative Rules (since 1993); Jt. Com. on Information Policy (also 1995); Judiciary and Consumer Affairs; Child Abuse and Neglect Prevention Bd. (since 1993). **1997** — Education and Financial Institutions (chp., eff. 4/21/98, also 1995); Business, Economic Development and Urban Affairs (eff. 4/21/98, also 1995); Judiciary (eff. 4/21/98, also 1995); Labor, Transportation and Financial Institutions; Education Comn. of the States (eff. 4/30/98, also 1995).

Telephone: Office: (608) 266-5830; E-mail: Sen.Darling@legis.wisconsin.gov

Voting address: River Hills 53217.

Mailing address: Office: Room 317 East, State Capitol, P.O. Box 7882, Madison 53707-7882.

Representative   **Representative**   **Representative**
PRIDEMORE   **J. OTT**   **KNODL**

Don Pridemore (Rep.), 22nd Assembly District

Born Milwaukee, October 20, 1946; married; 3 sons. Graduate Milwaukee Lutheran H.S. 1964; B.S.E.E. Marquette U. 1977. Full-time legislator. Former electronics research technician, electronics design engineer, senior electronics project engineer, holder of 4 U.S. patents, and amateur ABATE chili judge. Awarded the Vietnam Service Medal in 1968; served in U.S. Air Force 1965-69. Member: Hartford Lions; Hartford Area Taxpayers Assn. (com. mbr., fmr. pres.); Greater Hartford Optimists Club (charter bd. mbr., fmr. pres.); Land-O-Hills Baseball League (fmr. 14-yr. commissioner); Erin Baseball Club (fmr. 15-yr. pres.); Washington and Waukesha Co. Republican Party; American Legion; VFW; NRA; Senior Friends (Hartford). Former member: IEEE; Wis. Citizens for Legal Reform (st. dir.); BSA Troop 741 (former ASM). Erin Park Bd. 1995-2010.

Elected to Assembly 2004; reelected since 2006. Biennial committee assignments: **2013** — Urban Education (chp.); Campaigns and Elections (vice chp.); Education (also 2011); Veterans; Workforce Development (also 2007, 2005). **2011** — Children and Families (chp., also mbr. 2009); Colleges and Universities; Election and Campaign Reform (also 2009). **2009** — Education Reform (chp. 2007, mbr. 2005). **2007** — Children and Family Law (vice chp.); Judiciary and Ethics; Urban and Local Affairs (vice chp. 2005); Ways and Means (also 2005). **2005** — Budget Review.

Telephone: Office. (608) 267-2367; (888) 534-0099 (toll free); Fax: (608) 282-3699; District: (262) 670-0638.

E-mail: Rep.Pridemore@legis.wisconsin.gov

Voting address: Hartford 53027.

Mailing address: Office: Room 318 North, State Capitol, P.O. Box 8953, Madison 53708.

Jim Ott (Rep.), 23rd Assembly District

Born Milwaukee, June 5, 1947; married; 2 sons, 1 grandchild. Graduate Milwaukee Washington H.S. 1965; B.S. UW-Milwaukee 1970; M.S. UW-Milwaukee 1975; J.D. Marquette U. 2000. Full-time legislator. Former broadcast meteorologist and instructor at UW-Parkside. Served in U.S. Army, 1970-73; Vietnam veteran. Member: State Bar of Wisconsin; American Meteorological Society; Mequon/Thiensville Noon Rotary; Mequon/Thiensville Chamber of Commerce; American Legion; Ozaukee County Republican Party; North Shore Branch Milwaukee Co. Republican Party; Lumen Christi Catholic Church (past parish council pres.). Recipient: National Weather Service *Public Service Award* 2006; Archbishops Vatican II *Service Award* 1999; Vietnam Campaign Medal and Meritorious Unit Citation; Emerging Political Leaders Program; BILLD Leadership Fellow.

Elected to Assembly 2006; reelected since 2008. Biennial committee assignments: **2013** — Judiciary (chp.); Constitution and Ethics; Criminal Justice; Urban and Local Affairs; Veterans; Judicial Council (also 2011); Law Revision Com. (co-chp., also 2011). **2011** — Judiciary and Ethics (chp.); Jt. Com. for Review of Admin. Rules (co-chp.); Natural Resources (through 5/23/11, also 2009, vice chp. 2007). **2009** — Education Reform (also 2007); Fish and Wildlife. **2007** — Elections and Constitutional Law; Workforce Development.

Telephone: Office: (608) 266-0486; (888) 534-0023 (toll free); District: (262) 240-0808.

E-mail: Rep.OttJ@legis.wisconsin.gov

Voting address: Mequon 53092.

Mailing address: Office: Room 317 North, State Capitol, P.O. Box 8953, Madison 53708-8953.

Dan Knodl (Rep.), 24th Assembly District

Born Milwaukee, December 14, 1958; 4 children. Graduate Menomonee Falls East H.S. 1977; attended UW-Madison. Resort owner. Member: Washington Co. Convention and Visitors Bureau; Ozaukee/Washington Land Trust; Pike Lake Sportsmans Club. Pike Lake Protection District 2000-present (secy.). Washington County Board 2006-08.

Elected to Assembly 2008; reelected since 2010. Assistant Majority Leader 2011. Biennial committee assignments: **2013** — Labor (chp., mbr. 2009); Jobs, Economy and Mining (vice chp.); Government Operations and State Licensing; State Affairs; Urban Education; Workforce Development. **2011** — Aging and Long-Term Care (chp.); Jt. Survey Com. on Tax Exemptions (co-chp.); Assembly Organization; Colleges and Universities; Rules; Ways and Means (also 2009); Jt. Com. on Legislative Organization. **2009** — State Affairs and Homeland Security.

Telephone: Office: (608) 266-3796; (888) 529-0024 (toll free); District: (262) 502-0118.

Voting address: N101 W14475 Ridgefield Court, Germantown 53022.

Mailing address: Office: Room 218 North, State Capitol, P.O. Box 8952, Madison 53708.

9th SENATE DISTRICT

**Senator
LEIBHAM**

Detail Map: City of Sheboygan

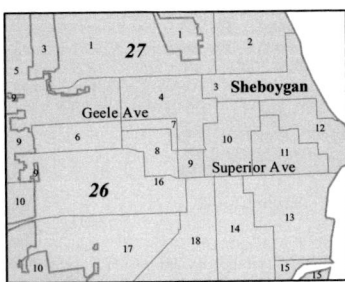

Joseph K. Leibham (Rep.), 9th Senate District

Born Sheboygan, June 6, 1969; married; 3 children. Graduate Sheboygan Area Lutheran H.S.; B.A. UW-Madison 1991; attended UW-La Crosse 1987-89 and Ealing College (London, England) 1990. Former food service industry account executive and manager/membership development, Sheboygan County Chamber of Commerce. Member: Sheboygan/Manitowoc Rebuilding Together; Friends of Sheboygan Senior Center; Citizen's Police Academy (graduate); Boy Scouts of America (Eagle Scout); Elder, Usher at Trinity Lutheran Church. Sheboygan City Council 1993-2000 (pres. 1995-96).

Elected to Assembly 1998-2000; elected to Senate 2002; reelected since 2006. President Pro Tempore 2013, 2011; Minority Caucus Chairperson 2009; Assistant Minority Leader 2007; Majority Caucus Vice Chairperson 2003. Biennial Senate committee assignments: **2013** — Elections and Urban Affairs (vice chp.); Transportation, Public Safety, and Veterans and Military Affairs (vice chp.); Jt. Com. for Review of Administrative Rules (vice chp., also 2011, co-chp. 2003, mbr. 2007); Economic Development and Local Government; Jt. Com. on Finance (also 2011, 2005); Jt. Legis. Council. **2011** — Transportation and Elections (vice chp.). **2009** — Economic Development; Transportation, Tourism, Forestry, and Natural Resources; Veterans and Military Affairs, Biotechnology and Financial Institutions (also 2007); Jt. Com. on Information Policy and Technology. **2007** — Ethics Reform and Government Operations; Transportation, Tourism and Insurance; Jt. Com. on Legis. Org. **2005** — Jt. Com. for Review of Criminal Penalties (co-chp.); Energy, Utilities and Information Technologies (through 6/13/05); Higher Education and Tourism (eff. 6/13/05). **2003** — Transportation and Information Infrastructure (chp.); Energy and Utilities. Assembly committee assignments: **2001** — Jt. Legis. Audit (co-chp.); Census and Redistricting (vice chp., also 1999); Tax and Spending Limitations (vice chp.); Energy and Utilities; State and Local Finance; Transportation (also 1999). **1999** — Utilities (vice chp.); Small Business and Economic Development; State Affairs.

Telephone: Office: (608) 266-2056; (888) 295-8750 (toll free); District: (920) 457-7367.

E-mail: Sen.Leibham@legis.wisconsin.gov

Internet address: leibhamsenate.com

Voting address: Sheboygan 53083.

Mailing address: Office: Room 15 South, State Capitol, P.O. Box 7882, Madison 53707-7882

Representative   **Representative**   **Representative**
TITTL   **ENDSLEY**   **KESTELL**

Paul Tittl (Rep.), 25th Assembly District

Born Delavan, November 23, 1961; married; 2 children, 2 grandchildren. Graduate Lincoln High (Manitowoc) 1980. Owner, Vacuum and Sewing Center. Member: National Rifle Association; Eagles Manitowoc; Manitowoc Co. Home Builders Association. Former member: Economic Development Authority; Wastewater Treatment Facility Bd.; Manitowoc Crime Prevention Com.; Community Development Authority; Safety Traffic and Parking Commission; Wisconsin Utility Tax Assn., 2009-13; WCA Taxation and Finance Steering Com., 2010-13; WCA Judicial and Public Safety Steering Com., 2010-13. Manitowoc City Council 2004-08 (pres. 2006-07); Manitowoc Co. Bd. of Supervisors 2006-13 (chm. 2010-12).

Elected to Assembly 2012. Biennial committee assignments: **2013** — Consumer Protection (vice chp.); Family Law; Small Business Development; State and Federal Relations; Veterans.

Telephone: Office: (608) 266-0315; (888) 529-0025 (toll free); District: (920) 682-6203 (home).

E-mail: Rep.Tittl@legis.wisconsin.gov

Voting address: Manitowoc 54220.

Mailing address: Office: Room 21 North, State Capitol, P.O. Box 8953, Madison 53708.

Mike Endsley (Rep.), 26th Assembly District

Born Sheboygan, March 4, 1962; 2 children. Graduate Sheboygan Falls H.S. 1980; B.S. UW-Platteville 1984. Full-time legislator. Former sales manager. Member: St. Paul Lutheran Church; Wis. Right to Life; Sheboygan Co. Right to Life; Pro Life Wis.; Sheboygan Co. Republican Party; Sheboygan Co. Chamber of Commerce; Sheboygan Senior Activity Center (Advisory Bd.).

Elected to Assembly 2010; reelected 2012. Biennial committee assignments: **2013** — Aging and Long Term Care (chp.); Small Business Development (vice chp.); Children and Families; Tourism; Transportation (also 2011); Veterans. **2011** — Jobs, Economy and Small Business (vice chp.); Ways and Means.

Telephone: Office: (608) 266-0656; (888) 529-0026 (toll free).

E-mail: Rep.Endsley@legis.wisconsin.gov

Voting address: 1829 North 27th Place, Sheboygan 53081.

Mailing address: Office: Room 219 North, State Capitol, P.O. Box 8952, Madison 53708.

Steve Kestell (Rep.), 27th Assembly District

Born Town of Lyndon, Sheboygan Co., June 15, 1955; married; 3 adult children and grandchildren. Graduate Plymouth H.S. Bowhay Institute of Legislative Leadership 2000. Full-time legislator. Former retail manager and regional sales manager. Member: Sheboygan Co. Republican Party. Former member: Family Resource Center of Sheboygan County (bd. mbr.); Gov.'s Council on Highway Safety; Howards Grove Jaycees; ADA Volunteer Firefighters; 4-H project leader; Junior Achievement instructor. Howards Grove School Bd. 1981-84, 1986-98 (pres. 1995-98).

Elected to Assembly since 1998. Biennial committee assignments: **2013** — Education (chp., also 2011, vice chp. 2005, mbr. 1999-2005); Family Law (vice chp., also 2005, mbr. 2003, 2001); State and Local Finance; Urban Education; Ways and Means; Wis. Historical Soc. Bd. of Curators (since 2007). **2011** — Children and Families; Criminal Justice and the Courts; Insurance. **2009** — Children and Families (chp. 2001-2005, mbr. 1999); Corrections and the Courts; Workforce Development; Wis. Aerospace Auth. (also 2007). **2007** — Jt. Com. on Finance; Legis. Coun. Spec. Com. on Strengthening Wis. Families (chp.). **2005** — Rural Development (also 2003); Legis. Coun. Spec. Com. on Adoption and Termination of Parental Rights; Child Abuse and Neglect Prevention Bd. (since 4/7/2000). **2003** — Agriculture (since 1999). **2001** — Small Business and Consumer Affairs; Legis. Coun. Com. on Relative Caregivers (co-chp.). **1999** — Government Operations (vice chp.); Transportation; Legis. Coun. Spec. Com. on Navigable Waters Recodification.

Telephone: Office: (608) 266-8530; (888) 529-0027 (toll free); District: (920) 565-2044.

E-mail: Rep.Kestell@legis.wisconsin.gov

Voting address: Elkhart Lake 53020.

Mailing address: Office: 212 North, State Capitol, P.O. Box 8952, Madison 53708.

10th SENATE DISTRICT

Senator
HARSDORF

Detail Map: Town of Richmond

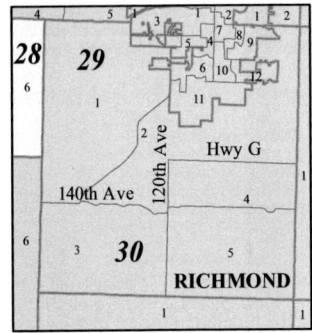

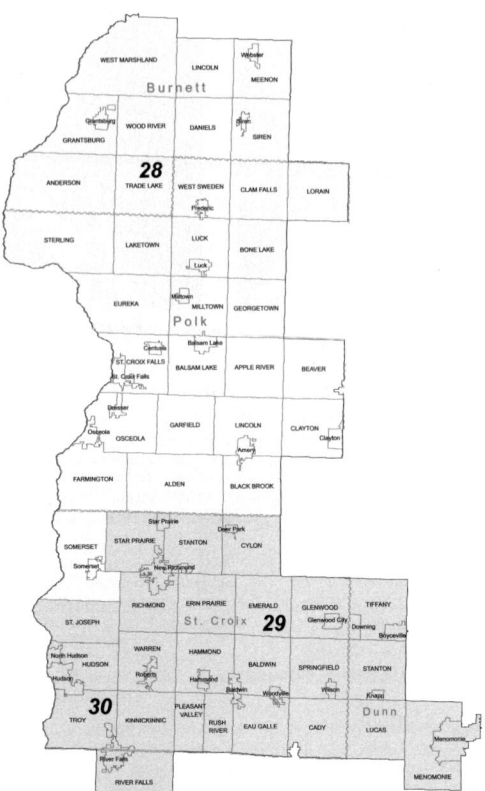

Sheila E. Harsdorf (Rep.), 10th Senate District

Born St. Paul, MN, July 25, 1956; 1 son. Graduate River Falls H.S.; B.S. in animal science, U. of Minnesota 1978; Wis. Rural Leadership Program, grad. of 1st class (1986). Member: Pierce Co. Republican Party; Pierce Co. Farm Bureau (former dir. and treas.); Luther Memorial Church. Former member: Wis. State FFA Sponsors Bd. (chp.); Wis. Conservation Corps Bd. (secy.); Kinnickinnic River Land Trust Bd.; Pierce Co. Dairy Promotion Com. (past chm.); Wis. State ASCS Com.; Adv. Council on Small Business, Agriculture, Labor for Federal Reserve Bank of Minneapolis.

Elected to Assembly 1988-96; elected to Senate 2000; reelected since 2004. Majority Caucus Vice Chairperson 2013, 2011; Minority Caucus Vice Chairperson 2009; Majority Caucus Sergeant at Arms 2005. Biennial Senate committee assignments: **2013** — Universities and Technical Colleges (chp.); Jt. Com. on Information Policy and Technology (co-chp., also 2011, mbr. 2001); Agriculture, Small Business and Tourism; Energy, Consumer Protection and Government Reform; Jt. Com. on Finance (also 2011, 2003); Midwestern Higher Education Comn. (vice chp., also 2011, mbr. 2003-07). **2011** — State and Federal Relations and Information Technology (chp.); Agriculture, Forestry, and Higher Education (vice chp.). **2009** — Agriculture and Higher Education (also 2007); Commerce, Utilities, Energy, and Rail; Jt. Legislative Council (also 2007, 2003); Mississippi River Parkway Commission (since 2001); World Dairy Center Authority (since 2003). **2007** — Commerce, Utilities and Rail. **2005** — Higher Education and Tourism (chp., also 2003); Jt. Survey Com. on Tax Exemptions (co-chp., mbr. 2003); Education (also 2001); Housing and Financial Institutions. **2003** — Law Revision Com. (also 2001). **2001** — 2001-2003 Biennial Budget; Labor and Agriculture; Environmental Education Bd.; Ad. Bd. for Midwest Center for Agricultural Research, Education, and Disease and Injury Prevention; Jt. Legis. Council Special Com. on the Public Health System's Response to Terrorism and Public Health Emergencies. Assembly committee assignments: **1997** — Jt. Com. on Finance (also 1995). **1993** — Agriculture, Forestry and Rural Affairs; Colleges and Universities (ranking minority mbr. since 1991); Natural Resources (since 1989); Veterans and Military Affairs (eff. 4/26/93); Educational Communications Bd. (since 1989). **1991** — Agriculture, Aquaculture and Forestry; State Affairs (also 1989). **1989** — Agriculture and its Subcom. on Aquaculture.

Telephone: Office: (608) 266-7745; (800) 862-1092 (toll free); Fax: (608) 267-0369.

E-mail: Sen.Harsdorf@legis.wisconsin.gov

Voting address: Town of River Falls 54022.

Mailing address: Office: Room 18 South, P.O. Box 7882, Madison 53707-7882.

Representative
SEVERSON

Representative
MURTHA

Representative
KNUDSON

Erik Severson (Rep.), 28th Assembly District

Born Duluth, MN, February 3, 1974; married; 2 children. Graduate Esko H.S. 1992; B.S. U. of Minnesota-Duluth 1993; M.D. Mayo Medical School 2002; medical internship U. of North Dakota 2002-03; family medicine residency U. of Minnesota 2003-05. Physician. Member: NRA.

Elected to Assembly 2010; reelected 2012. Biennial committee assignments: **2013** — Health (chp., vice chp. 2011); Criminal Justice; Education; Energy and Utilities (also 2011); Workforce Development; Jt. Survey Com. on Retirement Systems. **2011** — Natural Resources.

Telephone: Office: (608) 267-2365; (888) 529-0028 (toll free).

E-mail: Rep.Severson@legis.wisconsin.gov

Voting address: Star Prairie 54026.

Mailing address: Office: Room 221 North, State Capitol, P.O. Box 8953, Madison 53708.

John Murtha (Rep.), 29th Assembly District

Born Baldwin, August 8, 1951; married; 4 children. Graduate St. Croix Central H.S. (Hammond) 1969; Chippewa Valley Tech. (Eau Claire) wood tech. 1970. Self employed. Member: NRA; AOPA. Town of Eau Galle Board (St. Croix Co.) supervisor 1999-2003, chairman 2003-09.

Elected to Assembly 2006; reelected since 2008. Majority Caucus Vice Chairperson 2013, 2011. Biennial committee assignments: **2013** — Housing and Real Estate (chp.); Agriculture (since 2007); International Trade and Commerce; Public Safety and Homeland Security; Rules (also 2011); Rural Affairs. **2011** — Housing (chp., mbr. 2009); Forestry; Rural Economic Development and Rural Affairs. **2009** — Rural Economic Development (also 2007). **2007** — Small Business (vice chp.); Labor and Industry.

Telephone: Office: (608) 266-7683; (888) 529-0029 (toll free).

E-mail: Rep.Murtha@legis.wisconsin.gov

Voting address: Baldwin 54002.

Mailing address: Office: Room 309 North, State Capitol, P.O. Box 8953, Madison 53708.

Dean Knudson (Rep.), 30th Assembly District

Born Mayville, ND, April 29, 1961; married; 2 children. Graduate May-Port H.S. (Mayville, ND) 1979; attended Mayville St. College, North Dakota St. U.; D.V.M. Iowa St. U. 1986. Veterinarian. Member: Hudson Daybreak Rotary (fmr. pres.); Trinity Lutheran Church; Hudson Area Chamber of Commerce (fmr. pres.); Am. Veterinary Medical Assn.; Wisconsin Veterinary Medical Assn.; Minnesota Veterinary Medical Assn.; Republican Party of Wis.; Republican Party of St. Croix Co. (fmr. chm.); Republican Party of Pierce Co.; Hudson SAFE Senior Graduation Party (fmr. chm.); Iowa St. U. Alumni Assn.; Omega Tau Sigma. Mayor of Hudson 2008-10; Alderperson, Hudson 1996-2002; Hudson Library Bd. 1996-2002; Hudson Plan Commission 2008-10; St. Croix Business Park Bd. 2010.

Elected to Assembly 2010; reelected 2012. Biennial committee assignments: **2013** — Colleges and Universities (vice chp. 2011); Jt. Com. on Finance. **2011** — Education; Urban and Local Affairs.

Telephone: Office: (608) 266-1526; (888) 529-0030 (toll free); District: (715) 690-9225.

E-mail: Rep.Knudson@legis.wisconsin.gov

Voting address: 1753 Laurel Avenue, Hudson 54016.

Mailing address: Office: Room 320 East, State Capitol, P.O. Box 8952, Madison 53708.

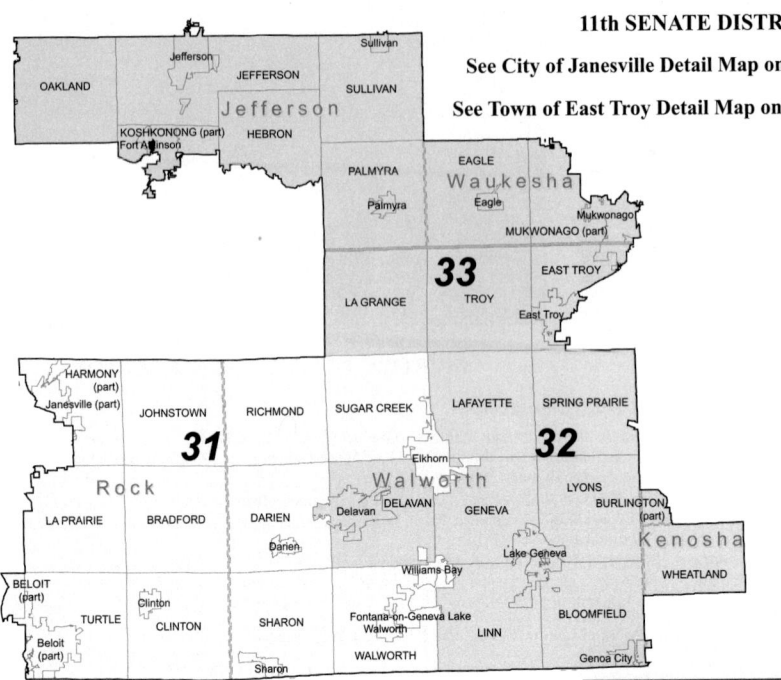

11th SENATE DISTRICT

See City of Janesville Detail Map on p. 48

See Town of East Troy Detail Map on p. 74

See Waukesha County Detail
Map on pp. 94 & 95

**Senator
KEDZIE**

Neal J. Kedzie (Rep.), 11th Senate District

Born Waukesha, January 27, 1956; married; 3 children. Graduate Oak Creek H.S.; B.S. UW-Whitewater 1978; graduate school UW-Whitewater. Full-time legislator. Member: Civil Air Patrol (rank of major); Walworth, Waukesha, and Jefferson Co. Republican Parties; Walworth Co. Farm Bureau; Walworth Co. Historical Society; Walworth Co. L.E.P.C.; UW-Whitewater Communications Advisory Committee (2004-present); Black Point Historic Preserve Bd. (2011-present). Former member: Lauderdale-La Grange Volunteer Fire Dept. (secy.). La Grange Town Board 1987-98 (chm. 1988-98); La Grange Planning and Zoning Comn. (chm.).

Elected to Assembly 1996-2000; elected to Senate 2002; reelected since 2006. Assistant Senate Majority Leader 2005. Biennial Senate committee assignments: **2013** — Natural Resources (chp.); Energy, Consumer Protection and Government Reform (vice chp.); Jt. Review Com. on Criminal Penalties (co-chp.); Government Operations, Public Works, and Telecommunications; Leg. Coun. Spec. Com. on Legal Interventions for Persons with Alzheimer's Disease and Related Dementias; State of Wis. Building Comn.; Sporting Heritage Council; Wis. Environmental Education Bd. **2011** — Natural Resources and Environment (chp.); Mining Jobs, Select Com. on (chp., eff. 9/30/11); Energy, Biotechnology and Consumer Protection (vice chp., eff. 8/26/11); Judiciary, Utilities, Commerce, and Government Operations (vice chp.); Jt. Survey Com. on Retirement Systems (co-chp., eff. 8/26/11); Agriculture, Forestry, and Higher Education; Leg. Coun. Spec. Com. on Review of the Managed Forest Land Program. **2009** — Children and Families and Workforce Development; Commerce, Utilities, Energy, and Rail; Environment; Transportation, Tourism, Forestry, and Natural Resources; Wis. Environmental Education Bd. (since 1999). **2007** — Commerce, Utilities and Rail; Environment and Natural Resources (chp. 2003); Small Business, Emergency Preparedness, Workforce Development, Technical Colleges and Consumer Protection; Leg. Council Spec. Com. on Great Lakes Water Resources Compact (chp.). **2005** — Natural Resources and Transportation (chp.); Agriculture and Insurance; Campaign Finance Reform and Ethics; Energy, Utilities and Information Technology (eff. 6/13/05); Higher Education and Tourism (through 6/13/05); Organization; Jt. Com. on Legislative Organization; Gov.'s Council on Highway Safety (eff. 1/23/06); Wis. Rustic Roads Bd. **2003** — Environment and Natural Resources (chp.); Agriculture, Financial Institutions and Insurance; Labor, Small Business Development and Consumer Affairs; Transportation and Information Infrastructure. Assembly committee assignments: **2001** — Environment (chp., also 1999, mbr. 1997); Aging and Long-Term Care; Financial Institutions (since 1997); Natural Resources (also 1999); Jt. Survey Com. on Tax Exemptions. **1999** — Conservation and Land Use (vice chp.); Housing (vice chp. 1997); Urban and Local Affairs. **1997** — Rural Affairs (vice chp.); State-Federal Relations; Legis. Coun. Com. on Utility Public Benefit Programs.

Telephone: Office: (608) 266-2635; (800) 578-1457 (toll free); District: (262) 742-2025.

E-mail: Sen.Kedzie@legis.wisconsin.gov

Voting address: Elkhorn 53121.

Mailing address: Office: Room 313 South, State Capitol, P.O. Box 7882, Madison 53707-7882.

Representative
LOUDENBECK

Representative
AUGUST

Representative
NASS

Amy Loudenbeck (Rep.), 31st Assembly District

Born Midland, MI, September 29, 1969; married. Graduate Hinsdale Central H.S. (Hinsdale, IL) 1987; B.A. political science, international relations UW-Madison 1991; studied abroad in Kingston, Jamaica. Former chamber of commerce executive, compliance manager, environmental/engineering services project manager. Member: State Line World Trade Assn. (pres.); Clinton Community Historical Soc.; Clinton Fencehoppers Snowmobile Club; International Miniature Zebu Cattle Assn.; Wis. DNR Green Tier Advisory Bd.; Friends of Clinton Public Library. Former member: Town of Linn Fire Dept. Town of Clinton supervisor 2010-12.

Elected to Assembly 2010; reelected 2012. Biennial committee assignments: **2013** — Workforce Development (chp.); Children and Families (vice chp.); Environment and Forestry; International Trade and Commerce; State and Federal Relations; Jt. Legis. Council; State Capitol and Executive Residence Bd. (also 2011); Wis. Housing and Economic Development Authority. **2011** — Tourism, Recreation and State Properties (vice chp.); Jobs, Economy and Small Business; Public Health and Public Safety.

Telephone: Office: (608) 266-9967; District: (262) 296-1030.
E-mail: Rep.Loudenbeck@legis.wisconsin.gov
Voting address: 10737 South State Road 140, Clinton 53525.
Mailing address: Office: Room 209 North, State Capitol, P.O. Box 8952, Madison 53708.

Tyler August (Rep.), 32nd Assembly District

Born Wisconsin, January 26, 1983; single. Graduate Big Foot H.S. 2001; attended UW-Eau Claire and UW-Madison; completed 2012 Emerging Leader Program at Univ. of Virginia Darden School of Business. Full-time legislator. Former chief of staff to Rep. Thomas Lothian. Member: Republican Party of Wis. (fmr. bd. mbr.); Republican Party of 1st Congressional Dist. (fmr. chm.); Republican Party of Walworth Co. (fmr. chm, vice-chm.); National Rifle Association. Recipient: American Conservative Union *Defender of Liberty* 2012; GOPAC *Emerging Leader* 2012.

Elected to Assembly 2010; reelected 2012. Biennial committee assignments: **2013** — Government Operations and State Licensing (chp.); Jt. Survey Com. on Tax Exemptions (co-chp.); Labor (vice chp.); Health; Judiciary; State Affairs; Jt. Com. for Review of Admin. Rules. **2011** — Consumer Protection and Personal Privacy (vice chp.); Homeland Security and State Affairs; Insurance.

Telephone: Office: (608) 266-1190.
E-mail: Rep.August@legis.wisconsin.gov
Voting address: Lake Geneva 53147.
Mailing address: Office: Room 119 West, State Capitol, P.O. Box 8952, Madison 53708.

Stephen L. Nass (Rep.), 33rd Assembly District

Born Whitewater, October 7, 1952. Graduate Whitewater H.S.; B.S. UW-Whitewater 1978; M.S. Ed. in school business management UW-Whitewater 1990. Former payroll benefits analyst and information analyst/negotiator. Member of Wis. Air National Guard (retired, 33 years of service), served in Operations Desert Shield and Desert Storm. Member: American Legion; Veterans of Foreign Wars; Wis. State Assn. of Parliamentarians; Mukwonago Business Breakfast Club; Jefferson Co. Agribusiness Club. Whitewater City Council 1977-81; UW-Whitewater Bd. of Visitors 1979-89.

Elected to Assembly since 1990. Biennial committee assignments: **2013** — Colleges and Universities (chp., also 2011, 2007, mbr. since 2003); Education (vice chp. 1995-2001, mbr. since 1991); Government Operations and State Licensing; Housing and Real Estate; Labor; State and Local Finance. **2011** — Ways and Means (vice chp., also 2005, mbr. 2009, 2003); Labor and Workforce Development (also 2001). **2009** — Labor (chp. 2005, 2003). **2007** — Education Reform (vice chp., also 2003, chp. 2001, mbr. since 1999); Labor and Industry. **2005** — Property Rights and Land Management (vice chp.). **2001** — Personal Privacy; Education Commission of the States (also 1999). **1999** — Government Operations; Labor and Employment (vice chp. 1997, mbr. 1995); Jt. Com. on Audit. **1997** — Mandates (chp.); Criminal Justice and Corrections; Rural Affairs; Legis. Coun. Com. on Services for Visually Handicapped Students.

Telephone: Office: (608) 266-5715; (888) 529-0033 (toll free); District: (262) 495-3424.
E-mail: Rep.Nass@legis.wisconsin.gov
Voting address: Whitewater 53190.
Mailing address: Office: Room 12 West, State Capitol, P.O. Box 8953, Madison 53708.

12th SENATE DISTRICT

Senator
TIFFANY

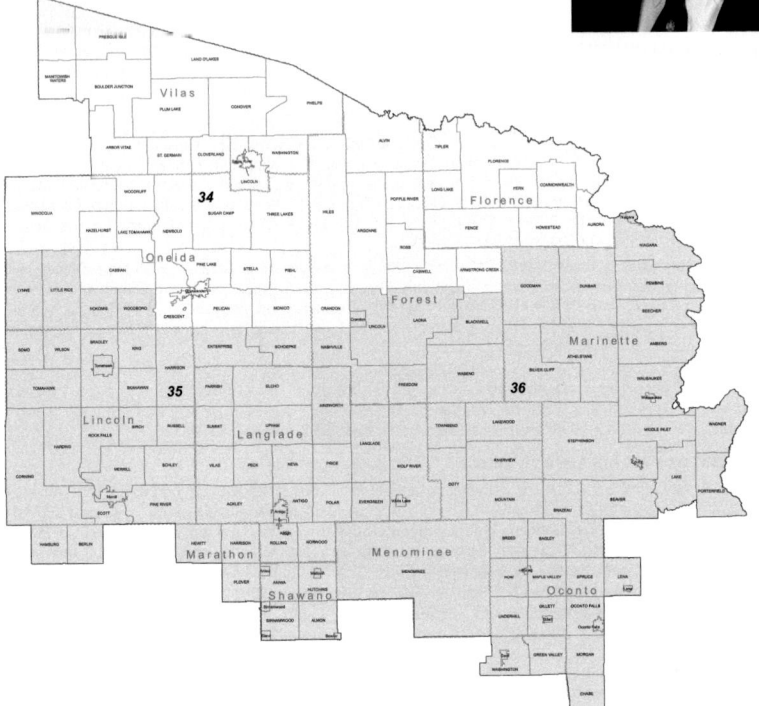

Tom Tiffany (Rep.), 12th Senate District

Born Wabasha, MN, December 30, 1957; married; 3 children. Graduate Elmwood H.S. 1976; B.S. Agricultural economics UW-River Falls 1980. Owner of excursion boat company and dam tender. Member: Minocqua Chamber of Commerce; Tomahawk Chamber of Commerce; Rhinelander Chamber of Commerce; National Rifle Association; Tavern League of Wisconsin; Ruffed Grouse Society. Former member: Oneida Co. Economic Development Corporation; Wisconsin Restaurant Assn. (bd. of dir.). Town supervisor 2009-13.

Elected to Assembly 2010; elected to Senate 2012. Biennial Senate committee assignments: **2013** — Workforce Development, Forestry, Mining, and Revenue (chp.); Agriculture, Small Business, and Tourism (vice chp.); Natural Resources; Jt. Com. for Review of Administrative Rules; Jt. Survey Com. on Tax Exemptions. Assembly committee assignments: **2011** — Forestry (vice chp.); Natural Resources; Tourism, Recreation and State Properties.

Telephone: Office: (608) 266-2509.

E-mail: Sen.Tiffany@legis.wisconsin.gov

Voting address: Town of Little Rice, Oneida County.

Mailing address: Office: Room 409 South, State Capitol, P.O. Box 7882, Madison 53708-7882.

Representative
SWEARINGEN

Representative
CZAJA

Representative
MURSAU

Rob Swearingen (Rep.), 34th Assembly District

Born Oneida Co., July 23, 1963; married; 2 children. Graduate Rhinelander H.S. 1981. Restaurant owner/operator. Member: Tavern League of Wisconsin (former pres., zone vice pres., district director); American Beverage Licensees (former member, bd. of dir.); Oneida Co. Tavern League (former pres., vice pres.); Rhinelander Chamber of Commerce; Oneida County Republican Party.

Elected to Assembly 2012. Biennial committee assignments: **2013** — State Affairs (vice chp.); Housing and Real Estate; Natural Resources and Sporting Heritage; Public Safety and Homeland Security; Small Business Development; Tourism.

Telephone: Office: (608) 266-7141; (888) 534-0034 (toll free); District: (715) 369-5493.

E-mail: Rep.Swearingen@legis.wisconsin.gov

Voting address: 4485 Oakview Lane, Rhinelander 54501.

Mailing address: Office: Room 19 North, State Capitol, P.O. Box 8953, Madison 53708.

Mary J. Czaja (Rep.), 35th Assembly District

Born Tomahawk, September 25, 1963; 4 children. Graduate Tomahawk H.S. 1981; B.S. in finance and economics UW-River Falls 1986. Insurance agency owner. Member: Tomahawk Main St. Inc. (fmr. pres.); Tomahawk Regional Chamber of Commerce; Tomahawk Child Care (fmr. pres.); National Alliance for Insurance Education and Research (bd. mbr.). Former member: Professional Insurance Agents of Wis. (secy., treas., vice pres., pres., national dir.).

Elected to Assembly 2012. Biennial committee assignments: **2013** — Aging and Long Term Care (vice chp.); Environment and Forestry; Insurance; Small Business Development; Tourism.

Telephone: Office: (608) 266-7694; (888) 534-0035 (toll free).

E-mail: Rep.Czaja@legis.wisconsin.gov

Voting address: Irma 54442.

Mailing address: Office: Room 15 West, State Capitol, P.O. Box 8952, Madison 53708; District: P.O. Box 321, Tomahawk 54487.

Jeffrey L. Mursau (Rep.), 36th Assembly District

Born Oconto Falls, June 12, 1954; married; 4 sons, 8 grandchildren. Graduate Coleman H.S. 1972; attended UW-Oshkosh. Small business owner; electrical contractor. Member: Crivitz Ski Cats waterski team (advisor, former pres.); Crivitz Lions Club; Crivitz, WI – Crivitz, Germany Sister City Organization (fmr. dir.); Wings over Wisconsin; St. Mary's Catholic Church; 4th Degree Knights of Columbus; Friends of Gov. Thompson State Park; Master Loggers Certifying Bd. Recipient: Crivitz Business Association *Citizen of the Year* 1994. Crivitz Village President 1991-2004.

Elected to Assembly 2004; reelected since 2006. Biennial committee assignments: **2013** — Environment and Forestry (chp.); Agriculture (also 2011, 2007); Natural Resources and Sporting Heritage; Rural Affairs; State and Federal Relations; Spec. Com. on State-Tribal Relations (chp., also 2011, 2007, vice chp. 2009); Gov. Council on Forestry; Wis. Environmental Education Bd. **2011** — Forestry (chp., vice chp. 2007, mbr. since 2005); Natural Resources (chp., mbr. since 2005). **2009** — Workforce Development. **2007** — Rural Economic Development (chp.); Consumer Protection and Personal Privacy. **2005** — Tourism (vice chp.); Rural Development; Small Business.

Telephone: Office: (608) 266-3780; (888) 534-0036 (toll free).

Voting address: 4 Oak Street, Crivitz 54114.

Mailing address: Office: Room 18 North, State Capitol, P.O. Box 8953, Madison 53708.

13th SENATE DISTRICT

See City of Hartford Detail Map on p. 58

See Village of DeForest Detail Map on p. 46

See Waukesha County Detail Map on pp. 94 & 95

Senator
FITZGERALD

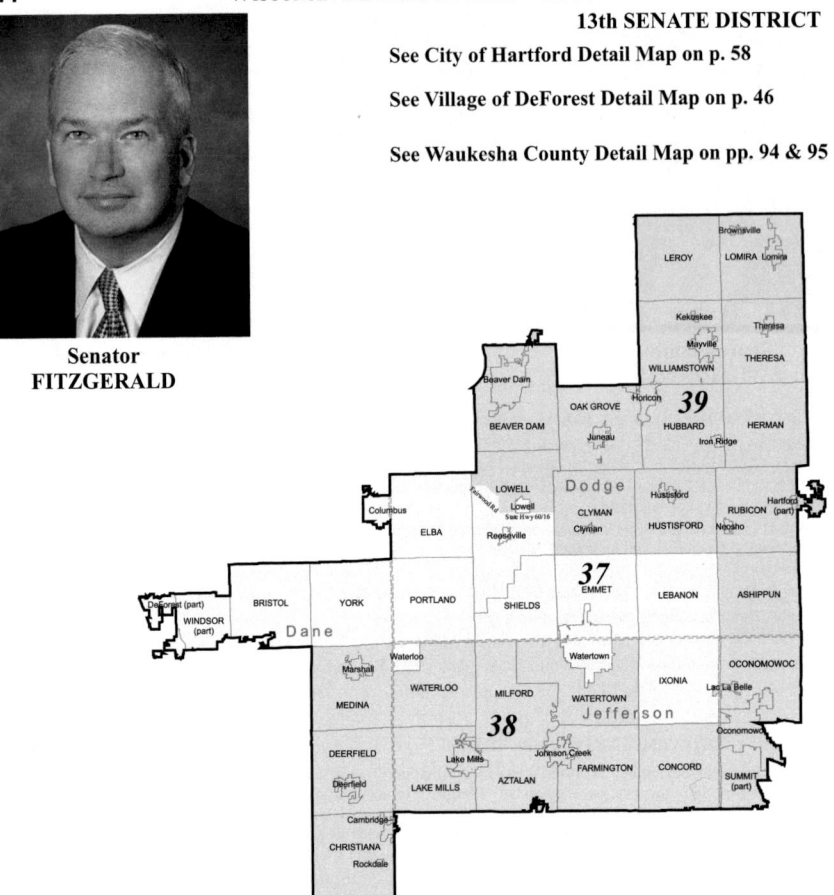

Scott L. Fitzgerald (Rep.), 13th Senate District

Born Chicago, IL, November 16, 1963; married; 3 children. Graduate Hustisford H.S. 1981; B.S. in journalism UW-Oshkosh 1985; U.S. Army Armor Officer Basic Course 1985; U.S. Army Command and General Staff College. Former associate newspaper publisher; U.S. Army Reserve Lt. Colonel (ret.). Member: Dodge Co. Republican Party (chm. 1992-94); Juneau Lions Club; Reserve Officers Assn.; Knights of Columbus.

Elected to Senate 1994; reelected since 1998. Majority Leader 2013, 2011(through 7/24/12); Minority Leader 2011 (eff. 7/24/12), 2009, 2007; Majority Leader 9/17/04 to 11/10/04. Biennial committee assignments: **2013** — Senate Org. (chp. since 2011, mbr. since 2007); Jt. Com. on Employment Relations (since 2007); Jt. Com. on Legis. Org. (since 2007); Jt. Legislative Council (since 2005). **2005** — Jt. Com. on Finance (co-chp., mbr. since 2003); Jt. Legis. Audit. **2003** — Jt. Com. for Review of Criminal Penalties (co-chp.); Education, Ethics and Elections; Homeland Security, Veterans and Military Affairs and Government Reform; Judiciary, Corrections and Privacy; Claims Bd. (eff. 12/5/03); Education (eff. 4/21/98); Health, Utilities, Veterans and Military Affairs; Judiciary, Consumer Affairs, and Campaign Finance Reform; Privacy, Electronic Commerce and Financial Institutions (also 1999); Wis. Housing and Economic Development Authority. **1999** — Economic Development, Housing and Government Operations (member to 2/24/99, also 1997); Rural Economic Development Bd. (also 1997). **1997** — State Government Operations and Corrections (chp., eff. 4/21/98); Education (eff. 1/7/98); Health, Human Services, Aging, Corrections, Veterans and Military Affairs (1/15/97 to 4/20/98); Government Effectiveness (eff. 4/21/98, also 1995); Human Resources, Labor, Tourism, Veterans and Military Affairs (eff. 4/21/98); Jt. Com. on Information Policy (eff. 4/21/98, also 1995); Legis. Coun. Coms. on Local Government Spending (vice chp.), on the School Calendar. **1995** — Business, Economic Development and Urban Affairs (member to 6/96); Agriculture, Transportation, Utilities and Financial Institutions; Legis. Coun. Coms. on Americans with Disabilities Act (co-chp.), on Recodification of Fish and Game Laws.

Telephone: Office: (608) 266-5660; E-mail: Sen.Fitzgerald@legis.wisconsin.gov

Voting address: Juneau 53039.

Mailing address: Office: Room 211 South, State Capitol, P.O. Box 7882, Madison 53707-7882.

Representative	Representative	Representative
JAGLER	**KLEEFISCH**	**BORN**

John Jagler (Rep.), 37th Assembly District

Born Louisville, KY, November 4, 1969; married; 3 children. Graduate Oak Creek H.S. 1987; graduate Trans-American School of Broadcasting (Madison) 1989; attended UW-Parkside 1987-88. Owner, communications consulting company. Former radio morning show host, news anchor; communications director, assembly speaker Jeff Fitzgerald. Member: Down Syndrome Association of Wisconsin; Wisconsin Upside Down; Honorable Order of Kentucky Colonels; National Rifle Assn.; Watertown Elks Club. Former member: RTNDA – Radio TV News Directors Assn.; Milwaukee Press Club.

Elected to Assembly 2012. Biennial committee assignments: **2013** — Education (vice chp.); Constitution and Ethics; Consumer Protection; Housing and Real Estate; Insurance; Urban Education.

Telephone: Office: (608) 266-9650; (888) 534-0037 (toll free).

E-mail: Rep.Jagler@legis.wisconsin.gov

Voting address: Watertown 53094.

Mailing address: Office: Room 316 North, State Capitol, P.O. Box 8952, Madison 53708.

Joel Kleefisch (Rep.), 38th Assembly District

Born Waukesha, June 8, 1971; married; 2 children. Graduate Waukesha North H.S. 1989; B.A. Pepperdine U. 1993. Former investigative television news reporter for WISN-TV; legislative policy advisor and constituent director. Member: Watertown Elks Club; Watertown Moose Club; Stone Bank Lions Club; Ducks Unlimited; National Wild Turkey Federation; National Rifle Assn.; Wings Over Wisconsin; Lakewatch Volunteer Organization (founder).

Elected to Assembly 2004; reelected since 2006. Minority Caucus Vice Chairperson 2009. Biennial committee assignments: **2013** — Criminal Justice (chp., also 2007, mbr. 2009); Natural Resources and Sporting Heritage (vice chp.); Corrections; Labor; State Affairs (vice chp. 2007, mbr. 2005); Tourism. **2011** — Jt. Review Com. on Criminal Penalties (co-chp.); Natural Resources; Jt. Com. on Finance. **2009** — Consumer Protection; Rules; State Affairs and Homeland Security. **2007** —Children and Family Law; Colleges and Universities. **2005** — Financial Institutions; Judiciary; State-Federal Relations.

Telephone: Office: (608) 266-8551; (888) 534-0038 (toll free).

E-mail: Rep.Kleefisch@legis.wisconsin.gov

Voting address: Oconomowoc 53066.

Mailing address: Office: Room 307 North, State Capitol, P.O. Box 8952, Madison 53708; District: P.O. Box 273, Okauchee 53069.

Mark L. Born (Rep.), 39th Assembly District

Born Beaver Dam, April 14, 1976; married; 1 child. Graduate Beaver Dam H.S. 1994; B.A. political science and history, Gustavus Adolphus College (St. Peter, MN) 1998. Full-time legislator. Former corrections supervisor, Dodge Co. Sheriff Dept. Member: Dodge Co. Historical Society (vice pres.); Leadership Beaver Dam Steering Com.; Beaver Dam Lake Improvement Assn. (fmr. vice pres.); Republican Party of Dodge Co. (fmr. chm.); Beaver Dam Elks Lodge 1540; St. John's Lutheran Church, Beaver Dam. Beaver Dam Fire and Police Commission 1993-95; Beaver Dam City Council 1995-99.

Elected to Assembly 2012. Biennial committee assignments: **2013** — State and Local Finance (vice chp.); Financial Institutions; Insurance; Natural Resources and Sporting Heritage; Tourism; Workforce Development.

Telephone: Office: (608) 266-2540; District: (920) 887-2202.

E-mail: Rep.Born@legis.wisconsin.gov

Voting address: Beaver Dam 53916.

Mailing address: Office: Room 312 North, State Capitol, P.O. Box 8952, Madison 53708.

14th SENATE DISTRICT

**Senator
OLSEN**

Detail Map: Village of DeForest

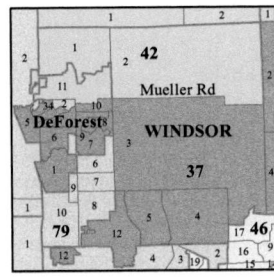

Luther S. Olsen (Rep.), 14th Senate District

Born Berlin, February 26, 1951; married. Graduate Berlin H.S. 1969; B.S. UW-Madison 1973; Wis. Rural Leadership Program Group IV 1990-92. Partner in farm supply dealerships. Member: Green Lake Co. Republican Party; Waushara Co. Republican Party; Education Commission of the States (bd. of dir.); NCSL Education Committee Co-Chair, 2012-14. Former member: Waushara Co. Fair Bd. (dir.); Family Health/La Clinica director (1995-99); Berlin Area School Board 1976-97 (pres. 1986-95).

Elected to Assembly 1994-2002; elected to Senate 2004; reelected since 2008. Biennial Senate committee assignments: **2013** — Education (chp., also 2011, 2005, mbr. 2009, 2007); Jt. Com. on Finance (vice chp., also 2011, mbr. since 2005); Insurance and Housing (also 2011); Educ. Communications Bd. (since 2005); State Capitol and Executive Residence Bd. (since 2009). **2011** — Leg. Coun. Spec. Coms. on Health Care Access (chp.), on Review of Spousal Maintenance Awards in Divorce Proceedings; University of Wisconsin Hospitals and Clinics Authority Bd. (also 2007, 2005). **2009** — Environment. **2007** — Jt. Survey Com. on Retirement Systems; Child Abuse and Neglect Prevention Bd. (also 2005). **2005** — Agriculture and Insurance; Legis. Coun. Spec. Com. on School Aid Formula (chp.). Assembly committee assignments: **2003** — Education (chp. since 1997, mbr. 1995); Education Reform (since 1999, vice chp. 2001); Health (since 1997); Housing; Rural Affairs; Workforce Development. **2001** — Ways and Means; Migrant Labor Council (since 1995). **1999** — Tourism and Recreation; Legis. Coun. Coms. on Dental Care Access, on Navigable Waters Recodification. **1997** — Colleges and Universities; State-Federal Relations; Gov.'s Council on Model Academic Standards; Legis. Coun. Coms. on Services for Visually Handicapped Students (chp.), on Children at Risk Program, on the School Calendar. **1995** — Government Operations (vice chp.); Jt. Com. for Review of Administrative Rules; Agriculture; Mandates; State Supported Programs Study and Adv. Com.; Legis. Coun. Coms. on Public Libraries, on Public School Open Enrollment, on the School Aid Formula.

Telephone: Office: (608) 266-0751; (800) 991-5541 (toll free).

E-mail: Sen.Olsen@legis.wisconsin.gov

Voting address: Ripon 54971.

Mailing address: Room 319 South, State Capitol, P.O. Box 7882, Madison 53707-7882.

Representative **Representative** **Representative**
PETERSEN **BALLWEG** **RIPP**

Kevin David Petersen (Rep.), 40th Assembly District

Born Waupaca, December 14, 1964; married; 2 children. Graduate Waupaca H.S. 1983; B.S.M.E. U. of New Mexico 1989. Co-owner family-run electronics corporation. Served in U.S. Navy sub service, 1983-94, Persian Gulf War veteran. Member U.S. Naval Reserve 1994-2008. Member: Waupaca Co. Republican Party; VFW Post 1037 (life member); Amvets Post 1887 (life member); American Legion Post 161; United States Submarine Veterans, Inc.; Waupaca Area Chamber of Commerce; New London Chamber of Commerce; National Rifle Association. Town of Dayton Supervisor 2001-07.

Elected to Assembly 2006; reelected since 2008. Biennial committee assignments: **2013** — Insurance (chp., also 2011); Energy and Utilities (vice chp. 2007, mbr. 2011, 2009); Health (also 2011); Jobs, Economy and Mining; State and Federal Relations; Jt. Com. on Information Policy and Technology. **2011** —Ways and Means; Jt. Com. on Audit. **2009** — Aging and Long-Term Care (also 2007); Veterans and Military Affairs (also 2007). **2007** — Homeland Security and State Preparedness.

Telephone: Office; (608) 266-3794; (888) 947-0040 (toll free).
E-mail: Rep.Petersen@legis.wisconsin.gov
Voting address: Waupaca 54981.
Mailing address: Office: Room 105 West, State Capitol, P.O. Box 8953, Madison 53708.

Joan Ballweg (Rep.), 41st Assembly District

Born Milwaukee, March 16, 1952; married; 3 children. Graduate Nathan Hale H.S. (West Allis) 1970; attended UW-Waukesha; B.A. Elementary Education UW-Stevens Point 1974. Co-owner of farm equipment business. Former 1st grade teacher. Member: Markesan Chamber of Commerce (former treas.); Waupun Chamber of Commerce; Green Lake County Farm Bureau; Waupun Memorial Hospital (bd. of dir., fmr. chp.); Agnesian HealthCare Enterprises, LLC management com. (fmr. secy.); volunteer, Markesan District Schools; Markesan PTA (fmr. pres.); Markesan AFS Chapter (hosting coordinator, pres., fmr. host family, liaison). Former member: FEMA V Regional Advisory Council. Recipient: Markesan District Education Assn. *Friend of Education Award* 1990. Markesan City Council 1987-91; Mayor of Markesan 1991-97.

Elected to Assembly 2004; reelected since 2006. Majority Caucus Chairperson 2013, 2011. Biennial committee assignments: **2013** — Jt. Legis. Council (co-chp., also 2011); Colleges and Universities (vice chp. 2007, 2005, mbr. 2011, 2009); Assembly Org. (also 2011); Rules (also 2011); Tourism; Leg. Coun. Spec. Com. on 911 Communications (chp.). **2011** — Labor and Workforce Development (chp.); Homeland Security and State Affairs; Leg. Coun. Spec. Com. on Review of Higher Education Financial Aid Programs (chp.). **2009** — Renewable Energy and Rural Affairs; State Affairs and Homeland Security; Leg. Coun. Spec. Com. on Emergency Management and Continuity of Government (vice chp.). **2007** — Homeland Security and State Preparedness (chp.); Insurance (also 2005); Public Health; Small Business (also 2005); Leg. Coun. Spec. Com. on Disaster Preparedness Planning (chp.). **2005** — Family Law; Rural Affairs and Renewable Energy.

Telephone: Office: (608) 266-8077; (888) 534-0041 (toll free); District: (920) 398-3708.
E-mail: Rep.Ballweg@legis.wisconsin.gov
Voting address: 170 West Summit Street, Markesan 53946.
Mailing address: Office: Room 210 North, State Capitol, P.O. Box 8952, Madison 53708.

Keith Ripp (Rep.), 42nd Assembly District

Born Madison, November 13, 1961; married; 3 children. Graduate Lodi H.S. 1980; UW-Madison farm and industry short course 1981. Farmer and small business owner. Member: Wis. Soybean Marketing Bd. (fmr. pres., vice pres.); Badger Agvest LLC (fmr. pres. and co-founder); Wis. Corn Growers Assn. (fmr. pres., vice pres.); Wis. Farm Bureau; Lodi FFA Alumni (fmr. pres., co-founder); Columbia and Dane Co. Republican Party; Yellow Thunder Snowmobile Club; Ducks Unlimited. Town of Dane Supervisor 2006-08.

Elected to Assembly 2008; reelected since 2010. Biennial committee assignments: **2013** — Transportation (chp., mbr. since 2009); Agriculture (also 2011); Rural Affairs; Small Business Development; State Affairs; Ways and Means. **2011** — Consumer Protection and Personal Privacy (chp.); Rural Economic Development and Rural Affairs; State Fair Park Bd. **2009** — Criminal Justice; Renewable Energy and Rural Affairs.

Telephone: Office: (608) 266-3404.
Voting address: Lodi 53555.
Mailing address: Office: Room 223 North, State Capitol, P.O. Box 8953, Madison 53708.

15th SENATE DISTRICT

Detail Map: City of Janesville

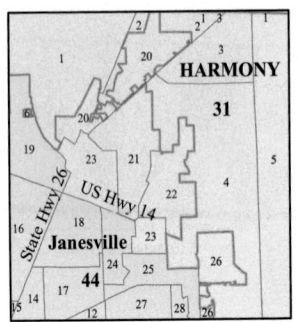

**Senator
CULLEN**

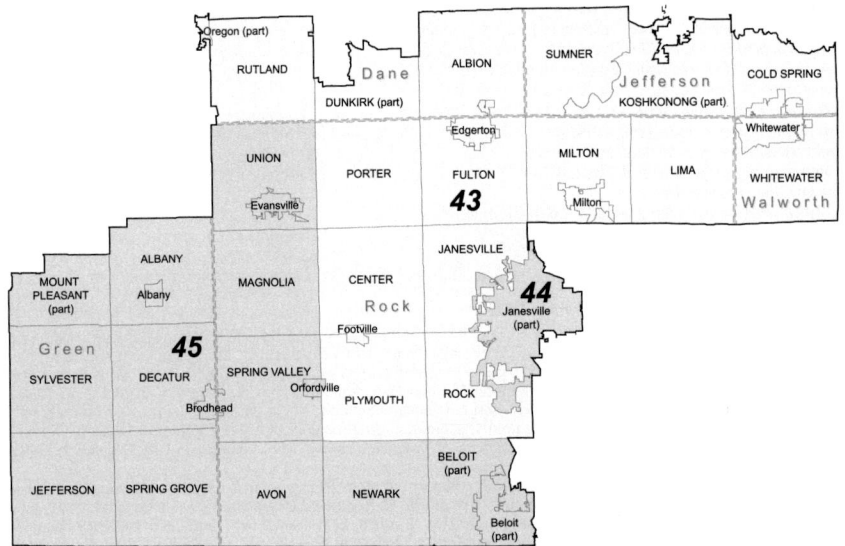

Tim Cullen (Dem.), 15th Senate District

Born Janesville, February 25, 1944; married; 4 step-children, 2 children. Graduate Janesville H.S. 1962; B.S. UW-Whitewater 1966; graduate work Northern Ill. U. Full-time legislator. Secy. of Wis. Dept. of Health and Social Services 1987-88. Former vice president, senior vice president, Blue Cross/Blue Shield 1988-2007. Served in U.S. Army Reserve. Member: Les Aspin School of Gov't. Bd. of Visitors; Echo (bd. mbr.); Janesville Teacher Diversity Bd. (chp.). Former member: Common Cause (fmr. bd. mbr.); Wisconsin Eye (bd. mbr.); Janesville YMCA (bd. mbr.). Janesville city council 1970-71. Janesville School Bd. 2007-10.

Elected to Senate 1974-1986; reelected 2010. Majority Leader 1985, 1983, 1981 (eff. 5/26/82). Biennial committee assignments: **2013** — Education; Insurance and Housing. **2011** — Mining (chp.); Venure Capital and Small Business (chp.); Agriculture, Elections and UW System; Education and Corrections; Health, Revenue, Tax Fairness, and Insurance; Economic Development, Veterans and Military Affairs; State and Federal Relations and Information Technology; Workforce Development, Small Business, and Tourism; Jt. Legislative Council.

Telephone: Office: (608) 266-2253; (800) 334-1468 (toll free).

E-mail: Sen.Cullen@legis.wisconsin.gov

Voting address: Janesville 53545.

Mailing address: Office: Room 108 South, State Capitol, P.O. Box 7882, Madison 53707-7882.

Representative
JORGENSEN

Representative
KOLSTE

Representative
RINGHAND

Andy Jorgensen (Dem.), 43rd Assembly District

Born Berlin, September 10, 1967; married; 3 children. Graduate Omro H.S. 1986; Brown Institute (MN) 1987. Former morning radio personality, assembly line operator, UAW shop steward, General Motors Janesville, worked on family dairy farm. Bd. member: Respite Care Assn. of Wis.; Jefferson Co. Local Emergency Planning Council; Jefferson Co. Agribusiness Club. Member: Rock Co. Farm Bureau; Trinity Lutheran Church, Fort Atkinson.

Elected to Assembly 2006; reelected since 2008. Minority Caucus Chairperson 2013. Biennial committee assignments: **2013** — Agriculture (since 2007); Assembly Organization; International Trade and Commerce; Rules; Rural Affairs (also 2007); Small Business Development. **2011** — Rural Economic Development and Rural Affairs; Transportation; Jt. Legis. Audit (vice chp. 2009). **2009** — Renewable Energy and Rural Affairs (chp.); Rural Economic Development (vice chp.); Labor. **2007** — Biofuels and Sustainable Energy; Consumer Protection and Personal Privacy.

Telephone: Office: (608) 266-3790; (888) 534-0043 (toll free).

E-mail: Rep.Jorgensen@legis.wisconsin.gov

Voting address: 1534 Joyce Road, Fort Atkinson 53538.

Mailing address: Office: Room 113 North, State Capitol, P.O. Box 8952, Madison 53708.

Debra Kolste (Dem.), 44th Assembly District

Born O'Neill, NE, June 20, 1953; married; 3 children. Graduate Kimball Co. H.S. (Kimball, NE) 1971; B.S. medical technology U. of Nebraska 1975. Full-time legislator. Former medical technologist. Member: YMCA of Northern Rock Co. (bd. mbr.); Health Net of Rock Co.; League of Women Voters; Friends of Rotary Gardens. Former member: Mercy Health Systems Volunteers (pres.); Rock Futbol Soccer League (founding bd. mbr.); PTO Bd.; PTA Bd. Janesville School Board, 2000-09.

Elected to Assembly 2012. Biennial committee assignments: **2013** — Health; Small Business Development; Transportation; Workforce Development.

Telephone: Office: (608) 266-7503; (888) 947-0044 (toll free); District: (608) 756-4311.

E-mail: Rep.Kolste@legis.wisconsin.gov

Voting address: Janesville 53546.

Mailing address: Office: Room 8 North, State Capitol, P.O. Box 8952, Madison 53708.

Janis Ringhand (Dem.), 45th Assembly District

Born Madison, February 13, 1950; married; 2 children, 5 grandchildren. Graduate Evansville H.S. 1968; Associate Degree Madison Area Tech. Coll. 1985. Full-time legislator. Former accountant for small businesses, executive director of nonprofit. Member: Stoughton Hospital Bd. (chp.); Rock Co. Literacy Connection (vice pres.); Evansville Chamber of Commerce; VFW Auxiliary Post 6905 (secy.); Evansville Energy Independence Team. Former member: Creekside Place, Inc. (bd. of dir.); Evansville Community Partnership (secy.). Evansville City Council 1998-2002, 2008-10. Mayor of Evansville 2002-06.

Elected to Assembly 2010; reelected 2012. Minority Caucus Secretary 2013. Biennial committee assignments: **2013** — Government Operations and State Licensing; Small Business Development; Urban and Local Affairs (also 2011); Veterans; Workforce Development. **2011** — Rural Economic Development and Rural Affairs; Veterans and Military Affairs.

Telephone: Office: (608) 266-1192; (888) 534-0080 (toll free); District: (608) 882-5879.

E-mail: Rep.Ringhand@legis.wisconsin.gov

Voting address: 412 Fowler Circle, Evansville 53536.

Mailing address: Office: Room 321 West, State Capitol, P.O. Box 8953, Madison 53708.

16th SENATE DISTRICT

**Senator
MILLER**

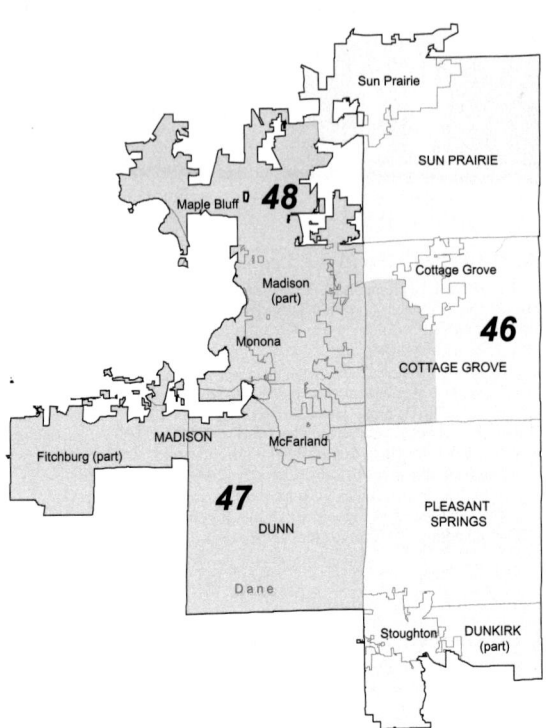

See Madison Area Detail Map on pp. 90 & 91

Mark Miller (Dem.), 16th Senate District

Born Boston, MA, February 1, 1943. Graduate Middleton H.S.; B.S. UW-Madison; Bowhay Institute for Legislative Leadership Development (BUILLD) 1999; Flemming Fellows Leadership Institute 2002. Former military pilot; Wis. Air National Guard, 1966-95 (ret. Lt. Colonel); former real estate property manager. Dane County Bd. of Health 1998-2004; Bd. of Health for Madison and Dane Co. 2004-07. Dane Co. Board of Supervisors 1996-2000.

Elected to Assembly 1998-2002; elected to Senate 2004; reelected since 2008. Minority Leader 2011; Majority Caucus Chairperson 2007. Biennial Senate committee assignments: **2013** — Elections and Urban Affairs; Energy, Consumer Protection, and Government Reform; Natural Resources; Jt. Legislative Council (since 2005). **2011** — Senate Org.; Jt. Com. on Employment Relations; Jt. Com. on Legislative Organization. **2009** — Environment (chp.); Jt. Com. on Finance (co-chp. since 11/5/07, mbr. 2007). **2007** — Environment and Natural Resources (chp.). **2005** — Agriculture and Insurance; Campaign Finance Reform and Ethics; Jt. Com. for Review of Administrative Rules; Child Abuse and Neglect Prevention Bd. (also 2003). Assembly committee assignments: **2003** — Children and Families (since 1999); Health (since 1999); Natural Resources (also 2001); Veterans and Military Affairs; Environmental Education Bd. (also 2001). **2001** — Environment. **1999** — Campaigns and Elections; Consumer Affairs; Public Health.

Telephone: Office: (608) 266-9170; District: (608) 221-2701.

E-mail: Sen.Miller@legis.wisconsin.gov

Voting address: Monona 53716.

Mailing address: Office: Room 7 South, State Capitol, P.O. Box 7882, Madison 53707-7882.

Representative
HEBL

Representative
KAHL

Representative
SARGENT

Gary Alan Hebl (Dem.), 46th Assembly District

Born Madison, May 15, 1951; married; 3 children; 1 grandson. Graduate Sun Prairie H.S. 1969; B.A. Political Science UW-Madison 1973; Gonzaga U. Law School 1976. Bowhay Institute for Legislative Leadership Development 2008. Attorney and owner of a title insurance company. Member: Wis. League of Conservation Voters; Dane Co. Bar Assn.; Wis. Bar Assn.; Sun Prairie Optimist Club (youth coordinator, fmr. pres.); Sun Prairie Chamber of Commerce (pres. elect 2014, pres.); U.W. Flying Club (chm., bd. of dir.); Aircraft Owners Assn.; Experimental Aircraft Assn.; Knights of Columbus (4th deg. mbr.); Sun Prairie Cable Access Bd.; YMCA (bd. of dir., fmr. pres.); Sun Prairie Public Library Bd. of Trustees (fmr. pres.); Sacred Heart Parish Council (fmr. trustee); Sun Prairie Quarterback Club (fmr. pres.). Recipient: State Bar of Wis. *Scales of Justice Award* 2009-10; Wis. Dietetic Assn. *Nutrition Champion Award* 2010; Pharmacy Society of Wis. *Legislator of the Year* 2010, 2009; Sun Prairie *Star* poll *Best Attorney in Sun Prairie* 2010, 2009, 2008, 2004, 2003, 2002; *James J. Reininger Award* for lifetime achievement 2008; Wis. Assn. of PEG Channels *Friend of Access Award* 2010, 2007; Wis. League of Conservation Voters *Conservation Champion* 2011-12, 2009-10, 2005-06; Madison Magazine *One of Madison's Best Real Estate Attorneys* 2002; Sun Prairie Exchange Club *Book of Golden Deeds Award* 2003; Chamber of Commerce *Judith Krivsky Business Person of the Year Award* 2002; Sun Prairie Business and Education Partnership *Outstanding Small Business of the Year* 2001.

Elected to Assembly 2004; reelected since 2006. Biennial committee assignments: **2013** — Family Law; Judiciary (ranking mbr.); Natural Resources and Sporting Heritage; Tourism; Jt. Com. for Review of Administrative Rules (ranking mbr., mbr. since 2009). **2011** — Consumer Protection and Personal Privacy; Criminal Justice and Corrections (eff. 5/11/11); Judiciary and Ethics (ranking mbr., chp. 2009); Tourism, Recreation and State Properties (eff. 2/7/12); Leg. Coun. Spec. Com. on Judicial Discipline and Recusal (co-chp.). **2009** — Ways and Means (chp. eff. 9/18/09, vice chp., mbr. since 2005); Insurance; Natural Resources (since 2005). **2007** — Housing; Small Business (also 2005). **2005** — Property Rights and Land Management.

Telephone: Office: (608) 266-7678.
E-mail: Rep.Hebl@legis.wisconsin.gov
Voting address: Sun Prairie 53590.
Mailing address: Office: Room 120 North, State Capitol, P.O. Box 8952, Madison 53708.

Robb Kahl (Dem.), 47th Assembly District

Born Menomonee Falls, January 5, 1972; married; 4 children. Graduate L.P. Goodrich H.S. (Fond du Lac) 1990; B.A. *cum laude* Ripon College 1994; J.D. *cum laude* U. of Wisconsin Law School 1997; attended Syracuse College of Law 1994-95. Attorney, small business owner. Member: State Bar of Wis.; Democratic Party of Wis.; Monona Chamber of Commerce; Fitchburg Chamber of Commerce; McFarland Chamber of Commerce; Monona Grove Businessmen's Assn.; International Union of Operating Engineers; Ripon College Bd. of Trustees. Law clerk, Wis. court of appeals 1997-98; Wis. Transportation Finance and Policy Commission 2011-13; Monona Community Development Authority (chair) 2011-13; Monona City Council 2001-03; Mayor of Monona 2003-11.

Elected to Assembly 2012. Biennial committee assignments: **2013** — Aging and Long Term Care; Children and Families (eff. 5/10/13); Energy and Utilities; Insurance; State Affairs; Jt. Com. for Review of Administrative Rules.

Telephone: Office: (608) 266-8570; District: (608) 224-0342.
Voting address: Monona 53716.
Mailing address: Office: Room 7 West, State Capitol, P.O. Box 8952, Madison 53708.

Melissa Sargent (Dem.), 48th Assembly District

Born Madison, March 28, 1969; married; 4 sons. Graduate Madison East H.S. 1987; B.A. UW-Madison 1991. Small business owner. Member: Wis. League of Conservation Voters; Sierra Club; Democratic Party; Wis. Business Alliance; Emerge Wis.; NARAL Pro-Choice Wis.; Make Room for Youth; Friends of Cherokee Marsh. Former member: Midwest Shiba Inu Dog Rescue (pres.); Gompers PTO (pres.). Dane Co. Bd. of Supervisors 2010-present.

Elected to Assembly 2012. Biennial committee assignments: **2013** — Aging and Long Term Care; Financial Institutions; International Trade and Commerce; Small Business Development; Jt. Legis. Audit Com.

Telephone: Office: (608) 266-0960.
E-mail: Rep.Sargent@legis.wisconsin.gov
Voting address: 1638 Mayfield Lane, Madison 53704.
Mailing address: Office: Room 8 West, State Capitol, P.O. Box 8953, Madison 53708.

17th SENATE DISTRICT

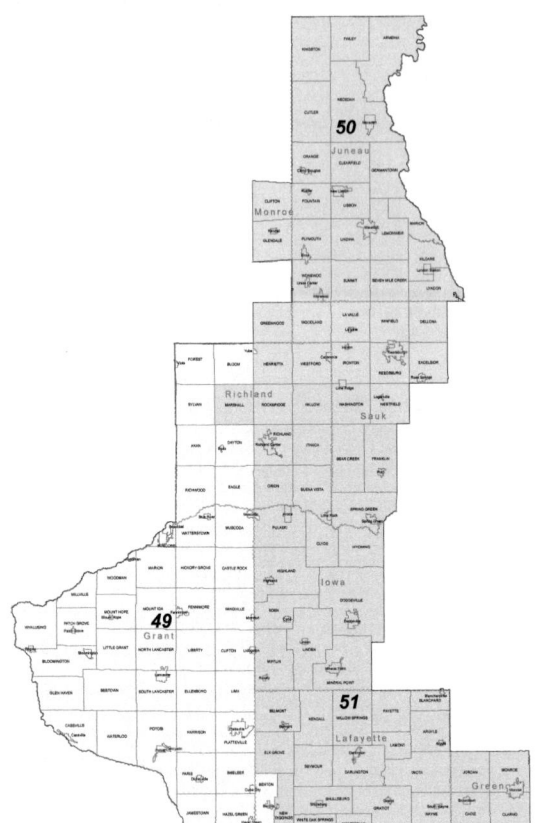

Senator
SCHULTZ

Dale W. Schultz (Rep.), 17th Senate District

Born Madison, June 12, 1953; married; 2 children. Graduate Madison West H.S.; B.B.A. UW-Madison 1975. Farm manager and real estate broker. Member: National Conference of State Legislatures; National Conference of Insurance Legislators; Sauk Co. Farm Bureau; Masons; Shrine; Lions; Hillpoint Rod and Gun Club. Awards: Military Order of the Purple Heart *Legislator of the Year* 2002; Wisconsin Wetlands Association and Sierra Club *Conservation Award* 2002; Deer and Elk Farmers Association *Legislator of the Year* 2002; WMC *Outstanding Legislator Award* 2001; Tavern League of Wisconsin *Top Shelf Award* 2000; Neighborhood Housing Services *Legislative Leadership Award* 2000; *Excellence in Education Award* 2000; *Friend of Grocers Award* 2010, 2006, 2004; AFSCME Local 2748 *Appreciation Award* 1998; Wis. Sheriffs and Deputy Sheriffs Assn. *Commendation* 1997; Wis. Counties Assn. *Friend of County Government* 2004; Council of State Governments *Toll Fellow* 1996, 1995; Wis. Hospitals Assn. *Health Care Leadership Award* 2003; Wis. Farm Bureau Federation *Friend of Agriculture* 2006, 2004; Wis. Federation of Cooperatives *Friend of Cooperatives* 2003; Wis. Pharmacists Assn. *Outstanding Legislator;* Wis. Assn. of Health Underwriters *Insuring Freedom Award* 2004; Wis. Medical Society *Health Leadership Award* 2004; Wis. Ethanol Producers Assn. and Wis. Corn Growers Assn. *Legislator of the Year* 2006; Wis. Dept. of Veterans Affairs *Iron Mike Award* 2006; Wis. Community Action Program Assn. *William Steiger Human Services Award* 2008.

Elected to Assembly 1982-91 (resigned 10/7/91); elected to Senate in September 1991 special election; reelected since 1994. Majority Leader 2005, 2003 (eff. 11/9/04). Biennial committee assignments: **2013** — Financial Institutions and Rural Issues (chp., also 2011); Universities and Technical Colleges (vice chp.); Agriculture, Small Business and Tourism; Insurance and Housing (vice chp. 2011); State and Federal Relations; Jt. Legis. Coun. (since 2009, also 2005); Jt. Survey Com. on Retirement Systems (also 2009, co-chp. 2003); State Historical Soc. Bd. of Curators (since 2001). **2011** — State of Wis. Building Comn. **2009** — Public Health, Senior Issues, Long-Term Care, and Job Creation. **2007** — Environment and Natural Resources; Public Health, Senior Issues, Long-Term Care and Privacy; Transportation, Tourism and Insurance. **2005** — Organization (chp.); Jt. Com. on Employment Relations; Jt. Com. on Legislative Organization; State and Federal Relations; State Capitol and Executive Residence Bd. (since 1999). **2003** — Agriculture, Financial Institutions and Insurance (chp.); Health, Children, Families, Aging and Long Term Care; Higher Education and Tourism; Transportation Projects Commission (also 2001).

Telephone: Office: (608) 266-0703; (800) 978-8008 (toll free); District: (608) 647-4614.
E-mail: Sen.Schultz@legis.wisconsin.gov
Voting address: Richland Center 53581.
Mailing address: Office: Room 122 South, State Capitol, P.O. Box 7882, Madison 53707-7882.

Representative
TRANEL

Representative
BROOKS

Representative
MARKLEIN

Travis Tranel (Rep.), 49th Assembly District

Born Dubuque, IA, September 12, 1985; married; 3 children. Graduate Wahlert Catholic H.S. (Dubuque, IA) 2004; B.A. Loras College (Dubuque, IA) 2007. Dairy farmer, small business owner. Member: St. Joseph Sinsinawa Parish Council, 2010-12 (pres., 2011-12); Wis. Farm Bureau; Knights of Columbus; National Rifle Association; Ducks Unlimited; Platteville Area Chamber of Commerce; Southwest Wis. Young Professionals; Grant Co. Republican Party. Recipient: DBA *Legislative Excellence Award* 2012; WMC *Working for Wisconsin Award* 2012; MMAC *Champion of Commerce Award* 2012.

Elected to Assembly 2010; reelected 2012. Biennial committee assignments: **2013** — State and Federal Relations (chp.); Agriculture (vice chp. 2011); Campaigns and Elections; Family Law; Insurance (also 2011). **2011** —Financial Institutions.

Telephone: Office: (608) 266-1170; (888) 872-0049 (toll free).

E-mail: Rep.Tranel@legis.wisconsin.gov

Voting address: Cuba City 53807.

Mailing address: Office: Room 308 North, State Capitol, P.O. Box 8953, Madison 53708.

Ed Brooks (Rep.), 50th Assembly District

Born Baraboo, July 1, 1942; married; 3 children; 5 grandchildren. Graduate Webb H.S. (Reedsburg) 1960; B.S. agricultural economics UW-Madison 1965. Dairy producer. Former co. sup. f/USDA, FmHA, loan officer f/PCA Madison. Served in U.S. Army Reserve 1965-71. Member: Wis. Fed. of Co-ops (fmr. chairman); Wis. Farm Bureau; American Legion Post 350. Former member: C.A.L.S. B.O.V.; Endeavor 4-H Club (leader); St. John Lutheran Church (past pres. church council). Recipient: *Friend of Cooperatives* 2012; *Friend of Wisconsin Towns* 2011; WMC *Working for Wisconsin* 2011-12; *Friend of Education* 1998; *Friend of Extension*. Town supervisor 1979-1985; town chairman 1985-present.

Elected to Assembly 2008; reelected since 2010. Biennial committee assignments: **2013** — Urban and Local Affairs (chp., also 2011); Public Safety and Homeland Security (vice chp.); Agriculture (since 2009); Corrections; Veterans. **2011** — Criminal Justice and Corrections. **2009** — Corrections and the Courts; Criminal Justice.

Telephone: Office: (608) 266-8531; (877) 947-0050 (toll free); District: (608) 524-2406.

E-mail: Rep.Brooks@legis.wisconsin.gov

Voting address: Reedsburg 53959.

Mailing address: Office: Room 20 North, State Capitol, P.O. Box 8952, Madison 53708.

Howard Marklein (Rep.), 51st Assembly District

Born Madison, October 3, 1954; married; 2 children, 3 stepchildren, 3 grandchildren. Graduate River Valley H.S. (Spring Green) 1972; B.A. UW-Whitewater 1976. Certified public accountant; certified fraud examiner. Member: St. John's Catholic Church, Spring Green (fin. com. mbr.); Taliesin Preservation Inc. Bd. of Trustees (treas.); Wis. Academy of Science Arts and Letters (treas.); UW-Whitewater Natl. Alumni Assn. (pres); UW-Whitewater Foundation (bd. of dir. pres.); Wis. Academy Foundation Bd. of Dir. (treas.). Former member: Fort Health Care Bd. of Dir. (chp., treas.); Fort Atkinson Rotary Club (pres.); Fort Atkinson Chamber of Commerce (pres.); Whitewater Chamber of Commerce (pres.); Dodgeville Chamber of Commerce (vice pres.).

Elected to Assembly 2010; reelected 2012. Biennial committee assignments: **2013** — Ways and Means (chp.); Agriculture (also 2011); Education (vice chp. 2011); Financial Institutions (also 2011); Rural Affairs; Jt. Legis. Audit Com.; Small Business Regulatory Review Bd. (chp.). **2011** — UW Hospitals and Clinics Authority.

Telephone: Office: (608) 266-7502; (888) 534-0051 (toll free); District: (608) 588-5632.

E-mail: Rep.Marklein@legis.wisconsin.gov

Voting address: S11665 Soeldner Road, Spring Green 53588.

Mailing address: Office: Room 214 North, State Capitol, P.O. Box 8953, Madison 53708.

18th SENATE DISTRICT

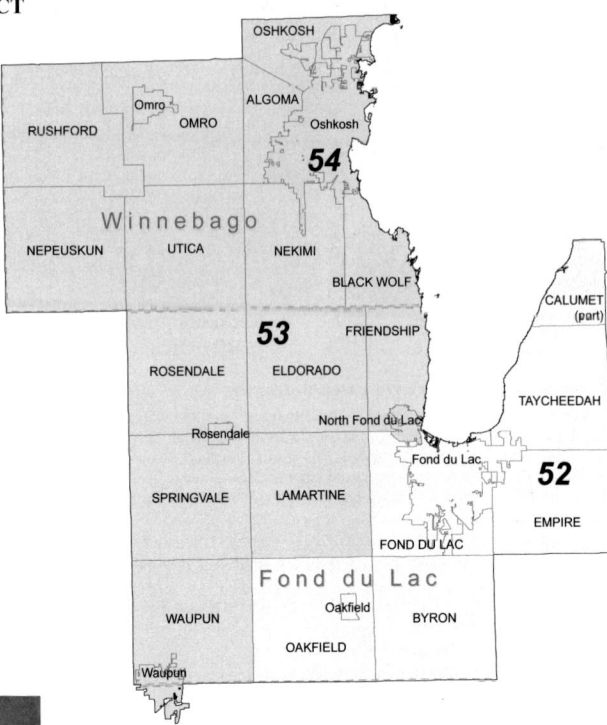

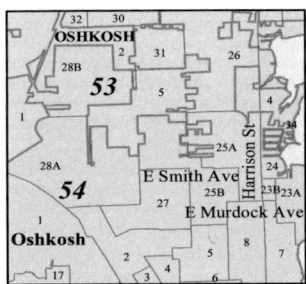

Detail Map: Oshkosh Area

**Senator
GUDEX**

Rick Gudex (Rep.), 18th Senate District

Born Fond du Lac, July 23, 1968. Graduate St. Mary Springs H.S. (Fond du Lac) 1986. Full-time legislator. Former production manager. Member: Knights of Columbus Council 664; Elks Club BPOE #57. Mayor of Mayville 1998-2000. Fond du Lac City Council 2009-12.

Elected to Senate 2012. Biennial committee assignments: **2013** — Economic Development and Local Government (chp.); Government Operations, Public Works, and Telecommunications (vice chp.); Education; Universities and Technical Colleges; Jt. Com. on Information Policy and Technology.

Telephone: Office: (608) 266-5300; (888) 736-8720 (toll free); District (920) 922-1383.

E-mail: Sen.Gudex@legis.wisconsin.gov

Voting address: Fond du Lac 54935.

Mailing address: Office: Room 415 South, State Capitol, P.O. Box 7882, Madison 53707-7882. District: P.O. Box 1381, Fond du Lac 54936-1381.

| Representative | Representative | Representative |
| THIESFELDT | SCHRAA | HINTZ |

Jeremy Thiesfeldt (Rep.), 52nd Assembly District

Born Fond du Lac, November 22, 1966; married; 4 children. Graduate Kettle Moraine Lutheran H.S. (Jackson) 1985; B.S. Elementary education Dr. Martin Luther College 1989. Full-time legislator. Former teacher. Member: Thrivent Financial for Lutherans; Americans for Prosperity; Fond du Lac Noon Rotary; Fond du Lac County Rep. Party; Redeemer Lutheran Church. Former member: Camp Croix (1995-96); Minnesota District Lutheran Teachers' Conf. (1989-96); Wisconsin Area Lutheran Educators' Conf. (1999-2010); Wisconsin Lutheran State Teachers' Conf. (1996-99). Fond du Lac city council 2005-10 (vice pres. 2006-09).

Elected to Assembly 2010; reelected 2012. Biennial committee assignments: **2013** — Consumer Protection (chp.); Transportation (vice chp.); Urban Education (vice chp.); Campaigns and Elections; Corrections; Education (also 2011). **2011** — Urban and Local Affairs (vice chp.); Children and Families; Criminal Justice and Corrections (eff. 5/23/11).

Telephone: Office: (608) 266-3156; (888) 529-0052 (toll free); District: (920) 933-2086.

E-mail: Rep.Thiesfeldt@legis.wisconsin.gov

Voting address: Fond du Lac 54935.

Mailing address: Office: Room 16 West, State Capitol, P.O. Box 8953, Madison 53708.

Michael Schraa (Rep.), 53rd Assembly District

Born Fort Carson, CO, April 17, 1961; married; 3 children. Graduate Oshkosh North H.S. 1979; attended UW-Oshkosh 1980-82. Restaurant owner. Former stock broker/investment advisor. Member: Winnebago Co. Republican Party (ex. bd.); Fond du Lac Co. Republican Party; Southwest Rotary (Oshkosh); Oshkosh Chamber of Commerce; Portico Church (Oshkosh); Fond du Lac Co. Farm Bureau; NFIB; Wis. Ind. Business; NRA. Former member: Oshkosh Jaycees; Big Brothers/Big Sisters; Exchange Club.

Elected to Assembly 2012. Biennial committee assignments: **2013** — Corrections (vice chp.); Agriculture; Children and Families; Colleges and Universities; Rural Affairs; Small Business Development.

Telephone: Office: (608) 267-7990; District: (920) 267-0217.

Voting address: Oshkosh 54904.

Mailing address: Office: Room 22 West, State Capitol, P.O. Box 8953, Madison 53708; District: P.O. Box 2253, Oshkosh 43903-2253.

Gordon Hintz (Dem.), 54th Assembly District

Born Oshkosh, November 29, 1973; single. Graduate Oshkosh North H.S. 1992; B.A. Hamline U. (St. Paul, Minn.) 1996; M.P.A. UW-Madison 2001. Municipal consultant. Former legislative staff assistant, U.S. Representative Jay Johnson, U.S. Senator Herb Kohl; management and budget analyst, City of Long Beach, CA; instructor, political science dept., UW-Oshkosh. Member: Oshkosh Rotary Club; First Congregational Church; Propel; Oshkosh Chamber of Commerce; Winnebago Co. Democratic Party; 6th Congressional Dist. Democratic Party (chm.). Former member: International City/County Management Assn.

Elected to Assembly 2006; reelected since 2008. Biennial committee assignments: **2013** — Financial Institutions (ranking min. mbr., mbr. 2011); Urban and Local Affairs (ranking min. mbr., mbr. 2009, 2007); Jobs, Economy and Mining; State and Local Finance; Building Comn. (also 2011); State Capitol and Executive Residence Bd. **2011** — Education; Labor and Workforce Development (eff. 4/26/11). **2009** — Colleges and Universities (since 2007); Consumer Protection (chp.); Workforce Development (vice chp.); Jobs, the Economy, and Small Business. **2007** — Aging and Long-Term Care; Judiciary and Ethics.

Telephone: Office: (608) 266-2254; (888) 534-0054 (toll free); District: (920) 232-0805.

E-mail: Rep.Hintz@legis.wisconsin.gov

Voting address: 1209 Waugoo Avenue, Oshkosh 54901.

Mailing address: Office: Room 109 North, State Capitol, P.O. Box 8952, Madison 53708.

See Fox Cities Detail Map on p. 98

Detail Map: Grand Chute

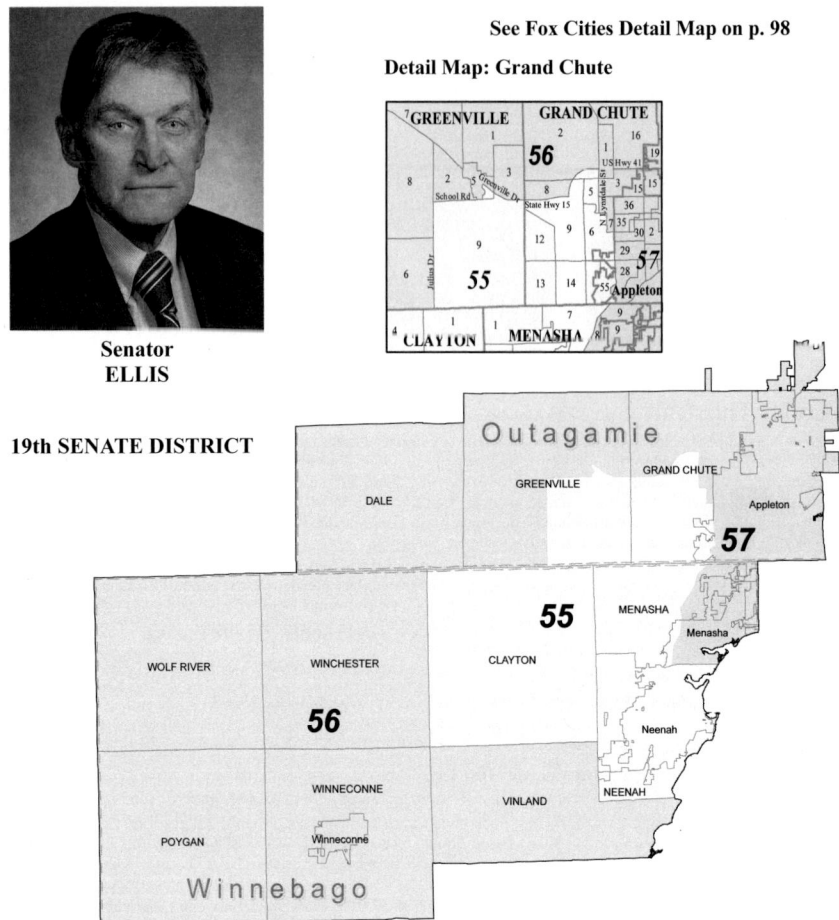

Senator
ELLIS

19th SENATE DISTRICT

Michael G. Ellis (Rep.), 19th Senate District

Born Neenah; married. Graduate Neenah H.S.; B.S. in secondary education UW-Oshkosh 1965. Legislator and farmer. Neenah City Council 1969-75.

Elected to Assembly 1970-80; elected to Senate since 1982. President of the Senate 2013, 2011 (through 7/17/12); Minority Leader 1999 (resigned 1/25/00), 1997 (1/15/97 to 4/20/98), 1995 (eff. 6/96); Majority Leader 1997 (eff. 4/21/98), 1995 (eff. 1/95 to 6/96), 1993 (eff. 4/20/93); Assistant Minority Leader 1987, 1985. Biennial committee assignments: **2013** — State and Federal Relations (chp.); Jt. Com. on Employment Relations (co-chp., also 2011, also mbr. 1989-1999, res. 1/25/00); Jt. Com. on Legislative Organization (co-chp., also 2011, also mbr. 1985-1999, res. 1/25/00); Senate Organization (chp. 1997, eff. 4/21/98, also 1/95 to 6/96, 1993, mbr. 2011, 1985-1999, resigned 1/25/00). **2011** — Jt. Legislative Council (co-chp., also mbr. 1989 to 1999, res. 1/25/00). **2009** — Ethics Reform and Government Operations (also 2007); Jt. Survey Com. on Tax Exemptions (co-chp. 2003, mbr. 2007, 2001). **2005** — Campaign Finance Reform and Ethics (chp.); State and Federal Relations (chp.). **2003** — Education, Ethics and Elections (chp.). **2001** — Jt. Survey Com. on Retirement Systems (also 1999); Retirement Research Com. (also 1999); Universities, Housing, and Government Operations. **1995** — Jt. Com. on Information Policy (resigned 12/5/95); Spec. Com. on State and Federal Relations (vice chp. 6/96, chp. 1/95 to 6/96); School Funding Commission. **1993** — Senate Rules (mbr. 1987 to 4/20/93). **1991** — Legis. Coun. Coms. on Drainage District Laws, on Issues Relating to Hunger Prevention, on Oversight of Community Mental Health Services, on Private Forest Land Programs. **1987** — Urban Affairs, Energy, Environmental Resources and Elections; Housing, Government Operations and Cultural Affairs (resigned 4/21/87); Legis. Coun. Com. on Natural and Recreational Resources. **1985** — Energy and Environmental Resources (also 1983); Tourism, Revenue, Financial Institutions and Forestry; Child Labor Coun. **1983** — Transportation; Legis. Coun. Peace Officer Study Com.

Telephone: Office: (608) 266-0718; District: (920) 751-4801.

Voting address: Neenah 54956.

Mailing address: Office: Room 220 South, State Capitol, P.O. Box 7882, Madison 53707-7882; District: 429 South Commercial Street, Neenah 54956.

| Representative | Representative | Representative |
| KAUFERT | MURPHY | BERNARD SCHABER |

Dean R. Kaufert (Rep.), 55th Assembly District

Born Outagamie County, May 23, 1957; married; 2 children, 2 grandchildren. Graduate Neenah H.S. Trophy and Awards store owner. EMT-B (NREMT) Mountain Ambulance and Rescue Volunteer. Member: Winnebago Co. Republican Party; Neenah-Menasha Noon Optimists; Neenah-Menasha Elks Club; Fox Cities Chamber of Commerce; Governor's Council on Domestic Abuse 2001-07. Neenah City Council 1985-91.

Elected to Assembly since 1990. Majority Caucus Sergeant at Arms 1997, 1995; Minority Caucus Sergeant at Arms 1993. Biennial committee assignments: **2013** — Tourism (chp.); Financial Institutions (vice chp. 2007, chp. 1995, mbr. 2011, 2009, 1993); Small Business Development; Transportation; Jt. Com. for Review of Admin. Rules. **2011** — Tourism, Recreation and State Properties (chp., also 2007, mbr. 2009); Health; Jt. Legislative Council (since 2003); State Building Comn. (since 2007); Governor's Council on Tourism (also 2009). **2007** — Corrections and the Courts. **2005** — Jt. Com. on Finance (co-chp., also 2003, mbr. since 1997); Jt. Legis. Audit (vice chp. 2003); Jt. Com. on Employment Relations (also 2003). **1999** — Jt. Com. on Information Policy (also 1997). **1997** — Legis. Coun. Com. on Local Government Funding. **1995** — Housing (vice chp., mbr. 1993, 1991); Criminal Justice and Corrections; Mandates; Small Business and Economic Development (also 1993); Spec. Com. on Gambling Oversight (vice chp.). **1993** — Criminal Justice and Public Safety (also 1991). **1991** — Environmental Resources, Utilities and Mining; Small Business and Education or Training for Employment; Legis. Coun. Com. on Energy Resources; Task Force on Regulatory Barriers to Affordable Housing.

Telephone: Office: (608) 266-5719; (888) 534-0055 (toll free); District: (920) 729-0521.

E-mail: Rep.Kaufert@legis.wisconsin.gov

Voting address: 1360 Alpine Lane, Neenah 54956.

Mailing address: Office: Room 15 North, State Capitol, P.O. Box 8952, Madison 53708.

Dave Murphy (Rep.), 56th Assembly District

Born Appleton, November 26, 1954; married; 2 children. Graduate Hortonville H.S. 1972; attended UW-Fox Valley 1972-74. Full-time legislator. Former owner, fitness center and agri-business; real estate broker. Member: Fox Valley Lutheran Homes (delegate); Greenville Lions Club. Former member: Zion Lutheran Church Council (pres.); Paper Valley Soccer Club (vice-pres.).

Elected to Assembly 2012. Biennial committee assignments: **2013** — Colleges and Universities (vice chp.); Constitution and Ethics; Housing and Real Estate; Insurance; Urban and Local Affairs.

Telephone: Office: (608) 266-7500; District: (920) 378-1424.

Voting address: Greenville 54942.

Mailing address: Office: Room 304 North, State Capitol, P.O. Box 8953, Madison 53708.

Penny Bernard Schaber (Dem.), 57th Assembly District

Born Mundelein, IL November 5, 1953; married. Graduate Mundelein H.S. 1971; Associate Degree, Physical Therapist Assistant, Southern Illinois U. 1973; B.S. Physiology Southern Illinois U. 1977; B.S. Physical Therapy Northwestern U. 1980; Associate Degree, Natural Resources Technology, Fox Valley Technical Coll. 1986. Full-time legislator. Retired physical therapist, last 10 years as a school physical therapist. Peace Corps volunteer, Campino Grande Brazil 1977-78. Member: Fox Valley Sierra Group (former chp., membership chair); John Muir Chapter, Sierra Club (former chp., outings and membership chair); Wis. League of Conservation Voters; American Physical Therapy Assn.; Wis. Physical Therapy Assn. Former member: Master Gardener, Outagamie Co.; Historic Hearthstone (bd. of dir.).

Elected to Assembly since 2008. Minority Caucus Vice Chairperson 2011 (eff. 2/15/12), Minority Caucus Secretary 2011. Biennial committee assignments: **2013** — Aging and Long Term Care (also 2011, eff. 12/6/11); Jobs, Economy and Mining; State Affairs; Transportation (also 2011); Jt. Survey Com. on Tax Exemptions. **2011** —Jobs, Economy and Small Business (vice chp. 2009); Public Health and Public Safety. **2009** — Health and Health Care Reform; Public Health.

Telephone: Office: (608) 266-3070; (888) 534-0057 (toll free); District: (920) 739-6041.

E-mail: Rep.BernardSchaber@legis.wisconsin.gov

Voting address: 815 East Washington Street, Appleton 54911.

Mailing address: Office: Room 126 North, State Capitol, P.O. Box 8952, Madison 53708.

20th SENATE DISTRICT

Detail Map: City of Hartford

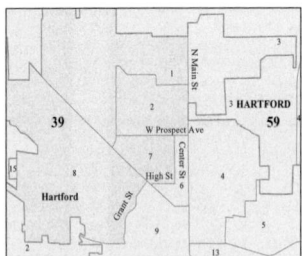

Detail Map: Town of Trenton

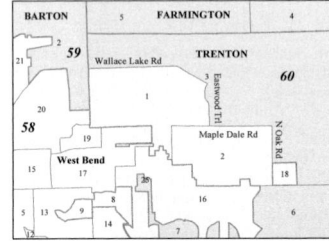

Senator
GROTHMAN

Glenn Grothman (Rep.), 20th Senate District

Born Milwaukee, July 3, 1955. Graduate Homestead H.S. (Mequon); B.B.A.; J.D. UW-Madison. Former practicing attorney. Member: Kiwanis-West Bend Early Risers; Washington Co. Bar Assn.; Loyal Order of the Moose-West Bend; UW-Madison Alumni Assn. of Washington Co.; Kettle Moraine Symphony (bd. member). Recipient: Milwaukee Co. Rep. Party *Assembly Tax Cutter of the Year* 2002; Ind. Bus. Assn. *Legislator of the Year* 2000; Wis. Counties Assn. *Outstanding Legislator Award* 1997-98; Wis. Right to Life *Pro-Life Hero Award* 1996, *Sanctity of Life Award* 2004; Pro-Life Wis. *Legislator of the Year* 2010, 1995; Wis. Grocers Assn. *Friend of Grocers Award* 1997-2012; Wis. Farm Bureau *Friend of Agriculture Award* 1995-2007; Wis. Dairy Business Assn. *Milk Bottle Award* 2006, 2004; Wis. Curves for Women *Legislator of the Year Award* 2003; Wis. Builders Assn. *Friend of Housing Award* 2001-07, *Legislator of the Year* 2005; Apartment Assoc. *Legislator of the Year* 2000; Nat'l Fed. of Independent Businesses *Guardian of Small Business Award* 1999-2000, 2005-06; WMC *Working for Wisconsin Award* 1998-2006, *Exemplar Award* for work on manufacturing tax credit 2012; Wis. Guild of Midwives *Legislator of the Year* 2006; Eagle Forum *Leadership Award* 2007; Wis. Bear Hunters Assn. *Hero Award* 2010; *Friends of Wis. Craft Brewers Award* 2012; Milw. Metropolitan Assn. of Commerce *Champion of Commerce Award* 2012.

Elected to Assembly in December 1993 special election; reelected 1994-2002; elected to Senate 2004; reelected since 2008. Assistant Majority Leader 2013, 2011; Assistant Minority Leader 2009; Minority Caucus Chairperson 2007; Majority Caucus Vice Chairperson 2003, 2001, 1999. Biennial Senate committee assignments: **2013** — Judiciary and Labor (chp.); Senate Org. (since 2009); Workforce Development, Forestry, Mining, and Revenue; Jt. Com. on Finance (also 2011); Jt. Com. on Leg. Org. (since 2009). **2011** — Labor, Public Safety, and Urban Affairs (vice chp.); Education (since 2005); Jt. Com. for Review of Administrative Rules (since 2009, co-chp. 2005). **2009** — Judiciary, Corrections, Insurance, Campaign Finance Reform and Housing; Labor, Elections and Urban Affairs (also 2007); Transportation, Tourism, Forestry, and Natural Resources; WHEDA Bd. (also 2007). Assembly committee assignments: **2003** — Jt. Com. for Review of Administrative Rules (co-chp. since 1995); Campaigns and Elections; Judiciary (vice chp. 1997, also 1995, mbr. 1993); Labor; Rules (since 1999); Law Revision Com. (co-chp. since 1997, mbr. 1995). **2001** — Children and Families (also 1999); Education Reform (also 1999). **1999** — Legis. Coun. Com. on Use of Prescription Drugs for Children (co-chp.). **1997** — Income Tax Review. **1993** — Spec. Com. on Welfare Reform.

Telephone: Office: (608) 266-7513; (800) 662-1227 (toll free); District: (262) 338-8061.

E-mail: Sen.Grothman@legis.wisconsin.gov

Voting address: 151 University Drive 312-N, West Bend 53095.

Mailing address: Office: Room 10 South, State Capitol, P.O. Box 7882, Madison 53707-7882.

Representative	Representative	Representative
STRACHOTA	**LeMAHIEU**	**STROEBEL**

Pat Strachota (Rep.), 58th Assembly District

Born Cuyahoga Co., Ohio, June 29, 1955; married; 4 children. Graduate Glen Oak/Gimour Academy 1973; B.A. Government, minor in American History, certificate in Urban Planning, St. Mary's College (Notre Dame, Ind.) 1977. Full-time legislator. Member: West Bend Noon Rotary; Kettle Moraine YMCA (bd. mbr.); West Bend Chamber of Commerce; Washington Co. Ag. and Industry Society; Washington Co. Historical Society; Friend of West Bend Art Gallery; St. Frances Cabrini Parish; West Bend Community Foundation (bd. mbr.). Former member: West Bend Economic Development Corp. (bd. mbr.); West Bend/Jackson Boys & Girls Club (bd. mbr.); Great Blue Heron Girl Scout Council (bd. mbr.). Washington Co. Board 1986-2002. Southeast Wisconsin Regional Planning Comn. 1986-2002.

Elected to Assembly 2004; reelected since 2006. Majority Caucus Vice Chairperson 2007. Biennial committee assignments: **2013** — Jt. Com. on Finance (vice chp., mbr. 2011); Health (also 2011, 2005). **2009** — Health and Health Care Reform (also 2007); Jobs, the Economy and Small Business; Public Health. **2007** — Jobs and the Economy (chp.); Workforce Development (vice chp.); Aging and Long-Term Care (also 2005); Rules; Ways and Means (also 2005). **2005** — Medicaid Reform (vice chp.); Southeast Wisconsin Freeways.

Telephone: Office: (608) 264-8486; District: (262) 338-3790.

E-mail: Rep.Strachota@legis.wisconsin.gov

Voting address: West Bend 53095.

Mailing address: Office: Room 324 East, State Capitol, P.O. Box 8953, Madison 53708.

Daniel R. LeMahieu (Rep.), 59th Assembly District

Born Sheboygan, November 5, 1946; married; 3 children. Graduate Oostburg H.S. 1964; attended UW-Sheboygan and UW-Milwaukee. Former publisher of Lakeshore Weekly. Vietnam Era veteran; served in Army, 1969-71. Member: Oostburg Business Association (past pres.); Oostburg Kiwanis Club (past pres.). Recipient: *Friend of Agriculture Award* 2005-06, 2003-04; Wis. Counties Assn. *Legislator of the Year* 2008, *Outstanding Legislator Award* 2005-06, 2003-04; Wis. Grocers Assn. *Friend of Grocers Award* 2011-12, 2009-10, 2007-08, 2003-04; *Friend of the Dairy Industry Award* 2011-12, 2005-06, 2003-04; Wis. Pro-Life *Legislator of the Year* 2005; Wis. Builders Assn. *Friend of the Housing Industry Award* 2011, 2010, 2009, 2008, 2007, 2006, 2005; Metropolitan Milwaukee Assn. of Commerce *Champion of Commerce Award* 2011-12, 2007-08, 2005-06; NFIB *Guardian of Small Business Award* 2007-08; Wis. Manufacturing and Commerce *Working for Wisconsin Award* 2011-12. Sheboygan Co. Bd. 1988-Dec. 2002 (chm. 2000-Dec. 2002).

Elected to Assembly since 2002. Biennial committee assignments: **2013** — Jt. Com. for Review of Administrative Rules (co-chp., also 2007, vice chp. 2005, mbr. since 2005); Jt. Com. on Finance (also 2011). **2009** — Corrections and the Courts (since 2005); Natural Resources (also 2007); Urban and Local Affairs (vice chp. 2007, 2003, chp. 2005). **2007** — Aging and Long-Term Care (also 2003). **2003** — Rural Development; Small Business.

Telephone: Office: (608) 266-9175; (888) 534-0059 (toll free); District: (920) 528-8679.

E-mail: Rep.LeMahieu@legis.wisconsin.gov

Voting address: W6284 Lake Ellen Drive, P.O. Box 277, Cascade 53011.

Mailing address: Office: Room 304 East, State Capitol, P.O. Box 8952, Madison 53708.

Duey Stroebel (Rep.), 60th Assembly District

Born Cedarburg, September 1, 1959; married; 8 children. Graduate Cedarburg H.S. 1978; B.B.A. UW-Madison 1984; M.S. UW-Madison 1987. Real estate. Member: Ozaukee Board of Realtors; Cedarburg Chamber of Commerce; Greater Cedarburg Foundation (fmr. pres.); City of Cedarburg Downtown Ad Hoc Committee; Concordia University President's Council. Former member: Ozaukee Bank and Cornerstone Bank (bd. of dir.). Town of Cedarburg Parks Commission 2001-04; Town of Cedarburg Planning Commission 2003-05; Cedarburg School Board 2007-12.

Elected to Assembly in May 2011 special election; reelected 2012. Biennial committee assignments: **2013** — State and Local Finance (chp.); Jt. Survey Com. on Retirement Systems (co-chp.); Colleges and Universities; Environment and Forestry; Financial Institutions (also 2011); Insurance (also 2011). **2011** — Natural Resources.

Telephone: Office: (608) 267-2369; (888) 534-0060 (toll free) District: (262) 424-2583.

E-mail: Rep.Stroebel@legis.wisconsin.gov

Voting address: Cedarburg 53012.

Mailing address: Office: Room 207 North, State Capitol, P.O. Box 8953, Madison 53708.

21st SENATE DISTRICT

See Racine Area Detail Map on p. 98

**Senator
LEHMAN**

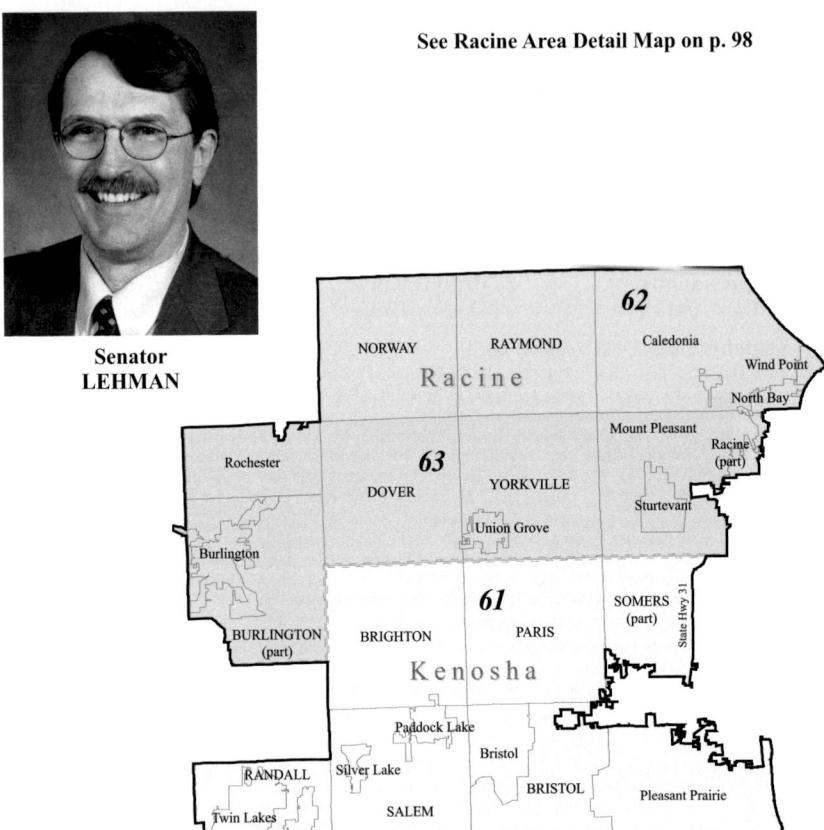

John W. Lehman (Dem.), 21st Senate District

Born Rhinelander, August 2, 1945; married; 3 daughters. Graduate Washington Park H.S. (Racine); B.A. Luther College 1967; M.Ed. Carthage College 1979; attended UW-Parkside and UW-Madison. Full-time legislator. Former high school history and economics teacher. Member: Racine Co. Democratic Party; Prader-Willi Syndrome Assn. of Wis.; Racine Heritage Museum; Friends of the Library, Racine Public Library; Clean Wisconsin; Sierra Club; Southeastern Wis. Educator Hall of Fame; Washington Park H.S. Hall of Fame. Former member: Racine Public Library Bd. (former pres.); Racine Sister City Planning Council; Racine Bd. of Health; Racine Education Association. Recipient: Luther College *Distinguished Service Award* 2007; Wis. League of Conservation Voters *Conservation Champion* 2007-08, 2005-06. Racine City Council 1988-2000 (former pres.).

Elected to Assembly 1996-2004; elected to Senate 2006; reelected in June 2012 special election. Majority Caucus Chairperson 2009. Biennial Senate committee assignments: **2013** — Education (chp. 2009, mbr. 2007); Workforce Development, Forestry, Mining, and Revenue; Jt. Legis. Audit Com.; Jt. Survey Com. on Tax Exemptions. **2011** — Education and Corrections (chp.); Children and Families, Disability Rights, and Housing Sustainability (vice chp.); Job Training, Technical Colleges, and Workforce Development; Labor, Consumer Buying Power and Consumer Protection; Jt. Com. on Finance (also 2009). **2009** —Economic Development; Labor, Elections and Urban Affairs; Jt. Com. for Review of Admin. Rules (vice co-chp. 2007). **2007** — Economic Development, Job Creation, Family Prosperity and Housing (vice chp.). Assembly committee assignments: **2005** — Education (since 1997); Education Reform (since 2001); Insurance (also 2003); Workforce Development (also 2003). **2001** — Environment; Natural Resources (also 1999); Public Health (eff. 11/19/01); Small Business and Consumer Affairs; Legis. Coun. Spec. Com. on Mental Health Parity. **1999** — Family Law; Small Business and Economic Development (also 1997). **1997** — Urban and Local Affairs; Legis. Coun. Com. on the School Calendar.

Telephone: Office: (608) 266-1832; (866) 615-7510 (toll free); District: (262) 632-3330.

E-mail: Sen.Lehman@legis.wisconsin.gov

Voting address: 708 Orchard Street, Racine 53405-2354.

Mailing address: Office: Room 5 South, State Capitol, P.O. Box 7882, Madison 53707-7882.

Representative	Representative	Representative
KERKMAN	WEATHERSTON	VOS

Samantha Kerkman (Rep.), 61st Assembly District

Born Burlington, March 6, 1974; 2 children. Graduate Wilmot H.S.; B.A. UW-Whitewater 1996. Member: Kenosha Area Business Alliance; Twin Lakes Chamber and Area Business Assn.; Twin Lakes American Legion Auxiliary Post 544; VFW Auxiliary, Bloomfield Center Post 5830; St. Alphonsus Catholic Church. Former member: Burlington Area Chamber of Commerce; Powers Lake Sportsmen Club.

Elected to Assembly since 2000. Majority Caucus Sergeant at Arms 2013, 2011. Biennial committee assignments: **2013** — Jt. Legis. Audit Com. (co-chp., also 2011, mbr. since 2001); Ways and Means (vice chp., chp. 2011, 2007, mbr. since 2001); Children and Families; Judiciary (also 2001-05). **2011** — Financial Institutions (also 2003, 2001); Judiciary and Ethics (since 2007). **2007** — Homeland Security and State Preparedness (vice chp.); Consumer Protection and Personal Privacy; Jobs and the Economy. **2005** — Budget Review (chp., also 2003); State-Federal Relations (vice chp.); Southeast Wisconsin Freeways. **2001** — Urban and Local Affairs (vice chp.); Government Operations.

Telephone: Office: (608) 266-2530; (888) 529-0061 (toll free); District: (262) 279-1037,

E-mail: Rep.Kerkman@legis.wisconsin.gov

Internet: www.legis.state.wi.us/assembly/asm66/news/default.htm

Voting address: Town of Randall.

Mailing address: Office: Room 315 North, State Capitol, P.O. Box 8952, Madison 53708; District: P.O. Box 156, Powers Lake 53159.

Thomas Weatherston (Rep.), 62nd Assembly District

Born Buffalo, NY, February 15, 1950; married; 1 child. Graduate Williamsville Central H.S. 1968; A.A.S. construction management, Erie Community College 1975; B.S. industrial engineering State University College of NY at Buffalo 1977. Full-time legislator. Former director of facilities management at Modine Manufacturing Company, and adjunct instructor at Gateway Technical College. Vietnam veteran, served in U.S. Air Force 1968-72. Member: Kiwanis; Vietnam Veterans of America Chapter 767; Veterans of Foreign Wars Post 10301. Former member: Racine Area Veterans Inc. (pres.); St. Catherine H.S. (bd. mbr.); Salvation Army (advisory bd.). Caledonia Utility District Commission 2011-13. Caledonia Village Trustee 2010-13.

Elected to Assembly 2012. Biennial committee assignments: **2013** — Veterans (vice chp.); Colleges and Universities; Consumer Protection; State and Local Finance; Workforce Development.

Telephone: Office: (608) 266-0731; (888) 534-0062 (toll free); District: (262) 989-3424.

E-mail: Rep.Weatherston@legis.wisconsin.gov

Voting address: Racine 53402.

Mailing address: Office: Room 109 West, State Capitol, P.O. Box 8953, Madison 53708.

Robin J. Vos (Rep.), 63rd Assembly District

Born Burlington, July 5, 1968. Graduate Burlington H.S. 1986; UW-Whitewater 1991. Owner of several small businesses. Former congressional district director; former legislative assistant. Member: Rotary Club (past pres.); Ducks Unlimited; Racine/Kenosha Farm Bureau; Knights of Columbus; Racine Co. Rep. Party; Racine Area Manufacturers and Commerce; NFIB (leadership council mbr.); Union Grove Chamber of Commerce; Burlington Chamber of Commerce. UW Board of Regents 1989-91. Racine Co. Board 1994-2004 (former chp. of Finance and Personnel Com.).

Elected to Assembly 2004; reelected since 2006. Speaker of the Assembly 2013. Biennial committee assignments: **2013** — Assembly Organization (chp.); Jt. Com. on Legis. Organization (co-chp.); Jt. Com. on Employment Relations (co chp., mbr. 2011); Rules (vice chp.); Jt. Legislative Council (since 2009). **2011** — Jt. Com. on Finance (co-chp., mbr. since 2007); Jt. Com. on Audit. **2009** — Insurance. **2007** — Elections and Constitutional Law (vice chp. eff. 1/3/08); Jobs and the Economy (eff. 1/17/08).

Telephone: Office: (608) 266-3387; (888) 534-0063 (toll free); Fax: (608) 282-3663; District: (262) 514-2597.

E-mail: Rep.Vos@legis.wisconsin.gov

Voting address: 960 Rock Ridge Road, Burlington 53105.

Mailing address: Office: Room 217 West, State Capitol, P.O. Box 8953, Madison 53708.

22nd SENATE DISTRICT

Detail Map: City of Kenosha

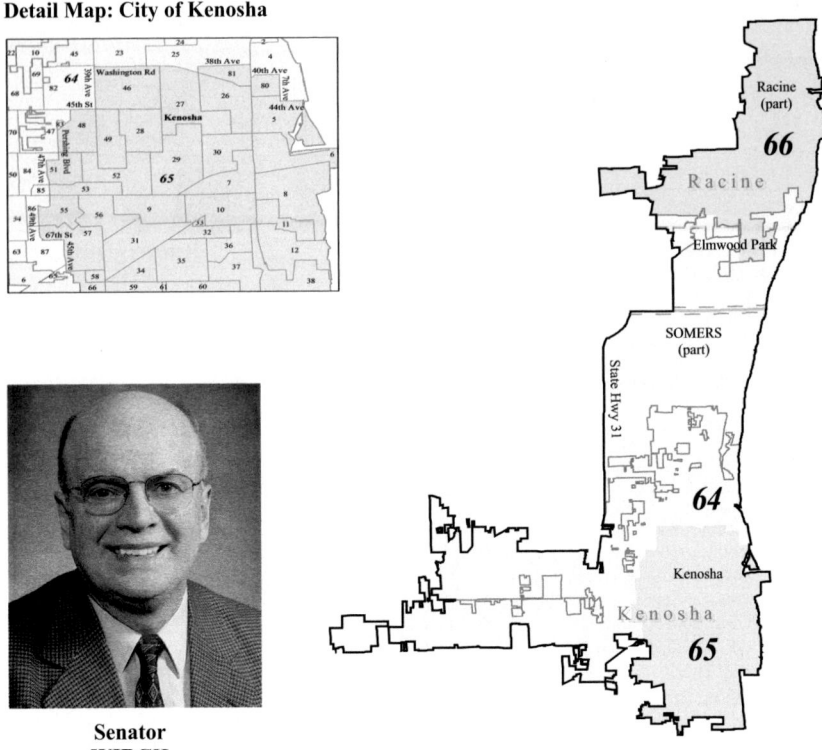

Senator
WIRCH

Robert W. Wirch (Dem.), 22nd Senate District

Born Kenosha, November 16, 1943; married; 2 children. Graduate Mary D. Bradford H.S.; B.A. UW-Parkside 1970. Full-time legislator. Former factory worker and liaison to JTPA programs. Served in Army Reserve 1965-71. Member: Danish Brotherhood; Kenosha Sport Fishing and Conservation Assn.; Friends of the Museum; Kenosha Scout Leaders Rescue Squad Advisory Council; Democratic. Party of Wis. Former member: Kenosha Boys and Girls Club (bd. of dir.). Kenosha County supervisor 1986-94 (served on Health and Human Services Com., Welfare Bd., and Developmental Disabilities Bd.).

Elected to Assembly 1992; reelected 1994; elected to Senate since 1996. Minority Caucus Chairperson 2003. Biennial committee assignments: **2013** — Government Operations, Public Works, and Telecommunications; Natural Resources; Jt. Com. on Finance (also 2001). **2011** — Energy, Biotechnology, and Consumer Protection; Labor, Public Safety, and Urban Affairs; Natural Resources and Environment. **2009** — Small Business, Emergency Preparedness, Technical Colleges, and Consumer Protection (chp.); Jt. Survey Com. on Retirement Systems (co-chp., also 2007, 2001, 1999, mbr. since 1997); Commerce, Utilities, Energy and Rail; Environment; Labor, Elections and Urban Affairs (vice chp. 2007); Jt. Legislative Council. **2007** — Small Business, Emergency Preparedness, Workforce Development, Technical Colleges and Consumer Protection (chp.); Commerce, Utilities and Rail; Environment and Natural Resources. **2005** — Energy, Utilities and Information Technology; Natural Resources and Transportation; Veterans, Homeland Security, Military Affairs, Small Business and Government Reform; Retirement Research Com. (since 1997). **2003** — Energy and Utilities; Environment and Natural Resources; Homeland Security, Veterans and Military Affairs, and Government Reform. **2001** — Environmental Resources; Human Services and Aging (also 1999); Judiciary, Consumer Affairs, and Campaign Finance Reform. **1999** — Economic Development, Housing and Government Operations (chp.); Agriculture, Environmental Resources and Campaign Finance Reform; State of Wis. Building Comn.; Law Revision Com.; Transportation Projects Comn. **1997** — Jt. Legis. Audit (co-chp., eff. 1/15/97 to 4/20/98); Jt. Com. for Review of Administrative Rules (eff. 1/15/97 to 1/5/98, also 1995); Agriculture and Environmental Resources (eff. 1/15/97 to 4/20/98); Health, Family Services and Aging (eff. 4/21/98); Health, Human Services, Aging, Corrections, Veterans and Military Affairs (eff. 1/15/97 to 1/7/98); Judiciary, Campaign Finance Reform and Consumer Affairs (chp., eff. 1/5/98); Council on Workforce Excellence.

Telephone: Office: (608) 267-8979; District: (262) 694-7379; Office Hotline: (888) 769-4724.

E-mail: Sen.Wirch@legis.wisconsin.gov

Voting address: Somers 53144.

Mailing address: Office: Room 127 South, State Capitol, P.O. Box 7882, Madison 53707-7882.

Representative
BARCA

Representative
OHNSTAD

Representative
MASON

Peter W. Barca (Dem.), 64th Assembly District

Born Kenosha, August 7, 1955; married; 2 children. Graduate Mary D. Bradford H.S. 1973; B.S. UW-Milwaukee 1977; attended Harvard U.; M.A. UW-Madison 1983. Past president, Aurora Assoc. International. Former CEO, Northpointe Resources; National Ombudsman, USSBA; Midwest Regional Administrator, USSBA. Member: Foundation Bd. of Dir., UW-Parkside; Society for ISCTR (co-founder); WISITALIA (past pres.); Former member: Lake County Econ. Dev. Com. on Small Business (chp.); Com. to Found the Boys and Girls Club of Kenosha (chp.); Lake County Partnership on Econ. Dev. (exec. com.); Small Business Forum of DNC (nat'l co-chair); Kenosha Family and Aging Soc. (bd. mbr.); Kenosha Incubator Assn. (chm.).

Elected to Assembly 1984-1992 (resigned 6/8/93 upon election to U.S. Congress); reelected since 2008. Minority Leader 2013, 2011; Majority Caucus Chairperson 2009, 1993, 1991. Biennial committee assignments: **2013** — Assembly Organization (since 2009, also 1993, 1991); Rules (since 2009, also 1993, 1991); Jt. Com. on Employment Relations (also 2011); Jt. Com. on Information Policy and Technology; Jt. Legislative Council (also 2011); Jt. Com. on Legislative Organization (also 2011); Wisconsin Economic Development Corporation Bd. (also 2011). **2009** — Jt. Legis. Audit Com. (co-chp.); Financial Institutions; Jobs, the Economy and Small Business.

Telephone: Office: (608) 266-5504; (888) 534-0064 (toll free).

E-mail: Rep.Barca@legis.wisconsin.gov

Voting address: Kenosha 53144.

Mailing address: Office: Room 201 West, State Capitol, P.O. Box 8952, Madison 53708.

Tod Ohnstad (Dem.), 65th Assembly District

Born Eau Claire, May 21, 1952; married. Graduate Altoona Public H.S. 1970; attended UW-Parkside. Former member: UAW Local 72 (chm. of trustees, shop committeeman, bargaining committee, executive bd.). City of Kenosha Alderman 2008-present.

Elected to Assembly 2012. Biennial committee assignments: **2013** — Insurance; Jobs, Economy and Mining; Labor; Tourism.

Telephone: Office: (608) 266-0455; (888) 534-0065 (toll free); District: (262) 764-1950.

E-mail: Rep.Ohnstad@legis.wisconsin.gov

Voting address: Kenosha 53140.

Mailing address: Office: Room 420 North, State Capitol, P.O. Box 8953, Madison 53708.

Cory Mason (Dem.), 66th Assembly District

Born Racine, January 25, 1973; married; 2 daughters, 1 son. Graduate Case H.S. (Racine); B.A. in philosophy UW-Madison. Full-time legislator. Member: River Alliance of Wis. (fmr. bd. mbr.); UW Center for Tobacco Research and Intervention (fmr. bd. mbr.); League of Conservation Voters; Racine Heritage Museum; Root River Council; I-94 Labor Development Com. (fmr. co-chp.); Wis. Coastal Management Bd. Former member: Racine Rotary West. Redevelopment Authority of Racine 2005-11 (commissioner).

Elected to Assembly 2006; reelected since 2008. Biennial committee assignments: **2013** — Jt. Com. on Finance (ranking min. mbr, also 2011 eff. 1/12/12, mbr. 2009); Jt. Legis. Council. **2011** — Jobs, Economy and Small Business; Natural Resources (ranking min. mbr., mbr. since 2007); Tourism, Recreation and State Properties; Legis. Coun. Spec. Com. on Infant Mortality. **2009** — Jt. Com. on Information Policy and Technology; Spec. Com. on Clean Energy Jobs; UW Hospitals and Clinics Authority Board; Groundwater Work Group. **2007** — Education; Jobs and the Economy.

Telephone: Office: (608) 266-0634; (888) 534-0066 (toll free).

Voting address: 1948 Michigan Boulevard, Racine 53402.

Mailing address: Office: Room 6 North, State Capitol, P.O. Box 8953, Madison 53708.

23rd SENATE DISTRICT
See Eau Claire Area Detail Map on p. 97

Detail Map: City of Marshfield

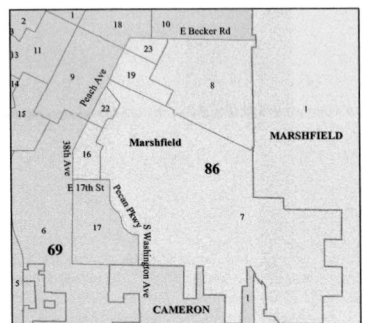

Senator
MOULTON

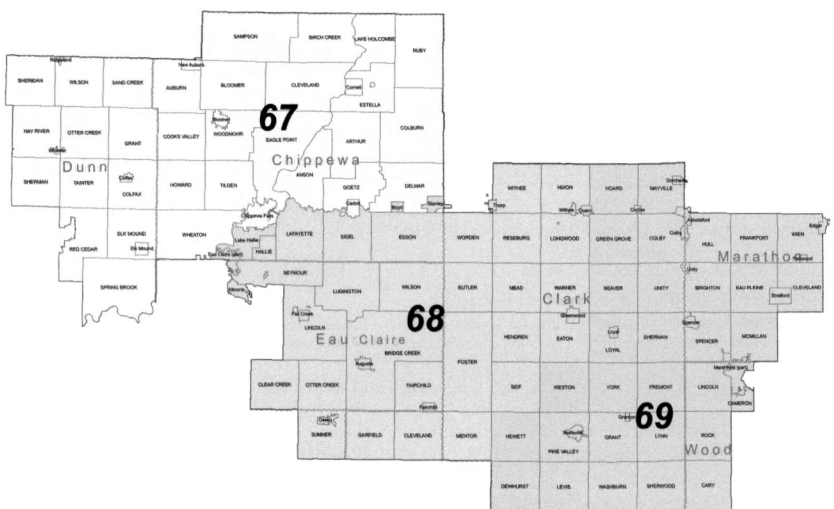

Terry Moulton (Rep.), 23rd Senate District

Born Whitefish, MT, July 19, 1946; married; 2 children, 8 grandchildren. Graduate Chippewa Falls H.S. 1964; attended UW-Eau Claire. Owner of archery and tackle shop and fishing tackle manufacturer. Former hospital accountant and business manager. Member: Chippewa Falls and Eau Claire Chambers of Commerce; Archery Range and Retailers Organization; Muskies, Inc.; Chippewa Bowhunters; Chippewa Rod and Gun; Eau Claire Archers; Eau Claire Rod and Gun Club.

Elected to Assembly 2004, 2006; elected to Senate 2010. Biennial committee assignments: **2013** — Agriculture, Small Business, and Tourism (chp.); Health and Human Services (vice chp.); Natural Resources (vice chp.); Small Business Regulatory Review Bd. (also 2011); State of Wis. Building Comn.; Council on Tourism (also 2011). **2011** — Workforce Development, Small Business, and Tourism (chp.); Natural Resources and Environment (vice chp.); Agriculture, Forestry, and Higher Education; Health.

Telephone: Office: (608) 266-7511; (888) 437-9436 (toll free).

E-mail: Sen.Moulton@legis.wisconsin.gov

Voting address: Chippewa Falls 54729.

Mailing address: Office: Room 306 South, State Capitol, P.O. Box 7882, Madison 53707-7882.

| Representative | Representative | Representative |
| LARSON | BERNIER | SUDER |

Tom Larson (Rep.), 67th Assembly District

Born Eau Claire, February 11, 1948; married; 3 children. Graduate Colfax H.S. 1966; attended Chippewa Valley Tech. Coll. Full-time legislator. Master electrician, licensed designer. Member: NFIB; Chippewa Valley Home Builders; ABC of Wisconsin; Colfax Kiwanis; Int'l. Assn. of Electrical Inspectors; Menomonie Chamber of Commerce; Colfax Sportsman Club; NRA; Chippewa Falls Chamber of Commerce.

Elected to Assembly 2010; reelected 2012. Biennial committee assignments: **2013** — Family Law (chp.); Energy and Utilities (vice chp., mbr. 2011); Jobs, Economy and Mining; Judiciary; Small Business Development; Transportation. **2011** — Judiciary and Ethics (vice chp.); Rural Economic Development and Rural Affairs.

Telephone: Office: (608) 266-1194; (888) 534-0067 (toll free); District: (715) 962-3030.

E-mail: Rep.Larson@legis.wisconsin.gov

Voting address: Colfax 54730.

Mailing address: Office: Room 18 West, State Capitol, P.O. Box 8952, Madison 53708.

Kathy Bernier (Rep.), 68th Assembly District

Born Eau Claire, April 29, 1956; 3 children, 6 grandchildren. Graduate Chippewa Falls Senior H.S. 1974; B.A. UW-Eau Claire; certificate in public management essentials, UW-Green Bay 2005. Member: American Legislative Exchange Council; Chippewa Falls Chamber of Commerce; Lake Hallie Optimists Club; Wis. Women in Government; National Federation of Women Legislators. Former member: Wis. County Clerks Assn. (legis. chair, fmr. treas.); Wis. County Constitutional Officers; Chippewa County Humane Assn.; Kiwanis Noon Club. Village of Lake Hallie trustee 2007-present. Chippewa County Clerk 1999-2011.

Elected to Assembly 2010; reelected 2012. Biennial committee assignments: **2013** — Campaigns and Elections (chp.); Rural Affairs (vice chp.); Aging and Long-Term Care (also 2011); Public Safety and Homeland Security; Workforce Development. **2011** — Election and Campaign Reform (vice chp.); Tourism, Recreation and State Properties.

Telephone: Office: (608) 266-9172; (888) 534-0068 (toll free).

E-mail: Rep.Bernier@legis.wisconsin.gov

Voting address: 10923 40th Avenue, Chippewa Falls 54729.

Mailing address: Office: Room 107 West, State Capitol, P.O. Box 8952, Madison 53708.

Scott Suder (Rep.), 69th Assembly District

Born Medford, September 28, 1968. Graduate Abbotsford H.S.; B.A. UW-Eau Claire 1991. Former legislative aide. Member of Wis. Air National Guard, 2003-2010; veteran of Operation Iraqi Freedom (3 tours). Member: Abbotsford Sportsman Club; NRA (lifetime mbr.); NRA-ILA; Natl. Assn. of Sportsmen Legislators; Abbotsford American Legion; Wis. Farm Bureau; NWTF; Abbotsford Lions Club. Recipient: MMAC *Champion of Commerce* 2010; Wis. Builders Assn. *Friend of Housing* 2008; Dairy Business Assn. *Legislative Excellence Award* 2010; Wis. Academy of Pediatrics *Legislator of the Year Award* 2008; Wis. Housing Alliance Outstanding *Legislative Leader Award* 2006; NCSL *Medal of Civic Honor* 2007; Wis. Council of the Blind and Visually Impaired *Outstanding Leadership Award* 2007; Am. Acad. of Pediatrics *Legislator of the Year* 2007; Wis. Bearhunters Assn. *Legislator of the Year* 2006; Wis. Coalition Against Sexual Assault *Voices of Courage Public Policy Award* 2006; Wis. Coalition Against Domestic Abuse *Legislative Champion Award* 2010, *Partner in Social Justice Award* 2003; NWTF *Legislator of the Year* 2002; Amer. Police Hall of Fame *Distinguished Service Award;* NFIB *Guardian of Small Business Award; Friend of Wis. Grocers Award;* NRA *Defender of Freedom Award; Friend of Agriculture Award* 2000-04. Abbotsford City Coun. 1996-2001.

Elected to Assembly since 1998. Majority Leader 2013, 2011; Minority Caucus Chairperson 2009. Biennial committee assignments: **2013** — Rules (chp., also 2011, mbr. 2009); Assembly Organization (vice chp., also 2011, mbr. 2009); Veterans; Jt. Com. on Employment Relations (also 2011); Jt. Legis. Council (also 2011); Jt. Com. on Legis. Organization (also 2011). **2009** — Fish and Wildlife; Insurance; Personal Privacy. **2007** — Jt. Com. on Finance; Rural Economic Development Bd. (since 2003). **2005** — Criminal Justice and Homeland Security (chp.); Rural Development (vice chp., also 2003); Agriculture (since 1999); Corrections and the Courts (vice chp. 1999-2001, mbr. 2003); Transportation (since 1999). **2003** — Criminal Justice (chp. and mbr. since 2001); Law Revision Com. (also 2001). **2001** — Census and Redistricting. **1999** — Campaigns and Elections (vice chp.); Highway Safety (eff. 10/12/99); Judiciary and Personal Privacy; Waste Cutters Task Force (chp.)

Telephone: Office: (608) 266-2401; (888) 534-0069 (toll free); District: (715) 223-6964.

E-mail: Rep.Suder@legis.wisconsin.gov

Voting address: 102 South 4th Avenue, Abbotsford 54405.

Mailing address: Office: Room 115 West, State Capitol, P.O. Box 8953, Madison 53708.

24th SENATE DISTRICT   **Detail Map: Town of Grant**

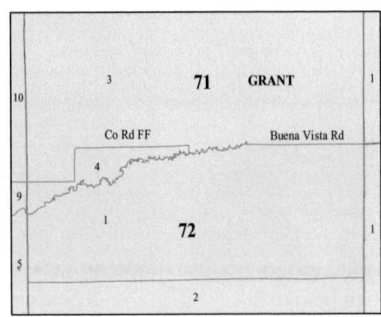

**Senator
LASSA**

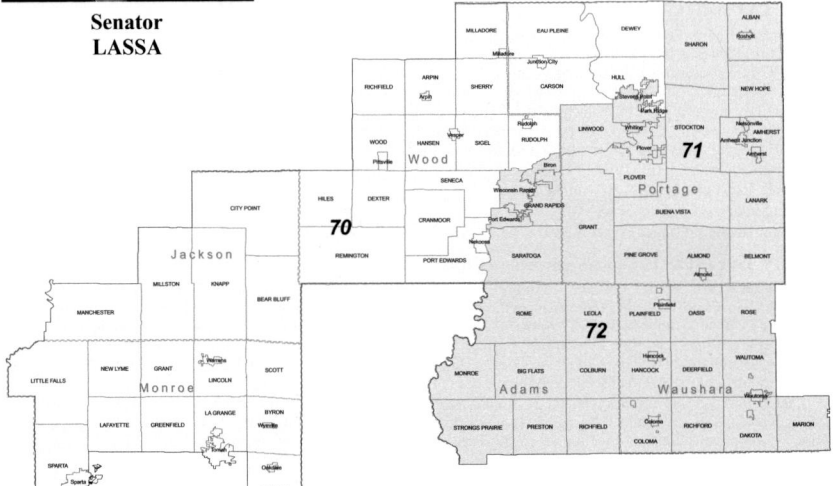

Julie M. Lassa (Dem.), 24th Senate District

Born Stevens Point, October 21, 1970; married; 3 children. Graduate Stevens Point Area Senior H.S.; B.S. in political science and public administration UW-Stevens Point 1993; UW-Madison La Follette Institute of Public Affairs graduate work. Full-time legislator. Former legislative aide and executive director, Plover Area Business Assn. Member: Heart of Wisconsin Business and Economic Alliance; Adams County Chamber of Commerce; Sparta Area Chamber of Commerce; Greater Tomah Area Chamber of Commerce; Black River Area Chamber of Commerce; Waushara Area Chamber of Commerce; Portage Co. Democratic Party (former chp.); Portage Co. Business Council; Small Business Environmental Council; Workforce Innovation Council. Dewey Town Board 1993-94.

Elected to Assembly 1998-2002 (resigned eff. 5/9/03); elected to Senate in April 2003 special election; reelected since 2004. Minority Caucus Chairperson 2013, 2011; Minority Caucus Secretary 1999. Biennial Senate committee assignments: **2013** — Agriculture, Small Business, and Tourism; Economic Development and Local Government; Financial Institutions and Rural Affairs; Wisconsin Economic Development Corporation Bd.; Child Abuse and Neglect Prevention Bd. (since 2007, also 2003, 2001). **2011** — Economic Development, Veterans and Military Affairs; Financial Institutions and Rural Issues; Jt. Legislative Audit (also 2007, 2005). **2009** — Economic Development (chp.); Children and Families and Workforce Development; Health, Health Insurance, Privacy, Property Tax Relief, and Revenue; Jt. Com. on Finance. **2007** — Economic Development, Job Creation, Family Prosperity and Housing (chp.); Agriculture and Higher Education (vice chp.); Campaign Finance Reform, Rural Issues and Information Technology. **2005** — Housing and Financial Institutions; Job Creation, Economic Development and Consumer Affairs (ranking min. mbr.). **2003** — Agriculture, Financial Institutions and Insurance; Jt. Com. for Review of Administrative Rules. Assembly committee assignments: **2003** — Agriculture (since 1999); Budget Review (ranking min. mbr.); Economic Development (ranking minority mbr., 2001); Financial Institutions; Rural Affairs. **2001** — Colleges and Universities (also 1999); Labor and Workforce Development. **1999** — Small Business and Economic Development; Transportation; World Dairy Center Authority.

Telephone: Office: (608) 266-3123; (800) 925-7491 (toll free); District: (715) 342-3806.

E-mail: Sen.Lassa@legis.wisconsin.gov

Voting address: Stevens Point 54482.

Mailing address: Office: Room 126 South, State Capitol, P.O. Box 7882, Madison 53707-7882.

Representative
VRUWINK

Representative
SHANKLAND

Representative
KRUG

Amy Sue Vruwink (Dem.), 70th Assembly District

Born Wisconsin Rapids, May 22, 1975; married; 2 children. Graduate Auburndale H.S. 1993; B.S. Marian University (Fond du Lac) 1997. Full-time legislator. Former legislative aide to U.S. Representative David R. Obey and Area Program Director for the Minnesota Farm Bureau. Member: Sparta Area Chamber of Commerce; Tomah Area Chamber of Commerce; Wood County Farm Bureau; National Rifle Association; Wisconsin Bear Hunters; Central Wisconsin Fair Association. Recipient: Wis. Builders Assn. *Friend of Housing* 2013, 2012, 2010; Auburndale FFA *Friend of the FFA* 2011-12; School Nutrition Assn. of Wis. *Star Advocate* 2010; Wis. Assn. of Fairs *Grand Champion Supporter* 2010; Aldo Leopold Audubon Society *Outstanding Conservation Voting Record* 2009-10; DBA *Distinguished Leadership Award* 2009; WPA *Friend of the Industry* 2009; Wis. Federation of Cooperatives *Friend of Cooperatives* 2008; Wis. Community Action Program Assn. *Jacqueline Lawrence Outstanding Advocate Award* 2007; Wis. Housing Alliance *Outstanding Legislative Leader* 2006; DBA *Friend of the Wis. Dairy Industry* 2005-06; Marian University *Distinguished Alumni Award* 2005; Wis. Farm Bureau Federation *Friend of Agriculture* 2005-06, 2003-04; Am. Cancer Society *Certificate of Recognition* 2004; Wis. Bear Hunters Assn. *Appreciation* (2-time).

Elected to Assembly since 2002. Minority Caucus Secretary 2005, 2003. Biennial committee assignments: **2013** — Agriculture (ranking min. mbr, also 2011, chp. 2009, mbr. since 2003); Rural Affairs (ranking min. mbr.); Transportation (since 2003); Veterans; Educational Communications Bd. (also 2011); Transportation Projects Commission (also 2003-2007). **2011** — Rural Economic Development and Rural Affairs. **2009** — Fish and Wildlife; Health and Health Care Reform (since 2007); Personal Privacy; Renewable Energy and Rural Affairs; Rural Economic Development Bd. (since 2005). **2005** — Aging and Long-Term Care (also 2003); Health (also 2003); Rural Affairs and Renewable Energy.

Telephone: Office: (608) 266-8366; (888) 534-0070 (toll free); District: (715) 652-2909.

E-mail: Rep.Vruwink@legis.wisconsin.gov

Voting address: 9425 Flower Lane, Milladore 54454.

Mailing address: Office: Room 112 North, State Capitol, P.O. Box 8953, Madison 53708.

Katrina Shankland (Dem.), 71st Assembly District

Born Wausau, August 4, 1987; single. Graduate Wittenberg-Birnamwood H.S. 2005; B.A. political science UW-Madison 2009; attended UW-Marathon Co. 2004-05, Marquette U. 2005-06. Full-time legislator. Former field organizer and programs coordinator at renewable energy nonprofit. Member: Portage Co. Democratic Party.

Elected to Assembly 2012. Biennial committee assignments: **2013** — Constitution and Ethics; Energy and Utilities; Natural Resources and Sporting Heritage; State Affairs (eff. 4/29/13); Workforce Development.

Telephone: Office: (608) 267-9649; (888) 534-0071 (toll free); District: (715) 881-1880.

E-mail: Rep.Shankland@legis.wisconsin.gov

Voting address: 833 Clark Street, Apt. G, Stevens Point 54481.

Mailing address: Office: Room 418 North, State Capitol, P.O. Box 8953, Madison 53708.

Scott S. Krug (Rep.), 72nd Assembly District

Born Wisconsin Rapids, September 16, 1975; married; 5 children. Graduate Lincoln H.S. 1993; attended UW-Stevens Point; A.D. Mid-State Tech. Coll. 1999; B.A.S. psychology UW-Green Bay 2009. Employment training specialist. Former Wood Co. jail discharge planner, Juneau Co. law enforcement officer. Member: Heart of Wisconsin Business and Economic Alliance; Wisconsin Rapids Rotary. Former member: WINR Advisory Bd.; ICS Self-sufficiency Committee. Recipient: WMC *Working for Wisconsin Award* 2012; Dairy Business Assn. *Legislative Excellence Award* 2012; 3rd Congressional District *State Legislator of the Year* 2012.

Elected to Assembly 2010; reelected 2012. Biennial committee assignments: **2013** — Children and Families (chp, vice chp. 2011); Environment and Forestry (vice chp.); Colleges and Universities; Corrections; Rural Affairs. **2011** — Criminal Justice and Corrections; Rural Economic Development and Rural Affairs.

Telephone: Office: (608) 266-0215; (888) 529-0072 (toll free); District: (715) 459-2267.

E-mail: Rep.Krug@legis.wisconsin.gov

Voting address: Town of Rome 54457.

Mailing address: Office: Room 208 North, State Capitol, P.O. Box 8952, Madison 53708.

25th SENATE DISTRICT

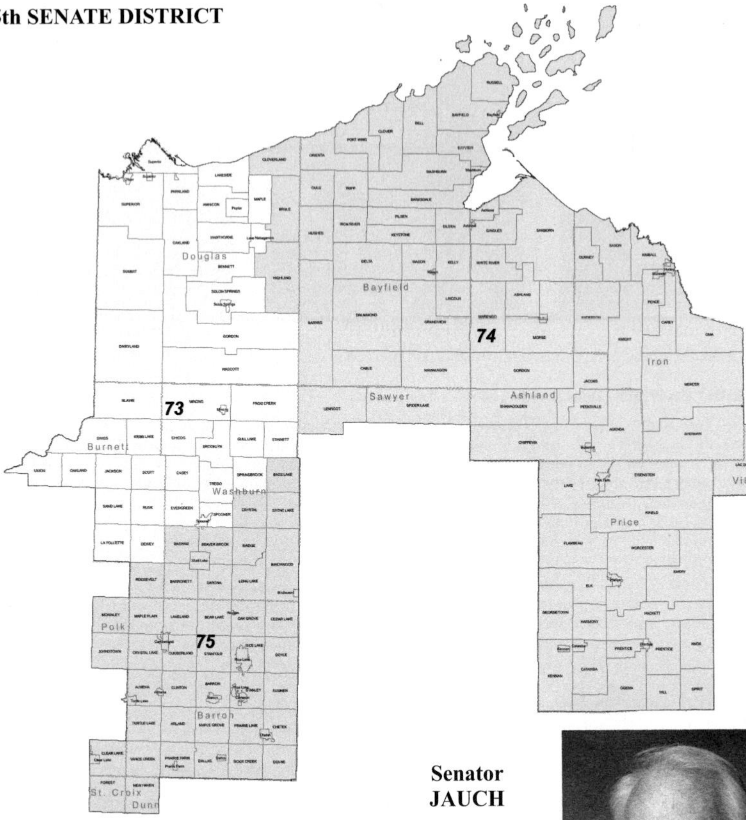

74

73

75

Senator
JAUCH

Robert Jauch (Dem.), 25th Senate District

Born Wheaton, IL, November 22, 1945; married; 2 children. Graduate Wheaton Central H.S.; attended UW-Eau Claire 1968-71, UW-Superior 1973. Full-time legislator. Former field rep. for Congressman David Obey. Veteran; served in Army 1964-68. Member: Vietnam Veterans of America; VFW; NCSL.

Elected to Assembly 1982, 1984; elected to Senate since 1986. Minority Leader 1995, 1993 (eff. 5/12/93). Biennial committee assignments: **2013** — Financial Institutions and Rural Issues; Workforce Development, Forestry, Mining, and Revenue. **2011** — Education (vice chp. 2009, mbr. 2005, 1993-2001); Public Health, Human Services, and Revenue; Jt. Com. on Finance (also 2007, 1991-99, Asm. mbr. 1985, 1983 eff. 10/7/83); Jt. Survey Com. for Retirement Systems (also mbr. and co-chp. 1987 to 4/20/93). **2009** — Children and Families and Workforce Development (chp.); Environment; Rural Issues, Biofuels, and Information Technology; Jt. Legis. Audit; Jt. Com. on Information Policy and Technology (also 2007, co-chp. 2001). **2007** — Tax Fairness and Family Prosperity (chp., eff. 11/5/07); Jt. Com. for Review of Administrative Rules (co-chp., mbr. 1987-1993); Environment and Natural Resources (vice chp.). **2005** — Jt. Survey Com. on Tax Exemptions. **2003** — Education, Ethics and Elections; Health, Children, Families, Aging and Long Term Care. **2001** — 2001-03 Biennial Budget (chp.); Economic Development and Corrections (chp.); Privacy, Electronic Commerce and Financial Institutions (also 1999); Legis. Adv. Com. to the Minn.-Wis. Boundary Area Comn. (since 1997). **1999** — Jt. Com. on Information Policy (co-chp., also 1997, eff. 1/15/97 to 4/20/98, 1995). **1997** — Education and Financial Institutions (eff. 4/21/98); Insurance, Tourism and Rural Affairs (eff. 1/15/97 to 4/20/98); Jt. Legislative Council (also 1995); Education Comn. of the States (also 1995); Submerged Cultural Resources Council (also 1995); Midwestern Higher Education Comn.; Legis. Coun. Coms. on Children at Risk Program, on School Discipline and Safety. **1995** — Jt. Com. on Employment Relations (resigned 10/17/95, also 1993); Jt. Com. on Legislative Organization (resigned 10/17/95, also 1993); Insurance (eff. 12/95-6/96); Insurance, Tourism, Veterans and Military Affairs (eff. 6/96); Senate Organization (resigned 10/17/95, also 1993); School Funding Comn.; Spec. Com. on State and Federal Relations (vice chp., resigned 10/17/95); Council on Alcohol and Other Drug Abuse; Disability Bd.; Legis. Coun. Com. on Lead Poisoning and Control. **1993** — Student Readiness Study Com.; Retirement Research Com. (mbr. and co-chp. 1987-4/20/93); Legis. Coun. Coms. on AISC, on Children in Need of Protection or Services, on State Fire Programs.

Telephone: Office: (608) 266-3510; (800) 469-6562 (toll free).
E-mail: Sen.Jauch@legis.wisconsin.gov
Voting address: Poplar 54864-9126.
Mailing address: Office: Room 310 South, State Capitol, P.O. Box 7882, Madison 53707-7882.

Representative   **Representative**   **Representative**
MILROY   **BEWLEY**   **SMITH**

Nick Milroy (Dem.), 73rd Assembly District

Born Duluth, MN, April 15, 1974; married; 3 children. Graduate Superior Senior H.S. 1992; B.S. UW-Superior 1998; attended UW-Eau Claire 1999-2000. Full-time legislator. Former fisheries biologist. Served in U.S. Navy 1992-94, U.S. Naval Reserve 1994-2000; deployed to Persian Gulf during Operation Southern Watch. Member: Douglas Co. Democratic Party (former secy.). Former member: Lake Superior Bi-national Forum; St. Louis River Watershed TMDL Partnership (bd. of dir.); Am. Fisheries Soc.; Duluth-Superior Metropolitan Interstate Council (policy bd. mbr.); Head of the Lakes Fair (bd. of dir.). Superior City Council 2005-09.

Elected to Assembly 2008; reelected since 2010. Biennial committee assignments: **2013** — Environment and Forestry; Natural Resources and Sporting Heritage; Rural Affairs; Veterans; Leg. Council Spec. Com. on State-Tribal Relations (also 2011). **2011** — Forestry (also 2009); Natural Resources (also 2009); Veterans and Military Affairs (also 2009). **2009** — Fish and Wildlife (vice chp.).

Telephone: Office: (608) 266-0640; (888) 534-0073 (toll free); District: (715) 392-8690.

E-mail: Rep.Milroy@legis.wisconsin.gov

Voting address: 4543 South Sam Anderson Road, South Range 54874.

Mailing address: Office: Room 11 West, State Capitol, P.O. Box 8953, Madison 53708.

Janet Bewley (Dem.), 74th Assembly District

Born Painesville, OH, November 10, 1951; married; 5 children. Graduate James Ford Rhodes H.S. (Cleveland, OH) 1969; B.A. Case Western Reserve U. 1973; M. Ed. U. of Maine 1977. Full-time legislator. Former Community Relations Officer, WHEDA. Ashland City Council 2007-09.

Elected to Assembly 2010; reelected 2012. Biennial committee assignments: **2013** — Colleges and Universities; Housing and Real Estate; Public Safety and Homeland Security; Rural Affairs; Transportation Projects Comn.; Leg. Coun. Spec. Com. on State-Tribal Relations (also 2011). **2011** — Forestry; Homeland Security and State Affairs; Housing; Transportation.

Telephone: Office: (608) 266-7690; (888) 534-0074 (toll free); District: (715) 682-0285.

E-mail: Rep.Bewley@legis.wisconsin.gov

Voting address: 810 Chapple Avenue, Ashland 54806.

Mailing address: Office: Room 322 West, State Capitol, P.O. Box 8952, Madison 53708.

Stephen Smith (Dem.), 75th Assembly District

Born Minneapolis, MN, August 31, 1951; married; 3 children. Graduate St. John's Preparatory (Collegeville, MN) 1969; B.S. accounting, UW-Superior 1973; attended UW-Madison 1971, UW Center-Barron Co. 1969-71. Full-time legislator. Owner of home center. Former owner of school bus company and accountant. Member: Shell Lake Lions Club; Elks Lodge 1441; Knights of Columbus Council 2137. Former member: Boys and Girls Club of Rice Lake Bd. (founding mbr.); Wis. School Bus Assn. Bd. (1982-2006, pres. 1991-93); Rice Lake Jaycees; Apple Valley Jaycees (state dir.); Eagan, Minn. Jaycees (pres.); Phi Beta Lambda. Shell Lake Zoning Bd. of Appeals 2008-present. Rice Lake Airport Commission 2001-06. Rice Lake Zoning Bd. of Appeals 2002-06. Barron Co. Bd. of Supervisors 1986-88.

Elected to Assembly 2012. Biennial committee assignments: **2013** — Agriculture; Rural Affairs; Small Business Development.

Telephone: Office: (608) 266-2519; (888) 534-0075 (toll free); District: (715) 468-4075.

E-mail: Rep.Smith@legis.wisconsin.gov

Voting address: Shell Lake 54871.

Mailing address: Office: Room 4 West, State Capitol, P.O. Box 8953, Madison 53708.

26th SENATE DISTRICT

See Madison Area Detail Map on pp. 90 & 91

Senator
RISSER

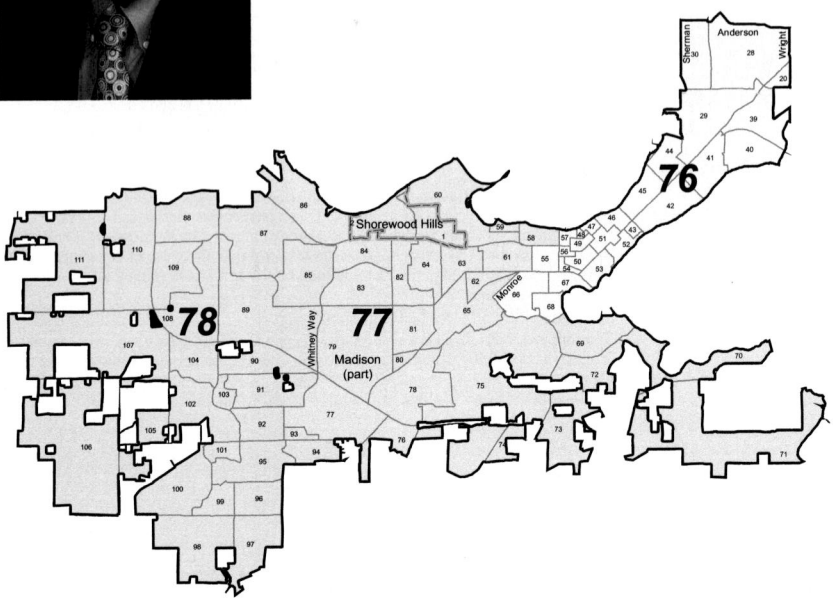

Fred Risser (Dem.), 26th Senate District

Born Madison, May 5, 1927; married; 3 children. Attended Carleton College (MN), UW-Madison; B.A. U. of Oregon 1950; LL.B. U. of Oregon 1952. Attorney. World War II veteran; Navy. Member: State Bar of Wis. and Oregon and Dane Co. Bar Assns.; NCSL (past mbr. Natl. Exec. Com.); CSG (past mbr. Natl. Exec. Com., Midwestern Conf. chp. 1993, 1982). Presidential Elector 2012, 2008, 1964.

Elected to Assembly 1956-60; elected to Senate in 1962 special election; reelected since 1964. Longest serving legislator in Wisconsin history and longest serving state legislator in U.S. President of the Senate 2011 (eff. 7/17/12), 2009, 2007, 2001, 1999, 1997 (eff. 1/15/97 to 4/20/98), 1995 (eff. 7/9/96), also 1979 to 4/20/93; Co-Majority Leader 2001 (eff. 10/22/02); Assistant Minority Leader 1995 (eff. 1/5/95 to 7/12/96), 1993 (eff. 4/20/93, also 1965); Sen. Pres. Pro Tempore 1977, 1975; Minority Ldr. 1967-73. Biennial committee assignments: **2013** —Judiciary and Labor; State and Federal Relations; Joint Legislative Council (co-chp. 2011 eff. 7/17/12, also 2007, 2001, 1999, 1997, chp. 1987, 1983, 1971, mbr. 1967-2009); State of Wis. Building Comn. (vice chp. 2009, 2007, 2001, 1999, 1971 to 5/19/93, mbr. since 1969); State Capitol and Executive Residence Bd. (chp. since 2003, co-chp. 1989 to 4/20/98, mbr. since 1983). **2011** — Judiciary, Utilities, Commerce, and Government Operations; Senate Organization (chp. 1987 to 4/20/98, also chp. 1977-1981, mbr. 2011 eff. 7/17/12, 2009, 2007, 1967-2003); Jt. Com. on Legislative Organization (co-chp. eff. 7/17/12, also 2009, 2007, 2001, 1999, 1997, eff. 1/15/97 to 4/20/98, also 1977 to 4/20/93, mbr. 1967-2003); Jt. Com. for Review of Admin. Rules (also 2009); Jt. Com. on Employment Relations (co-chp. eff. 7/17/12, also 2009, 2007, 2001, 1999, 1997, eff. 1/6/97 to 4/20/98, also 1995, eff. 7/9/96, also 1979 to 4/20/93, mbr. 1973-2009); Jt. Com. on Information Policy and Technology; Comn. on Uniform State Laws (since 2005). **2009** — Ethics Reform and Government Operations (chp., also 2007); State Historical Society Bd. of Curators (since 1983). **2007** — Wis. Environmental Education Bd. (also 2005). **2005** — Campaign Finance Reform and Ethics; Judiciary, Corrections and Privacy (eff. 4/1/05); State and Federal Relations. **2003** — Environment and Natural Resources. **2001** — Judiciary, Consumer Affairs, and Campaign Finance Reform; Disability Bd. (since 1997). For committee activities prior to 2001, see previous editions of the *Wisconsin Blue Book.*

Telephone: Office: (608) 266-1627; District: (608) 238-5008.

E-mail: Sen.Risser@legis.wisconsin.gov

Voting address: Madison 53703.

Mailing address: Office: Room 130 South, State Capitol, P.O. Box 7882, Madison 53707-7882.

Representative
TAYLOR

Representative
BERCEAU

Representative
HULSEY

Chris Taylor (Dem.), 76th Assembly District

Born January 13, 1968, Los Angeles, CA; married; 2 children. Graduate Birmingham H.S. (Van Nuys, CA) 1986; B.A. U. of Pennsylvania 1990; J.D. U. of Wisconsin Law School 1995. Full-time legislator. Former public policy director, Planned Parenthood of Wisconsin and practicing attorney. Member: State Bar of Wisconsin; Wisconsin League of Conservation Voters; Planned Parenthood Advocates of Wisconsin; Planned Parenthood Federation; Sierra Club; Lowell Home School Association; Democratic Party of Wisconsin. Former member: Public Interest Law Bd. (legislative subcom. chair).

Elected to Assembly in August 2011 special election; reelected 2012. Biennial committee assignments: **2013** — Children and Families; Family Law; Health (also 2011); Labor; Jt. Legis Council Law Revision Com. (also 2011), Steering Com. for Symposia Series on State Income Tax. **2011** — Labor and Workforce Development; Ways and Means.

Telephone: Office: (608) 266-5342; E-mail: Rep.Taylor@legis.wisconsin.gov
Voting address: Madison 53704.
Mailing address: Office: State Capitol, P.O. Box 8953, Madison 53708.

Terese Berceau (Dem.), 77th Assembly District

Born Green Bay, August 23, 1950. B.S. UW-Madison 1973; graduate studies in Urban and Regional planning UW-Madison. Staff, UW-Madison Robert M. La Follette School; staff, Wis. Counties Assn.; real estate sales; substitute teacher. Member: Dane Co. Dem. Party; Planned Parenthood Advocates of Wisconsin; Madison Civics Club; League of Conservation Voters. Former member: Monona Terrace Community and Convention Center Bd.; Greater Madison Convention and Visitors Bureau Bd.; Gov.'s Coun. on Domestic Abuse. Recipient: Wis. Coalition Against Domestic Violence *Legislative Champion Award* 2010; Wis. Women's Network *Stateswoman of the Year* 2006; Wis. League of Conservation Voters Award 2002-2010; Wis. Council of the Blind *Legislator of the Year* 2005; Wis. Coalition Against Sexual Assault *Voices of Courage Award* 2005; Wis. Alliance of Cities *Urban Families Recognition* 2004; Domestic Abuse Intervention Services *Certificate of Recognition* 2004; Wis. Coalition Against Domestic Violence *"DV Diva" Award* 2003; Domestic Abuse Intervention Service *Public Service Award* 2002; National Alliance for the Mentally Ill – Dane County *Community Action Citizen Award* 2003. City of Madison Community Development Authority (chp. 1989-92); Dane Co. Bd. of Supervisors 1992-2000.

Elected to Assembly since 1998. Biennial committee assignments: **2013** — Campaigns and Elections; Colleges and Universities; Insurance; State and Local Finance; Jt. Survey Com. on Retirement Systems; Jt. Legislative Council; State Coun. on Alcohol and Other Drug Abuse. **2011** — Children and Families; Wis. State Historical Society Curator. **2009** — Urban and Local Affairs (chp.).

Telephone: Office: (608) 266-3784; District: (608) 225-8193; E-mail: Rep.Berceau@legis.wisconsin.gov
Web site: http://www.terese.org
Voting address: Madison 53711.
Mailing address: Office: Room 104 North, State Capitol, P.O. Box 8952, Madison 53708.

Brett Hulsey (Dem.), 78th Assembly District

Born April 28, 1959, Oklahoma City, OK; one son, one daughter. Attended UW, Dartmouth College, Oklahoma State, and Colorado State U. B.A. Middlebury College 1982; M.S. Natural Science U. of Oklahoma 1988. Founder-owner of energy and environmental consulting firm. Former VISTA volunteer for Alaska state division of energy; environmental policy advisor and assistant political director for the 1992 Clinton-Gore campaign; union leader; stonemasons asst. foreman, Rocky Mountain Institute; Sierra Club: senior Midwest rep., Great Lakes program dir., coordinator of Challenge to Sprawl campaign, Protect Our Families from Floods Project; former middle and H.S. teacher, Cross Academy, Norman, OK. Member: Democratic Party; AARP; Sierra Club; Clean Wisconsin; Wis. Wildlife Federation; YMCA; Spring Harbor Middle School PTO; NACo Green Government Advisory Com.; Madison Nordic Ski Club (fmr. pres.). Former member: Stephens Elem. PTO (co-pres.); First Unitarian Soc. Recipient: FEMA *Outstanding Public Service Award;* ARC of Dane Co. *Elected Official Award for work with people with disability challenges;* Men's Fitness Magazine *Clean Water Champion.* Four-time Wis. Ironman, college cross country team captain, nationally ranked cross country ski racer, Eagle Scout. Dane Co. supervisor 1998-2011, Personnel and Finance Com. (chp.), Strategic Growth Com. (chp.), Lakes and Watersheds Comn., Manure Management Subcom., Transportation Com. (vice chp.), Transportation Planning Bd., Public Protection and Judiciary Com., Long Range Trans. Planning Com., Recycling and Solid Waste Comn.

Elected to Assembly 2010; reelected 2012. Biennial committee assignments: **2013** — Energy and Utilities (also 2011); Government Operations and Licensure (ranking mbr.); Jobs, Economy and Mining; Tourism; Ways and Means (ranking mbr.). **2011** — Natural Resources; Tourism, Recreation, and State Properties (eff. 9/30/11).

Telephone: Office: (608) 266-7521; E-mail: Rep.Hulsey@legis.wisconsin.gov
Voting address: 21 Merrill Crest Drive, Madison 53705.
Mailing address: Office: Room 5 North, State Capitol, P.O. Box 8952, Madison 53708.

Senator
ERPENBACH

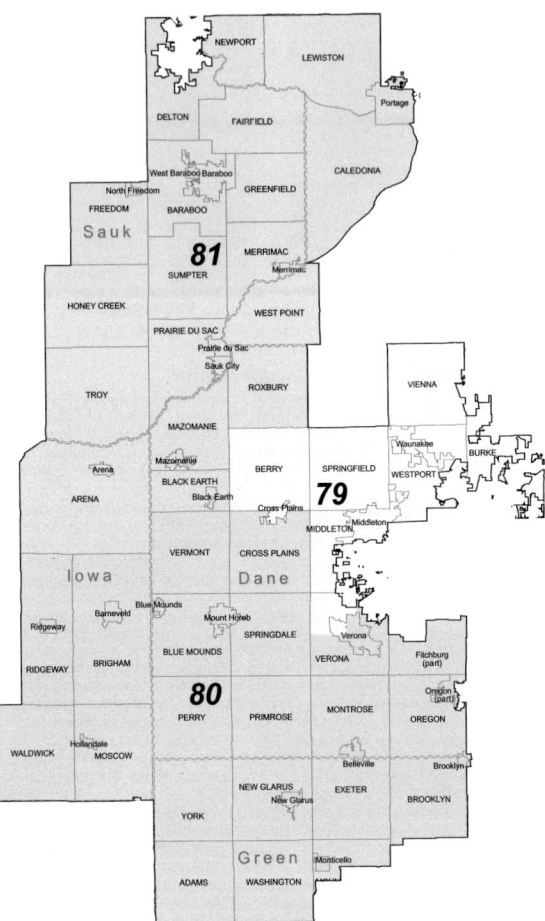

Jon B. Erpenbach (Dem.), 27th Senate District

Born Middleton, January 28, 1961; 2 children. Graduate Middleton H.S.; attended UW-Oshkosh 1979-81. Former communications director, legislative aide, radio personality, short order cook, meat packer, truck driver, and City of Middleton recreation instructor.

Elected to Senate 1998; reelected since 2002. Minority Leader 2003 session. Biennial committee assignments: **2013** — Health and Human Services (chp. 2007); Insurance and Housing; Universities and Technical Colleges. **2011** — Health; Judiciary, Utilities, Commerce, and Government Operations; Transportation and Elections; Jt. Legis. Coun. (also 2003, 1999). **2009** — Health, Health Insurance, Privacy, Property Tax Relief, and Revenue (chp.); Jt. Survey Com. on Tax Exemptions (co-chp., also 2007); Commerce, Utilities, Energy, and Rail; Education (vice chp. 2007, mbr. 2005, 2001, 1999); Judiciary, Corrections, Insurance, Campaign Finance Reform, and Housing. **2007** — Campaign Finance Reform, Rural Issues and Information Technology (vice chp.); Transportation, Tourism and Insurance. **2005** — Agriculture and Insurance; Health, Children, Families, Aging and Long-Term Care. **2003** — Jt. Com. on Employment Relations; Jt. Com. on Legislative Organization; Senate Organization; Jt. Legis. Coun. Spec. Com. on Review of Open Records Law (co-chp. since 2001). **2001** — Privacy, Electronic Commerce and Financial Institutions (chp., also 1999); 2001-03 Biennial Budget; Health, Utilities, Veterans and Military Affairs (also 1999); Jt. Com. on Information Policy and Technology; Law Revision Committee (also 1999); Legis. Coun. Com. on Condominium Law Review (co-chp. since 1999). **1999** — Jt. Committee on Information Policy; Lambeau Field; Jt. Survey Committee on Retirement Systems; Census Education Bd.; Governor's Blue Ribbon Task Force on Passenger Rail.

Telephone: Office: (608) 266-6670; District: (888) 549-0027 (toll free).

E-mail: Sen.Erpenbach@legis.wisconsin.gov

Voting address: 7194 Belle Fontaine Boulevard, Middleton 53562.

Mailing address: Office: Room 104 South, State Capitol, P.O. Box 7882, Madison 53707-7882.

**Representative
HESSELBEIN**

**Representative
POPE**

**Representative
CLARK**

Dianne Hesselbein (Dem.), 79th Assembly District

Born Madison, March 10, 1971; married; 3 children. Graduate La Follette H.S. (Madison) 1989; B.S. UW-Oshkosh 1993; M.A. Edgewood College 1996. Full-time legislator. Member: Dane Co. Democratic Party; Friends of Pheasant Branch; Clean WI; Wis. League of Conservation Voters; Middleton Action Team; VFW Ladies Auxiliary Council. Former member: Parent Teacher Organization (pres.); Boy Scouts of America (cubmaster); Girl Scout troop leader. Middleton-Cross Plains Area School District Bd. 2005-08. Dane Co. Bd. 2008-present.

Elected to Assembly 2012. Biennial committee assignments: **2013** — Colleges and Universities; Education; Natural Resources and Sporting Heritage; Tourism; Veterans.

Telephone: Office: (608) 266-5340; (888) 534-0079 (toll free).

E-mail: Rep.Hesselbein@legis.wisconsin.gov

Voting address: Middleton 53562.

Mailing address: Office: Room 9 North, State Capitol, P.O. Box 8952, Madison 53708.

Sondy Pope (Dem.), 80th Assembly District

Born Madison, April 27, 1950; married. Graduate River Valley H.S.; attended Madison Area Technical College and Edgewood College. Former Associate Director of the Foundation for Madison's Public Schools. Member: Natl. Caucus of Environmental Legislators; Honorary Life Member, Wis. Congress of Parents and Teachers. Fellow, Bowhay Institute, La Follette School, UW-Madison; Fellow, Flemming Institute, Center for Policy Alternatives; School and District Accountability Team 2011-13; Educator Effectiveness Coordinating Council 2011-13. Oakhill Correctional Institute Advisory Bd.; State Superintendent's Entrepreneurship Task Force (co-chp.) 2009-11.

Elected to Assembly since 2002. Biennial committee assignments: **2013** — Consumer Protection (also 2009); Education (chp. 2009, mbr. since 2003); Rules; Urban Education; Jt. Legis. Council Spec. Com. on Improving Educational Opportunities in High School. **2011** — Children and Families (also 2009); Housing; Jt. Leg. Council Spec. Com. on Infant Mortality. **2009** — Corrections and the Courts (since 2005); State Affairs and Homeland Security; Leg. Coun. Spec. Com. on School Safety. **2007** — Aging and Long-Term Care (since 2003); Education Reform. **2005** — Medicaid Reform. **2003** — Rural Affairs; Small Business.

Telephone: Office: (608) 266-3520; (888) 534-0080 (toll free).

E-mail: Rep.Pope@legis.wisconsin.gov

Voting address: 9262 Moen Road, Cross Plains 53528.

Mailing address: Office: Room 111 North, State Capitol, P.O. Box 8953, Madison 53708.

Fred Clark (Dem.), 81st Assembly District

Born Ann Arbor, MI, May 14, 1959; 1 child. Graduate Huron H.S. (Ann Arbor, MI) 1977; attended Michigan Tech. U.; B.S. Michigan State U. 1985; M.S. UW-Madison 1992. Forester. Small business owner, forestry contractor. Member: Society of American Foresters (chair, southwest Wis. chapter); Great Lakes Timber Professionals Assn.; Wis. League of Conservation Voters; Pheasants Forever; Wis. Council on Forestry.

Elected to Assembly 2008; reelected since 2010. Biennial committee assignments: **2013** — Education (also 2011); Environment and Forestry; Jobs, Economy and Mining; Natural Resources and Sporting Heritage. **2011** — Natural Resources (also 2009); Rules; Tourism, Recreation and State Properties (vice chp. 2009); Transportation Projects Comn. **2009** — Forestry (chp., eff. 12/4/09); Rural Economic Development; Wis. Council on Tourism.

Telephone: Office: (608) 266-7746; (888) 534-0081 (toll free).

Voting address: 938 Water Street #202, Sauk City 53583.

Mailing address: Room 122 North, State Capitol, P.O. Box 8952, Madison 53708.

28th SENATE DISTRICT

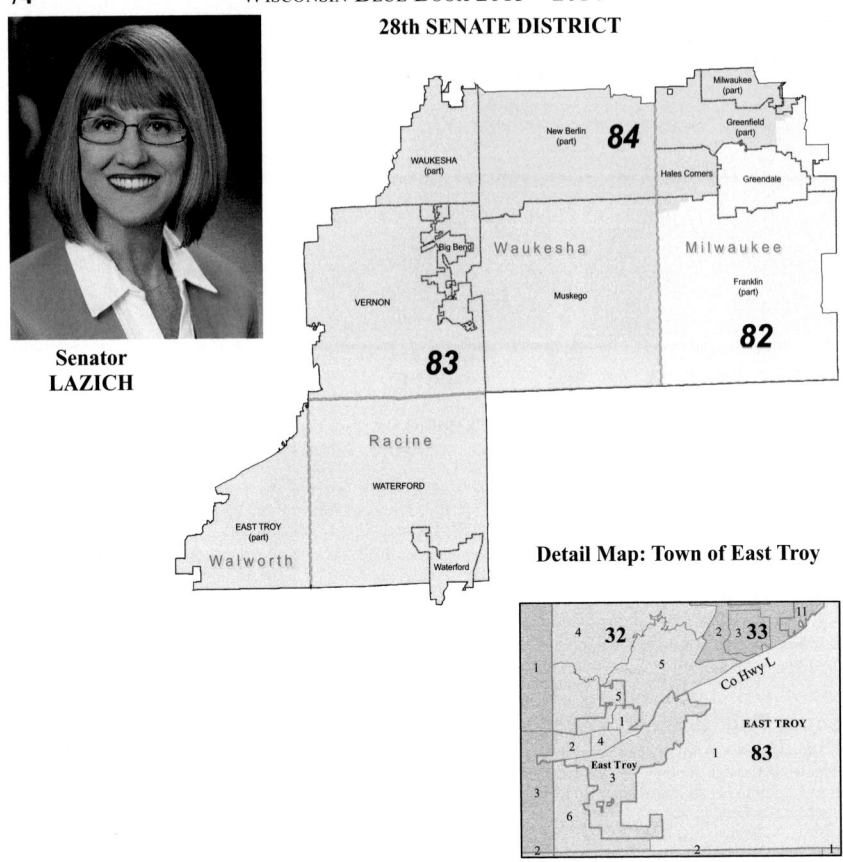

**Senator
LAZICH**

Detail Map: Town of East Troy

See Milwaukee Area Detail Map on pp. 92 & 93
See Waukesha County Area Detail Map on pp. 94 & 95

Mary A. Lazich (Rep.), 28th Senate District

Born Loyal, October 3, 1952; married; 3 children. B.A. UW-Milwaukee, *summa cum laude.* Former county board supervisor and city council member. Member: Waukesha Co. Republican Party; Waukesha Co. Republican Women's Club; New Berlin Lioness; New Berlin Historical Society; Boy Scout Advisory Com., Potawatomi Area Council. Waukesha Co. Board supervisor 1990-93, and mbr. of its Legislative, Intergovernmental and Education Com., Health and Human Services Com., Transportation Com., and Community Development Block Grant Bd.; New Berlin City Council 1986-92 (former president, chm. of Finance Com., chm. of Board of Public Works, mbr. of Planning Commission and Crime Prevention Com.).

Elected to Assembly 1992-96 (resigned eff. 4/20/98); elected to Senate in April 1998 special election; reelected since 2000. Majority Caucus Chairperson 2003. Biennial Senate committee assignments: **2013** — Elections and Urban Affairs (chp.); Health and Human Services (also 2007); Jt. Com. on Finance (also 2005, 2003); Jt. Legis. Audit (since 2009, 2001, 1999, co-chp. 1997 eff. 4/21/98). **2011** — Transportation and Elections (chp.); Public Health, Human Services, and Revenue (vice chp.); Labor, Public Safety, and Urban Affairs; Jt. Legis. Council. **2009** — Health, Health Insurance, Privacy, Property Tax Relief, and Revenue; Small Business, Emergency Preparedness, Technical Colleges, and Consumer Protection. **2007** — Education (also 2001, 1999); Judiciary and Corrections; Sentencing Comn. **2005** — Labor and Election Process Reform; Women's Council (also 1999, 1997). **2003** — Jt. Com. on Administrative Rules; Energy and Utilities; Law Revision Com. (co-chp.). **2001** — Health, Utilities, Veterans and Military Affairs; Jt. Com. on Information Policy and Technology. **1999** — Council on Highway Safety. **1997** — Education and Financial Institutions; Government Effectiveness; State Government Operations and Corrections; Forward Wisconsin, Inc. Assembly committee assignments: **1997** — Jt. Legis. Audit (co-chp., also 1995); Working Families (vice chp.); Financial Institutions; Health (since 1993); Labor and Employment (also 1995). **1995** — Insurance, Securities and Corporate Policy; Urban Education (also 1993); Welfare Reform; Legis. Coun. Com. on Health Care Information. **1993** — Excise and Fees; Judiciary; Transportation; Legis. Coun. Com. on Child Care Economics.

Telephone: Office: (608) 266-5400; (800) 334-1442 (toll free); District: (414) 425-9452.
E-mail: Sen.Lazich@legis.wisconsin.gov
Voting address: New Berlin 53151.
Mailing address: Office: Room 8 South, State Capitol, P.O. Box 7882, Madison 53707-7882.

Representative
STONE

Representative
CRAIG

Representative
KUGLITSCH

Jeff Stone (Rep.), 82nd Assembly District

Born Topeka, KS, January 28, 1961; married. Graduate West Muskingum H.S. (Zanesville, OH); B.A. in political science and history, Washburn U. (Topeka) *magna cum laude* and Phi Kappa Phi 1983. Printing business owner. Member: Partners of Parks, Greenfield; South Suburban Chamber of Commerce; Greendale Chamber of Commerce; Greenfield Chamber of Commerce (past secy.); Greendale Lions. Awards: NFIB *Guardian of Small Business Award* 2011-12; Wis. Troopers Assn. *Legislator of the Year* 2007; Wis. Counties Assn. *Outstanding Legislator Award* 2005-06; TDA *Transportation Service Award* 2005; MMAC *Champion of Commerce* 2011-12; *Friend of YMCA of Metropolitan Milwaukee* 2006; Aggregate Producers of Wis. 2005; Wis. Builders Assn. *Friend of the Housing Industry* 2001-12; Milwaukee Co. Republican Party *Taxcutter of the Year* 2001; *Legislative Leadership National Com. Against Drunk Driving Award* 2000; Wisconsin Manufacturers and Commerce *Working for Wisconsin* 2012, 2004, 2002, 2000. Greenfield City Council 1994-98.

Elected to Assembly in April 1998 special election; reelected since November 1998. Biennial committee assignments: **2013** — Small Business Development (chp.); Health (vice chp., chp 2011); Jobs, Economy and Mining, Transportation (since 2009, chp. 2001, vice chp. 1999); Ways and Means; Jt. Legis. Council; Wis. Economic Development Corp. Bd. **2011** — Election and Campaign Reform; Jobs, Economy and Small Business; Legis. Coun. Spec. Com. on Local Service Consolidation. **2009** — Elections and Campaign Finance Reform; Health and Healthcare Reform. **2007** — Jt. Com. on Finance (since 2003); Leg. Coun. Spec. Com. on Airport Authorities (chp.); Wis. Center District Bd. (eff 4/29/08). **2005** — University of Wis. Hospitals and Clinics Authority.

Telephone: Office: (608) 266-8590; (888) 534-0082 (toll free); District: (414) 529-1100.

E-mail: Rep.Stone@legis.wisconsin.gov

Voting address: 5535 Grandview Drive, Greendale 53129.

Mailing address: Office: Room 314 North, State Capitol, P.O. Box 8953, Madison 53708.

David Craig (Rep.), 83rd Assembly District

Born Waukesha, March 16, 1979; married; 5 children. Graduate Wisconsin Lutheran H.S. 1997; attended UW-Waukesha; B.A. UW-Milwaukee 2002. Licensed real estate agent. Former aide to Congressman Paul Ryan. Village of Big Bend trustee 2008-10.

Elected to Assembly in May 2011 special election; reelected 2012. Biennial committee assignments: **2013** — Financial Institutions (chp., mbr. 2011); Campaigns and Elections; Family Law; Government Operations and State Licensing; Insurance (also 2011); Judiciary. **2011** — Judiciary and Ethics.

Telephone: Office: (608) 266-3363; (888) 534-0083 (toll free).

E-mail: Rep.Craig@legis.wisconsin.gov

Voting address: P.O. Box 323, Big Bend 53103.

Mailing address: Office: Room 127 West, State Capitol, P.O. Box 8952, Madison 53708.

Michael Kuglitsch (Rep.), 84th Assembly District

Born Milwaukee, February 3, 1960; married; 4 children. Graduate New Berlin West H.S. 1978; B.A. Business UW-Whitewater 1983. Business consultant. Former member: Wisconsin Restaurant Assn. (pres.); Wisconsin Bowling Centers Assn. (pres.); New Berlin Chamber of Commerce (pres.).

Elected to Assembly 2010; reelected 2012. Biennial committee assignments: **2013** — State Affairs (chp.); International Trade and Commerce (vice chp.); Jobs, Economy and Mining; Labor; Workforce Development. **2011** — Homeland Security and State Affairs (vice chp.); Jobs, Economy and Small Business; Labor and Workforce Development.

Telephone: Office: (608) 267-5158.

E-mail: Rep.Kuglitsch@legis.wisconsin.gov

Voting address: New Berlin 53146.

Mailing address: Office: Room 129 West, State Capitol, P.O. Box 8952, Madison 53708.

29th SENATE DISTRICT

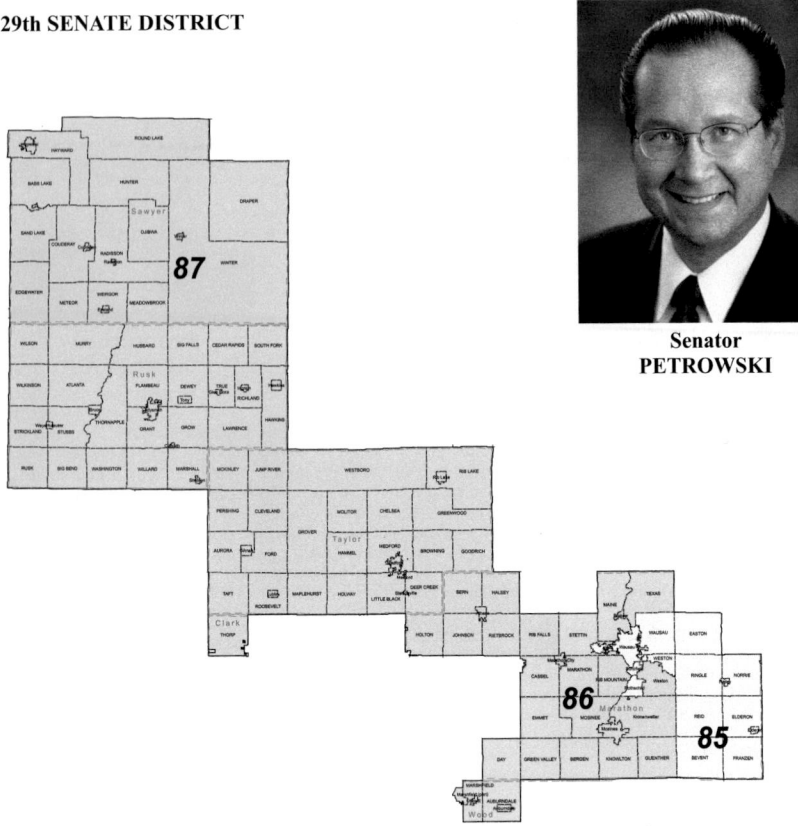

Senator
PETROWSKI

See City of Marshfield Detail Map on p. 64

Jerry Petrowski (Rep.), 29th Senate District

Born Wausau, June 16, 1950; married; 4 children, 2 grandchildren. Graduate Newman H.S. (Wausau); attended UW-Marathon County and Northcentral Technical College. Former ginseng, dairy, and beef farmer. Served in Army Reserve 1968-74. Member: 7th Congressional District, Marathon, Wood, Taylor, Rusk, Sawyer, Price, Lincoln, Portage, and Shawano County Republican Parties; Farm Bureau; Natl. Rifle Assn.; Friends of Rib Mountain; Marathon Lions. Former member: Wis. Rifle and Pistol Assn.; Internatl. Brotherhood of Electrical Workers Local #1791; Childcare Connection Bd.; DOT Law Enforcement Adv. Coun.; Marathon County Hunger Coalition. Recipient: Wis. Vietnam Veterans' *Legislator of the Year Award* 2002; Wis. Dept. of Veterans Affairs *Certificate of Commendation* 2005; Wis. Towns Assn. *Friend of Wis. Towns Award* 2011; Wis. Dental Assn. *Award of Honor (Mission of Mercy)* 2011; Wis. Farm Bureau's *Friend of Agriculture Award* 2006, 2004; Wis. Dairy Business Assn. *Award* 2012, 2010, 2008; 3M *Award of Appreciation* 2001; Wis. Paper Council *Champion of Paper Award* 2007; UWSP Paper Science Foundation *Friends of the Foundation Award* 2005; Amer. Academy of Pediatrics *Childhood Legislator Advocate of the Year* 2005; Wis. Grocers Assn. *Friend of the Grocers Award* 2012, 2008, 2006, WMC *Working for Wisconsin Award* 2012, 2002, 2000; Wis. Builders Assn. *Friend of Housing Award* 2006; State Farm Insurance *Golden Car Seat Award* 2007; Wis. Troopers Assn. *Legislator of the Year Award* 2003; Wis. County Police Assn. *Legislative Merit Award* 2007; Allied Health Chiropractic Centers *Commitment and Dedication to the Chiropractic Profession Award* 2004; Wis. Ginseng Board *Assistance to the Wis. Ginseng Industry Award* 2005; Wis. Bear Hunters Assn. *Hero Award* 2012.

Elected to Assembly 1998-2010; elected to Senate in June 2012 special election. Majority Caucus Sergeant at Arms 2003-2007. Biennial Senate committee assignments: **2013** — Transportation, Public Safety, and Veterans and Military Affairs (chp.); Economic Development and Local Government (vice chp.); Agriculture, Small Business, and Tourism; Financial Institutions and Rural Issues; Joint Legislative Council; State Councils on: Interstate Compact on Educational Opportunity for Military Children; Military and State Relations; Highway Safety; Transportation Projects Commission. Assembly committee assignments: **2011** — Transportation (chp., also 2007, vice chp. 2001-05, mbr. 2009, 1999); Public Health and Public Safety; Rural Economic Development and Rural Affairs; Veterans and Military Affairs (since 2007, also 1999-2003). **2009** — Renewable Energy and Rural Affairs. **2007** — Rural Affairs; State Affairs (since 1999); Gov.'s Council on Highway Safety (since 2003).

Telephone: Office: (608) 266-2502.
E-mail: Sen.Petrowski@legis.wisconsin.gov
Voting address: Marathon 54448.
Mailing address: Office: Room 123 South, State Capitol, P.O. Box 7882, Madison 53707.

Representative **WRIGHT**   Representative **SPIROS**   Representative **WILLIAMS**

Mandy Wright (Dem.), 85th Assembly District

Born Wausau, June 7, 1977; married; 3 children. Graduate Wausau East H.S. 1995; B.A. English and Norwegian, St. Olaf (Northfield, MN) 1999; ELL and English teacher's certification, Concordia 2004; M.A. education Viterbo 2008. Full-time legislator. Former Wausau school district teacher and soccer coach; teen coordinator, Boys and Girls Club, case manager, Big Brothers/Big Sisters. Member: League of Conservation Voters; Leigh Yawkey Woodson Art Museum; Wis. Farmer's Union; Democratic Party of Wis.; Noon Optimists; Wausau Nordic Ski Club; Friends of Rib Mountain; Wausau Region Chamber of Commerce; Sierra Club; YMCA; Stoney Acres Community Farm; Hmong 18 Clan Council of Wisconsin (adv.); Religion Education Teachers (vol.); YMCA Horizon Mentor (vol.); Safe Schools Ambassador Family Leader (vol.).

Elected to Assembly 2012. Biennial committee assignments: **2013** — Agriculture; Consumer Protection; Education; Small Business Development.

Telephone: Office: (608) 266-0654; (888) 534-0085 (toll free).

E-mail: Rep.Wright@legis.wisconsin.gov

Voting address: Wausau 54403.

Mailing address: Office: Room 10 West, State Capitol, P.O. Box 8953, Madison 53708.

John Spiros (Rep.), 86th Assembly District

Born Akron, Ohio, July 28, 1961; married; 5 children. Graduate Marietta H.S. (Marietta, Ohio) 1979; A.A.S. criminal justice MTCC (Omaha, NE) 1985. Vice president, safety and claims management for a transport company. Served in U.S. Air Force 1979-85. Member: Trucking Industry Defense Assn. (bd. mbr.); Wis. Farm Bureau; Central Wis. State Fair (bd. mbr.). Former member: Marshfield Rotary Club. City of Marshfield Alderman 2005-13.

Elected to Assembly 2012. Biennial committee assignments: **2013** — Criminal Justice (vice chp.); Children and Families; Transportation; Ways and Means.

Telephone: Office: (608) 266-1182; (888) 534-0086 (toll free).

E-mail: Rep.Spiros@legis.wisconsin.gov

Voting address: Marshfield 54449.

Mailing address: Office: Room 17 North, State Capitol, P.O. Box 8953, Madison 53708.

Mary Williams (Rep.), 87th Assembly District

Born Phillips, July 8, 1949; married; 3 children, 4 grandchildren. Graduate Phillips H.S. 1967; associate degree Taylor Co. Teachers Coll. 1969; B.S. elementary ed. UW-Stevens Point 1974. Restaurant owner. Former elementary teacher, Medford Area School Dist. Member: Farm Bureau; Dairy Promotion Com.; Dairy Breakfast Com.; Pri-Ru-Ta RC&D (pres.); Taylor Co. Safe & Stable Families; Wis. Restaurant Assn.; Natl. Fed. of Ind. Businesses; Chamber of Commerce; We Whittlesey Whizzers Snowmobile Club; Taylor Co. Local Emergency Planning Com. Former member: Big Brothers/Big Sisters of Taylor Co. (pres.); Restorative Justice of Taylor Co. (pres.); Intl. Trade, Business and Economic Development Council – Tourism Com. (chp.); Price Waterways Assn.; Taylor Co. Cooperative Youth Fair; WEAC; NEA. Recipient: State Bar of Wis. *Scales of Justice Award* 2011-12; Wis. Forestry Council *Distinguished Service Award* 2008; Wis. Bear Hunters *Hero Award;* Wis. Builders Assn. *Friend of Housing; Friend of Wis. Dairy Industry;* WCCO *Legislator of the Year* 2004, 2003; Natl. MS Society *Outstanding Volunteer Advocate* 2003. Taylor Co. Tourism Council. Taylor Co. Bd. 1992-96.

Elected to Assembly since 2002. Majority Caucus Secretary 2013, 2011, 2007; Minority Caucus Secretary 2009. Biennial committee assignments: **2013** — Jobs, Economy and Mining (chp.); Aging and Long Term Care; Family Law; International Trade and Commerce; Natural Resources and Sporting Heritage; Rules (since 2007). **2011** — Jobs, Economy and Small Business (chp., mbr. 2009); Children and Families; Forestry (also 2003-07); Natural Resources (also 2003-07).

Telephone: Office: (608) 266-7506; (888) 534-0087 (toll free); District: (715) 748-5980.

E-mail: Rep.WilliamsM@legis.wisconsin.gov

Voting address: 542 Billings Avenue, Medford 54451.

Mailing address: Office: Room 17 West, State Capitol, P.O. Box 8953, Madison 53708.

30th SENATE DISTRICT

Senator
HANSEN

Detail Map: City of De Pere

See Green Bay Area Detail Map on p. 96

Dave Hansen (Dem.), 30th Senate District

Born Green Bay, December 18, 1947; married; 3 children, 11 grandchildren. Graduate Green Bay West H.S.; B.S. UW-Green Bay 1971. Full-time legislator. Former teacher. Former truck driver for Green Bay Department of Public Works. Former Teamster's Union steward. Former member: Brown Co. Human Services Bd. (chp.); N.E.W. Zoo Advisory Bd.; Brown Co. Education and Recreation Com. (chp.); Great Lakes Compact Commission. Brown Co. Bd. Supervisor 1996-2002.

Elected to Senate 2000; reelected since 2004. Assistant Minority Leader 2013, 2011, 2005, 2003; Majority Leader 2009 (eff. 12/15/10); Assistant Majority Leader 2011 (eff. 7/24/12); 2009, 2007. Biennial committee assignments: **2013** — Agriculture, Small Business and Tourism; Energy, Consumer Protection and Government Reform; Senate Organization (since 2003); Transportation, Public Safety, and Veterans and Military Affairs; Jt. Com. on Legislative Organization (since 2003); Jt. Survey Com. on Retirement Systems (co-chp. 2011, eff. 7/24/12). **2011** — Transportation, Infrastructure, Financial Institutions and Retirement Security (chp.); Job Creation, Energy & Utilities, and Rural Affairs (vice chp.); Agriculture, Forestry, and Higher Education; Energy, Biotechnology, and Consumer Protection; State and Federal Relations and Information Technology; Jt. Com. on Finance (eff. 7/24/12, 2009, vice co-chp. 2007). **2009** — Education (since 2005); Transportation, Tourism, Forestry, and Natural Resources; Jt. Leg. Coun. Spec. Com. on State-Tribal Relations; Claims Bd.; Transportation Projects Commission (also 2001); Women's Council. **2007** — Commerce, Utilities and Rail; Transportation, Tourism and Insurance. **2005** — Agriculture and Insurance; Labor and Election Process Reform. **2003** — Jt. Legis. Audit (through 5/23/03); Agriculture, Financial Institutions and Insurance; Education, Ethics and Elections; Labor, Small Business Development and Consumer Affairs. **2001** — Labor and Agriculture (chp.); Jt. Com. for Review of Administrative Rules; Environmental Resources; Human Services and Aging; Universities, Housing, and Government Operations; Law Revision Committee; Unemployment Insurance Advisory Council (*ex officio* member).

Telephone: Office: (608) 266-5670; (866) 221-9395 (toll free); District: (920) 391-2000.

E-mail: Sen.Hansen@legis.wisconsin.gov

Voting address: 3489 Blackwolf Run, Green Bay 54311.

Mailing address: Office: Room 106 South, State Capitol, P.O. Box 7882, Madison 53707-7882.

Representative
KLENKE

Representative
NYGREN

Representative
GENRICH

John L. Klenke (Rep.), 88th Assembly District

Born Green Bay, April 25, 1958; married; 6 children. Graduate Green Bay Southwest H.S. 1976; B.A. accounting/finance 1980; M.S. Taxation 1982. Full-time legislator. Former treasurer, vice president corporate strategy, division president, and director of corporate tax for interstate trucking firm. Member: St. Bernards and St. Phillips Catholic Parish.

Elected to Assembly 2010; reelected 2012. Biennial committee assignments: **2013** — Jt. Com. on Finance. **2011** — Energy and Utilities (vice chp.); Jobs, Economy and Small Business; Tourism, Recreation and State Properties.

Telephone: Office: (608) 266-0485; (888) 534-0088 (toll free); District: (920) 469-8599.

E-mail: Rep.Klenke@legis.wisconsin.gov

Voting address: 3463 Yorkshire Road, Green Bay 54311.

Mailing address: Office: Room 306 East, State Capitol, P.O. Box 8952, Madison 53708.

John Nygren (Rep.), 89th Assembly District

Born Marinette, February 27, 1964; married; 3 children. Graduate Marinette H.S. 1982; attended UW-Marinette. Insurance and financial representative. Former restaurant owner and operator. Member: Jaycees (lifetime mbr., fmr. chapter, state, U.S. pres.); Marinette Kiwanis (fmr. pres.); Marinette Co. GOP (fmr. chm.). City of Marinette Recreation and Planning Bd. 2003-06.

Elected to Assembly 2006; reelected since 2008. Biennial committee assignments: **2013** — Jt. Com. on Finance (co-chp., mbr. 2011); Jt. Com. on Audit; Jt. Legis. Council; Jt. Com. on Employment Relations. **2011** — Insurance (also 2009, vice chp. 2007). **2009** — Education (also 2007); Health and Health Care Reform (also 2007). **2007** — Jobs and the Economy.

Telephone: Office: (608) 266-2343; (888) 534-0089 (toll free).

E-mail: Rep.Nygren@legis.wisconsin.gov

Voting address: Marinette 54143.

Mailing address: Office: Room 309 East, State Capitol, P.O. Box 8953, Madison 53708.

Eric Genrich (Dem.), 90th Assembly District

Born Green Bay, October 8, 1979; married; 2 children. Graduate Notre Dame Academy 1998; B.A. UW-Madison 2002; MLIS UW-Milwaukee 2010. Full-time legislator. Former librarian and legislative aide. Member: Neighbor-Works Green Bay; Democratic Party of Brown County; Fisk Addition Neighborhood Assn.; AFSCME Local 1901B; Current Young Professionals Network.

Elected to Assembly 2012. Biennial committee assignments: **2013** — Financial Institutions; Housing and Real Estate; Ways and Means.

Telephone: Office: (608) 266-0616; (888) 534-0090 (toll free); District: (920) 593-8528.

E-mail: Rep.Genrich@legis.wisconsin.gov

Voting address: 1089 Division Street, Green Bay 54303.

Mailing address: Office: Room 304 West, State Capitol, P.O. Box 8952, Madison 53708.

31st SENATE DISTRICT

**Senator
VINEHOUT**

See Eau Claire Area Detail Map on p. 97

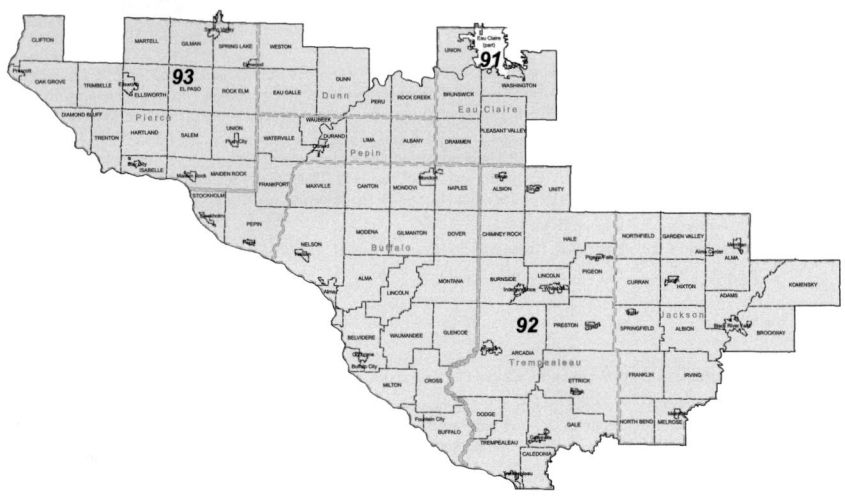

Kathleen Vinehout (Dem.), 31st Senate District

Born June 16, 1958; married; 1 child. B.S. with honors in education Southern Illinois U. 1980; M.P.H. St. Louis U. 1982; Ph.D. St. Louis U. 1987; A.D. in agriculture. Organic farmer. Former dairy farmer, university professor, health care manager. Member: Wis. Farmers Union; Wis. Farm Bureau Federation (fmr. bd. mbr., Buffalo Co.); Alma Chamber of Commerce; Democratic Party of Buffalo Co. (fmr. chp.); Andrew Blackfoot American Legion Auxiliary Post 129. Former member: Buffalo Co. Agricultural Fair Assn. (bd. mbr.); American Federation of Teachers (treas., Local 4100). Recipient: Wis. Farmers Union *Friend of Farmers Union Award* 2013; Wis. Congress of Parents and Teachers *Joan Dykstra Friends of Children Award* 2012; Wis. Aquaculture Assn. *Friend of Wisconsin Aquaculture* 2011; La Crosse Area Development Council *Triangle of Achievement;* AFSCME Council 40 *Protector of Quality Services Award* 2010; School Administrators Alliance *Legislator of the Year* 2010; Wis. Academy of Family Physicians *Friend of Family Medicine;* Wis. Grocers Assn. *Friend of Grocers* 2010; Wis. Crop Production Assn. *Outstanding Service to Agriculture Award;* Wis. Assn. of County Homes 2010 *Outstanding Legislative Service Award;* Wis. Troopers Assn. *Legislator of the Year* 2010; Wis. League of Conservation Voters *Conservation Champion* 2008; Wis. Assn. of PEG Channels *Friend of Access* 2008; Wis. Assn. of FFA *Honorary State FFA Degree* 2008; Pharmacy Soc. of Wis. *Legislator of the Year* 2008; Wis. Federation of Cooperatives *Friend of Cooperatives* 2008. Mississippi River Regional Planning Commission 2004-present.

Elected to Senate 2006; reelected 2010. Minority Caucus Vice Chairperson 2013, 2011; Majority Caucus Vice Chairperson 2009. Biennial committee assignments: **2013** — Agriculture, Small Business and Tourism; Education (also 2011); Jt. Com. on Information Policy and Technology; Jt. Com. for Review of Admin. Rules; Jt. Legislative Audit Com. (co.-chp., 2011 eff. 7/24/12, 2009); Mississippi River Parkway Comn. (also 2011). **2011** — Agriculture, Forestry, and Higher Education; Financial Institutions and Rural Issues. **2009** — Agriculture and Higher Education (chp., also 2007); Children, Families and Workforce Development; Economic Development; Public Health, Senior Issues, Long-Term Care, and Job Creation. **2007** — Health and Human Services (vice chp.); Economic Development, Job Creation, Family Prosperity and Housing; Judiciary and Corrections.

Telephone: Office: (608) 266-8546; (877) 763-6636 (toll free).

E-mail: Sen.Vinehout@legis.wisconsin.gov

Voting address: Alma 54610.

Mailing address: Office: Room 22 South, State Capitol, P.O. Box 7882, Madison 53707-7882.

Representative WACHS	Representative DANOU	Representative PETRYK

Dana Wachs (Dem.), 91st Assembly District

Born Eau Claire, August 25, 1957; married; 3 children. Graduate Memorial H.S. (Eau Claire) 1975; attended UW-Eau Claire 1975-76; B.S. Marquette U. 1981; J.D. Valparaiso U. 1985. Attorney. Member: American Bar Assn.; Wis. State Bar; Eau Claire County Bar Assn; Wis. Assn. of Justice; Rotary; Chippewa Valley Jazz Orchestra (bd. mbr.); Wis. Farmers Union; Muskies, Inc. Eau Claire City Council 2009-12 – Eau Claire City County Bd. of Health, Eau Claire Transit Comn., Eau Claire Affirmative Action Com., Eau Claire Parks and Waterways Com., L.E. Phillips Memorial Library (bd. mbr.), Eau Claire Economic Policy Adv. Com.

Elected to Assembly 2012. Biennial committee assignments: **2013** — Colleges and Universities; Constitution and Ethics; Judiciary; Workforce Development.

Telephone: Office: (608) 266-7461; (888) 534-0091 (toll free); District (715) 552-1439.

E-mail: Rep.Wachs@legis.wisconsin.gov

Voting address: Eau Claire 54701.

Mailing address: Office: Room 302 North, State Capitol, P.O. Box 8953, Madison 53708.

Chris Danou (Dem.), 92nd Assembly District

Born Bloomington, IL, 1967; married; 2 children. Graduate Columbus H.S. (Marshfield) 1985; A.A. UW-Marsh-field/Wood Co. 1987; B.A. with distinction UW-Madison 1990; M.A. international affairs The American U. (Washington, D.C.) 1991; M.S. natural resources UW-Stevens Point 1997. Full-time legislator. Former police officer, City of Onalaska. Member: Wis. Farm Bureau Fed.; Ducks Unlimited; National Farmers Union; Pheasants Forever; Trout Unlimited; The Nature Conservancy. Former member: Onalaska Professional Police Assn. (pres.); Wis. Professional Police Assn; Wis. Crime Victims Council. Recipient: Wisconsin Professional Police Association *Legislator of the Year* 2009-10; *Friend of Grocers* 2012, 2010.

Elected to Assembly 2008; reelected since 2010. Biennial committee assignments: **2013** — Agriculture (since 2009); Environment and Forestry; Insurance; Natural Resources and Sporting Heritage; Transportation. **2011** — Homeland Security and State Affairs; Natural Resources (vice chp. 2009); Rural Economic Development and Rural Affairs. **2009** — Fish and Wildlife; Renewable Energy and Rural Affairs.

Telephone: Office: (608) 266-7015; (888) 534-0091 (toll free); District: (608) 534-5016.

E-mail: Rep.Danou@legis.wisconsin.gov

Voting address: Trempealeau 54661.

Mailing address: Office: Room 107 North, State Capitol, P.O. Box 8952, Madison 53708.

Warren Petryk (Rep.), 93rd Assembly District

Born Eau Claire, January 24, 1955; single. Graduate Boyceville H.S. 1973; attended UW-Stout; B.A. with highest honors UW-Eau Claire 1978. Eagle Scout, November 1969. Worked in community relations for United Cerebral Palsy of West Central Wis.; co-founder of musical entertainment group "The Memories". Member: Eau Claire, Menomonie, Ellsworth, and Prescott Chambers of Commerce; National Rifle Association; Eau Claire Rod and Gun Club; Cleghorn Lions Club; Chippewa Valley Council of Boy Scouts of America (bd. dir.).

Elected to Assembly 2010; reelected 2012. Biennial committee assignments: **2013** — Veterans (chp.); Workforce Development (vice chp.); Aging and Long-Term Care (vice chp. 2011); Jobs, Economy and Mining; Natural Resources and Sporting Heritage; Jt. Com. on Information Policy and Technology. **2011** — Jobs, Economy and Small Business; Veterans and Military Affairs.

Telephone: Office: (608) 266-0660; (888) 534-0093 (toll free); District (715) 878-4002.

E-mail: Rep.Petryk@legis.wisconsin.gov

Voting address: Eleva 54738.

Mailing address: Office: Room 306 North, State Capitol, P.O. Box 8953, Madison 53708.

32nd SENATE DISTRICT

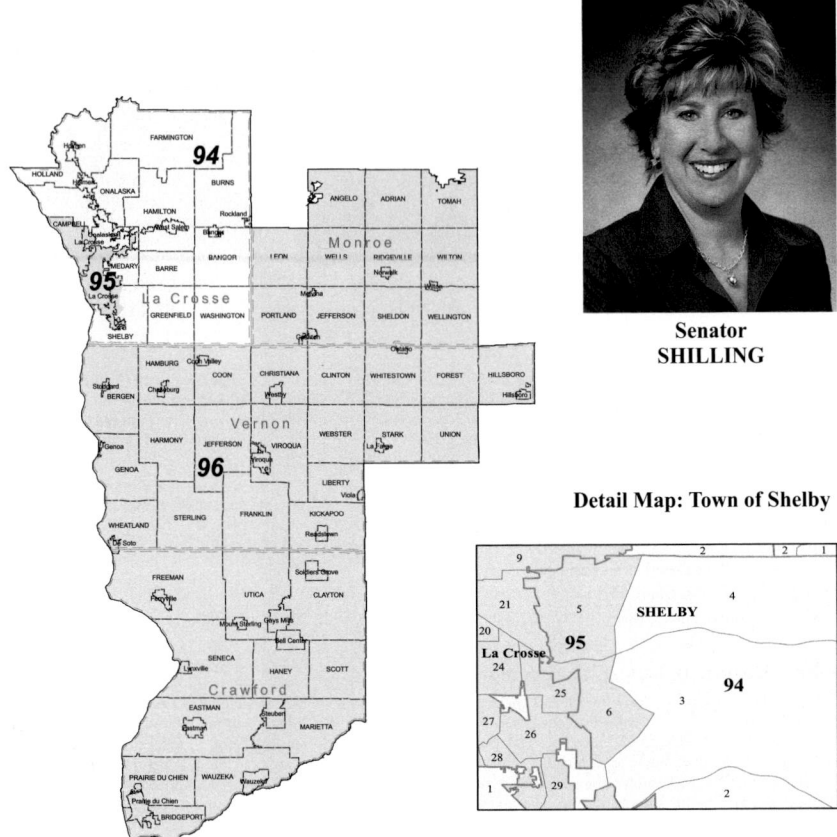

Senator
SHILLING

Detail Map: Town of Shelby

Jennifer Shilling (Dem.), 32nd Senate District

Born Oshkosh, July 4, 1969; married; 2 children. Graduate Buffalo Grove, IL H.S.; B.A. in political science and public administration, UW-La Crosse 1992. Former congressional aide and legislative aide. Member: UW-La Crosse Alumni Assn. (fmr. pres.); La Crosse Co. League of Women Voters; La Crosse Co. Democratic Party (former chp.); UW-La Crosse Chancellor's Community Council; Viterbo University Bd. of Advisors; La Crosse Area Chamber of Commerce; La Crosse County Local Emergency Planning Com.; La Crosse Area Habitat for Humanity Women Build; Vernon Women's Alliance; Viroqua Chamber Main Street; Riverfront La Crosse Community Advisory Bd. La Crosse Co. Bd. 1990-92.

Elected to Assembly 2000-10; elected to Senate in special election August 2011; reelected 2012. Minority Caucus Sergeant at Arms 2005. Biennial Senate committee assignments: **2013** — Government Operations, Public Works, and Telecommunications; Universities and Technical Colleges; Jt. Com. on Finance (also 2011). Assembly committee assignments: **2011** — Jt. Com. on Finance (also 2009). **2009** — Health and Health Care Reform (also 2007); Rules. **2007** — Colleges and Universities (since 2003); Workforce Development; State of Wisconsin Building Commission (also 2005). **2005** — Financial Institutions (since 2001); Health (since 2001); Highway Safety (also 2003). **2003** — Insurance (also 2001). **2001** — Personal Privacy; Legis. Adv. Com. to the Minn.-Wis. Boundary Area Comn.

Telephone: Office: (608) 266-5490; (800) 385-3385 (toll free).

E-mail: Sen.Shilling@legis.wisconsin.gov

Voting address: La Crosse 54601.

Mailing address: Office: Room 20 South, State Capitol, P.O. Box 7882, Madison 53707-7882.

| Representative | Representative | Representative |
| DOYLE | BILLINGS | NERISON |

Steve Doyle (Dem.), 94th Assembly District

Born La Crosse, May 21, 1958; married; 2 children. Graduate Aquinas H.S. 1976; B.A. UW-La Crosse 1980; J.D. U. of Wisconsin Law School 1986. Attorney. Former instructor, UW-La Crosse. Former member: Family Resource Center (bd. mbr.); Family and Childrens Center (bd. mbr.); Coulee Region Humane Society (bd. mbr., pres.). La Crosse Co. Bd. 1986-present (chairperson 2002-11).

Elected to Assembly in May 2011 special election; reelected 2012. Biennial committee assignments: **2013** — Corrections; Insurance (also 2011); Tourism; Transportation (also 2011). **2011** — Rural Economic Development and Rural Affairs; Tourism, Recreation and State Properties.

Telephone: Office: (608) 266-0631; (888) 534-0094 (toll free); District: (608) 783-1204; (608) 784-7299.

E-mail: Rep.Doyle@legis.wisconsin.gov

Voting address: N5525 Hauser Road, Onalaska 54650.

Mailing address: Office: Room 124 North, State Capitol, P.O. Box 8952, Madison 53708.

Jill Billings (Dem.), 95th Assembly District

Born Rochester, MN, January 19, 1962; 2 children. Graduate Stewartville H.S. 1980; B.A. Augsburg College, Minneapolis, MN 1989. Council of State Governments BILLD Fellow 2012. Full-time legislator. Former teacher of English and Citizenship to Hmong adults. Member: Viterbo University Board of Advisors; UW-La Crosse Chancellor's Community Council; La Crosse County League of Women Voters; La Crosse County Democratic Party. Former member: Wisconsin Counties Association County Ambassador Program; La Crosse Area Family Policy Board; Stepping Stones Children's Advocacy Center; La Crosse County Economic Development Fund; La Crosse Community Foundation Granting Advisory Board. La Crosse County Board 2004-12.

Elected to the Assembly in November 2011 special election; reelected 2012. Biennial committee assignments: **2013** — Constitution and Ethics (co-chp.); Children and Families; Colleges and Universities; Tourism; Workforce Development; Legis. Coun. Spec. Com. on Permanency for Young Children in the Child Welfare System. **2011** — Public Health and Safety; Consumer Protection and Personal Privacy.

Telephone: Office: (608) 266-5780; (888) 534-0095 (toll free).

Voting address: 403 South 13th Street, La Crosse 54601.

Mailing address: Office: Room 307 West, State Capitol, P.O. Box 8952, Madison 53708.

Lee Nerison (Rep.), 96th Assembly District

Born La Crosse, July 31, 1952; married; 3 children, 3 grandchildren. Graduate Viroqua H.S. 1970; UW-Madison Farm and Industry Short Course 1971. Farmer. Former dairy farmer. Former member: Coon Valley Lions. Former member: Vernon Co-op Oil and Gas (bd. mbr., secretary); Viroqua FFA Alumni (reporter); Westby FFA Alumni; Church Council (vice pres., treasurer). Vernon Co. Board 1998-2006 (chairperson 2002-06).

Elected to Assembly 2004; reelected since 2006. Biennial committee assignments: **2013** — Agriculture (chp., also 2011, vice chp. 2007, 2005, mbr. 2009); Aging and Long-Term Care; Consumer Protection; Natural Resources and Sporting Heritage; Veterans. **2011** — Natural Resources (since 2007); Veterans and Military Affairs. **2009** — Public Safety; Rural Economic Development. **2007** — Rural Affairs (chp.); Energy and Utilities (also 2005); Public Health. **2005** — Rural Affairs and Renewable Energy; Tourism.

Telephone: Office: (608) 266-3534; District: (608) 634-4562.

Voting address: Westby 54667.

Mailing address: Office: Room 310 North, State Capitol, P.O. Box 8953, Madison 53708.

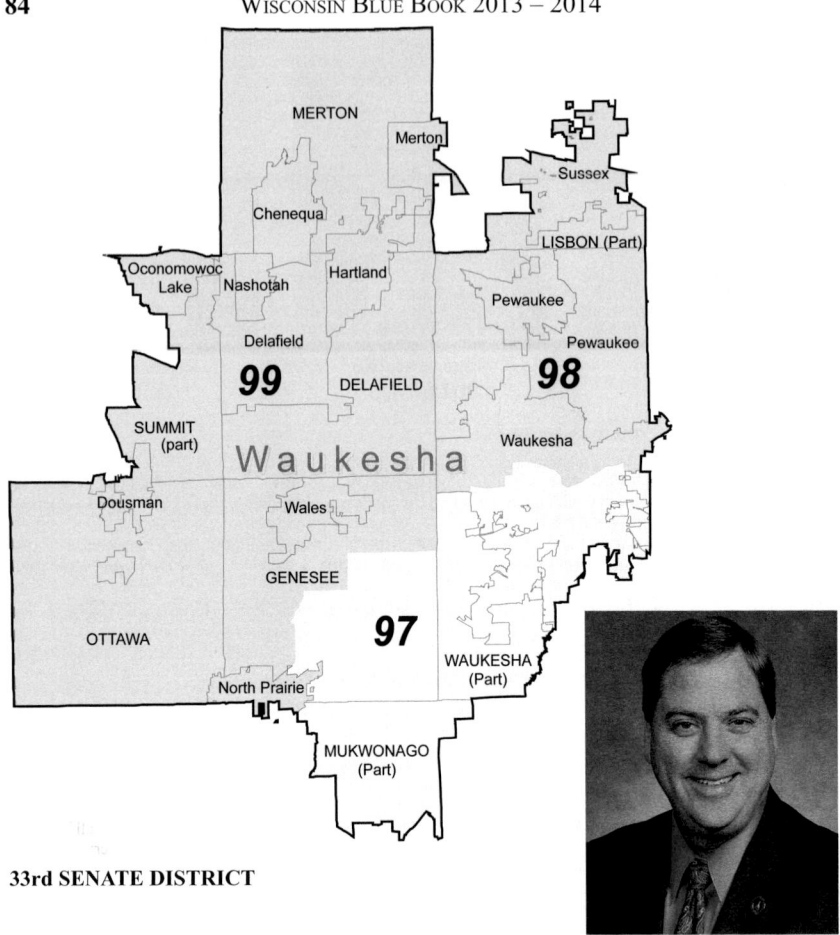

33rd SENATE DISTRICT

See Waukesha County Detail Map on pp. 94 & 95

See Waukesha Area Detail Map on p. 97

Senator
FARROW

Paul Farrow (Rep.), **33rd Senate District**

Born Milwaukee, 1964; married; 2 children. Graduate Marquette U. H.S. 1982; A.D. Waukesha Co. Tech. Coll. 1987; B.A. Carroll Coll. 1991. Self employed. Partner in a radon mitigation company. Former owner of home inspection business. Member: Pewaukee Chamber of Commerce; Presidential Advisory Council, Carroll U.; Waukesha Co. Business Alliance; Waukesha Co. Republican Party. Former member: National Assn. of Home Inspectors; World Muskie Hunt (past pres.).

Elected to Assembly 2010; elected to Senate in December 2012 special election. Biennial Senate committee assignments: **2013** — Government Operations, Public Works, and Telecommunications (chp.); Education (vice chp.); Judiciary and Labor; Jt. Survey Com. on Retirement Systems. Assembly committee assignments: **2011** — Transportation (vice chp.); Colleges and Universities; Housing.

Telephone: Office: (608) 266-9174.

E-mail: Sen.Farrow@legis.wisconsin.gov

Voting address: Pewaukee 53072.

Mailing address: Office: Room 323 South, State Capitol, P.O. Box 7882, Madison 53707.

Representative	Representative	Representative
KRAMER	NEYLON	KAPENGA

Bill Kramer (Rep.), 97th Assembly District

Born Waukesha, January 21, 1965; single. Graduate Waukesha South H.S. 1983; B.B.A. in accounting, *magna cum laude,* UW-Whitewater 1987; J.D. Duke U. School of Law 1994. Certified financial planner, attorney, and certified public accountant. Member: Waukesha Elks; Free and Accepted Mason, Waukesha Lodge #37; Waukesha Chamber of Commerce; St. Mary's Parish; Waukesha Co. Republican Party. Waukesha Co. Board 1998-99, 2004-07.

Elected to Assembly 2006; reelected since 2008. Speaker Pro Tempore 2013, 2011. Biennial committee assignments: **2013** — Assembly Organization (also 2011); Financial Institutions (chp. 2011, mbr. since 2007); Rules (also 2011); Jt. Legis. Council. **2011** — Jt. Survey Com. on Retirement Systems (co-chp.). **2009** — Criminal Justice (also 2007); Judiciary and Ethics (vice chp. 2007); Jt. Legis. Audit. **2007** — Aging and Long-Term Care; Elections and Constitutional Law; Insurance.

Telephone: Office: (608) 266-8580; District: (262) 546-4603.

Voting address: S39 W27465 Brookhill Drive, Waukesha 53189.

Mailing address: Office: Room 103 West, State Capitol, P.O. Box 8952, Madison 53708.

Adam Neylon (Rep.), 98th Assembly District

Born Elgin, IL, December 30, 1984; single. Graduate H.D. Jacobs H.S. 2003; B.A. Carroll U. 2008. Small business owner. Former legislative staffer for U.S. Rep. Jim Sensenbrenner and State Rep. Bill Kramer. Member: Presidents Advisory Council at Carroll U.; Waukesha Co. Business Alliance; Republican Party of Waukesha Co. (fmr. youth chm.); National Rifle Association.

Elected to Assembly in April 2013 special election. Biennial committee assignments: **2013** — Children and Families; Energy and Utilities; Government Operations and State Licensing; State Affairs; State Supported Programs Study and Advisory Com.

Telephone: Office: (608) 266-5120.

E-mail: Rep.Neylon@legis.wisconsin.gov

Voting address: Pewaukee 53072.

Mailing address: Office: Room 121 West, State Capitol, P.O. Box 8953, Madison 53708.

Chris Kapenga (Rep.), 99th Assembly District

Born Zeeland, MI, February 19, 1972; married; 2 children. Graduate Holland Christian (Holland, MI) 1990. B.S. in accountancy, Calvin College (Grand Rapids, MI) 1994. Business owner. Former certified public accountant. Member: Elmbrook Church Financial Counseling (dir.). Former member: WSCA School Bd. (vice chm., treas., secy.); WICPA; Metro-Milwaukee Chamber of Commerce; Institute of Management Accountants (bd. mbr.).

Elected to Assembly 2010; reelected 2012. Biennial committee assignments: **2013** — Constitution and Ethics (chp.); Financial Institutions (vice chp.); Health; Jobs, Economy and Mining; Labor. **2011** — Labor and Workforce Development (vice chp.); Insurance; Jobs, Economy and Small Business; Ways and Means.

Telephone: Office: (608) 266-3007; (888) 529-0099 (toll free).

Voting address: Delafield 53018.

Mailing address: Office: Room 220 North, State Capitol, P.O. Box 8952, Madison 53708.

Jeffrey Renk: Senate Chief Clerk

Born Wauwatosa, January 31, 1960; married; 1 child. Graduate Wauwatosa West H.S. 1978; attended UW-Milwaukee 1978-80; B.S. political science UW-Madison 1984. Former Senate assistant chief clerk 2004-12; computer programmer, Legislative Technology Services Bureau 1998-2004; Assembly chief clerk staff 1988-98; Assembly messenger 1983-88. Member: American Society of Legislative Clerks and Secretaries. Former member: National Association of Legislative Information Technology.

Elected Senate Chief Clerk 2013.

Telephone: Office: (608) 266-2517.

Voting address: Fitchburg 53719.

Mailing address: Office: Room B20 Southeast, State Capitol, P.O. Box 7882, Madison 53707-7882.

Edward (Ted) A. Blazel: Senate Sergeant at Arms

Born Quincy, IL, June 14, 1972; married; 2 children. Graduate Quincy Senior H.S. 1990; B.A. St. Norbert College (De Pere) 1994; M.A. Marquette U. (Milwaukee) 1998. Former legislative aide. Member: National Legislative Service and Security Assn.; Heritage Heights Community Assn.

Elected Senate Sergeant at Arms 2003; reelected since 2005.

Telephone: Office: (608) 266-1801.

Voting address: Madison 53714.

Mailing address: Office: Room B35 South, State Capitol, P.O. Box 7882, Madison 53707-7882.

Patrick E. Fuller: Assembly Chief Clerk

Born Toledo, Ohio, February 24, 1954; married; 1 child. Graduate St. Francis de Sales H.S. (Toledo) 1972; B.E. U. of Toledo 1980; M.B.A. Touro University International (Los Alamitos, CA) 2001. Former director Wisconsin Troops to Teachers Program, Wis. Dept. of Veterans Affairs 1998-2000. Vietnam Era and Operation Desert Storm veteran. Served in U.S. Marine Corps 1972-86; U.S. Army 1986-97. Member: NRA; Second Marine Division Assn.; Veterans of Foreign Wars; Disabled Veterans of America; American Legion; Force Recon Association; 75th Ranger Regiment Association.

Elected Assembly Chief Clerk 2003; reelected since 2005.

Telephone: Office: (608) 266-5811.

E-mail address: Patrick.Fuller@legis.wisconsin.gov

Voting address: 214 Grove Street, Ridgeway 53582.

Mailing address: Office: Suite 401, 17 West Main Street, Risser Justice Center, Madison 53708-8952.

Anne Tonnon Byers: Assembly Sergeant at Arms

Born Green Bay, December 14, 1968; married; 2 children. Graduate Green Bay East H.S. 1987; attended UW-Green Bay; B.S. UW-Madison 1991; UW Certified Public Management Program 2001. Former Assistant Assembly Sergeant at Arms 1998-2010; Office Manager for Assembly Sergeant 1993-98. Member: Cub Scout Pack 53.

Elected Assembly Sergeant at Arms 2011; reelected 2013.

Telephone: Office: (608) 266-1503.

E-mail address: anne.tonnonbyers@legis.wisconsin.gov

Voting address: Village of McFarland.

Mailing address: Office: Room 411 West, State Capitol, P.O. Box 8952, Madison 53708-8952.

SENATE DISTRICTS

Enacted by 2011 Wisconsin Act 43

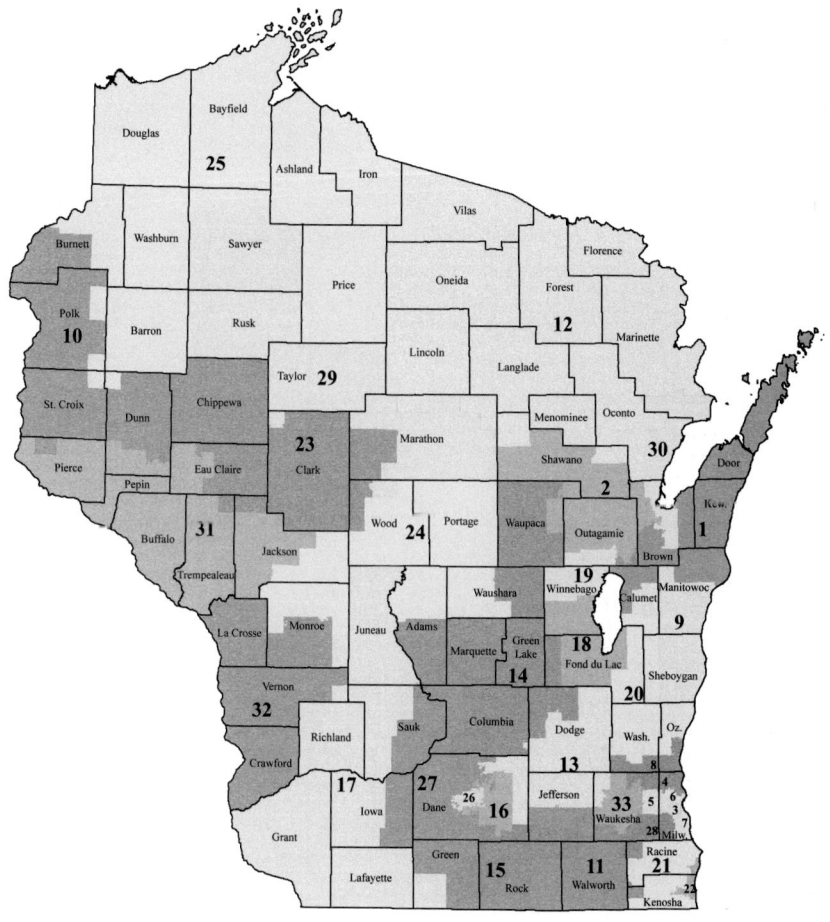

ASSEMBLY DISTRICTS

Enacted by 2011 Wisconsin Act 43

(As modified by the U.S. District Court for the Eastern
District of Wisconsin in *Baldus vs. Members of the Wisconsin
Government Accountability Board*, Case No. 11-CV-562)

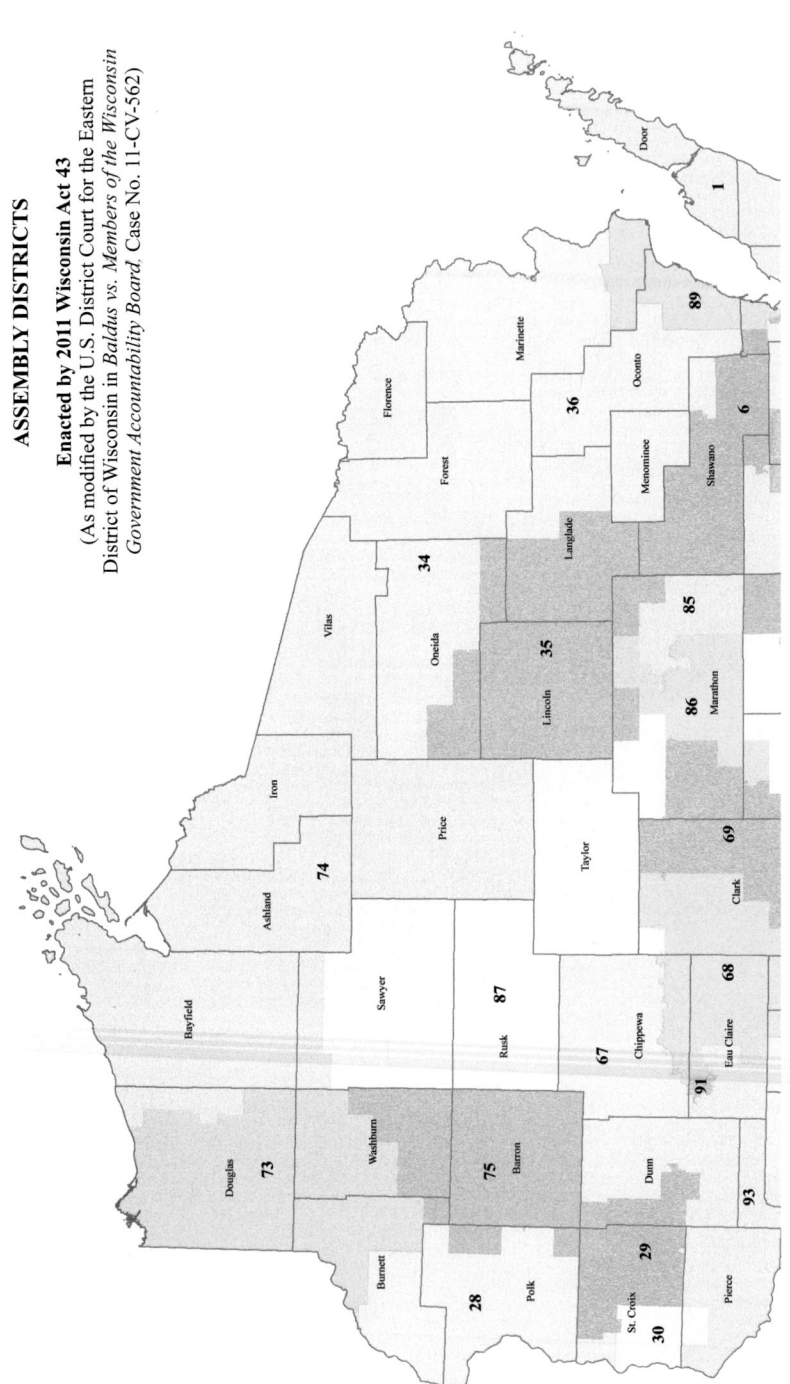

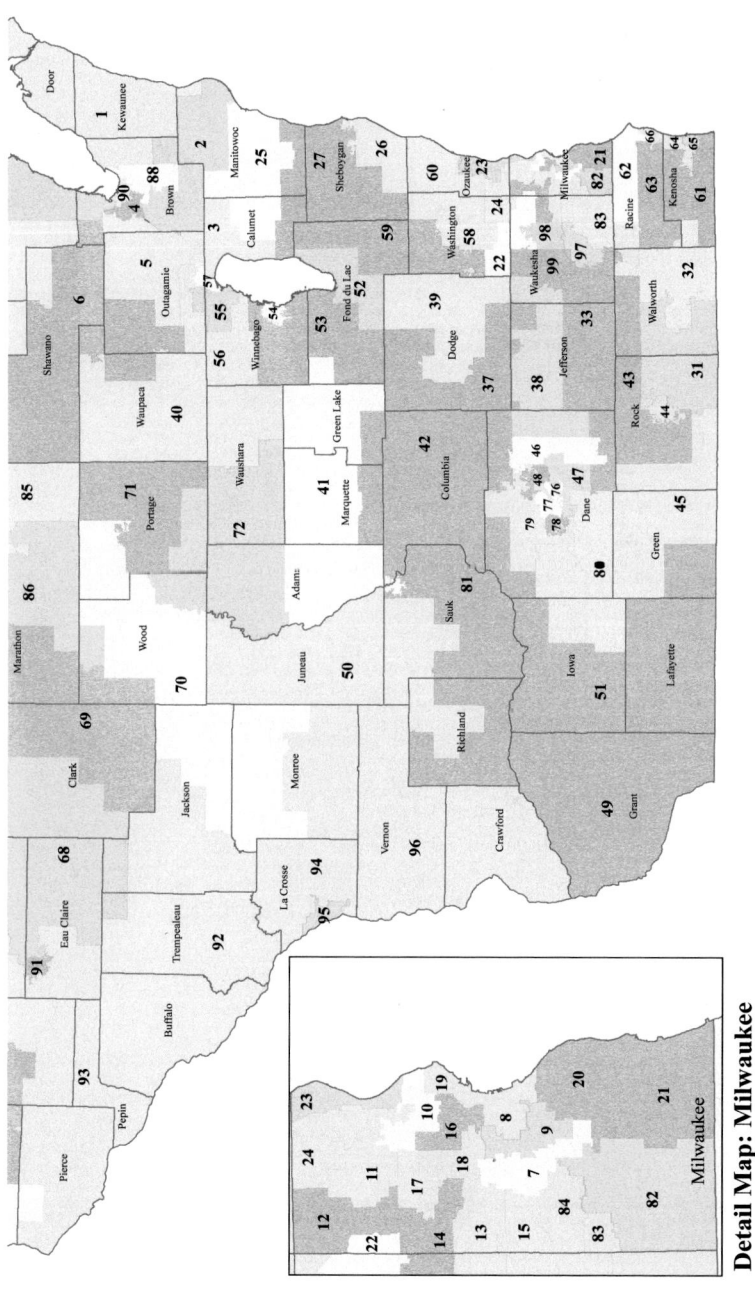

Detail Map: Milwaukee

Detail Map: Madison Area

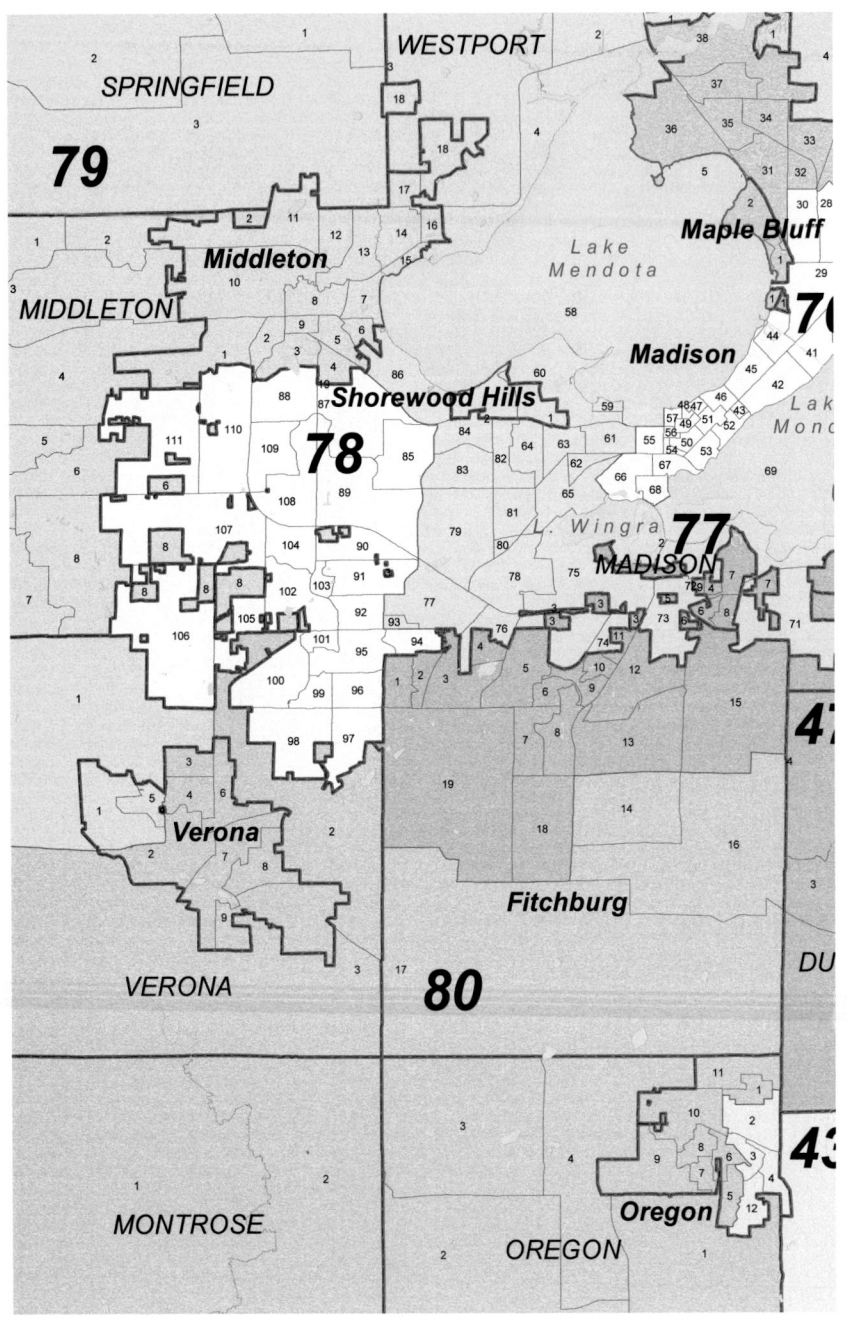

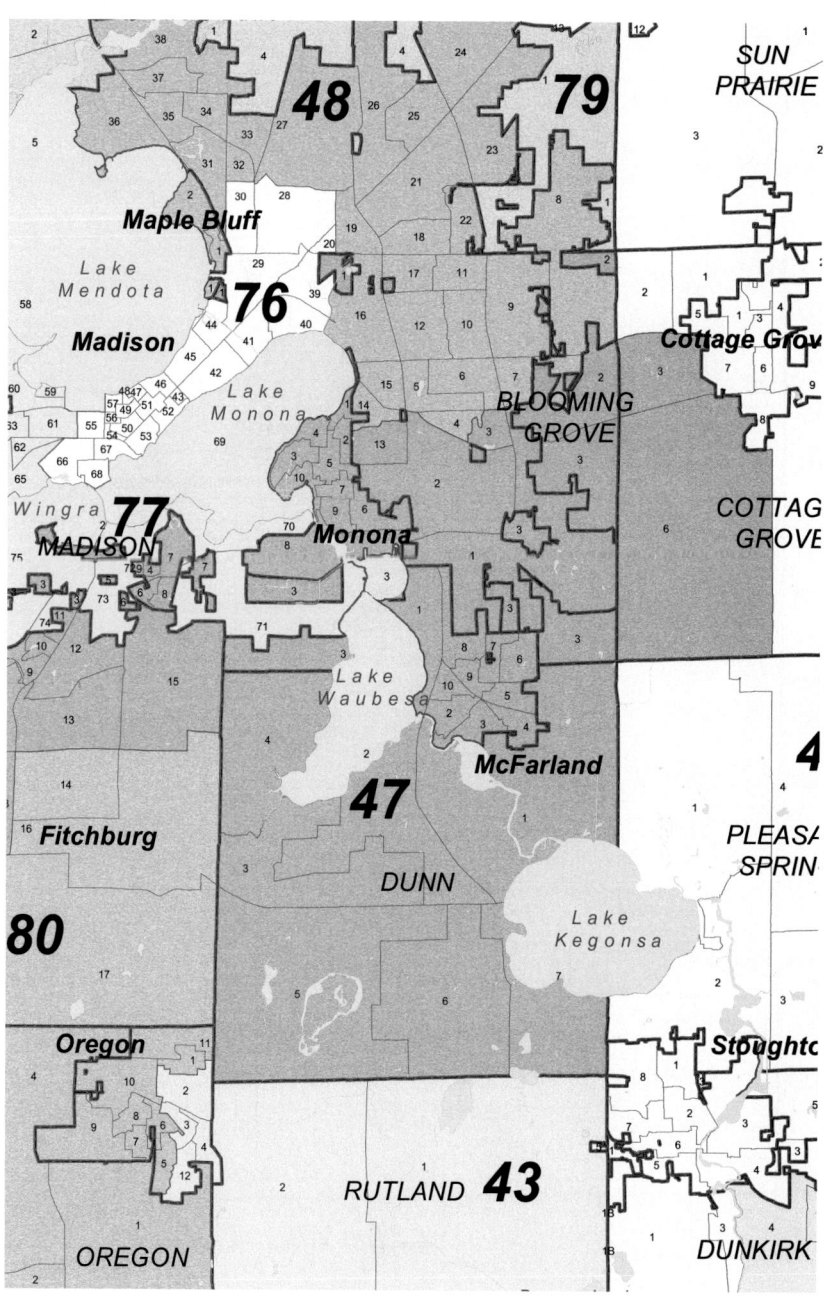

Detail Map: Milwaukee County (North)

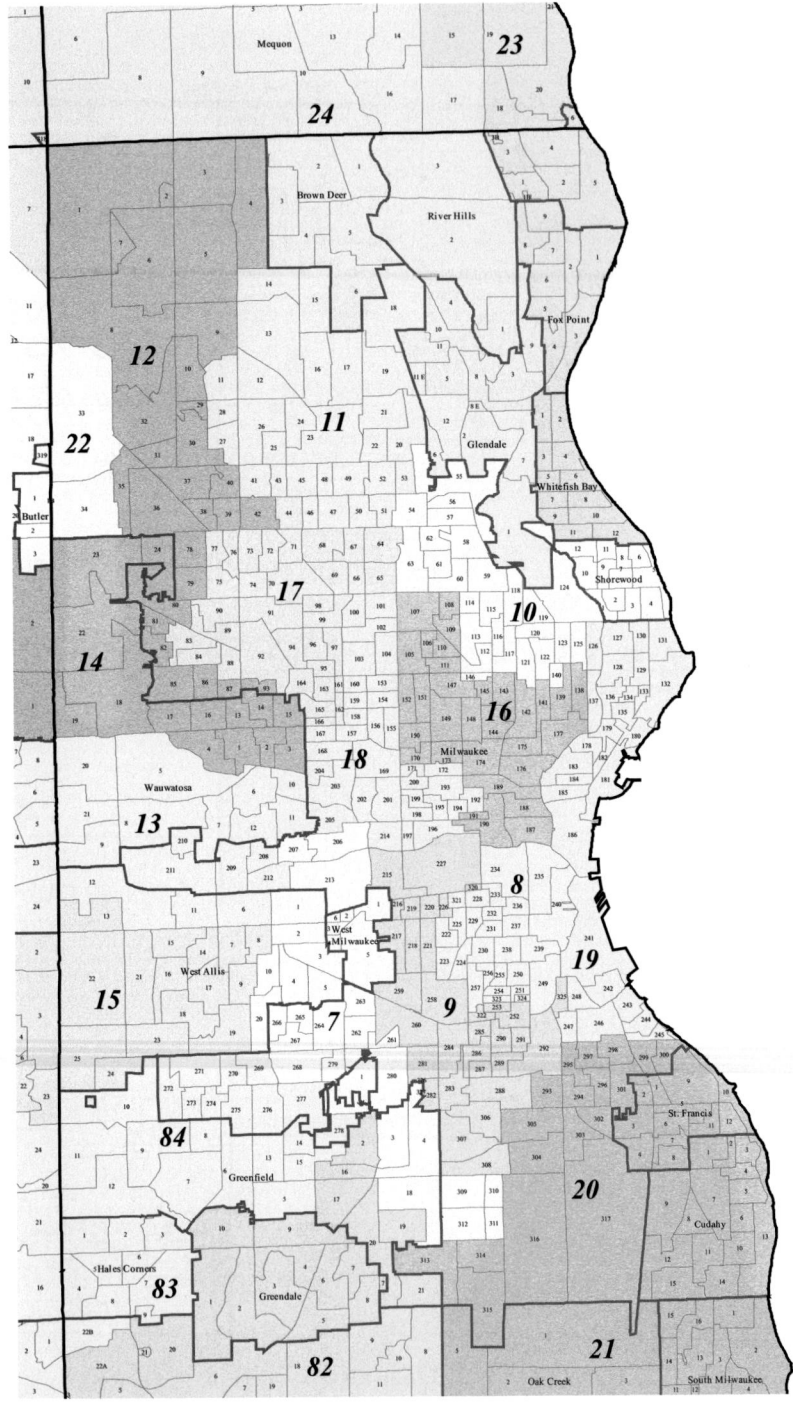

Detail Map: Milwaukee County (South)

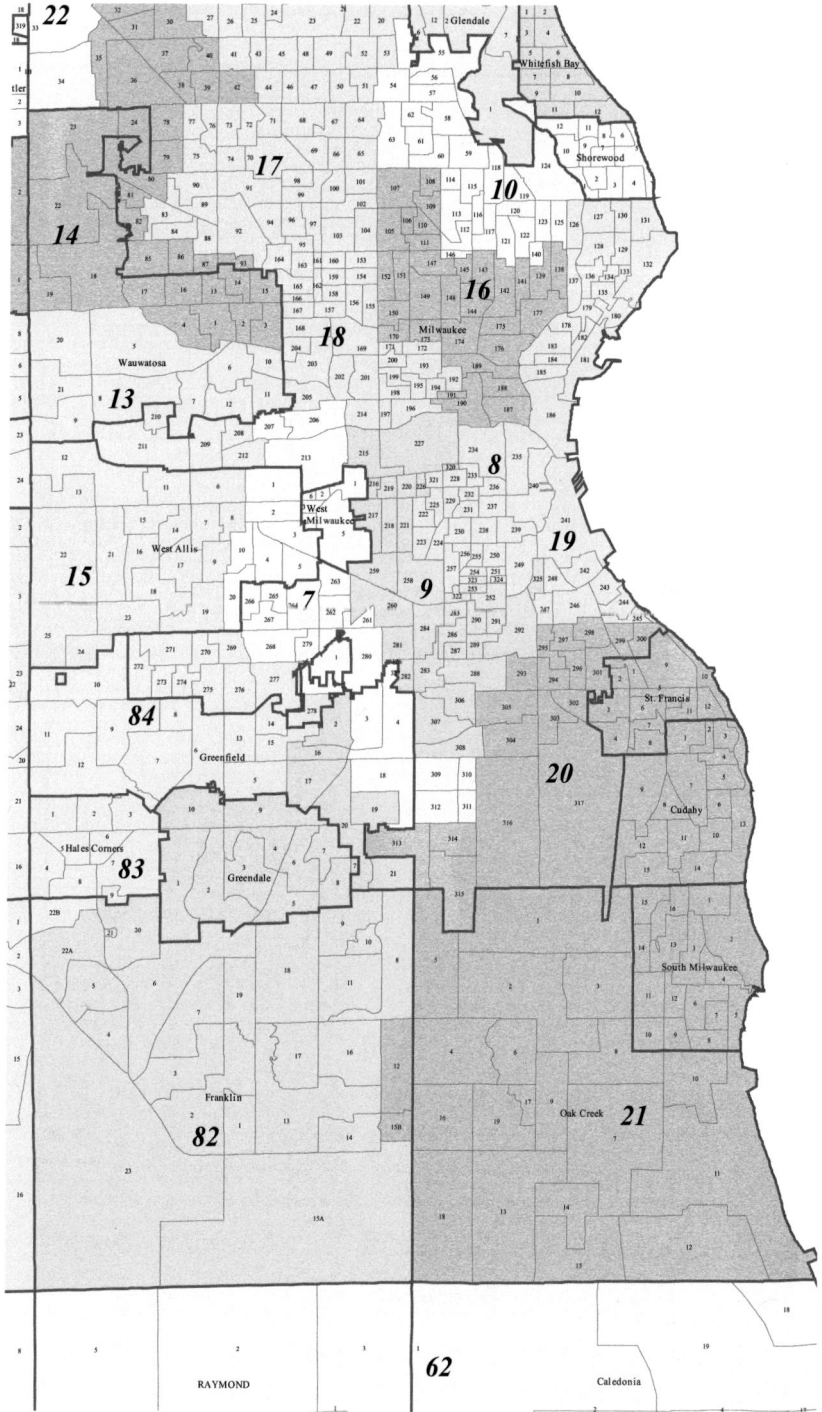

Detail Map: Waukesha County (West)

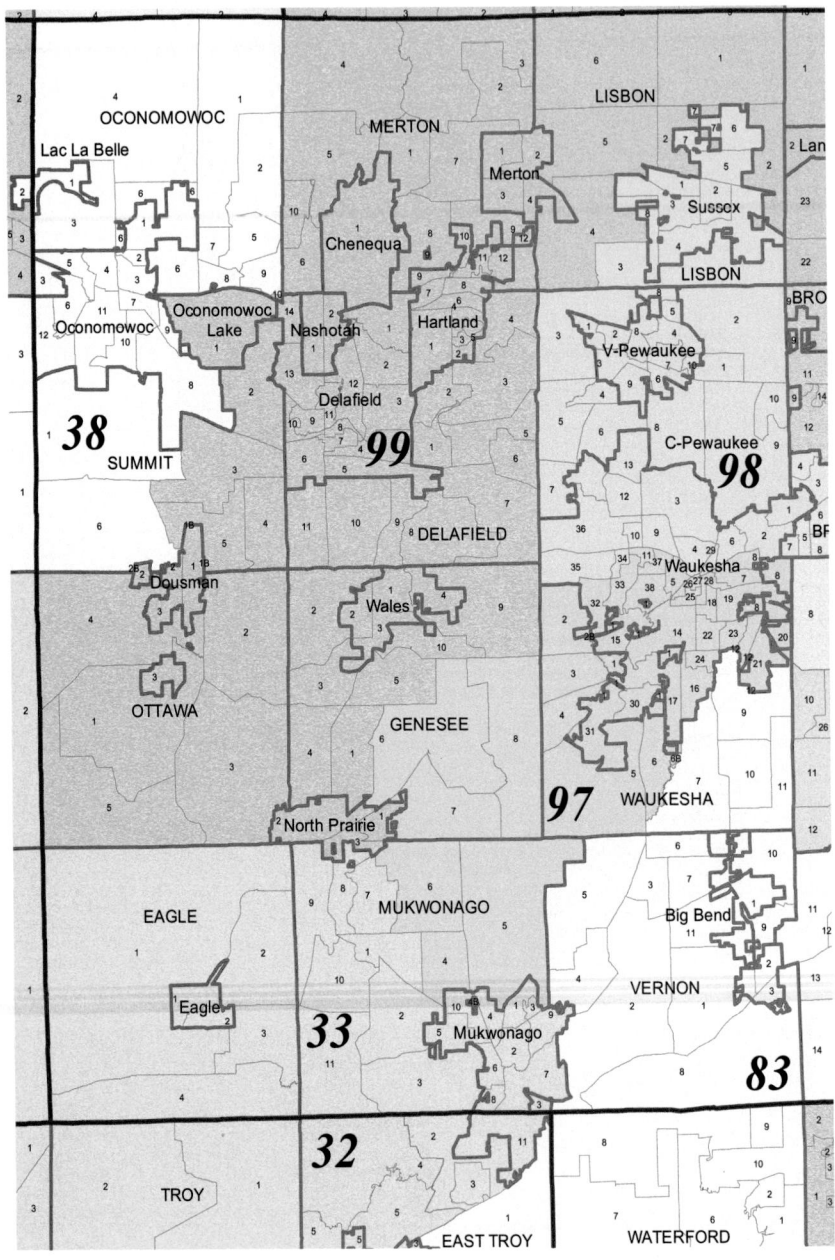

Detail Map: Waukesha County (East)

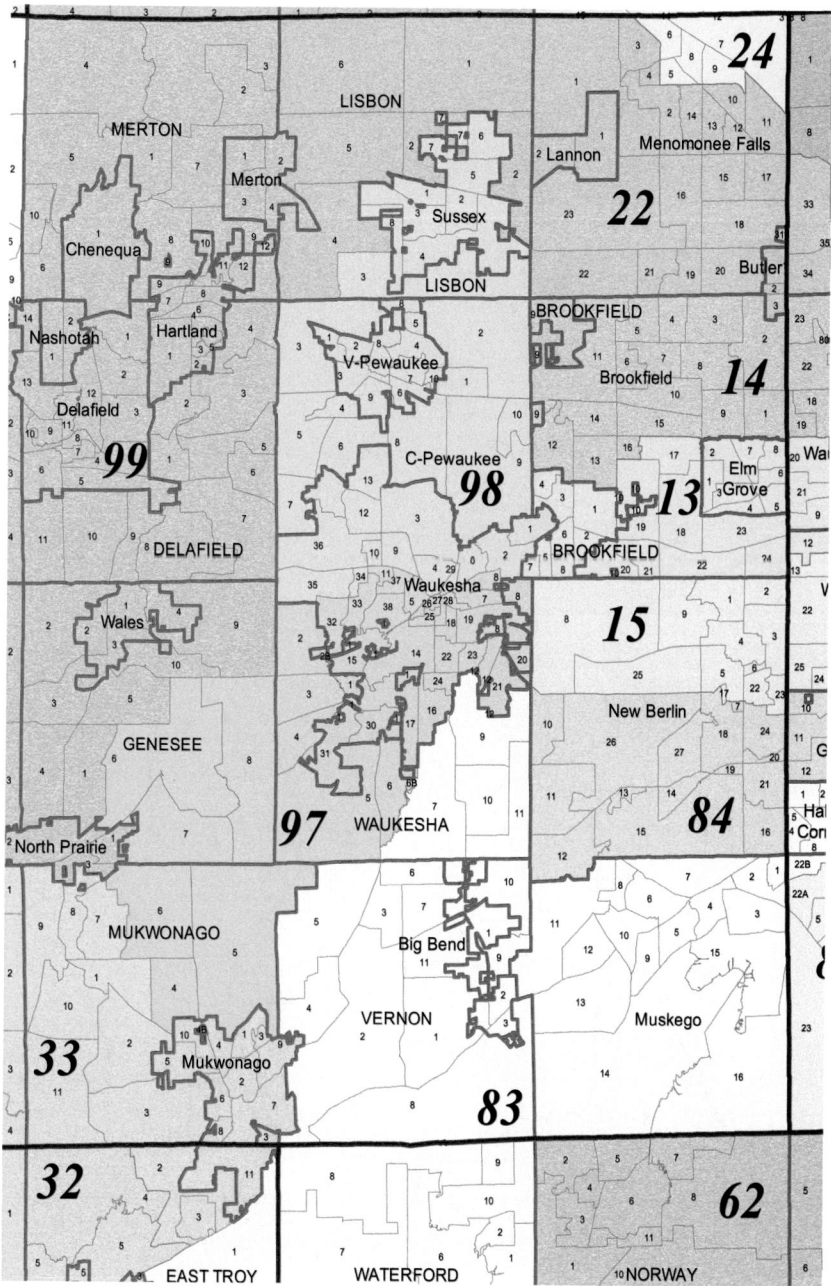

Detail Map: Green Bay Area

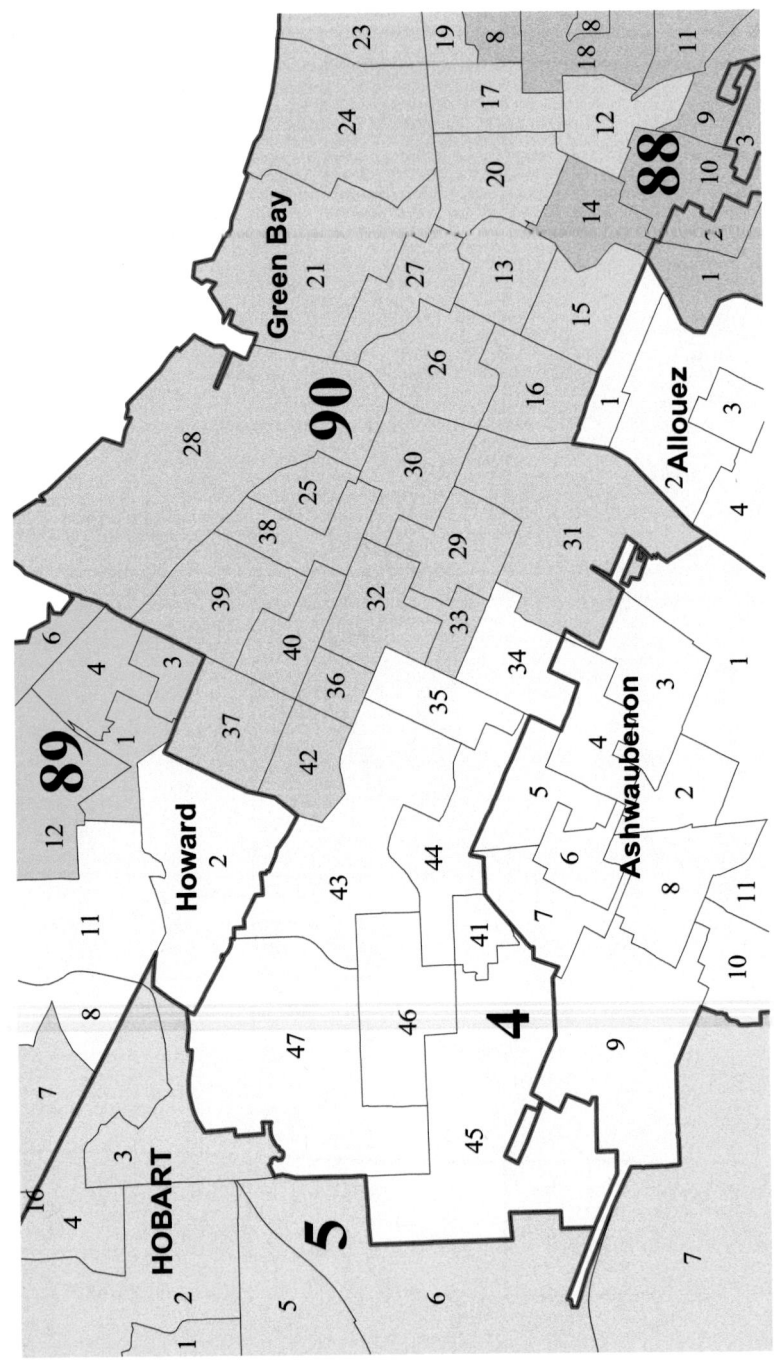

Detail Map: Eau Claire Area

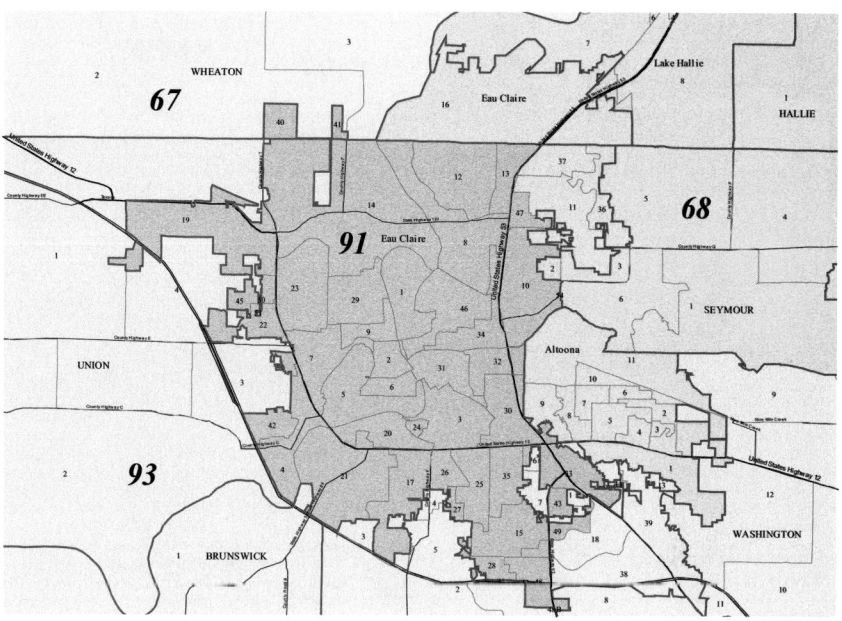

Detail Map: Waukesha Area

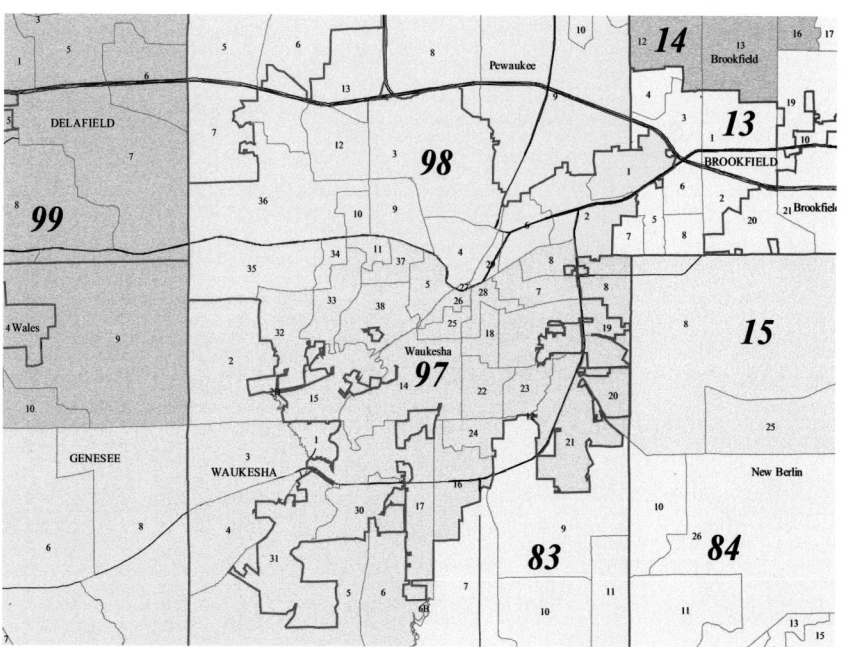

Detail Map: Racine Area

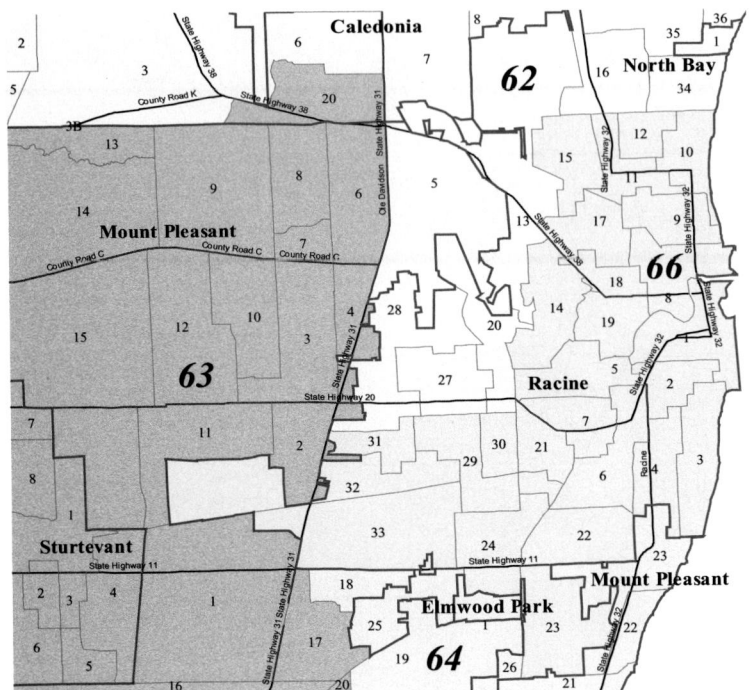

Detail Map: Fox Cities

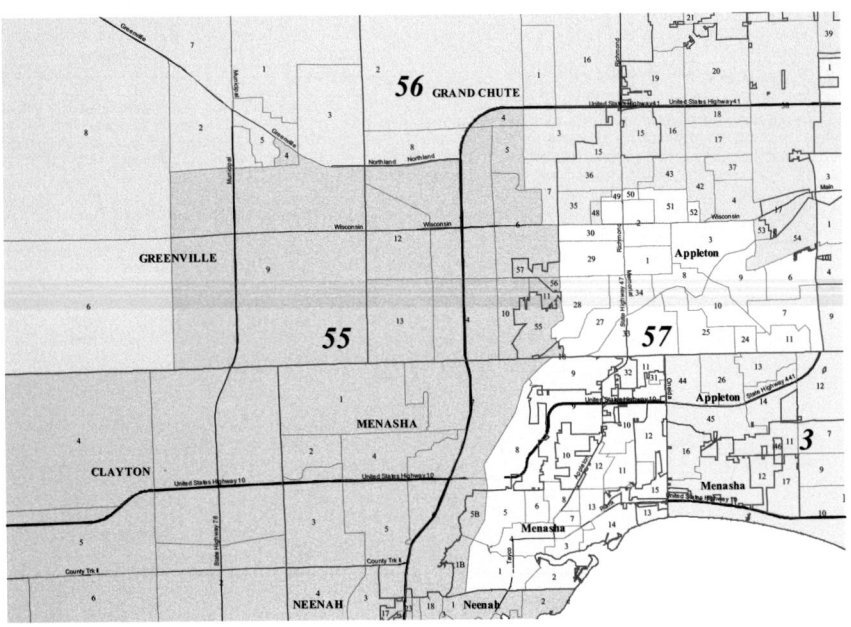

Feature
Article

The Wisconsin Historical Society: Collecting, Preserving, and Sharing Stories Since 1846

The headquarters building of the Wisconsin Historical Society on the University of Wisconsin-Madison campus, as seen from Langdon Street. *(Wisconsin Historical Society photo by Robert Granflaten)*

The Wisconsin Historical Society: Collecting, Preserving, and Sharing Stories Since 1846

By John Zimm

With contributions by Michael Edmonds, Helmut Knies, and Michael Stevens

Graphic Design by Lynn Lemanski
Wisconsin Legislative Reference Bureau

Background Frame by Sarah Girkin

Table of Contents

The Wisconsin Historical Society: Collecting, Preserving, and Sharing Stories Since 1846

Appropriately enough, the roots of Wisconsin's world-class historical society can be traced back to a conversation between two pioneers. In the autumn of 1845, Richard Magoon, an early settler of Lafayette County and a Black Hawk War veteran, happened upon Chauncey Britt, the editor of the Mineral Point *Democrat*. Magoon was concerned about losing the history of the territory he had helped to settle and suggested to Britt that the time was right for the organization of "an Historical Society, to collect, from the pioneers then alive, such facts in regard to the early history of Wisconsin, as they might possess, as well as to treasure up those occurring in the future."

The Wisconsin Historical Society headquarters building, Madison, Wisconsin. (Wisconsin Historical Society photo by Robert Granflaten)

Chauncey Britt felt that Magoon's idea was a good one and printed an unassuming little article in the *Democrat* calling for assistance from his "brethren of the press." Britt reasoned: "There are hundreds of men now in Wisconsin who could furnish much valuable information relative to the early history of the Territory . . . A few years more, and they will have passed away, and the future people of Wisconsin will seek in vain for the information which they can now communicate."

Image of the Eben Peck cabin, painted by Isabella Dengel in 1891. Built in 1837, the Peck cabin was the first building in Madison, the city where only nine years later the Wisconsin Historical Society would be. (WHi Image ID 2859)

Magoon's suggestion and Britt's forward-looking appeal set in motion the creation of the Wisconsin Historical Society, which today has grown into one of the largest, most active, and most diversified state historical societies in the nation. The Wisconsin Historical Society – older by two years than the state itself – possesses an extraordinary library and manuscript collection. A host of archival materials are made widely accessible to Wisconsinites via 14 Area Research Centers which are scattered throughout the state. A vast majority of the state's residents are within an hour and a half's drive of a center. The society has cultivated a network of nearly 400 affiliated local historical societies, operates 11 historic sites as well as the Wisconsin Historical Museum, and boasts a vigorous publishing program that produces an average of 15 new titles annually on a wide range of Wisconsin-related themes. The society preserves historically and archaeologically significant places in a variety of ways: protecting historic properties by administering Wisconsin's portion of the National Register of Historic Places and the State Register of Historic Places, providing guidance on the restoration and repair of significant properties, and protecting burial sites throughout the state.

The Wisconsin Historical Society has long been a pioneering institution with a unique relationship to the people of Wisconsin. In 1853, the Wisconsin Historical Society became the first historical society in America to receive state funding; thus, because it is a public institution it is the society's responsibility to "treasure up" the stories of people from all walks of life. In this way, 167 years ago the society laid the foundations for a social history, which has enriched our knowledge of the past through the preservation and sharing of stories that include women, American Indians, African Americans, laborers, and many others traditionally ignored in historical accounts. The society preserves and shares the lives and objects of people from every corner of the state. Membership is open to all who pay annual dues, and the society's collections belong to the people of Wisconsin.

Unlikely as it may have seemed, this all began in a frontier territory with no railroads, in a capital city with dirt streets where wolves and prairie fires were still hazards – in short, a place where history seemed more to be made rather than preserved. The creation of the Wisconsin Historical Society is a manifold tale of pioneers, perseverance, and forward-looking vision.

The Early Years

Chauncey Britt printed another entreaty in September 1846, this time in the pages of the *Milwaukee Courier*. Britt's appeal came just as delegates from around Wisconsin prepared to gather in Madison for the state's first constitutional convention. Britt captured the attention of several delegates, and quietly a series of meetings took place, first at Morrison's American Hotel on the Capitol Square and later in the Capitol library. Little is known about these meetings, the source having vanished with an attendee who shortly thereafter moved to California and promptly died. Yet a basic organizational structure was created and officers were elected. Among the officers of the society were some prominent men of the Territory: businessmen Solomon Juneau and Byron Kilbourn, banker Samuel Marshall, and former Territorial Governor James Duane Doty. Plans were made for a meeting to be held in Madison in January 1847.

Some of the first officers of the Wisconsin Historical Society. From left: Solomon Juneau (WHi Image ID 2733), Byron Kilbourn (WHi Image ID 27655), Sam Marshall (WHi Image ID 1835), and James Duane Doty (WHi Image ID 10020)

This first annual meeting of the Wisconsin Historical Society in January 1847 was representative of the early years of the organization. Former governor Doty, one of the society's vice presidents, was selected to deliver an address before the assemblage, which he did not. Officers were elected to serve for the following year, but otherwise there was little activity. As one participant recounted, "I do not think much was done other than making an organization."

In January 1849, the society was reorganized and became more active. A constitution was adopted, which established the aim of the society to "preserve the materials for a complete history of Wisconsin embracing the antiquities, and the history of the Indian tribes." Resolutions were adopted, among them a request

Increase Lapham, one of Wisconsin's most note-worthy scientists, was one of the charter members and cofounders of the Wisconsin Historical Society. Lapham's many accomplishments include writing a pioneering work on the destruction of forests in 1867, helping establish the Milwaukee public high school program, and helping establish the National Weather Bureau, the forerunner of today's National Weather Service. (WHi Image ID 1944)

by Increase Lapham that "surveyors throughout this state be requested to furnish this Society with sketches from actual measurements of the ancient mounds and artificial earth-works in their vicinity." Governor Nelson Dewey was made president of the society, and the bright and ambitious Lapham, future state geologist and father of the United States Weather Bureau, was made corresponding secretary. A library was begun, starting with the *Laws* and *Journals* of the Territory and government documents from New York State and the Smithsonian. With the arrival of Lyman Draper in 1852, the Wisconsin Historical Society was set on a path of growth and innovation that within a few decades would make it the envy of older institutions.

Lyman Copeland Draper was born September 4, 1815, in Erie County, New York, on a farm at the mouth of Eighteen Mile Creek, so named because it was 18 miles from Buffalo. Lyman's father, Luke Draper, was a restless man, a sometime tavern keeper and farmer who had a keen interest in medicine. Luke and his family moved several times, seeking different opportunities along the eastern shore of Lake Erie before settling in Lockport, New York, in 1821. Luke kept a tavern in Lockport, in which young Lyman heard accounts from his father's patrons of adventure and war on the western frontier. Lyman also absorbed the stories of his grandfather Jonathan Draper, who had been one of the Minutemen at Lexington during the Revolutionary War and who later did sporadic duty in the New Hampshire militia combating British raiding parties. Lyman's father was also a veteran, seeing occasional service in the War of 1812 as it played out on New York's western frontier. Luke Draper was captured by the British, came under cannon fire while sailing with a couple of companions, and served with the New York militia that was disbanded rather than used to defend Fort George. On his way home from Fort George, Luke and another man were captured again by the British and hauled to Montreal for imprisonment.

As he grew, young Lyman heard these tales of high adventure and lamented the fact that he did not find accounts such as these in the books he read or in the words of orators. In time, Lyman would resolve to remedy this neglect, and to save from oblivion the stories and lives of the lesser-known men who, in Lyman's words, "suffered more, and were honored less, than almost any equal number of adventurers in any country or age."

Lyman inherited his mother's diminutive frame, growing to only five feet tall and 100 pounds, hardly bigger than a schoolboy. "I am a small bit of a fellow," he would one day explain. A correspondent later joked that Draper could "jump into one of my pockets and [I'll] carry you all over the plantation . . . taking care you don't fall out and break your neck." His younger brothers quickly grew larger and more robust than he, and the restlessness and vigor he inherited from his father were directed toward the mind and the imagination. Draper read voraciously, did well in the intermittent schooling he received as a youth, and won the respect of the locals in Lockport through his learnedness.

At 17 Draper began trying his hand at writing, showing even at that age an unusual devotion to accuracy. Yet writing seemed to afflict the fragile little man with an odd array of ailments. As he matured and his ambitions grew, Draper planned to write a magnificent series of biographies of the pioneers, works that would go mostly unwritten as hypochondria got the better of him. Time and again he postponed his writing to collect more material or to treat a variety of maladies. Ultimately, Draper would complete very few works; it is as a collector that he is remembered.

As a teenager in the 1830s Draper began corresponding with pioneers and their descendants, a lifelong custom he practiced right until his death. In 1840, Draper began to supplement this written correspondence with interviews. To accomplish this, Draper traveled extensively through the Alleghenies and the South, finding old pioneers and recording their reminiscences. Explaining his inspiration to go to these great lengths, Draper once wrote to a friend: "I am very passionately devoted to the Pioneer history of the romantic West – I keep delving away at it, more for the real love I have for the thing itself than anything else." Throughout his early adulthood Draper would try his hand at several careers, clerking and farming, even testing the waters of the newspaper business for a short time in Mississippi, and studied at two different colleges, but history and collecting were his first loves, and to them he would return whenever possible. In

Lyman Draper directed the society for over three decades, during which he built notable library and manuscript collections, as well as assembling a museum, or "cabinet," as it was then called. (WHi Image ID 2629)

the fall of 1852, Draper found an opportunity to devote himself more or less full time to his scholarly pursuits.

A college friend, Judge Charles Larrabee, had for years attempted to lure Draper to Wisconsin, dangling various potential jobs before him: as state librarian, or as a professor at the state university, or with the nascent state historical society. By the time he arrived in Madison in October 1852, however, Draper discovered that Larrabee was out of power, a state librarian had been appointed, and the university needed no more professors. Meanwhile, the Wisconsin Historical Society's founders were at a crossroads, unable to settle on a direction for the organization.

Despite unfavorable career prospects, Draper remained in Madison. He was supported by a modest inheritance from an uncle and found a congenial reception among his fellow Baptists. Thanks to his inheritance, Draper needed only part-time employment to supplement his income; between times, he was free to work on his biography of a backwoods surveyor and adventurer named Daniel Boone. With an eye still trained on gainful employment, Draper introduced himself to influential members of the Wisconsin Historical Society, whom he impressed with his erudition and ideas to expand the society's activities.

STATE HOUSE, WISCONSIN.

The Wisconsin Historical Society's first home was in the State Capitol, pictured here as the building looked in 1859. (WHi Image ID 3965)

Draper later reflected that the historical society in 1852 was going through stages similar to those experienced by "kindred institutions – an early organization by the foresight of a hopeful few, followed by neglect, a brief sickly existence, and an early death . . . resuscitated again and again." While a handful of the founders of the Wisconsin Historical Society expected it to grow into a sort of private club open only to members, others dreamed of a public institution devoted to all citizens of the state. Unsurprisingly for a western historian, Draper likened the society to "the old Kentucky hunter, his trusty gun . . . once accidentally failing him, he would 'pick the flint, and try the old rifle again.'"

As it turned out, Draper was just the man to "pick the flint, and try the old rifle again." In January 1853, having endeared himself to several prominent society members including Governor Leonard Farwell, then president of the society, Draper was admitted as a member and named to its executive committee. That winter, Draper sat down with Charles Larrabee to write a charter for the society, in which they stated, "The object of the Society shall be to collect, embody, arrange, and preserve in authentic form a library of books, pamphlets, maps, charts, manuscripts, papers, paintings, statuary, and other materials illustrative of the History of the State." They went on to establish that the Wisconsin Historical Society should "exhibit faithfully the antiquities of the past and present condition and resources of Wisconsin. It should promote the study of history by lectures, and diffuse and publish information relating to the description and history of the state." Under this charter, the society was authorized to collect broadly, open its doors to everyone, and receive substantial funding from the state.

What began as a club of history-minded amateurs seven years earlier was about to undertake a remarkable period of growth and innovation. For the next three decades the society would be guided by Draper's forward-looking, democratic vision and matchless leadership. Though he did not have much to begin with, Draper did find one thing awaiting him at the Wisconsin Historical Society: a library, albeit one in embryonic form.

The Wisconsin Historical Society Library and Archives

In 1853, Draper found a few dozen government documents housed in a glass-front bookcase, as well as a few manuscripts donated to the society some years earlier. From these humble beginnings, the library and archives of the Wisconsin Historical Society has grown into one of the finest collections for the study of North American history in the United States. Consisting of more than three million items including books, pamphlets, newspapers, and microfilm, the library has particularly strong genealogy, labor union, North American exploration, African American, and Native American holdings. It serves as the North American history library for the University of Wisconsin-Madison and houses one of the premier collections of Wisconsin, federal, and Canadian government publications. Each year the library adds over 7,000 books; an equal number of government documents including books, pamphlets, and reports; hundreds of newspapers; and 2,000 rolls of microfilm. In the society's headquarters, the library reading room, which was refurbished in 2010, hosts upward of 100,000 visitors a year. The library's digital collections hosted on the society Web site are viewed 35,000 times each day.

The society's archives comprise 105,000 cubic feet of diaries, journals, memoirs, photographs, assorted government documents, rare books, sound and film recordings, and a wealth of other materials filling 37 miles of shelves. The archives have notably strong collections in a variety of areas, including film and theater, labor history, mass communications, maps, the McCormick-International Harvester collection, social action, and the well-known Draper Manuscripts, which is a collection of documents concerning the frontier west of the Appalachian Mountains. Most of this material is available to researchers through the network of 14 area research centers located on University of Wisconsin System campuses around the state and the Northern Great Lakes Visitor Center outside Ashland. Additionally, the society serves as the state archives, preserving state and local government records and making these records accessible to the public.

When Draper was named the corresponding secretary of the Wisconsin Historical Society in January 1854, he set out at once to increase the size and scope of the society's research collections. Though he had little money, Draper was able

Map showing the locations of the 14 Area Research Centers in Wisconsin. They are located on UW campus libraries throughout the state as well as at the Northern Great Lakes Visitor Center in Ashland.

to accumulate volumes by appealing to the vanity of others. He wrote to dozens of prominent historians and public figures, named them honorary members of the society, and solicited contributions of their works. Twenty books came in that first month, 37 the next, and 45 the third, from such notable people as Francis Parkman, William H. Prescott, George Bancroft, and Emma Willard. Draper used a substantial portion of the first of the society's state funds to purchase a remarkable collection of Americana, including 17th-century French accounts of Canada and early editions recounting Jonathan Carver and Alexander Mackenzie's travels

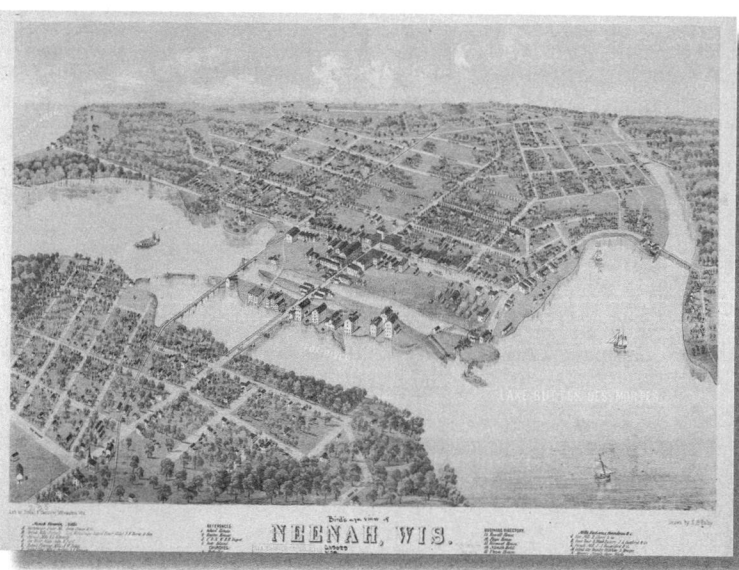

Bird's-eye map of Neenah, Wisconsin (WHi Image ID 22648)

through the interior. Draper also convinced the legislature to print extra copies of government publications so he could exchange volumes with other institutions. In his first year at the helm, the library grew to more than 2,000 books and pamphlets, necessitating a move from the Capitol to the basement of Madison's First Baptist Church, where it occupied 2,700 square feet for the next decade.

Draper also gathered manuscripts, collecting beyond state borders. A typical appeal for manuscripts was added to Draper's first annual report in 1854, in which he submitted a list of "Objects of Collection Desired by the Society." Items on his list included "Manuscript statements and narratives of pioneer settlers – old letters and journals relative to the early history and settlement of Wisconsin, and of the Black Hawk War; biographical notices of our pioneers, and of eminent citizens, deceased; and facts illustrative of our Indian tribes, their history, characteristics, sketches of their prominent chiefs, orators and warriors."

History, to Draper, was a literary activity that should focus on elegantly written, factually accurate depictions of the heroic deeds of great men. While dreaming of the tomes he would craft about the lives of the pioneers, Draper desired to get as close as possible to the actual events, to record in minute and precise detail the lives he wished to celebrate. Accordingly, Draper continued to search far and wide for pioneers and their children, to gather their stories, diaries, records, and reminiscences. Draper's definition of a hero was also broad, seeing greatness in the men and women who settled the frontier: the wives and farmers, shopkeepers, and militiamen who had built their lives under difficult circumstances. Never shy about asking for materials, at the beginning of the Civil War Draper sent a circulating letter to a number of officers from Wisconsin's gathering regiments requesting they send him relics and curiosities. He also encouraged soldiers to keep diaries for a large Civil War collection he planned to assemble, with which he planned to write an illustrated history of Wisconsin's involvement in the war. Like his other writing projects, this never came to fruition.

Draper gathered maps (many of them rare), daguerreotypes, portraits, and prints. He also sought perishable items such as newspapers, broadsides, pamphlets, magazines, and sheet music – items all too often here one day and gone the next – documenting contemporary life in America, knowing that in time these materials would be sources for history. "No sectarian feelings, no political prejudices," Draper wrote, "have turned us aside from the high purpose we have had in view – to provide for all classes of honest and earnest investigators, facts and information upon almost all conceivable subjects of interest, profit and culture."

Draper simultaneously collected for the Wisconsin Historical Society and for his own personal manuscript library, which was bequeathed to the society upon his death in 1891. This collection, known colloquially as the Draper Manuscripts, consisted of original documents, Draper's transcriptions of documents, interview notes, Draper's correspondence, extracts from newspapers and other published sources, muster rolls, military records, and more, covering primarily the period between the French and Indian War and the War of 1812 (ca. 1755-1815). Society staff organized the mass of partially sorted papers into 491 volumes divided into 50 series of varying lengths, arranged by geographic area, subject, and individual. Contained in the Draper Manuscripts are personal papers of some legendary figures in early American history, including Daniel Boone, Simon Kenton, Mohawk chief Joseph Brant, and George Rogers Clark, among many others. The Draper

Painting of La Pointe, Madeline Island, Wisconsin, showing buildings of the American Fur Company and both of the Mission churches, ca. 1842. (WHi Image ID 42457)

Manuscripts soon became the society's most famous and extensively used collection. In 1940, the society began putting the collection on microfilm to make it more widely available, and even published a guide for the collection that numbers almost 500 pages.

By the end of the Civil War, the library had grown to more than 20,000 volumes, which had the shelves in the Baptist church filled to overflowing, and stacks of books piled to the ceiling. Relief from overcrowding came in 1866, when the society was given three rooms on the second floor of the south wing of the new State Capitol. After the move, the society's visibility increased as well. As many as 15,000 patrons visited the library and museum every year, with legislators, attorneys, newspaper editors, clergymen, visiting scholars, and dozens of university students navigating the collections daily. Draper was so well-known by this time that important cultural institutions around the nation happily exchanged materials with him. The library began comprehensively collecting publications of the United States government in 1870, and by the centennial year of 1876 the society had the largest library west of Washington, DC, holding 65,000 items; in 1883, it passed the 100,000 mark.

Librarian Daniel S. Durrie seated in the two-story-high gallery that the Historical Society occupied in the old South Wing of the State Capitol from 1866 until 1883. (WHi Image ID 23291)

Incredibly, Draper accomplished this with only a few hundred dollars per year, a thousand miles away from the center of the book trade, and with the majority of new acquisitions coming as gifts. More importantly, Draper's collecting was innovative and unbiased. Not only were the standard newspapers of the day acquired, but also hundreds of volumes of colonial papers and then-esoteric journals such as the *Cherokee Pioneer* (the first Native American periodical) and *The African Repository* (an early African American journal). Draper's imaginative view of what "history" meant, as well as his universal tastes, laid the foundations of one of the nation's richest research collections. The principles of broad and impartial collecting have guided all succeeding generations of the society's librarians and archivists.

In 1887, Lyman Draper retired, and his hand-picked successor, Reuben Gold Thwaites, took over operations of the society. Energetic, enthusiastic, and, like his predecessor, diminutive (he once remarked, "My length from the top of my collar to the top of my heel is four feet, seven inches"), Thwaites differed from Draper in that he was systematic and orderly in his collecting. Thwaites adopted new practices in acquisitions, cataloging, research, and conservation of printed material. He established an antiquarian fund to gather money to buy items, and then planned a series of trips to obtain manuscripts that would fill gaps in the current collections of the society. Thwaites coordinated with potential donors, planned his itinerary carefully, and set a rigorous schedule. He detailed all he accomplished after one trip through the Fox Valley, noting the acquisition of "old letter-books, diaries, memoranda and letters, fully 2,000 documents in all, illustrative of olden times, particularly the fur trade and the conduct of Indian affairs."

Prioritizing Wisconsin's legacy in collecting items, Thwaites successfully solicited and acquired the papers of notable Wisconsinites while also conducting interviews in order to create oral histories. Thwaites instituted the practice of sending society staff to libraries in other states, and later to Canada, England, and France, for the purpose of copying documents relating to Wisconsin. He himself went on two trips to Europe for this purpose. Thwaites also worked to gather records of contemporary society, especially those sources describing the history of localities and local matters, believing these to be important not only as historical records, but because they satisfied a genuine public interest.

As the 19th century drew to a close the Wisconsin Historical Society enjoyed a reputation as one of the leading historical societies in America. In 1893, future president Theodore Roosevelt praised the society as "the father of all

Stacks of the society library in 1898, when the society occupied rooms in the third Capitol building. At one time, gas light fixtures were used in this space, allowing an open flame to burn perilously close to flammable items like the newspaper collection. (WHi Image ID 23287)

Frederick Jackson Turner's history seminar at work in an alcove at the society in 1893, when the society was still housed in the third Capitol building. (WHi Image ID 1910)

such societies in the West." Roosevelt continued, "Every American scholar, and in particular every American historian, is under a debt to your Society, and a debt to the State of Wisconsin, for having kept it up." The next year another future president, Professor Woodrow Wilson of Princeton College, commented on legislative support for the society library, writing, "I have no hesitation in saying that its loss or impairment would be nothing less than a national calamity, so far as the scholarship of the country is concerned . . . Certainly no legislative grant could more directly contribute to the best interests of scholarship and patriotism than a grant to preserve such records as you possess."

Thwaites realized early on that most of the users of the society's collections were college students. Accordingly, he consciously, and programmatically, chose to "hitch the Society's star" to the future development of the university. Students were coming to Madison in greater numbers as enrollment increased fivefold in the last 15 years of the 19th century. Moreover, university faculty emphasized the consultation of a wide array of primary documents that were generally not available at the university library. Thwaites offered students unlimited access to the society's library stacks and opened additional rooms for study. Noted historian Frederick Jackson Turner, who regularly led his "little band of investigators" to the society, later wrote that this greater freedom for their work "was the opening of a new life."

Ties between the Wisconsin Historical Society and the University of Wisconsin grew stronger in 1900 with the construction of a shared library building on the university campus. The imposing neoclassical structure was filled with marble staircases, mosaic floors, mahogany furniture, and state-of-the-art technology such as telephones and electric lights. Manuscripts, newspapers, and government publications were housed in their own reading rooms on the ground floor. From the main second floor hallway, researchers passed a massive card catalog and an elegant reference desk before entering the monumental reading room, with its 30-foot columns and stained-glass skylights. Initially, books from both the society and the university libraries were shelved in a single six-story stack wing. A decade later a second stack wing on the north was constructed to house the university's books. Advanced students and university faculty made up the lion's share of users, while undergraduates were tolerated and curious visitors were referred to a balcony where they would not disturb the scholars working below. For the next half century the society library would serve as the university's principal research collection.

Reuben Gold Thwaites, 1899. Thwaites assumed leadership of the society in 1887 from the legendary Lyman Draper. During his 26-year tenure, Thwaites created his own legend, increasing the society's scope, modernizing its operations, and forging close ties with the University of Wisconsin. (WHi Image ID 62768)

In 1907, the society began to take on new responsibilities with regard to state and local governments when the Wisconsin Legislature passed Chapter 88, Laws of 1907, the Wisconsin Archives Act. This act paved the way for the society to house and administer the state archives. Before this time, a great deal of effort had gone into collecting personal manuscripts, diaries, letters and the like, but little had been done in Wisconsin to preserve government documents. A survey of Wisconsin's government records was done by the American Historical Association's Public Archives Commission in 1904, the same year the state capitol building burned down. The report of this survey stated that, although damage to government documents had been limited by the fireproof vaults in which they'd been stored, the fire necessitated emergency storage that exposed these materials to a variety of hazards. Rather than create a new department of archives or wait to construct a new fireproof building for storage, the report's author suggested that non-current records be given to the Wisconsin Historical Society, "which has so amply shown its ability to care for them." Through numerous changes to the law, the society today still has the responsibility to collect, maintain, and make available for use the records of the state over 100 years later.

This period just before World War I has been described as the library's golden era. From Thwaites's arrival until 1913, the library's endowment more than doubled, the collections tripled in size, and state support quadrupled. The staff grew from 4 to 31, and the number of users had risen almost tenfold. In the various offices and reading rooms, a dozen highly motivated librarians – mostly female, since women could be paid lower wages than men – were the core of the institution. They worked seven hours on weekdays and half-days on Saturday, with 26 vacation days in addition to the usual holidays. In the second floor administrative

Annie Nunns, one of the library matriarchs who guided the society through the difficult years from World War I through the Great Depression. (WHi Image ID 97811)

suite, Thwaites cultivated donors and legislators while in adjacent offices others worked to stretch the budget, select books, and compile bibliographies.

On October 22, 1913, Thwaites died suddenly, having groomed no one to take his place. Even when the society was still housed at the state capitol, Thwaites had begun hiring a team of "young and devoted" librarians who were recent university graduates. They were an "exceptionally intelligent, well-trained, and agreeable body of young women" who took their professional responsibilities seriously and viewed their accomplishments with pride, and whom Thwaites held to strict standards and high expectations. Chief among these colleagues was Annie Nunns, whom Thwaites had hired in the late 1880s, the first of his female hires. In another era, Nunns, who was now assistant superintendent, would probably have been made society director; as it was, she, along with Mary Stuart Foster (known as "Mary, Queen of Stacks") and Iva Welsh controlled virtually all aspects of library policy and operation for the next 30 years.

Referring to themselves as "the Big Three," Nunns, Foster, and Welsh served the society during intensely difficult times, working long hours for little pay. Nunns would serve as the assistant superintendent, handling a litany of administrative matters, until her death in January 1942. Foster was the head of reference from 1904 until 1944, known for enforcing strict rules governing decorum in the reading room, creating the impression that transgressors who "whispered or even cleared a throat would be at least summarily ejected and at worst held for execution at dawn." Welsh was the head of cataloging from 1909 until 1944 and was remembered for her expert knowledge of rare books, meticulous attention to detail, and "undeviating adherence to established procedure." Together the Big Three guided the library through the First World War, the Great Depression, and into the Second World War, when budgets were tight, staffing was short, and demands upon the library increased with a growing university to serve.

Succeeding Thwaites as society director was Milo Quaife, a scholar

One of the professional young women Reuben Gold Thwaites hired was librarian Emma Hawley, shown here working on a typewriter she modified to accommodate library catalog cards. This 1892 photo was taken by Thwaites, who was also an amateur photographer. (WHi Image ID 23318)

with high academic credentials. Arriving from the Lewis Institute in Chicago, and needing to fill very large shoes, Quaife chose to continue and improve on Thwaites's collecting programs. He expanded efforts to secure out-of-state records by employing a staff member to comb the files of various federal departments in Washington, looking for documents relating to Wisconsin. In 1915, the society's field representative sent back 10,000 photostatic copies that first year. Unfortunately the cost for this work was considerable, and the project had to be scaled back in its second year. Quaife also used the authority granted by the 1907 Wisconsin Archives Act to solicit records of the executive department and other agencies.

Quaife's tenure lasted for only six years, his successes mitigated by the debilitating impact of World War I and his legacy clouded by controversies with society members and legislators that caused him to leave Wisconsin. Quaife's

Milo Quaife was just 33 years old when he was hired as society director in January 1914. Under Quaife's leadership, the society began publishing the Wisconsin Magazine of History, which continues to this day. (WHi Image ID 98885)

successor, Joseph C. Schafer, another impeccable scholar, headed the society for the next two decades. He saw the organization as a well-oiled machine that required only ongoing maintenance, and he made no radical changes or innovations beyond those prompted by his personal scholarly interests. When confronted by the Great Depression, this hands-off approach resulted in a significant decline in the society's operations and its abilities to collect and process donations.

By the time the matriarchs passed from the scene in the mid-1940s, decades of poverty and neglect had left the library in desperate straits. Both the society library and the university library were "disgracefully overcrowded," with too many books, not enough room for students, and overcrowded staff work rooms. A 1943 report concluded that the university needed its own library and a doubling of its book budget. To alleviate overcrowding, staffs of the society and university libraries worked out coordinated collecting procedures to reduce duplication. Additionally, society director Edward Alexander enthusiastically embraced microfilm. The library bought its first newspapers on microfilm in 1942, and the next year Alexander employed library staff to microfilm the society's newspaper holdings. Within a year the library contained more than 1,000 reels of microfilm. All hard-copy subscriptions to out-of-state newspapers ended in 1945 and were replaced with papers available on film.

In 1953, the university library moved into the new Memorial Library on the block next to the Wisconsin Historical Society. Society collections were promptly redistributed into the vacated space, and construction crews began renovating the interior of the 1900 building. The separate first-floor reading rooms for manu-

The American Library Association group portrait, 1901, outside the society headquarters building. The organization's meeting happened in Madison because Thwaites wanted to draw attention to the Wisconsin Historical Society's new building. (WHi Image ID 45544)

scripts, government publications, and newspapers became museum galleries, and all library materials were now serviced from a central desk in the large second-floor reading room. The reconstruction that ended in 1955 also expanded the library's shelving space by 40 percent and created 50 study carrels in the stacks for graduate students. That same year, the society donated approximately 100,000 books and pamphlets from its non-American materials to Memorial Library. The society continued to serve as the university's North American research collection, a role the Wisconsin Historical Society library still fulfills today.

The post-World War II era also saw a renewed effort to modernize and expand the archives. Under the direction of Clifford Lord, the society began collecting historical records at the national level in broad topical areas. Most significantly, he acquired the records of the Cyrus McCormick family and the McCormick-Deering company (later International Harvester). Lord also expanded a state-level effort to collect union records to national levels with the acquisition of the records of the American Federation of Labor and large industrial unions. But most significantly for the long term, Lord created a national collecting program for the records of mass communication, including broadcasting, print journalism, and advertising as well as film and theater studies. The generally stated purpose behind collecting in all of these areas was the same as for state and local history: to collect, preserve, and provide access to important historical records that provide critical, and unbiased, information to Americans about their history, politics, and economy.

In 1962, several government document repositories on scattered university campuses around Wisconsin were converted into active research centers. This gave birth to the society's Area Research Center program. Each of the 14 centers serves a specific geographic region and houses records created in, and focused on, that region. Staffing is provided to help users navigate collections, and a courier system allows all the centers to share their collections with each other. This system makes the collections much more accessible than they were previously. Today, the society's Area Research Center system leads the nation in the size, scope, and usage of its network. The research centers benefit both the society

McCormick poster, ca. 1882. The McCormick-International Harvester Company Collection contains documents, publications, photographs and films related to Cyrus Hall McCormick and the International Harvester Company. The collection includes more than 12 million pages or items dating from 1753 to 1985. These items document the history of the agricultural equipment industry, the McCormick family, and many other topics in fields as diverse as the histories of advertising, technology, labor, business, rural life, philanthropy, architecture, Virginia, and Chicago. (WHi Image ID 3600)

and the University of Wisconsin System. Campuses aid the society by providing staffing and facilities to house records, while the society enables campuses to provide access to primary documents for undergraduates, high school students, and university faculty.

The Wisconsin Historical Society has documented some of the most pressing issues of the 20th century, including socialism, communism, Social Security and entitlements, civil liberties and free speech. During the turbulent decade of the 1960s, the society actively documented social reform movements. Field services staff gathered materials covering the anti-Vietnam War movement, the New Left, and the battles over reproductive rights and abortion, to name only a few. The society also collected letters, records, photographs, and other materials document-

A Student Nonviolent Coordinating Committee poster reading "One Man, One Vote," part of the society's extensive collection of materials documenting the civil rights movement. (WHi Image ID 53039)

ing the civil rights movement. Among these acquisitions were materials from more than 75 "Freedom Summer" volunteers, including activist Andrew Goodman. Goodman was one of three young civil rights workers who went south in the summer of 1964 to work on voter registration and freedom school initiatives, only to die at the hands of white supremacists. The story of their civil rights activism and their murders formed the storyline for the 1988 film *Mississippi Burning*.

The society's Library-Archives Division also holds more than 450 collections with oral history content, including some interviews that were collected by society staff. The topics of these interviews reflect the collecting areas of the Library-Archives Division: local history of cities, towns, and villages in Wisconsin, immigration, heritage and ethnicity, politics, military service, agriculture, logging, forestry and conservation, and mass communication and performing arts. Researchers can listen to any recording at no charge in the headquarters building in Madison or purchase a CD for themselves. Highlights of the collection include the Beloit bicentennial oral history project interviews, conducted in 1976, concerning the migration of blacks to the city after World War I; and the Barneveld tornado oral history project, interviews conducted after that town's devastating tornado of June 8, 1984.

The 1970s saw a dramatic shift in the clientele the library and archives served as the Bicentennial of the American Revolution in 1976 awakened many Americans to their own family history. For most of the 20th century fully 90 percent of the library's users had been students and scholars; however, by the late 1970s genealogists made up half of the library's patrons. Students and amateur researchers were competing for seats in the reading room, while university researchers wanting a vacant microfilm reader needed to arrive as soon as the library doors opened. Many of the genealogists had no experience navigating primary

Woman and young girl holding signs opposing school segregation, Milwaukee, ca. 1964. (WHi Image ID 4993)

documents, so library staff began teaching classes and publicizing the society's genealogical collections.

As the library and archives entered the computer age in the 1980s, library users' expectations began to shift. The initiation of a campuswide computerized catalog in the mid-1980s brought students to the library looking not for esoteric tomes or primary documents, but for information, often concerning current events. When the library catalog became available over the internet in 1993, researchers around the country and the world began to discover the extent of the society's collections. Consequently, society staff began fielding more and more calls from Hollywood writers, fact-checkers at national news outlets such as CNN, and attorneys arguing cases on each coast. Library patrons were no longer just academic historians – they were customers in a nationwide information marketplace.

Modern times bring new challenges and opportunities. Additional national- and state-level collecting programs have come and usually stayed. The statutes and procedures that govern the acquisition of the records of state and local governments have expanded as government's role has increased and as the records being created have moved increasingly into electronic formats. The staff follows detailed procedures for the appraisal, acquisition, and management of collections. Computer technology and the Internet have revolutionized intellectual and physical access to historical records. Nearly 300,000 pages from rare books, manuscripts, photographs, and other historical documents are posted on the society's Web site and receive more than 35,000 views a day. Another 6.4 million pages have been scanned by Google Books through a partnership with the University of Wisconsin and other major universities. And the society has licensed

Longtime society archivist Harry Miller examining Land Office records in the Archives stacks. (Wisconsin Historical Society photo by Robert Granflaten)

millions of pages of microfilmed newspaper content dating back to the Colonial era for access through online subscription services.

To implement these changes, the staff and organization of both the archives and the library have also undergone major adaptations. Most significantly, the two separate divisions were merged in 1999 and reorganized along functional lines to improve services and operate more efficiently. Over the past decade increasing portions of the staff's work has migrated to acquiring, managing, preserving, and providing access to digital content. In coming years, this trend will most likely accelerate. At the same time, major investments will occur to ensure that the existing record of Wisconsin and national history found in the many books, photographs, and documents collected over the centuries is protected and preserved.

In no way could Lyman Draper or Reuben Gold Thwaites, who worked to "treasure up" handbills, newspapers, letters, and similar ephemera, have anticipated the scope and demands of the digital age and its complex technologies. However, their commitment to the important work of history lives on in the present day, and their spirit infuses the efforts of the librarians and archivists who work to preserve and share the story of this state and its people.

Revitalization and Outreach

In the 20th century, the Wisconsin Historical Society was deeply affected by the worldwide economic collapse that resulted in the Great Depression, forcing programs to contract as resources grew scarce. Yet even amid the political upheavals of midcentury, the society experienced a rebirth and successfully adapted to new user demands. The struggles against Fascism and Communism highlighted the need for Americans to better understand their national history, while Wisconsinites' renewed interest in their own heritage created a demand for genealogical information and local history materialsf. Responding to these and other demands of the mid-20th century, the society under its next two directors, Edward Alexander and Clifford Lord, would modernize older programs while also reaching out to Wisconsinites on the local level in a variety of new ways.

Following Joseph Schafer's death in 1941, Edward P. Alexander of the New York State Historical Association was hired to be the "young man in a hurry" who would jump-start the society into a new era. Alexander renewed the society's dynamic, ambitious vision that had gone dormant for the preceding two decades. Alexander refreshed the museum and the publications programs to make both more appealing to the public. Additionally, he reached out to local communities, strengthening ties with local historical societies and expanding the membership program. Underlying all of these efforts was Alexander's conviction that "a historical society must have popular appeal if it is to have influence in its particular community."

In 1946, Clifford Lord took the helm as director following the departure of Alexander. Lord brought big ideas and the conviction that things should happen quickly. There was little that Lord did not want the society to tackle, and less that he thought could not be resolved before lunch if everyone just put their hearts and minds to the task. Lord's political and cultural education was molded by the Depression, the New Deal, World War II, and the burgeoning Cold War. Lord and his new assistants, mostly young World War II veterans, put their distinctive stamp on the century-old State Historical Society.

Lord and his staff believed that they were not just running a historical agency; they were making history in their own time. They faced both new opportunities and fresh problems, including the challenge of "relevance." What useful purpose did the historical society serve in the new atomic age? What endeavors would justify the expense of maintaining it? The answers for these men, and especially for Lord, lay in recasting the society as an institution that would address modern problems.

Dr. Clifford Lord, who here examines a book in the society's manuscript collection, directed the society from 1946 until 1958. An ambitious, energetic, and creative man, Lord was instrumental in reviving the society after the strains of two world wars and the Great Depression. (WHi Image ID 98886)

Lord viewed history as part of the great "battle for the minds and souls of men," a requirement for citizens to "know and understand" the basis of American democracy. As he said in an address on the importance of state and local history: "The study of history . . . clearly demonstrates the power of the individual to make his contribution, to shape or help shape the course of events; to make history where history is made – at the local level." Society president George Banta Jr. made those goals even clearer in 1951 when he argued, "For those interested in combating Marxism . . . the serious study of state and local history can supply one of the most effective ways of blunting one of the major intellectual weapons of our adversaries."

Reaching larger popular audiences was crucial if Lord and his staff wanted to achieve this goal. Lord and his assistants went so far as to create a mythical staff member, "the plumber from Kenosha," who was "called into every policy conference, into the discussion of every new program, every promotional or publicity release." Lord noted this fictitious plumber was a helpful addition to the staff, if a slightly aggravating person to reach. As Lord wrote, "We do wonder a bit . . . just how does one capture his imagination, his interest, his appreciation, his enthusiasm?" The society would still serve the university scholars and professional academics, but a renewed society needed also to reach men and women of all backgrounds and professions to be fully relevant in the mid-20th century.

The Wisconsin Historical Museum

One of the tools Alexander, and later, Lord, would end up using to reach the public was a rejuvenated museum. When he joined the society in 1941, Alexander saw the latent potential of the museum, noting, "The treasures of the Society's Library and Museum . . . were crying out to be used." The society had been collecting artifacts and displaying them from its very beginning. The ravages of the Depression had taken a harsh toll on the efforts to build and maintain a museum collection. It took Alexander's vision to rebuild that program.

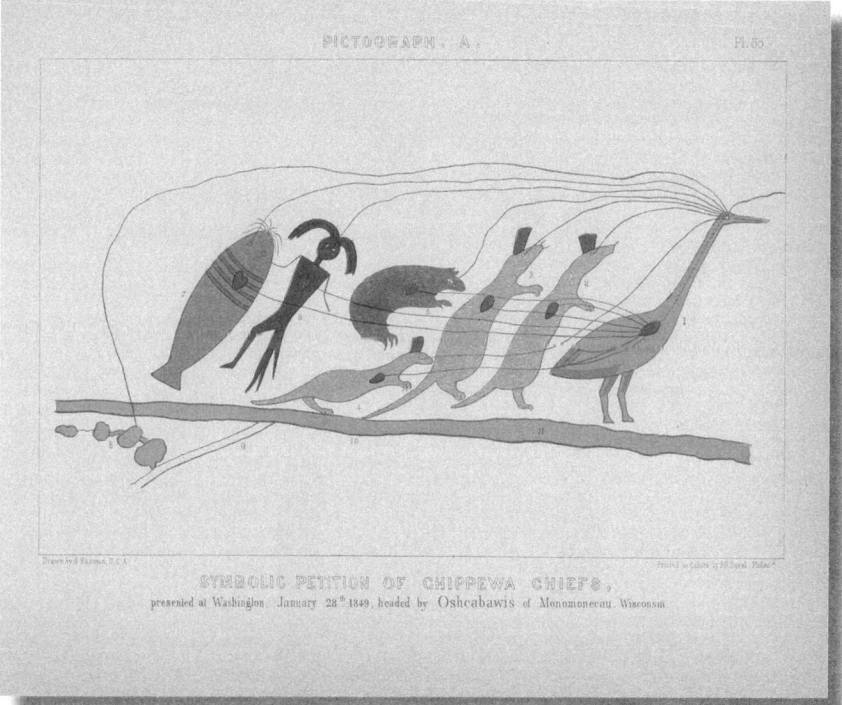

Nineteenth-century petition from Ojibwe clan chiefs. The animal figures represent clan leaders, the thick line represents Lake Superior, and the four small ovals represent rice beds. This petition indicates that the Ojibwe are of one mind and one heart and do not wish to be removed from their wild rice beds near Lake Superior. (WHi Image ID 1871)

The creation of a museum, or "cabinet," as the parlance of the time put it, was one of four functions outlined in the Wisconsin Historical Society's 1853 charter. The cabinet lacked definition and purpose in the early days of its existence, but by the 1870s it had become a noteworthy part of the society's holdings. A significant acquisition was the Perkins Collection, a 9,000-item assortment of Native American stone and copper implements obtained in 1875. Visitors also were drawn to the gallery of painted portraits and the cabinet's assortment of "curiosities," which included a silken tassel from the bed of Mary, Queen of

Scots; a fragment of the famous warship *Constitution*; and a rosary of olive wood from the Mount of Olives. Yearly attendance in the 1870s was estimated between 20,000 and 35,000 visitors.

In 1900, when the society moved to its new building on the University of Wisconsin campus, additional space was dedicated to the museum. The fourth floor of the new building became the museum's home, with handsome glass cases displaying notable objects from the cabinet. Separate rooms were available for

Commemorative roster of Company G of the 12th regiment, Wisconsin Volunteer Infantry, created October 1861. (WHi Image ID 28378)

displays of the state's "ethnology, war history, photographs and engravings, bric-a-brac, and curiosities." Yet the fourth-floor location was still problematic, being fairly inaccessible to the public and unbearably hot in the summer months. Additionally, the only staff devoted to the museum was a janitor assigned to the society in its old quarters at the state capitol.

While public funding was sought to support other programs, Thwaites relied on private donations to support the museum. In early 1892, Thwaites convinced the society's curators to establish an antiquarian fund. Money for the fund came from membership dues and the sale of duplicate volumes from the society's library. By 1907, the antiquarian fund had reached $10,000, from which the society's executive committee voted $400 annually to fund museum acquisitions. That same year the Wisconsin Legislature increased the society's budget, which enabled Thwaites to lure Charles E. Brown away from the Milwaukee Public Museum to head a newly created Museum Department.

Painting by Cal Peters depicting the battle of Bad Axe at the Wisconsin River on August 2, 1832. (WHi Image ID 4522)

Brown immediately brought direction and order to the museum. Under his guidance the collections were classified and rearranged, an accessioning system was installed, field collecting began in earnest, and special exhibits became a regular occurrence. Brown also prescribed limits on what would be collected, generally limiting items to the broad fields of history, ethnology, archaeology, and art. Though these were not enforced strictly, they did help bring focus to the museum collections. Meanwhile, Brown overhauled the displays in each of the rooms of the museum to make them more attractive, which helped draw more visitors. The displays in turn influenced collecting as Brown identified and obtained items needed for new exhibits. Special effort was made to secure materials on Wisconsin's ethnic groups, religion, and obsolete farm implements as well as items pertaining to the post office, lumbering, or firefighting. Photographic collections also increased rapidly, as a flood of donations came in, including a complete set of photographs of Union generals, 465 photographs of Confederate officers, and numerous photographs of American Indians.

For the next 20 years museum attendance grew. Brown gladly gave talks and guided tours of the museum exhibits to school groups that visited in great numbers. University classes came to study cooking methods of Wisconsin pioneers and Indians, while engineers studied early farm implements and industrial machinery. Women's groups, Boy Scout troops, delegates from any number of state conventions held in Madison, and a host of other visitors came through the doors as attendance swelled to between 60,000 and 80,000 people a year.

The Wisconsin Historical Museum's reach also expanded beyond Madison. Brown prepared displays of artifacts, implements, and photographs to circulate throughout the state. He also traveled around Wisconsin talking to schools, advising local museums and historical societies, and giving interviews to newspapers and, in the 1930s, on the radio. Brown worked with several groups, including the University of Wisconsin and the Madison Park and Pleasure Drive Association, among others, to mark and preserve Indian mounds in various parts of Madison and elsewhere in southern Wisconsin. Thanks to these vigorous activities in the museum, the society's visibility grew among several audiences, including schoolchildren and their parents and teachers, as well as the donors whose funding made the acquisitions and exhibits possible. Additional funding from the Wisconsin Legislature kept the museum functioning well until the Great Depression.

In 1932, the legislature cut the society's budget, just as the Great Depression dried up private donations. The society's executive committee and Superintendent Schafer struggled to find ways to maintain essential services. Brown turned his attention to his work with a Works Progress Administration project, and the museum was at a standstill for the next decade until the arrival of Alexander.

Alexander rejuvenated the museum in several ways. New exhibits kept modern concepts in mind, taking into account "structure, space, form, color, and light as a unified whole." Alexander hired additional staff for the museum and revised collection policies. For the first time, exhibits were placed in the first-floor galleries. Patrons passed these on their way to the library, making them more prominent than the fourth-floor galleries, which still held long-standing exhibits. Believing that "museums need not look like morgues," Alexander installed lighted cases to improve viewing of the displays. Exhibits changed frequently, covering a variety of themes including the circus and turn-of-the-century "do-it-yourself" projects. Once again, attendance soared. Although wartime travel restrictions and tight resources led to a decline in acquisitions, the immediate postwar years were encouraging in that the museum received greater funding. The extensive remodel of the headquarters building completed in 1956 effectively doubled the size of the museum as additional galleries on the first floor were cleared to make way for museum exhibits.

The theme of museum exhibits often coincided with special events or dates. In the fall of 1947, exhibits were planned and prepared illustrating a chronological history of Wisconsin in anticipation of the centennial of statehood the next year. The "Draper Centennial Year," commemorating Draper's hiring as corresponding secretary, was celebrated in 1954 with an exhibit featuring some of his works. In the early 1960s, the museum created displays titled "Meet Mr. Lincoln" and "Wisconsin in the Civil War" as the state observed the Civil War Centennial.

In 1967, the Wisconsin Historical Society began another remodeling project, a major addition to its headquarters building. The construction affected the museum more than any other society program. Displays in the first-floor galleries had to be moved occasionally to accommodate construction. Remodeling of

A T-shaped addition to the society headquarters under construction, 1967. (WHi Image ID 98620)

the fourth floor substantially reduced the available exhibit space as the gallery was converted into the archives reading room. One exhibit, a popular display on pharmacy, had stood in a fourth-floor gallery for close to 60 years. Even in the midst of the construction, the museum opened an exhibit titled "The Black Community: Its Culture and Heritage" that had been a year in planning and research. Planning also went forward for future exhibits celebrating famous Wisconsin women and another about Philip Fox La Follette, whose papers the society made available to the public in the summer of 1970.

Although the 1967 addition afforded more space to store books, manuscripts, and museum objects, just six years later society director James Morton Smith wrote that the building "already lacks space for library materials, museum and … archival materials." An inventory of its collections found that the museum held about 50,000 objects, and even more items were anticipated with the opening of Old World Wisconsin in 1976. Austerity delayed movement on a solution to overcrowding until the late 1970s, when a long-range planning report identified the society's major need as "space for the continued growth and proper care of the collections." The society began to search for a building where the museum could move, to alleviate overcrowding at the headquarters building.

On July 18, 1980, under the leadership of director Richard Erney, the society purchased a vacant building on the Capitol Square in Madison that was the long-time home of the Wolff, Kubly and Hirsig hardware store. Over the next several years the building was renovated to house museum exhibits, fabrication facilities, and museum education staff and facilities. The museum relocated to the Capitol Square in 1985 and has called the location home ever since. Through displays titled "People of the Woodlands," "Frontier Wisconsin," "The Immigrant State,"

Ojibwe beaded moccasins, made by Francis Weyman (Pywasit) as a gift for Mrs. Charles E. Lunberg. (WHS Museum #1954.241,a)

"Making a Living," and "Sense of Community," visitors to the Wisconsin Historical Museum can learn about the history and shared experiences of the many cultures that settled Wisconsin.

Today, the museum's collections contain more than 110,000 historical objects and nearly 400,000 archaeological artifacts documenting the history of Wisconsin from prehistoric times to the present. The museum has notable collections in the fields of anthropology, business and technology, costumes, textiles and personal artifacts, domestic life, and political and military life. These collections help visitors understand important trends and events of daily life within diverse social, ethnic, and religious backgrounds. The Wisconsin Historical Museum building comprises four stories. A museum store, an auditorium, and exhibits space occupy the first floor, while the other three floors house exhibits of various display objects and artifacts relating to a particular area of Wisconsin's past.

The Wisconsin Historical Museum, in addition to its exhibits, also holds events celebrating various facets of Wisconsin life, including music, beer, and quilting. The museum operates a vibrant foodways program; the popular History Sandwiched In is an informal brown-bag lunch-and-lecture series that covers a breadth of historical subjects. Museum visitors can enjoy topics such as Paul Bunyan's Northwoods folklore and the maritime history of Door County, enabling them to make connections between Wisconsin's past and contemporary issues of today. The Taste Traditions of Wisconsin programs, begun in the early 2000s, explore the rich culinary history, indigenous ingredients, and remarkable ethnic foodways of Wisconsin. Taste Traditions events pair noteworthy speakers with delicious meals, creating a unique experience for museum visitors. These events are routinely sold out.

The museum has gained national exposure, notably a 2012 episode of the Travel Channel's *Mysteries at the Museum*

The Wisconsin Historical Museum collects a variety of objects, from clothing to firearms, toys to furniture. (WHi Image ID 98887)

Curator Joe Kapler holds the enormous Potter Knife. The 31-pound, six-foot-long knife was presented to Wisconsin congressman John Potter by members of the Missouri Republican Party in 1860, after Potter stood up for an antislavery representative from Illinois. (WHS Museum #1957.1122; photo by Joel Heiman)

featuring the twisted engine block from the truck used in the 1970 Sterling Hall bombing on the University of Wisconsin campus. In 2011, the Travel Channel's *Bert the Conqueror* received a tour of the museum's *Odd Wisconsin* exhibit, which highlighted some of the state's quirkier accomplishments, from snake oils and other objects of general quackery to the banjo-ukulele used by jingle composer Richard Trentlage in the first recording of the Oscar Mayer Wiener Song in 1962. Though the need for more modern facilities has once again become apparent, the Wisconsin Historical Museum continues to foster an appreciation of Wisconsin's past among the tens of thousands of visitors who pass through its doors annually.

The Wisconsin Historical Society Press

*Y*et another program needing rejuvenation after the difficult Great Depression era was the Wisconsin Historical Society Press. The Wisconsin Historical Society Press is the oldest publisher in the State of Wisconsin, having published its first book in 1855. Now the press has grown into an award-winning publisher, offering an average of 15 new titles each year on Wisconsin history and culture. Since 1917, the press has published a quarterly journal, *The Wisconsin Magazine of History*. The press has explored a variety of formats beyond books and magazines, including posters, textbooks, books for young readers, audio books, and e-books. While today the society press' titles appeal to a broad audience of general readers, since 1855 the press has played a key role in supporting the society's mission to connect people to the past, while at the same time preserving in print Wisconsin's unique and varied history.

When Lyman Draper took the helm as the society's corresponding secretary, he brought to the organization the conviction that the documents he and others collected deserved to be published and read, analyzed, and put to work helping us know and understand our past. Draper also envisioned a plan that would accomplish two goals at once, printing the raw material of history and using it to build the society's library. In 1855 the society printed its first book, properly titled *First Annual Report and Collections of the State Historical Society of Wisconsin for the Year 1854,* a 147-page compilation of documents. Among the documents published in this volume were reports from the executive committee and treasurer of the society, as well as a dozen articles and documents on topics including the French and Indian War and recollections from Green Bay in 1816-1817. Scattered throughout the volume were Draper's annotations, revealing the expertise he had acquired in Wisconsin history after only a few years in the state. The *Wisconsin Historical Collections* was designated as a departmental report, which meant that the state funded the printing costs for the 8,000 copies, and it became a significant tool Draper would use for barter.

Every two or three years a new volume of the *Wisconsin Historical Collections* was issued, containing an increasing amount of memoirs, journals, narratives, interviews, and other eyewitness accounts of Wisconsin's past. By the time Draper retired from the society in 1887, the *Wisconsin Historical Collections* numbered 10 volumes and the society's reputation had grown steadily. Thwaites published 10 more volumes – 11,000 pages containing over a thousand documents – before the series was discontinued in 1915. Among the treasures in the *Wisconsin Historical Collections* are more than 100 pioneer reminiscences from fur traders, farmwomen, and Indian elders as well as diaries from travelers, soldiers, immigrants, and missionaries, written while significant events in Wisconsin's development were unfolding, making it the single most comprehensive record of life in Wisconsin during the colonial era.

THE
WISCONSIN MAGAZINE
OF
HISTORY
SEPTEMBER   1917

VOLUME I
NUMBER 1

PUBLISHED QUARTERLY
BY THE STATE HISTORICAL
SOCIETY OF WISCONSIN

The first issue of the Wisconsin Magazine of History, *September 1917. (WHi Image ID 98888)*

During his time as director, Thwaites was also the secretary and editor of the Wisconsin History Commission, which was formed to commemorate the semicentennial of the Civil War. The Wisconsin History Commission would usher into print some titles of lasting significance, including Frank Haskell's account of the Battle of Gettysburg and Ethel Hurn's *Wisconsin Women in the War*, a remarkable volume detailing the various, and sometimes surprising, roles women played during the Civil War. While Thwaites came to be known as a first-rate editor, the bulk of his most impressive editorial work was done for other publishers, including the monumental *Jesuit Relations* and the *Journals of Lewis and Clark*. In all, Thwaites edited 170 volumes and wrote 15 others.

After Thwaites's untimely death in 1913, his successor, the youthful and much maligned Quaife, brought the press into the 20th century in significant ways.

Quaife was only 33 years old when hired to direct the society, yet he came equipped with ideas that showed he was well ahead of his time. Quaife proposed publishing a dictionary of Wisconsin biography, which was ultimately completed in 1960, and his idea for a historical atlas of the state was fulfilled by the University of Wisconsin Press in 1998. The society's publications expanded during

Quaife's tenure to include monographs and secondary histories as well as miscellaneous reference works. Quaife also ended the long-running *Wisconsin Historical Collections* series, replacing it with a quarterly membership magazine titled *The Wisconsin Magazine of History*.

Quaife introduced the magazine to readers in 1917, noting that because "the historical interests of the professional scholars among our membership are catered to by numerous historical reviews," the magazine was meant to appeal to the intelligent layman "without sacrificing in any way the scholarly ideals of the society." The magazine was a decisive step into a new era for the press, connecting the society with Wisconsinites more closely than before. Every three months when a new issue of the magazine arrived, readers were given history in a more accessible format than the primary documents published until then. After nearly 100 years the *Wisconsin Magazine of History* has published over two thousand feature articles totaling more than 30,000 pages and continues to be an important part of the society and the press. In 2000, the *Wisconsin Magazine of History* was substantially redesigned for the first time since 1973. The switch to a full-color format was done to make the magazine "more attractive, more varied, and more appealing to a wider audience." In 2010, it won the Award of Merit from the American Association for State and Local History, having been called "a model for the field" and "the best magazine of its kind in the country."

Les Fishel, society director from 1959 to 1969. (WHi Image ID 79582)

After Quaife's ouster as director in 1919 he stayed on for another three years as chief of research and publications. Throughout much of the next two decades the press was less active as Wisconsin suffered through the Great Depression. With the rejuvenation of the society that came with the hiring of Alexander, press publications were modernized. The *Wisconsin Magazine of History* was revamped to look more appealing to the average reader and to make it more informative. Historians were commissioned to write a series of biographies on notable Wisconsinites. The press hired additional staff in 1948 and was able to produce over the next decade "the most distinguished shelf of publications ever to appear over the society's imprimatur." A closer relationship with the University of Wisconsin in the postwar era sparked the creation of Logmark Editions, an imprint of the society press that printed notable graduate theses.

In 1960, society director Les Fishel revealed to select members of the society and the University of Wisconsin that the press was planning to create a multivolume history of the state, beginning with the earliest times and stretching up to the modern day. Each volume would be approximately 400 pages and would encompass a significant period in Wisconsin's development: volume 1, *From Exploration to Statehood*; volume 2, *The Civil War Era*; volume 3, *Urbanization* and *Industrialization*; volume 4, *The Progressive Era*; volume 5, *War, a New Era, and Depression*; and volume 6, *Continuity and Change*. The History of Wisconsin Series was an ambitious project, ultimately involving six authors and dozens of researchers, and has become the standard reference work for Wisconsin history. The first volume of the series was published in 1973, just in time for the farewell party for the volume's distinguished author, Alice E. Smith. Twenty-five years later, the sixth and final volume was published, coincidentally during Wisconsin's sesquicentennial year.

In 1976, the press published the first books in a series that continues to this day, the *Documentary History of the Ratification of the Constitution*, the flagship project of the National Historical Records and Publications Commission. Upon publication of the first two volumes of this series in May 1976, society director James Morton Smith, along with the press director and several of the series editors, traveled to Washington, DC, to present copies to Warren Burger, then Chief Justice of the Supreme Court. The press has since published 22 more volumes in the series and has at least seven more volumes in development. Following in the tradition of documentary publishing established by Lyman Draper, the series is a standard reference work employed by judges and constitutional historians nationwide and has gar-

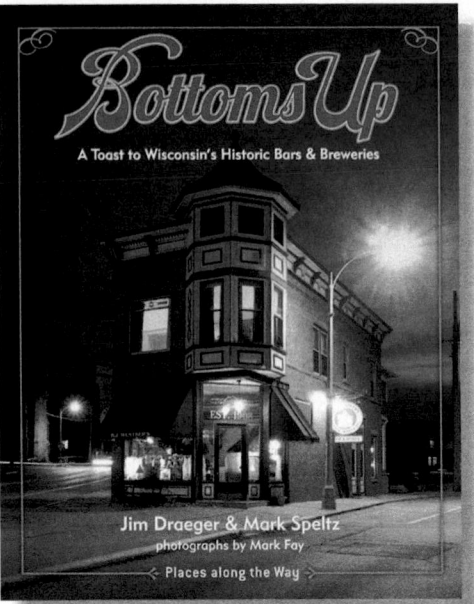

Bottoms Up: A Toast to Wisconsin's Historic Bars and Breweries, *by Jim Draeger and Mark Speltz, takes readers on a tour of 70 distinctive bars and breweries around the state.*

Green Bay Packers: Trials, Triumphs, and Tradition, *by William Povletich, tells the story of how one small American city came to host one of football's most iconic teams.*

nered rare praise, being called "the most important editorial project in the nation" as well as "a world treasure."

Throughout the 1970s and 1980s, the society press produced half a dozen books annually, issued the *Wisconsin Magazine of History* four times a year, made a catalog annually and generated mailing lists, and promoted the books whenever possible. A former editor from the time recalled that the editors "periodically hauled [books] to historical conventions in places as distant as New York and Washington in the society's station wagon," all with a staff of five or so. Over the past quarter century, the press has attempted to find a synthesis between engaging larger audiences while not sacrificing scholarship in the process. While titles such as Peter J. Coleman's *Debtors and Creditors in America: Insolvency, Imprisonment for Debt, and Bankruptcy, 1607-1900* contributed to a scholarly understanding of the American past, appealing narratives of the lives, events, and cultural elements that have contributed to Wisconsin's makeup today have provided a way to engage a wider audience. Topics such as architecture and preservation, sports and favorite pastimes, cooking and foodways, popular culture, biography, memoir, and military history have predominated and have helped the press expand its readership within and even beyond Wisconsin's borders.

The press has fostered a number of partnerships with external organizations to develop content and promote titles, which has led to an increasing number of books covering a diverse swath of Wisconsin history and culture. The press recently partnered with the Oneida Tribe of Indians of Wisconsin to create *A Nation within a Nation: Voices of the Oneidas in Wisconsin*; with the Wisconsin Milk Marketing Board on *Creating Dairyland*; and with the Special Olympics of Wisconsin and Wisconsin's Board for People with Developmental Disabilities to publish and promote *Cindy Bentley: Spirit of a Champion*, to name just a few projects. Wisconsin Public Television has been an active partner with the press, resulting in projects like *Wisconsin Vietnam War Stories* as well as programs based on press titles, including *Fill 'Er Up* and *Bottoms Up: A Toast to Wisconsin's Historic Bars & Breweries*, which are part of the press's Places Along the Way series. Working with these and other organizations has helped the press tell a variety of new stories and reach new audiences.

At the heart of the press's recent efforts is the conviction that quality stories, well told, shared in print, have the power to move and engage readers. As an example, in the early 1990s, fewer than 20 years after the fall of Saigon, the society launched a project to collect and publish the letters and diaries of Wisconsin Vietnam War veterans. The project ultimately resulted in the society press book *Voices from Vietnam*, edited by Michael Stevens. Veterans often found it difficult to share their stories with their loved ones, yet many answered the call for materials. Donald Thies, who served in the 101st Airborne Division in 1971, was one of them. Among the materials Thies donated was a photograph of himself and several of his comrades taken just before a challenging mission that lasted several days. When the press reprinted this title recently, this photograph was selected to be on the cover. Thies was so touched by the use of his image that he contacted all of the veterans shown in the photo and had them sign a poster-sized image of the cover. He later presented the poster to Wisconsin Historical Society Director Ellsworth Brown.

Local History

Vietnam War veteran Donald Thies presented this signed poster-sized book cover replica to society director Ellsworth Brown in 2012. (Wisconsin Historical Society Press)

In every community around Wisconsin there are people who are interested in the stories that make up their shared history – stories about schools, churches, businesses, and families, as well as about the events that have shaped their community's identity. Local historical societies abound in Wisconsin, groups that have been busily engaged in preserving objects and accounts of the lives that influenced their particular experience.

In anticipation of the state's semicentennial celebration in 1898, society director Thwaites successfully advocated for legislation that would allow the establishment of affiliates by exempting them from the payment of filing fees for their articles of organization. It authorized the society to provide uniform bylaws and require an annual report to the society. Thwaites urged local groups and libraries to collect materials – diaries, letters, journals, books, and the like – relating to the history of their locale. He also spoke at gatherings, encouraging local leadership to build research centers, place historical markers, and develop museums, and promoting cooperation between local societies and schools in an effort to foster an interest in history among teachers and students. In 1899, Green Bay and Ripon became the first two local historical societies to affiliate with the Wisconsin Historical Society.

A generation later, as World War II raged in Europe, Edward Alexander noted, "Institutions which do not immediately serve the war effort tend to decline rapidly and nearly all educational projects have hard sledding." Alexander believed that the study of local history "inculcates the highest kind of patriotism," explaining, "America is big and impersonal and thus difficult to understand and appreciate as a whole." On the other hand, a local community was "warm and human and personal, especially when its personality has been made known." Clifford Lord pointed out the international importance of local history, writing, "We are engaged today in the greatest battle for the minds and souls of men and women which the modern world has witnessed … Study local history and we dissipate the fog of intangibles … We come to appreciate the significance of the American experiment. We see the essential elements it has to offer to all men everywhere as a model and an inspiration. We begin to comprehend why democracy is still potentially the greatest revolutionary force on the face of the earth."

Even in wartime, Wisconsin's local historical societies had successfully kept their members interested and involved, whether through planning new displays at local museums or gathering new items for display. Alexander did what he could to encourage the local societies, publishing accounts of their activities in the *Wisconsin Magazine of History* and working to codify stronger partnerships with the local societies. Alexander hoped, among other things, to circulate displays from the society's museum collections to local museums around the state to "help them become even more active educational forces." The Wisconsin Historical Society also began sending out instructional pamphlets to individuals wanting advice on operation of a local society and published articles in the *Wisconsin Magazine of History* to offer suggestions and encouragement to local societies.

A large measure of Lord's program to revitalize the society after World War II focused on aiding local societies and local historians to better understand their localities. The study of local history, Lord wrote, "cannot help but make us better citizens," while it also had the power to "make us better people, for it cannot help but give us insight into how human beings act and react." Most importantly, however, the study of local history would restore the importance of the individual in a sometimes all-too-impersonal world. As Lord explained, "When you get back to the locality you see that history, with God's help, is made by men. We witness it every day. It is so obvious we overlook it." Appropriately, then, Lord worked to improve the relationship between the Wisconsin Historical Society and the local historical societies that had become affiliated with it.

The award-winning Wisconsin Magazine of History *publishes well-researched, well-written, and lavishly illustrated articles on a wide variety of Wisconsin history topics.*

In 1961, the society's board of curators created the Wisconsin Council for Local History to help promote communication and cooperation among local history groups. The Wisconsin Council for Local History brings together the almost 400 affiliated organizations from all parts of Wisconsin, representing a variety of geographic locales such as counties, reservations, cities, villages, townships, and neighborhoods.

The council also includes organizations with specialized interests such as railroads, labor history, cemeteries, and particular ethnic heritages.

Also in the 1960s, the society created an Office of Local History to assist those who were interested in creating local historical societies, as well as to improve communication between the Wisconsin Historical Society and its affiliates. The Office of Local History soon began holding annual regional conventions, published a newsletter, *Exchange*, and produced a number of how-to pamphlets for local societies such as *A Cataloging System for Local Historical Society and Museums*. Today the society has two field representatives assisting local societies, one responsible for groups in northern Wisconsin and another for the southern part of the state.

One long standing program administered by the Office of Local History is the Historical Markers program. In 1944, Governor Walter Goodland, foreseeing the end of World War II and the increased tourist travel that would ensue in the state, appointed a committee to study how best to mark historic locations in Wisconsin. Just after the war, the state began marking historic locations such as the site of Nicolet's landing near Green Bay. In 1950, the Wisconsin Historical Sites and Markers Committee came up with a standardized design for new markers, made of cast aluminum and painted brown with cream-colored lettering and featuring a "ferocious-looking badger." The next year, the first of these standardized markers was placed at the Peshtigo Fire Cemetery.

The markers program has been another way the society and local communities work together. While the society approves new-marker applications, individuals and groups pay for the markers themselves and choose the subject matter. Markers must denote places of historical interest significant enough to warrant commemoration on a local, state, or national level and must also touch on one of a wide array of categories including archaeology, architecture, culture, events, ethnic groups and associations, geology, legends, and natural history.

Panther intaglio effigy mound historical marker in Fort Atkinson. (Wisconsin Historical Society)

Today more than 540 historical markers dot the state, with new marker applications being accepted regularly. Wisconsin's historical markers offer a unique insight into the breadth of the state's history, showcasing how interests have changed over time and bringing the past to light with an immediacy that is not easy to replicate with other media. Travelers can see the place in Ashland County where Pierre Radisson and Medan Groseilliers built a crude stockade in 1659, or know when they stop at a wayside in Chippewa County that they are on the site of the old McCann farm where Old Abe, the War Eagle,

The society's Historymobile brought displays and artifacts to communities around the state, beginning in the mid-1950s and continuing until the late 1970s. (WHi Image ID 98830)

spent his early years. Markers engage the imagination in a specific time and place, helping us commemorate events while bringing us closer to the features that have helped shape our state.

One of the society's most distinctive and popular venues for connecting with local communities was the Historymobile. Called "one of the Society's most innovative and important educational services," the Historymobile consisted of a Ford pickup and a mobile home modified to host museum exhibits. In April 1954, the Historymobile set out from the state capital on its first tour of Wisconsin, carrying an exhibit titled "History through Our Historic Sites." For more than two decades the society sent a new traveling exhibit on the road for up to 230 days each year, parking at schools and village halls where residents would line up to walk through exhibits with titles such as "Wisconsin: Wilderness, Territory, Frontier State"; "Sawdust and Spangles: The Circus in Wisconsin"; or "Signers of the Declaration of Independence." The society printed study guides for the exhibits, one version for students and another for teachers. The curators who called the Historymobile home while on the road were also on hand to answer questions and interpret the exhibits. No admission was charged to view the traveling museum. A visit from the Historymobile was a special event for most communities. The local papers would announce its impending arrival, and schoolchildren as well as adults toured its exhibits with great enthusiasm. During its 23-year existence, the Historymobile traveled close to 80,000 miles and hosted an estimated three million people.

Today, the Wisconsin Historical Society provides a wide array of services for the almost 400 local societies with which it is affiliated. Local society members regularly consult with staff about preserving or renovating historic buildings, establishing or improving museums, or preserving archaeological sites. Society representatives arrange regional conferences as well as an annual statewide conference where local society members can meet to share ideas and discuss common issues. In turn, local societies share in the mission and responsibility of preserving Wisconsin's heritage. Together, the society and its local affiliates have preserved a countless number of artifacts, photographs, maps, manuscripts, oral histories, and other documentation. Beyond the shared mission of preservation, they have worked together to educate the public about the past and have collaborated on special projects to enhance historical efforts in Wisconsin.

Reaching Out to Schools

The Historymobile was only one of a number of society programs that appealed to young people over the years. The society's first attempts to be useful to schools began with Thwaites, who saw the society as an engine for popular education whose influence ought to extend to the borders of the state. He reached out to Wisconsin's schools, regularly giving talks to teachers in schools and at state conventions. In Green Bay, he sowed the idea of having a story hour at a local library, with stories ranging from Jamestown to the Civil War. Ever the newspaperman, Thwaites issued a bulletin of information and reported the idea to the *Library Journal*.

Like many of its outreach programs, the society's first school program began under the directorship of Clifford Lord. Intending "to increase greatly the tangible service we render to the people of the State," in 1947 the society launched an ambitious, multifaceted program for young people. In the spring of that year, the society helped establish prototype junior chapters in six schools to work out methods and experiment with teaching local history for young people. Membership in a junior club entitled members to *Badger History* magazine, a newsletter, a membership card, buttons, and a chapter charter. Dues ranged from 25 cents for groups of five or more to 75 cents for children not part of an organized chapter. Additionally, the society circulated copies of the *Wisconsin Teacher Newsletter* to teachers leading junior chapters. The newsletter reported on new chapters as well as program ideas developed in the various chapters and "conveyed a sense of participation in a state-wide program."

In October 1947, the first issue of the monthly *Badger History* was published. The magazine featured brief but informative articles on people and events in Wisconsin's past written by society staff and other experts, as well as articles written by schoolchildren. The magazine also printed suggestions detailing how children could be historians themselves by preserving objects, reading appropriate history books, or visiting historic places. The magazine had two distinct sections, one aimed at elementary grades and the other at the intermediate grades. Editors of *Badger History* aimed to connect with children by promising that "this new BADGER HISTORY magazine is yours … Our magazine will be written FOR you and BY you. We shall print your stories, essays, poems, histories, pictures, hobbies, cartoons – all about your community, your county, your state."

Enthusiasm for Wisconsin history ran high with the statehood centennial only a year away. Yet little could society staff have known how popular the junior program would be. In December 1947, Director Lord reported that the junior program had 102 chapters and close to 2,000 members. By the end of the program's first year there were over 14,000 members. Most importantly, the junior chapters were active in a number of projects. Several chapters wrote histories of their school districts or of notable farms in their areas, while others wrote about local churches or cemeteries. Chapters wrote often to the editors of *Badger History* to tell of achievements. A chapter in Waupaca reported that they were helping with a Danish Waupaca program, including compiling a cookbook and holding a literary benefit program. Another chapter reported, perhaps with a bit of hyperbole: "We also made a complete study of Wisconsin, learning everything we possibly could about it." At the conclusion of the first year of the program, Lord reported proudly: "The activities of our juniors would quite literally fill a book."

A decade later, Wisconsin had one of the most active junior historian programs in the nation. Membership had grown to include 20,687 students in 1,156 chapters. The society's director of the program noted with pride that in the first decade of its existence, *Badger History* had printed 1,100 articles written by schoolchildren. Growth in the students was also palpable, as the program director wrote: "The past is tied to the present in the child's mind as he finds, through interviewing and reading and writing, that history is real and alive." The society encouraged junior chapters by awarding prizes for group projects, essays, models of historic buildings, oratory and audiovisual projects, posters, murals, and scrapbooks. Up to six conventions were held at different locations in the state, drawing thousands of children to see skits and pageants, or to tour historic sites. By 1960, the society regularly fielded questions from several states seeking advice on how to start a similar program.

Participants reaped many benefits from the junior historian program. The conventions made "history palpable and alive – not merely dates and places in a book" for participating children. The program director noted the junior historians had the opportunity "to make new friends, find out what other chapters are doing, enter genial competition, gain poise in programs where they appear on the same platform with mayors, Chamber of Commerce presidents – even the governor." As they interviewed grandparents for special projects, children rescued stories that may have been forever lost; in addition, they sometimes found antiques and historic objects when visiting older people to talk about earlier times. Some young historians borrowed objects to create a museum in their schools, which developed an interest in history throughout the community.

Changes to Wisconsin's school system in the 1960s put an end to this promising program. As early as 1963, membership was declining, for which the program's directors commonly blamed school consolidation. Fewer teachers were inclined to invest time outside of the classroom to the project after consolidation, and larger schools provided more clubs to students, which also chipped away at membership. More problematic for the junior historian program was the institution of new guidelines for teaching social studies that most school districts adopted in the fall of 1965.

The new Wisconsin Social Studies Curriculum moved the teaching of Wisconsin history from middle grades to the fourth grade, which rendered obsolete much of the material available in *Badger History*. Responding to these new guidelines, *Badger History* was changed from a monthly magazine into social studies resource units. The society published four new issues of *Badger History* each school year. Each issue covered a unique topic in Wisconsin history using language, pictures, and activities meant to appeal to fourth-grade students. Without the support of *Badger History*, where middle and high school students had formerly seen their work displayed, and where teachers could see the work of other chapters, enthusiasm for the program eroded further.

Some elements of the junior historian program held on for several years after the program's decline began. Membership cards were still available to junior historian chapters, but they were not advertised. *Badger History* in its new format continued publication until 1980, when it was halted altogether. Local historical societies were encouraged to create their own junior programs, with limited success. One school district in Walworth County continued to have an annual essay contest, a remnant of the junior history program, but this too had ended by the late 1980s.

The activities of the junior historian clubs foreshadowed a similar program begun in the 1990s: National History Day. National History Day has become one of the most fruitful venues through which the society engages younger audiences. Through National History Day in Wisconsin, schoolchildren from grades 6 to 12 are given a topic to research by examining historical issues, ideas, people, and events. Students' research is then presented in various ways, including exhibits, performances, documentaries, Web sites, and research papers. Presentations are judged at regional events, with winners advancing to the statewide competition in Madison. From these, a select number of participants are chosen to represent Wisconsin at a national competition, held each summer at the University of Maryland. In 2001, the program's first year in Wisconsin, almost 2,000 students participated in the program with the help of 41 teachers. During the 2011-2012

It's obvious which state these National History Day participants are representing! (Wisconsin Historical Society)

academic year, participation had grown to 9,000 students and 229 teachers at 103 different schools.

Participation in National History Day activities benefits students in many ways. They develop skills in research, writing, and critical thinking and have the chance to express themselves creatively. Student interest in history increases considerably as scholars do their own research, form their own opinions, and present their findings in the manner they choose. Moreover, students become aware of how relevant the past is to their modern lives. In the words of one participant: "History will never be just words on a page now that I have had the opportunity to do my own research through National History Day. It is a story that continues through everyone's lives and paves the way for the future."

In 1991, as the result of advocacy by local historical societies, the legislature provided authorization and funding for an expanded school services program to assist schools in the teaching of state history. In addition to holding workshops and training programs for teachers, the society began to develop new curricular material related to state history. In the 1990s, the Wisconsin Historical Society Press renewed its publishing efforts to provide teachers and students with quality books for young readers. Working with the school services staff, the press began the New Badger History series. Books in this series covered a wide array of topics in Wisconsin history including immigration, archaeology, and land use, in a format and vocabulary appropriate for elementary to middle school-aged students. The press also produced teacher guides, which made the books more useful and accessible for Wisconsin

Wisconsin, Our State, Our Story, the fourth-grade history textbook, was produced by the Wisconsin Historical Society Press in both English and Spanish versions. (Wisconsin Historical Society)

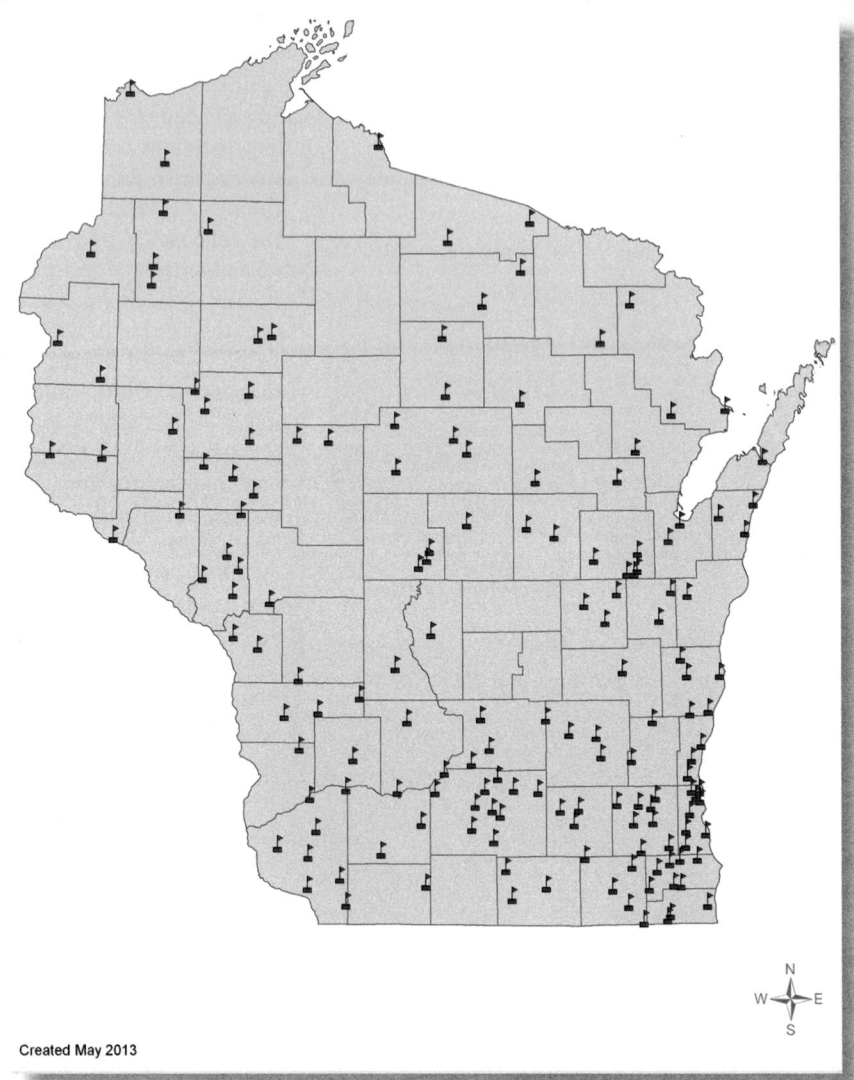

Created May 2013

Map showing the school districts in Wisconsin that have adopted the textbook Wisconsin: Our State, Our Story, *produced by the Wisconsin Historical Society Press, for use in fourth-grade classrooms. (Wisconsin Historical Society map)*

classrooms. These books were the forerunners of two additional projects that would see light in the early part of the 21st century: the Badger Biographies series and *Wisconsin: Our State, Our Story*, the press's fourth-grade textbook.

The Badger Biographies series started in 2005 with the publication of *Mai Ya's Long Journey*. Recounting the story of a young Hmong woman whose parents fled Laos during the Vietnam War, the narrative follows Mai Ya from her childhood in Thailand's Ban Vinai refugee camp to her new home in Wisconsin. The Badger Biographies series now numbers more than 20 titles and deals with a diverse set of lives, from famous Wisconsinites Curly Lambeau and Les Paul to lesser-known citizens such as Casper Jaggi, a Swiss cheese maker from Monroe, and Dr. Kate Pelham Newcomb, who worked as a doctor in Minocqua in the early to mid-20th century. Books in this series have been used in children's classrooms as well as in a variety of literacy programs around the state for adults learning to read English.

Wisconsin: Our State, Our Story is a full-color, comprehensive textbook presenting Wisconsin history to fourth graders utilizing the "Thinking Like a Historian" method, an inquiry-based method showing students how to investigate the past by asking questions. Artifacts, documents, and vintage photographs illustrate the textbook, giving students a window into the past and the people, buildings, and objects that comprised Wisconsin in former times, while the lessons align with cross-curricular Wisconsin Model Academic Standards. To reach the state's growing Latino population, the press partnered with Milwaukee Public Schools to create a Spanish-language edition of the textbook, *Wisconsin: Nuestro Estado, Nuestra Historia*.

Keeping up with new technologies in the classroom, the society is now creating interactive whiteboard activities for use with *Wisconsin: Our State, Our Story*. These lessons are designed to conform to Wisconsin education standards and provide a wealth of instruction opportunities. Students who may struggle with plain text will find pictures, video, audio, and more to help guide them toward a better understanding of the content. Built-in vocabulary and assessment tools give educators a fun and engaging way to tackle difficult concepts as well as provide a snapshot of how well the students understand the material.

Innovations

Just as social movements and political upheaval gave impetus to revitalization of the Wisconsin Historical Society in the mid-20th century, technological advances profoundly affected the way the society preserved and shared history with Wisconsinites. The society built upon Americans' love of the automobile by providing destinations for vacationing families as it began to acquire historic sites in the 1950s. Soon, however, it became clear that not every historic structure, place, or neighborhood could be owned and operated by one organization. The historic preservation movement of the second half of the twentieth century ultimately enabled the society to share tools and incentives with individuals and interested groups to preserve their properties. What's more, as the state historic preservation office, the society has stimulated hundreds of millions of dollars in economic growth by providing property owners with block grants and tax incentives to revitalize historic places.

As technology gave birth to new broadcast media through the 20th century, the society eagerly embraced these new forms to share history. The society first experimented with radio broadcasting in the 1930s and started producing television programs and films in the 1950s. More recently, a revitalized partnership with Wisconsin Public Television has brought a steady stream of programming across the state, while the internet, social media, and new classroom tools have enabled the society to be a daily presence in the lives of Wisconsin citizens via the society Web site, multiple Facebook pages and Twitter feeds, blogs, and interactive lessons prepared to supplement the society's classroom materials.

Wisconsin Historic Sites

Automobiles helped grow Wisconsin's economy in the 20th century, creating jobs in manufacturing and in tourism. State and local governments improved roads, while resort owners and small-town boosters sent out promotional materials to attract travelers by showing the many pastimes and recreations available just off Wisconsin's highways. At the same time, a new trend in museum design began to take root: the historic site. Originally conceived in the 19th century as a new way to display artifacts in a historically rich environment, historic sites in the early 20th century evolved into places where people could experience "a feeling of historical mood, a haunting impression of having passed this way before." Just after World War II, the society began acquiring historic sites, giving automobile travelers a historic destination for day trips and places to visit while on vacation.

The Dousman family and friends on the east porch of Villa Louis, ca. 1898. (WHi Image ID 60079)

Since the 1950s, Wisconsin's Historic Sites have proven an innovative way to kindle public interest in history by letting people see the homes, accoutrements, clothing, and foodways of earlier generations. The Wisconsin Historical Society operates 11 historic sites: Circus World Museum, First Capitol, H.H. Bennett Studio, Madeline Island Museum, Old World Wisconsin, Pendarvis, Reed School, Stonefield, Villa Louis, Wade House, and Black Point Estate. The society's Historic Sites are much more than just places on a map where significant structures are preserved; they are gateways into other times and places where history is experienced and the senses are engaged, bringing visitors closer to the men and women who helped shape Wisconsin's development.

Early Days in Wisconsin

Some of the first Europeans to set foot in Wisconsin were fur trappers and traders. The early 1600s saw a variety of French explorers skirt lands that would one day become part of Wisconsin. Étienne Brûlé is thought to have traveled along Lake Superior's south shore in 1622, while Jean Nicolet is known to have landed near the future site of Green Bay in 1634 while searching for a water route to the Pacific Ocean. Instead of a route to the spice-rich East, Nicolet found furs that could be made into the hats then fashionable in Europe. For the next two hundred years, the fur trade reigned in Wisconsin. Indian trappers and hunters provided furs to Europeans, who paid for them with metal knives, guns, flints, awls, and ammunition. Riches were plentiful for the traders who kept a steady stream of furs going east.

To protect this trading system, forts were built throughout the Great Lakes region. One of these was Fort Crawford, built in 1816 by the young United States government, on the Mississippi River's St. Feriole Island on the site of a battle occurring two years earlier between the British and the Americans in the War of 1812. Situated in a channel of the river in Prairie du Chien, the island was strategically important but ultimately a poor choice for a fort. The island flooded often, which the soldiers garrisoning Fort Crawford found out in 1821, 1822, and 1826. The 1826 flood caused so much damage that Fort Crawford was abandoned and the site sold to Hercules Dousman, a representative for John Jacob Astor's American Fur Company. Dousman's rapport with local Indian tribes, as well as his keen business sense, made him indispensable to Fort Crawford and, ultimately, very wealthy as he later branched out into the lumber trade and land

Interior view of the front hallway of Villa Louis. (WHi Image ID 42006)

speculation. Dousman bought the site knowing that a mound on St. Feriole Island was safe from the floodwaters and would be a beautiful location for an estate he planned to build.

Standing in this spot today is Villa Louis, the Wisconsin Historical Society's first historic site acquisition. In the 1840s Dousman had built an elegant, stylish home on the estate. After his death the property passed to his son Louis, who in 1870 tore down his father's original home, recycled some of the materials, and constructed a new residence in the Italian Villa style. In 1885, he added stables, barns, a racetrack, and other buildings to the estate and remodeled the interior of the villa to embody the principles of the British Arts and Crafts movement. The Arts and Crafts movement, which began as a reaction against industrialization and machine-produced goods, stressed simpler ornamentation, quality materials, and traditional construction techniques in which craftsmen took pride in their work and creative expression rather than laboring in the difficult factory conditions of the day. Louis Dousman died shortly after the 1885 remodel at only 37 years old. The Villa stood little used or empty for several years when Louis's widow remarried and moved east.

Descendants of Hercules and Louis Dousman renovated the Villa in the early 1930s and offered the property to the Wisconsin Historical Society. The society at the time was struggling to weather the difficult Depression years, so the family arranged to have the city of Prairie du Chien operate the villa as a museum. As the society began its post-Depression rebirth, the family once again offered it Villa Louis, and on January 1, 1950, the society finally acquired the title to the property. Two years later, in April 1952, Villa Louis opened to the public. Subsequent donations and purchases of Dousman family papers, photographs, furnishings, and accessories original to the house help preserve the story of the Villa and even aided a major restoration of the estate that began in 1994.

Villa Louis today brings to life unique chapters in Wisconsin's past, from the days of the fur trade to the grandeur of the Victorian Era. Visitors to Villa Louis can experience such diverse activities as watching a reenactment of the Battle of Prairie du Chien and helping prepare breakfast in a Victorian kitchen. During the annual Carriage Classic, carriage drivers in period clothes test their skill at navigating obstacles or simply drive out for a country picnic – a favorite leisure activity in Victorian-era Wisconsin – bringing St. Feriole Island to life with beautiful horses and ornate carriages.

The Villa Louis Carriage Classic is a pleasure-driving show held on the beautiful grounds of the historic site in Prairie du Chien. This show hosts one of the finest carriage-driving competitions in the Midwest. (Wisconsin Historical Society)

At the other end of the state, Madeline Island was also touched by the fur trade. Situated in Lake Superior at the northern tip of Wisconsin, Madeline Island is the largest of the Apostle Islands and one of the first places in Wisconsin that missionaries and trappers saw as they traversed the Great Lakes in search of furs and souls. Island history includes a number of legendary names, such as French explorers Pierre-Esprit Radisson and Medard Chouart des Groseilliers, Jesuit missionary Father Claude Jean Allouez, and the fur trader Astor, who became America's first millionaire with the help of Wisconsin furs. By the turn of the 20th century, the fur trade having died decades earlier, Madeline Island emerged as a destination for tourists. One of the many who rode the rails from St. Paul was Leo Capser, who first visited the island in 1903.

An interpreter at the Madeline Island Museum shows a pelt to a visiting family. (Wisconsin Historical Society)

Capser was so taken by the beauty of the island he returned often after that first visit. He and wife Bella eventually became summer residents of Madeline Island and dedicated themselves to preserving its unique story. In 1955, the Capsers bought four historic structures on the island: a small 1835 warehouse from the historic American Fur Company complex, the former La Pointe town jail, a Scandinavian-style barn, and the Old Sailors' Home, originally built as a memorial to a drowned sailor. The Capsers moved the buildings and joined them to form the Madeline Island Museum. With the help of local historians the Capsers built an impressive collection of artifacts documenting the history of the island.

The society acquired and assumed operations of the Madeline Island Museum in 1968. In 1991, the museum expanded by adding the Capser Center and, in 2005, the Walkway Gallery, connecting the new facility with the original museum. The Capser Center houses changing exhibits on island and regional history, an auditorium, a museum store, space for collections storage and exhibit fabrication, and staff offices. Thanks to the Capsers and their love of Madeline Island, visitors today can still see a wealth of objects from every chapter of the island's long story, from Native and voyageur artifacts from the fur trade era, to objects and photographs that detail the daily lives of the 19th- and early 20th-century settlers. Also on display are tools and equipment used in a number of industries once performed on the island, including logging, boat building, commercial fishing, and barrel making.

Even before Wisconsin achieved statehood, miners established a foothold in what would become the southwest corner of the state. In the 1830s, miners from Cornwall, in southwestern England, began settling in Mineral Point and throughout the Upper Mississippi lead region. Before they built the small limestone homes similar to those they had left in England, many miners burrowed into hillsides like badgers, giving Wisconsin its renowned mascot. Mineral Point enjoyed a boom as a thriving commercial center that continued into early Wisconsin statehood when the lead deposits were finally exhausted. Many miners left the state in 1849 when word reached that gold had been found in California.

Almost a hundred years later, Robert Neal and Edgar Hellum found Mineral Point's history and heritage endangered. In 1935, Neal and Hellum decided to rehabilitate several original structures from Mineral Point's colorful past. They named their first restoration Pendarvis, after an estate in Cornwall. In the Cornish tradition, Neal and Hellum gave names to the other houses they acquired and renovated: Polperro and Trelawny. They also planted gardens around Pendarvis

Pendarvis House, one of several houses restored by Robert Neal and Edgar Hellum. (Wisconsin Historical Society)

similar to those Cornish settlers planted when they first came to Mineral Point. Needing money to live and continue their renovations, Neal and Hellum opened the Pendarvis House Restaurant, specializing in authentic Cornish fare such as cakes, preserves, and pasties. The *Saturday Evening Post* once named Pendarvis House one of the seven finest restaurants in the United States.

In 1970, Neal and Hellum retired, and the Wisconsin Historical Society acquired Pendarvis, which has grown into a collection of 10 structures. The next year, the society began operating Pendarvis as a unique historic site telling the story of Cornish settlement and the heyday of lead mining in Wisconsin. The society also acquired 40 acres of land across Shake Rag Street containing the Merry Christmas Mine. In addition to preserving tangible evidence of Wisconsin's mining days, Pendarvis keeps Cornish heritage alive through Cornish language classes as well as special events featuring Cornish dishes prepared in the same way they were in Neal and Hellum's restaurant for 35 years. Visitors can also enjoy a 43-acre prairie that features native flowers and grasses similar to those that welcomed Cornish settlers to Wisconsin so long ago.

At the same time the Cornish miners were settling the lead-mining region, Wisconsin was inching closer to statehood. During the fall and winter of 1836, near the picturesque hamlet of Belmont, Wisconsin's first territorial legislature established a government. One of the acts of this legislature was to make Madison the capital, after which many people and businesses left Belmont and the surrounding area. Two buildings used during the 1836 Territorial Legislative session – the Council House where the legislators met and a lodging house for the legislators – survived the ensuing decades, both eventually being used as residences. Initial work preserving and restoring the First Capitol buildings began in the early 1900s, led by the Wisconsin Federation of Women's Clubs. First Capitol State Park was originally established in 1924, and operated by the state of Wisconsin. More than 70 years later, the society acquired the buildings. After some restoration work, First Capitol opened as a historic site in 1996. Here visitors can see the buildings where lawmakers convened for just over a month in the late fall of 1836 and put 42 laws on the books. At First Capitol, in addition to making Madison the permanent capital, the legislature established Wisconsin's judicial system and called for building roads and a railroad.

Daily Life in Wisconsin's Past

Wisconsin's path from its earliest days to the present has been shaped and influenced by innumerable acts of daily life undertaken by Wisconsinites of all backgrounds. Our ways of working and building a life are always changing. We continually employ new tools and methods as we develop the means of using them. By collecting and maintaining places, implements, and machines from days gone by, several of Wisconsin's historic sites give us a vibrant window through which we can experience the lives of those who helped shape our state.

In a state that's now crisscrossed by numerous interstate and county highways, with rail lines and airports serving many of its larger cities, it can be difficult to imagine how complicated it was to travel here in the mid-1800s. Roads were generally tortuous and in poor repair, making travel a lengthy, often grueling affair. Inns along the way provided respite to weary travelers. Some, like Wade House in Greenbush, became themselves a destination for locals who gathered to talk about the affairs of the day, share a meal or a drink, and maybe sing a song or two.

Wade House, a three-story Greek Revival stagecoach inn that became the society's second historic site in 1953, was built by Sylvanus Wade in 1850 near the Mullet River, which powered the sawmill where boards for the inn were cut. Wade House became a regular meeting place and was the scene of countless cotillions and caucuses. With the construction of a new plank road between Sheboygan and Fond du Lac, the bustling village of Greenbush seemed to have a bright future. However, little more than a decade later the railroad bypassed Greenbush, and the inevitable decline of the once-ascendant town began. Wade House remained in business until 1910. It then served as a private residence until 1941, when the owners sold it to a family friend who planned to restore the house.

When money ran out in 1950, the owners sold Wade House to Marie Kohler, daughter of the Kohler Company founder, and her sister-in-law Ruth De Young

Wade House, built in Greenbush in 1850. (Wisconsin Historical Society)

Kohler. The Kohlers began a three-year-long, top-to-bottom restoration of the old inn. Marie died before the restoration began, yet it was ably directed by Ruth, who sought to deed the property to the society upon completion of the project. Sadly, Ruth died three months shy of the grand opening, at age 46. On June 6, 1953, with poet Carl Sandburg on hand, Wade House opened to the public. In the ensuing years the society made additions to the grounds of Wade House. The Wesley Jung Carriage House Museum opened to the public in 1968, displaying the handiwork of several carriage makers. In 1999, builders and craftsmen working under the supervision of the Wisconsin Historical Society constructed a replica of the Herrling Sawmill, which stood near the inn in the late 19th century. The mill can be operated using water power or with the help of a motor when water is low.

Wade House preserves and interprets a truly unique chapter from Wisconsin's past as a place where travelers found rest and a good meal. Wade House also keeps alive Wisconsin's Civil War heritage with an annual Civil War weekend, where attendees can stroll through a Union army campsite, buy products at a number of merchants' tents, and see a reenactment of a Civil War battle. A new visitor center and the Wesley Jung Carriage Museum greet visitors and welcome them into a vibrant slice of 19th-century Wisconsin life.

The society's third historic site, Stonefield, located north of Cassville in southwestern Wisconsin, preserves and interprets Wisconsin's rich agricultural heritage. The grounds of Stonefield once housed the mansion of Nelson Dewey, Wisconsin's first governor, who moved to the state in 1836 to practice law. Dewey also worked to build the village of Cassville on the Mississippi River, believing it would be a major city one day. After completing his two terms as governor, Dewey again turned his attention, and his not inconsiderable fortune, toward Cassville's development, including construction of a mansion on 2,000 acres of land near the Mississippi River. Dewey lost most of his fortune in the panic of 1873. The same year, his beloved mansion burned to the ground. A few years later the property was sold and a modest summer residence was built on the foundations of Dewey's incinerated mansion. The state acquired Stonefield in 1936 and managed it as Nelson Dewey State Park.

As early as 1932, the society and the University of Wisconsin's School of Agriculture began working on a plan to develop a farm museum in the state. Society director Joseph Schafer was keenly interested in the idea, and several conferences were convened throughout the state in the ensuing years to flesh out plans for the museum. The Great Depression effectively stifled any concrete progress beyond the planning stages for nearly two decades, but the idea was never extinguished completely. The society and the School of Agriculture proposed several sites in and around Madison for the museum, and each organization began collecting tools and implements. In 1953, the Wisconsin Legislature designated Stonefield as the state farm and craft museum, to be administered by the society.

Although Dewey had not been known for his agricultural expertise, the site of his estate offered ample space for a farm museum on a historically significant property. With state funding and the cooperation of local government, the society began to construct Stonefield Village. By 1961, Stonefield Village had grown to 30 buildings, comprising a re-created village with shops and offices emblematic of 19th-century Wisconsin rural life. Today, the State Agricultural Museum at Stonefield displays rare farm tools, implements, tractors, and wagons, while a re-created farmstead based on a Department of Agriculture plan from 1901 shows visitors how farmers led their daily lives before 20th century innovations such as electrification and television reshaped home life. The life of Nelson Dewey is remembered in the brick home built in 1879 on the foundation of his mansion. Costumed interpreters lead visitors through the residence's two floors, where

A young visitor to Stonefield gets an up-close look at a blacksmith's work.
(Wisconsin Historical Society)

items that once belonged to Dewey give a vivid glimpse into the life of the 19th-century upper class.

Agriculture and daily life also play a big part in Eagle, where the society's largest historic site is located. In the same way that a historian uses a variety of source material to craft a narrative of the past, from diaries and letters to newspapers and governmental reports, Old World Wisconsin draws on a wide range of buildings, backgrounds, and experiences to tell the story of several ethnic groups that played prominent roles in Wisconsin's development.

Above: The hardworking oxen at Old World Wisconsin in Eagle are a perennial favorite with visitors. (Wisconsin Historical Society)

Below: The Kruza house at Old World Wisconsin is an example of a Polish farmstead from the late 19th century. It is an example of stove-wood construction, a European building technique wherein logs are cut into short, uniform sections and stacked to resemble piles of firewood. (Wisconsin Historical Society)

A decade of planning and collecting resulted in the 576-acre outdoor museum, which opened its doors in the bicentennial year of 1976. The society identified and collected more than 60 historic buildings from around the state. Each was carefully dismantled, moved to Eagle, and reconstructed. These farm buildings demonstrate the unique ways Norwegian, Polish, Danish, German, and Finnish immigrants built their lives in Wisconsin. The compelling story of a group of African Americans who settled in Wisconsin before the Civil War is told through the reconstruction of the Pleasant Ridge Chapel and the United Brethren Church.

Visitors to Old World Wisconsin are brought into a world where women washed clothes by hand and prepared food with fire rather than electricity, and farmers worked their fields with the help of horses and oxen rather than tractors. Various historic animal breeds common to 19th-century Wisconsin call Old World home, including horses, pigs, and the always popular oxen. Crossroads Village re-creates a typical Wisconsin town of the 1870s, complete with stores, shoemakers, blacksmiths, and services at St. Peter's Church. A variety of domestic arts from bygone eras are preserved and shared, from the wheelwright's craft to spinning wool into yarn. Kids can see how their forebears were educated in a one-room schoolhouse, where one teacher taught all grades.

Farther north, in Neillsville, Reed School also preserves Wisconsin's educational heritage. The society's 10th historic site opened to the public in 2007 after a significant renovation of the nearly century-old, one-room schoolhouse. Reed School was built in 1915, at a time when most Wisconsin children were educated in a similar one-room environment. First through eighth graders continued to get their education at Reed School until 1951, when schools in Wisconsin were rapidly consolidating. Gordon Smith, a former student at Reed School, bought the building and with the help of the Wisconsin Historical Society restored it to its 1939 appearance, the year Smith attended Reed School. The school is furnished with restored original and historically appropriate desks

Reed School, near Neillsville, interprets a 1939 one-room schoolhouse. (Wisconsin Historical Society)

and chairs, while on the grounds visitors can see a restored baseball field where schoolchildren spent countless recesses at play.

Leisure in Wisconsin

Wisconsinites have long harbored a healthy respect not only for work, but for leisure time and recreation as well. Even in the 19th century, shorter workweeks and easier travel via trains and automobiles inspired a new middle class to find ways to stay entertained and escape everyday life. Before television, radio, and movies, people sought out live shows at the theater. Traveling circuses were also

Noted Wisconsin photographer H.H. Bennett took this famous photograph of his son Ashley leaping the chasm at Stand Rock, Wisconsin Dells, in 1886. H.H. Bennett's studio is now operated as an historic site. (WHi Image ID 2101)

popular. Numerous places around Wisconsin – from Bayfield to Lake Geneva – have long been destinations of choice for people wanting to escape the cities. Yet one of the first places that comes to mind when we think of recreation in Wisconsin is the Wisconsin Dells, a place made famous by photographer H.H. Bennett.

In 1874, a writer voyaging down the Wisconsin River near Kilbourn City wrote of the excessive natural beauty he saw, exclaiming, "We move on from one spot which we think the most lovely to another that excels, and on through inexhaustible beauties, in a state of unalloyed rapture at the exquisite scenery." This same scenery had already captivated photographer Henry Hamilton Bennett, who in 1865 purchased a tintype portrait studio in Kilbourn City. Bennett began selling stereoscopic views of the rugged riverbanks and stony outcroppings so characteristic of the Dells of the Wisconsin River. Bennett's work appeared in guidebooks and other promotional literature that drew travelers to the area. In 1875, Bennett built a new photography studio in Kilbourn City, where he developed his distinctive photographs and sold them to tourists. Bennett was on the cutting edge of photographic technology of the time, and even conceived several inventions that made his trade easier, including a revolving solar printing house and a portable darkroom. Bennett also created a stop-action shutter that enabled him to photograph moving objects clearly.

Bennett died in 1908 and Kilbourn City was renamed the Wisconsin Dells in the 1930s, but the lasting beauty of Bennett's work is preserved and celebrated in the H.H. Bennett Studio, which became a historic site in 2000. An earlier restoration had returned Bennett's studio to its 1908 appearance. The studio now houses some of Bennett's own handmade cameras, glass plate negatives, and many

One of the beautifully restored circus wagons at Circus World. (Wisconsin Historical Society)

original Bennett photographs. New technologies at the Bennett Studio bring his work to life, as visitors view stereoscopic images in 3D on high-resolution monitors through liquid crystal spectacles. Visitors can also see Bennett's photographs documenting the Ho-Chunk Indians, who made their lives around the Wisconsin River and nearby waterways.

At the same time as Bennett was working in his photographic studio, five brothers named Albert, Otto, Alfred, Charles, and John Ringling worked to perfect their circus act. After seeing their first circus as boys in the 1870s in McGregor, Iowa, the Ringlings were inspired to start their own act. In 1882, the Ringling brothers performed their first show in Mazomanie, Wisconsin, and two years later founded the Ringling Brothers Circus in Baraboo. Within a few years the brothers were touring throughout the state and Midwest and had welcomed their two other brothers, Henry and Gus, into the family business. By the turn of the century, the Ringling Brothers Circus had more than 1,000 employees, 335 horses, 26 elephants, and 16 camels, all of which needed 92 railcars to transport. Though they traveled around the country, Baraboo was the site of the circus's winter quarters, which the locals referred to as "Ringlingville."

Circus World Museum joined the society's growing family of historic sites in 1959 and is the nation's premier institution preserving circus history. While the society owns the land, buildings, equipment, and collections at Circus World Museum (with the exception of modern rolling equipment like trucks and trailers), the site is managed by Circus World Museum Foundation Inc., a nonprofit organization, via a lease-management agreement. Among the 30 buildings on the 64-acre site are several original buildings the Ringlings used between 1897 and 1916, as well as the remnants of a footbridge that once carried employees over the

Circus World houses more than 8,650 colorful circus posters. (Circus World Museum)

Baraboo River. Circus World houses more than two-thirds of the original circus wagons still in existence today, as well as an unparalleled archival collection documenting circus history, including circus ads and posters, journals, business records, paintings, handbills and heralds, costumes, rare photographs, films, and much more. Circus World Museum shares circus performances, magic shows, and animal performances, keeping alive crowd-pleasing Gilded Age entertainments. A popular feature for young visitors is the chance to create and perform in their own big-top production in the Kid's World Interactive Circus.

On October 8, 1871, there seemed to be what one Wisconsin lumberman described as "fire in the air." As fire devastated millions of acres around Peshtigo, the Great Chicago Fire raged to the south, while lesser-known blazes erupted in

Black Point Estate Historic House and Gardens, the society's newest historic site. (Wisconsin Historical Society)

Michigan, all of which caused incalculable loss of property and unfathomable loss of life. Needing somewhere to go while their houses and businesses were rebuilt, many wealthy Chicagoans sought refuge in Lake Geneva, Wisconsin. Some of these families chose to stay year-round, while others maintained summer homes on the picturesque lake. By the 1880s, Lake Geneva was a favorite retreat for the well-to-do who needed some time away from the city.

Chicago brewer Conrad Seipp was one of the lucky ones. The Great Chicago Fire spared his business, and for a time he was Chicago's largest brewer. His success allowed him the means to build a family retreat in Lake Geneva. In 1888, work was completed on Black Point, a Queen Anne-style "cottage" with 20 rooms, including 13 bedrooms but only one bathroom. Black Point is surrounded

Vintage base ball at Old World Wisconsin is the re-creation of the styles, speech, rules, and terminology of the 1860s game. It's not only a competitive game, but also a reenactment of baseball life, similar to an American Civil War reenactment. It is a fast-growing sport in the United States, with 225 clubs in 32 states. (Wisconsin Historical Society)

by eight acres, much of which is adorned with lush gardens, and has 620 feet of shoreline on Geneva Lake. Four generations of the Seipp family enjoyed the site before a descendant donated it to the state in 2005. While each generation added its own touch to Black Point, they kept all the older household items. As a result the cottage's furnishings vary in style from Victorian to the modern era. After a $1.9 million restoration, Black Point opened to the public in 2007, being run by a board of volunteers. On January 1, 2013, the Wisconsin Historical Society assumed management of the site.

Each year the sites and museum draw in more than half a million visitors, and they will continue to be an important resource to connect Wisconsinites to the past. The immediate future holds bright promise. In June 2013, 60 years after Wade House first opened, a new Learning and Visitor Center opened, offering a multitiered orientation to the historic site, including a large room for public and private functions, classroom and workshop space, a museum store, and a café. Additionally, this new facility is the home of the Wesley W. Jung Carriage Museum, which houses the state's largest collection of antique carriages and working wagons. A new interpreter-training center at Old World Wisconsin was recently completed, just the first step in a lengthy project to update and improve this site.

The sites offer visitors the unique opportunity to engage so many senses: the sight of historic barns, houses, and gardens, or beasts of burden toiling in fields in much the same way that oxen and draft horses broke the fields in pioneer Wisconsin; the tastes of food prepared using authentic ethnic recipes, traditional ingredients and tools and served in an historic setting; the sounds of a game of vintage baseball, or exploding musketry, or music performed on an antique piano. Schoolchildren often rave about their visit to their parents, teachers, and friends long after experiencing one of the sites. One young visitor to Old World Wisconsin named Maddie was so moved by her experience that she wrote to Old World's director to thank him for the "amazing tour," and continued that her "favorite part (though I had so many) was probably getting to act like a child from the 1800s farm life." Maddie closed her letter by writing, "I hope to return again."

Historic Preservation

The society's early history focused on owning historic resources – books, manuscripts, and artifacts. In the 20th century, the society added historic sites to its collections. The last third of the 20th century added a new dimension to the society's efforts. Throughout the nation, recognition grew that it was neither feasible nor prudent for every historic building to be owned by a government or historical agency. Instead, the society and its state and federal partners began to develop new tools and incentives that enabled others to better preserve our heritage.

With the passage of the National Historic Preservation Act in 1966, the society became the federally des-

The key to the renovation of the Stoughton Opera House was a spirit of civic volunteerism, a phased restoration plan, and persistent fund-raising efforts. The refurbished theater was rededicated on February 22, 2001 – the 100th anniversary of its original opening. (Wisconsin Historical Society)

ignated State Historic Preservation Office (SHPO), an active role that continues today. The society nominates places of architectural, historic, and archaeological significance to the National Register of Historic Places in partnership with the National Park Service and manages the State Register of Historic Places. The society also reviews federal, state, and local projects for their impact on historic and archaeological properties, administers state and federal tax credit programs, and administers the state's burial sites protection program.

As in other states around the nation, Wisconsin's first steps in historic preservation were undertaken by private groups and individuals. In 1903, people concerned about preserving Native American artifacts and sites in Wisconsin founded the Wisconsin Archaeological Society. The group primarily focused on Indian mounds and by the 1920s had helped save 500 mounds throughout the state. In 1908, the Wisconsin Federation of Women's Clubs partnered with the Wisconsin Archaeological Society and the Sauk County Historical Society to purchase Man Mound near Baraboo, the only surviving human effigy mound in the United States. Other projects typically involved the purchase of historically significant buildings, such as the Old Agency House and Fort Winnebago in Portage, the Little White Schoolhouse in Ripon, St. Augustine Church in New Diggings, and historic Hazelwood in Green Bay, the home of the principal author of Wisconsin's constitution. A significant legislative step toward preservation in Wisconsin came when Wisconsin enacted the Integrated

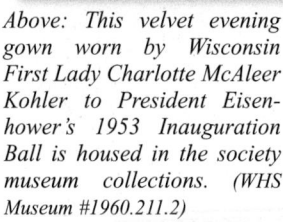

Above: This velvet evening gown worn by Wisconsin First Lady Charlotte McAleer Kohler to President Eisenhower's 1953 Inauguration Ball is housed in the society museum collections. (WHS Museum #1960.211.2)

Top left: Dorothy Gregory Koltes prom dress, ca. 1927. (WHS Museum #1969.193.2)

Bottom left: Dorothy Turner Main dress, ca. 1926. (WHS Museum #1979.262.1)

Park Act, Chapter 549, Laws of 1947, which made it possible for the state to purchase, restore, and develop properties of historic and archaeological significance. The first property purchased under this legislation in 1952 was a portion of the 1,000-year-old site of Aztalan.

In the post-World War II era, urban renewal and interstate highway projects threatened historically significant places and inspired preservationists to take action. A 1965 report titled "With Heritage So Rich" identified a number of preservation initiatives, including the identification and registration of historically significant properties and partnership on preservation issues at all levels of government. One year later, Congress enacted the National Historic Preservation Act (NHPA). The act established state historic preservation offices in every state. It also established the National Register of Historic Places, which defined criteria for determining the importance of a property. These standards have helped make the process of historic preservation more efficient, effective, and accessible.

The society's SHPO documents historic properties, reviews projects for effects on historically and culturally significant properties, and aids in preservation capabilities through workshops, grants, and training seminars. To date, Wisconsin has approximately 2,300 listings on the National Register of Historic Places. These listings encompass roughly 25,000 buildings. In addition, the state is home to 42 National Historic Landmarks, highlighting the important national historical and architectural contributions of the state, such as Taliesin and the Ringling Brothers winter quarters in Baraboo. These listings recognize properties as varied as rural one-room schools and major university buildings, the homes of workers, and the northwoods compounds of industrialists.

In addition to documenting the historic significance of places, listing provides opportunities such as tax credits and grants to help preserve the property. The society has worked with Wisconsin businesses and homeowners to ensure that they qualify for federal and state tax credits. As a result, nearly $1 billion has been invested in Wisconsin since the mid-1970s for work to preserve the state's built heritage. Since 1976, the society certified nearly 500 projects that helped preserve income-producing buildings, which in turn brought $150 million in federal tax credits back to the state. A similar program for homeowners has, since 1992, resulted in 2,166 projects with total investment in excess of $100 million. Through the program, abandoned warehouses and schools have been turned into desirable apartments, and empty downtown storefronts now house restaurants and shops, adding a renewed vibrancy to Wisconsin cities and villages.

To help citizens, the State Historic Preservation Office created the Wisconsin Architecture and History Inventory (AHI), a digital source of information on more than 133,000 historic buildings, structures, and objects throughout Wisconsin. Types of places listed in the inventory include round barns, log houses, metal truss bridges, small-town commercial buildings, and Queen Anne houses that reflect Wisconsin's distinct cultural landscape. Each property has a digital record providing basic information about the property, and most include exterior images. More than 200,000 images of these properties are available online.

The society also began providing grants and technical advice to help communities across the state identify and protect historic resources. Municipal governments began adopting historic preservation ordinances and designating local landmarks and districts in the 1960s and 1970s. The first community in Wisconsin to develop a historic preservation ordinance and appoint a historic preservation commission was Milwaukee in 1963. Similar action took place in Madison in 1970, Fond du Lac in 1971, and Mineral Point in 1972. Today, a total of 68 units of local government have followed suit and are working to protect their historic resources with the assistance of the society.

In 1985, a group of state legislators, developers, architects, and attorneys formed the Wisconsin Historic Preservation Task Force. The group developed a comprehensive historic preservation legislative packet, much of which was enacted in 1987. These initiatives included the establishment of a Wisconsin State Register of Historic Places, a state tax credit program, and zoning and funding programs to support historic preservation. These improved programs help save irreplaceable historic resources in Wisconsin and also serve as ways of promoting investment within the state's borders.

The Wisconsin Historical Society works to protect archaeological resources as well. Early in the 20th century, the society's museum director began to gather archaeological information, which is still used today. However, the first major program at the society to focus on archaeology started 10 years before the passage of the National Historic Preservation Act. Federal legislation in 1956 initiated the interstate highway system, and the law provided for the protection and recovery

One-thousand-year-old American Indian burial mounds shaped like birds and animals grace a hilltop in the Wisconsin River Valley in southwestern Wisconsin. (Wisconsin Department of Natural Resources)

of historic, archaeological, and paleontological resources. Although the act did not make state compliance with these provisions mandatory, Wisconsin's Highway Department nonetheless created a procedure to allow limited archaeological research before highway construction. Federal law also required each state to select an institutional sponsor for archaeology, and the society assumed that role in Wisconsin.

In 1958, the society negotiated its first cooperative agreement with the State Highway Commission. The State Highway Commission provided money for field survey and excavation and the society agreed to prepare the reports and provide the storage for artifacts. As a result, the society improved its ability to tell stories from ancient Wisconsin. A decade of intensive fieldwork made significant progress. For example, archaeologists excavated the Millville Site in

Grant County and discovered the remains of 14 Native American circular houses that formed a community that was 1,600 years old. The success of the highway program led to negotiations with the Department of Natural Resources, which resulted in support for work at Wisconsin's most famous archaeological site, Aztalan, located along on the west bank of the Crawfish River east of Lake Mills in Jefferson County. Society archaeologists worked at Aztalan for three years focusing on the stockade, the pyramidal mound, and the village area.

The most important federal legislation affecting public archaeology was the National Historic Preservation Act of 1966. This legislation created the Section 106 compliance process, which required that agencies using federal funds consider archaeological sites in project development. As a result, the society began to increase its archaeological field research on a contract basis with federal and state agencies. For example, in 1971, funded by the Army Corps of Engineers, the society began the first large-scale archaeological survey ever conducted in the state, the La Farge Reservoir Project. This was a 10-year study to locate archaeological sites in the Kickapoo River Valley in Vernon County. The La Farge survey identified over 200 archaeological sites, providing the first complete sequence of more than 10,000 years of human occupation in Wisconsin.

The state's 1985 burial sites protection law, Act 316, and the 1987 historic preservation law, Act 395, provided greater support for protection of both burials and archaeological sites. It also placed greater responsibility on state agencies to consider the impact of their construction projects and land-management practices on historical resources. In the past 25 years, the society has expanded on and added new efforts that advance knowledge of the past and protect historical locations for the future. The society maintains records on burials and archaeological sites, issues permits for investigations on public land, and administers a property tax exemptions program for owners who agree to protect important sites. In addition, educational programs raise awareness of ways that citizens can protect, enjoy, and respect local landmarks.

As a state abutted by two of the Great Lakes, with thousands of smaller lakes within its borders, many of which have been used for transportation, commerce, and leisure, not all of Wisconsin's archaeological sites are under dry land. The society administers a nationally recognized underwater archaeology program. As part of this program, society archaeologists document, study, and promote tourism. Wisconsin waters hold a wide variety of objects to be explored, documented and preserved, from an 1,800-year-old dugout canoe to 19th- and 20th-century shipwrecks. Naturally, since Wisconsin waters have witnessed 700 shipwrecks, downed vessels comprise many underwater archaeological sites. But several hundred other prehistoric and historic sites are known to exist on the beds of Wisconsin's lakes and rivers. The society's underwater archaeology program has conducted investigations on nearly 80 archaeological sites throughout the state. These efforts have resulted in 17 Wisconsin shipwrecks being placed on the National Register of Historic Places. With 860 miles of Great Lakes shoreline, 14,000 inland lakes, and thousands of miles of rivers and streams, the underwater archaeology program has a wide-ranging responsibility for studying and protecting all of the underwater archaeological resources that lie beneath the state's waters.

Wisconsin Historical Society underwater archaeologist exploring a Lake Superior shipwreck. (Wisconsin Historical Society photo by Tamara Thomsen)

The Wisconsin Historical Society's historic preservation efforts have had visible and lasting effects across Wisconsin. From a Finnish farmstead in Oulu in Bayfield County, to the Jeffris Flats apartments in Janesville, the society has aided the renovation and revitalization of buildings and neighborhoods around the state. One recent example is the renovation of the historic Pabst Brewery complex, which the State Historic Preservation Office is assisting through federal income tax credits. The first building to be completed on the 21-acre Pabst Brewery site is the Blue Ribbon Loft Apartments, a three-story, 140,000-square-foot brick building originally called the Washhouse and Cooper Shop. This building was converted into a 95-unit live/work loft-style rental apartment community. During construction, the developer reserved a percentage of the jobs to train unskilled workers from the surrounding neighborhood in the construction trades. This development has revived one of Milwaukee's most iconic buildings while supporting new businesses, providing affordable housing, and allowing residents to live and work downtown. Additionally, the project has been the catalyst for future development of the historically significant Pabst Brewery site and has brought federal dollars to Wisconsin. Through efforts like the Pabst Brewery renovation, the society preserves significant structures while also stimulating job creation, investment, and economic growth around the state.

Radio, Television, and the Internet

Throughout the 20th century, the society embraced new technologies to share Wisconsin history in new ways. Soon after the introduction of radio in the 1920s, society experts took to the airwaves. In the 1950s, television was the new thing, and the society was active in creating programs seen on public television stations around the state. The society's partnership with Wisconsin Public Television has led in recent years to several history-related programs as well as television documentaries based on Wisconsin Historical Society Press books. In the late 1990s, the society launched a Web site, *www.wisconsinhistory. org*, currently in its third generation, which has enabled the society to share Wisconsin and North American history with patrons around the globe.

As early as the 1930s, Wisconsin Historical Society staff used the radio as a way to reach out to the public. Charles Brown of the museum staff and Louise Kellogg, a researcher, writer, and historian who worked in the society library, both appeared on WHA radio occasionally, with Brown making nine appearances on the station in 1932. Ten years later society director Edward Alexander gave a course of 32 lectures on Wisconsin history over the two state radio stations then broadcasting, WHA in Madison and WLBL in Stevens Point. The centennial of Wisconsin's statehood in 1948 revived interest in history, and society staff made regular appearances for radio interviews. By the 1950s, radio was being explored as a means of better communication between the society and local history groups, including talks by experts to local groups broadcast over FM radio, and book discussions and study groups following assignments and lectures delivered by the society.

In the 1950s, the society also began to create television programs. In 1953, the society launched a 27-minute color film, *The Presence of Our Past*, which documented the wide-ranging activities of the Wisconsin Historical Society. With the advent of WHA-TV, the state's public television station, the society began to work with the new station to produce several programs, including a panel quiz show, *TV Museum*; 15 children's programs, such as *Grandma's Attic*; as well

Wisconsin Historical Society staff members working on a show with WHA-TV. (WHi Image ID 98936)

as numerous five-minute short programs. On *Lori's Log Cabin*, a program for children that aired on public television in the 1960s, a society staffer played the role of a new settler in early Wisconsin who would ask other settlers for advice and help.

Throughout the 1960s, the society remained active in radio and television. Society staff created hundreds of programs for radio and television, including a public television series titled *Wisconsin Windows* that covered a broad array of topics ranging from the Civil War centennial to the historic sites. For several years society staff produced a series of programs on Wisconsin writers, while special programs for radio and television were regularly recorded in and around the society's headquarters building. The society at this time had on staff a coordinator for programming who worked on scripts, recorded numerous radio and television programs, and traveled around the state filming historic sites and other notable locations for use in a variety of radio and television shows.

The society and Wisconsin Public Television renewed their partnership in the mid-1990s as the sesquicentennial of statehood neared. *Sesquicentennial Wisconsin Stories* was a five-part installment of programs created by Wisconsin Public Television and the Wisconsin Historical Society in 1998. With episodes titled "This Place We Call Wisconsin," "Finding a Home," "Laboratory of Democracy," "Building a State," and "Time to Play," the series documented the people, places, and politics that helped make Wisconsin what it is today. The society and WPT collaborated on a series of 52 one-minute programs titled *Sesquicentennial Minutes*, documenting very briefly a wide assortment of topics, from Billy Mitchell to the Underground Railroad. The society continues to work

Ho-Chunk group in traditional dress, 1900. From the Charles Van Schaick collection. This is one of more than 75,000 images available online at wisconsinhistory.org. (WHi Image ID 61591)

with Wisconsin Public Television, regularly collaborating on documentaries for the *Wisconsin Hometown Stories* series, as well as documentaries based on society press titles, like the popular *Bottoms Up*, which has garnered national attention. The society and Wisconsin Public Television have additionally created Wisconsin-focused documentaries on World War II and the Korean and Vietnam Wars, as well as two new programs with agricultural historian Jerry Apps about the heritage of life on the farm.

Launched in 1997, the society's Web site, *www.wisconsinhistory.org*, plays an increasing role in making history accessible to people not only in Wisconsin, but worldwide. The amount of information available on the internet is already difficult to enumerate, and is growing steadily. Since 1998, more than 10 million pages from society collections have been shared on the Web. There are 163,000 pages from society collections appearing on University of Wisconsin Web sites, while 6.4 million appear in Google books. Another 3.8 million have been licensed to commercial firms for use in subscription-only newspaper collections. The society also sells copies of vital records and images through ecommerce applications. About 6,800 orders are placed each year, 26 per day, 80% of which are for genealogical records and 20% for image reproductions. Sales and licensing of online content generates about $250,000 per year. As the internet has become a standard tool for researchers and history enthusiasts, the Web site will only grow in the future, while the challenge will always be to determine relevant content that meets user expectations.

Entrepreneurship and the Wisconsin Historical Foundation

The Wisconsin Historical Society is unusual in that it is both a membership organization and a state agency. The society received a charter from the legislature in 1853 as a private corporation with a public purpose, and received funding from the state for the first time in 1854 to support society operations. In 1949, state statutes recognized that the society "had become a state agency through increased legislative control over the activities of the society." This law recognized that the society slowly evolved into a state agency by gradually transferring control to the state over various functions. The society started depositing its funds in the state treasury in 1920, its employees were subject to the civil service laws, its operations and funding were largely controlled by state statute, and the society held all property as a trustee for the state.

The society has always had to supplement the funds it receives from the state with other sources. These include membership dues, admission charges at historic sites, sales of books and copies of documents, photo reproduction licenses, and other fees. Private gifts, collected since 1954 by the Wisconsin Historical Foundation, and federal grants also help cover expenses. Volunteers have become an invaluable resource for the society. In 2010, 64% of the society's budget was covered by state tax revenue, including funding for 106.5 full-time positions. That same year, volunteers provided approximately 250,000 hours of labor, or the equivalent of 120 full-time positions.

The Wisconsin Historical Society has cultivated the support of private philanthropy for over 150 years. In his annual report of the society for 1856, Draper expressed "the hope that many of our liberal and wealthy citizens may be induced to bestow a portion of their surplus wealth upon our society that it may . . . have an endowment to place it beyond the reach" of the caprices of nature and economic strain. While every director since Draper has actively sought private donations to increase the society's activities and reach, an important development in this work came in 1954 with the creation of the Wisconsin Historical Foundation.

A group of society supporters established the Wisconsin Historical Foundation in 1954 as a nonprofit organization to assist the society in securing private sources of funding. For its first 50 years, the foundation had a board of directors that met, secured donations, and invested to grow the money it collected. While the state has, since 1854, provided generous financial support to the society, growing budgetary demands on the state steadily increased the need for private funding sources as the 20th century came to a close. Recognizing the need for more vigorous fund-raising, the Wisconsin Historical Foundation hired its first paid employee in 1998. The staff has since grown to 15, and the foundation performs four distinct functions for the society: financial stewardship, administering the society's membership program, securing major gifts to the society, and strategic financial support for society initiatives.

In 2006, the foundation embarked on its first major philanthropic effort, *Forward! The Campaign for the Wisconsin Historical Society*. While the Forward Campaign set a goal of raising $77 million, it was also envisioned as a movement to get a broad coalition of people involved in actively using history to understand their own stories and world, and to pass these on to the next generation. To accomplish this, the Forward Campaign set four fundamental objectives: transform the historic sites to provide engaging and educational experiences that are authentic, varied, and unique; update the society's digital collections and services, including modernizing the society Web site; preserve the society's world-class collections by securing renovations to the society's headquarters building, as well as the construction of a new storage and preservation facility to store collections and master evolving conservation techniques; and create a far-reaching community of members, donors, advocates, volunteers, and leaders to take a more active role in discovering and appreciating their history.

The effects of the Forward Campaign are visible throughout the state and offer a compelling vision of the superb things that can be accomplished through the combined efforts of involved citizens and state support. In April 2010, the society was able to celebrate the completion of a $2.9 million restoration of the library reading room. During the seven-month project, the room regained its original magnificence through the replacement of fluorescent lights with a reconstructed stained glass skylight, new furnishings, lighting, and shelving, and the restoration of many historic details obscured or missing since an earlier renovation in 1955. The restoration was celebrated as one of the biggest successes of the Forward Campaign to date in 2010, and more exciting projects are still in the works.

On November 8, 2011, the society broke ground for a new visitor center and the Wesley W. Jung Carriage Museum on the grounds of historic Wade House in Greenbush. The 38,000-square-foot, $13.5 million building overlooking bustling Highway 23 midway between Sheboygan and Fond du Lac is a year-round, state-of-the-art facility showcasing Wade House's outstanding collections and serving as a powerful tool for education and service to the community. Notably, the project received about 55% of its funding from the state, with the remaining 45% was paid by private donations. The Forward Campaign was also instrumental in funding a new 3,060-square-foot multipurpose facility at Old World Wisconsin, housing a number of functions from curatorial to administrative staff spaces to training areas for costumed interpreters.

Increasing support for the society will be crucial in ensuring that this age is remembered not merely as a bright period in the Wisconsin Historical Society's long history, but also as the foundation for a society of permanently greater stability, strength, and scope. While a lot has been accomplished, the society has high aspirations for the future as it embraces new technologies, safeguards its world-class collections, transforms its historic sites, and, perhaps most importantly, seeks to engage the broadest possible public audience.

Conclusion

A former director of the Wisconsin Historical Society once noted, "The varied programs of the society make it a state version of the Library of Congress, the National Archives, and the Smithsonian Institution, all rolled into one." The society has grown from a small gathering of pioneers in 1846 into a complex organization performing a wide range of functions. Yet the

Robert La Follette Sr. and Robert La Follette Jr. (WHi Image ID 28147)

basic mission of the society has remained largely unchanged: to collect, preserve, and share Wisconsin's stories.

The Wisconsin Historical Society has long been a leader and innovator among America's historical societies. Unlike historical societies on the eastern seaboard that had restrictive memberships, the society since 1846 has been supported by a membership open to anyone willing to pay dues. At a time when history was largely the tale of past politics and battlefield glory, the society has documented the lives of rich and poor, famous and unknown. Collecting contemporary history has been a constant focus, whether it be Lyman Draper collecting the papers of land speculator Daniel Boone or efforts of archivists to collect Web sites on contemporary politics. The society's collections and efforts have served as a model for other states, which have developed programs that were first tried in Wisconsin.

Historical gardeners at Old World Wisconsin plant heirloom varieties of flowers and vegetables in re-creating early settler gardens. (Photo courtesy Nancy L. Klemp)

While commonalities over time abound, the society has remained responsive to changing circumstances. Draper built a world-class library and manuscript collection without the help of a wealthy benefactor, instead securing regular state funding, making the Wisconsin Historical Society the oldest publicly funded historical society in America. Reuben Gold Thwaites transformed the Progressive Era society into an engine of public education, leading the way for similar changes in historical societies around the nation. Clifford Lord transitioned the society from a largely scholarly research institution into a public service institution aiming to be of service to as many people, in as many ways, as possible. Under subsequent leaders, the society employed the latest technologies – radio, television, and the Internet – to connect to a broader public and reach out to young and old alike to share in Wisconsin's outstanding past.

Today, the Wisconsin Historical Society is one of the most active and varied historical societies in the nation. It faces new challenges, as it has in every generation since 1846. Time, technologies, social trends, and heightened expectations transform how the society collects, preserves, and shares our common history. It represents a covenant between generations. Just as those earlier pioneers worked to share the record of their successes and failures with subsequent generations, so the society of today ensures that generations yet unborn will know the events of our own time. It is a solemn trust, and one that the Wisconsin Historical Society has carried out well over the past 167 years.

The library reading room at the society headquarters is a popular location for university students to prepare for finals. (Photo by John Nondorf)

Special Articles in Prior Blue Books 1970 to 2009

For 1919 to 1933 *Blue Books:* see 1954 *Blue Book,* pp. 177-182.

For 1935 to 1962 *Blue Books:* see 1964 *Blue Book,* pp. 227-232.

For 1964 to 1968 *Blue Books:* see 2007-2008 *Blue Book,* pp. 192-193.

Commerce and Culture

The Indians of Wisconsin, by William H. Hodge, 1975 *Blue Book,* pp. 95-192.

Wisconsin Business and Industry, by James J. Brzycki, Paul E. Hassett, Joyce Munz Hach, Kenneth S. Kinney, and Robert H. Milbourne, 1987-1988 *Blue Book,* pp. 99-165.

Wisconsin Writers, by John O. [Jack] Stark, 1977 *Blue Book,* pp. 95-185.

Wisconsin's People: A Portrait of Wisconsin's Population on the Threshold of the 21st Century, by Paul R. Voss, Daniel L. Veroff, and David D. Long, 2003-2004 *Blue Book,* pp. 99-174.

Education

Education for Employment: 70 Years of Vocational, Technical and Adult Education in Wisconsin, by Kathleen A. Paris, 1981-1982 *Blue Book,* pp. 95-212.

The Wisconsin Idea: The University's Service to the State, by Jack Stark, 1995-1996 *Blue Book,* pp. 99-179.

The Wisconsin Idea for the 21st Century, by Alan B. Knox and Joe Corry, 1995-1996 *Blue Book,* pp. 180-192.

Environment

Exploring Wisconsin's Waterways, by Margaret Beattie Bogue, 1989-1990 *Blue Book,* pp. 99-297.

Protecting Wisconsin's Environment, by Selma Parker, 1973 *Blue Book,* pp. 97-161.

Wisconsin's Troubled Waters, by Selma Parker, 1973 *Blue Book,* pp. 102-136.

Government

The Budget - State Fiscal Policy Document, by Dale Cattanach and Terry A. Rhodes, 1970 *Blue Book,* pp. 261-272.

The Changing World of Wisconsin Local Government, by Susan C. Paddock, 1997-1998 *Blue Book,* pp. 99-172.

Equal Representation: A Study of Legislative and Congressional Apportionment in Wisconsin, by H. Rupert Theobald, 1970 *Blue Book,* pp. 70-260.

The Legislative Process in Wisconsin, by Richard L. Roe, Pamela J. Kahler, Robin N. Kite, and Robert P. Nelson, 1993-1994 *Blue Book,* pp. 99-194.

Local Government in Wisconsin, by James R. Donoghue, 1979-1980 *Blue Book,* pp. 95-218.

Rules and Rulings: Parliamentary Procedure from the Wisconsin Perspective, by H. Rupert Theobald, 1985-1986 *Blue Book,* pp. 99-215.

The Wisconsin Court System: Demystifying the Judicial Branch, by Robin Ryan and Amanda Todd, 2005-2006 *Blue Book,* pp. 99-184.

History

Capitals and Capitols in Early Wisconsin, by Stanley H. Cravens, 1983-1984 *Blue Book,* pp. 99-167.

A History of the Property Tax and Property Tax Relief in Wisconsin, by Jack Stark, 1991-1992 *Blue Book,* pp. 99-165.

Progressivism Triumphant: The 1911 Wisconsin Legislature, by John D. Buenker, 2011-2012 *Blue Book,* pp.99-169.

Restoring the Vision: The First Century of Wisconsin's Capitol, by Michael J. Keane, 2001-2002 *Blue Book,* pp. 99-188.

Ten Events That Shaped Wisconsin's History, by Norman K. Risjord, 1999-2000 *Blue Book,* pp. 99-146.

Those Who Served: Wisconsin Legislators 1848-2007, by Michael J. Keane, 2007-2008 *Blue Book,* p. 99-191.

Wisconsin at 150 Years, by Michael J. Keane and Daniel F. Ritsche, 1997-1998 *Blue Book,* color supplement.

Wisconsin at the Frontiers of Astronomy: A History of Innovation and Exploration, by Peter Susalla and James Lattis, 2009-2010 *Blue Book,* pp. 99-189.

Wisconsin Celebrates 150 Years of Statehood: A Photographic Review, 1999-2000 *Blue Book,* color supplement.

Capitol Visitor's Guide

Hours:
Building open daily 8 a.m. - 6 p.m.·
The Capitol closes at 4 p.m. weekends and holidays.

Information Desk
Located in the rotunda, ground floor.

Tours
Daily Monday - Saturday at 9, 10, and 11 a.m., 1, 2, and 3 p.m.; Sundays at 1, 2, and 3 p.m. A 4 p.m. tour is offered weekdays between Memorial Day and Labor Day. Tours start at the Information Desk in the rotunda and last 45 to 50 minutes. Reservations are required for groups of 10 or more. Call (608) 266-0382 7:30 a.m. - 4:30 p.m. Monday - Friday, or visit the Web site at http://tours.wisconsin.gov/pub/Reservations.

Observation Deck
6th Floor, accessible from 4th floor via NW or W stairways. Open daily from Memorial Day to Labor Day. There is a small museum devoted to the Capitol at the entrance to the observation deck.

Souvenirs
Available at the Information Desk, include books,
postcards, miniatures, and tour videos.

Capitol Police
Room B2 North.

Handicapped Entrances
At Martin Luther King Jr. Blvd., East Washington Avenue,
Wisconsin Avenue, and West Washington Avenue.

Parking
Limited parking (meters) on the Capitol Square.
Several public ramps are located within two blocks of the Capitol.

Senate Chamber
South wing, 2nd floor; visitors gallery, 3rd floor.

Assembly Chamber
West wing, 2nd floor; visitors gallery, 3rd floor.

Supreme Court Hearing Room
East wing, 2nd floor.

Governor's Office & Conference Rm
East wing, 1st floor.

Lieutenant Governor's Office
East wing, ground floor.

Attorney General's Office
East wing, 1st floor.

Legislative Offices
To find a specific office, check one of the Capitol Directories
located in the rotunda and on the ground floor of each wing.

Hearings
Information about the time and location of public hearings
is posted at the entrance to each legislative chamber.

Hearing Rooms
North Hearing Room, North wing, 2nd floor.

Grand Army of the Republic Hall, Room 417 North.
Joint Committee on Finance, Room 412 East.
Senate Hearing Room, Room 411 South.
Additional hearing rooms are located on the 2nd and 3rd floors.

Capitol Facts & Figures

Construction Chronology

West wing: 1906 – 1909

East wing: 1908 – 1910

Central portion: 1910 – 1913

South wing: 1909 – 1913

North wing: 1914 – 1917

First meeting of legislature in building: 1909

Dedication: July 8, 1965

Renovation: 1990 – 2001

Statistics

Height of each wing: 61 feet

Height of observation deck: 92 feet

Height of dome mural: 184 feet, 3 inches

Height of dome (to top of statue): 284 feet, 9 inches

Length of building from N to S & E to W:
483 feet, 9 inches

Floor space: 448,297 square feet

Volume: 8,369,665 cubic feet

Original cost: $7,203,826.35
(including grounds, furnishings, and
power plant)

Wisconsin Constitution

3

Wisconsin Constitution: text as amended through April 2013 and votes on constitutional amendments and statewide referenda submitted to the people

Horses on Treadmill, Old World Wisconsin

(Wisconsin Historical Society)

WISCONSIN CONSTITUTION
As amended through April 2013 *

TABLE OF CONTENTS

WISCONSIN CONSTITUTION

As amended through April 2013 *

Preamble

We, the people of Wisconsin, grateful to Almighty God for our freedom, in order to secure its blessings, form a more perfect government, insure domestic tranquility and promote the general welfare, do establish this constitution.

ARTICLE I.
DECLARATION OF RIGHTS

Equality; inherent rights. SECTION 1. [*As amended April 1986*] All people are born equally free and independent, and have certain inherent rights; among these are life, liberty and the pursuit of happiness; to secure these rights, governments are instituted, deriving their just powers from the consent of the governed. [*1983 AJR-9; 1985 AJR-9*]

Equality; inherent rights. SECTION 1. [*As amended November 1982*] All people are born equally free and independent, and have certain inherent rights; among these are life, liberty and the pursuit of happiness; to serve these rights, governments are instituted, deriving their just powers from the consent of the governed. [*1979 AJR-76; 1981 AJR-35; submit: May '82 Spec.Sess. AJR-1*]

Equality; inherent rights. SECTION 1. [*Original form*] All men are born equally free and independent, and have certain inherent rights; among these are life, liberty and the pursuit of happiness; to secure these rights, governments are instituted among men, deriving their just powers from the consent of the governed.

Slavery prohibited. SECTION 2. There shall be neither slavery, nor involuntary servitude in this state, otherwise than for the punishment of crime, whereof the party shall have been duly convicted.

Free speech; libel. SECTION 3. Every person may freely speak, write and publish his sentiments on all subjects, being responsible for the abuse of that right, and no laws shall be passed to restrain or abridge the liberty of speech or of the press. In all criminal prosecutions or indictments for libel, the truth may be given in evidence, and if it shall appear to the jury that the matter charged as libelous be true, and was published with good motives and for justifiable ends, the party shall be acquitted; and the jury shall have the right to determine the law and the fact.

Right to assemble and petition. SECTION 4. The right of the people peaceably to assemble, to consult for the common good, and to petition the government, or any department thereof, shall never be abridged.

Trial by jury; verdict in civil cases. SECTION 5. [*As amended November 1922*] The right of trial by jury shall remain inviolate, and shall extend to all cases at law without regard to the amount in controversy; but a jury trial may be waived by the parties in all cases in the manner prescribed by law. Provided, however, that the legislature may, from time to time, by statute provide that a valid verdict, in civil cases, may be based on the votes of a specified number of the jury, not less than five-sixths thereof. [*1919 AJR-26; 1921 AJR-14; 1921 c. 504*]

Trial by jury. SECTION 5. [*Original form*] The right of trial by jury shall remain inviolate; and shall extend to all cases at law, without regard to the amount in controversy;

but a jury trial may be waived by the parties in all cases, in the manner prescribed by law.

Excessive bail; cruel punishments. SECTION 6. Excessive bail shall not be required, nor shall excessive fines be imposed, nor cruel and unusual punishments inflicted.

---

* Current provisions of the constitution are printed the full width of the page, and previous wordings (if any) follow each active provision in double-column format. Any section not indicated as having been amended and not followed by two-column text still exists as ratified by the people of Wisconsin when they adopted the Wisconsin Constitution on March 13, 1848.

Rights of accused. SECTION 7. In all criminal prosecutions the accused shall enjoy the right to be heard by himself and counsel; to demand the nature and cause of the accusation against him; to meet the witnesses face to face; to have compulsory process to compel the attendance of witnesses in his behalf; and in prosecutions by indictment, or information, to a speedy public trial by an impartial jury of the county or district wherein the offense shall have been committed; which county or district shall have been previously ascertained by law.

Prosecutions; double jeopardy; self-incrimination; bail; habeas corpus. SECTION 8. [*As amended per certification of the Board of State Canvassers dated April 7, 1982*] (1) No person may be held to answer for a criminal offense without due process of law, and no person for the same offense may be put twice in jeopardy of punishment, nor may be compelled in any criminal case to be a witness against himself or herself.

(2) All persons, before conviction, shall be eligible for release under reasonable conditions designed to assure their appearance in court, protect members of the community from serious bodily harm or prevent the intimidation of witnesses. Monetary conditions of release may be imposed at or after the initial appearance only upon a finding that there is a reasonable basis to believe that the conditions are necessary to assure appearance in court. The legislature may authorize, by law, courts to revoke a person's release for a violation of a condition of release.

(3) The legislature may by law authorize, but may not require, circuit courts to deny release for a period not to exceed 10 days prior to the hearing required under this subsection to a person who is accused of committing a murder punishable by life imprisonment or a sexual assault punishable by a maximum imprisonment of 20 years, or who is accused of committing or attempting to commit a felony involving serious bodily harm to another or the threat of serious bodily harm to another and who has a previous conviction for committing or attempting to commit a felony involving serious bodily harm to another or the threat of serious bodily harm to another. The legislature may authorize by law, but may not require, circuit courts to continue to deny release to those accused persons for an additional period not to exceed 60 days following the hearing required under this subsection, if there is a requirement that there be a finding by the court based on clear and convincing evidence presented at a hearing that the accused committed the felony and a requirement that there be a finding by the court that available conditions of release will not adequately protect members of the community from serious bodily harm or prevent intimidation of witnesses. Any law enacted under this subsection shall be specific, limited and reasonable. In determining the 10-day and 60-day periods, the court shall omit any period of time found by the court to result from a delay caused by the defendant or a continuance granted which was initiated by the defendant.

(4) The privilege of the writ of habeas corpus shall not be suspended unless, in cases of rebellion or invasion, the public safety requires it. [*June 1980 Spec.Sess. AJR-9; 1981 AJR-5*]

Prosecutions; second jeopardy; self-incrimination; bail; habeas corpus. SECTION 8. [*As amended November 1870*] No person shall be held to answer for a criminal offense without due process of law, and no person for the same offense shall be put twice in jeopardy of punishment, nor shall be compelled in any criminal case to be a witness against himself. All persons shall, before conviction, be bailable by sufficient sureties, except for capital offenses when the proof is evident or the presumption great; and the privilege of the writ of habeas corpus shall not be suspended unless when, in cases of rebellion or invasion, the public safety may require it. [*1869 AJR-6; 1870 SJR-3; 1870 c. 118*]

Criminal procedure. SECTION 8. [*Original form*] No person shall be held to answer for a criminal offense, unless on the presentment, or indictment of a grand jury, except in cases of impeachment, or in cases cognizable by justices of the peace, or arising in the army or navy, or in the militia when in actual service in time of war, or public danger; and no person for the same offence shall be put twice in jeopardy of punishment, nor shall be compelled in any criminal case to be a witness against himself; all persons shall, before conviction, be bailable by sufficient sureties except for capital offences when the proof is evident, or the presumption great; and the privilege of the writ of habeas corpus shall not be suspended unless when, in cases of rebellion, or invasion, the public safety may require.

Remedy for wrongs. SECTION 9. Every person is entitled to a certain remedy in the laws for all injuries, or wrongs which he may receive in his person, property, or character; he ought to obtain justice freely, and without being obliged to purchase it, completely and without denial, promptly and without delay, conformably to the laws.

Victims of crime. SECTION 9m. [*As created April 1993*] This state shall treat crime victims, as defined by law, with fairness, dignity and respect for their privacy. This state shall ensure that crime victims have all of the following privileges and protections as provided by law: timely disposition of the case; the opportunity to attend court proceedings unless the trial court finds sequestration is necessary to a fair trial for the defendant; reasonable protection from the accused throughout the criminal justice process; notification of court proceedings; the opportunity to confer with the prosecution; the opportunity to make a statement to the court at disposition; restitution; compensation; and information about the outcome of the case and the release of the accused. The legislature shall provide remedies for the violation of this section. Nothing in this section, or in any statute enacted pursuant to this section, shall limit any right of the accused which may be provided by law. [*1991 SJR-41; 1993 SJR-3*]

Treason. Section 10. Treason against the state shall consist only in levying war against the same, or in adhering to its enemies, giving them aid and comfort. No person shall be convicted of treason unless on the testimony of two witnesses to the same overt act, or on confession in open court.

Searches and seizures. Section 11. The right of the people to be secure in their persons, houses, papers, and effects against unreasonable searches and seizures shall not be violated; and no warrant shall issue but upon probable cause, supported by oath or affirmation, and particularly describing the place to be searched and the persons or things to be seized.

Attainder; ex post facto; contracts. Section 12. No bill of attainder, ex post facto law, nor any law impairing the obligation of contracts, shall ever be passed, and no conviction shall work corruption of blood or forfeiture of estate.

Private property for public use. Section 13. The property of no person shall be taken for public use without just compensation therefor.

Feudal tenures; leases; alienation. Section 14. All lands within the state are declared to be allodial, and feudal tenures are prohibited. Leases and grants of agricultural land for a longer term than fifteen years in which rent or service of any kind shall be reserved, and all fines and like restraints upon alienation reserved in any grant of land, hereafter made, are declared to be void.

Equal property rights for aliens and citizens. Section 15. No distinction shall ever be made by law between resident aliens and citizens, in reference to the possession, enjoyment or descent of property.

Imprisonment for debt. Section 16. No person shall be imprisoned for debt arising out of or founded on a contract, expressed or implied.

Exemption of property of debtors. Section 17. The privilege of the debtor to enjoy the necessary comforts of life shall be recognized by wholesome laws, exempting a reasonable amount of property from seizure or sale for the payment of any debt or liability hereafter contracted.

Freedom of worship; liberty of conscience; state religion; public funds. Section 18. [*As amended November 1982*] The right of every person to worship Almighty God according to the dictates of conscience shall never be infringed; nor shall any person be compelled to attend, erect or support any place of worship, or to maintain any ministry, without consent; nor shall any control of, or interference with, the rights of conscience be permitted, or any preference be given by law to any religious establishments or modes of worship; nor shall any money be drawn from the treasury for the benefit of religious societies, or religious or theological seminaries. [*1979 AJR-76; 1981 AJR-35; submit: May '82 Spec.Sess. AJR-1*]

Freedom of worship; liberty of conscience; state religion; public funds. Section 18. [*Original form*] The right of every man to worship Almighty God according to the dictates of his own conscience shall never be infringed; nor shall any man be compelled to attend, erect or support any place of worship, or to maintain any ministry, against his consent; nor shall any control of, or interference with, the rights of conscience be permitted, or any preference be given by law to any religious establishments or modes of worship; nor shall any money be drawn from the treasury for the benefit of religious societies, or religious or theological seminaries.

Religious tests prohibited. Section 19. No religious tests shall ever be required as a qualification for any office of public trust under the state, and no person shall be rendered incompetent to give evidence in any court of law or equity in consequence of his opinions on the subject of religion.

Military subordinate to civil power. Section 20. The military shall be in strict subordination to the civil power.

Rights of suitors. Section 21. [*As amended April 1977*] (1) Writs of error shall never be prohibited, and shall be issued by such courts as the legislature designates by law.

(2) In any court of this state, any suitor may prosecute or defend his suit either in his own proper person or by an attorney of the suitor's choice. [*1975 AJR-11; 1977 SJR-9*]

Writs of error. SECTION 21. [*Original form*] Writs of error shall never be prohibited by law.

Maintenance of free government. SECTION 22. The blessings of a free government can only be maintained by a firm adherence to justice, moderation, temperance, frugality and virtue, and by frequent recurrence to fundamental principles.

Transportation of school children. SECTION 23. [*As created April 1967*] Nothing in this constitution shall prohibit the legislature from providing for the safety and welfare of children by providing for the transportation of children to and from any parochial or private school or institution of learning. [*1965 AJR-70; 1967 AJR-7*]

Use of school buildings. SECTION 24. [*As created April 1972*] Nothing in this constitution shall prohibit the legislature from authorizing, by law, the use of public school buildings by civic, religious or charitable organizations during nonschool hours upon payment by the organization to the school district of reasonable compensation for such use. [*1969 AJR-74; 1971 AJR-10*]

Right to keep and bear arms. SECTION 25. [*As created November 1998*] The people have the right to keep and bear arms for security, defense, hunting, recreation or any other lawful purpose. [*1995 AJR-53; 1997 AJR-11*]

Right to fish, hunt, trap, and take game. SECTION 26. [*As created April 2003*] The people have the right to fish, hunt, trap, and take game subject only to reasonable restrictions as prescribed by law. [*2001 SJR-2; 2003 AJR-1*]

ARTICLE II.
BOUNDARIES

State boundary. SECTION 1. It is hereby ordained and declared that the state of Wisconsin doth consent and accept of the boundaries prescribed in the act of congress entitled "An act to enable the people of Wisconsin territory to form a constitution and state government, and for the admission of such state into the Union," approved August sixth, one thousand eight hundred and forty-six, to wit: Beginning at the northeast corner of the state of Illinois - that is to say, at a point in the center of Lake Michigan where the line of forty-two degrees and thirty minutes of north latitude crosses the same; thence running with the boundary line of the state of Michigan, through Lake Michigan, Green Bay, to the mouth of the Menominee river; thence up the channel of the said river to the Brule river; thence up said last-mentioned river to Lake Brule; thence along the southern shore of Lake Brule in a direct line to the center of the channel between Middle and South Islands, in the Lake of the Desert; thence in a direct line to the head waters of the Montreal river, as marked upon the survey made by Captain Cram; thence down the main channel of the Montreal river to the middle of Lake Superior; thence through the center of Lake Superior to the mouth of the St. Louis river; thence up the main channel of said river to the first rapids in the same, above the Indian village, according to Nicollet's map; thence due south to the main branch of the river St. Croix; thence down the main channel of said river to the Mississippi; thence down the center of the main channel of that river to the northwest corner of the state of Illinois; thence due east with the northern boundary of the state of Illinois to the place of beginning, as established by "An act to enable the people of the Illinois territory to form a constitution and state government, and for the admission of such state into the Union on an equal footing with the original states," approved April 18th, 1818.

Alternate boundary. [*An additional paragraph, adopted by the convention as part of Art. II, sec. 1, was rejected by the act which admitted Wisconsin into the Union (9 U.S. Stat. Ch. L, pp. 233-235)*]: Provided, however, that the following alteration of the foresaid boundary be, and hereby is proposed to the congress of the United States as the preference of the state of Wisconsin, and if the same shall be assented and agreed to by the congress of the United States, then the same shall be and forever remain obligatory on the state of Wisconsin, viz.: Leaving the aforesaid boundary line at the foot of the rapids of the St. Louis river; thence in a direct line, bearing south-westerly, to the mouth of the Iskodewabo, or Rum river, where the same empties into the Mississippi river, thence down the main channel of said Mississippi river as prescribed in the aforesaid boundary.

Enabling act accepted. SECTION 2. [*As amended April 1951*] The propositions contained in the act of congress are hereby accepted, ratified and confirmed, and shall remain irrevocable without the consent of the United States; and it is hereby ordained that this state shall never interfere with the primary disposal of the soil within the same by the United States, nor with any regulations congress may find necessary for securing the title in such soil to bona fide purchasers thereof; and in no case shall nonresident proprietors be taxed higher than residents. Provided, that nothing in this constitution, or in the act of congress aforesaid, shall in any manner prejudice or affect the right of the state of Wisconsin to 500,000 acres of land granted to said state, and to be hereafter selected and located by and under the act of congress entitled "An act to appropriate the proceeds of the sales of the public lands, and grant pre-emption rights," approved September fourth, one thousand eight hundred and forty-one. [*1949 AJR-64; 1951 AJR-7*]

Enabling act accepted. SECTION 2. [*Original form*] The propositions contained in the act of congress are hereby accepted, ratified and confirmed, and shall remain irrevocable without the consent of the United States; and it is hereby ordained that this state shall never interfere with the primary disposal of the soil within the same by the United States, nor with any regulations congress may find necessary for securing the title in such soil to bona fide purchasers thereof; and no tax shall be imposed on land the property of the United States; and in no case shall

nonresident proprietors be taxed higher than residents. Provided, that nothing in this constitution, or in the act of congress aforesaid, shall in any manner prejudice or affect the right of the state of Wisconsin to five hundred thousand acres of land granted to said state, and to be hereafter selected and located by and under the act of congress entitled "An act to appropriate the proceeds of the sales of the public lands, and grant pre-emption rights," approved September fourth, one thousand eight hundred and forty-one.

ARTICLE III.
SUFFRAGE

Electors. SECTION 1. [*As created April 1986*] Every United States citizen age 18 or older who is a resident of an election district in this state is a qualified elector of that district. [*1983 AJR-33; 1985 AJR-3*]

Implementation. SECTION 2. [*As created April 1986*] Laws may be enacted:

(1) Defining residency.

(2) Providing for registration of electors.

(3) Providing for absentee voting.

(4) Excluding from the right of suffrage persons:

(a) Convicted of a felony, unless restored to civil rights.

(b) Adjudged by a court to be incompetent or partially incompetent, unless the judgment specifies that the person is capable of understanding the objective of the elective process or the judgment is set aside.

(5) Subject to ratification by the people at a general election, extending the right of suffrage to additional classes. [*1983 AJR-33; 1985 AJR-3*]

Secret ballot. SECTION 3. [*As created April 1986*] All votes shall be by secret ballot. [*1983 AJR-33; 1985 AJR-3*]

Revision of Article III. The original 6 sections of Article III of the constitution were repealed in April 1986 when the wording of the article was reorganized into the 3 new sections shown above.

Electors. SECTION 1. [*As amended November 1934*] Every person, of the age of twenty-one years or upwards, belonging to either of the following classes, who shall have resided in the state for one year next preceding any election, and in the election district where he offers to vote such time as may be prescribed by the legislature, not exceeding thirty days, shall be deemed a qualified elector at such election: (1) Citizens of the United States.

(2) Persons of Indian blood, who have once been declared by law of congress to be citizens of the United States, any subsequent law of congress to the contrary notwithstanding.

(3) The legislature may at any time extend, by law, the right of suffrage to persons not herein enumerated; but no such law shall be in force until the same shall have been submitted to a vote of the people at a general election, and approved by a majority of all the votes cast on that question at such election; and provided further, that the legislature may provide for the registration of electors, and prescribe proper rules and regulations therefor. [*1931 AJR-52; 1933 SJR-74*]

Termination of voting by resident aliens. [*Subdivision 2* (of the text adopted in 1882), *as amended November*

1908] 2. Persons of foreign birth who, prior to the first day of December, A.D. 1908, shall have declared their intentions to become citizens conformable to the laws of the United States on the subject of naturalization, provided that the rights hereby granted to such persons shall cease on the first day of December, A.D. 1912. [*1905 AJR-16; 1907 AJR-47; 1907 c. 661*]

Qualifications of electors. SECTION 1. [*As amended November 1882*] Every male person of the age of twenty-one years or upwards, belonging to either of the following classes, who shall have resided in the state for one year next preceding any election, and in the election district where he offers to vote such time as may be prescribed by the legislature not exceeding thirty days shall be deemed a qualified elector at such election. 1. Citizens of the United States. 2. Persons of foreign birth who shall have declared their intention to become citizens, conformably to the laws of the United States on the subject of naturalization. 3. Persons of Indian blood who have once been declared by law of congress to be citizens of the United States, any subsequent law of congress to the contrary notwithstanding. 4. Civilized persons of Indian descent not members of any tribe; provided that the legislature may at any time extend, by law, the right of suffrage to persons not herein enumerated, but no such law shall be in force until the same shall have been submitted to a vote of the people at a general election, and approved by a majority of all the votes cast at such election; and provided further, that in incorporated cities and villages, the legislature may provide for the registration of electors and prescribe proper rules and regulations therefor. [*1881 AJR-26; 1882 SJR-18; 1882 c. 272*]

Equal suffrage to colored persons. In *Gillespie v. Palmer,* 20 Wis. (1866) 544, the Wisconsin Supreme Court ruled that Chapter 137, Laws of 1849, extending *equal suffrage to colored persons,* was approved by the voters on November 6, 1849.

Qualifications of electors. Section 1. [*Original form*] Every male person of the age of twenty-one years or upwards belonging to either of the following classes, who shall have resided in the state for one year next preceding any election, shall be deemed a qualified elector at such election:

[*First.*] White citizens of the United States.

[*Second.*] White persons of foreign birth who shall have declared their intention to become citizens, conformably to the laws of the United States on the subject of naturalization.

[*Third.*] Persons of Indian blood who have once been declared by law of congress to be citizens of the United States, any subsequent law of congress to the contrary notwithstanding.

[*Fourth.*] Civilized persons of Indian descent, not members of any tribe. Provided, that the legislature may at any time extend, by law, the right of suffrage to persons not herein enumerated, but no such law shall be in force until the same shall have been submitted to a vote of the people at a general election, and approved by a majority of all the votes cast at such election.

Who not electors. Section 2. [*Original form*] No person under guardianship, non compos mentis or insane shall be qualified to vote at any election; nor shall any person convicted of treason or felony be qualified to vote at any election unless restored to civil rights.

Votes to be by ballot. Section 3. [*Original form*] All votes shall be given by ballot except for such township officers as may by law be directed or allowed to be otherwise chosen.

Section 4. [*Repealed. 1983 JR-30; 1985 JR-14; vote April 1986*]

Residence saved. Section 4. [*Original form*] No person shall be deemed to have lost his residence in this state by reason of his absence on business of the United States or of this state.

Section 5. [*Repealed. 1983 JR-30; 1985 JR-14; vote April 1986*]

Military stationing does not confer residence. Section 5. [*Original form*] No soldier, seaman or marine in the army or navy of the United States shall be deemed a resident of this state in consequence of being stationed within the same.

Section 6. [*Repealed. 1983 JR-30; 1985 JR-14; vote April 1986*]

Exclusion from suffrage. Section 6, [*Original form*] Laws may be passed excluding from the right of suffrage all persons who have been or may be convicted of bribery or larceny, or of any infamous crime, and depriving every person who shall make or become directly or indirectly interested in any bet or wager depending upon the result of any election from the right to vote at such election.

ARTICLE IV.
LEGISLATIVE

Legislative power. Section 1. The legislative power shall be vested in a senate and assembly.

Legislature, how constituted. Section 2. The number of the members of the assembly shall never be less than fifty-four nor more than one hundred. The senate shall consist of a number not more than one-third nor less than one-fourth of the number of the members of the assembly.

Apportionment. Section 3. [*As amended November 1982*] At its first session after each enumeration made by the authority of the United States, the legislature shall apportion and district anew the members of the senate and assembly, according to the number of inhabitants. [*1979 AJR-76; 1981 AJR-35; submit: May '82 Spec.Sess. AJR-1*]

Apportionment. Section 3. [*As amended November 1962*] At their first session after each enumeration made by the authority of the United States, the legislature shall apportion and district anew the members of the senate and assembly, according to the number of inhabitants, excluding soldiers and officers of the United States army and navy. [*1959 SJR-12; 1961 SJR-11*]

Senate district area factor. Sections 3, 4 and 5. [*Approved by voters April 1953*] An amendment to Art. IV, secs. 3, 4, 5, relating to senate apportionment based on area and population, was approved by 1951 SJR-50 and 1953 AJR-7. However, the Supreme Court held the amendment not validly submitted to the voters in *State ex rel. Thomson v. Zimmerman,* 264 W. 644, 60 NW (2d) 416.

Apportionment. Section 3. [*As amended November 1910*] At their first session after each enumeration made by the authority of the United States, the legislature shall apportion and district anew the members of the senate and assembly, according to the number of inhabitants, excluding Indians not taxed, soldiers and officers of the United States army and navy. [*1907 SJR-18; 1909 SJR-35; 1909 c. 478*]

Census and apportionment. Section 3. [*Original form*] The legislature shall provide by law for an enumeration of the inhabitants of the state in the year one thousand eight hundred and fifty-five, and at the end of every ten years thereafter; and at their first session after such enumeration, and also after each enumeration made by the authority of the United States, the legislature shall apportion and district anew the members of the senate and assembly, according to the number of inhabitants, excluding Indians not taxed, and soldiers and officers of the United States army and navy.

Representatives to the assembly, how chosen. Section 4. [*As amended November 1982*] The members of the assembly shall be chosen biennially, by single districts, on the Tuesday succeeding the first Monday of November in even-numbered years, by the qualified electors of the several districts, such districts to be bounded by county, precinct, town or ward lines, to consist of contiguous territory and be in as compact form as practicable. [*1979 AJR-76; 1981 AJR-35; submit: May '82 Spec.Sess. AJR-1*]

Representatives to the assembly, how chosen. SECTION 4. [*As amended November 1881*] The members of the assembly shall be chosen biennially, by single districts, on the Tuesday succeeding the first Monday of November after the adoption of this amendment, by the qualified electors of the several districts, such districts to be bounded by county, precinct, town or ward lines, to consist of contiguous territory and be in a compact form as practicable. [*1880*

SJR-9; 1881 AJR-7; 1881 c. 262]

Assemblymen, how chosen. SECTION 4. [*Original form*] The members of the assembly shall be chosen annually by single districts, on the Tuesday succeeding the first Monday of November, by the qualified electors of the several districts. Such districts to be bounded by county, precinct, town, or ward lines, to consist of contiguous territory, and be in as compact form as practicable.

Senators, how chosen. SECTION 5. [*As amended November 1982*] The senators shall be elected by single districts of convenient contiguous territory, at the same time and in the same manner as members of the assembly are required to be chosen; and no assembly district shall be divided in the formation of a senate district. The senate districts shall be numbered in the regular series, and the senators shall be chosen alternately from the odd and even-numbered districts for the term of 4 years. [*1979 AJR-76; 1981 AJR-35; submit: May '82 Spec.Sess. AJR-1*]

Senators, how chosen. SECTION 5. [*As amended November 1881*] The senators shall be elected by single districts of convenient contiguous territory, at the same time and in the same manner as members of the assembly are required to be chosen, and no assembly district shall be divided in the formation of a senate district. The senate districts shall be numbered in the regular series, and the senators shall be chosen alternately from the odd and even-numbered districts. The senators elected or holding over at the time of the adoption of this amendment shall continue in office till their successors are duly elected and qualified; and after the adoption of this amendment all senators shall be chosen for the term of four years. [*1880 SJR-9; 1881*

AJR-7; 1881 c. 262]

Senators, how chosen. SECTION 5. [*Original form*] The senators shall be chosen by single districts of convenient contiguous territory, at the same time and in the same manner as members of the assembly are required to be chosen, and no assembly district shall be divided in the formation of a senate district. The senate districts shall be numbered in regular series, and the senators chosen by the odd-numbered districts shall go out of office at the expiration of the first year, and the senators chosen by the even-numbered districts shall go out of office at the expiration of the second year, and thereafter the senators shall be chosen for the term of two years.

Qualifications of legislators. SECTION 6. No person shall be eligible to the legislature who shall not have resided one year within the state, and be a qualified elector in the district which he may be chosen to represent.

Organization of legislature; quorum; compulsory attendance. SECTION 7. Each house shall be the judge of the elections, returns and qualifications of its own members; and a majority of each shall constitute a quorum to do business, but a smaller number may adjourn from day to day, and may compel the attendance of absent members in such manner and under such penalties as each house may provide.

Rules; contempts; expulsion. SECTION 8. Each house may determine the rules of its own proceedings, punish for contempt and disorderly behavior, and with the concurrence of two-thirds of all the members elected, expel a member; but no member shall be expelled a second time for the same cause.

Officers. SECTION 9. [*As amended April 1979*] Each house shall choose its presiding officers from its own members. [*1977 SJR-51; 1979 SJR-1*]

Officers. SECTION 9. [*Original form*] Each house shall choose its own officers, and the senate shall choose a

temporary president when the lieutenant governor shall not attend as president, or shall act as governor.

Journals; open doors; adjournments. SECTION 10. Each house shall keep a journal of its proceedings and publish the same, except such parts as require secrecy. The doors of each house shall be kept open except when the public welfare shall require secrecy. Neither house shall, without consent of the other, adjourn for more than three days.

Meeting of legislature. SECTION 11. [*As amended April 1968*] The legislature shall meet at the seat of government at such time as shall be provided by law, unless convened by the governor in special session, and when so convened no business shall be transacted except as shall be necessary to accomplish the special purposes for which it was convened. [*1965 AJR-5; 1967 AJR-15*]

Meeting of legislature. SECTION 11. [*As amended November 1881*] The legislature shall meet at the seat of government at such time as shall be provided by law, once in two years, and no oftener, unless convened by the governor, in special session, and when so convened no business shall be transacted except as shall be necessary to

accomplish the special purposes for which it was convened. [*1880 SJR-9; 1881 AJR-7; 1881 c. 262*]

Place and time of meeting. SECTION 11. [*Original form*] The legislature shall meet at the seat of government, at such time as shall be provided by law, once in each year and not oftener, unless convened by the governor.

Ineligibility of legislators to office. SECTION 12. No member of the legislature shall, during the term for which he was elected, be appointed or elected to any civil office in the state, which shall have been created, or the emoluments of which shall have been increased, during the term for which he was elected.

Ineligibility of federal officers. SECTION 13. [*As amended April 1966*] No person being a member of congress, or holding any military or civil office under the United States, shall be eligible to a seat in the legislature; and if any person shall, after his election as a member of the legislature, be elected to congress, or be appointed to any office, civil or military, under the government of the United States, his acceptance thereof shall vacate his seat. This restriction shall not prohibit a legislator from accepting short periods of active duty as a member of the reserve or from serving in the armed forces during any emergency declared by the executive. [*1963 SJR-24; 1965 SJR-15*]

Ineligibility of federal officers. SECTION 13. [*Original form*] No person being a member of congress, or holding any military or civil office under the United States, shall be eligible to a seat in the legislature; and if any person shall, after his election as a member of the legislature, be elected to congress, or be appointed to any office, civil or military, under the government of the United States, his acceptance thereof shall vacate his seat.

Filling vacancies. SECTION 14. The governor shall issue writs of election to fill such vacancies as may occur in either house of the legislature.

Exemption from arrest and civil process. SECTION 15. Members of the legislature shall in all cases, except treason, felony and breach of the peace, be privileged from arrest; nor shall they be subject to any civil process, during the session of the legislature, nor for fifteen days next before the commencement and after the termination of each session.

Privilege in debate. SECTION 16. No member of the legislature shall be liable in any civil action, or criminal prosecution whatever, for words spoken in debate.

Enactment of laws. SECTION 17. [*As amended April 1977*] (1) The style of all laws of the state shall be "The people of the state of Wisconsin, represented in senate and assembly, do enact as follows:".

(2) No law shall be enacted except by bill. No law shall be in force until published.

(3) The legislature shall provide by law for the speedy publication of all laws. [*1975 AJR-11; 1977 SJR-9*]

Style of laws; bills. SECTION 17. [*Original form*] The style of the laws of the state shall be "The people of the state of Wisconsin, represented in senate and assembly, do enact as follows:" and no law shall be enacted except by bill.

Title of private bills. SECTION 18. No private or local bill which may be passed by the legislature shall embrace more than one subject, and that shall be expressed in the title.

Origin of bills. SECTION 19. Any bill may originate in either house of the legislature, and a bill passed by one house may be amended by the other.

Yeas and nays. SECTION 20. The yeas and nays of the members of either house on any question shall, at the request of one-sixth of those present, be entered on the journal.

SECTION 21. [*Repealed. 1927 SJR-61; 1929 SJR-7; vote April 1929*]

Compensation of members. SECTION 21. [*As amended November 1881*] Each member of the legislature shall receive for his services, for and during a regular session, the sum of five hundred dollars, and ten cents for every mile he shall travel in going to and returning from the place of meeting of the legislature on the most usual route. In case of an extra session of the legislature, no additional compensation shall be allowed to any member thereof, either directly or indirectly, except for mileage to be computed at the same rate as for a regular session. No stationery, newspapers, postage or other perquisite except the salary and mileage above provided, shall be received from the state by any member of the legislature for his services, or in any other manner as such member. [*1880 SJR-9; 1881 AJR-7; 1881 c. 262*]

Compensation of members. SECTION 21. [*As amended November 1867*] Each member of the legislature shall receive for his services three hundred and fifty dollars per annum and ten cents for every mile he shall travel in going to and returning from the place of the meeting of the legislature on the most usual route. In case of an extra session of the legislature no additional compensation shall be allowed to any member thereof either directly or indirectly. [*1865 SJR-26; 1866 SJR-16; 1867 c. 25*]

Compensation of members. SECTION 21. [*Original form*] Each member of the legislature shall receive for his services two dollars and fifty cents for each day's attendance during the session, and ten cents for every mile he shall travel in going to and returning from the place of the meeting of the legislature, on the most usual route.

Powers of county boards. SECTION 22. The legislature may confer upon the boards of supervisors of the several counties of the state such powers of a local, legislative and administrative character as they shall from time to time prescribe.

Town and county government. SECTION 23. [*As amended April 1972*] The legislature shall establish but one system of town government, which shall be as nearly uniform as practicable; but the legislature may provide for the election at large once in every 4 years of a chief executive officer in any county with such powers of an administrative character as they may from time to time prescribe in accordance with this section and shall establish one or more systems of county government. [*1969 SJR-58; 1971 SJR-4*]

Uniform town and county government. SECTION 23. [*As amended April 1969*] The legislature shall establish but one system of town and county government, which shall be as nearly uniform as practicable, except that the requirement of uniformity shall not apply to the administrative means of exercising powers of a local legislative character conferred by section 22 upon the boards of supervisors of the several counties; but the legislature may provide for the election at large once in every 4 years of a chief executive officer in any county with such powers of an administrative character as they may from time to time prescribe in accordance with this section. [*1967 AJR-18; 1969 SJR-8*]

Uniform town and county government. SECTION

23. [*As amended November 1962*] The legislature shall establish but one system of town and county government, which shall be as nearly uniform as practicable; but the legislature may provide for the election at large once in every four years of a chief executive officer in any county having a population of five hundred thousand or more with such powers of an administrative character as they may from time to time prescribe in accordance with this section. [*1959 AJR-121; 1961 AJR-61*]

Uniform town and county government. SECTION 23. [*Original form*] The legislature shall establish but one system of town and county government, which shall be as nearly uniform as practicable.

Chief executive officer to approve or veto resolutions or ordinances; proceedings on veto. SECTION 23a. [*As amended April 1969*] Every resolution or ordinance passed by the county board in any county shall, before it becomes effective, be presented to the chief executive officer. If he approves, he shall sign it; if not, he shall return it with his objections, which objections shall be entered at large upon the journal and the board shall proceed to reconsider the matter. Appropriations may be approved in whole or in part by the chief executive officer and the part approved shall become law, and the part objected to shall be returned in the same manner as provided for in other resolutions or ordinances. If, after such reconsideration, two-thirds of the members-elect of the county board agree to pass the resolution or ordinance or the part of the resolution or ordinance objected to, it shall become effective on the date prescribed but not earlier than the date of passage following reconsideration. In all such cases, the votes of the members of the county board shall be determined by ayes and noes and the names of the members voting for or against the resolution or ordinance or the part thereof objected to shall be entered on the journal. If any resolution or ordinance is not returned by the chief executive officer to the county board at its first meeting occurring not less than 6 days, Sundays excepted, after it has been presented to him, it shall become effective unless the county board has recessed or adjourned for a period in excess of 60 days, in which case it shall not be effective without his approval. [*1967 AJR-18; 1969 SJR-8*]

Chief executive officer to approve or veto resolutions or ordinances; proceedings on veto. SECTION 23a. [*Created November 1962*] Every resolution or ordinance passed by the county board in any county having a population of five hundred thousand or more shall, before it becomes effective, be presented to the chief executive officer. If he approves, he shall sign it; if not, he shall return it with his objections, which objections shall be entered at large upon the journal and the board shall proceed to reconsider the matter. Appropriations may be approved in whole or in part by the chief executive officer and the part approved shall become law, and the part objected to shall be returned in the same manner as provided for in other resolutions or ordinances. If, after such reconsideration, two-thirds of the members-elect of the county board agree to pass

the resolution or ordinance or the part of the resolution or ordinance objected to, it shall become effective on the date prescribed but not earlier than the date of passage following reconsideration. In all such cases, the votes of the members of the county board shall be determined by ayes and nays and the names of the members voting for or against the resolution or ordinance or the part thereof objected to shall be entered on the journal. If any resolution or ordinance is not returned by the chief executive officer to the county board at its first meeting occurring not less than six days, Sundays excepted, after it has been presented to him, it shall become effective unless the county board has recessed or adjourned for a period in excess of sixty days, in which case it shall not be effective without his approval. [*1959 AJR-121; 1961 AJR-61*]

Gambling. SECTION 24. [*As amended April 1993*] (1) Except as provided in this section, the legislature may not authorize gambling in any form.

(2) Except as otherwise provided by law, the following activities do not constitute consideration as an element of gambling:

(a) To listen to or watch a television or radio program.

(b) To fill out a coupon or entry blank, whether or not proof of purchase is required.

(c) To visit a mercantile establishment or other place without being required to make a purchase or pay an admittance fee.

(3) [*As amended April 1999*] The legislature may authorize the following bingo games licensed by the state, but all profits shall accrue to the licensed organization and no salaries, fees or profits may be paid to any other organization or person: bingo games operated by religious, charitable, service, fraternal or veterans' organizations or those to which contributions are deductible for federal or state income tax purposes. All moneys received by the state that are attributable to bingo games shall be used for property tax relief for residents of this state as

provided by law. The distribution of moneys that are attributable to bingo games may not vary based on the income or age of the person provided the property tax relief. The distribution of moneys that are attributable to bingo games shall not be subject to the uniformity requirement of section 1 of article VIII. In this subsection, the distribution of all moneys attributable to bingo games shall include any earnings on the moneys received by the state that are attributable to bingo games, but shall not include any moneys used for the regulation of, and enforcement of law relating to, bingo games. [*1997 AJR-80; 1999 AJR-2*]

(3) The legislature may authorize the following bingo games licensed by the state, but all profits shall accrue to the licensed organization and no salaries, fees or profits may be paid to any other organization or person: bingo games operated by religious, charitable, service, fraternal or veterans' organizations or those to which contributions are deductible for federal or state income tax purposes.

(4) The legislature may authorize the following raffle games licensed by the state, but all profits shall accrue to the licensed local organization and no salaries, fees or profits may be paid to any other organization or person: raffle games operated by local religious, charitable, service, fraternal or veterans' organizations or those to which contributions are deductible for federal or state income tax purposes. The legislature shall limit the number of raffles conducted by any such organization.

(5) [*As amended April 1999*] This section shall not prohibit pari-mutuel on-track betting as provided by law. The state may not own or operate any facility or enterprise for pari-mutuel betting, or lease any state-owned land to any other owner or operator for such purposes. All moneys received by the state that are attributable to pari-mutuel on-track betting shall be used for property tax relief for residents of this state as provided by law. The distribution of moneys that are attributable to pari-mutuel on-track betting may not vary based on the income or age of the person provided the property tax relief. The distribution of moneys that are attributable to pari-mutuel on-track betting shall not be subject to the uniformity requirement of section 1 of article VIII. In this subsection, the distribution of all moneys attributable to pari-mutuel on-track betting shall include any earnings on the moneys received by the state that are attributable to pari-mutuel on-track betting, but shall not include any moneys used for the regulation of, and enforcement of law relating to, pari-mutuel on-track betting. [*1997 AJR-80; 1999 AJR-2*]

(5) This section shall not prohibit pari-mutuel on-track betting as provided by law. The state may not own or operate any facility or enterprise for pari-mutuel betting, or lease any state-owned land to any other owner or operator for such purposes.

(6) (a) [*As amended April 1999*] The legislature may authorize the creation of a lottery to be operated by the state as provided by law. The expenditure of public funds or of revenues derived from lottery operations to engage in promotional advertising of the Wisconsin state lottery is prohibited. Any advertising of the state lottery shall indicate the odds of a specific lottery ticket to be selected as the winning ticket for each prize amount offered. The net proceeds of the state lottery shall be deposited in the treasury of the state, to be used for property tax relief for residents of this state as provided by law. The distribution of the net proceeds of the state lottery may not vary based on the income or age of the person provided the property tax relief. The distribution of the net proceeds of the state lottery shall not be subject to the uniformity requirement of section 1 of article VIII. In this paragraph, the distribution of the net proceeds of the state lottery shall include any earnings on the net proceeds of the state lottery. [*1997 AJR-80; 1999 AJR-2*]

(6) (a) The legislature may authorize the creation of a lottery to be operated by the state as provided by law. The expenditure of public funds or of revenues derived from lottery operations to engage in promotional advertising of the Wisconsin state lottery is prohibited. Any advertising of the state lottery shall indicate the odds of a specific lottery ticket to be selected as the winning ticket for each prize amount offered. The net proceeds of the state lottery shall be deposited in the treasury of the state, to be used for property tax relief as provided by law.

(b) The lottery authorized under par. (a) shall be an enterprise that entitles the player, by purchasing a ticket, to participate in a game of chance if: 1) the winning tickets are randomly predetermined and the player reveals preprinted numbers or symbols from which it can be immediately determined whether the ticket is a winning ticket entitling the player to win a prize as prescribed in the features and procedures for the game, including an opportunity to win a prize in a secondary or subsequent chance drawing or game; or 2) the ticket is evidence of the numbers or symbols selected by the player or, at the player's option, selected by a computer, and the player becomes entitled to a prize as prescribed in the features and procedures for the game, including an opportunity to win a prize in a secondary or subsequent chance drawing or game if some or all of the player's symbols or numbers are selected in a chance drawing or game, if the player's ticket is randomly selected by the computer at the time of purchase or if the ticket is selected in a chance drawing.

(c) Notwithstanding the authorization of a state lottery under par. (a), the following games, or games simulating any of the following games, may not be conducted by the state as a lottery: 1) any game in which winners are selected based on the results of a race or sporting event; 2) any banking card game, including blackjack, baccarat or chemin de fer; 3) poker; 4) roulette; 5) craps or any other game that involves rolling dice; 6) keno; 7) bingo 21, bingo jack, bingolet or bingo craps; 8) any game of chance that is placed on a slot machine or any mechanical, electromechanical or electronic device that is generally available to be played at a gambling casino; 9) any game or device that is commonly known as a video game of chance or a video gaming machine or that is commonly considered to be a video gambling machine, unless such machine is a video device operated by the state in a game authorized under par. (a) to permit the sale of tickets through retail outlets under contract with the state and the device does not determine or indicate whether the player has won a prize, other than by verifying that the player's ticket or some or all of the player's symbols or numbers on the player's ticket have been selected in a chance drawing, or by verifying that the player's ticket has been randomly selected by a central system computer at the time of purchase; 10) any game that is similar to a game listed in this paragraph; or 11) any other game that is commonly considered to be a form of gambling and is not, or is not substantially similar to, a game conducted by the state under par. (a). No game conducted by the state under par. (a) may permit a player of the game to purchase a ticket, or to otherwise participate in the game, from a residence by using a computer, telephone or other form of electronic, telecommunication, video or technological aid. [*(1), (2)(intro.) amended; (6) (b), (c) created; June 1992 AJR-1; 1993 SJR-2*]

Lotteries and divorces. SECTION 24. [*As amended April 1987*] (1) Except as provided in this section, the legislature shall never authorize any lottery or grant any divorce.

(2) Except as otherwise provided by law, the following activities do not constitute consideration as an element of a lottery:

(a) To listen to or watch a television or radio program.

(b) To fill out a coupon or entry blank, whether or not proof of purchase is required.

(c) To visit a mercantile establishment or other place without being required to make a purchase or pay an admittance fee.

(3) The legislature may authorize the following bingo games licensed by the state, but all profits shall accrue to the licensed organization and no salaries, fees or profits may be paid to any other organization or person: bingo games operated by religious, charitable, service, fraternal or veterans' organizations or those to which contributions are deductible for federal or state income tax purposes.

(4) The legislature may authorize the following raffle games licensed by the state, but all profits shall accrue to the licensed local organization and no salaries, fees or profits may be paid to any other organization or person: raffle games operated by local religious, charitable, service, fraternal or veterans' organizations or those to which contributions are deductible for federal or state income tax purposes. The legislature shall limit the number of raffles conducted by any such organization.

(5) This section shall not prohibit pari-mutuel on-track betting as provided by law. The state may not own or operate any facility or enterprise for pari-mutuel betting, or lease any state-owned land to any other owner or operator for such purposes.

(6) The legislature may authorize the creation of a lottery to be operated by the state as provided by law. The expenditure of public funds or of revenues derived from lottery operations to engage in promotional advertising of the Wisconsin state lottery is prohibited. Any advertising of the state lottery shall indicate the odds of a specific lottery ticket to be selected as the winning ticket for each prize amount offered. The net proceeds of the state lottery shall be deposited in the treasury of the state, to be used for property tax relief as provided by law. [*Pari-mutuel: 1985 AJR-45; 1987 AJR-2. State lottery: 1985 SJR-1; 1987 AJR-3.*]

Lotteries and divorces. SECTION 24. [*As amended April 1977*] The legislature shall never authorize any lottery or grant any divorce. (1) The legislature may authorize bingo games licensed by the state, and operated by religious, charitable, service, fraternal or veterans' organizations or those to which contributions are deductible for federal or state income tax purposes. All profits must inure to the licensed organization and no salaries, fees or profits shall be paid to any other organization or person. (2) The legislature may authorize raffle games licensed by the state, and operated by local religious, charitable, service, fraternal or veterans' organizations or those to which contributions are deductible for federal or state income tax purposes. The legislature shall limit the number of raffles conducted by any such organization. All profits must inure to the licensed local organization and no salaries, fees or profits shall be paid to any other organization or person. (3) Except as the legislature may provide otherwise, the following activities do not constitute consideration as an element of a lottery: (a) To listen to or watch a television or radio program. (b) To fill out a coupon or entry blank, whether or not proof of purchase is required. (c) To visit a mercantile establishment or other place without being required to make a purchase or pay an admittance fee. [*1975 AJR-43; 1977 AJR-10*]

Lotteries and divorces. SECTION 24. [*As amended April 1973*] The legislature shall never authorize any lottery, or grant any divorce, but may authorize bingo games licensed by the state, and operated by religious, charitable, service, fraternal or veterans' organizations or those to which contributions are deductible for federal or state income tax purposes. All profits must inure to the licensed organization and no salaries, fees or profits shall be paid to any other organization or person. Except as the legislature may provide otherwise, to listen to or watch a television or radio program, to fill out a coupon or entry blank, whether or not proof of purchase is required, or to visit a mercantile establishment or other place without being required to make a purchase or pay an admittance fee does not constitute consideration as an element of a lottery. [*1971 SJR-13; 1973 AJR-6*]

Lotteries and divorces. SECTION 24. [*As amended April 1965*] The legislature shall never authorize any lottery, or grant any divorce. Except as the legislature may provide otherwise, to listen to or watch a television or radio program, to fill out a coupon or entry blank, whether or not proof of purchase is required, or to visit a mercantile establishment or other place without being required to make a purchase or pay an admittance fee does not constitute consideration as an element of a lottery. [*1963 SJR-42; 1965 SJR-13*]

Lotteries and divorces. SECTION 24. [*Original form*] The legislature shall never authorize any lottery, or grant any divorce.

Stationery and printing. SECTION 25. The legislature shall provide by law that all stationery required for the use of the state, and all printing authorized and required by them to be done for their use, or for the state, shall be let by contract to the lowest bidder, but the legislature may establish a maximum price; no member of the legislature or other state officer shall be interested, either directly or indirectly, in any such contract.

Extra compensation; salary change. SECTION 26. [*As amended April 1992*] (1) The legislature may not grant any extra compensation to a public officer, agent, servant or contractor after the services have been rendered or the contract has been entered into.

(2) Except as provided in this subsection, the compensation of a public officer may not be increased or diminished during the term of office:

(a) When any increase or decrease in the compensation of justices of the supreme court or judges of any court of record becomes effective as to any such justice or judge, it shall be effective from such date as to every such justice or judge.

(b) Any increase in the compensation of members of the legislature shall take effect, for all senators and representatives to the assembly, after the next general election beginning with the new assembly term.

(3) Subsection (1) shall not apply to increased benefits for persons who have been or shall be granted benefits of any kind under a retirement system when such increased benefits are provided by a legislative act passed on a call of ayes and noes by a three-fourths vote of all the members elected to both houses of the legislature and such act provides for sufficient state funds to cover the costs of the increased benefits. [*1989 AJR-47; 1991 AJR-16*]

Extra compensation; salary change. SECTION 26. [*As amended April 1977*] The legislature shall never grant any extra compensation to any public officer, agent, servant or contractor, after the services shall have been rendered or the contract entered into; nor shall the compensation of any public officer be increased or diminished during his term of office except that when any increase or decrease provided by the legislature in the compensation of the justices of the supreme court or judges of any court of record shall become effective as to any such justice or judge, it shall be effective from such date as to each of such justices or judges. This section shall not apply to increased benefits for persons who have been or shall be granted benefits of any kind under a retirement system when such increased benefits are provided by a legislative act passed on a call of ayes and noes by a three-fourths vote of all the members elected to both houses of the legislature, which act shall provide for sufficient state funds to cover the costs of the increased benefits. [*1975 AJR-11; 1977 SJR-9*]

Extra compensation; salary change. SECTION 26. [*As amended April 1974*] The legislature shall never grant any extra compensation to any public officer, agent, servant or contractor, after the services shall have been rendered or the contract entered into; nor shall the compensation of any public officer be increased or diminished during his term of office except that when any increase or decrease provided by the legislature in the compensation of the justices of the supreme court, or judges of the circuit court shall become effective as to any such justice or judge, it shall become effective from such date as to each of such justices or judges. This section shall not apply to increased benefits for persons who have been or shall be granted benefits of any kind under a retirement system when such increased benefits are provided by a legislative act passed on a call of yeas and nays by a three-fourths vote of all the members elected to both houses of the legislature, which act shall provide for sufficient state funds to cover the costs of the

increased benefits. [*1971 SJR-3; 1973 SJR-15*]

Extra compensation; salary change. SECTION 26. [*As amended April 1967*] The legislature shall never grant any extra compensation to any public officer, agent, servant or contractor, after the services shall have been rendered or the contract entered into; nor shall the compensation of any public officer be increased or diminished during his term of office except that when any increase or decrease provided by the legislature in the compensation of the justices of the supreme court, or judges of the circuit court shall become effective as to any such justice or judge, it shall be effective from such date as to each of such justices or judges. This section shall not apply to increased benefits for teachers under a teachers' retirement system when such increased benefits are provided by a legislative act passed on a call of yeas and nays by a three-fourths vote of all the members elected to both houses of the legislature. [*1965 AJR-162; 1967 AJR-17*]

Extra compensation; salary change. SECTION 26. [*As amended April 1956*] The legislature shall never grant any extra compensation to any public officer, agent, servant or contractor, after the services shall have been rendered or the contract entered into; nor shall the compensation of any public officer be increased or diminished during his term of office. This section shall not apply to increased benefits for teachers under a teachers' retirement system when such increased benefits are provided by a legislative act passed on a call of yeas and nays by a three-fourths vote of all the members elected to both houses of the legislature. [*1953 SJR-21; 1955 SJR-8*]

Extra compensation; salary change. SECTION 26. [*Original form*] The legislature shall never grant any extra compensation to any public officer, agent, servant or contractor after the services shall have been rendered or the contract entered into; nor shall the compensation of any public officer be increased or diminished during his term of office.

Suits against state. SECTION 27. The legislature shall direct by law in what manner and in what courts suits may be brought against the state.

Oath of office. SECTION 28. Members of the legislature, and all officers, executive and judicial, except such inferior officers as may be by law exempted, shall before they enter upon the duties of their respective offices, take and subscribe an oath or affirmation to support the constitution of the United States and the constitution of the state of Wisconsin, and faithfully to discharge the duties of their respective offices to the best of their ability.

Militia. SECTION 29. The legislature shall determine what persons shall constitute the militia of the state, and may provide for organizing and disciplining the same in such manner as shall be prescribed by law.

Elections by legislature. SECTION 30. [*As amended November 1982*] All elections made by the legislature shall be by roll call vote entered in the journals. [*1979 AJR-76; 1981 AJR-35; submit: May '82 Spec.Sess. AJR-1*]

Elections by legislature. SECTION 30. [*Original form*] In all elections to be made by the legislature the members thereof shall vote viva voce, and their votes shall be entered on the journal.

Special and private laws prohibited. SECTION 31. [*As amended April 1993*] The legislature is prohibited from enacting any special or private laws in the following cases:

(1) For changing the names of persons, constituting one person the heir at law of another or granting any divorce.

(2) For laying out, opening or altering highways, except in cases of state roads extending into more than one county, and military roads to aid in the construction of which lands may be granted by congress.

(3) For authorizing persons to keep ferries across streams at points wholly within this state.

(4) For authorizing the sale or mortgage of real or personal property of minors or others under disability.

(5) For locating or changing any county seat.

(6) For assessment or collection of taxes or for extending the time for the collection thereof.

(7) For granting corporate powers or privileges, except to cities.

(8) For authorizing the apportionment of any part of the school fund.

(9) For incorporating any city, town or village, or to amend the charter thereof. [*(1) amended; June 1992 AJR-1; 1993 SJR-2*]

Special and private laws prohibited. SECTION 31. [*As amended November 1892*] The legislature is prohibited from enacting any special or private laws in the following cases:

1st. For changing the name of persons or constituting one person the heir at law of another.

2d. For laying out, opening or altering highways, except in cases of state roads extending into more than one county, and military roads to aid in the construction of which lands may be granted by congress.

3d. For authorizing persons to keep ferries across streams at points wholly within this state.

4th. For authorizing the sale or mortgage of real or personal property of minors or others under disability.

5th. For locating or changing any county seat.

6th. For assessment or collection of taxes or for extending the time for the collection thereof.

7th. For granting corporate powers or privileges, except to cities.

8th. For authorizing the apportionment of any part of the school fund.

9th. For incorporating any city, town or village, or to amend the charter thereof. [*1889 SJR-13; 1891 SJR-13; 1891 c. 362*]

Special or private laws. SECTION 31. [*Created November 1871*] The legislature is prohibited from enacting any special or private laws in the following cases:

1st. For changing the name of persons or constituting one person the heir at law of another.

2d. For laying out, opening or altering highways, except in cases of state roads extending into more than one county, and military roads to aid in the construction of which lands may be granted by congress.

3d. For authorizing persons to keep ferries across streams at points wholly within this state.

4th. For authorizing the sale or mortgage of real or personal property of minors or others under disability.

5th. For locating or changing any county seat.

6th. For assessment or collection of taxes or for extending the time for the collection thereof.

7th. For granting corporate powers or privileges, except to cities.

8th. For authorizing the apportionment of any part of the school fund.

9th. For incorporating any town or village or to amend the charter thereof. [*1870 SJR-14; 1871 AJR-29; 1871 c. 122*]

General laws on enumerated subjects. SECTION 32. [*As amended April 1993*] The legislature may provide by general law for the treatment of any subject for which lawmaking is prohibited by section 31 of this article. Subject to reasonable classifications, such laws shall be uniform in their operation throughout the state. [*June 1992 AJR-1; 1993 SJR-2*]

General laws on enumerated subjects. SECTION 32. [*Created November 1871*] The legislature shall provide general laws for the transaction of any business that may be prohibited by section thirty-one of this article, and all such laws shall be uniform in their operation throughout the   state. [*1870 SJR-14; 1871 AJR-29; 1871 c. 122*]

Auditing of state accounts. SECTION 33. [*Created November 1946*] The legislature shall provide for the auditing of state accounts and may establish such offices and prescribe such duties for the same as it shall deem necessary. [*1943 SJR-35; 1945 SJR-24*]

Continuity of civil government. SECTION 34. [*Created April 1961*] The legislature, in order to ensure continuity of state and local governmental operations in periods of emergency resulting from enemy action in the form of an attack, shall (1) forthwith provide for prompt and temporary succession to the powers and duties of public offices, of whatever nature and whether filled by election or appointment, the incumbents of which may become unavailable for carrying on the powers and duties of such offices, and (2) adopt such other measures as may be necessary and proper for attaining the objectives of this section. [*1959 AJR-48; 1961 SJR-1*]

ARTICLE V.
EXECUTIVE

Governor; lieutenant governor; term. SECTION 1. [*As amended April 1979*] The executive power shall be vested in a governor who shall hold office for 4 years; a lieutenant governor shall be elected at the same time and for the same term. [*1977 SJR-51; 1979 SJR-1*]

Governor; lieutenant governor; term. SECTION 1. [*Original form*] The executive power shall be vested in a governor, who shall hold his office for two years; a lieutenant governor shall be elected at the same time, and for the same term.

SECTION 1m. [*Repealed. 1977 SJR-51; 1979 SJR-1; vote April 1979*]

Governor; 4-year term. SECTION 1m. [*Created April 1967*] Notwithstanding section 1, beginning with the general election in 1970 and every four years thereafter, there shall be elected a governor to hold office for a term of four years. [*1965 AJR-4; 1967 AJR-9 and SJR-12*]

SECTION 1n. [*Repealed. 1977 SJR-51; 1979 SJR-1; vote April 1979*]

Lieutenant governor; 4-year term. SECTION 1n. [*Created April 1967*] Notwithstanding section 1, beginning with the general election in 1970 and every four years thereafter, there shall be elected a lieutenant governor to hold office for a term of four years. [*1965 AJR-4; 1967 AJR-9 and SJR-12*]

Eligibility. SECTION 2. No person except a citizen of the United States and a qualified elector of the state shall be eligible to the office of governor or lieutenant governor.

Election. SECTION 3. [*As amended April 1967*] The governor and lieutenant governor shall be elected by the qualified electors of the state at the times and places of choosing members of the legislature. They shall be chosen jointly, by the casting by each voter of a single vote applicable to both offices beginning with the general election in 1970. The persons respectively having the highest number of votes cast jointly for them for governor and lieutenant governor shall be elected; but in case two or more slates shall have an equal and the highest number of votes for governor and lieutenant governor, the two houses of the legislature, at its next annual session shall forthwith, by joint ballot, choose one of the slates so having an equal and the highest number of votes for governor and lieutenant governor. The returns of election for governor and lieutenant governor shall be made in such manner as shall be provided by law. [*1965 AJR-3; 1967 AJR-8 and SJR-11*]

Election. SECTION 3. [*Original form*] The governor and lieutenant governor shall be elected by the qualified electors of the state at the times and places of choosing members of the legislature. The persons respectively having the highest number of votes for governor and lieutenant governor shall be elected; but in case two or more shall have an equal and the highest number of votes for governor, or lieutenant governor, the two houses of the legislature, at its next annual session shall forthwith, by joint ballot, choose one of the persons so having an equal and the highest number of votes for governor, or lieutenant governor. The returns of election for governor and lieutenant governor shall be made in such manner as shall be provided by law.

Powers and duties. SECTION 4. The governor shall be commander in chief of the military and naval forces of the state. He shall have power to convene the legislature on extraordinary occasions, and in case of invasion, or danger from the prevalence of contagious disease at the seat of government, he may convene them at any other suitable place within the state. He shall communicate to the legislature, at every session, the condition of the state, and recommend such matters to them for their consideration as he may deem expedient. He shall transact all necessary business with the officers of the government, civil and military. He shall expedite all such measures as may be resolved upon by the legislature, and shall take care that the laws be faithfully executed.

Section 5. [*Repealed. 1929 SJR-81; 1931 SJR-6; vote November 1932*]

Compensation of governor. Section 5. [*As amended November 1926*] The governor shall receive, during his continuance in office, an annual compensation of not less than five thousand dollars, to be fixed by law, which shall be in full for all traveling or other expenses incident to his duties. The compensation prescribed for governor immediately prior to the adoption of this amendment shall continue in force until changed by the legislature in a manner consistent with the other provisions of this constitution. [*1923 AJR-88; 1925 AJR-50; 1925 c. 413*]

Compensation of governor. Section 5. [*As amended November 1869*] The governor shall receive during his continuance in office, an annual compensation of five thousand dollars which shall be in full for all traveling or other expenses incident to his duties. [*1868 AJR-13; 1869 SJR-6; 1869 c. 186*]

Compensation of governor. Section 5. [*Original form*] The governor shall receive during his continuance in office, an annual compensation of one thousand two hundred and fifty dollars.

Pardoning power. Section 6. The governor shall have power to grant reprieves, commutations and pardons, after conviction, for all offenses, except treason and cases of impeachment, upon such conditions and with such restrictions and limitations as he may think proper, subject to such regulations as may be provided by law relative to the manner of applying for pardons. Upon conviction for treason he shall have the power to suspend the execution of the sentence until the case shall be reported to the legislature at its next meeting, when the legislature shall either pardon, or commute the sentence, direct the execution of the sentence, or grant a further reprieve. He shall annually communicate to the legislature each case of reprieve, commutation or pardon granted, stating the name of the convict, the crime of which he was convicted, the sentence and its date, and the date of the commutation, pardon or reprieve, with his reasons for granting the same.

Lieutenant governor, when governor. Section 7. [*As amended April 1979*] (1) Upon the governor's death, resignation or removal from office, the lieutenant governor shall become governor for the balance of the unexpired term.

(2) If the governor is absent from this state, impeached, or from mental or physical disease, becomes incapable of performing the duties of the office, the lieutenant governor shall serve as acting governor for the balance of the unexpired term or until the governor returns, the disability ceases or the impeachment is vacated. But when the governor, with the consent of the legislature, shall be out of this state in time of war at the head of the state's military force, the governor shall continue as commander in chief of the military force. [*1977 SJR-51; 1979 SJR-1*]

Lieutenant governor, when governor. Section 7. [*Original form*] In case of the impeachment of the governor, or his removal from office, death, inability from mental or physical disease, resignation, or absence from the state, the powers and duties of the office shall devolve upon the lieutenant governor for the residue of the term or until the governor, absent or impeached, shall have returned, or the disability shall cease. But when the governor shall, with the consent of the legislature, be out of the state in time of war, at the head of the military force thereof, he shall continue commander in chief of the military force of the state.

Secretary of state, when governor. Section 8. [*As amended April 1979*] (1) If there is a vacancy in the office of lieutenant governor and the governor dies, resigns or is removed from office, the secretary of state shall become governor for the balance of the unexpired term.

(2) If there is a vacancy in the office of lieutenant governor and the governor is absent from this state, impeached, or from mental or physical disease becomes incapable of performing the duties of the office, the secretary of state shall serve as acting governor for the balance of the unexpired term or until the governor returns, the disability ceases or the impeachment is vacated. [*1977 SJR-51; 1979 SJR-1*]

Lieutenant governor president of senate; when secretary of state to be governor. Section 8. [*Original form*] The lieutenant governor shall be president of the senate, but shall have only a casting vote therein. If, during a vacancy in the office of the governor, the lieutenant governor shall be impeached, displaced, resign, die, or from mental or physical disease become incapable of performing the duties of his office, or be absent from the state, the secretary of state shall act as governor until the vacancy shall be filled or the disability shall cease.

Section 9. [*Repealed. 1929 SJR-82; 1931 SJR-7; vote November 1932*]

Compensation of lieutenant governor. Section 9. [*As amended November 1869*] The lieutenant governor shall receive during his continuance in office an annual compensation of one thousand dollars. [*1868 AJR-13; 1869 SJR-6; 1869 c. 186*]

Compensation of lieutenant governor. Section 9. [*Original form*] The lieutenant governor shall receive double the per diem allowance of members of the senate, for every day's attendance as president of the senate, and the same mileage as shall be allowed to members of the legislature.

Governor to approve or veto bills; proceedings on veto. Section 10. [*As amended April 1990; April 2008*] (1) (a) Every bill which shall have passed the legislature shall, before it becomes a law, be presented to the governor.

(b) If the governor approves and signs the bill, the bill shall become law. Appropriation bills may be approved in whole or in part by the governor, and the part approved shall become law.

(c) In approving an appropriation bill in part, the governor may not create a new word by rejecting individual letters in the words of the enrolled bill, and may not create a new sentence by combining parts of 2 or more sentences of the enrolled bill. [*2005 SJR-33; 2007 SJR-5*]

Governor to approve or veto bills; proceedings on veto. SECTION 10. [*As amended April 1990*] (c) In approving an appropriation bill in part, the governor may not create a new word by rejecting individual letters in the words of the enrolled bill.

(2) (a) If the governor rejects the bill, the governor shall return the bill, together with the objections in writing, to the house in which the bill originated. The house of origin shall enter the objections at large upon the journal and proceed to reconsider the bill. If, after such reconsideration, two-thirds of the members present agree to pass the bill notwithstanding the objections of the governor, it shall be sent, together with the objections, to the other house, by which it shall likewise be reconsidered, and if approved by two-thirds of the members present it shall become law.

(b) The rejected part of an appropriation bill, together with the governor's objections in writing, shall be returned to the house in which the bill originated. The house of origin shall enter the objections at large upon the journal and proceed to reconsider the rejected part of the appropriation bill. If, after such reconsideration, two-thirds of the members present agree to approve the rejected part notwithstanding the objections of the governor, it shall be sent, together with the objections, to the other house, by which it shall likewise be reconsidered, and if approved by two-thirds of the members present the rejected part shall become law.

(c) In all such cases the votes of both houses shall be determined by ayes and noes, and the names of the members voting for or against passage of the bill or the rejected part of the bill notwithstanding the objections of the governor shall be entered on the journal of each house respectively.

(3) Any bill not returned by the governor within 6 days (Sundays excepted) after it shall have been presented to the governor shall be law unless the legislature, by final adjournment, prevents the bill's return, in which case it shall not be law. [*1987 AJR-71; 1989 SJR-11*]

Governor to approve or veto bills; proceedings on veto. SECTION 10. [*As amended November 1930*] Every bill which shall have passed the legislature shall, before it becomes a law, be presented to the governor; if he approve, he shall sign it, but if not, he shall return it, with his objections, to that house in which it shall have originated, who shall enter the objections at large upon the journal and proceed to reconsider it. Appropriation bills may be approved in whole or in part by the governor, and the part approved shall become law, and the part objected to shall be returned in the same manner as provided for other bills. If, after such reconsideration, two-thirds of the members present shall agree to pass the bill, or the part of the bill objected to, it shall be sent, together with the objections, to the other house, by which it shall likewise be reconsidered, and if approved by two-thirds of the members present it shall become a law. But in all such cases the votes of both houses shall be determined by yeas and nays, and the names of the members voting for or against the bill or the part of the bill objected to, shall be entered on the journal of each house respectively. If any bill shall not be returned by the governor within six days (Sundays excepted) after it shall have been presented to him, the same shall be a law unless the legislature shall, by their adjournment, prevent its return, in which case it shall not be a law. [*1927 SJR-35; 1929 SJR-40*]

Approval of bills. SECTION 10. [*As amended November 1908*] Every bill which shall have passed the legislature shall, before it becomes a law, be presented to the governor; if he approve, he shall sign it, but if not, he shall return it, with his objections, to that house in which it shall have originated, who shall enter the objections at large upon the journal and proceed to reconsider it. If, after such reconsideration, two-thirds of the members present shall agree to pass the bill, it shall be sent, together with the objections to the other house, by which it shall likewise be reconsidered, and if approved by two-thirds of the members

present it shall become a law. But in all such cases the votes of both houses shall be determined by yeas and nays, and the names of the members voting for or against the bill shall be entered on the journal of each house respectively. If any bill shall not be returned by the governor within six days (Sundays excepted) after it shall have been presented to him, the same shall be a law unless the legislature shall, by their adjournment, prevent its return, in which case it shall not be a law. [*1905 AJR-45; 1907 AJR-46; 1907 c. 661*]

Approval of bills. SECTION 10. [*Original form*] Every bill which shall have passed the legislature shall, before it becomes a law, be presented to the governor; if he approve, he shall sign it, but if not, he shall return it, with his objections, to that house in which it shall have originated, who shall enter the objections at large upon the journal, and proceed to reconsider it. If, after such reconsideration two-thirds of the members present shall agree to pass the bill, it shall be sent, together with the objections, to the other house, by which it shall likewise be reconsidered, and if approved by two-thirds of the members present, it shall become a law. But in all such cases the votes of both houses shall be determined by yeas and nays, and the names of the members voting for or against the bill, shall be entered on the journal of each house respectively. If any bill shall not be returned by the governor within three days (Sundays excepted) after it shall have been presented to him, the same shall be a law, unless the legislature shall, by their adjournment, prevent its return, in which case it shall not be a law.

ARTICLE VI.
ADMINISTRATIVE

Election of secretary of state, treasurer and attorney general; term. SECTION 1. [*As amended April 1979*] The qualified electors of this state, at the times and places of choosing the members of the legislature, shall in 1970 and every 4 years thereafter elect a secretary of state, treasurer and attorney general who shall hold their offices for 4 years. [*1977 SJR-51; 1979 SJR-1*]

Election of secretary of state, treasurer and attorney-general; term. SECTION 1. [*Original form*] There shall be chosen by the qualified electors of the state, at the times and places of choosing the members of the legislature, a secretary of state, treasurer and attorney-general, who shall severally hold their offices for the term of two years.

SECTION 1m. [*Repealed. 1977 SJR-51; 1979 SJR-1; vote April 1979*]

Secretary of state; 4-year term. SECTION 1m. [*Created April 1967*] Notwithstanding section 1, beginning with the general election in 1970 and every four years thereafter, there shall be chosen a secretary of state to hold office for a term of four years. [*1965 AJR-4; 1967 AJR-9 and SJR-12*]

SECTION 1n. [*Repealed. 1977 SJR-51; 1979 SJR-1; vote April 1979*]

Treasurer; 4-year term. SECTION 1n. [*Created April 1967*] Notwithstanding section 1, beginning with the general election in 1970 and every four years thereafter, there shall be chosen a treasurer to hold office for a term of four years. [*1965 AJR-4; 1967 AJR-9 and SJR-12*]

SECTION 1p. [*Repealed. 1977 SJR-51; 1979 SJR-1; vote April 1979*]

Attorney general; 4-year term. SECTION 1p. [*Created April 1967*] Notwithstanding section 1, beginning with the general election in 1970 and every four years thereafter, there shall be chosen an attorney general to hold office for a term of four years. [*1965 AJR-4; 1967 AJR-9 and SJR-12*]

Secretary of state; duties, compensation. SECTION 2. [*As amended November 1946*] The secretary of state shall keep a fair record of the official acts of the legislature and executive department of the state, and shall, when required, lay the same and all matters relative thereto before either branch of the legislature. He shall perform such other duties as shall be assigned him by law. He shall receive as a compensation for his services yearly such sum as shall be provided by law, and shall keep his office at the seat of government. [*1943 SJR-35; 1945 SJR-24*]

Secretary of state. SECTION 2. [*Original form*] The secretary of state shall keep a fair record of the official acts of the legislature and executive department of the state, and shall, when required, lay the same and all matters relative thereto, before either branch of the legislature. He shall be ex officio auditor, and shall perform such other duties as shall be assigned him by law. He shall receive as a compensation for his services yearly, such sum as shall be provided by law, and shall keep his office at the seat of government.

Treasurer and attorney general; duties, compensation. SECTION 3. The powers, duties and compensation of the treasurer and attorney general shall be prescribed by law.

County officers; election, terms, removal; vacancies. SECTION 4. [*As amended April 2005*] (1) (a) Except as provided in pars. (b) and (c) and sub. (2), coroners, registers of deeds, district attorneys, and all other elected county officers, except judicial officers, sheriffs, and chief executive officers, shall be chosen by the electors of the respective counties once in every 2 years.

(b) Beginning with the first general election at which the governor is elected which occurs after the ratification of this paragraph, sheriffs shall be chosen by the electors of the respective counties, or by the electors of all of the respective counties comprising each combination of counties combined by the legislature for that purpose, for the term of 4 years and coroners in counties in which there is a coroner shall be chosen by the electors of the respective counties, or by the electors of all of the respective counties comprising each combination of counties combined by the legislature for that purpose, for the term of 4 years.

(c) Beginning with the first general election at which the president is elected which occurs after the ratification of this paragraph, district attorneys, registers of deeds, county clerks, and treasurers shall be chosen by the electors of the respective counties, or by the electors of all of the respective counties comprising each combination of counties combined by the legislature for that purpose, for the term of 4 years and surveyors in counties in which the office of surveyor is filled by election shall be chosen by the electors of the respective counties, or by the electors of all of the respective counties comprising each combination of counties combined by the legislature for that purpose, for the term of 4 years.

(2) The offices of coroner and surveyor in counties having a population of 500,000 or more

are abolished. Counties not having a population of 500,000 shall have the option of retaining the elective office of coroner or instituting a medical examiner system. Two or more counties may institute a joint medical examiner system.

(3) (a) Sheriffs may not hold any other partisan office.

(b) Sheriffs may be required by law to renew their security from time to time, and in default of giving such new security their office shall be deemed vacant.

(4) The governor may remove any elected county officer mentioned in this section except a county clerk, treasurer, or surveyor, giving to the officer a copy of the charges and an opportunity of being heard.

(5) All vacancies in the offices of coroner, register of deeds or district attorney shall be filled by appointment. The person appointed to fill a vacancy shall hold office only for the unexpired portion of the term to which appointed and until a successor shall be elected and qualified.

(6) When a vacancy occurs in the office of sheriff, the vacancy shall be filled by appointment of the governor, and the person appointed shall serve until his or her successor is elected and qualified. [*2003 AJR-10; 2005 SJR-2*]

County officers; election, terms, removal; vacancies. SECTION 4. [*As amended November 1998*] (1) Except as provided in sub. (2), coroners, registers of deeds, district attorneys, and all other elected county officers except judicial officers, sheriffs and chief executive officers, shall be chosen by the electors of the respective counties once in every 2 years.

(2) The offices of coroner and surveyor in counties having a population of 500,000 or more are abolished. Counties not having a population of 500,000 shall have the option of retaining the elective office of coroner or instituting a medical examiner system. Two or more counties may institute a joint medical examiner system.

(3) (a) Sheriffs may not hold any other partisan office.

(b) Sheriffs may be required by law to renew their security from time to time, and in default of giving such new security their office shall be deemed vacant.

(c) Beginning with the first general election at which the governor is elected which occurs after the ratification of this paragraph, sheriffs shall be chosen by the electors of the respective counties once in every 4 years.

(4) The governor may remove any elected county officer mentioned in this section, giving to the officer a copy of the charges and an opportunity of being heard.

(5) All vacancies in the offices of coroner, register of deeds or district attorney shall be filled by appointment. The person appointed to fill a vacancy shall hold office only for the unexpired portion of the term to which appointed and until a successor shall be elected and qualified.

(6) When a vacancy occurs in the office of sheriff, the vacancy shall be filled by appointment of the governor, and the person appointed shall serve until his or her successor is elected and qualified. [*1995 AJR-37; 1997 SJR-43*]

County officers; election, terms, removal; vacancies. SECTION 4. [*As amended April 1982*] (1) Sheriffs, coroners, registers of deeds, district attorneys, and all other elected county officers except judicial officers and chief executive officers, shall be chosen by the electors of the respective counties once in every 2 years.

(2) The offices of coroner and surveyor in counties having a population of 500,000 or more are abolished. Counties not having a population of 500,000 shall have the option of retaining the elective office of coroner or instituting a medical examiner system. Two or more counties may institute a joint medical examiner system.

(3) Sheriffs shall hold no other office. Sheriffs may be required by law to renew their security from time to time, and in default of giving such new security their office shall be deemed vacant.

(4) The governor may remove any elected county officer mentioned in this section, giving to the officer a copy of the charges and an opportunity of being heard.

(5) All vacancies in the offices of sheriff, coroner,

register of deeds or district attorney shall be filled by appointment. The person appointed to fill a vacancy shall hold office only for the unexpired portion of the term to which appointed and until a successor shall be elected and qualified. [*1979 AJR-99; 1981 AJR-7*]

County officers; election, terms, removal; vacancies. SECTION 4. [*As amended April 1972*] Sheriffs, coroners, register of deeds, district attorneys, and all other county officers except judicial officers and chief executive officers, shall be chosen by the electors of the respective counties once in every two years. The offices of coroner and surveyor in counties having a population of 500,000 or more are abolished. Counties not having a population of 500,000 shall have the option of retaining the elective office of coroner or instituting a medical examiner system. Two or more counties may institute a joint medical examiner system. Sheriffs shall hold no other office; they may be required by law to renew their security from time to time, and in default of giving such new security their office shall be deemed vacant, but the county shall never be made responsible for the acts of the sheriff. The governor may remove any officer in this section mentioned, giving to such a copy of the charges against him and an opportunity of being heard in his defense. All vacancies shall be filled by appointment, and the person appointed to fill a vacancy shall hold only for the unexpired portion of the term to which he shall be appointed and until his successor shall be elected and qualified. [*1969 SJR-63; 1971 SJR-38*]

County officers; election, terms, removal; vacancies. SECTION 4. [*As amended April 1967*] Sheriffs, coroners, registers of deeds, district attorneys, and all other county officers except judicial officers and chief executive officers, shall be chosen by the electors of the respective counties once in every two years. The offices of coroner and surveyor in counties having a population of 500,000 or more are abolished at the conclusion of the terms of office during which this amendment is adopted. Sheriffs shall hold no other office; they may be required by law to renew their security from time to time, and in default of giving such new security their office shall be deemed vacant, but the county shall never be made responsible for the acts of the sheriff. The governor may remove any officer in this section mentioned, giving to such a copy of the charges against him and an opportunity of being heard in his defense. All vacancies shall be filled by appointment, and the person appointed to fill a vacancy shall hold only for the unexpired portion of the term to which he shall be appointed and until his successor shall be elected and qualified. [*1965 AJR-72; 1967 SJR-7*]

County officers; election, terms, removal; vacancies. SECTION 4. [*As amended April 1965*] Sheriffs, coroners, register of deeds, district attorneys, and all other county officers except judicial officers and chief executive officers, shall be chosen by the electors of the respective counties once in every two years. The offices of coroner and surveyor in counties having a population of 500,000 or more are abolished at the conclusion of the terms of office during which this amendment is adopted. Sheriffs shallhold no other office, and shall not serve more than two terms or parts thereof in succession; they may be required by law to renew their security from time to time, and in default of giving such new security their office shall be deemed vacant, but the county shall never be made responsible for the acts of the sheriff. The governor may remove any officer in this section mentioned, giving to such a copy of the charges against him and an opportunity of being heard in his defense. All vacancies shall be filled by appointment, and the person appointed to fill a vacancy shall hold only for the unexpired portion of the term to which he shall be appointed and until his successor shall be elected and qualified. [*1963 AJR-14; 1965 SJR-17*]

County officers; election, terms, removal; vacancies. SECTION 4. [*As amended November 1962*] Sheriffs, coroners, registers of deeds, district attorneys, and all other county officers except judicial officers and chief executive officers, shall be chosen by the electors of the respective counties once in every two years. Sheriffs shall hold no other office, and shall not serve more than two terms or parts thereof in succession; they may be required by law to renew their security from time to time, and in default of giving such new security their office shall be deemed vacant, but the county shall never be made responsible for the acts of the sheriff. The governor may remove any officer in this section mentioned, giving to such a copy of the charges against him and an opportunity of being heard in his defense. All vacancies shall be filled by appointment, and the person appointed to fill a vacancy shall hold only for the unexpired portion of the term to which he shall be appointed and until his successor shall be elected and qualified. [*1959 AJR-121; 1961 AJR-61*]

County officers; election, terms, removal; vacancies. SECTION 4. [*As amended April 1929*] Sheriffs, coroners, registers of deeds, district attorneys, and all other county officers except judicial officers, shall be chosen by the electors of the respective counties once in every two years. Sheriffs shall hold no other office, and shall not serve more than two terms or parts thereof in succession; they may be required by law to renew their security from time to time,

and in default of giving such new security their office shall be deemed vacant, but the county shall never be made responsible for the acts of the sheriff. The governor may remove any officer in this section mentioned, giving to such a copy of the charges against him and an opportunity of being heard in his defense. All vacancies shall be filled by appointment, and the person appointed to fill a vacancy shall hold only for the unexpired portion of the term to which he shall be appointed and until his successor shall be elected and qualified. [*1927 AJR-8; 1929 AJR-8*]

County officers. SECTION 4. [*As amended November 1882*] Sheriffs, coroners, registers of deeds, district attorneys, and all other county officers, except judicial officers shall be chosen by the electors of the respective counties, once in every two years. Sheriffs shall hold no other office and be ineligible for two years next succeeding the termination of their offices; they may be required by law to renew their security from time to time, and in default of giving such new security their office shall be deemed vacant, but the county shall never be made responsible for the acts of the sheriff. The governor may remove any officer in this section mentioned, giving to such a copy of the charges against him and an opportunity of being heard in his defense. All vacancies shall be filled by appointment and the person appointed to fill a vacancy shall hold only for the unexpired portion of the term to which he shall be appointed, and until his successor shall be elected and qualified. [*1881 AJR-16; 1882 SJR-20; 1882 c. 290*]

County officers. SECTION 4. [*Original form*] Sheriffs, coroners, registers of deeds and district attorneys shall be chosen by the electors of the respective counties, once in every two years, and as often as vacancies shall happen; sheriffs shall hold no other office, and be ineligible for two years next succeeding the termination of their offices. They may be required by law, to renew their security from time to time; and in default of giving such new security, their offices shall be deemed vacant. But the county shall never be made responsible for the acts of the sheriff. The governor may remove any officer in this section mentioned, giving to such officer a copy of the charges against him, and an opportunity of being heard in his defence.

ARTICLE VII.
JUDICIARY

Impeachment; trial. SECTION 1. [*As amended November 1932*] The court for the trial of impeachments shall be composed of the senate. The assembly shall have the power of impeaching all civil officers of this state for corrupt conduct in office, or for crimes and misdemeanors; but a majority of all the members elected shall concur in an impeachment. On the trial of an impeachment against the governor, the lieutenant governor shall not act as a member of the court. No judicial officer shall exercise his office, after he shall have been impeached, until his acquittal. Before the trial of an impeachment the members of the court shall take an oath or affirmation truly and impartially to try the impeachment according to evidence; and no person shall be convicted without the concurrence of two-thirds of the members present. Judgment in cases of impeachment shall not extend further than to removal from office, or removal from office and disqualification to hold any office of honor, profit or trust under the state; but the party impeached shall be liable to indictment, trial and punishment according to law. [*1929 SJR-103; 1931 SJR-8*]

Impeachments. SECTION 1. [*Original form*] The court for the trial of impeachments shall be composed of the senate. The house of representatives shall have the power of impeaching all civil officers of this state, for corrupt conduct in office, or for crimes and misdemeanors; but a majority of all the members elected shall concur in an impeachment. On the trial of an impeachment against the governor, the lieutenant governor shall not act as a member of the court. No judicial officer shall exercise his office, after he shall have been impeached, until his

acquittal. Before the trial of an impeachment, the members of the court shall take an oath or affirmation, truly and impartially to try the impeachment according to evidence; and no person shall be convicted without the concurrence of two-thirds of the members present. Judgment in cases of impeachment shall not extend further than to removal from office, or removal from office and disqualification to hold any office of honor, profit or trust under the state; but the party impeached shall be liable to indictment, trial and punishment according to law.

Court system. SECTION 2. [*As amended April 1977*] The judicial power of this state shall be vested in a unified court system consisting of one supreme court, a court of appeals, a circuit court, such trial courts of general uniform statewide jurisdiction as the legislature may create by law, and a municipal court if authorized by the legislature under section 14. [*1975 AJR-11; 1977 SJR-9*]

Judicial power, where vested. SECTION 2. [*As amended April 1966*] The judicial power of this state, both as to matters of law and equity, shall be vested in a supreme court, circuit courts, and courts of probate. The legislature may also vest such jurisdiction as shall be deemed necessary in municipal courts, and may authorize the establishment of inferior courts in the several counties, cities, villages or towns, with limited civil and criminal jurisdiction. Provided, that the jurisdiction which may be vested in municipal courts shall not exceed in their respective municipalities that of circuit courts in their respective circuits as prescribed in this constitution; and that the legislature shall provide as well for the election of judges of the municipal courts as of the judges of inferior courts, by the qualified electors of the respective jurisdictions. The term of office of the judges of the said municipal and inferior courts shall not be longer than that of the judges of the circuit courts. [*1963 SJR-32; 1965 SJR-26*]

Judicial power, where vested. SECTION 2. [*Original form*] The judicial power of this state, both as to matters of law and equity, shall be vested in a supreme court, circuit courts, courts of probate, and in justices of the peace. The legislature may also vest such jurisdiction as shall be deemed necessary in municipal courts, and shall have power to establish inferior courts in the several counties, with limited civil and criminal jurisdiction. Provided, that the jurisdiction which may be vested in municipal courts shall not exceed in their respective municipalities that of circuit courts in their respective circuits as prescribed in this constitution; and that the legislature shall provide as well for the election of judges of the municipal courts as of the judges of inferior courts, by the qualified electors of the respective jurisdictions. The term of office of the judges of the said municipal and inferior courts shall not be longer than that of the judges of the circuit courts.

Supreme court: jurisdiction. SECTION 3. [*As amended April 1977*] (1) The supreme court shall have superintending and administrative authority over all courts.

(2) The supreme court has appellate jurisdiction over all courts and may hear original actions and proceedings. The supreme court may issue all writs necessary in aid of its jurisdiction.

(3) The supreme court may review judgments and orders of the court of appeals, may remove cases from the court of appeals and may accept cases on certification by the court of appeals. [*1975 AJR 11; 1977 SJR-9*]

Supreme court, jurisdiction. SECTION 3. [*Original form*] The supreme court, except in cases otherwise provided in this constitution, shall have appellate jurisdiction only, which shall be coextensive with the state; but in no case removed to the supreme court shall a trial by jury be allowed. The supreme court shall have a general superintending control over all inferior courts; it shall have power to issue writs of habeas corpus, mandamus, injunction, quo warranto, certiorari, and other original and remedial writs, and to hear and determine the same.

Supreme court: election, chief justice, court system administration. SECTION 4. [*As amended April 1977*] (1) The supreme court shall have 7 members who shall be known as justices of the supreme court. Justices shall be elected for 10-year terms of office commencing with the August 1 next succeeding the election. Only one justice may be elected in any year. Any 4 justices shall constitute a quorum for the conduct of the court's business.

(2) The justice having been longest a continuous member of said court, or in case 2 or more such justices shall have served for the same length of time, the justice whose term first expires, shall be the chief justice. The justice so designated as chief justice may, irrevocably, decline to serve as chief justice or resign as chief justice but continue to serve as a justice of the supreme court.

(3) The chief justice of the supreme court shall be the administrative head of the judicial system and shall exercise this administrative authority pursuant to procedures adopted by the supreme court. The chief justice may assign any judge of a court of record to aid in the proper disposition of judicial business in any court of record except the supreme court. [*1975 AJR-11; 1977 SJR-9*]

Supreme court justices; term; election; quorum. SECTION 1 [4]. [*As amended April 1903*] The chief justice and associate justices of the supreme court shall be severally known as the justices of said court, with the same terms of office of ten years respectively as now provided. The supreme court shall consist of seven justices, any four of whom shall be a quorum, to be elected as now provided, not more than one each year. The justice having been longest a continuous member of said court, or in case two or more such senior justices shall have served for the same length of time, then the one whose commission first expires shall be ex officio, the chief justice. [*1901 AJR-33; 1903 AJR-5; 1903 c. 10*]

Supreme court, how constituted. SECTION 1 [4]. [*As amended April 1889*] The chief justice and associate justices of the supreme court shall be severally known as justices of said court with the same terms of office, respectively, as now provided. The supreme court shall consist of five justices (any three of whom shall be a quorum), to be elected as now provided. The justice having been longest a continuous member of the court (or in case two or more of such senior justices having served for the same length of time, then the one whose commission first expires), shall be ex officio the chief justice. [*1887 SJR-19; 1889 AJR-7; 1889 c. 22*]

Supreme court, how constituted. SECTION 4. [*As amended November 1877*] The supreme court shall consist of one chief justice and four associate justices, to be elected by the qualified electors of the state. The legislature shall at its first session after the adoption of this amendment provide by law for the election of two associate justices of said court to hold their offices respectively for terms ending two and four years respectively after the end of the term of the justice of the said court, then last to expire. And thereafter the chief justice and associate justices of the said court shall be elected and hold their offices respectively for the term of ten years. [*1876 SJR-16; 1877 SJR-2; 1877 c. 48*]

Supreme court, how constituted. SECTION 4. [*Original form*] For the term of five years, and thereafter until the legislature shall otherwise provide, the judges of the several circuit courts, shall be judges of the supreme court, four of whom shall constitute a quorum, and the concurrence of a majority of the judges present shall be necessary to a decision. The legislature shall have power, if they should think it expedient and necessary to provide by law, for the organization of a separate supreme court, with the jurisdiction and powers prescribed in this constitution, to consist of one chief justice, and two associate justices, to be elected by the qualified electors of the state, at such time and in such manner as the legislature may provide.

The separate supreme court when so organized, shall not be changed or discontinued by the legislature; the judges thereof shall be so classified that but one of them shall go out of office at the same time; and their term of office shall be the same as is provided for the judges of the circuit court. And whenever the legislature may consider it necessary to establish a separate supreme court, they shall have power to reduce the number of circuit court judges to four, and subdivide the judicial circuits, but no such subdivision or reduction shall take effect until after the expiration of the term of some one of said judges, or till a vacancy occur by some other means.

SECTION 5. [*Repealed. 1975 AJR-11; 1977 SJR-9; vote April 1977*]

Judicial circuits. SECTION 5. [*Original form*] The state shall be divided into five judicial circuits, to be composed as follows: The first circuit shall comprise the counties of Racine, Walworth, Rock and Green; the second circuit, the counties of Milwaukee, Waukesha, Jefferson and Dane; the third circuit, the counties of Washington, Dodge, Columbia, Marquette, Sauk and Portage; the fourth circuit, the counties of Brown, Manitowoc, Sheboygan, Fond

du Lac, Winnebago and Calumet; and the fifth circuit shall comprise the counties of Iowa, LaFayette, Grant, Crawford and St. Croix; and the county of Richland shall be attached to Iowa, the county of Chippewa to the county of Crawford, and the county of La Pointe to the county of St. Croix, for judicial purposes, until otherwise provided by the legislature.

Court of appeals. SECTION 5. [*Created April 1977*] (1) The legislature shall by law combine the judicial circuits of the state into one or more districts for the court of appeals and shall designate in each district the locations where the appeals court shall sit for the convenience of litigants.

(2) For each district of the appeals court there shall be chosen by the qualified electors of the district one or more appeals judges as prescribed by law, who shall sit as prescribed by law. Appeals judges shall be elected for 6-year terms and shall reside in the district from which elected. No alteration of district or circuit boundaries shall have the effect of removing an appeals judge from office during the judge's term. In case of an increase in the number of appeals judges, the first judge or judges shall be elected for full terms unless the legislature prescribes a shorter initial term for staggering of terms.

(3) The appeals court shall have such appellate jurisdiction in the district, including jurisdiction to review administrative proceedings, as the legislature may provide by law, but shall have no original jurisdiction other than by prerogative writ. The appeals court may issue all writs necessary in aid of its jurisdiction and shall have supervisory authority over all actions and proceedings in the courts in the district. [*1975 AJR-11; 1977 SJR-9*]

Circuit court: boundaries. SECTION 6. [*As amended April 1977*] The legislature shall prescribe by law the number of judicial circuits, making them as compact and convenient as practicable, and bounding them by county lines. No alteration of circuit boundaries shall have the effect of removing a circuit judge from office during the judge's term. In case of an increase of circuits, the first judge or judges shall be elected. [*1975 AJR-11; 1977 SJR-9*]

Alteration of circuits. SECTION 6. [*Original form*] The legislature may alter the limits or increase the number of circuits, making them as compact and convenient as practicable, and bounding them by county lines; but no such alteration or increase shall have the effect to remove

a judge from office. In case of an increase of circuits, the judge or judges shall be elected as provided in this constitution and receive a salary of not less than that herein provided for judges of the circuit court.

Circuit court: election. SECTION 7. [*As amended April 1977*] For each circuit there shall be chosen by the qualified electors thereof one or more circuit judges as prescribed by law. Circuit judges shall be elected for 6-year terms and shall reside in the circuit from which elected. [*1975 AJR-11; 1977 SJR-9*]

Circuit judges; election, eligibility, term, salary. SECTION 7. [*As amended November 1924*] For each circuit there shall be chosen by the qualified electors thereof one circuit judge, except that in any circuit in which there is a county that had a population in excess of eighty-five thousand, according to the last state or United States census, the legislature may, from time to time, authorize additional circuit judges to be chosen. Every circuit judge shall reside in the circuit from which he is elected, and shall hold his office for such term and receive such compensation as the legislature shall prescribe. [*1921 SJR-24; 1923 SJR-27; 1923 c. 408*]

Circuit judges, election. SECTION 7. [*As amended April 1897*] For each circuit there shall be chosen by the qualified

electors thereof, one circuit judge, except that in any circuit composed of one county only, which county shall contain a population, according to the last state or United States census, of one hundred thousand inhabitants or over, the legislature may from time to time authorize additional circuit judges to be chosen. Every circuit judge shall reside in the circuit from which he is elected and shall hold his office for such term and receive such compensation as the legislature shall prescribe. [*1895 SJR-9; 1897 SJR-10; 1897 c. 69*]

Circuit judges, election. SECTION 7. [*Original form*] For each circuit there shall be a judge chosen by the qualified electors therein, who shall hold his office as is provided in this constitution, and until his successor shall be chosen and qualified; and after he shall have been elected, he shall reside in the circuit for which he was elected. One of said judges shall be designated as chief justice in such manner as the legislature shall provide. And the legislature shall at its first session provide by law as well for the election of, as for classifying the judges of the circuit court to be

elected under this constitution, in such manner that one of said judges shall go out of office in two years, one in three years, one in four years, one in five years and one in six years, and thereafter the judge elected to fill the office shall hold the same for six years.

Circuit court: jurisdiction. SECTION 8. [*As amended April 1977*] Except as otherwise provided by law, the circuit court shall have original jurisdiction in all matters civil and criminal within this state and such appellate jurisdiction in the circuit as the legislature may prescribe by law. The circuit court may issue all writs necessary in aid of its jurisdiction. [*1975 AJR-11; 1977 SJR-9*]

Circuit court, jurisdiction. SECTION 8. [*Original form*] The circuit courts shall have original jurisdiction in all matters civil and criminal within this state, not excepted in this constitution, and not hereafter prohibited by law; and appellate jurisdiction from all inferior courts and tribunals, and a supervisory control over the same. They shall also

have the power to issue writs of habeas corpus, mandamus, injunction, quo warranto, certiorari, and all other writs necessary to carry into effect their orders, judgments and decrees, and give them a general control over inferior courts and jurisdictions.

Judicial elections, vacancies. SECTION 9. [*As amended April 1977*] When a vacancy occurs in the office of justice of the supreme court or judge of any court of record, the vacancy shall be filled by appointment by the governor, which shall continue until a successor is elected and qualified. There shall be no election for a justice or judge at the partisan general election for state or county officers, nor within 30 days either before or after such election. [*1975 AJR-11; 1977 SJR-9*]

Vacancies; judicial elections. SECTION 9. [*As amended April 1953*] When a vacancy shall happen in the office of judge of the supreme or circuit courts, such vacancy shall be filled by an appointment of the governor, which shall continue until a successor is elected and qualified, and a supreme court justice when so elected shall hold his office for a term of 10 years and a circuit judge when so elected shall hold his office for such term as the legislature prescribes for circuit judges elected under section seven of this article. There shall be no election for a judge or judges at any general election for state or county officers, nor

within 30 days either before or after such election. [*1951 SJR-3; 1953 SJR-5*]

Vacancies; judicial elections. SECTION 9. [*Original form*] When a vacancy shall happen in the office of judge of the supreme or circuit courts, such vacancy shall be filled by an appointment of the governor, which shall continue until a successor is elected and qualified; and when elected such successor shall hold his office the residue of the unexpired term. There shall be no election for a judge or judges at any general election for state or county officers, nor within thirty days either before or after such election.

Judges: eligibility to office. SECTION 10. [*As amended April 1977*] (1) No justice of the supreme court or judge of any court of record shall hold any other office of public trust, except a judicial office, during the term for which elected. No person shall be eligible to the office of judge who shall not, at the time of election or appointment, be a qualified elector within the jurisdiction for which chosen.

(2) Justices of the supreme court and judges of the courts of record shall receive such compensation as the legislature may authorize by law, but may not receive fees of office. [*1975 AJR-11; 1977 SJR-9*]

Compensation and qualifications of judges. SECTION 10. [*As amended November 1912*] Each of the judges of the supreme and circuit courts shall receive a salary, payable at such time as the legislature shall fix, of not less than one thousand five hundred dollars annually; they shall receive no fees of office, or other compensation than their salary; they shall hold no office of public trust, except a judicial office, during the term for which they are respectively elected, and all votes for either of them for any office, except a judicial office, given by the legislature or the people, shall be void. No person shall be eligible to the office of judge who shall not, at the time of his election, be a citizen of the United States and have attained the age of twenty-five years, and be a qualified elector within the jurisdiction for which he may be chosen. [*1909 AJR-36;*

1911 AJR-26; 1911 c. 665]

Compensation and qualifications of judges. SECTION 10. [*Original form*] Each of the judges of the supreme and circuit courts shall receive a salary, payable quarterly, of not less than one thousand five hundred dollars annually; they shall receive no fees of office, or other compensation than their salaries; they shall hold no office of public trust, except a judicial office, during the term for which they are respectively elected, and all votes for either of them for any office, except a judicial office, given by the legislature or the people, shall be void. No person shall be eligible to the office of judge, who shall not, at the time of his election, be a citizen of the United States, and have attained the age of twenty-five years, and be a qualified elector within the jurisdiction for which he may be chosen.

SECTION 11. [*Repealed. 1975 AJR-11; 1977 SJR-9; vote April 1977*]

Terms of courts; change of judges. SECTION 11. [*Original form*] The supreme court shall hold at least one term annually, at the seat of government of the state, at such time as shall be provided by law. And the legislature may provide for holding other terms and at other places when

they may deem it necessary. A circuit court shall be held at least twice in each year in each county of this state rganized for judicial purposes. The judges of the circuit court may hold courts for each other, and shall do so when required by law.

Disciplinary proceedings. SECTION 11. [*Created April 1977*] Each justice or judge shall be subject to reprimand, censure, suspension, removal for cause or for disability, by the supreme court pursuant to procedures established by the legislature by law. No justice or judge removed

for cause shall be eligible for reappointment or temporary service. This section is alternative to, and cumulative with, the methods of removal provided in sections 1 and 13 of this article and section 12 of article XIII. [*1975 AJR-11; 1977 SJR-9*]

Clerks of circuit and supreme courts. SECTION 12. [*As amended April 2005*] (1) There shall be a clerk of circuit court chosen in each county organized for judicial purposes by the qualified electors thereof, who, except as provided in sub. (2), shall hold office for two years, subject to removal as provided by law.

(2) Beginning with the first general election at which the governor is elected which occurs after the ratification of this subsection, a clerk of circuit court shall be chosen by the electors of each county, for the term of 4 years, subject to removal as provided by law.

(3) In case of a vacancy, the judge of the circuit court may appoint a clerk until the vacancy is filled by an election.

(4) The clerk of circuit court shall give such security as the legislature requires by law.

(5) The supreme court shall appoint its own clerk, and may appoint a clerk of circuit court to be the clerk of the supreme court. [*2003 AJR-10; 2005 SJR-2*]

Clerks of circuit and supreme courts. SECTION 12. [*As amended November 1882*] There shall be a clerk of the circuit court chosen in each county organized for judicial purposes by the qualified electors thereof, who shall hold his office for two years, subject to removal as shall be provided by law; in case of a vacancy, the judge of the circuit court shall have power to appoint a clerk until the vacancy shall be filled by an election; the clerk thus elected or appointed shall give such security as the legislature may require. The supreme court shall appoint its own clerk, and a clerk of the circuit court may be appointed a clerk of the supreme court. [*1881 AJR-16; 1882 SJR-20; 1882 c. 290*]

Clerks of courts. SECTION 12. [*Original form*] There shall be a clerk of the circuit court chosen in each county organized for judicial purposes, by the qualified electors thereof, who shall hold his office for two years, subject to removal, as shall be provided by law. In case of a vacancy, the judge of the circuit court shall have the power to appoint a clerk until the vacancy shall be filled by an election. The clerk thus elected or appointed shall give such security as the legislature may require; and when elected shall hold his office for a full term. The supreme court shall appoint its own clerk, and the clerk of a circuit court may be appointed clerk of the supreme court.

Justices and judges: removal by address. SECTION 13. [*As amended April 1977*] Any justice or judge may be removed from office by address of both houses of the legislature, if two-thirds of all the members elected to each house concur therein, but no removal shall be made by virtue of this section unless the justice or judge complained of is served with a copy of the charges, as the ground of address, and has had an opportunity of being heard. On the question of removal, the ayes and noes shall be entered on the journals. [*1975 AJR-11; 1977 SJR-9*]

Removal of judges. SECTION 13. [*As amended April 1974*] Any judge of the supreme, circuit, county or municipal court may be removed from office by address of both houses of the legislature, if two-thirds of all the members elected to each house concur therein, but no removal shall be made by virtue of this section unless the judge complained of shall have been served with a copy of the charges against him, as the ground of address, and shall have had an opportunity of being heard in his defense. On the question of removal, the ayes and noes shall be entered on the journals. [*1971 AJR-31; 1973 AJR-55*]

Removal of judges. SECTION 13. [*Original form*] Any judge of the supreme or circuit court may be removed from office by address of both houses of the legislature, if two-thirds of all the members elected to each house concur therein, but no removal shall be made by virtue of this section unless the judge complained of shall have been served with a copy of the charges against him, as the ground of address, and shall have had an opportunity of being heard in his defense. On the question of removal, the ayes and noes shall be entered on the journals.

Municipal court. SECTION 14. [*As amended April 1977*] The legislature by law may authorize each city, village and town to establish a municipal court. All municipal courts shall have uniform jurisdiction limited to actions and proceedings arising under ordinances of the municipality in which established. Judges of municipal courts may receive such compensation as provided by the municipality in which established, but may not receive fees of office. [*1975 AJR-11; 1977 SJR-9*]

Judges of probate. SECTION 14. [*Original form*] There shall be chosen in each county, by the qualified electors thereof, a judge of probate, who shall hold his office for two years and until his successor shall be elected and qualified, and whose jurisdiction, powers and duties

shall be prescribed by law. Provided, however, that the legislature shall have power to abolish the office of judge of probate in any county, and to confer probate powers upon such inferior courts as may be established in said county.

SECTION 15. [*Repealed. 1963 SJR-32; 1965 SJR-26; vote April 1966*]

Justices of the peace. SECTION 15. [*As amended April 1945*] The electors of the several towns at their annual town meeting, and the electors of cities and villages at their charter elections except in cities of the first class, shall, in such manner as the legislature may direct, elect justices of the peace, whose office shall be for 2 years and until their successors in office shall be elected and qualified. In case of an election to fill a vacancy occurring before the expiration of a full term, the justice elected shall hold

for the residue of the unexpired term. Their number and classification shall be regulated by law. And the tenure of 2 years shall in no wise interfere with the classification in the first instance. The justices thus elected shall have such civil and criminal jurisdiction as shall be prescribed by law. [*1943 SJR-9; 1945 SJR-6*]

Justices of the peace. SECTION 15. [*Original form*] The electors of the several towns, at their annual town meeting, and the electors of cities and villages, at their charter elections, shall in such manner as the legislature may direct, elect justices of the peace, whose term of office shall be for two years, and until their successors in office shall be elected and qualified. In case of an election to fill a vacancy, occurring before the expiration of a full term, the justice elected shall hold for the residue of the unexpired term. Their number and classification shall be regulated by law. And the tenure of two years shall in no wise interfere with the classification in the first instance. The justices, thus elected, shall have such civil and criminal jurisdiction as shall be prescribed by law.

SECTION 16. *[Repealed. 1975 AJR-11; 1977 SJR-9; vote April 1977]*

Tribunals of conciliation. SECTION 16. *[Original form]* The legislature shall pass laws for the regulation of tribunals of conciliation, defining their powers and duties. Such tribunals may be established in and for any township, and shall have power to render judgment to be obligatory on the parties when they shall voluntarily submit their matter in difference to arbitration, and agree to abide the judgment or assent thereto in writing.

SECTION 17. *[Repealed. 1975 AJR-11; 1977 SJR-9; vote April 1977]*

Style of writs; indictments. SECTION 17. *[Original form]* The style of all writs and process shall be, "The state of Wisconsin;" all criminal prosecutions shall be carried on in the name and by the authority of the same, and all indictments shall conclude against the peace and dignity of the state.

SECTION 18. *[Repealed. 1975 AJR-11; 1977 SJR-9; vote April 1977]*

Suit tax. SECTION 18. *[Original form]* The legislature shall impose a tax on all civil suits commenced or prosecuted in the municipal, inferior or circuit courts, which shall constitute a fund to be applied toward the payment of the salary of judges.

SECTION 19. *[Repealed. 1975 AJR-11; 1977 SJR-9; vote April 1977]*

Testimony in equity suits; master in chancery. SECTION 19. *[Original form]* The testimony in causes in equity shall be taken in like manner as in cases at law, and the office of master in chancery is hereby prohibited.

SECTION 20. *[Repealed. 1975 AJR-11; 1977 SJR-9; vote April 1977]* See Art. 1, sec. 21.

Rights of suitors. SECTION 20. *[Original form]* Any suitor, in any court of this state, shall have the right to prosecute or defend his suit either in his own proper person, or by an attorney or agent of his choice.

SECTION 21. *[Repealed. 1975 AJR-11; 1977 SJR-9; vote April 1977]* See Art. IV, sec. 17.

Publication of laws and decisions. SECTION 21. *[Original form]* The legislature shall provide by law for the speedy publication of all statute laws, and of such judicial decisions, made within the state, as may be deemed expedient. And no general law shall be in force until published.

SECTION 22. *[Repealed. 1975 AJR-11; 1977 SJR-9; vote April 1977]*

Commissioners to revise code of practice. SECTION 22. *[Original form]* The legislature, at its first session after the adoption of this constitution, shall provide for the appointment of three commissioners, whose duty it shall be to inquire into, revise and simplify the rules of practice, pleadings, forms and proceedings, and arrange a system adapted to the courts of record of this state, and report the same to the legislature, subject to their modification and adoption; and such commission shall terminate upon the rendering of the report, unless otherwise provided by law.

SECTION 23. *[Repealed. 1975 AJR-11; 1977 SJR-9; vote April 1977]*

Court commissioners. SECTION 23. *[Original form]* The legislature may provide for the appointment of one or more persons in each organized county, and may vest in such persons such judicial powers as shall be prescribed by law. Provided, that said power shall not exceed that of a judge of a circuit court at chambers.

Justices and judges: eligibility for office; retirement. SECTION 24. *[As amended April 1977]* (1) To be eligible for the office of supreme court justice or judge of any court of record, a person must be an attorney licensed to practice law in this state and have been so licensed for 5 years immediately prior to election or appointment.

(2) Unless assigned temporary service under subsection (3), no person may serve as a supreme court justice or judge of a court of record beyond the July 31 following the date on which such person attains that age, of not less than 70 years, which the legislature shall prescribe by law.

(3) A person who has served as a supreme court justice or judge of a court of record may, as provided by law, serve as a judge of any court of record except the supreme court on a temporary basis if assigned by the chief justice of the supreme court. *[1975 AJR-11; 1977 SJR-9]*

Retirement and eligibility for office of justices and circuit judges. SECTION 24. *[As amended April 1968]* No person seventy years of age or over may take office as a supreme court justice or circuit judge. No person may take or hold such office unless he is licensed to practice law in this state and has been so licensed for five years immediately prior to his election or appointment. No supreme court justice or circuit judge may serve beyond the July 31 following the date on which he attains the age of seventy. A person who has served eight or more years as a supreme court justice or circuit judge may serve temporarily, on appointment by the chief justice of the supreme court or by any associate justice designated by the supreme court, as a judge of a circuit court, under such general laws as the legislature may enact. *[1965 SJR-36; 1967 SJR-96]*

Retirement and eligibility for office of justices and circuit judges. SECTION 24. *[Created April 1955]* No person seventy years of age or over may take office as a supreme court justice or circuit judge. No person may take or hold such office unless he is licensed to practice law in this state and has been so licensed for five years immediately prior to his election or appointment. No supreme court justice or circuit judge may serve beyond the end of the month in which he attains the age of seventy, but any such justice or judge may complete the term in which he is serving or to which he has been elected when this section takes effect. Any person retired under the provisions of this section may, at the request of the chief justice of the supreme court, serve temporarily as a circuit judge and shall be compensated as the legislature provides. This section shall take effect on July first following the referendum at which it is approved. *[1953 SJR-6; 1955 SJR-10]*

ARTICLE VIII.
FINANCE

Rule of taxation uniform; income, privilege and occupation taxes. SECTION 1. [*As amended April 1974*] The rule of taxation shall be uniform but the legislature may empower cities, villages or towns to collect and return taxes on real estate located therein by optional methods. Taxes shall be levied upon such property with such classifications as to forests and minerals including or separate or severed from the land, as the legislature shall prescribe. Taxation of agricultural land and undeveloped land, both as defined by law, need not be uniform with the taxation of each other nor with the taxation of other real property. Taxation of merchants' stock-in-trade, manufacturers' materials and finished products, and livestock need not be uniform with the taxation of real property and other personal property, but the taxation of all such merchants' stock-in-trade, manufacturers' materials and finished products and livestock shall be uniform, except that the legislature may provide that the value thereof shall be determined on an average basis. Taxes may also be imposed on incomes, privileges and occupations, which taxes may be graduated and progressive, and reasonable exemptions may be provided. [*1971 AJR-2; 1973 AJR-1*]

Rule of taxation uniform; income, privilege and occupation taxes. SECTION 1. [*As amended April 1961*] The rule of taxation shall be uniform but the legislature may empower cities, villages or towns to collect and return taxes on real estate located therein by optional methods. Taxes shall be levied upon such property with such classifications as to forests and minerals including or separate or severed from the land, as the legislature shall prescribe. Taxation of merchants' stock-in-trade, manufacturers' materials and finished products, and livestock need not be uniform with the taxation of real property and other personal property, but the taxation of all such merchants' stock-in-trade, manufacturers' materials and finished products and livestock shall be uniform, except that the legislature may provide that the value thereof shall be determined on an average basis. Taxes may also be imposed on incomes; privileges and occupations, which taxes may be graduated and progressive, and reasonable exemptions may be provided. [*1959 AJR-120; 1961 SJR-34*]

Rule of taxation uniform; income, privilege and occupation taxes. SECTION 1. [*As amended April 1941*]. The rule of taxation shall be uniform but the legislature may empower cities, villages or towns to collect and return taxes on real estate located therein by optional methods. Taxes shall be levied upon such property with such classifications

as to forests and minerals including or separate or severed from the land, as the legislature shall prescribe. Taxes may also be imposed on incomes, privileges and occupations, which taxes may be graduated and progressive, and reasonable exemptions may be provided. [*1939 AJR-37; 1941 AJR-15*]

Rules of taxation; income taxes. SECTION 1. [*As amended April 1927*] The rule of taxation shall be uniform, and taxes shall be levied upon such property with such classifications as to forests and minerals, including or separate or severed from the land, as the legislature shall prescribe. Taxes may also be imposed on incomes, privileges and occupations, which taxes may be graduated and progressive, and reasonable exemptions may be provided. [*1925 AJR-51; 1927 AJR-3*]

Uniform rule of taxation; income tax. SECTION 1. [*As amended November 1908*] The rule of taxation shall be uniform, and taxes shall be levied upon such property as the legislature shall prescribe. Taxes may also be imposed on incomes, privileges and occupations, which taxes may be graduated and progressive, and reasonable exemptions may be provided. [*1905 AJR-12; 1907 SJR-19; 1907 c. 661*]

Uniform rule of taxation. SECTION 1. [*Original form*] The rule of taxation shall be uniform, and taxes shall be levied upon such property as the legislature shall prescribe.

Appropriations; limitation. SECTION 2. [*As amended November 1877*] No money shall be paid out of the treasury except in pursuance of an appropriation by law. No appropriation shall be made for the payment of any claim against the state except claims of the United States and judgments, unless filed within six years after the claim accrued. [*1876 SJR-14; 1877 SJR-5; 1877 c. 158*]

Appropriations. SECTION 2. [*Original form*] No money shall be paid out of the treasury, except in pursuance of an

appropriation by law.

Credit of state. SECTION 3. [*As amended April 1975*] Except as provided in s. 7 (2) (a), the credit of the state shall never be given, or loaned, in aid of any individual, association or corporation. [*1973 AJR-145; 1975 AJR-1*]

Credit of state. SECTION 3. [*Original form*] The credit of the state shall never be given, or loaned, in aid of any

individual, association or corporation.

Contracting state debts. SECTION 4. The state shall never contract any public debt except in the cases and manner herein provided.

Annual tax levy to equal expenses. SECTION 5. The legislature shall provide for an annual tax sufficient to defray the estimated expenses of the state for each year; and whenever the expenses of any year shall exceed the income, the legislature shall provide for levying a tax for the ensuing year, sufficient, with other sources of income, to pay the deficiency as well as the estimated expenses of such ensuing year.

Public debt for extraordinary expense; taxation. SECTION 6. For the purpose of defraying extraordinary expenditures the state may contract public debts (but such debts shall never in the aggregate exceed one hundred thousand dollars). Every such debt shall be authorized by law, for some purpose or purposes to be distinctly specified therein; and the vote of a majority of all the members elected to each house, to be taken by yeas and nays, shall be necessary to the passage of such law; and every such law shall provide for levying an annual tax sufficient to pay the annual interest of such debt and the principal within five years from the passage of such law, and shall specially appropriate the proceeds of such taxes to the payment of such principal and interest; and such appropriation shall not be repealed, nor the taxes be postponed or diminished, until the principal and interest of such debt shall have been wholly paid.

Public debt for public defense; bonding for public purposes. SECTION 7. [*As amended April 1992*] (1) The legislature may also borrow money to repel invasion, suppress insurrection, or defend the state in time of war; but the money thus raised shall be applied exclusively to the object for which the loan was authorized, or to the repayment of the debt thereby created.

(2) Any other provision of this constitution to the contrary notwithstanding:

(a) The state may contract public debt and pledges to the payment thereof its full faith, credit and taxing power:

1. To acquire, construct, develop, extend, enlarge or improve land, waters, property, highways, railways, buildings, equipment or facilities for public purposes.

2. To make funds available for veterans' housing loans.

(b) The aggregate public debt contracted by the state in any calendar year pursuant to paragraph (a) shall not exceed an amount equal to the lesser of:

1. Three-fourths of one per centum of the aggregate value of all taxable property in the state; or

2. Five per centum of the aggregate value of all taxable property in the state less the sum of: a. the aggregate public debt of the state contracted pursuant to this section outstanding as of January 1 of such calendar year after subtracting therefrom the amount of sinking funds on hand on January 1 of such calendar year which are applicable exclusively to repayment of such outstanding public debt and, b. the outstanding indebtedness as of January 1 of such calendar year of any entity of the type described in paragraph (d) to the extent that such indebtedness is supported by or payable from payments out of the treasury of the state.

(c) The state may contract public debt, without limit, to fund or refund the whole or any part of any public debt contracted pursuant to paragraph (a), including any premium payable with respect thereto and any interest to accrue thereon, or to fund or refund the whole or any part of any indebtedness incurred prior to January 1, 1972, by any entity of the type described in paragraph (d), including any premium payable with respect thereto and any interest to accrue thereon.

(d) No money shall be paid out of the treasury, with respect to any lease, sublease or other agreement entered into after January 1, 1971, to the Wisconsin State Agencies Building Corporation, Wisconsin State Colleges Building Corporation, Wisconsin State Public Building Corporation, Wisconsin University Building Corporation or any similar entity existing or operating for similar purposes pursuant to which such nonprofit corporation or such other entity undertakes to finance or provide a facility for use or occupancy by the state or an agency, department or instrumentality thereof.

(e) The legislature shall prescribe all matters relating to the contracting of public debt pursuant to paragraph (a), including: the public purposes for which public debt may be contracted; by vote of a majority of the members elected to each of the 2 houses of the legislature, the amount of public debt which may be contracted for any class of such purposes; the public debt or other indebtedness which may be funded or refunded; the kinds of notes, bonds or other evidence of public debt which may be issued by the state; and the manner in which the aggregate value of all taxable property in the state shall be determined.

(f) The full faith, credit and taxing power of the state are pledged to the payment of all public debt created on behalf of the state pursuant to this section and the legislature shall provide by appropriation for the payment of the interest upon and instalments of principal of all such public debt as the same falls due, but, in any event, suit may be brought against the state to compel such payment.

(g) At any time after January 1, 1972, by vote of a majority of the members elected to each of the 2 houses of the legislature, the legislature may declare that an emergency exists and submit to the people a proposal to authorize the state to contract a specific amount of public debt for a purpose specified in such proposal, without regard to the limit provided in paragraph (b). Any such authorization shall be effective if approved by a majority of the electors voting thereon. Public debt contracted pursuant to such authorization shall thereafter be deemed to have been contracted pursuant to paragraph (a), but neither such public debt nor any public debt contracted to fund or refund such public debt shall be considered in computing the debt limit provided in paragraph (b). Not more than one such authorization shall be thus made in any 2-year period. [*1989 SJR-76; 1991 SJR-30*]

Public debt for public defense; bonding for public purposes. SECTION 7. [*As amended April 1975*] (1) The legislature may also borrow money to repel invasion, suppress insurrection, or defend the state in time of war; but the money thus raised shall be applied exclusively to the object for which the loan was authorized, or to the repayment of the debt thereby created.

(2) Any other provision of this constitution to the contrary notwithstanding:

(a) The state may contract public debt and pledges to the payment thereof its full faith, credit and taxing power:

1. To acquire, construct, develop, extend, enlarge or improve land, waters, property, highways, buildings, equipment or facilities for public purposes.

2. To make funds available for veterans' housing loans.

(b) The aggregate public debt contracted by the state in any calendar year pursuant to paragraph (a) shall not exceed an amount equal to the lesser of:

1. Three-fourths of one per centum of the aggregate value of all taxable property in the state; or

2. Five per centum of the aggregate value of all taxable property in the state less the sum of: a. the aggregate public debt of the state contracted pursuant to this section outstanding as of January 1 of such calendar year after subtracting therefrom the amount of sinking funds on hand on January 1 of such calendar year which are applicable exclusively to repayment of such outstanding public debt and, b. the outstanding indebtedness as of January 1 of such calendar year of any entity of thetype described in paragraph (d) to the extent that such indebtedness is supported by or payable from payments out of the treasury of the state.

(c) The state may contract public debt, without limit, to fund or refund the whole or any part of any public debt contracted pursuant to paragraph (a), including any premium payable with respect thereto and any interest to accrue thereon, or to fund or refund the whole or any part of any indebtedness incurred prior to January 1, 1972, by any entity of the type described in paragraph (d), including any premium payable with respect thereto and any interest to accrue thereon.

(d) No money shall be paid out of the treasury, with respect to any lease, sublease or other agreement entered into after January 1, 1971, to the Wisconsin State Agencies Building Corporation, Wisconsin State Colleges Building Corporation, Wisconsin State Public Building Corporation, Wisconsin University Building Corporation or any similar entity existing or operating for similar purposes pursuant to which such nonprofit corporation or such other entity undertakes to finance or provide a facility for use or occupancy by the state or an agency, department or instrumentality thereof.

(e) The legislature shall prescribe all matters relating to the contracting of public debt pursuant to paragraph (a), including: the public purposes for which public debt may be contracted; by vote of a majority of the members elected to each of the 2 houses of the legislature, the amount of public debt which may be contracted for any class of such purposes; the public debt or other indebtedness which may be funded or refunded; the kinds of notes, bonds or other evidence of public debt which may be issued by the state; and the manner in which the aggregate value of all taxable property in the state shall be determined.

(f) The full faith, credit and taxing power of the state are pledged to the payment of all public debt created on behalf of the state pursuant to this section and the legislature shall provide by appropriation for the payment of the interest upon and instalments of principal of all such public debt as the same falls due, but, in any event, suit may be brought against the state to compel such payment.

(g) At any time after January 1, 1972, by vote of a majority of the members elected to each of the 2 houses of the legislature, the legislature may declare that an emergency exists and submit to the people a proposal to authorize the state to contract a specific amount of public debt for a purpose specified in such proposal, without regard to the limit provided in paragraph (b). Any such authorization shall be effective if approved by a majority of the electors voting thereon. Public debt contracted pursuant to such authorization shall thereafter be deemed to have been contracted pursuant to paragraph (a), but neither such public debt nor any public debt contracted to fund or refund such public debt shall be considered in computing the debt limit provided in paragraph (b). Not more than one such authorization shall be thus made in any 2-year period. [*1973 AJR-145; 1975 AJR-1*]

Public debt for public defense; bonding for public purposes. SECTION 7. [*As amended April 1969*] (1) The legislature may also borrow money to repel invasion, suppress insurrection, or defend the state in time of war; but the money thus raised shall be applied exclusively to the object for which the loan was authorized, or to the repayment of the debt thereby created.

(2) Any other provision of this constitution to the contrary notwithstanding:

(a) The state may contract public debt and pledges to the payment thereof its full faith, credit and taxing power to acquire, construct, develop, extend, enlarge or improve land, waters, property, highways, buildings, equipment or facilities for public purposes.

(b) The aggregate public debt contracted by the state in any calendar year pursuant to paragraph (a) shall not exceed an amount equal to the lesser of:

1. Three-fourths of one per centum of the aggregate value of all taxable property in the state; or

2. Five per centum of the aggregate value of all taxable property in the state less the sum of: a. the aggregate public debt of the state contracted pursuant to this section outstanding as of January 1 of such calendar year after subtracting therefrom the amount of sinking funds on hand on January 1 of such calendar year which are applicable exclusively to repayment of such outstanding public debt and, b. the outstanding indebtedness as of January 1 of such calendar year of any entity of the type described in paragraph (d) to the extent that such indebtedness is supported by or payable from payments out of the treasury of the state.

(c) The state may contract public debt, without limit, to fund or refund the whole or any part of any public debt contracted pursuant to paragraph (a), including any premium payable with respect thereto and any interest to accrue thereon, or to fund or refund the whole or any part of any indebtedness incurred prior to January 1, 1972, by any entity of the type described in paragraph (d), including any premium payable with respect thereto and any interest to accrue thereon.

(d) No money shall be paid out of the treasury, with

respect to any lease, sublease or other agreement entered into after January 1, 1971, to the Wisconsin State Agencies Building Corporation, Wisconsin State Colleges Building Corporation, Wisconsin State Public Building Corporation, Wisconsin University Building Corporation or any similar entity existing or operating for similar purposes pursuant to which such nonprofit corporation or such other entity undertakes to finance or provide a facility for use or occupancy by the state or an agency, department or instrumentality thereof.

(e) The legislature shall prescribe all matters relating to the contracting of public debt pursuant to paragraph (a), including: the public purposes for which public debt may be contracted; by vote of a majority of the members elected to each of the 2 houses of the legislature, the amount of public debt which may be contracted for any class of such purposes; the public debt or other indebtedness which may be funded or refunded; the kinds of notes, bonds or other evidence of public debt which may be issued by the state; and the manner in which the aggregate value of all taxable property in the state shall be determined.

(f) The full faith, credit and taxing power of the state are pledged to the payment of all public debt created on behalf of the state pursuant to this section and the legislature shall provide by appropriation for the payment of the interest

upon and instalments of principal of all such public debt as the same falls due, but, in any event, suit may be brought against the state to compel such payment.

(g) At any time after January 1, 1972, by vote of a majority of the members elected to each of the 2 houses of the legislature, the legislature may declare that an emergency exists and submit to the people a proposal to authorize the state to contract a specific amount of public debt for a purpose specified in such proposal, without regard to the limit provided in paragraph (b). Any such authorization shall be effective if approved by a majority of the electors voting thereon. Public debt contracted pursuant to such authorization shall thereafter be deemed to have been contracted pursuant to paragraph (a), but neither such public debt nor any public debt contracted to fund or refund such public debt shall be considered in computing the debt limit provided in paragraph (b). Not more than one such authorization shall be thus made in any 2-year period. [*1967 AJR-1; 1969 AJR-1*]

Public debt for public defense. SECTION 7. [*Original form*] The legislature may also borrow money to repel invasion, suppress insurrection, or defend the state in time of war; but the money thus raised shall be applied exclusively to the object for which the loan was authorized, or to the repayment of the debt thereby created.

Vote on fiscal bills; quorum. SECTION 8. On the passage in either house of the legislature of any law which imposes, continues or renews a tax, or creates a debt or charge, or makes, continues or renews an appropriation of public or trust money, or releases, discharges or commutes a claim or demand of the state, the question shall be taken by yeas and nays, which shall be duly entered on the journal; and three-fifths of all the members elected to such house shall in all such cases be required to constitute a quorum therein.

Evidences of public debt. SECTION 9. No scrip, certificate, or other evidence of state debt, whatsoever, shall be issued, except for such debts as are authorized by the sixth and seventh sections of this article.

Internal improvements. SECTION 10. [*As amended April 1992*] Except as further provided in this section, the state may never contract any debt for works of internal improvement, or be a party in carrying on such works.

(1) Whenever grants of land or other property shall have been made to the state, especially dedicated by the grant to particular works of internal improvement, the state may carry on such particular works and shall devote thereto the avails of such grants, and may pledge or appropriate the revenues derived from such works in aid of their completion.

(2) The state may appropriate money in the treasury or to be thereafter raised by taxation for:

(a) The construction or improvement of public highways.

(b) The development, improvement and construction of airports or other aeronautical projects.

(c) The acquisition, improvement or construction of veterans' housing.

(d) The improvement of port facilities.

(e) The acquisition, development, improvement or construction of railways and other railroad facilities.

(3) The state may appropriate moneys for the purpose of acquiring, preserving and developing the forests of the state. Of the moneys appropriated under the authority of this subsection in any one year an amount not to exceed two-tenths of one mill of the taxable property of the state as determined by the last preceding state assessment may be raised by a tax on property. [*1989 SJR-76; 1991 SJR-30*]

Internal improvements. SECTION 10. [*As amended April 1968*] The state shall never contract any debt for works of internal improvement, or be a party in carrying on such works; but whenever grants of land or other property shall have been made to the state, especially dedicated by the grant to particular works of internal improvement, the state may carry on such particular works and shall devote thereto the avails of such grants, and may pledge or appropriate the revenues derived from such works in aid of their completion. Provided, that the state may appropriate

money in the treasury or to be thereafter raised by taxation for the construction or improvement of public highways or the development, improvement and construction of airports or other aeronautical projects or the acquisition, improvement or construction of veterans' housing or the improvement of port facilities. Provided, that the state may appropriate moneys for the purpose of acquiring, preserving and developing the forests of the state; but of the moneys appropriated under the authority of this section in any one year an amount not to exceed two-tenths of one mill of the taxable property of the state as determined by the last preceding state assessment may be raised by a tax on property. [*1965 SJR-28; 1967 SJR-18*]

Internal improvements. SECTION 10. [*As amended April 1960*] The state shall never contract any debt for works of internal improvement, or be a party in carrying on such works; but whenever grants of land or other property shall have been made to the state, especially dedicated by the grant to particular works of internal improvement, the state may carry on such particular works and shall devote thereto the avails of such grants, and may pledge or appropriate the revenues derived from such works in aid of their completion. Provided, that the state may appropriate money in the treasury or to be thereafter raised by taxation for the construction or improvement of public highways or the development, improvement and construction of airports or other aeronautical projects or the acquisition, improvement or construction of veterans' housing or the improvement of port facilities. Provided, that the state may appropriate moneys for the purpose of acquiring, preserving and developing the forests of the state; but there shall not be appropriated under the authority of this section in any one year an amount to exceed two-tenths of one mill of the taxable property of the state as determined by the last preceding state assessment. [*1957 AJR-39; 1959 SJR-20*]

Internal improvements. SECTION 10. [*As amended April 1949*] The state shall never contract any debt for works of internal improvement, or be a party in carrying on such works; but whenever grants of land or other property shall have been made to the state, especially dedicated by the grant to particular works of internal improvement, the state may carry on such particular works and shall devote thereto the avails of such grants, and may pledge or appropriate the revenues derived from such works in aid of their completion. Provided, that the state may appropriate money in the treasury or to be thereafter raised by taxation for the construction or improvement of public highways or the development, improvement and construction of airports or other aeronautical projects or the acquisition, improvement or construction of veterans' housing. Provided, that the state may appropriate moneys for the purpose of acquiring, preserving and developing the forests of the state; but there shall not be appropriated under the authority of this section in any one year an amount to exceed two-tenths of one mill of the taxable property of the state as determined by the last preceding state assessment. [*1948 Spec.Sess. SJR-2; 1949 SJR-5*]

Internal improvements. SECTION 10. [*As amended April 1945*] The state shall never contract any debt for works of internal improvement, or be a party in carrying on such works; but whenever grants of land or other property shall have been made to the state, especially dedicated by the grant to particular works of internal improvement, the state may carry on such particular works, and shall devote thereto the avails of such grants, and may pledge or appropriate the revenues derived from such works in aid of

their completion. Provided, that the state may appropriate money in the treasury or to be thereafter raised by taxation for the construction or improvement of public highways or the development, improvement and construction of airports or other aeronautical projects. Provided, that the state may appropriate moneys for the purpose of acquiring, preserving and developing the forests of the state; but there shall not be appropriated under the authority of this section in any one year an amount to exceed two-tenths of one mill of the taxable property of the state as determined by the last preceding state assessment. [*1943 SJR-16; 1945 SJR-7*]

Internal improvements. SECTION 10. [*As amended November 1924*] The state shall never contract any debt for works of internal improvement, or be a party in carrying on such works; but whenever grants of land or other property shall have been made to the state, especially dedicated by the grant to particular works of internal improvement, the state may carry on such particular works, and shall devote thereto the avails of such grants, and may pledge or appropriate the revenues derived from such works in aid of their completion. Provided, that the state may appropriate money in the treasury or to be thereafter raised by taxation for the construction or improvement of public highways. Provided, that the state may appropriate moneys for the purpose of acquiring, preserving and developing the forests of the state; but there shall not be appropriated under the authority of this section in any one year an amount to exceed two-tenths of one mill of the taxable property of the state as determined by the last preceding state assessment. [*1921 SJR-30; 1923 AJR-70; 1923 c. 289*]

Water power and forests. SECTION 10. [*Approved by voters November 1910*] An amendment to Art. VIII, sec. 10, authorizing a state property tax of two-tenths of one mill to finance appropriations for acquisition and development of water power and forests was approved by 1907 SJR-43. There was no "second consideration" resolution but 1909 SB\553 enacted the proposal into law as Chap. 514, Laws of 1909. The procedure was declared invalid by the Supreme Court in *State ex rel. Owen v. Donald*, 160 W 21, 151 NW 331.

Public highways. [*As amended November 1908, a new sentence was added at the end of the section*] Provided, that the state may appropriate money in the treasury or to be thereafter raised by taxation for the construction or improvement of public highways. [*1905 SJR-14; 1907 SJR-22; 1907 c. 238*]

Internal improvements. SECTION 10. [*Original form*] The state shall never contract any debt for works of internal improvement, or be a party in carrying on such works, but whenever grants of land or other property shall have been made to the state, especially dedicated by the grant to particular works of internal improvements, the state may carry on such particular works, and shall devote thereto the avails of such grants, and may pledge or appropriate the revenues derived from such works in aid of their completion.

ARTICLE IX.
EMINENT DOMAIN AND PROPERTY OF THE STATE

Jurisdiction on rivers and lakes; navigable waters. SECTION 1. The state shall have concurrent jurisdiction on all rivers and lakes bordering on this state so far as such rivers or lakes shall form a common boundary to the state and any other state or territory now or hereafter to be formed, and bounded by the same; and the river Mississippi and the navigable waters leading into the Mississippi and St. Lawrence, and the carrying places between the same, shall be common highways and forever free, as well to the inhabitants of the state as to the citizens of the United States, without any tax, impost or duty therefor.

Territorial property. SECTION 2. The title to all lands and other property which have accrued to the territory of Wisconsin by grant, gift, purchase, forfeiture, escheat or otherwise shall vest in the state of Wisconsin.

Ultimate property in lands; escheats. SECTION 3. The people of the state, in their right of sovereignty, are declared to possess the ultimate property, in and to all lands within the jurisdiction of the state; and all lands the title to which shall fail from a defect of heirs shall revert or escheat to the people.

ARTICLE X.
EDUCATION

Superintendent of public instruction. SECTION 1. [*As amended November 1982*] The supervision of public instruction shall be vested in a state superintendent and such other officers as the legislature shall direct; and their qualifications, powers, duties and compensation shall be prescribed by law. The state superintendent shall be chosen by the qualified electors of the state at the same time and in the same manner as members of the supreme court, and shall hold office for 4 years from the succeeding first Monday in July. The term of office, time and manner of electing or appointing all other officers of supervision of public instruction shall be fixed by law. [*1979 AJR-76; 1981 AJR-35; submit: May '82 Spec.Sess. AJR-1*]

Superintendent of public instruction. SECTION 1. [*As amended November 1902*] The supervision of public instruction shall be vested in a state superintendent and such other officers as the legislature shall direct; and their qualifications, powers, duties and compensation shall be prescribed by law. The state superintendent shall be chosen by the qualified electors of the state at the same time and in the same manner as members of the supreme court, and shall hold his office for four years from the succeeding first Monday in July. The state superintendent chosen at the general election in November, 1902, shall hold and continue in his office until the first Monday in July, 1905, and his successor shall be chosen at the time of the judicial election in April, 1905. The term of office, time and manner of electing or appointing all other officers of supervision of public instruction shall be fixed by law. [*1899 SJR-21; 1901 SJR-24; 1901 c. 258*]

Superintendent of public instruction. SECTION 1. [*Original form*] The supervision of public instruction shall be vested in a state superintendent, and such other officers as the legislature shall direct. The state superintendent shall be chosen by the qualified electors of the state, in such manner as the legislature shall provide; his powers, duties and compensation shall be prescribed by law. Provided, that his compensation shall not exceed the sum of twelve hundred dollars annually.

School fund created; income applied. SECTION 2. [*As amended November 1982*] The proceeds of all lands that have been or hereafter may be granted by the United States to this state for educational purposes (except the lands heretofore granted for the purposes of a university) and all moneys and the clear proceeds of all property that may accrue to the state by forfeiture or escheat; and the clear proceeds of all fines collected in the several counties for any breach of the penal laws, and all moneys arising from any grant to the state where the purposes of such grant are not specified, and the 500,000 acres of land to which the state is entitled by the provisions of an act of congress, entitled "An act to appropriate the proceeds of the sales of the public lands and to grant pre-emption rights," approved September 4, 1841; and also the 5 percent of the net proceeds of the public lands to which the state shall become entitled on admission into the union (if congress shall consent to such appropriation of the 2 grants last mentioned) shall be set apart as a separate fund to be called "the school fund," the interest of which and all other revenues derived from the school lands shall be exclusively applied to the following objects, to wit:

(1) To the support and maintenance of common schools, in each school district, and the purchase of suitable libraries and apparatus therefor.

(2) The residue shall be appropriated to the support and maintenance of academies and normal schools, and suitable libraries and apparatus therefor. [*1979 AJR-76; 1981 AJR-35; submit: May '82 Spec.Sess. AJR-1*]

School fund created; income applied. SECTION 2. [*Original form*] The proceeds of all lands that have been or hereafter may be granted by the United States to this state for educational purposes (except the lands heretofore granted for the purpose of a university) and all moneys and the clear proceeds of all property that may accrue to the state by forfeiture or escheat, and all moneys which may be paid as an equivalent for exemption from military duty; and the clear proceeds of all fines collected in the several counties for any breach of the penal laws, and all moneys arising from any grant to the state where the purposes of such grant are not specified, and the five hundred thousand acres of land to which the state is entitled by the provisions of an act of congress, entitled "An act to appropriate the proceeds of the sales of the public lands and to grant pre-emption rights," approved the fourth day of September, one thousand eight hundred and forty-one; and also the five per centum of the net proceeds of the public lands to which the state shall become entitled on her admission into the union (if congress shall consent to such appropriation of the two grants last mentioned) shall be set apart as a separate fund to be called "the school fund," the interest of which and all other revenues derived from the school lands shall be exclusively applied to the following objects, to wit:

1. To the support and maintenance of common schools, in each school district, and the purchase of suitable libraries and apparatus therefor.

2. The residue shall be appropriated to the support and maintenance of academies and normal schools, and suitable libraries and apparatus therefor.

District schools; tuition; sectarian instruction; released time. SECTION 3. [*As amended April 1972*] The legislature shall provide by law for the establishment of district schools, which shall be as nearly uniform as practicable; and such schools shall be free and without charge for tuition to all children between the ages of 4 and 20 years; and no sectarian instruction shall be allowed therein; but the legislature by law may, for the purpose of religious instruction outside the district schools, authorize the release of students during regular school hours. [*1969 AJR-41; 1971 AJR-17*]

District schools; tuition; sectarian instruction. SECTION 3. [*Original form*] The legislature shall provide by law for the establishment of district schools, which shall be as nearly uniform as practicable; and such schools shall be free and without charge for tuition to all children between the ages of four and twenty years; and no sectarian instruction shall be allowed therein.

Annual school tax. SECTION 4. Each town and city shall be required to raise by tax, annually, for the support of common schools therein, a sum not less than one-half the amount received by such town or city respectively for school purposes from the income of the school fund.

Income of school fund. SECTION 5. Provision shall be made by law for the distribution of the income of the school fund among the several towns and cities of the state for the support of common schools therein, in some just proportion to the number of children and youth resident therein between the ages of four and twenty years, and no appropriation shall be made from the school fund to any city or town for the year in which said city or town shall fail to raise such tax; nor to any school district for the year in which a school shall not be maintained at least three months.

State university; support. SECTION 6. Provision shall be made by law for the establishment of a state university at or near the seat of state government, and for connecting with the same, from time to time, such colleges in different parts of the state as the interests of education may require. The proceeds of all lands that have been or may hereafter be granted by the United States to the state for the support of a university shall be and remain a perpetual fund to be called "the university fund," the interest of which shall be appropriated to the support of the state university, and no sectarian instruction shall be allowed in such university.

Commissioners of public lands. SECTION 7. The secretary of state, treasurer and attorney general, shall constitute a board of commissioners for the sale of the school and university lands and for the investment of the funds arising therefrom. Any two of said commissioners shall be a quorum for the transaction of all business pertaining to the duties of their office.

Sale of public lands. SECTION 8. Provision shall be made by law for the sale of all school and university lands after they shall have been appraised; and when any portion of such lands shall be sold and the purchase money shall not be paid at the time of the sale, the commissioners shall take security by mortgage upon the lands sold for the sum remaining unpaid, with seven per cent interest thereon, payable annually at the office of the treasurer. The commissioners shall be authorized to execute a good and sufficient conveyance to all purchasers of such lands, and to discharge any mortgages taken as security, when the sum due thereon shall have been paid. The commissioners shall have power to withhold from sale any portion of such lands when they shall deem it expedient, and shall invest all moneys arising from the sale of such lands, as well as all other university and school funds, in such manner as the legislature shall provide, and shall give such security for the faithful performance of their duties as may be required by law.

ARTICLE XI.
CORPORATIONS

Corporations; how formed. SECTION 1. [*As amended April 1981*] Corporations without banking powers or privileges may be formed under general laws, but shall not be created by special act, except for municipal purposes. All general laws or special acts enacted under the provisions of this section may be altered or repealed by the legislature at any time after their passage. [*1979 AJR-53; 1981 AJR-13*]

Corporations; how formed. SECTION 1. [*Original form*] Corporations without banking powers or privileges may be formed under general laws, but shall not be created by special act, except for municipal purposes, and in cases where, in the judgment of the legislature, the objects of the corporation cannot be attained under general laws. All general laws or special acts enacted under the provisions of this section may be altered or repealed by the legislature at any time after their passage.

Property taken by municipality. SECTION 2. [*As amended April 1961*] No municipal corporation shall take private property for public use, against the consent of the owner, without the necessity thereof being first established in the manner prescribed by the legislature. [*1959 AJR-22; 1961 SJR-8*]

Property taken by municipality. SECTION 2. [*Original form*] No municipal corporation shall take private property for public use, against the consent of the owner, without the necessity thereof being first established by the verdict of a jury.

Municipal home rule; debt limit; tax to pay debt. SECTION 3. [*As amended April 1981*] (1) Cities and villages organized pursuant to state law may determine their local affairs and government, subject only to this constitution and to such enactments of the legislature of statewide concern as with uniformity shall affect every city or every village. The method of such determination shall be prescribed by the legislature.

(2) No county, city, town, village, school district, sewerage district or other municipal corporation may become indebted in an amount that exceeds an allowable percentage of the taxable property located therein equalized for state purposes as provided by the legislature. In all cases the allowable percentage shall be 5 percent except as specified in pars. (a) and (b):

(a) For any city authorized to issue bonds for school purposes, an additional 10 percent shall be permitted for school purposes only, and in such cases the territory attached to the city for school purposes shall be included in the total taxable property supporting the bonds issued for school purposes.

(b) For any school district which offers no less than grades one to 12 and which at the time of incurring such debt is eligible for the highest level of school aids, 10 percent shall be permitted.

(3) Any county, city, town, village, school district, sewerage district or other municipal corporation incurring any indebtedness under sub. (2) shall, before or at the time of doing so, provide for the collection of a direct annual tax sufficient to pay the interest on such debt as it falls due, and also to pay and discharge the principal thereof within 20 years from the time of contracting the same.

(4) When indebtedness under sub. (2) is incurred in the acquisition of lands by cities, or by counties or sewerage districts having a population of 150,000 or over, for public, municipal purposes, or for the permanent improvement thereof, or to purchase, acquire, construct, extend, add to or improve a sewage collection or treatment system which services all or a part of such city or county, the city, county or sewerage district incurring the indebtedness shall, before or at the time of so doing, provide for the collection of a direct annual tax sufficient to pay the interest on such debt as it falls due, and also to pay and discharge the principal thereof within a period not exceeding 50 years from the time of contracting the same.

(5) An indebtedness created for the purpose of purchasing, acquiring, leasing, constructing, extending, adding to, improving, conducting, controlling, operating or managing a public utility of a town, village, city or special district, and secured solely by the property or income of such public utility, and whereby no municipal liability is created, shall not be considered an indebtedness of such town, village, city or special district, and shall not be included in arriving at the debt limitation under sub. (2). [*1979 SJR-28; 1981 SJR-5*]

Municipal home rule; debt limit; tax to pay debt. SECTION 3. [*As amended April 1966*] Cities and villages organized pursuant to state law are hereby empowered, to determine their local affairs and government, subject only to this constitution and to such enactments of the legislature of state-wide concern as shall with uniformity affect every city or every village. The method of such determination shall be prescribed by the legislature. No county, city, town, village, school district or other municipal corporation may become indebted in an amount that exceeds an allowable percentage of the taxable property located therein equalized for state purposes as provided by the legislature. In all cases the allowable percentage shall be five per centum except as follows: (a) For any city authorized to issue bonds for school purposes, an additional ten per centum shall be permitted for school purposes only, and in such cases the territory attached to the city for school purposes shall be included in the total taxable property supporting the bonds issued for school purposes. (b) For any school district which offers no less than grades one to twelve and which at the time of incurring such debt is eligible for the highest level of school aids, ten per centum shall be permitted. Any county, city, town, village, school district, or other municipal corporation incurring any indebtedness as aforesaid, shall before or at the time of doing so, provide for the collection of a direct annual tax sufficient to pay the interest on such debt as it falls due, and also to pay and discharge the principal thereof within twenty years from the time of contracting the same; except that when such indebtedness is incurred in the acquisition of lands by cities, or by counties having a population of one hundred fifty thousand or over, for public, municipal purposes, or for the permanent improvement thereof, the city or county incurring the same shall, before or at the time of so doing, provide for the collection of a direct annual tax sufficient to pay the interest on such debt as it falls due, and also to pay and discharge the principal thereof within a period not exceeding fifty years from the time of contracting the same. An indebtedness created for the purpose of purchasing, acquiring, leasing, constructing, extending, adding to, improving, conducting, controlling, operating or managing a public utility of a town, village, city or special district, and secured solely by the property or income of such public utility, and whereby no municipal liability is created, shall not be considered an indebtedness of such town, village, city or special district, and shall not be included in arriving at such debt limitation. [*1963 SJR-59; 1965 AJR-10*]

Municipal home rule; debt limit; tax to pay debt.
SECTION 3. [*As amended April 1963*] Cities and villages organized pursuant to state law are hereby empowered, to determine their local affairs and government, subject only to this constitution and to such enactments of the legislature of state-wide concern as shall with uniformity affect every city or every village. The method of such determination shall be prescribed by the legislature. No county, city, town, village, school district or other municipal corporation may become indebted in an amount that exceeds an allowable percentage of the taxable property located therein equalized for state purposes as provided by the legislature. In all cases the allowable percentage shall be five per centum except as follows: (a) For any city authorized to issue bonds for school purposes, an additional ten per centum shall be permitted for school purposes only, and in such cases the territory attached to the city for school purposes shall be included in the total taxable property supporting the bonds issued for school purposes. (b) For any school district which offers no less than grades one to twelve and which at the time of incurring such debt is eligible for the highest level of school aids, ten per centum shall be permitted. Any county, city, town, village, school district, or other municipal corporation incurring any indebtedness as aforesaid, shall before or at the time of doing so, provide for the collection of a direct annual tax sufficient to pay the interest on such debt as it falls due, and also to pay and discharge the principal thereof within twenty years from the time of contracting the same; except that when such indebtedness is incurred in the acquisition of lands by cities, or by counties having a population of one hundred fifty thousand or over, for public, municipal purposes, or for the permanent improvement thereof, the city or county incurring the same shall, before or at the time of so doing, provide for the collection of a direct annual tax sufficient to pay the interest on such debt as it falls due, and also to pay and discharge the principal thereof within a period not exceeding fifty years from the time of contracting the same. An indebtedness created for the purpose of purchasing, acquiring, leasing, constructing, extending, adding to, improving, conducting, controlling, operating or managing a public utility of a town, village or city, and secured solely by the property or income of such public utility, and whereby no municipal liability is created, shall not be considered an indebtedness of such town, village or city, and shall not be included in arriving at such five or eight per centum debt limitation. [*1961 AJR-92; 1963 AJR-19*]

Municipal home rule; debt limit; tax to pay debt.
SECTION 3. [*As amended April 1961*] Cities and villages organized pursuant to state law are hereby empowered, to determine their local affairs and government, subject only to this constitution and to such enactments of the legislature of state-wide concern as shall with uniformity affect every city or every village. The method of such determination shall be prescribed by the legislature. No county, city, town, village, school district, or other municipal corporation shall be allowed to become indebted in any manner or for any purpose to any amount, including existing indebtedness, in the aggregate exceeding five per centum on the value of the taxable property therein, to be ascertained, other than for school districts and counties having a population of 500,000 or over, by the last assessment for state and county taxes previous to the incurring of such indebtedness and for school districts and counties having a population of 500,000 or over by the value of such property as equalized for state purposes; except that for any city which is authorized to issue bonds for school purposes the total indebtedness of such city shall not exceed in the aggregate eight per centum of the value of such property as equalized for state purposes and except that for any school district offering no less than grades one to twelve and which is at the time of incurring such debt eligible for the highest level of school aids, the total indebtedness of such school district shall not exceed ten per centum of the value of such property as equalized for state purposes; the manner and method of determining such equalization for state purposes to be provided by the legislature. Any county, city, town, village, school district, or other municipal corporation incurring any indebtedness as aforesaid, shall, before or at the time of doing so, provide for the collection of a direct annual tax sufficient to pay the interest on such debt as it falls due, and also to pay

and discharge the principal thereof within twenty years from the time of contracting the same; except that when such indebtedness is incurred in the acquisition of lands by cities, or by counties having a population of one hundred fifty thousand or over, for public, municipal purposes, or for the permanent improvement thereof, the city or county incurring the same shall, before or at the time of so doing, provide for the collection of a direct annual tax sufficient to pay the interest on such debt as it falls due, and also to pay and discharge the principal thereof within a period not exceeding fifty years from the time of contracting the same. An indebtedness created for the purpose of purchasing, acquiring, leasing, constructing, extending, adding to, improving, conducting, controlling, operating or managing a public utility of a town, village or city, and secured solely by the property or income of such public utility, and whereby no municipal liability is created, shall not be considered an indebtedness of such town, village or city, and shall not be included in arriving at such five or eight per centum debt limitation. [*1959 SJR-6; 1961 AJR-1*]

Municipal home rule; debt limit; tax to pay debt.
SECTION 3. [*As amended November 1960*] Cities and villages organized pursuant to state law are hereby empowered, to determine their local affairs and government, subject only to this constitution and to such enactments of the legislature of state-wide concern as shall with uniformity affect every city or every village. The method of such determination shall be prescribed by the legislature. No county, city, town, village, school district, or other municipal corporation shall be allowed to become indebted in any manner or for any purpose to any amount, including existing indebtedness, in the aggregate exceeding five per centum on the value of the taxable property therein, to be ascertained, other than for school districts and counties having a population of 500,000 or over, by the last assessment for state and county taxes previous to the incurring of such indebtedness and for school districts and counties having a population of 500,000 or over by the value of such property as equalized for state purposes; except that for any city which is authorized to issue bonds for school purposes the total indebtedness of such city shall not exceed in the aggregate eight per centum of the value of such property as equalized for state purposes; the manner and method of determining such equalization for state purposes to be provided by the legislature. Any county, city, town, village, school district, or other municipal corporation incurring any indebtedness as aforesaid, shall, before or at the time of doing so, provide for the collection of a direct annual tax sufficient to pay the interest on such debt as it falls due, and also to pay and discharge the principal thereof within twenty years from the time of contracting the same; except that when such indebtedness is incurred in the acquisition of lands by cities, or by counties having a population of one hundred fifty thousand or over, for public, municipal purposes, or for the permanent improvement thereof, the city or county incurring the same shall, before or at the time of so doing, provide for the collection of a direct annual tax sufficient to pay the interest on such debt as it falls due, and also to pay and discharge the principal thereof within a period not exceeding fifty years from the time of contracting the same. Providing, that an indebtedness created for the purpose of purchasing, acquiring, constructing, extending, adding to, improving, conducting, controlling, operating or managing a public utility of a town, village or city, and secured solely by the property or income of such public utility, and whereby no municipal liability is created, shall not be considered an indebtedness of such town, village or city, and shall not be included in arriving at such five or eight per centum debt limitation. [*1957 SJR-47; 1959 SJR-53*]

Municipal home rule; debt limit; tax to pay debt.
SECTION 3. [*As amended April 1955*] Cities and villages organized pursuant to state law are hereby empowered, to determine their local affairs and government, subject only to this constitution and to such enactments of the legislature of state-wide concern as shall with uniformity affect every city or every village. The method of such determination shall be prescribed by the legislature. No county, city, town, village, school district, or other municipal corporation shall be allowed to become indebted in any manner or for any purpose to any amount, including existing indebtedness, in

the aggregate exceeding five per centum on the value of the taxable property therein, to be ascertained, other than for school district, by the last assessment for state and county taxes previous to the incurring of such indebtedness and for school districts by the value of such property as equalized for state purposes; except that for any city which is authorized to issue bonds for school purposes the total indebtedness of such city shall not exceed in the aggregate eight per centum of the value of such property as equalized for state purposes; the manner and method of determining such equalization for state purposes to be provided by the legislature. Any county, city, town, village, school district, or other municipal corporation incurring any indebtedness as aforesaid, shall, before or at the time of doing so, provide for the collection of a direct annual tax sufficient to pay the interest on such debt as it falls due, and also to pay and discharge the principal thereof within twenty years from the time of contracting the same; except that when such indebtedness is incurred in the acquisition of lands by cities, or by counties having a population of one hundred fifty thousand or over, for public, municipal purposes, or for the permanent improvement thereof, the city or county incurring the same shall, before or at the time of so doing, provide for the collection of a direct annual tax sufficient to pay the interest on such debt as it falls due, and also to pay and discharge the principal thereof within a period not exceeding fifty years from the time of contracting the same. Providing, that an indebtedness created for the purpose of purchasing, acquiring, leasing, constructing, extending, adding to, improving, conducting, con- trolling, operating or managing a public utility of a town, village or city, and secured solely by the property or income of such public utility, and whereby no municipal liability is created, shall not be considered an indebtedness of such town, village or city, and shall not be included in arriving at such five or eight per centum debt limitation. [*1953 SJR-17; 1955 AJR-18*]

Municipal home rule; debt limit; tax to pay debt. Section 3. [*As amended April 1951*] Cities and villages organized pursuant to state law are hereby empowered, to determine their local affairs and government, subject only to this constitution and to such enactments of the legislature of state-wide concern as shall with uniformity affect every city or every village. The method of such determination shall be prescribed by the legislature. No county, city, town, village, school district, or other municipal corporation shall be allowed to become indebted in any manner or for any purpose to any amount, including existing indebtedness, in the aggregate exceeding 5 per centum on the value of the taxable property therein, to be ascertained by the last assessment for state and county taxes previous to the incurring of such indebtedness; except that for any city which is authorized to issue bonds for school purposes the total indebtedness of such city shall not exceed in the aggregate 8 per centum of the value of such property. Any county, city, town, village, school district, or other municipal corporation incurring any indebtedness as aforesaid, shall, before or at the time of doing so, provide for the collection of a direct annual tax sufficient to pay the interest on such debt as it falls due, and also to pay and discharge the principal thereof within 20 years from the time of contracting the same; except that when such indebtedness is incurred in the acquisition of lands by cities, or by counties having a population of 150,000 or over, for public, municipal purposes, or for the permanent improvement thereof, the city or county incurring the same shall, before or at the time of so doing, provide for the collection of a direct annual tax sufficient to pay the interest on such debt as it falls due, and also to pay and discharge the principal thereof within a period not exceeding 50 years from the time of contracting the same. Providing, that an indebtedness created for the purpose of purchasing, acquiring, leasing, constructing, extending, adding to, improving, conducting, controlling, operating or managing a public utility of a town, village or city, and secured solely by the property or income of such public utility, and whereby no municipal liability is created, shall not be considered an indebtedness of such town, village or city, and shall not be included in arriving at such 5 or 8 per centum debt limitation. [*1949 SJR-11; 1951 SJR-9*]

Municipal home rule; debt limit; tax to pay debt.

Section 3. [*As amended November 1932*] Cities and villages organized pursuant to state law are hereby empowered, to determine their local affairs and government, subject only to this constitution and to such enactments of the legislature of state-wide concern as shall with uniformity affect every city or every village. The method of such determination shall be prescribed by the legislature. No county, city, town, village, school district, or other municipal corporation shall be allowed to become indebted in any manner or for any purpose to any amount, including existing indebtedness, in the aggregate exceeding five per centum on the value of the taxable property therein, to be ascertained by the last assessment for state and county taxes previous to the incurring of such indebtedness. Any county, city, town, village, school district, or other municipal corporation incurring any indebtedness as aforesaid, shall, before or at the time of doing so, provide for the collection of a direct annual tax sufficient to pay the interest on such debt as it falls due, and also to pay and discharge the principal thereof within twenty years from the time of contracting the same; except that when such indebtedness is incurred in the acquisition of lands by cities, or by counties having a population of one hundred fifty thousand or over, for public, municipal purposes, or for the permanent improvement thereof, the city or county incurring the same shall, before or at the time of so doing, provide for the collection of a direct annual tax sufficient to pay the interest on such debt as it falls due, and also to pay and discharge the principal thereof within a period not exceeding fifty years from the time of contracting the same. Providing, that an indebtedness created for the purpose of purchasing, acquiring, leasing, constructing, extending, adding to, improving, conducting, controlling, operating or managing a public utility of a town, village or city, and secured solely by the property or income of such public utility, and whereby no municipal liability is created, shall not be considered an indebtedness of such town, village or city, and shall not be included in arriving at such five per centum debt limitation. [*1929 AJR-61; 1931 AJR-14*]

Municipal home rule; debt limit; tax to pay debt. Section 3. [*As amended November 1924*] Cities and villages organized pursuant to state law are hereby empowered, to determine their local affairs and government, subject only to this constitution and to such enactments of the legislature of state-wide concern as shall with uniformity affect every city or every village. The method of such determination shall be prescribed by the legislature. No county, city, town, village, school district, or other municipal corporation shall be allowed to become indebted in any manner or for any purpose to any amount, including existing indebtedness, in the aggregate exceeding five per centum on the value of the taxable property therein, to be ascertained by the last assessment for state and county taxes previous to the incurring of such indebtedness. Any county, city, town, village, school district, or other municipal corporation incurring any indebtedness as aforesaid, shall, before or at the time of doing so, provide for the collection of a direct annual tax sufficient to pay the interest on such debt as it falls due, and also to pay and discharge the principal thereof within twenty years from the time of contracting the same; except that when such indebtedness is incurred in the acquisition of lands by cities, or by counties having a population of one hundred fifty thousand or over, for public, municipal purposes, or for the permanent improvement thereof, the city or county incurring the same shall, before or at the time of so doing, provide for the collection of a direct annual tax sufficient to pay the interest on such debt as it falls due, and also to pay and discharge the principal thereof within a period not exceeding fifty years from the time of contracting the same. [*1921 SJR-5; 1923 SJR-18; 1923 c. 203*]

Organization of cities and villages. Section 3. [*As amended November 1912*] It shall be the duty of the legislature, and they are hereby empowered to provide for the organization of cities and incorporated villages, and to restrict their power of taxation, assessment, borrowing money, contracting debts, and loaning their credit, so as to prevent abuses in assessments and taxation, and in contracting debts by such municipal corporations. No county, city, town, village, school district, or other municipal corporation shall be allowed to become indebted in any manner or for any purpose to any amount, including existing indebtedness, in the aggregate exceeding five per centum on the value of the taxable property therein, to be ascertained by the last assessment for state and county taxes previous to the incurring of such indebtedness. Any county, city, town, village, school district, or other municipal corporation incurring any indebtedness as aforesaid, shall, before or at the time of doing so, provide for the collection of a direct annual tax sufficient to pay the interest on such debt as it falls due, and also to pay and discharge the principal thereof within twenty years from the time of contracting the same; except that when such indebtedness is incurred in the acquisition of lands by cities, or by counties having a population of one hundred fifty thousand or over, for public, municipal purposes, or for the permanent improvement thereof, the city or county incurring the same shall, before or at the time of so doing, provide for the collection of a direct annual tax sufficient to pay the interest on such debt as it falls due, and also to pay and discharge the principal thereof within a period not exceeding fifty years from the time of contracting the same. [*1909 SJR-32; 1911 SJR-26; 1911 c. 665*]

Municipal debt limit. [*An amendment approved by the voters in November 1874 added two new paragraphs at the end of the section*] No county, city, town, village, school district, or other municipal corporation shall be allowed to become indebted in any manner or for any purpose to any amount including existing indebtedness, in the aggregate exceeding five per centum on the value of the taxable property therein to be ascertained by the last assessment for state and county taxes previous to the incurring of such indebtedness. Any county, city, town, village, school district or other municipal corporation incurring any indebtedness as aforesaid, shall before or at the time of doing so provide for the collection of a direct annual tax sufficient to pay the interest on said debt as it falls due, and also to pay and discharge the principal thereof within twenty years from the time of contracting the same. [*1872 AJR-17; 1873 SJR-6; 1874 c. 3*]

Organization of cities and villages. SECTION 3. [*Original form*] It shall be the duty of the legislature, and they are hereby empowered, to provide for the organization of cities and incorporated villages, and to restrict their power of taxation, assessment, borrowing money, contracting debts and loaning their credit, so as to prevent abuses in assessments and taxation, and in contracting debts by such municipal corporations.

Acquisition of lands by state and subdivisions; sale of excess. SECTION 3a. [*As amended April 3, 1956*] The state or any of its counties, cities, towns or villages may acquire by gift, dedication, purchase, or condemnation lands for establishing, laying out, widening, enlarging, extending, and maintaining memorial grounds, streets, highways, squares, parkways, boulevards, parks, playgrounds, sites for public buildings, and reservations in and about and along and leading to any or all of the same; and after the establishment, layout, and completion of such improvements, may convey any such real estate thus acquired and not necessary for such improvements, with reservations concerning the future use and occupation of such real estate, so as to protect such public works and improvements, and their environs, and to preserve the view, appearance, light, air, and usefulness of such public works. If the governing body of a county, city, town or village elects to accept a gift or dedication of land made on condition that the land be devoted to a special purpose and the condition subsequently becomes impossible or impracticable, such governing body may by resolution or ordinance enacted by a two-thirds vote of its members elect either to grant the land back to the donor or dedicator or his heirs or accept from the donor or dedicator or his heirs a grant relieving the county, city, town or village of the condition; however, if the donor or dedicator or his heirs are unknown or cannot be found, such resolution or ordinance may provide for the commencement of proceedings in the manner and in the courts as the legislature shall designate for the purpose of relieving the county, city, town or village from the condition of the gift or dedication. [*1953 SJR-29; 1955 SJR-9*]

Acquisition of lands by state and cities; sale of excess. SECTION 3a. [*Created November 1912*] The state or any of its cities may acquire by gift, purchase, or condemnation lands for establishing, laying out, widening, enlarging, extending, and maintaining memorial grounds, streets, squares, parkways, boulevards, parks, playgrounds, sites for public buildings, and reservations in and about and along and leading to any or all of the same; and after the establishment, layout, and completion of such improvements, may convey any such real estate thus acquired and not necessary for such improvements, with reservations concerning the future use and occupation of such real estate, so as to protect such public works and improvements, and their environs, and to preserve the view, appearance, light, air, and usefulness of such public works. [*1909 SJR-63; 1911 SJR-25; 1911 c. 665*]

General banking law. SECTION 4. [*As amended April 1981*] The legislature may enact a general banking law for the creation of banks, and for the regulation and supervision of the banking business. [*1979 AJR-53; 1981 AJR-13*]

General banking law. SECTION 4. [*Created November 1902. This section was adopted to replace original sections 4 and 5 of this article*] The legislature shall have power to enact a general banking law for the creation of banks, and for the regulation and supervision of the banking business, provided that the vote of two-thirds of all the members elected to each house, to be taken by yeas and nays, be in favor of the passage of such law. [*P1899 AJR-16; 1901 SJR-25; 1901 c. 73*]

Legislature prohibited from incorporating banks. SECTION 4. [*Original form, repealed November 1899. 1899 AJR-16; 1901 SJR-25; 1901 c. 73*] The legislature shall not have power to create, authorize or incorporate, by any general, or special law, any bank, or banking power or privilege, or any institution or corporation having any banking power or privilege whatever, except as provided in this article.

SECTION 5. [*Repealed. 1899 JR-13; 1901 JR-2; 1901 c.73; vote November 1902*]

Referendum on banking laws. SECTION 5. [*Original form, repealed November 1902. 1899 AJR-16; 1901 SJR-25; 1901 c. 73*] The legislature may submit to the voters, at any general election, the question of "bank," or "no bank," and if at any such election a number of votes equal to a majority of all the votes cast at such election on that subject shall be in favor of banks, then the legislature shall have power to grant bank charters, or to pass a general banking law, with such restrictions and under such regulations as they may deem expedient and proper for the security of the bill holders. Provided, that no such grant or law shall have any force or effect until the same shall have been submitted to a vote of the electors of the state, at some general election, and been approved by a majority of the votes cast on that subject at such election.

ARTICLE XII
AMENDMENTS

Constitutional amendments. SECTION 1. Any amendment or amendments to this constitution may be proposed in either house of the legislature, and if the same shall be agreed to by a majority of the members elected to each of the two houses, such proposed amendment or amendments shall be entered on their journals, with the yeas and nays taken thereon, and referred to the legislature to be chosen at the next general election, and shall be published for three months previous to the time of holding such election; and if, in the legislature so next chosen, such proposed amendment or amendments shall be agreed to by a majority of all the members elected to each house, then it shall be the duty of the legislature to submit such proposed amendment or amendments to the people in such manner and at such time as the legislature shall prescribe; and if the people shall approve and ratify such amendment or amendments by a majority of the electors voting thereon, such amendment or amendments shall become part of the constitution; provided, that if more than one amendment be submitted, they shall be submitted in such manner that the people may vote for or against such amendments separately.

Constitutional conventions. SECTION 2. If at any time a majority of the senate and assembly shall deem it necessary to call a convention to revise or change this constitution, they shall recommend to the electors to vote for or against a convention at the next election for members of the legislature. And if it shall appear that a majority of the electors voting thereon have voted for a convention, the legislature shall, at its next session, provide for calling such convention.

ARTICLE XIII.
MISCELLANEOUS PROVISIONS

Political year; elections. SECTION 1. *[As amended April 1986]* The political year for this state shall commence on the first Monday of January in each year, and the general election shall be held on the Tuesday next succeeding the first Monday of November in even-numbered years. *[1983 AJR-33; 1985 AJR-3]*

Political year; elections. SECTION 1. *[As amended November 1882]* The political year for the state of Wisconsin shall commence on the first Monday in January in each year, and the general election shall be holden on the Tuesday next succeeding the first Monday in November. The first general election for all state and county officers, except judicial officers, after the adoption of this amendment, shall be holden in the year A.D. 1884, and thereafter the general election shall be held biennially. All state, county or other officers elected at the general election in the year 1881, and whose term of office would otherwise expire on the first Monday of January in the year 1884, shall hold and continue in such offices respectively until the first Monday in January in the year 1885. *[1881 AJR-16; 1882 SJR-20; 1882 c. 290]*

Political year; general election. SECTION 1. *[Original form]* The political year for the state of Wisconsin shall commence on the first Monday in January in each year, and the general election shall be holden on the Tuesday succeeding the first Monday in November in each year.

SECTION 2. *[Repealed. 1973 SJR-6; 1975 SJR-4; vote April 1975]*

Dueling. SECTION 2. *[Original form]* Any inhabitant of this state who may hereafter be engaged, either directly or indirectly, in a duel, either as principal or accessory, shall forever be disqualified as an elector, and from holding any office under the constitution and laws of this state, and may be punished in such other manner as shall be prescribed by law.

Eligibility to office. SECTION 3. *[As amended November 1996]* (1) No member of congress and no person holding any office of profit or trust under the United States except postmaster, or under any foreign power, shall be eligible to any office of trust, profit or honor in this state.

(2) No person convicted of a felony, in any court within the United States, no person convicted in federal court of a crime designated, at the time of commission, under federal law as a misdemeanor involving a violation of public trust and no person convicted, in a court of a state, of a crime designated, at the time of commission, under the law of the state as a misdemeanor involving a violation of public trust shall be eligible to any office of trust, profit or honor in this state unless pardoned of the conviction.

(3) No person may seek to have placed on any ballot for a state or local elective office in this state the name of a person convicted of a felony, in any court within the United States, the

name of a person convicted in federal court of a crime designated, at the time of commission, under federal law as a misdemeanor involving a violation of public trust or the name of a person convicted, in a court of a state, of a crime designated, at the time of commission, under the law of the state as a misdemeanor involving a violation of public trust, unless the person named for the ballot has been pardoned of the conviction. [*1993 AJR-3; 1995 AJR-16*]

Eligibility to office. SECTION 3. [*Original form*] No member of congress, nor any person holding any office of profit or trust under the United States (postmasters excepted) or under any foreign power; no person convicted of any infamous crime in any court within the United States; and no person being a defaulter to the United States or to this state, or to any county or town therein, or to any state or territory within the United States, shall be eligible to any office of trust, profit or honor in this state.

Great seal. SECTION 4. It shall be the duty of the legislature to provide a great seal for the state, which shall be kept by the secretary of state, and all official acts of the governor, his approbation of the laws excepted, shall be thereby authenticated.

SECTION 5. [*Repealed. 1983 AJR-33; 1985 SJR-3; vote April 1986*]

Residents on Indian lands, where to vote. SECTION 5. [*Original form*] All persons residing upon Indian lands, within any county of the state, and qualified to exercise the right of suffrage under the constitution, shall be entitled to vote at the polls which may be held nearest their residence, for state, United States or county officers. Provided, that no person shall vote for county officers out of the county in which he resides.

Legislative officers. SECTION 6. The elective officers of the legislature, other than the presiding officers, shall be a chief clerk and a sergeant at arms, to be elected by each house.

Division of counties. SECTION 7. No county with an area of nine hundred square miles or less shall be divided or have any part stricken therefrom, without submitting the question to a vote of the people of the county, nor unless a majority of all the legal voters of the county voting on the question shall vote for the same.

Removal of county seats. SECTION 8. No county seat shall be removed until the point to which it is proposed to be removed shall be fixed by law, and a majority of the voters of the county voting on the question shall have voted in favor of its removal to such point.

Election or appointment of statutory officers. SECTION 9. All county officers whose election or appointment is not provided for by this constitution shall be elected by the electors of the respective counties, or appointed by the boards of supervisors, or other county authorities, as the legislature shall direct. All city, town and village officers whose election or appointment is not provided for by this constitution shall be elected by the electors of such cities, towns and villages, or of some division thereof, or appointed by such authorities thereof as the legislature shall designate for that purpose. All other officers whose election or appointment is not provided for by this constitution, and all officers whose offices may hereafter be created by law, shall be elected by the people or appointed, as the legislature may direct.

Vacancies in office. SECTION 10. [*As amended April 1979*] (1) The legislature may declare the cases in which any office shall be deemed vacant, and also the manner of filling the vacancy, where no provision is made for that purpose in this constitution.

(2) Whenever there is a vacancy in the office of lieutenant governor, the governor shall nominate a successor to serve for the balance of the unexpired term, who shall take office after confirmation by the senate and by the assembly. [*1977 SJR-51; 1979 SJR-1*]

Vacancies in office. SECTION 10. [*Original form*] The legislature may declare the cases in which any office shall be deemed vacant, and also the manner of filling the vacancy, where no provision is made for that purpose in this constitution.

Passes, franks and privileges. SECTION 11. [*As amended November 1936*] No person, association, copartnership, or corporation, shall promise, offer or give, for any purpose, to any political committee, or any member or employe thereof, to any candidate for, or incumbent of any office or position under the constitution or laws, or under any ordinance of any town or municipality, of this state, or to any person at the request or for the advantage of all or any of them, any free pass or frank, or any privilege withheld from any person, for the traveling accommodation or transportation of any person or property, or the transmission of any message or communication.

No political committee, and no member or employe thereof, no candidate for and no incumbent of any office or position under the constitution or laws, or under any ordinance of any town or municipality of this state, shall ask for, or accept, from any person, association, copartnership, or corporation, or use, in any manner, or for any purpose, any free pass or frank, or any privilege withheld from any person, for the traveling accommodation or transportation of any person or property, or the transmission of any message or communication.

Any violation of any of the above provisions shall be bribery and punished as provided by law, and if any officer or any member of the legislature be guilty thereof, his office shall become vacant.

No person within the purview of this act shall be privileged from testifying in relation to anything therein prohibited; and no person having so testified shall be liable to any prosecution or punishment for any offense concerning which he was required to give his testimony or produce any documentary evidence.

Notaries public and regular employes of a railroad or other public utilities who are candidates for or hold public offices for which the annual compensation is not more than three hundred dollars to whom no passes or privileges are extended beyond those which are extended to other regular employes of such corporations are excepted from the provisions of this section. [*1933 AJR-50; 1935 AJR-67*]

Free passes forbidden. SECTION 11. [*Created November 1902*] No person, association, co-partnership, or corporation, shall promise, offer or give, for any purpose, to any political committee, or any member or employee thereof, to any candidate for, or incumbent of any office or position under the constitution or laws, or under any ordinance of any town or municipality, of this state, or to any person at the request for the advantage of all or any of them, any free pass or frank, or any privilege withheld from any person, for the traveling accommodation or transportation of any person or property, or the transmission of any message or communication.

No political committee, and no member or employee thereof, no candidate for and no incumbent of any office or position under the constitution or laws, or under any ordinance of any town or municipality of this state, shall ask for, or accept, from any person, association, co-partnership, or corporation, or use, in any manner, or for any purpose,

any free pass or frank, or any privilege withheld from any person, for the traveling accommodation or transportation of any person or property, or the transmission of any message or communication.

Any violation of any of the above provisions shall be bribery and punished as provided by law, and if any officer or any member of the legislature be guilty thereof, his office shall become vacant.

No person within the purview of this act shall be privileged from testifying in relation to anything therein prohibited; and no person having so testified shall be liable to any prosecution or punishment for any offense concerning which he was required to give his testimony or produce any documentary evidence.

The railroad commissioner and his deputy in the discharge of duty are excepted from the provisions of this amendment. [*1899 SJR-12; 1901 AJR-8; 1901 c. 437*]

Recall of elective officers. SECTION 12. [*As amended April 1981*] The qualified electors of the state, of any congressional, judicial or legislative district or of any county may petition for the recall of any incumbent elective officer after the first year of the term for which the incumbent was elected, by filing a petition with the filing officer with whom the nomination petition to the office in the primary is filed, demanding the recall of the incumbent.

(1) The recall petition shall be signed by electors equaling at least twenty-five percent of the vote cast for the office of governor at the last preceding election, in the state, county or district which the incumbent represents.

(2) The filing officer with whom the recall petition is filed shall call a recall election for the Tuesday of the 6th week after the date of filing the petition or, if that Tuesday is a legal holiday, on the first day after that Tuesday which is not a legal holiday.

(3) The incumbent shall continue to perform the duties of the office until the recall election results are officially declared.

(4) Unless the incumbent declines within 10 days after the filing of the petition, the incumbent shall without filing be deemed to have filed for the recall election. Other candidates may file for the office in the manner provided by law for special elections. For the purpose of conducting elections under this section:

(a) When more than 2 persons compete for a nonpartisan office, a recall primary shall be held. The 2 persons receiving the highest number of votes in the recall primary shall be the 2 candidates in the recall election, except that if any candidate receives a majority of the total number of votes cast in the recall primary, that candidate shall assume the office for the remainder of the term and a recall election shall not be held.

(b) For any partisan office, a recall primary shall be held for each political party which is by law entitled to a separate ballot and from which more than one candidate competes for the party's nomination in the recall election. The person receiving the highest number of votes in the recall primary for each political party shall be that party's candidate in the recall election.

Independent candidates and candidates representing political parties not entitled by law to a separate ballot shall be shown on the ballot for the recall election only.

(c) When a recall primary is required, the date specified under sub. (2) shall be the date of the recall primary and the recall election shall be held on the Tuesday of the 4th week after the recall primary or, if that Tuesday is a legal holiday, on the first day after that Tuesday which is not a legal holiday.

(5) The person who receives the highest number of votes in the recall election shall be elected for the remainder of the term.

(6) After one such petition and recall election, no further recall petition shall be filed against the same officer during the term for which he was elected.

(7) This section shall be self-executing and mandatory. Laws may be enacted to facilitate its operation but no law shall be enacted to hamper, restrict or impair the right of recall. [*1979 SJR-5; 1981 SJR-2*]

Recall of elective officers. SECTION 12. [*Created November 1926*] The qualified electors of the state or of any county or of any congressional, judicial or legislative district may petition for the recall of any elective officer after the first year of the term for which he was elected, by filing a petition with the officer with whom the petition for nomination to such office in the primary election is filed, demanding the recall of such officer. Such petition shall be signed by electors equal in number to at least twenty-five per cent of the vote cast for the office of governor at the last preceding election, in the state, county or district from which such officer is to be recalled. The officer with whom such petition is filed shall call a special election to be held not less than forty nor more than forty-five days from the filing of such petition. The officer against whom such petition has been filed shall continue to perform the duties of his office until the result of such special election shall have been officially declared. Other candidates for such office may be nominated in the manner as is provided by law in primary elections. The candidate who shall receive the highest number of votes shall be deemed elected for the remainder of the term. The name of the candidate against whom the recall petition is filed shall go on the ticket unless he resigns within ten days after the filing of the petition. After one such petition and special election, no further recall petition shall be filed against the same officer during the term for which he was elected. This article shall be self-executing and all of its provisions shall be treated as mandatory. Laws may be enacted to facilitate its operation, but no law shall be enacted to hamper, restrict or impair the right of recall. [*1923 SJR-39; 1925 SJR-12; 1925 c. 270*]

Marriage. SECTION 13. [*Created November 2006*] Only a marriage between one man and one woman shall be valid or recognized as a marriage in this state. A legal status identical or substantially similar to that of marriage for unmarried individuals shall not be valid or recognized in this state. [*2003 AJR-66; 2005 SJR-53*]

ARTICLE XIV.

SCHEDULE

Effect of change from territory to state. SECTION 1. That no inconvenience may arise by reason of a change from a territorial to a permanent state government, it is declared that all rights, actions, prosecutions, judgments, claims and contracts, as well of individuals as of bodies corporate, shall continue as if no such change had taken place; and all process which may be issued under the authority of the territory of Wisconsin previous to its admission into the union of the United States shall be as valid as if issued in the name of the state.

Territorial laws continued. SECTION 2. All laws now in force in the territory of Wisconsin which are not repugnant to this constitution shall remain in force until they expire by their own limitation or be altered or repealed by the legislature.

SECTION 3. [*Repealed. 1979 AJR-76; 1981 AJR-35; submit: May'82 Spec.Sess. AJR-1; vote November 1982*]

Territorial fines accrue to state. SECTION 3. [*Original form*] All fines, penalties, or forfeitures accruing to the territory of Wisconsin shall enure to the use of the state.

SECTION 4. [*Repealed. 1979 AJR-76; 1981 AJR-35; submit: May'82 Spec.Sess. AJR-1; vote November 1982*]

Rights of action and prosecution saved. SECTION 4. [*Original form*] All recognizances heretofore taken, or which may be taken before the change from territorial to a permanent state government, shall remain valid, and shall pass to and may be prosecuted in the name of the state; and all bonds executed to the governor of the territory, or to any other officer or court in his or their official capacity, shall pass to the governor or state authority and their successors in office, for the uses therein respectively expressed, and may be sued for and recovered accordingly; and all the estate, or property, real, personal or mixed, and all judgments, bonds, specialties, choses in action and claims or debts of whatsoever description of the territory of Wisconsin, shall enure to and vest in the state of Wisconsin, and may be sued for and recovered in the same manner and to the same extent by the state of Wisconsin as the same could have been by the territory of Wisconsin. All criminal prosecutions and penal actions which may have arisen, or which may arise before the change from a territorial to a state government, and which shall then be pending, shall be prosecuted to judgment and execution in the name of the state. All offenses committed against the laws of the territory of Wisconsin before the change from a territorial to a state government, and which shall not be prosecuted before such change, may be prosecuted in the name and by the authority of the state of Wisconsin with like effect as though such change had not taken place; and all penalties

incurred shall remain the same as if this constitution had not been adopted. All actions at law and suits in equity which may be pending in any of the courts of the territory of Wisconsin at the time of the change from a territorial to a state government may be continued and transferred to any court of the state which shall have jurisdiction of the subject matter thereof.

SECTION 5. [*Repealed. 1979 AJR-76; 1981 AJR-35; submit: May '82 Spec.Sess. AJR-1; vote November 1982*]

Existing officers hold over. SECTION 5. [*Original form*] All officers, civil and military, now holding their offices under the authority of the United States or of the territory

of Wisconsin shall continue to hold and exercise their respective offices until they shall be superseded by the authority of the state.

SECTION 6. [*Repealed. 1979 AJR-76; 1981 AJR-35; submit: May '82 Spec.Sess. AJR-1; vote November 1982*]

Seat of government. SECTION 6. [*Original form*] The first session of the legislature of the state of Wisconsin shall commence on the first Monday in June next, and shall be

held at the village of Madison, which shall be and remain the seat of government until otherwise provided by law.

SECTION 7. [*Repealed. 1979 AJR-76; 1981 AJR-35; submit: May '82 Spec.Sess. AJR-1; vote November 1982*]

Local officers hold over. SECTION 7. [*Original form*] All county, precinct, and township officers shall continue to hold their respective offices, unless removed

by the competent authority, until the legislature shall, in conformity with the provisions of this constitution, provide for the holding of elections to fill such offices respectively.

SECTION 8. [*Repealed. 1979 AJR-76; 1981 AJR-35; submit: May '82 Spec.Sess. AJR-1; vote November 1982*]

Copy of constitution for president. SECTION 8. [*Original form*] The president of this convention shall, immediately after its adjournment, cause a fair copy of this constitution, together with a copy of the act of the legislature of this territory, entitled "An act in relation to the formation of a state government in Wisconsin, and to change the time of holding the annual session of the

legislature," approved October 27, 1847, providing for the calling of this convention, and also a copy of so much of the last census of this territory as exhibits the number of its inhabitants, to be forwarded to the president of the United States to be laid before the congress of the United States at its present session.

SECTION 9. [*Repealed. 1979 AJR-76; 1981 AJR-35; submit: May '82 Spec.Sess. AJR-1; vote November 1982*]

Ratification of constitution; election of officers. SECTION 9. [*Original form*] This constitution shall be submitted at an election to be held on the second Monday in March next, for ratification or rejection, to all white male persons of the age of twenty-one years or upwards, who shall then be residents of this territory and citizens of the United States, or shall have declared their intention to become such in conformity with the laws of congress on the subject of naturalization; and all persons having such qualifications shall be entitled to vote for or against the adoption of this constitution, and for all officers first elected under it. And if the constitution be ratified by the said electors it shall become the constitution of the state of Wisconsin. On such of the ballots as are for the constitution shall be written or printed the word "yes," and

on such as are against the constitution the word "no." The election shall be conducted in the manner now prescribed by law, and the returns made by the clerks of the boards of supervisors or county commissioners (as the case may be) to the governor of the territory at any time before the tenth day of April next. And in the event of the ratification of this constitution by a majority of all the votes given, it shall be the duty of the governor of this territory to make proclamation of the same, and to transmit a digest of the returns to the senate and assembly of the state on the first day of their session. An election shall be held for governor, lieutenant governor, treasurer, attorney-general, members of the state legislature, and members of congress, on the second Monday of May next; and no other for further notice of such election shall be required.

SECTION 10. [*Repealed. 1979 AJR-76; 1981 AJR-35; submit: May '82 Spec.Sess. AJR-1; vote November 1982*]

Congressional apportionment. SECTION 10. [*Original form*] Two members of congress shall also be elected on the second Monday of May next; and until otherwise provided by law, the counties of Milwaukee, Waukesha, Jefferson, Racine, Walworth, Rock and Green, shall constitute the first congressional district, and elect one member; and the

counties of Washington, Sheboygan, Manitowoc, Calumet, Brown, Winnebago, Fond du Lac, Marquette, Sauk, Portage, Columbia, Dodge, Dane, Iowa, LaFayette, Grant, Richland, Crawford, Chippewa, St. Croix and La Pointe, shall constitute the second congressional district, and shall elect one member.

SECTION 11. [*Repealed. 1979 AJR-76; 1981 AJR-35; submit: May '82 Spec.Sess. AJR-1; vote November 1982*]

First elections. SECTION 11. [*Original form*] The several elections provided for in this article shall be conducted according to the existing laws of the territory; provided, that no elector shall be entitled to vote except in the town, ward or precinct where he resides. The returns of election for senators and members of assembly shall be transmitted to the clerk of the board of supervisors or county commissioners, as the case may be; and the votes shall be canvassed and certificates of election issued as now provided by law. In the first senatorial district the returns of the election for senator shall be made to the proper officer in the county of Brown; in the second senatorial

district to the proper officer in the county of Columbia; in the third senatorial district to the proper officer in the county of Crawford; in the fourth senatorial district to the proper officer in the county of Fond du Lac; and in the fifth senatorial district to the proper officer in the county of Iowa. The returns of election for state officers and members of congress shall be certified and transmitted to the speaker of the assembly, at the seat of government, in the same manner as the vote for delegate to congress are required to be certified and returned by the laws of the territory of Wisconsin, to the secretary of said territory, and in such time that they may be received on the first

Monday in June next; and as soon as the legislature shall be organized the speaker of the assembly and the president of the senate shall, in the presence of both houses, examine the

returns and declare who are duly elected to fill the several offices hereinbefore mentioned, and give to each of the persons elected a certificate of his election.

SECTION 12. [*Repealed. 1979 AJR-76; 1981 AJR-35; submit: May'82 Spec.Sess. AJR-1; vote November 1982*]

Legislative apportionment. SECTION 12. [*Original form*] Until there shall be a new apportionment, the senators and members of the assembly shall be apportioned among the several districts, as hereinafter mentioned,

and each district shall be entitled to elect one senator or member of the assembly, as the case may be. [*Enumeration of districts omitted as obsolete: see R.S. 1849 pp. 40-43; R.S. 1858 pp. 49-53*]

Common law continued in force. SECTION 13. Such parts of the common law as are now in force in the territory of Wisconsin, not inconsistent with this constitution, shall be and continue part of the law of this state until altered or suspended by the legislature.

SECTION 14. [*Repealed. 1979 AJR-76; 1981 AJR-35; submit: May'82 Spec.Sess. AJR-1; vote November 1982*]

Officers, when to enter on duties. SECTION 14. [*Original form*] The senators first elected in the even-numbered senate districts, the governor, lieutenant governor and other state officers first elected under this constitution, shall enter upon the duties of their respective offices on the first Monday of June next, and shall continue in office

for one year from the first Monday of January next; the senators first elected in the odd-numbered senate districts, and the members of the assembly first elected, shall enter upon their duties respectively on the first Monday of June next, and shall continue in office until the first Monday in January next.

SECTION 15. [*Repealed. 1979 AJR-76; 1981 AJR-35; submit: May'82 Spec.Sess. AJR-1; vote November 1982*]

Oath of office. SECTION 15. [*Original form*] The oath of office may be administered by any judge or justice of the

peace until the legislature shall otherwise direct.

Implementing revised structure of judicial branch. SECTION 16. [*As affected November 1982*] (1), (2), (3) and (5) [*Repealed*]

(4) [*Amended*] The terms of office of justices of the supreme court serving on August 1, 1978, shall expire on the July 31 next preceding the first Monday in January on which such terms would otherwise have expired, but such advancement of the date of term expiration shall not impair any retirement rights vested in any such justice if the term had expired on the first Monday in January. [*1979 AJR-76; 1981 AJR-35; submit: May'82 Spec.Sess. AJR-1*]

Implementing revised structure of judicial branch. SECTION 16. [*Created April 1977*] (1) The 1975/1977 amendment relating to a revised structure of the judicial branch shall take effect on August 1 of the year following the year of ratification by the voters.

(2) All county courts and the branches thereof in existence on the effective date of this amendment shall, as trial courts of general uniform statewide jurisdiction, continue after such effective date with the same jurisdiction, powers and duties conferred by law upon such courts and the branches and judges thereof until the legislature by law alters or abolishes such county courts and their jurisdiction, powers and duties.

(3) Subject to the jurisdiction established in section 14 of article VII, municipal courts and municipal court judges shall continue after the effective date of this amendment with the same jurisdiction, powers and duties as conferred upon suc h courts and judges as of the effective date until the legislature acts under sections 2 and 14 of article VII to alter or abolish such municipal courts and their jurisdiction, powers and duties.

(4) The terms of office of justices of the supreme court serving on the effective date shall expire on the July 31 next preceding the first Monday in January on which such terms would otherwise have expired, but such advancement of the date of term expiration shall not impair any retirement rights vested in any such justice if the term had expired on the first Monday in January.

(5) Prior to the effective date of this amendment the legislature shall by law establish one or more appeals court districts, provide for the election of appeals judges in such districts, and determine the jurisdiction of the court of appeals under section 21 of article I and section 5 of article VII as affected by this amendment, so that the court of appeals shall become operative on the effective date. [*1975 AJR-11; 1977 SJR-9*]

Note: Attached resolutions and signatures appear at the end of the constitution as printed in the *Revised Statutes* of 1849 and 1858.

HISTORY OF CONSTITUTIONAL AMENDMENTS
April 2, 2013

Art.	Sec.	Subject	First Approval	Second Approval	Submission to People	Date of Election	For	Against	Total Vote for Governor
IV	4	Assemblymen, 2-year terms	Ch.95, 1853	Ch.89, 1854	Ch.89, 1854	Nov. 1854	6,549	11,580	[1]
IV	5	Senators, 4-year terms	″	″	″	″	6,348	11,885	″
IV	11	Biennial legislative sessions					6,752	11,589	″
V	5	Governor's salary, changed from $1,250 to $2,500 a year	SJR 35 / JR 4, 1861	SJR 15 / JR 6, 1862		Nov. 1862	14,519	32,612	
IV	21	*Change legislators' pay to $350 a year	SJR 26 / JR 9, 1861	SJR 16 / JR 3, 1862	Ch.202, 1862	″	58,363	24,418	142,522 [1]
V	5	*Change governor's salary from $1,250 to $5,000 a year	AJR 13 / JR 9, 1865	SJR 6 / JR 2, 1866	Ch.25, 1867	Nov. 1867	47,353	41,764	130,781
V	9	*Change lieutenant governor's salary to $1,000 a year	″ , 1868	″ / JR 3, 1869	Ch.186, 1869	Nov. 1869	48,894	18,606	146,953 [2]
I	8	*Grand jury system modified	AJR 6 / JR 7, 1869	SJR 3 / JR 1, 1870	Ch.118, 1870	Nov. 1870	54,087	3,675	147,274
IV	31,32	*Private and local laws, prohibited on 9 subjects	SJR 14 / JR 13, 1870	AJR 29 / JR 8, 1871	Ch.122, 1871	Nov. 1871	16,272	29,755	[1]
VII	4	Supreme court, 1 chief and 4 associate justices	SJR 12 / JR 2, 1871	AJR 16 / JR 4, 1872	Ch.111, 1872	Nov. 1872	66,061	1,509	
XI	3	*Indebtedness of municipalities limited to 5%	AJR 17 / JR 11, 1872	SJR 6 / JR 1, 1873	Ch.37, 1873	Nov. 1874	79,140	16,763	178,122
VII	4	*Supreme court, 1 chief and 4 associate justices	SJR 16 / JR 10, 1876	SJR 2 / JR 4, 1877	Ch.48, 1877	Nov. 1877	33,046	3,371	″
VIII	2	*Claims against state, 6-year limit	SJR 14 / JR 7, 1876	SJR 5 / none³, 1877	Ch.158, 1877	″	53,532	13,936	171,856
IV	4,5,11	*Biennial sessions; assemblymen 2-year, senators 4-year terms	SJR 9 / none³, 1880	AJR 7 / none³, 1881	Ch.262, 1881	Nov. 1881	36,223	5,347	″
IV	21	*Change legislators' pay to $500 a year	″ , 1881	″ , 1882	Ch.272, 1882		60,091	8,089	
III	1	*Voting residence 30 days; in municipalities voter registration	AJR 26 / JR 5, 1881	SJR 18 / JR 3, 1882	Ch.290, 1882	Nov. 1882			
VI	4	*County officers except judicial, vacancies filled by appointment	AJR 16 / JR 4, 1881	SJR 20 / ″, 1882		″			
VII	12	*Clerk of court, full term election	″	″					
XIII	1	*Political year; biennial elections	″	″					
X	1	State superintendent, qualifications and pay fixed by legislature	AJR 16 / JR 34, 1885	AJR 2 / JR 4, 1887	Ch.357, 1887	Nov. 1888	12,967	18,342	354,714
VII	4	*Supreme court, composed of 5 justices of supreme court	SJR 19 / JR 5, 1887	AJR 7 / JR 3, 1889	Ch.22, 1889	Apr. 1889	125,759	14,712	211,111 [4]
IV	31	*Cities incorporated by general law	SJR 13 / JR 4, 1889	SJR 13 / JR 4, 1891	Ch.362, 1891	Nov. 1892	15,718	9,015	371,559
X	1	State superintendent, pay fixed by law	AJR 15 / JR 10, 1893	SJR 7 / JR 2, 1895	Ch.177, 1895	Nov. 1896	38,752	56,506	444,110
VII	7	*Circuit judges, additional in populous counties	SJR 9 / JR 8, 1895	SJR 10 / JR 9, 1897	Ch.69, 1897	Apr. 1897	45,823	41,513	119,572 [4]
X	1	*State superintendent, nonpartisan 4-year term, pay fixed by law	SJR 21 / JR 16, 1899	SJR 24 / JR 3, 1901	Ch.258, 1901	Nov. 1902	71,550	57,411	365,676
XI	4	*General banking law authorized	AJR 16 / JR 13, 1899	SJR 25 / JR 2, 1901	Ch.73, 1901	″	64,836	44,620	″
XI	5	*Banking law referenda requirement repealed	″	″			67,781	40,697	
XIII	11	*Free passes prohibited	SJR 12 / JR 8, 1899	AJR 8 / JR 9, 1901	Ch.437, 1901	Apr. 1903	51,377	39,857	114,468 [4]
VII	4	*Supreme court, 7 justices, 10-year terms	AJR 33 / JR 8, 1901	AJR 5 / JR 7, 1903	Ch.10, 1903	Nov. 1908	85,838	36,733	449,656
III	1	*Suffrage for full citizens only	AJR 16 / JR 15, 1905	AJR 47 / JR 25, 1907	Ch.661, 1907	″	85,958	27,270	″
V	10	*Governor's approval of bills in 6 days	AJR 45 / JR 14, 1905	AJR 46 / JR 13, 1907		″	85,696	37,729	″
VIII	1	*Income tax	AJR 12 / JR 12, 1905	SJR 19 / JR 29, 1907			116,421	46,739	
VIII	10	*Highways, appropriations for	SJR 14 / JR 11, 1905	SJR 22 / JR 18, 1907	Ch.238, 1907	Nov. 1910	54,932	52,634	319,522
IV	3	*Apportionment after each federal census	SJR 18 / JR 30, 1907	SJR 35 / JR 55, 1909	Ch.478, 1909	″	44,153	76,278	″
IV	21	Change legislators' pay to $1,000 a year	AJR 8 / JR 35, 1907	AJR 33 / JR 7, 1909	Ch.508, 1909	″			
VIII	10	*Water power and forests, appropriations for⁵	SJR 43 / JR 31, 1907	″ / Ch.514, 1909	Ch.514, 1909		62,468 [5]	45,924 [5]	
VII	10	*Judges' salaries, time of payment	AJR 36 / JR 34, 1909	AJR 26 / JR 24, 1911	Ch.665, 1911	Nov. 1912	44,855	34,865	393,849

HISTORY OF CONSTITUTIONAL AMENDMENTS
April 2, 2013–Continued

Art.	Sec.	Subject	First Approval			Second Approval			Submission to People		Date of Election	For	Against	Total Vote for Governor
XI	3	*City or county debt for lands, discharge within 50 years	SJR 32	JR 44	1909	SJR 26	JR 42	1911	''	''	''	45,369	34,975	''
XI	3a	*Public parks, playgrounds, etc.	SJR 63	JR 38	1909	SJR 25	JR 48	1911	''	''	''	43,424	33,931	''
IV	1	Initiative and referendum	AJR 36	JR 74	1911	AJR 4	JR 22	1913	Ch.770	1913	Nov. 1914	84,934	148,536	325,430
IV	21	Change legislators' pay to $600 a year, 2 cents a mile for additional round trips	AJR 78	JR 66	1911	AJR 8	JR 24	1913	''	1913	''	68,907	157,202	''
VII	6,7	Judicial circuits, decreased number, additional judges	AJR 134	JR 67	1911	AJR 11	JR 26	1913	Ch. 770	1913	Nov. 1914	63,311	154,827	''
VIII	new	State annuity insurance	SJR 72	JR 65	1911	AJR 38	JR 35	1913	''	1913	''	59,909	170,338	325,430
VIII	new	State insurance	AJR 119	JR 56	1911	AJR 9	JR 12	1913	''		''	58,490	165,966	''
XI	new	Home rule of cities and villages	SJR 31	JR 73	1911	SJR 19	JR 21	1913	''		''	86,020	141,472	''
XI	new	Municipal power of condemnation	AJR 104	JR 37	1911	AJR 10	JR 25	1913	''		''	61,122	154,945	''
XII	1	Constitutional amendments, submission after 3/5 approval by one legislature	SJR 57	JR 71	1911	SJR 22	JR 17	1913	''		''	71,734	160,761	''
XII	new	Constitution amended upon petition	AJR 36	JR 74	1911	AJR 4	JR 22	1913	''		''	68,435	150,215	''
XIII	new	Recall of civil officers	SJR 9	JR 41	1911	SJR 18	JR 15	1913	''		''	81,628	144,386	''
IV	21	Legislators' pay fixed by law	AJR 16	JR 23	1917	AJR 13	JR 37	1919	Ch.480	1919	Apr. 1920	126,243	132,258	''
VII	6,7	Judicial circuits, decreased number, additional judges	AJR 74	JR 20	1917	SJR 100	JR 92	1919	Ch.604	1919	Nov. 1922	113,786	116,436	''
I	5	*Jury verdict, 5/6 in civil cases	AJR 26	JR 58	1919	AJR 39	JR 14	1921	Ch.504	1921	Nov. 1922	171,433	156,820	481,828
VI	4	Municipal indebtedness for public utilities	AJR 22	JR 38	1919	AJR 39	JR 36	1921	Ch.437	1921	''	161,832	207,594	''
IV	new	Change legislators' pay to $750 a year	AJR 21	JR 54	1919	AJR 16	JR 37	1921	Ch.566	1921	''	105,234	219,639	''
IV	21	Change legislators' pay to $750 a year	SJR 8	JR 28	1921	SJR 5	JR 18	1923	Ch.241	1923	Apr. 1924	189,635	250,236	344,137[4]
VII	7	*Circuit judges, additional in populous counties	SJR 24	JR 24	1921	SJR 27	JR 64	1923	Ch.408	1923	Nov. 1924	240,207	226,562	796,432
VIII	10	*Forestry, appropriations for	SJR 30	JR 29	1921	AJR 70	JR 57	1923	Ch.289	1923	''	336,360	173,563	''
XI	3	*Home rule for cities and villages	SJR 5	JR 39	1921	SJR 18	JR 34	1923	Ch.203	1923	''	299,792	190,165	''
V	5	*Governor's salary fixed by law	AJR 88	JR 79	1923	AJR 50	JR 52	1925	Ch.413	1925	Nov. 1926	202,156	188,302	552,912
XIII	12	*Recall of elective officials	SJR 39	JR 39	1923	SJR 12	JR 16	1925	Ch.270	1925	''	205,868	201,125	''

Note: JR 41 of 1925, which became Joint Rule 16 of the Wisconsin Legislature, established a new procedure to incorporate the "submission to the people" clause into the proposal at second approval.

Art.	Sec.	Subject	First Approval			Second Approval			Date of Election	For	Against	Total Vote for Governor
IV	21	Change legislators' pay to $1,000 for session	AJR 16	JR 33	1925	AJR 2	JR 12	1927	Apr. 1927	151,736	199,260	308,885[4]
VIII	1	*Severance tax: forests, minerals	AJR 51	JR 61	1925	AJR 3	JR 13	1927	''	179,217	141,888	''
IV	21	*Legislators' salary repealed; to be fixed by law	SJR 61	JR 57	1927	AJR 3	JR 6	1929	Apr. 1929	237,250	212,846	397,912[2]
VI	4	*Sheriffs succeeding themselves for 2 terms	AJR 8	JR 24	1927	AJR 8	JR 13	1929	''	259,881	210,964	''
V	10	*Item veto on appropriation bills	SJR 35	JR 37	1927	SJR 40	JR 43	1929	Nov. 1930	252,655	153,703	606,825
V	5	*Governor's salary provision repealed; fixed by law	SJR 81	JR 69	1929	SJR 6	JR 52	1931	Nov. 1932	452,605	275,175	1,124,502
V	9	*Lieutenant governor's salary repealed; fixed by law	SJR 82	JR 70	1929	SJR 7	JR 53	1931	''	427,768	267,120	''

Art.	Sec.	Subject	First Approval			Second Approval			Date of Election	Vote		Total Vote for Governor
										For	Against	
VII	1	*Wording of section corrected	SJR 103	JR 72	1929	SJR 8	JR 58	1931	"	436,113	221,563	"
XI	3	*Municipal indebtedness for public utilities	AJR 61	JR 74	1929	AJR 14	JR 71	1931	"	401,194	279,631	"
III	1	*Women's suffrage	AJR 52	JR 91	1931	SJR 74	JR 76	1933	Nov. 1934	411,088	166,745	953,797
XIII	1	*Free passes, permitted as specified	AJR 50	JR 63	1933	AJR 67	JR 98	1935	Nov. 1936	365,971	361,799	1,237,095
VIII	1	*Installment payment of real estate taxes	AJR 37	JR 88	1939	AJR 15	JR 18	1941	Apr. 1941	330,971	134,808	547,213[2]
VII	15	*Justice of peace, abolish office in first class cities	SJR 9	JR 27	1943	SJR 6	JR 2	1945	Apr. 1945	160,965	113,408	381,192[4]
VIII	10	*Aeronautical program	SJR 16	JR 37	1943	SJR 7	JR 3	1945	"	187,111	101,169	"
IV	4	Sheriffs, no limit on successive terms	AJR 6	JR 36	1943	AJR 10	JR 47	1945	Apr. 1946	121,144	170,131	306,354[4]
IV	33	*Auditing of state accounts	SJR 35	JR 60	1943	SJR 24	JR 73	1945	Nov. 1946	480,938	308,072	1,040,444
VI	2	*Auditing (part of same proposal)	SJR 35	JR 60	1943	SJR 24	JR 73	1945	"			"
X	2	Public transportation of school children to any school	SJR 48	JR 73	1943	SJR 19	JR 78	1945	"	437,817	545,475	"
XI	3a	Repeal; relating to exercise of eminent domain by municipalities	SJR 30	JR 89	1945	SJR 15	JR 48	1947	"	210,086	807,318	"
II	2	Prohibition on taxing federal lands repealed	AJR 26	JR 33	1947	SJR 6	JR 2	1949	"	245,412	297,237	"
VIII	10	*Allow internal improvement debt for veterans' housing	SJR 2	JR 1	SS '48[36]	SJR 5	JR 1	1949	Nov. 1948	311,576	290,736	1,266,139
II	2	*Prohibition on taxing federal lands repealed	AJR 64	JR 11	1949	AJR 7	JR 7	1949	Apr. 1949	305,612	186,284	633,606[4]
XI	3	*City debt limit 8% for combined city and school purposes	SJR 11	JR 12	1949	AJR 7	JR 6	1951	"	313,739	191,897	"
IV	3,4,5	Apportionment based on area and population[7]	SJR 50	JR 59	1951	AJR 7	JR 7	1951	Apr. 1951	433,043[7]	406,133[7]	515,822[4]
VII	9	*Judicial elections to full terms	SJR 3	JR 41	1951	SJR 5	JR 5	1953	Apr. 1951	386,972	345,094	515,822[4]
VII	24	*Judges: qualifications, retirement	SJR 6	JR 46	1953	SJR 10	JR 10	1953	Apr. 1953	380,214	177,929	735,860[4]
VI	3	*School debt limit, equalized value	SJR 17	JR 47	1953	AJR 18	JR 12	1953	"	320,376	228,641	"
IV	26	*Teachers' retirement benefits	SJR 21	JR 41	1953	SJR 8	JR 17	1955	"	365,560	255,284	"
VI	4	Sheriffs, no limit on successive terms	AJR 13	JR 23	1953	AJR 22	JR 22	1955	Apr. 1955	269,722	328,603	520,554[4]
XI	3a	*Municipal acquisition of land for public purposes	SJR 29	JR 35	1953	SJR 9	JR 36	1955	"	376,692	193,544	"
XIII	11	Free passes, not for public use	AJR 12	JR 61	1953	AJR 47	JR 54	1955	"	188,715	380,207	"
VIII	10	*Port development	AJR 39	JR 58	1957	SJR 20	JR 15	1959	Apr. 1956	472,177	451,045	740,411[4]
XI	3	*Debt limit in populous counties, 5% of equalized valuation	SJR 47	JR 59	1957	SJR 53	JR 32	1959	"	686,104	529,467	"
IV	26	Salary increases during term for various public officers	SJR 21	JR 29	1959	SJR 6	JR 11	1961	"	297,066	307,575	"
IV	34	*Continuity of civil government	AJR 48	JR 50	1959	SJR 1	JR 10	1961	"	498,869	132,728	"
IV	4	Sheriffs, no limit on successive terms	AJR 31	JR 48	1959	AJR 7	JR 9	1961	"	283,495	388,238	"
VIII	1	*Personal property classified for tax purposes	AJR 120	JR 77	1959	SJR 34	JR 13	1961	Apr. 1960	381,881	220,434	1,182,160[8]
XI	2	*Municipal eminent domain, abolished jury verdict of necessity	AJR 22	JR 47	1959	SJR 8	JR 12	1961	Nov. 1960	348,406	259,566	1,728,009
XI	3	*Debt limit 10% of equalized valuation for integrated aid school district	SJR 6	JR 35	1959	AJR 1	JR 8	1961	Apr. 1961	409,963	224,783	765,807[4]
VIII	3	**"Indians not taxed" exclusion removed from apportionment formula	AJR 121	JR 68	1959	SJR 11	JR 32	1961	"	631,296	259,577	"
IV	23	*County executive: 4-year term	"	"	"	AJR 61	JR 64	1961	"	527,075	331,393	"
IV	4	*County executive: 2-year terms	"	"	"	"	"	"	"			"
IV	23a	*County executive veto power	"	"	"	"	"	"	"	524,240	319,378	"
IV	3	Time for apportionment of seats in the state legislature	AJR 162	JR 96	1961	AJR 23	JR 9	1963	Nov. 1962	232,851	277,014	1,265,900
IV	26	Salary increases during term for justices and judges	SJR 76	JR 68	1961	SJR 4	JR 7	1963	"	216,205	335,774	"
XI	3	*Equalized value debt limit	AJR 92	JR 71	1961	AJR 19	JR 8	1963	Apr. 1963	285,296	231,702	635,510[4]
VIII	10	Maximum state appropriation for forestry increased	AJR 133	JR 90	1961	AJR 73	JR 32	1963	"	440,978	536,724	"
XI	3	Property valuation for debt limit adjusted	AJR 134	JR 91	1961	AJR 74	JR 33	1963	Apr. 1964	336,994	572,276	1,046,801[4]

HISTORY OF CONSTITUTIONAL AMENDMENTS
April 2, 2013–Continued

Art.	Sec.	Subject	First Approval	Second Approval	Date of Election	Vote For	Vote Against	Total Vote for Governor
XII	1	Constitutional amendments, submission of related items in a single proposition	SJR 15, JR 30, 1961	SJR 1, JR 1, SS '63[6], 1965	"	317,676	582,045	"
VI	4	*Coroner and surveyor abolished in counties of 500,000	AJR 14, JR 30, 1963	SJR 17, JR 5, 1965	Apr. 1965	380,059	215,169	738,831[4]
IV	24	*Lotteries, definition revised	SJR 42, JR 35, 1963	SJR 13, JR 2, 1965	"	454,390	194,327	"
IV	13	*Legislators on active duty in armed forces	SJR 24, JR 34, 1963	SJR 15, JR 14, 1965	Apr. 1966	362,935	189,641	564,132[4]
VII	2	*Establishment of inferior courts	SJR 32, JR 48, 1963	SJR 26, JR 50, 1965	"	321,434	216,341	"
VII	15	*Justices of the peace abolished	"	"	"	"	"	"
XI	3	*Special district public utility debt limit	SJR 59, JR 44, 1963	SJR 11, JR 51, 1967	"	307,502	199,919	"
I	23	*Transportation of children to private schools	AJR 70, JR 46, 1965	AJR 10, JR 58, 1967	Apr. 1967	494,236	377,107	856,650[4]
I	26	*Judicial salary increased during term	AJR 162, JR 96, 1965	AJR 7, JR 13, 1967	"	489,989	328,292	"
IV	1m,1n	*4-year term for governor and lieutenant governor	AJR 4, JR 80, 1965	AJR 17, JR 17, 1967	"	534,368	310,478	"
V	3	*Joint election of governor and lieutenant governor	AJR 3, JR 45, 1965	SJR 12, JR 10, 1967	"	507,339	312,267	"
VI	1m	*4-year term for secretary of state	AJR 4, JR 80, 1965	SJR 11, JR 11, 1967	"	520,326	311,974	"
VI	1n	*4-year term for state treasurer	AJR 4, JR 80, 1965	AJR 8, JR 14, 1967	"	514,280	314,873	"
VI	1p	*4-year term for attorney general	AJR 4, JR 80, 1965	SJR 12, JR 10, 1967	"	515,962	311,603	"
VI	4	*Sheriffs, no limit on successive terms	AJR 72, JR 61, 1965	SJR 12, JR 10, 1967	Apr. 1967	508,242	324,544	856,650[4]
IV	11	*Legislative sessions, more than one permitted in biennium	AJR 5, JR 57, 1965	SJR 7, JR 12, 1967	Apr. 1968	670,757	267,997	884,996[4]
VII	24	*Uniform retirement date for justices and circuit judges	SJR 36, JR 101, 1965	AJR 15, JR 48, 1967	"	734,046	215,455	"
VII	24	*Temporary appointment of justices and circuit judges	SJR 36, JR 101, 1965	SJR 96, JR 56, 1967	"	"	"	"
VIII	10	*Forestry appropriation from sources other than property tax	SJR 28, JR 43, 1965	SJR 96, JR 56, 1967	"	678,249	245,807	"
IV	23	*Uniform county government modified	AJR 18, JR 49, 1965	SJR 18, JR 25, 1967	"	652,705	286,512	"
IV	23a	*County executive to have veto power	AJR 1, JR 58, 1967	SJR 8, JR 2, 1969	Apr. 1969	326,445	321,851	706,324[2]
VIII	7	*State public debt for specified purposes allowed	AJR 74, JR 38, 1969	AJR 1, JR 3, 1969	"	411,062	258,366	"
I	24	*Private use of school buildings	SJR 58, JR 32, 1969	AJR 10, JR 27, 1971	Apr. 1972	871,707	298,016	⌉[1]
IV	23	*County government systems authorized	SJR 63, JR 33, 1969	SJR 4, JR 13, 1971	"	571,285	515,255	
IV	4	*Coroner/medical examiner option	AJR 41, JR 37, 1969	SJR 38, JR 21, 1971	"	795,497	323,930	
X	3	*Released time for religious instruction	AJR 140, JR 44, 1971	AJR 17, JR 28, 1971	"	595,075	585,511	
I	25	*Equality of the sexes	SJR 13, JR 31, 1971	AJR 21, JR 5, 1973	Apr. 1973	447,240	520,936	1,008,553[2]
I	24	*Charitable bingo authorized	SJR 3, JR 12, 1971	AJR 6, JR 3, 1973	Apr. 1974	645,544	391,499	758,587[4]
IV	26	*Increased benefits for retired public employes	AJR 31, JR 30, 1971	SJR 15, JR 15, 1973	"	396,051	315,545	"
VII	13	*Removal of judges by 2/3 vote of legislature for cause	AJR 1, JR 39, 1971	AJR 55, JR 25, 1973	"	493,496	193,867	"
VIII	1	*Taxation of agricultural lands	AJR 145, JR 38, 1973	AJR 1, JR 29, 1973	Apr. 1975	353,377	340,518	699,043[4]
VIII	3,7	*Public debt for veterans' housing	AJR 133, JR 37, 1973	AJR 1, JR 3, 1975	"	385,915	300,232	"
VIII	7,10	*Internal improvements for transportation facilities[9]	AJR 44, JR 32, 1971	AJR 2, JR 2, 1975	"	342,596[4]	341,291[9]	"
XI	3	*Exclusion of certain debt from municipal debt limit	SJR 44, JR 32, 1971	SJR 55, JR 133, 1973	"	310,434	337,925	"
XIII	2	*Dueling: repeal of disenfranchisement	SJR 6, JR 10, 1973	SJR 4, JR 4, 1975	"	395,616	282,726	"

Art.	Sec.	Subject	First Approval	Second Approval	Date of Election	Vote For	Vote Against	Total Vote for Governor
XI	3	Municipal indebtedness increased up to 10% of equalized valuation	AJR 58, JR 35, 1973	AJR 6, JR 6, 1975	Apr. 1976	328,097	715,420	1,168,606[4]
VIII	7(2) (a),10	Internal improvements for transportation facilities[9]	AJR 133, JR 37, 1973	AJR 2, JR 2, 1975	Nov. 1976[9]	722,658	935,152	1,332,220[8]
IV	24	*Charitable raffle games authorized	AJR 43, JR 19, 1975	AJR 10, JR 6, 1977	Apr. 1977	483,518	300,473	775,490[4]
VII	2	*Unified court system [also changed I-21; IV-17 and 26; VII-3 to 11, 14, 16 to 23; XIV-16(1) to (4)]	AJR 11, JR 13, 1975	SJR 9, JR 7, 1977	"	490,437	215,939	"
VII	5	*Court of appeals created [also changed I-21(1); VII-2 and 3(3); XIV-16(5)]	"	"	"	455,350	229,316	"
VII	11,13	*Court system disciplinary proceedings	"	"	"	565,087	151,418	"
VII	24	*Retirement age for justices and judges set by law	"	"	"	506,207	244,170	"
IV	23	Town government uniformity	AJR 22, JR 15, 1977	AJR 20, JR 18, 1977	Apr. 1978	179,011	383,395	"
V	7,8	*Gubernatorial succession	SJR 51, JR 32, 1977	SJR 1, JR 3, 1979	Apr. 1979	538,959	187,440	840,166[4]
XIII	10	*Lieutenant governor vacancy	"	"	"	540,186	181,497	"
IV	9	*Senate presiding officer [also changed 5-8]	"	"	"	372,734	327,008	"
V	1	*4-year constitutional officer terms (improved wording) [also changed V-1m and 1n; VI-1, 1m, 1n and 1p]	"	"	"	533,620	164,768	"
I	8	*Right to bail[10]	AJR 9, JR 76, SS'80[6]	AJR 5, JR 8, 1981	Apr. 1981	505,092[10]	185,405[10]	
XI	1,4	*Obsolete corporation and banking provisions	AJR 53, JR 21, 1979	AJR 13, JR 9, 1981	"	418,997	186,898	
XI	3	*Indebtedness period for sewage collection or treatment systems	SJR 28, JR 43, 1979	SJR 5, JR 7, 1981	"	386,792	250,866	
XIII	12	*Primaries in recall elections	SJR 5, JR 41, 1979	SJR 2, JR 6, 1981	"	366,635	259,820	
VI	4	*Counties responsible for acts of sheriff	AJR 99, JR 38, 1979	AJR 7, JR 15, 1981	Apr. 1982	316,156	219,752	
I	1,18	*Gender-neutral wording (also changed X-1 and 2)	AJR 76, JR 36, 1979	AJR 35, JR 29, 1981	Nov. 1982	771,267	479,053	1,580,344
IV	3	*Military personnel treatment in redistricting	"	"	"	834,188	321,331	"
IV	4,5	*Obsolete 1881 amendment reference	AJR 76, JR 36, 1979	AJR 35, JR 29, 1981	Nov. 1982	919,349	238,884	1,580,340
IV	30	*Elections by legislature	"	"	"	977,438	193,679	"
X	1	*Obsolete reference to election and term of superintendent of public instruction	AJR 76, JR 36, 1979	AJR 35, JR 29, 1981	Nov. 1982	934,236	215,961	"
X	2	*Obsolete reference to military draft exemption purchase; school fund	"	"	"	887,488	295,693	"
XIV	3	*Obsolete transition from territory to statehood (also changed XIV-4 to 12; XIV-14, 15)	"	"	"	926,875	223,213	"
XIV	16(1)	*Obsolete transitional provisions of 1977 court reorganization [also changed XIV-16(2), (3), (5)]	"	"	"	882,091	237,698	"
XIV	16(4)	*Terms on supreme court effective date provision	AJR 9, JR 40, 1983	AJR 9, JR 21, 1985	Apr. 1986	960,540	190,366	"
I	1	*Rewording to parallel Declaration of Independence	AJR 9, JR 40, 1983	AJR 3, JR 14, 1985	"	419,699	65,418	461,118[4]
III	1-6	*Revision of suffrage defined by general law	AJR 33, JR 30, 1983	AJR 3, JR 14, 1985	"	401,911	83,183	"
XIII	5	*Modernizing constitutional text	"	"	"	404,273	82,512	"
XIII	5	*Obsolete suffrage right on Indian land	"	"	"	381,339	102,090	"
IV	24(5)	*Permitting pari-mutuel on-track betting	AJR 45, JR 36, 1985	AJR 2, JR 3, 1987	Apr. 1987	580,089	529,729	837,747[4]
IV	24(6)	*Authorizing the creation of a state lottery	SJR 1, JR 35, 1985	AJR 3, JR 4, 1987	Apr. 1987	739,181	391,942	"
VIII	1	Authorizing income tax credits or refunds for property or sales taxes	AJR 117, JR 74, 1987	SJR 9, JR 2, 1989	Apr. 1989	405,765	406,863	882,784[4]
V	10	*Redefining the partial veto power of the governor	SJR 71, JR 76, 1987	SJR 11, JR 39, 1989	Apr. 1990	387,068	252,481	685,878[4]
VIII	10	Providing housing for persons of low or moderate income	AJR 101, JR 55, 1989	AJR 7, JR 2, 1991	Apr. 1991	295,823	402,921	"
VIII	7(2)(a)1	*Railways and other railroad facilities (also created VIII-10)	SJR76, JR 52, 1989	SJR 30, JR 9, 1991	Apr. 1992	650,592	457,690	⌐[1]
IV	26	*Legislative and judiciary compensation, effective date	AJR 47, JR54, 1989	AJR 16, JR 13, 1991	"	736,832	348,645	"

HISTORY OF CONSTITUTIONAL AMENDMENTS
April 2, 2013–Continued

Art.	Sec.	Subject	First Approval	Second Approval	Date of Election	Vote For	Vote Against	Total Vote for Governor
VIII	1	Residential property tax reduction	AJR 81, JR 76, 1989	SJR 12, JR 14, 1991	Nov. 1992	675,876	1,536,975	2,531,114[8]
I	9m	*Crime victims	SJR 41, JR 17, 1991	SJR 3, JR 2, 1993	Apr. 1993	861,405	163,087	1,075,386[2]
IV	24	*Gambling, limiting "lottery"; divorce under general law (also amended IV-31,32)	AJR 1, JR 27, SS'92[6]	SJR 2, JR 3, 1993	"	623,987	435,180	"
I	3	Removal of unnecessary references to masculine gender [also amended 1-3, 7, 9, 19, 21(2); IV-6, 12, 13, 23a; V-4, 6; VI-2; VII-1, 12; XI-3a; XIII-4, 11, 12(6)]	AJR 121, JR 21, 1993	AJR 12, JR 3, 1995	Apr. 1995	412,032	498,801	939,676[4]
IV	24(6)(a)	Authorizing sports lottery dedicated to athletic facilities	SJR 49, JR 27, 1993	SJR 3, JR 2, 1995	Apr. 1995	348,818	618,377	"
VII	10(1)	Removal of restriction on judges holding nonjudicial public office after resignation during the judicial term	AJR 81, JR 20, 1993	AJR 15, JR 4, 1995	Apr. 1995	390,744	503,239	"
XIII	3	*Eligibility to seek or hold public office if convicted of a felony or a misdemeanor involving violation of a public trust	AJR 3, JR 19, 1993	AJR 16, JR 28, 1995	Nov. 1996	1,292,934	543,516	2,196,169[8]
I	25	*Guaranteeing the right to keep and bear arms	AJR 53, JR 27, 1995	AJR 11, JR 21, 1997	Nov. 1998	1,205,873	425,052	1,756,014
VI	4(1)(3)(5)(6)	*4-year term for sheriff; sheriffs permitted to hold nonpartisan office; allowed legislature to provide for election to fill vacancy during term	AJR 37, JR 23, 1995	SJR 43, JR 18, 1997	Nov. 1998	1,161,942	412,508	"
IV	24(3)(5)(6)	Distributing state lottery, bingo and pari-mutuel proceeds for property tax	AJR 80, JR 19, 1997	AJR 2, JR 2, 1999	Apr. 1999	648,903	105,976	758,965[4]
I	26	*Right to fish, hunt, trap, and take game	SJR 2, JR 16, 2001	AJR 1, JR 8, 2003	Apr. 2003	668,459	146,182	800,785[4]
VI	4(1)(3)(4)	*4-year term for county clerks, treasurers, clerks of circuit court, district attorneys, coroners, elected surveyors, and registers of deeds (also amended VII-12)	AJR 10, JR 12, 2003	SJR 2, JR 2, 2005	Apr. 2005	534,742	177,037	552,790[4]
XIII	13	*Marriage between one man and one woman	AJR 66, JR 29, 2003	SJR 53, JR 30, 2005	Nov. 2006	1,264,310	862,924	2,161,700
V	10(1)(c)	*Gubernatorial partial veto power	SJR 33, JR 46, 2005	SJR 5, JR 26, 2007	Apr. 2008	575,582	239,613	830,450[4]

*Ratified.

[1]No election for statewide office. [2]Total vote for State Superintendent. [3]No number assigned to joint resolution. [4]Total vote for Justice of Supreme Court. [5]Ratified but declared invalid by Supreme Court in State ex rel. Owen v. Donald, 160 Wis. 21 (1915). [6]Special session: July 1948, December 1964, June 1980, and August 1992. [7]Ratified but declared invalid by Supreme Court in State ex rel. Thomson v. Zimmerman, 264 Wis. 644 (1953). [8]Total vote for presidential delegate election. [9]Recount resulted in rejection (342,132 to 342,309). However, the Dane County Circuit Court ruled the recount invalid due to election irregularities and required that the referendum be resubmitted to the electorate. Resubmitted to the electorate November 1976 by the 1975 Wisconsin Legislature through Ch. 224, s.145r, Laws of 1975. [10]As a result of a Dane County Circuit Court injunction, vote totals were certified April 7, 1982, by the Board of State Canvassers.

Sources: Official records of the Government Accountability Board; Laws of Wisconsin, 2011 and previous volumes.

SUMMARY – CHANGING THE WISCONSIN CONSTITUTION

To amend the Wisconsin Constitution, it is necessary for two consecutive Wisconsin Legislatures to adopt an identical amendment (known as "first consideration" and "second consideration") and for a majority of the electorate to ratify the amendment at a subsequent election. See Art. XII, Sec. 1.

Since the adoption of the Wisconsin Constitution in 1848, the electorate has voted 143 out of 194 times to amend a total of 126 sections of the constitution (excluding the same vote for more than one item but including a vote that was later resubmitted by the legislature and two votes that were declared invalid by the courts). The Wisconsin Legislature adopted 156 acts or joint resolutions to submit these changes to the electorate.

STATEWIDE REFERENDA ELECTIONS OTHER THAN CONSTITUTIONAL AMENDMENTS

Question	Law Submitting	Year	Date of Election	Vote For	Vote Against
Territorial					
*Formation of a state government.	Territorial Laws 1846, page 5 (Jan.31)		Apr. 1846	12,334	2,487
Ratification of first constitution.	Art. XIX, Sec. 9 of 1846 Constitution		Apr. 1847	14,119	20,231
Extend suffrage to colored persons[1]	Supl. resolution to 1846 Constitution		Apr. 1847	7,664	14,615
*Ratification of second constitution	Art. XIV, Sec. 9 of 1848 Constitution		Mar. 1848	16,799	6,384
State					
*Extend suffrage to colored persons[2]	Ch.137	1849	Nov. 1849	5,265	4,075
*State banks; advisory referendum	Ch.143	1851	Nov. 1851	31,289	9,126
*General banking law	Ch.479	1852	Nov. 1852	32,826	8,711
*Liquor prohibition; advisory referendum.	Ch.101	1853	Nov. 1853	27,519	24,109
Extend suffrage to colored persons.	Ch.44	1857	Nov. 1857	28,235	41,345
*Amend general banking law; redemption of bank notes	Ch.98	1858	Nov. 1858	27,267	2,837
*Amend general banking law; circulation of bank notes	Ch.242	1861	Nov. 1861	57,646	2,515
*Amend general banking law; interest rate 7% per year	Ch.203	1862	Nov. 1862	46,269	7,794
Extend suffrage to colored persons[2]	Ch.414	1865	Nov. 1865	46,588	55,591
*Amend general banking law; taxing shareholders	Ch.102	1866	Nov. 1866	49,714	19,151
*Abolish office of bank comptroller.	JR12	1867			
*Incorporation of savings banks and savings societies	Ch.28	1868	Nov. 1868	15,499	1,948
*Women's suffrage upon school matters	Ch.384	1876	Nov. 1876	4,029	3,069
Revise 1897 banking law; banking department under commission	Ch.211	1885	Nov. 1886	43,581	38,998
*Primary election law	Ch.303	1897	Nov. 1898	86,872	92,607
Pocket ballots and coupon voting systems	Ch.451	1903	Nov. 1904	130,366	80,102
Women's suffrage	Ch.522	1905	Apr. 1906	45,958	111,139
*Soldiers' bonus financed by 3-mill property tax and income tax.	Ch.227	1911	Nov. 1912	135,545	227,024
*Wisconsin prohibition enforcement act	Ch.667	1919	Sept. 1919	165,762	57,324
*U.S. prohibition act (Volstead Act); memorializing Congress to amend.	Ch.556	1919	Nov. 1920	419,309	199,876
*Repeal of Wisconsin prohibition enforcement act	SJR42 JR47	1925	Nov. 1926	349,443	177,603
"	"	"	"	350,337	196,402
*Modification of Wisconsin prohibition enforcement act; advisory referendum	SJR14 JR16	1929	Apr. 1929	321,688	200,545
County distribution of auto licenses; advisory referendum	SJR26 JR11	1931	Apr. 1931	183,716	368,674
*Sunday blue law repeal; advisory referendum.	AJR116 JR114	1931	Apr. 1932	396,436	271,786
*Old-age pensions; advisory referendum	AJR42 JR64	SS'33	Apr. 1934	531,915	154,729
*Teacher tenure law repeal; advisory referendum.	AJR67 JR100	1939	Apr. 1940	403,782	372,524
Property tax levy for high school aid; 2 mills of assessed valuation.	Ch.525	1943	Apr. 1944	131,004	410,315
Daylight saving time; advisory referendum	SJR24 JR4	1947	Apr. 1947	313,091	379,740
3% retail sales tax for veterans bonus; advisory referendum	SJR58 JR62	1947	Nov. 1948	258,497	825,990
4-year term for constitutional officers; advisory referendum	SJR11 JR13	1951	Apr. 1951	210,821	328,613
Apportionment of legislature by area and population; advisory referendum	Ch.728	1951	Nov. 1952	689,615	753,092
*New residents entitled to vote for president and vice president	Ch.76	1953	Nov. 1954	550,056	414,680

STATEWIDE REFERENDA ELECTIONS OTHER THAN CONSTITUTIONAL AMENDMENTS-Continued

Question	Law Submitting		Date of Election	Vote For	Vote Against
Statewide educational television tax-supported; advisory referendum	AJR74	JR66	1953	Nov. 1954	308,385	697,262
*Daylight saving time		Ch.6	1957	Apr. 1957	578,661	480,656
*Ex-residents entitled to vote for president and vice president		Ch.512	1961	Nov. 1962	627,279	229,375
Gasoline tax increase for highway construction; advisory referendum	AJR3	JR3	SS'63	Apr. 1964	150,769	889,364
*New residents entitled to vote after 6 months		Chs.88,89	1965	Nov. 1966	582,389	256,246
State control and funding of vocational education; advisory referendum	AJR12	JR4	1969	Apr. 1969	292,560	409,789
*Recreational lands bonding; advisory referendum	AJR17	JR5	1969	Apr. 1969	361,630	322,882
*Water pollution abatement bonding; advisory referendum	"	"	"	"	446,763	246,968
*New residents entitled to vote after 10 days		Ch.85	1975	Nov. 1976	1,017,887	660,875
*Presidential voting revised		Ch.394	1977	Nov. 1978	782,181	424,386
*Overseas voting revised		"	"	"	658,289	524,029
*Public inland lake protection and rehabilitation districts		Ch.299	1979	Nov. 1980	1,210,452	355,024
*Nuclear weapons moratorium and reduction; advisory referendum	AJR99	JR38	1981	Sept. 1982	641,514	205,018
*Nuclear waste site locating; advisory referendum	AJR5	JR5	1983	Apr. 1983	78,327	628,414
*Gambling casinos on excursion vessels; advisory referendum		WisAct 321	1991	Apr. 1993	465,432	604,289
*Gambling casino restrictions; advisory referendum		"	"	"	646,827	416,722
*Video poker and other forms of video gambling allowed; advisory referendum		"	"	"	358,045	702,864
*Pari-mutuel on-track betting continuation; advisory referendum		"	"	"	548,580	507,403
*State-operated lottery continuation; advisory referendum		"	"	"	773,306	287,585
*Extended suffrage in federal elections to adult children of U.S. citizens living abroad		WisAct 182	1999	Nov. 2000	1,293,458	792,975
*Death penalty; advisory referendum	SJR5	JR58	2005	Nov. 2006	1,166,571	934,508

*Ratified.

[1]For text of resolution, see Wisconsin State Historical Society, Constitutional Series, Volume II, *The Convention of 1846*, edited by Milo M. Quaife, p. 755.

[2]In *Gillespie v. Palmer*, 20 Wis. 544 (1866), the Wisconsin Supreme Court ruled that Chapter 137, Laws of 1849, extending suffrage to colored persons, was ratified November 6, 1849.

Sources: Official records of the Government Accountability Board; *Laws of Wisconsin*, 2011 and previous volumes.

SUMMARY – STATEWIDE REFERENDA ELECTIONS

Statewide referendum questions are submitted to the electorate by the Wisconsin Legislature to 1) to ratify a law extending the right of suffrage (as required by the state constitution); 2) to ratify a law that has been passed contingent on voter approval; or 3) to seek voter opinion through an advisory referendum. Since 1848, the Wisconsin Legislature has presented 53 referendum questions to the Wisconsin electorate through the passage of acts or joint resolutions; 39 were ratified. During territorial times, the territorial legislature sent 4 questions to the electorate. Two of these passed: one to ratify the state constitution and one to allow the formation of a state government.

Framework of Government

4

The framework of Wisconsin government: an overall view of Wisconsin government, a chart of its organization, and a map of state agencies

Red Power Roundup at Wisconsin Historical Society, July 2009

(Wisconsin Historical Society)

LOCATION OF STATE AGENCIES IN MADISON
January 3, 2013

State Agency	Street Address	Map Locator Number
Administration, Department of	101 E. Wilson St.	13
Agriculture, Trade and Consumer Protection, Department of	2811 Agriculture Dr.	—
Attorney General, Office of the	State Capitol, Rm. 114 East	1
Children and Families, Department of	201 E. Washington Ave., 2nd Floor	9
Corrections, Department of	3099 E. Washington Ave.	—
Educational Approval Board	201 W. Washington Ave., 3rd Floor	16
Educational Communications Board	3319 W. Beltline Hwy.	—
Emergency Management, Wisconsin	2400 Wright St.	—
Employee Trust Funds, Department of	801 W. Badger Rd.	—
Employment Relations Commission	1457 E. Washington Ave., Suite 101	—
Financial Institutions, Department of	201 W. Washington Ave., Suite 500	16
Government Accountability Board	212 E. Washington Ave., 3rd Floor	17
Governor, Office of the	State Capitol, Rm. 115 East	1
Health Services, Department of	1 W. Wilson St.	14
Higher Educational Aids Board	131 W. Wilson St., Suite 902	15
Housing and Economic Development Authority	201 W. Washington Ave., Suite 700	16
Insurance, Commissioner of	125 S. Webster St.	11
Investment Board	121 E. Wilson St.	12
Justice, Department of	17 W. Main St.	5
Legislative Audit Bureau	22 E. Mifflin St., Suite 500	2
Legislative Council	1 E. Main St., Suite 401	4
Legislative Fiscal Bureau	1 E. Main St., Suite 301	4
Legislative Reference Bureau	1 E. Main St., Suite 200	4
Legislative Technology Services Bureau	17 W. Main St., Suite 200	5
Lieutenant Governor, Office of the	State Capitol, Rm. 19 East	1
Military Affairs, Department of	2400 Wright St.	—
Natural Resources, Department of	101 S. Webster St.	10
Public Instruction, Department of	125 S. Webster St.	11
Public Service Commission	610 N. Whitney Way.	—
Railroads, Office of the Commissioner	610 N. Whitney Way, Rm. 110	—
Revenue, Department of	2135 Rimrock Rd.	—
Safety and Professional Services, Department of	1400 E. Washington Ave., Rm. 112	—
Secretary of State, Office of the	30 W. Mifflin St., 10th Floor.	8
State Courts, Director of	State Capitol, Rm. 16 East	1
State Employment Relations, Office of	101 E. Wilson St., 4th Floor	13
State Law Library	120 Martin Luther King, Jr. Blvd.	5
State Historical Society Museum	30 N. Carroll St.	7
State Historical Society of Wisconsin	816 State St.	—
State Public Defender, Office of the	315 N. Henry St., 2nd Floor	6
State Treasurer, Office of the	1 S. Pinckney St., Suite 360	3
Supreme Court	State Capitol, Rm. 16 East	1
Technical College System	4622 University Ave.	—
Tourism, Department of	201 W. Washington Ave.	16
Transportation, Department of	4802 Sheboygan Ave.	—
University of Wisconsin System	1220 Linden Dr.	—
Veterans Affairs, Department of	201 W. Washington Ave.	16
Wisconsin Economic Development Corporation	201 W. Washington Ave.	16
Wisconsin Veterans Museum	30 W. Mifflin St.	8
Workforce Development, Department of	201 E. Washington Ave.	9

Source: List of State Agencies, at: http://www.wisconsin.gov/state/core/agency_index.html [January 2013].

CENTRAL MADISON LOCATOR MAP

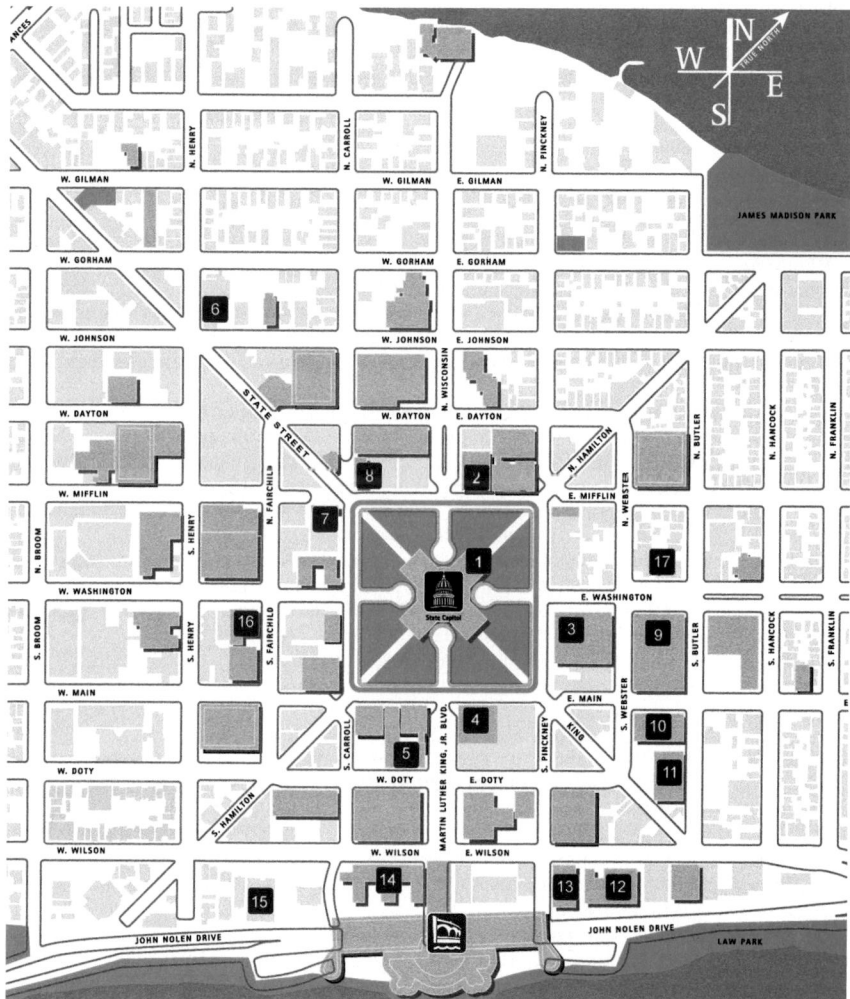

Base map: City of Madison, Planning Division.

THE FRAMEWORK OF WISCONSIN GOVERNMENT

Government at a Glance

Wisconsin state government is divided into three branches: legislative, executive, and judicial. The legislative branch includes the Wisconsin Legislature, which is composed of the senate and the assembly, and the service agencies and staff that assist the legislators. The executive branch, headed by the governor, includes five other elected constitutional officers, as well as 17 departments and 11 independent agencies created by statute. The judicial branch consists of the Wisconsin Supreme Court, the Court of Appeals, circuit courts, and municipal courts, as well as the staff and advisory groups that assist the courts. Each of the three branches is described in detail in its respective section of the *Blue Book.*

Local units of government in Wisconsin include 72 counties, 190 cities, 405 villages, 1,256 towns, and several hundred special districts.

Origins of the 30th State

Wisconsin's original residents were Native American hunters who arrived here about 14,000 years ago. The area's first farmers appear to have been the Hopewell people who raised corn, squash, and pumpkins about 2,000 years ago. They also were hunters and fishers, and their trade routes stretched to the Atlantic Coast and the Gulf of Mexico. Later arrivals included the Chippewa, Ho-Chunk (Winnebago), Mahican/Munsee, Menominee, Oneida, Potawatomi, and Sioux.

From Wilderness to Statehood. The first Europeans to reach Wisconsin were French explorers, fur trappers, and missionaries. Wisconsin was included in the French sphere of influence from the 1630s until the signing of the 1763 Treaty of Paris, which concluded the French and Indian War and ceded the land encompassing Wisconsin to Great Britain. At the end of the Revolutionary War, 20 years later, the British ceded the vast, unsettled territory west of the Appalachian Mountains to the new United States of America. (Actual British control of the area did not end, however, until 1814 at the conclusion of the War of 1812.)

As a U.S. territory, Wisconsin was initially governed by the Northwest Ordinance of 1787, and then sequentially by the laws of the Indiana Territory, the Illinois Territory, the Michigan Territory and, finally in 1836, the Wisconsin Territory.

On August 6, 1846, the Congress of the United States authorized the people living in what was then called the Territory of Wisconsin "to form a constitution and State government, for the purpose of being admitted into the Union". Based on this enabling act, the people of the territory called a constitutional convention in Madison to draft a fundamental law for governing the new state. The first proposal for a constitution was drafted in 1846 and submitted to the people on April 6, 1847, but the voters rejected it on a 20,231-to-14,119 vote because of several controversial provisions involving banking, voting rights, property rights of married women, and homesteading.

On March 13, 1848, a second convention submitted its draft, which was ratified by a vote of 16,799 to 6,384. The constitution then adopted remains in force to this day, although it has been amended on numerous occasions.

On May 29, 1848, Wisconsin became the 30th state admitted to the Union.

State Powers and Prohibitions. The enabling act passed by the U.S. Congress in 1846 declared that the Territory of Wisconsin was authorized to form a constitution and state government "on an equal footing with the original States in all respects whatsoever". From the moment of its birth, like the original states, the State of Wisconsin, its people, its lawmaking bodies, its administrative machinery, and its courts were subject to the U.S. Constitution.

In ratifying the U.S. Constitution, the 13 original states specifically delegated a number of powers to the U.S. Congress. Wisconsin agreed to this delegation when joining the Union. Congress is given the authority to regulate interstate and foreign commerce, maintain armed forces, declare war, coin money, establish a postal system, and grant patents and copyrights. Congress also has power to "make all laws which shall be necessary and proper" for carrying out its responsibilities.

The Tenth Amendment to the U.S. Constitution specifies: "The powers not delegated to the United States by the constitution, nor prohibited by it to the States, are reserved to the States, respectively, or to the people." Although the powers delegated to the federal government and the powers reserved to the states might appear to be neatly delineated, government responsibilities and activities have not been that clear-cut. In fact, many powers are exercised concurrently by the federal government and the states. Through judicial interpretation and laws enacted in response to changing societal needs, the powers exercised by Congress have been greatly expanded to include many activities once considered reserved to the states, as well as new authority not even imagined by the drafters, such as regulation of television and radio or development of a space exploration program. Likewise, the states have broadened their functions as society and technology have evolved.

The Many Sources of State Law

On April 20, 1836, the U.S. Congress passed the Organic Law establishing the Wisconsin Territory, as of July 3, 1836. It prescribed that the existing laws of the Territory of Michigan, to which Wisconsin had belonged, were to be "extended over the said territory . . . subject, nevertheless, to be altered, modified or repealed, by the governor and legislative assembly".

The Wisconsin Constitution continued the laws of the Territory of Wisconsin, by providing in Section 2 of Article XIV: "All laws now in force in the territory of Wisconsin which are not repugnant to this constitution shall remain in force until they expire by their own limitation or be altered or repealed by the legislature."

In addition to the provisions of the U.S. and Wisconsin Constitutions, the citizens of this state are governed by the wide-ranging laws contained in more than 7,000 pages of the Wisconsin Statutes. Even this body of law is not detailed enough. The Wisconsin Legislature has found that some areas are so technically complex that implementation of legislative policy must be left to certain state agencies with the power to issue administrative rules that have the effect of state law.

Notwithstanding the detailed wording of statutory law and administrative rules, there will still be specific provisions that are subject to various interpretations. In these cases, formal law is further defined by courts or administrative commissions authorized to interpret state law.

Making State Government Work

According to the general division of state government powers, the legislative branch enacts the laws; the executive branch carries them out (or *executes* them); and the judicial branch interprets them. This very simple description of state government tells only part of the story. Actually, all three branches play a part in establishing public policy, determining the meaning of the law, and ensuring that the laws are faithfully administered.

When most people think of "the law", they tend to regard it as something restrictive – a rule prohibiting certain actions. Although this may be one outcome, the real reason for the existence of law in a democratic system is to give the greatest benefit to the greatest number of people while protecting the individual rights prescribed by the federal and state constitutions. The only manner in which this can be achieved is by establishing a specific set of rules that attempt to prescribe for all citizens the limits of their rights and obligations.

Developing Public Policy. Policy cannot become law without legislative action. Each member of the legislature may introduce bills proposing new laws, joint resolutions proposing constitutional amendments, or simple and joint resolutions dealing with other matters, and each may offer amendments to proposals introduced by other members.

The governor also plays a major role in the development of formal public policy. The Wisconsin Constitution requires the governor to "communicate to the legislature, at every session, the condition of the state, and recommend such matters . . . for their consideration as he may deem expedient." This is done in the State of the State message, the budget message, and in special messages focusing on particular matters. In cases where a specific problem needs immediate legislative attention, the governor may call the legislature into a special session focusing on the matter. Before a bill becomes law, it must be passed by the legislature and signed by the governor. If the governor vetoes the bill instead of signing it, it can only become law if it is approved a second time by a two-thirds vote in each house of the legislature. In the case of appropriation bills that authorize spending, such as a budget, the governor can use the "partial veto" and veto only parts of the bill rather than the whole proposal. The veto power gives the governor a great deal of control over the content of any new law.

Once a new proposal is enacted, the governor, as the chief executive officer of the state, takes an active part in implementing the policy through oversight of the agencies involved in day-to-day administration of the law. According to the constitution, the governor "shall expedite all such measures as may be resolved upon by the legislature, and shall take care that the laws be faithfully executed."

The judicial branch also has an official role to play in the development of public policy. Although courts are not involved in the enactment of new laws, they do resolve conflicts about existing law – that is, they interpret the law. A court decision may occasionally result in an interpretation of a law that has quite a different effect from what the legislature originally intended. The legislature can redraft and clarify that law if it disagrees with the interpretation.

The opinions and concerns voiced by citizens of Wisconsin constitute the major source of ideas for new legislation. New policy proposals often result from everyday situations citizens encounter in their own communities. If they think that greater property tax relief is needed or that health insurance is unaffordable or that the business climate could be improved, they may determine "there ought to be a law". An individual may decide to write a letter to the editor of a newspaper, contact a legislator, or tell the governor about it. An association to which the person belongs may hire a spokesperson, called a "lobbyist", to recommend legislation or appear at legislative hearings.

State agencies are another primary source of public policy ideas. While administering current programs, departments are in a natural position to see how policies are working and whether they need to be changed, expanded, or abolished. Department heads have opportunities to discuss their insights with the governor, especially during development of the biennial budget, and they may be invited to contribute expert testimony at legislative hearings.

Increasing Services. In 1848, when Wisconsin became a state, government services were relatively simple. In his annual report of 1849, the secretary of state reported payments to only 14 people within the state's executive branch, and that included the constitutional officers. In 2012, state employment totaled 69,263 full-time equivalent positions.

This growth is primarily the result of the increasing size and complexity of today's society. At one time, many Wisconsin residents had little opportunity for formal schooling; in 2012, the University of Wisconsin System enrolled 180,969 students and public elementary and secondary enrollments totaled 872,436. In 2011, the Technical College System served 362,619 students. Once, the wooden Watertown Plank Road constituted an unequaled technological advancement over the muddy wagon trails of the day; by 2013, Wisconsin had 115,095 miles of highways and streets, more than 79% of them paved. In 2012, the state had 98 publicly owned airports. In 1900, the average U.S. life expectancy at birth was 47.3 years; by 2010, it had reached 78.7 years (76.2 for males and 81.0 for females). As Wisconsin's population increases in numbers and lives longer, the state faces many challenges, including improving education, renovating mature industries, developing the economy, protecting the environment, and improving transportation and health care.

Local Units of Government

In order to carry out its numerous responsibilities, every state has created subordinate units of local government. In most cases, these are legal, rather than constitutional, creations. This means the legislature may abolish them, change them, or give them increased or decreased powers and duties, as it chooses. In Wisconsin, the local units of government consist of counties, cities, villages, towns, and school districts. Special districts may be formed to handle regional concerns. Within the limits of statutory law, each unit has the power to tax and to make legally binding rules governing its own affairs.

Counties. Wisconsin has 72 counties. Together, they cover the entire territory of the state. The government offices for each county are located in a municipality within the county designated as the "county seat". The governing body of the county is the board of supervisors. The number of supervisors may vary from county to county, but within a particular county each supervisor must represent, as nearly as practicable, an equal number of inhabitants. County supervisors are elected in the spring nonpartisan elections for 2-year terms. (Milwaukee County Board Supervisors are elected to 2-year terms beginning in 2016. Current supervisors serve 4-year terms.) Other county officials, all of whom are elected in the fall partisan elections for 4-year terms, include the sheriff, the district attorney, clerk, treasurer, coroner, register of deeds, and clerk of circuit courts. As permitted by law, counties may employ a registered land surveyor in lieu of electing a surveyor, and the majority do. An appointed county medical examiner system may be substituted for an elected coroner. (Milwaukee County must appoint a medical examiner and a registered land surveyor.)

Since January 1, 1987, counties have been required to have a central administrative officer. Counties with a population of 500,000 or more (currently only Milwaukee County) must elect a "county executive", who is chosen for a 4-year term in the spring nonpartisan elections. Counties with a population of less than 500,000 may choose to have a "county administrator" appointed by the county board. If the county has neither an executive nor an administrator, the board must designate an elected or appointed official to serve as "administrative coordinator" for the county. The county board chairperson often is chosen for this post. There are 10 counties with elected executives; 25 have appointed administrators; and 33 have an appointed administrative coordinator.

Cities and Villages. Wisconsin's 190 cities and 405 villages are incorporated under general law. Based on a constitutional amendment ratified in 1924, they have "home rule" powers to determine their local affairs. In general, minimum population for incorporation as a village is 150 residents for an isolated village and 2,500 for a metropolitan village located in a more densely populated area. For cities, the minimums are 1,000 and 5,000, respectively, but an existing village that exceeds 1,000 population may opt for city status. Depending on population, a city qualifies to be in one of four classes. However, an increase or decrease in population does not automatically move a city to a different classification. In order to move from one class to another, a city whose population makes it eligible to be in a different class may initiate the action by making the required changes in governmental structure and by the mayor publishing a proclamation to that effect. For example, Milwaukee currently is the only "first class" city. Although Madison meets the population requirements to change from "second class" to "first class", it has not chosen to do so.

Wisconsin cities currently use two forms of executive organization. The vast majority elect a mayor and a city common council, but 10 operate under a council-manager system, in which the elected council selects the manager to serve as chief executive. In those cities with the mayor-council form of government, 93 have also appointed full- or part-time city administrators. City alderpersons are elected for 2-year terms in the spring nonpartisan elections, except in Milwaukee, where alderpersons serve 4-year terms.

In most villages, executive power is vested in the village president, who presides over the village board of trustees and votes as an *ex officio* trustee, but 10 villages use a village manager form of government with the manager chosen by the elected board. An additional 97 have created full- or part-time village administrators. Village trustees are elected for 2-year terms in the spring nonpartisan elections.

Towns. Town governments govern those areas of Wisconsin that are not included inside the corporate boundaries of either a city or a village. Wisconsin has 1,256 towns, including the entire County of Menominee, which is designated as a town. Towns have only those powers granted by the Wisconsin Statutes. In addition to their traditional responsibility for local road maintenance, town governments carry out a variety of functions and, in some instances, even undertake urban-type services. The town board is usually composed of 3 supervisors, but if a board is authorized to exercise village powers or if the town population is 2,500 or more it may have up to 5 members. (Menominee County has 7 town board members, who also serve as the county board of supervisors.) Town supervisors are elected for 2-year terms in the spring nonpartisan election. They perform a number of administrative functions, and the town board chairperson has certain executive powers and duties. A town board may also create the position of town administrator.

Supervisors are expected to carry out the policies set at the annual town meeting. The annual meeting is held on the third Tuesday of April (or another date set by the electors), and during the meeting all qualified voters of the town are entitled to discuss and vote on matters specified by state law.

School Districts. There are 426 school districts in Wisconsin. These are special units of government organized to carry out a single function, the operation of the public schools. Each district is run by an elected school board, which appoints the district administrators.

WISCONSIN STATE GOVE
July

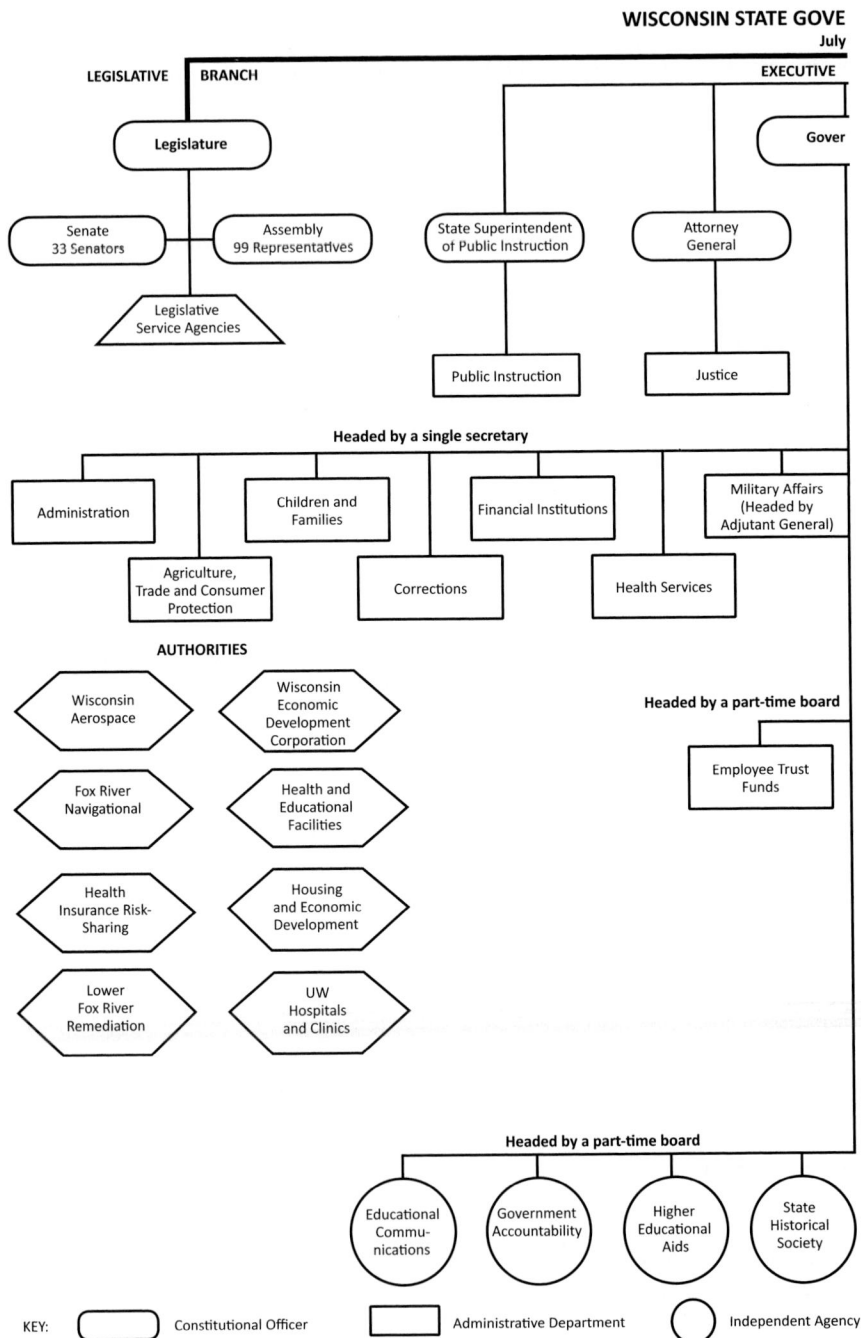

LEGISLATIVE   BRANCH

EXECUTIVE

Legislature

Gover

Senate
33 Senators

Assembly
99 Representatives

State Superintendent
of Public Instruction

Attorney
General

Legislative
Service Agencies

Public Instruction

Justice

Headed by a single secretary

Administration

Children and
Families

Financial Institutions

Military Affairs
(Headed by
Adjutant General)

Agriculture,
Trade and Consumer
Protection

Corrections

Health Services

AUTHORITIES

Wisconsin
Aerospace

Wisconsin
Economic
Development
Corporation

Headed by a part-time board

Fox River
Navigational

Health and
Educational
Facilities

Employee Trust
Funds

Health
Insurance Risk-
Sharing

Housing
and Economic
Development

Lower
Fox River
Remediation

UW
Hospitals
and Clinics

Headed by a part-time board

Educational
Commu-
nications

Government
Accountability

Higher
Educational
Aids

State
Historical
Society

KEY: Constitutional Officer   Administrative Department   Independent Agency

RNMENT ORGANIZATION
2013

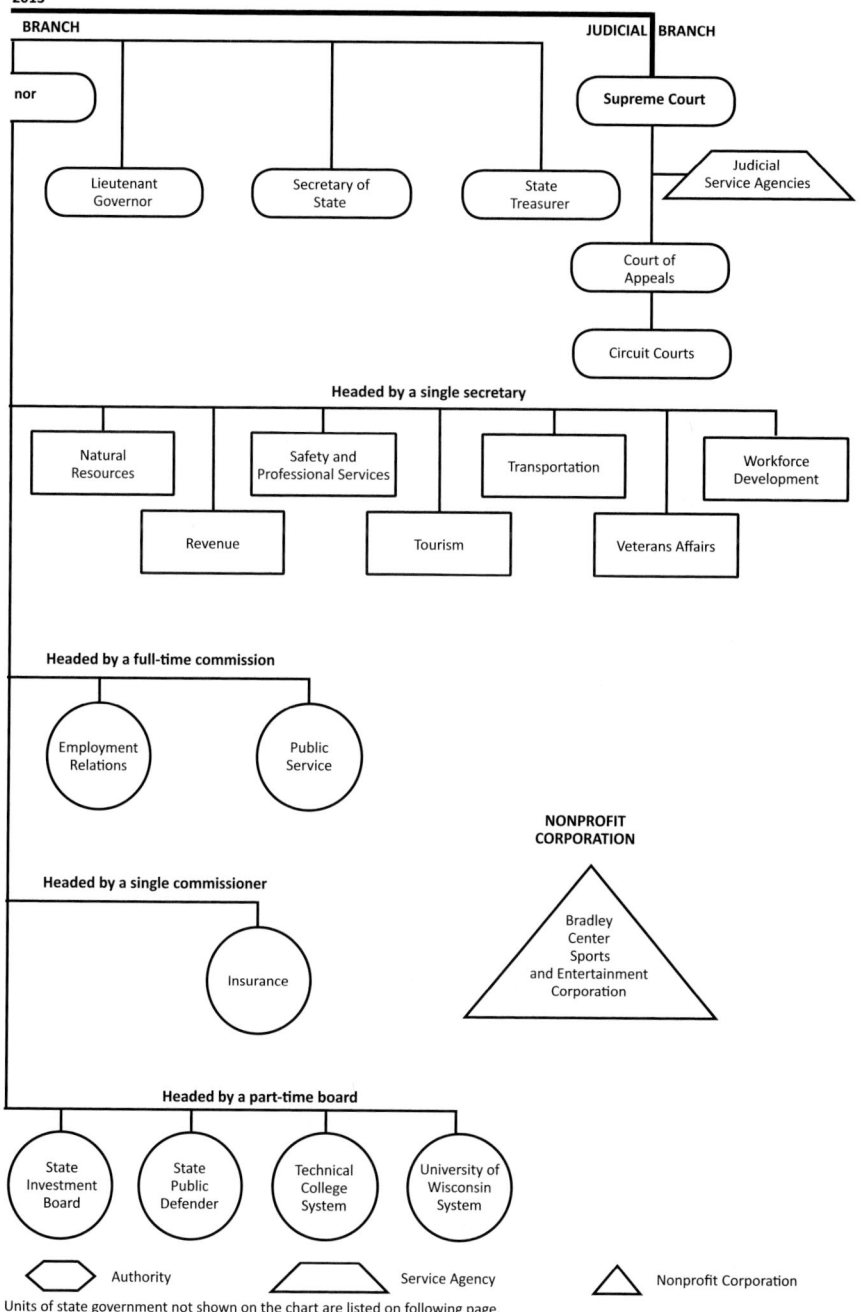

BRANCH

JUDICIAL BRANCH

nor

Supreme Court

Lieutenant Governor

Secretary of State

State Treasurer

Judicial Service Agencies

Court of Appeals

Circuit Courts

Headed by a single secretary

Natural Resources

Safety and Professional Services

Transportation

Workforce Development

Revenue

Tourism

Veterans Affairs

Headed by a full-time commission

Employment Relations

Public Service

NONPROFIT CORPORATION

Headed by a single commissioner

Insurance

Bradley Center Sports and Entertainment Corporation

Headed by a part-time board

State Investment Board

State Public Defender

Technical College System

University of Wisconsin System

Authority   Service Agency   Nonprofit Corporation

Units of state government not shown on the chart are listed on following page.

Units of State Government Not Shown on Organization Chart

The following units of state government are independent entities, which are attached to the agencies indicated for administrative purposes under Section 15.03 of the statutes.

Boards

Board on Aging and Long-Term Care (DOA)

Building Inspector Review Board (DSPS)

Burial Sites Preservation Board (State Historical Society)

Child Abuse and Neglect Prevention Board (DCF)

Claims Board (DOA)

College Savings Program Board (DOA)

Crime Victims Rights Board (DOJ)

Depository Selection Board (DOA)

Disability Board (Governor)

Educational Approval Board (Technical College System)

Emergency Medical Services Board (DHS)

Environmental Education Board (UW)

Historic Preservation Review Board (State Historical Society)

Incorporation Review Board (DOA)

Information Technology Management Board (DOA)

Interstate Adult Offender Supervision Board (DOC)

State Board for Interstate Juvenile Supervision (DOC)

Investment and Local Impact Fund Board (DOR)

Kickapoo Reserve Management Board (Tourism)

Lake Michigan Commercial Fishing Board (DNR)

Lake Superior Commercial Fishing Board (DNR)

Land and Water Conservation Board (DATCP)

Law Enforcement Standards Board (DOJ)

Livestock Facility Siting Review Board (DATCP)

Lower Wisconsin State Riverway Board (Tourism)

National and Community Service Board (DOA)

Board for People with Developmental Disabilities (DOA)

Prison Industries Board (DOC)

Public Records Board (DOA)

Small Business Regulatory Review Board (DOA)

State Capitol and Executive Residence Board (DOA)

State Fair Park Board (Tourism)

State Use Board (DOA)

Veterinary Diagnostic Laboratory Board (UW)

Volunteer Fire Fighter and Emergency Medical Technician Service Award Board (DOA)

Waste Facility Siting Board (DOA)

Commissions

Labor and Industry Review Commission (DWD)

Tax Appeals Commission (DOA)

Wisconsin Waterways Commission (DNR)

Councils

Bioenergy Council (DATCP)

Electronic Recording Council (DOA)

Groundwater Coordinating Council (DNR)

Interoperability Council (DOA)

Invasive Species Council (DNR)

Milwaukee Child Welfare Partnership Council (DCF)

Council on Offender Reentry (DOC)

Council on Physical Disabilities (DHS)

Council on Recycling (DNR)

Council on Utility Public Benefits (DOA)

Women's Council (DOA)

Divisions

Division of Hearings and Appeals (DOA)

Division of Trust Lands and Investments (DOA)

Offices

Office of Business Development (DOA)

Office of Credit Unions (DFI)

Office of Justice Assistance (DOA)

Office of the Commissioner of Railroads (PSC)

Office of State Employment Relations (DOA)

Legislative Branch

5

The legislative branch: profile of the legislative branch, description of the legislative process, summary of 2011-12 legislation, and description of legislative committees and service agencies

Pendarvis

(Wisconsin Historical Society)

OFFICERS OF THE 2013 LEGISLATURE

SENATE

President . . . . .Senator Michael G. Ellis
President pro tempore . . . . Senator Joseph K. Leibham
Chief clerk . . . . Honorable Jeffrey Renk
Sergeant at arms . . . . Honorable Edward A. Blazel

Majority Party Officers		**Minority Party Officers**
Leader	Senator Scott L. Fitzgerald	Senator Chris Larson
Assistant leader	Senator Glenn Grothman	Senator Dave Hansen
Caucus chairperson . .	Senator Frank G. Lasee	Senator Julie M. Lassa
Caucus vice chairperson	Senator Sheila E. Harsdorf	Senator Kathleen Vinehout
Caucus sergeant at arms	None	Senator Nikiya Harris

Chief Clerk: Mailing Address: P.O. Box 7882, Madison 53707-7882; Location: B20 South East, State Capitol; Telephone: (608) 266-2517.

Sergeant at Arms: Mailing Address: P.O. Box 7882, Madison 53707-7882; Location: B35 South, State Capitol; Telephone: (608) 266-1801.

ASSEMBLY

Speaker. . . . . Representative Robin J. Vos
Speaker pro tempore. . . . . Representative Bill Kramer
Chief clerk . . . . Honorable Patrick E. Fuller
Sergeant at arms . . . . Honorable Anne Tonnon Byers

Majority Party Officers		**Minority Party Officers**
Leader	Representative Scott Suder	Representative Peter W. Barca
Assistant leader	Representative Jim Steineke	Representative Sandy Pasch
Caucus chairperson . .	Representative Joan Ballweg	Representative Andy Jorgensen
Caucus vice chairperson	Representative John Murtha	Representative JoCasta Zamarripa
Caucus secretary. . . .	Representative Mary Williams	Representative Janis Ringhand
Caucus sergeant at arms	Representative Samantha Kerkman	Representative Josh Zepnick

Chief Clerk: Mailing Address: P.O. Box 8952, Madison 53708-8952; Location: 17 West Main Street, Suite 401; Telephone: (608) 266-1501.

Sergeant at Arms: Mailing Address: P.O. Box 8952, Madison 53708-8952; Location: 411 West, State Capitol; Telephone: (608) 266-1503.

LEGISLATIVE HOTLINE: Monday-Friday, 8:15 a.m.-4:45 p.m.; Telephone: Madison Area: 266-9960; Outside Madison Area: (800) 362-9472.

LEGISLATIVE INTERNET ADDRESS: http://www.legis.wisconsin.gov

LEGISLATIVE
BRANCH

A PROFILE OF THE LEGISLATIVE BRANCH

The legislative branch consists of the bicameral Wisconsin Legislature, made up of the senate with 33 members and the assembly with 99 members, together with the service agencies created by the legislature and the staff employed by each house. The legislature's main responsibility is to make policy by enacting state laws. Its service agencies assist it by performing fiscal analysis, research, bill drafting, auditing, statute editing, and information technology functions.

A new legislature is sworn into office in January of each odd-numbered year, and it meets in continuous biennial session until its successor is sworn in. The 2013 Legislature is the 101st Wisconsin Legislature. It convened on January 7, 2013, and will continue until January 5, 2015.

U.S. and Wisconsin Constitutions Grant Broad Legislative Powers. The power to determine the state's policies and programs lies primarily in the legislative branch of state government. According to the Wisconsin Constitution: "The legislative power shall be vested in a senate and assembly." This power is quite extensive, but certain limitations are imposed by both the U.S. Constitution and the Wisconsin Constitution. In addition, the legislature's power is restricted by the governor's authority to veto legislation, but a veto may be overridden by a two-thirds vote in both houses of the legislature.

All actions taken by the legislature must conform with the U.S. Constitution. For example, the U.S. Congress has exclusive powers to regulate foreign affairs and coin money, and states are denied the power to make treaties with foreign countries. In addition, state legislation may not abridge the rights guaranteed in the U.S. Bill of Rights. Powers that are not granted exclusively to the U.S. Congress or denied the states are considered to be reserved for the individual states.

In addition to the boundaries set by the U.S. Constitution, the legislature's authority is also limited by the state constitution. For instance, the Wisconsin Constitution requires the legislature to establish as uniform a system of town government as practicable, prevents it from enacting private or special laws on certain subjects, and prohibits laws that would infringe on the rights of Wisconsin citizens, as protected by the Declaration of Rights of the Wisconsin Constitution.

Biennial Sessions: 4-Year Senate Terms; 2-Year Assembly Terms. Originally, members of the assembly served for one year, while senators served for 2 years. An 1881 constitutional amendment doubled the respective terms to the current 2 and 4 years and converted the legislature from annual to biennial sessions.

Since its adoption on March 13, 1848, the Wisconsin Constitution has provided that the membership of the assembly shall be not less than 54 nor more than 100, and the membership of the senate shall consist of not more than one-third nor less than one-fourth of the number of assembly members. The first legislature had 85 members – 19 senators and 66 assemblymen. (Assembly members were renamed "representatives to the assembly" in 1969.) The number increased several times until the legislature became a 133-member body in 1862, with the constitutionally permitted maximums of 33 in the senate and 100 in the assembly. Over a century later, membership dropped to 132 in the 1973 Legislature, when the number of representatives was reduced to 99 so that each of the 33 senate districts would encompass 3 assembly districts. This is the current number and structure.

THE WISCONSIN LEGISLATURE

Number of Positions 2013 Legislature: Senate: 33 members, 202 employees (including senators); Assembly: 99 members, 317 employees (including representatives).

Total Budget 2011-13: $150,455,400 (including service agencies).

Constitutional Reference: Article IV.

Statutory Reference: Chapter 13, Subchapter I.

   Election of Legislators. All members of the legislature are elected from single-member districts. At the general election on the first Tuesday after the first Monday in November of even-numbered years, the voters of Wisconsin elect all members of the assembly and approximately one-half of the senators. These legislators-elect assume office in January of the following odd-numbered year when they convene to open the new legislative session at the State Capitol, together with the "holdover" senators who still have 2 years remaining of their 4-year terms. When a midterm vacancy occurs in any legislative office, it is filled through a special election called by the governor.

   The 33 senators are elected for 4-year terms from districts numbered 1 through 33. The 16 senators representing even-numbered districts are elected in the years in which a presidential election occurs. The 17 senators who represent odd-numbered districts are elected in the years in which a gubernatorial election is held.

   Since statehood in 1848, the Wisconsin Constitution has required the legislature, after each U.S. decennial census, to redraw the districts for both houses "according to the number of inhabitants". Thus, Wisconsin was following this practice long before the U.S. Supreme Court decided in 1962 that all states must redistrict according to the "one person, one vote" principle.

   Under the campaign finance reporting law enacted by the 1973 Legislature, candidates for the legislature, as well as for other public offices, are required to make full, detailed disclosure of their campaign contributions and expenditures. Candidates must make this disclosure to the Elections Division of the Government Accountability Board. Limits are placed on the amounts of contributions received from individuals and various committees. State law also requires legislators and candidates for legislative office to file a statement of their economic interests with the Ethics and Accountability Division of the Government Accountability Board.

   Political Parties in the Legislative Process. Partisan political organizations play an important role in the Wisconsin legislative process. Since 1949, all legislators, with rare exceptions, have been affiliated with either the Democratic Party or the Republican Party. The strongest representation of other parties was between 1911 and 1937, when there were one or more Socialists in the legislature, and between 1933 and 1947, when the Progressives maintained an independent party. In fact, in 1937 the Progressive Party had a plurality in both houses.

   Party organization in the legislature is based on the party group called the "caucus". In each house, all members of a particular political party form that party's caucus. Thus, there are four caucuses related to the party divisions in the two houses. The primary purpose of a caucus is to help party members maintain a unified position on critical issues. Party leaders, however, do not expect to secure party uniformity on every measure under consideration.

   Caucus meetings may be held at regular intervals or whenever convened by party leaders, and occasionally the senate and assembly caucuses of the same party meet in joint caucus. A caucus meeting is scheduled shortly after the general election and before the opening of the session to select candidates for the various leadership positions in each house. Although each party caucus nominates a slate of officers, the positions are usually won by the nominees of the majority party when a vote is taken in the full house.

   Legislative Officers and Leadership. The Wisconsin Constitution originally required the lieutenant governor to serve as president of the senate. As a result of an April 1979 constitutional amendment, the senate now selects its own president from among its members. When the president of the senate is absent or unable to preside, the president pro tempore, elected from the membership, may preside as substitute president.

   The presiding officer of the assembly is the speaker, who is elected by majority vote of the assembly membership. The speaker supervises all other officers of the chamber and appoints

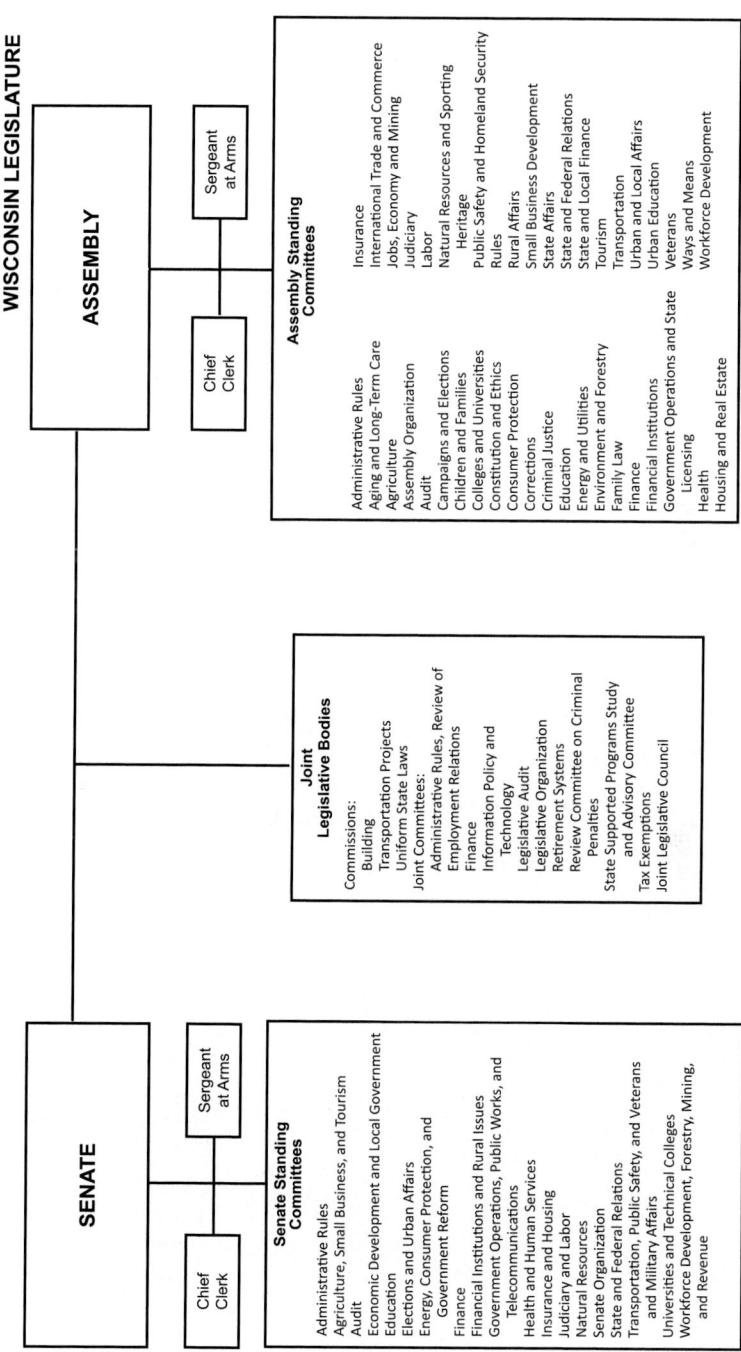

WISCONSIN LEGISLATURE

LEGISLATURE

SENATE

Chief Clerk

Sergeant at Arms

Senate Standing Committees

Administrative Rules
Agriculture, Small Business, and Tourism
Audit
Economic Development and Local Government
Education
Elections and Urban Affairs
Energy, Consumer Protection, and Government Reform
Finance
Financial Institutions and Rural Issues
Government Operations, Public Works, and Telecommunications
Health and Human Services
Insurance and Housing
Judiciary and Labor
Natural Resources
Senate Organization
State and Federal Relations
Transportation, Public Safety, and Veterans and Military Affairs
Universities and Technical Colleges
Workforce Development, Forestry, Mining, and Revenue

Joint Legislative Bodies

Commissions:
  Building
  Transportation Projects
  Uniform State Laws
Joint Committees:
  Administrative Rules, Review of
  Employment Relations
  Finance
  Information Policy and Technology
  Legislative Audit
  Legislative Organization
  Retirement Systems
  Review Committee on Criminal Penalties
  State Supported Programs Study and Advisory Committee
  Tax Exemptions
Joint Legislative Council

ASSEMBLY

Chief Clerk

Sergeant at Arms

Assembly Standing Committees

Administrative Rules
Aging and Long-Term Care
Agriculture
Assembly Organization
Audit
Campaigns and Elections
Children and Families
Colleges and Universities
Constitution and Ethics
Consumer Protection
Corrections
Criminal Justice
Education
Energy and Utilities
Environment and Forestry
Family Law
Finance
Financial Institutions
Government Operations and State Licensing
Health
Housing and Real Estate
Insurance
International Trade and Commerce
Jobs, Economy and Mining
Judiciary
Labor
Natural Resources and Sporting Heritage
Public Safety and Homeland Security
Rules
Rural Affairs
Small Business Development
State Affairs
State and Federal Relations
State and Local Finance
Tourism
Transportation
Urban and Local Affairs
Urban Education
Veterans
Ways and Means
Workforce Development

committees. When the speaker is absent or unable to preside, the speaker pro tempore, who is also elected from the membership, may substitute.

Each party in each house elects floor leaders, respectively known as the majority leader and assistant majority leader and the minority leader and assistant minority leader. To varying degrees, these party officers play powerful roles in directing and coordinating legislative activities.

Each house has a chief clerk and a sergeant at arms, who are elected by, but are not themselves members of, the legislature. The chief clerk serves as the clerk of the house when it is in session and supervises the preparation of legislative records. In conjunction with the presiding officers, the chief clerks supervise personnel and administrative functions for their respective houses. The sergeants at arms maintain order in and about the chambers and supervise the messengers.

Legislative Compensation. When the 2013 Legislature convened on January 7, 2013, all members were eligible for a salary of $49,943 per year. The process for setting legislative salaries requires the Director of the Office of State Employment Relations to submit proposed changes as part of the state compensation plan to the legislature's Joint Committee on Employment Relations. If the committee approves the plan, the new salary goes into effect for all legislators at the next inauguration. The committee also sets the salaries of the chief clerks and the sergeants at arms of the two houses within a range established under civil service procedures.

Members of the legislature, the chief clerks, and the sergeants at arms are entitled to an allowance not to exceed $88 per day ("per diem") for living expenses for each day spent in Madison on legislative business if they certify by affidavit that they have established temporary residence at the state capital. Those who choose not to establish temporary residence are entitled to half that amount. All members are reimbursed for one weekly round trip from the capital to their homes. They also are reimbursed for expenses incurred while serving as legislative members of a state or interstate agency or when specifically authorized to attend meetings of such agencies as nonmembers. The Speaker of the Assembly also receives a stipend, currently $25 per month.

Legislators receive allowances for their office and mailing expenses while attending legislative sessions. If the legislature is in session three or fewer days in a particular month, legislative

Senators Michael Ellis (left) and Fred Risser are approaching a combined 100 years of legislative service, a milestone unique in Wisconsin history. Ellis, a Republican, is President of the Senate; since 1979, Risser has served as President during periods of Democratic control. (Jay Salvo, Legislative Photographer)

leadership may authorize an interim expense allowance to cover postage and clerical assistance ($25 for representatives and $75 for senators).

Legislative Sessions. Members of each new legislature convene in the State Capitol at 2 p.m. on the first Monday in January of each odd-numbered year to take the oath of office, select officers, and organize for business. The initial meeting occurs on January 3 if the first Monday falls on January 1 or 2. The previous legislature usually holds its adjournment meeting on the same day, just prior to the convening of the new legislature. Thus, there is almost no interim between the two.

Originally, the constitution required the legislature to meet once during each annual session. An 1881 amendment restricted the body to one meeting in the two years comprising the biennial session. As a result, the legislature scheduled its meetings in a continuing biennial session with periodic recesses. It would meet in regular session from January through June of the odd-numbered year and then recess after completing the major portion of its work. It then might reconvene from time to time in the remainder of the year, as needed. When a legislature had completed its work for the biennium, it adjourned *sine die,* meaning it did not set a date to reconvene. At that point, the session was over even though only a portion of its two-year term had elapsed, and the legislature could not return unless called into special session by the governor.

In 1968, the state constitution was amended to permit the legislature to determine its own meeting schedule for the biennium. Beginning with the 1971 Legislature, annual sessions were formally initiated by law with the requirement that regular sessions begin in January of each year. Early in each biennium, the Joint Committee on Legislative Organization develops a work schedule for the 2-year period and submits it to the legislature in the form of a joint resolution. The 2013-2014 session schedule, for example, is structured around 15 floorperiods, with periods of committee work interspersed throughout the biennium.

Meetings of the respective houses of the legislature are held in the senate and assembly chambers in the State Capitol. Usually, the legislature meets Tuesday through Thursday of each week. Toward the end of many floorperiods, however, the houses may meet continuously during the day Tuesday through Friday and hold evening sessions. Unless otherwise ordered, daily sessions begin at 10 a.m. for the senate and 9 a.m. for the assembly (10 a.m. on the first legislative day of the week). Daily sessions usually extend beyond noon, especially later in the legislative session. If business permits, afternoons may be devoted to committee hearings or a combination of hearings and late afternoon sessions.

As illustrated in the foregoing description, the word "session" has several meanings. The "legislative session" usually refers to the 2-year period that comprises a particular legislature. If the legislature is "not in session", that may mean it is in an interim period between floorperiods. Saying that either the senate or assembly is "not in session", however, may mean that the house has adjourned for the day or that it has recessed until a later hour of the same day.

Extraordinary and Special Sessions. Beginning in 1962, the legislature adopted procedures that would permit it to reassemble through a petition signed by a majority of the members of each house. An amendment to the 1977 Joint Rules codified this procedure by allowing the legislature to call itself into an "extraordinary session". The legislature may convene in extraordinary session or extend a floorperiod at the direction of the majority of the members of the organization committee in each house, by passage of a joint resolution, or by a joint petition signed by the majority of members of each house.

In addition, the governor has the authority to call a "special session", in which the legislature can act only upon matters specifically mentioned in the governor's call. As of the adjournment of the 2011 Legislature, there had been 90 special sessions since Wisconsin became a state in 1848. It is possible for a regular session and a special session to be scheduled at different times during a week or even on the same day. Because special sessions may occur at any time during the legislative biennium, enactments resulting from a special session are now numbered within the regular sequence of biennial laws.

Session Records. Each house of the legislature keeps a record of its actions known as the daily journal. This record differs from the federal *Congressional Record* in that it does not provide a transcript or abbreviated account of speeches made on the floor. It is, instead, an outline

2013-2014 SESSION SCHEDULE

January 7, 2013	2013 Inauguration
January 9 and 10, 2013	Floorperiod
January 15 to 17, 2013	Floorperiod
January 29 to 31, 2013	Floorperiod
February 12 to 14, 2013	Floorperiod
February 26 to March 7, 2013	Floorperiod
March 21, 2013	Deadline for sending bills to governor
April 9 to 18, 2013	Floorperiod
May 7 to 16, 2013	Floorperiod
June 4 to 28, 2013 (or until passage of the budget)	Floorperiod
August 8, 2013	Deadline for sending nonbudget bills to governor
August 8, 2013 (or later)	Deadline for sending budget bill to governor*
September 17 to 19, 2013	Floorperiod
October 8 to 17, 2013	Floorperiod
November 5 to 14, 2013	Floorperiod
December 12, 2013	Deadline for sending bills to governor
January 14 to 23, 2014	Floorperiod
February 11 to 20, 2014	Floorperiod
March 11 to 20, 2014	Floorperiod
April 1 to 3, 2014	Last general-business floorperiod
April 24, 2014	Deadline for sending bills to governor
April 29 to May 1, 2014	Limited-business floorperiod
May 8, 2014	Deadline for sending bills to governor
May 20 and 21, 2014	Veto review floorperiod
May 2, 2014 to January 5, 2015	Interim committee work
June 4, 2014	Deadline for sending bills to governor
January 5, 2015	2015 Inauguration

Any floorperiod may be convened earlier or extended beyond its scheduled dates by majority action of the membership or the organization committees of the two houses. The Committee on Senate Organization may schedule sessions outside floorperiods for senate action on gubernatorial nominations, but the assembly does not have to hold skeleton sessions during these appointment reviews. The legislature may call itself into extraordinary session or the governor may call a special session during a floorperiod or on any intervening day.

*Deadline for budget bill will depend on bill's passage.

Source: 2013 Senate Joint Resolution 1.

record of the business before the house, including procedural actions taken on all measures considered on that particular day, roll call votes, communications received from the governor or the other house, special committee reports, and miscellaneous items.

The *Bulletin of the Proceedings of the Wisconsin Legislature* is issued periodically during the legislative session as needed. Each issue contains a cumulative record of actions taken on bills, joint resolutions, and resolutions by both houses, listed by bill or resolution number. It includes a subject and author index to legislation; a subject index to the legislative journals; a subject index to new laws and enrolled bills and joint resolutions; a numeric listing of statute sections affected by these laws; changes made to statutory court rules by supreme court orders; and the complete text of constitutional amendments ratified since the most recent publication of the *Wisconsin Statutes*. Another part indexes and reports action on administrative rule changes. The final edition of the *Bulletin* at the end of each biennium also includes a directory of lobbying organizations, licensed lobbyists, and legislative liaisons from state agencies.

Each week during the session, the chief clerks jointly issue a *Weekly Schedule of Committee Activities*, listing the business scheduled by the various committees for the coming week, together with the time and place of each hearing and advanced notices on hearings deemed to be of special interest. Each house also issues a daily calendar indicating the business to be taken up on the floor that day.

Complete texts of bills, amendments, and resolutions; bill histories; a subject index to legislation; hearing notices and calendars; and other information on the legislature are available on the Internet at www.legis.state.wi.us. Reference copies of all these legislative documents are available at the Legislative Reference Bureau, and numerous libraries throughout the state also receive them. Individuals and organizations may subscribe to receive printed versions of legislative documents. (See the table on Legislative Service in this section for fees and details.)

Senator Dale Schultz (R-Richland Center) addresses the Senate on the mining bill, February 27, 2013. (Jay Salvo, Legislative Photographer)

Standing Committees. To a large extent, the legislature does its work in committees. In the 2013 Legislature, the senate has 17 standing committees, the assembly 41, and there are 10 joint standing committees, composed of members from both houses. Joint standing committees are created in the statutes and membership is determined by law. Regular standing committees are created under the rules of their respective houses.

The standing committees in the individual houses consist of legislators only and operate throughout the biennium. Each committee is concerned with one or more broad subject areas related to government functions. It may hold public hearings on measures introduced in the legislature, conduct studies and investigations, and generally review matters within its area of concern. Legislative committees may also appoint subcommittees or study groups.

Senate rules require that each senator serve on at least one standing committee, and the Committee on Senate Organization sets the number of members on each committee. Usually the two major political parties are represented on the committees in proportion to their membership in the senate. The chairperson of the organization committee, who is also the majority leader, makes the appointments to committees. Committee nominations for individual members of the minority party are proposed by that party. An exception to the general method of appointment is the Committee on Senate Organization. It is an *ex officio* committee, consisting of members in leadership positions: the president, the majority and minority leaders, and the assistant leaders.

In the assembly, the speaker determines the number of members of each committee and the division of membership between the majority and minority parties. Under assembly rules, the speaker appoints majority party committee members directly and minority party committee members upon nomination by the assembly minority leader. Customarily, every member serves on at least one committee, although the rules are silent on the distribution of committee assignments. The speaker may appoint himself or herself to one or more standing committees and is a nonvoting member of all others. By rule, the Committee on Assembly Organization is composed of the speaker, the speaker pro tempore, the majority and minority leaders, the assistant leaders, and the caucus chairpersons. The Committee on Rules includes all members of the organization committee plus one majority and one minority party member appointed by the speaker.

Temporary Special Committees. In addition to the standing committees, special committees may be appointed during a legislative session to study specific problems or conduct designated investigations and report to the legislature before the conclusion of the session.

Prior to 1947, the legislature created interim committees to investigate particular subjects. They functioned between legislative sessions and reported their findings and recommendations to the next legislature. Since 1947, almost all interim studies have been referred to the Joint Legislative Council, which coordinates a program of study and investigation after deciding which topics it will consider. The council usually appoints separate committees to study specific matters, and these committees include nonlegislative members.

Employees of the Legislature. Each house of the legislature provides staff services, which are managed by the respective chief clerk and sergeant at arms under the supervision of the Committee on Senate Organization or the speaker of the assembly. Although senate and assembly employees are not part of the classified service, they are paid in accordance with the compensation and classification plan established for employees in the classified service and within pay ranges approved by the Joint Committee on Legislative Organization.

The legislature is assisted by five service agencies responsible for financial and program audits, fiscal information and analysis, bill drafting, research services, statutory revision, legal counsel and policy assistance, and computer and telecommunications services.

An early priority of the 2013 Legislature was the passage of legislation to reform the state's mining laws. The bill, Senate Bill 1, received a public hearing on January 23, 2013. (Jay Salvo, Legislative Photographer)

NEWS MEDIA CORRESPONDENTS
COVERING THE 2013 LEGISLATURE
January 7, 2013

Organization	Correspondents	Telephone
Newspaper and Wire Services		
Appleton Post-Crescent	Ben Jones	255-9256
Associated Press	Scott Bauer, Todd Richmond	255-3679
Capital Times	Jack Craver, Jessica VanEgeren	262-6438/262-6424
Capitol News Service	Stan Milam	(608) 774-8584
Isthmus	Judith Davidoff	251-5627
Milwaukee Journal Sentinel	Patrick Marley, Jason Stein	258-2262/258-2274
Wheeler News Service	Thom Gerretsen	(715) 389-2373
Wheeler Reports	Gwyn Guenther, Trevor Guenther	287-0130
Wisconsin Catholic Newspapers	John Huebscher	257-0004
Wisconsin State Journal	Dee Hall, Mary Spicuzza	252-6132/252-6122
Radio and Television		
WIBA-AM and FM (Madison)	John Colbert	251-1978/274-2995/ (608) 438-6853
WISC-TV (Madison)	Jessica Arp, Colin Benedict	(608) 332-9453/277-5246
WKOW-TV (Madison)	Tony Galli, Jennifer Kliese, Greg Neumann, Joseph Radske Robyn Turner	273-2727
WMTV-TV (Madison)	Ryan Lobenstein, Zac Schultz	274-1500
WNWC-FM (Madison)	Bruce Barrows	271-1025
WOLX-FM (Madison)	Kitty Dunn	826-0077
Wisconsin Public Radio	Gilman Halsted, Shawn Johnson, Michael Leland, Shamane Mills	263-4358/263-7985
Wisconsin Public Television	Kathy Bissen, Frederica Freyberg, Andy Moore, Adam Schrager, Zac Schultz, Christine Sloan-Miller, Andy Soth, Joel Waldinger	263-2121/263-8496/ 265-6646/263-5628/ 263-8585/263-6023/ 263-7124/263-4599/ 890-2840
Wisconsin Radio Network	Andrew Beckett, Bob Hague, Jackie Johnson, Brian Moon	251-3900
Internet News Service		
Wispolitics.com	J.R. Ross, Mike Schramm, Jason Smathers, Andy Szal	441-8418

Sources: Assembly Sergeant at Arms.

THE LEGISLATURE ON THE INTERNET

Legislative Information

The Wisconsin Legislature's Internet home page at **http://legis.wisconsin.gov** provides extensive information regarding the legislature and the legislative process. Follow the links under Legislative Activity to access basic information on current legislative activity. **Request text and history of legislative proposals** allows users to access legislative documents by bill or act number for the current or recent sessions. The **Spotlight** link provides a weekly update on recent actions in the legislature. In addition, the **legislative service agencies** have individual home pages where many of their publications are available.

Documents enables users to search for specific acts, bills, or statutes from 1995 to date. It also offers access to a variety of other legislative documents and indexes, which can also be searched by word.

The legislature's home page links to individual legislator's home pages, which include e-mail addresses, district maps, committee assignments, and biographical information. Some legislators also provide brief audio clips and personally designed pages to communicate with their constituents.

Live Video and Audio – WisconsinEye

WisconsinEye, a private, nonprofit public affairs network, began offering exclusive live video and audio of legislative floor sessions and certain other legislative activities in May 2007. Links to live video and audio, as well as archives of past activity, are available at **http://wiseye.org**.

Legislative Notification Service

This service allows citizens to track legislation by creating a profile of items of interest. Profiles may include specific proposals identified by author, committee, or subject matter and may specify activity occurring at various stages of the legislative process. After a profile is filed on the Web site **http://notify.legis.state.wisconsin.gov**, users will receive daily or weekly e-mails of relevant activities.

Senator Joseph Leibham (R-Sheboygan), President Pro Tempore of the Senate, is responsible for taking the gavel when the President is absent or participating in floor debate. (Jay Salvo, Legislative Photographer)

2010 POPULATION OF LEGISLATIVE DISTRICTS
As Created by 2011 Wisconsin Act 43[1]
2010 State Population – 5,686,986

District	2010 Population	Deviation from Ideal[2] Total	Percent	District	2010 Population	Deviation from Ideal[2] Total	Percent
SD-1	172,313	−20	−0.01%	SD-18	171,722	−611	−0.35%
AD-1 . . .	57,220	−224	−0.39	AD-52. . .	57,232	−212	−0.37
AD-2 . . .	57,649	205	0.36	AD-53. . .	57,240	−204	−0.36
AD-3 . . .	57,444	0	0.00	AD-54. . .	57,250	−194	−0.34
SD-2	172,461	128	0.07	SD-19	172,576	243	0.14
AD-4 . . .	57,486	42	0.07	AD-55. . . .	57,493	49	0.08
AD-5 . . .	57,470	26	0.04	AD-56. . .	57,582	138	0.24
AD-6 . . .	57,505	61	0.11	AD-57. . .	57,501	57	0.10
SD-3	171,977	−356	−0.21	SD-20	172,003	−330	−0.19
AD-7 . . .	57,498	54	0.09	AD-58. . .	57,227	−217	−0.38
AD-8[1] . . .	57,196	−248	−0.43	AD-59. . .	57,391	−53	−0.09
AD-9[1] . . .	57,283	−161	−0.28	AD-60. . .	57,385	−59	−0.10
SD-4	172,425	92	0.05	SD-21	172,324	−9	−0.01
AD-10. . .	57,428	−16	−0.03	AD-61. . .	57,614	170	0.30
AD-11. . .	57,503	59	0.10	AD-62. . .	57,345	−99	−0.17
AD-12. . .	57,494	50	0.09	AD-63. . .	57,365	−79	−0.14
SD-5	172,421	88	0.05	SD-22	172,270	−63	−0.04
AD-13. . .	57,452	8	0.01	AD-64. . .	57,270	−174	−0.30
AD-14. . .	57,597	153	0.27	AD-65. . .	57,455	11	0.02
AD-15. . .	57,372	−72	−0.13	AD-66. . .	57,545	101	0.18
SD-6	172,292	−41	−0.02	SD-23	172,149	−184	−0.11
AD-16. . .	57,458	14	0.02	AD-67. . .	57,239	−205	−0.36
AD-17. . .	57,354	−90	−0.16	AD-68. . .	57,261	−183	−0.32
AD-18. . .	57,480	36	0.06	AD-69. . .	57,649	205	0.36
SD-7	172,423	90	0.05	SD-24	172,520	187	0.11
AD-19. . .	57,546	102	0.18	AD-70. . .	57,552	108	0.19
AD-20. . .	57,428	−16	−0.03	AD-71. . .	57,519	75	0.13
AD-21. . .	57,449	5	0.01	AD-72. . .	57,449	5	0.01
SD-8	172,356	23	0.01	SD-25	172,409	76	0.04
AD-22. . .	57,495	51	0.09	AD-73. . .	57,453	9	0.02
AD-23. . .	57,579	135	0.23	AD-74. . .	57,494	50	0.09
AD-24. . .	57,282	−162	−0.28	AD-75. . .	57,462	18	0.03
SD-9	172,439	106	0.06	SD-26	172,596	263	0.15
AD-25. . .	57,322	−122	−0.21	AD-76. . .	57,617	173	0.30
AD-26. . .	57,581	137	0.24	AD-77. . .	57,433	−11	−0.02
AD-27. . .	57,536	92	0.16	AD-78. . .	57,546	102	0.18
SD-10	172,245	−88	−0.05	SD-27	172,449	116	0.07
AD-28. . .	57,467	23	0.04	AD-79. . .	57,461	17	0.03
AD-29. . .	57,537	93	0.16	AD-80. . .	57,585	141	0.24
AD-30. . .	57,241	−203	−0.35	AD-81. . .	57,403	−41	−0.07
SD-11	172,329	−4	−0.00	SD-28	172,218	−115	−0.07
AD-31. . .	57,240	−204	−0.36	AD-82. . .	57,430	−14	−0.02
AD-32. . .	57,524	80	0.14	AD-83. . .	57,423	−21	−0.04
AD-33. . .	57,565	121	0.21	AD-84. . .	57,365	−79	−0.14
SD-12	172,381	48	0.03	SD-29	172,292	−41	−0.02
AD-34. . .	57,387	−57	−0.10	AD-85. . .	57,480	36	0.06
AD-35. . .	57,562	118	0.20	AD-86. . .	57,454	10	0.02
AD-36. . .	57,432	−12	−0.02	AD-87. . .	57,358	−86	−0.15
SD-13	172,387	54	0.03	SD-30	172,798	465	0.27
AD-37. . .	57,507	63	0.11	AD-88. . .	57,556	112	0.19
AD-38. . .	57,493	49	0.08	AD-89. . .	57,634	190	0.33
AD-39. . .	57,387	−57	−0.10	AD-90. . .	57,608	164	0.28
SD-14	171,988	−345	−0.20	SD-31	172,338	5	0.00
AD-40. . .	57,366	−78	−0.14	AD-91. . .	57,359	−85	−0.15
AD-41. . .	57,337	−107	−0.19	AD-92. . .	57,431	−13	−0.02
AD-42. . .	57,285	−159	−0.28	AD-93. . .	57,548	104	0.18
SD-15	172,496	163	0.09	SD-32	172,122	−211	−0.12
AD-43. . .	57,443	−1	−0.00	AD-94. . .	57,266	−178	−0.31
AD-44. . .	57,395	−49	−0.09	AD-95. . .	57,372	−72	−0.13
AD-45. . .	57,658	214	0.37	AD-96. . .	57,484	40	0.07
SD-16	172,429	96	0.06	SD-33	172,288	−45	−0.03
AD-46. . .	57,458	14	0.02	AD-97. . .	57,279	−165	−0.29
AD-47. . .	57,465	21	0.04	AD-98. . .	57,513	69	0.12
AD-48. . .	57,506	62	0.11	AD-99. . .	57,496	52	0.09
SD-17	172,550	217	0.13				
AD-49. . .	57,346	−98	−0.17				
AD-50. . .	57,624	180	0.31				
AD-51. . .	57,580	136	0.24				

[1]This table reflects modifications made to Assembly Districts 8 and 9 by the U.S. District Court for the Eastern District of Wisconsin in its decision in *Baldus vs. Members of the Wisconsin Government Accountability Board,* Case No. 11-CV-562, April 11, 2012.

[2]Ideal Senate District: 172,333. Ideal Assembly District: 57,444.

Sources: U.S. Census Bureau, 2010 Census Redistricting Data (Public Law 94-171) Summary File, March 2011; *Appendix to: 2011 Wisconsin Act 43.* Assembly Districts 8 and 9 population and deviations calculated by the Wisconsin Legislative Reference Bureau.

HOW A BILL BECOMES A LAW

The legislature decides policy by passing bills. A bill must pass both houses of the legislature and be signed by the governor before it becomes law. Other proposals introduced in the legislature also support the body's policy making function. Joint resolutions, which must pass both houses, may propose constitutional amendments, develop a session schedule, or modify the rules that govern both houses. They do not require the governor's signature. Simple resolutions, which are adopted by only one house, may organize the house at the beginning of the session, propose changes to house rules, or ask the attorney general for a legal opinion on a bill.

Introducing a Bill. A bill that proposes to change existing law will usually amend, create, repeal, renumber, renumber and amend, or repeal and recreate one or more sections of the *Wisconsin Statutes*. After the Legislative Reference Bureau (LRB) drafts a bill, it is ready for introduction in one of the legislative houses. Each measure must go through regular procedures and be passed by the house of origin before it can go to the other house, where the process is repeated.

No one but individual legislators or legislative committees may introduce a bill. However, the statutes direct the Joint Committee on Finance to introduce the governor's executive budget bill without change. The legislator who introduces a bill is its "author"; others in the house of origin who support the bill may sign on as "coauthors". The measure may also list "cosponsors" from the second house.

When passing laws, legislators act as the representatives of the people. Therefore, the constitution requires that every bill introduced in the legislature begin with the words: "The people of the state of Wisconsin, represented in senate and assembly, do enact as follows:".

Fiscal Estimates and Bill Analyses. Fiscal estimates put a price tag on legislation. In 1953, Wisconsin pioneered fiscal estimates, often called "fiscal notes", and many other states have copied this important legislative tool. Every measure that increases or decreases state or general local government revenues or expenditures must be accompanied by a reliable estimate of its short-range and long-range fiscal effects. Agencies that would ultimately administer the proposed program or be affected by the measure, should it be enacted, prepare most fiscal notes. In the highly technical area of public retirement systems, the Joint Survey Committee on Retirement Systems prepares fiscal estimates with the assistance of Legislative Council staff. In these cases, the note must evaluate not only the fiscal effect of a proposal but also its legality under state and federal law and its desirability as a matter of public policy.

Since 1967, the LRB has prepared an analysis of each bill introduced in the legislature, explaining in plain language the existing law and how it will change if the bill becomes law. The analysis is printed in the bill immediately following the title. As a general rule, analyses are not updated to reflect amendments approved during the legislative process, so they usually describe only the content of the bill at introduction.

Introduction, First Reading, and Referral to Committee. A bill is introduced when the chief clerk of the author's house assigns it a number and records the introduction for the house journal. Traditionally, the "first reading" took place when the clerk read that part of the proposal's title known as the "relating clause" – the clause that briefly describes the subject matter of the bill, e.g., "relating to the powers and duties of state traffic patrol officers and motor vehicle inspectors" when the house was meeting. In recent times, the clerk usually distributes a report showing the numbers and relating clauses of proposals offered for introduction which takes the place of an actual reading. After first reading, the presiding officer usually refers the proposal to the appropriate standing committee for review. Generally bills that appropriate money, provide for revenue, or relate to taxation are referred to the Joint Committee on Finance before they can be enacted into law.

Committee Hearings. All committee proceedings are open to the general public. Neither assembly nor senate rules require a chairperson to schedule a hearing. If a hearing is held, anyone may speak to the committee to support or oppose a measure or merely to present information to the committee without taking a position. Persons may also register for or against a proposal or submit written comments or petitions without making an oral presentation.

Committees do not keep verbatim transcripts of their hearings, but they do maintain appearance records listing persons who testify or register at the hearing, together with any printed

Representative Evan Goyke, a freshman Democrat from Milwaukee, speaks in committee. Goyke's father, Gary, served in the Wisconsin Senate from 1975-1983. (Jay Salvo, Legislative Photographer)

information those parties submit relative to bills and resolutions before the committee. Records for the current legislative session are filed in the office of the committee chairperson. Copies of appearance records for prior sessions, beginning with the 1951 session, are filed in the LRB. Records from 1997 to the present are available on the legislature's Web site.

The chairperson of a committee decides whether or not to take action on a particular proposal. If the decision is to act, the chairperson will call an "executive session" of the committee. In the session, committee members discuss the bill and may ask questions of persons in attendance, but no further public testimony is taken. At the close of the executive session, the committee decides whether to recommend passage of the bill as originally introduced, passage with amendments, or rejection. If the result is a tie vote, the committee can report the bill without recommendation. A committee's decision is contained in a brief report to the house. (Bills that receive a negative recommendation are almost never reported to the floor.)

The following is an example of a committee report to the assembly from the *Assembly Journal*, March 1, 2013:

The committee on **Workforce Development** reports and recommends:

Assembly Bill 15

Relating to: payment of unemployment insurance benefits under a work-sharing program.

Assembly Amendment 1 adoption:

Ayes: 16 – Representatives Loudenbeck, Petryk, Honadel, Pridemore, Knodl, Bernier, Kuglitsch, Severson, Born, Weatherston, Ringhand, Billings, Barnes, Kolste, Shankland and Wachs.

Noes: 0.

Passage as amended.

Ayes: 10 – Representatives Loudenbeck, Petryk, Honadel, Pridemore, Knodl, Bernier, Kuglitsch, Severson, Born and Weatherston.

Noes: 6 – Representatives Ringhand, Billings, Barnes, Kolste, Shankland and Wachs.

To calendar of March 6, 2013

Amy Loudenbeck
Chairperson

Committee chairpersons determine the scheduling of committee hearings. A committee is allowed a reasonable period of time to consider matters referred to it. A majority of the members of the assembly may withdraw a bill not reported by an assembly committee 21 days after the date of referral by motion or petition. In the senate, a majority may vote to withdraw a bill from a committee at any time but not during the 7 days preceding any scheduled committee hearing nor the 7 days following the date on which the hearing was held. In both houses, when an attempt is unsuccessful, all subsequent motions to withdraw the same proposal require at least a two-thirds vote of the members. In practice, bills are very rarely withdrawn from committees without a committee report.

Scheduling Debate. Both the senate and assembly make use of a daily calendar to schedule proposals for consideration. In the 2013 Legislature, all proposals reported by senate standing committees are referred to the Committee on Senate Organization; in the assembly, they are referred to the Committee on Rules. These committees schedule business for floor debate.

Parliamentary Procedure. The rules of parliamentary procedure, which are guides for each house, facilitate the legislative process and are printed in pamphlets, titled "Senate Rules" and "Assembly Rules". Each house may create new rules and amend or repeal its current rules by passage of a simple resolution. "Joint Rules" deal with the relations between the houses and with administrative proceedings common to both. Changes in joint rules require the passage of a joint resolution.

Parliamentary process may seem unduly cumbersome to the onlooker, but it helps the houses operate in an organized fashion. The process is designed to protect the minority in its right to be heard and to promote careful deliberation and orderly consideration of all legislation. For particularly difficult procedural questions, the presiding officer of each house has access to such standard sources as *Mason's Manual of Legislative Procedure, Jefferson's Manual,* and *Rulings of the Chair.*

Second Reading. Once a bill is scheduled for house action, the clerk gives it a second reading by title. The purpose of a second reading is to consider amendments. An amendment may be a "simple" amendment, which makes changes within the bill, or a "substitute amendment", which

Any citizen may offer their opinion on legislation when it receives a public hearing in the committee to which it has been referred. Here the Assembly Committee on Campaigns and Elections takes testimony. (Jay Salvo, Legislative Photographer)

completely replaces the original bill. Members may offer, debate, and vote upon amendments at any time prior to a vote to "engross" the measure and read it a third time. Engrossment of a bill incorporates all adopted amendments and all approved technical corrections into a proposal in its house of origin. The rules of both houses require a formal delay after the proposal is engrossed, which gives legislators time to reconsider the issues raised by the bill. In many cases, however, the rules are suspended by unanimous consent or a two-thirds vote so that second and third readings can occur on the same legislative day.

Third Reading. The purpose of the third reading is to make a final decision on a proposal itself. After a third reading, the proposal is put to the house for a vote with the following questions: "This bill having been read 3 separate times, the question is, 'Shall the bill pass?'" (for the senate) or "Shall the bill be passed?" (for the assembly). Members can debate the bill's contents at this point, but it is not subject to amendment. When all members finish speaking they vote. A bill may pass on a voice vote, unless a roll call vote is required by the state constitution, by law or legislative rule, or by request of a prescribed number of members.

Action in the Second House. If the bill passes, it is "messaged" (sent) to the other house, where it goes through substantially the same procedure as in the first house. In the second house, however, the bill may be referred directly to the daily calendar without referral to a standing committee. When the second house concurs in the bill, whether with or without additional amendments, the measure is messaged back to the house of origin.

If the second house amends the bill before concurring, the house of origin must vote upon those amendments. If the original house rejects amendments or further amends the bill, the resulting proposal may be sent back to the second house. The bill may pass repeatedly between the two houses, or the legislature may create a conference committee made up of members representing both houses, where attempts are made to iron out the differences between the 2 versions. The compromise version, drawn up by the conference committee, cannot be amended in either house when it is brought to a vote. When both houses have agreed on identical wording of a bill, the LRB "enrolls" it in its final form, incorporating any amendments and corrections approved by both houses, and the measure is forwarded for the governor's signature.

On average about 1,600 bills were introduced in each of the past 10 legislatures, but only about 20% of those passed. Bills fail for many reasons: the house of origin may vote to "indefinitely postpone" or "table" a bill and then never take it up again; the second house may vote to "nonconcur" or may concur but with amendments unacceptable to the house of origin; or the proposal may "die in committee" and never be reported back to the house. An unsuccessful proposal does not carry over to the following legislature. A member must reintroduce it as a new bill.

Action of the Governor. The governor has 6 days (excluding Sundays) in which to act on the bill by: 1) signing it, in which case it becomes law; 2) vetoing it in whole or, if an appropriation bill, in part; or 3) failing to sign it within 6 days, in which case it becomes law without the governor's signature. Partial veto of words or numbers within a bill is permitted in the case of bills which contain an appropriation. If the governor signs the bill but vetoes part of it, the portion not vetoed becomes law.

Bills are not sent to the office of the governor immediately following passage but are presented when the governor calls for them. The legislative session schedule, however, provides deadlines after each floorperiod when all bills not yet called for must be sent to the governor. It also provides a specific floorperiod for final legislative review of the governor's vetoes.

If the governor vetoes a bill, in whole or part, the vetoed parts must be returned to the house of origin with the governor's written objections. A vetoed bill or part of a bill can become law despite the governor's objections, but it requires a two-thirds vote in each house to override the veto. If either house fails to muster the sufficient number of votes, the governor's veto is sustained, and the vetoed bill or portion dies.

Session Laws. Each new law is numbered as a Wisconsin Act, based on the year of the legislative session and its order of enactment, e.g., 2013 Wisconsin Act 1. The date of enactment is the date the governor approves the act, the date it becomes a law without the governor's signature, or the date the legislature votes to override the governor's veto. The following day is the new law's official date of publication. On or before that date, copies of the act must be available to the public electronically. The secretary of state must publish the act's number, title, and original bill number within 10 working days after the date of enactment in the newspaper designated as the official state paper for publication of legal notices (currently the *Wisconsin State Journal*). The notice contains the date of enactment and date of publication and states the act is available for public distribution. The act takes effect the day after its official publication date, unless another effective date is specified in the law itself.

Ultimately, the LRB compiles all the laws enacted during the biennium into bound volumes, called the "Laws of Wisconsin". The LRB incorporates any portions of these laws that make changes in the statutes into the edition of the "Wisconsin Statutes" dated for that legislative biennium. Thus, the edition identified as the *2011-2012 Wisconsin Statutes* includes all statutory changes resulting from laws enacted by the 2011 Legislature.

The Budget Bill. The budget bill is the longest and most complex bill of the session. Because Wisconsin's budget covers a 2-year period from July 1 of one odd-numbered year through June 30 of the next, its development involves a chain of events stretching over almost a year. In the fall of every even-numbered year, state agencies must submit funding requests to the Department of Administration. Their funding requests include estimates of the cost of existing services over the next 2 years and may propose changes they hope are made in their programs. The Department of Administration's state budget office then compiles the data for review by the governor or governor-elect. While developing the budget, the governor may hold a hearing on any department's budget request to get additional input.

State law requires the governor to deliver the budget message to the new legislature on or before the last Tuesday in January, although the legislature may extend the deadline at the governor's request. The state budget report and the biennial executive budget bill or bills accompany the message.

In the legislature, the Joint Committee on Finance holds hearings on the departmental requests and governor's program initiatives. When these are completed, it reports the budget bill to the house of the legislature in which it was introduced. The committee's report takes the form of a substitute amendment. The bill then follows the normal legislative procedure through both houses of the legislature and is submitted for the governor's approval. The governor may sign the budget bill, veto it in its entirety (which would be unlikely), or use partial vetoes, as is usually the case. To meet the state's budgetary cycle, the new budget law should be effective by July 1 of the odd-numbered year, but there sometimes is a delay of several days, or even weeks or months, during which state agencies continue to operate at their levels of appropriation from the preceding budget.

Further Reading. The preceding section has provided a brief description of how a bill becomes a law in Wisconsin. In practice, legislative procedure is more complex than explained here. The feature article in the *1993-1994 Wisconsin Blue Book* contains a more detailed description and uses a case study approach to further illustrate the legislative process. It may be accessed via the *Wisconsin Blue Book* link on the Legislative Reference Bureau's Web site: http://legis.state.wi.us/lrb/pubs/bluebook.htm.

2013-2014 LEGISLATIVE SERVICE

The complete 2013-2014 Legislative Service consists of 6 parts, which may be ordered by subscription from the Document Sales office:

Bills, resolutions, and amendments (complete text of each as introduced).

Acts are the laws enacted in bill form by the legislature and signed by the governor or passed over the governor's veto. The acts are distributed separately as "slip laws".

Journals are a daily record of the business conducted in each house, but they are not verbatim accounts. The service provides preliminary editions of the journals (published on the morning after the legislative day on yellow paper for senate journals and green paper for assembly journals) and the final corrected editions (printed on white paper and distributed two or three weeks later).

The **Bulletin of Proceedings** contains a numerical listing of all bills and other measures introduced in each house of the legislature and a cumulative record of actions taken on each. It includes a subject index to all measures introduced and to all acts, a list of proposals introduced by each legislator, and a numerical listing of statutory sections affected by acts and enrolled bills. It is issued as needed during the biennial session.

The **Weekly Schedule of Committee Activities** lists the time and place of legislative committee hearings for the coming week and advanced notices for hearings on issues of special interest.

Administrative Rules lists the administrative rules submitted by executive branch agencies by clearinghouse rule number. It includes a subject index, a list of agency contacts, and a cumulative record of actions taken on each proposal.

To obtain all or part of the legislative service, contact Document Sales, Wisconsin Department of Administration, 4622 University Avenue, Madison 53705-2156 or call (608) 266-3358, or (800) 362-7253 for an order form. E-mail Document Sales at docsales@doa.state.wi.us. Any part may be ordered separately. Prepayment is required on all orders. Faxed orders are accepted at (608) 261-8150 when paying with a credit card. Subscribers receive their documents through the mail. All subscriptions to the 2013-2014 Legislative Service will expire on December 31, 2014.

SERVICE	Interdepartmental Delivery*	United Parcel Service (UPS) and U.S. Postal Service*
Complete service, including daily calendars . . .	$500	$845
Bills, resolutions, and amendments	160	335
Acts (slip laws)	20	85
Journals	55	145
Bulletin of Proceedings	200	350
Weekly Schedule of Committee Activities . . .	15	85
Administrative Rules	65	95

*All sales are subject to the 5% state sales tax, 0.5% county sales tax, and 0.5% or 0.1% stadium tax, where applicable.

Governor Scott Walker greeted members on his way to the podium to deliver his biennial budget address. (Jay Salvo, Legislative Photographer)

Senator Nikiya Harris (D-Milwaukee) participates in Senate debate. Harris began her first legislative session in January 2013. (Jay Salvo, Legislative Photographer)

EXECUTIVE VETOES, 1931 – 2011 SESSIONS

Session	Bills Vetoed in Entirety			Bills Partially Vetoed			Partial Vetoes Contained in Biennial Budget Bills	
	Number Vetoed	Vetoes Sustained	Vetoes Overridden	Number Partially Vetoed	All Partial Vetoes Sustained	One or More Partial Vetoes Overridden	Number of Partial Vetoes[1]	Vetoes Overridden
1931	58	58	—	2	2	—	12	0
1933	15	15	—	1	1	—	12	0
1935	27	27	—	4	4	—	0	0
1937	10	10	—	1	1	—	0	0
1939	22[2]	22	—	4	4	—	1	0
1941	17	17	—	1	1	—	1	0
1943	39	19	20	1	—	1	0	0
1945	30	25	5	2	1	1	1	0
1947	10	9	1	1	1	—	2	0
1949	17	15	2	2	1	1	0	0
1951	18	18	—	2	2	—	0	0
1953	31	28	3	4[3]	4	—	2	0
1955	38	38	—	—	—	—	0	0
1957	35	34	1	3	3	—	2	0
1959	36	32	4	1	1	—	0	0
1961	70	68	2	3	3	—	2	0
1963	72	68	4	1	1	—	0	0
1965	24	23	1	4	4	—	1	0
1967	18	18	—	5	5	—	0	0
1969	34	33	1	11	11	—	27	0
1971	32	29	3	8	8	—	12	0
1973	13	13	—	18	15	3	38	2
1975	37	31	6	22	18	4	42	5
1977	21	17	4	16	13	3	67	21
1979	19	16	3	9	7	2	45	1
1981	11	9	2	11	10	1	121[4]	0
1983	3	3	—	11	10	1	70	6
1985	7	7	—	7	6	1	78	2
1987	38	38	—	20	20	—	290	0
1989	35	35	—	28	28	—	203	0
1991	33	33	—	13	13	—	457	0
1993	8	8	—	24	24	—	78	0
1995	4	4	—	21	21	—	112	0
1997	3	3	—	8	8	—	152	0
1999	5	5	—	9	9	—	255	0
2001	—	—	—	3	3	—	315	0
2003	54	54	—	10	10	—	131	0
2005	47	47	—	2	2	—	139	0
2007	1	1	—	4	4	—	33	0
2009	6	6	—	5	5	—	81	0
2011	—	—	—	3	3	—	50	0

Note: The legislature is not required to act on vetoes. Any veto not acted upon is counted as sustained, including pocket vetoes. "Vetoes sustained" includes the following pocket vetoes: 1931 (20); 1937 (5); 1941 (12); 1943 (4); 1951 (14); 1955 (10); 1957 (1); 1973 (1). A "pocket veto" resulted if the governor took no action on a bill after the legislature had adjourned *sine die*. (*Sine die*, from the Latin for "without a day", means the legislature adjourns without setting a date to reconvene.) With this type of adjournment, the legislature concluded all its business for the biennium, and there was no opportunity for it to sustain or override the veto (see Article V, Section 10, *Wisconsin Constitution*). Under current legislative session schedules, in which the legislature usually adjourns on the final day of its existence, just hours before the newly elected legislature is seated, the pocket veto is unlikely.

[1]The number of individual veto statements in the governor's veto message.

[2]Attorney general ruled veto of 1939 SB-43 was void and it became law (see Vol. 28, *Opinions of the Attorney General*, p. 423).

[3]1953 AB-141, partially vetoed in two separate sections by separate veto messages, is counted as one.

[4]Attorney general ruled several vetoes "ineffective" because the governor failed to express his objections (see Vol. 70, *Opinions of the Attorney General*, p. 189).

Source: Compiled by Wisconsin Legislative Reference Bureau from the *Bulletin of the Proceedings of the Wisconsin Legislature* and the Assembly and Senate *Journals*.

POLITICAL COMPOSITION OF THE
WISCONSIN LEGISLATURE
1885 – 2013

Legislative Session[1]	Senate							Assembly						
	D	R	P	S	SD	M[4]	Vacant	D	R	P	S	SD	M[5]	Vacant
1885	13	20	—	—	—	—	—	39	61	—	—	—	—	—
1887	6	25	—	—	—	2	—	30	57	—	—	—	13	—
1889	6	24	—	—	—	3	—	29	71	—	—	—	—	—
1891	19	14	—	—	—	—	—	66	33	—	—	—	1	—
1893	26	7	—	—	—	—	—	56	44	—	—	—	—	—
1895	13	20	—	—	—	—	—	19	81	—	—	—	—	—
1897	4	29	—	—	—	—	—	8	91	—	—	—	1	—
1899	2	31	—	—	—	—	—	19	81	—	—	—	—	—
1901	2	31	—	—	—	—	—	18	82	—	—	—	—	—
1903	3	30	—	—	—	—	—	25	75	—	—	—	—	—
1905	4	28	—	—	1	—	—	11	85	—	—	4	—	—
1907	5	27	—	—	1	—	—	19	76	—	—	5	—	—
1909	4	28	—	—	1	—	—	17	80	—	—	3	—	—
1911	4	27	—	—	2	—	—	29	59	—	—	12	—	—
1913	9	23	—	—	1	—	—	37	57	—	—	6	—	—
1915	11	21	—	—	1	—	—	29	63	—	—	8	—	—
1917	6	24	—	3	—	—	—	14	79	—	7	—	—	—
1919	2	27	—	4	—	—	—	5	79	—	16	—	—	—
1921	2	27	—	4	—	—	—	2	92	—	6	—	—	—
1923	—	30	—	3	—	—	—	1	89	—	10	—	—	—
1925	—	30	—	3	—	—	—	1	92	—	7	—	—	—
1927	—	31	—	2	—	—	—	3	89	—	8	—	—	—
1929	—	31	—	2	—	—	—	6	90	—	3	—	1	—
1931	1	30	—	2	—	—	—	2	89	—	9	—	—	—
1933	9	23	—	1	—	—	—	59	13	24	3	—	1	—
1935	13	6	14	—	—	—	—	35	17	45	3	—	—	—
1937	9	8	16	—	—	—	—	31	21	46	2	—	—	—
1939	6	16	11	—	—	—	—	15	53	32	—	—	—	—
1941	3	24	6	—	—	—	—	15	60	25	—	—	—	—
1943	4	23	6	—	—	—	—	14	73	13	—	—	—	—
1945	6	22	5	—	—	—	—	19	75	6	—	—	—	—
1947	5	27	1	—	—	—	—	11	88	—	—	—	—	1
1949	3	27	—	—	—	—	3	26	74	—	—	—	—	—
1951	7	26	—	—	—	—	—	24	75	—	—	—	—	1
1953	7	26	—	—	—	—	—	25	75	—	—	—	—	—
1955	8	24	—	—	—	—	1	36	64	—	—	—	—	—
1957	10	23	—	—	—	—	—	33	67	—	—	—	—	—
1959	12	20	—	—	—	—	1	55	45	—	—	—	—	—
1961	13	20	—	—	—	—	—	45	55	—	—	—	—	—
1963	11	22	—	—	—	—	—	46	53	—	—	—	—	1
1965	12	20	—	—	—	—	1	52	48	—	—	—	—	—
1967	12	21	—	—	—	—	—	47	53	—	—	—	—	—
1969	10	23	—	—	—	—	—	48	52	—	—	—	—	—
1971	12	20	—	—	—	—	1	67	33	—	—	—	—	—
1973	15	18	—	—	—	—	—	62	37	—	—	—	—	—
1975	18	13	—	—	—	—	2	63	36	—	—	—	—	—
1977	23	10	—	—	—	—	—	66	33	—	—	—	—	—
1979	21	10	—	—	—	—	2	60	39	—	—	—	—	—
1981	19	14	—	—	—	—	—	59	39	—	—	—	—	1
1983	17	14	—	—	—	—	2	59	40	—	—	—	—	—
1985	19	14	—	—	—	—	—	52	47	—	—	—	—	—
1987	19	11	—	—	—	—	3	54	45	—	—	—	—	—
1989	20	13	—	—	—	—	—	56	43	—	—	—	—	—
1991	19	14	—	—	—	—	—	58	41	—	—	—	—	—
1993[2]	15	15	—	—	—	—	3	52	47	—	—	—	—	—
1995[2]	16	17	—	—	—	—	—	48	51	—	—	—	—	—
1997[2]	17	16	—	—	—	—	—	47	52	—	—	—	—	—
1999	17	16	—	—	—	—	—	44	55	—	—	—	—	—
2001	18	15	—	—	—	—	—	43	56	—	—	—	—	—
2003	15	18	—	—	—	—	—	41	58	—	—	—	—	—
2005	14	19	—	—	—	—	—	39	60	—	—	—	—	—
2007	18	15	—	—	—	—	—	47	52	—	—	—	—	—
2009	18	15	—	—	—	—	—	52	46	—	—	—	1	—
2011[3]	14	19	—	—	—	—	—	38	60	—	—	—	1	—
2013	15	18	—	—	—	—	—	39	59	—	—	—	—	1

Note: The number of assembly districts was reduced from 100 to 99 beginning in 1973.

Key: Democrat (D); Progressive (P); Republican (R); Socialist (S); Social Democrat (SD); Miscellaneous (M).

[1]Political composition at inauguration.

[2]In the 1993, 1995, and 1997 Legislatures, majority control of the senate shifted during the session. On 4/20/93, vacancies were filled resulting in a total of 16 Democrats and 17 Republicans; on 6/16/96, there were 17 Democrats and 16 Republicans; and on 4/19/98, there were 16 Democrats and 17 Republicans.

[3]A series of recall elections during the session resulted in a switch in majority control of the senate, with 17 Democrats and 16 Republicans as of 7/16/12.

[4]Miscellaneous = one Independent and one People's (1887); one Independent and 2 Union Labor (1889).

[5]Miscellaneous = 3 Independent, 4 Independent Democrat, and 6 People's (1887); one Union Labor (1891); one Fusion (1897); one Independent (1929, 2009, 2011); one Independent Republican (1933).

Sources: Pre-1943 data is taken from the Secretary of State, *Officers of Wisconsin: U.S., State, Judicial, Congressional, Legislative and County Officers*, 1943 and earlier editions, and the *Wisconsin Blue Book*, various editions. Later data compiled from Wisconsin Legislative Reference Bureau sources.

STATUTES, SESSION LAWS, AND ADMINISTRATIVE CODE

Printed Materials

The printed state documents listed below are available from Document Sales, 4622 University Avenue, Madison 53705-2156; telephone (608) 266-3358; Fax: (608) 261-8150.

Prices listed do not reflect 5% state sales tax and, where applicable, 0.5% county sales tax and/or 0.5% or 0.1% stadium tax. Taxes must be included with payment. Prepayment is required for all orders. Make check or money order payable to Wisconsin Department of Administration. For MasterCard or Visa orders, call (800) 362-7253.

Wisconsin Statutes 2011-12:

Hardcover 6-volume set – $86 (picked up); $94 (shipped)

Softcover 6-volume set – $51 (picked up); $59 (shipped)

2011 Laws of Wisconsin: Hardcover 2-volume set – $44.15 (picked up); $48.85 (shipped)

Wisconsin Administrative Code, including loose-leaf *Administrative Register.* Subscriptions are available for the entire code or individual code books. Contact Document Sales at (608) 266-3358 for current pricing information.

Machine-Readable Data

WisLaw, the computer-searchable CD-ROM, contains the Wisconsin Statutes and Annotations, plus the Wisconsin and U.S. Constitutions, Supreme Court Rules, Wisconsin Acts, recent Opinions of the Attorney General, the Administrative Code and Register, executive orders, and town law forms.

WisLaw is continuously updated and is available only by annual subscription. (The number of CD updates released in any 12-month period may vary.) The CD will only be delivered upon receipt of a signed end-user license, subscription form, and full payment. Subscription forms and *WisLaw* end-user licenses are available at Document Sales (see address above) or through the Legislative Reference Bureau home page, at: **http:// legis.wisconsin.gov/rsb/order.htm**

Sources: Wisconsin Department of Administration, *Document Sales Catalog,* and Legislative Reference Bureau.

The 2013 Legislature continued an initiative to modify administrative procedure and tighten legislative oversight of rule-making. Representative Daniel LeMahieu (R-Cascade), cochairperson of the Joint Committee for Review of Administrative Rules, explained the initiative to the press. (Jay Salvo, Legislative Photographer)

STANDING COMMITTEES
OF THE 2013 WISCONSIN LEGISLATURE

All standing committees of the 2013 Wisconsin Legislature are described in this section. The standing committees of the senate are created by the Committee on Senate Organization while standing committees of the assembly are enumerated in Assembly Rule 9. In the case of each standing committee listed below, the names of committee officers are followed by those of the majority party and minority party, separated by a semicolon. An * indicates the ranking minority member.

The committee process offers legislators an opportunity to critically examine legislation in a less formal setting than the floor of a legislative chamber. Senator Julie Lassa questioned a witness before the Senate Committee on Economic Development and Local Government. (Greg Anderson, Legislative Photographer)

SENATE STANDING COMMITTEES

Administrative Rules — VUKMIR, *chairperson;* LEIBHAM, TIFFANY; HARRIS*, VINEHOUT.

Agriculture, Small Business, and Tourism — MOULTON, *chairperson;* TIFFANY, *vice chairperson;* HARSDORF, SCHULTZ, PETROWSKI; VINEHOUT*, HANSEN, LASSA, TAYLOR.

Audit — COWLES, *chairperson;* DARLING, LAZICH; VINEHOUT*, LEHMAN.

Economic Development and Local Government — GUDEX, *chairperson;* PETROWSKI, *vice chairperson;* LEIBHAM; LASSA*, TAYLOR.

Education — OLSEN, *chairperson;* FARROW, *vice chairperson;* VUKMIR, DARLING, GUDEX; LEHMAN*, CULLEN, HARRIS, VINEHOUT.

Elections and Urban Affairs — LAZICH, *chairperson;* LEIBHAM, *vice chairperson;* LASEE; TAYLOR*, MILLER.

Energy, Consumer Protection, and Government Reform — COWLES, *chairperson;* KEDZIE, *vice chairperson;* HARSDORF; HANSEN*, MILLER.

Finance — DARLING, *chairperson;* OLSEN, *vice chairperson;* HARSDORF, GROTHMAN, LEIBHAM, LAZICH; SHILLING*, WIRCH.

Financial Institutions and Rural Issues — SCHULTZ, *chairperson;* LASEE, *vice chairperson;* PETROWSKI; LASSA*, JAUCH.

Government Operations, Public Works, and Telecommunications — FARROW, *chairperson;* GUDEX, *vice chairperson;* LASEE, KEDZIE; WIRCH*, HARRIS, SHILLING.

Health and Human Services — VUKMIR, *chairperson;* MOULTON, *vice chairperson;* LAZICH; ERPENBACH*, CARPENTER.

Insurance and Housing — LASEE, *chairperson;* OLSEN, *vice chairperson;* SCHULTZ; CULLEN*, ERPENBACH.

Judiciary and Labor — GROTHMAN, *chairperson;* VUKMIR, *vice chairperson;* FARROW; RISSER*, HARRIS.

Natural Resources — KEDZIE, *chairperson;* MOULTON, *vice chairperson;* TIFFANY; MILLER*, WIRCH.

Senate Organization — FITZGERALD, *chairperson;* ELLIS, GROTHMAN; LARSON*, HANSEN.

State and Federal Relations — ELLIS, *chairperson;* COWLES, *vice chairperson;* SCHULTZ; CARPENTER*, RISSER.

Transportation, Public Safety, and Veterans and Military Affairs — PETROWSKI, *chairperson;* LEIBHAM, *vice chairperson;* COWLES; CARPENTER*, HANSEN.

Universities and Technical Colleges — HARSDORF, *chairperson;* SCHULTZ, *vice chairperson;* GUDEX; SHILLING*, ERPENBACH.

Workforce Development, Forestry, Mining, and Revenue — TIFFANY, *chairperson;* DARLING, *vice chairperson;* GROTHMAN; JAUCH*, LEHMAN.

ASSEMBLY STANDING COMMITTEES

Administrative Rules — LeMAHIEU, *chairperson;* KAUFERT, *vice chairperson;* AUGUST; HEBL*, KAHL.

Aging and Long-Term Care — ENDSLEY, *chairperson;* CZAJA, *vice chairperson;* WILLIAMS, BERNIER, PETRYK, NERISON; BERNARD SCHABER*, SARGENT, KAHL.

Agriculture — NERISON, *chairperson;* TAUCHEN, *vice chairperson;* MARKLEIN, A. OTT, MURTHA, MURSAU, RIPP, TRANEL, BROOKS, SCHRAA; VRUWINK*, JORGENSEN, DANOU, SMITH, GOYKE, WRIGHT.

Assembly Organization — VOS, *chairperson;* SUDER, *vice chairperson;* STEINEKE, KRAMER, BALLWEG; BARCA*, PASCH, JORGENSEN.

Audit — KERKMAN, *chairperson;* MARKLEIN, *vice chairperson;* NYGREN; RICHARDS*, SARGENT.

Campaigns and Elections — BERNIER, *chairperson;* PRIDEMORE, *vice chairperson;* THIESFELDT, WEININGER, TRANEL, CRAIG; ZAMARRIPA*, KESSLER, BERCEAU.

Children and Families — KRUG, *chairperson;* LOUDENBECK, *vice chairperson;* ENDSLEY, SCHRAA, SPIROS, KERKMAN, NEYLON (eff. 4/16/13); TAYLOR*, BILLINGS, JOHNSON, KAHL (eff. 5/10/13).

Colleges and Universities — NASS, *chairperson;* MURPHY, *vice chairperson;* KNUDSON, WEATHERSTON, STROEBEL, BALLWEG, KRUG, SCHRAA; BEWLEY*, BILLINGS, HESSELBEIN, WACHS, BERCEAU.

Constitution and Ethics — KAPENGA, *cochairperson,* BILLINGS, *cochairperson;* JAGLER, J. OTT, TAUCHEN, MURPHY; WACHS*, SHANKLAND.

Consumer Protection — THIESFELDT, *chairperson;* TITTL, *vice chairperson;* A. OTT, NERISON, WEATHERSTON, JAGLER; POPE*, JOHNSON, WRIGHT.

Corrections — BIES, *chairperson;* SCHRAA, *vice chairperson;* BROOKS, KRUG, THIESFELDT, KLEEFISCH; DOYLE*, PASCH, ZAMARRIPA.

Criminal Justice — KLEEFISCH, *chairperson;* SPIROS, *vice chairperson;* JACQUE, J. OTT, SEVERSON, BIES; KESSLER*, GOYKE, JOHNSON.

Education — KESTELL, *chairperson;* JAGLER, *vice chairperson;* SEVERSON, NASS, PRIDEMORE, MARKLEIN, THIESFELDT; POPE*, CLARK, WRIGHT, HESSELBEIN.

Energy and Utilities — HONADEL, *chairperson;* LARSON, *vice chairperson;* JACQUE, WEININGER, SEVERSON, KLENKE, PETERSEN, NEYLON (eff. 4/16/13); ZEPNICK*, HULSEY, KAHL, SHANKLAND.

Environment and Forestry — MURSAU, *chairperson;* KRUG, *vice chairperson;* CZAJA, LOUDENBECK, STROEBEL; DANOU*, MILROY, CLARK.

Family Law — LARSON, *chairperson;* KESTELL, *vice chairperson;* WILLIAMS, TITTL, CRAIG, TRANEL; TAYLOR*, PASCH, HEBL.

Finance — NYGREN, *chairperson;* STRACHOTA, *vice chairperson;* LEMAHIEU, KOOYENGA, KNUDSON, KLENKE; MASON*, RICHARDS.

Financial Institutions — CRAIG, *chairperson;* KAPENGA, *vice chairperson;* STROEBEL, SANFELIPPO, KRAMER, KAUFERT, MARKLEIN, WEININGER, BORN; HINTZ*, ZEPNICK, YOUNG, RICHARDS, GENRICH, SARGENT.

Government Operations and State Licensing — AUGUST, *chairperson;* CRAIG, *vice chairperson;* KNODL, NASS, KOOYENGA, HUTTON, NEYLON (eff. 4/16/13); HULSEY*, SINICKI, RINGHAND, KESSLER (eff. 4/29/13).

Health — SEVERSON, *chairperson;* STONE, *vice chairperson;* SANFELIPPO, STRACHOTA, AUGUST, KAPENGA, PETERSEN; PASCH*, TAYLOR, KOLSTE, RIEMER.

Housing and Real Estate — MURTHA, *chairperson;* SANFELIPPO, *vice chairperson;* NASS, MURPHY, JAGLER, SWEARINGEN; YOUNG*, BEWLEY, GENRICH.

Insurance — PETERSEN, *chairperson;* WEININGER, *vice chairperson;* CZAJA, JAGLER, HONADEL, CRAIG, TRANEL, BORN, MURPHY, STROEBEL; DANOU*, BERCEAU, YOUNG, DOYLE, KAHL, OHNSTAD.

International Trade and Commerce — WEININGER, *chairperson;* KUGLITSCH, *vice chairperson;* WILLIAMS, LOUDENBECK, TAUCHEN, MURTHA; JORGENSEN*, RIEMER, SARGENT.

Jobs, Economy and Mining — WILLIAMS, *chairperson;* KNODL, *vice chairperson;* LARSON, SANFELIPPO, KAPENGA, KUGLITSCH, PETRYK, PETERSEN, STONE, JACQUE; CLARK*, BERNARD SCHABER, ZAMARRIPA, HINTZ, HULSEY, OHNSTAD.

Judiciary — J. OTT, *chairperson;* JACQUE, *vice chairperson;* AUGUST, CRAIG, KERKMAN, LARSON; HEBL*, WACHS, GOYKE.

Labor — KNODL, *chairperson;* AUGUST, *vice chairperson;* KAPENGA, NASS, KUGLITSCH, KLEEFISCH; SINICKI*, TAYLOR, OHNSTAD.

Natural Resources and Sporting Heritage — A. OTT, *chairperson;* KLEEFISCH, *vice chairperson;* BORN, BIES, WILLIAMS, MURSAU, NERISON, PETRYK, STEINEKE, SWEARINGEN; MILROY*, DANOU, CLARK, HEBL, SHANKLAND, HESSELBEIN.

Public Safety and Homeland Security — JACQUE, *chairperson;* BROOKS, *vice chairperson;* MURTHA, BERNIER, SWEARINGEN; KESSLER*, ZAMARRIPA, BEWLEY.

Rules — SUDER, *chairperson;* VOS, *vice chairperson;* KRAMER, STEINEKE, BALLWEG, MURTHA, WILLIAMS; BARCA*, PASCH, JORGENSEN, ZAMARRIPA, POPE.

Rural Affairs — TAUCHEN, *chairperson;* BERNIER, *vice chairperson;* KRUG, MURTHA, RIPP, SCHRAA, MURSAU, MARKLEIN; VRUWINK*, JORGENSEN, MILROY, BEWLEY, SMITH.

Small Business Development — STONE, *chairperson;* ENDSLEY, *vice chairperson;* HUTTON, KAUFERT, SWEARINGEN, LARSON, RIPP, CZAJA, SCHRAA, TITTL; JORGENSEN*, RINGHAND, SARGENT, SMITH, WRIGHT, KOLSTE.

State Affairs — KUGLITSCH, *chairperson;* SWEARINGEN, *vice chairperson;* AUGUST, KLEEFISCH, KNODL, RIPP, NEYLON (eff. 4/16/13); ZAMARRIPA*, BERNARD SCHABER, KAHL, SHANKLAND (eff. 4/29/13).

State and Federal Relations — TRANEL, *cochairperson;* YOUNG, *cochairperson;* MURSAU, PETERSEN, TITTL, LOUDENBECK; ZEPNICK*, BARNES.

State and Local Finance — STROEBEL, *chairperson;* BORN, *vice chairperson;* KESTELL, WEATHERSTON, NASS, TAUCHEN; ZEPNICK*, HINTZ, BERCEAU.

Tourism — KAUFERT, *chairperson;* BIES, *vice chairperson;* CZAJA, KLEEFISCH, ENDSLEY, BORN, A. OTT, SWEARINGEN, BALLWEG; BILLINGS*, HULSEY, DOYLE, HEBL, OHNSTAD.

Transportation — RIPP, *chairperson;* THIESFELDT, *vice chairperson;* SPIROS, A. OTT, SANFELIPPO, ENDSLEY, LARSON, KAUFERT, STONE; BERNARD SCHABER*, VRUWINK, DOYLE, DANOU, RIEMER, KOLSTE.

Urban and Local Affairs — BROOKS, *chairperson;* HUTTON, *vice chairperson;* JACQUE, J. OTT, HONADEL, MURPHY; HINTZ*, RINGHAND, BARNES.

Urban Education — PRIDEMORE, *chairperson;* THIESFELDT, *vice chairperson;* JAGLER, KESTELL, KNODL, WEININGER, HUTTON, SANFELIPPO; SINICKI*, POPE, PASCH, BARNES, JOHNSON.

Veterans — PETRYK, *chairperson;* WEATHERSTON, *vice chairperson;* SUDER, BIES, ENDSLEY, NERISON, PRIDEMORE, BROOKS, J. OTT, TITTL; RINGHAND*, MILROY, SINICKI, VRUWINK, HESSELBEIN, GOYKE.

Ways and Means — MARKLEIN, *chairperson;* KERKMAN, *vice chairperson;* RIPP, SPIROS, STONE, HONADEL, KESTELL; HULSEY*, RIEMER, BARNES.

Workforce Development — LOUDENBECK, *chairperson;* PETRYK, *vice chairperson;* HONADEL, KUGLITSCH, SEVERSON, PRIDEMORE, WEATHERSTON, BORN, BERNIER, KNODL; RINGHAND*, BILLINGS, KOLSTE, BARNES, SHANKLAND, WACHS.

The Wisconsin Assembly has seen unusually large freshmen classes in each of the last two sessions. A majority of the members of the 2013 Assembly are in their first or second terms. Representative Dianne Hesselbein (D-Middleton) is one of 25 freshmen in 2013. (Jay Salvo, Legislative Photographer)

PERSONAL DATA ON WISCONSIN LEGISLATORS
2003 – 2013 Sessions

	2003		2005		2007		2009		2011		2013	
	Sen.	Rep.	Sen.	Rep.	Sen.	Rep.	Sen.	Rep.*	Sen.	Rep.*	Sen.	Rep.
Party affiliation												
Democrat	15	41	14	39	18	47	18	52	14	38	15	39
Republican	18	58	19	60	15	52	15	46	19	60	18	60
Number with previous legislative service												
In senate	27	0	28	0	29	0	31	0	26	0	30	0
In assembly	22	84	23	81	23	82	23	86	23	69	25	74
Highest number of prior sessions in same house	20	16	21	17	22	18	23	19	24	14	25	13
Occupations												
Full-time legislator	13	39	11	39	12	38	11	39	12	32	12	35
Attorney	3	8	2	11	3	11	3	12	3	8	3	7
Farmer	3	9	3	9	3	5	3	5	2	6	2	4
Other	14	43	17	40	15	45	16	43	16	53	16	53
Education												
High school only	4	12	4	9	2	7	1	7	0	4	1	5
Beyond high school	29	87	29	90	31	92	32	92	33	95	32	94
Bachelor's or associate degree	25	67	26	70	28	69	29	69	29	73	28	72
Advanced degree	7	32	8	34	10	37	11	35	10	27	9	27
Number with experience on local governing body												
County board	4	19	4	18	4	17	4	15	6	16	7	18
Municipal board	8	35	10	28	12	25	12	30	9	29	11	30
Age												
Oldest	75	75	77	77	79	79	81	80	83	72	85	72
Youngest	33	27	34	28	36	28	38	29	30	25	32	25
Average	51	49	52	50	54	50	55	50	56	49	57	49
Veterans	4	13	4	13	2	16	2	16	2	13	2	10
Marital status												
Single	5	17	10	25	8	25	9	24	7	18	9	22
Married	28	80	23	70	25	69	24	71	26	79	24	77
Widowed	0	2	0	4	0	5	0	4	0	2	0	0
Number of women	8	27	8	26	8	22	7	22	8	23	9	24

*Includes one Independent.

Sen. – Senators; Rep. – Representatives.

Note: Most data are recorded as of the date on which the legislature first convened; ages are determined as of January 1.

Sources: *Wisconsin Blue Book*, various issues, and data collected by the Wisconsin Legislative Reference Bureau, January 2013.

Representatives David Craig (R-Big Bend), Travis Tranel (R-Cuba City), and Chad Weininger (R-Green Bay) are all members of the large 2011 freshman class that have returned for a second term.
(Jay Salvo, Legislative Photographer)

JOINT LEGISLATIVE COMMITTEES AND COMMISSIONS

Joint committees and commissions are created by statute and include members from both houses. Three joint committees include nonlegislative members. Names of committee officers are followed by those of the majority and minority party, separated by a semicolon. The ranking minority member is indicated by an *. Commissions also include gubernatorial appointees and, in 2 cases, the governor. All telephone numbers that do not include an area code are Madison numbers, area code 608.

JOINT COMMITTEE FOR REVIEW OF
ADMINISTRATIVE RULES

Members: SENATOR VUKMIR, REPRESENTATIVE LEMAHIEU, *cochairpersons;* SENATORS LEIBHAM, TIFFANY; HARRIS*, VINEHOUT; REPRESENTATIVES KAUFERT, AUGUST; HEBL*, KAHL.

Mailing Addresses: Senator Vukmir, Room 131 South, State Capitol, P.O. Box 7882, Madison 53707-7882; Representative LeMahieu, Room 304 East, State Capitol, P.O. Box 8952, Madison 53708-8952.

Telephones: Senator Vukmir, 266-2512; Representative LeMahieu, 266-9175.

E-mail: sen.vukmir@legis.wisconsin.gov; rep.lemahieu@legis.wisconsin.gov

Statutory References: Sections 13.56, 227.19, 227.24, 227.26, 227.40 (5), and 806.04 (11).

Agency Responsibility: The Joint Committee for Review of Administrative Rules must review proposed rules and may object to the promulgation of rules as part of the legislative oversight of the rule-making process. It also may suspend rules that have been promulgated; suspend or extend the effective period of emergency rules; and order an agency to put unwritten policies in rule form.

Following standing committee review, a proposed rule must be referred to the joint committee. The committee must meet to review proposed rules that receive standing committee objections, and may meet to review any rule received without objection. The joint committee has 30 days to review the rule, but that period may be extended for an additional 30 days. The joint committee may uphold or reverse the standing committee's action or may, on its own accord, object to a proposed rule or portion of a rule. If it objects or concurs with a standing committee's objection, it introduces bills concurrently in both houses to prevent promulgation of the rule. If either bill is enacted, the agency may not adopt the rule unless specifically authorized to do so by subsequent legislative action. If the joint committee disagrees with a standing committee's objection, it may overrule the standing committee and allow the agency to adopt the rule. The joint committee may also request the agency to modify a proposed rule.

The joint committee may suspend a rule after holding a public hearing, but suspension must be based on one or more of the following reasons: absence of statutory authority; an emergency related to public health or welfare; failure to comply with legislative intent; conflict with existing state law; a change in circumstances since passage of the law that authorized the rule; a rule that is arbitrary or capricious or imposes undue hardship; or a rule affecting construction of a dwelling that would increase the cost of construction by more than $1,000. Within 30 days following the suspension, the committee must introduce bills concurrently in both houses to repeal the suspended rule. If either bill is enacted, the rule is repealed and the agency may not promulgate it again unless authorized by the legislature. If both bills fail to pass, the rule remains in effect and may not be suspended again except for rules increasing the cost of construction of a dwelling by more than $1,000; these are suspended until specific legislation authorizing them is enacted.

The joint committee receives notice of any action in a circuit court for declaratory judgments about the validity of a rule and may intervene in the action with the consent of the Joint Committee on Legislative Organization.

Organization: The joint committee consists of 5 senators and 5 representatives, and the membership from each house must include representatives of both the majority and minority parties.

Speaker Robin Vos (R-Burlington) (left) listens to Democrat Andy Jorgensen of Fort Atkinson make his point. (Jay Salvo, Legislative Photographer)

History: The Joint Committee for Review of Administrative Rules was one of the first of its kind in the country, and it has served as a model widely copied by other states. Chapter 221, Laws of 1955, revised administrative rules procedures and created the committee with "advisory powers only". It could investigate complaints about rules and recommend changes to rule-making agencies but could not directly affect the rule-making process. Chapter 659, Laws of 1965, granted the committee authority to suspend a rule based on testimony at a public hearing. With enactment of Chapter 34, Laws of 1979, the joint committee acquired the power to review proposed rules based on the objections of a legislative standing committee. Further modifications occurred when 1985 Wisconsin Act 182 authorized the joint committee to extend its 30-day review period and allowed it to negotiate with agencies to modify existing rules. 2011 Wisconsin Act 21 modified the legislative review of proposed rules to require referral of all proposed rules to the joint committee.

State of Wisconsin
BUILDING COMMISSION

Members: GOVERNOR WALKER, *chairperson;* REPRESENTATIVE KAUFERT, *vice chairperson;* SENATORS KEDZIE, MOULTON; RISSER; REPRESENTATIVES BALLWEG; HINTZ; BOB BRANDHERM (citizen member appointed by governor). Nonvoting advisory members from Department of Administration: MICHAEL HUEBSCH (departmental secretary), GILBERT FUNK (chief engineer), vacancy (chief architect).

Secretary: SUMMER R. SHANNON-BRADLEY, *administrator,* Division of State Facilities, Department of Administration.

Mailing Address: P.O. Box 7866, Madison 53707-7866.

Location: 101 East Wilson Street, 7th Floor, Madison.

Telephone: 266-1031.

Fax: 267-2710.

Statutory Reference: Section 13.48.

Agency Responsibility: The State of Wisconsin Building Commission coordinates the state building program which includes the necessary lands, new buildings, all facilities and equipment required, and the remodeling, reconstruction, maintenance, and reequipping of existing buildings and facilities. The commission determines the projects to be incorporated into the long-range program and recommends a biennial building program to the legislature, including the amount to be appropriated in the biennial budget. The state building program for 2011-13 was $966,977,300. The commission oversees all state construction, except highway development. In addition, the commission may authorize expenditures from the State Building Trust Fund for construction, remodeling, maintenance, and planning of future development. The commission is the only state body that can authorize the contracting of state debt. All transactions for the sale of instruments that result in a state debt liability must be approved by official resolution of the commission.

Organization: The 8-member commission includes 6 legislators. Both the majority and minority parties in each house must be represented, and one legislator from each house must also be a member of the State Supported Programs Study and Advisory Committee. The governor serves as chairperson; one citizen member serves at the pleasure of the governor. In addition, three officials from the Department of Administration – the secretary, the head of the engineering function, and the ranking architect – serve as nonvoting, advisory members.

History: The State of Wisconsin Building Commission was created by Chapter 563, Laws of 1949, to establish a long-range public building program. Another 1949 law (Chapter 604) gave the commission authority to organize the quasi-public Wisconsin State Public Building Corporation. This legal device, familiarly known as a "dummy building corporation", was used to finance public buildings to house state agencies because the Wisconsin Constitution prevented direct borrowing by the state for such projects. The quasi-public corporation was first used in 1925, when the University Building Corporation was developed to permit construction of revenue-producing facilities on the Madison campus, including dormitories and athletic buildings. The State Agencies Building Corporation, a similar entity, was formed in 1958 (Chapter 593, Laws of 1957) to finance nonrevenue-producing buildings, such as classroom facilities, and Chapter 267, Laws of 1961, extended the corporation's authority to the financing of public welfare buildings.

In 1969, voters amended the constitution, and the legislature passed Chapter 259, which provided for direct state borrowing and ended the use of the various building corporations. The law enlarged the powers of the commission to finance capital facilities for all state agencies.

A separate State Bond Board, including 4 members of the Building Commission, was established by Chapter 259 to supervise the contracting of state debt. Chapter 90, Laws of 1973, abolished the bond board and returned its duties and responsibilities to the Building Commission.

Joint Review Committee on
CRIMINAL PENALTIES

Members: SENATORS KEDZIE, TAYLOR; REPRESENTATIVES JACQUE, GOYKE; J.B. VAN HOLLEN (attorney general); EDWARD F. WALL (secretary of corrections); KELLI S. THOMPSON (state public defender); JAMES T. BAYORGEON, DAVID G. DEININGER (reserve judges appointed by supreme court); BRADLEY GEHRING, MAURY STRAUB (public members appointed by governor).

Mailing Address: Senator Kedzie, Room 313 South, State Capitol, P.O. Box 7882, Madison 53707-7882; Representative Jacque, Room 123 West, State Capitol, P.O. Box 8952, Madison 53708.

Telephones: Senator Kedzie, 266-2635; Representative Jacque, 266-9870.

E-mail: sen.kedzie@legis.wisconsin.gov; rep.jacque@legis.wisconsin.gov

Statutory Reference: Section 13.525.

Agency Responsibility: The Joint Review Committee on Criminal Penalties, created by 2001 Wisconsin Act 109, reviews any bill that creates a new crime or revises a penalty for an existing crime when requested to do so by a chairperson of a standing committee in the house of origin to which the bill was referred. The presiding officer in the house of origin may also request a report from the joint committee if the bill is not referred to a standing committee.

Committee reports on bills submitted for its review concern the costs or savings to public agencies; the consistency of proposed penalties with existing penalties; whether alternative language is needed to conform the proposed penalties to existing penalties; and whether any acts prohibited by the bill are already prohibited under existing law.

Once a report is requested for a bill, a standing committee may not vote on the bill and the house of origin may not pass the bill before the joint committee submits its report or before the 30th day after the request is made, whichever is earlier.

Organization: Legislative members include one majority and one minority party member from each house; the members from the majority parties serve as cochairpersons. One reserve judge must reside somewhere within judicial administrative districts one through 5, and the other in districts 6 through 10. Public members must include an individual with law enforcement experience and one who is an elected county official.

Joint Committee on
EMPLOYMENT RELATIONS

SENATOR ELLIS (senate president), REPRESENTATIVE VOS (assembly speaker), SENATORS FITZGERALD (majority leader), LARSON (minority leader); REPRESENTATIVES SUDER (majority leader), BARCA (minority leader); SENATOR DARLING, REPRESENTATIVE NYGREN (joint finance committee cochairpersons).

A break in the action gave Senator Tim Cullen (D-Janesville) the opportunity to chat with Senator Lena Taylor (D-Milwaukee). (Greg Anderson, Legislative Photographer)

Mailing Address: Legislative Council Staff, P.O. Box 2536, Madison 53701-2536.

Location: 1 East Main Street, Suite 401, Madison.

Telephone: 266-1304.

Statutory References: Sections 13.111, 20.923 (4), and 230.12; Chapter 111, Subchapter V.

Agency Responsibility: The Joint Committee on Employment Relations approves all changes to the collective bargaining agreements that cover state employees represented by unions, and the compensation plans for nonrepresented state employees. These plans and agreements include pay adjustments; fringe benefits; performance awards; pay equity adjustments; and other items related to wages, hours, and conditions of employment. The committee also approves the assignment of unclassified positions to the executive salary group ranges.

In the case of unionized employees, the Office of State Employment Relations or, for certain University of Wisconsin bargaining units, the Board of Regents, submits tentative agreements negotiated between it and certified labor organizations to the committee. If the committee disapproves an agreement, it is returned to the bargaining parties for renegotiation.

When the committee approves an agreement for unionized employees, it introduces those portions requiring legislative approval in bill form and recommends passage without change. If the legislature fails to pass the bill, the agreement is returned to the bargaining parties for renegotiation.

The Office of State Employment Relations also submits the compensation plans for nonrepresented employees to the committee. One plan covers all nonrepresented classified employees and certain officials outside the classified service, including legislators, justices of the supreme court, court of appeals judges, circuit court judges, constitutional officers, district attorneys, heads of executive agencies, division administrators, and others designated by law. The faculty and academic staff of the UW System are covered by a separate compensation plan, which is based on recommendations made by the UW Board of Regents.

After public hearings on the nonrepresented employee plans, the committee may modify the office's recommendations, but the committee's modifications may be disapproved by the governor. The committee may set aside the governor's disapproval by a vote of 6 committee members.

Organization: The committee, which was established by Chapter 270, Laws of 1971, is a permanent joint legislative committee comprised of 8 members. It is assisted in its work by the Legislative Council Staff and the Legislative Fiscal Bureau.

Joint Committee on
FINANCE

SENATOR DARLING, REPRESENTATIVE NYGREN, SENATORS OLSEN, HARSDORF, LEIBHAM, LAZICH, GROTHMAN; SHILLING*, WIRCH; REPRESENTATIVES STRACHOTA, KOOYENGA, KNUDSON, LeMAHIEU, KLENKE; MASON*, RICHARDS.

Mailing Addresses: Senator Darling, Room 317 East, State Capitol, P.O. Box 7882, Madison 53707-7882; Representative Nygren, Room 309 East, State Capitol, P.O. Box 8953, Madison 53708-8953.

Telephones: Senator Darling, 266-5830; Representative Nygren, 266-2343.

E-mail: sen.darling@legis.wisconsin.gov; rep.nygren@legis.wisconsin.gov

Statutory References: Sections 13.09-13.11, 16.47, 16.505, 16.515, and 20.865 (4).

Agency Responsibility: The Joint Committee on Finance examines all legislation that deals with state income and spending. It also gives final approval to a wide variety of state payments and assessments. Any bill introduced in the legislature that appropriates money, provides for revenue, or relates to taxation must be referred to the joint committee.

The joint committee introduces the biennial budget as recommended by the governor. After holding a series of public hearings and executive sessions, it submits its own version of the budget as a substitute amendment to the governor's budget bill for consideration by the legislature.

Arguably the most important committee in the legislature is the Joint Committee on Finance. The most prominent of its many duties is the detailed review of the governor's biennial budget bill. The cochairpersons this session are Representative John Nygren (R-Marinette) and Senator Alberta Darling (R-River Hills). (Jay Salvo, Legislative Photographer)

At regularly scheduled quarterly meetings, the joint committee considers agency requests to adjust their budgets. It may approve a request for emergency funds if it finds that the legislature has authorized the activities for which the appropriation is sought. It may also transfer funds between existing appropriations and change the number of positions authorized to an agency in the budget process.

When required, the joint committee introduces legislation to pay claims against the state, resolve shortages in funds, and restore capital reserve funds of the Wisconsin Housing and Economic Development Authority to the required level. As an emergency measure, it may reduce certain state agency appropriations when there is a decrease in state revenues.

The joint committee gives final approval for a variety of fiscal operations including: disposition of federal block grant funds and private gifts, grants, and bequests; changes in supplemental security income payment levels if approved by the governor; plans to deal with shortfalls in state agency fund accounts; disposition of oil overcharge funds; and expenditure plans for federal low-income assistance funds. In addition, the committee may inquire into the operations of any state agency for the purpose of improving agency efficiency.

Organization: The committee is a joint standing committee composed of the 8 senators on the Senate Finance Committee and the 8 representatives on the Assembly Finance Committee. It generally includes members of the majority and minority party in each house. Cochairpersons of the joint committee are appointed in the same manner as are standing committees of their respective houses.

History: The use of a joint standing committee to consider appropriation bills dates back to 1857 when the legislature created the Joint Committee on Claims. In 1911 (Chapter 6), the Joint Committee on Finance replaced the claims committee and was given the responsibility to consider all bills related to revenue and taxation. Chapter 609, Laws of 1915, authorized the governor, secretary of state, and state treasurer to approve emergency appropriations when the legislature was not in session to permit departments with insufficient funds to carry out their normal duties. Chapter 97, Laws of 1929, transferred this function to a new Emergency Board, which consisted of the governor and the cochairpersons of the joint finance committee. The power to approve supplemental appropriations, transfer funds between appropriations, and handle other interim fiscal matters was given to a joint legislative committee called the Board on Government Operations (BOGO) by Chapter 228, Laws of 1959. BOGO's functions were transferred to the Joint Committee on Finance by Chapter 39, Laws of 1975.

<hr />

Joint Committee on
INFORMATION POLICY AND TECHNOLOGY

Members: SENATOR HARSDORF, REPRESENTATIVE PETERSEN, *cochairpersons;* SENATORS COWLES, GUDEX; CARPENTER, VINEHOUT; REPRESENTATIVES PETRYK, WEININGER; BARCA, GENRICH.

Statutory Reference: Section 13.58.

Agency Responsibility: The Joint Committee on Information Policy and Technology reviews information management practices of state and local units of government to ensure economic and efficient service, maintain data security and integrity, and protect the privacy of individuals who are subjects of the databases. It studies the effects of proposals by the state to expand existing information technology or implement new technologies. With concurrence of the Joint Committee on Finance, it may direct the Department of Administration to report on any information technology system project that could cost $1 million or more in the current or succeeding biennium. The committee may direct the Department of Administration to prepare reports or conduct studies and may make recommendations to the governor, the legislature, state agencies, or local governments based on this information. The University of Wisconsin Board of Regents is required to submit a report to the committee twice annually, detailing each information technology project in the University of Wisconsin System costing more than $1 million or deemed "high-risk" by the board. The committee may make recommendations on the identified projects to the governor and the legislature. The committee is composed of 3 majority and 2 minority party members from each house of the legislature. It was created by 1991 Wisconsin Act 317 and its membership was revised by 1999 Wisconsin Act 29.

The Joint Legislative Audit Committee oversees the legislature's constitutional mandate to provide for the auditing of state accounts. Representative Samantha Kerkman and Senator Robert Cowles are cochairpersons of this important committee. (Jay Salvo, Legislative Photographer)

Joint
LEGISLATIVE AUDIT COMMITTEE

Members: SENATOR COWLES, REPRESENTATIVE KERKMAN, *cochairpersons;* SENATOR DARLING, REPRESENTATIVE NYGREN (joint finance committee cochairpersons); SENATORS LAZICH; VINEHOUT*, LEHMAN; REPRESENTATIVES MARKLEIN; RICHARDS*, SARGENT.

Mailing Addresses: Senator Cowles, Room 118 South, State Capitol, P.O. Box 7882, Madison 53707-7882; Representative Kerkman, Room 315 North, State Capitol, P.O. Box 8952, Madison 53708-8952.

Telephones: Senator Cowles, 266-0484; Representative Kerkman, 266-2530.

E-mail: sen.cowles@legis.wisconsin.gov; rep.kerkman@legis.wisconsin.gov

Statutory Reference: Section 13.53.

Agency Responsibility: The Joint Legislative Audit Committee, which was created by Chapter 224, Laws of 1975, advises the Legislative Audit Bureau, subject to general supervision of the Joint Committee on Legislative Organization. Its members include the cochairpersons of the Joint Committee on Finance, plus 2 majority and 2 minority party members from each house of the legislature. The committee evaluates candidates for the office of state auditor and makes recommendations to the Joint Committee on Legislative Organization, which selects the auditor.

The committee may direct the state auditor to undertake specific audits and review requests for special audits from individual legislators or standing committees, but no legislator or standing committee may interfere with the auditor in the conduct of an audit.

The committee reviews each report of the Legislative Audit Bureau and then confers with the state auditor, other legislative committees, and the audited agencies on the report's findings. It may propose corrective action and direct that followup reports be submitted to it.

The committee may hold hearings on audit reports, ask the Joint Committee on Legislative Organization to investigate any matter within the scope of the audit, and request investigation of any matter relative to the fiscal and performance responsibilities of a state agency. If an audit report cites financial deficiencies, the head of the agency must report to the Joint Legislative Audit Committee on remedial actions taken. Should the agency head fail to report, the committee may refer the matter to the Joint Committee on Legislative Organization and the appropriate standing committees.

When the committee determines that legislative action is needed, it may refer the necessary information to the legislature or a standing committee. It can also request information from a committee on action taken or seek advice of a standing committee on program portions of an audit. The committee may introduce legislation to address issues covered in audit reports.

JOINT LEGISLATIVE COUNCIL

Members: SENATOR OLSEN (designated by senate president), REPRESENTATIVE BALLWEG (designated by assembly speaker), *cochairpersons;* SENATORS LEIBHAM (president pro tempore), FITZGERALD (majority leader), LARSON (minority leader), DARLING (cochairperson, Joint Committee on Finance), SHILLING (ranking minority member, Joint Committee on Finance), SCHULTZ, FARROW, PETROWSKI, RISSER, MILLER; REPRESENTATIVES VOS (assembly speaker), KRAMER (speaker pro tempore), SUDER (majority leader), BARCA (minority leader), NYGREN (cochairperson, Joint Committee on Finance), MASON (ranking minority member, Joint Committee on Finance), LOUDENBECK, STONE, BERCEAU, PASCH. (Members designated by title serve *ex officio.*)

Director of Legislative Council Staff: TERRY C. ANDERSON, terry.anderson@legis.wisconsin.gov

Deputy Director: LAURA D. ROSE, laura.rose@legis.wisconsin.gov

Legislative Council Rules Clearinghouse: SCOTT GROSZ, *codirector,* scott.grosz@legis.wisconsin.gov; JESSICA KARLS-RUPLINGER, *codirector,* jessica.karls@legis.wisconsin.gov

Mailing Address: P.O. Box 2536, Madison 53701-2536.

Location: 1 East Main Street, Suite 401, Madison.

Telephone: 266-1304.

Fax: 266-3830.

Internet Address: http://www.legis.wisconsin.gov/lc

Publications: General Report of the Joint Legislative Council to the Legislature; State Agency Staff Members With Responsibilities Related to the Legislature; Wisconsin Legislator Briefing Book; Directory of Joint Legislative Council Committees; Comparative Retirement Study; rules clearinghouse reports; staff briefs; information memoranda on substantive issues considered by council committees; staff memoranda; amendment and act memoranda.

Number of Employees: 34.17.

Total Budget 2011-13: $8,035,800.

Statutory References: Sections 13.81-13.83, 13.91, and 227.15.

Agency Responsibility: The Joint Legislative Council creates special committees made up of legislators and interested citizens to study various problems of state and local government. Study topics are selected from requests presented to the council by law, joint resolution, individual legislators, and others. After research and public hearings, the study committees draft proposals and submit them to the council, which must approve those drafts it wants introduced in the legislature as council bills.

The council is assisted in its work by the Legislative Council staff, a bureau created in Section 13.91, Wisconsin Statutes. The staff provides legal counsel and scientific and policy research assistance to all of the legislature's substantive standing committees and joint statutory committees (except the Joint Committee on Finance) and assists individual legislators on request. The staff operates the rules clearinghouse to review proposed administrative rules and assists standing committees in their oversight of rulemaking. The staff also assists the legislature in identifying and responding to issues relating to the Wisconsin Retirement System.

By law, the Legislative Council staff must be "strictly nonpartisan" and must observe the confidential nature of the research and drafting requests received by it. The law requires that state agencies and local governmental units cooperate fully with the council staff in its carrying out of its statutory duties.

Organization: The council consists of 22 legislators. The majority of them serve *ex officio,* and the remainder are appointed as are members of standing committees. The president of the senate and the speaker of the assembly serve as cochairpersons of the council, but each may designate another member to assume that office or decline to serve on the council. The council operates two permanent statutory committees and various special committees appointed to study selected subjects. The Legislative Council staff director is appointed from outside the classified service by the Joint Committee on Legislative Organization, and the director makes staff appointments from outside the service.

History: Chapter 444, Laws of 1947, created the council to conduct interim studies on subjects affecting the general welfare of the state. The first council was organized later that year with 12 members. In 1967, the council began to appoint staff members to provide legal counsel and technical assistance to legislative standing committees. The 1979 executive budget (Chapter 34) assigned the administrative rules clearinghouse function to the council. 1993 Wisconsin Act 52 made a number of reorganizational changes. The act renamed the council the Joint Legislative Council and designated the president of the senate and the speaker of the assembly (or their designees) cochairpersons. Under Act 52, the council was directed to reorganize at the beginning of the biennial session, instead of May 1 of the odd-numbered year, and its support agency was officially named the Legislative Council Staff. 2005 Wisconsin Act 316 transferred the functions of the retirement research director to the council staff, making the staff responsible

Majority Leader Scott Suder (left) discusses the day's agenda with Representatives JoCasta Zamarripa and Mandela Barnes, both Milwaukee Democrats. (Jay Salvo, Legislative Photographer)

for supporting the Joint Survey Committee on Retirement Systems and the legislature regarding legislation involving the Wisconsin Retirement System.

PERMANENT STATUTORY COMMITTEES

Special Committee on State-Tribal Relations

Members: REPRESENTATIVE MURSAU, *chairperson;* SENATOR VINEHOUT, *vice chairperson;* SENATOR SCHULTZ; REPRESENTATIVES BEWLEY, MILROY, STEINEKE, STROEBEL; WILLIAM MORROW (Lac Courte Oreilles Band of Lake Superior Chippewa Indians of Wisconsin), DEE ANN ALLEN (Lac du Flambeau Band of Lake Superior Chippewa Indians), MARVIN DEFOE (Red Cliff Band of Lake Superior Chippewas), JORDAN S. MARTINSON (St. Croix Chippewa Indians of Wisconsin), CHRIS MCGESHICK (Sokaogon Chippewa Community), JON GREENDEER (Ho-Chunk Nation), GARY BESAW (Menominee Indian Tribe of Wisconsin), MELINDA DANFORTH (Oneida Tribe of Indians of Wisconsin), HAROLD G. FRANK (Forest County Potawatomi Community).

The Special Committee on State-Tribal Relations is appointed by the Joint Legislative Council each biennium to study issues related to American Indians and the Indian tribes and bands in this state and develop specific recommendations and legislative proposals relating to such issues. Legislative membership includes not fewer than 6 nor more than 12 members with at least one member of the majority and the minority party from each house. The council appoints no fewer than 6 and no more than 11 members from names submitted by federally recognized Wisconsin Indian tribes or bands or the Great Lakes Inter-Tribal Council. The council may not appoint more than one member recommended by any one tribe or band or the Great Lakes Inter-Tribal Council. The committee has its origins in the Menominee Indians Committee, created in 1955 to study the governmental status of the Menominee Indian Tribe at that time. Chapter 39, Laws of 1975, replaced that committee with the more broadly focused Native American Study Committee. Its name was changed to the American Indian Study Committee in 1982. 1999 Wisconsin Act 60 gave it its current name and revised the membership. The committee's composition and duties are prescribed in Section 13.83 (3) of the statutes.

. . .Technical Advisory Committee

Members: LOA PORTER (Department of Children and Families), GAIL NAHWAHQUAW (Department of Health Services), TOM BELLAVIA (Department of Justice), QUINN WILLIAMS (Department of Natural Resources), DAVID O'CONNOR (Department of Public Instruction), THOMAS D. OURADA (Department of Revenue), KELLY JACKSON (Department of Transportation), TRISTAN COOK (Department of Workforce Development).

Under Section 13.83 (3) (f), Wisconsin Statutes, as created by Chapter 39, Laws of 1975, the Technical Advisory Committee, consisting of representatives of 8 major executive agencies, assists the Special Committee on State-Tribal Relations.

Law Revision Committee

Members: vacancy.

The Law Revision Committee is appointed each biennium by the Joint Legislative Council. The membership of the committee is not specified, but it must include majority and minority party representation from each house. The committee reviews minor nonsubstantive remedial changes to the statutes as proposed by state agencies and reviews attorney general's opinions and court decisions declaring a Wisconsin statute unconstitutional, ambiguous, or otherwise in need of revision. It considers proposals by the Legislative Reference Bureau to correct statutory language and session laws that conflict or need revision, and it may submit recommendations for major law revision projects to the Joint Legislative Council. It serves as the repository for interstate compacts and agreements and makes recommendations to the legislature regarding revision of such agreements. The committee was created by Chapter 204, Laws of 1979, as a combination of the Judiciary Committee, which had its origins in a 1951 mandate to prepare a criminal code, and the Remedial Legislation Committee, created in 1959. Its composition and duties are prescribed in Section 13.83 (1) of the statutes.

Special Committees Reporting in 2013

Special Committee on Improving Educational Opportunities in High School

Members: Senator Olsen, *chairperson;* Senator Farrow, *vice chairperson;* Senators Cullen, Grothman; Representative Pope; Joni Burgin, Bill Fitzpatrick, Joe Garza, Robert Hein, Patricia Hoben, William Hughes, Mark Kaiser, Suzanne Kelley, Jim Leef, Jeff Monday, Harry Muir, Patricia Neudecker, Sheila Ruhland, Stephen Mark Tyler.

The special committee is directed to develop legislation to create and enhance opportunities for both lower and higher achieving students in high school. The committee shall: evaluate current options available to high school students for both career and technical education and post-secondary enrollment, including the Youth Options Program; examine both career and technical education and post-secondary enrollment options available to high school students in other states; and determine how to promote coordination between high schools, technical colleges, universities, and employers to ensure that high school students have the skills necessary to meet the workforce needs of employers in this state.

Special Committee on Legal Interventions for Persons with Alzheimer's Disease and Related Dementias

Members: Representative Knodl, *chairperson;* Representative Bernard Schaber, *vice chairperson;* Senators Kedzie, Wirch; Suzanne Bottum-Jones, Kathi Cauley, William Hanrahan, Tom Hlavacek, Gina Koeppl, Robert Lightfoot II, Rob Mueller, Wanda Plachecki, Brian Purtell, Tom Reed, Kenneth Robbins, Chrystal Rosso.

The special committee is directed to review and develop legislation to clarify the statutes regarding guardianship, protective placement, involuntary commitment, and involuntary treat-

JOINT LEGISLATIVE COUNCIL

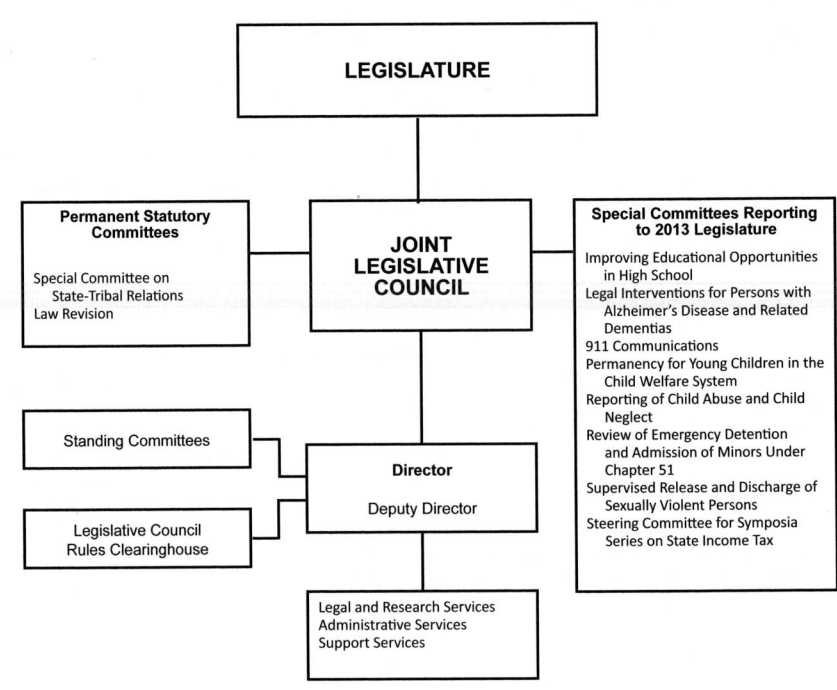

Legislators serve a unique intermediary role – being an integral part of the government in Madison, but at the same time citizens of their districts. Senator Neal Kedzie greeted a group of visitors from his district at his capitol office. (Jay Salvo, Legislative Photographer)

ment as they apply to vulnerable adults with a dementia diagnosis who may or may not have a co-occurring psychiatric diagnosis.

Special Committee on 911 Communications

Members: REPRESENTATIVE BALLWEG, *chairperson;* SENATOR JAUCH, *vice chairperson;* SENATOR MOULTON; REPRESENTATIVE VRUWINK; JIM BACKUS, THOMAS BYCHINSKI, TRACEY FROILAND, PAUL GEISZLER, JAMES JERMAIN, KEITH KESLER, BRIAN LANDERS, PAM MCINNIS, TODD NEHLS, JEFF RANOUS, VICKI SANFELIPO, RICHARD TUMA, BRADLEY WELP.

The special committee is directed to review 911 public safety communications in Wisconsin and develop legislation as needed to strengthen and improve the system. The special committee shall study: a) creation of a statewide entity to provide coordination and long-term planning for the system; b) existing funding sources and projected costs of the system; c) the training curriculum and requirements for 911 dispatch personnel; d) establishment of a minimum 911 service standard; e) methods to upgrade multiline telephone system technology to enable responders to locate calls originating from large or multilocation facilities; and f) best practices around the county for potential implementation in Wisconsin.

Special Committee on Permanency for Young Children in the Child Welfare System

Members: REPRESENTATIVE KERKMAN, *chairperson;* SENATOR LAZICH, *vice chairperson;* REPRESENTATIVE BILLINGS; COLLEEN ELLINGSON, CHRIS FOLEY, TAMARA GRIGSBY, MARK GUMZ, AMY HERBST, MOLLY JASMER, ESIE LEOSO-CORBINE, LAURA MAKI, JESSICA MURPHY, ROBIN NEESON, RÄNDI OTHROW, RON ROGERS, MICHELLE SNEAD, MARY SOWINSKI.

The special committee is directed to study current law relating to permanency for children under the age of eight who are placed or at risk of being placed outside of their home, such as in foster care, to determine whether modifications could be made to reduce the length of time it takes to achieve permanency and to improve outcomes for these children. The special committee shall also determine how current law may be modified to encourage the placement of younger children with a relative as an option for permanency or support.

Special Committee on Reporting of Child Abuse and Child Neglect

Members: SENATOR DARLING, *chairperson;* SENATOR SHILLING, *vice chairperson;* REPRESENTATIVES BERCEAU, THIESFELDT; SUSAN DREYFUS, KRISTEN INIGUEZ, KATHARINE KUCHARSKI, BILL ORTH, HENRY PLUM, MICHAEL SCHMIDTKNECHT, LYNN SHEETS, MARY TRIGGIANO.

The special committee is directed to conduct a recodification of Section 48.981, Wisconsin Statutes, Wisconsin's child abuse and child neglect reporting requirements, to reorganize the statute in a logical manner, renumber and retitle certain subsections, consolidate related provisions, modernize language, resolve ambiguities in language, and make other necessary organizational changes. The special committee shall also: recommend changes to current law regarding who is required to report suspected abuse or neglect of children and the circumstances under which such a report is mandated; and study the reporting of suspected abuse of students at institutions of higher education.

Special Committee on Review of Emergency Detention and Admission of Minors Under Chapter 51

Members: SENATOR LAZICH, *chairperson;* REPRESENTATIVE PASCH, *vice chairperson;* SENATOR HANSEN; REPRESENTATIVE BALLWEG; MICHAEL J. BACHHUBER, JON S. BERLIN, KRISTIN M. KERSCHENSTEINER, GEORGE KERWIN, MICHAEL KIEFER, GINA KOEPPL, TALLY MOSES, BRIAN A. SHOUP, GALEN STREBE, BRENDA E. WESLEY, CARIANNE YERKES.

The special committee is directed to review the following provisions in Chapter 51, Wisconsin Statutes: a) the appropriateness of, and inconsistencies in, the utilization of emergency detention procedures under Section 51.15, Wisconsin Statutes, across this state, and the availability and cost of emergency detention facilities; b) the inconsistent statutory approaches to emergency detention between Milwaukee County and other counties in the state; and c) the inconsistent application of procedures relating to admission of minors under Section 51.13, Wisconsin Statutes, as modified by 2005 Wisconsin Act 444.

Senator Scott Fitzgerald (R-Juneau) (center), as Senate Majority Leader, sets the agenda for the upper house of the legislature. Here he confers with members of the majority caucus Leah Vukmir of Wauwatosa and Joe Leibham of Sheboygan. (Jay Salvo, Legislative Photographer)

Special Committee on Supervised Release and Discharge of Sexually Violent Persons

Members: REPRESENTATIVE STRACHOTA, *chairperson;* SENATOR DARLING, *vice chairperson;* SENATORS CULLEN, LAZICH; MARK BENSEN, MICHAEL BOHREN, RON CRAMER, REBECCA DALLAT, SHARI HANNEMAN, IAN HENDERSON, FRANK LISKA, LOUIS MOLEPSKE, JR., RICK OLIVA, ANTHONY RIOS.

The special committee is directed to review the current process for granting supervised release and discharging persons who have been committed as sexually violent persons under Chapter 980, Wisconsin Statutes. The special committee shall: determine what level of judicial input regarding the determination whether to grant a sexually violent person supervised release or discharge from a civil commitment under Chapter 980 is appropriate; review the criteria for determining whether a person is fit for supervised release and determine whether this criteria should be modified; and review the criteria for determining whether a person should be discharged from his or her civil commitment to determine whether the criteria are appropriate.

Steering Committee for Symposia Series on State Income Tax

Members: REPRESENTATIVE VOS, *chairperson;* REPRESENTATIVE KOOYENGA, *vice chairperson;* SENATORS GROTHMAN, TAYLOR, VINEHOUT; REPRESENTATIVES RICHARDS, TAYLOR; BOB ZIEGELBAUER.

The steering committee is directed to conduct information symposia and develop recommendations regarding Wisconsin's income tax code. The committee shall: review Wisconsin's current income tax code, the income tax codes of other states, and previously proposed methods for state tax code reform; consider the social and economic effects of tax code reforms as applied to individual and corporate taxpayers as well as the fiscal effects on state revenues; and develop recommendations, in the form of a committee report, for income tax reform that would improve economic growth for residents and businesses in the State of Wisconsin.

Joint Committee on
LEGISLATIVE ORGANIZATION

Members: SENATOR ELLIS (senate president), REPRESENTATIVE VOS (assembly speaker), *cochairpersons;* SENATORS FITZGERALD (majority leader), LARSON (minority leader), GROTHMAN (assistant majority leader), HANSEN (assistant minority leader); REPRESENTATIVES SUDER (majority leader), BARCA (minority leader), STEINEKE (assistant majority leader), PASCH (assistant minority leader).

Mailing Address: Legislative Council Staff, P.O. Box 2536, Madison 53701-2536.

Location: 1 East Main Street, Suite 401, Madison.

Telephone: 266-1304.

Statutory References: Sections 13.80 and 13.90.

Agency Responsibility: The Joint Committee on Legislative Organization is the policy-making body for the legislative service bureaus: the Legislative Audit Bureau, the Legislative Fiscal Bureau, the Legislative Reference Bureau, and the Legislative Technology Services Bureau. In this capacity, it assigns tasks to each bureau, approves bureau budgets, and sets the salary of bureau heads. The joint committee selects the four bureau heads, but it acts on the recommendation of the Joint Legislative Audit Committee when appointing the state auditor. The joint committee also selects the director of the Legislative Council Staff.

The committee may inquire into misconduct by members and employees of the legislature. It oversees a variety of operations, including the work schedule for the legislative session, computer use, space allocation for legislative offices and legislative service agencies, parking on the State Capitol Park grounds, and sale and distribution of legislative documents. The joint committee recommends which newspaper should serve as the official state newspaper for publication of state legal notices. It advises the Government Accountability Board on its operations and, upon recommendation of the Joint Legislative Audit Committee, may investigate any problems the Legislative Audit Bureau finds during its audits. The committee may employ outside consultants to study ways to improve legislative staff services and organization.

Organization: The 10-member joint committee is a permanent body, consisting of the presiding officers and party leadership of both houses. The committee has established a Subcommittee on Legislative Services to advise it on matters pertaining to the legislative institution, including the review of computer technology purchases. The Legislative Council Staff provides staff assistance to the committee.

History: The joint committee was created by Chapter 149, Laws of 1963, as part of a legislative reorganization proposed by the Committee on Legislative Organization and Procedure under the authority of Chapter 686, Laws of 1961. The 1963 law also transferred the Legislative Reference Bureau and the Statutory Revision Bureau to the legislative branch and placed them under the supervision of the joint committee. The three other service agencies were placed under the committee's authority by later legislation: the Legislative Audit Bureau in Chapter 659, Laws of 1965; the Legislative Fiscal Bureau in Chapter 215, Laws of 1971; and the Legislative Technology Services Bureau in 1997 Wisconsin Act 27. 2007 Wisconsin Act 20 eliminated the Revisor of Statutes Bureau and transferred its duties to the Legislative Reference Bureau.

In 1966, the joint committee was empowered to investigate misconduct by legislators and legislative staff. Actions by subsequent legislatures expanded the joint committee's supervision of legislative operations to include legislative office space, legislative computer operations, and publication of notices and documents.

Joint Survey Committee on
RETIREMENT SYSTEMS

Members: Senator Schultz, Representative Stroebel, *cochairpersons;* Senators Farrow; Hansen; Representatives Severson; Berceau; Charlotte Gibson (assistant attorney general appointed by attorney general), *secretary;* Robert J. Conlin (secretary of employee trust funds), Ted Nickel (insurance commissioner); Tim Pederson (public member appointed by governor).

Mailing Address: Legislative Council Staff, P.O. Box 2536, Madison 53701-2536.

Telephone: 266-1304.

Statutory Reference: Section 13.50.

Agency Responsibility: The Joint Survey Committee on Retirement Systems makes recommendations on legislation that affects retirement and pension plans for public officers and employees, and its recommendations must be attached as an appendix to each retirement bill. Neither house of the legislature may consider such a bill until the joint survey committee submits a written report that describes the proposal's purpose, probable costs, actuarial effect, and desirability as a matter of public policy.

Organization: The 10-member joint survey committee includes majority and minority party representation from each legislative house. An experienced actuary from the Office of the Commissioner of Insurance may be designated to serve in the commissioner's place on the committee. The public member cannot be a participant in any public retirement system in the state and is expected to "represent the interests of the taxpayers". Appointed members serve 4-year terms unless they lose the status upon which the appointment was based. The joint survey committee is assisted by the Joint Legislative Council staff in the performance of its duties, but may contract for actuarial assistance outside the classified service.

Joint Legislative
STATE SUPPORTED PROGRAMS
STUDY AND ADVISORY COMMITTEE

Members: Senator Kedzie, 4 vacancies; Representative Neylon, 5 vacancies.

Statutory Reference: Section 13.47.

Minority Leader Chris Larson, the youngest member of the Wisconsin Senate, enjoyed inauguration day with his family. *(Greg Anderson, Legislative Photographer)*

Agency Responsibility: Members of the Joint Legislative State Supported Programs Study and Advisory Committee visit and inspect the State Capitol and all institutions and office buildings owned or leased by the state. They are granted free and full access to all parts of the buildings, the surrounding grounds, and all persons associated with the buildings. The committee may also examine any institution, program, or organization that receives direct or indirect state financial support.

Organization: The committee consists of 5 senators and 6 representatives. Members appointed from each house must represent the two major political parties, and one legislator from each house must also be a member of the State of Wisconsin Building Commission. Assistance to the committee is provided by the Legislative Council Staff.

History: The use of a legislative committee to visit and supervise the use of state institutions and property dates back to 1881. The current joint committee was created by Chapter 266, Laws of 1973. It replaced the Committee to Visit State Properties, which had combined the functions of the Committee to Visit State Institutions, created in 1947 to inspect state property and state institutions, and the Committee on Physical Plant Maintenance, created in 1957 to manage the State Capitol and the single state office building then in existence.

Joint Survey Committee on
TAX EXEMPTIONS

Members: SENATOR LASEE, REPRESENTATIVE AUGUST, *cochairpersons;* SENATORS TIFFANY, LEHMAN*; REPRESENTATIVES HONADEL, BERNARD SCHABER*; RICHARD G. CHANDLER (secretary of revenue); STEVEN MEANS (Department of Justice representative appointed by attorney general); KIMBERLY SHAUL (public member appointed by governor).

Mailing Address: Legislative Council Staff, P.O. Box 2536, Madison 53701-2536.

Telephone: 266-1304.

Statutory Reference: Section 13.52.

Agency Responsibility: The Joint Survey Committee on Tax Exemptions, created by Chapter 153, Laws of 1963, considers all legislation related to the exemption of persons or property from state or local taxes. It is assisted by the Legislative Council Staff.

Any legislative proposal that affects tax exemptions must be referred to the committee immediately upon introduction. Budget bills containing tax exemptions are referred simultaneously to the joint survey committee and the Joint Committee on Finance. The joint survey committee must report within 60 days on the tax exemptions contained within a budget bill. Neither house of the legislature may consider tax exemption proposals until the joint survey committee has issued its report, attached as an appendix to the bill, describing the proposal's legality, desirability as public policy, and fiscal effect. In the course of its review, the committee is authorized to conduct investigations, hold hearings, and subpoena witnesses.

Organization: The 9-member committee includes representation from each house of the legislature with 2 members from the majority party and one from the minority party. The public member must be familiar with the tax problems of local government. Members' terms expire on January 15 of odd-numbered years.

Robin Vos, Speaker of the Assembly, is the first speaker from Racine County since 1860. (Jay Salvo, Legislative Photographer)

TRANSPORTATION PROJECTS COMMISSION

Members: GOVERNOR WALKER, *chairperson;* SENATORS PETROWSKI, LEIBHAM, COWLES; CULLEN, CARPENTER; REPRESENTATIVES SPIROS, RIPP, ENDSLEY; BEWLEY, VRUWINK; THOMAS CARLSEN, BARBARA FLEISNER LAMUE, MICHAEL RYAN (citizen members appointed by governor). Nonvoting member: MARK GOTTLIEB (secretary of transportation).

Commission Secretary: SHARON BREMSER, sharon.bremser@dot.wi.gov

Mailing Address: P.O. Box 7913, Madison 53707-7913.

Location: Hill Farms State Transportation Building, 4802 Sheboygan Avenue, Room 901, Madison.

Telephone: 266-5408.

Fax: 267-1856.

Statutory Reference: Section 13.489.

Agency Responsibility: The Transportation Projects Commission, created by 1983 Wisconsin Act 27, includes representation from each house of the legislature with 3 members from the majority party and 2 from the minority party. The commission reviews Department of Transportation recommendations for major highway projects. The department must report its recommendations to the commission by September 15 of each even-numbered year, and the commission, in turn, reports its recommendations to the governor or governor-elect, the legislature, and the Joint Committee on Finance before December 15 of each even-numbered year. The department must also provide the commission with a status report on major transportation projects every 6 months. The commission also approves the preparation of environmental impact or assessment statements for potential major highway projects.

Commission on
UNIFORM STATE LAWS

Members: JOANNE HUELSMAN, *chairperson;* RICHARD A. CHAMPAGNE (designated by chief, Legislative Reference Bureau), *secretary,* SENATOR RISSER; REPRESENTATIVE GOYKE, JUSTICE DAVID PROSSER, JR.; TERRY ANDERSON (director, Legislative Council Staff); JOHN MACY, JUSTICE PATIENCE ROGGENSACK (public members appointed by governor).

Mailing Address: 1 East Main Street, Suite 200, Madison 53701-2037.

Telephone: 266-9930.

Fax: 264-6948.

Statutory Reference: Section 13.55.

Agency Responsibility: The Commission on Uniform State Laws advises the legislature on uniform laws and model laws. It examines subjects on which interstate uniformity is desirable and the best methods for achieving it, cooperates with the National Conference of Commissioners on Uniform State Laws in preparing uniform acts, and prepares bills adapting the uniform acts to Wisconsin. The commission reports biennially to the Law Revision Committee of the Joint Legislative Council.

Organization: The commission consists of 8 members, including 2 public members appointed by the governor for 4-year terms. Legislative members serve 2-year terms, must represent the 2 major political parties, and must be state bar association members. A legislative seat may be filled by a former legislator if no current legislator meets the criteria, or if no eligible legislator is willing or able to accept the appointment. In addition to the members prescribed by law, the commission may include a number of life-members.

History: The commission was originally created by Chapter 83, Laws of 1893, which authorized the governor to appoint 3 members to serve as the Commissioners for the Promotion of Uniformity of Legislation in the United States. In 1931, Chapter 67 designated the Revisor of Statutes as the sole Wisconsin commissioner. Chapter 173, Laws of 1941, added the chief of the Legislative Reference Library as a commissioner. The commission was created in its present form by Chapter 312, Laws of 1957, and its membership was expanded to include 2 members of the State Bar appointed by the governor. Chapter 135, Laws of 1959, added the director (then called the executive secretary) of the Legislative Council Staff as a member. Chapter 294, Laws of 1979, added 4 legislative members and deleted the requirement that public members appointed by the governor be members of the State Bar. 2003 Wisconsin Act 2 added a requirement that legislative members must be state bar association members. 2007 Wisconsin Act 20 eliminated the Revisor of Statutes, reducing the total membership to 8.

LEGISLATIVE SERVICE AGENCIES

LEGISLATIVE AUDIT BUREAU

State Auditor: JOE CHRISMAN, joe.chrisman@

Special Assistant to the State Auditor: JOSH SMITH, joshua.smith@

Deputy State Auditor for Financial Audit: BRYAN NAAB, bryan.naab@

Deputy State Auditor for Program Evaluation: PAUL STUIBER, paul.stuiber@

Audit Directors: DIANN L. ALLSEN, diann.allsen@; SHERRY HAAKENSON, sherry.haakenson@; CAROLYN STITTLEBURG, carolyn.stittleburg@; DEAN SWENSON, dean.swenson@

Mailing Address: 22 East Mifflin Street, Suite 500, Madison 53703-2512.

Telephones: 266-2818; Fraud, waste, and mismanagement hotline: (877) FRAUD-17.

Fax: 267-0410.

Internet Address: http://www.legis.wisconsin.gov/lab

E-mail Address: leg.audit.info@legis.wisconsin.gov

Address e-mail by combining the user ID and the state extender: userid@**legis.wisconsin.gov**

Publications: Audit reports of individual state agencies and programs; biennial reports.

Number of Employees: 86.80.

Total Budget 2011-13: $16,174,200.

Statutory Reference: Section 13.94.

Agency Responsibility: The Legislative Audit Bureau is responsible for conducting financial and program audits to assist the legislature in its oversight function. The bureau performs financial audits to determine whether agencies have conducted and reported their financial trans-

LEGISLATIVE SERVICE AGENCIES

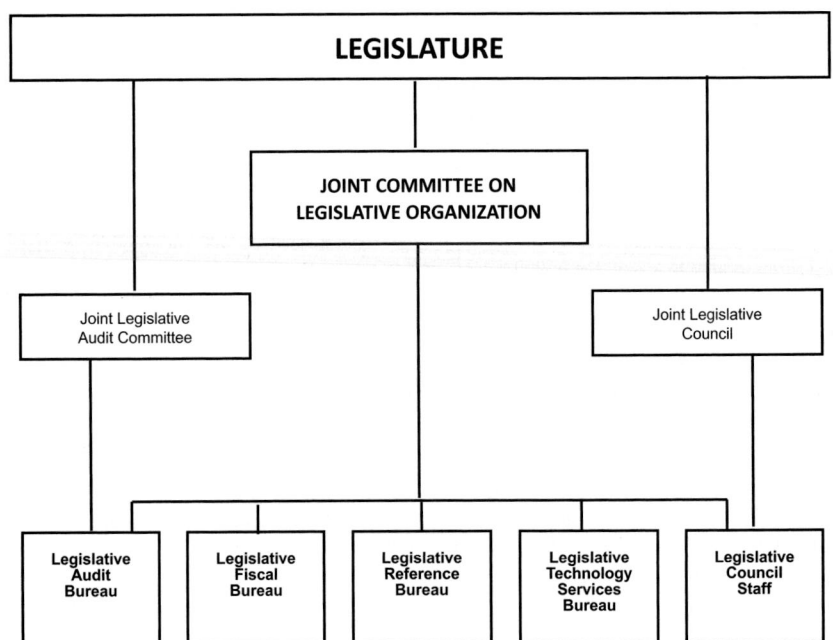

actions legally and properly. It undertakes program audits to analyze whether agencies have managed their programs efficiently and effectively and have carried out the policies prescribed by law.

The bureau's authority extends to executive, legislative, and judicial agencies; authorities created by the legislature; special districts; and certain service providers that receive state funds. The bureau may audit any county, city, village, town, or school district at the request of the Joint Legislative Audit Committee.

The bureau provides an annual audit opinion on the state's comprehensive financial statements by the Department of Administration and prepares audits and reports on the financial transactions and records of state agencies at the state auditor's discretion or at the direction of the Joint Legislative Audit Committee. The bureau maintains a toll-free number (1-877-FRAUD-17) to receive reports of fraud, waste, and mismanagement in state government.

Typically, the bureau's program audits are conducted at the request of the Joint Legislative Audit Committee, initiated by the State Auditor, or required by legislation. The reports are reviewed by the Joint Legislative Audit Committee, which may hold hearings on them and may introduce legislation in response to audit recommendations.

Organization: The director of the bureau is the State Auditor, who is appointed by the Joint Committee on Legislative Organization upon the recommendation of the Joint Legislative Audit Committee. Both the State Auditor and the bureau's staff are appointed from outside the classified service and are strictly nonpartisan.

History: The bureau was created as a legislative service agency under the jurisdiction of the Joint Committee on Legislative Organization by Chapter 659, Laws of 1965. It replaced the Department of State Audit, which was created by Chapter 9, Laws of 1947, as an executive agency. This followed a 1946 constitutional amendment that removed auditing powers from the secretary of state and authorized the legislature to provide for state audits by law.

Representative Peter W. Barca (D-Kenosha) is the Assembly Minority Leader. It is the difficult task for the minority leader to articulate and adroitly advance the minority's position within the rules despite a numerical disadvantage. (Jay Salvo, Legislative Photographer)

Statutory Advisory Council

Municipal Best Practices Reviews Advisory Council: STEVE O'MALLEY, ADAM PAYNE (representing the Wisconsin Counties Association); MARK ROHLOFF (representing the League of Wisconsin Municipalities); RICHARD NAWROCKI (representing the Wisconsin Towns Association). (All are appointed by the State Auditor.)

The 4-member Municipal Best Practices Reviews Advisory Council advises the State Auditor on the selection of county and municipal service delivery practices to be reviewed by the State Auditor. The State Auditor is required to conduct periodic reviews of procedures and practices used by local governments in the delivery of governmental services; identify variations in costs and effectiveness of such services between counties and municipalities; and recommend practices to save money or provide more effective service delivery. Council members are chosen from candidates submitted by the organizations represented. The council was created by 1999 Wisconsin Act 9 in Section 13.94 (8), Wisconsin Statutes, and succeeds the council created by 1995 Wisconsin Act 27.

LEGISLATIVE COUNCIL STAFF

See Joint Legislative Council pp. 273-275

Floor debate gives members an opportunity to state their position on pending legislation, and to improve it by offering amendments. Here Senator Tim Cullen addresses his colleagues. (Greg Anderson, Legislative Photographer)

LEGISLATIVE FISCAL BUREAU

Director: ROBERT WM. LANG.

Program Supervisors: FRED AMMERMAN, JERE BAUER, DARYL HINZ, DAVID LOPPNOW, CHARLES MORGAN, ROB REINHARDT.

Administrative Assistant: VICKI HOLTEN.

Mailing Address: 1 East Main Street, Suite 301, Madison 53703.

Telephone: 266-3847.

Fax: 267-6873.

Internet Address: www.legis.state.wi.us/lfb

E-mail Address: fiscal.bureau@legis.wisconsin.gov

Publications: Biennial budget and budget adjustment: summaries of state agency budget requests; cumulative and comparative summaries of the governor's proposals, Joint Committee on Finance provisions and legislative amendments, and separate summaries of legislative amendments when necessary; summary of governor's partial vetoes. Informational reports on various state programs, budget issue papers, and revenue estimates. (Reports and papers available on the Internet or upon request.)

Number of Employees: 35.00.

Total Budget 2011-13: $7,912,400.

Statutory Reference: Section 13.95.

Agency Responsibility: The Legislative Fiscal Bureau develops fiscal information for the legislature, and its services must be impartial and nonpartisan. One of the bureau's principal duties is to staff the Joint Committee on Finance and assist its members. As part of this responsibility, the bureau studies the state budget and its long-range implications, reviews state revenues and expenditures, suggests alternatives to the committee and the legislature, and prepares a report detailing earmarks in the budget bill. In addition, the bureau provides information on all other bills before the joint committee and analyzes agency requests for new positions and appropriation supplements outside of the budget process.

The bureau provides fiscal information to any legislative committee or legislator upon request. On its own initiative, or at legislative direction, the bureau may conduct studies of any financial issue affecting the state. To aid the bureau in performing its duties, the director or designated employees are granted access, with or without notice, to all state departments and to any records maintained by the agencies relating to their expenditures, revenues, operations, and structure.

Organization: The Joint Committee on Legislative Organization is the policy-making body for the Legislative Fiscal Bureau, and it selects the bureau's director. The director is assisted by program supervisors responsible for broadly defined subject areas of government budgeting and fiscal operations. The director and all bureau staff are chosen outside the classified service.

History: The bureau was created by Chapter 154, Laws of 1969. It evolved from the legislative improvement study that was initiated by Chapter 686, Laws of 1961, using a Ford Foundation grant and state funding. Through the improvement program, the legislature developed its own fiscal staff, known as the Legislative Budget Staff, under the supervision of the Legislative Programs Study Committee. In February 1968, the study committee renamed the budget staff the Legislative Fiscal Bureau and specified its functions. Chapter 215, Laws of 1971, transferred responsibility for the bureau's supervision to the Joint Committee on Legislative Organization.

LEGISLATIVE REFERENCE BUREAU

Chief: STEPHEN R. MILLER, 267-2175, steve.miller@legis.wisconsin.gov

Administrative Services: CATHLENE M. HANAMAN, *deputy chief,* 267-9810, cathlene.hanaman@legis.wisconsin.gov

Legal Services: PETER R. GRANT, JEFFREY T. KUESEL, MARC E. SHOVERS, REBECCA C. TRADEWELL, *managing attorneys.*

Legislative Research and Library: JULIE POHLMAN, *manager,* 266-0344, julie.pohlman@legis.wisconsin.gov

Mailing Address: P.O. Box 2037, Madison 53701-2037.

Location: 1 East Main Street, Suite 200.

Telephones: Legal: 266-3561; Research: 266-0341; Library: 266-7040.

Fax: Legal: 264-6948; Research and Library: 266-5648.

Internet Address: www.legis.wisconsin.gov/lrb

Publications: *Wisconsin Blue Book; Capitol Headlines;* Laws of Wisconsin; *Selective List of Recent Acquisitions;* various sections of the *Bulletin of the Proceedings of the Wisconsin Legislature;* Wisconsin Statutes and Annotations; Wisconsin Administrative Code and Register; Wisconsin Town Law Forms; *WisLaw* on compact disc; informational reports.

Number of Employees: 60.00.

Total Budget 2011-13: $12,452,200.

Statutory Reference: Section 13.92.

Agency Responsibility: The Legislative Reference Bureau provides nonpartisan, confidential bill drafting, research, and library services to the legislature. The bureau also serves public officials, students of government, and citizens.

By statute, the bureau drafts all legislative proposals and amendments for introduction in the legislature. Legislative attorneys also prepare plain language analyses that are printed with all bills and most resolutions. A significant portion of the bureau's work involves the drafting of the state's biennial budget.

The bureau also publishes each Wisconsin act and produces the bound volumes of session laws enacted during the biennial legislative session.

The bureau incorporates newly enacted laws into the existing statutes. The bureau prints updated Wisconsin Statutes and Annotations every two years when the legislature completes its session and publishes quarterly updated versions of the statutes on its Internet site and on compact disc.

The bureau publishes the Wisconsin Administrative Code and the Wisconsin Administrative Register. It also prepares the Wisconsin Town Law Forms.

The reference and library section provides a broad range of information to aid legislators and other government officials. It also publishes reports on subjects of legislative concern and the *Wisconsin Blue Book,* the official almanac of Wisconsin government. Legislative analysts respond to inquiries about the work of the legislature and state government in general. The bureau also offers seminars on legislative procedure to students and civic groups.

The Theobald Legislative Library contains an extensive collection of material pertaining to government and public policy issues. The library staff prepares the *Index to the Bulletin of the Proceedings of the Wisconsin Legislature* which includes a subject index to legislation, author indexes, and subject indexes to legislative journals, administrative rules, and Wisconsin acts.

The bureau keeps the drafting records of all legislation introduced and uses those records to provide information on legislative history. Drafting records, beginning with the 1927 session, are available to the public as part of the bureau's noncirculating reference collection.

Organization: The Joint Committee on Legislative Organization is the policy-making body for the bureau, and it selects the bureau chief.

History: The creation of the Legislative Reference Bureau, originally the Legislative Reference Library, by Chapter 168, Laws of 1901, was the first organized effort in the nation to provide a state legislature with professional staff assistance. Initially under the governance of the Free Library Commission, the bureau soon began providing bill drafting services to the legislature, a task officially assigned by Chapter 508, Laws of 1907. The bureau acquired the duty of editing the *Wisconsin Blue Book* in 1929 (Chapter 194). In 1963, the legislature renamed the agency the Legislative Reference Bureau and placed it under the direction of the Joint Committee on Legislative Organization. In 2008, the legislature transferred statutory revision duties to the bureau.

The Wisconsin Blue Book, *produced by the Legislative Reference Bureau, is a useful guide to Wisconsin government for citizens of all ages. (Greg Anderson, Legislative Photographer)*

LEGISLATIVE TECHNOLOGY SERVICES BUREAU

Director: JEFF YLVISAKER.
Administration Manager: PAM BENISCH.
Enterprise Operations Manager: MATT HARNED.
Geographic Information Systems Manager: TONY VAN DER WIELEN.
Software Development Manager: DOUG DEMUTH.
Technical Support Manager: NATE ROHAN.
Mailing Address: 17 West Main Street, Suite 200, Madison 53703.
Telephone: 264-8582.
Fax: 267-6763.
Internet Address: http://www.legis.wisconsin.gov/ltsb
Publications: *Wisconsin Legislative Biennial Strategic Technology Plan,* 2011-2012.
Number of Employees: 43.00.
Total Budget 2011-13: $8,311,600.
Statutory Reference: Section 13.96.

Agency Responsibility: The Legislative Technology Services Bureau (LTSB) provides confidential, nonpartisan information technology services and support to the Wisconsin Legislature. These services include legislative office automation, e-mail, web publishing, training, project management, custom software creation, and management of the information technology infrastructure.

LTSB creates, maintains, and enhances specialized software used for bill drafting, production of the *Wisconsin Statutes* and *Administrative Code,* and publication of the *Wisconsin Blue Book.* It supports the publication of legislative documents including bills and amendments, house journals, daily calendars, and the Bulletin of the Proceedings.

The bureau also maintains network infrastructure, data center operations, electronic communications, desktop computers, laptops, printers, and other technology devices. It keeps an inventory of computer hardware and software assets and manages technology replacement schedules. It provides redistricting services following each decennial U.S. Census and mapping services throughout the decade.

LTSB also provides specialized software for managing constituent interactions, delivers audio and video services, supports the legislature during floor sessions including the voting systems, manages the technology for the Wisconsin Legislature's Internet site, and offers training services for legislators and staff in the use of information technology.

Organization: The Joint Committee on Legislative Organization is the policy-making body for the bureau. It selects the director and is specifically responsible for reviewing and approving all information technology proposals. The director appoints bureau staff. Both the director and the staff serve outside the classified service.

History: The bureau was statutorily created by 1997 Wisconsin Act 27 as the Integrated Legislative Information Staff and was renamed by 1997 Wisconsin Act 237.

Representative Bill Kramer (R-Waukesha), serving his second term as Speaker Pro Tempore, normally presides over the Assembly. (Jay Salvo, Legislative Photographer)

SUMMARY OF SIGNIFICANT LEGISLATION
ENACTED BY THE 2011 LEGISLATURE

This section highlights significant legislation enacted by the 2011 Wisconsin Legislature in the biennial session that began January 3, 2011, and concluded January 7, 2013. The legislation is categorized by subject matter and in cases when an act affects more than one area of state law, such as 2011 Wisconsin Act 32 (the budget act), significant provisions are separately described under multiple subject headings. The section concludes with a summary of major proposals that failed to be enacted or adopted.

The following table summarizes activity in recent legislative sessions:

	Legislative Session				
	2003-04	2005-06	2007-08	2009-10	2011-12
Total Drafting Requests	9,560	10,134	7,919	9,447	7,312
Bills Introduced	1,568	1,971	1,581	1,723	1,400
Assembly Bills.	998	1,232	988	997	786
Senate Bills	570	739	593	726	614
Acts	327	491	242	406	286
Percentage of Bills Enacted . . .	20.9%	24.9%	15.3%	23.6%	20.4%
Bills Totally Vetoed	54	47	1	5	0
Bills Partially Vetoed	10	2	4	6	3

SIGNIFICANT 2011-2012 LEGISLATION

Administrative Law

Act 21 (*January 2011 Special Session AB-8*) makes the following changes relating to promulgating administrative rules:

- Prohibits a state agency from implementing a standard, requirement, or threshold unless a statute or rule explicitly requires or permits the standard, requirement, or threshold.

- Provides that a legislative intent statement or a description of a state agency's general powers or duties does not confer rule-making authority beyond what the legislature explicitly confers and that a statutory standard, requirement, or threshold does not confer the authority to promulgate by rule a more restrictive standard, requirement, or threshold.

- Requires gubernatorial approval of the statement of the scope and the final draft of a proposed rule, including an emergency rule, and permits the Joint Committee for Review of Administrative Rules to review any proposed rule.

- Extends to all state agencies the requirement that an economic impact analysis be prepared for a proposed rule, expands the information that must be included in an economic impact analysis, and requires Department of Administration (DOA) approval of a proposed rule if the proposed rule would incur $20 million or more in implementation and compliance costs.

- Provides that the venue for a declaratory judgment action on the validity of a rule is in the county where the party asserting the invalidity of the rule resides or has its principal place of business or, if that party does not reside in Wisconsin, in the county where the dispute arose. Under former law, venue for such an action was in Dane County.

Beverages

Act 32 (*AB-40*) authorizes the Department of Revenue (DOR) instead of municipalities to issue beer wholesaler's permits. Under the act, a brewer may not hold a wholesaler's permit but may, under its brewer's permit, sell, ship, transport, and deliver its own beer to wholesalers; transport beer between the brewery premises and the brewer's warehouse; and, if the brewer annually produces 300,000 or fewer barrels of beer, sell, ship, and deliver its own beer to retailers. Under the act, a brewer may not also hold a retail license, but the brewer's permit authorizes the brewer to make retail sales at the brewery premises and at one off-site retail outlet the brewer establishes.

At these two retail locations, the brewer may make retail sales of its own beer and of other Wisconsin-made beer and, if the brewer held a retail liquor license on June 1, 2011, intoxicating liquor. The act also eliminates a provision that restricted some brewers from operating restaurants and instead authorizes a brewer to operate two restaurants, one on the brewery premises and one at an off-site retail outlet.

Business and Consumer Law

Act 7 (*January 2011 Special Session SB-6*) creates the Wisconsin Economic Development Corporation (WEDC), an authority charged with developing and implementing economic programs to provide business support and expertise and financial assistance to companies that invest and create jobs in Wisconsin and to support new business start-ups and business expansion and growth in Wisconsin.

Act 32 (*AB-40*) makes the following changes to the laws relating to economic development:

- Eliminates the Department of Commerce.
- Transfers several programs related to economic development from the former Department of Commerce to WEDC, including the State Main Street Program; the Brownfields Grant Program; and numerous programs for the administration of tax credits.
- Eliminates a number of programs related to economic development that were administered by the Department of Commerce, including grants to the Women's Business Initiative Corporation; community development block grants; the Capital Access Program; renewable energy grants and loans; loans to manufacturing businesses; gaming economic diversification grants and loans; grants to the Center for Advanced Technology and Innovation; the Economic Adjustment Program; the Business Employees' Skills Training Grant Program; entrepreneurial assistance grants; the Wisconsin Trade Project Program; the Rural Economic Development Program; manufacturing extension center grants; grants to the Wisconsin Angel Network; the Technology Commercialization Grant and Loan Program; manufacturing investment tax credits; administration of the Forward Innovation Fund and the Wisconsin Development Fund; and the Economic Liaison Program with American Indians.

Children

Act 270 (*SB-173*) requires a juvenile court to make its confidential electronic records available to criminal courts, municipal courts, and other juvenile courts; prosecutors of cases in those courts; and attorneys and guardians ad litem (GALs) for parents and children who are parties to municipal or juvenile court proceedings and to make such records relating to a delinquency proceeding available to law enforcement agencies. The act permits such records made available to be used by a court only for conducting or preparing for court proceedings; by a prosecutor, attorney, or GAL only for performing official duties relating to a court proceeding; and by a law enforcement agency only for investigating alleged criminal or delinquent activity.

Correctional System

Act 38 (*SB-57*) eliminates programs that allowed prisoners to earn, for days spent in confinement without incident, "positive adjustment time" that would have reduced the number of days of incarceration. The act also eliminates the court's ability to shorten a person's sentence based on a court determination that the person would benefit from the reduced sentence, the opportunity for certain prisoners to be released from incarceration early if they are within 12 months of release, and early discharge from community supervision.

Act 38 eliminates the Earned Release Review Commission, restores the Parole Commission, and authorizes the Parole Commission, at its discretion, to release to community supervision certain prisoners who have served a portion of their sentences confined in prison. Under the act, the sentencing court determines whether certain prisoners who have served either 75 percent or 85 percent of their confinement sentences may be released to community supervision. The act allows a sentencing court to grant certain offenders early release from probation.

Act 94 (*AB-69*) creates a presumption of immunity from civil liability for a person who used deadly force against another if all of the following apply:

- The person against whom the force was used was attempting to enter, or had unlawfully and forcefully entered, the dwelling, motor vehicle, or place of business of the person who used the force.
- The person who used the force was in that dwelling, motor vehicle, or place of business.
- The person who used the force knew or reasonably believed that an unlawful and forcible entry was occurring or had occurred.

Act 94 does not provide a presumption of immunity to a person who used the deadly force if the person was engaged in a criminal activity or was using his or her dwelling, motor vehicle, or place of business to further a criminal activity or if the person against whom the force was used had identified himself or herself as a public safety worker, or should have been known to be a public safety worker, and was performing his or her official duties. The act entitles a person who is civilly immune to recover his or her attorney fees, court costs, and other expenses related to defending against the suit.

The Majority Leader is responsible for the efficient conduct of Assembly floor sessions in advancement of the majority party's agenda. This session, that role again falls to Scott Suder of Abbotsford. (Jay Salvo, Legislative Photographer)

Education

Primary and Secondary Education

Act 32 (*AB-40*) makes the following changes to the Milwaukee Parental Choice Program (MPCP), under which certain low-income pupils who reside in the city of Milwaukee may attend a private school at state expense:

- Eliminates the cap on the number of pupils that may participate in the MPCP.
- Requires the Department of Public Instruction (DPI) to provide information obtained through the application process to DOR and requires DOR to determine whether a pupil is eligible to participate in the MPCP on the basis of family income.
- Increases the family income limit from 175 percent of the federal poverty level

to 300 percent of the federal poverty level.

- Permits family income for a married family to be reduced by $7,000 before determining income eligibility.
- Permits a pupil to remain eligible to participate in the MPCP if the pupil's family income increases.
- Permits any private school, not just private schools located in the city of Milwaukee, to participate.
- Permits participating private schools to charge tuition and fees, in addition to the state choice payment, to a participating pupil in grades 9 to 12 if the pupil's family income exceeds 220 percent of the federal poverty level.
- Requires DPI to notify each participating private school of any proposed changes to the MPCP prior to the beginning of the school year in which the changes are to take place.
- Allows a private school seeking to participate in the MPCP to obtain preaccreditation from any statutorily recognized accrediting agency.

In addition, Act 32 creates a Parental Choice Program for Eligible School Districts having all of the same characteristics as the MPCP except for the following:

- Any school district located in a city of the second class and meeting certain criteria related to income and state aid, as determined by DPI, may participate in the program and may continue to participate in future years. The Racine Unified School District is the only eligible school district DPI identified for the 2011-12 school year.
- A pupil may participate if the pupil was enrolled in the eligible district in the previous school year; was not enrolled in school in the previous school year; was enrolled in the program in the previous school year; or is enrolling in kindergarten, first grade, or ninth grade in a school participating in the program in the current school year.
- Pupil participation is limited to 250 pupils in the first school year of the program

Representative Dave Murphy (at left, R-Greenville), serving his first term, chats with the Assembly's most senior member, Al Ott. Ott (R-Forest Junction) first served in the 1987 session. (Jay Salvo, Legislative Photographer)

and 500 pupils in the second school year of the program, but is not limited in any subsequent school year.

Act 32 also eliminates the limit of 5,250 pupils who may attend a virtual charter school under the Open Enrollment Program.

Act 32 directs DPI to establish a student information system to collect and maintain information about public school pupils and ensure that within five years every school district is using the system.

Act 32 requires DPI to replace the statewide knowledge and concepts examinations with pupil assessments developed by the Smarter Balanced Assessment Consortium or by an entity DPI selects.

Act 125 (*SB-353*) prohibits a public school employee and certain other individuals who provide services for a public school from using seclusion or physical restraint on a pupil except under certain conditions. Seclusion may be used only if the pupil's behavior presents a clear, present, and imminent risk to physical safety; it is the least restrictive intervention available; it lasts only as long as is necessary; an employee maintains constant supervision of the pupil; the seclusion room or area is free from objects that may injure the pupil; the pupil has access to a bathroom, water, necessary medications, and meals; and no door connecting the room or area to other rooms or areas is capable of being locked. Physical restraint may be used only if the pupil's behavior presents a clear, present, and imminent risk to physical safety; it is the least restrictive intervention available; the degree of force used and the duration of the restraint are reasonable and no more than necessary; there are no medical contraindications to its use; certain specified maneuvers and techniques are not employed; it does not constitute corporal punishment; and neither mechanical nor chemical restraints are used.

Act 166 (*SB-461*) makes the following changes:

- Creates a segregated fund, the Read to Lead Development Fund, to support literacy and early childhood development programs, and the Read to Lead Development Council.
- Requires each school board and each charter school annually to assess pupils enrolled in kindergarten for reading readiness. The school board or charter school must provide a pupil at risk of reading difficulty with interventions or remedial reading services.
- Prohibits DPI from issuing an initial license to teach in grades kindergarten to 5, in special education, or as a reading specialist unless the applicant passes an examination identical to the Foundations of Reading test administered in 2012 as part of the Massachusetts Tests for Educator Licensure.
- Requires DPI to work in consultation with the governor's office and others to determine how the performance of persons who have recently completed teacher education and preparatory programs and who have been recommended for licensure will be used to evaluate the effectiveness of the programs. The act requires DPI to share certain information obtained about these persons from the programs with the public and requires the programs to share this information with prospective applicants.
- Requires DPI to develop an educator effectiveness evaluation system and an equivalency process. The act requires school districts to use either the system or the process to evaluate teacher and principal performance beginning in the 2014-15 school year and, using information obtained from the evaluation, place teachers and principals in one of multiple performance categories.

Act 172 (*AB-259*) requires DPI to develop guidelines to educate athletic coaches and pupil athletes and their parents about the nature and risk of concussion and head injury in youth athletic activities. The bill requires that a person who is suspected of sustaining a concussion or head injury in a youth athletic activity be removed from the activity. A person who has been removed may not participate in a youth athletic activity until a health care provider gives him or her written clearance to do so.

Act 215 (*SB-174*) closes the parental choice program for eligible school districts (currently open only to the Racine Unified School District) to additional school districts.

Elections

Act 23 (*AB-7*) provides, with certain exceptions, that an individual must present proof of identification in order to vote in an election. The act permits a number of specified documents to be used as proof, including a Wisconsin driver's license or identification card. With limited exceptions, a document must contain a photograph of the individual. With certain exceptions, an individual voting absentee must provide a copy of the proof with his or her application. The act permits an elector who does not have proof of identification to vote provisionally. A provisional ballot is valid only if the elector who casts the ballot presents the required proof to the municipality in which he or she resides by 4 p.m. on the Friday after an election. The act also increases to 28 days the durational residency requirement for electors to vote in an election, requires most electors who vote at polling places to provide their signatures when voting, eliminates the option of using a single action to vote a straight party ticket, shortens the period for late registration and absentee voting in person before election day, and eliminates corroboration of an elector's residence by another elector of the same municipality as acceptable proof of residence for registration.

Act 43 (*SB-148*) redistricts this state's legislative districts in accordance with the 2010 U.S. census of population.

Act 44 (*SB-149*) redistricts this state's congressional districts in accordance with the 2010 U.S. census of population.

Act 75 (*SB-116*) changes the date of the September primary election to the second Tuesday in August and renames it the partisan primary. The act also changes the dates for related election occurrences in accordance with that date change.

Employment

Act 10 (*January 2011 Special Session AB-11*) limits the scope of collective bargaining for state and municipal employees, except police officers and fire fighters, to bargaining over a base wage increase that does not exceed the increase in the consumer price index. The act also prohibits municipal governments from collectively bargaining with employees in a manner inconsistent with the Municipal Employment Relations Act (MERA) and eliminates collective bargaining for University of Wisconsin (UW) System employees, employees of the UW Hospitals and Clinics Authority, and certain home care and child care providers. The act also requires each public sector collective bargaining unit, except units containing police officers or fire fighters, to annually certify its collective bargaining representative in order to bargain collectively, limits to one year the duration of collective bargaining agreements covering all state or municipal employees except police officers or fire fighters, and prohibits local governments and the state from deducting labor organization dues from the earnings of an employee who is not a police officer or fire fighter.

Act 10 makes the following changes to the laws relating to public employment and fringe benefits for public employees:

- Requires public employees under the Wisconsin Retirement System (WRS) to pay one-half of all actuarially required contributions to fund their retirement benefits and prohibits the employer, with exceptions, from paying this amount in behalf of the employees. Protective occupation participants (who are generally law enforcement and fire fighting personnel) must pay the same percentage of earnings as public employees who are not protective occupation participants, but the employer must pay these amounts in behalf of the employee if required by a collective bargaining agreement. Former law allowed the employer to pay these contributions for all employees.

- Requires the director of Office of State Employment Relations (OSER) to set the amount that the employer must pay for state employee health insurance costs. The act specifies that the employer may not pay more than 88 percent of the average premium costs of health insurance plans offered in the tier with the lowest employee premium costs by the Group Insurance Board (GIB).

- Decreases the formula multiplier that is used to calculate an annuity for elected and executive participating employees in the WRS from 2 percent to 1.6 percent, resulting in a 20 percent reduction in the value of a WRS annuity calculated according to the formula methodology. This decrease applies only to

Senator Dave Hansen, Assistant Minority Leader, talks with colleagues Fred Risser (left) and Mark Miller. *(Jay Salvo, Legislative Photographer)*

future years of service earned by the employees.

- Provides that, under the local government health insurance program offered to local government employers by the GIB, the employer may not pay more than 88 percent of the average premium costs of health insurance plans offered in the tier with the lowest employee premium costs.

- With exceptions, requires employees in retirement systems of counties having a population of 500,000 or more (currently, only Milwaukee County) to pay half of all actuarially required contributions for funding benefits under the retirement system and prohibits the employer from paying these contributions in behalf of the employees.

- With exceptions, requires employees in retirement systems of first class cities (currently, only the city of Milwaukee) to pay all employee-required contributions for funding benefits under the retirement system and prohibits the employer from paying these contributions in behalf of the employees.

- Creates 37 unclassified division administrator positions in executive branch state agencies and permits the appointing authority in these agencies to designate any managerial position as an administrator position.

- Permits an appointing authority of a state agency to reassign a career executive employee to a career executive position in any state agency if the appointing authority in the agency to which the employee is to be reassigned approves of the reassignment.

- Permits an appointing authority of a state agency, during a state of emergency declared by the governor, to discharge any employee who fails to report to work as scheduled for any three days or any employee who participates in a strike or certain other work actions.

Assistant Majority Leader Glenn Grothman (R-West Bend) exchanges views with Senator Kathleen Vinehout (D-Alma). (Jay Salvo, Legislative Photographer)

- Requires the GIB to design health care coverage plans for 2012 for state employees that, after inflation adjustments, reduces premium costs by at least 5 percent from the costs of such plans during 2011.

Act 32 (*AB-40*) modifies Act 10 to allow municipal transit employees to bargain over wages, hours, and conditions of employment if the state would lose federal funding if the employees were limited to bargaining over the base wage increase under Act 10. Under the act, the Wisconsin Employment Relations Commission must determine which employees qualify. The act prohibits police officers and fire fighters hired on or after July 1, 2011, from bargaining over the requirement that they pay the employee share of retirement contributions and prohibits municipal police and fire fighters hired on or after July 1, 2011, from bargaining over the design and selection of their health care coverage plans.

Health and Social Services

Act 217 (*SB-306*) makes various changes to abortion laws, including:

- Requiring a physician who is to perform or induce an abortion to determine whether the woman's consent is voluntary by speaking to the woman in person, out of the presence of anyone other than a person working for or with the physician. If the physician suspects that the woman is in danger of physical harm by anyone coercing her to consent to an abortion, the physician must inform the woman of domestic abuse services and provide her private access to a telephone.
- Prohibiting giving an abortion-inducing drug to a woman unless the physician who prescribed the abortion-inducing drug performs a physical exam on the woman and is physically present in the room at the time the abortion-inducing drug is given to the woman.

Act 32 (*AB-40*) makes changes related to Medical Assistance (MA), including allowing the Department of Health Services (DHS), until January 1, 2015, to establish policies to make certain changes to the laws related to MA including policies that conflict with or supersede certain statutes. DHS must seek any necessary federal approval by MA state plan amendment or waiver of federal Medicaid law and may not implement the policy if the federal government does not approve. Before implementing a policy that conflicts with a statute and before seeking federal approval, DHS must submit the proposed policy along with estimates of cost savings to the Joint Committee on Finance (JCF) for review. The act also requires DHS to request a waiver of federal Medicaid law so that DHS does not have to maintain effort in the MA program. If the federal government does not approve the waiver of maintenance of effort, DHS must reduce income levels for the purposes of determining eligibility for MA programs to 133 percent of the federal poverty line to the extent permitted under the federal Patient Protection and Affordable Care Act. The act supersedes the related provisions in Act 10.

Justice

Act 35 (*SB-93*) requires DOJ to issue a license to carry a concealed and dangerous weapon, including a handgun, to an applicant who is a Wisconsin resident, who is at least 21 years of age, who submits proof of training, and who is not subject to prohibitions against possessing a firearm. The act also permits persons to prohibit others from carrying a firearm in residences, including in common areas of residential buildings; on nonresidential grounds and in nonresidential buildings; at certain special events; in local government buildings; and in buildings on the grounds of a university or college. A person who violates the prohibitions is guilty of trespassing and subject to a civil forfeiture.

Local Law

Act 32 (*AB-40*) does the following:
- Prohibits a county from using its own workforce to perform a highway improvement project on a highway under the jurisdiction of another county or a municipality that is located in a different county.
- Prohibits a city or village with a population of 5,000 or more from having a county workforce perform a highway improvement project unless the project is under the local roads improvement program.

Natural Resources

Act 169 (*SB-411*) requires the Department of Natural Resources (DNR) to establish a wolf harvesting season and to issue wolf harvesting licenses that authorize both hunting and trapping if the wolf is not on the Wisconsin or U.S. list of endangered or threatened species. If the number of license applications exceeds the number of licenses that DNR makes available for a year, DNR must issue 50 percent of the licenses by random selection and 50 percent through a cumulative preference system. The act authorizes DNR to close the season if necessary to effectively manage the wolf population. The act authorizes the use of dogs to hunt wolves, the hunting of wolves at night for part of the season, and the baiting of wolves with certain types of bait. The act establishes a wolf depredation program, under which payments may be made for the death or injury caused by wolves to livestock or pets, except for dogs being used to hunt wolves. The wolf hunting license fees that DNR collects are used to make the payments under this program.

Act 118 (*SB-368*) restructures the laws regarding discharges into wetlands and wetland mitigation. The changes include:
- Specifying that the issuance of a wetland permit by DNR replaces a water quality certification that is required by federal law.
- Requiring DNR to issue certain general wetland permits, including general permits for commercial, residential, municipal, agricultural, or recreational purposes, if the area of wetland to be affected does not exceed 10,000 square feet.
- Authorizing DNR to issue general permits that prohibit discharges into certain types of wetlands, such as calcareous and boreal rich fens and marshes containing wild rice.
- Establishing steps DNR must take in reviewing an application for an individual permit and requirements to be met to minimize adverse impacts to wetlands and to ensure there will not be a significant adverse impact.
- Requiring that mitigation be performed under each individual permit DNR

issues and eliminating the restriction that mitigation may not be used for discharges into areas of special natural resource interest.

- Requiring DNR to establish a mitigation program that includes the use of mitigation banks; participation in a process under which a payment may be made for creating or otherwise improving other wetlands, if DNR establishes such a process; and completion of actual mitigation within a certain distance from the discharge. The act requires that the ratio of mitigation be at least 1.2 acres improved for each acre affected.

Public Utilities

Act 22 (*January 2011 Special Session SB-13*) makes various changes to the Public Service Commission's (PSC) regulation of telecommunications providers, including the following:

- Limiting the PSC's authority to regulate both telecommunications utilities (TUs), which are telecommunications providers that resulted from the breakup of the Bell System under federal antitrust regulation in the 1970s and 1980s, and alternative telecommunications utilities (ATUs), which compete with TUs. The act generally subjects both TUs and ATUs to the same level of regulation by creating exemptions from requirements that applied to TUs under former law, limiting the requirements that the PSC was allowed to impose on ATUs under former law, eliminating price regulation and other types of alternative regulation of TUs, and allowing a TU to require that the PSC regulate the TU like an ATU.
- Imposing limitations on the intrastate switched access rates that telecommunications providers may charge each other. The requirements depend on the number of the telecommunications provider's access lines, and on the date the PSC initially certified the telecommunications provider as a TU or ATU. In general, the requirements impose deadlines by which a telecommunications provider's intrastate switched access rates may not exceed the interstate switched access rates that the telecommunications provider is allowed to charge under federal law.
- Requiring TUs and ATUs to file tariffs for intrastate switched access service and allowing the filing of tariffs for other services. The act also limits the PSC's authority regarding tariffs that TUs and ATUs elect to file with the PSC.
- Exempting interconnected voice over Internet protocol service from PSC regulation, except for requirements relating to interconnection agreements, intrastate switched access rates, and certain assessments.
- Limiting the PSC's authority to ensure universal access to telecommunications services and imposing requirements regarding the availability of basic voice service.
- Making changes to requirements for the use of another person's transmission equipment and property by public utilities and telecommunications providers.

State Government

State Finance

Act 32 (*AB-40*) removes the statutory limit on the total amount the Investment Board may annually assess the funds it manages for its share of the Investment Board's operating expenditures. Instead, the Investment Board may establish and monitor its own budget for operating expenditures and must report quarterly on its operating expenditures.

Transportation

Act 23 (*AB-7*) and **Act 32** (*AB-40*) allow the Department of Transportation (DOT), upon implementation of the federal REAL ID Act in Wisconsin, to issue driver's licenses and identification cards that are not compliant with REAL ID standards if they clearly state on their face that they cannot be accepted as identification for any official federal purpose and if they use a unique design or color to alert federal authorities that they are not REAL ID compliant. Various requirements, however, still apply to applications and application processing for REAL ID noncompliant driver's licenses and identification cards. The acts also create a religious belief exception to the requirement that a photograph appear on a driver's license or identification card, although after the implementation of the federal REAL ID Act the exception applies only to REAL ID noncompliant driver's licenses and identification cards. The acts lengthen the valid period of a driving receipt issued by DOT, and create a similar identification card receipt issued by DOT, which serve as a temporary license or identification card while an application is being processed. The acts specify that DOT may not issue an identification card to a person who holds a driver's license from another state.

Act 32 (*AB-40*) modifies DOT's major highway projects program to establish two different categories of major highway projects. The first category encompasses major highway projects, as contemplated under preexisting law, except that the minimum total cost criteria is increased from $5 million to $30 million, adjusted for inflation. For these major highway projects, the act allows DOT to perform engineering and design work prior to legislative approval of the project. The second category of major highway projects encompasses projects that do not fall within the first category and that have a minimum total cost of $75 million, adjusted for inflation. For these projects, the act allows DOT to prepare an environmental impact statement or environmental assessment for a project without approval by the Transportation Projects Commission (TPC), creates a different TPC review and approval process, and allows DOT to proceed with construction of a project upon TPC approval without additional legislative approval.

Act 32 also creates a category of highway projects called "southeast Wisconsin freeway megaprojects," which are projects on southeast Wisconsin freeways that have a total cost of more than $500 million, adjusted for inflation. These projects may be funded only from specified appropriations, including bond proceeds, and no funding for construction of these projects may be provided without legislative approval. The act approves DOT's I-94 north-south corridor project and Zoo interchange project as southeast Wisconsin freeway megaprojects, authorizes approximately $150 million in additional general obligation bonding to fund these two projects, and requires DOT to submit a report to JCF relating to financing the Zoo interchange project. Under preexisting law, these two projects were approved as southeast Wisconsin freeway rehabilitation projects. The act also transfers certain funds from the southeast Wisconsin freeway

The Wisconsin Assembly has invited many dignitaries to address it in the past, from Theodore Roosevelt (1911) to the Crown Prince of Norway (1939). In May 2013, the 14th Dalai Lama of Tibet addressed the body. (Jay Salvo, Legislative Photographer)

The Senate Chamber. *(Greg Anderson, Legislative Photographer)*

rehabilitation program to the southeast Wisconsin freeway megaprojects program.

Act 32 also creates a category of projects called "high-cost state highway bridge projects," which are projects involving the construction or rehabilitation of a bridge on the state trunk highway system that have a total cost of more than $150 million, but which exclude certain types of projects. The act creates a separate funding source for these projects. However, the act also authorizes DOT to fund preliminary costs for the Hoan Bridge project in Milwaukee County, in the 2011-13 fiscal biennium, from DOT's programs for major highway projects, state highway rehabilitation projects, and southeast Wisconsin freeway megaprojects.

Act 32 also requires DOT, in issuing a certificate when there is a security interest in the titled vehicle, to issue the certificate in the name of the vehicle owner but to deliver the certificate to the secured party rather than the vehicle owner. The certificate may be in an electronic or digital form.

Act 32 also eliminates the Southeastern Regional Transit Authority (SERTA) and eliminates authorization to create a Dane County Regional Transit Authority (RTA), a Chippewa Valley RTA, and a Chequamegon Bay RTA, all of which were created or authorized in 2009 Wisconsin Act 28. The act also eliminates the Southeast Wisconsin Transit Capital Assistance Program, under which DOT was formerly authorized to award grants from bond proceeds to the SERTA for transit capital improvements.

Act 91 (*SB-96*) does the following:

- Adds several items to an existing list of violations for which a motor vehicle manufacturer, importer, or distributor (distributor) may be subject to license revocation or a suit for damages.
- Requires a distributor to compensate a motor vehicle dealer for motor vehicle service work based on the dealer's effective nonwarranty labor rate and average percentage markup over dealer cost for parts. The act also specifies the method by which these rates are determined and contested.
- Requires a distributor to pay termination benefits to a dealer when the distributor terminates a franchise that may constitute less than the entire agreement between the distributor and the dealer.
- Requires a distributor to pay a dealer the franchise's fair market value if a franchise is terminated because the distributor discontinued a line make.
- Adds several items to an existing list of termination benefits that a distributor must pay to a dealer upon termination of a franchise.
- Provides several exceptions to the requirement that a distributor pay termination benefits.
- Requires a distributor to indemnify a dealer against certain claims alleging defective or negligent manufacture or design of a motor vehicle or accessory.

The act does not apply to motorcycle manufacturers, importers, or distributors.

MAJOR PROPOSALS THAT FAILED ENACTMENT OR ADOPTION

Business and Consumer Law

Assembly Bill 129 and *Senate Bill 94* would have established the Wisconsin Venture Capital Authority, as well as an investment fund and investment programs to be administered by the authority to invest in venture capital funds and Wisconsin start-up and other businesses.

Constitutional Amendments

Assembly Joint Resolution 63, proposed by the 2011 legislature on first consideration, would have allowed the recall of a public officer only if that officer had been charged with a crime punishable by imprisonment of one year or more, or against whom a finding of probable cause of violation of the state code of ethics had been made.

Assembly Joint Resolution 100, proposed by the 2011 legislature on first consideration, would have required the state to account for all funds it receives or spends in accordance with generally accepted accounting principles and to gradually extinguish any deficit in a state fund.

Senate Joint Resolution 16, proposed to the 2011 legislature on second consideration, would have imposed restrictions on a county executive's partial veto power over appropriations that are identical to the restrictions imposed on the governor's partial veto power over appropriations.

Senate Joint Resolution 60, proposed to the 2011 legislature on second consideration, would have prohibited the governor, in exercising his or her partial veto power over appropriation bills, from vetoing part of a section of a bill without rejecting the entire section.

Education

Assembly Bill 51 and *Senate Bill 22* would have made extensive changes to laws relating to charter schools, including creating the Charter School Authorizing Board, allowing additional charter school authorizers, and eliminating the limit on the number of pupils who may attend virtual charter schools.

Assembly Bill 110 and *Senate Bill 486* would have created the Special Needs Scholarship Program, providing scholarships to disabled pupils to allow them to attend a private school or a public school located outside their school district of residence.

Environment

Assembly Bill 426 and *Senate Bill 488* would have established requirements for iron mining separate from those for mining for other metallic minerals.

Public Utilities

Assembly Bill 72 and *Senate Bill 50* would have repealed rules promulgated by the PSC regarding wind energy systems.

Executive Branch

6

The executive branch: profile of the executive branch and descriptions of constitutional offices, departments, independent agencies, state authorities, regional agencies, and interstate agencies and compacts

Craftsman Applying Gold Leaf During the Wisconsin Historical Society Reading Room Renovation

(Wisconsin Historical Society, 94.1.60)

ELECTIVE CONSTITUTIONAL EXECUTIVE STATE OFFICERS

Office	Officer/Party	Residence[1]	Term Expires	Annual Salary[2]
Governor.	Scott Walker (Republican)	Milwaukee	January 5, 2015	$144,423
Lieutenant Governor.	Rebecca Kleefisch (Republican)	Oconomowoc	January 5, 2015	76,261
Secretary of State	Douglas J. La Follette (Democrat)	Kenosha	January 5, 2015	68,556
State Treasurer.	Kurt W. Schuller (Republican)	Eden	January 5, 2015	68,556
Attorney General.	J.B. Van Hollen (Republican)	Waunakee	January 5, 2015	140,147
Superintendent of Public Instruction	Tony Evers (nonpartisan office)	Madison	July 3, 2017	120,111

[1]Residence when originally elected.

[2]Annual salary as established for term of office by the Wisconsin Legislature.

Sources: 2011-12 Wisconsin Statutes; Wisconsin Legislative Reference Bureau, Wisconsin Brief 12-9, *Wisconsin State Officers*, November 2012, and Wisconsin Brief 12-11, *Salaries of State Elected Officials*, December 2012.

The Capitol Square can be enjoyed by Wisconsin residents and visitors during all seasons. (Greg Anderson, Legislative Photographer and Sarah Girkin)

EXECUTIVE BRANCH

A PROFILE OF THE EXECUTIVE BRANCH

Structure of the Executive Branch

The structure of Wisconsin state government is based on a separation of powers among the legislative, executive, and judicial branches. The legislative branch sets broad policy and establishes the general structures and regulations for carrying them out. The executive branch administers the programs and policies, while the judicial branch is responsible for adjudicating any conflicts that may arise from the interpretation or application of the laws.

Constitutional Officers. The executive branch includes the state's six constitutional officers – the governor, lieutenant governor, secretary of state, state treasurer, attorney general, and state superintendent of public instruction. Originally, the term of office for all constitutional officers was two years, but since the 1970 elections, their terms have been four years. All, except the state superintendent, are elected on partisan ballots in the fall elections of the even-numbered years at the midpoint between presidential elections. Though originally a partisan officer, the superintendent is now elected on a nonpartisan ballot in the April election.

The governor, as head of the executive branch, is constitutionally required to "take care that the laws be faithfully executed". In Article V of the state constitution, as ratified in 1848, the people of Wisconsin provided for the election of a governor and a lieutenant governor who would become "acting governor" in the event of a vacancy in the governor's office. Originally, the lieutenant governor was also the presiding officer of the senate. (By subsequent amendments, the lieutenant governor was relieved of senate duties and now assumes the full title of "governor" if the office is vacated.)

In Article VI, the constitution provided for three additional elected officers to assist in administering the laws of the new state. The first session of the legislature in 1848 authorized the secretary of state to keep official records, including enrolled laws and various state papers, and to act as state auditor by examining the treasurer's books and preparing budget projections for the legislature. The state treasurer was given responsibility for receiving all money and tax collections and paying out only those amounts authorized by the legislature for the operation of state government. The attorney general was to provide legal advice to the legislature and other constitutional officers and represent the state in legal matters tried in the courts of this state, other states, and the federal government.

The sixth officer, created by Article X of the constitution, was the state superintendent of public instruction. The first legislature gave the superintendent very specific duties, including the mandate to travel throughout the state inspecting common schools and advocating good public schools. The superintendent was to recommend texts, take a census of school age children, collect statistics on existing schools, and determine the apportionment of school aids.

The simplicity of administering state government in the early years is illustrated by the fact that total expenditures for 1848 government operations were only $13,472, which included the expenses of the legislature and circuit courts. As prescribed by the constitution and state law, the salaries of all six constitutional officers totaled $5,050 that year. (The lieutenant governor did not receive a salary, but he was given a double legislative per diem.) The state's annual budget totaled $32.5 billion in fiscal year 2012-13, and many of the duties first assigned to the constitutional officers are now carried out by specialized state agencies.

1967 Reorganization. Over a century later, the Wisconsin Committee on the Reorganization of the Executive Branch, in its report to the 1967 Legislature, concluded that state government could no longer be neatly divided into precise legislative, executive, and judicial domains. In many instances the subjects of legislation had become so technically complex that the legislature found it necessary to grant rule-making authority to the administrative agencies. The courts had also encountered a staggering load of technical detail and had come to depend on administrative agencies to use their quasi-judicial powers to assist the judicial branch.

Although the Wisconsin Constitution delegated ultimate responsibility for state administration to the governor, the proliferation of agencies over the years had made it increasingly difficult for one official to exercise effective executive control. The committee identified 85 state agencies within the executive branch of Wisconsin state government, many of which had no direct relationship to the governor. Chapter 75, Laws of 1967, attempted to integrate agencies by function and make them responsive to the elected chief executive, by drastically reducing the number of executive agencies from 85 to 32. Like everything else, however, state government does not remain static. Since the 1967 reorganization, the legislature has created new state agencies, while abolishing or consolidating others. In addition, there have been numerous changes to the duties and responsibilities of the various agencies. The following sections describe the current organization of the executive branch.

Departments. The term "department" is used to designate a principal administrative agency within the executive branch. Within a department, the major subunit is the division, which is headed by an administrator. Each division, in turn, is divided into bureaus, headed by directors. Bureaus may include sections, headed by chiefs, and smaller units, headed by supervisors. There currently are 17 departments in the executive branch.

Wisconsin Administrative Departments

Administration	Natural Resources
Agriculture, Trade and Consumer Protection	Public Instruction
Children and Families	Revenue
Corrections	Safety and Professional Services
Employee Trust Funds	Tourism
Financial Institutions	Transportation
Health Services	Veterans Affairs
Justice	Workforce Development
Military Affairs	

In the majority of cases, the departments are headed by a secretary appointed by the governor with the advice and consent of the senate. Only the Department of Employee Trust Funds and the Department of Veterans Affairs are headed by boards that select the secretary. When administrators are personally chosen by and serve at the pleasure of the governor, they usually work in close cooperation with the chief executive.

Debate about whether the governor should directly appoint department heads continues. Public administration theory has long held that a governor can be the chief executive only if he or she has the authority to hold department heads directly accountable. On the other hand, the original purpose of a board was to insulate a department from politics, thereby enabling its head and staff to develop expertise and a sense of professionalism.

Independent Agencies. In addition to constitutional offices and administrative departments, there are 11 units of the executive branch that have been specifically designated as independent agencies.

Independent Executive Agencies

Educational Communications Board	State Historical Society of Wisconsin
Employment Relations Commission	State Investment Board
Government Accountability Board	State Public Defender Board
Higher Educational Aids Board	Technical College System
Office of the Commissioner of Insurance	University of Wisconsin System
Public Service Commission	

Although the independent agencies are usually headed by part-time boards or multiple commissioners, the governor appoints most of these officials, with advice and consent of the senate, which serves to strengthen executive control of these units.

Authorities. In some instances, the legislature has decided to create corporate public bodies, known as "authorities", to handle specific functions. Although they are agencies of the state, the authorities operate outside the regular government structure and are intended to be financially self-sufficient. Currently, there are 9 authorities provided for by Wisconsin law, 8 of which are active – the Wisconsin Aerospace Authority (WAA), the Wisconsin Economic Development Corporation, the Fox River Navigational System Authority, the Lower Fox River Remediation Authority, the Wisconsin Health and Educational Facilities Authority (WHEFA), the Health Insurance Risk-Sharing Plan Authority, the Wisconsin Housing and Economic Development Authority (WHEDA), and the University of Wisconsin Hospitals and Clinics Authority. WAA, the Lower Fox River Remediation Authority, WHEDA, WHEFA, and UW Hospitals and Clinics Authority are authorized to issue bonds to finance their respective activities. Most authority members are appointed by the governor with advice and consent of the senate, but some are chosen from the legislature or serve as *ex officio* members.

Nonprofit Corporation. In 1985, the legislature created the Bradley Center Sports and Entertainment Corporation, a public, nonprofit corporation, which operates the Bradley Center in Milwaukee, the home of the Milwaukee Bucks, the Milwaukee Admirals hockey team, and the Marquette University basketball team. The corporation is headed by a board of directors appointed by the governor.

Special Districts. The legislature may create special districts that serve "a statewide public purpose." These districts oversee the management of facilities for exposition centers, sports teams, and the cultural arts. Members of the governing boards are appointed by public officials. Currently, the Wisconsin Center, Miller Park, Lambeau Field, and the Madison Overture Center operate as special districts.

Boards, Councils, and Committees. Many departments and agencies have subordinate part-time boards, councils, and committees that carry out specific tasks or act in an advisory capacity. Boards may function as policy-making units, and some are granted policy-making or quasi-judicial powers. Examining boards set the standards of professional competence and conduct for the professions they supervise, and they are authorized to examine new practitioners, grant licenses, and investigate complaints of alleged unprofessional conduct. Councils function on a continuing basis to study and recommend solutions for problems arising in a specified functional area of state government. Committees usually are short-term bodies, appointed to study a specific problem and to recommend solutions or policy alternatives.

Boards are always created by statute. Councils are usually created by statute, but committees, because of their temporary nature, are created by session law rather than being written into the statutes. In addition, agency heads may create and appoint their own councils or committees as needed. The *Blue Book* describes only those units created by statute.

Attached Units. Under the 1967 reorganization, certain boards, commissions, and councils were attached to departments or independent agencies for administrative purposes only. These units are sometimes referred to as "15.03 units" because of the statutory section number that defines them. The larger agencies are expected to provide various services, such as budgeting and program coordination, but the 15.03 units exercise their statutory powers independently of the department or agency to which they are attached.

Government Employment

Classified Service. An important feature of Wisconsin state government employment is the merit system. Wisconsin's civil service, which is called "classified service", is designed to ensure that the most qualified person is hired for the job, based on test results and experience, rather than political affiliation. In 1905, Wisconsin was one of the first states to adopt such a system, and the Wisconsin classified service was considered one of the strongest because it encompassed the major portion of state personnel.

Since the 1967 reorganization of the executive branch, the trend has been to make top agency positions, including deputy secretaries, executive assistants, and division administrators, unclassified appointments. Despite this change at the top levels, most state employees, with the principal exception of legislative staff and the University of Wisconsin faculty and academic appointments, are hired and promoted through the classified service on the basis of merit.

Salaries. Positions in the classified service are categorized so that those involving similar duties, responsibilities, and qualifications are paid on the same basis. The Office of State Employment Relations (OSER) is directed to apply the principle of equal pay for equivalent skills and responsibilities when assigning a classification to a pay range.

Each biennium, OSER establishes the compensation plan of classifications and related salary ranges for classified employees subject to modification by the Joint Committee on Employment Relations. The governor may veto the committee's actions, although the vote of six committee members can override a veto. Some provisions of the compensation plan, as approved by the committee, may require changes in existing law, in which case they must be presented in bill form to the legislature for enactment.

Number of State Employees. The increasing size and complexity of state government is reflected in the number of employees. To illustrate this, a total of 1,924 people worked for Wisconsin state government in 1906. By contrast, according to the Legislative Fiscal Bureau, 69,263 full-time equivalent employee positions were authorized for fiscal year 2012-13.

Housing State Government

The first capitol in Madison was built during the Wisconsin Territory days at a cost of more than $60,000. Construction began in 1837 but was not completed until 1845. The building, which served as the first state capitol, was demolished in 1863 to make way for a larger second capitol, which was completed in 1866. When the second state capitol was extensively damaged by fire in 1904, construction of the current capitol began. The present capitol, which was completed in 1917 for $7,203,826.35, has undergone extensive restoration and renovation, costing more than $140 million, completed in 2001.

Today, the agencies of state government in Madison are housed in the capitol and various state-owned office buildings, with additional space leased from private landlords. There are also state office buildings in Eau Claire, Green Bay, La Crosse, Milwaukee, Waukesha, and Wisconsin Rapids, plus district offices maintained throughout the state for the field units of many of the operating departments.

Besides its office buildings, the state owns or maintains a variety of educational, correctional, and mental health institutions across Wisconsin. The University of Wisconsin System operates 13 degree-granting institutions and 13 two-year colleges that feature freshman-sophomore instruction.

The state's adult corrections program, under the direction of the Department of Corrections, currently operates 5 maximum security prisons, 11 medium security prisons, 2 minimum security institutions, a prison for women, and 16 correctional centers. The department's juvenile corrections program operates Lincoln Hills School for male juveniles and Copper Lake School for Girls, both at Irma.

Through the Department of Health Services, the state operates 4 mental health institutions at Madison, Mauston, and Winnebago, and 3 centers for the developmentally disabled at Madison, Chippewa Falls, and Union Grove. The department also operates the Mendota Juvenile Treatment Center, a secure juvenile correctional facility in an inpatient mental hospital setting.

The Department of Public Instruction maintains a school that offers special training for blind and visually impaired students at Janesville and a similar school for the deaf and hard-of-hearing at Delavan. The Wisconsin Veterans Homes at Chippewa Falls in Chippewa County, King in Waupaca County, and Union Grove in Racine County are operated by the state to serve eligible Wisconsin veterans and qualifying spouses.

Functions of the Executive Branch

Governor and Lieutenant Governor. The governor, as Wisconsin's chief executive officer, represents all the people of the state. Because of this, the Office of the Governor is the focal point for receiving suggestions and complaints about state affairs. Administratively, the governor exercises authority through the power of appointment, consultation with department heads, and execution of the executive budget after its enactment by the legislature. The governor plays a key role in the legislative process through drafting the initial version of the biennial budget, which is submitted to the legislature in the form of a bill. Other opportunities to influence legislative action arise in the chief executive's state of the state message and special messages to the legislature about topics of concern. The governor also shapes the legislative process through the power to veto bills, call special sessions of the legislature, and appoint committees or task forces to study state problems and make recommendations for changes in the law.

Based on a 1979 amendment, the constitution provides that if the incumbent governor dies, resigns, or is removed from office, the lieutenant governor becomes governor for the unexpired term. The lieutenant governor serves temporarily as "acting governor" when the governor is impeached, incapacitated, or absent from the state.

Commerce. While the U.S. Constitution specifically delegates to Congress the regulation of interstate commerce, each state regulates intrastate commerce within its borders. The definitions of interstate and intrastate commerce overlap at times, and over the years the U.S. Supreme Court has greatly broadened the meaning of the "commerce clause" in the federal constitution. Despite this broad interpretation, the states continue to exercise considerable authority over commerce.

Commerce involves goods, services, and commercial documents, as well as transportation and communication, so the state's involvement in regulating commerce is broad. The state's primary objective is to protect the public as consumers and as participants in financial transactions. Wisconsin state government is also interested in maintaining a stable, orderly market for carrying out commercial activities and for promoting the state's economic development.

One aspect of consumer protection is the inspection of farm products and the conditions under which they are produced. The state inspects cattle for infectious diseases, conducts research in animal and plant diseases, regulates the use of pesticides, grades fruits and vegetables for marketing, and sets standards for processed food. Explicit standards are set by law or in the administrative rules promulgated by the Department of Agriculture, Trade and Consumer Protection. The department is concerned not only with the conditions of growing and processing food but also with fair trade practices in its sale.

Another important aspect of consumer protection is the licensing of various trades and professions. Individuals working in certain professions must achieve state-mandated levels of training and proficiency before they can offer their services to the public. Examples include professions affecting public health, such as doctors and nurses, or public safety, such as architects and engineers. The Department of Safety and Professional Services assists a variety of examining boards associated with various trades and professions and directly regulates certain types of professional activity.

The state protects consumers by maintaining an orderly market in which the public can conduct business. State activities include specifying methods of fair competition, regulating rates for public utilities, setting standards for the operation of financial institutions, regulating gambling, and regulating the sale of securities and insurance. The Department of Financial Institutions regulates banks, savings institutions, credit unions, and the sale of securities. It also registers trademarks, corporations, and other organizations and files Uniform Commercial Code documents. The Office of the Commissioner of Insurance regulates the sale of insurance. The Public Service Commission regulates public utility rates and services. The Gaming Division in the Department of Administration regulates racing and charitable gambling and oversees gaming compacts between Indian tribes and the state. The Department of Revenue administers the Wisconsin Lottery.

The state is concerned with promoting economic development. The Wisconsin Economic Development Corporation develops and implements programs to provide business support and expertise and financial assistance to companies that are investing and creating jobs in Wisconsin and to promote new business start-ups and business growth and expansion in the state. The Department of Tourism promotes travel to Wisconsin's scenic, historic, artistic, educational, and recreational sites. It stimulates the development of private commercial tourist facilities and encourages local tourist-related businesses.

In the interests of public safety and welfare, the state enforces laws that regulate public and private buildings. The Department of Safety and Professional Services enforces dwelling codes, reviews construction plans for new buildings, inspects subsystems that serve buildings, and performs training and consulting services for the building industry.

Education. Wisconsin officially recognized the importance of education within a democratic society at statehood in 1848 when it provided for the establishment of local schools in the state constitution and required that education be free to all children. The constitution further directed the legislature to establish a state university at Madison and colleges throughout the state as needed.

Wisconsin's public educational institutions now enroll an estimated one million students each year. In fall 2012, there were 872,436 pupils in the public elementary (606,754) and secondary (265,682) schools and 180,969 students enrolled in the University of Wisconsin System. The Technical College System enrolled 132,535 students in its associate degree programs for the 2011-12 school year and 230,084 in its other programs.

Wisconsin relies on 426 local school districts to administer its elementary and secondary programs. Twelve cooperative educational service agencies (CESAs) furnish support activities to the local districts on a regional basis, and the Department of Public Instruction, headed by the State Superintendent of Public Instruction, a nonpartisan constitutional officer, provides supervision and consultation for the districts.

In 1970 the state was divided into 16 vocational, technical, and adult education districts. These districts, renamed technical college districts, are each supervised by a district board that has taxing power. At the state level, the Technical College System Board supervises the districts.

Governor Scott Walker is joined by elected officials and representatives of the Wisconsin and Minnesota Departments of Transportation on May 28, 2013 in a symbolic groundbreaking to mark the beginning of the construction of a new crossing over the St. Croix River that will replace the 1931 Stillwater Lift Bridge. The $629 million project is expected to be completed in 2016, after which the lift bridge will become a hiking and biking trail. (Office of the Governor)

At the collegiate level, all state-financed institutions of higher education are integrated into a single University of Wisconsin System. The system's two largest campuses at Madison and Milwaukee offer programs leading to doctoral degrees. Eleven other degree-granting institutions provide 4-year courses of baccalaureate study, and 13 UW Colleges provide 2-year courses of college-level study. State funding also supports Wisconsin residents enrolled at the Medical College of Wisconsin, Inc.

Three other state agencies perform educational functions. The Higher Educational Aids Board administers federal and state student financial assistance programs. The Educational Communications Board operates the state's networks for educational radio and educational television. The State Historical Society of Wisconsin maintains the state historical library, museum, and various historic sites.

Environmental Resources and Transportation. From a wilderness inhabited by 305,391 people in 1850, the state has evolved into a complex society with a population of 5,686,986 in April 2010, according to the U.S. decennial census. Most of Wisconsin is not densely populated, and the state has a comparatively large amount of open space. However, population growth, higher levels of consumption, and industrial development have increased environmental pollution.

Once pioneers could come to a wilderness, cut the forests, clear the land, and hunt and fish with little thought of damage to the soil, streams, or wildlife. Now these resources must be protected from destruction, depletion, or extinction. The Department of Natural Resources administers numerous programs that control water quality, air pollution, and solid waste disposal. Under state regulations, municipalities and industries cannot dump untreated sewage or industrial wastes into surface waters; smokestacks and automobiles must meet air pollution limits; farmers are encouraged to preserve soil and groundwater quality; and solid waste disposal facilities must meet construction and operation standards. The department regulates hunting and fishing to protect fish and wildlife resources and manages other programs designed to conserve and restore endangered and threatened species. It also promotes recreational and educational opportunities through state parks, forests, trails, and natural areas.

The Department of Transportation administers a variety of programs related to environmental resources. The highways that crisscross the state have a major impact on land use and people's lifestyles. Urban freeways and interstate highways greatly affect the use and development of surrounding land. They determine where people live, work, and play. When state government plans the location and financing of highways and roads, it must carefully consider both short- and long-range consequences.

The state's highway system consists of approximately 12,000 miles of interstate highways, state highways, county trunk highways, town roads, city and village streets, and park and forest roads. The state is concerned not only with building and maintaining adequate roads to meet demands, but also with providing for the safety of travelers using those roads. In 2013, more than 5.4 million vehicles were registered in Wisconsin, and approximately 4.5 million residents were licensed to drive. With 601 traffic fatalities in 2012, traffic safety is a constant concern.

The department must ensure that licensed drivers know the laws, are physically fit to drive, and have the required driving skills. It keeps track of drivers' records and can suspend the licenses of those who prove hazardous to themselves or others. It oversees highway construction and maintenance, highway patrol, and enforcement of driver and vehicle standards. The department is also involved in developing aviation and airports in Wisconsin and with promoting mass transit and passenger rail transportation.

Human Relations and Resources. Besides protecting the environment, the state must also protect its citizens directly. Population growth that affects the quality of land, water, and air resources has an increasingly complex effect on people themselves and their relationships to each other and their government. The inhabitants of a state are its prime resource, and government must ensure their general welfare. Records of birth, marriage, divorce, and death are collected and used to identify trends and potential problems.

In the state's early days, public health was primarily concerned with preventing the spread of communicable diseases. Today, the work of the Department of Health Services includes protection from biological terrorist attacks, disease prevention and detection, health education programs, and maintenance of institutions for the care and treatment of the mentally handicapped or mentally ill. The department is also responsible for a broad range of social services for the aged, the handicapped, and children.

A wide range of work-related issues are subject to state regulation. Minimum wages and maximum hours are set by law. If a worker is injured on the job, state worker's compensation may be available; unemployment compensation helps many workers faced with loss of a job. If a worker is seeking a job, the state (in partnership with the federal government) provides a job service to help the individual find work or to acquire the skills necessary for employment. If a worker suspects job discrimination because of age, race, creed, color, handicap, marital status, sex, national origin, ancestry, sexual orientation, or arrest or conviction record, the state may investigate the matter. The Department of Workforce Development is responsible for protecting and assisting workers and provides employment and assistance to rehabilitate the handicapped. The Department of Children and Families provides training and other services to help welfare recipients join the labor market under the state's Wisconsin Works (W-2) program. The Employment Relations Commission mediates or arbitrates labor disputes between workers and their employers.

The Department of Veterans Affairs has grant and loan programs to help eligible veterans acquire a home, business, or education, and it provides personal and medical care for eligible elderly veterans and their spouses at the Wisconsin Veterans Homes at Chippewa Falls, King, and Union Grove.

The state also protects its citizens from society's lawless elements by maintaining stability and order. Law enforcement is largely a local matter, but the Department of Corrections is responsible for segregating convicted adult and juvenile offenders in its penal institutions and rehabilitating them for eventual return to society. The Office of the State Public Defender represents indigents in trial and postconviction legal proceedings. The Department of Justice furnishes legal services to state agencies and technical assistance and training to local law enforcement agencies. It also enforces state laws against gambling, arson, child pornography, and narcotic drugs.

The state maintains an armed military force, the Wisconsin National Guard, to protect the populace in times of state or national emergency, whether natural or human caused, and to supplement the federal armed forces in time of war. These activities come under the jurisdiction of the Department of Military Affairs.

General Executive Functions. The services described so far are direct services to the public. In order for the state to perform these functions, it must also perform certain "staff" functions. The state requires general departments that oversee the hiring of agency personnel and provide space, equipment, salaries, and a retirement system for them. It must levy and collect taxes to support its activities, manage these state funds, and ensure that they are spent according to law. It also evaluates agency operations to assure that the various departments are performing their assigned tasks and preparing for future needs.

Some agencies are designed to perform staff functions almost exclusively. The Department of Administration, for example, is called the state's "housekeeping" department. Its duties include state budgeting, preauditing, engineering and facilities management, state planning, and data processing. The Office of State Employment Relations operates the state's classified service system. The Department of Revenue collects taxes levied by state law, distributes part of that revenue to local units of government, and calculates the equalized value of the property that has been assessed by local government.

The Department of Employee Trust Funds manages the state's retirement systems and the employee insurance programs that cover state and local government workers. At any one time, the state must have large sums of money in its employee trust funds to meet its obligations. The Investment Board invests these funds in stocks, bonds, and real estate in order to earn the maximum amount of interest possible until the funds are needed. The Department of Administration processes the receipt and disbursement of these and other state moneys.

The Office of the Secretary of State handles general executive duties, such as keeping various state records and affixing the state seal on certain records. The Government Accountability Board oversees the state's election processes, monitors campaign expenditures, keeps election records, administers a code of ethics for state public officials, and regulates lobbyists and their employers.

This introduction illustrates how state government both benefits and regulates dozens of aspects of life in Wisconsin. The following sections describe in detail the agencies that make up the executive branch of state government and the numerous services they perform each day.

Total Budget, under each agency's entry, reflects the dollars budgeted during the 2011-12 legislative session for the 2011-13 fiscal biennium (July 1, 2011 to June 30, 2013). These figures are based on the final published appropriation schedule under Chapter 20, Wisconsin Statutes, and do not include statutorily-directed funding modifications or supplemental funding adjustments.

Number of Employees are the number of full-time equivalent positions authorized in the agency's 2012-13 "adjusted base", which is the set of figures each agency uses to begin budgeting for the next biennium.

Budget and employee data provided by the Legislative Fiscal Bureau. Telephone numbers listed without an area code are Madison numbers in area code 608.

Daniel Chester French's statue, "Wisconsin", will mark it's 100th year atop the Capitol dome in 2014, spanning the administration of 22 Wisconsin governors. (Greg Anderson, Legislative Photographer)

OFFICE OF THE GOVERNOR

Governor: SCOTT WALKER.

Chief of Staff: ERIC SCHUTT.

Deputy Chief of Staff: RICH ZIPPERER.

Chief Legal Counsel: BRIAN HAGEDORN.

Senior Advisor: WAYLON HURLBURT.

Communications Director: JOCELYN WEBSTER.

Press Secretary: THOMAS EVENSON.

Senior Director of Legislative Affairs: CINDY POLZIN.

Senior Policy Advisors: KIMBERLY LIEDL, EILEEN SCHOENFELDT.

Policy Advisors: MICHAEL BRICKMAN, PATRICK HUGHES.

Budget Director: BRIAN HAYES.

Gubernatorial Appointments Director: ERIC ESSER.

Director of Constituent Services: ALAN COLVIN.

Proclamations Director: BOB NENO.

Executive Assistant: DOROTHY MOORE.

Deputy Chief of Staff for External Operations: SCOTT MATEJOV.

Director of External Communications: ANDREW DAVIS.

Director of Wisconsin Office in Washington, D.C.: WENDY RIEMANN, (202) 624-5870; 444 North Capitol Street NW, Suite 613, Washington, D.C. 20001.

Mailing Address: P.O. Box 7863, Madison 53707-7863.

Location: 115 East, State Capitol, Madison.

Telephone: 266-1212.

Office E-mail: govgeneral@wisconsin.gov

Fax: General: 267-8983.

Internet Address: www.wisgov.state.wi.us

Number of Employees: 37.25.

Total Budget 2011-13: $8,871,600.

Constitutional Reference: Article V.

Statutory Reference: Chapter 14, Subchapter I.

Agency Responsibility: As the state's chief executive, the governor represents all the people and is responsible for safeguarding the public interest. The constitution sets certain limits on the governor's powers, but the increased size and complexity of state government have given the governor's office many more responsibilities than it originally had.

The governor gives policy direction to the state and plays an important role in the legislative process. Through the biennial budget, developed and administrated in conjunction with the Department of Administration and various agency heads, the governor ultimately reviews and directs the activities of all administrative agencies. Major policy changes are highlighted in the governor's annual state of the state message and other special messages to the legislature.

The governor has other specialized powers related to the legislative process. The chief executive may call a special legislative session to deal with specific legislation, may veto an entire bill, or may veto parts of appropriation bills. In the case of either whole or partial vetoes, a two-thirds vote of the members present in each house of the legislature is required to override the governor's action.

Although various administrators direct the day-to-day operations of state agencies, the governor is considered the head of the executive branch. For the most part, the individuals, commissions, or part-time boards that head the major administrative departments are appointed by,

Governor Scott Walker greets children at La Casa de Esperanza, a community-based social and economic services organization in Waukesha, in April 2013. (Office of the Governor)

and serve at the pleasure of the governor, although many of these appointments require senate confirmation.

As the state's chief administrative officer, the governor must approve federal aid expenditures; state land purchases; highway and airport construction; land or building leases for state use; and numerous state contracts, including compacts negotiated with Indian gaming authorities. The governor may request the attorney general to protect the public interest in various legal actions.

The statutes authorize the governor to create special advisory committees or task forces to conduct studies and make recommendations. These committees frequently attract experienced citizens from many fields, who donate their time and expertise as a public service. The governor also appoints over 1,000 persons to various councils and boards, which are created by law to advise and serve state government, and personally serves on selected bodies, such as the State of Wisconsin Building Commission.

If a vacancy occurs in the state senate or assembly, state law directs the governor to call a special election. Vacancies in elective county offices and judicial positions can be filled by gubernatorial appointment for the unexpired terms or until a successor is elected. The governor may dismiss sheriffs, district attorneys, coroners, or registers of deeds for proven malfeasance.

The governor serves as commander in chief of the Wisconsin National Guard when it is called into state service during emergencies, such as natural disasters and civil disturbances. (When National Guard units perform national service, they are under command of the U.S. President.)

The chief executive has sole power to extradite a person charged with a criminal offense and to exercise executive clemency by granting a pardon, reprieve, or sentence commutation to a convicted criminal offender. The nonstatutory Pardon Advisory Board, which was created by executive order in 1980 to expedite the pardon process, reviews applications for executive clemency and makes recommendations to the governor.

History: Before Wisconsin entered the Union, the U.S. President appointed the territorial governor, but the state constitution, adopted in 1848, gave executive powers to an elected governor. Debate during the constitutional conventions revealed reluctance to change the duties traditionally performed by the chief executive. Questions regarding the post of governor concentrated instead on the amount of salary, length of term, location of residence and, above all, veto power. An effort to divest the governor of veto power failed, as did attempts to vest pardoning power in the legislature and to deny the governor power to remove county officials from office for cause.

There have been several constitutional amendments adopted over the years affecting the authority of the governor. A 1967 amendment lengthened the governor's term from 2 to 4 years, effective 1971. A constitutional amendment, ratified in 1930, empowered the governor to approve appropriation bills in part, thereby creating the partial veto. Another amendment, ratified in 1990, restricted the partial veto power by forbidding the governor to create new words by striking individual letters within words. An amendment ratified in 2008 further restricted the partial veto power by forbidding the governor from creating a new sentence by combining parts of two or more sentences.

Statutory Councils

State Council on Alcohol and Other Drug Abuse: CRAIG HARPER (designated to represent governor), SENATORS 2 vacancies; REPRESENTATIVES BIES, PASCH; TINA VIRGIL (attorney general designee), STEVE FERNAN (superintendent of public instruction designee), KEVIN MOORE (secretary of health services designee), ROGER FRINGS (commissioner of insurance designee), DENNIS BASKIN (secretary of corrections designee), RANDY ROMANSKI, SONYA SIDKY (secretary of transportation designees), CHARLOTTE RASMUSSEN (chairperson of Pharmacy Examining Board designee), DOUG ENGLEBERT (Controlled Substances Board representative), REBECCA WIGG-NINHAM (Governor's Commission on Law Enforcement and Crime representative), MICHAEL WAUPOOSE (service provider representative), SUE SHEMANSKI (nominated by Wisconsin County Human Service Association, Inc.); NORMAN BRIGGS, SANDY HARDIE, JOYCE O'DONNELL, MARY RASMUSSEN, DUNCAN SHROUT, SCOTT STOKES (public members). (All except *ex officio* members or their designees are appointed by governor.)

The State Council on Alcohol and Other Drug Abuse recommends, coordinates, and reviews the efforts of state agencies to control and prevent alcohol and drug abuse. It evaluates program effectiveness, recommends improved programming, issues reports to educate people about the dangers of drug abuse, and allocates responsibility for various alcohol and drug abuse programs among state agencies. The council also recommends legislation, cooperates with federal agencies, and receives federal funds.

The 22-member council includes 6 members with a professional, research, or personal interest in alcohol and other drug abuse problems, appointed for 4-year terms, and one of them must be a consumer representing the public. It was created by Chapter 384, Laws of 1969, as the Drug Abuse Control Commission. Chapter 219, Laws of 1971, changed its name to the Council on Drug Abuse and placed the council in the executive office. It was renamed the Council on Alcohol and Other Drug Abuse by Chapter 370, Laws of 1975, and the State Council on Alcohol and Other Drug Abuse by Chapter 221, Laws of 1979. Its composition and duties are prescribed in Sections 14.017 (2) and 14.24 of the statutes.

Council on Military and State Relations: LARRY OLSON (representative of the department of military affairs); LINDA FOURNIER (representative of Fort McCoy, Monroe County); vacancy (appointed by senate majority leader); vacancy (appointed by senate minority leader); vacancy (appointed by assembly speaker); vacancy (appointed by assembly minority leader); JAMIE AULIK (representative of the governor). (All except legislative members appointed by the governor.)

The 7-member Council on Military and State Relations assists the governor by working with the state's military installations, commands and communities, state agencies, and economic development professionals to develop and implement strategies designed to enhance those installations. It advises and assists the governor on issues related to the location of military installations and assists and cooperates with state agencies to determine how those agencies can better serve military communities and families. It also assists the efforts of military families and their support groups regarding quality-of-life issues for service members and their families. The council was created by 2005 Wisconsin Act 26 and its composition and duties are prescribed in Section 14.017 (4) of the statutes.

Read to Lead Development Council: SCOTT WALKER (governor), *chairperson;* TONY EVERS (state superintendent of public instruction), *vice chairperson;* SENATOR OLSEN (chair of senate education committee); vacancy (ranking minority member of senate education committee); REPRESENTATIVE KESTELL (chair of assembly education committee); vacancy (ranking minority member of assembly education committee); MARA BROWN, LAURA PILS (elementary and secondary education teachers or principals); vacancy (preschool teacher); MARY READ, 2 vacancies (philanthropic community representatives); TONY PEDRIANA, 2 vacancies (business community representatives); KATHY CHAMPEAU (Wisconsin State Reading Association representative); STEVE DYKSTRA (Wisconsin Reading Coalition representative); MARCIA HENRY (International Dyslexia Association representative); MICHELE ERIKSON (Wisconsin Literacy, Inc., representative); vacancy (Wisconsin Library Association representative); RACHEL LANDER (research community representative); vacancy (representative of organization serving children with disabilities). (All except *ex officio* and legislative members appointed by the governor.)

The 22-member Read to Lead Development Council makes recommendations to the governor and state superintendent of public instruction regarding recipients of literacy and early childhood development grants. It annually submits a report on its operation to the appropriate standing committees of the legislature. All except *ex officio* and legislative members are appointed by the governor to 3-year terms. The council was created by 2011 Wisconsin Act 166 and its composition and duties are prescribed in Sections 14.017 (5) and 14.20 (1m) of the statutes.

Standards Development Council: Inactive.

The 7-member Standards Development Council, created by 1997 Wisconsin Act 27, was directed to submit to the governor, by November 14, 1997, recommendations relating to pupil academic standards in mathematics, science, reading and writing, geography, and history. The act provided that if the governor approved the standards, he or she was authorized to issue them as an executive order. The council is directed to periodically review the standards and recommend changes to the governor. The composition and duties of the council are prescribed in Sections 14.017 (3) and 14.23 of the statutes.

INDEPENDENT UNIT ATTACHED FOR BUDGETING, PROGRAM COORDINATION, AND RELATED MANAGEMENT FUNCTIONS BY SECTION 15.03 OF THE STATUTES

DISABILITY BOARD

Disability Board: GOVERNOR SCOTT WALKER, CHIEF JUSTICE SHIRLEY ABRAHAMSON, SENATOR ELLIS (senate president), SENATOR LARSON (senate minority leader), REPRESENTATIVE VOS (assembly speaker), REPRESENTATIVE BARCA (assembly minority leader), ROBERT GOLDEN (dean, UW Medical School).

Statutory References: Sections 14.015 (1) and 17.025.

Agency Responsibility: The Disability Board is authorized by law to determine when a temporary disability exists in any of the constitutional offices because the incumbent is incapacitated due to illness or injury, and it may fill a temporary vacancy. The board, which was created by Chapter 422, Laws of 1969, originally had similar powers for supreme court justices and circuit court judges, but these were repealed by Chapter 449, Laws of 1977, and Chapter 332, Laws of 1975, respectively.

GOVERNOR'S APPOINTMENTS TO MISCELLANEOUS COMMITTEES AND ORGANIZATIONS

Wisconsin Humanities Council

Members: Gubernatorial appointees: JOYCE ERICKSON, MARY C. KNAPP. (The governor appoints 6 members to the council. Other members are elected by the council.)

Executive Director: DENA WORTZEL.

Address: 222 South Bedford Street, Suite F, Madison 53703-3688.

Telephone: (608) 262-0706.

Fax: (608) 263-7970.

E-mail Address: contact@wisconsinhumanities.org

Internet Address: www.wisconsinhumanities.org

Publications: Grant guidelines and a periodic newsletter.

The Wisconsin Humanities Council, an independent, nonprofit organization, was established in 1972 under the provisions of federal Public Law 89-209. Members of the council include civic leaders; representatives of business, government, labor, professional, cultural, and educational institutions; and scholars and teachers in the humanities. The council receives annual funding from the National Endowment for the Humanities, the State of Wisconsin, and other sources. It creates, and through its grant program, supports programming that uses history, culture, and discussion to strengthen community life for everyone in Wisconsin. Any nonprofit organization or institution may apply to the council for project support. In planning and presenting public programs, applicant organizations must ordinarily involve scholars with graduate degrees in the humanities.

The Medical College of Wisconsin, Inc.

Board of Trustees: Gubernatorial appointees: ELIZABETH BRENNER, CURT S. CULVER, CORY L. NETTLES, GREG WESLEY, EDWARD J. ZORE. (The governor appoints two members of the board of trustees with senate consent.)

President: JOHN RAYMOND, SR.

Mailing Address: 8701 Watertown Plank Road, P.O. Box 26509, Milwaukee 53226-0509.

Telephone: (414) 456-8225.

Fax: (414) 456-6560.

State Appropriation 2011-13: $13,858,200.

Publications: *Alumni News,* annual reports, directory of physician consultants, *Facts, Medical College of Wisconsin News, World.*

Statutory Reference: Sections 13.106, 39.15, and 39.155.

The Medical College of Wisconsin, Inc., is a private nonprofit educational corporation located in Milwaukee. The college receives a specified sum under the "student capitation" program for each Wisconsin resident it enrolls. The Higher Educational Aids Board determines whether applicants qualify as state residents. The college also receives state funds for its family medicine residency program.

The governor appoints two board of trustees members for 6-year terms. The college is required to fulfill certain reporting requirements, and the Legislative Audit Bureau conducts postaudits of expenditures made under state appropriations.

In September 1967, Marquette University terminated its sponsorship of the college, then known as the Marquette School of Medicine, Inc. To increase the supply of physicians in Wisconsin, the legislature enacted Chapter 3, Laws of 1969, which appropriated funds to the school provided Wisconsin residents received first preference for admission. The legislature made a token appropriation to test the law's constitutionality, and the Wisconsin Supreme Court ruled the law constitutional in *State ex rel. Warren v. Rueter,* 44 Wis. 2d 201 (1969). Chapter 185, Laws of 1969, fully funded state support for the college. In 1970, the college's name was changed to The Medical College of Wisconsin, Inc.

GOVERNOR'S SPECIAL COMMITTEES
June 30, 2013

The committees described in this section include those Governor Scott Walker created or continued. Most of the committees were created under Section 14.019, Wisconsin Statutes, which provides that "the governor may, by executive order, create nonstatutory committees in such number and with such membership as desired, to conduct such studies and to advise the governor in such matters as directed." Committee members serve at the pleasure of the governor.

Unless terminated sooner, a special committee expires automatically on the fourth Monday of January of the year in which a new gubernatorial term begins. The governor may, however, provide for its continued existence by executive order. In that event, existing members continue to serve unless they resign or until the governor replaces them.

The law also provides that the governor may designate an employee of the Office of the Governor or of the Department of Administration to coordinate the activities of nonstatutory committees. In some cases, the governor has ordered other state agencies to staff and financially support committees.

When a new gubernatorial term begins, each committee is required to submit a final report to the governor or governor-elect prior to the new term. Copies of each final report and any other report a special committee prepared must be submitted to the Reference and Loan Library in the Department of Public Instruction for distribution under Section 35.83 (3), Wisconsin Statutes.

Section 20.505 (1) (ka), Wisconsin Statutes, provides for the expenses of special committees created by executive order. In addition, certain committees receive specific state appropriations, and some receive federal funds because they are established in response to federal program requirements.

The special committees are listed in alphabetical order by the key word in each committee name.

Council on Autism

Members: NISSAN BAR-LEV, WENDY COOMER, TERRI ENTERS, VIVIAN HAZELL, ROSALIA HELMS, MILANA MILLAN, GLEN SALLOWS, PAM STOIKA, BRADLEY THOMPSON, MICHAEL WILLIAMS.

Contact person: JULIE BRYDA, julie.bryda@wisconsin.gov

Address: Department of Health Services, 1 West Wilson Street, P.O. Box 7851, Madison 53707-7851.

Telephone: (414) 874-1681.

Governor Jim Doyle created the council in Executive Order 94, April 5, 2005, to meet quarterly and advise the Department of Health Services on strategies for implementing statewide supports and services for children with autism. It was recreated by Governor Walker in Executive Order 6, January 21, 2011. Of the maximum 15 members appointed by the governor to the council, at least a majority must be parents of children with autism or autism spectrum disorders. The remaining members may be providers of services to children with autism, local government officials, persons who are knowledgeable of autism issues, or simply members of the general public.

Bicycle Coordinating Council

Members: DAVID SPIEGELBERG (designated by secretary of tourism); BRIGIT BROWN (designated by secretary of natural resources); JILL MROTEK GLENZINSKI (designated by secretary of transportation); RANDY THIEL (designated by state superintendent of public instruction); JON MORGAN (designated by secretary of health services); LARRY CORSI (designated by director, Department of Transportation, Bureau of Transportation Safety); SENATOR OLSEN (appointed by senate majority leader), SENATOR SHILLING (appointed by senate minority leader); REPRESENTATIVE RIPP (appointed by assembly speaker), REPRESENTATIVE HULSEY (appointed by assembly minority leader); CHRISTOPHER S. FORTUNE, KEVIN HARDMAN, CRAIG A. HEYWOOD, KRYSTYNA KORNILOWICZ, BRENDA MAXWELL (public members).

Contact person: JILL MROTEK GLENZINSKI, jill.mrotekglenzinski@dot.wi.gov

Governor Scott Walker and Adjutant General Don Dunbar tour forest fire damage in Bayfield and Douglas Counties in May 2013. (Office of the Governor)

Address: Department of Transportation, P.O. Box 7913, Madison 53707-7913.

Telephone: 267-7757.

Governor Tommy G. Thompson created the council in Executive Order 122, June 24, 1991, and Governor Walker most recently recreated it in Executive Order 6, January 21, 2011. A similar council was originally created by Governor Patrick J. Lucey in June 1977 under Executive Order 43, and it has been recreated several times since. The council consists of not more than 17 members. The council considers all matters relating to: efforts of state agencies to encourage the use of the bicycle as an alternative means of transportation; promoting bicycle safety and education; promoting safe bicycling to school; promoting bicycling as a recreational and tourist activity; and disseminating information on state and federal funding for bicycle programs. The council also reviews the bicycle programs of state agencies, issues reports to the governor and the legislature, and makes recommendations concerning pertinent legislation.

State of Wisconsin Citizen Corps Council

Members: appointments pending.

Contact person: MICHAEL JORDAN, Office of Justice Assistance, 261-7529.

Governor Jim Doyle created the council in Executive Order 67, September 8, 2004. It was most recently recreated by Governor Walker in Executive Order 9 on January 25, 2011, to act as a statewide advisory council to encourage community participation in domestic preparedness through public education, training, and volunteer service. The council provides information and recommendations to the governor, the legislature, and the public regarding the operation, program priorities, and allocation of funds for the Wisconsin Citizen Corps initiative.

Wisconsin Coastal Management Council

Members: LARRY MACDONALD, *chairperson;* vacancy, *vice chairperson;* SENATOR WIRCH; REPRESENTATIVE WEATHERSTON; JAMES P. HURLEY (UW System representative), ED EBERLE (designated by secretary of administration), STEPHEN GALARNEAU (designated by secretary of natural resources), SHERI WALZ (designated by secretary of transportation); ERVIN SOULIER (tribal government representative); Sharon Cook (City of Milwaukee representative); Robert D. Browne, John Dickert, Patricia Hoeft, Kenneth L. Leinbach, William Schuster.

Contact person: Mike Friis.

Address: Wisconsin Coastal Management Program, Department of Administration, 101 East Wilson Street, 9th Floor, P.O. Box 8944, Madison 53708-8944.

Telephone: 267-7982.

Fax: 267-6917.

Internet Address: http://coastal.wisconsin.gov

Acting Governor Martin J. Schreiber established the council in Executive Order 49, October 7, 1977. It has been recreated or revised several times, and was continued most recently by Governor Walker in Executive Order 6, January 21, 2011. It succeeded the Coastal Coordinating and Advisory Council appointed by Governor Patrick J. Lucey in 1974. The 1977 council was created to comply with provisions of the federal Coastal Zone Management Act of 1972 and to implement Wisconsin's official Coastal Management Program, which received federal approval on May 22, 1978. The council advises the governor on issues pertaining to the Great Lakes coasts and assists in providing policy direction for Wisconsin's coastal management efforts. Members represent the legislature, state agencies, units of local government, tribal governments, and citizens. To provide opportunities for full participation in the program, the governor encouraged the council to establish citizens' committees to advise the council on key issues affecting the coasts. The council endorsed "Wisconsin Coastal Management Program: Needs Assessment and Multi-Year Strategy, 2011-2015" in February 2011. Annually since 2002, the program has produced the *Wisconsin Great Lakes Chronicle.* Archived copies are available from the Wisconsin Coastal Management Program's Web site.

College and Workforce Readiness Council

Members: Tim Sullivan (governor's designee), *chairperson;* Senator Fitzgerald (senate majority leader); Senator Larson (senate minority leader); Representative Farrow (speaker's designee); Representative Barca (assembly minority leader); Tony Evers (superintendent of public instruction); Eloise Anderson (secretary of children and families); Reggie Newson (secretary of workforce development); Renée Wachter (President, UW System designee); Annette Severson (Wisconsin technical college board president designee); Rolf Wegenke (Wisconsin Association of Independent Colleges and Universities president); James Crawford (tribal representative); Laura Cataldo (worker representative); John Zorbini (employer representative); Jeffrey Clark (small business representative).

Governor Walker created the council in Executive Order 56, January 13, 2012, to recommend policies and programs to improve student readiness for college or a career in the state. The council is charged with prioritizing improvement in the reduction of dropout and remediation rates, along with income and racial achievement gaps; increasing the overall number of degrees and certificates awarded; expanding dual enrollment and credit opportunities to middle and high school students; designing shorter, less costly degree programs to fill highly-needed positions while promoting and supporting technical career pathways for students; and easing the transition between institutions, specifically through credit transfer and the granting of credit for on-the-job training and work experience.

The council is made up of 15 members, including the governor, the leadership of the state legislature, the state superintendent, the secretaries of the department of workforce development and the department of children and families, the presidents of the UW system; technical college system and Wisconsin Association of Independent Colleges and Universities (or the designees of all of the former), as well as four members appointed by and serving at the pleasure of the governor, including representatives of Wisconsin tribes, workers, employers, and the small business community.

Statewide Criminal Justice Coordinating Council

Members: Edward F. Wall (secretary of corrections), *cochairperson;* J.B. Van Hollen (attorney general), *cochairperson;* John Murray (executive director, Office of Justice Assistance); Kelli Thompson (State Public Defender); Matthew Joski (county sheriff); Brad

KEIL (chief of police); DAVID O'LEARY (district attorney); JOHN VOELKER (director of state courts); REGGIE NEWSON (secretary of workforce development); ELOISE ANDERSON (secretary of children and families); KITTY RHOADES (secretary of health services); C. WILLIAM FOUST (chair of chief judges of circuit courts); MARK ABELES-ALLISON (county administrator); vacancy (county criminal justice coordinating council representative); JANE JENNINGS (crime victims representative); MARK CLEMENTS, MALLORY O'BRIEN (public members); PATTI JO SEVERSON (mental health and criminal justice representative); RICH VAN BOXTEL (tribal representative).

Address: Office of Justice Assistance, 1 South Pinckney Street, Suite 615, Madison 53703-3220.

Telephone: 266-3323.

Internet Address: oja.state.wi.us/policy/statewide-criminal-justice-coordinating-council

The statewide council was created by Governor Walker in Executive Order 65 on April 9, 2012. It is tasked with developing criminal justice policy recommendations to strengthen public safety and the justice system; investigate effective and innovative criminal justice-related programs employed at the county level, encourage the development of county or multi-county criminal justice coordinating councils; provide recommendations on the collection and synthesis of real-time criminal justice data, and with the aid of all executive branch agencies, develop and make recommendations to implement a reporting system to track key criminal justice indicators on a monthly basis; promote the evaluation of new and current criminal justice policies; and provide strategic planning and guidance for the management of federal grants.

The council must submit an annual report to the governor, the chief justice, and the chief clerk of each house. It meets on a quarterly basis. The Office of Justice Assistance provides staff and support for the council.

Governor's Committee for People With Disabilities

Members: JOSEPH MIELCZAREK, JR., *chairperson;* JEFF FOX (Council on Physical Disabilities), *vice chairperson;* JOANNE STEPHENS (Council on Mental Health); RAMSEY LEE (Board for People with Developmental Disabilities); ALEX H. SLAPPEY (Council for the Deaf and Hard of Hearing); MARK JANOWIAK (Council on Blindness); vacancy (State Council on Alcohol and Other Drug Abuse); WAYNE COREY, THOMAS FELL, DANIEL LAATSCH, NANCY LEIPZIG, JOHN W. OLSON, SANDRA POPP (at-large members). Nonvoting *ex officio* member: LT. GOVERNOR KLEEFISCH.

Address: 1 West Wilson Street, Room 518, Madison 53703.

Telephone: 266-7816.

Fax: 266-3386.

The Wisconsin Governor's Committee for People with Disabilities in its present form was established in March of 1976 by Governor Patrick J. Lucey, and has been reauthorized through executive order by every governor since that time. It was most recently recreated by Governor Walker in Executive Order 6 on January 21, 2011. The original executive order provided initial guidance for the committee to advise the governor's office on a broad range of issues affecting people with disabilities. The committee's mission, "to enhance the health and general well-being of disabled citizens in Wisconsin", was created out of a realization that state government lacked a process of systematically communicating the needs of people with disabilities to responsible state and local officials. In an effort to enhance the value of the committee, the executive order was rewritten in 2004 to support a focus on issues, policies, and programs that will encourage involvement in the workforce.

The committee consists of the Lieutenant Governor as a nonvoting, *ex officio* member, and not more than 20 members, appointed by the governor to serve at his pleasure. The committee as a whole includes Wisconsin residents with disabilities and individuals that have demonstrated interest in the concerns of all disability groups. All serve as unpaid volunteers. Six of the committee members represent specific disability constituencies: 1) Council on Blindness; 2) Wisconsin Council for the Deaf and Hard of Hearing; 3) Wisconsin Board for People with Developmental Disabilities; 4) Wisconsin Council on Mental Health; 5) State Council on Alcohol and Other Drug Abuse; and 6) Council on Physical Disabilities.

The committee meets quarterly, usually in March, June, September, and December. In addition to the Executive Committee, the Governor's Committee also has two subcommittees: the Business Leadership Network Subcommittee and the Youth Leadership Forum Subcommittee.

Early Childhood Advisory Council

Members: ELOISE ANDERSON (secretary of children and families), TONY EVERS (state superintendent of public instruction), *cochairpersons;* THERESE AHLERS, NANCY ARMBRUST, JOHN ASHLEY, FREDI BOVE, SHEILA BRIGGS, DAN BURKHALTER, DAVE EDIE, MORNA FOY, DELORES GOKEE-RINDAL, BESSIE GRAY, JILL HOITING, JENNIFER JONES, JILL KEENLANCE, PETER KELLY, KIA LABRACKE, LINDA LEONHART, MARY MADSEN, LUPE MARTINEZ, KEVIN MOORE, JUDY NORMAN-NUNNERY, GAIL PROPSOM, KEVIN REILLY, CAROLYN STANFORD TAYLOR, JON STELLMACHER, ANN TERRELL, JENNIFER THAYER, EDWARD F. WALL, ROLF WEGENKE.

Internet Address: dcf.wi.gov/ecac

Governor Jim Doyle created the council in Executive Order 269 on October 30, 2008, in accordance with Federal Public Law 110-134. It was recreated by Governor Walker in Executive Order 6, on January 21, 2011. The council makes recommendations to the governor regarding development of a comprehensive statewide early childhood system. Responsibilities of the council include the following: conducting needs assessments; identifying barriers to collaboration between federal and state programs; developing recommendations for increasing participation of children in early childhood services; developing recommendations for a unified data collection system; supporting professional development; assessing the capacity of higher education to support the development of early childhood professionals; and making recommendations to improve early learning standards.

Early Intervention Interagency Coordinating Council

Members: CINDY FLAUGER, *chairperson;* LAURICE LINCOLN, *vice chairperson;* vacancy (state legislator); JULIE WALSH (designated by commissioner of insurance), LINDA HUFFER (Department of Health Services, Division of Long-Term Care designee), SHARON FLEISCHFRESSER (Department of Health Services, Division of Public Health designee), LAURA SATERFIELD (State Office of Child Care designee), JENNY GILES (Department of Public Instruction designee); WILLIAM BARREAU, VICTORIA DEER, TERRI ENTERS, LARA KAIN, LINDA LEONHART, THERESA VINCENT.

Contact person: JACQUELINE MOSS, jacqueline.moss@dhs.wisconsin.gov

Address: Department of Health Services, 1 West Wilson Street, P.O. Box 7851, Madison 53707-7851.

Governor Tommy G. Thompson first established the council in Executive Order 17, June 26, 1987, and recreated it in Executive Order 334, May 21, 1998. Governor Walker most recently recreated it in Executive Order 6, January 21, 2011. Often called the "Birth to Three" Council, it was created to comply with the federal Individuals With Disabilities Education Act of 1986 and recreated to comply with the federal Individuals With Disabilities Education Act of 1997. The council advises and assists the Department of Health Services in the development and administration of early intervention services for infants and toddlers with developmental delays and their families. It consists of at least 15 members and is directed by the governor to include at least 4 parents of infants, toddlers, or children aged 12 or younger with disabilities; at least 4 private or public providers of early intervention services; at least one state legislator; at least one member involved in personnel training; at least one representative of a Head Start agency or program; and other members representing state agencies that provide services or payment for early intervention services to infants and toddlers and their families. Members, other than those serving *ex officio,* serve 3-year terms. Administrative and support services are provided to the council by the Department of Health Services. The council issues an annual report for each federal fiscal year.

Governor's Council on Financial Literacy

Members: WENDY BAUMANN, PETER BILDSTEN, JENNIFER BLOCK, JO ANNE BURRIS, J. MICHAEL COLLINS, RAYMOND DEPERRY, TONY EVERS, KRISTINE HACKBARTH HORN, JAIMES JOHNSON, AMY KERWIN, ALEXANDER KIEFER, KENNETH KING, HOWARD MARKLEIN, MERIDEE MAYNARD, MARY

Ann McCoshen, Ted Nickel, M. Scott Niederjohn, Rita O'Brien, Luther Olsen, James Podewils, Victor Rodriquez, Pablo Sanchez, Alejo Torres.

Governor Jim Doyle created the council in Executive Order 92, March 30, 2005, to work with existing state agencies, private entities, and nonprofit associations in improving the financial literacy of Wisconsin citizens. It was recently recreated by Governor Walker in Executive Order 24, April 6, 2011. The council is directed to collaborate with the Office of the Commissioner of Insurance, implement research and policy initiatives, and serve as sounding board for the Office of the Governor and the Office of Financial Literacy in the Department of Financial Institutions to provide guidance and develop strategies to improve financial literacy among Wisconsin's citizens. The council will also promote the statewide financial literacy awareness and education campaign entitled Money Smart Week Wisconsin. The council consists of 25 members or less, with a chairperson, and two vice chairpersons selected from within the group. The Secretary of the Department of Financial Institutions is required to submit an annual progress report on the council.

Historical Records Advisory Board

Members: Menzi L. Behrnd-Klodt, Clayborn Benson, Matthew Blessing, Anita T. Doering, Maria Escalante, Jane M. Pederson, Rick Pifer, Jane Schetter, Michelle Sweetser, Kenneth J. Wirth.

Coordinator: Matthew Blessing, matt.blessing@wisconsinhistory.org

Address: 816 State Street, Madison 53706.

Telephone: 264-6480.

Governor Patrick J. Lucey created the advisory board on April 4, 1977. It was most recently continued by Governor Walker in Executive Order 6, January 21, 2011. That action enables the state to participate in the grants program of the National Historical Publications and Records Commission, which coordinates the preservation of historic records in the United States and approves federal grants to qualified Wisconsin institutions and to the state advisory board. The board promotes the availability and use of historical records as keys to improved understanding of our cultural heritage. Members serve staggered 3-year terms.

Homeland Security Council

Members: Brigadier General Donald P. Dunbar, *chairperson;* Henry Anderson, Susan Buroker, David Cagigal, David Erwin, Stephen Fitzgerald, Gregory Leck, Bradley Liggett, David Mahoney, Dave Matthews, Phil Montgomery, John Murray, Steven Riffel, Brian Satula, Edward F. Wall, David Woodbury.

Contact persons: Randi Milsap, randi.milsap@wisconsin.gov; Lori Getter, lori.getter@wisconsin.gov

Address: 2400 Wright Street, P.O. Box 14587, Madison 53708.

Telephones: 242-3072 or 242-3239.

Fax: 242-3082.

Internet Address: http://homelandsecurity.wi.gov

Governor Jim Doyle created the council in Executive Order 7, March 18, 2003, to advise the governor and to coordinate the efforts of state and local agencies regarding the prevention of, and response to, potential threats to the homeland security of the state. It was recently recreated by Governor Walker in Executive Order 101 on May 3, 2013. The council's 16 members are appointed by and serve at the pleasure of the governor. The council works with federal, state, and local agencies, nonprofit organizations, and private industry to prevent and respond to any threat of terrorism, promote personal preparedness, and make recommendations to the governor on additional steps to further enhance Wisconsin's homeland security.

Independent Living Council of Wisconsin

Members: Tim Sheehan (director of a center for independent living); Tamara Jandrowski (independent living program representative); Stephen J. West (representative of the directors of Native American Vocational Rehabilitation programs); Marilee Adamski-Smith, Benjamin

Governor Scott Walker visits with employees at Rust-Oleum in Pleasant Prairie in June 2013. *(Office of the Governor)*

BARRETT, CYNTHIA BENTLEY, PETER EARLE, CHRIS HENDRICKSON, DEBRA LANGHAM, RON JANSEN, AUGUST KRIESER, LEWIS TYLER, vacancy. Nonvoting members: KATHLEEN ENDERS (representing Department of Workforce Development, Division of Vocational Rehabilitation), vacancy (representing Department of Health Services), STEVEN KRIESER (representing Department of Transportation), vacancy (representing Department of Administration, Division of Housing).

Contact person: MIKE BACHHUBER.

Address: 3810 Milwaukee Street, Madison 53714.

Telephones: 256-9257; (866) 656-4010 (toll free); TTY: use 711 telecommunications relay.

Fax: 256-9301.

Internet Address: www.ilcw.org

Governor Tommy G. Thompson created the council in Executive Order 212, January 10, 1994, to comply with the 1992 amendments to the federal Rehabilitation Act of 1973. In 2004, Governor Jim Doyle issued Executive Order 65, which outlines the current membership and established the council as a nonprofit entity. Governor Walker most recently recreated the council in Executive Order 6, January 21, 2011. In coordination with the Division of Vocational Rehabilitation, the council has the responsibility to develop and submit the state plan for independent living services for people with disabilities to state and federal agencies; monitor, review, and evaluate the state plan; and related purposes.

The council currently consists of 14 voting members and 4 *ex officio* members representing the Department of Workforce Development, the Department of Health Services, the Department of Transportation, and the Department of Administration's Division of Housing. The majority of members must be persons with disabilities who do not work for a center for independent living or the State of Wisconsin. At least one member must be a director of a center for independent living chosen by centers for independent living, and at least one must be a representative of the directors of Native American vocational rehabilitation programs. Voting members of the council serve staggered 3-year terms and may serve no more than two consecutive terms.

Governor's Information Technology Executive Steering Committee

Members: CHRIS SCHOENHERR (department of administration representative), *chairperson;* JOAN HANSEN (department of children and families representative); SCOTT LEGWOLD (department of corrections representative); JONATHAN BARRY (department of workforce development representative); KEVIN MOORE (department of health services representative); MATT MORONEY (department of natural resources representative); JACK JABLONSKI (department of revenue representative); SUSAN BUROKER (department of agriculture, trade and consumer protection representative); MICHAEL BERG (department of transportation representative); DAVID CAGIGAL (State Chief Information Officer).

Contact person: VICKY HALVERSON, vicky.halverson@wisconsin.gov

Telephone: 264-9578.

The committee was created by Governor Walker's Executive Order 99 on April 26, 2013. It is a governance body responsible for the effective and efficient application of information technology (IT) assets across the state for the delivery of services to the constituents of the state. Specifically its purpose is to establish enterprise IT and IT procurement strategies, policies direction, and standards for state agencies.

The members consist of senior executive business leaders from the departments of Administration, Children and Families, Corrections, Workforce Development, Health Services, Natural Resources, Revenue, Agriculture, Trade and Consumer Protection, Transportation, and the State Chief Information Officer, or the designees of any. All cabinet-level agencies are directed to consult and align their IT efforts with the committee. The Department of Administration's Division of Enterprise Technology provides staff support to the committee.

Governor's Judicial Selection Advisory Committee

Members: MICHAEL BRENNAN, *chairperson;* WILLIAM CURRAN, DONALD DAUGHERTY, STEVEN GIBBS, KATHERINE LONGLEY, LON ROBERTS.

Contact person: BRIAN HAGEDORN, brian.hagedorn@wisconsin.gov

Address: Office of the Governor, Room 115 East, State Capitol, P.O. Box 7863, Madison 53707-7863.

Telephone: 266-1212.

Governor Anthony Earl established the Governor's Advisory Council on Judicial Selection in Executive Order 1, January 6, 1983. Governor Walker most recently recreated and restructured it as an advisory committee in Executive Order 29, May 11, 2011. The council makes recommendations to the governor on filling vacancies in the state court system. The committee consists of any number of individuals as determined by the governor. Members serve for 12-month renewable terms. The governor designates the chairperson, who has discretion to determine the method by which applicants are considered and recommended. The chairperson also has the authority to appoint temporary members.

Governor's Juvenile Justice Commission

Members: CARL ASHLEY, THEODORE ENGELBART, ANDREW FABRY, JOSE FLORES, TIERNEY GILL, STEVEN GLAMM, DAVID HUESEMANN, EDDIE JACKSON, TASHA JENKINS, JESSICA JIMENEZ, KENDALL KELLEY, TED LEWIS, KATHLEEN MALONE, ERIC MEAUX, JAMES MOESER, WILLIAM NEITZEL, DAVID NORTHCUTT, JANET PROCTOR, EDWARD ROSS, CARI TAYLOR, MINDY TEMPELIS, HANNAH VOGEL, ANNETTE ZIEGLER.

Address: Office of Justice Assistance, 1 South Pinckney Street, Suite 600, Madison 53702-0001.

Telephone: 266-3323.

Fax: 266-6676.

Governor Tommy G. Thompson created the commission as the Juvenile Justice Advisory Group in Executive Order 55, January 30, 1989, repealed and recreated it as the Governor's Juvenile Justice Commission in Executive Order 110, February 6, 1991, and Governor Walker continued it most recently in Executive Order 8, January 25, 2011. The commission awards funds received by the state under the federal Juvenile Justice and Delinquency Prevention Act, the Juvenile Accountability Block Grant, and other state and federal programs. It also advises the governor and the legislature on juvenile justice issues. The Office of Justice Assistance provides staff and pays the expenses of the commission.

Pardon Advisory Board

Members: Inactive.

Governor Lee Sherman Dreyfus originally created the Pardon Advisory Board in Executive Order 39, March 6, 1980. Governor Walker most recently recreated the board in Executive Order 20, March 16, 2011.

Governor's Council on Physical Fitness and Health

Members: KENNETH BERG, AMY DELONG, LEROY DEPAS, ELIZABETH FARAH, CARL HEIGL, JILL HOITING, SUSAN KUNFERMAN, SHANYN LANCASTER, LINDA LEE, KIMBERLY LIEDL (designated by governor), ERIN LORANG, KAREN MCKEOWN (designated by secretary of health services).

Contact persons: KAREN MCKEOWN, karen.mckeown@dhs.wisconsin.gov

Address: Department of Health Services, 1 West Wilson Street, Madison 53703.

Telephones: 267-7828.

Governor Anthony Earl established the council in Executive Order 10, April 19, 1983, and Governor Walker most recently recreated it in Executive Order 73, June 18, 2012. The council is directed to develop policy recommendations to improve the status of children's health, physical fitness and nutritional intake, as well as educate the public and media on the importance of those goals. It is also to encourage stakeholder and community leaders to assist in preventing obesity in all state residents throughout their lives.

The Department of Health Services provides staff support to the council, which consists of no less than nine members and no more than 15. Members include the governor, the secretary of Health Services or the designees of both, and citizen members appointed and serving at the pleasure of the governor.

State Rehabilitation Council

Members: LINDA VEGOE (client assistance programs), *chairperson;* JAMES DOBRINSKA (business, industry and labor representative), *vice chairperson;* ROBERT BUETTNER (disability advocacy groups), *secretary/treasurer;* MATTHEW ZELLMER (parent training and information center); ALVIN HILL (community rehabilitation program service provider); RONALD JANSEN (Statewide Independent Living Council); JULIE FERCHOFF (vocational rehabilitation counselor); ROXAN PEREZ (business, industry and labor representative); CAYTE ANDERSON, STEPHANIE DRUM, JODI HANNA, KRISTIN STERN (disability advocacy groups); PATRICIA LERCH (Native American vocational rehabilitation); WENDI DAWSON (Department of Public Instruction). Nonvoting member: MICHAEL GRECO (administrator, Division of Vocational Rehabilitation).

Contact person: KRISTIN ROLLING, kristin.rolling@dwd.wisconsin.gov

Address: Division of Vocational Rehabilitation, 201 East Washington Avenue, P.O. Box 7852, Madison 53707-7852.

Telephone: 261-0077.

Governor Tommy G. Thompson created the council in Executive Order 363, January 30, 1999, to advise the Department of Workforce Development on the statewide vocational rehabilitation plan for disabled individuals required under 29 U.S. Code Section 720, *et seq.* Governor Walker most recently continued the council in Executive Order 6, January 21, 2011. The council is similar to one established in Executive Order 196, July 1, 1993, as the State Rehabilitation Advisory Council. Council members serve 3-year terms. A majority must be individuals with disabilities not employed by the Department of Workforce Development, Division of Vocational Rehabilitation Services. The administrator of that division is a nonvoting *ex officio* member of the council.

Wisconsin Technology Committee

Members: Wisconsin Technology Council chair, vice chair, president, secretary and treasurer.

Contact person: TOM STILL, *president.*

Address: 455 Science Drive, Suite 240, Madison 53711.

Telephone: 442-7557.

The committee was created Governor Walker in Executive Order 51, November 4, 2011. It is an advisory committee consisting of the members of the Wisconsin Technology Council, which was created by state legislation as non-profit corporation, but removed from the statutes with the repeal of the Department of Commerce. Creation of the committee allows the Council to coordinate with state government. The Council assists the state in promoting the creation, development and retention of science- and technology-based businesses by developing programs that stimulate innovation and entrepreneurial activity. It also provides policy guidance to lawmakers. It provides an annual report to the appropriate standing committee of each house of the legislature.

The five members of the committee include the chair, vice-chair, president, secretary and treasurer of the Wisconsin Technology Council.

Telecommunications Relay Service Council

Members: THOMAS E. HARBISON, *chairperson;* RONALD E. BYINGTON, MARGARET CALTEAUX, JILL COLLINS, CHERI FRENCH, DAVID FRIGEN, KAREN E. JORGENSEN, TOM MEITNER, HELEN RIZZI, vacancy.

Contact person: JACK R. CASSELL, jack.cassell@wisconsin.gov

Address: Division of Enterprise Technology, Department of Administration, 101 East Wilson Street, 8th Floor, P.O. Box 7844, Madison 53707-7844.

Telephones: 234-4781; TTY: 267-6934.

Fax: 266-2164.

Governor Tommy G. Thompson created the council in Executive Order 95, June 19, 1990, recreated it in Executive Order 131, October 2, 1991, and Governor Walker continued it most recently in Executive Order 6, January 21, 2011. The council was directed to advise the Bureau of Telecommunications Management in the Department of Administration on the feasibility or desirability of: establishing requirements and procedures for a telecommunications relay service; requiring the service to be available 24 hours a day, 7 days a week; requiring users to pay rates that are no greater than rates for functionally equivalent voice telecommunications service; prohibiting relay service operators from refusing or limiting the length of calls; prohibiting relay service operators from disclosing the contents of calls, keeping records of their contents beyond the duration of the calls, and intentionally altering the content of a call; requiring relay service operators to take training on the problems faced by hearing-impaired and speech-impaired persons using the service; and authorizing the establishment by contract of a statewide telecommunications relay service. The council consists of not more than 11 members, 4 of whom must use a telecommunications relay service. These must include one speech-impaired person, one hearing-impaired person, one speech- and hearing-impaired person, and one person not having a speech or hearing impairment. Five of the members must include one representative each from the Wisconsin Association of the Deaf, Wisconsin Telecommunications, Inc., Wisconsin State Telephone Association, a local exchange telecommunications utility, and an interexchange telecommunications utility doing business in this state.

Governor's Council on Workforce Investment

Members: MARY ISBISTER, *chairperson;* MICHAEL LASZKIEWICZ, *vice chairperson;* REGGIE NEWSON, *executive director;* DAVID BRUKARDT, ALLEN BUECHEL, JEFFREY CLARK, TONY EVERS, MORNA FOY, ROBERT GERBITZ, DANIEL HARTUNG, GRAILING JONES, THERESA JONES, JULIE LASSA, TERRY McGOWAN, DAN MELLA, DAVID MITCHELL, ALAN OLSON, ALAN PETELINSEK, WARREN PETRYK, DAWN PRATT, MARK REIHL, SARIT SINGHAL, HOWARD TEETER, TOM TIFFANY, ROBIN VOS, DANIEL P. VRAKAS, BRIAN WHITE, WYMAN WINSTON, JOSH ZEPNICK.

Contact person: LISA BOYD, lisa.boyd@dwd.wisconsin.gov

Address: Department of Workforce Development, P.O. Box 7946, Madison 53707-7946.

Telephone: 266-3485.

Governor Tommy G. Thompson created the council in Executive Order 385, November 17, 1999, and Governor Walker most recently continued it in Executive Order 100, May 2, 2013, to qualify the state to receive federal funds allotted under the Workforce Investment Act (WIA) of 1998. The council consists of members appointed in accordance with federal law and additional members the governor may designate. As specified by law, the majority of members are from the private sector. The governor directed the council to carry out the duties and functions prescribed in WIA, Public Law 105-220; to advise the governor on workforce development strategy and policy, and undertake research and other activities to assist the governor in enhancing the operation and performance of workforce programs in the state; and advance other initiatives to support a skilled workforce. The governor further directed that all appropriate state agencies work together on the council and at the local level to develop a strong, skilled workforce for Wisconsin's future.

Governor Scott Walker delivers the State of the State Address in the Assembly Chamber in the State Capitol on January 15, 2013. (Office of the Governor)

STATE OFFICERS APPOINTED BY THE GOVERNOR
AS REQUIRED BY STATUTE
June 30, 2013

Officers[1]	Name	Home Address[2]	Term Expires[3]	Salary or Per Diem[4]
*Accounting Examining Board	Steve Corbeille	Marinette	July 1, 2013	$25 per day
	Glenn Michaelsen	Brookfield	July 1, 2013	$25 per day
Secs. 15.08, 15.405 (1)	Kathleen LaBrake[5]	Wausau	July 1, 2014	$25 per day
	Marion Wozniak	Edgerton	July 1, 2014	$25 per day
	John Scheid[5]	Milwaukee	July 1, 2015	$25 per day
	Todd Craft[5]	Hartland	July 1, 2016	$25 per day
	Gerald Denor[5]	Menomonee Falls	July 1, 2017	$25 per day
Adjutant General Sec. 15.31	Brig. Gen Donald P. Dunbar		Sept. 1, 2012	Group 4
*Administration, Dept. of, Secy. Secs. 15.05 (1) (a), 15.10	Michael Huebsch	West Salem	Pleasure of Gov.	Group 8
Adult Offender Supervision Board, Interstate	Tamara Grigsby	Milwaukee	May 1, 2011	None
	Gregory Potter	Wisconsin Rapids	May 1, 2013	None
Sec. 15.145 (3)	Karalyn Downing	Madison	May 1, 2015	None
	Colleen Winston	Verona	May 1, 2015	None
Adult Offender Supervision Board, Interstate Compact Administrator Sec. 304.16 (2)(d)	Tracy Hudrlik	Madison	May 1, 2017	None
*Aerospace Authority, Wis.	Thomas Crabb	Middleton	June 30, 2010	None
Sec. 114.61	Judith Schieble	Sheboygan	June 30, 2010	None
	Thomas Mullooly	Wauwatosa	June 30, 2011	None
	Edward Wagner	Marshfield	June 30, 2011	None
	Mark Hanna	Sheboygan	June 30, 2012	None
	Mark Lee	Middleton	June 30, 2012	None
Affirmative Action, Council on	David Dunham	Madison	July 1, 2011	None
	Eileen Hocker	Madison	July 1, 2011	None
Secs. 15.09 (1)(a),	Sandra Ryan	Madison	July 1, 2011	None
15.105 (29)(d)	Ronald Shaheed	Milwaukee	July 1, 2011	None
	Nancy Vue	Madison	July 1, 2011	None
	Thresessa Childs	Milwaukee	July 1, 2012	None
	Janice Hughes	Fitchburg	July 1, 2012	None
	John Magerus	Racine	July 1, 2012	None
	James Parker	La Crosse	July 1, 2012	None
	Yolanda Santos Adams	Kenosha	July 1, 2012	None
	Lakshmi Bharadwaj	Milwaukee	July 1, 2013	None
*Aging and Long-Term Care, Board on	Dale Taylor	Eau Claire	May 1, 2015	None
	Terry Lynch	Racine	May 1, 2016	None
Secs. 15.07 (1)(b) 9,	Eva Arnold[5]	Beloit	May 1, 2017	None
15.105 (10)	Barbara Bechtel	Brown Deer	May 1, 2017	None
	Tanya Meyer[5]	Gleason	May 1, 2017	None
	Michael Brooks[5]	Oshkosh	May 1, 2018	None
	James Surprise	Wautoma	May 1, 2018	None
*Agriculture, Trade and Consumer Protection,	Richard Cates	Spring Green	May 1, 2013	Not exc. $35 per day nor $1,000 per yr.
Board of	Michael Dummer	Holmen	May 1, 2015	Not exc. $35 per day nor $1,000 per yr.
Secs. 15.07 (1)(a), 15.07 (5)(d), 15.13	John Koepke	Oconomowoc	May 1, 2015	Not exc. $35 per day nor $1,000 per yr.
	Andre Diercks	Coloma	May 1, 2017	Not exc. $35 per day nor $1,000 per yr.
	Miranda Leis	Cashton	May 1, 2017	Not exc. $35 per day nor $1,000 per yr.
	Mark Schleitwiler	Green Bay	May 1, 2017	Not exc. $35 per day nor $1,000 per yr.
	Dennis Badtke	Rosendale	May 1, 2019	Not exc. $35 per day nor $1,000 per yr.
	Nicole Hansen[5]	Necedah	May 1, 2019	Not exc. $35 per day nor $1,000 per yr.
	Dean Strauss	Sheboygan Falls	May 1, 2019	Not exc. $35 per day nor $1,000 per yr.
*Agriculture, Trade and Consumer Protection, Dept. of, Secy. Secs. 15.05 (1)(d), 15.07 (1)	Ben Brancel	Endeavor	Pleas. of Gov.	Group 6
Alcohol and Other Drug Abuse, State Council on	Craig Harper	Whitefish Bay	Pleas. of Gov.	None
	Mark C. Seidl	Algoma	Pleas. of Gov.	None
Secs. 14.017 (2), 15.09	Michael Waupoose	Madison	Pleas. of Gov.	None
	Rebecca Wigg-Ninham	Green Bay	Pleas. of Gov.	None
	Norman Briggs	Baraboo	July 1, 2015	None
	Sandy Hardie	Eden	July 1, 2015	None
	Duncan Shrout	Wauwatosa	July 1, 2015	None
	Joyce O'Donnell	West Allis	July 1, 2017	None
	Mary Rasmussen	Boyceville	July 1, 2017	None
	Scott A. Stokes	Clintonville	July 1, 2017	None

Officers[1]	Name	Home Address[2]	Term Expires[3]	Salary or Per Diem[4]
*Architects, Landscape Architects, Professional Engineers, Designers and Land Surveyors, Board of Secs. 15.08, 15.405 (2)	James E. Rusch	New Richmond	July 1, 2006	$25 per day
	Ryan Klippel	Sun Prairie	July 1, 2009	$25 per day
	Steven Nielsen	Luck	July 1, 2009	$25 per day
	Scott Berg	Appleton	July 1, 2011	$25 per day
	Julia DeCicco	Milwaukee	July 1, 2011	$25 per day
	Matthew Janiak	Mondovi	July 1, 2011	$25 per day
	Ruth Johnson	Madison	July 1, 2011	$25 per day
	Michael Kinney	River Falls	July 1, 2012	$25 per day
	Gary Kohlenberg	Oconomowoc	July 1, 2012	$25 per day
	Nancy Ragland	Madison	July 1, 2012	$25 per day
	Daniel Fedderly	Boyceville	July 1, 2013	$25 per day
	Thomas Gasperetti	Milwaukee	July 1, 2013	$25 per day
	Charles Kopplin	Milwaukee	July 1, 2013	$25 per day
	Lawrence Schnuck	Milwaukee	July 1, 2013	$25 per day
	Rosheen Styczinski	Milwaukee	July 1, 2013	$25 per day
	Steven Tweed	Monona	July 1, 2013	$25 per day
	Mark Cook	Cambridge	July 1, 2014	$25 per day
	Michael Eberle	Middleton	July 1, 2014	$25 per day
	Steven Hook	Milwaukee	July 1, 2014	$25 per day
	James Mickowski	Stoughton	July 1, 2014	$25 per day
	Mark Mayer	Menasha	July 1, 2014	$25 per day
	Andrew Albright	Sun Prairie	July 1, 2015	$25 per day
	Andrew Gersich	Madison	July 1, 2015	$25 per day
	Joseph Eberle[5]	Pewaukee	July 1, 2017	$25 per day
	4 vacancies			
*Artistic Endowment Foundation Chap. 247	Inactive			
Arts Board Sec. 15.445 (1)	Nick Meyer	Eau Claire	May 1, 2011	None
	Barbara Munson	Mosinee	May 1, 2011	None
	Susan Friebert	Milwaukee	May 1, 2012	None
	John Hendricks	Sparta	May 1, 2012	None
	Sharon Stewart	Washburn	May 1, 2013	None
	Ann Brunner	Kewaunee	May 1, 2014	None
	Mary Gielow	Mequon	May 1, 2014	None
	Brian Kelsey	Fish Creek	May 1, 2014	None
	LaMoine MacLaughlin	Clayton	May 1, 2015	None
	Heather McDonell	Madison	May 1, 2015	None
	Robert Wagner	Mequon	May 1, 2015	None
	Bruce Bernberg	Racine	May 1, 2016	None
	Ron Madich	La Pointe	May 1, 2016	None
	Kevin Miller	Fond du Lac	May 1, 2016	None
	Matthew Wallock	Madison	May 1, 2016	None
*Athletic Trainers Affiliated Credentialing Board Sec. 15.406 (4)	Ryan Berry	Appleton	July 1, 2013	$25 per day
	Carolynn Leaman	Milwaukee	July 1, 2014	$25 per day
	James Nesbit	Phillips	July 1, 2014	$25 per day
	Kurt Fielding[5]	Green Bay	July 1, 2015	$25 per day
	Shanyn C. Lancaster[5]	Milwaukee	July 1, 2016	$25 per day
	Gregory Vergamini[5]	Superior	July 1, 2016	$25 per day
*Auctioneer Board Sec. 15.504 (3)	Patrick McNamara[5]	Lancaster	May 1, 2010	$25 per day
	Kathryn Daley	Green Bay	May 1, 2011	$25 per day
	Timothy Sweeney	Green Lake	May 1, 2012	$25 per day
	Ronald Polacek	Prairie du Sac	May 1, 2013	$25 per day
	Jerry Thiel	Chilton	May 1, 2014	$25 per day
	James Wenzler	Oak Creek	May 1, 2015	$25 per day
	Randy Stockwell[5]	Dorchester	May 1, 2016	$25 per day
*Banking Review Board Secs. 15.07 (1)(b) 1, 15.185 (1), 15.555 (1)	Debra R. Lins	Sauk City	May 1, 2014	$25 per day, not exc. $1,500 per yr.
	Ralph Tenuta	Kenosha	May 1, 2015	$25 per day, not exc. $1,500 per yr.
	Thomas Spitz	Sun Prairie	May 1, 2016	$25 per day, not exc. $1,500 per yr.
	Douglas Farmer	La Crosse	May 1, 2017	$25 per day, not exc. $1,500 per yr.
	Robert C. Gorsuch[5]	Fitchburg	May 1, 2018	$25 per day, not exc. $1,500 per yr.
*Bradley Center Sports and Entertainment Corporation, Bd. of Directors of the Sec. 232.03	Gail A. Lione	Milwaukee	July 1, 2006	None
	Marc Marotta	Mequon	July 1, 2013	None
	Rolen L. Womack	Brown Deer	July 1, 2013	None
	Ted Kellner	Milwaukee	July 1, 2016	None
	Gary Sweeney	Milwaukee	July 1, 2016	None
	Michael Spector	Milwaukee	July 1, 2017	None
	Patrick Lawton[5]	Oconomowoc	July 1, 2018	None
	Matthew Parlow[5]	Milwaukee	July 1, 2018	None
	Andrew Petzold	Mequon	July 1, 2018	None
	Michael Grebe[5]	Milwaukee	July 1, 2020	None
Building Commission Sec. 13.48 (2)	Robert Brandherm	Verona	Pleas. of Gov.	None

Officers[1]	Name	Home Address[2]	Term Expires[3]	Salary or Per Diem[4]
Building Inspector Review Board Sec. 15.405 (1m)	Martin Rifken	Madison	May 1, 2013	None
	James Micech	Jackson	May 1, 2015	None
Burial Sites Preservation Board Secs. 15.07 (5)(o), 15.705 (1)	Corina Williams	Oneida	July 1, 2010	$25 per day
	Robert Powless	Odanah	July 1, 2012	$25 per day
	Kathryn Eagan-Bruhy	Minocqua	July 1, 2013	$25 per day
	David Grignon	Keshena	July 1, 2014	$25 per day
	Cynthia Stiles	Rhinelander	July 1, 2014	$25 per day
	Kathleen M. Foley-Winkler	Shorewood	July 1, 2015	$25 per day
*Cemetery Board Sec. 15.405 (3m)	Kathleen Cantu	Madison	July 1, 2012	$25 per day
	Cecelia Timmons	Madison	July 1, 2012	$25 per day
	Ed Greenfield	Green Bay	July 1, 2013	$25 per day
	Mary Lehman	Appleton	July 1, 2014	$25 per day
	Francis Groh	Appleton	July 1, 2016	$25 per day
	Clyde Rupnow	Watertown	July 1, 2016	$25 per day
Child Abuse and Neglect Prevention Board Secs. 15.07 (1)(a), 15.195 (4)	Nancy Armbrust	Green Bay	May 1, 2011	None
	James Leonhart	Madison	May 1, 2011	None
	Michael Bloedorn	West Bend	May 1, 2012	None
	Barbara Knox	Cross Plains	May 1, 2013	None
	Jennifer Moyes	Madison	May 1, 2013	None
	Dimitri Topitzes	Milwaukee	May 1, 2013	None
	Jeffrey Lamont	Wausau	May 1, 2014	None
	Jesus Mireles	Waukesha	May 1, 2014	None
	Teri Zywicki	Milwaukee	May 1, 2015	None
	Kimberly Liedl	Madison	Pleas. of Gov.	None
	2 vacancies			
*Children and Families, Dept. of, Secy. Secs. 15.20	Eloise Anderson	Sacramento, CA	Pleas. of Gov.	Group 6
*Chiropractic Examining Board Secs. 15.08, 15.405 (5)	Mania Moore	New Richmond	July 1, 2009	$25 per day
	Kathleen Schneider	Minocqua	July 1, 2012	$25 per day
	John Church	Janesville	July 1, 2013	$25 per day
	James Koshick[5]	New Berlin	July 1, 2013	$25 per day
	Michael McMahon[5]	Eau Claire	July 1, 2013	$25 per day
	Jodi Griffith	Cumberland	July 1, 2015	$25 per day
	Patricia Schumacher[5]	Marshfield	July 1, 2015	$25 per day
*Circus World Museum Foundation Secs. 44.16 (2)	David Hoffman[5]	Black River Falls	Pleas. of Gov.	None
Claims Board Secs. 15.07 (2)(e), 15.105 (2)	Brian Hagedorn	Madison	Pleas. of Gov.	None
*College Savings Program Board 15.07 (1)(b), 15.105 (25m), 16.641	Patrick Sheehy	Mequon	May 1, 2013	None
	Robert Kieckhefer	Mequon	May 1, 2015	None
	William Oemichen	Madison	May 1, 2015	None
	John Wheeler[5]	Middleton	May 1, 2015	None
	Alberta Darling[5]	River Hills	May 1, 2017	None
	Kimberly Shaul[5]	Cottage Grove	May 1, 2017	None
Controlled Substances Board Sec. 15.405 (5g)	Alan Bloom	Fox Point	May 1, 2014	None
	Gunnar Larson	Milwaukee	May 1, 2016	None
Conveyance Safety Code Council Sec. 15.157 (14)(a)	Jesse Kaysen	Madison	July 1, 2009	None
	Paul Rosenberg	Mequon	July 1, 2013	None
	Kenneth Smith	Madison	July 1, 2013	None
	Andrew Zielke	Madison	July 1, 2013	None
	Michael Dauck	Mazomanie	July 1, 2014	None
	Kelvin Nord	Slinger	July 1, 2014	None
	Adam Smith	Madison	July 1, 2014	None
	Brian Hornung	Middleton	July 1, 2015	None
*Cosmetology Examining Board Sec. 15.405 (17))	Vicky McNally	Edgerton	July 1, 2016	None
*Corrections, Dept. of, Secy. Secs. 15.05 (1)(a), 15.14	Edward Wall[5]	Windsor	Pleas. of Gov.	Group 6
*Credit Union Review Board Secs. 15.07 (1)(b) 3, 15.07 (5)(s), 15.185 (7)(b)	Dennis Degenhardt	West Bend	May 1, 2014	$25 per day, not exc. $1,500 per yr.
	Brian Prunty	Antigo	May 1, 2015	$25 per day, not exc. $1,500 per yr.
	J. David Christenson	Wausau	May 1, 2016	$25 per day, not exc. $1,500 per yr.
	Colleen Woggon	Kendall	May 1, 2017	$25 per day, not exc. $1,500 per yr.
	Lisa M. Greco[5]	Brookfield	May 1, 2018	$25 per day, not exc. $1,500 per yr.
*Credit Unions, Office of, Director Sec. 15.185 (7)(a)	Suzanne T. Cowan	Oregon	Pleas. of Gov.	Group 3
Crematory Authority Council Sec. 15.407 (8)	Paul Haubrich	Bayside	July 1, 2008	None
	Kelly Coleman-Kohorn	Germantown	July 1, 2010	None
	Gary Langendorf	Racine	July 1, 2011	None
	Linda Reid	Whitewater	July 1, 2011	None
	Scott Brainard	Wausau	July 1, 2012	None
	Adam Casper	West Salem	July 1, 2012	None
	William Cress	Stoughton	July 1, 2013	None

Officers[1]	Name	Home Address[2]	Term Expires[3]	Salary or Per Diem[4]
Crime Victims Rights Bd. Sec. 15.255 (2)	Carmen Pitre	Milwaukee	Pleas. of Gov.	None
Criminal Penalties, Joint Review Committee on Sec. 13.525 (1)	Bradley Gehring	Appleton	Pleas. of Gov.	None
	Maury Straub	Port Washington	Pleas. of Gov.	None
Deaf and Hard of Hearing, Council for the Secs. 15.09 (1)(a), 15.197 (8)	Mary Griffin	Eau Claire	July 1, 2013	None
	Billy Mauldin	Madison	July 1, 2013	None
	Tracy Haas	Watertown	July 1, 2015	None
	Deborah A. Herczog	Stoddard	July 1, 2015	None
	Denise Johnson	Milwaukee	July 1, 2015	None
	Steven Smart	Waukesha	July 1, 2015	None
	Gary Ebben	Waukesha	July 1, 2017	None
	Nicole Everson	Eau Claire	July 1, 2017	None
	Justin Vollmar	Delavan	July 1, 2017	None
*Deferred Compensation Board Secs. 15.07 (1)(b) 14, 15.07 (5)(f), 15.165 (4)	Edward Main	Madison	July 1, 2012	None
	John Nelson	Middleton	July 1, 2013	None
	Gail Hanson	Madison	July 1, 2014	None
	Michael Gracz	Oregon	July 1, 2015	None
	vacancy			
*Dentistry Examining Board Secs. 15.08, 15.405 (6)	Mark Braden	Lake Geneva	July 1, 2014	$25 per day
	Eileen Donohoo	Wauwatosa	July 1, 2014	$25 per day
	Lyndsay N. Knoell	Mt. Pleasant	July 1, 2014	$25 per day
	Sandra Linhart	La Crosse	July 1, 2014	$25 per day
	Beth Welter	Prairie du Chien	July 1, 2014	$25 per day
	William Anderson[5]	South Range	July 1, 2016	$25 per day
	Debra Beres[5]	Waukesha	July 1, 2016	$25 per day
	Leonardo Huck	Thiensville	July 1, 2017	$25 per day
	Timothy McConville[5]	Verona	July 1, 2017	$25 per day
	Wendy Pietz[5]	Milwaukee	July 1, 2017	$25 per day
	vacancy			
Developmental Disabilities, Bd. for People with Secs. 15.09 (1)(a), 15.105 (8)	Debra Glover	Milwaukee	July 1, 2007	$50 per day
	Susan Kay Nutter	La Crosse	July 1, 2007	$50 per day
	Roxanne M. Price	La Crosse	July 1, 2007	$50 per day
	Cindy Zellner-Ehlers	Sturgeon Bay	July 1, 2007	$50 per day
	Gerald Born	Madison	July 1, 2010	$50 per day
	Jackie Wenkman	Jefferson	July 1, 2010	$50 per day
	Joan Burns	Madison	July 1, 2011	$50 per day
	Kevin Fech	Cudahy	July 1, 2011	$50 per day
	Jonathan Donnelly	Madison	July 1, 2012	$50 per day
	Katherine Maloney Perhach	Whitefish Bay	July 1, 2012	$50 per day
	Barbara Gadbois	Bayfield	July 1, 2013	$50 per day
	Pam Malin	De Pere	July 1, 2013	$50 per day
	Andrew Gerbitz	Oconomowoc	July 1, 2014	$50 per day
	Ramsey A. Lee	Hudson	July 1, 2014	$50 per day
	Patrick Young	Germantown	July 1, 2014	$50 per day
	Robert Kuhr	Menasha	July 1, 2016	$50 per day
	David Pinno	New London	July 1, 2016	$50 per day
	L. Lynn Stansberry-Brusnahan	Shorewood	July 1, 2016	$50 per day
	Elsa Diaz Bautista	Milwaukee	July 1, 2017	$50 per day
	Judith Quigley	Elm Grove	July 1, 2017	$50 per day
	Sheila Thornton	Tomah	July 1, 2017	$50 per day
*Dietitians Affiliated Credentialing Board Sec. 15.406 (2)	Donna Loveland	Onalaska	July 1, 2014	$25 per day
	Patricia Roblee	Oshkosh	July 1, 2014	$25 per day
	Scott Krueger	Shawano	July 1, 2015	$25 per day
	Gail Underbakke[5]	Madison	July 1, 2015	$25 per day
*Domestic Abuse, Council on Secs. 15.09 (1)(a), 15.197 (16)	Maytong Chang	Milwaukee	July 1, 2011	None
	Mariana Rodriguez	Milwaukee	July 1, 2011	None
	Gene Redhail	Oneida	July 1, 2012	None
	Terese Berceau	Madison	July 1, 2013	None
	Rachel Rodriguez	Waunakee	July 1, 2013	None
	Kara Schurman[5]	Milwaukee	July 1, 2013	None
	L. Kevin Hamberger[5]	Franklin	July 1, 2014	None
	Jamie Kratz-Gullickson	Beaver Dam	July 1, 2014	None
	Renee Schulz-Stangl[5]	Marshfield	July 1, 2014	None
	Susan Sippel[5]	Manitowoc	July 1, 2014	None
	Jennifer Shilling[5]	La Crosse	July 1, 2015	None
Dry Cleaner Environmental Response Council Sec. 15.347 (2)	Jill Fitzgerald	Muskego	July 1, 2011	None
	Jim Fitzgerald	Butler	July 1, 2013	None
	Richard Klinke	Madison	July 1, 2013	None
	Kevin Braden	Brookfield	July 1, 2014	None
	Brett Donaldson	Neenah	July 1, 2015	None
	Jeanne Tarvin	Slinger	July 1, 2015	None

Officers[1]	Name	Home Address[2]	Term Expires[3]	Salary or Per Diem[4]
Dwelling Code Council	Thomas Doleschy	Muskego	July 1, 2010	None
Secs. 15.09 (1)(a), 15.157 (3)	Michael Mueller	Greendale	July 1, 2010	None
	Jeffrey Bechard	Eau Claire	July 1, 2011	None
	Robert Jakel	Kaukauna	July 1, 2011	None
	Steven Levine	Madison	July 1, 2012	None
	Frank Opatik	Wausau	July 1, 2012	None
	Dennis Bauer	McFarland	July 1, 2013	None
	Amy Bliss	Cottage Grove	July 1, 2013	None
	Michael Coello	New Berlin	July 1, 2013	None
	Peter Krabbe	Seymour	July 1, 2013	None
	Robert Premo	Hartland	July 1, 2013	None
	Brian Wert	Hudson	July 1, 2013	None
	Philip Borchardt	Merrill	July 1, 2014	None
	David Dolan-Wallace	Green Bay	July 1, 2014	None
	Steven Gryboski	Green Bay	July 1, 2014	None
	Mary L. Schroeder	Brookfield	July 1, 2014	None
	Gary Zajicek	Prairie du Sac	July 1, 2014	None
*Economic Development Corp.	Daniel Ariens	Green Bay	Pleas. of Gov.	None
Authority, Wis.	Raymond Drager	Colfax	Pleas. of Gov.	None
Sec. 238.02 (1)	Corey Hoze	Milwaukee	Pleas. of Gov.	None
	Lisa Mauer	Wauwatosa	Pleas. of Gov.	None
	Paul Radspinner	Madison	Pleas. of Gov.	None
	vacancy			
*Economic Development Corp. Authority, Wis. Chief Exec. Officer Sec. 238.02(3)	Reed Hall	Minocqua	Pleas. of Gov.	—[6]
Education Commission	Jessica Doyle	Madison	Pleas. of Gov.	None
of the States	Tony Evers	Madison	Pleas. of Gov.	None
Sec. 39.76	Tracie Happel	Onalaska	Pleas. of Gov.	None
	Bette Lang	Beloit	Pleas. of Gov.	None
	Demond Means	Mequon	Pleas. of Gov.	None
Educational Approval	Christy L. Brown	Bayside	Pleas. of Gov.	$25 per day
Board	Robert Hein	Janesville	Pleas. of Gov.	$25 per day
Sec. 15.945 (1)	Donald Madelung	Windsor	Pleas. of Gov.	$25 per day
	Jo Oyama-Miller	Monona	Pleas. of Gov.	$25 per day
	William Roden	Grafton	Pleas. of Gov.	$25 per day
	Katie Thiry	Prescott	Pleas. of Gov.	$25 per day
	Monica Williams	Appleton	Pleas. of Gov.	$25 per day
*Educational Communications	Thomas Basting	Madison	May 1, 2013	None
Board	Diane Everson	Edgerton	May 1, 2013	None
Secs. 15.07 (1)(a) 5, 15.57	Karen Schroeder[5]	Birchwood	May 1, 2015	None
	Rolf Wegenke[5]	Sun Prairie	May 1, 2015	None
	Eileen Littig	Green Bay	Pleas. of Gov.	None
Electronic Recording Council	Craig Haskins	Milwaukee	July 1, 2012	None
Sec. 15.107 (6)	Kristi Chlebowski	Madison	July 1, 2013	None
	Marcia Drouin-Howe	Monona	July 1, 2013	None
	Marge Geissler	Chippewa Falls	July 1, 2013	None
	John Wilcox	Eau Claire	July 1, 2013	None
	Tyson Fettes	Burlington	July 1, 2015	None
	Jodi Helgeson	Grand Marsh	July 1, 2015	None
*Emergency Management Div., Administrator of Sec. 15.313 (1)	Brian Satula	Oak Creek	Pleas. of Gov.	Group 1
Emergency Medical Services	Melinda Allen	Juda	May 1, 2014	None
Board	Jerry Biggart	Milwaukee	May 1, 2014	None
Sec. 15.195 (8)	Kathleen Bruss	Milwaukee	May 1, 2014	None
	Mark Fredrickson	Hilbert	May 1, 2014	None
	Gregory West	Muskego	May 1, 2014	None
	Steven Bane	West Allis	May 1, 2015	None
	Mario Colella	Milwaukee	May 1, 2015	None
	Les Luder	Superior	May 1, 2015	None
	James Austad	Oshkosh	May 1, 2016	None
	Cecile D'Huyvetter	Onalaska	May 1, 2016	None
	Carrie Meier	Waunakee	May 1, 2016	None
*Employee Trust Funds Board Secs. 15.07 (1)(a) 3, 15.07 (5)(f), 15.16 (1) (c)	Victor Shier	Kewaskum	May 1, 2013	None
*Employment Relations, Office of, Dir. Sec. 15.105 (29)	Gregory L. Gracz	Verona	Pleas. of Gov.	Group 6
*Employment Relations Comn.	Judith Neumann	Madison	March 1, 2013	Group 5
Secs. 15.06 (1), 15.58	James Scott	Dousman	March 1, 2015	Group 5
	Rodney Pasch	Fond du Lac	March 1, 2017	Group 5
Federal-State Relations Office, Director Sec. 16.548 (1)	Jen Jinks	Washington, D.C.	Pleas. of Gov.	Group 3
*Financial Institutions, Dept. of Secy. of Secs. 15.05 (1)(a), 15.18	Peter Bildsten	Baraboo	Pleas. of Gov.	Group 6

Officers[1]	Name	Home Address[2]	Term Expires[3]	Salary or Per Diem[4]
Forestry, Council on Sec. 15.347 (19)	R. Bruce Allison	Verona	Pleas. of Gov.	None
	Michael Bolton.	Plover	Pleas. of Gov.	None
	Dennis G. Brown	Rhinelander	Pleas. of Gov.	None
	Troy Brown	Antigo	Pleas. of Gov.	None
	Randy Champeau	Rosholt	Pleas. of Gov.	None
	Matt Dallman	Tomahawk	Pleas. of Gov.	None
	Paul J. DeLong.	Madison	Pleas. of Gov.	None
	Donald Friske	Merrill	Pleas. of Gov.	None
	James Heerey	New Auburn	Pleas. of Gov.	None
	Jeanne Higgins.	Chequamegon	Pleas. of Gov.	None
	Thomas Hittle	Rhinelander	Pleas. of Gov.	None
	James Hoppe.	Rhinelander	Pleas. of Gov.	None
	William J. Horvath.	Stevens Point	Pleas. of Gov.	None
	Mary Hubler	Rice Lake	Pleas. of Gov.	None
	James Kerkman	Bangor	Pleas. of Gov.	None
	Kimberly Quast	Fond du Lac	Pleas. of Gov.	None
	Mark Rickenbach	Madison	Pleas. of Gov.	None
	Robert Rogers	Custer	Pleas. of Gov.	None
	Henry Schienebeck	Butternut	Pleas. of Gov.	None
	Jane Severt.	Merrill	Pleas. of Gov.	None
	Jeffrey C. Stier.	Madison	Pleas. of Gov.	None
	Paul Strong.	Hazelhurst	Pleas. of Gov.	None
	Tom Tiffany	Hazelhurst	Pleas. of Gov.	None
	Kathleen Vinehout	Alma	Pleas. of Gov.	None
	Virgil Waugh.	Milton	Pleas. of Gov.	None
	Richard Wedepohl	Madison	Pleas. of Gov.	None
*Fox River Navigational System Authority Sec. 237.02	John Vette	Oshkosh	July 1, 2013	None
	William Raaths.	Menasha	July 1, 2014	None
	S. Timothy Rose	Appleton	July 1, 2014	None
	John Shier	Green Bay	July 1, 2014	None
	Ron Van De Hey	Kaukauna	July 1, 2014	None
	vacancy			None
*Funeral Directors Examining Board Secs. 15.08, 15.405 (16)	Michele Moore.	La Crosse	July 1, 2009	$25 per day
	Brian Langendorf	Racine	July 1, 2014	$25 per day
	Kristen Piehl	Kenosha	July 1, 2014	$25 per day
	Thomas Bradley	Antigo	July 1, 2015	$25 per day
	Eric Lengell	Milwaukee	July 1, 2016	$25 perday
	Dean Stensberg[5]	Middleton	July 1, 2017	$25 per day
*Geologists, Hydrologists and Soil Scientists, Examining Board of Professional Secs. 15.08, 15.405 (2m)	Patricia Trochlell.	Blue Mounds	July 1, 2009	$25 per day
	Ruth Johnson.	Madison	July 1, 2010	$25 per day
	John Hahn	Elm Grove	July 1, 2011	$25 per day
	Brenda Halminiak	Rhinelander	July 1, 2012	$25 per day
	Randall Hunt.	Cross Plains	July 1, 2012	$25 per day
	Frederick Madison.	Lodi	July 1, 2012	$25 per day
	Kenneth Bradbury	Madison	July 1, 2013	$25 per day
	Sue Bridson	Madison	July 1, 2013	$25 per day
	William Mode	Neenah	July 1, 2013	$25 per day
	Richard Beilfuss	Baraboo	July 1, 2014	$25 per day
	James Robertson	Madison	July 1, 2014	$25 per day
*Government Accountability Board Secs. 15.07 (1)(a) 2, 15.60	Thomas Cane	Wausau	May 1, 2013	None
	Michael Brennan.	Marshfield	May 1, 2014	None
	Thomas Barland	Eau Claire	May 1, 2015	None
	David Deininger[5].	Monroe	May 1, 2016	None
	Timothy Vocke[5]	Rhinelander	May 1, 2017	None
	Gerald Nichol[5]	Madison	May 1, 2018	None
Great Lakes Comn. Sec. 14.78 (1)	Dave Hansen	Green Bay	July 1, 2013	None
	Dean Haen	Green Bay	July 1, 2016	None
	Ken Johnson	Madison	Pleas. of Gov.	None
*Great Lakes Protection Fund Sec. 14.84	Ken Johnson	Madison	Jan. 12, 2014	None
	Richard Meeusen	Pewaukee	Jan. 9, 2015	None
Groundwater Coordinating Council Secs. 15.09 (5)(f), 15.347 (13)	George Kraft.	Amherst	July 1, 2013	None
Group Insurance Board Secs. 15.07 (1)(b), 15.07 (5)(f), 15.165 (2)	Brian Yerges	Plymouth	May 1, 2013	$25 per day
	Nancy Thompson	Waterloo	May 1, 2014	$25 per day
	Terri Carlson	Edgerton	May 1, 2015	$25 per day
	Herschel Day.	Altoona	May 1, 2015	$25 per day
	Michael Farrell.	Bristol	May 1, 2015	$25 per day
	Charles Grapentine.	Madison	May 1, 2015	$25 per day
	Jon Litscher	Beaver Dam	Pleas. of Gov.	None
*Health and Educational Facilities Authority, Wis. Sec. 231.02 (1)	Bruce Colburn	Milwaukee	July 1, 2014	None
	Richard Canter.	Milwaukee	July 1, 2015	None
	Richard Keintz.	Madison	July 1, 2016	None
	Kevin Flaherty.	Milwaukee	July 1, 2017	None
	Tim Size	Madison	July 1, 2018	None
	James Dietsche.	De Pere	July 1, 2019	None
	Robert Van Meeteren[5]	Reedsburg	July 1, 2020	None
Health Care Liability Insurance Plan/Injured Patients and Families Compensation Fund Bd. of Governors Sec. 619.04 (3), 655.27 (2)	Dennis Conta.	Milwaukee	May 1, 2010	None
	Carla Borda	Hubertus	May 1, 2015	None
	Christopher Flatter.	Rothschild	May 1, 2015	None
	Kathryn Osborne.	Madison	May 1, 2015	None
	Susan Engler	Milwaukee	May 1, 2016	None

Officers[1]	Name	Home Address[2]	Term Expires[3]	Salary or Per Diem[4]
*Health Insurance Risk-Sharing Plan Authority Sec. 149.41 (1)	Annette Stebbins	Madison	May 1, 2013	None
	Cathy Winters[5]	Wausau	May 1, 2013	None
	Ellen Henningsen	Madison	May 1, 2014	None
	Larry Rambo	Hartland	May 1, 2014	None
	John Russell[5]	Columbus	May 1, 2014	None
	Thomas Wagner	Oshkosh	May 1, 2014	None
	Steven Youso[5]	Auburndale	May 1, 2014	None
	Wendy Arnone[5]	Menomonee Falls	May 1, 2015	None
	Michele Bachhuber[5]	Marshfield	May 1, 2015	None
	Christianna Hanson[5]	Hortonville	May 1, 2015	None
	Peter Todd Catlin[5]	Nashotah	May 1, 2016	None
	Linda Hoff[5]	Mt. Horeb	May 1, 2016	None
	Joseph A. Kachelski[5]	Verona	May 1, 2016	None
*Health Services, Dept. of, Secy. Secs. 15.05 (1)(a), 15.19	Kitty Rhoades	Hudson	Pleas. of Gov.	Group 9
*Hearing and Speech Examining Board Secs. 15.08, 15.405 (6m)	Melanie Blechl	Neenah	July 1, 2012	$25 per day
	Okie Allen	Eau Claire	July 1, 2013	$25 per day
	Samuel Gubbels	Madison	July 1, 2013	$25 per day
	Edward Korabic	Milwaukee	July 1, 2013	$25 per day
	Peter Zellmer	Appleton	July 1, 2013	$25 per day
	Patricia Willis	Waukesha	July 1, 2014	$25 per day
	Steven Klapperich	St. Cloud	July 1, 2015	$25 per day
	Mary Polenske	Sun Prairie	July 1, 2015	$25 per day
	Thomas Sather[5]	Eau Claire	July 1, 2015	$25 per day
	Doreen Jensen	Oshkosh	July 1, 2016	$25 per day
Higher Educational Aids Board Secs. 15.07 (1)(a) 1, 15.67 (1)	Teresa Rutherford	Rice Lake	May 1, 2011	None
	Mary Jo Green	Nekoosa	May 1, 2012	None
	Ann Greenheck	Lone Rock	May 1, 2012	None
	James Palmer	Madison	May 1, 2012	None
	Randall McCready	Kenosha	May 1, 2013	None
	Laramie Wieseman	Lake Geneva	May 1, 2013	None
	Steven DiSalvo	Fond du Lac	May 1, 2014	None
	Gary Roberts	Onalaska	May 1, 2014	None
	Timothy Rindahl	Arcadia	May 1, 2015	None
	Steven Midthun	Greendale	May 1, 2016	None
Higher Educational Aids Board, Exec. Secy. Sec. 39.29	John Reinemann	Madison	Pleas. of Gov.	Group 3
Highway Safety, Council on Secs. 15.09 (1)(a), 15.467 (3)	Robert Barten	Stevens Point	July 1, 2013	None
	Brian Lueth	De Pere	July 1, 2013	None
	LaVerne Hermann	Waterloo	July 1, 2014	None
	Randall Thiel	Sheboygan	July 1, 2014	None
	John Corbin	Madison	July 1, 2015	None
	Stephen Fitzgerald	Madison	July 1, 2015	None
	Patrick Hughes	Milwaukee	July 1, 2015	None
	Kurt Schultz	Spring Green	July 1, 2015	None
	Richard G. Van Boxtel	Oneida	July 1, 2015	None
	Jeff Plale	South Milwaukee	July 1, 2016	None
Historic Preservation Review Board Sec. 15.705 (2)	Anne Biebel	Cross Plains	July 1, 2013	None
	Kelly Jackson	Lac du Flambeau	July 1, 2013	None
	Kubet Luchterhand	Ellison Bay	July 1, 2013	None
	Carlen Hatala	Milwaukee	July 1, 2014	None
	Daniel Joyce	Kenosha	July 1, 2014	None
	Valentine Schute	La Crosse	July 1, 2014	None
	Daniel Stephans	Madison	July 1, 2014	None
	Donna Zimmerman	Amherst Junction	July 1, 2014	None
	Carol Johnson	Black Earth	July 1, 2015	None
	David V. Mollenhoff	Madison	July 1, 2015	None
	Neil Prendergast	Stevens Point	July 1, 2015	None
	Sissel Schroeder	Madison	July 1, 2015	None
	Paul Wolter	Baraboo	July 1, 2015	None
	Bruce Block	Milwaukee	July 1, 2016	None
	Robert Gough	Eau Claire	July 1, 2016	None
Historical Society Endowment Fund Council Secs. 15.09 (1)(a), 15.707 (3)	Inactive			
*Housing and Economic Development Authority, Wis. Sec. 234.02 (1)	Perry Armstong	Madison	Jan. 1, 2014	None
	Bradley Guse	Arpin	Jan. 1, 2014	None
	Daniel Lee	Waunakee	Jan. 1, 2015	None
	Lee Swanson	Cross Plains	Jan. 1, 2015	None
	Sue Shore	Wausau	Jan. 1, 2016	None
	McArthur Weddle	Milwaukee	Jan. 1, 2016	None
*Housing and Economic Development Authority, Wis., Executive Director Sec. 234.02 (3)	Wyman Winston	Madison	Jan. 3, 2015	Group 6
Information Technology Management Board Sec. 15.215 (1)	Carla Cross	Milwaukee	May 1, 2011	None
	Gina Frank	Madison	May 1, 2013	None
	Sean Dilweg	Madison	Pleas. of Gov.	None
	Lorrie Heinemann	Madison	Pleas. of Gov.	None
*Insurance, Commissioner of Secs. 15.06 (1) (b), (3)(a) 1, 15.06 (3)(b), 15.73	Ted Nickel	Merrill	Pleas. of Gov.	Group 5

Officers[1]	Name	Home Address[2]	Term Expires[3]	Salary or Per Diem[4]
Interoperability Council	Melinda Allen	Juda	May 1, 2009	None
Sec. 15.107 (18)	Richard Van Boxtel	Oneida	May 1, 2012	None
	Thomas Czaja	Milwaukee	May 1, 2013	None
	Steven Hansen	Racine	May 1, 2013	None
	Lynn Schubert	Burlington	May 1, 2013	None
	Jon Freund	Sun Prairie	May 1, 2015	None
	Matthew Joski	Kewaunee	May 1, 2015	None
	James Koleas	Milwaukee	May 1, 2015	None
	William Stolte	Grafton	May 1, 2015	None
Invasive Species Council	Charles Henriksen	Green Bay	July 1, 2012	None
Sec. 15.347 (18)	James Kerkman	Bangor	July 1, 2012	None
	Kenneth F. Raffa	Madison	July 1, 2013	None
	Patricia Morton	Whitewater	July 1, 2014	None
	James Reinartz	Saukville	July 1, 2015	None
	Thomas Bressner	Madison	July 1, 2017	None
	Gregory Long	New Berlin	July 1, 2017	None
	Paul Schumacher	Sturgeon Bay	July 1, 2017	None
Investment and Local Impact Fund Board Sec. 15.435	Inactive			
*Investment Board, State of Wis.	Thomas Boldt	Appleton	May 1, 2015	$50 per day
Secs. 15.07 (1)(a) 4,	Bruce Colburn	Milwaukee	May 1, 2015	$50 per day
15.07 (2)(a), 15.07 (5)(a),	William H. Levit, Jr.	Milwaukee	May 1, 2015	$50 per day
15.76	Norman Cummings	Brookfield	May 1, 2017	$50 per day
	Lon Roberts	Wausau	May 1, 2017	$50 per day
	vacancy			
*Judicial Commission	Saied Assef	Green Bay	Aug. 1, 2014	$25 per day
Sec. 757.83	Mark Barrette	Beaver Dam	Aug. 1, 2014	$25 per day
	Eileen Burnett	De Pere	Aug. 1, 2014	$25 per day
	William Cullinan	New Berlin	Aug. 1, 2014	$25 per day
	Lynn Leazer	Verona	Aug. 1, 2015	$25 per day
Judicial Council	Dennis Myers	Germantown	July 1, 2015	None
Secs. 15.09 (1)(a), 758.13 (1)	Benjamin Pliskie	Brookfield	July 1, 2016	None
	Brad Schimel	Waukesha	Pleas. of Gov.	None
Justice Assistance, Office of Exec. Staff Director Sec. 15.105 (19)	vacancy		Pleas. of Gov.	Group 2
*Kickapoo Reserve Management Board	Senn Brown	Madison	May 1, 2012	$25 per day
Secs. 15.07 (1)(b) 20,	Tracy Littlejohn	La Crosse	May 1, 2012	$25 per day
15.07 (5)(y), 15.445 (2)	Susan Cushing	La Farge	May 1, 2013	$25 per day
	Adlai Mann	Black River Falls	May 1, 2013	$25 per day
	David Maxwell	Westby	May 1, 2013	$25 per day
	Ron Johnson	La Farge	May 1, 2014	$25 per day
	William Quackenbush	Black River Falls	May 1, 2014	$25 per day
	Richard Wallin	Viroqua	May 1, 2014	$25 per day
	Paul Hayes	Westby	May 1, 2015	$25 per day
	Brandon Hysel	La Farge	May 1, 2015	$25 per day
	Alan Szepi	Norwalk	May 1, 2016	$25 per day
*Labor and Industry Review Commission	Robert Glaser	Johnson Creek	March 1, 2015	Group 5
	Laurie McCallum	Lodi	March 1, 2017	Group 5
Secs. 15.06 (2)(a), 15.225 (1)	Clarence Jordahl	Middleton	March 1, 2019	Group 5
Labor and Management Council Secs. 15.09 (1)(a), 15.227 (17)	Inactive			
Laboratory of Hygiene Bd.	Michael Cavanagh	Madison	May 1, 2012	None
Sec. 15.915 (2)	David Taylor	Madison	May 1, 2012	None
	Darryll Farmer	Eau Claire	May 1, 2013	None
	Barry Irmen	Edgerton	May 1, 2013	None
	Michael Ricker	De Pere	May 1, 2013	None
	Jeffery Kindrai	Lancaster	May 1, 2014	None
	Robert Corliss	Oregon	May 1, 2016	None
Lake Michigan Commercial Fishing Board	Charles W. Henriksen	Baileys Harbor	Pleas. of Gov.	None
Sec. 15.345 (3)	Richard R. Johnson	Ellison Bay	Pleas. of Gov.	None
	Michael Le Clair	Two Rivers	Pleas. of Gov.	None
	Mark Maricque	Green Bay	Pleas. of Gov.	None
	Dan Pawlitzke	Two Rivers	Pleas. of Gov.	None
	Neil A. Schwarz	Sheboygan	Pleas. of Gov.	None
	Dean Swaer	Oconto	Pleas. of Gov.	None
Lake States Wood Utilization Consortium Sec. 26.37 (1)	Inactive			
Lake Superior Commercial Fishing Board	Jeff Bodin	Bayfield	Pleas. of Gov.	None
Sec. 15.345 (2)	Bill Damberg	Bayfield	Pleas. of Gov.	None
	Maurine Halvorson	Bayfield	Pleas. of Gov.	None
	Craig Hoopman	Bayfield	Pleas. of Gov.	None
	vacancy			
*Land and Water Conservation Bd.	Eric Birschbach	Verona	May 1, 2014	$25 per day
Secs. 15.07 (1)(b) 10,	Dennis Caneff	Madison	May 1, 2014	$25 per day
15.07 (1)(cm), 15.07 (5)(h),	Lynn Harrison	Elk Mound	May 1, 2015	$25 per day
15.135 (4)(am)	Mark Cupp	Muscoda	May 1, 2016	$25 per day
	vacancy			

Officers[1]	Name	Home Address[2]	Term Expires[3]	Salary or Per Diem[4]
Law Enforcement Standards Board Sec. 15.255 (1)	Gary Cuskey	Spooner	May 1, 2014	None
	Lisa Gerbig	La Crosse	May 1, 2014	None
	Teresa Smocyzk	Rhinelander	May 1, 2014	None
	James Arts	Green Bay	May 1, 2015	None
	Joseph Collins	Two Rivers	May 1, 2015	None
	Nathan Henriksen	DeForest	May 1, 2015	None
	Jon Koch	Brussels	May 1, 2015	None
	Jean Galasinski	Trempealeau	May 1, 2016	None
	Laura Messner-Washer	Elkhorn	May 1, 2016	None
	Kim Gaffney	Oxford	May 1, 2017	None
	Jennifer Harper	Richland Center	May 1, 2017	None
Library and Network Development, Council on Secs. 15.09 (1)(a), 15.377 (6)	Francis Cherney	Milladore	July 1, 2011	None
	Calvin Potter	Sheboygan Falls	July 1, 2012	None
	Kris Wendt	Rhinelander	July 1, 2012	None
	Michael Bahr	Germantown	July 1, 2013	None
	Ewa Barczyk	Milwaukee	July 1, 2013	None
	Nita Burke	Darlington	July 1, 2013	None
	Bob Koechley	Fitchburg	July 1, 2013	None
	Sandra Melcher	Milwaukee	July 1, 2013	None
	Annette Smith	Milton	July 1, 2013	None
	Kristi Williams	Cottage Grove	July 1, 2013	None
	Cara Cavin	Verona	July 1, 2014	None
	Joshua Cowles	Oconomowoc	July 1, 2014	None
	Miriam Erickson	Fish Creek	July 1, 2014	None
	Patrick Wilkinson	Oshkosh	July 1, 2014	None
	Rhonda Gould	Burlington	July 1, 2015	None
	Douglas Lay	Suamico	July 1, 2015	None
	Joan Robb	Green Bay	July 1, 2015	None
	Emily Rogers	De Pere	July 1, 2015	None
*Lower Fox River Remediation Authority Secs. 279.02	Gregory B. Conway	De Pere	June 30, 2011	None
	Patrick Schillinger	De Pere	June 30, 2011	None
	Robert Cowles	Green Bay	June 30, 2013	None
	Dave Hansen	Green Bay	June 30, 2013	None
	David Stegeman	Mequon	June 30, 2016	None
	James Wall	Green Bay	June 30, 2016	None
	vacancy			
Lower Wisconsin State Riverway Board Secs. 15.07 (1)(b) 15, 15.07 (5)(w), 15.445 (3)	Frederick Madison	Lodi	May 1, 2013	$25 per day
	George Arimond	La Crosse	May 1, 2014	$25 per day
	Don Greenwood	Spring Green	May 1, 2014	$25 per day
	Ronald Leys	Prairie du Chien	May 1, 2014	$25 per day
	Ritchie Brown	Black River Falls	May 1, 2015	$25 per day
	Robert Cary	Blue River	May 1, 2015	$25 per day
	Melody Moore	Mazomanie	May 1, 2015	$25 per day
	Gerald Dorscheid	Arena	May 1 2016	$25 per day
	David O. Martin	Muscoda	May 1, 2016	$25 per day
Madison Cultural Arts District Board Secs. 71.05 (1)(c) 6, 229.842	Carol Toussaint	Madison	July 1, 2014	None
	Diane Kay Ballweg	Madison	July 1, 2016	None
	Sheryl Theo	Madison	July 1, 2017	None
	Susan Hamblin	Madison	Pleas. of Gov.	None
Managed Forest Land Board Sec. 15.345 (6)	Eugene Roark	Madison	May 1, 2009	None
	Kevin Koth	Tomahawk	May 1, 2011	None
	Elroy Zemke	Rothschild	May 1, 2011	None
	Neil Paulson	Drummond	May 1, 2013	None
*Marriage and Family Therapy, Professional Counseling, and Social Work, Examining Board of Secs. 15.08 (7), 15.405 (7c)	Nancy Clark	Seymour	July 1, 2011	$25 per day
	Mary Jo Walsh	Mukwonago	July 1, 2011	$25 per day
	Arlie Albrecht	Green Bay	July 1, 2012	$25 per day
	Darryl Wood	La Crosse	July 1, 2012	$25 per day
	Alice Hanson-Drew[5]	Shorewood	July 1, 2013	$25 per day
	Peter Fabian	Madison	July 1, 2014	$25 per day
	Allison Gordon[5]	Waukesha	July 1, 2014	$25 per day
	Nick Smiar	Eau Claire	July 1, 2014	$25 per day
	Linda Pellmann	Oconomowoc	July 1, 2015	$25 per day
	Barbara Viste-Johnson	Luxemburg	July 1, 2015	$25 per day
	Elizabeth Krueger[5]	Waukesha	July 1, 2016	$25 per day
	Charles V. Lindsey[5]	Sun Prairie	July 1, 2016	$25 per day
*Massage Therapy and Bodywork Therapy Affiliated Credentialing Board Sec. 15.406 (6)	Carie Martin	Eau Claire	July 1, 2011	None
	Amy Connell	Madison	July 1, 2012	None
	Lillian Pounds	Milwaukee	July 1, 2012	None
	Xiping Zhou	Madison	July 1, 2012	None
	June Motzer	Hudson	July 1, 2013	None
	John E. Anderson	Rothschild	July 1, 2014	None
	Elizabeth Krizenesky	Neenah	July 1, 2014	None
	Carole Ostendorf	West Allis	July 1, 2014	None
	Wendy Wettengel Perrigoue	De Pere	July 1, 2014	None
	Cindy C. Spitza	Muskego	July 1, 2014	None
	Barbara Yetter	Manitowoc	July 1, 2014	None
	vacancy			
*Medical College of Wis., Inc., Board of Trustees of the Sec. 39.15	Linda Mellowes	Milwaukee	May 1, 2009	None
	Sheldon Lubar	Milwaukee	May 1, 2011	None
	Chris Abele	Milwaukee	May 1, 2012	None
	Cory Nettles	Milwaukee	May 1, 2013	None
	Edward Zore	Milwaukee	May 1, 2014	None
	Elizabeth Brenner	Waukesha	May 1, 2015	None
	Gregory Wesley	Milwaukee	May 1, 2015	None
	Curt S. Culver	Milwaukee	May 1, 2016	None
	3 vacancies			

Officers[1]	Name	Home Address[2]	Term Expires[3]	Salary or Per Diem[4]
Medical Education Review Committee Sec. 39.16	Inactive (7 members)			
*Medical Examining Board Secs. 15.08, 15.405 (7)	Gene Musser	Madison	July 1, 2013	$25 per day
	Timothy Swan	Marshfield	July 1, 2013	$25 per day
	Mary Jo Capodice[5]	Sheboygan	July 1, 2014	$25 per day
	Jude Genereaux	Ellison Bay	July 1, 2014	$25 per day
	Kenneth Simons	Mequon	July 1, 2014	$25 per day
	Rodney Erickson[5]	Tomah	July 1, 2015	$25 per day
	Suresh Misra	Mequon	July 1, 2015	$25 per day
	James Barr	Chetek	July 1, 2016	$25 per day
	Greg Collins[5]	De Pere	July 1, 2016	$25 per day
	Sridhar Vasudevan[5]	Belgium	July 1, 2016	$25 per day
	Timothy Westlake[5]	Hartland	July 1, 2016	$25 per day
	Russell Yale[5]	Fox Point	July 1, 2016	$25 per day
	Carolyn Ogland Vukich	Madison	July 1, 2017	$25 per day
Mental Health, Council on Secs. 15.09 (1)(a), 15.197 (1)	Corrie Briggs	Hudson	July 1, 2010	None
	Jackie Baldwin	St. Germain	July 1, 2012	None
	William Benedict	Madison	July 1, 2013	None
	Nic Dibble	Madison	July 1, 2013	None
	Shel Gross	Madison	July 1, 2013	None
	Jennifer Lowenberg	Verona	July 1, 2013	None
	Mishelle O'Shasky	Wisconsin Rapids	July 1, 2013	None
	Jodell Pelishek	Rice Lake	July 1, 2013	None
	Don Pirozzoli	Belleville	July 1, 2013	None
	Ann Catherine Veierstahler	Milwaukee	July 1, 2013	None
	Judith Wilcox	Madison	July 1, 2013	None
	Carol Keen	Milwaukee	July 1, 2014	None
	Mary Neubauer	Cudahy	July 1, 2014	None
	Joann Stephens	Westfield	July 1, 2014	None
	Edward F. Wall	Windsor	July 1, 2014	None
	Kathleen Enders	Waukesha	July 1, 2015	None
	Richard Immler		July 1, 2015	None
	Dave Sommers	Menomonie	July 1, 2015	None
	David Stepien	Madison	July 1, 2015	None
	Donna Wrenn	Madison	July 1, 2015	None
	Julie-Anne Braun	Waterford	July 1, 2016	None
	Walter D. Nencka	Hubertus	July 1, 2016	None
	Matthew Strittmater	La Crosse	July 1, 2016	None
*Merit Recruitment and Selection Administrator, Division of (OSER) Sec. 15.173 (1)(b)	John R. Lawton	Madison	March 26, 2014	Group 3
*Midwest Interstate Low-Level Radioactive Waste Comn., Wis. Commissioner Sec. 14.81 (1)	Stanley York	Middleton	Pleas. of Gov.	None
Midwest Interstate Passenger Rail Commission Sec. 14.86 (1)	Craig Anderson	Waukesha	Jan. 5, 2015	None
	Mark Gottlieb	Madison	Jan. 5, 2015	None
Midwestern Higher Educ. Comn. Sec. 14.90 (1)	Rolf Wegenke	Madison	July 1, 2014	None
	Gerald Whitburn	Wausau	July 1, 2014	None
	Don Madelung	Madison	Pleas. of Gov.	None
Migrant Labor, Council on Secs. 15.09 (1)(a), 15.227 (8)	Enrique Figueroa	Milwaukee	July 1, 2012	None
	James Kern	Mondovi	July 1, 2012	None
	Lupe Martinez	Pewaukee	July 1, 2012	None
	Liliana Parodi	Darien	July 1, 2013	None
	Teresa Tellez-Giron	Madison	July 1, 2013	None
	Steve Ziobro	Waterloo	July 1, 2013	None
	John Bauknect	Cross Plains	July 1, 2014	None
	Erica Kunze	Star Prairie	July 1, 2014	None
	Kevin Magee	Madison	July 1, 2014	None
	Richard W. Okray	Plover	July 1, 2015	None
	Guadalupe Rendon	Racine	July 1, 2016	None
Military and State Relations, Council on Sec. 14.017 (4)	Jamie Aulik	Manitowoc	Pleas. of Gov.	None
	Linda Fournier	Sparta	Pleas. of Gov.	None
	Larry Olson	Madison	Pleas. of Gov.	None
Milwaukee Child Welfare Partnership Council Secs. 15.09 (1)(a), 15.197 (24)	Deborah Blanks	Milwaukee	July 1, 2011	
	Tamara Grigsby	Milwaukee	July 1, 2013	None
	Christine Holmes	Milwaukee	July 1, 2013	None
	Marshall Murray	Wauwatosa	July 1, 2013	None
	Michael Skwierawski	Milwaukee	July 1, 2013	None
	Colleen Ellingson	Milwaukee	July 1, 2014	None
	Francine Feinberg	Whitefish Bay	July 1, 2014	None
	Mallory O'Brien	Milwaukee	July 1, 2014	None
	Linda Davis	Thiensville	July 1, 2015	None
	Willie Johnson	Milwaukee	July 1, 2015	None
	Kimberly Kampschroer	Milwaukee	July 1, 2015	None
	Russell Stamper II	Milwaukee	July 1, 2015	None
	John F. Weishan	Milwaukee	July 1, 2015	None
	Earnestine Willis	Milwaukee	July 1, 2015	None

Officers[1]	Name	Home Address[2]	Term Expires[3]	Salary or Per Diem[4]
Milwaukee River Revitalization Council Secs. 15.09 (1)(a), 15.347 (15)	Richard Flood	Cedarburg	July 1, 2008	None
	Jon Richards	Milwaukee	July 1, 2009	None
	Cheryl Brickman	Mequon	July 1, 2010	None
	Raymond Krueger	Milwaukee	July 1, 2010	None
	Christine Nuernberg	Mequon	July 1, 2010	None
	Nancy Frank	Elkhorn	July 1, 2011	None
	Ronald Stadler	Cedarburg	July 1, 2011	None
	Caroline Icks Torinus	West Bend	July 1, 2011	None
	Dan Small	Belgium	July 1, 2012	None
	Christopher Svoboda	Milwaukee	July 1, 2012	None
	vacancy			
Mississippi River Parkway Commission Sec. 14.85 (1)(a)	Frank Fiorenza	Potosi	Feb. 1, 2012	None
	Dennis Donath	Prescott	Feb. 1, 2016	None
	Jean Galasinski	Trempealeau	Feb. 1, 2016	None
	Joachim Kostrau	Bagley	Feb. 1, 2016	None
	Alan Lorenz	La Crosse	Feb. 1, 2016	None
	Robert Miller	Alma	Feb. 1, 2016	None
	Anne Muirhead	Genoa	Feb. 1, 2016	None
	Sherry Quamme	Ferryville	Feb. 1, 2016	None
	David Smith	Pepin	Feb. 1, 2016	None
Multifamily Dwelling Code Council Secs. 15.09 (1)(a), 15.157 (12)	Korinne Schneider	Milwaukee	July 1, 2007	None
	Michael Morey	Madison	July 1, 2008	None
	Kraig Biefeld	Ixonia	July 1, 2011	None
	Edward Gray	Kenosha	July 1, 2011	None
	Jeffery Brohmer	La Crosse	July 1, 2012	None
	Beth Gonnering	Kenosha	July 1, 2012	None
	David Nitz	Berlin	July 1, 2012	None
	Mark Scott	Pewaukee	July 1, 2012	None
	James Klett	Milwaukee	July 1, 2013	None
	Kevin Wipperfurth	McFarland	July 1, 2013	None
	Scott Burkart	Eau Claire	July 1, 2014	None
	Peter Scheuerman	Plymouth	July 1, 2014	None
	3 vacancies			
National and Community Service Board Sec. 15.105 (24)	Larry Kleinsteiber	Madison	May 1, 2008	None
	Maia Pearson	Madison	May 1, 2010	None
	Martha Kerner	Madison	May 1, 2012	None
	Rachel Graham	Madison	May 1, 2013	None
	Thi Le	Madison	May 1, 2013	None
	Sondra LeGrand	La Crosse	May 1, 2013	None
	Yia Thao	Green Bay	May 1, 2013	None
	Lisa Delmore	Wisconsin Dells	May 1, 2014	None
	Marguita Fox	Middleton	May 1, 2014	None
	Scott Fromader	Madison	May 1, 2014	None
	Sue Grady	Madison	May 1, 2014	None
	Robert Griffith	Kenosha	May 1, 2014	None
	Kathleen Groat	Appleton	May 1, 2014	None
	James Langdon	Madison	May 1, 2014	None
	Amy McDowell	Madison	May 1, 2014	None
	Mark Mueller	Lake Mills	May 1, 2014	None
	John Scocos	Madison	May 1, 2014	None
	Bob Guenther	Sheboygan	May 1, 2015	None
	Angela Kringle	Shawano	May 1, 2015	None
	Margaret Moore	Whitefish Bay	May 1, 2015	None
	Donald P. Dunbar	Madison	May 1, 2016	None
	Anthony F. Hallman	Three Lakes	May 1, 2016	None
*Natural Resources, Dept. of, Secy. Sec. 15.05 (1)(c)	Cathy Stepp	Sturtevant	Pleas. of Gov.	Group 7
*Natural Resources Board Secs. 15.07 (1)(a), 15.34	Christine Thomas	Plover	May 1, 2015	None
	Jane Wiley	Wausau	May 1, 2015	None
	William Bruins	Waupun	May 1, 2017	None
	Terry Hilgenberg	Shawano	May 1, 2017	None
	Gregory Kazmierski	Mukwonago	May 1, 2017	None
	Preston D. Cole[5]	Milwaukee	May 1, 2019	None
	Gary Zimmer	Laona	May 1, 2019	None
Nonmotorized Recreation and Transportation Trails Council Sec. 15.347 (20)	Rod Bartlow	Slinger	Pleas. of Gov.	None
	William Hauda	Dodgeville	Pleas. of Gov.	None
	Dana Johnson	Waukesha	Pleas. of Gov.	None
	Anne Murphy	Poynette	Pleas. of Gov.	None
	Joel Patenaude	Middleton	Pleas. of Gov.	None
	Debbie Peterson	Balsam Lake	Pleas. of Gov.	None
	David Phillips	Madison	Pleas. of Gov.	None
	Geoffrey Snudden	Green Bay	Pleas. of Gov.	None
	Blake Theisen	Madison	Pleas. of Gov.	None
	Ned Zuelsdorff	Madison	Pleas. of Gov.	None
*Nursing, Board of Secs. 15.01 (6), 15.08, 15.405 (7g)	Maria Joseph	Madison	July 1, 2013	$25 per day
	Gretchen Lowe	Madison	July 1, 2013	$25 per day
	Kay Coppens	West Bend	July 1, 2014	$25 per day
	Julia Nelson	Boscobel	July 1, 2014	$25 per day
	Carol Ott	Mequon	July 1, 2014	$25 per day
	Julie Ellis	New Berlin	July 1, 2015	$25 per day
	Rachelle Lancaster	Fond du Lac	July 1, 2015	$25 per day
	Lillian Nolan[5]	Fond du Lac	July 1, 2015	$25 per day
	Jeffrey Miller[5]	Cedarburg	July 1, 2016	$25 per day

Officers[1]	Name	Home Address[2]	Term Expires[3]	Salary or Per Diem[4]
*Nursing Home Administrator Examining Board Secs. 15.08, 15.405 (7m)	David Egan.	Kenosha	July 1, 2007	$25 per day
	Susan Kinast-Porter	Monroe	July 1, 2009	$25 per day
	Kenneth Arneson.	Oshkosh	July 1, 2010	$25 per day
	Loreli Dickinson.	Oconto	July 1, 2011	$25 per day
	Mary Lease.	Oregon	July 1, 2011	$25 per day
	Mary Pike	Madison	July 1, 2011	$25 per day
	Mary Ann Clark	Cumberland	July 1, 2013	$25 per day
	Earlene Ronk.	Jefferson	July 1, 2014	$25 per day
	Heather Sheehan.	Hayward	July 1, 2014	$25 per day
*Occupational Therapists Affiliated Credentialing Board Sec. 15.406 (5)	Mylinda Barisas-Matula	Sheboygan	July 1, 2010	$25 per day
	Deborah McKernan-Ace.	Stoughton	July 1, 2010	$25 per day
	David Cooper	Slinger	July 1, 2011	$25 per day
	Dorothy Olson	Appleton	July 1, 2011	$25 per day
	Gail Slaughter	Two Rivers	July 1, 2011	$25 per day
	Brian Holmquist	Madison	July 1, 2013	$25 per day
	Corliss Rice	Milwaukee	July 1, 2013	$25 per day
Offender Reentry, Council on Sec. 15.145 (5)	Melinda Danforth	Oneida	July 1, 2011	None
	Jerry Hancock	Madison	July 1, 2011	None
	Janine Geske	Milwaukee	July 1, 2012	None
	Chuck Brendel	Sheboygan	July 1, 2014	None
	John Chisholm	Milwaukee	July 1, 2014	None
	Robert Pedersen	Menasha	July 1, 2014	None
	Michael Tobin	Madison	July 1, 2014	None
	Arline Hillestad	Stevens Point	July 1, 2015	None
	Mark Podoll	Berlin	July 1, 2015	None
	Jason Witt	Onalaska	July 1, 2015	None
*Optometry Examining Bd. Secs. 15.08, 15.405 (8)	Swaminat Balachandran	Verona	July 1, 2010	$25 per day
	Gregory Foster.	Neillsville	July 1, 2013	$25 per day
	Ann Meier Carli	Green Bay	July 1, 2014	$25 per day
	Brian Hammes	Fond du Lac	July 1, 2015	$25 per day
	Mark Jinkins[5]	Sturgeon Bay	July 1, 2016	$25 per day
	Robert Schulz[5]	Appleton	July 1, 2016	$25 per day
	Richard L. Fogg[5]	La Crosse	July 1, 2017	$25 per day
*Parole Commission, Chairperson Secs. 15.145 (1), 17.07 (3m)	Kathleen Nagle.	Fond du Lac	March 1, 2015	Group 2
Perfusionists Examining Council Sec. 15.407 (2m)	David Cobb	Madison	July 1, 2010	$25 per day
*Pharmacy Examining Board Secs. 15.08, 15.405 (9)	Suzette Renwick	La Crosse	July 1, 2012	$25 per day
	Gregory Weber.	Milwaukee	July 1, 2014	$25 per day
	Charlotte Rasmussen.	Stanley	July 1, 2015	$25 per day
	Thaddeus Schumacher.	Fitchburg	July 1, 2015	$25 per day
	Franklin LaDien[5].	Menomonee Falls	July 1, 2016	$25 per day
	Kristi Sullivan[5].	Fitchburg	July 1, 2016	$25 per day
	Philip Trapskin[5]	Fitchburg	July 1, 2017	$25 per day
	Cathy Winters[5]	Wausau	July 1, 2017	$25 per day
Physical Disabilities, Council on Secs. 15.09 (1)(a), 15.197 (4)	Sandra Stokes	Green Bay	July 1, 2010	None
	Christine Duranceau	Rothschild	July 1, 2011	None
	Jeffrey Fox	Gordon	July 1, 2011	None
	Jon Baltmanis	Waupaca	July 1, 2012	None
	Benjamin Barrett.	Trego	July 1, 2013	None
	Karen Secor	Montreal	July 1, 2013	None
	Lewis Tyler	Brookfield	July 1, 2013	None
	Charles Vandenplas	Clintonville	July 1, 2013	None
	Joanne Zimmerman	Bayside	July 1, 2013	None
	Roberto Escamilla II.	Cudahy	July 1, 2015	None
	John Meissner	Little Chute	July 1, 2015	None
	Joey Torkelson	Delavan	July 1, 2015	None
	Noah Hershkowitz	Madison	July 1, 2016	None
	vacancy			
*Physical Therapy Examining Board Sec. 15.405 (7r)	Thomas Murphy[5].	De Pere	July 1, 2013	$25 per day
	Jane Stroede	Wisconsin Dells	July 1, 2013	$25 per day
	Michele Thorman[5]	La Crosse	July 1, 2015	$25 per day
	Shari Berry.	Tomah	July 1, 2016	$25 per day
	Lori Dominiczak[5]	Brown Deer	July 1, 2017	$25 per day
Physician Assistants, Council on Secs. 15.08, 15.407 (2)	Mary Pangman Schmitt[5].	Waterford	July 1, 2008	None
*Podiatry Affiliated Credentialing Board Secs. 15.406 (3)	Gary Brown	Kenosha	July 1, 2014	$25 per day
	William Weis.	Franklin	July 1, 2015	$25 per day
	Jeffery Giesking[5].	Menomonie	July 1, 2016	$25 per day
	Thomas Komp[5].	Suamico	July 1, 2017	$25 per day
*Prison Industries Board Secs. 15.07 (1)(b) 12, 15.145 (2)	Lyle Balistreri	Wauwatosa	May 1, 2008	None
	James Langdon.	DeForest	May 1, 2011	None
	Debra Pickett.	Darlington	May 1, 2011	None
	Bill Holley	Middleton	May 1, 2012	None
	Jose Carrillo	Janesville	May 1, 2014	None
	Tracey Isensee	Black River Falls	May 1, 2014	None
	Helen McCain[5].	Madison	May 1, 2015	None
	Bill Smith	Madison	May 1, 2015	None
	Edward F. Wall.	Windsor	May 1, 2015	None

Officers[1]	Name	Home Address[2]	Term Expires[3]	Salary or Per Diem[4]
*Psychology Examining Board Secs. 15.08, 15.405 (10m)	Teresa Rose	Hazelhurst	July 1, 2012	$25 per day
	Melissa Westendorf	South Milwaukee	July 1, 2013	$25 per day
	Rebecca Anderson	Milwaukee	July 1, 2014	$25 per day
	Bruce Erdmann[5]	Madison	July 1, 2015	$25 per day
	Daniel Schroeder[5]	Hartland	July 1, 2015	$25 per day
	vacancy			
*Public Defender Board Secs. 15.07 (1)(a), 15.78	Joe Morales	Racine	May 1, 2012	None
	James Brennan	Milwaukee	May 1, 2013	None
	Ellen Thorn	Sparta	May 1, 2013	None
	Daniel M. Berkos	Mauston	May 1, 2014	None
	John J. Hogan	Rhinelander	May 1, 2014	None
	Michael Maxwell	Waukesha	May 1, 2014	None
	David Coon	Brookfield	May 1, 2015	None
	Mai N. Xiong[5]	Kronenwetter	May 1, 2015	None
	Regina Dunkin[5]	Beloit	May 1, 2016	None
Public Health Council Sec. 15.197 (13)	Mary Jo Baisch	Milwaukee	July 1, 2011	None
	Catherine Frey	Madison	July 1, 2011	None
	Gary Gilmore	La Crosse	July 1, 2011	None
	Deborah Miller	Dorchester	July 1, 2011	None
	A. Charles Post	Milwaukee	July 1, 2011	None
	Ayaz Samadani	Beaver Dam	July 1, 2011	None
	Julie Willems Van Dijk	Wausau	July 1, 2011	None
	Mark Villalpando	Sturtevant	July 1, 2011	None
	Bevan Baker	Milwaukee	July 1, 2012	None
	John Bartkowski	Milwaukee	July 1, 2012	None
	Bridget Clementi	Waukesha	July 1, 2012	None
	Faye Dodge	Keshena	July 1, 2012	None
	Terri Kramolis	Ashland	July 1, 2012	None
	Douglas Nelson	Milwaukee	July 1, 2012	None
	Thai Vue	La Crosse	July 1, 2012	None
	Amy Bremel	Fish Creek	July 1, 2013	None
	Susan Garcia Franz	Neenah	July 1, 2013	None
	Corazon Loteyro	Mercer	July 1, 2013	None
	Gretchen Sampson	Balsam Lake	July 1, 2013	None
	James Sanders	Milwaukee	July 1, 2013	None
	Lynn Sheets	Milwaukee	July 1, 2013	None
	William Keeton	Oconomowoc	July 1, 2016	None
Public Records Board Sec. 15.105 (4)	Carl Buesing	Sheboygan	Pleas. of Gov.	None
	Carol Hemersbach	Greenwood	Pleas. of Gov.	None
	Scott Kowalski	Madison	Pleas. of Gov.	None
	Sandra Rudd	Pardeeville	Pleas. of Gov.	None
	Peter Sorce	Germantown	Pleas. of Gov.	None
*Public Service Commission Secs. 15.06 (1), 15.79	Eric Callisto	Madison	March 1, 2015	Group 5
	Phil Montgomery	Green Bay	March 1, 2017	Group 5
	Ellen Nowak[5]	Mequon	March 1, 2019	Group 5
*Radiography Examining Bd. Sec. 15.407 (7e)	Mary Jafari	Onalaska	May 1, 2012	None
	Kelley Grant	Sturtevant	May 1, 2013	None
	James Lemerond	Cleveland	May 1, 2014	None
	Gregg Bogost	Madison	May 1, 2015	None
	Susan Sanson[5]	Greenfield	May 1, 2016	None
	2 vacancies			
*Railroads, Commissioner of Secs. 15.06 (1)(ar), 15.795 (1)	Jeff Plale	South Milwaukee	March 1, 2017	Group 5
*Real Estate Appraisers Board Secs. 15.07 (1)(b) 17, 15.07 (1)(cm), 15.07 (5)(x), 15.405 (10r)	Henry F. Simon	Middleton	May 1, 2009	$25 per day
	Marla Britton	Westby	May 1, 2011	$25 per day
	Jose Perez	Milwaukee	May 1, 2011	$25 per day
	Lawrence Nicholson	Hartland	May 1, 2014	$25 per day
	Scott Brunner[5]	Wauwatosa	May 1, 2016	$25 per day
	Carl Clementi	Hartland	May 1, 2016	$25 per day
	vacancy			
Real Estate Curriculum and Examinations, Council on Secs. 15.09 (1)(a), 15.407 (5)	Susan E. Hamer	Green Bay	July 1, 2004	None
	Lawrence Sager	Madison	July 1, 2004	None
	Paul G. Hoffman	Waukesha	July 1, 2006	None
	Peter Sveum	Stoughton	July 1, 2006	None
	Richard Hinsman	Racine	July 1, 2007	None
	Peggy Lovejoy	West Salem	July 1, 2007	None
	Barbara McGill	Waukesha	July 1, 2010	None
*Real Estate Examining Board Sec. 15.405 (11m)	Dennis Pierce	Kenosha	July 1, 2013	$25 per day
	Stephen Beers[5]	Fontana	July 1, 2014	$25 per day
	Michael Mulleady	Minocqua	July 1, 2014	$25 per day
	Charles Szafir III.	Milwaukee	July 1, 2016	$25 per day
	Marie Hetzer	Sun Prairie	July 1, 2016	$25 per day
	Randal Savaglio	Racine	July 1, 2017	$25 per day
	Tammy Wagner	Stevens Point	July 1, 2017	$25 per day
Recycling, Council on Secs. 15.09 (1)(b), 15.347 (17)	James Birmingham	Greendale	Jan. 5, 2015	None
	George Hayducsko, Jr.	Menomonie	Jan. 5, 2015	None
	Charles Larscheid	Green Bay	Jan. 5, 2015	None
	Joseph Liebau, Jr.	Milwaukee	Jan. 5, 2015	None
	Rick Meyers	Milwaukee	Jan. 5, 2015	None
	Neil Peters-Michaud	Middleton	Jan. 5, 2015	None
	William Waltz	Oconomowoc	Jan. 5, 2015	None
Respiratory Care Practitioners Examining Council Secs. 15.08, 15.407 (1m)	vacancy			

Officers[1]	Name	Home Address[2]	Term Expires[3]	Salary or Per Diem[4]
Retirement Board, Wis. Secs. 15.07 (1)(a), 15.165 (3)(b)	John David	Watertown	May 1, 2008	$25 per day
	Wayne E. Koessl	Kenosha	May 1, 2009	$25 per day
	Herbert Stinski	Milton	May 1, 2012	$25 per day
	Jamie Aulik	Manitowoc	May 1, 2013	$25 per day
	Mary Von Ruden	Sparta	May 1, 2013	$25 per day
	Steven Wilding	Oak Creek	May 1, 2016	$25 per day
	2 vacancies			
Retirement Systems, Jt. Survey Com. on Sec. 13.50 (1)(c)	Tim Pederson	Hartland	Feb. 14, 2015	None
*Revenue, Dept. of, Secy. Secs. 15.05 (1)(a), 15.43	Richard Chandler	Madison	Pleas. of Gov.	Group 7
*Rural Health Development Council Sec. 15.917 (1)	Erica Hoven	Westby	July 1, 2009	None
	Linda L. McFarlin	Friendship	July 1, 2009	None
	Byron Crouse	Madison	July 1, 2012	None
	Tim Size	Sauk City	July 1, 2013	None
	Charlie Walker	Chippewa Falls	July 1, 2014	None
	Jeremy Normington-Slay	Friendship	July 1, 2015	None
	Syed Ahmed	Brookfield	July 1, 2016	None
	James O'Keefe	Mauston	July 1, 2016	None
	Blane Christman	Chippewa Falls	July 1, 2017	None
	Jacalyn Szehner	Plover	July 1, 2018	None
	3 vacancies			
*Safety and Professional Services, Dept. of, Secy. Secs. 15.05 (1)(a), 15.40	Dave Ross	Superior	Pleas. of Gov.	Group 4
*Savings Institutions Review Board Sec. 15.185 (3)	George Gary	Milwaukee	May 1, 2014	$10 per day
	Robert Holmes	Tomah	May 1, 2014	$10 per day
	James Olson	Appleton	May 1, 2014	$10 per day
	Paul Adamski	Stevens Point	May 1, 2017	$10 per day
	Charles Schmalz	Appleton	May 1, 2017	$10 per day
*Sign Language Interpreter Council Sec. 15.407 (9)(a)	Debra Gorra Barash	Bayside	July 1, 2014	None
	Carlos Jaramillo	Madison	July 1, 2014	None
	Joel Mankowski	Greenfield	July 1, 2014	None
	Faye Jordan Peters	Appleton	July 1, 2014	None
	Joseph Riggio	Madison	July 1, 2014	None
	Steven Smart	Waukesha	July 1, 2014	None
	Christopher Woodfill	Delavan	July 1, 2014	None
Small Business Environmental Council Secs. 15.09 (1)(a), 15.347 (8)	Michael Simpson	Milwaukee	July 1, 2012	None
	Jeanne Whitish	Cross Plains	July 1, 2013	None
	Amy Litscher	Lake Mills	July 1, 2014	None
Small Business Regulatory Review Board Sec. 15.155 (5)	James Ring	Madison	May 1, 2014	None
	Kimberly Vele	Bowler	May 1, 2014	None
	Thomas Wulf	Sturgeon Bay	May 1, 2014	None
	Steven Davis	Oshkosh	May 1, 2015	None
	Erich Korth	Neenah	May 1, 2015	None
	Guy Wood	New Auburn	May 1, 2015	None
*Snowmobile Recreational Council Secs. 15.09 (1)(a), 15.347 (7)	Karen Carlson	Frederic	July 1, 2013	None
	Mike Cerny	Sharon	July 1, 2013	None
	Beverly Dittmar	Eagle River	July 1, 2013	None
	Patrick Schmutzer	Franksville	July 1, 2013	None
	Michael Willman	Merrill	July 1, 2013	None
	Jon Schweitzer	Black River Falls	July 1, 2013	None
	Jerry Green	Black River Falls	July 1, 2014	None
	Samuel Landes	Dane	July 1, 2014	None
	Robert Lang	Cable	July 1, 2014	None
	Andrew Malecki	Green Bay	July 1, 2014	None
	David Newman	Unity	July 1, 2014	None
	Thomas Chwala[5]	Lake Mills	July 1, 2015	None
	Larry Erickson[5]	Hurley	July 1, 2015	None
	Dale Mayo[5]	Conover	July 1, 2015	None
	Lee Van Zeeland[5]	Appleton	July 1, 2015	None
*Southeast Wis. Professional Baseball Park Dist. Board Sec. 229.66 (2)	Gerardo Gonzalez	Mequon	July 1, 2015	None
	Erik Johnson[5]	Madison	July 1, 2015	None
	Tracey Klein	Brookfield	July 1, 2015	None
	William L. McReynolds[5]	Racine	July 1, 2015	None
	Kristine O'Meara[5]	West Bend	July 1, 2015	None
	Don Smiley	Milwaukee	July 1, 2015	None
Sporting Heritage Council Sec. 15.347 (21)	William Torhorst	Oregon	May 1, 2016	None
State Capitol and Executive Residence Board Sec. 15.105 (5)	Laurel McManus Brown	Fitchburg	May 1, 2013	None
	Ronald Siggelkow	Madison	May 1, 2013	None
	Jay Fernholz	Holmen	May 1, 2015	None
	Arlan Kay	Madison	May 1, 2015	None
	Kathryn Neitzel	Verona	May 1, 2017	None
	Marijo Reed	Oconomowoc	May 1, 2017	None
State Employees Suggestion Board Sec. 15.105 (29)(c) 1.	David M. Vriezen	Waterloo	May 1, 2011	None
	Sandy Drew	Madison	May 1, 2013	None
	vacancy			

Officers[1]	Name	Home Address[2]	Term Expires[3]	Salary or Per Diem[4]
*State Fair Park Board Secs. 15.07 (1)(b), 15 15.07 (5)(j), 15.445 (4)	Jim Sullivan	Wauwatosa	Jan. 1, 2012	None
	Leah Vukmir	Wauwatosa	Jan. 1, 2013	None
	Keith Ripp	Lodi	Jan. 1, 2013	None
	Dan Devine	Milwaukee	May 1, 2014	$10 per day, not exc. $600 per year
	James Villa[5]	West Allis	May 1, 2014	$10 per day, not exc. $600 per year
	Aldo Madrigrano	Sussex	May 1, 2015	$10 per day, not exc. $600 per year
	Mary Maas	Tomah	May 1, 2016	$10 per day, not exc. $600 per year
	John Yingling	Mequon	May 1, 2015	$10 per day, not exc. $600 per year
	Sue Rupnow[5]	Wausau	May 1, 2017	$10 per day, not exc. $600 per year
	Susan Crane[5]	Burlington	May 1, 2018	$10 per day, not exc. $600 per year
*State Historical Society of Wisconsin Board of Curators Sec. 15.70	Elizabeth Adelman	Mukwonago	July 1, 2013	None
	Trig Solberg	Woodruff	July 1, 2014	None
	William Van Sant[5]	Bayfield	July 1, 2015	None
	Dave Anderson	Malone	Pleas. of Gov.	None
State Trails Council Secs. 15.09 (1)(a), 15.347 (16)	Thomas Huber	Madison	July 1, 2007	None
	Jim Joque	Mosinee	July 1, 2011	None
	Lindor Maletzke	Mountain	July 1, 2013	None
	Bryan Much	Oconomowoc	July 1, 2013	None
	David Phillips	Madison	July 1, 2013	None
	Robbie Webber	Madison	July 1, 2013	None
	Ken Carpenter	Fort Atkinson	July 1, 2015	None
	Randy Harden	Sheboygan	July 1, 2015	None
	Doug Johnson	DeForest	July 1, 2015	None
	Phillip Johnsrud	Iola	July 1, 2015	None
	LuAna Schneider	DeForest	July 1, 2015	None
	Michael McFadzen	Plymouth	July 1, 2017	None
State Use Board Secs. 15.07 (1)(b), 15.105 (22)	Michael Casey	Bloomington	May 1, 2011	None
	Nickolas George, Jr.	Madison	May 1, 2011	None
	Bill Smith	Madison	May 1, 2011	None
	Jean Zweifel	Albany	May 1, 2011	None
	Tim Casper	Madison	May 1, 2013	None
	Marie Danforth	Madison	May 1, 2013	None
	David Dumke	Brule	May 1, 2013	None
	Enid Glenn	Madison	May 1, 2013	None
	Helen McCain	Madison	May 1, 2017	None
*Tax Appeals Commission Secs. 15.01 (2), 15.06 (1)(a), 15.06 (3)(a) 2, 15.105 (1)	Thomas McAdams	Greendale	March 1, 2013	Group 4
	Roger LeGrand	La Crosse	March 1, 2015	Group 4
	Lorna Hemp Boll	Madison	March 1, 2017	Group 4
Tax Exemptions, Jt. Survey Com. on Sec. 13.52 (1) (d)	Kimberly Shaul	Cottage Grove	Jan. 15, 2013	None
Teachers Retirement Board Secs. 15.07 (5)(f), 15.165 (3)(a)	Sandra Claflin-Chalton	Menomonie	May 1, 2012	$25 per day
	Daniel Nerad	Madison	May 1, 2013	$25 per day
	Roberta Rasmus	Chippewa Falls	May 1, 2013	None
	Susan Harrison	Menomonie	May 1, 2014	$25 per day
*Technical College System Board Secs. 15.07 (1)(a), 15.07 (5)(e), 15.94	Mary Cuene	Green Bay	May 1, 2013	$100 per year
	Natalie Cruz	Hartland	May 1, 2013	$100 per year
	Phillip Neuenfeldt	Milwaukee	May 1, 2013	$100 per year
	Stan Davis	Sun Prairie	May 1, 2015	$100 per year
	Becky Levzow	Rio	May 1, 2015	$100 per year
	Andrew Petersen	Verona	May 1, 2015	$100 per year
	Philip Baranowski	Green Lake	May 1, 2017	$100 per year
	John Schwantes	Elkhart Lake	May 1, 2017	$100 per year
	Stephen Willett	Phillips	May 1, 2017	$100 per year
	Stephen Mark Tyler[5]	Woodville	May 1, 2019	$100 per year
Tourism, Council on Secs. 15.09 (1)(a), 15.447 (1)	Paul Cunningham	Fond du Lac	July 1, 2014	None
	Stanton Peter Helland, Jr.	Wisconsin Dells	July 1, 2014	None
	Aimee Juan	Cumberland	July 1, 2014	None
	Joe Klimczak	Blue Mounds	July 1, 2014	None
	Deborah Archer	Cross Plains	July 1, 2015	None
	James Bolen	Cable	July 1, 2015	None
	Kathy Kopp	Platteville	July 1, 2015	None
	Paul Upchurch	Milwaukee	July 1, 2015	None
	Stacey Watson	Milwaukee	July 1, 2015	None
	Cindy L. Burzinski	Eagle River	July 1, 2016	None
	Allyson Gommer	Eau Claire	July 1, 2016	None
	Brian Kelsey	Fish Creek	July 1, 2016	None
	Scott Krause	Green Lake	July 1, 2016	None
	Lola L. Roeh	Elkhart Lake	July 1, 2016	None
*Tourism, Dept. of, Secy. Secs. 15.05 (1)(a), 15.44	Stephanie Klett	Beloit	Pleas. of Gov.	Group 6
*Transportation, Dept. of, Secy. Secs. 15.05 (1)(a), 15.46	Mark Gottlieb	Port Washington	Pleas. of Gov.	Group 7
Transportation Projects Commission Sec. 13.489 (1)	Thomas Carlsen	Verona	Pleas. of Gov.	None
	Barbara Fleisner	Mosinee	Pleas. of Gov.	None
	Michael Ryan	Waunakee	Pleas. of Gov.	None

Officers[1]	Name	Home Address[2]	Term Expires[3]	Salary or Per Diem[4]
Uniform State Laws, Commission on Sec. 13.55 (1)	Patience Roggensack	Madison	May 1, 2015	None
	John Macy	Waukesha	May 1, 2017	None
*Univ. of Wis. Hospitals and Clinics Authority Sec. 233.02	Carol L. Booth	Madison	Pleas. of Gov.	None
	Richard W. Choudoir	Columbus	Pleas. of Gov.	None
	Thomas Basting	Madison	July 1, 2014	None
	Richard Fetherston	Verona	July 1, 2014	None
	Mike Weiden[5]	Madison	July 1, 2014	None
	Lisa Reardon	Nashotah	July 1, 2015	None
	Humberto Vidaillet	Marshfield	July 1, 2015	None
	Pablo Sanchez[5]	Madison	July 1, 2017	None
*Univ. of Wis. System, Bd. of Regents of the Secs. 15.07 (1)(a), 15.91	Katherine Pointer	De Pere	May 1, 2013	None
	John Drew	Milwaukee	May 1, 2014	None
	Tracy Hribar	Franksville	May 1, 2014	None
	Gary Roberts	Onalaska	May 1, 2014	None
	Michael Falbo	Franklin	May 1, 2015	None
	David Walsh	Madison	May 1, 2015	None
	Chuck Pruitt	Milwaukee	May 1, 2016	None
	Jose Vasquez	Milwaukee	May 1, 2016	None
	Mark Bradley	Wausau	May 1, 2017	None
	Ed Manydeeds	Eau Claire	May 1, 2017	None
	Tim Higgins	Appleton	May 1, 2018	None
	Gerald Whitburn	Wausau	May 1, 2018	None
	John Behling	Eau Claire	May 1, 2019	None
	Regina Millner	Madison	May 1, 2019	None
	Margaret Farrow[5]	Pewaukee	May 1, 2020	None
	Janice Mueller[5]	Madison	May 1, 2020	None
Utility Public Benefits Council on Sec. 15.107 (17)	James Boullion	Madison	July 1, 2011	None
	Janis Ringhand	Evansville	July 1, 2013	None
*Veterans Affairs, Board of Secs. 15.07 (1)(a), 15.49	John Townsend	Fond du Lac	May 1, 2013	None
	Daniel Naylor	Waupaca	May 1, 2013	None
	Alan Richards	Grafton	May 1, 2013	None
	Marvin Freedman	Middleton	May 1, 2015	None
	Carl Krueger	Cudahy	May 1, 2015	None
	Peter Moran	Superior	May 1, 2015	None
	Daniel Bohlin	Stitzer	May 1, 2017	None
	Ben Collins	Lake Geneva	May 1, 2017	None
	John Gaedke	Merrimac	May 1, 2017	None
	Cathy Gorst[5]	Marshfield	May 1, 2017	None
	Kevin Nicholson	Wauwatosa	May 1, 2017	None
*Veterans Affairs, Dept. of, Secy. Sec. 15.05 (1m), 15.49	John Scocos	Fitchburg	Pleas. of Gov.	Group 6
Veterinary Diagnostic Laboratory Board Sec. 15.915 (1)	Sandra Larson	Evansville	May 1, 2014	None
	Alissa Grenawalt	Beloit	May 1, 2015	None
	Steven Van Lannen	Suamico	May 1, 2015	None
	James Meronek	Prairie du Sac	May 1, 2016	None
	Ray Pawlisch	Brodhead	May 1, 2016	None
	Sheryl Shaw	Middleton	Pleas. of Gov.	None
*Veterinary Examining Bd. Secs. 15.08, 15.405 (12)	Theresa Waage	Argyle	July 1, 2012	$25 per day
	William Rice	Milwaukee	July 1, 2013	$25 per day
	Robert R. Spencer	La Crosse	July 1, 2013	$25 per day
	Wesley Elford	Mayville	July 1, 2014	$25 per day
	Brenda Nemec	Pewaukee	July 1, 2014	$25 per day
	Sheldon Schall	Waunakee	July 1, 2014	$25 per day
	Philip Johnson	Wineconne	July 1, 2015	$25 per day
	Neil Wiseley[5]	Mayville	July 1, 2016	$25 per day
Volunteer Fire Fighter and Emergency Medical Technician Service Award Board Sec. 15.105 (26)	Robert H. Seitz	Monticello	May 1, 2005	None
	Kristen Halverson	Monona	May 1, 2009	None
	Allen Schraeder	Ripon	May 1, 2012	None
	Melinda Allen	Monroe	May 1, 2013	None
	John Scherer	Middleton	May 1, 2013	None
	Kenneth A. Bartz	Dodgeville	May 1, 2015	None
	vacancy			
*Waste Facility Siting Board Secs. 15.07 (1)(b) 11, 15.07 (5)(t), 15.105 (12)	James Schuerman	Wisconsin Rapids	May 1, 2013	$35 per day
	Dale Shaver	Waukesha	May 1, 2014	$35 per day
	Jeanette DeKeyser	Neenah	May 1, 2015	$35 per day
*Waterways Commission, Wis. Secs. 15.01 (2), 15.06 (1)(ag), 15.06 (3)(a) 3, 15.345 (1)	Roger Walsh	Wauwatosa	March 1, 2013	None
	Maureen Kinney	La Crosse	March 1, 2014	None
	James Rooney	Racine	March 1, 2014	None
	Lee Van Zeeland	Appleton	March 1, 2015	None
	vacancy			
Wisconsin Center District Board of Directors Sec. 229.42 (4)(e)	Franklyn Gimbel	Milwaukee	May 1, 2012	None
	Thomas Linscott	Milwaukee	May 1, 2013	None
	Stephen H. Marcus	River Hills	May 1, 2016	None
Wisconsin Compensation Rating Committee Sec. 626.31 (1)(b)	James Buchen	Verona	Pleas. of Gov.	None
	Daniel Burazin	Waterford	Pleas. of Gov.	None

Officers[1]	Name	Home Address[2]	Term Expires[3]	Salary or Per Diem[4]
Women's Council Secs. 15.09 (1)(a), 15.107 (11)	Renee Boldt	Appleton	July 1, 2011	None
	Jane Clark	Madison	July 1, 2011	None
	Nicole Bowman-Farrell	Shawano	July 1, 2012	None
	Mary Jo Baas.	Brookfield	July 1, 2014	None
	Jessie Nicholson	Milwaukee	July 1, 2014	None
	Patricia Cadorin	Hartland	July 1, 2015	None
	Karen Katz.	Wausau	July 1, 2015	None
	Michelle Mettner.	Madison	July 1, 2015	None
*Workforce Development, Dept. of, Secy. Secs. 15.05 (1)(a), 15.22	Reginald Newson	Milwaukee	Pleas. of Gov.	Group 6

*Nominated by the governor and appointed with the advice and consent of the senate. Senate confirmation is required for secretaries of departments, members of commissions and commissioners, governing boards, examining boards, and other boards as designated by statute.

[1]List includes *only* appointments made by the governor. Additional members frequently serve *ex officio* or are appointed by other means. The governor also appoints members of intrastate regional agencies and nonstatutory committees and makes temporary appointments under statute Chapter 17 to elected state and county offices when vacancies occur. For complete membership list of unit, including officers, see full description elsewhere in the *Blue Book*. Section numbers under each entry refer to statute sections authorizing appointment by the governor. Statute Section 21.18 provides for the governor's military staff.

[2]Home address is the municipality from which the officer was appointed to a full-time office or the current address of part-time officials.

[3]Terms are specified by the following statute sections or as otherwise provided by law: Sec. 15.05 (1) - secretaries; Sec. 15.06 (1) - commissioners; Sec. 15.07 (1) - governing boards and attached boards; Sec. 15.08 (1) - examining boards and councils; Sec. 15.09 (1) - councils.

[4]Members of boards and councils are reimbursed for actual and necessary expenses incurred in performing their duties. In addition, examining board members receive $25 per day for days worked, and members of certain other boards under statute Section 15.07 (5) receive a per diem as noted in the table. Statute Section 20.923 places state officials in one of 10 executive salary groups (ESG) for which salary ranges have been established. Group salary ranges for the period June 30, 2013 through June 27, 2015, are: Group 1: $60,001-$93,935; Group 2: $64,801-$101,450; Group 3: $69,986-$109,566; Group 4: $75,586-$118,333; Group 5: $81,632-$127,802; Group 6: $88,164-$138,029; Group 7: $95,217-$149,073; Group 8: $102,836-$160,999; Group 9: $111,065-$173,880; Group 10: $119,951-$187,793.

[5]Nominated by governor but not yet confirmed by senate.

[6]Compensation set by Economic Development Corporation Board.

Source: Appointment lists maintained by governor's office and received by the Legislative Reference Bureau on or before June 30, 2013.

Lieutenant Governor Kleefisch talks to pupils about the importance of disaster preparedness at the Student Tools for Emergency Planning (STEP) program at Woodlands School in Milwaukee. Also in attendance was General Don Dunbar, the state Adjutant General and head of the Department of Military Affairs, which contains the Wisconsin Division of Emergency Management. (Office of the Lieutenant Governor)

OFFICE OF THE LIEUTENANT GOVERNOR

Lieutenant Governor: REBECCA KLEEFISCH.

Chief of Staff and Media Inquiries: CASEY HIMEBAUCH.

Scheduling and Operations Director: MARGARET RING.

Policy Advisor: ROBERT SCHLAEGER.

Mailing Address: P.O. Box 2043, Madison 53702-2043.

Location: Room 19 East, State Capitol, Madison.

Telephone: 266-3516.

Fax: 267-3571.

Agency E-mail Address: ltgov@wisconsin.gov

Internet Address: www.ltgov.state.wi.us

Number of Employees: 4.00.

Total Budget 2011-13: $787,0000.

Constitutional References: Article V, Sections 1, 2, 3, 7, and 8; Article XIII, Section 10.

Statutory Reference: Chapter 14, Subchapter II.

Agency Responsibility: The lieutenant governor is the state's second-ranking executive officer, a position comparable to that of the Vice President of the United States. If the incumbent governor dies, resigns, or is removed from office, the lieutenant governor becomes governor for the balance of the unexpired term. (Prior to a constitutional amendment in April 1979, the lieutenant governor was considered only "acting governor" in those circumstances.) The lieutenant governor serves as acting governor when the governor is temporarily unable to perform the duties of the office due to impeachment, incapacitation, or absence from the state. If the lieutenant governor becomes governor, he or she must nominate a new lieutenant governor and the successor must be confirmed by the senate and the assembly.

The governor may designate the lieutenant governor to represent the governor's office on any statutory board, commission, or committee on which the governor is entitled to membership. Under such designation, the lieutenant governor has all the authority and responsibility granted by law to the governor. The governor may also designate the lieutenant governor to represent the chief executive's office on any nonstatutory committee or intergovernmental body created to maintain relationships with federal, state, and local governments or regional agencies. The lieutenant governor participates in national organizations of lieutenant governors and may be asked by the governor to coordinate specific state services and programs.

Organization: From 1848 until 1970, the lieutenant governor was elected for a 2-year term on a separate ballot in the November general election of even-numbered years. Since 1970, following amendment of the Wisconsin Constitution, voters have elected the governor and lieutenant governor on a joint ballot to a 4-year term. Candidates are nominated independently in the partisan August primary, but voters cast a combined ballot for the two offices in the November election.

History: The Territory of Wisconsin had no lieutenant governor, but the secretary of the territory was authorized to act as governor in the event of the governor's death or absence. The Wisconsin Constitution of 1848 provided for the post of lieutenant governor after considerable debate. Some delegates to the convention argued that the president of the senate, chosen from the membership of that body, should succeed the governor, with the secretary of state second in line of succession. The convention delegates who objected to a person's becoming governor without being elected on a statewide basis prevailed, however, and the post of lieutenant governor was included in the constitution.

Originally, the lieutenant governor was also the president of the senate and could cast a deciding vote in case of a tie. In 1979, the voters ratified a constitutional amendment enabling the senate to choose its own presiding officer from among its members, beginning in 1981.

Department of
ADMINISTRATION

Address e-mail by combining the user ID and the state extender: userid@**wisconsin.gov**
All telephone numbers are 608 area code unless otherwise indicated.

Secretary of Administration: MIKE HUEBSCH, 266-1741, mike.huebsch@
Deputy Secretary: Chris Schoenherr, 266-1741, chris.schoenherr@
Executive Assistant: Wendy Coomer, 266-1741, wendy.coomer@
Chief Legal Counsel: Gregory Murray, 267-0202, gregory.murray@
Communications Director: Stephanie Marquis, 267-7874, stephanie.marquis@
Mailing Address: P.O. Box 7864, Madison 53707-7864.
Location: State Administration Building, 101 East Wilson Street, Madison.
Telephone: (608) 266-1741.
Fax: (608) 267-3842.
Internet Address: www.doa.wi.gov
Number of Employees: 921.58.
Total Budget 2011-13: $2,032,248,000.
Statutory References: Sections 15.10 and 15.103; Chapter 16.

Administrative Services, Division of: James Langdon, *administrator,* 267-1001,
   james.langdon@; Fax: 264-9500; P.O. Box 7869, Madison 53707-7869.
   Financial Management, Bureau of: Jana Steinmetz, *director,* 266-1359, jana.steinmetz@
   Personnel, Bureau of: Kim Pomeroy, *director,* 266-0653, kim.pomeroy@
   State Prosecutors Office: Philip Werner, *director,* 267-2700, phil.werner@
Capitol Police, Division of: David Erwin, *police chief and administrator,* 266-7546,
   david.erwin@; Fax: 267-9343; B2N State Capitol, Madison 53702.
Energy Services, Division of: Kevin Vesperson, *administrator,* 261-6357, kevin.vesperson@;
   Susan S. Brown, *deputy administrator,* 266-2035, susan.brown@; Fax: 267-6931; P.O. Box
   7868, Madison 53707-7868.
   Home Energy Plus, Bureau of: Barb Klug Sieja, *director,* 267-0227, barbara.klugsieja@
   State Energy Office: David J. Jenkins, *program manager,* 264-7651, davidj.jenkins@
Enterprise Operations, Division of: Helen McCain, *administrator,* 267-9634, helen.mccain@;
   Fax: 267-0600; P.O. Box 7867, Madison 53707-7867.
   Enterprise Fleet, Bureau of: John Marx, *director,* 267-7693, john.marx@
   Procurement, Bureau of: Rick Hughes, *director,* 266-1558, rick.hughes@
   State Risk Management, Bureau of: Rollie Boeding, *director,* 266-1866, rollie.boeding@;
      Fax: 264-8250.
Enterprise Technology, Division of: David Cagigal, *administrator and state chief information
   officer,* 261-8406, david.cagigal@; Herb Thompson, *deputy administrator,* 261-7750,
   herb.thompson@; Fax: 267-0626; P.O. Box 7844, Madison 53707-7844.
   Business Application Support, Bureau of: Kathy Skiera, *director,* 261-9570,
      kathy.skiera@
   Business Services, Bureau of: James Sylla, *acting director,* 264-6186, james.sylla@
   District Attorneys Information Technology, Bureau of: Laura Radke, *director,* 261-6614,
      laura.radke@
   Infrastructure Support, Bureau of: Jim Schmolesky, *director,* 224-3777,
      jim.schmolesky@
   Publishing and Distribution, Bureau of: Timothy Smith, *director,* 266-5800,
      timothy.smith@

DEPARTMENT OF ADMINISTRATION

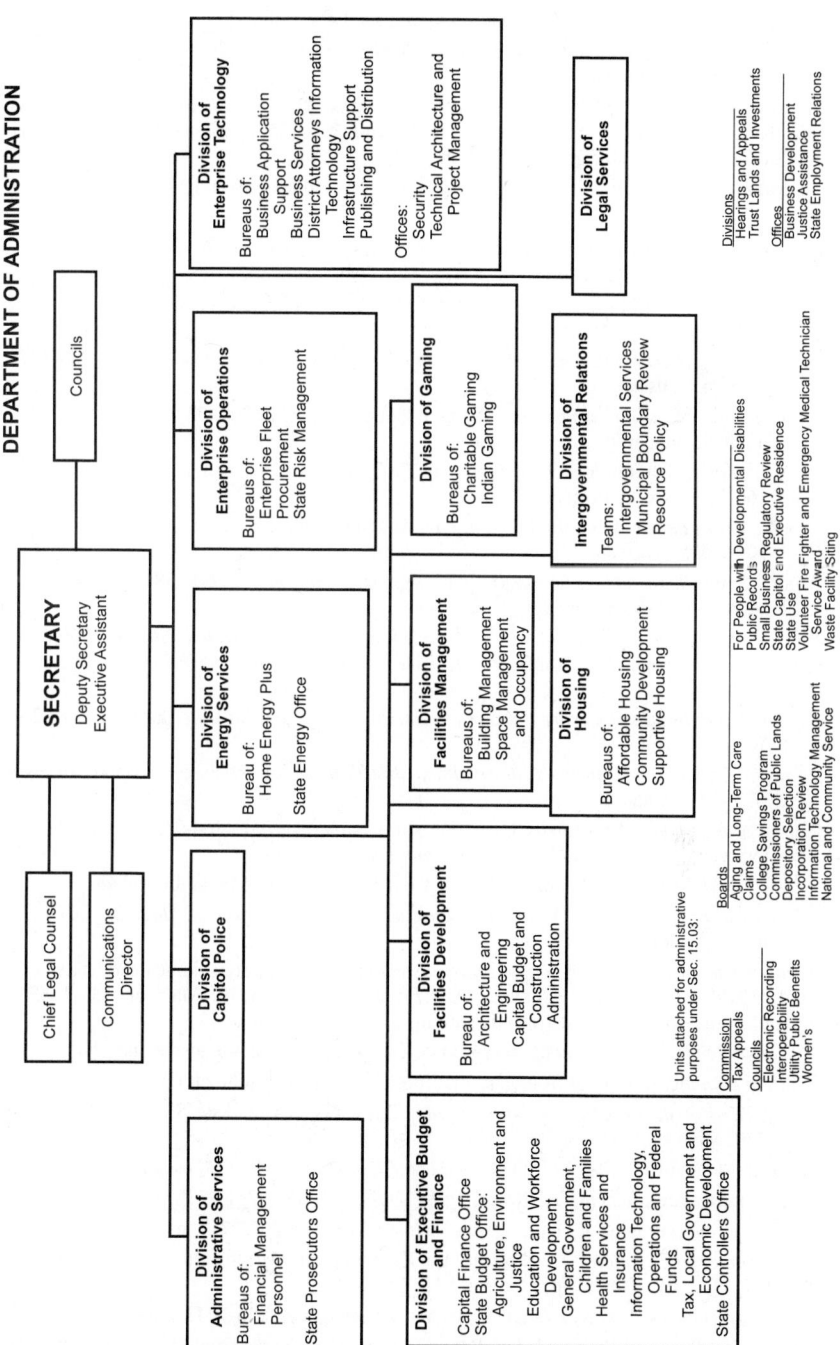

Councils

SECRETARY
Deputy Secretary
Executive Assistant

Chief Legal Counsel

Communications
Director

**Division of
Administrative Services**

Bureaus of:
Financial Management
Personnel

State Prosecutors Office

**Division of
Capitol Police**

**Division of Executive Budget
and Finance**

Capital Finance Office
State Budget Office:
  Agriculture, Environment and
    Justice
  Education and Workforce
    Development
  General Government,
    Children and Families
  Health Services and
    Insurance
  Information Technology,
    Operations and Federal
    Funds
  Tax, Local Government and
    Economic Development
State Controllers Office

**Division of
Facilities Development**

Bureau of:
  Architecture and
    Engineering
  Capital Budget and
    Construction
    Administration

**Division of
Energy Services**

Bureau of:
  Home Energy Plus

State Energy Office

**Division of
Facilities Management**

Bureaus of:
  Building Management
  Space Management
    and Occupancy

**Division of
Housing**

Bureaus of:
  Affordable Housing
  Community Development
  Supportive Housing

**Division of
Enterprise Operations**

Bureaus of:
  Enterprise Fleet
  Procurement
  State Risk Management

Division of Gaming

Bureaus of:
  Charitable Gaming
  Indian Gaming

**Division of
Intergovernmental Relations**

Teams:
  Intergovernmental Services
  Municipal Boundary Review
  Resource Policy

**Division of
Enterprise Technology**

Bureaus of:
  Business Application
    Support
  Business Services
  District Attorneys Information
    Technology
  Infrastructure Support
  Publishing and Distribution

Offices:
  Security
  Technical Architecture and
    Project Management

**Division of
Legal Services**

Divisions
  Hearings and Appeals
  Trust Lands and Investments

Offices
  Business Development
  Justice Assistance
  State Employment Relations

Units attached for administrative
purposes under Sec. 15.03:

Boards
  Aging and Long-Term Care
  Claims
  College Savings Program
  Commissioners of Public Lands
  Depository Selection
  Incorporation Review
  Information Technology Management
  National and Community Service
  For People with Developmental Disabilities
  Public Records
  Small Business Regulatory Review
  State Capitol and Executive Residence
  Statute
  Volunteer Fire Fighter and Emergency Medical Technician
    Service Award
  Waste Facility Siting

Commission
  Tax Appeals

Councils
  Electronic Recording
  Interoperability
  Utility Public Benefits
  Women's

ADMINISTRATION

Security, Office of: BILL NASH, *acting director,* 224-3779, bill.nash@

Technical Architecture and Project Management, Office of: JIM HENNING, *director,* 266-5055, james.henning@

Executive Budget and Finance, Division of: BRIAN HAYES, *administrator,* 266-1035, brian.hayes@; KIRSTEN GRINDE, *deputy administrator,* 266-1353, kirsten.grinde@; Fax: 267-0372; P.O. Box 7864, Madison 53707-7864.

    Capital Finance Office: KEVIN TAYLOR, *director,* 266-2305, kevin.taylor@

    State Budget Office:

        Agriculture, Environment and Justice: CAITLIN MORGAN FREDERICK, *team leader,* 266-2081, caitlin.frederick@

        Education and Workforce Development: SARA HYNEK, *team leader,* 266-1037, sara.hynek@

        General Government, Children and Families: JENNIFER KRAUS, *team leader,* 266-5878, jennifer.kraus@

        Health Services and Insurance: MICHELLE GAUGER, *team leader,* 266-3420, michelle.gauger@

        Information Technology, Operations and Federal Funds: SCOTT THORNTON, *team leader,* 266-5051, scott.thornton@

        Tax, Local Government and Economic Development: PAUL ZIEGLER, *team leader,* 266-1040, paul.ziegler@

    State Controller's Office: STEPHEN J. CENSKY, *state controller,* 266-8158, steve.censky@; P.O. Box 7932, Madison 53707-7932.

Facilities Development, Division of: SUMMER SHANNON-BRADLEY, *administrator,* 266-1031, summer.shannonbradley@; NAOMI R. DE MERS, *advisor to the administrator,* 266-2646, naomi.demers@

    Architecture and Engineering, Bureau of: GIL FUNK, *director and state chief engineer,* 266-3783, gill.funk@

    Capital Budget and Construction Administration, Bureau of: ROBINSON J. BINAU, *director,* 267-6927, rj.binau@

Facilities Management, Division of: CINDY TORSTVEIT, *administrator,* 264-9503, cindy.torstveit@; vacancy, *advisor to the administrator.*

    Building Management, Bureau of: KEITH BECK, *director,* 266-2645, keith.beck@

    Space Management and Occupancy, Bureau of: CRAIG BARKELAR, *director,* 261-0602, craig.barkelar@

Gaming, Division of: STEVE KNUDSON, *administrator,* 270-2555, steve.knudson@; Fax: 270-2564; 3319 West Beltline Highway, First Floor, P.O. Box 8979, Madison 53708-8979; Internet Address: www.doa.state.wi.us/gaming

    Charitable Gaming, Bureau of: JOSEPH GASTEL, *director,* 270-2546, joseph.gastel@

    Indian Gaming, Bureau of: JOHN DILLETT, *director,* 270-2533, john.dillett@

Housing, Division of: LISA MARKS, *administrator,* 267-0770, lisa.marks@; Fax: 266-5381; P.O. Box 7970, Madison 53707-7970.

    Affordable Housing, Bureau of: OSCAR HERRERA, *director,* 264-6152, oscar.herrera@

    Community Development, Bureau of: TOM CLIPPERT, *director,* 261-7538.

    Supportive Housing, Bureau of: MARTY EVANSON, *director,* 267-2713, marty.evanson@

Intergovernmental Relations, Division of: ED EBERLE, *administrator,* 267-1824, ed.eberle@; Fax: 267-6917; P.O. Box 8944, Madison 53707-8944.

    Intergovernmental Services Team: DAWN VICK, *team leader,* 266-7043, dawn.vick@

    Municipal Boundary Review Team: RENEE POWERS, *team leader,* 266-3200, renee.powers@

    Resource Policy Team: MIKE FRIIS, *team leader,* 267-7982, mike.friis@

Legal Services, Division of: GREGORY MURRAY, *chief legal counsel and administrator,* 267-0202, gregory.murray@

Publications: Agency Budget Requests and Revenue Estimates; Annual Fiscal Report; Biennial Report; Budget in Brief; Budget Message; Capital Budget Recommendations; Comprehensive Annual Financial Report; Continuing Disclosure Annual Report; Decisions of Tax Appeals Commission; Executive Budget; Summary of Tax Exemption Devices; Wisconsin Energy Statistics; Wisconsin Population Estimates.

Agency Responsibility: The Department of Administration (DOA) provides a wide range of support services to other state agencies. One of the chief duties of the department is to provide the governor with fiscal management information and the policy alternatives required for preparation of Wisconsin's biennial budget. It analyzes administrative and fiscal issues facing the state and recommends solutions. The department also coordinates telecommunications, energy, and land use planning and community development. It regulates racing, charitable gaming, and Indian gaming. It is responsible for managing the state's buildings and leased office space, as well as statewide facilities project planning and analysis. The department maintains a federal-state relations office in Washington, D.C.

Organization: The department is administered by a secretary appointed by the governor with the advice and consent of the senate. The secretary must be appointed "on the basis of recognized interest, administrative and executive ability, training and experience in and knowledge of problems and needs in the field of administration." The secretary appoints the department's division administrators from outside the classified service.

Unit Functions: The *Division of Administrative Services* provides numerous support services to the department and agencies attached for administrative support, including human resources, records and forms, space and property management, financial management, mail, printing, business recovery, and management planning. Other major functions are to prepare and administer the departmental budget, advise the secretary on policies and procedures, and perform internal audits. It pays the salaries and any associated fringe benefits for all district attorneys and their staff attorneys. It also reviews and pays the compensation of special prosecutors for the 71 district attorneys' offices. (Menominee and Shawano Counties share a district attorney.)

The *Division of Capitol Police* uses officers working in Madison and Milwaukee to provide a wide range of investigative, security, and related public safety services to state agencies, employees, and others. It protects state facilities; conducts criminal investigations; and provides protective services to the governor and visiting dignitaries.

The *Division of Energy Services* administers federal and statewide low-income household energy assistance programs involving conservation, weatherization, and bill payment. In coordination with local government and community action agencies, the division distributes more than $140 million in annual energy assistance and approximately $60 million annually to fund weatherization measures to approximately 215,000 low-income households throughout Wisconsin.

The State Energy Office is federally funded and administers federal funds received from the U.S. Department of Energy under the State Energy Program Strategic Plan and various federal laws. It develops policy options for consideration by the governor and state agencies, coordinates activities with other state agencies, identifies federal funding opportunities and facilitates applications for funding by state and local governments and private entities, and performs duties necessary to maintain federal designation and funding.

The *Division of Enterprise Operations* manages state procurement policies and contracts, auto and air fleet transportation, and risk management. The division handles statewide contracts, DOA and consolidated agency purchasing, municipal cooperative purchasing, work center contracting, federal and state surplus property disposition, state agency recycling and waste reduction programs, and minority business contracting. It oversees fleet policies, records management, interdepartmental mail, and state agency document sales and distribution. It also manages the state's self-funded programs for liability, property, and worker's compensation, and assists agencies in controlling and reducing risk management losses.

The *Division of Enterprise Technology* manages the state's information technology (IT) assets and uses technology to improve government efficiency and service delivery. It provides

Department of Administration employees repair outdoor lighting at the State Capitol. *(Greg Anderson, Legislative Photographer)*

computer services to state agencies and operates the statewide voice data and video telecommunications network. In consultation with business and IT managers from state agencies and local governments, the division develops strategies, policies, and standards for cross-agency and multijurisdictional use of IT resources. The division provides centralized security training, research, and print and mail services to other state agencies and provides statewide computer systems for district attorneys. Through the Geographic Information Office, the division coordinates Wisconsin's geospatial information activities and provides geographic information systems (GIS) services to state agencies, service organizations, and local governments.

The *Division of Executive Budget and Finance* provides fiscal and policy analysis to the governor for development of executive budget proposals and assists agencies in the technical preparation of budget requests. It reviews legislation and coordinates the fiscal estimates that accompany all expenditure bills. It also advises the State of Wisconsin Building Commission and the governor on the issuance of state debt and administers finances for the clean water revolving loan fund program. The division provides program and management evaluation and maintains the management information system for authorized state employee positions. It establishes accounting policies and procedures, maintains the state's central payroll and accounting systems, monitors agency internal control procedures, produces the state's annual fiscal and financial reports, and administers the state's Section 529 College Savings programs and the local government investment pool.

The *Division of Facilities Development* develops and administers the state building program under the direction of the State of Wisconsin Building Commission. Its functions include: statewide facilities project planning and analysis; architectural and engineering selection and design oversight; construction contract bidding and administration, and project management; and field supervision of construction projects. The division also oversees: management and operations of statewide heating plants and centralized fuel procurement; the energy conservation bonding program; and all real estate transactions requiring State Building Commission approval.

The *Division of Facilities Management* operates and maintains 30 major buildings in 7 cities throughout the state including the State Capitol, the Executive Residence, and state office buildings in Madison. The division is responsible for building management, tenant improvements, building service contracts, space planning and occupancy, parking administration, all state leasing and real estate transactions, and property acquisition and disposition.

The *Division of Gaming* regulates bingo, raffles, and Class III Indian gaming pursuant to state/ tribal gaming compacts. The division licenses and regulates bingo games and raffles conducted by nonprofit, charitable, religious, fraternal, and service organizations. It conducts tribal gaming compliance reviews and payment audits and certifies vendors to conduct gaming business in accordance with state/tribal compacts and federal law.

The *Division of Housing* offers a broad range of financial and technical assistance to improve and expand housing, increase affordable housing opportunities, and provide services to people without housing. The variety of federal and state programs it manages benefits persons with disabilities, low- and moderate-income residents, and homeless populations. The division partners with local governments, homeless service providers, developers, and housing organizations throughout the state to improve housing conditions for low- to moderate-income Wisconsin residents. It distributes over $30 million annually.

The *Division of Intergovernmental Relations* provides a variety of services to the public and state, local, and tribal governments. It advises the department and the governor on state, local, and tribal relationships and coordinates the state's efforts to influence federal legislation. It manages the Coastal Management Program, provides population estimates and projections, and does demographic research.

The division administers the Comprehensive Planning and Land Information Grants. Working with the Incorporation Review Board, the division reviews and issues determinations on pe titions to incorporate towns into villages or cities. It oversees the Municipal Boundary Review Program and the Plat Review Program, and administers the municipal service payment program which reimburses local governments for providing police, fire, and solid waste services to state facilities.

The *Division of Legal Services,* created in Section 15.103 (1g) by 2009 Wisconsin Act 28, provides legal services to state agencies and to the Department of Administration. It provides legal assistance and advice on issues such as procurement, contracting, construction, budget development, and other common activities with the goal of bringing about greater agencywide consistency on such matters. The division is available to support and consult with agencies on contract development, negotiation, and other areas of legal expertise.

History: The legislature created the Department of Administration in Chapter 228, Laws of 1959, and authorized it to provide centralized staff services to the governor, to assume common administrative functions for other executive agencies, and to coordinate the state's business affairs. Chapter 228 also abolished the Bureaus of Engineering, Personnel, and Purchases; the Department of Budget and Accounts; and the Division of Departmental Research in the Office of the Governor. Their functions and personnel were transferred to the new department.

Since its creation, the department has assumed additional duties. State comprehensive planning responsibilities and population estimation were added in 1967 and 1972, respectively. 1976 Executive Order 36 moved the Office of Emergency Energy Assistance from the Office of the Governor to the department's State Planning Office and broadened its responsibilities to include energy policy planning and program management. The 1989 executive budget created the Division of Housing (subsequently repealed in 2003) and gave the department responsibility for grant and loan programs for low- and moderate-income housing. The 1991 executive budget created the Division of Information Technology Services (now the Division of Enterprise Technology) to consolidate and manage the state's computer and telecommunications resources.

Other functions assigned to the department have included the Coastal Management Program (1981), low-income weatherization assistance (1991), low-income energy assistance (1995), a college tuition prepayment program (1995) (transferred to the Office of the State Treasurer by 1999 Wisconsin Act 9), municipal boundary and plat review (1997), and the Wisconsin Fresh Start Program (1998).

Over the years, legislation has transferred various functions out of the department. Chapter 645, Laws of 1961, created a separate Personnel Board to review departmental decisions. Chapter 196, Laws of 1977, transferred the administration of civil service, collective bargaining, and classification and compensation to the newly created Department of Employment Relations. The Division of Emergency Government, which became part of the department in 1979, was moved to the Department of Military Affairs by 1989 Wisconsin Act 31. Regulation of mobile home dealers and mobile parks was transferred to the Department of Commerce by 1999 Wisconsin Act 9. With the repeal of the Division of Housing, 2003 Wisconsin Act 33 transferred grant and loan programs for low- and moderate-income housing to the Department of Commerce. Housing programs were transferred from the Department of Commerce back to DOA by 2011 Wisconsin Act 32.

Gaming Regulation. 1997 Wisconsin Act 27 repealed the Wisconsin Gaming Board and created the Division of Gaming in the department to monitor gaming on Indian lands and regulate pari-mutuel wagering, racing, and charitable gaming.

Originally, the Wisconsin Constitution stated: "The legislature shall never authorize any lottery." This provision was interpreted as prohibiting all forms of gambling. Following a 1973 constitutional amendment to allow charitable bingo, the legislature enacted Chapter 156, Laws of 1973, to permit bingo games and create the Bingo Control Board in the Department of Regulation and Licensing. Charitable raffles were permitted by a 1977 constitutional amendment, and the legislature assigned their regulation to the Bingo Control Board in Chapter 426, Laws of 1977.

Pari-mutuel on-track wagering and the state lottery were permitted by constitutional amendments in 1987. The legislature created the Racing Board to regulate the sport in 1987 Wisconsin Act 354. The Wisconsin Lottery, originally operated by the Lottery Board, was created by 1987 Wisconsin Act 119.

The Wisconsin Gaming Commission, created by 1991 Wisconsin Act 269, replaced the Lottery Board and the Racing Board and also assumed responsibility for Indian gaming, charitable gaming (bingo and raffles), and crane games. The Wisconsin Gaming Board, created by 1995 Wisconsin Act 27, replaced the Gaming Commission. (That act also transferred responsibility for management of the Wisconsin Lottery to the Department of Revenue.) 1997 Wisconsin Act 27 transferred gaming duties, except for lottery regulation, to the Department of Administration. 2011 Wisconsin Act 32 eliminated the Office of Energy Independence and transferred to DOA from the Office of the State Treasurer responsibility for the state's Section 529 College Savings programs and the local government investment pool.

Statutory Councils

Acid Deposition Research Council: Inactive.

The 7-member Acid Deposition Research Council makes recommendations on types and levels of funding for acid deposition research and reviews "acid rain" research. The council was created by 1985 Wisconsin Act 296, and its composition and duties are prescribed in Sections 15.107 (5) and 16.02 of the statutes.

Certification Standards Review Council: David Kliber (commercial laboratory representative), *chairperson;* Susan Hill (appointed by UW-Madison chancellor to represent Laboratory of Hygiene), *vice chairperson;* Steve Jossart (industrial laboratory representative), *secretary;* Randall Thater (large municipal wastewater plant representative); Judy Tholen (small municipal wastewater plant representative); Kirsti Sorsa (public water utility representative); vacancy (solid and hazardous waste disposal facility representative); Chris Groh (demonstrated interest in laboratory certification); vacancy (livestock farmer). (Unless otherwise designated, all are appointed by secretary of administration.)

The 9-member Certification Standards Review Council reviews the Department of Natural Resources laboratory certification and registration program and makes recommendations to the department about its programs for testing water, wastewater, waste material, soil, and hazardous waste. The council's members serve 3-year terms, and no member may serve more than two consecutive terms. The council was created by 1983 Wisconsin Act 410, and its composition and duties are prescribed in Sections 15.107 (12) and 299.11 (3) of the statutes.

Small Business, Veteran-Owned Business and Minority Business Opportunities, Council on: Mohammed Hashim, *chairperson;* Aggo Akyea, Craig A. Anderson, David W. Aragon,

NORMAN BARRIENTOS, WILLIAM BECKETT, TINA CHANG, WILLIAM JOHNSON, JR., BRIAN MITCHELL, ALLEN R. SCHRAEDER, 3 vacancies. (All are appointed by secretary of administration.) Nonvoting secretary: HELEN MCCAIN (Department of Administration designee).

The 13-member Council on Small Business, Veteran-Owned Business and Minority Business Opportunities advises the department on the participation of its constituent groups in state purchasing. Its members are appointed for 3-year terms and may not serve more than two consecutive full terms. The law prescribes minimum membership numbers for the types of businesses represented on the council: racial minority-owned (2); owned by handicapped person (1); nonprofit for rehabilitation of disabled (1); and veteran-owned (2). At least one member must represent the Department of Safety and Professional Services and one must be a consumer member. The council was created by Chapter 419, Laws of 1977, and its name and membership were amended by 1991 Wisconsin Act 170 to include veteran-owned business. Its composition and duties are prescribed in Sections 15.107 (2) and 16.755 of the statutes.

INDEPENDENT UNITS ATTACHED FOR BUDGETING, PROGRAM COORDINATION, AND RELATED MANAGEMENT FUNCTIONS BY SECTION 15.03 OF THE STATUTES

BOARD ON AGING AND LONG-TERM CARE

Members: EVA ARNOLD, BARBARA BECHTEL, TERRY LYNCH, TANYA L. MEYER, JAMES SURPRISE, DALE TAYLOR, vacancy (appointed by governor with senate consent).

Executive Director: HEATHER A. BRUEMMER, (608) 246-7014, heather.bruemmer@wisconsin.gov

Mailing Address: 1402 Pankratz Street, Suite 111, Madison 53704.

Telephones: (608) 246-7013; Ombudsman Program: (800) 815-0015; Medigap Helpline: (800) 242-1060.

Fax: (608) 246-7001.

E-mail Address: boaltc@wisconsin.gov

Publications: Biennial Report.

Number of Employees: 37.00.

Total Budget 2011-13: $5,543,100.

Statutory References: Sections 15.07 (1)(b) 9., 15.105 (10), and 16.009.

Agency Responsibility: The 7-member Board on Aging and Long-Term Care reports biennially to the governor and the legislature on long-term care for the aged and disabled; state involvement in long-term care; program recommendations; and actions taken by state agencies to carry out the board's recommendations. The board monitors the development and implementation of federal, state, and local laws and regulations related to long-term care facilities. The board's ombudsman service investigates complaints from persons receiving long-term care concerning improper treatment or noncompliance with federal or state law and serves as mediator or advocate to resolve disputes between patients and institutions.

The board operates the Medigap Helpline, which provides information and counseling on various types of insurance, including health, hospital indemnity, cancer, nursing home, and long-term care and nursing home policies designed to supplement Medicare. Helpline information also covers the Health Insurance Risk-Sharing Plan (HIRSP), group insurance continuation and conversion rights, and health maintenance organization plans for Medicare beneficiaries.

The board members, who serve staggered 5-year terms, must have demonstrated a continuing interest in the problems of providing long-term care for the aged and disabled. At least four must be public members with no interest in or affiliation with any nursing home. The board appoints the executive director from the classified service.

The board was created by Chapter 20, Laws of 1981, which merged the Board on Aging and the Governor's Ombudsman Program for the Aging and Disabled, as the result of a legislative study. Predecessor agencies included the State Commission on Aging, created by Chapter 581, Laws of 1961, followed in 1967 (Chapters 75 and 327) by the Council on Aging in the Department of Health and Social Services, which was subsequently renamed the Board on Aging in Chapter 332, Laws of 1971.

OFFICE OF BUSINESS DEVELOPMENT

Director: NANCY MISTELE, 267-7873, nancy.mistele@; JOE KNILANS, *deputy director,* 267-7394, joe.knilans@

Mailing Address: P.O. Box 7864, Madison 53707.

Fax: (608) 267-3842.

Statutory References: Sections 15.105 (32) and 16.28.

Agency Responsibility: The Office of Business Development provides administrative support to the Small Business Regulatory Review Board to review, reduce, or remove burdens that unnecessary laws and rules place on small business in Wisconsin, and performs other functions determined by the secretary of administration. The office is under the direction and supervision of a director appointed by and serving at the pleasure of the governor. The deputy director is also appointed by the governor to serve at his or her pleasure. The office was created by 2011 Wisconsin Act 32.

CLAIMS BOARD

Members: STEVE MEANS (Department of Justice representative designated by attorney general), *chairperson;* GREG MURRAY (Department of Administration representative designated by secretary of administration); SENATOR LEIBHAM (designated by chairperson, Senate Committee on Finance), REPRESENTATIVE STRACHOTA (designated by chairperson, Assembly Committee on Finance); BRIAN HAGEDORN (representative of the Office of the Governor designated by governor).

Secretary: GREG MURRAY.

Mailing Address: P.O. Box 7864, Madison 53707-7864.

Location: State Administration Building, 101 East Wilson Street, 10th Floor, Madison.

Telephone: (608) 264-9595.

E-mail Address: patricia.reardon@wisconsin.gov

Internet Address: www.claimsboard.wi.gov

Number of Employees: 0.00.

Total Budget 2011-13: $190,000.

Statutory References: Sections 15.07 (2)(e), 15.105 (2), and 16.007.

Agency Responsibility: The 5-member Claims Board investigates and pays, denies, or makes recommendations on all money claims against the state of $10 or more, when such claims are referred to it by the Department of Administration. The findings and recommendations of the board are reported to the legislature and no claim may be considered by the legislature until the board has made its recommendation.

Originally, the statutory procedure for making claims against the state was to file the claim with the Director of Budget and Accounts or to have a legislator introduce it as a bill. The legislature created the Claims Commission in Chapter 669, Laws of 1955, to handle these matters. Under the 1967 executive branch reorganization, the commission was renamed the Claims Board, and it absorbed the Commission for the Relief of Innocent Persons and the Judgment Debtor Relief Commission.

COLLEGE SAVINGS PROGRAM BOARD

Members: WILLIAM OEMICHEN, *chairperson;* MIKE HUEBSCH (secretary of administration); DEBORAH DURCAN (designated by UW Board of Regents president); ROLF WEGENKE (president of the Wisconsin Association of Independent Colleges and Universities); KEN JOHNSON (designated by the chairperson of the Investment Board); JAMES ZYLSTRA (designated by the president of the Technical College System Board); Paul C. Adamski, Alberta Darling, Robert Kieckhafer, Patrick Sheehy, John Wheeler. (All except *ex officio* members are appointed by the governor with senate consent.)

Mailing Address: P.O. Box 7864, Madison 53707-7871.

Telephone: 264-7899.

Fax: 266-7647.

E-mail Address: edvest@wisconsin.gov

Internet Address: www.edvest.com and www.tomorrowsscholar.com

Statutory References: Sections 15.07 (1) (b) 2., 15.105 (25m), and 16.641.

Agency Responsibility: The 11-member College Savings Program Board was created by 1999 Wisconsin Act 44 and its members serve 4-year terms. It administers the EdVest and Tomorrow's Scholar college savings program that provides for tax-sheltered investment accounts held in a trust fund to cover future higher education expenses. Originally attached to the Office of the State Treasurer, it was attached to the Department of Administration by 2011 Wisconsin Act 32.

DEPOSITORY SELECTION BOARD

Members: Kurt Schuller (state treasurer), Mike Huebsch (secretary of administration), Richard G. Chandler (secretary of revenue).

Statutory References: Sections 15.105 (3) and 34.045.

Agency Responsibility: The 3-member Depository Selection Board, as created by Chapter 418, Laws of 1977, establishes procedures to be used by state agencies in the selection of depositories for public funds and in contracting for their banking services. The board's *ex officio* members may designate others to serve in their place. The secretary of revenue replaced the executive director of the investment board as a member as a result of 2001 Wisconsin Act 16.

ELECTRONIC RECORDING COUNCIL

Members: Tyson Fettes (register of deeds), *chairperson;* Craig Haskins (representing an association of title insurance), *vice chairperson;* Kristi Chlebowski, Marge Geissler, Jodi Helgeson (registers of deeds); Marcia Drouiin-Howe (representing an association of bankers); John F. Wilcox (representing attorneys who practice real property law). (All members are appointed by governor).

Agency Responsibility: The 7-member Electronic Recording Council recommends standards regarding the electronic recording of real estate documents for adoption by rules promulgated by the Department of Administration. The council was created by 2005 Wisconsin Act 421, and its composition and duties are prescribed in Sections 15.107 (6) and 706.25 (4) of the statutes.

DIVISION OF HEARINGS AND APPEALS

Acting Administrator: Wayne Wiedenhoeft, wayne.wiedenhoeft@wisconsin.gov

Mailing Address: 5005 University Avenue, Suite 201, Madison 53705-5400.

Telephone: (608) 266-8007.

Fax: Madison: (608) 264-9885; Milwaukee: (414) 227-3818; Eau Claire: (715) 831-3235.

E-mail Address: dhamail@wisconsin.gov

Internet Address: http://dha.state.wi.us

Number of Employees: 49.93.

Total Budget 2011-13: $11,602,600.

Statutory References: Sections 15.103 (1), 50.04 (4)(e), 227.43, 301.035, and 949.11.

Agency Responsibility: The Division of Hearings and Appeals conducts quasi-judicial hearings for several state agencies. It must decide contested administrative proceedings for the Department of Natural Resources, cases arising under the Department of Justice's Crime Victim Compensation Program, and appeals related to actions of the Departments of Health Services,

Children and Families, Safety and Professional Services, and Agriculture, Trade and Consumer Protection. It also hears appeals from the Department of Transportation, including those related to motor vehicle dealer licenses, highway signs, motor carrier regulation, and disputes arising between motor vehicle dealers and manufacturers. The division conducts hearings for the Department of Corrections regarding probation, parole, and extended supervision revocation and juvenile aftercare supervision. It also handles contested cases for the Department of Public Instruction, the Department of Employee Trust Funds, and the Low-Income Home Energy Assistance Program of the Department of Administration. Other agencies may contract with the division for hearing services.

The secretary of administration appoints the division's administrator from the classified service. By law, the division operates independently of the department except for certain budgeting and management functions. 1983 Wisconsin Act 27 created the division by combining the Division of Natural Resources Hearings and the Division of Nursing Home Forfeiture Appeals, both originating with the 1977 Legislature. In 1986, the division received jurisdiction over crime victim compensation hearings and cases involving protection of human burial sites. With the creation of the Department of Corrections in 1990, the legislature transferred a portion of the Office of Administrative Hearings from the Departments of Health and Social Services to the division, making the division responsible for parole, probation, and juvenile aftercare revocation. When the Office of the Commissioner of Transportation was abolished in 1993, the legislature transferred many Department of Transportation hearing functions to the division. Contested administrative hearings for the Department of Health and Family Services and the Department of Workforce Development were transferred to the division by 1995 Wisconsin Act 370.

INCORPORATION REVIEW BOARD

Members: ED EBERLE (designated by secretary of administration), *chairperson;* TERRENCE J. McMAHON, LONNIE MULLER (appointed by Wisconsin Towns Association); PAUL FISK (appointed by League of Wisconsin Municipalities); RICH EGGELSTON (appointed by Wisconsin Alliance of Cities).

Contact person: ERICH SCHMIDTKE, Planning Analyst, Division of Intergovernmental Relations.

Mailing Address: 101 East Wilson Street, 9th Floor, Madison 53702.

Telephone: (608) 264-6102.

Statutory References: Sections 15.07 (2)(m), 15.105 (23), 16.53 (4), 66.0203, and 66.0207.

The 5-member Incorporation Review Board reviews petitions to incorporate territory as a city or village to determine whether the petition meets certain public interest statutory standards. These standards may include characteristics of the proposed municipality's territory, that part of the territory beyond its most densely populated core, its ability to provide services and generate revenue, and its impact on neighboring jurisdictions. The board is also charged with prescribing and collecting an incorporation review fee. The board must present its findings to the Division of Intergovernmental Relations within 180 days after receipt of referral from a circuit court unless the court sets a different time limit or all parties agree to a stay to allow time for an alternative dispute resolution of any disagreements. Any board member who owns property in, or resides in the town that is the subject of the incorporation petition, or a contiguous city or village, must be replaced for purposes of reviewing that petition. Members serve at the pleasure of the appointing authority and, with the exception of the DOA representative, serve only in an advisory capacity. The board was created by 2003 Wisconsin Act 171.

INFORMATION TECHNOLOGY MANAGEMENT BOARD

Members: Inactive.

Agency Responsibility: The Information Technology Management Board advises the Department of Administration on strategic information technology plans submitted by state agencies, the management of the state's information technology assets, and progress made on agency projects. The board may review the department's decisions on appeal from other state agencies. The board's membership includes the governor, the cochairpersons of the legislature's Joint Committee on Information Policy and Technology or their designees, a member of the minority party from the senate and the assembly, the secretary of administration or designee, 2 heads of departments or independent agencies appointed by the governor, and 2 other members appointed by the governor to 4-year terms. The board was created by 2001 Wisconsin Act 16 and attached to the Department of Administration by 2003 Wisconsin Act 33. Its composition and duties are prescribed in Sections 15.105 (28) and 16.978 of the statutes.

INTEROPERABILITY COUNCIL

Members: DAVID STEINGRABER (Office of Justice Assistance designee), *chairperson;* JOHNNIE LEE SMITH (adjutant general designee); RANDY STARK (secretary of natural resources designee); STEPHEN FITZGERALD (secretary of transportation designee); DAVID CAGIGAL (department of administration information technology representative); TOM CZAJA (chief of police); MATTHEW JOSKI (sheriff); STEVE HANSEN (fire chief); MINDY ALLEN (emergency medical services director); JON FREUND (local government elected official); WILLIAM STOLTE (local government emergency management director); RICHARD VANBOXTEL (American Indian tribe or band representative); LYNN SCHUBERT (hospital representative); vacancy (local health department representative) vacancy (person with experience or expertise in interoperable communications).

Agency Responsibility: The 15-member Interoperability Council recommends goals, standards, timelines, guidelines, and procedures for achieving a statewide public safety interoperable communication system. The system will enable the exchange of voice, data, and video communications among public safety agencies and associated resources including public works and transportation agencies, hospitals, and volunteer emergency services agencies. It assists the Office of Justice Assistance in obtaining and allocating funding, including for homeland security. The council, which receives staff support from the Office of Justice Assistance, was created by 2007 Wisconsin Act 79, and its composition and duties are prescribed in Sections 15.107 (18) and 15.9645 of the statutes.

OFFICE OF JUSTICE ASSISTANCE

Executive Director: DARCY VARESE.

Mailing Address: 1 South Pinckney Street, Suite 615, Madison 53703.

Telephone: (608) 266-3323.

Fax: (608) 266-6676.

Internet Address: www.oja.wi.gov

Publications: Crime in Wisconsin, Arrests in Wisconsin, Sexual Assaults in Wisconsin; Juvenile Justice Improvement Plan; Wisconsin Justice Information Sharing annual report, Violence Against Women Plan; Wisconsin Homeland Security Strategic Plan, Byrne Justice Assistance Grants strategic plan.

Number of Employees: 43.30.

Total Budget 2011-13: $129,681,300.

Statutory References: Sections 15.105 (19), 16.964, 16.971 (9).

Agency Responsibility: The Office of Justice Assistance (OJA) is an independent state agency with an executive director appointed by the governor. It is almost entirely federally funded. OJA promotes improvement of public safety in Wisconsin through a variety of criminal justice and antiterrorism programs. OJA advises the governor and other public officials on criminal justice, juvenile justice, and homeland security issues. OJA provides financial and technical assistance to public safety, first response and emergency management agencies, local and tribal governments, and nonprofit organizations throughout the state.

OJA is the state's administering agency (SAA) for federal criminal justice and homeland security grant funds including the federal Juvenile Justice Delinquency Prevention Act, Violence Against Women Act, Justice Assistance Grant program, and State Homeland Security Grant program. OJA is the applicant agency for federal discretionary criminal justice and homeland security grant programs including Grants to Encourage Arrests, National Criminal History Improvement Program, National Instant Criminal Background Check System, Residential Substance Abuse Treatment program, and others. State funded grant programs include Beat Patrol; Treatment Alternatives and Diversion; Child Advocacy Centers; and Youth Diversion grants.

OJA's has primary responsibility for carrying out the state coordination of automated justice information systems among state and local criminal justice agencies. OJA's Wisconsin Justice Information Sharing (WIJIS) program provides a statewide strategic vision of justice information sharing as well as innovative technical solutions that improve information sharing between law enforcement and justice agencies, and the flow of electronic information through the justice system.

OJA's Statistical Analysis Center (SAC) conducts research and publishes reports on high visibility justice issues. The SAC manages the state's Uniform Crime Reporting and Incident-based Reporting programs, Juvenile Secure Detention Records database, and Treatment Alternatives and Diversion data analysis.

OJA is responsible for the development and implementation of the statewide public safety interoperable communication system. OJA develops the Statewide Homeland Security Plan, and leads efforts to identify gaps in the state's protection, set priorities for use of federal funds to fill those gaps and awards grants to increase the capacity of first responders and communities to prevent, respond to, and recover from catastrophic events, including terrorist attacks.

OJA also assists in locating and registering sex offenders who have not complied with the state's sex offender registry requirements.

Several advisory groups and gubernatorial appointed commissions advise OJA on its programs and funding decisions, including the Governor's Juvenile Justice Commission, Interoperability Council, Violence Against Women Act Advisory Committee, WIJIS Policy Advisory Group, Treatment Alternatives and Diversion advisory group, and numerous other justice and grant advisory groups.

The Office of Justice Assistance originally was known as the Wisconsin Council on Criminal Justice, created by executive order in 1969 in the Department of Justice as the state planning body required by the federal Law Enforcement Assistance Administration. In 1971, the council was transferred by executive order to the governor's office. Chapter 418, Laws of 1977, created the council as a statutory agency in the governor's office. 1983 Wisconsin Act 27 created the council as an independent statutory body and attached it to the Department of Administration. The council was repealed and recreated under its current name by 1987 Wisconsin Act 27.

NATIONAL AND COMMUNITY SERVICE BOARD

Members: ANTHONY HALLMAN (public member), *president;* MARK MUELLER (youth education, training and development representative), *vice president;* MAIA PEARSON (youth representative); MARGUITA FOX (older adult volunteer representative); KATHLEEN GROAT (private, nonprofit organization representative and local government representative); SUE GRADY (superintendent of public instruction designee); JIM LANGDON (secretary of administration designee); ROBERT GUENTHER (organized labor representative); THI LE (national service youth representative); vacancy (national service program representative); RACHEL GRAHAM, SONDRA LEGRAND, MARGARET MOORE, 3 vacancies (public members). Nonvoting members: LINDA SUNDE (Corporation for National and Community Service); JOHN SCOCOS (Department of Veterans Affairs), AMY McDOWELL (Department of Health Services), MICHAEL HINMAN (Department of Military Affairs), SCOTT FROMADER (Department of Workforce Development). (All except *ex officio* members are appointed by governor.)

Executive Director: THOMAS H. DEVINE.

Mailing Address: 1 West Wilson Street, Room B274, Madison 53703.

Telephones: (608) 261-6716; (800) 620-8307 (toll free).

Internet Address: www.servewisconsin.org

Number of Employees: 5.00.

Total Budget 2011-13: $8,498,400.

Statutory References: Sections 15.105 (24) and 16.22.

Agency Responsibility: The National and Community Service Board, created by 1993 Wisconsin Act 437, in accordance with the federal National and Community Trust Act of 1993, oversees the planning and implementation of community service programs in Wisconsin that meet previously unmet human, public safety, educational, environmental, and homeland security needs. The board is authorized to receive and distribute funds from governmental and private sources, and it acts as an intermediary between the Corporation for National and Community Service (CNCS) and local agencies providing funding for AmeriCorps State programs.

The board oversees 25 AmeriCorps programs consisting of 1,200 AmeriCorps members serving in over 300 placement sites statewide. After completing a successful year of service, AmeriCorps members in Wisconsin are eligible for Federal Education Awards that can be used to pay tuition or pay back student loans.

The board's voting members, who must number at least 16, are appointed to serve 3-year terms. No more than 4 of them may be state officers and employees, and no more than 9 may be members from the same political party. To the extent practicable, membership should be diverse in terms of race, national origin, age, sex, and disability. Nonvoting members appointed by the governor must include the state representative of the CNCS and may include representatives of state agencies providing community social services.

BOARD FOR PEOPLE WITH DEVELOPMENTAL DISABILITIES

Members: BARBARA KATZ, *chairperson;* MICHAEL GRECO (designated by secretary of workforce development); BETH WROBLESKI (designated by secretary of health services); SUZAN VAN BEAVER (designated by state superintendent of public instruction); DAN BIER (designated by UW Waisman Center Director); BARBARA BECKERT (designated by Disability Rights Wisconsin); ALIZA CLAIRE BIBLE, LYNN CARUS, KEVIN FECH, BARB GADBOIS, WENDY GAHN-ACKLEY, ANDREW GERBITZ, DEBRA GLOVER, ROBERT KUHR, RAMSEY LEE, NATHANIEL LENTZ, PAM MALIN, KATHERINE PERHACH, QYLA PERSON, DAVID PINNO, BARBARA SORENSEN, LYNN STANSBERRY-BRUSNAHAN, CAROLE STUEBE, PATRICK YOUNG, CINDY ZELLNER-EHLERS (all appointed by governor).

Executive Director: BETH SWEDEEN.

Mailing Address and Location: 101 East Wilson Street, Room 219, Madison 53703-2796.

Telephones: 266-7826; (888) 332-1677 (toll free); TTY: 266-6660.

Fax: 267-3906.

Internet Address: www.wi-bpdd.org

E-mail Address: bpddhelp@wi-bpdd.org

Number of Employees: 6.75.

Total Budget 2011-13: $2,603,400.

Statutory References: Sections 15.09 (1)(a), 15.105 (8), and 51.437 (14r).

Agency Responsibility: The board, formerly the Council on Developmental Disabilities, advises the Department of Administration, other state agencies, the legislature, and the governor on matters related to developmental disabilities. The statutes do not specify the exact number of board members, but all who serve are appointed to staggered 4-year terms, must be state residents, represent all geographic areas of the state, and the state's diversity with respect to race and ethnicity. The public members appointed by the governor must include representatives of public and private nonprofit agencies that provide direct services at the local level to persons with developmental disabilities. At least 60% of the board's members must be persons who have developmental disabilities or are the parents, relatives, or guardians of such individuals, but these members may not be associated with public or private agencies that receive federal funding. The members appointed by agency heads represent the relevant agencies of the state that administer federal funds related to individuals with disabilities. The Council on Developmental Disabilities was created within the Department of Health and Family Services by Chapter 322, Laws of 1971, and made an independent unit by Chapter 29, Laws of 1977. 2007 Wisconsin Act 20 renamed it the Board for People with Developmental Disabilities, renumbered it from s. 15.197 (11n), and attached it to the Department of Administration under s. 15.03.

BOARD OF COMMISSIONERS OF PUBLIC LANDS

Commissioners: DOUGLAS J. LA FOLLETTE (secretary of state), KURT SCHULLER (state treasurer), J.B. VAN HOLLEN (attorney general). (All serve as *ex officio* members.)

DIVISION OF TRUST LANDS AND INVESTMENTS

Executive Secretary: TIA NELSON, 266-8369, tia.nelson@wisconsin.gov; TOM GERMAN, *deputy secretary,* 267-2233, tom.german@wisconsin.gov

Mailing Address: P.O. Box 8943, Madison 53708-8943.

Location: 101 East Wilson Street, 2nd Floor, Madison.

Telephone: (608) 266-1370.

Fax: (608) 267-2787.

Internet Address: http://bcpl.wisconsin.gov

Email Address: bcplinfo@wisconsin.gov

District Office: JOHN SCHWARZMANN, *administrator,* john.schwarzmann@bcpl.wisconsin.gov, P.O. Box 277, 7271 Main Street, Lake Tomahawk 54539-0277, (715) 277-3366; Fax: (715) 277-3363.

Publications: Biennial Report; Common School Fund/Normal School Fund Brochure; Trust Assets and Programs Fact Sheet; State Trust Fund Loan Program Brochure.

Number of Employees: 8.50.

Total Budget 2011-13: $3,094,400.

Constitutional Reference: Article X, Sections 2, 5, 6, 7, and 8.

Statutory References: Section 15.103 (4) and Chapter 24.

Agency Responsibility and History: The Board of Commissioners of Public Lands and its Division of Trust Lands and Investments manage the state's remaining trust lands, manage trust funds primarily for the benefit of public education, and maintain the state's original 19th century land survey and land sales records.

The board was created in 1848 by Article X of the Wisconsin Constitution to manage and sell lands that were granted to the state by the federal government for the purposes of supporting public education and developing the state's infrastructure. Nearly all of the approximately 3.6 million acres from federal land grants that were placed into trust for the benefit of public education have been sold. The agency still holds title to about 76,000 acres of trust lands. Of those remaining lands, almost 71,000 acres are Normal School Trust Lands and nearly 5,200 acres are Common School Trust Lands. The School Trust Lands are managed for timber production, natural area preservation, and public use.

The constitution established "a board of commissioners for the sale of school and university lands and for the investment of funds arising therefrom" consisting of the Secretary of State, State Treasurer, and Attorney General. The Revised Statutes of 1849 created the Board of Commissioners of the School and University Lands. In 1878, the board was renamed the Board of Commissioners of Public Lands. Chapter 75, Laws of 1967, created the Division of Trust Lands and Investments, under the supervision of the board, to serve as the board's operating agency. The board appoints an executive secretary outside the classified service to administer the division. The division was originally attached to the Department of Natural Resources. Since then, the legislature has successively attached the division to the Department of Justice (Chapter 34, Laws of 1979), the Department of Administration (1993 Wisconsin Act 16), the Office of the State Treasurer (1995 Wisconsin Act 27), and again to the Department of Administration (1997 Wisconsin Act 27).

The agency manages four "trust funds", the largest of which is the Common School Fund. The principal of this fund continues to grow through the collection of fees, fines, and forfeitures that accrue to the state. Most of the trust fund assets are invested in loans to Wisconsin municipalities and school districts through the State Trust Fund Loan Program. The loans finance a wide variety of public purpose projects statewide while providing the trust funds with a reasonable rate of return at low risk. Over the last five years, Wisconsin citizens have benefited from $625.76 million in trust fund loans used to support community, public safety, economic development, and school projects. Trust assets that are not invested in trust fund loans are invested in state and municipal bonds and the State Investment Fund.

The net earnings of the Common School Fund are distributed annually by the Department of Public Instruction to all Wisconsin public school districts. During the 2012 and 2013 fiscal years, a total of $62.6 million in earnings were distributed from the Common School Fund to support public school libraries throughout Wisconsin. The other small trust funds are used to support the University of Wisconsin and the state's general fund. 2005 Wisconsin Act 352 enables the board to use the proceeds of the state of trust lands to purchase other property to improve timberland management, prevent forest fragmentation, or increase public access to existing land holdings. Over the last five years, the agency has increased lands managed for timber by 10%, decreased unproductive lands by 17%, and increased public access by 16%. In the process of realigning trust land ownership, 8,234 acres of high quality natural areas and wildlife habitat have been transferred to the Department of Natural Resources.

PUBLIC RECORDS BOARD

Members: MATTHEW BLESSING (representing the director, state historical society), *chairperson;* SCOTT KOWALSKI (small business representative), *vice chairperson;* SANDRA BORADY-RUDD (designee of governor), *secretary;* MELISSA SCHMIDT (representing the joint legislative council staff director); MARY BURKE (designee of attorney general); BRYAN NAAB (designee of state auditor); CARL BUESING (representative of school board or governing body of a municipality); PETER SORCE (other member). (Representatives are appointed by the respective officers or the governor.)

Executive Secretary: GEORGIA THOMPSON, georgia.thompson@wisconsin.gov

Mailing Address: 4622 University Avenue, Room 10A, Madison 53702.

Telephone: (608) 266-2770.

Fax: (608) 266-5050.

Internet Address: http://publicrecordsboard.wi.gov

Publications: General Schedules for Records Common to State Agencies and Local Units of Government; miscellaneous training and records materials.

Statutory References: Sections 15.105 (4) and 16.61.

Agency Responsibility: The Public Records Board is responsible for the preservation of important state records, the cost-effective management of records by state agencies, and the orderly disposition of state records that have become obsolete. State agencies must have written approval from the board to dispose of records they generate or receive.

1991 Wisconsin Acts 39 and 269 directed the board to create a registry of those record series that contain personally identifiable information and made it the repository for general information about state computer matching programs.

Originally created by Chapter 316, Laws of 1947, as the Committee on Public Records and placed under the State Historical Society, the agency was transferred to the governor's office by Chapter 547, Laws of 1957. The committee was renamed the Public Records Board and attached to the Department of Administration by Chapter 75, Laws of 1967. Chapter 350, Laws of 1981, changed the board's name to the Public Records and Forms Board and added forms management to its duties. In 1995, Wisconsin Act 27 designated the board's current name and removed its forms management duties.

SMALL BUSINESS REGULATORY REVIEW BOARD

Members: SENATOR MOULTON (senate small business committee chairperson), REPRESENTATIVE MARKLEIN (assembly small business committee chairperson); STEVE DAVIS, ERICH KORTH, JIM RING, MINOO SEIFODDINI, KIMBERLY VELE, GUY WOOD, THOMAS WULF (appointed by governor).

Statutory References: Sections 15.105 (33), and 227.30.

Agency Responsibility: The 9-member Small Business Regulatory Review Board may determine that a newly filed emergency rule would have a significant fiscal impact on small businesses, defined as ones that employ 25 or fewer full-time employees or have gross annual sales of less than $5 million. The board may further determine whether the issuing agency has complied with statutory provisions that seek to reduce the impact of rules on small businesses and whether the data used to propose a rule is accurate. If the board finds an agency has not complied with the law, it may request compliance from that agency, and, in addition, suggest changes to the proposed rule. The board may also review state agency rules and guidelines to determine whether they place an unnecessary burden on small businesses. If the board determines a rule or guideline does place an undue burden on small businesses, it submits a report and recommendations to the Joint Committee for Review of Administrative Rules.

The 7 members the governor appoints represent small business and serve 3-year terms. The senate majority leader and assembly speaker each appoint one chairperson from standing committees concerned with small business. The board was created by 2003 Wisconsin Act 145 and its membership was revised by 2007 Wisconsin Act 20 and 2011 Wisconsin Acts 32 and 46.

STATE CAPITOL AND EXECUTIVE RESIDENCE BOARD

Members: CINDY TORSTVEIT (designated by secretary of administration); JIM DRAEGER (designated by director, state historical society); vacancy (engineer employed by the Department of Administration and appointed by secretary); SENATORS OLSEN, RISSER, SCHULTZ; REPRESENTATIVES HINTZ, LOUDENBECK, STROEBEL; ARLAN K. KAY, RON SIGGLEKOW (architects); JOHN J. FERNHOLZ (landscape architect); DEBRA ALTON, LAUREL BROWN, MARIJO REED (interior designers); KATHRYN NEITZEL (citizen member or architect, landscape architect, or interior designer). (All except *ex officio* members and their designees are appointed by governor.)

Statutory References: Sections 15.105 (5) and 16.83.

Agency Responsibility: The 16-member State Capitol and Executive Residence Board, created by Chapter 183, Laws of 1967, includes 7 citizen members with specified expertise, appointed by the governor to serve staggered 6-year terms. The purpose of the board is to direct the continuing and consistent maintenance of the property, decorative furniture, and furnishings of the capitol and executive residence. No renovations, repairs (except of an emergency nature), installation of fixtures, decorative items, or furnishings for the ground and buildings of the capitol or executive residence may be performed by or become the property of the state by purchase wholly or in part from state funds, or by gift, loan or otherwise, until approved by the board as to design, structure, composition, and appropriateness.

Office of State
EMPLOYMENT RELATIONS

Director: GREGORY L. GRACZ.

Deputy Director: JESSICA O'DONNELL, 266-9820, jessica.odonnell@

Legal Counsel: WILLIAM RAMSEY, 266-0047, william.ramsey@

State Employee Suggestion Program: SHELLY WEBER, *coordinator,* (608) 266-0664; Program e-mail: wiemployeesuggestionprogram@; Program Internet address: http://suggest.wi.gov

Affirmative Action, Division of: JEANETTE JOHNSON, *administrator,* 266-3017.

Compensation, Classification and Labor Relations, Division of: KATHY KOPP, *administrator,* 266-1860.

    Compensation, Bureau of: vacancy, *director,* 266-1729.

    Labor Relations, Bureau of: JIM UNDERHILL, *director,* 266-9564, jim.underhill@

Merit Recruitment and Selection, Division of: JOHN R. LAWTON, *administrator,* 266-1499, jack.lawton@

    Agency Services, Bureau of: LINDA BRENNAN, *director,* 267-0344, linda.brennan@

    Outreach Services, Bureau of: JENNIFER GEBERT, *director,* 267-2155, jennifer.gebert@

Mailing Address: P.O. Box 7855, Madison 53707-7855.

Address e-mail by combining the user ID and the state extender: userid@**wisconsin.gov**

Location: 101 East Wilson Street, 4th Floor, Madison.

Telephone: State job information: (608) 266-1731.

Fax: (608) 267-1020.

Internet Address: http://oser.state.wi.us

Publications: Council on Affirmative Action Report; Wisc.Jobs Bulletin; Veterans Employment Report; W-2 Hiring Report; Workforce Planning and Fact Book; Written Hiring Reasons Report.

Number of Employees: 48.65.

Total Budget 2011-13: $11,321,200.

Statutory References: Sections 15.105 (29); Chapter 111, Subchapter V, and Chapter 230.

Agency Responsibility: The Office of State Employment Relations is responsible for personnel and employment relations policies and programs for state government employees. The office administers the state's classified service, which is designed to staff state governmental agencies with employees chosen on the basis of merit. It evaluates job categories, determines employee performance and training needs, and assists managers in their supervisory duties. The office sets standards for and ensures compliance with affirmative action plans and provides training on human resource programs to supervisors, managers, human resource staff, and other state employees. It represents the executive branch in its role as an employer under the state's employment relations statutes.

A director, appointed by the governor, administers the office. The director appoints the administrators of the Division of Affirmative Action and Workforce Planning and the Division of Compensation, Classification and Labor Relations from outside the classified service. The governor appoints the administrator of the Division of Merit Recruitment and Selection to a 5-year term, with the advice and consent of the senate, based on a competitive examination. The governor may appoint the administrator for subsequent 5-year terms with the senate's consent.

Unit Functions: The *Division of Affirmative Action* administers the state's equal employment opportunity/affirmative action (EEO/AA) program and reports annually to the governor and legislature about the affirmative action accomplishments of state agencies. It develops state EEO/AA policies, procedures and programs; establishes state standards for agencies, the University of Wisconsin System, and legislative service agencies; approves and monitors agency EEO/AA plans, analyzes state workforce data for use in developing EEO/AA reports and recommendations. It monitors the effect of personnel transactions, hiring processes and employment conditions at state agencies to ensure that AA group members are not adversely affected, provides information and technical assistance to agencies to assist in the development of innovative personnel programs to increase the effectiveness of state EEO/AA efforts, assists in compliance investigations, helps state agencies in the recruitment for hard-to-fill positions, provides EEO/AA and diversity training to supervisors and managers, and provides support staff to the Council on Affirmative Action.

The *Division of Compensation, Classification and Labor Relations* administers the state's compensation plan and leave statutes and policies. It also assists in state agency compliance with the federal and state family and medical leave acts. The division represents the state as the employer in negotiating wages, benefits, and working conditions with the certified labor unions that represent state employees, and those contracts must then be ratified by the legislature. The division serves the state in arbitration proceedings and conducts labor relations training programs for state management representatives. It assigns nonrepresented classifications to pay ranges and assigns certain represented classifications to pay ranges as part of the collective bargaining process. It also assists in state agency compliance with protective occupation determinations and the federal Fair Labor Standards Act.

The *Division of Merit Recruitment and Selection,* created in Section 15.105 (29)(b) in 2003 Wisconsin Act 33, administers the state's civil service system by coordinating the recruiting, testing, evaluating, and hiring of applicants. It conducts and coordinates training for state managers and human resources staff. The division assists agencies in workforce planning and administers layoffs, transfers, and reinstatements of nonrepresented classified employees. It allocates positions to classifications and administers the state's performance evaluation program. The division operates Wisconsin Personnel Partners, which provides personnel services to local government units, and the Wisconsin Certification Examination Services, which provides licensure examination services to agencies on a fee basis. The division also oversees the administration of employee assistance programs in all state agencies, under which state employees and their families may receive assistance with personal or work-related problems.

History: An office that administers state employment procedures dates back to the creation of a State Civil Service Commission in Chapter 363, Laws of 1905. The law declared that appointments to and promotions in the civil service would be made only according to merit. Chapter 456, Laws of 1929, reconstituted the commission as the Personnel Board within the newly created Bureau of Personnel. This structure continued for 30 years until the legislature placed the board and bureau in the new Department of Administration, created in Chapter 228, Laws of 1959.

In 1972, Governor Patrick Lucey issued an executive order creating an affirmative action unit in the Bureau of Personnel. The order also directed the head of every state agency to encourage women and minorities to apply for promotions and to designate an affirmative action officer responsible for developing an affirmative action plan.

Chapter 196, Laws of 1977, created the Department of Employment Relations and transferred to it from the Department of Administration the organizational units and functions of the Employee Relations Division, including affirmative action, personnel, collective bargaining, and human resources services.

The legislature reorganized personnel functions in 1983 Wisconsin Act 27 by assigning classification and compensation responsibility to the secretary and recruitment and examination responsibility to a statutorily created Division of Merit Recruitment and Selection. The same law created the Personnel Board as an independent agency to review civil service rules and investigate and report on their impact. 1989 Wisconsin Act 31 abolished the Personnel Board and transferred its functions to the department. The 2003-05 biennial budget, Act 33, abolished the department and created the Office of State Employment Relations attached to the Department of Administration.

Statutory Council and Board

Affirmative Action, Council on: JAMES PARKER (appointed by governor), *chairperson;* CHRISTOPHER ZENCHENKO (appointed by senate president); ROGER L. PULLIAM (appointed by assembly speaker); vacancy (appointed by senate minority leader), ANNETTE WILLIAMS (appointed by assembly minority leader); YOLANDA SANTOS ADAMS, LAKSHMI BHARADWAJ, JANICE K. HUGHES, JOHN MAGERUS, SANDRA RYAN, RONALD SHAHEED, NANCY VUE, 3 vacancies (appointed by governor).

Contact person: vacancy, *administrator,* Division of Affirmative Action and Workforce Planning, 266-3017.

The 15-member Council on Affirmative Action advises the director of state employment relations, evaluates affirmative action programs throughout the classified service, seeks compliance with state and federal regulations, and recommends improvements in the state's affirmative action efforts. The council must report annually to the legislature and governor. It may recommend legislation, consult with agency personnel and other interested groups, and conduct hearings. Council members serve 3-year terms. A majority of them must be public members, and a majority must represent minority persons, women, and people with disabilities. The council was created by Chapter 196, Laws of 1977, in the Department of Employment Relations and is located in the Office of State Employment Relations (2003 Wisconsin Act 33). Its composition and duties are prescribed in Sections 15.105 (29)(d) and 230.46 of the statutes.

State Employees Suggestion Board: SANDY DREW, *chairperson;* DAVID M. VRIEZEN, vacancy (all appointed by governor).

Internet Address: http://suggest.wi.gov

The 3-member State Employees Suggestion Board administers an awards program to encourage unusual and meritorious suggestions and accomplishments by state employees that promote economy and efficiency in government services. Board members are appointed for 4-year terms, and at least one of them must be a state officer or employee. The board was created by Chapter 278, Laws of 1953, as the Wisconsin State Employees Merit Award Board and renamed in 1987 Wisconsin Act 142. It has been successively located in the Bureau of Personnel, the

Department of Administration, the Department of Employment Relations (1989 Wisconsin Act 31), and the Office of State Employment Relations (2003 Wisconsin Act 33). Its composition and duties are prescribed in Sections 15.105 (29)(c) and 230.48 of the statutes.

STATE USE BOARD

Members: JEAN ZWEIFEL (work center representative), *chairperson;* MICHAEL CASEY, vacancy (public members); MARIE DANFORTH (mental health services representative, Department of Health Services); vacancy (vocational rehabilitation representative, Department of Workforce Development); NICKOLAS C. GEORGE, JR. (private business representative); HELEN McCAIN (Department of Administration representative); BILL G. SMITH (small business representative). (All are appointed by governor.)

Mailing Address: Bureau of Procurement, Division of Enterprise Operations, P.O. Box 7867, Madison 53707-7867.

Telephone: (608) 266-5462.

Fax: (608) 267-0600.

Publication: Annual Report to the Secretary.

Number of Employees: 1.50.

Total Budget 2011-13: $247,200.

Statutory References: Sections 15.105 (22) and 16.752.

Agency Responsibility: The 8-member State Use Board was created by 1989 Wisconsin Act 345. Its members, who serve 4-year terms, oversee state purchases from work centers certified by the board. To be certified, centers must meet certain conditions: 1) the work center must make a product or provide a service the state needs; 2) it must offer these goods or services at a fair market price; and 3) it must employ individuals with severe disabilities for at least 75% of the direct labor used in providing the goods or services.

TAX APPEALS COMMISSION

Commissioners: LORNA HEMP BOLL, ROGER W. LEGRAND, vacancy (appointed by governor with senate consent).

Legal Assistant: NANCY BATZ, 266-9754, nancy.batz@wisconsin.gov

Mailing Address: 5005 University Avenue, Suite 110, Madison 53705.

Telephone: (608) 266-1391.

Fax: (608) 261-7060.

Number of Employees: 5.00.

Total Budget 2011-13: $1,075,200.

Statutory References: Sections 15.01 (2), 15.06 (1), 15.105 (1), and 73.01.

Publications: Decisions are at: www.wisbar.org/taxappeals.

Agency Responsibility: The 3-member Tax Appeals Commission hears and decides appeals of persons and entities of assessments of the Department of Revenue involving all major state-imposed taxes, including individual and corporate income taxes, homestead and farmland preservation tax credits, real estate transfer fees, and sales and use taxes, as well as appeals of state assessments of manufacturing property. The commission also decides disputes between persons or entities and the Department of Transportation regarding certain motor vehicle taxes and fees. The commission's decisions may be appealed to circuit court.

Commissioners serve staggered 6-year terms and must be experienced in tax matters. The chairperson, who is designated by the governor to serve a 2-year term, must not serve on or under any committee of a political party. Employees of the commission are appointed by the chairperson from the classified service.

The Tax Appeals Commission was created as the Board of Tax Appeals by Chapter 412, Laws of 1939. Before 1939, individuals took appeals of income and property taxes to the local county board of review with appeal permitted to the state Tax Commission. Corporations took their appeals to the Commissioner of Taxation with appeal to the circuit court. The board was renamed the Tax Appeals Commission by Chapter 75, Laws of 1967. 1985 Wisconsin Act 29 provided that the commission include a small claims division.

COUNCIL ON UTILITY PUBLIC BENEFITS

Members: Inactive

The 11-member Council on Utility Public Benefits advises the Department of Administration on issues related to energy efficiency, conservation programs, and energy assistance to low-income households, including weatherization, payment of energy bills, and early identification and prevention of energy crises. Services are provided through community action agencies, nonprofit corporations, or local governments. Grants are also awarded to nonprofit corporations for energy conservation and efficiency services, renewable resources in the least competitive sectors of the energy conservation market, and programs that promote environmental protection, electric system reliability, or rural economic development. The council was created by 1999 Wisconsin Act 9, and its composition and duties are prescribed in Sections 15.107 (17) and 16.957 of the statutes.

VOLUNTEER FIRE FIGHTER AND EMERGENCY MEDICAL TECHNICIAN SERVICE AWARD BOARD

Members: ROBERT H. SEITZ (fire chiefs statewide organization representative), *chairperson;* MELINDA R. ALLEN (volunteer emergency medical service technician), KENNETH A. BARTZ (volunteer fire fighters statewide organization representative), KRISTEN HALVERSON, ALLEN R. SCHRAEDER, vacancy (representatives of municipalities using volunteer fire fighters), ED EBERLE (secretary of administration designee), JOHN SCHERER (individual experienced in financial planning). (All but *ex officio* members are appointed by governor.)

Contact person: DAWN VICK, 267-1824.

Mailing Address: 101 East Wilson Street, 6th Floor, Madison 53703.

Telephone: (608) 266-7043.

Number of Employees: 0.00.

Total Budget 2011-13: $3,803,000.

Statutory References: Sections 15.105 (26) and 16.25.

The Service Award Program operates under the direction of an 8-member Volunteer Fire Fighter and Emergency Medical Technician Service Award Board appointed by the governor. It establishes by rule a tax-deferred benefit program for volunteer fire fighters, emergency medical technicians, and first responders based on their length of service to a community. The program is designed to assist municipalities in retaining volunteers. The board contracts with qualified organizations to provide investment plans and administrative services to municipalities that choose to participate in the service awards program, and the communities make payments directly to the plan providers. In appointing the board members, who serve 3-year terms, the governor must seek representatives from different regions of the state and from municipalities of different sizes. Representatives of the fire chiefs and volunteer fire fighters organizations must be volunteer fire fighters themselves. The board was created by 1999 Wisconsin Act 105.

WASTE FACILITY SITING BOARD

Members: JAMES W. SCHUERMAN (town official), *chairperson;* ALLEN A. JANSEN (town official), *vice chairperson;* PATRICIA M. TRAINER (designated by secretary of transportation), *secretary;* PETER L. NAUTH (designated by secretary of agriculture, trade and consumer protection), vacancy (designated by secretary of safety and professional services); DALE SHAVER (county official). (Town and county officials are appointed by governor with senate consent.)

Executive Director: DAVID H. SCHWARZ.

Mailing Address: 5005 University Avenue, Suite 201, Madison 53705-5400.

E-mail Address: dhamail@wisconsin.gov

Internet Address: http://dha.state.wi.us

Telephone: (608) 261-6564.

Fax: (608) 264-9885.

Number of Employees: 0.00.

Total Budget 2011-13: $91,000.

Statutory References: Sections 15.07 (1)(b) 11., 15.105 (12), 289.33, and 289.64.

Agency Responsibility: The 6-member Waste Facility Siting Board supervises a mandated negotiation-arbitration procedure between applicants for new or expanded solid or hazardous waste facility licenses and local committees composed of representatives from the municipalities affected by proposed facilities. It is authorized to make final awards in arbitration hearings and can enforce legal deadlines and other obligations of applicants and local committees during the process.

Town and county officials serve staggered 3-year terms, and the governor, when making these appointments, must consider timely recommendations of the Wisconsin Towns Association and the Wisconsin Counties Association. The board appoints an executive director who is authorized to request assistance from any state agency in helping the board fulfill its duties. The board is funded by a fee on each ton of waste disposed of in a licensed solid or hazardous waste facility. The board was created by Chapter 374, Laws of 1981.

WOMEN'S COUNCIL

Members: MARY JO BAAS (public member appointed by governor), *chairperson;* SENATORS HANSEN, SHILLING (appointed by senate majority leader); REPRESENTATIVES PASCH, vacancy (appointed by assembly speaker); MICHELLE METTNER (designated by governor); SARAH BRIGANTI, HEATHER SMITH (public members appointed by senate president); HEIDI GREEN, KIM NICKEL (public members appointed by assembly speaker); RENEE BOLDT, NICOLE BOWMAN-FARRELL, PATTY CADORIN, KAREN KATZ, JESSIE NICHOLSON (public members appointed by governor).

Executive Director: CHRISTINE LIDBURY.

Mailing Address: 101 East Wilson Street, 8th Floor, Madison 53702.

Telephone: (608) 266-2219.

Fax: (608) 267-0626.

E-mail Address: womenscouncil@wisconsin.gov

Internet Address: http://womenscouncil.wi.gov

Publications: Numerous publications related to the council's mission.

Number of Employees: 1.00.

Total Budget 2011-13: $279,800.

Statutory References: Sections 15.107 (11) and 16.01.

Agency Responsibility: The 15-member Women's Council is charged with identifying barriers that prevent women in Wisconsin from participating fully and equally in all aspects of life. The council promotes public and private sector initiatives that empower women through educational opportunity; provides a clearinghouse for information relating to women's issues; works in cooperation with related groups and organizations; and promotes opportunities for partnerships with various organizations to address issues affecting Wisconsin women. The council advises state agencies about the impact upon women of current and emerging state policies, laws, and rules; recommends changes to the public and private sectors and initiates legislation to further women's economic and social equality and improve this state's tax base and economy; and disseminates information on the status of women in this state.

The governor or governor's designee serves a 4-year term on the council; all other members serve 2-year terms. The governor appoints 6 public members, one of whom the governor designates as chairperson. The Women's Council was created by 1983 Wisconsin Act 27. It was preceded by a nonstatutory commission, the Governor's Commission on the Status of Women, which was created in 1964 and abolished in 1979.

Department of
AGRICULTURE, TRADE AND CONSUMER PROTECTION

Address e-mail by combining the user ID and the state extender: userid@**wisconsin.gov**
All telephone numbers are 608 area code unless otherwise indicated.

Board of Agriculture, Trade and Consumer Protection: DENNIS BADTKE, RICHARD CATES, ANDREW DIERCKS, MICHAEL DUMMER, JOHN KOEPKE, MIRANDA LEIS, vacancy (agricultural representatives); MARK SCHLEITWILER, DEAN STRAUSS (consumer representatives) (appointed by governor with senate consent).

Secretary of Agriculture, Trade and Consumer Protection: BEN BRANCEL, 224-5015.

Deputy Secretary: JEFF LYON, 224-5035.

Executive Assistant: SUSAN BUROKER, 224-5001.

Wisconsin Agricultural Statistics Service: GREG BUSSLER, *state agricultural statistician,* 224-4838, greg.bussler@nass.usda.gov

Legal Counsel, Office of: DAVID MEANY, *chief counsel,* 224-5022, david.meany@

Mailing Address: P.O. Box 8911, Madison 53708-8911.

Location: 2811 Agriculture Drive, Madison.

Telephones: Consumer Protection Hotline: (800) 422-7128; Farm and Rural Services Hotline: (800) 942-2474; Wisconsin Telemarketing No-Call List sign-up: (866) 966-2255.

Fax: Office of the Secretary: 224-5034; Division of Agricultural Development: 224-5110; Division of Agricultural Resource Management: 224-4656; Division of Animal Health: 224-4871; Division of Food Safety: 224-4710; Division of Management Services: 224-4737; Division of Trade and Consumer Protection: 224-4963.

Internet Address: www.datcp.wi.gov

Departmental E-mail Address: datcp_web@wisconsin.gov

Agricultural Development, Division of: MIKE POWERS, *administrator,* 224-5142, mike.powers@
  Agricultural Business and Sector Development Bureau: vacancy, *director.*
  Agricultural Market Development Bureau: JEN PINO-GALLAGHER, *director,* 224-5125, jen.pinogallagher@
  Farm and Rural Services Bureau: KATHY SCHMITT, *director,* 224-5048, kathy.schmitt@
  County Fair Coordinator: ROBERT WILLIAMS, 224-5131, robert.williams@

Agricultural Resource Management, Division of: JOHN PETTY, *administrator,* 224-4567, john.petty@
  Agrichemical Management, Bureau of: LORI BOWMAN, *director,* 224-4550, lori.bowman@
  Land and Water Resources, Bureau of: KATHY PIELSTICKER, *director,* 224-4621, kathy.pielsticker@
  Plant Industry, Bureau of: BRIAN KUHN, *director and assistant division administrator,* 224-4590, brian.kuhn@

Animal Health, Division of: PAUL MCGRAW, *state veterinarian, administrator,* 224-4884, paul.mcgraw@
  Administrative Services, Bureau of: vacancy, *director.*
  Animal Disease Control, Bureau of: vacancy, *director,* 224-4884.
  State Humane Officer: YVONNE M. BELLAY, 224-4888, yvonne.bellay@

Food Safety, Division of: STEVEN C. INGHAM, *administrator,* 224-4701, steven.ingham@
  Food Safety and Inspection, Bureau of: PETER HAASE, *director,* 224-4711, peter.haase@
  Meat Safety and Inspection, Bureau of: CINDY KLUG, *director,* 224-4729, cindy.klug@

Management Services, Division of: SUSAN BUROKER, *interim administrator,* 224-5001, susan.buroker@

DEPARTMENT OF AGRICULTURE, TRADE AND CONSUMER PROTECTION

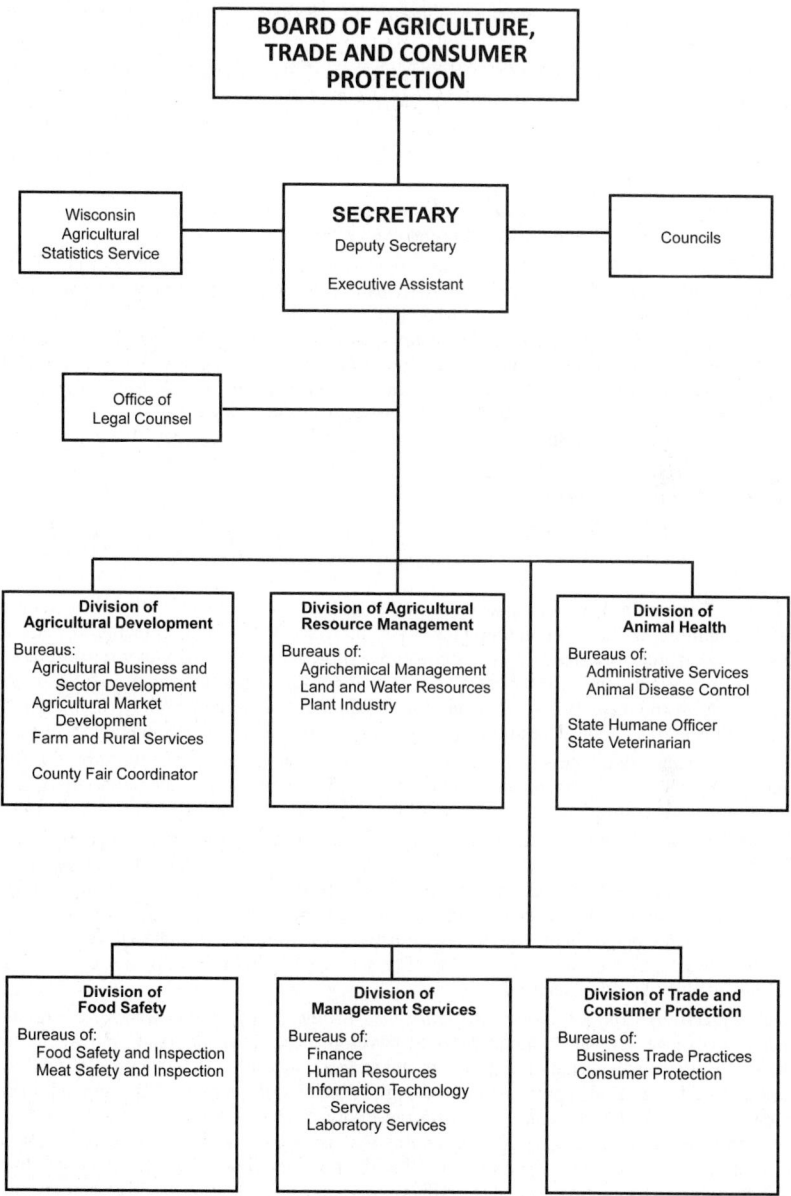

BOARD OF AGRICULTURE, TRADE AND CONSUMER PROTECTION

Wisconsin Agricultural Statistics Service

SECRETARY

Deputy Secretary

Executive Assistant

Councils

Office of Legal Counsel

Division of Agricultural Development

Bureaus:
　Agricultural Business and
　　Sector Development
　Agricultural Market
　　Development
　Farm and Rural Services

County Fair Coordinator

Division of Agricultural Resource Management

Bureaus of:
　Agrichemical Management
　Land and Water Resources
　Plant Industry

Division of Animal Health

Bureaus of:
　Administrative Services
　Animal Disease Control

State Humane Officer
State Veterinarian

Division of Food Safety

Bureaus of:
　Food Safety and Inspection
　Meat Safety and Inspection

Division of Management Services

Bureaus of:
　Finance
　Human Resources
　Information Technology
　　Services
　Laboratory Services

Division of Trade and Consumer Protection

Bureaus of:
　Business Trade Practices
　Consumer Protection

Units attached for administrative purposes under Sec. 15.03:　Bioenergy Council
Land and Water Conservation Board
Livestock Facility Siting Review Board

Finance, Bureau of: JASON GHERKE, *director,* 224-4748, jason.gherke@

Human Resources, Bureau of: BARRY WANNER, *director,* 224-4760, barry.wanner@

Information Technology Services, Bureau of: KAREN ARRIOLA, *director,* 224-4770, karen.arriola@

Laboratory Services, Bureau of: STEVEN M. SOBEK, *director,* 267-3500, steve.sobek@

Trade and Consumer Protection, Division of: SANDRA CHALMERS, *administrator,* 224-4920, sandra.chalmers@

> *Business Trade Practices, Bureau of:* JEREMY S. MCPHERSON, *director,* 224-4922, jeremy.mcpherson@
>
> *Consumer Protection, Bureau of:* MICHELLE REINEN, *director and assistant division administrator,* 224-4965, michelle.reinen@

Publications: Agricultural Land Sales; *Chloroacetanilide Herbicide Metabolites in Wisconsin Groundwater; Complaint Guide for the Wisconsin Consumer;* Farm Transfers in Wisconsin – A Guide for Farmers; *Groundwater Protection: An Evaluation of Wisconsin's Atrazine Rule; Groundwater Quality – Agricultural Chemicals in Wisconsin Groundwater May 2002;* Guide to Wisconsin Cheese Factory Outlets and Tours; *Landlord and Tenants: The Wisconsin Way; Livestock Guidance: Local Planning for Livestock Operations in Wisconsin; Planning for Agriculture in Wisconsin: A Guide for Communities; Preventing Senior Citizen Rip-offs;* Wisconsin Agricultural Statistics; Wisconsin Dairy Plant Directory; Wisconsin Nursery Directory; Wisconsin Pest Bulletin.

Number of Employees: 594.89.

Total Budget 2011-13: $203,739,500.

Statutory References: Sections 15.13, 15.135, and 15.137; Chapters 88, 91-100, 127, and 136.

Agency Responsibility: The Department of Agriculture, Trade and Consumer Protection regulates agriculture, trade, and commercial activity in Wisconsin for the protection of the state's citizens. It enforces the state's primary consumer protection laws, including those relating to deceptive advertising, unfair business practices, and consumer product safety. The department oversees enforcement of Wisconsin's animal health and disease control laws and conducts a variety of programs to conserve and protect the state's vital land, water, and plant resources.

The department administers financial security programs to protect agricultural producers, facilitates the marketing of Wisconsin agricultural products in interstate and international markets, and promotes agricultural development and diversification.

Organization: The 9 members of the Board of Agriculture, Trade and Consumer Protection serve staggered 6-year terms. Of the board members, 2 must be consumer representatives and 7 must have an agricultural background. Appointments to the board must be made "without regard to party affiliation, residence or interest in any special organized group". The board directs and supervises the department, which is administered by a secretary appointed by the governor with the advice and consent of the senate. The secretary appoints the division administrators from outside the classified service.

Unit Functions: The *Division of Agricultural Development* provides services to assist producers, agribusinesses, and organizations to develop local, state, national, and international markets for Wisconsin agricultural products and to foster agricultural development and diversification in the state. It also provides counseling and mediation services to farmers, administers a rural electric power service program with the Public Service Commission, and oversees the operation of producer-elected marketing boards that assess fees within their respective groups for promotion, research, and education related to their commodities. The division also administers Agricultural Development and Diversification grants, a federal-state market news program, the "Something Special from Wisconsin" and Alice in Dairyland marketing programs, as well as the state aid programs for county and district fairs, the Livestock Breeders Association, and World Dairy Expo.

The *Division of Agricultural Resource Management* administers programs designed to protect the state's agricultural resources, as well as public health and the environment. It works to pre-

The Department of Agriculture, Trade and Consumer Protection enforces rules regarding fair business practices and promotes the health of consumers by working to ensure the safety of plants and animals. (Department of Agriculture, Trade and Consumer Protection)

vent agricultural practices that contaminate surface water and groundwater and jointly administers a nonpoint source pollution control program with the Department of Natural Resources. It directs programs related to farmland preservation and soil and land conservation, agricultural chemical cleanup, drainage districts, and agricultural impact statements. It regulates the sale and use of pesticides, animal feed, fertilizers, seed, and soil and plant additives and conducts programs to prevent and control plant pests, such as the gypsy moth.

The *Division of Animal Health* works closely with agricultural producers and veterinarians to diagnose, prevent, and control serious domestic animal diseases that threaten public health and the food chain. It licenses and inspects animal dealers and markets, regulates the import and export of animals across state lines, acts to prevent the spread of animal diseases, and assists in the enforcement of state humane laws. Through the Premises Identification Program, it registers persons who keep livestock and assigns an identification code to each place at which livestock are kept to facilitate animal disease control. It also regulates emerging industries, such as aquaculture and farm-raised deer.

The *Division of Food Safety* protects the state's food supply. From production through processing, packaging, distribution, and retail sale, the division works to ensure safe and wholesome food and to prevent fraud and misbranding in food sales. It licenses and inspects dairy plants, food and beverage processing establishments, meat slaughter and processing facilities, food warehouses, grocery stores, and other food establishments. The division inspects all dairy farms; inspects and samples food products; oversees food grading; and regulates the advertising, packaging, and labeling of food products.

The *Division of Management Services* provides administrative services to the department, including budget and accounting; facilities and fleet management; shipping, mailing, and printing; human resource management; and information technology services. The division also operates a general laboratory that provides analytical support to departmental inspection and sampling programs.

The *Division of Trade and Consumer Protection* enforces a wide range of consumer protection laws and handles nearly 200,000 consumer complaints and inquiries annually. It promulgates and enforces rules pertaining to deceptive advertising, consumer fraud, consumer product safety, landlord-tenant practices, home improvement, telecommunications, telemarketing, motor vehicle repair, fair packaging and labeling, weights and measures, and many other aspects of marketing. To promote fair and open competition in the marketplace, the division investigates and regulates unfair and anticompetitive business practices. It monitors the financial condition and business practices of dairy plants, grain warehouses, food processing plants, and public storage warehouses in order to protect agricultural producers and depositors. It also administers the state's Telemarketing No-Call List.

History: The present form of the Department of Agriculture, Trade and Consumer Protection is largely the result of the consolidation of several related agencies in 1929, but the department traces its lineage and responsibilities back to pre-statehood days.

From its beginnings, Wisconsin has been concerned with agriculture; food quality, safety, and labeling; plant and animal health; unfair business and trade practices; and consumer protection, and has taken steps to protect the public. The 1839 territorial legislature provided for the inspection of certain food and other products and established a program to regulate weights and measures. County inspectors were responsible for certifying the grade, wholesomeness, quantity, and proper packaging of food and distilled spirits, with county treasurers charged with enforcing the weights and measures standards. The 1867 Legislature, in Chapter 176, authorized the governor to appoint a treasury agent to enforce the laws relating to itinerant sales by "hawkers and peddlers". The 1889 Legislature, in Chapter 452, created the Office of the Dairy and Food Commissioner to enforce food safety, food labeling, and weights and measures laws. Other legislation over the years created various related functions such as the State Veterinarian, the State Board of Agriculture, the Inspector of Apiaries, the State Orchard and Nursery Inspector, the State Supervisor of Illuminating Oils, and the State Humane Agent.

The Department of Agriculture was created by Chapter 413, Laws of 1915, which combined the functions of several prior entities including the Board of Agriculture, Livestock Sanitary Board, State Veterinarian, Inspector of Apiaries, and Orchard and Nursery Inspector. Under the control and supervision of a Commissioner of Agriculture appointed by the governor with senate consent, the department had the responsibility to promote the interests of agriculture, dairying, horticulture, manufactures, and the domestic arts. It collected and published farm crop, livestock, and other statistics relating to state resources and regulated the practice of veterinary medicine. Through its own informational publications and paid advertisements in print media both inside the country and in foreign lands, it also sought to further the "development and enrichment" of the state by attracting "desirable immigrants" and "capital seeking profitable investment". These efforts were intended to promote the advantages and opportunities offered by the state "to the farmer, the merchant, the manufacturer, the home seeker, and the summer visitor".

The Division of Markets was created within the Department of Agriculture by Chapter 670, Laws of 1919. The duty of the division was to promote, in the interest of the producer, distributor, and consuming public, the economical and efficient distribution of farm products. Responsibilities included devising systems for marketing, grading, standardization, and storage of farm products; preventing deceptive practices; maintaining a market news service for collecting and reporting information on the supply, demand, prices, and commercial movement of farm products; and designing copyrighted trademarks, labels, and brands for Wisconsin farm products. A separate Department of Markets was created by Chapter 571, Laws of 1921, under the direction of a commissioner of markets appointed by the governor with senate consent. The department retained most of the duties of the former division, but was allowed to give assistance to cooperative associations and was specifically charged with regulating unfair methods of competition in business and unfair trade practices.

The modern department had its inception when Chapter 479, Laws of 1929, created the Department of Agriculture and Markets by consolidation of the Department of Agriculture, the Department of Markets, the Dairy and Food Commissioner, the State Treasury Agent, the State Supervisor of Inspectors of Illuminating Oils, and the State Humane Agent. The department, which was under the control of three commissioners appointed by the governor with senate consent, assumed all duties performed by the component agencies. The department was reorganized and renamed the Department of Agriculture by Chapter 85, Laws of 1939, but its basic mission and authority was not changed. The department was overseen by a 7-member State Board of Agriculture, whose members, appointed by the governor with senate consent, in turn appointed the department's director. All members of the board were required to be persons experienced in farming.

The department's name was changed to the current Department of Agriculture, Trade and Consumer Protection by Chapter 29, Laws of 1977. This law also specified that one of the 7 board members must be a consumer representative.

1995 Wisconsin Act 27 directed the governor, rather than the board, to appoint the department secretary with senate consent, and expanded the board's membership to 8, including 2 consumer representatives. The board continues to set policy for the agency. Act 27 also consolidated the administration of most consumer protection activities within the department by transferring some staff and functions from the Department of Justice. However, the Department of Justice cooperates in the enforcement of consumer protection laws by providing legal services such as civil litigation. 1997 Wisconsin Act 95 added a ninth board member to represent agriculture.

In recent decades, the legislature has expanded the department's responsibilities related to land and water resources, including the areas of soil conservation, drainage districts, groundwater protection, nonpoint source pollution abatement, pesticides, animal disease control, and agricultural chemical storage and cleanup. It has allowed the department to create marketing boards for agricultural commodities, to promote agricultural development and diversification, and promote the state's agricultural products in interstate and international markets. The department also conducts programs for protecting producers against catastrophic financial defaults, farmland preservation, and farm mediation.

Statutory Councils

Agricultural Education and Workforce Development Council: KATHY SCHMITT (secretary of agriculture, trade and consumer protection designee); SHARON WENDT (state superintendent of public instruction designee); MIKE GRECO (secretary of workforce development designee); REED HALL (chief executive officer of the Wisconsin Economic Development Corporation); CARRIE MICKELSON (secretary of natural resources designee); JOHN SHUTSKE (president of the University of Wisconsin System designee); DAN CLANCY (director of the technical college system); DAVID WILLIAMS (chancellor of the University of Wisconsin-Extension designee); MICHAEL COMPTON (member chosen jointly by deans of specified UW System colleges and UW-Madison School of Veterinary Medicine); KAREN KNOX (technical college system director appointed by director of the technical college system); DAVID SHONKWEILER (technical college dean with authority over agricultural programs appointed by director of technical college system); SENATOR OLSEN (chairperson of a senate standing committee concerned with education); REPRESENTATIVE KESTELL (chairperson of an assembly standing committee concerned with education); SENATOR MOULTON (chairperson of a senate standing committee concerned with agriculture); REPRESENTATIVE NERISON (chairperson of an assembly standing committee concerned with agriculture); PAUL LARSON (Wisconsin Association of Agricultural Educators representative); DARLENE ARNESON, BECKY LEVZOW (general agriculture representatives); SAM SKEMP, DOUG WILSON (agribusiness representatives); GERRY MICH (representative environmental stewardship); EARL GUSTAFSON (representative of businesses related to natural resources); vacancy (representative of businesses related to plant agriculture); RICHARD MILLER (representative of landscaping, golf course, greenhouse, floral, and related businesses); MARK MACPHAIL (representative of food product and food processing businesses); ANDREA BROSSARD (representative of businesses related to animal agriculture); CAL DALTON (representative of businesses related to renewable energy); PAM JAHNKE (representative of agricultural communication interests); AL HERRMAN (representative of businesses providing engineering, mechanical, electronic, and power services relating to agriculture); vacancy (board of agriculture, trade and consumer protection representative); DAVE KRUSE (teacher of science, vocational technology, business, math, or a similar field, appointed by superintendent of

A food safety inspector checks food preparation equipment during a routine inspection at a grocery store. (Department of Agriculture, Trade and Consumer Protection)

public instruction); NATALIE KILLION (school guidance counselor, appointed by superintendent of public instruction); RICHARD AUSTIN (school board member, appointed by superintendent of public instruction); GREGORY PEYER (school district administrator, appointed by superintendent of public instruction) (all except *ex officio* members, legislators, and those appointed by the superintendent of public instruction are appointed by the secretary of agriculture, trade and consumer protection).

The mission of the 34-member Agricultural Education and Workforce Development Council is to recommend policies and other changes to improve the efficiency of the development and provision of agricultural education across educational systems and to support employment in industries related to agriculture, food, and natural resources by seeking to increase the hiring and retention of well-qualified employees and promote the coordination of educational systems to develop, train, and retrain employees for current and future careers. It also advises state agencies on matters relating to integrating agricultural education and workforce development systems. All except *ex officio* members and legislators are appointed for staggered 3-year terms and may not serve more than 2 consecutive terms. The council was created by 2007 Wisconsin Act 223 and its composition and duties are prescribed in Sections 15.137 (2) and 93.33 of the statutes.

Agricultural Producer Security Council: CRAIG MYRHE (Farmer's Educational and Cooperative Union of America, Wisconsin Division, representative), NICHOLAS GEORGE (Midwest Food Processor's Association, Inc., representative), RON STATZ (National Farmer's Organization, Inc., representative), vacancy (Wisconsin Agri-Service Association, Inc., representative), JOHN UMHOEFER (Wisconsin Cheese Makers Association representative), JIM ZIMMERMAN (representative of both the Wisconsin Corn Growers Association, Inc., and the Wisconsin Soybean Association, Inc.), LOUISE HEMSTEAD (Wisconsin Dairy Products Association, Inc., representative), DAVE DANIELS (Wisconsin Farm Bureau Federation representative), JOHN MANSKE (Wisconsin Federation of Cooperatives representative), DUANE MAATZ (Wisconsin Potato and Vegetable Growers Association, Inc., representative) (appointed by the secretary of agriculture, trade and consumer protection).

The 10-member Agricultural Producer Security Council advises the Department of Agriculture, Trade and Consumer Protection (DATCP) on the administration and enforcement of agricultural producer security programs. All members are appointed by the secretary of DATCP for 3-year terms. The council was created by 2001 Wisconsin Act 16 and its composition and duties are prescribed in Sections 15.137 (1) and 126.90 of the statutes.

Farm to School Council: vacancy (department of agriculture, trade and consumer protection employee appointed by secretary of agriculture, trade and consumer protection), SUSAN UTTECH (department of health services employee appointed by secretary of department of health services), JUNE PAUL (department of public instruction employee appointed by superintendent of public instruction), LAURA BROWN, MAUREEN CASSIDY, DIANE CHAPETA, JILL GASKEL, BRIDGET HOLCOMB, MARY JANSSEN, JACK KLOPPENBURG, KIM LAPACEK, DUANE MAATZ, PETE McGESHICK III, KYMM MUTCH, CHERYL PEIL, SUSAN PETERMAN, PATRICK REMINGTON, MARY JO TUCKWELL (appointed by secretary of agriculture, trade and consumer protection).

The Farm to School Council advises the Department of Agriculture, Trade and Consumer Protection regarding the promotion and administration of farm to school programs. The secretary of DATCP appoints an employee of the department and appoints an unspecified number of farmers, experts in child care, school food service personnel, and other persons with interests in agriculture, nutrition, and education. The secretary of health services appoints an employee of the department of health services and the superintendent of public instruction appoints an employee of the department of public instruction. The council was created by 2009 Wisconsin Act 293 and its composition and duties are prescribed in Sections 15.137 (3) and 93.49 of the statutes.

Fertilizer Research Council: Voting members: MIKE MLEZIVA, JEFF SOMMERS, vacancy (industry representatives nominated by fertilizer industry); TOM CRAVE, RANDY VOLLRATH, vacancy (crop producing farmer representatives); ANDREW CRAIG (water quality expert appointed by secretary of natural resources). (All except the water quality expert are appointed jointly by secretary of agriculture, trade and consumer protection and dean of UW-Madison College of Agricultural and Life Sciences.) Nonvoting members: BEN BRANCEL (secretary of agriculture, trade and consumer protection), CATHY STEPP (secretary of natural resources), MOLLY JAHN (dean, UW-Madison College of Agricultural and Life Sciences).

Mailing Address: P.O. Box 8911, Madison 53708-8911.

Telephone: 224-4614.

The 10-member Fertilizer Research Council meets annually to review and recommend projects involving research on soil management, soil fertility, plant nutrition, and for research on surface and groundwater problems related to fertilizer use. The secretary of agriculture, trade and consumer protection grants final approval for project funding. These research projects are granted to the UW System and are financed through funds generated from the sale of fertilizer and soil or plant additives in Wisconsin. The council's voting members are appointed for 3-year terms and may not serve more than 2 consecutive terms. The council was created by Chapter 418, Laws of 1977, and its composition and duties are prescribed in Sections 15.137 (5) and 94.64 (8m) of the statutes.

INDEPENDENT UNITS ATTACHED FOR BUDGETING, PROGRAM COORDINATION, AND RELATED MANAGEMENT FUNCTIONS BY SECTION 15.03 OF THE STATUTES

BIOENERGY COUNCIL

Members: TIM CLAY, JAMIE DERR, DAVID DONOVAN, ANDREW FIENE, DICK GORDER, RON TEHASSI HILL, JEFF LANDIN, T.J. MORICE, TROY RUNGE, BOB SATHER, HENRY SCHIENEBECK, PETER TAGLIA, KEVIN WALLENFANG, JULIAN ZELAZNY. (All members are appointed by the secretary of agriculture, trade and consumer protection.)

Statutory References: Sections 15.137 (6) and 93.47.

Agency Responsibility: The Bioenergy Council is responsible for identifying voluntary best management practices for sustainable biomass and biofuels production.

The number of members of the council is not specified, and all are appointed by the secretary of agriculture, trade and consumer protection to serve at the pleasure of the secretary. The council was created by 2009 Wisconsin Act 401.

LAND AND WATER CONSERVATION BOARD

Members: LEAH WAVRUNEK (secretary of administration designee), MARY ANNE LOWNDES (secretary of natural resources designee), JOHN PETTY (secretary of agriculture, trade and consumer protection designee); PATRICK LAUGHRIN, TOM RUDOLPH, CHARLES WAGNER (county land conservation committee members); RYAN SCHROEDER (public member); ROBIN LEARY (resident of city of 50,000 or more); MARK F. CUPP (representing governmental unit involved in river management); LYNN HARRISON (farmer); DENNIS CANEFF (representing charitable natural resources organization). (All except *ex officio* members or designees are appointed by governor with senate consent.)

Advisory Members: PATRICIA LEAVENWORTH (U.S. Department of Agriculture, Natural Resources Conservation Service); SUSAN BUTLER, BRAD PFAFF (U.S. Department of Agriculture, Farm Service Agency); WILLIAM BLAND (designated by dean of the UW-Madison College of Agricultural and Life Sciences); KEN GENSKOW (appointed by director of UW-Extension); KURT CALKINS, JIM VANDENBROOK (designated by staff of county land conservation committees).

Statutory References: Sections 15.135 (4), 91.06, and 92.04.

Agency Responsibility: The 11-member Land and Water Conservation Board advises the secretary and department regarding soil and water conservation, animal waste management, and farmland preservation. As part of its farmland preservation duties, the board certifies agricultural preservation plans and zoning ordinances. It reviews and makes recommendations to the department on county land and water resource plans, local livestock regulations, agricultural shoreland management ordinances, and funding allocations to county land conservation committees. The board also advises the UW System annually about needed research and education programs related to soil and water conservation. In addition, it assists the Department of Natural Resources with issues related to runoff from agriculture and other rural sources of pollution.

The board's 3 county land conservation committee members are chosen by the Wisconsin Land and Water Conservation Association, Inc., to serve 2-year terms. The 4 members who must fulfill statutorily defined categories serve staggered 4-year terms. The undesignated member serves a 2-year term. In addition, the board must invite the appointment of advisory members from agencies or organizations specified by statute.

The board was originally created as the Land Conservation Board by Chapter 346, Laws of 1981, which also abolished the Agricultural Lands Preservation Board and transferred its functions to the new board. Chapter 346 also transferred administration of the state's soil and water conservation program from the UW System to the department but continued the university's responsibility for soil and water conservation research and educational programs. 1993 Wisconsin Act 16 changed the name of the board to the Land and Water Conservation Board.

LIVESTOCK FACILITY SITING REVIEW BOARD

Members: LEE ENGELBRECHT (representing towns); ANDY JOHNSON (representing counties); BOB SELK (representing environmental interests); vacancy (representing livestock farming interests); FRAN BYERLY, JEROME GASKA, BOB TOPEL (public members). (All nominated by the secretary of agriculture, trade and consumer protection and appointed by the governor with senate consent.)

Telephone: 224-4500.

The 7-member Livestock Facility Siting Review Board may review certain decisions made by political subdivisions relating to the siting or expansion of livestock facilities, such as feedlots. An aggrieved person may challenge the decision of a city, village, town, or county government approving or disapproving the siting or expansion of a livestock facility by requesting the board to review the decision. If the board determines that a challenge is valid, it shall reverse the decision of the governmental body. The decision of the board is binding on the political subdivision, but either party may appeal the board's decision in circuit court. All members are appointed for 5-year terms. The four members representing specific interests are selected from lists of names submitted by the Wisconsin Towns Association, Wisconsin Counties Association, environmental organizations, and statewide agricultural organizations, respectively. The board was created by 2003 Wisconsin Act 235 and its composition and duties are prescribed in Sections 15.135 (1) and 93.90 of the statutes.

Department of
CHILDREN AND FAMILIES

Address e-mail by combining the user ID and the state extender: userid**@wisconsin.gov**
All telephone numbers are 608 area code unless otherwise indicated.

Secretary of Children and Families: ELOISE ANDERSON, 266-8684.

Deputy Secretary: JOAN HANSEN, 266-8684, joan.hansen@

Executive Assistant: SARA BUSCHMAN, 266-8684, sara.buschman@

Communications Director: JOE SCIALFA, 266-8684, joe.scialfa@

Chief Legal Counsel: RANDALL KEYS, 266-8684, randall.keys@

Legislative Director: CYNTHIA ARCHER, 266-8684, cynthia1.archer@

Tribal Liaison: LOA PORTER, 266-8684, loa.porter@

Mailing Address: P.O. Box 8916, Madison 53708-8916.

Location: 201 East Washington Avenue, Second Floor, Madison.

Telephone: 267-3905.

Fax: 261-6972.

Internet Address: www.dcf.wisconsin.gov

Department E-mail Address: dcfweb@wisconsin.gov

Publications: Annual fiscal reports; Biennial reports; Reports and informational brochures (available through divisions).

Number of Employees: 778.00.

Total Budget 2011-13: $1,217,922,800.

Statutory References: Section 15.20; Chapter 46.

Early Care and Education, Division of: JUDY NORMAN-NUNNERY, *administrator,* 261-8684 judy.normannunnery@; JILL CHASE, *acting deputy administrator,* 261-8684, jill.chase@

    Child Care Administration, Bureau of: vacancy, *director.*

    Early Care Regulation, Bureau of: CINDA STRICKER, *acting director,* 266-8842, cinda.stricker@

    Quality Improvement, Bureau of: LAURA SATERFIELD, *director,* 261-8684, laura.saterfield@

    Milwaukee Early Care Administration: HOLLY DAVIS, *director,* (414) 289-5830, holly.davis@

Family and Economic Security, Division of: KRIS RANDAL, *administrator,* 266-8719, kris.randal@; JOHN CHAPIN, *deputy administrator,* 266-8719, john.chapin@

    Child Support, Bureau of: JACQUELINE SCHARPING, *director,* 267-8978, jacqueline.scharping@

    Working Families, Bureau of: JANICE PETERS, *director,* 267-0513, janice.peters@

Management Services, Division of: RON HUNT, *administrator,* 266-9718, ron.hunt@; MELISSA WAVELET, *deputy administrator,* 266-9718, melissa.wavelet@

    Budget and Policy, Bureau of: ROBERT NIKOLAY, *director,* 266-9718, robert.nikolay@

    Finance, Bureau of: HOPE KOPROWSKI, *director,* 266-3059, hope.koprowski@

    Human Resources, Bureau of: LYNN WIESER, *director,* 266-9936, lynn.wieser@

    Information Technology Services, Bureau of: STEVE MCDOWELL, *director,* 264-9831, steve.mcdowell@

DEPARTMENT OF CHILDREN AND FAMILIES

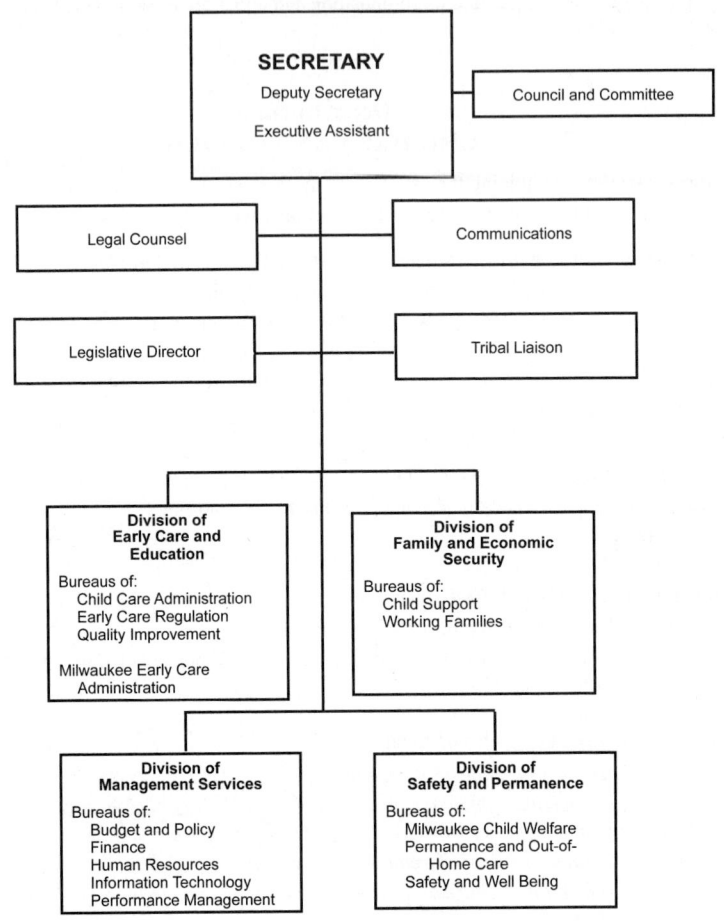

SECRETARY
Deputy Secretary
Executive Assistant

Council and Committee

Legal Counsel

Communications

Legislative Director

Tribal Liaison

Division of Early Care and Education

Bureaus of:
  Child Care Administration
  Early Care Regulation
  Quality Improvement

Milwaukee Early Care
  Administration

Division of Family and Economic Security

Bureaus of:
  Child Support
  Working Families

Division of Management Services

Bureaus of:
  Budget and Policy
  Finance
  Human Resources
  Information Technology
  Performance Management

Division of Safety and Permanence

Bureaus of:
  Milwaukee Child Welfare
  Permanence and Out-of-
    Home Care
  Safety and Well Being

Units attached for administrative purposes under Sec. 15.03:   Child Abuse and Neglect Prevention Board
Milwaukee Child Welfare Partnership Council

Performance Management, Bureau of: REBECCA SCHWEI, *director,* 267-9328, rebecca.schwei@

Regional Operations, Bureau of: JOHN TUOHY, *director,* 261-8084, john.tuohy@

Safety and Permanence, Division of: FREDI-ELLEN BOVE, *administrator,* 266-8717, frediellen.bove@; JOHN ELLIOTT, *deputy administrator,* 266-8717, john.elliott@

Milwaukee Child Welfare, Bureau of: ARLENE HAPPACH, *director,* (414) 220-7063, arlene.happach@

Permanence and Out-of-Home Care, Bureau of: RON HERMES, *director,* 266-8717, ron.hermes@

Safety and Well Being, Bureau of: ROBERT WILLIAMS, *director,* 266-9293, robertb.williams@

Agency Responsibility: The Department of Children and Families provides or oversees county provision of various services to assist children, youth, and families, including services for children in need of protection or services for their families, adoption and foster care services, licensing of facilities that care for children, background investigations of child caregivers, and child abuse and neglect investigations. It administers the Wisconsin Works (W-2) program, including the child care subsidy program, child support enforcement and paternity establishment, and programs related to the Temporary Assistance to Needy Families (TANF) income support program. The department works to ensure families have access to high quality and affordable early care and education and also administers the licensing and regulation of day care centers.

Organization: The department is administered by a secretary who is appointed by the governor with the advice and consent of the senate. The secretary appoints the division administrators from outside the classified service.

Unit Functions: The *Division of Early Care and Education* is responsible for the child care licensing and quality improvement programs, including YoungStar; administers the Wisconsin Shares program; and manages the Milwaukee Early Care Administration.

The *Division of Family and Economic Security* is responsible for the W-2, child support, and refugee services programs.

The *Division of Management Services* oversees the department's budget, financial management, information systems and technology; regional operations; human resource services and employment relations; affirmative action and civil rights compliance; purchasing and contract administration; facilities management; project management; and other administrative services.

The *Division of Safety and Permanence* directly administers child welfare services in Milwaukee County, supervises county-administered child welfare services in the balance of the state, and manages related programs including prevention services and the Special Needs Adoption program.

History: By the time the federal government entered the field of public welfare during the Great Depression of the 1930s, Wisconsin had already pioneered a number of programs, including aid to children and pensions for the elderly (enacted in 1931). The Wisconsin Children's Code, enacted by Chapter 439, Laws of 1929, was one of the most comprehensive in the nation. The state's initial response to federal funding was to establish separate departments to administer social security funds and other public welfare programs. After several attempts at reorganization and a series of studies, the legislature established the State Department of Public Welfare in Chapter 435, Laws of 1939, to provide unified administration of all existing welfare functions. Public health and care for the aged were delegated to separate agencies.

The executive branch reorganization act of 1967 created the Department of Health and Social Services. The Board of Health and Social Services, appointed by the governor, directed the new department and appointed the departmental secretary to administer the agency, whose responsibilities included public welfare. In Chapter 39, Laws of 1975, the legislature abolished the board and replaced it with a secretary appointed by the governor with the advice and consent of the senate. That same law called for a reorganization of the department, which was completed by July 1977. The Department of Health and Social Services was renamed the Department of Health and Family Services (DHFS), effective July 1, 1996.

The decades of the 1960s and 1970s saw an expansion of public welfare and health services at both the federal and state levels. Especially notable were programs for medical care for the needy and aged (Medical Assistance and Medicare), drug treatment programs, food stamps, and Aid to Families with Dependent Children Program (AFDC). DHFS was assigned additional duties during the 1980s in the areas of child support, child abuse and neglect, and welfare reform.

1995 Wisconsin Act 27 revised AFDC and transferred it and other income support programs including Medical Assistance eligibility and food stamps to the Department of Workforce Development (DWD). (Wisconsin Works, known as W-2, replaced AFDC in 1995 Wisconsin Act 289.) Existing welfare reform programs, including Job Opportunities and Basic Skills (JOBS), Learnfare, Parental Responsibility, and Work-Not-Welfare, were also transferred to DWD, along with child and spousal support, the Children First Program, Older American Community Service Employment, refugee assistance programs, and vocational rehabilitation functions. Health care

The Department of Children and Families held a "flash mob" at the State Capitol in May 2013 to kick off the new foster care recruitment campaign for Foster Care Awareness Month. Participating was Tonette Walker, the wife of Governor Scott Walker. (Department of Children and Families)

facilities plan review was transferred from the Department of Industry, Labor and Human Relations to DHFS by 1995 Wisconsin Act 27. Act 27 also transferred laboratory certification to the Department of Agriculture, Trade and Consumer Protection and low-income energy assistance to the Department of Administration.

As a result of 1995 Wisconsin Act 303, DHFS assumed responsibility for direct administration and operation of Milwaukee County child welfare services. 2001 Wisconsin Act 16 transferred the Medical Assistance Eligibility Program and the Food Stamp Program to DHFS from the Department of Workforce Development.

2007 Wisconsin Act 20 created the Department of Children and Families (DCF), beginning July 1, 2008. It also changed the name of DHFS to the Department of Health Services and split the responsibilities of DHFS between the two departments. Act 20 transferred from DHFS to DCF the duty to provide or oversee county supervision of various services to assist children and families, including services for children in need of protection or services and their families, adoption services, licensing of facilities that provide care for children, child caregiver background investigations, and child abuse and neglect investigations. The act also transferred from DWD to DCF administration of Wisconsin Works, including the child care subsidy program, child support enforcement and paternity establishment, and programs related to temporary assistance for needy families (TANF).

Statutory Council and Committee

Domestic Abuse, Council on: REPRESENTATIVE JACQUE (designated by assembly speaker), JAMIE KRATZ-GULLICKSON (designated by assembly minority leader), vacancy (designated by senate majority leader), SENATOR SHILLING (designated by senate minority leader); L. KEVIN HAMBERGER, GENE REDHAIL, MARIANA RODRIGUEZ, RENEE SCHULTZ-STANGL, KARA SCHURMAN, SUSAN SIPPEL, 3 vacancies (members not designated by legislative leadership are nominated and appointed by governor with senate consent.)

The 13-member Council on Domestic Abuse makes recommendations to the secretary on domestic abuse, reviews grant applications, advises the department and legislature on domestic abuse policy, and, in conjunction with the Judicial Conference, develops forms for filing petitions for domestic abuse restraining orders and injunctions. Members are appointed for staggered 3-year terms. Members designated by legislative leadership do not have to be legislators. The council was created by Chapter 111, Laws of 1979, and it was transferred from the Department of Health and Family Services to the Department of Children and Families by 2007 Wisconsin Act 20. Its composition and duties are prescribed in Sections 15.207 (16) and 49.165 (3) of the statutes.

Rate Regulation Advisory Committee: Tongenell Campbell (VIC Living Center), Jill Chaffee (Northwest Passage); Dave Fritsch (Clinicare); Linda Hall (Wisconsin Association of Family and Children Agencies); Ron Hauser (Lutheran Social Services of Wisconsin and Upper Michigan, Inc.); Ron Hermes (Department of Children and Families); Katie Herrem (Department of Corrections); Beverly Johnson (AJA Enterprise, LLC); Bruce Kamradt (Milwaukee WrapAround); James Kania (Department of Children and Families, Bureau of Milwaukee Child Welfare); Rachel Karow (Family Works); Teresa Kovach (Portage County Department of Human Services); Jeremy Krall (Brown County Department of Human Services); Patricia Lancour (Fond du Lac County Department of Social Services); Hugh Meyers (Orion Family Services); Jesus Mireles (Waukesha County Department of Health and Human Services); Jacqueline Moen-Kadlec (Ho-Chunk Tribe); Cheri Salava (Rock County Human Services); John Solberg (Rawhide, Inc.); Renee Soroko (Winnebago County Human Services); Alan Stauffer (Waupaca County Department of Health and Human Services); Chrya Trost (LaCausa, Inc.); Ruth Wiseman (Chileda); Dawn Woodward (Columbia County Human Services) (appointed by secretary of children and families).

The secretary of children and families appoints members to a committee to advise the department regarding rates for child placing agencies, residential care centers and group homes. Committee membership includes purchasers; county departments of social services or human services; the Bureau of Milwaukee Child Welfare; tribes; consumers; and a statewide association of private, incorporated family and children's social services agencies representing all groups of providers that are affected by the rate regulation process. The committee was created by 2009 Wisconsin Act 335. Its composition and duties are prescribed in Section 49.343 (5) of the statutes.

Independent Units Attached for Budgeting, Program Coordination, and Related Management Functions by Section 15.03 of the Statutes

CHILD ABUSE AND NEGLECT PREVENTION BOARD

Members: Barbara Knox (public member), *chairperson;* Michael Bloedorn (public member), *vice chairperson;* Kimberly Liedl (designated by governor), Jill Karofsky (designated by attorney general), Kevin Moore (designated by secretary of health services), Sheila Briggs (designated by state superintendent of public instruction), Melissa Roberts (designated by secretary of corrections), Sara Buschman (designated by secretary of children and families); Representative Kleefisch (representative to the assembly appointed by speaker), vacancy (representative to the assembly appointed by assembly minority leader), Senator Grothman (senator appointed by president of senate), Senator Lassa (senator appointed by senate minority leader); Nancy Armbrust, Jeffrey Lamont, Sandra McCormick, Jesus Mireles, Jennifer Noyes, Jane Pirsig, Dimitri Topitzes, Teri Zywicki (public members appointed by governor).

Interim Executive Director: Jennifer Jones, jennifer.jones@wisconsin.gov

Mailing Address: 110 East Main Street, Suite 810, Madison 53703-3316.

Telephone: 266-6871.

Fax: 266-3792.

Internet Address: wichildrentrustfund.org

Publications: ACES in Wisconsin; Child Sexual Abuse Prevention: Tips for Parents; Positive Parenting: Tips on Discipline; Shaken Baby Syndrome Prevention materials.

Number of Employees: 6.00.

Total Budget 2011-13: $5,996,400.

Statutory References: Sections 15.205 (4) and 48.982.

Agency Responsibility: The 20-member Child Abuse and Neglect Prevention Board administers the Children's Trust Fund. The board recommends policies to the legislature, governor, and state agencies to protect children and support prevention activities. The board supports, funds, and evaluates evidence-informed and innovative strategies that are effective in helping Wisconsin communities prevent child maltreatment through culturally competent, family-centered, coordinated approaches to the delivery of support services that strengthen families. The board also implements consumer education and social marketing campaigns and provides education on prevention and positive parenting through printed materials and informational seminars. Funding is derived through charges on duplicate birth certificates, federal matching funds, and private contributions. In 2001, the board created a nonprofit corporation, the Celebrate Children Foundation with funds from the sale of the Celebrate Children special license plates to raise additional money for improving the lives of children and families in Wisconsin.

The board's 10 public members serve staggered 3-year terms. The board appoints the executive director and staff from the classified service. It was created by 1983 Wisconsin Act 27, and it was transferred from the Department of Health and Family Services to the Department of Children and Families by 2007 Wisconsin Act 20.

MILWAUKEE CHILD WELFARE PARTNERSHIP COUNCIL

Members: LINDA DAVIS (public member), *chairperson;* WILLIE JOHNSON, JR., RUSSELL STAMPER, JOHN WEISHAN (Milwaukee County board members nominated by Milwaukee County Executive), vacancy (representative to the assembly appointed by assembly speaker), REPRESENTATIVE JOHNSON (representative to the assembly appointed by assembly minority leader), SENATOR DARLING (senator appointed by senate president), vacancy (senator appointed by senate minority leader); COLLEEN ELLINGSON, FRANCINE FEINBERG, TAMARA GRIGSBY, CHRISTINE HOLMES, KIM KAMPSCHROER, MARSHALL MURRAY, MALLORY O'BRIEN, MICHAEL SKWIERAWSKI, EARNESTINE WILLIS (public members); 2 vacancies (children's services network nominees). (All but legislators are appointed by governor.)

Contact Person: ARLENE HAPPACH.

Mailing Address: 1555 North Rivercenter Drive, Suite 220, Milwaukee 53212.

Telephone: (414) 220-7029.

Statutory References: Sections 15.207 (24) and 46.562.

Agency Responsibility: The 19-member Milwaukee Child Welfare Partnership Council makes recommendations to the Department of Children and Families and the legislature regarding policies and plans to improve the child welfare system in Milwaukee County, including a neighborhood-based system for delivery of services. It may also recommend funding priorities and identify innovative public and private funding opportunities. The 15 nonlegislative members are appointed to 3-year terms, and the governor designates one of the public members as chairperson. At least 6 public members must be residents of Milwaukee County. The council was created by 1995 Wisconsin Act 303, and it was transferred from the Department of Health and Family Services to the Department of Children and Families by 2007 Wisconsin Act 20.

Department of
CORRECTIONS

Address e-mail by combining the user ID and the state extender: userid@**wisconsin.gov**
All telephone numbers are 608 area code unless otherwise indicated.

Secretary of Corrections: EDWARD WALL, 240-5055, edward.wall@

Deputy Secretary: DEIRDRE MORGAN, 240-5055, deirdre.morgan@

Executive Assistant: SCOTT LEGWOLD, 240-5055, scott.legwold@

Office of Legal Counsel: KATHRYN ANDERSON, *chief,* 240-5049, kathryn.anderson@

Director of Public Affairs: vacancy, 240-5060.

Legislative Liaison: MELISSA ROBERTS, 240-5056, melissab.roberts@

Policy Initiatives Advisor: TONY STREVELER, 240-5801, anthony.streveler@

Detention Facilities, Office of: KRISTI DIETZ, *director,* 240-5052, kristi.dietz@; Milwaukee: (414) 227-5199.

Victim Services, Office of: COLLEEN JO WINSTON, *director,* 240-5888, colleenj.winston@

Prison Rape Elimination Act Director: MARION MORGAN, 240-5113, marion.morgan@

Reentry Director: JULE CAVANAUGH, 240-5015, jule.cavanaugh@

Mailing Address: P.O. Box 7925, Madison 53707-7925.

Location: 3099 East Washington Avenue, Madison 53704.

Telephone: 240-5000.

Fax: 240-3300.

Internet Address: www.doc.wi.gov

Number of Employees: 10,254.37.

Total Budget 2011-13: $2,468,594,500.

Statutory References: Section 15.14; Chapter 301.

Adult Institutions, Division of: CATHY JESS, *administrator,* 240-5104, cathy.jess@; JOHN PAQUIN, *assistant administrator,* john.paquin@; LARRY JENKINS, *assistant administrator,* larry. jenkins@; vacancy, *security chief,* 240-5105; 3099 East Washington Avenue, Madison 53704; Division Fax: 240-3310.

Correctional Enterprises, Bureau of: vacancy, *director,* 240-5201; Fax: 240-3320.

Health Services, Bureau of: JAMES GREER, *director,* 240-5122, james.greer@; Fax: 240-3311.

Offender Classification and Movement, Bureau of: MARK HEISE, *director,* 240-5800, mark.heise@; Fax: 240-3350.

Program Service, Bureau of: vacancy, *director,* 240-5160; Fax: 240-3310.

Planning and Operations Unit: TIM LEMONDS, *director,* 240-5180, tim.lemonds@; Fax: 240-3310.

PRISONS

Maximum Security:

  Columbia Correctional Institution: MICHAEL MEISNER, *warden,* P.O. Box 950, Portage 53901-0950, (608) 742-9100; Fax: (608) 742-9111.

  Dodge Correctional Institution: JIM SCHWOCKERT, *warden,* P.O. Box 661, Waupun 53963-0661, (920) 324-5577; Fax: (920) 324-6297.

  Green Bay Correctional Institution: MIKE BAENEN, *warden,* P.O. Box 19033, Green Bay 54307-9033, (920) 432-4877; Fax: (920) 448-6545.

  Waupun Correctional Institution: WILLIAM POLLARD, *warden,* P.O. Box 351, Waupun 53963-0351, (920) 324-5571; Fax: (920) 324-7250.

  Wisconsin Secure Program Facility: TIM HAINES, *warden,* P.O. Box 1000, Boscobel 53805-0900, (608) 375-5656; Fax: (608) 375-5434.

Medium Security:

  Fox Lake Correctional Institution: MARC CLEMENTS, *warden,* P.O. Box 147, Fox Lake 53933-0147, (920) 928-3151; Fax: (920) 928-6981.

  Jackson Correctional Institution: LIZZIE TEGELS, *warden,* P.O. Box 232, Black River Falls 54615-0232, (715) 284-4550; Fax: (715) 284-7335.

  Kettle Moraine Correctional Institution: BRIAN FOSTER, *warden,* P.O. Box 31, Plymouth 53073-0031, (920) 526-3244; Fax: (920) 526-9320.

  Milwaukee Secure Detention Facility: FLOYD MITCHELL, *warden,* 1015 North 10th Street, P.O. Box 05740, Milwaukee 53205-0740, (414) 212-3535; Fax: (414) 212-6811.

DEPARTMENT OF CORRECTIONS

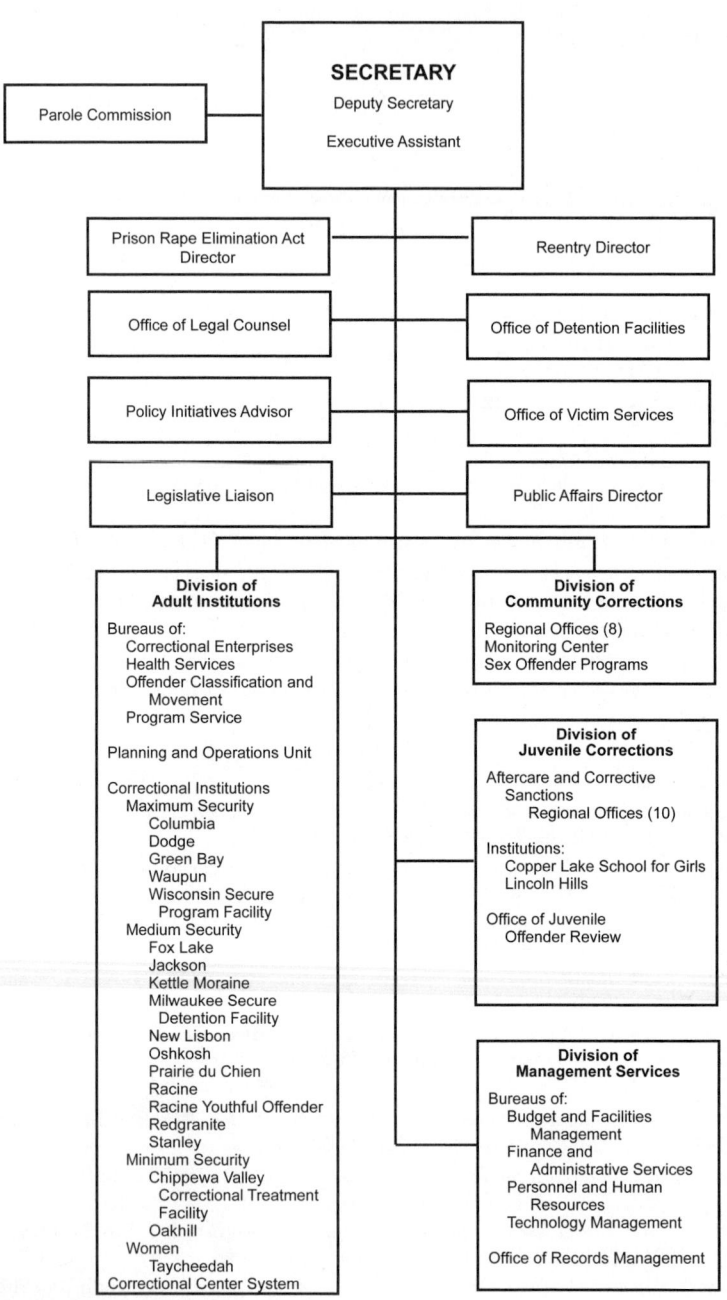

SECRETARY

Deputy Secretary

Executive Assistant

Parole Commission

Prison Rape Elimination Act Director

Reentry Director

Office of Legal Counsel

Office of Detention Facilities

Policy Initiatives Advisor

Office of Victim Services

Legislative Liaison

Public Affairs Director

Division of Adult Institutions

Bureaus of:
    Correctional Enterprises
    Health Services
    Offender Classification and
        Movement
    Program Service

Planning and Operations Unit

Correctional Institutions
    Maximum Security
        Columbia
        Dodge
        Green Bay
        Waupun
        Wisconsin Secure
            Program Facility
    Medium Security
        Fox Lake
        Jackson
        Kettle Moraine
        Milwaukee Secure
            Detention Facility
        New Lisbon
        Oshkosh
        Prairie du Chien
        Racine
        Racine Youthful Offender
        Redgranite
        Stanley
    Minimum Security
        Chippewa Valley
            Correctional Treatment
            Facility
        Oakhill
    Women
        Taycheedah
    Correctional Center System

Division of Community Corrections

Regional Offices (8)
Monitoring Center
Sex Offender Programs

Division of Juvenile Corrections

Aftercare and Corrective
    Sanctions
        Regional Offices (10)

Institutions:
    Copper Lake School for Girls
    Lincoln Hills

Office of Juvenile
    Offender Review

Division of Management Services

Bureaus of:
    Budget and Facilities
        Management
    Finance and
        Administrative Services
    Personnel and Human
        Resources
    Technology Management

Office of Records Management

Units attached for administrative purposes under Sec. 15.03:
Interstate Adult Offender Supervision Board
Council on Offender Reentry

Prison Industries Board
State Board for Interstate Juvenile Supervision

New Lisbon Correctional Institution: TIMOTHY DOUMA, *warden,* P.O. Box 2000, New Lisbon 53950-2000, (608) 562-6400; Fax: (608) 562-6410.

Oshkosh Correctional Institution: JUDY SMITH, *warden,* P.O. Box 3530, Oshkosh 54903-3530, (920) 231-4010; Fax: (920) 236-2615/2626.

Prairie du Chien Correctional Facility: GARY BOUGHTON, *warden,* P.O. Box 6000, Prairie du Chien 53821, (608) 326-7828; Fax: (608) 326-5960.

Racine Correctional Institution: PAUL KEMPER, *warden,* 2019 Wisconsin Street, Sturtevant 53177-1829, (262) 886-3214; Fax: (262) 886-3514.

Racine Youthful Offender Correctional Institution: ROBERT HUMPHREYS, *warden,* P.O. Box 2200, Racine 53404-2713, (262) 638-1999; Fax: (262) 638-1777.

Redgranite Correctional Institution: MICHAEL A. DITTMANN, *warden,* 1006 County Road EE, P.O. Box 900, Redgranite 54970-0925, (920) 566-2600; Fax: (920) 566-2610.

Stanley Correctional Institution: JEFFREY PUGH, *warden,* 100 Corrections Drive, Stanley 54768-6500, (715) 644-2960; Fax: (715) 644-2966.

Minimum Security:

Chippewa Valley Correctional Treatment Facility: PAMELA WALLACE, *warden,* 2909 East Park Avenue, Chippewa Falls 54729, (715) 720-2850; Fax: (715) 720-2859.

Oakhill Correctional Institution: DAN WESTFIELD, *warden,* P.O. Box 140, Oregon 53575-0140, (608) 835-3101; Fax: (608) 835-9196.

Women:

Taycheedah Correctional Institution: DEANNE SCHAUB, *warden,* 751 County Road K, P.O. Box 1947, Fond du Lac 54936-1947, (920) 929-3800; Fax: (920) 929-2946.

CENTER SYSTEM

QUALA CHAMPAGNE, *warden, Wisconsin Correctional Center System,* 3099 East Washington Avenue, P.O. Box 7969, Madison 53707-7969, 240-5310; Fax: 240-3335.

Black River Correctional Center: MATTHEW GERBER, superintendent, W6898 East Staffon Road, Route #5, Black River Falls 54615-6426, (715) 333-5681; Fax: (715) 333-2708.

John C. Burke Correctional Center: MARK RICE, *superintendent,* 900 South Madison Street, P.O. Box 900, Waupun 53963-0900, (920) 324-3460; Fax: (920) 324-4575.

Felmers Chaney Correctional Center: MICHAEL COCKROFT, *superintendent,* 2825 North 30th Street, Milwaukee 53210, (414) 874-1600; Fax: (414) 874-1695.

Drug Abuse Correctional Center: JEFF JAEGER, *superintendent,* Kempster Hall/Winnebago Mental Health Institute, 1305 North Drive, P.O. Box 36, Winnebago 54985-0036, (920) 236-2700; Fax: (920) 426-5601.

Robert E. Ellsworth Correctional Center: MICHELLE J. HOFFMAN, *superintendent,* 21425-A Spring Street, Union Grove 53182-9408, (262) 878-6000; Fax: (262) 878-6015.

Flambeau Correctional Center: vacancy, *superintendent,* N671 County Road M, Hawkins 54530-9400, (715) 585-6394; Fax: (715) 585-6563.

Gordon Correctional Center: WAYNE OLSON, *superintendent,* 10401 East County Road G, Gordon 54838, (715) 376-2680; Fax: (715) 376-4361.

Kenosha Correctional Center: ANN KRUEGER, *superintendent,* 6353 14th Avenue, Kenosha 53143, (262) 653-7099; Fax: (262) 653-7241.

McNaughton Correctional Center: BRAD KOSBAB, *superintendent,* 8500 Rainbow Road, Lake Tomahawk 54539-9558, (715) 277-2484; Fax: (715) 277-2293.

Milwaukee Women's Correctional Center: PAMELA ZANK, *superintendent,* 615 West Keefe Avenue, Milwaukee 53212, (414) 267-6101; Fax: (414) 267-6130.

Oregon Correctional Center: vacancy, *superintendent,* 5140 Highway M, P.O. Box 25, Oregon 53575-0025, (608) 835-3233; Fax: (608) 835-3145.

Sanger B. Powers Correctional Center: PATRICK MELMAN, *superintendent,* N8375 County Line Road, Oneida 54155-9300, (920) 869-1095; Fax: (920) 869-2650.

St. Croix Correctional Center: JoANN SKALSKI, *superintendent,* 1859 North 4th Street, P.O. Box 36, New Richmond 54017-0036, (715) 246-6971; Fax: (715) 246-3680.

Marshall E. Sherrer Correctional Center: GARY MITCHELL, *superintendent,* 1318 North 14th Street, Milwaukee 53205-2596, (414) 343-5000; Fax: (414) 343-5039.

Thompson Correctional Center: DEWAYNE STREET, *superintendent,* 434 State Farm Road, Deerfield 53531-9562, (608) 423-3415; Fax: (608) 423-9852.

Winnebago Correctional Center: SUSAN ROSS, *superintendent,* 4300 Sherman Road, P.O. Box 128, Winnebago 54985-0128, (920) 424-0402; Fax: (920) 424-0430.

Community Corrections, Division of: DENISE SYMDON, *administrator,* 240-5300; SHIRLEY STORANDT, *assistant administrator,* 3099 East Washington Avenue, Madison 53704; Fax: 240-3330.

Region 1: LANCE WIERSMA, *chief,* 3319 West Beltline Highway, Suite W300, Madison 53704, 261-7441; Fax: 261-7450.

Region 2: LISA YEATES, *chief,* 9531 Rayne Road, Suite 2, Sturtevant 53177-1833, (262) 884-3780; Fax: (262) 884-3799.

Region 3: NIEL THORESON, *chief,* 4160 North Port Washington Road, Milwaukee 53212, (414) 229-0600; Fax: (414) 229-0584.

Region 4: ROSE SNYDER-SPAAR, *chief,* 1360 American Drive, Neenah 54956, (920) 751-4623; Fax: (920) 751-4601.

Region 5: GENA JARR, *chief,* 770 Technology Way, Suite 500, Chippewa Falls 54729-4516, (715) 738-3001; Fax: (715) 738-3000.

Region 6: MICKEY MCCASH, *chief,* 2187 North Stevens Street, Suite B, Rhinelander 54501-0497, (715) 365-2587; Fax: (715) 369-5255.

Region 7: SALLY TESS, *chief,* 141 Northwest Barstow Street, Room 126, Waukesha 53188-3756, (262) 521-5157; Fax: (262) 548-8697.

Region 8: RON KALMUS, *chief,* 427 East Tower Drive, Suite 200, Wautoma 54982-6927, (920) 787-5500; Fax: (920) 787-5589.

Monitoring Center: vacancy, *director,* 3099 East Washington Avenue, Madison 53704, 240-5850.

Sex Offender Programs: GRACE ROBERTS, *director,* 3099 East Washington Avenue, Madison 53704, 240-5820.

Juvenile Corrections, Division of: CARI J. TAYLOR, *administrator,* 240-5900, cari.taylor@; RANDALL HEPP, *assistant administrator,* 240-5902, randall.hepp@; 3099 East Washington Avenue, Madison 53704; Division Fax: 240-3370.

Aftercare and Corrective Sanctions:

Appleton: 2107 Spencer Street, Appleton 54914-4638, (920) 997-3870.

Eau Claire: 718 West Clairemont Avenue, Room 140, Eau Claire 54701-6143, (715) 836-6683.

Green Bay: 200 North Jefferson Street, Suite 134, Green Bay 54301, (920) 448-6548.

Madison: 2909 Landmark Place, Suite 104, Madison 53713, 288-3350.

Milwaukee: 4200 North Holton Street, Suite 120, Milwaukee 53212, (414) 229-0701.

Neenah: 1356 American Drive, Neenah 54956, (920) 729-3900.

Schofield: 1699 Schofield Avenue, Suite 120, Schofield 54476-1021, (715) 241-8890.

Sheboygan: 3422 Wilgus Avenue, Sheboygan 53081, (920) 456-6548.

Sparta: 820 Industrial Drive, Suite 6, Sparta 54656, (608) 269-1921.

Sturtevant: 9531 Rayne Road, Suite 3, Sturtevant 53177-1833, (262) 884-3748.

Institutions:

Copper Lake School for Girls: PAUL J. WESTERHAUS, *superintendent,* W4380 Copper Lake Road, Irma 54442-9720, (715) 536-8386; Fax: (715) 536-8236, paul.westerhaus@

Lincoln Hills School: PAUL J. WESTERHAUS, *superintendent,* W4380 Copper Lake Road, Irma 54442-9720, (715) 536-8386; Fax: (715) 536-8236, paul.westerhaus@

Juvenile Offender Review, Office of: SHELLEY HAGAN, *director,* 240-5918; Fax: 240-3370, shelley.hagan@

Management Services, Division of: STACEY ROLSTON, *administrator,* 240-5401, stacey.rolston@; TIM LEFAVE, *assistant administrator,* 240-5400, tim.lefave@; Division Fax: 240-3340.

Budget and Facilities Management, Bureau of: ROLAND COUEY, *director,* 240-5405, roland.couey@

Finance and Administrative Services, Bureau of: JERRY SALVO, *director,* 240-5412, jerry.salvo@

Personnel and Human Resources, Bureau of: KARI HEILMAN, *director,* 240-5460 kari.heilman@

Records Management, Office of: BILL CLAUSIUS, *director,* 240-5407, bill.clausius@

Technology Management, Bureau of: CURT TAYLOR, *director,* 240-5752, curt.taylor@

Agency Responsibility: The Department of Corrections administers Wisconsin's state prisons, community corrections, and juvenile corrections programs. It supervises the custody and discipline of all inmates in order to protect the public and seeks to rehabilitate offenders and reintegrate them into society. The department currently operates 19 correctional facilities and 16 correctional centers for adults, and 2 facilities for juveniles. It also supervises offenders on probation, parole, and extended supervision; monitors compliance with deferred prosecution programs; and may make recommendations for pardons or commutations of sentence when requested by the governor. The department maintains the sex offender registry for those who are required by law to register. The department also monitors sex offenders who are required by law to be on lifetime GPS.

Organization: The department is headed by a secretary who is appointed by the governor with the advice and consent of the senate. The secretary appoints the division administrators from outside the classified service.

Unit Functions: The *Office of the Secretary* ensures the overall mission of the department is achieved. Services and initiatives directly supervised by the Office of the Secretary include legal counsel, public information, reentry, and the Prison Rape Elimination Act. The reentry initiative is a crime prevention strategy designed to increase the number of offenders who live productive, law-abiding lives from admission to custody through supervision in the community.

The *Office of Detention Facilities,* in the office of the secretary, is responsible for the inspection and evaluation of all local detention facilities, including jails, houses of correction, secure juvenile detention centers, and municipal lockups. It provides technical assistance and training on various detention issues.

The *Division of Adult Institutions* supervises adult inmates in a variety of correctional settings. It assigns inmates to one of 6 security classifications, based on their records, backgrounds, and the risk they may pose to the public, correctional officers, and other inmates.

Security classifications include 2 levels each of maximum, medium, and minimum security. These levels determine how closely inmates are guarded, how restricted their movements are within the institution, and the programs in which they may participate. Although prisons are classified by the highest level of security for which the facility is built and administered, an individual facility may contain several security levels.

The prison program is designed to offer offenders opportunities to develop skills necessary to lead law-abiding lives upon release. Services include evaluation of an offender's background and needs and the provision of programs to meet those needs. Programs include academic and vocational education, alcohol and other drug abuse treatment, other clinical treatment, work, and religious observance. The division offers job training for inmates through Badger State

Industries, which produces various items, including furniture, textiles and linens, license plates, and signs.

The division also administers 16 minimum security correctional centers across the state. Center staff work closely with probation and parole agents to assist the transition of inmates back into the community. Center programming includes basic education, alcohol and drug counseling, work experience, and work release.

The *Division of Community Corrections* supervises persons released on parole and extended supervision, as well as those placed on probation by the court. The supervision is community-based to strengthen family and community ties, encourage lawful behavior, and provide local treatment programs. Probation and parole agents hold offenders accountable for their behavior, provide direct services, and refer their clients to community service agencies. They also provide investigative services to the courts, the Division of Adult Institutions, and the Parole Commission to aid in sentencing, institutional programming, and parole planning. Under limited circumstances, agents supervise juveniles released to aftercare programs, persons conditionally released from mental health facilities, and sexually violent persons placed on supervised release. The division is also responsible for the sex offender registry and the electronic monitoring center.

The *Division of Juvenile Corrections,* created in Section 301.025, Wisconsin Statutes, by 1995 Wisconsin Act 27, administers programs to treat and rehabilitate delinquent youth and protect the public. It operates the state's juvenile corrections institutions and community corrections programs. Through its Juvenile Offender Review Program, the division determines whether offenders in the institutions are eligible for release, oversees the aftercare services of those who are released, and selects the participants for intensive surveillance under the Corrective Sanctions Program. The division also administers the Community Youth and Family Aids Program, which offers financial incentives to counties to divert juveniles from state institutions and into less restrictive community rehabilitation programs, and it awards grants to counties that participate in the Intensive Aftercare Program, which offers a wide range of social, educational, and employment assistance.

The *Division of Management Services* provides budgeting, research, data processing, personnel, and telecommunications services and oversees accounting, procurement, and facilities management.

History: In Chapter 288, Laws of 1851, the legislature established a commission to locate and supervise the building and administration of a state prison. The commissioners chose Waupun as the site and the facility was opened in 1852. Waupun housed both male and female offenders until 1933 when the Wisconsin Prison for Women opened in Taycheedah.

From 1853 to 1874 an elected state prison commissioner ran the prison. Beginning in 1874, the governor appointed three state prison commissioners to hire a warden and direct state prison operation. In 1881, prisons and other public welfare functions were placed under the supervision of the State Board of Supervision of Wisconsin Charitable, Reformatory and Penal Institutions, subsequently renamed the State Board of Control of the Wisconsin Reformatory, Charitable and Penal Institutions in 1891. Both adult and juvenile facilities came under the board's control.

By 1939, the Division of Corrections within the newly created Department of Public Welfare had assumed supervision of prisons, juvenile institutions, and probation and parole. Under the 1967 executive branch reorganization, the division became part of the Department of Health and Social Services. The division was reorganized as a separate Department of Corrections in 1989 Wisconsin Act 31, but responsibility for juvenile offenders remained with the Department of Health and Social Services until 1995 Wisconsin Act 27 transferred juvenile corrections and related services to the Department of Corrections.

Waupun was the state's only prison until 1898, when the Wisconsin State Reformatory for prisoners from 16 to 30 years-of-age opened at Green Bay. The age limitation was repealed in 1966 and the facility was renamed the Green Bay Correctional Institution in 1978. A separate facility for women, the Industrial Home for Women, began operations in Taycheedah in 1921. The Wisconsin Prison for Women at Taycheedah opened in 1933. Fox Lake Correctional Institution opened in 1962. Further expansion of the state prison system occurred when Kettle

Moraine Boys School was converted to an adult institution in 1975, followed by the conversion of Oregon School for Girls to a minimum security prison (Oakhill) in 1977. Dodge Correctional Institution, which serves as reception and evaluation center for all adult male felons sentenced by Wisconsin courts, opened in 1978. Rapid growth of the prison population led to the opening of Columbia and Oshkosh Correctional Institutions in 1986, Racine Correctional Institution in 1991, Jackson Correctional Institution in 1996, the Wisconsin Secure Program Facility located in Boscobel, in 1999, Redgranite Correctional Institution in 2001, Stanley Correctional Institution in 2003, and New Lisbon Correctional Institution in 2004. The department opened a minimum security facility to serve the needs of inmates with alcohol and other drug abuse problems in Chippewa Falls in 2004.

While the capacity of Wisconsin prisons had grown considerably since 1986, the number of inmates confined to adult institutions grew from just over 6,000 in 1989 to more than 15,000 in 1995. As a result, 1995 Wisconsin Act 344 authorized the department to contract with other states to house Wisconsin inmates. 1997 Wisconsin Act 27 authorized housing state inmates in private prisons in other states. By the end of 2002, out-of-state prisons housed more than 3,400 Wisconsin inmates. Near the end of 2004, fewer than 300 inmates were located out-of-state, due to new institutions, an increased number of beds at existing prisons, expanded contracting with county sheriffs to house inmates in county jails, and expanded noninstitutionalization options created in 2003 Wisconsin Act 33. By 2006, all out-of-state inmates were returned to Wisconsin facilities.

Wisconsin's first juvenile institution for boys opened in 1860 at Waukesha and was replaced by Kettle Moraine at Plymouth in 1963. A second facility, Wisconsin School for Boys, which was subsequently renamed the Ethan Allen School, opened at Wales in 1959. Lincoln Hills School for Boys began operations in 1970. (It was opened to girls in 1976 and the school was renamed.) The first juvenile institution for girls was established in 1875 in Milwaukee as a private agency that received state aid. The Wisconsin School for Girls, later renamed the Oregon School for Girls, opened in 1931 and closed in 1976. Girls were then sent to Lincoln Hills. In response to concerns about overcrowding at Lincoln Hills and the need for treatment programs for girls, the legislature authorized a separate facility, which opened as Southern Oaks Girls School at Union Grove in 1994. Another juvenile facility was opened in Prairie du Chien in 1997, but it has been converted into a medium security adult prison. 2011 Wisconsin Act 32 closed the Ethan Allen School and the Southern Oaks Girls School, with the boys from Ethan Allen school transferred to Lincoln Hills and the girls from Southern Oaks transferred to a new Copper Lake Girls School located on the Lincoln Hill grounds.

Probation and parole were unknown in the early years of statehood. Criminal sentences were for definite periods of time and to be fully served. Until 1860, executive pardons were the only means for early release. Chapter 324, Laws of 1860, established early releases for good behavior, known as "good time". Calculations of good time ended with the adoption of mandatory release dates for crimes committed after May 31, 1984. Parole was first enacted in 1889, but was apparently invalidated by the Wisconsin Supreme Court. New parole provisions were enacted in 1897 for the Green Bay Reformatory and for the Waupun State Prison in Chapter 110, Laws of 1907. That law allowed the State Board of Control to parole inmates with the governor's approval, but the approval requirement was removed in 1947. The State Board of Control was also given supervisory responsibility for offenders placed on probation in 1909. Currently, the Parole Commission, created in 1989, has final authority in granting discretionary paroles. Under 1997 Wisconsin Act 283, a person who is convicted of a felony committed on or after December 31, 1999, and sentenced to prison must serve a specified time in prison followed by a specified period of extended supervision in the community. Persons given this bifurcated sentence were not eligible for parole. The Earned Release Review Commission was created by 2009 Wisconsin Act 28. It authorized the commission to consider eligible inmates to be considered for release from incarceration to extended supervision depending on the nature of the crime, the time it was committed, and other factors such as the health or age of the inmate. Most incarcerated prisoners were able to earn "positive adjustment time" (sometimes referred to as "good time") for complying with prison regulations or performing assigned duties. 2011

Wisconsin Act 38 again renamed the body the Parole Commission and substantially repealed most early release provisions.

Statutory Commission

Parole Commission: KATHLEEN NAGLE (appointed by governor with senate consent), *chairperson;* EMILY DAVIDSON, DOUG DRANKIEWICZ, WILLIAM FRANCIS, DANIELLE LACOST, STEVEN LANDREMAN, 2 vacancies (appointed by chairperson from classified service).

Address: 3099 East Washington Avenue, P.O. Box 7960, Madison 53707-7960.

Telephone: 240-7280.

Fax: 240-7299.

The 8-member Parole Commission conducts regularly scheduled interviews to consider the parole of eligible inmates confined in a state correctional institution, a contracted county jail facility, or a county house of corrections or inmates transferred to mental health institutions.

The governor appoints the commission's chairperson, with senate consent, who serves at the pleasure of the governor for a 2-year term. The other members, who shall have knowledge of or experience in corrections or criminal justice, are appointed by the chairperson from the classified service.

The commission's statutory predecessor, the Parole Board, was created by Chapter 221, Laws of 1979, to advise the secretary of health and social services, and its members were appointed by the secretary. The Parole Commission was created by 1989 Wisconsin Act 107. The Earned Release Review Commission was created by 2009 Wisconsin Act 28. It authorized the commission to consider eligible inmates to be considered for release from incarceration to extended supervision depending on the nature of the crime, the time it was committed, and other factors such at the health or age of the inmate. Most incarcerated prisoners were able to earn "positive adjustment time" (some-times referred to as "good time") for complying with prison regulations or performing assigned duties. 2011 Wisconsin Act 38 again renamed the body the Parole Commission and substantially repealed most early release provisions. The commission's composition and duties are prescribed in Sections 15.145 (1), 17.07 (3m), 304.01, and 304.06 of the statutes.

INDEPENDENT UNITS ATTACHED FOR BUDGETING, PROGRAM COORDINATION, AND RELATED MANAGEMENT FUNCTIONS BY SECTION 15.03 OF THE STATUTES

INTERSTATE ADULT OFFENDER SUPERVISION BOARD

Members: TRACY HUDRLIK (compact administrator); vacancy (legislative branch representative); vacancy (judicial branch representative); BRIAN HAGEDORN (executive branch representative); COLLEEN WINSTON (victims' group representative). (All are appointed by governor).

Statutory References: Sections 15.145 (3) and 304.16 (4).

Agency Responsibility: The 5-member Interstate Adult Offender Supervision Board officially appoints the Wisconsin representative to the national commission. The board advises the department on its participation in the compact and on the operation of the compact within this state. The representatives serve 4-year terms while the compact administrator serves at the pleasure of the governor. It was created by 2001 Wisconsin Act 96.

COUNCIL ON OFFENDER REENTRY

Members: JULE CAVANAUGH (reentry director), *chairperson;* SCOTT LEGWOLD (secretary of corrections designee); vacancy (secretary of workforce development designee); LINDA HARRIS (secretary of health services designee); ELOISE ANDERSON (secretary of children and families); TAQWANYA SMITH (secretary of transportation designee); DEAN STENSBERG (attorney general designee); KATHLEEN NAGLE (chairperson of the Parole Commission or designee); CAROLYN STANFORD TAYLOR (state superintendent of public instruction designee); LISA STARK (current or former judge appointed by director of state courts); JEROME DILLARD (current or former incarcerated convict appointed by the secretary of corrections); MARK PODOLL (law enforcement officer); ARLINE HILLESTAD (representative of a crime victim's rights or crime victim services organization); vacancy (representative of a faith-based organization involved with community reintegration of offenders); JASON WITT (representative of a county department of human services); vacancy (tribal representative); vacancy (representative of a nonprofit organization involved with community reintegration that is not a faith-based organization); JOHN CHISHOLM (a district attorney); MIKE TOBIN (representative of the office of the state public defender); vacancy (an academic professional in the field of criminal justice); CHUCK BRENDEL (a representative of the Wisconsin Technical College System) (all except *ex officio* members appointed by governor).

Statutory References: Sections 15.145 (5) and 301.095.

Agency Responsibility: All except *ex officio* members, or as otherwise provided, of the 21-member Council on Offender Reentry are appointed by the governor for 3-year terms to coordinate reentry initiatives across the state, including promotion and collaboration of training opportunities, funding sources, and information sharing. The board was created by 2009 Wisconsin Act 28.

PRISON INDUSTRIES BOARD

Members: BILL G. SMITH, 2 vacancies (private business and industry representatives); JOSE CARILLO, 2 vacancies (private labor organization representatives); TRACEY ISENSEE (Technical College System representative); EDWARD HALL (Department of Corrections representative); HELEN MCCAIN (Department of Administration representative). (All are appointed by governor.)

Statutory References: Sections 15.145 (2) and 303.015.

Agency Responsibility: The 9-member Prison Industries Board advises Prison Industries. It develops a plan for the manufacturing and marketing of prison industry products, the provision of prison industry services, and research and development activities. No prison industry may be established or permanently closed without board approval. The board reviews the department's budget request for Prison Industries and may make recommendations to the governor for changes. The board gives prior approval for Prison Industries purchases exceeding $250,000. Members are appointed for 4-year terms. It was created by 1983 Wisconsin Act 27.

STATE BOARD FOR INTERSTATE JUVENILE SUPERVISION

Members: SHELLEY HAGAN (administrator of Interstate Compact for Juveniles); vacancy (deputy compact administrator or designee); REPRESENTATIVE BIES (representative(s) of legislative branch); MARY WAGNER (representative(s) of judicial branch); CHRISTOPHER LEE (representative(s) of executive branch); TANYA NELSON (representative of victims groups) (all appointed by governor).

Statutory References: Sections 15.145 (4) and 938.999 (9).

Agency Responsibility: The members of the State Board for Interstate Juvenile Supervision are appointed by the governor for 3-year terms to advise and exercise oversight and advocacy concerning the state's participation in activities of the Interstate Compact for Juveniles and may exercise any other statutorily authorized duties including the development of policy concerning the operations and procedures of the compact within the state. The board consists of at least six members, as more than one member may be appointed to represent the legislative, judicial, and executive branches of the state. The board was created by 2005 Wisconsin Act 234.

EDUCATIONAL COMMUNICATIONS BOARD

Board Members: ROLF WEGENKE (private schools representative), *chairperson;* TONY EVERS (superintendent of public instruction), *vice chairperson;* SENATORS HARRIS, OLSEN; REPRESENTATIVES KESTELL, VRUWINK; MIKE HUEBSCH (secretary of administration), KEVIN P. REILLY (president, UW System), MORNA FOY (director, Technical College System), THOMAS J. BASTING, SR., EILEEN LITTIG (public members); KAREN SCHROEDER (public schools representative), REGINA MILLNER (appointed by UW System Board of Regents), ANNE KATZ (president, Wisconsin Public Radio Association), DIANE EVERSON (educational TV coverage area representative), Ellis Bromberg (appointed by Technical College System Board). (Public members and representatives of public and private schools are appointed by governor.)

Executive Director: GENE PURCELL, 264-9666, gpurcell@ecb.state.wi.us

Deputy Director: Larry Dokken, 264-9669, Fax: 264-9622, ldokken@ecb.state.wi.us

Education, Division of: Marta Bechtol, *administrator,* 264-9733, Fax: 264-9622, mbechtol@ecb.state.wi.us

Engineering Services, Division of: Terrence Baun, *administrator,* 264-9746, Fax: 264-9622, tbaun@ecb.state.wi.us

Public Radio, Division of: Mike Crane, *director,* 821 University Avenue, Madison 53706, 265-3378, Fax: 263-9763, mike.crane@wpr.org

Public Television, Division of: James Steinbach, *director,* 821 University Avenue, Madison 53706, 263-1232, Fax: 263-9763, james.steinbach@wpt.org

Mailing Address: 3319 West Beltline Highway, Madison 53713-4296.

Telephone: (608) 264-9600.

Fax: (608) 264-9622.

Internet Address: www.ecb.org

Publications: Biennial report; Television Program Guide; WPR Annual Report; WPT Annual Report; teachers' manuals and guides for instructional multimedia programs.

Number of Employees: 56.68.

Total Budget 2011-13: $35,980,800.

Statutory References: Section 15.57; Chapter 39, Subchapter I.

Agency Responsibility: The Educational Communications Board oversees the statewide public broadcasting system, its instructional telecommunications programming, and public service media for the cultural and educational needs of the state's citizens. The board plans, constructs, and operates the state's public radio and television networks, and it is the licensee for the state's 17 public radio stations and 5 public television stations. The board operates the Emergency Alert System, the Amber Alert System, National Weather Service Transmitters, a telecommunication operations center, satellite facilities, and an educational broadband system (EBS).

The board shares responsibility for public broadcasting with the University of Wisconsin Board of Regents. Programming is produced through UW facilities or acquired from national, regional, state, and local sources. The board also is affiliated with public television stations licensed to Milwaukee Area Technical College, television station WSDE in Duluth, and several public radio stations.

Educational services include selection, acquisition or production, implementation, and evaluation of K-12 educational media and accompanying materials in cooperation with teachers in public and private schools, the Cooperative Educational Service Agencies, the Department of Public Instruction, the Technical College System, and the UW System.

Organization: The board includes 16 members. Those appointed by the governor, the UW Board of Regents, and the Technical College System Board serve 4-year terms. Legislative members must represent the majority and minority party in each house. The board appoints an executive director from outside the classified service. Division administrators and other agency staff are appointed by the executive director.

Unit Functions: The *Division of Education* operates the Wisconsin Media Lab which provides a wide variety of K-12 educational media for use by Wisconsin educators and students. Programming is delivered to the state via Public Television and online.

The *Division of Engineering Services* develops, operates, and maintains the statewide telecommunication systems used to receive and deliver instructional, educational, and cultural programming. It coordinates broadcasting of the Emergency Alert System, the National Weather Service, and the Amber Alert System.

During the summer of 2012, the Educational Communications Board constructed a 400-ft. replacement tower for WHSA-FM, Brule. Here, a tower crew erects the new tower (right) which is next to the old tower (left). Built in 1952, the old tower was the last of the original "state station" towers built by the State Radio Council. The old tower was taken down following the completion of the new tower. In addition to WHSA-FM, a Wisconsin Public Radio station, the tower site provides a base for Wisconsin Public Television and public safety equipment. (Educational Communications Board)

The *Division of Public Radio* operates the statewide Wisconsin Public Radio service in partnership with the UW Board of Regents (through UW-Colleges and UW-Extension). Wisconsin Public Radio service includes three networks: 1) the News and Classical Music Network, 2) the Wisconsin Ideas Network, and 3) an HD-2 Classical Network – all of which offer national, regional, and local programming.

The *Division of Public Television* operates the statewide Wisconsin Public Television service in partnership with the UW Board of Regents (through UW-Colleges and UW-Extension). Daytime broadcast hours are devoted to children's and instructional programming and evening hours to cultural, informational, and entertainment programs. Wisconsin Public Television delivers national programming from the Public Broadcasting Service and focuses on producing local programs on topics of regional and state interest.

History: Wisconsin's history in educational broadcasting dates back to the oldest public radio station in the nation. The University of Wisconsin's research in "wireless" communication led to the beginning of scheduled radio broadcasting in 1917 on Station 9XM, which was renamed WHA-AM in 1922. Wisconsin made a commitment to statewide educational broadcasting in 1945. Chapter 570, Laws of 1945, created the State Radio Council to plan, produce, and transmit educational, cultural, and service programs over a statewide FM radio network. Over the next two decades, the council constructed and activated 10 radio transmitters. In Chapter 360, Laws of 1953, the council also assumed responsibility for research in educational television.

The 1967 executive branch reorganization renamed the council the Educational Broadcasting Board, created the Educational Broadcasting Division under its supervision, and attached the board and the division to the Coordinating Council for Higher Education. The name was changed to the Educational Communications Board in Chapter 276, Laws of 1969. With the demise of the Coordinating Council, the Educational Communications Board became an independent agency in Chapter 100, Laws of 1971. In 1971, the board began to extend educational television to the entire state, and it had constructed 5 UHF television stations by 1977. Signal translator facilities erected in the 1980s extended service to areas of the state beyond the reach of regular transmitters. Most recently, the Educational Communications Board has begun to offer HD Radio services and expanded television programming through WPT Create and WPT The Wisconsin Channel. The board has worked cooperatively with the UW Board of Regents to enhance public broadcasting service for the state's citizens.

Department of
EMPLOYEE TRUST FUNDS

Address e-mail by combining the user ID and the state extender: userid**@etf.wi.gov**
All telephone numbers are 608 area code unless otherwise indicated.

Employee Trust Funds Board: WAYNE E. KOESSL (Wisconsin Retirement Board member), *chairperson;* JOHN DAVID (Wisconsin Retirement Board member), *vice chairperson;* ROBERT M. NIENDORF (Teachers Retirement Board member), *secretary;* WILLIAM FORD (elected by WRS annuitants); KIMBERLY HALL (Technical College or educational support personnel employee); JON LITSCHER (governor's designee on Group Insurance Board); JESSICA O'DONNELL (designee of director, Office of State Employment Relations); MICHAEL LANGYEL, ROBERTA RASMUS, DAVID WILTGEN (Teachers Retirement Board members); MARY VON RUDEN, vacancy (Wisconsin Retirement Board members); VICTOR SHIER (appointed by governor with senate confirmation). (Board representatives are appointed by their respective boards; the annuitant member and the technical college or public school educational support employee are elected by the constituency groups.)

Secretary of Employee Trust Funds: BOB CONLIN, 266-0301, bob.conlin@

Deputy Secretary: ROB MARCHANT, 266-9854, robert.marchant@

Budget and Trust Finance, Office of: vacancy, *director.*

Communications Director: MARK LAMKINS, 266-3641, mark.lamkins@

Deferred Compensation Director: SHELLY SCHUELLER, 266-6611, shelly.schueller@

Internal Audit, Office of: JOHN VINCENT, *director,* 261-7942, john.vincent@

Insurance Services, Division of: LISA ELLINGER, *administrator,* 264-6627, lisa.ellinger@

Legal Services, Office of: DAVID NISPEL, *general counsel,* 264-6936, david.nispel@

Legislative Liaison: TARNA HUNTER, 267-0908, tarna.hunter@

Management Services, Division of: PAM HENNING, *administrator,* 267-2929, pamela.henning@

Policy and Compliance, Office of: STEVE HURLEY, *director,* 267-2847, steve.hurley@

Retirement Services, Division of: MATT STOHR, *administrator,* 266-1210, matthew.stohr@

Mailing Address: P.O. Box 7931, Madison 53707-7931.

Location: 801 West Badger Road, Madison.

Telephones: Member services: (608) 266-3285 (Madison) or (877) 533-5020; Self-service line: (877) 383-1888; Wisconsin Relay Service 7-1-1 or (800) 947-3529 (English) or (800) 833-7813 (Spanish).

Internet Address: http://etf.wi.gov (includes e-mail inquiry form).

Publications: *Comprehensive Annual Financial Report; Employer Bulletin; WRS News;* and various employer manuals and employee brochures on the Wisconsin Retirement System, the group insurance plans, the deferred compensation program, and the employee reimbursement account program.

Number of Employees: 260.20.

Total Budget 2011 13: $69,667,300.

Statutory References: Sections 15.16 and Chapter 40.

Agency Responsibility: The Department of Employee Trust Funds administers various employee benefit programs, including the retirement, group insurance, disability, and deferred compensation programs and employee reimbursement and commuter benefits accounts. It serves all state employees and teachers and most municipal employees, with the notable exceptions of employees of the City and County of Milwaukee.

Organization: The 13-member Employee Trust Funds Board provides direction and supervision to the department and the Wisconsin Retirement System (WRS). Board membership includes 2 *ex officio* members and 11 members who are appointed or elected for 4-year terms to represent employers, members, employees, taxpayers, and annuitants. The member appointed by the governor to represent taxpayers must have specific professional experience and cannot be a WRS participant. The board approves all administrative rules; authorizes payment of all retirement annuities, except those for disability; and hears appeals of benefit determinations. It appoints the secretary from outside the classified service, and the secretary selects the deputy from outside the service. Division and office heads are appointed from within the classified service by the secretary.

Unit Functions: The *Division of Insurance Services* is responsible for policy development and implementation of health, life, disability, and long-term care insurance; accumulated sick leave conversion credit; and the employee reimbursement and commuter benefits accounts.

The *Division of Management Services* provides support services for human resources, payroll, information technology, facility management, capital budget and inventory, records management, document design, mail and supplies, board liaisons, library, and telecommunications.

The *Division of Retirement Services* develops and implements retirement policies and services for the members of the retirement system, including calculation and payment of retirement and related benefits, and the deferred compensation program.

History: The 1891 Legislature initiated pension coverage for local government employees when it required Milwaukee to create a pension fund for retired and disabled police and fire fighters in Chapter 287. Sixteen years later, the legislature extended pension coverage to protective service employees of smaller cities through Chapter 671, Laws of 1907. The 1909 Legislature authorized a pension system for City of Milwaukee teachers in Chapter 510; and Chapter 323, Laws of 1911, created a retirement system for those school districts throughout the rest of the state that wished to enroll their teachers. With enactment of Chapter 459, Laws of 1921, Wisconsin established a mandatory, joint contributory, statewide teachers' pension system, covering virtually all teachers in public schools (outside of Milwaukee), normal schools, and the University of Wisconsin.

The legislature first provided retirement plans for general municipal employees outside of Milwaukee in Chapter 175, Laws of 1943. In the same session, a retirement system was created for general employees by Chapter 176, Laws of 1943. Local fire and police pension funds were closed to new members by Chapter 206, Laws of 1947, and these employees have since been covered with the general employees. Chapter 60, Laws of 1951, created the Public Employees Social Security Fund, making Wisconsin the first state in the nation to permit some state and local government employees to be covered by Social Security.

Chapter 211, Laws of 1959, created group life and group health insurance programs for state employees, a group life insurance program for municipal employees, and the Group Insurance Board to monitor the administration of the programs. The 1967 executive branch reorganization created the Department of Employee Trust Funds to administer the various retirement funds, and the Group Insurance Board was attached to it.

Chapter 280, Laws of 1975, initiated the merger of the existing, separate retirement funds that covered all publicly employed teachers in the state and all state and local public employees, except employees of the City of Milwaukee and Milwaukee County who have their own systems. The legislature transferred local police and fire pension funds to the overall general employee system in Chapter 182, Laws of 1977. The implementation of the merged Wisconsin Retirement System was completed, effective January 1, 1982, by Chapter 96, Laws of 1981.

Statutory Boards

Deferred Compensation Board: EDWARD D. MAIN, *chairperson;* JOHN NELSON, *vice chairperson;* GAIL HANSON, *secretary;* MARTIN BEIL, MICHAEL GRACZ (appointed by governor with senate consent).

The 5-member Deferred Compensation Board establishes rules for offering deferred compensation plans to state and local employees and contracts with deferred compensation plan providers. Its members are appointed for 4-year terms. The board was created by 1989 Wisconsin Act 31, and its composition and duties are prescribed in Sections 15.165 (4) and 40.80 of the statutes.

Group Insurance Board: JON LITSCHER (designated by governor), *chairperson;* BONNIE CYGANEK (designated by attorney general), *vice chairperson;* JESSICA O'DONNELL (designated by Director of the Office of State Employment Relations), *secretary;* HERSCHEL DAY (WRS-insured teacher participant); BRIAN HAYES (designated by secretary of administration); DANIEL SCHWARTZER (designated by commissioner of insurance); JANE NIKOLAI (WRS-insured nonteacher participant); CHARLES GRAPENTINE (retired WRS-insured participant); BRIAN YERGES (WRS-insured local government participant); NANCY THOMPSON (chief executive or member of local government participating in WRS); MICHAEL FARRELL (appointed by governor, no membership requirement). (All except *ex officio* members are appointed by governor.)

The 11-member Group Insurance Board oversees the group health, life, income continuation, and other insurance programs offered to state employees, covered local employees, and retirees. The board's 5 appointed members serve 2-year terms. The board was created by Chapter 211, Laws of 1959, and its composition and duties are prescribed in Sections 15.165 (2) and 40.03 (6) of the statutes.

Teachers Retirement Board: MICHAEL LANGYEL (Milwaukee teacher), *chairperson;* ROBIN STARCK (public school teacher), *vice chairperson;* SUSAN HARRISON (UW System teacher representative appointed by governor), *secretary;* SANDRA CLAFLIN-CHALTON (UW System teacher representative appointed by governor); JON JOSLIN, BETSY M. KIPPERS, MARY JO MEIER, PATRICK PHAIR, DAVID WILTGEN (public school teachers); vacancy (public school administrator appointed by governor); R. THOMAS PEDERSEN (technical college teacher); ROBERTA RASMUS (school board member appointed by governor); DENNIS MURPHY (teacher annuitant). (Members not appointed by governor are elected by their constituent groups.)

The 13-member Teachers Retirement Board advises the Employee Trust Funds Board about retirement matters related to teachers, recommends and approves or rejects administrative rules, authorizes payment of disability annuities for teachers, and hears appeals of staff determinations of disability. Board members serve staggered 5-year terms; the 2 UW System representatives may not be from the same campus. The board was created by Chapter 204, Laws of 1953, and its composition and duties are prescribed in Sections 15.165 (3) (a) and 40.03 (7) of the statutes.

Wisconsin Retirement Board: WAYNE E. KOESSL (county or town governing body member), *chairperson;* JOHN DAVID (city or village chief executive or governing board member), *vice chairperson;* MARY VON RUDEN (participating employee of local employer other than city or village), *secretary;* JAMIE AULIK (county clerk or deputy); TED NICKEL (commissioner of insurance); HERBERT STINSKI (participating city or village finance officer); STEVEN WILDING (participating city or village employee); vacancy (not a participant or beneficiary of the WRS); vacancy (participating state employee). (All, except insurance commissioner or designee, are appointed by governor.)

The 9-member Wisconsin Retirement Board advises the Employee Trust Funds Board about retirement matters related to state and local general and protective employees and performs the same functions for these employees as the Teachers Retirement Board does for teachers. The board's appointed members serve staggered 5-year terms, and the municipal official and county board member are nominated by their respective statewide associations. The board was created by Chapter 96, Laws of 1981, and its composition and duties are prescribed in Sections 15.165 (3) (b) and 40.03 (8) of the statutes.

EMPLOYMENT RELATIONS COMMISSION

Address e-mail by combining the user ID and the state extender: userid**@wisconsin.gov**
All telephone numbers are 608 area code unless otherwise indicated.

Commissioners: JAMES R. SCOTT, *chairperson,* 266-0354, james.scott@; RODNEY G. PASCH, rodney.pasch@, 266-3297; vacancy (appointed by governor with senate consent).

General Counsel: PETER G. DAVIS, 266-2993, peterg.davis@

Team Leader: WILLIAM C. HOULIHAN, 266-0147, william.houlihan@

Election Coordinator: GEORGANN KRAMER, 266-9287, georgann.kramer@

Mailing Address: P.O. Box 7870, Madison 53707-7870.

Location: 1457 East Washington Avenue, Suite 101, Madison.

Telephone: (608) 266-1381.

Fax: (608) 266-6930.

Agency E-mail Address: werc@werc.state.wi.us

Internet Address: http://werc.wi.gov

Publications: Biennial reports; complaint procedures manual; agency decisions.

Number of Employees: 25.50.

Total Budget 2011-13: $6,396,000.

Statutory References: Sections 15.58, 230.44, and 230.45; Chapter 111.

Agency Responsibility: The Employment Relations Commission promotes collective bargaining and peaceful labor relations in the private and public sectors. It processes various types of labor relations cases, including elections, bargaining unit clarifications, union security referenda, mediations, interest arbitrations, grievance arbitrations, prohibited or unfair labor practices, and declaratory rulings. The commission also issues decisions arising from state employee civil service appeals, including appeals relating to certain classification, examination, and appointment issues, disciplinary actions, hazardous employment injury benefits, and noncontractual grievances. The commission's decisions are subject to review in state court. In addition to mediating labor disputes, the commission provides training and assistance to parties interested in labor/management cooperation and a consensus approach to resolving labor relations issues.

Organization: The 3 full-time commissioners are chosen for staggered 6-year terms, and the governor designates one commissioner to serve as chairperson for a 2-year term. The chairperson functions as the agency administrator. The general counsel provides advice to the commission, commission staff, advocates, and citizens and serves as liaison to the legislature and to the attorney general, who represents the commission in court.

History: Chapter 51, Laws of 1937, created the Wisconsin Labor Relations Board as an independent agency in the executive branch. Chapter 57, Laws of 1939, replaced the board with the Employment Relations Board and amended state laws governing labor relations. The 1967 Legislature renamed the board the Employment Relations Commission and continued it as an independent agency.

Chapter 509, Laws of 1959, authorized municipal employees to organize and be represented by labor organizations in negotiating wages, hours, and conditions of employment. Chapter 124, Laws of 1971, gave municipal employees the right to bargain collectively and made a municipal employer's refusal to bargain a prohibited practice. Chapters 246 and 247, Laws of 1971, established compulsory interest arbitration for police and firefighters in Milwaukee and other municipalities. Chapter 270, Laws of 1971, gave state employees the right to bargain collectively. 2003 Wisconsin Act 33 abolished the Personnel Commission and transferred to the Employment Relations Commission responsibility for various civil service appeals related to state employment. 2011 Wisconsin Acts 10 and 32 amended all collective bargaining laws administered by the commission.

Department of
FINANCIAL INSTITUTIONS

Address e-mail by combining the user ID and the state extender: userid**@wisconsin.gov**
All telephone numbers are 608 area code unless otherwise indicated.

Secretary of Financial Institutions: PETER J. BILDSTEN, 267-1709,
  peter.bildsten@; Fax: 261-4334.

Deputy Secretary: RAY ALLEN, 267-1719, ray.allen@

Executive Assistant: GEORGIA E. MAXWELL, 267-1718, georgia.maxwell@

Communications Director: GEORGE ALTHOFF, 261-4504, george.althoff@

Chief Legal Counsel: CHRISTOPHER GREEN, 266-7968, chris.green@; Fax: 261-4334.

Mailing Address: P.O. Box 8861, Madison 53708-8861.

Location: 201 West Washington Avenue, Suite 500, Madison.

Telephones: 261-9555; TDY: 266-8818.

Fax: 261-4334.

Internet Address: www.wdfi.org

Number of Employees: 136.54.

Total Budget 2011-13: $35,256,500.

Statutory References: Sections 15.18 and 182.01; Chapters 224, Subchapter II, and 421-427.

Administrative Services and Technology, Division of: CHERYLL OLSON-COLLINS, *administrator,* 267-1707, cheryll.olsoncollins@; P.O. Box 7876, Madison 53707-7876; Division Fax: 261-7200.

  Budget and Fiscal Services, Bureau of: SUSAN J. DIETZEL, *director,* 267-0399, susan.dietzel@

  Information Technology, Bureau of: JOHN AMUNDSON, *director,* 267-1714, john.amundson@

Banking, Division of: MICHAEL MACH, *administrator,* 266-0451, mike.mach@; P.O. Box 7876, Madison 53707-7876; Division Fax: 267-6889.

  Consumer Affairs, Bureau of: PAUL EGIDE, *director,* 267-3518, paul.egide@; Consumer Act inquiries: 264-7969, (800) 452-3328 in Wisconsin; P.O. Box 8041, Madison 53708-8041.

Licensed Financial Services Bureau: JEAN PLALE, *director,* 266-0447, jean.plale@

Mortgage Banking Bureau: JEAN PLALE, *director,* 266-0447, jean.plale@

Corporate and Consumer Services, Division of: GEORGE PETAK, *administrator,* 266-6810, george.petak@; P.O. Box 7846, Madison 53707-7846; Division Fax: 267-6813.

Corporations, Bureau of: JENNIFER ACKER, *supervisor,* 264-7801, jennifer.acker@; Corporations inquiries: 261-7577; P.O. Box 7846, Madison 53707-7846.

Financial Literacy, Office of: DAVID D. MANCL, *director,* 261-9540, david.mancl@

Uniform Commercial Code, Bureau of: DEANNA GRAHN, *supervisor,* 267-6811, deanna.grahn@; Uniform Commercial Code inquiries: 261-9543; P.O. Box 7847, Madison 53707-7847.

Securities, Division of: PATRICIA STRUCK, *administrator,* 266-3432, patricia.struck@; P.O. Box 1768, Madison 53701-1768; Division Fax: 264-7979.

Publications: Internet only: Annual Report; Annual Report on Condition of Wisconsin Banks; Annual Report on Condition of Wisconsin Savings and Loan Associations and Savings Banks; Annual Report on Payday Lending; Quarterly Report on Condition of Wisconsin Banks; credit and consumer protection information; industry bulletins, newsletters, and forms.

Agency Responsibility: The Department of Financial Institutions regulates state-chartered banks, savings and loans associations, and savings banks, as well as various operations of the

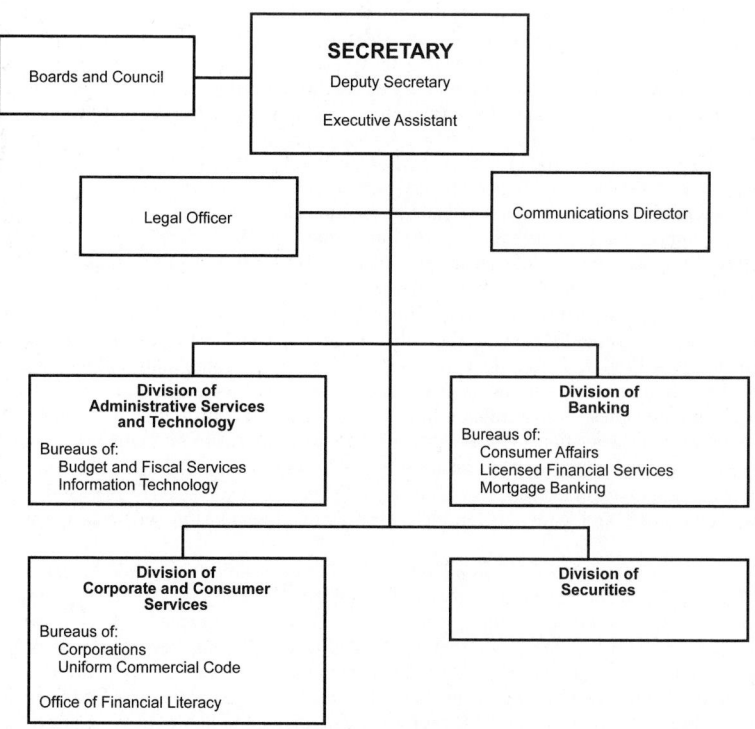

DEPARTMENT OF FINANCIAL INSTITUTIONS

Unit attached for administrative purposes under Sec. 15.03: Office of Credit Unions securities industry. It examines and files charters and other documents of businesses and organizations and registers and regulates the mortgage banking industry and other financial service providers. It oversees Uniform Commercial Code filings. It administers the Wisconsin Consumer Act and registers merchants who extend credit. It also issues notary public commissions and registers trademarks, trade names, and brands. The department is self-supporting through program revenue derived from fees and assessments paid by regulated entities and individuals.

Organization: The department is administered by a secretary, who is appointed by the governor with the advice and consent of the senate. The secretary appoints the administrators for 3 of the 4 divisions from outside the classified service and the administrator of the Division of Administrative Services and Technology from the classified service.

Unit Functions: The *Office of Financial Literacy* (OFL), in the Division of Corporate and Consumer Services, promotes financial literacy to the public as a vital life skill. It emphasizes financial and economic literacy for Wisconsin's youth. The OFL works closely with the Governor's Council on Financial Literacy (GCFL) in a statewide effort to improve the financial literacy of students, employees, and families, with special attention to fraud prevention and encouraging the "unbanked" to take advantage of the important services offered by financial institutions. The OFL takes the lead role in producing the GCFL's Money Smart Week Wisconsin (MSWW) campaign in conjunction with the Federal Reserve Bank of Chicago. MSWW is the nation's first-ever financial literacy campaign to focus on an entire state. The OFL also has a lead role in the National Institute of Financial and Economic Literacy, a nationally recognized, graduate-level, teacher-training program consisting of three week-long programs each summer.

The *Division of Administrative Services and Technology* provides support services to the department through its administration of the agency's budget, personnel, procurement, and information technology services.

The *Division of Banking,* created in Section 15.183 (1), Wisconsin Statutes, by 1995 Wisconsin Act 27, is advised by the Banking Review Board. It regulates and supervises state-chartered banks and consumer financial service industries under statutory Chapters 220 through 224. In addition to chartering and regularly examining state banks, the division licenses loan companies, mortgage bankers, mortgage brokers, loan originators, collection agencies, community currency exchanges, sales finance companies, adjustment service companies, sellers of checks, insurance premium finance companies, and credit services organizations. It also regulates auto dealers' installment sales contracts. The division investigates applications for expanded banking powers, new financial products, and interstate bank acquisitions and mergers. It may conduct joint examinations with Federal Reserve System examiners and with the Federal Deposit Insurance Corporation. With Banking Review Board approval, the administrator may establish uniform rules for savings programs and fiduciary operations.

The division supervises state-chartered savings and loan associations and savings banks and enforces the laws governing them under statutory Chapters 214 and 215 with the advice of the Savings Institutions Review Board. It works to resolve consumer complaints and reviews and approves applications for acquisitions, new branches and other offices, and the organization of mutual holding companies. It may rule on interstate mergers or acquisitions. It also conducts joint examinations of associations with the federal Office of Thrift Institutions and may examine savings banks with the Federal Deposit Insurance Corporation.

The division administers the Wisconsin Consumer Act, which resolves consumer complaints and advises consumers and lenders regarding their rights and responsibilities under consumer law.

The *Division of Corporate and Consumer Services* is responsible for examining and filing business records for corporations and other organizations. It examines charters, documents that affect mergers, consolidations, and dissolutions, and reviews the annual reports of various businesses, including partnerships, corporations, limited liability companies, cooperatives, and foreign corporations. It also examines and files documents under the Uniform Commercial Code, including statements of business indebtedness, consignments, terminations, and financing statements and maintains the statewide Uniform Commercial Code lien system. The division prepares certified copies of the records in its custody and responds to inquiries about corporations and other business entities and organizations for which it has records. It also issues notary public commissions and registers trademarks, trade names, and brands. The division is also responsible for the issuance of state video franchise authority certificates.

The *Division of Securities,* created in Section 15.183 (3), Wisconsin Statutes, by 1995 Wisconsin Act 27, regulates the sale of investment securities and franchises under statutory Chapters 551, 552, and 553. It examines and registers the offerings and may bar them from registration in this state. The division licenses and monitors the activities of broker-dealers, securities agents, investment advisers, and investment adviser representatives. It conducts field audits and investigates complaints. When violations are detected, it initiates the appropriate administrative, injunctive, or criminal action. The division also regulates corporate takeovers.

History: The Department of Financial Institutions (DFI) was created in 1995 Wisconsin Act 27. The act reorganized formerly independent offices of the commissioners of banking, savings and loan, and securities as divisions and transferred them to the department. In addition, Act 27 transferred the responsibility for business organization filings and the Uniform Commercial Code lien information filings to the department from the Office of the Secretary of State. The same act transferred the regulation of mortgage bankers and loan originators and solicitors to the department from the Department of Regulation and Licensing. 2007 Wisconsin Act 42 replaced cable television franchises granted by municipalities with statewide video service franchises granted by DFI. 2011 Wisconsin Act 32 transferred to DFI the notary and trademark functions formerly performed by the Office of the Secretary of State. The Mortgage Loan Originator Council was repealed by 2011 Wisconsin Act 233.

Banking. For the first five years of statehood, no regular commercial banks existed in Wisconsin. Prior to amendment in 1902, Article XI of the Wisconsin Constitution required that any banking law must be approved in a statewide referendum. Bank regulation began when the legislature created the Office of Bank Comptroller in Chapter 479, Laws of 1852, and the voters approved the law in 1853. That law allowed any group meeting state requirements to go into the banking business. It was designed primarily to regulate the issuance of bank notes. Bank supervision was transferred to the state treasurer in 1868 and remained with that office until 1903.

The 1902 constitutional amendment gave the legislature the power to enact general banking laws without a referendum. In Chapter 234, Laws of 1903, the legislature created the State Banking Department. The department also supervised savings and loan associations until 1947 and credit unions until 1972. Under the 1967 executive branch reorganization, the department continued as an independent agency and was renamed the Office of the Commissioner of Banking. 1995 Wisconsin Act 27 reorganized the agency as the Division of Banking and transferred it to the Department of Financial Institutions.

Savings Institutions. Attempts to register and examine savings and loan associations date back to the 1850s in Wisconsin, but there are no records of any associations incorporating under these laws. In 1876, the legislature passed Chapter 384 to require that savings banks and savings societies register with the county registers of deeds and the secretary of state. Voters approved the law in November 1876. Several associations incorporated shortly afterward. Beginning with Chapter 368, Laws of 1897, building and loan associations were regulated by the bank examiner in the state treasurer's office.

In 1903, responsibility for regulating savings and loan associations was transferred to the State Banking Department. Chapter 411, Laws of 1947, moved regulation from that department to the newly created Savings and Loan Association Department. The law also created the forerunner of the current Savings Institutions Review Board. In 1967, the executive branch reorganization act renamed the department the Office of the Commissioner of Savings and Loan. In 1991 Wisconsin Act 221, the office assumed responsibility for chartering, regulating, and examining savings banks. The same law created the Savings Bank Review Board. 1995 Wisconsin Act 27 reorganized the agency as the Division of Savings and Loan and transferred it to the Department of Financial Institutions. It was renamed the Division of Savings Institutions in 1999 and repealed in 2003 Wisconsin Act 33. Its duties were transferred to the Division of Banking.

Securities. Laws enacted by states to protect the public against securities fraud are commonly referred to as "blue sky" laws. (The term "blue sky" is believed to have originated when a judge ruled that a particular stock had about the same value as a patch of blue sky.) Wisconsin's first "blue sky" law was Chapter 756, Laws of 1913. This law was revised successively in 1919,

1933, 1941, 1969, and 2007. The current Wisconsin Uniform Securities Law, effective January 1, 2009, was enacted as 2007 Wisconsin Act 196, and it is based upon the Uniform Securities Act of 2002. From 1913 until 1939, the regulation of securities came under the jurisdiction first of the Railroad Commission (and its successor the Public Service Commission) and later the State Banking Department. The Department of Securities was created by Chapter 68, Laws of 1939, to regulate the sale of stocks, bonds, and other forms of business ownership or debt. It was renamed the Office of the Commissioner of Securities by Chapter 75, Laws of 1967. 1995 Wisconsin Act 27, reorganized the agency as the Division of Securities and transferred it to the Department of Financial Institutions.

Statutory Boards

Banking Review Board: DEBRA R. LINS, *chairperson;* DOUGLAS L. FARMER, AMELIA E. MACARENO, THOMAS E. SPITZ, RALPH J. TENUTA (appointed by governor with senate consent).

The 5-member Banking Review Board advises the Division of Banking regarding the banking industry in Wisconsin and reviews the division's administrative actions. Members are appointed for staggered 5-year terms, and at least 3 of them must each have at least 5 years' banking experience. No member may act in any matter involving a bank of which the member is an officer, director, or stockholder or to which that person is indebted. The board was created by Chapter 10, Laws of Special Session 1931-32, under the State Banking Department (renamed the Office of the Commissioner of Banking in 1967), and transferred to the Department of Financial Institutions by 1995 Wisconsin Act 27. Its composition and duties are prescribed in Sections 15.185 (1) and 220.035 of the statutes.

Savings Institutions Review Board: PAUL C. ADAMSKI, *chairperson;* GEORGE E. GARY, ROBERT W. HOLMES, JAMES K. OLSON, CHARLES SCHMALZ (appointed by governor with senate consent).

The 5-member Savings Institutions Review Board advises the Division of Banking on matters impacting savings and loan associations and savings banks in Wisconsin. It reviews division orders and determinations, hears appeals on certain actions taken by the division, and may act on any matter submitted by the division. Members serve 5-year terms. At least 3 of them must each have a minimum of 5 years' experience in the savings and loan or savings bank business in this state. Chapter 441, Laws of 1974, created the board as the Savings and Loan Review Board in the Savings and Loan Association Department (renamed the Office of the Commissioner of Savings and Loan in 1967) and 1995 Wisconsin Act 27 transferred it to the Department of Financial Institutions. In 2003, Act 33 renamed the board and eliminated the Savings Bank Review Board. Its composition and duties are prescribed in Sections 15.185 (3) and 215.04 of the statutes.

INDEPENDENT UNIT ATTACHED FOR BUDGETING, PROGRAM COORDINATION, AND RELATED MANAGEMENT FUNCTIONS BY SECTION 15.03 OF THE STATUTES

OFFICE OF CREDIT UNIONS

Director: KIM SANTOS, 267-2608, kim.santos@

Mailing Address: P.O. Box 14137, Madison 53708-0137.

Location: 201 West Washington Avenue, Suite 500, Madison.

Telephone: 261-9543.

Fax: 267-0479.

Internet Address: www.wdfi.org

Publications: Quarterly Credit Union Bulletin.

Statutory References: Section 15.185 (7) (a); Chapter 186.

Agency Responsibility: The Office of Credit Unions regulates credit unions chartered to do business in Wisconsin. It charters new credit unions, examines credit union records and assets, consents to consolidation of credit unions within the state and, in cooperation with similar agencies in neighboring states, approves interstate mergers. If a credit union is not in compliance with state law, the office may remove its officers, suspend operations, or take possession of the credit union's business. The director is appointed by the governor and must have at least 3 years' experience either in the operation of a credit union or in a credit union supervisory agency or a combination of both. All personnel and budget requests by the office must be processed and forwarded without change by the department, unless the office requests or concurs in a change.

History: Regulation of credit unions began in 1913 (Chapter 733) when the legislature passed a law that required "cooperative credit associations" to obtain their charters from the State Banking Department. That law was repealed by Chapter 334, Laws of 1923, which required the department to charter and regulate "credit unions". The Office of the Commissioner of Credit Unions was created in Chapter 193, Laws of 1971, as a separate agency by removing the credit union division and its advisory board from the Office of the Commissioner of Banking and giving it expanded powers. 1995 Wisconsin Act 27 created the Office of Credit Unions and attached it to the Department of Financial Institutions under Section 15.03, Wisconsin Statutes.

Statutory Board

Credit Union Review Board: J. David Christenson, Dennis Degenhardt, Lisa Greco, Brian Prunty, Colleen Woggon (appointed by governor with senate consent).

The 5-member Credit Union Review Board advises the Office of Credit Unions regarding credit unions in Wisconsin. It reviews rules and regulations issued by the office, acts as an appeals board for persons aggrieved by any act of the office, and may require the office to submit its actions for approval. Members serve staggered 5-year terms and each must have at least 5 years' experience in credit union operations. The board was created within the State Banking Department by Chapter 411, Laws of 1947, then transferred to the Office of the Commissioner of Credit Unions in 1971, and later made part of the Office of Credit Unions in 1995 Wisconsin Act 27. Its composition and duties are prescribed in Sections 15.185 (7) (b) and 186.015 of the statutes.

GOVERNMENT ACCOUNTABILITY BOARD

Address e-mail by combining the user ID and the state extender: userid@**wisconsin.gov**
All telephone numbers are 608 area code unless otherwise indicated.

Members: Timothy Vocke, *chairperson;* Gerald Nichol, *vice chairperson;* Michael Brennan, *secretary;* Thomas Barland, Thomas Cane, David Deininger. (All members are former judges appointed to staggered terms by the governor, and confirmed by two-thirds vote of the senate.)

Director and General Counsel: KEVIN J. KENNEDY, 266-8005, kevin.kennedy@

Mailing Address: P.O. Box 7984, Madison 53707-7984.

Location: 212 East Washington Avenue, Third Floor, Madison.

Telephones: Elections: 266-8005; Campaign Finance, Ethics, and Lobbying: 266-8005.

Fax: 267-0500.

E-Mail Address: gab@wi.gov

Internet Address: http://gab.wi.gov

Elections Division: Michael Haas, *administrator,* 266-0136, michael.haas@

Ethics and Accountability Division: Jonathan Becker, *administrator,* 266-8123, jonathan.becker@

Number of Employees: 53.75.

Total Budget 2011-13: $11,188,900.

Statutory References: Chapters 5-12, Subchapter III of Chapter 13, and Subchapter III of Chapter 19.

Agency Responsibility: The Government Accountability Board (GAB) administers the state's campaign finance, elections, ethics, and lobby laws, investigates alleged violations of those laws, and brings civil actions to collect forfeitures. It may subpoena records and notify the district attorney or attorney general of any grounds for civil or criminal prosecution. The GAB issues advisory opinions to officials, local governments, and others asking about their own conduct; promulgates administrative rules; and conducts training for local election officials, campaign and lobby registrants, and state public officials.

The GAB maintains the campaign finance registration and reporting system which limits and requires full disclosure of contributions and disbursements made on behalf of every candidate for public office. The statutes specify which candidates, individuals, political parties, and groups must register and file detailed financial statements. Registration and reporting are required for nonresident committees that make contributions and for all individuals who make independent disbursements. The GAB administers the electronic filing of campaign finance reports of all registrants that receive contributions in excess of $20,000 in a campaign period for candidate committees or in excess of $20,000 in a biennium for other registrants.

The GAB administers the state elections code along with implementing the federal Help America Vote Act of 2002 that establishes certain election requirements regarding the conduct of federal elections in the state. The director and general counsel serves as the chief state election official. The GAB is responsible for the design and maintenance of the Statewide Voter Registration System (SVRS) which is required to be used by all municipalities in the state to administer federal, state, and local elections.

The GAB also has compliance review authority over local election officials' actions relating to ballot preparation, candidate nomination, voter qualifications, recall, conduct of elections, and election administration. The GAB holds information and training meetings with local election officials to promote uniform election procedures. The GAB is responsible for the training and certification of all municipal clerks and chief election inspectors in the state.

The GAB administers the Code of Ethics for State Public Officials and Wisconsin's lobbying law. The intent of the ethics code is to forbid a state official from using a public position to obtain anything of value for the personal benefit of the official, the official's family, or the official's private business. Wisconsin's lobbying law prohibits lobbyists and the organizations that employ them from furnishing anything of value to a state official or employee except in a limited number of well-defined circumstances. The GAB collects and makes available information about the financial interests of state officials, candidates, and nominees; and compiles and disseminates on its Web sites information about organizations' efforts to influence legislation and administrative rules as well as the time and money spent by those organizations in lobbying activities.

Organization: The 6 members of the board, each of whom must have formerly been elected to and served as a judge of a court of record in Wisconsin, are appointed to 6-year terms by the governor from nominations submitted by a nominating committee called the Governmental Accountability Candidate Committee. The committee consists of one court of appeals judge from each of the court of appeals districts, chosen by lot by the chief justice of the supreme court in the presence of the other justices.

Board members may not be involved in partisan political activities and may not hold another state office or position except that of reserve judge of a circuit court or court of appeals. The board appoints a legal counsel outside the classified service as agency head to perform legal and administrative functions for the board. The board includes an Elections Division and an Ethics and Accountability Division, each of which is under the direction and supervision of an administrator appointed by the board. The board designates an employee to serve as the chief election officer of the state.

History: The Government Accountability Board was created by 2007 Wisconsin Act 1. Act 1 abolished the State Ethics and Elections Boards and their functions were merged into the new agency, effective after January 10, 2008.

The Elections Board was created as an independent agency by Chapter 334, Laws of 1973, which transferred administration of the state's election laws from the secretary of state and created the campaign finance registration and reporting system.

The Ethics Board was created by Chapter 90, Laws of 1973, to administer the ethics code applicable to public officials and employees created by the act. Lobbying has been regulated in Wisconsin since 1858. The secretary of state was made responsible for the enforcement of lobbying laws by Chapter 278, Laws of 1977, and this regulation was transferred to the Ethics Board by 1989 Wisconsin Act 338.

Statutory Council

Election Administration Council: LISA WEINER (Milwaukee County Board of Election Commissioners); NEIL ALBRECHT (City of Milwaukee Board of Election Commissioners); SUE ERTMER (Winnebago County Clerk); NAN KOTTKE (Marathon County Clerk); MARILYN K. BHEND (Johnson Town Clerk); JULEE HELT (Waunakee Village Clerk); DIANE HERMANN-BROWN (Sun Prairie City Clerk); MIKE HOPPENRATH (Watertown City Clerk); SUE PECK (Marshall Village Clerk); AUDREY RUE (Brigham Town Clerk); HOWARD SEIFERT (citizen representative); ALICIA M. BOEHME (Disability Rights Wisconsin); ANDREA KAMINSKI (Executive Director, League of Women Voters of Wisconsin); SANDI WESOLOWSKI (Clerk, City of Franklin); ANITA JOHNSON (Election Administration Advocate, Citizen Action of Wisconsin, Milwaukee); MAUREEN RYAN (Wisconsin Coalition of Independent Living Centers).

The Election Administration Council assists the Government Accountability Board in preparing and revising, as necessary, a state plan that meets the requirements of Public Law 107-252, the federal "Help America Vote Act of 2002", which will enable participation by the state in federal financial assistance programs authorized under that law. The members of the council are appointed by the GAB elections division administrator. The membership must include the clerk or executive director of the board of election commissioners of the two counties or municipalities having the largest population, one or more election officials of other counties or municipalities, representatives of organizations that advocate for the interests of the voting public, and other electors of Wisconsin. The council was created by 2003 Wisconsin Act 265 in the Elections Board, and was attached to the GAB by 2007 Wisconsin Act 1. The composition and duties of the council are specified in Sections 5.05 (10), 5.68 (3m), and 15.607 (1) of the statutes.

Department of
HEALTH SERVICES

Address e-mail by combining the user ID and the state extender: userid@**wisconsin.gov**
All telephone numbers are 608 area code unless otherwise indicated.

Secretary of Health Services: KITTY RHOADES, 266-9622, kitty.rhoades@

Deputy Secretary: KEVIN MOORE, 266-9622, kevin.moore@

Executive Assistant: ANDREW HITT, 266-9622, andrew.hitt@

Communications Director: STEPHANIE SMILEY, 266-5862, stephanie.smiley@

  Area Administration: vacancy, *director,* 261-9334.

  Tribal Affairs: GAIL NAHWAHQUAW, *director,* 267-5068, gail.nahwahquaw@

Legislative Liaison: ALEX IGNATOWSKI, 266-3262, alex.ignatowski@

Legal Counsel, Office of: SANDRA ROWE, *chief legal counsel,* 266-0355, sandra.rowe@

Inspector General, Office of: ALAN WHITE, *inspector general,* 266-2521, alan.white@; LORI THORNTON, *deputy inspector general,* 261-8308, lori.thornton@

Office of Free Market Health Care: 266-9622.

Policy Initiatives and Budget, Office of: vacancy, *director,* 266-2907; ANDREW FORSAITH, *budget director,* 266-7684, andrew.forsaith@; Fax: (608) 267-0358.

Mailing Address: P.O. Box 7850, Madison 53707-7850.

Location: Wilson Street State Human Services Building, 1 West Wilson Street, Madison.

Telephone: 266-1865.

Internet Address: http://dhs.wisconsin.gov

Publications: Annual fiscal reports; Biennial reports; Reports and informational brochures (available through divisions).

Number of Employees: 5,923.80.

Total Budget 2011-13: $17,653,817,300.

Statutory References: Section 15.19; Chapter 46.

Enterprise Services, Division of: vacancy, *administrator,* 261-6837; CHERYL K. JOHNSON, *deputy administrator,* 266-5869, cherylk.johnson@; Fax: 267-6749.

    Continuity Management, Facilities and Operations, Bureau of: RITA PRIGIONI, *director,* 266-8472, rita.prigioni@

    Fiscal Services, Bureau of: AMY MCDOWELL, *director,* 266-2019, amy.mcdowell@

    Human Resources, Bureau of: SCOTT C. THOMPSON, *director,* 266-8999, scottc.thompson@

    Information and Technology Services, Bureau of: THOMAS D. WIEGERS, *acting director,* 261-6837, thomas.wiegers@

    Agency Project Management, Office of: PATRICK W. COOPER, *director,* 267-2846, patrick.cooper@

    Strategic Sourcing, Bureau of: JACQUELINE SOMMERS SMITH, *supervisor,* 266-0509, jacqueline.sommerssmith@

Health Care Access and Accountability, Division of: BRETT H. DAVIS, *administrator,* 266-8922, brett.davis@; MARLIA MATTKE, *deputy administrator,* 266-9749, marlia.mattke@; P.O. Box 309, Madison 53701-0309, Fax: 266-6786.

    Benefits Management, Bureau of: RACHEL CURRANS-HENRY, *deputy director,* 267-1421, rachel.curranshenry@

    Disability Determination Bureau: SALLY FITZER, *director,* 266-0490, sally.fitzer@ssa.gov

    Enrollment Policy and Systems, Bureau of: SHAWN SMITH, *director,* 266-1935, shawn.smith@

    Fiscal Management, Bureau of: CURTIS CUNNINGHAM, *director,* 261-6858, curtis.cunningham@

    Operational Coordination, Bureau of: CHERYL JATCZAK, *director,* 267-7118, cheryl.jatczak@

    Milwaukee Enrollment Services: EDWARD KAMIN, *director,* (414) 289-6535, edward.kamin@

Long Term Care, Division of: BRIAN SHOUP, *administrator,* 266-0554, brian.shoup@; BETH WROBLEWSKI, *deputy administrator,* 261-5987, beth.wroblewski@; Fax: 261-6079.

    Family Care Expansion, Office of: MARGARET KRISTAN, *director,* 261-6393, margaret.kristan@

    Aging and Disability Resources, Bureau of: vacancy, *director,* 266-3840.

    Center Operations, Bureau of: THEODORE BUNCK, *director,* 301-9200, theodore.bunck@

        Central Wisconsin Center for the Developmentally Disabled: JANICE HOLLING, *director,* 317 Knutson Drive, Madison 53704-1197, 301-9200, Fax: 301-9438, janice.holling@

        Northern Wisconsin Center for the Developmentally Disabled: JACQUELINE NEUROHR, *director,* 2820 East Park Avenue, P.O. Box 340, Chippewa Falls 54729-0340, (715) 723-5542, Fax: (715) 723-8464, jacqueline.neurohr@

        Southern Wisconsin Center for the Developmentally Disabled: JIM HENKES, *director,* 2415 Spring Street, P.O. Box 100, Union Grove 53182-0100, (262) 878-2411, Fax: (262) 878-2922, james.henkes@

    Financial Management Services, Bureau of: TOM LAWLESS, *director,* 261-7810, thomas.lawless@

    Long Term Support, Bureau of: GAIL PROPSOM, *director,* 267-5987, gail.propsom@

Mental Health and Substance Abuse Services, Division of: LINDA HARRIS, *administrator,* 266-2717, linda.harris@; PATRICK CORK, *deputy administrator,* 266-2717, patrick.cork@

    Client Rights Office: JAMES YEADON, *supervisor,* 266-5525, james.yeadon@

    Prevention, Treatment and Recovery, Bureau of: JOYCE ALLEN, *director,* 266-2717, joyce.allen@

        Mendota Mental Health Institute: GREGORY VAN RYBROEK, *director,* 301 Troy Drive, Madison 53704-1599, 301-1000, Fax: 301-1390, gregory.vanrybroek@

DEPARTMENT OF HEALTH SERVICES

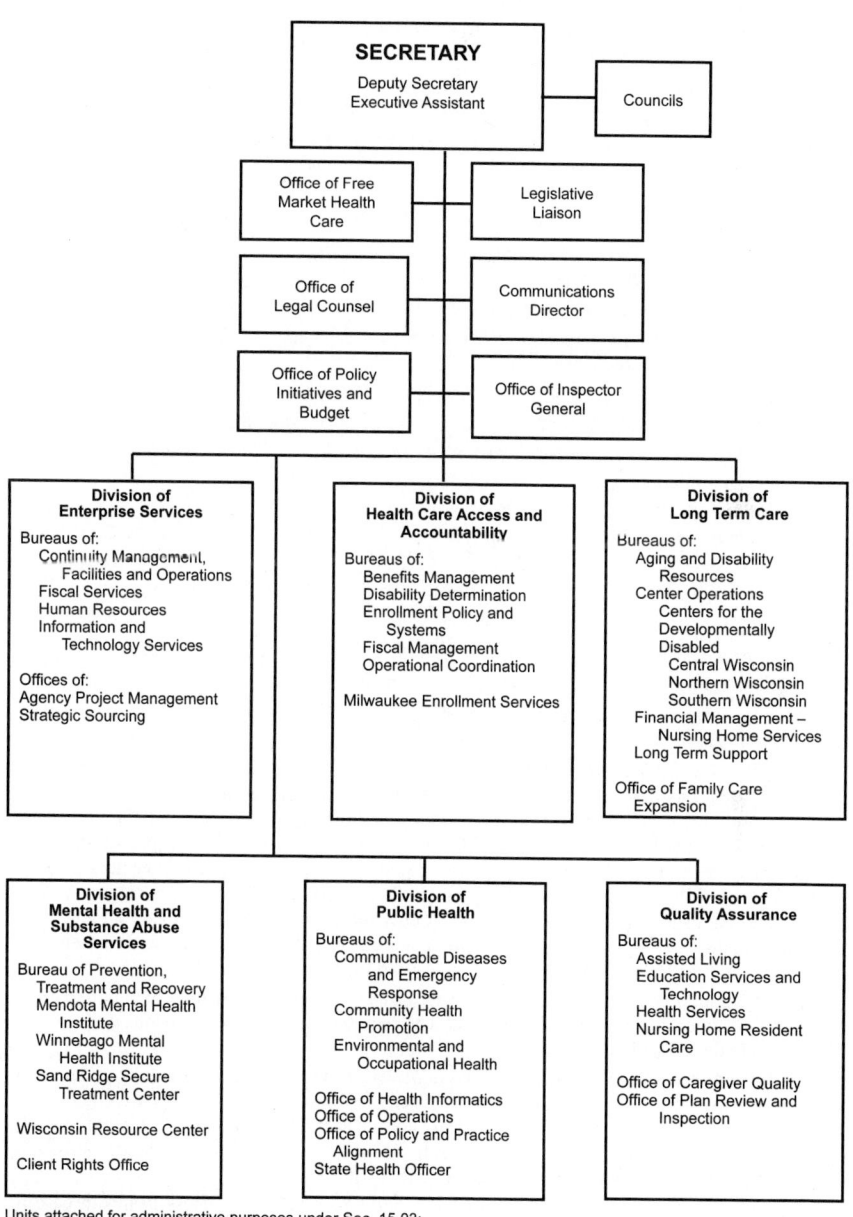

SECRETARY
Deputy Secretary
Executive Assistant

Councils

Office of Free Market Health Care

Legislative Liaison

Office of Legal Counsel

Communications Director

Office of Policy Initiatives and Budget

Office of Inspector General

Division of Enterprise Services

Bureaus of:
Continuity Management,
Facilities and Operations
Fiscal Services
Human Resources
Information and
Technology Services

Offices of:
Agency Project Management
Strategic Sourcing

Division of Health Care Access and Accountability

Bureaus of:
Benefits Management
Disability Determination
Enrollment Policy and
Systems
Fiscal Management
Operational Coordination

Milwaukee Enrollment Services

Division of Long Term Care

Bureaus of:
Aging and Disability
Resources
Center Operations
Centers for the
Developmentally
Disabled
Central Wisconsin
Northern Wisconsin
Southern Wisconsin
Financial Management –
Nursing Home Services
Long Term Support

Office of Family Care
Expansion

Division of Mental Health and Substance Abuse Services

Bureau of Prevention,
Treatment and Recovery
Mendota Mental Health
Institute
Winnebago Mental
Health Institute
Sand Ridge Secure
Treatment Center

Wisconsin Resource Center

Client Rights Office

Division of Public Health

Bureaus of:
Communicable Diseases
and Emergency
Response
Community Health
Promotion
Environmental and
Occupational Health

Office of Health Informatics
Office of Operations
Office of Policy and Practice
Alignment
State Health Officer

Division of Quality Assurance

Bureaus of:
Assisted Living
Education Services and
Technology
Health Services
Nursing Home Resident
Care

Office of Caregiver Quality
Office of Plan Review and
Inspection

Units attached for administrative purposes under Sec. 15.03:
Emergency Medical Services Board
Council on Physical Disabilities

Winnebago Mental Health Institute: THOMAS J. SPEECH, *director,* P.O. Box 9, Winnebago 54985-0009, (920) 235-4910, Fax: (920) 237-2043, thomas.speech@

Sand Ridge Secure Treatment Center: DEBORAH J. MCCULLOCH, *director,* 1111 North Road, Mauston 53948, (608) 847-4438, Fax: (608) 847-1790, deborah.mcculloch@

Wisconsin Resource Center: BYRAN BARTOW, *director,* 1505 North Street, P.O. Box 16, Winnebago 54985-0016, (920) 426-4310, Fax: (920) 236-4199, byran.bartow@

Public Health, Division of: KAREN MCKEOWN, *administrator,* 267-7828, karen.mckeown@; SANDY BREITBORDE, *deputy administrator,* 266-9780, sandra.breitborde@; P.O. Box 2659, Madison 53701-2659, Fax: 266-6988, TTY: (888) 701-1253.

  State Health Officer: DR. HENRY ANDERSON, 266-1253, henry.anderson@

  Communicable Diseases and Emergency Response, Bureau of: DIANE CHRISTEN, *director,* 267-9363, diane.christen@

  Community Health Promotion, Bureau of: SUSAN UTTECH, *director,* 267-3561, susan.uttech@

  Environmental and Occupational Health, Bureau of: CHARLES WARZECHA, *director,* 264-9880, charles.warzecha@

  Health Informatics, Office of: OSKAR ANDERSON, *director,* 267-7279, oskar.anderson@

  Operations, Office of: DONNA MOORE, *director,* 261-9434, donnaj.moore@

  Policy and Practice Alignment, Office of: PATRICIA GUHLEMAN, *director,* 266-1347, patricia.guhleman@

Quality Assurance, Division of: OTIS WOODS, *administrator,* 267-7185, otis.woods@; vacancy, *deputy administrator,* 266-7952; Fax: 267-0352; Milwaukee office: 819 North Sixth Street, Milwaukee 53203, (414) 227-5000.

  Caregiver Quality, Office of: LAURIE ARKENS, *director,* 264-9876, laurie.arkens@

  Assisted Living, Bureau of: ALFRED JOHNSON, *director,* 266-8598, alfred.johnson@

  Education Services and Technology, Bureau of: vacancy, *director,* 266-2055.

  Health Services, Bureau of: CREMEAR MIMS, *director,* (414) 227-4556, cremear.mims@

  Nursing Home Resident Care, Bureau of: JUAN FLORES, *interim director,* 267-0351, juan.flores@

  Plan Review and Inspection, Office of: DAVID SOENS, *director,* 266-9675, david.soens@

Agency Responsibility: The Department of Health Services administers a wide range of services to clients in the community and at state institutions, regulates certain care providers, and supervises and consults with local public and voluntary agencies. Its responsibilities span public health; mental health and substance abuse; long-term support and care; services to people who have a disability, medical assistance, and children's services; aging programs; physical and developmental disability services; sensory disability programs; operation of care and treatment facilities; quality assurance programs; nutrition supplementation programs; medical assistance; and health care for low-income families, elderly, and disabled persons.

Organization: The department is administered by a secretary who is appointed by the governor with the advice and consent of the senate. The secretary appoints the division administrators from outside the classified service.

Unit Functions: The *Division of Enterprise Services* oversees financial management, information systems and technology, personnel and employment relations, affirmative action and civil rights compliance, purchasing and contract administration, facilities management, continuity of operations planning, project management, and other administrative services. It handles billing, collection, and related accounting for state institutions.

The *Division of Health Care Access and Accountability* provides access to health care for low-income persons, the elderly, and people with disabilities. It administers the Medical Assistance (Medicaid), BadgerCare Plus, SeniorCare, Chronic Disease Aids, General Relief, and FoodShare programs.

The *Division of Long Term Care* administers a variety of programs that provide long-term support for the elderly and people with disabilities. These programs include Family Care, Aging and Disability Resource Centers, Community Relocation Initiative, Community Integration Initiative, Pathways to Independence, and the Community Options Program. The division manages nursing home funding, nursing home policies, and reimbursement and auditing services. The division also includes the Offices for the Deaf and Hard of Hearing and the Blind or Visually Impaired as well as programs for Autism and Brain Injury. The division supports the Birth to 3 Interagency Coordinating Council and the Assistive Technology Council as required by federal law. In addition, it operates three state centers for persons with developmental disabilities: Northern Wisconsin Center (Chippewa Falls), Central Wisconsin Center (Madison), and Southern Wisconsin Center (Union Grove).

The *Division of Mental Health and Substance Abuse Services* administers programs to meet mental health and substance abuse prevention, diagnosis, early intervention, and treatment needs, as well as the Community Forensic Programs for individuals in need of competency evaluation and treatment and community-based treatment for persons found not guilty by reason of mental disease or defect when community treatment is ordered by the court. It administers the state's institutional programs for persons whose mental health needs or developmental disabilities cannot be met in a community setting. The two mental health institutes, Mendota Mental Health Institute and Winnebago Mental Health Institute, provide treatment for persons with mental health needs which require inpatient hospitalization including medical, psychological, social, and rehabilitative services. Mendota Mental Health Institute houses a secure treatment unit to meet the mental health needs of male adolescents from the Department of Corrections' juvenile institutions. The division operates the Wisconsin Resource Center as a medium security facility for mentally ill prison inmates whose treatment needs cannot be met by the Department of Corrections. It also provides treatment at the Sand Ridge Secure Treatment Center for individuals civilly committed under the sexually violent persons law, and provides services for persons placed on supervised release.

The *Division of Public Health* promotes and protects public health in Wisconsin through various services and regulations. It administers programs that address environmental and occupational health, family and community health, chronic and communicable disease prevention and control, and programs relating to maternal and child health, including the Women, Infants and Children (WIC) Supplemental Food Program. It licenses emergency medical service providers and technicians and approves and supervises their training. The division is also responsible for inspecting restaurants, hotels and motels, bed and breakfast establishments, camps and campgrounds, food vendors, and swimming pools. The division performs vital recordkeeping functions including providing birth, death, marriage, and divorce certificates and the gathering, analysis and publishing of statistical information related to the health of the state's population. The division conducts formal statutory reviews of all local health departments every five years.

The *Division of Quality Assurance* licenses and regulates over 40 different programs and facilities that provide health, long-term care, and mental health and substance abuse services including assisted living facilities, nursing homes, community-based residential facilities home health agencies, and facilities serving people with developmental disabilities. It also performs caregiver background checks and investigations.

History: The Department of Health Services combines supervision of many state and local functions that had developed separately in the 1800s. For more than two decades after statehood, Wisconsin created separate governing boards and institutions for the care of prisoners; juveniles; and blind, deaf, and mentally ill persons. By 1871, there were six such institutions. The first attempt to institute overall supervision of these services came when the legislature passed Chapter 136, Laws of 1871, creating the State Board of Charities and Reform. Its duties included examination of the operations of state institutions and their boards and investigation of practices in local asylums, jails, and schools for the blind and deaf.

In Chapter 298, Laws of 1881, the legislature abolished the separate institutional boards and combined their functions under the State Board of Supervision of Wisconsin Charitable, Reformatory and Penal Institutions. The State Board of Charities and Reform continued to operate until 1891. In that year, the two boards were combined as the State Board of Control of the Wisconsin Reformatory, Charitable and Penal Institutions in Chapter 221, Laws of 1891, thus completing the consolidation of public welfare activities.

The Department of Health Services building undergoes window replacement in 2013 as part of a $14.5 million, 18-month, restoration project. Construction on the building, which is on the National Register of Historic Places, was begun in 1930, and is built of granite from the State Quarry in Amberg, Wisconsin. (Department of Health Services)

In the early days of statehood, public health was primarily a function of local governments. In Chapter 366, Laws of 1876, the legislature established the State Board of Health to "study the vital statistics of this state, and endeavor to make intelligent and profitable use of the collected records of death and sickness among the people." The board was directed to "make sanitary investigations and inquiries respecting the causes of disease, and especially of epidemics; the causes of mortality, and the effects of localities, employments, conditions, ingesta, habits and circumstances on the health of the people." This directive defines much of the work still done in public health. Later legislation required the board to take responsibility for tuberculosis care (1905), to direct its efforts toward preventing blindness in infants (1909), and to inspect water and sewerage systems to prevent typhoid and dysentery (1919). In addition, at various times, the board licensed restaurants, health facilities, barbers, embalmers, and funeral directors.

By the time the federal government entered the field of public welfare during the Great Depression of the 1930s, Wisconsin had already pioneered a number of programs, including aid to children and pensions for the elderly (enacted in 1931). The Wisconsin Children's Code, enacted by Chapter 439, Laws of 1929, was one of the most comprehensive in the nation. The state's initial response to federal funding was to establish separate departments to administer social security funds and other public welfare programs. After several attempts at reorganization and a series of studies, the legislature established the State Department of Public Welfare in Chapter 435, Laws of 1939, to provide unified administration of all existing welfare functions. Public health and care for the aged were delegated to separate agencies.

The executive branch reorganization act of 1967 created the Department of Health and Social Services. The Board of Health and Social Services, appointed by the governor, directed the new department and appointed the departmental secretary to administer the agency. In addition to combining public welfare, public health, and care for the aged in the reorganization act, the 1967 Legislature added the Division of Vocational Rehabilitation in Chapter 43. In Chapter 39, Laws of 1975, the legislature abolished the board and replaced it with a secretary appointed by the governor with the advice and consent of the senate. That same law called for a reorganization of the department, which was completed by July 1977. The Department of Health and Social Services was renamed the Department of Health and Family Services (DHFS), effective July 1, 1996.

The decades of the 1960s and 1970s saw an expansion of public welfare and health services at both the federal and state levels. Especially notable were programs for medical care for the needy and aged (Medical Assistance and Medicare), drug treatment programs, food stamps, Aid to Families with Dependent Children Program (AFDC), and increased regulation of hospitals and nursing homes.

While continuing to administer its established programs, the department was assigned additional duties during the 1980s in the areas of child support, child abuse and neglect, programs for the handicapped, and welfare reform. However, 1989 Wisconsin Acts 31 and 107 created a separate Department of Corrections to administer adult corrections institutions and programs, and 1995 Wisconsin Act 27 transferred responsibility for juvenile offenders to that department.

1995 Wisconsin Act 27 revised AFDC and transferred it and other income support programs including Medical Assistance eligibility and food stamps to the Department of Workforce Development (DWD). (Wisconsin Works, known as W-2, replaced AFDC in 1995 Wisconsin Act 289.) Existing welfare reform programs, including Job Opportunities and Basic Skills (JOBS), Learnfare, Parental Responsibility, and Work-Not-Welfare, were also transferred to DWD, along with child and spousal support, the Children First Program, Older American Community Service Employment, refugee assistance programs, and vocational rehabilitation functions. Health care facilities plan review was transferred from the Department of Industry, Labor and Human Relations to DHFS by 1995 Wisconsin Act 27. Act 27 also transferred laboratory certification to the Department of Agriculture, Trade and Consumer Protection and low-income energy assistance to the Department of Administration.

As a result of 1995 Wisconsin Act 303, the department assumed responsibility for direct administration and operation of Milwaukee County child welfare services. Primary responsibility for the Health Insurance Risk-Sharing Program (HIRSP) was transferred to the department from the Office of the Commissioner of Insurance by 1997 Wisconsin Act 27. 2001 Wisconsin Act 16 transferred the Medical Assistance Eligibility Program and the Food Stamp Program to DHFS from the Department of Workforce Development.

2007 Wisconsin Act 20 changed the name of the department to the Department of Health Services beginning July 1, 2008. Act 20 also created a separate Department of Children and Families and split the responsibilities of DHFS between the two departments.

The Office of Free Market Health Care, which is jointly directed by the Department of Health Services and the Office of the Commissioner of Insurance, was established by Executive Order 10 on January 27, 2011. The responsibilities of the office include developing plans that encourage competition in health care benefits and insurance plans through free-market, consumer driven approaches.

Statutory Councils and Committees

Birth Defect Prevention and Surveillance, Council on: LINDSAY ZETZSCHE (UW Medical School representative), WILLIAM RHEAD (Medical College of Wisconsin, Inc., representative), vacancy (pediatric nurse representative), MICHELLE KEMPF-WEIBEL (children and youth with special health care needs DHS program representative), CAROL NODDINGS-EICHINGER (early intervention services DHS program representative), ANN BUEDEL (Vital Records Office, health statistics research and analysis DHS representative), PHILIP GIAMPIETRO (State Medical Society representative), vacancy (Wisconsin Health and Hospital Association representative), KERRY BALDWIN JEDELE (Wisconsin Chapter, American Academy of Pediatrics representative), vacancy (Council on Developmental Disabilities representative), MIR BASIR (nonprofit organization representative), LISA B. NELSON (parent/guardian of child with a birth defect), CYNTHIA DESTEFFEN (local health department representative) (appointed by secretary of health services).

Contact Person: PEGGY HELM-QUEST, 267-2945, peggy.helmquest@

The 13-member Council on Birth Defect Prevention and Surveillance makes recommendations to the department regarding the administration of the Wisconsin Birth Defects Registry. The registry documents diagnoses and counts the number of birth defects for children up to age two. The council advises what birth defects are to be reported; the content, format, and procedures for reporting; and the contents of the aggregated reports. Members are appointed by the secretary of health services to 4-year terms. The UW Medical School and Medical College of Wisconsin, Inc., representatives must have expertise in birth defects epidemiology. Nurse representatives must specialize in pediatrics or have expertise in birth defects. The program representatives are from the appropriate subunits in the department. The nonprofit representative must be from an organization whose primary purpose is birth defect prevention and which does not promote abortion as a method of prevention. The department has added a nonstatutory council member to represent parents or guardians of children born with birth defects. The council was created by 1999 Wisconsin Act 114. Its duties and composition are prescribed in Sections 15.197 (12) and 253.12 (4) of the statutes. Additional information is available at: http://www.cbdps.state.wi.us/index.html.

Blindness, Council on: ELEANOR LOOMANS, *chairperson;* BILL GALLIK, *vice chairperson;* JOHN HARTMAN, KELLI HUGHES, BRUCE PARKINSON, CHARMAINE PIQUETTE, ROBERTO TORREZ, EDWARD H. WEISS, JOAN J. WUCHERER; DAVID HYDE (nonvoting member) (appointed by secretary of health services).

The 9-member Council on Blindness makes recommendations to the department and other state agencies on policies, procedures, services, programs, and research that affect blind or visually impaired people. Members are appointed by the secretary of health services for staggered 3-year terms, and 7 of them must be blind or visually impaired. Originally, the council was created by Chapter 305, Laws of 1947, as the Advisory Committee of the Blind to advise the Board of Public Welfare and the State Superintendent of Public Instruction. The current council was created in the Department of Health and Social Services by Chapter 366, Laws of 1969. Its composition and duties are prescribed in Sections 15.197 (2) and 47.03 (9) of the statutes. Additional information is available at: http://www.blindnesscouncil.wisconsin.gov.

Deaf and Hard of Hearing, Council for the: WILLIAM MAULDIN, *chairperson;* MARY JANE GRIFFIN, DANIEL HOULIHAN, TAMERA L. KLINK, ALEX SLAPPEY, 4 vacancies (all appointed by governor).

The 9-member Council for the Deaf and Hard of Hearing advises the department on the provision of effective services to deaf, hard-of-hearing, late-deafened, and deaf-blind people. Members are appointed by the governor for staggered 4-year terms. The council was created by Chapter 34, Laws of 1979, as the Council for the Hearing Impaired and renamed by 1995 Wisconsin Act 27. Its duties and composition are prescribed in Sections 15.09 (5) and 15.197 (8) of the statutes. Additional information is available at: http://www.dhhcouncil.state.wi.us.

Medicaid Pharmacy Prior Authorization Advisory Committee: BRETT DAVIS, *chairperson;* RACHEL CURRANS-HENRY, *vice chairperson;* ROSANNE BARBER, JAMES BOBLIN, WARD BROWN, CATHERINE DECKER, RONALD DIAMOND, LAWRENCE FLEMING, KEVIN IZARD, AL LIEGEL, STEVE MAIKE, WILLIAM RADUEGE, PAT TOWERS, ALICIA WALKER, MICHAEL WITKOVSKY (appointed by secretary of health services).

The Medicaid Pharmacy Prior Authorization Advisory Committee advises the department on issues related to prior authorization decisions concerning prescription drugs on behalf of medical assistance recipients. Section 49.45 (49) (a) of the statutes directs the secretary of health services to establish a committee, of at least 5 members, including 2 physicians, 2 pharmacists, and an advocate for recipients of medical assistance who has sufficient medical background to evaluate a prescription drug's effectiveness. Members are appointed by the secretary. Information is available at: www.forwardhealth.wi.gov/wiportal/tab/42/icscontent/provider/pac/index. htm.spage.

Mental Health, Council on: SHELDON GROSS, *chairperson;* WILLIAM BENEDICT, JULIE-ANNE BRAUN, COREN BRIGGS, NIC DIBBLE, KIM EITHUN-HARSHNER, KATHLEEN ENDERS, LINDA HARRIS, RICHARD IMMLER, CAROL KEEN, DAVID NENCKA, MARY NEUBAUER, MISHELLE O'SHASKY, JODELL PELISHEK, DAVID SOMMERS, JOANNE STEPHENS, MATTHEW STRITTMATER, ANN CATHERINE VEIERSTAHLER, EDWARD WALL, JUDITH WILCOX, DONNA WRENN (appointed by secretary of health services).

The Council on Mental Health is composed of not less than 21 or more than 25 members nominated by the secretary of health services and appointed by the governor for 3-year terms. Persons appointed shall include representatives of groups and a proportion of members as specified in 42 USC 300x-3 (c), as amended in April 2, 2008. The council advises the department, governor, and legislature on mental health programs; provides recommendations on the expenditure of federal mental health block grants; reviews the department's plans for mental health services; and serves as an advocate for the mentally ill. The council was created by 1983 Wisconsin Act 439, and its membership was amended by 2007 Wisconsin Act 20. Its composition and duties are prescribed in Sections 15.197 (1) and 51.02 of the statutes. Additional information is available at: http://www.mhc.state.wi.us.

Newborn Screening Advisory Group: Umbrella Committee: DAVID ALLEN, MEI BAKER, JEFFREY BRITTON, CHARLES BROKOPP, DAVID DIMMOCK, MICHELLE FARRELL, GARY HOFFMAN, TAMI HORZEWSKI, MURRAY KATCHER, MICHELLE KEMPF-WEIBEL, KAREN MICHALSKI, JILL PARADOWSKI, JILL RADOWICZ, GREG RICE, MICHAEL ROCK, JOHN ROUTES, J. PAUL SCOTT, TAMMY TIMMLER, AUDREY TLUCZEK, SANDRA VAN CALCAR, LUANN WEIK (appointed by secretary of health services).

The Newborn Screening Advisory Umbrella Committee advises the department regarding the statutorily required program, which generally provides that infants receive blood or other diagnostic tests for congenital and metabolic disorders. Newborn screening has been required since 1978, and is a joint effort of the Department of Health Services and the State Laboratory of Hygiene. Section 253.13 (5) of the statutes requires the department to periodically consult appropriate experts in reviewing and evaluation of the state's newborn screening programs. The number and qualifications of committee members is not specified. Members are appointed by the secretary. Information is available at: http://www.slh.wisc.edu/newborn/guide/advisory.dot.

Public Health Council: JULIE WILLEMS VAN DIJK (local health representative), *chairperson;* JOHN BARTKOWSKI, CATHERINE FREY, CORAZON LOTEYRO, DOUGLAS NELSON, THAI VUE (health care consumer representatives); MARY JO BAISCH, S. GARCIA FRANZ, JOHN MEUER, DEBORAH MILLER, CHARLES POST, AYAZ SAMADANI, JAMES SANDERS (health care provider representatives); BRIDGET CLEMENTI, GARY GILMORE, LYNN SHEETS (health professions educator representatives); BEVAN BAKER, TERRI KRAMOLIS, GRETCHEN SAMPSON (local health departments and boards representatives); FAYE DODGE (tribal representative); AMY BREMEL, MARK VILLALPANDO (public safety representatives); vacancy.

The 23-member Public Health Council advises the department, the governor, the legislature, and the public on progress made in the implementation of the department's 10-year public health plan and coordination of responses to public health emergencies. Members are nominated by the secretary of health services and appointed by the governor to serve 3-year terms and must include representatives of health care consumers, health care providers, health professions educators, local health departments and boards, federally recognized American Indian tribes or bands in this state, public safety agencies, and, if established by the secretary of health services, the Public Health Advisory Committee. 2003 Wisconsin Act 186 created the council and its composition and duties are prescribed in Sections 15.197 (13) and 250.07 (1m) of the statutes.

Trauma Advisory Council: ALEX BEUNING, GABY ISKANDER, 2 vacancies (physicians); CHERYL PAAR, vacancy (registered nurses); 2 vacancies (emergency medical service providers); MERRILEE CARLSON, vacancy (rural hospital representatives); NIRAV PATEL, vacancy (urban hospital representatives); BRENDA FELLENZ (EMS Board representative).

The 13-member Trauma Advisory Council, all appointed by the secretary of health services, advises the department on developing and implementing a statewide trauma care system. Membership must include physicians, registered nurses, prehospital emergency medical service providers, urban and rural hospital personnel, and the medical services board. They must represent "all geographical areas of the state". Physician appointees must represent urban and rural areas, and one of the prehospital emergency medical service providers must represent a municipality. The council was created by 1997 Wisconsin Act 154 and its composition and duties are prescribed in Sections 15.197 (25) and 146.56 (1) of the statutes. Additional information is available at: http://www.dhs.wisconsin.gov/trauma/councils/index.htm.

INDEPENDENT UNITS ATTACHED FOR BUDGETING, PROGRAM COORDINATION, AND RELATED MANAGEMENT FUNCTIONS BY SECTION 15.03 OF THE STATUTES

EMERGENCY MEDICAL SERVICES BOARD

Members: TROY HAASE, *chairperson;* STEVE BANE, *vice chairperson;* MINDY ALLEN, JIM AUSTAD, JERRY BIGGART, BRENDA FELLENZ, MARK FREDRICKSON, KENNETH JOHNSON, LES LUDER, GLORIA MURAWSKY, vacancy (voting members appointed by governor). *Ex officio* nonvoting members: BRIAN LITZA (designated by secretary of health services), JANET NODORFT (designated by secretary of transportation), TIMOTHY WEIR (designated by state director, Technical College System Board), MICHAEL KIM (state medical director for emergency medical services).

Mailing Address: P.O. Box 2659, Madison 53701-2659.

Telephone: 266-1568.

Statutory References: Sections 15.195 (8) and 146.55 (3).

Agency Responsibility: The 15-member Emergency Medical Services Board appoints an advisory committee of physicians to advise the department on the selection of the state medical director for emergency medical services and to review that person's performance. It also advises the director on medical issues; reviews emergency medical service statutes and rules concerning the transportation of patients; and recommends changes to the Department of Health Services and the Department of Transportation. The board includes personnel from the appropriate state agencies and related emergency services in its deliberations.

The board includes 11 voting members, appointed by the governor for 3-year terms, who must "represent the various geographical areas of the state" and various types of emergency medical service providers. The board, which was created by 1993 Wisconsin Act 16, replaced the Emergency Medical Services Assistance Board, created by 1989 Wisconsin Act 102.

COUNCIL ON PHYSICAL DISABILITIES

Members: BEN BARRETT, *chairperson;* JON BALTMANIS, *vice chairperson;* JOANNE ZIMMERMAN, *secretary;* JORJAN BORLIN, CLAIRE DRAEGER, CHRISTINE DURANCEAU, JEFF FOX, MARGE LIBERSKI, JOHN MEISSNER, KAREN SECOR, SANDRA STOKES, LEWIS TYLER, CHARLES VANDENPLAS; vacancy (governor's representative) (all members are appointed by governor).
Coordinator: DAN JOHNSON.
Mailing Address: 1 West Wilson Street, Room 437, Madison 53703.
Telephones: 267-9582; TTY 267-9880.
E-mail Address: dan.johnson@
Internet Address: http://www.pdcouncil.state.wi.us
Statutory References: Sections 15.197 (4) and 46.29.
Agency Responsibility: The 14-member Council on Physical Disabilities develops and modifies the state plan for services to persons with physical disabilities. It advises the secretary of health services, recommends legislation, encourages public understanding of the needs of persons with physical disabilities, and promotes programs to prevent physical disability. The 13 appointed members are appointed by the governor to serve 3-year terms and must be state residents. At least 6 members must be persons with physical disabilities; 2 may be parents, guardians, or relatives of persons with physical disabilities; and at least one must be a service provider. The council must include equitable representation for sex, race, and urban and rural areas. The council was created by 1989 Wisconsin Act 202.

HIGHER EDUCATIONAL AIDS BOARD

Members: GARY ROBERTS (UW System Board of Regents member); vacancy (Technical College System Board member); RANDALL MCCREADY (UW System financial aids administrator); MARY JO GREEN (Technical College System financial aids administrator); TIMOTHY RINDAHL (UW System student representative); vacancy (Technical College System student representative); STEVEN DISALVO (independent colleges and universities board of trustees representative); STEVE MIDTHUN (independent colleges and universities financial aid administrator); MIKE BORMETT (designated by superintendent of public instruction); LARAMIE WIESEMAN (independent colleges and universities student representative); JAMES PALMER (public member); VERNA FOWLER (nonstatutory nonvoting representative of tribal higher educational institutions). (All members, except *ex officio* member and tribal representative, are appointed by governor.)
Executive Secretary: JOHN REINEMANN.
Mailing Address: P.O. Box 7885, Madison 53707-7885.
Location: 131 West Wilson Street, Suite 902, Madison.
Telephone: (608) 267-2206.
Fax: (608) 267-2808.
Agency E-mail Address: HEABmail@wisconsin.gov
Internet Address: http://heab.wi.gov
Publications: Biennial report; Report on Financial Aid Programs; various board reports.
Number of Employees: 11.00.
Total Budget 2011-13: $284,551,700.
Statutory References: Section 15.67; Chapter 39, Subchapter III.
Agency Responsibility: The Higher Educational Aids Board is responsible for the management and oversight of the state's student financial aid system for Wisconsin residents attending institutions of higher education. It also enters into interstate agreements and performs student loan collection services.

The board establishes policies for the state's student financial aid programs, including academic excellence scholarships, Wisconsin tuition grants, Wisconsin higher education grants, talent incentive grants, Wisconsin Covenant grant, handicapped student grants, Indian student grants, minority student grants (private sector and Technical College System), teacher education loans, minority teacher loans, nursing loans, and interstate reciprocity. It administers the contracts for medical and dental education services and the Wisconsin Health Education Loan Program and approves the participants in the Medical College of Wisconsin, Inc., per capita grant program. It administers the John R. Justice loan repayment grant program which provides loan repayment assistance for local, state, and federal public defenders and local and state prosecutors.

Organization: The 11 statutory members of the board include the superintendent of public instruction or designee, 7 members who serve 3-year terms, and 3 student members who serve 2-year terms. The students must be at least 18 years old, residents of this state, enrolled at least half-time, and in good academic standing. The UW and private nonprofit institution students must be undergraduates. The governor appoints the board's executive secretary. In 2005, the board added a nonstatutory nonvoting member to represent tribal institutions of higher education.

History: The Higher Educational Aids Board originated as the State Commission for Academic Facilities. It was created by Chapter 573, Laws of 1963, to administer Title I of the Federal Higher Education Facilities Act of 1963, which funded grants for university and college building programs in Wisconsin. Chapter 264, Laws of 1965, gave the commission student financial aid responsibilities and changed its name to the State Commission for Higher Educational Aids. Chapter 313, Laws of 1967, authorized the commission to organize the Wisconsin Higher Education Corporation to administer the federal Guaranteed Student Loan Program. The corporation was given an independent board of directors as a private nonstock corporation in 1984. Chapter 276, Laws of 1969, renamed the commission the Higher Educational Aids Board. The Higher Educational Aids Board was inadvertently repealed by 1995 Wisconsin Act 27, but was continued as the Higher Educational Aids Council by Executive Order 283. The legislature recreated the board in 1997 Wisconsin Act 27.

STATE HISTORICAL SOCIETY OF WISCONSIN

For e-mail combine the user ID and the state extender: userid@**wisconsinhistory.org**
All telephone numbers are 608 area code unless otherwise indicated.

Board of Curators: CONRAD GOODKIND, *president;* BRIAN RUDE, *president-elect;* DAVID ANDERSON (designated by governor); REPRESENTATIVE KESTELL (designated by assembly speaker); SENATOR SCHULTZ (designated by senate president), SENATOR RISSER (minority party senator), REPRESENTATIVE KESSLER (minority party representative to the assembly); R. WILLIAM VAN SANT (appointed by governor with senate consent); JON ANGELI, ANGELA BARTELL, CHRIS BERRY, SID BREMER, LAURA CRAMER, LAURIE DAVIDSON, LANE EARNS, NORBERT HILL, JR., JOHN O. HOLZHUETER, GREG HUBER, ELLEN LANGILL, CAROL MCCHESNEY JOHNSON, WILL JONES, CHLORIS LOWE, JR., WILLIAM O'CONNOR, LOWELL PETERSON, JERRY PHILLIPS, WALT RUGLAND, MICHAEL SCHMUDLACH, SAM SCINTA, THOMAS SHRINER, JR., TERRY THIESSEN, JOHN THOMPSON, AHARON ZOREA. (Unless otherwise indicated, curators are elected by the membership of the state historical society or serve *ex officio.*)

Board Secretary: ELLSWORTH H. BROWN.

Director: ELLSWORTH H. BROWN, 264-6440, ellsworth.brown@

   Information Technology: PAUL E. HEDGES, *coordinator,* 264-6451, paul.hedges@

   Public Information: ROBERT L. GRANFLATEN, *coordinator,* 264-6586, bob.granflaten@

   State Historian and Special Projects: ALICIA L. GOEHRING, *coordinator,* 264-6515, alicia.goehring@

Administrative Services, Division of: GREG T. PARKINSON, *administrator,* 264-6581, greg.parkinson@

   Facility Maintenance: JOHN D. KEES, *coordinator,* 264-6431, john.kees@

   Financial Services: PAUL J. HAMILTON, *coordinator,* 264-6426, paul.hamilton@

   Human Resources: KATE J. JOCHIMSEN, *coordinator,* 264-6448, katej.jochimsen@

Historic Preservation – Public History, Division of: vacancy, *administrator and state historic preservation officer.*

Historic Preservation Section: JAMES R. DRAEGER, *section chief,* 264-6511, jim.draeger@;
  state archaeologist: JOHN H. BROIHAHN, 264-6496, john.broihahn@
Society Press: KATHRYN BORKOWSKI, *editorial director,* 264-6461, kathy.borkowski@
Library – Archives, Division of: MATTHEW T. BLESSING, *administrator and state archivist,*
  264-6480, matt.blessing@; MICHAEL I. EDMONDS, *deputy administrator,* 264-6538, michael.
  edmonds@
  Collection Development: HELMUT M. KNIES, *coordinator,* 264-6478, helmut.knies@

STATE HISTORICAL SOCIETY

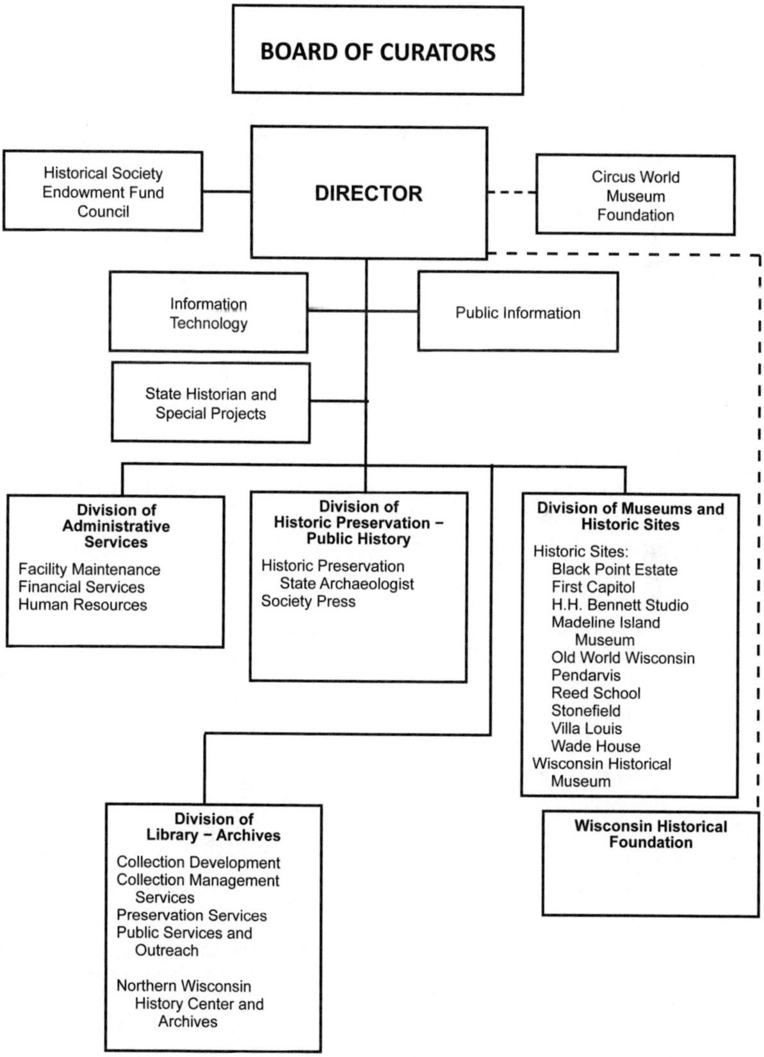

BOARD OF CURATORS

Historical Society
Endowment Fund
Council

DIRECTOR

Circus World
Museum
Foundation

Information
Technology

Public Information

State Historian and
Special Projects

**Division of
Administrative
Services**

Facility Maintenance
Financial Services
Human Resources

**Division of
Historic Preservation –
Public History**

Historic Preservation
  State Archaeologist
Society Press

**Division of Museums and
Historic Sites**

Historic Sites:
  Black Point Estate
  First Capitol
  H.H. Bennett Studio
  Madeline Island
    Museum
  Old World Wisconsin
  Pendarvis
  Reed School
  Stonefield
  Villa Louis
  Wade House
Wisconsin Historical
  Museum

**Division of
Library – Archives**

Collection Development
Collection Management
  Services
Preservation Services
Public Services and
  Outreach

Northern Wisconsin
  History Center and
  Archives

**Wisconsin Historical
Foundation**

Units attached for administrative purposes under Sec.
15.03:

Burial Sites Preservation Board
Historic Preservation Review Board

Collection Management Services: MAIJA S. CRAVENS, *coordinator,* 264-6522, maija.cravens@

Preservation Services: KATIE D. MULLEN, *coordinator,* 264-6489, kathleen.mullen@

Public Services and Outreach: RICHARD L. PIFER, *coordinator,* 264-6477, rick.pifer@

Northern Wisconsin History Center and Archives at the Northern Great Lakes Visitor Center: LINDA L. MITTLESTADT, *archivist,* (715) 685-2649; 29270 County Highway G, Ashland 54806; linda.mittlestadt@

Museums and Historic Sites, Division of: CHERYL E. SULLIVAN, *administrator,* 264-6434, cheryl.sullivan@; DAWN ST. GEORGE, *assistant administrator,* 261-9350, dawn.stgeorge@

Black Point Estate: DAVID A. DESIMONE, *site director,* (262) 248-1888; W4270 Southland Road, Lake Geneva 53147; david.desimone@

First Capitol: ALLEN L. SCHROEDER, *site director,* (608) 987-2122; Highway G, Belmont 53510; allen.schroeder@

H.H. Bennett Studio: vacancy, *site director,* (608) 253-3523; 215 Broadway, P.O. Box 147, Wisconsin Dells 53965.

Madeline Island Museum: STEVE R. COTHERMAN, *site director,* (715) 747-2415; La Pointe 54850; steve.cotherman@

Old World Wisconsin: DAN FREAS, *site director,* (262) 594-6302; W372 S9727 Highway 67, P.O. Box 69, Eagle 53119; dan.freas@

Pendarvis: ALLEN L. SCHROEDER, *site director,* (608) 987-2122; 114 Shake Rag Street, Mineral Point 53565; allen.schroeder@

Reed School: vacancy, *site director,* (608) 253-3523; U.S. Highway 10 and Cardinal Avenue, Neillsville 54456; reedschool@

Stonefield: ALLEN L. SCHROEDER, *site director,* (608) 725-5210; P.O. Box 125, Cassville 53806; allen.schroeder@

Villa Louis: SUSAN CAYA-SLUSSER, *site director,* (608) 326-2721; P.O. Box 65, Prairie du Chien 53821; susan.cayaslusser@

Wade House: DAVID M. SIMMONS, *site director,* (920) 526-3271; P.O. Box 34, Greenbush 53026; david.simmons@

Wisconsin Historical Museum: JENNIFER L. KOLB, *museum director,* 261-2461, jennifer.kolb@

Museum Archaeology: KELLY E. HAMILTON, *coordinator,* 264-6560, kelly.hamilton@

Wisconsin Historical Foundation: WESLEY E. MOSMAN BLOCK, *co-director and chief operating officer,* 264-6443, wesley.mosmanblock@; DIANE L. NIXA, co-*director and chief advancement officer,* 261-1378, diane.nixa@

Main Information Desk: (608) 264-6400.

Mailing Address: 816 State Street, Madison 53706-1417.

Archives and Library Location: 816 State Street, Madison.

Archives Telephone: 264-6460; Archives Fax: 264-6472; Library Telephone: 264-6534; Library Fax: 264-6520.

Museum Location: 30 North Carroll Street, Madison 53703-2707.

Museum Information: 264-6555; Museum Tours: 264-6557; Museum Fax: 264-6575.

Internet Address: www.wisconsinhistory.org

Publications: *Columns; Wisconsin Magazine of History.* The society also publishes books, research guides, and miscellaneous brochures. Recent publications include *Bottoms Up: A Toast to Wisconsin's Historic Bars and Breweries; Green Bay Packers: Trials, Triumphs, and Tradition; Return to Wake Robin: One Cabin in the Heyday of Northwoods Resorts.*

Number of Employees: 131.54.

Total Budget 2011-13: $41,461,200.

Statutory References: Section 15.70; Chapter 44, Subchapters I and II.

Agency Responsibility: The mission of the State Historical Society of Wisconsin, known informally as the Wisconsin Historical Society, is to help connect people to the past. The society has a statutory duty to collect and preserve historical and cultural resources related to Wisconsin and to make them available to the public. To meet these objectives, the society maintains a major history research collection in Madison and in 14 area research centers; operates 11 historic sites and museums, an office at the Northern Great Lakes Visitor Center, a field services office in Eau Claire, and statewide school services programs. It owns Circus World Museum, which is managed by the Circus World Museum Foundation. It provides public history programming such as National History Day and collaborates with other agencies such as Wisconsin Public Television to deliver history programming to the public. It provides technical services and advice to 383 affiliated local historical societies throughout the state. It conducts, publishes, and disseminates research on Wisconsin and U.S. history, and serves as the state's historic preservation office, which regulates the designation of historic structures and archaeological sites by administering the state and national registers of historic places. The society is also responsible for implementation of the state's Burial Sites Preservation Law.

Organization: The society is both a state agency and a membership organization. The society's Board of Curators includes 8 statutory appointments and up to 30 members who are elected according to the society's constitution and bylaws. The 3 members appointed by the governor with senate consent serve staggered 3-year terms. The board selects the society's director, who serves as administrative head and as secretary to the board.

Unit Functions: The *Division of Administrative Services* provides management and program support in the areas of accounting, financial services, budgeting, human resources, purchasing, and facility maintenance of the society's headquarters building.

The *Division of Historic Preservation – Public History* helps make the history of Wisconsin more accessible to state residents and awards historic designations to places of historic value. It administers Wisconsin's portion of the National Register of Historic Places in partnership with the National Park Service and manages the State Register of Historic Places. It nominates places of architectural, historic, and archaeological significance to the registers. It reviews federal, state, and local projects for their effect on historic and archaeological properties. The division certifies historic building rehabilitation projects for state and federal income tax credits, archaeological sites for property tax exemptions, and historic buildings as eligible for the state historic building code. The division administers the historical markers program, identifies and promotes underwater archaeological sites, and administers the state's burial sites preservation program. The division, through the Wisconsin Historical Society Press, edits and publishes most of the materials issued by the society, including books and a quarterly magazine of history. The division offers instructional materials and programs to schools and teachers to assist them in teaching the history of Wisconsin (including the state history textbook for fourth graders), coordinates the state's National History Day program, and provides technical assistance to local historical societies affiliated with the society through the Wisconsin Council for Local History. It also operates a field services office in Eau Claire to serve northern Wisconsin.

The *Division of Library – Archives* maintains notable collections in Wisconsin and North American history including areas such as genealogy; labor; business and industry; social action, including civil rights, antiwar movements, and reproductive rights issues; mass communications; and dramatic arts, including theater, motion pictures, and television. The library and archives serve as the North American history research collection for the UW-Madison. The library acts as regional depository for U.S. government publications and official depository for Wisconsin state government publications. The archives program acquires, catalogs, preserves, and makes available primary source materials, including manuscripts, maps, newspapers, photographs, sound recordings, films, videos, and other records pertaining to Wisconsin history and selected fields of U.S. history. It serves as the state archives, collecting and providing access to permanent records of state and local government. In partnership with the University of Wisconsin System, the archives operates 14 Area Research Centers throughout Wisconsin to bring its archival holdings on regional history closer to the public. It also makes available the collections of the Wisconsin Center for Film and Theater Research, which is administered jointly by the society and the UW-Madison.

The *Division of Museums and Historic Sites* operates 11 historic sites and museums: Black Point Estate, First Capitol, H.H. Bennett Studio, Madeline Island Museum, Old World Wisconsin, Pendarvis, Reed School, Stonefield, Villa Louis, Wade House, and the Wisconsin Historical Museum. The division collects and preserves the material culture of Wisconsin and interprets the state's history and prehistory for the public. The sites contain historic structures and visitor service buildings that reflect major themes of Wisconsin history, such as ethnic pioneer settlement, mining, farming, fur trade, exploration, transportation, rural life, and town development. The museum in Madison addresses the history of Wisconsin with exhibits covering all of these themes. The division fulfills its educational role through exhibitions, tours, school visits, and a variety of public programs conducted at the museum in Madison, the historic sites, and other venues throughout the state. The division supervises the preservation and development of artifact collections, and operates an archaeology program under a cooperative agreement with the Department of Transportation and the Department of Natural Resources.

The society owns an additional historic site in Baraboo, Circus World, which is operated by the Circus World Museum Foundation. This museum offers an extensive collection of circus memorabilia, unique circus wagons, and it operates a circus in Baraboo during the summer months.

The *Wisconsin Historical Foundation* is a 501 (c) (3) corporation and the advancement arm of the Wisconsin Historical Society. The foundation receives and administers gifts on behalf of the society and manages the society's membership program. The foundation has a separate board of directors.

History: The Wisconsin Historical Society was originally founded as a private association in 1846, two years before statehood. It was chartered by the Wisconsin Legislature in Chapter 17, Laws of 1853, which made the society responsible for the preservation and care of all records, articles, and other materials of historic interest to the state. The society has received state funding since 1854 (Chapter 16) – longer than any other state historical society in the nation.

The legislature expanded the state's historic preservation program in Chapter 29, Laws of 1977, by making the society responsible for preservation activities associated with the designation, restoration, and repair of historic properties. Chapter 341, Laws of 1981, provided statutory support for local ordinances designed to preserve historic buildings. It set up a framework for a state historic building code with alternative standards for the preservation or restoration of historic structures. 1987 Wisconsin Act 395 strengthened the state's historic preservation laws by creating the State Register of Historic Places to protect historic and prehistoric properties. This law and 1987 Wisconsin Act 399 provided state tax credits and exemptions for owners of certain historic and archaeological properties.

1985 Wisconsin Act 29 formalized the practice of allowing the historical society to enter into a lease agreement with a nonprofit corporation, now called the Circus World Museum Foundation, for the purpose of operating the Circus World Museum.

Statutory Council

Historical Society Endowment Fund Council: Inactive.

The Historical Society Endowment Fund Council advises the state historical society regarding the raising and disbursement of funds used to support the society's historical and cultural preservation services and educational activities. The 10-member council must include representation from the Wisconsin Arts Board, the State Historical Society of Wisconsin, the Wisconsin Academy of Science, Arts and Letters, the Wisconsin Humanities Council, Wisconsin Public Radio and Wisconsin Public Television, and 4 public members, all appointed by the governor. The council was created by 1997 Wisconsin Act 27 and its composition and duties are prescribed in Section 15.707 (3) of the statutes.

INDEPENDENT UNITS ATTACHED FOR BUDGETING, PROGRAM COORDINATION, AND RELATED MANAGEMENT FUNCTIONS BY SECTION 15.03 OF THE STATUTES

BURIAL SITES PRESERVATION BOARD

Burial Sites Preservation Board: ELLSWORTH H. BROWN (state historical society director); KATHERINE C. EGAN-BRUHY, KATHLEEN FOLEY, CYNTHIA STILES (nominated by Wisconsin Archaeological Survey); DAVID J. GRIGNON, CORINA MROZINSKI, vacancy (nominated by the Great Lakes Inter-Tribal Council, Inc., and the Menominee Tribe). Nonvoting members: vacancy (state historic preservation officer), JOHN H. BROIHAHN (state archaeologist). (All except *ex officio* members are appointed by governor.)

Mailing Address: 816 State Street, Madison 53706-1417.

Telephones: (608) 264-6505; (800) 342-7834 (within Wisconsin).

Statutory References: Section 15.705 (1); Chapter 157, Subchapter III.

Agency Responsibility: The Burial Sites Preservation Board was created to protect all the interests related to human burial sites and to ensure equal treatment and respect for all human burials, regardless of ethnic origin, cultural background, or religious affiliation. The board develops detailed policies to implement the burial sites preservation program; reviews decisions of the director or the administrative hearing examiner concerning applications for permits to disturb cataloged burial sites; and reviews the director's decisions regarding the disposition of human remains and burial objects removed from a burial site. This program was created by 1985 Wisconsin Act 316.

Organization: The 9-member board includes 3 members with professional qualifications in archaeology, physical anthropology, or history and 3 members of federally recognized Indian nations in Wisconsin who have a knowledge of tribal preservation planning, history, or archaeology or who serve as elders, traditional persons, or spiritual leaders of a tribe. The 6 appointed members serve 3-year terms.

HISTORIC PRESERVATION REVIEW BOARD

Historic Preservation Review Board: ANNE E. BIEBEL, BRUCE T. BLOCK, ROBERT J. GOUGH, CARLEN HATALA, KELLY S. JACKSON, CAROL MCCHESNEY JOHNSON, DAN J. JOYCE, KUBET LUCHTERHAND, DAVID V. MOLLENHOFF, NEIL PREDERGAST, SISSEL SCHROEDER, VALENTINE J. SCHUTE, JR., DANIEL J. STEPHANS, PAUL WOLTER, DONNA ZIMMERMAN (all appointed by governor).

Mailing Address: 816 State Street, Madison 53706-1417.

Telephone: (608) 264-6498.

Statutory References: Section 15.705 (2); Chapter 44, Subchapter II.

Agency Responsibility: The Historic Preservation Review Board approves nominations to the Wisconsin State Register of Historic Places and the National Register of Historic Places upon recommendation of the State Historic Preservation Officer. (By statute, the director of the State Historical Society serves as the state officer or designates someone to do so.) The board approves the distribution of federal grants-in-aid for preservation; advises the state historical society; and requests comments from planning departments of affected municipalities, local landmark commissions, and local historical societies regarding properties being considered for nomination to the state and national registers. The board was created by Chapter 29, Laws of 1977.

Organization: The board consists of 15 members appointed by the governor to staggered 3-year terms. At least 9 must be professionally qualified in the areas of architecture, archaeology, art history, and history. Up to 6 members may be qualified in related fields, such as landscape architecture, urban and regional planning, law, or real estate.

Office of the Commissioner of
INSURANCE

> Address e-mail by combining the user ID and the state extender: userid@**wisconsin.gov**
> All telephone numbers are 608 area code unless otherwise indicated.

Commissioner: TED NICKEL, 267-3782, ted.nickel@

Deputy Commissioner: DAN SCHWARTZER, 267-1233, dan.schwartzer@

Insurance Administrator for Funds and Program Management: LOUIS CORNELIUS, 264-8113, louis.cornelius@

Legal Counsel: MOLLIE ZITO, 264-6017, mollie.zito@

Public Information Officer and Legislative Liaison: J.P. WIESKE, 266-2493, jp.wieske@

Regulation and Enforcement, Division of: GINA FRANK, *administrator,* 267-4384, gina.frank@

> *Financial Analysis and Examinations, Bureau of:* REBECCA EASLAND, *director,* 261-8562, rebecca.easland@

> *Market Regulation, Bureau of:* vacancy, *director.*

Mailing Address: P.O. Box 7873, Madison 53707-7873.

Location: 125 South Webster Street, Madison 53702.

Telephones: General: 266-3585; Agent licensing: 266-8699; Insurance complaint hotline: (800) 236-8517; Local Government Property Insurance Fund: (877) 229-0009 (Wisconsin only); State Life Insurance Fund: (800) 562-5558.

Fax: 266-9935.

Internet Address: http://oci.wi.gov

Publications: Annual reports; *Wisconsin Insurance News;* various pamphlets and materials for consumers, insurance companies, and agents. (Contact the Office of the Commissioner of Insurance.)

Number of Employees: 152.30.

Total Budget 2011-13: $208,169,400.

Statutory References: Section 15.73; Chapter 601.

Agency Responsibility: The Office of the Commissioner of Insurance supervises the insurance industry in Wisconsin. The office is responsible for examining insurance industry financial practices and market conduct, licensing insurance agents, reviewing policy forms for compliance with state insurance statutes and regulations, investigating consumer complaints, and providing consumer information. Its goals are to ensure the financial soundness of insurers doing business in Wisconsin; secure fair treatment by insurance companies and agents of policyholders and claimants; encourage industry self-regulation; emphasize loss prevention as part of good insurance practice; and educate the public on insurance issues.

The office administers two segregated insurance funds. The State Life Insurance Fund offers up to $10,000 of low-cost life insurance protection to any Wisconsin resident who meets prescribed risk standards. The Local Government Property Insurance Fund provides mandatory coverage for local governments against fire loss, as well as optional coverage for certain property damage they may incur.

The agency oversees activities of the Health Care Liability Insurance Plan, which provides liability coverage for hospitals, physicians, and other health care providers in Wisconsin, and the Injured Patients and Families Compensation Fund, which provides medical malpractice coverage for qualified health care providers on claims in excess of a provider's underlying coverage.

Organization: The commissioner of insurance is appointed by the governor with the advice and consent of the senate. The commissioner cannot be a candidate for public office and there are stringent restrictions on the commissioner's political activities. The commissioner appoints the deputy commissioner from outside the classified service and the division administrators from the classified service.

Unit Functions: The *Funds and Program Management Organizational Unit* contains the Management Analysis and Planning Section, the Information Technology Section, the Local Government Property Insurance Fund, and the State Life Insurance Fund. The first two sections are responsible for providing a variety of administrative services in support of all agency programs and employees. These services include budget, finance and accounting, receivables, certain procurement tasks, training and employee development, project management, and all IT services including help desk, applications development and support, security, e-mail, and network management. The two funds operate state programs providing property insurance for local units of government in Wisconsin, and basic life insurance for Wisconsin residents, respectively.

The *Division of Regulation and Enforcement* conducts field reviews of insurer underwriting, rating, claim handling, and marketing practices. It investigates insurance agent activities, prepares enforcement proceedings, and, in conjunction with the legal unit, prosecutes offenders. It helps consumers resolve problems with insurers and agents, and carries out the agency's consumer education program. Other duties include review of premium rates and insurance policy forms and contracts filed with the office to ensure their compliance with state law; review of insurer advertising files; and licensing and testing of insurance agents.

The division also conducts field examinations of the financial condition of insurers domiciled in Wisconsin and monitors the financial condition of insurers doing business in the state. It oversees insurer rehabilitations and liquidations, and audits and collects insurer taxes and fees. It incorporates the formation of new insurers and is responsible for the licensing of nondomestic insurers that want to do business in the state. It reviews and approves, as appropriate, transactions that result in the change of control or financial structure of domestic insurers. It also administers the fire department dues program in cooperation with the Department of Safety and Professional Services, whereby dues paid by insurers who provide fire coverage are disbursed to municipalities for fire protection and the fire fighters' pension and disability funds.

History: State regulation of insurance dates back to 1870 when Chapter 56 created a Department of Insurance in the secretary of state's office to license agents and, upon complaint, examine the books of fire and inland navigation insurance companies. In 1878 (Chapter 214), the legislature created a separate Department of Insurance, headed by a commissioner appointed by the governor, to perform these functions. From 1881 to 1911, based on Chapter 300, Laws of 1881, an elected commissioner administered the insurance department. With the enactment of Chapter 484, Laws of 1911, the insurance commissioner was again made an appointee. The 1967 executive branch reorganization act renamed the department the Office of the Commissioner of Insurance and continued it as an independent regulatory agency.

Other highlights include the development of the standard fire insurance contract in Chapter 195, Laws of 1891, and stricter regulation of the life insurance industry in 1907 to prevent fraud and misrepresentation. In 1911 and 1913, Wisconsin added coverage of local governments' property and buildings under the State Insurance Fund.

Wisconsin became the only state to establish a state life insurance fund for its residents under Chapter 577, Laws of 1911, which authorized the Department of Insurance to issue life insurance and annuity contracts. Since 1947 (Chapters 487 and 521), the office's responsibilities have included the review of all insurance policy forms and the filing of most premium rates. Wisconsin's current insurance laws are largely the result of a recodification developed between 1967 and 1979 by the Legislative Council and they have served as a basis for the model acts adopted by the National Association of Insurance Commissioners (an association of state insurance regulators).

Statutory Boards and Council

Insurance Security Fund, Board of Directors of the: TED NICKEL (insurance commissioner), J.B. VAN HOLLEN (attorney general), KURT SCHULLER (state treasurer); MARK J. BACKE, JOHN F. CLEARY, JAMES E. CRIST, DAVID G. DIERCKS, KENNETH ERLER, PETER C. FARROW, J. STANLEY HOFFERT, ALLEN OGILVIE, JANIS POTTER, SCOTT SEYMOUR, TOD J. ZACHARIAS (insurance industry representatives appointed by commissioner).

The Board of Directors of the Insurance Security Fund administers a fund that protects certain insurance policyholders and claimants from excessive delay and loss in the event of insurer liquidation. The fund consists of life, allocated annuity, health, HMO, property and casualty, and administrative accounts. The fund supports continuation of coverage under many life, annuity, and health policies. It is financed by assessments paid by most insurers in this state. The board may consist of 12 to 14 members but must include the attorney general, state treasurer, and insurance commissioner or their designees. The industry members must be chosen from representatives of insurers who are subject to the security fund law, and one member must be a representative of a service insurance corporation. The board's advice and recommendations to the commissioner are not subject to the state's open records law. The board was originally created in Chapter 144, Laws of 1969, with substantial revisions in Chapter 109, Laws of 1979, and its composition and duties are prescribed in Sections 646.12 and 646.13 of the statutes.

Injured Patients and Families Compensation Fund/Wisconsin Health Care Liability Insurance Plan, Board of Governors of the: TED NICKEL (insurance commissioner), *chairperson;* RANDY BLUMER, DAVID MAURER, LESLIE SVOBODA (insurance industry representatives appointed by commissioner); JOHN WALSH (named by State Bar of Wisconsin); M. ANGELA DENTICE (named by Wisconsin Association for Justice); ROBERT JAEGER, LINDA SYTH (named by Wisconsin Medical Society); RALPH TOPINKA (named by Wisconsin Hospital Association); CARLA BORDA, SUSAN ENGLER, CHRISTOPHER FLATTER, KATHRYN OSBORNE (public members appointed by governor).

The 13-member Board of Governors of the Injured Patients and Families Compensation Fund/Wisconsin Health Care Liability Insurance Plan oversees the health care liability plans for licensed physicians and nurse anesthetists, medical partnerships and corporations, cooperative sickness care associations, ambulatory surgery centers, hospitals, some nursing homes, and certain other health care providers. The board also supervises the Injured Patients and Families Compensation Fund, which pays medical malpractice claims in excess of a provider's underlying coverage. The 4 public members serve staggered 3-year terms, and at least 2 of them must not be attorneys or physicians nor be professionally affiliated with any hospital or insurance company. The insurance commissioner or the commissioner's designee, who must be an employee of the office of the commissioner, serves as chairperson. The board was created by the medical malpractice law, Chapter 37, Laws of 1975, and its composition and duties are prescribed in Sections 619.04 (3) and 655.27 of the statutes.

Injured Patients and Families Compensation Fund Peer Review Council: JOHN KELLY, *chairperson;* SANDRA OSBORN, vacancy (physicians); TOM KIRSCHBAUM, JEFF RENIER (public members).

The 5-member Injured Patients and Families Compensation Fund Peer Review Council reviews within one year of the first payment on a claim each claim for damages arising out of medical care provided by a health care provider or provider's employee, if the claim is paid by any of the following: the Patients Compensation Fund, a mandatory health care risk-sharing plan, a private health care liability insurer, or a self-insurer. The council can recommend adjustments in fees paid to the Injured Patients and Families Compensation Fund and the Wisconsin Health Care Liability Insurance Plan or premiums paid to private insurers, if requested by the insurer. The Board of Governors of the Injured Patients and Families Compensation Fund/Wisconsin Health Care Liability Insurance Plan appoints the council and designates its officers and the terms of the members. Not more than 3 members may be physicians. The chairperson must be a physician, who also serves as an *ex officio* nonvoting member of the Medical Examining Board. The council was created by 1985 Wisconsin Act 340, and its composition and duties are prescribed in Section 655.275 of the statutes.

State of Wisconsin
INVESTMENT BOARD

Members: LON ROBERTS, *chairperson;* THOMAS BOLDT, *vice chairperson;* DAVID A. STELLA (noneducator participant appointed by Wisconsin Retirement Board), *secretary;* MIKE HUEBSCH (secretary of administration); NORMAN CUMMINGS (representing Local Government Investment Pool participants); WAYNE D. MCCAFFERY (educator participant appointed by Teachers Retirement Board); BRUCE COLBURN, WILLIAM H. LEVIT, JR., vacancy. (Except as noted, the governor appoints the members with senate consent.)

Executive Director: MICHAEL WILLIAMSON, 266-9451.

Chief Financial Officer: CINDY KLIMKE, 266-9909.

Chief Investment Officer: DAVID VILLA, 266-9734.

Chief Legal Officer: JANE HAMBLEN, 266-8824.

Chief Operating Officer: LORI WERSAL, 266-2042.

Internal Audit Director: BRANDON BRICKNER, 261-6787.

Public Information Officer: VICKI HEARING, 261-2415, vicki.hearing@swib.state.wi.us

Mailing Address: P.O. Box 7842, Madison 53707-7842.

Location: 121 East Wilson Street, Madison.

Telephone: (608) 266-2381; Toll-Free Beneficiary Hotline: (800) 424-7942.

Fax: (608) 266-2436.

Internet Address: www.swib.state.wi.us

Agency E mail Address: info@swib.state.wi.us

Publications: Annual Report; Schedule of Investments.

Number of Employees: 145.10.

Total Budget 2011-13: $57,777,200.

Statutory References: Section 15.76; Chapter 25.

Agency Responsibility: The State of Wisconsin Investment Board is responsible for investing the assets of the Wisconsin Retirement System, the State Life Insurance Fund, the Local Government Property Insurance Fund, the State Historical Society of Wisconsin Endowment Trust Fund, the Injured Patients and Families Compensation Fund, the Tuition Trust Fund, and the State Investment Fund.

For purposes of investment, the retirement system's assets are divided into two funds. The Core Retirement Investment Trust is a broadly diversified portfolio of domestic and international common stocks, corporate and government bonds, and private markets that include real estate and private debt and equity. The Variable Retirement Investment Trust is invested primarily in common stocks. On December 31, 2012, Wisconsin Retirement System trust funds constituted 93% of the $91.1 billion managed by the Investment Board.

The State Investment Fund invests the commingled cash balances of various state and local government funds in short-term investments with earnings and losses distributed on a pro rata basis to the individual component funds. The fund encompasses the cash balance of the state's general fund and about 68 separate state funds, including the Children's Trust Fund, the Lottery Fund, the Recycling Fund, the Tuition Trust Fund, and the Wisconsin Election Campaign Fund, as well as various state agency accounts. Authorized local governments may participate by depositing moneys in the Local Government Investment Pool, which is a separate fund within the State Investment Fund.

Organization: Except for the secretary of administration, appointments to the 9-member board, which is a body corporate with power to sue and be sued, in its name, are for 6-year terms. The secretary of administration is an *ex officio* member. At least 4 of the 5 general members must have a minimum of 10 years investment experience, and none may have a financial interest in or be employed by a dealer or broker in securities, mortgages, or real estate investments. The sixth member appointed by the governor must have 10 years of financial experience and be an employee of a government that participates in the Local Government Investment Pool.

The board appoints the executive director and the internal auditor from outside the classified service. The executive director, with the participation of the board, appoints the chief investment officer, and the managing and investment directors from outside the classified service. All other professional employees are also appointed by the executive director from outside the classified service. Board employees may not have any direct or indirect financial interest in any firm engaged in the sale or marketing of real estate or investments or give paid investment advice to others.

History: Chapter 459, Laws of 1921, created a mandatory pension system for teachers and three separate boards to invest the annuity funds of public school, normal school, and university teachers. The 1929 Legislature created the State Annuity and Investment Board and made it responsible for investing the assets of the teachers' pension funds and other state funds, except the school funds that remained under control of the Commissioners of Public Lands (Chapter 491). The board also assumed oversight and asset management of funds for the newly created state employee pension system as the result of Chapter 176, Laws of 1943.

Chapter 511, Laws of 1951, replaced the three teacher retirement boards and the Annuity and Investment Board with the State Teachers Retirement Board and the State Investment Board, which was responsible for investing the assets of all non-Milwaukee teachers. Chapter 511 also granted the State Investment Board authority to invest the assets of the nonteaching, non-Milwaukee public employees who were covered under the Wisconsin Retirement Fund. Chapter 430, Laws of 1957, brought the funds of the Milwaukee teachers under the control of the State Investment Board. Chapter 96, Laws of 1981, consolidated all public employee retirement plans, with the exception of the City and County of Milwaukee, into the Wisconsin Retirement System, and the State Investment Board has continued to invest the retirement system funds. As a result of the consolidation, the retirement system is the ninth largest public pension fund in the U.S. and the 30th largest public or private pension fund worldwide.

Chapter 449, Laws of 1925, created a State Board of Deposits to insure state funds on deposit in state banks through a deposit fund, managed by the state treasurer under the direction of the board. The board's duties were to designate the banks in which state funds could be deposited and to specify the maximum amount of state funds each could receive. Participating banks paid into the deposit fund, which was designed to reimburse any losses incurred through bank failure.

Chapter 511, Laws of 1951, authorized the State Investment Board to invest the state's operating funds and directed it to carry out the investment functions of the State Board of Deposits. Although state funds had been invested since 1911, the 1951 reorganization increased the types of investments the board could consider for the funds it managed. Previously, the state's operating funds had been placed in noninterest bearing accounts. In 1957, the legislature created the State Investment Fund, which merged all state funds except for a handful that are reported separately. The Local Government Pooled-Investment Fund, created in 1976, allows local governments to invest their idle cash at competitive rates of return and withdraw it on a two-day notice with no penalty.

The position of chief investment officer was created by 1995 Wisconsin Act 274, which also provided for an internal audit function.

Although the board has always been subject to the prudent expert fiduciary standard of responsibility, the statutes specified a legal list of authorized investments until 2007. 2007 Wisconsin Act 212 made the prudent expert fiduciary standard the prevailing standard with respect to assets of the Wisconsin Retirement System, thereby overriding the legal list and other provisions in law that previously constrained the board's investment authority.

Department of
JUSTICE

Attorney General: J.B. VAN HOLLEN, 266-1221.

Deputy Attorney General: Kevin M. St. John, 266-1221.

Executive Assistant: Steven P. Means, 266-1221.

Communications, Office of: Dana Brueck, 266-1221.

Legislative Liaison, Office of: Mark Rinehart, 266-1221.

Public Affairs and Policy: Dean F. Stensberg, *director,* 266-1221.

Mailing Address: P.O. Box 7857, Madison 53707-7857.

Location: Attorney General's Office, 114 East, State Capitol; Department of Justice, 17 West Main Street, Madison.

Telephones: General: 266-1221; Arson Tip Line: (800) 362-3005; Office of Crime Victim Services: (800) 446-6564; Drug Tip Helpline: (800) 622-DRUG (622-3784); Amber Alert Hotline: (866) 65AMBER (652-6237); Consumer Protection: (800) 998-0700.

Fax: 267-2779.

Internet Address: www.doj.state.wi.us

Number of Employees: 609.49.

Total Budget 2011-13: $186,190,000.

Constitutional References: Article VI, Sections 1 and 3.

Statutory References: Section 15.25; Chapter 165.

Crime Victim Services, Office of: Jill J. Karofsky, *executive director,* 266-0109; Fax: 267-1938.

   Crime Victim Services: Kathy Zupan, *director,* 264-9484.

   Program Assistance and Administration: Cindy Grady, *director,* 264-6209.

   Victim Services: Christine Nolan, *director,* 267-5251.

Criminal Investigation, Division of: David Matthews, *administrator,* 266-1671; Patrick Mitchell, *deputy administrator,* 266-1671; Fax: 267-2777.

   Field Operations Bureau, Eastern Region: David Spakowicz, *director,* 266-1671.

   Field Operations Bureau, Western Region: Tina R. Virgil, *director,* 266-1671.

   Special Operations: Jody Wormet, *director,* 266-1671.

   State Fire Marshal: Michael L. Rindt, 266-1671.

Law Enforcement Services, Division of: Brian R. O'Keefe, *administrator,* 266-7052; David Zibolski, *deputy administrator,* 267-2232; Fax: 266-1656.

   Crime Information Bureau: Walter M. Neverman, *director,* 264-6207.

   Crime Laboratory System: Kevin E. Jones, *director,* 267-2224.

   Locations:

      Madison: 266-2031, 4626 University Avenue, Madison 53705-2174.

      Milwaukee: (414) 382-7500, 1578 South 11th Street, Milwaukee 53204-2860.

      Wausau: (715) 845-8626, 7100 West Stewart Avenue, Wausau 54401.

   Training and Standards Bureau: Tony Barthuly, *director,* 266-9606.

Legal Services, Division of: Kevin C. Potter, *administrator,* 266-0332.

   Civil Litigation Unit: Corey Finkelmeyer, *director,* 266-7234.

   Consumer Protection and Antitrust Unit: John Greene, *director,* 267-2162.

   Criminal Appeals Unit: Gregory Weber, *director,* 267-2167.

   Criminal Litigation and Public Integrity Unit: Roy Korte, *director,* 266-1447.

   Environmental Protection Unit: Thomas Dawson, *director,* 264-9442.

   Medicaid Fraud Control and Elder Abuse Unit: Thomas Storm, *director,* 266-9222.

DEPARTMENT OF JUSTICE

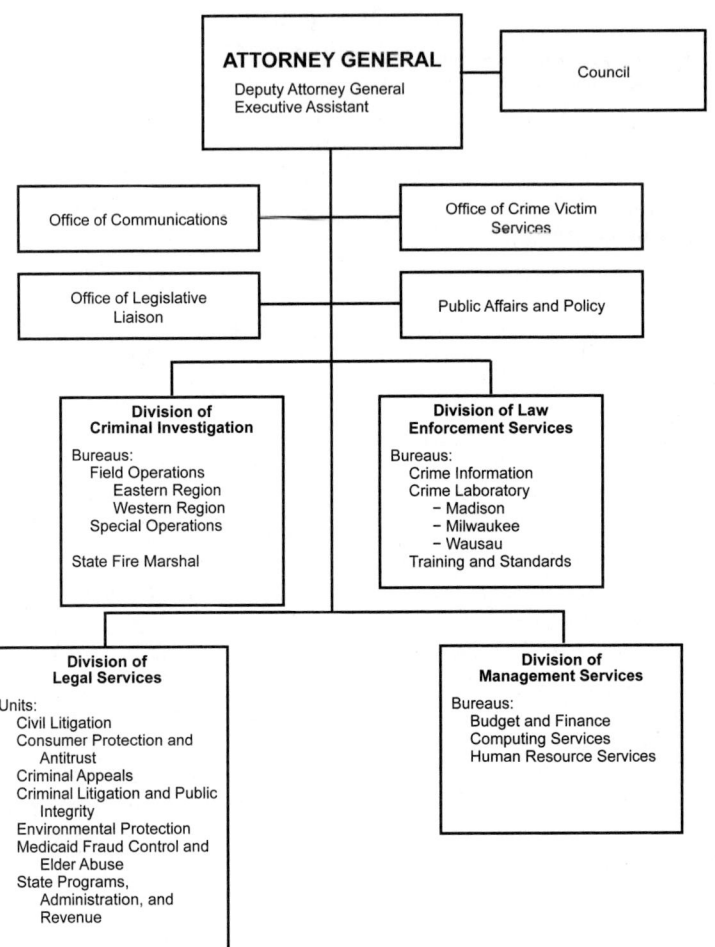

ATTORNEY GENERAL
Deputy Attorney General
Executive Assistant

Council

Office of Communications

Office of Crime Victim Services

Office of Legislative Liaison

Public Affairs and Policy

Division of Criminal Investigation

Bureaus:
Field Operations
    Eastern Region
    Western Region
Special Operations

State Fire Marshal

Division of Law Enforcement Services

Bureaus:
Crime Information
Crime Laboratory
    – Madison
    – Milwaukee
    – Wausau
Training and Standards

Division of Legal Services

Units:
Civil Litigation
Consumer Protection and
    Antitrust
Criminal Appeals
Criminal Litigation and Public
    Integrity
Environmental Protection
Medicaid Fraud Control and
    Elder Abuse
State Programs,
    Administration, and
    Revenue

Division of Management Services

Bureaus:
Budget and Finance
Computing Services
Human Resource Services

Units attached for administrative purposes under Sec. 15.03:   Crime Victims Rights Board
Law Enforcement Standards Board

State Programs, Administration, and Revenue Unit: CHARLOTTE GIBSON, *director,* 266-3952.

Management Services, Division of: BONNIE CYGANEK, *administrator,* 267-1300; Fax: 266-1656.

Budget and Finance, Bureau of: KAREN VAN SCHOONHOVEN, *director,* 267-6714.

Computing Services, Bureau of: vacancy, *director,* 266-7076.

Human Resource Services, Bureau of: MARY CASEY, *director,* 266-0461.

Publications: Opinions of the Attorney General; Annual Report; Criminal Investigation and Physical Evidence Handbook; Domestic Abuse Incident Report; Law Enforcement Bulletin; Safe Schools Legal Resource Manual; *When Crime Strikes: Injured Victims Can Get Help;* Wisconsin Law Enforcement Film Catalog; *Wisconsin Open Meetings Law: A Citizen's Guide; Wisconsin Open Meetings Law: A Compliance Guide; Wisconsin Public Records Law;* Wisconsin Prosecutor's Newsletter; Wisconsin Resource Directory for Crime Victims.

Agency Responsibility: The Department of Justice provides legal advice and representation, criminal investigation, and various law enforcement services for the state. It represents the state in civil cases and handles criminal cases that reach the Wisconsin Court of Appeals or the Wisconsin Supreme Court. It also represents the state in criminal cases on appeal in federal courts and participates with other states in federal cases that are important to Wisconsin. The department provides legal representation in lower courts when expressly authorized by law or requested by the governor, either house of the legislature, or a state agency head. It also represents state agencies in court reviews of their administrative decisions.

Organization: The Department of Justice is supervised by the attorney general, a constitutional officer who is elected on a partisan ballot to a 4-year term. The attorney general appoints the deputy attorney general, the executive assistant, the department's division administrators, and the executive director of the Office of Crime Victim Services. With the exception of the administrator of the Division of Criminal Investigation, which is a classified position, all of these positions serve at the pleasure of the attorney general.

Unit Functions: The *Office of Crime Victim Services* administers state and federal funding to programs that assist victims of crime. Three programs receive full or partial funding from surcharges assessed against convicted criminals: the Crime Victim Compensation Program reimburses eligible victims and their dependents for medical and other qualifying expenses; the Sexual Assault Victim Services (SAVS) Program provides grants to nonprofit organizations that offer services to sexual assault victims; and the Victim/Witness Assistance Program partially reimburses counties for their costs of providing services to crime victims and witnesses. Federal funding supports four programs: the Wisconsin Victim Resource Center, which assists victims in understanding and exercising their statutory and constitutional crime victims' rights, the Victims of Crime Act (VOCA) Program that provides grants to programs to provide direct services to innocent victims of crime; the Children's Justice Act, which supports improved investigation, prosecution, and judicial handling of child abuse and neglect; and the Crime Victim Compensation Program.

The *Division of Criminal Investigation,* created in Section 15.253 (2), Wisconsin Statutes, by 1991 Wisconsin Act 269, investigates crimes that are statewide in nature or importance. Special agents work closely with local officials to investigate and prosecute crimes involving homicide, arson, drug trafficking, illegal gaming, crimes against children, financial crimes, multijurisdictional crimes, computer crimes, homeland security, public integrity, and government fraud. The division provides extensive training to local, state, and federal officers.

The *Division of Law Enforcement Services* provides advanced technical services, information, and training to state and local law enforcement agencies and jails. It maintains central fingerprint identification records and computerized criminal history information, operates the Handgun Hotline, and provides criminal history background check services. The statewide telecommunications system links Wisconsin criminal justice agencies to national, state, and local crime files and databases. The crime laboratory system with locations in Madison, Milwaukee, and Wausau, analyzes forensic evidence for the Wisconsin criminal justice system and provides crime scene response in major cases.

The division administers standards and basic recruit training for statewide criminal justice professionals including law enforcement, tribal law enforcement, jail, and secure juvenile detention officers. The division maintains and enforces certification and annual recertification training standards for law enforcement, jail, and secure detention officers, instructors, and training academies. It collaborates extensively with advisory committees and criminal justice training professionals in developing and delivering law enforcement curriculum. It also promotes and provides timely and accurate training, records, reimbursements, and reference information for law enforcement, jail, and secure detention officers.

The *Division of Legal Services* provides legal representation and advice to the governor, legislature, other state officers and agencies, district attorneys, and county corporation counsels. It also provides training and education to all district attorneys and assistant district attorneys. It enforces state environmental, antitrust, employment, consumer protection, and Medicaid fraud laws. It also prosecutes economic crimes and represents the state in all felony appeals and litigation brought by prison inmates. At the request of district attorneys, the division provides special prosecutors in complex homicide, drug, and white collar and other criminal cases. It defends the state in civil lawsuits filed against the state or its officers and employees and handles matters related to public records, Indian law, and fair housing.

The *Division of Management Services* prepares the agency budget; manages agency personnel, finances, and facilities; and provides information technology services.

History: When Wisconsin became a territory in 1836, the U.S. President appointed the attorney general. In 1839, a territorial act gave the governor the power to appoint the attorney general with the consent of the Legislative Council (the upper house of the territorial legislature) to a term of 3 years. The Wisconsin Constitution, as adopted in 1848, provided for an elected attorney general with a 2-year term. A constitutional amendment ratified in 1967 increased the term to 4 years, effective in 1971.

Chapter 75, Laws of 1967, named the agency headed by the attorney general the Department of Justice and transferred to its control the State Crime Laboratory, the arson investigation program from the Commissioner of Insurance, and the criminal investigation functions of the Beverage and Cigarette Tax Division of the Department of Revenue. The 1975 Legislature returned alcohol and tobacco tax enforcement to the Department of Revenue.

The 1969 Legislature added enforcement of certain laws related to dangerous drugs, narcotics, and organized crime to the duties of the department and created the public intervenor to intervene in or initiate proceedings to protect public rights in water and other natural resources. In Chapter 189, Laws of 1979, the legislature transferred the crime victims program from the Department of Industry, Labor and Human Relations to the Department of Justice. 1995 Wisconsin Act 27 transferred the public intervenor to the Department of Natural Resources and consumer protection functions to the Department of Agriculture, Trade and Consumer Protection.

Attorney General J.B. Van Hollen speaks at the Wisconsin State Crime Laboratory in Milwaukee. The news conference was held to promote the national Prescription Drug "Take Back" Day, designed to combat prescription drug abuse. Also participating were representatives from the federal Drug Enforcement Administration, the Wisconsin Department of Natural Resources, and local law enforcement authorities. (Department of Justice)

Statutory Council

Crime Victims Council: MICHELLE G. ARROWOOD, GAYLE M. PATRAW (victim services representatives); KURT D. HEUER (law enforcement representative); BRAD D. SCHIMEL (district attorney representative); SCOTT L. HORNE (judicial representative); AVE M. BIE, CHRIS H. DANOU, TOM EAGON, CHARLES S. MCGEE, MARION MORGAN, MALLORY E. O'BRIEN, MICHAEL S. ROGOWSKI, ANNA M. RUZINSKI, WILLIAM SWANSON, vacancy (citizen members). (All are appointed by attorney general.)

The 15-member Crime Victims Council provides advice and recommendations on victims' rights issues and legislation. Members are appointed for staggered 3-year terms, and the 10 citizen members must have demonstrated sensitivity and concern for crime victims. The council was created by Chapter 189, Laws of 1979, as the Crime Victims Compensation Council. It was renamed in Chapter 20, Laws of 1981, and its duties and composition are prescribed in Sections 15.09 (5) and 15.257 (2) of the statutes.

INDEPENDENT UNITS ATTACHED FOR BUDGETING, PROGRAM COORDINATION, AND RELATED MANAGEMENT FUNCTIONS BY SECTION 15.03 OF THE STATUTES

CRIME VICTIMS RIGHTS BOARD

Members: TIMOTHY GRUENKE (district attorney appointed by Wisconsin District Attorneys' Association); PAUL SUSIENKA (local law enforcement representative appointed by the attorney general); TRISHA ANDERSON (county provider of victim and witness services appointed by attorney general); CHARLES S. MCGEE (citizen member appointed by the Crime Victims Council); CARMEN PITRE (citizen member appointed by governor).

Statutory References: Sections 15.255 (2) and 950.09.

The 5-member Crime Victims Rights Board may review and investigate complaints filed by victims of crime regarding their rights. The board is an independent agency. The Department of Justice provides staff to help administer the duties of the board, but actions of the board are not subject to approval or review by the attorney general. The board may issue a private or public reprimand against a public official or agency that violates a crime victim's rights; refer a possible violation of a victim's rights by a judge to the judicial commission; seek appropriate relief on behalf of a crime victim necessary to protect that person's rights; or seek a forfeiture up to $1,000 against a public officer or agency for intentional violations. The board can also issue reports and recommendations regarding victims' rights and service provision.

Members serve 4-year terms. The 2 citizen members may not be employed in law enforcement, by a district attorney, or by a county board to provide crime victim's services. The board was created by 1997 Wisconsin Act 181.

LAW ENFORCEMENT STANDARDS BOARD

Members: TERRI SMOCZYK (law enforcement representative), *chairperson;* JOSEPH COLLINS (law enforcement representative), *vice chairperson;* LISA GERBIG, NATHAN HENRIKSEN, SCOTT E. PEDLEY, LAURA WASHER (law enforcement representatives); TIMOTHY BAXTER (district attorney); GARY CUSKEY, JON KOCH (local government representatives); JEAN GALASINSKI (public member); STEVEN FITZGERALD (designated by secretary of transportation), BRIAN O'KEEFE (designated by attorney general), JOHN MURRAY (executive director, Office of Justice Assistance), RANDY STARK (designated by secretary of natural resources). Nonvoting member: G.B. JONES (special agent in charge, Milwaukee FBI Office). (All except *ex officio* members are appointed by governor.)

Secretary: BRIAN O'KEEFE, *administrator,* Division of Law Enforcement Services, P.O. Box 7857, Madison 53707-7857.

Statutory References: Sections 15.255 and 165.85.

Agency Responsibility: The 15-member Law Enforcement Standards Board sets minimum employment, education, and training standards for law enforcement, tribal law enforcement, and jail and secure detention officers. It certifies persons who meet professional standards as qualified to be officers. The board consults with other government agencies regarding the development of training schools and courses, conducts research to improve law enforcement and jail administration and performance, and evaluates governmental units' compliance with standards. Its appointed members serve staggered 4-year terms. The law enforcement representatives must include at least one sheriff and one chief of police. The public member cannot be employed in law enforcement. Chapter 466, Laws of 1969, created the board.

Curriculum Advisory Committee: DANIEL BURGESS, KURT HEUER, JOHN MORRISSEY, RICHARD OLIVA, MICHAEL STEFFES (police chiefs); DARRELL BERGLIN, RON CRAMER, DAVID GRAVES, DAVID PETERSON, TERRY VOGEL, RANDY WRIGHT (sheriffs); CHRISTOPHER NEUMAN (training director, Wisconsin State Patrol); CLARK PAGEL (nonvoting consultant representing Wisconsin Technical College System) (police chiefs and sheriffs appointed by Law Enforcement Standards Board).

The 13-member Curriculum Advisory Committee advises the Law Enforcement Standards Board on the establishment of curriculum requirements for training of law enforcement, tribal law enforcement, and jail and secure detention officers. The statutes do not stipulate length of terms. Chapter 466, Laws of 1969, created the committee and its composition and duties are prescribed in Section 165.85 (3) (d) of the statutes.

Department of
MILITARY AFFAIRS

Commander in Chief: GOVERNOR SCOTT WALKER.

Adjutant General: BRIGADIER GENERAL DONALD P. DUNBAR, 242-3001, donald.p.dunbar@us.army.mil

Deputy Adjutant General for Army: BRIG. GEN. MARK E. ANDERSON, 242-3010, mark.e.anderson2@us.army.mil

Deputy Adjutant General for Air: BRIG. GEN. GARY L. EBBEN, 242-3020, gary.l.ebben@ang.af.mil

Executive Assistant: MICHAEL T. HINMAN, 242-3009, michael.t.hinman@us.army.mil

Mailing Address: P.O. Box 8111, Madison 53708-8111.

Location: 2400 Wright Street, Madison 53704-2572.

Telephones: General: 242-3000; Division of Emergency Management: 242-3232; 24-hour hotline for emergencies and hazardous materials spills: (800) 943-0003.

Fax: 242-3111; Division of Emergency Management: 242-3247.

Internet Address: Department of Military Affairs and Wisconsin National Guard: http://dma.wi.gov; Wisconsin Emergency Management: http://emergencymanagement.wi.gov; Wisconsin Homeland Security: http://homelandsecurity.wi.gov

Number of State Employees: 416.56.

Total State Budget 2011-13: $165,185,800.

Total Federal Budget: Approximately $306 million annually.

Constitutional References: Article IV, Section 29; Article V, Section 4.

Statutory References: Sections 15.31 and 15.313; Chapters 321, 322, and 323.

Adjutant General Staff:

Assistant Adjutant General – Readiness and Training: BRIG. GEN. MARK J. MICHIE, mark.j.michie.mil@mail.mil

U.S. Property and Fiscal Office: COL. JOHN VAN DE LOOP, (608) 427-7266, john.vandeloop@us.army.mil

Inspector General: COL. DAVID M. SEARS, 242-3086, david.m.sears6.mil@mail.mil

Director of Communications: MAJ. PAUL RICKERT, 242-3050, paul.j.rickert.mil@mail.mil

Staff Judge Advocate: LT. COL. DAVID M. DZIOBKOWSKI, 242-3073, david.m.dziobkowski.mil@mail.mil

DEPARTMENT OF MILITARY AFFAIRS

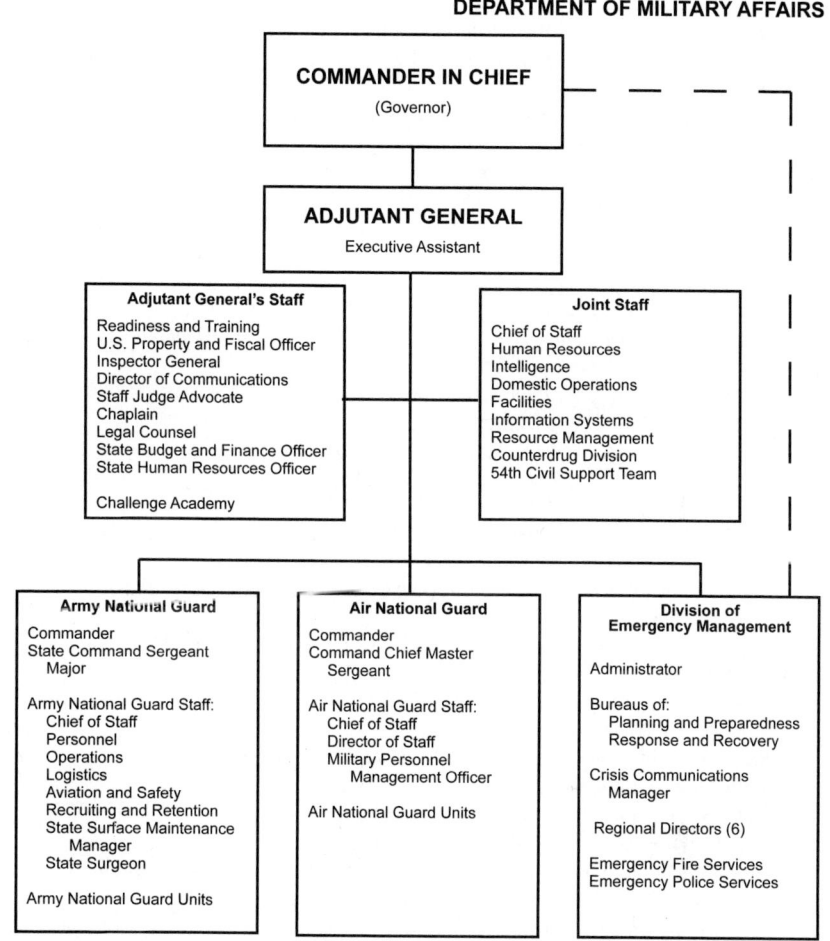

COMMANDER IN CHIEF
(Governor)

ADJUTANT GENERAL
Executive Assistant

Adjutant General's Staff

Readiness and Training
U.S. Property and Fiscal Officer
Inspector General
Director of Communications
Staff Judge Advocate
Chaplain
Legal Counsel
State Budget and Finance Officer
State Human Resources Officer

Challenge Academy

Joint Staff

Chief of Staff
Human Resources
Intelligence
Domestic Operations
Facilities
Information Systems
Resource Management
Counterdrug Division
54th Civil Support Team

Army National Guard

Commander
State Command Sergeant
 Major

Army National Guard Staff:
 Chief of Staff
 Personnel
 Operations
 Logistics
 Aviation and Safety
 Recruiting and Retention
 State Surface Maintenance
  Manager
 State Surgeon

Army National Guard Units

Air National Guard

Commander
Command Chief Master
 Sergeant

Air National Guard Staff:
 Chief of Staff
 Director of Staff
 Military Personnel
  Management Officer

Air National Guard Units

**Division of
Emergency Management**

Administrator

Bureaus of:
 Planning and Preparedness
 Response and Recovery

Crisis Communications
 Manager

Regional Directors (6)

Emergency Fire Services
Emergency Police Services

Chaplain: MAJ. DOUGLAS HEDMAN, 242-3450, douglas.hedman@us.army.mil

Legal Counsel: RANDI WIND MILSAP, 242-3072, randi.milsap@wisconsin.gov

State Budget and Finance Officer: BRETT COOMBER, 242-3155, brett.coomber@wisconsin.gov

State Human Resources Officer: LYNN E. BOODRY, 242-3163, lynn.boodry@wisconsin.gov

Wisconsin National Guard Challenge Academy (Fort McCoy): COL. (RET.) MARK MURPHY, *director,* (608) 269-9000, director@challenge.dma.state.wi.us

Joint Staff:

Chief of Staff: BRIG. GEN. JOHN E. MCCOY, 242-3006, john.mccoy@us.army.mil

Human Resources (J1), Director of Manpower and Personnel: COL. JOHN SCHROEDER, 242-3552, john.schroeder@us.army.mil

Intelligence (J2), Director of Security and Intelligence: LT. COL. VIRGINIA L. EGLI, 242-3038, virginia.l.egli.mil@mail.mil

Domestic Operations (J3/5/7), Director of Domestic Operations and Strategic Plans: COL. JULIE M. GERETY, 242-3530, julie.m.gerety.mil@mail.mil

Facilities (J4), Director of Installation Management: COL. JEFFREY J. LIETHEN, 242-3365, jeffrey.liethen@wisconsin.gov

Information Systems (J6), Director of Information Systems: COL. STEVEN LEWIS, 242-3650, steven.lewis2@us.army.mil

Resource Management, Director of Property and Fiscal Operations: COL. DANIEL SAILER, (608) 427-7212, daniel.sailer@us.army.mil

Director of Counterdrug Division: COL. TIM C. LAWSON, 242-3540, tim.c.lawson.mil@mail.mil

Commander, 54th Civil Support Team (CST): LT. COL. DAVID W. MAY, 245-8431, david.w.may16.mil@mail.mil

Wisconsin Army National Guard: BRIG. GEN. MARK E. ANDERSON, *assistant adjutant general for the army,* 242-3010, mark.e.anderson2@us.army.mil

    State Command Sergeant Major: COMMAND SGT. MAJ. BRADLEY SHIELDS, 242-3012, bradley.j.shields.mil@mail.mil

    Army National Guard Staff:

      Chief of Staff, Army Staff: COL. KENNETH A. KOON, 242-3030, kenneth.koon@us.army.mil

      Deputy Chief of Staff for Personnel (G1): COL. JOANE K. MATHEWS, 242-3444, joni.mathews@us.army.mil

      Deputy Chief of Staff for Operations (G3): LT. COL. PETER ANDERSON, 242-3500, peter.k.anderson@us.army.mil

      Deputy Chief of Staff for Logistics (G4): LT. COL. GALEN D. WHITE, 242-3584, galen.d.white.mil@mail.mil

      Deputy Chief of Staff for Aviation and Safety: LT. COL. RUSSELL J. SWEET, 242-3140, russell.j.sweet@us.army.mil

      Recruiting and Retention Command: LT. COL. ERIC J. KILLEN, 242-3804, eric.killen@us.army.mil

      State Surface Maintenance Manager: LT. COL. KENNETH G. UTING, (608) 427-7223, kenneth.g.uting.mil@mail.mil

      State Surgeon: COL. KENNETH K. LEE, 242-3443, kenneth.k.lee@us.army.mil

    Army National Guard Units (major commands):

      32nd Infantry Brigade Combat Team (Camp Douglas): COL. TIM C. LAWSON, *commander,* tim.c.lawson.mil@mail.mil; LT. COL. MICHAEL J. GEORGE, *administrative officer,* (608) 427-7349, michael.j.george@us.army.mil

      157th Maneuver Enhancement Brigade (Milwaukee): COL. JOHN SCHROEDER, *commander,* (414) 961-8682, john.schroeder@us.army.mil

      64th Troop Command (Madison): COL. PAUL F. RUSSELL, *commander and administrative officer,* 242-3840, paul.f.russell@us.army.mil

      426th Regiment (Wisconsin Military Academy) (Fort McCoy): COL. RICHARD J. BORKOWSKI, *commander;* LT. COL. GARY R. THOMPSON, *administrative officer,* (608) 388-9990, gary.r.thompson1@us.army.mil

Wisconsin Air National Guard: BRIG. GEN. GARY L. EBBEN, *assistant adjutant general for air,* 242-3020, gary.l.ebben@ang.af.mil

    Command Chief Master Sergeant: COMMAND CHIEF MASTER SGT. GREGORY A. CULLEN, gregory.a.cullen@ang.af.mil

    Air National Guard Staff:

      Chief of Staff, Air Staff: BRIG. GEN. JOHN E. MCCOY.

      Director of Staff: COL. JOHN PUTTRE, 242-3120, john.puttre@ang.af.mil

Military Personnel Management Officer: LT. COL. BRIAN S. BUHLER, 242-3122, brian.buhler@ang.af.mil

Air National Guard Units (major commands):

  115th Fighter Wing (Madison): COL. JEFFREY WIEGAND, *commander,* 245-4501, jeffrey.j.wiegand.mil@mail.mil

  128th Air Refueling Wing (Milwaukee): COL. EDWARD E. METZGAR, *commander,* (414) 944-8333, edward.metzgar@ang.af.mil

  Volk Field Combat Readiness Training Center (Camp Douglas): COL. DAVID L. ROMUALD, *commander,* (608) 427-1200, david.romuald@ang.af.mil

Emergency Management, Division of: BRIAN M. SATULA, *administrator,* 242-3210, brian.satula@wisconsin.gov

  Planning and Preparedness, Bureau of: GREG ENGLE, *director,* 242-3203, greg.engle@wisconsin.gov

  Response and Recovery, Bureau of: PATRICK O'CONNOR, *director,* 242-3204, patrick.oconnor@wisconsin.gov

  Response Section Supervisor: MARK GREENWOOD, 242-3336, mark.greenwood@wisconsin.gov

  Crisis Communications Manager: LORI GETTER, 242-3239, lori.getter@wisconsin.gov

  Southwest Regional Office (Madison): PAUL FRANCE, *director,* 242-5389, paul.france@wisconsin.gov

  East Central Regional Office (Fond du Lac): STEVE FENSKE, *director,* (920) 929-3730, steve.fenske@wisconsin.gov

  Northeast Regional Office (Wausau): MICHELLE HARTNESS, *director and response section supervisor,* (715) 845-9517, michelle.hartness@wisconsin.gov

  Northwest Regional Office (Spooner): RANDY BOOKS, *director,* (715) 635-8704, randy.books@wisconsin.gov

  Southeast Regional Office (Waukesha): BEN SCHLIESMAN, *director,* (262) 782-1515, ben.schliesman@wisconsin.gov

  West Central Regional Office (Eau Claire): LISA OLSON MCDONALD, *director,* (715) 839-3825, lisa.olsonmcdonald@wisconsin.gov

  Emergency Fire Services: KEITH TVEIT, *coordinator,* (608) 220-6049, keith.tveit@wisconsin.gov

  Emergency Police Services: vacancy, *coordinator,* (608) 444-0003.

Publications: *@Ease Express;* Wisconsin Emergency Management *Digest;* Wisconsin Homeland Security *Homefront.*

Agency Responsibility: The Department of Military Affairs provides an armed military force through the Wisconsin National Guard, which is organized, trained, equipped, and available for deployment under official orders in state and national emergencies. The federal mission of the National Guard is to provide trained units to the U.S. Army and U.S. Air Force in time of war or national emergency. Its state mission is to assist civil authorities, protect life and property, and preserve peace, order, and public safety in times of natural or human-caused emergencies.

The *Division of Emergency Management* is headed by a division administrator appointed by the governor with the advice and consent of the senate. It coordinates the development and implementation of the state emergency operations plan; provides assistance to local jurisdictions in the development of their programs and plans; administers private and federal disaster and emergency relief funds; administers the Wisconsin Disaster Fund; and maintains the state's 24-hour duty officer reporting and response system. The division also conducts training programs in emergency planning for businesses and state and local officials, as well as educational programs for the general public. Under Title III of the federal 1986 Superfund Amendments and Reauthorization Act and 1987 Wisconsin Act 342, the division requires public and private entities that possess hazardous substances to file reports on these substances. It establishes local

A Wisconsin Army National Guard UH-60 Black Hawk helicopter from the Madison-based Army Aviation Support Facility 2 drops water on hot spots in the Douglas County wildfire in May 2013. Two helicopters from the unit supported local firefighting efforts. (Department of Natural Resources)

emergency response committees and oversees implementation of their plans and corresponding state plans. The division administers emergency planning performance grants that assist local emergency planning committees in complying with state and federal law. In addition, the division contracts with regional hazardous materials response teams which respond to the most dangerous levels of hazardous substance releases. It also coordinates planning and training for off-site radiological emergencies at nuclear power plants in and near Wisconsin. The Emergency Police Services (EPS) program provides support to law enforcement in times of crisis. The program coordinates state law enforcement response to emergencies, including coordination of mutual aid for law enforcement assistance in natural disasters, prison disturbances, and other emergencies. The Emergency Fire Services Coordinator enhances fire service emergency response throughout the state and coordinates intrastate mutual aid through the Mutual Aid Box Alarm System (MABAS).

A key resource within Wisconsin Emergency Management (WEM) is its system of 6 regional offices located throughout the state. The regional offices are co-located with the Wisconsin State Patrol regional posts in Waukesha, Fond du Lac, Eau Claire, Spooner, and Wausau, and at WEM's central office in Madison. Each office is assigned to work with a group of 8 to 14 counties. Regional directors are knowledgeable in each of the division's programs, and support both municipal and county programs in planning, training, exercising, response and recovery activities, as well as the coordination of administrative activities between the division and local governments. When disasters and emergencies strike, regional directors are the division's initial responders, serving as field liaisons for the State Emergency Operations Center.

Organization: The Wisconsin Constitution designates the governor as the commander in chief of the Wisconsin National Guard. The department is directed by the adjutant general, who is appointed by the governor for a 5 year term and may serve successive terms. The adjutant general must be an officer actively serving in the Army or Air National Guard of Wisconsin who has attained at least the rank of colonel and is fully qualified to hold the rank of major general in either the Army or Air National Guard.

In addition to state support, the Wisconsin National Guard is also funded and maintained by the federal government, and when it is called up in an active federal duty status, the president of the United States becomes its commander in chief. The federal government provides arms and ammunition, equipment and uniforms, major outdoor training facilities, pay for military and support personnel, and training and supervision. The state provides personnel; conducts training as required under the National Defense Act; and shares the cost of constructing, maintaining, and operating armories and other military facilities. The composition of Wisconsin Army and Air National Guard units is authorized by the U.S. secretary of defense through the National Guard Bureau. All officers and enlisted personnel must meet the same physical, education, and other eligibility requirements as members of the active-duty U.S. Army or U.S. Air Force.

History: Until the 20th century, the United States relied heavily on military units organized by the states to fight its wars. Known as "minutemen" in the American Revolution, state militias, which could be called up on brief notice, provided soldiers for the Revolutionary War, the Mexican War, the Civil War, and the Spanish-American War.

In 1792, the U.S. Congress passed a law that required all able-bodied men between 18 and 45 years of age to serve in local militia units, a provision that was incorporated into the territorial statutes of Wisconsin. The Wisconsin Constitution, as adopted in 1848, authorized the legislature to determine the composition, organization, and discipline of the state militia.

The 1849 Wisconsin Statutes specified the procedure for the organization of locally controlled "uniform companies". Each uniform company included 30 men who had to equip themselves with arms and uniforms.

By 1858 (Chapter 87), the legislature provided for the organization of the state militia, which ultimately replaced the uniform companies. As commander in chief of the militia, the governor appointed the adjutant general and the general officers and issued commissions to the elected officers of uniform companies. The governor could provide arms for the officers, but they were required to supply their own uniforms and horses. Not until 1873 (Chapter 202) was money appropriated from the general fund to help support militia companies. Chapter 208, Laws of 1879, changed the militia's name to the Wisconsin National Guard.

Federal supervision of and financial responsibility for the National Guard came with Congressional passage of the Dick Act in 1903. Congress passed the law in response to the lack of uniformity among state units, which became evident during the Spanish-American War and subsequent occupation of the Philippines. The act set standards for Guard units, granted federal aid, and provided for inspections by regular U.S. Army officers.

The National Defense Act of 1933 formally created the National Guard of the United States, a reserve component of the U.S. Army. The act allowed the mobilization of intact National Guard units through their simultaneous dual enlistment as state and federal military forces. This permitted Guard personnel to mobilize for federal duty directly from state status in event of a federal emergency, rather than being discharged to enlist in the federal forces, as was done in World War I. A 1990 U.S. Supreme Court case upheld the authority of the U.S. Congress to send Army National Guard units (under U.S. Army command) out of the country to train for their federal mission.

Wisconsin National Guard troops fought in the Civil War, the Spanish-American War, World War I, and World War II. Wisconsin troops from the "Iron Brigade" gained national recognition in the Civil War, and the 32nd "Red Arrow" Infantry Division won fame for its combat record in both World Wars. The Wisconsin Air National Guard became a separate service in 1947, and members of the Wisconsin Air Guard served in the Korean War. Over the past 50 years, Wisconsin units have been called to active federal service on numerous occasions. In 1961, the 32nd Division was activated during the Berlin Crisis. More than 1,400 Guard members from Wisconsin were sent to the Persian Gulf to participate in Operations Desert Shield and Desert Storm in 1990-91. Beginning in 1996, units were called to support peacekeeping efforts in the Balkans. Wisconsin Air National Guard units were deployed to enforce U.N. no-fly zones in Southwest Asia in the 1990s, and two units were called to support Operation Allied Force, the NATO air operations over Kosovo in 1999.

Within hours of the September 11, 2001, terrorist attacks on America, the Wisconsin National Guard began yet another period of extensive support to U.S. military operations. Air National Guard units in Wisconsin have provided fighter aircraft to patrol the skies over major U.S. cities and critical national infrastructure, tanker aircraft to refuel patrolling fighters and U.S. military aircraft overseas, and critical radar support to North American Aerospace Defense Command and the Federal Aviation Administration.

Wisconsin Army National Guard units began mobilizing into active federal service in December 2001. Since then, nearly every unit in the Wisconsin Army and Air National Guard has been ordered to active duty in support of operations in Afghanistan (Operation Enduring Freedom) and Iraq (Operation Iraqi Freedom and Operation New Dawn), as well as homeland defense missions in the United States (Operation Noble Eagle) and continuing operations in the Balkans. In 2009, nearly 4,000 Wisconsin Guard members deployed in support of the Global War on Terror including 3,200 members of the 32nd Infantry Brigade Combat Team who conducted the largest operational deployment of the Wisconsin National Guard since World War II. Since 2001, nearly 13,000 Wisconsin Guard members have deployed in support of the Global War on Terror.

However, while the soldiers and airmen of the state's militia continue to deploy overseas and serve in harm's way when America calls, they remain available to answer the call to service in Wisconsin and throughout the nation when a natural disaster strikes or in response to domestic emergencies. The Wisconsin National Guard has provided domestic support to the citizens of Wisconsin since the 1880s. It has assisted state and local authorities with personnel and equipment during natural disasters such as forest fires, floods, tornadoes, and snowstorms. It has also assisted local authorities in restoring order during periods of civil unrest during the late 1960s and early 1970s, as well as provided support to 25 state institutions during a state employee strike in 1977. The Wisconsin National Guard has provided assistance to other states and nations for such major catastrophic events as Hurricane Katrina and the 2010 Haiti earthquake. The most recent large-scale domestic service of the Wisconsin National Guard occurred in June 2008 when over 1,000 Wisconsin Guard members assisted state and local authorities in the response to widespread flooding across the southern part of the state.

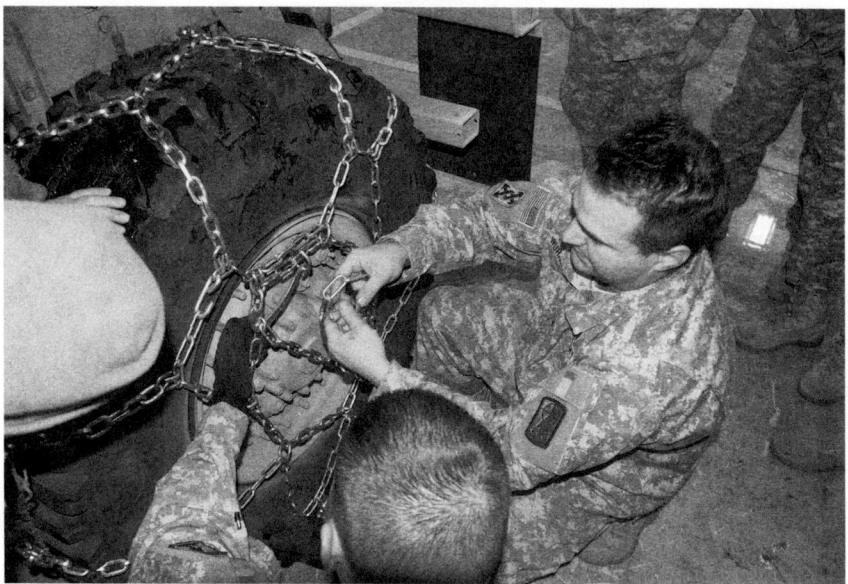

Soldiers from the Wisconsin National Guard's 108th Forward Support Company and Battery A, 1st Battalion, 121st Field Artillery in Sussex, Wisconsin, place tire chains on a military vehicle in preparation for supporting Division of Emergency Management efforts during a major snowstorm that hit the state in December 2012. (Wisconsin National Guard photo by 1st Lt. Joe Trovato)

The **Division of Emergency Management** originated as the Office of Civil Defense, which was developed to administer emergency programs in case of enemy attack and was located in the governor's office under Chapter 443, Laws of 1951. Its predecessors include the Wisconsin Council of Defense, organized by executive order of Governor Julius P. Heil in 1940, and the State Council on Civil Defense, created in the governor's office by Chapter 9, Laws of 1943. The 1943 council was abolished in 1945 and its functions transferred to the adjutant general, who was appointed director of the Office of Civil Defense by the governor, as permitted in the 1951 law.

Chapter 628, Laws of 1959, renamed the office the Bureau of Civil Defense and added responsibilities for natural and human-caused disasters. The 1967 executive branch reorganization transferred the bureau to the Department of Local Affairs and Development as the Division of Emergency Government. In Chapter 361, Laws of 1979, the division was transferred to the Department of Administration. The division became part of the Department of Military Affairs in 1989 Wisconsin Act 31 and was renamed by 1995 Wisconsin Act 247. When 1997 Wisconsin Act 27 abolished the State Emergency Response Board, the division assumed the board's responsibilities pertaining to hazardous chemical substances and spills and the contracts with regional hazardous materials response teams. Since 1997, Wisconsin Emergency Management has coordinated the state's terrorism preparedness efforts by working to deter, prevent, respond to, and recover from terrorist attacks. The Wisconsin Homeland Security Council was initially created in March 2003 (Executive Order 7) and recreated in January 2011 (Executive Order 6) to advise the governor and coordinate the efforts of state and local officials regarding the prevention of, and response to, potential threats to the homeland security of the state.

Department of
NATURAL RESOURCES

Address e-mail by combining the user ID and the state extender: userid@**wisconsin.gov**
All telephone numbers are 608 area code unless otherwise indicated.

Natural Resources Board: PRESTON COLE (southern member), *chairperson;* TERRY N. HILGENBERG (northern member), *vice chairperson;* GREGORY KAZMIERSKI (southern member), *secretary;* JANE WILEY, GARY ZIMMER (northern members); CHRISTINE L. THOMAS (southern member), WILLIAM BRUINS (at-large member). (All are appointed by governor with senate consent.)

Secretary of Natural Resources: CATHY L. STEPP, 267-7556, DNRSecretary@

Deputy Secretary: MATT MORONEY, 264-6266, matt.moroney@

Executive Assistant: SCOTT GUNDERSON, 267-9521, scott.gunderson@

Legislative and Policy Advisor: PAUL HEINEN, 266-2120, paul.heinen@

Legislative Liaison: MICHAEL BRUHN, 266-5375, michael.bruhn@

Legal Services, Bureau of: TIMOTHY A. ANDRYK, *director,* 264-9228, tim.andryk@

Business Support and Sustainability, Office of: AL SHEA, *director,* 266-5896, allen.shea@

Communication, Office of: WILLIAM COSH, *director,* 267-2773, william.cosh@

Cooperative Environmental Assistance, Bureau of: vacancy, *director,* 267-3125.

Energy, Transportation and Environmental Analysis, Bureau of: DAVID R. SIEBERT, *director,* 264-6048, david.siebert@

Management and Budget, Bureau of: JOSEPH P. POLASEK, JR., director, 266-2794, joseph.polasekjr@

Mailing Address: P.O. Box 7921, Madison 53707-7921.

Location: State Natural Resources Building (GEF 2), 101 South Webster Street, Madison.

Telephones: Customer and General Information: (888) WDNRINFO (936-7463) or (608) 266-2621; Violation Hotline (to confidentially report suspected wildlife, recreational, and environmental violations): (800) TIP-WDNR (847-9367) or #367 by cellular phone; Hazardous Substance Spill Line: (800) 943-0003; Outdoor Report (recorded message): (608) 266-2277; Daily Air Quality: (866) 324-5924; Gypsy Moth: (800) 642-6684; Emerald Ash Borer: (800) 462-2803; Firewood: (877) 303-9663; Burning Permits (888) WIS-BURN (947-2876).

TTY: Access via relay 711.

Internet Address: dnr.wi.gov

Air, Waste, and Remediation & Redevelopment, Division of: PAT STEVENS, *administrator,* 264-9210, pat.stevens@; SUZANNE BANGERT, *deputy administrator,* 266-0014, suzanne.bangert@

   Air Management, Bureau of: BART SPONSELLER, *director,* 267-8537, bart.sponseller@

   Remediation and Redevelopment, Bureau for: MARK F. GIESFELDT, *director,* 267-7562, mark.giesfeldt@

   Waste and Materials Management, Bureau of: ANN COAKLEY, *director,* 261-8449, ann.coakley@

Customer and Employee Services, Division of: JULIE SAUER, *administrator,* 266-2241, julie.sauer@; MICHELE YOUNG, *deputy administrator,* 266-7566, michele.young@

   Community Financial Assistance, Bureau of: MARY ROSE TEVES, *director,* 267-7683, mary.teves@

   Customer Service and Outreach, Bureau of: DIANE L. BROOKBANK, *director,* 267-7799, diane.brookbank@

   Finance, Bureau of: TIMOTHY SELL, *acting director,* 267-9601, timothy.sell@

   Human Resources, Bureau of: ROBERT MASNADO, *director,* 266-6999, robert.masnado@

   Technology Services, Bureau of: MICHAEL KESSENICH, *acting director,* 275-3469, michael.kessenich@

DEPARTMENT OF NATURAL RESOURCES

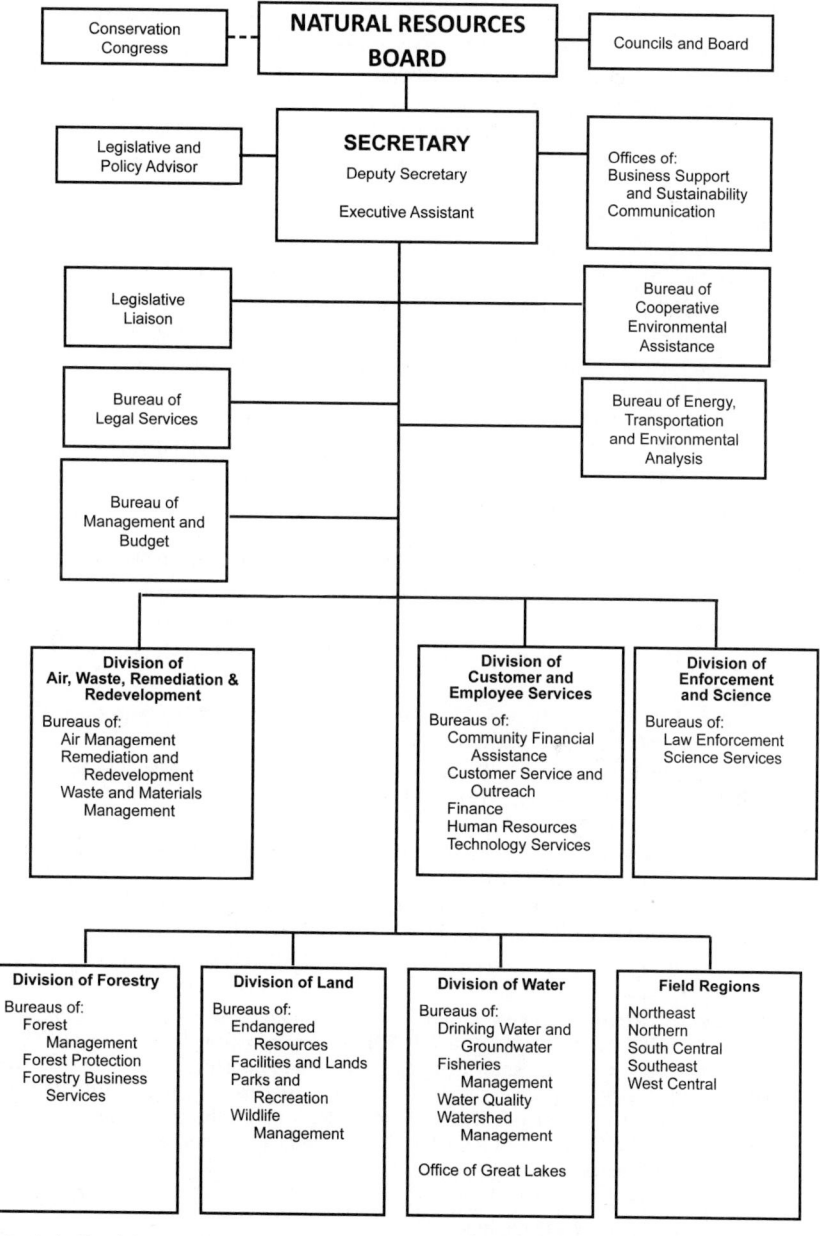

Conservation Congress

NATURAL RESOURCES BOARD

Councils and Board

Legislative and Policy Advisor

SECRETARY
Deputy Secretary
Executive Assistant

Offices of:
Business Support and Sustainability
Communication

Legislative Liaison

Bureau of Cooperative Environmental Assistance

Bureau of Legal Services

Bureau of Energy, Transportation and Environmental Analysis

Bureau of Management and Budget

Division of Air, Waste, Remediation & Redevelopment

Bureaus of:
Air Management
Remediation and Redevelopment
Waste and Materials Management

Division of Customer and Employee Services

Bureaus of:
Community Financial Assistance
Customer Service and Outreach
Finance
Human Resources
Technology Services

Division of Enforcement and Science

Bureaus of:
Law Enforcement
Science Services

Division of Forestry

Bureaus of:
Forest Management
Forest Protection
Forestry Business Services

Division of Land

Bureaus of:
Endangered Resources
Facilities and Lands
Parks and Recreation
Wildlife Management

Division of Water

Bureaus of:
Drinking Water and Groundwater
Fisheries Management
Water Quality
Watershed Management

Office of Great Lakes

Field Regions

Northeast
Northern
South Central
Southeast
West Central

Units attached for administrative purposes under Sec. 15.03:   Groundwater Coordinating Council
Invasive Species Council
Lake Michigan Commercial Fishing Board
Lake Superior Commercial Fishing Board
Council on Recycling
Wisconsin Waterways Commission

Enforcement and Science, Division of: TIM LAWHERN, *administrator,* 264-6133, timothy.lawhern@

   Law Enforcement, Bureau of: RANDALL J. STARK, *director,* 266-1115, randall.stark@

   Science Services, Bureau of: JOHN R. SULLIVAN, *director,* 267-9753, john.r.sullivan@

Forestry, Division of: PAUL DELONG, *administrator and State Forester,* 264-9224, paul.delong@; DARRELL E. ZASTROW, *deputy administrator,* 266-0290, darrell.zastrow@

   Forest Management, Bureau of: ROBERT J. MATHER, *director,* 266-1727, robert.mather@

   Forest Protection, Bureau of: TRENT L. MARTY, *director,* 266-7978, trent.marty@

   Forestry Business Services, Bureau of: WENDY M. MCCOWN, *director,* 266-7510, wendy.mccown@

Land, Division of: KURT THIEDE, *administrator,* 266-5833, kurt.thiede@; SANJAY OLSON, *deputy administrator,* 261-6453, sanjay.olson@

   Endangered Resources, Bureau of: ERIN CRAIN, *director,* 267-7479, erin.crain@

   Facilities and Lands, Bureau of: STEVEN W. MILLER, *director,* 266-5782, steven.miller@

   Parks and Recreation, Bureau of: DANIEL J. SCHULLER, *director,* 266-2185, daniel.schuller@

   Wildlife Management, Bureau of: THOMAS M. HAUGE, *director,* 266-2193, tom.hauge@

Water, Division of: KENNETH JOHNSON, *administrator,* 264-6278, kenneth.johnson@; RUSSELL A. RASMUSSEN, *deputy administrator,* 267-7651, russell.rasmussen@

   Drinking Water and Groundwater, Bureau of: JILL D. JONAS, *director,* 267-7545, jill.jonas@

   Fisheries Management, Bureau of: MICHAEL D. STAGGS, *director,* 267-0796, mike.staggs@

   Great Lakes, Office of: STEVE GALARNEAU, *director,* 266-1956, steven.galarneau@

   Water Quality, Bureau of: SUSAN SYLVESTER, *director,* 266-1099, susan.sylvester@

   Watershed Management, Bureau of: PAM BIERSACH, *director,* 261-8447, pamela.biersach@

Field Regions:

   Northeast: JEAN ROMBACK-BARTELS, *director,* (920) 662-5114, 2984 Shawano Avenue, Green Bay 54313-6727, jean.rombackbartels@

   Northern: JOHN F. GOZDZIALSKI, *director,* (715) 635-4002, 810 West Maple Street, Spooner 54801; Co-regional office: (715) 369-8900, 107 Sutliff Avenue, Rhinelander 54501, john.gozdzialski@

   South Central: MARK D. AQUINO, *director,* (608) 275-3262, 3911 Fish Hatchery Road, Fitchburg 53711, mark.aquino@

   Southeast: ERIC NITSCHKE, *director,* (414) 263-8570, 2300 North Dr. Martin Luther King Jr. Drive, Milwaukee 53212, eric.nitschke

   West Central: DAN BAUMANN, *director,* (715) 839-3722, 1300 West Clairemont Avenue, Eau Claire 54702, dan.baumann@

Publications: *Wisconsin Natural Resources* (bimonthly magazine by subscription – call (608) 267-7410 or (800) 678-9472); parks newspapers and visitor guides; hunting, fishing, trapping, snowmobiling, ATV, and boating regulations; various brochures, fact sheets, and reports (lists available). Teachers may write to the Office of Communication for a list of publications. Individuals may subscribe to receive weekly e-mail links to the DNR Weekly News, DNR Outdoor Report, and other topics at: dnr.wi.gov Search: news.

Number of Employees: 2,658.94.

Total Budget 2011-13: $1,044,909,900.

Statutory References: Sections 15.05 (1) (c), 15.34, and 15.343; Chapters 23, 26-33, 87, 88, and 160.

Agency Responsibility: The Department of Natural Resources (DNR) is responsible for implementing state and federal laws that protect and enhance Wisconsin's natural resources, including its air, land, water, forests, wildlife, fish, and plants. It coordinates the many state-administered programs that protect the environment and provides a full range of outdoor recreational opportunities for Wisconsin residents and visitors.

Organization: The 7 members of the Natural Resources Board serve staggered 6-year terms. At least 3 of them must be from the northern part of the state and at least 3 from the southern part. Effective May 1, 2017, at least one member is required to have an agricultural background, and at least 3 members must have held an annual hunting, fishing, or trapping license in at least 7 of the 10 years previous to being nominated. Board members are subject to restrictions on holding DNR permits or depending on permit holders for a significant portion of their income. The board directs and supervises the department and acts as a formal point of contact for citizens.

The department is administered by a secretary appointed by the governor with the advice and consent of the senate. The secretary appoints the department's division administrators from outside the classified service. The regional directors, who are appointed from the classified service, manage all of the agency's field operations for their respective areas and report directly to the secretary. The Office of Business Support and Sustainability focuses on proactive business support, organizational effectiveness, and sustainability. It provides focal points within the department to better balance job creation and economic vitality with the department's environmental and conservation mission; streamline regulations, improve operational and management systems, undertake organizational efficiencies, and improve customer service; and expand the department's capacity to support business and local government efforts to become more sustainable.

Unit Functions: The *Division of Air, Waste, and Remediation & Redevelopment* protects the state's air quality and general environmental health through air pollution control, cleanup and redevelopment of contaminated property, and solid and hazardous waste management in cooperation with the federal Environmental Protection Agency, international agencies, local governments, private industry, and citizens. It develops air quality implementation plans, monitors air quality, conducts inspections, operates a permit program, and initiates compliance actions in accordance with state and federal requirements. The division's waste and materials management program implements Wisconsin's waste management laws to help ensure adequate waste treatment and disposal capacity for Wisconsin citizens and businesses; efficiently regulates waste, materials, and mining facilities to minimize their impact on human health and the environment; implements waste and recycling laws to minimize waste, conserve energy, and make productive use of material resources; and ensures Wisconsin citizens and businesses have the knowledge, opportunity, and mechanisms to safely and economically minimize, reuse, recycle, manage, and dispose of the waste and materials/byproducts they generate. The division's remediation and redevelopment program is responsible for the cleanup and redevelopment of contaminated sites that fall under the following legislation: the hazardous substances spills law, the environmental repair law, the abandoned container law, the federal Superfund and Brownfields laws, the state land recycling law, and the Resource Conservation and Recovery Act. The remediation and redevelopment program also responds to emergency contamination incidents.

The *Division of Customer and Employee Services* provides a variety of customer services including the sale of hunting and fishing licenses, boat, ATV, and snowmobile registration, environmental education programs, and public information. It oversees distribution of financial aids for environmental programs that benefit local governments and nonprofit conservation organizations, such as the Clean Water Fund and the Stewardship Fund, and acts as liaison to federal and state agencies. The division also provides a variety of management services for the department, including budgetary and financial services, personnel and human resource management, computer and information technology support, affirmative action, employee assistance, training, and telecommunication services.

The *Division of Enforcement and Science* is responsible for enforcing the state's conservation, hunting, fishing, environmental, and recreational safety laws, for providing scientific research and environmental analyses to inform agency policy and operational decisions on natural resource issues, for providing interagency coordination of the review of transportation infrastructure projects, and for providing a central point of contact for the regulated community on energy-related projects.   The division's wardens and environmental staff promote safety and compliance with the law through enforcement and educational outreach programs, such as classes in hunting, boating, snowmobile, and all-terrain vehicle safety, and community involvement programs such as the Learn to Hunt Program.   The division reviews major public and private proposals under the federal and state Environmental Policy Acts, and certifies laboratories and laboratory operators for wastewater treatment systems, water supply systems, incinerators, sanitary landfills, and septage services.   The division is also responsible for provision of agency laboratory services (analytical chemistry and biological) through the Wisconsin State Laboratory of Hygiene and other private contract laboratories as necessary.   The division also conducts biological and social science research, provides technical writing, editing, and publication of research results, and provides expertise to assist other divisions and guide the department in policy formation.

The *Division of Forestry,* created by 1999 Wisconsin Act 9, is responsible for the administration and implementation of programs that protect and manage the state's forest resources in a sustainable manner so as to provide economic, ecological, social, recreational, and cultural benefits.   The division is involved with the management of about 16 million acres of public and private forest land and millions of urban trees in the state.   All of the 500,000 acres of state forest land were certified in 2004 as sustainably managed by third party auditors from the Forest Stewardship Council and Sustainable Forestry Initiative.   More than 2 million acres of county forest lands, which DNR works in partnership with 29 counties to manage, were certified in 2005, as were over 2 million acres of private lands managed under the Managed Forest Law program.   Foresters provide assistance to private woodlot owners; offer expertise in urban forestry; manage and monitor forest insects and diseases; operate three tree nurseries; provide public education and awareness activities; and work in partnership with local governments, the timber industry, environmental groups, and recreation interests.   The division administers grants and loans to county forests, urban forestry grants to communities, forest landowner grants to woodland owners, and forest fire protection grants to fire departments.   The fire management program

Department of Natural Resources workers test the effectiveness of a fire break prepared around the perimeter of a prescribed burn unit with a test fire. (Department of Natural Resources)

is responsible for forest fire protection on 18 million acres of forest, brush, and grassland and coordinates with local fire departments to prevent and control forest fires.

The *Division of Land* has major responsibility for protecting and conserving the state's biological diversity and providing nature-based recreational opportunities. The division administers programs related to wildlife; state lands, parks, trails, southern forests, and recreation areas; rare and endangered animal and plant species, and natural communities; and outdoor recreational resources. The division operates educational programs and helps private landowners manage their lands for the benefit of wildlife and rare resources. It manages wildlife and habitats on about 1.5 million acres of land owned or leased by the state and works with federal, county, and other local government authorities to protect and manage the resources on an additional 3.6 million acres of public lands, including national and county forests. The wildlife program manages populations such as deer, bear, furbearers, waterfowl and birds, and maintains and restores habitats such as wetlands, grasslands, and prairies. The endangered resources program conserves Wisconsin's rare and declining species and natural communities through the State Natural Areas program and the Nongame and Endangered Species program work that is supported primarily by funds derived from voluntary contributions designated by taxpayers on their state income tax returns and through purchase of the Endangered Resources license plate. The Endangered Resources program also supports ecosystem management decision-making in the department through the Citizen-Based Monitoring Program, the Natural Heritage Inventory Program, and the Aquatic and Terrestrial Resources inventory. Parks personnel manage the state's extensive parks, southern forests, recreation areas, and trails systems, including the Ice Age and North Country National Scenic Trails, which are designed for the conservation of natural resources and a wide variety of recreational activities including biking, hiking, snow mobiling, and camping. The division is also responsible for land acquisition for parks, trails, southern forests, recreation areas, wildlife areas, fishery areas, natural areas, and other state wildlife-related recreation lands, as well as property planning and the development of public use facilities on state lands. It coordinates the Stewardship Program, which provides grants for the purchase of lands for natural and recreational areas, wildlife habitats, urban green spaces, local parks, trails, and riverways.

The *Division of Water* works with many partners to protect public health and safety, and the quality and quantity of Wisconsin's groundwater, surface water, and aquatic ecosystems. The division is responsible for implementing the Clean Water Act in order to achieve the goal of fishable and swimmable waters throughout Wisconsin. Division staff works to prevent or regulate water pollution from industries, municipal sewage treatment facilities, construction sites, large farms, and urban areas. The division monitors compliance, sets water quality standards, and provides financial and technical assistance. Division programs protect drinking water and groundwater resources for both human and ecosystem health, and ensure the safety and security of the state's drinking water systems and private wells. The division strives to enhance and restore outstanding fisheries in Wisconsin's waters. It regulates sport and commercial fishing through licensing and provides fish hatchery services, fish stocking and surveying, aquatic habit improvement, angler education, and public access programs. The division helps protect the waters of the state that are held in trust for all the people of the state through the Public Trust Doctrine. Division staff oversees the placement of structures in state waters, wetland management and restoration, shoreland zoning, and floodplain management. The division helps local government units to protect lives and property through floodplain management and dam safety inspections. The division cooperates with many states and Canada to protect the water quality, quantity, and ecosystems of the Mississippi River and Great Lakes basins. The division also houses the Office of Great Lakes, which is responsible for restoring five designated Areas of Concern (AOC) in and along the Great Lakes.

The *Field Regions* enable the department to make its programs accessible to the general public. (Most DNR field staff work within county assignments.) This structure combines employees with different types of expertise into interdisciplinary teams responsible for assessing natural resource and environmental needs from a broader perspective.

History: Today, the Department of Natural Resources has dual responsibility for both traditional conservation duties and environmental protection. Its history and structure reflect more than a century of government and citizen involvement with these concerns. Wisconsin's earliest conservation legislation focused on fish, game, and forests. Chapter 253, Laws of 1874, created a Board of Fish Commissioners charged with hatching fish eggs received from the federal government and distributing the fry to Wisconsin waters. The governor was authorized in 1885 by Chapter 455 to appoint 3 fish wardens to enforce fishing regulations and collect statistics from commercial fishermen. Chapter 456, Laws of 1887, directed the governor to appoint 4 game wardens to enforce all laws protecting fish and game.

Chapter 229, Laws of 1897, established a 3-member commission to develop legislation creating a forestry department. The commission was directed to devise ways to use the state's forest resources without harming the climate or water supplies and to preserve forest resources without retarding the state's economic development. The report of this commission led to Chapter 450, Laws of 1903, which established a Department of State Forestry with a superintendent appointed by the Board of State Forest Commissioners. Chapter 495, Laws of 1907, created a State Park Board with authority to acquire and manage land for park purposes.

Chapter 406, Laws of 1915, consolidated all park and conservation functions under a 3-member Conservation Commission of Wisconsin, appointed by the governor with senate approval. From then until 1995, the management and conservation of Wisconsin's natural resources was directed by a part-time commission or board, except for the period 1923 to 1927, when a single full-time commissioner was created by Chapter 118, Laws of 1923, to head the Department of Conservation. Since the enactment of 1995 Wisconsin Act 27, which provided that the secretary would be appointed by the governor with senate consent rather than appointed by the board, the current board's role has been an advisory one.

The 1960s saw major changes in conservation legislation. Chapter 427, Laws of 1961, created a committee charged with developing a long-range plan for acquiring and improving outdoor recreation areas. It initiated the Outdoor Recreation Act Program (ORAP) to fund land acquisitions. In 1969, Chapter 353 expanded ORAP and authorized the state to incur debt up to $56 million between 1969 and 1981 for the purpose of providing outdoor recreation opportunities. With enactment of 1989 Wisconsin Act 31, the legislature created the Stewardship Program, which authorized up to $250 million in state debt to acquire and develop land for recreational uses, wildlife habitats, fisheries, and natural areas.

Wisconsin's antipollution efforts date back to Chapter 412, Laws of 1911, when the legislature gave the State Board of Health investigative powers in water pollution cases. Prior to that, such investigations were primarily the responsibility of local government. In Chapter 264, Laws of 1927, the legislature created a committee to supervise the water pollution control activities carried out by several state agencies, including the Conservation Commission. The Department of Resource Development, which had been created by Chapter 442, Laws of 1959, assumed water pollution control duties under Chapter 614, Laws of 1965, and statewide air pollution regulation with Chapter 83, Laws of 1967.

In the 1967 executive branch reorganization, the legislature created the Department of Natural Resources by combining the Department of Conservation and the Department of Resource Development. The new department was given authority to regulate air and water quality, as well as solid waste disposal, and directed to develop an integrated program to protect air, land, and water resources.

Chapter 274, Laws of 1971, required all state agencies to report on the environmental impacts of proposed actions that could significantly affect environmental quality. Chapter 275, Laws of 1971, provided for state protection of endangered fish and wildlife, and Chapter 370, Laws of 1977, placed nongame species and endangered wild plants under state protection. A program protecting surface waters from nonpoint source pollution was created by Chapter 418, Laws of 1977, and a groundwater protection program, based on numerical standards for polluting substances, was created by 1983 Wisconsin Act 410. In Wisconsin Act 335, the 1989 Legislature made major changes in the laws governing recycling, source reduction, and disposal of solid wastes.

Statutory Board and Councils

Dry Cleaner Environmental Response Council: vacancy (small dry cleaning operation); BRETT DONALDSON, RICHARD W. KLINKE (large dry cleaning operation); KEVIN BRADEN (wholesale distributor of dry cleaning solvent); JEANNE TARVIN (engineer, professional geologist, hydrologist, or soil scientist); JIM FITZGERALD (manufacturer or seller of dry cleaning equipment) (appointed by governor).

The 6-member Dry Cleaner Environmental Response Council advises the department on matters related to the Dry Cleaner Environmental Response Program, which is administered by DNR and provides awards to dry cleaning establishments for assistance in the investigation and cleanup of environmental contamination. Council members are appointed for staggered 3-year terms. The council, which is scheduled to sunset on June 30, 2032, was created by 1997 Wisconsin Act 27, as amended by 1997 Wisconsin Act 300. Its composition and duties are prescribed in Sections 15.347 (2) and 292.65 (13) of the statutes.

Council on Forestry: PAUL DELONG (chief state forester); SENATORS TIFFANY, vacancy; REPRESENTATIVES CLARK, MURSAU; TOM HITTLE (forest products company which owns and manages large forest land tracts representative); RICHARD WEDEPOHL (owners of nonindustrial, private forest land representative); JANE SEVERT (counties containing county forests representative); JIM HOPPE (paper and pulp industry representative); TROY BROWN (lumber industry representative); MATT DALLMAN (nonprofit conservation organization representative); KIMBERLY QUAST (forester who provides consultation services); MARK RICKENBACH (school of forestry representative); RANDY CHAMPEAU (conservation education representative); vacancy (forestry-affiliated labor union representative); ALLISON BRUCE (urban and community forestry representative); JAMES KERKMAN (Society of American Foresters representative); HENRY SCHIENBECK (timber producer organization representative); VIRGIL WAUGH (secondary wood industry representative); PAUL STRONG (nonvoting member, Federal Department of Agriculture representative).

The 20-member Council on Forestry advises the governor, the legislature, the Department of Natural Resources, and other state agencies on topics relating to forestry in Wisconsin including: protection from fire, insects, and disease; sustainable forestry; reforestation and forestry genetics; management and protection of urban forests; increasing the public's knowledge and awareness of forestry issues; forestry research; economic development and marketing of forestry products; legislation affecting forestry; and staff and funding needs for forestry programs. The council shall submit a biennial report on the status of the state's forestry resources and industry to the governor and the appropriate standing committees of the legislature by June 1 of each odd-numbered year. All members are appointed by the governor. Lengths of terms are not specified by law. The council was created by 2001 Wisconsin Act 109. Its composition and duties are prescribed in Sections 15.347 (19) and 26.02 of the statutes.

Managed Forest Land Board: Inactive.

The 5-member Managed Forest Land Board administers the program established by the Department of Natural Resources to award grants to nonprofit conservation organizations, to local governmental units, and to the department to acquire land, including conservations easements on land, to be used for hunting, fishing, hiking, sightseeing, and cross-country skiing. The department consults with the board to promulgate administrative rules establishing requirements for awarding grants. Appointed board members serve 3-year terms. The board was created by 2007 Wisconsin Act 20, and its composition and duties are prescribed in Sections 15.345 (6) and 77.895 of the statutes.

Metallic Mining Council: Inactive.

The 9-member Metallic Mining Council advises the department on matters relating to the reclamation of mined land. Its members are appointed by the secretary of natural resources for staggered 3-year terms, and they are expected to represent "a variety and balance of economic, scientific, and environmental viewpoints." The council was created by Chapter 377, Laws of 1977, and its composition and duties are prescribed in Sections 15.347 (12) and 289.08 of the statutes.

Milwaukee River Revitalization Council: Inactive.

The 13-member Milwaukee River Revitalization Council advises the legislature, governor, and department on matters related to environmental, recreational, and economic revitalization of the Milwaukee River Basin, and it assists local governments in planning and implementing projects. It is also responsible for developing and implementing a plan that encourages multiple recreational, entrepreneurial, and cultural activities along the streams of the Milwaukee River Basin. Its 11 appointed members serve 3-year terms. Each of the priority watersheds in the basin must be represented by at least one council member. The council was created by 1987 Wisconsin Act 399, and its composition and duties are prescribed in Sections 15.347 (15) and 23.18 of the statutes.

Natural Areas Preservation Council: MICHAEL STRIGEL (appointed by council of the Wisconsin Academy of Sciences, Arts and Letters), *chairperson;* JAMES P. BENNETT (representing University of Wisconsin System, appointed by board of regents), *vice chairperson;* ERIN E. CRAIN (representing Department of Natural Resources, appointed by the board of natural resources), *secretary;* THOMAS L. EDDY, JAMES W. PERRY (appointed by council of the Wisconsin Academy of Sciences, Arts and Letters); OWEN D. BOYLE (representing Department of Natural Resources, appointed by the board of natural resources); EVELYN HOWELL, PATRICK ROBINSON, JOY ZEDLER (representing University of Wisconsin System, appointed by board of regents); DENNIS YOCKERS (representing the Department of Public Instruction, appointed by the state superintendent of public instruction); SUSAN BORKIN (representing Milwaukee Public Museum, appointed by MPM board of directors).

The 11-member Natural Areas Preservation Council advises the department on matters pertaining to the protection of natural areas that contain native biotic communities and habitats for rare species. It also makes recommendations about gifts or purchases for the state natural areas system. The council was created by Chapter 566, Laws of 1951, as the State Board for Preservation of Scientific Areas. It was renamed the Scientific Areas Preservation Council in Chapter 327, Laws of 1961, and given its current name in 1985 Wisconsin Act 29. One of the appointments from the Wisconsin Academy of Sciences, Arts and Letters must represent private colleges in the state. Its composition and duties are prescribed in Sections 15.347 (4) and 23.26 of the statutes.

Nonmotorized Recreation and Transportation Trails Council: ROD BARTLOW, WILLIAM HAUDA, DANA JOHNSON, ANNE MURPHY, JOEL PATENAUDE, DEBBIE PETERSON, DAVID PHILLIPS, GEOFFREY SNUDDEN, BLAKE THIESEN, NED ZUELSDORFF (appointed by governor).

The Nonmotorized Recreation and Transportation Trails Council carries out studies and advises the governor, the legislature, and the Department of Natural Resources and the Department of Transportation on matters related to nonmotorized recreation and transportation trails. The size of the council is not specified. Council members are appointed by the governor to serve at the pleasure of the governor. Membership is to represent geographic diversity and to consist of those who personally undertake nonmotorized activities or who participate in organizations that own or maintain nonmotorized trails or that promote nonmotorized trail activities. Members should be appointed to represent as many as possible of the following groups: pedestrians; persons who represent local forests or parks; persons who are interested in tourism promotion; persons who represent tribal lands; persons with physical disabilities; persons who engage in nature-based activities such as bird watching, nature study, hunting, and fishing; and persons who engage in activities on water trails, horseback riding or buggy driving, long-distance hiking, snow sports, and bicycling. The council was created by 2009 Wisconsin Act 394 and its composition and duties are prescribed in Sections 15.347 (20) and 23.177 of the statutes.

Small Business Environmental Council: JEANNE WHITISH (appointed by senate president); RICHARD KLINKE (appointed by senate minority leader); SHANE LAUTERBACH (appointed by assembly speaker); AMY LITSCHER (appointed by assembly minority leader); VINCE RUFFOLO (appointed by secretary of natural resources); ANDRE JACQUE, AL SHEA, vacancy (representing general public and appointed by governor).

The 8-member Small Business Environmental Council advises the Department of Natural Resources on the effectiveness of assistance programs to small businesses that enable them to comply with the federal Clean Air Act. It also advises on the fairness and effectiveness of air pollution rules promulgated by the Department of Natural Resources and the U.S. Environmental Protection Agency regarding the impact on small businesses. Members are appointed to 3-year terms. The 4 members appointed by legislative officers must own or represent owners of small business stationary air pollution sources. The 3 members appointed by the governor may not own or represent small business stationary sources. The council was created by 1991 Wisconsin Act 302, and it was transferred from the Department of Commerce to the Department of Natural Resources by 2011 Wisconsin Act 32. Its composition and duties are prescribed in Sections 15.347 (8) and 285.795 of the statutes.

Snowmobile Recreational Council: KAREN CARLSON, BEVERLY DITTMAR, LARRY ERICKSON, ROBERT LANG, ANDREW MALECKI, DAVE NEWMAN, MICHAEL WILLMAN (northern representatives); MIKE CERNY, THOMAS CHWALA, JERRY GREEN, SAMUEL LANDES, DALE MAYO, PATRICK SCHMUTZER, JON SCHWEITZER, LEE VAN ZEELAND (southern representatives). (All are appointed by governor with senate consent.)

The 15-member Snowmobile Recreational Council carries out studies and makes recommendations to the governor, the legislature, and the Department of Natural Resources and the Department of Transportation regarding all matters affecting snowmobiling. Council members are appointed for staggered 3-year terms. At least 5 must represent the northern part of the state, and at least 5 must represent the southern part. The council was created by Chapter 277, Laws of 1971, and its composition and duties are prescribed in Sections 15.347 (7) and 350.14 of the statutes.

Sporting Heritage Council: SCOTT GUNDERSON (designated by secretary of natural resources), *chairperson;* WILLIAM TORHORST (appointed by governor), SENATORS KEDZIE, WIRCH; REPRESENTATIVES MILROY, STEINEKE; RALPH FRITSCH (representing deer hunters); ANDY PANTZLAFF (representing bear hunters); MARK LABARBERA (representing bird hunters); BENJAMIN GRUBER (representing anglers); SCOTT ZIMMERMAN (representing furbearing animal hunters and trappers); JOE CAPUTO (Conservation Congress member).

The 12-member Sporting Heritage Council advises the governor, the legislature, and the natural resources board about issues relating to hunting, trapping, fishing, and other types of outdoor recreation activities, including ways improve the recruitment and retention of hunters, trappers, and anglers; to improve the management and protection of natural resources; ways to promote and implement youth outdoor recreation activities; and ways to improve access to public and private land and lakes. It is required to submit a biennial report on the status of the recruitment and retention of hunters, trappers, and anglers to the governor, the legislature, and the chairperson of the natural resources board by July 1 of each even-numbered year. Five members are appointed by the natural resources board from nominations provided by sporting organizations that have as their primary objective the promotion of hunting, fishing, or trapping, with one member each representing the interests of deer hunters, bear hunters, bird hunters, anglers, and furbearing animal hunters and trappers. Members other than the secretary of natural resources are appointed for 3-year terms. The council was created by 2011 Wisconsin Act 168 and its composition and duties are prescribed in Sections 15.347 (21) and 29.036 of the statutes.

State Trails Council: ROBBIE WEBBER, *chairperson;* BRYAN MUCH, *vice chairperson;* SKIP MALETZKE, *secretary;* KEN L. CARPENTER, RANDY HARDEN, DOUG JOHNSON, PHIL JOHNSRUD, MIKE MCFADZEN, DAVID PHILLIPS, LUANA SCHNEIDER, vacancy (appointed by governor).

The 11-member State Trails Council advises the department about the planning, acquisition, development, and management of state trails. Its members are appointed for 4-year terms. It was created by 1989 Wisconsin Act 31, and its composition and duties are prescribed in Sections 15.347 (16) and 23.175 (2) (c) of the statutes. 2011 Wisconsin Act 104 added two members and required that they be knowledgeable, and engage in, one or more of the various recreational uses of trails.

Independent Organization — Conservation Congress

Conservation Congress Executive Council: RICK OLSON, JOE WEISS (District 1); ALLAN BROWN, DAVID LARSON (District 2); BEN LOMA, MARCELL WIELOCH (District 3); JOHN ASCHENBRENNER, BOB ELLINGSON (District 4); KEVIN SMABY, AL SUCHLA (District 5); STAN BROWNELL, DAVID

A Department of Natural Resources worker inoculates a chestnut tree with a slurry of hypovirus. The virus is intended to kill off the fungus that causes American chestnut blight. (Department of Natural Resources)

PUHL (District 6); DALE MAAS, ARLYN SPLITT (District 7); LARRY BONDE, DAVID MILLER (District 8); LEE FAHRNEY, MIKE ROGERS (District 9); AL PHELAN, KEN RISLEY (District 10); ROBERT BOHMANN, ALLEN SHOOK (District 11); JOSH HENNLICH, MICHAEL KUHR (District 12).

The Conservation Congress is a 360-member publicly elected citizen advisory group, and its 24-member executive council advises the Natural Resources Board on all matters under the board's jurisdiction. The Conservation Congress is organized into 12 districts statewide. Each district elects 2 members to one-year terms on the executive council. The congress originated in 1934 and received statutory recognition in Chapter 179, Laws of 1971. Its duties are prescribed in Section 15.348 of the statutes.

INDEPENDENT UNITS ATTACHED FOR BUDGETING, PROGRAM COORDINATION, AND RELATED MANAGEMENT FUNCTIONS BY SECTION 15.03 OF THE STATUTES

GROUNDWATER COORDINATING COUNCIL

Groundwater Coordinating Council: KEN JOHNSON (designated by secretary of natural resources), *chairperson;* ERIC SCOTT (designated by secretary of safety and professionals services), JOHN PETTY (designated by secretary of agriculture, trade and consumer protection), HENRY ANDERSON (designated by secretary of health services), DAN SCUDDER (designated by secretary of transportation), JAMES HURLEY (designated by president, UW System), JAMES ROBERTSON (state geologist), GEORGE KRAFT (representing governor).

Statutory References: Sections 15.347 (13) and 160.50.

Agency Responsibility: The 8-member Groundwater Coordinating Council advises state agencies on the coordination of nonregulatory programs related to groundwater management. Member agencies exchange information regarding groundwater monitoring, budgets for groundwater programs, data management, public information efforts, laboratory analyses, research, and state appropriations for research. The council reports annually to the legislature, governor, and agencies represented regarding the council's activities and recommendations and its assessment of the current state of groundwater resources and related management programs. Persons designated to serve on behalf of their agency heads must be agency employees with "sufficient authority to deploy agency resources and directly influence agency decision making." The governor's representative serves a 4-year term. The council was created by 1983 Wisconsin Act 410.

INVASIVE SPECIES COUNCIL

Invasive Species Council: JACK SULLIVAN (designated by secretary of natural resources); TRAVIS OLSON (designated by secretary of administration); BRIAN KUHN (designated by secretary of agriculture, trade and consumer protection); DANIELLE JOHNSON (designated by secretary of tourism); TODD MATHESON (designated by secretary of transportation); THOMAS BRESSNER, JAMES KERKMAN, GREGORY LONG, PATRICIA MORTON, KENNETH RAFFA, JAMES REINARTZ, PAUL SCHUMACHER (appointed by governor).

The 12-member Invasive Species Council conducts studies related to controlling invasive species and makes recommendations to the Department of Natural Resources regarding a system for classifying invasive species under the department's statewide invasive species control program and procedures for awarding grants to public and private agencies engaged in projects to control invasive species. All except *ex officio* members or their designees are appointed by the governor to 5-year terms to represent public and private interests affected by the presence of invasive species in the state. The council was created by 2001 Wisconsin Act 109. Its composition and duties are prescribed in Sections 15.347 (18) and 23.22 of the statutes.

LAKE MICHIGAN COMMERCIAL FISHING BOARD

Lake Michigan Commercial Fishing Board: CHARLES W. HENRIKSEN, RICHARD R. JOHNSON, MICHAEL LECLAIR, MARK MARICQUE, DEAN SWAER (licensed, active commercial fishers); NEIL A. SCHWARZ (licensed, active wholesale fish dealer); DAN PAWLITZKE (state citizen). (All are appointed by governor.)

Statutory References: Sections 15.345 (3) and 29.33 (7).

Agency Responsibility: The 7-member Lake Michigan Commercial Fishing Board was created by Chapter 418, Laws of 1977. Its members must live in counties contiguous to Lake Michigan. The 5 commercial fishers must represent fisheries in specific geographic areas. The board reviews applications for transfers of commercial fishing licenses between individuals, establishes criteria for allotting catch quotas to individual licensees, assigns catch quotas when the department establishes special harvest limits, and assists the department in establishing criteria for identifying inactive license holders.

LAKE SUPERIOR COMMERCIAL FISHING BOARD

Lake Superior Commercial Fishing Board: MAURINE HALVORSON, CRAIG HOOPMAN, vacancy (licensed, active commercial fishers); JEFF BODIN (licensed, active wholesale fish dealer); vacancy (state citizen). (All are appointed by governor.)

Statutory References: Sections 15.345 (2) and 29.33 (7).

Agency Responsibility: The 5-member Lake Superior Commercial Fishing Board was created by Chapter 418, Laws of 1977. Its members must live in counties contiguous to Lake Superior. The board reviews applications for transfers of commercial fishing licenses between individuals, establishes criteria for allotting catch quotas to individual licensees, assigns catch quotas when the department establishes special harvest limits, and assists the department in establishing criteria for identifying inactive license holders.

COUNCIL ON RECYCLING

Council on Recycling: JAMES BIRMINGHAM, GEORGE HAYDUCSKO, JR., CHARLES LARSCHEID, JOSEPH LIEBAU, JR., RICK MEYERS, NEIL PETERS-MICHAUD, WILLIAM WALTZ (appointed by governor).

Statutory References: Sections 15.347 (17) and 159.22.

Agency Responsibility: The 7 members of the Council on Recycling are appointed to 4-year terms that coincide with that of the governor. The council, which was created by 1989 Wisconsin Act 335, promotes implementation of the state's solid waste reduction, recovery, and recycling programs; helps public agencies coordinate programs and exchange information; advises state agencies about creating administrative rules and establishing priorities for market development; and advises the DNR and the UW System about education and research related to solid waste recycling. The council also promotes a regional and interstate marketing system for recycled materials and reports to the legislature about market development and research to encourage recycling. The council advises the department about statewide public information activities and advises the governor and the legislature.

WISCONSIN WATERWAYS COMMISSION

Wisconsin Waterways Commission: JAMES F. ROONEY (Lake Michigan area), *chairperson;* ROGER WALSH (inland area), *vice chairperson;* DAVID KEDROWSKI (Lake Superior area), MAUREEN KINNEY (Mississippi River area), LEE VAN ZEELAND (Lake Winnebago watershed). (All are appointed by governor with senate consent.)

Mailing Address: P.O. Box 7921, Madison 53707.

Location: State Natural Resources Building (GEF 2), 101 South Webster Street, Madison.

Telephone: (715) 822-8583.

Statutory References: Sections 15.345 (1) and 30.92.

Agency Responsibility: The 5-member Wisconsin Waterways Commission was created by Chapter 274, Laws of 1977. Its members serve staggered 5-year terms, and each must represent a specific geographic area and be knowledgeable about that area's recreational water use problems. The commission may have studies conducted to determine the need for recreational boating facilities; approve financial aid to local governments for development of recreational boating projects, including the acquisition of weed harvesters; and recommend administrative rules for the recreational facilities boating program.

Office of the
STATE PUBLIC DEFENDER

For e-mail combine the user ID and the state extender: userid**@opd.wi.gov**
All telephone numbers are 608 area code unless otherwise indicated.

Public Defender Board: DANIEL M. BERKOS, *chairperson;* REGINA DUNKIN (public member), *vice chairperson;* JAMES M. BRENNAN, DAVID COON, JOHN HOGAN, MICHAEL MAXWELL, ELLEN THORN; MAI NENG XIONG (public member), vacancy. (Except as indicated, all are state bar members. All are appointed by governor with senate consent.)

State Public Defender: KELLI THOMPSON, 266-0087, thompsonk@

Deputy State Public Defender: MICHAEL TOBIN, 266-8259, tobinm@

Legislative Liaison: ADAM PLOTKIN, 264-8572, plotkina@

Budget Director: ANNA OEHLER, 267-0311, oehlera@

Communications Director: RANDY KRAFT, 267-3587, kraftr@

Information Technology Director: GAIL ZAUCHA, 261-0621, zauchag@

Legal Counsel: DEVON LEE, 261-0633, leed@

Administrative Services Division: vacancy, *director,* 266-9447.

Appellate Division: MARLA J. STEPHENS, *director,* Madison: 264-8573; Milwaukee: (414) 227-4891; stephensm@

Assigned Counsel Division: KATHLEEN PAKES, *director,* 261-8856, pakesk@

Training Division: GINA PRUSKI, *director,* 266-6782, pruskig@

Trial Division: CATHERINE DORL, *director,* 267-9588, dorlc@; JENNIFER BIAS, *deputy director and affirmative action officer,* Milwaukee: (414) 227-4028; biasj@

Mailing Address: P.O. Box 7923, Madison 53707-7923.

Location: 315 North Henry Street, 2nd Floor, Madison.

Telephone: 266-0087.

Fax: 267-0584; Assigned Counsel Division Fax: 261-0625.

Internet Address: www.wisspd.org

Number of Employees: 579.85.

Total Budget 2011-13: $165,096,500.

Statutory References: Section 15.78; Chapter 977.

Agency Responsibility: The Office of the State Public Defender makes determinations of indigence and provides legal representation for persons in specified types of proceedings who are unable to afford a private attorney. The state public defender, who must be a member of the state bar, serves at the pleasure of the Public Defender Board.

Organization: The 9-member Public Defender Board appoints the state public defender, promulgates rules for determining indigence, and establishes procedures for certifying lists of private attorneys who can be assigned as counsel. Board members are appointed for staggered 3-year terms, and at least 5 of these must be members of the State Bar of Wisconsin. Members may not be or be employed by a judicial or law enforcement officer, a district attorney, a corporation counsel, or the state public defender.

Unit Functions: The *Administrative Services Division* oversees accounting, purchasing, payroll services, budget preparation, case management, and fiscal analysis.

The *Appellate Division* uses both program staff and private attorneys to provide post-judgement legal representation to the indigent and minors in criminal, civil commitment, juvenile code, and children's code cases in the trial and appellate courts.

The *Assigned Counsel Division* oversees a variety of functions related to appointment of private attorneys to represent indigent clients in cases not handled by staff, including certification and training, logistical support, and payment of fees.

The *Trial Division* provides legal representation at the trial level to indigent persons who have been charged with adult felony crimes or misdemeanors punishable by imprisonment. It also represents minors charged with juvenile offenses, persons subject to a petition for civil commitment, and individuals involved in termination of parental rights.

History: Both the United States Constitution (Sixth and Fourteenth Amendments) and the Wisconsin Constitution (Article I, Section 7), as interpreted by the U.S. and Wisconsin Supreme Courts, guarantee the right to publicly-provided counsel for poor people charged with crimes or facing potential deprivations of liberty. In 1859, the Wisconsin Supreme Court ruled, in *Carpenter and Sprague vs. the County of Dane* (9 Wis. 274), that a county is liable to pay for an attorney provided by the court in a criminal case to represent an indigent defendant who cannot otherwise afford representation.

The position of state public defender was created in 1966 by Chapter 479, Laws of 1965, under the supervision of the Wisconsin Supreme Court and funded, in part, by a private grant from the Ford Foundation. The duties of the office were originally confined to appellate defense, and its mission was to pursue post-conviction appeals for indigents before the appropriate courts, including the U.S. Supreme Court. Defense of indigents at the trial court level remained a county responsibility, dependent upon court-appointed private counsel paid by the county or privately funded public defender services.

Chapter 29, Laws of 1977, transferred the state public defender from the judicial branch to the executive branch as an independent agency under the Public Defender Board, which was authorized to appoint the defender to a 5-year renewable term with removal only for cause. (Chapter 356, Laws of 1979, later provided that the public defender serve at the pleasure of the board.) Chapter 29 also transferred the responsibility for defense of indigents at the trial level from the counties to the public defender's office, but representation by the defender's staff was limited, based on funding and statutory criteria. Client representation was, and continues to be, divided between staff attorneys and private counsel paid by the public defender.

Chapter 29, Laws of 1977, directed the public defender to determine the percentage of cases that private counsel would handle in each county. Chapter 356, Laws of 1979, established those percentages by law with the public defender staff assuming various portions of the caseloads in 47 counties and private counsel responsible for all cases in the remaining 25 counties. 1985

Wisconsin Act 29 expanded the use of public defender staff attorneys to all 72 counties and repealed the sunset provision enacted in 1979, which would have abolished the agency, effective November 15, 1985.

1995 Wisconsin Act 27 directed the public defender to enter into annual fixed fee contracts with private counsel and limited the number of trial-level cases assigned to private attorneys to one-third of all cases handled. It also eliminated public defender representation in some cases, including certain matters related to prison and jail conditions, sentence modifications, probation and parole revocations, child support, and parents of children in need of protection or services (CHIPS).

2009 Wisconsin Act 164 revised the financial criteria for public defender representation and provided for additional staff positions to provide services to 75% of the additional clients who will qualify for representation. Act 164 was designed to reduce the number of cases in which the courts appoint an attorney at county expense and to enhance consistency in appointment of attorneys statewide.

Department of
PUBLIC INSTRUCTION

Address e-mail by combining the user ID and the state extender: userid@**dpi.wi.gov**
All telephone numbers are 608 area code unless otherwise indicated.

State Superintendent: TONY EVERS, 266-1771, anthony.evers@

Deputy State Superintendent: MIKE THOMPSON, 266-1771, michael.thompson@

Executive Assistant: JESSICA JUSTMAN, 266-1771, jessica.justman@

Special Assistant: SCOTT JONES, 266-1771, scott.jones@

Legal Services, Office of: JANET JENKINS, *chief legal counsel,* 266-9353, janet.jenkins@

Education Information Services: JOHN JOHNSON, *director,* 266-1098, john.johnson@

Policy Initiatives Advisor Executive: vacancy, 266-1771.

Legislative Liaison: JENNIFER KAMMERUD, 266-7073, jennifer.kammerud@

Mailing Address: P.O. Box 7841, Madison 53707-7841.

Location: State Education Building (GEF 3), 125 South Webster Street, Madison.

Telephones: 266-3390; (800) 441-4563; TDD: 267-2427.

Fax: 267-5188.

Internet Addresses: Departmental: www.dpi.wi.gov; BadgerLink: www.badgerlink.net

Number of Employees: 635.57.

Total Budget 2011-13: $11,990,588,800.

Constitutional Reference: Article X, Section 1.

Statutory References: Section 15.37; Chapters 43 and 115-121.

Academic Excellence, Division for: SHEILA BRIGGS, *assistant superintendent,* 266-3361, sheila.briggs@; Division Fax: 267-9275.

    Career and Technical Education: SHARON WENDT, *director,* 267-9251, sharon.wendt@

    Common Core State Standards Implementation: EMILIE AMUNDSON, *director,* 267-3726, emilie.amundson@

    Content and Learning: REBECCA VAIL, *director,* 266-2364, rebecca.vail@

    Educator Effectiveness: JULIE BRILLI, *director,* 267-9551, julie.brilli@

    Teacher Education, Professional Development, and Licensing: TAMMY HUTH, *director,* 266-0986, tammy.huth@

Finance and Management, Division for: BRIAN PAHNKE, *assistant superintendent,* 267-9124, brian.pahnke@; Division Fax: 266-3644.

DEPARTMENT OF PUBLIC INSTRUCTION

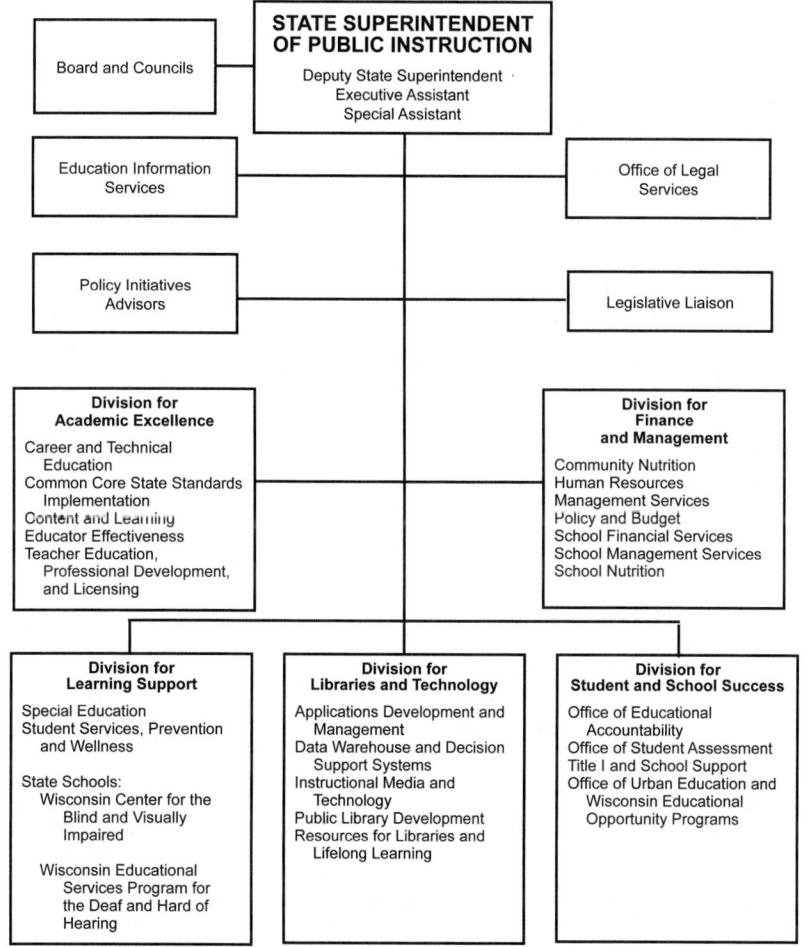

Community Nutrition: AMANDA KANE, *director,* 267-9123, amanda.kane@

Human Resources: KATHERINE KNUDSON, *director,* 267-9200, katherine.knudson@

Management Services: SUE LINTON, *director,* 266-3320, suzanne.linton@

Policy and Budget: MICHAEL BORMETT, *director,* 266-2804, michael.bormett@

School Financial Services: ROBERT SOLDNER, *director,* 266-6968, robert.soldner@

School Management Services: vacancy, *director,* 266-7475.

School Nutrition: JESSICA SHARKUS, *director,* 267-9121, jessica.sharkus@

Learning Support, Division for: CAROLYN STANFORD TAYLOR, *assistant superintendent,* 266-1649, carolyn.stanford.taylor@; Division Fax: 267-3746, Division TTY: 267-2427.

Special Education: STEPHANIE PETSKA, *director,* 266-1781, stephanie.petska@

Student Services, Prevention and Wellness: DOUGLAS WHITE, *director,* 266-5198, douglas.white@

Wisconsin Center for the Blind and Visually Impaired: Peter Dally, *director,* 1700 West State Street, Janesville 53546-5399, (608) 758-6100, (800) 832-9784, Fax: (608) 758-6161, peter.dally@

Wisconsin Educational Services Program for the Deaf and Hard of Hearing: Alex Slappey, *director,* 309 West Walworth Avenue, Delavan 53115-1099, (262) 740-2066, voice: (877) 973-3323, TTY: (877) 973-3324, Fax: (262) 728-7160, alex.slappey@

Libraries and Technology, Division for: Kurt Kiefer, *assistant superintendent,* 266-2205, kurt.kiefer@; Division Fax: 267-9207.

Division Internet Address: http://dlt.dpi.wi.gov/

> *Applications Development and Management:* Dan Retzlaff, *manager,* 267-2285, daniel.retzlaff@
>
> *Data Warehouse and Decision Support Systems:* Melissa Straw, *manager,* 266-1089, melissa.straw@
>
> *Instructional Media and Technology:* Jeff Knutsen, *director,* 266-3856, jeffrey.knutsen@
>
> *Public Library Development:* John DeBacher, *director,* 267-9225, john.debacher@
>
> *Resources for Libraries and Lifelong Learning:* Martha Berninger, *director,* 224-6161, martha.berninger@

Student and School Success, Division for: Lynette Russell, *assistant superintendent,* 266-5450, lynette.russell@; Division Fax: 267-9142.

> *Educational Accountability, Office of:* Laura Pinsonneault, *director,* 267-1072, laura.pinsonneault@
>
> *Student Assessment, Office of:* Troy Couillard, *director,* 267-1072, troy.couillard@
>
> *Title I and School Support:* Mary Kleusch, *director,* 267-3163, mary.kleusch@
>
> *Urban Education, Office of* and *Wisconsin Educational Opportunity Programs:* Kevin Ingram, *director,* (414) 227-4413, kevin.ingram@

Publications: Biennial Report; Wisconsin School Directory; various curriculum, instruction, library and student services publications and research studies. Electronic publications include *Channel Weekly, DPI-ConnectED,* various program area newsletters and Web sites, including the School Performance Report and Wisconsin Information Network for Successful Schools (WINSS), available on the department's Internet site.

Agency Responsibility: The Department of Public Instruction provides direction and technical assistance for public elementary and secondary education in Wisconsin. The department offers a broad range of programs and professional services to local school administrators and staff. It distributes state school aids and administers federal aids to supplement local tax resources, improves curriculum and school operations, ensures education for children with disabilities, offers professional guidance and counseling, and develops school and public library resources.

Organization: The department is headed by the State Superintendent of Public Instruction, a constitutional officer who is elected on the nonpartisan spring ballot for a term of 4 years. The state superintendent appoints a deputy state superintendent and assistant state superintendents from outside the classified service. The assistant superintendents are responsible for administering the operating divisions of the department. The superintendent also appoints the director of the Office of Educational Accountability, which was created in Section 15.374 (1), Wisconsin Statutes, by 1993 Wisconsin Act 16.

Unit Functions: The *Division for Academic Excellence (DAE)* provides leadership and professional development regarding curriculum development, academic and technical skills standards, and instructional methods and strategies, as well as professional learning and support to a variety of content area educators. The division is comprised of five teams: Career and Technical Education; Common Core State Standards Implementation; Content and Learning; Educator Effectiveness; and Teacher Education, Professional Development and Licensing. A service orientation and culturally responsive view guide the teams' work to provide technical assistance to educators, parents, communities, and professional organizations.

The division reviews and approves educator preparation programs and licenses teachers, pupil services personnel, administrators, and library professionals. The division monitors school district and vocational education compliance with state nondiscrimination laws and rules.

The division administers a variety of programs that provide assistance and grants to public school students and teachers on the basis of merit and need, as well as provides consultation and leadership for multicultural education. These programs include: American Indian Studies Program, American Indian Language and Culture Education, Herb Kohl Educational Foundation Award Program, Presidential Awards for Mathematics and Science Teachers, U.S. Senate Youth Program, Urban Teacher World Program, as well as international partnerships with Germany, China, Japan, Thailand, and France. DAE also directs youth options, education for employment, the career and technical student organizations, and administers the high school equivalency/general educational development (HSED/GED) program for state residents who have not completed high school.

DAE administers federal programs that provide assistance for world languages, advanced placement, and alternative education. The division administers funds for school districts under the Carl D. Perkins Career and Technical Education Act of 2006 to enhance and improve career and technical educational programs. DAE also administers part of the state and federally funded Bilingual/English as a Second Language Program.

The division provides a cradle-to-career focus for instructional leaders and educators through work done by the Office of Early Learning and by providing standards and supports through high school and the transition to postsecondary work. The division curates and creates high quality resources to assist with Common Core State Standards implementation. Resources and technical assistance are provided around career and technical education standards and other core academic standards. Gifted and Talented education support can also be found in the Division for Academic Excellence.

The division is leading efforts to develop and implement a statewide educator effectiveness system, where all educators will be evaluated based upon multiple measures. This complex system factors in educator practice and student performance in providing feedback to educators around their strengths and areas for improvement.

The *Division for Finance and Management* distributes state and federal school aids and grants; administers school district revenue limits; monitors the Milwaukee Parental Choice Program and the interdistrict open enrollment program; prescribes school financial accounting methods; consults with school districts on their budgets; and collects, analyzes, and publishes school finance data. Consulting services are provided to assist districts and charter schools with management and planning, school district reorganization, pupil transportation, private school relations, school board elections and duties, and finance and asset management. The division is responsible for both state and federally funded school food and nutrition services, nonschool child care food services, and elderly nutrition programs. It also provides support services to the department for financial management, human resources, budget preparation, educational policy and administrative rule development, and legislative analysis.

The *Division for Learning Support,* created in Section 15.373 (1), Wisconsin Statutes, as the Division for Handicapped Children by Chapter 327, Laws of 1967, formerly named in 1993 Wisconsin Act 335, as the Division for Learning Support: Equity and Advocacy, and most recently renamed in 2011 Wisconsin Act 158, provides technical assistance, leadership, advocacy, staff development, training, and education to help meet the diverse cultural, emotional, social, health, and educational needs of Wisconsin's youth. The mission is met through collaboration with federal, state, and local groups. The division manages state and federal resources, monitors and evaluates programs and practices, and facilitates school-district and community efforts to meet specific needs of students. The division administers programs involving school nursing, social work, psychological services, and school counseling services; alcohol, tobacco, and other drug abuse; suicide prevention; alcohol and traffic safety; school-age parents; school violence prevention; prevention of HIV and other sexually transmitted diseases; pregnancy prevention; health education; physical education and activity; coordinated school health programs; compulsory school attendance; and after-school programs.

The division offers technical assistance and financial support to help school districts provide a free appropriate public education for students with disabilities, combat educational discrimination, and train professional staff. It is responsible for special educational programs and services for students with disabilities. It must ensure that all students with disabilities are identified, evaluated, and provided appropriate education and services. It supervises all special education programs and checks their compliance with departmental standards and state and federal law. The division provides consultation for and supervision of the Pupil Nondiscrimination Program.

The division administers the Wisconsin Educational Services Program for the Deaf and Hard of Hearing (WESP-DHH) and the Wisconsin Center for the Blind and Visually Impaired (WCBVI). Each program operates a residential school for state residents who are ages 3 to 21, have a visual or hearing impairment, and need individualized instruction. Both schools provide academic and vocational education on site at no cost to families. Both programs also offer instructional and technical assistance, teaching materials, and evaluations of pupils to local school districts and other agencies.

The *Division for Libraries and Technology (DLT)*, created as the Division for Library Services in Section 15.373 (2), Wisconsin Statutes, by Chapter 327, Laws of 1967, renamed as the Division for Libraries, Technology, and Community Learning in 2001 Wisconsin Act 48, and most recently renamed the Division for Libraries and Technology in 2011 Wisconsin Act 158, provides assistance for the development and improvement of public and school libraries; fosters interlibrary cooperation and resource sharing; and promotes information and instructional technology in schools and libraries. The division administers the state aid program for Wisconsin's 17 public library systems. It also administers the federal Library Services and Technology Act. The division facilitates interlibrary loan and reference services to the state's libraries and manages WISCAT (www.WISCAT.net), the interlibrary loan management system and electronic union and virtual catalog of Wisconsin library holdings. The division also acts as a state-level clearinghouse for interlibrary loan requests; administers BadgerLink (www.badgerlink.net), the statewide full-text database project that allows access to thousands of magazines, newsletters, newspapers, pamphlets, and historical documents; and, in collaboration with other Wisconsin library organizations, manages BadgerLearn, the statewide portal of training and professional development materials created by the Wisconsin library community. The division manages contracts with library organizations necessary to the provision of interlibrary loan services, library service to the blind and visually impaired, and enhancing awareness of high quality children's literature in the school and library communities. The division directs the public librarian certification program, and the summer library reading program, and provides planning and coordination for the development of libraries in schools and Wisconsin communities, as well as regional public library systems.

DLT also serves as the information technology team for the entire agency. One of the division's teams implements and supports a new statewide K-12 data warehouse and dashboard system; this data warehouse system aggregates data from a variety of data collections and information systems into an easy-to-use interface for every school district across Wisconsin known as WISEdash. The division provides information and resources for and about schools through WINSS (Wisconsin Information Network for Successful Schools), SDPR (School District Performance Report), and other department resources. DLT also provides guidance and oversight to instructional technology efforts in all Wisconsin school districts. The DLT staff has led the development of a statewide digital learning strategic plan with the state superintendent's Digital Learning Advisory Council, creating a roadmap for all school districts. Project efforts include creation of a statewide learning management system and virtual professional learning community portal. In addition, DLT provides guidance on development of local technology and library media program plans and utilization of the Common School Fund, and consults on school library media program staff licensure. The staff also facilitates professional learning activities associated with education technology integration within schools.

The *Division for Student and School Success* is responsible for ensuring that all children attain proficiency in meeting the Wisconsin Model Academic Standards. The four teams in this division, Educational Accountability, Student Assessment, Title I and School Support, and Wisconsin Educational Opportunity Programs and Urban Education, have as a major focus closing the achievement gap that exists among children of color, the economically disadvantaged, and their peers.

The Office of Educational Accountability provides data to assist district and school person-nel in evaluating and making decisions related to educational planning and programming. This team provides accountability outcomes via School and District Report Cards related to state and federal legislation and gives technical assistance in evaluating results and developing approach-es to using data to inform decisions ensuring students are prepared for college and careers.

The Office of Student Assessment provides statewide assessments which measure student proficiency related to the Wisconsin Model Academic Standards and the Common Core State Standards. Assessments also include screening measures in early literacy and English language proficiency. The data from these assessments are compiled into reports for district and school improvement efforts as well as meeting the expectations of state and federal reporting require-ments.

The Title I and School Support Team provides a multitude of resources to districts and schools that include a number of programs under the federal Elementary and Secondary Education Act of 1965 and the No Child Left Behind Act of 2001, including programs under Title I-Part A, Even Start, Migrant Education, Neglected and Delinquent Youth, McKinney-Vento Homeless Assistance Act, the VISTA program, and the state class size reduction program Student Achieve-ment Guarantee in Education (SAGE).

The Wisconsin Educational Opportunity Programs and Urban Education Team focuses on improving high school graduation rates, reducing dropouts and encouraging nontraditional, mi-nority, disadvantaged, and low-income students with college potential to pursue postsecondary education. Programs to achieve team objectives include state and federal Talent Search, Talent Incentive Program, Early Identification Program, Pre-College Scholarship Program, Gear Up, and Upward Bound Program. The Urban Education program was established in 1995 to provide services to urban areas including Beloit, Kenosha, Milwaukee, and Racine to facilitate coopera-tive efforts to address the challenges and equity needs facing families, children, and educators in an urban setting. Programs to achieve team objectives include Special Education, Title I, and Urban Staff Development and Teacher Education Program Review.

History: The Wisconsin Constitution, as adopted in 1848, required the state legislature to pro-vide by law for the establishment of district schools that would be free to all children between the ages of 4 and 20 years. It also created a State Superintendent of Public Instruction to super-vise public education. Under the 1849 Wisconsin Statutes, the superintendent was ordered to visit schools in all the counties, recommend textbooks and courses of instruction, and distribute state money for public schools to the counties.

Originally, the superintendent was elected to a 2-year term at the partisan general election in November. With the adoption of a constitutional amendment in 1902, the superintendent was placed on the nonpartisan April ballot and given a 4-year term of office.

In the early years of statehood, the hiring of teachers was entirely a local matter. In 1861, the legislature created county superintendents of schools with the power to license teachers begin-ning in 1862. The state superintendent was also given licensing authority in 1868 (Chapter 169). Local districts and county superintendents continued to license teachers until 1939, when the legislature gave that power exclusively to the Department of Public Instruction.

For a number of years, state support of public education consisted of money derived prin-cipally from the sale of public lands that the federal government had granted to the state. In Chapter 287, Laws of 1885, the legislature levied a one-mill (one-tenth of a cent) state property tax to be collected by the state and distributed to counties for school support. The state's first attempt to equalize tax support for schools in property-poor districts was the Wisconsin El-ementary Equalization Law of 1927 (Chapter 536). It was promoted by State Superintendent John Callahan, who also urged a 40% level of state support for local school costs – a figure not reached until after 1970. The 1995 Legislature enacted a law to ensure that state aids and school levy tax credits would cover two-thirds of local school revenues, but subsequently repealed that requirement in 2003.

Originally, Wisconsin only required tax support for elementary schools. Individual cities, such as Racine and Kenosha, funded their own high schools. The legislature enacted public support for high schools in 1875 (Chapter 323). Kindergarten originated in 1856 when Margarethe Schurz started a German-speaking program for children 2 through 5 years of age in Watertown, Wisconsin. The first public school kindergarten opened in Manitowoc in 1873 for 4- and 5-year-old children. The program continued to spread until, in 1973, the legislature required school districts to provide a 5-year-old kindergarten. In the 1990s, an increasing number of school districts offered full-day programs for 5-year-old children and kindergarten programs for 4-year-olds.

Although state law had contained some curriculum requirements as early as 1849, the legislature did not establish high school graduation requirements until 1983. In 1985, it prescribed a detailed set of standards local districts must meet to be eligible for state aid. The 1997 Legislature mandated that school boards adopt pupil academic standards in certain subjects, a series of examinations to measure pupil achievement in 4th, 8th, and 10th grades, and a high school graduation examination. The 2003 Legislature eliminated the high school graduation examination.

State concern for special education began with the establishment of the Wisconsin Institute for Education of the Blind in Janesville in 1850 and a school for the deaf in Delavan in 1852. These schools were administered by public welfare agencies until transferred to the Department of Public Instruction in 1947. The 1927 Legislature enacted laws to provide aid for special classes for "crippled children" and increased aid for districts to educate mentally handicapped children. Funding for education of all handicapped children was enacted in 1973 to comply with federal law.

While state administration of school libraries fell under the jurisdiction of the superintendent, the Free Library Commission set standards for public libraries. In 1965, the legislature transferred this function to the department.

Statutory Board and Councils

Alcohol and Other Drug Abuse Programs, Council on: GARY ALBRECHT, *chairperson;* ARTHUR ANDERSON, CHRISTINE CLAIR, MARCIA CREASEY, JIM HICKEY, JOSEPH KUCAK, CARRIE KULINSKI, DENISE SATHER, WENDELL WAUKAU, 9 vacancies (appointed by state superintendent).

The Council on Alcohol and Other Drug Abuse Programs advises the state superintendent about programs to prevent or reduce alcohol, tobacco, and other drug abuse by minors. The council consists of 18 members (by administrative rule) who serve at the pleasure of the state superintendent. The council was created by Chapter 331, Laws of 1979, and its duties are prescribed in Section 115.36 of the statutes.

Blind and Visual Impairment Education Council: NISSAN BAR-LEV (special education director), *chairperson;* STEPHANIE KLAS, PATRICIA MATHEWS, ERIN RANDALL-CLARK (parents of visually impaired children); JULIE HAPEMAN, CHERYL ORGAS, CHRIS ZENCHENKO (members of organizations affiliated with visually impaired); DAWN SOTO (licensed teacher of visually impaired); SADIQUA WHITE-HARPER (licensed teacher of orientation and mobility); vacancy (licensed general education teacher); NANCY THOMPSON (school board member); vacancy (school district administrator); FRED WOLLENBURG (CESA representative); MARY KAREN OUDEANS (higher education representative); MARY ANN DAMM, MARY SPIDELL, vacancy (other members) (all appointed by superintendent).

The 17-member Blind and Visual Impairment Education Council advises the state superintendent on statewide activities that will benefit visually impaired pupils; makes recommendations for improvements in services provided by the Wisconsin Center for the Blind and Visually Impaired; and proposes ways to improve the preparation of teachers and staff and coordination between the department and other agencies that offer services to the visually impaired. Members serve 3-year terms. At least one must be certified by the Library of Congress as a Braille transcriber. The higher education representative must either have experience as an educator of the visually impaired or an educator of teachers of the visually impaired. At least one of the three remaining members must be visually impaired. The council was created as the Council on the Blind by Chapter 276, Laws of 1969, renamed as the Council on the Education of the Blind in Chapter 292, Laws of 1971, and renamed and substantially revised by 1999 Wisconsin Act 9. Its composition and duties are prescribed in Sections 15.377 (1) and 115.37 of the statutes.

Deaf and Hard-of-Hearing Education Council: DAVID COLLINS, MICHELLE KIHNTOPF (parents of hearing impaired children); POLLY ANN WILLIAMS-SLAPPEY (teacher of hearing impaired pupils); PAULA MINIX (licensed speech-language pathologist); BRIAN ANDERSON (school district special education director); BETH LARIMER (licensed audiologist with expertise in educational audiology); AMY OTIS-WILBORN (educator of hearing impaired teachers); vacancy (interpreter training instructor); THERESA KAMENICK (educational interpreter); ROBIN BARNES, ANDREW KONKEL, JOAN-NA COOKIE ROANG (other members); MICHELLE PANDIAN (itinerate teacher); KORYN KONEAZNY (regular education teacher) (all appointed by state superintendent).

The Deaf and Hard-of-Hearing Education Council advises the state superintendent on issues related to pupils who are hearing impaired. It informs the superintendent on services, programs, and research that could benefit those students. The council makes recommendations for improving services provided by the Wisconsin Educational Services Program for the Deaf and Hard of Hearing; reviews and makes recommendations on the level of quality and services available to hearing-impaired pupils; proposes ways to improve the preparation of teachers and other staff who provide services to the hearing impaired; and proposes ways to improve coordination between the department and providers of services to the hearing impaired. The council's 12 statutory members serve 3-year terms. It was created by 2001 Wisconsin Act 57, and its composition and duties are prescribed in Sections 15.377 (2) and 115.372 of the statutes.

Library and Network Development, Council on: SANDRA MELCHER (public member), *chairperson;* ANNETTE SMITH (professional member), *vice chairperson;* KRISTI WILLIAMS (public member), *secretary;* EWA BARCZYK, NITA BURKE, JOSHUA COWLES, RHONDA GOULD, ROBERT KOECHLEY, JOAN ROBB, EMILY ROGERS, vacancy (professional members); BARBARA ARNOLD, MICHAEL BAHR, CARA CAVIN, FRANCIS CHERNEY, MIRIAM ERICKSON, DOUGLAS H. LAY, CALVIN POTTER, KRIS ADAMS WENDT (public members) (appointed by governor).

The 19-member Council on Library and Network Development advises the state superintendent and the administrator of the Division for Libraries and Technology on the performance of their duties regarding library service. Members serve 3-year terms. The professional members represent various types of libraries and information services. The public members must demonstrate an interest in libraries and other types of information services. The council was created by Chapter 347, Laws of 1979, and its composition and duties are prescribed in Sections 15.377 (6) and 43.07 of the statutes.

Professional Standards Council for Teachers: ARTHUR ANDERSON (public school pupil services professional), *chairperson;* TERRY SCHOESSOW (public school teacher), *vice chairperson;* WILLIAM DALLAS (public school teacher), *secretary;* LINDA LUEDTKE (public school pupil services professional); LISA BENZ, PAULA HASE, KATHERINE SWAIN, vacancy (public school teachers); STEPHANIE ARMSTRONG (public school special education teacher); SUE NELSON (private school teacher); KARIN EXO (public school principal); JOHN GAIER (public school district administrator); KATY HEYNING, JULIE UNDERWOOD (UW System educational faculty members); JAMES JUERGENSEN (private college education faculty member); JOHN HASLAM, vacancy (public school board members); AMY STEPHENSON (parent of public school child); ALEXANDRA AGAR (student enrolled in teacher preparatory program) (appointed by state superintendent with senate consent).

The 19-member Professional Standards Council for Teachers advises the state superintendent regarding licensing and evaluating teachers; evaluation and approval of teacher education programs; the status of teaching in Wisconsin; school board practices to develop effective teaching; peer mentoring; evaluation systems; and alternative dismissal procedures.

Members serve 3-year terms, except the student member, who serves for 2 years. Public school teachers and pupil service professionals are recommended by the largest statewide labor organization representing teachers. The private school teacher is recommended by the Wisconsin Council of Religious and Independent Schools. The public school administrator and principal are recommended by their statewide organizations. Faculty members are recommended by the UW System president and the Wisconsin Association of Independent Colleges and Universities. The council was created by 1997 Wisconsin Act 298, and its composition and duties are prescribed in Sections 15.377 (8) and 115.425 of the statutes.

School District Boundary Appeal Board: TONY EVERS (superintendent of public instruction); DAVID AMUNDSON, PATRICK DORIN, RICHARD ELORANTA, MARY KATHLEEN MALONEY, STEVEN PATE, SPENCER ROTZEL, PETER SEVERSON, PATRICIA SILVER, THERESE TRAVIA, 3 vacancies (appointed by state superintendent).

The 13-member School District Boundary Appeal Board hears appeals from persons aggrieved by actions taken under Chapter 117, Wisconsin Statutes, providing for school district reorganization. The appointed members include 4 each from large, medium, and small district school boards, who are appointed for staggered 2-year terms. No two members may live within the boundaries of the same CESA. The board was created by 1983 Wisconsin Act 27, and its composition and duties are prescribed in Sections 15.375 (2) and 117.05 of the statutes.

Special Education, Council on: JOHN PETERSON, *chairperson;* NICOLA CIURRO, *vice chairperson;* MARGARET CARPENTER, KATHRYN CHARLAND, JIM DIMOCK, NANCY DONAHUE, MICHAEL GRECO, CLAUDIA WEAVER HENDRICKSON, PATRICIA LANCOUR, SUE LARSON, PATRICIA LUEBKE, DON NIELSEN, LORI PETTIBONE, COURTNEY SALZER, STACY SKONING, DIANE SLIVKA, CHERI SYLLA, LAURA WEAVER, CARLA WITKOWSKI (appointed by state superintendent).

The Council on Special Education advises the state superintendent on programs for children with disabilities. It assists in developing evaluations, and reporting data to the U.S. Department of Education, developing policies, and advising the state superintendent regarding the needs of children with disabilities. The number of council members is unspecified, but the following categories must be represented: regular and special education teachers; institutions of higher education that train special education personnel; state and local education officials; administrators of programs for children with disabilities; agencies involved in financing or delivery of related services; private schools and charter schools; a vocational, community, or business organization that provides transitional services; the Department of Corrections; parents of children with disabilities; and individuals with disabilities. Council members are appointed for 3-year terms, and the majority must be individuals with disabilities or parents of children with disabilities. The council was created as the Council on Exceptional Education by Chapter 89, Laws of 1973, and renamed and revised by 1997 Wisconsin Act 164. Its composition and duties are prescribed in Section 15.377 (4) of the statutes.

PUBLIC SERVICE COMMISSION

Address e-mail by combining the user ID and the state extender: userid@**wisconsin.gov**
All telephone numbers are 608 area code unless otherwise indicated.

Commissioners: PHIL MONTGOMERY, 267-7897, phil.montgomery@, *chairperson;* ERIC CALLISTO, 267-7898, eric.callisto@; ELLEN NOWAK, 267-7899, ellen.nowak@ (appointed by governor with senate consent).

Executive Assistant to the Chairperson: R.J. PIRLOT, 267-7897, rj.pirlot@

Secretary to the Commission: SANDRA PASKE, 266-1265, sandra.paske@

Administrative Law Judge, Office of: MICHAEL NEWMARK, *administrative law judge,* 261-8523, michael.newmark@

Governmental and Public Affairs, Office of: NATHAN CONRAD, *director,* 266-9600, nathan.conrad@

General Counsel: CYNTHIA SMITH, 266-1264, cynthia.smith@

Legislative Liaison: ELISE NELSON, 267-3589, elise.nelson@

Administrative Services, Division of: SARAH KLEIN, *administrator,* 266-3587, sarah.klein@

Natural Gas and Energy Division: ROBERT NORCROSS, *administrator,* 266-0699, robert.norcross@

Telecommunications Division: vacancy, *administrator.*

Water, Compliance and Consumer Affairs, Division of: vacancy, *administrator,* 266-3767.

Mailing Address: P.O. Box 7854, Madison 53707-7854.

Location: Public Service Commission Building, 610 North Whitney Way, Madison.

Telephones: General inquiries: (888) 816-3831 (in-state only) or 266-5481; Consumer affairs (800) 225-7729; Complaints: (800) 225-7729 (in-state only) or 266-2001; Media relations: 266-9600; TTY: (800) 251-8345 (in-state only) or 267-1479.

Fax: 266-3957.

E-mail Address: pscrecs@psc.wi.gov

Internet Address: http://psc.wi.gov

Publications: Biennial report; strategic energy assessment; various statistics on electric utilities, gas utilities, and telephone companies and guides for utility customers, including publications for consumers related to electricity, natural gas, water, and telephone services.

Number of Employees: 147.10.

Total Budget 2011-13: $46,980,200.

Statutory References: Sections 15.06 and 15.79; Chapter 196.

Agency Responsibility: The Public Service Commission (PSC) is responsible for regulating Wisconsin's public utilities and ensuring that utility services are provided to customers at prices reasonable to both ratepayers and utility owners. The commission regulates the rates and services of electric, gas distribution, heating, water, and combined water and sewer utilities. The commission has limited jurisdiction over landline telecommunications providers and services. In most instances, the commission's jurisdiction does not extend to the activities of electric cooperatives, wireless telephone providers, cable television, or Internet service.

Responsibilities of the commission include setting utility rates, determining levels for adequate and safe service, and utility bond sales and stock offerings. It confirms or rejects utility applications for major construction projects, such as power plants, transmission lines, and wind farms. In addition to ensuring utility compliance with statutes, administrative codes, and recordkeeping requirements, the commission's staff investigates and mediates thousands of consumer complaints annually. During the complaint process, commission staff reviews all pertinent information to make certain that the utility's handling of the complaint is in compliance with the applicable rules. The commission also rules on proposed mergers between utility companies.

The commission certifies various types of telecommunications providers, manages the Universal Service Fund, handles some wholesale disputes between providers including interconnection agreement filings and disputes, and administers telephone numbering resources.

Organization: The governor appoints the 3 full-time commissioners, with senate approval, to serve staggered 6-year terms, but an individual commissioner holds office until a successor is appointed and qualified. No commissioner may have a financial interest in a railroad or public utility or water carrier or serve on or under a political party committee. By work rule, no employee or immediate family member may own stock in a utility or any entity regulated by the commission. The governor designates a chairperson who, in turn, may appoint division administrators from outside the classified service.

Unit Functions: The *Division of Administrative Services* provides the commission's human resources and personnel management, budget development, financial management, information technology, staff development, facilities management, intervenor financing coordination, procurement, and grants administration. Its central records management staff provides agency staff with printing, mail, and case file services.

The *Natural Gas and Energy Division* is responsible for all aspects of regulating electric utilities and the provision of natural gas service. PSC approval is required for utilities to change rates, build power plants, or construct major transmission lines. The division looks at need, alternatives, costs, and environmental impacts for construction cases and reviews finances, corporate structure, and affiliated interests in rate cases. It also provides the commissioners with information they need in order to make decisions regarding construction and rate cases.

The *Telecommunications Division* is responsible for oversight of the telecommunication industry in Wisconsin and resolution of disputes involving those services that are within PSC jurisdiction. The PSC promotes competition in the state's telecommunications markets in order to ensure access to modern and affordable service throughout the state. The PSC works to resolve disputes between service providers, administers universal service programs, administers telephone numbering resources, and advises the Federal Communications Commission on matters pertaining to Wisconsin's interests in federal telecommunications policy. The division also undertakes the PSC's efforts on broadband infrastructure mapping and planning.

The *Division of Water, Compliance and Consumer Affairs* is responsible for regulating water and sewer public utilities in Wisconsin and ensuring utility compliance with the consumer sections of the state administrative code and statutes. The division offers assistance to all of the state's utilities for compliance with the statutes, code, and record-keeping requirements and the development of consumer affairs policies. The division also coordinates consumer information and mediates resolutions to consumer complaints.

History: Public utility regulation in Wisconsin followed and was closely related to railroad regulation. Railroads were the first modern enterprise to have their rates regulated, and Wisconsin became one of the first states to pass such laws. Chapter 273, Laws of 1874, established a railroad rate structure and provided for 3 appointed railroad commissioners to supervise rail freight operations. Two years later in Chapter 57, Laws of 1876, the legislature repealed much of the 1874 law and established a single appointed commissioner of railroads. The commissioner was made an elected official in 1881 (Chapter 300).

The forerunner of today's commission dates from Chapter 362, Laws of 1905, which created an appointed 3-member Railroad Commission to supervise rail operations, appraise railroad property, and set rates. With the enactment of Chapter 499, Laws of 1907, which extended the powers of the Railroad Commission, Wisconsin became the first state to regulate all public utilities.

Chapter 183, Laws of 1931, renamed the agency the Public Service Commission of Wisconsin and made it responsible for comprehensive motor carrier regulation in 1933 (Chapter 488). The 1967 executive branch reorganization continued the commission as an independent agency. Chapter 29, Laws of 1977, transferred the commission's railroad and motor carrier regulatory functions to the Transportation Commission (recreated in 1982 as the now defunct Office of the Commissioner of Transportation). Railroad regulation was assigned to the newly created Office of the Commissioner of Railroads by 1993 Wisconsin Act 123.

Laws passed in 1985 provided for a partial deregulation of public utility holding companies and telecommunications service. 1993 Wisconsin Act 496 significantly altered the regulation of telecommunications utilities, particularly regarding rate-setting procedures. 2011 Wisconsin Act 22 established a new regulatory framework for telecommunications utilities, which eliminated the commission's authority to regulate the prices utilities charge telecommunications customers, as well as removing the commission's authority to investigate most consumer complaints involving retail telecommunications issues.

Statutory Councils

Telecommunications Privacy Council: Inactive.

The Telecommunications Privacy Council advises the commission on guidelines designed to protect the privacy of users of telecommunications services. The number of members on the council is not specified, but all must represent telecommunications providers or consumers. The council was created by 1993 Wisconsin Act 496 and its composition and duties are prescribed in Section 196.209 of the statutes.

Universal Service Fund Council: DAVID BYERS, JILL COLLINS, JAMES COSTELLO, PAM HOLMES, GWEN JACKSON, JOANNE JOHNSON, BOB JONES, ROBERT KELLERMAN, JEAN PAUK, CHRIS RASCH, KATHY SCHMITT, PAMELA SHERWOOD, PAULETTE WATFORD (appointed by Public Service Commission).

Universal Service Fund Manager: JEFF RICHTER, Public Service Commission, P.O. Box 7854, Madison 53707-7854; Telephone: 267-9624; Fax: 266-3957; TTY: (800) 251-8345 (in-state only) or 267-1479; jeff.richter@

The Universal Service Fund Council advises the commission on the administration of the Universal Service Fund, which assists low-income customers, disabled customers, and customers in areas where telecommunication service costs are relatively high, in obtaining affordable access to basic telecommunication services. The Universal Service Fund manager acts as liaison between the commission and the council. The number of members on the council is not specified. All must represent telecommunication service providers or consumers, but the majority of members must be consumers. The council was created by 1993 Wisconsin Act 496 and its composition and duties are prescribed in Section 196.218 (6) of the statutes.

Wind Siting Council: TOM GREEN, WILLIAM RAKOCY (representing wind energy system developers); GLEN SCHWALBACH (town representative); SCOTT GODFREY (county representative); DAN EBERT, ANDY HESSELBACH (representing the energy industry); TYSON COOK, MICHAEL VICKERMAN (representing environmental groups); GEORGE KRAUSE, JR., TOM MEYER (representing realtors); JAMES AMSTADT, JARRED SEARLS (adjacent or nearby landowners not receiving compensation for hosting wind energy systems); JENNIFER HEINZEN, CARL KUEHNE (public members); vacancy (University of Wisconsin System faculty member with expertise regarding health impacts of wind energy systems) (appointed by Public Service Commission).

The 15-member Wind Siting Council advises the commission on promulgation of rules relating to restrictions a political subdivision may impose on the installation of a wind energy system including setback requirements that provide reasonable protection from any health effects. The council also surveys the peer-reviewed scientific research regarding the health impacts of wind energy systems and studies state and national regulatory developments regarding the siting of wind energy systems. The members of the council are appointed by the commission for 3-year terms. The council was created by 2009 Wisconsin Act 40 and its composition and duties are prescribed in Sections 15.797 (1) and 196.378 (4g) of the statutes.

INDEPENDENT UNIT ATTACHED FOR BUDGETING, PROGRAM COORDINATION, AND RELATED MANAGEMENT FUNCTIONS BY SECTION 15.03 OF THE STATUTES

OFFICE OF THE COMMISSIONER OF RAILROADS

Commissioner of Railroads: JEFF PLALE, 266-3182, jeff.plale@

Legal Counsel: DOUGLAS S. WOOD, 266-9536, doug.wood@

Legislative/Public Policy Analyst: HEATHER GRAVES, 266-0276, heather.graves@

Rail Safety Analyst: TOM CLAUDER, 266-2874, thomas.clauder@

Mailing Address: P.O. Box 7854, Madison 53707-7854.

Location: 610 North Whitney Way, Suite 110, Madison.

Telephone: 266-0276.

Fax: 261-8220.

Internet Address: http://ocr.wi.gov

Number of Employees: 6.00.

Total Budget 2011-13: $1,166,000.

Statutory References: Sections 15.06 (1) (a) and 15.795 (1); Chapters 189-192 and 195.

Agency Responsibility: The Office of the Commissioner of Railroads enforces regulations related to railway safety and determines the safety of highway crossings including the adequacy of railroad warning devices. The office also retains authority over the rates and services of intrastate water carriers. The office is funded by assessments on railroads.

The governor appoints the commissioner with senate consent to a 6-year term and the commissioner holds the office until a successor is appointed. The commissioner may not have a financial interest in railroads or water carriers and may not serve on or under any committee of a political party. The office was created by 1993 Wisconsin Act 123 as an independent regulatory agency to assume the functions relating to railroad regulation that 1993 Wisconsin Act 16 had transferred to the Public Service Commission when the Office of the Commissioner of Transportation was eliminated. The responsibility for regulating water carriers was added by 2005 Wisconsin Act 179.

Department of
REVENUE

Address e-mail by combining the user ID and the state extender: userid@**revenue.wi.gov**
All telephone numbers are 608 area code unless otherwise indicated.

Secretary of Revenue: RICHARD G. CHANDLER, 266-6466, richard.chandler@; Fax: 266-5718.

Deputy Secretary: JACK JABLONSKI, 266-6466, jackl.jablonski@

Executive Assistant: JENNIFER WESTERN, 266-6466, jennifer.western@

General Counsel, Office of: DANA J. ERLANDSEN, *chief counsel,* 267-8970, dana.erlandsen@

Communications Director: LAUREL PATRICK, 266-2300, laurele.patrick@; Fax: 266-5718.

Legislative Advisor: MICHAEL WAGNER, 266-7817, michaelw.wagner@

Enterprise Services Division: PATRICIA LASHORE, *administrator,* 264-8175, patricia.lashore@; Division Fax: 266-2825.

> *Privacy and Records Management Officer:* PAUL RIEHEMANN, 264-6863, paul.riehemann@

> *Budget and Business Services Bureau:* vacancy, *director,* 266-3347.

> *Financial Management Services Bureau:* BLANCA RIVERA, *director,* 266-8469, blanca.rivera@

> *Human Resource Services Bureau:* JON RENEAU, *director,* 261-8979, jon.reneau@

Income, Sales and Excise Tax Division: DIANE L. HARDT, *administrator,* 266-6798, diane.hardt@; VICKI GIBBONS, *deputy administrator,* 266-3612, vicki.gibbons@; Division Fax: 261-6240.

> *Audit Bureau:* WENDY MILLER, *director,* 261-5154, wendy.miller@

> *Compliance Bureau:* CATHERINE BINK, *director,* 266-7879, catherine.bink@

> *Customer Service Bureau:* JULIE RENEAU, *director,* 266-1179, julie.reneau@

>> *Criminal Investigations Section:* JUSTIN SHEMANSKI, *chief,* 266-0286, justin.shemanski@

>> *Technical Services Section:* NATHANIEL WEBER, *chief,* 266-8025, nathaniel.weber@

> *Tax Operations Bureau:* ERIN EGAN, *director,* 261-5235, erinb.egan@

Lottery Division: MICHAEL J. EDMONDS, *administrator,* 267-4500, michael.edmonds@; JEAN ADLER, *deputy administrator,* 261-6888, jean.adler@; Division Fax: 267-4505.

> *Administrative Services and Communications Bureau:* ANDREW BOHAGE, *director,* 264-6604, andrew.bohage@

> *Product Development and Marketing Bureau:* SAVERIO MAGLIO, *director,* 267-4817, saverio.maglio@

> *Retailer Relations and Sales Bureau:* COLLEEN DVORAK, *director,* 267-0976, jean.dvorak@

Research and Policy Division: JOHN KOSKINEN, *administrator and chief economist,* 267-8973, john.koskinen@; Division Fax: 266-6240.

> *Income Tax Policy and Economic Team:* vacancy, *leader,* 266-6785.

> *Sales and Property Tax Policy Team:* vacancy, *leader,* 266-5773.

State and Local Finance Division: CLAUDE LOIS, *administrator,* 266-0939, claude.lois@; JESSICA IVERSON, *deputy administrator,* 266-9759, jessica.iverson@; Division Fax: 264-6887.

> *Equalization Bureau:* vacancy, *director,* 261-5275.

> *Local Government Services Bureau:* VALEAH FOY, *director,* 261-5360, valeah.foy@

> *Manufacturing and Utility Bureau:* TIMOTHY DRASCIC, *director,* 266-3845, timothy.drascic@

> *Office of Technical and Assessment Services:* SCOTT SHIELDS, *director,* 266-8223, office telephone: 266-7750, scott.shields@

DEPARTMENT OF REVENUE

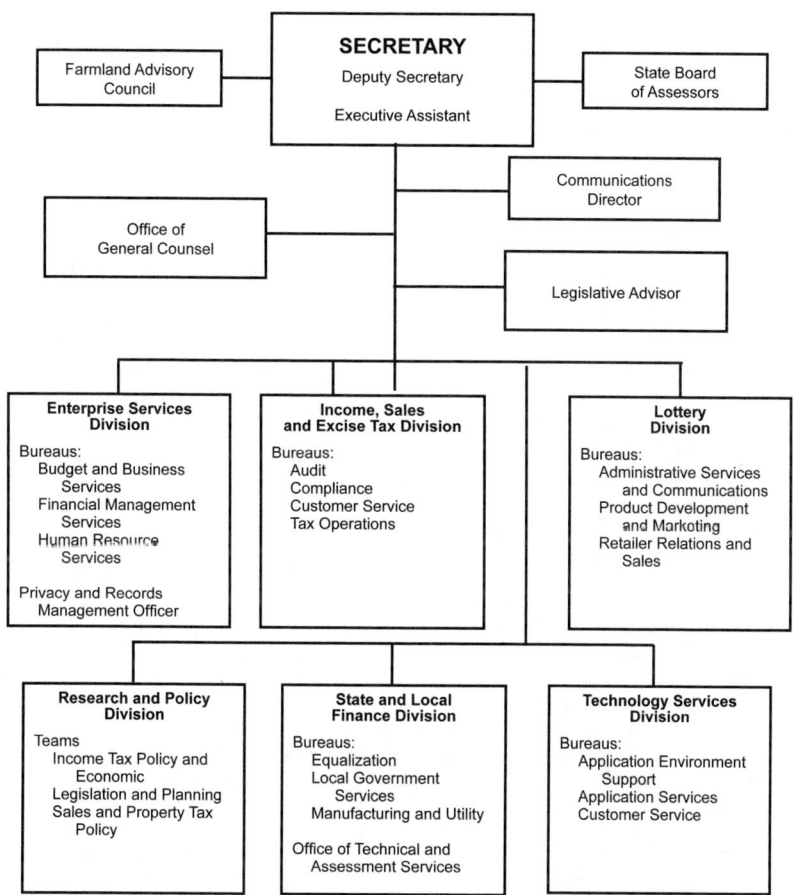

Unit attached for administrative purposes under Sec. 15.03:   Investment and Local Impact Fund Board

---

Technology Services Division: RICHARD OFFENBECHER, *administrator,* 261-2276, richard.offenbecher@; Division Fax: 266-9923.

    Application Environment Support Bureau: PATRICK GRANT, *director,* 266-9751, patrick.grant@

    Application Services Bureau: NEERAJ KULKARNI, *director,* 261-5183, neeraj.kulkarni@

    Customer Service Bureau: JULIE RAES, *director,* 264-6879, julie.raes@

Mailing Address: P.O. Box 8933, Madison 53708-8933.

Locations: 2135 Rimrock Road, Madison, and regional offices in Appleton, Eau Claire, Green Bay, Milwaukee, Wausau, and Chicago, Illinois.

Telephones: (608) 266-2486 – individuals; (608) 266-2776 – businesses; Telecommunications Relay Service dial "711" or visit Wisconsin Relay for more information.

Fax: (608) 267-1030.

Internet Address: www.revenue.wi.gov

Publications: *Agricultural Assessment Guide;* biennial report; *County and Municipal Revenues and Expenditures;* A Guide for Property Owners; *Quarterly Economic Outlook;* Summary of Tax Exemption Devices; *Town, Village, and City Taxes; Wisconsin Tax Bulletin;* and various brochures and publications on specific issues.

Number of Employees: 1,052.08.

Total Budget 2011-13: $349,903,700.

Statutory References: Sections 15.43 and 15.435; Chapters 70-79, 125, and 139.

Agency Responsibility: The Department of Revenue administers all major state tax laws (except the insurance premiums tax) and enforces the state's alcohol beverage and tobacco laws. It estimates state revenues, forecasts state economic activity, helps formulate tax policy, and administers the Wisconsin Lottery. It also determines equalized value of taxable property and assesses manufacturing property. It administers local financial assistance programs and assists local governments in their property assessments and financial management.

Organization: The department is administered by a secretary who is appointed by the governor with the advice and consent of the senate. The secretary appoints the administrators of the Income, Sales and Excise Tax Division and the Technology Services Division from the classified service and the other division administrators from outside the classified service.

Unit Functions: The *Office of General Counsel* provides legal counsel and opinions; reviews tax legislation and administrative rules; and represents the department in all cases brought before the Tax Appeals Commission, in collections actions brought before state circuit courts and federal bankruptcy courts, and in nontax cases before administrative agencies. It also is responsible for providing a prompt and impartial review of all assessments appealed by individuals, partnerships, trusts, and corporations relating to income, franchise, sales, use, withholding, and gift taxes and the homestead tax credit.

The *Enterprise Services Division* provides departmentwide services in the areas of administration, budget and financial management, business services, printing, records management, personnel, affirmative action, equal opportunity, employee development, employment relations, and other management services.

The *Income, Sales and Excise Tax Division* administers tax laws relating to income, withholding, franchise, sales and use, local exposition, premier resort area, estate, fiduciary, liquor, beer, wine, cigarette and tobacco products, motor vehicles, alternate and aviation fuel taxes, rental vehicles, dry cleaning, and police and fire protection fees; and ambulatory surgical center assessment. The division also administers the homestead credit, earned income tax credit, and farmland preservation credit programs. The division drafts and reviews tax legislation, administrative rules, tax forms/instructions and publications; processes tax returns and payments; audits tax returns; provides taxpayer and practitioner assistance; collects delinquent taxes; and conducts criminal investigations.

The *Lottery Division* administers the Wisconsin Lottery. It manages the design, distribution, and sale of lottery products; conducts lottery game drawings; handles media relations; assists retailers with marketing lottery products; makes payment on winning tickets; provides product information through informational advertisements and its Web site (www.wilottery.com); and answers players' questions.

The *Research and Policy Division* provides detailed analyses of fiscal and economic policies to the departmental secretary, the governor, and other state officials. It assesses the impact of current and proposed tax laws, prepares official general fund tax collection estimates used to develop the state budget, issues quarterly forecasts of the state's economy, and develops statistical reports.

The *State and Local Finance Division* establishes the state's equalized values; assesses all manufacturing and telecommunications company property for property tax purposes; assesses and collects taxes on utilities, railroads, airlines, mining, and other special properties; and provides financial management and technical assistance to municipal and county governments. It administers the state municipal and county aid program, property tax relief for municipal services, the lottery credit program, and tax incremental financing programs. It provides property assessment administration and certifies assessment personnel.

The *Technology Services Division* administers technology services for all parts of the department, including data administration, applications development, workstation support, data collection, and technology planning.

The department also administers the state's unclaimed property program.

History: The antecedents of the Department of Revenue date back at least to Chapter 130, Laws of 1868, which created a State Board of Assessors, composed of the secretary of state and the entire state senate, to perform the state's taxing functions. At that time, the property tax was the state's primary source of revenue.

Chapter 235, Laws of 1873, changed the board's composition to the secretary of state, state treasurer, and attorney general. The 1899 Legislature created the Office of Tax Commissioner (Chapter 206) to supervise the state's taxation system and made the commissioner a member and presiding officer of the State Board of Assessors.

The composition of the State Board of Assessors was changed again in Chapter 237, Laws of 1901, when the legislature replaced the constitutional officers with two assistant commissioners. The 1905 Legislature abolished the State Board of Assessors (Chapter 380) and assigned its functions to a 3-member Tax Commission, appointed by the governor with the advice and consent of the senate. This structure lasted until Chapter 412, Laws of 1939, created the Department of Taxation, headed by a single commissioner. Chapter 75, Laws of 1967, renamed the agency the Department of Revenue and the commissioner became the secretary.

Throughout the years, certain tax-related functions have been moved from one agency or level of government to another. For example, local officials originally assessed manufacturing property, but the 1973 Legislature gave the department responsibility for assessing all manufacturing property in the state.

Similarly, the 1939 Legislature made the Department of Taxation responsible for performing audits upon the request of local governmental units. After assignment to several other agencies, the legislature returned this function to the Department of Revenue in 1971. In 1983, the legislature repealed the department's mandatory municipal audit functions but left intact its discretionary oversight of municipal accounting.

The department currently is responsible for administration of the Wisconsin Lottery. The lottery was originally created by 1987 Wisconsin Act 119 and administered by the Lottery Board. It was later managed by the Wisconsin Gaming Commission. 1995 Wisconsin Act 27, which transferred the State Lottery to the Department of Revenue, also repealed the commission and created the Gaming Board. The Gaming Board was repealed in 1997 Wisconsin Act 27.

Statutory Board and Council

State Board of Assessors: TIM DRASCIC, *chairperson;* TONYA BUCHNER, KELLY COULSON, KURT KELLER (Department of Revenue employees appointed by secretary).

The State Board of Assessors investigates objections to the amount, valuation, or taxability of real or personal manufacturing property, as well as objections to the penalties issued for late filing or nonfiling of required manufacturing property report forms. The number of board members is determined by the secretary, but all must be department employees. The board was created by Chapter 90, Laws of 1973, and its composition and duties are prescribed in Section 70.995 (8) of the statutes.

Farmland Advisory Council: RICHARD CHANDLER (secretary of revenue), *chairperson;* vacancy (agribusiness), CARL AXNESS (knowledgeable about agricultural lending practices), BRUCE JONES (UW System agricultural economist), TIM HANNA (mayor of a city of 40,000 or more population), vacancy (environmental expert), vacancy (representing nonagricultural business), STEPHEN HINTZ (urban studies professor), HERB TAUCHEN (farmer) (all appointed by secretary of revenue); MELVIN RAATZ (assessor) (appointed by secretary of revenue as an advisor to council).

Agency Responsibility: The 9-member Farmland Advisory Council advises the Department of Revenue on implementing use-value assessment of agricultural land and reducing urban sprawl. It is required to report annually to the legislature on the usefulness of use-value assessment as a way to preserve farmland, discourage urban sprawl, and reduce the conversion of farmland to other uses. It also recommends changes to the shared revenue formula to compensate local governments adversely affected by use-value assessment. In carrying out its duties, it cooperates with the Wisconsin Strategic Growth Task Force of the State Interagency Land Use Council. The council was created by 1995 Wisconsin Act 27, and its composition and duties are prescribed in Section 73.03 (49) of the statutes.

INDEPENDENT BOARD ATTACHED FOR BUDGETING, PROGRAM COORDINATION, AND RELATED MANAGEMENT FUNCTIONS BY SECTION 15.03 OF THE STATUTES

INVESTMENT AND LOCAL IMPACT FUND BOARD ("Mining Board")

Investment and Local Impact Fund Board: Inactive.

The 11-member Investment and Local Impact Fund Board administers the Investment and Local Impact Fund, created to help municipalities alleviate costs associated with social, educational, environmental, and economic impacts of metalliferous mineral mining. The board certifies to the Department of Administration the amount of the payments to be distributed to municipalities from the fund. It also provides guidance and funding to local governments throughout the development of a mining project.

In addition to the secretary of revenue and the chief executive officer of the Wisconsin Economic Development Corporation, or their designees, the board's 9 appointed members serve staggered 4-year terms. They include 3 public members; the 5 local officials recommended by: the League of Wisconsin Municipalities (1), the Wisconsin Towns Association (1), the Wisconsin Association of School Boards (1), and the Wisconsin Counties Association (2); and a Native American member is recommended by the Great Lakes Inter-Tribal Council, Inc. Certain board members must meet qualifications based on residence in or adjacent to a county or municipality with a metallic minerals ore body or mineral development. The board was created by Chapter 31, Laws of 1977, and its composition and duties are specified in Sections 15.435 (1) and 70.395 (2), Wisconsin Statutes.

Department of
SAFETY AND PROFESSIONAL SERVICES

Secretary of Safety and Professional Services: DAVE ROSS, 266-1352, dave.ross@wisconsin.gov

Deputy Secretary: BILL WENDLE, 267-2435, bill.wendle@wisconsin.gov

Executive Assistant: GREG GASPER, 266-8608, greg.gasper@wisconsin.gov

General Counsel: MICHAEL BERNDT, 266-0011, michael.berndt@wisconsin.gov

Mailing Address: P.O. Box 8935, Madison 53708-8935.

Location: 1400 East Washington Avenue, Madison.

Telephones: 266-2112 (for operator, select menu option "6"); TTY: 267-2416.

Internet Address: http://dsps.wi.gov

Fax: 267-0644.

Number of Employees: 369.60.

Total Budget 2011-13: $132,258,800.

Statutory References: Sections 15.08, 15.085, 15.40, and 15.405-15.407; Chapters 101, 145, 440-462, 472, and 480.

Industry Services, Division of: THOMAS WIGHTMAN, *administrator,* 267-9152, thomas.wightman@wisconsin.gov; Division Fax: 267-1381; Regional Fax: Green Bay: (920) 492-5604; Hayward: (715) 634-5150; La Crosse: (608) 785-9330; Stevens Point: (715) 345-5269; Waukesha: (262) 548-8614.

Legal Services and Compliance, Division of: CHAD KOPLIEN, *administrator,* 266-3445, chad.koplien@wisconsin.gov

DEPARTMENT OF SAFETY AND PROFESSIONAL SERVICES

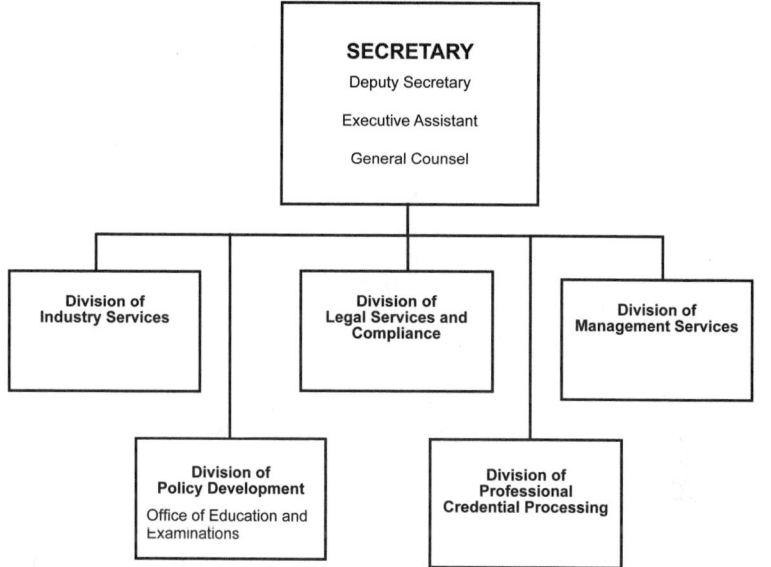

Management Services, Division of: KELLI KAALELE, *administrator,* 261-4466, kelli.kaalele@wisconsin.gov

Policy Development, Division of: KATHERINE KOSCHNICK, *administrator,* 266-8419, katherine.koschnick@wisconsin.gov

Education and Examinations, Office of: JILL REMY, *program manager,* 266-7703, jill.remy@wisconsin.gov

Professional Credential Processing, Division of: ANGELA HERL, *administrator,* 266-0557, angela.herl@wisconsin.gov

Examining Boards (Statutory Authority of Examining Boards) and Assigned Staff:

Accounting Examining Board: JOHN S. SCHEID (accountant), *chairperson;* TODD C. CRAFT (accountant), *vice chairperson;* MARION R. WOZNIAK (accountant), *secretary;* GERALD E. DENOR, KIM L. TREDINNICK (accountants); STEVEN A. CORBEILLE*; GLENN MICHAELSEN*. *Executive Director:* ANGELA HELLENBRAND, 261-5406, angie.hellenbrand@wisconsin.gov.

Architects, Landscape Architects, Professional Engineers, Designers and Land Surveyors, Examining Board of: ROSHEEN STYCZINSKI (landscape architect), *chairperson;* JAMES F. MICKOWSKI (designer), *vice chairperson;* CHARLES W. KOPPLIN (engineer), *secretary.* The 5 professional sections listed below comprise the examining board for a total of 15 professional members and 10 public members. *Executive Director:* ANGELA HELLENBRAND, 261-5406, angie.hellenbrand@wisconsin.gov.

Architect Section: LAWRENCE J. SCHNUCK (architect), *chairperson;* JULIA A. DeCICCO*, *vice chairperson;* JAMES GERSICH (architect), *secretary;* MICHAEL EBERLE (architect); GARY KOHLENBERG*.

Designer Section: JAMES F. MICKOWSKI (designer), *chairperson;* THOMAS J. GASPERETTI*, *vice chairperson;* STEVEN T. TWEED (designer), *secretary;* MARK A. COOK (designer); vacancy*.

Engineer Section: CHARLES W. KOPPLIN (engineer), *chairperson;* STEVEN J. HOOK*, *vice chairperson;* JOSEPH W. EBERLE (engineer), *secretary;* MARK E. MAYER (engineer); vacancy*.

Landscape Architect Section: ROSHEEN M. STYCZINSKI (landscape architect), *chairperson;* MICHAEL J. KINNEY*, *vice chairperson;* ANDREW ALBRIGHT (landscape architect), *secretary;* BERNIE A. ABRAHAMSON*; vacancy (landscape architect).

Land Surveyor Section: MATTHEW J. JANIAK (land surveyor), *chairperson;* JAMES E. RUSCH (land surveyor), *vice chairperson;* DANIEL FEDDERLY (land surveyor), *secretary;* RUTH G. JOHNSON*; vacancy*.

Chiropractic Examining Board: JAMES P. KOSHICK (chiropractor), *chairperson;* JOHN E. CHURCH (chiropractor), *vice chairperson;* JODI GRIFFITH (chiropractor), *secretary;* PATRICIA A. SCHUMACHER (chiropractor); KATHLEEN A. SCHNEIDER*; vacancy*. *Executive Director:* THOMAS RYAN, 261-2378, thomas.ryan@wisconsin.gov.

Cosmetology Examining Board: JEFFREY A. PATTERSON (aesthetician/cosmetologist), *chairperson;* SUSAN KOLVE-FEEHAN (private school of cosmetology representative), *vice chairperson;* GERALDINE L. REUTER (public school of cosmetology representative), *secretary;* VICKY L. MCNALLY, HOWARD TWAIT, vacancy (aestheticians/cosmetologists); CHERYL A. PEARSE*; vacancy (electrologist); vacancy*. *Executive Director:* ANGELA HELLENBRAND, 261-5406, angie.hellenbrand@wisconsin.gov.

Dentistry Examining Board: LYNDSAY KNOELL (dentist), *chairperson;* JOHN W. GRIGNON (dentist), *vice chairperson;* SANDRA E. LINHART (dental hygienist), *secretary;* MARK T. BRADEN, ADRIANA JARAMILLO, KIRK R. RITCHIE, BETH R. WELTER (dentists); DEBRA J. BERES, EILEEN DONHOO (dental hygienists); 2 vacancies*. *Executive Director:* ANGELA HELLENBRAND, 261-5406, angie.hellenbrand@wisconsin.gov.

Funeral Directors Examining Board: BRIAN LANGENDORF (funeral director/embalmer), *chairperson;* DEAN STENSBERG*, *vice chairperson;* THOMAS BRADLEY (funeral director/ embalmer), *secretary;* MICHELE M. MOORE, KRISTEN A. PIEHL (funeral director/ embalmer); ERIC LENGELL*. *Executive Director:* ANGELA HELLENBRAND, 261-5406, angie.hellenbrand@wisconsin.gov.

Geologists, Hydrologists and Soil Scientists, Examining Board of Professional: WILLIAM N. MODE (geologist), *chairperson;* BRENDA S. HALMINIAK (geologist), *vice chairperson;* RICHARD BEILFUSS (hydrologist), *secretary.* The 3 professional sections listed below comprise the examining board for a total of 9 professional members and 3 public members. *Executive Director:* DAN WILLIAMS, 267-7223, dan1.williams@wisconsin.gov.

Geologist Section: WILLIAM N. MODE (geologist), *chairperson;* BRENDA S. HALMINIAK (geologist), *vice chairperson;* SUE E. BRIDSON*, *secretary;* JAMES M. ROBERTSON (geologist).

Hydrologist Section: RANDALL J. HUNT (hydrologist), *chairperson;* KENNETH R. BRADBURY (hydrologist), *vice chairperson;* RUTH G. JOHNSON*, *secretary;* RICHARD D. BEILFUSS (hydrologist).

Soil Scientist Section: PATRICIA A. TROCHLELL (soil scientist), *vice chairperson;* JOHN A. HAHN*, *secretary;* vacancy (soil scientist); vacancy*.

Hearing and Speech Examining Board: STEVEN J. KLAPPERICH (hearing instrument specialist), *chairperson;* DOREEN E. JENSEN (audiologist), *vice chairperson;* SAMUEL P. GUBBELS (otolaryngologist), *secretary;* OKIE E. ALLEN, PETER J. ZELLMER (hearing instrument specialists); EDWARD W. KORABIC (audiologist); THOMAS W. SATHER, PATRICIA L. WILLIS (speech-language pathologists); 2 vacancies*. *Executive Director:* ANGELA HELLENBRAND, 261-5406, angie.hellenbrand@wisconsin.gov.

Marriage and Family Therapy, Professional Counseling and Social Work Examining Board: NICHOLAS P. SMIAR (social worker), *chairperson;* CHARLES V. LINDSEY (professional counselor), *vice chairperson;* LINDA G. PELLMANN (marriage and family therapist), *secretary.* The following 3 sections comprise the examining board, for a total of 10 professional members and 3 public members. *Executive Director:* DAN WILLIAMS, 267-7223, dan1.williams@wisconsin.gov.

Marriage and Family Therapist Section: ARLIE J. ALBRECHT (marriage and family therapist), *chairperson;* ALICE HANSON-DREW*, *vice chairperson;* PETER FABIAN (marriage and family therapist), *secretary;* LINDA G. PELLMANN (marriage and family therapist).

Professional Counselor Section: CHARLES V. LINDSEY (professional counselor), *chairperson;* ALLISON L. GORDON (professional counselor), *vice chairperson;* LESLIE D. MIRKIN (professional counselor), *secretary;* NANCY CLARK*.

Social Worker Section: NICHOLAS P. SMIAR (independent social worker), *chairperson;* BARBARA L. VISTE-JOHNSON (clinical social worker), *vice chairperson;* ELIZABETH A. KRUEGER (government social worker), *secretary;* vacancy (advanced practice social worker); vacancy*.

Medical Examining Board: SHELDON A. WASSERMAN (physician), *chairperson;* KENNETH B. SIMONS (physician), *vice chairperson;* JUDE GENEREAUX*, *secretary;* MARY JO CAPODICE, RODNEY A. ERICKSON, SURESH K. MISRA, GENE MUSSER, TIMOTHY L. SWAN, SRIDHAR V. VASUDEVAN, TIMOTHY W. WESTLAKE, RUSSELL S. YALE (physicians); JAMES BARR*, GREG M. COLLINS*. *Executive Director:* THOMAS RYAN, 261-2378, thomas.ryan@wisconsin.gov (includes following boards).

Athletic Trainers Affiliated Credentialing Board: STEVEN J. NASS (athletic trainer), *chairperson;* RYAN A. BERRY (athletic trainer), *vice chairperson;* JEANNE M. BROWN (athletic trainer), *secretary;* JAMES W. NESBIT (athletic trainer); GREGORY L. LANDRY (physician), vacancy*.

Dietitians Affiliated Credentialing Board: GAIL L. UNDERBAKKE, *chairperson;* SCOTT M. KRUEGER, *vice chairperson;* DONNA C. LOVELAND, *secretary;* PATRICIA M. ROBLEE*.

Massage Therapy and Bodywork Therapy Affiliated Credentialing Board: ELIZABETH C. KRIZENESKY (massage therapist & body worker), *chairperson;* CAROLE G. OSTENDORF*, *vice chairperson;* BARBARA YETTER (massage therapist & body worker), *secretary;* JOHN E. ANDERSON (school representative); CINDY SPITZA, vacancy (massage therapists & body workers); WENDY M. WETTENGEL-PERRIGOUE (technical college representative).

Occupational Therapists Affiliated Credentialing Board (266-2112): BRIAN B. HOLMQUIST (occupational therapist), *chairperson;* CORLISS A. RICE*, *vice chairperson;* DAVID COOPER*, *secretary;* MYLINDA BARISAS-MATULA, GAIL C. SLAUGHTER (occupational therapists); DEBORAH A. MCKERNAN-ACE, DOROTHY J. OLSON (occupational therapist assistants).

Podiatry Affiliated Credentialing Board: WILLIAM W. WEIS (podiatrist), *chairperson;* THOMAS R. KOMP (podiatrist), *vice chairperson;* GARY BROWN*, *secretary;* JEFFERY L. GIESKING (podiatrist).

Nursing, Board of: JULIA A. NELSON (registered nurse), *chairperson;* GRETCHEN R. LOWE*, *vice chairperson;* LILLIAN NOLAN*, *secretary;* JULIE L. ELLIS, RACHELLE J. LANCASTER, JEFFREY G. MILLER, CAROL H. OTT (registered nurses); MARIA JOSEPH, vacancy (licensed practical nurses). *Executive Director:* DAN WILLIAMS, 267-7223, dan1.williams@wisconsin.gov.

Licensed Practical Nurses, Examining Council on: (Inactive).

Registered Nurses, Examining Council on: (Inactive).

Nursing Home Administrator Examining Board: DAVID M. EGAN (nursing home administrator), *chairperson;* KENNETH D. ARNESON (nursing home administrator), *vice chairperson;* MARY K. LEASE (registered nurse), *secretary;* EARLENE RONK (nursing home administrator); SUSAN KINAST-PORTER (physician); LORELI DICKINSON*, MARY F. PIKE*; PAUL H. PESHEK (designated by secretary of health services); 2 vacancies (nursing home administrators). *Executive Director:* THOMAS RYAN, 261-2378, thomas.ryan@wisconsin.gov.

Optometry Examining Board: GREGORY A. FOSTER (optometrist), *chairperson;* ANN MEIER CARLI (optometrist), *vice chairperson;* KATHI L. LEACH (optometrist), *secretary;* RICHARD L. FOSS, BRIAN J. HAMMES (optometrists); MARK A. JINKINS*, vacancy*. *Executive Director:* ANGELA HELLENBRAND, 261-5406, angie.hellenbrand@wisconsin.gov.

Pharmacy Examining Board: THADDEUS J. SCHUMACHER (pharmacist), *chairperson;* FRANKLIN J. LADIEN (pharmacist), *vice chairperson;* CHARLOTTE RASMUSSEN*, *secretary;* JEANNE M. SEVERSON, JASON D. WALKER-CRAWFORD, GREGORY C. WEBER (pharmacists); KRISTI SULLIVAN*. *Executive Director:* DAN WILLIAMS, 267-7223, dan1.williams@wisconsin.gov. *Pharmacist Advisory Council:* (Inactive).

Physical Therapy Examining Board: MICHELE A. THORMAN (physical therapist), *chairperson;* LORI H. DOMINICZAK (physical therapist), *vice chairperson;* SHARI L. BERRY (physical therapist), *secretary;* JANE L. STROEDE (physical therapist assistant); THOMAS MURPHY*. *Executive Director:* THOMAS RYAN, 261-2378, thomas.ryan@wisconsin.gov.

Psychology Examining Board: BRUCE R. ERDMANN (psychologist), *chairperson;* MELISSA J. WESTENDORF (psychologist), *vice chairperson;* REBECCA ANDERSON (psychologist), *secretary;* DANIEL A. SCHROEDER (psychologist); 2 vacancies*. *Executive Director:* DAN WILLIAMS, 267-7223, dan1.williams@wisconsin.gov.

Radiography Examining Board: SUSAN SANSON (radiographer), *chairperson;* JAMES LEMEROND (radiographer), *vice chairperson;* KELLEY GRANT (radiographer), *secretary;* GREGG A. BOGOST (physician-radiologist); MARY ELLEN JAFARI (radiologic physicist); 2 vacancies*. *Executive Director:* THOMAS RYAN, 261-2378, thomas.ryan@wisconsin.gov.

Real Estate Examining Board: STEPHEN P. BEERS (real estate salesperson/ broker), *chairperson;* MICHAEL J. MULLEADY (real estate salesperson/broker), *vice chairperson;* RANDAL F. SAVAGLIO (real estate sales/broker), *secretary;* MARIE H. HETZER, TAMMY L. WAGNER (real estate salesperson/brokers); DENNIS M. PIERCE*, vacancy*. *Executive Director:* ANGELA HELLENBRAND, 261-5406, angie.hellenbrand@wisconsin.gov.

Veterinary Examining Board: ROBERT R. SPENCER (veterinarian), *chairperson;* WILLIAM S. RICE (veterinarian), *vice chairperson;* NEIL A. WISELEY (veterinarian), *secretary;* WESLEY G. ELFORD, PHILIP C. JOHNSON (veterinarians); BRENDA A. NEMEC (veterinarian technician); SHELDON SCHALL*, vacancy*. *Executive Director:* THOMAS RYAN, 261-2378, thomas. ryan@wisconsin.gov.

Boards (Statutory Authority of Boards) and Assigned Staff:

Auctioneer Board: TIMOTHY D. SWEENY (auctioneer), *chairperson;* JERRY L. THIEL (auctioneer/auction company representative), *vice chairperson;* JAMES C. WENZLER*, *secretary;* RANDY J. STOCKWELL (auctioneer); PATRICK J. MCNAMARA, (auctioneer/auction company representative); RONALD J. POLACEK*, vacancy*. *Executive Director:* ANGELA HELLENBRAND, 261-5406, angie.hellenbrand@wisconsin.gov.

Building Inspectors Review Board (attached by s. 15.03): DON ESPOSITO (senate majority leader designee); DAVID HUEBSCH (speaker of assembly designee); GARY ROEHRIG (secretary of safety and professional services designee); MARTIN RIFKEN (representing building contractors and building developers); vacancy (certified building inspector). Except as indicated, all members appointed by governor with senate consent. *Executive Director:* JEFF WEIGAND, 267-9794, jeffrey.weigand@wisconsin.gov.

Cemetery Board: CLYDE W. RUPNOW (licensed cemetery authority business representative), *chairperson;* FRANCIS J. GROH (licensed cemetery authority business representative), *vice chairperson;* MARY B. LEHMAN (licensed cemetery authority business representative), *secretary;* WILLIAM E. GREENFIELD (licensed cemetery authority business representative); KATHLEEN M. CANTU*; vacancy*. *Executive Director:* ANGELA HELLENBRAND, 261-5406, angie.hellenbrand@wisconsin.gov.

Controlled Substances Board: DOUG ENGELBERT (designated by secretary of health services), *chairperson;* ALAN BLOOM (pharmacologist), *vice chairperson;* YVONNE M. BELLAY (designated by secretary of agriculture, trade and consumer protection), *secretary;* FRANKLIIN J. LADIEN (designated by pharmacy examining board); MARTIN G. KOCH (designated by attorney general); vacancy (psychiatrist). *Executive Director:* DAN WILLIAMS, 267-7223, dan1.williams@wisconsin.gov.

Real Estate Appraisers Board: MARLA L. BRITTON (assessor), *chairperson;* SHARON R.

FIEDLER (certified residential appraiser), *vice chairperson;* LAWRENCE R. NICHOLSON (certified general appraiser), *secretary;* CARL N. CLEMENTI (licensed appraiser); JOSE PEREZ*, HENRY F. SIMON*; vacancy*. *Executive Director:* THOMAS RYAN, 261-2378, thomas.ryan@wisconsin.gov.

Councils (Statutory Authority of Councils) and Assigned Staff:

Anesthesiologists Assistants, Council on: JAMES R. MESROBIAN (anesthesiologist), *chairperson;* CAROLYN J. FARRELL (anesthesiologist); MARCY SALZER*; KENNETH B. SIMONS (Medical Examining Board designee); ROBERT J. STUPI (anesthesiologist assistant). *Executive Director:* JEFF WEIGAND, 267-9794, jeffrey.weigand@wisconsin.gov.

Automatic Fire Sprinkler System Contractors and Journeymen Council: JEFF WEIGAND (department of safety and professional services), *secretary;* DAN DRIEBEL, CHRIS SCHOENBECK (licensed journeymen automatic fire sprinkler fitters); JEFF BATEMAN, GREG HINTZ (licensed automatic fire sprinkler contractors). *Executive Director:* JEFF WEIGAND, 267-9794, jeffrey.weigand@wisconsin.gov.

Contractor Certification Council: CRAIG RAKOWSKI (building contractor representing Wisconsin Builders Association), JAY STATZ (building contractor representing National Association of Remodeling Contractors), JOSEPH WELCH (building contractor representing Wisconsin State Council of Carpenters). *Executive Director:* JEFF WEIGAND, 267-9794, jeffrey.weigand@wisconsin.gov.

Conveyance Safety Code Council: ANDREW ZIEKLE (manufacturer of elevators); KENNETH SMITH (elevator servicing business representative); PAUL ROSENBERG (architectural design or elevator consulting profession representative); KELVIN NORD (labor organization representative); ADAM SMITH (city, village, town, or county representative); MICHAEL DAUCK (owner or manager of a building containing an elevator); vacancy*; BRIAN HORNUNG (commercial construction building contractor); BRIAN RAUSCH (designated by secretary of safety and professional services); JIM QUAST (department employee familiar with commercial building inspectors designated by secretary of safety and professional services), *nonvoting secretary.* *Executive Director:* JEFF WEIGAND, 267-9794, jeffrey. weigand@wisconsin.gov.

Crematory Authority Council: SCOTT K. BRAINARD, WILLIAM R. CRESS, GARY A. LANGENDORF (funeral director crematory authority); ADAM J. CASPER, KELLY L. COLEMAN-KOHORN, PAUL A. HAUBRICH (cemetery crematory authority); LINDA A. REID*; JEFF WEIGAND (designated by secretary of safety and professional services), *executive director and nonvoting member:* 267-9794, jeffrey.weigand@wisconsin.gov.

Dwelling Code Council: DENNIS BAUER (remodeling contractor); GARY ZAJICEK (building contractor); PHILIP BORCHARDT, ROBERT PREMO, BRIAN WERT (certified building inspectors employed by local government); MICHAEL COELLO, PETER KRABBE (construction material supply representatives); AMY BLISS (manufactured housing representative); DAVID DOLAN-WALLACE (architect, engineer, or designer); STEVEN GRYBOSKI, MARY L. SCHROEDER, vacancy (building trade labor organization representatives); vacancy (person with disabilities); vacancy (fire prevention professional); JEFF WEIGAND (department of safety and professional services), *executive director and nonvoting secretary:* 267-9794, jeffrey.weigand@wisconsin.gov.

Manufactured Housing Code Council: JAY MCDONALD, ROB MOBLEY (manufacturers); BART HUNTINGTON, MARK THIEDE (manufactured home dealers); ROB GULOTTA, vacancy (owners of manufactured home communities); ANTHONY WIDOWSKI, vacancy (installers); ROSS KINZLER (industry association representative); vacancy (supplier of materials or services); CHUCK ONSUM (public member); STEVE BREITLOW (labor representative); DAN CURRAN (inspector); JEFF WEIGAND (department of safety and professional services), *executive director and nonvoting secretary:* 267-9794, jeffrey.weigand@wisconsin.gov.

Multifamily Dwelling Code Council: EDWARD R. GRAY, MARK SCOTT (skilled building trades labor organization representatives); DAVID A. NITZ (municipal inspector: county with population less than 50,000); PETER SCHEUERMAN (municipal inspector: county with population over 50,000); SCOTT BURKART, vacancy (fire service workers); BETH

A. GONNERING, vacancy (multifamily dwelling contractors and developers); KEVIN WIPPERFURTH, 2 vacancies (materials manufacturers and finished product suppliers); JAMES R. KLETT (architects, engineers, and designers representative); 2 vacancies*; JEFF WEIGAND (department of safety and professional services), *executive director and nonvoting secretary:* 267-9794, jeffrey.weigand@wisconsin.gov.

Perfusionists Examining Council: SHAWN E. MERGEN (perfusionist), *chairperson;* JEFFREY P. EDWARDS (perfusionist), *vice chairperson;* GARY TSAROVSKY (perfusionist), *secretary;* DAVID F. COBB*; vacancy (physician). Parent-board: Medical Examining Board.

Plumbers Council: vacancy (department employee), *secretary;* DAVE JONES (master plumber); SCOTT HAMILTON (journeyman plumber). *Executive Director:* JEFF WEIGAND, 267-9794, jeffrey.weigand@wisconsin.gov.

Physician Assistants, Council on: ANNE B. HLETKO (physician assistant), *chairperson;* JODY L. WILKINS (physician assistant), *vice chairperson;* JEREMIAH L. BARRETT (designated by vice chancellor for health sciences of UW-Madison); JULIE A. DOYLE (physician assistant); MARY PANGMAN SCHMITT*. Parent-board: Medical Examining Board.

Respiratory Care Practitioners Examining Council: WILLIAM D. ROSANDICK (respiratory care practitioner), *chairperson;* LYNN R. WALDERA (respiratory care practitioner), *vice chairperson;* ANN M. MEICHER (respiratory care practitioner), *secretary;* vacancy (physician with a specialty in cardiothoracic surgeon or cardiovascular anesthesiologist); vacancy*. Parent-board: Medical Examining Board.

Sign Language Interpreter Council: JOEL E. MANOKOWSKI (deaf or hard of hearing member), *chairperson;* STEVE SMART (interpreter member), *vice chairperson;* FAY JORDAN-PETERS (deaf or hard of hearing member), *secretary;* SUZETTE GARAY, JOSEPH RIGGIO, vacancy (deaf or hard of hearing members); DEBRA GORRA BARASH (interpreter member); CARLOS JARAMILLO (interpreter services member). *Executive Director:* JEFF WEIGAND, 267-9794, jeffrey.weigand@wisconsin.gov.

---

*Asterisk indicates public member. Other members represent the profession regulated, unless otherwise noted. The governor appoints all examining board and council members with the advice and consent of the senate, unless otherwise indicated.

Visit the Department of Safety and Professional Services Web site at http://dsps.wi.gov for the latest information on board memberships.

Boards and Councils Within the Department of Safety and Professional Services

Unit	Statutory Citation	Significant Session Laws Affecting	Duties Specified in Wisconsin Statutes
Accounting Examining Board	S. 15.405 (1)	1913 c. 337; 1967 c. 327; 1981 c. 356	Ch. 442
Architects, Landscape Architects, Professional Engineers, Designers and Land Surveyors, Examining Board of	S. 15.405 (2)	1917 c. 644; 1931 c. 486; 1955 c. 547; 1969 c. 446; 1993 a. 463, a. 465; 1997 a. 300	Ch. 443
Auctioneer Board	S. 15.405 (3)	1993 a. 102	Ch. 480
Automatic Fire Sprinkler System Contractors and Journeymen Council	S. 15.407 (17)	1971 c. 255; 1979 c. 221; 1995 a. 27; 2011 a. 32	S. 145.17 (2)
Cemetery Board	S. 15.405 (3m)	2005 a. 25	Ch. 440, Subchap.IX
Chiropractic Examining Board	S. 15.405 (5)	1925 c. 408	Ch. 446
Contractor Certification Council	S. 15.407 (11)	2005 a. 200; 2011 a. 32	S. 101.625
Controlled Substances Board	S. 15.405 (5g)	1969 c. 384; 1971 c. 219; 1995 a. 305	Ch. 961
Conveyance Safety Code Council	S. 15.407 (14)	2005 a. 456; 2011 a. 32	S. 101.986
Cosmetology Examining Board	S. 15.405 (17)	1939 c. 431; 1987 a. 265 (combined with barbering); 2005 a. 314; 2011 a. 190 (separated from barbering)	Ch. 454, Subchap.I
Crematory Authority Council	S. 15.407 (8)	2005 a. 31	S. 15.09 (5)
Dentistry Examining Board	S. 15.405 (6)	1885 c. 129; 1997 a. 96	Ch. 447
Dwelling Code Council	S. 15.407 (10)	1975 c. 404; 1995 a. 27; 2011 a. 32, a. 146	S. 101.62, 101.72
Funeral Directors Examining Board	S. 15.405 (16)	1905 c. 420; 1975 c. 39; 1983 a. 485	Ch. 445
Geologists, Hydrologists and Soil Scientists, Examining Board of Professional	S. 15.405 (2m)	1997 a. 300	Ch. 470
Hearing and Speech Examining Board	S. 15.405 (6m)	1969 c. 300; 1989 a. 316; 2003 a. 270	Ch. 459
Manufactured Housing Code Council	S. 15.407 (13)	2005 a. 45; 2011 a. 32	S. 101.933
Marriage and Family Therapy, Professional Counseling, and Social Work Examining Board	S. 15.405 (7c)	1991 a. 160; 2001 a. 80	Ch. 457
Medical Examining Board	S. 15.405 (7)	1897 c. 264; 1903 c. 426; 1953 c. 325; 1985 a. 340; 1993 a. 16	Ch. 448, Subchap.II
Anesthesiologist Assistants, Council on	S. 15.407 (7)	2011 a. 160	S. 448.23
Athletic Trainers Affiliated Credentialing Board	S. 15.406 (4)	1999 a. 9	Ch. 448, Subchap.VI
Dietitians Affiliated Credentialing Board	S. 15.406 (2)	1993 a. 443; 1997 a. 75	Ch. 448, Subchap.V
Massage Therapy and Bodywork Therapy Affiliated Credentialing Board	S. 15.406 (6)	2001 a. 74; 2009 a. 355	Ch. 460
Occupational Therapists Affiliated Credentialing Board	S. 15.406 (5)	1999 a. 180	Ch. 448, Subchap.VII
Perfusionists Examining Council	S. 15.407 (2m)	2001 a. 89	S. 448.40 (2)
Physician Assistants, Council on	S. 15.407 (2)	1973 c. 149; 1977 c. 418; 2011 a. 146	S. 448.20
Podiatry Affiliated Credentialing Board	S. 15.406 (3)	1997 a. 175; 2009 a. 113	Ch. 448, Subchap.IV

**Boards and Councils Within the Department of Safety and Professional Services –
Continued**

Unit	Statutory Citation	Significant Session Laws Affecting	Duties Specified in Wisconsin Statutes
Respiratory Care Practitioners Examining Council	S. 15.407 (1m)	1989 a. 229	S. 15.407 (1m)
Midwives Advisory Committee, Licensed	S. 440.987	2005 a. 292	S. 440.987
Multifamily Dwelling Code Council	S. 15.407 (12)	1991 a. 39; 1995 a. 27; 2011 a. 32	S. 101.972
Nursing, Board of	S. 15.405 (7g)	1911 c. 346; 1967 c. 327	Ch. 441, Subchap.I
Registered Nurses, Examining Council on	S. 15.407 (3)(a)	1921 c. 365	S. 441.05
Licensed Practical Nurses, Examining Council on	S. 15.407 (3)(b)	1949 c. 402	S. 441.10
Nursing Home Administrator Examining Board	S. 15.405 (7m)	1969 c. 478	Ch. 456
Optometry Examining Board	S. 15.405 (8)	1915 c. 488	Ch. 449
Pharmacy Examining Board	S. 15.405 (9)	1882 c. 167	Ch. 450
Pharmacist Advisory Council	S. 15.407 (6)	1997 a. 68	S. 450.025
Physical Therapy Examining Board	S. 15.405 (7r)	1967 c. 327; 1993 a. 107; 2001 a. 70; 2009 a. 149	Ch. 448, Subchap.III
Plumbers Council	S. 15.407 (16)	1967 c. 327; 1979 c. 221; 1995 a. 27; 2011 a. 32	S. 145.02 (4)
Psychology Examining Board	S. 15.405 (10m)	1969 c. 290	Ch. 455
Radiography Examining Board	S. 15.405 (7e)	2009 a. 106	Ch. 462
Real Estate Appraisers Board	S. 15.405 (10r)	1989 a. 340; 1991 a. 78	Ch. 458
Real Estate Examining Board	S. 15.405 (11m)	1919 c. 656; 1981 c. 94; 2011 a. 32	Ch. 452
Real Estate Curriculum and Examinations, Council on	S. 15.407 (5)	1989 a. 341; 1989 a. 359	S. 452.06 (2)
Sign Language Interpreter Council	S. 15.407 (9)	2009 a. 360	S. 440.032
Veterinary Examining Board	S. 15.405 (12)	1961 c. 294; 1995 a. 321	Ch. 453
Attached by S. 15.03 Building Inspector Review Board	S. 15.405 (1m)	2005 a. 457; 2011 a. 32	S. 101.596

Under Section 440.042, Wisconsin Statutes, the secretary of the department of safety and professional services may appoint advisory committees to advise the department and its boards on matters relating to the regulation of credential holders. Professions for which an advisory committee may be created are as follows: acupuncture; athletic agent; behavior analysts; boxing; charitable organizations; home inspector; interior designer; licensed midwife; music, art and dance therapy; peddler; private detective; private security person; professional employer organizations; professional fund raiser; professional fund raising council; real estate contractual forms; real estate appraisers application; real estate appraisers education and experience; registered sanitarian; substance abuse counselor.

Publications: Biennial reports; Consumer Complaints; Other Resources; The Impaired Professionals Procedure; Information About Your Hearing; Wisconsin Directory of Accredited Schools of Nursing; plus informational bulletins for credential holders, monthly disciplinary reports, and statute/rules codebooks.

Agency Responsibility: The Department of Safety and Professional Services is responsible for ensuring the safe and competent practice of licensed professionals in Wisconsin. The department also administers and enforces laws to assure safe and sanitary conditions in public and private buildings and regulates petroleum products and petroleum storage tank systems. It provides administrative services to the state occupational regulatory authorities responsible for regulation of occupations and offers policy assistance in such areas as evaluating and establishing new professional licensing programs, creating routine procedures for legal proceedings, and adjusting policies in response to public needs. Currently, the department and regulatory authorities are responsible for regulating more than 430,000 credential holders and 200 types of credentials.

The department investigates and prosecutes complaints against credential holders and assists with drafting statutes and administrative rules. The Professional Assistance Procedure (PAP) program enforces participation agreements with credential holders who are chemically impaired, allowing them to retain their professional credentials if they comply with requirements, including treatment for chemical dependency.

The department provides direct regulation and licensing of certain occupations and activities. Numerous boards and regulatory authorities attached to the department have independent responsibility for the regulation of specific professions in the public interest. Within statutory limits, they determine the education and experience required for credentialing, develop and evaluate examinations, and establish standards for professional conduct. These standards are set by administrative rule and enforced through legal action upon complaints from the public. The regulatory authorities may reprimand a credential holder; limit, suspend, or revoke the credential of a practitioner who violates laws or board rules; and, in some cases, impose forfeitures.

Regulatory authority members must be state residents, and they cannot serve more than two consecutive terms. No member may be an officer, director, or employee of a private organization that promotes or furthers the profession or occupation regulated by that board.

Organization: The governor appoints the secretary of the department with the advice and consent of the senate. The secretary appoints a deputy secretary, an executive assistant, and the heads of various subunits from outside the classified service.

The boards and councils attached to the department consist primarily of members of the professions and occupations they regulate. In 1975, the legislature mandated that at least one public member serve on each board. In 1984, it required an additional public member on most boards. Public members are prohibited from having ties to the profession they regulate. In most cases, the governor appoints all members of the licensing and regulatory boards with the advice and consent of the senate. However, in some cases, council members are appointed by the governor without senate confirmation, by the secretary of the department, or by their related examining boards.

Unit Functions: The *Division of Industry Services* is divided into three bureaus and an administrative services section. The Bureau of Environmental Services administers the Petroleum Environmental Cleanup Fund Award (PECFA) and Petroleum Products and Tanks programs. The Bureau of Field Services provides services related to the construction and operation of buildings, along with ensuring compliance with health and safety codes. The Bureau of Technical Services provides services such as plan review, consultation, and product evaluation. The Administrative Services Section provides administrative support to internal and external stakeholders.

The *Division of Legal Services and Compliance* (DLSC) is a public law office providing legal services to professional boards and regulated industries. As part of these services, DLSC is organized into legal teams which include complaint intake personnel, consumer protection investigators, paralegals, prosecutors and designated board counsel. The division inspects business establishments of credential holders, audits specific trust accounts and financial records, monitors compliance with disciplinary orders and administers the Professional Assistance Procedure – a confidential monitoring program for impaired professionals.

The *Division of Management Services* provides administrative and technical support assistance to the department and boards, including information technology, budget and fiscal services, human resources, and administrative support services.

The *Division of Policy Development* provides professional and administrative support to over 60 regulatory boards, councils, and committees. This includes: preparing agendas, transcribing meeting minutes, and researching and analyzing issues related to the regulated professions and programs. The division facilitates the drafting of administrative code and implementation of new laws, rules, and policies.

The *Division of Professional Credential Processing* receives applications for licenses and permits, creates applicant records, and determines whether credential criteria have been met.

History: The 2011-13 biennial budget, 2011 Wisconsin Act 32, created the Department of Safety and Professional Services (DSPS) by combining the Department of Regulation and Licensing (DRL) and the Divisions of Safety and Buildings and Environmental and Regulatory Services from the Department of Commerce.

Chapter 75, Laws of 1967, created DRL and attached to it 14 separate examining boards that had been independent agencies. The 1967 reorganization also transferred to the department some direct licensing and registration functions not handled by boards, including those for private detectives and detective agencies, charitable organizations, and professional fund-raisers and solicitors.

DRL's responsibilities changed significantly since its creation. Initially, it performed routine housekeeping functions for the examining boards, which continued to function as independent agencies. Subsequently, a series of laws required the department to assume various substantive administrative functions previously performed by the boards and to provide direct regulation of several professions.

DSPS's Division of Safety and Buildings traces its roots to 1911 when the Legislature created the Industrial Commission in Chapter 485 to set standards for a safe place of employment. This "safe place" statute was extended in Chapter 588, Laws of 1913, to include public buildings, defined as "any structure used in whole or in part as a place of resort, assemblage, lodging, trade, traffic, occupancy, or use by the public, or by three or more tenants." The commission adopted its first building code in 1914. Programs added over the years include plumbing, heating, ventilation, air conditioning, energy conservation, private on-site waste treatment systems, accessibility for people with disabilities, and electrical inspection and certification. These responsibilities and the job of administering various other laws relating to the promotion of safety in public and private buildings, including enforcing building codes, and the licensure of occupations such as electricians and plumbers, were ultimately assumed by the Department of Commerce.

DSPS's Division of Environmental and Regulatory Services was created by 1995 Wisconsin Act 27 which transferred the PECFA program and the safety and buildings functions from the Department of Industry, Labor and Human Relations to the Department of Commerce. It was removed as a statutory requirement under 2011 Wisconsin Act 32.

Office of the
SECRETARY OF STATE

Secretary of State: DOUGLAS La FOLLETTE, 266-8888.

Deputy Secretaries of State: SUSAN CHURCHILL, SHARON RICKORDS, 266-3470.

Government Records Division: ANN BLOCZYNSKI, *administrator,* 266-1437.

Mailing Address: P.O. Box 7848, Madison 53707-7848.

Location: 30 West Mifflin Street, 10th Floor, Madison 53703.

Telephone: (608) 266-8888.

Fax: (608) 266-3159.

Internet Address: www.sos.state.wi.us

E-mail Address: statesec@wi.gov

Number of Employees: 4.0.

Total Budget 2011-13: $1,027,200.

Constitutional References: Article VI, Sections 1 and 2.

Statutory Reference: Chapter 14, Subchapter III.

Agency Responsibility: The Office of the Secretary of State performs a variety of services for state government and Wisconsin municipalities. Wisconsin's Constitution requires the secretary of state to maintain the official acts of the legislature and governor, and to keep the Great Seal of the State of Wisconsin and affix it to all official acts of the governor.

Organization: The secretary of state, a constitutional officer elected on a partisan ballot in the November general election, heads the Office of the Secretary of State.

Unit Functions: The *Government Records Division* keeps the Great Seal of the State of Wisconsin and affixes it to all official acts of the governor, coordinates the publication of state laws with the Legislative Reference Bureau, records official acts of the legislature and the governor, and files oaths of office. It also files deeds for state lands and buildings, issues authentications and apostilles (a form of international authentication of notaries public), preserves the original copies of all enrolled laws and resolutions, and files annexations, charter ordinances, and incorporation papers for villages and cities. Municipal records and deeds can be accessed via the agency Web site.

History: The 1836 congressional act that organized the Territory of Wisconsin provided for a secretary of the territory to be appointed by the President of the United States. This office was the forerunner of the post of secretary of state created by the Wisconsin Constitution. Delegates to the constitutional conventions of 1846 and 1848 determined that the secretary of state would be a constitutional officer. From the beginning of statehood until 1970, the secretary of state was elected for a 2-year term. Pursuant to a constitutional amendment ratified in 1967 and effective since the 1970 election, the term was extended to 4 years.

In the early days of statehood, the secretary of state personally performed a broad range of duties that are now delegated to other state agencies. Chapter 276, Laws of 1969, created the Office of the Secretary of State to assist the secretary.

Office of the
STATE TREASURER

State Treasurer: KURT SCHULLER, 266-1714, kurt.schuller@wi.gov

Deputy State Treasurer: SCOTT FELDT, 266-7982, scott.feldt@wi.gov

Mailing Address: P.O. Box 7871, Madison 53707-7871.

Location: One South Pinckney Street, Suite 360, Madison.

Telephones: (608) 266-1714, Toll-free (855) 375-2274; Unclaimed property: (608) 267-7977, Toll-free (877) 699-9211.

Fax: (608) 266-2647.

Internet Address: www.statetreasury.wisconsin.gov; www.wismissingmoney.com

Publications: Monthly newsletter for legislators and their staffs; periodic newsletter for local clerks and treasurers; a blog http://wistatetreasury.wordpress.com/, semiannual classified listing of unclaimed property owners.

Number of Employees: 9.95.

Total Budget 2011-13: $9,722,200.

Constitutional References: Article VI, Sections 1 and 3.

Statutory Reference: Chapter 14, Subchapter IV.

Agency Responsibility: The Office of the State Treasurer serves citizens and local government by providing for receipt, custody, oversight, and disbursement of unclaimed property reported to the state.

Organization: The state treasurer, a constitutional officer elected for a 4-year term by partisan ballot in the November general election, heads the Office of the State Treasurer and is the fiscal trustee for the State of Wisconsin.

Functions: The state treasurer participates in the promotion of the state's unclaimed property program administered by the Department of Revenue, and signs certain checks and other financial instruments.

History: The territorial treasurer, an office created in 1839, was appointed by the governor, but the Wisconsin Constitution, adopted in 1848, made the office an elective partisan position. From 1848 through 1968, the state treasurer was elected to a 2-year term in the November general election. Since 1970, following ratification of a constitutional amendment in April 1967, the state treasurer has been elected to a 4-year term. Chapter 276, Laws of 1969, created the Office of the State Treasurer to assist the treasurer.

TECHNICAL COLLEGE SYSTEM

Address e-mail by combining the user ID and the state extender: userid@**wtcsystem.edu**
All telephone numbers are 608 area code unless otherwise indicated.

Technical College System Board: S. MARK TYLER (public member), *president;* ANDREW PETERSEN (public member), *vice president;* JOHN SCHWANTES (public member), *secretary;* REGGIE NEWSON (secretary of workforce development), TONY EVERS (superintendent of public instruction), JOSE VASQUEZ (designated by UW System Board of Regents President); PHILLIP L. NEUENFELDT (employee member); STEPHEN D. WILLET (employer member); BECKY LEVZOW (farmer member); NATALIE CRUZ (student member); PHILIP BARANOWSKI, MARY QUINNETTE CUENE, STAN DAVIS (public members). (All except *ex officio* members are appointed by governor.)

President and State Director: MORNA K. FOY, 266-1770, morna.foy@

Executive Vice President: JAMES ZYLSTRA, 266-1739, james.zylstra@

  Management Services, Office of: NORMAN KENNEY, *associate vice president,* 266-1766, norman.kenney@

  Technology and Data Governance, Office of: KELLY GALLAGHER, *associate vice president,* 266-2947, kelly.gallagher@

Provost and Vice President of Student Success: KATHLEEN CULLEN, 266-9399, kathleen.cullen@

  Instruction, Office of: ANNETTE SEVERSON, *associate vice president,* 267-9064, annette.severson@

  Student Development and Assessment, Office of: WILLA PANZER, *associate vice president,* 267-9065, willa.panzer@

Strategic Partnerships and External Relations: CONOR SMYTH, *director,* 266-2991, conor.smyth@

Mailing Address: P.O. Box 7874, Madison 53707-7874.

Location: 4622 University Avenue, Madison.

Telephone: 266-1207.

Fax: 266-1690.

Internet Address: www.wtcsystem.edu

Publications: *Wisconsin Technical Colleges;* Technical College Facts; annual and biennial reports; annual evaluation reports of technical college offerings and services; cost allocation summaries; employer satisfaction reports; graduate follow-up reports.

Number of Employees: 58.00

Total Budget 2011-13: $291,429,800.

Statutory References: Section 15.94; Chapter 38.

  Agency Responsibility: The Technical College System Board is the coordinating agency for the Technical College System. The board establishes statewide policies and standards for the educational programs and services provided by the 16 technical college districts that cover the state. The district boards, in turn, are responsible for the direct operation of their respective schools and programs. They are empowered to levy property taxes, provide for facilities and equipment, employ staff, and contract for services. The districts set academic and grading standards, appoint the district directors, hire instructional and other staff, and manage the district budget.

  The system board supervises district operations through reporting and audit requirements and consultation, coordination, and support services. It sets standards for building new schools and adding to current facilities. It also provides assistance to districts in meeting the needs of target groups, including services for the disadvantaged, the disabled, women, dislocated workers, the incarcerated, and minorities.

The board administers state and federal aids. It works with the Department of Public Instruction to coordinate secondary and postsecondary vocational and technical programs. It also cooperates with the University of Wisconsin System to establish coordinated programming to make the services of the two agencies fully available to state residents. The board cooperates with the Department of Workforce Development to provide training for apprentices.

Organization: The 13-member Technical College System Board includes 9 members appointed by the governor to serve staggered 6-year terms and a technical college student appointed for a 2-year term. The student must be 18 years of age and a state resident who is enrolled at least half-time and in good academic standing. The governor may not appoint a student member from the same technical college in any two consecutive terms. No person may serve as board president for more than two successive annual terms. A 1971 opinion of the attorney general held that a member of a technical college district board could not serve concurrently on the state board (60 *OAG* 178). The board appoints a director, called the "system president", from outside the classified service to serve at its pleasure, and the system president selects the executive assistant and division administrators from outside the classified service.

The 16 technical college districts encompass 48 campuses. Each district is headed by a board of 9 members who serve staggered 3-year terms. For all districts except Milwaukee, district boards include 2 employers, 2 employees, a school district administrator, a state or local elected official, and 3 additional members as defined by statute. A district appointment committee, composed of county board chairpersons or school board presidents, appoints the board members, subject to approval of the state system board. Each district is administered by a director, called a "president", appointed by the district board.

For Milwaukee, 7 of the 9 board members must be residents of Milwaukee County. The board's 9 members include: 5 persons that represent employers (3 with 15 or more employees, 2 with 100 or more employees, and at least 2 manufacturers); one school district administrator; one elected official who holds a state or local office; and 2 additional members. Milwaukee board members are appointed by a committee composed of the county executive of Milwaukee County and the chairpersons of the Milwaukee, Ozaukee, and Washington County boards of supervisors.

Unit Functions: The *Strategic Advancement Team* provides leadership for systemwide policy analysis and development, public outreach, and federal and state government relations. It is responsible for coordination of systemwide budgeting and planning; research; and labor market information.

The *Offices of Management Services* and *Technology and Data Governance* have oversight responsibility for internal operations including accounting, budgeting, procurement, payroll, human resources, facilities, and information technology. In addition, the division provides guidance to the technical colleges in developing financial policies and standards, distributes state aid, and assists the board in determining student fees and tuition rates and approving district facility development projects. The offices are also responsible for management information and oversight of district budgets and enrollments.

The *Office of Instruction* has responsibility for program definition, approval, evaluation, and review. It focuses on programs in agriculture, office services, marketing, home economics (including family and consumer education), health occupations, trade and industry (including apprenticeship, fire service, law enforcement, safety, and technical and vocational training), general education, personnel certification, and environmental education. It also serves as a liaison to secondary schools

The *Office of Student Development and Assessment* is responsible for coordination of state and federal grant programs, student financial aid, federal projects for the disabled and disadvantaged, adult and continuing education outreach, adult basic education and English language learning, and Workforce Investment Act projects. It serves as a liaison to business and industry.

History: Laws passed in 1907 permitted cities to operate trade schools for persons age 16 or older as part of the public school system (Chapter 122), and allowed them to establish technical schools or colleges, under the control of either the school board or a special board (Chapter 344). In Chapter 616, Laws of 1911, Wisconsin was the first state to establish a system of state aid and support for industrial education. The law required every community with a population of 5,000 or more to establish an industrial education board, which was authorized to levy a property tax. It created the State Board of Industrial Education and an assistant for industrial education in the office of the State Superintendent of Public Instruction.

In the Laws of 1911, Wisconsin was the first state to set up apprenticeship agreements (Chapter 347) and require employers to release 14- to 16-year-olds for part-time attendance in continuation schools for apprentices, if such schooling was available (Chapter 505). Hours in class were to count as part of the total paid work hours. The schools, established through the work of Charles McCarthy, first director of the present-day Legislative Reference Bureau, emphasized general cultural and vocational education, as well as trade skills.

Due in part to the efforts of McCarthy, the U.S. Congress passed the Smith-Hughes Act in 1917, the first federal legislation specifically designed to promote vocational education, which it modeled on Wisconsin's vocational training programs. The act offered financial aid to states to help pay teachers' and administrators' salaries and provided funds for teacher training.

Chapter 494, Laws of 1917, changed the name of the State Board of Industrial Education to the State Board of Vocational Education, authorized it to employ a state director, and designated it as the sole agency to work with the newly created federal board.

During the Great Depression, Wisconsin tightened its compulsory school attendance laws, which resulted in more 14- to 18-year-olds attending vocational school. The demand for adult education also increased, as recognized by Chapter 349, Laws of 1937, which renamed the board the State Board of Vocational and Adult Education. During that same period, the vocational school in Milwaukee began to offer college transfer courses.

Events of the 1960s transformed the Wisconsin vocational-technical system into the postsecondary system of today. Federal vocational school legislation affected business education and emphasized training for the unemployed. The federal Vocational Education Act, passed in 1963, helped the local boards build new facilities. Chapter 51, Laws of 1961, authorized the state board to offer associate degrees for 2-year technical courses. The 1965 Legislature passed Chapter 292, which required a system of vocational, technical and adult education (VTAE) districts covering the entire state by 1970 and changed the board's name to the State Board of Vocational, Technical and Adult Education. (Chapter 327, Laws of 1967, dropped "State" from the name.) College transfer programs were authorized in Madison, Milwaukee, and Rhinelander.

As a result of federal and state legislative changes in the 1960s, VTAE enrollments more than doubled to 466,000 between 1967 and 1982. The 1970s also saw significant increases in the number of associate degree programs. Other major statutory changes included the requirement that VTAE schools charge tuition and that they improve cooperation and coordination with the University of Wisconsin System.

In the past two decades, the system has increased its focus on lifelong learning; education for economic development; and services for groups that formerly had less access to education, including people in rural areas, women, and minorities. The system has placed special emphasis on assisting the unemployed, displaced homemakers, and those with literacy problems.

1993 Wisconsin Act 399 renamed the VTAE system, changing the name to the Technical College System, and designated the state board as the Technical College System Board. District VTAE schools became "technical colleges".

Since the mid-1990s, the Wisconsin Technical College System (WTCS) has experienced sustained, unprecedented enrollment growth. Six-month placement rates for WTCS graduates remained very strong, even during periods of historic economic recession. The colleges continued to develop flexible delivery options, including online offerings and career pathways that make it easy for individuals to return for training and credentials over the course of a career. In 2011, the WTCS celebrated its centennial.

INDEPENDENT BOARD ATTACHED FOR BUDGETING, PROGRAM COORDINATION, AND RELATED MANAGEMENT FUNCTIONS BY SECTION 15.03 OF THE STATUTES

EDUCATIONAL APPROVAL BOARD

Members: DON MADELUNG, *chairperson;* JO OYAMA-MILLER, *vice chairperson;* ROBERT HEIN, *secretary;* WILLIAM RODEN, KATIE THIRY, MONICA WILLIAMS (appointed by governor).

Executive Secretary: DAVID C. DIES, 267-7733.

Mailing Address: 201 West Washington Avenue, Madison 53703.

Telephone: (608) 266-1996.

Fax: (608) 264-8477.

Internet Address: http://eab.state.wi.us

E-mail: eabmail@eab.wisconsin.gov

Publications: A Guide to the EAB; School and Program Approval Guide; Wisconsin Directory of Private Postsecondary Schools.

Number of Employees: 5.00.

Total Budget 2011-13: $1,160,800.

Statutory References: Sections 15.945 (1) and 38.50.

Agency Responsibility: The Educational Approval Board (EAB) is an independent state agency responsible for protecting Wisconsin's consumers and supporting quality educational options, by regulating and evaluating for-profit postsecondary business, trade, or distance learning schools; out-of-state, nonprofit colleges and universities; and in-state, nonprofit institutions incorporated after 1991. The board currently oversees more than 200 schools serving approximately 60,000 adults in 800+ degree and nondegree programs.

The board consists of not more than 7 members who serve at the pleasure of the governor and represent state agencies and others interested in educational programs. It employs the executive secretary and other staff from the classified service. Originally formed by order of the governor in 1944, the legislature created the agency in Chapter 137, Laws of 1953, as the Governor's Educational Advisory Committee to approve and supervise schools and educational courses that trained veterans under various federal laws. A 1957 law (Chapter 438) directed the committee to certify those private vocational schools that offered adequate courses and to prevent fraud and misrepresentation. Chapter 568, Laws of 1963, gave the committee responsibility for licensing agents of private vocational schools, and Chapter 595, Laws of 1965, renamed it the Educational Approval Council. It was renamed the Educational Approval Board and administratively attached to the Department of Public Instruction by Chapter 214, Laws of 1967. The board was attached to the Board of Vocational, Technical and Adult Education by Chapter 125, Laws of 1971.

The Educational Approval Board was repealed by 1995 Wisconsin Act 27, as part of an initiative to create a state Department of Education. The Wisconsin Supreme Court ruled the measure unconstitutional and the agency's functions were continued under Executive Orders 283 and 287 which created the Educational Approval Council. The legislature recreated the board in 1997 Wisconsin Act 27 and attached it to the Higher Educational Aids Board. In 1999 Wisconsin Act 9, the board was attached to the Department of Veterans Affairs. 2001 Wisconsin Act 16 repealed statutory language which specifically made the board responsible for approving schools and courses of instruction for veterans and war orphans. The board was attached to the Wisconsin Technical College System Board (WTCSB) by 2005 Wisconsin Act 25. Under EAB's administrative attachment, budgeting, program operations, and related management functions are conducted with the help of the WTCSB. However, the EAB is treated as a distinct unit of government that exercises its powers, duties, and functions prescribed by law, including rule making, licensing and regulation, and operational planning independently of the WTCSB.

Department of
TOURISM

For e-mail combine the user ID and the state extender: userid@**travelwisconsin.com**
All telephone numbers are 608 area code unless otherwise indicated.

Secretary of Tourism: STEPHANIE KLETT, 266-2345, sklett@

Deputy Secretary: DAVID FANTLE, 266-8773, dfantle@

Mailing Address: P.O. Box 8690, Madison 53708-8690.

Location: 201 West Washington Avenue, 2nd Floor, Madison.

Telephones: 266-2161; Personalized trip planning publications and travel information: (800) 432-8747, M-F 8:00 a.m.-4:30 p.m.

Fax: 266-3403.

Tourism Information Internet Address: www.travelwisconsin.com

Industry Internet Address: http://industry.travelwisconsin.com

Industry Relations and Services, Bureau of: SARAH KLAVAS, *director,* 266-3750, sklavas@

Marketing and Communications, Bureau of: DAVID FANTLE, *marketing director,* 266-8773, dfantle@; LISA MARSHALL, *communications director,* 267-3773, lmarshall@

Technology and Customer Services, Bureau of: JOELLYN MERZ, *director,* 261-8214, jmerz@

Number of Employees: 27.00.

Total Budget 2011-13: $30,400,700.

Statutory References: Section 15.44; Chapter 41.

Publications: *Travel Wisconsin Activity Guide; Wisconsin Travel Guide;* guides for seasonal events and recreation.

Agency Responsibility: The Department of Tourism promotes travel to Wisconsin's scenic, historic, artistic, educational, and recreational sites. Travel sectors targeted by the department include leisure, meetings and conventions, sports, group tours, and international. Through planning, research, and assistance it provides guidance to the tourism and recreation industry to aid in the development of facilities. It also assists cooperative projects between profit and nonprofit tourism ventures. The department encourages local tourism development through the Joint Effort Marketing Grant Program, the "Ready, Set, Go" Sports Marketing Grant Program, Meetings Mean Business Grant Program, and the Travel Information Center Grant Program.

Organization: The governor appoints the secretary, with the advice and consent of the senate, to direct the department. The secretary appoints the bureau directors from the classified service.

Unit Functions: The Secretary's Office provides administrative support to the department and to its attached boards, including budget, policy planning and analysis, and accounting.

The *Bureau of Industry Relations and Services* provides a direct communication link between the tourism industry and the Department of Tourism through a field staff team that works with destinations, businesses, and associations statewide. Public agencies, private sector entities, and economic development organizations can take advantage of a variety of tools and partnerships offered through this bureau. The bureau also coordinates the grant programs, market research, publications development, graphic design, produces the annual Governor's Conference on Tourism along with special events throughout the state, and niche market development (meetings and conventions, sports groups, and international).

The *Bureau of Marketing and Communications* promotes and advertises Wisconsin as "the Midwest's premier travel destination". Through market research, coordinated advertising, promotional campaigns, and publications targeted to travelers' interests, the bureau works to attract in-state and out-of-state tourists and associated travel dollars. The Communications team works with the news media worldwide to develop positive stories about Wisconsin as a travel destination.

The *Bureau of Technology and Customer Services* delivers Wisconsin travel information to visitors through various channels, including publication distribution, telephone travel assistance, and travelwisconsin.com, the official travel and tourism Web site for the State of Wisconsin. The bureau also coordinates several programs to collect local travel information from destination marketing organizations around the state, and makes the details on more than 13,000 attractions, restaurants, accommodations, and events readily available to potential visitors.

History: State tourism promotion originated in the Department of Natural Resources to encourage travel to state parks and commercial recreational sites. Chapter 39, Laws of 1975, transferred tourism functions to the Department of Business Development and created the Division of Tourism as a statutory entity within the department. Chapter 361, Laws of 1979, created the Department of Development, which absorbed the division, through a merger of the Department of Business Development and the Department of Local Affairs and Development. 1995 Wisconsin Act 27 reorganized the division as the Department of Tourism, effective January 1, 1996.

Statutory Board and Council

Arts Board: BRUCE BERNBERG, *chairperson;* ROBERT WAGNER, *vice chairperson;* SUSAN FRIEBERT, MARY GIELOW, JOHN HENDRICKS, BRIAN KELSEY, LAMOINE MACLAUGHLIN, RON MADICH, HEATHER A. MCDONELL, NICK MEYER, KEVIN MILLER, BARBARA E. MUNSON, GLENDA P. NOEL-NEY, SHARON STEWART, MATTHEW WALLOCK (appointed by governor).

Executive Director: GEORGE TZOUGROS, 267-2006, george.tzougros@wisconsin.gov

Mailing Address: P.O. Box 8690, Madison 53708-8690.

Telephone: 266-0190.

Fax: 267-0380.

E-mail Address: artsboard@wisconsin.gov

Internet Address: artsboard.wisconsin.gov

Devils Lake State Park near Baraboo, Wisconsin. (R.J. and Linda Miller)

Publications: Internet only: Annual Report; Guide to Programs and Services; grant applications (all programs); Wisconsin Folks Web Site; Portal Wisconsin; Web site in collaboration with the Cultural Coalition of Wisconsin.

Number of Employees: 4.00.

Total Budget 2011-13: $3,161,700.

Statutory References: Section 15.445 (1); Chapter 44, Subchapter III.

Agency Responsibility: The legislature directs the Arts Board to study and assist artistic and cultural activities in the state, assist communities in developing their own arts programs, and plan and implement funding programs for groups or individuals engaged in the arts.

As a funding agency, the board assists arts organizations and individual artists through a variety of programs designed to provide broad public access to the arts, strengthen the state's artistic resources, and create opportunities for individuals of exceptional talent. Financial support programs for individuals and organizations include apprenticeships, artists-in-education programs, challenge grants, community activities, fellowships, opportunity grants, program assistance and support, and programs for presenters. The board also provides matching grants to local arts agencies and municipalities through the Wisconsin Regranting Program.

The board aids Wisconsin's artistic community through an information program that includes workshops, conferences, research projects, and publications. The board regularly produces and distributes materials on local, state, and national arts activities for both the arts community and the general public. It arranges for the governor's official portrait.

The 15 board members serve staggered 3-year terms and must be state residents with a concern for the arts. Each geographic quadrant of the state must be represented by at least 2 members. The board selects the executive director from outside the classified service. Chapter 90, Laws of 1973, created the board and attached it to the Department of Administration to succeed the Governor's Council on the Arts, which Governor Gaylord Nelson had established in 1963. 1995 Wisconsin Act 27 attached the board to the Department of Tourism for administrative purposes. 2011 Wisconsin Act 32 provided that the Arts Board was in the Department of Tourism.

Council on Tourism: Paul Upchurch, *chairperson;* Deb Archer, Aimee Awonohapy, James Bolen, Cindy Burzinski, Paul Cunningham, Allyson Gommer, S. Peter Helland, Jr., Brian Kelsey, Joe Klimczak, Kathy Kopp, Scott Krause, Lola Roeh, Stacey Watson; Stephanie Klett (secretary of tourism); Senators Hansen, Moulton; Representatives Billings, Kaufert; George Tzougros (executive director, Arts Board); Ellsworth Brown (director, state historical society). (All except *ex officio* members are appointed by governor.)

The 21-member Council on Tourism advises the secretary about tourism and encourages Wisconsin private companies to promote the state in their advertisements. The 14 appointed members serve 3-year terms and assist the secretary in formulating a statewide marketing plan. Nominations for public member appointments must be sought from (but are not limited to) multicounty regional associations engaged in promoting tourism; statewide associations of businesses related to tourism; area visitor and convention bureaus; arts organizations; the Great Lakes Inter-Tribal Council, Inc., and other agencies with knowledge of American Indian tourism; and persons engaged in businesses catering to tourists. Nominees must have experience in marketing and promotion strategy and must represent the different geographical areas of the state and the diversity of the tourism industry. The council was created by 1987 Wisconsin Act 1 in the Department of Development and transferred to the Department of Tourism by 1995 Wisconsin Act 27. Its composition and duties are prescribed in Sections 15.447 (1) and 41.12 of the statutes.

Independent Units Attached for Budgeting, Program Coordination, and Related Management Functions by Section 15.03 of the Statutes

KICKAPOO RESERVE MANAGEMENT BOARD

Members: Susan C. Cushing, Brandon Hysel, Ronald M. Johnson, Alan Szepi (residents of specified municipalities and school districts within watershed); Paul Frei, Richard T. Wallin (watershed residents outside specified units); William L. Quackenbush (nonresident

Kayaking in the Apostle Islands. *(R.J. and Linda Miller)*

environmental advocate); vacancy (nonresident education representative); DAVE MAXWELL (nonresident recreation and tourism representative); TRACY LITTLEJOHN, ADLAI J. MANN (members with knowledge of watershed's cultural resources, nominated by Ho-Chunk Nation) (appointed by governor).

Executive Director: MARCY WEST, marcy.west@wisconsin.gov

Mailing Address: S 3661 State Highway 131, La Farge 54639.

Telephone: (608) 625-2960.

Fax: (608) 625-2962.

E-mail Address: kickapoo.reserve@wisconsin.gov

Internet Address: http://kvr.state.wi.us

Publications: Kickapoo Valley Reserve Visitors' Guide.

Number of Employees: 4.00.

Total Budget 2011-13: $1,928,808.

Statutory References: Sections 15.07 (1) (b) 20., 15.445 (2), 41.40, and 41.41.

Agency Responsibility: The 11-member Kickapoo Reserve Management Board manages 8,569 acres in the Kickapoo Valley Reserve to preserve and enhance the area's environmental, scenic, and cultural features; provides facilities for the use and enjoyment of visitors; and promotes the reserve as a destination for vacationing and recreation. Subject to the approval of the governor, the board may purchase land for inclusion in the reserve and trade land in the reserve under certain conditions. The Kickapoo Valley Reserve Visitor Center offers meetings and classrooms, interactive exhibits, educational programs, and tourist information.

The board also may lease land for purposes consistent with the management of the reserve or for agricultural purposes; authorize, license, regulate, and collect and spend revenue from private concessions in the reserve; accept gifts, grants, and bequests; and cooperate with and provide matching funds to nonprofit groups organized to provide assistance to the reserve.

The board may not authorize mining in the reserve or on any land acquired by the board and may not sell land that is in the reserve. It has authority to promulgate rules about use of the waters, land, and facilities under its jurisdiction, and the Department of Tourism is responsible for enforcement of state laws and rules relating to the reserve.

The governor appoints board members for staggered 3-year terms. Four members must be residents of villages, towns, and school districts in the immediate vicinity of the reserve; 2 must be residents of the Kickapoo River watershed outside of the immediate vicinity of the reserve; and 3 members who are not residents of the watershed are appointed by the governor to represent education, environment, and tourism issues. In addition, 2 members are nominated by the Ho-Chunk Nation who have an interest in and knowledge of the cultural resources within the watershed. Various state agencies must appoint nonmember liaisons to the board, and the board may request that any federally recognized American Indian tribe or band in this state, other than the Ho-Chunk Nation, appoint a nonmember liaison. The board appoints the executive director from outside the classified service. The board was created as the Kickapoo Valley Governing Board by 1993 Wisconsin Act 349 and attached to the Department of Administration. 1995 Wisconsin Act 27 attached the board to the Department of Tourism, and it was renamed by 1995 Wisconsin Act 216. The board's membership was revised by 2005 Wisconsin Act 396.

LOWER WISCONSIN STATE RIVERWAY BOARD

Members: DONALD GREENWOOD (Sauk County), *chairperson;* FRED MADISON (recreational user group representative), *vice chairperson;* RONALD LEYS (Crawford County), *secretary;* MELODY K. MOORE (Dane County), ROBERT CARY (Grant County), GERALD DORSCHEID (Iowa County), GREG GREENHECK (Richland County); GEORGE ARIMOND, RITCHIE J. BROWN (recreational user groups' representatives appointed by governor with senate consent). (County representatives are nominated by respective county boards and appointed by governor.)

Executive Director: MARK E. CUPP, 202 North Wisconsin Avenue, P.O. Box 187, Muscoda 53573-0187, mark.cupp@wisconsin.gov

Telephones: (608) 739-3188; (800) 221-3792.

Sherwood Point Lighthouse in Door County.   (Door County Convention and Visitors Bureau)

Fax: (608) 739-4263.

Internet Address: http://lwr.state.wi.us

Publications: Summary of regulations, Strategic Plan, Biennial Report.

Number of Employees: 2.00.

Total Budget 2011-13: $405,200.

Statutory References: Section 15.445 (3); Chapter 30, Subchapter IV.

Agency Responsibility: The 9-member Lower Wisconsin State Riverway Board is responsible for protecting and preserving the scenic beauty and natural character of the riverway. The board reviews permit applications for buildings, walkways, timber harvests, utility facilities, bridges, and other structures in the riverway and issues permits for activities that meet established standards.

Board members serve staggered 3-year terms. Each of the 6 county representatives must be either an elected official or a resident of a city or village that abuts the Lower Wisconsin State Riverway or of a town located at least in part in the riverway. The 3 members representing recreational user groups may not reside in any of the 6 specified counties. The board was created by 1989 Wisconsin Act 31 and attached to the Department of Natural Resources. 1995 Wisconsin Act 27 attached the board to the Department of Tourism.

STATE FAIR PARK BOARD

Members: JOHN YINGLING, *chairperson;* SUSAN CRANE (general business representative); SENATORS CARPENTER, FARROW; REPRESENTATIVES RIPP, vacancy (legislative members recommended by party leadership and appointed by governor); MARY MAAS (general business experience); vacancy (business technology experience); DAN DEVINE (West Allis resident); SUE RUPNOW (agriculture business representative); ALDO MADRIGRANO (state resident); BEN BRANCEL (secretary of agriculture, trade and consumer protection); STEPHANIE KLETT (secretary of tourism). (All except *ex officio* members or designees are appointed by governor with senate consent.)

Chief Executive Officer: RICK FRENETTE, (414) 266-7020.

Executive Assistant: MARIAN SANTIAGO-LLOYD, (414) 266-7021.

Mailing Address: 640 South 84th Street, West Allis 53214.

Telephones: (414) 266-7000; (414) 266-7100 (ticket office); (800) 884-FAIR (recorded announcement of events).

Fax: (414) 266-7007.

E-mail Address: wsfp@wisconsin.gov

Internet Address: www.wistatefair.com

Publications: *A Brief History of the Wisconsin State Fair;* WSFP cook book; fair brochures. Daily events schedule and premium books available at www.wistatefair.com.

Number of Employees: 39.90.

Total Budget 2011-13: $41,314,800.

Statutory References: Section 15.445 (4); Chapter 42.

Agency Responsibility: The State Fair Park Board manages the State Fair Park and supervises its use for fairs, exhibits, or promotional events for agricultural, commercial, educational, and recreational purposes. It also leases or licenses the property at reasonable rates for other uses when not needed for public purposes. The board is directed to develop new facilities at State Fair Park and to provide a permanent location for an annual Wisconsin State Fair, major sports events, agricultural and industrial expositions, and other programs of civic interest.

Organization: The State Fair Park Board consists of 13 members. Legislative members, who represent the majority and minority parties, are nominated by party leadership and appointed by the governor. The 7 citizen members serve staggered 5-year terms. The departmental secretaries may designate members to serve in place of the secretaries. The board appoints the park director from outside the classified service.

History: Beginning with the first Wisconsin State Fair at Janesville in October 1851, the event has served as a showcase for Wisconsin agriculture and commerce. The State Agricultural Society, which sponsored the first fair, continued to operate it through 1897. In that year, Chapter 301 created the Wisconsin State Board of Agriculture and placed operation of the fair under its control. When the Department of Agriculture was created in 1915, the state fair became part of the new department.

In Chapter 149, Laws of 1961, the independent Wisconsin Exposition Department, headed by a 7-member board, was created to manage the fair and the park's year-round operation. Under the 1967 executive branch reorganization, the Exposition Department became the Wisconsin Exposition Council in the Department of Local Affairs and Development.

Chapter 125, Laws of 1971, created a 3-member State Fair Park Board, appointed by the governor and attached to the Department of Agriculture for administrative purposes. In 1985 Wisconsin Act 20, the legislature increased board membership to 5, specified 5-year terms of service, and required senate confirmation of the governor's nominees.

In 1990, as provided by 1989 Wisconsin Act 219, the State Fair Park Board became an independent body. 1995 Wisconsin Act 27 attached the board to the Department of Tourism, and 1999 Wisconsin Act 197 revised and increased board membership.

Over the years, the location of the state fair was debated and even its continued existence was in doubt. At various times between 1851 and 1885, Fond du Lac, Janesville, Madison, Milwaukee, and Watertown hosted the fair. Milwaukee was chosen as the state fair site from 1886 through 1891, and the fairs held there were so successful that a permanent site was purchased in what is now West Allis, a Milwaukee suburb. That site, first used for the 1892 fair, is included in the state fair's location today.

Several studies published during the 1960s recommended that the fair be moved to a larger site in the Milwaukee area. Chapter 125, Laws of 1971, decided the fair would remain at its site (partially in West Allis, partially in Milwaukee), with updated or new facilities being funded through self-amortizing state bonds. Fair operations have been self-financed since 1935. 1999 Wisconsin Act 9 provided funding for substantial construction and renovation of park facilities. 1999 Wisconsin Act 197 authorized the board to create a nonprofit corporation to raise funds and provide support and contract with that same corporation for operation and development of the park. Act 197 also authorized the park board to permit private individuals to construct facilities on fair grounds under a lease agreement with the board.

Today, State Fair Park draws more than 2 million visitors to its events and activities each year, and the Wisconsin State Fair, with attendance of more than 900,000, remains the state's oldest and largest annual event.

Department of
TRANSPORTATION

Address e-mail by combining the user ID and the state extender: userid@**dot.wi.gov**
All telephone numbers are 608 area code unless otherwise indicated.

Secretary of Transportation: MARK GOTTLIEB, 266-1114, mark.gottlieb@

Deputy Secretary: MICHAEL J. BERG, 266-1114, michael.berg@

Executive Assistant: STEVE KRIESER, 266-1114, steven.krieser@

General Counsel, Office of: JOHN J. SCHULZE, JR., *chief legal counsel,* 266-8928, johnj.schulzejr@

Policy, Budget and Finance, Office of: PAUL M. HAMMER, *director,* 267-9618, paul.hammer@

Public Affairs, Office of: PEG SCHMITT, *director,* 266-5599, peg.schmitt@, Fax: 266-7186.

Mailing Address: P.O. Box 7910, Madison 53707-7910.

Location: Hill Farms State Transportation Building, 4802 Sheboygan Avenue, Madison.

Internet Address: www.dot.wisconsin.gov

Number of Employees: 3,350.04.

Total Budget 2011-13: $5,647,297,700.

Statutory References: Sections 15.46, 15.465, and 15.467; Chapters 82-86, 110, 114, 340-349, and 351.

Business Management, Division of: DENISE SOLIE, *administrator,* 266-2090, denise.solie@; JON KRANZ, *deputy administrator,* 264-7700, jonathan.kranz@

  Business Services, Bureau of: PATRICIA JACKSON-WARD, *director,* 267-4479, patricia.jacksonward@

  Human Resource Services, Bureau of: RANDY SARVER, *director,* 266-0507, randy.sarver@

  Information Technology Services, Bureau of: ANN SCHWARTZ, *director,* 266-0033, ann.schwartz@

Motor Vehicles, Division of: LYNNE B. JUDD, *administrator,* 266-7079, lynne.judd@; PATRICK FERNAN, *deputy administrator,* 261-8605, patrick.fernan@

  Driver Services, Bureau of: DONNA BROWN-MARTIN, *director,* 266-9890, donna.brownmartin@

  Field Services, Bureau of: KRISTINA BOARDMAN, *director,* 266-5082, kristina.boardman@; vacancy, *deputy director,* 266-2743.

  Vehicle Services, Bureau of: MITCHELL WARREN, *director,* 267-5121, mitchell.warren@

    Vehicle Emission Testing (Southeast Wisconsin): (800) 242-7510; Milwaukee/Waukesha area: (414) 266-1080.

  Motor Vehicle Regional Managers:

    North Central Region: JILL GEOFFROY, (715) 355-4613, 5301 Rib Mountain Drive, Wausau 54401, jill.geoffroy@

    Northeast Region: DONALD GENIN, (920) 960-9092, 711 West Association Drive, Appleton 54914, donald.genin@

    Northwest Region: PATRICIA NELSON, (715) 234-3773, 735 West Avenue, Rice Lake 54868-1359, patricia.nelson@

    Southeast Region: SANDRA BRISCO, (414) 227-3288, 1001 West St. Paul Avenue, 2nd Floor, Milwaukee 53233, sandra.brisco@

    Southwest Region: DONALD REINCKE, (608) 789-4630, 9477 Highway 16 East, Onalaska 54650-9903, donald.reincke@

State Patrol, Division of: STEPHEN FITZGERALD, *superintendent,* 266-0454, stephen.fitzgerald@; COLONEL BEN H. MENDEZ, 266-3908, benjamin.mendez@

  Division Mailing Address: P.O. Box 7912, Madison 53707-7912.

  Telephones: General: (608) 266-3212; Road Condition Reports: Madison: (608) 246-7580; Milwaukee: (414) 785-7140; elsewhere in Wisconsin: (800) 762-3947.

  Fax: 267-4495.

  Field Operations, Bureau of: MAJOR BRIAN K. RAHN, 266-0184, brian.rahn@

    State Patrol Region Captains/Executive Officers:

      North Central Region:

        Wausau Post: NICHOLAS R. WANINK, *captain,* (715) 845-1143, nicholas.wanink@; STEVEN G. KRUEGER, *executive officer,* (715) 845-1143, steven.krueger@; Fax: (715) 848-9255; 2805 Martin Avenue, Wausau 54401-7172.

      Northeast Region:

        Fond du Lac Post: NICK SCORCIO, JR., *captain,* (920) 929-3700, nick.scorcio@; ANTHONY L. BURRELL, *executive officer,* (920) 929-3700, anthony.burrell@; Fax: (920) 929-7666; 851 South Rolling Meadows Drive, P.O. Box 984, Fond du Lac 54936-9927.

      Northwest Region:

        Eau Claire Post: JEFFREY J. FRENETTE, *captain,* (715) 839-3800, jeffrey.frenette@;

DEPARTMENT OF TRANSPORTATION

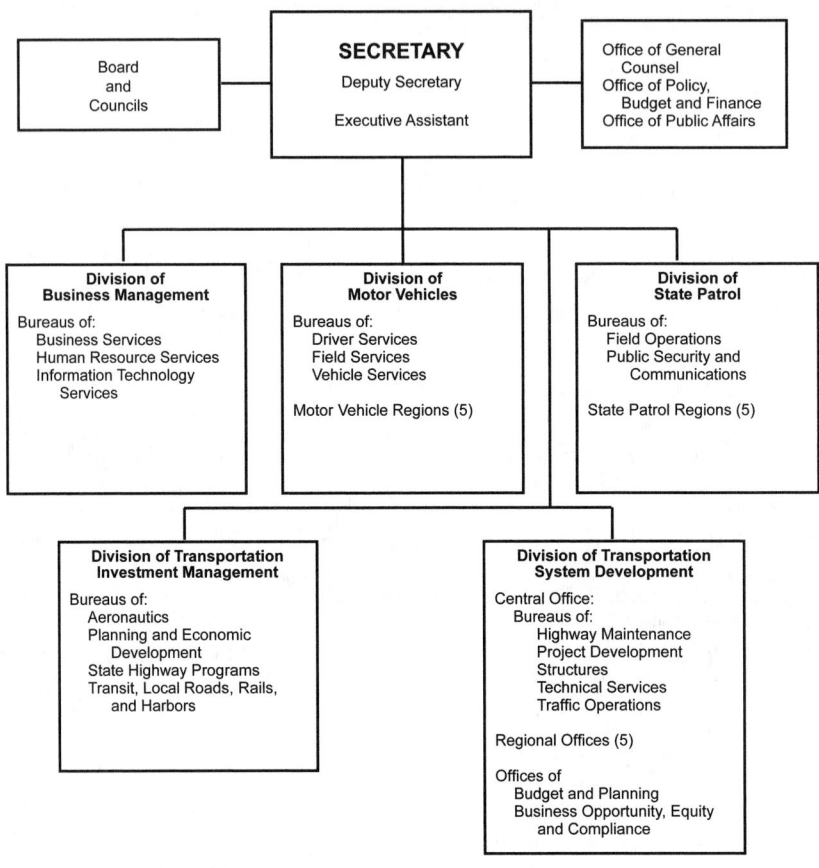

Fax: (715) 839-3841; JEFFREY D. LORENTZ, *executive officer,* (715) 839-3800, jeffrey.lorentz@; Fax: (715) 839-3873; 5005 Highway 53 South, Eau Claire 54701-8846.

Spooner Post: DORI L. PETZNICK, *executive officer,* (715) 635-2141, dori.petznick@; Fax: (715) 635-6373; W7102 Green Valley Road, Spooner 54801.

Southeast Region:

Waukesha Post: TIMOTHY L. CARNAHAN, *captain,* (262) 785-4700, timothy.carnahan@; JAMES M. KICMOL, *executive officer,* (262) 785-4700, james.kicmol@; Fax: (262) 785-4722; 21115 Highway 18, Waukesha 53186-2985.

Southwest Region:

DeForest Post: CHARLES R. TEASDALE, *captain,* (608) 846-8500, charles.teasdale@; BRAD ALTMAN, *executive officer,* (608) 846-8500, brad.altman@; Fax: (608) 846-8536; 911 West North Street, DeForest 53532-1971.

Tomah Post: PAUL D. MATL, *executive officer,* (608) 374-0513, paul.matl@; Fax: (608) 374-0599; 23928 Lester McMullin Drive, Tomah 54660-5376.

Public Security and Communications, Bureau of: MAJOR J.D. LIND, *director,* 267-9522.

Transportation Investment Management, Division of: AILEEN SWITZER, *administrator,* 266-5791, aileen.switzer@; Fax: 266-0686; P.O. Box 7913, Madison 53707-7913.

Aeronautics, Bureau of: DAVID GREENE, *director,* 266-2480, david.greene@

Planning and Economic Development, Bureau of: SANDRA BEAUPRÉ, *director,* 266-7575, sandra.beaupre@

State Highway Programs, Bureau of: JOSEPH NESTLER, *director,* 266-9495, joseph.nestler@

Transit, Local Roads, Rails, and Harbors, Bureau of: ADAM BOARDMAN, *director,* 266-2963, adam.boardman@

Transportation System Development, Division of: DANIEL GRASSER, *administrator,* 267-7111, daniel.grasser@; Division Fax: 264-6667.

Division Mailing Address: 4802 Sheboygan Avenue, Room 451, P.O. Box 7965, Madison 53707-7965.

Division E-mail Address: dotdtsddivision-office@dot.wi.gov

Deputy Administrator – Statewide Bureaus: RORY RHINESMITH, 266-2392, rory.rhinesmith@; Fax: 264-6667.

Highway Maintenance, Bureau of: DAVID I. VIETH, *director,* 267-8999, david.vieth@; Fax: 267-7856.

Project Development, Bureau of: BETH CANNESTRA, *director,* 266-3707, beth.cannestra@; Fax: 266-8459.

Structures, Bureau of: SCOT BECKER, *director,* 266-5161, scot.becker@; Fax: 261-6277.

Technical Services, Bureau of: REBECCA BURKEL, *director,* 246-5399, rebecca.burkel@; Fax: 267-0307.

Traffic Operations, Bureau of: JOHN M. CORBIN, *director,* 266-0459, john.corbin@; Fax: 261-6295.

Budget and Planning, Office of: MARIETTA SMITH, *chief,* 266-2836, marietta.smith@; Fax: 264-6667.

Business Opportunity, Equity and Compliance, Office of: AGGO AKYEA, *director,* 267-9527, aggo.akyea@

Deputy Administrator – Regions: DONALD J. MILLER, 264-6677, donald.miller@; Fax: 264-6667.

North Central Region, Rhinelander: RUSS HABECK, *director,* (715) 365-3490, russ.habeck@; Fax: (715) 365-5780; TTY: (715) 365-5719; 1681 Second Avenue South, Wisconsin Rapids 54495; KEN WICKHAM, *deputy director,* (715) 421-8300, kenneth.wickham@; Fax: (715) 423-0334; 510 North Hanson Lake Road, Rhinelander 54501-5108.

Northeast Region, Green Bay: WILL DORSEY, *director,* (920) 492-5643, will.dorsey@; Fax: (920) 492-5640; TTY: (920) 492-5673; 944 Vanderperren Way, P.O. Box 28080, Green Bay 54324-0080; COLLEEN HARRIS, *deputy director,* (920) 492-5678, colleen.harris@

Northwest Region, Eau Claire: DONALD GUTKOWSKI, *director,* (715) 836-2891, donald.gutkowski@; Fax: (715) 836-2807; TTY: (715) 836-6578; 718 West Clairemont Avenue, Eau Claire 54701-5108; JERALD MENTZEL, *deputy director,* (715) 392-7925, jerald.mentzel@; Fax: (715) 392-7863; TTY Relay Service: (800) 947-3529; 1701 North Fourth Street, Superior 54880-1068.

Southeast Region, Waukesha: DEWAYNE JOHNSON, *director,* (262) 548-5884, dewayne.johnson@; Fax: (414) 548-5662; TTY: (414) 548-8801; 141 Northwest Barstow Street, Waukesha 53187-0798; BRETT WALLACE, *deputy director,* (262) 548-5884, brett.wallace@; Fax: (414) 548-5662; 151 Northwest Barstow Street, Waukesha 53187-0798.

Southwest Region, La Crosse: JOSEPH OLSON, *director,* (608) 785-9022, joseph.olson@; Fax: (608) 785-9969; TTY: (608) 789-7862; 3550 Mormon Coulee Road, La Crosse

54601-6767; Rose Phetteplace, *deputy director,* (608) 246-3801, rose.phetteplace@; Fax: (608) 246-7996; TTY: (608) 246-5385; 2101 Wright Street, Madison 53704-2583.

Publications: Biennial Report; Connections 2030; Five-Year Airport Improvement Program (online; updated monthly); Motorcyclist Handbook for Wisconsin (online); *Rustic Roads;* Six-Year Highway Improvement Program; Traffic Safety Reporter; *Trucking Wisconsin Style;* Wisconsin Aeronautical Chart (even-numbered years); Wisconsin Airport Directory (odd-numbered years); Wisconsin Alcohol Traffic Facts; Wisconsin Commercial Drivers' Manual (online); Wisconsin Drivers' Book (online); Wisconsin Highway Map; Wisconsin Motorcycle Crash Facts; Wisconsin Motorists' Handbook and Study Guide (online); Wisconsin Traffic Crash Facts (annual).

Agency Responsibility: The Department of Transportation is responsible for the planning, promotion, and protection of all transportation systems in the state. Its major responsibilities involve highways, motor vehicles, motor carriers, traffic law enforcement, railroads, waterways, mass transit, and aeronautics.

The department works with several federal agencies in the administration of federal transportation aids. It also cooperates with departments at the state level in travel promotion, consumer protection, environmental analysis, and transportation services for elderly and handicapped persons.

Organization: The secretary is appointed by the governor with the advice and consent of the senate and has overall management responsibility for the department. The secretary appoints the deputy secretary, executive assistant, and all division administrators from outside the classified service.

Unit Functions: The *Division of Business Management* plans and administers the department's programs for accounting and auditing, information technology, human resources, purchasing, vehicle fleet, facilities, and management services.

The *Division of Motor Vehicles* issues vehicle titles and registrations, individual identification cards, and handicapped parking permits; examines and licenses drivers, commercial driving instructors, and vehicle salespersons; certifies commercial driver examiners; licenses motor car-

A bicycle and pedestrian bridge serves travelers in Fitchburg. (Department of Transportation)

riers, commercial driving schools, vehicle dealers, manufacturers, and distributors; and investigates consumer complaints about vehicle sales and trade practices. It keeps the records of drivers' traffic violations and demerit points. It is responsible for the vehicle emissions inspection program, and it administers reciprocal trucking agreements with other states and the Canadian provinces and provides traffic accident data to law enforcement officials, highway engineers, and traffic safety and media representatives. The division operates 5 regional offices, 81 customer service centers, and 11 travel locations to support the state's approximately 4.5 million licensed drivers and ID card holders and over 5.4 million registered vehicles.

The *Division of State Patrol* promotes highway safety by enforcing state traffic laws regarding motor vehicles and motor carriers. The State Patrol also has criminal law enforcement powers and can assist local law enforcement agencies by providing emergency police services. It operates the statewide mobile data communications network, which is available to local law enforcement agencies, and it makes annual inspections of Wisconsin's school buses and ambulances. The division oversees 5 regional offices and a law enforcement training academy open to all federal, state, county, local, and tribal law enforcement officers.

The *Division of Transportation Investment Management* performs statewide planning for highways, railroads, harbors, airports, and mass transit and promotes a multimodal transportation system to best serve state citizens and businesses. The division directs data collection; provides service to local governments and planning agencies; and manages state road aids, highway finance, and other transportation assistance programs. The division is responsible for uniform statewide direction in the planning, design, construction, maintenance, and operation of Wisconsin's airports, harbors, highways, and railroads. The division is involved with the state's 132 public use airports, 3,600 miles of railroad tracks, 29 commercial water ports, and harbors, and the approximately 12,000 miles of roads and streets in the State Trunk Highway (STH) system, including 743 miles of Interstate highways within the state. The division administers all state and federal funding for airport, railroad, and harbor development projects in Wisconsin.

The *Division of Transportation System Development* performs development, maintenance, and operations functions related to the STH system. The division is split into two basic areas: Statewide Bureaus and Regional Operations. It provides uniform direction in planning, design, and construction phases of project delivery as well as improving the safety and efficiency of the STH system. The division also provides leadership in the protection of public interests and resources through public and local interactions.

The five state statewide bureaus include: 1) Highway Maintenance, 2) Project Development, 3) Structures, 4) Technical Services, and 5) Traffic Operations. These statewide bureaus advise the regional offices as well as other divisions regarding engineering, economic, environmental, and social standards and practices. The division also monitors the quality and efficiency of the department's various programs and assures compliance with federal and state laws and regulations. The five regional offices manage the operation and development of state highways and participate in the development, management, and implementation of local road and nonhighway transportation projects. They also maintain working relationships with local units of government, represent the department in local and regional planning efforts, and represent local and regional needs in departmental processes.

History: The history of the Department of Transportation mirrors the evolution of 20th century transportation. The Highway Commission was created when Chapter 337, Laws of 1911, authorized state aid for public highways. Later, Chapter 410, Laws of 1939, consolidated registration, licensing, inspection, enforcement, and highway safety promotion in the Motor Vehicle Department. The legislature established the Aeronautics Commission in Chapter 513, Laws of 1945, and directed it to cooperate with the federal government and other states to "prepare for the generally expected extensive expansion of aviation following the termination of World War II."

The Department of Transportation was created by Chapter 75, Laws of 1967, which merged the Highway Commission, the Aeronautics Commission, and the Motor Vehicle Department. Chapter 500, Laws of 1969, required three divisions within the department: aeronautics, highways, and motor vehicles. The department was strengthened by Chapter 29, Laws of 1977, which vested accountability at the departmental, instead of divisional, level and gave the secretary, rather than the governor, the authority to appoint division heads. The secretary was also allowed to reorganize the department with the governor's approval.

Statutory Board and Councils

Highway Safety, Council on: RANDALL R. THIEL (state officer), *chairperson;* RICHARD VAN BOXTEL (citizen member), *vice chairperson;* SENATORS LEIBHAM, PETROWSKI; REPRESENTATIVES RIPP, STONE, THIESFELDT; JOHN CORBIN, STEPHEN FITZGERALD, PATRICK HUGHES, JEFF PLALE (state officers); ROBERT BARTEN, LAVERNE E. HERMANN, BRIAN LUETH, KURT SCHULTZ (citizen members). (All except legislators are appointed by governor.)

The 15-member Council on Highway Safety advises the secretary about highway safety matters. The council consists of 2 senators and 3 representatives. At least one senator and at least one representative must serve on standing committees that deal with transportation matters. The other 10 members, who serve staggered 3-year terms, include 5 state officers with transportation and highway safety duties and 5 citizen members. The council was originally created in the Office of the Governor by Chapter 276, Laws of 1969, and was moved to the Department of Transportation by Chapter 34, Laws of 1979. Its composition and duties are prescribed in Sections 15.467 (3) and 85.07 (2) of the statutes.

Rustic Roads Board: MARION FLOOD, *chairperson;* DANIEL FEDDERLY, *vice chairperson;* SENATOR PETROWSKI; REPRESENTATIVE RIPP; RAYMOND DEHAHN, ROBERT HANSEN, BRUCE LINDGREN, ALAN LORENZ, CHARLES RAYALA, THOMAS SOLHEIM. (Nonlegislative members are appointed by secretary of transportation.)

The 10-member Rustic Roads Board oversees the application and selection process of locally-nominated county highways and local roads for inclusion in the Rustic Roads network. Established in 1973, the Rustic Roads Program is a partnership between local officials and state government to showcase some of Wisconsin's most picturesque and lightly-traveled roadways for the leisurely enjoyment of hikers, bikers, and motorists. The board includes the chairpersons of the senate and assembly committees with jurisdiction over transportation matters. Its 8 nonlegislative members serve staggered 4-year terms, and at least 4 of them must be nominees of the Wisconsin Counties Association. The board was created by Chapter 142, Laws of 1973, and its composition and duties are prescribed in Sections 15.465 (2) and 83.42 of the statutes.

Uniformity of Traffic Citations and Complaints, Council on.

The 10-member Council on Uniformity of Traffic Citations and Complaints recommends forms used for traffic violations. The council was created by Chapter 292, Laws of 1967, as the Uniform Traffic Citation and Complaint Committee and renamed by 1985 Wisconsin Act 145. Its composition and duties are prescribed in Sections 15.467 (4) and 345.11 of the statutes.

The council meets on an as-needed basis, and members are designated when required. Members include the secretary of transportation or designee, a member of the Department of Transportation responsible for law enforcement, a member designated by the Director of State Courts, and members designated by the presidents of the following: the Wisconsin Sheriffs and Deputy Sheriffs Association, the County Traffic Patrol Association, the Chiefs of Police Association, the State Bar of Wisconsin, the Wisconsin Council of Safety, the Wisconsin District Attorneys Association, and the Judicial Conference.

UNIVERSITY OF WISCONSIN SYSTEM

Board of Regents: MICHAEL J. FALBO, *president;* REGINA MILLNER, *vice president;* TONY EVERS (superintendent of public instruction), S. MARK TYLER (president, Technical College System Board); JOHN R. BEHLING, MARK J. BRADLEY, JOHN DREW, MARGARET FARROW, TIM HIGGINS, EDMUND MANYDEEDS, JANICE MUELLER, CHARLES PRUITT, GARY ROBERTS, JOSÉ VÁSQUEZ, DAVID G. WALSH, GERALD WHITBURN; TRACY HRIBAR, vacancy (students). (All except *ex officio* members are appointed by governor with senate consent.)

Secretary to the Board: JANE RADUE, 1860 Van Hise Hall, 1220 Linden Drive, Madison 53706-1557, (608) 262-2324.

Mailing Address: Central administrative offices for the UW System and the UW Colleges are located in Madison. Individual universities and 2-year UW Colleges can be reached by contacting them directly. Administrative offices for UW-Extension are in Madison; Extension representatives are located at each county seat.

Publications: biennial and annual reports; *Fact Book; Introduction to the University of Wisconsin System;* unit bulletins, catalogs, reports, circulars; periodicals and books.

Number of Employees: 34,366.21.

Total Budget 2011-13: $10,971,928,100.

Constitutional Reference: Article X, Section 6.

Statutory References: Section 15.91; Chapter 36.

System Administration

1220 Linden Drive, Madison 53706-1559
General Telephone: (608) 262-2321
Internet Address: www.wisconsin.edu

President of the University of Wisconsin System: KEVIN P. REILLY, 1720 Van Hise Hall, 1220 Linden Drive, Madison 53706-1559, (608) 262-2321.

Senior Vice President for Administration and Fiscal Affairs: DAVID L. MILLER, 1752 Van Hise Hall, 262-4048.

Senior Vice President for Academic and Student Affairs: MARK NOOK, 1730 Van Hise Hall, 262-3826.

Vice President for Finance: DEBORAH A. DURCAN, 1624 Van Hise Hall, 262-1311.

General Counsel: TOMAS STAFFORD, 1856 Van Hise Hall, 262-6497.

UW-Madison

161 Bascom Hall, 500 Lincoln Drive, Madison 53706
General Telephone: (608) 262-1234
Internet Address: www.wisc.edu

Chancellor: REBECCA BLANK, 161 Bascom Hall, 500 Lincoln Drive, Madison 53706, 262-9946.

Provost and Vice Chancellor for Academic Affairs: PAUL M. DELUCA, JR., 150 Bascom Hall, 262-1304.

Vice Chancellor for Finance and Administration: DARRELL BAZZELL, 100 Bascom Hall, 263-2467.

Vice Chancellor for University Relations: VINCENT J. SWEENEY, JR., 92 Bascom Hall, 265-2822.

Interim Director of the Office of Administrative Legal Services: MICHAEL S. WEIDEN, 361 Bascom Hall, 263-7400.

Vice Chancellor for Medical Affairs: ROBERT GOLDEN, 4129 Health Sciences Learning Center, 750 Highland Avenue, 263-4910.

Dean of Agricultural and Life Sciences: KATHRYN VANDENBOSCH, 140 Agricultural Hall, 262-4930.

Dean of Business: FRANCOIS ORTALO-MAGNE, 4339 Grainger Hall, 262-7867.

UNIVERSITY OF WISCONSIN SYSTEM

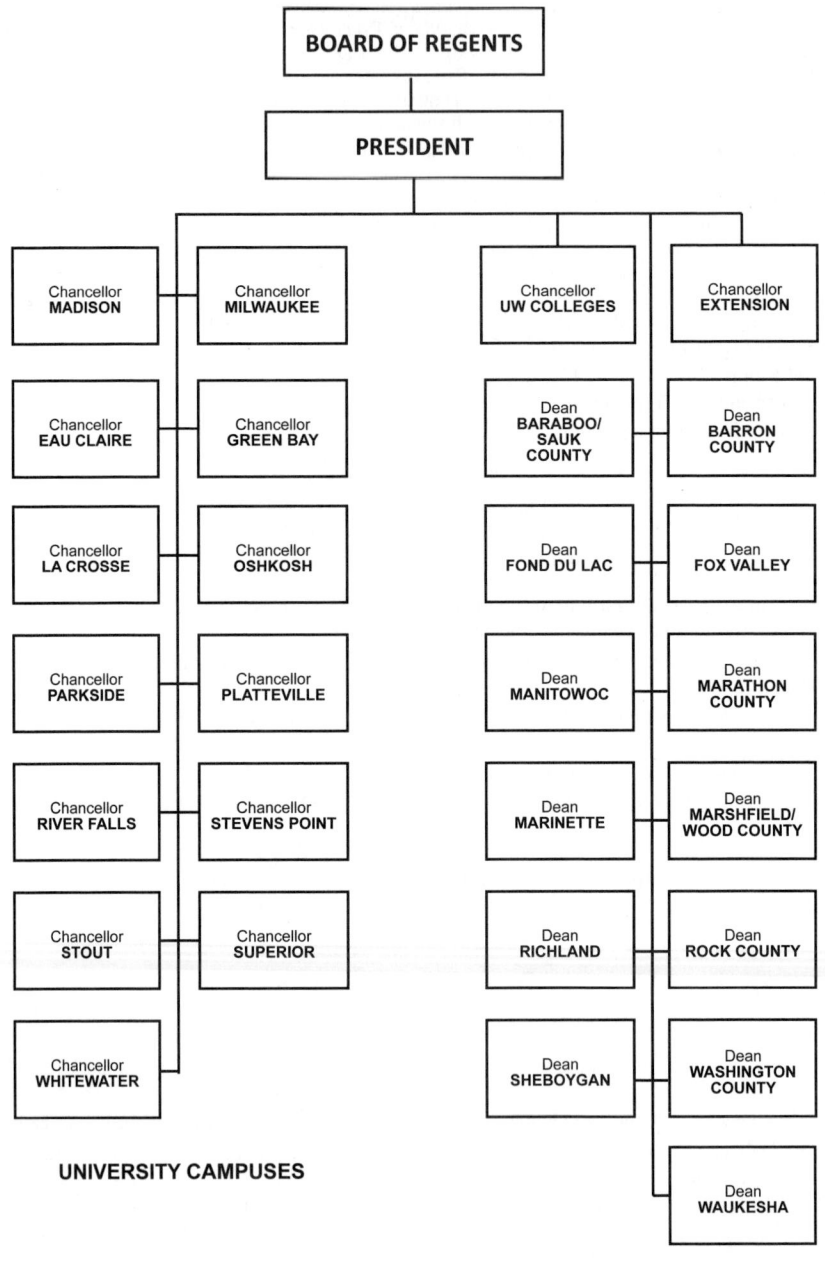

BOARD OF REGENTS

PRESIDENT

| Chancellor MADISON | Chancellor MILWAUKEE | | Chancellor UW COLLEGES | Chancellor EXTENSION |

Chancellor EAU CLAIRE — Chancellor GREEN BAY

Chancellor LA CROSSE — Chancellor OSHKOSH

Chancellor PARKSIDE — Chancellor PLATTEVILLE

Chancellor RIVER FALLS — Chancellor STEVENS POINT

Chancellor STOUT — Chancellor SUPERIOR

Chancellor WHITEWATER

UNIVERSITY CAMPUSES

Dean BARABOO/ SAUK COUNTY — Dean BARRON COUNTY

Dean FOND DU LAC — Dean FOX VALLEY

Dean MANITOWOC — Dean MARATHON COUNTY

Dean MARINETTE — Dean MARSHFIELD/ WOOD COUNTY

Dean RICHLAND — Dean ROCK COUNTY

Dean SHEBOYGAN — Dean WASHINGTON COUNTY

Dean WAUKESHA

TWO-YEAR COLLEGES

Units attached for administrative purposes under Sec. 15.03:
Environmental Education Board
Veterinary Diagnostic Laboratory Board

Dean of Education: JULIE UNDERWOOD, 377 Education Building, 262-1763.

Dean of Engineering: IAN ROBERTSON, 2610 Engineering Hall, 262-3482.

Vice Chancellor for Research and Dean of the Graduate School: MARTIN CADWALLADER, 333 Bascom Hall, 262-1044.

Dean of Human Ecology: SOYEON SHIM, 141 Human Ecology Building, 262-4847.

Interim Dean of International Studies and Programs: GUIDO PODESTA, 268 Bascom Hall, 262-6823.

Dean of Law: MARGARET RAYMOND, 5211 Law Building, 262-0618.

Dean of Letters and Science: vacancy, 105 South Hall, 263-2303.

Director of Libraries: EDWARD VAN GEMERT, 372 Memorial Library, 262-2600.

Dean of Medicine and Public Health: ROBERT GOLDEN, 4129 Health Sciences Learning Center, 750 Highland Avenue, 263-4910.

Dean of Nursing: KATHARYN MAY, BX2455 Clinical Science Center-Module K6, 263-9725.

Dean of Pharmacy: JEANETTE ROBERTS, 1126B Rennebohm Hall, 262-1414.

Dean of Veterinary Medicine: MARK D. MARKEL, 2015 Linden Drive West, 263-6716.

Dean of Students: LORI BERQUAM, 75 Bascom Hall, 263-5702.

Dean of Continuing Studies and Associate Vice Chancellor: JEFFREY S. RUSSELL, 21 North Park Street, 7th Floor, 262-5821.

Interim Secretary of the Academic Staff: JO ANN CARR, 270 Bascom Hall, 263-2985.

Secretary of the Faculty: ANDREA POEHLING, 133 Bascom Hall, 265-4562.

Director of Undergraduate Admissions and Recruitment: ADELE C. BRUMFIELD, 702 West Johnson Street, 264-0464.

Director of Visitor and Information Programs: STEVE AMUNDSON, 329 Union South, 1308 West Dayton Street, 265-9501.

Vice Provost of Enrollment Management and Registrar: JOANNE BERG, Room 11601, 333 East Campus Mall, 262-3964.

Registrar: SCOTT OWCZAREK, Room 10101, 333 East Campus Mall, 262-3964.

UW-Milwaukee
P.O. Box 413, Milwaukee 53201-0413
General Telephone: (414) 229-1122
Internet Address: www.uwm.edu

Chancellor: MICHAEL R. LOVELL, 202 Chapman Hall, P.O. Box 413, Milwaukee 53201, 229-4331.

Provost/Vice Chancellor: JOHANNES BRITZ, 215 Chapman Hall, 229-4501.

Interim Vice Chancellor, Finance and Administrative Affairs: ROBIN VAN HARPEN, 310 Chapman Hall, 229-2629.

Interim Vice Chancellor for Research and Dean of the Graduate School: DAVID YU, 249 Mitchell Hall, 229-2866.

Vice Chancellor for Student Affairs: MICHAEL LALIBERTE, 132 Chapman Hall, 229-4038.

Vice Chancellor, University Relations and Communications: THOMAS LULJAK, 180A Chapman Hall, 229-5024.

Dean, College of Engineering and Applied Science: BRETT PETERS, 524 Engineering and Mathematical Sciences Building, 229-4126.

Dean, College of Letters and Science: RODNEY SWAIN, 218A Holton Hall, 229-5895.

Dean, College of Health Sciences: CHUKUKA ENWEMEKA, 897 Enderis Hall, 229-4712.

Dean, School of Architecture and Urban Planning: ROBERT C. GREENSTREET, 241 Architecture and Urban Planning Building, 229-4016.

Dean, Peck School of the Arts: SCOTT EMMONS, 284 Arts Building, 229-4762.

Dean, School of Business Administration: TIMOTHY SMUNT, N425 Business Administration Building, 229-6256.

Interim Dean, School of Education: BARBARA DALY, 595 Enderis Hall, 229-4181.

Interim Dean, School of Information Studies: JEONG WOOSEOB, Northwest Quadrant Building, 3598, 229-4709.

Dean, School of Nursing: SALLY LUNDEEN, 767B Cunningham Hall, 229-4189.

Dean, School of Social Welfare: STAN STOJKOVIC, 1095 Enderis Hall, 229-4400.

Interim Dean, School of Continuing Education: SAMMIS WHITE, 161 West Wisconsin Avenue, 53203, 227-3326.

Dean, Joseph J. Zilber School of Public Health: MAGDA PECK, 1240 North 10th Street, 227-4128.

Dean, School of Freshwater Sciences: DAVID GARMAN, 600 East Greenfield Avenue, 53204, 382-1700.

Acting Director of Admissions: JEFF MEECE, 222 Mellencamp Hall, 229-6164.

Secretary of the University: TRUDY TURNER, 225 Mitchell Hall, 229-5989.

UW-Eau Claire

105 Garfield Avenue, P.O. Box 4004, Eau Claire 54702-4004
General Telephone: (715) 836-4636
Internet Address: www.uwec.edu

Chancellor: JAMES C. SCHMIDT, 836-2327.
Provost and Vice Chancellor, Academic Affairs: PATRICIA A. KLEINE, 836-2320.
Vice Chancellor for Student Affairs: BETH HELLWIG, 836-5992.

UW-Eau Claire's significant conservation and sustainability initiatives have been recognized by the Princeton Review's Guide to 322 Green Colleges for the past two years. (University of Wisconsin-Eau Claire)

Vice Chancellor for Administration and Finance: DAVID GESSNER, 836-5182.
Dean of Students: BRIAN CARLISLE, 836-5992.
Interim Dean, College of Arts and Sciences: DAVID BAKER, 836-2542.
Dean, College of Education and Human Sciences: GAIL P. SCUKANEC, 836-3264.
Dean, College of Business: DIANE HOADLEY, 836-2500.
Dean, College of Nursing and Health Sciences: LINDA YOUNG, 836-5287.
Assistant Chancellor of Facilities and University Relations: MIKE RINDO, 836-3331.
President of UWEC Foundation and Executive Director of University Advancement: KIM WAY, 836-5630.
Executive Director, Enrollment Services and Admissions: KRISTINA C. ANDERSON, 836-5415.
Registrar: TESSA PERCHINSKY, 836-3887.

UW-Green Bay
2420 Nicolet Drive, Green Bay 54311-7001
General Telephone: (920) 465-2000
Internet Address: www.uwgb.edu

Chancellor: THOMAS K. HARDEN, 465-2207.
Provost and Vice Chancellor for Academic Affairs: JULIA E. WALLACE, 465-5161.
Vice Chancellor, Business and Finance: KELLY FRANZ, 465-2210.
Assistant Chancellor for University Advancement: BEVERLY C. CARMICHAEL, 465-2074.
Dean of Enrollment Services: MICHAEL C. STEARNEY, 465-2236.
Dean of Students: BRENDA AMENSON-HILL, 465-2159.
Dean, College of Liberal Arts and Sciences: SCOTT FURLONG, 465-2336.
Dean, College of Professional Studies: SUE JOSEPH MATTISON, 465-2050.
Director of University Communications: CHRISTOPHER SAMPSON, 465-2527.
Media Relations Coordinator: KELLY MCBRIDE, 465-2526.
Registrar: AMANDA HRUSKA, 465-2155.

UW-La Crosse
1725 State Street, La Crosse 54601-9959
General Telephone: (608) 785-8000
Internet Address: www.uwlax.edu

Chancellor: JOE GOW, 785-8004.
Provost/Vice Chancellor: HEIDI MACPHERSON, 785-8042.
Vice Chancellor, Administration and Finance: BOB HETZEL, 785-8021.
President, UW-L Foundation: ALLEN TRAPP, 785-8489.
Affirmative Action Officer: NIZAM ARAIN, 785-8541.
Associate Dean, Campus Climate and Diversity: BARBARA STEWART, 785-5092.
Associate Vice Chancellor for Academic Affairs: BOB HOAR, 785-8159.
Director, Human Resources: MADELINE HOLZEM, 785-8013.
Interim Executive Director, Facilities Planning and Management: SCOTT SCHUMACHER, 785-8916.
Chief Information Officer: MOHAMED ELHINDI, 785-8662.
Vice Chancellor, Student Affairs: PAULA M. KNUDSON, 785-8062.
Assistant Chancellor, University Advancement: GREG REICHERT, 785-8672.
Dean, College of Business Administration: BRUCE MAY, 785-8091.
Dean, College of Liberal Studies: RUTHANN E. BENSON, 785-8113.
Dean, College of Science and Health: BRUCE V. RILEY, 785-8218.
Director, Admissions: COREY SJOQUIST, 785-8939.
Registrar: CHRISTINE S. BAKKUM, 785-8577.

UW-Oshkosh

800 Algoma Boulevard, Oshkosh 54901-8617
General Telephone: (920) 424-1234
Internet Address: www.uwosh.edu

Chancellor: RICHARD H. WELLS, 424-0200.
Provost/Vice Chancellor: LANE EARNS, 424-0300.
Vice Chancellor, Student Affairs: PETRA M. ROTER, 424-4000.
Assistant Vice Chancellor for Student Engagement and Success/Dean of Students: SHARON KIPETZ, 424-3100.
Assistant Vice Chancellor, Academic Support: vacancy, 424-3080.
Dean, Graduate Studies: SUSAN CRAMER, 424-3095.
Vice Chancellor, Administrative Services: THOMAS G. SONNLEITNER, 424-3030.
Associate Vice Chancellor, Administrative Services: LORI WORM, 424-3033.
Dean, College of Business: WILLIAM TALLON, 424-1424.
Dean, College of Education and Human Services: FREDERICK L. YEO, 424-3322.
Dean, College of Letters and Science: JOHN J. KOKER, 424-1210.
Dean, College of Nursing: ROSEMARY SMITH, 424-3089.
Director, Admissions: JILL M. ENDRIES, 424-0228.
Registrar: LISA M. DANIELSON, 424-3007.

UW-Parkside

P.O. Box 2000, Kenosha 53141-2000
General Telephone: (262) 595-2345
Internet Address: www.uwp.edu

Chancellor: DEBORAH L. FORD, 595-2211.
Interim Provost/Vice Chancellor for Academic Affairs: FRED EBEID, 595-2261.
Associate Provost: DENNIS ROME, 595-2364.
Vice Chancellor, Administrative and Fiscal Affairs: MEL KLINKNER, 595-2141.
Dean of Students: TAMMY MCGUCKIN, 595-2598.
Assistant Chancellor for University Relations and Advancement: JOHN JARACZEWSKI, 595-2591.
Assistant Vice Chancellor for Institutional Effectiveness: KIMBERLY KELLEY, 595-2553.
Associate Vice Chancellor for Enrollment Management: DEANN POSSEHL, 595-2454.
Dean, College of Arts and Humanities: DEAN YOHNK, 595-2188.
Interim Dean, College of Business, Economics and Computing: DIRK BALDWIN, 595-2243.
Dean, College of Natural and Health Science: EMMANUEL OTU, 595-2973.
Dean, College of Social Sciences and Professional Studies: WALTER JACOBS, 595-2993.
Director, Institute for Professional Education Development: vacancy.
Executive Director, Center for Community Partnerships: JANE SCHAEFER, 595-2208.
Senior Diversity Officer: EDWARD TWYMAN, 595-2039.
Registrar: RHONDA KIMMEL, 595-2237.

UW-Platteville

1 University Plaza, Platteville 53818-3099
General Telephone: (608) 342-1491
Internet Address: www.uwplatt.edu

Chancellor: DENNIS J. SHIELDS, 342-1234.
Chief Diversity and Inclusion Officer: JENNIFER DECOSTE, 342-6152.
Provost and Vice Chancellor for Academic Affairs: MITTIE DEN HERDER, 342-1261.
Assistant Vice Chancellor for Academic Affairs: D. JOANNE WILSON, 342-1262.
Associate Vice Chancellor: DAVID VAN BUREN, 342-1262.

Vice Chancellor for Administrative Services: ROBERT G. CRAMER, 342-1226.
Assistant Vice Chancellor for Student Affairs: LAURA BAYLESS, 342-1854.
Director of Admissions and Enrollment Services: ANGELA UDELHOFEN, 342-1125.
Dean, College of Business, Industry, Life Science and Agriculture: WAYNE WEBER, 342-1547.
Dean, College of Engineering, Mathematics, and Science: WILLIAM HUDSON, 342-1561.
Dean, College of Liberal Arts and Education: ELIZABETH THROOP, 342-1151.
Dean, School of Graduate Studies: vacancy, 342-1262.
Registrar: DAVID KIECKHAFER, 342-1321.

UW-River Falls

410 South Third Street, River Falls 54022-5001
General Telephone: (715) 425-3911
Internet Address: www.uwrf.edu

Chancellor: DEAN VAN GALEN, 425-3201.
Provost/Vice Chancellor for Academic Affairs: FERNANDO DELGADO, 425-3700.
Assistant Chancellor, Business and Finance: ELIZABETH FRUEH, 425-3737.
Executive Director of Advancement: CHRIS MUELLER, 425-3545.
Dean, College of Agriculture, Food and Environmental Sciences: DALE GALLENBERG, 425-3841.
Dean, College of Arts and Sciences: BRADLEY CASKEY, 425-3777.
Dean, College of Education and Professional Studies: LARRY SOLBERG, 425-3774.
Dean, College of Business and Economics: GLENN POTTS, 425-3335.
Associate Vice Chancellor for Enrollment and Student Success: KRISTINA ANDERSON, 425-3202.
Associate Vice Chancellor for Student Affairs: GREGG HEINSELMAN, 425-4444.
Associate Vice Chancellor for Academic Affairs: MICHAEL MILLER, 425-0699.
Director of Admissions: MARK MEYDAM, 425-3500.
Registrar: DAN VANDE YACHT, 425-3342.

The University Center on the UW-River Falls campus is the gathering place for the campus community. (Kathy M. Helgeson/ UW-River Falls Communications)

UW-Stevens Point

Room 213 Old Main, 2100 Main Street, Stevens Point 54481-3897
General Telephone: (715) 346-0123
Internet Address: www.uwsp.edu

Chancellor: Bernie L. Patterson, 346-2123.
Provost/Vice Chancellor, Academic Affairs: Gregory Summers, 346-4686.
Vice Chancellor, Business Affairs: Gregory Diemer, 346-2641.
Vice Chancellor, Student Affairs: Al Thompson, Jr., 346-2481.
Vice Chancellor, University Advancement: Christopher Richards, 346-3812.
Associate Vice Chancellor, Personnel, Budget, and Grants: Katie Jore, 346-3710.
Interim Associate Vice Chancellor, Teaching, Learning and Academic Programs: James Sage, 346-4625.
Chief Information Officer, Information Technology: Marsha Henfer, 346-2727.
Executive Director, University Relations and Communication: Kate Worster, 346-3827.
Dean, College of Fine Arts and Communication: Jeffrey Morin, 346-4920.
Dean, College of Letters and Science: Christopher Cirmo, 346-4224.
Dean, College of Natural Resources: Christine Thomas, 346-4617.
Dean, College of Professional Studies: Marty Loy, 346-3169.
Director, Admissions: Terri Crumley, 346-2441.
Registrar: Daniel Kellogg, 346-4301.

UW-Stout

P.O. Box 790, Menomonie 54751-0790
General Telephone: (715) 232-1122
Internet Address: www.uwstout.edu

Chancellor: Charles W. Sorensen, 232-2441.
Provost/Vice Chancellor, Academic and Student Affairs: Joseph Bessie, 232-2421.
Vice Chancellor, Administrative and Student Life Services: Phil Lyons, 232-1683.
Vice Chancellor, University Advancement and Marketing: Mark Parsons, 232-1151.
Associate Vice Chancellor, Academic and Student Affairs: Jacalyn Weissenburger, 232-2421.
Dean, College of Arts, Humanities and Social Sciences: Maria Alm, 232-2596.
Dean, College of Education, Health and Human Sciences: Mary Hopkins-Best, 232-1088.
Dean, College of Management: Abel Adekola, 232-1234.
Dean, College of Science, Technology, Engineering and Mathematics: Jeffrey Anderson, 232-4053.
Dean of Students: Joan Thomas, 232-1181.
Executive Director of Enrollment Management: Pamela Holsinger-Fuchs, 232-2639.
Registrar: Scott Correll, 232-1233.

UW-Superior

Belknap and Catlin Street, P.O. Box 2000, Superior 54880-4500
General Telephone: (715) 394-8101
Internet Address: www.uwsuper.edu

Chancellor: Renee Wachter, 394-8221.
Provost: Faith C. Hensrud, 394-8449.
Vice Chancellor for Administration and Finance: Janet K. Hanson, 394-8014.
Vice Chancellor for Campus Life/Dean of Students: Vicki Hajewski, 394-8241.
Vice Chancellor, University Advancement: Jeanne Thompson, 394-8598.
Interim Assistant to the Chancellor for EO/AA and Diversity: Peggy Fecker, 394-8365.
Assistant Vice Chancellor for Enrollment Management: vacancy, 394-8306.

Interim Dean of Faculties: LIZ BLUE, 394-8131.
Registrar: DIANE DOUGLAS, 394-8218.

UW-Whitewater
Hyer Hall, 800 West Main Street, Whitewater 53190-1790
General Telephone: (262) 472-1234
Internet Address: www.uww.edu

Chancellor: RICHARD J. TELFER, 472-1918.
Provost/Vice Chancellor for Academic Affairs: BEVERLY A. KOPPER, 472-1672.
Vice Chancellor, Administrative Affairs: D. JEFF ARNOLD, 472-1922.
Vice Chancellor for Student Affairs: THOMAS R. RIOS, 472-1051.
Associate Vice Chancellor for Academic Affairs: GREG COOK, 472-1077.
Dean, College of Arts and Communication: MARK L. MCPHAIL, 472-1221.
Dean, College of Business and Economics: CHRISTINE CLEMENTS, 472-1343.
Dean, College of Education: KATHARINA E. HEYNING, 472-1101.
Dean, College of Letters and Sciences: MARY A. PINKERTON, 472-1712.
Dean, Graduate School, Continuing Education and Summer Session: JOHN F. STONE, 472-1006.
Assistant Vice Chancellor, Enrollment and Retention: MATT ASCHENBRENER, 472-1512.
Registrar: JODI M. HARE, 472-1570.

UW Colleges and UW-Extension
432 North Lake Street, Madison 53706-1498
General Telephone: (608) 262-3786

Chancellor: RAYMOND W. CROSS, (608) 262-3786.
Assistant to the Chancellor: BARB SANDRIDGE, (608) 262-3786.

UW Colleges
Internet Address: www.uwc.edu/
Provost/Vice Chancellor: GREG LAMPE, (608) 263-1794.
Vice Chancellor, Administrative and Financial Services: STEVEN WILDECK, (608) 265-3040.
Associate Vice Chancellor for Administrative and Financial Services: COLLEEN GODFRIAUX, (608) 265-9807
Associate Vice Chancellor for Academic Affairs: LISA SEALE, (608) 263-7217.
Associate Vice Chancellor for Student Services and Enrollment Management: RICHARD BARNHOUSE, (608) 265-0476.
Interim Chief Information Officer: WERNER GADE, (608) 262-7832.
Registrar: LARRY GRAVES, (608) 262-9048.
Baraboo/Sauk County: 1006 Connie Road, Baraboo 53913-1098, (608) 355-5200, www.baraboo.uwc.edu
  CEO/Dean: TOM PLEGER.
Barron County: 1800 College Drive, Rice Lake 54868-2497, (715) 234-8176, www.barron.uwc.edu
  CEO/Dean: PAUL CHASE.
Fond du Lac: 400 University Drive, Fond du Lac 54935-2998, (920) 929-1100, www.fdl.uwc.edu
  CEO/Dean: JOHN SHORT.
Fox Valley: 1478 Midway Road, Menasha 54952-1297, (920) 832-2600, www.fox.uwc.edu
  CEO/Dean: MARTIN RUDD.

Manitowoc: 705 Viebahn Street, Manitowoc 54220-6699, (920) 683-4700,
www.manitowoc.uwc.edu
CEO/Dean: CHARLES CLARK.

Marathon County: 518 South 7th Avenue, Wausau 54401-5396, (715) 261-6100,
www.uwmc.uwc.edu
CEO/Dean: KEITH MONTGOMERY.

Marinette: 750 West Bay Shore Street, Marinette 54143-4299, (715) 735-4300,
www.marinette.uwc.edu
CEO/Dean: PAULA LANGTEAU.

Marshfield/Wood County: 2000 West 5th Street, Marshfield 54449-0150, (715) 389-6500,
www.marshfield.uwc.edu
CEO/Dean: PATRICIA STUHR.

Richland: 1200 Highway 14 West, Richland Center 53581-1399, (608) 647-6186,
www.richland.uwc.edu
CEO/Dean: PATRICK HAGEN.

Rock County: 2909 Kellogg Avenue, Janesville 53546-5699, (608) 758-6565,
www.rock.uwc.edu
CEO/Dean: CARMEN WILSON.

Sheboygan: One University Drive, Sheboygan 53081-4789, (920) 459-6600,
www.sheboygan.uwc.edu
CEO/Dean: JACKIE JOSEPH-SILVERSTEIN.

Washington County: 400 University Drive, West Bend 53095-3699, (262) 335-5200,
www.washington.uwc.edu
CEO/Dean: PAUL PRICE.

Waukesha: 1500 North University Drive, Waukesha 53188-2799, (262) 521-5200,
www.waukesha.uwc.edu
CEO/Dean: HARRY MUIR.

UW-Extension

Internet Address: www.uwex.edu
Interim Vice Chancellor/Provost: AARON BROWER, (608) 262-6151.
Associate Vice Chancellor: GREG HUTCHINS, (608) 263-7810.
Vice Chancellor, Administrative and Financial Services: STEVEN WILDECK, (608) 265-3040.
Dean, Outreach and E-Learning Extension: DAVID SCHEJBAL, (608) 262-1034.
Dean and Director, Cooperative Extension: RICK KLEMME, (608) 263-2775.
Associate Vice Chancellor for Administrative and Financial Services: MARK DORN, (608) 262-5975.
Director, Broadcasting and Media Innovations: MALCOLM BRETT, (608) 263-9598.
Executive Director, Entrepreneurship and Economic Development: MARK LANGE, (608) 263-7794.
Interim Chief Information Officer: WERNER GADE, (608) 262-7832.
Interim Secretary of the Faculty/Academic Staff: DAN HILL, (608) 262-4387.

Officers and Units Required by Statute

State Cartographer: HOWARD VEREGIN, (608) 262-6852, 384 Science Hall, 550 North Park Street, Madison 53706-1491.

State Geologist: JAMES ROBERTSON, (608) 263-7384, Geological and Natural History Survey, 3817 Mineral Point Road, Madison 53705-5100.

Agricultural Safety and Health Center: CHERYL SKJOLAAS, *interim director,* (608) 265-0568, 460 Henry Mall, Madison 53706.

Center for Environmental Education: JEREMY SOLIN, *interim director,* (715) 346-4973, 110 College of Natural Resources, 403 Learning Resources Center, Stevens Point 54481.

Geological and Natural History Survey: JAMES ROBERTSON, *state geologist,* (608) 262-1705, 3817 Mineral Point Road, Madison 53705-5100.

Area Health Education Center: NANCY SUGDEN, *director,* (608) 263-4927, 203 Bradley Memorial, 1300 University Avenue, Madison 53706.

Wisconsin State Herbarium: KENNETH CAMERON, *director,* (608) 262-2792, Department of Botany, Room 160, Birge Hall, Madison 53706-1381.

Psychiatric HealthEmotions Research Institute: NED KALIN, *director,* (608) 263-6079, 6001 Research Park Boulevard, Madison 53719.

Robert M. La Follette Institute of Public Affairs: THOMAS DELEIRE, *director,* (608) 262-4531, 1225 Observatory Drive, Madison 53706.

State Soils and Plant Analysis Laboratory: JOHN PETERS, *director,* (608) 262-4364, 8452 Mineral Point Road, Madison 53705.

Institute for Excellence in Urban Education: GAIL SCHNEIDER, *associate dean for academic affairs,* (414) 229-5253, School of Education, P.O. Box 413, UW-Milwaukee, Milwaukee 53201.

James A. Graaskamp Center for Real Estate: MICHAEL BRENNAN, *executive director,* (608) 263-4392, 975 University Avenue, Room 5262, Grainger Hall, Madison 53706,

School of Veterinary Medicine: MARK D. MARKEL, *dean,* (608) 262-3573, 2015 Linden Drive West, Madison 53706-1102.

Agency Responsibility: The prime responsibilities of the University of Wisconsin System are teaching, public service, and research. The system provides postsecondary academic education for more than 180,000 students, including 137,000 full-time equivalent undergraduates.

Organization: The UW System consists of 13 four-year universities, 13 two-year colleges, and statewide extension programs. UW-Madison and UW-Milwaukee offer bachelor's, master's, doctoral, and professional degrees. Eleven other universities in the UW System offer associate, bachelor's, and master's degree programs: UW-Eau Claire, UW-Green Bay, UW-La Crosse, UW-Oshkosh, UW-Parkside, UW-Platteville, UW-River Falls, UW-Stevens Point, UW-Stout, UW-Superior, and UW-Whitewater.

The two-year UW Colleges serve local and commuter students by providing freshman-sophomore university course work that is transferable to other campuses. In addition, the colleges offer general education associate degrees. While UW colleges faculty and staff are employed by the UW System, municipalities and/or counties own the campuses and buildings in which the UW Colleges are located.

UW-Extension provides noncredit and for-credit classroom and distance learning courses, as well as continuing education and a wide range of public service programs.

The 18-member Board of Regents of the University of Wisconsin System establishes policies to govern the system and plans for the future of public higher education in Wisconsin. Two members serve *ex officio;* the student members serve staggered 2-year terms; and the other 14 members serve staggered 7-year terms. The governor may not appoint a student member from the same institution in any 2 consecutive terms.

The board appoints the president of the UW System, the chancellors of the 13 universities, the chancellor of UW-Extension and the UW Colleges, and the deans of the 13 UW Colleges. All appointees serve at the pleasure of the board. The board also sets admission standards, reviews and approves university budgets, and establishes the regulatory framework within which the individual units operate.

Unit Functions: The president of the University of Wisconsin System has full executive responsibility for system operation and management. This officer carries out the duties prescribed by statute; implements the policies established by the Board of Regents; manages and

Instructor Tom Turbon describes a neural stem cell differentiation procedure during a class held at the Embedded Teaching Labs at the University of Wisconsin-Madison. Eighteen students and five teachers from nine rural Wisconsin high schools are participating in the Summer Science Camp outreach program. (Jeff Miller/UW-Madison)

coordinates the system's administrative offices; and exercises fiscal control through budget development, management-planning programs, and coordination and evaluation of the academic programs on all campuses.

Each chancellor serves as executive head of a particular campus or program, administers board policies under the direction of the system's president, and is accountable to the board of regents. Subject to board policy, the chancellors, in consultation with their faculties, design curricula and set degree requirements; determine academic standards and establish grading systems; define and administer institutional standards for faculty peer evaluation; screen candidates for appointment, promotion, and tenure; administer auxiliary services; and control all funds allocated to or generated by their respective programs. One chancellor administers both UW Colleges and UW-Extension.

History: Today's UW System is the product of the 1971 merger of two existing university boards – the Board of Regents of the University of Wisconsin and the Board of Regents of the State Universities – and the institutions they governed.

From earliest times, Wisconsin lawmakers recognized the need for a tax-supported university. The territorial legislature passed laws in 1836, 1838, and 1839 regarding establishment and location of a university, and Article X, Section 6, of the state constitution ratified in 1848, provided for a state university at or near the seat of state government. Chapter 20, Laws of 1848, which implemented the constitutional provision, delegated university administration to a board of regents and classes began in 1849. Critical to the university's early development was Chapter 114, Laws of 1866, which reorganized the board of regents, expanded its authority, and authorized the governor to appoint the regents. The 1866 reorganization provided for instruction in agriculture on the Madison campus and an experimental farm, thereby making the university eligible, as Wisconsin's land-grant institution, to receive the proceeds derived from sale of lands granted by the federal government to support agricultural education and research.

The State Universities originated with Chapter 82, Laws of 1857, which provided funds for a system of 2-year normal schools to train teachers and created the Board of Regents of Normal Schools. The first normal school opened at Platteville in 1866 and the ninth 50 years later at Eau Claire. In 1929, the 9 normal schools became "state teachers colleges" and were authorized to offer baccalaureate degree programs. They were renamed state colleges in 1951 and state universities in 1964. Chapter 75, Laws of 1967, renamed the governing body, designating it the Board of Regents of State Universities.

Chapter 100, Laws of 1971, mandated the merger of Wisconsin's two systems of public higher education to form the University of Wisconsin System. Chapter 335, Laws of 1973, recreated Chapter 36 of the statutes and provided a single statutory charter to govern public higher education in Wisconsin. The University of Wisconsin Colleges, which were previously called UW Centers, were renamed by 1997 Wisconsin Act 237.

Statutory Council:

Rural Health Development Council: vacancy (designated by secretary of health services); BYRON J. CROUSE (UW Medical School representative); SYED AHMED (Medical College of Wisconsin, Inc., representative); TIM SIZE (Wisconsin Health and Educational Facilities Authority representative); vacancy (private rural lender representative); JIM O'KEEFE (rural hospital representative); vacancy (physician practicing in rural area); BLANE CHRISTMAN (dentist practicing in rural area); JACALYN SZEHNER (nurse practicing in rural area); vacancy (dental hygienist practicing in rural area); vacancy (public health services representative); KATHY SCHMITT (designated by secretary of agriculture, trade and consumer protection); TOM WALSH (designated by secretary of workforce development); CHARLIE WALKER (rural economic development representative), vacancy (public member from rural area); JEREMY NORMINGTON (rural health clinic representative); 2 vacancies. (All except *ex officio* members or their designees are appointed by governor with senate consent.)

Mailing Address: Wisconsin Office of Rural Health, UW School of Medicine and Public Health, 310 N. Midvale Boulevard, Suite 301, Madison 53705.

Telephone: 261-1883, (800) 385-0005 (toll free).

The 18-member Rural Health Development Council advises the board of regents regarding administration of the health professions loan assistance program, delivery of health care and improvement of facilities in rural areas, and coordination of state and federal programs available to assist rural health facilities. Appointed members serve 5-year terms. The council was created by 1989 Wisconsin Act 317 in the Department of Commerce and moved to the University System under 2009 Wisconsin Act 28. Its composition and duties are prescribed in Sections 15.917 and 36.62 of the statutes.

ORGANIZATION CREATED BY STATUTE
WITHIN THE UNIVERSITY OF WISCONSIN SYSTEM

LABORATORY OF HYGIENE

Laboratory of Hygiene Board: DARRELL BAZZELL (designated by chancellor of UW-Madison), SANDRA BREITBORDE (designated by secretary of health services), JACK SULLIVAN (designated by secretary of natural resources), SUSAN BUROKER (designated by secretary of agriculture, trade and consumer protection); JEFF KINDRAI (local health department representative); BERNARD POESCHEL (physician representing clinical laboratories); MICHAEL RICKER (representing private environmental testing laboratories); MICHAEL CAVANAGH (representing occupational health laboratories); BARRY IRMEN (medical examiner or coroner); DARRYLL FARMER, DAVID TAYLOR (public members). Nonvoting member: CHARLES D. BROKOPP (director, Laboratory of Hygiene). (All except *ex officio* officers or designees are appointed by governor.)

Director: CHARLES D. BROKOPP.

Medical Director: DANIEL F. KURTYCZ.

Associate Director: SHERRY GEHL.

Mailing Address: 465 Henry Mall, Madison 53706-1578; 2601 Agriculture Drive, Madison 53707-7996 (Environmental Health Division).

Telephones: (608) 262-1293; Customer service: (800) 442-4618; Administrative office: (608) 262-3911; Wisconsin Occupational Health Laboratory: (608) 224-6210, (800) 446-0403; Proficiency Testing Program: (608) 890-1800, (800) 462-5261; Environmental Health Division: (608) 224-6202, (800) 442-4618.

Internet Address: www.slh.wisc.edu

Division Fax: (608) 262-3257; Environmental Health Division Fax: (608) 224-6213.

Publications: Newborn Screening Newsletter; Occupational Health Newsletter; reference manual; annual report; research annual report, fee schedules; assorted special publications.

Number of Employees: 309.75.

Total Budget 2011-13: $65,729,600.

Statutory References: Sections 15.07 (1), 15.915 (2), and 36.25 (11).

Agency Responsibility: The Laboratory of Hygiene, headed by a director appointed by the UW Board of Regents, provides complete laboratory services for appropriate state agencies and local health departments in the areas of water quality, air quality, public health, and contagious diseases. It performs laboratory tests and consultation for physicians, health officers, local agencies, private citizens, and resource management officials to prevent and control diseases and environmental hazards. As part of the UW-Madison, the laboratory provides facilities for teaching and research in the fields of public health and environmental protection.

The laboratory operates under the direction and supervision of the Laboratory of Hygiene Board, composed of 11 members, 7 of whom are appointed by the governor to serve 3-year terms.

History: Chapter 344, Laws of 1903, created the Laboratory of Hygiene at the University of Wisconsin to examine water supplies, investigate contagious and infectious diseases, and function as the official laboratory of the State Board of Health. The executive branch reorganization act of 1967 extended the laboratory's services to the Department of Natural Resources.

INDEPENDENT UNITS ATTACHED FOR BUDGETING, PROGRAM COORDINATION, AND RELATED MANAGEMENT FUNCTIONS BY SECTION 15.03 OF THE STATUTES

ENVIRONMENTAL EDUCATION BOARD

Environmental Education Board: SCOTT ASHMANN (higher education institutions faculty representative), *chairperson;* SENATORS KEDZIE, RISSER; REPRESENTATIVES DANOU, MURSAU; ROBIN HARRIS (designated by president, UW System), CARRIE MORGAN (designated by secretary of natural resources), VICTORIA RYDBERG (designated by superintendent of public instruction), RANDY ZOGBAUM (designated by president, Technical College System Board); DARLENE ARNESON (agricultural representative), BETH CARRENO (nature centers, museums, zoos representative), JIM JENSON (business and industry representative), CONNIE LAWNICZAK (energy representative), RUTH ANN LEE (conservation and environmental organizations representative), THERESA LEHMAN (labor representative), DONALD PETERSON (forestry representative), DEBRA WEITZEL (environmental educators representative). (Unless otherwise designated, members are appointed by president of UW System.)

Mailing Address: 110H Trainer Natural Resources Building, UW-Stevens Point, 800 Reserve Street, Stevens Point 54481.

Telephone: (715) 346-3805.

Internet Address: www.uwsp.edu/cnr/weeb

Statutory References: Sections 15.915 (6), 36.54.

Agency Responsibility: The Environmental Education Board awards matching grants to public agencies and nonprofit corporations to develop and distribute environmental education programs. The board consults with the state's educational agencies, the Department of Natural Resources, and other state agencies to identify needs and establish priorities for environmental education. Its 17 members include 9 representatives of educational institutions and nongovernmental interest groups who are appointed to serve 3-year terms. The senate and assembly members must represent the majority and the minority parties in their respective houses. The board was created by 1989 Wisconsin Act 299 and was transferred from the Department of Public Instruction to the UW System by 1997 Wisconsin Act 27.

VETERINARY DIAGNOSTIC LABORATORY BOARD

Veterinary Diagnostic Laboratory Board: SANDRA LARSON (livestock producer), *chairperson;* BEN BRANCEL (secretary of agriculture, trade and consumer protection), DARRELL BAZZELL (designated by chancellor of UW-Madison), MARK MARKEL (dean of the UW-Madison School of Veterinary Medicine), SHERRY SHAW (veterinarian employed by the federal government); ALISSA GRENAWALT (livestock producer); JAMES MERONEK, STEVE VAN LANNEN (representing animal agriculture); vacancy (practicing veterinarian); THOMAS McKENNA (laboratory director) (nonvoting member). (All except *ex officio* members are appointed by governor.)

Mailing Address: 445 Easterday Lane, Madison 53706.

Telephone: (608) 262-5432.

Fax: (847) 574-8085.

Statutory References: Sections 15.915 (1) and 36.58.

Agency Responsibility: The Veterinary Diagnostic Laboratory Board oversees the Veterinary Diagnostic Laboratory, which provides animal health testing and diagnostic services on a statewide basis for all types of animals. The board has 10 members, 6 of whom are appointed by the governor. Five of these members serve staggered 3-year terms, while one member, a veterinarian employed by the federal government, serves at the pleasure of the governor. The board prescribes policies for the laboratory's operation, develops its biennial budget, and sets fees for laboratory services. It also consults with the UW-Madison chancellor on the appointment of the laboratory director.

History: Both the board and the laboratory were created by 1999 Wisconsin Act 107, which transferred the laboratory's facilities and employees from the Department of Agriculture, Trade and Consumer Protection to the UW System, effective July 1, 2000.

Department of
VETERANS AFFAIRS

Address e-mail by combining the user ID and the state extender: userid@**dva.wisconsin.gov**
All telephone numbers are 608 area code unless otherwise indicated.

Board of Veterans Affairs: JOHN TOWNSEND (6th district), *chairperson;* JOHN M. GAEDKE (2nd district), *vice chairperson;* DANIEL BOHLIN (3rd district), *secretary;* BENJAMIN COLLINS (1st district), CATHY GORST (7th district), CARL KRUEGER (4th district), DANIEL J. NAYLOR (8th district), KEVIN NICHOLSON (5th district); ALAN RICHARDS (at-large member). (All are veterans appointed by governor with senate consent. At least one member must represent each congressional district.)

Secretary of Veterans Affairs: JOHN A. SCOCOS, 266-1315, john.scocos@

Deputy Secretary: MICHAEL TREPANIER, 266-1315, michael.trepanier@

Executive Assistant: JENNA HOMBURG, 266-1315, jenna.homburg@

Legal Counsel, Office of: JAMES STEWART, *chief legal counsel,* 266-3733, jimmy.stewart@

Budget, Finance and Facilities, Office of: JAMES A. PARKER, *chief financial officer,* 266-1843, james.parker@

Public Affairs, Office of: CARLA VIGUE, *communications director,* 266-0517, carla.vigue@

Wisconsin Veterans Museum: MICHAEL TELZROW, *director,* 266-1009, michael.telzrow@

Mailing Address: P.O. Box 7843, Madison 53707-7843.

Location: 201 West Washington Avenue, Madison.

Telephone: 266-1311, toll free: 1-800-WIS-VETS (800-947-8387).

Fax: 264-7616.

DEPARTMENT OF VETERANS AFFAIRS

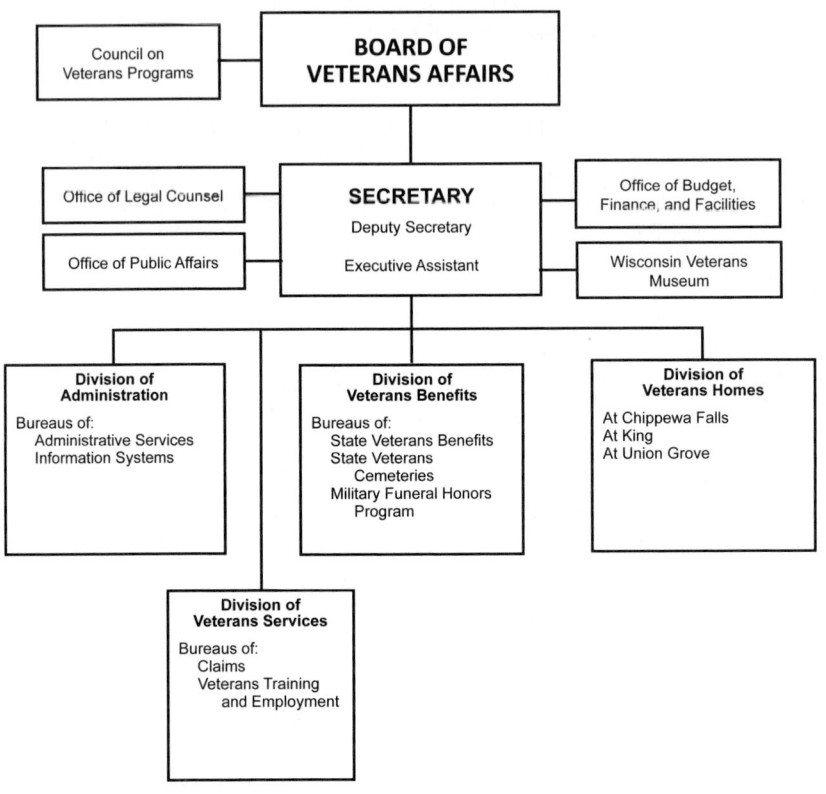

Internet Address: www.wisvets.com

Number of Employees: 1,136.10.

Total Budget 2011-13: $299,449,100.

Statutory References: Section 15.49; Chapter 45.

Administration, Division of: Kenneth G. Grant, *administrator,* 267-7207, kenneth.grant@; Fax: 264-6089.

> *Administrative Services, Bureau of:* Amy Franke, *director,* 267-1796, amy.franke@; Fax 266-5414.

> *Information Systems, Bureau of:* Chris Apfelbeck, *director,* 267-1794, chris.apfelbeck@

Veterans Benefits, Division of: Tom Rhatican, *administrator,* 266-2778, thomas.rhatican@; Fax: 267-0403.

> *State Veterans Benefits, Bureau of:* vacancy, *director,* 266-6783.

> *State Veterans Cemeteries, Bureau of:* Marian Lewandowski, *director,* (262) 878-6742, marian.lewandowski@

> *Military Funeral Honors Program:* (877) 944-6667, Fax: (866) 454-0356.

Veterans Homes, Division of: RANDALL NITSCHKE, *administrator,* 264-7619, randall.nitschke@

Wisconsin Veterans Home, Chippewa Falls, 2175 East Park Avenue, Chippewa Falls 54729; MARK WILSON, *commandant,* (715) 299-0189, mark.wilson@

Wisconsin Veterans Home, King 54946-0600, Fax: (715) 258-5736; JIM KNIGHT, *commandant,* (715) 258-4241, jim.knight@; DIANE JAHNKE, *deputy commandant,* (715) 258-4241, diane.jahnke@; vacancy, *adjutant,* (715) 258-4249; *Public Information/ Volunteer Coordinator:* AMBER MICHEL, (715) 258-4247, amber.michel@

Wisconsin Veterans Home, Union Grove, 21425D Spring Street, Union Grove 53182; REID AARON, *commandant,* (262) 878-6752, reid.aaron@

Veterans Services, Division of: JAMES BOND, *administrator,* 266-7916, james.bond@

Claims, Bureau of: KIM MICHALOWSKI, *director,* VA Regional Office, 5400 West National Avenue, BM 157, Milwaukee 53214, (414) 902-5757; Fax: (414) 902-9421.

Veterans Training and Employment, Bureau of: DOMINGO LEGUIZAMON, *director,* 267-7329.

Publications: *The Bugle; The Courier;* brochures on the state veterans' programs and services for Wisconsin veterans, Wisconsin Veterans Museum (Madison), the Wisconsin Veterans Home (King), the Wisconsin Veterans Home (Union Grove), and Wisconsin's veterans memorial cemeteries.

Agency Responsibility: The Department of Veterans Affairs works on behalf of Wisconsin's veterans community – veterans, their families and their survivors – in recognition of their service and sacrifice to our sate and nation. It oversees veterans benefits, programs, and services in the areas of education, health care, and federal claims assistance, among others. It also operates the Wisconsin veterans homes at Chippewa Falls, King, and Union Grove, the Wisconsin Veterans Museum in Madison, the Southern Wisconsin Veterans Memorial Cemetery at Union Grove, the Northern Wisconsin Veterans Memorial Cemetery near Spooner, and the Central Wisconsin Veterans Memorial Cemetery at King. The department currently serves an estimated 397,000 veterans living in Wisconsin.

Organization: The department is headed by a secretary who directs and supervises departmental activities. The secretary, who must be a veteran, is nominated by the governor after personally consulting with the presiding officers of at least 6 Wisconsin veterans organizations and appointed with advice and consent of the senate. The board of veterans affairs consists of 9 members appointed by the governor with senate consent who serve staggered 4-year terms. All board members must be veterans, as defined by statute, and there must be at least one member of the board who is a resident of each congressional district. The secretary, after consulting with the board, may promulgate administrative rules necessary to carry out the powers and duties of the department.

Unit Functions: The *Division of Administration* administers information technology, information systems, infrastructure management, human resources, personnel benefits, and training.

The *Division of Veterans Benefits* administers loan and emergency grant programs offered by the state, state veteran cemeteries, and the state military funeral honors program.

Emergency grants are available to provide subsistence aid for qualified veterans who have experienced a loss of income due to illness or disability, and veterans who require health care that cannot be obtained through other means. These grants have strict income and asset limits.

The division provides administration for the veterans memorial cemeteries. These cemeteries provide burial space for veterans, their spouses, and eligible family members. Veterans can be buried free of charge; non-veteran spouses and family members are charged a burial fee. As part of the Bureau of State Veterans Cemeteries, the Veterans Assistance Program operates veterans assistance centers in Chippewa Falls, King, and Union Grove. Through the centers, homeless veterans and veterans at risk of becoming homeless receive education, job training, and rehabilitative services to enable them to obtain steady employment and affordable housing. The program is a joint effort with the U.S. Department of Veterans Affairs and community-based agencies and is supplemented by service delivery support and outreach to veterans service organizations, veterans health care facilities, and correctional institutions.

The division administers the military funeral honors program, coordinating the efforts of veterans service organizations, the active duty military and reserve forces, as well as the Wisconsin National Guard. The division provides training of veteran organizations and military units who provide military funeral honors requested by the family. The division has limited capability to provide military funeral honors teams with departmental staff.

The *Division of Veterans Homes* administers the state's facilities for eligible veterans who are permanently incapacitated from performing any substantially gainful employment due to age or physical disability and who may be admitted if they meet service and residency criteria. Applicants must apply their income and resources to the cost of their care as required by Medicaid eligibility standards. The spouses and parents of eligible veterans may also be admitted.

The Wisconsin Veterans Home at Chippewa Falls is a 72-bed skilled nursing facility.

The Wisconsin Veterans Home at King serves 721 members. It includes four licensed skilled nursing care buildings and the Central Wisconsin Veterans Memorial Cemetery. Residents receive complete medical and nursing care, along with therapeutic treatments and social services. Veterans and spouses or surviving spouses may be admitted at King.

The Wisconsin Veterans Home at Union Grove is capable of serving 197 members by providing a 39-bed assisted living residence and a 158-bed skilled nursing facility. This continuum of care is available to veterans and their spouses and offers assistance with health care, daily living needs, memory care, short-term rehabilitation, and long-term care.

The *Division of Veterans Services* administers education and employment services programs, claims services, and transition assistance programs. The division also provides an array of employment and educational services to include transition assistance, grants, job referrals, academic credit for military experience programs, and assistance in obtaining teaching credentials through the Troops to Teachers Program.

The State Approving Agency coordinates programs and approves schools to assist veterans to effectively use their GI Bill benefits.

The *Wisconsin Veterans Museum* in Madison is dedicated to Wisconsin veterans of all wars. It houses and exhibits artifacts related to Wisconsin's participation in U.S. military actions from the Civil War to the present and offers programs to the public on the history of Wisconsin's war efforts.

History: Legislation to benefit Wisconsin veterans dates back to the post-Civil War era. Most of the enactments between the Civil War and World War I were concerned with providing relief for destitute veterans and their families. In 1887, the Grand Army of the Republic (GAR), the prominent Civil War veterans' organization, founded the Grand Army Home at King, supported by private donations and federal and state subsidies. Now called the Wisconsin Veterans Home, the institution was first operated by the GAR and later by a state board and the adjutant general's office. Further recognition of Civil War veterans came in 1901, when the legislature established a Grand Army of the Republic headquarters and museum in the State Capitol. In 1993, the state opened the Wisconsin Veterans Museum in a separate building on the Capitol Square. The Southern Wisconsin Veterans Home at Union Grove, authorized in 1999 Wisconsin Act 9, opened in 2001.

After World War I, the 1919 Legislature granted a cash bonus, or alternatively an education bonus, to soldiers who fought in the war. It also created a fund for the relief of sick, wounded, or disabled veterans, administered by the Service Recognition Board and later its successor, the Soldiers' Rehabilitation Board. Other legislation between World Wars I and II provided funds for hospitalization, memorials, and free courses through the University of Wisconsin-Extension.

Chapter 443, Laws of 1943, created the Veterans Recognition Board to provide medical, hospital, educational, and economic assistance to returning Wisconsin veterans of World War II and their dependents.

The creation of the Department of Veterans Affairs by Chapter 580, Laws of 1945, brought all veterans programs under a single agency. The department absorbed the Grand Army Home, the GAR Memorial Hall, the veterans claim services, and the Soldiers' Rehabilitation Board. The department was assigned the economic aid, hospital care, and education grants programs.

It also took over three segregated veterans funds that were combined into the Veterans Trust Fund in 1961.

Two major new programs relating to housing and education were implemented after World War II. Beginning with legislation in 1947, programs were established to help veterans finance home loans through a trust fund. The state supreme court declared earmarking liquor tax moneys for the fund unconstitutional under the internal improvements clause, but a constitutional amendment, approved by the voters in 1949, resolved the problem. Chapter 627, Laws of 1949, authorized loans to qualified veterans for a portion of the value of their housing. The legislature converted this program to a second mortgage home loan program in 1973, when it established the Primary Home Loan Program that is financed with general obligation bonds. The state's use of general obligation bonding to offer home loans to veterans raised constitutional concerns. The legislature responded by proposing an amendment to the Wisconsin Constitution, which the voters ratified in April 1975.

1997 Wisconsin Act 27 expanded eligibility for state veterans benefits to any person who has served on active duty in the U.S. armed forces for two continuous years or the full period of the individual's initial service obligation, whichever is less, regardless of when or where the service occurred, including during peacetime. Previously, to be considered a "veteran" for the purposes of state benefits, a person must generally have performed active service for 90 days or more during a designated war period or a period of duty during specified conflicts or peacekeeping operations.

1999 Wisconsin Act 136 required the department to administer a program to coordinate the provision of military funeral honors to eligible deceased veterans. 2003 Wisconsin Act 102 authorized the department to develop and operate residential, treatment, and nursing care facilities in northwestern Wisconsin, on surplus land located at the Northern Wisconsin Center for the Developmentally Disabled in Chippewa Falls.

2011 Wisconsin Act 36 placed the direction and supervision of the department under the secretary of veterans affairs, rather than the board. It also increased the size of the board from 7 to 9 members, reduced their terms of office from 6 to 4 years, and required that at least one member of the board be a resident of each congressional district.

Statutory Council

Council on Veterans Programs: ROGER FETTERLY (Military Officers Association of America), *chairperson;* ROBERT PIARO (Vietnam Veterans of America), *vice chairperson;* MARK GRAMS (Marine Corps League), *secretary;* CHARLES ROLOFF (American Legion), ALBERT W. LABELLE, JR. (Disabled American Veterans), MICHAEL FURGAL (Veterans of Foreign Wars), RUSS ALSTEEN (Navy Club), DAVID SCHMIDT (Veterans of World II – AMVETS), DON HEILIGER (American Ex-Prisoners of War), MARK FOREMAN (Vietnam Veterans Against the War), vacancy (Catholic War Veterans of the U.S.A.), BEN BERLIN (Jewish War Veterans of the U.S.A.), KEN WENDT (Polish Legion of American Veterans), WILLIAM SIMS (National Association for Black Veterans, Inc.), PAUL FINE (Army Navy Union), MIKE GOURLIE (Wisconsin Association of Concerned Veterans Organizations), ELIZABETH BENN (United Women Veterans, Inc.), WALTER STENAVICH (U.S. Submarine Veterans of World War II), WILLIAM HUSTAD (Wisconsin Vietnam Veterans, Inc.), RICK CHERONE (Military Order of the Purple Heart), MICHEL SOEHNER (American Red Cross), VERN LOVLEY (County Veterans Service Officers Association), KEN NESS (Wisconsin Chapter of the Paralyzed Veterans of America), LENNY SHIER (Retired Enlisted Association), RICK DEMOYA (American GI Forum), GARY TRAYNOR (Blinded Veterans Association of Wisconsin). (All are appointed by their respective organizations).

The 26-member Council on Veterans Programs studies and presents policy alternatives and recommendations to the Board of Veterans Affairs. It is comprised of representatives appointed for one-year terms by organizations that have a direct interest in veterans' affairs. The council was created by Chapter 443, Laws of 1943, and its composition and duties are prescribed in Sections 15.497 and 45.35 (3d) of the statutes.

Department of
WORKFORCE DEVELOPMENT

Address e-mail by combining the user ID and the state extender: userid@**dwd.wisconsin.gov**
All telephone numbers are 608 area code unless otherwise indicated.

Secretary of Workforce Development: REGGIE NEWSON, 267-1410, reggie.newson@

Deputy Secretary: JONATHAN BARRY, 267-3200, jonathan.barry@

Executive Assistant: JOHN FANDRICH, 266-2284, johnp.fandrich@

Legal Counsel: HOWARD BERNSTEIN, 266-9427, howard.bernstein@

Communications Director: JOHN DIPKO, 266-6753, john.dipko@

Legislative Liaison: CONNIE SCHULZE, 266-1756, connie.schulze@

Office of Skills Development: SCOTT JANSEN, *director,* 266-3252, scott.jansen@

Mailing Address: P.O. Box 7946, Madison 53707-7946.

Location: 201 East Washington Avenue, Madison.

Telephone: (608) 266-3131.

Fax: (608) 266-1784.

Internet Address: www.dwd.wisconsin.gov

Publications: Contact individual divisions for publications.

Number of Employees: 1,744.81.

Total Budget 2011-13: $658,531,000.

Statutory References: Sections 15.22, 15.223, 15.225, and 15.227; Chapters 47, 102-106, 108, 109, and 111.

Administrative Services Division: KATHLEEN REED, *administrator,* 261-4599, kathleen.reed@; LARRY STUDESVILLE, *deputy administrator,* 261-2138, larry.studesville@

　Financial Management, Bureau of: TAMARA MOE, *director,* 261-4582, tami.moe@

　General Services, Bureau of: MARGARET MCGRATH, *director,* 266-1777, margaret.mcgrath@

　Human Resource Services, Bureau of: LYNDA HANOLD, *director,* 266-6496, lynda.hanold@

　Information Technology Services, Bureau of: STEVE MUELLER, *director and CIO,* 264-8800, steve.mueller@

Employment and Training, Division of: LISA BOYD, *administrator,* 266-3485, lisa.boyd@; vacancy, *deputy administrator,* 266-3623.

　Apprenticeship Standards, Bureau of: KAREN P. MORGAN, *director,* 266-3133, karen.morgan@

　Job Service, Bureau of: BRIAN SOLOMON, *director,* 267-7514, brian.solomon@

　Program Management and Special Populations, Bureau of: JUAN JOSE LOPEZ, *director,* 266-0002, juan.lopez@

　Workforce Training, Bureau of: vacancy, *director.*

　Veterans Services, Office of: GARY MEYER, *acting manager,* 267-7277, gary.meyer@

　Economic Advisors, Office of: DENNIS WINTERS, 267-3262, dennis.winters@

Equal Rights Division: JOE HANDRICK, *administrator,* 266-0946, joseph.handrick@; JIM CHIOLINO, *deputy administrator,* 266-3345, jim.chiolino@; Division TTY: 264-8752.

　Civil Rights, Bureau of: LARRY JAKUBOWSKI, *director,* (414) 227-4396, larry.jakubowski@

　Labor Standards, Bureau of: JIM CHIOLINO, *director,* 266-3345, jim.chiolino@

　Support Services, Office of: JULIE BABLER, *manager,* 266-7560, juliea.babler@

Unemployment Insurance, Division of: ROBERT RODRIGUEZ, *administrator,* 266-8533, robert.rodriguez@; BENJAMIN PEIRCE, *deputy administrator,* 266-3635, benjamin.peirce@

DEPARTMENT OF WORKFORCE DEVELOPMENT

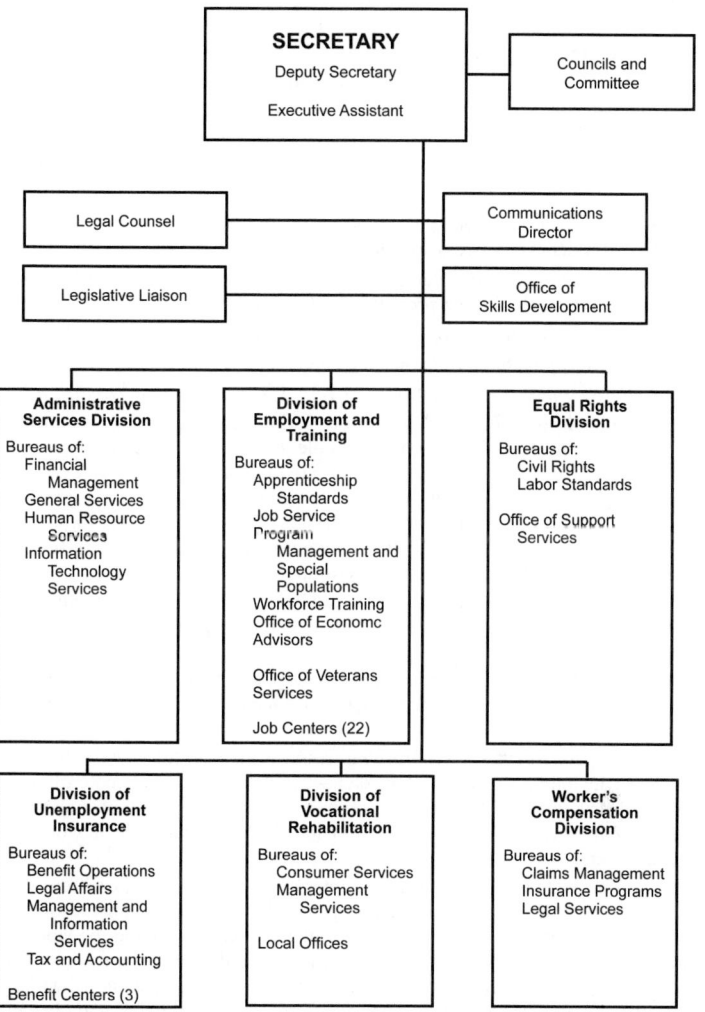

Unit attached for administrative purposes under Sec. 15.03:   Labor and Industry Review Commission

Benefit Operations, Bureau of: Lutfi Shahrani, *director,* 266-8211, lutfi.shahrani@

Legal Affairs, Bureau of: Janell Knutson, *director,* 266-1639, janell.knutson@

Management and Information Services, Bureau of: Pamela James, *director,* 266-6904, pamela.james@

Tax and Accounting, Bureau of: Thomas McHugh, *director,* 266-3130, thomas.mchugh@

Benefit Centers:

   Madison: Initial claims: (608) 232-0678; Employee inquiries: (608) 232-0824; Employer inquiries: (608) 232-0633.

Milwaukee: Initial claims: (414) 438-7700; Employee inquiries: (414) 438-7713; Employer inquiries: (414) 438-7705.

Statewide: Initial claims: (800) 822-5246; Employee inquiries: (800) 494-4944; Employer inquiries: (800) 247-1744.

Vocational Rehabilitation, Division of: MICHAEL GRECO, *administrator,* 261-4576, michael.greco@; JOANNA RICHARD, *deputy administrator,* 261-0074, joanna.richard@; Division TTY: 243-5601.

   Consumer Services, Bureau of: JOHN HAUGH, *director,* 261-2126, john.haugh@

   Management Services, Bureau of: ENID GLENN, *director,* 261-0073, enid.glenn@

   Local Offices: To contact a local DVR office, call (800) 442-3477 or visit http://dwd.wisconsin.gov/dvr/locations/default.htm

Worker's Compensation Division: JOHN METCALF, *administrator,* 266-6841, john.metcalf@; BRIAN KRUEGER, *deputy administrator,* 267-4415, brian.krueger@

   Claims Management, Bureau of: TRACY AIELLO, *director,* 267-9407, tracy.aiello@

   Insurance Programs, Bureau of: vacancy, *director.*

   Legal Services, Bureau of: JIM O'MALLEY, *director,* 267-6704, jim.omalley@

Agency Responsibility: The Department of Workforce Development conducts a variety of work-related programs designed to connect people with employment opportunities in Wisconsin. It has major responsibility for the state's employment and training services; job centers; job training and placement services provided in cooperation with private sector employers; apprenticeship programs; and employment-related services for people with disabilities. It oversees the unemployment insurance and worker's compensation programs and is also responsible for adjudicating cases involving employment discrimination, housing discrimination, and labor law.

Organization: The department is administered by a secretary who is appointed by the governor with the advice and consent of the senate. The secretary appoints the division administrators from outside the classified service.

Unit Functions: The *Administrative Services Division* provides management and program support to the other divisions, including facilities, finance, human resources, and information technology services.

The *Division of Employment and Training* oversees all workforce services administered by the department including the state labor exchange system (www.jobcenterofwisconsin.com); analyzes and distributes labor market information; monitors migrant worker services; and operates the state apprenticeship program. The division also has a statewide network of 22 comprehensive job centers.

The *Equal Rights Division,* created by Chapter 327, Laws of 1967, enforces state laws that protect citizens from discrimination in employment, housing, and public accommodations. It also administers the enforcement of family and medical leave laws and the labor laws relating to hours, conditions of work, minimum wage standards, and timely payment of wages. It determines prevailing wage rates and enforces them for state and municipal public works projects not including highway projects. The division also enforces child labor laws and plant closing laws.

The *Division of Unemployment Insurance* administers programs to pay benefits to unemployed workers, collect employer taxes, resolve contested benefit claims and employer tax issues, detect unemployment insurance fraud, and collect unemployment insurance overpayments and delinquent taxes. The division also collects wage information for national and Wisconsin New Hire Directory databases.

The *Division of Vocational Rehabilitation* provides employment services to individuals who have significant physical and mental disabilities that create barriers in obtaining, maintaining, or improving employment. Each person is counseled and may receive medical, psychological, and vocational evaluations and training services. Employment programs, which are supported through state and federal funding, include vocational rehabilitation for eligible persons with disabilities; supported employment, including job coaching for individuals with severe disabilities; and the Business Enterprise Program, which establishes business or vending stand locations for individuals who are legally blind.

The *Worker's Compensation Division* administers programs designed to ensure that injured workers receive required benefits from insurers or self-insured employers; encourage rehabilitation and reemployment for injured workers; and promote the reduction of work-related injuries, illnesses, and deaths.

History: In response to the state's industrialization, which began in the 1880s, Wisconsin took the lead nationally in adjusting labor laws to modern industrial conditions. Based on European models, the legislature adopted social insurance, whereby the costs of correcting labor problems, such as worker injuries and unemployment, were imposed on employers as an inducement to prevent the problems.

Wisconsin's laws, enacted during the early part of the 20th century, dealt with minimum wages, conditions of employment for women and children, worker's compensation, free public employment offices, apprenticeship standards, and job safety regulations. Many of these programs served as models for legislation in other states. Wisconsin's original worker's compensation act (Chapter 50, Laws of 1911) was the first state law of its kind in the nation. In the 1930s, Wisconsin led in developing the unemployment compensation system (Chapter 20, Laws of Special Session 1931) and issued the first benefit check in the nation in 1936.

Since World War II, Wisconsin has enacted legislation prohibiting discrimination in employment on the basis of race, sex, creed, national origin, marital status, ancestry, arrest or conviction record, off-duty use of lawful products, membership in military reserve, sexual orientation, age, and disability. Similar laws now protect access to housing and public accommodations.

Early in the 20th century, the state delegated labor law administration to a politically independent body of experts, the State Industrial Commission, and its advisory committees. The commission was encouraged to solve problems through administrative decision making and the development of administrative rules to supplement the laws. A close tie between state government and the University of Wisconsin enabled the governor and legislature to translate reforms conceived in the academic arena into law. This cooperative meshing of academic research and government action came to be known as "The Wisconsin Idea".

The Department of Workforce Development evolved from the Wisconsin Bureau of Labor Statistics, which was created in 1883. The bureau was succeeded by the State Industrial Commission in 1911. Following the 1967 executive branch reorganization, the commission directed the new Department of Industry, Labor and Human Relations (DILHR) and was renamed the Industry, Labor and Human Relations Commission by Chapter 276, Laws of 1969. The commission was replaced by a secretary in Chapter 29, Laws of 1977.

Effective July 1, 1996, the Department of Industry, Labor and Human Relations was renamed the Department of Industry, Labor and Job Development by 1995 Wisconsin Act 29, but the department was given the option of using the name Department of Workforce Development in 1995 Wisconsin Act 289. It formally chose to exercise that option beginning July 1, 1996, and the legislature officially recognized the name choice in 1997 Wisconsin Act 3.

The department was significantly altered by 1995 Wisconsin Act 27. It assumed many duties formerly performed by other agencies, in particular supervision of welfare and income maintenance programs and vocational rehabilitation services, which were transferred from the former Department of Health and Social Services. At the same time, the Division of Safety and Buildings was transferred out of the department to the new Department of Commerce. 1997 Wisconsin Act 191 assigned the department primary responsibility for establishing and operating a statewide system for enforcing child, family, and spousal support obligations, including expanded authority to deny, revoke, or suspend various licenses, permits, and credentials of delinquent payers.

The statutes provide that the minimum wage is set through the administrative rules process, which includes legislative review. In January 2004, the secretary established the Minimum Wage Advisory Council to recommend an appropriate increase in the minimum wage. The council was comprised of representatives from business, labor organizations, the university system, and the legislature, and issued its final report on May 1, 2004.

2007 Wisconsin Act 20 created the Department of Children and Families (DCF), beginning July 1, 2008. It also changed the name of the Department of Health and Family Services

(DHFS) to the Department of Health Services and split the responsibilities of DHFS between the two departments. Act 20 also transferred from the Department of Workforce Development to DCF administration of Wisconsin Works, including the child care subsidy program, child support enforcement and paternity establishment, and programs related to temporary assistance to needy families (TANF).

Statutory Councils and Committee

Wisconsin Apprenticeship Council: Not appointed at the time of publication.

> Mailing Address: P.O. Box 7972, Madison 53707-7972.

> Telephone: (608) 266-3133.

The 23-member Wisconsin Apprenticeship Council advises the department on matters pertaining to Wisconsin's apprenticeship system. The council consists of nine representatives of employers and nine representatives of employees appointed by the secretary of workforce development, one representative of the technical college system appointed by the director of the technical college system, one representative of the Department of Public Instruction appointed by the superintendent of public instruction, two members appointed to represent the public interest appointed by the secretary of workforce development, and one permanent classified Department of Workforce Development employee appointed by the secretary of workforce development to serve as the nonvoting chairperson. The council was created by Chapter 29, Laws of 1977, and its duties and composition are prescribed in Sections 15.09 (5) and 15.227 (13) of the statutes.

Labor and Management Council: Inactive.

The 21-member Labor and Management Council provides a forum for labor, management, and public sector representatives to discuss issues that affect the state's economy and to foster positive labor-management relations in the workplace. Council members serve 5-year terms. The council was created by 1987 Wisconsin Act 27, and its composition and duties are prescribed in Section 15.227 (17) of the statutes.

Lt. Governor Rebecca Kleefisch and Department of Workforce Development Secretary Reggie Newson joined Walgreens executives in Oconomowoc in February 2013 to announce an expansion of the company's Retail Employees with Disabilities Initiative, an innovative job training program for people with disabilities. (Department of Workforce Development)

Migrant Labor, Council on: LUPE MARTINEZ (migrant representative), *acting chairperson/ vice chairperson;* SENATOR WIRCH, vacancy; REPRESENTATIVE ZAMARRIPA, vacancy; JOHN I. BAUKNECHT, ENRIQUE FIGUEROA, KEVIN MAGEE, GUADALUPE RENDON, TERESA TELLEZ-GIRON (migrant representatives); JAMES KERN, ERICA KUNZE, RICHARD W. OKRAY, LILIANA PARODI, STEVE ZIOBRO, vacancy (migrant employer representatives). (All except legislative members are appointed by governor.)

The 16-member Council on Migrant Labor advises the department and other state officials about matters affecting migrant workers. The council's 4 legislator members represent the two major political parties and are appointed "to act as representatives of the public". The nonlegislative members serve 3-year terms. The council was created by Chapter 17, Laws of 1977, and its composition and duties are prescribed in Sections 15.227 (8), 103.967, and 103.968 of the statutes.

Self-Insurers Council: MICHAEL FONTAINE, JILL E. JOSWIAK, RICK KANTE, DANIEL KUGLER, CHRISTINE MCKINZIE (appointed by secretary of workforce development).

The 5-member Self-Insurers Council advises the department about matters related to companies that cover their own worker's compensation losses rather than insuring them with an insurance carrier. Members are appointed for 3-year terms by the secretary of the department. The council was created by Chapter 29, Laws of 1977, and its duties and composition are prescribed in Sections 15.09 (5) and 15.227 (11) of the statutes.

Unemployment Insurance, Council on: JANELL KNUTSON (permanent classified employee of department) (nonvoting member), *chairperson;* JAMES BUCHEN, MICHAEL GOETZLER, EARL GUSTAFSON, JAMES LACOURT (employer representatives); EDWARD LUMP (employer representative, small business owner or representing small business association); SALLY FEISTEL, TERRANCE MCGOWAN, PHILLIP NEUENFELDT, ANTHONY RAINEY, MARK REIHL (employee representatives). (All are appointed by secretary of workforce development.)

The 11-member Council on Unemployment Insurance advises the legislature and the department about unemployment compensation matters. It includes 5 employers and 5 labor representatives who are appointed for 6-year terms, plus a permanent, classified employee of the department who acts as the council's nonvoting chairperson. In making council appointments, the secretary must consider "balanced representation of the industrial, commercial, construction, nonprofit and public sectors of the state's economy." One employer representative must be a small business owner or represent a small business association. The council was created as the Council on Unemployment Compensation by Chapter 327, Laws of 1967. Its name was changed by 1997 Wisconsin Act 39. Its composition and duties are prescribed in Sections 15.227 (3) and 108.14 (5) of the statutes.

Worker's Compensation, Council on: JOHN METCALF (nonvoting member), *chairperson;* JEFFREY J. BEIRIGER, JEFFREY BRAND, JAMES A. BUCHEN, MARY NUGENT, CHRISTINE PEHLER (employer representatives); STEPHANIE BLOOMINGDALE, RON KENT, SCOTT REDMAN, BRAD SCHWANDA, MONICA THOMAS (employee representatives); BILL BRANDL, DAVID COLLINGWOOD, STEVEN GINSBURG (nonvoting insurance company representatives). (All are appointed by secretary of workforce development.)

The 14-member Council on Worker's Compensation is appointed by the secretary of the department to advise the legislature and the department about worker's compensation and related matters. The council was created by Chapter 281, Laws of 1963, as the Advisory Committee on Workmen's Compensation, appointed by the Industrial Commission. It was given its current name and located in the Department of Industry, Labor and Human Relations by Chapter 327, Laws of 1967. The council includes three nonvoting representatives of insurers authorized to do worker's compensation insurance business in Wisconsin and a department employee acting as chairperson. The council's composition and duties are prescribed in Sections 15.227 (4) and 102.14 (2) of the statutes.

Health Care Provider Advisory Committee: JOHN METCALF (administrator, worker's compensation division), *chairperson;* DAVID BRYCE, GINA BUONO, MARY JO CAPODICE, MAJA JURISIC, MIKE LISCHAK, vacancy (medical doctors); JEFF LYNE, PETER SCHUBBE (chiropractors); AMANDA GILLILAND, KAREN SEIDL (hospital representatives); BARB JANUSIAK (registered nurse);

Jennifer Pollak (physical therapist); Ron H. Stark, Sri Vasudevan (at-large members). (All are appointed pursuant to Section 102.16 (2m) (g), Wisconsin Statutes, and Section DWD 81.14 (1), Wisconsin Administrative Code.)

The Health Care Provider Advisory Committee advises the department and the Council on Worker's Compensation on modifications to treatment standards (treatment guidelines) contained in Chapter DWD 81, Wisconsin Administrative Code, for determining necessity of treatment disputes pursuant to Section 102.16 (2m), Wisconsin Statutes. Section 102.15 (2m) (g), created by 2005 Wisconsin Act 172, directs the department to establish the committee, but does not specify its membership. Section DWD 81.14 (1), Wisconsin Administrative Code, created in the Wisconsin Administrative Register of October 2007, Number 622, provides that the committee is to be composed of the administrator of the worker's compensation division as chairperson, and 14 other members: 6 doctors of different specialties, 2 chiropractors, 2 hospital representatives, 1 registered nurse, 1 physical therapist, and 2 at-large members. All except the chairperson must be licensed and practicing in Wisconsin, and provide treatment under Section 102.42. Appointments are made by the department from a consensus list of 24 names submitted by the Wisconsin Medical Society, the Wisconsin Chiropractic Association, and the Wisconsin Hospital Association, with the exception of the 2 at-large members selected by the department.

Independent Unit Attached for Program Coordination and Related Management Functions by Section 15.03 of the Statutes

LABOR AND INDUSTRY REVIEW COMMISSION

Labor and Industry Review Commission: Laurie McCallum, *chairperson;* C. William Jordahl, vacancy (appointed by governor with senate consent).

General Counsel: Tracey L. Schwalbe, tracey.schwalbe@dwd.wisconsin.gov

Mailing Address: P.O. Box 8126, Madison 53708-8126.

Location: Public Broadcasting Building, 3319 West Beltline Highway, Madison.

Telephone: (608) 266-9850.

Fax: (608) 267-4409.

E-mail Address: lirc@dwd.wisconsin.gov

Internet Address: http://dwd.wisconsin.gov/lirc

Publications: Informational brochure.

Number of Employees: 25.50.

Total Budget 2011-13: $6,390,000.

Statutory References: Sections 15.225 and 103.04.

Agency Responsibility: The 3-member Labor and Industry Review Commission is a quasi-judicial body, created by Chapter 29, Laws of 1977, which handles petitions seeking review of the decisions of the Department of Workforce Development related to unemployment insurance, worker's compensation, fair employment, and public accommodations. It also hears appeals about discrimination in postsecondary education involving a person's physical condition or developmental disability. Commission decisions may be appealed to the circuit court. Commission decisions are enforced by the Department of Justice or the commission's legal staff. Commission members serve full-time for staggered 6-year terms, and they select a chairperson from their membership to serve for a 2-year period. By law, the commission's budget must be transmitted to the governor by the department without modification, unless the commission agrees to the change.

STATE AUTHORITIES

Authorities are public, corporate bodies created for specific purposes.

WISCONSIN AEROSPACE AUTHORITY

Members: THOMAS CRABB (public member), *chairperson;* MARK HANNA (public member), *vice chairperson;* THOMAS MULLOOLY (public member), *secretary-treasurer;* SENATOR LEIBHAM (appointed by senate president); REPRESENTATIVE KESTELL (appointed by assembly speaker); R. AILEEN YINGST (Wisconsin Space Grant Consortium director); MARK LEE, JUDITH SCHIEBLE, EDWARD WAGNER (public members).

Statutory References: Chapter 114, Subchapter II.

Agency Responsibility: The Wisconsin Aerospace Authority is directed to promote the state's aerospace industry by developing a business plan in cooperation with the Wisconsin Space Grant Consortium, securing adequate funding for spaceport facilities and services, sponsoring events to attract space-related businesses, advertising the use of spaceports to the public, and establishing a safety program.

Organization: The authority is a public corporation consisting of the director of the Wisconsin Space Grant Consortium and 8 members serving 3-year terms. One member is a state senator appointed by the president of the senate and one member is a state representative appointed by the speaker of the assembly. The 6 public members are nominated by the governor with the consent of the senate and must be Wisconsin residents with experience in the commercial space industry, education, finance, or some other significant experience related to the functions of the authority.

The authority was created by 2005 Wisconsin Act 335.

WISCONSIN ECONOMIC DEVELOPMENT CORPORATION

Board Members: GOVERNOR SCOTT WALKER, *chairperson;* DAN ARIENS, RAYMOND DREGER, CORY HOZE, LISA MAUER, PAUL RADSPINNER, vacancy (appointed by governor with senate consent); REPRESENTATIVE STONE (majority party representative appointed by speaker); REPRESENTATIVE BARCA (minority party representative appointed by speaker); SCOTT KLUG (private sector employee appointed by speaker); SENATOR LEIBHAM (majority party senator appointed by senate majority leader); SENATOR LASSA (minority party senator appointed by senate majority leader); C. THOMAS SYLKE (private sector employee appointed by senate majority leader); MICHAEL HUEBSCH (secretary of administration), RICHARD CHANDLER (secretary of revenue) (nonvoting members).

Chief Executive Officer: REED HALL, (608) 210-6700.

Mailing Address: P.O. Box 1687, Madison 53701.

Location: 201 West Washington Avenue, 6th Floor, Madison.

Telephone: (608) 266-1018.

Internet Address: inwisconsin.com

Statutory References: Chapter 238.

Agency Responsibility: The Wisconsin Economic Development Corporation (WEDC) develops and implements programs to provide business support and expertise and financial assistance to companies that are investing and creating jobs in Wisconsin and to promote new business start-ups and business expansion and growth in the state. The authority was established in 2011 to assume many of the functions previously performed by the former Department of Commerce.

Organization: The WEDC is an authority, which is a body corporate and politic. It is governed by a 15-member board composed of the governor, who shall serve as chairperson of the board; 6 members appointed by the governor with senate consent to serve at the pleasure of the

HATCO of Sturgeon Bay, the 2012 winner of the Governor's Export Achievement Award, has received technical assistance from the Wisconsin Economic Development Corporation developing global business development plans. (Wisconsin Economic Development Corporation)

governor; 3 members appointed by the speaker of the assembly, consisting of one majority and one minority party representative, and one person employed in the private sector to serve at the speaker's pleasure; and 3 members appointed by the senate majority leader, consisting of one majority and one minority party senator, and one person employed in the private sector to serve at the majority leader's pleasure. The secretary of administration and the secretary of revenue serve as nonvoting members.

The corporation is administered by a chief executive officer (CEO) nominated by the governor, and with the advice and consent of the senate appointed, to serve at the pleasure of the governor. The board may delegate to the CEO any powers and duties the board considers proper and determines the compensation and qualifications of the CEO and employees. Corporation employees are not state employees but may participate in the Wisconsin Retirement System.

History: The 1911 Legislature created the Industrial Commission in Chapter 485 to set standards for a safe place of employment. This "safe place" statute was extended in Chapter 588, Laws of 1913, to include public buildings. The commission adopted its first building code in 1914.

The state's promotion of business and economic development originated with the Division of Industrial Development, established in the governor's office by Chapter 271, Laws of 1955. The division was transferred to the newly created Department of Resource Development in 1959 and renamed the Division of Economic Development. Chapter 614, Laws of 1965, returned the division to the governor's office. While in the executive office, it absorbed the Office of Economic Opportunity (1966), which had been created in the Department of Resource Development to administer the federal antipoverty programs enacted in 1964. Under the 1967 executive branch reorganization, the division became part of the Department of Local Affairs and Development, and local and regional planning functions were integrated into it.

Chapter 125, Laws of 1971, created the Department of Business Development. The department absorbed the Division of Tourism from the Department of Natural Resources in 1975. Under Chapter 361, Laws of 1979, the Department of Business Development was combined with the Department of Local Affairs and Development to form the Department of Development, subsequently renamed the Department of Commerce (Commerce) by 1995 Wisconsin Act 27. The department's responsibility for state tourism promotion ended with the creation of the Department of Tourism by 1995 Wisconsin Act 27. Act 27 also transferred to Commerce the PECFA program and the safety and buildings functions from the Department of Industry, Labor and Human Relations; responsibility for plat review from the Department of Agriculture, Trade and Consumer Protection; municipal boundary review from the Department of Administration; and relocation assistance under eminent domain law from the Department of Industry, Labor and Human Relations. Responsibility for plat review and municipal boundary review was transferred to the Department of Administration by 1997 Wisconsin Act 27. Regulation of manufactured home dealers and manufactured home parks was transferred to the department from the Department of Administration by 1999 Wisconsin Act 9. Act 9 also transferred titling of manufactured homes from the Department of Transportation. Regulation of manufactured home park utilities was transferred from the Public Service Commission by 2001 Wisconsin Act 16. In 2003, Wisconsin Act 33 transferred housing programs to the department from the Department of Administration.

2009 Wisconsin Act 2 deleted five existing zone programs, including the Enterprise Development Zones, the Community Development Zones, the Agricultural Development Zones, the Technology Development Zones, and the Airport Development Zones, and created a new consolidated tax credit program to promote job creation, capital investment, employee training, and job retention in Wisconsin. Act 2 also increased substantially the amount of angel and early-stage seed investment tax credits available annually for high-technology, biotechnology, and nanotechnology start-up companies which had been initiated by 2003 Wisconsin Act 255.

2011 Wisconsin Act 7 created, effective February 24, 2011, the Wisconsin Economic Development Corporation to develop and administer economic development programs for the state. Act 7 required Commerce to provide staff or other resources to assist the WEDC in carrying out its duties, and for both entities to coordinate their economic development programs.

2011 Wisconsin Act 32 repealed the Department of Commerce effective July 1, 2011. The act transferred certain of Commerce's economic development and business promotion responsibilities, including grants, loans, and tax incentives, to the WEDC and housing programs to the Department of Administration. The administration of various other laws relating to the promotion of safety in public and private buildings, including enforcing building codes, and the licensure of occupations that had been regulated by Commerce, such as electricians and plumbers, were transferred to a new Department of Safety and Professional Services (DSPS), which was also created by Act 32. In addition to the safety and buildings responsibilities transferred from Commerce, the DSPS assumed the other functions previously performed by the Department of Regulation and Licensing, which was also repealed by Act 32.

FOX RIVER NAVIGATIONAL SYSTEM AUTHORITY

Board of Directors: RONALD VAN DE HEY (Outagamie County representative), *chairperson;* BILL RAATHS (Winnebago County representative), *vice chairperson;* TIMOTHY ROSE (Outagamie County representative); JOHN L. VETTE (Winnebago County representative); JOHN SHIER, vacancy (Brown County representatives); JEAN ROMBACK-BARTELS (designated by secretary of natural resources); WILL DORSEY (designated by secretary of transportation); JIM DRAEGER (designated by director, state historical society) (county residents are appointed by the governor).

Chief Executive Officer: HARLAN P. KIESOW.

Telephone: (920) 759-9833.

Internet Address: http://foxriverlocks.org

Total Budget 2011-13: $250,800.

Statutory References: Chapter 237.

Agency Responsibility: The Fox River Navigational System Authority is responsible for the rehabilitation, repair, and management of the navigation system on or near the Fox River in 3 counties. The federal government transferred ownership of the navigational system to the State of Wisconsin in 2004. The authority may enter into contracts with third parties to operate the system. It may not sublease all or any part of the navigational system without DOA approval. It may enter into contracts with nonprofit organizations to raise funds. The authority may charge fees for services provided to watercraft owners and users of navigational facilities. While the authority may contract debt, it may not issue bonds. It must submit an audited financial statement annually to DOA.

Organization: The Fox River Navigational System Authority is a public corporation consisting of 9 members. The 6 members the governor appoints serve 3-year terms. At least one member from each of the 3 counties must be a resident of a city, village, or town in which a navigational system lock is located. The board appoints the chief executive officer to serve at its pleasure. The authority was created by 2001 Wisconsin Act 16.

HEALTH INSURANCE RISK-SHARING PLAN AUTHORITY

Board of Directors: JOE KACHELSKI (Wisconsin Hospital Association, Inc., representative), *chairperson;* WENDY ARNONE, LINDA HOFF, LARRY RAMBO, STEVE YOUSO (represent insurers participating in the plan); MICHELLE BAUER (Wisconsin Medical Society representative); CATHY WINTERS (Pharmacy Society of Wisconsin representative); JOHN RUSSELL (health care providers representative); CHRIS HANSON (small business representative); ELLEN HENNINGSEN (professional consumer advocate); ANNETTE STEBBINS, TOM WAGNER (persons with coverage under plan). Nonvoting member: J.P. WIESKE (designated by commissioner of insurance).

Executive Director: AMIE GOLDMAN.

Mailing Address: 1 East Main Street, Suite 305, Madison 53703.

Telephone: (608) 441-5777.

Fax: (608) 441-5776.
Agency E-mail Address: info@hirsp.org
Internet Address: www.hirsp.org
Publications: Annual Report; Quarterly Newsletter "News from the HIRSP Authority".
Number of Employees: 4.00.
Statutory References: Chapter 149, Subchapter III.

Agency Responsibility: The Health Insurance Risk-Sharing Plan (HIRSP) Authority is responsible for the operation of state and federal HIRSP plans, which provide health insurance to Wisconsin residents who are unable to find adequate coverage in the private market due to their medical conditions or who have lost their employer-sponsored group health insurance. The authority can adopt policies for the operation of the plan, enter into contracts for the plan's administration, and pay the operating and administrative expenses from a designated fund. The authority is also tasked with maintaining the plan as a state pharmacy assistance program and reporting annually to both the legislature and the governor on the operation of the plan.

Organization: The authority is a public corporation consisting of a 13-member board of directors appointed by the governor, with the advice and consent of the senate, who serve for 3-year terms. Four of the members must represent participating insurers, 4 must represent certain health care providers, and 5 other members must include one small business representative, one professional consumer advocate, and at least 2 who have HIRSP coverage. The Commissioner of Insurance (or his or her designee) serves as a nonvoting member of the board. Annually, the governor appoints one of the voting members as the chairperson. The authority's board of directors can elect officers and appoint a nonboard member as the executive director. The authority was created by 2005 Wisconsin Act 74.

LOWER FOX RIVER REMEDIATION AUTHORITY

Members: TRIPP AHERN, GREGORY CONWAY, ROBERT COWLES, DAVE HANSEN, PATRICK SCHILLINGER, JAMES WALL, vacancy (all appointed by governor with advice and consent of the senate).
Statutory References: Chapter 279.

Agency Responsibility: The authority is authorized to issue assessment bonds for eligible waterway improvement costs, which generally include environmental investigation and remediation of the Fox River extending from Lake Winnebago to the mouth of the river in Lake Michigan, and including any portion of Green Bay in Lake Michigan containing sediments discharged from the river, as described in an administrative or judicial order or decree or an administrative or judicially approved agreement. A consenting landowner may submit an application to the authority to request it to issue bonds for eligible waterway improvement costs. The consenting landowner making application must agree to the levy of an assessment against affected property owned by the landowner for the bond repayment costs, costs of financing and associated administrative costs, fees, and reserves. The authority calculates the amount of the assessment and levies the assessment on the consenting landowner. The landowner pays the assessment to the authority. The authority uses the assessment to repay the bonds and associated costs. The state is not liable for the authority's bonds, and the bonds are not a debt of the state.

Organization: The authority is a public corporation consisting of 7 members appointed by the governor with the advice and consent of the senate, for 7-year terms. Members of the board must be Wisconsin residents and no more than 4 members may be from the same political party. The term of each member expires on June 30 or until a successor is appointed.

The authority was created by 2007 Wisconsin Act 20.

UNIVERSITY OF WISCONSIN HOSPITALS AND CLINICS AUTHORITY

Board of Directors: DAVID WALSH (UW Board of Regents member appointed by board president), *chairperson;* MICHAEL WEIDEN (appointed by governor with senate consent), *vice chairperson;* SENATOR OLSEN (designated by senate cochairperson, Joint Committee on Finance), REPRESENTATIVE MARKLEIN (designated by assembly cochairperson, Joint Committee on Finance); THOMAS BASTING, RICHARD FETHERSTON, LISA REARDON, PABLO SANCHEZ, HUMBERTO VIDAILLET (appointed by governor with senate consent); JEFFREY BARTELL, MICHAEL FALBO (UW Board of Regents members appointed by board president); REBECCA BLANK (chancellor, UW-Madison); ROBERT GOLDEN (dean, UW-Madison Medical School); GEORGE WILDING (departmental chairperson, UW-Madison Medical School, appointed by UW-Madison chancellor), KATHARYN MAY (UW health professions faculty, other than UW Medical School, appointed by UW-Madison chancellor); WENDY COOMER (designated by secretary of administration).

President and Chief Executive Officer: DONNA KATEN-BAHENSKY.

Mailing Address: 600 Highland Avenue, Room H4/810, Madison 53792-8350.

Location: 600 Highland Avenue, Madison.

Telephone: (608) 263-8025.

Fax: (608) 263-9830.

Publications: *Our UW Health; Kids Connections; Medical Directions; Ripple Effect.*

Number of Employees: 8,100 (not state funded).

Total Budget 2011-13: $2,480,575,000 (not state funded).

Statutory References: Chapter 233.

Agency Responsibility: The University of Wisconsin Hospitals and Clinics Authority operates the UW Hospital and Clinics, including the American Family Children's Hospital, and related clinics and health care facilities. Through the UW Hospital and Clinics and its other programs it delivers health care, including care for the indigent; provides an environment for instruction of physicians, nurses, and other health-related disciplines; sponsors and supports health care research; and assists health care programs and personnel throughout the state. Subject to approval by its board of directors, the authority may issue bonds to support its operations and may seek financing from the Wisconsin Health and Educational Facilities Authority.

Organization: The authority is a public corporation, which is self-financing. It derives much of its income from charges for clinical and hospital services. The 16-member board of directors includes 6 governor's appointees who serve 5-year terms. The board elects a chairperson annually and appoints the chief executive officer for the authority. The authority was created by 1995 Wisconsin Act 27, which separated UW Hospital and Clinics and their related services from the UW System, effective July 1, 1996.

WISCONSIN HEALTH AND EDUCATIONAL FACILITIES AUTHORITY

Members: RICHARD CANTER, *chairperson;* TIMOTHY K. SIZE, *vice chairperson;* BRUCE COLBURN, JAMES DIETSCHE, KEVIN FLAHERTY, RICHARD KEINTZ, ROBERT VAN MEETEREN (appointed by governor with senate consent).

Executive Director: DENNIS P. REILLY.

Mailing Address: 18000 West Sarah Lane, Suite 300, Brookfield 53045-5841.

Telephone: (262) 792-0466.

Fax: (262) 792-0649.

Agency E-mail Address: info@whefa.com

Internet Address: www.whefa.com

Publications: Annual Report; Quarterly Newsletter.

Number of Employees: 4.00 (not state funded).

Statutory Reference: Chapter 231.

Agency Responsibility: The Wisconsin Health and Educational Facilities Authority (WHEFA) issues bonds on behalf of qualifying tax-exempt health care and educational facilities to help them finance their capital costs. Since interest earned on the bonds is exempt from federal income taxation, they can be marketed at lower interest rates, which reduces the cost of borrowing. WHEFA has no taxing power and receives no general appropriations from the state; it supports its operations by imposing fees on participating institutions. WHEFA's bonds and notes are funded solely through loan repayments from the borrowing institution or sponsor. WHEFA's bonds are not a debt, liability, or obligation of the State of Wisconsin or any of its subdivisions.

WHEFA may issue bonds to finance any qualifying capital project, including new construction, remodeling, and renovation; expansion of current facilities; and purchase of new equipment or furnishings. WHEFA may also issue bonds to refinance outstanding debt of qualifying health care and educational institutions.

Organization: WHEFA is a public corporation. Its 7 members are appointed by the governor with consent of the senate for staggered 7-year terms, and no more than 4 may be members of the same political party. Each member's appointment remains in effect until a successor is appointed. The governor annually appoints one member as chairperson, and the members appoint the vice chairperson and executive director. The executive director and staff are employed outside the classified service and are not paid by state funds. The members receive no compensation.

History: WHEFA was created as the Wisconsin Health Facilities Authority by Chapter 304, Laws of 1973. Operations began in September 1979, after the Wisconsin Supreme Court found the law constitutional in *State ex rel. Wisconsin Health Facilities Authority v. Lindner*, 91 Wis. 2d 145 (1979), when it ruled that assistance to a religiously affiliated hospital does not advance religion or foster unnecessary entanglement between church and state. WHEFA issued its first debt in December 1979.

1987 Wisconsin Act 27 expanded the scope of WHEFA to include assistance to private, tax-exempt colleges and universities and continuing care retirement communities and changed its name to reflect the broader responsibilities. 1993 Wisconsin Act 438 added not-for-profit institutions that have health education as their primary purpose. 2003 Wisconsin Act 109 further expanded the scope of WHEFA to include the issuance of bonds for the benefit of private, tax-exempt elementary or secondary educational institutions. 2009 Wisconsin Act 2 allowed for WHEFA to include the issuance of bonds for the benefit of private, tax-exempt research facilities.

WISCONSIN HOUSING AND
ECONOMIC DEVELOPMENT AUTHORITY

Address e-mail by combining the user ID and the state extender: userid@**wheda.com**
All telephone numbers are 608 area code unless otherwise indicated.

Members: H. LEE SWANSON, *chairperson;* DANIEL F. LEE, *vice chairperson;* SENATORS CULLEN, GROTHMAN; REPRESENTATIVES LOUDENBECK, YOUNG; REED HALL (chief executive officer of Wisconsin Economic Development Corporation), MICHAEL HUEBSCH (secretary of administration); PERRY ARMSTRONG, BRADLEY GUSE, SUE SHORE, MCARTHUR WEDDLE. (All except legislative and *ex officio* members are appointed by governor with senate consent.)

Executive Director: WYMAN B. WINSTON, 266-2893, wyman.winston@

Executive Assistant: MARY ANN MCCOSHEN, 267-5200, mary_ann.mccoshen@

Executive Secretary: MAUREEN BRUNKER, 266-7354, maureen.brunker@

Mailing Address: P.O. Box 1728, Madison 53701-1728.

Location: 201 West Washington Avenue, Suite 700, Madison 53703; Milwaukee Office: 140 South 1st Street, Suite 200, Milwaukee 53204.

Telephones: Madison: (608) 266-7884; Milwaukee: (414) 227-4039; Toll free: (800) 334-6873.

Fax: Madison: (608) 267-1099; Milwaukee: (414) 227-4704.

Internet Address: www.wheda.com

Communications and Community Development: JENNIFER CONLIN, *director,* 266-7811, jennifer.conlin@

Economic Development: FARSHAD MALTES, *director,* 266-2027, farshad.maltes@

Financial Services: LAURA B. MORRIS, *chief financial officer,* 266-1640, laura.morris@

General Counsel: TIMOTHY RADELET, 266-2748, tim.radelet@

Human Resources and Administration: MARK EMMRICH, *director,* 267-2921, mark.emmrich@

Information Technology: vacancy.

Multifamily: MARY WRIGHT, *director,* 266-6622, mary.wright@

Operations: JOHN HOGAN, *chief operating officer,* 267-2307, john.hogan@

Single Family: GEOFFREY COOPER, *director,* 266-2184, geoffrey.cooper@

Publications: Annual Report; Dividends for Wisconsin.

Number of Employees: 158.00 (not state funded).

Total Budget 2012-13: $18,000,000 (not state funded).

Statutory Reference: Chapter 234.

Agency Responsibility: The Wisconsin Housing and Economic Development Authority (WHEDA) provides loans for low- and moderate-income housing, as well as financing programs for business and agricultural development. The authority finances most of its programs through the sale of bonds that are not an obligation of the State of Wisconsin. Since interest earned on the bonds is exempt from federal income taxation, they can be marketed at lower interest rates, which reduces the cost of borrowing.

WHEDA provides low-cost, 30-year fixed financing to low- and moderate-income home buyers who must meet specific income and loan limits eligibility requirements. WHEDA Advantage mortgages also provide access to down payment assistance, job loss mortgage payment protection, and education resources to help home buyers succeed long-term as homeowners. As an exclusive for WHEDA homeowners, the authority also offers low-cost home improvement loans to complete up to $10,000 in home repairs.

Both federally taxable and tax-exempt bonds are used to finance multifamily housing programs, which include homeless and special needs housing initiatives and loans to help with predevelopment of rental housing projects. In addition, the authority administers the federal Low-Income Housing Tax Credit Program (LIHTC) for developers of affordable rental housing.

WHEDA acts for the state in administering federally funded housing programs in coordination with the U.S. Department of Housing and Urban Development. Foremost among these are the Section 8 programs of the federal Housing and Community Development Act of 1979, which fund construction and rehabilitation of rental housing through rent subsidies to owners.

A companion organization, the WHEDA Foundation, makes grants to nonprofit organizations and local governments for housing projects that benefit persons-in-crisis. Grants are made to acquire and/or rehabilitate existing housing or construct new housing. The foundation also receives grant money on behalf of WHEDA.

WHEDA administers several economic development loan guarantee and financing programs that encourage job creation and economic growth. Agricultural loan guarantees include the Credit Relief Outreach Program (CROP) to help farmers obtain agricultural production loans; the Farm Asset Reinvestment Management (FARM) program to help farmers who want to start, expand, or modernize operations; and the Agribusiness loan guarantee to help businesses develop or expand production of products using Wisconsin's raw agricultural commodities.

The authority also provides the WHEDA Small Business Guarantee (WSBC) to acquire or expand a small business; the Contractors Loan Guarantee (CLG) to help contractors complete contracts to build their business; and the Neighborhood Business Revitalization Guarantee (NBRG), used to expand a business or to develop commercial real estate in an urban area.

WHEDA, as part of a Wisconsin based Community Development Entity (CDE), is responsible for allocating federal New Market Tax Credits (NMTC). Since 2004, $450 million in NMTCs have been received to help stimulate economic development and job growth in low-income Wisconsin communities. In addition, WHEDA received $22.4 million in federal funding from the State Small Business Credit Initiative (SSBCI) to create a small business lending program to help spur private sector job creation.

Organization: WHEDA is a public body corporate and politic consisting of 12 members. In addition to the secretary of administration and the CEO of the Wisconsin Economic Development Corporation, or their designees, there are 4 legislative members who must represent the majority and minority party in each house. The 6 public members serve staggered 4-year terms, and the governor selects one to serve as chairperson for a one-year term. The governor appoints WHEDA's executive director with the advice and consent of the senate for a 2-year term. Staff members are employed outside the classified service and are not paid from state funds.

History: WHEDA was created as the Wisconsin Housing Finance Authority by Chapter 287, Laws of 1971. Program operations began in July 1973, after the Wisconsin Supreme Court declared the Housing Finance Authority constitutional in *State ex rel. Warren v. Nusbaum,* 59 Wis. 2d 391 (1973). The authority issued its first debt instruments in March 1974. In 1983, Wisconsin Act 81 broadened the authority's mission to include financing for economic development projects and changed the name to the Wisconsin Housing and Economic Development Authority. In 1985 Wisconsin Acts 9 and 153 and 1987 Wisconsin Act 421, the legislature expanded WHEDA's powers to include the insuring and subsidizing of farm operating loans, drought assistance loan guarantees, and interest rate reductions. The legislature added loan guarantee programs for agricultural development and small businesses (1989 Wisconsin Act 31), recycling (1989 Wisconsin Act 335), tourism businesses (1989 Wisconsin Act 336), and businesses located in targeted areas of the state (1991 Wisconsin Act 39). 1993 Wisconsin Act 16 transferred the property tax deferral loan program to WHEDA from the Department of Administration. In 2005, WHEDA's Modernization Bill (2005 Wisconsin Act 75) was passed, representing the first comprehensive enhancement of WHEDA's programs in over 30 years. This legislation has increased WHEDA's financing capacity for affordable housing and business development. 2011 Wisconsin Act 79 expanded business eligibility and loan limits for WHEDA's business loan guarantee program. 2011 Wisconsin Act 214, signed into law in 2012, allowed the authority to issue federally tax-exempt bonds to finance new business expansion projects. In July 2012, WHEDA removed its first-time home buyer requirement for its home loans, enabling more Wisconsin families to qualify for an affordable mortgage.

NONPROFIT CORPORATIONS

A public nonprofit corporation is created by the legislature for a specific purpose.

BRADLEY CENTER SPORTS AND ENTERTAINMENT CORPORATION

Board of Directors: MARC J. MAROTTA, *chairperson;* GAIL A. LIONE, MATTHEW J. PARLOW, MICHAEL J. SPECTOR (nominated by Bradley Family Foundation); MICHAEL W. GREBE, TED D. KELLNER, PATRICK S. LAWTON, ANDREW A. PETZOLD, GARY D. SWEENEY. (All are appointed by governor.)

Mailing Address: 1001 North Fourth Street, Milwaukee 53203-1314.

Telephone: (414) 227-0400.

Fax: (414) 227-0497.

E-mail Address: scostello@bcsec.com

Internet Address: www.bmoharrisbradleycenter.com

Statutory Reference: Chapter 232.

Agency Responsibility: The Bradley Center Sports and Entertainment Corporation is a public nonprofit corporation, created by 1985 Wisconsin Act 26 as an instrumentality of the state to receive the donation of the Bradley Center, a sports and entertainment facility located in Milwaukee County, from the Bradley Center Corporation. Its responsibility is to own and operate the center for the economic and recreational benefit of the citizens of Wisconsin. The center is the home of the Milwaukee Bucks basketball team, the Milwaukee Admirals hockey team, and the Marquette University men's basketball team. Other tenants are family entertainment shows and concerts. The state and its political subdivisions are not liable for any debt or obligation of the corporation. The corporation may not divest itself of the center, nor may it dissolve unless the legislature directs it to do so by law. If the corporation is dissolved, all of its assets become state property.

State law exempts the corporation from most open records and open meeting laws applicable to state agencies, but the board must submit an annual financial statement to the governor and the legislature.

Organization: The corporation's board of directors is made up of 9 members appointed by the governor, serving staggered 7-year terms. Six members require senate consent, must "represent the diverse interests of the people of this state", and must be state residents. Three of those 6 must have executive and managerial business experience. The remaining 3 directors are nominated by the Bradley Family Foundation, Inc. No director may be an elected public official; the board selects it chairperson annually.

WISCONSIN ARTISTIC ENDOWMENT FOUNDATION

Members: Inactive.

Statutory Reference: Chapter 247.

Agency Responsibility: The Wisconsin Artistic Endowment Foundation was created as a nonprofit corporation to support the arts by converting donated property and art objects into cash and distributing these and other moneys to the arts board for programs that provide operating support to arts organizations.

Organization: The foundation was created by 2001 Wisconsin Act 16 and can only be dissolved by the legislature.

REGIONAL AGENCIES

The following agencies were created by state law to function in one specific area of the state, usually an area composed of more than one county.

REGIONAL PLANNING COMMISSIONS

Regional planning commissions advise local units of government on the planning and delivery of public services to the citizens of a defined region, and they prepare and adopt master plans for the physical development of the region they serve. Regional planning provides a way to address problems that transcend local government boundaries, and offers joint solutions for intergovernmental cooperation.

The commissions may conduct research studies; make and adopt plans for the physical, social, and economic development of the region; assist in grant writing for financial assistance; provide advisory services to local governmental units and other public and private agencies; and coordinate local programs that relate to their objectives. Many commissions serve as a one-stop source of statistical information for the local governments of their area.

Currently, there are nine regional planning commissions, serving all but five of the state's 72 counties. Their boundaries are based on such considerations as common topographical and geographical features; the extent of urban development; existence of special or acute agricultural, forestry, or other rural problems; or regional physical, social, and economic characteristics.

Among the many categories of projects developed or assisted by regional planning commissions are rail and air transportation, waste disposal and recycling, highways, air and water quality, farmland preservation and zoning, land conservation and reclamation, outdoor recreation, parking and lakefront studies, and land records modernization.

Chapter 466, Laws of 1955, created the statute that governs the state's regional planning commissions (Section 66.0309, Wisconsin Statutes) and authorized the governor (or a state agency designated by the governor) to create a regional planning commission upon petition by the local governing bodies.

Membership of regional planning commissions varies according to conditions defined by statute. Unless otherwise specified by a region's local governments, the term of office for a commissioner is six years. The commissions are funded through state and federal planning grants, contracts with local governments for special planning services, and a statutorily authorized levy of up to .003% of equalized real estate value charged to each local governmental unit.

As authorized by state law, Wisconsin's regional planning commissions have established the Association of Wisconsin Regional Planning Commissions. The association's purposes include assisting the study of common problems and serving as an information clearinghouse.

Bay-Lake Regional Planning Commission

Region: Brown, Door, Florence, Kewaunee, Manitowoc, Marinette, Oconto, and Sheboygan Counties.

Members: CHERYL R. MAXWELL (Marinette), *chairperson;* TOM SIEBER (Brown); KEN FISHER (Door); EDWIN A. KELLEY, YVONNE VAN PEMBROOK, vacancy (Florence); ERIC CORROY, BRUCE HEIDMANN, ROBERT WEIDNER (Kewaunee); CHUCK HOFFMAN, DONALD MARKWARDT, vacancy (Manitowoc); ALICE BAUMGARTEN, MARY G. MEYER (Marinette); DENNIS KROLL, THOMAS KUSSOW, vacancy (Oconto); MIKE HOTZ, ED PROCEK, TRACI ROBINSON (Sheboygan).

Executive Director: RICHARD HEATH, rheath@baylakerpc.org

Mailing Address: 441 South Jackson Street, Green Bay 54301.

Telephone: (920) 448-2820; Fax: (920) 448-2823.

Internet Address: www.baylakerpc.org

Capital Area Regional Planning Commission

Region: Dane County.

Members: Larry Palm (Mayor of Madison appointee), *chairperson;* Peter McKeever (Dane County Executive appointee), *vice chairperson;* Jeff Baylis, *secretary;* Kurt Sonnentag (Dane County Cities and Villages Association appointee), *treasurer;* Eric Hohol, Jason Kramar (Dane County Cities and Villages Association appointees); Martha Gibson, Caryl Terrell (Dane County Executive appointees); Susan Studz, Bob Wipperfurth (Dane County Towns Association appointees); Zach Brandon, Ken Golden, Warren Onken (Mayor of Madison appointees).

Executive Director: vacancy.

Deputy Director: Kamran Mesbah.

Mailing Address: City-County Building, 210 Martin Luther King Jr. Boulevard, Room 362, Madison 53703.

Telephone: 266-4137; Fax: 266-9117.

Internet Address: www.capitalarearpc.org; E-mail Address: info@capitalarearpc.org

East Central Wisconsin Regional Planning Commission

Region: Calumet, Fond du Lac*, Green Lake*, Marquette*, Menominee, Outagamie, Shawano, Waupaca, Waushara, and Winnebago Counties. *Inactive members.

Members: Robert Hermes (Menominee), *chairperson;* Donna Kalata (Waushara), *vice chairperson;* Bill Barribeau, Merlin Gentz, Pat Laughrin (Calumet); Muriel Bzdawka, Ruth M. Winter (Jeremy Johnson, alternate) (Menominee); Tim Hanna, Tom Nelson, Peter Stueck, Kevin Sturm, Michael R. Thomas (Outagamie); Ken Capelle, Jerry Erdmann, Marshal Geise (Shawano); Gary Barrington, DuWayne Federwitz, Dick Koeppen, Brian Smith (Waupaca); Neal Strehlow, Larry Timm (Waushara); David Albrecht, Ernie Bellin, Jim Erdman, Mark Harris, Ken Robl, Burk Tower (Mark Rohloff, alternate) (Winnebago).

Executive Director: Eric W. Fowle, efowle@ecwrpc.org

Mailing Address: 400 Ahnaip Street, Suite 100, Menasha 54952.

Telephone: (920) 751-4770; Fax: (920) 751-4771.

Internet Address: www.ecwrpc.org

Mississippi River Regional Planning Commission

Region: Buffalo, Crawford, Jackson, La Crosse, Monroe, Pepin, Pierce, Trempealeau, and Vernon Counties.

Members: Eugene Savage (Jackson), *chairperson;* Margaret M. Baecker (Trempealeau), *vice chairperson;* Vicki Burke (La Crosse), *secretary-treasurer;* Daniel Barr, John Schlesselman, James Scholmeier (Buffalo); Gerald F. Krachey, Ronald Leys, Greg Russell (Crawford); Ron Carney, James Christenson (Jackson); James Ehrsam, Tara Johnson (La Crosse); James Kuhn, Cedric Schnitzler, vacancy (Monroe); Norman Murray, Bruce Peterson, David Smith (Pepin); Richard Purdy, James Ross, William Schroeder (Pierce); Phillip Borreson, Ernest Vold (Trempealeau); Nancy Jaekel, James Neubauer, Jo Ann Nickelatti (Vernon).

Executive Director: Gregory D. Flogstad.

Mailing Address: 1707 Main Street, Suite 435, La Crosse 54601-3227.

Telephone: (608) 785-9396; Fax: (608) 785-9394.

Internet Address: www.mrrpc.com; E-mail Address: plan@mrrpc.com

North Central Wisconsin Regional Planning Commission

Region: Adams, Forest, Juneau, Langlade, Lincoln, Marathon, Oneida, Portage*, Vilas, and Wood Counties. *Inactive members.

Members: Erhard Huettl (Forest), *chairperson;* Bettye Nall (Marathon), *vice chairperson;* Ron Jacobson, Donald Krahn, Glenn Licitar (Adams); Jim Landru, Paul Millan (Forest); Edmund Wafle, Kenneth Winters, vacancy (Juneau); George Bornemann, Ronald Nye, Paul Schuman (Langlade); Robert Lussow, Frank Saal, Jr., Douglas Williams (Lincoln);

VIRGINIA HEINEMANN, CRAIG MCEWEN (Marathon); THOMAS RUDOLPH, 2 vacancies (Oneida); BOB EGAN, RALPH SITZBERGER, vacancy (Vilas); TOM HAFERMAN, GERALD NELSON, vacancy (Wood).

Executive Director: DENNIS L. LAWRENCE.

Mailing Address: 210 McClellan Street, Suite 210, Wausau 54403.

Telephone: (715) 849-5510; Fax: (715) 849-5110.

Internet Address: www.ncwrpc.org; E-mail Address: staff@ncwrpc.org

Northwest Regional Planning Commission

Region: Ashland, Bayfield, Burnett, Douglas, Iron, Price, Rusk, Sawyer, Taylor, and Washburn Counties and the Tribal Nations of Bad River, Lac Courte Oreilles, Lac du Flambeau, Red Cliff, and St. Croix.

Members: DOUGLAS FINN (Douglas), *chairperson;* RANDY TATUR (Rusk), *vice chairperson;* HAL HELWIG (Sawyer), *secretary-treasurer;* RICHARD PUFALL, WILLIAM WHALEN, DONNA WILLIAMSON (Ashland); JAMES CRANDALL, SHAWN MILLER (Bayfield); ED PETERSON, DON TAYLOR (Burnett); MARVIN FINNENDALE, BRUCE HAGEN, LARRY QUAM (Douglas); TOM INNES, JOSEPH PINARDI (Iron); RUSS KAPITZ, ROBERT KOPISCH, TOM RATZLAFF (Price); DAN GUDIS, vacancy (Rusk); KATHY MCCOY (Sawyer); JIM METZ, ROLLIE THUMS, MICHAEL WELLNER (Taylor); GARY CUSKEY, THOMAS MACKIE, STEVEN SATHER (Washburn); vacancy (Northwest Tribal nations representative); ROSE GURNOE-SOULIER (Red Cliff Tribal Council); GORDON THAYER (Lac Courte Oreilles Tribal Council); MARK WIGGINS, JR. (Bad River Tribal Council); STUART BEARHART (St. Croix Tribal Council).

Executive Director: MYRON SCHUSTER, mschuster@nwrpc.com

Mailing Address: 1400 South River Street, Spooner 54801-1390.

Telephone: (715) 635-2197; Fax: (715) 635-7262.

Internet Address: www.nwrpc.com

Southeastern Wisconsin Regional Planning Commission

Region: Kenosha, Milwaukee, Ozaukee, Racine, Walworth, Washington, and Waukesha Counties.

Members: DAVID L. STROIK (Washington), *chairperson;* WILLIAM R. DREW (Milwaukee), *vice chairperson;* ADELENE GREENE (Kenosha), *secretary;* NANCY RUSSELL (Walworth), *treasurer;* ROBERT W. PITTS, MICHAEL J. SKALITZKY (Kenosha); MARINA DIMITRIJEVIC, JOHN ROGERS (Milwaukee); THOMAS H. BUESTRIN, DAVID OPITZ, GUSTAV W. WIRTH, JR. (Ozaukee); GILBERT B. BAKKE, DAVE EBERLE, PEGGY SHUMWAY (Racine); CHARLES COLMAN, LINDA SEEMEYER, vacancy (Walworth); DANIEL S. SCHMIDT, DANIEL W. STOFFEL (Washington); MICHAEL CROWLEY, JOSE DELGADO, JAMES T. DWYER (Waukesha).

Executive Director: KENNETH R. YUNKER.

Mailing Address: W239 N1812 Rockwood Drive, P.O. Box 1607, Waukesha 53187-1607.

Telephone: (262) 547-6721; Fax: (262) 547-1103.

Internet Address: www.sewrpc.org; E-mail Address: sewrpc@sewrpc.org

Southwestern Wisconsin Regional Planning Commission

Region: Grant, Green, Iowa, Lafayette, and Richland Counties.

Members: ART CARTER (Green), *chairperson;* TIM MCGETTIGAN (Lafayette), *vice chairperson;* EILEEN NICKELS, JERRY WEHRLE, LARRY WOLF (Grant); NATHAN L. KLASSY, JOHN WAELTI (Green); SHIRLEY BARNES, DAVID BAUER, vacancy (Iowa); LANCE MCNAUGHTON, JACK SAUER (Lafayette); JEANETTA KIRKPATRICK, ROBERT NEAL SMITH, vacancy (Richland).

Executive Director: LAWRENCE T. WARD, l.ward@swwrpc.org

Mailing Address: 20 South Court Street, P.O. Box 262, Platteville 53818.

Telephone: (608) 342-1214; Fax: (608) 342-1220.

Internet Address: www.swwrpc.org

West Central Wisconsin Regional Planning Commission

Region: Barron, Chippewa, Clark, Dunn, Eau Claire, Polk, and St. Croix Counties.

Members: JESS MILLER (Barron), *chairperson;* LEE MCILQUHAM (Chippewa), *vice chairperson;* RICHARD CREASER (Dunn), *secretary-treasurer;* KEN JOST, BILL KOEPP (Barron); LEIGH DARROW, MICHAEL LEISZ (Chippewa); CHARLES HARWICK, CHARLES RUETH, JOE WAICHULIS, JR. (Clark); STEVE RASMUSSEN, ROBERT WALTER (Dunn); KATHLEEN CLARK, JOHN FRANK, GORDON STEINHAUER (Eau Claire); TOM ENGEL, WILLIAM JOHNSON IV, WARREN NELSON (Polk); AGNES RING, TRAVIS SCHACHTNER, LARRY WEISENBECK (St. Croix).

Executive Director: JAY TAPPEN.

Mailing Address: 800 Wisconsin Street, Mail Box 9, Eau Claire 54703-3606.

Telephone: (715) 836-2918; Fax: (715) 836-2886.

Internet Address: www.wcwrpc.org; E-mail Address: wcwrpc@wcwrpc.org

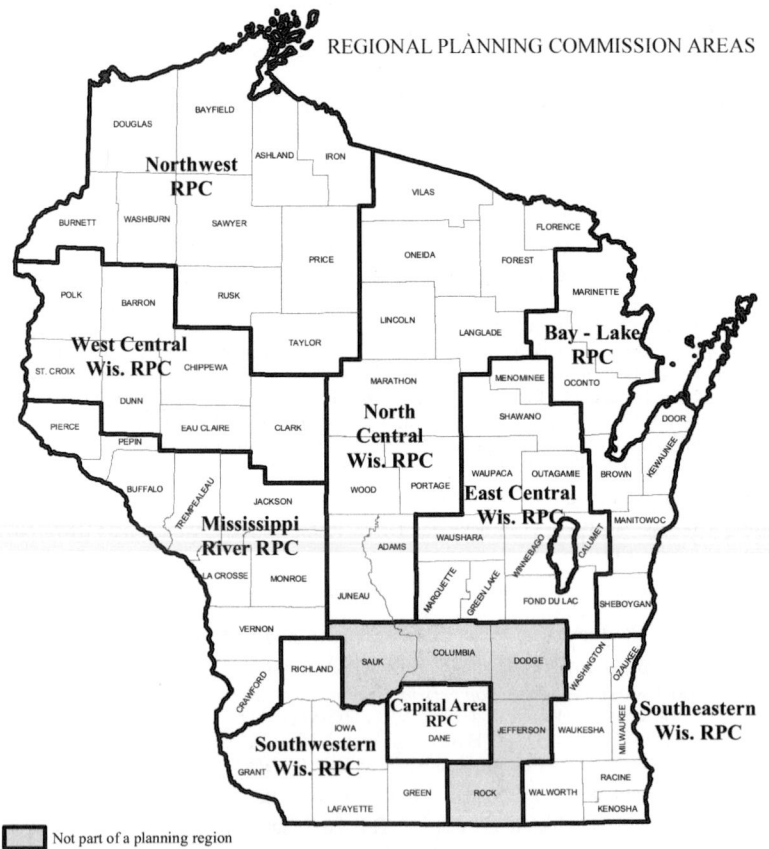

Map by Wisconsin Legislative Technology Services Bureau.

MADISON CULTURAL ARTS DISTRICT BOARD

District Board Members: SUSAN A. HAMBLIN (designated by governor); SHERYL THEO, CAROL T. TOUSSAINT, vacancy (appointed by governor); vacancy (designated by City of Madison Mayor); WILLIAM C. KEYS, vacancy (Madison School Board nominees appointed by City of Madison Mayor); ANTHONY AMATO, LINDA BALDWIN O'HERN, SCOTT RESNICK, MICHAEL E. VERVEER, SUSANNE VOELTZ (appointed by City of Madison Mayor); DIANE CHRISTIANSEN (designated by Dane County Executive); BRIAN E. BUTLER (appointed by Dane County Executive).

Statutory Reference: Chapter 229, Subchapter V.

Agency Responsibility: Arts districts are public corporations that may acquire, construct, operate, and manage cultural arts facilities. A local district may issue revenue bonds, invest funds, set standards for the use of facilities, and establish and collect fees for usage. The Madison Cultural Arts District Board's activities are suspended until requested otherwise.

PROFESSIONAL FOOTBALL STADIUM DISTRICT

Board Members: ANN PATTESON, *chairperson;* KEN GOLOMSKI, *vice chairperson;* CHUCK LAMINE, *secretary;* MARGARET JENSEN, *treasurer;* RON ANTONNEAU, ROBERT COWLES, KEITH ZIMMERMAN.

Statutory Reference: Chapter 229, Subchapter IV.

Agency Responsibility: The Professional Football Stadium District is an owner and landlord of Lambeau Field, the designated home of the Green Bay Packers football team. It is a public corporation that may acquire, construct, equip, maintain, improve, operate, and manage football stadium facilities or hire others to do the same. The district issued bonds for the redevelopment of Lambeau Field, which was substantially completed on July 31, 2003. All district debt was retired August 1, 2011. Maintenance and operation of the stadium is governed by provisions of the Lambeau Field Lease Agreement by and among the district, Green Bay Packers, Inc., and the City of Green Bay. The district currently imposes a 0.5% sales and use tax approved by Brown County voters in a referendum. Proceeds from the tax can be used for district administrative expenses, maintenance, and operating costs of stadium facilities and related purposes consistent with statutory limitations and lease provisions. In accordance with statutory provisions, the tax will be extinguished once sufficient funds are escrowed for maintenance and operation of the stadium and district administrative expenses. The district was created by 1999 Wisconsin Act 167.

SOUTHEAST WISCONSIN PROFESSIONAL BASEBALL PARK DISTRICT

District Board Members: DON SMILEY (Milwaukee County, appointed by governor), *chairperson;* DANIEL MCKEITHAN, JR. (Milwaukee County, appointed by chief executive officer), *vice chairperson;* MARK THOMSEN (City of Milwaukee representative appointed by mayor), *secretary;* KAREN MAKOUTZ (Ozaukee County, appointed by chief executive officer), *treasurer;* JERRY GONZALEZ (Ozaukee County), BILL MCREYNOLDS (Racine County), KRISTINE O'MEARA (Washington County), TRACEY KLEIN (Waukesha County) (county members appointed by governor); ERIK JOHNSON (at-large member, appointed by governor); MICHAEL GONZALEZ (Milwaukee County), DOUGLAS STANSIL (Racine County), MARK MCCUNE (Washington County), BILL MASLOWSKI (Waukesha County) (members appointed by county's chief executive officer).

Executive Director: MICHAEL R. DUCKETT.

Mailing Address: Miller Park, One Brewers Way, Milwaukee 53214.

Telephone: (414) 902-4040.

Fax: (414) 902-4033.

Internet Address: www.millerparkdistrict.com

Statutory Reference: Chapter 229, Subchapter III.

Agency Responsibility: The Southeast Wisconsin Professional Baseball Park District is majority owner of Miller Park, the home of the Milwaukee Brewers Baseball Club. It is a public corporation that may acquire, construct, maintain, improve, operate, and manage baseball park facilities which include parking lots, garages, restaurants, parks, concession facilities, entertainment facilities, and other related structures. The district may impose a sales tax and a use tax at a rate not to exceed 0.1%.

The district is also authorized to issue bonds for certain purposes related to baseball park facilities. A city or county within the district's jurisdiction may make loans or grants to the district, expend funds to subsidize the district, borrow money for baseball park facilities, or grant property to the state dedicated for use by a professional baseball park.

The district, which was created by 1995 Wisconsin Act 56, includes Milwaukee, Ozaukee, Racine, Washington, and Waukesha Counties. The district board consists of 13 members, 6 appointed by the governor, 6 appointed by the chief executive officers of each county in the district (2 from the most populous county), and one appointed by the mayor of Milwaukee. The governor appoints the chairperson. Members appointed by the governor must be confirmed by the senate. Members appointed by county executive officers or the mayor of Milwaukee must be confirmed by their respective county boards or the city council.

WISCONSIN CENTER DISTRICT

Board of Directors: WILLIE L. HINES, JR. (Milwaukee Common Council President), *secretary;* MARTIN MATSON (City of Milwaukee comptroller), *treasurer;* SENATOR DARLING (designated by senate cochairperson, Joint Committee on Finance), REPRESENTATIVE KOOYENGA (designated by assembly cochairperson, Joint Committee on Finance); CHRIS SCHOENHERR (designated by secretary of administration); STEPHEN H. MARCUS, 2 vacancies (private sector representatives appointed by governor); ANDY NUNEMAKER, JEFF SHERMAN (private sector representatives appointed by Milwaukee County Executive); KATHY EHLEY (mayor of city that contributes room taxes appointed by Milwaukee County Executive); ALDERMEN HAMILTON, PUENTE (public sector representatives appointed by Milwaukee Common Council President); JOEL BRENNAN, vacancy (private sector representative appointed by Mayor of City of Milwaukee).

President and CEO: RICHARD A. GEYER, (414) 908-6050, rgeyer@wcd.org

Mailing Address: 400 West Wisconsin Avenue, Milwaukee 53203.

Telephone: (414) 908-6000.

Fax: (414) 908-6010.

Internet Addresses: www.wcd.org, www.frontierairlinescenter.org, www.milwaukeetheatre.org, www.uscellulararena.com

Statutory Reference: Chapter 229, Subchapter II.

Agency Responsibility: The Wisconsin Center District (WCD) owns and operates the U.S. Cellular Arena, the Milwaukee Theatre, and the Frontier Airlines Center. The district is not supported by property taxes or state subsidies. It is funded by operating revenue and special sales taxes on hotel rooms, restaurant food and beverages, and car rentals within its taxing boundaries (Milwaukee County). The WCD is classified by law as a local exposition district that may acquire, construct, and operate an exposition center and related facilities; enter into contracts and grant concessions; mortgage district property and issue bonds; and invest funds as the district board considers appropriate. Local exposition districts are public corporations. Interest income on exposition district bonds is tax-exempt, and the district is exempt from state income and franchise taxes.

The board has 15 members, 13 of whom serve 3-year terms. Legislative members serve for terms concurrent with their term of office. Public officials can no longer serve after their term of office expires. Public sector representatives appointed by the Milwaukee Common Council President must be city residents. The 2 private sector representatives the Mayor of Milwaukee appoints must reside in the city. The private sector representatives the county executive appoints must live outside the City of Milwaukee. Of the 4 gubernatorial appointees, 2 must live in Milwaukee County but not in the City of Milwaukee. The governor's appointees must include the secretary of the state Department of Administration (or designee), a member who has significant involvement with the lodging industry, and a member who has significant involvement with the food and beverage industry. Local exposition districts were authorized by 1993 Wisconsin Act 263.

INTERSTATE AGENCIES AND COMPACTS

Wisconsin is party to a variety of interstate compacts. These agreements are binding on two or more states, and they establish uniform guidelines or procedures for agencies within the signatory states. The following section lists agencies created by enactment of enabling legislation in all of the participating states or by interstate agreement of their respective governors. It also describes interstate compacts that are expressly ratified in the Wisconsin Statutes but do not require appointment of delegates.

EDUCATION COMMISSION OF THE STATES

Wisconsin Delegates: GOVERNOR WALKER, *chairperson;* TONY EVERS (superintendent of public instruction); SENATOR OLSEN; REPRESENTATIVE KESTELL; TRACIE HAPPEL, DEMOND MEANS, vacancy (public members appointed by governor).

Mailing Address: National commission: Education Commission of the States, 700 Broadway, #810, Denver, Colorado 80203-3442.

Telephone: National Commission: (303) 299-3600.

Internet Address: www.ecs.org

Statutory References: Sections 39.75 and 39.76.

Agency Responsibility: The Education Commission of the States was established to foster national cooperation among executive, legislative, educational, and lay leaders of the various states. It offers a forum for discussing policy alternatives in the education field; provides an information clearinghouse about educational problems and their various solutions throughout the nation; and facilitates the improvement of state and local educational systems. The governor designates the chairperson of the 7-member delegation, and the Department of Administration provides staff services. Wisconsin's participation in the commission originated in Chapter 641, Laws of 1965, which established an interstate compact for education and specified the composition of the Wisconsin delegation.

GREAT LAKES COMMISSION

Wisconsin Members: KENNETH JOHNSON (state officer member), *chairperson;* STEVE GALARNEAU, DEAN HAEN (all appointed by governor).

Mailing Address: Great Lakes Commission: TIM A. EDER, *executive director,* 2805 South Industrial Highway, Suite 100, Ann Arbor, Michigan 48104.

Telephones: Wisconsin Delegation Chair: (608) 264-6278; Great Lakes Commission: (734) 971-9135.

Commission Fax: (734) 971-9150.

Internet Address: www.glc.org

Publications of the Great Lakes Commission: *Advisor; Annual Report.*

Statutory Reference: Section 14.78.

Agency Responsibility: A 3-member delegation represents Wisconsin on the 8-state Great Lakes Commission. The interstate commission promotes orderly development of the water resources of the Great Lakes Basin; offers advice on balancing industrial, commercial, agricultural, water supply, and residential and recreational uses of the lakes' water resources; and enables basin residents to benefit from public works, such as navigational aids.

Commissioners from the states of Illinois, Indiana, Michigan, Minnesota, New York, Ohio, Pennsylvania, and Wisconsin share information and coordinate state positions on issues of regional concern.

Organization: The governor appoints the 3 Wisconsin delegates to the Great Lakes Commission. The delegates are chosen on the basis of their knowledge of and interest in Great Lakes Basin problems. One commissioner, who must be a state officer or employee, is appointed to an indefinite term and serves as secretary of Wisconsin's compact commission and as a member of the executive committee of the interstate commission. Wisconsin's other commissioners serve 4-year terms.

History: The Great Lakes Commission was established in 1955 following enactment of enabling legislation by a majority of the Great Lakes states. It replaced the Deep Waterways Commission, established to promote the St. Lawrence Seaway project. With enactment of Chapter 275, Laws of 1955, Wisconsin ratified the Great Lakes Basin Compact and created the Wisconsin Great Lakes Compact Commission, consisting of the state members of the Great Lakes Commission. Congress recognized the Great Lakes Basin Compact in P.L. 90-419 on July 24, 1968.

GREAT LAKES PROTECTION FUND

Wisconsin Representatives: KENNETH JOHNSON, RICHARD MEEUSEN (appointed by governor with senate consent).

Mailing Address and Telephone: RUSS VAN HERIK, *executive director,* 1560 Sherman Avenue, Suite 880, Evanston, Illinois 60201, (847) 425-8150, Fax: (847) 424-9832.

Internet Address: www.glpf.org

Statutory Reference: Section 14.84.

Agency Responsibility: The Great Lakes Protection Fund was created by the Council of Great Lakes Governors to finance projects for the protection and cleanup of the Great Lakes. Priorities include the prevention of toxic pollution, the identification of effective clean-up ap-

Lake Superior entry lighthouse. (Department of Tourism)

proaches, the demonstration of natural resource stewardship, and the classification of health effects of toxic pollution.

In 1989, the governors of Illinois, Michigan, Minnesota, New York, Ohio, Pennsylvania, and Wisconsin signed the formal agreement creating the Great Lakes Protection Fund, and the Wisconsin Legislature approved the state's participation in 1989 Wisconsin Act 31. The fund was incorporated as a not-for-profit corporation, managed by a board of directors composed of 2 representatives from each member state. Each state's contribution to the original $100 million endowment was determined by estimating its proportion of Great Lakes water consumption. Wisconsin's share was $12 million.

GREAT LAKES-ST. LAWRENCE RIVER BASIN WATER RESOURCES COUNCIL

Wisconsin Members: GOVERNOR WALKER *(chair)*; CATHY STEPP (secretary of department of natural resources) (alternate).

Mailing Address: Great Lakes-St. Lawrence River Basin Water Resources Council, c/o Council of Great Lakes Governors: DAVID NAFTZGER, *executive director*, 20 North Wacker Drive, Suite 2700, Chicago, Illinois 60606.

Telephone: Secretariat, Council of Great Lakes Governors: (312) 407-0177.

Secretariat, Council of Great Lakes Governors Fax: (312) 407-0038.

E-mail Address: cglg@cglg.org

Internet Address: www.glslcompactcouncil.org

Statutory References: Sections 14.95, 281.343.

Agency Responsibility: The governor serves as Wisconsin's representative on the council. The council is charged with aiding and promoting the coordination of the activities and programs of the Great Lakes states concerned with water resources management in the Great Lakes basin. The council may promulgate and enforce rules and regulations as may be necessary for the implementation and enforcement of the Great Lakes-St. Lawrence River Basin Water Resources Compact. The compact governs withdrawals, consumptive uses, conservation and efficient use, and diversions of basin water resources.

Under the compact, the governors from the states of Illinois, Indiana, Michigan, Minnesota, New York, Ohio, Pennsylvania, and Wisconsin, jointly pursue intergovernmental cooperation and consultation to protect, conserve, restore, improve, and effectively manage the waters and water dependent natural resources of the basin.

Organization: The governors of all participating states are *ex officio* members of the council. The governor may designate the secretary of natural resources as his alternate to attend and vote at all meetings. Any other alternate must be nominated by the governor with the advice and consent of the senate. The alternate serves at the pleasure of the governor. The governor may also appoint an advisor to attend all meetings of the council. If the governor does appoint an advisor, that person must have knowledge of and experience with Great Lakes water management issues.

History: The council was created by the ratification of the Great Lakes-St. Lawrence River Basin Water Resources Compact. Wisconsin joined the compact with the passage and signing of 2007 Wisconsin Act 227. Congress ratified the compact in Public Law 110-342. The compact became effective as state and federal law on December 8, 2008.

GREAT LAKES-ST. LAWRENCE RIVER
WATER RESOURCES REGIONAL BODY

Wisconsin Members: GOVERNOR WALKER *(chair);* CATHY STEPP (secretary of department of natural resources), *designee.*

Mailing Address: Great Lakes-St. Lawrence River Basin Water Resources Council, c/o Council of Great Lakes Governors: DAVID NAFTZGER, *secretary,* 20 North Wacker Drive, Suite 2700, Chicago, Illinois 60606.

Telephone: Secretariat, Council of Great Lakes Governors: (312) 407-0177.

Secretariat, Council of Great Lakes Governors Fax: (312) 407-0038.

E-mail Address: cglg@cglg.org

Internet Address: www.glslregionalbody.org

Statutory Reference: Section 281.343.

Agency Responsibility: The governor serves as Wisconsin's representative on the regional body. The regional body is charged with aiding and promoting the coordination of the activities and programs of the Great Lakes states and provinces concerned with water resources management in the Great Lakes basin. The regional body may develop procedures for implementation of the Great Lakes-St. Lawrence River Basin Water Resources Sustainable Water Resources Agreement. The agreement is a good-faith agreement between Great Lakes states and provinces that governs withdrawals, consumptive uses, conservation and efficient use, and diversions of basin water resources.

Governors from the states of Illinois, Indiana, Michigan, Minnesota, New York, Ohio, Pennsylvania, and Wisconsin, and the premiers of Ontario and Quebec jointly pursue intergovernmental cooperation and consultation to protect, conserve, restore, improve, and manage the waters and water dependent natural resources of the basin.

Organization: The governors and premiers of all participating states are *ex officio* members of the regional body. The governor may designate an alternate to attend and vote at all meetings. The designee serves at the pleasure of the governor.

History: The regional body was created by Great Lakes governors and premiers by signing the Great Lakes-St. Lawrence River Basin Sustainable Water Resources Agreement on December 13, 2005. Parts of the agreement entered into force on the day the agreement was signed. Other parts will enter into force once all of the parties have enacted the necessary state or provincial measures.

INTERSTATE INSURANCE PRODUCT REGULATION COMMISSION

Wisconsin Member: TED NICKEL (commissioner of insurance).

Mailing Address: Commission: 444 North Capitol Street NW, Hall of the States, Suite 701, Washington, D.C. 20001-1509.

Telephone: Commission: (202) 471-3962.

Commission Fax: (816) 460-7476.

Internet Address: www.insurancecompact.org

Statutory References: Sections 14.82 and 601.58.

Agency Responsibility: The Interstate Insurance Product Regulation Commission is made up of the member states of the Interstate Insurance Product Regulation Compact. The compact's purposes are to develop uniform standards for life, annuity, disability income, and long-term care insurance products, create a central clearinghouse to provide prompt review of insurance products, approve product filings, long-term care advertisements and disability income and long-term care rate filings that satisfy uniform standards, and improve coordination of regulatory resources and expertise between state insurance departments. The commission establishes reasonable uniform standards for insurance products covered under the compact. As of June 2013, 42 states and Puerto Rico were members of the compact.

Organization: Wisconsin is represented on the commission by the state's commissioner of insurance or his or her designee. Each state member is entitled to one vote.

History: The commission reached its operational threshold in 2006. Wisconsin joined the commission with the signing of 2007 Wisconsin Act 168 in March 2008.

INTERSTATE COMMISSION FOR JUVENILES

Wisconsin Member: SHELLEY HAGAN, *compact administrator,* Office of Juvenile Offender Review, Division of Juvenile Corrections, Wisconsin Department of Corrections.

Mailing Address: 836 Euclid Avenue, Suite 322, Lexington, Kentucky 40502.

Telephone: (859) 721-1062.

E-mail Address: icjadmin@juvenilecompact.org

Internet Address: www.juvenilecompact.org

Statutory References: Sections 14.92 and 938.999.

Agency Responsibility: The Interstate Commission for Juveniles is designed to oversee, supervise, and coordinate the interstate movement of certain juveniles, delinquents, and run-away offenders. The commission has the authority to promulgate rules, which have the effect of statutory law, and enforce compliance with the Interstate Compact for Juveniles, including through judicial means. The commission is directed to resolve disputes between states regarding the compact, levy assessments against compacting states to cover its costs, and report annually on its activities. The commission is also directed to collect standardized data concerning the interstate movement of juveniles. The commission came into existence when 35 states ratified the Interstate Compact for Juveniles in August 2008.

Organization: The commission is composed of one commissioner from each of the compacting states. Each compacting state has one vote on the interstate commission. The commission will meet at least once per year. The Council of State Governments provides organizational support to the commission.

INTERSTATE WILDLIFE VIOLATOR COMPACT ADMINISTRATORS BOARD

Wisconsin Administrator: JENNIFER MCDONOUGH, jennifer.mcdonough@wisconsin.gov

Mailing Address: Wisconsin Department of Natural Resources, P.O. Box 7921, Madison 53707-7921.

Telephone: (608) 267-0859.

Statutory Reference: Section 29.03.

Agency Responsibility: The Interstate Wildlife Violator Compact establishes a process whereby wildlife law violations by a nonresident while in a member state may be handled as if the person were a resident in the state where the violation took place, meaning personal recognizance may be permitted instead of arrest, booking, and bonding. The process is aimed at increasing the efficiency of conservation wardens by allowing more time for enforcement duties rather than violator processing. The compact requires each member state to recognize the revocations and suspensions of individuals hunting, fishing, and trapping privileges from other member states that result from a wildlife related violation. The compact also requires each member state to revoke or suspend the hunting, fishing, and trapping licenses of any resident of that state who violates a wildlife related law in another member state and fails to resolve the matter by payment of the penalty or appearance in court. The board of compact administrators was established to serve as the governing body for the resolution of all matters relating to the operation of the compact.

Organization: The board is composed of one representative from each participating state. The Wisconsin representative is appointed by the secretary of natural resources. Each member of the board has one vote. As of June 2013, 38 states are members of the compact.

History: Wisconsin was authorized to develop administrative rules for Wisconsin's role in the Wildlife Violator Compact and apply to become a member of the compact with the signing of 2005 Wisconsin Act 282 in April 2006. Once the administrative rules were adopted and in effect, Wisconsin applied to become a member of the Wildlife Violator Compact and was accepted effective April 15, 2008.

LOWER ST. CROIX MANAGEMENT COMMISSION

Wisconsin Member: DAN BAUMANN (designated by secretary of natural resources).

Telephone and Mailing Address: Department of Natural Resources, West Central Region, 1300 West Clairemont Avenue, Eau Claire 54701, (715) 839-3700.

Agency Responsibility: The Lower St. Croix Management Commission was created to provide a forum for discussion of problems and programs associated with the Lower St. Croix National Scenic Riverway. It coordinates planning, development, protection, and management of the riverway for Wisconsin, Minnesota, and the U.S. government.

The commission was created by a cooperative agreement signed in 1973 by the National Park Service and the governors of Wisconsin and Minnesota. It consists of one member each from the National Park Service and the natural resources departments of the two states.

MIDWEST INTERSTATE LOW-LEVEL RADIOACTIVE WASTE COMMISSION

Wisconsin Member: STANLEY YORK (appointed by governor with senate consent).

Mailing Address: Chair and Executive Director Stanley York, Midwest Interstate Low-Level Radioactive Waste Commission, P.O. Box 2659, Madison 53701-2659.

Telephones: Wisconsin member: 230-3532; Commission: 267-4793.

E-Mail Address: Wisconsin member: stan.york@tds.net

Commission Fax: 267-4799.

Statutory References: Sections 14.81 and 16.11.

Agency Responsibility: The Midwest Interstate Low-Level Radioactive Waste Commission is responsible for the disposal of low-level radioactive wastes. Based on the Midwest Interstate Low-Level Radioactive Waste Compact, it may negotiate agreements for disposal of waste at facilities within or outside the region; appear as an intervenor before any court, board, or commission in any matter related to waste management; and review the emergency closure of a regional facility. The commission is directed to settle disputes between party states regarding the compact and adopt a regional management plan designating host states for the establishment of needed regional facilities.

Wisconsin's commission member must promote Wisconsin's interest in an equitable distribution of responsibilities among compact member states, encourage public access and participation in the commission's proceedings, and notify the governor and legislature if the commission proposes to designate a disposal facility site in this state.

Organization: The commission represents Indiana, Iowa, Minnesota, Missouri, Ohio, and Wisconsin, each of which has one voting member.

History: 1983 Wisconsin Act 393 ratified the Midwest Interstate Low-Level Radioactive Waste Compact, which provided for formation of the Midwest Low-Level Radioactive Waste Commission. The U.S. Congress encouraged the development of such compacts by enacting the Low-Level Radioactive Waste Policy Act in 1980, as amended by the Low-Level Radioactive Waste Policy Amendments Act of 1985.

Door County shore at sunset. *(Department of Tourism)*

MIDWEST INTERSTATE PASSENGER RAIL COMMISSION

Wisconsin Representatives: MARK GOTTLIEB (designated by governor); REPRESENTATIVE THIESFELDT (appointed by assembly speaker); SENATOR RISSER (appointed by senate president); CRAIG ANDERSON (private sector representative).

Mailing Address: Commission: LAURA KLIEWER, *director,* 701 East 22nd Street, Suite 110, Lombard, Illinois 60148.

Telephone: Commission: (630) 925-1922.

Commission Fax: (630) 925-1930.

Internet Address: www.miprc.org

Statutory References: Sections 14.86 and 85.067.

Agency Responsibility: The Midwest Interstate Passenger Rail Commission brings together state leaders from the members of the Midwest Interstate Passenger Rail Compact to advocate for the funding and authorization necessary to make passenger rail improvements. It also seeks to develop a long-term interstate plan for high-speed passenger rail service implementation. The current members are Illinois, Indiana, Kansas, Michigan, Minnesota, Missouri, Nebraska, North Dakota, Ohio, and Wisconsin. The commission is empowered to work with local and federal officials, to educate the public on the advantages of passenger rail, and to make recommendations to member states.

Organization: Wisconsin is represented by 4 members on the commission. Those members must be the governor or his or her designee; one assembly member appointed by the assembly speaker for a 2-year term; one senate member appointed by the senate president for a 2-year term; and one member representing the private sector, who serves for the governor's term of office. The members serve without compensation.

History: The Midwest Interstate Passenger Rail Compact became operational in 2000 when three states, Indiana, Minnesota, and Missouri, approved it. Wisconsin joined the compact and gained commission membership with the signing of 2007 Wisconsin Act 117 in April 2008.

MIDWESTERN HIGHER EDUCATION COMMISSION

Wisconsin Members: DON MADELUNG (designated by governor); SENATOR HARSDORF (appointed by senate president); REPRESENTATIVE NASS (appointed by assembly speaker); ROLF WEGENKE, GERALD WHITBURN; MORNA FOY, MICHAEL MORGAN (alternates) (appointed by governor).

Mailing Address: 105 Fifth Avenue South, Suite 450, Minneapolis, Minnesota 55401.

Telephone: (612) 677-2777; (855) 767-6432 (toll free).

Internet Address: http://mhec.org

Statutory References: Sections 14.90 and 39.80.

Agency Responsibility: The Midwestern Higher Education Commission was organized to further higher educational opportunities for residents of states participating in the Midwest Higher Education Compact. The commission may enter into agreements with member and non-member states, or their universities and colleges, to provide programs and services for students, including student exchanges and improved access. The commission also studies the effects of the compact on higher education and the needs and resources for programs in member states. The compact's three core functions are cost-savings initiatives, student access, and policy research and analysis.

Organization: The compact currently includes Illinois, Indiana, Iowa, Kansas, Michigan, Minnesota, Missouri, Nebraska, North Dakota, Ohio, South Dakota, and Wisconsin. Each state appoints 5 members to the governing commission, including the governor (or governor's designee) and 2 legislators, who serve 2-year terms. The 2 members appointed by the governor must be selected from the field of higher education. One serves a 4-year term and one serves a 2-year term. Any member state may withdraw from the compact 2 years after the passage of a law authorizing withdrawal.

History: Wisconsin ratified the Midwestern Higher Education Compact in 1993 Wisconsin Act 358, effective July 1, 1994.

MILITARY INTERSTATE CHILDREN'S COMPACT COMMISSION

State Council: TONY EVERS (state superintendent of public instruction); JOHN HENDRICKS (superintendent of school district with high concentration of children of military families, appointed by state superintendent); LT. COL. JOHN BLAHA (representative from a military installation, appointed by state superintendent); vacancy (appointed by assembly speaker); SENATOR PETROWSKI (appointed by senate majority leader). Nonvoting members: SHELLEY WEISS (appointed by state superintendent), compact commissioner; BECKY WALLEY (military family education liaison, appointed by state superintendent)

Contact: SHELLEY WEISS.

Mailing Address: 3014 Happy Valley Road, Sun Prairie 53590.

Telephone: (608) 698-2409.

Statutory References: Sections 14.91 and 115.997.

Agency Responsibility: The Military Interstate Children's Compact Commission oversees implementation of the Interstate Compact on Educational Opportunity for Military Children. The compact was enacted to facilitate the education of children of military families, and remove barriers to educational success imposed by frequent moves and the deployment of parents. The commission has the authority to promulgate rules, and enforce compliance with the compact, including through judicial means. The commission may provide for the resolution of disputes between states regarding the compact and issue advisory opinions concerning the meaning of the compact. As of June 2013, 43 states have ratified the compact.

Organization: The commission is composed of one commissioner from each of the compacting states. Each compacting state has one vote on the interstate commission. The commission will meet at least once per year. The Council of State Governments provides organizational support to the commission.

History: Wisconsin joined the compact upon passage of 2009 Wisconsin Act 329, effective May 26, 2010.

MISSISSIPPI RIVER PARKWAY COMMISSION

Wisconsin Commissioners: ALAN L. LORENZ (La Crosse County), *chairperson;* KATHLEEN GOODMAN (Buffalo County), *treasurer;* SENATORS SCHULTZ, VINEHOUT; REPRESENTATIVES NERISON, DANOU; SHERRY QUAMME (Crawford County); HANS KOSTRAU (Grant County); DENNIS DONATH (Pierce County); BRUCE QUINTON (Pepin County); JEAN GALASINSKI (Trempealeau County); MARK CLEMENTS (Vernon County). (Legislators are nominated by presiding officer and appointed by governor. County representatives are appointed by governor.) Nonvoting members: CATHY STEPP (secretary of natural resources), MARK GOTTLIEB (secretary of transportation), ELLSWORTH BROWN (director, state historical society), STEPHANIE KLETT (secretary of tourism).

Contact: ALAN L. LORENZ, alanlorenz@centurytel.net

Mailing Address: W4927 Hoeth Street, La Crosse 54601.

Telephone: (608) 788-8264.

Statutory Reference: Section 14.85.

Agency Responsibility: The Mississippi River Parkway Commission coordinates development and preservation of Wisconsin's portion of the Great River Road corridor along the Mississippi River. It assists and advises state and local agencies about maintaining and enhancing the scenic, historic, economic, and recreational assets within the corridor and cooperates with similar commissions in other Mississippi River states and the Province of Ontario. On June 15, 2000, the U.S. Secretary of Transportation designated the entire 250-mile length of the Wisconsin Great River Road as a National Scenic Byway, thereby recognizing it as an outstanding example of America's scenic beauty. It is Wisconsin's only National Scenic Byway.

Organization: The 16-member Wisconsin commission includes 12 voting members, appointed to 4-year terms, and 4 nonvoting *ex officio* members. The 4 legislative members represent the two major political parties in each house.

The commission selects its own chairperson who is Wisconsin's sole voting representative at national meetings of the Mississippi River Parkway Commission.

History: The Wisconsin commission is part of the Mississippi River Parkway Commission, which was given statutory recognition by Chapter 482, Laws of 1961. It dates back to 1939 when Wisconsin Governor Julius P. Heil appointed a 10-member committee to cooperate with agencies from other Mississippi River states in planning the Great River Road. This scenic route extends from the Gulf of Mexico to the Mississippi River's headwaters at Lake Itasca, Minnesota. North of Lake Itasca, the route connects with the Trans-Canada Highway and terminates at Minaki, Ontario.

The Federal Highway Aid Acts of 1973, 1976, and 1978 provided Wisconsin approximately $21 million in Great River Road funding. While categorical funding is no longer available, the Wisconsin Department of Transportation has continued improvements to Wisconsin's portion of the Great River Road, including pedestrian and bicycle trails, landscaping, preservation of historic sites, and other programs. Wisconsin has also received more than $7 million in discretionary grants from the National Scenic Byways Program from 2000 through 2008. These grants were matched with 20% state and local government funds. The commission also boasts an active Promotions Committee, comprised of volunteers and commissioners who are active in the Wisconsin tourism industry.

UPPER MISSISSIPPI RIVER BASIN ASSOCIATION

Wisconsin Representative: DAN BAUMANN, JAMES FISCHER (alternate) (appointed by governor).

Mailing Addresses: Wisconsin representative: 1300 West Clairemont Avenue, Eau Claire 54701. Upper Mississippi River Basin Association: DRU BUNTIN, *executive director,* 415 Hamm Building, 408 St. Peter Street, St. Paul, Minnesota 55102.

Telephones: Wisconsin: (715) 839-3722; Minnesota: (612) 224-2880.

Internet Address: www.umrba.org

Agency Responsibility: The Upper Mississippi River Basin Association is a nonprofit organization created by Illinois, Iowa, Minnesota, Missouri, and Wisconsin to facilitate cooperative action regarding the basin's water and related land resources. It sponsors studies of river-related issues, cooperative planning for use of the region's resources, and an information exchange. It also enables the member states to develop regional positions on resource issues and to advocate the basin states' collective interests before the U.S. Congress and federal agencies. The association has placed major emphasis on its Environmental Management Program, a partnership among the U.S. Army Corps of Engineers, the U.S. Fish and Wildlife Service, and the five states. This program, which was approved by the federal Water Resources Development Act of 1986, authorized habitat rehabilitation projects, resource inventory and analysis, recreation projects, and river traffic monitoring.

Organization: The association consists of one representative from each member state. The members annually elect one of their number to serve as chairperson. Five federal agencies with major water resources responsibilities serve as advisory members: the Environmental Protection Agency and the U.S. Departments of Agriculture, Army, Interior, and Transportation.

History: The Upper Mississippi River Basin Association was formed on December 2, 1981, when the articles of association were signed by representatives of the member states. In late 1983 and early 1984, executive orders were issued by four of the five governors reaffirming membership in the association.

Wisconsin has many scenic roadways that are especially beautiful in the fall, including this roadway in Marinette County. (Department of Tourism)

INTERSTATE COMPACTS

Interstate Compact on Adoption and Medical Assistance

The compact authorizes the Department of Children and Families, on behalf of this state, to enter into interstate agreements, including the interstate compact on adoption and medical assistance, with other states that enter into adoption assistance agreements. In these agreements, other states must provide Medical Assistance (MA) benefits, under its own laws, to children who were adopted as residents of Wisconsin, and Wisconsin must provide the same benefits to children who were adopted as residents of other states. Any interstate agreement is revocable upon written notice to the other state but remains in effect for one year after the date of the notice. Benefits already granted continue even if the agreement is revoked. The compact has been adopted by 49 states and the District of Columbia. (1985 Wisconsin Act 308)

Statutory Reference: Section 48.9985.

Administrator: Department of Children and Families.

Interstate Compact for Adult Offender Supervision

The compact creates cooperative procedures for individuals placed on parole, probation, or extended supervision in one state to be supervised in another state if certain conditions are met. The compact has been adopted by all 50 states, the District of Columbia, U.S. Virgin Islands, and Puerto Rico. (2001 Wisconsin Act 96)

Statutory Reference: Section 304.16.

Administrator: Department of Corrections (appointed by governor).

Corrections Compact

The compact allows Wisconsin to enter into contracts with states that are party to the compact to confine Wisconsin's inmates in the other state's correctional facilities or receive inmates from other states. The contract provides for inmate upkeep and special services. The compact has been adopted by 39 states and the District of Columbia. (Chapter 20, Laws of 1981)

Statutory Reference: Sections 302.25-302.26.

Administrator: Department of Corrections.

Agreement on Detainers

The agreement is designed to clear up indictments or complaints that serve as a basis for a detainer lodged against a prisoner incarcerated in one jurisdiction and wanted in another. The agreement allows the state making the request to obtain temporary custody of the prisoner to conduct a trial on outstanding charges. The agreement has been adopted by 48 states and the District of Columbia. (Chapter 255, Laws of 1969)

Statutory Reference: Sections 976.05 and 976.06.

Emergency Management Assistance Compact

The compact authorizes states that are members to provide mutual assistance to other member states in an emergency or disaster declared by the governor of the affected state. Under the compact, member states cooperate in emergency-related training and formulate plans for interstate cooperation in responding to a disaster. All 50 states now belong to the compact. (1999 Wisconsin Act 26)

Statutory Reference: Section 323.80.

Administrator: Division of Emergency Management, Department of Military Affairs.

Interstate Compact on Mental Health

The compact facilitates the proper and expeditious treatment of persons with mental illness or mental retardation by the cooperative action of the party states, to the benefit of the person, their families, and society. The compact (and enacting laws) provides for this to be done irrespective of the legal residence and citizenship status of the person. The compact has been adopted in 45 states and the District of Columbia. (Chapter 611, Laws of 1965)

Statutory Reference: Sections 51.75-51.80.

Administrator: Department of Health Services.

Nurse Licensure Compact

The compact allows a nurse licensed by a party state to practice nursing in any other party state without obtaining a license. It requires each party state to participate in a database of all licensed nurses. The compact has been adopted by Arizona, Arkansas, Colorado, Delaware, Idaho, Iowa, Kentucky, Maine, Maryland, Mississippi, Missouri, Nebraska, New Hampshire, New Mexico, North Carolina, North Dakota, Rhode Island, South Carolina, South Dakota, Tennessee, Texas, Utah, Virginia, and Wisconsin. (1999 Wisconsin Act 22)

Statutory Reference: Section 441.50.

Administrator: Department of Safety and Professional Services.

Interstate Compact on Placement of Children

The compact provides a legal framework to administer the compact law among the party states to ensure protection and services when a child is placed across state lines when under the jurisdiction of that state and the most suitable placement is in a different state. It requires notice and proof of appropriateness and safety before a placement is made; allocates legal and administrative responsibilities by the sending state for the duration of placement; provides a basis for enforcement of rights; and authorizes joint actions to improve operations and services. All states have adopted the compact. (Chapter 354, Laws of 1977)

Statutory Reference: Sections 48.988 and 48.989.

Administrator: Department of Children and Families.

Interstate Agreement on Qualification of Educational Personnel

The agreement authorizes the State Superintendent of Public Instruction to enter into contracts with party states to accept their educational personnel. These agreements allow Wisconsin to offer initial licenses to teachers from contracting states and allows other states to accept Wisconsin-trained teachers on the same basis. The agreement has been adopted by 35 states and the District of Columbia. (Chapter 42, Laws of 1969)

Statutory Reference: Sections 115.46-115.48.

Administrator: State Superintendent of Public Instruction.

Judicial Branch

7

The judicial branch: profile of the judicial branch, summary of recent significant supreme court decisions, and descriptions of the supreme court, court system, and judicial service agencies

Koepsell Farm, Old World Wisconsin

(Wisconsin Historical Society)

WISCONSIN SUPREME COURT

Justice	First Assumed Office	Began First Elected Term	Current Term Expires July 31
Shirley S. Abrahamson, Chief Justice	1976*	August 1979	2019
Ann Walsh Bradley	1995	August 1995	2015
N. Patrick Crooks	1996	August 1996	2016
David T. Prosser, Jr.	1998*	August 2001	2021
Patience Drake Roggensack	2003	August 2003	2013**
Annette K. Ziegler	2007	August 2007	2017
Michael J. Gableman	2008	August 2008	2018

*Initially appointed by the governor.
**Justice Roggensack was reelected to a new term beginning August 1, 2013 and expiring July 31, 2023.
Source: Director of State Courts, departmental data, June 2013.

Seated, from left to right are Justice Annette K. Ziegler, Justice David T. Prosser, Jr., Justice Ann Walsh Bradley, Chief Justice Shirley S. Abrahamson, Justice N. Patrick Crooks, Justice Patience D. Roggensack, and Justice Michael J. Gableman. (Wisconsin Supreme Court)

JUDICIAL BRANCH

A PROFILE OF THE JUDICIAL BRANCH

Introducing the Court System. The judicial branch and its system of various courts may appear very complex to the nonlawyer. It is well-known that the courts are required to try persons accused of violating criminal law and that conviction in the trial court may result in punishment by fine or imprisonment or both. The courts also decide civil matters between private citizens, ranging from landlord-tenant disputes to adjudication of corporate liability involving many millions of dollars and months of costly litigation. In addition, the courts act as referees between citizens and their government by determining the permissible limits of governmental power and the extent of an individual's rights and responsibilities.

A court system that strives for fairness and justice must settle disputes on the basis of appropriate rules of law. These rules are derived from a variety of sources, including the state and federal constitutions, legislative acts and administrative rules, as well as the "common law", which reflects society's customs and experience as expressed in previous court decisions. This body of law is constantly changing to meet the needs of an increasingly complex world. The courts have the task of seeking the delicate balance between the flexibility and the stability needed to protect the fundamental principles of the constitutional system of the United States.

The Supreme Court. The judicial branch is headed by the Wisconsin Supreme Court of 7 justices, each elected statewide to a 10-year term. The supreme court is primarily an appellate court and serves as Wisconsin's "court of last resort". It also exercises original jurisdiction in a small number of cases of statewide concern. There are no appeals to the supreme court as a matter of right. Instead, the court has discretion to determine which appeals it will hear.

In addition to hearing cases on appeal from the court of appeals, there also are three instances in which the supreme court, at its discretion, may decide to bypass the appeals court. First, the supreme court may review a case on its own initiative. Second, it may decide to review a matter without an appellate decision based on a petition by one of the parties. Finally, the supreme court may take jurisdiction in a case if the appeals court finds it needs guidance on a legal question and requests supreme court review under a procedure known as "certification".

The Court of Appeals. The Court of Appeals, created August 1, 1978, is divided into 4 appellate districts covering the state, and there are 16 appellate judges, each elected to a 6-year term. The "court chambers", or principal offices for the districts, are located in Madison (5 judges), Milwaukee (4 judges), Waukesha (4 judges), and Wausau (3 judges).

In the appeals court, 3-judge panels hear all cases, except small claims actions, municipal ordinance violations, traffic violations, and mental health, juvenile, and misdemeanor cases. These exceptions may be heard by a single judge unless a panel is requested.

Circuit Courts. Following a 1977-78 reorganization of the Wisconsin court system, the circuit court became the "single level" trial court for the state. Circuit court boundaries were revised so that, except for 3 combined-county circuits (Buffalo-Pepin, Florence-Forest, and Menominee-Shawano), each county became a circuit, resulting in a total of 69 circuits.

In the more populous counties, a circuit may have several branches with one judge assigned to each branch. As of August 1, 2012, Wisconsin had a combined total of 249 circuits or circuit branches and the same number of circuit judgeships, with each judge elected to a 6-year term. For administrative purposes, the circuit court system is divided into 10 judicial administrative districts, each headed by a chief judge appointed by the supreme court. The circuit courts are funded with a combination of state and county money. For example, state funds are used to pay the salaries of judges, and counties are responsible for most court operating costs.

A final judgment by the circuit court can be appealed to the Wisconsin Court of Appeals, but a decision by the appeals court can be reviewed only if the Wisconsin Supreme Court grants a petition for review.

Municipal Courts. Individually or jointly, cities, villages, and towns may create municipal courts with jurisdiction over municipal ordinance violations that have monetary penalties. There are more than 200 municipal courts in Wisconsin. These courts are not courts of record, and they have limited jurisdiction. Usually, municipal judgeships are not full-time positions.

Selection and Qualification of Judges. In Wisconsin, all justices and judges are elected on a nonpartisan ballot in April. The Wisconsin Constitution provides that supreme court justices and appellate and circuit judges must have been licensed to practice law in Wisconsin for at least 5 years prior to election or appointment. While state law does not require that municipal judges be attorneys, municipalities may impose such a qualification in their jurisdictions.

Supreme court justices are elected on a statewide basis; appeals court and circuit court judges are elected in their respective districts. The governor may make an appointment to fill a vacancy in the office of justice or judge to serve until a successor is elected. When the election is held, the candidate elected assumes the office for a full term.

Since 1955, Wisconsin has permitted retired justices and judges to serve as "reserve" judges. At the request of the chief justice of the supreme court, reserve judges fill vacancies temporarily or help to relieve congested calendars. They exercise all the powers of the court to which they are assigned.

Judicial Agencies Assisting the Courts. Numerous state agencies assist the courts. The Wisconsin Supreme Court appoints the Director of State Courts, the State Law Librarian and staff, the Board of Bar Examiners, the director of the Office of Lawyer Regulation, and the Judicial Education Committee. Other agencies that assist the judicial branch include the Judicial Commission, Judicial Council, and the State Bar of Wisconsin.

The shared concern of these agencies is to improve the organization, operation, administration, and procedures of the state judicial system. They also function to promote professional standards, judicial ethics, and legal research and reform.

Court Process in Wisconsin. Both state and federal courts have jurisdiction over Wisconsin citizens. State courts generally adjudicate cases pertaining to state laws, but the federal government may give state courts jurisdiction over specified federal questions. Courts handle two types of cases – civil and criminal.

Civil Cases. Generally, civil actions involve individual claims in which a person seeks a remedy for some wrong done by another. For example, if a person has been injured in an automobile accident, the complaining party (plaintiff) may sue the offending party (defendant) to compel payment for the injuries.

In a typical civil case, the plaintiff brings an action by filing a summons and a complaint with the circuit court. The defendant is served with copies of these documents, and the summons directs the defendant to respond to the plaintiff's attorney. Various pretrial proceedings, such as pleadings, motions, pretrial conferences, and discovery, may be required. If no settlement is reached, the matter goes to trial. The U.S. and Wisconsin Constitutions guarantee trial by jury, except in cases involving an equitable action, such as a divorce action. In civil actions, unless a party demands a jury trial and pays the required fee, the trial may be conducted by the court without a jury. The jury in a civil case consists of 6 persons unless a greater number, not to exceed 12, is requested. Five-sixths of the jurors must agree on the verdict. Based on the verdict, the court enters a judgment for the plaintiff or defendant.

Wisconsin law provides for small claims actions that are streamlined and informal. These actions typically involve the collection of small personal or commercial debts and are limited to questions of $10,000 or less except for third party complaints, personal injury claims, and actions based in torts where the limit is $5,000 or less. Small claims cases are decided by the circuit court judge, unless a jury trial is requested. Attorneys commonly are not used.

Criminal Cases. Under Wisconsin law, criminal conduct is an act prohibited by state law and punishable by a fine or imprisonment or both. There are two types of crime – felonies and misdemeanors. A felony is punishable by confinement in a state prison for one year or more; all other crimes are misdemeanors punishable by imprisonment in a county jail. Misdemeanors have a maximum sentence of 12 months unless the violator is a "repeater" as defined in the statutes.

Because a crime is an offense against the state, the state, rather than the crime victim, brings action against the defendant. A typical criminal action begins when the district attorney, an elected official, files a criminal complaint in the circuit court stating the essential facts concerning the offense charged. The defendant may or may not be arrested at that time. If the defendant has not yet been arrested, generally the judge or a court commissioner then issues an "arrest warrant" in the case of a felony or a "summons" in the case of a misdemeanor. A law enforcement officer then must serve a copy of the warrant or summons on an individual and, in the case of a warrant, make an arrest.

Once in custody, the defendant is taken before a circuit judge or court commissioner, informed of the charges, and given the opportunity to be represented by a lawyer at public expense if he or she cannot afford to hire one. Bail is usually set at this time. In the case of a misdemeanor, a trial date is set. In felony cases, the defendant has a right to a preliminary examination, which is a hearing before the court to determine whether the state has probable cause to charge the individual.

If the preliminary examination is waived, or if it is held and probable cause found, the district attorney files an information (a sworn accusation on which the indictment is based) with the court. The arraignment is then held before the circuit court judge, and the defendant enters a plea ("guilty", "not guilty", "no contest subject to the approval of the court", or "not guilty by reason of mental disease or defect").

Following further pretrial proceedings, if a plea agreement is not reached, the case goes to trial in circuit court. Criminal cases are tried by a jury of 12, unless the defendant waives a jury trial or there is agreement for fewer jurors. The jury considers the evidence presented at the trial, determines the facts and renders a verdict of guilty or not guilty based on instructions given by the circuit judge. If the jury issues a verdict of guilty, a judgment of conviction is entered and the court determines the sentence. In a felony case the court may order a presentence investigation before pronouncing sentence.

In a criminal case, the jury's verdict to convict the defendant must be unanimous. If not, the defendant is acquitted (cleared of the charge) or, if the jury is unable to reach a unanimous verdict, the court may declare a mistrial and the prosecutor may seek a new trial. Once acquitted, a person cannot be tried again in criminal court for the same charge, based on provisions in both the federal and state constitutions that prevent double jeopardy. Aggrieved parties may, however, bring a civil action against the individual for damages, based on the incident.

History of the Court System. The basic powers and framework of the court system were established by Article VII of the state constitution when Wisconsin gained statehood in 1848. At that time, judicial power was vested in a supreme court, circuit courts, courts of probate, and justices of the peace. Subject to certain limitations, the legislature was granted power to establish inferior courts and municipal courts and determine their jurisdiction.

The constitution originally divided the state into five judicial circuit districts. The five judges who presided over those circuit courts were to meet at least once a year at Madison as a "Supreme Court" until the legislature established a separate court. The Wisconsin Supreme Court was instituted in 1853 with 3 members chosen in statewide elections – one was elected as chief justice and the other 2 as associate justices. In 1877, a constitutional amendment increased the number of associate justices to 4. An 1889 amendment prescribed the current practice under which all court members are elected as justices. The justice with the longest continuous service presides as chief justice, unless that person declines, in which case the office passes to the next justice in terms of seniority. Since 1903, the constitution has required a court of 7 members.

Over the years, the legislature created a large number of courts with varying types of jurisdiction. As a result of numerous special laws, there was no uniformity among the counties. Different types of courts in a single county had overlapping jurisdiction, and procedure in the various courts was not the same. A number of special courts sprang up in heavily urbanized areas, such as Milwaukee County, where the judicial burden was the greatest. In addition, many municipalities established police justice courts for enforcement of local ordinances, and there were some 1,800 justices of the peace.

The 1959 Legislature enacted Chapter 315, effective January 1, 1962, which provided for the initial reorganization of the court system. The most significant feature of the reorganization was the abolition of special statutory courts (municipal, district, superior, civil, and small claims). In addition, a uniform system of jurisdiction and procedure was established for all county courts.

The 1959 law also created the machinery for smoother administration of the court system. One problem under the old system was the imbalance of caseloads from one jurisdiction to another. In some cases, the workload was not evenly distributed among the judges within the same jurisdiction. To correct this, the chief justice of the supreme court was authorized to assign circuit and county judges to serve temporarily as needed in either type of court. The 1961 Legislature took another step to assist the chief justice in these assignments by creating the post of Administrative Director of Courts. This position has since been redefined by the supreme court and renamed the Director of State Courts. In recent years, the director has been given added administrative duties and increased staff to perform them.

The last step in the 1959 reorganization effort was the April 1966 ratification of two constitutional amendments that abolished the justices of the peace and permitted municipal courts. At this point the Wisconsin system of courts consisted of the supreme court, circuit courts, county courts, and municipal courts.

In April 1977, the court of appeals was authorized when the voters ratified an amendment to Article VII, Section 2, of the Wisconsin Constitution, which outlined the current structure of the state courts:

The judicial power of this state shall be vested in a unified court system consisting of one supreme court, a court of appeals, a circuit court, such trial courts of general uniform statewide jurisdiction as the legislature may create by law, and a municipal court if authorized by the legislature under section 14.

In June 1978, the legislature implemented the constitutional amendment by enacting Chapter 449, Laws of 1977, which added the court of appeals to the system and eliminated county courts.

The chief justice speaks to new legislators at the beginning of the 2013 legislative session. Justice Prosser is seen in the foreground. (Supreme Court)

SUPREME COURT

Chief Justice: SHIRLEY S. ABRAHAMSON
Justices: ANN WALSH BRADLEY
N. PATRICK CROOKS
DAVID T. PROSSER, JR.
PATIENCE DRAKE ROGGENSACK
ANNETTE K. ZIEGLER
MICHAEL J. GABLEMAN

Mailing Address: Supreme Court and Clerk: P.O. Box 1688, Madison 53701-1688.

Locations: Supreme Court: Room 16 East, State Capitol, Madison; Clerk: 110 East Main Street, Madison.

Telephone: 266-1298.

Fax: 261-8299.

Internet Address: www.wicourts.gov

Clerk of Supreme Court: DIANE FREMGEN, 266-1880, Fax: 267-0640.

Court Commissioners: NANCY KOPP, MARK NEUSER, JULIE RICH, DAVID RUNKE; 266-7442.

Number of Positions: 38.50.

Total Budget 2011-13: $10,472,200.

Constitutional References: Article VII, Sections 2-4, 9-13, and 24.

Statutory Reference: Chapter 751.

Responsibility: The Wisconsin Supreme Court is the final authority on matters pertaining to the Wisconsin Constitution and the highest tribunal for all actions begun in the state, except those involving federal issues appealable to the U.S. Supreme Court. The court decides which cases it will hear, usually on the basis of whether the questions raised are of statewide importance. It exercises "appellate jurisdiction" if 3 or more justices grant a petition to review a decision of a lower court. It exercises "original jurisdiction" as the first court to hear a case if 4 or more justices approve a petition requesting it to do so. Although the majority of cases advance from the circuit court to the court of appeals before reaching the supreme court, the high court may decide to bypass the court of appeals. The supreme court can do this on its own motion or at the request of the parties; in addition, the court of appeals may certify a case to the supreme court, asking the high court to take the case directly from the circuit court.

The supreme court does not take testimony. Instead, it decides cases on the basis of written briefs and oral argument. It is required by statute to deliver its decisions in writing, and it may publish them in the *Wisconsin Reports* as it deems appropriate.

The supreme court sets procedural rules for all courts in the state, and the chief justice serves as administrative head of the state's judicial system. With the assistance of the director of state courts, the chief justice monitors the status of judicial business in Wisconsin's courts. When a calendar is congested or a vacancy occurs in a circuit or appellate court, the chief justice may assign an active judge or reserve judge to serve temporarily as a judge of either type of court.

Organization: The supreme court consists of 7 justices elected to 10-year terms. They are chosen in statewide elections on the nonpartisan April ballot and take office on the following August 1. The Wisconsin Constitution provides that only one justice can be elected in any single year, so supreme court vacancies are sometimes filled by gubernatorial appointees who serve until a successor can be elected. The authorized salary for supreme court justices for 2013 is $144,495. The chief justice receives $152,495.

The justice with the most seniority on the court serves as chief justice unless he or she declines the position. In that event, the justice with the next longest seniority serves as chief justice. Any 4 justices constitute a quorum for conducting court business.

The court staff is appointed from outside the classified service. It includes the director of state courts who assists the court in its administrative functions; 4 commissioners who are attorneys and assist the court in its judicial functions; a clerk who keeps the court's records; and a marshal who performs a variety of duties. Each justice has a secretary and one law clerk.

WISCONSIN COURT SYSTEM – ADMINISTRATIVE STRUCTURE

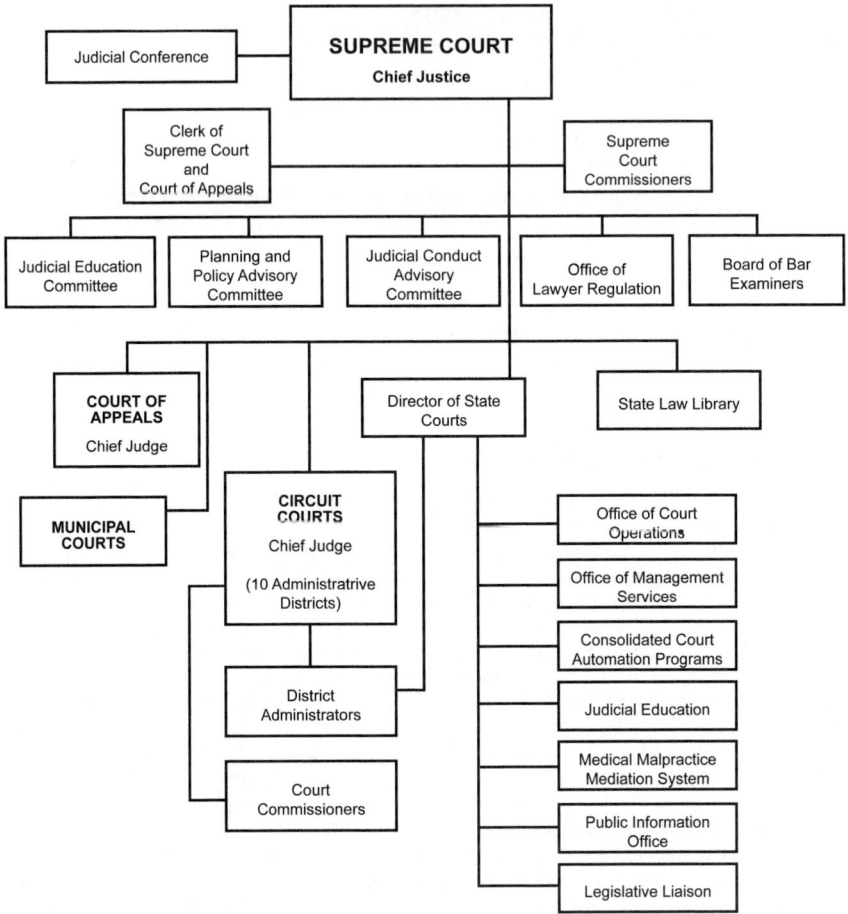

Independent Bodies: Judicial Commission; Judicial Council
Associated unit: State Bar of Wisconsin

COURT OF APPEALS

Judges: District I: KITTY B. BRENNAN (2015)
PATRICIA S. CURLEY* (2014)
RALPH ADAM FINE (2018)
JOAN F. KESSLER (2016)
District II: RICHARD S. BROWN** (2018)
MARK D. GUNDRUM (2019)
LISA S. NEUBAUER* (2014)
PAUL F. REILLY (2016)
District III: MICHAEL W. HOOVER* (2015)
MARK A. MANGERSON (2018)
LISA K. STARK (2019)
District IV: BRIAN W. BLANCHARD (2016)
PAUL B. HIGGINBOTHAM (2017)
JOANNE F. KLOPPENBURG (2018)
PAUL LUNDSTEN* (2013)
GARY E. SHERMAN (2014)

Note: *Indicates the presiding judge of the district. **Indicates chief judge of the court of appeals. The judges' current terms expire on July 31 of the year shown.

Court of Appeals Clerk: DIANE M. FREMGEN, P.O. Box 1688, Madison 53701-1688; Location: 110 East Main Street, Suite 215, Madison, 266-1880, Fax: 267-0640.

Staff Attorneys: 10 East Doty Street, 7th Floor, Madison 53703, 266-9320.

Internet Address: www.wicourts.gov/courts/appeals/index.htm

Number of Positions: 75.50.

Total Budget 2011-13: $20,954,000.

Constitutional Reference: Article VII, Section 5.

Statutory Reference: Chapter 752.

Organization: A constitutional amendment ratified on April 5, 1977, mandated the Court of Appeals, and Chapter 187, Laws of 1977, implemented the amendment. The court consists of 16 judges serving in 4 districts (4 judges each in Districts I and II, 3 judges in District III, and 5 judges in District IV). The Wisconsin Supreme Court appoints a chief judge of the court of appeals to serve as administrative head of the court for a 3-year term, and the clerk of the supreme court serves as the clerk for the court.

Appellate judges are elected for 6-year terms in the nonpartisan April election and begin their terms of office on the following August 1. They must reside in the district from which they are chosen. Only one court of appeals judge may be elected in a district in any one year. The authorized salary for appeals court judges for 2013 is $136,316.

Functions: The court of appeals has both appellate and supervisory jurisdiction, as well as original jurisdiction to issue prerogative writs. The final judgments and orders of a circuit court may be appealed to the court of appeals as a matter of right. Other judgments or orders may be appealed upon leave of the appellate court.

The court usually sits as a 3-judge panel to dispose of cases on their merits. However, a single judge may decide certain categories of cases, including juvenile cases; small claims; municipal ordinance and traffic violations; and mental health and misdemeanor cases. No testimony is taken in the appellate court. The court relies on the trial court record and written briefs in deciding a case, and it prescreens all cases to determine whether oral argument is needed. Both oral argument and "briefs only" cases are placed on a regularly issued calendar. The court gives criminal cases preference on the calendar when it is possible to do so without undue delay of civil cases. Staff attorneys, judicial assistants, and law clerks assist the judges.

Decisions of the appellate court are delivered in writing, and the court's publication committee determines which decisions will be published in the *Wisconsin Reports.* Only published opinions have precedential value and may be cited as controlling law in Wisconsin. Unpublished opinions that are authored by a judge and issued after July 1, 2009, may be cited for their persuasive value.

District I: 330 East Kilbourn Avenue, Suite 1020, Milwaukee 53203-3161. Telephone: (414) 227-4680.

District II: 2727 North Grandview Boulevard, Suite 300, Waukesha 53188-1672. Telephone: (262) 521-5230.

District III: 2100 Stewart Avenue, Suite 310, Wausau 54401. Telephone: (715) 848-1421.

District IV: 10 East Doty Street, Suite 700, Madison 53703-3397. Telephone: (608) 266-9250.

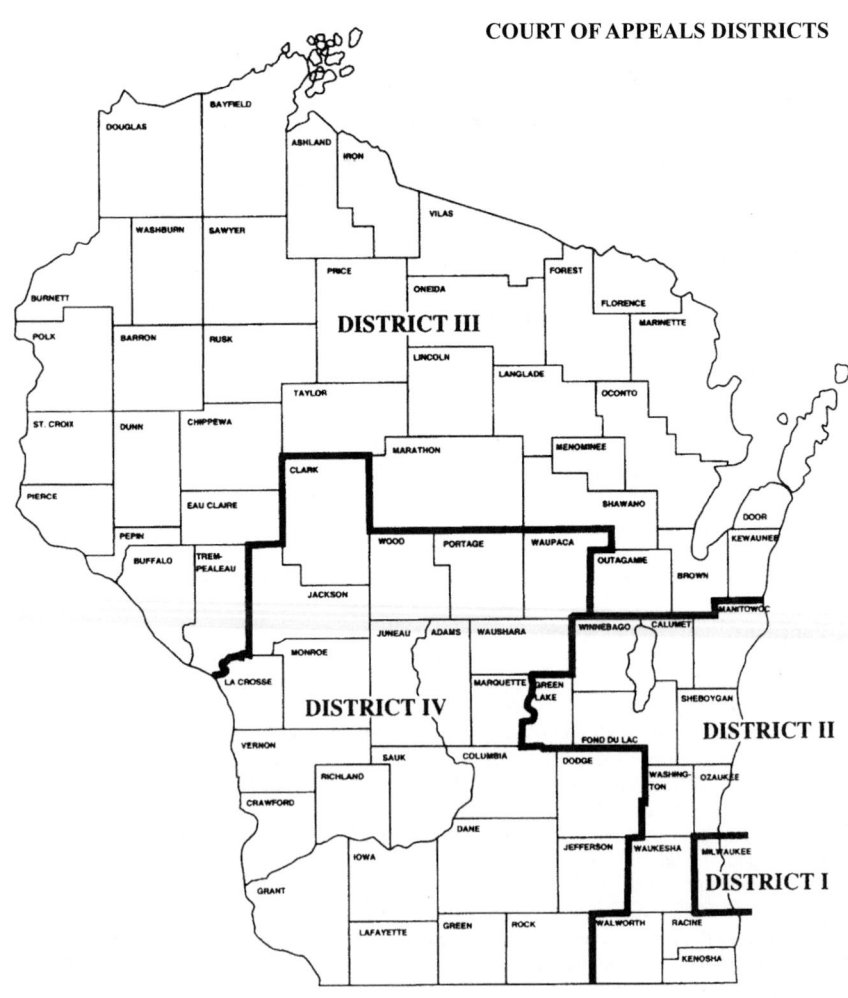

COURT OF APPEALS DISTRICTS

CIRCUIT COURTS

District 1: Milwaukee County Courthouse, 901 North 9th Street, Room 609, Milwaukee 53233-1425. Telephone: (414) 278-5113; Fax: (414) 223-1264.
Chief Judge: JEFFREY KREMERS.
Administrator: BRUCE HARVEY.

District 2: Racine County Courthouse, 730 Wisconsin Avenue, Racine 53403-1274. Telephone: (262) 636-3133; Fax: (262) 636-3437.
Chief Judge: MARY K. WAGNER.
Administrator: ANDREW GRAUBARD.

District 3: Waukesha County Courthouse, 515 West Moreland Boulevard, Room 359, Waukesha 53188-2428. Telephone: (262) 548-7209; Fax: (262) 548-7815.
Chief Judge: RANDY KOSCHNICK.
Administrator: MICHAEL NEIMON.

District 4: 404 North Main Street, Suite 105, Oshkosh 54901-4901.
Telephone: (920) 424-0028; Fax: (920) 424-0096.
Chief Judge: ROBERT WIRTZ.
Administrator: JON BELLOWS.

District 5: Dane County Courthouse, 215 South Hamilton Street, Madison 53703-3290. Telephone: 267-8820; Fax: 267-4151.
Chief Judge: JAMES P. DALEY.
Administrator: GAIL RICHARDSON.

District 6: 3317 Business Park Drive, Suite A, Stevens Point 54481-8834.
Telephone: (715) 345-5295; Fax: (715) 345-5297.
Chief Judge: GREGORY POTTER.
Administrator: RON LEDFORD.

District 7: La Crosse County Law Enforcement Center, 333 Vine Street, Room 3504, La Crosse 54601-3296. Telephone: (608) 785-9546; Fax: (608) 785-5530.
Chief Judge: JAMES J. DUVALL.
Administrator: PATRICK BRUMMOND.

District 8: 414 East Walnut Street, Suite 100, Green Bay 54301-5020.
Telephone: (920) 448-4281; Fax: (920) 448-4336.
Chief Judge: DONALD ZUIDMULDER.
Administrator: JOHN POWELL.

District 9: 2100 Stewart Avenue, Suite 310, Wausau 54401.
Telephone: (715) 842-3872; Fax: (715) 845-4523.
Chief Judge: NEAL NIELSEN.
Administrator: SUSAN BYRNES.

District 10: 4410 Golf Terrace, Suite 150, Eau Claire 54701-3606.
Telephone: (715) 839-4826; Fax: (715) 839-4891.
Chief Judge: SCOTT NEEDHAM.
Administrator: SCOTT JOHNSON.

Internet Address: www.wicourts.gov/courts/circuit/index.htm

State-Funded Positions: 527.00.

Total Budget 2011-13: $193,063,700.

Constitutional References: Article VII, Sections 2, 6-13.

Statutory Reference: Chapter 753.

Responsibility: The circuit court is the trial court of general jurisdiction in Wisconsin. It has original jurisdiction in both civil and criminal matters unless exclusive jurisdiction is given to another court. It also reviews state agency decisions and hears appeals from municipal courts. Jury trials are conducted only in circuit courts.

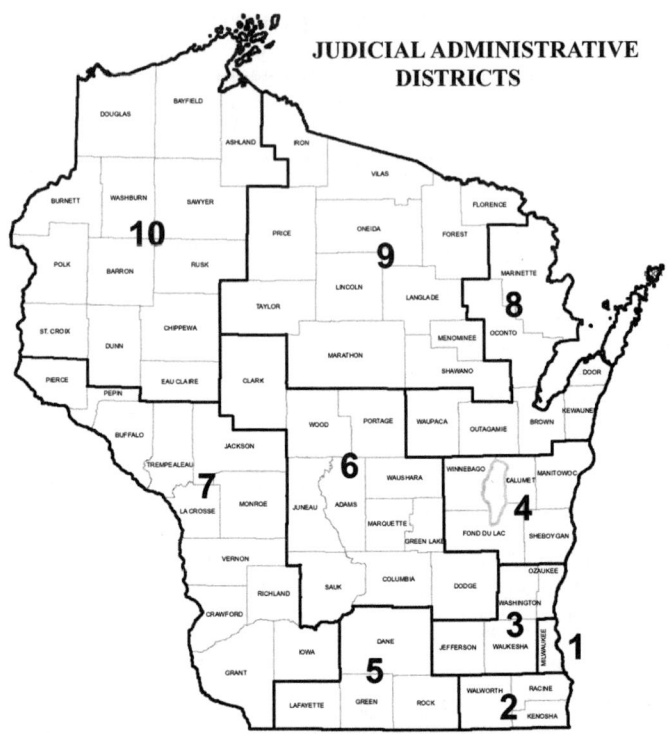

JUDICIAL ADMINISTRATIVE DISTRICTS

The constitution requires that a circuit be bounded by county lines. As a result, each circuit consists of a single county, except for 3 two-county circuits (Buffalo-Pepin, Florence-Forest, and Menominee-Shawano). Where judicial caseloads are heavy, a circuit may have several branches, each with an elected judge. Statewide, 40 of the state's 69 judicial circuits had multiple branches as of August 1, 2012, for a total of 249 circuit judgeships.

Organization: Circuit judges, who serve 6-year terms, are elected on a nonpartisan basis in the county in which they serve in the April election and take office the following August 1. The governor may fill circuit court vacancies by appointment, and the appointees serve until a successor is elected. The authorized salary for circuit court judges for 2012 is $128,600. The state pays the salaries of circuit judges and court reporters. It also covers some of the expenses for interpreters, guardians ad litem, judicial assistants, court-appointed witnesses, and jury per diems. Counties bear the remaining expenses for operating the circuit courts.

Administrative Districts. Circuit courts are divided into 10 administrative districts, each supervised by a chief judge, appointed by the supreme court from the district's circuit judges. A judge usually cannot serve more than 3 successive 2-year terms as chief judge. The chief judge has authority to assign judges, manage caseflow, supervise personnel, and conduct financial planning.

The chief judge in each district appoints a district court administrator from a list of candidates supplied by the director of state courts. The administrator manages the nonjudicial business of the district at the direction of the chief judge.

Circuit Court Commissioners are appointed by the circuit court to assist the court, and they must be attorneys licensed to practice law in Wisconsin. They may be authorized by the court to conduct various civil, criminal, family, small claims, juvenile, and probate court proceedings. Their duties include issuing summonses, arrest warrants, or search warrants; conducting initial appearances; setting bail; conducting preliminary examinations and arraignments; imposing monetary penalties in certain traffic cases; conducting certain family, juvenile, and small claims court proceedings; hearing petitions for mental commitments; and conducting uncontested probate proceedings. On their own authority, court commissioners may perform marriages, administer oaths, take depositions, and issue subpoenas and certain writs.

The statutes require Milwaukee County to have full-time family, small claims, and probate court commissioners. All other counties must have a family court commissioner, and they may employ other full- or part-time court commissioners as deemed necessary.

In a collaborative effort between two branches of government, the Supreme Court and two legislative committees hold a joint meeting to discuss issues related to justice. Chief Justice Shirley Abrahamson is seated next to Senator Glenn Grothman, chairperson of the Senate Committee on Judiciary and Labor. (Supreme Court)

JUDGES OF CIRCUIT COURT
June 1, 2013

County Circuits	Court Location	Judges	Term Expires July 31
Adams	Friendship	Charles A. Pollex	2015
Ashland	Ashland	Robert E. Eaton	2018
Barron			
Branch 1	Barron	James C. Babler	2016
Branch 2	Barron	Timothy M. Doyle	2014
Branch 3	Barron	James D. Babbitt	2014
Bayfield	Washburn	John P. Anderson	2015
Brown			
Branch 1	Green Bay	Donald R. Zuidmulder	2015
Branch 2	Green Bay	Tom Walsh	2018
Branch 3	Green Bay	Tammy Jo Hock[1,2]	2013
Branch 4	Green Bay	Kendall M. Kelley	2015
Branch 5	Green Bay	Marc A. Hammer	2015
Branch 6	Green Bay	John P. Zakowski	2018
Branch 7	Green Bay	Timothy A. Hinkfuss[3]	2013
Branch 8	Green Bay	William M. Atkinson	2015
Buffalo-Pepin	Alma	James J. Duvall	2018
Burnett	Siren	Kenneth Kutz	2015
Calumet	Chilton	Jeffrey S. Froehlich	2018
Chippewa			
Branch 1	Chippewa Falls	Roderick A. Cameron	2014
Branch 2	Chippewa Falls	James Isaacson	2015
Branch 3	Chippewa Falls	Steven R. Cray	2014
Clark	Neillsville	Jon M. Counsell	2018
Columbia			
Branch 1	Portage	Daniel S. George	2015
Branch 2	Portage	W. Andrew Voigt	2017
Branch 3	Portage	Alan White[3]	2013
Crawford	Prairie du Chien	James P. Czajkowski	2016
Dane			
Branch 1	Madison	John Markson	2014
Branch 2	Madison	Maryann Sumi	2017
Branch 3	Madison	John C. Albert	2018
Branch 4	Madison	Amy Smith	2016
Branch 5	Madison	Nicholas J. McNamara	2016
Branch 6	Madison	Shelley J. Gaylord	2015
Branch 7	Madison	William E. Hanrahan	2014
Branch 8	Madison	Frank D. Remington	2018
Branch 9	Madison	Richard Niess	2017
Branch 10	Madison	Juan B. Colas	2015
Branch 11	Madison	Ellen K. Berz	2018
Branch 12	Madison	David T. Flanagan	2018
Branch 13	Madison	Julie Genovese	2015
Branch 14	Madison	C. William Foust	2016
Branch 15	Madison	Stephen Ehlke	2016
Branch 16	Madison	Rebecca Rapp St. John[1,4]	2013
Branch 17	Madison	Peter C. Anderson	2016
Dodge			
Branch 1	Juneau	Brian A. Pfitzinger	2014
Branch 2	Juneau	John R. Storck[3]	2013
Branch 3	Juneau	Andrew P. Bissonnette[5]	2013
Branch 4	Juneau	Steven Bauer	2014
Door			
Branch 1	Sturgeon Bay	D. Todd Ehlers	2018
Branch 2	Sturgeon Bay	Peter C. Diltz	2018
Douglas			
Branch 1	Superior	Kelly J. Thimm	2015
Branch 2	Superior	George L. Glonek	2015
Dunn			
Branch 1	Menomonie	William C. Stewart, Jr.	2016
Branch 2	Menomonie	Rod W. Smeltzer	2015
Eau Claire			
Branch 1	Eau Claire	Lisa K. Stark	2018
Branch 2	Eau Claire	Michael Schumacher	2014
Branch 3	Eau Claire	William M. Gabler, Sr.	2018
Branch 4	Eau Claire	Jon M. Theisen	2018
Branch 5	Eau Claire	Paul J. Lenz	2018
Florence-Forest	Crandon	Leon D. Stenz	2014
Fond du Lac			
Branch 1	Fond du Lac	Dale L. English	2014
Branch 2	Fond du Lac	Peter L. Grimm	2016
Branch 3	Fond du Lac	Richard J. Nuss	2015
Branch 4	Fond du Lac	Gary R. Sharpe	2016
Branch 5	Fond du Lac	Robert J. Wirtz	2017
Forest (see *Florence-Forest*)			
Grant			
Branch 1	Lancaster	Robert P. VanDeHey	2017
Branch 2	Lancaster	Craig R. Day	2015
Green			
Branch 1	Monroe	Jim Beer	2015
Branch 2	Monroe	Thomas J. Vale	2015
Green Lake	Green Lake	Mark Slate	2017
Iowa	Dodgeville	William D. Dyke	2016
Iron	Hurley	Patrick John Madden	2017

JUDGES OF CIRCUIT COURT
June 1, 2013–Continued

County Circuits	Court Location	Judges	Term Expires July 31
Jackson	Black River Falls	Thomas Lister	2015
Jefferson			
Branch 1	Jefferson	Jennifer L. Weston	2015
Branch 2	Jefferson	William F. Hue[3]	2013
Branch 3	Jefferson	vacancy	—
Branch 4	Jefferson	Randy R. Koschnick	2017
Juneau			
Branch 1	Mauston	John Pier Roemer	2016
Branch 2	Mauston	Paul S. Curran	2014
Kenosha			
Branch 1	Kenosha	David Mark Bastianelli	2015
Branch 2	Kenosha	Jason A. Rossell	2018
Branch 3	Kenosha	Bruce E. Schroeder	2014
Branch 4	Kenosha	Anthony Milisauskas	2017
Branch 5	Kenosha	Wilbur W. Warren III	2015
Branch 6	Kenosha	Mary K. Wagner	2015
Branch 7	Kenosha	S. Michael Wilk	2018
Branch 8	Kenosha	Chad G. Kerkman	2015
Kewaunee	Kewaunee	Dennis J. Mleziva	2016
La Crosse			
Branch 1	La Crosse	Ramona A. Gonzalez[3]	2013
Branch 2	La Crosse	Elliott Levine[3]	2013
Branch 3	La Crosse	Todd Bjerke[3]	2013
Branch 4	La Crosse	Scott L. Horne[3]	2013
Branch 5	La Crosse	Dale T. Pasell	2017
Lafayette	Darlington	William D. Johnston	2015
Langlade	Antigo	Fred W. Kawalski	2017
Lincoln			
Branch 1	Merrill	Jay R. Tlusty	2016
Branch 2	Merrill	John Yackel[1,6]	2013
Manitowoc			
Branch 1	Manitowoc	vacancy[7]	—
Branch 2	Manitowoc	Gary Bendix	2018
Branch 3	Manitowoc	Jerome L. Fox	2017
Marathon			
Branch 1	Wausau	Jill N. Falstad	2015
Branch 2	Wausau	Gregory Huber	2016
Branch 3	Wausau	vacancy	—
Branch 4	Wausau	Gregory Grau[3]	2013
Branch 5	Wausau	Mike Moran	2017
Marinette			
Branch 1	Marinette	David G. Miron	2014
Branch 2	Marinette	James A. Morrison[1,2]	2013
Marquette	Montello	Richard O. Wright[8]	2013
Menominee-Shawano			
Branch 1	Shawano	James R. Habeck	2014
Branch 2	Shawano	William F. Kussel, Jr.	2018
Milwaukee			
Branch 1	Milwaukee	Maxine Aldridge White	2017
Branch 2	Wauwatosa	Joe Donald	2015
Branch 3	Milwaukee	Clare L. Fiorenza	2015
Branch 4	Milwaukee	Mel Flanagan	2018
Branch 5	Milwaukee	Mary Kuhnmuench	2016
Branch 6	Milwaukee	Ellen Brostrom	2015
Branch 7	Milwaukee	Jean W. DiMotto	2015
Branch 8	Milwaukee	William Sosnay	2018
Branch 9	Milwaukee	Paul R. Van Grunsven	2017
Branch 10	Milwaukee	Timothy G. Dugan	2017
Branch 11	Milwaukee	Dominic S. Amato[9]	2013
Branch 12	Milwaukee	David L. Borowski	2015
Branch 13	Milwaukee	Mary Triggiano	2017
Branch 14	Milwaukee	Christopher R. Foley	2016
Branch 15	Milwaukee	J.D. Watts	2015
Branch 16	Wauwatosa	Michael J. Dwyer	2015
Branch 17	Milwaukee	Carolina Maria Stark	2018
Branch 18	Wauwatosa	Pedro Colón	2017
Branch 19	Wauwatosa	Dennis R. Cimpl	2017
Branch 20	Milwaukee	Dennis P. Moroney	2018
Branch 21	Milwaukee	William Brash III	2014
Branch 22	Milwaukee	Timothy M. Witkowiak	2015
Branch 23	Milwaukee	Lindsey Grady	2018
Branch 24	Milwaukee	Charles F. Kahn, Jr.	2016
Branch 25	Milwaukee	Stephanie Rothstein	2016
Branch 26	Milwaukee	William Pocan[3]	2013
Branch 27	Milwaukee	Kevin E. Martens	2014
Branch 28	Wauwatosa	Mark A. Sanders	2018
Branch 29	Milwaukee	Richard J. Sankovitz	2015
Branch 30	Milwaukee	Jeffrey A. Conen	2015
Branch 31	Milwaukee	Daniel A. Noonan	2014
Branch 32	Milwaukee	Michael D. Guolee	2014
Branch 33	Milwaukee	Carl Ashley	2017
Branch 34	Milwaukee	Glenn H. Yamahiro	2016
Branch 35	Milwaukee	Frederick C. Rosa	2017
Branch 36	Milwaukee	Jeffrey A. Kremers	2017

JUDGES OF CIRCUIT COURT
June 1, 2013–Continued

County Circuits	Court Location	Judges	Term Expires July 31
Branch 37	Wauwatosa	Karen Christenson	2016
Branch 38	Milwaukee	Jeffrey A. Wagner	2018
Branch 39	Milwaukee	Jane Carroll	2018
Branch 40	Milwaukee	Rebecca Dallett	2014
Branch 41	Wauwatosa	John J. DiMotto	2014
Branch 42	Milwaukee	David A. Hansher	2015
Branch 43	Milwaukee	Marshall B. Murray	2018
Branch 44	Milwaukee	Daniel L. Konkol	2016
Branch 45	Wauwatosa	Rebecca G. Bradley[1,2]	2013
Branch 46	Milwaukee	Bonnie L. Gordon	2018
Branch 47	Milwaukee	John Siefert	2017
Monroe			
Branch 1	Sparta	Todd L. Ziegler[3]	2013
Branch 2	Sparta	Mark L. Goodman	2016
Branch 3	Sparta	J. David Rice	2016
Oconto			
Branch 1	Oconto	Michael T. Judge	2017
Branch 2	Oconto	Jay N. Conley	2016
Oneida			
Branch 1	Rhinelander	Patrick F.O'Melia	2014
Branch 2	Rhinelander	Michael H. Bloom	2018
Outagamie			
Branch 1	Appleton	Mark McGinnis	2017
Branch 2	Appleton	Nancy J. Krueger	2014
Branch 3	Appleton	Mitchell J. Metropulos	2014
Branch 4	Appleton	Greg Gill, Jr.	2018
Branch 5	Appleton	Michael W. Gage	2015
Branch 6	Appleton	Dee R. Dyer	2018
Branch 7	Appleton	John A. Des Jardins	2018
Ozaukee			
Branch 1	Port Washington	Paul V. Malloy	2015
Branch 2	Port Washington	Thomas R. Wolfgram[10]	2013
Branch 3	Port Washington	Sandy A. Williams	2015
Pepin (see *Buffalo-Pepin*)			
Pierce	Ellsworth	Joe Boles	2016
Polk			
Branch 1	Balsam Lake	Molly E. GaleWyrick	2014
Branch 2	Balsam Lake	Jeff Anderson	2017
Portage			
Branch 1	Stevens Point	Thomas B. Eagon	2018
Branch 2	Stevens Point	John V. Finn[3]	2013
Branch 3	Stevens Point	Thomas T. Flugaur	2018
Price	Phillips	Douglas T. Fox	2014
Racine			
Branch 1	Racine	Gerald P. Ptacek[3]	2013
Branch 2	Racine	Eugene Gasiorkiewicz	2016
Branch 3	Racine	Emily S. Mueller	2017
Branch 4	Racine	John S. Jude	2016
Branch 5	Racine	Mike Piontek	2018
Branch 6	Racine	Wayne J. Marik	2015
Branch 7	Racine	Charles H. Constantine	2014
Branch 8	Racine	Faye M. Flancher	2015
Branch 9	Racine	Allan B. Torhorst	2015
Branch 10	Racine	Timothy D. Boyle	2018
Richland	Richland Center	Andrew Sharp	2018
Rock			
Branch 1	Janesville	James P. Daley	2014
Branch 2	Janesville	Alan Bates	2016
Branch 3	Janesville	Michael Fitzpatrick	2015
Branch 4	Janesville	Daniel T. Dillon[3]	2013
Branch 5	Janesville	Kenneth Forbeck	2015
Branch 6	Janesville	Richard T. Werner	2015
Branch 7	Janesville	Barbara W. McCrory	2018
Rusk	Ladysmith	Steven P. Anderson	2016
St. Croix			
Branch 1	Hudson	Eric J. Lundell	2014
Branch 2	Hudson	Edward F. Vlack III[3]	2013
Branch 3	Hudson	Scott R. Needham	2018
Branch 4	Hudson	Howard Cameron	2014
Sauk			
Branch 1	Baraboo	Patrick J. Taggart	2018
Branch 2	Baraboo	James Evenson	2016
Branch 3	Baraboo	Guy D. Reynolds	2018
Sawyer	Hayward	Jerry Wright	2015
Shawano (see *Menominee-Shawano*)			
Sheboygan			
Branch 1	Sheboygan	L. Edward Stengel	2015
Branch 2	Sheboygan	Timothy M. Van Akkeren[3]	2013
Branch 3	Sheboygan	Angela Sutkiewicz	2017
Branch 4	Sheboygan	Terence T. Bourke	2015
Branch 5	Sheboygan	James J. Bolgert	2018
Taylor	Medford	Ann Knox-Bauer	2015
Trempealeau	Whitehall	John A. Damon[3]	2013
Vernon	Viroqua	Michael J. Rosborough	2017

JUDGES OF CIRCUIT COURT
June 1, 2013–Continued

County Circuits	Court Location	Judges	Term Expires July 31
Vilas	Eagle River	Neal A. Nielsen	2016
Walworth			
Branch 1	Elkhorn	Phillip A. Koss	2018
Branch 2	Elkhorn	James L. Carlson	2016
Branch 3	Elkhorn	John R. Race	2015
Branch 4	Elkhorn	David M. Reddy	2016
Washburn	Shell Lake	Eugene D. Harrington	2015
Washington			
Branch 1	West Bend	James Pouros	2017
Branch 2	West Bend	James K. Muehlbauer	2014
Branch 3	West Bend	Todd Martens	2017
Branch 4	West Bend	Andrew T. Gonring	2018
Waukesha			
Branch 1	Waukesha	Michael O. Bohren[3]	2013
Branch 2	Waukesha	Jennifer Dorow	2018
Branch 3	Waukesha	Ralph M. Ramirez	2017
Branch 4	Waukesha	Lloyd V. Carter	2017
Branch 5	Waukesha	Lee Sherman Dreyfus, Jr.	2014
Branch 6	Waukesha	Patrick C. Haughney	2014
Branch 7	Waukesha	J. Mac Davis	2015
Branch 8	Waukesha	James R. Kieffer	2015
Branch 9	Waukesha	Donald J. Hassin, Jr.[3]	2013
Branch 10	Waukesha	Linda M. Van De Water	2015
Branch 11	Waukesha	William Domina	2017
Branch 12	Waukesha	Kathryn W. Foster	2018
Waupaca			
Branch 1	Waupaca	Philip M. Kirk	2017
Branch 2	Waupaca	John P. Hoffmann	2016
Branch 3	Waupaca	Raymond S. Huber	2018
Waushara	Wautoma	Guy Dutcher	2017
Winnebago			
Branch 1	Oshkosh	Thomas J. Gritton	2018
Branch 2	Oshkosh	Scott C. Woldt	2017
Branch 3	Oshkosh	Barbara Hart Key	2016
Branch 4	Oshkosh	Karen L. Seifert	2018
Branch 5	Oshkosh	John Jorgensen	2016
Branch 6	Oshkosh	Daniel J. Bissett	2017
Wood			
Branch 1	Wisconsin Rapids	Gregory J. Potter	2014
Branch 2	Wisconsin Rapids	Nicholas J. Brazeau, Jr.	2018
Branch 3	Wisconsin Rapids	Todd P. Wolf	2015

[1]Appointed by the governor.

[2]Newly elected on April 2, 2013, for a 6-year term to commence on August 1, 2013.

[3]Reelected on April 2, 2013, for a 6-year term to commence on August 1, 2013.

[4]Rhonda L. Lanford was newly elected on April 2, 2013, for a 6-year term to commence on August 1, 2013.

[5]Joseph G. Sciascia was newly elected on April 2, 2013, for a 6-year term to commence on August 1, 2013.

[6]Robert Russell was newly elected on April 2, 2013, for a 6-year term to commence on August 1, 2013.

[7]Mark R. Rohrer was newly elected on April 2, 2013, for a 6-year term to commence on August 1, 2013.

[8]Bernard Ben Bult was newly elected on April 2, 2013, for a 6-year term to commence on August 1, 2013.

[9]Dave Swanson was newly elected on April 2, 2013, for a 6-year term to commence on August 1, 2013.

[10]Joe Voiland was newly elected on April 2, 2013, for a 6-year term to commence on August 1, 2013.

Sources: *2011-2012 Wisconsin Statutes;* Government Accountability Board, departmental data, April 2013; governor's appointment notices; *The Third Branch* newsletter, Winter 2013 and previous issues.

MUNICIPAL COURTS

Constitutional References: Article VII, Sections 2 and 14.

Statutory References: Chapters 755 and 800.

Internet Address: www.wicourts.gov/courts/municipal/index.htm

Responsibility: The Wisconsin Legislature authorizes cities, villages, and towns to establish municipal courts to exercise jurisdiction over municipal ordinance violations that have monetary penalties. In addition, the Wisconsin Supreme Court ruled in 1991 (*City of Milwaukee v. Wroten,* 160 Wis. 2d 107) that municipal courts have authority to rule on the constitutionality of municipal ordinances.

As of May 1, 2013, there were 245 municipal courts with 243 municipal judges. Courts may have multiple branches; the City of Milwaukee's municipal court, for example, has 3 branches. (Milwaukee County, which is the only county authorized to appoint municipal court commissioners, had 3 part-time commissioners as of May 2013.) Two or more municipalities may agree to form a joint court, and there are 61 joint courts, serving up to 15 municipalities each. Besides Milwaukee, Madison is the only city with a full-time municipal court.

Upon convicting a defendant, the municipal court may order payment of a forfeiture plus costs and surcharges, or, if the defendant agrees, it may require community service in lieu of a forfeiture. In general, municipal courts may also order restitution up to $10,000. Where local ordinances conform to state drunk driving laws, a municipal judge may suspend or revoke a driver's license.

If a defendant fails to pay a forfeiture or make restitution, the municipal court may suspend the driver's license or commit the defendant to jail. Municipal court decisions may be appealed to the circuit court of the county where the offense occurred.

Organization: Municipal judges are elected at the nonpartisan April election and take office May 1. The term of office is 4 years and the governing body determines the position's salary. There is no state requirement that the office be filled by an attorney, but a municipality may enact such a qualification by ordinance.

If a municipal judge is ill, disqualified, or unavailable, the chief judge of the judicial administrative district containing the municipality may transfer the case to another municipal judge. If none is available, the case will be heard in circuit court.

History: Chapter 276, Laws of 1967, authorized cities, villages, and towns to establish municipal courts after the forerunner of municipal courts (the office of the justice of the peace) was eliminated by a constitutional amendment, ratified in April 1966. A constitutional amendment ratified in April 1977, which reorganized the state's court system, officially granted the legislature the power to authorize municipal courts.

STATEWIDE JUDICIAL AGENCIES

A number of statewide administrative and support agencies have been created by supreme court order or legislative enactment to assist the Wisconsin Supreme Court in its supervision of the Wisconsin judicial system.

DIRECTOR OF STATE COURTS

Director of State Courts: A. JOHN VOELKER, 266-6828, john.voelker@

Deputy Director for Court Operations: SARA WARD-CASSADY, 266-3121, sara.ward-cassady@

Deputy Director for Management Services: PAM RADLOFF, 266-8914, pam.radloff@

Consolidated Court Automation Programs: JEAN BOUSQUET, *director,* 267-0678, jean.bousquet@

Fiscal Officer: BRIAN LAMPRECH, 266-6865, brian.lamprech@

Judicial Education: DAVID H. HASS, *director,* 266-7807, david.hass@

Medical Malpractice Mediation System: RANDY SPROULE, *director,* 266-7711, randy.sproule@

Public Information Officers: AMANDA TODD, 264-6256, amanda.todd@; TOM SHEEHAN, 261-6640, tom.sheehan@

Legislative Liaison: NANCY ROTTIER, 267-9733, nancy.rottier@

Address e-mail by combining the user ID and the state extender: userid@**wicourts.gov**

Mailing Address: Director of State Courts: P.O. Box 1688, Madison 53701-1688; Staff: 110 East Main Street, Madison 53703.

Location: Director of State Courts: Room 16 East, State Capitol, Madison; Staff: 110 East Main Street, Madison.

Fax: 267-0980.

Internet Address: www.wicourts.gov

Number of Employees: 129.25.

Total Budget 2011-13: $40,335,300.

References: Wisconsin Statutes, Chapter 655, Subchapter VI, and Section 758.19; Supreme Court Rules 70.01-70.08.

Responsibility: The Director of State Courts administers the nonjudicial business of the Wisconsin court system and informs the chief justice and the supreme court about the status of judicial business. The director is responsible for supervising state-level court personnel; developing the court system's budget; and directing the courts' work on legislation, public information, and information systems. This office also controls expenditures; allocates space and equipment; supervises judicial education, interdistrict assignment of active and reserve judges, and planning and research; and administers the medical malpractice mediation system.

The director is appointed by the supreme court from outside the classified service. The position was created by the supreme court in orders, dated October 30, 1978, and February 19, 1979. It replaced the administrative director of courts, which had been created by Chapter 261, Laws of 1961.

STATE LAW LIBRARY

State Law Librarian: JULIE TESSMER, 261-2340, julie.tessmer@wicourts.gov

Deputy Law Librarian: AMY CROWDER, 267-2253, amy.crowder@wicourts.gov

Mailing Address: P.O. Box 7881, Madison 53707-7881.

Location: 120 Martin Luther King, Jr. Blvd., 2nd Floor, Madison.

Telephones: General Information and Circulation: 266-1600; Reference Assistance: 267-9696; (800) 322-9755 (toll-free).

Fax: 267-2319.

Internet Address: http://wilawlibrary.gov

Reference E-mail Address: wsll.ref@wicourts.gov

Publications: *WSLL @ Your Service* (monthly e-newsletter), at:
http://wilawlibrary.gov/newsletter/index.html

Number of Employees: 16.50.

Total Budget 2011-13: $6,022,600.

References: Wisconsin Statutes, Section 758.01; Supreme Court Rule 82.01.

Responsibility: The State Law Library is a public library open to all citizens of Wisconsin. It serves as the primary legal resource center for justices, judges, and staff of the entire Wisconsin court system. The library is administered by the supreme court, which appoints the library staff and determines the rules governing library use. The library acts as a consultant and resource for county law libraries throughout the state. Milwaukee County and Dane County contract with the State Law Library for management and operation of their courthouse libraries (the Milwaukee Legal Resource Center and the Dane County Legal Resource Center).

The library's 140,000-volume collection features session laws, statutory codes, court reports, administrative rules, legal indexes, and case law digests of the U.S. government, all 50 states and U.S. territories. It also includes selected documents of the federal government, legal and bar periodicals, legal treatises, and legal encyclopedias. The collection circulates to judges and court staff, attorneys, legislators, and government personnel.

The library offers reference, basic legal research and document delivery services, and training in the use of legal research Web sites and databases.

OFFICE OF LAWYER REGULATION

Board of Administrative Oversight: ROD ROGAHN (lawyer), *chairperson;* MARK A. PETERSON (lawyer), *vice chairperson;* BARRETT J. CORNEILLE, MARGADETTE DEMET, CHARLES P. DYKMAN, JOHN MCNAMARA, JOSEPH E. REDDING, HARVEY WENDEL (lawyers); DEANNA M. HOSIN, CLAUDE GILMORE, SHARON SCHMELING, vacancy (nonlawyers). (All members are appointed by the supreme court.)

Preliminary Review Committee: EDWARD HANNAN (lawyer), *chairperson;* ROBERT J. ASTI (lawyer), *vice chairperson;* JOHN W. CAMPION, MARTIN W. HARRISON, FRANK LO COCO, WILLIAM MUNDT, TIMOTHY NIXON, JAMES R. SMITH, vacancy (lawyers); DENNIS BLASIUS, JOHN FLANNERY, CLAIRE FOWLER, MICHAEL KINDSCHI, MICHAEL D. NOVAK (nonlawyers). (All members are appointed by the supreme court.)

Special Preliminary Review Panel: THOMAS A. CABUSH, CATHERINE LA FLEUR, ROBERT A. MATHERS, vacancy (lawyers); DANIEL ADAMS, JOHN DRIESSEN, DEE KITTLESON (nonlawyers). (All members are appointed by the supreme court.)

Sixteen District Committees (all members are appointed by the supreme court):

District 1 Committee (serves Jefferson, Kenosha, and Walworth Counties): MARK BROMLEY (lawyer), *chairperson;* PATRICK ANDERSON, BRENDA J. DAHL, ROBERT I. DUMEZ, TIMOTHY GERAGHTY, C. BENNETT PENWELL, CHRISTINE TOMAS (lawyers); JOHN G. BRAIG, WILLIAM J. BRYDGES, RANDALL J. HAMMETT, JEROME HONORE, JEROME K. LAURENT (nonlawyers).

District 2 Committee (serves Milwaukee County): JULIE A. O'HALLORAN (lawyer), *chairperson;* ROBERT C. MENARD (lawyer), *vice chairperson;* COLLEEN D. BALL, ELIOT BERNSTEIN, REBECCA BLEMBERG, SARAH FRY BRUCH, JACQUES C. CONDON, CEDRIC CORNWALL, ROBIN DORMAN, BRADLEY FOLEY, MICHELE FORD, HEATHER GATEWOOD, JAMES GEHRKE, DAVID B. KARP, LYNN LAUFENBERG, MICHAEL LAUFENBERG, BRETT LUDWIG, CHRISTOPHER J. MACGILLIS, THOMAS MERKLE, JAMES MOCZYDLOWSKI, ROBERT E. NAILEN, KEITH O'DONNELL, RAYMOND E.H. SCHRANK, DAVID W. SIMON, WILLIAM T. STUART, FRANK TERSCHAN, MONTE WEISS, JOSEPH WELCENBACH, THOMAS WHIPP (lawyers); ARLYN ADAMS, J. STEPHEN ANDERSON, FRANK VALENTINE BIALEK, RON BLAZEL, CARLOS A. BURITICA, NEILAND COHEN, RICHARD IPPOLITO, J. DAIN MADDOX, GARY NOSACEK, DANICA OLSON, HOLLY PATZER, KEITH J. ROBERTS, DEEDEE RONGSTAD, JOHN E. SUNDEEN, WILLIAM WARD, JAMES C. WENZLER (nonlawyers).

District 3 Committee (serves Fond du Lac, Green Lake, and Winnebago Counties): STEVEN R. SORENSON (lawyer), *chairperson;* PETER CULP, KENNARD N. FRIEDMAN, KRISTI L. FRY, ELIZABETH J. NEVITT, BETH OSOWSKI, DAVID J. SCHULTZ, KATHERINE SEIFERT, TIMOTHY R. YOUNG, JOHN S. ZARBANO (lawyers); KRISTY BRADISH, JOHN FAIRHURST, MARY JO KEATING, THOMAS E. KELROY, SUSAN T. VETTE (nonlawyers).

District 4 Committee (serves Calumet, Door, Kewaunee, Manitowoc, and Sheboygan Counties): NATASHA TORRY-MORGAN (lawyer), *chairperson;* BARRY S. COHEN, MARY LYNN DONOHUE, WILLIAM F. FALE, ROBERTA A. HECKES, ROBERT LANDRY (lawyers); DONALD A. SCHWOBE, JAMES STECKER, SUZANNE J. WEGNER, ALAN WHITE, RICHARD YORK (nonlawyers).

District 5 Committee (serves Buffalo, Clark, Crawford, Jackson, La Crosse, Monroe, Pepin, Richland, Trempealeau, and Vernon Counties): KARA M. BURGOS (lawyer), *chairperson;* MICHAEL C. ABLAN, DANIEL C. ARNDT, BRUCE J. BROVOLD, CHRISTOPHER DOERFLER, STEPHANIE HOPKINS, PAUL B. MILLIS, DAVID RUSSELL, JON D. SEIFERT (lawyers); DAVID CAMPBELL, JAMES W. GEISSNER, JAMES HANSON, RICHARD KYTE, PAUL R. LORENZ, RICHARD A. MERTIG, REED POMEROY, LARRY D. WYMAN (nonlawyers).

District 6 Committee (serves Waukesha County): GARY KUPHALL (lawyer), *chairperson;* LINDA S. COYLE, MARTIN DITKOF, ROSEMARY JUNE GORETA, MICHAEL JASSAK, RAMON A. KLITZKE, BRAD A. MARKVART, DANIEL MURRAY, PAUL E. SCHWEMER, NELSON E. SHAFER, MARGARET G. ZICKUHR (lawyers); RICHARD GASSO, ROBERT HAMILTON, THERESA M. PETERMAN, JOHN SCHATZMAN (nonlawyers).

District 7 Committee (serves Adams, Columbia, Juneau, Marquette, Portage, Sauk, Waupaca, Waushara, and Wood Counties): THOMAS M. KUBASTA (lawyer), *chairperson;* KAYE ANDERSON, STEPHEN D. CHIQUOINE, LEO L. GRILL, JOHN KRUSE (lawyers); PHILIP BAEBLER, LAVINDA CARLSON, DAVID A. KORTH, SUSAN G. MARTIN, ALAN K. PETERSON (nonlawyers).

District 8 Committee (serves Dunn, Eau Claire, Pierce, and St. Croix Counties): ROBERT L. LOBERG (lawyer), *chairperson;* JAY E. HEIT, MARK N. MATHIAS, GREGORY S. NICASTRO, CAROL N. SKINNER, PHILLIP M. STEANS, TRACY N. TOOL, R. MICHAEL WATERMAN (lawyers); KRISTEN AINSWORTH, JOHN DEROSIER, EDWARD HASS, THERESA JOHNSON, WILLIAM O'GARA, PAUL W. SCHOMMER (nonlawyers).

District 9 Committee (serves Dane County): THOMAS W. SHELLANDER (lawyer), *chairperson;* ANNE M. BLOOD, ANDREW CLARKOWSKI, JESUS G.Q. GARZA, AARON HALSTEAD, THOMAS S. HORNIG, ROBERT KASIETA, JENNIFER SLOAN LATTIS, DAVID MINKO, JENNIFER E. NASHOLD, BRIANE F. PAGEL, JR., MICHELE PERREAULT, LAWRENCE P. PETERSON, BRUCE AL. SCHULTZ, MEGAN A. SENATORI, DENNIS M. SULLIVAN, JAMES R. TROUPIS, JANICE K. WEXLER (lawyers); PATRICIA BASS, PATRICK DELMORE, NORMAN JENSEN, LYNN M. LEAZER, LARRY MCCRAY, BARBARA MORTENSEN, LARRY NESPER, ROBERT G. OWENS, THERON E. PARSONS, KATHLEEN M. RAAB, RICHARD C. SEAMAN, CONSUELO LOPEZ SPRINGFIELD, KENNETH YUSKA, JOHN ZERBE (nonlawyers).

District 10 Committee (serves Marinette, Menominee, Oconto, Outagamie, and Shawano Counties): GALE MATTISON (lawyer), *chairperson;* MICHAEL F. BROWN, TONY A. KORDUS, ROBERT SISSON, LAURA C. SMYTHE, GERALD WILSON (lawyers); GUY T. GOODING, TERRY HILGENBERG, JOHN W. HILL, CONNIE M. SEEFELDT, STEPHEN C. WARE (nonlawyer).

District 11 Committee (serves Ashland, Barron, Bayfield, Burnett, Chippewa, Douglas, Iron, Polk, Price, Rusk, Sawyer, Taylor, and Washburn Counties): CRAIG HAUKAAS (lawyer), *chairperson;* DEBORAH ASHER, ANNETTE M. BARNA, JOHN R. CARLSON, PARRISH J. JONES, TIMOTHY T. SEMPF, AMANDA L. WIECKOWIC (lawyers); GENE ANDERSON, JOHN BENNETT, ELIZABETH ESSER, DIANE FJELSTAD, ERNY HEIDEN, MARY ANN KING (nonlawyers).

District 12 Committee (serves Grant, Green, Iowa, Lafayette, and Rock Counties): JAMES A. CARNEY (lawyer), *chairperson;* JODY L. COOPER, DAN D. GARTZKE, THOMAS H. GEYER, ROBERT HOWARD, MELISSA B. JOOS, MARGARET M. KOEHLER, CAROLYN L. SMITH, JAMES D. WICKHEM (lawyers); LORI R. BIENEMA, DENNIS L. EVERSON, MICHAEL FURGAL, WILLIAM HUSTAD, MICHAEL F. METZ, ROBERT D. SPOODEN, LARRY WOLF (nonlawyers).

District 13 Committee (serves Dodge, Ozaukee, and Washington Counties): Joseph G. Doherty (lawyer), *chairperson;* John A. Best, Michael P. Herbrand, Christine Eisenmann Knudtson, Daniel L. Vande Zande, Annamarie A. Wineke (lawyers); Robert Blazich, Mark L. Born, Ramona Larson, Bonnie L. Schwid (nonlawyers).

District 14 Committee (serves Brown County): Bruce R. Bachhuber (lawyer), *chairperson;* Robert Gagan, Terry Gerbers, Mark A. Pennow, Thomas V. Rohan, Edward J. Vopal (lawyers); Richard Allcox, Debra L. Bursik, Jim Marshall, Joseph Neidenbach (nonlawyers).

District 15 Committee (serves Racine County): Mark F. Nielsen (lawyer), *chairperson;* John J. Buchakliam, Kristin Cafferty, Patricia J. Hanson, Mark R. Hinkston, Robert W. Keller, Timothy J. Pruitt, Robert K. Weber (lawyers); Thomas Chryst, Mark Gleason, Patricia Hoffman, Frank Konieska, Peter Smet (nonlawyers).

District 16 Committee (serves Forest, Florence, Langlade, Lincoln, Marathon, Oneida, and Vilas Counties): William D. Mansell (lawyer), *chairperson;* Lisa Brouillette, Laura K. Fitzsimmons, Douglas Klingberg, Dawn R. Lemke, Ginger Murray (lawyers); John P. Coleman, Monty Raskin, Dianne M. Weiler, Yvonne H. Weiler (nonlawyers).

Office of Lawyer Regulation: Keith L. Sellen, *director,* keith.sellen@wicourts.gov; John O'Connell, *deputy director,* john.o'connell@wicourts.gov; Elizabeth Estes, *deputy director,* elizabeth.estes@wicourts.gov; Bill Weigel, *litigation counsel,* bill.weigel@wicourts.gov; Mary Hoeft Smith, *trust account program administrator,* mary.hoeftsmith@wicourts.gov

Telephone: 267-7274; Central Intake toll-free (877) 315-6941.

Fax: 267-1959.

Mailing Address: 110 East Main Street, Suite 315, Madison 53703-3383.

Number of Employees: 27.50.

Total Budget 2011-13: $5,648,200.

References: Supreme Court Rules, Chapters 21 and 22.

Responsibility: The Office of Lawyer Regulation was created by order of the supreme court, effective October 1, 2000, to assist the court in fulfilling its constitutional responsibility to supervise the practice of law and protect the public from professional misconduct by members of the State Bar of Wisconsin. This agency assumed the attorney disciplinary functions that had previously been performed by the Board of Attorneys Professional Responsibility and, prior to January 1, 1978, by the Board of State Bar Commissioners.

The director of the Office of Lawyer Regulation is appointed by the supreme court and must be admitted to the practice of law in Wisconsin no later than six months following appointment. The Board of Administrative Oversight and the Preliminary Review Committee perform oversight and adjudicative responsibilities under the supervision of the supreme court.

The Board of Administrative Oversight consists of 12 members, 8 lawyers and 4 public members. Board members are appointed by the supreme court to staggered 3-year terms and may not serve more than two consecutive terms. The board monitors the overall system for regulating lawyers but does not handle actions regarding individual complaints or grievances. It reviews the "fairness, productivity, effectiveness and efficiency" of the system and reports its findings to the supreme court. After consultation with the director, it proposes the annual budget for the agency to the supreme court.

The Office of Lawyer Regulation receives and evaluates all complaints, inquiries, and grievances related to attorney misconduct or medical incapacity. The director is required to investigate any grievance that appears to support an allegation of possible attorney misconduct, and the attorney in question must cooperate with the investigation. District investigative committees are appointed in the 16 State Bar districts by the supreme court to aid the director in disciplinary investigations, forward matters to the director for review, and provide assistance when grievances can be settled at the district level.

After investigation, the director decides whether the matter should be forwarded to a panel of the Preliminary Review Committee, be dismissed, or be diverted for alternative action. This

14-member committee consists of 9 lawyers and 5 public members, who are appointed by the supreme court to staggered 3-year terms and may not serve more than two consecutive terms.

If a panel of the Preliminary Review Committee determines there is cause to proceed, the director may seek disciplinary action, ranging from private reprimand to filing a formal complaint with the supreme court that requests public reprimand, license suspension or revocation, monetary payment, or imposing conditions on the continued practice of law. An attorney may be offered alternatives to formal disciplinary action, including mediation, fee arbitration, law office management assistance, evaluation and treatment for alcohol and other substance abuse, psychological evaluation and treatment, monitoring of the attorney's practice or trust account procedures, continuing legal education, ethics school, or the multistate professional responsibility examination.

Formal disciplinary actions for attorney misconduct are filed by the director with the supreme court, which appoints a referee from a permanent panel of attorneys and reserve judges to hear discipline cases, make disciplinary recommendations to the court, and to approve the issuance of certain private and public reprimands. Referees conduct hearings on complaints of attorney misconduct, petitions alleging attorney medical incapacity, and petitions for reinstatement. They make findings, conclusions, and recommendations and submit them to the supreme court for review and appropriate action. Only the supreme court has the authority to suspend or revoke a lawyer's license to practice law in the State of Wisconsin.

Allegations of misconduct against the director, a lawyer member of staff, retained counsel, a lawyer member of a district committee, a lawyer member of the preliminary review committee, a lawyer member of the board of administrative oversight, or a referee are assigned by the director for investigation by a special investigator. The special investigator may close a matter if there is not enough information to support an allegation of possible misconduct. If there is enough information to support an allegation of possible misconduct an investigation is commenced. The investigator can then dismiss the matter after investigation or submit an investigative report to the special preliminary review panel which will ultimately decide whether or not there is cause to proceed. The special preliminary review panel consists of 7 members, 4 lawyers and 3 public members appointed by the supreme court who serve staggered 3-year terms and may not serve more than two consecutive terms. If cause is found, the special investigator can proceed to file a complaint with the supreme court and prosecute the matter personally or may assign that responsibility to counsel retained by the director for such purposes.

BOARD OF BAR EXAMINERS

Board of Bar Examiners: DANIEL D. BLINKA (Marquette University Law School faculty), *chairperson;* CHARLES P. DYKMAN (State Bar member), *vice chairperson;* KENNETH KUTZ (circuit court judge); KURT D. DYKSTRA, MARK R. FREMGEN, W. CRAIG OLAFSSON, vacancy (State Bar members); STEVEN M. BARKAN (UW Law School faculty); JAMES A. COTTER, PATRICIA EVANS, BONNIE L. SCHWID (public members). (All members are appointed by the supreme court.)

Director: JACQUELYNN B. ROTHSTEIN, 266-9760; Fax: 266-1196.

Mailing Address: 110 East Main Street, Suite 715, P.O. Box 2748, Madison 53701-2748.

E-mail Address: bbe@wicourts.gov

Internet Address: www.wicourts.gov/about/organization/offices/bbe.htm

Number of Employees: 8.00.

Total Budget 2011-13: $1,586,400.

References: Supreme Court Rules, Chapters 30, 31, and 40.

Responsibility: The 11-member Board of Bar Examiners manages all bar admissions by examination or by motion on proof of practice; conducts character and fitness investigations of all candidates for admission to the bar, including diploma privilege graduates; and administers the Wisconsin mandatory continuing legal education requirement for attorneys.

The board was formed from two Supreme Court Boards: the Board of Continuing Legal Education and the Board of Bar Commissioners. The Board of Continuing Legal Education was created effective January 1, 1976, to administer the Wisconsin Supreme Court's mandatory continuing legal education requirements for lawyers. Effective January 1, 1978, the Board of Continuing Legal Education was renamed the Board of Attorneys Professional Competence and continued to be charged with administering mandatory continuing legal education.

The Board of Bar Commissioners was charged with administering bar admission and compliance with the Code of Professional Responsibility. Effective January 1, 1978, the Board of Bar Commissioners' duties with respect to bar admission were transferred to the Board of Attorneys Professional Competence. Effective January 1, 1991, the Board of Attorneys Professional Competence was renamed the Board of Bar Examiners.

Members are appointed for staggered 3-year terms, but no member may serve more than two consecutive full terms. The number of public members was increased from one to 3 by a supreme court order, effective January 1, 2001.

JUDICIAL CONDUCT ADVISORY COMMITTEE

Judicial Conduct Advisory Committee: D. TODD EHLERS (circuit court or reserve judge serving in a rural area); DONALD ZUIDMULDER (judicial administrative district chief judge); LISA S. NEUBAUER (court of appeals judge); WAYNE MARIK (circuit court or reserve judge serving in an urban area); BRUCE GOODNOUGH (municipal court judge); MORIA KRUEGER (reserve judge); ANTON JAMIESON (circuit court commissioner); ROGER PETTIT (State Bar member); RANDY MORRISSETTE II (public member). (All members are selected by the supreme court.)

Mailing Address: P.O. Box 1688, Madison 53701-1688.

Internet Address: www.wicourts.gov/courts/committees/judicialconduct.htm

Telephone: 266-6828.

Fax: 267-0980.

Reference: Supreme Court Rules, Chapter 60 Appendix.

Responsibility: The Wisconsin Supreme Court established the Judicial Conduct Advisory Committee as part of its 1997 update to the Code of Judicial Conduct. The 9-member committee gives formal advisory opinions and informal advice regarding whether actions judges are contemplating comply with the code. It also makes recommendations to the supreme court for amendment to the Code of Judicial Conduct or the rules governing the committee.

JUDICIAL CONFERENCE

Members: All supreme court justices, court of appeals judges, circuit court judges, reserve judges, 3 municipal court judges (designated by the Wisconsin Municipal Judges Association), 3 judicial representatives of tribal courts (designated by the Wisconsin Tribal Judges Association), one circuit court commissioner designated by the Family Court Commissioner Association, and one circuit court commissioner designated by the Judicial Court Commissioner Association.

Internet Address: www.wicourts.gov/courts/committees/judicialconf.htm

References: Sections 758.171-758.18, Wisconsin Statutes; Supreme Court Rule 70.15.

Responsibility: The Judicial Conference, which was created by the Wisconsin Supreme Court, meets at least once a year to recommend improvements in administration of the justice system, conduct educational programs for its members, adopt the revised uniform traffic deposit and misdemeanor bail schedules, and adopt forms necessary for the administration of certain court proceedings. Since its initial meeting in January 1979, the conference has devoted sessions to family and children's law, probate, mental health, appellate practice and procedures, civil law, criminal law, truth-in-sentencing, and traffic law.

Judicial Conference bylaws have created a Nominating Committee and five standing committees. Committee members are elected by the Judicial Conference. The standing committees include: the Civil Jury Instructions Committee, the Criminal Jury Instructions Committee, the Juvenile Jury Instructions Committee, the Legislative Committee, and the Uniform Bond Committee. Chairpersons of each standing committee are selected annually by the committee members. The Nominating Committee is made up of the judges who chair the standing committees and the secretary of the Judicial Conference.

The Judicial Conference may create study committees to examine particular topics. These study committees must report their findings and recommendations to the next annual meeting of the Judicial Conference. Study committees usually work for one year, unless extended by the Judicial Conference.

JUDICIAL EDUCATION COMMITTEE

Judicial Education Committee: SHIRLEY S. ABRAHAMSON (supreme court chief justice); MICHAEL W. HOOVER (designated by appeals court chief judge); A. JOHN VOELKER (director of state courts); JEFFREY A. CONEN, MOLLY E. GALEWYRICK, TIMOTHY A. HINKFUSS, SCOTT L. HORNE, CHAD G. KERKMAN, 3 vacancies (circuit court judges appointed by supreme court); REBECCA PERSICK, ALICE A. RUDEBUSCH (circuit court commissioners appointed by supreme court); JINI M. RABAS (designated by dean, UW Law School); THOMAS HAMMER (designated by dean, Marquette University Law School). *Ex officio* member: LISA K. STARK (dean, Wisconsin Judicial College).

Office of Judicial Education: DAVID H. HASS, *director,* david.hass@wicourts.gov

Mailing Address: Office of Judicial Education, 110 East Main Street, Room 200, Madison 53703.

Telephone: 266-7807.

Fax: 261-6650.

E-mail Address: JED@wicourts.gov

Internet Address: www.wicourts.gov/courts/committees/judicialed.htm

Reference: Supreme Court Rules, Chapters 32, 33, and 75.05.

Responsibility: The 16-member Judicial Education Committee approves educational programs for judges and court personnel. The 8 circuit court judges and 2 circuit court commissioners on the committee serve staggered 2-year terms and may not serve more than two consecutive terms. The dean of the Wisconsin Judicial College is an *ex officio* member of the committee and has voting privileges.

In 1976, the supreme court issued Chapter 32 of the Supreme Court Rules, which established a mandatory program of continuing education for the Wisconsin judiciary, effective January 1, 1977. This program applies to all supreme court justices and commissioners, appeals court judges and staff attorneys, circuit court judges, and reserve judges. Each person subject to the rule must obtain a specified number of credit hours of continuing education within a 6-year period. The Office of Judicial Education, which the supreme court established in 1971, administers the program. It also sponsors initial and continuing educational programs for municipal judges and circuit court clerks.

PLANNING AND POLICY ADVISORY COMMITTEE

Planning and Policy Advisory Committee: SHIRLEY S. ABRAHAMSON (supreme court chief justice), *chairperson;* JUAN COLÁS (circuit court judge), *vice chairperson;* BRIAN BLANCHARD (appeals court judge selected by court); RICHARD BATES, JAMES BOLGERT, DAVID BOROWSKI, WILLIAM BRASH, THOMAS FLUGAUR, EUGENE HARRINGTON, TIMOTHY HINKFUSS, ELLIOTT LEVINE, PAT MADDEN, WILLIAM POCAN, DAVID REDDY, LINDA VAN DE WATER (circuit court judges elected by judicial administrative districts); DANIEL KOVAL (municipal judge elected by

Wisconsin Municipal Judges Association); JAMES BOLL, MARY WOLVERTON (selected by State Bar Board of Governors); GREGG MOORE (nonlawyer, elected county official); LINDA HOSKINS, DIANE TREIS-RUSK (nonlawyers); KELLI THOMPSON (public defender); ANDREW GRAUBARD (court administrator); JEFFREY ALTENBURG (prosecutor); CARLO ESQUEDA (circuit court clerk); DOLORES BOMRAD (circuit court commissioner). (Unless indicated otherwise, members are appointed by the chief justice.) Nonvoting associates: MARY WAGNER (chief judge liaison), A. JOHN VOELKER (director of state courts).

Planning Subcommittee: MICHAEL ROSBOROUGH (circuit court judge), *chairperson;* LISA NEUBAUER (appeals court judge); KATHRYN FOSTER, PAT MADDEN, MARY TRIGGIANO (circuit court judges); ANDREW GRAUBARD (court administrator); vacancy (circuit court clerk); DOLORES BOMRAD (circuit court commissioner); JOSEPH HEIM (public member). *Ex officio* members: SHIRLEY S. ABRAHAMSON (supreme court chief justice), JUAN COLÁS (circuit court judge, vice chairperson of Planning and Policy Advisory Committee), A. JOHN VOELKER (director of state courts).

Staff Policy Analyst: BONNIE MACRITCHIE, bonnie.macritchie@wicourts.gov

Mailing Address: 110 East Main Street, Room 410, Madison 53703.

Telephone: 261-7550.

Fax: 267-0911.

Internet Address: www.wicourts.gov/courts/committees/ppac.htm

Reference: Supreme Court Rule 70.14.

Responsibility: The 26-member Planning and Policy Advisory Committee advises the Wisconsin Supreme Court and the Director of State Courts on planning and policy and assists in a continuing evaluation of the administrative structure of the court system. It participates in the budget process of the Wisconsin judiciary and appoints a subcommittee to review the budget of the court system. The committee meets at least quarterly, and the supreme court meets with the committee annually. The Director of State Courts participates in committee deliberations, with full floor and advocacy privileges, but is not a member of the committee and does not have a vote.

This committee was created in 1978 as the Administrative Committee of the Courts and renamed the Planning and Policy Advisory Committee in December 1990.

WISCONSIN JUDICIAL SYSTEM — INDEPENDENT BODIES

JUDICIAL COMMISSION

Members: MICHAEL J. APRAHAMIAN, FRANK J. DAILY (State Bar members); SAIED ASSEF, MARK BARRETTE, EILEEN BURNETT, WILLIAM E. CULLINAN, LYNN M. LEAZER (nonlawyers); EMILY S. MUELLER (circuit court judge); PAUL F. REILLY (appeals court judge). (Judges and State Bar members appointed by supreme court. Nonlawyers are appointed by governor with senate consent.)

Executive Director: JAMES C. ALEXANDER.

Administrative Assistant: LAURY BUSSAN.

Mailing Address: 110 East Main Street, Suite 700, Madison 53703-3328.

Telephone: 266-7637.

Fax: 266-8647.

Agency E-mail: judcmm@wicourts.gov

Internet Address: www.wicourts.gov/judcom

Publication: Annual Report.

Number of Employees: 2.00.

Total Budget 2011-13: $649,200.

Statutory References: Sections 757.001, 757.81-757.99.

Responsibility: The 9-member Judicial Commission conducts investigations for review and action by the supreme court regarding allegations of misconduct or permanent disability of a judge or court commissioner. Members are appointed for 3-year terms but cannot serve more than two consecutive full terms.

The commission's investigations are confidential. If an investigation results in a finding of probable cause that a judge or court commissioner has engaged in misconduct or is disabled, the commission must file a formal complaint of misconduct or a petition regarding disability with the supreme court. Prior to filing a complaint or petition, the commission may request a jury hearing of its findings before a single appellate judge. If it does not request a jury hearing, the chief judge of the court of appeals selects a 3-judge panel to hear the complaint or petition.

The commission is responsible for prosecution of a case. After the case is heard by a jury or panel, the supreme court reviews the findings of fact, conclusions of law, and recommended disposition. It has ultimate responsibility for determining appropriate discipline in cases of misconduct or appropriate action in cases of permanent disability.

History: In 1972, the Wisconsin Supreme Court created a 9-member commission to implement the Code of Judicial Ethics it had adopted. The code enumerated standards of personal and official conduct and identified conduct that would result in disciplinary action. Subject to supreme court review, the commission had authority to reprimand or censure a judge.

A constitutional amendment approved by the voters in 1977 empowered the supreme court, using procedures developed by the legislature, to reprimand, censure, suspend, or remove any judge for misconduct or disability. With enactment of Chapter 449, Laws of 1977, the legislature created the Judicial Commission and prescribed its procedures. The supreme court abolished its own commission in 1978.

JUDICIAL COUNCIL

Members: PATIENCE DRAKE ROGGENSACK (justice designated by supreme court); BRIAN W. BLANCHARD (judge designated by court of appeals); A. JOHN VOELKER (director of state courts); GERALD P. PTACEK, JEFFREY A. WAGNER, MARY K. WAGNER, MAXINE A. WHITE (circuit court judges designated by Judicial Conference); SENATOR GROTHMAN (chairperson, senate judicial committee); REPRESENTATIVE J. OTT (chairperson, assembly judicial committee); GREG M. WEBER (designated by attorney general); TRACY K. KUCZENSKI (designated by Legislative Reference Bureau Chief); DAVID E. SCHULTZ (faculty member, UW Law School, designated by dean); THOMAS L. SHRINER, JR. (adjunct professor, Marquette University Law School, designated by dean); MARLA J. STEPHENS (designated by state public defender); CHRISTINE REW BARDEN (State Bar member, designated by president-elect); THOMAS W. BERTZ, WILLIAM GLEISNER, CATHERINE A. LA FLEUR (State Bar members selected by State Bar); BRAD SCHIMEL (district attorney appointed by governor); DENNIS MYERS, BENJAMIN J. PLISKIE (public members appointed by governor).

Mailing Address: 110 East Main Street, Suite 822, Madison 53703.

Telephone: 261-8290.

Fax: 261-8289.

Number of Employees: 1.00.

Total Budget 2011-13: $139,400.

Statutory References: Section 758.13.

Responsibility: The Judicial Council, created by Chapter 392, Laws of 1951, assumed the functions of the Advisory Committee on Rules of Pleading, Practice and Procedure, created by the 1929 Legislature. The 21-member council is authorized to advise the supreme court, the governor, and the legislature on any matter affecting the administration of justice in Wisconsin, and it may recommend legislation to change the procedure, jurisdiction, or organization of the courts. The council studies the rules of pleading, practice, and procedure and advises the supreme court about changes that will simplify procedure and promote efficiency.

Several council members serve at the pleasure of their appointing authorities. The 4 circuit judges selected by the Judicial Conference serve 4-year terms. The 3 members selected by the State Bar and the 2 citizen members appointed by the governor serve 3-year terms. The council is supported by one staff attorney.

WISCONSIN JUDICIAL SYSTEM — ASSOCIATED UNIT

STATE BAR OF WISCONSIN

Board of Governors (effective July 1, 2013): *Officers:* PATRICK J. FIEDLER, *president;* ROBERT R. GAGAN, *president-elect;* KEVIN G. KLEIN, *past president;* JENNIFER A. STUBER, *secretary;* KEVIN J. LYONS, *treasurer;* SHERRY COLEY, *chair of the board. District members:* BRIAN L. ANDERSON, ROBERT G. BARRINGTON, ANDREW P. BEILFUSS, BRUCE J. BROVOLD, DOUGLAS S. BUCK, JOSEPH M. CARDAMONE, MICHAEL J. COHEN, RAYMOND M. DALL'OSTO, JOHN E. DANNER, WILLIAM F. FALE, MARTIN P. GAGNE, MARGARET W. HICKEY, DAVID E. JONES, JILL M. KASTNER, LISA M. LAWLESS, STEVEN A. LEVINE, BRETT H. LUDWIG, JOHN R. ORTON, NILESH P. PATEL, THOMAS J. PHILLIPS, GREGORY A. PITTS, SARAH A. PONATH, DEBORAH BROWN PRICE, CHRISTOPHER E. ROGERS, ANIQUE N. RUIZ, THOMAS P. SCHWABA, RONALD J. SONDERHOUSE, GEORGE K. STEIL, JR., RICHARD J. SUMMERFIELD, PAUL G. SWANSON, LAURA SKILTON VERHOFF, R. MICHAEL WATERMAN, NICHOLAS C. ZALES. *Young Lawyers Division:* LEE D. TURONIE. *Government Lawyers Division:* ANN MARIE MOLITOR. *Nonresident Lawyers Division:* ANTHONY J. GRAY, DEBRA E. KUPER, DANIEL F. RINZEL, TODD R. SEELMAN. *Senior Lawyers Division:* THOMAS J. DROUGHT. *Nonlawyer members:* SUSAN K. MILLER, LELAND WIGG-NINHAM. *Minority Bar Liaisons:* ROBIN DALTON, ADRIA D. MADDALENI (nonvoting members).

Executive Director: GEORGE C. BROWN.

Mailing Address: P.O. Box 7158, Madison 53707-7158.

Location: 5302 Eastpark Boulevard, Madison.

Internet Address: www.wisbar.org; www.facebook.com/statebarofwi; www.twitter.com/statebarofwi

Telephones: General: 257-3838; Lawyer Referral and Information Service: (800) 362-9082.

Agency E-mail: service@wisbar.org

Publications: *WisBar InsideTrack; Wisconsin Lawyer Directory; Wisconsin Lawyer Magazine; Wisconsin News Reporter's Legal Handbook; Rotunda Report;* various legal practice handbooks and resources; various consumer pamphlets and videotapes, including *A Gift to Your Family: Planning Ahead for Future Health Care Needs.*

References: Supreme Court Rules, Chapters 10 and 11.

Responsibility: The State Bar of Wisconsin is an association of persons authorized to practice law in Wisconsin. It works to raise professional standards, improve the administration of justice and the delivery of legal services, and provide continuing legal education to lawyers. The State Bar conducts legal research in substantive law, practice, and procedure and develops related reports and recommendations. It also maintains the roll of attorneys, collects mandatory assessments imposed by the supreme court for supreme court boards and to fund civil legal services for the poor, and performs other administrative services for the judicial system.

Attorneys may be admitted to the State Bar by the full Wisconsin Supreme Court or by a single justice. Members are subject to the rules of ethical conduct prescribed by the supreme court, whether they practice before a court, an administrative body, or in consultation with clients whose interests do not require court appearances.

Organization: Subject to rules prescribed by the Wisconsin Supreme Court, the State Bar is governed by a board of governors, of not fewer than 52 members, consisting of the board's 6 officers, not fewer than 35 members selected by State Bar members from the association's 16 districts, 8 members selected by divisions of the State Bar, and 3 nonlawyers appointed by the supreme court. The board of governors selects the executive director, the executive committee, and the chairperson of the board.

History: In 1956, the Wisconsin Supreme Court ordered the organization of the State Bar of Wisconsin, effective January 1, 1957, to replace the formerly voluntary Wisconsin Bar Association, organized in 1877. All judges and attorneys entitled to practice before Wisconsin courts were required to join the State Bar. Beginning July 1, 1988, the Wisconsin Supreme Court suspended its mandatory membership rule, and the State Bar temporarily became a voluntary membership association, pending the disposition of a lawsuit in the U.S. Supreme Court. The Supreme Court ruled in *Keller v. State Bar of California,* 496 U.S. 1 (1990) that it is permissible to mandate membership provided certain restrictions are placed on the political activities of the mandatory State Bar. Effective July 1, 1992, the Wisconsin Supreme Court reinstated the mandatory membership rule upon petition from the State Bar Board of Governors.

Justice is not confined to the State Capitol. The Supreme Court travels to local courthouses for its Justice on Wheels program. (Supreme Court)

SUMMARY OF SIGNIFICANT DECISIONS OF THE WISCONSIN SUPREME COURT AND COURT OF APPEALS

June 2011 – June 2013

Alexis Blanco, Michael Duchek, Peggy Hurley, Elisabeth Shea, Robert Nelson, Legislative Reference Bureau

CONSTITUTIONAL LAW

Validity of the Domestic Partnership Statutes

In *Appling v. Doyle,* 2013 WI App 3, 345 Wis. 2d 762, 826 N.W.2d 666 (2012), the court of appeals concluded that the legal status provided by Wisconsin's domestic partnership statutes is not substantially similar to the legal status of marriage. The domestic partnership law, found in Chapter 770, Wisconsin Statutes, allows couples, including same-sex couples, to enter into domestic partnerships and acquire certain rights and responsibilities. The court found that the domestic partnership law does not violate the state's constitution, which was recently amended to restrict same-sex marriage.

In 2006, Wisconsin voters ratified an amendment to the Wisconsin Constitution related to same-sex couples and marriage, under Article XIII, Section 13. One provision of the amendment provided that a legal status substantially similar to or identical to marriage would not be recognized in the state for unmarried couples. Another provision of the amendment provided that only a marriage between one man and one woman would be recognized in this state.

In 2009, the Wisconsin Legislature passed the domestic partnership statutes which provided a number of rights and responsibilities similar to those offered in marriage. Several plaintiffs, including Julaine Appling, filed suit the same year challenging the constitutionality of the domestic partnership law. Originally, the case was filed with the Wisconsin Supreme Court, but the supreme court declined to take on the case and it was instead filed with the circuit court. The plaintiffs argued that the domestic partnership law created a legal status "similar to that of marriage" that violated the constitutional amendment. Advocacy group Fair Wisconsin, along with a number of same-sex couples, filed a motion to intervene and defend against the suit after the attorney general declined to do so. The circuit court found that the domestic partnership law was not in violation of the marriage amendment. Appling appealed the circuit court's ruling and the court of appeals affirmed. The court of appeals, citing previous cases, wrote that the burden was on Appling to prove beyond a reasonable doubt that the intention of the marriage amendment was to forbid the particular type of domestic partnership created by the legislature. Appling failed to meet the burden, the court said.

The plaintiffs argued that the term "legal status" referred only to "the eligibility and formation requirements of marriages and domestic partnerships, not the rights and obligations that come with these relationships." The plaintiffs further reasoned that the eligibility and formation requirements for domestic partnerships were the same as, or similar to, those for marriage.

To determine the meaning of the constitutional amendment, the court said it was required to look at three sources: the plain meaning of the language, the constitutional debates regarding the amendment, and the earliest interpretations of the amendment's provisions by the legislature. The court, looking at the plain meaning of the language of the amendment, held that "legal status ... of marriage" encompasses the rights and obligations provided to couples who enter into domestic partnerships, as well as the eligibility, formation, and termination requirements in marriage. As a whole, the court wrote, the two rights afforded to the two groups "are not substantially similar" to one another. The rights and responsibilities provided to couples in domestic partnerships are limited and include the ability to take family medical leave to care for an injured or sick partner, and the right to inherit a partner's estate in the absence of a will, among others. Some rights and responsibilities not granted to couples in domestic partnerships include the "presumption that all property of married couples is marital property" and the right to "adopt children jointly."

The court, when looking at the debate regarding the proposed amendment, found that the proponents said that the amendment did not prohibit the legislature from giving certain benefits to

The East Wing of the State Capitol is home to the Supreme Court. Kenyon Cox's mosaic of Justice adorns the rotunda. (Clarissa Pohlman)

same-sex partners, rather it prohibited providing those partnerships with the same benefits and status as married couples. Memos provided to the proponents by legislative attorneys also supported this position, said the court. In addition, some plaintiffs in this case were quoted saying that the amendment was intended to prevent marriage by another name, said the court. Finally, looking at the only legislative interpretation of the amendment, the domestic partnership law, the court held that it would not look to it for guidance on the meaning of the amendment.

The court affirmed the domestic partnership law because it conferred a legal status that was considerably different than that conferred by marriage.

Warrantless Search

In *State of Wisconsin v. St. Martin,* 2011 WI 44, 334 Wis. 2d 290, 800 N.W.2d 858 (2011), the supreme court considered the constitutionality of a warrantless search of St. Martin's apartment, weighing St. Martin's refusal to give consent to the search against his co-tenant's approval of the search. The court had two United States Supreme Court decisions to guide them, each coming to a different conclusion depending on whether the person who refuses to grant consent is "physically present" at the residence when he or she makes the refusal.

The Supreme Court held, in *George v. Randolph,* 547 U.S. 103 (2006), that if the consenting and the nonconsenting residents are both present at the dwelling when consent is sought, a warrantless search may not be conducted. However, in *United States v. Matlock,* 415 U.S. 164 (1974), the Court held that the objection to a search by an absent, albeit nearby, resident could not trump the consent to a search given by a resident who is present at the residence when consent is sought by the police. Applying the case it felt most closely matched the facts of the instant case, the court held that the search of St. Martin's apartment was constitutional.

The case came before the supreme court on certification from the court of appeals. The certification question was stated as follows: whether the rule regarding consent to search a shared dwelling which states that a warrantless search cannot be justified when a physically present resident expressly refuses consent, applies where the physically present resident is taken forcibly from his residence by law enforcement officers but remains in close proximity to the residence such that the refusal is made directly to law enforcement on the scene? Looking carefully at the specific facts in the instant case, the supreme court held that the *Randolph* case did not apply where, as here, the person objecting was not physically present at the residence when permission for the warrantless search was sought by law enforcement. Instead, the court felt that the facts more closely resembled those of *Matlock*, where the nonconsenting resident was nearby, but not physically present at, the dwelling, and therefore unable to trump the consent given by the resident who was at the dwelling.

The court noted that the Supreme Court, in reaching a different conclusion in *Randolph* from the one it had reached in *Matlock*, acknowledged that the distinction between the circumstances in the two cases was fine. The court noted that in order to establish a useful and pragmatic guideline, the law, in this case, is "unapologetically formalistic" and that admittedly small differences in the fact scenarios are dispositive.

The court found that under the facts of this case, St. Martin was not "physically present" when he refused consent. St. Martin lived in a residence with his girlfriend, LaToya. LaToya went to the police, stating that St. Martin had beaten her, and that she suspected he had cocaine in their home. The police accompanied LaToya back to her home, where they met St. Martin. The court noted that St. Martin stood at the door when the police arrived and gave no objection to their entry. St. Martin was arrested for the alleged battery and placed in a squad car at the scene. At that time, LaToya consented to search of the home; when an officer approached the squad car to ask St. Martin for his consent, he refused. The officers conducted the search and found cocaine and currency.

The court concluded that, while St. Martin was indisputedly near his residence, he was not "at the door and objecting" to the search, nor was he physically present in the home for the "threshold colloquy" seeking consent to search. The court noted that St. Martin had been properly arrested and taken into custody when he was questioned, and that there was nothing to suggest that St. Martin's removal from the home was merely a pretext to deny him a threshold colloquy.

The court found that, in order for the *Randolph* case to control, St. Martin would have had to be more than merely nearby: he would have had to have been physically present in the home, and that he would have had to refuse consent pursuant to a colloquy that took place while he was physically present. The court rejected the notion that the police officer's attempt to obtain consent while St. Martin was outside of the home constituted a "threshold colloquy", noting that other courts had applied the *Randolph* case in a similarly narrow manner. The court concluded, therefore, that the facts in the instant case more closely resembled those in the *Matlock* case, which held that the refusal to consent to a search by a physically absent resident who had been arrested and was in a squad car some distance from the home could not trump the consent to search given by another resident of the home.

Two justices writing to dissent looked at the same facts and concluded that St. Martin was physically present for the purposes of determining whether *Randolph* applied, and that the warrantless search was therefore unlawful. The dissent agreed that *Randolph* applies only if the person is physically present when he or she objects to a warrantless search, but rejected that notion that "physical presence" required the objecting person to be squarely within the home. Instead the dissent argued that a more reasonable interpretation is that a person may object to a search of his or her home when he or she is physically present "at the scene" and not necessarily inside the home.

CRIMINAL LAW

Constitutionality of Warrantless Searches as a Condition of Extended Supervision

In *State v. Rowan*, 2012 WI 60, 341 Wis. 2d 281, 814 N.W.2d 854 (2012), the supreme court was asked to consider whether the Fourth Amendment to the U.S. Constitution, or its counterpart in the Wisconsin Constitution, permitted a court to impose upon a defendant a condition of extended supervision allowing "any law enforcement officer to search the defendant's person, vehicle, or residence for firearms, at any time and without probable cause or reasonable suspicion." The court held that such a condition did not violate Rowan's constitutional rights because the court had made an individualized determination that the condition was necessary, based upon the facts of that particular case.

The case originated in March 2008, when Rowan was observed by a police officer driving erratically and running a stop sign. Rowan subsequently crashed into a pole. At the scene of the accident, Rowan appeared intoxicated and agitated. She also reached to the floor of her vehicle and asked where her gun was. Police subsequently located a semiautomatic handgun and a box of ammunition in the vehicle. Rowan was taken to a hospital for emergency treatment, where she acted aggressively toward hospital staff and a law enforcement officer and made additional threats. As a law enforcement officer attempted to restrain Rowan, Rowan injured the officer's hand. Rowan was charged with five counts and convicted on each count at a jury trial. For one of the counts, battery to a law enforcement officer, the court, acting under its statutory authority to impose conditions of extended supervision, imposed a condition that Rowan, her residence, and her vehicle would be subject to search for a firearm at any time by law enforcement without probable cause or reasonable suspicion. Rowan appealed, arguing that the condition violated her constitutional rights. The court of appeals certified the case to the supreme court, which voted unanimously to affirm the judgment of the circuit court.

Writing the court's opinion, Justice Crooks began with a statement of the test used to determine whether a condition of release is constitutionally permissible, which is that courts will uphold a condition as long as it is both: 1) not overly broad and 2) reasonably related to the person's rehabilitation. In addressing the first part of the test, the court noted the United States Supreme Court's holding in *Samson v. California*, which addressed a California law subjecting all parolees to suspicionless searches at any time, day or night. In contrast, the court wrote, the condition placed upon Rowan was specifically based upon evidence that Rowan had made numerous threats, including a subsequent threat against a judge, and had purchased several firearms subsequent to her arrest. Noting that the condition was limited to searches for firearms and that the searches had to be performed in a reasonable manner, the supreme court concluded that the condition was not overly broad. Addressing the second part of the test, the court wrote of the interconnection between encouraging lawful conduct and protecting the public. Again citing Rowan's history with firearms and making threats, the court wrote that providing Rowan with an incentive to refrain from possessing firearms was reasonably related to her rehabilitation, which would also serve the interest of public safety. For these reasons, the court held that the condition imposed by the court did not violate constitutional protections afforded to Rowan.

The court also rejected a separate argument made by Rowan that her conviction for battery to a law enforcement officer was invalidated by the fact that the officer was not acting in an official capacity at the time of the battery, which is an element of the offense. Rowan had argued that because the officer was assisting a nurse who was performing a blood draw on Rowan, the officer was not acting in an official capacity. The court rejected this argument, noting that there was ample evidence from which the jury could have concluded that the officer was acting in an official capacity at the time of the battery.

CIVIL LAW
Can an Unmodifiable Agreement for Child Support be Enforceable?

In *In re marriage of May*, 2012 WI 35, 339 Wis. 2d 626, 813 N.W.2d 179 (2012), the Wisconsin Supreme Court considered a stipulated agreement between two divorced parents that required the father to pay, for a period of 33 months, a fixed amount of child support that amounted to 72% of his income. After entering into the stipulation, the father sought to have it modified as being unfair to him and against public policy. The supreme court, looking at all of the circumstances surrounding the agreement, weighing public policy concerns, and considering the changed circumstances from the time the parties entered into the agreement, rejected the father's arguments and ruled that the agreement may be enforced.

The Mays were divorced in October 2005. After the divorce, the parties wrangled in court over the next couple of years on a variety of child-related issues, including payment of child support, visitation arrangements, scheduling conflicts, and payment of various child care costs. In January 2008, the court entered an order based on a stipulation entered into between the Mays. The stipulation required the father to pay a minimum of $1,203 a month for child support and prohibited the father from seeking a reduction of that amount for 33 months. In an apparent exchange for that arrangement, the mother assumed certain child care costs and agreed that the father could make temporarily decreased payments on child support arrearages that had accumulated.

After approximately 18 months, the father sought to reduce the child support payments. The mother argued that, in light of the stipulation between the parties that child support would be "unmodifiable" for at least 33 months, the father was equitably estopped from seeking reduction in the payments until that period of time passed. The circuit court agreed with the mother; the father appealed, and the court of appeals certified the issue to the supreme court, which agreed to decide the matter.

The supreme court set forth the questions on review: does the stipulation and order establishing unmodifiable minimum child support payments for 33 months violate public policy, and did the circuit court err when it estopped the father from seeking a modification of the child support order? The supreme court turned first to the discussion of whether the stipulation and order violates public policy.

The court held that, while parties are generally free to enter into stipulations regarding the amounts paid for child support, certain agreements tend to undermine the paramount consideration, the best interests of the child, and may therefore be voided as against public policy. For example, an unmodifiable stipulation and order that set a maximum amount of child support for a particular period of time would violate public policy, as would a stipulation and order that set a minimum amount of child support with no durational limit. Looking at the stipulation and order in the instant case, however, the court found that it did not violate public policy.

The court declined to adopt a rule that unmodifiable floors that are limited in duration are invalid per se. The court noted that the parties are generally free to enter into a stipulation so long as the stipulation is made knowingly and intentionally, and was fair to the parties when they entered into it. The court found that those things were all true in the *May* case. The court noted that, although the percentage of the father's income due as child support appears high, the father's income was the same when he brought the challenge as it was when he freely entered into the stipulation. The court also observed that the father's income had fluctuated significantly over the years since the couple had divorced and the stipulation was limited in duration. All of these factors, coupled with the fact that the mother gave up certain things in exchange for the stipulation and relied upon the stipulation being unmodifiable, factored into the court's decision to uphold it. Further, the court stated that an unmodifiable stipulation can have the advantage of keeping parties out of court, at least for the duration of the stipulation; the court noted that the tension created by repetitive litigation tends to be against the best interests of the children involved.

However, the court held that even if a stipulation for child support was entered into freely and knowingly, was fair when it was entered into, and not against public policy, the court retained its equitable jurisdiction to consider whether the stipulation is in the best interests of the child. Reiterating that its primary purpose in litigation involving child support is to promote and protect the best interests of the children involved, the court observed that courts are obligated to ensure that every court order reflects this purpose and to consider all of the circumstances surrounding a stipulation, when it was entered into and when it is challenged, before deciding whether to uphold the stipulation. Looking at the *May* case, the court found that the father failed to demonstrate any changed circumstances or other equitable considerations that would justify a refusal to enforce the stipulation.

A Circuit Court Lacks Authority to Order a School District to Provide Educational Services to Expelled Students

In *Madison Metropolitan School District v. Circuit Court for Dane County,* 2011 WI 72, 336 Wis. 2d 95, 800 N.W.2d 442 (2011), the supreme court affirmed a court of appeals decision that a circuit court does not have authority to order a school district to provide alternative educational services to a juvenile who has been adjudicated delinquent and lawfully expelled from school. A circuit court may, however, order the juvenile to attend educational programs that a school district offers.

On June 5, 2009, a 15-year-old student (referred to as M.T.) was arrested for bringing nine bags of marijuana to school, and charged with possession of marijuana with the intent to deliver.

The Madison Metropolitan School District (MMSD) filed a complaint seeking the expulsion of M.T. from the district. After two hearings, the hearing officer ordered that M.T. be expelled for up to three semesters with the opportunity to return to school after one semester if specific conditions were met. The order of expulsion denied M.T. any educational programing from MMSD for at least one semester.

Due to the drug-related charges, M.T. was also subject to a delinquency proceeding in Dane County circuit court. Upon finding M.T. to be delinquent, the court ordered the Dane County Department of Human Services to prepare a pre-dispositional report under Section 938.33 (1), Wisconsin Statutes. The report included a plan for M.T. to attend school regularly without unexcused absences while under the jurisdiction of the juvenile court. The court adopted this provision in its dispositional order and notified the school district that it had a duty to provide educational programming. MMSD refused to provide any educational programming, including "home school materials."

In an order to show cause to MMSD, the circuit court stated that it could not fulfill its statutory duties if the school district refused to provide any educational programming, and that MMSD's actions were contributing to M.T.'s delinquency. The school district objected to the order to show cause by letter, stating that the order undermined its statutory authority to designate the terms of an expulsion. Following a hearing, the circuit court ordered MMSD to develop an educational program for M.T. MMSD complied, but, after its motion for reconsideration was denied, appealed the circuit court's decision. The court of appeals construed the appeal as a petition for a supervisory writ. The court of appeals agreed with MMSD that the circuit court had gone beyond its authority under the Juvenile Justice Code, granted a supervisory writ, and vacated the circuit court's order.

On review, the supreme court evaluated a circuit court's authority under the Juvenile Justice Code and a school district's statutory authority and duties in a situation where a juvenile has been expelled and adjudicated delinquent but not committed to an institution or program that is required to provide educational services. The supreme court held that MMSD had the authority to expel M.T. and encouraged it to provide alternative educational services, but held that a circuit court may not require a school district to do so. The court also held that Section 938.34, Wisconsin Statutes, allows a circuit court to order a delinquent juvenile to attend educational programs that a school district offers, but does not require the school district to create a particular program or enter into a contract for one.

Finally, the court addressed the circuit court's claim that, when a school district refuses to provide educational programming to a delinquent juvenile, this act contributes to the delinquency of the juvenile under Section 938.45, Wisconsin Statutes. The circuit court argued that this gave it the authority to order the school district to provide educational services. The supreme court disagreed with the circuit court's reasoning. Section 938.45, Wisconsin Statutes concerns "persons" who contribute to the delinquency of the juvenile, which, the court held, means natural persons, not entities such as school districts.

Justice Crooks, joined by Chief Justice Abrahamson and Justice Bradley, dissented, arguing that the 1996 Juvenile Justice Code expanded the circuit court's authority to develop a range of dispositions to address juvenile crime. The dissent concluded that this expanded authority includes the authority to order a district to provide educational services to an expelled juvenile that the circuit court has adjudged delinquent.

The Cost of Redacting Public Records

In *Milwaukee Journal Sentinel v. City of Milwaukee,* 2012 WI 65, 341 Wis. 2d 607, 815 N.W.2d 367 (2012), the supreme court was asked to address whether the public records law permitted authorities, such as cities, to charge for the cost of deleting or redacting nondisclosable information included within a public record. The supreme court held that charging for such costs was not permitted under the public records law.

The case originated with public records requests made by two reporters from the *Milwaukee Journal Sentinel* (the newspaper) for police dispatch and incident reports for crimes in the City of Milwaukee (the city). After complying with a number of requests, the city asked for prepayment of costs to comply with the requests, including costs to delete or redact nondisclosable information from the records. The newspaper filed suit in response, conceding that the city was required by law to redact certain information from the records, but contending that the newspaper was not liable for payment for the costs of performing the redactions. The circuit court ruled that the newspaper was liable under the public records law for payment of all actual, necessary, and direct costs incurred by the city to comply with the requests, including the costs of deleting or redacting nondisclosable information. The newspaper filed a petition to bypass the court of appeals and have the supreme court directly review the ruling of the circuit court, and the supreme court granted the petition.

In her lead opinion, joined by two other justices, Chief Justice Abrahamson examined the text of various provisions of the public records law. She noted that the legislature in 1981 had specifically contemplated that information would need to be redacted from certain records, but had not provided that an authority could charge for time spent redacting the records. She wrote that while the public records law allowed authorities to charge for the actual, necessary, and direct costs of other specific tasks associated with complying with a public records request, deleting or redacting information did not fit neatly within any of those enumerated tasks. Specifically, she wrote that redacting information from a record was not part of "locating" or "reproducing" a record, both of which are tasks for which an authority may charge under the law.

Chief Justice Abrahamson also declined to read into the statute authority to charge for redacting, citing the declaration in the public records law of a policy in favor of access to records. She noted that increasing the costs of public records requests may inhibit access to public records or render them completely inaccessible, which would be inconsistent with that declaration of policy. Finally, the chief justice cited a 1983 Attorney General's opinion consistent with the court's opinion and noted that, in spite of the Attorney General's opinion, the legislature had not amended the law to allow authorities to charge for the costs of redaction or deletion.

Justice Prosser and Justice Roggensack both wrote opinions to concur with the result of the lead opinion, but declined to join it. They wrote separately to urge the legislature to revisit the issue presented by the case. Justice Roggensack, whose opinion was considered the majority opinion on the policy issue, wrote that the court's holding could result either in unfulfilled requests or high costs to taxpayers. Her opinion was joined by three other justices.

The Difference Between a Zoning Ordinance and a Nonzoning Police Power Ordinance

In *Zwiefelhofer v. Town of Cooks Valley,* 2012 WI 7, 338 Wis. 2d 488, 809 N.W.2d 362 (2012), the supreme court was asked to determine whether a town's nonmetallic mining ordinance was a zoning ordinance or a nonzoning police power ordinance. The court held that the ordinance was not a zoning ordinance because it did not share many of the fundamental characteristics of traditional zoning.

The Cooks Valley town board enacted an ordinance regulating nonmetallic mining (commercial sand and gravel pits) and associated activities. The town had adopted village powers under Section 60.22 (3), Wisconsin Statutes, and therefore had police power, including the power to enact a zoning ordinance. However, Chippewa County, in which the town was located, had enacted countywide zoning under Section 59.69, Wisconsin Statutes, and therefore the town could not adopt a zoning ordinance without county board approval. Town residents brought a declaratory action against the town seeking a declaration that the ordinance was invalid because, as a zoning ordinance, the town did not seek county board approval before enacting it.

The ordinance required a permit to operate a nonmetallic mine. An application for a permit would be considered by the town plan commission, which would make a recommendation to the town board. The town board would hold a public hearing on the application and grant the permit if it determined the application was complete, the mine was in the best interests of the citizens of the town and consistent with protection of public health, safety and welfare, and the applicant received federal, state, and county permits. The board could grant a permit with or without certain types of conditions. The ordinance exempted mines in existence prior to its enactment, but applied to any expansion of those mines.

Instead of creating a bright-line rule distinguishing a zoning ordinance from a nonzoning police power ordinance, the court used a functional approach, cataloguing the characteristics of traditional zoning and zoning's commonly accepted purposes and comparing these to the town's ordinance. The court identified a list of six characteristics that typically exist in traditional zoning, though not always: 1) division of a geographic area into multiple zones or districts; 2) within a district, established permitted uses and prohibited uses; 3) the purpose of controlling the location of an activity, rather than the manner in which an activity takes place; 4) classification of uses and attempt to comprehensively regulate all possible uses; 5) fixed determination of permitted uses rather than case-by-case determination of conditionally permitted uses; and 6) allowance of nonconforming uses that existed at the time the zoning ordinance was adopted.

The court compared the characteristics of the town's ordinance to these six traditional zoning characteristics. It held that, unlike traditional zoning, the ordinance applied throughout the town, rather than creating districts or zones; that it included no permitted uses; that it was aimed at regulating nonmetallic mining regardless of its location; that it applied only to nonmetallic mining instead of regulating a comprehensive set of uses in the town; and that it applied only on a case-by-case basis. The court noted that, like traditional zoning, the ordinance "grandfathered" mines in existence at the time of the ordinance's adoption. However, the court held that a nonzoning police power ordinance can also exempt preexisting uses. Despite the fact that the ordinance was a significant regulation on the use of land, the court held this was not dispositive. Its overall lack of similarity to traditional zoning led the court to conclude that the ordinance was not a zoning ordinance.

While noting that there have been several formulations of the general purpose of zoning, the court identified the most appropriate one to be the separation of incompatible land uses. The court concluded that the ordinance did not share this purpose because it did not identify or separate incompatible land uses, and that its purpose was instead to simply regulate nonmetallic mines

Hospital-Owned Offsite Outpatient Clinic Is Tax-Exempt

In *Covenant Healthcare System, Inc. v. City of Wauwatosa*, 2011 WI 80, 336 Wis. 2d 522, 800 N.W.2d 906 (2011), the supreme court held that an off-site outpatient clinic owned and operated by a hospital was exempt from property taxes.

Covenant Healthcare System, Inc. (Covenant) was the sole member of St. Joseph Regional Medical Center (St. Joseph), which owned and operated St. Joseph Hospital in Milwaukee. In 2003, Covenant built a 5-story building five miles away from the hospital and transferred ownership to St. Joseph. St. Joseph Outpatient Clinic (Outpatient Clinic) was operated on three of the five floors, and Covenant filed a tax exemption request for these three floors of the building for each year between 2003 and 2006. The City of Wauwatosa denied each request, Covenant paid the assessment, and brought an action to recover the amount it had been assessed. The circuit court found in favor of Covenant. The court of appeals reversed, holding the Outpatient Clinic was not tax-exempt. The supreme court reversed.

The supreme court addressed four issues relating to property tax exemption under Section 70.11 (4m) (a), Wisconsin Statutes. First, to qualify for the exemption the Outpatient Clinic must have been used exclusively for the purpose of a hospital. The court held that the Outpatient Clinic had been built in order to move and expand services currently provided at the hospital to a new space and free up space at the hospital. It also held that the Outpatient Clinic and the hospital's records and billing system were fully integrated, that they shared the same department heads, the same physicians, and operated under the same hospital license. Therefore, the court held that the Outpatient Clinic essentially served as a department of the hospital, and was used exclusively for the purpose of a hospital.

Second, if the Outpatient Clinic was determined to be a doctor's office, it would not qualify for the tax exemption. The city urged the court to consider whether the Outpatient Clinic resembled a doctor's office from the perspective of a patient. However, the court looked instead at factors such as how physicians were compensated, whether they had offices, whether they owned or leased the building or equipment, whether clinic billing software was separate from the hospital's, and the existence of a gift shop and cafeteria. Based on these factors the court concluded that the Outpatient Clinic was not a doctor's office.

Third, to be eligible for the property tax exemption, the Outpatient Clinic could not be "used for commercial purposes." The court rejected the city's proposal to focus on the generation of profits, meaning revenues in excess of costs, as an oversimplification of "commercial purposes." It noted that this formula would require not-for-profits to operate at a loss or break-even in order to qualify for a property tax exemption. Instead, the court held that "commercial" means "having profit as the primary aim." The court said that the Outpatient Clinic's primary goal was diagnosing, treating, and caring for the sick, injured, and disabled, therefore it was not used for commercial purposes.

Finally, the Outpatient Clinic would be precluded from a property tax exemption if any part of its net earnings inured to the benefit of a "shareholder, *member*, director or officer...." Section 70.11 (4m) (a) (emphasis added by court). Therefore, the court had to determine if Covenant was a "member" as contemplated in the statute. The court reasoned that if a "member" included a not-for-profit corporation, a not-for-profit hospital would have to rewrite its bylaws to exclude a not-for-profit member from the distribution of its assets upon dissolution, or the hospital would never qualify for tax-exempt status. In the case of St. Joseph, this would mean it would have to assign its assets to go to an unrelated not-for-profit corporation upon dissolution, which would give the unrelated organization an interest in the hospital's failure. The court held that this is an unreasonable construction of the statute's language. It held that the term "member" does not include not-for-profit entities like Covenant.

Justice Abrahamson dissented, arguing that, given that property is presumed taxable and that exemptions are strictly construed, Covenant had not met its burden to prove that the Outpatient Clinic was not used as a doctor's office.

Local Regulation of Livestock Facility Siting Preempted

In *Adams v. State Livestock Facilities Siting Review Bd.,* 2012 WI 85, 342 Wis. 2d 444, 820 N.W.2d 404 (2012), the supreme court held that the livestock facility siting law, Section 93.90, Wisconsin Statutes, (Siting Law) preempts local government's authority to impose on a livestock siting permit any conditions outside of those the Siting Law allows.

In 1977, the Town of Magnolia (Town) adopted a zoning ordinance, including water quality protections prohibiting the discharge of pollutants exceeding the minimum standards set for navigable waters under the Wisconsin Administrative Code. In 2004, the legislature enacted the Siting Law, and in 2005 the Town adopted it as part of its zoning ordinance. On May 1, 2006, the Department of Agriculture, Trade and Consumer Protection (DATCP) promulgated Wisconsin Administrative Code Chapter ATCP 51 (ATCP 51), which provided more detailed guidelines for the permitting process, as required by the Siting Law. On May 2, 2006, Larson Acres, Inc. (Larson) filed with the Town an application for a conditional use permit (CUP) for a livestock facility to house 1,500 animal units. On May 24, 2006, the Town revised the water quality provision of its zoning ordinance to also apply the standards for groundwater and drinking water under the Wisconsin Administrative Code and applicable federal drinking water regulations.

On March 27, 2007 the Town granted Larson a CUP with seven conditions relating to informing the town of Larson's pollutant minimization and nutrient management plans, allowing the Town access for water quality testing, sharing information with the Town that was required to be provided to the Department of Natural Resources (DNR), and allowing the Town to annually review Larson's compliance with the CUP. Larson challenged five of the seven conditions in an appeal to the State Livestock Facilities Siting Review Board (Siting Board). The Siting Board affirmed the permit but found that the conditions that were not based on the standards incorporated into ATCP 51 to be beyond the Town's authority to impose. The Siting Board modified or struck those conditions accordingly.

The Town appealed to the circuit court, which found that the Siting Law only required a political subdivision to comply with certain procedures in order to impose standards more stringent than the states. Because the court found that the Town's conditions were all based upon the state's administrative code, it concluded that the Town had the authority to impose these conditions without following the Siting Law's procedures. The court also found that the Siting Board did not have the authority to modify a permit, but rather could only affirm or reverse a permit in its entirety.

Larson appealed, and the court of appeals reversed. It determined that the Siting Law preempted the Town from imposing the challenged conditions, and that the Town had not followed the Siting Law procedures required to impose conditions more stringent than state's. It also held that the Siting Board had the authority to modify conditions to a permit.

The supreme court reviewed the Siting Board's decision de novo and affirmed the court of appeals' decision. First, the court reviewed Wisconsin's preemption doctrine to determine how to analyze the Siting Law's language. It concluded that livestock facility siting presented a mixed issue of statewide and local concern, and that the analysis was whether any of four factors was met: 1) whether the legislature has expressly withdrawn the power of a political subdivision to act; or whether the political subdivision's actions 2) logically conflict with the legislation; 3) defeat the purpose of the legislation; or 4) are contrary to the spirit of the legislation.

Second, the court determined that the plain language of the Siting Law expressly withdrew a political subdivision's power to regulate livestock facility siting. It came to this conclusion after noting that the Siting Law required DATCP to promulgate uniform statewide livestock siting standards, that it prohibited a political subdivision from disapproving a livestock facility siting permit, except in narrow circumstances, and that it limited the conditions a political subdivision may impose on livestock siting permits to those consistent with the statewide standards, except in narrow circumstances.

Third, the court determined that the conditions the Town imposed on Larson's CUP were not consistent with the Siting Law, and did not satisfy the narrow exception allowing more stringent conditions because the Town did not base them on an adopted "fact-finding". Finally, the court held that the authority to modify the conditions of a siting permit, while not expressly conferred, is necessarily implied by the statutes under which the Siting Board operates. It held that the purpose of the Siting Law and ATCP 51 was to facilitate timely approval of proper permit applications, and it would frustrate that purpose to invalidate a Siting Board decision to correct an error in an efficient manner.

Justice Abrahamson dissented for three reasons, the third of which Justice Bradley joined. First, she argued that the Siting Law limits but does not expressly withdraw the ability of a political subdivision to regulate livestock facility siting, and concluded that the majority therefore used the wrong preemption analysis. Second, she reasoned that the conditions imposed on the permit were not prohibited because the Town has the power, under a separate statute, to impose similar conditions to regulate the operations of a livestock facility. Finally, she concluded that the plain language of the Siting Law prohibited the Siting Board from modifying the Town's conditions and, even if it may lead to absurd results, it is the legislature's job to amend this language, not the court's.

Medical Malpractice; Providing Information to Patient

In *Jandre v. Injured Patients & Families Compensation Fund,* 2012 WI 39, 340 Wis. 2d 31, 813 N.W.2d 627 (2012), the court was asked to interpret the informed consent statute, Section 448.30, Wisconsin Statutes, that requires a doctor to inform a patient about the availability of alternative, viable medical treatments and the benefits and risks of those treatments. In this case, Jandre was taken to the emergency room after he began drooling, had slurred speech, and the left side of his face drooped. The emergency room doctor performed a physical examination and made a preliminary determination that Jandre may have had a mini-stroke, a stroke, a tumor, or suffered from Bell's palsy. She used a stethoscope to detect any sign of a blocked artery, but did not order a diagnostic, noninvasive test that was more reliable, and did not inform him of the availability of this other test. The doctor made a final diagnosis of Bell's palsy, prescribed medication, and sent Jandre home with instructions to see a neurologist. When admitted to the hospital 11 days later with the stroke, his right carotid artery was 95 percent blocked. Jandre brought an action for negligent misdiagnosis and for failure to inform the patient about available diagnostic tests not used. The circuit court jury found that the doctor was not negligent in her diagnosis of Bell's palsy, but was negligent for failure to inform the patient as required under Section 448.30, Wisconsin Statutes. The court of appeals affirmed the jury's decisions.

The supreme court affirmed the court of appeals while declining to establish a bright-line rule suggested by the defendants that as a matter of law a doctor has no duty to inform a patient about conditions unrelated to the one identified in the doctor's nonnegligent diagnosis. The court said the statutory requirement to disclose other available diagnostic tests is based on the facts and circumstances of the particular case, so a bright-line rule is not appropriate. Instead, the doctor is required to give the patient information that a reasonable person under the circumstance confronting the patient would like to know. This duty is limited, said the court; the doctor has no duty to inform the patient unless the doctor has, or should have had, sufficient knowledge about the patient's condition to trigger an awareness that the information was reasonably necessary for the patient to make an informed decision regarding his or her care. In addition, the court said, the statute limits the doctor's duty, including having no duty to inform the patient of detailed technical information or of extremely remote possibilities that might falsely alarm the patient.

The court emphasized that this duty is not one of strict liability. Instead doctors are only liable if they fail to disclose information that is necessary for a reasonable person to make an intelligent decision about treatment or diagnosis choices. Under the statute and the case law, the scope of the duty of informed consent is shaped by objective, negligence-based standards. The court noted the strict liability argument appears to suggest that juries' hindsight sympathy for a patient would inhibit the jurors from applying the reasonable patient standard; but it rejected that suggestion, saying if juries cannot be trusted to apply the law in this situation, the role of the jury in all negligence cases would need to be reconsidered.

The court also rejected the position that the doctor's duty to inform the patient is determined by the generally accepted customs of the medical profession. Rather, based on earlier court decisions, it held that the doctor's disclosure must be measured by the patient's objective need for information to make an intelligent decision. The court went on to hold that "...negligence in failing to abide by the professional standard of care and negligence in failing to obtain informed consent are two separate and distinct forms of malpractice, with two different standards of care." Thus, there is no inconsistency in holding that a reasonable patient may want information about alternative diagnostic techniques when the doctor was not negligent in using one of a multitude of alternative nonnegligent diagnostic techniques. The standard of care for treatment, said the court, is a professional, reasonable doctor standard, while the standard for informed consent is the reasonable patient standard.

The court said that the duty to inform was needed in this case because the available procedure not used by the doctor was noninvasive, and more importantly, more conclusive than the diagnostic procedure used by the doctor, and could verify a condition that involved potentially serious risks. No tests for Bell's Palsy exist, said the court, and the symptoms exhibited by Jandre were atypical of the symptoms for Bell's Palsy. That diagnosis, said the court, can only be reached by excluding other conditions. These facts, said the court, "...led the jury to find that a reasonable person in the patient-plaintiff's position would have wanted to know about the alternate diagnostic procedures." The reasonable patient standard, emphasized the court, does not require the doctor to disclose all information, only what a reasonable patient would find necessary to make an intelligent, informed decision. "The point is that the physician's duty to inform the patient depends on the facts and circumstances of each case. The question of breach of the physician's duty to inform a patient is quintessentially a jury question."

Justice Prosser concurred in the lead decision saying that there was ample evidence to support the verdict; to reverse the court of appeals decision would require the court to overrule or withdraw language from earlier cases, and that action was not warranted on the facts presented in this case. He went on to suggest that since much has changed since Section 448.30, Wisconsin Statutes, was enacted, perhaps a committee should be created to review this issue.

Justice Roggensack, joined by Justices Ziegler and Gableman, wrote a dissent saying that the lead opinion, had it garnered the vote of four justices, would have imposed strict liability for missed diagnosis under a new concept that the legislature did not codify by "...expanding a patient's right of informed consent under Section 448.30 from a right to be informed about the risks and benefits of treatments and procedures that *were recommended* by the physician into a right to be informed about all treatments and procedures that *were not recommended* by the physician, but which may be relevant to whether the correct diagnosis was made."

Proper Placement of a Patient with Alzheimer's Disease

In the *Matter of Mental Commitment of Helen E.F.*, 2012 WI 50, 340 Wis. 2d 500, 814 N.W.2d 179 (2012), the supreme court addressed whether a patient with Alzheimer's disease was a proper subject for involuntary commitment under Chapter 51 of the Wisconsin Statutes or whether she was a more proper subject for protective placement and services under Chapter 55 of the Wisconsin Statutes. The supreme court ruled that because the patient's Alzheimer's disease was likely to be a permanent, untreatable condition, protective placement under Chapter 55 was more appropriate.

The facts of the case were undisputed. Helen E.F. (Helen) was an 85-year-old nursing home resident who suffered from Alzheimer's disease with progressive dementia, memory loss, and a limited ability to communicate. After beginning to exhibit aggressive behavior at the nursing home where she lived, Helen was subsequently transported to an emergency room in Fond du Lac for treatment. A police officer placed Helen in the hospital's behavioral health unit pursuant to Chapter 51 and the county began a Chapter 51 proceeding to involuntarily commit Helen for treatment. The court commissioner, finding no probable cause to commit Helen under Chapter 51, converted the petition to an action under Chapter 55 for protective placement and issued a 30-day order for protective placement. Following the expiration of that 30-day period, the county again filed a Chapter 51 petition. Based on one physician's testimony that Helen's disturbances were controllable with medication, the court granted the Chapter 51 petition for a six-month involuntary commitment. Helen appealed to the court of appeals, which reversed the circuit court. The court of appeals determined that, because Alzheimer's was not a condition that could ultimately be treated, Helen was not a proper subject for commitment under Chapter 51. The county appealed and the supreme court granted review.

The supreme court began with a discussion of the differences between Chapter 51 and Chapter 55. The court noted that, in order to be eligible for protective services under Chapter 55, a circuit court had to find a number of elements. Among these are that the individual is so incapable of providing for her own care as to create a substantial risk of serious harm to herself because of a developmental disability, degenerative brain disorder, serious and persistent mental illness, or other incapacity and the individual must have a disability that is permanent or likely permanent. Chapter 55, the court observed, is intended to provide for long-term care of individuals with incurable disorders. In contrast, the court wrote, the purpose of Chapter 51 is to provide individuals with treatment and rehabilitation for mental illnesses, substance abuse problems, and other conditions on a temporary, not long-term, basis. The court noted that, unlike Chapter 51, Chapter 55 provides for placements with the least restrictions and specifically prohibits placements in units for the acutely mentally ill. The court also observed that Chapter 55 requires the appointment of a guardian ad litem, which would have provided Helen with an individualized, long-term advocate and would have advised the court about Helen's best interests regarding the administration of psychotropic medication.

The court wrote that "given the current state of medical science, Helen's Alzheimer's Disease is incurable and untreatable." Although some of Helen's symptoms might respond to treatment, the court wrote, the underlying condition, and most of the other associated symptoms, would not. Examining Alzheimer's disease in light of the differences between Chapter 51, which can be utilized for individuals who could ultimately be returned to society, and 55, which envisions long-term care for individuals who could not be so returned, the court affirmed the court of appeals in ruling that Helen's case was more appropriate for proceedings under Chapter 55.

Chief Justice Abrahamson wrote separately in concurrence, joined by Justice Bradley, to emphasize the tensions between examining individuals based upon their precise conditions and examining them based upon their behavior and symptoms. She wrote that it may be time for the legislature to revisit the goals and intended scopes of the two chapters at issue in the case.

Termination of Parental Rights-Default Judgment

The case, *Dane County Department of Human Services v. Mable K.*, 2013 WI 28, 346 Wis. 2d 396, 828 N.W.2d 198 (2013), concerned the use of default judgments in cases involving the termination of parental rights. In this case, Dane County petitioned the circuit court to terminate Mable K.'s parental rights for her two children, as well as the parental rights of the fathers of the two children. Ms. K. was ordered to appear at the hearing regarding the allegations leading to the petition for termination of her parental rights. Ms. K. was present for the first day of the hearing but failed to appear at the second day of the hearing. Her attorney asked the court to delay the hearing, which it did, and called Ms. K., telling her to come to the hearing. Meanwhile, Dane County asked the court to grant a default judgment terminating Ms. K.'s parental rights. The court recessed the hearing to allow Ms. K. to appear, but when she did not arrive, the court granted Dane County's motion for the default judgment. Before granting that motion, Ms. K.'s attorney asked to present evidence on her client's behalf; the court denied that request but allowed the attorney to cross-examine the county's witnesses. Upon Ms. K.'s arrival, her attorney asked the court to reconsider its entry of a default judgment. The court allowed Ms. K. to testify as to why she failed to appear, but found her reasons insufficient to support vacating the default judgment.

Four months later, at the hearing to finalize the disposition of the matter, the court entered an order terminating Ms. K.'s parental rights. She appealed, and the appellate court ordered the circuit court to first decide the post-dispositional motions. At the hearing on those motions, the attorney for Ms. K. again asked to introduce evidence that contradicted the county's testimony. The court refused, but decided that it had deprived Ms. K. of her statutory right to an attorney when it barred her attorney from adding evidence that tended to refute the county's evidence. The circuit court said the way to remedy its error was to continue the case at the point where the county had provided its evidence and to allow Ms. K.'s attorney to present evidence to the court, not a jury, regarding the petition to terminate her parental rights.

The case went back to the court of appeals, where it was dismissed. The case was then appealed to the supreme court to determine if the circuit court's actions were correct. The supreme court, relying on previous decisions, held that the circuit court should have allowed Ms. K.'s attorney to present evidence on her client's behalf even if the client failed to appear. "A parent's attorney may act on behalf of a parent who does not appear in person." That statutory right to an attorney is preserved even after the entry of a default judgment, the court said. The court went on to say the circuit court should have heard the additional evidence offered by Ms. K.'s attorney before entering a default judgment terminating Ms. K.'s parental rights.

The supreme court said that the remedy suggested by the circuit court to correct its own errors, to continue the matter by letting Ms. K.'s attorney present evidence to the court, not the jury, was incorrect. Continuing the case half way through the proceedings, said the court, is fundamentally unfair because the jury is gone, a new one cannot hear only half of the testimony, and Ms. K. will be required to have another attorney appointed who would have to argue against a default judgment that the circuit court has twice entered. Rebutting evidence that is over two years old would put the burden on Ms. K. to prove she is not an unfit mother, which is in conflict with the requirement that the government has the burden to prove that the mother is unfit, the court held. The court also held that the circuit court was in error when it removed her statutory right to a jury trial. The supreme court remanded the case to the circuit court for a new fact-finding hearing before a jury

Justice Ziegler, joined by Justices Roggensack and Gableman, dissented, saying that the majority decision undercuts the authority of circuit courts to sanction a nonappearing parent by ordering the trying of the case before the court instead of a jury. In addition, this decision fails to consider the interest of the children, who have not lived with their biological mother for years, and now must wait even longer for a decision.

What is "Compensation"?

In *Cramer and Lokken v. Eau Claire County,* 2013 WI App 67 (to be published), the Court of Appeals, District III, was asked to determine what is meant by the term "compensation" in Section 59.22 (1) (a) 1., Wisconsin Statutes. The statute requires a county board to establish the total annual compensation to be paid to elected county officials before their term of office begins, and prohibits the county board from altering that compensation during the official's term in office.

The county board, in response to state legislation requiring local governmental employees to pay the employee share of contributions to their retirement program, deducted those amounts from the official's paychecks. The county also deducted money from their paycheck to pay for increased health insurance premiums. The officials sued, saying the deductions resulted in a reduction in their compensation, in violation of the state law.

The circuit court found for the officials, but the court of appeals reversed. The court of appeals relied on the wording of Section 59.22 (1) (a) 1., saying that the court must look to the common meaning of the words and the words must be interpreted in context, to avoid absurd results. The second sentence of the statute, said the court, provides that compensation is composed of sal-

The Supreme Court greets legislative committee members at a reception outside the hearing room.
(Supreme Court)

ary, fees, or a combination of those two components. This definition of what compensation is composed of, said the court, is what must be used when interpreting the language of that statute.

The court, rejecting the official's attempt to look to other statutory sections to determine what is meant by "salary", said that the definition in one statute need not be the same as in another statute that is intended for a different purpose. The court said that the plain meaning of "salary" in this statute is fixed compensation for a set period of time, not take-home pay, which is an amount that, because of various deductions, is beyond the control of the county board. The statute, said the court, requires the board to set the compensation before the term of office begins, not the take-home pay.

The language of Section 59.22 (1) (a) 1., said the court, specifies that compensation is comprised of salary and fees, and because salary is fixed compensation for a set period of time, the official's only possible argument is that fringe benefits are within the category of "fees" mentioned in the statute, which the court noted was not argued by the officials, and would not be a reasonable interpretation of the statute.

The court went on to review the history of the statute, including a research document that discussed the revision of the statute in 1945, which the court said was consistent with the current version. That document supports the conclusion of the court that compensation is composed of salary and fees. Additionally, said the court, during the period when this statute was created, pensions and insurance contributions were excluded from the definition of compensation, and the terms "salary" and "compensation" had the same meaning. The court concluded that if fringe benefits, such as pension payments, are to be included in the compensation paid to county officials, the legislature can make that change, not the court.

Statistics

8

Statistical information about Wisconsin: agriculture, associations, commerce and industry, conservation and recreation, education, employment and income, geography and climate, history, local and state government, military and veterans affairs, news media, population and vital statistics, post offices, social services, state and local finance, and transportation

Early Construction of the Wisconsin Historical Society Headquarters

(Wisconsin Historical Society)

HIGHLIGHTS OF AGRICULTURE IN WISCONSIN

Farm Production — In 2011, Wisconsin ranked first nationally in the production of cheese (including leading the nation with 38% of domestic Muenster production, 30% of Italian production, and 19% of American production) and dry whey products and second to California in the production of milk and butter. In crop production, it ranked first in corn for silage, oats, cranberries, and snap beans for processing. It was among the top five producers of forage, potatoes, tart cherries, maple syrup, carrots for processing, sweet corn for processing, green peas for processing, and cucumbers for pickles. Wisconsin is also the leading producer of mink pelts and milk goats in the country. As befits the state known as "America's Dairyland", Wisconsin had more milk cows than any other state in the nation except California, with over 1.26 million head, about 14% of the nation's total.

Cash Receipts and Income — Total net Wisconsin farm income was $3.8 billion in 2011, an increase of almost $1.5 billion since 2007. Wisconsin ranked 11th nationally in total net farm income in 2011, up from 24th in 2009. California led the nation in farm income for 2011 with about $16.3 billion, while Alaska, with a total net income of $8.8 million, ranked last.

Total cash receipts for Wisconsin farm products marketed in 2011 amounted to over $11.7 billion. California led the nation that year in total cash receipts from farm marketings at $43.5 billion. Dairy products accounted for 44.7% of Wisconsin's cash receipts from farm marketings in 2011, with feed, oil, and food crops providing 27.1% and meat animals 11.7%.

Number and Size of Farms — From 2007 to 2011, the number of farms in the nation increased by 94,490 to 2,170,000; in Wisconsin, the number increased from about 76,000 to 76,800. Until the 1990s, the number of Wisconsin's farms had decreased fairly steadily from a peak of 199,877 in 1935, but the decline slowed in recent years, and has now begun to reverse itself. Wisconsin farmland decreased from 23.5 million acres to 15 million acres between 1935 and 2011, and the average farm size increased from 117 acres to 195 acres over the same period.

Value of Farms and Farmland — Land and buildings on Wisconsin farms were valued at about $61 billion in 2011, an increase of $4 billion or 7% from 2010. The average value per farm increased from $725,961 in 2010 to $788,961 in 2011. The average value per acre in 2011 was $4,050, an increase of $325 compared to 2010 values.

The average price for agricultural land sold in Wisconsin during 2011 was $4,332 per acre, an increase of almost $400 from the $3,953 average selling price in 2010. Land continuing in agricultural use after sale sold for a statewide average of $4,288 per acre in 2011; agricultural land that sold for other uses was purchased for an average price of $5,818 per acre.

Farm Assets and Debts — Wisconsin farms recorded assets of $907,925 per farm in 2011 and debt of $117,865 per farm for a debt-to-asset ratio of 13%.

The following tables present selected data. Consult footnoted sources for more detailed information on agriculture.

NUMBER, SIZE AND VALUE OF FARMS IN WISCONSIN
1935 – 2011

Year	Number of Farms	Land in Farms (acres)	Average Size of Farm (acres)	Value of Land and Buildings Total (in millions)	Value of Land and Buildings Average per Farm	Value of Land and Buildings Average per Acre
1935	200,000	23,500,000	117	$1,246	$6,228	$53
1940	187,000	22,900,000	123	1,191	6,368	52
1945	178,000	23,600,000	133	1,440	8,088	61
1950	174,000	23,600,000	136	2,100	12,071	89
1955	155,000	23,200,000	150	2,343	15,117	101
1960	138,000	22,200,000	161	2,953	21,396	133
1965	124,000	21,400,000	173	3,317	26,750	155
1970	110,000	20,100,000	183	4,663	42,393	232
1975	100,000	19,300,000	193	8,376	83,762	434
1980	93,000	18,600,000	200	18,674	200,800	1,004
1985	83,000	17,900,000	216	16,898	203,586	944
1990	80,000	17,600,000	220	14,098	176,220	801
1995	80,000	16,800,000	210	17,472	218,400	1,040
1996	79,000	16,600,000	210	18,758	237,443	1,130
1997	79,000	16,500,000	209	19,305	244,367	1,170
1998	78,000	16,300,000	209	20,212	259,128	1,240
1999	78,000	16,200,000	208	23,490	301,154	1,450
2000	77,500	16,000,000	206	27,200	350,968	1,700
2001	77,000	15,800,000	205	30,810	400,130	1,950
2002	77,000	15,700,000	204	33,755	438,377	2,150
2003	76,500	15,600,000	204	35,880	469,020	2,300
2004	76,500	15,500,000	203	38,750	507,500	2,500
2005	76,500	15,400,000	201	43,890	573,725	2,850
2006	76,000	15,300,000	201	48,960	644,210	3,200
2007	78,500	15,200,000	194	57,760	735,796	3,800
2008	78,000	15,200,000	195	58,520	750,256	3,850
2009	78,000	15,200,000	195	57,000	730,769	3,750
2010	78,000	15,200,000	195	56,625	725,961	3,725
2011	77,000	15,000,000	195	60,750	788,961	4,050

Notes: "Farm" is currently defined as a place that sells, or would normally sell, at least $1,000 of agricultural products during the year. The actual number of farms in Wisconsin peaked at 199,877 in 1935. Total Value Average per Farm figures calculated by Wisconsin Legislative Reference Bureau. Prior year's numbers have been revised to reflect updated source data

Sources: U.S. Department of Agriculture, National Agricultural Statistics Service, "Farms, Land in Farms, and Livestock Operations" February 2012,"and "Agricultural Land Values and Cash Rents", August 2012.

2011 WISCONSIN CASH RECEIPTS FROM FARM MARKETINGS
(Percent of Major Commodities)

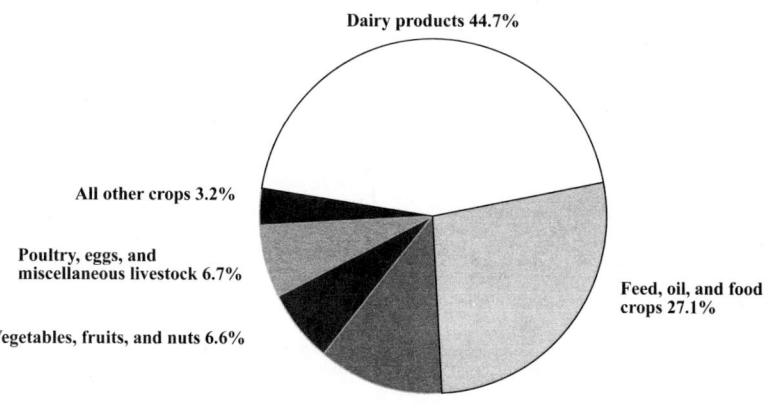

Dairy products 44.7%

All other crops 3.2%

Poultry, eggs, and miscellaneous livestock 6.7%

Vegetables, fruits, and nuts 6.6%

Feed, oil, and food crops 27.1%

Meat animals 11.7%

WISCONSIN CASH RECEIPTS FROM FARM MARKETINGS
By Commodity, 2007 – 2011
(In Thousands)

Commodity	2007	2008	2009	2010	2011
ALL COMMODITIES	**$8,873,018**	**$9,517,709**	**$7,571,132**	**$9,224,147**	**$11,740,787**
LIVESTOCK, DAIRY, AND POULTRY	**6,332,681**	**6,340,399**	**4,800,035**	**5,893,742**	**7,410,388**
Meat animals	**972,826**	**938,366**	**826,221**	**983,689**	**1,374,014**
Cattle and calves	856,056	820,222	726,337	859,514	1,235,729
Hogs	111,262	112,800	94,619	115,936	138,285
Sheep and lambs	5,508	5,344	5,265	8,239	NA
Dairy products	**4,594,365**	**4,571,532**	**3,270,677**	**4,147,199**	**5,245,114**
Poultry and eggs	**430,320**	**467,125**	**358,669**	**397,164**	**408,203**
Broilers	91,530	99,866	87,927	95,243	93,200
Farm chickens	235	306	281	327	335
Chicken eggs	89,263	102,910	78,301	78,316	86,112
Other poultry	71,840	NA	NA	NA	NA
Miscellaneous livestock	**335,170**	**363,376**	**344,468**	**365,690**	**383,057**
Honey	6,149	6,960	5,972	6,881	6,464
Wool	204	198	188	200	298
Aquaculture	**NA**	**NA**	**NA**	**NA**	**NA**
Trout	1,590	1,421	1,791	1,624	1,857
Other aquaculture	9,620	NA	10,040	10,235	10,550
Other livestock	317,606	NA	326,477	346,750	363,888
Mink pelts	43,086	60,056	37,777	57,685	72,353
All other livestock*	274,520	NA	288,700	289,065	291,535
CROPS	**2,540,337**	**3,177,310**	**2,771,097**	**3,330,405**	**4,330,399**
Food grains	**95,561**	**155,150**	**101,159**	**78,456**	**148,585**
Wheat	94,373	153,036	99,945	76,996	146,276
Feed crops	**1,078,106**	**1,333,223**	**1,022,520**	**1,461,300**	**2,188,098**
Barley	1,567	3,175	1,134	1,283	1,001
Corn	1,002,828	1,209,099	934,451	1,371,889	2,101,508
Hay	61,933	107,209	76,326	77,524	74,902
Oats	11,779	13,740	10,609	10,605	10,686
Tobacco	**NA**	**NA**	**NA**	**NA**	**NA**
Oil crops	**366,256**	**475,445**	**572,140**	**779,206**	**845,048**
Soybeans	365,468	475,065	572,140	779,206	845,048
Vegetables	**438,688**	**574,530**	**536,383**	**463,068**	**546,387**
Beans, dry	3,452	6,063	5,554	4,755	5,637
Potatoes, fall	208,829	283,722	256,886	227,916	252,768
Beans, snap, processing	31,297	61,862	52,613	41,028	58,434
Cabbage	14,788	9,982	NA	NA	NA
Carrots	5,140	6,207	6,927	5,064	7,133
Corn, sweet	64,577	95,800	78,323	58,653	80,144
Cucumbers, processing	9,217	8,363	8,649	8,085	7,151
Onions, storage	6,902	4,985	8,366	5,076	4,618
Peas, green, processing	18,739	20,222	24,847	22,784	35,679
Miscellaneous vegetables	74,370	75,100	75,505	75,240	76,535
Fruits and nuts	**232,473**	**287,091**	**205,769**	**203,381**	**228,343**
Apples	22,595	25,036	22,687	15,382	17,362
Cherries, tart	2,842	210	2,263	1,611	1,910
Cranberries	193,518	247,670	166,404	172,896	195,356
Strawberries, spring	6,528	7,105	7,285	6,437	6,440
Other berries	5,020	5,070	5,110	5,065	5,230
Miscellaneous fruits and nuts	1,970	2,000	2,020	1,990	2,045
All other crops	**329,253**	**351,871**	**333,127**	**344,994**	**373,938**
Maple product	3,392	5,865	7,340	4,622	5,627
Other seeds	14,490	NA	16,165	16,215	16,630
Mint	4,438	3,616	3,041	4,267	5,360
Other field crops	48,985	71,650	NA	NA	NA
Greenhouse/nursery	**255,090**	**253,560**	**237,560**	**240,570**	**247,685**
Christmas trees	14,830	14,800	13,500	13,800	14,300
Other greenhouse	240,260	238,760	224,060	226,770	233,385

Note: Bold figures indicate category totals of the commodities immediately following and indicate categories included in next
higher level of aggregation. Category totals may include amounts for specific commodities not listed separately or that are
not listed to provide confidentiality to large producers in concentrated industries. Prior year's numbers have been revised
to reflect updated source data.

NA indicates data is not available.

*Horses and mules are included in "all other livestock."

Source: U.S. Department of Agriculture, Economic Research Service, "Farm Cash Receipts, 2007-2011," at:
http://www.ers.usda.gov/data-products/farm-income-and-wealth-statistics.aspx [March 20, 2013].

CASH RECEIPTS AND INCOME FROM FARMING
By State, 2011
(In Millions)

State	Cash Receipts			Government Payments[1]	Income	
	Livestock and Products	Crops	Total		Net	Rank
Alabama	$3,682.9	$1,167.5	$4,850.5	$115.8	$547.2	35
Alaska	6.8	24.9	31.7	11.3	8.8	50
Arizona.	1,819.4	2,494.5	4,313.9	58.1	1,581.1	23
Arkansas	4,414.1	4,001.8	8,415.9	364.8	1,422.7	26
California	12,358.0	31,186.0	43,544.0	259.1	16,304.9	1
Colorado	4,154.5	2,921.6	7,076.1	235.4	1,669.7	22
Connecticut	196.6	363.5	560.1	10.5	143.7	45
Delaware	761.0	320.0	1,081.0	21.0	197.1	44
Florida	1,498.0	6,764.5	8,262.5	175.1	2,260.9	18
Georgia.	4,826.1	3,528.2	8,354.4	222.3	2,463.2	16
Hawaii	89.9	629.6	719.5	16.9	231.2	42
Idaho	3,981.1	3,347.3	7,328.3	113.4	2,441.2	17
ILLINOIS	2,600.1	17,220.2	19,820.3	627.4	6,099.7	4
Indiana	3,291.8	8,544.7	11,836.5	300.5	3,803.9	10
IOWA	12,349.9	17,542.2	29,892.1	811.9	10,813.2	2
Kansas	8,913.9	6,944.6	15,858.5	542.8	5,191.2	7
Kentucky	2,748.2	2,170.1	4,918.3	273.8	1,508.7	25
Louisiana.	1,058.3	2,402.2	3,460.6	210.1	1,192.2	29
Maine	344.5	373.3	717.9	17.4	236.3	41
Maryland.	1,110.9	980.5	2,091.4	41.1	551.1	34
Massachusetts	117.8	397.8	515.6	21.0	128.6	46
MICHIGAN	3,018.9	5,027.5	8,046.3	156.6	3,347.9	12
MINNESOTA	7,001.0	11,535.4	18,536.4	487.9	5,784.6	5
Mississippi	2,909.8	2,448.2	5,358.1	245.6	1,254.8	28
Missouri	4,199.4	5,510.4	9,709.8	367.2	3,333.2	13
Montana	1,420.1	2,122.1	3,542.2	298.7	846.6	31
Nebraska	10,061.0	11,754.0	21,815.0	470.3	7,456.7	3
Nevada	399.3	281.2	680.5	10.4	223.6	43
New Hampshire	96.0	93.5	189.5	12.9	29.3	48
New Jersey	126.8	994.6	1,121.4	17.1	387.5	37
New Mexico	3,297.9	807.9	4,105.8	88.1	1,347.4	27
New York	3,208.2	2,053.0	5,261.2	57.4	1,776.1	21
North Carolina	6,931.6	3,611.6	10,543.2	401.2	3,006.9	14
North Dakota.	1,127.6	6,209.4	7,337.0	460.8	2,171.1	19
Ohio	3,120.0	6,528.3	9,648.2	256.7	3,886.4	9
Oklahoma	5,755.1	1,301.2	7,056.3	341.8	1,510.3	24
Oregon	1,351.1	3,272.5	4,623.6	110.8	1,029.2	30
Pennsylvania	4,377.3	2,312.3	6,689.6	73.8	2,041.6	20
Rhode Island	11.4	51.3	62.7	3.9	11.4	49
South Carolina	1,417.9	1,177.3	2,595.2	113.6	445.7	36
South Dakota.	3,452.7	5,957.7	9,410.4	303.4	4,619.9	8
Tennessee	1,405.2	2,095.6	3,500.8	140.3	799.1	32
Texas	15,817.7	6,863.6	22,681.3	917.4	5,343.9	6
Utah	1,096.7	510.3	1,607.0	35.1	293.7	39
Vermont	637.2	119.7	756.8	17.8	261.4	40
Virginia	2,121.6	1,182.5	3,304.0	100.4	752.5	33
Washington.	2,354.7	6,311.0	8,665.6	231.2	2,985.4	15
West Virginia.	460.3	104.2	564.5	14.3	32.0	47
WISCONSIN	7,410.4	4,330.4	11,740.8	196.0	3,802.7	11
Wyoming.	1,087.3	362.2	1,449.5	41.3	330.1	38
UNITED STATES[2]. . . .	$165,997.9	$208,253.8	$374,251.7	$10,421.4	$117,907.7	

[1]Includes both cash payments and payments-in-kind (PIK).

[2]Detail may not add due to rounding.

Source: U.S. Department of Agriculture, Economic Research Service, Income and Production Expenses, at: http://www.ers.usda.gov/Data/FarmIncome/FinfidmuXls.htm [June 21, 2013].

WISCONSIN'S RANK IN AGRICULTURE, 2011

Commodity	Unit	United States (000s)	Wisconsin (000s)	Percent of U.S.	Rank in U.S.	Leading State in U.S.
CASH RECEIPTS						
ALL COMMODITIES		$374,251,708	$11,740,787	3.1%	9	California
Livestock and livestock products . .		165,997,906	7,410,388	4.5	6	Texas
Crops		208,253,802	4,330,399	2.1	16	California
PRODUCTION						
DAIRY						
Milk production	Lbs	196,245,000	26,117,000	13.3	2	California
Cheese (excluding cottage cheese)	Lbs	10,597,030	2,634,683	24.9	1	**Wisconsin**
American	Lbs	4,267,341	794,538	18.6	1	**Wisconsin**
Muenster	Lbs	131,237	50,108	38.2	1	**Wisconsin**
Mozzarella	Lbs	3,560,665	898,721	25.2	2	California
Italian	Lbs	4,560,139	1,348,636	29.6	2	California
Dry whey, human food	Lbs	950,863	294,202	30.9	1	**Wisconsin**
LIVESTOCK AND POULTRY						
Cattle and calves, all[1]	Head	90,769	3,400	3.7	9	Texas
Milk cows[2]	Head	9,194	1,265	13.8	2	California
Hogs and pigs, all[3]	Head	66,361	340	0.5	19	Iowa
Sheep[1]	Head	5,345	84	1.6	17	Texas
Milk goats[1]	Head	360	44	12.2	1	**Wisconsin**
Chickens[3]	Head	447,251	6,030	1.3	19	Iowa
Broilers	Head	8,607,600	46,500	0.5	19	Georgia
Trout, sold 12" or longer	Lbs	45,416	450	1.0	8	Idaho
Mink pelts	Pelts	3,091	1,051	34.0	1	**Wisconsin**
Honey	Lbs	148,357	3,591	2.4	9	North Dakota
Eggs	Eggs	91,855,000	1,277,000	1.4	18	Iowa
CROPS						
Corn for grain	Bu	12,358,412	517,920	4.2	7	Iowa
Corn for silage	Tons	108,926	15,698	14.4	1	**Wisconsin**
Oats	Bu	53,649	7,130	13.3	1	**Wisconsin**
Soybeans	Bu	3,056,032	73,600	2.4	13	Iowa
Wheat, all	Bu	1,999,347	21,775	1.1	22	Kansas
Barley	Bu	155,780	705	0.5	17	Idaho
Forage (dry equivalent), all	Tons	89,438	8,596	9.6	3	California
Hay (dry only), all	Tons	131,144	4,075	3.1	13	South Dakota
Potatoes, all	Cwt	427,406	25,000	5.8	3	Idaho
Dry edible beans	Cwt	19,833	110	0.6	16	North Dakota
Cherries, tart	Lbs	231,700	6,700	2.9	4	Michigan
Apples	Lbs	9,420,000	51,400	0.5	12	Washington
Strawberries	Cwt	28,946	40	0.1	6	California
Maple syrup	Gals	2,794	155	5.5	4	Vermont
Cranberries	Bbl	7,712	4,410	57.2	1	**Wisconsin**
Mint for oil	Lbs	8,856	225	2.5	6	Washington
Onions	Cwt	54,627	555	1.0	9	Washington
Cabbage for fresh market	Cwt	21,129	896	4.2	9	California
Sweet corn for fresh market	Cwt	28,089	694	2.5	10	Florida
Carrots for processing	Tons	339	92	27.1	2	Washington
Sweet corn for processing	Tons	2,627	596	22.7	3	Washington
Green peas for processing	Tons	295	73	24.7	2	Washington
Snap beans for processing	Tons	681	301	44.2	1	**Wisconsin**
Cucumbers for pickles	Tons	482	31	6.4	4	Michigan

Abbreviations: Bbl = barrels, Bu = bushels, Cwt = hundredweight, Gals = gallons, Lbs = pounds.

[1]January 1, 2012 inventory.

[2]Average number during year, excluding heifers not yet fresh.

[3]December 1, 2011 inventory.

Source: National Agriculture Statistics Service, U.S. Department of Agriculture, Wisconsin's Rank in the Nation's Agriculture, 2011, at: http://www.nass.usda.gov/Statistics_by_State/Wisconsin/Publications/Annual_Statistical_Bulletin/bulletin2012_web.pdf [June 7, 2013].

NUMBER AND ACREAGE OF FARMS
By State, 2007 and 2012

State	Number of Farms		Farm Acreage (in thousands)		Average Farm Size (acres)	
	2007	2012	2007	2012	2007	2012
Alabama	43,000	46,500	8,600	8,850	200	190
Alaska	660	680	900	880	1,364	1,294
Arizona.	10,000	15,500	26,000	26,100	2,600	1,684
Arkansas	46,500	47,800	14,300	13,500	308	282
California	75,000	80,500	26,200	25,400	349	316
Colorado	31,000	36,300	30,700	31,300	990	862
Connecticut	4,200	4,900	360	400	86	82
Delaware	2,200	2,500	515	490	234	196
Florida	40,000	47,500	10,000	9,250	250	195
Georgia.	47,500	47,000	10,000	10,400	211	221
Hawaii	5,500	7,500	1,300	1,110	236	148
Idaho	24,500	24,500	11,700	11,400	478	465
ILLINOIS	72,500	74,300	27,300	26,600	377	358
Indiana	58,800	60,000	15,000	14,700	255	245
IOWA	88,400	92,200	31,500	30,700	356	333
Kansas	63,800	65,500	47,200	46,000	740	702
Kentucky.	83,000	85,500	13,700	14,000	165	164
Louisiana.	26,800	29,000	7,800	7,950	291	274
Maine	7,100	8,100	1,360	1,350	192	167
Maryland.	12,000	12,800	2,035	2,050	170	160
Massachusetts	6,100	7,700	520	520	85	68
MICHIGAN	52,800	54,700	10,000	9,900	189	181
MINNESOTA	79,000	79,400	27,400	26,800	347	338
Mississippi.	41,700	42,300	11,000	11,150	264	264
Missouri	104,500	106,000	30,000	29,000	287	274
Montana	28,300	28,600	60,000	58,800	2,120	2,056
Nebraska	47,300	46,700	45,600	45,500	964	974
Nevada	3,000	2,950	6,300	5,840	2,100	1,980
New Hampshire	3,400	4,150	450	470	132	113
New Jersey.	9,800	10,200	790	730	81	72
New Mexico	18,000	23,800	45,000	43,900	2,500	1,845
New York	34,200	36,000	7,500	7,000	219	194
North Carolina	48,000	50,000	8,800	8,500	183	170
North Dakota.	30,100	31,600	39,400	39,600	1,309	1,253
Ohio	75,700	73,400	14,200	13,550	188	185
Oklahoma	82,500	85,500	33,700	34,800	408	407
Oregon	38,300	38,100	17,000	16,500	444	433
Pennsylvania.	58,000	62,100	7,650	7,700	132	124
Rhode Island	850	1,220	60	70	71	57
South Carolina	24,700	26,700	4,850	4,800	196	180
South Dakota.	31,300	31,000	43,700	43,650	1,396	1,408
Tennessee	79,000	76,000	11,400	10,800	144	142
Texas.	229,000	244,700	129,500	128,000	566	523
Utah	15,000	16,400	11,600	11,100	773	677
Vermont	6,200	7,000	1,220	1,220	197	174
Virginia.	47,100	46,200	8,510	8,050	181	174
Washington.	33,000	39,300	15,100	14,800	458	377
West Virginia.	21,400	22,100	3,600	3,620	168	164
WISCONSIN	76,000	76,800	15,200	15,000	200	195
Wyoming.	8,800	10,800	34,400	30,200	3,909	2,796
UNITED STATES	2,075,510	2,170,000	930,920	914,000	449	421

Note: "Farm" is currently defined as a place that sells, or would normally sell, at least $1,000 of agricultural products during the year.

Sources: U.S. Department of Agriculture, National Agricultural Statistics Service "Farms, Land in Farms, and Livestock Operations", 2013, and earlier editions.

WISCONSIN AGRICULTURAL LAND SALES
By County, 2010 and 2011

County[1]	Total Agricultural Land Sales[2]				Land Continuing in Agricultural Use		Agricultural Land Diverted to Other Uses	
	Number		Dollar Avg. per Acre		Dollar Avg. per Acre		Dollar Avg. per Acre	
	2010	2011	2010	2011	2010	2011	2010	2011
Adams	9	18	$3,258	$4,022	$3,258	$4,022	—	—
Ashland	4	1	1,085	1,571	1,126	1,571	$850	—
Barron	50	37	2,777	2,369	2,573	2,374	4,462	$2,201
Bayfield	17	16	1,197	1,448	1,198	1,429	1,164	27,200
Brown	22	34	6,302	8,085	6,330	7,156	5,135	16,250
Buffalo	25	20	2,945	4,282	2,941	4,282	2,965	—
Burnett	12	10	2,745	1,982	2,791	2,011	2,139	1,350
Calumet	20	20	5,232	6,422	5,232	6,422	—	—
Chippewa	42	52	3,076	2,476	3,076	2,494	—	1,655
Clark	49	78	2,688	2,926	2,688	2,927	—	2,867
Columbia	29	33	4,244	5,757	4,244	5,437	—	7,732
Crawford	26	27	2,940	2,821	2,927	2,826	3,030	2,784
Dane	48	49	6,463	7,243	6,463	7,186	6,400	8,199
Dodge	46	55	5,014	5,966	5,002	5,827	5,181	9,812
Door	5	13	3,846	4,125	3,846	4,125	—	—
Douglas	6	7	2,352	897	2,352	889	—	1,100
Dunn	43	50	2,751	3,571	2,890	3,611	1,767	1,616
Eau Claire	20	26	3,713	3,584	3,078	3,580	8,411	3,736
Florence	—	2	—	4,307	—	4,307	—	—
Fond du Lac	27	63	4,967	4,958	4,803	4,958	10,000	—
Forest	2	2	3,832	1,982	3,832	2,267	—	1,300
Grant	48	66	4,079	4,176	4,079	4,177	—	4,000
Green	24	43	4,027	4,595	3,831	4,595	5,784	—
Green Lake	26	8	4,980	5,478	5,022	5,478	700	—
Iowa	39	30	3,576	4,696	3,569	4,638	3,688	7,222
Iron	—	—	—	—	—	—	—	—
Jackson	23	28	2,557	3,509	2,557	3,456	—	4,849
Jefferson	17	30	5,954	5,439	5,643	5,391	16,294	6,604
Juneau	14	22	2,754	2,967	2,754	2,900	—	5,161
Kenosha	4	14	11,644	6,562	6,925	6,562	27,600	—
Kewaunee	17	12	4,392	4,900	4,325	4,667	5,670	6,485
La Crosse	18	15	5,233	3,594	5,558	3,594	4,029	—
Lafayette	41	40	4,643	4,319	4,573	4,319	7,528	—
Langlade	6	13	1,743	2,390	1,743	2,390	—	—
Lincoln	3	13	4,000	2,829	4,000	2,649	—	4,152
Manitowoc	32	39	5,133	5,744	5,133	5,721	—	6,946
Marathon	75	61	2,717	2,920	2,668	2,915	3,719	3,509
Marinette	15	16	3,046	2,911	3,077	2,917	1,765	2,600
Marquette	13	12	2,902	2,741	2,908	2,793	2,400	2,590
Milwaukee	—	1	—	8,500	—	8,500	—	—
Monroe	33	54	3,329	3,825	3,329	3,396	—	14,642
Oconto	22	27	2,872	2,881	2,869	2,881	3,000	—
Oneida	2	4	1,590	2,788	1,590	2,592	—	5,029
Outagamie	18	34	4,424	5,500	4,424	5,466	—	7,500
Ozaukee	5	16	5,070	7,261	5,070	7,261	—	—
Pepin	15	9	3,162	3,763	3,162	3,763	—	—
Pierce	37	39	3,971	4,052	3,282	3,969	7,651	6,218
Polk	24	35	2,717	2,850	2,388	2,857	9,971	2,185
Portage	14	20	2,527	2,708	2,548	2,711	2,405	2,634
Price	5	10	2,755	2,654	3,170	2,756	2,017	1,512
Racine	9	26	5,943	5,992	5,273	5,992	11,292	—
Richland	27	37	2,697	3,086	2,697	3,075	—	3,727
Rock	39	52	5,234	6,526	5,234	6,514	—	10,500
Rusk	25	20	1,797	1,713	1,726	1,630	2,058	2,524
St. Croix	49	55	3,943	3,886	3,910	3,929	5,291	2,421
Sauk	15	24	4,614	4,123	4,614	3,784	—	5,549
Sawyer	4	3	2,569	2,079	2,569	2,092	—	1,400
Shawano	34	32	3,604	4,382	3,609	4,443	2,055	2,740
Sheboygan	15	36	4,762	5,536	4,614	5,546	5,991	5,000
Taylor	30	24	2,096	2,086	2,036	2,116	5,619	1,544
Trempealeau	39	45	3,097	3,202	3,092	3,181	3,503	4,650
Vernon	47	34	3,414	3,622	3,420	3,653	3,038	2,473
Vilas	1	1	2,000	7,614	2,000	7,614	—	—
Walworth	28	40	6,169	6,883	6,164	6,728	8,700	12,462
Washburn	18	7	1,782	1,957	1,736	1,957	2,322	—
Washington	9	20	8,298	7,782	8,244	7,782	8,649	—
Waukesha	6	10	13,924	9,236	14,800	9,236	13,848	—
Waupaca	12	24	3,775	3,158	3,385	3,116	19,621	6,274
Waushara	13	16	3,087	2,889	3,087	2,880	—	3,105
Winnebago	17	22	4,755	4,926	4,755	4,870	—	6,960
Wood	25	35	2,947	3,191	2,719	3,242	3,948	2,795
STATE	1,554	1,887	$3,953	$4,332	$3,861	$4,288	$5,909	$5,818

[1]Menominee County had no agricultural sales in years shown.

[2]Includes land with and without buildings and other improvements.

Source: U.S. Department of Agriculture, National Agricultural Statistics Service, "Agricultural Land Sales, Total Agricultural Land, Wisconsin, 2011" and earlier editions, at: http://www.nass.usda.gov/Statistics_by_State/Wisconsin/Publications/Land_Sales/ [May 2, 2013].

WISCONSIN NET FARM INCOME, 2007 – 2011

	2007	2008	2009	2010	2011
Number of farms.	78,500	78,000	78,000	77,500	77,000
Average net farm income per farm (dollars).	$29,975	$25,939	$10,187	$27,095	$49,386
		Income (in thousands)			
Value of crop production.	$2,620,123	$3,113,499	$2,996,040	$3,247,276	$4,335,088
Value of livestock production	6,281,825	6,353,373	4,877,488	5,966,786	7,370,139
Revenues from services and forestry	1,331,562	1,388,109	1,390,297	1,293,557	1,285,330
VALUE OF AGRICULTURAL SECTOR OUTPUT[1]. . .	$10,233,510	$10,854,981	$9,263,825	$10,507,619	$12,990,557
Less: Purchased inputs[2]	4,923,390	5,690,325	5,470,518	5,384,756	6,154,566
Less: Motor vehicle registration and licensing	14,018	13,882	15,077	12,795	12,792
Less: Property taxes	390,000	360,000	380,000	410,000	360,000
Plus: Direct Government payments	207,974	229,991	405,870	259,289	196,027
GROSS VALUE ADDED	$5,114,077	$5,020,764	$3,804,099	$4,959,358	$6,659,225
Less: Capital consumption (depreciation) .	1,252,552	1,327,838	1,390,003	1,415,756	1,481,372
NET VALUE ADDED[3]	$3,861,525	$3,692,926	$2,414,096	$3,543,602	$5,177,853
Less: Payments to stakeholders[4].	1,508,453	1,669,689	1,619,513	1,443,702	1,375,121
NET FARM INCOME[5]	$2,353,072	$2,023,237	$794,583	$2,099,900	$3,802,732

Note: Average net farm income calculated by Wisconsin Legislative Reference Bureau. Prior year's numbers have been revised to reflect updated source data.

[1]Value of agricultural sector output is the gross value of the commodities and services produced within a year.

[2]Includes purchases of feed, livestock, poultry, and seed; outlays for fertilizers and lime, pesticides, fuel and electricity; capital repair and maintenance; and marketing, storage, transportation, contract labor, and other expenses.

[3]Net value added is the sector's contribution to the national economy and is the sum of the income from production earned by all factors of production, regardless of ownership.

[4]Includes compensation for hired labor, net rent received by nonoperator landlords, and interest payments.

[5]Net farm income is the farm operators' share of income from the sector's production activities.

Sources: U.S. Department of Agriculture, Economic Research Service, "Number of Farms, U.S. and states", and "Value added to the U.S. economy by the agricultural sector via the production of goods and services, Wisconsin", at: http://www.ers.usda.gov/Data/FarmIncome/FinfidmuXls.htm [May 7, 2013].

FARM ASSETS AND LIABILITIES
By Leading Agricultural States, 2011

State	Number of Farms[1]	Average Assets Per Farm[2]	Average Liability Per Farm[2]	Average Equity Per Farm[2]	Debt as Percentage of Assets[3]
Arkansas	48,301	$643,059	$64,717	$578,342	10.1%
California	81,501	1,843,522	168,532	1,674,990	9.1
Florida	47,501	NA	72,131	NA	NA
Georgia.	47,001	758,085	56,405	701,680	7.4
ILLINOIS	74,602	1,460,435	129,636	1,330,799	8.9
Indiana	62,000	1,087,922	107,879	980,043	9.9
IOWA	92,300	1,844,869	164,384	1,680,484	8.9
Kansas	65,501	1,082,004	126,847	955,158	11.7
MINNESOTA	79,802	1,161,716	113,500	1,048,216	9.8
Missouri	106,502	720,493	50,008	670,485	6.9
Nebraska	46,802	1,866,478	181,428	1,685,050	9.7
North Carolina	50,401	727,517	50,011	677,506	6.9
Texas	245,002	964,465	35,661	928,804	3.7
Washington.	39,501	1,025,863	93,806	932,057	9.1
WISCONSIN	77,001	907,925	117,865	790,060	13.0

NA: Asset and equity data for Florida not available.

[1]"Farm" is currently defined as a place that sells, or would normally sell, at least $1,000 of agricultural products during the year.

[2]Dollar amounts represent farm businesses, excluding household assets and debts.

[3]Debt does not include all financial obligations that are contained in the liabilities column. Percent calculated by Wisconsin Legislative Reference Bureau.

Source: U.S. Department of Agriculture, Economic Research Service, "Farm Business and Household Survey Data: Customized Data Summaries From ARMS", at: http://www.ers.usda.gov/Data/ARMS/app/Farm.aspx [June 2013].

STATEWIDE ASSOCIATIONS OF WISCONSIN
Listed by Key Word

AAA Wisconsin, Inc.
Tom Frymark, Regional Pres.
P.O. Box 33, Madison 53701-0033
(608) 836-6555 www.aaa.com

Academic Staff Professionals Representative Org.
Janet Swandby, Exec. Dir.
10 E. Doty St., Suite 519, Madison 53703
(608) 286-9599 aspro@aspro.net www.aspro.net

Academy of Sciences, Arts and Letters, Wis.
Jane Elder, Exec. Dir.
1922 University Ave., Madison 53726
(608) 263-1692 info@wisconsinacademy.org
www.wisconsinacademy.org

Accountants, Wis. Inst. of Certified Public
Dennis Tomorsky, Pres./CEO
235 N. Executive Dr., Suite 200, Brookfield 53005
(262) 785-0445 dennis@wicpa.org www.wicpa.org

ACOG (American College of Obstetricians and
Gynecologists), Wis. Section
Jennifer Hallett, Assn. Services Dir.
563 Carter Ct., Suite B, Kimberly 54136
(920) 560-5636 jennifer@badgerbay.co www.acog.org

Activity Professionals, Wis. Representatives of (WRAP)
Cindy Tewalt, Pres.
3604 Wilden St., Eau Claire 54703
(715) 834-3976 cindytewalt@gmail.com www.wrap-wi.org

AFT – Wisconsin (Federation of Teachers)
Bryan Kennedy, Pres.
6602 Normandy Ln., Madison 53719
(608) 662-1444 kennedy@aft-wisconsin.org
www.aft-wisconsin.org

Aging Groups, Coalition of Wis.
A.J. Nino Amato, Pres.
2850 Dairy Dr., Suite 100, Madison 53718
(608) 224-0606 namato@cwag.org www.cwag.org

Agri-Business Assn., Wis.
Tom Bressner, Exec. Dir.
6000 Gisholt Dr., Suite 208, Madison 53713-4816
(608) 223-1111 tom@wiagribusiness.org
www.wiagribusiness.org

Agribusiness Council, Wis.
Ferron Havens, Pres.
P.O. Box 46100, Madison 53744
(877) 947-2474 fhavenswac@mhtc.net wisagri.com

Agricultural Educators, Wis. Assn. of
Bridgett Neu, Exec. Dir.
1172 Hummingbird Ln., Plymouth 53073
(262) 224-7553 bridgett@waae.com www.waae.com

Agriculture, Wis. Women for
Lisa Condon, Pres.
W5763 Prospect Rd., Horicon 53032
(920) 485-4329 lisacondon@mac.com
americanagriwomen.org

Agronomy, Amer. Soc. of
Ellen Bergfeld, CEO
5585 Guilford Rd., Madison 53711
(608) 268-4979 ebergfeld@sciencesocieties.org
www.agronomy.org

Alcohol Problems Council of Wis.
Jim Cotter, Secy.
222 S. Dickason Blvd., Columbus 53925
(920) 623-3625 jcotter@wisconsinmc.org
alcoholproblemswi.org

American Fed. Of State, County and Municipal Employees,
AFL-CIO
Debbie Garcia, Area Field Serv. Dir.
8033 Excelsior Dr., Suite A, Madison 53717-1903
(608) 836-6666 dgarcia@afscme.org

American Legion, Dept. of Wis.
David A. Kurtz, Adj.
2930 American Legion Dr., P.O. Box 388,
Portage 53901-0388
(608) 745-1090 info@wilegion.org www.wilegion.org

American Legion Aux. (Dept. of Wis.)
Bonnie Dorniak, Secy./Treas.
P.O. Box 140, 2930 American Legion Dr.,
Portage 53901-0124
(608) 745-0124 alawi@amlegionauxwi.org
amlegionauxwi.org

Amusement and Music Operators, Wis.
Maxine D. O'Brien, Exec. Dir.
P.O. Box 250, Poynette 53955
(608) 635-4316 wamomax@aol.com www.wamo.net

Amvets (Dept. of Wis.)
Michael H. Mahoney, Exec. Dir.
750 N. Lincoln Memorial Dr., Rm. 306,
War Memorial Center, Milwaukee 53202
(414) 273-5288 amvetswi@yahoo.com www.amvets-wi.org

Amvets Ladies Aux., Dept. of Wis.
Candice Endres, Pres.
5331 N. 107th St., Milwaukee 53225
(414) 466-0048 candy.endres@yahoo.com
www.amvets-wi.org/auxiliary.htm

Anesthetists, Wis. Assn. of Nurse, Inc.
Debra Dahlke, Pres.
7117 Elderberry Rd., Middleton 53562
(608) 220-4486 president@wiana.com wiana.com

Animals, Alliance for
Lynn Pauly, Rick Bogle, Co-Directors
P.O. Box 1632, Madison 53701-1632
(608) 257-6333 Alliance@AllAnimals.org
www.allanimals.org

Animals, Citizens United for
Tia Bransted, Pres.
P.O. Box 511321, Milwaukee 53203-0221
(262) 353-8347 info@cufa-wi.org www.cufa-wi.org

Apartment Assn., Wis.
Kristy Weinke, Admin. Asst.
627 Bayshore Dr., Oshkosh 54901
(920) 230-9221 admin@waaonline.org www.waaonline.org

Apple Growers Assn., Wis.
Anna M. Maenner, Exec. Dir.
211 Canal Rd., Waterloo 53594
(920) 478-4277 office@waga.org www.waga.org

Aquaculture Assn., Inc., Wis.
Cinty Johnson, Secy.
P.O. Box 37, Star Prairie 54026
(715) 248-3657 cindy@wisconsinaquaculture.com
www.wisconsinaquaculture.com

Arabian Horse Assn., Wis.
Nancy Miller, Pres.
6301 Fox Run, Sun Prairie 53590
(608) 825-9986 nmfr7@charter.net
www.wisconsinarabian.com

Arborist Assn., Wis.
Larry Axlen, Jr., Legis. Chair
1830 S. West Ave., Waukesha 53189
(262) 574-3149 www.waa-isa.org/index.htm

Arc – Wisconsin, Disability Assoc. Inc., The
James Hoegemeier, Exec. Dir.
2800 Royal Ave., #209, Madison 53713
(608) 222-8907 arcw@att.net www.arc-wisconsin.org

Architects, Wis. Society of
William Babcock, Exec. Dir.
321 S. Hamilton St., Madison 53703-4000
(608) 257-8477 aiaw@aiaw.org www.aiaw.org

Army and Navy Union
Howard Cole, Cmdr.
5000 W. National Ave, Bldg. 70 C-7, Milwaukee 53295
(414) 384-2000, ext. 46420 howard.cole@va.gov

Art Therapy Association, Wis.
Marianne Huebner, Pres.
P.O. Box 1765, Milwaukee 53201-1765
info@wiarttherapy.org www.wiarttherapy.org

Arthritis Foundation, Upper Midwest Region
Kristin Beres, Regional Finance Director
1650 S. 108th St., West Allis 53214
(800) 333-1380 info.wi@arthritis.org www.arthritis.org

Artists Assn., Wis. Regional
Mary Ann Inman, Pres.
316 Church St., Clinton 53525
(608) 676-4853 inman_ma@yahoo.com
www.wraawrap.org

Asphalt Pavement Assn., Wis., Inc.
Scot Schwandt, Exec. Dir.
620 Water Street, Prairie du Sac 53578
(608) 255-3114 scot@wispave.org www.wispave.org

Auctioneers Assn., Inc., Wis.
Carol Wagenson, Exec. Dir.
P.O. Box 2908, La Crosse 54602-2908
(608) 558-5041 info@wisconsinauctioneers.org
www.wisconsinauctioneers.org

Automatic Merchandising Council, Wis.
David Kwarciany, Jr., Govt. Affairs Chm.
16300 W. Silver Spring Dr., Menomonee Falls 53051
(262) 781-8507

Automobile and Truck Dealers Assn., Inc., Wis.
William Sepic, Pres.
150 E. Gilman St., Suite A, Madison 53703
(608) 251-5577 wsepic@watda.org www.watda.org

Automotive Aftermarket Association, Wis.
Gary Manke, Exec. Dir.
5330 Wall St., Suite 100, Madison 53718-7929
(608) 240-2065 gmanke@medaassn.com www.waaa.info

Automotive Historians, Soc. of (Wis. Ch.)
Kenneth E. Nimocks, Pres.
3765 Spring Green Rd., Green Bay 54313-7565
(920) 865-4004 knimocks@netnet.net

Automotive Parts Assn., Inc., Wis.
Gary W. Manke, CAE, Exec. Dir.
5330 Wall St., Suite 100, Madison 53718-7929
(608) 240-2066 gmanke@medaassn.com
www.wapaonline.com

Bandmasters' Assn., Inc., Wis.
Donna M. Wirth, Exec. Secy.
14544 Squire Ln., Kiel 53042
(920) 894-3991 wbasec.dwirth@gmail.com

Bankers Assn., Wis.
Rose Oswald Poels, Pres./CEO
4721 S. Biltmore Lane, Madison 53718
(608) 441-1200 ropoels@wisbank.com www.wisbank.com

Bankers Assn., Wis. Mortgage
Justin Laxton, Assn. Manager
P.O. Box 1606, Madison 53701-1606
(608) 255-4180 info@wimba.org www.wimba.org

Bankers of Wis., Community
Daryll J. Lund, Pres. & CEO
455 Cty Rd. M., Suite 101, Madison 53719
(608) 833-4229 daryll@communitybankers.org
www.communitybankers.org

Beef Council, Inc., Wis.
John W. Freitag, Exec. Dir.
632 Grand Canyon Dr., Madison 53719
(608) 833-9940 jwf@beeftips.com beeftips.com

Beer Distributors Assn., Inc., Wis.
Eric Jensen, Exec. Dir.
1 S. Pinckney Street, Suite 318, Madison 53703
(608) 287-3282 eric@wisbeer.com www.wisbeer.org/

Berry Growers Assn., Inc., Wis.
Anna Maenner, Exec. Dir.
211 Canal Rd., Waterloo 53594
(920) 478-3852 info@wiberries.org wiberries.org

Beverage Assn., Wis.
Kelly McDowell, Exec. Secy.
33 E. Main St., Suite 701, Madison 53703
(608) 852-7555 kellymmcdowell@gmail.com
wibeverage.com

Blind and Visually Impaired, Inc., Wis. Council of the
Loretta Himmelsbach, Exec. Dir.
754 Williamson St., Madison 53703
(608) 255-1166 lhimmelsbach@wcblind.org
www.wcblind.org

Botanical Club of Wis
Theodore S. Cochrane, Secy.
Room 251 Birge Hall, 430 Lincoln Dr.,
UW-Madison Herbarium, Madison 53706-1381
(608) 262-2792 tscochra@wisc.edu
wisplants.uwsp.edu/BCW

Bowhunters Assn., Wis., Inc.
Michael Brust, Pres.
P.O. Box 240, Clintonville 54929
(715) 823-4670 office@wisconsinbowhunters.org
www.wisconsinbowhunters.org

Bowling Assn., Wis. State USBC
Donald Hildebrand, Assn. Mgr.
P.O. Box 91418, Glendale 53209
(414) 446-9988 donh@wibowl.com wibowl.com

Bowling Centers Association of Wis.
Gary Hartel, Exec. Dir.
21140 W. Capitol Dr., Suite 5, Pewaukee 53072
(262) 783-4292 bcaw@bowlwi.com www.bowlwi.com

Brain Injury Alliance of Wis., Inc.
Lori Schultz, Exec. Dir.
21100 W. Capitol Dr., Suite 5, Pewaukee 53072
(262) 790-9660 lschultz@biaw.org www.biaw.org

Breeders Assn., Wis. Brown Swiss
Barbara Muenzenberger, Secy./Treas.
W561 Muenzenberger Rd., Coon Valley 54623
(608) 486-2297 bovalleyswiss@aol.com
www.allbreedaccess.com/wibrownswiss

Breeders Assn., Wis. Draft Horse
Nancy LaCrosse, Secy.
E2767 Nuclear Rd., Kewaunee 54216
(920) 776-1239 mnpjalacrosse@tds.net

Breeders Assn., Wis. Guernsey
Deb Lakey, Secy./Treas.
W23375 11th St., Trempealeau 54661
(608) 484-0416 wisgba@yahoo.com www.wiguernsey.org

Breeders Assn., Wis. Livestock
Jill Alf, Exec. Dir.
7811 N Consolidated School Rd., Edgerton 53534
(608) 868-2505 alfhamp@centurytel.net
www.wisconsinlivestockbreeders.com

Breeder's Assn., Wis. Shorthorn
Melinda Orebaugh, Secy.
W5306 County Rd. W, Holmen 54636
(608) 526-2578 info@wisconsinshorthorns.com
www.wisconsinshorthorns.com

Broadcasters Assn., Wis.
Michelle Vetterkind, Pres./CEO
44 E. Mifflin St., Suite 900, Madison 53703-2800
(608) 255-2600 mvetterkind@wi-broadcasters.org
www.wi-broadcasters.org

Buck and Bear Club, Inc., Wis.
Steve Ashley, Dir. Of Records
P.O. Box 478, Stevens Point 54481
(877) 273-6408 info@wi-buck-bear.org
www.wi-buck-bear.org

Builders and Contractors of Wis., Inc., Associated
John Mielke, Pres.
5330 Wall St., Madison 53718
(608) 244-5883 jmielke@abcwi.org www.abcwi.org

Builders Assn. of Wis., Master
John R. Topp, Exec. Secy
17100 W. Bluemound Rd., Suite 102, Brookfield 53005
(262) 785-1430 john@buildacea.org www.buildacea.org

Builders Assn., Wis.
Jerry Deschane, Exec. Vice Pres.
4868 High Crossing Blvd., Madison 53704-7403
(608) 242-5151 jdeschane@wisbuild.org www.wisbuild.org

Burial Vault Assn., Wis.
Mark Lipscomb, Jr., Exec. Dir.
2602 W. Silver Spring Dr., Glendale 53209
(414) 276-5763 marklipscombjr@sbcglobal.net

Business Assn. of Wis., Independent
Steve Kohlmann, Exec. Dir.
960 Timber Pass, Brookfield 53045
(262) 844-0333 ibawoffice@gmail.com www.ibaw.com

Business, Natl. Federation of Independent (Wis. Ch.)
Bill G. Smith, State Director
10 E. Doty St., Suite 519, Madison 53703
(608) 255-6083 Bill.Smith@nfib.org www.nfib.com/wi

Businesses, Inc., Wis. Independent
John Gard, Pres.
122 West Washington Avenue, Suite 650, Madison 53703
(800) 362-9644 johngard@wibiz.org www.wibiz.org

Cable Communications Assn., Wis.
Thomas E. Moore, Exec. Dir.
22 E. Mifflin St., Suite 1010, Madison 53703
(608) 256-1683 www.wicable.tv

Camp Assn., American, Wis.
Kim Rathsack, Section Exec.
N9659 Hopfensperger Rd., Appleton 54915
(765) 342-8456 ext. 529 krathsack@acacamps.org
www.acawisconsin.org

Campground Owners, Wis. Assn. of
Lori Severson, Exec. Dir.
P.O. Box 228, Ettrick 54627
(608) 525-2327 director@wisconsincampgrounds.com
wisconsincampgrounds.com

Cancer Soc., Inc., Amer. (Midwest Div.)
Jari Allen, Exec. Vice Pres.
P.O. Box 902, Pewaukee 53072-0902
(262) 312-4015 jari.allen@cancer.org www.cancer.org

Carpenters, Wis. State Council of
Mark S. Reihl, Exec. Dir.
115 W. Main St., Madison 53703
(608) 256-1206 marksreihl@gmail.com

Cast Metals Assn., Wis.
Steve Lewallen, Exec. Dir.
111 Woodside Ct., Neenah 54956
(920) 727-9949 selewallen@gmail.com
www.wicastmetals.com

Cattlemen's Assn., Wis.
Arin Crooks, Pres.
2 E. Mifflin Street, Suite 601, Madison 53703
(608) 228-1457 wisbeef@yahoo.com
www.wisconsincattlemen.com

Cattlewomen's Council, Wis.
Kathy Miller, Pres.
8434 198th Ave., Bristol 53104
(262) 857-7168 kjmiller7@frontier.com
www.wisconsincattlemen.com

Cemetery and Cremation Assn., Wisconsin
Glen Porter, Pres.
14875 W. Greenfield Ave., Highland Memorial Park,
New Berlin 53151
(262) 786-6450 egporter@highlandmemorial.com

Charter Schools Assn., Wis.
Carrie Bonk, Exec. Dir.
P.O. Box 1704, Madison 53701-1704
(414) 215-9272 info@wicharterschools.org
www.wicharterschools.org

Children and Families, Inc., Wis. Council on
Ken Taylor, Exec. Dir.
555 W. Washington Ave., Suite 200, Madison 53703
(608) 284-0580 ktaylor@wccf.org www.wccf.org

Children of the American Revolution, Wis. St. Soc.
Mrs. Ivan Niedling, Honorary Sr. State Pres.
700 3rd St., Plover 54467
(715) 341-1996

Children with Behavioral Disorders, Inc., Wis. Council for
Debbie Brent, Prog. Chair
P.O. Box 1993, Waukesha 53187-1993
(262) 370-2434 debbrent@att.net www.wiccbd.com

Children's Service Soc. of Wis.
Bob Duncan, Pres.
620 S. 76th Street, Suite 120, Milwaukee 53214
(414) 337-8634 rduncan@chw.org www.cssw.org

Chiropractic Assn., Wis.
Karen Rockwell, Exec. Dir.
521 E. Washington Ave., Madison 53703
(608) 256-7023 krockwell@wichiro.org www.wichiro.org

Christmas Tree Producers Assn., Inc., Wis.
Cheryl Nicholson, Exec. Secy.
W9833 Hogan Rd., Portage 53901-9279
(608) 742-8663 info@christmastrees-wi.org
www.christmastrees-wi.org

Churches, Wis. Council of
Scott Anderson, Exec. Dir.
750 Windsor St., Suite 301, Sun Prairie 53590-2149
(608) 837-3108 sanderson@wichurches.org
www.wichurches.org

City/County Management Assn., Wis.
Karen Matze, Interim Exec. Dir.
2949 Yellow Jasmine Way, Suamico 54313
(920) 544-0009 kmatze@wcma-wi.org www.wcma-wi.org

Civil Air Patrol, Wis. Wing
Col. Clarence A. Peters, Commander
2400 Wright St., Madison 53704-2572
(608) 242-3067 terry.norby@wisconsin.gov wiwgcap.org

Civil Liberties Union of Wis., Inc., American
Christopher Ahmuty, Exec. Dir.
207 E. Buffalo St., No. 325, Milwaukee 53202-5774
(414) 272-4032 liberty@aclu-wi.org www.aclu-wi.org

Clerks of Circuit Court Assn., Wis.
Pam Radtke, Pres.
333 Vine St., La Crosse 54601
(608) 785-9590 pam.radtke@wicourts.gov

Collectors Assn., Inc., Wis.
Mona Sen, Exec. Secy.
P.O. Box 6275, Madison 53716
(608) 620-5922 wcaexecutivesecretary@gmail.com
http://wisconsincollectorsassociation.org

Colleges and Universities, Wis. Assn. of Independent
Rolf Wegenke, Pres.
122 W. Washington Ave., Suite 700, Madison 53703
(608) 256-7761 mail@waicu.org www.waicu.org

Collegiate DECA, Wis.
Mae Laatsch, State Dir.
130 Keyes, P.O. Box 85, Lake Mills 53551
(608) 358-1448 mlaatsch@madisoncollege.edu
www.wicollegiatedeca.org

Colonial Wars in the State of Wis., Society of
Jerry P. Hill, Gov.
5677 N. Consaul Pl., Milwaukee 53217-4818
(414) 332-9479 jerryp@wi.rr.com

Common Cause in Wis.
Jay Heck, Exec. Dir.
P.O. Box 2597, Madison 53701-2597
(608) 256-2686 ccwisjwh@itis.com
www.commoncausewisconsin.org

Communication, International Training in
Priscilla W. Bartoloth, Chair
8728 Jackson Park Blvd., Wauwatosa 53226-2710
(414) 774-6812 pbartoloth@wi.rr.com

Community Action Program Assn., Inc., Wis.
Robert Jones, Exec. Dir.
1310 Mendota St., Suite 107, Madison 53714-1039
(608) 244-4422 bjones@wiscap.org www.wiscap.org

Concrete Assn., Wis. Precast
Katie Boycks, Assn. Manager
10 E. Doty Street, Suite 523, Madison 53703
(608) 441-1436 kboycks@kpasllc.com www.wiprecast.org

Concrete Assn., Wis. Ready Mixed
Cherish Schwenn, Exec. Dir.
44 E. Mifflin St., Suite 305, Madison 53703
(608) 250-6304 info@wrmca.com www.wrmca.com

Concrete Paving Assn., Wis.
Kevin McMullen, Pres.
2423 American Ln., Suite 2, Madison 53704
(608) 240-1020 kmcmullen@wisconcrete.org
www.wisconcrete.org

Construction Employers Assn., Inc., Allied
John Topp, CEO
17100 W. Bluemound Rd., Suite 102, Brookfield 53005
(262) 785-1430 john@buildacea.org www.buildacea.org

Consulting Foresters Assn., Wis.
Kimberly K. Quast, Chair
W6861 Pastwood Rd., Fond du Lac 54937
(920) 238-9027 kquastforestry@charter.net
www.wi-consultingforesters.com

Contractors Assn. of Wis., Mechanical
Jeff Gaecke, Exec. Vice Pres.
3315 N. Ballard, Suite D, Appleton 54911
(920) 734-3148 jeff@omswi.com

Contractors Assn., Inc., Wis. Underground
Jeff Weakly, Pres.
2835 N. Mayfair Rd., Suite 22, Milwaukee 53222-4405
(414) 778-1050 wuca@wuca.org www.wuca.org

Cooperative Network
William Oemichen, Pres./CEO
1 S. Pinckney St., Suite 810, Madison 53703-2869
(608) 258-4400 bill.oemichen@cooperativenetwork.coop
cooperativenetwork.coop

Corn Promotion Board, Inc., Wis.
Bob Oleson, Exec. Dir.
W1360 Hwy 106, Palmyra 53156
(262) 495-2232 wicorn@centurytel.net www.wicorn.org

Counties Assn., Wis.
Mark D. O'Connell, Exec. Dir.
22 E. Mifflin St., Suite 900, Madison 53703
(608) 663-7188 mail@wicounties.org www.wicounties.org

Counties Mineral Resources Assn., Inc., Wis.
Erhard Huettl, Chm.
6116 Evergreen Ln., Wabeno 54566-9631
(715) 473-5314

Counties Utility Tax Assn., Wis.
Alice O'Connor, Exec. Dir.
2 E. Mifflin St., Suite 600, Madison 53703
(608) 255-8891 aoc@dewittross.com

County Agricultural Agents, Wis. Assn.
Katie Wantoch, Pres.
800 Wilson Ave., Rm 330, Dunn County UW Extension,
Menomonie 54751
(715) 232-1636 katie.wantoch@ces.uwex.edu
www.uwex.edu/ces/wacaa

County and Municipal Employees, Wis. Council 40
AFSCME, AFL-CIO
Rick Badger, Exec. Dir.
8033 Excelsior Dr., Suite B, Madison 53717
(608) 836-4040 www.afscme40.org

County Clerks Assn., Wis.
Sue Ertmer, Pres.
P.O. Box 2808, 415 Jackson St., Oshkosh 54903
(920) 236-4890 sertmer@co.winnebago.wi.us
www.wccawebsite.com

County Code Administrators, Wis.
Michelle Staff, Secy./Treas.
320 S. Main St., Rm. 201, Jefferson 53549
(920) 774-4537 wccadm@yahoo.com www.wccadm.com

County Constitutional Officers Assn., Inc., Wis.
Jay Zahn
421 Nebraska, Door County Treasurer, Sturgeon Bay 54235
(920) 746-2286

County Forests Assn., Inc., Wis.
Jane Severt, Exec. Dir.
P.O. Box 70, 3243 Golf Course Rd., Rhinelander 54501
(715) 282-5951 wcfa@frontier.com
www.wisconsincountyforests.com

County Officers, Wis. Assn. of
Shawn Handland, Treas.
400 4th St. N., Rm. 1290, Administrative Center,
La Crosse 54601-3200
(608) 785-9712 shandland@lacrossecounty.org

County Planning and Zoning Directors Assn., Wis.
Scott Godfrey, Pres.
222 N. Iowa St., Iowa County Courthouse, Dodgeville 53533
(608) 935-0398 scott.godfrey@iowacounty.org

County Police Assn. Ltd., Wis.
Robert Wierenga, Exec. Dir.
P.O. Box 764, Delavan 53115
(262) 749-1301 info@wcpawi.com www.wcpawi.com

County Surveyors Assn., Inc., Wis.
Kathleen E. Swingle, Secy.
5251 County Rd. C, Danbury 54830
(715) 866-8420 www.sco.wisc.edu

County Treasurers' Assn., Wis.
Louise Ketterer, Pres.
111 S. Jefferson St., P.O. Box 430, Lancaster 53813
(608) 723-2604 lketterer@co.grant.wi.gov
http://wicountytreasurers.com

County Veterans Service Officers Assn. of Wis.
Laura Moore, Secy.
225 N. Beaumont Rd., Suite 137, Prairie du Chien 53821
(608) 326-0204 lmoore@crawfordcoutywi.org
www.wicvso.org

Court Reporters Assn., Wis.
Susan Kay, Pres.
735 N. Water St., M185, Milwaukee 53202
(414) 224-9533 skay@brownjones.com
www.wicourtreporters.org

Credit Union League, Wis.
Tom Liebe, Vice Pres.
1 E. Main St., Suite 101, Madison 53703
(608) 514-0082 tliebe@theleague.coop
www.theleague.coop

Crop Improvement Assn., Inc., Wis.
Jack Kaltenberg, Pres.
1575 Linden Dr., 554 Moore Hall, UW-Madison,
Madison 53706-1514
(608) 262-1341 wcia@mailplus.wisc.edu
www.wcia.wisc.edu

Crop Science Society of America
Ellen Bergfeld, CEO
5585 Guilford Rd., Madison 53711
(608) 268-4979 ebergfeld@sciencesocieties.org
www.crops.org

Dahlia Soc., Badger State
Monique Volden, Secy.
1167 State Rd. 78, Mt. Horeb 53572
(608) 437-6846 jamavolden@aol.com
www.midwestdahliaconference.org/

Dahlia Society of Wis., Inc.
John Thiermann, Secy.
7728 W. Plainfield Ave., Greenfield 53220-2837
(414) 327-1759 jthiermann@wi.rr.com

Dairy Products Assn., Inc., Wis.
Brad Legreid, Exec. Dir.
8383 Greenway Blvd., Middleton 53562-3506
(608) 836-3336 info@wdpa.net www.wdpa.net

Dance Council, Wis.
Richard Clark, Pres.
P.O. Box 707, Madison 53701-0707
info@wisconsindancecouncil.org
www.wisconsindancecouncil.org

Democratic Party of Wis.
Mike Tate, Chair
110 King St., Suite 203, Madison 53703
(608) 255-5172 info@wisdems.org www.wisdems.org

Diabetes Assn., Amer. - Wisconsin
Sally Sheperdson, Exec. Dir.
375 Bishops Way, Suite 220, Brookfield 53005-6200
(414) 778-5500 ssheperdson@diabetes.org
www.diabetes.org

Disability Rights Wisconsin
Tom Masseau, Exec. Dir.
131 W. Wilson St., Suite 700, Madison 53703-2716
(608) 267-0214 tom.masseau@drwi.org
www.disabilityrightswi.org

Domestic Violence, Wis. Coalition Against
Patti Seger, Exec. Dir.
307 S. Paterson St., Suite 1, Madison 53703
(608) 255-0539 pattis@wcadv.org www.wcadv.org

Driver and Traffic Safety Education Assn., Wis.
Dick Bilda, Pres.
1417 Crystal Lake Dr., Oconomowoc 53066
(262) 567-3816 bilda3d@hotmail.com
www.adtsea.org/wisconsin/

Easter Seals Wisconsin, Inc.
Christine Fessler, Pres./CEO
101 Nob Hill Rd., Suite 301, Madison 53713-3969
(608) 277-8288 info@eastersealswisconsin.com
www.eastersealswisconsin.com

Economic Development Assn., Wis.
Kristen Fish, Exec. Dir.
10 E. Doty St., Suite 500, Madison 53703
(608) 255-5666 weda@weda.org www.weda.org

Economic Education, Inc., Wis. Council on
James P. Injeski, Pres.
7635 W. Bluemound Rd., Suite 106, Milwaukee 53213
(414) 221-9400 econed@economicswisconsin.org
www.economicswisconsin.org

Education Assn., Council, Wis.
P.O. Box 8003, Office of WEAC Executive Director,
Madison 53708-8003
(608) 276-7711 www.weac.org

Education Association, Creation
Eugene A. Sattler, Dir.
W2228 Badger Ave., Pine River 54965-9640
(920) 987-5979 creationed.com

Educators' Assn., Inc., Wis. Retired
David L. Bennett, Exec. Dir.
6405 Century Ave., Suite 201, Middleton 53562
(608) 831-5115 dbennett@wrea.net www.wrea.net

Egg Producers Assn., Wis.
N9416 Tamarack Rd., Whitewater 53190
(414) 495-6220

Electric Cooperative Assn., Wis.
Share Brandt, Mgr.
1 S. Pinckney St., Suite 810, Madison 53703
(608) 258-4400 share.brandt@cooperativenetwork.coop
www.weca.coop

Electric Utilities of Wis., Municipal
Zachary Bloom, Exec. Dir.
725 Lois Drive, Sun Prairie 53590
(608) 837-2263 zbloom@meuw.org www.meuw.org

Electrical Contractors Assn., Inc., National (Wis. Chap.)
Loyal O'Leary, Exec. Vice-Pres.
2200 Kilgust Rd., Madison 53713
(608) 221-4650 loyal@wisneca.com www.wisneca.com

Electronic Service Assn., Wis.
Sandra Neuens, Treas.
P.O. Box 125, Sussex 53089-0125
(262) 246-6495 snlneuens@wi.rr.com www.wesa.org

EMS Assn., Wis.
Mindy Allen, Exec. Dir.
26422 Oakridge Dr., Wind Lake 53185-9769
(800) 793-6820 WEMSA@wisconsinems.com
www.wisconsinems.com

Engineering Assn., State
Larry Legro, Pres.
4510 Regent St., Madison 53705-4963
(608) 233-4696 wisea@wisea.org www.wisea.org

Engineering Companies of Wis., Amer. Coun. Of
Jayne Martinko, Pres.
3 S. Pinckney St., Suite 800, Madison 53703
(608) 257-9223 acecwi@acecwi.org www.acecwi.org

Environment Wis., Inc.
Megan Severson, State Advocate
122 State St., Suite 310, Madison 53703
(608) 268-0511 www.wisconsinenvironment.org

Environmental Education, Inc., Wis. Assn. for
Jodi Hermsen, Admin.
800 Reserve St., Stevens Point 54481
(715) 346-2796 waee@uwsp.edu www.waee.org

Environmental Technologists, Inc., Federation of (FET)
Barbara Hurula, Exec. Dir.
W175 N11081 Stonewood Dr., #203, Germantown 53022
(262) 437-1700 info@fetinc.org www.fetinc.org

Equipment Dealers Assn., Midwest
Gary W. Manke, CAE, CEO
5330 Wall St., Suite 100, Madison 53718-7929
(608) 240-4700 gmanke@medaassn.com
www.medaassn.com

Ex-POWS, American
Edward Wojahn, Adj.
1553 W. Young Dr., Onalaska 54650
(608) 783-3670

Fabricare Institute, Wis.
Brian Swingle, Exec. Dir.
12342 W. Layton Ave., Greenfield 53228
(414) 529-4707 bswingle@toriiphillips.com
www.wiscleaners.com

Fairs, Wis. Assn. of
Jayme Buttke, Exec. Secy.
5320 County Road F, Merrill 54452
(715) 536-0246 wifairs@sbcglobal.net www.wifairs.com

Family Action, Inc., Wis.
Julaine K. Appling, Pres.
P.O. Box 1327, Madison 53701-1327
(608) 268 5074 info@wifamilyaction.org
www.wifamilyaction.org

Family and Children's Agencies, Wis. Assn. of
Linda A. Hall, Exec. Dir.
131 W. Wilson St., Suite 901, Madison 53703
(608) 257-5939 lhall@wafca.org www.wafca.org

Family Court Commissioners Assn., Inc., Wis.
Sandra Grady, Exec. Secy.
901 N. 9th St., Rm. 707, Milwaukee 53233
(414) 278-4428 sandra.grady@wicourts.gov

Family Ties, Inc., Wis.
Hugh Davis, Exec. Dir.
16 N. Carroll St., Suite 230, Madison 53703
(608) 267-6888 info@wifamilyties.org
www.wifamilyties.org

Farm Bureau Federation, Cooperative, Wis.
Roger Cliff, CAO
P.O. Box 5550, 1241 John Q. Hammons Dr.,
Madison 53705-0550
(608) 828-5703 www.wfbf.com

Farmers Union, Wis.
Darin Von Ruden, Pres.
117 W. Spring St., Chippewa Falls 54729-2359
(715) 723-5561 dvonruden@wisconsinfarmersunion.com
wisconsinfarmersunion.com

Fathers for Children and Families, Wis. (WFCF)
Peter Kerr, Pres.
P.O. Box 1742, Madison 53701-1742
(608) 255-3237 5050dad@gmail.com wisconsinfathers.org

FFA, Wis. Assn. Of
Jeff Hicken, State Advisor
P.O. Box 7841, Madison 53707-7841
(608) 267-9255 jeffrey.hicken@dpi.wi.gov
dpi.wi.gov/ffa/ffa.html

Financial Services Assn., Wis.
Thomas E. Moore, Exec. Dir.
22 E. Mifflin St., Suite 1010, Madison 53703
(608) 256-6413

Fire Fighters of Wis., Inc., Professional
Mahlon Mitchell, Pres.
7 N. Pinckney St., Suite 200, Madison 53703
(608) 251-5832 president@pffw.org www.pffw.org

Firefighters Assn., Inc., Wis. State
Larry Plumer, Pres.
P.O. Box 126, Durand 54736-0126
(800) 588-2989 plumer@wi-state-fighters.org
www.wi-state-firefighters.org

Fisheries Soc., Amer. (Wis. Chap.)
Justine Hasz, Secy./Treas.
P.O. Box 1846, Madison 53701
(715) 421-7845 secretary-treasurer@wi-afs.org
www.wi-afs.org

Food Processors Assn., Inc., Midwest
Nicholas C. George, Jr., Pres.
4600 American Parkway, Suite 210, Madison 53718
(608) 255-9946 info@mwfpa.org www.mwfpa.org

Food Protection, Inc., Wis. Assn. For
Leslie F. Lamb, Secy./Treas.
P.O. Box 620705, Middleton 53562
(608) 469-3290 leslamb@charter.net
www.wifoodprotection.org

Forest History Association of Wis., Inc.
Sara Connor, Pres.
P.O. Box 424, Two Rivers 54241-0424
http://chipsandsawdust.com

Forest Industry Safety and Training Alliance, Inc.
Henry Schienebeck, Exec. Dir.
P.O. Box 714, Rhinelander 54501
(800) 551-2656 info@fistausa.org www.fistausa.org

Foresters, Inc., Assn. of Consulting, Wis. Chap.
David L. Dhaseleer, Chair
856 N. Fourth St., Steigerwaldt Land Services, Inc.,
Tomahawk 54487-2127
(715) 453-3274 sls@slstomahawk.com
www.acf-foresters.org

Forty (40) Hommes et 8 Chevaux, La Societe des
Thomas J. Orval, Grand Corres.
312 Hillside Circle, Johnson Creek 53038
(920) 699-5676 wigrandvoiture@tds.net fortyandeight.org

Fresh Market Vegetable Growers Assn., Wis.
Anna Maenner, Exec. Dir.
211 Canal Rd., Waterloo 53594
(920) 478-3852 info@wisconsinfreshproduce.org
www.wisconsinfreshproduce.org

Funeral Directors Assn., Wis.
22 E. Mifflin St., Suite 1010, Madison 53703
(608) 256-1757 info@wfda.org www.wfda.org

Funeral Services and Cremation Alliance of Wis.
Erin Krueger, Exec. Dir.
P.O. Box 67, Madison 53701
(608) 204-0306 info@fsawisconsin.org
www.fsawisconsin.org

Genealogical Society, Inc., Wis. State
Chris Klauer, Admin. Asst.
P.O. Box 5106, Madison 53705-0106
(920) 397-7219 wsgs@wsgs.org www.wsgs.org

GI Forum, Wis. Amer.
Rick Demoya, Cmdr.
P.O. Box 620288, Middleton 53562
(608) 695-8762 demoyas@charter.net

Ginseng Board of Wisconsin
Anne Buntrock, Office Mgr.
668 Maratech Ave., Suite E, Marathon 54448
(715) 443-2444 ginseng@ginsengboard.com
www.ginsengboard.com

Gold Star Wives of America, Inc.
Crystal Wenum, Pres.
692 Baker Rd., Hudson 54016-7946
(715) 386-8615 goldstarwives.org

Golf Assn., Inc., Wis. State
Rob Jansen, Exec. Dir.
11350 W. Theo Trecker Way, West Allis 53214
(414) 443-3560 info@wsga.org www.wsga.org

Golf Course Supts. Assn., Inc., Wis.
Brett Grams, Chap. Exec.
N1922 Virginia Dr., Waupaca 54981
(920) 643-4888 bgrams@wgcsa.com www.wgcsa.com

Grange, Wis. State
Duane Scott, Master
N2552 Strunk Rd., Fort Atkinson 53538-9025
(920) 723-6660 wisconsingrange@gmail.com

Great Lakes Graphics Assn.
Joseph E. Lyman, Pres.
W232 N2950 Roundy Circle East, Suite 200, Pewaukee
53072-4110
(262) 522-2210 info@glga.info www.glga.info

Green Industry Federation, Inc., Wis.
Brian Swingle, Exec. Dir.
12342 W. Layton Ave., Greenfield 53228
(414) 529-4705 bswingle@toriiphillips.com www.wgif.net

Grocers Assn., Inc., Wis.
Brandon Scholz, Pres.
33 E. Main St., Suite 701, Madison 53703
(608) 244-7150 brandon@wisconsingrocers.com
www.wisconsingrocers.com

Hazardous Materials Responders, Inc., Wis. Assn.
Doug Rohn, Pres.
6517 Bettys Lane, Madison 53711
(608) 274-3949 madinstr@tds.net www.wahmr.com

Head Start Assn., Wis.
Dan Stickler, Exec. Dir.
122 E. Olin Ave., Suite 110, Madison 53713
(608) 442-6879 cousin@whsaonline.org
www.whsaonline.org

Health and Physical Education, Wis.
Keith Bakken, Exec. Dir.
1725 State St., 24 Mitchell Hall, UW-La Crosse,
La Crosse 54601
(608) 785-8175 whpe@uwlax.edu www.whpe.us

Health Care Assn., Wis.
James McGinn, Dir. of Govt. Rel.
131 W. Wilson St., Suite 1001, Madison 53703
(608) 257-0125 jim@whca.com

Health Care Assn., Wis. Primary
Stephanie Harrison, Exec. Dir.
5202 Eastpark Blvd., Suite 109, Madison 53718
(608) 277-7477 wphca@wphca.org www.wphca.org

Health Charities of Wis., Community
Gary Ross, Pres./CEO
6737 W. Washington St., Suite 2253, West Allis 53214
(414) 918-9100 or (800) 783-0242
gross@healthcharities.org
www.healthcharities.org/wisconsin

Health Information Management Assn., Wis.
Cassandra Bissen, Exec. Dir.
2350 South Ave., Suite 107, La Crosse 54601-6272
(608) 787-0168 whima@whima.org whima.org

Health Plans, Wis. Assn. Of
Nancy J. Wenzel, CEO
10 E. Doty St., Suite 503, Madison 53703
(608) 255-8599 nancy@wihealthplans.org
www.wihealthplans.org

Health Underwriters, Wis. Assn. of
Alice O'Connor, Exec. Dir.
2 E. Mifflin St., #600, Madison 53703
(608) 268-0200 aoc@dewittross.com www.ewahu.org

Hearing Professionals, Wis. Alliance of
Doug Johnson, Exec. Dir.
123 W. Washington Ave., Suite 201, Madison 53703-2558
(608) 201-7965 dqj@jjassociates.com www.wahpinfo.org

Heart Assn., American (Midwest Affiliate)
Maureen Cassidy, Vice. Pres of Advocacy
2850 Dairy Dr., Suite 300, Madison 53718
(608) 221-8866, ext. 2333 maureen.cassidy@heart.org
www.heart.org

Hereford Assn., Wis.
Ruth Espenscheid, Secy.
12044 Hwy 78, P.O. Box 296, Argyle 53504-0296
(608) 543-3788 wlbaosf@mhtc.net wisconsinherefords.org

History, Wis. Council for Local
Terry Thiessen, Pres.
1707 Pilgrim Way, New Holstein 53061-1246
(920) 948-7748 tethiessen@frontier.com
wisconsinhistory.org

Holstein Assn., Wis.
Larry Nelson, Exec. Dir.
902 Eighth Ave., Baraboo 53913
(800) 223-4269 or (608) 356-2114 larryn@wisholsteins.com
www.wisholsteins.com

Home Health United/Visiting Nurse Service, Inc.
Rick Bourne, Pres./CEO
4639 Hammersley Rd., Madison 53711
(608) 241-6950 rbourne@hhuvns.org
www.homehealthunited.org

Honey Producers Assn., Wis.
Derald Kettelwell, Pres.
10432 W. Norwich Ave., Greenfield 53228
(414) 545-5514 deraldk@prodigy.net www.wihoney.com

Horse Club, Inc., Wis. Morgan
Marie Stewart, Pres.
9099 Colby Rd., Mt. Horeb 53572-2704
(608) 832-6559 xroads@tds.net
www.wisconsinmorganhorseclub.org

Horse Council, Wis. State, Inc.
Pam Pritchard, Adm. Asst.
121 S. Ludington St., Columbus 53925
(920) 623-0393 pam@wisconsinstatehorsecouncil.org
www.wisconsinstatehorsecouncil.org

Horse Trail Assn., Inc., Glacial Drumlin
Ken Carpenter, Pres.
P.O. Box 82, Deerfield 53531-0082
(608) 576-4104 witrails@gmail.com www.gdhta.org

Hospice Organization and Palliative Experts of Wis. (HOPE)
Melanie G. Ramey, Exec. Dir.
3240 University Ave., Suite 2, Madison 53705-3570
(608) 233-7166 MELR217@aol.com
www.wisconsinhospice.org

Hospital Assn., Inc., Wis.
Steve Brenton, Pres.
P.O. Box 2590389, Madison 53725-9038
(608) 274-1820 www.wha.org

Hotel and Lodging Assn., Wis.
Trisha A. Pugal, Pres., CEO
1025 S. Moorland Rd., Suite 200, Brookfield 53005
(262) 782-2851 pugal@wisconsinlodging.org
www.wisconsinlodging.org

Housing Alliance, Wis.
Ross Kinzler, Exec. Dir.
301 N. Broom St., Suite 101, Madison 53703
(608) 255-3131 info@housingalliance.us
www.housingalliance.us

Humane Societies, Inc., Wis. Federated
Pam McCloud Smith, Bd. Pres.
5132 Voges Rd., Madison 53718
(608) 838-0413, ext. 111 pmsmith@giveshelter.org
www.wisconsinfederatedhs.org

Humanities Council, Wis.
Dena Wortzel, Exec. Dir.
222 S. Bedford St., Suite F, Madison 53703-3688
(608) 262-0706 contact@wisconsinhumanities.org
wisconsinhumanities.org

Insulation Contractors Assn., Inc., Wis.
Mark Borchardt, Pres.
4916 S. 79th St., Greenfield 53220
(414) 791-3005 debbiewanta@hotmail.com

Insurance Agents of Wis., Inc., Professional
Ronald Von Haden, Exec. Vice-Pres.
6401 Odana Rd., Madison 53719-1126
(608) 274-8188 rvonhaden@piaw.org www.piaw.org

Insurance Agents of Wisconsin, Independent
Matthew G. Banaszynski, Exec. Vice-Pres.
725 John Nolen Dr., Madison 53713-1421
(608) 256-4429 iiaw@iiaw.com www.iiaw.com

Insurance Alliance, Wis.
Andrew J. Franken, Pres.
44 E. Mifflin St., Suite 901, Madison 53703
(608) 255-1749 contact@wial.com wial.com

Insurance Companies, Wis. Assn. of Mutual
James Tlusty, Pres.
5315 Wall St., Suite 205, Madison 53718
(608) 246-2552 wamic@chorus.net www.wamic.org

International Institute of Wis., Inc.
Alexander P. Durtka, Jr., Pres.
1110 N. Old World 3rd St., Milwaukee 53203-1117
(414) 225-6220 info@iiwisconsin.org

Interscholastic Athletic Assn., Wis.
David J. Anderson, Exec. Dir.
5516 Vern Holmes Dr., Stevens Point 54482
(715) 344-8580 danderson@wiaawi.org www.wiaawi.org

Japan-America Soc. of Wis., Inc.
Alexander P. Durtka, Jr., Pres.
1110 W. 3rd St., Suite 420, Milwaukee 53203-1117
(414) 225-6220 jasw@iiwisconsin.org

JCI Wisconsin, Inc.
Steve Moddie, Exec. Vice Pres.
P.O. Box 1547, Appleton 54912-1547
(920) 731-7681 evp@jciwisconsin.org
www.jciwisconsin.org

Judges Assn., Wis. Municipal
Jodi A. Sanfelippo, Secy./Treas.
219 N. Milwaukee St., Suite 2B, Milwaukee 53202
(414) 287-9875 secretary-treasurer@wmja.net
www.wmja.net

Kidney Foundation of Wis., Inc., Natl.
Cynthia A. Huber, CEO
16655 W. Bluemound Rd., Suite 240, Brookfield 53005-5923
(262) 821-0705 or (800) 543-6393 nkfw@kidneywi.org
www.kidneywi.org

Labor and Employment Relations Assn. (Wis. Ch.)
Suzanne Clement, Secy./Treas.
3477 N. Cramer St., Milwaukee 53211
(414) 962-1203 sueclera@gmail.com
http://www4.uwm.edu/Org/lera/

Labor History Society, Wis.
Steve Cupery, Pres.
6333 W. Bluemound Rd., Milwaukee 53213
(414) 771-0700, ext. 20 info@wisconsinlaborhistory.org
www.wisconsinlaborhistory.org

Laborers' Dist. Council, Wis.
John J. Schmitt, Pres. and Bus. Mgr.
4633 Liuna Way, Suite 101, DeForest 53532
(608) 846-8242 jschmitt@wilaborers.org
www.wilaborers.org

Land and Water Conservation Assn., Inc., Wis.
Jim VandenBrook, Exec. Dir.
702 E. Johnson St., Madison 53703-1533
(608) 441-2677 jim@wlwca.org www.wlwca.org

Language Teachers, Wis. Assn. for (WAFLT)
Keely Lake, Pres.
101 N. University Ave., Wayland Academy,
Beaver Dam 53916
(920) 885-3376 president@waflt.org www.waflt.org

Law Librarians Assn. of Wis., Inc.
Emily Koss, Pres.
1000 N. Water St., Suite 1700,
Reinhart Boerner Van Deuren, SC, Milwaukee 53202
(414) 298-8510 ekoss@reinhartlaw.com
www.aallnet.org/chapter/llaw

Lawns of Wisconsin Network (LaWN)
Karl Schimmel, Pres.
8170 N. Granville Woods Rd., Milwaukee 53223
(815) 351-1224 kschimmel@carlinsales.com

Lawyers Assistance Program, Wis.
Linda Albert, Mgr.
5302 E. Park Blvd., P.O. Box 7158, Madison 53707
(608) 250-6172 lalbert@wisbar.org www.wisbar.org/wislap

Lawyers, Assn. for Women
Dana Kader Robb, Admin.
3322 N. 92nd St., Milwaukee 53222
(414) 750-4404 dana@barefoot-marketing.com
www.associationforwomenlawyers.org

Lawyers, Wis. Assn. for Justice
Jane E. Garrott
44 E. Mifflin St., Suite 402, Madison 53703-2897
(608) 257-5741 jgarrott@wisjustice.org www.wisjustice.org

League of Women Voters of Wis. Education Network, Inc.
Andrea Kaminski, Exec. Dir.
612 W. Main St., #200, Madison 53703
(608) 256-0827 kaminski@lwvwi.org www.lwvwi.org

Learning Disabilities Assn. of Wis.
Diane Sixel, Pres.
7625 Lechler Ln., Kiel 53042
info@ldawisconsin.org ldawisconsin.com

Legal Assn. for Women
Ashley Richter, Pres.
P.O. Box 2121, Madison 53701-2121
www.wisbar.org/bars/law

Letter Carriers' Assn., Wis. Rural
Ron Berg, Secy./Treas.
402 Dalogasa Dr., Arena 53503
(608) 220-4855 sec.treas2@frontiernet.net wirlca.org

Leukemia and Lymphoma Soc. (Wis. Chap.)
Chris Watry, Operations Asst.
200 S. Executive Dr., Suite 203, Brookfield 53005
(262) 785-4251 chris.watry@lls.org www.lls.org/wi

Libertarian Party of Wisconsin
Terry Gray, Chair
5113 Starker Ave., Madison 53716-1915
(800) 236-9236, ext.2 chair@lpwi.org www.lpwi.org/

Lions Clubs Internatl. (MD-27 - Wi.)
Kathleen Gruna, Office Manager
3834 County Rd. A, Rosholt 54473
(715) 677-4764 lionstat@wi-net.com wisconsinlions.org

Liquid Waste Carriers Assn., Wis.
Katie Boycks, Assn. Manager
10 E. Doty Street, Suite 523, Madison 53703
(608) 441-1436 kboycks@kpasllc.com www.wlwca.com

Lobbyists, Inc., Assn. of Wis.
Justin Laxton, Assn. Manager
10 E. Doty Street, Suite 523, Madison 53703
(608) 442-7295 awl@wisconsinlobbyists.com
www.wisconsinlobbyists.com

LSLA Education, Inc.
Tim Kassis, Pres.
P.O. Box 160, Antigo 54409
(715) 623-5410 lsla@lakestateslumber.com

Lung Assn. in Wis., Amer.
Dona Wininsky, Dir. Of Public Policy and Comm.
13100 W. Lisbon Rd., Suite 700, Brookfield 53005
(262) 703-4840 dona.wininsky@lungwi.org
www.lungwi.org

Lupus Foundation of Amer., Inc., Wis. Chap.
Dawn Thomas-Semanko, Exec. Dir.
2600 N. Mayfair Rd., Suite 320, Milwaukee 53226
(414) 443-6400 lupuswi@lupuswi.org www.lupuswi.org

Make-A-Wish Foundation of Wis.
Patti Gorsky, Pres. And CEO
13195 W. Hampton Ave., Butler 53007
(262) 781-4445 info@wisconsin.wish.org
www.wisconsin.wish.org

Manufacturers' Agents, Inc., Wis. Assn. of
Stewart Oliver, Pres.
11801 W. Silver Spring Dr. #200, Milwaukee 53225
(414) 778-0640 wama@wama.org wama.org

Manufacturers and Commerce, Wis.
Kurt Bauer, Pres./CEO
P.O. Box 352, Madison 53701-0352
(608) 258-3400 wmc@wmc.org www.wmc.org

Maple Syrup Producers Assoc., Wis.
Gretchen Grape, Exec. Dir.
33186 Cty Hwy W, Holcombe 54745
(715) 447-5758 gretchen_grape@yahoo.com
www.wismaple.org

Marine Corps League Auxiliary
Eleanor Maller, Pres.
431 15th St., Racine 53403
(262) 637-3403

Marine Corps League, Dept. of Wis.
Lynn Sabel, Commandant
1614 S. Carriage Ln., Unit A, New Berlin 53151
(262) 424-2183 lynn.f.sabel@usbank.com

Masonry Alliance, Wis.
Jane Svinicki, Exec. Dir.
6737 W. Washington St., Suite 1300, Milwaukee 53214
(414) 276-0667 info@wma-online.org
www.wma-online.org

Mayflower Descendants, Wis., Soc. Of
Mrs. Robert R. Pekowsky, Historian
1629 North Golf Glen, Unit D, Madison 53704-7074
(608) 467-6646 martell135@charter.net
www.mayflowerwi.org

Meat Processors, Inc., Wis. Assn. of
Peter Drone, Exec. Secy.
P.O. Box 331, Bloomington 53804
(608) 994-2559 peter@wi-amp.com www.wi-amp.com

Medical Society, Wis.
William R. Abrams, CEO
P.O. Box 1109, Madison 53701-1109
(608) 442-3800 communications@wismed.org
www.wisconsinmedicalsociety.org

Military Officers Assn. of America, Wis. Council of Chapters
Col. Robert J. Gadwill, Pres.
1327 Glades Dr., Altoona 54720
(715) 834-1498 bdgrcreek@aol.com moaa.org

Milk Marketing Board, Wis.
James Robson, CEO
8418 Excelsior Dr., Madison 53717
(608) 836-8820 www.eatwisconsincheese.com

Mining Impact Coalition of Wis., Inc.
Frank Koehn, Pres.
P.O. Box 834, Ashland 54806
(608) 233-8455 burroak15@gmail.com

Mothers Against Drunk Driving (MADD)
Becky DrewsDebuque, Victim Advocate
P.O. Box 284, Beloit 53512
(262) 347-4026 becky.drews@madd.org madd.org

Motor Carriers Assn., Wis.
Thomas Howells, Pres.
562 Grand Canyon Dr., Madison 53719-1033
(608) 833-8200 thowells@witruck.org

Movers Assn., Wis.
Cherie Houser, Vice Pres.
562 Grand Canyon Dr., Madison 53719-1033
(608) 833-8200 chouser@witruck.org www.wismovers.org

MRA - The Management Assn., Inc.
Susan M. Fronk, Pres.
N19 W24400 Riverwood Dr., Waukesha 53188
(262) 523-9090 www.mranet.org

Muck Farmers Assn., Wis.
Rod Gumz, Pres.
N570 6th Court, Endeavor 53930
(608) 981-2488

Multiple Sclerosis Soc., Natl. (Wis. Chap.)
Colleen G. Kalt, Pres./CEO
1120 James Dr., Suite A, Hartland 53029
(262) 369-4400 or (800) 242-3358 info.wisms@nmss.org
www.wisms.org

Municipalities, League of Wis.
Dan Thompson, Exec. Dir.
122 W. Washington Ave., Suite 300, Madison 53703
(608) 267-2380 league@lwm-info.org www.lwm-info.org

Music Educators Assn., Inc., Wis.
Timothy J. Schaid, Exec. Dir.
1005 Quinn Dr., Waunakee 53597
(608) 850-3566 mgeorge@wsmamusic.org
www.wmeamusic.org

Myasthenia Gravis Foundation of Amer. (Wis. Chapter)
Bryn Feyen, Chp.
2474 S. 96th St., West Allis 53227
(262) 938-9800 wisconsin@myasthenia.org
myasthenia.org/wisconsin

NAIFA Wisconsin
Lynda J. Patterson, Exec. Dir
22 N. Carroll St., Suite 300, Madison 53703
(608) 244-3131 info@naifa.wisconsin.org
www.naifawisconsin.org

NAMI Wisconsin, Inc.
Julianne Carbin, Exec. Dir.
4233 W. Beltline Hwy, Madison 53711
(608) 268-6000 or (800) 236-2988 julianne@
namiwisconsin.org www.namiwisconsin.org

National Farmers Organization, Wis.
Don Hamm, State Pres.
955 17th St., Prairie du Sac 53578
(608) 643-3341, ext. 222 dhamm@nfo.org

National Guard Assn., Inc., Wis.
Ronald R. Wagner, Exec. Dir.
2400 Wright St., Rm. 208, Madison 53704-2572
(608) 242-3114 wingainc@att.net www.winga.org

National Guard Enlisted Assn., Inc., Wis.
Robert Serrahn, Exec. Dir.
2400 Wright St., Madison 53704-2572
(608) 242-3112 wngea@yahoo.com wngea.org

Natural Food Associates, Inc., Wis.
Michael Hittner, Pres.
910 W. Grand Ave., Wisconsin Rapids 54495
(715) 421-2061 wisconsinnaturalfoods.org

Nature Conservancy, Wis. Chap.
Mary Jean Huston, State Dir.
633 W. Main St., Madison 53703
(608) 251-8140 wisconsin@tnc.org nature.org

Navy Club of USA
Nellie P. Debaker, Cmdr.
N7197 County Road H, Luxemburg 54217-9221
(920) 845-5033 n9691@yahoo.com

Newspaper Assn., Inc., Wis.
Beth Bennett, Exec. Dir.
1901 Fish Hatchery Road, Madison 53713
(608) 283-7621 beth.bennett@WNAnews.com
www.wnanews.com

Nursery Assn., Wis.
Brian Swingle, Exec. Dir.
12342 W. Layton Ave., Greenfield 53228
(414) 529-4705 bswingle@toriiphillips.com www.wgif.net

Nurses Assn., Wis.
Gina Dennik-Champion, Exec. Dir.
6117 Monona Dr., Suite 1, Madison 53716-3995
(608) 221-0383 gina@wisconsinnurses.org
www.wisconsinnurses.org

Nurses, Wis. Assn. of Licensed Practical
JoAnn Shaw, Pres.
22 E. Mifflin St., Suite 1010, Madison 53703
(608) 256-5299 jslpn@sbcglobal.net

Nursing Home Social Workers Assn., Wis.
Jeff McCabe, Pres.
3300 W. Brewster St., c/o Brewster Village, Appleton 54914
(920) 225-1985 jeff.mccabe@outagamie.org wnhswa.org

Nursing, Inc., Wis. League for
Debra Turtenwald, Admin. Asst.
P.O. Box 653, Germantown 53022
(414) 454-9561 info@wisconsinwln.org
www.wisconsinwln.org

Nutrition and Dietetics, Wis. Academy of
Kelly Nuckolls, Media Spokesperson
563 Carter Court, Suite B, Kimberly 54136
(888) 232-8631 eatrightwisc@gmail.com
www.eatrightwisc.org

Occupational Therapy Assn., Inc., Wis.
Teri Black, Pres.
122 E. Olin Ave., Suite 165, Madison 53713
(608) 287-1606 wota@wota.net www.wota.net

Ophthalmology, Wis. Academy of
Richard H. Paul, Exec. Dir.
10 W. Phillip Rd., Suite 120, Vernon Hills, IL 60061
(800) 838-3527 richardpaul@dls.net www.wieyemd.org

Orchid Soc., Wis.
Bruce Efflandt
3518 North 98th St., Milwaukee 53222
(262) 327-9373 berniesfloral@mail.com
www.wisconsinorchidsociety.com

Ornithology, Inc., Wis. Soc. for
Christine Reel, Treas.
2022 Sherryl Ln., Waukesha 53188-3142
(262) 844-8187 wso1939@hotmail.com www.wsobirds.org

Orthodontists, Wis. Soc. of
Dr.David L. Olsen, Pres.
145 W. Calumet St., Appleton 54915-4934
(920) 731-2777 olsenortho@newbc.rr.com

Otolaryngology - Head and Neck Surgery, Wis Soc. of
Diane Heatley, Secy./Treas.
600 Highland Ave., K4/766, Madison 53792-7375
(608) 262-7181 secy-treasurer@wiscoto.org
www.wiscoto.org

Outdoor Advertising Assoc. of Wis.
Janet Swandby, Exec. Dir.
10 E. Doty St., Suite 518, Madison 53703
(608) 286-0764 swandby@swandby.com www.oaaw.org

Paper Council, Wis.
Jeffrey G. Landin, Pres.
5485 Grande Market Dr., Suite B, Appleton 54913
(920) 574-3752 landin@wipapercouncil.org
www.wisconsinpapercouncil.org

Paratransit Provider, Wis. Rural and
Julie Deaton, Pres.
P.O. Box 618, Rhinelander 54501
(715) 369-1337 jdeaton@headwaterinc.com
www.witransportation.org

Parents and Teachers Inc., Wis. Congress of
Heather Leckey, Pres.
4797 Hayes Rd., Suite 102, Madison 53704-3288
(608) 244-1455 info@wisconsinpta.org
www.wisconsinpta.org

Park and Recreation Assn., Inc., Wis.
Steven J. Thompson, Exec. Dir.
6601-C Northway, Greendale 53129
(414) 423-1210 sthompson@wpraweb.org

Pathologists, Wis. Soc. of
Eric Ostermann, Exec. Dir.
563 Carter Ct., Suite B, Kimberly 54136
(920) 560-5634 eric@badgerbay.co www.wispath.com

Peace and Justice, Wis. Network for
Diane Farsetta, Exec. Dir.
122 State St., No. 405A, Madison 53703-2500
(608) 250-9240 diane@wnpj.org www.wnpj.org

Pediatric Dentists, Wis. Soc. of
Cesar D. Gonzalez, DDS, Pres.
1801 W. Wisconsin Ave., Marquette University School of Dentistry, Milwaukee 53233
(414) 288-6391 cesar.gonzalez@marquette.edu

Perinatal Care, Wis. Assn. for
Ann E. Conway, Exec. Dir.
211 S. Paterson St., Suite 250, Madison 53703
(608) 285-5858 wapc@perinatalweb.org
www.perinatalweb.org

Perinatal Foundation
Ann E. Conway, Exec. Dir.
211 S. Paterson St., Suite 250, Madison 53703
(608) 285-5858 foundation@perinatalweb.org
www.perinatalweb.org

Petroleum Marketers & Convenience Store Assn., Wis.
Matthew C. Hauser, Pres.
121 S. Pinckney St., Suite 300, Madison 53703
(608) 256-7555 info@wpmca.org www.wpmca.org

Pharmacy Soc. of Wis.
Christopher Decker, CEO and Exec. Vice Pres.
701 Heartland Tr., Madison 53717
(608) 827-9200 chrisd@pswi.org www.pswi.org

PHCC/Master Plumbers – Wis. Assn.
Jeffrey J. Beiriger, Exec. Dir.
P.O. Box 833, Germantown 53022
(888) 782-6815 mail@phcc-wi.org www.phcc-wi.com

Phenological Soc., Wis.
Mark Schwartz, Pres.
4484 North Woodburn St., Shorewood 53211
(414) 229-3740 mds@uwm.edu www.wps.uwm.edu

Physical Medicine and Rehabilitation, Wis. Soc. of
James W. Leonard, D.O., Pres.
1685 Highland Ave., 6th Floor, Madison 53705
(608) 263-8632 leonard@rehab.wisc.edu www.wispmr.org

Physical Therapy Assn., Wis.
Karen Curran, Exec. Dir.
3510 E. Washington Ave., Madison 53704
(608) 221-9191 wpta@wpta.org www.wpta.org

Physician Assistants, Wis. Academy of
Jeff Oryall
563 Carter Ct., Suite B, Kimberly 54136
(920) 560-5630 wapa@wapa.org www.wapa.org

Physicians, Am. College of Emergency (Wis. Ch.)
Richard H. Paul, Exec. Dir.
10 W. Phillip Rd., Suite 120, Vernon Hills, IL 60061-1330
(800) 838-3627 richardpaul@dls.net
www.wisconsinacep.org

Physicians, Wis. Academy of Family
Larry Pheifer, Exec. Dir.
210 Green Bay Rd., Thiensville 53092
(262) 512-0606 academy@wafp.org www.wafp.org

Pipe Welding Bureau, Natl. Certified (Wis. Chap.)
Timothy A. Penno, Exec. Dir.
5940 Seminole Centre Ct., Suite 102, Madison 53711
(608) 288-1414 tim.penno@mechanicalindustries.org

Podiatric Medicine, Wis. Soc. of
Steven Frydman, DPM, Exec. Dir.
7929 N. 76th St., Milwaukee 53223
(414) 371-2468 wspm@aol.com
www.wisconsinpodiatrists.com

Police Assn., Wis. Chiefs of
Donald Thaves, Exec. Dir.
River Ridge - 1141 South Main St., Shawano 54166
(715) 524-8283 dthaves@shawanonet.net
www.wichiefs.org

Police Assn., Wis. Professional
James L. Palmer, Exec. Dir.
660 John Nolen Dr., Suite 300, Madison 53713
(608) 273-3840 palmer@wppa.com www.wppa.com

Pork Assn., Wis. Cooperative
Tammy Vaassen, Dir. of Operations
P.O. Box 327, Lancaster 53813-0327
(608) 723-7551 wppa@wppa.org www.wppa.org

Postal History Soc., Wis.
Darren Mueller, Pres.
P.O. Box 343, Oak Creek 53154
(414) 429-3750 darren.mueller@juno.com
www.wfscstamps.org/Clubs/WisconsinPostalHistory/

Postsecondary Agricultural Students
Paul Cutting, State Director
1800 Bronson Blvd., Fennimore 53809
(800) 362-3322, ext. 2467 pcutting@swtc.edu
www.wipas.org

Potato and Vegetable Growers Assn., Wis.
Duane Maatz, Exec. Dir.
P.O. Box 327, Antigo 54409-0327
(715) 623-7683 wpvga@wisconsinpotatoes.com
www.wisconsinpotatoes.com

Potato Growers Aux., Inc., Wis.
Lynn Isherwood, Pres.
P.O. Box 327, Antigo 54409-0327
(715) 623-7683 wpvga@wisconsinpotatoes.com

Potato Improvement Assn., Wis. Seed
P.O. Box 173, Antigo 54409-0173
(715) 623-7683 www.potatoseed.org

Prevent Blindness Wis., Inc.
Barbara Armstrong, Exec. Dir
759 N. Milwaukee St., Suite 305, Milwaukee 53202
(414) 765-0505 info@preventblindnesswisconsin.org
www.preventblindness.org/wi

Preventive Medicine, Wis., Soc. for
Henry A. Anderson, M.D., Pres.
200 Lakewood Blvd., Madison 53704-5916
(608) 266-1253 anderha@sbcglobal.net

Psychological Assn., Wis.
Sarah Bowen, Exec. Dir.
126 S. Franklin St., Madison 53703
(608) 251-1450 wispsych@execpc.com
www.wipsychology.org

Purple Heart, Military Order of the (Dept. of Wis.)
William J. Lobeck, Dept. Adjutant
16510 Ridgeview Ln., Viola 54664
(608) 538-3194 lzwest@mwt.net

Quality, Amer. Soc. For
Paul E. Borawski, CEO
600 N. Plankinton Ave., Milwaukee 53203
(414) 272-8575 cs@asq.org www.asq.org

Radiologic Technologists, Wis. Soc. of
Marnet Zimmer, Secy.
3711 S. Iowa Ave., St. Francis 53235
(414) 769-1239 margaret.zimmer@sbcglobal.net
www.wsrt.net

Radiological Soc., Wis.
Jane Svinicki, Exec. Dir.
6737 W. Washington St., Suite 1300, Milwaukee 53214
(414) 755-6293 jane@svinicki.com www.wi-rad.org

Railroad Passengers, Wis. Assn. of
Mark Weitenbeck, Treas.
3385 S. 119th St., West Allis 53227-3943
(414) 541-1112 wisarp@hotmail.com www.wisarp.org

Reading Assn., Wis. State
Sue Bradley, Admin. Asst.
N7902 E. Friesland Rd., Randolph 53956
(920) 326-6280 wsra@wsra.org www.wsra.org

Real Property Listers Assn., Wis.
Michelle Schultz, Pres.
51 S. Main St., Janesville 53545
(608) 757-5610 schultz@co.rock.wi.us www.wrpla.org

Red Cross, Amer.
Patty Flowers, Reg. CEO
2600 W. Wisconsin Ave., Milwaukee 53233
(414) 342-8680 www.redcross.org

Register of Deeds Assn., Wis.
Michael Mazemke, Pres.
P.O. Box 307, Waupaca 54981
(715) 258-6322 www.wrdaonline.org

Rehabilitation For Wisconsin, Inc.
Thomas Cook, Exec. Dir.
2000 Engel St., Suite 100, Madison 53713
(608) 244-5310 rfw@rfw.org http://www.rfwia.org/

Republican Party of Wis.
Stephan Thompson, Exec. Dir.
148 E. Johnson St., Madison 53703
(608) 257-4765 info@wisgop.org www.wisgop.org

Reserve Officers Assn. of the U.S. (Dept. of Wis.)
LTC Timothy Lubinsky, Exec. Secy.
728 Newbury St., Ripon 54971
(920) 450-3951 tlubinsky19@hotmail.com www.roa.org

Residential Services Association of Wis.
Jennifer Rzepka, Exec. Dir.
6737 W. Washington St., Suite 1300, Milwaukee 53214
(414) 276-9273 info@rsawisconsin.org
www.rsawisconsin.org

Restaurant Assn., Wis.
Edward J. Lump, Pres./CEO
2801 Fish Hatchery Rd., Madison 53713
(608) 270-9950 elump@wirestaurant.org
www.wirestaurant.org

Retired Enlisted Assn., The
Holly Hoppe, Pres.
Courthouse, 301 Washington St., Oconto 54153
(920) 834-6817 cvso@co.oconto.wi.us www.trea.org

RID (Remove Intoxicated Drivers)
Mardy Meacham, Coord.
122 Eagle Lake Ave., Mukwonago 53149
(262) 363-5554 christysmom@aol.com www.rid-usa.org

Right to Life, Inc., Wis.
Barbara L. Lyons, Exec. Dir.
9730 W. Bluemound Rd., Suite 200, Milwaukee 53226-2331
(877) 855-5007 admin@wrtl.org www.wrtl.org

Runaway Services, Wis. Assn. for
Patricia Balke, Exec. Dir.
2318 E. Dayton St., Madison 53704
(608) 241-2649 pbalke@sbcglobal.net wahrs.org

Saddlebred Assn. of Wis., Amer.
Vicky Holston, Pres.
35660 W. Lake Dr., Oconomowoc 53066
(262) 560-9764 vholston@msn.com www.asaw.org

Safety Patrols Inc., Wis.
Joann Solberg, Exec. Dir.
P.O. Box 620584, Middleton 53562
(608) 332-5480 wisconsinsafetypatrols@gmail.com
www.wisconsinsafetypatrol.com

St. Francis Children's Center, Inc.
Gerald Coon, Exec. Dir.
6700 N. Port Washington Rd., Milwaukee 53217-3919
(414) 351-0450 gcoon@sfcckids.org www.sfcckids.org

Sanitary Engineering, Amer. Soc. of (Wis. Chap.)
Ervin Mirr, Secy.
4610 Raven Ct., Brookfield 53005-1242
(262) 781-4725

School Administrators, Assn. of Wis.
Jim Lynch, Exec. Dir.
4797 Hayes Rd., Suite 103, Madison 53704-3288
(608) 241-0300 jimlynch@awsa.org www.awsa.org

School Attorneys Assn., Wis.
Andrea Voelker, Pres.-Elect.
P.O. Box 1030, 3624 Oakwood Hills Pky.,
Eau Claire 54702-1030
(715) 839-7786 avoelker@wrpr.com
www.wasb.org/websites/wsaa/index.php?p=216

School Boards, Inc., Wis. Assn. of
John Ashley, Exec. Dir.
122 W. Washington Ave., Suite 400, Madison 53703
(608) 257-2622 jashley@wasb.org www.wasb.org

School Bus Assn., Wis.
Michael McManus, Exec. Dir.
7044 S. 13th St., Oak Creek 53154
(414) 908-4956, ext.119 m.mcmanus@wi-sba.org
www.wi-sba.org

School Music Assn., Inc., Wis.
Timothy J. Schaid, Exec. Dir.
1005 Quinn Dr., Waunakee 53597
(608) 850-3566 mgeorge@wsmamusic.org wsmamusic.org

School Music, Wis. Foundation for
Timothy J. Schaid, Exec. Dir.
1005 Quinn Dr., Waunakee 53597
(608) 850-3566 mgeorge@wsmamusic.org
wsmamusic.com/foundation

Schools Accreditation, Wis. Religious and Independent, Inc.
Beatrice Weiland, Exec. Dir.
P.O. Box 685, Muskego 53150
(262) 895-3679 wrisa@wrisa.net www.wrisa.net

Schools, Wis. Assn. of Christian
Matt Williams, Exec. Dir.
1840 Bond St., Green Bay 54303
(920) 499-5561 office@wacschools.org
www.wacschools.org

Seasonal Residents Assn.
Nick Kaufmann
P.O. Box 46108, Madison 53744
(800) 880-9944 info@wisra.org www.wisra.org

SEIU Healthcare, Wis.
Dian Palmer, Pres.
4513 Vernon Rd., Madison 53705-2366
(608) 277-1199 dianp@seiuhcwi.org www.seiuhcwi.org

Seniors of Wis., Inc., United
Dorothy Seeley, Pres.
4515 W. Forest Home Ave., Milwaukee 53219-4837
(414) 321-0220 www.unitedseniorsofwisconsin.org

Sexual Assault, Wis. Coalition Against
Pennie Meyers, Interim Exec. Dir.
600 Williamson St., Suite N2, Madison 53703
(608) 257-1516 wcasa@wcasa.org www.wcasa.org

Sheriffs and Deputy Sheriffs Assn., Wis.
James Cardinal, Exec. Dir.
P.O. Box 145, Chippewa Falls 54729-0145
(715) 723-7173 jcardinal@wsdsa.org www.wsdsa.org

Sheriff's Assn., Badger State
Dean Meyer, Exec. Dir.
P.O. Box 394, Bruce 54819
(715) 415-2412 badgersheriff@brucetel.net
www.badgersheriff.com

Sign Assn., Wis.
Christopher Ruditys, Exec. Dir.
11801 W. Silver Spring Dr., #200, Milwaukee 53225
(414) 271-9277 ruditys@wamllc.net
www.wisconsinsign.com

Sister Relationships, Inc., Wis.
Alexander P. Durtka, Jr., Pres.
1110 N. Old World Third St., Milwaukee 53203-1102
(414) 225-6220 wisci@iiwisconsin.org

SkillsUSA - Post Secondary
Dale A. Drees, State Dir.
1825 N. Bluemound Dr., P.O. Box 2277,
Fox Valley Technical College, Appleton 54912
(920) 735-2489 drees@fvtc.edu skillsusa.org

Soccer Assn., Inc., Wis.
William Sandoval, Pres.
6520 W. Layton Ave., Suite 201, Greenfield 53220
(414) 281-1300 president@wisoccer.org www.wisoccer.org

Social Workers, Inc., Natl. Assn. of (Wis. Chap.)
Marc Herstand, Exec. Dir.
131 W. Wilson St., Suite 903, Madison 53703
(608) 257-6334 naswwi@naswwi.org www.naswwi.org

Socialist Party of Wis.
Robert A. McMullen, Secy.
1001 E. Keefe Ave., Milwaukee 53212
(414) 332-0654

Sod Producers Assn., Wis.
Gina Halter, Exec. Secy.
22920 Hanson Rd., Union Grove 53182
(262) 895-6820 haltersod@prodigy.net

Soil Science Soc. of America
Ellen Bergfeld, CEO
5585 Guilford Rd., Madison 53711
(608) 273-8080 ebergfeld@sciencesocieties.org
www.soils.org

Soybean Assn., Wis.
R. Karls, Exec. Dir.
2976 Triverton Pike Dr., Madison 53711-5840
wisoybean.org

Specialized Medical Vehicle Assn. of Wisconsin
Jim Brown, Pres.
2703 Industrial St., Wisconsin Rapids 54495
(800) 423-7818 woi_rcc@wctc.net

Speech-Language Pathology and Audiology Assn., Wis.
Mary Bahr Schwenke, Pres.
2448 South 102nd Street, Suite 340, Milwaukee 53277
(414) 329-2500 wsha@wisha.org www.wisha.org

Spinal Cord Injury Assn., Natl. (Wis. Chapter)
Kim Nerone, Fund Dev. Coord.
540 S. 1st Street, Milwaukee 53204-1516
(414) 384-4022 office@spinalcordwi.org
www.spinalcordwi.org

Stamp Clubs, Inc., Wis. Federation of
Allen Vick, Treas.
2090 River Estate Lane, Stoughton 53589
(608) 873-3481 norskelodge@aol.com
www.wfscstamps.org

State Employees Union, Wis. (AFSCME Council 24,
AFL-CIO)
Marty Beil, Exec. Dir.
8033 Excelsior Dr., Suite C, Madison 53717-1903
(608) 836-0024 mbeil@wseu-24.org wseu-24.org

Student Financial Aid Administrators, Wis. Assn. of
Wendy Hilvo, Pres.
4425 N. Port Washington Rd., Columbia College of Nursing,
FAO, Glendale 53212
(414) 326-2337 wendy.hilvo@ccon.edu www.wasfaa.net

Students, Inc., United Council of UW
Courtney Morse, Exec. Dir.
14 W. Mifflin St., Suite 212, Madison 53703
(608) 263-3422, ext.11 ed@unitedcouncil.net.
www.unitedcouncil.net

Supporting Families Together Assn.
Jill Hoiting, Exec. Dir.
700 Ray-O-Vac Drive, Suite 6, Madison 53711
(608) 443-2490 info@supportingfamiliestogether.org
www.supportingfamiliestogether.org

Surgeons, Wis. Soc. of Plastic
Chris Hussussian, Pres.
8700 West Watertown Plank Rd., Milwaukee 53226
(414) 805-5440 jlogiudice@mcw.edu
wisocietyplasticsurgery.com

Surveyors, Inc., Wis. Soc. of Land
Francis R. Thousand, Exec. Dir.
5113 Spaanem Ave., Madison 53716
(608) 770-9759 fthousant@charter.net www.wsls.org

Taxicab Owners, Wis. Assn. of
Richard Running, Pres.
318 W. Decker St., Viroqua 54665
(608) 637-2599 richard@runninginc.net
www.witransportation.org

Taxpayers Alliance, Wis.
Todd A. Berry, Pres.
401 North Lawn Ave., Madison 53704-5033
(608) 241-9789 wistax@wistax.org www.wistax.org

Taxpayers Assn., Inc., Wis. Property
Mike Marsch, Pres.
P.O. Box 1493, Madison 53701-1493
(608) 255-7473 wisproptax@yahoo.com wptonline.org

Teachers, American Assn. of Physics (Wis. Section)
Erik Hendrickson, Secy./Treas.
UW-Eau Claire, Dept. of Physics and Astronomy,
Eau Claire 54702-4004
(715) 836-5834 hendrije@uwec.edu www.wapt.org

Teamsters Joint Council No.39, Wis.
Anthony Cornelius, Secy./Treas.
1546 Main St., Green Bay 54302
(920) 435-8895 tcornelius662@new.rr.com

Telecommunications Assn., Wis. State
William C. Esbeck, Exec. Dir.
122 W. Washington Ave., Suite 1050, Madison 53703
(608) 256-8866 bill.esbeck@wsta.info www.wsta.info

Telemedia Council, Inc., Natl.
Marieli Rowe, Exec. Dir.
1922 University Ave., Madison 53726
(608) 218-1182 ntelemedia@aol.com
www.nationaltelemediacouncil.org

Textile Services, Wis. Assn. of
Brian Swingle, Exec. Dir.
12342 W. Layton Ave., Greenfield 53228
(414) 529-4703 bswingle@toriiphillips.com

Theatre Owners of Wis., Natl. Assn. of
Paul J. Rogers, Pres.
W168 N8936 Appleton Ave., Menomonee Falls 53051
(262) 532-0017 nato@natoofwiup.org www.natoofwiup.org

Timber Professionals Assn., Great Lakes
Henry Schienebeck, Exec. Dir.
P.O. Box 1278, Rhinelander 54501-1278
(715) 282-5828 henry@newnorth.net www.timberpa.com

Title Assn., Inc., Wis. Land
Karen E. Gilster, Exec. Dir.
P.O. Box 873, West Salem 54669
(608) 786-2336 kgilster@wlta.org www.wlta.org

Tool Die and Machining Association of Wis.
Becky Fisher, Acct. Mgr.
W175 N11117 Stonewood Dr., Suite 204,
Germantown 53022
(262) 532-2440 toolmaker@tdmaw.org www.tdmaw.org

Tourism Federation, Wis.
Julia Hertel
P.O. Box 393, Sun Prairie 53590
(608) 335-0019 info@witourismfederation.org
www.witourismfederation.org

Towing Assoc., Wis.
Tom Howells, Pres.
P.O. Box 44849, Madison 53744-4849
(608) 833-8200 thowells@witruck.org www.witow.org

Towns Assn., Wis.
Richard J. Stadelman, Exec. Dir.
W7686 County Rd. MMM, Shawano 54166
(715) 526-3157 wtowns@frontiernet.net
www.wisctowns.com

Translators and Interpreters Guild, AFL-CIO (Wis. Chap.)
Rick Kissell
P.O. Box 1101, Milwaukee 53201-1101
(414) 617-8039 rick@kissell.org www.ttig.org

Transportation Builders Assn., Wis.
Patrick Goss, Exec. Dir.
1 South Pinckney St., Suite 300, Madison 53703
(608) 256-6891 pgoss@wtba.org www.wtba.org

Transportation Development Assn. of Wis., Inc.
Craig Thompson, Exec. Dir.
10 E. Doty St., Suite 201, Madison 53703
(608) 256-7044 craig.thompson@tdawisconsin.org
www.tdawisconsin.org

Transportation Union, United
Craig C. Peachy, State Dir.
7 N. Pinckney St., Suite 320, Madison 53703-4262
(608) 251-4120 utulo56@gmail.com wisconsin.utu.org

Tree Farm Com., Wis.
David J. Czysz, Admin.
P.O. Box 285, Stevens Point 54481
(715) 252-2001 witreefarm@gmail.com
www.witreefarm.org

Trees For Tomorrow, Inc.
Maggie Bishop, Exec. Dir.
P.O. Box 609, Eagle River 54521-0609
(715) 479-6456 learning@treesfortomorrow.com
www.treesfortomorrow.com

University of Wis. Foundation
Michael M. Knetter, Pres./CEO
1848 University Ave., Madison 53726
(608) 263-4545 www.supportuw.org

Utilities Assn., Inc., Wis.
William R. Skewes, Exec. Dir.
44 E. Mifflin St., Suite 202, Madison 53703
(608) 257-3151 bskewes@wiutilities.org
www.wiutilities.org

Utility Investors, Inc., Wis.
Robert Seitz, Exec. Dir.
10 E. Doty St., Suite 500, Madison 53703-3397
(608) 663-5813 info@wuiinc.org http://wuiinc.org

Utility Tax Assn., Wis.
Jan DeKeyser, Secy.
1655 County Rd. A, Neenah 54956
(920) 725-3284 jdekeyser@netzero.net

Veteran Organizations, Wis. Assn. of Concerned
Bob Buhr, Secy.
510 3rd St., Clear Lake 54005
(715) 220-6988 bobbuhr@cltcomm.net www.wacvo.org

Veterans Against the War, Vietnam
John Zutz, Coord.
2922 N. Booth St., Milwaukee 53212-2537
www.vvaw.org

Veterans Foundation, Wis.
James Mullarkey, Secy.
P.O. Box 1917, Waukesha 53187-1917
(414) 640-6616 jmullarkey@wivf.org
www.wisconsinveteransfoundation.org

Veterans' Memorial, Clear Lake
Douglas Cahow, Pres.
P.O. Box 450, Clear Lake 54005
(612) 716-7478 teachdoug@aol.com
www.clvetsmemorial.com

Veterans of Amer., Vietnam (Wis. State Council)
James Mullarkey, Secy.
P.O. Box 1917, Waukesha 53187-1917
(414) 640-6616 jmullarkey@vvawi.org www.vvawi.org

Veterans of America, Wis. Paralyzed
Paul Lehman, Exec. Dir.
2311 S. 108th St., West Allis 53227-1901
(414) 328-8910 lehmanp@wisconsinpva.org
www.wisconsinpva.org

Veterans of Foreign Wars (Auxiliary)
Rita Byers, Secy.
547 Front St, Cashton 54619
(608) 654-7970 rb.wi.lavfw@gmail.com
www.wiladiesvfwaux.org

Veterans of Foreign Wars (Dept. of Wis.)
Stephen Pepper, State QM
P.O. Box 6128, Monona 53716
(608) 221-5276 wivfw@att.net http://vfwofwi.com

Veterans, Blinded, Assn. of Wis.
Gary Traynor, Pres.
2216 21st St., Rice Lake 54868
(715) 864-1900 gstraynor@aol.com

Veterans, Catholic War (Wis. Dept.)
Ray Woznick, Cmdr.
P.O. Box 1492, Fond du Lac 54936-1492
(920) 251-2278 raywoz@charter.net www.cwv.org

Veterans, Catholic War, Aux. (Wis. Dept.)
Susan Jane Schwartz, Rep.
645 W. Scott St., #102, Fond du Lac 54937
(920) 251-0210

Veterans, Disabled Amer. (Dept. of Wis.)
Ken Kuehnl, Adj.
1253 Scheuring Rd., Suite A, De Pere 54115
(920) 338-8620 gbdav@sbcglobal.net davwi.org

Veterans, Disabled Amer., Aux. (Dept. of Wis.)
Patty Davis, St. Adj
455 W. Sunnyview Dr, #104, Oak Creek 53154
(414) 731-1312 iamdavaproud@gmail.com
www.davawi.org

Veterans, Jewish War - Dept. of Wis.
Sam Gingold, Cmdr.
1906 E. Shorewood Blvd., #345, Shorewood 53222-2633
(414) 332-4717 sgingold@sbcglobal.net

Veterans, Natl. Assn. for Black (Wis. Chap.)
William Sims, State Pres.
P.O. Box 11432, Milwaukee 53211-0432
(800) 842-4597 chakaris.buckley@cvivet.org nabvets.org

Veterans, Polish Legion of American
Daniel Klosowski, Cmdr.
9015 W. Rochelle Ave., Milwaukee 53224
(414) 379-2637 wiplavvetspost11@gmail.com

Veterans, United Women
Elizabeth Benn, Pres.
163 Amber Tr., Sun Prairie 53590
(608) 235-3901 beth@adneynet.com

Veterans, Wis. Vietnam
William F. Hustad, St. Secy.
W4489 Exeter Crossing Rd., Monticello 53570
(608) 527-2942 wfhus1@tds.net www.wivietnamvets.org

Veterans, Wisconsin Submarine
Owen W. Williams, Cmdr.
309 Gibson St., Apt. N, Mukwonago 53149
(262) 363-7330 barbss220@gmail.com

Veterinary Medical Assn., Wis.
Kim Brown Pokorny, Exec. Dir.
2801 Crossroads Dr., Suite 1200, Madison 53718
(608) 257-3665 kpokorny@wvma.org www.wvma.org

Vision Forward Assn.
Patrick Brown, Exec. Dir.
912 N. Hawley Rd., Milwaukee 53213-3292
(414) 615-0100 info@vision-forward.org
www.vision-forward.org

Water Recycling Assn., Wis. Onsite
Katie Boycks, Assn. Manager
10 E. Doty Street, Suite 523, Madison 53703
(608) 441-1436 info@wowra.com www.wowra.com

Water Well Assoc., Inc., Wis.
Cynthia Denman, Exec. Dir.
P.O. Box 565, Prairie du Chien 53821
(608) 326-0935 cdenwiwater@wisconsinwaterwell.com
www.wisconsinwaterwell.com

WEA Credit Union
Mark Schrimpf, Pres.
P.O. Box 8003, Madison 53708-8003
(608) 274-9828 www.weacu.com

Wetlands Assn., Wis.
Tracy Hames, Exec. Dir.
214 N. Hamilton St., #201, Madison 53703
(608) 250-9971 info@wisconsinwetlands.org
www.wisconsinwetlands.org

Wildlife Society, Wis. Chapter
Pres.
P.O. Box 863, Madison 53701-0863
joomla.wildlife.org/Wisconsin/

Wine and Spirit Inst., Wis.
Eric Petersen, Exec. Dir.
22 N. Carroll St., Suite 200, Madison 53703
(608) 256-5223

Wisconsin Defense Counsel
Jane Svinicki, CAE, Exec. Dir.
6737 W. Washington St., Suite 1300, Milwaukee 53214
(414) 276-1881 info@wdc-online.org www.wdc-online.org

Wisconsin Information Network (WIN)
Dottie Feder, Pres.
17305 Oak Park Row, Brookfield 53045
(262) 786-6200 dottiebrkf@sbcglobal.net

Wisconsin Intercollegiate Athletic Conference
Gary F. Karner, Commissioner
780 Regent St., Madison 53715
(608) 263-4402 gkarner@uwsa.edu www.wiacsports.com

Wisconsin Lakes
Karen von Huene, Exec. Dir.
4513 Vernon Blvd., Suite 101, Madison 53705
(608) 661-4313 info@wisconsinlakes.org
www.wisconsinlakes.org

WisconsinAIRS, Inc.
Marie Lehman, Pres.
P.O. Box 8082, Janesville 53547-8082
(608) 297-3124 info@wisconsinairs.org
www.wisconsinairs.com

Women Highway Safety Leaders, Inc., Wis. Assn. of
LaVerne Hoerig, National Rep.
1321 Clara Ave., Sheboygan 53081-5261
(920) 452-0905

Women, Wis. National Organization for
Karen L. Godshall, Pres.
P.O. Box 45671, Madison 53744
(608) 313-4669 admin@winow.org winow.org

Women's Network, Wis.
Emily Winecke, Administrator
612 W. Main St., Suite 200, Madison 53703
(608) 255-9809 info@wiwomensnetwork.org
wiwomensnetwork.org

Woodland Owners Assn., Inc., Wis.
Nancy C. Bozek, Exec. Dir.
P.O. Box 285, Stevens Point 54481-0285
(715) 346-4798 wwoa@uwsp.edu
www.wisconsinwoodlands.org

Writers, Inc., Council for Wis.
Geoff Gilpin, Pres.
6973 Heron Way, DeForest 53532
(608) 846-2812 geoff.gilpin@charter.net
www.wisconsinwriters.org

WWOA Foundation, Inc.
(Wisconsin Woodland Owners Assn.)
Kendra Johncock, Pres.
3606 Dyer Lake Rd., Burlington 53105
(262) 539-3222 senocenter@senocenter.org
www.senocenter.org

Source: This list was compiled from a questionnaire mailed to known statewide associations in Fall 2012.

NOTE
If you know of any additional PERMANENT, STATEWIDE, NONPROFIT associations – other than religious or fraternal – please send the information to the Blue Book Editor, Legislative Reference Bureau, P.O. Box 2037, Madison, Wisconsin 53701-2037. New associations which meet the stated criteria will be included in the next edition of the *Wisconsin Blue Book*.

HIGHLIGHTS OF COMMERCE AND INDUSTRY IN WISCONSIN

Manufacturing — Value added by manufacture in Wisconsin totaled $67.6 billion in 2010, an decrease of $4.3 billion since 2006. The industry groups with the highest value added in 2010 were food, $11.8 billion; machinery, $8.9 billion; fabricated metal products, $7 billion; and paper, $6.3 billion.

Wisconsin ranked 10th among the states in value added by manufacture in 2010. Leaders in this category were California, $224.4 billion; Texas, $189.0 billion; and Ohio, $107.2 billion. The national total for value added was $2.161 trillion in 2010, a decrease of $125 billion since 2006.

Energy Consumption — In 2010, Wisconsin's total energy use per capita reached 286.4 million Btu, 1% higher than the usage rate in 1990 and 10% higher than in 1970. Seen from a national perspective, Wisconsin has gone from consuming energy at about 85% of the U.S. average in 1970 to about 95% the national average in 2010. Compared to various national averages, Wisconsin places a much heavier reliance on coal for its energy usage, but uses less petroleum, natural gas, nuclear power, and renewable energy. As energy consumption has increased, Wisconsin, which was an exporter of electricity in the 1970s, has increasingly become a net importer. Of the petroleum consumed in Wisconsin in 2010, the largest portion, about 87.3%, was used for transportation, followed by residential (5.6%), agricultural (4%), and commercial (1.75%) usage.

Gasoline Usage and Tax — In 2011, each automobile in Wisconsin was driven an average of 11,782 miles. This is 2,017 miles, or about 11%, more than the national average of 10,614 miles per year. Wisconsin automobiles averaged 23.2 miles per gallon of gasoline, nearly the same as the national average of 23.1 mpg.

The state motor fuel tax was indexed annually prior to April 1, 2006. Since indexing began on April 1, 1985, the average annual adjustment in state tax was typically between 0.4 and 0.8 cents. After April 1, 2006, the state motor fuel tax can only be changed by legislative action. The current tax has not increased since then, when it was indexed to a total of 30.9 cents per gallon. The federal government's gasoline tax has also remained at 18.4 cents per gallon since that date, for a total of 49.3 cents per gallon in federal and state taxes.

Exports and Markets — In 2012, Wisconsin's leading exports were industrial machinery, including computers, $7.3 billion; electric machinery, $2.3 billion; and scientific and medical instruments, $2.3 billion. The leading market for Wisconsin exports in 2012 was Canada ($7.6 billion), followed by Mexico ($2.2 billion), and China ($1.5 billion). The total of all exports from Wisconsin to all markets in 2012 was $23.1 billion.

Financial Institutions — The number of banks operating in Wisconsin has decreased from the post-Depression high of 647 in 1982 to 295 in 2012. Over the same period, deposits increased from $22.5 billion to $132.8 billion. In 2012, Wisconsin's 35 state and federally chartered savings institutions had total deposits of $13.2 billion.

In 2012, Wisconsin had 187 state-chartered credit unions with almost 2.3 million members and $23.4 billion in assets.

Corporations — In 2012, a total of 2,817 foreign corporations were licensed in Wisconsin, a 100% increase from 1,408 in 1990. Incorporation and licensing fees collected by the state in 2012 totaled $19.6 million.

The following tables present selected data. Consult footnoted sources for more detailed information about commerce and industry.

WISCONSIN USE OF PETROLEUM 1970 – 2010
(In Trillions of Btu)

Year	Total[1]	Transportation	Residential	Industrial	Agricultural	Commercial	Electric Utility
1970	457.7	271.2	107.9	21.1	18.1	31.5	7.9
1975	475.0	314.0	87.6	19.3	18.8	27.5	7.8
1980	454.4	329.2	71.2	13.2	21.4	14.6	4.8
1985	412.0	314.4	51.7	9.4	19.2	16.0	1.4
1990	444.4	347.7	42.6	22.1	16.0	15.0	1.0
1995	475.4	386.2	40.8	18.5	15.6	13.4	0.8
1996	490.8	395.4	43.5	20.9	15.9	14.2	0.9
1997	495.1	403.8	40.5	20.8	15.3	13.1	1.6
1998	494.3	414.2	33.9	19.1	14.5	10.8	1.8
1999	511.6	425.2	36.6	21.2	15.0	11.6	2.0
2000	507.5	419.8	38.8	20.5	14.7	12.1	1.6
2001	509.6	421.0	36.7	25.0	14.2	11.6	1.3
2002	519.3	433.7	38.0	19.3	14.5	11.8	2.1
2003	506.9	434.4	37.3	8.7	14.6	10.6	1.3
2004	515.8	442.8	36.6	10.8	14.3	9.8	1.5
2005	499.2	417.9	34.5	18.2	13.6	13.3	1.8
2006	493.5	412.5	35.3	16.6	17.2	10.5	1.4
2007	498.1	415.2	32.8	18.5	19.0	10.7	1.9
2008	476.4	399.7	32.5	13.4	17.9	11.8	1.1
2009	452.7	383.1	29.4	7.4	21.6	10.6	0.6
2010[2]	455.7	398.0	25.5	5.3	18.5	8.0	0.5

Note: The numbers for year 2003 to the present have been revised to reflect updated source data.

[1]Detail may not add to total due to rounding.

[2]Preliminary estimates.

Source: Wisconsin Office of Energy Independence, *Wisconsin Energy Statistics, 2011,* "Wisconsin Petroleum Use, by Economic Sector, 1970-2010", at: http://www.stateenergyoffice.wi.gov/docview.asp?docid=24003&locid=160 [January 7, 2013].

WISCONSIN AND U.S. ENERGY CONSUMPTION BY RESOURCE
1970 – 2010
(In Millions of Btu per Capita)

Energy Resource	1970	1975	1980	1985	1990	1995	2000	2005	2010[1]
Petroleum									
U.S.	126.1	133.2	128.0	112.8	113.9	109.9	116.0	116.0	100.9
Wisconsin	103.6	104.0	96.6	86.8	90.8	92.2	93.9	89.4	74.5
Wisconsin as % of U.S. per capita. . .	82.2%	78.1	75.4	77.0	79.7	83.9	80.9	77.0	73.9
Natural Gas									
U.S.	106.3	92.4	89.1	74.4	78.5	85.1	84.4	76.3	79.7
Wisconsin	74.7	80.0	73.2	64.3	62.6	74.2	73.3	73.8	65.7
Wisconsin as % of U.S. per capita. . .	69.7%	87.3	82.1	86.2	79.8	87.2	86.9	96.6	82.4
Coal									
U.S.	59.8	58.6	67.9	73.5	76.8	75.4	80.0	77.1	67.5
Wisconsin	80.4	57.4	69.0	78.9	84.1	90.3	96.8	95.2	92.0
Wisconsin as % of U.S. per capita. . .	134.5%	98.0	101.6	107.4	109.5	119.7	121.0	123.5	136.2
Nuclear									
U.S.	1.2	8.8	12.1	17.1	24.5	26.6	27.9	27.6	27.3
Wisconsin	0.4	24.3	22.7	25.0	24.8	23.1	23.1	14.6	25.2
Wisconsin as % of U.S. per capita. . .	32.5%	276.7	188.7	145.9	101.3	86.9	82.8	53.1	92.3
Renewable[2]									
U.S.	19.9	21.9	24.1	26.0	24.9	25.2	22.2	21.7	26.0
Wisconsin	7.4	7.9	12.3	13.5	13.1	13.4	10.3	11.2	14.9
Wisconsin as % of U.S. per capita. . .	31.1%	29.4	43.1	42.1	41.3	38.4	46.3	51.7	57.3
Electric Imports[3]									
Wisconsin	−6.4	−4.5	−1.4	−0.4	8.1	14.9	18.3	22.3	14.1
Total Resource Use									
U.S.	313.2	314.8	321.1	303.8	318.6	322.3	330.5	318.7	301.5
Wisconsin	260.1	269.2	272.4	268.1	283.5	308.1	315.7	306.5	286.4
Wisconsin as % of U.S. per capita. . .	82.5%	85.3	84.2	87.4	91.2	97.3	95.5	96.2	95.0

Note: Previous years' numbers have been updated to reflect revisions in source.

[1]Preliminary data.

[2]Includes wood, waste, alcohol, and other biomass energy; hydroelectric; geothermal; solar; and wind.

[3]Import of electricity reflects estimated resource energy used in other states or Canada to produce electricity imported into Wisconsin. This resource energy is estimated assuming 11,300 Btu per k Wh imported into Wisconsin. A negative number indicates energy used in Wisconsin to produce electricity exported out of state.

Source: Wisconsin Office of Energy Independence, "Wisconsin Energy Statistics 2011", at: http://energyindependence.wi.gov/subcategory.asp?linksubcatid=3527&linkcatid=2847&linkid=1451&locid=160. Percentages calculated by Division of Energy.

AUTOMOBILE USAGE AND GASOLINE MILEAGE
Wisconsin and United States, 1980 – 2011

Year	Average Miles Driven Per Auto		Average Auto Miles Per Gallon of Gasoline	
	Wisconsin	U.S.	Wisconsin	U.S.
1980	9,782	8,813	16.1	16.0
1985	10,455	9,419	17.6	17.5
1990	11,659	10,504	20.3	30.2
1995	12,435	11,203	21.2	21.1
2000	13,293	11,976	22.0	21.9
2001	13,132	11,831	22.2	22.1
2002	13,544	12,202	22.1	22.0
2003	13,681	12,325	22.3	22.2
2004	13,831	12,460	22.6	22.5
2005	13,886	12,510	22.2	22.1
2006	13,858	12,485	22.6	22.5
2007	11,888	10,710	23.0	22.9
2008	11,422	10,290	23.8	23.7
2009	11,534	10,391	23.6	23.5
2010	11,822	10,650	23.4	23.3
2011*	11,782	10,614	23.2	23.1

Note: Wisconsin and U.S. figures are derived from different sources and may not be strictly compatible.
*Preliminary data.
Source: Wisconsin Office of Energy Independence, *Wisconsin Energy Statistics, 2011*, "Energy Efficiency Indices", at: http://www.stateenergyoffice.wi.gov/subcategory.asp?linksubcatid=3527&linkcatid=2847&linkid=1451&locid=160 [June 2013].

WISCONSIN MOTOR VEHICLE FUEL TAX
1925 – 2013

Date of Change	Gasoline Tax Per Gallon[1]	Change	
		Amount	Percent
April 1, 1925.	2.0¢	2.0¢	—
April 1, 1931.	4.0	2.0	100.0%
July 1, 1955	6.0	2.0	50.0
July 1, 1966	7.0	1.0	16.7
May 1, 1980	9.0	2.0	28.6
August 1, 1981.	13.0	4.0	44.4
August 1, 1983.	15.0	2.0	15.4
July 1, 1984	16.0	1.0	6.7
April 1, 1985[2]	16.5	0.5	3.1
August 1, 1987[3]	20.0	2.0	11.1
April 1, 1990.	21.5	0.7	3.4
April 1, 1991.	22.2	0.7	3.3
April 1, 1993[4]	23.2	1.0	4.5
April 1, 1994.	23.1	(0.1)	(0.4)
April 1, 1995[5]	23.4	0.3	1.3
April 1, 1996[5]	23.7	0.3	1.3
April 1, 1997.	23.8	0.1	0.4
November 1, 1997[6].	24.8	1.0	4.2
April 1, 2000.	26.4	0.6	2.3
April 1, 2001.	27.3	0.9	3.4
April 1, 2002.	28.1	0.8	2.9
April 1, 2003.	28.5	0.4	1.4
April 1, 2004.	29.1	0.6	2.1
April 1, 2005.	29.9	0.8	2.7
April 1, 2006[7]	30.9	1.0	3.3
April 1, 2007.	30.9	0.0	0.0
April 1, 2008.	30.9	0.0	0.0
April 1, 2009.	30.9	0.0	0.0
April 1, 2010.	30.9	0.0	0.0
April 1, 2011.	30.9	0.0	0.0
April 1, 2012.	30.9	0.0	0.0
April 1, 2013.	30.9	0.0	0.0

[1]Tax rates for some alternate fuels are based on energy density. The rates effective April 1, 2005, are 21.9 cents for LPG (liquefied petroleum gas) and 23.9 cents for CNG (compressed natural gas). E85 (85% fuel ethanol) is taxed at the same rate as gasoline.
[2]Beginning in April 1985, the state motor fuel tax was indexed (1983 Wisconsin Act 27) to take into account fuel consumption and inflation. By law, the tax increase or decrease is automatically calculated annually, based on the inflation rate from the National Highway Maintenance and Operations Cost Index and the percentage change in motor fuel consumption. (The federal gasoline tax has been 18.4 cents per gallon since October 1, 1993.)
[3]Statutory adjustment (1987 Wisconsin Act 27).
[4]1991 Wisconsin Act 119 postponed further fuel tax indexing until April 1, 1993.
[5]1993 Wisconsin Act 16 set aside the calculation of the consumption factor for 1995 and 1996 and provided fixed consumption factors for each year.
[6]1997 Wisconsin Act 27 increased the motor fuel tax rate and modified the indexing formula to take into account only the change to the cost index.
[7]2005 Wisconsin Act 85 ended annual motor fuel tax indexing as of April 1, 2006.
Sources: Session laws of the Wisconsin Legislature; Wisconsin Department of Revenue, *Motor Vehicle Fuel Tax Information*, April 2005 and previous years, and Motor Vehicle Fuel Tax FAQ, at: http://www.dor.state.wi.us/faqs/ise/mofuel.html [February 26, 2013].

VALUE ADDED BY MANUFACTURING
By State, 2006 and 2010
(In Thousands)

State	Value Added 2006	Value Added 2010	2010 State Rank	State	Value Added 2006	Value Added 2010	2010 State Rank
Alabama	$40,508,374	$39,477,873	21	Montana	$3,473,829	$2,551,517	47
Alaska	1,591,723	2,251,546	49	Nebraska	15,442,084	17,009,023	35
Arizona	27,434,381	26,643,385	28	Nevada	7,461,470	7,690,060	41
Arkansas	27,227,220	21,683,165	32	New Hampshire	9,184,912	10,144,986	38
California	237,839,913	224,414,400	1	New Jersey	51,717,072	46,867,229	17
Colorado	20,827,682	22,000,214	31	New Mexico	9,556,167	11,468,005	37
Connecticut	32,714,281	29,699,369	26	New York	92,045,545	79,844,983	9
Delaware	8,861,847	6,979,762	42	North Carolina	106,995,548	92,607,471	7
District of Columbia	170,703	135,839	51	North Dakota	3,874,006	3,785,572	46
Florida	50,783,649	44,507,515	18	Ohio	124,940,967	107,236,102	3
Georgia	61,846,157	58,451,517	11	Oklahoma	23,845,537	20,711,003	34
Hawaii	2,049,067	1,391,356	50	Oregon	39,460,642	35,045,461	24
Idaho	7,241,625	12,115,046	36	Pennsylvania	108,927,106	97,690,975	5
ILLINOIS	107,367,302	105,002,676	4	Rhode Island	7,829,237	5,550,639	43
Indiana	90,202,790	96,508,166	6	South Carolina	38,048,632	35,006,713	25
IOWA	40,930,701	38,131,344	22	South Dakota	5,385,977	5,535,544	44
Kansas	26,021,290	27,726,365	27	Tennessee	62,013,449	51,771,552	15
Kentucky	42,967,301	37,738,939	23	Texas	194,846,489	189,009,164	2
Louisiana	64,354,626	55,745,964	13	Utah	17,667,739	24,988,541	29
Maine	7,746,705	7,768,924	40	Vermont	5,079,245	4,463,017	45
Maryland	22,807,831	22,058,204	30	Virginia	50,648,560	54,182,680	14
Massachusetts	48,427,263	44,290,520	19	Washington	48,861,784	55,972,688	12
MICHIGAN	88,161,261	83,358,808	8	West Virginia	10,467,886	9,352,792	39
MINNESOTA	48,943,285	49,139,587	16	WISCONSIN	71,864,921	67,556,120	10
Mississippi	20,697,706	21,260,120	33	Wyoming	3,417,945	2,369,969	48
Missouri	45,147,536	43,838,741	20	UNITED STATES	$2,285,928,967	$2,160,731,149	

Note: State amounts may not sum to United States total due to rounding.

Source: U.S. Census Bureau, *Annual Survey of Manufactures, Geographic Area Statistics,* 2006 and 2010 and previous editions.

VALUE ADDED BY MANUFACTURING IN WISCONSIN
By Industry Group, 2006 – 2010
(In Thousands)

Industry Group	2006	2007	2008	2009	2010
Food	$8,646,704	$10,207,676	$10,188,266	$11,072,812	$11,803,511
Machinery	8,164,613	8,519,730	8,544,226	7,398,648	8,892,883
Fabricated metal products	6,989,573	7,412,932	7,729,408	6,114,096	7,044,906
Paper	6,843,929	6,568,651	6,084,473	6,493,854	6,282,072
Computer and electronic products	7,255,171	7,493,530	3,051,036	3,470,347	4,505,598
Chemicals	4,617,007	4,900,506	4,361,656	4,086,818	4,412,094
Transportation equipment	6,531,169	7,175,246	5,281,142	3,258,691	4,266,036
Plastics and rubber products	3,416,351	3,716,292	3,389,629	3,410,687	3,538,204
Electrical equipment, appliances, and components	4,006,418	4,334,847	4,028,508	3,160,027	3,332,508
Printing and related support activities	3,283,212	3,579,769	3,481,046	2,878,478	2,828,336
Miscellaneous manufacturing	2,011,878	1,596,556	1,553,723	1,648,507	2,109,667
Wood products	2,220,368	2,156,074	1,788,501	1,276,614	1,398,897
Primary metal industries	2,535,149	2,880,961	2,670,040	1,388,119	1,884,770
Nonmetallic mineral products	1,907,558	1,811,218	1,812,054	1,640,656	1,671,836
Furniture and related products	1,442,194	1,660,034	1,915,966	1,200,314	1,272,418
Beverage and tobacco products	916,413	888,963	616,592	1,113,492	1,187,555
Textile mills	312,817	237,269	187,455	194,451	227,046
Leather and allied products	100,373	149,784	173,927	135,317	159,205
Textile products	159,648	151,981	58,561	75,114	110,277
Apparel	101,287	69,184	—[2]	—[2]	64,144
TOTAL[1]	$71,864,921	$75,761,615	$67,080,030	$60,331,031	$67,251,209

[1]Total may not add due to the exclusion of certain manufacturing catagories that have very little presence in the state.

[2]Apparel manufacturers in Wisconsin declined to report data for 2008 and 2009 for competitive reasons.

Source: U.S. Census Bureau, *Annual Survey of Manufactures, Geographic Area Statistics,* 2011, and previous editions.

WISCONSIN EXPORTS
By Leading Export, 2010 – 2012

Export*	2010	2011	2012	% Change, 2011 to 2012
Industrial machinery	$6,353,498,067	$6,869,779,937	$7,304,737,915	6.33%
Electrical machinery	2,262,904,433	2,487,013,353	2,321,465,123	–6.66
Scientific and medical instruments . . .	2,174,608,360	2,145,253,878	2,301,217,693	7.27
Vehicles (not railway)	1,091,412,582	1,415,927,802	1,732,203,124	22.34
Paper and paperboard	835,342,003	943,360,064	904,405,035	–4.13
Plastic	749,638,219	792,817,207	875,159,864	10.39
Iron and steel products	309,044,242	415,433,064	477,937,108	15.05
Books and newspapers	340,687,690	434,850,663	422,780,348	–2.78
Beverages	101,462,803	317,966,680	399,966,034	25.79
Furniture and bedding	257,627,063	316,672,588	332,230,857	4.91
Aircraft and spacecraft	233,150,205	357,036,059	329,848,211	–7.61
Miscellaneous food	200,625,452	249,784,817	289,687,708	15.97
Dairy, eggs, honey, etc.	213,039,647	231,178,247	281,824,315	21.91
Pharmaceutical products	220,281,846	230,390,054	258,858,890	12.36
Miscellaneous chemical products	243,058,717	251,935,840	252,031,268	0.04
Baking related	176,633,004	227,894,353	220,085,501	–3.43
Mineral fuel and oil	247,030,706	250,248,072	213,340,978	–14.75
Preserved food	130,513,476	158,919,025	200,192,953	25.97
Wood	184,190,374	208,706,177	194,964,562	–6.58
Cereals	515,968,693	382,845,660	184,793,187	–51.73
TOTAL – Leading Exports	$16,840,717,582	$18,688,013,540	$19,497,730,674	4.33%
TOTAL – All Exports	$19,789,522,286	$22,055,118,359	$23,097,184,710	4.72%

Note: This table has been revised following changes to the source. It is not strictly compatible with previous export tables.
*Export categories based on U.S. Census Bureau commodity codes.
Source: Wisconsin Economic Development Corporation, departmental data, March 2013.

WISCONSIN EXPORTS
By Leading Market, 2010 – 2012

Market	2010	2011	2012	% Change, 2011 to 2012
Canada	$6,052,797,469	$7,145,027,282	$7,618,107,579	6.62%
Mexico	2,009,980,927	1,986,950,427	2,165,245,186	8.97
China	1,333,238,575	1,380,660,109	1,543,696,686	11.81
Australia	582,899,292	762,377,660	865,494,864	13.53
Japan	730,827,773	736,207,537	862,523,938	17.16
Germany	747,256,649	879,127,526	714,953,199	–18.67
United Kingdom	615,436,206	624,073,474	614,788,124	–1.49
Chile	422,408,249	614,356,677	553,833,208	–9.85
France	557,416,293	533,248,396	509,156,230	–4.52
Brazil	558,698,006	574,460,220	497,732,368	–13.36
India	235,751,537	329,446,327	456,402,055	38.54
Belgium	376,832,120	365,977,342	410,783,047	12.24
Korean Republic	360,266,013	420,777,130	406,004,982	–3.51
Netherlands	353,796,080	365,947,076	394,850,368	7.90
Singapore	251,690,646	235,082,729	329,856,506	40.32
Saudi Arabia	238,029,177	282,688,181	312,128,407	10.41
United Arab Emirates	106,260,114	167,604,812	305,205,819	82.10
Hong Kong	285,498,875	303,332,818	289,205,563	–4.66
Italy	301,088,370	317,100,126	270,690,820	–14.64
Peru	130,794,278	179,486,421	234,093,892	30.42
TOTAL – Leading Markets	$16,250,966,649	$18,203,932,270	$19,354,752,841	6.32%
TOTAL – All Markets*	$19,789,522,286	$22,055,118,359	$23,097,184,710	4.72%

Note: This table has been revised following changes to the source. It is not strictly compatible with previous export tables.
*Includes markets not individually identified in this table.
Source: Wisconsin Economic Development Corporation, departmental data, March 2013.

BASIC DATA ON WISCONSIN CORPORATIONS
1905 – 2012

| | Transactions[1] | | | Fees | | | |
| | Domestic | | | | | | |
Year[2]	Articles of Incorporation Filed[3]	Amdts. and Restated Articles	Foreign Corporations Licensed[3]	Fees for Articles of Incorporation	Fees for Foreign Corporation[4]	Other Corporation Fees[5]	Total Fees Collected
Calendar							
1905	98	—	95	—	—	—	$69,312
1915	1,043	382	112	$28,287	$3,743	$89,695	121,725
1925	1,438	896	198	57,614	11,139	78,153	146,906
1935	1,272	439	176	30,839	8,956	41,631	81,426
1945	1,120	680	131	31,823	4,826	113,963	150,612
1955	2,537	874	287	89,951	31,146	175,973	297,070
1965	4,063	1,320	401	344,906	120,506	193,844	659,256
Fiscal							
1975	5,976	1,483	663	361,013	386,061	594,498	1,341,572
1980	7,334	1,978	753	373,220	753,461	788,204	1,914,885
1985	7,605	2,359	1,018	485,835	1,142,129	1,371,476	2,999,440
1990	8,387	2,525	1,408	546,550	2,368,900	1,491,104	4,406,554
1995	10,031	2,716	1,507	829,555	4,208,178	2,538,521	7,576,254
2000	21,133	3,088	2,464	2,265,455	6,403,447	3,548,264	12,217,166
2001	20,461	3,064	2,394	2,631,375	6,901,290	3,257,622	12,790,287
2002	22,734	3,145	2,314	2,735,390	6,330,109	3,408,267	12,473,766
2003	26,629	3,057	2,436	3,223,455	7,379,300	5,262,635	15,865,390
2004	31,440	3,644	2,566	3,820,735	6,253,800	6,406,280	16,480,815
2005	33,589	3,595	2,787	4,092,782	6,043,400	5,509,178	15,645,000
2006	33,829	3,711	3,010	4,084,800	8,693,800	4,149,400	16,928,000
2007	32,555	3,596	3,067	1,525,538	5,406,350	6,208,548	17,113,116
2008	31,943	3,401	2,900	1,488,312	5,871,084	7,264,855	18,534,351
2009	27,212	2,273	2,459	5,074,039	7,554,100	5,079,361	17,707,500
2010	27,349	2,231	2,495	5,247,361	8,311,900	5,291,939	18,851,200
2011	28,535	2,210	2,706	10,303,300	7,696,300	723,400	18,723,000
2012	30,014	2,166	2,817	10,599,880	8,345,500	700,200	19,645,500

[1]Includes only those corporate entities for which the reporting agency is the office of record.
[2]Since 1975, data is computed on a fiscal year basis, ending June 30 of year shown.
[3]Beginning in 1997, includes limited liability companies.
[4]Since 1975, totals include fees for foreign corporation annual reports.
[5]Includes fees for filing annual reports and corporation charter documents other than articles of incorporation.
Sources: Wisconsin Department of Financial Institutions, departmental data for 2000-2012, June 2012; previous data from the Office of the Wisconsin Secretary of State.

FINANCIAL INSTITUTIONS OPERATING IN WISCONSIN
Number and Deposits, 1900 – 2012

Year*	Number	Total Deposits (in thousands)	Year*	Number	Total Deposits (in thousands)
1900	349	$124,892	2001	337	$78,567,000
1910	630	268,766	2002	328	83,602,000
1920	976	767,534	2003	319	95,909,000
1930	936	935,006	2004	322	96,111,000
1940	574	993,155	2005	318	100,643,000
1950	556	2,965,580	2006	320	103,511,000
1960	561	4,385,838	2007	316	109,734,000
1970	602	8,750,823	2008	307	114,838,000
1980	634	24,763,910	2009	302	125,785,000
1990	504	37,588,879	2010	299	126,660,000
1995	449	59,591,000	2011	296	128,628,000
2000	365	75,379,000	2012	295	132,812,000

*Beginning in 1994, data includes federal charter savings associations and state-chartered savings associations, supervised by the U.S. Office of Thrift Supervision, and institutions operating in Wisconsin but headquartered outside the state. Deposits for these years are rounded to nearest thousands of dollars.
Sources: **1950 and earlier:** Board of Governors of the Federal Reserve System, *All-Bank Statistics, U.S.,* 1959; **1960:** Wisconsin Commissioner of Banks, agency data, December 1965; **1970:** Federal Deposit Insurance Corporation, *Assets and Liabilities – Commercial and Mutual Savings Banks,* June 1971; **1980:** Federal Deposit Insurance Corporation, corporate data; **1981-93:** Federal Deposit Insurance Corporation, *Data Book: Operating Banks and Branches,* Book 3, June 30, 1993, and previous issues; **1994 to date:** *Federal Deposit Insurance Corporation, Summary of Deposits,* "State Totals by Charter Class for All Institution Deposits, Deposits of All FDIC-Insured Institutions Operating in Wisconsin", June 30, 2012, and previous issues.

FDIC-INSURED INSTITUTIONS OPERATING IN WISCONSIN
By County, June 30, 2012

County	Commercial Banks			Savings Institutions		
	Number of		Deposits	Number of		Deposits
	Institutions	Offices	(in Millions)	Institutions	Offices	(in Millions)
Adams	5	6	$210	1	1	$3
Ashland	5	10	299	0	0	0
Barron	10	21	787	3	4	126
Bayfield	5	11	208	0	0	0
Brown	18	77	4,793	3	15	405
Buffalo	4	10	298	1	1	7
Burnett	3	8	216	0	0	0
Calumet	8	14	442	2	2	49
Chippewa	9	18	620	4	8	169
Clark	8	15	389	2	4	116
Columbia	10	25	992	2	2	62
Crawford	6	11	373	1	1	44
Dane	32	150	12,346	8	35	2,196
Dodge	16	34	943	4	4	175
Door	4	13	576	2	4	111
Douglas	6	9	519	1	3	51
Dunn	8	21	368	2	3	38
Eau Claire	14	29	1,421	3	9	234
Florence	3	6	91	0	0	0
Fond du Lac	12	33	1,553	5	6	243
Forest	2	6	140	0	0	0
Grant	11	38	1,088	1	3	88
Green	10	18	777	1	2	66
Green Lake	9	12	540	2	2	33
Iowa	7	13	363	1	1	36
Iron	1	2	73	0	0	0
Jackson	3	9	266	1	1	3
Jefferson	14	30	1,111	0	0	0
Juneau	7	15	385	0	0	0
Kenosha	12	38	2,021	3	4	33
Kewaunee	5	14	401	0	0	0
La Crosse	13	40	1,903	0	0	0
Lafayette	9	13	332	0	0	0
Langlade	5	6	125	0	0	0
Lincoln	5	9	290	2	2	105
Manitowoc	12	25	1,533	1	2	45
Marathon	22	58	2,645	2	5	227
Marinette	11	20	711	1	4	87
Marquette	6	9	197	0	0	0
Milwaukee	23	203	39,702	12	77	3,298
Monroe	11	17	716	0	0	0
Oconto	7	17	326	0	0	0
Oneida	9	18	741	0	0	0
Outagamie	21	43	2,579	6	18	753
Ozaukee	11	38	1,850	3	10	215
Pepin	3	3	211	0	0	0
Pierce	7	14	475	1	1	50
Polk	8	14	529	1	1	14
Portage	14	26	1,147	2	3	140
Price	5	8	171	1	1	87
Racine	11	54	2,773	4	12	252
Richland	7	8	230	1	1	22
Rock	16	41	1,949	3	5	166
Rusk	5	8	211	1	1	43
St. Croix	14	28	923	1	1	22
Sauk	14	34	1,280	1	1	7
Sawyer	6	9	321	1	1	25
Shawano	9	17	442	2	2	36
Sheboygan	13	40	1,832	2	5	41
Taylor	4	6	262	2	2	162
Trempealeau	10	19	555	0	0	0
Vernon	9	18	398	1	1	18
Vilas	10	15	443	0	0	0
Walworth	16	41	1,566	2	3	48
Washburn	5	9	265	1	1	18
Washington	12	34	1,877	5	20	739
Waukesha	28	149	9,002	11	46	1,556
Waupaca	10	26	1,009	0	0	0
Waushara	11	14	254	1	1	23
Winnebago	13	33	1,910	5	10	238
Wood	12	27	1,315	5	8	482
TOTAL*	260	1,927	$119,608	35	360	$13,204

*Total number of institutions is an unduplicated total for institutions operating in more than one county. Deposit figures do not add to state totals due to rounding.

Note: Menominee County did not report separately.

Source: Federal Deposit Insurance Corporation, "Deposits of all FDIC-Insured Institutions Operating in Wisconsin: State Totals by County, as of June 30, 2012".

WISCONSIN FINANCIAL INSTITUTIONS
June 30, 2012

Type of Institution or Branch	Insured Commercial Banks and Trust Companies				Insured Savings Institutions		
	Total	National Charter	State Charter		Total	Federal Charter	State Charter
			Federal Reserve System				
			Member	Nonmember			
Headquartered in state	271	35	21	181	34	18	16
Headquartered outside of state. . . .	24	9	3	11	1	1	0
Total institutions	295	44	24	192	35	19	16
Total offices	2,287	990	184	753	360	295	65
Total deposits (in millions)	$132,812	$80,758	$8,262	$30,588	$13,204	$10,085	$3,119

Source: Federal Deposit Insurance Corporation, Summary of Deposits, June 30, 2012, "Individual State Tables – Charter Class".

WISCONSIN STATE-CHARTERED CREDIT UNIONS
Number, Members, and Assets
1930 – 2012

Year		Membership		Assets	
	Credit Unions	Total Members	Annual % Change	Total Assets (in millions)	Annual % Change
1930	22	4,659	—	$0.5	—
1935	383	57,847	—	2.9	—
1940	592	153,849	—	11.2	—
1945	536	144,524	—	19.1	—
1950	542	193,296	—	42.9	—
1955	696	292,552	—	120.6	—
1960	733	363,444	—	206.4	—
1965	781	493,399	—	346.6	—
1970	766	628,543	—	480.4	—
1975	673	805,123	—	875.5	—
1980	618	1,060,292	—	1,403.8	—
1985	550	1,261,407	—	2,831.4	—
1990	440	1,485,109	4.3%	4,148.8	8.6%
1991	427	1,596,547	7.5	4,495.6	8.4
1992	418	1,608,412	0.7	4,991.5	11.0
1993	406	1,646,847	2.4	5,360.1	7.4
1994	394	1,714,182	4.1	5,755.1	7.4
1995	384	1,744,696	1.8	6,179.2	7.4
1996	375	1,773,611	1.7	6,569.9	6.3
1997	369	1,803,529	1.7	7,175.4	9.2
1998	358	1,834,944	1.7	8,192.4	14.2
1999	350	1,887,429	2.9	8,737.3	6.7
2000	340	1,918,729	1.7	9,425.9	7.9
2001	326	1,883,387	-1.8	10,439.4	10.8
2002	308	1,937,867	2.9	11,665.6	11.7
2003	298	1,966,929	1.5	12,772.5	9.5
2004	287	1,992,238	1.3	13,684.4	7.1
2005	280	2,047,031	2.8	14,805.3	8.2
2006	267	2,086,700	1.9	15,656.2	5.7
2007	260	2,083,319	-0.2	16,543.3	5.7
2008	250	2,118,505	1.7	18,182.3	9.9
2009	236	2,164,648	2.2	19,719.6	8.5
2010	223	2,186,471	1.0	20,685.4	4.9
2011	203	2,225,892	1.8	21,915.6	5.9
2012	187	2,264,788	1.7	23,353.8	6.6

Note: Annual percentage increase not available for years preceding 1990.

Source: Wisconsin Department of Financial Institutions, Office of Credit Unions, *Year-End 2012 Bulletin*, at:
https://www.wdfi.org/_resources/indexed/site/fi/cu/QuarterlyReports/2012/2012YearEndBulletinA.pdf [March 2013] and previous editions. Percentages calculated by Wisconsin Legislative Reference Bureau.

HIGHLIGHTS OF CONSERVATION AND RECREATION IN WISCONSIN

Recreation — Wisconsin currently operates 48 state parks, 13 state forests, and 5 recreation areas. The parks range in size from Devil's Lake with 18,275 acres to Lakeshore with 22 acres. The largest single state recreational facility is the Northern Highland-American Legion Forest with 223,283 acres. A total of 36 state trails are open to the public.

Visitors to Wisconsin's state parks, forests, trails, and recreation areas numbered nearly 15.6 million in 2012.

Hunting and fishing are major recreational activities. In recent years, approximately 33 million fish and between 2 and 4 million game animals of various species have been harvested annually. Over 664,000 resident annual fishing licenses were sold in 2011. In addition, resident husband and wife fishing licenses totaled nearly 229,000, and nonresident fishing licenses totaled approximately 280,000. Almost 630,000 boats were registered in 2011.

Land Acquisition — Three land acquisition programs have been established to acquire land for recreational purposes. From 1961 through 1992, the Outdoor Recreation Act Program (ORAP) acquired 555,816 acres for the state's conservation and recreation programs at a cost of almost $172 million. From fiscal year 1990, when the legislature created the Warren Knowles-Gaylord Nelson Stewardship Program, through fiscal year 1999, the stewardship fund spent over $124 million to acquire an additional 167,000 acres. From fiscal years 2000 through 2012, the Stewardship 2000 Fund acquired over 397,000 acres and spent nearly $450 million.

Natural Resources Funding and Expenditures — The Department of Natural Resources spent over $467 million on conservation and recreation programs in fiscal year 2011-12, down from $500 million in fiscal year 2010-11. Funding comes from the state's general fund and segregated funds, including registration and licensing fees, park stickers, and federal aids.

The following tables present selected data. Consult footnoted sources for more detailed information about conservation and recreation.

FISH AND GAME HARVESTED AND STOCKED, 2011-2012

Catch and Harvest Data for Wisconsin Fish[1]

	Catch	Harvest
All fish species.	88,000,000	33,000,000
Great Lakes trout.		147,039
Great Lakes salmon		473,553

Harvest Indicators

	Harvest		Harvest
Wild Turkey	49,666	Raccoon[2].	310,586
Pheasant[2].	178,722	Red fox[2]	14,729
Ruffed grouse[2]	336,530	Gray fox[2].	12,266
Gray partridge[2].	247	Coyotes[2]	67,969
Bobwhite quail[2]	164	Deer (with guns).	274,047
Woodcock[2].	87,059	Deer (with bows).	94,267
Squirrels[2].	338,782	Bear	4,646
Cottontail rabbit[2].	85,086	Ducks[3]	445,700
Snowshoe hare[2]	6,494	Canada geese.	38,898
Doves[3]	72,426		

Furbearer Harvest

	Harvest		Harvest
Muskrats[2].	324,980	Bobcat	357
Mink[2].	11,716	Opossum[2]	2,278
Beaver[2].	46,413	Skunk[2]	1,468
River otter	1,487	Fisher.	1,338
Total value of all pelts purchased by licensed Wisconsin fur buyers			$5,805,598

Fish and Wildlife Stocked

Game farm pheasants released.	53,875
Warmwater fish, produced and distributed (includes fry)	8,594,357
Coldwater fish	4,298,573

[1]Harvest is the actual number of fish caught and kept; catch is the estimate of all fish caught, including those released. All fish species estimated from mail survey conducted in 2006. Great Lakes totals estimated by on site creel surveys in 2011 and 2012.

[2]Estimates based on hunter surveys.

[3]Harvest data from U.S. Fish and Wildlife Service, Division of Migratory Bird Management. Data is for the 2010-2011 hunting season.

Source: Wisconsin Department of Natural Resources, departmental data, April 2013.

FISH AND GAME LICENSES AND RECREATION PERMITS
Number Issued, 2006 – 2011

	2006	2007	2008	2009	2010	2011
Boats registered	626,740	620,169	634,779	627,263	616,175	629,886
Snowmobiles registered	178,195	219,688	224,539	228,081	235,374	218,736
All terrain vehicles registered	272,773	277,113	218,539	277,279	279,263	307,582
Deer hunting and license tags including nonresident[1] . .	505,620	508,854	514,156	519,236	501,746	504,732
Small game hunting license tags including nonresident[1]	127,216	137,012	133,443	129,262	132,510	128,770
Resident annual fishing licenses[2]	638,171	649,662	665,027	708,003	688,046	664,146
Resident husband and wife fishing licenses	221,925	229,513	226,519	238,523	233,526	228,747
Nonresident annual fishing licenses	94,810	92,084	88,798	94,075	90,879	82,361
Nonresident family annual fishing licenses	61,998	64,825	67,568	72,190	69,789	66,416
15-day nonresident family fishing licenses	16,414	18,270	36,809	37,253	36,216	32,794
15-day nonresident fishing licenses	33,232	35,197	34,705	36,085	34,631	32,988
4-day nonresident fishing licenses	109,855	98,329	96,513	99,534	94,805	65,445
Resident sports licenses	75,811	72,057	69,113	63,953	58,943	58,943
Nonresident sports licenses	3,400	3,748	3,847	3,825	3,667	3,684
2-day Great Lakes fishing licenses	32,158	34,278	32,450	32,445	31,379	26,911
Resident archer's licenses[1].	189,331	193,339	195,333	196,793	197,598	200,695
Nonresident archer's licenses[1]	8,285	8,797	8,913	8,816	8,654	8,858
Guide licenses (residents only)	1,457	1,452	1,355	1,477	1,458	1,454
Conservation patron licenses	59,914	56,559	55,159	50,752	46,837	44,952
Nonresident patron licenses	864	957	937	1,005	925	921

[1]Includes 10- and 11-year-old mentored licenses.

[2]Includes senior and junior fishing licenses.

Source: Wisconsin Department of Natural Resources, departmental data, April 2013.

Wisconsin State Parks, Forests, and Trails

State Parks & Recreation Areas

State Forests

State Trails

Ice Age National Scientific Reserve Unit

Ice Age National and State Scenic Trail

North Country National Scenic and State Trail

State Park/Forest/Trail/ Recreation Area under development. Please see our website for development and progress updates.

Source: Wisconsin Department of Natural Resources, departmental data, May 2013. Map provided by Wisconsin Department of Tourism. For park updates, see dnr.wi.gov/topic/parks/.

WISCONSIN STATE FORESTS, PARKS, TRAILS, AND RECREATION AREAS

Name	Location	Dominant Features	Established	Acres	Number of Visitors[1]				
					2000	2005	2010	2011	2012
NORTHERN FORESTS[2]									
Black River	SE of Black River Falls US 12, STH 27 & 54	Abundance of wildlife and scenery	1957	68,431	195,579	23,611	12,644	3,926	12,603
Brule River	S of Brule STH 27	Excellent fishing and canoeing	1907	47,386	125,339	9,945	7,264	9,680	8,480
Flambeau River	23 mi. W of Phillips CTH W	Outstanding canoeing river	1931	90,742	162,665	20,091	4,624	4,824	4,368
Governor Knowles	1 mi. W of Grantsburg STH 70	River scenery	1970	20,608	89,714	20,219	3,728	2,492	2,836
Northern Highland-American Legion	SE Iron, WC Vilas, NC Oneida Counties	Scenic lakes and forests	1925	232,352	2,050,151	53,737	203,024	198,860	193,428
Peshtigo River	5 mi. W of Crivitz, N of CTH W	Diverse natural communities and rivers	2001	11,143	NA	NA	4,656	1,448	1,180
TOTAL				470,662	2,623,448	127,603	235,940	221,230	222,895
SOUTHERN FORESTS									
Havenwoods	Milwaukee, N. Hopkins St.	A nature preserve in the city	1978	237	49,581	51,774	47,761	42,299	40,619
Kettle Moraine North	N of Kewaskum STH 45, 23 & 67	Glacial formations	1936	29,498	620,903	700,774	541,628	530,472	610,961
Kettle Moraine South	Whitewater USH 12, STH 59/67	Glacial topography	1936	21,241	1,230,519	805,340	1,135,702	1,101,843	1,294,945
Lapham Peak	S of Delafield CTH C	Highest point in county, glacial formations	1985	1,006	250,681	261,930	319,957	331,407	345,236
Loew Lake	10 mi. W of Menomonee Falls CTH Q	Kettle lake, glacial valley	1987	1,086	NA	NA	NA	NA	NA
Pike Lake	2 mi. E of Hartford STH 60	Glacial lake	1960	678	156,325	201,217	188,136	170,774	233,889
Point Beach	4 mi. N of Two Rivers STH 42	Sand beach, natural history	1938	2,903	407,066	406,800	376,556	373,855	390,760
TOTAL				56,648	2,715,075	2,427,835	2,609,740	2,550,650	2,916,410
STATE PARKS									
Amnicon Falls	10 mi. SE of Superior USH 2	Scenic waterfalls, covered bridge	1961	825	84,773	86,680	87,983	87,211	86,100
Aztalan	4 mi. E of Lake Mills CTH Q	Ancient Native American village	1947	172	60,565	59,695	42,387	39,069	44,000
Belmont Mound[3]	2 mi. N of Belmont CTH G & B	Wide vista from hilltop tower	1961	254	8,484	40,607	NA	NA	NA
Big Bay	On Madeline Island in Lake Superior	Sand beach, natural history	1963	2,418	108,365	129,435	142,913	142,705	159,969
Big Foot Beach	1 mi. S of Lake Geneva STH 12 & 120	A beach park	1949	271	177,963	178,567	192,913	184,982	177,429
Blue Mound	1 mi. NW of Blue Mounds STH 18 & 151	Highest point in southern Wisconsin	1959	1,153	178,962	153,202	141,870	134,660	148,722
Brunet Island	Northwest of Cornell	River island park	1936	1,225	107,590	161,150	155,175	152,266	154,837
Buckhorn	13 mi. N of Mauston STH 58, CTH G	River scenery	1971	2,637	NA	127,735	132,845	131,755	142,422
Capital Springs	5 mi SE of Madison on Lake Farm Rd.	Shoreline and trails	2000	323	NA	NA	61,548	NA	NA
Copper Culture[3]	0.5 mi. W of Oconto on N. River Rd.	Archaeological site	1959	42	NA	NA	NA	NA	NA
Copper Falls	4 mi. N of Mellen STH 13 & 169	River gorge, waterfalls	1929	2,716	125,080	145,087	140,324	136,811	139,631
Council Grounds	1 mi. NW of Merrill STH 107	River scenery	1938	509	213,411	221,033	224,933	201,502	193,088
Devil's Lake	3 mi. S of Baraboo STH 123	Bluffs, mountain scenery	1911	18,275	1,317,275	1,207,001	1,817,710	1,728,679	2,236,888
Governor Dodge	3 mi. N of Dodgeville STH 23	Rocky promontories	1948	5,149	407,629	442,856	504,752	531,324	521,527
Governor Nelson	5 mi. E of Middleton CTH M	Wooded lakeshore, Native American effigy mounds	1975	422	218,015	184,961	196,805	192,106	189,185
Governor Thompson	25 miles NW of Crivitz	Lakeshore and trout streams	2000	2,450	NA	NA	46,907	59,750	55,700
Harrington Beach	10 mi. N of Port Washington I 43, CTH D	Lake Michigan shoreline	1966	637	114,912	140,769	168,915	170,611	176,941
Hartman Creek	6 mi. W of Waupaca STH 54	Lake scenery, pine plantation	1962	1,417	239,539	143,575	155,001	166,990	132,118
Heritage Hill[3]	S Green Bay STH 57	Restored early American buildings	1973	55	36,528	NA	NA	NA	NA
High Cliff	9 mi. E of Menasha STH 114	Wooded bluffs, Lake Winnebago	1954	1,145	820,560	830,080	451,346	416,996	456,380
Interstate	St. Croix Falls USH 8	River gorge, rocky bluffs, glacial features	1900	1,330	354,715	270,995	290,381	260,743	292,876
Kinnickinnic	6 mi. W of River Falls CTH F	River scenery	1972	1,239	207,900	217,600	169,300	162,800	171,200
Kohler-Andrae	4 mi. S of Sheboygan STH 141	Lake Michigan sand dunes	1928	1,848	378,483	417,568	414,850	393,057	418,373
Lake Kegonsa	3 mi. N of Stoughton CTH N	Prairie and lakeshore	1962	343	187,782	189,639	184,350	176,134	196,457
Lake Wissota	5 mi. NE of Chippewa Falls STH 29, CTH K & O	Lake scenery	1962	1,062	108,222	102,032	118,121	110,654	106,505

WISCONSIN STATE FORESTS, PARKS, TRAILS, AND RECREATION AREAS—Continued

Name	Location	Dominant Features	Established	Acres	Number of Visitors[1]				
					2000	2005	2010	2011	2012
Lakeshore	Milwaukee, N. Harbor Dr.	Urban oasis, marina, Lake Michigan	1998	22	NA	NA	89,455	88,600	112,880
Merrick	1 mi. N of Fountain City STH 35	Mississippi River, birds	1932	322	101,609	83,346	82,556	77,975	85,759
Mill Bluff	4 mi. W of Camp Douglas USH 12/16	Rocky bluffs	1936	1,337	49,541	54,854	56,104	56,627	58,678
Mirror Lake	1 mi. S of Lake Delton	Lake scenery	1962	2,200	341,452	326,198	367,834	346,960	353,017
Natural Bridge	15 mi. NW of Sauk City CTH C	Natural rock bridge	1972	530	57,454	30,600	7,724	10,527	24,772
Nelson Dewey	1 mi. N of Cassville CTH VV	Home of first governor, river bluffs	1935	756	51,456	39,541	24,871	28,029	38,857
New Glarus Woods	1 mi. S of New Glarus STH 69 & CTH NN	Wooded valleys, natural oak woods	1934	415	48,276	177,322	56,900	52,073	51,535
Newport	2 mi. SE of Gills Rock STH 42	Lake scenery, forests	1964	2,373	177,194	153,986	137,088	136,298	136,914
Pattison	10 mi. S of Superior STH 35	Highest waterfall in Wisconsin	1920	1,436	167,221	184,579	197,627	181,684	196,715
Peninsula	N of Fish Creek STH 42	Green Bay, limestone bluffs	1910	3,777	1,105,651	1,018,868	1,077,397	1,028,954	1,145,943
Perrot	1 mi. N of Trempealeau STH 35	River scenery, wooded bluffs	1918	1,270	208,537	269,061	317,519	292,567	324,777
Potawatomi	2 mi. NW of Sturgeon Bay STH 42	Limestone bluffs	1928	1,221	228,909	201,379	209,390	202,655	200,205
Rib Mountain	4 mi. SW of Wausau CTH N	State's 4th highest place, spectacular views	1927	1,503	208,670	234,685	154,387	176,398	294,720
Roche-A-Cri	2 mi. N of Friendship STH 13	Woodlands, 300-foot-high rock outcropping	1948	492	72,232	110,884	48,314	51,171	46,165
Rock Island	Ferry (no vehicles) from Washington Island	Island scenery, historic stone buildings	1965	912	16,998	15,811	25,859	25,108	25,930
Rocky Arbor	1 mi. NW of Wisconsin Dells USH 12	Rocky ledges, wooded valleys	1932	244	57,545	65,674	69,876	69,015	72,015
Straight Lake	5 mi. NE of Luck via SH 35 & 270th Ave.	Wooded wilderness and lake	2002	NA	NA	NA	NA	NA	NA
Tower Hill	3 mi. SE of Spring Green STH 23 & CTH C	Historic shot tower, panoramic views	1922	77	51,031	76,226	14,644	14,284	12,621
Whitefish Dunes	10 mi. NE of Sturgeon Bay STH 57	Lake Michigan, sand dunes	1967	864	189,778	167,092	205,987	203,029	208,427
Wildcat Mountain	3 mi. S of Ontario STH 33	Bluff lands, Kickapoo River	1948	3,628	173,100	186,994	214,048	193,647	211,957
Willow River	NE of Hudson CTH A	River scenery, waterfalls, lake	1967	2,854	354,470	347,691	479,050	479,850	575,050
Wyalusing	12 mi. S of Prairie du Chien USH 18 & CTH C & X	Junction of Wisconsin and Mississippi rivers	1917	2,628	173,439	180,429	207,498	198,075	239,726
Yellowstone Lake	7 mi. NW of Argyle CTH N	Lake	1970	890	260,981	275,163	278,160	228,090	291,133
TOTAL				77,665	9,706,425	9,650,650	10,163,131	9,722,421	10,908,144
STATE TRAILS[4]									
"400"	Reedsburg STH 23/33 to Elroy STH 80/82	22 miles of trail, bluffs	1988	441	35,125	43,470	47,235	46,010	42,395
Ahnapee[3]	Sturgeon Bay STH 42/57 to E of Luxemburg CTH A	18.6-mile trail, river scenery	1970	571	NA	NA	NA	NA	NA
Badger	Madison to Freeport IL, STH 69	40 miles of trail, former railroad grade	2000	534	NA	NA	122,133	118,953	215,963
Bearskin-Hiawatha	Minocqua to CH K & Heafford Jct. to Tomahawk	24.6 miles of trail, forests	1973	787	115,200	136,500	157,720	156,720	103,000
Buffalo River	Fairchild to Mondovi US 10	36.4 miles of trail, rural scenery	1976	556	39,280	38,307	38,307	38,307	38,307
Capital City[3]	Madison, Dempsey Rd to USH 18/151 Frontage Rd.	Asphalt path through woods, fields, and city	2001	NA	NA	NA	NA	NA	NA
Cattail[3]	Amery SH 46 to Almena CTH P	17.8-mi. trail through forests, farms, wetlands	1999	405	NA	NA	NA	NA	NA
Chippewa River	Eau Claire SW to Red Cedar Trail, STH 85	20 miles of trail, river scenery	1990	387	334,607	109,240	56,502	55,460	47,025
Elroy-Sparta	Elroy STH 80/82 to Sparta STH 71	32.5 miles of trail, hills, valleys, tunnels	1965	674	60,075	59,495	65,187	63,187	56,755
Fox River[3]	Trailhead at Porlier and Adams Streets, Green Bay	Fox River bridge, 14-mi. trail along river	1991	298	NA	NA	NA	NA	NA
Friendship[3]	Brillion – Forest Junction parallel to USH 10	6 miles of trail past farms and woods	2000	8	NA	NA	NA	NA	NA
Gandy Dancer[3]	St. Croix Falls USH 8 to S of Superior CTH C	66 miles of trail, forests, connects to MN	1989	810	177,939	234,248	245,411	248,950	259,953
Glacial Drumlin	Waukesha CTH X to NE of Jefferson CTH Y	49 miles of trail, views of Ice Age features	1984	930	65,572	58,849	73,245	66,016	65,809
Great River[3]	Onalaska USH 53 to NW of Trempealeau STH 35/54	24 miles of trail, Mississippi River, bluffs	1986	304	NA	NA	NA	NA	NA
Green Circle[5]	Circles Stevens Point area	River scenery	1992	0	NA	NA	NA	NA	NA

WISCONSIN STATE FORESTS, PARKS, TRAILS, AND RECREATION AREAS–Continued

Name	Location	Dominant Features	Established	Acres	Number of Visitors[1]				
					2000	2005	2010	2011	2012
Hank Aaron	Milwaukee, Menomonee River Valley	Menomonee River Valley	1996	60	NA	NA	NA	NA	NA
Hillsboro[3]	Union Center to Hillsboro STH 33/80/82	4.2 miles of trail, rural scenery	1988	66	NA	NA	NA	NA	NA
Ice Age Trail[5]	Sturgeon Bay to St. Croix Falls	Moraines and other glacial features	1988	5,097	NA	NA	NA	NA	NA
La Crosse River[3]	Sparta STH 16 to NE of La Crosse	24.5-mile trail, broad river valley	1978	396	37,150	45,695	53,020	51,685	46,775
Mascoutin Valley[3]	Ripon to Berlin STH 49	19-mi. trail, farms, woods, and wetlands	1996	45	NA	NA	NA	NA	NA
Military Ridge	Madison USH 18/151 to Dodgeville STH 23	39.6 miles of trail, most on crest of ridge	1981	635	67,224	115,797	123,735	126,057	108,039
Mountain-Bay[3]	Wausau CTH SS to Green Bay CTH HS	80.5-mile trail, varied landscape	1993	1,083	NA	NA	NA	NA	NA
Nicolet[3]	Gillett to Townsend STH 32	Forests, streams	1999	1,171	NA	NA	NA	NA	NA
North Country[5]	Douglas, Bayfield, Ashland, and Iron counties	Footpath across Northern Wisconsin	2000	546	—	NA	NA	NA	NA
Oconto River[3]	Oconto US 41 to Stiles Junction US 141	8-mi. trail along Oconto River	1997	91	NA	NA	NA	NA	NA
Old Abe[4]	NE of Chippewa Falls CTH S to Cornell STH 27/64	17-mi. trail, Chippewa River	1990	243	NA	NA	NA	NA	NA
Pecatonica[3]	Belmont E to Calamine CTH G	10 miles of trail, stream	1974	242	NA	NA	NA	NA	NA
Red Cedar	Menomonie STH 29 S to Chippewa River Trail	14.5 miles of trail, river, bluffs	1973	822	45,760	53,380	46,479	47,905	52,480
Saunders[3]	S of Superior CTH C SW to MN border	8.4 miles of trail, wet woods	1991	207	NA	NA	NA	NA	NA
Sugar River[3]	New Glarus STH 39/69 to Brodhead STH 11	23.5 miles of trail, farms, prairies, woods	1972	302	45,362	67,812	40,196	35,783	30,170
Tomorrow River[3]	Plover to Amherst Junction	15 miles of trail, glacial terrain	1996	389	NA	NA	NA	NA	NA
Tuscobia	Park Falls CTH B to Rice Lake CTH SS	74 miles of trail, forests	1966	1,393	44,150	46,783	10,009	8,460	12,747
White River[3]	Elkhorn CTH H to Racine Cty., Spring Valley Rd.	10-mile trail, farmlands and historic town	1999	247	NA	NA	NA	NA	NA
Wild Goose[3]	Fond du Lac USH 41/151 to STH 60 S of Juneau	32 miles of trail, Horicon Marsh	1986	418	NA	NA	NA	NA	NA
Wild Rivers[3]	Solon Springs CTH A to Rice Lake	63.5 miles of trail, woods	1993	1,139	NA	NA	NA	NA	NA
Wiouwash[3]	Oshkosh-Hortonville, Split Rock-Aniwa	51.6 miles of trail, prairies, woods	1992	283	NA	NA	NA	NA	NA
TOTAL				21,579	1,067,444	1,009,576	1,079,179	1,063,493	1,079,418
STATE RECREATION AREAS									
Richard Bong	8 mi. SE of Burlington STH 142	Small lakes, open space, varied recreation	1963	4,537	462,274	220,045	331,232	330,839	337,612
Browntown-Cadiz Springs	6 mi. W of Monroe STH 11	Spring-fed lakes	1970	644	99,191	44,833	59,044	61,645	52,737
Chippewa Moraine Ice Age[6]	6 mi. E of New Auburn CTH M	Kettle lakes, other glacial features	1974	3,224	17,737	24,984	24,718	23,684	24,535
Fischer Creek[2]	1 mi. N of Cleveland on Lakeshore Rd.	Lake Michigan shoreline, scenic bluffs	1991	124	NA	NA	NA	NA	NA
Hoffman Hills[3]	8 mi. NE of Menomonie CTH B or E	Wooded hills	1980	707	32,460	32,880	33,290	31,290	36,460
TOTAL				9,235	611,662	322,742	448,284	447,458	451,344

Abbreviations: USH – U.S. highway; STH – state trunk highway; CTH – county trunk highway; NA – not available.

[1]Visitor numbers are estimates.

[2]Northern Forests figures for 2005-present are camping attendance only, not day-use visitors.

[3]Operated locally or by county; no attendance information available.

[4]Not accessible by vehicle.

[5]Various owners and operators (National Scenic Trails).

Source: Wisconsin Department of Natural Resources, Bureau of Parks and Recreation, departmental data, April 2013.

DEPARTMENT OF NATURAL RESOURCES SOURCES OF FUNDING
Fiscal Years 2007-08 – 2011-12
(In Thousands)

Source of Funding	2007-08	2008-09	2009-10	2010-11	2011-12
Segregated funds					
All-terrain vehicle registration fees	$4,698	$4,683	$4,461	$3,979	$4,286
Boat registration fees	5,442	6,032	5,775	5,525	5,645
Dry cleaner fund	717	1,082	3,352	2,016	1,582
Endangered resources voluntary payments	826	1,205	1,700	886	811
Environmental improvement fund	2,368	2,151	1,227	1,873	959
Environmental management account	17,637	16,052	16,994	24,707	42,320
Federal aids	48,989	59,346	49,715	61,609	53,483
Fishing, hunting licenses and permits	76,173	72,287	66,814	68,168	65,057
Forestry mill tax	96,145	99,915	103,138	99,341	94,462
Gifts and donations	338	327	448	390	543
Heritage State Parks and Forests Trust Fund	36	—	—	—	—
Nonpoint source account	3,887	4,336	7,258	11,241	13,046
Park stickers and fees	13,418	13,581	13,837	13,997	16,057
Petroleum storage environmental cleanup fund . . .	5,358	5,294	5,147	5,223	5,722
Program revenue	33,506	32,201	31,951	31,400	31,006
Recycling fund	35,334	31,988	31,992	21,214	—
Snowmobile registration fees	4,231	3,953	4,108	4,172	3,570
Waste management fund	116	9	—	—	—
Water resources account	13,490	12,741	12,371	12,553	12,606
Wisconsin Natural Resources Magazine	891	833	865	746	663
TOTAL	$363,601	$368,015	$361,153	$369,039	$351,820
General funds					
General purpose revenue	$141,250	$143,755	$51,401	$67,305	$52,616
Program revenues	21,913	21,536	20,516	19,926	18,161
Program revenue – services	12,318	12,442	12,055	13,340	10,934
Federal aids	25,952	26,753	29,081	30,624	33,978
TOTAL	$201,432	$204,486	$113,052	$131,194	$115,690
GRAND TOTAL	$565,033	$572,501	$474,205	$500,234	$467,510

Source: Wisconsin Department of Natural Resources, departmental data, April 2013.

DEPARTMENT OF NATURAL RESOURCES EXPENDITURES
Fiscal Years 2007-08 – 2011-12
(In Thousands)

Program	2007-08	2008-09	2009-10	2010-11	2011-12
Land Management	**$114,512***	**$117,588***	**$113,693***	**$115,341***	**$114,012***
Wildlife management	21,344	21,927	20,244	21,006	21,595
Forestry	53,693	55,552	53,117	53,448	51,928
Southern forests	5,599	5,740	5,594	5,826	5,834
Parks	17,892	17,865	18,372	17,654	18,155
Endangered resources	5,023	5,005	5,287	5,905	5,941
Facilities and lands	9,968	10,412	10,107	10,376	9,596
Lands program management	992	1,087	971	1,126	962
Air and Waste Management	**$36,191***	**$36,296***	**$37,889***	**$40,110***	**$35,990***
Air management	15,893	16,114	17,195	16,426	14,712
Cooperative environmental assistance	875	917	827	853	828
Remediation and redevelopment	11,184	10,866	11,675	14,374	12,126
Waste management	7,405	7,182	7,347	7,444	7,330
Air/waste program management	834	1,217	845	1,014	992
Enforcement and Science	**$41,793***	**$43,769***	**$44,003***	**$46,824***	**$45,068***
Law enforcement	30,871	32,090	32,465	33,453	31,326
Integrated science services	10,102	10,684	10,759	12,490	12,785
Enforcement/science program management	820	995	779	882	957
Water Management	**$80,773***	**$76,488***	**$72,424***	**$75,515***	**$76,876***
Fisheries management and habitat protection	28,344	26,409	24,116	26,523	25,619
Watershed management	39,002	36,145	35,201	35,511	37,888
Drinking and groundwater	12,338	12,159	12,011	12,314	12,304
Water program management	1,096	1,734	1,096	1,168	1,065
Conservation Aids	**$43,483***	**$45,574***	**$43,284***	**$42,323***	**$42,044***
Fish and wildlife aids	1,568	811	702	570	989
Forestry aids	10,265	11,214	10,522	10,640	9,205
Recreational aids	16,092	15,992	13,576	12,533	12,506
Aids in lieu of taxes	10,944	12,362	13,767	13,783	14,369
Enforcement aids	2,020	2,166	2,277	2,277	2,277
Wildlife damage aids	2,594	3,030	2,441	2,520	2,697
Environmental Aids	**$42,831***	**$42,018***	**$42,978***	**$31,890***	**$32,350***
Water quality aids	3,544	5,610	5,728	6,112	6,551
Solid and hazard waste aids	35,337	32,219	31,476	21,401	22,526
Environmental aids	822	1,022	3,355	2,439	1,761
Environmental planning aids	302	441	210	287	283
Nonpoint aids	2,826	2,727	2,209	1,651	1,229
Debt Service	**$124,833***	**$127,252***	**$45,268***	**$70,456***	**$52,963***
Resource	48,071	51,566	26,205	34,012	27,725
Environmental	3,531	3,698	4,250	3,957	4,376
Water quality	69,456	67,581	10,011	27,240	15,585
Administrative facility	3,775	4,407	4,802	5,248	5,276
Acquisition and Development	**$11,937***	**$18,915***	**$9,107***	**$13,519***	**$8,128***
Wildlife	795	559	1,270	1,466	644
Fish	3,359	6,219	1,980	1,203	481
Forestry	2,558	5,465	1,411	4,612	818
Southern forests	497	202	182	167	234
Parks	2,539	3,864	1,312	1,487	1,229
Endangered resources	917	1,369	1,464	2,753	1,482
Facilities and lands	1,159	1,216	1,467	1,819	3,237
CAES (Customer and Employee Services)	72	6	9	—	1
Water resources	42	15	13	13	2
Administration	**$25,816***	**$20,547***	**$23,273***	**$23,279***	**$21,286***
Administration	1,563	1,261	1,266	1,386	1,464
Legal services	2,353	2,241	2,147	2,182	2,029
Management and budget	770	520	422	395	502
Facility rental	6,564	5,515	7,036	7,144	7,149
Nonbudget accounts	14,567	11,011	12,402	12,173	10,142
Customer and Employee Relations (CAER)	**$42,856***	**$44,093***	**$42,285***	**$40,975***	**$38,795***
Enterprise and technology/technology services	9,051	9,000	7,735	8,816	7,699
Finance	6,011	5,907	5,884	6,141	6,193
Human resources	3,694	4,268	3,889	3,767	3,873
Communication and education strategy	3,561	3,742	4,034	3,231	1,519
Community financial assistance	5,201	5,234	5,754	5,348	5,308
Customer service and licensing	12,114	12,711	11,950	10,705	11,327
CAER program management	3,224	3,230	3,038	2,967	2,877
TOTAL	**$565,033**	**$572,501**	**$474,205**	**$500,234**	**$467,510**

*Total of detail immediately following. Totals do not add due to rounding.

Source: Wisconsin Department of Natural Resources, departmental data, April 2013.

NATURAL RESOURCES LAND ACQUISITIONS
Fiscal Years 1990 – 2012*

Fiscal Year	Fisheries Mgmnt.	Northern Forests	Parks	Natural Areas	Southern Forests	Wildlife Mgmnt.	Wild Rivers	Other	Total
				ACRES ACQUIRED					
			WARREN KNOWLES-GAYLORD NELSON STEWARDSHIP PROGRAM						
1990	2,333	975	683	1,278	283	4,269	2,490	10	12,311
1991	1,671	930	1,352	4,745	1,567	5,997	11,832	61	28,155
1992	1,787	791	362	3,176	157	3,940	15,067	226	25,506
1993	1,475	721	624	3,166	298	5,160	4,328	245	16,018
1994	2,879	396	1,820	3,288	306	3,137	3,191	563	15,580
1995	8,093	373	271	1,985	370	5,052	835	633	17,612
1996	2,344	977	1,248	5,830	398	3,566	2,012	368	16,743
1997	1,548	213	884	2,038	161	2,929	2,003	332	10,110
1998	1,133	278	107	1,467	81	4,045	9,944	317	17,372
1999	600	815	641	1,904	513	2,501	775	209	7,957
				STEWARDSHIP 2000 PROGRAM					
2000	2,808	496	3,705	3,301	110	11,800	16,135	136	38,489
2001	2,773	149	4,295	1,063	194	5,191	3,558	683	17,905
2002	1,595	5,525	1,349	3,174	208	4,997	607	258	17,713
2003	1,880	35,464	2,029	5,801	0	3,765	2,406	86	51,432
2004	1,177	4,132	3,060	1,747	159	7,513	2,132	156	20,076
2005	2,308	6,578	3,842	7,477	475	5,385	10,692	329	37,086
2006	957	18,799	1,823	2,592	103	6,022	767	414	31,476
2007	982	45,075	713	2,948	171	3,247	8,793	192	62,121
2008	915	8,722	1,641	2,288	12	6,515	2,589	454	23,136
2009	837	7,943	1,876	1,844	1,024	2,150	1,867	358	17,899
2010	785	8,547	1,000	3,498	37	3,767	818	73	18,525
2011	1,786	27,070	3,525	5,845	297	5,560	2,729	5	46,818
2012	587	10,866	619	1,804	0	892	184	7	14,958
TOTAL. . . .	43,253	185,835	37,471	72,258	6,923	107,402	105,754	6,114	564,999
				COST TO ACQUIRE (in thousands)					
			WARREN KNOWLES-GAYLORD NELSON STEWARDSHIP PROGRAM						
1990	$1,951	$395	$727	$610	$490	$1,880	$2,216	$1	$8,269
1991	1,498	385	384	2,133	1,675	3,027	6,245	1,557	16,902
1992	1,530	416	461	1,195	398	2,735	5,537	48	12,320
1993	1,359	547	547	1,473	249	1,636	1,950	31	7,791
1994	2,315	178	902	724	793	2,118	1,843	148	9,021
1995	3,688	640	762	3,472	1,315	3,872	1,120	219	15,087
1996	2,596	542	2,758	3,108	1,036	2,832	1,413	441	14,726
1997	1,757	378	1,168	589	617	2,439	1,321	80	8,349
1998	1,513	137	337	2,077	293	4,331	11,005	1,307	21,001
1999	1,534	941	1,548	1,075	1,170	3,693	580	336	10,878
				STEWARDSHIP 2000 PROGRAM					
2000	$2,861	$550	$2,734	$3,472	$403	$9,061	$12,633	$352	$32,066
2001	5,247	533	8,605	2,156	873	4,251	739	420	22,824
2002	4,156	13,575	3,244	2,955	1,105	5,635	1,095	3,822	35,587
2003	3,976	7,680	4,105	3,603	0	3,908	3,807	117	27,196
2004	3,054	13,474	5,727	2,770	579	8,490	4,629	130	38,853
2005	5,034	2,418	16,693	4,993	3,050	8,164	3,591	401	44,345
2006	3,919	9,852	3,247	3,642	1,220	5,574	1,526	81	29,061
2007	3,529	20,147	6,760	4,039	1,081	7,227	15,864	254	58,901
2008	2,529	8,734	3,222	3,004	246	10,016	5,777	135	33,663
2009	2,236	6,534	8,069	1,849	11,325	4,250	3,729	128	38,122
2010	2,232	5,867	2,881	5,448	272	6,693	2,119	122	25,635
2011	4,277	12,974	4,762	7,153	2,023	10,144	5,416	35	46,782
2012	1,657	7,426	2,605	1,836	0	2,736	369	0	16,628
TOTAL. . . .	$64,448	$114,323	$82,248	$63,376	$30,213	$114,711	$94,524	$10,165	$574,008

*The Warren Knowles-Gaylord Nelson Stewardship Program replaced the Outdoor Recreation Act Program (ORAP) in 1990.
Source: Wisconsin Department of Natural Resources, Bureau of Facilities and Lands, departmental data, April 2013.

CONSERVATION AND RECREATION LAND IN WISCONSIN
Acres By Ownership

County	Wisconsin Department of Natural Resources – 2013								U.S. Forest Service 2012[2]	Total
	Forests	Wild Rivers	Natural Areas	Parks	Fisheries	Wildlife	Other	Total DNR		
Adams	—	—	7,579	492	1,518	7,511	640	17,740	—	17,740
Ashland	756	—	325	5,998	489	7,523	142	15,233	182,192	197,425
Barron	60	—	1	343	1,185	6,183	47	7,818	—	7,818
Bayfield	2,693	—	12,076	—	11,474	952	214	27,409	273,848	301,257
Brown	—	—	171	511	416	2,423	99	3,620	—	3,620
Buffalo	—	—	418	399	22	13,166	—	14,004	—	14,004
Burnett	15,316	—	1	251	3,941	52,142	222	71,872	—	71,872
Calumet	—	—	43	1,277	14	10,569	18	11,921	—	11,921
Chippewa	—	—	898	7,468	1,908	3,136	45	13,455	—	13,455
Clark	224	—	1	—	163	495	1	883	—	883
Columbia	—	123	599	657	1,783	19,954	22	23,138	—	23,138
Crawford	—	8,012	3,914	—	1,027	7,250	199	20,402	—	20,402
Dane	—	4,662	1,131	2,691	5,241	10,843	264	24,831	39	24,870
Dodge	—	—	1	223	654	24,538	292	25,708	—	25,708
Door	—	—	4,394	9,406	245	3,508	119	17,672	—	17,672
Douglas	86,581	129	304	4,119	7,225	1,014	532	99,905	—	99,905
Dunn	—	—	2,406	1,278	1,059	11,999	—	16,742	—	16,742
Eau Claire	—	—	568	146	475	2,103	50	3,342	—	3,342
Florence	36,323	11,495	8,988	177	123	40	45	57,190	85,252	142,442
Fond du Lac	10,697	—	100	410	51	17,211	112	28,581	—	28,581
Forest	24,809	—	121	635	269	3,609	2	29,444	346,177	375,621
Grant	623	13,892	634	3,410	1,590	—	308	20,456	—	20,456
Green	—	—	231	1,327	127	4,022	—	5,707	—	5,707
Green Lake	—	—	548	—	753	17,651	—	18,952	—	18,952
Iowa	85	10,551	721	6,601	2,587	2,037	146	22,728	—	22,728
Iron	33,403	35,603	7,137	63	1	10,775	172	87,153	—	87,153
Jackson	68,227	—	606	113	4,740	3,254	166	77,106	—	77,106
Jefferson	3,580	—	103	836	173	16,255	4	20,951	—	20,951
Juneau	—	—	1,485	5,447	536	5,140	53	12,661	—	12,661
Kenosha	—	—	479	4,537	192	2,034	26	7,268	—	7,268
Kewaunee	—	—	1	495	26	2,729	—	3,251	—	3,251
La Crosse	2,992	127	62	372	629	3,719	—	7,901	—	7,901
Lafayette	—	—	234	1,418	725	4,048	3	6,428	—	6,428
Langlade	18,515	—	407	304	13,993	2,831	212	36,260	32,727	68,987
Lincoln	20,149	2,425	81	2,833	3,113	4,641	233	33,474	—	33,474
Manitowoc	2,943	—	297	424	11	6,568	946	11,189	—	11,189
Marathon	1,724	—	1	3,008	2,508	23,017	9	30,267	—	30,267
Marinette	26,807	4,730	1,957	7,663	1,722	8,878	1,016	52,773	—	52,773
Marquette	—	—	1,747	—	4,498	7,137	2	13,384	—	13,384
Menominee[1]	—	—	1	—	—	—	16	17	—	17
Milwaukee	304	—	1	109	—	58	76	547	—	547
Monroe	—	—	115	1,607	4,077	361	98	6,256	—	6,256
Oconto	632	—	271	772	1,117	4,502	204	7,498	141,744	149,242
Oneida	69,199	29,297	8,253	584	717	7,770	196	116,016	11,312	127,328
Outagamie	—	—	1,504	327	331	9,525	57	11,744	—	11,744
Ozaukee	—	—	1,721	714	90	1,464	50	4,040	—	4,040
Pepin	—	—	1,947	—	17	3,798	—	5,762	—	5,762
Pierce	—	—	411	1,445	795	1,227	883	4,761	—	4,761
Polk	5,584	—	879	4,029	1,924	13,295	104	25,816	—	25,816
Portage	—	—	366	838	5,351	28,017	205	34,777	—	34,777
Price	9,287	—	1	263	321	9,805	20	19,696	151,626	171,322
Racine	—	—	11	99	632	3,375	37	4,155	—	4,155
Richland	—	6,957	54	—	2,462	3,083	—	12,556	—	12,556
Rock	—	—	530	1	339	8,429	218	9,517	—	9,517
Rusk	15,289	—	41	—	446	2,990	148	18,913	—	18,913
St. Croix	—	—	139	2,953	1,125	7,209	713	12,138	—	12,138
Sauk	—	5,883	5,567	17,726	1,424	3,927	1,143	35,670	—	35,670
Sawyer	84,049	14,181	345	658	2,534	6,684	345	108,798	129,183	237,981
Shawano	—	—	232	957	328	14,325	87	15,930	—	15,930
Sheboygan	16,114	—	129	964	2,078	3,438	59	22,781	—	22,781
Taylor	—	—	250	17	275	8,832	81	9,455	125,234	134,689
Trempealeau	58	—	1	1,612	1,140	4,357	43	7,212	—	7,212
Vernon	52	—	454	3,785	2,214	221	877	7,603	—	7,603
Vilas	142,075	—	3,830	—	369	7,188	82	153,543	54,568	208,111
Walworth	7,624	—	1,940	522	721	5,676	105	16,587	—	16,587
Washburn	5,331	2,250	443	501	3,575	2,537	158	14,794	—	14,794
Washington	5,120	—	1	759	378	7,288	82	13,628	—	13,628
Waukesha	12,344	—	303	357	295	5,533	323	19,156	—	19,156
Waupaca	—	—	646	1,284	5,520	3,575	286	11,311	—	11,311
Waushara	—	—	631	850	12,704	5,442	259	19,885	—	19,885
Winnebago	—	—	133	2	198	13,833	126	14,291	—	14,291
Wood	173	—	15	—	513	15,268	44	16,012	—	16,012
STATE	729,740	150,315	91,939	119,061	131,216	543,932	13,486	1,779,688	1,533,902	3,313,590

[1] Land in Menominee County that is not privately owned is held by the Menominee Nation.

[2] Federal lands controlled by the U.S. Forest Service as of September 30, 2012.

Sources: U.S. Forest Service, "Land Areas of the National Forest System as of September 30, 2012", January 2013; Wisconsin Department of Natural Resources, departmental data, April 2013.

HIGHLIGHTS OF EDUCATION IN WISCONSIN

Universities and Colleges — A total of 180,969 students enrolled in the University of Wisconsin System for the 2012 fall semester. The system's 2012 summer school enrollment was 51,951, and the UW-Extension's credit outreach enrolled 43,514 students in the 2011-12 fiscal year.

Wisconsin's private institutions of higher education encompass a broad range of schools, including 7 universities, 11 colleges, 6 technical and professional schools, 3 theological seminaries, and 2 tribal colleges. Over the past five years, enrollments in private institutions have stayed steady with a total of 67,430 students in 2011-12.

Technical Colleges — Wisconsin's Technical College System had a total enrollment of 362,619 students in 2011-12. Enrollments for individual institutions that year ranged from 7,479 at Nicolet Area Technical College to 51,097 at Fox Valley Technical College.

Elementary and Secondary Schools — Following a peak enrollment of 999,921 in 1971-72, public school registrations declined to a low of 767,542 in 1984-85. In the last 10 years, enrollments have remained midway between those levels, with a total of 872,436 in 2012-13.

In the 2012-13 school year, 122,949 students, or 12.4% of Wisconsin's estimated 1 million elementary and secondary pupils, were enrolled in private schools. Over the last 10 years, private school enrollments have decreased by almost 20,000 students.

Teachers — Of Wisconsin's 56,800 public school teachers employed in the 2012-13 school year, 40,055 taught in elementary grades and 16,745 were secondary teachers. In the 2012-13 school year, Wisconsin's average salary for all teachers was $55,171. Nationally, Wisconsin ranked 21st for the 2011-12 school year. New York had the highest average salary that year at an estimated $73,398. South Dakota's average salary was the lowest at $38,804.

Educational Alternatives — Reported enrollment in Wisconsin home-based private education programs reached a peak of 21,288 students during 2002-03, and has steadily declined to 16,979 in 2012-13. In the 2012-13 school year, Wisconsin charter school enrollments totaled 43,529 students.

Educational Expenditures — State and local expenditures for education in Wisconsin for 2011-12 totaled $16.8 billion, or $2,949 per capita, based on Wisconsin's estimated population. Wisconsin ranked 18th in the nation with total expenditures per pupil of $11,453 in the 2009-10 fiscal year, while New York was first ($18,167) and Utah was 50th ($6,452). In fiscal year 2011-12, school costs in Wisconsin totaled $10.6 billion. The 2011-12 cost per pupil was $12,375.

Educational Attainment — For 2010-11, Wisconsin schools conferred 2,418 doctoral-level degrees, 9,695 master's degrees, and 35,279 bachelor's degrees. In the same year, it awarded 63,600 public high school diplomas.

The following tables present selected data. Consult footnoted sources for more detailed information about education.

UNIVERSITY OF WISCONSIN SYSTEM
Fall Enrollment 2007 – 2012

Institution	2007-08	2008-09	2009-10	2010-11	2011-12	2012-13	2012-13 Detail Female	2012-13 Detail Male
Universities*	**160,364**	**161,781**	**165,120**	**167,705**	**166,699**	**166,862**	**89,048**	**77,814**
Eau Claire	10,854	11,140	11,216	11,413	11,234	11,047	6,466	4,581
Green Bay	6,110	6,286	6,638	6,636	6,665	6,790	4,409	2,381
La Crosse	9,994	9,880	10,009	10,135	10,258	10,380	6,092	4,288
Madison*	41,563	41,620	41,654	42,180	42,065	42,463	21,699	20,764
Undergraduate*	30,166	30,362	29,925	30,169	30,014	30,507	15,694	14,813
Agricultural and Life Sciences	2,301	2,365	2,453	2,579	2,834	3,162	1,873	1,289
Business	1,321	1,403	1,682	1,748	1,906	1,795	765	1,030
Education	1,902	1,861	1,803	1,855	1,980	1,870	1,353	517
Engineering	3,156	3,396	3,510	3,733	3,786	4,045	791	3,254
Human Ecology	874	991	910	879	907	752	610	142
Letters and Science	18,032	17,843	17,003	16,829	16,117	16,382	8,747	7,635
Medicine & Public Health	239	211	166	100	36	2	2	0
Nursing	714	691	730	779	775	746	659	87
Pharmacy	22	16	19	25	38	44	23	21
University Special†	1,605	1,585	1,649	1,642	1,635	1,709	871	838
Graduate	8,876	8,733	9,130	9,375	9,325	9,385	4,600	4,785
Law	871	830	880	857	879	755	314	441
Med. & Pub. Health, Other Clinical	819	863	867	922	991	963	536	427
Pharmacy	518	519	529	540	538	532	308	224
Veterinary Medicine	313	313	323	317	318	321	247	74
Milwaukee*	29,338	29,215	30,418	30,470	29,726	29,114	15,313	13,801
Undergraduate*	24,395	24,299	25,204	25,239	24,639	24,175	12,396	11,779
Academic Opportunity Center	1,332	1,223	1,348	1,332	1,290	1,171	660	511
College of Health Sciences	1,556	1,635	1,658	1,696	1,754	1,749	1,177	572
College of Letters and Science	7,845	7,857	8,170	8,238	8,012	8,008	4,181	3,827
College of Nursing	1,062	983	1,021	1026	1,042	1,041	877	164
Engineering & Applied Science	1,451	1,454	1,500	1,538	1,583	1,553	138	1,415
Joint Programs L&S and CEAS	—	—	—	—	6	10	1	9
Global Studies Interdisciplinary	144	176	192	200	201	185	115	70
Helen Bader/Social Welfare	982	942	998	1083	1,205	1,158	663	495
Lubar School of Business	3,957	3,990	4,007	3,844	3,673	3,631	1,280	2,351
Peck School of the Arts	1,944	2,017	2,002	2,009	1,847	1,733	950	783
School Arch. & Urban Planning	702	707	635	586	568	504	161	343
School of Education	1,794	1,747	1,794	1,854	1,679	1,530	1,118	412
School of Information Studies	168	178	228	230	304	412	116	296
University Special†	1,458	1,390	1,651	1,603	1,475	1,490	959	531
Graduate	4,943	4,916	5,214	5,231	5,087	4,939	2,917	2,022
Oshkosh	12,772	12,753	13,192	13,629	13,513	13,519	8,025	5,494
Parkside	5,010	5,167	5,303	5,160	4,887	4,769	2,486	2,283
Platteville	7,189	7,512	7,803	7,928	8,262	8,678	3,154	5,524
River Falls	6,452	6,555	6,728	6,902	6,788	6,447	3,937	2,510
Stevens Point	9,115	9,163	9,209	9,500	9,477	9,677	5,132	4,545
Stout	8,477	8,839	9,017	9,339	9,356	9,247	4,655	4,592
Superior	2,753	2,689	2,794	2,856	2,825	2,700	1,576	1,124
Whitewater	10,737	10,962	11,139	11,557	11,643	12,031	6,104	5,927
Colleges*	**13,029**	**13,275**	**13,789**	**14,385**	**14,570**	**14,107**	**7,574**	**6,533**
Baraboo/Sauk County	666	679	597	594	617	597	319	278
Barron	606	627	679	715	706	634	349	285
Fond du Lac	751	736	779	794	749	692	369	323
Fox Valley	1,745	1,650	1,731	1,830	1,822	1,799	900	899
Manitowoc	594	543	550	614	666	614	355	259
Marathon County	1,368	1,364	1,388	1,410	1,368	1,275	652	623
Marinette	459	469	569	526	461	464	257	207
Marshfield/Wood County	636	628	674	711	715	628	393	235
Richland	449	474	495	454	476	523	282	241
Rock County	912	1,058	1,175	1,215	1,289	1,305	749	556
Sheboygan	725	782	856	875	896	836	422	414
Washington County	1,018	1,018	1,040	1,117	1,037	998	490	508
Waukesha	2,038	2,035	2,093	2,240	2,248	2,118	980	1,138
Online Courses	1,062	1,212	1,163	1,290	1,520	1,624	1,057	567
SYSTEM TOTAL	173,393	175,056	178,909	182,090	181,269	180,969	96,622	84,347

*Total of detail immediately following.

†"University Special" designates students at UW-Madison and UW-Milwaukee who are allowed to take courses without having to qualify as degree candidates.

Sources: University of Wisconsin System, Office of Policy Analysis and Research, departmental data and Student Statistics reports, at: http://www.uwsa.edu/opar/ssb/ [March 2013]; *2011-12 UW System Fact Book*.

UNIVERSITY OF WISCONSIN SYSTEM
Summer Session Enrollment 2007 – 2012

Institution	2007	2008	2009	2010	2011	2012	2012 Detail Female	2012 Detail Male
Universities*	**45,650**	**46,030**	**47,907**	**49,364**	**48,669**	**47,809**	**27,593**	**20,216**
Eau Claire	2,524	2,464	2,598	2,607	2,591	2,738	1,831	907
Green Bay	1,615	1,887	2,087	2,213	2,260	2,236	1,543	693
La Crosse	2,888	2,931	2,918	3,156	2,899	3,068	2,053	1,015
Madison	12,540	12,123	12,632	12,587	12,642	12,269	5,946	6,323
Undergraduate*	7,464	7,118	7,597	7,342	7,334	6,995	3,259	3,736
Agricultural and Life Sciences	536	578	549	549	643	676	279	397
Business	322	345	347	432	426	339	197	142
Education	441	379	415	405	462	413	118	295
Engineering	684	666	707	668	755	860	654	206
Human Ecology	385	385	339	341	325	272	72	200
Letters and Science	3,427	3,292	3506	3,296	3,234	3,030	1,448	1,582
Medicine & Public Health	112	109	110	74	27	0	0	0
Nursing	85	73	84	104	117	105	16	89
Pharmacy	4	2	1	0	4	4	2	2
University Special†	1,468	1,289	1539	1,473	1,341	1,296	473	823
Graduate	4,510	4,435	4,448	4,559	4,570	4,622	2,424	2,198
Law	182	171	191	226	224	205	118	87
Med. & Pub. Health, Other Clinical	159	198	199	230	272	232	69	163
Pharmacy	145	129	127	139	150	136	60	76
Veterinary Medicine	80	72	70	91	92	79	16	63
Milwaukee	8,707	9,072	9,238	9,770	9,358	8,838	5,199	3,639
Undergraduate*	6,563	6,849	6,938	7,411	7,194	6,787	3,822	2,965
Academic Opportunity Center	155	144	171	194	187	154	87	67
College of Health Sciences	477	507	498	553	600	619	450	169
College of Letters and Science	1,670	1,787	1,785	1,940	1,852	1,723	991	732
College of Nursing	248	282	264	279	278	265	210	55
Engineering & Applied Science	358	382	375	429	420	433	38	395
Joint Programs L&S and CEAS	0	0	0	0	2	2	0	2
Global Studies Interdisciplinary	33	41	45	55	65	61	40	21
Helen Bader/Social Welfare	261	254	265	290	349	319	204	115
Lubar School of Business	1,188	1,243	1,268	1,255	1,159	1,032	389	643
Peck School of the Arts	315	367	335	372	347	297	195	102
School Arch. & Urban Planning	79	78	90	65	53	60	24	36
School of Education	485	466	485	535	493	454	356	98
School of Information Studies	47	52	71	73	111	130	45	85
University Special†	1,247	1,246	1,286	1,371	1,278	1,238	793	445
Graduate	2,144	2,223	2,300	2,359	2,164	2,051	1,377	674
Oshkosh	2,309	2,292	2,781	3,052	2,938	2,846	1,851	995
Parkside	1,342	1,362	1,675	1,692	1,438	1,308	761	547
Platteville	1,792	1,854	2,014	1,951	1,867	2,018	985	1,033
River Falls	1,849	1,798	1,714	1,723	1,832	1,909	1,275	634
Stevens Point	3,447	3,673	2,529	2,514	2,586	2,517	1,455	1,062
Stout	2,587	2,494	3,687	3,784	3,938	3,953	2,271	1,682
Superior	796	691	706	824	862	761	506	255
Whitewater	3,254	3,389	3,328	3,491	3,458	3,348	1,917	1,431
Colleges*	**3,769**	**3,880**	**4,134**	**4,157**	**4,068**	**4,142**	**2,579**	**1,563**
Baraboo/Sauk County	107	111	66	124	103	83	41	42
Barron	59	61	61	86	74	80	48	32
Fond du Lac	191	167	150	170	158	162	99	63
Fox Valley	355	379	343	382	316	284	145	139
Manitowoc	147	109	119	135	143	123	88	35
Marathon County	178	242	221	195	176	140	85	55
Marinette	77	69	87	76	72	91	61	30
Marshfield/Wood County	147	134	144	137	132	133	84	49
Richland	76	24	51	43	43	38	23	15
Rock County	179	157	236	242	223	256	141	115
Sheboygan	109	132	136	131	149	128	80	48
Washington County	221	178	178	197	162	134	92	42
Waukesha	860	778	843	807	746	662	369	293
Online Courses	1,063	1,339	1,499	1,432	1,571	1,828	1,223	605
SYSTEM TOTAL	49,419	49,910	52,041	53,521	52,737	51,951	30,172	21,779

*Total of detail immediately following.

†"University Special" designates students at UW-Madison and UW-Milwaukee who are allowed to take courses without having to qualify as degree candidates.

Source: University of Wisconsin System, Office of Policy Analysis and Research, May 2013.

UNIVERSITY OF WISCONSIN – EXTENSION PROGRAMS
2007-08 – 2011-12

Program type	2007-08	2008-09	2009-10	2010-11	2011-12
Broadcasting and Media Innovations[1]					
Wisconsin Public Radio (listeners per week)	424,000	467,000	456,800	439,300	476,400
Wisconsin Public Television (viewers per week)	527,560	493,785	420,000	561,000	560,000
Wisconsin Public Television telecourses (hours)	250	32	32	30	59
Interactive conferencing hours.	203,766	218,825	208,221	184,225	169,980
Continuing Education, Outreach and E-Learning					
Online courses	301	294	297	338	379
Online certificate and degree programs	16	10	11	11	12
Online enrollments.	3,891	3,896	4,406	5,026	5,517
Number of enrollments[2]	40,649	39,344	44,152	46,001	43,514
Noncredit programs	5,664	5,845	5,915	5,970	5,700
Noncredit enrollments	146,097	142,506	144,110	160,000	144,092
UW HELP (Higher Education Location Program) contacts. . . .	32,900	29,632	26,598	28,481	22,469
Learner Support Services contacts.	144,929	97,775	104,996	133,525	144,179
Online applications to UW System Campuses	151,000	159,753	165,948	177,375	177,985
Independent Learning Enrollments[3]	2,551	2,063	1,697	1,402	1,400
Cooperative Extension Teaching Contacts[4]					
Agriculture/Agribusiness	274,013	407,938	316,799	253,563	265,911
Community, Natural Resources and Economic Development. .	113,856	117,971	113,013	145,702	84,533
Family Living Programs.	431,633	430,267	518,270	496,816	543,406
4-H/Youth Development	274,715	308,258	339,538	340,030	376,375
Leadership Wisconsin (leadership development program) . . .	—	418	492	772	927
Wisconsin Geological and Natural History Survey	15,228	8,859	9,305	14,486	16,786
Entrepreneurship and Economic Development[5]					
Counseling and technical assistance clients	2,951	2,784	3,118	3,343	2,468
Business Answerline-assisted clients	2,668	2,259	2,220	1,864	1,787
Counseling and technical assistance hours	23,942	20,503	22,726	23,219	16,898
Training programs	1,261	865	1,091	935	623
Training program participants	17,337	12,792	13,763	12,956	6,547
Business startups.	—	76	119	167	122
Extension Conference Centers					
J.F. Friedrick Center[6]**, The Lowell Center, The Pyle Center**					
Conference participants	74,816	73,675	74,572	75,870	64,162
Events	2,024	1,744	1,947	2,939	2,665

[1]Wisconsin Public Radio and Wisconsin Public Television are cooperative services of the University of Wisconsin-Extension and the Wisconsin Educational Communications Board.

[2]Undergraduate and Graduate enrollments combined.

[3]Adjusted for student withdrawals.

[4]Cooperative Extension data are for the calendar year, except Wisconsin Geological and Natural History Survey numbers for 2011-12. In addition, its faculty and staff offer contacts through publications, telephone, mass media, and the World Wide Web.

[5]Formerly called Business and Manufacturing Extension.

[6]The J.F. Friedrick Center closed June 22, 2008.

Source: The UW Colleges and UW-Extension *2012 Annual Report,* at: http://www.uwex.uwc.edu/publications [March 2012] and previous editions.

ENROLLMENT IN WISCONSIN TECHNICAL COLLEGE SYSTEM

Annual Enrollment Summary, 2000-01 – 2011-12

School Year	Total[1]	College Parallel	Associate Degree	Technical Diploma	Vocational Adult	Non-Post Secondary[2]	Community Services
2002-03	429,355	19,064	113,253	40,098	232,766	81,860	13,277
2003-04	416,857	19,282	115,675	41,125	221,283	79,265	12,156
2004-05	406,323	20,181	115,422	39,291	214,948	76,870	10,817
2005-06	409,380	20,242	117,408	38,305	219,584	74,556	10,631
2006-07	400,057	21,053	117,028	39,045	210,396	72,951	10,206
2007-08	390,272	22,142	117,722	38,583	203,493	70,585	9,113
2008-09	375,944	24,080	122,773	39,025	182,713	73,198	8,760
2009-10	382,006	27,139	133,602	39,011	178,257	76,325	10,082
2010-11	370,588	27,938	136,232	36,101	167,135	72,176	13,181
2011-12	362,619	27,636	132,535	34,452	166,463	65,506	14,112

[1]Unduplicated student headcount.

[2]Includes Basic Education.

Source: Wisconsin Technical College System, *Fact Book 2013,* at: http://www.wtcsystem.edu/reports/data/factbook/index.htm and previous issues.

Annual Enrollment Summary, By Technical College – 2011-12

Technical College	Total[1]	College Parallel	Associate Degree	Technical Diploma	Vocational Adult	Non-Post Secondary[2]	Community Services
Blackhawk	11,126	—	3,987	1,100	5,749	1,640	361
Chippewa Valley	15,709	980	6,587	1,898	7,455	1,971	—
Fox Valley	51,097	—	16,060	3,150	32,785	2,479	814
Gateway	22,689	—	11,744	2,451	7,069	5,976	—
Lakeshore	13,495	—	3,588	997	8,202	1,825	221
Madison Area	39,222	11,230	15,709	4,155	9,839	6,365	3,940
Mid-State.	8,488	—	3,876	1,185	3,442	1,782	20
Milwaukee Area	41,601	13,552	20,915	3,212	7,227	21,540	18
Moraine Park.	17,279	—	7,495	2,493	6,193	3,149	1,017
Nicolet Area	7,479	901	1,324	534	3,910	707	1,713
Northcentral	17,969	—	6,032	1,463	8,472	5,027	—
Northeast Wisconsin	43,890	—	13,866	4,082	26,608	4,119	215
Southwest Wisconsin . . .	11,195	—	3,438	1,201	6,925	2,195	174
Waukesha County	23,491	—	8,183	2,627	11,925	2,933	1,672
Western.	15,916	973	6,018	1,805	7,081	2,425	963
Wisconsin Indianhead . . .	21,973	—	3,713	2,099	13,581	1,373	2,984
TOTAL.	362,619	27,636	132,535	34,452	166,463	65,506	14,112

[1]Unduplicated student headcount.

[2]Includes Basic Education.

Source: Wisconsin Technical College System, *Fact Book 2013,* at: http://www.wtcsystem.edu/reports/data/factbook/index.htm and previous issues.

WISCONSIN PRIVATE INSTITUTIONS OF HIGHER EDUCATION
Fall Enrollment, 2007-08 – 2011-12

Institution (Location)	2007-08	2008-09	2009-10	2010-11	2011-12
Universities and Colleges					
Alverno College (Milwaukee)	2,654	2,782	2,815	2,759	2,605
Beloit College (Beloit)	1,366	1,388	1,407	1,397	1,385
Cardinal Stritch University (Milwaukee)	6,277	6,242	6,276	5,842	5,358
Carroll University (Waukesha)	3,325	3,318	3,115	3,396	3,522
Carthage College (Kenosha)	2,778	2,816	3,137	3,144	3,082
Concordia University Wisconsin (Mequon)	5,933	6,549	7,178	7,484	7,618
Edgewood College (Madison)	2,582	2,544	2,549	2,626	2,658
Lakeland College (Sheboygan)	3,695	3,744	3,932	3,936	3,881
Lawrence University (Appleton)	1,433	1,496	1,495	1,557	1,487
Marian University (Fond du Lac)	2,957	2,891	2,841	2,881	2,615
Marquette University (Milwaukee)	11,516	11,633	11,689	11,806	12,002
Mount Mary College (Milwaukee)	1,681	1,862	2,008	1,957	1,738
Northland College (Ashland)	687	695	612	603	534
Ripon College (Ripon)	1,000	1,057	1,065	1,065	991
Saint Norbert College (De Pere)	2,169	2,137	2,175	2,241	2,225
Silver Lake College (Manitowoc)	832	853	704	720	635
Viterbo University (La Crosse)	3,088	2,944	3,287	3,238	3,092
Wisconsin Lutheran College (Milwaukee)	706	753	776	840	1,022
Technical and Professional					
Bellin College of Nursing (Green Bay)	304	289	331	329	310
Herzing University* (Madison & Kenosha campuses)	1,803	1,902	NA	4,526	3,745
Medical College of Wisconsin (Milwaukee)	1,235	1,228	817	1,277	1,257
Milwaukee Institute of Art & Design (Milwaukee)	636	675	660	700	727
Milwaukee School of Engineering (Milwaukee)	2,516	2,621	2,648	2,589	2,486
Wisconsin School of Professional Psychology (Milwaukee)	60	75	78	75	83
Theological Seminaries					
Maranatha Baptist Bible College (Watertown)	897	866	901	962	1,019
Nashotah House (Nashotah)	98	107	108	114	119
Sacred Heart School of Theology (Hales Corners)	170	175	139	107	102
Tribal Colleges					
College of the Menominee Nation (Keshena)	505	512	634	615	699
Lac Courte Oreilles Ojibwa Community College (Hayward)	574	478	561	489	433
TOTAL	63,477	64,632	63,938	69,275	67,430

*For-profit institution.

Sources: National Center for Education Statistics, Integrated Postsecondary Education Data System, at: http://nces.ed.gov/ipeds/datacenter; U.S. Department of Education, Office of Postsecondary Education, Database of Accredited Postsecondary Institutions and Programs, accredited by the Higher Learning Commission of the North Central Association of Colleges and Schools, at: http://ope.ed.gov/accreditation/; individual school registrars.

DIPLOMAS AND EARNED DEGREES
By State 2010-11

State	High School Diplomas[1] Public[2]	Higher Education			
		Associate Degree	Bachelor's Degree	Master's Degree	Doctorate Level Degrees (Ph.D., M.D., J.D. etc.)
Alabama	44,520	11,795	27,248	11,888	2,144
Alaska	7,720	1,523	1,770	693	46
Arizona.	66,490	58,991	50,928	36,231	2,937
Arkansas	28,440	10,181	13,259	4,793	813
California	386,220	107,675	169,623	67,439	17,140
Colorado	51,820	16,145	29,540	14,246	2,170
Connecticut	38,450	6,079	19,735	9,131	1,808
Delaware.	8,190	1,820	5,877	2,705	546
District of Columbia	3,260	555	8,402	10,078	3,458
Florida	163,620	86,254	86,281	31,766	9,297
Georgia.	92,160	17,949	45,075	17,533	4,005
Hawaii	11,070	3,766	5,751	2,062	529
Idaho	17,390	3,919	9,171	1,790	321
ILLINOIS	132,670	40,009	71,580	43,011	7,846
Indiana	65,460	18,603	43,519	14,337	3,386
IOWA	33,710	19,290	36,266	9,982	3,112
Kansas	31,320	9,501	18,191	7,227	1,476
Kentucky.	41,930	13,029	21,078	8,350	1,812
Louisiana.	34,450	7,236	21,509	7,017	2,236
Maine	14,030	3,309	7,347	1,766	367
Maryland.	57,900	13,921	29,247	16,975	2,652
Massachusetts	63,820	12,900	53,749	33,905	7,637
MICHIGAN	110,300	30,859	56,217	21,252	5,807
MINNESOTA	59,720	20,480	33,386	21,823	4,352
Mississippi	26,930	11,440	13,230	4,676	1,170
Missouri	62,470	18,534	41,648	20,697	4,656
Montana	9,690	2,058	5,512	1,201	357
Nebraska.	19,620	5,351	13,510	4,684	1,371
Nevada.	24,990	4,997	7,556	2,720	839
New Hampshire	14,300	3,062	9,479	3,666	448
New Jersey.	95,200	21,124	37,087	14,427	3,101
New Mexico	19,080	6,552	8,179	3,266	583
New York	185,930	66,644	127,205	70,225	14,230
North Carolina	87,370	25,154	48,670	16,226	4,116
North Dakota.	7,110	2,552	5,674	1,572	456
Ohio	108,010	33,479	63,882	22,636	6,033
Oklahoma	38,120	10,710	19,511	6,356	1,611
Oregon	35,410	10,945	19,542	7,326	1,849
Pennsylvania	132,100	29,241	88,205	36,016	9,316
Rhode Island	9,880	3,461	10,863	2,545	709
South Carolina	39,880	9,771	23,034	5,849	1,606
South Dakota.	8,550	2,601	5,211	1,427	300
Tennessee	62,520	12,478	31,026	11,099	2,989
Texas	279,970	58,609	107,438	42,039	9,705
Utah	30,340	12,398	24,461	6,995	1,087
Vermont	6,790	1,223	6,100	2,377	388
Virginia.	81,600	24,193	49,077	20,697	4,923
Washington.	66,580	27,045	31,398	9,850	2,412
West Virginia.	17,300	4,688	12,978	5,884	1,007
WISCONSIN	63,600	15,012	35,279	9,695	2,418
Wyoming.	5,570	3,216	1,860	482	188
UNITED STATES . . .	3,103,540	942,327	1,715,913[3]	730,635[3]	163,765

[1]Private school data unavailable at time of publication.

[2]Projected.

[3]Total includes U.S. Service schools: 3,549 Bachelor's Degrees and 2 Master's Degrees granted.

Sources: U.S. Department of Education, Institute of Education Sciences, National Center for Education Statistics, *Digest of Education Statistics 2012,* advanced release tables, at: http://nces.ed.gov/programs/digest/2012menu_tables.asp; U.S. Department of Education, National Center for Education Statistics [June 2013].

WISCONSIN SCHOOL DISTRICT FINANCIAL DATA
1990-91 to 2012-13

Fiscal Year	State School Aid Amount[2] (in millions)	State School Aid Percent Change	Gross School Levy Amount[2] (in millions)	Gross School Levy Percent Change	Total School Costs[1] Amount[2] (in millions)	Total School Costs[1] Percent Change	Cost Per Pupil Amount	Cost Per Pupil Percent Change
1990-91	$1,857.4	—	$2,356.4	—	$4,555.7	—	$5,712	—
1991-92	1,950.4	5.0%	2,568.0	9.0%	4,877.1	7.1%	5,987	4.8%
1992-93	2,046.0	4.9	2,843.8	10.7	5,287.9	8.4	6,375	6.5
1993-94	2,186.6	6.9	2,988.1	5.1	5,527.1	4.5	6,549	2.7
1994-95	2,462.0	12.6	2,995.7	0.3	5,848.2	5.8	6,796	3.8
1995-96	2,705.2	9.9	3,023.6	0.9	6,150.2	5.2	7,068	4.0
1996-97	3,566.1	31.8	2,528.1	−16.4	6,546.8	6.4	7,447	5.4
1997-98	3,804.7	6.7	2,590.4	2.5	6,939.0	6.0	7,874	5.7
1998-99	3,989.4	4.9	2,735.8	5.6	7,250.7	4.5	8,244	4.7
1999-2000	4,226.3	5.9	2,794.9	2.2	7,546.9	4.1	8,376	1.6
2000-01	4,463.3	5.6	2,928.1	4.8	7,899.5	4.7	8,765	4.6
2001-02	4,602.4	3.1	3,071.8	4.9	8,347.5	5.7	9,571	9.2
2002-03	4,775.2	3.8	3,192.0	3.9	8,749.9	4.8	10,023	4.7
2003-04	4,806.3	0.7	3,367.6	5.5	8,911.2	1.8	10,229	2.1
2004-05	4,857.9	1.1	3,610.7	7.2	9,216.2	3.4	10,605	3.7
2005-06	5,159.1	6.2	3,592.3	−0.5	9,539.4	3.5	10,989	3.6
2006-07	5,294.4	2.6	3,787.8	5.4	9,902.9	3.8	11,413	3.9
2007-08	5,340.1	0.9	4,066.6	7.4	10,265.1	3.7	11,894	4.2
2008-09	5,462.4	2.3	4,279.0	5.2	10,623.3	3.5	12,346	3.8
2009-10	5,315.4	−2.7	4,537.6	6.0	10,833.7	2.0	12,624	2.3
2010-11	5,325.0	0.2	4,692.9	3.4	11,161.9	3.0	13,020	3.1
2011-12	4,893.5	−8.1	4,646.7	−1.0	10,584.9	−5.2	12,375	−5.0
2012-13	4,964.4	1.4	4,656.1	0.2	NA	—	NA	—

NA – Not available.

[1]Includes the gross costs of general operations, special projects, debt service, and food service; the net cost of capital projects; and the costs of CESA and County Children with Disabilities Education Board operations.

[2]1996-97 through 2012-13 are appropriated amounts.

Sources: Wisconsin Department of Public Instruction, School Financial Services, at: http://sfs.dpi.wi.gov/, May 2013 and previous years; Wisconsin Legislative Fiscal Bureau, *Comparative Summary of Budget Recommendations (2011 Act 32)*, August 2011; Informational Paper #24, *State Aid to School Districts*, January 2013.

WISCONSIN SCHOOL DISTRICT ENROLLMENT LEVELS

Number of Districts by Total Enrollment Level, 2007-08 – 2012-13

Enrollment Level[1]	2007-08	2008-09	2009-10	2010-11	2011-12	2012-13
1-499	113	113	113	114	120	123
500-999	128	124	124	123	121	122
1,000-1,999	100	101	102	102	99	98
2,000-2,999	37	39	37	35	33	29
3,000-3,999	25	25	26	27	30	32
4,000-4,999	12	11	12	11	10	11
5,000-9,999	20	20	19	21	21	21
10,000 and above	11	11	11	11	11	11
TOTAL	446	444	444	444	445	447

[1]Enrollment data includes nondistrict-sponsored charter schools.

Number of Districts by 9-12 Enrollment Level, 2007-08 – 2012-13

Enrollment Level[1]	2007-08	2008-09	2009-10	2010-11	2011-12	2012-13
0[2]	59	59	60	61	61	62
1-299	165	163	169	171	174	180
300-499	71	73	68	68	69	64
500-999	73	71	68	69	73	72
1,000-1,999	55	55	57	54	45	47
2,000 and above	23	23	22	21	23	22
TOTAL	446	444	444	444	445	447

[1]Enrollment data includes nondistrict-sponsored charter schools.

[2]This group includes the K3-8 districts, which do not have secondary level students.

Source: Wisconsin Department of Public Instruction, "Public School Enrollment Data – Public Enrollment by District by Grade", at: http://lbstat.dpi.wi.gov/lbstat_pubdata3 [February 2013].

ENROLLMENT IN WISCONSIN PUBLIC AND PRIVATE ELEMENTARY AND SECONDARY SCHOOLS

Public Schools, 2002-03 – 2012-13

Grade Level	2002-03	2003-04	2004-05*	2005-06	2006-07	2007-08	2008-09	2009-10	2010-11	2011-12	2012-13
Pre-kindergarten	26,092	26,668	27,444	31,218	33,821	37,773	43,153	47,054	50,200	54,438	55,008
Kindergarten	57,670	59,372	58,724	60,382	60,408	59,590	60,373	61,094	60,721	60,875	62,422
1	58,538	58,368	58,521	59,593	60,696	60,474	59,779	60,197	61,262	60,572	61,037
2	58,628	58,877	57,807	58,978	59,703	60,807	60,486	59,557	60,226	60,984	60,585
3	60,819	59,196	58,874	58,664	59,554	60,000	60,969	60,661	59,981	60,216	61,243
4	62,436	61,744	59,267	59,984	59,356	59,995	60,308	61,242	61,015	60,094	60,670
5	64,213	62,970	61,493	60,304	60,261	59,581	60,222	60,413	61,420	60,958	60,253
6	66,925	65,762	62,557	62,737	61,257	60,827	60,235	60,656	61,053	61,818	61,369
7	68,631	68,192	66,095	65,153	63,938	62,030	61,588	61,748	61,264	61,442	62,310
8	67,751	68,663	67,168	66,985	65,606	64,135	62,305	61,814	61,337	61,413	61,857
9	77,508	77,798	76,173	76,674	75,282	73,746	71,662	69,323	68,383	67,542	67,699
10	73,022	72,043	71,196	73,409	72,425	70,788	69,395	68,291	66,490	65,510	64,507
11	70,284	70,989	69,928	71,428	73,694	72,507	71,326	70,144	69,076	66,851	66,346
12	68,714	69,389	69,510	69,665	70,699	72,380	71,785	71,242	69,858	68,392	67,130
TOTAL	881,231	880,031	864,757	875,174	876,700	874,633	873,586	872,436	872,286	871,105	872,436

Private Schools, 2002-03 – 2012-13

Grade Level	2002-03	2003-04	2004-05	2005-06	2006-07	2007-08	2008-09	2009-10	2010-11	2011-12	2012-13
Pre-kindergarten	13,487	13,604	14,434	14,431	14,662	15,008	14,814	13,646	14,737	14,793	14,982
Kindergarten	11,736	11,191	11,517	11,440	10,890	10,663	10,483	10,161	9,893	9,797	9,994
1	12,021	11,201	10,950	10,896	11,017	10,714	10,306	9,975	9,810	9,767	9,492
2	11,888	11,460	10,970	10,756	10,629	10,764	10,376	10,006	9,744	9,703	9,487
3	11,807	11,412	11,187	10,698	10,466	10,484	10,481	10,026	9,648	9,635	9,462
4	11,896	11,304	11,114	10,866	10,522	10,338	10,187	10,179	9,659	9,542	9,320
5	11,865	11,309	11,047	10,800	10,641	10,412	10,078	9,957	9,927	9,587	9,450
6	11,286	10,994	10,824	10,564	10,325	10,368	9,961	9,672	9,486	9,555	9,233
7	11,193	10,408	10,420	10,164	9,984	9,952	9,775	9,377	9,223	9,192	9,157
8	10,682	10,683	10,247	10,092	9,841	9,876	9,563	9,486	9,072	9,078	8,909
9	6,414	6,112	6,332	6,300	6,306	6,414	6,287	5,980	6,089	5,939	6,159
10	6,076	6,214	5,950	6,275	6,134	6,153	6,072	6,043	5,789	5,866	5,917
11	5,949	5,880	5,925	5,825	5,936	5,923	5,857	5,770	5,796	5,534	5,677
12	6,073	5,750	5,665	5,616	5,559	5,599	5,555	5,496	5,583	5,442	5,217
Ungraded Elementary and Secondary	246	330	210	310	507	938	1,005	1,038	916	1,238	493
TOTAL	142,619	137,852	136,792	135,033	133,419	133,066	130,800	126,812	125,372	124,668	122,949

*Major changes were implemented for data collection in 2004-05. Data from 2004-05 is not comprehensive.

Sources: Wisconsin Department of Public Instruction, *Basic Facts About Wisconsin Elementary and Secondary Schools, 2003-2004,* and previous issues; departmental data, April 2005; 2004-05 to 2012-13 Public School Enrollment Data, at: http://lbstat.dpi.wi.gov/lbstat_pubdata3 [February 2013]; Non-Public (Private) School Enrollment Data, at: http://lbstat.dpi.wi.gov/lbstat_privdata [March 2013].

WISCONSIN PUBLIC HIGH SCHOOL COMPLETION RATES
By CESA District and Race, 2010-11

						Student Detail by Race					
						Am. Indian/	Asian/				Combined/
		Total Students and Rates				Alaskan	Pacific		Hispanic/		Small
CESA	Total[1]	Rate	Female	Rate	Male	Rate	Native	Islander	Black	Latino	White	Groups[2]
1	15,559	80.1	7,923	83.4	7,636	77.0	9	501	3,001	1,632	9,379	380
2	8,811	88.1	4,432	90.8	4,379	85.6	0	189	383	479	6,646	846
3	1,612	96.1	805	97.1	807	95.1	0	0	0	0	501	1,111
4	2,281	93.6	1,128	93.2	1,153	93.9	6	108	13	9	969	967
5	2,922	92.2	1,399	92.6	1,523	91.7	16	37	6	72	2,562	925
6	6,885	91.8	3,383	93.9	3,502	89.8	0	228	49	135	5,331	1,048
7	4,846	91.6	2,448	93.8	2,398	89.5	40	71	30	209	3,310	1,230
8	1,609	91.2	833	93.0	776	89.3	41	0	0	7	873	696
9	1,677	92.3	821	93.4	856	91.3	38	210	13	0	1,072	543
10.	2,448	89.5	1,254	91.1	1,194	87.9	0	10	18	12	1,481	963
11.	3,357	90.9	1,631	91.2	1,726	90.5	4	0	20	18	1,705	1,295
12.	926	90.2	439	92.8	487	87.9	78	0	0	0	669	293
TOTAL.	61,653	87.6	30,820	89.8	30,833	85.5	746	2,272	4,443	3,449	50,151	—

Notes: Percent completion calculated by number of combined completions (diplomas, HSED, certificate) divided by number of students expected to complete high school. Rates calculated by the Wisconsin Legislative Reference Bureau. Students identified by two or more races: CESA 1 – 70; 2 – 112; 3 – 0; 4 – 6; 5 – 18; 6 – 0; 7 – 8; 8 – 0; 9 – 0; 10 – 5; 11 – 30; 12 – 0; total – 592. This table is based on 4-year adjusted cohort completion rates, as required by federal law, and may not be comparable to tables in prior Blue Books.

[1]Includes students who have earned certificates, HSED, and regular diplomas. Details may not sum to total because of privacy rules on identifying small groups.

[2]This group includes members of racial and ethnic and/or gender groups not identified as such because of privacy rules.

Source: Wisconsin Department of Public Instruction's WINSS Web site, at: http://data.dpi.state.wi.us/data/.

WISCONSIN CHARTER SCHOOL ENROLLMENTS
By CESA District and Race, 2012-13

					Asian/			
		Total Students		American	Pacific			
CESA	Total	Female	Male	Indian	Islander	Black	Hispanic	White
1	24,104	12,123	11,981	105	1,569	10,159	5,345	6,578
2	4,538	2,263	2,275	51	126	380	760	3,060
3	373	176	197	0	1	2	6	353
4	992	482	510	9	39	18	47	841
5	2,115	1,021	1,094	20	61	34	102	1,863
6	5,471	2,760	2,711	37	338	140	303	4,575
7	1,913	969	944	11	182	65	240	1,365
8	326	168	158	31	1	1	8	279
9	1,299	591	708	11	15	16	25	1,197
10.	573	253	320	9	9	17	16	492
11.	1,469	753	716	19	18	42	48	1,317
12.	356	176	180	56	6	3	1	281
TOTAL. . . .	43,529	21,735	21,794	359	2,365	10,877	6,901	22,201

Note: Students identified by two or more races: CESA 1 – 348; 2 – 161; 3 – 11; 4 – 38; 5 – 35; 6 – 78; 7 – 50; 8 – 6; 9 – 35; 10 – 30; 11 – 25; 12 – 9; total – 826.

Sources: Wisconsin Department of Public Instructions's WINSS site, at: http://data.dpi.state.wi.us/data/, and departmental data [March 2013].

Wisconsin Cooperative Educational Service Agency (CESA) Districts

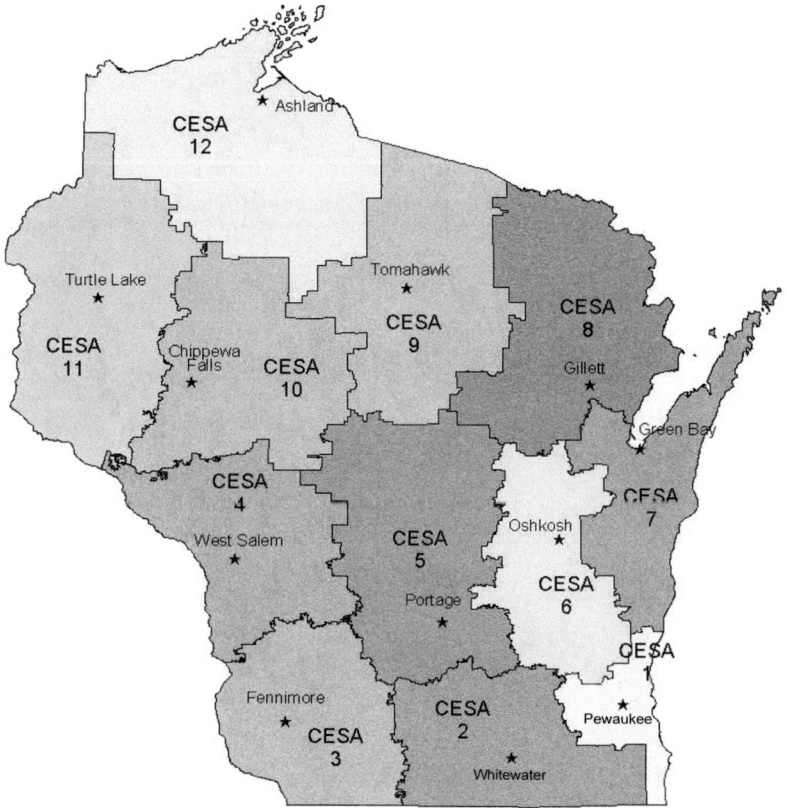

Source: Wisconsin Department of Public Instruction.

WISCONSIN PUBLIC SCHOOL SALARIES
Instructional Staff Employment and Average Salaries 2008-09 to 2012-13

| | | | Instructional Staff | | | |
| | | Avg. Salary | | Non- | | Avg. Salary |
Year	Total	of Total	Principals	supervisory	Teachers	of Teachers
2008-09	65,459	$55,633	2,495	3,509	59,455	$51,121
2009-10	64,903	55,193	2,478	3,576	58,849	51,264
2010-11	63,948	58,159	2,434	3,473	58,041	54,195
2011-12	61,850	57,649	2,383	3,287	56,180	53,792
2012-13	62,698	58,999	2,467	3,431	56,800	55,171

Detail: Elementary and Secondary Teachers 2008-09 to 2012-13

| | Elementary | | | Secondary | | |
| | | | Avg. | | | Avg. |
Year	Men	Women	Salary	Men	Women	Salary
2008-09	7,287	33,518	$51,173	8,593	10,057	$51,008
2009-10	7,213	33,176	51,240	8,505	9,954	51,317
2010-11	7,232	33,571	53,750	7,849	9,389	55,248
2011-12	7,054	32,564	53,551	7,484	9,078	54,369
2012-13	7,132	32,923	55,171	7,567	9,178	55,171

Sources: National Education Association, *Rankings of the States 2012 and Estimates of School Statistics 2013*, at: www.nea.org/home/44479.htm, December 2012, and previous issues.

AVERAGE SALARIES OF PUBLIC SCHOOL TEACHERS
By State, 2011-12

| | Average | State | | Average | State |
State	Salary	Rank	State	Salary	Rank
Alabama	$48,003	37	Montana	$48,546*	33
Alaska	62,425	8	Nebraska	48,154	36
Arizona.	48,691*	31	Nevada	54,559*	18
Arkansas	46,314	44	New Hampshire	54,177*	19
California	68,531	5	New Jersey	67,078	6
Colorado	49,049	29	New Mexico	45,622	47
Connecticut	69,465	3	New York	73,398	1
Delaware	58,800*	12	North Carolina	45,947	46
District of Columbia	68,720*	4	North Dakota.	46,058	45
Florida	46,479	42	Ohio	56,715	16
Georgia.	52,938	22	Oklahoma	44,391	49
Hawaii	54,070	20	Oregon	57,348	14
Idaho	48,551*	32	Pennsylvania	61,934	10
ILLINOIS	57,636	13	Rhode Island	62,186*	9
Indiana	50,516	25	South Carolina	47,428	38
IOWA	50,240	26	South Dakota.	38,804	51
Kansas	46,718	41	Tennessee	47,082	40
Kentucky.	49,730	28	Texas	48,373	34
Louisiana.	50,179*	27	Utah	48,159*	35
Maine	47,338	39	Vermont	51,306*	24
Maryland.	63,634	7	Virginia.	48,703*	30
Massachusetts	71,721	2	Washington.	52,232	23
MICHIGAN	61,560	11	West Virginia.	45,320*	48
MINNESOTA	54,959*	17	**WISCONSIN**	53,792	21
Mississippi	41,646*	50	Wyoming.	57,222	15
Missouri	46,406*	43	UNITED STATES	$55,418*	

*Data estimated.

Source: National Education Association, *Rankings and Estimates: Rankings of the States 2012 and Estimates of School Statistics 2013,* at: www.nea.org/home/44479.htm, December 2012.

STATE AND LOCAL EDUCATION PAYROLLS
Instructional Employees, By State, March 2011

| | Kindergarten-12 | | | | Higher Education | | | |
| | FTE Employees* | | Payroll | | FTE Employees* | | Payroll | |
State	Number	Rank	(in thousands)	Rank	Number	Rank	(in thousands)	Rank
Alabama	70,369	26	$254,182	26	12,085	23	$78,970	21
Alaska	13,503	47	65,886	44	1,667	49	12,327	46
Arizona.	72,629	22	255,630	25	14,485	18	90,897	19
Arkansas	55,622	30	186,050	32	8,112	33	52,234	32
California	415,060	2	2,350,957	1	63,193	1	518,874	1
Colorado	70,875	25	290,158	22	15,304	16	100,225	17
Connecticut	67,094	27	357,501	19	6,787	34	46,885	34
Delaware	11,355	50	54,213	48	2,756	42	17,631	42
District of Columbia	6,809	51	38,484	51	365	51	2,116	51
Florida	245,953	4	857,538	7	31,957	4	206,055	4
Georgia.	161,676	8	641,114	9	18,754	12	114,451	14
Hawaii	19,711	42	82,984	41	3,859	38	25,080	38
Idaho	22,962	41	75,244	43	3,525	39	18,533	40
ILLINOIS	189,632	5	945,751	5	30,745	5	180,490	6
Indiana	89,022	17	365,180	17	24,079	8	121,121	12
IOWA	50,146	32	196,555	31	10,356	27	68,556	24
Kansas	63,784	29	218,611	28	9,799	29	61,096	30
Kentucky.	72,541	23	249,105	27	12,475	22	74,711	23
Louisiana.	73,958	21	271,515	23	10,270	28	65,134	25
Maine	29,194	38	80,812	42	2,504	44	13,684	45
Maryland.	93,691	15	516,844	14	15,539	15	104,092	16
Massachusetts	112,892	13	563,426	12	10,491	26	61,458	29
MICHIGAN	120,057	12	605,167	10	28,772	7	208,851	3
MINNESOTA	81,480	19	364,024	18	14,880	17	92,389	18
Mississippi	51,141	31	163,058	33	9,609	30	52,030	33
Missouri	90,910	16	341,150	20	13,396	21	75,340	22
Montana	16,572	43	60,657	45	2,040	47	11,529	48
Nebraska	36,658	35	141,107	34	4,725	36	28,591	36
Nevada	33,910	37	140,506	35	2,876	41	21,287	39
New Hampshire	28,860	39	106,872	39	2,438	45	16,468	43
New Jersey.	161,271	9	970,430	4	14,339	19	128,714	11
New Mexico	35,786	36	126,225	37	5,540	35	26,838	37
New York	341,851	3	1,931,782	2	28,778	6	203,421	5
North Carolina	155,340	10	543,010	13	32,345	3	167,608	8
North Dakota.	12,451	49	46,978	49	2,900	40	17,898	41
Ohio	162,901	7	747,825	8	23,894	9	155,163	9
Oklahoma	64,379	28	205,788	29	8,763	32	54,024	31
Oregon	48,196	33	200,347	30	14,137	20	88,590	20
Pennsylvania.	181,226	6	865,826	6	22,127	10	175,490	7
Rhode Island	15,964	44	88,943	40	2,525	43	15,511	44
South Carolina	71,891	24	264,132	24	10,753	25	62,466	28
South Dakota.	14,882	46	46,584	50	2,123	46	12,326	47
Tennessee	94,074	14	329,245	21	11,984	24	62,891	27
Texas	484,096	1	1,843,586	3	55,450	2	393,512	2
Utah	40,005	34	133,888	36	9,540	31	63,378	26
Vermont	15,732	45	56,710	47	1,416	50	10,881	50
Virginia.	135,835	11	564,096	11	19,586	11	141,644	10
Washington.	75,065	20	390,144	15	16,072	14	118,684	13
West Virginia.	28,221	40	108,009	38	4,719	37	29,355	35
WISCONSIN	88,156	18	379,893	16	17,967	13	108,534	15
Wyoming.	13,442	48	58,023	46	1,953	48	11,182	49
UNITED STATES	4,708,795		$20,741,744		694,752		$4,589,214	

Note: State payroll detail may not sum to U.S. total due to rounding.

*FTE = Full-time equivalent employees.

Source: U.S. Department of Commerce, Bureau of the Census, "Government Employment and Payroll", at:
http://www.census.gov/govs/apes [January 2013]. Rank calculated by Wisconsin Legislative Reference Bureau.

EXPENDITURES PER PUPIL
By State and Source
2006-07 – 2009-10

State	Expenditures per Pupil				2009-10 State Rank	Revenue Sources for 2009-10 Pupil Expenditure		
	2006-07	2007-08	2008-09	2009-10		Federal	State	Local
Alabama	$8,398	$9,197	$8,964	$8,907	40	16.1%	52.5%	31.4%
Alaska	12,324	14,641	15,363	15,829	4	15.8	62.5	21.7
Arizona.	7,338	7,727	8,022[2]	7,968[2]	47	18.8	38.7	42.5
Arkansas	8,391	8,677	8,854[2]	9,281[2]	34	15.9	52.1	32.1
California	8,952[1]	9,706[1,2]	9,503[2]	9,300[2]	33	13.8	54.2	32.0
Colorado	8,286	9,152	8,782	8,926	39	8.3	43.6	48.1
Connecticut	13,659	14,610[2]	15,353[2]	15,698[2]	5	8.6	35.0	56.4
Delaware	11,760	12,153	12,109	12,222	13	12.2	58.6	29.1
District of Columbia . . .	15,511	16,353[2]	19,698	20,910	—	9.1	—	90.9
Florida	8,567	9,084[2]	8,867[2]	8,863[2]	41	16.1	31.5	52.3
Georgia.	9,102	9,718	9,649[2]	9,432[2]	32	14.8	37.9	47.2
Hawaii	11,060	11,800	12,400	11,714	16	14.9	81.6	3.5
Idaho	6,648	6,951[2]	7,118[2]	7,100[2]	49	20.8	57.8	21.4
ILLINOIS	9,596	10,353[2]	11,097[2]	11,739[2]	14	12.4	28.4	59.2
Indiana	9,080	8,867[2]	9,254[2]	9,479[2]	31	11.1	47.2	41.7
IOWA	8,791	9,520	9,704	9,748	27	13.4	40.0	46.6
Kansas	9,243	9,883	10,204	9,972	26	11.7	52.7	35.6
Kentucky.	7,940[1]	8,740	8,786	8,957	38	16.6	52.1	31.3
Louisiana.	8,937	10,006[2]	10,625[2]	10,701[2]	20	19.1	43.0	37.9
Maine	11,644	11,761	12,183[2]	12,452[2]	12	11.9	40.9	47.2
Maryland.	11,975	13,235[2]	13,737[2]	14,007[2]	9	7.8	41.5	50.7
Massachusetts	12,857	13,667	14,534[2]	14,699[2]	8	7.5	41.6	50.9
MICHIGAN	9,922	10,075	10,373	10,447	25	13.3	54.2	32.5
MINNESOTA	9,589	10,048[2]	10,983[2]	10,665[2]	21	12.5	59.3	28.2
Mississippi.	7,459	7,890[2]	8,064[2]	8,104[2]	46	21.3	47.5	31.2
Missouri	8,848	9,532	9,617[2]	9,721[2]	28	14.9	29.3	55.8
Montana	9,191	9,786	10,120	10,565	23	16.0	46.6	37.3
Nebraska	10,068	10,565	10,846	11,460	17	12.7	33.0	54.3
Nevada	7,806	8,187	8,321	8,376	43	8.5	32.6	58.8
New Hampshire	11,037	11,951	12,583	13,072	10	12.5	32.1	55.4
New Jersey.	16,163	17,620[2]	16,973	17,379	2	9.4	36.4	54.2
New Mexico	8,849	9,291	9,648	9,621	29	21.0	63.4	15.6
New York	15,546	16,794[2]	17,746[2]	18,167[2]	1	9.0	41.0	50.0
North Carolina	7,878	7,798[2]	8,463	8,225	44	15.3	58.2	26.5
North Dakota.	8,671	9,324	9,802	10,519	24	22.1	44.0	33.9
Ohio	9,940	10,340	10,669	11,224	19	10.8	44.1	45.1
Oklahoma	7,430	7,683	7,878	7,929	48	17.2	47.8	35.0
Oregon	8,958	9,565	9,611	9,268	35	13.2	47.4	39.4
Pennsylvania.	10,905	11,741	12,299	12,729	11	10.9	35.8	53.3
Rhode Island	13,453	14,459	14,719[2]	14,723[2]	7	11.5	34.9	53.6
South Carolina	8,566	9,060	9,228	9,080	36	13.9	43.8	42.3
South Dakota.	8,064	8,535	8,543	9,020	37	19.5	31.1	49.4
Tennessee	7,129[2]	7,820[2]	7,992	8,117	45	13.6	45.1	41.4
Texas	7,850	8,350[2]	8,562	8,788	42	15.6	39.4	45.0
Utah	5,706	5,978	6,612	6,452	50	12.6	51.2	36.3
Vermont	13,629	14,421	15,096	16,006	3	10.6	81.6	7.8
Virginia.	10,214	10,664	10,928	10,594	22	10.4	37.3	52.3
Washington.	8,524[2]	9,058[2]	9,585[2]	9,497[2]	30	11.9	58.7	29.5
West Virginia.	9,727	10,059[2]	10,606[2]	11,730[2]	15	15.6	55.4	29.0
WISCONSIN	10,367	10,791	11,183	11,453	18	10.5	44.8	44.7
Wyoming.	13,266	13,856	14,628	15,232	6	7.3	51.6	41.2
UNITED STATES . .	$9,683[1,2]	$10,297[1,2]	$10,540[2]	$10,652[2]		12.7%	43.5%	43.8%

[1]Prekindergarten students imputed, affecting total student count and per pupil expenditure calculation.

[2]Value affected by redistribution of reported expenditure values to correct for missing data items, and/or to distribute state direct support expenditures.

Source: U.S. Department of Education, Institute of Education Sciences, National Center for Education Statistics, *Revenues and Expenditures for Public Elementary and Secondary Education: School Year 2009-10 (Fiscal Year 2010),* November 2012, and previous NCES publications. Rank calculated by Wisconsin Legislative Reference Bureau. Detail may not add to total due to rounding.

STATE AND LOCAL PER CAPITA EDUCATION EXPENDITURES
By State, Fiscal Year 2009-10

State	All Education Amount	All Education Rank	Elementary and Secondary Amount	Elementary and Secondary Rank	Higher Education Amount	Higher Education Rank	Other Education* Amount	Other Education* Rank
Alabama	$2,762	25	$1,609	37	$993	12	$161	17
Alaska	4,501	1	3,323	2	1,018	10	160	18
Arizona.	2,095	48	1,299	50	687	36	108	39†
Arkansas	2,716	29†	1,787	27	789	31	140	25†
California	2,745	26	1,749	30	866	20	130	30
Colorado	2,611	37	1,664	34	857	22	90	47
Connecticut	3,161	10	2,326	7	676	37	159	19
Delaware	3,330	7	1,927	16†	1,141	4	262	2
District of Columbia	3,934	3	3,677	1	258	51	–	–
Florida	2,034	50	1,409	48	484	50	141	24
Georgia.	2,570	40	1,802	26	564	46	204	9†
Hawaii	2,387	45	1,536	41	800	30	51	50
Idaho	2,100	47	1,293	51	702	33	105	43
ILLINOIS	2,706	32	1,908	18	674	38	125	34
Indiana	2,550	41	1,558	40	839	24	153	22
IOWA	3,042	13	1,846	23	1,063	7	133	28
Kansas	2,989	14	1,943	13	952	15	94	46
Kentucky.	2,587	38	1,518	42	859	21	209	7
Louisiana.	2,651	35	1,767	29	697	34	187	12
Maine	2,581	39	1,852	22	563	47	166	15†
Maryland.	3,140	11	2,098	8	926	18	117	36
Massachusetts	2,764	23	1,971	12	635	41	158	20
MICHIGAN	2,944	17	1,815	24	1,022	8†	107	41†
MINNESOTA	2,887	19	1,868	20	824	27	195	11
Mississippi.	2,524	42	1,493	44	903	19	128	31†
Missouri	2,365	46	1,627	35	616	43	122	35
Montana	2,612	36	1,626	36	820	28	166	15†
Nebraska	3,128	12	1,983	11	1,009	11	136	27
Nevada	2,054	49	1,479	45	485	49	89	48
New Hampshire	2,716	29†	1,991	10	613	44	112	38
New Jersey.	3,610	6	2,809	5	629	42	171	13
New Mexico	3,162	9	1,814	25	1,180	3	168	14
New York	3,654	5	2,877	4	669	39†	108	39†
North Carolina	2,480	44	1,456	46	927	17	97	45
North Dakota.	3,203	8	1,769	28	1,285	1	149	23
Ohio	2,844	21	1,892	19	712	32	240	5
Oklahoma	2,720	28	1,592	38	988	14	140	25†
Oregon	2,716	29†	1,588	39	1,022	8†	107	41†
Pennsylvania.	2,763	24	1,936	14	669	39†	157	21
Rhode Island.	2,876	20	2,076	9	574	45	225	6
South Carolina	2,653	34	1,710	32	694	35	250	4
South Dakota.	2,481	43	1,516	43	834	25	131	29
Tennessee	2,010	51	1,358	49	526	48	126	33
Texas	2,954	15	1,927	16†	940	16	86	49
Utah	2,657	33	1,438	47	1,106	6	113	37
Vermont	3,748	4	2,353	6	1,139	5	255	3
Virginia.	2,907	18	1,933	15	845	23	128	31†
Washington.	2,722	27	1,685	33	829	26	207	8
West Virginia.	2,838	22	1,732	31	816	29	289	1
WISCONSIN	2,952	16	1,861	21	991	13	100	44
Wyoming.	4,369	2	2,980	3	1,185	2	204	9†
UNITED STATES . . .	$2,780		$1,856		$785		$140	

Note: Per capita amounts are based on population figures as of July 2010.

*Includes assistance and subsidies to individuals and private elementary and secondary schools, and colleges and universities, as well as miscellaneous education expenditures.

†Tied.

Source: U.S. Department of Education, Institute of Education Sciences, National Center for Education Statistics, *Digest of Education Statistics 2012* [March 2013], at: http://nces.ed.gov/programs/digest/d12/tables/dt12_032.asp. Rank calculated by Wisconsin Legislative Reference Bureau. Detail may not add to total due to rounding.

EDUCATION EXPENDITURES
BY STATE AND LOCAL GOVERNMENTS
By State, Fiscal Year 2009-10
(In Millions)

State	Total Expenditures[1]	Higher Education	Elem. & Secondary Schools	State	Total Expenditures[1]	Higher Education	Elem. & Secondary Schools
Alabama – State	$5,521	$4,751	—	Montana – State	$933	$769	—
Local	7,697	—	$7,697	Local	1,655	44	$1,611
Alaska – State	1,300	714	472	Nebraska – State	1,786	1,537	—
Local	1,914	13	1,901	Local	3,939	310	3,629
Arizona – State	3,740	3,046	—	Nevada – State	1,554	1,312	—
Local	9,695	1,362	8,333	Local	4,000	—	4,000
Arkansas – State	2,714	2,305	—	New Hampshire – State	955	808	—
Local	5,221	—	5,221	Local	2,622	—	2,622
California – State	27,596	22,419	334	New Jersey – State	8,380	4,108	2,765
Local	74,904	9,923	64,981	Local	23,387	1,431	21,956
Colorado – State	4,670	4,215	—	New Mexico – State	2,437	2,089	—
Local	8,511	111	8,401	Local	4,096	348	3,748
Connecticut – State	2,991	2,418	5	New York – State	11,883	9,794	—
Local	8,311	—	8,311	Local	58,988	3,180	55,807
Delaware – State	1,323	1,027	61	North Carolina – State	8,209	6,968	311
Local	1,673	—	1,673	Local	15,500	1,891	13,610
Florida – State	8,784	6,137	—	North Dakota – State	968	867	—
Local	29,530	2,989	26,541	Local	1,193	—	1,193
Georgia – State	7,425	5,443	—	Ohio – State	10,353	7,586	—
Local	17,538	33	17,505	Local	22,459	629	21,830
Hawaii – State	3,254	1,091	2,094	Oklahoma – State	4,248	3,715	7
Local	0+	—	0+	Local	5,979	—	5,979
Idaho – State	1,087	922	—	Oregon – State	3,300	2,890	—
Local	2,212	180	2,032	Local	7,126	1,033	6,094
ILLINOIS – State	7,601	5,995	—	Pennsylvania – State	9,406	7,406	—
Local	27,155	2,656	24,499	Local	25,731	1,106	24,625
Indiana – State	6,436	5,445	—	Rhode Island – State	894	604	53
Local	10,115	1	10,115	Local	2,132	—	2,132
IOWA – State	2,837	2,430	—	South Carolina – State	4,594	3,216	219
Local	6,442	812	5,630	Local	7,708	—	7,708
Kansas – State	2,243	1,974	—	South Dakota – State	708	601	—
Local	6,301	747	5,554	Local	1,318	80	1,238
Kentucky – State	5,220	3,734	575	Tennessee – State	4,145	3,342	—
Local	6,025	—	6,025	Local	8,632	—	8,632
Louisiana – State	4,416	3,169	399	Texas – State	21,893	19,195	514
Local	7,633	—	7,633	Local	52,709	4,555	48,154
Maine – State	980	748	12	Utah – State	3,383	3,071	—
Local	2,446	—	2,446	Local	3,991	—	3,991
Maryland – State	4,812	4,136	0+	Vermont – State	873	713	—
Local	13,356	1,220	12,136	Local	1,473	—	1,473
Massachusetts – State	5,171	4,127	10	Virginia – State	7,652	6,624	—
Local	12,949	39	12,910	Local	15,670	156	15,514
MICHIGAN – State	9,503	8,388	62	Washington – State	6,990	5,592	—
Local	19,571	1,709	17,862	Local	11,362	—	11,362
MINNESOTA – State	5,410	4,375	—	West Virginia – State	2,050	1,514	—
Local	9,920	—	9,920	Local	3,213	—	3,213
Mississippi – State	2,371	1,990	—	WISCONSIN – State	4,896	4,325	—
Local	5,126	693	4,433	Local	11,907	1,316	10,591
Missouri – State	3,621	2,887	0+	Wyoming – State	546	431	0+
Local	10,561	804	9,757	Local	1,921	238	1,682
				U.S. TOTAL – State	$254,063	$202,964	$7,892
				Local[2]	$605,902	$39,765	$566,137

Note: State payments to local governments for education aids appear as local government expenditures.

[1]"Total expenditures" includes "other education" expenditures not reported separately here. Figures may not add to total due to rounding by Wisconsin Legislative Reference Bureau.

[2]Includes District of Columbia expenditures: Total = $2,380; Higher Ed. = $156; Elem & Sec. = $2,224 (in millions).

Source: U.S. Department of Commerce, Bureau of the Census, "State and Local Government Finances by Level of Government and by State: 2009-2010", at: http://www.census.gov/govs/estimate/ [September 2012].

STATE AND LOCAL EXPENDITURES FOR PUBLIC EDUCATION IN WISCONSIN
2007-08 – 2011-12
(In Millions)

Agency/Program	2007-08	2008-09	2009-10	2010-11	2011-12
Public elementary and secondary schools[1]	$10,265.1	$10,623.3	$10,833.7	$11,161.9	$10,584.9
Department of Public Instruction	95.6	96.9	97.7	100.5	99.5
University of Wisconsin System	4,438.1	4,488.0	4,643.4	5,546.7	5,556.4
Wisconsin Technical College System Board	175.2	176.0	176.8	178.3	138.8
Public libraries (local expenditures)[2]	216.0	224.5	231.5	233.9	236.7
Other:					
Arts Board (Department of Tourism)	4.0	3.9	4.2	4.9	0
Educational Communications Board	16.0	16.1	15.0	14.9	15.3
Higher Educational Aids Board	120.7	132.9	123.5	148.7	136.8
Medical College of Wisconsin, Inc. (state funding)	6.6	6.8	6.1	6.1	5.7
State Historical Society	20.0	20.7	19.5	20.2	19.6
TOTAL	$15,357.3	$15,789.1	$16,151.4	$17,416.1	$16,793.7
Per capita expenditures[3]	$2,719	$2,782	$2,840	$3,062	$2,949

[1]Includes the gross costs of general operations, special projects, debt service, and food service; the net cost of capital projects; and the costs of CESA and County Children with Disabilities Education Board operations.

[2]Expenditures are for calendar year ending in the fiscal year shown.

[3]Based on total state population. Wisconsin Census total for 2010: 5,686,986; population estimate for January 1, 2011: 5,694,236.

Sources: Wisconsin Department of Administration, *Annual Fiscal Report, Appendix (Budgetary Basis) 2011-12*, 2012 and previous issues; Wisconsin Department of Administration, Demographic Services Center, *Time Series of the Final Official Population Estimates and Census Counts for Wisconsin Counties* [June 2013]; Wisconsin Department of Public Instruction, Library Service Data, 2011 and previous data; Wisconsin Department of Public Instruction, departmental data. Per capita data calculated by Wisconsin Legislative Reference Bureau.

WISCONSIN HOME-BASED PRIVATE EDUCATIONAL PROGRAMS
2003-04 to 2012-13 Enrollments

Grade Level	2003-04	2004-05	2005-06	2006-07	2007-08	2008-09	2009-10	2010-11	2011-12	2012-13
1	1,403	1,423	1,428	1,375	1,356	1,357	1,409	1,127	1,136	1,086
2	1,377	1,415	1,368	1,352	1,317	1,317	1,335	1,164	1,142	983
3	1,522	1,402	1,338	1,350	1,376	1,350	1,322	1,179	1,076	1,033
4	1,453	1,476	1,369	1,389	1,349	1,385	1,365	1,098	1,137	992
5	1,427	1,446	1,417	1,320	1,383	1,334	1,326	1,155	1,050	1,039
6	1,457	1,360	1,430	1,447	1,332	1,412	1,343	1,189	1,078	1,002
7	1,487	1,482	1,387	1,376	1,424	1,286	1,367	1,160	1,070	994
8	1,512	1,475	1,427	1,393	1,314	1,390	1,232	1,149	1,027	916
9	1,488	1,516	1,428	1,422	1,273	1,259	1,316	1,042	1,038	862
10	1,616	1,446	1,507	1,538	1,375	1,300	1,183	1,144	917	895
11	1,592	1,551	1,370	1,453	1,397	1,246	1,184	1,064	1,004	725
12	1,241	1,233	1,212	1,036	1,134	1,076	967	891	703	719
Ungraded	3,459	3,518	3,642	3,706	3,695	3,646	3,700	6,214	5,901	5,733
TOTAL	21,034	20,743	20,323	20,157	19,725	19,358	19,049	19,576	18,279	16,979

Note: A home-based private educational program is a program of educational instruction provided to a child by a child's parent or guardian or by a person designated by the parent or guardian. These programs must provide at least 875 hours of instruction each school year and must offer a sequentially progressive curriculum of fundamental instruction in reading, language arts, mathematics, social studies, science, and health.

Source: Wisconsin Department of Public Instruction, "Home-Based Private Educational Program Enrollment Trends: Enrollment by Grade," at: http://sms.dpi.wi.gov/sms_hbstats [February 2013].

WISCONSIN STATE DOCUMENT DEPOSITORY LIBRARIES

Depository libraries collect publications issued by the federal government and Wisconsin state agencies through the Department of Public Instruction's document depository program. State depository libraries are designated to receive copies of all collected publications. Regional depository libraries receive approximately three-quarters of all collected publications, and selective depository libraries receive two-thirds.

City	Library	Internet Address
STATE LEVEL DEPOSITORY		
Madison	Legislative Reference Bureau	www.legis.wi.gov/lrb
Madison	State Historical Society of Wisconsin	www.wisconsinhistory.org
Madison	Resources for Libraries and Lifelong Learning, Department of Public Instruction	rl3.dpi.wi.gov
REGIONAL DEPOSITORY		
Appleton	Appleton Public Library	www.apl.org
Eau Claire	McIntyre Library, UW-Eau Claire	www.uwec.edu/library
Green Bay	Cofrin Library, UW-Green Bay	www.uwgb.edu/library
La Crosse	La Crosse Public Library	www.lacrosselibrary.org
Milwaukee	Milwaukee Public Library	www.mpl.org
Platteville	Karrmann Library, UW-Platteville	www.uwplatt.edu/library
Racine	Racine Public Library	www.racinelibrary.info
River Falls	Chalmer Davee Library, UW-River Falls	www.uwrf.edu/library
Stevens Point. . .	UW-Stevens Point Library	www.uwsp.edu/library
Superior	Superior Public Library	superiorlibrary.org
SELECTIVE DEPOSITORY		
Appleton	Seeley G. Mudd Library, Lawrence University	www.lawrence.edu/library
Beloit.	Morse Library, Beloit College	www.beloit.edu/library
Eau Claire	L.E. Phillips Memorial Public Library	www.ecpubliclibrary.info
Fond du Lac . . .	Fond du Lac Public Library	www.fdlpl.org
Green Bay	Brown County Library	www.co.brown.wi.us/library
Hayward	Lac Courte Oreilles Ojibwa College Community Library	www.lco.edu/dept/libcul
Janesville.	Gary J. Lenox Library, UW-Rock County	rock.uwc.edu/library-technology
Kenosha	UW-Parkside Library	www.uwp.edu/departments/library
La Crosse	Murphy Library, UW-La Crosse	www.uwlax.edu/murphylibrary
Madison	Madison Public Library	www.madisonpubliclibrary.org
Manitowoc. . . .	Manitowoc Public Library	www.manitowoclibrary.org
Marshfield	UW-Marshfield/Wood County Library	www.marshfield.uwc.edu/library
Menomonie . . .	UW-Stout Library	www.uwstout.edu/lib
Milwaukee	Golda Meir Library, UW-Milwaukee	www.uwm.edu/library
Oshkosh	Polk Library, UW-Oshkosh	www.uwosh.edu/library
Oshkosh	Oshkosh Public Library	www.oshkoshpubliclibrary.org
Portage.	Portage Public Library	www.scls.lib.wi.us/por
Rhinelander . . .	Richard J. Brown Library, Nicolet Area Technical College	library.nicoletcollege.edu
Ripon.	Lane Library, Ripon College	www.ripon.edu/library
Shawano	Shawano City-County Library	www.shawanolibrary.org
Superior	Jim Dan Hill Library, UW-Superior	www.uwsuper.edu/library
Two Rivers. . . .	Lester Public Library	www.lesterlibrary.org
Waukesha	UW-Waukesha County Library	waukesha.uwc.edu/library
Waukesha	Waukesha Public Library	www.waukesha.lib.wi.us
Wauwatosa. . . .	Wauwatosa Public Library	wauwatosalibrary.org
West Bend	UW-Washington County Library	washington.uwc.edu/library
Whitewater. . . .	Andersen Library, UW-Whitewater	library.uww.edu
Wisconsin Rapids	McMillan Memorial Library	www.mcmillanlibrary.org

Source: Wisconsin Department of Public Instruction, Resources for Libraries and Lifelong Learning, *Wisconsin Document Depository Program State Depository Libraries,* at: http://rl3.dpi.wi.gov/svc_depository_liblist [December 6, 2012].

WISCONSIN PUBLIC LIBRARY SYSTEMS, 2011

Library System	Resource Library	Address	Counties or Cities Served	2011 Total Service Population	Circulation	State Aid for 2011
Arrowhead	Hedberg Public Library (608) 758-6600	316 S. Main Street Janesville, WI 53545-3971	Rock	160,298	2,078,840	$490,327
Eastern Shores	Mead Public Library (920) 459-3400 Ext. 3414	710 N. 8th Street Sheboygan, WI 53081-4563	Ozaukee, Sheboygan	201,913	2,607,374	631,058
Indianhead Federated	L.E. Phillips Memorial Public Library (715) 839-5001	400 Eau Claire Street Eau Claire, WI 54701-3799	Barron, Chippewa, Dunn, Eau Claire, Pepin, Pierce, Polk, Price, Rusk, St. Croix	457,336	5,420,305	1,565,182
Kenosha County	Kenosha Public Library (262) 564-6324	812 56th Street P.O. Box 1414 Kenosha, WI 53141-1414	Kenosha	166,626	1,339,772	468,705
Lakeshores	Racine Public Library (262) 636-9170	75 Seventh Street Racine, WI 53403-1200	Racine, Walworth	286,148	2,429,942	728,057
Manitowoc-Calumet	Manitowoc Public Library (920) 686-3000	707 Quay Street Manitowoc, WI 54220-4539	Calumet, Manitowoc	117,174	1,176,243	392,538
Mid-Wisconsin Federated	West Bend Community Memorial Library (262) 335-5151	630 Poplar Street West Bend, WI 53095-3246	Dodge, Jefferson, Washington City of Whitewater	320,194	3,316,983	1,246,824
Milwaukee County Federated	Milwaukee Public Library (414) 286-3000	814 W. Wisconsin Avenue Milwaukee, WI 53233-2309	Milwaukee	948,458	7,805,626	4,201,906
Nicolet Federated	Brown County Library (920) 448-4400	515 Pine Street Green Bay, WI 54301-5194	Brown, Door, Florence, Kewaunee, Marinette, Menominee, Oconto, Shawano	429,883	4,133,609	1,187,660
Northern Waters Library Service	Superior Public Library (715) 394-8860	1530 Tower Avenue Superior, WI 54880-2563	Ashland, Bayfield, Burnett, Douglas, Iron, Sawyer, Vilas, Washburn	150,496	1,422,966	577,600
Outagamie Waupaca	Appleton Public Library (920) 832-6170	225 N. Oneida Street Appleton, WI 54911-4780	Outagamie, Waupaca	240,051	3,150,488	675,557
South Central	Madison Public Library (608) 266-6363	201 W. Mifflin Street Madison, WI 53703-2597	Adams, Columbia, Dane, Green, Portage, Sauk, Wood	813,488	13,095,009	2,341,961
Southwest Wisconsin	Platteville Public Library (608) 348-7441	65 S. Elm Street Platteville, WI 53818-3139	Crawford, Grant, Iowa, Lafayette, Richland	126,654	1,057,228	404,040
Waukesha County Federated.	Waukesha Public Library (262) 524-3680	321 Wisconsin Avenue Waukesha, WI 53186-4786	Waukesha	390,371	5,107,172	1,065,150
Winding Rivers	La Crosse Public Library (608) 789-7100	800 Main Street La Crosse, WI 54601-4122	Buffalo, Jackson, Juneau, La Crosse, Monroe, Trempealeau, Vernon	279,252	3,122,175	866,558
Winnefox.	Oshkosh Public Library (920) 236-5210	106 Washington Avenue Oshkosh, WI 54901-4985	Fond du Lac, Green Lake, Marquette, Waushara, Winnebago	325,273	4,615,504	1,331,345
Wisconsin Valley Library Service	Marathon County Public Library (715) 261-7200	300 N. First Street Wausau, WI 54403-5405	Clark, Forest, Langlade, Lincoln, Marathon, Oneida, Taylor	280,621	2,697,567	1,112,088
TOTAL				5,694,236	64,576,803	$19,286,556

Sources: Wisconsin Department of Public Instruction, Public Library Statistics, "Statistics at the State and System Level, 2011: 2011 Wisconsin Public Library Service Data", at: http://pld.dpi.wi.gov/pld_dm-lib-stat and *Wisconsin Public Library Directory, 2012*, June 2012, at: http://pld.dpi.wi.gov/files/pld/pdf/wipldir.pdf.

HIGHLIGHTS OF EMPLOYMENT AND INCOME IN WISCONSIN

Labor Force — An average of about 2,840,300 workers were employed in Wisconsin in 2012. Another 211,400 were part of the available workforce but were unemployed, resulting in an average unemployment rate of 6.9% for 2012. Since 1970, Wisconsin's labor force has increased by over 1.1 million workers from 1,941,700 to 3,051,700 in 2012. Based on January figures, the state's highest unemployment rate for that period occurred in 1983 when it reached 11.7%.

Employment by Industry — An average of 2.78 million Wisconsin workers were engaged in nonfarm employment in 2012. The greatest number worked in trade, transportation, and utilities (511,100); and manufacturing (454,900).

Nationally, 129.8 million were employed in nonfarm work in 2010. Trade, transportations, and utilities, with 24.6 million workers; and government, with 22.5 million, were the largest segments.

In March 2011, manufacturing and retail trade together accounted for approximately one-third of the number of employees in Wisconsin. The majority (84.5%) of the 138,045 business establishments in the state had fewer than 20 employees in March 2011. Manufacturing accounted for the greatest number of large-sized firms, 327 out of 1,075 establishments with 250 or more employees.

Income by Industry — Earned income, which consists of wages and salaries, labor income, and proprietor's income, totaled $167.7 billion in Wisconsin in 2012. Service industries provided the greatest percentage of Wisconsin's earned income during that year, about 33.3%, with manufacturing at 19.7%. Government (all levels) and government enterprises were third at 14.1%.

Personal Income — Personal income in Wisconsin totaled $232.1 billion in 2012. Wisconsin's per capita personal income of $40,537 lags behind the national average of $42,693, ranking Wisconsin 26th among the states. Connecticut had the highest per capita personal income ($58,908 in 2012, or about 138% of the national average). Mississippi had the lowest per capita personal income in 2012 at $33,073, about 77.5% of the national average.

Wisconsin's total adjusted gross income (total income reported for tax purposes) in 2011 was about $142 billion, or $47,640 per tax return. Ozaukee County had the highest per return AGI in 2011 at $89,490, followed by Waukesha County at $73,460. St. Croix County is third ($59,350), and Dane County is fourth ($59,040). Rusk County ($30,620), Forest County ($29,210), and Menominee County ($16,130) had the lowest per return adjusted gross incomes.

Unemployment Benefits — In an average month in 2012, Wisconsin reported that 88,900 persons (about 42% of the 211,400 unemployed) received unemployment compensation. Nationally, 3.4 million people, or 27% of the 12.5 million unemployed, received benefits during an average month. The average weekly benefit in Wisconsin was $271.07, less than the national average of $302.67. The highest average weekly benefit of $420.85 was paid in Hawaii, followed by New Jersey ($395.88), and Massachusetts ($391.68). Lowest in the nation were Alabama ($204.31), Louisiana ($198.95), and Mississippi ($192.86).

The following tables present selected data. Consult footnoted sources for more detailed information about employment and income.

EMPLOYMENT IN WISCONSIN, BY INDUSTRY
Annual Average, 2008 – 2012
(In Thousands)

	2008	2009	2010	2011	2012
Civilian Labor Force.	3,087.3	3,100.5	3,062.6	3,063.5	3,051.7
Unemployed	150.6	271.2	255.3	230.7	211.4
Percentage of labor force unemployed . .	4.9%	8.7%	8.3%	7.5%	6.9%
Employed	2,936.7	2,829.3	2,807.3	2,832.8	2,840.3
Total nonfarm	2,878.1	2,752.4	2,735.3	2,758.6	2,784.6
Service providing	2,263.4	2,211.3	2,207.8	2,217.9	2,233.2
Goods producing.	614.7	541.1	527.5	540.7	551.4
Trade, transportation, and utilities	540.7	517.3	508.3	510.6	511.1
Manufacturing	492.9	436.4	430.6	445.0	454.9
Educational and health services	406.6	414.7	418.3	410.8	418.0
Professional and business services. . . .	281.4	258.5	268.0	284.8	289.7
Local government	288.4	290.8	291.8	288.8	286.3
Leisure and hospitality.	259.5	252.7	250.9	252.4	257.4
Financial activities.	164.1	161.2	157.5	160.6	162.6
Other services, except public services . .	139.0	138.1	137.6	137.2	137.5
State government	103.8	99.9	97.6	96.6	95.5
Construction	118.4	101.7	94.0	92.7	93.0
Information	50.2	48.0	46.6	46.8	46.2
Federal government	29.6	30.1	31.2	29.4	29.0
Natural resources and mining	3.4	3.0	2.9	3.0	3.5

Sources: Wisconsin Department of Workforce Development, Bureau of Workforce Information, Labor Market Information,
"Local Area Unemployment Statistics (LAUS) Program Data", 2012 and previous years, at:
http://worknet.wisconsin.gov/worknet/dalaus.aspx?menuselection=da [May 7, 2013],
and "Current Employment Statistics (CES) Program Data", 2012 and previous years, at:
http://worknet.wisconsin.gov/worknet/daces.aspx?menuselection=da [May 7, 2013].

MANUFACTURING EMPLOYMENT IN WISCONSIN
By Industry Group, 2006 – 2011

Industry Group	2006	2007	2008	2009	2010	2011
Food	57,187	60,345	62,590	61,712	62,789	63,000
Fabricated metal products	65,529	70,118	69,673	59,580	58,349	63,015
Machinery	61,331	64,016	63,545	55,865	53,951	57,541
Paper.	32,283	32,302	31,046	28,389	29,590	29,848
Plastics and rubber products	26,305	30,663	29,237	29,292	28,993	29,268
Printing and related support activities	32,925	32,881	30,925	27,578	25,691	26,401
Transportation equipment	33,980	34,159	31,083	23,291	23,354	25,374
Computer and electronic products.	19,785	22,246	22,318	22,872	21,333	21,529
Electrical equipment, appliances, and components . .	25,494	24,594	24,099	20,234	19,444	19,547
Primary metal industries.	20,344	22,417	20,162	15,363	16,657	18,503
Wood products.	28,981	26,833	24,443	17,729	16,848	17,194
Miscellaneous manufacturing	18,063	14,881	14,062	14,136	14,571	14,855
Furniture and related products.	15,891	17,467	16,617	16,136	13,932	13,524
Chemicals	13,125	14,634	14,199	12,993	12,056	12,779
Nonmetallic mineral products	10,593	10,784	9,600	8,211	7,829	7,809
Beverage and tobacco products	2,691	2,599	2,546	2,559	2,704	2,832
Textile products	1,844	1,492	1,286	1,106	1,237	1,184
Leather and allied products	1,418	1,685	1,728	1,518	1,377	1,388
Textile mills	1,481	1,834	1,680	1,068	1,095	1,104
Apparel.	1,369	1,074	—*	—*	—*	—*
TOTAL.	471,262	487,573	472,422	420,890	413,190	427,906

*Industries with fewer than 950 employees not individually reported after 2007.
Source: U.S. Census Bureau, "2011 Annual Survey of Manufactures, Geographic Area Statistics" and prior years.

EMPLOYMENT TRENDS IN WISCONSIN
January 1990 – January 2013 (In Thousands)

Month and Year	Civilian Labor Force*	Employed	Unemployed	Unemployment Rate	Total Nonfarm Employment	Service Producing	Goods Producing	Manu- facturing	Trade, Trans- portation, and Utilities
Jan. 1990	2,592.8	2,483.8	109.0	4.2%	2,206.7	1,615.2	591.5	513.7	448.0
Jan. 1991	2,625.2	2,486.9	138.3	5.3	2,232.9	1,650.1	582.8	505.9	454.4
Jan. 1992	2,651.7	2,521.4	130.3	4.9	2,269.0	1,684.2	584.8	504.0	456.2
Jan. 1993	2,715.1	2,587.4	127.7	4.7	2,324.9	1,726.8	598.1	513.5	459.8
Jan. 1994	2,803.4	2,674.9	128.5	4.6	2,383.8	1,772.9	610.9	523.1	473.4
Jan. 1995	2,867.6	2,763.6	104.1	3.6	2,476.9	1,828.9	648.0	556.5	489.7
Jan. 1996	2,898.7	2,791.0	107.7	3.7	2,523.8	1,873.7	650.1	555.9	500.2
Jan. 1997	2,942.3	2,837.3	104.9	3.6	2,559.9	1,900.6	659.3	559.9	504.2
Jan. 1998	2,970.9	2,875.1	95.8	3.2	2,625.2	1,941.6	683.6	583.2	512.5
Jan. 1999	2,975.8	2,881.0	94.7	3.2	2,686.4	1,993.0	693.4	586.5	526.7
Jan. 2000	2,987.7	2,897.3	90.3	3.0	2,748.9	2,047.6	701.3	590.2	541.4
Jan. 2001	3,019.4	2,907.2	112.1	3.7	2,770.7	2,081.2	689.5	577.0	549.2
Jan. 2002	3,030.7	2,869.9	160.8	5.3	2,719.4	2,075.9	643.5	531.6	533.0
Jan. 2003	3,041.0	2,873.0	168.0	5.5	2,710.5	2,089.4	621.1	509.3	528.3
Jan. 2004	3,037.8	2,877.2	160.6	5.3	2,718.1	2,111.1	607.0	493.5	529.5
Jan. 2005	3,024.4	2,877.9	146.5	4.8	2,757.2	2,145.2	612.0	496.6	532.0
Jan. 2006	3,060.2	2,915.8	144.4	4.7	2,790.0	2,171.2	618.8	501.1	536.0
Jan. 2007	3,109.6	2,959.9	149.6	4.8	2,814.4	2,200.0	614.4	498.7	541.3
Jan. 2008	3,096.4	2,959.2	137.2	4.4	2,828.3	2,221.5	606.8	495.8	539.9
Jan. 2009	3,107.3	2,884.5	222.7	7.2	2,755.1	2,193.7	561.4	464.9	520.6
Jan. 2010	3,080.5	2,798.0	282.4	9.2	2,658.2	2,153.9	504.3	419.8	501.3
Jan. 2011	3,045.3	2,819.3	226.0	7.4	2,679.5	2,169.4	510.1	432.1	503.5
Jan. 2012	3,060.1	2,845.8	214.2	7.0	2,698.7	2,169.4	529.3	446.7	505.5
Feb. 2012	3,059.0	2,847.3	211.7	6.9	2,713.2	2,186.1	527.1	446.2	498.6
Mar. 2012	3,058.1	2,847.2	210.9	6.9	2,741.7	2,208.7	533.0	448.4	500.7
Apr. 2012	3,056.4	2,844.8	211.6	6.9	2,775.6	2,231.6	544.0	450.4	502.8
May 2012	3,053.9	2,840.5	213.4	7.0	2,809.1	2,257.7	551.4	452.6	510.5
Jun. 2012	3,050.8	2,836.1	214.7	7.0	2,826.3	2,259.6	566.7	462.6	514.1
Jul. 2012	3,048.1	2,833.3	214.8	7.0	2,798.9	2,227.7	571.2	465.7	511.5
Aug. 2012	3,046.4	2,833.3	213.1	7.0	2,804.8	2,233.5	571.3	465.4	513.0
Sept. 2012	3,045.8	2,835.6	210.2	6.9	2,812.3	2,248.8	563.5	459.5	511.9
Oct. 2012	3,046.5	2,838.8	207.7	6.8	2,817.6	2,258.8	558.8	453.9	514.9
Nov. 2012	3,047.3	2,841.6	205.7	6.7	2,816.8	2,262.8	554.0	454.4	525.5
Dec. 2012	3,049.0	2,844.5	204.6	6.7	2,799.7	2,253.7	546.0	453.1	524.2
Jan. 2013	3,050.7	2,838.4	212.2	7.0	2,725.6	2,191.4	534.2	452.3	504.0

Note: Data are estimates that are revised monthly and annually and are seasonally adjusted. Industry classifications in this table are defined by the North American Industry Classification System (NAICS), and are not directly comparable to the Standard Industrial Classification (SIC) codes used previously.

*Civilian labor force includes both employed and unemployed persons, age 16 and over, and excludes current military personnel and other institutionalized individuals.

Sources: Wisconsin Department of Workforce Development, Wisconsin Worknet, "Current Employment Statistics", at: http://worknet.wisconsin.gov/worknet/daces.aspx?menuselection=da [May 14, 2013], and "Local Area Unemployment Statistics", at: http://worknet.wisconsin.gov/worknet/dalaus.aspx?menuselection=da [May 14, 2013].

WISCONSIN PERSONAL EARNED INCOME
By Source, 2008 – 2012
(In Millions)

Industry	2008	2009	2010	2011	2012
Services*	$50,361	$50,074	$52,000	$54,378	$55,906
Manufacturing	32,091	28,703	29,824	31,672	33,064
Government and government enterprises	22,449	23,083	24,002	24,263	23,686
Finance and insurance	9,607	9,571	10,660	10,996	10,961
Retail trade	9,717	9,373	9,724	10,023	10,295
Construction	9,724	8,180	8,421	8,475	8,739
Wholesale trade	8,650	8,127	8,211	8,675	9,135
Transportation and warehousing	5,934	5,637	5,373	5,544	5,655
Information	3,583	3,479	3,295	3,431	3,565
Real estate and rental and leasing	1,527	1,502	1,547	1,564	1,505
Utilities	1,298	1,334	1,483	1,500	1,644
Farm earnings	1,886	1,008	1,944	2,983	2,805
Agricultural services, forestry, and fishing	353	364	453	476	536
Mining	272	242	190	209	233
TOTAL	$157,453	$150,682	$157,126	$164,189	$167,730

Note: Total may not add due to rounding.

*Services includes the following NAICS classification categories: Professional and technical services; Management of companies and enterprises; Administrative and waste services; Educational services; Health care and social assistance; Arts, entertainment, and recreation; Accommodation and food services; and Other services except public administration.

Source: U.S. Department of Commerce, Bureau of Economic Analysis, Income and employment tables by NAICS industry, 2010, 2011, and 2012, *Table SA05N: Personal Income and Detailed Earnings by Industry – Wisconsin*, at: http://www.bea.gov/iTable/iTable.cfm?reqid=70&step=1#reqid=70&step=1&isuri=1 [May 17, 2013].

DISTRIBUTION OF WISCONSIN BUSINESS ESTABLISHMENTS
By Number of Employees and Establishments, March 2011

Industry[1]	Total Employees[2]		Number of Establishments by Employment Size					
		Total	1 to 19	20 to 49	50 to 99	100 to 249	250 to 499	500 or more
Forestry, fishing, hunting and agricultural support	2,881	498	480	13	2	1	1	1
Mining	2,330	154	126	17	5	6	0	0
Utilities	13,265	305	187	59	28	22	3	6
Construction	86,205	13,810	13,031	560	140	61	12	6
Manufacturing	424,211	8,939	5,586	1,466	892	668	211	116
Food, beverage, and tobacco products[3]	65,899	1,058	580	202	124	90	39	23
Textiles, textile products, apparel and leather and allied products[4]	4,169	233	190	25	4	13	1	0
Wood products	18,065	581	394	103	47	29	5	3
Paper	30,995	223	53	46	42	49	23	10
Printing and related support activities	27,513	765	557	91	58	37	14	8
Petroleum and coal products	510	23	15	6	1	1	0	0
Chemicals	12,646	339	207	72	38	16	2	4
Plastics and rubber products	27,041	452	195	104	80	57	10	6
Nonmetallic mineral products	7,505	380	303	48	12	12	5	0
Primary metal	18,054	179	63	27	42	28	10	9
Fabricated metal products	62,697	1,942	1,259	338	185	133	24	3
Machinery	53,585	1,037	597	202	113	81	28	16
Computer and electronic products	25,152	240	124	35	34	26	9	12
Electrical equipment, appliances, and components	18,963	188	84	29	23	26	16	10
Transportation equipment	24,525	242	124	36	32	29	12	9
Furniture and related products	14,269	454	352	51	25	18	6	2
Miscellaneous manufacturing	12,623	603	489	51	32	23	7	1
Wholesale trade	108,847	7,063	5,814	819	260	132	29	9
Durable goods	66,691	4,244	3,446	551	164	62	16	5
Nondurable goods	37,127	1,965	1,546	248	89	68	11	3
Retail trade	295,401	19,447	16,384	1,877	654	452	73	7
Motor vehicles and parts	34,455	2,478	2,043	284	120	29	2	0
Furniture and home furnishings	7,534	1,022	946	67	7	2	0	0
Electronics and appliances	7,927	942	884	25	15	18	0	0
Building materials and garden supplies	26,565	1,881	1,600	168	43	70	0	0
Food and beverages	51,905	2,057	1,485	199	222	143	8	0
Health and personal care	16,979	1,353	1,024	304	23	2	0	0
Gasoline stations	22,732	2,433	2,185	235	12	1	0	0
Clothing and clothing accessories	21,328	2,122	1,861	218	40	3	0	0
Sporting goods, hobbies, books and music	10,849	1,127	996	101	27	2	1	0
General merchandise	63,047	823	428	52	115	168	59	1
Miscellaneous retail	14,232	2,012	1,848	147	17	0	0	0
Nonstore retailers (including online)	17,848	1,197	1,084	77	13	14	3	6
Transportation and warehousing	94,808	5,195	4,311	528	192	126	19	19
Truck transportation	49,147	3,459	3,014	285	94	49	8	9
Couriers and messengers	8,865	258	188	25	17	24	2	2
Transit and ground passenger service	13,913	506	314	118	46	25	3	0
Warehousing and storage	13,707	297	205	43	18	21	4	6
Information	53,964	2,303	1,850	273	91	62	11	16
Publishing	17,641	533	400	80	22	24	3	4
Motion pictures and sound recording	3,422	264	206	42	15	1	0	0
Broadcasting	4,207	188	130	33	17	8	0	0
Telecommunications	17,817	1,086	944	86	30	14	6	6
Data processing, hosting and related services	9,793	165	107	31	6	14	2	5
Other information services	1,084	67	63	1	1	1	0	1
Finance and insurance	140,381	9,212	8,369	520	159	95	36	33
Real estate and rental and leasing	23,556	4,363	4,176	131	37	17	1	1
Professional, scientific, and technical services	106,554	11,270	10,286	659	201	96	19	9
Management of companies and enterprises	66,105	969	626	138	74	69	31	31
Administrative support and waste management	133,637	6,725	5,704	502	240	185	58	36
Educational services	54,659	1,495	1,111	235	86	39	5	19
Health care and social services	383,665	14,491	11,678	1,547	600	455	124	87
Ambulatory health care	124,883	8,153	7,058	684	225	129	40	17
Hospitals	111,179	154	5	3	7	37	43	59
Nursing and residential care	81,311	2,438	1,630	355	227	195	25	6
Social assistance	66,292	3,746	2,985	505	141	94	16	5
Arts, entertainment, and recreation	40,548	2,676	2,285	237	76	61	13	4
Accommodations and food services	216,515	14,063	10,662	2,600	671	107	15	8
Accommodations	31,418	1,481	1,155	227	46	34	12	7
Food services and drinking places	185,097	12,582	9,507	2,373	625	73	3	1
Other services (except public administration)	106,376	14,725	13,733	767	169	50	2	4
Repair and maintenance	21,292	4,221	4,070	125	23	3	0	0
Personal and laundry services	26,827	4,155	3,942	167	33	12	1	0
Religious, grantmaking, civic, professional, and like organizations	58,257	6,349	5,721	475	113	35	1	4
TOTAL[5]	2,354,284	138,045	116,741	12,948	4,577	2,704	663	412

[1]Industry categories and the total include subcategories not reported separately.

[2]Number of employees for the week including March 12, 2011. Excludes most government and railroad employees and self-employed persons.

[3]Beverage and tobacco product manufacturers report number of employees using employment-size class of 2,500 to 4,999, which is not included in industry group total.

[4]Apparel manufacturers report number of employees using employment-size class of 1,000 to 2,499, which is not included in industry group total.

[5]Includes 342 unclassified establishments with 1 to 19 employees.

Source: U.S. Census Bureau, "County Business Patterns, Wisconsin: 2011", at: http://www.census.gov/econ/cbp/ [June 3, 2013].

EMPLOYEES IN NONAGRICULTURAL
Average by
(In

State	Total[1]	Other Services	Profes- sional and Business Services	Education and Health Services	Manu- facturing	Finance, Insurance, and Real Estate
Alabama	1,869.0	79.9	208.3	214.4	236.1	91.9
Alaska	324.4	11.5	26.2	41.7	12.7	15.0
Arizona.	2,377.3	88.4	339.4	344.0	147.8	162.5
Arkansas	1,163.2	43.5	118.0	165.9	160.1	48.8
California	13,891.8	484.7	2,069.4	1,786.9	1,242.4	759.8
Colorado	2,220.1	92.9	329.2	264.8	125.2	143.7
Connecticut	1,608.0	60.6	189.9	307.1	166.0	135.0
Delaware	412.7	19.7	54.5	64.8	26.2	42.7
District of Columbia	710.9	64.6	148.7	108.4	1.3	26.6
Florida	7,174.9	310.8	1,035.5	1,079.0	306.9	469.7
Georgia.	3,826.3	153.4	519.4	486.1	344.4	203.6
Hawaii	586.9	26.4	71.4	75.8	12.9	26.9
Idaho	602.9	21.3	73.4	84.0	53.0	28.9
ILLINOIS	5,610.7	254.4	799.0	832.5	558.8	360.8
Indiana	2,793.0	107.3	275.4	425.0	446.2	130.1
IOWA	1,469.2	57.0	121.6	213.5	200.1	101.4
Kansas	1,323.0	51.5	141.8	180.4	159.6	70.8
Kentucky.	1,769.8	70.6	179.7	250.0	209.1	86.0
Louisiana.	1,884.4	66.0	192.5	271.1	137.7	92.7
Maine	592.5	19.8	55.6	119.0	50.9	31.3
Maryland.	2,513.2	114.9	385.8	400.0	114.6	142.6
Massachusetts	3,186.3	118.7	461.0	664.4	254.0	207.5
MICHIGAN	3,861.4	166.6	514.3	617.0	474.4	186.7
MINNESOTA	2,637.2	114.6	313.4	458.4	292.1	171.1
Mississippi	1,089.5	34.8	91.8	132.3	135.8	44.9
Missouri	2,647.1	117.0	318.6	405.8	242.7	163.3
Montana	428.2	16.9	39.0	63.8	16.4	21.2
Nebraska	939.4	37.0	101.2	135.6	91.6	68.5
Nevada	1,115.6	33.8	135.7	99.9	37.7	52.1
New Hampshire	622.6	21.3	64.3	110.3	65.7	35.5
New Jersey.	3,854.5	160.1	582.2	605.5	257.7	253.5
New Mexico	801.6	28.5	98.2	119.9	29.0	32.9
New York	8,553.3	364.8	1,100.0	1,703.7	456.8	665.9
North Carolina	3,861.9	156.2	481.0	539.2	431.1	199.2
North Dakota.	375.6	15.6	28.4	54.9	22.7	20.4
Ohio	5,030.6	211.0	622.7	842.6	619.7	274.1
Oklahoma	1,526.4	60.7	169.1	203.9	123.1	80.0
Oregon	1,599.9	57.5	181.3	228.4	163.8	92.7
Pennsylvania.	5,615.5	250.3	685.1	1,136.0	560.6	311.9
Rhode Island	458.8	22.1	53.2	101.9	40.4	30.5
South Carolina	1,805.2	68.5	213.9	212.8	207.4	97.4
South Dakota.	402.8	15.7	27.3	64.4	36.9	28.7
Tennessee	2,612.5	100.5	304.6	372.9	297.8	137.8
Texas	10,342.0	360.9	1,273.1	1,387.6	810.7	622.5
Utah	1,181.0	33.8	152.5	155.0	111.3	67.9
Vermont	297.5	9.9	23.1	59.2	30.9	12.2
Virginia.	3,627.2	185.1	647.8	456.2	230.4	177.7
Washington.	2,777.4	104.5	326.0	375.2	257.8	135.1
West Virginia.	746.1	55.0	60.7	120.7	49.1	28.2
WISCONSIN	2,735.3	137.6	268.0	418.3	430.6	157.5
Wyoming.	282.6	11.5	17.2	26.3	8.7	10.8
UNITED STATES[3].	129,818.0	5,364.0	16,688.0	19,564.0	11,524.0	7,630.0

[1]Includes natural resources and mining, not shown separately.

[2]Construction includes natural resources and mining for Delaware, District of Columbia, Hawaii, Maryland, Nebraska, South Dakota, and Tennessee.

[3]State totals do no sum to U.S. totals because of differing methodologies.

Source: U.S. Census Bureau, "Statistical Abstract of the United States, 2012, Table 631. Employees in Nonfarm Establishments – States: 2010", at: http://www.census.gov/compendia/statab/2012/tables/12s0631.pdf [June 18, 2013].

ESTABLISHMENTS
State, 2010
Thousands)

Trade, Trans-portation, and Utilities	Con-struction[2]	Govern-ment	Leisure and Hospi-tality	Inform-ation	State
360.1	87.5	386.8	167.9	24.0	. . . . .Alabama
62.8	16.0	85.2	31.5	6.4	. . . . .Alaska
467.8	111.1	416.5	252.5	36.4	. . . . Arizona
234.4	48.5	218.2	99.9	15.5	. . . . Arkansas
2,616.9	559.8	2,422.5	1,493.7	429.0	. . . . California
397.2	114.9	393.4	263.1	71.4	. . . . Colorado
289.1	49.6	244.7	133.8	31.7	. . . . Connecticut
73.9	19.3	63.8	41.9	6.0	. . . . Delaware
27.1	10.5	245.7	59.4	18.6	. . . . District of Columbia
1,454.6	345.6	1,114.5	917.7	135.4	. . . . .Florida
808.3	148.6	678.1	373.9	101.3	. . . . Georgia
109.4	28.8	125.2	100.0	10.2	. . . . .Hawaii
120.9	31.3	118.9	58.1	9.6	. . . . Idaho
1,124.5	198.6	857.0	514.2	101.7	. . . . .ILLINOIS
541.3	115.3	438.0	272.1	35.7	. . . . Indiana
299.9	61.6	253.6	129.9	28.6	. . . . IOWA
251.0	53.5	262.0	113.1	31.2	. . . . .Kansas
359.2	67.7	331.4	167.8	26.1	. . . . Kentucky
364.2	121.9	366.3	194.0	26.2	. . . . Louisiana
116.8	24.3	103.4	59.8	9.1	. . . . Maine
437.6	144.1	500.9	228.8	43.9	. . . . Maryland
543.8	106.4	438.1	305.8	85.5	. . . . .Massachusetts
708.9	121.7	635.8	374.0	54.9	. . . . .MICHIGAN
490.4	86.4	416.7	233.9	54.3	. . . . .MINNESOTA
212.7	48.9	248.9	118.5	12.4	. . . . Mississippi
510.3	105.4	450.5	271.1	58.1	. . . . .Missouri
86.9	22.7	90.5	55.8	7.4	. . . . .Montana
196.0	42.5	169.4	80.7	16.9	. . . . Nebraska
208.8	59.1	155.0	308.9	12.5	. . . . Nevada
132.2	21.2	96.8	62.9	11.6	. . . . .New Hampshire
808.0	129.5	642.5	334.6	79.7	. . . . New Jersey
133.3	44.0	199.3	83.7	14.4	. . . . New Mexico
1,456.7	305.5	1,509.9	732.9	252.0	. . . . New York
710.6	176.0	704.3	390.4	68.2	. . . . North Carolina
80.3	21.3	79.9	34.4	7.3	. . . . North Dakota
946.5	167.6	782.3	475.5	77.5	. . . . .Ohio
276.5	66.9	339.6	138.3	25.0	. . . . .Oklahoma
308.2	67.8	299.5	161.8	32.2	. . . . Oregon
1,079.6	216.3	756.9	498.8	93.4	. . . . Pennsylvania
73.2	15.9	61.8	49.6	10.1	. . . . Rhode Island
344.4	78.9	345.2	206.9	25.7	. . . . South Carolina
80.6	20.9	78.7	43.1	6.6	. . . . South Dakota
554.7	105.4	431.9	261.9	44.9	. . . . Tennessee
2,049.5	569.7	1,860.3	1,006.1	195.3	. . . . Texas
229.4	65.1	216.4	110.1	29.2	. . . . .Utah
55.8	13.4	54.6	32.3	5.4	. . . . .Vermont
619.9	182.7	702.8	338.0	76.3	. . . . Virginia
516.5	141.1	546.7	265.8	102.9	. . . . Washington
134.5	32.6	152.6	72.3	10.3	. . . . West Virginia
508.3	94.0	420.6	250.9	46.6	. . . .**WISCONSIN**
51.5	22.5	72.6	32.4	3.9	. . . . Wyoming
24,605.0	5,526.0	22,482.0	13,020.0	2,711.0	. . . . . . .UNITED STATES[3]

UNEMPLOYMENT, UNEMPLOYMENT RATES, AND
UNEMPLOYMENT INSURANCE BENEFITS
By State, 2012

| | | Unemployment | | Insured as | Unemployment Insurance Benefits | |
| | | Persons (in thousands) | | | Average | Total Paid |
State	Rate[1]	Total[2]	Insured[3]	% of Total	Weekly	(in thousands)
Alabama	7.3%	157.1	37.0	24%	$204.31	$302,736
Alaska	7.0	25.6	12.8	50	244.60	159,664
Arizona.	8.3	251.7	52.4	21	212.34	453,334
Arkansas	7.3	98.8	33.4	34	289.16	347,499
California	10.5	1,934.5	511.7	26	294.95	6,524,647
Colorado	8.0	219.7	46.2	21	346.52	598,624
Connecticut	8.4	157.1	56.1	36	336.83	879,947
Delaware	7.1	31.6	10.0	32	244.98	116,623
District of Columbia	8.9	32.3	5.5	17	296.06	152,127
Florida	8.6	806.8	134.7	17	231.54	1,261,145
Georgia.	9.0	434.5	82.8	19	271.89	825,532
Hawaii	5.8	37.9	13.2	35	420.85	241,770
Idaho	7.1	54.6	18.1	33	252.90	174,056
ILLINOIS	8.9	585.0	160.0	27	314.41	2,323,652
Indiana	8.4	264.0	54.9	21	284.28	676,644
IOWA	5.2	85.7	29.1	34	324.68	416,953
Kansas	5.7	85.5	27.7	32	328.68	384,115
Kentucky.	8.2	170.9	37.4	22	289.73	476,162
Louisiana.	6.5	134.4	34.9	26	198.95	267,045
Maine	7.3	51.6	14.7	28	279.26	171,931
Maryland.	6.8	213.1	61.7	29	326.74	778,506
Massachusetts	6.7	233.7	98.4	42	391.68	1,740,999
MICHIGAN	9.2	426.0	110.5	26	292.12	1,353,535
MINNESOTA	5.7	167.7	59.3	35	360.91	853,923
Mississippi.	9.2	122.1	27.4	22	192.86	190,534
Missouri	6.9	207.4	53.1	26	239.38	514,547
Montana	6.0	30.5	12.5	41	270.42	123,405
Nebraska	4.0	40.2	13.8	34	265.04	138,005
Nevada.	11.1	152.5	35.7	23	303.80	478,523
New Hampshire	5.5	41.1	11.0	27	280.31	118,224
New Jersey.	9.5	436.2	141.7	32	395.88	2,507,238
New Mexico	6.9	64.6	19.3	30	300.87	260,767
New York	8.5	814.7	261.4	32	304.74	3,440,854
North Carolina	9.5	447.9	109.5	24	297.99	1,321,514
North Dakota.	3.1	12.2	3.6	29	353.52	64,192
Ohio	7.2	413.0	97.8	24	305.08	1,417,137
Oklahoma	5.2	93.8	23.7	25	274.06	267,751
Oregon	8.7	171.2	58.4	34	301.78	743,892
Pennsylvania	7.9	513.2	214.2	42	348.27	2,912,340
Rhode Island	10.4	58.3	14.9	26	377.42	250,847
South Carolina	9.1	197.1	41.2	21	241.83	305,377
South Dakota.	4.4	19.6	3.0	15	264.05	31,469
Tennessee	8.0	249.4	43.3	17	235.17	528,145
Texas	6.8	854.9	167.7	20	325.41	2,313,364
Utah	5.7	77.4	17.1	22	325.55	231,418
Vermont	5.0	17.8	6.9	39	306.25	98,947
Virginia.	5.9	247.0	48.3	20	289.61	591,827
Washington.	8.2	284.2	80.7	28	377.98	1,298,488
West Virginia.	7.3	59.1	18.3	31	273.30	224,599
WISCONSIN	6.9	211.4	88.9	42	271.07	945,893
Wyoming.	5.4	16.4	4.6	28	346.51	83,585
UNITED STATES[3]. . .	8.1%	12,506.0	3,357.4	27%	$302.67	$43,107,604

Note: Unemployment and unemployment insurance data include Puerto Rico and U.S. Virgin Islands, not listed separately.

[1]Total unemployed as a percentage of civilian workforce in the state.

[2]Insured unemployed are unemployed persons receiving unemployment benefits.

[3]Because of separate processing and weighting procedures, U.S. totals may differ from the sum of state data.

Source: U.S. Department of Labor, Employment and Training Administration, "Unemployment Insurance Data Summary – 4th Quarter 2012", at: http://workforcesecurity.doleta.gov/unemploy/content/data_stats/datasum12/DataSum_2012_4.pdf [June 7, 2013].

WISCONSIN ADJUSTED GROSS INCOME
By County, 2007 – 2011

County	2011 AGI[1]	Per Return AGI					2011 Rank
		2007	2008	2009	2010	2011	
Adams	$304,546,860	$33,264	$32,135	$30,966	$31,993	$32,100	69
Ashland	257,166,520	33,352	32,557	32,309	32,470	33,770	64
Barron	933,475,320	36,654	36,451	35,198	38,045	40,800	42
Bayfield	294,025,590	41,841	39,351	37,355	37,119	39,040	47
Brown	6,460,325,310	50,773	51,821	49,849	52,449	52,610	7
Buffalo	254,065,560	36,696	35,356	34,552	35,429	37,730	53
Burnett	244,439,480	33,279	34,191	33,492	33,022	33,550	66
Calumet	1,199,435,170	53,155	55,562	52,883	54,140	55,780	6
Chippewa	1,212,091,080	41,857	43,081	39,541	41,431	41,700	39
Clark	560,988,640	37,165	35,389	35,250	36,119	38,430	48
Columbia	1,337,456,720	45,434	45,453	43,953	45,344	46,990	17
Crawford	275,647,570	33,799	32,874	32,250	33,404	35,600	59
Dane	14,824,154,180	57,270	57,434	55,453	57,050	59,040	4
Dodge	1,947,199,970	43,922	44,255	42,404	45,276	46,950	19
Door	633,059,860	44,934	43,435	39,535	41,728	42,140	37
Douglas	803,970,930	39,143	39,646	38,953	39,609	39,840	45
Dunn	796,547,120	40,826	40,911	40,234	42,064	42,720	33
Eau Claire	2,210,234,040	44,499	59,323	60,252	62,822	45,410	23
Florence	78,664,390	36,526	37,314	35,127	36,548	37,410	55
Fond du Lac	2,322,091,580	46,302	46,808	45,142	47,092	46,920	20
Forest	128,468,630	29,563	29,247	28,201	29,166	29,210	71
Grant	856,414,150	37,098	37,155	35,594	39,483	37,930	51
Green	842,837,670	44,415	46,125	42,223	44,874	46,650	21
Green Lake	405,652,640	41,778	40,865	38,273	40,440	42,660	34
Iowa	513,530,600	43,126	42,876	42,190	42,626	44,550	28
Iron	102,561,110	33,376	30,920	30,987	30,885	33,080	68
Jackson	398,896,980	38,978	36,467	37,312	35,278	42,800	32
Jefferson	1,787,187,750	45,137	45,610	43,678	44,439	45,260	25
Juneau	428,229,140	34,796	34,414	33,147	34,233	34,850	62
Kenosha	3,559,057,610	46,273	47,125	45,603	45,517	46,330	22
Kewaunee	437,204,050	41,926	43,088	40,569	41,963	43,900	29
La Crosse	2,671,933,460	47,334	47,649	46,518	47,408	48,580	11
Lafayette	312,832,860	35,570	36,146	34,737	37,307	39,920	44
Langlade	350,868,760	35,163	35,013	34,374	35,408	35,570	60
Lincoln	552,753,130	40,332	44,247	39,283	39,949	39,530	46
Manitowoc	1,810,783,130	44,076	44,132	41,826	43,569	44,940	26
Marathon	3,148,162,590	47,695	48,265	46,421	47,448	48,140	13
Marinette	774,430,340	36,077	36,648	35,455	36,974	37,990	50
Marquette	266,646,610	36,703	35,000	34,453	34,521	35,930	57
Menominee	19,360,100	16,442	15,677	14,881	15,226	16,130	72
Milwaukee	19,613,282,100	43,390	43,557	41,704	41,932	42,830	31
Monroe	826,781,580	36,288	37,916	37,473	38,490	40,010	43
Oconto	752,593,220	40,145	40,842	39,146	40,814	41,420	40
Oneida	784,715,280	41,605	42,834	40,674	42,412	42,040	38
Outagamie	4,607,467,980	50,774	50,998	49,434	51,151	51,180	9
Ozaukee	3,878,750,470	89,593	86,785	79,263	82,425	89,490	1
Pepin	165,880,710	40,582	40,171	38,866	42,771	47,420	16
Pierce	927,920,510	50,450	51,169	49,643	50,850	52,480	8
Polk	866,082,810	41,332	41,333	39,716	40,802	42,610	35
Portage	1,469,119,750	45,844	45,584	44,604	45,700	45,340	24
Price	250,835,140	36,441	36,642	33,948	42,428	35,410	61
Racine	4,572,819,760	49,266	50,061	46,215	47,358	48,530	12
Richland	286,834,530	40,487	34,644	33,397	34,422	35,710	58
Rock	3,288,628,460	46,611	46,180	44,326	43,766	43,120	30
Rusk	202,707,780	31,584	30,805	29,034	30,749	30,620	70
St. Croix	2,322,617,700	58,028	58,254	56,188	57,854	59,350	3
Sauk	1,331,621,440	41,573	41,035	39,684	40,535	40,960	41
Sawyer	265,199,450	33,280	32,670	31,607	33,140	33,600	65
Shawano	716,105,630	37,435	36,947	35,251	36,605	36,920	56
Sheboygan	2,717,431,360	47,428	47,781	45,992	46,388	47,820	14
Taylor	345,259,760	39,179	38,613	35,154	34,614	38,120	49
Trempealeau	679,346,370	60,573	45,000	43,009	46,328	46,960	18
Vernon	495,711,950	36,088	35,912	34,724	36,662	37,760	52
Vilas	364,469,190	38,704	38,042	36,181	34,812	33,470	67
Walworth	2,250,709,280	47,237	47,110	44,436	45,834	47,700	15
Washburn	287,619,310	35,822	36,348	31,643	35,325	34,590	63
Washington	3,754,416,550	56,652	56,705	54,610	55,966	57,580	5
Waukesha	14,459,867,420	75,958	72,179	68,711	71,071	73,460	2
Waupaca	1,087,614,210	41,063	41,409	40,929	41,208	42,240	36
Waushara	422,060,760	37,261	33,810	34,871	33,539	37,510	54
Winnebago	3,951,632,310	49,459	48,202	46,629	47,813	49,220	10
Wood	1,681,742,140	43,726	43,946	42,294	43,316	44,710	27
STATE[2]	$142,023,000,000	$48,985	$47,046	$45,372	$46,958	$47,640	

Note: This table previously reported AGI on a per capita, rather than per return, basis. The change to a per return basis should result in more useful data because it will reflect the AGI of each taxpayer, rather than the AGI of the entire population, many of whom pay no taxes.

[1]"Wisconsin adjusted gross income" (AGI) is Wisconsin income as reported to the Wisconsin Department of Revenue for income tax purposes and is based on the federal income tax definition of gross income as modified by certain additions and subtractions required by state law.

[2]State totals and state per capita figures include amounts not allocated to a particular county.

Source: Wisconsin Department of Revenue, "Wisconsin Municipal Income Per Return Report, 2011" and earlier volumes, at: http://www.dor.state.wi.us/report/i.html#income [March 27, 2013]. Rankings calculated by Wisconsin Legislative Reference Bureau.

EARNED INCOME BY INDUSTRY,
(In

State	Earned Income Total[1]	Rank per Capita[2]	Farm Earnings	Agricultural Services Forestry Fishing and Other[3]	Mining	Utilities	Construction	Manufacturing
Alabama	$171,782.9	43	$504.8	$780.2	$846.6	$1,869.6	$7,131.9	$15,941.8
Alaska	34,215.6	11	9.7	340.2	2,340.1	288.8	2,184.1	776.0
Arizona.	235,780.7	42	876.5	463.2	1,259.9	1,721.6	9,508.1	14,181.7
Arkansas	102,402.6	46	1,765.2	603.7	856.2	904.3	3,761.8	8,751.3
California	1,711,100.3	16	15,617.9	7,968.4	5,446.9	10,743.2	60,842.5	131,958.9
Colorado	234,142.3	14	1,027.2	331.0	5,345.2	1,357.9	10,544.5	11,239.8
Connecticut	211,499.8	2	187.9	70.9	127.4	1,139.0	7,049.3	17,550.6
Delaware	38,462.7	24	126.4	NA	NA	291.5	1,505.3	1,994.8
District of Columbia	47,240.6	1	0.0	NA	3.9	253.1	1,183.6	136.7
Florida	779,338.8	28	2,403.5	1,849.7	463.1	3,121.1	22,992.2	23,726.2
Georgia.	365,740.2	41	2,536.1	854.7	405.9	2,534.3	12,658.2	25,621.4
Hawaii	61,294.8	18	264.4	56.3	34.1	482.2	3,112.3	777.6
Idaho	53,853.7	50	2,310.3	481.9	247.0	350.7	2,351.4	3,830.1
ILLINOIS	577,008.5	17	3,980.9	500.5	1,064.1	3,883.8	19,095.7	51,372.2
Indiana	241,242.5	40	2,311.5	440.0	726.8	1,841.0	11,210.1	38,006.7
IOWA	129,503.3	23	7,935.7	523.3	136.9	833.1	5,818.9	14,863.4
Kansas	120,732.3	25	2,648.4	557.9	1,336.3	1,007.1	4,705.2	12,439.7
Kentucky.	153,494.8	45	976.4	358.3	1,917.5	739.1	5,572.8	15,666.3
Louisiana.	181,372.6	30	1,424.8	597.1	6,154.4	1,155.1	10,550.3	13,165.7
Maine	52,477.6	29	209.0	480.0	14.7	217.8	2,266.0	3,568.9
Maryland.	305,826.8	6	496.1	135.4	181.1	2,022.7	14,216.0	10,136.7
Massachusetts	363,459.3	3	150.0	437.7	112.3	1,794.7	13,487.6	26,264.1
MICHIGAN	370,598.6	36	2,701.8	458.4	828.4	3,151.4	11,422.6	44,335.2
MINNESOTA	248,662.4	12	6,151.9	569.9	719.7	1,781.5	9,034.4	24,442.1
Mississippi	98,721.7	51	1,793.7	590.0	912.6	840.0	4,254.2	8,267.1
Missouri	235,153.7	32	1,608.2	408.6	409.6	1,551.9	9,710.4	18,500.7
Montana	37,561.9	37	746.3	254.5	953.2	405.4	1,894.8	1,094.0
Nebraska	80,052.4	21	4,868.7	281.3	118.7	633.2	3,783.1	5,702.3
Nevada	103,076.3	38	178.3	45.8	1,656.2	593.6	4,493.1	2,881.9
New Hampshire . . .	62,150.2	10	30.0	144.8	40.7	414.4	2,698.7	5,458.7
New Jersey.	475,393.1	4	395.8	178.9	222.0	2,668.6	15,495.3	26,400.7
New Mexico	73,159.2	44	1,367.3	125.7	2,347.6	497.5	2,913.8	2,299.7
New York	1,019,514.1	5	1,605.1	437.3	783.6	6,294.2	32,251.0	37,794.1
North Carolina	361,301.3	39	2,541.2	846.1	198.5	1,743.1	13,808.0	32,215.2
North Dakota.	36,305.8	7	3,643.6	162.9	2,669.2	450.2	2,612.9	1,550.6
Ohio	453,556.3	31	2,885.1	382.7	1,687.8	2,720.8	16,367.2	50,671.6
Oklahoma	148,799.0	33	1,442.0	300.3	9,608.2	1,682.7	5,708.2	10,278.5
Oregon	151,241.1	34	1,407.0	1,367.3	139.5	722.5	6,215.0	14,436.4
Pennsylvania	556,692.4	20	1,773.3	620.7	3,862.7	3,495.8	22,592.9	43,260.9
Rhode Island	47,253.1	15	17.6	NA	NA	161.9	1,653.4	2,826.3
South Carolina	161,863.7	49	349.1	383.9	86.7	1,525.1	6,090.1	15,638.8
South Dakota.	36,383.7	19	3,520.5	211.8	66.5	213.7	1,478.0	2,354.1
Tennessee	243,256.5	35	527.3	404.5	315.5	369.8	10,505.2	22,832.3
Texas	1,080,709.6	26	5,265.6	1,652.3	53,137.7	9,542.9	61,133.4	81,657.2
Utah	98,797.2	47	230.4	73.5	1,234.1	551.3	5,485.6	8,255.5
Vermont	26,914.6	22	205.5	92.4	43.2	294.8	1,286.9	2,251.2
Virginia.	385,403.8	9	597.5	395.4	1,169.4	1,717.3	14,135.4	16,957.9
Washington	313,212.0	13	3,171.9	2,481.8	193.2	647.3	12,965.9	25,455.9
West Virginia.	63,968.5	48	−70.8	112.8	3,363.2	624.5	2,992.9	3,617.8
WISCONSIN	232,129.1	27	2,804.9	535.8	233.0	1,644.2	8,738.6	33,064.4
Wyoming.	28,053.7	8	215.6	55.8	3,149.3	321.8	1,884.6	770.2
UNITED STATES	$13,401,868.7		$99,737.1	$31,488.5	$119,203.4	$85,813.0	$525,353.3	$987,242.0

NA – Not available.

[1]Includes wages and salaries, other labor income, and proprietor's income.

[2]Per capita rank calculated by the Wisconsin Legislative Reference Bureau.

[3]"Other" consists of income of U.S. residents employed by international organizations and foreign embassies and consulates in the United States.

[4]"Services" consists of the following NAICS industry categories: Professional and technical services; Management of companies and enterprises; Administrative and waste services; Educational services; Health care and social assistance; Arts, entertainment, and recreation; Accommodation and food services; and Other services, except public administration.

Source: U.S. Department of Commerce, Bureau of Economic Analysis, Regional Economic Accounts, 2012, Table SA05N, at: http://www.bea.gov/iTable/iTable.cfm?reqid=70&step=1#reqid=70&step=1&isuri=1 [June 24, 2013].

BY STATE – 2012
Millions)

Wholesale Trade	Retail Trade	Trans-portation	Information	Finance and Insurance	Real Estate and Rentals	Services[4]	Government and Government Enterprises	State
$5,403.6	$8,078.2	$3,872.3	$1,558.3	$5,537.3	$1,446.8	$37,160.2	$25,994.5	Alabama
464.4	1,559.7	1,672.0	493.4	864.3	406.1	7,812.0	9,059.8	Alaska
8,644.3	12,921.3	5,110.3	3,132.6	11,061.5	4,093.7	62,204.3	28,991.8	Arizona
3,598.1	4,906.9	3,586.3	1,060.5	2,516.2	1,113.8	21,756.0	13,081.9	Arkansas
60,912.5	77,145.3	34,803.5	69,802.1	75,487.6	22,187.1	480,378.3	206,251.9	California
9,177.5	10,218.5	4,883.6	10,663.0	11,995.2	4,609.0	67,019.7	31,077.7	Colorado
7,047.3	8,264.9	2,832.1	4,366.6	22,899.9	2,627.8	54,870.6	19,233.0	Connecticut
1,264.0	1,795.2	703.8	562.7	3,977.4	525.1	12,049.0	4,699.5	Delaware
684.4	799.0	416.9	2,414.4	2,597.2	1,268.6	40,268.9	36,043.2	District of Columbia
27,338.7	38,198.5	15,310.1	12,919.6	33,365.1	11,805.7	200,196.7	79,286.8	Florida
18,245.1	17,051.6	12,474.7	12,459.9	16,706.2	4,908.8	96,229.1	50,357.2	Georgia
1,154.0	2,701.2	1,485.3	677.0	1,345.6	956.2	15,785.8	15,751.4	Hawaii
1,812.9	2,939.3	1,173.3	588.9	1,699.3	424.1	12,424.0	6,780.7	Idaho
28,489.6	23,179.2	17,923.6	10,274.7	37,111.4	7,575.5	168,719.8	63,416.7	ILLINOIS
8,589.7	10,740.8	7,275.1	2,531.1	7,350.9	2,061.5	56,888.0	25,087.3	Indiana
5,098.5	6,016.6	3,592.4	1,813.8	8,034.3	871.9	24,645.2	14,815.0	IOWA
4,757.4	5,308.5	3,204.2	2,432.8	4,952.5	890.7	27,115.6	17,671.8	Kansas
5,330.2	7,205.5	5,767.9	1,702.5	5,357.2	1,144.1	33,811.7	24,344.2	Kentucky
5,736.4	8,489.1	6,867.5	1,715.3	4,714.7	2,365.8	42,500.1	23,467.1	Louisiana
1,417.9	2,930.4	893.0	500.2	1,969.7	466.2	13,384.5	6,485.3	Maine
7,965.5	11,580.0	4,659.2	5,673.9	11,445.3	3,658.5	83,054.0	54,094.3	Maryland
12,994.8	13,325.1	4,854.5	10,567.1	28,480.2	4,050.5	126,182.3	33,392.1	Massachusetts
13,845.5	16,211.2	7,671.5	4,472.1	12,889.8	2,807.1	100,083.6	40,171.6	MICHIGAN
12,379.9	10,022.2	5,595.2	4,756.1	15,620.3	3,105.3	69,056.4	25,165.1	MINNESOTA
2,283.1	4,866.3	2,522.2	765.9	2,353.0	663.8	18,952.9	15,714.9	Mississippi
9,407.7	11,342.9	6,135.2	6,588.2	10,753.4	2,135.7	65,400.2	28,208.7	Missouri
1,092.4	2,096.7	1,062.0	394.0	1,120.7	318.3	8,612.7	5,567.9	Montana
2,932.9	3,639.4	4,260.3	1,314.2	4,240.6	542.7	18,668.8	10,389.3	Nebraska
2,716.7	5,459.6	3,259.2	1,011.8	3,647.9	1,350.7	33,781.3	12,215.1	Nevada
2,638.6	3,959.0	712.9	1,275.4	2,938.8	609.6	16,425.6	5,605.7	New Hampshire
22,919.2	20,831.4	11,180.3	11,065.7	27,271.4	4,828.6	127,889.8	49,653.6	New Jersey
1,429.6	3,461.3	1,388.1	842.6	1,539.9	641.9	17,456.8	13,706.7	New Mexico
33,586.3	39,977.4	15,514.2	43,117.5	135,500.1	16,822.5	302,513.8	115,843.6	New York
13,626.9	16,897.8	6,846.9	6,397.1	16,972.6	3,343.8	90,061.6	55,914.5	North Carolina
2,033.1	1,760.6	1,789.2	518.5	1,099.4	482.2	6,999.3	4,816.9	North Dakota
18,257.6	20,664.4	11,526.2	5,926.3	18,025.8	5,248.5	125,452.6	50,131.1	Ohio
4,345.7	7,192.4	5,244.5	1,829.9	4,349.4	1,573.4	30,239.8	22,713.8	Oklahoma
7,106.3	7,293.4	3,310.3	2,927.0	4,940.2	1,664.8	38,777.1	18,248.3	Oregon
20,572.5	23,297.2	13,814.1	11,713.8	25,568.7	5,383.1	166,226.3	51,121.5	Pennsylvania
1,475.7	1,840.6	568.6	1,070.0	2,673.2	383.0	13,111.4	5,805.2	Rhode Island
4,925.5	8,157.3	2,935.5	1,919.0	5,713.8	1,596.2	36,186.8	25,009.0	South Carolina
1,350.5	1,789.8	726.8	379.4	1,573.1	239.5	7,381.1	4,492.1	South Dakota
9,470.6	12,970.1	9,746.2	3,282.7	9,958.5	2,657.1	70,505.7	25,881.0	Tennessee
53,472.2	50,153.7	40,172.0	19,689.0	50,242.8	16,366.5	271,050.6	125,460.9	Texas
3,702.0	5,949.8	3,070.2	2,302.2	4,738.4	1,362.0	25,909.5	14,173.9	Utah
687.0	1,456.9	391.1	304.5	755.7	240.8	6,831.6	3,387.2	Vermont
9,941.9	14,714.7	7,105.2	8,162.0	14,086.9	4,317.2	121,218.0	72,668.9	Virginia
11,140.5	15,576.0	6,802.5	18,093.7	9,849.3	3,332.5	74,671.6	45,314.6	Washington
1,521.0	2,978.9	1,436.6	696.0	1,142.3	516.7	13,569.1	9,485.0	West Virginia
9,135.5	10,294.8	5,655.4	3,565.3	10,960.8	1,505.1	55,906.1	23,685.9	WISCONSIN
694.7	1,196.5	1,061.3	222.3	587.8	379.4	4,427.1	4,644.0	Wyoming
$504,817.9	$601,407.2	$324,865.4	$322,510.8	$700,583.7	$163,875.6	$3,621,823.0	$1,674,579.0	UNITED STATES

PERSONAL INCOME IN WISCONSIN
1929 – 2012

	Wisconsin	Wisconsin				United States				
	Personal	Per			As % of	Per				
	Income	Capita	Annual	State	National	Capita				
Year	(in millions)[1]	Amount	% Change	Rank	Average	Amount	High[2]	State	Low	State
1929	$1,975	$673	—	18	96%	$700	$1,152	New York	$271	S.C.
1930	1,733	588	—	18	95	620	1,035	New York	202	Miss.
1935	1,416	461	—	19	97	474	722	Delaware	177	Miss.
1940	1,720	547	—	21	92	595	1,027	New York	215	Miss.
1945	3,499	1,182	—	22	96	1,237	1,644	Delaware	629	Miss.
1950	5,178	1,506	—	24	100	1,510	2,075	Nevada	770	Miss.
1955	6,899	1,875	—	21	98	1,911	2,527	Conn.	1,045	Miss.
1960	8,948	2,258	—	20	99	2,276	2,926	Conn.	1,237	Miss.
1965	11,803	2,789	—	22	98	2,859	3,583	Conn.	1,688	Miss.
1970	17,609	3,979	—	21	97	4,085	5,263	Alaska	2,617	Miss.
1975	27,810	6,086	—	25	99	6,172	10,683	Alaska	4,203	Miss.
1980	47,623	10,107	—	20	100	10,114	14,866	Alaska	7,007	Miss.
1985	65,709	13,840	—	28	94	14,758	20,321	Alaska	9,892	Miss.
1990	88,635	18,072	—	24	93	19,477	26,504	Conn.	13,089	Miss.
1991	92,124	18,557	2.7%	25	93	19,892	26,512	Conn.	13,702	Miss.
1992	98,917	19,683	6.1	24	94	20,854	28,362	Conn.	14,559	Miss.
1993	103,379	20,331	3.3	23	95	21,346	28,975	Conn.	15,290	Miss.
1994	109,927	21,413	5.3	23	97	22,172	29,693	Conn.	16,291	Miss.
1995	115,180	22,215	3.7	24	96	23,076	31,045	Conn.	16,885	Miss.
1996	121,718	23,273	4.8	25	96	24,175	32,424	Conn.	17,702	Miss.
1997	129,099	24,514	5.3	22	97	25,334	34,375	Conn.	18,550	Miss.
1998	138,667	26,175	6.8	20	97	26,883	36,822	Conn.	19,545	Miss.
1999	144,702	27,135	3.7	20	97	27,939	38,332	Conn.	20,053	Miss.
2000	153,548	28,570	5.3	20	96	29,845	41,489	Conn.	21,005	Miss.
2001	158,888	29,392	2.9	21	96	30,575	42,920	Conn.	21,950	Miss.
2002	162,866	29,937	1.9	21	97	30,804	42,521	Conn.	22,511	Miss.
2003	167,979	30,685	2.5	22	97	31,472	42,972	Conn.	23,466	Miss.
2004	177,154	32,157	4.8	22	98	32,937	45,398	Conn.	24,650	Miss.
2005	183,948	33,278	3.5	21	97	34,471	47,388	Conn.	24,664	Louis.
2006	192,818	34,701	4.3	22	96	36,276	49,852	Conn.	26,535	Miss.
2007	203,084	36,272	4.5	26	94	38,615	54,981	Conn.	28,541	Miss.
2008	209,999	37,314	2.9	28	94	39,751	56,248	Conn.	29,569	Miss.
2010[3]	218,564	38,432	3.0	28	95	40,584	56,001	Conn.	31,186	Miss.
2011	226,042	39,575	4.1	27	95	41,560	57,902	Conn.	32,000	Miss.
2012	232,129	40,537	2.4	26	95	42,693	58,908	Conn.	33,073	Miss.

Note: Alaska and Hawaii were not included in U.S. totals before 1950.

[1]Personal income includes all forms of income received by persons from business establishments; federal, state, and local governments; households and institutions; and foreign countries. Allowance is made for "in kind" income not received as cash.

[2]High shown is for the 50 states. In the following years, jurisdictions other than states had higher per capita personal income: 1950: Alaska (pre-statehood) – $2,400, District of Columbia – $2,228; 1991: District of Columbia – $27,567; 1992: District of Columbia – $28,916; 1993: District of Columbia – $29,996; 1994: District of Columbia – $30,835; 1995: District of Columbia – $31,266; 1996: District of Columbia – $32,786; 1997: District of Columbia – $34,488; 2001: District of Columbia – $44,827; 2002: District of Columbia – $46,407; 2003: District of Columbia – $48,446; 2004: District of Columbia – $51,803; 2005: District of Columbia – $52,811; 2006: District of Columbia – $55,755; 2007: District of Columbia – $62,484; 2008: District of Columbia – $64,991; 2010: District of Columbia – $71,220; 2011: District of Columbia – $73,783; 2012: District of Columbia – $74,710.

[3]2009 data not available.

Source: U.S. Department of Commerce, Bureau of Economic Analysis, Regional Accounts Data, "Annual State Personal Income", 2012 and previous editions, at: http://www.bea.gov/regional/spi/ [April 4, 2013].

HIGHLIGHTS OF GEOGRAPHY AND CLIMATE IN WISCONSIN

Land and Water Area — According to the U.S. Census Bureau, Wisconsin encompasses 65,496 square miles, of which 54,158 square miles is land. At 11,339 square miles, Wisconsin has the fourth largest water area in the United States, behind Alaska, Michigan, and Florida.

Lakes — The largest lake in Wisconsin is Lake Winnebago (206 square miles), which covers parts of three counties. The deepest natural lake is Green Lake in Green Lake County with a maximum depth of 236 feet. Most of Wisconsin's largest lakes are concentrated in the northern two-thirds of the state, and they include artificial bodies of water created by dams. Wisconsin has 15,074 documented lakes, of which approximately 40% are named. Green County has only five lakes while Vilas County has 1,318.

High Points — The state's highest recorded elevation is Timms Hill in Price County, at 1,951.5 feet. There are several other recorded elevations of at least 1,900 feet in Forest, Langlade, Lincoln, Marathon, Price, and Vilas Counties.

Temperature — In 2012, the annual statewide average temperature was 47.4° Fahrenheit. Across the state, average regional temperatures varied from 44.4° in the north central area to 50.3° in the southwest. In all regions of the state, average temperatures in 2012 were significantly higher than normal temperature figures, which are the averages for the period 1981-2010, based on computations by the State Climatology Office.

Precipitation — In 2012, the total statewide average rainfall was 27.99 inches. Regional precipitation averages varied from a high of 29.91 inches in the east central area to a low of 26.71 inches in the south central area. In all regions of the state, rainfall totals in 2012 were significantly lower than normal precipitation figures, which correspond to the averages for the period 1981-2010, according to the State Climatology Office.

The following tables present selected data. Consult footnoted sources for more detailed information about geography and climate.

WISCONSIN'S LARGEST WATER AREAS

Name	County[1]	Area in Acres
Lake Winnebago	Winnebago (also Calumet and Fond du Lac)	131,939
Lake Pepin	Pepin (also Buffalo and Pierce)	24,550
Petenwell Lake	Juneau (also Adams and Wood)	23,173
Lake Chippewa (Chippewa Flowage)	Sawyer	14,593
Lake Poygan	Winnebago (also Waushara)	14,024
Castle Rock Lake	Juneau (also Adams)	12,981
Turtle-Flambeau Flowage	Iron	12,942
Lake Koshkonong	Rock (also Dane and Jefferson)	10,595
Lake Mendota	Dane	9,781
Lake Butte des Morts	Winnebago	8,581
Lake Onalaska	La Crosse	8,391
Green Lake (Big Green)[2]	Green Lake	7,920
Lake St. Croix	St. Croix (also Pierce)	7,696
Lake Wisconsin	Sauk (also Columbia)	7,197
Beaver Dam Lake	Dodge (also Juneau)	6,718
Big Eau Pleine Reservoir	Marathon	6,348
Shawano Lake	Shawano	6,215
Lake Wissota	Chippewa	6,148
Geneva Lake	Walworth	5,401
Lac Courte Oreilles	Sawyer	5,139
Puckaway Lake	Green Lake (also Marquette)	5,013
Lake Du Bay	Portage (also Marathon)	4,649
Lake Winneshiek	Crawford	4,635
Lake Winneconne	Winnebago	4,553
Willow Flowage	Oneida	4,217
Lac Vieux Desert	Vilas	4,017
Wigwam Slough	La Crosse (also Vernon)	3,988
Trout Lake	Vilas	3,864
Pelican Lake	Oneida	3,545
Fence Lake	Vilas	3,483
Long Lake	Washburn	3,478
Tomahawk Lake	Oneida	3,462
Lake Monona	Dane	3,359
Round Lake	Sawyer	3,294
Lake Kegonsa	Dane	3,200
Grindstone Lake	Sawyer	3,176
Rainbow Flowage	Oneida	3,153
Gile Flowage	Iron	3,138

Note: Wisconsin's largest water areas are limited to those that are named, as determined by the Wisconsin Geographic Names Council.

[1]County listed first contains the water's source of origin. Other counties covered by the water area are shown in parentheses.

[2]Green Lake, at a maximum depth of 236 feet, is Wisconsin's deepest natural lake. Including artificial water areas, Lake Wazee is Wisconsin's deepest lake with a maximum depth of 350 feet.

Source: Wisconsin Department of Natural Resources, departmental data, at: http://dnr.wi.gov/lakes/lakepages/Results.aspx [February 14, 2013].

LAND AND INLAND LAKE AREA OF WISCONSIN COUNTIES

| County | Total Land Area | | Inland Lakes[1] | | | |
	Acres[2]	Rank	Number[2]	Number Rank	Acres[2]	Acres Rank
Adams	413,213	43	46	43	2,302	53
Ashland	668,822	11	157	23	5,936	38
Barron	552,135	24	369	17	17,748	15
Bayfield	945,832	2	962	4	22,629	9
Brown	339,013	56	22	61	170	71
Buffalo	429,846	42	8	69	196	70
Burnett	525,982	28	509	8	31,258	7
Calumet	203,671	68	8	70	98	72
Chippewa	645,358	13	449	11	20,027	13
Clark	774,282	7	32	54	1,076	58
Columbia	489,939	34	56	41	3,095	49
Crawford	365,222	52	77	34	6,243	35
Dane	766,233	8	63	37	21,788	11
Dodge	560,400	22	29	56	14,246	20
Door	308,466	59	25	60	3,254	48
Douglas	834,647	4	431	14	14,113	21
Dunn	544,067	26	20	63	3,953	43
Eau Claire	408,309	44	20	64	2,838	52
Florence	312,445	58	259	19	7,261	32
Fond du Lac	460,514	40	41	44	1,650	55
Forest	649,003	12	824	6	22,531	10
Grant	733,983	9	33	51	1,569	56
Green	373,732	50	5	72	350	63
Green Lake	223,640	65	36	49	17,120	16
Iowa	488,051	35	15	66	685	60
Iron	485,231	36	494	10	29,368	8
Jackson	632,141	15	135	26	5,004	40
Jefferson	356,143	53	33	52	3,710	44
Juneau	490,832	33	57	39	45,950	5
Kenosha	174,074	69	34	50	3,674	45
Kewaunee	219,212	66	15	67	251	66
La Crosse	289,079	61	19	65	8,568	30
Lafayette	405,496	46	8	71	620	61
Langlade	557,210	23	841	5	9,122	28
Lincoln	562,543	21	729	7	15,585	17
Manitowoc	377,013	48	101	31	1,492	57
Marathon	988,789	1	194	22	19,762	14
Marinette	895,582	3	442	12	13,735	22
Marquette	291,585	60	93	32	5,736	39
Menominee	228,869	64	128	28	4,044	42
Milwaukee	154,497	70	41	45	197	69
Monroe	576,496	19	119	29	3,433	47
Oconto	638,712	14	378	16	11,053	26
Oneida	712,301	10	1,129	2	68,447	3
Outagamie	408,015	45	33	53	213	68
Ozaukee	149,169	71	38	46	703	59
Pepin	148,469	72	29	57	278	64
Pierce	367,198	51	38	47	6,016	37
Polk	584,936	17	437	13	20,900	12
Portage	512,434	29	137	25	12,215	24
Price	802,800	6	388	15	15,048	19
Racine	212,801	67	22	62	3,030	51
Richland	375,137	49	9	68	251	67
Rock	459,611	41	75	35	11,159	25
Rusk	584,694	18	250	20	7,854	31
St. Croix	462,291	39	63	38	3,653	46
Sauk	531,777	27	28	58	10,993	27
Sawyer	804,675	5	495	9	56,587	4
Shawano	571,557	20	134	27	8,912	29
Sheboygan	327,210	57	69	36	2,106	54
Taylor	623,921	16	284	18	6,183	36
Trempealeau	469,097	38	26	59	409	62
Vernon	506,611	32	57	40	256	65
Vilas	548,227	25	1,318	1	93,889	2
Walworth	355,281	54	37	48	12,798	23
Washburn	510,152	30	964	3	31,265	6
Washington	275,650	63	53	42	3,072	50
Waukesha	351,727	55	117	30	15,133	18
Waupaca	478,536	37	240	21	7,152	33
Waushara	400,738	47	138	24	4,623	41
Winnebago	278,072	62	30	55	169,755	1
Wood	507,595	31	78	33	6,245	34
STATE	34,660,994		15,074		982,574	

[1]Lake Superior and Lake Michigan not included in totals.

[2]Land area statistics reported by the U.S. Census Bureau; lake statistics provided by Wisconsin Department of Natural Resources.

Sources: Wisconsin Department of Natural Resources, *Wisconsin Lakes, 2009,* at: http://dnr.wi.gov/lakes/lakebook/wilakes2009bma.pdf; U.S. Department of Commerce, Census Bureau, 2010 Census of Population and Housing, *Summary Population and Housing Characteristics, Wisconsin,* Table 16. Rank calculated by Wisconsin Legislative Reference Bureau. State totals may not add due to rounding.

WISCONSIN'S HIGH POINTS

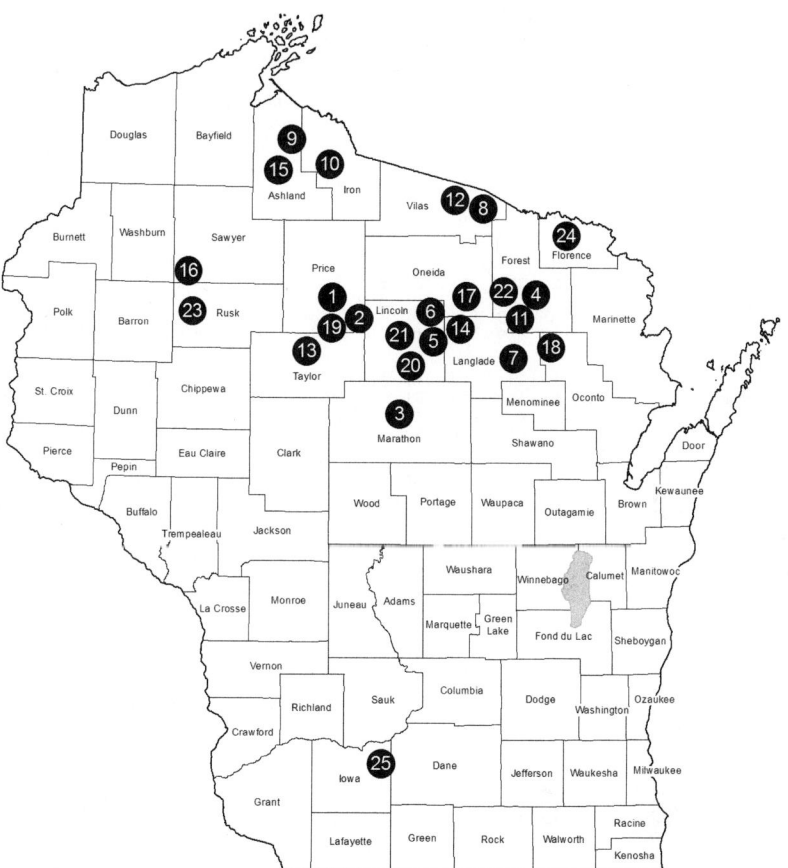

Rank	Name	County	Elevation in Feet
1	Timms Hill	Price	1,951.5
2	Pearson Hill	Price	1,951.0
3	Rib Mountain	Marathon	1,941.8
4	Sugarbush Hill	Forest	1,939.0
5	Lookout Mountain	Lincoln	1,920.0
6	Harrison Hills	Lincoln	1,910.0
7	Kent Lookout Tower	Langlade	1,903.0
8	Unnamed	Vilas	1,900.0
9	Mount Whittlesey	Ashland	1,872.0
10	Penokee Range	Iron	1,870.0
11	East Hill	Forest	1,850.0
12	Military Hill	Vilas	1,848.0
13	Unnamed	Taylor	1,840.0
14	Baldy Hill	Langlade	1,831.0
15	Gogebic Range	Ashland	1,820.0
16	Meteor Hill	Sawyer	1,801.0
17	Unnamed	Oneida	1,800.0
18	Carter Hills	Oconto	1,781.0
19	Spokes Hill	Price	1,780.0
20	Irma Hill	Lincoln	1,770.0
21	Chase Hill	Lincoln	1,760.0
22	West Hill	Forest	1,750.0
23	Blue Hills	Rusk	1,750.0
24	Unnamed	Florence	1,730.0
25	Blue Mounds	Iowa	1,719.0

Note: Elevations are not field verified. The highest points for individual counties are available on the Wisconsin State
  Cartographer's Office Web site, at: http://www.sco.wisc.edu/mapping-topics/wisconsin-high-points.html.
Source: Wisconsin State Cartographer's Office, departmental data, May 2013.

WISCONSIN TEMPERATURES AND PRECIPITATION,
By Region and Month, 2012

	Jan.	Feb.	Mar.	Apr.	May	June	July	Aug.	Sept.	Oct.	Nov.	Dec.	Annual[1]
Statewide													
2012 Temperature (°F). . .	20.8	26.1	45.4	44.9	59.2	67.1	74.7	67.2	57.7	45.1	34.6	25.6	47.4
Normal Temperature[2] . . .	15.4	19.8	30.6	44.0	55.1	64.6	69.2	67.3	58.8	46.5	33.4	19.9	43.7
2012 Precipitation (inches)	1.05	0.37	1.99	2.68	4.71	3.23	3.28	2.31	1.52	3.85	1.17	1.83	27.99
Normal Precipitation[2] . . .	1.13	1.06	1.79	2.97	3.55	4.22	4.05	4.00	3.72	2.84	2.18	1.45	32.96
Regions[3]													
Northwest													
2012 Temperature	18.5	24.3	42.7	44.3	57.5	65.2	73.0	65.9	56.8	42.9	32.6	21.9	45.5
Normal Temperature. . . .	12.0	16.9	28.5	42.4	54.1	63.1	68.3	66.3	57.5	44.9	31.0	16.8	41.8
2012 Precipitation	0.84	0.25	1.62	2.64	6.44	5.42	3.05	1.74	1.23	2.43	0.95	1.24	27.85
Normal Precipitation. . . .	0.95	0.88	1.61	2.65	3.37	4.04	4.14	4.05	3.97	3.07	1.96	1.21	31.89
North Central													
2012 Temperature	16.9	22.4	42.3	42.2	56.5	64.6	71.7	64.4	54.6	42.3	32.0	23.0	44.4
Normal Temperature. . . .	12.5	16.6	27.3	41.3	52.9	62.2	66.6	64.7	56.3	43.8	30.8	17.2	41.0
2012 Precipitation	1.23	0.43	1.44	2.21	4.76	4.48	3.64	1.93	1.81	4.17	1.48	1.33	28.91
Normal Precipitation. . . .	1.14	0.96	1.67	2.61	3.40	4.00	4.00	3.78	4.00	3.22	2.10	1.44	32.32
Northeast													
2012 Temperature	20.0	25.4	43.2	43.1	57.3	65.1	72.1	65.7	55.7	44.1	33.0	25.2	45.8
Normal Temperature. . . .	14.4	18.4	28.6	42.1	53.2	62.7	67.1	65.2	56.8	44.7	32.3	19.3	42.1
2012 Precipitation	0.86	0.28	1.77	1.69	3.67	3.58	4.81	1.91	1.87	4.98	1.37	1.63	28.42
Normal Precipitation. . . .	1.15	0.99	1.75	2.63	3.34	3.86	3.68	3.39	3.60	3.06	2.20	1.51	31.15
West Central													
2012 Temperature	21.5	26.8	48.1	47.4	61.9	69.1	75.8	67.7	59.0	45.8	35.4	24.3	48.6
Normal Temperature. . . .	15.3	20.2	31.8	46.0	57.1	66.6	70.9	68.6	60.0	47.5	33.5	19.6	44.8
2012 Precipitation	0.83	0.40	1.51	2.93	5.27	4.06	2.32	2.50	1.11	2.91	1.12	1.82	26.78
Normal Precipitation. . . .	0.96	0.93	1.84	3.11	3.80	4.44	4.34	4.57	3.89	2.49	2.09	1.24	33.71
Central													
2012 Temperature	21.9	27.3	47.1	45.7	60.7	68.3	76.3	68.4	58.5	46.2	35.5	26.8	48.6
Normal Temperature. . . .	16.8	21.2	31.9	45.5	56.5	66.0	70.3	68.1	59.6	47.3	34.4	20.9	44.9
2012 Precipitation	1.01	0.27	2.47	3.26	5.39	2.09	1.89	3.35	1.43	4.66	1.19	1.83	28.84
Normal Precipitation. . . .	1.12	1.06	1.81	3.03	3.68	4.40	4.21	3.99	3.61	2.56	2.18	1.41	33.06
East Central													
2012 Temperature	24.0	28.5	44.7	44.1	58.0	67.2	74.9	68.4	58.9	46.8	37.0	29.7	48.5
Normal Temperature. . . .	18.9	22.2	31.7	43.8	54.3	64.4	69.6	68.3	60.3	48.2	36.2	23.6	45.1
2012 Precipitation	1.20	0.37	2.70	2.65	4.24	2.30	4.41	2.89	1.12	4.99	0.89	2.15	29.91
Normal Precipitation. . . .	1.37	1.21	1.79	2.88	3.19	3.80	3.42	3.51	3.30	2.66	2.33	1.60	31.07
Southwest													
2012 Temperature	23.0	28.4	49.5	47.9	62.5	69.7	78.6	70.1	60.4	47.8	37.1	28.0	50.3
Normal Temperature. . . .	17.8	22.7	33.9	46.9	57.6	67.2	71.3	69.2	60.8	48.6	35.6	22.0	46.1
2012 Precipitation	1.22	0.28	2.20	3.68	3.74	1.19	2.89	2.56	1.95	3.65	1.51	2.03	26.90
Normal Precipitation. . . .	1.09	1.12	1.94	3.63	4.02	4.90	4.47	4.56	3.48	2.50	2.29	1.49	35.49
South Central													
2012 Temperature	23.7	28.7	49.1	46.8	62.3	70.1	78.4	69.5	60.0	47.6	36.9	29.8	50.2
Normal Temperature. . . .	18.8	23.3	34.0	46.7	57.6	67.3	71.4	69.3	61.0	48.8	36.5	23.0	46.5
2012 Precipitation	1.23	0.57	2.73	2.94	3.31	0.48	3.39	2.34	1.52	4.24	1.02	2.94	26.71
Normal Precipitation. . . .	1.30	1.42	2.05	3.53	3.76	4.68	4.14	4.15	3.51	2.73	2.44	1.76	35.46
Southeast													
2012 Temperature	25.4	29.5	48.0	45.2	60.0	68.6	77.4	69.4	60.3	47.6	37.7	31.5	50.1
Normal Temperature. . . .	20.8	24.9	34.5	45.9	56.0	66.2	71.1	69.7	61.8	49.7	38.0	25.1	47.0
2012 Precipitation	1.40	0.72	3.19	2.49	3.25	0.75	3.26	2.44	1.81	3.82	0.55	3.29	26.97
Normal Precipitation. . . .	1.58	1.49	2.02	3.46	3.62	4.02	3.80	4.00	3.41	2.71	2.56	1.92	34.59

[1]Annual temperature reflects the average of the monthly figures; annual precipitation is the total for the year.

[2]Normal temperatures and normal precipitation are the averages for the period 1981-2010, based on data computed by the State Climatology Office.

[3]The counties in each region are:

Northwest — Barron, Bayfield, Burnett, Chippewa, Douglas, Polk, Rusk, Sawyer, and Washburn.

North Central — Ashland, Clark, Iron, Lincoln, Marathon, Oneida, Price, Taylor, and Vilas.

Northeast — Florence, Forest, Langlade, Marinette, Menominee, Oconto, and Shawano.

West Central — Buffalo, Dunn, Eau Claire, Jackson, La Crosse, Monroe, Pepin, Pierce, St. Croix, and Trempealeau.

Central — Adams, Green Lake, Juneau, Marquette, Portage, Waupaca, Waushara, and Wood.

East Central — Brown, Calumet, Door, Fond du Lac, Kewaunee, Manitowoc, Outagamie, Sheboygan, and Winnebago.

Southwest — Crawford, Grant, Iowa, Lafayette, Richland, Sauk, and Vernon.

South Central — Columbia, Dane, Dodge, Green, Jefferson, and Rock.

Southeast — Kenosha, Milwaukee, Ozaukee, Racine, Walworth, Washington, and Waukesha.

Source: Wisconsin State Climatology Office, departmental data [June 2013].

HIGHLIGHTS OF HISTORY IN WISCONSIN

History — On May 29, 1848, Wisconsin became the 30th state in the Union, but the state's written history dates back more than 300 years to the time when the French first encountered the diverse Native Americans who lived here. In 1634, the French explorer Jean Nicolet landed at Green Bay, reportedly becoming the first European to visit Wisconsin. The French ceded the area to Great Britain in 1763, and it became part of the United States in 1783. First organized under the Northwest Ordinance, the area was part of various territories until creation of the Wisconsin Territory in 1836.

Since statehood, Wisconsin has been a wheat farming area, a lumbering frontier, and a preeminent dairy state. Tourism has grown in importance, and industry has concentrated in the eastern and southeastern part of the state.

Politically, the state has enjoyed a reputation for honest, efficient government. It is known as the birthplace of the Republican Party and the home of Robert M. La Follette, Sr., founder of the progressive movement.

Political Balance — After being primarily a one-party state for most of its existence, with the Republican and Progressive Parties dominating during portions of the state's first century, Wisconsin has become a politically competitive state in recent decades. The Republicans gained majority control in both houses in the 1995 Legislature, an advantage they last held during the 1969 session. Since then, control of the senate has changed several times. In 2009, the Democrats gained control of both houses for the first time since 1993; both houses returned to Republican control in 2011.

Scott Walker's victory in the 2010 gubernatorial race placed the governor's office in Republican hands after the 8 year tenure of Democrat Jim Doyle. Since 1958, a year that marked an end to GOP dominance in state politics, the Republicans have won the governor's office 9 times, and the Democrats 8 times. In the last 50 years, Wisconsin's two main urban areas – Milwaukee and Madison – have provided over half of the state's constitutional officers. During this period, 11 women have served as constitutional officers: three as lieutenant governor, one as attorney general, two as secretary of state, three as state treasurer, and two as superintendent of public instruction.

National Office — Although the Democratic candidate has carried Wisconsin six times in a row, presidential elections in the state tend to be close. In fact, in 2008 Barack Obama became the first candidate to win a majority (56%) of the presidential vote since 1988; he duplicated that feat in 2012 with just under 53%. This has resulted in Wisconsin being regarded as a hotly contested "swing state" in many recent presidential elections.

Wisconsin voters tend to retain their U.S. Senators in office for long periods of time. Since 1900, seven senators have served three terms or more, topped by Senator William Proxmire's 32 years in office. Democrats have usually held both of Wisconsin's U.S. Senate seats over the past 50 years, but currently each party holds one seat.

Currently, five Republicans and three Democrats represent Wisconsin in the U.S. House of Representatives, and two of the current members have been elected 15 or more times in regular elections but no other member has served more than nine terms. Democrats held the majority of seats from 1973 to 1991. The Republicans held the majority from 1991 to 1997, but lost it to the Democrats again in 1997. The Congressional delegation was evenly divided from 2003 to 2007. Democrats regained the majority in 2007, but Republicans won it back in the 2010 election. Certain congressional districts have traditionally been represented by one party or the other with little relationship to statewide politics.

Voter Turnout — Turnout in presidential and gubernatorial elections may vary as much as a half million votes from election to election. Although individual elections have been up and down, the trend has been upward. Over 3 million votes were cast in the last presidential election.

Supreme Court — Although justices of the Wisconsin Supreme Court are elected officials, they sometimes are first named to the court by gubernatorial appointment to fill a vacancy. Subsequently, the appointees must be elected to the office if they wish to stay on the court; most have been successful. Among the current seven justices, two came to the court by the appointment route. The first woman justice to serve the court, Shirley S. Abrahamson, was appointed in 1976. She was elected in 1979 and became chief justice in 1996.

SIGNIFICANT EVENTS IN WISCONSIN HISTORY

Under the Flag of France

Although American Indians lived in the area of present-day Wisconsin for several thousand years before the arrival of the French – numbering about 20,000 when the French arrived – the written history of the state began with the accounts of French explorers. The French explored the area, named places and established trading posts, but left relatively little mark on it. They were interested in the fur trade, rather than agricultural settlement, and were never present in large numbers.

1634 — Jean Nicolet: First known European to reach Wisconsin. Sought Northwest Passage.

1654-59 — Pierre Esprit Radisson and Medart Chouart des Groseilliers: First of the fur traders in Wisconsin.

1661 — Father Rene Menard: First missionary to Wisconsin Indians.

1665 — Father Claude Allouez founded mission at La Pointe.

1666 — Nicholas Perrot opened fur trade with Wisconsin Indians.

1672 — Father Allouez and Father Louis Andre built St. Francois Xavier mission at De Pere.

1673 — Louis Jolliet and Father Jacques Marquette discovered Mississippi River.

1678 — Daniel Greysolon Sieur du Lhut (Duluth) explored western end of Lake Superior.

1685 — Perrot made Commandant of the West.

1690 — Perrot discovered lead mines in Wisconsin and Iowa.

1701-38 — Fox Indian Wars.

1755 — Wisconsin Indians, under Charles Langlade, helped defeat British General Braddock.

1763 — Treaty of Paris. Wisconsin became part of British colonial territory.

Under the Flag of England

Wisconsin experienced few changes under British control. It remained the western edge of European penetration into the American continent, important only because of the fur trade. French traders plied their trade and British and colonial traders began to appear, but Europeans continued to be visitors rather than settlers.

1761 — Fort at Green Bay accepted by English.

1763 — Conspiracy of Pontiac. Two Englishmen killed by Indians at Muscoda.

1764 — Charles Langlade settled at Green Bay. First permanent settlement.

1766 — Jonathan Carver visited Wisconsin seeking Northwest Passage.

1774 — Quebec Act made Wisconsin a part of Province of Quebec.

1781 — Traditional date of settlement at Prairie du Chien.

1783 — Second Treaty of Paris. Wisconsin became United States territory.

Achieving Territorial Status

In spite of the Treaty of Paris, Wisconsin remained British in all but title until after the War of 1812. In 1815, the American army established control. Gradually, Indian title to the southeastern half of the state was extinguished. Lead mining brought the first heavy influx of settlers and ended the dominance of the fur trade in the economy of the area. The lead mining period ran from about 1824 to 1861. Almost half of the 11,683 people who lived in the territory in 1836 were residents of the lead mining district in the southwestern corner of the state.

1787 — Under the Northwest Ordinance of 1787, Wisconsin was made part of the Northwest Territory. The governing units for the Wisconsin area prior to statehood were:

1787-1800 — Northwest Territory.

1800-1809 — Indiana Territory.

1809-1818 — Illinois Territory.

1818-1836 — Michigan Territory.

1836-1848 — Wisconsin Territory.

1795 — Jacques Vieau established trading posts at Kewaunee, Manitowoc, and Sheboygan. Made headquarters at Milwaukee.

1804 — William Henry Harrison's treaty with Indians at St. Louis. United States extinguished Indian title to lead region (a cause of Black Hawk War).

1814 — Fort Shelby built at Prairie du Chien. Captured by English and name changed to Fort McKay.

1815 — War with England concluded. Fort McKay abandoned by British.

1816 — Fort Shelby rebuilt at Prairie du

Chien (renamed Fort Crawford). Astor's American Fur Company began operations in Wisconsin.

1818 — Solomon Juneau bought trading post of Jacques Vieau at Milwaukee.

1820 — Rev. Jedediah Morse preached first Protestant sermon in Wisconsin at Fort Howard (Green Bay) July 9. Henry Schoolcraft, James Duane Doty, Lewis Cass made exploration trip through Wisconsin.

1822 — New York Indians (Oneida, Stockbridge, Munsee, and Brothertown) moved to Wisconsin. First mining leases in southwest Wisconsin.

1825 — Indian Treaty established tribal boundaries.

1826-27 — Winnebago Indian War. Surrender of Chief Red Bird.

1828 — Fort Winnebago begun at Portage.

1832 — Black Hawk War.

1833 — Land treaty with Indians cleared southern Wisconsin land titles. First newspaper, *Green Bay Intelligencer,* established.

1834 — Land offices established at Green Bay and Mineral Point. First public road laid out.

1835 — First steamboat arrived at Milwaukee. First bank in Wisconsin opened at Green Bay.

1836 — Act creating Territory of Wisconsin signed April 20 by President Andrew Jackson. (Provisions of Ordinance of 1787 made part of the act.)

Wisconsin Territory

Wisconsin's population reached 305,000 by 1850. About half of the new immigrants were from New York and New England. The rest were principally from England, Scotland, Ireland, Germany, and Scandinavia. New York's Erie Canal gave Wisconsin a water outlet to the Atlantic Ocean and a route for new settlers. Wheat was the primary cash crop for most of the newcomers.

State politics revolved around factions headed by James Doty and Henry Dodge. As political parties developed, the Democrats proved dominant throughout the period.

1836 — Capital located at Belmont — Henry Dodge appointed governor, July 4, by President Andrew Jackson. First session of legislature. Madison chosen as permanent capital.

1837 — Madison surveyed and platted. First Capitol begun. Panic of 1837 – all territorial banks failed. Winnebago Indians ceded all claims to land in Wisconsin. Imprisonment for debt abolished.

1838 — Territorial legislature met in Madison. Milwaukee and Rock River Canal Company chartered.

1840 — First school taxes authorized and levied.

1841 — James D. Doty appointed governor by President John Tyler.

1842 — C.C. Arndt shot and killed in legislature by James R. Vineyard.

1844 — Nathaniel P. Tallmadge appointed governor. Wisconsin Phalanx (a utopian colony) established at Ceresco (Ripon).

1845 — Dodge reappointed governor. Mormon settlement at Voree (Burlington). Swiss colony came to New Glarus.

1846 — Congress passed enabling act for admission of Wisconsin as state. First Constitutional Convention met in Madison.

1847 — Census population 210,546. First Constitution rejected by people. Second Constitutional Convention.

1848 — Second Constitution adopted. President James K. Polk signed bill on May 29 making Wisconsin a state.

Early Statehood

Heavy immigration continued after statehood. The state remained largely agricultural with wheat the primary crop. Slavery, banking laws, and temperance were the major issues of the period. Despite the number of foreign immigrants and a shift from Democratic control to Republican control, most political leaders continued to have ties to the northeastern United States. New York state laws and institutions provided models for much of the activity of the early legislative sessions.

1848 — Legislature met June 5. Governor Nelson Dewey inaugurated June 7. State university incorporated. First telegram reached Milwaukee. Large scale German immigration began.

1849 — School code adopted. First free, tax-supported, graded school with high school at Kenosha.

1850 — Bond Law for controlling sale of liquor passed. State opened the Wisconsin Institute for Education of the Blind at Janesville.

1851 — First railroad train – Milwaukee to Waukesha. First state fair at Janesville.

1852 — School for deaf opened at Delavan. Prison construction begun at Waupun.

1853 — Impeachment of Judge Levi Hubbell. Capital punishment abolished (third state to take action).

1854 — Republican Party named at a meeting in Ripon. First class graduated at state university. Joshua Glover, fugitive slave, arrested in Racine, and the Wisconsin Supreme Court, in related matter, declared Fugitive Slave Law of 1850 unconstitutional. Milwaukee and Mississippi Railroad reached Madison.

Harrison Ludington, Governor of Wisconsin, 1876-1878. (State Historical Society of Wisconsin, 46742)

1856 — Bashford-Barstow election scandal. Legislative report on maladministration of school funds.

1857 — Railroad completed to Prairie du Chien. First high school class graduated at Racine. Industrial School for Boys opened at Waukesha.

1858 — Legislative investigation of bribery in 1856 Legislature.

1859 — Abraham Lincoln spoke at state fair in Milwaukee.

1861 — Beginning of Civil War. Governor called for volunteers for military service. Bank riot in Milwaukee. Office of county superintendent of schools created.

1862 — Governor Louis P. Harvey drowned.

Draft riots. Edward G. Ryan's address at Democratic Convention criticized Lincoln's conduct of war.

1864 — Cheese factory started at Ladoga, Fond du Lac County, by Chester Hazen.

1865 — 96,000 Wisconsin soldiers served in Civil War; losses were 12,216.

The Maturing Commonwealth

After the Civil War Wisconsin matured into a modern political and economic entity. Heavy immigration continued throughout the period. The mix of immigrants remained similar to that prior to the Civil War until the end of the century, when Poles began to appear in large numbers.

The Republican Party remained in control of state government throughout the period, but was challenged by Grangers, Populists, Socialists, and Temperance candidates in addition to the Democratic Party and dissidents within the Republican Party. Temperance, the use of foreign languages in schools, railroad regulation, and currency reform were major issues in the state throughout the period.

Wheat culture gradually declined in importance in Wisconsin as more fertile wheatlands were opened to cultivation in the north and west. In the 1880s and 1890s, dairying gradually became the primary agricultural pursuit in the state. The agricultural school at the university developed into a national leader in the field of dairy science. From the 1870s through the 1890s, lumbering prospered in the northern half of the state. At its peak from 1888 to 1893, it accounted for one-fourth of all wages paid in the state. By the end of the period, Milwaukee and the southeastern half of the state had developed a thriving heavy machinery industry. The paper industry was established in the Fox River Valley by the end of the century. The tanning and the brewing industries were also prominent.

1866 — First state normal school opened at Platteville. Agricultural College at university reorganized under Morrill Act.

1871 — Peshtigo fire burned over much of 6 counties in northeast Wisconsin, resulting in over 1,000 deaths.

1872 — Wisconsin Dairymen's Association organized at Watertown.

1873 — Invention of typewriter by C. Latham Sholes. The Patrons of Husbandry, an agricultural organization nicknamed the Grangers, elected Governor William R.

Taylor.

1874 — Potter Law limiting railroad rates passed.

1875 — Free high school law passed; women eligible for election to school boards. State Industrial School for Girls established at Milwaukee. Republicans defeated Grangers. Oshkosh almost destroyed by fire.

1876 — Potter Law repealed. Hazel Green cyclone.

1877 — John T. Appleby patented knotter for twine binders.

1882 — Constitution amended to make legislative sessions biennial. First hydroelectric plant established at Appleton.

1883 — Major hotel fire at the Newhall House in Milwaukee killed 71. South wing of Capitol extension collapsed; 7 killed. Agricultural Experiment Station established at university.

1885 — Gogebic iron range discoveries made Ashland a major shipping port.

1886 — Strikes related to the 8-hour work day movement at Milwaukee culminate in confrontation with militia at Bay View; 5 killed. Agricultural Short Course established at university.

1887 — Marshfield almost destroyed by fire.

1889 — Bennett Law, requiring classroom instruction in English, passed. Wisconsin Supreme Court in the "Edgerton Bible case", prohibited reading and prayers from the King James Bible in public schools. Arbor Day authorized. Former Governor Jeremiah Rusk became first U.S. Secretary of Agriculture.

1890 — Stephen M. Babcock invented quick, easy, accurate test for milk butterfat content.

1891 — Bennett Law repealed after bitter opposition from German Protestants and Catholics.

1893 — Wisconsin Supreme Court ordered state treasurer to refund to the state interest on state deposits, which had customarily been retained by treasurers.

1894 — Forest fires in northern and central Wisconsin.

1897 — Corrupt practice act passed.

1898 — Wisconsin sent 5,469 men to fight in Spanish-American War; losses were 134.

1899 — Antipass law prohibited railroads from giving public officials free rides. Tax commission created. New Richmond tornado.

Capitol Square, 1897. (State Historical Society of Wisconsin, 40205)

The Progressive Era

The state's prominent role in the reform movements which swept the country at the beginning of the century gave Wisconsin national fame and its first presidential candidate. Republicans dominated the state legislature, but Progressive and Stalwart factions fought continually for control of the party. Milwaukee consistently returned a strong Socialist contingent to the legislature.

Large-scale European immigration ended during this period, but ethnic groups retained strong individual identities and remained a significant force in the politics and culture of the state. Important social issues were reflected in the calendar of progressive legislation enacted during the period. The 2 world wars caused great stress because of the large German population of the state.

Heavy machinery manufacturing, paper products and dairying consolidated their position as the leading economic activities. As the last virgin forests in the northern half of the state were cut over, lumbering faded in importance. Brewing temporarily disappeared with the advent of Prohibition.

1900 — Wisconsin's first state park, Interstate near St. Croix Falls, established.

1901 — First Wisconsin-born Governor, Robert M. La Follette, inaugurated.

Milwaukee engineer Bornett L. Bobroff pioneered the development of electronic voting in legislative bodies in the Wisconsin Assembly in 1917. Here he demonstrates his invention to Congress. (State Historical Society of Wisconsin, 7320)

Teaching of agriculture introduced into rural schools. Legislative Reference Library, which served as a model for other states and the Library of Congress, established – later renamed the Legislative Reference Bureau.

1904 — Primary election law approved by referendum vote. State Capitol burned.

1905 — State civil service established; auto license law passed; tuberculosis sanitoria authorized. Forestry Board created. Railroad Commission, regulating railroads and subsequently utilities, created.

1907 — Current Capitol begun.

1908 — Income tax amendment adopted.

1910 — Milwaukee elected Emil Seidel first Socialist mayor. Eau Claire first Wisconsin city to adopt commission form of government.

1911 — First income tax law; teachers' pension act; vocational schools authorized; Industrial and Highway Commissions created; workmen's compensation act enacted.

1913 — Direct election of Wisconsin's U.S. senators approved.

1915 — Conservation Commission, State Board of Agriculture, and State Board of Education created.

1917 — Capitol completed, cost $7,258,763. 120,000 Wisconsin soldiers served in World War I; losses were 3,932. Wisconsin first state to meet draft requirements; 584,559 registrations.

1919 — Eighteenth Amendment (Prohibition) ratified.

1920 — Nineteenth Amendment (women's suffrage) ratified; first state to deliver ratification to Washington.

1921 — Equal rights for women and prohibition laws enacted.

1923 — Military training made optional at university.

1924 — La Follette won Wisconsin's vote for president as Progressive Party candidate. Reforestation amendment to state constitution adopted.

1925 — Senator La Follette died on June 18.

1929 — Professor Harry Steenbock of University of Wisconsin patented radiation of Vitamin D. Legislature repealed all Wisconsin laws for state enforcement of Prohibition.

1932 — Forest Products Laboratory erected at Madison.

1933 — Dairy farmers undertook milk strike to protest low prices. Wisconsin voted for repeal of 18th Amendment (Prohibition) to U.S. Constitution.

1934 — Wisconsin Progressive Party formed.

1942 — Governor-elect Loomis died;

1933: Wisconsin wets its whistle after 14 long, dry years. (State Historical Society of Wisconsin, 3493)

Supreme Court decided Lieutenant Governor Goodland to serve as acting governor.

1941-45 — Wisconsin enrolled 375,000 for World War II; casualties 7,980.

1946 — Wisconsin Progressive Party dissolved and rejoined Republican Party.

The Middle Years of the Twentieth Century

After the demise of the Progressives, the Democratic Party began a gradual resurgence and, by the late 1950s, became strongly competitive for the first time in over a century. With the decline in foreign immigration, the traditional ethnic differences became muted, but significant numbers of blacks appeared in the urban areas of the state for the first time. Discrimination in housing and employment became matters of concern. Other important issues included the growth in the size of state government, radicalism on the university campuses, welfare programs and environmental questions. Tourism emerged as a major industry during this period.

1948 — Centennial Year.

1949 — Legislature enacted new formula for distribution of state educational aids and classified school districts for this purpose.

1950 — Wisconsin enrolled 132,000 for the Korean Conflict; 800 casualties.

1951 — First major legislative reapportionment since 1892.

1957 — Legislation prohibited lobbyists from giving anything of value to a state employee.

1958 — Professor Joshua Lederberg, UW geneticist, Nobel prize winner in medicine.

1959 — Gaylord Nelson, first Democratic governor since 1933, inaugurated. Circus World Museum established at Baraboo. Frank Lloyd Wright, architect, died.

1960 — Mrs. Dena Smith elected state treasurer, first woman elected to statewide office in Wisconsin.

1961 — Legislation enacted to initiate long-range program of acquisition and improvement of state recreation facilities (ORAP program). Federal supervision of Menominee Indian tribe terminated on April 29; reservation became 72nd county.

1962 — Selective sales tax and income tax withholding enacted. Kohler Company strike, which began in 1954, settled.

1963 — John Gronouski, state tax commissioner, appointed U.S. Postmaster General. State expenditures from all funds for 1963-64 fiscal year top $1 billion for first time.

1964 — Wisconsin Supreme Court redistricted legislature after legislature and governor failed to agree on a plan. Two National Farmers Organization members killed in demonstration at Bonduel stockyard. Legislature enacted property tax relief for aged. The office of county superintendent of schools abolished, but Cooperative Educational Service Agencies (CESAs) created to provide regional services.

1965 — School compulsory attendance age raised to 18. All parts of state placed into vocational school districts. County boards reapportioned on population basis. State law prevented discrimination in housing. The State Capitol, in use since 1917, officially dedicated, after extensive remodeling and cleaning.

1966 — 1965 Legislature held first full even-year regular session since 1882. Governor Warren P. Knowles called out National Guard to keep order during civil rights demonstrations in Wauwatosa. Wisconsin Supreme Court upheld Milwaukee Braves baseball team move to Atlanta. Grand jury investigation of illegal lobbying activities in the legislature resulted in 13 indictments.

1967 — Executive branch reorganized along functional lines. Ban on colored oleomargarine repealed. Racial rioting in Milwaukee in July-August. Marathon marches demonstrate for Milwaukee open housing ordinance. Antiwar protests at the University of Wisconsin in Madison culminate in riot with injuries.

1968 — Constitutional amendment permitted the legislature to meet as provided by law rather than once a biennium, resulting in annual sessions. Ninety black students expelled from Wisconsin State University-Oshkosh when December demonstration damaged the administration building. Wisconsin's first heart transplant performed at St. Luke's Hospital in Milwaukee; first successful bone marrow transplant performed by team of scientists and surgeons at the University of Wisconsin in Madison.

1969 — Selective sales tax became general sales tax. On opening day of special legislative session on welfare and urban aids, welfare mothers and UW-Madison students, led by Father James Groppi, took over the Assembly Chamber; National Guard called to protect Capitol. Groppi cited for contempt and jailed; contempt charge upheld by Wisconsin Supreme Court. Student strikes at UW in Madison demanded Black studies department; National Guard activated to restore order. Congressman Melvin R. Laird appointed U.S. Secretary of Defense. Wisconsin's portion of Interstate Highway System completed.

1970 — Army Mathematics Research Building at the UW in Madison bombed by antiwar protestors, resulting in one death. "Old Main" at Wisconsin State University-Whitewater burned down in apparent arson. First elections to 4-year terms in Wisconsin history for all constitutional officers, based on constitutional amendment ratified in 1967. UW scientists, headed by Dr. Har Gobind Khorana, succeeded in the first total synthesis of a gene.

1971 — The legislature, now meeting in regular session throughout the biennium, enacted major shared tax redistribution, merger of University of Wisconsin and State University systems, revision of municipal employee relations laws.

1972 — Legislature enacted comprehensive consumer protection act, lowered the age of majority from 21 to 18, required environmental impact statement for all legislation affecting the environment, repealed railroad full crew law, and ratified the unsuccessful "equal rights" amendment to U.S. Constitution. Record highway death toll, 1,168.

1973 — State constitutional amendment permitting bingo adopted. Barbara Thompson first woman to hold the elective office of State Superintendent of Public Instruction. The 1954 Menominee Termination Act repealed by Congress. Legislature enacted state ethics code, repealed oleomargarine tax, funded programs for the education of all handicapped children, and established procedures for informal probate of simple estates.

1974 — Legislature enacted comprehensive campaign finance act and strengthened open meetings law. Democrats swept all constitutional offices and gained control of both houses of the 1975 Legislature for first time since 1893. Kathryn Morrison first woman elected to the state senate. Striking teachers fired in Hortonville.

1964-1975 — 165,400 Wisconsinites served in Vietnam; 1,239 were killed.

The Late Twentieth Century

Democrats lost control of the senate in 1993 for the first time since 1974, and in 1995 they lost control of the assembly for the first time since 1970. Control of the senate has changed several times since then. Women began to be widely represented in the legislature for the first time in the 90s.

Health care reform, restructuring welfare, the business climate in the state, taxation, education, and prisons were the chief concerns of policymakers in the 90s.

California challenged Wisconsin's dominance of the dairy industry. After an economic downturn in the 80s, the 90s saw a robust economy throughout most of the state with Madison leading the entire country in employment for several months. The farm sector and brewing industry continued to experience difficulties, however.

Litigation and demonstrations over off-reservation resource rights of the Chippewa Indians continued throughout the 80s to be replaced by controversy over Indian gaming in the 90s and into the new century.

1975 — Menominee Indians occupied Alexian Brothers Novitiate. Legislature made voter registration easier, established property tax levy limits on local governments, and eliminated statutory distinctions based on sex. UW-Madison scientist, Dr. Howard Temin, shared 1975 Nobel Prize in physiology-medicine.

1976 — U.S. District Court ordered integration of Milwaukee public schools. Ice storm damage reached $50.4 million. Wisconsin Legislature established a system for compensating crime victims. Exxon discovered sulfide zinc and copper deposits in Forest County. Shirley S. Abrahamson was appointed first woman on the Wisconsin Supreme Court. Wisconsin Supreme Court declared negative school aids law unconstitutional.

1977 — Governor Patrick J. Lucey appointed Ambassador to Mexico, and Lieutenant Governor Martin Schreiber became "acting governor". First state employees union strike lasted 15 days; National Guard ran prisons.

Constitutional amendments authorized raffle games and revised the structure of the court system by creating a Court of Appeals. Legislation enacted included public support of elections campaigns, no-fault divorce, and implied consent law for drunk driving.

1978 — Wisconsin Supreme Court allowed cameras in state courtrooms. Vel Phillips elected secretary of state, first black constitutional officer. Laws enacted included a hazardous waste management program.

1979 — Constitutional amendment removed lieutenant governor from serving as president of the senate. Moratorium on tax collections gave state taxpayers a 3-month "vacation" from taxes. Shirley S. Abrahamson, became the first woman elected to Wisconsin Supreme Court after serving by appointment for 3 years. Legislature established school of veterinary medicine at the UW-Madison.

1980 — Eric Heiden of Madison won five Olympic gold medals for ice speed skating, named winner of the Sullivan Award as best amateur athlete in the country. 15,000 Cuban refugees housed for the summer at Fort McCoy. Former Governor Lucey ran as independent candidate for U.S. Vice President. State revenue shortfall led to 4.4 percent cuts in state spending.

1981 — U.S. Supreme Court ruled against Wisconsin's historic open primary. Laws enacted included stronger penalties for drunk driving and changes in mining taxes.

1982 — State unemployment hit highest levels since the Great Depression. Voters endorsed first statewide referendum in nation calling for a freeze on nuclear weapons. Jos. Schlitz Brewing Co. acquired by Stroh Brewing Co. of Detroit, all Milwaukee operations closed.

1983 — Continued recession forced adoption of budget including a 10 percent tax surcharge and a pay freeze for state employees. Law raising minimum drinking age to 19 passed (effective 7/1/85). In one-day uprising, inmates at Waupun State Prison took 15 hostages, but released them uninjured. Laws enacted included a "lemon law" on motor vehicle warranties, changes in child support collection procedures and levels. UW-Madison School of Veterinary Medicine enrolled its first class.

1984 — Most powerful U.S. tornado of 1984

destroyed Barneveld; 9 dead. Democratic party chose presidential convention delegates in caucuses rather than by presidential preference primary as a result of the Democratic National Committee rules changes. Indian treaty rights to fish and hunt caused controversy. Economic conditions began to improve from the low-point of the previous 2 years.

1985 — Milwaukee air crash killed 31. Major consolidation of state banks by large holding companies. First state tax amnesty program.

1986 — Farm land values dropped across the state. Exxon dropped plans to develop copper mine near Crandon. Laws enacted raised the drinking age to 21, and limited damages payable in malpractice actions.

1987 — Voters approved constitutional amendments allowing pari-mutuel betting and a state lottery. Laws enacted included a mandatory seatbelt law, antitakeover legislation, gradual end to the inheritance and gift taxes, and a "learnfare" program designed to keep in school the children of families receiving Aid to Families With Dependent Children (AFDC). G. Heileman Brewing Company taken over by Alan Bond.

1988 — Driest summer since the 1930s. The first state lottery games began. Chrysler Corporation's automobile assembly plant in Kenosha, the nation's oldest car plant, closed. Laws enacted included mandatory family leave for employees.

1989 — Laws enacted included creation of Department of Corrections, the Lower Wisconsin State Riverway, and a statewide land stewardship program.

1990 — More than 1,400 Wisconsin National Guard and Reserve soldiers were called to active duty in Persian Gulf crisis, 11 casualties. The number of Milwaukee murders set a new record, raising demands for crime and drug controls. Laws enacted included a major recycling law and Milwaukee Parental Choice voucher program for public and nonsectarian private schools.

1991 — The price of raw milk hit lowest point since 1978. First Indian gambling compacts signed. Governor Tommy G. Thompson vetoed a record 457 items in the state budget.

1992 — Train derailment caused major spill of toxic chemicals and evacuation of over 22,000 people in Superior. Thousands of opponents, including children, staged protests at 6 abortion clinics in Milwaukee throughout the summer. Laws enacted included parental consent for abortion, health care reform, and creation of a 3-member Gaming Commission.

1993 — Wisconsin Congressman Les Aspin and UW-Madison President Donna Shalala named President Bill Clinton's Secretary of Defense and Secretary of Health and Human Services, respectively. Thousands in Milwaukee became ill as a result of cryptosporidium in the water supply. California passed Wisconsin in milk production. Republicans won control of state senate for the first time since 1974. Laws enacted included a 1999 sunset for traditional welfare programs, a cap on school spending, and permission to organize limited liability companies.

1994 — Laws enacted included removal of about $1 billion in public school operating taxes from property tax by 1997, a new regulatory framework for Public Service Commission regulation of telecommunication utilities, and granting towns most of the same powers exercised by cities and villages.

1995 — Republicans won control of state assembly for the first time since 1970. Elk reintroduced in northern Wisconsin. July heat wave contributed to 172 deaths.

1996 — Governor Thompson's new welfare reform plan, known as Wisconsin Works (W-2), received national attention. Train derailment forced evacuation of Weyauwega. Pabst Brewing closed 152-year-old brewery in Milwaukee. Senator George Petak was removed from office in the first successful legislative recall election in state history.

1997 — Groundbreaking for controversial new Miller Park, future home of the Milwaukee Brewers baseball team.

1998 — Tammy Baldwin became first Wisconsin woman elected to the U.S. Congress. U.S. Supreme Court upheld constitutionality of extension of Milwaukee Parental Choice school vouchers to religious schools. Second state tax amnesty program. Laws enacted included a mining moratorium, new penalties for failure to pay child support, truth-in-sentencing, and protection of fetuses.

1999 — Governor Tommy Thompson began record fourth term. Laws enacted included "smart growth", graduated drivers licensing, a sales tax rebate. Supermax, the state's high security prison, opened at Boscobel. Record low unemployment.

2000 — Legislature approved a local sales tax and revenue bonds for renovation of Lambeau Field, home of the Green Bay Packers.

Recent Years

2001 — Governor Thompson ended a record 14 years in office and assumed post of U.S. Secretary of Health and Human Services. Lt. Governor Scott McCallum became governor and appointed State Senator Margaret Farrow as the first woman to serve as lieutenant governor. Chronic Wasting Disease discovered in the state's deer herd. Extensive Mississippi River flooding. Miller Park opened. Laws enacted included telemarketing "no call" list, wetland protection, and the "senior care" prescription drug assistance plan.

2002 — Barbara Lawton became the first woman elected lieutenant governor and Peggy A. Lautenschlager became first woman elected attorney general. Deadliest single traffic accident in state history killed 10 and injured 40 near Sheboygan. Investigation into legislative caucus staffs resulted in criminal charges against five legislators. Seven Milwaukee County board members recalled over pension scandal.

2003 — Jim Doyle became first Democratic governor in 16 years. The Crandon mine issue was apparently resolved when local Indian tribes purchased the ore deposits. The renovated Lambeau Field opened. Senator Gary George became the second legislator in Wisconsin history to be recalled. A number of Wisconsin Guard and Reserve units were activated for service in the Iraq war. Wisconsin held its first mourning dove hunt.

2004 — Louis Butler, Jr., became the first black member of the Wisconsin Supreme Court. State government began to reduce its automobile fleet after allegations of misuse. Significant legislation included a livestock facility siting law and revision to clean air and water laws intended to spur job creation. Voter turnout in the fall election was 73%, the highest in many years.

2005 — The state minimum wage was increased. Wisconsin experienced a record 62 tornadoes during the year, including a

Civil War reenactment, Wade House Historic Site. (State Historical Society of Wisconsin)

record 27 in one day – August 18, when tornadoes hit Viola, Stoughton, and other communities resulting in one death, 27 injuries, and $40 million in damage. Several current and former members of the legislature were convicted of illegal campaign activities.

2006 — Continued participation in the Iraq War by Wisconsin National Guard and Reserve units was a potent issue, as was immigration reform. The legislature limited the use of condemnation power for the benefit of private individuals. Voters approved a constitutional amendment limiting marriage to persons of the opposite sex in November. An advisory referendum in favor of the death penalty was also approved by the voters.

2007 — Ethics laws and elections regulation procedures were modified. Milwaukee-based Miller Brewing merged with Denver's Coors brewery. The state budget did not pass until late October, one of the latest budgets in state history.

2008 — Louis Butler became the first sitting Supreme Court justice to be defeated at the polls in 40 years, losing to Michael Gableman. Severe flooding hit southern Wisconsin in June. Failure of an embankment caused Lake Delton to drain, destroying three homes. The Great Lakes Compact received state and federal approval, regulating the use of Great Lakes water outside their watershed. A sharp downturn in the economy caused a rise in unemployment and the closing of the General Motors plant in Janesville, ending a chapter in Wisconsin's 100-year involvement in auto assembly.

2009 — Democrats opened the 99th Legislature with control of the governor's office and both houses of the legislature for the first time since the 1985 session. The ongoing economic crisis resulted in a projected budget deficit of $6 billion for the next biennium. In the largest activation since the Berlin Crisis of 1961, 3,000 soldiers of the Wisconsin National Guard prepared for mobilization to Iraq. A severe

influenza outbreak resulted in 47 deaths.

2010 — A number of powerful tornadoes hit southern Wisconsin on June 21. Among the areas sustaining severe damage was the Old World Wisconsin historic site. The Republican Party swept the November elections, capturing the governor's office and both houses of the legislature. It was the first time in over 70 years that partisan control of all three switched in the same election. Governor-Elect Walker declined to accept $810 million in federal funds to build a high speed rail line between Madison and Milwaukee.

2011 — Governor Walker's proposal to curtail collective bargaining rights for public workers led 14 Democrats to leave the state in order to deny the senate a quorum. Thousands of protesters surrounded the Capitol to oppose the legislation, which was delayed for weeks before being enacted. Wisconsin remained in a state of political agitation into the summer as nine senators were the subject of recall elections; two were defeated. The legislature enacted a legislative redistricting plan for the first time in three decades; revamped the state's economic development efforts and expanded the parental school choice program.

2012 — Governor Walker, Lt. Gov. Kleefisch, and four senators were the subject of recall elections in ongoing ill-feeling over the 2011 collecting bargaining law. Walker, Kleefisch, and two senators were retained; one senator resigned and one was defeated giving the Democrats control of the senate. A period of severe heat and drought afflicted the state during June and July. Democrat Tammy Baldwin was elected Wisconsin's first female U.S. Senator in the fall election, but Republicans regained control of the state senate.

2013 — The legislature enacted revised regulations for the mining of metallic ferrous minerals, easing the way for construction of an iron mine in northern Wisconsin's Gogebic Range.

Sources: State Historical Society, *The Thirtieth Star, 1948; The 1958 Compton Yearbook* and succeeding editions; *The Americana Annual – 1967;* Robert C. Nesbit, *Wisconsin, A History;* Wisconsin Legislative Reference Bureau, *Clippings: Wisconsin History.*

FAMOUS CITIZENS OF WISCONSIN

Edward P. Allis (1824-1889), industrialist — developed the steel rolling mill.

Don Ameche* (1908-1993), actor — began career in radio, appeared in 56 movies; won Academy Award for *Cocoon*.

Roy Chapman Andrews* (1884-1960), explorer — found first dinosaur egg in the Gobi Desert.

Les Aspin* (1938-1995), political leader — President Clinton's first secretary of defense, January 1993 – December 1993; served 22 years in the U.S. Congress.

Stephen M. Babcock (1843-1931), chemist — devised butterfat content test.

John Bardeen* (1908-1991), physicist — twice winner of the Nobel Prize for development of the transistor and for the theory of superconductivity.

John Bascom (1827-1911), educator — president, University of Wisconsin 1874-1887; leader in upgrading the university to a nationally recognized institution.

Aaron Bohrod (1907-1992), painter — twice winner of the Guggenheim Fellowship; artist-in-residence at the University of Wisconsin-Madison.

Richard Ira "Dick" Bong* (1920-1945), aviator — leading World War II pilot; shot down 40 enemy planes to become America's "all time ace"; awarded Congressional Medal of Honor.

Olympia Brown (1835-1926), minister and publisher — first ordained woman minister in U.S.; key figure in women's rights movement.

Jerome I. Case (1819-1891), manufacturer — leader in mechanization of agriculture.

Carrie Chapman Catt* (1859-1947), suffragist — President of the National American Woman Suffrage Association, which she reorganized as the League of Women Voters with 2 million members after passage of the 19th amendment guaranteed women the vote.

Bernard J. Cigrand* (1866-1932), activist — leader in the movement to celebrate Flag Day.

Laurel Blair Salton Clark* (1961-2003), astronaut and naval flight surgeon — mission specialist died in crash of space shuttle Columbia.

John R. Commons (1862-1945), economist — drafted Wisconsin civil service law.

Seymour Cray* (1925-1996), computer scientist — called the "father of the supercomputer".

Leo T. Crowley (1889-1972), banker — structured the Federal Deposit Insurance Corporation as its chairperson, 1934-1945.

Patrick Cudahy (1849-1919), businessman — founder of a leading meat-packing company.

August Derleth* (1909-1971), author — noted for many contributions to literature about Wisconsin.

Ole Evinrude (1877-1934), inventor — developed the first outboard motor designed for mass production.

Edna Ferber (1885-1968), author — received 1925 Pulitzer Prize for the novel, *So Big.*

Lynn Fontanne (1887-1983) and **Alfred Lunt***, acting couple — appeared in theater, motion pictures, and television; jointly awarded Presidential Medal of Freedom in 1964.

Zona Gale* (1874-1938), author — recipient of 1921 Pulitzer Prize in drama for the play, *Miss Lulu Bett.*

Hamlin Garland* (1860-1940), author — received 1922 Pulitzer Prize for the novel, *A Daughter of the Middle Border.*

Ezekiel Gillespie (1818-1892), activist — plaintiff in 1866 Wisconsin Supreme Court case which resulted in extension of suffrage to Wisconsin Blacks; one of the founders of the first African Methodist Episcopal church in Wisconsin.

William T. Green (1863-1911), activist — first Black attorney in Wisconsin; active in securing the 1895 passage of the first civil rights law in the state.

Owen J. Gromme* (1896-1991), painter — wildlife artist, author of *Birds of Wisconsin,* and painter of the 1945 federal duck stamp.

John A. Gronouski* (1919-1996), political leader — postmaster general under Presidents Kennedy and Johnson; one of the architects of the modern Democratic Party in Wisconsin.

Mildred Fish Harnack* (1902-1943), war hero — while instructor at the University of Berlin, organized resistance group and transmitted intelligence to Allies; executed by Nazis.

Cordelia Harvey (1824-1895), humanitarian — instrumental in establishing military hospitals in the North during the Civil War.

Woodrow Charles "Woody" Herman (1913-1987), musician — jazz clarinetist and one of the outstanding "big band" leaders.

William Dempster Hoard (1836-1918), farmer and governor — introduced the French version of the silo and the subearth vault for curing cheese.

Harry Houdini (1874-1926), magician — world-renowned escape artist.

J. Willard Hurst (1911-1997), legal scholar — University of Wisconsin-Madison professor of law; nationally recognized expert in legal history.

Samuel C. Johnson (1833-1919), industrialist — founded wax products firm.

George F. Kennan* (1904-2005), diplomat, scholar and statesman — architect of Cold War "containment policy".

Walter J. Kohler, Sr.* (1875-1940), industrialist and governor — founded plumbing equipment company.

Julius Frank Anthony "Pee Wee King" Kuczynski* (1914-2000), musician — member of the Country Music Hall of Fame; author of over 400 songs including "Tennessee Waltz", one of the state songs of the State of Tennessee.

Belle Case La Follette* (1859-1931), lawyer and editor — first woman to graduate from the University of Wisconsin Law School; leader in support of the rights of women and African Americans.

Robert M. La Follette, Sr.* (1855-1925), political leader — progressive reformer as governor and U.S. Senator.

Carl Laemmle (1867-1939), business executive — major figure in the growth of the motion picture industry; built Universal City Studios.

Earl L. "Curly" Lambeau (1898-1965), professional football coach — founder and coach of the Green Bay Packers; instrumental in establishing the National Football League.

Mary Lasker* (1901-1994), philanthropist — her financial donations and influence supported vast expansion of cancer research; awarded Presidential Medal of Freedom in 1969.

William D. Leahy* (1875-1959), fleet admiral U.S. Navy — Chief of Naval Operations and President Roosevelt's chief of staff during World War II; the only Wisconsinite to wear the 5 stars of fleet admiral.

Aldo Leopold (1887-1948), teacher and author — University of Wisconsin professor and prominent ecologist; wrote *Sand County Almanac.*

Wladziu Valentino Liberace* (1919-1986), musician — world famous pianist-singer; known for his showmanship.

Vince Lombardi (1913-1970), professional football coach — 1959-1968 coach of the Green Bay Packers, the first NFL team to win 3 consecutive championships.

Alfred Lunt* (1893-1977) and **Lynn Fontanne**, acting couple — appeared in theater, motion pictures, and television; jointly awarded Presidential Medal of Freedom in 1964.

Douglas MacArthur (1880-1964), general — served in World Wars I and II, noted for his Philippine campaign, led post-war occupation of Japan, commander of UN forces in Korea.

Frederic March* (1897-1975), actor — won Academy Awards for *Dr. Jekyll and Mr. Hyde* and *Best Years of Our Lives.*

Helen Farnsworth Mears* (1872-1916), sculptor — created the Frances Willard statue in Statuary Hall of the U.S. Capitol and "The Genius of Wisconsin" in the Wisconsin Capitol.

Charles McCarthy (1873-1921), government innovator — established and directed first legislative reference library in the nation (forerunner of the Legislative Reference Bureau); wrote *The Wisconsin Idea*; advocate of vocational schools.

Golda Meir (1898-1978), political leader — prime minister of Israel (1969-1974); was educated and taught school in Milwaukee.

William "Billy" Mitchell (1879-1936), brigadier general, U.S. Army — fervent advocate of a strong air force.

John Muir (1838-1914), naturalist — promoted the national parks system.

Gaylord Nelson* (1916-2005), state legislator, governor, and U.S. Senator — founder of Earth Day.

Lorine Niedecker* (1903-1970), poet — author of several books of poetry; featured in most anthologies of 20th century American poetry.

Albert Ochsner* (1858-1925), surgeon — pioneer in radium cancer treatment.

Georgia O'Keeffe* (1887-1986), artist — innovative painter of flowers and landscapes, awarded Presidential Medal of Freedom in 1977.

Les Paul* (1915-2009), musician — pioneered electric guitar design and multitrack recording.

George C. Poage (1880-1962), athlete — first Black athlete to compete in the modern Olympics; won bronze medals in the 200 and 400 meter hurdles in the 1904 Olympics at St. Louis.

William Proxmire (1915-2005), U.S. Senator — noted for his "Golden Fleece Award" condemning government waste.

Mitchel Red Cloud, Jr.* (1925-1950), Winnebago war hero — posthumously awarded Congressional Medal of Honor for service in Korea; first member of a Wisconsin tribe so honored.

William H. Rehnquist* (1924-2005), jurist — Chief Justice of the U.S. Supreme Court 1986-2005; Associate Justice 1972-1986.

Albert Ringling (1852-1916), circus promoter — merged Ringling Brothers Circus with Barnum and Bailey Circus to become the "Greatest Show On Earth".

Jeremiah Rusk (1830-1893), soldier, governor, and congressman — brigadier general in Union army, first U.S. Secretary of Agriculture.

Carl Schurz (1829-1906), political activist — German immigrant to Wisconsin and national supporter of German-American interests; served as brigadier general in Union army, U.S. Secretary of the Interior, U.S. Senator from Missouri, ambassador to Spain, newspaper owner, and writer.

Margaretha Meyer Schurz (1833-1876), educator — opened the first U.S. kindergarten in Watertown in 1856, married to Carl Schurz.

C. Latham Sholes (1819-1890), inventor and journalist — developed first practical typewriter.

Donald Kent "Deke" Slayton* (1924-1993), astronaut — flew the first joint U.S.-Soviet space mission; awarded NASA Distinguished Service Medal in 1965.

Walter W. "Red" Smith* (1905-1982), sports columnist and commentator — first sportswriter to receive the Pulitzer Prize (1976) for distinguished criticism as a reporter with the *New York Times*.

Tom Snyder* (1936-2007), broadcaster — hosted national late-night television talk shows.

Harry Steenbock* (1886-1967), biochemist — produced Vitamin D in food by irradiation with ultraviolet light.

Brooks Stevens* (1911-1995), industrial designer — one of the founders of the Industrial Designers Society of America; designer of many notable automobiles and other items including trains, motorcycles, and appliances.

Howard Temin (1934-1994), scientist — winner of 1975 Nobel Prize in physiology for work on the relationship between viruses and cancer.

Spencer Tracy* (1900-1967), actor — won Academy Award for *Boys Town* and *Captains Courageous.*

Frederick Jackson Turner* (1861-1932), historian — developed noted theories regarding the American frontier; won 1933 Pulitzer Prize for history.

Charles Van Hise* (1857-1929), educator — president, University of Wisconsin 1903-1918; promoted the expansion of the university into many new fields, influenced the organization of graduate study as a separate division, and saw university enrollment double.

Thorstein Veblen* (1857-1929), economist — wrote *The Theory of the Leisure Class.*

William Vilas (1840-1908), political leader — served as U.S. Postmaster General, Secretary of Interior, and U.S. Senator; organized the Rural Free Delivery (RFD) mail system.

Cadwallader C. Washburn (1818-1882), multimillionaire businessman, congressman, and governor — had extensive flour, rail, and lumber business interests.

Orson Welles* (1915-1986), actor and director — performed in theater, radio, television, and motion pictures; directed and starred in the highly acclaimed movie, *Citizen Kane.*

Laura Ingalls Wilder* (1867-1957), author of children's books — wrote a series of books, including *Little House on the Prairie*, based on her life growing up in the Midwest.

Thornton N. Wilder* (1897-1975), playwright and novelist — received Pulitzer Prize for the novel *The Bridge of San Luis Rey* (1928) and the plays *Our Town* (1938) and *The Skin of Our Teeth* (1942).

Frances Willard (1839-1898), social reformer — organized the Woman's Christian Temperance Union.

Daniel Hale Williams (1856-1931), doctor — first physician to perform open heart surgery; only African American fellow in the original American College of Surgeons; began study of medicine in Janesville.

Laura Ross Wolcott (1834-1915), physician and suffragist — first woman physician in Wisconsin; active in organizing and first president of the Wisconsin Woman's Suffrage Association.

Frank Lloyd Wright* (1867-1959), architect — internationally known innovative designer.

Note: Only deceased Wisconsin citizens are included in this list.

*Born in Wisconsin.

Sources: Encyclopedias, books, newspaper, and periodical accounts.

HISTORIC SITES IN WISCONSIN

Site	Location	Paid Attendance[1] 2008-09	2009-10	2010-11	2011-12	Revenue 2011-12[2]
Bennett Studios	Wisconsin Dells	2,873	2,283	1,593	2,579	$49,974
Madeline Island	La Pointe	11,604	11,422	11,414	11,306	112,369
Old World Wisconsin	Eagle	43,496	42,615	38,581	50,164	772,839
Pendarvis	Mineral Point	4,235	4,233	4,522	4,908	52,342
Stonefield	Cassville	4,123	4,682	4,133	8,485	40,865
Villa Louis	Prairie du Chien	11,483	12,002	10,763	10,321	122,817
Wade House	Greenbush	15,283	13,084	13,313	11,214	117,066
TOTAL		93,097	90,321	84,319	98,977	$1,268,272
Circus World Museum[3]	Baraboo	40,123	36,100	38,423	41,229	$835,781

[1]Sites are generally open from May to October. For current information: http://www.wisconsinhistory.org/sitesmuseum.asp.
[2]Revenues from admissions, rentals, and inside sales (such as museum stores, restaurants, and rides).
[3]Statistics are for calendar year. Owned by the State Historical Society of Wisconsin, but operated by a private, nonprofit foundation.
Source: Wisconsin Historical Society, departmental data, June, 2013.

OFFICIAL HISTORICAL MARKERS IN WISCONSIN
February 2013

County	Location/Nearest Community	Subject
Adams	At the Park, Hwy 13, 3 miles north of Friendship	Roche-a-Cri State Park
Adams	S. Arkdale Cemetery, 1801 Cypress Ave., Town of Strongs Prairie	Site of First Norwegian Evangelical Lutheran Church of Roche-a-Cri
Ashland	Bay View Park, Hwy 2, Ashland	Fleet Admiral William D. Leahy
Ashland	Northland College campus, Ellis Avenue, Ashland	Northland College
Ashland	In park on Hwy 2 at western limits of Ashland	Radisson-Groseilliers Fort
Ashland	La Pointe, Madeline Island	Madeline Island
Ashland	Hwy 13, 10 miles south of Mellen	Great Divide
Ashland	Hwy 2, Odanah	The Bad River
Barron	Rest Area #34, westbound Hwy 53, 2 mi. south of Chetek	Pine Was King (Pineries)
Barron	2411-23 Street, Rice Lake	Our Lady of Lourdes Catholic Church
Bayfield	Herbster Community Center, STH 13, one block south of Lenawee Rd., Herbster	"The Gym"
Bayfield	Hwy 13, 0.5 mile east of Cornucopia	Tragedy of the Siskiwit
Bayfield	Hwy 13, Port Wing	School Consolidation
Bayfield	Hwy 13, 2.3 miles north of Washburn	Madeline Island
Brown	Denmark War Memorial Pk., Wisconsin Ave. (CTH KB)	Denmark
Brown	In park at corner of Broadway and George Sts., De Pere	Marquette-Jolliet Expedition
Brown	In Voyageur Park, De Pere	Rapides des Peres – Voyageur Park
Brown	403 North Broadway, De Pere	White Pillars
Brown	222 South Baird Street, Green Bay	Cnesses Israel Synagogue
Brown	2630 South Webster Avenue, Green Bay	Cotton House – Baird Law Office
Brown	Outside Packer Hall of Fame, Green Bay	Green Bay Packers
Brown	1008 South Monroe Avenue, Green Bay	Hazelwood
Brown	2630 South Webster Avenue, Green Bay	Heritage Hill State Park
Brown	Fox River Trail near Main Street Bridge, U.S. 141 Green Bay	Historic Green Bay Road
Brown	Hwy 57, 5 miles northeast of Green Bay	Red Banks
Brown	2630 South Webster Avenue, Green Bay	Roi-Porlier-Tank Cottage
Brown	Holy Apostles Church Cemetery, 2937 Freedom Rd., Oneida	Revolutionary War Veteran (Powlis)
Buffalo	Hwy 35, 0.5 mile north of Alma	Beef Slough
Burnett	Crex Meadows Wildlife Area, off Hwy F, N. of Grantsburg	Crex Meadows
Calumet	Wayside #4, intersection of Hwys 55 and 151, Brothertown Town	Brothertown Indians of Wisconsin
Calumet	City Hall, 2110 Washington Street, New Holstein	New Holstein
Calumet	Junction of CTH T and Church Rd., New Holstein	St. Martins Church
Calumet	Stockbridge Harbor, CTH E, Village of Stockbridge	Stockbridge Harbor
Chippewa	Hwy 124, 3 miles north of Chippewa Falls	Nation's First Cooperative Generating Station
Chippewa	2820 East Park Avenue, Chippewa Falls	Northern WI Center for the Developmentally Disabled
Chippewa	Fairgrounds, 308 Jefferson Ave., Chippewa Falls	Northern Wisconsin State Fair
Chippewa	Cornell Mill Yard Park and Bridge St., Cornell	Cornell Pulpwood Stacker
Chippewa	West side of Hwy 178, near Hwy T	Cobban Bridge
Chippewa	Hwy 178, 0.5 mile north of Jim Falls	Old Abe, the War Eagle
Clark	2 blocks west of Hwy 13, Colby	Colby Cheese
Clark	St. Hedwig's Church, CR-X at Gorman Avenue Near Thorp	St. Hedwig's/Poznan Colony
Columbia	Rest Area #12, westbound I90-94, E. of WI River	The Circus
Columbia	711 West James Street, Columbus	Governor James Taylor Lewis
Columbia	Hwy 113 at Wisconsin River crossing	Merrimac Ferry
Columbia	120 N. Main Street, Portage	Historic Pardeeville
Columbia	Hwy 33, 0.5 mile east of Portage	Fort Winnebago
Columbia	West Wisconsin and Crook Streets, Portage	Frederick Jackson Turner
Columbia	Across from sheriff's office, Cook Street, Portage	Ketchum's Point
Columbia	Hwy 33, 0.5 mile east of Portage	Marquette
Columbia	Hwy CM, 5 miles northeast of Portage	Potters' Emigration Society
Columbia	Museum at The Portage, 804 MacFarlane Rd., Portage	Society Hill Historic District
Columbia	Commerce Plaza Park, 301 West Wisconsin St., Portage	Zona Gale
Columbia	Rest Area #11, eastbound I90-94, 0.5 mi. E. of WI River	Rest Areas on the I-Roads
Columbia	Hwy 51, 0.5 mile south of Poynette	John Muir View
Columbia	Old Settlers Park, near intersection of Thomas and John Street, Poynette	Wallis Rowan and His Cabin

OFFICIAL HISTORICAL MARKERS IN WISCONSIN
February 2013–Continued

County	Location/Nearest Community	Subject
Columbia	Hwy 16, 4 miles east of Wisconsin Dells	Kingsley Bend Indian Mounds
Columbia	314 Broadway, Wisconsin Dells	Stroud Bank
Columbia	Village Park, 150 Lovers Lane, Wyocena	Major Elbert Dickason/Dickason's "Hotel"
Crawford	US-35, near River View Park, 0.3 miles north of CTH C, Ferryville	Patrick Joseph Lucey
Crawford	Hwy 171, 0.5 mile east of Gays Mills	Gays Mills Apple Orchards
Crawford	Hwy 35, 1.2 miles south of Lynxville	Rafting on the Mississippi
Crawford	Cornelius Family Park, 211 S. Main St., Prairie du Chien	Black Hawk's Surrender
Crawford	Fort Crawford Museum, 717 S. Beaumont Rd., Prairie du Chien	Fort Crawford
Crawford	Mississippi River Bridge, Prairie du Chien	Pere Marquette and Sieur Jolliet
Crawford	Beaumont and Rice Streets, Prairie du Chien	Museum of Medical Progress
Crawford	Mississippi River Bridge, Prairie du Chien	Prairie du Chien
Crawford	At entrance, Villa Louis Road, Prairie du Chien	Villa Louis
Crawford	521 N. Villa Road, Prairie du Chien	Villa Louis
Crawford	In lawn west of the Villa, Villa Louis, Prairie du Chien	War of 1812
Crawford	Hwy 61, 0.5 mile south of Soldiers Grove	James Davidson
Crawford	Soldiers Grove Park, Mill and Main Sts., Soldiers Grove	Soldiers Grove Origin
Dane	In park off Hwy A, Albion	Albion Academy
Dane	8770 Ridge Drive, Belleville	Primrose Lutheran Church
Dane	1 mile northeast of Blue Mounds, Hwy F	Brigham Park
Dane	Quivey's Grove, 6261 Nesbitt Road, Fitchburg	Mann House
Dane	2915 Syene Rd., Fitchburg	McCoy House
Dane	Camp Randall Memorial Park, UW-Madison campus	Camp Randall
Dane	8-12 N. Blount St., Madison	Ceramic Art Studio of Madison
Dane	4718 Monona Dr., Madison	Nathaniel Dean, Dean House
Dane	Vilas Communication Hall, UW-Madison campus	9XM-WHA
Dane	Bascom Hill, UW-Madison campus	North Hall
Dane	GEF III, 125 S. Webster St., Madison	Peck Cabin
Dane	Resurrection Cemetery, 2705 Regent St., Madison	Site of Former Greenbush Cemetery Burials
Dane	Olbrich Park, 3330 Atwood Ave., Madison	Third Lake Passage
Dane	415 E. Wilson St., Madison	Tragedy of War
Dane	816 State Street, Madison	State Historical Society
Dane	501 South Thornton Avenue, Madison	Yahara River Parkway
Dane	Indian Lake County Park, Hwy 19, 1 mi. E. of Marxville	Indian Lake Passage
Dane	Village Park, 39 Brodhead Street, Mazomanie	Historic Mazomanie
Dane	Branch Creek Conservancy Pk, Pleasant Branch Rd., Middleton	Pheasant Branch Encampment
Dane	Indian Mound Pk., 6200 Bl. of Ridgewood Ave., Monona	Outlet Mound
Dane	2455 West Broadway, Monona	Royal Airport/Charles Lindbergh
Dane	Entrance to Prairie Mound Cemetery, CTH M, Vil. of Oregon	Revolutionary War Veteran
Dane	Hwy 51, east shore of Lake Waubesa	Stephen Moulton Babcock (1843-1931)
Dane	Yahara River Bridge, W. Main St., 381 E. Main St., Stoughton	Main Street Historic District
Dane	La Follette County Park, 3 miles north of Stoughton	Robert Marion La Follette, Sr. (1855-1925)
Dane	300 E. Main Street, Sun Prairie	Georgia O'Keeffe
Dodge	214-216 Front St., Beaver Dam	Frederick Douglas
Dodge	Adams Spring Park, Spring Street, Fox Lake	Bernard "Bunny" Berigan (1908-1942)
Dodge	Addie Joss Park, Juneau	Adrian "Addie" Joss
Dodge	105 N. River St., Lowell	Lowell Women Firefighters
Dodge	Rest Area #64, northbound Hwy 41	World War II
Dodge	Hwys 28 and 67, on Main Street, Mayville	Wisconsin's First Iron Smelter
Dodge	Hwy 175, Theresa	Solomon Juneau House
Dodge	Jct. Hwys 26 and 67, Waupun	Auto Race – Green Bay to Madison
Door	12171 Garrett Bay Rd., Ellison Bay	The Clearing
Door	Zion Lutheran Church, 6710 CTH T, Egg Harbor	Zion Evangelical Lutheran Church
Door	Noble Square, 4167 Main Street, Fish Creek	The Alexander Noble House
Door	Namur, Hwy 57	Belgian Settlement in Wisconsin
Door	6145 Cave Point Drive, Town of Jacksonport	Jacksonport United Methodist Church
Door	Olde Stone Quarry Park, CTH B, Town of Sevastopol	Leathem and Smith Quarry
Door	3434 CTH V, Sturgeon Bay	The Episcopal Church of the Holy Nativity
Door	Hwy 42, 0.5 mile north of junction with Hwy 57	The Orchards of Door County
Douglas	Hwy 2, Brule	Brule River
Douglas	Hwys F and B, Lake Nebagamon	Evergreen Park Cottage Sanatorium
Douglas	Hwy 2, Poplar	Major "Dick" Bong
Douglas	Hwy 53, 1.5 miles south of Solon Springs	Brule-St. Croix Portage
Douglas	Allouez (Superior), along Hwys 2, 13, and 53	Burlington Northern Ore Docks
Douglas	Rest Area #23, Hwys 2 & 53, southern limits of Superior	Northwest Portal of Wisconsin
Douglas	Memorial Park, Superior	Old Stockade Site
Douglas	Whaleback Museum, Barker's Island, Superior	*S. S. Meteor*, last of the Whalebacks
Douglas	Superior Central High School, 1015 Belknap St., Superior	Summer White House – 1928
Douglas	Harbor Entry, Wisconsin Point Road, Superior	The Superior Entry
Douglas	Between McCaskill and Holden Bldgs., UW-Superior	University of Wisconsin-Superior
Douglas	Tourist Information Center, City Park, Hwy 2, Superior	Wartime Shipbuilding
Dunn	Caddie Woodlawn Park, Hwy 25, Menomonie	Caddie Woodlawn
Dunn	Rest Area #61, eastbound I94, Menomonie	Chippewa Valley White Pine
Dunn	Evergreen Cemetery, Menomonie	Dr. Stephen Tainter – Revolutionary War Veteran
Dunn	Evergreen Cemetery, north end of Shorewood Dr., Menomonie	Earliest Evergreen Burials/Evergreen Cemetery
Dunn	205 Main Street, Menomonie	Mabel Tainter Memorial
Dunn	Rest Area #62, I94	World War I
Eau Claire	Dells Mills Museum, N. of Augusta on STH 27, Augusta	Dells Mills
Eau Claire	Wayside #4, Hwy 85, 0.5 mi. west of Hwy 37, Eau Claire	Silver Mine Ski Jump

OFFICIAL HISTORICAL MARKERS IN WISCONSIN
February 2013–Continued

County	Location/Nearest Community	Subject
Fond du Lac	Fond du Lac Co. Park, W11413 CTH TC, Brandon	The Raube Road Site
Fond du Lac	Kettle Moraine Scenic Drive (CR-GGG), just north of Campbellsport	Haskell Noyes Memorial Woods
Fond du Lac	Hwy 151, 6 miles north of Fond du Lac	Edward S. Bragg
Fond du Lac	Rolling Meadows Golf Course, 560 W. Rolling Meadows Dr., Fond du Lac	County Home Cemetery Fond du Lac
Fond du Lac	Main Street and Forest Avenue, Fond du Lac	Military Road
Fond du Lac	30 East 2nd Street, Fond du Lac	Wisconsin Progressive Party
Fond du Lac	St. John the Baptist Church, Hwy W, Johnsburg	Father Caspar Rehrl
Fond du Lac	Southeast corner of Blackburn and Blossom Sts., Ripon	Birthplace of Republican Party
Fond du Lac	Pedrick Wayside, Hwy 23, Ripon	Carrie Chapman Catt
Fond du Lac	In park on Union Street, 1 block south of Hwy 23, Ripon	Ceresco
Fond du Lac	Ripon College campus, Ripon	Ripon College
Fond du Lac	Taycheedah Correctional Institution, Tn. of Taycheedah	Home of Governor James Duane Doty
Fond du Lac	Hwy 49, 4 miles east of Waupun	Horicon Marsh
Forest	Hwy 8, 1.8 miles east of Crandon	Northern Highland
Forest	Hwy 32, 1 mile south of Laona	Laona School Forest
Forest	Hwy 55, 0.5 mile north of Mole Lake	Battle of Mole Lake
Grant	Hwy 61, 0.3 miles south of Boscobel	The Gideons
Grant	Cassville	Village of Cassville
Grant	117 East Front Street, Cassville	Old Denniston House
Grant	620 Lincoln Avenue, Fennimore	The "Dinky"
Grant	Hwy 80 at the WI-IL state line, south of Hazel Green	Point of Beginning (Survey Point)
Grant	Cemetery, 1 block west of Hwys 61, 35, and 81, Lancaster	Nelson Dewey
Grant	Highway 35 and Slabtown Rd., 5 miles west of Lancaster	Pleasant Ridge
Grant	Rountree Hall, UW-Platteville	First State Normal School
Grant	114-108 South Main St., Potosi	Village of Potosi
Green	English Settlement Cemetery, 300 North Main St., Albany	English Settlement Cemetery
Green	Monroe Arts Center, 1315 11th St., Monroe	First Methodist Episcopal Church
Green	Monticello Monument Wayside, Hwy 69, Monticello	Nickolaus Gerber
Green	Village Park, 300 Blk of 2nd St., Hwy O, New Glarus	Herbert Kubly
Green	Hwy 69, New Glarus	New Glarus
Green Lake	Nathan Strong Park, East Huron St. (Hwy 116), Berlin	Lucy Smith Morris
Green Lake	Riverside Park, Berlin	Upper Fox River
Iowa	Hwy 14, 3 miles east of Arena	Village of Dover
Iowa	CTH Y, 3 mi. S. of Dodgeville	Dodge's Grove and Fort Union
Iowa	Courthouse lawn, Hwy 151, Dodgeville	Iowa County Courthouse
Iowa	Hwy YZ, 4 miles east of Dodgeville	Old Military Road
Iowa	Water Tower Park, Hwy 151, Mineral Point	Historic Mineral Point
Iowa	Iowa Co. Fairgrounds, 900 Fair St., Mineral Point	Laurence F. Graber, "Mr. Alfalfa"
Iowa	114 Shake Rag Street, Mineral Point	Shake Rag
Iowa	Library Park, Mineral Point	Wisconsin Territory
Iowa	9 Fountain St., Mineral Point	Site of Fort Jackson
Iowa	Frank Lloyd Wright Visitor Ctr., CTH C, Spring Green	Military River Crossing
Iowa	Hwy 14, east of Wisconsin River, near Spring Green	Frank Lloyd Wright
Iowa	Tower Hill State Park, Hwy C, south of Hwy 14	Shot Tower
Iron	Hwy 2, 10 miles west of Hurley	Gogebic Iron Range
Iron	Wayside WI Info. Ctr., Hwy 51, 1 mile north of Hurley	Iron Mining in Wisconsin
Jackson	Hwys 121 and 95, 1.5 mile west of Alma Center	Silver Mound
Jackson	Bell Mound Scenic Overlook, 5 mi. S. of Black River Falls	Black River Valley Scenic Outlook
Jackson	Hwy 54, 5 miles east of Black River Falls	Mitchell Red Cloud, Jr. (1925-1950)
Jackson	Rest Area #8, westbound I94, 15 mi. SE Black River Falls	The Passenger Pigeon
Jackson	Rest Area #7, eastbound I94, 15 mi. SE Black River Falls	Sphagnum Moss
Jackson	Rest Area #6, westbound I94	Highground Veterans Memorial
Jackson	Hwy 27, 6 miles south of Black River Falls	Martin M. Torkelson
Jefferson	Aztalan Museum, N6284 Hwy Q, Tn. of Aztalan	Princess Burial Mound
Jefferson	In park, north off Hwy 12, just east of Cambridge	Lake Ripley – Ole Evinrude
Jefferson	Burnt Village Co. Park, Hwy N, 2 mi. SE of Ft. Atkinson	Black Hawk War Encampment "Burnt Village"
Jefferson	400 block of Milwaukee Avenue East, Fort Atkinson	Fort Koshkonong
Jefferson	Koshkonong Mounds Road, near Fort Atkinson	Lake Koshkonong Effigy Mounds
Jefferson	Blackhawk Island Road, Town of Sumner	Lorine Niedecker
Jefferson	Hwy 106, western city limits of Fort Atkinson	Panther Intaglio
Jefferson	Iola Mills, 300 North Main St., Iola	Iola Mills
Jefferson	Rest Area #14, westbound I94	In Service to Their Country
Jefferson	3 miles east of Lake Mills on Hwy B, south on Hwy Q	Aztalan State Park
Jefferson	Rest Area #13, eastbound I94, 1 mile east of Lake Mills	Drumlins
Jefferson	Bald Bluff Overlook, CTH H, 1 1/2 mi. S. of Palmyra	Black Hawk War Encampment
Jefferson	919 Charles St., Watertown	First Kindergarten
Jefferson	7 miles southeast of Watertown, Hwy 16	Highway Marking
Jefferson	Milwaukee Street at the Rock River, Watertown	Milwaukee Street Bridge
Jefferson	919 Charles Street, Watertown	Octagon House
Jefferson	One Main St. (at bridge), Watertown	Trail Discovery
Juneau	Hwy C, 0.5 mile east of Camp Douglas	Castle Rock
Juneau	Camp Williams, off I94	Wisconsin Military Reservation
Juneau	On the trail at the western edge of Elroy	Elroy-Sparta State Trail
Juneau	In village park, Hwy HH, Lyndon Station	Hop Raising
Juneau	Rest Area #10, westbound I90-94	The Sand Counties – Aldo Leopold Territory
Juneau	Rest Area #9, eastbound I90-94, near Mauston	The Wisconsin River
Juneau	Rest Area #9, eastbound I90-94, near Mauston	The Iron Brigade
Kenosha	Rest Area #126, I94	Cordelia A.P. Harvey
Kenosha	24th Ave. & 56th St., Kenosha	Auto Production in Kenosha
Kenosha	Hwy 31 eastbound at 95th St., Kenosha	Green Bay Ethnic Trail
Kenosha	Green Ridge Cemetery, 6604 Seventh Ave., Kenosha	John McCaffery Burial Site
Kenosha	6501 3rd Avenue, Kenosha	Kemper Hall

OFFICIAL HISTORICAL MARKERS IN WISCONSIN
February 2013–Continued

County	Location/Nearest Community	Subject
Kenosha	5117 – 4th Ave., Kenosha	Kenosha (Southport) Lighthouse
Kenosha	Library Park, Kenosha	Reuben Deming
Kenosha	Green Ridge Cemetery, 6604 Seventh Avenue, Kenosha	Revolutionary War Veterans
Kenosha	15620 12th St., Kenosha	Schaefer Mammoth Site
Kenosha	Hwy 32 at the southern edge of Kenosha	32nd Division Memorial Highway
Kenosha	Rest Area-Tourist Info. Ctr. #26, westbound I94, N of I11	The Name "Wisconsin"
Kenosha	SE corner of STHs 50, 75, and 83, Town of Salem	Brass Ball Corners
Kewaunee	Ferry yard, Kewaunee	Car-Ferry Service
La Crosse	Rest Area #15, eastbound I90	The Driftless Area
La Crosse	McGilvray Rd. Access, Van Loon State Wildlife Area	The McGilvray "Seven Bridges Road"
La Crosse	Halfway Creek Lutheran Church, 2.5 mi. E. of Holmen	Luther College
La Crosse	Bishop's View Overlook, Hwy 33, 5 mi. E. of La Crosse	The Coulee Region
La Crosse	Rest Area #31, I94, French Island, La Crosse	Major General C.C. Washburn
La Crosse	La Crosse	Red Cloud Park
La Crosse	Corner of Front and State Streets, La Crosse	Spence Park
La Crosse	Rest Area-Tourist Info. Ctr. #31, I90, La Crosse	Upper Mississippi
La Crosse	Hwy 16 Valley View Mall entrance, just N. of Medary	Valley View Site
La Crosse	Neshonoc Cemetery, West Salem	Hamlin Garland
La Crosse	Swarthout Lakeside Park, Hwy 16, West Salem	Village of Neshonoc
Lafayette	First Capitol State Park, Hwy G, 4 mi. northwest of Belmont	Belmont-Wisconsin Territory 1836
Lafayette	First Capitol State Park, Hwy G, 4 mi. northwest of Belmont	Gov. Tommy G. Thompson's 1998 Address at Wisconsin's First Capitol
Lafayette	First Capitol State Park, Hwy G, 4 mi. northwest of Belmont	1998 Wisconsin Assembly (Sesquicentennial Marker)
Lafayette	Hwy 11, 1 mile west of Benton	Father Samuel Mazzuchelli
Lafayette	Intersection of Hwys F, 78, & Madison St., Blanchardville	Zarahemia – Predecessor of Blanchardville
Lafayette	101 S. Main St., Blanchardville	Zenas Gurley
Lafayette	Hwy 23, 5 miles south of Mineral Point	Fort Defiance
Lafayette	Hwy 11, 1 mile west of Shullsburg	Wisconsin Lead Region
Langlade	Hwy 52, near junction with Hwy 64	Antigo Silt Loam, State Soil of Wisconsin
Langlade	Wayside, Hwy 45, 3 miles south of Antigo	Langlade County Forest, Wisconsin's First County Forest
Langlade	Junction of Hwys 55 and 64, Langlade	De Langlade
Langlade	Hwy 55, 3.5 miles north of Lily at Wolf River	Old Military Road
Lincoln	715 E. 2nd St., Merrill	Merrill City Hall
Lincoln	Hwy 64 over the Prairie River – 200 W. First St., Merrill	Three Arch Stone Bridge
Manitowoc	CTH R, 1/2 mile N. of Schley Rd.	Rock Mill
Manitowoc	Rest Area #51, southbound I43, S. of Brown County line	Wisconsin's Dairy Industry
Manitowoc	Rest Area #52, northbound I43, S. of Brown County line	Wisconsin's Maritime Industries
Manitowoc	Lake Michigan Carferry Dock, 700 S. Lakeview Dr., Manitowoc	S. S. *Badger*/Manitowoc and the Car Ferries
Manitowoc	Mariner's Park, S. 8th St., at the Manitowoc River	Manitowoc's Maritime Heritage
Manitowoc	Manitowoc Maritime Museum, 75 Maritime Drive	Manitowoc Submarines
Manitowoc	Silver Lake Park, Hwy 151, west of Manitowoc	Winnebago Trail
Manitowoc	924 Pinecrest Lane, Manitowoc Rapids	Collins Road Bridge Span
Manitowoc	Pioneer Rd. and CTH XX, Meeme	Meeme Poll House
Manitowoc	St. Nazianz Village Hall, 228 W. Main St., St. Nazianz	George Washington School
Manitowoc	108 W. Birch, St. Nazianz	St. Nazianz
Manitowoc	Central Park, Two Rivers	Ice Cream Sundae
Manitowoc	Point Beach State Park, N. of Two Rivers on County O	Rawley Point Lighthouse
Manitowoc	Valders Memorial Park, Hwy J, Valders	Thorstein Veblen
Marathon	Rothschild Pk., Grand Ave., Park & Kort Sts., Rothschild	Wisconsin's 1st Home-Built Flying Machine
Marathon	UW-Marathon County campus, Wausau	The First Teachers' Training School in Wisconsin
Marathon	Wayside, northbound Hwy 51, 1 mile south of Hwy 153	First Workers Compensation Policy
Marinette	Peshtigo Cemetery, Oconto Avenue, Peshtigo	Peshtigo Fire Cemetery
Marinette	N2155 USH 141, Town of Pound	Lena Road Schoolhouse
Marinette	W2349 County JJ, Wausaukee	McAllister State Graded School
Marquette	Hwy 22, 8 miles south of Montello	John Muir Country
Marquette	Rest Area #82, Hwy 51, 4 miles north of Westfield	Korean War
Marquette	Westfield Town Hall, W 7703 Ember Ave. at 4th	Russell Flats
Menominee	Hwys 47 and 55, 5 miles north of Shawano	Menominee Reservation
Menominee	Hwy, 55, 2.5 miles north of Keshena	Spirit Rock
Milwaukee	8801 West Grange Avenue, Greendale	Wisconsin's Lime Industry
Milwaukee	8685 West Grange Avenue, Greendale	Jeremiah Curtin House
Milwaukee	6500 Northway, Greendale	Village of Greendale
Milwaukee	Junction of 108th St. and Cold Spring Rd., Greenfield	Cold Spring Road
Milwaukee	92nd and Forest Home Ave., Greenfield	Janesville Plank Road
Milwaukee	7325 W. Forest Home Ave., Greenfield	Town of Greenfield
Milwaukee	Zillman Park, S. Kinnickinnic Ave., Milwaukee	Bay View's Immigrants
Milwaukee	South Superior Street and East Russell Ave., Milwaukee	Bay View's Rolling Mill
Milwaukee	2000 West Wisconsin Avenue, Milwaukee	Captain Frederick Pabst
Milwaukee	Zeidler Park, 300 block of West Michigan St., Milwaukee	Carl Frederick Zeidler
Milwaukee	East Hartford & North Maryland Aves., UW-Milwaukee	Carl Sandburg Hall
Milwaukee	1756 North Prospect Avenue, Milwaukee	Civil War Camp
Milwaukee	Lobby, 700 West Virginia Street, Milwaukee	The Cream City
Milwaukee	Grounds of VA Hospital, Wood (Milwaukee)	Erastus B. Wolcott, M.D.
Milwaukee	Fourth Street and Kilbourn Avenue, Milwaukee	First African-American Church Built in Wisconsin
Milwaukee	Foot of East Michigan Street, Milwaukee	First Milwaukee Cargo Pier
Milwaukee	Layton Avenue, Milwaukee	General Mitchell Field
Milwaukee	Golda Meir Library on UW-Milwaukee campus	Golda Meir
Milwaukee	4th and State Streets, Milwaukee	Invention of the Typewriter
Milwaukee	Marquette Law School, 1103 W. WI Ave., Milwaukee	Mabel Wanda Raimey
Milwaukee	Civic Center, Milwaukee	MacArthur Square

OFFICIAL HISTORICAL MARKERS IN WISCONSIN
February 2013–Continued

County	Location/Nearest Community	Subject
Milwaukee	Merrill Park, 461 North 35th St., Milwaukee	Merrill Park
Milwaukee	Currie Park, Wauwatosa	Milwaukee County's First Airport
Milwaukee	East Hartford and North Downer Avenues, Milwaukee	Milwaukee-Downer College
Milwaukee	231 West Michigan Street, Milwaukee	Milwaukee Interurban Terminal, 1905-1951
Milwaukee	Zablocki VA Medical Center, Hwy 59	National Soldiers Home
Milwaukee	At the lighthouse in Lake Park, Milwaukee	North Point Lighthouse
Milwaukee	East North Avenue, Milwaukee	Old North Point Water Tower
Milwaukee	Wells and Edison Streets, Milwaukee	Oneida Street Station, T.M.E.R. and L. Co.
Milwaukee	144 East Wells Street, Milwaukee	Pabst Theater
Milwaukee	Cathedral Square Park, northeast corner, Milwaukee	Rescue of Joshua Glover
Milwaukee	North Avenue and Lake Drive, Milwaukee	Saint John's Infirmary
Milwaukee	North Lake Drive, Milwaukee	St. Mary's School of Nursing
Milwaukee	North Water and East Erie Streets, Milwaukee	Sinking of the *Lady Elgin*
Milwaukee	200 North Broadway, Milwaukee	Third Ward Fire
Milwaukee	Mitchell Hall, UW-Milwaukee, North Downer Avenue	The University of Wisconsin-Milwaukee
Milwaukee	Miller Brewing Company, Milwaukee	Watertown Plank Road
Milwaukee	100 East Wisconsin Avenue, Milwaukee	Wisconsin's Oldest Newspaper: The *Milwaukee Sentinel*
Milwaukee	3500 block on N. Oakland Ave., Shorewood	Lueddeman's On-the-River
Milwaukee	4145 N. Oakland Ave., Shorewood	Shorewood Armory
Milwaukee	1701 E. Capitol Drive, Shorewood	Shorewood High School
Milwaukee	3930 N. Murray Ave., Shorewood	Shorewood Village Hall
Milwaukee	909 Menomonee Ave., South Milwaukee	Lawson Airplane Company
Milwaukee	Wauwatosa Cemetery, 2405-2485 Wauwatosa Ave., Wauwatosa	Revolutionary War Veteran (Morgan)
Milwaukee	State Fair Park, Main Gate, West Allis	Camp Harvey
Milwaukee	In triangle at 57th, Hayes, and Fillmore, West Allis	Meadowmere
Milwaukee	State Fair Park, Main Gate, West Allis	Wisconsin State Fair Park
Monroe	Hwy 12, 4 miles west of Camp Douglas	Mesas and Buttes
Monroe	Rest Area #16, westbound I90, 5 miles east of Bangor	Coulee Country
Monroe	At the Kendall Depot, North Railroad Street, Kendall	Elroy-Sparta State Trail
Monroe	Old Leon School, 20638 Jameson Rd., Sparta	Donald "Deke" Slayton
Monroe	200 West Main Street, Sparta	Masonic Lodge
Monroe	112 South Court Street, Sparta	Monroe County Courthouse
Monroe	124 West Main Street, Sparta	Sparta Free Library
Monroe	123 West Main Street, Sparta	U.S. Post Office
Monroe	In park on Hwy 12, Tomah	Tomah
Oconto	Hwy F, 1.5 miles east of Lakewood	The Holt and Balcom Logging Camp No. 1
Oconto	Chicago and Main Streets, Oconto	First Church of Christ Scientist
Oconto	On Oconto River at Brazeau Avenue, Oconto	Mission of St. Francois Xavier
Oconto	Copper Culture State Park, Oconto	Old Copper Culture Cemetery
Oconto	1301 Main Street, Oconto	Stanley Toy Company
Oneida	Junction of CR-B and CR-Z, Pelican Lake	Mecikalski Stovewood Building
Oneida	Oneida County Courthouse grounds, Rhinelander	First Rural Zoning Ordinance
Oneida	Hodag Park, Rhinelander	The Hodag
Oneida	W. edge of National Forest, off Hwy 32 E. of Three Lakes	Nicolet National Forest
Outagamie	807 South Oneida Street, Appleton	First Electric Street Railway
Outagamie	600 Vulcan Street, Appleton	World's First Hydroelectric Central Station
Outagamie	North of jct. Hwys BB and 45, 4 miles west of Appleton	South Greenville Grange No. 225
Outagamie	Thelen Park, Kaukauna	Revolutionary War Veterans
Outagamie	Hwy 96, 0.1 mile west of Little Chute	Treaty of the Cedars
Outagamie	Beacon Avenue and Division Street, New London	Birthplace of the American Water Spaniel
Ozaukee	Intersection of CTHs R & C, Belgium	Wisconsin's Luxembourgers
Ozaukee	Columbia Rd. and Mequon Ave., Cedarburg	Cedar Creek
Ozaukee	City Hall, Washington Avenue, Cedarburg	Historic Cedarburg
Ozaukee	W62 N646 Washington Ave., Cedarburg	Interurban Bridge
Ozaukee	Doctor's Park, Washington Ave. and Mill St., Cedarburg	Washington Avenue Historic District
Ozaukee	Covered Bridge Road, 1 mile north of Five Corners	Last Covered Bridge
Ozaukee	Mequon City Hall, 11333 North Cedarburg Rd., Mequon	Wisconsin's German Settlers
Ozaukee	Ozaukee County Courthouse, 121 West Main Street, Port Washington	Port Washington Civil War Draft Riots
Ozaukee	102 East Pier Street, Port Washington	Port Washington Fire Engine House
Ozaukee	108 N. Lake St., Port Washington	The Wisconsin Chair Company Fire
Ozaukee	Triangle Park and Green Bay Rd., Saukville	The Saukville Trails
Ozaukee	Entrance Wall, 250 S. Main St., Thiensville	Historic Thiensville
Ozaukee	Junction of Hwys F and M, 3 miles west of Thiensville	The Oldest Lutheran Church in Wisconsin
Ozaukee	Hwy I, 0.5 mile east of Waubeka	Birthplace of Flag Day
Pepin	Washington Square, Durand	Pepin County Courthouse
Pepin	Hwy 35, 1 mile north of Stockholm	Maiden Rock
Pepin	Hwy 35, Pepin Park	Laura Ingalls Wilder
Pepin	Hwy 35, 3 miles northwest of Pepin	Site of Fort St. Antoine
Pierce	Hwy 35, 1 mile south of Hwy 63, southeast of Hager City	"Bow and Arrow"
Pierce	Hwy 35, 3 miles west of Maiden Rock	Lake Pepin
Pierce	Spring Pond Park, East Mill Rd., Plum City	Historic Plum City
Pierce	Hwy 65, 3 miles south of I94	Edgar Wilson Nye
Polk	Hwy 35, Luck	Danish Cooperative Company
Polk	City Park, St. Croix Falls	The Battle of St. Croix Falls
Polk	Interstate Park, St. Croix Falls	Gaylord Nelson
Polk	Interstate Park, Hwy 8, St. Croix Falls	State Park Movement in Wisconsin
Polk	Overlook Park, N. Washington (Main) St., St. Croix Falls	Where Are the Falls of the St. Croix?
Portage	County W, Buena Vista Marsh Wildlife Area	Wisconsin's Greater Prairie Chicken
Portage	Portage County Park, Hwy E, 3 miles south of Knowlton	Du Bay Trading Post
Portage	1700 block of Monroe St., Stevens Point	The Historic Southside Railroad Complex of Stevens Point
Price	Movrich Park, Willow Avenue, Town of Fifield	Historic Fifield

OFFICIAL HISTORICAL MARKERS IN WISCONSIN
February 2013–Continued

County	Location/Nearest Community	Subject
Price	Hwy 13, Phillips City Park, Phillips	Phillips Fire
Racine	Weimhoff-Jucker Park, Burlington	Mormons in Early Wisconsin
Racine	Hwy 31 at 5 Mile Rd., Town of Caledonia	Bohemian School House
Racine	936 South Main Street, Racine	The Blake House/Lucius Blake
Racine	Zoological Gardens, 2131 N. Main St., Racine	Northside Historic District of Cream Brick Cottages
Racine	Graceland and Mound Cemeteries, 1147 West Blvd., Racine	Soldiers of the American Revolution
Racine	Simonsen Park, Main & Fourteenth Sts., Racine	Southside Historic District
Racine	Hwy 11, western limits of Racine	The Spark
Racine	Racine Village Park, 4725 Lighthouse Dr., Racine	The Wind Point Lighthouse
Racine	1407 71st Drive, Union Grove	Revolutionary War Veteran
Racine	Heg Park Road, Waterford	Old Muskego
Richland	Boaz Park, Hwy 171, Boaz	Ocooch Mountains
Richland	Boaz Park, Hwy 171, Boaz	Richard M. Brewer
Richland	Wayside, Hwy 14, 1 mi. E. Gotham, Town of Buena Vista	The Pursuit West
Richland	Krouskop Park, 400 W. 6th St. (Hwy 14), Richland Center	Ada James
Richland	Krouskop Park, 400 W. 6th St. (Hwy 14), Richland Center	Birthplace of General Telephone and Electronics Corporation (GTE)
Richland	Hwy 14, 5 miles west of Richland Center	Boaz Mastodon
Richland	Pier County Park, Hwy 80, Rockbridge	Rockbridge
Richland	5 miles west of Richland Center on Hwy 14	Rural Electrification
Richland	Pier Co. Park, Hwy 80, Rockbridge	Troop Encampment
Rock	Beloit College campus, Beloit	Beloit College
Rock	Rock River Heritage Wky., Public Ave. & State St., Beloit	Black Hawk at Turtle Village
Rock	Tourist Info. Ctr. #22, westbound I90, south of Beloit	Black Hawk War
Rock	Rest Area-Tourist Information Center, westbound I90	Medal of Honor
Rock	I43 at I90, Beloit	Wisconsin's First Aviator
Rock	Hwy 140, 4 miles south of Clinton	Jefferson Prairie Settlement
Rock	11204 N. Church St., Cooksville	Historic Cooksville/Historic Waucoma
Rock	Mt. Philip Cemetery, west of Darien	Soldier of the American Revolution
Rock	Hwy 51, 0.5 miles south of Edgerton	Wisconsin's Tobacco Land
Rock	Blackhawk Golf Course Clubhouse, 2100 Palmer, Janesville	The Black Hawk War/Black Hawk's Grove
Rock	NW corner of Delavan Dr. and Beloit Ave., Janesville	Burr Robins Circus
Rock	In Courthouse Park on S. Atwood Ave., Janesville	First State Fair, October 1-2, 1851
Rock	Rock County Historical Society, 10 S. High St., Janesville	Janesville Tank Company
Rock	Rest Area #17, eastbound I90	Rock River Industry
Rock	Hwy 51, 3.8 miles south of Janesville	Route of Abraham Lincoln 1832 and 1859
Rock	18 South Janesville Street, Hwy 26, Milton	Milton House
Rock	On southwest bank of Storr's Lake, off Hwy 26, Milton	Storr's Lake, Milton
Rock	Beckman Mill Co. Park, Co. Rd. H, Town of Newark	How-Beckman Mill
Rock	Hwy J, Shopiere	Home of Governor Harvey
Rusk	Appolonia Cong. Church, Hwy 8 & Cemetery Rd., Bruce	Appolonia
Rusk	Hwy 8, Weyerhauser	Chippewa River and Menomonie Railway
St. Croix	Rest Area-Tourist Info. Ctr. #25, I94 east of Hudson	Brule-St. Croix Waterway
St. Croix	Hwy 35, 4.7 miles north of Hudson	St. Croix River
St. Croix	Campus Drive, Outlot #3, New Richmond	New Richmond Cyclone
Sauk	Devil's Lake State Park, S5975 Park Rd., Baraboo	Civilian Conservation Corps
Sauk	Hwy 33 at County U, 5 miles east of Baraboo	Lower Narrows
Sauk	Hwy 12, 1.5 miles south of Baraboo	Ringling Brothers Circus
Sauk	CTH A, near junction of Old County Hwy A and Dam Rd., Lake Delton	Lake Delton Catastrophe
Sauk	E8948 Diamond Hill Rd., North Freedom	Mid-Continent Railway Historical Society
Sauk	Reedsburg Area Historical Park, 3 mi. E. of Reedsburg	Clare A. Briggs, Cartoonist
Sauk	State Hwy 136, 0.75 mi. N of STH 154, Rock Springs	Van Hise Rock
Sauk	Derleth Park, Water Street, Sauk City	August W. Derleth
Sauk	Hwy 12, 5 miles northwest of Sauk City	The Baraboo Range
Sauk	Lower WI Riverway, Hwy 78, 2 mi. N. of Sauk City	Battle of Wisconsin Heights
Sauk	Lower WI Riverway, Hwy 60, 2 mi. E. of Spring Green	Western Escape
Sauk	Hwy A, 1.5 miles south of Wisconsin Dells	Dawn Manor – Site of Lost City of Newport
Sauk	Hwy 16, 0.1 mile west of Wisconsin Dells	Wisconsin Dells
Sawyer	Hwys 70 and 27, Couderay	Court Oreilles
Sawyer	Hwys 27 and 70, 7 miles west of Couderay	Radisson-Groseilliers
Sawyer	Hermans Landing, Cty Rd CC, at bridge, Hayward	The Chippewa Flowage
Sawyer	Lac Courte Oreilles Reservation, 13891 W. Mission Rd.	St. Francis Solanus Indian Mission
Sawyer	Hwy 27, 5.5 miles south of Hayward	Namekagon-Court Oreilles Portage
Sawyer	Hwy W, 6.75 miles southeast of Winter	John Deitz, "Battle of Cameron Dam"
Shawano	Hwy 22, 3.5 miles east of Shawano	Shawano
Shawano	Hwy 45 at city limits of Wittenberg	Homme Homes
Sheboygan	50 South Main Street, Cedar Grove	Early Dutch Settlers in Wisconsin
Sheboygan	Lake Street Café Beer Garden, N. of Vil. of Elkhart Lake	Elkhart Lake – Road Race Circuits
Sheboygan	Hwy 23, in the Park at Greenbush, 6 mi. W. of Plymouth	Old Wade House State Park
Sheboygan	Memorial Park, Garden Drive, 3 miles south of Oostburg	Dutch Settlement
Sheboygan	Heritage House Triangle Pk., Ctr. & N. 10th Sts., Oostburg	Historic Oostburg
Sheboygan	Greenleaf Historic Park, 900 Short Street, Random Lake	Nowack House
Sheboygan	Sheboygan North Point Park, North Point Dr., Sheboygan	The *Phoenix* Tragedy
Sheboygan	Wildwood Cemetery, 2026 New Jersey Ave., Sheboygan	Revolutionary War Veteran (David Waldo)
Sheboygan	Center Avenue and North Water Street, Sheboygan	Seils-Sterling Circus
Sheboygan	9th Street and Panther Avenue, Sheboygan	Sheboygan Indian Mound Park
Sheboygan	1138 Union Ave., Sheboygan	Veterans of Foreign Wars Post 1230
Sheboygan	Rochester Inn, 504 Water St., Sheboygan Falls	Cole Historic District
Sheboygan	Sheboygan River Dam, Broadway St., Sheboygan Falls	Downtown Sheboygan Falls Historic District
Taylor	Hwy 102, Rib Lake	Rib Lake Lumber Company
Taylor	Hwy 102, 3 miles northeast of Rib Lake	Rustic Road
Trempealeau	Hwy 53, 1.5 miles southeast of Galesville	Decorah Peak
Trempealeau	Junction of East Gale Avenue and Main Street, Galesville	Downtown Galesville Historic District

OFFICIAL HISTORICAL MARKERS IN WISCONSIN
February 2013–Continued

County	Location/Nearest Community	Subject
Trempealeau	STH 53 over Beaver Creek, Galesville	Galesville Bridge
Trempealeau	North of Main Hall, College Ave., Galesville	Galesville College
Trempealeau	Junction of West Ridge Ave. and Sixth St. near Cance Park, Galesville	Ridge Avenue Historic District
Trempealeau	Rest Area #5, eastbound I94, 2 miles southeast of Osseo	Winnebago Indians
Trempealeau	Great River State Tr., Hwy 35, 0.5 mi. E. of Trempealeau	The Mississippi River Parkway: First Project
Trempealeau	Perrot State Park	Brady's Bluff
Trempealeau	Perrot State Park, off Hwy 93	Perrot's Post
Vernon	Hwy 14, 0.5 mile west of Coon Valley	Nation's First Watershed Project
Vernon	Hwy 35, 2.5 miles north of De Soto	Battle of Bad Axe
Vernon	Hwy 35, 2 miles north of De Soto	Chief Win-no-shik, the Elder
Vernon	Hwy 35, Genoa	Dams on the Mississippi
Vernon	In power plant parking lot, west side of Hwy 35, Genoa	Wisconsin's First Nuclear-Fueled Generating Station
Vernon	Hwy 33, 0.1 mile west of Hillsboro	Admiral Marc A. Mitscher
Vernon	Hillsboro Lake Park, 300 Water Ave. at Hwys 80, 82, 33, Hillsboro	African American Settlers of the Cheyenne Valley
Vernon	Hwy 14, 0.5 mile north of Viroqua	Governor Rusk
Vernon	City Hall, 202 N. Main St., Viroqua	Viroqua's First Settler
Vilas	Hwy M, 6 miles south of Boulder Junction	First Forest Patrol Flight
Vilas	Trout Lake Nursery, Hwy M.	Forest Restoration – The Beginning
Vilas	Hwy 47, Flambeau Lake	Lac du Flambeau
Vilas	Lac Vieux Desert Park, West Shore Dr. near Land O'Lakes	Lac Vieux Desert
Vilas	Hwys 32 and 45, 0.5 mile south of Land O'Lakes	32nd Division Memorial Highway
Vilas	Hwy 45, 1.5 miles south of Land O'Lakes	Wisconsin River Headwaters
Vilas	Sayner Park, Sayner	Snowmobile
Walworth	Village Park, Allen Grove, on Hwy X, 3 mi. SW of Darien	Allen Family
Walworth	City of Delavan Parking Lot, 218 South 7th St., Delavan	Birthplace of "The Greatest Show on Earth"
Walworth	Horton Park, Hwy 11 in Delavan	Delavan's Circus Colony
Walworth	Tower Park, Walworth Ave., Delavan	Delavan's Historic Brick Street
Walworth	Grounds of State School for the Deaf, Hwy 11, Delavan	Wisconsin's First School for Deaf
Walworth	300 Church Street, East Troy	East Troy Railroad
Walworth	Veterans Memorial Park, Hwy 12, Genoa City	First Swedish Settlers in Wisconsin
Walworth	Hwy BB, 3.5 miles south of Lake Geneva	Wisconsin's First 4-H Club
Walworth	Oak Grove Cemetery, East Main Street, Whitewater	Revolutionary War Veterans
Walworth	Hwy 67 Industrial Park, N3440 STH 67 Williams Bay	755 Aircraft Control and Warning Squadron
Washburn	Hwy 70, 0.5 mile east of Spooner	Yellow River
Washburn	Junction of Hwys 53 and 63, Trego	Namekagon River
Washington	Dheinsville Park, Holy Hill Rd., Germantown	Dheinsville Settlement
Washington	Chandelier Ballroom, 700 South Main Street, Hartford	The Schwartz Ballroom
Washington	Hwy 83, Hartford	"Kissel"
Washington	South side of Hwy 33, 550 feet west of jct. with Hwy 144	Great Divide
Washington	At the park, Hwy A, E. of Hwy 114, NW of West Bend	Lizard Mound County Park
Waukesha	408 Main St., Delafield	Delafield Fish Hatchery
Waukesha	Southern Kettle Moraine State Forest, County C, Delafield	Lapham Peak
Waukesha	Mission Road at Mill Road, west of Delafield	Nashotah Mission
Waukesha	1101 North Genesee Street, Delafield	St. John's Northwestern Military Academy
Waukesha	Hwy 18, near Dousman	Masonic Home
Waukesha	Main Street, Lannon	Lannon Stone
Waukesha	N51 W34922 Wisconsin Ave., Okauchee	Historic Okauchee
Waukesha	Carroll College campus, Waukesha	Carroll College
Waupaca	Municipal Airport, Clintonville	Birthplace of an Airline
Waupaca	Walter Olen Park, Clintonville	Four-Wheel Drive
Waupaca	Marden Memorial Center, WI Veterans Home, King	General Charles King
Waupaca	Marden Memorial Center, WI Veterans Home, King	Grand Army Home
Waupaca	Triangle Park, Jct. of Hwy 22 with 110 and Hwy B, Manawa	Melvin O. Handrich – Medal of Honor Recipient
Waupaca	Hwy 110, 3.5 miles south of Marion	Chief Waupaca
Waushara	County J, 2 miles south of Almond	Sir Henry Wellcome
Waushara	State Hwy 49, Auroraville	The Auroraville Fountain
Waushara	6th Ave., Town of Hancock	Whistler Mound Group and Enclosure
Winnebago	9088 Clayton Avenue, Town of Menasha	Fox-Irish Cemetery
Winnebago	Menasha Hotel, Main and Mills Streets, Menasha	Wisconsin Central Railroad
Winnebago	Fritsie Park, Menasha	Butte des Morts
Winnebago	Interior walkway, 135 W. Wisconsin Ave., Neenah	Wisconsin Avenue Commercial Historic District
Winnebago	Scott Park, 515 E. Main St., Omro	Historic Omro
Winnebago	1619 Oshkosh Avenue, Oshkosh	Coles Bashford House
Winnebago	Oshkosh Public Museum, 1331 Algoma Blvd., Oshkosh	Edgar Sawyer House
Winnebago	Rainbow Park, Oshkosh	Knaggs Ferry
Winnebago	Wittman Field Airport, 20th Street Road, Oshkosh	S.J. Wittman
Winnebago	UW-Oshkosh campus, Oshkosh	University of Wisconsin-Oshkosh
Winnebago	Town of Winchester Cemetery, 1 mi. SW of Winchester	Samuel N. Rogers, Sr., American Revolutionary Soldier
Winnebago	Hwy B, west of Winneconne	Poygan Paygrounds
Wood	Wayside #4, junction of Hwys 10 and 13	Prisoners of War
Wood	West 100 Block of North Central Ave., Marshfield	Founder's Square
Wood	Riverside Park, Hwys 54 and 73, Nekoosa	Point Basse
Wood	Hwy 54, 5 miles west of Port Edwards	Cranberry Culture
Wood	Hwys 54 and 73, southern city limits of Wisconsin Rapids	Centralia Pulp and Paper Mill
Wood	South Wood County Historical Museum, 540 3rd Street S, Wisconsin Rapids	Myron "Grim" Natwick

Sources: State Historical Society of Wisconsin, Historical Markers Council, *A Guide to Wisconsin Historical Markers,* 1982; Division of Historic Preservation, departmental data, June 2013.

WISCONSIN VOTE IN PRESIDENTIAL ELECTIONS
1848 – 2012

Key:
A – American (Know Nothing)	LR – Liberal Republican	Soc – Socialist
AFC – America First Coalition	NA – New Alliance	SocUSA – Socialist Party USA
Cit – Citizens	Nat – National	SoD – Southern Democrat
Com – Communist	ND – National Democrat	SPW – Socialist Party of Wis.
Con – Constitution	NER – National Economic Recovery	SW – Socialist Worker
CU – Constitutional Union	NL – Natural Law	Tax – U.S. Taxpayers
D – Democrat	People's – People's (Populist)	TBL – The Better Life
ER – Independents for Economic Recovery	Pop – Populist	3rd – Third Party
FS – Free Soil	PP – People's Progressive	U – Union
G – Greenback	Prog – Progressive	UL – Union Labor
Gr – Grassroots	Proh – Prohibition	USL – U.S. Labor
Grn – Green	R – Republican	W – Whig
Ind – Independent	Rfm – Reform	WG – Wisconsin Greens
IP – Ind. Progressive	SD – Social Democrat	WIA – Wis. Independent Alliance
IS – Ind. Socialist	SE – Socialist Equality	Workers – Workers
ISL – Ind. Socialist Labor	SL – Socialist Labor	WtP – We, the People
ISW – Ind. Socialist Worker	S&L – Party for Socialism and	WW – Worker's World
LF – Labor–Farm/Laborista-Agrario	Liberation	
Lib – Libertarian		

Note: The party designation listed for a candidate is taken from the Congressional Quarterly *Guide to U.S. Elections*. A candidate whose party did not receive 1% of the vote for a statewide office in the previous election or who failed to meet the alternative requirement of Section 5.62, Wisconsin Statutes, must be listed on the Wisconsin ballot as "independent". In this listing, candidates whose party affiliations appear as "Ind", followed by a party designation, were identified on the ballot simply as "independent" although they also provided a party designation or statement of principle.

Under the Electoral College system, each state is entitled to electoral votes equal in number to its total congressional delegation of U.S. Senators and U.S. Representatives.

1848 (4 electoral votes)
Lewis Cass (D)	15,001
Zachary Taylor (W)	13,747
Martin Van Buren (FS)	10,418
TOTAL	39,166

1852 (5 electoral votes)
Franklin Pierce (D)	33,658
Winfield Scott (W)	22,210
John P. Hale (FS)	8,814
TOTAL	64,682

1856 (5 electoral votes)
John C. Fremont (R)	66,090
James Buchanan (D)	52,843
Millard Fillmore (A)	579
TOTAL	119,512

1860 (5 electoral votes)
Abraham Lincoln (R)	86,113
Stephen A. Douglas (D)	65,021
John C. Breckinridge (SoD)	888
John Bell (CU)	161
TOTAL	152,183

1864 (8 electoral votes)
Abraham Lincoln (R)	83,458
George B. McClellan (D)	65,884
TOTAL	149,342

1868 (8 electoral votes)
Ulysses S. Grant (R)	108,857
Horatio Seymour (D)	84,707
TOTAL	193,564

1872 (10 electoral votes)
Ulysses S. Grant (R)	104,994
Horace Greeley (D & LR)	86,477
Charles O'Conor (D)	834
TOTAL	192,305

1876 (10 electoral votes)
Rutherford B. Hayes (R)	130,668
Samuel J. Tilden (D)	123,927
Peter Cooper (G)	1,509
Green Clay Smith (Proh)	27
TOTAL	256,131

1880 (10 electoral votes)
James A. Garfield (R)	144,398
Winfield S. Hancock (D)	114,644
James B. Weaver (G)	7,986
John W. Phelps (A)	91
Neal Dow (Proh)	68
TOTAL	267,187

1884 (11 electoral votes)
James G. Blaine (R)	161,157
Grover Cleveland (D)	146,477
John P. St. John (Proh)	7,656
Benjamin F. Butler (G)	4,598
TOTAL	319,888

1888 (11 electoral votes)
Benjamin Harrison (R)	176,553
Grover Cleveland (D)	155,232
Clinton B. Fisk (Proh)	14,277
Alson J. Streeter (UL)	8,552
TOTAL	354,614

1892 (12 electoral votes)
Grover Cleveland (D)	177,325
Benjamin Harrison (R)	171,101
John Bidwell (Proh)	13,136
James B. Weaver (People's)	10,019
TOTAL	371,581

1896 (12 electoral votes)
William McKinley (R)	268,135
William J. Bryan (D)	165,523
Joshua Levering (Proh)	7,507
John M. Palmer (ND)	4,584
Charles H. Matchett (SL)	1,314
Charles E. Bentley (Nat)	346
TOTAL	447,409

1900 (12 electoral votes)
William McKinley (R)	265,760
William J. Bryan (D)	159,163
John G. Wooley (Proh)	10,027
Eugene V. Debs (SD)	7,048
Joseph F. Malloney (SL)	503
TOTAL	442,501

1904 (13 electoral votes)
Theodore Roosevelt (R)	280,164
Alton B. Parker (D)	124,107
Eugene V. Debs (SD)	28,220
Silas C. Swallow (Proh)	9,770
Thomas E. Watson (People's)	530
Charles H. Corregan (SL)	223
TOTAL	443,014

1908 (13 electoral votes)
William H. Taft (R)	247,747
William J. Bryan (D)	166,632
Eugene V. Debs (SD)	28,164
Eugene W. Chafin (Proh)	11,564
August Gillhaus (SL)	314
TOTAL	454,421

WISCONSIN VOTE IN PRESIDENTIAL ELECTIONS
1848 – 2012–Continued

1912 (13 electoral votes)

Woodrow Wilson (D)	164,230
William H. Taft (R)	130,596
Theodore Roosevelt (Prog)	62,448
Eugene V. Debs (SD)	33,476
Eugene W. Chafin (Proh)	8,584
Arthur E. Reimer (SL)	632
TOTAL	399,966

1916 (13 electoral votes)

Charles E. Hughes (R)	220,822
Woodrow Wilson (D)	191,363
Allan Benson (Soc)	27,631
J. Frank Hanly (Proh)	7,318
TOTAL	447,134

1920 (13 electoral votes)

Warren G. Harding (R)	498,576
James M. Cox (D)	113,422
Eugene V. Debs (Soc)	80,635
Aaron S. Watkins (Proh)	8,647
TOTAL	701,280

1924 (13 electoral votes)

Robert M. La Follette (Prog)	453,678
Calvin Coolidge (R)	311,614
John W. Davis (D)	68,096
William Z. Foster (Workers)	3,834
Herman P. Faris (Proh)	2,918
TOTAL	840,140

1928 (13 electoral votes)

Herbert Hoover (R)	544,205
Alfred E. Smith (D)	450,259
Norman Thomas (Soc)	18,213
William F. Varney (Proh)	2,245
William Z. Foster (Workers)	1,528
Verne L. Reynolds (SL)	381
TOTAL	1,016,831

1932 (12 electoral votes)

Franklin D. Roosevelt (D)	707,410
Herbert Hoover (R)	347,741
Norman Thomas (Soc)	53,379
William Z. Foster (Com)	3,112
William D. Upshaw (Proh)	2,672
Verne L. Reynolds (SL)	494
TOTAL	1,114,808

1936 (12 electoral votes)

Franklin D. Roosevelt (D)	802,984
Alfred M. Landon (R)	380,828
William Lemke (U)	60,297
Norman Thomas (Soc)	10,626
Earl Browder (Com)	2,197
David L. Calvin (Proh)	1,071
John W. Aiken (SL)	557
TOTAL	1,258,560

1940 (12 electoral votes)

Franklin D. Roosevelt (D)	704,821
Wendell Willkie (R)	679,206
Norman Thomas (Soc)	15,071
Earl Browder (Com)	2,394
Roger Babson (Proh)	2,148
John W. Aiken (SL)	1,882
TOTAL	1,405,522

1944 (12 electoral votes)

Thomas Dewey (R)	674,532
Franklin D. Roosevelt (D)	650,413
Norman Thomas (Soc)	13,205
Edward Teichert (Ind)	1,002
TOTAL	1,339,152

1948 (12 electoral votes)

Harry S Truman (D)	647,310
Thomas Dewey (R)	590,959
Henry Wallace (PP)	25,282
Norman Thomas (Soc)	12,547
Edward Teichert (Ind)	399
Farrell Dobbs (ISW)	303
TOTAL	1,276,800

1952 (12 electoral votes)

Dwight D. Eisenhower (R)	979,744
Adlai E. Stevenson (D)	622,175
Vincent Hallinan (IP)	2,174
Farrell Dobbs (ISW)	1,350
Darlington Hoopes (IS)	1,157
Eric Hass (ISL)	770
TOTAL	1,607,370

1956 (12 electoral votes)

Dwight D. Eisenhower (R)	954,844
Adlai E. Stevenson (D)	586,768
T. Coleman Andrews (Ind Con)	6,918
Darlington Hoopes (Ind Soc)	754
Eric Hass (Ind SL)	710
Farrell Dobbs (Ind SW)	564
TOTAL	1,550,558

1960 (12 electoral votes)

Richard M. Nixon (R)	895,175
John F. Kennedy (D)	830,805
Farrell Dobbs (Ind SW)	1,792
Eric Hass (Ind SL)	1,310
TOTAL	1,729,082

1964 (12 electoral votes)

Lyndon B. Johnson (D)	1,050,424
Barry M. Goldwater (R)	638,495
Clifton DeBerry (Ind SW)	1,692
Eric Hass (Ind SL)	1,204
TOTAL	1,691,815

1968 (12 electoral votes)

Richard M. Nixon (R)	809,997
Hubert H. Humphrey (D)	748,804
George C. Wallace (Ind A)	127,835
Henning A. Blomen (Ind SL)	1,338
Frederick W. Halstead (Ind SW)	1,222
TOTAL	1,689,196

1972 (11 electoral votes)

Richard M. Nixon (R)	989,430
George S. McGovern (D)	810,174
John G. Schmitz (A)	47,525
Benjamin M. Spock (Ind Pop)	2,701
Louis Fisher (Ind SL)	998
Gus Hall (Ind Com)	663
Evelyn Reed (Ind SW)	506
TOTAL	1,851,997

1976 (11 electoral votes)

Jimmy Carter (D)	1,040,232
Gerald R. Ford (R)	1,004,987
Eugene J. McCarthy (Ind)	34,943
Lester Maddox (A)	8,552
Frank P. Zeidler (Ind Soc)	4,298
Roger L. MacBride (Ind Lib)	3,814
Peter Camejo (Ind SW)	1,691
Margaret Wright (Ind Pop)	943
Gus Hall (Ind Com)	749
Lyndon H. LaRouche, Jr. (Ind USL)	738
Jules Levin (Ind SL)	389
TOTAL	2,104,175

WISCONSIN VOTE IN PRESIDENTIAL ELECTIONS
1848 – 2012–Continued

1980 (11 electoral votes)	
Ronald Reagan (R)	1,088,845
Jimmy Carter (D)	981,584
John Anderson (Ind)	160,657
Ed Clark (Ind Lib)	29,135
Barry Commoner (Ind Cit)	7,767
John Rarick (Ind Con)	1,519
David McReynolds (Ind Soc)	808
Gus Hall (Ind Com)	772
Deidre Griswold (Ind WW)	414
Clifton DeBerry (Ind SW)	383
TOTAL	2,273,221

1984 (11 electoral votes)	
Ronald Reagan (R)	1,198,800
Walter F. Mondale (D)	995,847
David Bergland (Lib)	4,884
Bob Richards (Con)	3,864
Lyndon H. LaRouche, Jr. (Ind)	3,791
Sonia Johnson (Ind Cit)	1,456
Dennis L. Serrette (Ind WIA)	1,007
Larry Holmes (Ind WW)	619
Gus Hall (Ind Com)	597
Melvin T. Mason (Ind SW)	445
TOTAL	2,212,018

1988 (11 electoral votes)	
Michael S. Dukakis (D)	1,126,794
George Bush (R)	1,047,499
Ronald Paul (Ind Lib)	5,157
David E. Duke (Ind Pop)	3,056
James Warren (Ind SW)	2,574
Lyndon H. LaRouche, Jr. (Ind NER)	2,302
Lenora B. Fulani (Ind NA)	1,953
TOTAL	2,191,612

1992 (11 electoral votes)	
Bill Clinton (D)	1,041,066
George Bush (R)	930,855
Ross Perot (Ind)	544,479
Andre Marrou (Lib)	2,877
James Gritz (Ind AFC)	2,311
Ron Daniels (LF)	1,883
Howard Phillips (Ind Tax)	1,772
J. Quinn Brisben (Ind Soc)	1,211
John Hagelin (NL)	1,070
Lenora B. Fulani (Ind NA)	654
Lyndon H. LaRouche, Jr. (Ind ER)	633
Jack Herer (Ind Gr)	547
Eugene A. Hem (3rd)	405
James Warren (Ind SW)	390
TOTAL	2,531,114

1996 (11 electoral votes)	
Bill Clinton (D)	1,071,971
Bob Dole (R)	845,029
Ross Perot (Rfm)	227,339
Ralph Nader (Ind WG)	28,723
Howard Phillips (Tax)	8,811
Harry Browne (Lib)	7,929
John Hagelin (Ind NL)	1,379
Monica Mooerhead (Ind WW)	1,333
Mary Cal Hollis (Ind Soc)	848
James E. Harris (Ind SW)	483
TOTAL	2,196,169

2000 (11 electoral votes)	
Al Gore (D)	1,242,987
George W. Bush (R)	1,237,279
Ralph Nader (WG)	94,070
Pat Buchanan (Ind Rfm)	11,446
Harry Browne (Lib)	6,640
Howard Phillips (Con)	2,042
Monica G. Moorehead (Ind WW)	1,063
John Hagelin (Ind Rfm)	878
James Harris (Ind SW)	306
TOTAL	2,598,607

2004 (10 electoral votes)	
John F. Kerry (D)	1,489,504
George W. Bush (R)	1,478,120
Ralph Nader (Ind TBL)	16,390
Michael Badnarik (Lib)	6,464
David Cobb (WG)	2,661
Walter F. Brown (Ind SPW)	471
James Harris (Ind SW)	411
TOTAL	2,997,007

2008 (10 electoral votes)	
Barack Obama (D)	1,677,211
John McCain (R)	1,262,393
Ralph Nader (Ind)	17,605
Bob Barr (Lib)	8,858
Chuck Baldwin (Ind Con)	5,072
Cynthia McKinney (WG)	4,216
Jeffrey J. Wamboldt (Ind WtP)	764
Brian Moore (Ind Soc USA)	540
Gloria La Riva (Ind S&L)	237
TOTAL	2,983,417

2012 (10 electoral votes)	
Barack Obama (D)	1,620,985
Mitt Romney (R)	1,407,966
Gary Johnson (Ind Lib)	20,439
Jill Stein (Ind Grn)	7,665
Virgil Goode (Con)	4,930
Jerry White (Ind SE)	553
Gloria La Riva (Ind S&L)	526
TOTAL	3,068,434

Note: Some totals include scattered votes for other candidates.

Sources: Official records of the Government Accountability Board, Elections Division and Congressional Quarterly, *Guide to U.S. Elections*, 1994.

VOTE FOR GOVERNOR IN GENERAL ELECTIONS
1848 – 2012

Key:

A – American	IPR – Independent Prohibition Republic	Prog – Progressive
C – Conservative	ISL – Independent Socialist Labor	Proh – Prohibition
Com – Communist	ISW – Independent Socialist Worker	R – Republican
Con – Constitution	IW – Independent Worker	Soc – Socialist
D – Democrat	L – Labor	SD – Social Democrat
DS – Democratic Socialist	LF – Labor-Farm/Laborista-Agrario	SDA – Social Democrat of America
G – Greenback	Lib – Libertarian	SL – Socialist Labor
Ind – Independent	Nat – National	SW – Socialist Worker
IC – Independent Communist	NR – National Republic	Tax – U.S. Taxpayers
ID – Independent Democrat	People's – People's (Populist)	U – Union
IL – Independent Labor	PLS – Progressive Labor Socialist	UL – Union Labor
IP – Independent Prohibition	PP – People's Progressive	W – Whig

Note: A candidate whose party did not receive 1% of the vote for a statewide office in the previous election or who failed to meet the alternative requirement of Section 5.62, Wisconsin Statutes, is listed on the Wisconsin ballot as "independent". When a candidate's party affiliation is listed as "independent" and a party designation is shown in italics, "independent" was the official ballot listing, but a party designation was found by the Wisconsin Legislative Reference Bureau in newspaper reports.

1848

Nelson Dewey (D)[1]	19,875
John Hubbard Tweedy (W)[1]	14,621
Charles Durkee (Ind)[1]	1,134
TOTAL	35,309

1849

Nelson Dewey (D)	16,649
Alexander L. Collins (W)	11,317
Warren Chase (Ind)	3,761
TOTAL	31,759

1851

Leonard James Farwell (W)	22,319
Don Alonzo Joshua Upham (D)	21,812
TOTAL	44,190

1853

William Augustus Barstow (D)	30,405
Edward Dwight Holton (R)	21,886
Henry Samuel Baird (W)	3,304
TOTAL	55,683

1855

William Augustus Barstow (D)[2]	36,355
Coles Bashford (R)	36,198
TOTAL	72,598

1857

Alexander William Randall (R)	44,693
James B. Cross (D)	44,239
TOTAL	90,058

1859

Alexander William Randall (R)	59,999
Harrison Carroll Hobart (D)	52,539
TOTAL	112,755

1861

Louis Powell Harvey (R)	53,777
Benjamin Ferguson (D)	45,456
TOTAL	99,258

1863

James Taylor Lewis (R)	72,717
Henry L. Palmer (D)	49,053
TOTAL	122,029

1865

Lucius Fairchild (R)	58,332
Harrison Carroll Hobart (D)	48,330
TOTAL	106,674

1867

Lucius Fairchild (R)	73,637
John J. Tallmadge (D)	68,873
TOTAL	142,522

1869

Lucius Fairchild (R)	69,502
Charles D. Robinson (D)	61,239
TOTAL	130,781

1871

Cadwallader Colden Washburn (R)	78,301
James Rood Doolittle (D)	68,910
TOTAL	147,274

1873

William Robert Taylor (D)	81,599
Cadwallader Colden Washburn (R)	66,224
TOTAL	147,856

1875

Harrison Ludington (R)	85,155
William Robert Taylor (D)	84,314
TOTAL	170,070

1877

William E. Smith (R)	78,759
James A. Mallory (D)	70,486
Edward Phelps Allis (G)	26,216
Collin M. Campbell (Soc)	2,176
TOTAL	178,122

1879

William E. Smith (R)	100,535
James G. Jenkins (D)	75,030
Reuben May (G)	12,996
TOTAL	189,005

1881

Jeremiah McLain Rusk (R)	81,754
N.D. Fratt (D)	69,797
T.D. Kanouse (Proh)	13,225
Edward Phelps Allis (G)	7,002
TOTAL	171,856

1884

Jeremiah McLain Rusk (R)	163,214
N.D. Fratt (D)	143,945
Samuel Dexter Hastings (Proh)	8,545
William L. Utley (G)	4,274
TOTAL	319,997

1886

Jeremiah McLain Rusk (R)	133,247
Gilbert Motier Woodward (D)	114,529
John Cochrane (People's)	21,467
John Myers Olin (Proh)	17,089
TOTAL	286,368

1888

William Dempster Hoard (R)	175,696
James Morgan (D)	155,423
E.G. Durant (Proh)	14,373
D. Frank Powell (L)	9,196
TOTAL	354,714

1890

George Wilbur Peck (D)	160,388
William Dempster Hoard (R)	132,068
Charles Alexander (Proh)	11,246
Reuben May (UL)	5,447
TOTAL	309,254

1892

George Wilbur Peck (D)	178,095
John Coit Spooner (R)	170,497
Thomas C. Richmond (Proh)	13,185
C.M. Butt (People's)	9,638
TOTAL	371,559

1894

William H. Upham (R)	196,150
George Wilbur Peck (D)	142,250
D. Frank Powell (People's)	25,604
John F. Cleghorn (Proh)	11,240
TOTAL	375,449

1896

Edward Scofield (R)	264,981
Willis C. Silverthorn (D)	169,257
Joshua H. Berkey (Proh)	8,140
Christ Tuttrop (SL)	1,306
Robert Henderson (Nat)	407
TOTAL	444,110

VOTE FOR GOVERNOR IN GENERAL ELECTIONS
1848 – 2012–Continued

1898	
Edward Scofield (R)	173,137
Hiram Wilson Sawyer (D)	135,353
Albinus A. Worsley (People's)	8,518
Eugene Wilder Chafin (Proh)	8,078
Howard Tuttle (SDA)	2,544
Henry Riese (SL)	1,473
TOTAL	329,430

1900	
Robert Marion La Follette (R)	264,419
Louis G. Bomrich (D)	160,674
J. Burritt Smith (Proh)	9,707
Howard Tuttle (SD)	6,590
Frank R. Wilke (SL)	509
TOTAL	441,900

1902	
Robert Marion La Follette (R)	193,417
David Stuart Rose (D)	145,818
Emil Seidel (SD)	15,970
Edwin W. Drake (Proh)	9,647
Henry E.D. Puck (SL)	791
TOTAL	365,676

1904	
Robert Marion La Follette (R)	227,253
George Wilbur Peck (D)	176,301
William A. Arnold (SD)	24,857
Edward Scofield (NR)	12,136
William H. Clark (Proh)	8,764
Charles M. Minkley (SL)	249
TOTAL	449,570

1906	
James O. Davidson (R)	183,558
John A. Aylward (D)	103,311
Winfield R. Gaylord (SD)	24,437
Ephraim L. Eaton (Proh)	8,211
Ole T. Rosaas (SL)	455
TOTAL	320,003

1908	
James O. Davidson (R)	242,935
John A. Aylward (D)	165,977
H.D. Brown (SD)	28,583
Winfred D. Cox (Proh)	11,760
Herman Bottema (SL)	393
TOTAL	449,656

1910	
Francis Edward McGovern (R)	161,619
Adolph H. Schmitz (D)	110,442
William A. Jacobs (SD)	39,547
Byron E. Van Keuren (Proh)	7,450
Fred G. Kremer (SL)	430
TOTAL	319,522

1912	
Francis Edward McGovern (R)	179,360
John C. Karel (D)	167,316
Carl D. Thompson (SD)	34,468
Charles Lewis Hill (Proh)	9,433
William H. Curtis (SL)	3,253
TOTAL	393,849

1914	
Emanuel Lorenz Philipp (R)	140,787
John C. Karel (D)	119,509
John James Blaine (Ind)	32,560
Oscar Ameringer (SD)	25,917
David W. Emerson (Proh)	6,279
John Vierthaler (Ind)	352
TOTAL	325,430

1916	
Emanuel Lorenz Philipp (R)	229,889
Burt Williams (D)	164,555
Rae Weaver (Soc)	30,649
George McKerrow (Proh)	9,193
TOTAL	434,340

1918	
Emanuel Lorenz Philipp (R)	155,799
Henry A. Moehlenpah (D)	112,576
Emil Seidel (SD)	57,523
William C. Dean (Proh)	5,296
TOTAL	331,582

1920	
John James Blaine (R)	366,247
Robert McCoy (D)	247,746
William Coleman (Soc)	71,126
Henry H. Tubbs (Proh)	6,047
TOTAL	691,294

1922	
John James Blaine (R)	367,929
Arthur A. Bentley (ID)	51,061
Louis A. Arnold (Soc)	39,570
M.L. Welles (Proh)	21,438
Arthur A. Dietrich (ISL)	1,444
TOTAL	481,828

1924	
John James Blaine (R)	412,255
Martin L. Lueck (D)	317,550
William F. Quick (Soc)	45,268
Adolph R. Bucknam (Proh)	11,516
Severi Alanne (IW)	4,107
Farrand K. Shuttleworth (IPR)	4,079
Jose Snover (SL)	1,452
TOTAL	796,432

1926	
Fred R. Zimmerman (R)	350,927
Charles Perry (Ind)	76,507
Virgil H. Cady (D)	72,627
Herman O. Kent (Soc)	40,293
David W. Emerson (Proh)	7,333
Alex Gorden (SL)	4,593
TOTAL	552,912

1928	
Walter Jodok Kohler, Sr. (R)	547,738
Albert George Schmedeman (D)	394,368
Otto R. Hauser (Soc)	36,924
Adolph R. Bucknam (Proh)	6,477
Joseph Ehrhardt (IL)	1,938
Alvar J. Hayes (IW)	1,420
TOTAL	989,143

1930	
Philip Fox La Follette (R)	392,958
Charles E. Hammersley (D)	170,020
Frank B. Metcalfe (Soc)	25,607
Alfred B. Taynton (Proh)	14,818
Fred Bassett Blair (IC)	2,998
TOTAL	606,825

1932	
Albert George Schmedeman (D)	590,114
Walter Jodok Kohler, Sr. (R)	470,805
Frank B. Metcalfe (Soc)	56,965
William C. Dean (Proh)	3,148
Fred Bassett Blair (Com)	2,926
Joe Ehrhardt (SL)	398
TOTAL	1,124,502

1934	
Philip Fox La Follette (Prog)	373,093
Albert George Schmedeman (D)	359,467
Howard Greene (R)	172,980
George A. Nelson (Soc)	44,589
Morris Childs (IC)	2,454
Thomas W. North (PR)	857
Joe Ehrhardt (ISL)	332
TOTAL	953,797

1936	
Philip Fox La Follette (Prog)	573,724
Alexander Wiley (R)	363,973
Arthur W. Lueck (D)	268,530
Joseph F. Walsh (U)	27,934
Joseph Ehrhardt (SL)	1,738
August F. Fehlandt (Proh)	1,008
TOTAL	1,237,095

1938	
Julius Peter Heil (R)	543,675
Philip Fox La Follette (Prog)	353,381
Harry Wilbur Bolens (D)	78,446
Frank W. Smith (U)	4,564
John Schleier, Jr. (ISL)	1,459
TOTAL	981,560

1940	
Julius Peter Heil (R)	558,678
Orland Steen Loomis (Prog)	546,436
Francis Edward McGovern (D)	264,985
Fred Bassett Blair (Com)	2,340
Louis Fisher (SL)	1,158
TOTAL	1,373,754

1942	
Orland Steen Loomis (Prog)	397,664
Julius Peter Heil (R)	291,945
William C. Sullivan (D)	98,153
Frank P. Zeidler (Soc)	11,295
Fred Bassett Blair (IC)	1,092
Georgia Cozzini (ISL)	490
TOTAL	800,985

VOTE FOR GOVERNOR IN GENERAL ELECTIONS
1848 – 2012–Continued

1944	
Walter Samuel Goodland (R)	697,740
Daniel W. Hoan (D)	536,357
Alexander O. Benz (Prog)	76,028
George A. Nelson (Soc)	9,183
Georgia Cozzini (Ind–ISL)	1,122
TOTAL	1,320,483

1946	
Walter Samuel Goodland (R)	621,970
Daniel W. Hoan (D)	406,499
Walter H. Uphoff (Soc)	8,996
Sigmund G. Eisenscher (IC)	1,857
Jerry R. Kenyon (ISL)	959
TOTAL	1,040,444

1948	
Oscar Rennebohm (R)	684,839
Carl W. Thompson (D)	558,497
Henry J. Berquist (PP)	12,928
Walter H. Uphoff (Soc)	9,149
James E. Boulton (ISW)	356
Georgia Cozzini (ISL)	328
TOTAL	1,266,139

1950	
Walter Jodok Kohler, Jr. (R)	605,649
Carl W. Thompson (D)	525,319
M. Michael Essin (PP)	3,735
William O. Hart (Soc)	3,384
TOTAL	1,138,148

1952	
Walter Jodok Kohler, Jr. (R)	1,009,171
William Proxmire (D)	601,844
M. Michael Essin (Ind)	3,706
TOTAL	1,615,214

1954	
Walter Jodok Kohler, Jr. (R)	596,158
William Proxmire (D)	560,747
Arthur Wepfer (Ind)	1,722
TOTAL	1,158,666

1956	
Vernon W. Thomson (R)	808,273
William Proxmire (D)	749,421
TOTAL	1,557,788

1958	
Gaylord Anton Nelson (D)	644,296
Vernon W. Thomson (R)	556,391
Wayne Leverenz (Ind)	1,485
TOTAL	1,202,219

1960	
Gaylord Anton Nelson (D)	890,868
Philip G. Kuehn (R)	837,123
TOTAL	1,728,009

1962	
John W. Reynolds (D)	637,491
Philip G. Kuehn (R)	625,536
Adolf Wiggert (Ind)	2,477
TOTAL	1,265,900

1964	
Warren P. Knowles (R)	856,779
John W. Reynolds (D)	837,901
TOTAL	1,694,887

1966	
Warren P. Knowles (R)	626,041
Patrick J. Lucey (D)	539,258
Adolf Wiggert (Ind)	4,745
TOTAL	1,170,173

1968	
Warren P. Knowles (R)	893,463
Bronson C. La Follette (D)	791,100
Adolf Wiggert (Ind)	3,225
Robert Wilkinson (Ind)	1,813
TOTAL	1,689,738

1970	
Patrick J. Lucey (D)	728,403
Jack B. Olson (R)	602,617
Leo James McDonald (A)	9,035
Georgia Cozzini (Ind–SL)	1,287
Samuel K. Hunt (Ind–SW)	888
Myrtle Kastner (Ind–PLS)	628
TOTAL	1,343,160

1974	
Patrick J. Lucey (D)	628,639
William D. Dyke (R)	497,189
William H. Upham (A)	33,528
Crazy Jim[3] (Ind)	12,107
William Hart (Ind–DS)	5,113
Fred Blair (Ind–C)	3,617
Georgia Cozzini (Ind–SL)	1,492
TOTAL	1,181,685

1978	
Lee Sherman Dreyfus (R)	816,056
Martin J. Schreiber (D)	673,813
Eugene R. Zimmerman (C)	6,355
John C. Doherty (Ind)	2,183
Adrienne Kaplan (Ind–SW)	1,548
Henry A. Ochsner (Ind–SL)	849
TOTAL	1,500,996

1982	
Anthony S. Earl (D)	896,872
Terry J. Kohler (R)	662,738
Larry Smiley (Lib)	9,734
James P. Wickstrom (Con)	7,721
Peter Seidman (Ind–SW)	3,025
TOTAL	1,580,344

1986	
Tommy G. Thompson (R)	805,090
Anthony S. Earl (D)	705,578
Kathryn A. Christensen (LF)	10,323
Darold E. Wall (Ind)	3,913
Sanford Knapp (Ind)	1,668
TOTAL	1,526,573

1990	
Tommy G Thompson (R)	802,321
Thomas A. Loftus (D)	576,280
TOTAL	1,379,727

1994	
Tommy G. Thompson (R)	1,051,326
Charles J.Chvala (D)	482,850
David S. Harmon (Lib)	11,639
Edward J. Frami (Tax)	9,188
Michael J. Mangan (Ind)	8,150
TOTAL	1,563,835

1998	
Tommy G. Thompson (R)	1,047,716
Ed Garvey (D)	679,553
Jim Mueller (Lib)	11,071
Edward J. Frami (Tax)	10,269
Mike Mangan (Ind)	4,985
A-Ja-mu Muhammad (Ind)	1,604
Jeffrey L. Smith (WG)	14
TOTAL	1,756,014

2002	
Jim Doyle (D)	800,515
Scott McCallum (R)	734,779
Ed Thompson (Lib)	185,455
Jim Young (WG)	44,111
Alan D. Eisenberg (Ind)	2,847
Ty A. Bollerud (Ind)	2,637
Mike Mangan (Ind)	1,710
Aneb Jah Rasta Sensas-Utcha Nefer-I (Ind) . .	929
TOTAL	1,775,349

2006	
Jim Doyle (D)	1,139,115
Mark Green (R)	979,427
Nelson Eisman (WG)	40,709
TOTAL	2,161,700

2010	
Scott Walker (R)	1,128,941
Tom Barrett (D)	1,004,303
Jim Langer (Ind)	10,608
James James (Ind)	8,273
TOTAL[4]	2,160,832

June 5, 2012 Recall Election	
Scott Walker (R)	1,335,585
Tom Barrett (D)	1,164,480
Hari Trivedi (Ind)	14,463
TOTAL	2,516,065

[1]Votes for Dewey and Tweedy are from *1874 Blue Book;* Durkee vote is based on county returns, as filed in the Office of the Secretary of State, but returns from Manitowoc and Winnebago Counties were missing. Without these 2 counties, Dewey had 19,605 votes and Tweedy had 14,514 votes. [2]Barstow's plurality was set aside in *Atty. Gen. ex rel. Bashford v. Barstow*, 4 Wis. 567 (1855) because of irregularities in the election returns. [3]Legal name. [4]Total includes 6,780 votes for the Libertarian ticket, which had a candidate for lieutenant governor, but no candidate for governor.
Source: Canvass reports and Government Accountability Board records. Totals include scattered votes for other candidates.

WISCONSIN GOVERNORS SINCE 1848

No.	Governor[1]	Political Party	Residence[2]	Service As Governor[3]		Born	Birthplace	Died	Burial Place
				Began	Ended				
1	Nelson Dewey	Democrat	Lancaster	6-7-1848	1-5-1852	12-19-1813	Lebanon, Conn.	7-21-1889	Lancaster, Wis.
2	Leonard James Farwell	Whig	Madison	1-5-1852	1-2-1854	1-5-1819	Watertown, N.Y.	4-11-1889	Grant City, Mo.
3	William Augustus Barstow	Democrat	Waukesha	1-2-1854	3-21-1856	9-13-1813	Plainfield, Conn.	12-13-1865	Cleveland, Ohio
4	Arthur MacArthur[4]	Democrat	Milwaukee	3-21-1856	3-25-1856	1-26-1815	Glasgow, Scotland	8-26-1896	Washington, D.C.
5	Coles Bashford	Republican	Oshkosh	3-25-1856	1-4-1858	1-24-1816	Putnam Co., N.Y.	4-25-1878	Oakland, Cal.
6	Alexander William Randall	Republican	Waukesha	1-4-1858	1-6-1862	10-31-1819	Ames, N.Y.	7-26-1872	Elmira, N.Y.
7	Louis Powell Harvey	Republican	Shopiere	1-6-1862	4-19-1862	7-22-1820	East Haddam, Conn.	4-19-1862	Madison, Wis.
8	Edward Salomon[5]	Republican	Milwaukee	4-19-1862	1-4-1864	8-11-1828	Stroebeck, Prussia	4-21-1909	Frankfurt, Germany
9	James Taylor Lewis	Republican	Columbus	1-4-1864	1-1-1866	10-30-1819	Clarendon, N.Y.	8-4-1904	Columbus, Wis.
10	Lucius Fairchild	Republican	Madison	1-1-1866	1-1-1872	12-27-1831	Kent, Ohio	5-23-1896	Madison, Wis.
11	Cadwallader Colden Washburn	Republican	La Crosse	1-1-1872	1-5-1874	4-22-1818	Livermore, Me.	5-14-1882	La Crosse, Wis.
12	William Robert Taylor	Democrat	Cottage Grove	1-5-1874	1-1-1876	7-10-1820	Woodbury, Conn.	3-17-1909	Madison, Wis.
13	Harrison Ludington	Republican	Milwaukee	1-1-1876	1-7-1878	7-30-1812	Ludingtonville, N.Y.	6-17-1891	Milwaukee, Wis.
14	William E. Smith	Republican	Milwaukee	1-7-1878	1-2-1882	6-18-1824	Near Inverness, Scotland	2-13-1883	Milwaukee, Wis.
15	Jeremiah McLain Rusk	Republican	Viroqua	1-2-1882	1-7-1889	6-17-1830	Morgan Co., Ohio	11-21-1893	Viroqua, Wis.
16	William Dempster Hoard	Republican	Fort Atkinson	1-7-1889	1-5-1891	10-10-1836	Stockbridge, N.Y.	11-22-1918	Ft. Atkinson, Wis.
17	George Wilbur Peck	Democrat	Milwaukee	1-5-1891	1-7-1895	9-28-1840	Henderson, N.Y.	4-16-1916	Milwaukee, Wis.
18	William Henry Upham	Republican	Marshfield	1-7-1895	1-4-1897	5-3-1841	Westminister, Mass.	7-2-1924	Marshfield, Wis.
19	Edward Scofield	Republican	Oconto	1-4-1897	1-7-1901	3-28-1842	Clearfield, Pa.	2-3-1925	Oconto, Wis.
20	Robert Marion La Follette, Sr.[6]	Republican	Madison	1-7-1901	1-1-1906	6-14-1855	Primrose, Dane Co., Wis.	6-18-1925	Madison, Wis.
21	James O. Davidson[6]	Republican	Soldiers Grove	1-1-1906	1-2-1911	2-10-1854	Sogn, Norway	12-16-1922	Madison, Wis.
22	Francis Edward McGovern	Republican	Milwaukee	1-2-1911	1-4-1915	1-21-1866	Elkhart Lake, Wis.	5-16-1946	Milwaukee, Wis.
23	Emanuel Lorenz Philipp	Republican	Milwaukee	1-4-1915	1-3-1921	3-25-1861	Honey Creek, Sauk Co., Wis.	6-15-1925	Milwaukee, Wis.
24	John James Blaine	Republican	Boscobel	1-3-1921	1-3-1927	5-4-1875	Wingville, Grant Co., Wis.	4-18-1934	Boscobel, Wis.
25	Fred R. Zimmerman	Republican	Milwaukee	1-3-1927	1-7-1929	11-20-1880	Milwaukee, Wis.	12-14-1954	Kohler, Wis.
26	Walter Jodok Kohler, Sr.	Republican	Kohler	1-7-1929	1-5-1931	3-3-1875	Sheboygan, Wis.	4-21-1940	Madison, Wis.
27	Philip Fox La Follette	Republican	Madison	1-5-1931	1-2-1933	5-8-1897	Madison, Wis.	8-18-1965	Madison, Wis.
28	Albert George Schmedeman	Democrat	Madison	1-2-1933	1-7-1935	11-25-1864	Madison, Wis.	11-26-1946	Madison, Wis.
29	Philip Fox La Follette	Progressive	Madison	1-7-1935	1-2-1939	5-8-1897	Madison, Wis.	8-18-1965	Madison, Wis.
30	Julius Peter Heil	Republican	Milwaukee	1-2-1939	1-4-1943	7-24-1876	Duesmond, Germany	11-30-1949	Milwaukee, Wis.
	Orland Steen Loomis[7]	Progressive	Mauston	Died prior to inauguration		11-2-1893	Mauston, Wis.	12-7-1942	Mauston, Wis.
31	Walter Samuel Goodland[7,8]	Republican	Racine	1-4-1943	3-12-1947	12-24-1862	Sharon, Wis.	3-12-1947	Racine, Wis.
32	Oscar Rennebohm[8]	Republican	Madison	3-12-1947	1-1-1951	5-25-1889	Leeds, Columbia Co., Wis.	10-15-1968	Madison, Wis.
33	Walter John Kohler, Jr.	Republican	Kohler	1-1-1951	1-7-1957	4-4-1904	Sheboygan, Wis.	3-10-1976	Kohler, Wis.
34	Vernon Wallace Thomson	Republican	Richland Center	1-7-1957	1-5-1959	11-5-1905	Richland Center, Wis.	4-2-1988	Richland Center, Wis.
35	Gaylord Anton Nelson	Democrat	Madison	1-5-1959	1-7-1963	6-4-1916	Clear Lake, Wis.	7-3-2005	Clear Lake, Wis.
36	John W Reynolds	Democrat	Green Bay	1-7-1963	1-4-1965	4-4-1921	Green Bay, Wis.	1-5-2002	Door County, Wis.
37	Warren Perley Knowles	Republican	New Richmond	1-4-1965	1-4-1971	8-19-1908	River Falls, Wis.	4-1-1993	River Falls, Wis.
38	Patrick Joseph Lucey[9]	Democrat	Madison	1-4-1971	7-6-1977	3-21-1918	La Crosse, Wis.		
39	Martin James Schreiber[9]	Democrat	Milwaukee	7-6-1977	1-1-1979	4-8-1939	Milwaukee, Wis.		
40	Lee Sherman Dreyfus	Republican	Stevens Point	1-1-1979	1-3-1983	6-20-1926	Milwaukee, Wis.	1-2-2008	Waukesha, Wis.
41	Anthony Scully Earl	Democrat	Madison	1-3-1983	1-5-1987	4-12-1936	Lansing, Mich.		
42	Tommy George Thompson[10]	Republican	Elroy	1-5-1987	2-1-2001	11-19-1941	Elroy, Wis.		
43	Scott McCallum[10]	Republican	Fond du Lac	2-1-2001	1-6-2003	5-2-1950	Fond du Lac, Wis.		
44	James Edward Doyle, Jr.	Democrat	Madison	1-6-2003	1-3-2011	11-23-1945	Washington, D.C.		
45	Scot Kevin Walker	Republican	Wauwatosa	1-3-2011		11-2-1967	Colorado Springs, Colo.		

[1]Includes those serving as acting governor when office is vacated. Administrations are numbered. [2]Residence at the time of election. [3]Article XIII, Section 1 of the Wisconsin Constitution was amended in November 1882 so that the term of office of all state and county officers began in January of odd-numbered years, rather than January of even-numbered years. [4]Served as acting governor during dispute over who won gubernatorial election. [5]Salomon became acting governor on death of Harvey on 4/19/62. [6]Davidson served as acting governor from La Follette's resignation until beginning the terms to which he was elected on 1/7/07. [7]Goodland became acting governor on death of Governor-elect Loomis and served entire 1943-44 term. [8]Rennebohm became acting governor on the death of Goodland on 3/12/47. [9]Schreiber became acting governor when Lucey resigned to become U.S. ambassador to Mexico. [10]McCallum became acting governor when Thompson resigned to become U.S. Secretary of Health and Human Services.

Sources: "Wisconsin's Former Governors", *1960 Wisconsin Blue Book*, pp. 69-206; Blue Book biographies.

WISCONSIN CONSTITUTIONAL OFFICERS, 1848 – 2013

Name	Term[1]	Residence
Governor		
(See separate table)		
Lieutenant Governors		
John E. Holmes (D)	1848-1850	Jefferson
Samuel W. Beall (D)	1850-1852	Taycheedah
Timothy Burns (D)	1852-1854	La Crosse
James T. Lewis (R)	1854-1856	Columbus
Arthur McArthur (D)[2]	1856-1858	Milwaukee
Erasmus D. Campbell (D)	1858-1860	La Crosse
Butler G. Noble (R)	1860-1862	Whitewater
Edward Salomon (R)[3]	1862-1864	Milwaukee
Wyman Spooner (R)	1864-1870	Elkhorn
Thaddeus C. Pound (R)	1870-1872	Chippewa Falls
Milton H. Pettit (R)[4]	1872-3/23/73	Kenosha
Charles D. Parker (D)	1874-1878	Pleasant Valley
James M. Bingham (R)	1878-1882	Chippewa Falls
Sam S. Fifield (R)	1882-1887	Ashland
George W. Ryland (R)	1887-1891	Lancaster
Charles Jonas (D)	1891-1895	Racine
Emil Baensch (R)	1895-1899	Manitowoc
Jesse Stone (R)	1899-1903	Watertown
James O. Davidson (R)[5]	1903-1907	Soldiers Grove
William D. Connor (R)	1907-1909	Marshfield
John Strange (R)	1909-1911	Oshkosh
Thomas Morris (R)	1911-1915	La Crosse
Edward F. Dithmar (R)	1915-1921	Baraboo
George F. Comings (R)	1921-1925	Eau Claire
Henry A. Huber (R)	1925-1933	Stoughton
Thomas J. O'Malley (D)	1933-1937	Milwaukee
Henry A. Gunderson (Prog)[6]	1937-10/16/37	Portage
Herman L. Ekern (Prog)[6]	5/16/1938-1939	Madison
Walter S. Goodland (R)[7]	1939-1945	Racine
Oscar Rennebohm (R)[8]	1945-1949	Madison
George M. Smith (R)	1949-1955	Milwaukee
Warren P. Knowles (R)	1955-1959	New Richmond
Philleo Nash (D)	1959-1961	Wisconsin Rapids
Warren P. Knowles (R)	1961-1963	New Richmond
Jack Olson (R)	1963-1965	Wisconsin Dells
Patrick J. Lucey (D)	1965-1967	Madison
Jack Olson (R)	1967-1971	Wisconsin Dells
Martin J. Schreiber (D)[9]	1971-1979	Milwaukee
Russell A. Olson (R)	1979-1983	Randall
James T. Flynn (D)	1983-1987	West Allis
Scott McCallum (R)[10]	1987-2001	Fond du Lac
Margaret A. Farrow (R)[10]	2001-2003	Pewaukee
Barbara Lawton (D)	2003-2011	Green Bay
Rebecca Kleefisch (R)	2011-	Oconomowoc
Secretaries of State		
Thomas McHugh (D)	1848-1850	Delavan
William A. Barstow (D)	1850-1852	Waukesha
Charles D. Robinson (D)	1852-1854	Green Bay
Alexander T. Gray (D)	1854-1856	Janesville
David W. Jones (D)	1856-1860	Belmont
Lewis P. Harvey (R)	1860-1862	Shopiere
James T. Lewis (R)	1862-1864	Columbus
Lucius Fairchild (R)	1864-1866	Madison
Thomas S. Allen (R)	1866-1870	Mineral Point
Llywelyn Breese (R)	1870-1874	Portage
Peter Doyle (D)	1874-1878	Prairie du Chien
Hans B. Warner (R)	1878-1882	Ellsworth
Ernst G. Timme (R)	1882-1891	Kenosha
Thomas J. Cunningham (D)	1891-1895	Chippewa Falls
Henry Casson (R)	1895-1899	Viroqua
William H. Froehlich (R)	1899-1903	Jackson
Walter L. Houser (R)	1903-1907	Mondovi
James A. Frear (R)	1907-1913	Hudson
John S. Donald (R)	1913-1917	Mt. Horeb
Merlin Hull (R)	1917-1921	Black River Falls
Elmer S. Hall (R)	1921-1923	Green Bay
Fred R. Zimmerman (R)	1923-1927	Milwaukee
Theodore Dammann (R)	1927-1935	Milwaukee
Theodore Dammann (Prog)	1935-1939	Milwaukee
Fred R. Zimmerman (R)[11]	1939-12/14/54	Milwaukee
Louis Allis (R)[11]	12/16/54-1/3/55	Milwaukee
Mrs. Glenn M. Wise (R)[11]	1/3/55-1957	Madison
Robert C. Zimmerman (R)	1957-1975	Madison
Douglas J. La Follette (D)	1975-1979	Kenosha
Mrs. Vel R. Phillips (D)	1979-1983	Milwaukee

WISCONSIN CONSTITUTIONAL OFFICERS, 1848 − 2013–Continued

Name	Term[1]	Residence
Douglas J. La Follette (D)	1983-	Madison
State Treasurers		
Jarius C. Fairchild (D)	1848-1852	Madison
Edward H. Janssen (D)	1852-1856	Cedarburg
Charles Kuehn (D)	1856-1858	Manitowoc
Samuel D. Hastings (R)	1858-1866	Trempealeau
William E. Smith (R)	1866-1870	Fox Lake
Henry Baetz (R)	1870-1874	Manitowoc
Ferdinand Kuehn (D)	1874-1878	Milwaukee
Richard Guenther (R)	1878-1882	Oshkosh
Edward C. McFetridge (R)	1882-1887	Beaver Dam
Henry B. Harshaw (R)	1887-1891	Oshkosh
John Hunner (D)	1891-1895	Eau Claire
Sewell A. Peterson (R)	1895-1899	Rice Lake
James O. Davidson (R)	1899-1903	Soldiers Grove
John J. Kempf (R)[12]	1903-7/30/04	Milwaukee
Thomas M. Purtell (R)[12]	7/30/04-1905	Cumberland
John J. Kempf (R)	1905-1907	Milwaukee
Andrew H. Dahl (R)	1907-1913	Westby
Henry Johnson (R)	1913-1923	Suring
Solomon Levitan (R)	1923-1933	Madison
Robert K. Henry (D)	1933-1937	Jefferson
Solomon Levitan (Prog)	1937-1939	Madison
John M. Smith (R)[4]	1939-8/17/47	Shell Lake
John L. Sonderegger (R)[13]	8/19/47-9/30/48	Madison
Clyde M. Johnston (appointed from staff)[13]	10/1/48-1949	Madison
Warren R. Smith (R)[4]	1949-12/4/57	Milwaukee
Mrs. Dena A. Smith (R)[13]	12/5/57-1959	Milwaukee
Eugene M. Lamb (D)	1959-1961	Milwaukee
Mrs. Dena A. Smith (R)[4]	1961-2/20/68	Milwaukee
Harold W. Clemens (R)[13]	2/21/68-1971	Oconomowoc
Charles P. Smith (D)	1971-1991	Madison
Cathy S. Zeuske (R)	1991-1995	Shawano
Jack C. Voight (R)	1995-2007	Appleton
Dawn Marie Sass (D)	2007-2011	Milwaukee
Kurt W. Schuller (R)	2011-	Eden
Attorneys General		
James S. Brown (D)	1848-1850	Milwaukee
S. Park Coon (D)	1850-1852	Milwaukee
Experience Estabrook (D)	1852-1854	Geneva
George B. Smith (D)	1854-1856	Madison
William R. Smith (D)	1856-1858	Mineral Point
Gabriel Bouck (D)	1858-1860	Oshkosh
James H. Howe (R)[14]	1860-1862	Green Bay
Winfield Smith (R)[14]	1862-1866	Milwaukee
Charles R. Gill (R)	1866-1870	Watertown
Stephen Steele Barlow (R)	1870-1874	Dellona
Andrew Scott Sloan (R)	1874-1878	Beaver Dam
Alexander Wilson (R)	1878-1882	Mineral Point
Leander F. Frisby (R)	1882-1887	West Bend
Charles E. Estabrook (R)	1887-1891	Manitowoc
James L. O'Connor (D)	1891-1895	Madison
William H. Mylrea (R)	1895-1899	Wausau
Emmett R. Hicks (R)	1899-1903	Oshkosh
Lafayette M. Sturdevant (R)	1903-1907	Neillsville
Frank L. Gilbert (R)	1907-1911	Madison
Levi H. Bancroft (R)	1911-1913	Richland Center
Walter C. Owen (R)[15]	1913-1918	Maiden Rock
Spencer Haven (R)[15]	1918-1919	Hudson
John J. Blaine (R)	1919-1921	Boscobel
William J. Morgan (R)	1921-1923	Milwaukee
Herman L. Ekern (R)	1923-1927	Madison
John W. Reynolds (R)	1927-1933	Green Bay
James E. Finnegan (D)	1933-1937	Milwaukee
Orlando S. Loomis (Prog)	1937-1939	Mauston
John E. Martin (R)[16]	1939-6/1/48	Madison
Grover L. Broadfoot (R)[16]	6/5/48-11/12/48	Mondovi
Thomas E. Fairchild (D)[16]	11/12/48-1951	Verona
Vernon W. Thomson (R)	1951-1957	Richland Center
Stewart G. Honeck (R)	1957-1959	Madison
John W. Reynolds (D)	1959-1963	Green Bay
George Thompson (R)	1963-1965	Madison
Bronson C. La Follette (D)	1965-1969	Madison
Robert W. Warren (R)[17]	1969-10/8/74	Green Bay
Victor A. Miller (D)[17]	10/8/74-11/25/74	St. Nazianz
Bronson C. La Follette (D)[17]	11/25/74-1987	Madison
Donald J. Hanaway (R)	1987-1991	Green Bay
James E. Doyle (D)	1991-2003	Madison
Peggy A. Lautenschlager (D)	2003-2007	Fond du Lac

WISCONSIN CONSTITUTIONAL OFFICERS, 1848 – 2013–Continued

Name	Term[1]	Residence
J.B. Van Hollen (R)	2007-	Waunakee
Superintendents of Public Instruction[18]		
Eleazer Root	1849-1852	Waukesha
Azel P. Ladd	1852-1854	Shullsburg
Hiram A. Wright	1854-1855	Prairie du Chien
A. Constantine Barry	1855-1858	Racine
Lyman C. Draper	1858-1860	Madison
Josiah L. Pickard	1860-1864	Platteville
John G. McMynn	1864-1868	Racine
Alexander J. Craig	1868-1870	Madison
Samuel Fallows	1870-1874	Milwaukee
Edward Searing	1874-1878	Milton
William Clarke Whitford	1878-1882	Milton
Robert Graham	1882-1887	Oshkosh
Jesse B. Thayer	1887-1891	River Falls
Oliver Elwin Wells	1891-1895	Appleton
John Q. Emery	1895-1899	Albion
Lorenzo D. Harvey	1899-1903	Milwaukee
Charles P. Cary	1903-1921	Delavan
John Callahan	1921-1949	Madison
George Earl Watson	1949-1961	Wauwatosa
Angus B. Rothwell[19]	1961-7/1/66	Manitowoc
William C. Kahl[19]	7/1/66-1973	Madison
Barbara Thompson	1973-1981	Madison
Herbert J. Grover[20]	1981-4/9/93	Cottage Grove
John T. Benson	1993-2001	Marshall
Elizabeth Burmaster	2001-2009	Madison
Tony Evers	2009-	Madison

[1]Article XIII, Section 1 of the Wisconsin Constitution was amended in 1882, to provide the terms for all partisan state officers would begin in odd-numbered, rather than even-numbered, years. The section was further amended in 1968 to change the term from 2 years to 4 years, effective with the November 1970 elections.

[2]Served as acting governor 3/21/1856 to 3/25/1856 during dispute over outcome of gubernatorial election.

[3]Became acting governor on the death of Governor Louis P. Harvey on 4/19/1862.

[4]Died in office.

[5]Became acting governor on 1/1/1906 when Robert M. La Follette, Sr., resigned to become U.S. Senator.

[6]Resigned to accept appointment to the State Tax Commission. Ekern appointed by Governor Philip La Follette to fill the unexpired term. Appointment ruled valid in *State ex rel. Martin v. Ekern*, 228 Wis. 645 (1937).

[7]Goodland reelected lieutenant governor, November 1942; became acting governor on 1/1/1943 for the term of deceased Governor-elect Orlando Loomis.

[8]Became acting governor on the death of Goodland on 3/12/1947.

[9]Became acting governor when Lucey resigned on 7/6/1977 to accept appointment as U.S. ambassador to Mexico.

[10]McCallum became governor on 2/1/2001 when Governor Tommy Thompson resigned to become U.S. Secretary of Health and Social Services. Farrow was appointed lieutenant governor on 5/9/2001.

[11]Died 12/14/1954 after being elected to a new 2-year term. Allis was appointed to fill the unexpired term. Wise was appointed to fill the full 2-year term.

[12]Appointed 7/30/1904 to fill a vacancy caused by the failure of Kempf to give the required bond.

[13]Appointed.

[14]Resigned in October 1862 to join the Union Army. Smith was appointed 10/7/1862 to replace him.

[15]Resigned 1/7/1918 after being elected to the Wisconsin Supreme Court. Haven was appointed to fill the unexpired term.

[16]Resigned to accept appointment to the Wisconsin Supreme Court. Broadfoot was appointed to fill the unexpired term. Broadfoot resigned to accept appointment to the Wisconsin Supreme Court, and Attorney General-elect Fairchild was appointed to fill the unexpired term.

[17]Resigned to accept appointment as U.S. District Judge for the Eastern District of Wisconsin. Miller appointed to fill the unexpired term. Bronson La Follette was elected to a full term and Miller resigned so that La Follette could be appointed to fill the rest of Warren's unexpired term.

[18]Prior to 1902, the state superintendent was elected on a partisan ballot in November, and the term began the first Monday in January. A constitutional amendment moved the election to the nonpartisan April ballot and the beginning of the term to the first Monday in July beginning in July 1905.

[19]Resigned to accept appointment to the Coordinating Committee for Higher Education. Kahl was appointed to fill the unexpired term.

[20]Resigned 4/9/1993. Lee Sherman Dreyfus was appointed to serve as "interim superintendent" for remainder of the unexpired term but did not officially become superintendent.

Source: Wisconsin Legislative Reference Bureau, *Wisconsin Blue Books,* various editions, and bureau records.

JUSTICES OF THE SUPREME COURT
1836 – 2013

Name	Term	Residence[1]
Judges During the Territorial Period		
Charles Dunn (Chief Justice)[2]	1836-1848	
William C. Frazier	1836-1838	
David Irvin	1836-1838	
Andrew G. Miller	1836-1848	
Circuit Judges Who Served as Justices 1848-53[3]		
Alexander W. Stow	1848-1851 (C.J.)	Fond du Lac
Levi Hubbell	1848-1853 (C.J. 1851)	Milwaukee
Edward V. Whiton	1848-1853 (C.J. 1852-53)	Janesville
Charles H. Larrabee	1848-1853	Horicon
Mortimer M. Jackson	1848-1853	Mineral Point
Wiram Knowlton	1850-1853	Prairie du Chien
Timothy O. Howe	1851-1853	Green Bay
Justices Since 1853		
Edward V. Whiton	1853-1859 (C.J.)	Janesville
Samuel Crawford	1853-1855	New Diggings
Abram D. Smith	1853-1859	Milwaukee
Orsamus Cole	1855-1892 (C.J. 1880-92)	Potosi
Luther S. Dixon[4]	1859-1874 (C.J.)	Portage
Byron Paine[4]	1859-1864, 1867-71	Milwaukee
Jason Downer[4]	1864-1867	Milwaukee
William P. Lyon[4]	1871-1894 (C.J. 1892-94)	Racine
Edward G. Ryan[4]	1874-1880 (C.J.)	Racine
David Taylor	1878-1891	Sheboygan
Harlow S. Orton	1878-1895 (C.J. 1894-95)	Madison
John B. Cassoday[4]	1880-1907 (C.J. 1895-07)	Janesville
John B. Winslow[4]	1891-1920 (C.J. 1907-20)	Racine
Silas U. Pinney	1892-1898	Madison
Alfred W. Newman	1894-1898	Trempealeau
Roujet D. Marshall[4]	1895-1918	Chippewa Falls
Charles V. Bardeen[4]	1898-1903	Wausau
Joshua Eric Dodge[4]	1898-1910	Milwaukee
Robert G. Siebecker[5]	1903-1922 (C.J. 1920-22)	Madison
James C. Kerwin	1905-1921	Neenah
William H. Timlin	1907-1916	Milwaukee
Robert M. Bashford[4]	Jan.-June 1908	Madison
John Barnes	1908-1916	Rhinelander
Aad J. Vinje[4]	1910-1929 (C.J. 1922-29)	Superior
Marvin B. Rosenberry[4]	1916-1950 (C.J. 1929-50)	Wausau
Franz C. Eschweiler[4]	1916-1929	Milwaukee
Walter C. Owen	1918-1934	Maiden Rock
Burr W. Jones[4]	1920-1926	Madison
Christian Doerfler	1921-1929	Milwaukee
Charles H. Crownhart[4]	1922-1930	Madison
E. Ray Stevens	1926-1930	Madison
Chester A. Fowler[4]	1929-1948	Fond du Lac
Oscar M. Fritz[4]	1929-1954 (C.J. 1950-54)	Milwaukee
Edward T. Fairchild[4]	1929-1957 (C.J. 1954-57)	Milwaukee
John D. Wickhem[4]	1930-1949	Madison
George B. Nelson[4]	1930-1942	Stevens Point
Theodore G. Lewis[4]	Nov. 15-Dec. 5, 1934	Madison
Joseph Martin[4]	1934-1946	Green Bay
Elmer E. Barlow[4]	1942-1948	Arcadia
James Ward Rector[4]	1946-1947	Madison
Henry P. Hughes	1948-1951	Oshkosh
John E. Martin[4]	1948-1962 (C.J. 1957-62)	Green Bay
Grover L. Broadfoot[4]	1948-1962 (C.J. Jan.-May 1962)	Mondovi
Timothy Brown[4]	1949-1964 (C.J. 1962-64)	Madison
Edward J. Gehl	1950-1956	Hartford
George R. Currie[4]	1951-1968 (C.J. 1964-68)	Sheboygan
Roland J. Steinle[4]	1954-1958	Milwaukee
Emmert L. Wingert[4]	1956-1959	Madison
Thomas E. Fairchild	1957-1966	Verona
E. Harold Hallows[4]	1958-1974 (C.J. 1968-74)	Milwaukee
William H. Dieterich	1959-1964	Milwaukee
Myron L. Gordon	1962-1967	Milwaukee
Horace W. Wilkie[4]	1962-1976 (C.J. 1974-76)	Madison
Bruce F. Beilfuss	1964-1983 (C.J. 1976-83)	Neillsville
Nathan S. Heffernan[4]	1964-1995 (C.J. 1983-95)	Sheboygan
Leo B. Hanley[4]	1966-1978	Milwaukee
Connor T. Hansen[4]	1967-1980	Eau Claire
Robert W. Hansen	1968-1978	Milwaukee
Roland B. Day[4]	1974-1996 (C.J. 1995-96)	Madison

JUSTICES OF THE SUPREME COURT
1836 – 2013–Continued

Name	Term	Residence[1]
Shirley S. Abrahamson[4]	1976- (C.J. 1996-)	Madison
William G. Callow	1978-1992	Waukesha
John L. Coffey	1978-1982	Milwaukee
Donald W. Steinmetz	1980-1999	Milwaukee
Louis J. Ceci[4]	1982-1993	Milwaukee
William A. Bablitch	1983-2003	Stevens Point
Jon P. Wilcox[4]	1992-2007	Wautoma
Janine P. Geske[4]	1993-1998	Milwaukee
Ann Walsh Bradley	1995-	Wausau
N. Patrick Crooks	1996-	Green Bay
David T. Prosser, Jr.[4]	1998-	Appleton
Diane S. Sykes[4]	1999-2004	Milwaukee
Patience D. Roggensack	2003-	Madison
Louis B. Butler, Jr.[4]	2004-2008	Milwaukee
Annette K. Ziegler	2007-	West Bend
Michael J. Gableman	2008-	Webster

Note: The structure of the Wisconsin Supreme Court has varied. There were 3 justices during the territorial period. From 1848 to 1853, circuit judges acted as supreme court judges (5 from 1848 to 1850 and 6 from 1850 to 1853). From 1853 to 1877, there were 3 elected justices. The number was increased to 5 by constitutional amendment in 1877. In 1903 the constitution was amended to raise the number to 7.

[1]Home address is the municipality from which the justice was originally appointed or elected.

[2]As a result of a constitutional amendment adopted in April 1889, the most senior justice serves as chief justice. Previously, the chief justice was elected or appointed to that position.

[3]Circuit judges acted as Supreme Court justices 1848-1853.

[4]Initially appointed to the court.

[5]Siebecker was elected April 7, 1903, but prior to inauguration for his elected term was appointed April 9, 1903, to fill the vacancy caused by the death of Justice Bardeen.

Sources: Wisconsin Legislative Reference Bureau, *Wisconsin Blue Books,* 1935, 1944, 1977; Government Accountability Board, Elections Division records; Wisconsin Supreme Court, *Wisconsin Reports,* various volumes.

SENATE PRESIDENTS PRO TEMPORE, SENATE PRESIDENTS AND ASSEMBLY SPEAKERS, 1848 – 2013

Legislative Session	Senate Presidents Pro Tempore or Presidents[1]	Residence	Assembly Speakers	Residence
1848	No permanent president pro tempore	—	Ninian E. Whiteside (D)	Lafayette County
1849	No permanent president pro tempore	—	Harrison C. Hobart (D)	Sheboygan
1850	No record	—	Moses M. Strong (D)	Mineral Point
1851	No record	—	Frederick W. Horn (D)	Cedarburg
1852	E.B. Dean, Jr. (D)	Madison	James M. Shafter (W)	Sheboygan
1853	Duncan C. Reed (D)	Milwaukee	Henry L. Palmer (D)	Milwaukee
1854	Benjamin Allen (D)	Hudson	Frederick W. Horn (D)	Cedarburg
1855	Eleazor Wakeley (D)	Whitewater	Charles C. Sholes (R)	Kenosha
1856	Louis Powell Harvey (R)	Shopiere	William Hull (D)	Grant County
1857	No permanent president pro tempore	—	Wyman Spooner (R)	Elkhorn
1858	Hiram H. Giles (R)	Stoughton	Frederick S. Lovell (R)	Kenosha County
1859	Dennison Worthington (R)	Summit	William P. Lyon (R)	Racine
1860	Moses M. Davis (R)	Portage	William P. Lyon (R)	Racine
1861	Alden I. Bennett (R)	Beloit	Amasa Cobb (R)	Mineral Point
1862	Frederick O. Thorp (D)	West Bend	James W. Beardsley (UD)	Prescott
1863	Wyman Spooner (R)	Elkhorn	J. Allen Barber (R)	Lancaster
1864	Smith S. Wilkinson (R)	Prairie du Sac	William W. Field (U)	Fennimore
1865	Willard H. Chandler (U)	Windsor	William W. Field (U)	Fennimore
1866	Willard H. Chandler (U)	Windsor	Henry D. Barron (U)	St. Croix Falls
1867	George F. Wheeler (U)	Nanuapa	Angus Cameron (U)	La Crosse
1868	Newton M. Littlejohn (R)	Whitewater	Alexander M. Thomson (R)	Janesville
1869	George C. Hazelton (R)	Boscobel	Alexander M. Thomson (R)	Janesville
1870	David Taylor (R)	Sheboygan	James M. Bingham (R)	Palmyra
1871	Charles G. Williams (R)	Janesville	William E. Smith (R)	Fox Lake
1872	Charles G. Williams (R)	Janesville	Daniel Hall (R)	Watertown
1873	Henry L. Eaton (R)	Lone Rock	Henry D. Barron (R)	St. Croix Falls
1874	John C. Holloway (R)	Lancaster	Gabriel Bouck (D)	Oshkosh
1875	Henry D. Barron (R)	St. Croix Falls	Frederick W. Horn (R)	Cedarburg
1876	Robert L.D. Potter (R)	Wautoma	Sam S. Fifield (R)	Ashland
1877	William H. Hiner (R)	Fond du Lac	John B. Cassoday (R)	Janesville
1878	Levi W. Barden (R)	Portage	Augustus R. Barrows (GB)	Chippewa Falls
1879	William T. Price (R)	Black River Falls	David M. Kelly (R)	Green Bay
1880	Thomas B. Scott (R)	Grand Rapids	Alexander A. Arnold (R)	Galesville
1881	Thomas B. Scott (R)	Grand Rapids	Ira B. Bradford (R)	Augusta
1882	George B. Burrows (R)	Madison	Franklin L. Gilson (R)	Ellsworth
1883	George W. Ryland (R)	Lancaster	Earl P. Finch (D)	Oshkosh
1885	Edward S. Minor (R)	Sturgeon Bay	Hiram O. Fairchild (R)	Marinette
1887	Charles K. Erwin (R)	Tomah	Thomas B. Mills (R)	Millston
1889	Thomas A. Dyson (R)	La Crosse	Thomas B. Mills (R)	Millston
1891	Frederick W. Horn (D)	Cedarburg	James J. Hogan (D)	La Crosse
1893	Robert J. MacBride (D)	Neillsville	Edward Keogh (D)	Milwaukee
1895	Thompson D. Weeks (R)	Whitewater	George B. Burrows (R)	Madison
1897	Lyman W. Thayer (R)	Ripon	George A. Buckstaff (R)	Oshkosh
1899	Lyman W. Thayer (R)	Ripon	George H. Ray (R)	La Crosse
1901	James J. McGillivray (R)	Black River Falls	George H. Ray (R)	La Crosse
1903-05	James J. McGillivray (R)	Black River Falls	Irvine L. Lenroot (R)	West Superior
1907	James H. Stout (R)	Menomonie	Herman L. Ekern (R)	Whitehall
1909	James H. Stout (R)	Menomonie	Levi H. Bancroft (R)	Richland Center
1911	Harry C. Martin (R)	Darlington	C.A. Ingram (R)	Durand
1913	Harry C. Martin (R)	Darlington	Merlin Hull (R)	Black River Falls
1915	Edward T. Fairchild (R)	Milwaukee	Lawrence C. Whittet (R)	Edgerton
1917	Timothy Burke (R)	Green Bay	Lawrence C. Whittet (R)	Edgerton
1919	Willard T. Stevens (R)	Rhinelander	Riley S. Young (R)	Darien
1921	Timothy Burke (R)	Green Bay	Riley S. Young (R)	Darien
1923	Henry A. Huber (R)	Stoughton	John L. Dahl (R)	Rice Lake
1925	Howard Teasdale (R)	Sparta	Herman Sachtjen (R)[2]	Madison
	Howard Teasdale (R)	Sparta	George A. Nelson (R)[2]	Milltown
1927	William L. Smith (R)	Neillsville	John W. Eber (R)	Milwaukee
1929	Oscar H. Morris (R)	Milwaukee	Charles B. Perry (R)	Wauwatosa
1931	Herman J. Severson (P)	Iola	Charles B. Perry (R)	Wauwatosa
1933	Orland S. Loomis (R)	Mauston	Cornelius T. Young (D)	Milwaukee
1935	Harry W. Bolens (R)	Port Washington	Jorge W. Carow (P)	Ladysmith
1937	Walter J. Rush (P)	Neillsville	Paul R. Alfonsi (P)	Pence
1939	Edward J. Roethe (R)	Fennimore	Vernon W. Thomson (R)	Richland Center
1941-43	Conrad Shearer (R)	Kenosha	Vernon W. Thomson (R)	Richland Center
1945	Conrad Shearer (R)	Kenosha	Donald C. McDowell (R)	Soldiers Grove

SENATE PRESIDENTS PRO TEMPORE, SENATE PRESIDENTS AND ASSEMBLY SPEAKERS, 1848 – 2013–Continued

Legislative Session	Senate Presidents Pro Tempore or Presidents[1]	Residence	Assembly Speakers	Residence
1947	Frank E. Panzer (R)	Brownsville	Donald C. McDowell (R)	Soldiers Grove
1949	Frank E. Panzer (R)	Brownsville	Alex L. Nicol (R)	Sparta
1951-53 . .	Frank E. Panzer (R)	Brownsville	Ora R. Rice (R)	Delavan
1955	Frank E. Panzer (R)	Brownsville	Mark Catlin, Jr. (R)	Appleton
1957	Frank E. Panzer (R)	Brownsville	Robert G. Marotz (R)	Shawano
1959	Frank E. Panzer (R)	Brownsville	George Molinaro (D)	Kenosha
1961	Frank E. Panzer (R)	Brownsville	David J. Blanchard (R)	Edgerton
1963	Frank E. Panzer (R)	Brownsville	Robert D. Haase (R)	Marinette
1965	Frank E. Panzer (R)	Brownsville	Robert T. Huber (D)	West Allis
1967-69 . .	Robert P. Knowles (R)	New Richmond	Harold V. Froehlich (R)	Appleton
1971	Robert P. Knowles (R)	New Richmond	Robert T. Huber (D)[3]	West Allis
	Robert P. Knowles (R)	New Richmond	Norman C. Anderson (D)[3]	Madison
1973	Robert P. Knowles (R)	New Richmond	Norman C. Anderson (D)	Madison
1975	Fred A. Risser (D)	Madison	Norman C. Anderson (D)	Madison
1977-81 . .	Fred A. Risser (D)[1]	Madison	Edward G. Jackamonis (D)	Waukesha
1983-89 . .	Fred A. Risser (D)	Madison	Thomas A. Loftus (D)	Sun Prairie
1991	Fred A. Risser (D)	Madison	Walter J. Kunicki (D)	Milwaukee
1993	Fred A. Risser (D)[4]	Madison	Walter J. Kunicki (D)	Milwaukee
	Brian D. Rude (R)[4]	Coon Valley	Walter J. Kunicki (D)	Milwaukee
1995	Brian D. Rude (R)[5]	Coon Valley	David T. Prosser, Jr. (R)	Appleton
	Fred A. Risser (D)[5]	Madison	David T. Prosser, Jr. (R)	Appleton
1997	Fred A. Risser (D)[6]	Madison	Ben Brancel (R)[7]	Endeavor
	Brian D. Rude (R)[6]	Coon Valley	Scott R. Jensen (R)[7]	Waukesha
1999	Fred A. Risser (D)	Madison	Scott R. Jensen (R)	Waukesha
2001	Fred A. Risser (D)	Madison	Scott R. Jensen (R)	Waukesha
2003-05 . .	Alan J. Lasee (R)	De Pere	John Gard (R)	Peshtigo
2007	Fred A. Risser (D)	Madison	Michael D. Huebsch (R)	West Salem
2009	Fred A. Risser (D)	Madison	Michael J. Sheridan (D)	Janesville
2011	Michael G. Ellis (R)[8]	Neenah	Jeff Fitzgerald (R)	Horicon
	Fred A. Risser (D)[8]	Madison	Jeff Fitzgerald (R)	Horicon
2013	Michael G. Ellis (R)	Neenah	Robin J. Vos (R)	Burlington

Note: Political party indicated is for session elected and is obtained from newspaper accounts for some early legislators.
Key: D-Democrat; GB-Greenback; P-Progressive; R-Republican; U-Union; UD-Union Democrat; W-Whig.
[1]Table lists the ranking legislator in each house, not the presiding officer. The "president pro tempore" is listed until May 1, 1979; "president of the senate" is listed after that date when the lieutenant governor's function as president was eliminated by a constitutional amendment adopted in April 1979. See separate table for a list of lieutenant governors.
[2]George A. Nelson (R), Polk County, was elected to serve at special session, 4/15/26 to 4/16/26, following the resignation of Herman Sachtjen after the regular session to accept circuit judge appointment.
[3]Anderson was elected speaker 1/18/72 to succeed Huber who resigned 12/13/71 to accept appointment as chairman of the Highway Commission.
[4]A new president was elected on 4/20/93 after a change in party control following two special elections.
[5]A new president was elected on 7/9/96 after a change in party control following a recall election.
[6]A new president was elected on 4/21/98 after a change in party control following a special election.
[7]Jensen was elected speaker 11/4/97 to succeed Brancel who resigned to become Wisconsin Secretary of Agriculture, Trade and Consumer Protection.
[8]A new president was elected on 7/17/12 after a change in party control following a recall election.
Sources: Senate and Assembly Journals; Wisconsin Legislative Reference Bureau records.

MAJORITY AND MINORITY LEADERS OF THE WISCONSIN SENATE AND ASSEMBLY, 1937 – 2013

Session	Senate Majority	Senate Minority	Assembly Majority	Assembly Minority
1937 . . .	Maurice P. Coakley (R)	NA	NA	NA
1939 . . .	Maurice P. Coakley (R)	Philip E. Nelson (P)	NA	Paul R. Alfonsi (P)
1941 . . .	Maurice P. Coakley (R)	Cornelius T. Young (D)	Mark S. Catlin, Jr. (R)	Andrew J. Biemiller (P)
				Robert E. Tehan (D)
1943 . . .	Warren P. Knowles (R)[1]	NA	Mark S. Catlin, Jr. (R)	Elmer L. Genzmer (D)
	John W. Byrnes (R)[1]			Lyall T. Beggs (P)
1945 . . .	Warren P. Knowles (R)	Anthony P. Gawronski (D)	Vernon W. Thomson (R)	Lyall T. Beggs (P)
				Leland S. McParland (D)
1947 . . .	Warren P. Knowles (R)	Robert E. Tehan (D)	Vernon W. Thomson (R)	Leland S. McParland (D)
1949 . . .	Warren P. Knowles (R)	NA	Vernon W. Thomson (R)	Leland S. McParland (D)
1951 . . .	Warren P. Knowles (R)	Gaylord Nelson (D)	Arthur O. Mockrud (R)	George Molinaro (D)
1953 . . .	Warren P. Knowles (R)	Henry W. Maier (D)	Mark S. Catlin, Jr. (R)	George Molinaro (D)
1955 . . .	Paul J. Rogan (R)[2]	Henry W. Maier (D)	Robert G. Marotz (R)	Robert T. Huber (D)
1957 . . .	Robert Travis (R)	Henry W. Maier (D)	Warren A. Grady (R)	Robert T. Huber (D)
1959 . . .	Robert Travis (R)	Henry W. Maier (D)	Keith Hardie (D)	David J. Blanchard (R)
1961 . . .	Robert Travis (R)	William R. Moser (D)[3]	Robert D. Haase (R)	Robert T. Huber (D)

MAJORITY AND MINORITY LEADERS OF THE
WISCONSIN SENATE AND ASSEMBLY, 1937 – 2013–Continued

Session	Senate Majority	Senate Minority	Assembly Majority	Assembly Minority
1963	Robert P. Knowles (R)	Richard J. Zaborski (D)	Paul R. Alfonsi (R)	Robert T. Huber (D)
1965	Robert P. Knowles (R)	Richard J. Zaborski (D)	Frank L. Nikolay (D)	Robert D. Haase (R)[4]
				Paul J. Alfonsi (R)[4]
1967	Jerris Leonard (R)	Fred A. Risser (D)	J. Curtis McKay (R)	Robert T. Huber (D)
1969	Ernest C. Keppler (R)	Fred A. Risser (D)	Paul R. Alfonsi (R)	Robert T. Huber (D)
1971	Ernest C. Keppler (R)	Fred A. Risser (D)	Norman C. Anderson (D)[5]	Harold V. Froehlich (R)
			Anthony S. Earl (D)[5]	
1973	Raymond C. Johnson (R)	Fred A. Risser (D)	Anthony S. Earl (D)	John C. Shabaz (R)
1975	Wayne F. Whittow (D)[6]	Clifford W. Krueger (R)	Terry A. Willkom (D)	John C. Shabaz (R)
	William A. Bablitch (D)[6]			
1977	William A. Bablitch (D)	Clifford W. Krueger (R)	James W. Wahner (D)	John C. Shabaz (R)
1979	William A. Bablitch (D)	Clifford W. Krueger (R)	James W. Wahner (D)[7]	John C. Shabaz (R)
			Gary K. Johnson (D)[7]	
1981	William A. Bablitch (D)[9]	Walter J. Chilsen (R)	Thomas A. Loftus (D)	John C. Shabaz (R)[8]
	Timothy F. Cullen (D)[9]			Tommy G. Thompson (R)[8]
1983	Timothy F. Cullen (D)	James E. Harsdorf (R)	Gary K. Johnson (D)	Tommy G. Thompson (R)
1985	Timothy F. Cullen (D)	Susan S. Engeleiter (R)	Dismas Becker (D)	Tommy G. Thompson (R)
1987	Joseph A. Strohl (D)	Susan S. Engeleiter (R)	Thomas A. Hauke (D)	Betty Jo Nelsen (R)
1989	Joseph A. Strohl (D)	Michael G. Ellis (R)	Thomas A. Hauke (D)	David T. Prosser (R)
1991	David W. Helbach (D)	Michael G. Ellis (R)	David M. Travis (D)	David T. Prosser (R)
1993	David W. Helbach (D)[10]	Michael G. Ellis (R)[10]	David M. Travis (D)	David T. Prosser (R)
	Michael G. Ellis (R)[10]	David W. Helbach (D)[10,11]		
		Robert Jauch (D)[11]		
1995	Michael G. Ellis (R)[13]	Robert Jauch (D)[12]	Scott R. Jensen (R)	Walter J. Kunicki (D)
		Charles Chvala (D)[12,13]		
	Charles Chvala (D)[13]	Michael G. Ellis (R)[13]		
1997	Charles Chvala (D)[14]	Michael G. Ellis (R)[14]	Steven M. Foti (R)	Walter J. Kunicki (D)[15]
	Michael G. Ellis (R)[14]	Charles Chvala (D)[14]		Shirley Krug (D)[15]
1999	Charles Chvala (D)	Michael G. Ellis (R)[16]	Steven M. Foti (R)	Shirley Krug (D)
		Mary E. Panzer (R)[16]		
2001	Charles Chvala (D)	Mary E. Panzer (R)	Steven M. Foti (R)	Shirley Krug (D)
	Russell S. Decker (D)[17]			Spencer Black (D)[18]
	Fred A. Risser (D)[17]			
	Jon B. Erpenbach (D)[17]			
2003	Mary E. Panzer (R)[19]	Jon B. Erpenbach (D)	Steven M. Foti (R)	James E. Kreuser (D)
	Scott L. Fitzgerald (R)[19]			
	Dale W. Schultz (R)[20]	Judith Biros Robson (D)[20]		
2005	Dale W. Schultz (R)	Judith Biros Robson (D)	Michael D. Huebsch (R)	James E. Kreuser (D)
2007	Judith Biros Robson (D)	Scott L. Fitzgerald (R)	Jeff Fitzgerald (R)	James E. Kreuser (D)
	Russell S. Decker (D)[21]			
2009	Russell S. Decker (D)[22]	Scott L. Fitzgerald (R)	Thomas M. Nelson (D)	Jeff Fitzgerald (R)
	Dave Hansen (D)[22]			
2011	Scott L. Fitzgerald (R)	Mark Miller (D)	Scott Suder (R)	Peter W. Barca (D)
	Mark Miller (D)[23]	Scott L. Fitzgerald (R)[23]		
2013	Scott L. Fitzgerald (R)	Chris Larson (D)	Scott Suder (R)	Peter W. Barca (D)

Note: Majority and minority leaders, who are chosen by the party caucuses in each house, were first recognized officially in the senate and assembly rules in 1963. Prior to the 1977 session, these positions were also referred to as "floor leader".

Key: (D) – Democrat; (P) – Progressive; (R) – Republican.

NA – Not available.

[1] Knowles granted leave of absence to return to active duty in U.S. Navy; Byrnes chosen to succeed him on 4/30/1943.
[2] Resigned after sine die adjournment.
[3] Resigned 1/30/1962.
[4] Haase resigned 9/15/1965; Alfonsi elected 10/4/1965.
[5] Earl elected 1/18/1972 to succeed Anderson who became Assembly Speaker.
[6] Whittow resigned 4/30/1976; Bablitch elected 5/17/1976.
[7] Wahner resigned 1/28/1980; Johnson elected 1/28/1980.
[8] Shabaz resigned 12/18/1981; Thompson elected 12/21/1981.
[9] Bablitch resigned 5/26/1982; Cullen elected 5/26/1982.
[10] Democrats controlled senate from 1/4/1993 to 4/20/1993 when Republicans assumed control after a special election.
[11] Helbach resigned 5/12/1993; Jauch elected 5/12/1993.
[12] Jauch resigned 10/17/1995; Chvala elected 10/24/1995.
[13] Republicans controlled senate from 1/5/1995 to 6/13/1996 when Democrats assumed control after a recall election.
[14] Democrats controlled the senate from 1/6/1997 to 4/21/1998 when Republicans assumed control after a special election.
[15] Kunicki resigned 6/3/1998; Krug elected 6/3/1998.
[16] Ellis resigned 1/25/2000; Panzer elected 1/25/2000.
[17] Decker and Risser elected co-leaders 10/22/2002. Erpenbach elected leader 12/4/2002.
[18] Black elected 5/1/2001.
[19] Panzer resigned 9/17/2004; Fitzgerald elected 9/17/2004.
[20] Schultz elected 11/9/2004; Robson elected 11/9/2004.
[21] Decker elected 10/24/2007.
[22] Hansen replaced Decker as leader, 12/15/2010.
[23] After a resignation on 3/16/12 resulted in a 16-16 split, Fitzgerald and Miller served as co-leaders. A recall election gave Democrats control of the senate as of 7/17/12.

Sources: *Wisconsin Blue Book*, various editions; newspaper accounts.

SENATE AND ASSEMBLY CHIEF CLERKS
AND SERGEANTS AT ARMS, 1848 – 2013

Legislative Session	Senate		Assembly	
	Chief Clerk	Sergeant at Arms	Chief Clerk	Sergeant at Arms
1848	Henry G. Abbey	Lyman H. Seaver	Daniel N. Johnson	John Mullanphy
1849	William R. Smith	F. W. Shollner	Robert L. Ream	Felix McLinden
1850	William R. Smith	James Hanrahan	Alex T. Gray	E. R. Hugunin
1851	William Hull	E. D. Masters	Alex T. Gray	C. M. Kingsbury
1852	John K. Williams	Patrick Cosgrove	Alex T. Gray	Elisha Starr
1853	John K. Williams	Thomas Hood	Thomas McHugh	Richard F. Wilson
1854	Samuel G. Bugh	J. M. Sherwood	Thomas McHugh	William H. Gleason
1855	Samuel G. Bugh	William H. Gleason	David Atwood	William Blake
1856	Byron Paine	Joseph Baker	James Armstrong	Egbert Mosely
1857	William Henry Brisbane	Alanson Filer	William C. Webb	William C. Rogers
1858	John L. V. Thomas	Nathaniel L. Stout	L. H. D. Crane	Francis Massing
1859	Hiram Bowen	Asa Kinney	L. H. D. Crane	Emmanual Munk
1860	J. H. Warren	Asa Kinney	L. H. D. Crane	Joseph Gates
1861	J. H. Warren	J. A. Hadley	L. H. D. Crane	Craig B. Peebe
1862	J. H. Warren	B. U. Caswell	John S. Dean	A. A. Huntington
1863	Frank M. Stewart	Luther Bashford	John S. Dean	A. M. Thompson
1864	Frank M. Stewart	Nelson Williams	John S. Dean	A. M. Thompson
1865	Frank M. Stewart	Nelson Williams	John S. Dean	Alonzo Wilcox
1866	Frank M. Stewart	Nelson Williams	E. W. Young	L. M. Hammond
1867	Leander B. Hills	Asa Kinney	E. W. Young	Daniel Webster
1868	Leander B. Hills	W. H. Hamilton	E. W. Young	C. L. Harris
1869	Leander B. Hills	W. H. Hamilton	E. W. Young	Rolin C. Kelly
1870	Leander B. Hills	E. M. Rogers	E. W. Young	Ole C. Johnson
1871	O. R. Smith	W. W. Baker	E. W. Young	Sam S. Fifield
1872	J. H. Waggoner	W. D, Hoard	E. W. Young	Sam S. Fifield
1873	J. H. Waggoner	Albert Emonson	E. W. Young	O. C. Bissel
1874	J. H. Waggoner	O. U. Aiken	George W. Peck	Joseph Deuster
1875	Fred A. Dennett	O. U. Aiken	R. M. Strong	J. W. Brackett
1876	A. J. Turner	E. T. Gardner	R. M. Strong	Elisha Starr
1877	A. J. Turner	C. E. Bullard	W. A. Nowell	Thomas B. Reid
1878	A. J. Turner[1]	L. J. Brayton	Jabez R. Hunter	Anton Klaus
	Charles E. Bross[1]			
1879	Charles E. Bross	Chalmers Ingersoll	John E. Eldred	Miletus Knight
1880	Charles E. Bross	Chalmers Ingersoll	John E. Eldred	D. H. Pulcifer
1881	Charles E. Bross	W. W. Baker	John E. Eldred	G. W. Church
1882	Charles E. Bross	A. T. Glaze	E. D. Coe	D. E. Welch
1883	Charles E. Bross	A. D. Thorp	I. T. Carr	Thomas Kennedy
1885	Charles E. Bross	Hubert Wolcott	E. D. Coe	John M. Ewing
1887	Charles E. Bross	T. J. George	E. D. Coe	William A. Adamson
1889	Charles E. Bross	T .J. George	E. D. Coe	F. E. Parsons
1891	J. P. Hume	John A. Barney	George W. Porth	Patrick Whelan
1893	Sam J. Shafer	John B. Becker	George W. Porth	Theodore Knapstein
1895	Walter L. Houser	Charles Pettibone	W. A. Nowell	B. F. Millard
1897	Walter L. Houser	Charles Pettibone	W. A. Nowell	C. M. Hambright
1889	Walter L. Houser	Charles Pettibone	W. A. Nowell	James H. Agen
1901	Walter L. Houser	Charles Pettibone	W. A. Nowell	A. M. Anderson
1903	Theodore W. Goldin	Sanfield McDonald	C. O. Marsh	A. M. Anderson
1905	L .K. Eaton	R. C. Falconer	C. O. Marsh	Nicholas Streveler
1907	A. R. Emerson	R. C. Falconer	C. E. Shaffer	W. S. Irvine
1909	F. E. Andrews	R. C. Falconer	C. E. Shaffer	W. S. Irvine
1911-13	F. M. Wylie	C. A. Leicht	C. E. Shaffer	W. S. Irvine
1915	O. G. Munson	F. E. Andrews	C. E. Shaffer	W. S. Irvine
1917	O. G. Munson	F. E. Andrews	C. E. Shaffer	T. G. Cretney
1919	O. G. Munson	John Turner	C. E. Shaffer	T. G. Cretney
1921	O. G. Munson	Vincent Kielpinski	C. E. Shaffer	T. G. Cretney
1923	F. W. Schoenfeld	C. A. Leicht	C. E. Shaffer	T. W. Bartingale
1925	F. W. Schoenfeld	C. A. Leicht	C. E. Shaffer	C. E. Hanson
1927-29	O. G. Munson	George W. Rickeman	C. E. Shaffer	C. F. Moulton
1931	R. A. Cobban	Emil A. Hartman	C. E. Shaffer	Gustave Rheingans
1933	R. A. Cobban	Emil A. Hartman	John J. Slocum	George C. Faust
1935-37	Lawrence R. Larsen	Emil A. Hartman	Lester H. Johnson	Gustave Rheingans
1939	Lawrence R. Larsen	Emil A. Hartman	John J. Slocum	Robert A. Merrill
1941-43	Lawrence R. Larsen	Emil A. Hartman	Arthur L. May	Norris J. Kellman
1945	Lawrence R. Larsen	Harold E. Damon	Arthur L. May	Norris J. Kellman
1947-53	Thomas M. Donahue	Harold E. Damon	Arthur L. May	Norris J. Kellman
1955-57	Lawrence R. Larsen	Harold E. Damon	Arthur L. May	Norris J. Kellman

SENATE AND ASSEMBLY CHIEF CLERKS
AND SERGEANTS AT ARMS, 1848 – 2013–Continued

Legislative	Senate		Assembly	
Session	Chief Clerk	Sergeant at Arms	Chief Clerk	Sergeant at Arms
1959	.Lawrence R. Larsen	Harold E. Damon	Norman C. Anderson	Thomas H. Browne
1961	.Lawrence R. Larsen	Harold E. Damon	Robert G. Marotz	Norris J. Kellman
1963	.Lawrence R. Larsen	Harold E. Damon	Kenneth E. Priebe	Norris J. Kellman
1965	.Lawrence R. Larsen[2]	Harold E. Damon	James P. Buckley	Thomas H. Browne
	William P. Nugent[2]			
1967	.William P. Nugent	Harry O. Levander	Arnold W. F. Langner[3]	Louis C. Romell
			Wilmer H. Struebing[3]	
1969	.William P. Nugent	Kenneth Nicholson	Wilmer H. Struebing	Louis C. Romell
1971	.William P. Nugent	Kenneth Nicholson	Thomas P. Fox	William F. Quick
1973	.William P. Nugent	Kenneth Nicholson	Thomas S. Hanson	William F. Quick
1975	.Glenn E. Bultman	Robert M. Thompson	Everett E. Bolle	Raymond J. Tobiasz
1977	.Donald J. Schneider	Robert M. Thompson	Everett E. Bolle	Joseph E. Jones
1979	.Donald J. Schneider	Daniel B. Fields	Marcel Dandeneau	Joseph E. Jones
1981	.Donald J. Schneider	Daniel B. Fields	David R. Kedrowski	Lewis T. Mittness
1983	.Donald J. Schneider	Daniel B. Fields	Joanne M. Duren	Lewis T. Mittness
1985	.Donald J. Schneider	Daniel B. Fields	Joanne M. Duren	Patrick Essie
1987	.Donald J. Schneider	Daniel B. Fields	Thomas T. Melvin	Patrick Essie
1989-91	.Donald J. Schneider	Daniel B. Fields	Thomas T. Melvin	Robert G. Johnston
1993	.Donald J. Schneider	Daniel B. Fields[4]	Thomas T. Melvin	Robert G. Johnston
		Jon H. Hochkammer[4]		
1995	.Donald J. Schneider	Jon H. Hochkammer	Thomas T. Melvin[5]	John A. Scocos
			Charles R. Sanders[5]	
1997	.Donald J. Schneider	Jon H. Hochkammer	Charles R. Sanders	John A. Scocos[6]
				Denise L. Solie[6]
1999	.Donald J. Schneider	Jon H. Hochkammer	Charles R. Sanders	Denise L. Solie
2001	.Donald J. Schneider	Jon H. Hochkammer[7]	John A. Scocos[7]	Denise L. Solie
2003	.Donald J. Schneider[8]	Edward A. Blazel	Patrick E. Fuller	Richard A. Skindrud
	Robert J. Marchant[8]			
2005-07	.Robert J. Marchant	Edward A. Blazel	Patrick E. Fuller	Richard A. Skindrud
2009	.Robert J. Marchant	Edward A. Blazel	Patrick E. Fuller	William M. Nagy
2011	.Robert J. Marchant[9]	Edward A. Blazel	Patrick E. Fuller	Anne Tonnon Byers
2013	.Jeffrey Renk	Edward A. Blazel	Patrick E. Fuller	Anne Tonnon Byers

[1]Bross elected 2/6/78; Turner resigned 2/7/78.

[2]Larsen died 3/2/65; Nugent elected 3/31/65.

[3]Langner resigned 5/2/67; Struebing elected 5/16/67.

[4]Fields served until 8/2/93. Randall Radtke served as Acting Sergeant from 8/3/93 to 11/3/93. Hochkammer was elected 1/25/94.

[5]Melvin retired 1/31/95; Sanders elected 5/24/95.

[6]Scocos resigned 9/25/97; Solie elected 1/15/98.

[7]Scocos resigned 2/25/02. Hochkammer resigned 9/2/02. No replacement was elected for either.

[8]Schneider resigned 7/4/03; Marchant elected 1/20/04.

[9]Marchant resigned 1/2/12.

Sources: Wisconsin Legislative Reference Bureau, *Wisconsin Blue Book,* various editions; journals and organizing resolutions of each house.

MEMBERS OF THE WISCONSIN LEGISLATURE, 1848 – 2007
See *2007-2008 Blue Book* Feature Article
"Those Who Served: Wisconsin Legislators 1848 – 2007," pp. 99-191.

WISCONSIN LEGISLATIVE SESSIONS, 1848 – 2011

Session	Opening and Adjournment Dates	Length of Session			Measures Introduced			Vetoes[1]		Laws Enacted
		Calendar Days[2]	Meeting Days[3] (S)	(A)	Bills	Jt. Res.	Res.	Bills Vetoed	Over-ridden	
1848	6/5-8/21	78	58	59	217	0	0	0	0	155
1849	1/10-4/2	83	69	65	428	0	0	1	1	220
1850	1/9-2/11	34	29	29	438	0	0	1	0	284
1851	1/8-3/17	69	59	59	707	0	0	9	0	407
1852	1/14-4/19	97	78	78	813	0	0	2	1	504
1853	1/12-4/4; 6/6-7/13	153	100	104	1,145	0	0	3	0	521
1854	1/11-4/3	83	66	66	880	0	0	2	0	437
1855	1/10-4/2	83	79	79	955	0	0	6	0	500
1856	1/9-3/31; 9/3-10/14	125	94	103	1,242	0	0	1	0	688
1857	1/14-3/9	55	46	46	895	0	0	0	0	517
1858	1/13-3/31; 4/10-5/17	116	95	97	1,364	157	342	28	0	436
1859	1/12-3/21	69	58	57	986	113	143	9	0	680
1860	1/11-4/2	83	66	67	1,024	69	246	2	0	489
1861	1/9-4/17	99	81	80	857	100	235	2	0	387
1861SS[4]	5/15-5/27	13	11	11	28	24	34	0	0	15
1862	1/8-4/7; 6/3-6/17	105	86	88	1,008	125	207	27	8	514
1862SS	9/10-9/26	17	15	15	43	25	37	0	0	17
1863	1/14-4/2	79	65	67	895	101	157	7	1	383
1864	1/13-4/4	83	68	69	835	66	141	0	0	509
1865	1/11-4/10	90	73	72	1,132	82	190	2	0	565
1866	1/10-4/2	83	75	74	1,107	64	208	5	0	733
1867	1/9-4/11	93	71	72	1,161	97	161	2	0	790
1868	1/8-3/6	59	46	45	987	73	119	2	0	692
1869	1/13-3/11	58	40	43	887	52	81	12	1	657
1870	1/12-3/17	65	51	51	1,043	54	89	2	0	666
1871	1/11-3/25	74	58	60	1,066	55	82	4	0	671
1872	1/10-3/26	77	61	60	709	79	124	2	0	322
1873	1/8-3/20	72	49	55	611	62	122	4	0	308
1874	1/14-3/12	58	50	49	688	91	111	2	0	349
1875	1/13-3/6	53	44	42	637	39	93	2	0	344
1876	1/12-3/14	63	50	50	715	57	115	2	0	415
1877	1/10-3/8	58	41	41	720	59	95	4	0	384
1878	1/9-3/21	72	55	55	735	79	134	2	0	342
1878SS	6/4-6/7	4	4	4	6	14	10	0	0	5
1879	1/8-3/5	57	43	43	610	49	105	0	0	256
1880	1/14-3/17	64	50	49	669	58	93	3	0	323
1881	1/12-4/14	93	63	64	780	104	100	3	0	334
1882	1/11-3/31	80	57	57	728	57	90	6	0	330
1883	1/10-4/4	85	57	67	705	75	100	2	0	360
1885	1/14-4/13	90	65	66	963	97	108	8	0	471
1887	1/12-4/15	94	69	68	1,293	114	60	10	0	553
1889	1/9-4/19	101	64	64	1,355	136	82	5	1	529
1891	1/14-4/25	102	68	69	1,216	137	91	8	1	483
1892SS	6/28-7/1	4	4	4	4	7	16	0	0	1
1892SS	10/17-10/27	11	9	9	8	6	14	0	0	2
1893	1/11-4/21	101	62	62	1,124	135	86	6	0	312
1895	1/9-4/20	102	70	70	1,154	139	88	0	0	387
1896SS	2/18-2/28	11	8	8	3	11	15	0	0	1
1897	1/13-4/21; 8/17-8/20	103	75	76	1,077	155	39	11	0	381
1899	1/11-5/4	114	78	77	910	113	40	4	0	357
1901	1/9-5/15	127	89	89	1,091	81	39	22	0	470
1903	1/14-5/23	130	87	89	1,115	65	81	23	0	451
1905	1/11-6/21	162	114	117	1,357	134	101	19	0	523
1905SS	12/4-12/19	16	12	14	24	15	26	0	0	17
1907	1/9-7/16	189	114	123	1,685	205	84	26	1	677
1909	1/13-6/18	157	100	101	1,567	213	49	24	0	550
1911	1/11-7/15	186	137	138	1,710	267	37	15	0	665
1912SS	4/30-5/6	7	6	6	41	7	6	0	0	22
1913	1/8-8/9	214	138	147	1,847	175	79	23	0	778
1915	1/13-8/24	224	147	148	1,560	220	79	15	0	637
1916SS	10/10-10/11	2	2	2	2	8	4	0	0	2
1917	1/10-7/16	188	130	133	1,439	229	115	18	0	679
1918SS	2/19-3/9	19	14	14	27	22	28	2	0	16
1918SS	9/24-9/25	2	2	2	2	6	9	0	0	2
1919	1/8-7/30	204	107	106	1,350	268	100	40	0	703
1919SS	9/4-9/8	5	4	3	7	4	6	0	0	7
1920SS	5/25-6/4	11	7	7	46	10	22	2	0	32
1921	1/12-7/14	184	116	116	1,199	207	93	41	1	591
1922SS	3/22-3/28	7	4	4	10	7	12	1	0	4
1923	1/10-7/14	186	114	120	1,247	215	93	52	0	449
1925	1/14-6/29	167	103	107	1,144	200	115	73	0	454
1926SS	4/15-4/16	2	2	2	1	8	12	0	0	1
1927	1/12-8/13	214	121	128	1,341	235	167	88	2	542
1928SS	1/24-2/4	12	9	8	20	35	23	0	0	5
1928SS	3/6-3/13	8	6	6	13	9	17	0	0	2
1929	1/9-9/20	255	137	135	1,366	278	185	44	0	530
1931	1/14-6/27	165	98	104	1,429	291	160	36	0	487
1931SS	11/24/31-2/5/32	74	48	42	99	93	83	2	0	31
1933	1/11-7/25	196	111	121	1,411	324	157	15	0	496
1933SS	12/11/33-2/3/34	55	30	34	45	160	53	0	0	20
1935	1/9-9/27	262	153	156	1,662	346	190	27	0	556
1937	1/13-7/2	171	97	114	1,404	228	127	10	0	432

WISCONSIN LEGISLATIVE SESSIONS, 1848 – 2011–Continued

Session	Opening and Adjournment Dates	Length of Session Calendar Days[2]	Meeting Days[3] (S)	(A)	Measures Introduced Bills	Jt. Res.	Res.	Vetoes[1] Bills Vetoed	Over-ridden	Laws Enacted
1937SS....	9/15-10/16	32	23	23	28	18	23	0	0	15
1939.....	1/11-10/6	269	154	154	1,559	268	133	22	0	535
1941.....	1/8-6/6	150	90	93	1,368	160	109	17	0	333
1943.....	1/13-8/3;	375	105	104	1,153	202	136	39	20	577
(1944: 1/12-1/22)										
1945.....	1/10-6/20; 9/5-9/6	240	97	93	1,156	208	109	31	5	590
1946SS...	7/29-7/30	2	2	2	2	6	14	0	0	2
1947.....	1/8-7/19; 9/9-9/11	247	114	114	1,220	195	97	10	1	615
1948SS....	7/19-7/20	2	2	2	0	5	11	0	0	0
1949.....	1/12-7/9; 9/12-9/13	245	105	106	1,432	188	86	17	2	643
1951.....	1/10-6/14	156	91	90	1,559	157	73	18	0	735
1953.....	1/14-6/12; 10/26-11/6	297	97	98	1,593	175	70	31	3	687
1955.....	1/12-6/24; 10/3-10/21	283	111	114	1,503	256	74	38	0	696
1957.....	1/9-6/28; 9/23-9/27	262	107	108	1,512	246	71	39	1	706
1958SS....	6/11-6/13	3	3	3	3	7	13	0	0	3
1959.....	1/14/59-5/27/60	500	159	163	1,769	272	84	36	4	696
(1959: 1/14-7/25, 11/3-12/23; 1960: 1/6-1/22, 5/16-5/27)										
1961.....	1/11/61-1/9/63	729	184	185	1,592	295	68	73	2	689
(1961: 1/11-8/12, 10/30-12/22; 1962: 1/8-1/12, 6/18-7/31, 12/27-12/29; 1963: 1/9)										
1963.....	1/9/63-1/13/65	736	150	142	1,619	241	110	72	4	580
(1963: 1/9-8/6, 11/4-11/21; 1964: 4/13-4/29, 11/9-11/11; 1965: 1/13)										
1963SS....	12/10-12/12	3	3	3	9	10	10	0	0	3
1965[5].....	1/13/65-1/2/67	720	161	157	1,818	293	86	24	1	666
(1965: 1/13-7/30, 10/4-11/4; 1966: 5/2-6/10; 1967: 1/2)										
1967.....	1/11/67-1/6/69	727	122	126	1,700	215	61	18	0	355
(1967: 1/11-3/9, 4/4-7/28, 10/17-11/16, 12/5-12/16; 1968: none; 1969: 1/6)										
1969.....	1/6/69-1/4/71	729	165	165	2,014	232	101	34	1	501
(1969: 1/6, 1/21-11/15; 1970: 1/5-1/16; 1971: 1/4)										
1969SS[6]...	9/29/69-1/17/70	111	28	18	5	5	8	0	0	1
1970SS....	12/22/70	1	1	1	0	1	5	0	0	0
1971.....	1/4/71-1/1/73	729	179	180	2,568	291	121	32	3	336
(1971: 1/4, 1/19-10/28; 1972: 1/18-3/10, 7/13-7/15; 1973: 1/1)										
1972SS....	4/19-4/28	10	5	6	9	4	4	0	0	6
1973.....	1/1/73-1/6/75	736	150	150	2,501	277	126	13	0	341
(1973: 1/1, 1/16-2/15, 3/13-7/26, 10/2-10/26; 1974: 1/29-3/29, 11/19-11/20; 1975: 1/6)										
1973SS....	12/17-12/21	5	5	5	3	2	6	0	0	2
1974SS....	4/29-6/13	46	17	21	12	1	4	0	0	6
1974SS[7]...	11/19-11/20	2	2	1	2	0	0	0	0	1
1975.....	1/6/75-1/3/77	729	124	125	2,325	169	88	36	6	414
(1975: 1/6, 1/1-2/20, 4/1-7/16, 9/2-9/26; 1976: 1/28-3/26, 6/15-6/17; 1977: 1/3)										
1975SS....	12/9-12/11	3	3	3	13	1	2	1	0	7
1976SS....	5/18	1	1	1	2	2	3	0	0	1
1976SS[7]...	6/15-6/17	3	3	3	13	4	3	0	0	8
1976SS....	9/8	1	1	1	4	1	1	0	0	2
1977.....	1/3/77-1/1/79	729	84	112	2,053	182	48	21	4	442
(1977: 1/3, 1/11-2/18, 3/29-7/1, 9/6-9/30; 1978: 1/24-1/26, 1/31-3/31, 6/13-6/15; 1979: 1/3)										
1977SS....	6/30	1	1	1	0	1	2	0	0	0
1977SS....	11/7-11/11	5	5	5	6	4	2	0	0	5
1978SS[7]...	6/13-6/15	3	3	3	2	5	2	0	0	2
1978SS....	12/20	1	1	1	2	4	2	0	0	2
1979.....	1/3/79-1/5/81	734	85	99	1,920	203	40	19	3	350
1979: 1/3, 1/9, 1/23-3/2, 4/17-6/29, 10/2-11/2; 1980: 1/29-4/2, 5/28-5/30; 1981: 1/5)										
1979SS....	9/5	1	1	1	10	3	2	0	0	5
1980SS[8]...	1/22-1/25	4	2	4	8	3	2	0	0	0
1980SS....	6/3- 7/3	31	13	12	20	14	2	0	0	7
1981.....	1/5/81-1/3/83	729	121	130	1,987	176	70	10	2	381
(1981: 1/5, 1/13, 1/27-2/20, 4/7-7/17, 9/30-10/30, 12/15-12/17;										

WISCONSIN LEGISLATIVE SESSIONS, 1848 – 2011–Continued

Session	Opening and Adjournment Dates	Length of Session Calendar Days[2]	Meeting Days[3] (S)	Meeting Days[3] (A)	Measures Introduced Bills	Jt. Res.	Res.	Vetoes[1] Bills Vetoed	Over-ridden	Laws Enacted
1982: 1/20-6/14;										
1983: 1/3)										
1981SS[9] . . . 11/4-11/17		14	8	7	6	3	2	0	0	3
1982SS[9] . . . 4/6-4/30, 5/5-5/20		45	18	21	4	2	2	1	0	1
1982SS[10] . . . 5/26-5/28		3	3	3	13	7	2	0	0	9
1983 . . . . . 1/3/83-1/7/85		736	72	80	1,902	173	50	3	0	521
(1983: 1/3, 1/25-1/28, 2/8-2/18,										
4/12-6/30, 10/4-10/28;										
1984: 1/31-4/6, 5/22-5/24;										
1985: 1/7)										
1983SS. . . . 1/4-1/6		3	3	1	2	2	1	0	0	2
1983SS. . . . 4/12-4/14		3	3	3	1	1	0	0	0	1
1983SS. . . . 7/11-7/14		4	4	4	5	3	1	0	0	4
1983SS. . . . 10/18-10/28		11	8	7	12	1	0	0	0	11
1984SS. . . . 2/2-4/4		63	18	13	2	1	0	0	0	0
1984SS. . . . 5/22-5/24		3	3	2	12	5	1	0	0	11
1985 . . . . . 1/7/85-1/7/87		331	68	66	1,624	171	41	7	0	293
(1985: 1/7, 1/15, 1/29-2/8, 3/19-3/21,										
4/23-6/29, 9/24-10/18;										
1986: 1/28-3/26, 5/20-5/22;										
1987: 1/5)										
1985SS. . . . 3/19-3/21		3	2	2	6	1	0	0	0	3
1985SS. . . . 9/24-10/19		26	11	7	21	1	0	0	0	17
1985SS. . . . 10/31		1	1	1	1	3	0	0	0	1
1985SS. . . . 11/20		1	1	1	24	2	0	0	0	12
1986SS. . . . 1/27-5/30		124	34	27	1	4	0	0	0	1
1986SS. . . . 3/24-3/26		3	3	3	1	1	0	0	0	1
1986SS. . . . 5/20-5/29		10	6	4	44	3	0	0	0	12
1986SS. . . . 7/15		1	1	1	3	1	0	0	0	2
1987[10] 1/5/87-1/3/89		730	60	73	1,628	199	21	35	0	412
(1987: 1/5, 1/13, 1/27-2/6, 3/17-3/19,										
4/21-7/2, 10/6-10/30;										
1988: 1/26-3/25, 5/17-5/19;										
1989: 1/3)										
1987SS. . . . 9/15-9/16		2	2	2	2	1	0	0	0	2
1987SS. . . . 11/18/87-6/7/88		203	9	11	19	3	0	3	0	5
1988SS. . . . 6/30		1	1	1	5	1	3	0	0	3
1989 . . . . . 1/3/89-1/7/91		735	68	70	1,557	244	45	35	0	361
(1989: 1/3, 1/4-1/9, 1/10, 1/11-1/23,										
1/24-2/3, 2/6-3/13, 3/14-3/16,										
3/17-4/24, 4/25-4/27, 4/28-5/15,										
5/16-6/30, 10/3-11/10, 11/13-12/31;										
1990: 1/1-1/22, 1/23-3/23, 3/26-5/14,										
5/15-5/17, 5/18-12/31;										
1991: 1/1-1/4, 1/7)										
1989SS. . . . 10/10/89-3/22/90		164	52	49	52	6	0	0	0	7
1990SS. . . . 5/15/90		1	1	1	7	1	0	0	0	0
1991 . . . . . 1/7/91-1/4/93		729	102	100	1,676	244	32	33	0	318
(1991: 1/7, 1/15, 1/29-3/14,										
4/16-5/16, 6/4-7/3, 10/1-11/8;										
1992: 1/28-3/27, 5/19-5/21;										
1993: 1/4)										
1991SS. . . . 1/29/-7/4		157	49	52	16	1	0	0	0	2
1991SS. . . . 10/15/91-5/21/92		220	50	47	9	2	0	0	0	1
1992SS[8] 4/14-6/4		52	20	17	7	1	2	0	0	2
1992SS. . . . 6/1		1	1	1	0	2	0	0	0	0
1992SS. . . . 8/25-9/15		22	7	7	1	1	2	0	0	1
1993 . . . . . 1/4/93-1/3/95		730	91	86	2,147	207	47	8	0	491
(1993: 1/4, 1/26-3/11, 4/20-7/16,										
10/5-10/28;										
1994: 1/25-3/25, 5/17;										
1995: 1/3)										
1994SS. . . . 5/18-5/19		2	2	2	6	1	0	0	0	3
1994SS[11] . . . 6/7-6/23		17	8	8	3	4	0	0	0	3
1995 . . . . . 1/3/95-1/6/97		735	78	90	1,780	163	38	4	0	467
(1995: 1/3-1/5, 1/17-2/2,										
2/14-3/9, 4/4-4/6, 5/16-6/29,										
9/19-10/12; 11/7-11/16;										
1996: 1/9-2/1, 3/5-3/28, 5/7-5/14, 7/9;										
1997: 1/6)										
1995SS. . . . 1/4		1	1	1	1	1	0	0	0	1
1995SS. . . . 9/5-10/12		36	12	13	1	1	0	0	0	1
1997 . . . . . 1/6/97-1/4/99		729	87	92	1,508	183	30	3	0	333
(1997: 1/6, 1/14, 1/28-1/30, 2/12, 2/25-2/26,										
3/4-3/20, 5/13-5/29, 6/10-9/30, 11/4-11/6,										
11/18-11/20;										
1998: 1/13-1/22, 2/3-2/12, 3/10-3/26,										
4/21-5/13;										
1999: 1/4)										
1998SS[12] . . . 4/21-5/21		31	13	12	13	2	2	0	0	5
1999[13] 1/4/99-1/3/01		731	97	101	1,498	168	52	5	0	196
(1999: 1/4, 1/14, 1/26-1/28, 2/16-2/18,										

WISCONSIN LEGISLATIVE SESSIONS, 1848 – 2011–Continued

Session	Opening and Adjournment Dates	Length of Session Calendar Days[2]	Meeting Days[3] (S)	(A)	Measures Introduced Bills	Jt. Res.	Res.	Vetoes[1] Bills Vetoed	Over-ridden	Laws Enacted
	3/2-3/4, 3/16-3/25, 5/11-10/6, 10/26-11/11;									
	2000: 1/25-2/10, 3/7-3/30, 5/2-5/4, 5/23-5/24;									
	2001: 1/3)									
1999SS[7] . . .	10/27-11/11	16	7	8	3	1	0	0	0	1
2000SS. . . .	5/4-5/9	8	3	3	2	2	1	0	0	1
2001	1/3/01-1/6/03	734	62	63	1,436	174	75	0	0	106
	(2001: 1/3, 1/30-2/1, 2/13-2/15, 3/6-3/22, 5/1-5/10, 6/5-7/26, 10/2-10/4, 10/16-11/8;									
	2002: 1/22-2/7, 2/26-3/14, 4/30-5/2, 5/14-5/15;									
	2003: 1/6)									
2001SS[7] . . .	5/1-5/3	3	1	2	1	0	0	0	0	1
2002SS[7] . . .	1/22-7/8	168	59	52	1	2	7	0	0	1
2002SS[7] . . .	5/13-5/15	3	3	2	2	0	0	0	0	1
2003[14]	1/6/03-1/3/05	729	104	94	1,567	164	78	54	0	326
	(2003: 1/6-1/7, 1/28-1/30, 2/18-2/20, 3/3-3/20, 4/29-5/8, 5/28-6/25, 9/23-10/2, 10/28-11/13;									
	2004: 1/20-2/5, 2/24-3/11, 4/27, 5/11-5/19;									
	2005: 1/3)									
2003SS	1/30-2/20	22	7	7	1	0	0	0	0	1
2005[15]	1/3/05-1/3/07	731	69	72	1,967	196	76	47	0	489
	(2005: 1/3, 1/11-1/27, 2/8, 2/15-2/24, 3/8-3/16, 4/5-4/12, 5/3-5/12, 5/31-6/30, 7/5, 7/20, 9/20-9/28, 10/25-11/9, 12/6-12/15;									
	2006: 1/17-2/2, 2/21-3/9, 4/25-5/17, 5/30-5/31, 7/12;									
	2007: 1/3)									
2005SS	1/12-1/20	9	4	1	2	0	0	0	0	1
2006SS. . . .	2/14-3/7	22	7	6	2	0	0	0	0	1
2007	1/3/07-1/5/09	733	91	89	1,574	230	50	1	0	239
	(2007: 1/3, 1/9, 1/30-2/1, 2/13, 2/20-3/1, 3/13-3/15, 4/17-4/26, 5/8-5/16, 5/29-11/8, 12/11;									
	2008: 1/15-1/31, 2/19-3/13, 5/6-5/8, 5/27-5/28;									
	2009: 1/5)									
2007SS. . . .	1/11-2/1	22	7	6	2	1	0	0	0	1
2007SS. . . .	10/15-10/23	9	5	3	2	0	0	0	0	0
2007SS. . . .	12/11/07, 1/15-5/14/08	156	38	39	1	1	0	0	0	0
2008SS. . . .	3/12-4/15	65	22	22	1	4	2	0	0	1
2008SS. . . .	4/17-5/15	29	11	11	1	4	2	0	0	1
2009[16]	1/5/09-1/3/11	729	59	60	1,720	221	44	6	0	406
	(2009: 1/5, 1/13, 1/27-2/26, 3/24-3/26, 4/21-4/30, 5/12-5/21, 6/9-6/30, 9/15-9/24, 10/20-11/5;									
	2010: 1/19-1/28, 2/16-3/4, 4/13-4/22, 5/4-5/6, 5/25-5/26, 12/15-12/16;									
	2011: 1/3)									
2009SS. . . .	6/24-6/27	4	4	3	1	0	0	0	0	0
2009SS. . . .	12/16-3/4/10	79	23	24	2	0	0	0	0	0
2011[17].	1/3/11-1/7/13	735	69	64	1,325	211	48	0	0	267
	(2011: 1/3, 1/11, 1/25-2/10, 2/22-3/10, 4/5-4/14, 5/10-5/19, 6/7-6/28, 7/19-8/2, 9/13-9/22, 10/18/-11/3;									
	2012: 1/17-1/26, 2/14-2/23, 3/6-3/15, 4/24, 5/22, 7/17;									
	2013: 1/7)									
2011SS. . . .	1/4-9/27	267	84	80	27	1	3	0	0	12
2011SS. . . .	9/29-12/8	71	22	22	48	0	0	0	0	7

Note: For 1836-1847 territorial sessions, see *1873 Blue Book*, p. 205.
[1]Partial vetoes not included. See Executive Vetoes table. [2]Number of calendar days from session opening date to final adjournment. [3]Number of days senate or assembly met, including "skeleton sessions" (those days on which the senate or assembly leadership calls the house in session *in absentia* to fulfill a procedural requirement). [4]SS denotes special session. Regular and special sessions may run concurrently with meetings held on the same day. Each is counted as a separate meeting day. [5]Although 1965 Legislature adjourned to 1/11/67, terms automatically expired on 1/2/67. [6]Senate adjourned the special session 11/15/69; assembly, 1/17/70. [7]Special session met concurrently with regular session. [8]1979 Legislature met concurrently in extraordinary and special session, 1/22/80 – 1/25/80. [9]Legislature met concurrently in special session and extended floorperiod. [10]Extraordinary sessions held in September 1987, and April, May and June 1988. May 1988 extraordinary session ran concurrently with May 1988 veto review period and also with June 1988 extraordinary session. [11]Extraordinary session held, 5/15/94 – 6/23/94. [12]Extraordinary session held in April 1998. [13]Extraordinary session held in April and May 2000. [14]Extraordinary sessions held in February, July, and August 2003; December 2003-February 2004; March 2004; May 2004; and July 2004. [15]Extraordinary sessions were held in July 2005 and April 2006. [16]Extraordinary sessions held in February, May, June, and December 2009 and in December 2010. [17]Extraordinary sessions were held in June and July 2011.
Sources: *Bulletin of the Proceedings of the Wisconsin Legislature,* various editions; and senate and assembly journals.

WISCONSIN MEMBERS, U.S. HOUSE OF REPRESENTATIVES
1848 – 2013

Name	Party	Residence	District	Term
Adams, Henry C	.Rep.	Madison	2	1903-1906
Amlie, Thomas R	.Rep., Prog.	Elkhorn	1	1931-1933; 1935-1939
Aspin, Les	.Dem.	East Troy	1	1971-1993
Atwood, David.	.Rep.	Madison	2	1870-1871
Babbitt, Clinton	.Dem.	Beloit	1	1891-1893
Babcock, Joseph W	.Rep.	Necedah	3	1893-1907
Baldus, Alvin.	.Dem.	Menomonie	3	1975-1981
Baldwin, Tammy.	.Dem.	Madison	2	1999-2013
Barber, J. Allen.	.Rep.	Lancaster	3	1871-1875
Barca, Peter W	.Dem.	Kenosha	1	1993-1995
Barnes, Lyman E.	.Dem.	Appleton	8	1893-1895
Barney, Samuel S	.Rep.	West Bend	5	1895-1903
Barrett, Thomas M.	.Dem.	Milwaukee	5	1993-2003
Barwig, Charles	.Dem.	Mayville	2	1889-1895
Beck, Joseph D.	.Rep.	Viroqua	7	1921-1929
Berger, Victor L	.Soc.	Milwaukee	5	1911-1913; 1919; 1923-1929
Biemiller, Andrew J	.Dem.	Milwaukee	5	1945-1947; 1949-1951
Billinghurst, Charles	.Rep.	Juneau	3	1855-1859
Blanchard, George W	.Rep.	Edgerton	1	1933-1935
Boileau, Gerald J.	.Rep., Prog.	Wausau	8,7	1931-1939
Bolles, Stephen	.Rep.	Janesville	1	1939-1941
Bouck, Gabriel.	.Dem.	Oshkosh	6	1877-1881
Bragg, Edward S.	.Dem.	Fond du Lac	5,2	1877-1883; 1885-1887
Brickner, George H	.Dem.	Sheboygan Falls	5	1889-1895
Brophy, John C.	.Rep.	Milwaukee	4	1947-1949
Brown, James S	.Dem.	Milwaukee	1	1863-1865
Brown, Webster E	.Rep.	Rhinelander	9,10	1901-1907
Browne, Edward E.	.Rep.	Waupaca	8	1913-1931
Burchard, Samuel D	.Dem.	Beaver Dam	5	1875-1877
Burke, Michael E	.Dem.	Beaver Dam	6,2	1911-1917
Bushnell, Allen R	.Dem.	Madison	3	1891-1893
Byrnes, John W	.Rep.	Green Bay	8	1945-1973
Cannon, Raymond J	.Dem.	Milwaukee	4	1933-1939
Cary, William J.	.Rep.	Milwaukee	4	1907-1919
Caswell, Lucien B	.Rep.	Fort Atkinson	2,1	1875-1883; 1885-1891
Cate, George W	.Reform	Stevens Point	8	1875-1877
Clark, Charles B	.Rep.	Neenah	6	1887-1891
Classon, David G	.Rep.	Oconto	9	1917-1923
Cobb, Amasa.	.Rep.	Mineral Point	3	1863-1871
Coburn, Frank P	.Dem.	West Salem	7	1891-1893
Cole, Orasmus	.Whig	Potosi	2	1849-1851
Cook, Samuel A	.Rep.	Neenah	6	1895-1897
Cooper, Henry Allen	.Rep.	Racine	1	1893-1919; 1921-1931
Cornell, Robert J.	.Dem.	De Pere	8	1975-1979
Dahle, Herman B	.Rep.	Mount Horeb	2	1899-1903
Darling, Mason C	.Dem.	Fond du Lac	2	1848-1849
Davidson, James H.	.Rep.	Oshkosh	6,8	1897-1913; 1917-1918
Davis, Glenn R.	.Rep.	Waukesha	2,9	1947-1957; 1965-1975
Deuster, Peter V	.Dem.	Milwaukee	4	1879-1885
Dilweg, La Vern R	.Dem.	Green Bay	8	1943-1945
Doty, James D	.Dem.	Neenah	3	1849-1853
Duffy, Sean P.	.Rep.	Ashland	7	2011-
Durkee, Charles	.Free Soil	Kenosha	1	1849-1853
Eastman, Ben C	.Dem.	Platteville	2	1851-1855
Eldredge, Charles A	.Dem.	Fond du Lac	4,5	1863-1875
Esch, John Jacob.	.Rep.	La Crosse	7	1899-1921
Flynn, Gerald T	.Dem.	Racine	1	1959-1961
Frear, James A	.Rep.	Hudson	10,9	1913-1935
Froehlich, Harold V	.Rep.	Appleton	8	1973-1975
Gehrmann, Bernard J	.Prog.	Mellen	10	1935-1943
Green, Mark A.	.Rep.	Green Bay	8	1999-2007
Griffin, Michael	.Rep.	Eau Claire	7	1894-1899
Griswold, Harry W.	.Rep.	West Salem	3	1939-1941
Guenther, Richard W.	.Rep.	Oshkosh	6,2	1881-1889
Gunderson, Steven.	.Rep.	Osseo	3	1981-1997
Hanchett, Luther	.Rep.	Plover	2	1861-1862
Haugen, Nils P.	.Rep.	Black River Falls	8,10	1887-1895
Hawkes, Charles, Jr	.Rep.	Horicon	2	1939-1941
Hazelton, George C	.Rep.	Boscobel	2	1877-1883
Hazelton, Gerry W.	.Rep.	Columbus	2	1871-1875
Henney, Charles W.	.Dem.	Portage	2	1933-1935
Henry, Robert K	.Rep.	Jefferson	2	1945-1947
Hopkins, Benjamin F	.Rep.	Madison	2	1867-1870
Hudd, Thomas R.	.Dem.	Green Bay	5	1886-1889
Hughes, James	.Dem.	De Pere	8	1933-1935
Hull, Merlin	.Prog.	Black River Falls	7,9	1929-1931; 1935-1953
Humphrey, Herman L	.Rep.	Hudson	7	1877-1883
Jenkins, John J.	.Rep.	Chippewa Falls	10,11	1895-1909
Johns, Joshua L	.Rep.	Appleton	8	1939-1943
Johnson, Jay.	.Dem.	New Franken	8	1997-1999
Johnson, Lester R	.Dem.	Black River Falls	9	1953-1965
Jones, Burr W	.Dem.	Madison	3	1883-1885
Kading, Charles A	.Rep.	Watertown	2	1927-1933
Kagen, Steve	.Dem.	Appleton	8	2007-2011
Kasten, Robert W., Jr	.Rep.	Waukesha	9	1975-1979
Kastenmeier, Robert W	.Dem.	Sun Prairie	2	1959-1991
Keefe, Frank B	.Rep.	Oshkosh	6	1939-1951
Kersten, Charles J	.Rep.	Whitefish Bay	5	1947-1949; 1951-1955
Kimball, Alanson M	.Rep.	Waushara	6	1875-1877
Kind, Ron	.Dem.	La Crosse	3	1997-
Kleczka, Gerald D	.Dem.	Milwaukee	4	1984-2005
Kleczka, John C	.Rep.	Milwaukee	4	1919-1923

WISCONSIN MEMBERS, U.S. HOUSE OF REPRESENTATIVES
1848 – 2013–Continued

Name	Party	Residence	District	Term
Klug, Scott L.	Rep.	Madison	2	1991-1999
Konop, Thomas F	Dem.	Kewaunee	9	1911-1917
Kopp, Arthur W	Rep.	Platteville	3	1909-1913
Kustermann, Gustav	Rep.	Green Bay	9	1907-1911
La Follette, Robert M., Sr	Rep.	Madison	3	1885-1891
Laird, Melvin R	Rep.	Marshfield	7	1953-1969
Lampert, Florian	Rep.	Oshkosh	6	1918-1930
Larrabee, Charles H	Dem.	Horicon	3	1859-1861
Lenroot, Irvine L.	Rep.	Superior	11	1909-1918
Lynch, Thomas.	Dem.	Antigo	9	1891-1895
Lynde, William Pitt	Dem.	Milwaukee	1,4	1848-1849; 1875-1879
Macy, John B	Dem.	Fond du Lac	3	1853-1855
Magoon, Henry S	Rep.	Darlington	3	1875-1877
McCord, Myron H	Rep.	Merrill	9	1889-1891
McDill, Alexander S	Rep.	Plover	8	1873-1875
McIndoe, Walter D.	Rep.	Wausau	6	1863-1867
McMurray, Howard J	Dem.	Milwaukee	5	1943-1945
Miller, Lucas M	Dem.	Oshkosh	6	1891-1893
Minor, Edward S.	Rep.	Sturgeon Bay	8,9	1895-1907
Mitchell, Alexander	Dem.	Milwaukee	1,4	1871-1875
Mitchell, John L	Dem.	Milwaukee	4	1891-1893
Monahan, James G.	Rep.	Darlington	3	1919-1921
Moody, James P	Dem.	Milwaukee	5	1983-1993
Moore, Gwen	Dem.	Milwaukee	4	2005-
Morse, Elmer A	Rep.	Antigo	10	1907-1913
Murphy, James W	Dem.	Platteville	3	1907-1909
Murray, Reid F.	Rep.	Ogdensburg	7	1939-1953
Nelson, Adolphus P	Rep.	Grantsburg	11	1918-1923
Nelson, John Mandt	Rep.	Madison	2,3	1906-1919; 1921-1933
Neumann, Mark W.	Rep.	Janesville	1	1995-1999
Obey, David R	Dem.	Wausau	7	1969-2011
O'Konski, Alvin E	Rep.	Mercer	10	1943-1973
O'Malley, Thomas D. P	Dem.	Milwaukee	5	1933-1939
Otjen, Theobald	Rep.	Milwaukee	4	1895-1907
Paine, Halbert E	Rep.	Milwaukee	1	1865-1871
Peavey, Hubert H	Rep.	Washburn	11,10	1923-1935
Petri, Thomas E	Rep.	Fond du Lac	6	1979-
Pocan, Mark	Dem.	Madison	2	2013-
Potter, John F	Rep.	East Troy	1	1857-1863
Pound, Thaddeus C	Rep.	Chippewa Falls	8	1877-1883
Price, Hugh H	Rep.	Black River Falls	8	1887
Price, William T	Rep.	Black River Falls	8	1883-1886
Race, John A.	Dem.	Fond du Lac	6	1965-1967
Randall, Clifford E.	Rep.	Kenosha	1	1919-1921
Rankin, Joseph	Dem.	Manitowoc	5	1883-1886
Reilly, Michael K	Dem.	Fond du Lac	6	1913-1917; 1930-1939
Reuss, Henry S.	Dem.	Milwaukee	5	1955-1983
Ribble, Reid J.	Rep.	Appleton	8	2011-
Roth, Toby	Rep.	Appleton	8	1979-1997
Rusk, Jeremiah M	Rep.	Viroqua	6,7	1871-1877
Ryan, Paul	Rep.	Janesville	1	1999-
Sauerhering, Edward.	Rep.	Mayville	2	1895-1899
Sauthoff, Harry.	Prog.	Madison	2	1935-1939; 1941-1945
Sawyer, Philetus	Rep.	Oshkosh	5,6	1865-1875
Schadeberg, Henry C	Rep.	Burlington	1	1961-1965; 1967-1971
Schafer, John C	Rep.	Milwaukee	4	1923-1933; 1939-1941
Schneider, George J	Rep., Prog.	Appleton	9,8	1923-1933; 1935-1939
Sensenbrenner, F. James, Jr	Rep.	Menomonee Falls	9,5	1979-
Shaw, George B	Rep.	Eau Claire	7	1893-1894
Sloan, A. Scott	Rep.	Beaver Dam	3	1861-1863
Sloan, Ithamar C	Rep.	Janesville	2	1863-1867
Smith, Henry.	Union Labor	Milwaukee	4	1887-1889
Smith, Lawrence H	Rep.	Racine	1	1941-1959
Somers, Peter J.	Dem.	Milwaukee	4	1893-1895
Stafford, William H	Rep.	Milwaukee	5	1903-1911; 1913-1919; 1921-1923; 1929-1933
Stalbaum, Lynn E	Dem.	Racine	1	1965-1967
Steiger, William A	Rep.	Oshkosh	6	1967-1978
Stephenson, Isaac	Rep.	Marinette	9	1883-1889
Stevenson, William H	Rep.	La Crosse	3	1941-1949
Stewart, Alexander.	Rep.	Wausau	9	1895-1901
Sumner, Daniel H	Dem.	Waukesha	2	1883-1885
Tewes, Donald E.	Rep.	Waukesha	2	1957-1959
Thill, Lewis D	Rep.	Milwaukee	5	1939-1943
Thomas, Ormsby B	Rep.	Prairie du Chien	7	1885-1891
Thomson, Vernon W	Rep.	Richland Center	3	1961-1975
Van Pelt, William K	Rep.	Fond du Lac	6	1951-1963
Van Schaick, Isaac W	Rep.	Milwaukee	4	1885-1887; 1889-1891
Voigt, Edward	Rep.	Sheboygan	2	1917-1927
Washburn, Cadwallader C	Rep.	Mineral Point, La Crosse	2 6	1855-1861; 1867-1871
Wasielewski, Thaddeus F	Dem.	Milwaukee	4	1941-1947
Weisse, Charles H	Dem.	Sheboygan Falls	6	1903-1911
Wells, Daniel, Jr	Dem.	Milwaukee	1	1853-1857
Wells, Owen A	Dem.	Fond du Lac	6	1893-1895
Wheeler, Ezra	Dem.	Berlin	5	1863-1865
Williams, Charles G	Rep.	Janesville	1	1873-1883
Winans, John.	Dem.	Janesville	1	1883-1885
Withrow, Gardner R	Rep., Prog.	La Crosse	7,3	1931-1939; 1949-1961
Woodward, Gilbert M	Dem.	La Crosse	7	1883-1885
Zablocki, Clement J	Dem.	Milwaukee	4	1949-1983

Sources: Wisconsin Legislative Reference Bureau, *Wisconsin Blue Book*, various editions; Congressional Quarterly, *Guide to U.S. Elections*, 1985; and official election records.

WISCONSIN MEMBERS, U.S. HOUSE OF REPRESENTATIVES
By District, 1943 – 2013

District	Name	Service	Party	Residence	Alphabetical Listing	
1st	Lawrence H. Smith	1941-59	Rep.	Racine	Aspin	1st
	Gerald T. Flynn	1959-61	Dem.	Racine	Baldus	3rd
	Henry C. Schadeberg	1961-65; 1967-71	Rep.	Burlington	Baldwin	2nd
	Lynn E. Stalbaum	1965-67	Dem.	Racine	Barca	1st
	Les Aspin[1]	1971-93	Dem.	East Troy	Barrett	5th
	Peter W. Barca[1]	1993-95	Dem.	Kenosha	Biemiller	5th
	Mark W. Neumann	1995-99	Rep.	Janesville	Brophy	4th
	Paul Ryan	1999-	Rep.	Janesville	Byrnes	8th
					Cornell	8th
2nd	Harry Sauthoff	1941-45	Prog.	Madison	Davis	2nd, 9th
	Robert K. Henry	1945-47	Rep.	Jefferson	Dilweg	8th
	Glenn R. Davis	1947-57	Rep.	Waukesha	Duffy	7th
	Donald E. Tewes	1957-59	Rep.	Waukesha	Flynn	1st
	Robert W. Kastenmeier	1959-91	Dem.	Sun Prairie	Froehlich	8th
	Scott L. Klug	1991-99	Rep.	Madison	Green	8th
	Tammy Baldwin	1999-2013	Dem.	Madison	Gunderson	3rd
	Mark Pocan	2013-	Dem.	Madison	Henry	2nd
					Hull	9th
3rd	William H. Stevenson	1941-49	Rep.	La Crosse	Johnson, J.	8th
	Gardner R. Withrow	1949-61	Rep.	La Crosse	Johnson, L.	9th
	Vernon W. Thomson	1961-75	Rep.	Richland Center	Kagen	8th
	Alvin Baldus	1975-81	Dem.	Menomonie	Kasten	9th
	Steven Gunderson	1981-97	Rep.	Osseo	Kastenmeier	2nd
	Ron Kind	1997-	Dem.	La Crosse	Keefe	6th
					Kersten	5th
4th	Thaddeus F. Wasielewski	1941-47	Dem.	Milwaukee	Kind	3rd
	John C. Brophy	1947-49	Rep.	Milwaukee	Kleczka	4th
	Clement J. Zablocki[2]	1949-83	Dem.	Milwaukee	Klug	2nd
	Gerald D. Kleczka[2]	1984-2005	Dem.	Milwaukee	Laird	7th
	Gwen Moore	2005-	Dem.	Milwaukee	McMurray	5th
					Moody	5th
5th[3]	Howard J. McMurray	1943-45	Dem.	Milwaukee	Moore	4th
	Andrew J. Biemiller	1945-47; 1949-51	Dem.	Milwaukee	Murray	7th
	Charles J. Kersten	1947-49; 1951-55	Rep.	Whitefish Bay	Neumann	1st
	Henry S. Reuss	1955-83	Dem.	Milwaukee	Obey	7th
	James P. Moody	1983-93	Dem.	Milwaukee	O'Konski	10th
	Thomas M. Barrett	1993-2003	Dem.	Milwaukee	Petri	6th
	F. James Sensenbrenner, Jr.	2003-	Rep.	Menomonee Falls	Pocan	2nd
					Race	6th
6th	Frank B. Keefe	1939-51	Rep.	Oshkosh	Reuss	5th
	William K. Van Pelt	1951-65	Rep.	Fond du Lac	Ribble	8th
	John A. Race	1965-67	Dem.	Fond du Lac	Roth	8th
	William A. Steiger[4]	1967-78	Rep.	Oshkosh	Ryan	1st
	Thomas E. Petri[4]	1979-	Rep.	Fond du Lac	Sauthoff	2nd
					Schadeberg	1st
7th	Reid F. Murray	1939-53	Rep.	Ogdensburg	Sensenbrenner	9th, 5th
	Melvin R. Laird[5]	1953-69	Rep.	Marshfield	Smith	1st
	David R. Obey[5]	1969-2011	Dem.	Wausau	Stalbaum	1st
	Sean P. Duffy	2011-	Rep.	Ashland	Steiger	6th
					Stevenson	3rd
8th	La Vern R. Dilweg	1943-45	Dem.	Green Bay	Tewes	2nd
	John R. Byrnes	1945-73	Rep.	Green Bay	Thomson	3rd
	Harold V. Froehlich	1973-75	Rep.	Appleton	Van Pelt	6th
	Robert J. Cornell	1975-79	Dem.	De Pere	Wasielewski	4th
	Toby Roth	1979-97	Rep.	Appleton	Withrow	3rd
	Jay Johnson	1997-99	Dem.	New Franken	Zablocki	4th
	Mark A. Green	1999-2007	Rep.	Green Bay		
	Steve Kagen	2007-2011	Dem.	Appleton		
	Reid J. Ribble	2011-	Rep.	Appleton		
9th[3,6]	Merlin Hull	1935-53	Prog.	Black River Falls		
	Lester R. Johnson	1953-65	Dem.	Black River Falls		
	Glenn R. Davis	1965-75	Rep.	Waukesha		
	Robert W. Kasten	1975-79	Rep.	Thiensville		
	F. James Sensenbrenner, Jr.	1979-2003	Rep.	Menomonee Falls		
10th[7]	Alvin E. O'Konski	1943-73	Rep.	Rhinelander		

[1]Aspin resigned 1/20/1993, to become U.S. Secretary of Defense. Barca was elected in a special election, 5/4/1993.
[2]Zablocki died 12/3/1983. Kleczka was elected in a special election, 4/3/1984.
[3]In the congressional reapportionment following the 2000 Census, Wisconsin's delegation was reduced from 9 to 8 members. The previous 4th, 5th, and 9th were reconfigured into the new 4th and 5th.
[4]Steiger died 12/4/1978, following his November 1978 election. Petri was elected in a special election, 4/3/1979.
[5]Laird resigned 1/21/1969, to become U.S. Secretary of Defense. Obey was elected in a special election, 4/1/1969.
[6]In the congressional redistricting based on the results of the 1960 Census of Population, the previous 9th District in western Wisconsin ceased to exist and a new 9th District was created in the Waukesha-Milwaukee metropolitan area.
[7]In the congressional reapportionment based on the results of the 1970 Census of Population, Wisconsin's delegation was reduced from 10 members to 9 members.
Sources: *1944 Wisconsin Blue Book* and Wisconsin Legislative Reference Bureau data.

U.S. SENATORS FROM WISCONSIN, 1848 – 2013

Class 1		Class 3	
Name	Service	Name	Service
Henry Dodge (D)	1848-1857	Isaac P. Walker (D).	1848-1855
James R. Doolittle (R)	1857-1869	Charles Durkee (UR)	1855-1861
Matthew H. Carpenter (R).	1869-1875	Timothy O. Howe (UR)	1861-1879
Angus Cameron (R)[1].	1875-1881	Matthew H. Carpenter (R).	1879-1881
Philetus Sawyer (R)	1881-1893	Angus Cameron (R)[1].	1881-1885
John Lendrum Mitchell (D)	1893-1899	John C. Spooner (R)	1885-1891
Joseph Very Quarles (R).	1899-1905	William F. Vilas (D)	1891-1897
Robert M. La Follette, Sr. (R)[2].	1906-1925	John C. Spooner (R)	1897-1907
Robert M. La Follette, Jr. (R)[3].	1925-1935	Isaac Stephenson (R)[5]	1907-1915
Robert M. La Follette, Jr. (P)	1935-1947	Paul O. Husting (D)	1915-1917
Joseph R. McCarthy (R).	1947-1957	Irvine L. Lenroot (R)[6]	1918-1927
William Proxmire (D)[4].	1957-1989	John J. Blaine (R)	1927-1933
Herbert H. Kohl (D)	1989-2013	F. Ryan Duffy (D)	1933-1939
Tammy Baldwin (D).	2013-	Alexander Wiley (R).	1939-1963
		Gaylord A. Nelson (D).	1963-1981
		Robert W. Kasten, Jr. (R)	1981-1993
		Russell D. Feingold (D)	1993-2011
		Ron Johnson (R).	2011-

Note: Each state has two U.S. Senators, and each serves a 6-year term. They were elected by their respective state legislatures until passage of the 17th Amendment to the U.S. Constitution on April 8, 1913, which provided for popular election. Article I, Section 3, Clause 2, of the U.S. Constitution divides senators into three classes so that one-third of the senate is elected every two years. Wisconsin's seats were assigned to Class 1 and Class 3 at statehood.

Key: Democrat (D); Progressive (P); Republican (R); Union Republican (UR)

[1]Not a candidate for reelection to Class 1 seat, but elected 3/10/1881 to fill vacancy caused by death of Class 3 Senator Carpenter on 2/24/1881.

[2]Elected 1/25/1905 but continued to serve as governor until 1/1/1906.

[3]Elected 9/29/1925 to fill vacancy caused by death of Robert La Follette, Sr., on 6/18/1925.

[4]Elected 8/27/1957 to fill vacancy caused by death of McCarthy on 5/2/1957.

[5]Elected 5/17/1907 to fill vacancy caused by resignation of Spooner on 4/30/1907.

[6]Elected 5/2/1918 to fill vacancy caused by death of Husting on 10/21/1917.

Source: Wisconsin Legislative Reference Bureau records.

HIGHLIGHTS OF LOCAL AND STATE GOVERNMENT IN WISCONSIN

Employment and Earnings — In March 2011, Wisconsin ranked 20th among the states in full-time equivalent (FTE) state and local government employees with 283,568. The State of Wisconsin employed 70,891 workers, while local government employed 212,677.

In March 2011, Wisconsin ranked 17th in average total payroll for state and local government employees with $1,207,565,776. California ranked first with a payroll of $9,858,934,440 and South Dakota ranked 50th with $150,276,139.

Units of Local Government — As of January 1, 2012, Wisconsin had 1,923 general units of local government – 72 counties, 190 cities, 405 villages, and 1,256 towns.

In 2012, counties varied in official population estimates from Milwaukee at 948,322 to Menominee with 4,214. These two counties were also highest and lowest in 2011 full value property assessments at $61 billion and $318 million, respectively. As determined by the U.S. Census Bureau in 2010, Marathon County is the largest in land area with 1,545 square miles and Ozaukee County the smallest with 232 square miles.

Based on the 2010 Census, Wisconsin's city residents totaled 3,150,339 in 2010, a 5.2% increase from the 2000 Census; village population was 869,587, a 26.6% increase; and town population was 1,667,060, a 0.1% decrease. As of April 1, 2010, a total of 92 Wisconsin municipalities had populations of 10,000 or more. The City of Milwaukee ranked first at 594,833, and the City of Elkhorn, with 10,084 residents, was smallest in the group.

Administration — Wisconsin cities may adopt a mayor, manager, or commission form of government. Of 190 cities, 10 have a city manager and 180 have a mayor. Currently, no city uses the commission form of government. Villages may use a president or manager form of government. Of 405 villages, only 10 have an appointed manager. Currently, 93 cities and 97 villages employ an administrator in a full-time or combined position.

Each county board is headed by a chairperson chosen by the board. In addition, 10 counties have an elected county executive, 25 have an appointed county administrator, and 33 have an appointed administrative coordinator.

The following tables present selected data. Consult footnoted sources for more detailed information about local and state government.

WISCONSIN STATE GOVERNMENT EMPLOYEES
By Status and Funding, 2002 – 2012

Employee Status[1]	2002	2007	2012	Type of Funding for Authorized Positions[3]	2002	2007	2012
Classified.	41,344	39,819	38,407	State appropriations . . .	36,019	34,756	35,730
Unclassified	22,019	21,079	22,035	User fees	17,644	18,011	16,725
Limited term	7,137	6,796	6,409	Federal appropriations .	8,913	9,564	10,107
Project	604	391	879	Segregated funds	6,209	5,145	5,081
Seasonal	114	76	56	TOTAL[4]	68,785	67,477	67,644
Other[2]	6,421	6,494	7,086				
TOTAL[4]	77,639	74,656	74,872				

[1]Headcount of employees working on a full- or part-time basis as of June 30.
[2]Includes UW System graduate assistants.
[3]Full-time equivalent positions authorized by legislature or under procedures authorized by the legislature as of June 30.
[4]Detail may not add to total due to rounding.
Source: Wisconsin Department of Administration, Division of Executive Budget and Finance, *State Employment Report,* June 2012, and previous issues.

WISCONSIN STATE CLASSIFIED SERVICE PROFILE
2000 – 2010

	2000		2005		2010	
	Number	Percent of Work Force	Number	Percent of Work Force	Number	Percent of Work Force
Category						
Permanent Classified Employees . . .	39,000	100.0%	39,604	100.0%	39,406	100.0%
Persons with Disabilities*	3,314	8.5	2,581	6.5	2,015	5.1
Women	20,044	51.4	20,264	51.2	20,211	51.3
Racial/ethnic minorities	3,067	7.9	3,583	9.0	4,107	10.4
Black	1,616	4.1	1,782	4.5	2,011	5.1
Hispanic	602	1.5	835	2.1	1,015	2.6
Asian	527	1.4	673	1.7	806	2.0
American Indian	322	0.8	293	0.7	271	0.7

*Total persons with disabilities includes persons with severe disabilities.

Source: Wisconsin State Office of Employment Relations, *Workforce Planning and Affirmative Action Report: Fiscal Year 2010,* and previous issues.

WISCONSIN STATE AND LOCAL GOVERNMENT EMPLOYMENT AND PAYROLLS
Employees and Payrolls by Function, March 2011

	Number of Employees			
	Full-time	Part-time	Full-time Equivalent (FTE)*	Total Payroll for FTE (in thousands)
Education	134,388	98,294	171,121	$719,118
Elementary and secondary	(97,831)	(42,602)	(117,884)	(467,716)
Higher education institutions	(34,195)	(52,456)	(49,381)	(237,550)
Libraries (local)	(1,530)	(3,017)	(2,866)	(9,016)
Other	(832)	(219)	(990)	(4,835)
Government administration (including courts)	14,351	17,094	18,255	79,294
Police protection	14,811	6,135	15,586	78,973
Public welfare and social insurance administration . .	12,560	4,016	14,915	55,879
Health and hospitals	9,702	4,345	11,823	49,365
Streets and highways	9,606	2,068	10,327	44,499
Corrections	13,134	986	13,637	58,479
Fire protection	4,125	5,354	4,659	25,056
Natural resources	2,805	1,213	3,226	12,911
Parks and recreation	2,269	3,166	3,231	11,371
Sewerage (local)	1,774	1,204	1,928	8,525
Transit	1,739	148	1,844	6,560
Utilities (electric and water supply)	2,018	155	2,052	10,055
Housing and community development	954	303	1,054	4,054
Solid waste management (local)	1,396	1,771	1,774	6,525
Other	7,015	4,740	7,735	35,129
TOTAL	232,647	150,992	283,167	$1,924,910

*Full-time Equivalent (FTE) is a derived statistic that provides an estimate of a government's total full-time employment by converting part-time employees to a full-time amount.

Source: U.S. Census Bureau, Government Employment and Payroll, *2011 Public Employment and Payroll Data: State and Local Government,* at: http://www2.census.gov/govs/apes/11stlwi.txt [November 2012].

Employment and Payrolls, 1990 – 2011

	Employees (full-time equivalents)			Monthly Payroll (in thousands)*		
Year	State	Local	Total	State	Local	Total
1990	66,541	183,318	249,859	$152,660	$409,907	$562,567
1997	64,709	201,633	266,342	204,267	569,193	773,460
1998	64,703	211,790	276,493	207,996	625,686	833,681
1999	63,185	207,587	270,772	214,684	628,043	842,727
2000	63,697	219,793	283,490	230,570	662,358	892,928
2001	69,428	218,824	288,252	257,605	676,935	934,540
2002	70,962	218,982	288,543	261,095	719,434	977,410
2003	71,040	217,004	288,044	268,249	739,031	1,007,280
2004	69,834	217,422	287,256	275,465	749,415	1,024,880
2005	70,189	223,523	293,712	275,824	809,593	1,085,417
2006	68,143	219,930	288,073	283,681	813,141	1,096,822
2007	68,714	212,931	281,645	295,616	788,590	1,084,207
2008	69,019	214,332	283,351	308,878	813,054	1,121,932
2009	70,457	222,214	292,671	322,316	846,922	1,169,238
2010	72,428	213,888	286,316	326,643	862,129	1,188,772
2011	70,891	212,677	283,568	328,658	878,908	1,207,566

*Prior to 1997, annual data reflected October payrolls. Beginning with the 1997 Annual Survey of Government Employment and Payroll, data reflects March payrolls.

Source: U.S. Census Bureau, Government Employment and Payroll, March 2011 and previous years, at: http://www.census. gov/govs/apes/ [December 5, 2012].

STATE AND LOCAL GOVERNMENT EMPLOYEES
Number and Earnings by State
March 2011 Payroll

State	Full-time Equivalent Employees Number Total	State	Local	Earnings March Payroll Total	State	Local
Alabama	284,778	89,768	195,010	$991,534,440	$364,099,942	$627,434,498
Alaska	54,743	26,747	27,996	275,423,127	138,369,425	137,053,702
Arizona	280,795	68,786	212,009	1,134,536,394	286,283,598	848,252,796
Arkansas	189,608	62,562	127,046	584,966,603	240,164,505	344,802,098
California	1,752,070	407,321	1,344,749	9,858,934,440	2,402,403,919	7,456,530,521
Colorado	270,166	72,113	198,053	1,166,933,953	354,879,191	812,054,762
Connecticut	185,209	62,090	123,119	963,706,365	350,952,385	612,753,980
Delaware	49,751	26,215	23,536	209,644,119	109,286,150	100,357,969
District of Columbia	42,502	—	42,502	254,516,962		254,516,962
Florida	888,159	184,237	703,922	3,449,849,606	706,917,692	2,742,931,914
Georgia	509,276	123,627	385,649	1,791,567,721	476,058,955	1,315,508,766
Hawaii	73,669	58,142	15,527	307,033,924	231,411,072	75,622,852
Idaho	78,569	21,773	56,796	274,395,383	93,059,379	181,336,004
ILLINOIS	626,921	131,153	495,768	2,929,636,994	658,956,332	2,270,680,662
Indiana	329,503	89,796	239,707	1,201,880,056	347,444,665	854,435,391
IOWA	177,268	50,378	126,890	730,599,260	260,866,014	469,733,246
Kansas	196,847	43,555	153,292	687,233,893	178,377,368	508,856,525
Kentucky	246,859	81,493	165,366	809,537,044	304,185,949	505,351,095
Louisiana	281,597	84,402	197,195	1,000,181,601	352,545,234	647,636,367
Maine	75,370	21,354	54,016	240,536,849	87,046,104	153,490,745
Maryland	307,031	86,714	220,317	1,496,593,379	405,812,305	1,090,781,074
Massachusetts	320,738	92,033	228,705	1,559,717,357	461,472,353	1,098,245,004
MICHIGAN	456,578	144,921	311,657	2,070,672,166	714,484,555	1,356,187,611
MINNESOTA	277,179	79,672	197,507	1,249,718,084	409,554,702	840,163,382
Mississippi	191,995	57,656	134,339	606,253,694	207,128,461	399,125,233
Missouri	317,310	87,361	229,949	1,100,835,932	300,022,538	800,813,394
Montana	57,874	20,795	37,079	208,635,954	81,145,471	127,490,483
Nebraska	120,974	32,065	88,909	463,991,843	121,974,906	342,016,937
Nevada	114,307	28,121	86,186	544,609,803	132,040,149	412,569,654
New Hampshire	72,273	19,394	52,879	278,743,721	84,735,208	194,008,513
New Jersey	488,114	146,801	341,313	2,651,583,489	847,805,398	1,803,778,091
New Mexico	125,664	46,794	78,870	446,700,556	178,395,559	268,304,997
New York	1,175,681	243,647	932,034	6,289,257,300	1,365,434,855	4,923,822,445
North Carolina	556,065	154,364	401,701	1,988,211,540	588,528,658	1,399,682,882
North Dakota	45,047	18,592	26,455	167,250,780	75,873,481	91,377,299
Ohio	594,695	139,049	455,646	2,470,876,106	653,416,073	1,817,460,033
Oklahoma	214,757	68,339	146,418	706,288,162	261,290,605	444,997,557
Oregon	197,299	65,542	131,757	867,511,165	300,712,302	566,798,863
Pennsylvania	591,926	168,548	423,378	2,560,498,334	776,728,636	1,783,769,698
Rhode Island	49,746	18,900	30,846	249,792,226	100,292,400	149,499,826
South Carolina	253,574	77,342	176,232	886,072,972	287,484,187	598,588,785
South Dakota	45,851	14,458	31,393	150,276,139	55,023,174	95,252,965
Tennessee	327,457	86,215	241,242	1,094,359,554	312,198,855	782,160,699
Texas	1,450,198	318,370	1,131,828	5,440,869,360	1,364,972,027	4,075,897,333
Utah	147,591	53,501	94,090	542,702,884	226,633,774	316,069,110
Vermont	39,649	14,419	25,230	156,139,842	66,639,510	89,500,332
Virginia	438,837	124,930	313,907	1,719,775,186	531,401,036	1,188,374,150
Washington	346,367	121,136	225,231	1,786,282,663	590,629,927	1,195,652,736
West Virginia	103,701	39,882	63,819	343,771,250	141,859,348	201,911,902
WISCONSIN	283,568	70,891	212,677	1,207,565,776	328,657,674	878,908,102
Wyoming	52,732	13,416	39,316	209,392,796	56,205,984	153,186,812
UNITED STATES	16,358,439	4,359,380	11,999,059	$70,377,598,748	$19,971,861,990	$50,405,736,758

Source: U.S. Department of Commerce, U.S. Census Bureau, 2011 Public Employment and Payroll data, at: http://www.census.gov/govs/apes/ [December 6, 2012].

LOCAL UNITS OF GOVERNMENT BY STATE AND TYPE – 2012

State	Total Units	Counties[1]	Municipalities[2]	Towns or Townships[3]	Special Districts	School Districts[4]
Alabama	1,208	67	461	—	548	132
Alaska	177	14	148	—	15	—
Arizona.	659	15	91	—	309	244
Arkansas	1,543	75	502	—	727	239
California	4,350	57	482	—	2,786	1,025
Colorado	2,818	62	271	—	2,305	180
Connecticut	644	—	30	149	448	17
Delaware	338	3	57	—	259	19
District of Columbia	2	—	1	—	1	—
Florida	1,554	66	410	—	983	95
Georgia.	1,365	153	535	—	497	180
Hawaii	21	3	1	—	17	—
Idaho	1,161	44	200	—	799	118
ILLINOIS	6,968	102	1,298	1,431	3,232	905
Indiana	2,694	91	569	1,006	737	291
IOWA	1,939	99	947	—	527	366
Kansas	3,806	103	626	1,268	1,503	306
Kentucky.	1,314	118	418	—	604	174
Louisiana.	530	60	304	—	97	69
Maine	841	16	22	466	238	99
Maryland.	347	23	157	—	167	—
Massachusetts	852	5	53	298	412	84
MICHIGAN	2,877	83	533	1,240	445	576
MINNESOTA	3,633	87	854	1,785	569	338
Mississippi	991	82	297	—	448	164
Missouri	3,752	114	955	312	1,837	534
Montana	1,240	54	129	—	736	321
Nebraska	2,581	93	530	419	1,267	272
Nevada.	190	16	19	—	138	17
New Hampshire	542	10	13	221	132	166
New Jersey.	1,344	21	324	242	234	523
New Mexico	854	33	103	—	622	96
New York	3,454	57	617	929	1,172	679
North Carolina	964	100	553	—	311	—
North Dakota.	2,666	53	357	1,314	759	183
Ohio	3,702	88	938	1,308	700	668
Oklahoma	1,854	77	590	—	637	550
Oregon	1,509	36	241	—	1,002	230
Pennsylvania.	4,905	66	1,015	1,546	1,764	514
Rhode Island	134	—	8	31	91	4
South Carolina	681	46	269	—	283	83
South Dakota.	1,979	66	311	907	543	152
Tennessee	920	92	345	—	469	14
Texas.	4,856	254	1,214	—	2,309	1,079
Utah	613	29	245	—	298	41
Vermont	728	14	43	237	143	291
Virginia.	497	95	229	—	172	1
Washington.	1,831	39	281	—	1,216	295
West Virginia.	658	55	232	—	316	55
WISCONSIN	3,123	72	595	1,255	761	440
Wyoming.	795	23	99	—	618	55
UNITED STATES	89,004	3,031	19,522	16,364	37,203	12,884

[1]Excludes areas corresponding to counties that have no organized government.

[2]"Municipalities" include cities, villages, boroughs (except in Alaska), and towns (except in Connecticut, Maine, Massachusetts, Minnesota, New Hampshire, New York, Rhode Island, Vermont, and Wisconsin).

[3]Includes both "townships" and "town" governments in the case of those states listed in footnote 2.

[4]Excludes systems operated as part of a state, county, municipal, or town government.

Source: U.S. Census Bureau, 2012 Census of Governments, *Local Governments by Type and State: 2012*, December 2012.

BASIC DATA ON WISCONSIN COUNTIES

County (year created)[1]	County Seat	Full Value 2011 Assessment (in thousands)[2]	Population 2012 Estimate	Pct. Change[3]	2012 Rank	Land Area in Sq. Miles[4]	2012 Density per Sq. Mile[5]
Adams (1848)	Friendship	$2,562,650	20,797	–0.4%	50	647.7	32.1
Ashland (1860). . . .	Ashland	1,236,153	16,063	–0.6	60	1,043.8	15.4
Barron (1859)	Barron	3,689,962	45,928	0.1	30	862.8	53.2
Bayfield (1845) . . .	Washburn	2,597,027	15,052	0.3	64	1,476.3	10.2
Brown (1818)	Green Bay	18,157,652	250,281	0.9	4	528.7	473.4
Buffalo (1853)	Alma	1,002,775	13,649	0.5	67	684.5	19.9
Burnett (1856)	Meenon[6]	2,687,878	15,457	0.0	62	821.5	18.8
Calumet (1836) . . .	Chilton	3,487,177	49,168	0.4	29	319.8	153.7
Chippewa (1845). . .	Chippewa Falls. . .	4,551,286	62,777	0.6	24	1,010.4	62.1
Clark (1853)	Neillsville	1,780,505	34,706	0.0	41	1,215.6	28.6
Columbia (1846). . .	Portage	5,027,684	56,835	0.0	26	773.8	73.4
Crawford (1818). . .	Prairie du Chien . .	1,097,301	16,638	0.0	59	572.7	29.1
Dane (1836)	Madison	50,195,950	491,555	0.7	2	1,201.9	409.0
Dodge (1836)	Juneau	6,040,549	88,692	–0.1	17	882.3	100.5
Door (1851)	Sturgeon Bay. . . .	7,169,425	27,867	0.3	45	482.7	57.7
Douglas (1854). . . .	Superior	3,406,406	44,191	0.1	33	1,309.1	33.8
Dunn (1854)	Menomonie	2,683,462	43,853	0.0	34	852.0	51.5
Eau Claire (1856) . .	Eau Claire	6,727,329	99,260	0.5	16	637.6	155.7
Florence (1881) . . .	Florence	598,773	4,358	–1.5	71	488.0	8.9
Fond du Lac (1836) .	Fond du Lac	6,965,438	101,955	0.3	15	722.9	141.0
Forest (1885).	Crandon	1,148,144	9,197	–1.2	68	1,014.1	9.1
Grant (1836).	Lancaster.	2,806,188	51,436	0.4	28	1,147.9	44.8
Green (1836).	Monroe.	2,625,141	36,863	0.1	39	584.0	63.1
Green Lake (1858). .	Green Lake.	2,452,746	19,106	0.3	55	354.3	53.9
Iowa (1829)	Dodgeville	1,871,064	23,726	0.2	48	762.7	31.1
Iron (1893).	Hurley	964,538	5,843	–1.2	70	757.2	7.7
Jackson (1853). . . .	Black River Falls. .	1,445,753	20,523	0.4	53	987.3	20.8
Jefferson (1836) . . .	Jefferson	6,583,896	83,857	0.2	20	557.0	150.6
Juneau (1856)	Mauston	1,965,190	26,878	0.8	46	767.6	35.0
Kenosha (1850) . . .	Kenosha	13,717,172	166,823	0.2	8	272.8	611.5
Kewaunee (1852) . .	Kewaunee	1,470,715	20,637	0.3	52	342.6	60.2
La Crosse (1851). . .	La Crosse	7,879,057	115,577	0.8	12	452.7	255.3
Lafayette (1846) . . .	Darlington	1,024,433	16,897	0.4	57	633.6	26.7
Langlade (1879). . .	Antigo	1,685,876	19,880	–0.5	54	872.7	22.8
Lincoln (1874). . . .	Merrill	2,381,381	28,856	0.4	44	883.3	32.7
Manitowoc (1836). .	Manitowoc.	5,374,268	81,437	0.0	21	591.5	137.7
Marathon (1850). . .	Wausau.	9,724,226	134,524	0.3	10	1,545.0	87.1
Marinette (1879). . .	Marinette.	3,647,216	41,718	–0.1	36	1,401.8	29.8
Marquette (1836) . .	Montello	1,591,145	15,394	–0.1	63	455.5	33.8
Menominee (1961). .	Keshena	318,242	4,214	–0.4	72	358.0	11.8
Milwaukee (1834). .	Milwaukee	61,099,029	948,322	0.1	1	241.6	3,925.2
Monroe (1854). . . .	Sparta	2,695,034	45,056	0.9	31	900.8	50.0
Oconto (1851)	Oconto	3,599,182	37,829	0.4	38	998.0	37.9
Oneida (1885)	Rhinelander	6,960,385	36,057	0.2	40	1,124.5	32.1
Outagamie (1851) . .	Appleton	13,314,090	178,150	0.8	6	640.3	278.2
Ozaukee (1853) . . .	Port Washington . .	10,706,478	86,635	0.3	18	232.0	373.4
Pepin (1858)	Durand	560,657	7,465	–0.1	69	232.3	32.1
Pierce (1853).	Ellsworth.	2,826,286	41,108	0.2	37	576.5	71.3
Polk (1853).	Balsam Lake	4,228,267	44,241	0.1	32	917.3	48.2
Portage (1836)	Stevens Point. . . .	4,932,212	70,806	1.1	23	806.3	87.8
Price (1879)	Phillips	1,466,119	14,055	–0.7	66	1,252.6	11.2
Racine (1836)	Racine	15,041,416	195,386	0.0	5	333.1	586.6
Richland (1842) . . .	Richland Center . .	1,084,105	18,043	0.1	56	586.2	30.8
Rock (1836)	Janesville.	9,861,961	160,129	–0.1	9	720.5	222.2
Rusk (1901)	Ladysmith	1,177,463	14,756	0.0	65	913.1	16.2
St. Croix (1840) . . .	Hudson.	7,335,670	84,856	0.6	25	721.8	117.6
Sauk (1840)	Baraboo	6,713,421	61,994	0.0	58	837.6	74.0
Sawyer (1883)	Hayward	3,580,825	16,659	0.6	35	1,256.4	13.3
Shawano (1853) . . .	Shawano	3,013,221	41,919	–0.1	13	892.5	47.0
Sheboygan (1836) . .	Sheboygan	8,894,481	115,549	0.0	19	513.6	225.0
Taylor (1875).	Medford	1,323,232	20,697	0.0	51	974.9	21.2
Trempealeau (1854) .	Whitehall.	1,806,682	28,986	0.6	43	734.1	39.5
Vernon (1851)	Viroqua.	1,771,843	29,865	0.3	42	794.9	37.6
Vilas (1893)	Eagle River.	7,344,419	21,485	0.3	49	873.7	24.6
Walworth (1836). . .	Elkhorn.	14,662,709	102,530	0.3	14	555.3	184.6
Washburn (1883). . .	Shell Lake	2,519,186	15,907	0.0	61	809.7	19.6
Washington (1836). .	West Bend	13,469,321	132,482	0.5	11	430.8	307.5
Waukesha (1846). . .	Waukesha	49,552,563	390,914	0.3	3	555.6	703.6
Waupaca (1851) . . .	Waupaca	3,827,192	52,381	–0.1	27	751.1	69.7
Waushara (1851). . .	Wautoma	2,487,428	24,506	0.0	47	626.0	39.1
Winnebago (1840) . .	Oshkosh	11,969,341	167,702	0.4	7	438.6	382.4
Wood (1856)	Wisconsin Rapids .	4,698,255	74,587	–0.2	22	792.8	94.1
State Total		$486,864,233	5,703,525	0.3%		54,310.1	105.0

[1]Counties are created by legislative act. Depending on the date, Wisconsin counties were created by the Michigan Territorial Legislature (1818-1836), the Wisconsin Territorial Legislature (1836-1848), or the Wisconsin State Legislature (after 1848). [2]Reflects actual market value of all taxable general property, including personal property and real estate, as determined by the Wisconsin Department of Revenue. [3]Change from 2010 U.S. Census. [4]Determined by 2010 Census. [5]2010 density calculated by Wisconsin Legislative Reference Bureau. [6]Town of Siren is used as a mailing address for county offices.

Sources: Wisconsin Department of Revenue, Division of State and Local Finance, *Town, Village, and City Taxes 2011: Taxes Levied 2011 – Collected 2012,* 2012; U.S. Census Bureau, Census 2010 Summary File 1, March 2013.

COUNTY OFFICERS IN WISCONSIN
June 30, 2013

County	Number of Supervisors	Chairperson	Administrator, Executive, or Administrative Coordinator[1]
Adams	20	John West	Trena Larson (AC)
Ashland	21	Pete Russo	Jeff Beirl (CA), Lori Schmidt (AC)
Barron	29	James Miller	Jeff French (CA)
Bayfield	13	Shawn Miller	Mark Abeles-Allison (CA)
Brown	26	Patrick W. Moynihan, Jr.	Brent Miller (CA)
Buffalo.	14	Del Twidt	Julie Lindstrom (AC)
Burnett.	24	Don Taylor	Candace Fitzgerald (CA)
Calumet	21	William Barribeau	Jay Shambeau (CA)
Chippewa	15	Paul Michels	Frank Pascarella (CA)
Clark	29	Wayne Hendrickson	Wayne Hendrickson (AC)
Columbia.	28	Andy Ross	Susan Moll (AC)
Crawford.	17	Peter Flesch	Dan McWilliams (AC)
Dane	37	John Hendrick	Joseph T. Parisi (CE)
Dodge	33	Russell Kottke	James Mielke (CA)
Door	21	Daniel Austad	Maureen Murphy (CA)
Douglas	21	Douglas G. Finn	Andrew Lisak (CA)
Dunn	29	Steven Rasmussen	Eugene Smith (AC)
Eau Claire	29	Gregg Moore	J. Thomas McCarty (CA)
Florence	12	Jeanette Bomberg	Donna Trudell (AC)
Fond du Lac	25	Martin F. Farrell	Allen J. Buechel (CE)
Forest.	21	Paul Millan	None
Grant	17	Larry Wolf	None
Green.	31	Arthur F. Carter	Michael J. Doyle (AC)
Green Lake.	19	John Meyers	Margaret R. Bostelmann (AC)
Iowa	21	David Bauer	Curt Kephart (CA)
Iron.	15	Joe Pinardi	Michael Saari (AC)
Jackson.	19	Dennis Eberhardt	Kyle Deno (AC)
Jefferson.	30	John Molinaro	Benjamin Wehmeier (CA)
Juneau	21	Alan K. Peterson	Alan K. Peterson (CA)
Kenosha	23	Jeffrey A. Gentz	James Kreuser (CE)
Kewaunee	20	Robert A. Weidner	Edward J. Dorner (CA)
La Crosse	29	Tara Johnson	Steve O'Malley (CA)
Lafayette.	16	Jack Sauer	Jack Sauer (AC)
Langlade	21	David Solin	Robin J. Stowe (AC)
Lincoln.	22	Robert Lussow	Randy Scholz (AC)
Manitowoc.	25	Paul Hansen	Robert Ziegelbauer (CE)
Marathon.	38	Gary Wyman	Brad Karger (CA)
Marinette.	30	Vilas Schroeder	Ellen C. Sorensen (CA)
Marquette	17	Paul Wade	Brenda Jahns-Grams (AC)
Menominee	7	Elizabeth Moses	Ronald Corn, Sr. (AC)
Milwaukee	18	Marina Dimitrijevic	Chris Abele (CE)
Monroe.	24	Bruce Humphrey	Catherine Schmit (CA)
Oconto	31	Lee Rymer	Kevin Hamann (AC)
Oneida	21	Ted Cushing	None
Outagamie	36	Judith A. Schuette	Thomas Nelson (CE)
Ozaukee	26	Lee Schlenvogt	Thomas W. Meaux (CA)
Pepin	12	Peter Adler	Larry Krcmar (AC)
Pierce.	17	Jeff Holst	Joann Miller (AC)
Polk	23	William Johnson IV	Dana Frey (CA)
Portage	25	O. Philip Idsvoog	Patty Dreier (CE)
Price	13	Robert Kopisch	Robert Kopisch (AC)
Racine	21	Peter Hansen	Jim Ladwig (CE)
Richland	21	Jeanetta Kirkpatrick	Victor V. Vlasak (AC)
Rock	29	J. Russell Podzilni	Craig Knutson (CA)
Rusk	21	Randy Tatur	Denise Wetzel (AC)
St. Croix	19	Daryl Standafer	Patrick J. Thompson (CA)
Sauk	31	Martin Krueger	Kathryn Schauf (CA)
Sawyer.	15	Hal Helwig	Hal Helwig (AC), Kris Mayberry (AC)
Shawano	27	Gerald Erdmann	Thomas Madsen (AC)
Sheboygan	25	Roger te Stroete	Adam Payne (CA)
Taylor	17	Jim Metz	None
Trempealeau	17	Ernest Vold	Paul L. Syverson (AC)
Vernon	29	Herbert Cornell	Ronald Hoff (AC)
Vilas	21	Stephen Favorite	David R. Alleman (AC)
Walworth.	11	Nancy Russell	David Bretl (CA)
Washburn	21	Steven Sather	None
Washington.	30	Herbert J. Tennies	Douglas Johnson (AC)
Waukesha	25	Paul Decker	Dan Vrakas (CE)
Waupaca	27	Dick Koeppen	Mary A. Robbins (AC)
Waushara.	11	Donna R. Kalata	Debra Behringer (AC)
Winnebago	36	David Albrecht	Mark Harris (CE)
Wood.	19	Lance Pliml	Lance Pliml (AC)

COUNTY OFFICERS IN WISCONSIN
June 30, 2013–Continued

County	Clerk	County Clerk Office Address
Adams	Cindy Phillippi (D)	400 N. Main St., Friendship 53934
Ashland	Heather W. Schutte (D)	201 W. Main St., Ashland 54806
Barron	DeeAnn Cook (R)	335 E. Monroe Av., #2130, Barron 54812
Bayfield	Scott S. Fibert (D)	P.O. Box 878, Washburn 54891
Brown	Sandra L. Juno (R)	P.O. Box 23600, Green Bay 54305-3600
Buffalo	Roxann M. Halverson (D)	407 S. 2nd St., P.O. Box 58, Alma 54610-0058
Burnett	Wanda Hinrichs (D)	7410 County Road K, #105, Siren 54872
Calumet	Beth A. Hauser (R)	206 Court St., Chilton 53014
Chippewa	Sandra L. Frion (D)	711 N. Bridge St., Chippewa Falls 54729
Clark	Christina M. Jensen (R)	517 Court St., Neillsville 54456
Columbia	Susan Moll (R)	400 DeWitt St., Portage 53901
Crawford	Janet L. Geisler (R)	225 N. Beaumont Rd., Suite 210, Prairie du Chien 53821
Dane	Scott McDonell (D)	210 Martin Luther King Jr. Blvd., Rm. 106A, Madison 53703
Dodge	Karen J. Gibson (R)	127 E. Oak St., Juneau 53039
Door	Jill M. Lau (R)	421 Nebraska St., Sturgeon Bay 54235
Douglas	Susan T. Sandvick (D)	1313 Belknap St., Superior 54880
Dunn	Marilyn Hoyt (D)	800 Wilson Av., Rm. 147, Menomonie 54751
Eau Claire	Janet K. Loomis (D)	721 Oxford Av., Eau Claire 54703
Florence	Donna Trudell (R)	501 Lake Av., P.O. Box 410, Florence 54121
Fond du Lac	Lisa Freiberg (R)	160 S. Macy St., Fond du Lac 54935
Forest	Lisa Kalata (D)	200 E. Madison St., Crandon 54520
Grant	Linda K. Gebhard (R)	111 S. Jefferson St., Lancaster 53813
Green	Michael J. Doyle (I)	1016 16th Av., Monroe 53566
Green Lake	Margaret R. Bostelmann (R)	P.O. Box 3188, Green Lake 54941-3188
Iowa	Gregory T. Klusendorf (D)	222 N. Iowa St., Dodgeville 53533
Iron	Michael Saari (D)	300 Taconite St., Suite 101, Hurley 54534
Jackson	Kyle Deno (D)	307 Main St., Black River Falls 54615
Jefferson	Barbara A. Frank (R)	320 S. Main St., Rm. 109, Jefferson 53549
Juneau	Kathleen Kobylski (R)	220 E. State St., Rm. 112, Mauston 53948
Kenosha	Mary Schuch-Krebs (D)	1010 56th St., Kenosha 53140
Kewaunee	Jamie Annoye (D)	810 Lincoln St., Kewaunee 54216
La Crosse	Ginny Dankmeyer (D)	400 4th St. N, Rm. 1210, La Crosse 54601
Lafayette	Linda Bawden (R)	626 Main St., P.O. Box 40, Darlington 53530
Langlade	Kathryn Jacob (D)	800 Clermont St., Antigo 54409
Lincoln	Christopher Marlowe (R)	801 N. Sales St., Suite 201, Merrill 54452-1632
Manitowoc	Jamie J. Aulik (D)	1010 S. 8th St., Manitowoc 54220
Marathon	Nan Kottke (D)	500 Forest St., Wausau 54403
Marinette	Kathy Brandt (R)	1926 Hall Av., Marinette 54143-1717
Marquette	Gary L. Sorensen (R)	P.O. Box 186, Montello 53949
Menominee	Ruth Waupoose (D)	P.O. Box 279, Keshena 54135
Milwaukee	Joseph Czarnezki (D)	901 N. 9th St., Rm. 105, Milwaukee 53233
Monroe	Shelley Bohl (R)	202 S. K St., Rm. 1, Sparta 54656
Oconto	Kim Pytleski (R)	301 Washington St., Oconto 54153-1699
Oneida	Mary Bartelt (D)	P.O. Box 400, Rhinelander 54501-0400
Outagamie	Lori O'Bright (R)	410 S. Walnut St., Appleton 54911
Ozaukee	Julianne B. Winkelhorst (R)	121 W. Main St., Port Washington 53074-0994
Pepin	Marcia R. Bauer (D)	740 7th Av. W., P.O. Box 39, Durand 54736
Pierce	Jamie R. Feuerhelm (D)	P.O. Box 119, Ellsworth 54011
Polk	Carole T. Wondra (D)	100 Polk County Plaza, Suite 110, Balsam Lake 54810
Portage	Shirley M. Simonis (D)	1516 Church St., Stevens Point 54481
Price	Jean Gottwald (D)	126 Cherry St., Rm. 106, Phillips 54555
Racine	Wendy M. Christensen (R)	730 Wisconsin Av., Racine 53403
Richland	Victor V. Vlasak (R)	P.O. Box 310, Richland Center 53581
Rock	Lori Stottler (D)	51 S. Main St., Janesville 53545
Rusk	Denise Wetzel (D)	311 E. Miner Av., Suite C150, Ladysmith 54848
St. Croix	Cindy Campbell (D)	1101 Carmichael Rd., Hudson 54016
Sauk	Rebecca A. DeMars (R)	505 Broadway, Rm. 144, Baraboo 53913
Sawyer	Kris Mayberry (R)	10610 Main St., Suite 10, Hayward 54843
Shawano	Rosemary Rueckert (R)	311 N. Main St., Shawano 54166
Sheboygan	Jon Dolson (R)	508 New York Av., Sheboygan 53081-4126
Taylor	Bruce P. Strama (D)	224 S. 2nd St., Medford 54451
Trempealeau	Paul L. Syverson (D)	36245 Main St., Whitehall 54773
Vernon	Ronald Hoff (R)	Courthouse Annex, Rm. 108, Viroqua 54665
Vilas	David R. Alleman (R)	330 Court St., Eagle River 54521
Walworth	Kimberly S. Bushey (R)	100 W. Walworth, Elkhorn 53121
Washburn	Lolita Olson (R)	P.O. Box 639, Shell Lake 54871
Washington	Brenda Jaszewski (R)	432 E. Washington St., West Bend 53095-7986
Waukesha	Kathleen Novack (R)	515 W. Moreland Blvd., #A120, Waukesha 53188
Waupaca	Mary A. Robbins (R)	811 Harding St., Waupaca 54981
Waushara	Melanie Rendon Stake (R)	P.O. Box 488, Wautoma 54982-0488
Winnebago	Susan Ertmer (R)	415 Jackson St., Oshkosh 54901
Wood	Cynthia Cepress (D)	P.O. Box 8095, Wisconsin Rapids 54495-8095

COUNTY OFFICERS IN WISCONSIN
June 30, 2013–Continued

County	Treasurer	Register of Deeds	Clerk of Circuit Court
Adams	Jani Zander (D)	Jodi Helgeson (R)	Kathleen Dye (D)
Ashland	Tracey A. Hoglund (R)	Karen M. Miller (D)	Kathleen R. Colgrove (R)
Barron	Yvonne K. Ritchie (R)	Margo Katterhagen (R)	Sharon Millermon (R)
Bayfield	Daniel Anderson (D)	Patricia Olson (D)	Kay Cederberg (D)
Brown	Kerry M. Blaney (D)	Cathy Williquette Lindsay (D)	Jason Beck (R)
Buffalo	Marilynn Sheahan (R)	Carol Burmeister (D)	Roselle Schlosser (R)
Burnett	Joanne Pahl (D)	Jeanine Chell (D)	Trudy Schmidt (D)
Calumet	Michael V. Schlaak (R)	Tamara Alten (R)	Barbara Van Akkeren (R)
Chippewa	Patricia Schimmel (D)	Marge Geissler (D)	Karen J. Hepfler (D)
Clark	Kathryn M. Brugger (D)	Peggy Walter (R)	Heather Bravener (D)
Columbia	Deborah A. Raimer (R)	Lisa Walker (R)	Susan Raimer (R)
Crawford	Martin E. Sprosty (D)	Melissa Nagel (D)	Donna M. Steiner (D)
Dane	Adam Gallagher (D)	Kristi Chlebowski (D)	Carlo Esqueda (D)
Dodge	Patti Hilker (R)	Christine Planasch (R)	Lynn Hron (R)
Door	Jay Zahn (R)	Carey Petersilka (R)	Nancy Robillard (R)
Douglas	Linda Helenius (D)	Gayle Wahner (D)	Joan Osty (D)
Dunn	Cindy Kopp (R)	Heather Kuhn (D)	Clara Minor (D)
Eau Claire	Larry C. Lokken (D)	Kathryn Christenson (D)	Kristina L. Aschenbrenner (R)
Florence	JoAnne Friberg (R)	Pattie Gehlhoff (R)	Paula Coraggio (R)
Fond du Lac	Julie M. Hundertmark (R)	Patricia Kraus (R)	Ramona Geib (A)
Forest	Amy T. Krause (D)	Cortney M. Britten (D)	Penny Carter (D)
Grant	Louise F. Ketterer (R)	Marilyn Pierce (R)	Kim K. Kohn (R)
Green	Sherri Hawkins (D)	Cynthia A. Meudt (R)	Carol Thompson (R)
Green Lake	Kathleen A. Morris (R)	Sarah Guenther	Susan J. Krueger (R)
Iowa	Jolene M. Millard (R)	Dixie L. Edge (D)	Lia N. Gust (R)
Iron	Mark Beaupré (R)	Dan Soine (D)	Karin Ransanici (D)
Jackson	JoAnne Forsting-Leonard (D)	Shari Marg (D)	Jan Moennig (D)
Jefferson	John E. Jensen (R)	Staci M. Hoffman (R)	Carla J. Robinson (R)
Juneau	Denise Giebel (R)	Christie L. Bender (R)	Loretta Roberts
Kenosha	Teri Jacobson (D)	JoEllyn M. Storz (D)	Rebecca Matoska-Mentink (D)
Kewaunee	Michelle M. Dax (R)	Janet L. Wolf (R)	Rebecca A. Deterville (D)
La Crosse	Shawn Handland (D)	Cheryl A. McBride (R)	Pamela Radtke (R)
Lafayette	Rebecca Taylor (R)	Joseph Boll (R)	Catherine McGowan (R)
Langlade	Ann Meyer (D)	Sandra M. Fischer (D)	Marilyn Baraniak (D)
Lincoln	Jan Lemmer (D)	Sara Koss (R)	Cindy Kimmons (R)
Manitowoc	Cheryl M. Duchow (D)	Preston Jones (D)	Lynn Zigmunt (D)
Marathon	Lorraine I. Beyersdorff (R)	Michael Sydow (D)	Diane Sennholz (D)
Marinette	Bev A. Noffke (R)	Renee Miller (R)	Linda L. Dumke-Marquardt (R)
Marquette	Diana Campbell (R)	Bette L. Krueger (R)	Shari Rudolph (R)
Menominee	Louise Davids (D)	Louise Davids (D)	Pamela Frechette (D)
Milwaukee	Daniel Diliberti (D)	John La Fave (D)	John Barrett (D)
Monroe	Annette M. Erickson (R)	Debra Brandt (R)	Shirley Chapiewsky (R)
Oconto	Tanya Peterson (R)	Annette Behringer (R)	Michael C. Hodkiewicz (R)
Oneida	Kris Ostermann (D)	Kyle J. Franson (R)	Brenda Behrle (D)
Outagamie	Dina Mumford (R)	Sarah Van Camp (R)	Lonnie Wolf (R)
Ozaukee	Karen L. Makoutz (R)	Ronald A. Voigt (R)	Mary Lou Mueller (R)
Pepin	Nancy Richardson (R)	Monica J. Bauer (R)	Audrey Lieffring (R)
Pierce	Phyllis J. Beastrom (D)	Vicki J. Nelson (R)	Peg M. Feuerhelm (D)
Polk	Amanda Nissen (D)	Laurie Anderson (D)	Joan Ritten
Portage	Stephanie Stokes (D)	Cynthia A. Wisinski (D)	Patricia Baker (D)
Price	Lynn M. Neeck (D)	Judith Chizek (D)	Chris Cress (D)
Racine	Jane F. Nikolai (R)	Tyson Fettes (R)	Roseanne Lee (R)
Richland	Julie Keller (R)	Susan Triggs (R)	Stacy Kleist (R)
Rock	Vicki Brown (D)	Randy Leyes (R)	Eldred Mielke (D)
Rusk	Verna Nielsen (R)	Carol Johnson (D)	Renae Baxter (D)
St. Croix	Laurie Noble (R)	Beth Pabst (D)	Lori Meyer (R)
Sauk	Elizabeth Geoghegan (R)	Brent Bailey (R)	Vicki Meister (R)
Sawyer	Dianne M. Ince (R)	Paula Chisser (R)	Anne Marie Swanson (R)
Shawano	Debra Wallace (R)	Amy Dillenburg (R)	Susan M. Krueger (R)
Sheboygan	Laura Henning-Lorenz (D)	Ellen Schleicher (D)	Nan Todd (D)
Taylor	Sarah Holtz (R)	Sara Nuernberger (D)	Margaret M. Gebauer (R)
Trempealeau	Laurie Halama (D)	Rose Oldun (D)	Michelle Weisenberger (D)
Vernon	Rachel Hanson (R)	Konna Spaeth (R)	Kathy Buros (R)
Vilas	Jerri Radtke (R)	Joan Hansen (R)	Jean Numrich (R)
Walworth	Valerie Etzel (R)	Donna Pruess (R)	Sheila Reiff (R)
Washburn	Janet L. Ullom (R)	Diane M. Poach (D)	Karen Nord (D)
Washington	Jane Merten (R)	Sharon Martin (R)	Theresa M. Russell (R)
Waukesha	Pamela Reeves (R)	Jim Behrend (R)	Kathy Madden (R)
Waupaca	Clyde Tellock (R)	Michael Mazemke (R)	Terrie Tews-Liebe (R)
Waushara	Elaine Wedell (R)	Heather Schwersenska (R)	Melissa M. Zamzow (R)
Winnebago	Mary Krueger (R)	Julie Pagel (R)	Melissa Konrad (R)
Wood	Karen Kubisiak (D)	Susan Ginter (R)	Cindy Joosten (R)

COUNTY OFFICERS IN WISCONSIN
June 30, 2013–Continued

County	District Attorney	Sheriff	Coroner/Medical Examiner
Adams	Tania Bonnett (I)	Sam Wollin (D)	Marilyn Rogers (ME)
Ashland	Kelly McNight (D)	Michael W. Brennan, Jr. (D)	Barbara Beeksma (R)
Barron	Angela Beranek (D)	Chris Fitzgerald (D)	Mary Ricci (ME)
Bayfield	Frederick Bourg (D)	Paul Susienka (D)	Gary Victorson (D)
Brown	David L. Lasee (R)	John Gossage (R)	Al Klimek (ME)
Buffalo	Thomas Clark (D)	Mike Schmidtknecht (R)	Peter Samb (R)
Burnett	William Norine (R)	Dean Roland (R)	Michael Maloney (ME)
Calumet	Nicholas Bolz (R)	Mark Ott (R)	Michael Klaeser (ME)
Chippewa	Steve Gibbs (R)	James Kowalczyk (D)	Ronald Patten (D)
Clark	Lyndsey Boon Brunette (D)	Greg Herrick (R)	Richard Schleifer (R)
Columbia	Jane E. Kohlwey (R)	Dennis Richards (R)	Angela Hinze (ME)
Crawford	Timothy Baxter (D)	Dale McCullick (D)	Joe Morovits (D)
Dane	Ismael Ozanne (D)	David Mahoney (D)	Vincent Tranchida (ME)
Dodge	Kurt Klomberg (R)	Patricia Ninmann (R)	Patrick Schoebel (ME)
Door	Raymond L. Pelrine (R)	Terry J. Vogel (R)	None
Douglas	Daniel Blank (D)	Thomas Dalbec (D)	Darrell Witt (ME)
Dunn	James M. Peterson (R)	Dennis Smith (D)	None
Eau Claire	Gary King (D)	Ron D. Cramer (R)	Thomas Thelen, R.N. (ME)
Florence	Douglas Drexler (D)	Jeff Rickaby (R)	Mary Johnson (R)
Fond du Lac	Eric Toney (R)	Mylan C. Fink, Jr. (R)	P. Douglas Kelley (ME)
Forest	Charles Simono (D)	John Dennee (D)	None
Grant	Lisa A. Riniker (R)	Nathan Dreckman (R)	Ronald A. Sturmer (R)
Green	Gary L. Luhman (R)	Jeff Skatrud (D)	Kris Hasse (R)
Green Lake	Kyle Sargent (R)	Mark A. Podoll (R)	Darlene Strey (R)
Iowa	Larry Nelson (D)	Steven R. Michek (R)	William Finley (D)
Iron	Martin Lipske (D)	Tony Furyk (D)	Diane Simonich (D)
Jackson	Gerald Fox (D)	Duane Waldera (D)	Karla Wood (R)
Jefferson	Susan Happ (D)	Paul Milbrath (R)	Patrick J. Theder (R)
Juneau	Michael Solovey (R)	Brent H. Oleson (R)	Kathleen Kohutko (R)
Kenosha	Robert Zapf (D)	David Beth (R)	Patrice Hall (ME)
Kewaunee	Andrew P. Naze (D)	Matthew J. Joski (R)	Rory Groessl (I)
La Crosse	Tim Gruenke (D)	Steven J. Helgeson (R)	John W. Steers (ME)
Lafayette	Kate Findley (D)	Scott Pedley (R)	Virginia Douglas (D)
Langlade	Ralph M. Uttke (D)	William Greening (D)	Larry E. Shadick (R)
Lincoln	Don Dunphy (R)	Jeff Jaeger (R)	Paul Proulx (R)
Manitowoc	Mark Rohrer (R)	Robert Hermann (D)	Curtis Green (D)
Marathon	Kenneth Heimerman (D)	Randy Hoenisch (D)	John Larson (ME)
Marinette	Allen R. Brey (D)	Jerry T. Sauve (R)	George F. Smith (R)
Marquette	Chad Hendee (R)	Kim Gaffney (R)	Thomas G. Wastart II (R)
Menominee	Gregory Parker (R)[2]	Robert Summers (D)	None
Milwaukee	John Chisholm (D)	David Clarke, Jr. (D)	Brian L. Peterson, M.D. (ME)
Monroe	Dan Cary (R)	Peter Quirin (R)	Toni Wissestad (ME)
Oconto	Ed Burke (R)	Michael R. Jansen (R)	Al Klimek (ME)
Oneida	Michael W. Schiek (R)	Grady Hartman (R)	Larry Mathein (ME)
Outagamie	Carrie Schneider (R)	Bradley Gehring (R)	Ruth Wulgaert (R)
Ozaukee	Adam Gerol (R)	Maury A. Straub (R)	John R. Holicek (R)
Pepin	Jon D. Seifert (D)	John Andrews (R)	Christy Rundquist (I)
Pierce	Sean Froelich (D)	Nancy Hove (D)	John Worsing (ME)
Polk	Daniel P. Steffen (D)	Pete Johnson (R)	Jonn Dinnies (ME)
Portage	Louis Molepske (D)	John Charewicz (D)	Scott Rifleman (R)
Price	Mark T. Fuhr (D)	Brian Schmidt (R)	James Dalbesio, III (D)
Racine	W. Richard Chiapete (R)	Christopher Schmaling (R)	Michael Payne (ME)
Richland	Jennifer M. Harper (R)	Darrell Berglin (R)	Mary E. Turner (R)
Rock	David O'Leary (D)	Robert Spoden (D)	Jenifer Keach (D)
Rusk	Andra Nodolf (R)	David Kaminski (D)	Kasi Ewert (R)
St. Croix	Eric Johnson (R)	John Shilts (R)	Patty Schachtner (ME)
Sauk	Kevin Calkins (R)	Chip Meister (R)	Greg L. Hahn (R)
Sawyer	Bruce Poquette (R)	Mark Kelsey (R)	Dave Dokkestul (R)
Shawano	Gregory Parker (R)[2]	Randall Wright (R)	Marcus Jesse (R)
Sheboygan	Joe DeCecco (D)	Todd W. Priebe (D)	David J. Leffin (R)
Taylor	Kristi Tlusty (D)	Bruce A. Daniels (D)	Scott Perrin (ME)
Trempealeau	Taavi McMahon (D)	Richard A. Anderson (D)	Bonnie Kindschy (D)
Vernon	Timothy Gaskell (R)	John Spears (R)	Janet Reed (R)
Vilas	Albert Moustakis (R)	Frank Tomlanovich (R)	Paul Tirpe (R)
Walworth	Dan Necci (R)	David Graves (R)	John Griebel (R)
Washburn	J. Michael Bitney (R)	Terry C. Dryden (R)	Karen L. Baker (R)
Washington	Mark D. Bensen (R)	Dale Schmidt (R)	Bob Posont (ME)
Waukesha	Brad Schimel (R)	Daniel Trawicki (R)	Lynda Biedrzycki (ME)
Waupaca	John P. Snider (R)	Brad Hardel (R)	Barry Tomaras (R)
Waushara	Scott Blader (R)	David R. Peterson (R)	Roland B. Handel (R)
Winnebago	Christian Gossett (R)	John Matz (R)	Barry Busby (R)
Wood	Craig Lambert	Thomas Reichert (D)	Garry Kronstedt (D)

COUNTY OFFICERS IN WISCONSIN
June 30, 2013–Continued

County	Surveyor[3]	County	Surveyor[3]
Adams	Gregory Rhinehart	Marathon	Emily Pierce
Ashland	David Carlson	Marinette	None
Barron	Mark Netterlund	Marquette	Jerol Smart
Bayfield	None	Menominee	None
Brown	Patrick J. Ford	Milwaukee	Kurt Bauer
Buffalo	Joe Nelsen (contracted)	Monroe	Gary Dechant
Burnett	Jason Towne	Oconto	Mark Teuteberg[4]
Calumet	Peter Hatas	Oneida	Michael Romportl
Chippewa	Sam Wenz	Outagamie	James Hebert
Clark	Wade Pettit	Ozaukee	Robert R. Dreblow
Columbia	Jim Grothman	Pepin	Ron Jasperson
Crawford	Rich Marx	Pierce	James Filkins
Dane	Dan Frick	Polk	Steve Geiger
Dodge	Jerry Thomasen	Portage	Joseph Glodowski (D)
Door	None	Price	Alfred Schneider
Douglas	Ben Klitzke	Racine	None
Dunn	Thomas Carlson	Richland	Matthew M. Filus
Eau Claire	Matt Janiak	Rock	Jason Houle
Florence	None	Rusk	None
Fond du Lac	Peter Kuen	St. Croix	Brian Halling
Forest	None	Sauk	Patrick Dederich (D)
Grant	Larry Austin	Sawyer	Dan Ploeger
Green	None	Shawano	None
Green Lake	Alan Shute	Sheboygan	None
Iowa	Bruce D. Bowden (R)	Taylor	Robert Meyer
Iron	None	Trempealeau	Joe Nelson
Jackson	Tim Jeatran	Vernon	None
Jefferson	Jim Morrow	Vilas	Thomas Boettcher (R)
Juneau	None	Walworth	None
Kenosha	None	Washburn	None
Kewaunee	None	Washington	Scott Schmidt
La Crosse	Bryan Meyer	Waukesha	Kurt Bauer
Lafayette	None	Waupaca	Joseph Glodowski
Langlade	David Tlusty	Waushara	Jerry Smart
Lincoln	Tony Dallman	Winnebago	None
Manitowoc	None	Wood	Kevin Boyer

Key: A – Appointed without party designation; AC – Administrative Coordinator; CA – County Administrator; CE – County Executive; D – Democrat; I – Independent; R – Republican; ME – Medical Examiner.

Note: All officers are elected countywide with the exception of the county board chairperson, county administrator, administrative coordinator, and medical examiner, who are elected or appointed by the county board. Elected county supervisors serve 2-year terms, except county executives who serve 4-year terms. All remaining county officers serve 4-year terms.

[1]Counties with a population of 500,000 or more are statutorily required to establish the office of county executive. Smaller counties may establish the office of county executive or name a county administrator. In counties without a county executive or county administrator, the county board must designate an elected or appointed official to serve as administrative coordinator.

[2]Menominee and Shawano County share a District Attorney.

[3]County boards are permitted to designate any registered land surveyor to perform the duties of the county surveyor. Surveyors are appointed unless party designation is shown.

[4]Surveyor/Land Information Systems Administrator.

Source: Data collected from county clerks by Wisconsin Legislative Reference Bureau, May 2013, and governor's appointment notices.

WISCONSIN CITIES
January 1, 2012

City (Year Incorporated)[1]	County	Population[4]				
		2010 Census	2012 Estimate	Percent Change	2010 Nonwhite[5]	2010 Hispanic or Latino Origin[6]
First Class Cities (150,000 or more) – 1 City						
Milwaukee (1846)	Milwaukee, Washington, Waukesha	594,833	595,425	0.1%	271,607	103,007
Second Class Cities (39,000 – 149,999) – 14 Cities						
Appleton (1857)	Calumet, Outagamie, Winnebago . .	72,623	72,810	0.3	7,124	3,643
Eau Claire (1872)[2]	Chippewa, Eau Claire	61,704	66,170	0.4	5,116	1,268
Fond du Lac (1852)[2] . . .	Fond du Lac	43,021	43,100	0.2	2,695	2,742
Green Bay (1854)	Brown	104,057	104,250	0.2	13,912	13,896
Janesville (1853)[2]	Rock	63,575	63,480	–0.1	3,689	3,421
Kenosha (1850)[3]	Kenosha	99,218	99,660	0.4	14,121	16,130
La Crosse (1856).	La Crosse	51,320	51,590	0.5	4,885	1,012
Madison (1856)	Dane	233,209	234,625	0.6	40,798	15,948
Oshkosh (1853)[2]	Winnebago	62,916	66,325	0.4	5,539	1,770
Racine (1848)[3]	Racine	78,860	78,830	0.0	20,362	16,309
Sheboygan (1853)	Sheboygan	49,288	49,110	–0.4	6,314	4,866
Waukesha (1895)[3]	Waukesha	70,718	71,020	0.4	5,321	8,529
Wauwatosa (1897)[3]	Milwaukee	46,396	46,320	–0.2	4,361	1,450
West Allis (1906)[3]	Milwaukee	60,411	60,300	–0.2	5,094	5,770
Third Class Cities (10,000 – 38,999) – 33 Cities						
Baraboo (1882)[3]	Sauk	12,048	11,952	–0.8	487	446
Beaver Dam (1856)	Dodge	16,214	16,333	0.7	502	1,210
Beloit (1857)[2]	Rock	36,966	36,850	–0.3	7,149	6,332
Brookfield (1954)	Waukesha	37,920	37,870	–0.1	3,545	853
Chippewa Falls (1869). . .	Chippewa	13,661	13,704	0.3	605	221
Cudahy (1906).	Milwaukee	18,267	18,247	–0.1	1,142	1,769
De Pere (1883)[3]	Brown	23,800	23,944	0.6	1,207	511
Fort Atkinson (1878)[2] . . .	Jefferson	12,368	12,380	0.1	315	1,128
Franklin (1956)	Milwaukee	35,451	35,520	0.2	4,168	1,592
Glendale (1950)[3]	Milwaukee	12,872	12,808	–0.5	2,499	465
Greenfield (1957)	Milwaukee	36,720	36,740	0.1	3,043	3,087
Hartford (1883)[3]	Dodge, Washington	14,223	14,258	0.2	425	686
Kaukauna (1885).	Outagamie	15,462	15,627	1.1	654	407
Manitowoc (1870)	Manitowoc	33,736	33,750	0.0	2,486	1,695
Marinette (1887).	Marinette	10,968	10,929	–0.4	271	149
Marshfield (1883)[3]	Marathon, Wood	19,118	19,061	–0.3	796	452
Menasha (1874)	Calumet, Winnebago.	17,353	17,407	0.3	954	1,204
Middleton (1963)[3]	Dane	17,442	17,903	2.6	1,764	984
Muskego (1964)[3].	Waukesha	24,135	24,217	0.3	529	545
Neenah (1873)	Winnebago.	25,501	25,723	0.9	1,163	967
New Berlin (1959).	Waukesha	39,584	39,770	0.5	2,256	1,036
Oak Creek (1955)[3]	Milwaukee	34,451	34,530	0.2	3,282	2,582
Oconomowoc (1875)[3] . . .	Waukesha	15,759	15,834	0.5	422	559
Pewaukee (1999)[3]	Waukesha	13,195	13,464	2.0	667	281
River Falls (1875)[3].	Pierce, St. Croix	15,000	15,040	0.3	673	270
Stevens Point (1858). . . .	Portage.	26,717	27,129	1.5	1,946	696
Sun Prairie (1958)[3].	Dane	29,364	29,840	1.6	3,749	1,253
Superior (1858)	Douglas	27,244	27,146	–0.4	2,166	382
Two Rivers (1878)[2]	Manitowoc	11,712	11,669	–0.4	536	224
Watertown (1853)	Dodge, Jefferson	23,861	23,891	0.1	706	1,731
Wausau (1872).	Marathon.	39,106	39,160	0.1	5,891	1,149
West Bend (1885)[3]	Washington.	31,078	31,380	1.0	1,049	1,213
Wisconsin Rapids (1869) .	Wood.	18,367	18,343	–0.1	1,186	535
Fourth Class Cities (Under 10,000) – 142 Cities						
Abbotsford (1965).	Clark, Marathon	2,310	2,300	–0.4	29	578
Adams (1926)[3].	Adams	1,967	1,946	–1.1	74	46
Algoma (1879)[3]	Kewaunee	3,167	3,171	0.1	84	91
Alma (1885)	Buffalo	781	816	4.5	9	5
Altoona (1887)[3]	Eau Claire	6,706	6,820	1.7	367	171
Amery (1919)[3]	Polk	2,902	2,940	1.3	49	65
Antigo (1885)[3]	Langlade	8,234	8,141	–1.1	288	226
Arcadia (1925).	Trempealeau	2,925	2,916	–0.3	48	914
Ashland (1887)[3]	Ashland, Bayfield	8,216	8,132	–1.0	986	176
Augusta (1885).	Eau Claire	1,550	1,545	–0.3	28	48
Barron (1887)	Barron	3,423	3,430	0.2	392	103
Bayfield (1913)	Bayfield	487	488	0.2	104	9
Berlin (1857)[3]	Green Lake, Waushara.	5,524	5,541	0.3	143	441

WISCONSIN CITIES
January 1, 2012–Continued

City (Year Incorporated)[1]	County	2010 Census	2012 Estimate	Percent Change	2010 Nonwhite[5]	2010 Hispanic or Latino Origin[6]
Black River Falls (1883)[3]	Jackson	3,622	3,609	–0.4	291	63
Blair (1949)	Trempealeau	1,366	1,370	0.3	17	52
Bloomer (1920)	Chippewa	3,539	3,539	0.0	59	27
Boscobel (1873)[3]	Grant	3,231	3,247	0.5	304	71
Brillion (1944)[3]	Calumet	3,148	3,183	1.1	60	89
Brodhead (1891)	Green, Rock	3,293	3,296	0.1	50	125
Buffalo City (1859)	Buffalo	1,023	1,017	–0.6	13	4
Burlington (1900)[3]	Racine, Walworth	10,464	10,496	0.3	327	898
Cedarburg (1885)[3]	Ozaukee	11,412	11,445	0.3	367	197
Chetek (1891)	Barron	2,221	2,221	0.0	36	39
Chilton (1877)	Calumet	3,933	3,932	0.0	83	169
Clintonville (1887)[3]	Waupaca	4,559	4,543	–0.4	132	149
Colby (1891)	Clark, Marathon	1,852	1,837	–0.8	37	221
Columbus (1874)[3]	Columbia, Dodge	4,991	5,026	0.7	143	164
Cornell (1956)[3]	Chippewa	1,467	1,471	0.3	33	3
Crandon (1898)	Forest	1,920	1,895	–1.3	244	40
Cuba City (1925)	Grant, Lafayette	2,086	2,088	0.1	17	10
Cumberland (1885)	Barron	2,170	2,166	–0.2	69	54
Darlington (1877)	Lafayette	2,451	2,443	–0.3	40	297
Delafield (1959)[3]	Waukesha	7,085	7,095	0.1	227	226
Delavan (1897)[3]	Walworth	8,463	8,442	–0.2	287	2,492
Dodgeville (1889)	Iowa	4,693	4,692	0.0	118	84
Durand (1887)[3]	Pepin	1,931	1,926	–0.3	29	16
Eagle River (1937)[3]	Vilas	1,398	1,381	–1.2	81	26
Edgerton (1883)[3]	Dane, Rock	5,461	5,481	0.4	157	222
Elkhorn (1897)[3]	Walworth	10,084	9,998	–0.9	307	1,108
Elroy (1885)[3]	Juneau	1,442	1,426	–1.1	29	32
Evansville (1896)[3]	Rock	5,012	5,051	0.8	159	179
Fennimore (1919)	Grant	2,497	2,506	0.4	31	31
Fitchburg (1983)[3]	Dane	25,260	25,246	–0.1	4,464	4,341
Fountain City (1889)	Buffalo	859	884	2.9	25	9
Fox Lake (1938)[3]	Dodge	1,519	1,514	–0.3	17	36
Galesville (1942)	Trempealeau	1,481	1,489	0.5	36	18
Gillett (1944)	Oconto	1,386	1,382	–0.3	65	70
Glenwood City (1895)	St. Croix	1,242	1,233	–0.7	16	24
Green Lake (1962)	Green Lake	960	974	1.5	11	18
Greenwood (1891)	Clark	1,026	1,022	–0.4	17	15
Hayward (1915)	Sawyer	2,318	2,348	1.3	354	59
Hillsboro (1885)[3]	Vernon	1,417	1,415	–0.1	19	32
Horicon (1897)	Dodge	3,655	3,649	–0.2	86	151
Hudson (1857)[3]	St. Croix	12,719	13,012	2.3	539	347
Hurley (1918)	Iron	1,547	1,513	–2.2	32	12
Independence (1942)	Trempealeau	1,336	1,339	0.2	11	172
Jefferson (1878)[3]	Jefferson	7,973	7,934	–0.5	203	937
Juneau (1887)	Dodge	2,814	2,776	–1.4	146	285
Kewaunee (1883)[3]	Kewaunee	2,952	2,951	0.0	66	53
Kiel (1920)[3]	Calumet, Manitowoc	3,738	3,742	0.1	83	74
Ladysmith (1905)[3]	Rusk	3,414	3,386	–0.8	106	53
Lake Geneva (1883)[3]	Walworth	7,651	7,654	0.0	237	1,323
Lake Mills (1905)[2]	Jefferson	5,708	5,742	0.6	122	216
Lancaster (1878)[3]	Grant	3,868	3,845	–0.6	58	31
Lodi (1941)	Columbia	3,050	3,049	0.0	77	62
Loyal (1948)	Clark	1,261	1,256	–0.4	15	13
Manawa (1954)	Waupaca	1,371	1,347	–1.8	24	27
Marion (1898)	Shawano, Waupaca	1,260	1,258	–0.2	26	22
Markesan (1959)	Green Lake	1,476	1,464	–0.8	5	109
Mauston (1883)[3]	Juneau	4,423	4,517	2.1	239	154
Mayville (1885)	Dodge	5,154	5,139	–0.3	92	138
Medford (1889)[3]	Taylor	4,326	4,338	0.3	106	54
Mellen (1907)	Ashland	731	719	–1.6	17	12

WISCONSIN CITIES
January 1, 2012–Continued

City (Year Incorporated)[1]	County	Population[4] 2010 Census	2012 Estimate	Percent Change	2010 Nonwhite[5]	2010 Hispanic or Latino Origin[6]
Menomonie (1882)[3]	Dunn	16,264	16,101	–1.0	1,176	276
Mequon (1957)[3]	Ozaukee	23,132	23,225	0.4	1,760	467
Merrill (1883)[3]	Lincoln	9,661	9,618	–0.4	248	196
Milton (1969)[3]	Rock	5,546	5,549	0.1	146	133
Mineral Point (1857)	Iowa	2,487	2,479	–0.3	47	17
Mondovi (1889)[3]	Buffalo	2,777	2,773	–0.1	73	40
Monona (1969)[3]	Dane	7,533	7,523	–0.1	459	232
Monroe (1882)[3]	Green	10,827	10,811	–0.1	252	526
Montello (1938)	Marquette	1,495	1,483	–0.8	65	43
Montreal (1924)	Iron	807	803	–0.5	16	13
Mosinee (1931)[3]	Marathon	3,988	3,989	0.0	75	50
Neillsville (1882)	Clark	2,463	2,438	–1.0	70	57
Nekoosa (1926)	Wood	2,580	2,570	–0.4	113	87
New Holstein (1926)	Calumet	3,236	3,234	–0.1	63	103
New Lisbon (1889)[3]	Juneau	2,554	2,567	0.5	439	109
New London (1877)[3]	Outagamie, Waupaca	7,295	7,300	0.1	168	500
New Richmond (1885)[3]	St. Croix	8,375	8,395	0.2	331	174
Niagara (1992)	Marinette	1,624	1,617	–0.4	27	19
Oconto (1869)[3]	Oconto	4,513	4,535	0.5	135	109
Oconto Falls (1919)[3]	Oconto	2,891	2,883	–0.3	96	35
Omro (1944)[3]	Winnebago	3,517	3,520	0.1	70	116
Onalaska (1887)	La Crosse	17,736	18,006	1.5	1,539	276
Osseo (1941)	Trempealeau	1,701	1,699	–0.1	28	27
Owen (1925)	Clark	940	939	–0.1	11	36
Park Falls (1912)	Price	2,462	2,464	0.1	122	24
Peshtigo (1903)	Marinette	3,502	3,510	0.2	101	41
Phillips (1891)	Price	1,478	1,447	–2.1	64	22
Pittsville (1887)	Wood	874	871	–0.3	16	7
Platteville (1876)[2]	Grant	11,224	11,338	1.0	535	179
Plymouth (1877)	Sheboygan	8,445	8,424	–0.2	213	205
Port Washington (1882)[3]	Ozaukee	11,250	11,287	0.3	457	347
Portage (1854)[3]	Columbia	10,324	10,298	–0.3	811	414
Prairie du Chien (1872)[3]	Crawford	5,911	5,901	–0.2	351	73
Prescott (1857)[3]	Pierce	4,258	4,258	0.0	137	87
Princeton (1920)[3]	Green Lake	1,214	1,207	–0.6	29	18
Reedsburg (1887)[3]	Sauk	9,200	9,259	0.6	241	393
Rhinelander (1894)[3]	Oneida	7,798	7,753	–0.6	334	104
Rice Lake (1887)[3]	Barron	8,438	8,405	–0.2	251	203
Richland Center (1887)	Richland	5,184	5,190	0.1	132	169
Ripon (1858)[3]	Fond du Lac	7,733	7,706	–0.3	183	388
St. Croix Falls (1958)[3]	Polk	2,133	2,130	–0.1	45	38
St. Francis (1951)[3]	Milwaukee	9,365	9,452	0.9	656	884
Schofield (1951)	Marathon	2,169	2,167	–0.1	206	39
Seymour (1879)	Outagamie	3,451	3,434	–0.5	156	70
Shawano (1874)[3]	Shawano	9,305	9,259	–0.5	1,438	286
Sheboygan Falls (1913)	Sheboygan	7,775	7,847	0.9	185	197
Shell Lake (1961)[3]	Washburn	1,347	1,352	0.4	29	8
Shullsburg (1889)	Lafayette	1,226	1,226	0.0	12	29
South Milwaukee (1897)[3]	Milwaukee	21,156	21,103	–0.3	1,100	1,699
Sparta (1883)[3]	Monroe	9,522	9,636	1.2	345	643
Spooner (1909)[3]	Washburn	2,682	2,667	–0.6	120	34
Stanley (1898)	Chippewa, Clark	3,608	3,583	–0.7	683	111
Stoughton (1882)	Dane	12,611	12,630	0.2	554	230
Sturgeon Bay (1883)[3]	Door	9,144	9,132	–0.1	315	251
Thorp (1948)[3]	Clark	1,621	1,636	0.9	18	14
Tomah (1883)[3]	Monroe	9,093	9,174	0.9	650	366
Tomahawk (1891)	Lincoln	3,397	3,384	–0.4	93	34
Verona (1977)[3]	Dane	10,619	10,856	2.2	617	258
Viroqua (1885)[3]	Vernon	4,362	4,339	–0.5	107	44
Washburn (1904)[3]	Bayfield	2,117	2,109	–0.4	230	33
Waterloo (1962)	Jefferson	3,333	3,331	–0.1	73	426
Waupaca (1875)[3]	Waupaca	6,069	6,040	–0.5	169	139
Waupun (1878)[3]	Dodge, Fond du Lac	11,340	11,432	0.8	1,651	217

WISCONSIN CITIES
January 1, 2012–Continued

		Population[4]				
City (Year Incorporated)[1]	County	2010 Census	2012 Estimate	Percent Change	2010 Nonwhite[5]	2010 Hispanic or Latino Origin[6]
Wautoma (1901)	Waushara.	2,218	2,185	–1.5	81	351
Westby (1920)	Vernon	2,200	2,229	1.3	29	22
Weyauwega (1939)[3]	Waupaca	1,900	1,930	1.6	26	115
Whitehall (1941)[3]	Trempealeau	1,558	1,573	1.0	22	66
Whitewater (1885)[2]	Jefferson, Walworth	14,390	14,757	2.6	1,009	1,372
Wisconsin Dells (1925) . .	Adams, Columbia, Juneau, Sauk . .	2,678	2,664	–0.5	108	198

Note: A city is not automatically reclassified based on changes in population but must take action to initiate a reclassification. Under Section 62.05 (2), Wisconsin Statutes, to change from one class to another a city must: 1) meet the required population size according to the last federal census; 2) fulfill required governmental changes; and 3) publish a mayoral proclamation.

[1]There are 190 cities in Wisconsin as of January 1, 2012.

[2]One of 10 cities with a city manager.

[3]One of 93 cities with a city administrator holding a full-time or combined position.

[4]Population estimates are based on the corrected totals. Race and ethnicity data have not been adjusted.

[5]In the 2010 U.S. Census, respondents were allowed to choose more than one race. The column "nonwhite" includes all who chose at least one race other than white.

[6]"Hispanic or Latino Origin" represents ethnicity and includes people of Cuban, Mexican, Puerto Rican, South or Central American, or other Spanish culture or origin, regardless of race.

Sources: Wisconsin Department of Administration, Demographic Services Center, *Official Final Estimates, 1/1/2012, Wisconsin Municipalities, with Comparison to Census 2010,* April 2013; League of Wisconsin Municipalities, *2011 Directory of Wisconsin City and Village Officials,* July 2011; and data compiled by Wisconsin Legislative Reference Bureau.

WISCONSIN VILLAGES
January 1, 2012

		Population				2010 Hispanic
Village (Year Incorporated)[1]	County	2010 Census	2012 Estimate	Percent Change	2010 Nonwhite	or Latino Origin[2]
Adell (1918).	Sheboygan	516	514	−0.4%	21	18
Albany (1883)	Green.	1,018	1,014	−0.4	25	24
Allouez (1986)[3]	Brown	13,975	13,959	−0.1	1,252	383
Alma Center (1902)	Jackson.	503	505	0.4	13	32
Almena (1945).	Barron	677	665	−1.8	23	5
Almond (1905).	Portage	448	449	0.2	5	59
Amherst (1899)	Portage	1,035	1,041	0.6	9	26
Amherst Junction (1912).	Portage	377	376	−0.3	0	2
Aniwa (1899)	Shawano	260	259	−0.4	1	2
Arena (1923).	Iowa	834	830	−0.5	14	15
Argyle (1903)	Lafayette	857	860	0.4	4	17
Arlington (1945)[3]	Columbia.	819	823	0.5	18	11
Arpin (1978)	Wood	333	331	−0.6	10	2
Ashwaubenon (1977)[3]	Brown	16,963	16,977	0.1	1,375	471
Athens (1901)	Marathon.	1,105	1,106	0.1	13	54
Auburndale (1881).	Wood.	703	702	−0.1	0	38
Avoca (1870).	Iowa	637	634	−0.5	19	12
Bagley (1919)	Grant	379	381	0.5	8	2
Baldwin (1875)[3]	St. Croix	3,957	3,953	−0.1	127	63
Balsam Lake (1905)	Polk	1,009	1,015	0.6	56	7
Bangor (1899)	La Crosse	1,459	1,470	0.8	30	23
Barneveld (1906)	Iowa	1,231	1,234	0.2	22	3
Bay City (1909)	Pierce.	500	499	−0.2	7	3
Bayside (1953)[4]	Milwaukee, Ozaukee.	4,389	4,380	−0.2	383	121
Bear Creek (1902)	Outagamie	448	447	−0.2	5	170
Belgium (1922)	Ozaukee	2,245	2,251	0.3	54	11 /
Bell Center (1901).	Crawford	117	117	0.0	2	0
Belleville (1892)[3]	Dane, Green	2,385	2,384	0.0	43	90
Bellevue (2003)[3]	Brown	14,570	14,650	0.5	970	1,359
Belmont (1894)	Lafayette.	986	988	0.2	10	7
Benton (1892)	Lafayette	973	971	−0.2	14	4
Big Bend (1928)	Waukesha	1,290	1,287	−0.2	26	30
Big Falls (1925)	Waupaca	61	61	0.0	0	1
Birchwood (1921)	Washburn	442	439	−0.7	8	5
Birnamwood (1895)	Marathon, Shawano	818	814	−0.5	18	15
Biron (1910)	Wood.	839	837	−0.2	8	7
Black Creek (1904)	Outagamie	1,316	1,316	0.0	36	28
Black Earth (1901)[3]	Dane	1,338	1,334	−0.3	39	17
Blanchardville (1890)	Iowa, Lafayette	825	823	−0.2	6	10
Bloomfield (2011)[5].	Walworth.	—	4,623	—	—	—
Bloomington (1880)	Grant	735	748	1.8	11	8
Blue Mounds (1912).	Dane	855	863	0.9	17	11
Blue River (1916)	Grant	434	437	0.7	10	8
Boaz (1939)	Richland	156	156	0.0	2	1
Bonduel (1916)	Shawano	1,478	1,481	0.2	52	25
Bowler (1923)	Shawano	302	300	−0.7	70	10
Boyceville (1922)	Dunn	1,086	1,087	0.1	15	19
Boyd (1891)	Chippewa	552	549	−0.5	8	4
Brandon (1881)	Fond du Lac	879	876	−0.3	19	44
Bristol (2009)[3]	Kenosha	4,914	4,924	0.2	84	118
Brokaw (1903)	Marathon.	251	244	−2.8	5	6
Brooklyn (1905).	Dane, Green	1,401	1,407	0.4	51	82
Brown Deer (1955)[4]	Milwaukee	11,999	12,065	0.6	4,358	471
Brownsville (1952)	Dodge	581	582	0.2	8	3
Browntown (1890).	Green.	280	282	0.7	9	5
Bruce (1901).	Rusk	779	778	−0.1	7	8
Butler (1913)[3]	Waukesha	1,841	1,837	−0.2	105	89
Butternut (1903)	Ashland	375	366	−2.4	18	4
Cadott (1895)	Chippewa	1,437	1,442	0.3	25	7
Caledonia (2005)[3]	Racine	24,705	24,731	0.1	1,563	1,303
Cambria (1866)	Columbia.	767	768	0.1	12	93
Cambridge (1891)	Dane, Jefferson.	1,457	1,463	0.4	40	25
Cameron (1894)	Barron	1,783	1,791	0.4	41	35
Camp Douglas (1893)	Juneau	601	607	1.0	10	5
Campbellsport (1902)	Fond du Lac	2,016	2,012	−0.2	32	20
Cascade (1914).	Sheboygan	709	707	−0.3	6	27
Casco (1920).	Kewaunee	583	584	0.2	30	44
Cashton (1901).	Monroe.	1,102	1,103	0.1	18	48
Cassville (1882)[4].	Grant	947	948	0.1	11	3
Catawba (1922)	Price	110	107	−2.7	0	1
Cazenovia (1902)	Richland, Sauk.	318	326	2.5	6	5
Cecil (1905)	Shawano	570	569	−0.2	31	12
Cedar Grove (1899)	Sheboygan	2,113	2,104	−0.4	36	70
Centuria (1904)	Polk	948	937	−1.2	37	5
Chaseburg (1922)	Vernon	284	286	0.7	5	5
Chenequa (1928)[3]	Waukesha	590	586	−0.7	18	6
Clayton (1909).	Polk	571	572	0.2	14	12
Clear Lake (1894)	Polk	1,070	1,071	0.1	18	30

WISCONSIN VILLAGES
January 1, 2012–Continued

Village (Year Incorporated)[1]	County	2010 Census	2012 Estimate	Percent Change	2010 Nonwhite	2010 Hispanic or Latino Origin[2]
Cleveland (1958)	Manitowoc	1,485	1,514	2.0	27	129
Clinton (1882)[3]	Rock	2,154	2,146	–0.4	42	173
Clyman (1924)	Dodge	422	422	0.0	19	20
Cobb (1902)	Iowa	458	461	0.7	7	1
Cochrane (1910)	Buffalo	450	448	–0.4	4	3
Coleman (1903)	Marinette	724	723	–0.1	22	23
Colfax (1904)	Dunn	1,158	1,147	–0.9	26	20
Coloma (1939)	Waushara	450	456	1.3	0	4
Combined Locks (1920)[3]	Outagamie	3,328	3,372	1.3	92	66
Conrath (1915)	Rusk	95	97	2.1	9	0
Coon Valley (1907)	Vernon	765	769	0.5	9	5
Cottage Grove (1924)[3]	Dane	6,192	6,230	0.6	416	185
Couderay (1922)	Sawyer	88	90	2.3	22	1
Crivitz (1974)	Marinette	984	980	–0.4	24	8
Cross Plains (1920)[3]	Dane	3,538	3,547	0.3	83	57
Curtiss (1917)	Clark	216	214	–0.9	1	112
Dallas (1903)	Barron	409	409	0.0	8	8
Dane (1899)	Dane	995	1,015	2.0	31	43
Darien (1951)[3]	Walworth	1,580	1,587	0.4	33	348
De Soto (1886)	Crawford, Vernon	287	290	1.0	1	0
Deer Park (1913)	St. Croix	216	214	–0.9	5	3
Deerfield (1891)[3]	Dane	2,319	2,354	1.5	79	76
DeForest (1891)[3]	Dane	8,936	9,003	0.7	467	325
Denmark (1915)[3]	Brown	2,123	2,127	0.2	60	52
Dickeyville (1947)	Grant	1,061	1,060	–0.1	4	12
Dorchester (1901)	Clark, Marathon	876	875	–0.1	10	112
Dousman (1917)	Waukesha	2,302	2,317	0.7	64	66
Downing (1909)	Dunn	265	264	–0.4	1	1
Doylestown (1907)	Columbia	297	294	–1.0	3	6
Dresser (1919)	Polk	895	895	0.0	11	17
Eagle (1899)	Waukesha	1,950	1,947	–0.2	17	41
East Troy (1900)[3]	Walworth	4,281	4,283	0.0	107	172
Eastman (1909)	Crawford	428	427	–0.2	5	0
Eden (1912)	Fond du Lac	875	881	0.7	20	41
Edgar (1898)[3]	Marathon	1,479	1,476	–0.2	18	30
Egg Harbor (1964)[3]	Door	201	202	0.5	1	9
Eland (1905)	Shawano	202	200	–1.0	11	5
Elderon (1917)	Marathon	179	178	–0.6	10	7
Eleva (1902)	Trempealeau	670	675	0.7	6	9
Elk Mound (1909)	Dunn	878	876	–0.2	75	22
Elkhart Lake (1894)	Sheboygan	967	960	–0.7	13	16
Ellsworth (1887)	Pierce	3,284	3,272	–0.4	80	48
Elm Grove (1955)[4]	Waukesha	5,934	5,930	–0.1	253	118
Elmwood (1905)	Pierce	817	815	–0.2	8	25
Elmwood Park (1960)	Racine	497	498	0.2	37	25
Embarrass (1895)	Waupaca	404	399	–1.2	11	3
Endeavor (1946)	Marquette	468	465	–0.6	27	21
Ephraim (1919)[3]	Door	288	289	0.3	1	7
Ettrick (1948)	Trempealeau	524	522	–0.4	4	11
Exeland (1920)	Sawyer	196	198	1.0	17	2
Fairchild (1880)	Eau Claire	550	546	–0.7	22	12
Fairwater (1921)	Fond du Lac	371	370	–0.3	6	24
Fall Creek (1906)	Eau Claire	1,315	1,311	–0.3	27	3
Fall River (1903)	Columbia	1,712	1,714	0.1	56	34
Fenwood (1904)	Marathon	152	149	–2.0	0	4
Ferryville (1912)	Crawford	176	178	1.1	1	4
Fontana-on-Geneva Lake (1924)[3]	Walworth	1,672	1,674	0.1	18	35
Footville (1918)	Rock	808	807	–0.1	6	8
Forestville (1960)	Door	430	429	–0.2	8	8
Fox Point (1926)[4]	Milwaukee	6,701	6,644	–0.9	538	162
Francis Creek (1960)	Manitowoc	669	670	0.1	14	3
Frederic (1903)[3]	Polk	1,137	1,134	–0.3	37	12
Fredonia (1922)	Ozaukee	2,160	2,160	0.0	50	39
Fremont (1882)	Waupaca	679	679	0.0	7	14
Friendship (1907)	Adams	725	702	–3.2	24	29
Friesland (1946)	Columbia	356	355	–0.3	7	15
Gays Mills (1900)[3]	Crawford	491	493	0.4	13	1
Genoa (1935)	Vernon	253	252	–0.4	7	0
Genoa City (1901)	Kenosha, Walworth	3,042	3,052	0.3	74	199
Germantown (1927)[3]	Washington	19,749	19,803	0.3	1,334	400
Gilman (1914)	Taylor	410	408	–0.5	1	2
Glen Flora (1915)	Rusk	92	91	–1.1	1	0
Glenbeulah (1913)	Sheboygan	463	463	0.0	2	5
Grafton (1896)[3]	Ozaukee	11,459	11,464	0.0	421	266
Granton (1916)	Clark	355	351	–1.1	4	4
Grantsburg (1887)	Burnett	1,341	1,334	–0.5	65	15

WISCONSIN VILLAGES
January 1, 2012–Continued

		Population				
Village (Year Incorporated)[1]	County	2010 Census	2012 Estimate	Percent Change	2010 Nonwhite	2010 Hispanic or Latino Origin[2]
Gratiot (1891)	Lafayette	236	234	–0.8	5	0
Greendale (1939)[4]	Milwaukee	14,046	14,123	0.5	805	667
Gresham (1908)[3]	Shawano	586	582	–0.7	178	19
Hales Corners (1952)[3]	Milwaukee	7,692	7,683	–0.1	311	333
Hammond (1880)	St. Croix	1,922	1,924	0.1	58	56
Hancock (1902)	Waushara	417	413	–1.0	6	46
Hartland (1891)[3]	Waukesha	9,110	9,118	0.1	377	262
Hatley (1912)	Marathon	574	589	2.6	27	14
Haugen (1918)	Barron	287	285	–0.7	13	5
Hawkins (1922)	Rusk	305	301	–1.3	9	0
Hazel Green (1867)	Grant, Lafayette	1,256	1,262	0.5	22	17
Hewitt (1973)	Wood	828	825	–0.4	8	8
Highland (1873)	Iowa	842	840	–0.2	19	8
Hilbert (1898)[3]	Calumet	1,132	1,130	–0.2	23	89
Hixton (1920)	Jackson	433	430	–0.7	20	6
Hobart (2003)[3]	Brown	6,182	6,501	5.2	1,261	140
Hollandale (1910)	Iowa	288	290	0.7	5	0
Holmen (1946)[3]	La Crosse	9,005	9,171	1.8	827	96
Hortonville (1894)[3]	Outagamie	2,711	2,705	–0.2	69	42
Howard (1959)[3]	Brown, Outagamie	17,399	18,166	4.4	919	410
Howards Grove (1967)	Sheboygan	3,188	3,199	0.3	50	28
Hustisford (1870)	Dodge	1,123	1,121	–0.2	24	33
Hustler (1914)	Juneau	194	193	–0.5	4	3
Ingram (1907)	Rusk	78	78	0.0	1	0
Iola (1892)	Waupaca	1,301	1,290	0.8	13	15
Iron Ridge (1913)	Dodge	929	930	0.1	12	29
Ironton (1914)	Sauk	253	252	–0.4	7	4
Jackson (1912)[3]	Washington	6,753	6,782	0.4	158	147
Johnson Creek (1903)[3]	Jefferson	2,738	2,806	2.5	94	204
Junction City (1911)	Portage	439	439	0.0	23	14
Kekoskee (1958)	Dodge	161	160	–0.6	0	3
Kellnersville (1971)	Manitowoc	332	329	–0.9	1	0
Kendall (1894)	Monroe	472	473	0.2	11	10
Kennan (1903)	Price	135	132	–2.2	0	1
Kewaskum (1895)[3]	Fond du Lac, Washington	4,004	4,006	0.0	88	117
Kimberly (1910)[3]	Outagamie	6,468	6,559	1.4	317	150
Kingston (1923)	Green Lake	326	326	0.0	1	9
Knapp (1905)	Dunn	463	461	–0.4	10	1
Kohler (1912)	Sheboygan	2,120	2,121	0.0	72	49
Kronenwetter (2002)[3]	Marathon	7,210	7,266	0.8	341	101
La Farge (1899)	Vernon	746	699	–6.3	20	3
La Valle (1883)	Sauk	367	362	–1.4	7	8
Lac La Belle (1931)	Jefferson, Waukesha	290	290	0.0	4	1
Lake Delton (1954)	Sauk	2,914	2,914	0.0	200	447
Lake Hallie (2003)	Chippewa	6,448	6,647	3.1	316	110
Lake Nebagamon (1907)	Douglas	1,069	1,075	0.6	40	8
Lannon (1930)	Waukesha	1,107	1,104	–0.3	28	44
Lena (1921)	Oconto	564	562	–0.4	15	10
Lime Ridge (1910)	Sauk	162	161	–0.6	1	0
Linden (1900)	Iowa	549	546	–0.5	9	6
Little Chute (1899)[3]	Outagamie	10,449	10,432	–0.2	337	327
Livingston (1914)	Grant, Iowa	664	662	–0.3	2	0
Loganville (1917)	Sauk	300	298	–0.7	3	4
Lohrville (1910)	Waushara	402	400	–0.5	14	16
Lomira (1899)	Dodge	2,430	2,434	0.2	57	111
Lone Rock (1886)	Richland	888	887	–0.1	24	17
Lowell (1894)	Dodge	340	337	–0.9	2	5
Lublin (1915)	Taylor	118	118	0.0	1	1
Luck (1905)[3]	Polk	1,119	1,101	–1.6	26	19
Luxemburg (1908)	Kewaunee	2,515	2,560	1.8	35	63
Lyndon Station (1903)	Juneau	500	500	0.0	8	16
Lynxville (1899)	Crawford	132	133	0.8	1	5
Maiden Rock (1887)	Pierce	119	119	0.0	4	1
Maple Bluff (1930)[3]	Dane	1,313	1,314	0.1	45	19
Marathon City (1884)[3]	Marathon	1,524	1,529	0.3	26	27
Maribel (1963)	Manitowoc	351	350	–0.3	3	1
Marquette (1958)	Green Lake	150	152	1.3	0	2
Marshall (1905)	Dane	3,862	3,864	0.1	137	429
Mason (1925)	Bayfield	93	93	0.0	16	3
Mattoon (1901)[4]	Shawano	438	437	–0.2	30	70
Mazomanie (1885)	Dane	1,652	1,661	0.5	64	39
McFarland (1920)[3]	Dane	7,808	7,839	0.4	365	176
Melrose (1914)	Jackson	503	498	–1.0	7	9
Melvina (1922)	Monroe	104	104	0.0	4	0

WISCONSIN VILLAGES
January 1, 2012–Continued

Village (Year Incorporated)[1]	County	2010 Census	2012 Estimate	Percent Change	2010 Nonwhite	2010 Hispanic or Latino Origin[2]
Menomonee Falls (1892)[4]	Waukesha	35,626	35,680	0.2	2,789	697
Merrillan (1881)	Jackson	542	539	–0.6	38	37
Merrimac (1899)[3]	Sauk	420	424	1.0	7	13
Merton (1922)[3]	Waukesha	3,346	3,384	1.1	113	72
Milladore (1933)	Portage, Wood	276	278	0.7	3	19
Milltown (1910)	Polk	917	916	–0.1	19	11
Minong (1915)	Washburn	527	527	0.0	12	32
Mishicot (1950)	Manitowoc	1,442	1,439	–0.2	32	13
Montfort (1893)	Grant, Iowa	718	716	–0.3	6	9
Monticello (1891)	Green	1,217	1,218	0.1	22	24
Mount Calvary (1962)	Fond du Lac	762	572	–24.9	82	83
Mount Hope (1919)	Grant	225	227	0.9	2	17
Mount Horeb (1899)[3]	Dane	7,009	7,026	0.2	231	116
Mount Pleasant (2003)[3]	Racine	26,197	26,220	0.1	2,714	2,181
Mount Sterling (1936)	Crawford	211	210	–0.5	1	0
Mukwonago (1905)[3]	Walworth, Waukesha	7,355	7,390	0.5	164	234
Muscoda (1894)[3]	Grant, Iowa	1,299	1,287	–0.9	14	11
Nashotah (1957)	Waukesha	1,395	1,387	–0.6	46	19
Necedah (1870)[3]	Juneau	916	925	1.0	21	26
Nelson (1978)	Buffalo	374	373	–0.3	5	5
Nelsonville (1913)	Portage	155	153	–1.3	3	2
Neosho (1902)	Dodge	574	572	–0.3	16	4
Neshkoro (1906)	Marquette	434	431	–0.7	8	20
New Auburn (1902)	Barron, Chippewa	548	545	–0.5	15	0
New Glarus (1901)[3]	Green	2,172	2,167	–0.2	37	57
Newburg (1973)	Ozaukee, Washington	1,254	1,251	–0.2	17	14
Nichols (1967)	Outagamie	273	271	–0.7	8	5
North Bay (1951)	Racine	241	239	–0.8	11	16
North Fond du Lac (1903)[3]	Fond du Lac	5,014	5,016	0.0	165	214
North Freedom (1893)	Sauk	701	696	–0.7	10	18
North Hudson (1912)[3]	St. Croix	3,768	3,768	0.0	110	70
North Prairie (1919)	Waukesha	2,141	2,145	0.2	23	43
Norwalk (1894)	Monroe	638	636	–0.3	11	224
Oakdale (1988)	Monroe	297	294	–1.0	5	0
Oakfield (1903)	Fond du Lac	1,075	1,080	0.5	26	19
Oconomowoc Lake (1959)[3]	Waukesha	595	594	–0.2	12	11
Ogdensburg (1912)	Waupaca	185	183	–1.1	7	0
Oliver (1917)	Douglas	399	418	4.8	14	1
Ontario (1890)	Vernon	554	553	–0.2	13	82
Oostburg (1909)	Sheboygan	2,887	2,889	0.1	65	94
Oregon (1883)[3]	Dane	9,231	9,308	0.8	344	204
Orfordville (1900)	Rock	1,442	1,453	0.8	23	63
Osceola (1886)[3]	Polk	2,568	2,573	0.2	75	53
Oxford (1912)	Marquette	607	604	–0.5	14	29
Paddock Lake (1960)[3]	Kenosha	2,992	2,987	–0.2	70	157
Palmyra (1866)	Jefferson	1,781	1,778	–0.2	28	184
Pardeeville (1894)	Columbia	2,115	2,112	–0.1	48	34
Park Ridge (1938)	Portage	491	496	1.0	42	2
Patch Grove (1921)	Grant	198	201	1.5	0	8
Pepin (1860)	Pepin	837	828	–1.1	9	2
Pewaukee (1876)[3]	Waukesha	8,166	8,178	0.1	517	286
Pigeon Falls (1956)	Trempealeau	411	415	1.0	3	5
Plain (1912)	Sauk	773	770	–0.4	18	14
Plainfield (1882)	Waushara	862	860	–0.2	16	155
Pleasant Prairie (1989)[3]	Kenosha	19,719	19,850	0.7	1,141	1,332
Plover (1971)[3]	Portage	12,123	12,373	2.1	684	393
Plum City (1909)	Pierce	599	602	0.5	6	34
Poplar (1917)	Douglas	603	607	0.7	33	0
Port Edwards (1902)[3]	Wood	1,818	1,796	–1.2	75	42
Potosi (1887)	Grant	688	687	–0.1	8	4
Potter (1980)	Calumet	253	251	–0.8	4	7
Pound (1914)	Marinette	377	376	–0.3	5	27
Poynette (1892)[3]	Columbia	2,528	2,529	0.0	82	40
Prairie du Sac (1885)[3]	Sauk	3,972	3,999	0.7	105	190
Prairie Farm (1901)	Barron	473	471	–0.4	2	10
Prentice (1899)	Price	660	652	–1.2	15	7
Pulaski (1910)[3]	Brown, Oconto, Shawano	3,539	3,541	0.1	108	69
Radisson (1953)	Sawyer	241	242	0.4	37	12
Randolph (1870)	Columbia, Dodge	1,811	1,811	0.0	25	86
Random Lake (1907)	Sheboygan	1,594	1,591	–0.2	39	71
Readstown (1898)	Vernon	415	421	1.4	14	5
Redgranite (1904)	Waushara	2,149	2,155	0.3	448	65
Reedsville (1892)	Manitowoc	1,206	1,200	–0.5	27	94
Reeseville (1899)	Dodge	708	708	0.0	23	19
Rewey (1902)	Iowa	292	290	–0.7	1	0
Rib Lake (1902)	Taylor	910	898	–1.3	11	9

WISCONSIN VILLAGES
January 1, 2012–Continued

Village (Year Incorporated)[1]	County	2010 Census	2012 Estimate	Percent Change	2010 Nonwhite	2010 Hispanic or Latino Origin[2]
Ridgeland (1921)	Dunn	273	273	0.0	7	0
Ridgeway (1902)	Iowa	653	651	−0.3	1	33
Rio (1887)	Columbia	1,059	1,057	−0.2	20	15
River Hills (1930)[4]	Milwaukee	1,597	1,591	−0.4	254	66
Roberts (1945)	St. Croix	1,651	1,654	0.2	74	34
Rochester (1912)	Racine	3,682	3,676	−0.2	59	103
Rockdale (1914)	Dane	214	214	0.0	12	3
Rockland (1919)	La Crosse	594	610	2.7	2	4
Rock Springs (1894)	Sauk	362	319	−11.9	33	4
Rosendale (1915)	Fond du Lac	1,063	1,057	−0.6	25	32
Rosholt (1907)	Portage	506	507	0.2	4	16
Rothschild (1917)	Marathon	5,269	5,276	0.1	294	61
Rudolph (1960)	Wood	439	431	−1.8	6	8
St. Cloud (1909)	Fond du Lac	477	473	−0.8	5	13
St. Nazianz (1956)	Manitowoc	783	783	0.0	14	13
Sauk City (1854)[3]	Sauk	3,410	3,424	0.4	74	170
Saukville (1915)[3]	Ozaukee	4,451	4,464	0.3	132	131
Scandinavia (1894)	Waupaca	363	365	0.6	4	8
Sharon (1892)	Walworth	1,605	1,599	−0.4	28	265
Sheldon (1917)	Rusk	237	235	−0.8	4	13
Sherwood (1968)[3]	Calumet	2,713	2,740	1.0	67	40
Shiocton (1903)	Outagamie	921	925	0.4	17	83
Shorewood (1900)[4]	Milwaukee	13,162	13,174	0.1	1,416	447
Shorewood Hills (1927)[3]	Dane	1,565	1,567	0.1	132	60
Silver Lake (1926)	Kenosha	2,411	2,404	−0.3	51	102
Siren (1948)[3]	Burnett	806	798	−1.0	66	19
Sister Bay (1912)[3]	Door	876	892	1.8	13	27
Slinger (1869)[3]	Washington	5,068	5,113	0.9	117	116
Soldiers Grove (1888)	Crawford	592	587	−0.8	2	3
Solon Springs (1920)	Douglas	600	599	−0.2	11	4
Somerset (1915)	St. Croix	2,635	2,647	0.5	107	135
South Wayne (1911)	Lafayette	489	488	−0.2	3	2
Spencer (1902)	Marathon	1,925	1,932	0.4	28	38
Spring Green (1869)	Sauk	1,628	1,632	0.2	40	13
Spring Valley (1895)[3]	Pierce, St. Croix	1,352	1,366	1.0	15	18
Star Prairie (1900)	St. Croix	561	558	−0.5	17	9
Stetsonville (1949)	Taylor	541	538	−0.6	4	6
Steuben (1900)	Crawford	131	130	−0.8	1	0
Stockbridge (1908)	Calumet	636	631	−0.8	8	5
Stockholm (1903)	Pepin	66	66	0.0	0	0
Stoddard (1911)[3]	Vernon	774	777	0.4	7	6
Stratford (1910)	Marathon	1,578	1,589	0.7	16	25
Strum (1948)[3]	Trempealeau	1,114	1,120	0.5	8	74
Sturtevant (1907)[3]	Racine	6,970	7,016	0.7	1,333	424
Suamico (2003)[3]	Brown	11,346	11,461	1.0	242	211
Sullivan (1915)	Jefferson	669	667	−0.3	9	11
Summit (2010)[3,6]	Waukesha	4,674	4,680	0.1	–	–
Superior (1949)	Douglas	664	663	−0.2	16	7
Suring (1914)	Oconto	544	543	−0.2	44	9
Sussex (1924)[3]	Waukesha	10,518	10,573	0.5	431	249
Taylor (1919)	Jackson	476	477	0.2	6	16
Tennyson (1940)	Grant	355	353	−0.6	2	0
Theresa (1898)	Dodge	1,262	1,259	−0.2	21	22
Thiensville (1910)[3]	Ozaukee	3,235	3,228	−0.2	189	90
Tigerton (1896)	Shawano	741	733	−1.1	44	14
Tony (1911)	Rusk	113	113	0.0	8	1
Trempealeau (1867)[3]	Trempealeau	1,529	1,576	3.1	22	21
Turtle Lake (1898)[3]	Barron, Polk	1,050	1,042	−0.8	75	18
Twin Lakes (1937)[3]	Kenosha	5,989	5,993	0.1	126	283
Union Center (1913)	Juneau	200	198	−1.0	3	1
Union Grove (1893)[3]	Racine	4,915	4,900	−0.3	132	158
Unity (1903)	Clark, Marathon	343	337	−1.7	1	5
Valders (1919)	Manitowoc	962	961	−0.1	5	61
Vesper (1948)	Wood	584	582	−0.3	18	6
Viola (1899)[3]	Richland, Vernon	699	700	0.1	9	4
Waldo (1922)	Sheboygan	503	503	0.0	31	12
Wales (1922)	Waukesha	2,549	2,547	−0.1	43	46
Walworth (1901)	Walworth	2,816	2,813	−0.1	56	502
Warrens (1973)	Monroe	363	359	−1.1	18	3
Waterford (1906)[3]	Racine	5,368	5,368	0.0	105	159
Waunakee (1893)[3]	Dane	12,097	12,277	1.5	416	269
Wausaukee (1924)	Marinette	575	573	−0.3	20	16
Wauzeka (1890)	Crawford	711	703	−1.1	22	13
Webster (1916)	Burnett	653	653	0.0	57	13
West Baraboo (1956)	Sauk	1,414	1,411	−0.2	77	70

WISCONSIN VILLAGES
January 1, 2012–Continued

		Population				2010 Hispanic or Latino
Village (Year Incorporated)[1]	County	2010 Census	2012 Estimate	Percent Change	2010 Nonwhite	Origin[2]
West Milwaukee (1906)[3]	Milwaukee	4,206	4,200	−0.1	665	1,068
West Salem (1893)[3]	La Crosse	4,799	4,827	0.6	139	59
Westfield (1902)	Marquette	1,254	1,256	0.2	32	46
Weston (1996)[3]	Marathon	14,868	15,051	1.2	1,670	301
Weyerhaeuser (1906)	Rusk	238	235	−1.3	2	3
Wheeler (1922)	Dunn	348	348	0.0	12	5
White Lake (1926)	Langlade	363	361	−0.6	12	9
Whitefish Bay (1892)[4]	Milwaukee	14,110	14,105	0.0	1,060	399
Whitelaw (1958)	Manitowoc	757	756	−0.1	18	20
Whiting (1947)	Portage	1,724	1,702	−1.3	53	45
Wild Rose (1904)	Waushara	725	719	−0.8	12	35
Williams Bay (1919)[3]	Walworth	2,564	2,577	0.5	58	167
Wilson (1911)	St. Croix	184	186	1.1	4	1
Wilton (1890)	Monroe	504	503	−0.2	12	37
Wind Point (1954)[3]	Racine	1,723	1,717	−0.3	69	40
Winneconne (1887)[3]	Winnebago	2,383	2,377	−0.3	40	32
Winter (1973)	Sawyer	313	314	0.3	16	16
Withee (1901)	Clark	487	484	−0.6	5	11
Wittenberg (1893)	Shawano	1,081	1,063	−1.7	53	77
Wonewoc (1878)[3]	Juneau	816	816	0.0	13	11
Woodman (1917)	Grant	132	131	−0.8	8	4
Woodville (1911)	St. Croix	1,344	1,354	0.7	34	31
Wrightstown (1901)[3]	Brown, Outagamie	2,827	2,842	0.5	91	123
Wyeville (1923)	Monroe	147	147	0.0	4	2
Wyocena (1909)	Columbia	768	756	−1.6	10	15
Yuba (1935)	Richland	74	73	−1.4	0	0

[1]There are 405 villages in Wisconsin as of January 1, 2012.

[2]"Hispanic or Latino Origin" represents ethnicity and includes people of Cuban, Mexican, Puerto Rican, South or Central American, or other Spanish culture or origin, regardless of race.

[3]One of 97 villages with an administrator, holding either a full-time or combination position.

[4]One of 10 villages operating under the manager form of government, holding either a full-time or combination position.

[5]The Town of Bloomfield became a village on December 12, 2011. Data is not available for 2010 Census, Percent Change, 2010 Nonwhite, and 2010 Hispanic or Latino Origin.

[6]The Town of Summit became a village on July 29, 2010. 2010 Census population reflects prior status as a town. Data is not available for 2010 Nonwhite, and 2010 Hispanic or Latino Origin.

Sources: Wisconsin Department of Administration, Demographic Services Center, *Official Final Estimates, 1/1/2012, Wisconsin Municipalities, with Comparison to Census 2010,* April 2013; and League of Wisconsin Municipalities, *2011 Directory of Wisconsin City and Village Officials,* July 2011.

WISCONSIN CITIES AND VILLAGES
OVER 10,000 POPULATION

City or Village (County)	2010 Census	2012 Estimate	Percent Change	2012 Rank	2010 Nonwhite	2010 Hispanic or Latino Origin[2]
Cities						
Appleton (Calumet, Outagamie, Winnebago)	72,623	72,810	0.3%	6	7,124	3,643
Baraboo (Sauk)	12,048	11,952	−0.8	70	487	446
Beaver Dam (Dodge)	16,214	16,333	0.7	48	502	1,210
Beloit (Rock).	36,966	36,850	−0.3	19	7,149	6,332
Brookfield (Waukesha)	37,920	37,870	−0.1	18	3,545	853
Burlington (Racine, Walworth)	10,464	10,496	0.3	82	327	898
Cedarburg (Ozaukee)	11,412	11,445	0.3	74	367	197
Chippewa Falls (Chippewa)	13,661	13,704	0.3	60	605	221
Cudahy (Milwaukee)	18,267	18,247	−0.1	42	1,142	1,769
De Pere (Brown)	23,800	23,944	0.6	34	1,207	511
Eau Claire (Chippewa, Eau Claire)	65,883	66,170	0.4	9	5,116	1,268
Fitchburg (Dane).	25,260	25,246	−0.1	31	4,464	4,341
Fond du Lac (Fond du Lac)	43,021	43,100	0.2	15	2,695	2,742
Fort Atkinson (Jefferson)	12,368	12,380	0.1	66	315	1,128
Franklin (Milwaukee)	35,451	35,520	0.2	22	4,168	1,592
Glendale (Milwaukee)	12,872	12,808	−0.5	64	2,499	465
Green Bay (Brown)	104,057	104,250	0.2	3	13,912	13,896
Greenfield (Milwaukee)	36,720	36,740	0.1	20	3,043	3,087
Hartford (Dodge, Washington).	14,223	14,258	0.2	56	425	686
Hudson (St. Croix).	12,719	13,012	2.3	63	539	347
Janesville (Rock).	63,575	63,480	−0.1	10	3,689	3,421
Kaukauna (Outagamie)	15,462	15,627	1.1	51	654	407
Kenosha (Kenosha)	99,218	99,660	0.4	4	14,121	16,130
La Crosse (La Crosse)	51,320	51,590	0.5	12	4,885	1,012
Madison (Dane)	233,209	234,625	0.6	2	40,798	15,948
Manitowoc (Manitowoc)	33,736	33,750	0.0	24	2,486	1,695
Marinette (Marinette)	10,968	10,929	−0.4	78	271	149
Marshfield (Marathon, Wood)	19,118	19,061	−0.3	40	796	452
Menasha (Calumet, Winnebago).	17,353	17,407	0.3	46	954	1,204
Menomonie (Dunn)	16,264	16,101	−1.0	49	1,176	276
Mequon (Ozaukee).	23,132	23,225	0.4	36	1,760	467
Middleton (Dane)	17,442	17,903	2.6	45	1,764	984
Milwaukee (Milwaukee, Washington, Waukesha). . . .	594,833	595,425	0.1	1	271,607	103,007
Monroe (Green)	10,827	10,811	−0.1	80	252	526
Muskego (Waukesha)	24,135	24,217	0.3	33	529	545
Neenah (Winnebago)	25,501	25,723	0.9	30	1,163	967
New Berlin (Waukesha)	39,584	39,770	0.5	16	2,256	1,036
Oak Creek (Milwaukee).	34,451	34,530	0.2	23	3,282	2,582
Oconomowoc (Waukesha).	15,759	15,834	0.5	50	422	559
Onalaska (La Crosse)	17,736	18,006	1.5	44	1,539	276
Oshkosh (Winnebago)	66,083	66,325	0.4	8	5,539	1,770
Pewaukee (Waukesha).	13,195	13,464	2.0	61	667	281
Platteville (Grant)	11,224	11,338	1.0	76	535	179
Port Washington (Ozaukee)	11,250	11,287	0.3	77	457	347
Portage (Columbia)	10,324	10,298	−0.3	84	811	414
Racine (Racine)	78,860	78,830	0.0	5	20,362	16,309
River Falls (Pierce, St. Croix)	15,000	15,040	0.3	53	673	270
Sheboygan (Sheboygan).	49,288	49,110	−0.4	13	6,314	4,866
South Milwaukee (Milwaukee)	21,156	21,103	−0.3	37	1,100	1,699
Stevents Point (Portage)	26,717	27,129	1.5	28	1,946	696
Stoughton (Dane)	12,611	12,630	0.2	65	554	230
Sun Prairie (Dane)	29,364	29,840	1.6	26	3,749	1,253
Superior (Douglas).	27,244	27,146	−0.4	27	2,166	382
Two Rivers (Manitowoc)	11,712	11,669	−0.4	71	536	224
Verona (Dane)	10,619	10,856	2.2	79	617	258
Watertown (Dodge, Jefferson)	23,861	23,891	0.1	35	706	1,731
Waukesha (Waukesha).	70,718	71,020	0.4	7	5,321	8,529
Waupun (Dodge, Fond du Lac)	11,340	11,432	0.8	75	1,651	217
Wausau (Marathon)	39,106	39,160	0.1	17	5,891	1,149
Wauwatosa (Milwaukee).	46,396	46,320	−0.2	14	4,361	1,450
West Allis (Milwaukee)	60,411	60,300	−0.2	11	5,094	5,770
West Bend (Washington).	31,078	31,380	1.0	25	1,049	1,213
Whitewater (Jefferson, Walworth).	14,390	14,757	2.6	54	1,009	1,372
Wisconsin Rapids (Wood)	18,367	18,343	−0.1	41	1,186	535

WISCONSIN CITIES AND VILLAGES
OVER 10,000 POPULATION–Continued

City or Village (County)	Population[1]					2010 Hispanic or Latino Origin[2]
	2010 Census	2012 Estimate	Percent Change	2012 Rank	2010 Nonwhite	
Villages						
Allouez (Brown)	13,975	13,959	–0.1	59	1,252	383
Ashwaubenon (Brown)	16,963	16,977	0.1	47	1,375	471
Bellevue (Brown)	14,570	14,650	0.5	55	970	1,359
Brown Deer (Milwaukee)	11,999	12,065	0.6	69	4,358	471
Caledonia (Racine)	24,705	24,731	0.1	32	1,563	1,303
Germantown (Washington)	19,749	19,803	0.3	39	1,334	400
Grafton (Ozaukee)	11,459	11,464	0.0	72	421	266
Greendale (Milwaukee)	14,046	14,123	0.5	57	805	667
Howard (Brown, Outagamie)	17,399	18,166	4.4	43	919	410
Little Chute (Outagamie)	10,449	10,432	–0.2	83	337	327
Menomonee Falls (Waukesha)	35,626	35,680	0.2	21	2,789	697
Mount Pleasant (Racine)	26,197	26,220	0.1	29	2,714	2,181
Pleasant Prairie (Kenosha)	19,719	19,850	0.7	38	1,141	1,332
Plover (Portage)	12,123	12,373	2.1	67	684	393
Shorewood (Milwaukee)	13,162	13,174	0.1	62	1,416	447
Suamico (Brown)	11,346	11,461	1.0	73	242	112
Sussex (Waukesha)	10,518	10,573	0.5	81	431	249
Waunakee (Dane)	12,097	12,277	1.5	68	416	269
Weston (Marathon)	14,868	15,051	1.2	52	1,670	301
Whitefish Bay (Milwaukee)	14,110	14,105	0.0	58	1,060	399

[1]Race and ethnicity data have not been adjusted since the 2010 Census. Population estimates are based on the corrected 2010 Census totals.

[2]"Hispanic or Latino Origin" represents ethnicity and includes people of Cuban, Mexican, Puerto Rican, South or Central American, or other Spanish culture or origin, regardless of race.

Source: Wisconsin Department of Administration, Demographic Services Center, *Official Final Estimates, 1/1/2012, Wisconsin Municipalities, with Comparison to Census 2010,* April 2013.

WISCONSIN TOWNS OVER 2,500 POPULATION
2012 Estimate and 2010 U.S. Census

Town (County)	2012 Estimate	2010 Census	Percent Change	Town (County)	2012 Estimate	2010 Census	Percent Change
Addison (Washington)	3,486	3,495	−0.3%	Menomonie (Dunn)	3,386	3,366	0.6%
Alden (Polk)	2,791	2,786	0.2	Merrill (Lincoln)	2,986	2,980	0.2
Algoma (Winnebago)	6,889	6,822	1.0	Merton (Waukesha)	8,361	8,338	0.3
Arbor Vitae (Vilas)	3,321	3,316	0.2	Middleton (Dane)	5,950	5,877	1.2
Ashippun (Dodge)	2,562	2,559	0.1	Milton (Rock)	2,939	2,923	0.5
Barton (Washington)	2,642	2,637	0.2	Minocqua (Oneida)	4,463	4,453	0.2
Beaver Dam (Dodge)	3,966	3,962	0.1	Mukwa (Waupaca)	2,937	2,930	0.2
Beloit (Rock)	7,654	7,662	−0.1	Mukwonago (Waukesha)	7,976	7,959	0.2
Bristol (Dane)	3,819	3,765	1.4	Neenah (Winnebago)	3,306	3,237	2.1
Brockway (Jackson)	2,821	2,828	−0.2	Newbold (Oneida)	2,727	2,719	0.3
Brookfield (Waukesha)	6,102	6,116	−0.2	Norway (Racine)	7,961	7,948	0.2
Buchanan (Outagamie)	6,903	6,755	2.2	Oakland (Jefferson)	3,097	3,100	−0.1
Burke (Dane)	3,308	3,284	0.7	Oconomowoc (Waukesha)	8,505	8,408	1.2
Burlington (Racine)	6,451	6,502	−0.8	Onalaska (La Crosse)	5,644	5,623	0.4
Campbell (La Crosse)	4,325	4,314	0.3	Oneida (Outagamie)	4,679	4,678	0.0
Cedarburg (Ozaukee)	5,778	5,760	0.3	Oregon (Dane)	3,192	3,184	0.3
Center (Outagamie)	3,416	3,402	0.4	Osceola (Polk)	2,863	2,855	0.3
Chase (Oconto)	3,027	3,005	0.7	Ottawa (Waukesha)	3,867	3,859	0.2
Clayton (Winnebago)	3,974	3,951	0.6	Pacific (Columbia)	2,705	2,707	−0.1
Cottage Grove (Dane)	3,877	3,875	0.1	Pelican (Oneida)	2,778	2,764	0.5
Dale (Outagamie)	2,751	2,731	0.7	Peshtigo (Marinette)	4,064	4,057	0.2
Dayton (Waupaca)	2,748	2,748	0.0	Pine Lake (Oneida)	2,743	2,740	0.1
Delafield (Waukesha)	8,195	8,400	−2.4	Pittsfield (Brown)	2,631	2,608	0.9
Delavan (Walworth)	5,268	5,285	−0.3	Pleasant Springs (Dane)	3,166	3,154	0.4
Dover (Racine)	3,979	4,051	−1.8	Pleasant Valley (Eau Claire)	3,083	3,044	1.3
Dunn (Dane)	4,930	4,931	0.0	Plymouth (Sheboygan)	3,202	3,195	0.2
Eagle (Waukesha)	3,514	3,507	0.2	Polk (Washington)	3,941	3,937	0.1
Eagle Point (Chippewa)	3,071	3,053	0.6	Randall (Kenosha)	3,184	3,180	0.1
East Troy (Walworth)	4,025	4,021	0.1	Raymond (Racine)	3,886	3,870	0.4
Ellington (Outagamie)	2,799	2,758	1.5	Rib Mountain (Marathon)	6,836	6,825	0.2
Empire (Fond du Lac)	2,806	2,797	0.3	Rice Lake (Barron)	3,061	3,060	0.0
Erin (Washington)	3,760	3,747	0.3	Richfield (Washington)	11,339	11,300	0.3
Farmington (Washington)	4,029	4,014	0.4	Richmond (St. Croix)	3,302	3,272	0.9
Farmington (Waupaca)	3,988	3,974	0.4	Rock (Rock)	3,195	3,196	0.0
Fond du Lac (Fond du Lac)	3,375	3,015	11.9	Rome (Adams)	2,728	2,720	0.3
Freedom (Outagamie)	5,910	5,842	1.2	St. Joseph (St. Croix)	3,852	3,842	0.3
Friendship (Fond du Lac)	2,691	2,675	0.6	Salem (Kenosha)	12,036	12,067	−0.3
Fulton (Rock)	3,257	3,252	0.2	Saratoga (Wood)	5,139	5,142	−0.1
Genesee (Waukesha)	7,331	7,340	−0.1	Scott (Brown)	3,567	3,545	0.6
Geneva (Walworth)	4,989	4,993	−0.1	Sevastopol (Door)	2,637	2,628	0.3
Grafton (Ozaukee)	4,086	4,053	0.8	Seymour (Eau Claire)	3,222	3,209	0.4
Grand Chute (Outagamie)	21,288	20,919	1.8	Sheboygan (Sheboygan)	7,376	7,271	1.4
Grand Rapids (Wood)	7,659	7,646	0.2	Shelby (La Crosse)	4,707	4,715	−0.2
Greenbush (Sheboygan)	2,575	2,565	0.4	Somers (Kenosha)	9,463	9,597	−1.4
Greenville (Outagamie)	10,602	10,309	2.8	Somerset (St. Croix)	4,054	4,036	0.4
Harmony (Rock)	2,576	2,569	0.3	Sparta (Monroe)	3,151	3,128	0.7
Harrison (Calumet)	10,912	10,839	0.7	Springfield (Dane)	2,749	2,734	0.5
Hartford (Washington)	3,600	3,609	−0.2	Stanley (Barron)	2,543	2,546	−0.1
Hayward (Sawyer)	3,569	3,567	0.1	Star Prairie (St. Croix)	3,515	3,504	0.3
Holland (La Crosse)	3,790	3,701	2.4	Stephenson (Marinette)	3,040	3,006	1.1
Hudson (St. Croix)	8,499	8,461	0.4	Stettin (Marathon)	2,557	2,554	0.1
Hull (Portage)	5,354	5,346	0.1	Stockton (Portage)	2,944	2,917	0.9
Ixonia (Jefferson)	4,483	4,385	2.2	Sugar Creek (Walworth)	3,938	3,943	−0.1
Jackson (Washington)	4,199	4,134	1.6	Taycheedah (Fond du Lac)	4,252	4,205	1.1
Janesville (Rock)	3,430	3,434	−0.1	Trenton (Washington)	4,727	4,732	−0.1
Koshkonong (Jefferson)	3,681	3,692	−0.3	Troy (St. Croix)	4,731	4,705	0.6
Lac du Flambeau (Vilas)	3,453	3,441	0.3	Union (Eau Claire)	2,694	2,663	1.2
Lafayette (Chippewa)	5,800	5,765	0.6	Vernon (Waukesha)	7,603	7,601	0.0
Lawrence (Brown)	4,416	4,284	3.1	Washington (Eau Claire)	7,187	7,182	0.1
Ledgeview (Brown)	6,967	6,555	6.3	Waterford (Racine)	6,338	6,344	−0.1
Lima (Sheboygan)	2,985	2,982	0.1	Waukesha (Waukesha)	9,142	9,133	0.1
Lisbon (Waukesha)	10,184	10,157	0.3	Wescott (Shawano)	3,195	3,183	0.4
Little Suamico (Oconto)	4,894	4,799	2.0	West Bend (Washington)	4,776	4,774	0.0
Lodi (Columbia)	3,281	3,273	0.2	Westport (Dane)	3,962	3,950	0.3
Lyons (Walworth)	3,693	3,698	−0.1	Wheatland (Kenosha)	3,360	3,373	−0.4
Madison (Dane)	6,278	6,279	0.0	Wheaton (Chippewa)	2,714	2,701	0.5
Medford (Taylor)	2,611	2,606	0.2	Wilson (Sheboygan)	3,356	3,330	0.8
Menasha (Winnebago)	18,545	18,498	0.3	Windsor (Dane)	6,469	6,345	2.0
Menominee (Menominee)	4,214	4,232	−0.4	Yorkville (Racine)	3,080	3,071	0.3

Source: Wisconsin Department of Administration, Demographic Services Center, *Official Final Estimates, 1/1/2012, Wisconsin Municipalities, with Comparison to Census 2010,* March 2013.

WISCONSIN POPULATION
BY COUNTY AND MUNCIPALITY
April 1, 2010 and January 1, 2012

County and Municipality	2010 Census	2012 Estimate	Percent Change	County and Municipality	2010 Census	2012 Estimate	Percent Change
ADAMS COUNTY	20,875	20,797	−0.37%	Barnes, town	769	771	0.26
Adams, city	1,967	1,946	−1.07	Bayfield, city	487	488	0.21
Adams, town	1,345	1,348	0.22	Bayfield, town	680	688	1.18
Big Flats, town	1,018	1,021	0.29	Bayview, town	487	485	−0.41
Colburn, town	223	225	0.90	Bell, town	263	265	0.76
Dell Prairie, town	1,590	1,604	0.88	Cable, town	825	828	0.36
Easton, town	1,130	1,135	0.44	Clover, town	223	221	−0.90
Friendship, village	725	702	−3.17	Delta, town	273	271	−0.73
Jackson, town	1,003	1,001	−0.20	Drummond, town	463	453	−2.16
Leola, town	308	307	−0.32	Eileen, town	681	681	0.00
Lincoln, town	296	292	−1.35	Grand View, town	468	471	0.64
Monroe, town	398	406	2.01	Hughes, town	383	386	0.78
New Chester, town	2,254	2,170	−3.73	Iron River, town	1,123	1,136	1.16
New Haven, town	655	660	0.76	Kelly, town	463	464	0.22
Preston, town	1,393	1,392	−0.07	Keystone, town	378	376	−0.53
Quincy, town	1,163	1,169	0.52	Lincoln, town	287	287	0.00
Richfield, town	158	158	0.00	Mason, town	315	315	0.00
Rome, town	2,720	2,728	0.29	Mason, village	93	93	0.00
Springville, town	1,318	1,319	0.08	Namakagon, town	246	247	0.41
Strongs Prairie, town	1,150	1,153	0.26	Orienta, town	122	122	0.00
Wisconsin Dells (part), city	61	61	0.00	Oulu, town	527	525	−0.38
				Pilsen, town	210	215	2.38
ASHLAND COUNTY	16,157	16,063	−0.58	Port Wing, town	368	373	1.36
Agenda, town	422	422	0.00	Russell, town	1,279	1,285	0.47
Ashland (part), city	8,216	8,132	−1.02	Tripp, town	231	237	2.60
Ashland, town	594	588	−1.01	Washburn, city	2,117	2,109	−0.38
Butternut, village	375	366	−2.40	Washburn, town	530	536	1.13
Chippewa, town	374	377	0.80				
Gingles, town	778	777	−0.13	BROWN COUNTY	248,007	250,281	0.92
Gordon, town	283	286	1.06	Allouez, village	13,975	13,959	−0.11
Jacobs, town	722	716	−0.83	Ashwaubenon, village	16,963	16,977	0.08
La Pointe, town	261	265	1.53	Bellevue, village	14,570	14,650	0.55
Marengo, town	390	395	1.28	De Pere, city	23,800	23,944	0.61
Mellen, city	731	719	−1.64	Denmark, village	2,123	2,127	0.19
Morse, town	493	495	0.41	Eaton, town	1,508	1,522	0.93
Peeksville, town	141	141	0.00	Glenmore, town	1,135	1,131	−0.35
Sanborn, town	1,331	1,325	−0.45	Green Bay, city	104,057	104,250	0.19
Shanagolden, town	125	127	1.60	Green Bay, town	2,035	2,047	0.59
White River, town	921	932	1.19	Hobart, village	6,182	6,501	5.16
				Holland, town	1,519	1,527	0.53
BARRON COUNTY	45,870	45,928	0.13	Howard (part), village	17,399	18,166	4.41
Almena, town	858	853	−0.58	Humboldt, town	1,311	1,309	−0.15
Almena, village	677	665	−1.77	Lawrence, town	4,284	4,416	3.08
Arland, town	789	809	2.53	Ledgeview, town	6,555	6,967	6.29
Barron, city	3,423	3,430	0.20	Morrison, town	1,599	1,597	−0.13
Barron, town	873	871	−0.23	New Denmark, town	1,541	1,552	0.71
Bear Lake, town	659	658	−0.15	Pittsfield, town	2,608	2,631	0.88
Cameron, village	1,783	1,791	0.45	Pulaski (part), village	3,321	3,323	0.06
Cedar Lake, town	948	961	1.37	Rockland, town	1,734	1,735	0.06
Chetek, city	2,221	2,221	0.00	Scott, town	3,545	3,567	0.62
Chetek, town	1,644	1,656	0.73	Suamico, village	11,346	11,461	1.01
Clinton, town	879	882	0.34	Wrightstown, town	2,221	2,231	0.45
Crystal Lake, town	757	754	−0.40	Wrightstown (part), village	2,676	2,691	0.56
Cumberland, city	2,170	2,166	−0.18				
Cumberland, town	876	873	−0.34	BUFFALO COUNTY	13,587	13,649	0.46
Dallas, town	565	567	0.35	Alma, city	781	816	4.48
Dallas, village	409	409	0.00	Alma, town	297	296	−0.34
Dovre, town	849	853	0.47	Belvidere, town	396	395	−0.25
Doyle, town	453	459	1.32	Buffalo, town	705	702	−0.43
Haugen, village	287	285	−0.70	Buffalo City, city	1,023	1,017	−0.59
Lakeland, town	975	983	0.82	Canton, town	305	308	0.98
Maple Grove, town	979	984	0.51	Cochrane, village	450	448	−0.44
Maple Plain, town	803	811	1.00	Cross, town	377	377	0.00
New Auburn (part), village	20	22	10.00	Dover, town	486	488	0.41
Oak Grove, town	948	952	0.42	Fountain City, city	859	884	2.91
Prairie Farm, town	573	576	0.52	Gilmanton, town	426	430	0.94
Prairie Farm, village	473	471	−0.42	Glencoe, town	485	480	−1.03
Prairie Lake, town	1,532	1,543	0.72	Lincoln, town	162	164	1.23
Rice Lake, city	8,419	8,405	−0.17	Maxville, town	309	304	−1.62
Rice Lake, town	3,060	3,061	0.03	Milton, town	534	542	1.50
Sioux Creek, town	655	650	−0.76	Modena, town	354	354	0.00
Stanfold, town	719	720	0.14	Mondovi, city	2,777	2,773	−0.14
Stanley, town	2,546	2,543	−0.12	Mondovi, town	469	472	0.64
Sumner, town	798	805	0.88	Montana, town	284	283	−0.35
Turtle Lake, town	624	625	0.16	Naples, town	691	697	0.87
Turtle Lake (part), village	957	950	−0.73	Nelson, town	571	581	1.75
Vance Creek, town	669	664	−0.75	Nelson, village	374	373	−0.27
				Waumandee, town	472	465	−1.48
BAYFIELD COUNTY	15,014	15,052	0.25				
Ashland (part), city	0	0	0.00	BURNETT COUNTY	15,457	15,457	0.00
Barksdale, town	723	724	0.14	Anderson, town	398	397	−0.25

WISCONSIN POPULATION
BY COUNTY AND MUNCIPALITY
April 1, 2010 and January 1, 2012–Continued

County and Municipality	2010 Census	2012 Estimate	Percent Change	County and Municipality	2010 Census	2012 Estimate	Percent Change
Blaine, town	197	196	-0.51	CLARK COUNTY	34,690	34,706	0.05
Daniels, town	649	649	0.00	Abbotsford (part), city	1,616	1,608	-0.50
Dewey, town	516	512	-0.78	Beaver, town	885	892	0.79
Grantsburg, town.	1,136	1,137	0.09	Butler, town	96	95	-1.04
Grantsburg, village.	1,341	1,334	-0.52	Colby (part), city	1,354	1,339	-1.11
Jackson, town	773	778	0.65	Colby, town	874	880	0.69
La Follette, town.	536	533	-0.56	Curtiss, village	216	214	-0.93
Lincoln, town	309	307	-0.65	Dewhurst, town	323	326	0.93
Meenon, town	1,163	1,158	-0.43	Dorchester (part), village	871	870	-0.11
Oakland, town	827	830	0.36	Eaton, town	712	710	-0.28
Roosevelt, town	199	199	0.00	Foster, town	95	96	1.05
Rusk, town	409	410	0.24	Fremont, town	1,265	1,261	-0.32
Sand Lake, town	531	534	0.56	Grant, town	916	920	0.44
Scott, town	494	501	1.42	Granton, village	355	351	-1.13
Siren, town	936	940	0.43	Green Grove, town	756	757	0.13
Siren, village	806	798	-0.99	Greenwood, city	1,026	1,022	-0.39
Swiss, town	790	793	0.38	Hendren, town	499	498	-0.20
Trade Lake, town	823	828	0.61	Hewett, town	293	292	-0.34
Union, town	340	340	0.00	Hixon, town	808	812	0.50
Webb Lake, town	311	312	0.32	Hoard, town	841	828	-1.55
Webster, village	653	653	0.00	Levis, town.	492	494	0.41
West Marshland, town	367	367	0.00	Longwood, town.	858	862	0.47
Wood River, town	953	951	-0.21	Loyal, city	1,261	1,256	-0.40
				Loyal, town	826	829	0.36
CALUMET COUNTY.	48,971	49,168	0.40	Lynn, town.	861	865	0.46
Appleton (part), city	11,088	11,080	-0.07	Mayville, town.	961	959	-0.21
Brillion, city	3,148	3,183	1.11	Mead, town	321	321	0.00
Brillion, town	1,486	1,494	0.54	Mentor, town.	584	586	0.34
Brothertown, town	1,329	1,323	-0.45	Neillsville, city.	2,463	2,438	-1.02
Charlestown, town	775	776	0.13	Owen, city	940	939	-0.11
Chilton, city	3,933	3,932	-0.03	Pine Valley, town.	1,157	1,165	0.69
Chilton, town.	1,143	1,140	-0.26	Reseburg, town.	776	780	0.52
[1]Harrison, town	10,839	10,912	0.67	Seif, town	172	172	0.00
Hilbert, village	1,132	1,130	-0.18	Sherman, town.	882	887	0.57
[1]Kaukauna (part), city	0	0	0.00	Sherwood, town	220	224	1.82
Kiel (part), city.	309	315	1.94	Stanley (part), city	6	6	0.00
Menasha (part), city	2,209	2,278	3.12	Thorp, city	1,621	1,636	0.93
New Holstein, city	3,236	3,234	-0.06	Thorp, town	808	818	1.24
New Holstein, town	1,508	1,510	0.13	Unity, town.	878	890	1.37
Potter, village	253	251	-0.79	Unity (part), village	139	137	-1.44
Rantoul, town	798	792	-0.75	Warner, town.	669	672	0.45
Sherwood, village	2,713	2,740	1.00	Washburn, town	290	294	1.38
Stockbridge, town	1,456	1,469	0.89	Weston, town.	699	698	-0.14
Stockbridge, village	636	631	-0.79	Withee, town.	966	974	0.83
Woodville, town	980	978	-0.20	Withee, village.	487	484	-0.62
				Worden, town	666	667	0.15
CHIPPEWA COUNTY	62,415	62,777	0.58	York, town	886	882	-0.45
Anson, town	2,076	2,090	0.67				
Arthur, town	759	765	0.79	COLUMBIA COUNTY	56,833	56,835	0.00
Auburn, town	697	696	-0.14	Arlington, town	806	801	-0.62
Birch Creek, town	517	520	0.58	Arlington, village	819	823	0.49
Bloomer, city	3,539	3,539	0.00	Caledonia, town	1,378	1,391	0.94
Bloomer, town	1,050	1,052	0.19	Cambria, village	767	768	0.13
Boyd, village	552	549	-0.54	Columbus (part), city	4,991	5,026	0.70
Cadott, village	1,437	1,442	0.35	Columbus, town	646	643	-0.46
Chippewa Falls, city	13,661	13,704	0.31	Courtland, town	525	529	0.76
Cleveland, town	864	865	0.12	Dekorra, town	2,311	2,309	-0.09
Colburn, town	856	862	0.70	Doylestown, village	297	294	-1.01
Cooks Valley, town	805	819	1.74	Fall River, village	1,712	1,714	0.12
Cornell, city	1,467	1,471	0.27	Fort Winnebago, town	825	821	-0.48
Delmar, town.	936	943	0.75	Fountain Prairie, town	887	885	-0.23
Eagle Point, town	3,053	3,071	0.59	Friesland, village.	356	355	-0.28
Eau Claire (part), city	1,981	1,980	-0.05	Hampden, town	574	572	-0.35
Edson, town	1,089	1,087	-0.18	Leeds, town	774	771	-0.39
Estella, town	433	430	-0.69	Lewiston, town.	1,225	1,227	0.16
Goetz, town	762	766	0.52	Lodi, city.	3,050	3,049	-0.03
Hallie, town	161	167	3.73	Lodi, town	3,273	3,281	0.24
Howard, town	798	795	-0.38	Lowville, town	1,008	1,010	0.20
Lafayette, town	5,765	5,800	0.61	Marcellon, town	1,102	1,094	-0.73
Lake Hallie, village	6,448	6,647	3.09	Newport, town.	586	586	0.00
Lake Holcombe, town	1,031	1,031	0.00	Otsego, town	693	694	0.14
New Auburn (part), village	528	523	-0.95	Pacific, town	2,707	2,705	-0.07
Ruby, town	494	489	-1.01	Pardeeville, village.	2,115	2,112	-0.14
Sampson, town.	892	901	1.01	Portage, city	10,324	10,298	-0.25
Sigel, town	1,044	1,042	-0.19	Poynette, village	2,528	2,529	0.04
Stanley (part), city	3,602	3,577	-0.69	Randolph, town	769	767	-0.26
Tilden, town	1,485	1,499	0.94	Randolph (part), village	472	470	-0.42
Wheaton, town.	2,701	2,714	0.48	Rio, village.	1,059	1,057	-0.19
Woodmohr, town.	932	941	0.97	Scott, town	905	911	0.66
				Springvale, town.	520	518	-0.38
				West Point, town.	1,955	1,970	0.77

WISCONSIN POPULATION
BY COUNTY AND MUNCIPALITY
April 1, 2010 and January 1, 2012–Continued

County and Municipality	2010 Census	2012 Estimate	Percent Change
Wisconsin Dells (part), city	2,440	2,432	–0.33
Wyocena, town.	1,666	1,667	0.06
Wyocena, village.	768	756	–1.56
CRAWFORD COUNTY.	16,644	16,638	–0.04
Bell Center, village.	117	117	0.00
Bridgeport, town	990	993	0.30
Clayton, town.	958	952	–0.63
De Soto (part), village.	108	108	0.00
Eastman, town	739	741	0.27
Eastman, village.	428	427	–0.23
Ferryville, village	176	178	1.14
Freeman, town	686	694	1.17
Gays Mills, village.	491	493	0.41
Haney, town	309	307	–0.65
Lynxville, village	132	133	0.76
Marietta, town	470	471	0.21
Mount Sterling, village	211	210	–0.47
Prairie du Chien, city	5,911	5,901	–0.17
Prairie du Chien, town.	1,073	1,070	–0.28
Scott, town.	462	458	–0.87
Seneca, town.	866	878	1.39
Soldiers Grove, village.	592	587	–0.84
Steuben, village	131	130	–0.76
Utica, town.	661	668	1.06
Wauzeka, town.	422	419	–0.71
Wauzeka, village.	711	703	–1.13
DANE COUNTY	488,073	491,555	0.71
Albion, town.	1,951	1,958	0.36
Belleville (part), village	1,848	1,850	0.11
Berry, town.	1,127	1,135	0.71
Black Earth, town	483	486	0.62
Black Earth, village	1,338	1,334	–0.30
Blooming Grove, town.	1,815	1,815	0.00
Blue Mounds, town	968	971	0.31
Blue Mounds, village	855	863	0.94
Bristol, town	3,765	3,819	1.43
Brooklyn (part), village	936	943	0.75
Burke, town	3,284	3,308	0.73
Cambridge (part), village	1,348	1,354	0.45
Christiana, town	1,235	1,238	0.24
Cottage Grove, town.	3,875	3,877	0.05
Cottage Grove, village.	6,192	6,230	0.61
Cross Plains, town	1,507	1,511	0.27
Cross Plains, village	3,538	3,547	0.25
Dane, town.	990	993	0.30
Dane, village.	995	1,015	2.01
Deerfield, town.	1,585	1,578	–0.44
Deerfield, village.	2,319	2,354	1.51
DeForest, village.	8,936	9,003	0.75
Dunkirk, town	1,945	1,945	0.00
Dunn, town.	4,931	4,930	–0.02
Edgerton (part), city	97	103	6.19
Fitchburg, city	25,260	25,246	–0.06
Madison, city.	233,209	234,625	0.61
Madison, town.	6,279	6,278	–0.02
Maple Bluff, village	1,313	1,314	0.08
Marshall, village	3,862	3,864	0.05
Mazomanie, town	1,090	1,091	0.09
Mazomanie, village.	1,652	1,661	0.54
McFarland, village.	7,808	7,839	0.40
Medina, town	1,376	1,377	0.07
Middleton, city.	17,442	17,903	2.64
Middleton, town	5,877	5,950	1.24
Monona, city.	7,533	7,523	–0.13
Montrose, town	1,081	1,084	0.28
Mount Horeb, village	7,009	7,026	0.24
Oregon, town.	3,184	3,192	0.25
Oregon, village.	9,231	9,308	0.83
Perry, town.	729	734	0.69
Pleasant Springs, town.	3,154	3,166	0.38
Primrose, town.	731	729	–0.27
Rockdale, village.	214	214	0.00
Roxbury, town	1,794	1,790	–0.22
Rutland, town	1,966	1,973	0.36
Shorewood Hills, village.	1,565	1,567	0.13
Springdale, town.	1,904	1,914	0.53
Springfield, town.	2,734	2,749	0.55
Stoughton, city.	12,611	12,630	0.15
Sun Prairie, city	29,364	29,840	1.62

County and Municipality	2010 Census	2012 Estimate	Percent Change
Sun Prairie, town.	2,326	2,315	–0.47
Vermont, town	819	818	–0.12
Verona, city	10,619	10,856	2.23
Verona, town.	1,948	1,966	0.92
Vienna, town.	1,482	1,490	0.54
Waunakee, village	12,097	12,277	1.49
Westport, town.	3,950	3,962	0.30
Windsor, town	6,345	6,469	1.95
York, town	652	655	0.46
DODGE COUNTY	88,759	88,692	–0.08
Ashippun, town	2,559	2,562	0.12
Beaver Dam, city	16,214	16,333	0.73
Beaver Dam, town.	3,962	3,966	0.10
Brownsville, village.	581	582	0.17
Burnett, town.	904	902	–0.22
Calamus, town.	1,048	1,046	–0.19
Chester, town.	687	690	0.44
Clyman, town	774	775	0.13
Clyman, village	422	422	0.00
Columbus (part), city	0	0	0.00
Elba, town.	996	996	0.00
Emmet, town.	1,302	1,307	0.38
Fox Lake, city	1,519	1,514	–0.33
Fox Lake, town	2,465	2,230	–9.53
Hartford (part), city	0	0	0.00
Herman, town	1,108	1,105	–0.27
Horicon, city.	3,655	3,649	–0.16
Hubbard, town.	1,774	1,777	0.17
Hustisford, town.	1,373	1,384	0.80
Hustisford, village.	1,123	1,121	–0.18
Iron Ridge, village.	929	930	0.11
Juneau, city	2,814	2,776	–1.35
Kekoskee, village	161	160	–0.62
Lebanon, town.	1,659	1,658	–0.06
Leroy, town	1,002	995	–0.70
Lomira, town.	1,137	1,137	0.00
Lomira, village.	2,430	2,434	0.16
Lowell, town.	1,190	1,194	0.34
Lowell, village.	340	337	–0.88
Mayville, city	5,154	5,139	–0.29
Neosho, village	574	572	–0.35
Oak Grove, town.	1,080	1,075	–0.46
Portland, town.	1,079	1,089	0.93
Randolph (part), village	1,339	1,341	0.15
Reeseville, village	708	708	0.00
Rubicon, town.	2,207	2,206	–0.05
Shields, town.	554	553	–0.18
Theresa, town	1,075	1,076	0.09
Theresa, village	1,262	1,259	–0.24
Trenton, town	1,293	1,305	0.93
Watertown (part), city	8,459	8,447	–0.14
Waupun (part), city	7,864	7,947	1.06
Westford, town.	1,228	1,231	0.24
Williamstown, town	755	762	0.93
DOOR COUNTY	27,785	27,867	0.30
Baileys Harbor, town	1,022	1,027	0.49
Brussels, town	1,136	1,135	–0.09
Clay Banks, town	382	383	0.26
Egg Harbor, town	1,342	1,349	0.52
Egg Harbor, village	201	202	0.50
Ephraim, village	288	289	0.35
Forestville, town.	1,096	1,101	0.46
Forestville, village.	430	429	–0.23
Gardner, town	1,194	1,208	1.17
Gibraltar, town.	1,021	1,030	0.88
Jacksonport, town	705	703	–0.28
Liberty Grove, town	1,734	1,743	0.52
Nasewaupee, town.	2,061	2,079	0.87
Sevastopol, town.	2,628	2,637	0.34
Sister Bay, village	876	892	1.83
Sturgeon Bay, city	9,144	9,132	–0.13
Sturgeon Bay, town	818	818	0.00
Union, town	999	999	0.00
Washington, town	708	711	0.42
DOUGLAS COUNTY	44,159	44,191	0.07
Amnicon, town.	1,155	1,164	0.78
Bennett, town	597	608	1.84
Brule, town.	656	665	1.37

WISCONSIN POPULATION
BY COUNTY AND MUNCIPALITY
April 1, 2010 and January 1, 2012–Continued

County and Municipality	2010 Census	2012 Estimate	Percent Change
Cloverland, town	210	209	-0.48
Dairyland, town	184	184	0.00
Gordon, town	636	637	0.16
Hawthorne, town	1,136	1,128	-0.70
Highland, town	311	312	0.32
Lake Nebagamon, village	1,069	1,075	0.56
Lakeside, town	693	701	1.15
Maple, town	744	749	0.67
Oakland, town	1,136	1,150	1.23
Oliver, village	399	418	4.76
Parkland, town	1,220	1,227	0.57
Poplar, village	603	607	0.66
Solon Springs, town	910	919	0.99
Solon Springs, village	600	599	-0.17
Summit, town	1,063	1,071	0.75
Superior, city	27,244	27,146	-0.36
Superior, town	2,166	2,186	0.92
Superior, village	664	663	-0.15
Wascott, town	763	773	1.31
DUNN COUNTY	43,857	43,853	-0.01
Boyceville, village	1,086	1,087	0.09
Colfax, town	1,186	1,212	2.19
Colfax, village	1,158	1,147	-0.95
Downing, village	265	264	-0.38
Dunn, town	1,524	1,532	0.52
Eau Galle, town	757	761	0.53
Elk Mound, town	1,792	1,816	1.34
Elk Mound, village	878	876	-0.23
Grant, town	385	386	0.26
Hay River, town	558	560	0.36
Knapp, village	463	461	-0.43
Lucas, town	764	765	0.13
Menomonie, city	16,264	16,101	-1.00
Menomonie, town	3,366	3,386	0.59
New Haven, town	677	676	-0.15
Otter Creek, town	501	501	0.00
Peru, town	242	242	0.00
Red Cedar, town	2,086	2,110	1.15
Ridgeland, village	273	273	0.00
Rock Creek, town	1,000	1,005	0.50
Sand Creek, town	570	569	-0.18
Sheridan, town	454	456	0.44
Sherman, town	849	860	1.30
Spring Brook, town	1,558	1,569	0.71
Stanton, town	791	794	0.38
Tainter, town	2,319	2,351	1.38
Tiffany, town	618	624	0.97
Weston, town	594	592	-0.34
Wheeler, village	348	348	0.00
Wilson, town	531	529	-0.38
EAU CLAIRE COUNTY	98,736	99,260	0.53
Altoona, city	6,706	6,820	1.70
Augusta, city	1,550	1,545	-0.32
Bridge Creek, town	1,900	1,896	-0.21
Brunswick, town	1,624	1,644	1.23
Clear Creek, town	821	832	1.34
Drammen, town	783	789	0.77
Eau Claire (part), city	63,902	64,190	0.45
Fairchild, town	343	345	0.58
Fairchild, village	550	546	-0.73
Fall Creek, village	1,315	1,311	-0.30
Lincoln, town	1,096	1,106	0.91
Ludington, town	1,063	1,064	0.09
Otter Creek, town	500	498	-0.40
Pleasant Valley, town	3,044	3,083	1.28
Seymour, town	3,209	3,222	0.41
Union, town	2,663	2,694	1.16
Washington, town	7,182	7,187	0.07
Wilson, town	485	488	0.62
FLORENCE COUNTY	4,423	4,358	-1.47
Aurora, town	1,036	1,018	-1.74
Commonwealth, town	399	399	0.00
Fence, town	192	185	-3.65
Fern, town	159	159	0.00
Florence, town	2,002	1,965	-1.85
Homestead, town	336	333	-0.89
Long Lake, town	157	156	-0.64
Tipler, town	142	143	0.70
FOND DU LAC COUNTY	101,633	101,955	0.32
Alto, town	1,045	1,041	-0.38
Ashford, town	1,747	1,749	0.11
Auburn, town	2,352	2,358	0.26
Brandon, village	879	876	-0.34
Byron, town	1,634	1,637	0.18
Calumet, town	1,470	1,475	0.34
Campbellsport, village	2,016	2,012	-0.20
Eden, town	1,028	1,033	0.49
Eden, village	875	881	0.69
Eldorado, town	1,462	1,467	0.34
Empire, town	2,797	2,806	0.32
Fairwater, village	371	370	-0.27
Fond du Lac, city	43,021	43,100	0.18
Fond du Lac, town	3,015	3,375	11.94
Forest, town	1,080	1,070	-0.93
Friendship, town	2,675	2,691	0.60
Kewaskum (part), village	0	0	0.00
Lamartine, town	1,737	1,740	0.17
Marshfield, town	1,138	1,141	0.26
Metomen, town	741	739	-0.27
Mount Calvary, village	762	572	-24.93
North Fond du Lac, village	5,014	5,016	0.04
Oakfield, town	703	702	-0.14
Oakfield, village	1,075	1,080	0.47
Osceola, town	1,865	1,865	0.00
Ripon, city	7,733	7,706	-0.35
Ripon, town	1,400	1,406	0.43
Rosendale, town	695	693	0.29
Rosendale, village	1,063	1,057	-0.56
St. Cloud, village	477	473	-0.84
Springvale, town	707	707	0.00
Taycheedah, town	4,205	4,252	1.12
Waupun (part), city	3,476	3,485	0.26
Waupun, town	1,375	1,380	0.36
FOREST COUNTY	9,304	9,197	-1.15
Alvin, town	157	157	0.00
Argonne, town	512	507	-0.98
Armstrong Creek, town	409	399	-2.44
Blackwell, town	332	319	-3.92
Caswell, town	91	89	-2.20
Crandon, city	1,920	1,895	-1.30
Crandon, town	650	643	-1.08
Freedom, town	345	345	0.00
Hiles, town	311	313	0.64
Laona, town	1,212	1,191	-1.73
Lincoln, town	955	948	-0.73
Nashville, town	1,064	1,059	-0.47
Popple River, town	44	43	-2.27
Ross, town	136	132	-2.94
Wabeno, town	1,166	1,157	-0.77
GRANT COUNTY	51,208	51,436	0.45
Bagley, village	379	381	0.53
Beetown, town	777	785	1.03
Bloomington, town	350	352	0.57
Bloomington, village	735	748	1.77
Blue River, village	434	437	0.69
Boscobel, city	3,231	3,247	0.50
Boscobel, town	376	374	-0.53
Cassville, town	416	412	-0.96
Cassville, village	947	948	0.11
Castle Rock, town	248	252	1.61
Clifton, town	385	387	0.52
Cuba City (part), city	1,877	1,875	-0.11
Dickeyville, village	1,061	1,060	-0.09
Ellenboro, town	525	528	0.57
Fennimore, city	2,497	2,506	0.36
Fennimore, town	612	611	-0.16
Glen Haven, town	417	418	0.24
Harrison, town	495	494	-0.20
Hazel Green, town	1,132	1,137	0.44
Hazel Green (part), village	1,243	1,249	0.48
Hickory Grove, town	455	457	0.44
Jamestown, town	2,076	2,102	1.25
Lancaster, city	3,868	3,845	-0.59
Liberty, town	553	556	0.54
Lima, town	805	808	0.37
Little Grant, town	283	282	-0.35
Livingston (part), village	657	655	-0.30

WISCONSIN POPULATION
BY COUNTY AND MUNCIPALITY
April 1, 2010 and January 1, 2012–Continued

County and Municipality	2010 Census	2012 Estimate	Percent Change	County and Municipality	2010 Census	2012 Estimate	Percent Change
Marion, town.	572	574	0.35	Dodgeville, town.	1,708	1,724	0.94
Millville, town	166	168	1.20	Eden, town	355	356	0.28
Montfort (part), village . .	622	620	–0.32	Highland, town.	750	757	0.93
Mount Hope, town	300	302	0.67	Highland, village.	842	840	–0.24
Mount Hope, village	225	227	0.89	Hollandale, village.	288	290	0.69
Mount Ida, town	561	566	0.89	Linden, town.	847	849	0.24
Muscoda, town.	769	765	–0.52	Linden, village.	549	546	–0.55
Muscoda (part), village . .	1,249	1,244	–0.40	Livingston (part), village . .	7	7	0.00
North Lancaster, town . . .	509	511	0.39	Mifflin, town.	585	586	0.17
Paris, town	702	703	0.14	Mineral Point, city	2,487	2,479	–0.32
Patch Grove, town	339	337	–0.59	Mineral Point, town	1,033	1,039	0.58
Patch Grove, village	198	201	1.52	Montfort (part), village . .	96	96	0.00
Platteville, city	11,224	11,338	1.02	Moscow, town.	576	583	1.22
Platteville, town	1,509	1,531	1.46	Muscoda (part), village . .	50	43	–14.00
Potosi, town	849	846	–0.35	Pulaski, town.	400	396	–1.00
Potosi, village	688	687	–0.15	Rewey, village	292	290	–0.68
Smelser, town	794	793	–0.13	Ridgeway, town	568	569	0.18
South Lancaster, town . . .	843	846	0.36	Ridgeway, village	653	651	–0.31
Tennyson, village	355	353	–0.56	Waldwick, town	473	473	0.00
Waterloo, town.	550	564	2.55	Wyoming, town	302	302	0.00
Watterstown, town	330	332	0.61				
Wingville, town	357	357	0.00	IRON COUNTY.	5,916	5,843	–1.23
Woodman, town	185	190	2.70	Anderson, town	58	57	–1.72
Woodman, village	132	131	–0.76	Carey, town	163	159	–2.45
Wyalusing, town	346	344	–0.58	Gurney, town.	159	159	0.00
				Hurley, city.	1,547	1,513	–2.20
GREEN COUNTY.	36,842	36,863	0.06	Kimball, town	498	487	–2.21
Adams, town.	530	535	0.94	Knight, town	211	207	–1.90
Albany, town.	1,106	1,109	0.27	Mercer, town.	1,407	1,399	–0.57
Albany, village.	1,018	1,014	–0.39	Montreal, city	807	803	–0.50
Belleville (part), village . .	537	534	–0.56	Oma, town	289	292	1.04
Brodhead (part), city. . . .	3,203	3,206	0.09	Pence, town	163	163	0.00
Brooklyn, town	1,083	1,089	0.55	Saxon, town	324	317	–2.16
Brooklyn (part), village . .	465	464	–0.22	Sherman, town	290	287	–1.03
Browntown, village	280	282	0.71				
Cadiz, town	815	809	–0.74	JACKSON COUNTY	20,449	20,523	0.36
Clarno, town	1,166	1,165	–0.09	Adams, town	1,342	1,357	1.12
Decatur, town	1,767	1,770	0.17	Albion, town	1,210	1,221	0.91
Exeter, town	2,023	2,035	0.59	Alma, town.	1,044	1,058	1.34
Jefferson, town.	1,217	1,223	0.49	Alma Center, village. . . .	503	505	0.40
Jordon, town	641	639	–0.31	Bear Bluff, town	138	137	–0.72
Monroe, city	10,827	10,811	–0.15	Black River Falls, city . . .	3,622	3,609	–0.36
Monroe, town	1,245	1,242	–0.24	Brockway, town	2,828	2,821	–0.25
Monticello, village.	1,217	1,218	0.08	City Point, town	182	180	–1.10
Mount Pleasant, town . . .	598	596	–0.33	Cleveland, town	481	486	1.04
New Glarus, town	1,335	1,342	0.52	Curran, town	343	343	0.00
New Glarus, village	2,172	2,167	–0.23	Franklin, town	448	455	1.56
Spring Grove, town	874	874	0.00	Garden Valley, town	422	424	0.47
Sylvester, town.	1,004	1,007	0.30	Garfield, town	638	649	1.72
Washington, town	809	816	0.87	Hixton, town	652	664	1.84
York, town	910	916	0.66	Hixton, village	433	430	–0.69
				Irving, town	751	758	0.93
GREEN LAKE COUNTY. . .	19,051	19,106	0.29	Knapp, town	299	304	1.67
Berlin (part), city.	5,435	5,450	0.28	Komensky, town	509	494	–2.95
Berlin, town	1,140	1,139	–0.09	Manchester, town	704	708	0.57
Brooklyn, town	1,826	1,835	0.49	Melrose, town	470	481	2.34
Green Lake, city	960	974	1.46	Melrose, village	503	498	–0.99
Green Lake, town	1,154	1,155	0.09	Merrillan, village.	542	539	–0.55
Kingston, town.	1,064	1,074	0.94	Millston, town	159	159	0.00
Kingston, village.	326	326	0.00	North Bend, town	488	498	2.05
Mackford, town	560	558	–0.36	Northfield, town.	639	643	0.63
Manchester, town	1,022	1,034	1.17	Springfield, town.	623	625	0.32
Markesan, city	1,476	1,464	–0.81	Taylor, village	476	477	0.21
Marquette, town	531	541	1.88				
Marquette, village	150	152	1.33	JEFFERSON COUNTY	83,686	83,857	0.20
Princeton, city	1,214	1,207	–0.58	Aztalan, town	1,457	1,459	0.14
Princeton, town	1,434	1,436	0.14	Cambridge (part), village .	109	109	0.00
St. Marie, town.	351	355	1.14	Cold Spring, town	727	724	–0.41
Seneca, town	408	406	–0.49	Concord, town	2,072	2,076	0.19
				Farmington, town	1,380	1,381	0.07
IOWA COUNTY.	23,687	23,726	0.16	Fort Atkinson, city	12,368	12,380	0.10
Arena, town	1,456	1,465	0.62	Hebron, town.	1,094	1,100	0.55
Arena, village	834	830	–0.48	Ixonia, town	4,385	4,483	2.23
Avoca, village	637	634	–0.47	Jefferson, city	7,973	7,934	–0.49
Barneveld, village	1,231	1,234	0.24	Jefferson, town.	2,178	2,180	0.09
Blanchardville (part),				Johnson Creek, village. . .	2,738	2,806	2.48
village	177	178	0.56	Koshkonong, town.	3,692	3,681	–0.30
Brigham, town	1,034	1,049	1.45	Lac La Belle (part), village	1	1	0.00
Clyde, town	306	307	0.33	Lake Mills, city	5,708	5,742	0.60
Cobb, village.	458	461	0.66	Lake Mills, town.	2,070	2,080	0.48
Dodgeville, city	4,693	4,692	–0.02	Milford, town	1,099	1,100	0.09

WISCONSIN POPULATION
BY COUNTY AND MUNCIPALITY
April 1, 2010 and January 1, 2012–Continued

County and Municipality	2010 Census	2012 Estimate	Percent Change	County and Municipality	2010 Census	2012 Estimate	Percent Change
Oakland, town	3,100	3,097	-0.10	Greenfield, town	2,060	2,072	0.58
Palmyra, town	1,186	1,182	-0.34	Hamilton, town	2,436	2,449	0.53
Palmyra, village	1,781	1,778	-0.17	Holland, town	3,701	3,790	2.40
Sullivan, town	2,208	2,208	0.00	Holmen, village	9,005	9,171	1.84
Sullivan, village	669	667	-0.30	La Crosse, city	51,320	51,590	0.53
Sumner, town	832	831	-0.12	Medary, town	1,461	1,482	1.44
Waterloo, city	3,333	3,331	-0.06	Onalaska, city	17,736	18,006	1.52
Waterloo, town	909	910	0.11	Onalaska, town	5,623	5,644	0.37
Watertown (part), city	15,402	15,444	0.27	Rockland, village	594	610	2.69
Watertown, town	1,975	1,968	-0.35	Shelby, town	4,715	4,707	-0.17
Whitewater (part), city	3,240	3,205	-1.08	Washington, town	558	555	-0.54
				West Salem, village	4,799	4,827	0.58
JUNEAU County	26,664	26,878	0.80				
Armenia, town	699	709	1.43	LAFAYETTE COUNTY	16,836	16,897	0.36
Camp Douglas, village	601	607	1.00	Argyle, town	436	435	-0.23
Clearfield, town	728	726	-0.27	Argyle, village	857	860	0.35
Cutler, town	326	330	1.23	Belmont, town	767	779	1.56
Elroy, city	1,442	1,426	-1.11	Belmont, village	986	988	0.20
Finley, town	97	97	0.00	Benton, town	504	506	0.40
Fountain, town	555	556	0.18	Benton, village	973	971	-0.21
Germantown, town	1,471	1,522	3.47	Blanchard, town	264	270	2.27
Hustler, village	194	193	-0.52	Blanchardville (part),			
Kildare, town	681	693	1.76	village	648	645	-0.46
Kingston, town	91	90	-1.10	Cuba City (part), city	209	213	1.91
Lemonweir, town	1,743	1,756	0.75	Darlington, city	2,451	2,443	-0.33
Lindina, town	718	715	-0.42	Darlington, town	875	884	1.03
Lisbon, town	912	916	0.44	Elk Grove, town	551	556	0.91
Lyndon, town	1,384	1,393	0.65	Fayette, town	376	384	2.13
Lyndon Station, village	500	500	0.00	Gratiot, town	550	544	-1.09
Marion, town	426	471	-1.17	Gratiot, village	236	234	-0.85
Mauston, city	4,423	4,517	2.13	Hazel Green (part), village	13	13	0.00
Necedah, town	2,327	2,347	0.86	Kendall, town	454	465	2.42
Necedah, village	916	925	0.98	Lamont, town	314	318	1.27
New Lisbon, city	2,554	2,567	0.51	Monticello, town	133	135	1.50
Orange, town	570	570	0.00	New Diggings, town	502	504	0.40
Plymouth, town	597	598	0.17	Seymour, town	446	450	0.90
Seven Mile Creek, town	358	354	-1.12	Shullsburg, city	1,226	1,226	0.00
Summit, town	646	649	0.46	Shullsburg, town	354	353	-0.28
Union Center, village	200	198	-1.00	South Wayne, village	489	488	-0.20
Wisconsin Dells (part), city	2	0		Wayne, town	490	494	0.82
Wonewoc, town	687	687	0.00	White Oak Springs, town	118	118	0.00
Wonewoc, village	816	816	0.00	Willow Springs, town	758	761	0.40
				Wiota, town	856	860	0.47
KENOSHA COUNTY	166,426	166,823	0.24				
Brighton, town	1,456	1,451	-0.34	LANGLADE COUNTY	19,977	19,880	-0.49
²Bristol, village	4,914	4,924	0.20	Ackley, town	524	526	0.38
Genoa City (part), village	6	6	0.00	Ainsworth, town	469	467	-0.43
Kenosha, city	99,218	99,660	0.45	Antigo, city	8,234	8,141	-1.13
Paddock Lake, village	2,992	2,987	-0.17	Antigo, town	1,412	1,410	-0.14
Paris, town	1,504	1,505	0.07	Elcho, town	1,233	1,236	0.24
Pleasant Prairie, village	19,719	19,850	0.66	Evergreen, town	495	493	-0.40
Randall, town	3,180	3,184	0.13	Langlade, town	473	476	0.63
Salem, town	12,067	12,036	-0.26	Neva, town	902	897	-0.55
Silver Lake, village	2,411	2,404	-0.29	Norwood, town	913	906	-0.77
Somers, town	9,597	9,463	-1.40	Parrish, town	91	89	-2.20
Twin Lakes, village	5,989	5,993	0.07	Peck, town	349	350	0.29
Wheatland, town	3,373	3,360	-0.39	Polar, town	984	986	0.20
				Price, town	228	226	-0.88
KEWAUNEE COUNTY	20,574	20,637	0.31	Rolling, town	1,504	1,505	0.07
Ahnapee, town	940	938	-0.21	Summit, town	163	163	0.00
Algoma, city	3,167	3,171	0.13	Upham, town	676	680	0.59
Carlton, town	1,014	1,020	0.59	Vilas, town	233	231	-0.86
Casco, town	1,165	1,172	0.60	White Lake, village	363	361	-0.55
Casco, village	583	584	0.17	Wolf River, town	731	737	0.82
Franklin, town	993	993	0.00				
Kewaunee, city	2,952	2,951	-0.03	LINCOLN COUNTY	28,743	28,856	0.39
Lincoln, town	948	939	-0.95	Birch, town	594	717	20.71
Luxemburg, town	1,469	1,466	-0.20	Bradley, town	2,408	2,421	0.54
Luxemburg, village	2,515	2,560	1.79	Corning, town	883	883	0.00
Montpelier, town	1,306	1,306	0.00	Harding, town	372	373	0.27
Pierce, town	833	832	-0.12	Harrison, town	833	838	0.60
Red River, town	1,393	1,397	0.29	King, town	855	857	0.23
West Kewaunee, town	1,296	1,308	0.93	Merrill, city	9,661	9,618	-0.45
				Merrill, town	2,980	2,986	0.20
LA CROSSE COUNTY	114,638	115,577	0.82	Pine River, town	1,869	1,869	0.00
Bangor, town	615	614	-0.16	Rock Falls, town	618	621	0.49
Bangor, village	1,459	1,470	0.75	Russell, town	677	678	0.15
Barre, town	1,234	1,235	0.08	Schley, town	934	930	-0.43
Burns, town	947	954	0.74	Scott, town	1,432	1,444	0.84
Campbell, town	4,314	4,325	0.25	Skanawan, town	391	394	0.77
Farmington, town	2,061	2,076	0.73	Somo, town	114	113	-0.88

WISCONSIN POPULATION
BY COUNTY AND MUNCIPALITY
April 1, 2010 and January 1, 2012–Continued

County and Municipality	2010 Census	2012 Estimate	Percent Change
Tomahawk, city	3,397	3,384	–0.38
Tomahawk, town.	416	418	0.48
Wilson, town.	309	312	0.97
MANITOWOC COUNTY. . .	81,442	81,437	–0.01
Cato, town	1,566	1,563	–0.19
Centerville, town.	645	644	–0.16
Cleveland, village	1,485	1,514	1.95
Cooperstown, town	1,292	1,296	0.31
Eaton, town	833	830	–0.36
Francis Creek, village . . .	669	670	0.15
Franklin, town	1,264	1,262	–0.16
Gibson, town.	1,344	1,350	0.45
Kellnersville, village. . . .	332	329	–0.90
Kiel (part), city.	3,429	3,427	–0.06
Kossuth, town	2,090	2,094	0.19
Liberty, town.	1,281	1,283	0.16
Manitowoc, city	33,736	33,750	0.04
Manitowoc, town.	1,083	1,091	0.74
Manitowoc Rapids, town .	2,150	2,140	–0.47
Maple Grove, town	835	834	–0.12
Maribel, village	351	350	–0.28
Meeme, town.	1,446	1,451	0.35
Mishicot, town.	1,289	1,284	–0.39
Mishicot, village	1,442	1,439	–0.21
Newton, town	2,264	2,272	0.35
Reedsville, village	1,206	1,200	–0.50
Rockland, town	1,001	1,001	0.00
St. Nazianz, village	783	783	0.00
Schleswig, town	1,963	1,979	0.82
Two Creeks, town	437	428	–2.06
Two Rivers, city	11,712	11,669	–0.37
Two Rivers, town	1,795	1,787	–0.45
Valders, village.	962	961	–0.10
Whitelaw, village	757	756	–0.13
MARATHON COUNTY . . .	134,063	134,524	0.34
Abbotsford (part), city . . .	694	692	–0.29
Athens, village	1,105	1,106	0.09
Bergen, town.	641	638	–0.47
Berlin, town	945	945	0.00
Bern, town	591	599	1.35
Bevent, town	1,118	1,124	0.54
Birnamwood (part), village	16	16	0.00
Brighton, town	612	610	–0.33
Brokaw, village	251	244	–2.79
Cassel, town	911	909	–0.22
Cleveland, town	1,488	1,497	0.60
Colby (part), city.	498	498	0.00
Day, town	1,085	1,092	0.65
Dorchester (part), village .	5	5	0.00
Easton, town	1,111	1,125	1.26
Eau Pleine, town.	773	770	–0.39
Edgar, village	1,479	1,476	–0.20
Elderon, town	606	612	0.99
Elderon, village	179	178	–0.56
Emmet, town.	931	936	0.54
Fenwood, village.	152	149	–1.97
Frankfort, town	670	667	–0.45
Franzen, town	578	582	0.69
Green Valley, town. . . .	541	540	–0.18
Guenther, town.	341	347	1.76
Halsey, town	651	647	–0.61
Hamburg, town.	918	912	–0.65
Harrison, town	374	375	0.27
Hatley, village	574	589	2.61
Hewitt, town	606	610	0.66
Holton, town	873	880	0.80
Hull, town	750	751	0.13
Johnson, town	985	985	0.00
Knowlton, town	1,910	1,911	0.05
Kronenwetter, village . . .	7,210	7,266	0.78
Maine, town	2,337	2,341	0.17
Marathon, town	1,048	1,045	–0.29
Marathon City, village . . .	1,524	1,529	0.33
Marshfield (part), city . . .	900	903	0.33
McMillan, town	1,968	1,987	0.97
Mosinee, city.	3,988	3,989	0.03
Mosinee, town	2,174	2,178	0.18
Norrie, town	976	977	0.10
Plover, town	689	687	–0.29

County and Municipality	2010 Census	2012 Estimate	Percent Change
Reid, town	1,215	1,224	0.74
Rib Falls, town.	993	996	0.30
Rib Mountain, town	6,825	6,836	0.16
Rietbrock, town	981	977	–0.41
Ringle, town	1,711	1,725	0.82
Rothschild, village	5,269	5,276	0.13
Schofield, city	2,169	2,167	–0.09
Spencer, town	1,581	1,591	0.63
Spencer, village	1,925	1,932	0.36
Stettin, town	2,554	2,557	0.12
Stratford, village.	1,578	1,589	0.70
Texas, town	1,615	1,610	–0.31
Unity (part), village	204	200	–1.96
Wausau, city	39,106	39,160	0.14
Wausau, town.	2,229	2,231	0.09
Weston, town.	639	651	1.88
Weston, village.	14,868	15,051	1.23
Wien, town.	825	832	0.85
MARINETTE COUNTY . . .	41,749	41,718	–0.07
Amberg, town	726	728	0.28
Athelstane, town.	504	507	0.60
Beaver, town	1,146	1,148	0.17
Beecher, town	724	724	0.00
Coleman, village.	724	723	–0.14
Crivitz, village.	984	980	–0.41
Dunbar, town.	1,094	1,005	–8.14
Goodman, town	619	614	–0.81
Grover, town	1,768	1,786	1.02
Lake, town	1,135	1,146	0.97
Marinette, city	10,968	10,929	–0.36
Middle Inlet, town	840	838	–0.24
Niagara, city	1,624	1,617	–0.43
Niagara, town	853	857	0.47
Pembine, town	889	890	0.11
Peshtigo, city.	3,502	3,510	0.23
Peshtigo, town	4,057	4,064	0.17
Porterfield, town	1,971	1,983	0.61
Pound, town	1,425	1,429	0.28
Pound, village	377	376	–0.27
Silver Cliff, town.	491	494	0.61
Stephenson, town	3,006	3,040	1.13
Wagner, town	681	684	0.44
Wausaukee, town	1,066	1,073	0.66
Wausaukee, village. . . .	575	573	–0.35
MARQUETTE COUNTY. . .	15,404	15,394	–0.06
Buffalo, town	1,221	1,223	0.16
Crystal Lake, town. . . .	484	485	0.21
Douglas, town	725	729	0.55
Endeavor, village.	468	465	–0.64
Harris, town	790	790	0.00
Mecan, town	686	688	0.29
Montello, city	1,495	1,483	–0.80
Montello, town.	1,033	1,034	0.10
Moundville, town	552	548	–0.72
Neshkoro, town	561	557	–0.71
Neshkoro, village	434	431	–0.69
Newton, town	547	548	0.18
Oxford, town.	885	887	0.23
Oxford, village.	607	604	–0.49
Packwaukee, town	1,416	1,412	–0.28
Shields, town.	550	551	0.18
Springfield, town.	830	834	0.48
Westfield, town.	866	869	0.35
Westfield, village.	1,254	1,256	0.16
MENOMINEE COUNTY . . .	4,232	4,214	–0.43
Menominee, town	4,232	4,214	–0.43
MILWAUKEE COUNTY . . .	947,735	948,322	0.06
Bayside (part), village . . .	4,300	4,292	–0.19
Brown Deer, village . . .	11,999	12,065	0.55
Cudahy, city	18,267	18,247	–0.11
Fox Point, village	6,701	6,644	–0.85
Franklin, city.	35,451	35,520	0.19
Glendale, city	12,872	12,808	–0.50
Greendale, village	14,046	14,123	0.55
Greenfield, city.	36,720	36,740	0.05
Hales Corners, village . . .	7,692	7,683	–0.12
Milwaukee (part), city . . .	594,833	595,425	0.10

WISCONSIN POPULATION
BY COUNTY AND MUNCIPALITY
April 1, 2010 and January 1, 2012–Continued

County and Municipality	2010 Census	2012 Estimate	Percent Change
Oak Creek, city	34,451	34,530	0.23
River Hills, village	1,597	1,591	-0.38
St. Francis, city	9,365	9,452	0.93
Shorewood, village	13,162	13,174	0.09
South Milwaukee, city	21,156	21,103	-0.25
Wauwatosa, city	46,396	46,320	-0.16
West Allis, city	60,411	60,300	-0.18
West Milwaukee, village	4,206	4,200	-0.14
Whitefish Bay, village	14,110	14,105	-0.04
MONROE COUNTY	44,673	45,056	0.86
Adrian, town	762	771	1.18
Angelo, town	1,296	1,297	0.08
Byron, town	1,342	1,345	0.22
Cashton, village	1,102	1,103	0.09
Clifton, town	690	694	0.58
Glendale, town	667	677	1.50
Grant, town	495	498	0.61
Greenfield, town	707	717	1.41
Jefferson, town	819	822	0.37
Kendall, village	472	473	0.21
La Grange, town	2,007	2,010	0.15
Lafayette, town	396	396	0.00
Leon, town	1,086	1,112	2.39
Lincoln, town	835	835	0.00
Little Falls, town	1,523	1,548	1.64
Melvina, village	104	104	0.00
New Lyme, town	168	173	2.98
Norwalk, village	638	636	-0.31
Oakdale, town	772	782	1.30
Oakdale, village	297	294	-1.01
Portland, town	808	821	1.61
Ridgeville, town	501	500	-0.20
Scott, town	135	137	1.48
Sheldon, town	727	736	1.24
Sparta, city	9,522	9,636	1.20
Sparta, town	3,128	3,151	0.74
Tomah, city	9,093	9,174	0.89
Tomah, town	1,400	1,416	1.14
Warrens, village	363	359	-1.10
Wellington, town	621	628	1.13
Wells, town	519	523	0.77
Wilton, town	1,027	1,038	1.07
Wilton, village	504	503	-0.20
Wyeville, village	147	147	0.00
OCONTO COUNTY	37,660	37,829	0.45
Abrams, town	1,856	1,862	0.32
Bagley, town	291	293	0.69
Brazeau, town	1,284	1,292	0.62
Breed, town	712	717	0.70
Chase, town	3,005	3,027	0.73
Doty, town	260	263	1.15
Gillett, city	1,386	1,382	-0.29
Gillett, town	1,043	1,038	-0.48
How, town	516	519	0.58
Lakewood, town	816	823	0.86
Lena, town	727	724	-0.41
Lena, village	564	562	-0.35
Little River, town	1,094	1,097	0.27
Little Suamico, town	4,799	4,894	1.98
Maple Valley, town	662	665	0.45
Morgan, town	984	986	0.20
Mountain, town	822	823	0.12
Oconto, city	4,513	4,535	0.49
Oconto, town	1,335	1,337	0.15
Oconto Falls, city	2,891	2,883	-0.28
Oconto Falls, town	1,265	1,263	-0.16
Pensaukee, town	1,381	1,380	-0.07
Pulaski (part), village	0	0	0.00
Riverview, town	725	725	0.00
Spruce, town	835	835	0.00
Stiles, town	1,489	1,491	0.13
Suring, village	544	543	-0.18
Townsend, town	979	986	0.72
Underhill, town	882	884	0.23
ONEIDA COUNTY	35,998	36,057	0.16
Cassian, town	985	983	-0.20
Crescent, town	2,033	2,037	0.20
Enterprise, town	315	317	0.63
Hazelhurst, town	1,273	1,278	0.39
Lake Tomahawk, town	1,043	1,034	-0.86
Little Rice, town	306	310	1.31
Lynne, town	141	142	0.71
Minocqua, town	4,453	4,463	0.22
Monico, town	309	311	0.65
Newbold, town	2,719	2,727	0.29
Nokomis, town	1,371	1,396	1.82
Pelican, town	2,764	2,778	0.51
Piehl, town	86	85	-1.16
Pine Lake, town	2,740	2,743	0.11
Rhinelander, city	7,798	7,753	-0.58
Schoepke, town	387	394	1.81
Stella, town	650	648	-0.31
Sugar Camp, town	1,694	1,708	0.83
Three Lakes, town	2,131	2,138	0.33
Woodboro, town	813	826	1.60
Woodruff, town	1,987	1,986	-0.05
OUTAGAMIE COUNTY	176,695	178,150	0.82
Appleton (part), city	60,045	60,240	0.32
Bear Creek, village	448	447	-0.22
Black Creek, town	1,259	1,256	-0.24
Black Creek, village	1,316	1,316	0.00
Bovina, town	1,145	1,151	0.52
Buchanan, town	6,755	6,903	2.19
Center, town	3,402	3,416	0.41
Cicero, town	1,103	1,103	0.00
Combined Locks, village	3,328	3,372	1.32
Dale, town	2,731	2,751	0.73
Deer Creek, town	637	640	0.47
Ellington, town	2,758	2,799	1.49
Freedom, town	5,842	5,910	1.16
Grand Chute, town	20,919	21,288	1.76
Greenville, town	10,309	10,602	2.84
Hortonia, town	1,097	1,094	-0.27
Hortonville, village	2,711	2,705	-0.22
Howard (part), village	0	0	0.00
Kaukauna (part), city	15,462	15,627	1.07
Kaukauna, town	1,238	1,249	0.89
Kimberly, village	6,468	6,559	1.41
Liberty, town	867	866	-0.12
Little Chute, village	10,449	10,432	-0.16
Maine, town	866	872	0.69
Maple Creek, town	619	612	-1.13
New London (part), city	1,610	1,614	0.25
Nichols, village	273	271	-0.73
Oneida, town	4,678	4,679	0.02
Osborn, town	1,170	1,181	0.94
Seymour, city	3,451	3,434	-0.49
Seymour, town	1,193	1,196	0.25
Shiocton, village	921	925	0.43
Vandenbroek, town	1,474	1,489	1.02
Wrightstown (part), village	151	151	0.00
OZAUKEE COUNTY	86,395	86,635	0.28
Bayside (part), village	89	88	-1.12
Belgium, town	1,415	1,416	0.07
Belgium, village	2,245	2,251	0.27
Cedarburg, city	11,412	11,445	0.29
Cedarburg, town	5,760	5,778	0.31
Fredonia, town	2,172	2,170	-0.09
Fredonia, village	2,160	2,160	0.00
Grafton, town	4,053	4,086	0.81
Grafton, village	11,459	11,464	0.04
Mequon, city	23,132	23,225	0.40
Newburg (part), village	97	97	0.00
Port Washington, city	11,250	11,287	0.33
Port Washington, town	1,643	1,649	0.37
Saukville, town	1,822	1,827	0.27
Saukville, village	4,451	4,464	0.29
Thiensville, village	3,235	3,228	-0.22
PEPIN COUNTY	7,469	7,465	-0.05
Albany, town	676	674	-0.30
Durand, city	1,931	1,926	-0.26
Durand, town	742	743	0.13
Frankfort, town	343	345	0.58
Lima, town	702	696	-0.85
Pepin, town	721	729	1.11
Pepin, village	837	828	-1.08

WISCONSIN POPULATION
BY COUNTY AND MUNCIPALITY
April 1, 2010 and January 1, 2012–Continued

County and Municipality	2010 Census	2012 Estimate	Percent Change
Stockholm, town	197	202	2.54
Stockholm, village	66	66	0.00
Waterville, town	831	831	0.00
Waubeek, town	423	425	0.47
PIERCE COUNTY	41,019	41,108	0.22
Bay City, village	500	499	−0.20
Clifton, town	2,012	2,017	0.25
Diamond Bluff, town	469	466	−0.64
El Paso, town	681	687	0.88
Ellsworth, town	1,146	1,153	0.61
Ellsworth, village	3,284	3,272	−0.37
Elmwood, village	817	815	−0.24
Gilman, town	959	967	0.83
Hartland, town	827	838	1.33
Isabelle, town	281	284	1.07
Maiden Rock, town	589	592	0.51
Maiden Rock, village	119	119	0.00
Martell, town	1,185	1,187	0.17
Oak Grove, town	2,150	2,157	0.33
Plum City, village	599	602	0.50
Prescott, city	4,258	4,258	0.00
River Falls (part), city	11,851	11,881	0.25
River Falls, town	2,271	2,276	0.22
Rock Elm, town	485	489	0.82
Salem, town	510	509	−0.20
Spring Lake, town	563	562	−0.18
Spring Valley (part), village	1,346	1,360	1.04
Trenton, town	1,829	1,834	0.27
Trimbelle, town	1,679	1,677	−0.12
Union, town	609	607	−0.33
POLK COUNTY	44,205	44,241	0.08
Alden, town	2,786	2,791	0.18
Amery, city	2,902	2,940	1.31
Apple River, town	1,146	1,152	0.52
Balsam Lake, town	1,411	1,407	−0.28
Balsam Lake, village	1,009	1,015	0.59
Beaver, town	835	836	0.12
Black Brook, town	1,325	1,333	0.60
Bone Lake, town	717	720	0.42
Centuria, village	948	937	−1.16
Clam Falls, town	596	600	0.67
Clayton, town	975	981	0.62
Clayton, village	571	572	0.18
Clear Lake, town	899	903	0.44
Clear Lake, village	1,070	1,071	0.09
Dresser, village	895	895	0.00
Eureka, town	1,649	1,649	0.00
Farmington, town	1,836	1,842	0.33
Frederic, village	1,137	1,134	−0.26
Garfield, town	1,692	1,690	−0.12
Georgetown, town	977	980	0.31
Johnstown, town	534	534	0.00
Laketown, town	961	962	0.10
Lincoln, town	2,208	2,177	−1.40
Lorain, town	284	283	−0.35
Luck, town	930	927	−0.32
Luck, village	1,119	1,101	−1.61
McKinley, town	347	353	1.73
Milltown, town	1,226	1,228	0.16
Milltown, village	917	916	−0.11
Osceola, town	2,855	2,863	0.28
Osceola, village	2,568	2,573	0.19
St. Croix Falls, city	2,133	2,130	−0.14
St. Croix Falls, town	1,165	1,167	0.17
Sterling, town	790	788	−0.25
Turtle Lake (part), village	93	92	−1.08
West Sweden, town	699	699	0.00
PORTAGE COUNTY	70,019	70,806	1.12
Alban, town	885	885	0.00
Almond, town	680	677	−0.44
Almond, village	448	449	0.22
Amherst, town	1,325	1,330	0.38
Amherst, village	1,035	1,041	0.58
Amherst Junction, village	377	376	−0.27
Belmont, town	616	620	0.65
Buena Vista, town	1,198	1,204	0.50
Carson, town	1,305	1,309	0.31
Dewey, town	932	934	0.21

County and Municipality	2010 Census	2012 Estimate	Percent Change
Eau Pleine, town	908	927	2.09
Grant, town	1,906	1,918	0.63
Hull, town	5,346	5,354	0.15
Junction City, village	439	439	0.00
Lanark, town	1,527	1,539	0.79
Linwood, town	1,121	1,127	0.54
Milladore (part), village	0	0	0.00
Nelsonville, village	155	153	−1.29
New Hope, town	718	719	0.14
Park Ridge, village	491	496	1.02
Pine Grove, town	937	940	0.32
Plover, town	1,701	1,710	0.53
Plover, village	12,123	12,373	2.06
Rosholt, village	506	507	0.20
Sharon, town	1,982	2,004	1.11
Stevens Point, city	26,717	27,129	1.54
Stockton, town	2,917	2,944	0.93
Whiting, village	1,724	1,702	−1.28
PRICE COUNTY	14,159	14,055	−0.73
Catawba, town	269	265	−1.49
Catawba, village	110	107	−2.73
Eisenstein, town	630	623	−1.11
Elk, town	988	992	0.40
Emery, town	297	295	−0.67
Fifield, town	901	895	−0.67
Flambeau, town	489	482	−1.43
Georgetown, town	171	171	0.00
Hackett, town	169	169	0.00
Harmony, town	222	223	0.45
Hill, town	333	332	−0.30
Kennan, town	356	355	−0.28
Kennan, village	135	132	−2.22
Knox, town	341	344	0.88
Lake, town	1,128	1,116	−1.06
Ogema, town	713	705	−1.12
Park Falls, city	2,462	2,464	0.08
Phillips, city	1,478	1,447	−2.10
Prentice, town	475	468	−1.47
Prentice, village	660	652	−1.21
Spirit, town	277	272	−1.81
Worcester, town	1,555	1,546	−0.58
RACINE County	195,408	195,386	−0.01
Burlington (part), city	10,464	10,496	0.31
Burlington, town	6,502	6,451	−0.78
Caledonia, village	24,705	24,731	0.11
Dover, town	4,051	3,979	−1.78
Elmwood Park, village	497	498	0.20
Mount Pleasant, village	26,197	26,220	0.09
North Bay, village	241	239	−0.83
Norway, town	7,948	7,961	0.16
Racine, city	78,860	78,830	−0.04
Raymond, town	3,870	3,886	0.41
Rochester, village	3,682	3,676	−0.16
Sturtevant, village	6,970	7,016	0.66
Union Grove, village	4,915	4,900	−0.31
Waterford, town	6,344	6,338	−0.09
Waterford, village	5,368	5,368	0.00
Wind Point, village	1,723	1,717	−0.35
Yorkville, town	3,071	3,080	0.29
RICHLAND COUNTY	18,021	18,043	0.12
Akan, town	403	405	0.50
Bloom, town	512	513	0.20
Boaz, village	156	156	0.00
Buena Vista, town	1,869	1,883	0.75
Cazenovia (part), village	314	313	−0.32
Dayton, town	693	698	0.72
Eagle, town	531	528	−0.56
Forest, town	352	352	0.00
Henrietta, town	493	492	−0.20
Ithaca, town	619	624	0.81
Lone Rock, village	888	887	−0.11
Marshall, town	567	573	1.06
Orion, town	579	582	0.52
Richland, town	1,379	1,373	−0.51
Richland Center, city	5,184	5,190	0.12
Richwood, town	533	527	−1.13
Rockbridge, town	734	732	−0.27
Sylvan, town	555	555	0.00

WISCONSIN POPULATION
BY COUNTY AND MUNCIPALITY
April 1, 2010 and January 1, 2012–Continued

County and Municipality	2010 Census	2012 Estimate	Percent Change	County and Municipality	2010 Census	2012 Estimate	Percent Change
Viola (part), village	477	479	0.42	Glenwood, town	785	788	0.38
Westford, town.	530	527	-0.57	Glenwood City, city . . .	1,242	1,233	-0.72
Willow, town.	579	582	0.52	Hammond, town	2,102	2,125	1.09
Yuba, village.	74	73	-1.35	Hammond, village	1,922	1,924	0.10
				Hudson, city	12,719	13,012	2.30
ROCK COUNTY	160,331	160,129	-0.13	Hudson, town	8,461	8,499	0.45
Avon, town.	608	606	-0.33	Kinnickinnic, town.	1,722	1,729	0.41
Beloit, city	36,966	36,850	-0.31	New Richmond, city . . .	8,375	8,395	0.24
Beloit, town	7,662	7,654	-0.10	North Hudson, village . .	3,768	3,768	0.00
Bradford, town.	1,121	1,108	-1.16	Pleasant Valley, town . . .	515	517	0.39
Brodhead (part), city. . . .	90	90	0.00	Richmond, town	3,272	3,302	0.92
Center, town	1,066	1,063	-0.28	River Falls (part), city . . .	3,149	3,159	0.32
Clinton, town.	930	934	0.43	Roberts, village	1,651	1,654	0.18
Clinton, village.	2,154	2,146	-0.37	Rush River, town.	508	507	-0.20
Edgerton (part), city	5,364	5,378	0.26	St. Joseph, town.	3,842	3,852	0.26
Evansville, city.	5,012	5,051	0.78	Somerset, town.	4,036	4,054	0.45
Footville, village.	808	807	-0.12	Somerset, village.	2,635	2,647	0.46
Fulton, town	3,252	3,257	0.15	Spring Valley (part), village	6	6	0.00
Harmony, town.	2,569	2,576	0.27	Springfield, town.	932	937	0.54
Janesville, city	63,575	63,480	-0.15	Stanton, town	900	900	0.00
Janesville, town	3,434	3,430	-0.12	Star Prairie, town	3,504	3,515	0.31
Johnstown, town.	778	781	0.39	Star Prairie, village.	561	558	-0.53
La Prairie, town	834	829	-0.60	Troy, town	4,705	4,731	0.55
Lima, town	1,280	1,277	-0.23	Warren, town.	1,591	1,600	0.57
Magnolia, town	767	763	-0.52	Wilson, village.	184	186	1.09
Milton, city.	5,546	5,549	0.05	Woodville, village	1,344	1,354	0.74
Milton, town	2,923	2,939	0.55				
Newark, town	1,541	1,535	-0.39	SAUK COUNTY	61,976	61,994	0.03
Orfordville, village.	1,442	1,453	0.76	Baraboo, city.	12,048	11,952	-0.80
Plymouth, town	1,235	1,186	3.97	Baraboo, town	1,672	1,673	0.06
Porter, town	945	956	1.16	Bear Creek, town	595	598	0.50
Rock, town.	3,196	3,195	-0.03	Cazenovia (part), village. .	4	13	225.00
Spring Valley, town	746	752	0.80	Dellona, town	1,552	1,565	0.84
Turtle, town	2,388	2,383	-0.21	Delton, town	2,391	2,408	0.71
Union, town	2,099	2,101	0.10	Excelsior, town.	1,575	1,576	0.06
				Fairfield, town	1,077	1,073	-0.37
RUSK COUNTY	14,755	14,756	0.01	Franklin, town	652	646	-0.92
Atlanta, town.	592	585	-1.18	Freedom, town.	447	451	0.89
Big Bend, town	358	360	0.56	Greenfield, town.	932	935	0.32
Big Falls, town.	140	139	-0.71	Honey Creek, town	733	734	0.14
Bruce, village	779	778	-0.13	Ironton, town.	660	658	-0.30
Cedar Rapids, town	41	41	0.00	Ironton, village.	253	252	-0.40
Conrath, village	95	97	2.11	La Valle, town	1,302	1,313	0.84
Dewey, town.	545	552	1.28	La Valle, village	367	362	-1.36
Flambeau, town	1,059	1,060	0.09	Lake Delton, village	2,914	2,914	0.00
Glen Flora, village.	92	91	-1.09	Lime Ridge, village	162	161	-0.62
Grant, town	813	811	-0.25	Loganville, village.	300	298	-0.67
Grow, town.	427	426	-0.23	Merrimac, town	942	955	1.38
Hawkins, town.	153	151	-1.31	Merrimac, village	420	424	0.95
Hawkins, village.	305	301	-1.31	North Freedom, village . .	701	696	-0.71
Hubbard, town	204	203	-0.49	Plain, village.	773	770	-0.39
Ingram, village.	78	78	0.00	Prairie du Sac, town . . .	1,144	1,141	-0.26
Ladysmith, city	3,414	3,386	-0.82	Prairie du Sac, village . .	3,972	3,999	0.68
Lawrence, town	311	309	-0.64	Reedsburg, city.	9,200	9,259	0.64
Marshall, town.	688	691	0.44	Reedsburg, town.	1,293	1,292	-0.08
Murry, town	277	279	0.72	Rock Springs, village . . .	362	319	-11.88
Richland, town.	232	234	0.86	Sauk City, village	3,410	3,424	0.41
Rusk, town.	525	539	2.67	Spring Green, town . . .	1,697	1,701	0.24
Sheldon, village	237	235	-0.84	Spring Green, village . . .	1,628	1,632	0.25
South Fork, town.	120	120	0.00	Sumpter, town	1,191	1,188	-0.25
Strickland, town	280	287	2.50	Troy, town	794	801	0.88
Stubbs, town	579	578	-0.17	Washington, town	1,007	1,005	-0.20
Thornapple, town	774	780	0.78	West Baraboo, village . . .	1,414	1,411	-0.21
Tony, village	113	113	0.00	Westfield, town.	571	569	-0.35
True, town	296	297	0.34	Winfield, town	856	859	0.35
Washington, town	339	344	1.47	Wisconsin Dells (part), city	175	171	-2.29
Weyerhaeuser, village . . .	238	235	-1.26	Woodland, town	790	796	0.76
Wilkinson, town	40	40	0.00				
Willard, town.	505	509	0.79	SAWYER COUNTY	16,557	16,659	0.62
Wilson, town.	106	107	0.94	Bass Lake, town	2,377	2,391	0.59
				Couderay, town	401	405	1.00
ST. CROIX COUNTY.	84,345	84,856	0.61	Couderay, village	88	90	2.27
Baldwin, town	928	922	-0.65	Draper, town.	204	206	0.98
Baldwin, village	3,957	3,953	-0.10	Edgewater, town	519	527	1.54
Cady, town.	821	827	0.73	Exeland, village	196	198	1.02
Cylon, town	683	680	-0.44	Hayward, city	2,318	2,348	1.29
Deer Park, village	216	214	-0.93	Hayward, town.	3,567	3,569	0.06
Eau Galle, town	1,139	1,148	0.79	Hunter, town	678	681	0.44
Emerald, town	853	850	-0.35	Lenroot, town	1,279	1,294	1.17
Erin Prairie, town	688	683	-0.73	Meadowbrook, town. . . .	131	137	4.58
Forest, town	629	627	-0.32	Meteor, town.	158	156	-1.27

WISCONSIN POPULATION
BY COUNTY AND MUNCIPALITY
April 1, 2010 and January 1, 2012–Continued

County and Municipality	2010 Census	2012 Estimate	Percent Change
Ojibwa, town.	249	252	1.20
Radisson, town.	405	403	–0.49
Radisson, village.	241	242	0.41
Round Lake, town	977	987	1.02
Sand Lake, town	813	820	0.86
Spider Lake, town	351	352	0.28
Weirgor, town	332	333	0.30
Winter, town	960	954	–0.63
Winter, village	313	314	0.32
SHAWANO COUNTY	41,949	41,919	–0.07
Almon, town.	584	585	0.17
Angelica, town.	1,793	1,810	0.95
Aniwa, town	541	538	–0.55
Aniwa, village	260	259	–0.38
Bartelme, town.	819	815	–0.49
Belle Plaine, town.	1,855	1,855	0.00
Birnamwood, town.	763	771	1.05
Birnamwood (part), village	802	798	–0.50
Bonduel, village	1,478	1,481	0.20
Bowler, village.	302	300	–0.66
Cecil, village.	570	569	–0.18
Eland, village	202	200	–0.99
Fairbanks, town	616	617	0.16
Germania, town	332	331	–0.30
Grant, town	991	990	–0.10
Green Valley, town.	1,089	1,093	0.37
Gresham, village.	586	582	–0.68
Hartland, town	904	902	–0.22
Herman, town	776	775	–0.13
Hutchins, town.	600	600	0.00
Lessor, town	1,263	1,267	0.32
Maple Grove, town	972	966	–0.62
Marion (part), city	25	26	4.00
Mattoon, village	438	437	–0.23
Morris, town	453	452	–0.22
Navarino, town.	446	445	–0.22
Pella, town	865	868	0.35
Pulaski (part), village . . .	218	218	0.00
Red Springs, town	925	928	0.32
Richmond, town	1,864	1,871	0.38
Seneca, town.	558	555	–0.54
Shawano, city	9,305	9,259	–0.49
Tigerton, village	741	733	–1.08
Washington, town	1,895	1,899	0.21
Waukechon, town	1,021	1,032	1.08
Wescott, town	3,183	3,195	0.38
Wittenberg, town.	833	834	0.12
Wittenberg, village.	1,081	1,063	–1.67
SHEBOYGAN COUNTY . . .	115,507	115,549	0.04
Adell, village.	516	514	–0.39
Cascade, village	709	707	–0.28
Cedar Grove, village. . . .	2,113	2,104	–0.43
Elkhart Lake, village. . . .	967	960	–0.72
Glenbeulah, village	463	463	0.00
Greenbush, town.	2,565	2,575	0.39
Herman, town	2,151	2,172	0.98
Holland, town	2,239	2,242	0.13
Howards Grove, village . .	3,188	3,199	0.35
Kohler, village	2,120	2,121	0.05
Lima, town.	2,982	2,985	0.10
Lyndon, town	1,542	1,546	0.26
Mitchell, town	1,304	1,303	–0.08
Mosel, town	790	790	0.00
Oostburg, village.	2,887	2,889	0.07
Plymouth, city	8,445	8,424	–0.25
Plymouth, town	3,195	3,202	0.22
Random Lake, village . . .	1,594	1,591	–0.19
Rhine, town	2,134	2,134	0.00
Russell, town.	377	378	0.27
Scott, town	1,836	1,835	–0.05
Sheboygan, city	49,288	49,110	–0.36
Sheboygan, town.	7,271	7,376	1.44
Sheboygan Falls, city . . .	7,775	7,847	0.93
Sheboygan Falls, town. . .	1,718	1,725	0.41
Sherman, town	1,505	1,498	–0.47
Waldo, village	503	503	0.00
Wilson, town.	3,330	3,356	0.78

County and Municipality	2010 Census	2012 Estimate	Percent Change
TAYLOR COUNTY	20,689	20,697	0.04
Aurora, town.	422	426	0.95
Browning, town	905	908	0.33
Chelsea, town	806	809	0.37
Cleveland, town	268	265	–1.12
Deer Creek, town	768	766	–0.26
Ford, town	268	271	1.12
Gilman, village.	410	408	–0 49
Goodrich, town	510	511	0.20
Greenwood, town	638	639	0.16
Grover, town	256	256	0.00
Hammel, town	713	711	–0.28
Holway, town	973	972	–0.10
Jump River, town	375	374	–0.27
Little Black, town	1,140	1,135	–0.44
Lublin, village	118	118	0.00
Maplehurst, town	335	335	0.00
McKinley, town	458	458	0.00
Medford, city.	4,326	4,338	0.28
Medford, town	2,606	2,611	0.19
Molitor, town	324	325	0.31
Pershing, town	180	179	–0.56
Rib Lake, town.	852	857	0.59
Rib Lake, village.	910	898	–1.32
Roosevelt, town	473	470	–0.63
Stetsonville, village	541	538	–0.55
Taft, town	430	428	–0.47
Westboro, town	684	691	1.02
TREMPEALEAU COUNTY .	28,816	28,986	0.59
Albion, town.	653	659	0.92
Arcadia, city	2,925	2,916	–0.31
Arcadia, town	1,779	1,796	0.96
Blair, city.	1,366	1,370	0.29
Burnside, town.	511	512	0.20
Caledonia, town	920	923	0.33
Chimney Rock, town . . .	241	239	–0.83
Dodge, town	389	392	0.77
Eleva, village.	670	675	0.75
Ettrick, town	1,237	1,234	–0.24
Ettrick, village	524	522	–0.38
Gale, town	1,695	1,708	0.77
Galesville, city	1,481	1,489	0.54
Hale, town	1,037	1,040	0.29
Independence, city	1,336	1,339	0.22
Lincoln, town	823	844	2.55
Osseo, city	1,701	1,699	–0.12
Pigeon, town.	891	892	0.11
Pigeon Falls, village	411	415	0.97
Preston, town.	953	961	0.84
Strum, village	1,114	1,120	0.54
Sumner, town	810	816	0.74
Trempealeau, town.	1,756	1,775	1.08
Trempealeau, village. . . .	1,529	1,576	3.07
Unity, town.	506	501	–0.99
Whitehall, city	1,558	1,573	0.96
VERNON COUNTY	29,773	29,865	0.31
Bergen, town.	1,364	1,364	0.00
Chaseburg, village	284	286	0.70
Christiana, town	931	937	0.64
Clinton, town.	1,358	1,373	1.10
Coon, town.	728	735	0.96
Coon Valley, village	765	769	0.52
De Soto (part), village . . .	179	182	1.68
Forest, town	634	631	–0.47
Franklin, town	1,140	1,160	1.75
Genoa, town	789	793	0.51
Genoa, village	253	252	–0.40
Greenwood, town	847	845	–0.24
Hamburg, town.	973	975	0.21
Harmony, town.	755	762	0.93
Hillsboro, city	1,417	1,415	–0.14
Hillsboro, town	807	806	–0.12
Jefferson, town.	1,143	1,140	–0.26
Kickapoo, town	626	636	1.60
La Farge, village	746	699	–6.30
Liberty, town.	252	257	1.98
Ontario, village	554	553	–0.18
Readstown, village.	415	421	1.45
Stark, town	363	363	0.00

WISCONSIN POPULATION
BY COUNTY AND MUNCIPALITY
April 1, 2010 and January 1, 2012–Continued

County and Municipality	2010 Census	2012 Estimate	Percent Change
Sterling, town	633	628	−0.79
Stoddard, village	774	777	0.39
Union, town	700	712	1.71
Viola (part), village	222	221	−0.45
Viroqua, city	4,362	4,339	−0.53
Viroqua, town	1,718	1,729	0.64
Webster, town	778	798	2.57
Westby, city	2,200	2,229	1.32
Wheatland, town	561	570	1.60
Whitestown, town	502	508	1.20
VILAS COUNTY	**21,430**	**21,485**	**0.26**
Arbor Vitae, town	3,316	3,321	0.15
Boulder Junction, town	933	938	0.54
Cloverland, town	1,029	1,032	0.29
Conover, town	1,235	1,235	0.00
Eagle River, city	1,398	1,381	−1.22
Lac du Flambeau, town	3,441	3,453	0.35
Land O'Lakes, town	861	865	0.46
Lincoln, town	2,423	2,432	0.37
Manitowish Waters, town	566	569	0.53
Phelps, town	1,200	1,204	0.33
Plum Lake, town	491	500	1.83
Presque Isle, town	618	627	1.46
St. Germain, town	2,085	2,083	−0.10
Washington, town	1,451	1,458	0.48
Winchester, town	383	387	1.04
WALWORTH COUNTY	**102,228**	**102,530**	**0.30**
[3]Bloomfield, town	6,278	1,611	-73.86
[3]Bloomfield, village	0	4,623	0.00
Burlington (part), city	0	0	0.00
Darien, town	1,693	1,696	0.18
Darien, village	1,580	1,587	0.44
Delavan, city	8,463	8,442	−0.25
Delavan, town	5,285	5,268	−0.32
East Troy, town	4,021	4,025	0.10
East Troy, village	4,281	4,283	0.05
Elkhorn, city	10,084	9,998	−0.85
Fontana on Geneva Lake, village	1,672	1,674	0.12
Geneva, town	4,993	4,989	−0.08
Genoa City (part), village	3,036	3,046	0.33
Lafayette, town	1,979	1,977	−0.10
La Grange, town	2,454	2,453	−0.04
Lake Geneva, city	7,651	7,654	0.04
Linn, town	2,383	2,398	0.63
Lyons, town	3,698	3,693	−0.14
Mukwonago (part), village	101	109	7.92
Richmond, town	1,884	1,889	0.27
Sharon, town	907	903	−0.44
Sharon, village	1,605	1,599	−0.37
Spring Prairie, town	2,181	2,181	0.00
Sugar Creek, town	3,943	3,938	−0.13
Troy, town	2,353	2,357	0.17
Walworth, town	1,702	1,692	−0.59
Walworth, village	2,816	2,813	−0.11
Whitewater (part), city	11,150	11,552	3.61
Whitewater, town	1,471	1,473	0.14
Williams Bay, village	2,564	2,577	0.51
WASHBURN COUNTY	**15,911**	**15,907**	**−0.03**
Barronett, town	442	438	−0.90
Bashaw, town	946	946	0.00
Bass Lake, town	505	512	1.39
Beaver Brook, town	713	714	0.14
Birchwood, town	478	481	0.63
Birchwood, village	442	439	−0.68
Brooklyn, town	254	255	0.39
Casey, town	353	356	0.85
Chicog, town	234	226	−3.42
Crystal, town	267	262	−1.87
Evergreen, town	1,135	1,133	−0.18
Frog Creek, town	130	132	1.54
Gull Lake, town	186	188	1.08
Long Lake, town	624	621	−0.48
Madge, town	508	512	0.79
Minong, town	917	923	0.65
Minong, village	527	527	0.00
Sarona, town	384	384	0.00
Shell Lake, city	1,347	1,352	0.37

County and Municipality	2010 Census	2012 Estimate	Percent Change
Spooner, city	2,682	2,667	−0.56
Spooner, town	706	711	0.71
Springbrook, town	445	441	−0.90
Stinnett, town	246	243	−1.22
Stone Lake, town	508	508	0.00
Trego, town	932	936	0.43
WASHINGTON COUNTY	**131,887**	**132,482**	**0.45**
Addison, town	3,495	3,486	−0.26
Barton, town	2,637	2,642	0.19
Erin, town	3,747	3,760	0.35
Farmington, town	4,014	4,029	0.37
Germantown, town	254	250	−1.57
Germantown, village	19,749	19,803	0.27
Hartford (part), city	14,223	14,258	0.25
Hartford, town	3,609	3,600	−0.25
Jackson, town	4,134	4,199	1.57
Jackson, village	6,753	6,782	0.43
Kewaskum, town	1,053	1,055	0.19
Kewaskum (part), village	4,004	4,006	0.05
Milwaukee (part), city	0	0	0.00
Newburg (part), village	1,157	1,154	−0.26
Polk, town	3,937	3,941	0.10
Richfield, village	11,300	11,339	0.35
Slinger, village	5,068	5,113	0.89
Trenton, town	4,732	4,727	−0.11
Wayne, town	2,169	2,182	0.60
West Bend, city	31,078	31,380	0.97
West Bend, town	4,774	4,776	0.04
WAUKESHA COUNTY	**389,891**	**390,914**	**0.26**
Big Bend, village	1,290	1,287	−0.23
Brookfield, city	37,920	37,870	−0.13
Brookfield, town	6,116	6,102	−0.23
Butler, village	1,841	1,837	−0.22
Chenequa, village	590	586	−0.68
Delafield, city	7,085	7,095	0.14
Delafield, town	8,400	8,195	−2.44
Dousman, village	2,302	2,317	0.65
Eagle, town	3,507	3,514	0.20
Eagle, village	1,950	1,947	−0.15
Elm Grove, village	5,934	5,930	−0.07
Genesee, town	7,340	7,331	−0.12
Hartland, village	9,110	9,118	0.09
Lac La Belle (part), village	289	289	0.00
Lannon, village	1,107	1,104	−0.27
Lisbon, town	10,157	10,184	0.27
Menomonee Falls, village	35,626	35,680	0.15
Merton, town	8,338	8,361	0.28
Merton, village	3,346	3,384	1.14
Milwaukee (part), city	0	0	0.00
Mukwonago, town	7,959	7,976	0.21
Mukwonago (part), village	7,254	7,281	0.37
Muskego, city	24,135	24,217	0.34
Nashotah, village	1,395	1,387	−0.57
New Berlin, city	39,584	39,770	0.47
North Prairie, village	2,141	2,145	0.19
Oconomowoc, city	15,759	15,834	0.48
Oconomowoc, town	8,408	8,505	1.15
Oconomowoc Lake, village	595	594	−0.17
Ottawa, town	3,859	3,867	0.21
Pewaukee, city	13,195	13,464	2.04
Pewaukee, village	8,166	8,178	0.15
Summit, village	4,674	4,680	0.13
Sussex, village	10,518	10,573	0.52
Vernon, town	7,601	7,603	0.03
Wales, village	2,549	2,547	−0.08
Waukesha, city	70,718	71,020	0.43
Waukesha, town	9,133	9,142	0.10
WAUPACA COUNTY	**52,410**	**52,381**	**−0.06**
Bear Creek, town	823	816	−0.85
Big Falls, village	61	61	0.00
Caledonia, town	1,627	1,641	0.86
Clintonville, city	4,559	4,543	−0.35
Dayton, town	2,748	2,748	0.00
Dupont, town	738	735	−0.41
Embarrass, village	404	399	−1.24
Farmington, town	3,974	3,988	0.35
Fremont, town	597	594	−0.50
Fremont, village	679	679	0.00

WISCONSIN POPULATION
BY COUNTY AND MUNCIPALITY
April 1, 2010 and January 1, 2012–Continued

County and Municipality	2010 Census	2012 Estimate	Percent Change	County and Municipality	2010 Census	2012 Estimate	Percent Change
Harrison, town	468	465	-0.64	Black Wolf, town	2,410	2,418	0.33
Helvetia, town	636	630	-0.94	Clayton, town	3,951	3,974	0.58
Iola, town	971	972	0.10	Menasha (part), city	15,144	15,129	-0.10
Iola, village	1,301	1,290	-0.85	Menasha, town	18,498	18,545	0.25
Larrabee, town	1,381	1,378	-0.22	Neenah, city	25,501	25,723	0.87
Lebanon, town	1,665	1,671	0.36	Neenah, town	3,237	3,306	2.13
Lind, town	1,579	1,584	0.32	Nekimi, town	1,429	1,428	-0.07
Little Wolf, town	1,424	1,419	-0.35	Nepeuskun, town	710	721	1.55
Manawa, city	1,371	1,347	-1.75	Omro, city	3,517	3,520	0.09
Marion (part), city	1,235	1,232	-0.24	Omro, town	2,116	2,127	0.52
Matteson, town	936	934	-0.21	Oshkosh, city	66,083	66,325	0.37
Mukwa, town	2,930	2,937	0.24	Oshkosh, town	2,475	2,470	-0.20
New London (part), city	5,685	5,686	0.02	Poygan, town	1,301	1,305	0.31
Ogdensburg, village	185	183	-1.08	Rushford, town	1,561	1,569	0.51
Royalton, town	1,434	1,437	0.21	Utica, town	1,299	1,304	0.38
St. Lawrence, town	710	707	-0.42	Vinland, town	1,765	1,757	-0.45
Scandinavia, town	1,066	1,065	-0.09	Winchester, town	1,763	1,772	0.51
Scandinavia, village	363	365	0.55	Winneconne, town	2,350	2,361	0.47
Union, town	806	811	0.62	Winneconne, village	2,383	2,377	-0.25
Waupaca, city	6,069	6,040	-0.48	Wolf River, town	1,189	1,192	0.25
Waupaca, town	1,173	1,184	0.94				
Weyauwega, city	1,900	1,930	1.58	**WOOD COUNTY**	74,749	74,587	-0.22
Weyauwega, town	583	577	-1.03	Arpin, town	929	938	0.97
Wyoming, town	329	333	1.22	Arpin, village	333	331	-0.60
				Auburndale, town	860	845	-1.74
WAUSHARA COUNTY	24,496	24,506	0.04	Auburndale, village	703	702	-0.14
Aurora, town	985	989	0.41	Biron, village	839	837	-0.24
Berlin (part), city	89	91	2.25	Cameron, town	511	488	-4.50
Bloomfield, town	1,052	1,058	0.57	Cary, town	424	425	0.24
Coloma, town	753	755	0.27	Cranmoor, town	168	165	-1.79
Coloma, village	450	456	1.33	Dexter, town	359	359	0.00
Dakota, town	1,227	1,229	0.16	Grand Rapids, town	7,646	7,659	0.17
Deerfield, town	737	742	0.68	Hansen, town	690	689	-0.14
Hancock, town	528	534	1.14	Hewitt, village	828	825	-0.36
Hancock, village	417	413	-0.96	Hiles, town	167	164	-1.80
Leon, town	1,439	1,440	0.07	Lincoln, town	1,564	1,569	0.32
Lohrville, village	402	400	-0.50	Marshfield (part), city	18,218	18,158	-0.33
Marion, town	2,038	2,036	-0.10	Marshfield, town	764	761	-0.39
Mount Morris, town	1,097	1,100	0.27	Milladore, town	690	691	0.14
Oasis, town	389	391	0.51	Milladore (part), village	276	278	0.72
Plainfield, town	550	550	0.00	Nekoosa, city	2,580	2,570	-0.39
Plainfield, village	862	860	-0.23	Pittsville, city	874	871	-0.34
Poy Sippi, town	931	929	-0.21	Port Edwards, town	1,427	1,422	-0.35
Redgranite, village	2,149	2,155	0.28	Port Edwards, village	1,818	1,796	-1.21
Richford, town	612	624	1.96	Remington, town	268	265	-1.12
Rose, town	640	644	0.63	Richfield, town	1,628	1,625	-0.18
Saxeville, town	986	986	0.00	Rock, town	855	858	0.35
Springwater, town	1,274	1,271	-0.24	Rudolph, town	1,028	1,028	0.00
Warren, town	668	669	0.15	Rudolph, village	439	431	-1.82
Wautoma, city	2,218	2,185	-1.49	Saratoga, town	5,142	5,139	-0.06
Wautoma, town	1,278	1,280	0.16	Seneca, town	1,120	1,121	0.09
Wild Rose, village	725	719	-0.83	Sherry, town	803	810	0.87
				Sigel, town	1,051	1,049	-0.19
WINNEBAGO COUNTY	166,994	167,702	0.42	Vesper, village	584	582	-0.34
Algoma, town	6,822	6,889	0.98	Wisconsin Rapids, city	18,367	18,343	-0.13
Appleton (part), city	1,490	1,490	0.00	Wood, town	796	793	-0.38

[1]Part of the Town of Harrison was annexed by the City of Kaukauna on October 19, 2010.

[2]Part of the Town of Bristol became the Village of Bristol on December 1, 2009. The village annexed the town remnant on July 4, 2010.

[3]Part of the Town of Bloomfield became the Village of Bloomfield on December 12, 2011.

Source: Wisconsin Department of Administration, Demographic Services Center, *January 1, 2012 Final Population Estimates*, October 2012.

HIGHLIGHTS OF MILITARY AND VETERANS AFFAIRS IN WISCONSIN

Military Service — More Wisconsinites served in World War II than in any other conflict, with Vietnam ranking second, but fatalities were heaviest in the Civil War. From the Civil War through the operations in Iraq and Afghanistan, about 26,800 Wisconsinites have lost their lives performing military service during times of conflict. Since September 11, 2001, nearly every unit in the Wisconsin Army and Air National Guard has been ordered to active duty in support of operations in Afghanistan (Operation Enduring Freedom) and Iraq (Operation Iraqi Freedom), as well as homeland defense missions in the United States (Operation Noble Eagle) and continuing operations in the Balkans. In 2009, nearly 4,000 Wisconsin National Guard members deployed in support of the Global War on Terror, including 3,200 members of the 32nd Infantry Brigade Combat Team who conducted the largest operational deployment of the Wisconsin National Guard since World War II.

As of June 2013, about 10,000 citizen-soldiers and airmen were serving in Wisconsin National Guard units at military facilities located in over 60 communities throughout the state.

Veterans' Programs — Since the end of World War II, about $3.6 billion in grants and loans have been provided to Wisconsin veterans. Historically, most of the grants have been for educational purposes, while the overwhelming number of loans were for housing. The grants have also covered subsistence and emergency health care assistance for needy veterans. Eligible veterans and, in some instances, spouses and dependent children of deceased veterans may qualify for personal loans to finance expenses, such as education, business start-ups or purchases, medical bills, debt consolidation, and mobile home purchases.

In 2012, Wisconsin veterans and their families received about $120 million in federal educational and vocational rehabilitation assistance. Wisconsin veterans received about $861 million in benefits through the compensation and pension programs. As of 2012, there were over 418,000 veterans living in the state.

The Wisconsin Veterans Homes at Chippewa Falls, King, and Union Grove had 953 members at the end of 2012. In general, to be eligible for residence, a veteran must have completed certain military service requirements and be a Wisconsin resident on the date of admission to a veterans home. In addition, he or she must have been a resident of Wisconsin at the time of entry into service or a resident of the state for any 5-year period after service and prior to application for admission. Depending on availability of space, spouses and surviving spouses or parents of qualifying veterans may also be admitted.

The following tables present selected data. Consult the footnoted sources for more detailed information about military and veterans affairs.

WISCONSIN'S MILITARY SERVICE

Military Action	Number Served	Number Killed
Civil War	91,379[1]	12,216
Spanish-American War	5,469	134[2]
Mexican Border Service	4,168	NA
World War I	122,215	3,932
World War II	332,200	8,390
Korean Conflict	132,000	729
Vietnam	165,400	1,239
Lebanon/Grenada	400	1
Panama	520	1
Operations Desert Shield/Desert Storm	10,400	11
Somalia	426	2
Bosnia/Kosovo	678	NA
Iraq and Afghanistan Theaters of Operations since September 11, 2001	33,904	123[3]

Note: Includes Wisconsin residents who served on active duty during declared wars and officially designated periods of hostilities.

NA – Not available.

[1]Total includes some who enlisted more than once. The net number of soldiers recruited in Wisconsin was about 80,000.

[2]Casualties only from Wisconsin 1st, 2nd, 3rd and 4th Regiments. No details available for Wisconsin residents serving in federal units.

[3]Includes one killed in attack on Pentagon on September 11, 2001.

Sources: U.S. Veterans Administration; U.S. Department of Defense; and Wisconsin Department of Veterans Affairs, departmental data, May 2, 2013.

DIRECT STATE BENEFITS TO WISCONSIN WAR VETERANS
1943 – 1961

Fiscal Year	Number of Grants and Loans	Total Benefits	Rehabilitation Trust Funds	Housing Fund
8/1/43-1946	6,359	$975,173	$975,173	—
1947	10,701	2,207,914	2,207,914	—
1948	9,578	3,511,527	3,511,527	—
1949	6,086	2,512,517	2,512,517	—
1950	5,867	3,463,058	2,040,658	$1,422,400
1951	6,137	5,178,106	2,104,550	3,073,556
1952	10,442	22,362,081	1,995,116	20,366,965
1953	5,099	8,842,780	1,331,140	7,511,640
1954	4,507	4,420,030	1,502,748	2,917,282
1955	3,482	4,236,298	1,112,173	3,124,125
1956	3,639	5,389,187	787,861	4,601,326
1957	2,890	4,246,004	730,452	3,515,552
1958	2,779	4,912,233	660,994	4,251,239
1959	2,954	5,419,609	670,262	4,749,347
1960	3,345	7,341,922	591,272	6,750,650
1961	3,081	6,654,189	584,426	6,069,763

Note: The 1961 Legislature merged all veterans' funds into the Veterans Trust Fund.

Source: Wisconsin Department of Veterans Affairs, departmental data, March 1995.

VETERANS BENEFITS, 1962 – 2012

Fiscal Year	Total Benefits	Grants				Personal Loan Program	Loans		
		Economic	Educational	Full-Time Educational Grants	Economic Assistance		Second Mortgage Housing	Revenue Bond Housing Loans	Gen. Obligation Bond Housing Loans
1962	$6,681,585	$53,891	$2,100	—	$515,008	—	$6,110,586	—	—
1965	3,737,259	100,751	13,654	—	359,705	—	3,263,149	—	—
1970	9,265,183	193,044	289,743	—	3,605,092	—	5,177,305	—	—
1975	69,554,865	607,279	1,240,917	$1,836,207	9,098,837	—	10,076,963	$46,694,662	—
1980	197,668,743	362,556	1,099,266	731,672	6,735,632	—	843,433	—	$187,896,184
1981	90,183,867	424,041	1,092,510	479,232	4,323,114	—	1,345,430	67,130,619	15,388,921
1982	16,221,058	378,614	1,159,025	469,347	3,656,939	—	1,062,015	8,400,780	1,094,338
1983	56,700,920	591,351	986,106	391,542	3,073,217	—	762,930	—	50,895,774
1984	58,137,350	469,314	1,227,239	328,036	3,116,789	—	782,463	—	52,213,509
1985	47,689,638	453,502	1,483,693	225,043	2,737,544	—	552,106	—	42,237,750
1986	19,297,133	378,999	1,255,252	157,379	3,678,759	—	243,147	—	13,583,597
1987	18,883,716	529,634	807,253	127,789	2,802,819	—	141,370	—	14,474,851
1988	28,134,558	426,595	696,352	91,392	2,405,642	—	289,606	—	24,224,971
1989	35,412,289	533,929	698,946	77,787	2,455,813	—	832,436	—	30,809,378
1990	44,837,433	636,434	683,355	62,025	2,776,835	—	327,819	—	40,350,965
1991	48,562,575	398,706	743,351	50,993	3,945,614	—	62,960	—	43,360,951
1992	35,155,551	381,312	526,215	137,799	4,192,505	—	18,799	—	29,898,921
1993	22,446,997	472,302	512,770	167,838	2,673,585	—	—	—	18,620,502
1994	58,337,813[1]	451,666	716,858	667	2,567,053	—	—	—	33,157,403
1995	126,009,594[1]	552,893	754,052	—	2,544,584	—	—	—	111,133,109
1996	80,581,789	601,030	1,609,350	—	3,189,625	—	—	—	75,181,784
1997	99,984,937	937,294	1,797,649	—	2,401,548	—	—	—	94,848,446
1998	160,760,389	783,664	1,680,881	—	666,575[2]	$10,215,928[2]	—	—	147,413,341
1999	139,857,465	2,263,317	1,447,882	—	—	11,837,974	—	—	124,908,352
2000	143,192,551	3,226,128	1,786,205	—	—	10,802,068	—	—	127,378,150
2001	73,390,596	1,205,846	1,768,452	—	—	9,034,356	—	—	61,381,942
2002	88,227,531	1,925,094	2,822,134	—	—	15,780,270	—	—	67,700,033
2003	83,866,773	1,752,733	2,909,812	—	—	19,792,680	—	—	59,411,548
2004	95,593,212	1,296,310	4,384,642	—	—	11,808,566	—	—	78,103,694
2005	37,428,288	413,564	5,698,107	—	—	2,271,942	—	—	29,044,675
2006	23,935,069	1,052,493	4,751,263	—	—	4,113,262	—	—	14,018,050
2007	48,026,312	678,109	3,715,648	—	—	5,933,810	—	—	37,698,745
2008	59,388,229	1,028,788	2,276,489	—	—	5,081,986	—	—	51,000,967
2009	43,587,113	961,497	1,694,312	—	—	2,764,736	—	—	38,166,568
2010	15,859,166	426,535	1,726,307	—	—	3,133,961	—	—	10,572,363
2011	4,011,393	682,235	1,271,083	—	—	2,058,075	—	—	—
2012	2,401,891	488,605	992,411	—	—	920,875	—	—	—

Note: The 1961 Legislature merged all veterans' funds into the Veterans Trust Fund.

[1]Includes $21,444,166 (FY94) and $11,024,956 (FY95) in consumer loans under the Veterans Trust Fund stabilization provision of 1993 Wisconsin Act 16.

[2]Personal loan program replaced economic assistance loans.

Source: Wisconsin Department of Veterans Affairs, departmental data, June 2013.

WISCONSIN NATIONAL GUARD

Joint Force Headquarters Wisconsin
Joint Force Headquarters Detachment – Madison
    54th Civil Support Team (WMD) – Madison

Headquarters, Wisconsin Army National Guard –
Madison
Joint Force Headquarters Separate Units
    Recruiting and Retention Battalion – Madison
    Det. 1, Recruiting and Retention Battalion – Madison
    Det. 2, Recruiting and Retention Battalion – Milwaukee
    Det. 52, Operational Support Airlift Command – Madison
    54th Civil Support Team – Madison
    505th Trial Defense Team
32nd Infantry Brigade Combat Team
    Headquarters and Headquarters Co. – Camp Douglas
    1st Battalion, 120th Field Artillery
    Headquarters and Headquarters Battery – Wisconsin
        Rapids
        Battery A – Marshfield
        Battery B – Stevens Point
    2nd Battalion, 127th Infantry
    Headquarters and Headquarters Co. (–) – Appleton
        Det. 1, Headquarters Co. – Clintonville
        Company A (–) – Waupun
        Det. 1, Co. A – Ripon
        Company B – Green Bay
        Company C – Fond du Lac
        Company D – Marinette
    1st Battalion, 128th Infantry
    Headquarters and Headquarters Co. (–) – Eau Claire
        Det. 1, Headquarters Co. – Abbotsford
        Company A – Menomonie
        Company B (–) – New Richmond
        Det. 1, Co. B – Rice Lake
        Company C (–) – Arcadia
        Det. 1, Co. C – Onalaska
        Company D – River Falls
    132nd Brigade Support Battalion
    Headquarters and Headquarters Co. – Portage
        Company A (–) (Distribution) – Janesville
        Det. 1, Co. A – Elkhorn
        Company B (Maintenance) – Mauston
        Company C (Medical) – Milwaukee
        Company D (–) (Forward Support) – Baraboo
        Det. 1, Co. D – Madison
        Company E (–) (Forward Support) – Waupaca
        Det. 1, Co. E – Appleton
        Company F (–) (Forward Support) – Neillsville
        Det. 1, Co. F – Eau Claire
        Company G (–) (Forward Support) – Mosinee
        Det. 1, Co. G – Wisconsin Rapids
    Brigade Special Troops Battalion
    Headquarters and Headquarters Co. (–) – Wausau
        Det. 1, Headquarters Co. – Merrill
        Company A (Engineer) – Onalaska
        Company B (Military Intelligence) – Madison
        Det. 1, Company B (TUAS Platoon) – Camp
            Douglas
        Company C (Signal) – Antigo
    1st Squadron, 105th Cavalry (Reconnaissance,
        Surveillance and Target Acquisition)
    Headquarters and Headquarters Troop – Madison
        Troop A – Fort Atkinson
        Troop B – Watertown
        Troop C – Reedsburg

64th Troop Command
Headquarters – Madison
    Wisconsin Medical Detachment – Camp Douglas
    732nd Combat Sustainment Support Battalion
    Headquarters and Headquarters Company – Tomah
        107th Maintenance Co. (–) – Sparta
            Det. 1, 107th Maintenance Co. – Viroqua
        1157th Transportation Co. – Oshkosh
        1158th Transportation Co. (–) – Beloit
            Det. 1, 1158th Trans. Co. – Black River Falls
    1st Battalion, 147th Aviation Regiment
    Headquarters and Headquarters Co. (–) – Madison
        Company A – Madison
        Det. 1, Co. C – Madison
        Company D (–) – Madison
        Company E (–) – Madison
    641st Troop Command Battalion
    Headquarters and Headquarters Detachment – Madison
        135th Medical Co. – Waukesha
        1967th Contingency Contracting Team – Camp
            Douglas
        273rd Engineer Co. (Wheeled Sapper) – Medford
        457th Chemical Co. (–) – Hartford
            Det. 1, 457th Chemical Co. – Burlington
        Det. 1, Co. B, 248th Aviation Support Bn. – West
            Bend
        Det. 1, Co. C, 2nd Battalion, 135th Aviation Regiment
            – West Bend
        Det. 2, Co. D, 2nd Battalion, 135th Aviation Regiment
            – West Bend
        Det. 2, Co. E, 2nd Battalion, 135th Aviation Regiment
            – West Bend
        Company F (–) 2nd Battalion, 238th Aviation
            Regiment – West Bend
        Det. 4, HHC, 2nd Battalion, 238th Aviation Regiment
            – West Bend
        Det. 5, Co. D, 2nd Battalion, 238th Aviation Regiment
            – West Bend
        Det. 5, Co. E, 2nd Battalion, 238th Aviation Regiment
            – West Bend
        112th Mobile Public Affairs Det. – Madison
        132 Army Band – Madison
157th Maneuver Enhancement Brigade
Headquarters and Headquarters Co. – Milwaukee
    1st Battalion, 121st Field Artillery (HIMARS)
    Headquarters and Headquarters Battery – Milwaukee
        Battery A – Racine
        Battery B – Plymouth
        Battery C – Sussex
        108th Forward Support Company (HIMARS) – Sussex
    257th Brigade Support Battalion
    Headquarters and Headquarters Det. – Oak Creek
        Company A (Distribution) – Whitewater
        Company B (Support Maintenance) – Kenosha
    924th Engineer Det. (Facilities) – Chippewa Falls
    32nd Military Police Company (–) – Milwaukee
        Det. 1, 32nd MP Company – Oconomowoc
    357th Signal Network Support Co. – Two Rivers
    949th Engineer Det. (Survey & Design Tm) – Chippewa
        Falls
    724th Engineer Battalion
        Headquarters and Headquarters Co. – Chippewa Falls

Company A – Hayward
106th Engineer Det. (Quarry Team) – Tomah
229th Engineer Co. (–) (Horizontal) – Prairie du Chien
   Det. 1, 229th Engineer Co. – Platteville
824th Engineer Det. (Concrete) – Richland Center
829th Engineer Co. (–) (Vertical) – Chippewa Falls
   Det. 1, 829th Engineer Co. – Richland Center
   Det. 2, 829th Engineer Co. – Ashland
950th Engineer Co. (–) (Clearance) – Superior
   Det. 1, 950th Engineer Co. – Spooner
   954th Engineer Platoon (Clearance) – Superior
951st Engineer Co. (–) (Wheeled Sapper) – Tomahawk

   Det. 1, 951st Engineer Co. – Rhinelander
426th Regiment – Regional Training Institute (Wisconsin Military Academy)
Headquarters and Headquarters Det. – Fort McCoy
   Training Site Detachment – Fort McCoy
   1st Battalion, 426th Rgt. (Field Artillery) – Fort McCoy
   2nd Battalion, 426th Rgt. (Modular Training) – Fort McCoy

AIR UNITS

Headquarters, Wisconsin Air National Guard – Madison
115th Fighter Wing – Truax Field, Madison
   115th Operations Group
      176th Fighter Squadron
      115th Operations Support Flight
   115th Maintenance Group
      115th Aircraft Maintenance Squadron
      115th Maintenance Squadron
      115th Maintenance Operations Flight
   115th Mission Support Group
      115th Logistics Readiness Squadron
      115th Security Forces Squadron
      115th Mission Support Flight
      115th Services Flight
      115th Civil Engineer Squadron
      115th Communications Flight
   115th Medical Group

128th Air Refueling Wing – Mitchell Field, Milwaukee
   128th Operations Group
      126th Air Refueling Squadron
      128th Operations Support Flight
   128th Maintenance Group
      128th Aircraft Maintenance Squadron
      128th Maintenance Squadron
      128th Maintenance Operations Flight
   128th Mission Support Group
      128th Logistics Readiness Squadron
      128th Security Forces Squadron
      128th Mission Support Flight
      128th Services Flight
      128th Civil Engineer Squadron
      128th Communications Flight
      126th Weather Flight
   128th Medical Group
Volk Field Combat Readiness Training Center – Camp Douglas
   128th Air Control Squadron – Volk Field CRTC, Camp Douglas

---

Bold Face – Major Command
(–) – Headquarters of a split unit
Abbreviations:
Bn. – Battalion
Co. – Company
CRTC – Combat Readiness Training Center
Det. – Detachment

HIMARS – High-Mobility Artillery Rocket System
MP – Military Police
Rgt. – Regiment
Trans. – Transportation
TUAS – Tactical Unmanned Aircraft System
WMD – Weapons of Mass Destruction

Source: Wisconsin Department of Military Affairs, departmental data, May 2011.

MEMBERSHIP, WISCONSIN VETERANS HOMES
1888 – 2012

	Civil and Indian Wars	Spanish–American	World War I		World War II		Korean Conflict		Total
			Men	Women	Men	Women	Men	Women	
1888	72	—	—	—	—	—	—	—	72
1890	139	—	—	—	—	—	—	—	139
1900	680	—	—	—	—	—	—	—	680
1910	699	—	—	—	—	—	—	—	699
1920	532	—	—	—	—	—	—	—	532
1930	254	108	10	14	—	—	—	—	386
1940	89	196	101	130	—	—	—	—	516
1950	27	156	189	93	5	1	—	—	471
1960	4	74	203	94	40	5	—	—	450
1961	3	66	221	88	39	8	—	—	427
1962	3	66	223	82	52	9	—	—	431
1963	3	67	235	87	57	10	—	—	459
1964	3	63	237	105	61	16	—	—	485
1965	2	62	247	112	77	16	—	—	516
1966	1	56	258	112	86	21	—	—	534
1967	1	46	272	120	93	20	—	—	555
1968	1	48	253	123	93	16	—	—	534
1969	1	43	253	145	101	14	—	—	560
1970	1	35	279	146	153	20	1	0	635
1971	1	39	316	160	184	31	2	0	723
1972	0	28	279	155	199	39	2	0	702
1973	0	25	285	108	199	37	0	1	715
1974	0	21	279	175	185	37	0	2	699

	Spanish-American		World War I		World War II		Korean Conflict		Vietnam		Other Eras[1]		Total
	Vets.	Deps.	Vets.	Deps.	Vets.	Deps.	Vets.	Deps.	Vets.	Deps.	Vets.	Deps.	
1975	1	18	272	171	198	40	3	2	0	0	0	0	705
1976	1	14	254	167	209	40	2	2	0	0	0	0	689
1977	1	13	270	164	205	41	4	2	0	0	0	0	700
1978	1	11	261	158	218	38	3	2	0	0	0	0	692
1979	1	11	244	146	227	37	4	1	0	0	0	0	672
1980	1	8	242	144	241	36	5	1	0	0	0	0	678
1981	0	8	224	139	264	40	8	2	0	0	0	0	685
1982	0	7	189	124	282	43	11	2	0	0	0	0	658
1983	0	5	171	111	297	42	14	2	1	0	0	0	643
1984	0	4	144	97	316	47	21	2	3	0	0	0	634
1985	0	4	129	102	329	54	28	0	5	0	0	0	651
1986	0	4	117	92	348	56	35	5	7	0	0	0	664
1987	0	2	108	84	384	60	36	4	8	0	0	0	686
1988	0	1	84	76	395	55	45	7	8	0	0	0	671
1989	0	2	62	75	399	67	50	7	9	1	0	0	672
1990	0	2	49	65	431	76	62	8	10	1	3	0	707
1991	0	2	43	57	440	74	69	10	10	2	3	0	710
1992	0	1	33	44	442	77	82	10	12	1	2	0	704
1993	0	1	23	41	463	73	94	9	11	1	2	0	718
1994	0	1	14	33	488	83	99	11	12	2	1	0	744
1995	0	1	8	31	484	84	99	12	16	2	1	0	738
1996	0	1	4	24	489	79	103	12	25	1	1	0	739
1997	0	1	3	20	479	82	107	11	38	1	3	0	744
1998	0	0	1	17	460	83	123	12	39	1	9	0	745
1999	0	0	0	12	445	87	128	11	41	3	13	1	741
2000	0	0	0	10	423	94	132	12	47	4	21	2	745
2001[2]	0	0	0	9	414	95	133	10	51	3	25	2	742
2002	0	0	0	8	404	103	130	11	54	3	29	2	744
2003	0	0	0	7	433	105	140	13	67	3	35	2	805
2004	0	0	0	3	416	99	148	15	72	3	40	2	798
2005	0	0	0	2	350	103	144	15	71	3	40	2	730
2006	0	0	0	1	407	119	164	17	87	5	50	4	854
2007	0	0	0	1	475	135	173	26	100	8	3	0	921
2008	0	0	0	1	417	123	177	26	115	7	4	0	870
2009	0	0	0	1	389	130	193	21	122	8	8	0	947
2010	0	0	0	1	356	127	176	22	122	8	10	0	892
2011	0	0	0	1	339	124	170	19	154	12	12	0	904
2012	0	0	0	1	330	121	180	32	178	11	19	2	953

Deps. – Dependents.

[1]Other periods of hostilities for which expeditionary medals were awarded.

[2]The Wisconsin Veterans Home at King was established in 1887, and the home at Union Grove opened in 2001. Data starting in 2001 includes both homes.

Source: Wisconsin Department of Veterans Affairs, departmental data, May 2013.

FEDERAL EXPENDITURES FOR VETERANS
By State, Federal Fiscal Year 2012

State	Veteran Population[1]	Total Expenditures	Compensation and Pension[2]	Medical Care[3]	Education and Vocational Rehabilitation/ Employment
Alabama	418,035	$2,415,560	$1,362,005	$807,118	$174,031
Alaska	74,513	410,052	178,264	166,961	53,712
Arizona	531,910	2,712,810	1,179,562	1,059,215	306,312
Arkansas	252,279	1,674,467	802,324	724,198	73,423
California	1,844,803	10,274,754	4,219,749	4,194,246	1,393,887
Colorado	395,613	2,111,996	1,011,092	650,528	284,980
Connecticut	215,316	889,948	309,790	464,585	74,104
Delaware	78,687	309,215	145,450	122,487	29,797
District of Columbia	31,839	2,099,018	66,819	164,821	22,122
Florida	1,543,496	8,889,429	4,067,030	3,521,811	782,267
Georgia	776,205	3,928,851	2,090,187	1,260,142	388,892
Hawaii	116,844	607,054	268,665	177,283	132,202
Idaho	138,320	635,946	287,723	279,402	48,246
ILLINOIS	764,203	3,237,715	1,180,084	1,623,723	280,998
Indiana	498,944	2,001,898	873,835	913,962	131,325
IOWA	238,236	994,001	425,818	471,990	67,379
Kansas	226,916	1,042,004	458,118	452,914	87,107
Kentucky	342,370	1,904,184	946,643	765,257	119,126
Louisiana	319,349	1,774,088	873,881	669,506	109,907
Maine	130,196	776,817	420,454	290,632	37,663
Maryland	450,401	1,991,533	825,856	813,581	273,254
Massachusetts	388,539	1,978,766	810,371	913,653	153,620
MICHIGAN	680,417	2,768,689	1,391,510	1,101,665	171,896
MINNESOTA	369,295	1,978,159	863,698	865,099	133,639
Mississippi	227,335	1,276,247	581,099	560,906	78,967
Missouri	505,729	2,527,524	1,153,182	1,012,336	161,337
Montana	102,246	537,303	258,791	228,308	34,722
Nebraska	141,102	887,641	427,268	342,330	58,708
Nevada	228,393	1,295,319	516,007	631,285	85,701
New Hampshire	113,101	516,990	221,888	228,792	51,111
New Jersey	441,820	1,633,179	774,174	629,453	164,539
New Mexico	172,085	1,129,055	596,324	433,359	63,130
New York	918,093	4,768,842	1,733,092	2,367,824	414,224
North Carolina	771,654	4,193,637	2,285,260	1,400,930	344,205
North Dakota	56,408	279,238	127,968	114,838	19,458
Ohio	899,615	5,805,377	1,583,125	1,818,697	268,769
Oklahoma	342,816	2,215,693	1,331,604	626,477	121,712
Oregon	328,138	1,915,327	924,333	784,387	120,664
Pennsylvania	980,529	4,075,364	1,720,685	1,754,069	296,410
Rhode Island	71,457	425,789	167,869	182,716	26,971
South Carolina	421,525	2,402,619	1,301,455	801,687	200,887
South Dakota	75,930	489,297	187,591	255,378	28,302
Tennessee	525,594	2,792,092	1,399,741	1,085,053	197,153
Texas	1,675,689	11,164,622	4,959,438	3,249,727	979,947
Utah	151,786	770,753	295,027	321,117	79,200
Vermont	49,905	241,641	105,307	105,226	16,312
Virginia	837,051	3,852,375	1,904,164	1,067,307	744,302
Washington	607,501	2,813,701	1,448,669	897,973	310,749
West Virginia	175,497	1,374,658	566,535	540,324	42,877
WISCONSIN	418,461	2,034,321	861,184	942,007	120,359
Wyoming	56,434	281,753	110,732	148,555	13,229
UNITED STATES	22,234,454	$120,404,628	$53,243,134	$45,521,300	$10,424,615

[1]Estimate as of September 30, 2012.

[2]Includes expenditures for the following programs: veterans' compensation for service-connected disabilities, dependency and indemnity compensation for service-connected deaths, veterans' pension for nonservice-connected disabilities, and burial and other benefits to veterans and their survivors.

[3]Includes expenditures for medical services, and other medical administrative and overhead items.

Source: Wisconsin Department of Veterans Affairs, departmental data, May 2013. United States totals include Puerto Rico and Guam.

WISCONSIN NEWSPAPERS
Daily Newspapers

Municipality	Newspaper[1]	Publisher	Web Address
Antigo	Antigo Daily Journal	Fred Berner	www.antigodailyjournal.com
Appleton	The Post-Crescent	Genia Lovett	www.postcrescent.com
Ashland	The Daily Press	David Thornberry	www.ashlandwi.com
Baraboo	Baraboo News Republic	Matt Meyers*	www.baraboonewsrepublic.com
Beaver Dam	Daily Citizen	Scott Zeinemann*	www.wiscnews.com/bdc/
Beloit	Beloit Daily News	Kent Eymann	www.beloitdailynews.com
Eau Claire	Leader-Telegram	Pieter Graaskamp	www.leadertelegram.com
Fond du Lac	The Reporter	Richard Roesgen	www.fdlreporter.com
Fort Atkinson	Daily Jefferson County Union	Brian Knox	www.dailyunion.com
Green Bay	Green Bay Press-Gazette	Kevin Corrado	www.greenbaypressgazette.com
Janesville	The Janesville Gazette	Skip Bliss	www.gazetteextra.com
Kenosha	Kenosha News	Kenneth Dowdell	www.kenoshanews.com
La Crosse	La Crosse Tribune	Rusty Cunningham	www.lacrossetribune.com
Madison	Wisconsin State Journal	Bill Johnston	www.madison.com/wsj/
Manitowoc	Herald Times Reporter	Kevin Corrado	www.htrnews.com
Marinette	EagleHerald	Dan White	www.ehextra.com
Marshfield	Marshfield News-Herald	Jonathan Gneiser*	www.marshfieldnewsherald.com
Milwaukee	The Daily Reporter	Ann Richmond	www.dailyreporter.com
Milwaukee	Milwaukee Journal Sentinel	Elizabeth Brenner	www.jsonline.com
Monroe	Monroe Times	Carl Hearing	www.themonroetimes.com
Oshkosh	Oshkosh Northwestern	Stewart Rieckman*	www.thenorthwestern.com
Portage	Portage Daily Register	Matt Meyers*	www.portagedailyregister.com
Racine	The Journal Times	Mark Lewis	www.journaltimes.com
Sheboygan	The Sheboygan Press	Nhia Yang*	www.sheboyganpress.com
Stevens Point	Stevens Point Journal	Michael Beck*	www.stevenspointjournal.com
Watertown	Watertown Daily Times	Kevin Clifford	www.wdtimes.com
Waukesha	The Freeman	Phil Paige	www.gmtoday.com
Wausau	Wausau Daily Herald	Michael Beck*	www.wausaudailyherald.com
West Bend	Daily News	Phil Paige	www.gmtoday.com
Wisconsin Rapids	Daily Tribune	Allen Hicks*	www.wisconsinrapidstribune.com

*General manager.

Other Newspapers

Municipality	Newspaper	Published	Publisher
Abbotsford 54405	Record-Review	Wed.	Kris O' Leary
Abbotsford 54405	The Tribune-Phonograph	Wed.	Kris O' Leary
Adams 53910	Adams-Friendship Times Reporter	Wed.	Dan & Mark Witte
Albany 53502	Hometown Herald	Thurs.	PJ Francis
Alma (Cochrane 54622)	Buffalo County Journal	Thurs.	Daniel, Michael, Gary Stumpf
Amery 54001	Amery Free Press	Tues.	Tom Stangl
Argyle 53504	Pecatonica Valley Leader	Thurs.	Michael & Patrick Reilly
Ashwaubenon (Green Bay 54304)	The Press	Fri.	Michael Aubinger
Augusta 54722	Augusta Area Times	Thurs.	Michael Stumpf
Baldwin 54002	The Baldwin Bulletin	Tues.	Thomas Hawley
Balsam Lake 54810	Lake County Ledger Press	Thurs.	Leslie Waggoner & Tom Miller
Barron 54812	Barron News-Shield	Wed.	Mark & James Bell
Berlin 54923	Berlin Journal	Thurs.	Ty Gonyo
Black Earth 53515	News-Sickle-Arrow	Thurs.	Dan & Mark Witte
Black River Falls 54615	Falls Banner Journal	Wed.	Dan & Mark Witte
Black River Falls 54615	Jackson County Chronicle	Wed.	Chris Hardie
Blair 54616	The Blair Press	Thurs.	Lee Henschel
Bloomer 54724	Bloomer Advance	Wed.	James Bell
Boscobel (Lancaster 53813)	The Boscobel Dial	Thurs.	John Ingebritsen
Brillion 54110	The Brillion News	Thurs.	Kristine Bastian
Brodhead 53520	The Independent Register	Wed.	Pete Cruger
Brookfield[2]	Brookfield-Elm Grove NOW	Thurs.	Hugh McGarry
Burlington 53105	Burlington Standard Press	Thurs.	Jack Cruger
Burlington 53105	Westline Report	Fri.	Cyndi Jensen (general manager)
Cambridge 53523	The Cambridge News	Thurs.	Brian Knox
Campbellsport 53010	Campbellsport News	Thurs.	Andrew Johnson
Cashton 54619	Cashton Record	Wed.	Paul Fanning
Cedarburg 53012	News Graphic	Tues. & Thurs.	Phil Paige
Chetek 54728	The Chetek Alert	Wed.	James Bell
Chilton 53014	Times-Journal	Thurs.	James H. Moran
Chippewa Falls 54729	The Chippewa Herald	Mon., Tues., Wed., Thurs.	Rusty Cunningham
Clinton 53525	The Clinton Topper	Thurs.	Jack Cruger
Clintonville 54929	Clintonville Chronicle	Tues.	Tricia Rose
Cochrane 54622	Cochrane-Fountain City Recorder	Thurs.	Daniel, Michael, Gary Stumpf
Colfax 54730	The Colfax Messenger	Wed.	Carlton DeWitt

WISCONSIN NEWSPAPERS
Other Newspapers–Continued

Municipality	Newspaper	Published	Publisher
Columbus (Beaver Dam 53916)	Columbus Journal	Sat.	Scott Zeinemann (general manager)
Cornell 54732	Courier Sentinel	Thurs.	Carol O'Leary
Cottage Grove 53527	The Herald-Independent	Thurs.	Brian Knox
Crandon 54520	The Forest Republican	Wed.	Hank Murphy
Cuba City 53807	Tri-County Press	Thurs.	John Ingebritsen
Cumberland 54829	Cumberland Advocate	Wed.	Paul Bucher
Darlington 53530	Republican Journal	Thurs.	Brian Lund
Deerfield 53531	The Independent	Thurs.	Brian Knox
DeForest 53532	DeForest Times-Tribune	Thurs.	Brian Knox
Delavan 53115	The Delavan Enterprise	Fri.	Vicky Wedig-Farence (editor)
Delavan 53115	Walworth - Fontana Times	Fri.	Cyndi Jensen (general manager)
Denmark 54208	Denmark News	Thurs.	Mark Hansen & Ryan Radue
De Pere (Green Bay 54305)	De Pere Journal	Thurs.	Kevin Corrado
Dodgeville 53533	The Dodgeville Chronicle	Thurs.	Michael & Patrick Reilly
Dousman[3]	Kettle Moraine Index	Thurs.	Steve Lyles
Durand 54736	The Courier-Wedge	Thurs.	Michael Stumpf
Eagle River 54521	Vilas County News-Review	Wed.	Kurt L. Krueger
East Troy 53120	East Troy News	Fri.	Vanessa Lenz (editor)
East Troy 53120	East Troy Times	Wed.	Vanessa Lenz (editor)
Eau Claire 54701	The Country Today	Wed.	Pieter Graaskamp
Edgar (Abbotsford 54405)	The Record-Review	Wed.	Kris O' Leary
Edgerton 53534	The Edgerton Reporter	Wed.	Diane & Helen Everson
Elkhorn 53121	Elkhorn Independent	Thurs.	Jack Cruger
Ellsworth 54011	Pierce County Herald	Wed.	Steven Dzubay
Elmwood (Spring Valley 54767)	Sun-Argus	Wed.	Paul Seeling
Elroy 53929	The Messenger of Juneau County	Thurs.	Bill Smith
Evansville 53536	The Evansville Review	Wed.	Kelly A., Stanley A., Danley C. Gildner
Fennimore (Lancaster 53813)	The Fennimore Times	Thurs.	John Ingebritsen
Florence 54121	The Florence Mining News	Wed.	Hank Murphy
Fox Lake 53933	Fox Lake Representative	Thurs.	Ty Gonyo
Frederic 54837	Inter-County Leader	Wed.	Douglas Panek
Gays Mills 54631	Crawford County Independent & The Kickapoo Scout	Thurs.	John Ingebritsen
Genoa City (Delavan 53115)	Genoa City Report	Thurs.	Alexandrea Dahlstrom (editor)
Germantown[2]	Germantown-Menomonee Falls NOW	Thurs.	Hugh McGarry
Glenwood City 54013	Tribune Press Reporter	Wed.	Carlton DeWitt
Glidden 54527	The Glidden Enterprise	Wed.	Chris Canfield
Grantsburg 54840	Burnett County Sentinel	Wed.	Randi L. Smith
Green Lake (Berlin 54923)	Green Lake Reporter	Thurs.	Ty Gonyo
Greenfield[2]	Greenfield-West Allis NOW	Thurs.	Hugh McGarry
Hammond (Roberts 54026)	Central St. Croix News	Thurs.	Jeff Redmon
Hartland[3]	Lake Country Reporter	Tues. & Thurs.	Steve Lyles
Hayward 54843	Sawyer County Record	Wed.	Janet Krokson
Hillsboro 54634	Hillsboro Sentry-Enterprise	Thurs.	John Ingebritsen
Hudson (River Falls 54022)	Hudson Star-Observer	Thurs.	Steven Dzubay
Hurley 54534	Iron County Miner	Thurs.	Ernest Moore
Juneau 53039	Dodge County Independent News	Thurs.	James Clifford
Kaukauna 54130	Times-Villager	Wed. & Sat.	Brian Roebke (editor)
Kenosha 53144	Labor Paper	Thurs.	Mark Onosko
Kewaskum 53040	The Statesman	Thurs.	Andrew & Nicole Kuehl
Kiel 53042	Tri-County News	Thurs.	Mike Mathes
Ladysmith 54848	Ladysmith News	Thurs.	James Bell
La Farge 54639	La Farge Episcope	Tues.	Lonnie Muller
Lake Geneva 53147	Lake Geneva Regional News	Thurs.	John Halverson (general manager)
Lake Mills 53551	Lake Mills Leader	Thurs.	Brian Knox
Lancaster 53813	Grant County Herald Independent	Thurs.	John Ingebritsen
Lodi 53555	Lodi Enterprise	Thurs.	Brian Knox
Loyal 54446	Tribune Record Gleaner	Wed.	Kris O'Leary & Kevin Flink
Luck 54853	Enterprise Press	Thurs.	Tom Miller
Madison 53713	The Capital Times	Wed.	Clayton Frink
Madison 53703	Isthmus	Thurs.	Vincent P. O'Hern
Marion 54950	The Marion Advertiser	Thurs.	Dan Brandenburg
Markesan 53946	Markesan Regional Reporter	Thurs.	Ty Gonyo
Mauston 53948	Juneau County Star-Times	Wed. & Sat.	Matt Meyers (general manager)
Mayville 53050	Dodge County Pionier	Thurs.	Andrew Johnson
McFarland 53558	McFarland Thistle & McFarland Community Life	Thurs.	Brian Knox
Medford 54405	The Star News	Thurs.	Carol O'Leary
Mellen 54546	The Mellen Weekly-Record	Wed.	James & Sandy Christl
Menomonie 54751	The Dunn County News	Sun. & Wed.	Rusty Cunningham
Merrill 54452	Merrill Courier	Fri.	Jeff Hovind
Middleton 53562	Middleton Times-Tribune	Thurs.	Dan & Mark Witte

WISCONSIN NEWSPAPERS
Other Newspapers–Continued

Municipality	Newspaper	Published	Publisher
Milton 53563.	Milton Courier	Thurs.	Brian Knox
Milwaukee 53202	Shepherd Express	Thurs.	Louis Fortis
Mineral Point 53565	The Democrat Tribune	Thurs.	Patrick & Michael Reilly
Minocqua 54548	The Lakeland Times	Tues. & Fri.	Gregg Walker
Mondovi 54755	Mondovi Herald News	Thurs.	Michael Stumpf
Montello 53949	The Marquette County Tribune	Thurs.	Dan & Mark Witte
Mosinee 54455.	The Mosinee Times	Thurs.	John Durst & James Kress
Mount Horeb 53572	Mount Horeb Mail	Thurs.	Dan & Mark Witte
Mukwonago 53149	Mukwonago Chief	Wed.	Steve Lyles
Muscoda (Lancaster 53813)	The Progressive	Thurs.	John Ingebritsen
Muskego[2]	Muskego-New Berlin NOW	Thurs.	Hugh McGarry
Neillsville 54456.	The Clark County Press	Wed.	Dan & Mark Witte
New Glarus 53574	Post Messenger Recorder	Thurs.	Dan & Mark Witte
New London 54961	County Post East	Thurs.	Trey Foerster
New Richmond 54017	New Richmond News	Thurs.	Steven Dzubay
North Shore[2]	North Shore NOW	Thurs.	Hugh McGarry
Oak Creek[2]	Oak Creek NOW	Thurs.	Hugh McGarry
Oconomowoc (Waukesha 53186)	Oconomowoc Enterprise	Thurs.	Phil Paige
Oconomowoc[3]	Oconomowoc Focus	Tues. & Thurs.	Steve Lyles
Oconto 54153	Oconto County Reporter	Wed.	Kevin Corrado
Oconto Falls 54154	Oconto County Times-Herald	Wed.	Greg Mellis
Omro 54963	Omro Herald	Thurs.	Ty Gonyo
Onalaska/Holmen	Courier-Life	Fri.	Chris Hardie
(La Crosse 54602)			
Ontario 54651	County Line	Thurs.	Karen Parker
Oregon 53575	The Oregon Observer	Thurs.	Lee Borkowski
			(general manager)
Osceola 54020	The Sun	Wed.	Randi Smith
Osseo 54758	Tri-County News.	Thurs.	Michael Stumpf
Park Falls 54552	The Park Falls Herald	Thurs.	Susan Kelley
Peshtigo 54157.	Peshtigo Times	Wed.	Mary Ann Gardon
Phillips 54555	The-Bee	Thurs.	Susan Kelley
Platteville 53818	The Platteville Journal	Wed.	John Ingebritsen
Plymouth 53073	The Review	Tues. & Thurs.	Barry & Christie Johanson
Port Washington 53074	Ozaukee Press	Thurs.	William F. Schanen III
Poynette (Sun Prairie 53590)	Poynette Press	Thurs.	Brian Knox
Prairie du Chien 53821	Courier Press	Mon. & Wed..	William H. Howe
Prescott 54021	Prescott Journal	Thurs.	John E. McLoone
Princeton (Berlin 54923).	Princeton Times-Republic	Thurs.	Ty Gonyo
Random Lake 53075.	The Sounder	Thurs.	Gary Feider (general manager)
Reedsburg 53959.	Reedsburg Independent	Thurs.	Dan & Mark Witte
Reedsburg 53959.	Reedsburg Times Press	Wed. & Sat.	Matt Meyers (general manager)
Rhinelander 54501.	The Northwoods River News	Tues., Thurs. & Sat.	Gregg Walker
Rice Lake 54868	The Chronotype	Wed.	Warren Dorrance
Richland Center 53581	The Richland Observer	Thurs.	John Ingebritsen
Ripon 54971	The Ripon Commonwealth Press	Wed.	Tim Lyke
River Falls 54022	River Falls Journal	Thurs.	Steven Dzubay
St. Croix Falls 54024	Standard-Press	Thurs.	Leslie Waggoner & Tom Miller
Sauk City 53913	Sauk Prairie Eagle	Wed.	Matt Meyers (general manager)
Sauk City 53583	Sauk Prairie Star	Thurs.	Dan & Mark Witte
Sharon (Delevan 53115)	Sharon Reporter	Fri.	Cyndi Jensen (general manager)
Shawano 54166	Shawano Leader	Wed., Thurs., Fri., & Sat.	Greg Mellis
Sheboygan (Plymouth 53073)	The Sheboygan Falls News	Wed.	Barry & Christie Johanson
Shell Lake 54871	Washburn County Register	Wed.	Douglas Panek
South Milwaukee[2]	South Shore NOW	Thurs.	Hugh McGarry
Sparta 54656	Monroe County Democrat	Thurs.	William Gleiss
Sparta 54656	The Sparta Herald	Mon.	Theodore C. Radde
Spooner 54801	Spooner Advocate	Thurs.	Janet Krokson
Spring Green 53588	Home News	Wed.	Dan & Mark Witte
Spring Valley 54767	Sun-Argus	Wed.	Paul Seeling
Stanley 54768	The Stanley Republican	Wed.	John E. McLoone
Stevens Point 54481	Portage County Gazette	Fri.	Pete Leahy
Stoughton 53589.	The Stoughton Courier Hub	Thurs.	Lee Borkowski
			(general manager)
Sturgeon Bay 54235	Door County Advocate	Wed. & Sat.	Kevin Corrado
Sun Prairie 53590	The Star	Thurs.	Brian Knox
Superior 54880.	Superior Telegram	Tues. & Fri.	Shelley Nelson (editor)
Sussex[3]	Sussex Sun	Wed.	Steve Lyles
Thorp 54771	The Thorp Courier	Wed.	Mark LaGasse
Three Lakes (Eagle River 54521)	The Three Lakes News	Wed.	Kurt L. Krueger
Tomah 54660.	The Tomah Journal and Monitor Herald.	Mon. & Thurs.	Chris Hardie
Tomahawk 54487	Tomahawk Leader	Tues.	Larry & Kathleen Tobin

WISCONSIN NEWSPAPERS
Other Newspapers–Continued

Municipality	Newspaper	Published	Publisher
Turtle Lake 54889	The Times	Thurs.	David Slack
Twin Lakes (Delevan 53115) . .	Twin Lakes Report.	Wed.	Cyndi Jensen (general manager)
Valders 54245	The Valders Journal	Thurs.	Brian Thomsen
Verona 53593	The Verona Press.	Thurs.	Lee Borkowski
			(general manager)
Viola 54664	Epitaph-News	Thurs.	Bonnie Howell-Sherman
Viroqua 54665	Vernon County Broadcaster	Thurs.	Chris Hardie
Washburn (Ashland 54806) . . .	The County Journal	Wed.	Wanda Moeller
Waterford (Delevan 53115) . . .	Waterford Post	Fri.	Cyndi Jensen (general manager)
Waterloo (Sun Prairie 53590) . .	The Courier	Thurs.	Brian Knox
Waukesha (Hartland 53029) . . .	Waukesha NOW	Thurs.	Steve Lyles
Waunakee (Sun Prairie 53590)	The Waunakee Tribune	Thurs.	Brian Knox
Waupaca 54981	County Post East	Thurs.	Stacy Knueppel
Waupaca 54981	County Post West	Thurs.	Kathy Banks
Wautoma 54982	Waushara Argus	Wed.	Mary Kunasch
Wauwatosa[2]	Wauwatosa NOW	Thurs.	Hugh McGarry
West Salem 54669	The Coulee News	Fri.	Chris Hardie
Westby 54667	Westby Times	Thurs.	Chris Hardie
Whitehall 54773	Trempealeau County Times	Thurs.	Dan & Mark Witte
Whitewater (Delevan 53115) . .	Whitewater Register	Thurs.	Cyndi Jensen (general manager)
Winneconne 54986.	The Winneconne News	Wed.	John Rogers
Winter 54896.	Sawyer County Gazette	Wed.	Sue Johnston
Wisconsin Dells (Portage 53901)	Wisconsin Dells Events	Wed. & Sat. . .	Matt Meyers (general manager)
Wisconsin Rapids 54495.	The Voice of Wisconsin Rapids	Fri.	Jeff Williams
Withee 54498	O-W Enterprise	Wed.	Mark Renderman
			& Mark Gorke
Wittenberg 54499	The Wittenberg Enterprise and		
	Birnamwood News.	Thurs.	Mariam Nelson
Woodville 54028.	The Woodville Leader	Wed.	Paul Seeling

[1]A "newspaper" is defined by Section 985.03 (1) (c), Wisconsin Statutes, as follows: "A newspaper, under this chapter, is a publication appearing at regular intervals and at least once a week, containing reports of happenings of recent occurrence of a varied character, such as political, social, moral and religious subjects, designed to inform the general reader . . .".

[2]Combined editorial office in Waukesha 53186.

[3]Combined editorial office in Hartland 53029.

Sources: Wisconsin Newspaper Association, *2013 Member Directory*; data compiled by Wisconsin Legislative Reference Bureau.

· WISCONSIN PERIODICALS

Name	Issued	Publishers
AAA Living/Wisconsin	Bimonthly	AAA Wisconsin, P.O. Box 33, Madison 53701-0033 wisconsin.aaa.com
Action Tracks	1 per year	Kurt Krueger, P.O. Box 1929, Eagle River 54521-1929 www.vilascountynewsreview.com
Agri-View	Weekly	Capital Newspapers, 1901 Fish Hatchery Rd., Madison 53713 www.agriview.com
Agronomy Journal	Bimonthly	American Society of Agronomy, 5585 Guilford Rd., Madison 53711 agron.scijournals.org
Airwaves	10 per year	Wisconsin Public Television, R. 1076 Vilas Hall, 821 University Ave., Madison 53706 www.wpt.org
American Orthoptic Journal	1 per year	UW Press, 1930 Monroe St., 3rd Floor, Madison 53711-2059 uwpress.wisc.edu/journals
Antique Trader	26 per year	F & W Media, Inc., 700 E. State St., Iola 54990-0001 www.antiquetrader.com
Arctic Anthropology	2 per year	UW Press, 1930 Monroe St., 3rd Floor, Madison 53711-2059 uwpress.wisc.edu/journals
Asphalt Contractor	10 per year	Amy Schwandt, 1233 Janesville Ave., Fort Atkinson 53538 www.forconstructionpros.com
Astronomy	Monthly	Kalmbach Publishing Co., P.O. Box 1612, Waukesha 53187-1612 www.astronomy.com
At Ease (web-based)	Bimonthly	Wisconsin National Guard, 2400 Wright St., Madison 53704 dma.wi.gov
Backyard Poultry Magazine	Bimonthly	Bart Smith, 145 Industrial Dr., Medford 54451 www.backyardpoultrymag.com
Badger Common 'Tater	Monthly	Wis. Potato and Vegetable Growers Assn., Inc., P.O. Box 327, Antigo 54409-0327 www.wisconsinpotatoes.com
Badger Herald	Daily (M-F)	Peter T. Hoeschele, 326 W. Gorham St., Madison 53703 www.badgerherald.com
Badger Legionnaire, The.	10 per year	Wisconsin American Legion, 2930 American Legion Dr., P.O. Box 388, Portage 53901 www.wilegion.org
Badger Rails	6 per year	Wis. Assn. of Railroad Passengers, 3385 S. 119th St., West Allis 53227 www.wisarp.org
Badger Sportsman	Monthly	Badger Sportsman LLC, 19 E. Main St., P.O. Box 1186, Oshkosh 54903-1186 www.badgersportsman.com
Bank Note Reporter	Monthly	F & W Media, Inc., 700 E. State St., Iola 54990-0001 numismaster.com
Beloit College Magazine.	3 per year	Beloit College, Office of Communications and Marketing, 700 College St., Beloit 53511-5595 www.beloit.edu/belmag
Beloit Fiction Journal	1 per year	Chris Fink, Beloit College, Box 11, 700 College St., Beloit 53511 www.beloit.edu/english/fictionjournal/
Benefits Magazine	Monthly	International Foundation of Employee Benefit Plans, 18700 W. Bluemound Rd., Brookfield 53045 www.ifebp.org/magazines
Benefits Quarterly	4 per year	International Soc. of Certified Employee Benefit Specialists, P.O. Box 209, Brookfield 53008-0209 www.iscebs.org
Blade	13 per year	F & W Media, Inc., 700 E. State St., Iola 54990-0001 www.blademag.com
Business Journal, The	Weekly	Mark J. Sabljak, 825 N. Jefferson St., Suite 200, Milwaukee 53202 milwaukee.bizjournals.com
Capitol Watch (e-Newsletter)	Weekly	Wisconsin Manufacturers & Commerce, P.O. Box 352, Madison 53701-0352 www.wmc.org
Catholic Financial Life Member Magazine	4 per year	Catholic Financial Life, 1100 West Wells St., Milwaukee 53233 www.catholicfinanciallife.org

WISCONSIN PERIODICALS–Continued

Name	Issued	Publishers
Cessna Owner Magazine. . . . . Monthly		Jones Publishing, Inc., N7528 Aanstad Rd., Iola 54945-5000 www.cessnaowner.org
Cheese Reporter . . . . Weekly		Dick Groves, 2810 Crossroads Dr., Suite 3000, Madison 53718 www.cheesereporter.com
Classic Toy Trains . . . . 9 per year		Kalmbach Publishing Co., P.O. Box 1612, Waukesha 53187-1612 www.classictoytrains.com
Coins . . . . Monthly		F & W Media, Inc., 700 E. State St., Iola 54990-0001 numismaster.com
Columns . . . . Quarterly		Wisconsin Historical Society, 816 State St. Madison 53706-1417 www.wisconsinhistory.org
Comics Buyer's Guide . . . . Monthly		F & W Media, Inc., 700 E. State St., Iola 54990-0001 www.cbgxtra.com
Concrete Contractor . . . . 7 per year		Nancy Terrill, 1233 Janesville Ave., Fort Atkinson 53538 www.forconstructionpros.com
Connection, The . . . . Semimonthly		Jeanne Gardner, P.O. Box 189, Iron River 54847 theconnectionnewspaper.com
Contemporary Literature. . . . . Quarterly		UW Press, 1930 Monroe St., 3rd Floor, Madison 53711-2059 uwpress.wisc.edu/journals
Corporate Report Wisconsin. . . . . 10 per year		Nei-Turner Media Group, Inc., 93 W. Geneva St., P.O. Box 1080, Williams Bay 53191 crwmag.com
Countryside and Small Stock Journal . . . . . Bimonthly		Bart Smith, 145 Industrial Dr., Medford 54451 www.countrysidemag.com
Courier, The . . . . Monthly		Wisconsin Veterans Home, N2665 County Rd. QQ, King 54946 dva.state.wi.us/PA-publications.asp
Crafts Report, The . . . . Monthly		Jones Publishing, Inc., N7528 Aanstad Rd., Iola 54945-5000 www.craftsreport.com
Credit Union Magazine . . . . Monthly		Doug Benzine, Credit Union National Assn., P.O. Box 431, Madison 53701-0431 creditunionmagazine.com
Crop Science. . . . . Bimonthly		Crop Science Soc. of Amer., 5585 Guilford Rd., Madison 53711-5801
Crop Weather . . . . Weekly (Apr.-Nov.)		Dept. of Agriculture, Trade and Consumer Protection, P.O. Box 8934, Madison 53708-8934 www.nass.usda.gov
Daily Cardinal . . . . Daily (M-F)		Daily Cardinal Media Corp., 821 University Ave., Madison 53706-1497 www.dailycardinal.com
Dairy Goat Journal. . . . . Bimonthly		Bart Smith, 145 Industrial Dr., Medford 54451 www.dairygoatjournal.com
Deer and Deer Hunting . . . . 11 per year		F & W Media, Inc., 700 E. State St., Iola 54990-0001 www.deeranddeerhunting.com
Director, The. . . . . Monthly		NFDA Services, Inc., 13625 Bishop's Dr., Brookfield 53005 www.nfda.org
Dolls . . . . 10 per year		Jones Publishing, Inc., N7528 Aanstad Rd., Iola 54945-5000 www.dollsmagazine.com
Drum Corps World. . . . . 18 per year		Sights & Sounds, Inc., 4926 N. Sherman Ave., Unit H, Madison 53704-8443 www.drumcorpsworld.com
EAA Sport Aviation . . . . Monthly		Experimental Aircraft Association, EAA Aviation Center, P.O. Box 3086, Oshkosh 54903-3086 www.eaa.org
Ecological Restoration. . . . . Quarterly		UW Press, 1930 Monroe St., 3rd Floor, Madison 53711-2059 uwpress.wisc.edu/journals
Equipment Today . . . . Monthly		Sean Dunphy, 1233 Janesville Ave., Fort Atkinson 53538 www.forconstructionpros.com
Exponent. . . . . Weekly		UW-Platteville, 102 Russell Hall, 1 University Plz., Platteville 53818-3012

WISCONSIN PERIODICALS–Continued

Name	Issued	Publishers
Feminist Collections: A Quarterly of Women's Studies Resources	Quarterly	UW System Women's Studies Librarian, 430 Memorial Library, 728 State St., Madison 53706 womenst.library.wisc.edu
Feminist Periodicals: A Current Listing of Contents	Quarterly/electronic	UW System Women's Studies Librarian, 430 Memorial Library, 728 State St., Madison 53706 womenst.library.wisc.edu/publications/feminist-periodicals.html
FineScale Modeler	10 per year	Kalmbach Publishing, 21027 Crossroads Cir., Waukesha 53186-4055 www.finescale.com
Fired Arts and Crafts	Monthly	Jones Publishing, Inc., N7528 Aanstad Rd., P.O. Box 5000, Iola 54945-5000 www.firedartsandcrafts.com
Flip Side	Biweekly (during school year)	UW-Eau Claire, Davies Center 132, Eau Claire 54701 www.flipsidepress.org
Focus	Biweekly	Wis. Taxpayers Alliance, 401 North Lawn Ave., Madison 53704-5033 www.wistax.org
Forward	4 per year	League of Women Voters of Wis., 612 W. Main St., #200, Madison 53703-2500 www.lwvwi.org
Forward in Christ	Monthly	Wis. Evangelical Lutheran Synod, 2929 N. Mayfair Rd., Milwaukee 53222-4398 www.wels.net/forwardinchrist
Foto News	Weekly	Tim Schreiber, 807 E. First St., Merrill 54452 www.merrillfotonews.com
Frame Building News	5 per year	F & W Media, Inc., 700 E. State St., Iola 54990-0001 www.fwmedia.com
Free Riders Press	Monthly	Daron Jensen, W5715 County Rd., Wautoma 54982-1126 freeriderspress.us
Freedom Pursuit	Semimonthly	Angie and Roger Griepentrog, P.O. Box 1016, Freedom 54131 www.thefreedompursuit.com
Freethought Today	10 per year	Freedom From Religion Foundation, Inc., P.O. Box 750, Madison 53701-0750 ffrf.org/fttoday
Gargoyle, The	2 per year	UW Law School, 975 Bascom Mall, Madison 53706 www.law.wisc.edu/alumni/gargoyle
GFWC-WI Clubwoman	Quarterly	Melisa Schmidt (editor), P.O. Box 272, Brodhead 53520 www.gfwc-wi.org
Goldmine	14 per year	F & W Media, Inc., 700 E. State St., Iola 54990-0001 www.goldminemag.com
Great Lakes TPA	Monthly	Hahn Printing/GLTPA, P.O. Box 1278, Rhinelander 54501 www.timberpa.com
Grow	3 per year	College of Agricultural and Life Sciences, 136 Agricultural Hall,1450 Linden Drive, Madison 53706 www.cals.wisc.edu/grow
Gun Digest, The Magazine	Biweekly	F & W Media, Inc., 700 E. State St., Iola 54990-0001 www.gundigest.com
Gwiazda Polarna Polish Biweekly Newspaper	Biweekly	Point Publications, Inc., 2804 Post Rd., Stevens Point 54481-6452 www.gwiazdapolarna.com
Hoard's Dairyman	Semimonthly	W.D. Hoard and Sons Co., 28 Milwaukee Ave., W., Fort Atkinson 53538-2018 www.hoards.com
Hocak Worak	Biweekly	Ho-Chunk Nation, P.O. Box 667, Black River Falls 54615 hocakworak.com
Hummingbird: Magazine of the Short Poem	2 per year	CX Dillhunt, 7129 Lindfield Rd., Madison 53717
Impact Magazine	Quarterly	Wis. Park and Recreation Assn., 6601-C Northway, Greendale 53129 www.wpraweb.org
In Business	Monthly	Jody Glynn Patrick, 200 River Place, #250, Madison 53716 ibmadison.com

WISCONSIN PERIODICALS–Continued

Name	Issued	Publishers
Independence	2 per year	Easter Seals Wisconsin, Inc., 101 Nob Hill Rd., Suite 301, Madison 53713-3969 eastersealswisconsin.com
Inside UW-Madison (Electronic only).	Biweekly (during school year)	University Communications and Marketing, 27 Bascom Hall, 500 Lincoln Dr., Madison 53706 http://insideuw.wisc.edu
JCI Journal	1 per year	JCI Wisconsin, Inc., P.O. Box 1547, Appleton 54912-1547 www.jciwisconsin.org
Journal of Environmental Quality	Bimonthly	American Society of Agronomy, 5585 Guilford Rd., Madison 53711 www.agronomy.org/publications/jeq
Journal of Human Resources	Quarterly	UW Press, 1930 Monroe St., 3rd Floor, Madison 53711-2059 uwpress.wisc.edu/journals
Journal of Natural Resources and Life Sciences Education	1 per year	American Society of Agronomy, 5585 Guilford Rd., Madison 53711 www.jnrlse.org
Journal of the Pharmacy Society of Wisconsin	6 per year	Pharmacy Society of Wisconsin, 701 Heartland Trail, Madison 53717 www.pswi.org
Kalihwisaks	Biweekly	Oneida Tribe of Indians of Wis., 909 Packerland Dr., P.O. Box 365, Oneida 54155 www.kalihwisaks.com
Land Economics	Quarterly	UW Press, 1930 Monroe St., 3rd Floor, Madison 53711-2059 uwpress.wisc.edu/journals
Landscape Journal	2 per year	UW Press, 1930 Monroe St., 3rd Floor, Madison 53711-2059 uwpress.wisc.edu/journals
Living Church, The	Biweekly	The Living Church Foundation, Inc., P.O. Box 514036, Milwaukee 53203-3436 www.livingchurch.org
Luso-Brazilian Review	2 per year	UW Press, 1930 Monroe St. 3rd Floor, Madison 53711-2059 uwpress.wisc.edu/journals
Madison Magazine.	Monthly	Michael D. Kornemann, 7025 Raymond Rd., Madison 53719 www.madisonmagazine.com
Marquette Law Review	Quarterly	Joe Christensen, Inc., P.O. Box 1881, Milwaukee 53201-1881 http://scholarship.law.marquette.edu/mulr/
Marquette Magazine	Quarterly	Marquette University, P.O. Box 1881, Milwaukee 53201-1881 www.marquette.edu/magazine
Menominee Nation News	Bimonthly	Menominee Indian Tribe, P.O. Box 910, Keshena 54135 www.menominee-nsn.gov
Metal Roofing	Bimonthly	F & W Media, Inc., 700 E. State St., Iola 54990-0001 www.fwmedia.com
Midwest Flyer Magazine	Bimonthly	Dave Weiman, P.O. Box 199, Oregon 53575-0199 www.midwestflyer.com
Military Trader.	Monthly	F & W Media, Inc., 700 E. State St., Iola 54990-0001 www.fwmedia.com
Milwaukee History.	Quarterly	Milwaukee County Historical Society, 910 N. Old World 3rd St., Milwaukee 53203-1591 milwaukeecountyhistsoc.org
Milwaukee Labor Press	Monthly	Milwaukee Area Labor Council, AFL-CIO Milwaukee, 633 S. Hawley Rd., #110, Milwaukee 53214 www.milwaukeelabor.org/in_the_news/labor_press/
Milwaukee Magazine	Monthly	Betty Quadracci, 126 N. Jefferson St., Suite 100, Milwaukee 53202 www.milwaukeemag.com
Model Railroader	Monthly	Terry Thompson, 20127 Crossroads Cir. P.O. Box 1612, Waukesha 53187-1612 www.modelrailroader.com
Monatshefte	Quarterly	UW Press, 1930 Monroe St., 3rd Floor, Madison 53711-2059 uwpress.wisc.edu/journals
N (Nude and Natural)	4 per year	The Naturist Society, LLC, 627 Bay Shore Dr., Suite 200, Oshkosh 54901 www.naturistsociety.com

WISCONSIN PERIODICALS–Continued

Name	Issued	Publishers
Native Plants Journal	3 per year	UW Press, 1930 Monroe St., 3rd Floor, Madison 53711-2059 uwpress.wisc.edu/journals
New Books on Women, Gender and Feminism	2 per year	UW System Women's Studies Librarian, 430 Memorial Library, 728 State St., Madison 53706 womenst.library.wisc.edu
New North B2B	Monthly	Sean Fitzgerald, P.O. Box 559, Oshkosh 54903-0559 www.newnorthb2b.com
North Woods Trader	Weekly	Kurt Krueger, P.O. Box 1929, Eagle River 54521-1929 www.vilascountynewsreview.com
Northbound	2 per year	Trees For Tomorrow, Natural Resources Education Center, 519 Sheridan E, P.O. Box 609, Eagle River 54521 www.treesfortomorrow.com
Numismatic News	Weekly	F & W Media, Inc., 700 E. State St., Iola 54990-0001 www.numismaticnews.com
Old Cars Report Price Guide	Bimonthly	F & W Media, Inc., 700 E. State St., Iola 54990-0001 www.oldcarsreport.com
Old Cars Weekly	Weekly	F & W Media, Inc., 700 E. State St., Iola 54990-0001 www.oldcarsweekly.com
On Premise	Bimonthly	Nei-Turner, 2817 Fish Hatchery Rd., Fitchburg 53713 tlw.org
On Wisconsin Magazine	Quarterly	Wis. Alumni Assn., 650 N. Lake St., Madison 53706-1476 onwisconsin.uwalumni.com
Passenger Pigeon, The	Quarterly	Wisconsin Society for Ornithology, 7680 Payvery Tr., Middleton 53562-4128 http://wsobirds.org
Pavement Maintenance & Reconstruction	8 per year	Amy Schwandt, 1233 Janesville Ave., Fort Atkinson 53538 www.forconstructionpros.com
Pharmacy in History	Quarterly	Amer. Institute of the History of Pharmacy, 77 Highland Ave., Madison 53705-2222 www.aihp.org
PhotoDaily	Daily	Rohn Engh, PhotoSource Internatl., Pine Lake Farm,1910 35th Rd., Osceola 54020-5602 www.photosource.com
PhotoLetter	Weekly	Rohn Engh, PhotoSource Internatl., Pine Lake Farm,1910 35th Rd., Osceola 54020-5602 www.photosource.com
PhotoStockNOTES	Weekly (on-line)	Rohn Engh, PhotoSource Internatl., Pine Lake Farm,1910 35th Rd., Osceola 54020-5602 www.photosource.com
Picture Post	Weekly (Memorial Day-Labor Day)	Kathy Banks, P.O. Box 609, Waupaca 54981 waupacanow.com
Pipers Magazine	Monthly	Jones Publishing, Inc., N7528 Aanstad Rd., Iola 54945-5000 www.piperowner.org
Progressive, The	Monthly	Matthew Rothschild, 409 E. Main St., Madison 53703-2863 www.progressive.org
Quality Progress	Monthly	American Society for Quality, 600 N. Plankinton Ave., Milwaukee 53201 www.qualityprogress.com
Renascence: Essays on Values in Literature	Quarterly	Marquette University, Raynor Memorial Libraries, M-164, P.O. Box 1881, Milwaukee 53201-1881 www.marquette.edu/renascence
Rental	7 per year	Eric Servais, 1233 Janesville Ave., Fort Atkinson 53538 www.forconstructionpros.com
Rethinking Schools	Quarterly	Rethinking Schools, Ltd., 1001 E. Keefe Ave., Milwaukee 53212 www.rethinkingschools.org
Royal Purple	Weekly (during semester)	UW-Whitewater, 800 W. Main St., 66 University Center, Whitewater 53190 www.royalpurplenews.com
Rural Builder	7 per year	F & W Media, Inc., 700 E. State St., Iola 54990-0001 www.fwmedia.com

WISCONSIN PERIODICALS–Continued

Name	Issued	Publishers
Sabbath Recorder, The.	Monthly	American Sabbath Tract and Comm. Council, P.O. Box 1678, Janesville 53547 www.seventhdaybaptist.org
Safety Zone (E-Newsletter)	Monthly	Wis. Safety Council, P.O. Box 352, Madison 53701-0352 www.wisafetycouncil.org
Sheep!	Bimonthly	Bart Smith, 145 Industrial Dr., Medford 54451 www.sheepmagazine.com
Silent Sports	Monthly	Pete Daniels, P.O. Box 558, Rhinelander 54501 silentsports.net
Soil Science Society of America Journal . . .	Bimonthly	Soil Science Society of America, 5585 Guilford Rd., Madison 53711-5801
Soo, The	Quarterly	Soo Line Historical and Technical Society, 2124 N. Locust St., Appleton 54914 sooline.org
Southeastern Wisconsin Regional Planning Commission Newsletter	Irregular	Southeastern Wis. Regional Planning Comn., P.O. Box 1607, Waukesha 53187-1607 www.sewrpc.org
Spanish Journal	Weekly	Spanish Journal, Inc., 611 W. National Ave., Suite 316, Milwaukee 53204 www.spanishjournal.com
Spectator	Weekly	UW-Eau Claire, 104 Hibbard Hall, Eau Claire 54701 www.spectatornews.com
Sports Collectors Digest	Weekly	F & W Media, Inc., 700 E. State St., Iola 54490-0001 sportscollectorsdigest.com
SubStance	3 per year	UW Press, 1930 Monroe St., 3rd Floor, Madison 53711-2059 uwpress.wisc.edu/journals
Teddy Bear Review	6 per year	Jones Publishing, Inc., P.O. Box 5000, Iola 54945-5000 www.teddybearreview.com
Today's Dads.	Quarterly	Peter Kerr, 1621 N. Willow Ct., Grafton 53024 wisconsinfathers.org
Trains Magazine	Monthly	Kalmbach Publishing Co., 21027 Crossroads Cir., P.O. Box 1612, Waukesha 53187-1612 www.trainsmag.com
Trapper and Predator Caller	10 per year	F & W Media, Inc., 700 E. State St., Iola 54990-0001 www.trapperpredatorcaller.com
Travel Wisconsin News (E-Newsletter)	Monthly	Wis. Dept. of Tourism, P.O. Box 8690, Madison 53708 industry.travelwisconsin.com/
Turkey & Turkey Hunting	6 per year	F & W Media, Inc., 700 E. State St., Iola 54990-0001 www.turkeyandturkeyhunting.com
Union Labor News.	Monthly	Union Labor News Publishers, Ltd., 1602 S. Park St., Madison 53715-2159 www.scfl.org
Update	2 per year	Wisconsin School of Business, 975 University Ave., Madison 53706 www.bus.wisc.edu
Vacation Week	Weekly (June-Aug.)	Kurt Krueger, P.O. Box 1929, Eagle River 54521-1929 www.vilascountynewsreview.com
Volume One	Bimonthly	Nick Meyer, 205 N. Dewey St., Eau Claire 54701 www.volumeone.org
Voyageur: NE Wisconsin's Historical Review	2 per year	Brown County Historical Society, P.O. Box 1411, Green Bay 54305-1411 www.voyageurmagazine.org
WEAC in Print.	Quarterly	Wis. Education Assn. Council, 33 Nob Hill Rd., Madison 53713-2199 www.weac.org
WFU News.	10 per year	Wis. Farmers Union, 117 W. Spring St., Chippewa Falls 54729-2359 www.wisconsinfarmersunion.com
Wisconservation	Monthly	Wisconsin Wildlife Federation, W7303 Cty Hwy CS & Q, Poynette 53955 www.wiwf.org
Wis. Agriculturist	Monthly	Farm Progress Companies, P.O. Box 236, Brandon 53919 www.wisconsinagriculturist.com

WISCONSIN PERIODICALS–Continued

Name	Issued	Publishers
Wis. Archeologist	Semiannual	Wis. Archeological Society, P.O. Box 44271, Madison 53744 www.wiarcheologicalsociety.org
Wis. Business Voice	Quarterly	Wisconsin Manufacturers & Commerce, P.O. Box 352, Madison 53701-0352 www.wmc.org
Wis. Counties	Monthly	Wis. Counties Assn., 22 E. Mifflin St., Suite 900, Madison 53703 www.wicounties.org
Wis. Economic Indicators	Monthly	Wis. Dept. of Workforce Development, 201 E. Washington Ave., Rm. A-400, Madison 53707 www.dwd.wisconsin.gov/oea
Wis. Energy Cooperative News	Monthly	Cooperative Network, 1 S. Pinckney St., Suite 810, Madison 53703 www.wecnmagazine.com
Wis. Farm Reporter	Semimonthly	Dept. of Agriculture, Trade and Consumer Protection, P.O. Box 8934, Madison 53708-8934 www.nass.usda.gov
Wis. Horsemen's News	Monthly	Journal Community Publishing Group, 600 Industrial Dr., Waupaca 54981 www.wishorse.com
Wis. International Law Journal	4 per year	UW Law School, 975 Bascom Mall, Madison 53706 http://hosted.law.wisc.edu/wordpress/wilj
Wis. Law Journal	Weekly	Ann Richmond, 225 E. Michigan St., Milwaukee 53203-3433 www.wislawjournal.com
Wis. Law Review	Bimonthly	Joe Christensen, Inc., 975 Bascom Mall, Madison 53706-1399 www.wisconsinlawreview.org
Wis. Lawyer	Monthly	State Bar of Wisconsin, P.O. Box 7158, Madison 53707-7158 www.wisbar.org
Wis. Lion.	Monthly	Wisconsin Lions, 3834 County Rd. A, Rosholt 54473 www.wisconsinlions.org/magazine
Wis. Magazine of History	Quarterly	State Historical Society of Wis., 816 State St., Madison 53706-1488 www.wisconsinhistory.org
Wis. Mapping Bulletin.	Electronic	State Cartographer's Office, 384 Science Hall, UW-Madison, 550 N. Park St., Madison 53706 news.sco.wisc.edu
Wis. Natural Resources	Bimonthly	Wisconsin Department of Natural Resources, P.O. Box 7921, Madison 53707-7921 www.wnrmag.com
Wis. People & Ideas	Quarterly	Wis. Academy of Sciences, Arts and Letters, 1922 University Ave., Madison 53726 www.wisconsinacademy.org
Wis. Police Journal.	Quarterly	Wis. Professional Police Assn., 660 John Nolen Dr., Suite 300, Madison 53713 www.wppa.com
Wis. Professional Agent	Monthly	PIA of Wisconsin, 6401 Odana Rd., Madison 53719-1126 www.piaw.org
Wis. Real Estate Magazine	Monthly	Wisconsin Realtors Assn., 4801 Forest Run Rd., Suite 201, Madison 53704 news.wra.org
Wis. Restaurateur	Quarterly	Wis. Restaurant Assn., 2801 Fish Hatchery Rd., Madison 53713-3120 www.wirestaurant.org
Wis. School Musician	3 per year	Wis. School Music Assn., 1005 Quinn Dr., Waunakee 53597 wsmamusic.org/wsm
Wis. School News	10 per year	Wis. Assn. of School Boards, Inc., 122 W. Washington Ave., Suite 400, Madison 53703-2718 www.wasb.org
Wis. State Farmer	Weekly	Terry Lodewegen, P.O. Box 609, Waupaca 54981 wisfarmer.com
Wis. State Genealogical Society Newsletter.	Quarterly	Wis. State Genealogical Soc., P.O. Box 5106, Madison 53705-0106 www.wsgs.org
Wis. Taxpayer, The.	11 per year	Wis. Taxpayers Alliance, 401 North Lawn Ave., Madison 53704-5033 www.wistax.org

WISCONSIN PERIODICALS–Continued

Name	Issued	Publishers
Wis. Trails	Bimonthly	Milwaukee Journal Sentinel, 333 W. State St., Milwaukee 53201 www.wisconsintrails.com
Wis. Waterfowl.	2 per year	Bast-Durbin, Inc., P.O. Box 427, Wales 53183 www.wisducks.org
Wisconsin Woodlands	Quarterly	Wisconsin Woodland Owners Assn., Inc., P.O. Box 285, Stevens Point 54481-0285 www.wisconsinwoodlands.org
WMJ (Wis. Medical Journal)	6 per year	Wisconsin Medical Society, P.O. Box 1109, Madison 53701-1109 www.wmjonline.org
Women in Higher Education.	Monthly	The Wenniger Company, 5376 Farmco Dr., Madison 53704 www.wihe.com
World Airshow News	6 per year	Sandra Parnau, Richardson Ventures, LTD, P.O. Box 975, East Troy 53120-0975 www.airshowmag.com
World Coin News	Monthly	F & W Media, Inc., 700 E. State St., Iola 54990-0001 www.numismaster.com

---

NOTE

If you know of any additional permanent Wisconsin publications that are published at periodic intervals, please send the information to the Blue Book Editor, Legislative Reference Bureau, P.O. Box 2037, Madison, Wisconsin 53701-2037.

BROADCASTING STATIONS IN WISCONSIN

Commercial Television Stations

City	Station	Digital Channel	Analog Channel	City	Station	Digital Channel	Analog Channel
Baraboo	W43BR	—	43	Madison	WMTV	19	15
Brookfield	WWRS	43	52	Milwaukee	WBME	48	49
Eau Claire	WEAU	13.1	13	Milwaukee	WCGV	25	24
Eau Claire	WEUX	49	48	Milwaukee	WDJT	46	58
Eau Claire	WQOW	15	18	Milwaukee	WISN	34	12
Glendale	WPXE	40	55	Milwaukee	WITI	33	6
Glendale	WTPX	46	—	Milwaukee	WMLW	13	—
Green Bay	WACY	27	32	Milwaukee	WTMJ	4	4
Green Bay	WBAY	23	2	Milwaukee	WYTU	17	—
Green Bay	WCWF	21	14	Milwaukee	WVCY	22	30
Green Bay	WFRV	39	5	Milwaukee	WVTV	18	18
Green Bay	WGBA	41	26	Rhinelander	WJFW	16	12
Green Bay	WLUK	11	11	Superior	KBJR	19	—
La Crosse	KQEG	23	—	Tomah	WIBU	51	—
La Crosse	WKBT	8	8	Wausau	WAOW	9.1	9
La Crosse	WLAX	17	25	Wausau	WYOW	9.2	—
La Crosse	WXOW	48	19	Wausau	WMOW	9.3	—
Madison	WBUW	32	57	Wausau	WFXS	31	55
Madison	WISC	50	3	Wausau	WSAW	7	7
Madison	TVW	14	—	West Allis	WBWT	557	—
Madison	WKOW	26	27				
Madison	WMSN	11	47				

Educational Television Stations

City	Station	Digital Channel	Analog Channel	City	Station	Digital Channel	Analog Channel
Green Bay	WPNE[1]	38	42	Milwaukee	WMVS	8	10
La Crosse	WHLA[1]	31	30	Milwaukee	WMVT[3]	35	36
Madison	WHA[2]	20	21	Park Falls	WLEF[1]	36	47
Menomonie	WHWC[1]	28	—	Wausau	WHRM[1]	20	24

Note: All analog broadcasting ended and was replaced by digital broadcasting on June 12, 2009.

Commercial Radio Stations

City	Station	Frequency	City	Station	Frequency
Adams	WDKM-FM	106.1	Eagle River	WERL	950
Altoona	WAXX-FM	104.5	Eagle River	WRJO-FM	94.5
Altoona	WAYY	790	Eau Claire	WATQ-FM	106.7
Altoona	WEAQ	1150	Eau Claire	WBIZ	1400
Altoona	WECL-FM	92.9	Eau Claire	WBIZ-FM	100.7
Altoona	WDRK-FM	99.9	Eau Claire	WISM-FM	98.1
Altoona	WIAL-FM	94.1	Eau Claire	WMEQ	880
Amery	WPCA-LP-FM	95.7	Eau Claire	WMEQ-FM	92.1
Amery	WXCE	1260	Eau Claire	WQRB-FM	95.1
Amery	WLMX-FM	104.9	Ephraim	WLGE-FM	106.9
Antigo	WACD-FM	106.1	Fond du Lac	KFIZ	1450
Antigo	WATK	900	Fond du Lac	WCLB	950
Appleton	WAPL-FM	105.7	Fond du Lac	WBJZ-FM	104.7
Appleton	WHBY	1150	Fond du Lac	WFDL-FM	97.7
Appleton	WRQE	93.5	Fond du Lac	WFON-FM	107.1
Appleton	WSCO	1570	Fond du Lac	WTCX-FM	96.1
Appleton	WXMM	92.9	Fort Atkinson	WFAW	940
Appleton	WYDR-FM	94.3	Fort Atkinson	WKCH-FM	106.5
Ashland	WATW	1400	Green Bay	WAUN-FM	92.7
Ashland	WBSZ-FM	93.3	Green Bay	WDUZ	1400
Ashland	WJJH-FM	96.7	Green Bay	WDUZ-FM	107.5
Ashland	WJJH-FM	102.3	Green Bay	WIXX-FM	101.1
Ashland	WNXR-FM	107.3	Green Bay	WKRU-FM	106.7
Baraboo	WBDL-FM	102.9	Green Bay	WKSZ-FM	95.9
Baraboo	WRPQ	740	Green Bay	WKZG-FM	104.3
Baraboo	WRPQ-FM	99.7	Green Bay	WNCY-FM	100.3
Beaver Dam	WBEV	1430	Green Bay	WNFL	1440
Beaver Dam	WTTN	1580	Green Bay	WOGB-FM	103.1
Beaver Dam	WXRO-FM	95.3	Green Bay	WPCK-FM	104.9
Beloit	WGEZ	1490	Green Bay	WQLH-FM	98.5
Berlin	WAUH-FM	102.3	Green Bay	WTAQ	1360
Berlin	WISS	1100	Green Bay	WTAQ-FM	97.5
Black River Falls	WWIS	1260	Green Bay	WZDR-FM	99.7
Black River Falls	WWIS-FM	99.7	Green Bay	WZOR-FM	94.7
Chippewa Falls	WCFW-FM	105.7	Greenfield	WISN	1130
Chippewa Falls	WOGO	680	Greenfield	WKKV-FM	100.7
Chippewa Falls	WWIB-FM	103.7	Greenfield	WOKY	920
Cleveland	WLKN-FM	98.1	Greenfield	WMIL-FM	106.1
Denmark	WGBW	1590	Greenfield	WRIT-FM	95.7
Denmark	WLWB	1530	Greenfield	WRNW-FM	97.3
Dickeyville	WVRE-FM	101.1	Hales Corners	WMYX-FM	99.1
Dodgeville	WDMP	810	Hales Corners	WSSP	1250
Dodgeville	WDMP-FM	99.3	Hales Corners	WXSS-FM	103.7
Durand	WRDN	1430	Hartford	WTKM	1540

BROADCASTING STATIONS IN WISCONSIN–Continued

City	Station	Frequency	City	Station	Frequency
Hartford	WTKM-FM	104.9	Oshkosh	WNAM	1280
Hayward	WHSM	910	Oshkosh	WOSH	1490
Hayward	WHSM-FM	101.1	Oshkosh	WPKR-FM	99.5
Hayward	WRLS-FM	92.3	Oshkosh	WVBO-FM	103.9
Hudson	WREY	630	Oshkosh	WWWX-FM	96.9
Hudson	WDGY	740	Park Falls	WCQM-FM	98.3
Hurley	WHRY	1450	Park Falls	WPFP	980
Janesville	WCLO	1230	Peshtigo	WSFQ-FM	96.3
Janesville	WJVL-FM	99.9	Pewaukee	WKSH	1640
Janesville	WSJY-FM	107.3	Platteville	WGLR	1280
Janesville	WWHG-FM	105.9	Platteville	WGLR-FM	97.7
La Crosse	WIZM	1410	Platteville	WPVL	1590
La Crosse	WIZM-FM	93.3	Platteville	WPVL-FM	107.1
La Crosse	WKBH-FM	100.1	Pleasant Prairie	WIIL-FM	95.1
La Crosse	WKTY	580	Pleasant Prairie	WLIP	1050
La Crosse	WLFN	1490	Plover	WBCV-FM	107.9
La Crosse	WLXR-FM	104.9	Plover	WGLX-FM	103.3
La Crosse	WQCC-FM	106.3	Plover	WHTQ-FM	96.7
La Crosse	WRQT-FM	95.7	Plover	WYTE-FM	106.5
Ladysmith	WJBL-FM	93.1	Plymouth	WJUB	1420
Ladysmith	WLDY	1340	Plymouth	WSTM-FM	91.3 & 103.3
Lake Geneva	WLKG-FM	96.1	Portage	WBKY-FM	95.9
Lake Geneva	WZRK	1550	Portage	WDLS	900
Madison	WIBA	1310	Portage	WDDC-FM	100.1
Madison	WIBA-FM	101.5	Portage	WNNO-FM	106.9
Madison	WHIT	1550	Portage	WPDR	1350
Madison	WJQM-FM	93.1	Prairie du Chien	WPRE	980
Madison	WLMV	1480	Prairie du Chien	WQPC-FM	94.3
Madison	WMAD-FM	96.3	Racine	WEZY-FM	92.1
Madison	WMGN-FM	98.1	Racine	WRJN	1400
Madison	WMMM-FM	105.5	Reedsburg	WNFM-FM	104.9
Madison	WOLX-FM	94.9	Reedsburg	WRDB	1400
Madison	WOZN	1670	Rhinelander	WCYE-FM	93.7
Madison	WOZN-FM	106.7	Rhinelander	WHDG-FM	97.3
Madison	WJJO-FM	94.1	Rhinelander	WLKD	1570
Madison	WMHX-FM	105.1	Rhinelander	WMQA-FM	95.9
Madison	WTLX-FM	100.5	Rhinelander	WOBT	1240 & 101.3
Madison	WTSO	1070	Rhinelander	WRHN-FM	100.1
Madison	WWQM-FM	106.3	Rhinelander	WRLO-FM	105.3
Madison	WXXM-FM	92.1	Rice Lake	WAQE	1090
Madison	WZEE-FM	104.1	Rice Lake	WAQE-FM	97.7
Manitowoc	WCUB	980	Rice Lake	WJMC	1240
Manitowoc	WLTU-FM	92.1	Rice Lake	WJMC-FM	96.1
Manitowoc	WOMT	1240	Rice Lake	WKFX-FM	99.1
Manitowoc	WQTC-FM	102.3	Richland Center	WRCO	1450
Marinette	WHYB-FM	103.7	Richland Center	WRCO-FM	100.9
Marinette	WSFQ-FM	96.3	Ripon	WRPN	1600
Marinette	WLST-FM	95.1	River Falls	WEVR	1550
Marinette	WMAM	570	River Falls	WEVR-FM	106.3
Marinette	WAGN	1340	Shawano	WJMQ-FM	92.3
Marshfield	WDLB	1450	Shawano	WOTE	1380
Marshfield	WOSQ-FM	92.3	Shawano	WOWN-FM	99.3
Marshfield	WYTE-FM	106.5	Shawano	WTCH	960
Mauston	WRJC	1270	Shawano	WTCH-FM	96.5
Mauston	WRJC-FM	92.1	Sheboygan	WBFM-FM	93.7
Mayville	WMDC-FM	98.7	Sheboygan	WHBL	1330
Medford	WIGM	1490	Sheboygan	WHBZ-FM	106.5
Medford	WKEB-FM	99.3	Sheboygan	WXER-FM	104.5 & 96.1
Menomonee Falls	WLDB-FM	93.3	Shell Lake	WCSW	940
Menomonee Falls	WLUM-FM	102.1	Shell Lake	WGMO-FM	95.3
Menomonee Falls	WMCS	1290	Shell Lake	WPLT-FM	106.3
Menomonie	WMEQ-FM	92.1	Siren	WXCX-FM	105.7
Merrill	WJMT	730	Sparta	WCOW-FM	97.1
Merrill	WMZK-FM	104.1	Sparta	WFBZ-FM	105.5
Milwaukee	WAUK	540	Sparta	WKLJ	1290
Milwaukee	WGLB	1560	Stevens Point	WPCN	1010
Milwaukee	WHQG-FM	102.9	Stevens Point	WPCN-FM	92.1
Milwaukee	WJMR-FM	98.3	Stevens Point	WKQH-FM	104.9
Milwaukee	WJYI	1340	Stevens Point	WSPT-FM	97.9
Milwaukee	WKLH-FM	96.5	Sturgeon Bay	WBDK-FM	96.7
Milwaukee	WLWK-FM	94.5	Sturgeon Bay	WDOR	910
Milwaukee	WNOV	860	Sturgeon Bay	WDOR-FM	93.9
Milwaukee	WNRG-FM	106.9	Sturgeon Bay	WRKU-FM	102.1
Milwaukee	WRRD	1510	Sturgeon Bay	WRLU-FM	104.1
Milwaukee	WTMJ	620	Sturgeon Bay	WSBW-FM	105.1
Milwaukee	WVCS-FM	90.1	Sturgeon Bay	WSRG-FM	97.7
Monroe	WEKZ	1260	Superior	KDWZ-FM	102.5
Monroe	WEKZ-FM	93.7	Superior	WEBC	560
Neillsville	WCCN	1370	Superior	WDSM	710
Neillsville	WCCN-FM	107.5	Superior	WGEE	970
Neillsville	WPKG-FM	92.7	Tomah	WBOG	1460
New Richmond	WDMO-FM	95.7	Tomah	WTMB-FM	94.5
New Richmond	WIXK	1590	Tomah	WXYM-FM	96.1
Oconto	WOCO	1260	Tomahawk	WJJQ	810
Oconto	WOCO-FM	107.1	Tomahawk	WJJQ-FM	92.5

BROADCASTING STATIONS IN WISCONSIN–Continued

City	Station	Frequency	City	Station	Frequency
Viroqua	WKPO-FM	105.9	Wausau	WSAU	550
Viroqua	WVRQ	1360	Wausau	WSAU-FM	99.9
Viroqua	WVRQ-FM	102.3	Wausau	WXCO	1230
Waupaca	WDUX	800	West Allis	WDDW-FM	104.7
Waupaca	WDUX-FM	92.7	West Allis	WJTI	1460
Waupun	WFDL	1170	West Bend	WBKV	1470
Wausau	WDEZ-FM	101.9	West Bend	WBWI-FM	92.5
Wausau	WDTX-FM	100.5	Whitehall	WHTL-FM	102.3
Wausau	WIFC-FM	95.5	Whitewater	WSLD-FM	104.5
Wausau	WOZZ-FM	94.7	Wisconsin Rapids	WFHR	1320
Wausau	WRIG	1390	Wisconsin Rapids	WRCW-FM	105.5

Noncommercial Radio Stations

City	Station	Frequency	City	Station	Frequency
Adams	WHAA-FM[1]	89.1	Milwaukee	WMMK-FM	88.1
Appleton	WEMI-FM	91.9	Milwaukee	WUWM-FM[2]	89.7
Appleton	WEMY-FM	91.5	Milwaukee	WVCX-FM	98.9
Appleton	WOVM-FM	91.1	Milwaukee	WVCY	690
Ashland	WRNC-LP-FM	97.7	Milwaukee	WVCY-FM	107.7
(Northland College)			Milwaukee	WVFL-FM	89.9
Ashland	WUWS[2]	90.9	Milwaukee	WVRN-FM	88.9
Auburndale	WLBL[1]	940	Milwaukee	WYMS-FM	88.9
Beloit	WBCR-FM	90.3	(Milwaukee Board of Education)		
(Beloit College)			Onalaska	WKBH	1570
Brule	WHSA-FM[1]	89.9	Oshkosh	WRST-FM[2]	90.3
Burlington	WBSD-FM	89.1	Oshkosh	WOCT-LP-FM	101.9
(Burlington Area School District)			Park Falls	WHBM-FM[1]	90.3
De Pere	WORQ-FM	90.1	Platteville	WSUP-FM[2]	90.5
Delafield	WHAD-FM[1]	90.7	Platteville	WSSW-FM	89.1
Eau Claire	WDVM	1050	Rhinelander	WXPR-FM	91.7
Eau Claire	WHEM-FM	91.3	Rhinelander	WXPW-FM	91.9
Eau Claire	WHWC-FM[1]	88.3	Ripon	WRPN-FM	90.1
Eau Claire	WUEC-FM[2]	89.7	(Ripon College)		
Eau Claire	WVCF-FM	90.5	River Falls	WRFW-FM[2]	88.7
Eau Claire	WVSS-FM[2]	90.7	Schofield	WCLQ-FM	89.5
Fond du Lac	WDKV-FM	91.7	Sheboygan	WSHS-FM	91.7
Green Bay	WHID-FM[2]	88.1	(Sheboygan Area School District)		
Green Bay	WJOK	1050	Sister Bay	WHDI-FM[1]	91.9
Green Bay	WPJP-FM	100.1	Sister Bay	WHND-FM[1]	89.7
Green Bay	WPNE-FM[1]	89.3	Sparta	WTPN-FM	103.9
Hayward	WOJB-FM	88.9	Stevens Point	WWSP-FM[2]	89.9
Highland	WHHI-FM[1]	91.3	Sturgeon Bay	WPFF-FM	90.5
Kenosha	WGTD-FM	91.1	Sturgeon Bay	WNLI-FM	88.5
(Gateway Technical College)			Superior	KUWS-FM[2]	91.3
La Crosse	WHLA-FM[1]	90.3	Superior	WHSA-FM[1]	89.9
La Crosse	WLSU-FM[2]	88.9	Superior	WSSU[1]	88.5
Lancaster	WJTY-FM	88.1	Suring	WHJL-FM	88.1
Madison	WERN-FM[1]	88.7	Suring	WMVM-FM	90.7
Madison	WHA[2]	970	Suring	WYVM-FM	90.9
Madison	WHFA	1240	Suring	WRVM-FM	102.7
Madison	WNWC	1190	Waukesha	WCCX-FM	104.5
(Northwestern College)			(Carroll College)		
Madison	WNWC-FM	102.5	Wausau	WHRM-FM[1]	90.9
(Northwestern College)			Wausau	WLBL-FM[1]	91.9
Madison	WORT-FM	89.9	Whitewater	WSUW-FM[2]	91.7
Madison	WSUM-FM[2]	91.7	Wisconsin Rapids	WMMA-FM	93.9
Manitowoc	WTSW-LP-FM	96.3	Wisconsin Rapids	WYNW-FM	92.9
Marinette	WLCJ-LP-FM	92.5			
Milladore	WGNV-FM	88.5			
Milwaukee	WEGZ-FM	105.9			
Milwaukee	WMSE-FM	91.7			
(Milwaukee School of Engineering)					

[1]Licensed to the Wisconsin Educational Communications Board.
[2]Licensed to the University of Wisconsin System Board of Regents.
[3]Operated by the Milwaukee Area Technical College Board.
Source: Wisconsin Broadcasters Association, *2013-2014 Directory*.

HIGHLIGHTS OF POPULATION AND VITAL STATISTICS IN WISCONSIN

State and County Population — Wisconsin's 2012 population was officially estimated to be 5,703,525, a .29% increase over the 2010 U.S. Census count of 5,686,986. The state grew 6.0% in the 2000s and 9.6% in the 1990s. By contrast, the growth in the preceding decade from 1980 to 1990 was less than 4% and represented the smallest increase in decennial census counts in state history. The greatest increase occurred between 1840 and 1850, the decade in which Wisconsin became a state, when population jumped 886.9% from 30,945 to 305,391.

Between 2000 and 2010, population increased over 20% in Calumet and St. Croix Counties, while population decreased in 19 counties. St. Croix County was the fastest growing county during the decade, with a population increase of 33.6%. Dane County had the largest absolute growth, adding 61,547 people, followed by Waukesha County, which grew by 29,124 people.

Population by Race and Age — In responding to the 2000 and 2010 U.S. Censuses of Population, individuals were given the opportunity to identify themselves as being of more than one race. About 1.2% and 1.8% of Wisconsin's population selected multiple races in 2000 and 2010, respectively. As a result, comparisons between the 2000 and 2010 Censuses and earlier censuses must be made with caution. It is not clear whether someone who selected Asian and white, for example, for the 2010 Census would have selected Asian or white in 1990. Only those who selected a single race are used in the following comparisons. Between 1890 and 2010, the nonwhite population in Wisconsin increased from 0.7% to over 13.8%. Wisconsin Indians were the largest minority group from 1890 until 1950; Blacks have been the largest since 1950. In 2010, Milwaukee County had the largest Black population at 253,764, followed by Dane County with 25,347, Racine County with 21,767, Kenosha County with 11,052, and Rock County with 7,978. 55.2% of the population of the City of Milwaukee was nonwhite. Wisconsin's Hispanic population increased by 74.2% from 2000 to 2010, reaching 336,056. The Asian population increased by 45.6% to 129,234.

The 2010 Wisconsin Indian population was 54,526, an increase of 15.5% over the 2000 population of 47,228. Wisconsin has 11 Indian reservations.

According to the 2010 Census, Wisconsin had a voting age population of 4,347,494 or 76.4% of the total population.

Vital Statistics — In 2011, Wisconsin recorded 30,287 marriages and 16,635 divorces and annulments. In 2011, the state had 67,736 live births (11.9 per 1,000 population), 427 infant deaths (6.3 per 1,000 live births), and 368 fetal deaths (5.4 per 1,000 deliveries). Total deaths in 2011 numbered 48,101 (8.4 per 1,000 population).

The following tables present selected data. Consult footnoted sources for more detailed information about population and vital statistics.

WISCONSIN POPULATION, 1840 – 2012

Year	Population	Increase	Percent Increase	Rural	Urban	Percent Urban	Density[1]
1840	30,945	—	—	30,945	—	—	0.6
1850	305,391	274,446	886.9%	276,768	28,623	9.4%	5.6
1860	775,881	470,490	154.1	664,007	111,874	14.4	14.1
1870	1,054,670	278,789	35.9	847,471	207,099	19.6	19.2
1880	1,315,497	260,827	24.7	998,293	317,204	24.1	24.0
1890	1,693,330	377,833	28.7	1,131,044	562,286	33.2	30.9
1900	2,069,042	375,712	22.2	1,278,829	790,213	38.2	37.4
1910	2,333,860	264,818	12.8	1,329,540	1,004,320	43.0	42.6
1920	2,632,067	298,207	12.8	1,387,209	1,244,858	47.3	47.6
1930	2,939,006	306,939	11.7	1,385,163	1,553,843	52.9	53.0
1940	3,137,587	198,581	6.7	1,458,443	1,679,144	53.5	57.3
1950	3,434,575	296,988	9.5	1,446,687	1,987,888[2]	57.9	62.7
1960	3,951,777	517,202	15.1	1,429,598	2,522,179	63.8	72.2
1970	4,417,821	466,044	11.8	1,507,313	2,910,418	65.9	81.3
1980	4,705,642	287,821	6.5	1,685,035	3,020,732	64.2	86.6
1990	4,891,769	186,127	4.0	1,679,813	3,211,956	65.7	90.1
2000	5,363,715	471,946	9.6	1,700,032	3,663,643	68.3	98.8
2010	5,686,986	323,271	6.0	NA	NA	NA	NA
2011[3]	5,694,236	7,250	0.1	NA	NA	NA	NA
2012[3]	5,703,525	9,289	0.2	NA	NA	NA	NA

NA – Not available.

[1]Population per square mile of land area.

[2]The "urban" definition was revised beginning with the 1950 census.

[3]Estimate from Wisconsin Department of Administration, Demographic Services Center.

Sources: U.S. Department of Commerce, U.S. Census Bureau; Wisconsin Department of Administration, Demographic Services Center, *Time Series of The Final Official Population Estimates and Census Counts for Wisconsin Counties,* October 1, 2012.

WISCONSIN POPULATION
2010 Census By Sex, Race, and Hispanic Origin

County	Total Population	Sex Male	Sex Female	White	Black or African American	American Indian and Alaska Native	Asian or Pacific Islander	Some Other Race	Two or More Races	Hispanic Origin (of any race)
Adams	20,875	11,221	9,654	19,409	633	205	86	266	276	783
Ashland . . .	16,157	8,082	8,075	13,662	48	1,791	63	56	537	302
Barron	45,870	22,814	23,056	44,076	407	406	226	236	519	862
Bayfield . . .	15,014	7,716	7,298	13,024	46	1,435	49	29	431	158
Brown	248,007	122,658	125,349	214,415	5,491	6,715	6,828	9,155	5,403	17,985
Buffalo	13,587	6,859	6,728	13,253	37	38	28	122	109	237
Burnett	15,457	7,806	7,651	14,163	81	718	55	67	373	194
Calumet . . .	48,971	24,543	24,428	46,187	246	203	1,047	705	583	1,690
Chippewa . .	62,415	32,404	30,011	59,504	982	310	788	182	649	800
Clark	34,690	17,577	17,113	33,338	80	174	135	773	190	1,292
Columbia. . .	56,833	28,935	27,898	54,468	717	277	330	441	600	1,444
Crawford. . .	16,644	8,575	8,069	16,080	296	39	66	36	127	150
Dane	488,073	241,411	246,662	413,631	25,347	1,730	23,201	12,064	12,100	28,925
Dodge	88,759	46,679	42,080	83,294	2,381	385	513	1,309	877	3,522
Door	27,785	13,679	14,106	26,839	144	162	116	249	275	671
Douglas . . .	44,159	22,087	22,072	41,166	486	868	384	82	1,173	494
Dunn	43,857	22,133	21,724	41,545	220	168	1,158	228	538	626
Eau Claire . .	98,736	48,351	50,385	91,946	874	471	3,328	519	1,598	1,804
Florence . . .	4,423	2,262	2,161	4,306	10	31	14	14	48	37
Fond du Lac .	101,633	49,926	51,707	95,674	1,305	471	1,169	1,700	1,314	4,368
Forest.	9,304	4,724	4,580	7,690	76	1,256	24	32	226	138
Grant	51,208	26,636	24,572	49,655	588	103	317	221	324	649
Green.	36,842	18,241	18,601	35,593	140	65	209	490	345	1,033
Green Lake. .	19,051	9,509	9,542	18,428	88	52	91	268	124	743
Iowa	23,687	11,878	11,809	23,127	87	36	134	102	201	336
Iron.	5,916	2,959	2,957	5,790	3	36	18	13	56	35
Jackson. . . .	20,449	10,874	9,575	18,258	400	1,271	73	144	303	519
Jefferson	83,686	41,638	42,048	78,632	681	257	578	2,479	1,059	5,555
Juneau	26,664	14,029	12,635	25,077	557	398	122	188	322	687
Kenosha . . .	166,426	82,444	83,982	139,416	11,052	814	2,482	7,880	4,782	19,592
Kewaunee . .	20,574	10,460	10,114	19,955	69	77	65	219	189	463
La Crosse . .	114,638	55,961	58,677	105,540	1,610	493	4,770	371	1,854	1,741
Lafayette . . .	16,836	8,582	8,254	16,292	39	48	58	303	96	522
Langlade . . .	19,977	10,032	9,945	19,267	72	191	63	100	284	324
Lincoln. . . .	28,743	14,412	14,331	27,929	157	100	134	131	292	340
Manitowoc. .	81,442	40,489	40,953	76,402	442	450	2,060	1,069	1,019	2,565
Marathon. . .	134,063	67,308	66,755	122,446	841	634	7,178	1,223	1,741	2,992
Marinette. . .	41,749	20,758	20,991	40,559	108	238	227	176	441	522
Marquette . .	15,404	7,808	7,596	14,920	77	86	68	126	127	391
Menominee .	4,232	2,098	2,134	451	19	3,701	1	6	54	178
Milwaukee. .	947,735	457,717	490,018	574,656	253,764	6,808	32,785	51,429	28,293	126,039
Monroe. . . .	44,673	22,648	22,025	41,940	512	510	329	764	618	1,661
Oconto	37,660	19,194	18,466	36,418	73	467	116	198	388	519
Oneida	35,998	17,993	18,005	34,787	152	323	193	82	461	385
Outagamie . .	176,695	88,130	88,565	161,238	1,736	2,982	5,294	2,728	2,717	6,359
Ozaukee . . .	86,395	42,340	44,055	82,010	1,177	208	1,529	483	988	1,956
Pepin	7,469	3,780	3,689	7,337	21	19	14	35	43	72
Pierce	41,019	20,420	20,599	39,614	232	151	308	201	513	623
Polk	44,205	22,177	22,028	42,807	96	454	166	226	456	656
Portage. . . .	70,019	34,984	35,035	65,981	383	265	1,983	546	861	1,853
Price	14,159	7,180	6,979	13,750	39	54	126	42	148	153
Racine	195,408	96,771	98,637	155,731	21,767	781	2,174	10,046	4,909	22,546
Richland . . .	18,021	9,042	8,979	17,540	82	46	99	119	135	360
Rock	160,331	78,815	81,516	140,513	7,978	516	1,669	5,948	3,707	12,124
Rusk	14,755	7,371	7,384	14,398	61	74	42	37	143	173
St. Croix . . .	84,345	42,218	42,127	80,914	552	313	923	483	1,160	1,692
Sauk	61,976	30,848	31,128	58,588	357	769	350	1,156	756	2,675
Sawyer. . . .	16,557	8,393	8,164	13,123	77	2,757	49	42	509	268
Shawano . . .	41,949	20,921	21,028	37,254	143	3,172	193	366	821	905
Sheboygan . .	115,507	58,010	57,497	103,861	1,684	444	5,345	2,297	1,876	6,329
Taylor	20,689	10,559	10,130	20,248	58	43	64	128	148	316
Trempealeau .	28,816	14,638	14,178	27,230	62	63	127	1,086	248	1,667
Vernon	29,773	14,854	14,919	29,085	109	61	99	145	274	394
Vilas	21,430	10,861	10,569	18,658	35	2,370	62	45	260	268
Walworth. . .	102,228	51,237	50,991	93,935	980	308	888	4,604	1,513	10,578
Washburn . .	15,911	7,924	7,987	15,343	36	186	65	49	232	208
Washington. .	131,887	65,393	66,494	126,317	1,155	401	1,445	1,052	1,517	3,385
Waukesha . .	389,891	191,355	198,536	363,963	4,914	1,066	10,852	4,041	5,055	16,213
Waupaca . . .	52,410	26,447	25,963	50,916	154	258	200	425	457	1,307
Waushara . .	24,496	12,893	11,603	23,012	454	131	108	509	282	1,329
Winnebago. .	166,994	83,952	83,042	154,445	2,975	1,036	3,880	2,188	2,470	5,784
Wood.	74,749	36,777	37,972	71,048	393	587	1,328	593	800	1,680
STATE . .	5,686,986	2,822,400	2,864,586	4,902,067	359,148	54,526	131,061	135,867	104,317	336,056

Sources: U.S. Department of Commerce, U.S. Census Bureau, P.L. 94-171 Redistricting File, processed by Wisconsin Demographic Services Center and the Applied Population Laboratory of UW-Madison, May 2011.

POPULATION CHANGES BY COUNTY, 2010-2012
State Increase: +0.3%

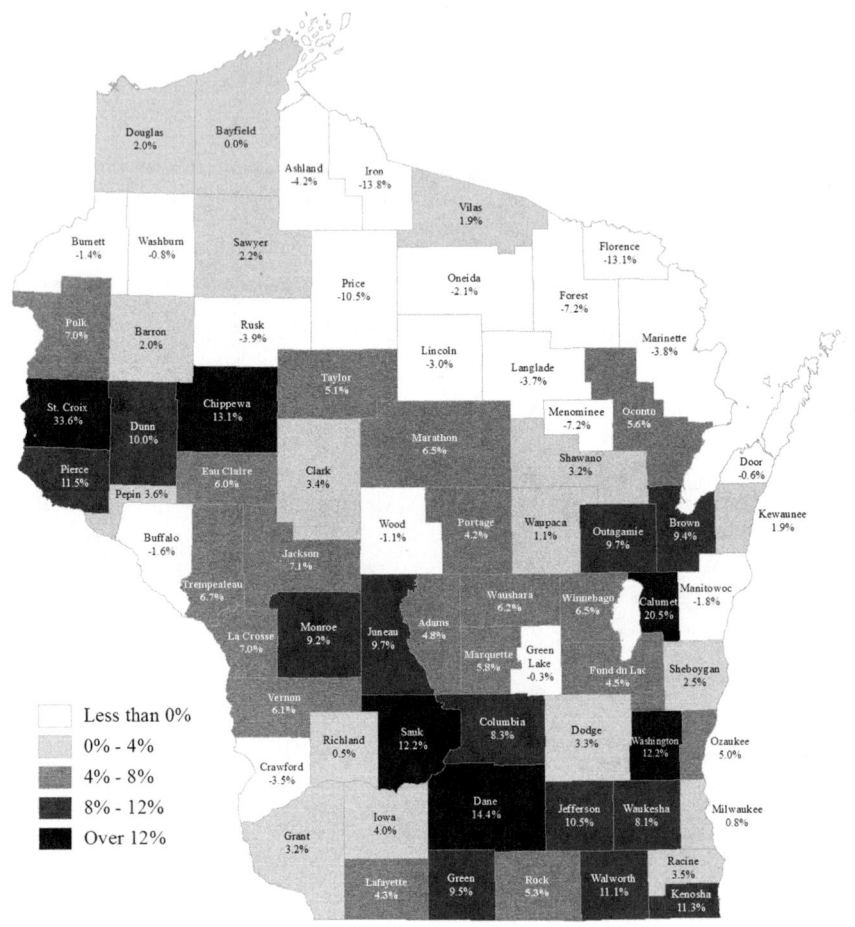

Less than 0%
0% - 4%
4% - 8%
8% - 12%
Over 12%

Source: Wisconsin Department of Administration, Demographic Services Center, *Official Population Estimates, January 1, 2012,* April 2013. Map produced by Wisconsin Legislative Technology Services Bureau.

WISCONSIN POPULATION, BY RACE, 1890 – 2011
Population Totals

U.S. Census Year	Total Population	White	Black	American Indian[1]	Asian[2]	Some Other Race	Two or More Races[3]	Hispanic or Latino Origin (of any race)[4]
1890	1,693,330	1,680,828	2,444	9,930	128	—	—	—
1900	2,069,042	2,057,911	2,542	8,372	217	—	—	—
1910	2,333,860	2,320,555	2,900	10,142	260	3	—	—
1920	2,632,067	2,616,938	5,201	9,611	314	3	—	—
1930	2,939,006	2,916,255	10,739	11,548	451	13	—	—
1940	3,137,587	3,112,752	12,158	12,265	388	24	—	—
1950	3,434,575	3,392,690	28,182	12,196	1,119	388	—	—
1960	3,951,777	3,858,903	74,546	14,297	2,836	1,195	—	—
1970[5]	4,417,933	4,258,959	128,224	18,924	6,557	5,067	—	62,875
1980[5]	4,705,642	4,443,035	182,592	29,320	22,043	41,788	—	62,782
1990	4,891,769	4,512,523	244,539	39,387	53,583	42,538	—	93,194
2000	5,363,675	4,769,857	304,460	47,228	90,393	84,842	66,895	192,921
2010	5,686,986	4,902,067	359,148	54,526	131,061	135,867	104,317	336,056
2011[6]	5,711,767	4,980,495	356,550	48,065	132,102	77,758	116,797	345,297

Population Percentages

U.S. Census Year	White	Black	American Indian[1]	Asian[2]	Some Other Race	Two or More Races[3]	Hispanic or Latino Origin (of any race)[4]
1890	99.3%	0.1%	0.6%	—	—	—	—
1900	99.5	0.1	0.4	—	—	—	—
1910	99.4	0.1	0.4	—	—	—	—
1920	99.4	0.2	0.4	—	—	—	—
1930	99.2	0.4	0.4	—	—	—	—
1940	99.2	0.4	0.4	—	—	—	—
1950	98.8	0.8	0.4	—	—	—	—
1960	97.6	1.9	0.4	0.1%	—	—	—
1970	96.4	2.9	0.4	0.2	0.1%	—	1.4%
1980	94.4	3.9	0.6	0.3	0.9	—	1.3
1990	92.2	5.0	0.8	1.2	0.9	—	1.9
2000	88.9	5.7	0.9	1.7	1.6	1.2%	3.6
2010	86.2	6.3	1.0	2.3	2.4	1.8	5.9
2011[6]	87.2	6.2	0.8	2.3	1.4	2.0	6.0

[1] Aleut and Eskimo populations included beginning in 1960.

[2] Native Hawaiian and Other Pacific Islanders are grouped with Asian.

[3] For the first time in the 2000 Census, individuals were allowed to select more than one race.

[4] The 1990 data on Hispanic/Spanish origin are generally comparable with those for the 1980 Census, but not the 1970 Census. In the 2000 Census, "Hispanic or Latino Origin" represents ethnicity and includes people of Cuban, Mexican, Puerto Rican, South or Central American, or other Spanish culture or origin, regardless of race.

[5] Total has been corrected by the U.S. Census Bureau. Details not adjusted to revised total.

[6] American Community Survey (ACS) is conducted every month on independent samples and produces annual or annual average estimates. These estimates consist of totals, proportions, percentages, means, medians, and ratios. The ACS provides annually updated data on demographic, socioeconomic, and housing characteristics.

Source: U.S. Department of Commerce, U.S. Census Bureau, *2011 American Community Survey 1-Year Estimates, Wisconsin ACS Demographic and Housing Estimates: 2011,* December 2012.

WISCONSIN POPULATION BY RACE AND HISPANIC ORIGIN
2011 Estimate[1]

Race	Total	Percent	Race	Total	Percent
		Total Wisconsin Population: 5,711,767			
One race	5,594,970	98.0%	Two or more races	116,797	2.0%
White	4,980,495	87.2	**Not Hispanic or Latino**[4]	5,366,470	94.0
Black or African American	356,550	6.2	One race	5,271,305	92.3
American Indian and Alaska Native	48,065	0.8	White	4,741,024	83.0
Asian	130,617	2.3	Black or African American	349,932	6.1
Asian Indian	26,626	0.5	American Indian and		
Chinese	19,174	0.3	Alaska Native	44,876	0.8
Filipino	8,279	0.1	Asian	130,040	2.3
Japanese	2,174	0.0	Native Hawaiian and Other		
Korean	7,361	0.1	Pacific Islander	1,413	0.0
Vietnamese	4,516	0.1	Some other race	4,020	0.1
Other Asian[2]	62,487	1.1	Two or more races	95,165	1.7
Native Hawaiian and Other Pacific					
Islander.	1,485	0.0	**Hispanic or Latino and Race**		
Native Hawaiian	388	0.0	Hispanic or Latino (of any race) .	345,297	6.0
Guamanian or Chamorro	460	0.0	Mexican	252,538	4.4
Samoan	92	0.0	Puerto Rican	51,488	0.9
Other Pacific Islander[3]	545	0.0	Cuban	3,322	0.1
Some other race	77,758	1.4	Other Hispanic or Latino . . .	37,949	0.7

[1]Information from U.S. Census Bureau American Community Survey (ACS). The ACS provides annually updated data on the characteristics of population and housing. It is conducted every month on independent samples, and produces annual or average estimates. The estimates consist of totals, proportions, percentages, means, medians, and ratios.

[2]Other Asian alone, or two or more Asian categories.

[3]Other Pacific Islander alone, or two or more Native Hawaiian and Other Pacific Islander categories.

[4]"Hispanic or Latino" refers to a person of Cuban, Mexican, Puerto Rican, South or Central American, or other Spanish culture or origin, regardless of race.

Source: U.S. Census Bureau, 2011 American Community Survey, *ACS Demographic and Housing Estimates: 2011 American Community Survey 1-Year Estimates,* December 2012.

WISCONSIN ASIAN POPULATION
1940 – 2011

	Total[1]	Asian Indian	Chinese	Filipino	Hmong	Japanese	Korean	Laotian	Vietnamese	Other Asian[2]
1940	388	NA	290	75	NA	23	NA	NA	NA	NA
1950	1,119	NA	590	NA	NA	529	NA	NA	NA	NA
1960	2,836	NA	1,010	401	NA	1,425	NA	NA	NA	NA
1970	6,557	NA	2,700	1,209	NA	2,648	NA	NA	NA	NA
1980	22,043	3,902	4,835	3,036	NA	2,123	2,900	NA	1,699	NA
1990	53,583	6,914	7,354	3,690	16,373	2,765	5,618	3,622	2,494	NA
2000	90,393	12,665	11,184	5,158	33,791	2,868	6,800	4,469	3,891	NA
2010	129,234	22,899	17,558	7,930	NA	2,729	7,919	NA	4,877	65,322
2011[3]	125,630	21,305	18,538	8,191	NA	2,449	8,760	NA	4,188	62,199

NA – Not available.

[1]Includes Native Hawaiian and Other Pacific Islander, and Other Asian, including Hmong and Laotian, not identified in the detailed categories.

[2]Other Asian alone, or two or more Asian categories.

[3]American Community Survey (ACS) is conducted every month on independent samples, and produces annual or annual average estimates. These estimates consist of totals, proportions, percentages, means, medians, and ratios. The ACS provides annually updated data on the characteristics of population and housing.

Source: U.S. Department of Commerce, U.S. Census Bureau, *2007-2011 American Community Survey 5-Year Estimates,* December 2012, and previous issues.

WISCONSIN INDIANS
Wisconsin Indian Population, 1900 – 2010

Year	Total	Male	Female
1900	8,372	4,321	4,051
1910	10,142	5,231	4,911
1920	9,611	4,950	4,661
1930	11,548	5,951	5,597
1940	12,265	6,354	5,911
1950	12,196	6,274	5,922
1960	14,297	7,195	7,102
1970	18,924	9,251	9,673
1980	29,320	14,489	14,831
1990	38,986	19,240	19,746
2000	47,228*	23,462	23,766
2010	54,526	27,212	27,314

*For the first time in the 2000 Census, individuals were allowed to select more than one race.
Source: U.S. Census Bureau, 2010 Census Summary File 1, July 2011, and previous issues.

Wisconsin Indian Reservations: Population and Acreage

Reservation Total/ County Detail	Tribe	2010 Reservation Population			June 2013 Acreage Ownership Status		
		Total	Indian	% Indian	Total[1]	Tribal	Individual
Bad River	Chippewa	1,479	1,089	73.63%	63,595.96	28,886.41	34,708.55
Ho-Chunk Nation	Ho-Chunk Nation	1,375	1,185	86.18	7,321.19	4,111.48	3,209.71
Lac Courte Oreilles	Chippewa	2,803	2,111	75.31	51,147.20	29,190.18	21,957.02
Lac du Flambeau	Chippewa	3,442	2,198	63.86	44,956.30	32,658.51	12,282.73
Menominee[2]	Menominee	3,141	2,967	94.46	235,374.35	229,705.35	5,669.00
Oneida (West)	Oneida	22,776	4,102	18.01	12,091.03	11,191.13	899.90
Potawatomi (Wisconsin)	Potawatomi	588	501	85.20	13,080.59	12,400.59	360.00
Red Cliff	Chippewa	1,123	943	83.97	8,109.15	6,189.75	1,904.75
St. Croix	Chippewa	768	622	80.99	2,327.05	2,327.05	0.00
Sokaogon	Chippewa	414	352	85.02	3,241.24	3,241.24	0.00
Stockbridge-Munsee	Mohican	644	511	79.35	16,997.66	16,864.43	133.23
TOTAL		38,553	16,581	43.01	458,241.72	376,766.12	81,124.89

[1]Totals include government land holdings for the following reservations: Bad River (1.00 acre), Lac du Flambeau (15.06 acres), Potawatomi (320.00 acres), and Red Cliff (14.65 acres).
[2]Public Law 93-107, the Menominee Restoration Act, effective on December 22, 1973, repealed the Menominee Termination Act of June 17, 1954 (P.L. 83-399) and acknowledged the Menominee Indian Tribe of Wisconsin as a federally recognized Indian tribe.
Sources: U.S. Census Bureau, Census 2010 Redistricting Data Summary File, March 2011; U.S. Bureau of Indian Affairs, departmental data, June 2013; Menominee Indian Tribe of Wisconsin, tribal data, May 2013. Acreage ownership totals, population totals, and percentages calculated by Wisconsin Legislative Reference Bureau.

Wisconsin Indian Land Holdings in Acres, By County, June 2013

County	Total Holdings	Tribal Land	Individual Land
Adams	121.35	0.35	121.00
Ashland	61,214.67	28,485.67	32,728.00
Barron	168.11	168.11	0.00
Bayfield	8,109.15	6,189.75	1,904.75
Brown	2,153.83	1,951.21	202.62
Burnett	1,358.74	1,358.74	0.00
Clark	926.82	369.08	557.74
Crawford	193.20	80.00	113.20
Dane	4.45	4.45	0.00
Douglas	516.27	0.00	516.27
Eau Claire	160.00	160.00	0.00
Forest	16,303.95	15,623.95	360.00
Iron	15,835.23	12,096.99	3,738.24
Jackson	1,428.37	719.45	708.92
Juneau	393.85	93.00	300.85
La Crosse	132.76	40.67	92.09
Langlade	200.48	200.48	0.00
Marathon	200.00	0.00	200.00
Marinette	40.00	0.00	40.00
Menominee	233,567.91	228,056.91	5,511.00
Milwaukee	19.58	19.58	0.00
Monroe	946.92	553.92	393.00
Oneida	345.93	176.07	169.86
Outagamie	9,937.20	9,239.92	697.28
Polk	851.80	851.80	0.00
Sauk	95.26	95.26	0.00
Sawyer	51,147.20	29,190.18	21,957.02
Shawano	19,344.40	18,727.68	616.72
Vilas	31,156.43	20,786.19	10,355.18
Vernon	1,200.00	1,200.00	0.00
Washburn	20.00	20.00	0.00
Wood	777.43	380.01	397.42

Note: Total holdings include government land in the following counties: Ashland (1.00 acre), Bayfield (14.65 acres), Forest (320.00 acres), and Vilas (15.06 acres).
Sources: U.S. Bureau of Indian Affairs, departmental data, June 2013; Menominee Indian Tribe of Wisconsin, tribal data, May 2013.

Tribal Chairpersons, Mailing Addresses, and Web Sites
May 2013

Tribe and Chairperson	Tribal Mailing Address and Web Sites
Bad River Band (Lake Superior Chippewa)	P.O. Box 39, Odanah 54861-0039, (715) 682-7111
Mike Wiggins, Jr.	http://www.badriver-nsn.gov
Forest County Potawatomi Community	P.O. Box 340, Crandon 54520-0346, (715) 478-7200
Gus Frank	http://www.fcpotawatomi.com
Ho-Chunk Nation	P.O. Box 667, Black River Falls 54615-0667, (715) 284-9343
Jon Greendeer (President)	http://www.ho-chunknation.com
Lac Courte Oreilles Band (Lake Superior Chippewa)	13394 W. Trepania Road, Hayward 54843-2186, (715) 634-8934
Gordon Thayer	http://www.lco-nsn.gov
Lac du Flambeau Band (Lake Superior Chippewa)	P.O. Box 67, Lac du Flambeau 54538-0067, (715) 588-3303
Tom Maulson (President)	http://www.ldftribe.com/
Menominee Tribe	P.O. Box 910, Keshena 54135-0910, (715) 799-5114
Craig Corn	http://www.menominee-nsn.gov
Oneida Nation	P.O. Box 365, Oneida 54155-0365, (920) 869-2214
Ed Delgado	http://www.oneidanation.org
Red Cliff Band (Lake Superior Chippewa)	88385 Pike Road, Hwy. 13, Bayfield 54814-0529, (715) 779-3700
Rose Soulier	http://www.redcliff-nsn.gov
St. Croix Chippewa Tribe	24663 Angeline Avenue, Webster 54893-9246, (715) 349-2195
Stuart Bearheart	http://www.stcciw.com/
Sokaogon Chippewa Community	3051 Sand Lake Road, Crandon 54520-8815, (715) 478-7500
Chris McGeshick	http://www.sokaogonchippewa.com
Stockbridge-Munsee Band (Mohican Nation)	P.O. Box 70, Bowler 54416-9801, (715) 793-4111
Wallace Miller (President)	http://www.mohican-nsn.gov

Sources: Wisconsin State Tribal Relations Initiative, http://witribes.wi.gov/ [May 2013] and individual tribal Web sites.

Wisconsin Tribal Gaming Facilities
May 2013

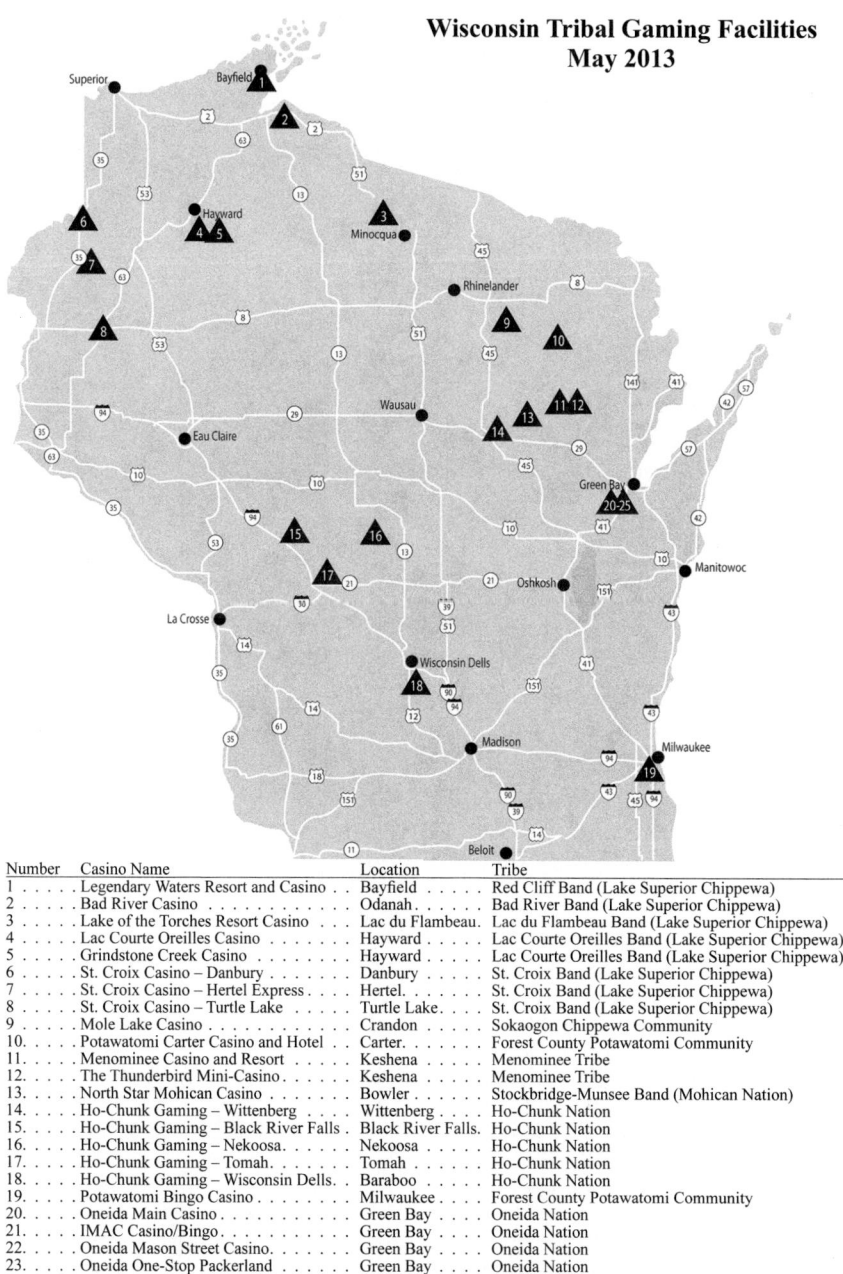

Number	Casino Name	Location	Tribe
1	Legendary Waters Resort and Casino	Bayfield	Red Cliff Band (Lake Superior Chippewa)
2	Bad River Casino	Odanah	Bad River Band (Lake Superior Chippewa)
3	Lake of the Torches Resort Casino	Lac du Flambeau.	Lac du Flambeau Band (Lake Superior Chippewa)
4	Lac Courte Oreilles Casino	Hayward	Lac Courte Oreilles Band (Lake Superior Chippewa)
5	Grindstone Creek Casino	Hayward	Lac Courte Oreilles Band (Lake Superior Chippewa)
6	St. Croix Casino – Danbury	Danbury	St. Croix Band (Lake Superior Chippewa)
7	St. Croix Casino – Hertel Express	Hertel.	St. Croix Band (Lake Superior Chippewa)
8	St. Croix Casino – Turtle Lake	Turtle Lake.	St. Croix Band (Lake Superior Chippewa)
9	Mole Lake Casino	Crandon	Sokaogon Chippewa Community
10	Potawatomi Carter Casino and Hotel	Carter.	Forest County Potawatomi Community
11	Menominee Casino and Resort	Keshena	Menominee Tribe
12	The Thunderbird Mini-Casino	Keshena	Menominee Tribe
13	North Star Mohican Casino	Bowler.	Stockbridge-Munsee Band (Mohican Nation)
14	Ho-Chunk Gaming – Wittenberg	Wittenberg	Ho-Chunk Nation
15	Ho-Chunk Gaming – Black River Falls	Black River Falls.	Ho-Chunk Nation
16	Ho-Chunk Gaming – Nekoosa	Nekoosa	Ho-Chunk Nation
17	Ho-Chunk Gaming – Tomah	Tomah	Ho-Chunk Nation
18	Ho-Chunk Gaming – Wisconsin Dells	Baraboo	Ho-Chunk Nation
19	Potawatomi Bingo Casino	Milwaukee	Forest County Potawatomi Community
20	Oneida Main Casino	Green Bay	Oneida Nation
21	IMAC Casino/Bingo	Green Bay	Oneida Nation
22	Oneida Mason Street Casino	Green Bay	Oneida Nation
23	Oneida One-Stop Packerland	Green Bay	Oneida Nation
24	Oneida Casino Travel Center	Oneida	Oneida Nation
25	Highway 54 Casino	Oneida	Oneida Nation

Note: Only Class III gaming facilities regulated by tribal compact are included, pursuant to P.L. 100-497, the Indian Gaming Regulatory Act, which divides gambling into three classes. An additional Ho-Chunk casino in Madison offers Class II gaming. Class I games are social games played solely for prizes of minimal value or traditional forms of Indian gaming played in connection with tribal ceremonies or celebrations. Class II includes bingo or bingo-type games, pull-tabs and punch-boards, and certain nonbanking card games, such as poker. Class III covers all other forms of gaming.
Source: Wisconsin Legislative Fiscal Bureau, *Informational Paper 88: Tribal Gaming in Wisconsin,* January 2013.

WISCONSIN VOTING AGE POPULATION BY RACE AND COUNTY
2010 Census and 2012 Estimate

County	2012 Total	2010 Total	White	Black/ African American	American Indian and Alaska Native	Asian	Native Hawaiian and Other Pacific Islander	Some Other Race	More Than One	Hispanic or Latino Origin*
Adams	17,460	17,454	15,935	598	203	90	6	8	26	588
Ashland	12,390	12,413	10,718	39	1,416	44	4	7	18	167
Barron	35,917	35,720	34,325	291	392	177	7	10	24	494
Bayfield . . .	12,244	12,161	10,812	22	1,170	43	4	9	10	91
Brown	188,653	186,184	162,483	3,705	5,076	4,470	92	96	196	10,066
Buffalo	10,663	10,566	10,306	18	60	26	1	17	2	136
Burnett	12,428	12,375	11,496	46	660	41	6	8	11	107
Calumet . . .	36,023	35,733	33,709	167	248	665	12	15	16	901
Chippewa . .	48,183	47,706	45,395	864	361	535	11	11	26	503
Clark	24,709	24,599	23,527	52	141	87	10	3	9	770
Columbia. . .	43,754	43,566	41,505	621	270	247	27	15	16	865
Crawford. . .	12,969	12,920	12,441	247	68	47	6	5	10	96
Dane	386,328	381,989	324,503	17,235	1,901	18,629	189	450	845	18,237
Dodge	69,389	69,180	63,961	2,241	441	369	38	30	46	2,054
Door	22,877	22,709	21,902	92	196	89	4	7	18	401
Douglas	34,867	34,694	32,579	376	1,047	336	14	20	38	284
Dunn	34,924	34,798	33,112	200	225	786	16	13	38	408
Eau Claire . .	78,613	77,864	73,172	653	572	2,232	35	40	82	1,078
Florence	3,611	3,649	3,560	7	41	20	2	0	0	19
Fond du Lac . .	79,207	78,589	73,638	937	549	754	23	34	57	2,597
Forest.	7,209	7,261	6,222	58	863	13	15	3	8	79
Grant	40,688	40,322	38,922	513	140	265	6	13	21	442
Green.	28,021	27,889	26,912	101	83	140	8	15	14	616
Green Lake. . .	14,770	14,663	14,027	5	4	3	2	0	0	1
Iowa	17,905	17,798	17,377	58	63	100	8	12	8	172
Iron.	4,895	4,935	4,845	5	48	15	0	0	4	18
Jackson.	15,941	15,818	14,148	379	878	46	19	8	15	325
Jefferson	64,222	63,829	59,160	502	318	470	16	32	40	3,291
Juneau	21,250	20,991	19,592	513	343	94	4	8	9	428
Kenosha	124,410	123,597	101,744	7,217	769	2,031	80	144	255	11,357
Kewaunee . . .	15,836	15,725	15,256	49	102	40	5	14	14	245
La Crosse . . .	91,283	90,176	83,999	1,149	576	3,172	33	58	100	1,089
Lafayette	12,584	12,487	12,053	18	53	37	0	0	4	322
Langlade	15,757	15,762	15,264	58	213	51	2	4	4	166
Lincoln	22,610	22,441	21,916	63	136	104	15	16	9	182
Manitowoc . .	63,499	63,232	59,800	272	439	1,247	25	33	50	1,366
Marathon . . .	101,972	101,194	94,081	527	625	4,105	43	41	97	1,675
Marinette. . . .	33,294	33,182	32,221	85	293	203	18	15	17	330
Marquette . . .	12,365	12,319	11,900	57	93	51	0	4	3	211
Menominee . .	2,853	2,853	423	10	2,338	1	0	0	1	80
Milwaukee. . .	714,853	711,358	433,061	168,280	5,644	23,660	331	790	2,476	77,116
Monroe.	33,429	33,003	31,038	366	420	229	34	13	22	881
Oconto	29,484	29,228	28,308	50	450	95	5	12	11	297
Oneida	29,536	29,359	28,454	134	373	150	16	7	10	215
Outagamie . . .	133,930	132,271	121,384	1,180	2,390	3,410	60	65	119	3,663
Ozaukee	66,489	66,023	62,520	878	239	1,123	26	32	65	1,140
Pepin	5,788	5,765	5,658	13	24	15	2	4	2	47
Pierce	32,065	31,860	30,766	187	185	280	6	17	17	402
Polk	33,876	33,705	32,677	77	394	119	5	23	26	384
Portage	56,338	55,472	52,322	325	309	1,325	20	31	49	1,091
Price	11,425	11,460	11,164	13	103	52	36	7	1	84
Racine	147,515	146,898	115,625	15,037	867	1,693	54	113	220	13,289
Richland	13,894	13,821	13,417	52	65	67	2	8	5	205
Rock	120,510	120,148	105,720	5,460	646	1,331	54	80	135	6,722
Rusk	11,490	11,440	11,158	28	97	40	2	1	6	108
St. Croix	62,099	61,462	59,021	394	358	638	19	36	44	952
Sauk	47,428	47,209	44,473	254	557	292	13	30	30	1,560
Sawyer	13,242	13,103	10,799	64	2,046	38	2	5	5	144
Shawano	32,504	32,387	29,227	84	2,371	155	18	4	25	503
Sheboygan . . .	88,346	87,925	79,347	1,305	499	3,064	32	48	78	3,552
Taylor	15,673	15,600	20,622	40	71	95	3	5	7	988
Trempealeau . .	22,059	21,831	20,622	40	71	95	3	5	7	988
Vernon	22,049	21,895	21,414	76	89	75	7	8	12	214
Vilas	17,743	17,621	15,816	33	1,533	66	3	9	4	157
Walworth. . . .	78,847	78,219	70,164	769	352	682	34	35	56	6,136
Washburn. . . .	12,727	12,679	12,231	22	246	46	2	2	7	123
Washington. . .	100,388	99,510	95,331	765	414	1,022	22	51	66	1,839
Waukesha . . .	298,149	296,081	273,899	3,256	1,160	7,769	112	143	256	9,486
Waupaca	40,691	40,540	39,216	111	303	152	7	9	10	732
Waushara	19,757	19,662	18,231	440	158	82	9	6	1	735
Winnebago. . .	131,980	130,862	121,239	2,336	1,105	2,655	58	62	132	9
Wood	57,864	57,745	55,161	240	2	2	0	0	0	3
STATE . . .	4,378,741	4,347,494	3,753,673	242,398	47,511	93,260	1,826	2,897	6,107	199,822

Note: The voting age population is 18 and older.

*"Hispanic or Latino Origin" represents ethnicity and includes people of Cuban, Mexican, Puerto Rican, South or Central American, or other Spanish culture or origin, regardless of race.

Sources: U.S. Department of Commerce, Census Bureau, P.L. 94-171 Redistricting File, as processed by the Wisconsin Legislative Technology Services Bureau, May 2011; Wisconsin Department of Administration, Demographic Services Center, *Official Final Estimates, 1/1/2012, Wisconsin Counties, with Comparison to Census 2010.*

WISCONSIN VITAL STATISTICS
1910 – 2011

Year	Marriages Number	Marriages Rate[3]	Divorces, Annulments Number[4]	Divorces, Annulments Rate[6]	Live Births Number	Live Births Rate[3]	Total Deaths[1] Number	Total Deaths[1] Rate[3]	Infant Deaths Number	Infant Deaths Rate[5]	Fetal Deaths[2] Number	Fetal Deaths[2] Rate[6]	Maternal Deaths Number	Maternal Deaths Rate[7]
1910	18,528	7.9	1,189	0.5	51,435	22.0	28,213	12.1	5,621	109.3	1,414	26.8	255	49.6
1915	17,833	7.2	1,721	0.7	58,014	23.3	26,676	10.7	4,520	77.9	1,711	28.6	291	50.2
1920	22,294	8.4	2,425	0.9	59,269	22.4	29,859	11.3	4,566	77.0	1,673	27.5	338	57.0
1925	16,385	5.8	2,467	0.9	58,024	20.7	29,380	10.5	3,861	66.5	1,712	28.7	294	50.7
1930	15,328	5.2	2,553	0.9	56,643	19.2	30,488	10.4	3,149	55.6	1,683	28.9	298	52.6
1935	21,075	6.9	3,543	1.2	52,402	17.2	30,404	10.0	2,413	46.0	1,257	23.4	193	36.8
1940	23,379	7.5	3,599	1.1	56,324	17.9	31,457	10.0	2,030	36.0	1,209	21.0	151	26.8
1945	25,269	8.5	6,393	2.2	61,577	20.9	31,776	10.7	1,890	30.7	1,141	18.2	81	13.2
1950	29,081	8.4	4,845	1.4	82,364	23.9	33,573	9.7	2,098	25.5	1,241	14.8	35	4.3
1955	25,543	7.0	4,720	1.3	92,333	25.2	35,250	9.6	2,175	23.6	1,233	13.2	22	2.4
1960	24,573	6.2	3,672	0.9	99,493	25.1	38,121	9.6	2,173	21.8	1,341	13.3	27	2.7
1965	28,410	6.7	5,232	1.2	82,919	19.7	40,146	9.5	1,829	22.1	1,042	12.4	13	1.6
1970	34,415	7.8	8,930	2.0	77,455	17.5	40,820	9.2	1,308	16.9	817	10.4	6	0.8
1975	35,888	7.8	13,187	2.9	65,145	14.3	39,916	8.8	881	13.5	530	8.1	3	0.5
1980	41,113	8.7	17,589	3.7	74,763	15.9	40,801	8.7	763	10.2	549	7.3	5	0.7
1985	40,014	8.4	16,596	3.5	73,647	15.4	41,434	8.7	674	9.2	471	6.4	4	0.5
1990	38,934	8.0	17,727	3.6	72,636	14.8	42,655	8.7	611	8.4	443	6.1	3	0.4
1995	36,354	7.1	17,313	3.4	67,493	13.2	45,037	8.7	493	7.3	403	5.9	2	0.3
1996	36,186	7.0	17,218	3.3	67,076	13.0	45,107	8.8	492	7.3	416	6.2	2	0.3
1997	35,546	6.8	17,289	3.3	66,490	12.7	44,860	8.6	431	6.5	361	5.4	2	0.3
1998	34,946	6.7	17,484	3.3	67,379	12.8	45,890	8.7	488	7.2	401	5.9	6	0.9
1999	35,754	6.8	17,302	3.3	68,181	12.9	46,571	8.7	456	6.7	353	5.2	6	0.9
2000	36,100	6.7	17,388	3.2	69,289	12.9	46,405	8.8	457	6.6	414	5.9	5	0.7
2001	34,790	6.5	17,457	3.3	69,012	12.7	46,537	8.7	491	7.1	375	5.4	4	0.6
2002	34,241	6.3	17,471	3.2	68,510	12.6	46,893	8.6	471	6.9	379	5.5	5	0.7
2003	34,220	6.3	17,150	3.1	69,999	12.7	46,040	8.4	454	6.5	344	4.9	9	1.3
2004	34,056	6.2	16,802	3.0	70,131	12.7	45,488	8.2	420	6.0	352	5.0	6	0.9
2005	33,876	6.1	16,297	2.9	70,934	12.7	46,544	8.3	469	6.6	363	5.1	15	2.1
2006	33,437	6.0	16,730	3.0	72,302	12.9	46,051	8.2	462	6.4	384	5.3	15	2.1
2007	32,159	5.7	16,458	2.9	72,757	12.9	46,117	8.2	469	6.4	386	5.3	15	2.1
2008	31,444	5.6	16,885	3.0	72,002	12.7	46,526	8.2	501	7.0	387	5.3	15	2.1
2009	30,057	5.3	16,705	2.9	68,708	12.5	45,598	8.0	426	6.0	341	4.8	13	1.2
2010	29,952	5.3	17,285	3.0	68,367	12.0	47,212	8.3	393	5.7	361	5.3	11	1.8
2011	30,287	5.3	16,635	2.9	67,736	11.9	48,101	8.4	427	6.3	368	5.4	13	1.9

[1]Excludes fetal deaths (20 weeks gestation and over).
[2]A fetal death report is not used for induced abortions.
[3]Per 1,000 population.
[4]Pre-1960 data includes legal separations.
[5]Per 1,000 live births.
[6]Per 1,000 deliveries (live births plus stillbirths of 20 weeks or more gestation).
[7]Per 10,000 live births.

Sources: Wisconsin Department of Health and Family Services, *Vital Statistics 1994*, and previous issues; Wisconsin Department of Health Services, *2012 Births to Wisconsin Residents by County*; *Wisconsin Births and Infant Deaths, 2010*, and previous issues; *Wisconsin Deaths, 2011*, and previous issues; *Wisconsin Marriages and Divorces, 2011*, and previous issues; departmental data, March 2013.

RESIDENT LIVE BIRTHS AND DEATHS IN WISCONSIN
By County, 1990 – 2010

County	Live Births					Deaths				
	1990	1995	2000	2005	2010	1990	1995[1]	2000	2005	2010[2]
Adams	175	167	158	159	135	182	185	226	225	255
Ashland	202	239	224	198	177	214	218	206	205	188
Barron	579	550	466	528	546	433	450	442	487	482
Bayfield	155	135	141	121	113	151	152	153	149	152
Brown	3,169	2,962	3,212	3,332	3,414	1,349	1,482	1,591	1,626	1,610
Buffalo	176	165	163	147	125	145	121	123	117	146
Burnett	143	171	136	159	138	159	179	183	182	135
Calumet	491	488	513	630	605	242	235	252	265	284
Chippewa	704	633	673	738	748	498	534	533	522	485
Clark	464	448	496	581	600	355	323	307	339	354
Columbia	610	607	616	691	600	450	532	508	498	514
Crawford	230	215	183	201	157	180	178	178	169	156
Dane	5,305	5,023	5,555	6,055	6,051	2,078	2,397	2,512	2,648	2,858
Dodge	985	947	994	910	872	765	810	848	826	913
Door	325	254	232	258	215	311	311	315	314	311
Douglas	540	493	513	466	487	440	455	454	425	397
Dunn	417	444	483	511	468	271	289	280	260	305
Eau Claire	1,208	1,118	1,116	1,178	1,114	658	664	639	704	703
Florence[3]	26	36	36	37	29	44	66	63	45	66
Fond du Lac	1,270	1,119	1,151	1,187	1,066	771	867	908	1,000	902
Forest[3]	132	137	114	114	117	122	109	131	103	109
Grant	661	561	540	559	545	493	465	495	484	504
Green	418	390	402	447	414	270	316	322	316	313
Green Lake	241	192	219	204	211	201	248	243	230	201
Iowa	318	296	263	320	290	195	191	195	177	208
Iron[3]	68	63	40	45	40	97	87	84	110	83
Jackson	217	189	233	237	237	187	187	219	189	180
Jefferson	873	852	931	1,028	923	541	579	608	608	615
Juneau	277	308	275	277	263	230	271	264	278	274
Kenosha	2,043	2,040	2,151	2,133	2,055	1,131	1,229	1,222	1,253	1,272
Kewaunee	237	218	224	232	205	184	193	189	182	147
La Crosse	1,416	1,267	1,234	1,292	1,345	836	869	888	818	923
Lafayette	227	176	174	207	207	172	147	144	130	146
Langlade	232	228	209	202	204	220	252	220	233	202
Lincoln	343	320	281	275	283	281	298	333	316	300
Manitowoc	1,072	898	894	855	805	774	819	852	742	824
Marathon	1,685	1,585	1,520	1,554	1,656	875	907	924	976	1,100
Marinette[3]	431	454	457	460	389	491	478	470	493	452
Marquette[3]	148	121	146	182	160	149	141	174	185	179
Menominee[3]	128	92	93	104	108	42	45	36	45	36
Milwaukee	17,013	15,067	14,846	14,906	14,310	9,282	9,200	9,063	8,605	8,147
Monroe	591	529	602	615	627	384	383	414	399	390
Oconto	398	388	383	388	368	272	331	357	327	356
Oneida	371	352	316	355	307	363	375	431	421	425
Outagamie	2,273	2,056	2,289	2,291	2,268	993	1,026	1,109	1,194	1,218
Ozaukee	945	934	869	852	774	497	541	583	605	744
Pepin	90	83	79	99	65	93	72	73	66	81
Pierce	477	403	412	443	425	237	235	244	229	231
Polk	529	470	454	506	457	352	380	376	401	401
Portage	913	788	805	726	749	398	438	404	491	477
Price	185	184	125	130	115	196	198	207	200	161
Racine	2,697	2,512	2,650	2,623	2,484	1,438	1,534	1,616	1,537	1,628
Richland	219	196	201	228	194	186	200	185	164	160
Rock	2,166	1,963	2,075	2,052	1,991	1,277	1,268	1,335	1,409	1,379
Rusk	213	192	148	163	138	157	183	168	191	170
St. Croix	840	725	908	1,193	1,119	375	438	444	429	541
Sauk	670	670	755	785	783	485	484	485	505	582
Sawyer	176	196	182	205	167	171	194	183	184	170
Shawano	525	456	470	478	447	418	444	476	448	449
Sheboygan	1,401	1,336	1,437	1,481	1,325	908	957	1,083	1,089	1,001
Taylor	289	221	247	246	238	195	191	176	196	198
Trempealeau	369	315	322	331	377	300	338	298	280	264
Vernon	332	351	390	403	399	290	311	330	324	270
Vilas	201	205	155	164	191	244	254	251	235	242
Walworth	996	952	1,102	1,209	1,077	651	710	826	860	836
Washburn	159	168	163	173	152	167	194	198	193	195
Washington	1,349	1,440	1,490	1,495	1,371	650	687	795	868	997
Waukesha	4,046	4,120	4,357	4,108	3,886	1,906	2,316	2,795	2,903	3,084
Waupaca	667	619	567	537	503	620	658	634	677	709
Waushara	245	240	225	241	232	223	242	243	237	259
Winnebago	1,936	1,838	1,926	1,826	1,872	1,094	1,271	1,194	1,258	1,397
Wood	1,039	923	878	868	839	646	704	695	745	762
STATE	72,661	67,493	69,289	70,934	68,367	42,655	45,036	46,405	46,544	47,212

[1]The total for 1995 includes one death with an unknown county of residence.
[2]The total for 2010 includes four deaths with unknown counties of residence.
[3]Since nearly all births and deaths occur in hospitals, the numbers for Florence, Forest, Iron, Marinette, Marquette, and Menominee Counties are small because they have no hospitals. Caution must be used in making inferences based on this data.

Sources: Wisconsin Department of Health Services, Division of Public Health, Office of Health Informatics, *Wisconsin Births and Infant Deaths, 2010*, at: http://www.dhs.wisconsin.gov/publications/P4/P45364-10.pdf, and previous issues; *Wisconsin Deaths, 2010*, at: http://www.dhs.wisconsin.gov/publications/P4/P45368-10.pdf, and previous issues.

MARRIAGE AND DIVORCE RATES BY STATE
1990 – 2011
(Rates per 1,000)[1]

State	Marriages[2]						Divorces[3]					
	1990	1995	2000	2005	2010	2011	1990	1995	2000	2005	2010	2011
Alabama	10.6	9.8	10.1	9.2	8.2	8.4	6.1	6.0	5.5	4.9	4.4	4.3
Alaska	10.2	9.0	8.9	8.2	8.0	7.8	5.5	5.0	3.9	4.3	4.7	4.8
Arizona.	10.0	8.8	7.5	6.6	5.9	5.7	6.9	6.2	4.6	4.2	3.5	3.9
Arkansas	15.3	14.4	15.4	12.9	10.8	10.4	6.9	6.3	6.4	6.0	5.7	5.3
California	7.9	6.3	5.8	6.4	5.8	5.8	4.3	NA	NA	NA	NA	NA
Colorado	9.8	9.0	8.3	7.6	6.9	7.0	5.5	NA	4.7	4.4	4.3	4.4
Connecticut	7.9	6.6	5.7	5.8	5.6	5.5	3.2	2.9	3.3	3.0	2.9	3.1
Delaware	8.4	7.3	6.5	5.9	5.2	5.2	4.4	5.0	3.9	3.8	3.5	3.6
District of Columbia	8.2	6.1	4.9	4.1	7.6	8.7	4.5	3.2	3.2	2.0	2.8	2.9
Florida	10.9	9.9	8.9	8.9	7.3	7.4	6.3	5.5	5.1	4.6	4.4	4.5
Georgia.	10.3	8.4	6.8	7.0	7.3	6.6	5.5	5.1	3.3	NA	NA	NA
Hawaii	16.4	15.7	20.6	22.6	17.6	17.6	4.6	4.6	3.9	NA	NA	NA
Idaho	13.9	13.1	10.8	10.5	8.8	8.6	6.5	5.8	5.5	5.0	5.2	4.9
ILLINOIS	8.8	6.9	6.9	5.9	5.7	5.6	3.8	3.2	3.2	2.6	2.6	2.6
Indiana	9.6	8.6	7.9	6.9	6.3	6.8	NA	NA	NA	NA	NA	NA
IOWA	9.0	7.7	6.9	6.9	6.9	6.7	3.9	3.7	3.3	2.7	2.4	2.4
Kansas	9.2	8.5	8.3	6.8	6.4	6.3	5.0	4.1	3.6	3.1	3.7	3.9
Kentucky	13.5	12.2	9.8	8.7	7.4	7.5	5.8	5.9	5.1	4.6	4.5	4.4
Louisiana.	9.6	9.3	9.1	8.0	6.9	6.4	NA	NA	NA	NA	NA	NA
Maine	9.7	8.7	8.8	8.2	7.1	7.2	4.3	4.4	5.0	4.1	4.2	4.2
Maryland.	9.7	8.4	7.5	6.9	5.7	5.8	3.4	3.0	3.3	3.1	2.8	2.9
Massachusetts	7.9	7.1	5.8	6.2	5.6	5.5	2.8	2.2	2.5	2.2	2.5	2.7
MICHIGAN	8.2	7.3	6.7	6.1	5.5	5.7	4.3	4.1	3.9	3.4	3.5	3.4
MINNESOTA	7.7	7.0	6.8	6.0	5.3	5.6	3.5	3.4	3.2	NA	NA	NA
Mississippi	9.4	7.9	6.9	5.8	4.9	4.9	5.5	4.8	5.0	4.4	4.3	4.0
Missouri	9.6	8.3	7.8	7.0	6.5	6.6	5.1	5.0	4.5	3.6	3.9	3.9
Montana	8.6	7.6	7.3	7.4	7.4	7.8	5.1	4.8	4.2	4.5	3.9	4.0
Nebraska	8.0	7.3	7.6	7.0	6.6	6.6	4.0	3.8	3.7	3.3	3.6	3.5
Nevada	99.0	85.2	72.2	57.4	38.3	36.9	11.4	7.8	9.9	7.4	5.9	5.6
New Hampshire	9.5	8.3	9.4	7.3	7.3	7.1	4.7	4.2	4.8	3.9	3.8	3.8
New Jersey	7.6	6.5	6.0	5.7	5.1	4.8	3.0	3.0	3.0	2.9	3.0	2.9
New Mexico	8.8	8.8	8.0	6.6	7.7	8.0	4.9	6.6	5.1	4.6	4.0	3.3
New York	8.6	8.0	7.1	6.8	6.5	6.9	3.2	3.0	3.0	2.9	2.9	2.9
North Carolina	7.8	8.4	8.2	7.3	6.6	6.7	5.1	5.0	4.5	4.1	3.8	3.7
North Dakota.	7.5	7.1	7.2	6.8	6.5	6.7	3.6	3.4	3.4	2.9	3.1	2.7
Ohio	9.0	8.0	7.8	6.5	5.8	5.9	4.7	4.3	4.2	3.5	3.4	3.4
Oklahoma	10.6	8.6	NA	7.3	7.2	6.9	7.7	6.6	NA	5.6	5.2	5.2
Oregon	8.9	8.1	7.6	7.3	6.5	6.6	5.5	4.7	4.8	4.2	4.0	3.8
Pennsylvania	7.1	6.2	6.0	5.8	5.3	5.3	3.3	3.2	3.1	2.3	2.7	2.8
Rhode Island	8.1	7.3	7.6	7.0	5.8	6.0	3.7	3.6	2.9	3.0	3.2	3.2
South Carolina	15.9	11.9	10.6	8.3	7.4	7.2	4.5	3.9	3.8	2.9	3.1	3.2
South Dakota.	11.1	9.9	9.4	8.4	7.3	7.5	3.7	3.9	3.5	2.8	3.4	3.3
Tennessee	13.9	15.5	15.5	10.9	8.8	9.0	6.5	6.2	5.9	4.6	4.2	4.3
Texas	10.5	9.9	9.4	7.8	7.1	7.1	5.5	5.2	4.0	3.3	3.3	3.2
Utah	11.2	10.7	10.8	9.8	8.5	8.6	5.1	4.4	4.3	4.1	3.7	3.7
Vermont	10.9	10.3	10.0	8.9	9.3	8.3	4.5	4.7	4.1	3.6	3.8	3.6
Virginia.	11.4	10.2	8.8	8.2	6.8	6.8	4.4	4.3	4.3	4.0	3.8	3.8
Washington.	9.5	7.7	6.9	6.5	6.0	6.1	5.9	5.4	4.6	4.3	4.2	4.1
West Virginia.	7.2	6.1	8.7	7.4	6.7	7.2	5.3	5.2	5.1	5.1	5.1	5.2
WISCONSIN	7.9	7.0	6.7	6.1	5.3	5.3	3.6	3.4	3.2	2.9	3.0	2.9
Wyoming.	10.7	10.6	10.0	9.3	7.6	7.8	6.6	6.6	5.8	5.2	5.1	4.8

NA – Not available.

[1]Rates are based on provisional counts of marriages and divorces by state of occurrence. Rates are per 1,000 total population residing in area. Population enumerated as of April 1 for 1990, 2000, and 2010, and estimated as of July 1 for all other years.
[2]Data includes nonlicensed marriages registered.
[3]Data includes annulments. Includes divorce petitions filed or legal separations for some counties or states.

Sources: Centers for Disease Control and Prevention, National Vital Statistics System, *Marriage rates by State: 1990, 1995, and 1999-2011*, at: http://www.cdc.gov/nchs/mardiv.htm [May 2013]; *Divorce rates by State: 1990, 1995, and 1999-2011*, at: http://www.cdc.gov/nchs/mardiv.htm [May 2013].

WISCONSIN DEATHS AND DEATH RATES – 2011

	Total		Males		Females	
Age Group	Deaths	Rate*	Deaths	Rate*	Deaths	Rate*
Under 1 year	425	643.3	229	678.2	196	607.0
1-4 years	72	25.0	38	25.8	34	24.2
5-9 years	30	8.2	21	11.2	9	5.0
10-14 years.	56	15.0	28	14.7	28	15.3
15-19 years.	177	44.5	122	59.9	55	28.4
20-24 years.	295	76.1	209	105.6	86	45.4
25-29 years.	313	84.4	227	120.6	86	47.1
30-34 years.	359	99.8	255	139.1	104	59.0
35-39 years.	390	117.5	240	142.7	150	91.6
40-44 years.	626	166.5	372	196.1	254	136.4
45-49 years.	1,133	269.0	692	328.4	441	209.4
50-54 years.	1,806	409.0	1,117	506.7	689	311.6
55-59 years.	2,519	635.2	1,573	794.2	946	476.6
60-64 years.	3,001	895.0	1,806	1,084.3	1,195	708.2
65-69 years.	3,281	1,401.9	1,932	1,708.1	1,349	1,115.5
70-74 years.	4,064	2,291.5	2,292	2,760.1	1,772	1,878.9
75-79 years.	4,956	3,520.9	2,649	4,237.7	2,307	2,948.2
80-84 years.	7,066	6,011.1	3,470	7,188.7	3,596	5,190.5
85-89 years.	8,092	10,409.0	3,426	12,503.6	4,666	9,269.0
90-94 years.	6,258	18,405.9	2,112	22,000.0	4,146	16,991.8
95 years and over . . .	3,180	31,673.3	680	34,343.4	2,500	31,017.4
ALL AGES.	48,101	843.4	23,490	829.5	24,609	857.0

*Per 100,000 population in that group.

Source: Wisconsin Department of Health Services, Division of Public Health, Office of Health Informatics, *Wisconsin Deaths, 2011,* March 2013, at: http://www.dhs.wisconsin.gov/publications/P4/P45368-11.pdf.

WISCONSIN POPULATION, BY AGE GROUP, 2010 and 2011

	Population of Group		Male		Female	
Age Group	2010 Census	2011	2010	2011	2010	2011
Under 5 years	358,443	354,582	183,391	181,311	175,052	173,271
5-9 years	368,617	366,125	188,286	187,096	180,331	179,029
10-14 years	375,927	374,737	192,232	191,369	183,695	183,368
15-19 years	399,209	398,138	204,803	204,123	194,406	194,015
20-24 years	386,552	388,090	196,897	198,230	189,655	189,860
25-29 years	372,347	371,212	189,349	188,531	182,998	182,681
30-34 years	349,347	360,156	178,120	183,627	171,227	176,529
35-39 years	345,328	332,465	174,619	168,412	170,709	164,053
40-44 years	380,338	376,468	191,738	190,023	188,600	186,445
45-49 years	437,627	421,951	218,539	211,062	219,088	210,889
50-54 years	436,126	442,287	218,303	220,805	217,823	221,482
55-59 years	385,986	397,161	192,952	198,366	193,034	198,795
60-64 years	313,825	335,775	155,756	166,788	158,069	168,987
65-69 years	227,029	234,369	109,168	113,246	117,861	121,123
70-74 years	173,467	177,590	81,067	83,123	92,400	94,467
75-79 years	141,252	140,950	62,181	62,596	79,071	78,354
80-84 years	117,061	117,749	47,549	48,350	69,512	69,399
85 years and over	118,505	121,962	37,450	39,034	81,055	82,928
STATE	5,686,986	5,711,767	2,822,400	2,836,092	2,864,586	2,875,675
Median age	38.5	38.7	37.3	37.5	39.6	39.9

Source: U.S. Census Bureau, Population Division, *Annual Estimates of the Resident Population by Sex and Age for Wisconsin: April 1, 2010 to July 1, 2011,* December 2012.

POSTAL ZIP CODES FOR WISCONSIN MUNICIPALITIES

Municipality and County	ZIP Code
Abbotsford, Clark	54405
Abrams, Oconto	54101
Adams, Adams	53910
Adell, Sheboygan	53001
Afton, Rock	53501
Alban, Portage (Rosholt)[1]	54473
Albany, Green	53502
Albertville, Dunn (Colfax)[1]	54730
Alden, St. Croix (New Richmond)[1]	54017
Algoma, Kewaunee	54201
Allenton, Washington	53002
Allouez, Brown	54301
Alma, Buffalo	54610
Alma Center, Jackson	54611
Almena, Barron	54805
Almond, Portage	54909
Altdorf, Wood (Vesper)[1]	54489
Altoona, Eau Claire	54720
Alvin, Florence	54542
Amberg, Marinette	54102
Amery, Polk	54001
Amherst, Portage	54406
Amherst Junction, Portage	54407
Angelica, Brown (Pulaski)[1]	54162
Aniwa, Marathon	54408
Antigo, Langlade	54409
Apostle Islands National Lake, Bayfield (Bayfield)[1]	54814
Appleton, Outagamie[2]	54911
Arbor Vitae, Oneida	54568
Arcadia, Trempealeau	54612
Arena, Iowa	53503
Argonne, Forest	54511
Argyle, Lafayette	53504
Arkansaw, Pepin	54721
Arkdale, Adams	54613
Arland, Polk (Clayton)[1]	54004
Arlington, Columbia	53911
Armstrong Creek, Forest	54103
Arnott, Portage (Stevens Point)[1]	54481
Arpin, Wood	54410
Ashippun, Dodge	53003
Ashland, Ashland	54806
Ashley, Marathon (Mosinee)[1]	54455
Ashwaubenon, Brown	54304
Athelstane, Marinette	54104
Athens, Marathon	54411
Atwood, Clark (Owen)[1]	54460
Auburndale, Wood	54412
Augusta, Eau Claire	54722
Auroraville, Green Lake (Berlin)[1]	54923
Avalon, Rock	53505
Avoca, Iowa	53506
Babcock, Wood	54413
Bagley, Grant	53801
Baileys Harbor, Door	54202
Bakerville, Wood (Marshfield)[1]	54449
Baldwin, St. Croix	54002
Balsam Lake, Polk	54810
Bancroft, Portage	54921
Bangor, La Crosse	54614
Baraboo, Sauk	53913
Barnes, Douglas	54873
Barneveld, Iowa	53507
Barre Mills, La Crosse (La Crosse)[1]	54601
Barron, Barron	54812
Barronett, Barron	54813
Bassett, Kenosha	53101
Bateman, Chippewa (Chippewa Falls)[1]	54729
Bay City, Pierce	54723
Bayfield, Bayfield	54814
Bayside, Milwaukee	53217
Bay Mills, Lincoln (Tomahawk)[1]	54487
Bay View, Milwaukee (Milwaukee)[3]	53207
Bear Creek, Outagamie	54922
Beaver, Marinette	54114
Beaver Dam, Dodge	53916
Beecher, Marinette (Pembine)[1]	54156
Beetown, Grant	53802
Beldenville, Pierce	54003
Belgium, Ozaukee	53004
Bell Center, Crawford (Gays Mills)[1]	54631

Municipality and County	ZIP Code
Belleville, Dane	53508
Bellevue, Brown	54311
Belmont, Lafayette	53510
Beloit, Rock[2]	53511
Benet Lake, Kenosha	53102
Bennett, Douglas	54873
Benoit, Bayfield	54816
Benton, Lafayette	53803
Berlin, Green Lake	54923
Bethel, Wood (Arpin)[1]	54410
Bevent, Marathon (Hatley)[1]	54440
Big Bend, Waukesha	53103
Big Falls, Waupaca	54926
Big Flats, Adams (Arkdale)[1]	54613
Birch, Lincoln (Irma)[1]	54442
Birchwood, Washburn	54817
Birnamwood, Shawano	54414
Biron, Wood (Wisconsin Rapids)[1]	54494
Black Brook, Polk (Clear Lake)[1]	54005
Black Creek, Outagamie	54106
Black Earth, Dane	53515
Black River Falls, Jackson	54615
Blackwell, Forest (Laona)[1]	54541
Blair, Trempealeau	54616
Blanchardville, Lafayette	53516
Blenker, Wood	54415
Bloom City, Vernon	54634
Bloomer, Chippewa	54724
Bloomingdale, Vernon (Westby)[1]	54667
Bloomington, Grant	53804
Bloomville, Lincoln (Gleason)[1]	54435
Blue Mounds, Dane	53517
Blue River, Grant	53518
Boardman, St. Croix (Hudson)[1]	54016
Boaz, Richland (Richland Center)[1]	53581
Bonduel, Shawano	54107
Boscobel, Grant	53805
Boulder Junction, Vilas	54512
Bowler, Shawano	54416
Boyceville, Dunn	54725
Boyd, Chippewa	54726
Brackett, Eau Claire (Fall Creek)[1]	54742
Branch, Manitowoc	54247
Brandon, Fond du Lac	53919
Brantwood, Price	54513
Briggsville, Marquette	53920
Brill, Barron	54818
Brillion, Calumet	54110
Bristol, Kenosha	53104
Brodhead, Green	53520
Brokaw, Marathon	54417
Brookfield, Waukesha[2]	53005
Brooklyn, Green	53521
Brooks, Marquette	53952
Brown Deer, Milwaukee[2]	53209
Brownsville, Dodge	53006
Browntown, Green	53522
Bruce, Rusk	54819
Brule, Douglas	54820
Brussels, Door	54204
Bryant, Langlade	54418
Buena Vista, Portage (Plover)[1]	54467
Buffalo City, Buffalo	54622
Burkhardt, St. Croix (Hudson)[1]	54016
Burlington, Racine	53105
Burnett, Dodge	53922
Butler, Waukesha	53007
Butte des Morts, Winnebago	54927
Butternut, Ashland	54514
Byron, Dodge	53006
Cable, Bayfield	54821
Cadott, Chippewa	54727
Cady, St. Croix (Wilson)[1]	54027
Caledonia, Racine	53108
Cambria, Columbia	53923
Cambridge, Dane	53523
Cameron, Barron	54822
Campbell, La Crosse (La Crosse)[1]	54601
Campbellsport, Fond du Lac	53010
Camp Douglas, Juneau[4]	54618
Camp Lake, Kenosha	53109
Canton, Barron	54868

Municipality and County	ZIP Code
Carey, Iron (Hurley)[1].	54534
Caroline, Shawano.	54928
Carson, Portage (Junction City)[1].	54443
Carter, Forest (Wabeno)[1].	54566
Caryville, Eau Claire (Eau Claire)[1]	54701
Cascade, Sheboygan.	53011
Casco, Kewaunee	54205
Cashton, Monroe.	54619
Cassian, Oneida (Harshaw)[1].	54529
Cassville, Grant	53806
Cataract, Monroe.	54620
Catawba, Price	54515
Cato, Manitowoc.	54230
Cavour, Forest	54511
Cayuga, Ashland (Mellen)[1]	54546
Cazenovia, Richland	53924
Cecil, Shawano	54111
Cedar, Iron (Saxon)[1]	54559
Cedar Falls, Dunn (Menomonie)[1]	54751
Cedarburg, Ozaukee	53012
Cedar Grove, Sheboygan	53013
Cedar Rapids, Rusk (Glen Flora)[1]	54526
Center Valley, Outagamie (Black Creek)[1]	54106
Centerville, Trempealeau (Galesville)[1]	54630
Centuria, Polk	54824
Chaseburg, Vernon.	54621
Chelsea, Taylor.	54451
Chenequa, Waukesha (Hartland)[1]	53029
Chetek, Barron.	54728
Chili, Clark.	54420
Chilton, Calumet.	53014
Chippewa Falls, Chippewa[4]	54729
Christie, Clark (Neillsville)[1]	54456
City Point, Wood (Pittsville)[1]	54466
Clam Falls, Polk	54837
Clam Lake, Ashland	54517
Clark, Clark (Withee)[1]	54498
Clayton, Polk.	54004
Clear Lake, Polk	54005
Clearwater Lake, Vilas (Eagle River)[1]	54521
Clearwater Lake, Oneida (Three Lakes)[1]	54562
Cleghorn, Trempealeau (Eleva)[1]	54738
Cleveland, Manitowoc.	53015
Clifton, Pierce (River Falls)[1]	54022
Clinton, Rock	53525
Clintonville, Waupaca	54929
Cloverland, Vilas (Eagle River)[1].	54521
Clyman, Dodge	53016
Cobb, Iowa.	53526
Cochrane, Buffalo	54622
Coddington, Portage (Plover)[1]	54467
Colby, Clark	54421
Coleman, Marinette	54112
Colfax, Dunn.	54730
Colgate, Washington.	53017
Collins, Manitowoc	54207
Coloma, Waushara	54930
Columbus, Columbia	53925
Combined Locks, Outagamie	54113
Comstock, Barron	54826
Connorsville, Dunn (Boyceville)[1]	54725
Conover, Vilas	54519
Conrath, Rusk	54731
Coon Valley, Vernon	54623
Cornell, Chippewa	54732
Corning, Lincoln (Merrill)[1]	54452
Cornucopia, Bayfield	54827
Cosy Valley, Ashland (Mellen)[1]	54546
Cottage Grove, Dane.	53527
Couderay, Sawyer.	54828
Crandon, Forest	54520
Cream, Buffalo (Alma)[1]	54610
Crescent, Chippewa (Cadott)[1]	54727
Crivitz, Marinette	54114
Cross Plains, Dane.	53528
Cuba City, Grant.	53807
Cudahy, Milwaukee	53110
Cumberland, Barron	54829
Curtiss, Clark	54422
Cushing, Polk	54006
Custer, Portage.	54423
Cutler, Juneau	54618
Cylon, St. Croix (New Richmond)[1]	54017

Municipality and County	ZIP Code
Dairyland, Burnett.	54830
Dale, Outagamie	54931
Dallas, Barron	54733
Dalton, Green Lake	53926
Danbury, Burnett.	54830
Dancy, Marathon (Mosinee)[1]	54455
Dane, Dane.	53529
Darien, Walworth	53114
Darlington, Lafayette	53530
Deerbrook, Langlade.	54424
Deerfield, Dane.	53531
Deer Park, St. Croix	54007
DeForest, Dane	53532
Delafield, Waukesha	53018
Delavan, Walworth.	53115
Dellwood, Adams	53927
Delta, Bayfield	54856
Denmark, Brown.	54208
De Pere, Brown	54115
Deronda, Polk	54001
De Soto, Vernon	54624
Deer Creek, Taylor (Stetsonville)[1]	54480
Dewey, Portage (Stevens Point)[1].	54481
Dexterville, Wood (Pittsville)[1]	54466
Diamond Bluff, Pierce (Hager City)[1]	54014
Dickeyville, Grant	53808
Dodge, Trempealeau.	54625
Dodgeville, Iowa[4]	53533
Donald, Taylor (Gilman)[1]	54433
Dorchester, Clark	54425
Dousman, Waukesha.	53118
Downing, Dunn	54734
Downsville, Dunn	54735
Doylestown, Columbia	53928
Dresser, Polk.	54009
Drummond, Bayfield.	54832
Dunbar, Marinette	54119
Durand, Pepin	54736
Dyckesville, Kewaunee (Luxemburg)[1]	54217
Eagle, Waukesha	53119
Eagle Point, Chippewa (Chippewa Falls)[1]. . . .	54729
Eagle River, Vilas	54521
Eagleton, Chippewa (Bloomer)[1].	54724
East Ellsworth, Pierce	54010
East Farmington, Polk (Osceola)[1]	54020
East Troy, Walworth	53120
Eastman, Crawford	54626
Eaton, Clark (Greenwood)[1]	54437
Eau Claire, Eau Claire[2]	54701
Eau Galle, Dunn	54737
Eau Pleine, Portage (Junction City)[1].	54443
Eden, Fond du Lac.	53019
Edgar, Marathon	54426
Edgerton, Rock	53534
Edgewater, Sawyer.	54834
Edmund, Iowa	53535
Edson, Chippewa (Boyd)[1]	54726
Egg Harbor, Door	54209
Eisenstein, Price (Park Falls)[1]	54552
El Paso, Pierce (Beldenville)[1]	54003
Eland, Marathon	54427
Elcho, Langlade	54428
Elderon, Marathon.	54429
Eldorado, Fond du Lac.	54932
Eleva, Trempealeau	54738
Elk, Price (Phillips)[1]	54555
Elk Creek, Trempealeau (Independence)[1]	54747
Elk Mound, Dunn	54739
Elkhart Lake, Sheboygan	53020
Elkhorn, Walworth.	53121
Ellis, Portage (Stevens Point)[1]	54481
Ellison Bay, Door	54210
Ellsworth, Pierce[4]	54011
Elm Grove, Waukesha	53122
Elmwood, Pierce.	54740
Elroy, Juneau.	53929
Elton, Langlade	54430
Embarrass, Waupaca	54933
Emerald, St. Croix	54013
Endeavor, Marquette.	53930
Ephraim, Door	54211
Erin, St. Croix (New Richmond)[1]	54017

Municipality and County	ZIP Code
Erin Prairie, St. Croix (Baldwin)[1]	54002
Esadore Lake, Taylor (Medford)[1]	54451
Ettrick, Trempealeau	54627
Eureka, Winnebago[4]	54963
Eureka Center, Polk (St. Croix Falls)[1]	54024
Evansville, Rock	53536
Exeland, Sawyer	54835
Fairchild, Eau Claire	54741
Fairwater, Fond du Lac	53931
Fall Creek, Eau Claire	54742
Fall River, Columbia	53932
Fence, Florence	54120
Fennimore, Grant	53809
Fenwood, Marathon	54426
Ferryville, Crawford	54628
Fifield, Price	54524
Figis, Wood (Marshfield)[1]	54472
Fish Creek, Door	54212
Fitchburg, Dane[2]	53575
Florence, Florence	54121
Fond du Lac, Fond du Lac[2]	54935
Fontana, Walworth	53125
Footville, Rock	53537
Forest Junction, Calumet	54123
Forestville, Door	54213
Fort Atkinson, Jefferson	53538
Fort McCoy, Monroe	54656
Foster, Trempealeau (Osseo)[1]	54758
Fountain City, Buffalo	54629
Foxboro, Douglas	54836
Fox Lake, Dodge	53933
Fox Point, Milwaukee	53217
Francis Creek, Manitowoc	54214
Franklin, Milwaukee	53132
Franksville, Racine	53126
Franzen, Shawano (Wittenberg)[1]	54499
Frederic, Polk	54837
Fredonia, Ozaukee	53021
Freedom, Outagamie[2]	54130
Fremont, Waupaca	54940
French Island, La Crosse (La Crosse)[1]	54601
Friendship, Adams	53934
Friesland, Columbia[4]	53923
Galesville, Trempealeau	54630
Galloway, Marathon	54432
Gays Mills, Crawford	54631
Genesee Depot, Waukesha	53127
Genoa, Vernon	54632
Genoa City, Walworth	53128
Germantown, Washington	53022
Gile, Iron	54525
Gillett, Oconto	54124
Gilman, Taylor[4]	54433
Gilmanton, Buffalo	54743
Gleason, Lincoln	54435
Glenbeulah, Sheboygan	53023
Glendale, Milwaukee[2]	53209
Glen Flora, Rusk	54526
Glen Haven, Grant	53810
Glenwood City, St. Croix	54013
Glidden, Ashland	54527
Goodman, Marinette	54125
Goodrich, Taylor (Medford)[1]	54451
Gordon, Douglas	54838
Gotham, Richland	53540
Grafton, Ozaukee	53024
Grand Chute, Outagamie (Appleton)[3]	54911
Grand Marsh, Adams	53936
Grand Rapids, Wood (Wisconsin Rapids)[1]	54494
Grand View, Bayfield	54839
Granton, Clark	54436
Grantsburg, Burnett	54840
Gratiot, Lafayette	53541
Green Bay, Brown[2]	54301
Green Grove, Clark (Owen)[1]	54460
Greenbush, Sheboygan	53026
Greendale, Milwaukee	53129
Greenfield, Milwaukee[2]	53219
Green Lake, Green Lake	54941
Greenleaf, Brown	54126
Green Valley, Shawano	54127

Municipality and County	ZIP Code
Greenville, Outagamie	54942
Greenwood, Clark	54437
Gresham, Shawano	54128
Gurney, Iron	54559
Hackett, Price (Phillips)[1]	54555
Hager City, Pierce	54014
Halder, Marathon (Mosinee)[1]	54455
Hales Corners, Milwaukee	53130
Hallie, Eau Claire (Eau Claire)[1]	54703
Hamburg, Marathon	54411
Hammond, St. Croix	54015
Hancock, Waushara	54943
Hannibal, Taylor	54439
Hanover, Rock	53542
Hansen, Wood (Vesper)[1]	54489
Harding, Lincoln (Merrill)[1]	54452
Harrison, Lincoln (Gleason)[1]	54435
Harshaw, Oneida	54529
Hartford, Washington	53027
Hartland, Waukesha	53029
Hatfield, Jackson (Merrillan)[1]	54754
Hatley, Marathon	54440
Haugen, Barron	54841
Haven, Sheboygan	53083
Hawkins, Rusk	54530
Hawthorne, Douglas	54842
Hayward, Sawyer	54843
Hazel Green, Grant	53811
Hazelhurst, Oneida	54531
Heafford Junction, Lincoln	54532
Helenville, Jefferson	53137
Hendren, Clark (Willard)[1]	54493
Herbster, Bayfield	54844
Hersey, St. Croix (Wilson)[1]	54027
Hertel, Burnett	54845
Hewitt, Wood	54441
High Bridge, Ashland	54846
Highland, Iowa	53543
Hilbert, Calumet	54129
Hiles, Forest	54511
Hillpoint, Sauk	53937
Hillsboro, Vernon	54634
Hillsdale, Barron	54733
Hingham, Sheboygan	53031
Hixton, Jackson	54635
Hoard, Clark (Curtiss)[1]	54422
Hobart, Brown[2]	54115
Hofa Park, Outagamie (Seymour)[1]	54165
Hogarty, Marathon (Aniwa)[1]	54408
Holcombe, Chippewa	54745
Hollandale, Iowa	53544
Hollister, Langlade (White Lake)[1]	54491
Holmen, La Crosse	54636
Honey Creek, Walworth	53138
Horicon, Dodge	53032
Hortonville, Outagamie	54944
Houlton, St. Croix	54082
Howard, Brown[2]	54303
Howards Grove, Sheboygan	53083
Hubertus, Washington	53033
Hudson, St. Croix	54016
Hull, Portage (Stevens Point)[1]	54481
Humbird, Clark	54746
Hunting, Shawano (Tigerton)[1]	54486
Huntington, St. Croix (New Richmond)[1]	54017
Hurley, Iron	54534
Hustisford, Dodge	53034
Hustler, Juneau	54637
Independence, Trempealeau	54747
Ingram, Rusk	54526
Institute, Door (Sturgeon Bay)[1]	54235
Iola, Waupaca[4]	54945
Irma, Lincoln	54442
Iron Belt, Iron	54536
Iron Ridge, Dodge	53035
Iron River, Bayfield	54847
Isaar, Outagamie (Seymour)[1]	54165
Island Lake, Chippewa (New Auburn)[1]	54757
Ixonia, Jefferson	53036
Jackson, Washington	53037

Municipality and County	ZIP Code
Jacksonport, Door (Sturgeon Bay)[1]	54235
Janesville, Rock[2]	53545
Jefferson, Jefferson	53549
Jeffris, Lincoln (Gleason)[1]	54435
Jersey City, Lincoln (Tomahawk)[1]	54487
Jewett, St. Croix (New Richmond)[1]	54017
Jim Falls, Chippewa	54748
Joel, Polk (Amery)[1]	54001
Johnson Creek, Jefferson[2]	53038
Jordon, Portage (Stevens Point)[1]	54481
Juda, Green	53550
Jump River, Taylor	54434
Junction City, Portage	54443
Juneau, Dodge	53039
Kaiser, Price (Park Falls)[1]	54552
Kansasville, Racine	53139
Kaukauna, Outagamie[4]	54130
Kellner, Wood (Wisconsin Rapids)[1]	54494
Kellnersville, Manitowoc	54215
Kelly, Marathon (Schofield)[1]	54476
Kempster, Langlade	54424
Kendall, Monroe	54638
Kennan, Price	54537
Kenosha, Kenosha[2]	53140
Keshena, Menominee	54135
Kewaskum, Washington	53040
Kewaunee, Kewaunee	54216
Kiel, Manitowoc	53042
Kieler, Grant	53812
Kimball, Iron (Hurley)[1]	54534
Kimberly, Outagamie	54136
King, Waupaca	54946
Kingston, Green Lake	53939
Kinnickinnic, Pierce (River Falls)[1]	54022
Knapp, Dunn	54749
Knowles, Dodge	53048
Knowlton, Marathon (Mosinee)[1]	54455
Kohler, Sheboygan	53044
Krakow, Shawano[2]	54137
Kronenwetter, Marathon	54455
Kunesh, Brown (Pulaski)[1]	54162
Lac du Flambeau, Vilas	54538
La Crosse, La Crosse[2]	54601
Ladysmith, Rusk	54848
La Farge, Vernon	54639
Lafayette, Chippewa (Chippewa Falls)[1]	54729
Lake, Price (Park Falls)[1]	54552
Lake Delton, Sauk	53940
Lake Emily, Portage (Amherst Junction)[1]	54407
Lake Geneva, Walworth	53147
Lake George, Oneida (Rhinelander)[1]	54501
Lake Hallie, Chippewa (Chippewa Falls)[1]	54729
Lake Holcombe, Chippewa (Holcombe)[1]	54745
Lake Mills, Jefferson	53551
Lake Nebagamon, Douglas	54849
Lake Tomahawk, Oneida	54539
Lake Wazeecha, Wood (Wisconsin Rapids)[1]	54494
Lake Windsor, Dane (Windsor)[1]	53598
Lake Wissota, Chippewa (Chippewa Falls)[1]	54729
Laketown, Polk (Cushing)[1]	54006
Lakewood, Oconto	54138
Lancaster, Grant	53813
Land O'Lakes, Vilas	54540
Lannon, Waukesha	53046
Laona, Forest	54541
La Pointe, Ashland	54850
Larsen, Winnebago	54947
La Valle, Sauk	53941
Lebanon, Dodge	53047
Lena, Oconto	54139
Leopolis, Shawano	54948
Lewis, Polk	54837
Lily, Langlade	54491
Lime Ridge, Sauk	53942
Linden, Iowa	53553
Lindsey, Wood (Marshfield)[1]	54449
Linwood, Portage (Stevens Point)[1]	54481
Lisbon, Waukesha	53089
Little Black, Taylor (Medford)[1]	54451
Little Chicago, Marathon (Marathon)[1]	54448
Little Chute, Outagamie	54140

Municipality and County	ZIP Code
Little Falls, Polk (Amery)[1]	54001
Little Suamico, Oconto	54141
Livingston, Grant	53554
Lodi, Columbia	53555
Loganville, Sauk	53943
Lohrville, Waushara (Redgranite)[1]	54970
Lomira, Dodge	53048
Lone Rock, Richland	53556
Long Lake, Florence	54542
Longwood, Clark (Withee)[1]	54498
Loomis, Marinette (Porterfield)[1]	54159
Loretta, Sawyer	54896
Lost Creek, Pierce (Ellsworth)[1]	54011
Lowell, Dodge	53557
Loyal, Clark	54446
Lublin, Taylor	54447
Luck, Polk	54853
Lugerville, Price (Phillips)[1]	54555
Luxemburg, Kewaunee	54217
Lymantown, Price (Park Falls)[1]	54552
Lyndon Station, Juneau	53944
Lynn, Clark (Granton)[1]	54436
Lynxville, Crawford[4]	54626
Lyons, Walworth	53148
Madison, Dane[2]	53703
Maiden Rock, Pierce	54750
Malone, Fond du Lac	53049
Manawa, Waupaca	54949
Manchester, Green Lake	53946
Manitowish Waters, Vilas	54545
Manitowoc, Manitowoc[4]	54220
Maple, Douglas	54854
Maple Bluff, Dane (Madison)[1]	53704
Maplehurst, Clark (Withee)[1]	54498
Maplewood, Door	54226
Marathon, Marathon	54448
Marathon City, Marathon (Marathon)[1]	54448
Marengo, Ashland[2]	54846
Maribel, Manitowoc	54227
Marinette, Marinette	54143
Marion, Waupaca	54950
Markesan, Green Lake	53946
Markton, Langlade (White Lake)[1]	54491
Marquette, Green Lake	53947
Marshall, Dane	53559
Marshfield, Wood[4]	54449
Martell, Pierce (Spring Valley)[1]	54767
Mason, Bayfield[4]	54856
Mather, Juneau	54641
Mattoon, Shawano	54450
Mauston, Juneau	53948
Mayville, Dodge	53050
Mazomanie, Dane	53560
McFarland, Dane	53558
McNaughton, Oneida	54543
McMillan, Wood (Marshfield)[1]	54449
Medford, Taylor	54451
Medina, Outagamie	54944
Mellen, Ashland	54546
Melrose, Jackson	54642
Menasha, Winnebago	54952
Menekaunee, Marinette (Marinette)[1]	54143
Menomonee Falls, Waukesha[4]	53051
Menomonie, Dunn	54751
Mequon, Ozaukee[2]	53092
Mercer, Iron	54547
Merrill, Lincoln	54452
Merrillan, Jackson	54754
Merrimac, Sauk	53561
Merton, Waukesha	53056
Middle Inlet, Marinette	54114
Middle Ridge, La Crosse (Bangor)[1]	54614
Middleton, Dane	53562
Mikana, Barron	54857
Milan, Marathon	54411
Milladore, Wood	54454
Millston, Jackson	54643
Milltown, Polk	54858
Milton, Rock	53563
Milwaukee, Milwaukee[2]	53201
Mindoro, La Crosse	54644
Mineral Point, Iowa	53565

Municipality and County	ZIP Code
Minocqua, Oneida	54548
Minong, Washburn	54859
Mishicot, Manitowoc	54228
Modena, Buffalo	54755
Moeville, Pierce (Ellsworth)[1]	54011
Mole Lake, Forest (Crandon)[1]	54520
Mondovi, Buffalo[4]	54755
Monico, Oneida	54501
Monona, Dane (Madison)[3]	53716
Monroe, Green	53566
Monroe Center, Adams (Arkdale)[1]	54613
Montello, Marquette	53949
Montfort, Grant	53569
Monticello, Green	53570
Montreal, Iron	54550
Moon, Marathon (Mosinee)[1]	54455
Moquah, Ashland	54806
Morris, Shawano (Tigerton)[1]	54486
Morrisonville, Dane	53571
Morse, Ashland (Mellen)[1]	54546
Mosinee, Marathon	54455
Mountain, Oconto	54149
Mount Calvary, Fond du Lac	53057
Mount Hope, Grant	53816
Mount Horeb, Dane	53572
Mount Pleasant, Racine[4]	53177
Mount Sterling, Crawford	54645
Mukwonago, Waukesha	53149
Muscoda, Grant	53573
Muskego, Waukesha	53150
Nashotah, Waukesha	53058
Nashville, Forest (Crandon)[1]	54520
Navarino, Shawano	54107
Necedah, Juneau	54646
Neenah, Winnebago[4]	54956
Neillsville, Clark	54456
Nekoosa, Wood	54457
Nelma, Forest	54542
Nelson, Buffalo	54756
Nelsonville, Portage	54458
Neopit, Menominee	54150
Neosho, Dodge	53059
Neshkoro, Marquette	54960
Neva Corners, Langlade (Deerbrook)[1]	54424
Newald, Forest	54511
New Auburn, Chippewa	54757
New Berlin, Waukesha[2]	53146
Newburg, Washington	53060
Newburg Corners, La Crosse (Bangor)[1]	54614
New Franken, Brown	54229
New Glarus, Green	53574
New Haven, Polk (Clear Lake)[1]	54005
New Holstein, Calumet[4]	53061
New Johannesburg, St. Croix (New Richmond)[1]	54017
New Lisbon, Juneau	53950
New London, Waupaca	54961
New Munster, Kenosha	53152
New Post, Sawyer	54828
New Richmond, St. Croix	54017
Newton, Manitowoc	53063
Niagara, Marinette	54151
Nichols, Outagamie	54152
Norrie, Shawano (Birnamwood)[1]	54414
North Fond du Lac, Fond du Lac (Fond du Lac)[3]	54935
North Freedom, Sauk	53951
North Hudson, St. Croix (Hudson)[1]	54016
North Lake, Waukesha	53064
North Menomonie, Dunn (Menomonie)[1]	54751
North Prairie, Waukesha	53153
North Woods Beach, Sawyer	54843
Northfield, Jackson	54635
Norwalk, Monroe	54648
Nye, Polk (Osceola)[1]	54020
Oak Creek, Milwaukee	53154
Oak Grove, Pierce (Prescott)[1]	54021
Oakdale, Monroe	54649
Oakfield, Fond du Lac	53065
Oconomowoc, Waukesha	53066
Oconto, Oconto	54153
Oconto Falls, Oconto	54154

Municipality and County	ZIP Code
Odanah, Ashland	54861
Ogdensburg, Waupaca	54962
Ogema, Price	54459
Ojibwa, Sawyer	54862
Okauchee, Waukesha	53069
Oliver, Douglas	54880
Oma, Iron (Hurley)[1]	54534
Omro, Winnebago	54963
Onalaska, La Crosse	54650
Oneida, Brown	54155
Ontario, Vernon	54651
Oostburg, Sheboygan	53070
Oregon, Dane	53575
Orfordville, Rock	53576
Osceola, Polk	54020
Oshkosh, Winnebago[2]	54901
Osseo, Trempealeau	54758
Owen, Clark	54460
Oxford, Marquette	53952
Packwaukee, Marquette	53953
Paddock Lake, Kenosha (Salem)[1]	53168
Padus, Forest (Wabeno)[1]	54566
Palmyra, Jefferson	53156
Pardeeville, Columbia	53954
Park Falls, Price	54552
Park Ridge, Portage (Stevens Point)[1]	54481
Parrish, Lincoln (Gleason)[1]	54435
Patch Grove, Grant	53817
Pearson, Langlade	54462
Pelican, Oneida (Rhinelander)[1]	54501
Pelican Lake, Oneida	54463
Pell Lake, Walworth	53157
Pembine, Marinette	54119
Pence, Iron	54550
Pensaukee, Oconto (Oconto)[1]	54153
Pepin, Pepin	54759
Peplin, Marathon (Mosinee)[1]	54455
Perkinstown, Taylor (Medford)[1]	54451
Peshtigo, Marinette	54157
Pewaukee, Waukesha	53072
Phelps, Vilas	54554
Phillips, Price	54555
Phlox, Langlade	54464
Pickerel, Langlade	54465
Pickett, Winnebago	54964
Pigeon Falls, Trempealeau	54760
Pine River, Waushara	54965
Pittsville, Wood	54466
Plain, Sauk	53577
Plainfield, Waushara	54966
Platteville, Grant	53818
Pleasant Lake, Waushara (Coloma)[1]	54930
Pleasant Prairie, Kenosha	53158
Pleasant Valley, St. Croix (Hammond)[1]	54015
Plover, Portage	54467
Plum City, Pierce	54761
Plum Lake, Vilas (Sayner)[1]	54560
Plymouth, Sheboygan	53073
Polar, Langlade	54418
Polley, Taylor (Gilman)[1]	54433
Polonia, Portage (Custer)[1]	54423
Poniatowski, Marathon (Edgar)[1]	54426
Poplar, Douglas	54864
Popple River, Florence (Long Lake)[1]	54542
Portage, Columbia	53901
Port Edwards, Wood	54469
Porterfield, Marinette	54159
Port Washington, Ozaukee	53074
Port Wing, Bayfield	54865
Poskin, Barron	54812
Post Lake, Langlade (Elcho)[1]	54428
Potosi, Grant	53820
Potter, Calumet	54160
Pound, Marinette	54161
Powers Lake, Kenosha	53159
Poynette, Columbia	53955
Poy Sippi, Waushara	54967
Prairie du Chien, Crawford	53821
Prairie du Sac, Sauk	53578
Prairie Farm, Barron	54762
Pray, Wood (Pittsville)[1]	54466
Preble, Brown (Green Bay)[1]	54302

Municipality and County	ZIP Code
Prentice, Price	54556
Prescott, Pierce	54021
Presque Isle, Vilas	54557
Princeton, Green Lake	54968
Pulaski, Brown	54162
Pulcifer, Oconto	54124
Racine, Racine[2]	53401
Radisson, Sawyer	54867
Randolph, Columbia[4]	53956
Random Lake, Sheboygan	53075
Range, Polk (Amery)[1]	54001
Readfield, Waupaca	54969
Readstown, Vernon	54652
Red Cliff, Bayfield (Bayfield)[1]	54814
Redgranite, Waushara	54970
Redville, Clark (Withee)[1]	54498
Reedsburg, Sauk[4]	53959
Reedsville, Manitowoc	54230
Reeseville, Dodge	53579
Reeve, Polk (Clayton)[1]	54004
Remington, Wood (Babcock)[1]	54413
Rewey, Iowa	53580
Rhinelander, Oneida	54501
Rib Falls, Marathon (Edgar)[1]	54426
Rib Lake, Taylor	54470
Rib Mountain, Marathon (Wausau)[1]	54401
Rice Lake, Barron	54868
Richardson, Polk (Clayton)[1]	54004
Richfield, Washington	53076
Richford, Waushara (Coloma)[1]	54930
Richland Center, Richland	53581
Ridgeland, Dunn	54763
Ridgeway, Iowa	53582
Ringle, Marathon	54471
Rio, Columbia	53960
Rio Creek, Kewaunee	54201
Riplinger, Marathon (Spencer)[1]	54479
Ripon, Fond du Lac	54971
River Falls, Pierce	54022
River Hills, Milwaukee (Milwaukee)[3]	53217
Roberts, St. Croix	54023
Rochester, Racine	53167
Rock Falls, Dunn	54764
Rockfield, Washington	53022
Rockland, La Crosse	54653
Rock Springs, Sauk	53961
Rome, Wood (Nekoosa)[1]	54457
Rosendale, Fond du Lac	54974
Rosholt, Portage	54473
Rothschild, Marathon	54474
Royalton, Waupaca	54961
Rozellville, Marathon (Stratford)[1]	54484
Rubicon, Dodge	53078
Rudolph, Wood	54475
Rush River, St. Croix (Baldwin)[1]	54002
Rusk, Dunn (Menomonie)[1]	54751
St. Cloud, Fond du Lac	53079
St. Croix Falls, Polk	54024
St. Francis, Milwaukee	53235
St. Germain, Vilas	54558
St. Nazianz, Manitowoc	54232
Salem, Kenosha	53168
Sanborn, Ashland	54806
Sand Creek, Dunn	54765
Sand Lake, Polk (Dresser)[1]	54009
Sarona, Washburn	54870
Sauk City, Sauk	53583
Saukville, Ozaukee	53080
Saxeville, Waushara	54976
Saxon, Iron	54559
Sayner, Vilas	54560
Scandinavia, Waupaca	54977
Schley, Lincoln (Merrill)[1]	54452
Schofield, Marathon	54476
Scott, Brown (Green Bay)[1]	54301
Seneca, Crawford	54654
Sevastopol, Door (Sturgeon Bay)[1]	54235
Sextonville, Richland	53584
Seymour, Outagamie	54165
Sharon, Walworth	53585
Shawano, Shawano	54166

Municipality and County	ZIP Code
Sheboygan, Sheboygan[2]	53081
Sheboygan Falls, Sheboygan	53085
Shelby, La Crosse (La Crosse)[1]	54601
Sheldon, Rusk	54766
Shell Lake, Washburn	54871
Shepley, Shawano (Wittenberg)[1]	54499
Sherman, Price (Park Falls)[1]	54552
Sherry, Wood (Milladore)[1]	54454
Sherwood, Calumet	54169
Shiocton, Outagamie	54170
Shorewood, Milwaukee (Milwaukee)[3]	53211
Shorewood Hills, Dane (Madison)[1]	53705
Shullsburg, Lafayette	53586
Silver Cliff, Marinette	54104
Silver Lake, Kenosha	53170
Sinsinawa, Grant	53824
Siren, Burnett	54872
Sister Bay, Door	54234
Skanawan, Lincoln (Irma)[1]	54442
Slinger, Washington	53086
Sobieski, Oconto	54171
Soldiers Grove, Crawford	54655
Solon Springs, Douglas	54873
Somers, Kenosha	53171
Somerset, St. Croix	54025
Soperton, Forest (Wabeno)[1]	54566
South Beaver Dam, Dodge (Beaver Dam)[1]	53916
South Byron, Fond du Lac	53006
South Chase, Brown (Pulaski)[1]	54162
South Fork, Rusk (Hawkins)[1]	54530
South Milwaukee, Milwaukee	53172
South Range, Douglas	54874
South Wayne, Lafayette	53587
Sparta, Monroe	54656
Spencer, Marathon	54479
Split Rock, Shawano (Tigerton)[1]	54486
Spokeville, Clark (Loyal)[1]	54446
Spooner, Washburn	54801
Springbrook, Washburn	54875
Springfield, Walworth	53176
Springstead, Price (Park Falls)[1]	54552
Spring Green, Sauk	53588
Spring Valley, Pierce	54767
Stangelville, Brown (Denmark)[1]	54208
Stanley, Chippewa	54768
Stanton, St. Croix (New Richmond)[1]	54017
Starks, Oneida (Rhinelander)[1]	54501
Stella, Oneida (Rhinelander)[1]	54501
Sterling, Polk (Cushing)[1]	54006
Star Lake, Vilas	54561
Star Prairie, St. Croix	54026
Stetsonville, Taylor	54480
Steuben, Crawford	54657
Stevens Point, Portage[4]	54481
Stiles, Oconto	54139
Stitzer, Grant	53825
Stockbridge, Calumet	53088
Stockholm, Pepin	54769
Stockton, Portage (Stevens Point)[1]	54481
Stoddard, Vernon	54658
Stone Lake, Sawyer	54876
Stoughton, Dane	53589
Stratford, Marathon	54484
Strum, Trempealeau	54770
Sturgeon Bay, Door	54235
Sturtevant, Racine[2]	53177
Suamico, Brown[2]	54173
Sugar Camp, Oneida (Rhinelander)[1]	54501
Sullivan, Jefferson	53178
Summit, Waukesha	53066
Summit Lake, Langlade	54485
Sun Prairie, Dane[4]	53590
Superior, Douglas	54880
Suring, Oconto	54174
Sussex, Waukesha	53089
Taycheedah, Fond du Lac	53935
Taylor, Jackson	54659
Theresa, Dodge	53091
Thiensville, Ozaukee	53092
Thornton, Shawano (Shawano)[1]	54166
Thorp, Clark	54771
Three Lakes, Oneida	54562

Municipality and County	ZIP Code
Tigerton, Shawano	54486
Tilden, Chippewa (Chippewa Falls)[1]	54729
Tilleda, Shawano	54978
Tipler, Florence	54542
Tisch Mills, Manitowoc	54240
Tomah, Monroe	54660
Tomahawk, Lincoln[4]	54487
Tony, Rusk	54563
Townsend, Oconto	54175
Trego, Washburn	54888
Trempealeau, Trempealeau	54661
Trevor, Kenosha[4]	53179
Trimbelle, Pierce (Ellsworth)[1]	54011
Tripoli, Oneida	54564
Troy, Pierce (River Falls)[1]	54022
Tunnel City, Monroe	54662
Turtle Lake, Barron	54889
Tustin, Waupaca (Fremont)[1]	54940
Twin Lakes, Kenosha	53181
Two Rivers, Manitowoc	54241
Ubet, Polk (Dresser)[1]	54009
Underhill, Oconto	54124
Union Center, Juneau	53962
Union Grove, Racine	53182
Unity, Marathon	54488
Upson, Iron	54565
Valders, Manitowoc	54245
Valmy, Door (Sturgeon Bay)[1]	54235
Van Dyne, Fond du Lac	54979
Veedum, Wood (Pittsville)[1]	54466
Vernon, Waukesha[2]	53186
Verona, Dane	53593
Vesper, Wood	54489
Victory, Vernon	54624
Viola, Vernon	54664
Viroqua, Vernon	54665
Wabeno, Forest	54566
Waldo, Sheboygan	53093
Wales, Waukesha	53183
Walworth, Walworth	53184
Wanderoos, Polk (Amery)[1]	54001
Warren, St. Croix (Roberts)[1]	54023
Warrens, Monroe	54666
Wascott, Douglas[4]	54838
Washburn, Bayfield	54891
Washington, Vilas (Eagle River)[1]	54521
Washington Island, Door	54246
Waterford, Racine	53185
Waterloo, Jefferson	53594
Watertown, Jefferson[2]	53094
Waubeka, Ozaukee	53021
Waukau, Winnebago	54980
Waukesha, Waukesha[2]	53186
Waumandee, Buffalo	54622
Waunakee, Dane	53597
Waupaca, Waupaca	54981
Waupun, Dodge	53963
Wausau, Marathon[4]	54401
Wausaukee, Marinette	54177
Wautoma, Waushara	54982
Wauwatosa, Milwaukee[2]	53208
Wauzeka, Crawford	53826
Wayside, Brown (Greenleaf)[1]	54126

Municipality and County	ZIP Code
Webb Lake, Burnett	54830
Webster, Burnett	54893
Wentworth, Douglas	54874
West Allis, Milwaukee[2]	53214
West Baraboo, Sauk (Baraboo)[1]	53913
West Bend, Washington[2]	53090
West Lima, Vernon	54639
West Milwaukee, Milwaukee (Milwaukee)[3]	53214
West Salem, La Crosse	54669
Westboro, Taylor	54490
Westby, Vernon	54667
Westfield, Marquette	53964
Weston, Marathon	54476
Westport, Dane	53597
Weurtsburg, Marathon (Athens)[1]	54411
Weyauwega, Waupaca	54983
Weyerhaeuser, Rusk	54895
Wheeler, Dunn	54772
Whitcomb, Shawano (Tigerton)[1]	54486
Whitefish Bay, Milwaukee[2]	53211
Whitehall, Trempealeau	54773
White Lake, Langlade	54491
Whitelaw, Manitowoc	54247
Whitewater, Walworth	53190
Whiting, Portage (Stevens Point)[1]	54481
Whittlesey, Taylor (Medford)[1]	54451
Wild Rose, Waushara	54984
Wildwood, St. Croix (Woodville)[1]	54028
Willard, Clark	54493
Williams Bay, Walworth	53191
Wilmot, Kenosha	53192
Wilson, St. Croix	54027
Wilton, Monroe	54670
Winchester, Vilas	54557
Winchester, Winnebago (Larsen)[1]	54947
Wind Lake, Racine	53185
Wind Point, Racine	53402
Windsor, Dane	53598
Winnebago, Winnebago	54985
Winneconne, Winnebago	54986
Winter, Sawyer	54896
Wisconsin Dells, Columbia	53965
Wisconsin Rapids, Wood[2]	54494
Withee, Clark	54498
Wittenberg, Shawano[4]	54499
Wonewoc, Juneau	53968
Woodboro, Oneida (Rhinelander)[1]	54501
Woodford, Lafayette	53599
Woodland, Dodge	53099
Woodman, Grant	53827
Woodruff, Oneida	54568
Woodville, St. Croix	54028
Woodworth, Kenosha	53194
Worcester, Price (Phillips)[1]	54555
Wrightstown, Brown	54180
Wyalusing, Grant (Bagley)[1]	53801
Wyeville, Monroe	54660
Wyocena, Columbia	53969
Yellow Lake, Burnett	54830
York, Clark (Granton)[1]	54436
Yuba, Richland	54634
Zachow, Shawano	54182
Zenda, Walworth	53195

[1]These locations no longer have post offices and mail should be addressed to municipality listed in parenthesis.

[2]Indicates multicoded city. To determine last 2 digits of ZIP code for any specific city street, consult the local post office. The ZIP code given is the general delivery ZIP code for the city.

[3]Post office is located in the city shown in parenthesis. ZIP code is listed as "acceptable" on USPS Web site.

[4]Indicates there is an additional ZIP code that is used for a specific P.O. Box, company or organization, or a military installation.

Source: U.S. Postal Service, at: http://www.usps.com [April 2013].

HIGHLIGHTS OF SOCIAL SERVICES IN WISCONSIN

Welfare — According to the U.S. Census Bureau, during 2009-10, almost $457 billion was spent nationally by state and local governments on a variety of public welfare programs. Wisconsin spent about $9.5 billion, or $1,670 per capita, which ranked it 11th among the states, compared to the national average of $1,476. New York's per capita expenditure was highest at $2,526 and Nevada the lowest at $811. Minnesota ($2,215) was 4th. State and local welfare expenditures represented $43.94 per $1,000 of personal income in Wisconsin, ranking it 15th among the states, above the national average ($37.11), while New Mexico ($66.02), Maine ($60.23), Alaska ($56.66), and Vermont ($56.54) ranked highest, with Wisconsin's neighbor Minnesota ($52.08) ranking 6th. Colorado ($20.00), Nevada ($22.68), and Virginia ($27.00) were the lowest.

Participation in Wisconsin Works (W-2), a program providing job subsidies to employers and cash and noncash benefits, such as job assistance and subsidized child care, to participants if they meet certain work requirements, has increased since the last decade but average payments have fallen. The average monthly caseload for W-2 was 15,350 households in 2011 and 14,156 in 2012, with a statewide average monthly payment of $518 in 2011 and $510 in 2012. Total W-2 expenditures fell from $157.2 million in 2011 to $146.8 million in 2012.

Medical Assistance and BadgerCare — Of the total combined Medical Assistance and BadgerCare provider payments of $7.00 billion in fiscal year 2011-12, $2.69 billion (38.5%) was spent on managed care/HMOs. The next highest payment category was $1.29 billion for other non-institutional fee-for-service (18.4%).

Medical assistance expenditures in Wisconsin in calendar year 2012 rose to $6.16 billion, from about $5.41 billion in 2011. A county breakdown of medical assistance for 2012 shows average expenditures of $3,011 per recipient. According to the Department of Health Services, the counties with the greatest percentage of recipients were Menominee (72.26%), Ashland (58.60%), Milwaukee (56.25%), Rusk (53.80%), and Washburn (53.50%). The counties with the smallest proportion of recipients were Ozaukee (15.76%), Waukesha (16.23%), Pierce (19.43%), and Washington (20.89%). The highest average expenditures per recipient were in Richland ($5,327), Pepin ($5,004), Waupaca ($4,731), and Pierce ($3,891) counties; Lafayette ($2,172), Burnett ($2,209), Vilas ($2,308), and Taylor ($2,349) counties were lowest.

Institutions — Since 2010, the average daily adult corrections population declined slightly from 22,643 in 2010 to 22,154 in 2011, and 21,911 in 2012. In 2012, a daily average of 47,178 persons were on probation and 20,593 on parole and mandatory release. Overall, more than 90,000 people were under the control of the Department of Corrections.

A per inmate state expenditure for corrections of $52,833 ranked Wisconsin 15th among the states in FY2011. As of December 31, 2011, Wisconsin had an incarceration rate of 372 persons per 100,000 population, not counting prisoners under local jurisdiction. Louisiana (865), Mississippi (687), Alabama (646), Oklahoma (640), Texas (639), Arizona (592), Georgia (553), Arkansas (548), and Florida (544) had the highest rates. Maine (147), Massachusetts (154), Minnesota (183), Rhode Island (197), New Hampshire (204), North Dakota (213), Utah (243), Nebraska (244), Vermont (259), Washington (264), New Jersey (277), Hawaii (285), and New York (287), had the lowest rates.

The total average daily number of persons in Wisconsin's care and treatment facilities declined from 1,622 in 2010 to 1,566 in 2011 and 2012.

The number of youths in the state's juvenile corrections institutions declined from 437 in 2010 to 321 in 2011 and to 287 in 2012.

The following tables present selected data. Consult footnoted sources for more detailed information about corrections and social services.

STATE AND LOCAL PUBLIC WELFARE EXPENDITURES
State Fiscal Years 2009-10

State	Amount (in thousands)			Per Capita*		Per $1,000 Personal Income*	
	State and Local	State	Local	Amount	Rank	Amount	Rank
Alabama	$6,025,626	$5,957,066	$68,560	$1,259.17	38	$37.35	25
Alaska	1,770,224	1,763,848	6,376	2,478.80	2	56.66	3
Arizona.	8,504,242	8,199,047	305,195	1,326.06	31	39.26	21
Arkansas	4,296,644	4,290,502	6,142	1,470.65	23	45.43	13
Caifornia	52,217,532	35,956,608	16,260,924	1,398.50	26	33.38	33
Colorado	4,249,944	3,467,391	782,553	841.96	49	20.00	50
Connecticut	5,604,860	5,488,262	116,598	1,567.57	17	28.28	47
Delaware	1,648,455	1,648,268	187	1,832.04	10	46.47	12
District of Columbia	2,679,348	—	2,679,348	4,429.32	—	62.19	—
Florida	22,178,186	20,793,953	1,384,233	1,177.27	43	30.70	40
Georgia.	9,706,016	9,473,668	232,348	999.37	47	28.94	46
Hawaii	2,033,570	1,960,207	73,363	1,491.59	21	36.42	29
Idaho	1,815,872	1,784,787	31,085	1,155.80	45	36.63	28
ILLINOIS	17,752,231	17,152,339	599,892	1,382.36	27	32.89	34
Indiana	8,181,466	7,977,461	204,005	1,260.51	37	37.04	26
IOWA	4,603,168	4,489,104	114,064	1,509.14	20	39.84	20
Kansas	3,376,695	3,341,630	35,065	1,181.02	42	30.64	41
Kentucky	7,092,873	7,051,254	41,619	1,631.59	13	50.20	10
Louisiana.	6,392,203	6,319,151	73,052	1,406.32	25	37.89	24
Maine	2,928,496	2,891,415	37,081	2,206.22	5	60.23	2
Maryland.	9,020,239	8,771,519	248,720	1,559.06	18	32.07	36
Massachusetts	13,553,990	13,476,069	77,921	2,067.59	8	40.43	18
MICHIGAN	12,941,011	11,760,002	1,181,009	1,310.20	33	38.17	23
MINNESOTA	11,761,955	10,201,049	1,560,906	2,214.78	4	52.08	6
Mississippi.	4,927,828	4,895,555	32,273	1,659.16	12	53.80	5
Missouri	7,405,047	7,244,251	160,796	1,235.06	39	33.92	31
Montana	1,319,490	1,266,671	52,819	1,331.53	30	38.70	22
Nebraska	2,314,922	2,241,729	73,193	1,264.89	36	32.07	35
Nevada	2,193,957	1,825,311	368,646	811.29	50	22.68	49
New Hampshire	2,049,091	1,848,009	201,082	1,556.11	19	35.39	30
New Jersey.	13,994,148	12,844,928	1,149,220	1,590.32	16	31.54	37
New Mexico	4,492,990	4,390,919	102,071	2,174.82	6	66.02	1
New York	48,985,427	37,955,024	11,030,403	2,525.65	1	51.42	7
North Carolina	11,186,485	9,671,551	1,514,934	1,170.11	44	33.81	32
North Dakota.	874,077	814,574	59,503	1,295.64	34	30.51	42
Ohio	18,387,909	15,294,488	3,093,421	1,593.69	15	44.35	14
Oklahoma	5,399,205	5,363,647	35,558	1,435.89	24	40.41	19
Oregon	5,066,544	4,827,724	238,820	1,319.99	32	36.76	27
Pennsylvania.	24,563,183	20,430,942	4,132,241	1,931.41	9	47.76	11
Rhode Island	2,258,013	2,249,657	8,356	2,145.32	7	51.08	8
South Carolina	6,206,150	6,131,641	74,509	1,338.37	29	41.57	17
South Dakota.	984,079	971,039	13,040	1,205.10	40	30.46	43
Tennessee	9,379,093	9,223,298	155,795	1,475.29	22	42.03	16
Texas	28,688,104	28,293,025	395,079	1,136.01	46	29.72	44
Utah	2,749,517	2,654,386	95,131	990.65	48	30.84	38
Vermont	1,406,131	1,404,772	1,359	2,246.54	3	56.54	4
Virginia.	9,560,406	8,001,889	1,558,517	1,191.48	41	27.00	48
Washington.	8,711,634	8,521,387	190,247	1,291.96	35	30.74	39
West Virginia.	3,006,049	3,000,075	5,974	1,621.06	14	50.97	9
WISCONSIN	9,506,838	8,015,692	1,491,146	1,670.31	11	43.94	15
Wyoming.	756,740	733,844	22,896	1,340.42	28	29.55	45
UNITED STATES	$456,707,902	$404,330,628	$52,377,274	$1,476.44		$37.11	

*Rates and rankings calculated by the Wisconsin Legislative Reference Bureau.

Sources: U.S. Department of Commerce, U.S. Census Bureau, Governments Division, "State and Local Government Finances by Level of Government and by State: 2009-10", at: http://www.census.gov/govs/local/ [April 25, 2013]; U.S. Department of Commerce, Bureau of Economic Analysis, "Regional Economic Accounts: Annual State Personal Income (SA1-3)", at: http://bea.gov/regional/index.htm [March 27, 2013] (2010 data used in calculations); and "Annual Estimates of the Population for the United States, States, and Puerto Rico: April 1, 2010 to July 1, 2011 (NST-EST2011-01)", at: http://www.census.gov/popest/data/historical/2010s/vintage_2011/index.html (July 1, 2010 estimates used in calculations).

WISCONSIN WORKS (W-2) EXPENDITURES, BY AGENCY
Calendar Years 2011 and 2012

W-2 Contract Agency	Total Expenditures 2011	2012	Counties Served by Consortia
County W-2 Agencies			
Bayfield	$91,820	$110,770	
Burnett	53,827	17,709	
Crawford	59,528	70,738	
Door	168,389	137,484	
Dunn	570,512	395,280	
Eau Claire	464,798	427,335	
Fond du Lac	631,326	860,418	
Green Lake	109,515	216,436	
Iron	44,069	91,131	
Jefferson	155,203	154,697	
Kenosha	6,091,671	6,323,747	
La Crosse	526,103	447,506	
Oconto	221,859	221,047	
Pepin	50,130	43,598	
Polk	123,714	192,571	
Racine	4,909,276	4,338,028	
Rock	2,007,135	1,702,153	
Taylor	105,370	98,408	
Waupaca	430,701	417,549	
Winnebago	2,274,256	2,124,640	
Subtotal	$19,089,201	$18,391,244	
County Agency Consortia			
Ashland Consortium	$299,496	$229,694	Ashland and Price
Capitol Consortium	8,348,689	7,944,981	Dane, Dodge, and Sauk
Lakeshore Consortium	1,194,986	950,607	Manitowoc and Sheboygan
Outagamie and Calumet County Consortium	1,211,993	1,158,970	Calumet and Outagamie
PAW Consortium	1,627,801	1,392,724	Adams, Portage, and Wood
Southwest Consortium	482,352	532,190	Grant, Green, Iowa, Lafayette, and Richland
Subtotal	$13,165,317	$12,209,165	
Private W-2 Agencies			
Kaiser Group – Walworth	$560,781	$538,762	
Policy Studies, Inc. – Milwaukee W-2 Employment Agency (NW)	21,238,012	20,016,354	
Social Development Commission – Milwaukee Eligibility and Assessment Agency	12,399,790	10,366,861	
United Migrant Opportunity Services – Milwaukee W-2 Employment Agency (SE)	18,805,010	17,597,931	
YWCA GM – Milwaukee W-2 Employment Agency (NE)	13,025,347	14,728,167	
Subtotal	$66,028,940	$63,248,075	
Private Agency Consortia			
Arbor Education and Training, LLC	$2,351,847	$2,285,161	Ozaukee, Washington, and Waukesha
Forward Service Corporation Consortium	6,437,154	7,555,514	Brown, Florence, Forest, Kewaunee, Langlade, Lincoln, Marathon, Marinette, Marquette, Menominee, Oneida, Shawano, Vilas, and Waushara
MAXIMUS – Milwaukee W-2 Employment Agency	37,244,149	30,953,642	Central and Southwest Milwaukee
Public Consulting Group, Inc. – Milwaukee SSI/SSDI Advocacy Agency	5,410,729	5,188,378	Central, Northeast, and Northwest Milwaukee
United Migrant Opportunity Services – Milwaukee SSI/SSDI Advocacy Agency	3,255,671	3,611,552	Southeast and Southwest Milwaukee
Workforce Connections Consortium	2,957,422	2,354,328	Buffalo, Columbia, Douglas, Jackson, Juneau, Monroe, Pierce, St. Croix, Sawyer, Trempealeau, Vernon, and Washburn
Workforce Resource, Inc. – West Central Consortium	1,256,349	1,042,267	Barron, Chippewa, Clark, and Rusk
Subtotal	$58,913,322	$52,990,843	
TOTAL	$157,196,780	$146,839,327	

Source: Wisconsin Department of Children and Families, departmental data, June 2013.

WISCONSIN WORKS (W-2) BENEFITS, BY COUNTY
Calendar Years 2011 and 2012

County	2011 Average Monthly Paid Caseload	2011 Average Monthly Benefit Payment	2012 Average Monthly Paid Caseload	2012 Average Monthly Benefit Payment	County	2011 Average Monthly Paid Caseload	2011 Average Monthly Benefit Payment	2012 Average Monthly Paid Caseload	2012 Average Monthly Benefit Payment
Adams	17	$450	22	$452	Marinette . . .	21	$449	32	$508
Ashland . . .	23	522	21	473	Marquette . .	23	462	17	490
Barron	45	557	33	538	Menominee .	30	397	26	457
Bayfield . . .	9	413	10	492	Milwaukee . .	10,476	534	9,471	524
Brown	304	420	232	393	Monroe	50	491	27	481
Buffalo	2	172	2	337	Oconto	10	441	16	476
Burnett	5	533	2	476	Oneida	44	476	53	502
Calumet . . .	13	496	16	428	Outagamie . .	128	485	122	483
Chippewa . .	18	550	17	429	Ozaukee . . .	25	473	20	478
Clark	26	569	28	531	Pepin	3	522	1	635
Columbia. . .	50	504	42	500	Pierce.	11	397	7	452
Crawford . . .	5	551	6	490	Polk	9	660	7	536
Dane	806	511	782	503	Portage	30	492	23	484
Dodge	57	460	41	456	Price	3	539	3	553
Door	15	527	10	596	Racine	627	464	550	466
Douglas . . .	48	456	16	517	Richland . . .	7	606	6	539
Dunn	50	550	40	565	Rock	221	499	206	508
Eau Claire . .	44	537	47	510	Rusk	22	576	14	584
Florence . . .	2	552	3	544	St. Croix . . .	36	496	37	533
Fond du Lac .	73	487	102	484	Sauk	9	403	4	471
Forest.	17	541	19	514	Sawyer	60	459	69	508
Grant	12	511	7	577	Shawano . . .	96	507	83	446
Green.	17	501	36	501	Sheboygan . .	22	391	8	431
Green Lake. .	12	418	23	477	Taylor	8	473	6	529
Iowa	6	474	4	450	Trempealeau .	8	414	9	446
Iron. , , , , ,	4	559	10	496	Vernon	6	383	6	383
Jackson. . . .	17	478	10	424	Vilas	6	530	6	559
Jefferson . . .	17	479	18	485	Walworth . .	45	535	44	523
Juneau	9	341	7	443	Washburn . .	7	471	4	260
Kenosha . . .	563	483	591	476	Washington. .	43	526	37	494
Kewaunee . .	16	558	17	451	Waukesha . .	155	485	139	502
La Crosse . .	57	453	45	426	Waupaca . . .	50	502	59	461
Lafayette . . .	4	505	4	498	Waushara. . .	12	382	12	368
Langlade . . .	28	506	47	476	Winnebago. .	284	495	268	479
Lincoln. . . .	47	412	67	484	Wood.	116	495	95	494
Manitowoc. .	35	513	28	475	TOTAL. . .	15,350	$518	14,156	$510
Marathon. . .	174	469	264	498					

Source: Wisconsin Department of Children and Families, departmental data, June 2013.

BADGERCARE AND MEDICAL ASSISTANCE IN WISCONSIN
By Type of Service, Fiscal Years 1999-2000 – 2011-12
(In Millions)

| | Long-Term Care | | | | Hospitals | | | | Physicians and Clinics | | Drugs | | Home Care[1] | | Managed Care (HMO)[2] | | Other Non-Institutional Fee-for-Service[3] | | Total Provider Payments[4,5] | |
| | Nursing Homes | | State Centers | | Inpatient | | Outpatient | | | | | | | | | | | | | |
Fiscal Year	Amount	% of Total	Amount	% of Total	Amount	% of Total	Amount	% of Total	Amount	% of Total	Amount	% of Total	Amount	% of Total	Amount	% of Total	Amount	% of Total	Amount	Annual % Change
1999-2000	$906.3	29.8%	$135.9	4.5%	$270.6	8.9%	$55.3	1.8%	$63.2	2.1%	$336.5	11.1%	$498.8	16.4%	$394.4	13.0%	$251.8	8.3%	$3,044.0	—
2000-01	916.2	27.8	115.3	3.5	297.8	9.0	58.7	1.8	72.4	2.2	373.6	11.4	522.2	15.9	523.6	15.9	280.1	8.5	3,291.8	8.1%
2001-02	980.6	26.5	126.9	3.4	333.2	9.0	69.6	1.9	78.7	2.1	432.5	11.7	528.4	14.3	681.8	18.4	319.2	8.6	3,700.9	12.4
2002-03	990.6	25.7	123.9	3.2	332.0	8.6	75.6	2.0	85.2	2.2	494.7	12.9	592.6	15.4	657.9	17.1	334.5	8.7	3,849.2	4.0
2003-04	972.2	21.3	143.0	3.1	338.0	7.4	91.6	2.0	116.9	2.6	700.5	15.4	636.8	14.0	1,013.6	22.2	381.8	8.4	4,558.9	18.4
2004-05	963.8	20.2	117.7	2.5	388.6	8.1	103.7	2.2	133.2	2.8	772.0	16.2	754.9	15.8	873.7	18.3	487.2	10.2	4,777.1	4.8
2005-06	940.1	20.7	115.5	2.5	357.0	7.9	85.8	1.9	104.9	2.3	459.6	10.1	789.2	17.4	1,068.0	23.5	424.2	9.3	4,546.3	-4.8
2006-07	878.2	18.3	111.4	2.3	372.6	7.7	81.6	1.7	111.0	2.3	389.7	8.1	773.6	16.1	1,307.5	27.2	472.3	9.8	4,809.4	5.8
2007-08	837.2	16.3	117.1	2.3	409.7	8.0	85.1	1.7	157.2	3.1	466.3	9.1	812.5	15.8	1,422.3	27.7	599.3	11.7	5,137.5	6.8
2008-09	890.7	14.4	92.0	1.5	602.2	9.7	162.2	2.6	152.6	2.5	621.5	10.0	747.9	12.1	2,089.3	33.8	637.2	10.3	6,188.6	20.5
2009-10	909.5	12.8	148.1	2.1	459.9	6.5	152.8	2.1	188.5	2.6	660.7	9.3	604.5	8.5	2,358.5	33.2	760.2	10.7	7,114.6	15.0
2010-11	842.9	11.2	112.5	1.5	502.5	6.7	188.2	2.5	151.9	2.0	617.6	8.2	599.5	8.0	3,457.1	46.0	1,050.7	14.0	7,522.8	5.7
2011-12	818.8	11.7	127.1	1.8	440.0	6.3	196.3	2.8	166.8	2.4	610.6	8.7	659.0	9.4	2,691.3	38.5	1,288.5	18.4	6,998.4	-7.0

Note: Enrollments in BadgerCare began in July 1999, and expenditures for the program are included in the Medical Assistance figures above. Medical Assistance expenditure data prior to BadgerCare can be found in previous *Blue Books*.

[1] Home Care includes HCBS waivers.

[2] Managed Care includes all capitated programs (BC/BS+, HMOs, CCF/WAM, SSI managed care, PACE/Partnership, Family Care).

[3] All non-institutional fee-for-service acute care care not otherwise captured plus local government plus Medicare crossovers.

[4] Does not include offsetting recoveries and collections, such as estate recoveries, drug rebates, etc.

[5] Total includes expenditures not listed separately.

Source: Wisconsin Department of Health Services, departmental data, July 2013. Data prior to 2006 is from Wisconsin Legislative Fiscal Bureau.

WISCONSIN MEDICAID AND BADGERCARE
Calendar Years 2011 and 2012

County	Recipients[1] 2011	Recipients[1] 2012	2012 % of Population	Rank	Expenditures[2] 2011	Expenditures[2] 2012	2012 Per Recipient Amount	Rank
Adams	8,522	8,448	40.62%	23	$18,210,400	$19,880,934	$2,353.33	68
Ashland	8,966	9,413	58.60	2	27,363,556	29,005,685	3,081.45	25
Barron	21,430	21,773	47.41	11	56,984,037	59,074,493	2,713.20	54
Bayfield	5,454	5,938	39.45	28	14,622,645	17,245,742	2,904.30	41
Brown	84,041	85,732	34.25	43	210,576,021	232,392,520	2,710.69	55
Buffalo	3,422	3,282	24.05	64	11,794,774	12,118,875	3,692.53	8
Burnett	6,720	6,996	45.26	12	14,566,350	15,455,141	2,209.14	71
Calumet	10,197	10,501	21.36	68	26,423,451	24,758,348	2,357.71	67
Chippewa	26,595	26,400	42.05	18	70,717,234	80,626,825	3,054.05	27
Clark	14,180	14,273	41.13	21	34,453,108	40,398,452	2,830.41	46
Columbia	15,976	16,319	28.71	59	52,363,077	57,686,282	3,534.92	12
Crawford	6,792	6,825	41.02	22	16,086,906	18,310,009	2,682.79	56
Dane	110,368	112,177	22.82	67	378,782,524	415,943,177	3,707.92	6
Dodge	25,016	24,851	28.02	60	73,710,453	80,100,467	3,223.23	21
Door	9,181	9,123	32.74	46	20,891,430	21,680,474	2,376.46	66
Douglas	19,622	19,602	44.36	14	49,764,543	54,500,795	2,780.37	51
Dunn	16,034	16,155	36.84	35	42,100,869	46,587,479	2,883.78	42
Eau Claire	38,082	38,470	38.76	31	111,434,565	124,022,035	3,223.86	20
Florence	1,172	1,040	23.86	65	3,862,551	3,870,682	3,721.81	5
Fond du Lac	31,126	30,791	30.20	56	82,402,359	97,805,398	3,176.43	22
Forest	4,292	4,829	52.51	6	11,859,536	12,731,005	2,636.36	58
Grant	16,473	16,365	31.82	48	45,368,172	50,164,251	3,065.34	26
Green	11,711	11,926	32.35	47	31,788,982	35,970,552	3,016.15	30
Green Lake	6,317	6,449	33.75	44	18,424,653	19,630,859	3,044.02	28
Iowa	7,377	7,448	31.39	51	18,359,503	20,729,004	2,783.16	49
Iron	3,054	2,868	49.08	8	9,097,584	9,611,445	3,351.27	14
Jackson	8,296	8,466	41.25	20	19,624,783	23,004,166	2,717.24	53
Jefferson	25,551	26,262	31.32	52	84,744,091	92,277,622	3,513.73	13
Juneau	11,544	11,773	43.80	15	27,059,342	30,867,131	2,621.86	60
Kenosha	65,651	67,425	40.42	24	150,140,289	175,082,212	2,596.70	61
Kewaunee	6,049	5,952	28.84	58	16,379,130	16,710,626	2,807.56	47
La Crosse	39,757	40,127	34.72	40	114,801,360	142,239,117	1,544.72	11
Lafayette	5,740	5,863	34.70	41	11,089,921	12,733,110	2,171.77	72
Langlade	9,909	9,782	49.21	7	21,772,420	24,293,993	2,483.54	63
Lincoln	11,648	11,413	39.55	27	30,278,236	33,852,931	2,966.17	33
Manitowoc	24,863	25,140	30.87	55	71,271,018	82,067,350	3,264.41	17
Marathon	48,674	49,424	36.74	37	122,510,733	145,692,588	2,947.81	36
Marinette	15,414	14,997	35.95	38	50,501,059	49,816,149	3,321.74	16
Marquette	5,550	5,669	36.83	36	14,856,296	16,138,745	2,846.84	43
Menominee	3,082	3,045	72.26	1	8,151,850	8,406,175	2,760.65	52
Milwaukee	517,096	533,467	56.25	3	1,296,985,847	1,588,649,864	2,977.97	32
Monroe	17,072	17,482	38.80	30	36,754,499	44,691,002	2,556.40	62
Oconto	12,862	12,671	33.50	45	34,394,229	38,329,622	3,024.99	29
Oneida	14,581	14,465	40.12	25	38,246,487	41,100,066	2,841.35	44
Outagamie	47,137	48,875	27.43	62	123,594,550	136,006,843	2,782.75	50
Ozaukee	13,419	13,656	15.76	72	44,941,135	48,908,956	3,581.50	9
Pepin	1,934	1,928	25.83	63	7,922,612	9,648,140	5,004.22	2
Pierce	8,198	7,989	19.43	70	29,829,042	31,083,378	3,890.77	4
Polk	12,390	12,248	27.68	61	44,190,912	45,262,043	3,695.46	7
Portage	22,429	22,461	31.72	49	52,628,094	66,295,171	2,951.57	35
Price	6,904	6,684	47.56	10	20,817,117	21,588,954	3,229.95	18
Racine	75,689	77,827	39.83	26	186,728,378	220,493,182	2,833.12	45
Richland	5,553	5,418	30.03	57	24,280,993	28,863,438	5,327.32	1
Rock	68,280	69,079	43.14	16	161,426,377	168,818,406	2,443.85	64
Rusk	8,025	7,938	53.80	4	20,095,059	23,132,931	2,914.20	39
St. Croix	20,239	19,883	23.43	66	61,231,546	62,697,515	3,153.32	23
Sauk	19,576	19,258	31.06	53	55,537,079	62,156,500	3,227.57	19
Sawyer	8,383	8,124	48.77	9	22,264,571	23,703,761	2,917.75	38
Shawano	15,819	16,307	38.90	29	39,232,683	42,794,754	2,624.32	59
Sheboygan	35,697	36,309	31.42	50	99,074,035	107,388,247	2,957.62	34
Taylor	8,842	8,650	41.79	19	20,094,414	20,317,453	2,348.84	69
Trempealeau	10,731	10,911	37.64	32	30,967,565	36,494,934	3,344.78	15
Vernon	10,947	11,104	37.18	33	27,341,227	32,331,693	2,911.72	40
Vilas	7,457	9,148	42.58	17	15,993,027	21,109,724	2,307.58	70
Walworth	34,576	35,445	34.57	42	83,468,288	93,758,648	2,645.19	57
Washburn	8,644	8,511	53.50	5	23,394,545	25,070,353	2,945.64	37
Washington	27,505	27,675	20.89	69	77,703,711	85,464,336	3,088.14	24
Waukesha	61,753	63,440	16.23	71	208,044,071	224,980,760	3,546.35	10
Waupaca	18,593	18,697	35.69	39	83,786,795	88,451,811	4,730.80	3
Waushara	9,183	9,083	37.06	34	20,985,834	22,154,286	2,439.09	65
Winnebago	50,809	51,923	30.96	54	125,314,257	144,913,227	2,790.93	48
Wood	32,231	33,275	44.61	13	80,520,711	99,901,787	3,002.31	31
Tribal totals[3]	7,837	3,674	—	—	15,747,157	4,139,659	1,126.74	—
STATE	—[1]	—[1]	—		$5,408,726,659	$6,164,184,283	$3,011.42	

[1]Unduplicated total of recipients by county or administrative agency, but individuals who moved during the year and received benefits from more than one county/administrative agency that year will be counted in the unduplicated tally for each county/administrative agency from which benefits were received. Statewide recipient totals are not included because the sum of the county statistics would overcount individuals who moved during the year. [2]The expenditure totals include benefits issued and individuals eligible under BadgerCare+/MA and subprograms CORE, BASIC, Family Planning Only Services, Medicaid Waiver. Costs include: Managed Care Capitation Payments, Fee For Service Payment to providers and Long Term Care waiver program payments. [3]Tribal agencies include Bad River Tribe, Lac du Flambeau Tribe, Oneida Nation, Potawatomi Tribe, Red Cliff Tribe, Sokaogon Tribe, and Stockbridge-Munsee Tribe.

Sources: Wisconsin Department of Health Services, departmental data, July 2013; Wisconsin Department of Administration, Division of Intergovernmental Relations, Demographic Services Center, *County Population Estimates, January 1, 2012.* Percentages and rankings calculated by Wisconsin Legislative Reference Bureau.

STATE CORRECTIONS AND HEALTH SERVICES INSTITUTIONS
Population, 1970 – 2012

	2012 Avg. Pop.	Rated Cap.[1]	Average Daily Population (Year ending June 30)					
Institutions			1970	1980	1990	2000	2010	2011
STATE CORRECTIONS POPULATION								
Maximum Security (Men)								
Assessment and Evaluation[2]	1,225	904	—	—	—	—	1,214	1,240
Columbia Correctional Institution	825	541	—	—	477	808	820	806
Dodge Correctional Institution[2].	337	261	—	88	551	1,377	341	335
Green Bay Correctional Institution	1,082	749	755	658	832	1,002	1,089	1,086
Wisconsin Secure Program Facility	478	501	—	—	—	101	461	470
Waupun Correctional Institution	1,235	882	954	1,087	1,126	1,225	1,237	1,229
	5,181	3,838	1,709	1,833	2,986	4,513	5,161	5,165
Medium Security								
Fox Lake Correctional Institution	1,170	979	553	570	785	1,112	1,046	1,034
Jackson Correctional Institution	969	837	—	—	—	971	977	969
Kettle Moraine Correctional Institution	1,160	783	293	368	542	1,233	1,160	1,156
New Lisbon Correctional Institution	1,014	950	—	—	—	—	1,009	999
Oshkosh Correctional Institution	2,026	1,494	—	—	444	1,859	2,031	2,011
Prairie du Chien Correctional Institution	507	326	—	—	—	297	500	500
Racine Correctional Institution	1,559	1,021	—	—	—	1,414	1,553	1,549
Racine Youthful Offender Correctional Facility . . .	446	400	—	—	—	395	445	444
Red Granite Correctional Institution	1,016	990	—	—	—	—	1,013	1,012
Stanley Correctional Institute.	1,521	1,500	—	—	—	—	1,509	1,512
	11,388	9,280	846	938	1,771	7,281	11,242	11,185
Minimum Security								
Chippewa Valley Correctional Treatment Center. . .	471	450	—	—	—	—	465	489
Fox Lake	109	288	—	—	—	—	280	274
Oakhill Correctional Institution.	676	344	—	198	368	564	677	662
Sturtevant Transitional Facility[3]	258	150	—	—	—	—	261	252
Wisconsin Correctional Center System (WCCS)[4] . . .	1,675	1,286	390	276	1,071	1,816	1,649	1,536
	3,188	2,230	390	474	1,439	2,380	3,332	3,213
Detention Facility								
Milwaukee Secure Detention Facility[3]	974	461	998	—	—	—	956	946
Wisconsin Women's Correctional System[4]								
Taycheedah Correctional Institution (medium/. . . . maximum)	686	653	141	123	203	644	579	683
Correctional Centers (minimum)	453	284					683	515
Contract Facilities								
Federal Contract	25	—	—	—	—	—	30	27
In-State	96	—	—	—	—	—	660	420
	121	—	—	—	78	4,665	690	447
Other Adults								
Community Residential Confinement	—	—	—	—	48	—	—	—
Division of Intensive Sanctions.	—	—	—	—	—	412	—	—
Parole and mandatory release[5]	20,593	—	4,329	3,045	4,217	8,951	19,783	20,321
Probation	47,178	—	4,530	16,797	25,907	55,046	48,340	47,370
	67,771	—	8,859	19,842	30,172	64,409	68,123	67,691
Juvenile Corrections[6]								
Copper Lake School[7]	23	29	—	—	—	—	—	—
Ethan Allen School[7].	—	—	365	306	320	438	207	144
Lincoln Hills School[7]	264	519	—	245	252	330	176	158
Southern Oaks Girls School	—	—	—	—	—	87	49	19
Youth Leadership Training Center[8]	—	—	—	—	—	40	—	—
Sprite Program	—	—	—	—	—	9	5	0
Juvenile Correctional Camp System	—	—	81	24	—	—	—	—
	287	538	446	575	572	904	437	321
Juvenile Aftercare.	69	—	—	—	—	—	76	71
Alternate Care.	38	—	—	—	—	174	49	41
Corrective Sanctions	114	—	—	—	—	134	140	135
TOTAL POPULATION	**90,270**	—	**12,391**	**23,785**	**37,221**	**84,796**	**91,840**	**90,413**

STATE CORRECTIONS AND HEALTH SERVICES INSTITUTIONS
Population, 1970 – 2012-Continued

Institutions	2012 Avg. Pop.	Rated Cap.[1]	1970	1980	1990	2000	2010	2011
			Average Daily Population (Year ending June 30)					
MENTAL HEALTH INSTITUTIONS (MHI)								
Mendota MHI	222	234	522	202	266	238	240	224
Winnebago MHI	171	169	574	310	266	279	291	174
Mendota Juvenile Treatment Center	29	29	—	—	—	43	29	29
Sand Ridge Secure Treatment Center.	360	400	—	—	—	72	286	287
Central State Hospital.	—	—	258	154	—	—	—	—
Wisconsin Resource Center[9]	366	389	—	—	161	421	427	416
CENTERS FOR DEVELOPMENTALLY DISABLED (CDD)								
Central Wisconsin CDD	245	340	1,070	731	606	380	258	254
Northern Wisconsin CDD.	16	30	1,421	676	495	189	12	16
Southern Wisconsin CDD.	157	210	1,207	735	576	274	178	166
TOTAL POPULATION	**1,566**	**1,801**	**5,052**	**2,808**	**2,370**	**1,896**	**1,622**	**1,566**

[1]DOC "rated capacity" is the original design capacity, based on industry standards, plus modifications and expansions. It excludes beds and multiple bunking to accommodate crowding. DHS Care and Treatment Facilities' capacity is "staffed capacity", based on staffing and other budgetary resources rather than number of beds.

[2]Dodge CI serves as the assessment and evaluation (A&E) center for sentenced adult felons. A&E for sentenced adult female felons moved from Dodge CI to Taycheedah CI December 2004.

[3]Milwaukee Secure Detention Facility includes capacity of 538 male and 40 female probation and parole holds.

[4]In July 2005, DOC designated the institutions for female offenders as the Wisconsin Women's Correctional System, which now includes Taycheedah CI and 2 of the minimum security Correctional Centers. John Burke CC became a male facility as of November 2011. A limited number of female inmates are housed outside WWCS at predominantly male St. Croix CC. WCCS population statistics prior to 2005 include both male and female inmates. Dodge CI infirmary had 1 female inmate and Milwaukee Secure Detention Facility had 31 females.

[5]Parole data through 1991 included juveniles; figures from 1992 to date do not include juvenile cases.

[6]JDOC has administered juvenile incarceration since July 1996.

[7]Ethan Allen and Southern Oaks closed in June 2011; Copper Lake opened in June 2011.

[8]Youth Leadership Training Camp program, formerly at Camp Douglas and closed in February 2002, is now part of the program at Lincoln Hills.

[9]Wisconsin Resource Center is administered by DHS in partnership with DOC as a specialized mental health facility.

Sources: Wisconsin Department of Corrections, *Fiscal Year Summary Report of Population Movement for 1991* and previous issues, and departmental data, June 2013 and prior years; Wisconsin Department of Health Services, departmental data, June 2013 and prior years.

PRISON POPULATION AND CORRECTIONAL EXPENDITURES
By State, 1980 – 2011

State	Total Confined as of Dec. 31[1]					Incarceration Rate[2]	State Corrections Expenditures FY2010-11		
	1980	1990	2000	2010	2011		Total (in thousands)	Per Inmate Amount	Rank
Alabama	6,543	15,665	26,034	30,739	31,271	646	$563,058	$18,317	49
Alaska[3]	822	2,622	2,128	2,775	2,901	393	283,764	102,257	2
Arizona[4]	4,372	14,261	25,412	38,423	38,370	592	906,213	23,585	42
Arkansas	2,911	6,766	11,851	16,147	16,037	548	411,436	25,481	39
California[4]	24,569	97,309	160,412	164,213	149,025	416	6,589,627	40,129	27
Colorado[5]	2,629	7,671	16,833	22,815	21,978	438	1,023,871	44,877	22
Connecticut[3]	4,308	10,500	13,155	13,308	12,549	361	698,030	52,452	16
Delaware[3,4]	1,474	3,471	3,937	3,961	4,003	439	266,666	67,323	6
Florida	20,735	44,387	71,318	104,306	103,055	544	2,465,017	23,633	40
Georgia.	12,178	22,345	44,141	54,685	53,955	553	1,462,044	26,736	37
Hawaii[3,6]	985	2,533	3,553	3,939	3,910	285	191,030	48,497	19
Idaho	817	1,961	5,535	7,431	7,739	479	219,042	29,477	35
ILLINOIS[5]	11,899	27,516	45,281	48,418	48,427	376	1,514,033	31,270	34
Indiana	6,683	12,736	19,811	28,012	28,890	437	661,358	23,610	41
IOWA[7]	2,481	3,967	7,955	9,388	9,057	301	332,291	35,395	31
Kansas	2,494	5,777	8,344	9,051	9,327	320	341,552	37,736	28
Kentucky.	3,588	9,023	14,919	19,937	20,952	468	518,890	26,026	38
Louisiana.	8,889	18,599	35,207	39,444	39,709	865	757,363	19,201	48
Maine	814	1,523	1,635	1,942	1,952	147	142,410	73,332	5
Maryland.	7,731	17,848	22,490	22,275	22,252	382	1,383,744	62,121	8
Massachusetts[8]	3,185	8,273	9,479	10,027	10,316	154	1,050,827	104,800	1
MICHIGAN	15,124	34,267	47,718	44,113	42,904	441	1,663,416	37,708	29
MINNESOTA	2,001	3,176	6,238	9,796	9,800	183	508,237	51,882	17
Mississippi.	3,902	8,375	19,239	20,366	20,585	687	354,626	17,413	50
Missouri	5,726	14,943	27,519	30,614	30,829	511	720,834	23,546	43
Montana	739	1,425	3,105	3,716	3,678	370	188,537	50,737	18
Nebraska	1,446	2,403	3,816	4,498	4,511	244	241,829	53,764	13
Nevada[9]	1,839	5,322	10,063	12,556	12,639	463	275,865	21,971	45
New Hampshire	326	1,342	2,257	2,761	2,614	204	112,666	40,806	25
New Jersey[5]	5,884	21,128	29,784	25,007	23,834	277	1,453,667	58,130	11
New Mexico	1,279	3,187	4,666	6,614	6,855	323	406,630	61,480	9
New York	21,815	54,895	70,199	56,461	55,262	287	2,995,539	53,055	14
North Carolina	15,513	18,411	27,043	35,436	35,102	365	1,422,868	40,153	26
North Dakota.	253	483	994	1,487	1,423	213	88,475	59,499	10
Ohio[5]	13,489	31,822	45,833	51,712	50,964	445	1,625,282	31,429	33
Oklahoma	4,796	12,285	23,181	24,514	24,024	640	530,853	21,655	46
Oregon	3,177	6,492	10,553	14,831	14,459	378	711,895	48,000	20
Pennsylvania.	8,171	22,290	36,844	51,075	51,390	402	1,910,065	37,397	30
Rhode Island[3,6]	813	2,392	1,966	2,086	2,065	197	181,796	87,151	3
South Carolina	7,862	17,319	21,017	22,822	22,233	481	445,612	19,526	47
South Dakota.	635	1,341	2,613	3,431	3,530	422	112,316	32,736	32
Tennessee	7,022	10,388	22,166	27,451	28,479	437	796,449	29,013	36
Texas	29,892	50,042	158,008	164,652	163,552	639	3,764,642	22,864	44
Utah	932	2,496	5,541	6,795	6,877	243	297,609	43,798	23
Vermont[3]	480	1,049	1,313	1,649	1,598	259	128,356	77,839	4
Virginia.	8,920	17,593	29,643	37,410	38,130	466	1,679,294	44,889	21
Washington[5]	4,399	7,995	14,666	18,212	17,808	264	1,002,442	55,043	12
West Virginia.	1,257	1,565	3,795	6,642	6,803	362	275,564	41,488	24
WISCONSIN[10]	3,980	7,362	20,336	21,973	20,559	372	1,160,898	52,833	15
Wyoming	534	1,110	1,680	2,112	2,183	378	127,318	65,113	7
UNITED STATES[1]. .	302,313	706,288	1,209,131	1,362,028	1,340,365	435	$46,976,046	$34,490	

[1]Except where noted otherwise, total confined refers to "sentenced prisoners" (more than one year) under a state's jurisdiction, regardless of where the prisoner is held. U.S. totals displayed do not include federal prisoners for December 31, 2010 (190,641) and December 31, 2011 (197,050). With federal prisoners included, the U.S. incarceration rate is 466. As of December 31, 2001, sentenced felons from the District of Columbia are the responsibility of the Federal Bureau of Prisons.

[2]Total state prisoners with a sentence of more than one year per 100,000 state residents. Rates for states with integrated systems are likely to be overstated compared to states that do not include jails in total population counts.

[3]Prisons and jails form one integrated system. Data include total jail and prison populations. Alaska includes persons in electronic and special monitoring programs.

[4]Prison jurisdiction population figures are based on custody counts. Arizona includes inmates in contracted beds. California includes out-of-state and other correctional facilities

[5]Includes some prisoners sentenced to one year or less. For Illinois and New Jersey, includes prisoners sentenced to one year.

[6]Counts include dual jurisdiction cases in which the inmate is currently housed in another jurisdiction's facilities.

[7]Iowa began including work release and operating while intoxicated status in 2009, jurisdiction only before 2009.

[8]Massachusetts offenders may be sentenced to up to 2.5 years in locally operated institutions and are excluded from the state count. Those excluded include 3,271 in the county system with sentences of over one year.

[9]2011 figure for Nevada is a preliminary estimate.

[10]Wisconsin count includes 722 temporary probation and parole placements.

Sources: U.S. Department of Justice, Office of Justice Programs, Bureau of Justice Statistics, "Prisoners in 2011", December 2012, at: http://www.bjs.gov/index.cfm?ty=pbdetail&iid=4559; U.S. Department of Commerce, U.S. Census Bureau, Governments Division, "2011 Annual Survey of State Government Finances", April 25, 2013, at: http://www.census.gov/govs/state; U.S. Department of Commerce, U.S. Census Bureau, "Annual Estimates of the Resident Population for the United States, Regions, States, and Puerto Rico: April 1, 2010 to July 1, 2011 (NST-EST2011-01)", at: http://www.census.gov/popest/data/historical/2010s/vintage_2011. Per inmate expenditure averages and rankings, and state incarceration rates calculated by Wisconsin Legislative Reference Bureau.

HIGHLIGHTS OF STATE AND LOCAL FINANCE IN WISCONSIN

Revenues and Expenditures — In the 2011-12 fiscal year, a large reduction of about $15.1 million in interest and investment income compared to the prior fiscal year accounted for most of the drop of almost $16.0 million in total Wisconsin state government revenues, which fell to $40.5 billion from all sources. Expenditures for 2011-12 totaled $41.5 billion. Of these expenditures, almost $27.4 billion were general fund and the remaining $14.2 billion were from special funds (such as the conservation and transportation funds), federal funding, pension and retirement funds, and other sources.

Of the total state budget allocations of $63.6 billion for the 2011-13 biennium, state operations accounted for 39.2% ($25.0 billion) and local assistance for 30.8% ($19.6 billion). The remaining 30.0% ($19.1 billion) comprised aids to individuals and organizations.

For the 2011-12 fiscal year, the agency with the single largest expenditure total was the Department of Health Services, almost $9.5 billion (23.0%). Expenditures by the Department of Public Instruction, including state aids to local schools, were $5.9 billion (14.3%). Shared revenue and tax relief of $2.4 billion accounted for 5.9%.

Total state tax revenues for 2011-12 were approximately $14.8 billion, including about $13.5 billion in general purpose revenue. Revenue from income taxes totaled about $7.9 billion, about $7.0 billion of which was individual income taxes and about $907 million in corporation income taxes, while sales and excise taxes were about $5.0 billion.

State-Local Finances — In 2009-10, Wisconsin ranked 23rd nationally in total per capita state and local government general revenues ($8,000, or lower than the U.S. average of $8,089). In total direct general state and local government per capita expenditures, Wisconsin also ranked 23rd ($8,091 compared to the U.S. average of $8,205). In 2009-10, Wisconsin ranked 21st in total state tax revenues at $63.53 per $1,000 personal income, compared to a national average of $59.50.

Wisconsin returned $1.63 billion to local units of government in property tax relief and shared revenue in fiscal year 2013 ($747.4 million as school levy credits and about $879.0 million in shared revenue).

Property Taxes — General property taxes levied in Wisconsin in 2011 totaled almost $10.4 billion for a net amount of about $9.6 billion after state property tax relief. Milwaukee ($25.59), Crawford ($23.77), Lafayette ($23.36), and Rock ($23.20) counties had the highest effective (full value equalized) net tax rate; Vilas ($9.45) and Sawyer ($10.58) counties were the lowest, compared to the state average of $19.79, a 2.1% increase from 2010. The share of property taxes paid by residential taxpayers was 70.2%. Commercial taxpayers paid 19.7%, and the share paid by manufacturing is 2.8%.

State-Federal Finances — Federal tax receipts from Wisconsin in fiscal year 2012 totaled about $41.5 billion, with the largest amount generated by individual income and employment taxes ($35.8 billion). Federal expenditures in Wisconsin – including grants to state and local government, salaries and wages, direct payments to individuals, procurement, and other programs – amounted to $9,648 per resident. This distribution, on a per capita basis, ranked Wisconsin 32nd among the states in federal funds received. Alaska was the highest at $17,762 per person, followed by Virginia ($17,008) and Maryland ($16,673). Nevada ($7,321) was the lowest, followed by Minnesota ($8,367), Utah ($8,519), Illinois ($8,571), and New Hampshire ($8,610). Direct federal aid to Wisconsin in 2011-12 totaled $10.9 billion, and about 53% of that applied to health services. Local units of government received about $1.39 billion for all functions. Those federal aid amounts are down substantially from 2010-11.

Indebtedness — Total outstanding state government debt in Wisconsin, as of May 31, 2013, amounted to $8.04 billion, of which $6.22 billion was tax-supported (general and segregated funds) and $1.82 billion was revenue-supported. Total state indebtedness at the end of 2011 constituted 1.62% of state-assessed valuation and amounted to $1,384.16 per capita. Local debt in 2011 totaled about $8.7 billion, about $4.5 billion of that for cities. School district and technical college district debt was almost $5.3 billion.

The following tables present selected data. Consult footnoted sources for more detailed information about state and local finance.

STATE BUDGET ALLOCATIONS
By Type of Revenue Source
Fiscal Years 2011-12 and 2012-13

Revenue Type and Allocation	2011-12	2012-13	2011-13 Total	% of Total – All Sources
GENERAL PURPOSE REVENUE	**$13,840,640,100**	**$14,755,176,400**	**$28,595,816,500**	**44.95%**
State operations	3,446,568,600	4,114,263,000	7,560,831,600	11.88
Local assistance	7,324,296,300	7,371,843,200	14,696,139,500	23.10
Aids to individuals and organizations	3,069,775,200	3,269,070,200	6,338,845,400	9.96
PROGRAM REVENUE – TOTAL	**$12,751,075,300**	**$13,001,392,000**	**$25,752,467,300**	**40.48%**
State operations	6,314,315,500	6,363,937,000	12,678,252,500	19.93
Local assistance	1,162,042,100	1,130,381,000	2,292,423,100	3.60
Aids to individuals and organizations	5,274,717,700	5,507,074,000	10,781,791,700	16.95
Program Revenue – Federal	**$8,394,938,800**	**$8,588,544,400**	**$16,983,483,200**	**26.69%**
State operations	2,381,945,500	2,366,355,000	4,748,300,500	7.46
Local assistance	1,097,797,500	1,065,777,700	2,163,575,200	3.40
Aids to individuals and organizations	4,915,195,800	5,156,411,700	10,071,607,500	15.83
Program Revenue – Service	**$796,202,100**	**$780,003,800**	**$1,576,205,900**	**2.48%**
State operations	607,804,400	593,440,500	1,201,244,900	1.89
Local assistance	39,680,800	39,779,500	79,460,300	0.12
Aids to individuals and organizations	148,716,900	146,783,800	295,500,700	0.46
Program Revenue – Other	**$3,559,934,400**	**$3,632,843,800**	**$7,192,778,200**	**11.31%**
State operations	3,324,565,600	3,404,141,500	6,728,707,100	10.58
Local assistance	24,563,800	24,823,800	49,387,600	0.08
Aids to individuals and organizations	210,805,000	203,878,500	414,683,500	0.65
SEGREGATED REVENUE – TOTAL	**$4,581,130,200**	**$4,691,390,900**	**$9,272,521,100**	**14.57%**
State operations	2,299,639,200	2,414,764,400	4,714,403,600	7.41
Local assistance	1,314,959,000	1,295,469,000	2,610,428,000	4.10
Aids to individuals and organizations	966,532,000	981,157,500	1,947,689,500	3.06
Segregated Revenue – Federal	**$899,567,900**	**$905,442,300**	**$1,805,010,200**	**2.84%**
State operations	666,852,600	672,727,000	1,339,579,600	2.11
Local assistance	227,923,500	227,923,500	455,847,000	0.72
Aids to individuals and organizations	4,791,800	4,791,800	9,583,600	0.02
Segregated Revenue – Local	**$108,559,400**	**$108,559,400**	**$217,118,800**	**0.34%**
State operations	7,393,700	7,393,700	14,787,400	0.02
Local assistance	92,971,500	92,971,500	185,943,000	0.29
Aids to individuals and organizations	8,194,200	8,194,200	16,388,400	0.03
Segregated Revenue – Service	**$192,898,100**	**$197,898,100**	**$390,796,200**	**0.61%**
State operations	192,898,100	197,898,100	390,796,200	0.61
Segregated Revenue – Other	**$3,380,104,800**	**$3,479,491,100**	**$6,859,595,900**	**10.78%**
State operations	1,432,494,800	1,536,745,600	2,969,240,400	4.67
Local assistance	994,064,000	974,574,000	1,968,638,000	3.09
Aids to individuals and organizations	953,546,000	968,171,500	1,921,717,500	3.02
FEDERAL REVENUE – TOTAL	**$9,294,506,700**	**$9,493,986,700**	**$18,788,493,400**	**29.53%**
State operations	3,048,798,100	3,039,082,000	6,087,880,100	9.57
Local assistance	1,325,721,000	1,293,701,200	2,619,422,200	4.12
Aids to individuals and organizations	4,919,987,600	5,161,203,500	10,081,191,100	15.85
TOTAL – ALL SOURCES	**$31,172,845,600**	**$32,447,959,300**	**$63,620,804,900**	**100.00%**
State operations	12,060,523,300	12,892,964,400	24,953,487,700	39.22
Local assistance	9,801,297,400	9,797,693,200	19,598,990,600	30.81
Aids to individuals and organizations	9,311,024,900	9,757,301,700	19,068,326,600	29.97

General purpose revenue: general taxes, miscellaneous receipts and revenues collected by state agencies that are paid into the general fund, lose their identity, and are available for appropriation by the legislature.

Program revenue: revenues paid into the general fund and credited by law to an appropriation used to finance a specific program or agency.

Segregated fund revenue: revenues deposited, by law, into funds other than the general fund and available only for the purposes for which such funds were created.

Federal revenue: money received from the federal government (may be disbursed either through a segregated fund or through the general fund).

Service revenue: money transferred between or within state agencies for reimbursement for services rendered or materials purchased.

State operations: amounts budgeted to operate programs carried out by state government.

Local assistance: amounts budgeted as state aids to assist programs carried out by local governmental units in Wisconsin.

Source: Wisconsin Department of Administration, State Budget Office, departmental data, June 2013.

WISCONSIN STATE REVENUES – ALL FUNDS
Fiscal Years 2009-10, 2010-11, 2011-12
(In Thousands)

	2009-10	2010-11	2011-12
TOTAL GENERAL FUND TAX REVENUES*	$12,156,840	$12,937,210	$13,541,842
TOTAL GPR TAX REVENUES*	$12,131,659	$12,911,865	$13,514,631
Income Taxes*	6,923,649	7,553,510	7,948,248
Individual	6,089,170	6,700,647	7,041,673
Corporation	834,479	852,863	906,575
Sales and Excise Taxes*	4,702,134	4,829,865	4,998,292
General sales and use	3,944,187	4,109,019	4,288,739
Cigarette	644,269	604,831	587,751
Other tobacco products	59,887	60,885	65,524
Liquor and wine	44,182	45,803	47,037
Malt beverage (beer)	9,609	9,327	9,241
Public Utility Taxes*	319,377	341,344	365,912
Private light, heat, and power	208,617	227,318	231,580
Municipal light, heat, and power	2,925	3,190	3,029
Telephone	70,031	67,022	80,976
Pipeline	23,052	27,108	33,674
Electric cooperative	10,395	11,554	11,164
Municipal electric	4,146	4,863	5,171
Conservation and regulation	211	288	312
Utility tax (refunds) interest and penalties	0	1	6
Inheritance and Estate Taxes	871	−128	323
Miscellaneous Taxes*	185,628	187,274	201,856
Insurance companies (premiums)	130,718	139,951	148,082
Real estate transfer fee	44,307	35,555	39,843
Lawsuits (courts)	10,492	11,670	13,832
Other	111	98	99
PROGRAM TAX REVENUES*	25,181	25,345	27,211
Fire dues	16,167	16,550	17,676
Pari-mutuel taxes	306	0	0
County expo tax administration	97	632	672
Baseball park administration fee	343	384	396
Business trust regulation fee	2,055	1,795	2,024
Other	6,213	5,984	6,443
TRANSPORTATION FUND*			
Motor fuel tax	971,786	988,265	983,859
Air-carrier tax	4,505	6,259	5,986
Railroad tax	24,056	24,880	28,087
Aviation fuel tax	1,188	1,278	1,141
Other taxes	7,146	8,229	8,234
CONSERVATION FUND*			
2/10 Mill forestry mill tax	86,896	84,235	82,655
Forest crop taxes	5,004	5,631	5,013
Motor fuel tax	3	2	1
MEDIATION FUND	2	2	2
PETROLEUM INSPECTION TAX	60,957	67,583	66,123
ECONOMIC DEVELOPMENT FUND TEMPORARY			
SERVICE CHARGES	20,610	25,865	27,527
TOTAL STATE TAX REVENUES	$13,338,993	$14,149,439	$14,750,470
TOTAL DEPARTMENT REVENUES*	32,137,971	41,527,063	25,029,052
Intergovernmental revenue	11,521,558	12,552,481	11,161,047
Licenses and permits	1,662,803	1,729,135	1,731,183
Charges for goods and services	3,426,455	3,601,172	3,811,937
Contributions	2,980,810	3,312,172	3,288,711
Interest and investment income	8,624,470	15,965,453	836,370
Gifts and donations	555,577	569,986	567,650
Proceeds from sale of bonds	1,233,951	1,515,997	1,379,104
Other revenues	1,921,317	2,009,216	2,101,309
Other transactions	211,030	271,451	151,741
TRANSFERS	761,716	824,559	737,888
TOTAL REVENUES	$46,238,680	$56,501,061	$40,517,410

*Total of subsequent detail.

Source: Wisconsin Department of Administration, *2012 Annual Fiscal Report,* October 15, 2012.

WISCONSIN STATE EXPENDITURES BY AGENCY
Fiscal Years 2010-11 and 2011-12

Agency	2010-11 Amount	2010-11 Percent	2011-12 Amount	2011-12 Percent
Administration, Department of (DOA)	$1,079,928,115.00	2.52%	$952,704,790.76	2.31%
Aging and Long Term Care, Board on.	2,604,722.69	0.01	2,537,826.42	0.01
Agriculture, Trade and Consumer Protection, Department of	87,883,681.32	0.21	83,578,171.54	0.20
Arts Board	4,900,180.94	0.01	−7,500.00	−0.00
Child Abuse and Neglect Prevention Board	3,075,619.95	0.01	2,386,181.93	0.01
Children and Families, Department of.	2,072,926,673.46	4.84	2,022,515,819.73	4.89
Commerce, Department of.	222,016,169.91	0.52	−125,758,485.49	−0.30
Corrections, Department of	1,270,637,570.65	2.97	1,194,381,789.11	2.89
District Attorneys (DOA)	49,841,505.60	0.12	48,432,280.76	0.12
Educational Communications Board	14,928,534.22	0.03	15,285,966.19	0.04
Employee Trust Funds, Department of	5,904,327,806.01	13.78	6,235,693,962.74	15.09
Employment Relations Commission.	3,019,244.05	0.01	2,757,237.41	0.01
Environmental Improvement Program (DOA)	217,032,112.00	0.51	157,791,831.83	0.38
Financial Institutions, Department of	15,233,415.76	0.04	15,179,320.89	0.04
Fox River Navigation System Authority.	125,400.00	0.00	125,400.00	0.00
Government Accountability Board	6,026,835.48	0.01	6,382,326.22	0.02
Governor, Office of the	3,716,363.79	0.01	3,743,189.39	0.01
Health Services, Department of	10,045,145,283.61	23.45	9,490,241,682.25	22.97
Higher Education Aids Board	148,702,262.44	0.35	136,825,522.50	0.33
Historical Society, State	20,198,776.19	0.05	19,550,205.68	0.05
Insurance, Office of the Commissioner of.	92,004,705.71	0.21	56,235,697.39	0.14
Investment Board	27,435,014.25	0.06	28,639,756.57	0.07
Justice, Department of.	100,031,626.76	0.23	98,419,109.70	0.24
Lieutenant Governor, Office of the	378,748.37	0.00	321,055.32	0.00
Lower Wisconsin Riverway	186,711.62	0.00	196,195.25	0.00
Medical College of Wisconsin.	6,056,559.33	0.01	5,701,507.17	0.01
Military Affairs, Department of	95,019,816.27	0.22	94,020,118.39	0.23
Natural Resources, Department of.	498,339,834.45	1.16	466,819,744.43	1.13
People with Developmental Disabilities, Board for . .	1,406,405.20	0.00	1,309,446.15	0.00
Public Defender, Office of the	77,667,043.91	0.18	90,642,902.90	0.22
Public Instruction, Department of	6,389,771,195.22	14.91	5,889,274,747.01	14.25
Public Lands, Board of Commissioners of	1,777,384.96	0.00	1,354,624.64	0.00
Public Service Commission	24,015,223.36	0.06	22,247,969.00	0.05
Regulation and Licensing, Department of.	15,170,206.11	0.04	63,192,081.05	0.15
Revenue, Department of.	455,998,598.54	1.06	491,992,951.80	1.19
Secretary of State, Office of the	690,783.40	0.00	475,952.18	0.00
State Employment Relations, Office of	4,741,648.72	0.01	4,441,886.33	0.01
State Fair Park Board	18,999,329.61	0.04	19,753,892.32	0.05
Technical College System Board	178,298,847.32	0.42	138,830,392.71	0.34
Tourism, Department of	14,311,308.67	0.03	16,330,000.77	0.04
Transportation, Department of.	2,761,384,437.21	6.45	2,842,774,729.51	6.88
Treasurer, Office of the State	3,867,335.91	0.01	3,057,661.88	0.01
University of Wisconsin System.	5,546,710,406.36	12.95	5,556,376,901.11	13.45
Veterans Affairs, Department of	201,273,950.07	0.47	156,838,824.11	0.38
Wisconsin Economic Development Corporation . . .	17,367,267.85	0.04	60,245,927.34	0.15
Workforce Development, Department of	364,967,798.86	0.85	398,234,226.26	0.96
TOTAL EXECUTIVE	$38,070,142,461.31	88.86%	$36,772,075,821.15	88.99%
TOTAL JUDICIAL	135,255,363.00	0.32	130,853,119.03	0.32
TOTAL LEGISLATIVE	66,263,678.86	0.15	64,463,115.44	0.16
Shared Revenue and Tax Relief	2,396,090,258.79	5.59	2,420,287,275.00	5.86
Miscellaneous Appropriations	91,124,559.84	0.21	162,455,526.52	0.39
Program Supplements	−546,543.23	−0.00	112,425,885.80	0.27
Public Debt.	720,436,075.81	1.68	766,326,491.56	1.85
Building Commission	6,469,717.64	0.02	5,971,105.99	0.01
BUILDING PROGRAM	1,358,553,161.15	3.17	888,536,805.68	2.15
GRAND TOTAL.	$42,843,788,733.17	100.00%	$41,323,395,146.17	100.00%

Source: Wisconsin Department of Administration, State Controller's Office, *Appendix to Annual Fiscal Report (Budgetary Basis),* October 2011 and 2012. Agency percentages calculated by Wisconsin Legislative Reference Bureau.

WISCONSIN STATE REVENUES AND EXPENDITURES
Fiscal Years 1970-71 – 2011-12
(In Thousands)

Fiscal Year	General Fund[1]		Other Funds[2]		Total – All Funds		Net Surplus[3]
Ending 6/30	Revenues	Expenditures	Revenues	Expenditures	Revenues	Expenditures	(or deficit)
1971	$1,790,957	$1,780,703	$929,124	$726,545	$2,720,081	$2,507,247	$34,840
1972	2,096,084	2,031,896	961,970	697,144	3,058,054	2,729,040	116,914
1973	2,480,748	2,296,679	1,112,600	791,657	3,593,347	3,088,337	217,404
1974	2,687,517	2,729,854	1,114,326	865,724	3,801,842	3,595,577	241,359
1975	2,966,532	3,148,968	1,252,422	924,455	4,218,954	4,073,423	78,120
1976	3,476,690	3,439,062	1,677,155	1,283,467	5,153,846	4,722,529	86,473
1977	3,807,748	3,712,595	1,887,150	1,376,726	5,694,898	5,089,322	166,587
1978	4,240,298	3,994,220	1,875,978	1,446,286	6,116,277	5,440,486	407,770
1979	4,622,611	4,696,263	2,200,365	1,620,899	6,822,976	6,317,162	280,561
1980	4,900,275	5,027,130	2,481,324	1,809,840	7,381,599	6,836,970	72,627
1981	5,335,427	5,452,247	2,738,491	1,922,648	8,073,918	7,374,895	14,065
1982	5,564,585	5,520,811	2,757,388	2,021,266	8,321,974	7,542,078	70,811
1983	6,036,016	6,302,575	3,905,944	2,288,804	9,941,961	8,591,379	(182,126)
1984	6,966,282	6,360,657	3,614,895	2,528,273	10,581,177	8,888,930	383,085
1985	7,160,174	7,237,716	4,908,582	2,743,287	12,068,756	9,981,002	314,084
1986	7,798,367	7,757,063	6,380,605	2,774,683	14,178,972	10,531,747	279,744
1987	8,133,265	8,205,100	5,061,597	2,693,737	13,194,863	10,898,836	232,733
1988	8,432,698	8,427,084	3,566,763	2,790,038	11,999,461	11,217,121	216,963
1989	9,030,466	8,809,189	5,778,125	3,094,116	14,808,591	11,903,305	375,016
1990	9,418,918	9,464,483	5,483,442	3,287,809	14,902,360	12,752,292	306,452
1991	10,184,183	10,350,332	5,930,658	3,706,452	16,114,839	14,056,784	113,609
1992	11,033,948	11,082,220	7,786,483	4,218,565	18,820,431	15,300,785	73,681
1993	11,828,599	11,708,360	8,192,793	4,596,981	20,021,392	16,305,341	153,540
1994	12,442,349	12,323,509	5,812,805	4,756,564	18,255,154	17,080,073	234,877
1995	13,259,772	13,094,450	9,823,810	4,963,553	23,083,582	18,058,003	400,881
1996	13,804,399	13,648,601	10,038,961	5,057,062	23,843,360	18,705,663	581,690
1997	14,669,320	14,932,404	12,741,438	5,144,002	27,410,758	20,076,406	386,558
1998	15,701,212	15,509,615	13,896,719	6,071,649	29,597,931	21,581,264	533,240
1999	16,252,539	16,098,587	11,847,678	6,864,567	28,100,217	22,963,154	737,748
2000	18,185,980	18,333,634	14,687,330	8,111,005	32,873,310	26,444,639	574,416
2001	19,285,734	19,448,417	2,990,770	8,719,341	22,276,504	28,167,758	445,999
2002	20,850,074	21,248,608	5,920,241	10,395,514	26,770,315	31,644,122	44,469
2003	20,683,921	20,956,485	10,598,486	11,025,745	31,282,407	31,982,230	(163,608)
2004	22,040,940	21,716,332	19,544,497	12,177,401	41,585,437	33,893,733	127,369
2005	21,191,600	21,488,178	15,827,541	10,772,231	37,019,141	32,260,409	(131,675)
2006	22,321,870	22,148,049	17,611,450	11,636,031	39,933,320	33,784,080	35,014
2007	23,123,424	23,205,243	23,140,557	11,329,591	46,263,981	34,534,834	36,467
2008	23,997,838	24,103,773	4,668,268	12,195,449	28,666,106	36,299,222	110,424
2009	25,078,246	25,280,016	(4,760,111)	13,216,367	20,318,135	38,496,383	(37,167)
2010	26,918,079	26,933,345	19,320,601	13,214,942	46,238,680	40,148,287	99,873
2011	28,926,518	28,951,824	27,574,543	13,974,915	56,501,061	42,926,739	305,584
2012	28,557,414	27,379,001	11,959,996	14,158,805	40,517,410	41,537,806	1,115,672

[1]Includes general purpose revenue (GPR), program revenue, and federal funding.

[2]Includes special revenue funds (such as conservation and transportation), federal funding, debt service, capital projects, pension and retirement funds, trust and agency funds, and others.

[3]Unappropriated (unreserved) balance of the general fund for the fiscal year.

Source: Wisconsin Department of Administration, Bureau of Financial Operations, *2012 Annual Fiscal Report,* October 15, 2012, and previous editions.

WISCONSIN TRANSPORTATION FUND
REVENUES AND EXPENDITURES[1]
Fiscal Years 2010-11 and 2011-12

	2010-11		2011-12	
	State Funds	Federal, Local, and Agency Funds	State Funds	Federal, Local, and Agency Funds
OPENING BALANCE	$230,822,777	($1,226,842,412)	$200,187,371	($1,036,984,858)
REVENUES				
Motor fuel taxes	988,264,444	—	983,859,809	—
Vehicle registration[2]	423,771,608	—	439,932,974	—
Drivers license fees	41,805,420	—	40,802,510	—
Motor carrier fees	4,175,633	—	2,452,000	—
Other motor vehicle fees	26,725,152	—	25,027,263	—
Overweight/oversize permits	5,202,142	—	5,555,176	—
Investment earnings (loss)	166,593	—	(186,054)	—
Aeronautical taxes and fees	8,143,956	—	7,619,936	—
Railroad property taxes	24,814,426	—	28,089,534	—
Dealers' licenses	557,612	—	679,447	—
Miscellaneous[3]	36,745,162	3,194,074	63,849,755	1,874,517
Service center operations	—	18,412,332	—	20,481,403
State and local highway facilities – Federal[4]	—	980,884,475	—	691,704,067
State and local highway facilities – Local	—	61,648,710	—	65,158,706
Major highway development – Revenue bonds	—	132,227,932	—	188,279,291
Highway administration and planning – Federal	—	3,639,234	—	2,801,391
Aeronautics – Federal	—	69,375,427	—	49,593,496
Aeronautics – Local	—	6,260,337	—	11,224,595
Railroad assistance – Federal	—	3,315,837	—	3,887,401
Railroad assistance – Local	—	6,229,213	—	10,224,573
Railroad passenger service – Federal	—	4,239,251	—	24,165,336
Railroad passenger service – Local	—	448,854	—	68,163
Transit assistance – Federal	—	27,741,947	—	24,837,790
Transit assistance – Local	—	880,223	—	848,586
Congestion mitigation air quality – Federal	—	3,153,848	—	1,630,778
Congestion mitigation air quality – Local	—	3,682,874	—	(161,034)
Surface transportation grants – Federal	—	—	—	50,914
Surface transportation grants – Local	—	—	—	12,729
Harbors assistance – Federal	—	1,748,868	—	120,079
Harbors assistance – Local	—	10,893	—	2,740
Safe routes to school – Federal	—	925,133	—	2,435,247
Safe routes to school – Local	—	811	—	18,238
Transportation enhancement activities – Federal[4]	—	16,810,740	—	9,121,099
Transportation enhancement activities – Local	—	3,280,729	—	2,639,584
Bicycle and pedestrian facilities – Federal	—	89,288	—	1,505,059
Bicycle and pedestrian facilities – Local	—	41,738	—	586,994
Transportation planning grants	—	1,535	—	—
General administration and planning – Federal	—	30,596,651	—	28,217,781
General administration and planning – Local	—	200,252	—	737,376
Administrative facilities – Revenue bonds	—	5,480,277	—	3,946,139
Highway safety – Federal	—	6,400,567	—	5,373,902
Gifts and grants	—	473,262	—	2,235,856
TOTAL REVENUES	$1,560,372,148	$1,391,395,312	$1,597,682,350	$1,153,622,796
TOTAL AVAILABLE	$1,791,194,925	$164,552,900	$1,797,869,721	$116,637,938

[1]The Transportation Fund is a multipurpose special revenue fund created to provide resources for transportation-related facilities and modes with revenues derived from users of transportation facilities. Transportation facilities and major highway projects are also funded with revenue bonds and general obligation bonds.

[2]Section 84.59, Wisconsin Statutes, provides that vehicle registration revenues derived under s. 341.25 are deposited with a trustee in a fund outside the state treasury. Only those revenues not required for the repayment of revenue bond obligations are considered income to the Transportation Fund. During FY 2011-12, $194.5 million was retained by the trustee and in FY 2010-11, $179.6 million was retained by the trustee.

[3]FY2011-12 Miscellaneous revenues – State funds includes a $22.9 million general fund transfer, $25.8 million petroleum inspection fund transfer and $0.4 million conservation fund transfer. FY2010-11 Miscellaneous revenues – State funds includes $2.3 million transferred from the general fund, $24.1 million from the petroleum inspection fund and $0.4 million from the conservation fund.

WISCONSIN TRANSPORTATION FUND
REVENUES AND EXPENDITURES[1]
Fiscal Years 2010-11 and 2011-12–Continued

	2010-11		2011-12	
	State Funds	Federal, Local, and Agency Funds	State Funds	Federal, Local, and Agency Funds
EXPENDITURES				
Local Assistance				
Highway aids	$442,678,274	—	$438,945,699	—
Local bridge and highway improvement[4]	32,934,832	$130,979,962	35,019,400	$125,527,451
Mass transit	128,894,698	26,037,541	132,444,939	16,155,201
Railroads	2,474,346	3,823,620	2,355,414	3,236,030
Special legislative projects (local grants)	(35,281)			
Aeronautics	15,608,902	77,011,014	16,791,130	63,290,536
Highway safety	—	5,792,759	—	6,248,941
Multimodal transportation studies	(12,613)	—	(34,339)	—
Rail passenger service	1,663,623	4,135,025	3,654,441	(3,601,328)
Harbors	1,686,582	1,872,961	67,682	19,251
Safe routes to school	—	3,015,425	—	2,405,496
Transportation planning grants to local governmental units	—	(6,565)	—	(48,897)
Transportation enhancement activities[4]	—	9,901,439	—	14,920,757
Bicycle and pedestrian facilities	1,081,494	1,093,119	1,055,957	1,021,040
Total Local Assistance	$626,974,857	$263,656,300	$630,300,323	$229,174,478
Aids to Individuals and Organizations				
Transportation facilities economic assistance and development	$2,679,961	$198,214	$1,753,495	$415,274
Railroad crossings	4,060,961	2,734,879	3,388,170	3,473,890
Elderly and disabled	828,290	2,083,939	537,470	779,101
Freight rail	—	(1,475,212)	—	4,310,011
Total Aids to Individuals and Organizations .	$7,569,212	$3,541,820	$5,679,135	$8,978,276
State Operations				
Highway improvements[4]	$439,789,012	$682,822,278	$558,319,720	$659,082,293
Major highway development – Revenue bonds . .	—	143,524,372	—	169,697,119
Highway maintenance, repair, and traffic operations	235,809,959	10,855,672	216,285,633	8,610,814
Highway administration and planning	15,019,247	3,194,757	13,063,355	3,047,444
Traffic enforcement and inspection	60,912,169	7,456,427	65,188,064	7,344,371
Transportation safety	975,034	4,999,113	1,235,402	4,375,156
General administration and planning	53,785,830	12,929,416	56,722,511	12,836,062
Administrative facilities – Revenue bonds	—	5,308,695	—	3,946,139
Vehicle registration and drivers licensing	65,665,612	2,236,956	72,017,091	2,216,659
Vehicle inspection and maintenance	3,470,300	—	3,193,300	—
Debt repayment and interest[5]	17,697,657	—	46,262,081	—
Service centers	—	16,900,196	—	16,727,392
Congestion mitigation air quality	—	1,751,344	—	7,770,843
Miscellaneous	2,588,362	42,360,412	2,376,791	7,606,227
Total State Operations	$895,713,182	$934,339,638	$1,034,663,948	$903,260,519
Transfers				
Conservation fund	$19,925,303	—	$19,862,291	—
General fund[6]	40,825,000	—	—	—
Total Transfers	$60,750,303	—	$19,862,291	—
TOTAL EXPENDITURES.	$1,591,007,554	$1,201,537,758	$1,690,505,697	$1,141,413,273
UNRESERVED FUND BALANCE	$200,187,371	($1,036,984,858)	$107,364,024	($1,024,775,335)

[4]The American Recovery and Reinvestment Act of 2009 (ARRA) provided $553.3 million in federal funding for highway improvement projects. ARRA-funded adjusted expenditures for highway projects totaled $0.2 million in FY 2011-12 and $47.3 million in FY 2010-11.

[5]2009 Wisconsin Act 28 (2009-2011 biennial budget act) authorized $565.0 million in general obligation bond funding for the I-94 North-South Freeway Reconstruction, state highway rehabilitation, and major highway projects. 2011 Wisconsin Act 32 (2011-2013 biennial budget act) authorized an additional $397.6 million. During FY 2011-12, $33.8 million in project costs were funded by general obligation bond proceeds and $300.6 million in FY 2010-11. 2009 Wisconsin Act 28 authorized the restructuring of general obligation bond debt, eliminating FY 2010-11 principal payments.

[6]The amounts provided in the above exhibit exclude financial activity relating to general obligation bond funded projects, which are reimbursed by the Capital Improvement Fund. As a result, amounts in this exhibit vary from amounts reported in Exhibit A-2 of the Annual Fiscal Report.

Source: Wisconsin Department of Administration, Division of Executive Budget and Finance, *2012 Annual Fiscal Report (Budgetary Basis) Appendix,* October 15, 2012.

WISCONSIN CONSERVATION FUND
REVENUES, EXPENDITURES, AND BALANCES
Fiscal Years 2007-08 – 2011-12

	2007-08	2008-09	2009-10	2010-11	2011-12
OPENING CASH BALANCE	$19,348,420	$16,832,895	$10,559,478	$22,619,142	$10,825,193
REVENUES	288,313,532	298,042,970	297,472,425	285,565,714	300,716,453
User fees (licenses, registration)	100,405,430	107,596,536	108,389,469	101,159,981	106,685,846
Forestry mill tax	84,529,264	87,364,228	86,895,392	84,234,712	82,655,049
Federal aids	49,679,136	46,923,176	45,100,915	45,200,151	58,397,301
Motor fuel tax formula	23,055,418	22,750,591	23,040,750	22,934,467	22,864,505
Severance tax	5,289,754	5,668,517	5,004,089	5,631,667	5,012,725
Other revenues (sales, services)	25,354,530	27,739,922	29,041,810	26,404,736	25,101,027
EXPENDITURES	290,829,057	304,316,387	285,412,761	297,359,663	280,892,205
Land and forestry – state	92,208,338	94,731,670	92,675,788	90,150,583	90,476,521
Land and forestry – federal	13,976,944	14,372,319	12,467,574	16,440,942	16,674,780
Enforcement/science – state	24,652,483	25,405,823	24,410,685	23,938,230	23,423,099
Enforcement/science – federal	7,688,614	8,824,216	9,993,173	12,031,891	10,951,402
Water management – state	25,739,492	23,519,983	20,957,121	23,809,609	21,556,060
Water management – federal	5,327,011	6,537,725	6,160,414	5,739,060	6,013,891
Conservation aids – state	31,762,786	31,348,827	28,787,757	30,006,477	29,707,704
Conservation aids – federal	1,585,027	4,723,021	5,708,759	5,058,713	4,266,992
Environmental aids – state	5,101,556	8,535,471	5,947,542	7,366,005	6,533,996
Development/debt service – state. . . .	18,984,845	19,294,504	25,112,458	22,818,234	20,162,288
Development/debt service – federal . .	8,313,349	14,551,103	4,420,490	9,681,827	3,110,679
Administrative services – state	14,650,722	807,338	2,520,441	2,516,843	2,415,405
Administrative services – federal	5,052,664	247,495	714,556	840,844	912,887
CAES management – state*	16,883,471	31,225,243	27,330,448	26,885,888	24,690,729
CAES management – federal*	532,502	4,548,908	4,802,268	4,607,284	5,535,743
Other activities – state	18,369,253	15,642,741	13,403,287	15,467,233	14,460,029
TRANSFER TO GENERAL FUND .	—	—	—	—	—
FUND BALANCE	$16,832,895	$10,559,478	$22,619,142	$10,825,193	$30,649,441

*CAES – Customer and Employee Services Division.

Note: The Conservation Fund is a segregated fund that provides funding for many activities of the Wisconsin Department of Natural Resources, including fish and wildlife management, forestry, parks and recreation, law enforcement, administrative activities, and a portion of the Wisconsin Conservation Corps program.

Source: Wisconsin Department of Administration, Bureau of Financial Operations, *2012 Annual Fiscal Report (Budgetary Basis) Appendix,* October 15, 2012, and previous issues.

STATE PAYMENTS TO LOCAL UNITS OF GOVERNMENT
Property Tax Relief and Shared Revenue
By County, Fiscal Year 2013

County[1]	School Levy Credits	Shared Revenue Payments	County Total	Per Capita Amount[2]	Rank
Adams	$3,847,611	$1,222,054	$5,069,665	$243.77	53
Ashland	1,739,875	6,011,888	7,751,763	482.58	1
Barron	5,810,440	6,975,763	12,786,203	278.40	34
Bayfield	2,938,928	1,428,373	4,367,301	290.15	29
Brown	28,170,156	26,890,890	55,061,046	220.00	66
Buffalo	1,475,775	2,796,184	4,271,959	312.99	16
Burnett	3,510,927	1,172,625	4,683,552	303.01	20
Calumet	4,979,265	3,634,048	8,613,313	175.18	72
Chippewa	6,268,779	10,786,646	17,055,425	271.68	38
Clark	2,604,085	8,006,650	10,610,735	305.73	18
Columbia	7,967,411	7,715,326	15,682,737	275.93	35
Crawford	1,713,183	3,554,503	5,267,686	316.61	15
Dane	86,330,927	25,097,872	111,428,799	226.69	62
Dodge	9,315,433	12,710,745	22,026,178	248.34	50
Door	5,943,906	1,354,581	7,298,487	261.90	44
Douglas	4,806,921	11,045,341	15,852,262	358.72	6
Dunn	4,481,101	7,874,221	12,355,322	281.74	32
Eau Claire	10,451,231	12,910,716	23,361,947	235.36	57
Florence	912,519	373,097	1,285,616	295.00	26
Fond du Lac	10,286,351	14,432,769	24,719,120	242.45	55
Forest	1,585,988	992,801	2,578,789	280.39	33
Grant	4,442,537	12,538,938	16,981,475	330.15	10
Green	4,739,159	3,955,454	8,694,613	235.86	56
Green Lake	3,093,094	3,078,428	6,171,522	323.01	11
Iowa	3,211,017	2,080,375	5,291,392	223.02	65
Iron	1,107,362	1,307,003	2,414,365	413.21	3
Jackson	1,944,653	3,069,726	5,014,379	244.33	52
Jefferson	10,143,223	9,241,475	19,384,698	231.16	60
Juneau	3,588,420	4,982,613	8,571,033	318.89	13
Kenosha	22,366,999	19,837,605	42,204,604	252.99	47
Kewaunee	1,974,410	4,220,429	6,194,839	300.18	22
La Crosse	13,197,650	18,340,601	31,538,251	272.88	37
Lafayette	1,761,082	4,474,926	6,236,008	369.06	5
Langlade	2,214,341	4,154,394	6,368,735	320.36	12
Lincoln	3,160,223	5,492,462	8,652,685	299.86	23
Manitowoc	7,301,141	16,699,321	24,000,462	294.71	27
Marathon	15,019,538	18,789,205	33,808,743	251.32	49
Marinette	5,472,219	9,394,609	14,866,828	356.36	8
Marquette	2,229,962	992,176	3,222,138	209.31	68
Menominee	465,043	622,061	1,087,104	257.97	46
Milwaukee	104,886,427	310,315,240	415,201,667	437.83	2
Monroe	3,597,252	8,210,251	11,807,503	262.06	43
Oconto	4,949,390	4,398,345	9,347,735	247.10	51
Oneida	8,037,849	1,846,867	9,884,716	274.14	36
Outagamie	19,114,324	22,782,015	41,896,339	235.17	58
Ozaukee	16,720,287	6,494,599	23,214,886	267.96	41
Pepin	1,023,496	1,348,976	2,372,472	317.81	14
Pierce	4,945,131	5,058,699	10,003,830	243.35	54
Polk	7,416,261	4,153,078	11,569,339	261.51	45
Portage	7,290,215	7,555,676	14,845,891	209.67	67
Price	2,056,011	2,911,593	4,967,604	353.44	9
Racine	22,151,872	33,708,491	55,860,363	285.90	31
Richland	1,716,742	3,774,824	5,491,566	304.36	19
Rock	14,721,573	32,208,023	46,929,596	293.07	28
Rusk	2,032,118	3,668,183	5,700,301	386.30	4
St. Croix	12,130,596	3,936,427	16,067,023	189.34	71
Sauk	9,167,459	4,944,013	14,111,472	227.63	61
Sawyer	3,875,192	953,767	4,828,959	289.87	30
Shawano	4,244,275	5,155,618	9,399,893	224.24	64
Sheboygan	13,657,795	17,667,953	31,325,748	271.10	40
Taylor	1,681,055	3,554,942	5,235,997	252.98	48
Trempealeau	2,744,173	6,225,807	8,969,980	309.46	17
Vernon	2,847,170	5,967,419	8,814,589	295.15	25
Vilas	7,191,309	513,233	7,704,542	358.60	7
Walworth	21,469,393	6,344,724	27,814,117	271.28	39
Washburn	3,456,193	1,282,456	4,738,649	297.90	24
Washington	19,369,050	5,731,248	25,100,298	189.46	70
Waukesha	80,434,596	10,778,277	91,212,873	233.33	59
Waupaca	5,672,659	8,173,074	13,845,733	264.33	42
Waushara	3,365,214	1,687,171	5,052,385	206.17	69
Winnebago	16,086,021	21,664,247	37,750,268	225.10	63
Wood	6,776,019	15,732,679	22,508,698	301.78	21
STATE	$747,400,002	$879,006,809	$1,626,406,811	$285.16	

[1]53 municipalities (cities and villages) are located in two or more counties. For municipalities that are in more than one county, payments are attributed to what the Department of Revenue determines to be the "primary" county. For example, payments to Appleton are attributed to Outagamie County even though parts of Appleton are also located in Calumet and Winnebago Counties.

[2]Per capita calculations are based on January 1, 2012 county population estimates, the most recent available at publication time.

Sources: Wisconsin Department of Revenue, Division of State and Local Finance, Bureau of Property Tax, Local Government Services Section, departmental data, June 2013; and Wisconsin Department of Administration, Division of Intergovernmental Relations, Demographic Services Center, *County Final Population Estimates, January 1, 2012* [October 2012]. Per capita amounts and rankings calculated by Wisconsin Legislative Reference Bureau.

SELECTED STATE TAX REVENUES
By State, Per $1,000 Personal Income
Fiscal Years Ending in 2012

State	Total Taxes[1] Amount	Rank	Sales and Gross Receipts Taxes General Sales	Motor Fuels	Selective Sales Taxes Public Utilities	Tobacco	Alcohol	Individual Income	Corporation Net Income	Motor Vehicle	Property
Alabama	$52.70	39	$13.24	$3.15	$4.29	$0.73	$1.01	$17.57	$2.41	$1.30	$1.89
Alaska	206.03	1	NA	1.20	0.12	1.97	1.18	NA	19.38	1.70	6.30
Arizona.	55.02	37	26.34	3.80	0.09	1.35	0.29	13.12	2.75	0.75	3.20
Arkansas	80.93	9	27.44	4.56	0.00	2.41	0.48	23.46	3.95	1.68	9.85
California	65.67	17	16.68	3.24	0.45	0.52	0.20	32.16	4.65	2.24	1.22
Colorado	43.78	47	9.83	2.69	0.05	0.87	0.17	20.82	2.10	2.08	NA
Connecticut	72.91	10	17.77	2.30	1.19	1.98	0.29	34.85	2.96	1.19	NA
Delaware	87.36	6	NA	2.94	1.55	3.14	0.46	34.10	6.82	1.43	NA
Florida	42.34	48	24.90	2.92	4.06	0.49	0.68	NA	2.57	2.12	0.00
Georgia.	45.32	45	14.50	2.41	0.00	0.62	0.48	22.26	1.62	0.97	0.19
Hawaii	89.99	5	44.02	1.52	2.46	1.99	0.80	25.14	1.31	3.37	NA
Idaho	62.66	25	22.74	4.40	0.06	0.90	0.15	22.53	3.50	2.59	NA
ILLINOIS	63.15	22	13.92	2.24	3.03	1.05	0.48	27.20	6.06	2.99	0.11
Indiana	65.10	19	27.45	3.25	0.90	1.93	0.18	19.75	3.97	2.25	0.00
IOWA	60.48	27	18.71	3.40	0.00	1.74	0.11	23.39	3.29	4.08	NA
Kansas	61.44	26	23.41	3.60	0.00	0.86	0.98	23.95	2.63	1.71	0.62
Kentucky.	68.23	15	19.88	5.15	0.42	1.80	0.77	22.88	3.75	1.33	3.45
Louisiana.	49.59	41	15.53	3.17	0.07	0.73	0.31	13.64	1.60	0.80	0.28
Maine	71.98	11	20.28	4.61	0.54	2.66	0.33	27.48	4.42	2.09	0.73
Maryland.	55.80	36	13.33	2.40	0.42	1.35	0.10	23.27	2.88	1.54	2.47
Massachusetts . . .	62.75	24	13.97	1.84	0.07	1.58	0.21	32.83	5.51	1.31	0.01
MICHIGAN	64.68	20	25.81	2.63	0.07	2.57	0.40	18.42	1.64	2.62	4.85
MINNESOTA . . .	82.68	8	19.87	3.42	0.00	1.70	0.32	32.12	4.29	2.72	3.25
Mississippi.	70.43	12	31.12	4.22	0.02	1.59	0.43	15.21	4.01	1.77	0.24
Missouri	45.93	44	13.20	3.01	0.00	0.45	0.15	21.82	1.28	1.21	0.12
Montana	65.47	18	NA	5.64	1.32	2.32	0.91	23.97	3.52	4.04	6.85
Nebraska	54.44	38	18.20	3.74	0.70	0.42	0.36	22.96	2.93	1.60	0.00
Nevada	65.73	16	33.31	2.83	0.22	1.00	0.40	NA	NA	1.77	2.28
New Hampshire . .	35.50	50	NA	2.31	1.35	3.46	0.16	1.31	8.39	1.72	6.13
New Jersey.	57.75	32	17.04	1.14	2.02	1.67	0.28	23.41	4.06	1.38	0.01
New Mexico	69.55	14	27.21	3.21	0.36	1.02	0.55	15.73	3.84	1.32	0.82
New York	70.18	13	11.68	1.57	0.92	1.60	0.23	38.03	4.48	1.52	NA
North Carolina . . .	62.87	23	15.43	5.15	1.06	0.82	0.89	28.74	3.38	1.92	NA
North Dakota. . . .	154.80	2	30.93	5.63	1.11	0.78	0.23	11.91	5.94	3.04	0.07
Ohio	57.16	34	18.24	3.71	2.32	1.86	0.22	19.91	0.26	1.76	NA
Oklahoma	59.32	29	16.24	2.99	0.26	1.97	0.70	18.65	3.00	4.57	NA
Oregon	57.52	33	NA	3.53	0.62	1.69	0.11	38.52	2.86	3.35	0.10
Pennsylvania. . . .	59.19	30	16.47	3.72	2.40	2.01	0.58	18.15	3.30	1.62	0.07
Rhode Island	59.37	28	17.76	2.49	2.15	2.77	0.27	22.53	2.59	1.22	0.04
South Carolina . . .	49.65	40	18.08	3.28	0.28	0.16	0.95	19.13	1.56	1.11	0.05
South Dakota. . . .	41.82	49	23.04	3.75	0.10	1.66	0.42	NA	1.64	1.88	NA
Tennessee	49.26	42	26.77	3.44	0.04	1.15	0.55	0.75	5.04	1.27	NA
Texas	44.97	46	22.67	2.94	0.57	1.36	0.87	NA	NA	1.82	NA
Utah	58.81	31	18.80	3.77	0.26	1.25	0.46	24.97	2.62	1.75	NA
Vermont	102.45	3	12.71	4.02	0.49	2.98	0.83	22.24	3.59	2.68	35.25
Virginia.	47.06	43	9.05	2.25	0.39	0.50	0.50	26.51	2.18	1.28	0.09
Washington.	56.27	35	33.89	3.76	1.47	1.50	1.11	NA	NA	1.73	6.06
West Virginia. . . .	83.73	7	19.97	6.05	2.43	1.71	1.36	27.45	3.01	1.68	0.09
WISCONSIN . . .	63.53	21	16.68	3.85	1.66	2.58	0.21	26.97	3.83	2.14	0.67
Wyoming.	90.93	4	35.44	2.37	0.16	0.93	0.06	NA	NA	2.42	11.29
UNITED STATES[2]	$59.50		$18.17	$2.99	$1.08	$1.28	$0.45	$20.99	$3.13	$1.89	$0.97

NA – Not applicable.

[1]Includes other taxes not listed separately.

[2]United States totals displayed exclude District of Columbia.

Sources: U.S. Census Bureau, Governments Division, "2012 Annual Survey of State Government Tax Collections", at http://www.census.gov/govs/statetax/; and U.S. Department of Commerce, Bureau of Economic Analysis, Regional Economic Information System, "SA1-3 – Personal Income Summary 2012", at: http://www.bea.gov/regional/docs/income. Amounts per $1,000 personal income and rankings calculated by Wisconsin Legislative Reference Bureau.

PER CAPITA STATE AND LOCAL REVENUES
Selected Sources, Fiscal Year 2009-10

State	Amount	Rank	Federal Sources Amount	Federal Sources Percent	State/Local Sources Amount[1]	State/Local Sources Percent	Total Taxes[2]	Property	Sales	Individual Income
Alabama	$7,043	41	$2,044	29.0%	$4,999	71.0%	$2,777	$538	$1,318	$564
Alaska	19,658	1	4,586	23.3	15,072	76.7	8,637	1,846	945	—
Arizona	6,564	47	2,110	32.1	4,454	67.9	3,063	1,141	1,358	377
Arkansas	6,932	42	2,162	31.2	4,770	68.8	3,248	595	1,641	715
California	8,742	13	1,989	22.8	6,753	77.2	4,624	1,443	1,391	1,223
Colorado	7,818	27	1,441	18.4	6,377	81.6	4,060	1,589	1,337	810
Connecticut	9,222	10	1,903	20.6	7,319	79.4	5,987	2,517	1,502	1,613
Delaware	9,517	6	2,278	23.9	7,239	76.1	3,979	739	526	1,008
District of Columbia	17,076	—	6,490	38.0	10,586	62.0	8,314	3,073	2,248	1,830
Florida	7,243	36	1,518	21.0	5,725	79.0	3,493	1,499	1,640	—
Georgia	6,499	48	1,782	27.4	4,717	72.6	3,100	1,091	1,131	722
Hawaii	8,965	11	2,072	23.1	6,893	76.9	4,837	1,021	2,377	1,120
Idaho	6,388	49	1,796	28.1	4,592	71.9	2,763	833	975	680
ILLINOIS	7,509	31	1,730	23.0	5,779	77.0	4,182	1,824	1,327	663
Indiana	7,139	38	1,663	23.3	5,476	76.7	3,595	1,179	1,332	836
IOWA	8,569	16	2,337	27.3	6,232	72.7	3,917	1,364	1,312	900
Kansas	7,965	24	1,698	21.3	6,266	78.7	3,993	1,375	1,375	941
Kentucky	7,103	39	2,244	31.6	4,859	68.4	3,168	682	1,204	964
Louisiana	8,932	12	3,161	35.4	5,771	64.6	3,554	744	1,918	503
Maine	8,403	18	2,527	30.1	5,877	69.9	4,398	1,788	1,260	982
Maryland	8,429	17	1,991	23.6	6,438	76.4	4,849	1,459	1,181	1,728
Massachusetts	9,396	9	2,257	24.0	7,139	76.0	5,100	1,978	1,067	1,543
MICHIGAN	7,740	29	2,126	27.5	5,615	72.5	3,615	1,455	1,321	594
MINNESOTA	8,726	14	2,042	23.4	6,683	76.6	4,587	1,408	1,535	1,216
Mississippi	8,140	20	3,088	37.9	5,052	62.1	3,022	852	1,410	456
Missouri	6,841	45	2,046	29.9	4,795	70.1	3,164	957	1,193	769
Montana	8,143	19	2,751	33.8	5,392	66.2	3,249	1,292	545	721
Nebraska	8,040	21	1,903	23.7	6,137	76.3	4,027	1,481	1,287	828
Nevada	6,651	46	1,256	18.9	5,394	81.1	3,749	1,293	1,893	—
New Hampshire	7,339	33	1,764	24.0	5,574	76.0	3,812	2,463	609	63
New Jersey	9,457	7	1,791	18.9	7,666	81.1	5,804	2,811	1,299	1,173
New Mexico	8,600	15	3,253	37.8	5,347	62.2	3,171	629	1,581	463
New York	12,237	3	2,871	23.5	9,367	76.5	7,023	2,274	1,778	2,190
North Carolina	7,066	40	1,834	26.0	5,232	74.0	3,422	897	1,231	956
North Dakota	10,317	4	2,805	27.2	7,512	72.8	5,158	1,020	1,598	450
Ohio	7,714	30	2,100	27.2	5,614	72.8	3,762	1,130	1,224	1,043
Oklahoma	7,253	35	2,219	30.6	5,034	69.4	3,032	638	1,271	592
Oregon	7,767	28	2,074	26.7	5,694	73.3	3,420	1,287	343	1,289
Pennsylvania	7,832	26	1,904	24.3	5,928	75.7	4,146	1,259	1,294	1,052
Rhode Island	9,404	8	2,892	30.8	6,512	69.2	4,570	2,083	1,348	864
South Carolina	7,220	37	1,722	23.9	5,497	76.1	2,839	1,017	980	577
South Dakota	7,343	32	2,403	32.7	4,940	67.3	3,166	1,136	1,698	—
Tennessee	6,367	50	1,921	30.2	4,446	69.8	2,870	791	1,630	27
Texas	6,913	43	1,795	26.0	5,118	74.0	3,427	1,549	1,518	0
Utah	6,879	44	1,819	26.4	5,059	73.6	2,999	829	1,124	758
Vermont	9,789	5	3,161	32.3	6,628	67.7	4,719	2,164	1,378	781
Virginia	7,323	34	1,352	18.5	5,971	81.5	3,885	1,401	1,029	1,079
Washington	8,027	22	1,862	23.2	6,164	76.8	3,970	1,249	2,403	—
West Virginia	7,876	25	2,481	31.5	5,395	68.5	3,490	744	1,309	821
WISCONSIN	8,000	23	1,901	23.8	6,099	76.2	4,287	1,695	1,239	1,018
Wyoming	14,325	2	3,962	27.7	10,362	72.3	6,166	2,623	1,925	—
UNITED STATES	$8,089		$2,016	24.9%	$6,072	75.1%	$4,105	$1,428	$1,394	$842

[1]Includes taxes, charges, and miscellaneous general revenues.

[2]Total taxes also include corporate income, motor vehicle license, and other taxes not listed separately.

Sources: U.S. Department of Commerce, U.S. Census Bureau, "Table 1. State and Local Government Finances by Level of Government and by State: 2009-10", at: http://www.census.gov/govs/local/ [April 25, 2013] and "Annual Estimates of the Population for the United States, Regions, States, and Puerto Rico: April 1, 2010 to July 1, 2012 (NST-EST2012-01)", at: http://www.census.gov/popest/data/historical/2010s/vintage_2011/index.html (July 1, 2010 estimates used in calculations). Per capita figures, percentages, and rankings calculated by Wisconsin Legislative Reference Bureau.

SELECTED PER CAPITA STATE AND LOCAL GOVERNMENT EXPENDITURES, BY FUNCTION
Fiscal Year 2009-10

	Direct General Expenditure* Amount	Rank	Education	Public Welfare	Health and Hospitals	Highways	Police and Fire	Correction	Parks and Natural Resources	Sewerage and Solid Waste
Alabama	$7,378	36	$2,762	$1,259	$1,122	$443	$335	$155	$152	$119
Alaska	17,825	1	4,501	2,479	841	2,435	682	384	826	336
Arizona.	6,729	45	2,095	1,326	490	412	509	259	199	240
Arkansas	6,702	46	2,716	1,471	433	435	262	169	172	190
California	9,112	9	2,745	1,399	853	443	605	346	312	258
Colorado	7,994	26	2,611	842	722	496	747	260	406	185
Connecticut	8,899	13	3,161	1,568	604	447	444	188	117	216
Delaware	9,309	8	3,330	1,832	521	703	352	291	173	292
District of Columbia	17,822	—	3,934	4,429	1,024	930	1,306	426	452	770
Florida	7,253	38	2,034	1,177	705	463	570	239	333	303
Georgia.	6,609	47	2,570	999	731	355	334	233	147	194
Hawaii	8,964	11	2,387	1,492	908	549	415	152	279	490
Idaho	6,578	48	2,100	1,156	647	619	336	192	247	207
ILLINOIS	8,059	24	2,706	1,382	442	640	535	153	236	211
Indiana	6,937	43	2,550	1,261	594	421	316	155	143	211
IOWA	8,390	18	3,042	1,509	1,029	757	274	140	250	225
Kansas	8,020	25	2,989	1,181	856	599	364	174	204	184
Kentucky.	7,325	37	2,587	1,632	620	521	258	165	158	218
Louisiana.	9,437	4	2,651	1,406	1,196	636	444	286	377	223
Maine	8,328	19	2,581	2,206	484	632	284	158	181	225
Maryland.	8,596	16	3,140	1,559	372	538	503	300	273	266
Massachusetts . . .	9,078	10	2,764	2,068	458	387	455	182	116	308
MICHIGAN	7,477	33	2,944	1,310	744	375	334	230	111	228
MINNESOTA . . .	8,848	14	2,887	2,215	558	696	388	162	358	203
Mississippi.	7,964	28	2,524	1,659	1,225	572	290	182	186	150
Missouri	6,975	42	2,365	1,235	762	533	402	150	212	171
Montana	8,106	22	2,612	1,332	386	927	345	250	351	170
Nebraska	7,989	27	3,128	1,265	690	677	308	196	371	165
Nevada	6,573	49	2,054	811	483	536	615	246	378	164
New Hampshire . . .	7,530	31	2,716	1,556	132	562	404	155	133	169
New Jersey.	9,400	7	3,610	1,590	493	456	484	245	182	297
New Mexico	9,420	5	3,162	2,175	815	596	456	305	300	183
New York	11,927	3	3,654	2,526	1,102	550	613	312	186	400
North Carolina	6,917	44	2,480	1,170	1,017	355	342	204	177	184
North Dakota.	8,900	12	3,203	1,296	306	1,205	265	145	561	243
Ohio	7,848	29	2,844	1,594	683	414	442	157	138	267
Oklahoma	7,077	41	2,720	1,436	493	671	353	183	176	129
Oregon	8,121	21	2,716	1,320	728	553	440	279	271	282
Pennsylvania.	8,316	20	2,763	1,931	534	673	298	251	157	286
Rhode Island.	8,673	15	2,876	2,145	248	375	633	181	94	203
South Carolina	7,550	30	2,653	1,338	1,277	352	315	155	143	193
South Dakota.	7,381	35	2,481	1,205	335	956	287	199	392	186
Tennessee	6,427	50	2,010	1,475	685	354	373	160	119	151
Texas	7,248	39	2,954	1,136	642	411	357	228	192	182
Utah	7,083	40	2,657	991	553	685	311	178	244	215
Vermont	9,403	6	3,748	2,247	297	839	297	199	188	209
Virginia.	7,499	32	2,907	1,191	624	405	392	271	140	240
Washington.	8,423	17	2,722	1,292	981	638	378	246	280	412
West Virginia.	7,398	34	2,838	1,621	356	667	236	166	202	192
WISCONSIN	8,091	23	2,952	1,670	533	633	397	267	246	229
Wyoming.	13,465	2	4,369	1,340	2,121	1,349	553	357	826	331
UNITED STATES	$8,205		$2,780	$1,476	$725	$504	$447	$236	$224	$245

*Includes amounts for categories not shown separately.

Sources: U.S. Department of Commerce, U.S. Census Bureau, "State and Local Government Finances by Level of Government and by State: 2009-10", at:: http://www.census.gov/govs/local/ [April 25, 2013] and "Annual Estimates of the Resident Population for the United States, Regions, States, and Puerto Rico: April 1, 2010 to July 1, 2011 (NST-EST2011-01)", at: http://www.census.gov/popest/data/historical/2010s/vintage_2011/index.html (July 1, 2010 estimates used in calculations). Per capita values and rankings calculated by Wisconsin Legislative Reference Bureau.

FEDERAL TAX COLLECTIONS
By State, Fiscal Year 2012
(In Thousands of Dollars)

State[1]	Total	Individual Income and Employment[2]	Corporate Income[3]	Estate and Gift[4]	Excise[5]
Alabama	$20,882,949	$19,500,672	$1,102,865	$92,170	$187,242
Alaska	4,898,780	4,640,174	191,060	16,221	51,325
Arizona	34,850,436	29,968,613	3,408,925	138,364	1,334,534
Arkansas	25,299,832	18,266,603	6,304,626	81,849	646,754
California	292,563,574	249,275,399	37,181,407	2,878,983	3,227,785
Colorado	41,252,701	36,113,422	3,968,517	170,608	1,000,154
Connecticut	47,262,702	40,875,490	5,431,458	265,176	690,578
Delaware	21,835,412	14,602,084	7,087,549	79,223	66,556
District of Columbia	20,747,652	20,139,227	392,793	192,193	23,439
Florida	122,249,635	113,188,889	6,609,351	1,544,804	906,591
Georgia	65,498,308	53,987,301	8,417,016	337,989	2,756,002
Hawaii	6,511,578	5,922,132	398,720	38,604	152,122
Idaho	7,622,490	7,169,783	367,921	49,778	35,008
ILLINOIS	124,431,227	103,654,375	17,337,038	678,260	2,761,554
Indiana	51,238,512	47,141,859	3,228,361	99,134	769,158
IOWA	18,753,596	17,210,796	1,315,070	57,434	170,296
Kansas	21,904,615	18,510,512	1,980,014	61,873	1,352,216
Kentucky	25,085,813	22,986,776	1,764,142	93,968	240,927
Louisiana	34,811,072	33,187,181	1,102,737	154,350	366,804
Maine	6,229,189	5,542,557	509,393	36,642	140,597
Maryland	48,107,002	45,186,159	2,626,431	233,856	60,556
Massachusetts	79,826,976	73,152,183	5,278,522	321,860	1,074,411
MICHIGAN	59,210,158	54,959,506	3,841,440	219,672	189,540
MINNESOTA	78,685,402	61,712,466	16,121,685	178,146	673,105
Mississippi	10,458,549	9,693,914	609,194	33,468	121,973
Missouri	48,413,247	40,997,767	6,082,671	262,763	1,070,046
Montana	4,383,777	4,147,270	156,415	22,238	57,804
Nebraska	19,795,254	13,470,845	6,149,516	71,152	103,741
Nevada	13,727,425	12,737,643	757,762	102,097	129,923
New Hampshire	8,807,691	8,370,452	205,260	25,715	206,264
New Jersey	111,377,490	92,020,482	17,459,934	337,572	1,559,502
New Mexico	7,866,206	7,494,229	150,549	47,007	174,421
New York	201,167,954	176,938,759	21,269,375	1,613,152	1,346,668
North Carolina	61,600,064	54,747,979	6,411,802	160,378	279,905
North Dakota	5,664,860	5,268,271	301,698	44,965	49,926
Ohio	111,094,276	95,611,009	11,604,143	442,510	3,436,614
Oklahoma	27,087,264	19,789,170	3,982,694	100,565	3,214,835
Oregon	22,716,602	21,131,294	1,229,807	99,919	255,582
Pennsylvania	108,961,515	94,747,441	11,222,657	479,816	2,511,601
Rhode Island	10,992,338	8,607,614	2,327,315	45,082	12,327
South Carolina	18,557,166	17,064,717	1,211,525	77,513	203,411
South Dakota	5,136,249	4,840,542	235,097	22,583	38,027
Tennessee	47,010,303	41,867,521	3,903,991	96,346	1,142,445
Texas	219,459,878	171,880,172	27,984,282	976,287	18,619,137
Utah	15,642,129	13,227,408	1,809,517	54,256	550,948
Vermont	3,524,887	3,236,379	255,605	9,814	23,089
Virginia	64,297,400	53,807,056	9,994,059	287,696	208,589
Washington	52,443,862	47,600,345	3,793,982	225,073	824,462
West Virginia	6,498,502	6,082,100	315,740	31,782	68,880
WISCONSIN	41,498,033	35,757,347	4,641,696	547,028	551,962
Wyoming	3,828,379	3,495,933	175,685	85,199	71,562
UNITED STATES[6]	$2,524,320,134	$2,172,233,368	$281,461,580	$14,450,249	$56,174,937

[1] Taxes may be collected in one state from residents of another state for a variety of reasons, and some corporations pay taxes from a principal office, although their operations may be located in several states.

[2] Collections of individual income tax (withheld and not withheld) include Old-Age, Survivors, Disability, and Hospital Insurance (OASDHI) taxes on salaries and wages under the Federal Insurance Contributions Act (FICA), and on self-employment income under the Self-Employment Insurance Contributions Act (SECA).

[3] Includes business income from tax-exempt organizations.

[4] The estate tax was temporarily repealed for deaths in calendar year 2010 before being reinstated retroactively with a $5 million exemption. The law also provided a $5 million exemption for the estates of 2011 decedents. These tax law changes significantly reduced estate tax gross collections in FY2011 relative to other fiscal years.

[5] Excludes excise taxes collected by the Customs Service and the Alcohol and Tobacco Tax and Trade Bureau.

[6] United States totals include international and undistributed totals not included in state listing for taxes filed by members of armed forces stationed overseas or other U.S. citizens abroad. Also included are returns from residents of Puerto Rico either with income from sources outside Puerto Rico or income earned as U.S. government employees. Corporation taxes include those paid by domestic and foreign businesses with principal offices outside the United States. Adjustments and credits are not shown by state, but are included in the U.S. totals. Detail may not add to totals due to rounding.

Source: U.S. Department of the Treasury, Internal Revenue Service, "Internal Revenue Service Data Book 2012," Publication 55B, March 2013.

PER CAPITA FEDERAL EXPENDITURES
By State, Fiscal Year 2010

State	Total Amount	Rank	Retirement and Disability	Grants	Procurement	Salaries and Wages	Other Direct Payments
Alabama	$11,819.83	11	$3,761.03	$1,940.15	$2,192.95	$1,174.37	$2,751.33
Alaska	17,762.29	1	2,239.71	4,878.99	3,469.69	5,709.52	1,464.38
Arizona.	10,079.26	27	2,899.67	2,246.71	2,004.55	779.16	2,149.17
Arkansas	9,912.49	30	3,554.14	2,346.79	600.49	829.16	2,581.91
California	8,960.37	44	2,277.43	2,117.06	1,544.45	659.92	2,361.52
Colorado	9,879.68	31	2,552.89	1,748.37	2,061.37	1,693.81	1,823.24
Connecticut	15,662.23	4	2,839.41	2,321.95	3,345.35	532.37	6,623.15
Delaware	8,994.35	42	3,403.17	2,288.76	403.88	788.01	2,110.54
District of Columbia . .	102,904.18	—	4,631.23	18,068.09	35,315.07	38,272.62	6,617.18
Florida	9,930.36	29	3,423.96	1,492.78	956.36	689.55	3,367.71
Georgia.	9,536.58	33	2,689.97	1,729.07	1,286.24	1,793.21	2,038.08
Hawaii	15,331.33	5	3,211.37	2,224.18	2,017.80	5,805.78	2,072.20
Idaho	9,091.54	39	2,907.82	1,900.71	1,679.87	794.39	1,808.76
ILLINOIS	8,570.70	47	2,637.77	1,875.20	904.13	619.57	2,534.03
Indiana	9,038.43	41	3,035.58	1,845.33	848.02	672.40	2,637.09
IOWA	9,315.67	35	3,106.61	2,099.04	778.83	624.45	2,706.74
Kansas	10,180.27	26	3,009.34	1,660.03	1,072.39	2,039.34	2,399.18
Kentucky.	13,197.90	7	3,419.04	2,189.78	1,725.17	2,121.21	3,742.70
Louisiana.	11,738.34	13	2,874.90	3,328.11	1,608.22	1,037.31	2,889.81
Maine	11,024.05	18	3,683.21	2,851.20	1,306.65	853.70	2,329.28
Maryland.	16,672.74	3	3,311.41	2,501.30	4,593.79	2,605.24	3,661.00
Massachusetts	12,592.89	9	2,812.04	3,413.73	2,441.70	688.18	3,237.25
MICHIGAN	9,199.15	38	3,278.50	2,081.96	654.27	485.47	2,698.95
MINNESOTA	8,366.58	49	2,691.02	1,984.92	556.28	635.07	2,499.31
Mississippi	10,588.38	22	3,297.28	2,652.63	898.43	1,016.65	2,723.39
Missouri	11,746.36	12	3,209.44	2,338.07	2,171.07	1,222.36	2,805.42
Montana	10,873.52	20	3,440.27	2,970.88	828.17	1,207.35	2,426.86
Nebraska	9,051.87	40	2,988.06	1,920.21	715.49	976.13	2,451.98
Nevada	7,321.11	50	2,682.81	1,370.74	891.35	719.00	1,657.20
New Hampshire	8,610.37	46	3,269.36	1,755.49	1,090.30	668.48	1,826.73
New Jersey.	9,211.90	37	2,823.48	1,758.07	1,164.29	634.43	2,831.63
New Mexico	13,577.73	6	3,219.07	3,263.54	3,641.68	1,344.23	2,109.22
New York	10,437.87	24	2,776.85	3,256.44	716.44	719.19	2,968.96
North Carolina	9,515.69	34	3,105.35	2,107.80	638.72	1,609.72	2,054.10
North Dakota.	12,929.83	8	3,278.44	3,326.42	1,018.83	1,610.89	3,695.25
Ohio	9,227.12	36	3,045.91	2,114.94	765.34	604.59	2,696.35
Oklahoma	10,256.30	25	3,351.19	2,093.86	899.62	1,486.25	2,425.38
Oregon	8,868.03	45	3,152.66	2,269.46	534.33	670.44	2,241.13
Pennsylvania	11,488.70	16	3,421.26	2,315.41	1,523.53	692.99	3,535.51
Rhode Island	11,172.13	17	3,166.59	2,994.62	951.39	946.99	3,112.54
South Carolina	10,070.16	28	3,443.10	1,775.10	1,766.64	998.39	2,086.93
South Dakota.	11,676.28	14	3,223.58	2,763.70	1,121.27	1,265.76	3,301.97
Tennessee	10,851.62	21	3,327.39	2,220.96	1,597.93	604.67	3,100.67
Texas	8,976.73	43	2,402.92	1,774.63	1,614.38	1,190.13	1,994.67
Utah	8,518.87	48	2,180.12	1,804.24	1,359.83	1,155.91	2,018.78
Vermont	11,833.69	10	3,207.26	3,803.34	1,488.86	1,157.10	2,177.13
Virginia.	17,008.19	2	3,537.60	1,528.25	7,291.27	2,638.68	2,012.39
Washington	10,474.69	23	3,046.03	2,189.80	1,493.16	1,715.89	2,029.82
West Virginia.	11,608.56	15	4,177.45	2,682.25	961.98	1,045.01	2,741.87
WISCONSIN	9,647.65	32	2,959.83	2,108.68	1,724.12	514.58	2,340.44
Wyoming.	11,019.09	19	2,916.81	3,999.34	1,010.22	1,258.41	1,834.32
UNITED STATES* . .	$10,459.69		$2,935.25	$2,187.11	$1,604.73	$1,099.28	$2,633.32

*Totals include the 50 states and District of Columbia. U.S. Outlying Areas are excluded.

Source: U.S. Department of Commerce, U.S. Census Bureau, *Consolidated Federal Funds Report for Fiscal Year 2010: State and County Areas,* September 2011.

FEDERAL REVENUE DISTRIBUTED
TO STATE AND LOCAL GOVERNMENTS
By State, Fiscal Year 2009-10

State	Per Capita Amount	Per Capita Rank	Intergovernmental Revenue (in thousands) to State Government	Intergovernmental Revenue (in thousands) to Local Government	Total	Percent of all State and Local General Revenue
Alabama	$2,044	26	$8,840,961	$940,975	$9,781,936	29.0%
Alaska	4,586	1	2,955,497	318,975	3,274,472	23.3
Arizona.	2,110	21	12,337,706	1,188,372	13,526,078	32.1
Arkansas	2,162	19	5,961,108	356,667	6,317,775	31.2
California	1,989	29	62,958,004	11,300,054	74,258,058	22.8
Colorado	1,441	48	6,294,236	983,068	7,277,304	18.4
Connecticut	1,903	32	6,217,632	588,654	6,806,286	20.6
Delaware.	2,278	15	1,976,903	72,466	2,049,369	23.9
District of Columbia	6,490	—	—	3,926,319	3,926,319	38.0
Florida	1,518	47	24,996,716	3,617,268	28,613,984	21.0
Georgia.	1,782	41	15,938,771	1,370,189	17,308,960	27.4
Hawaii	2,072	24	2,586,608	240,089	2,826,697	23.1
Idaho	1,796	38	2,659,457	161,250	2,820,707	28.1
ILLINOIS	1,730	43	18,956,139	3,254,513	22,210,652	23.0
Indiana	1,663	46	10,276,593	516,181	10,792,774	23.3
IOWA	2,337	14	6,535,811	592,149	7,127,960	27.3
Kansas	1,698	45	4,580,934	274,345	4,855,279	21.3
Kentucky.	2,244	17	9,117,626	635,616	9,753,242	31.6
Louisiana.	3,161	5	13,174,285	1,189,579	14,363,864	35.4
Maine	2,527	11	3,201,555	153,072	3,354,627	30.1
Maryland.	1,991	28	10,162,959	1,361,318	11,524,277	23.6
Massachusetts	2,257	16	13,126,642	1,689,596	14,816,238	24.0
MICHIGAN	2,126	20	19,320,406	1,675,998	20,996,404	27.5
MINNESOTA	2,042	27	9,930,013	916,858	10,846,871	23.4
Mississippi.	3,088	6	8,645,642	522,474	9,168,116	37.9
Missouri	2,046	25	11,444,588	824,041	12,268,629	29.9
Montana	2,751	10	2,498,169	227,362	2,725,531	33.8
Nebraska.	1,903	33	3,146,417	335,397	3,481,814	23.7
Nevada	1,256	50	2,758,834	637,705	3,396,539	18.9
New Hampshire	1,764	42	2,138,110	185,257	2,323,367	24.0
New Jersey.	1,791	40	14,753,302	1,016,296	15,769,598	18.9
New Mexico	3,253	3	6,065,367	651,566	6,716,933	37.8
New York	2,871	8	49,619,082	6,067,724	55,686,806	23.5
North Carolina	1,834	36	15,350,128	2,182,364	17,532,492	26.0
North Dakota.	2,805	9	1,687,395	204,101	1,891,496	27.2
Ohio	2,100	22	21,953,202	2,281,111	24,234,313	27.2
Oklahoma	2,219	18	7,892,192	449,517	8,341,709	30.6
Oregon	2,074	23	6,843,589	1,115,227	7,958,816	26.7
Pennsylvania	1,904	31	21,116,037	3,080,401	24,196,438	24.3
Rhode Island	2,892	7	2,851,196	193,692	3,044,888	30.8
South Carolina	1,722	44	7,499,023	484,586	7,983,609	23.9
South Dakota.	2,403	13	1,766,695	194,982	1,961,677	32.7
Tennessee	1,921	30	11,321,262	891,092	12,212,354	30.2
Texas	1,795	39	40,779,780	4,540,784	45,320,564	26.0
Utah	1,819	37	4,369,605	678,730	5,048,335	26.4
Vermont	3,161	4	1,902,523	75,998	1,978,521	32.3
Virginia.	1,352	49	9,221,138	1,627,797	10,848,935	18.5
Washington.	1,862	35	10,890,811	1,666,850	12,557,661	23.2
West Virginia.	2,481	12	4,353,106	247,551	4,600,657	31.5
WISCONSIN	1,901	34	10,229,562	586,215	10,815,777	23.8
Wyoming.	3,962	2	2,093,364	142,933	2,236,297	27.7
UNITED STATES	$2,016		$555,296,681	$68,435,323	$623,732,004	24.9%

Sources: U.S. Department of Commerce, U.S. Census Bureau, "State and Local Government Finances: 2009-10", at:
http://www.census.gov/govs/estimate/ and "Annual Estimates of the Resident Population for the United States, Regions,
States, and Puerto Rico: April 1, 2010 to July 1, 2012 (NST-EST2012-01)", at:
http://www.census.gov/popest/states/NST-ann-est.html. Per capita amounts, percentages, and rankings calculated by
Wisconsin Legislative Reference Bureau.

FEDERAL AIDS TO WISCONSIN
Fiscal Years 2010-11 and 2011-12
(In Thousands)

Agency Administering Aid	Federal Aid Received by Wisconsin 2011-12	2010-11	Disbursed to Local Governments 2011-12	2010-11	Aid to Individuals and Organizations 2011-12	2010-11
Administration, Department of . .	$402,439	$408,042	$168,938	$246,782	$132,450	$9,232
Agriculture, Trade and Consumer Protection, Department of	14,931	17,133	—	—	—	—
Arts Board	32	871	—	—	—	480
Child Abuse and Neglect Prevention Board	1,260	360	—	—	880	643
Children and Families, Department of	650,669	679,741	77,907	77,746	473,645	546,524
Clean Water Fund Program*	62,387	73,391	62,387	73,391	—	—
Commerce, Department of.	(33,609)	175,566	(12,868)	31,398	(107,076)	112,171
Corrections, Department of	2,803	2,758	—	—	—	—
Government Accountability Board	1,754	447	—	—	—	—
Health and Family Services, Department of	—	—	124,130	125,449	—	—
Health Services, Department of . .	5,790,567	6,669,285	—	—	5,362,587	6,300,211
Higher Educational Aids Board . .	25	1,580	—	—	—	1,593
Historical Society	1,223	1,078	—	—	—	—
Insurance, Office of the Commissioner of.	1,120	412	—	—	—	—
Justice, Department of	15,193	16,332	7,895	8,254	1,427	1,227
Military Affairs, Department of . .	62,781	63,863	15,981	20,882	313	433
Natural Resources, Department of	98,626	83,815	8,005	6,885	—	—
People with Developmental Disabilities, Board for	1,204	1,194	—	—	586	528
Public Instruction, Department of .	849,252	920,092	738,560	820,711	56,858	57,295
Public Lands Board	67	43	67	43	—	—
Public Service Commission	1,186	1,650	—	—	—	—
Regulation and Licensing, Department of	1,645	173	—	—	—	—
Revenue, Department of	11	—	—	—	—	—
State Fair Park Board	—	1	—	—	—	—
Supreme Court	747	760	—	—	—	—
Technical College System Board .	28,110	32,221	23,941	28,280	1,163	1,125
Tourism, Department of	999	—	—	—	585	—
Transportation, Department of. . .	845,444	1,148,921	170,465	209,453	3,580	4,081
University of Wisconsin System. .	1,859,744	1,836,679	—	—	—	1,035,942
Veterans Affairs, Department of . .	2,456	2,287	—	—	—	—
Workforce Development, Department of	235,677	263,318	—	—	97,624	104,508
TOTAL.	$10,898,743	$12,402,013	$1,385,408	$1,649,274	$6,024,622	$8,175,992

Note: Aid is not necessarily disbursed in the same fiscal year in which it is received by the agency. In some cases, aid is received as reimbursement for previous expenditures.

*Federal aid received by Wisconsin for Clean Water Fund (Environmental Improvement Program, DOA) also includes safe drinking water loan program appropriations.

Source: Wisconsin Department of Administration, State Controller's Office, *Annual Fiscal Report – Appendix*, October 2011 and October 2012.

STATE AND LOCAL PUBLIC DEBT, BY STATE
State Fiscal Years Ending Between July 1, 2009 and June 30, 2010

State	Debt Outstanding at End of Fiscal Year (in thousands)			Per Capita Debt Outstanding		Per Capita Interest		Interest as %	
	Total	State	Local	Amount	Rank	on Debt	Rank	of Debt	Rank
Alabama	$27,665,258	$8,785,245	$18,880,013	$5,781.18	42	$236.77	37	4.10%	19
Alaska	10,189,586	6,380,597	3,808,989	14,268.21	3	559.67	2	3.92	23
Arizona.	49,961,736	13,960,248	36,001,488	7,790.50	26	323.19	21	4.15	14
Arkansas	13,700,124	4,246,826	9,453,298	4,689.27	47	162.56	48	3.47	38
California	403,984,771	148,929,107	255,055,664	10,819.61	7	413.08	9	3.82	27
Colorado	50,727,291	16,709,540	34,017,751	10,049.60	12	456.69	6	4.54	4
Connecticut	40,826,112	30,215,550	10,610,562	11,418.30	5	513.18	5	4.49	5
Delaware	7,798,668	5,515,150	2,283,518	8,667.19	18	394.24	13	4.55	3
District of Columbia	10,330,553	—	10,330,553	17,077.78	—	699.18	—	4.09	—
Florida	150,579,163	41,324,398	109,254,765	7,993.11	23	256.07	34	3.20	45
Georgia	52,445,684	13,788,833	38,656,851	5,400.00	44	153.83	49	2.85	48
Hawaii	12,634,409	7,700,654	4,933,755	9,267.12	16	356.03	15	3.84	26
Idaho	6,123,748	3,872,453	2,251,295	3,897.74	50	169.46	46	4.35	7
ILLINOIS	135,991,102	61,411,694	74,579,408	10,589.57	8	452.85	7	4.28	11
Indiana	51,139,488	23,634,564	27,504,924	7,878.98	24	299.90	26	3.81	28
IOWA	14,951,113	5,140,385	9,810,728	4,901.68	46	193.24	42	3.94	22
Kansas	28,925,832	6,478,228	22,447,604	10,116.96	11	435.99	8	4.31	9
Kentucky	41,809,644	14,393,269	27,416,375	9,617.55	15	411.68	10	4.28	10
Louisiana	35,158,279	17,442,967	17,715,312	7,735.01	27	397.80	11	5.14	1
Maine	8,910,606	6,034,227	2,876,379	6,712.93	34	276.13	30	4.11	17
Maryland	42,542,143	24,474,671	18,067,472	7,353.01	33	305.41	23	4.15	13
Massachusetts	97,253,899	73,939,716	23,314,183	14,835.54	2	607.46	1	4.09	20
MICHIGAN	77,302,267	32,146,344	45,155,923	7,826.38	25	303.12	24	3.87	24
MINNESOTA	45,365,514	11,682,878	33,682,636	8,542.35	19	353.20	16	4.13	15
Mississippi	13,834,120	6,467,833	7,366,287	4,657.84	48	165.40	47	3.55	34
Missouri	44,522,972	20,421,226	24,101,746	7,425.80	32	271.86	32	3.66	31
Montana	5,992,979	4,400,044	1,592,935	6,047.66	39	229.96	38	3.80	29
Nebraska	13,872,229	2,330,277	11,541,952	7,579.87	29	177.36	45	2.34	50
Nevada	28,190,455	4,435,774	23,754,681	10,424.37	10	333.94	20	3.20	46
New Hampshire . . .	10,992,420	8,347,216	2,645,204	8,347.78	20	386.00	14	4.62	2
New Jersey	98,049,914	60,968,300	37,081,614	11,142.55	6	395.35	12	3.55	35
New Mexico	16,842,825	8,739,878	8,102,947	8,152.73	22	252.33	35	3.10	47
New York	316,667,489	129,529,501	187,137,988	16,327.10	1	542.42	3	3.32	41
North Carolina	51,831,576	18,853,155	32,978,421	5,421.58	43	225.90	39	4.17	12
North Dakota	4,467,955	2,198,282	2,269,673	6,622.83	37	286.93	29	4.33	8
Ohio	76,278,871	30,003,599	46,275,272	6,611.12	38	273.11	31	4.13	16
Oklahoma	18,696,692	9,963,419	8,733,273	4,972.28	45	182.94	44	3.68	30
Oregon	33,994,612	13,510,005	20,484,607	8,856.61	17	302.98	25	3.42	40
Pennsylvania	122,318,518	44,737,622	77,580,896	9,617.96	14	349.99	17	3.64	32
Rhode Island	12,197,342	9,498,115	2,699,227	11,588.62	4	515.52	4	4.45	6
South Carolina	38,092,072	15,770,780	22,321,292	8,214.62	21	270.04	33	3.29	43
South Dakota	5,464,956	3,483,142	1,981,814	6,692.35	35	238.09	36	3.56	33
Tennessee	38,352,539	5,835,113	32,517,426	6,032.71	40	200.32	40	3.32	42
Texas	249,881,304	42,033,571	207,847,733	9,894.93	13	346.31	18	3.50	37
Utah	18,386,132	6,477,933	11,908,199	6,624.49	36	182.98	43	2.76	49
Vermont	4,665,743	3,492,873	1,172,870	7,454.35	31	298.08	27	4.00	21
Virginia	61,775,699	25,046,936	36,728,763	7,698.91	28	295.92	28	3.84	25
Washington.	71,055,560	27,478,320	43,577,240	10,537.76	9	345.53	19	3.28	44
West Virginia.	10,771,691	7,144,323	3,627,368	5,808.82	41	200.28	41	3.45	39
WISCONSIN	43,090,155	22,318,551	20,771,604	7,570.75	30	311.16	22	4.11	18
Wyoming.	2,470,229	1,514,359	955,870	4,375.54	49	153.64	50	3.51	36
UNITED STATES	$2,829,074,037	$1,113,207,691	$1,715,866,346	$9,145.81		$341.77		3.74%	

Sources: U.S. Department of Commerce, U.S. Census Bureau, "State and Local Government Finances by Level of Government and by State: 2009-10", at: http://www.census.gov/govs/local/ [April 22, 2013] and "Annual Estimates of the Population for the United States, Regions, States, and Puerto Rico: April 1, 2010 to July 1, 2011", at: http://www.census.gov/popest/data/historical/2010s/vintage_2011/index.html (July 1, 2010, estimate used in calculations). Per capita values and rankings calculated by Wisconsin Legislative Reference Bureau.

PUBLIC INDEBTEDNESS IN WISCONSIN
Outstanding State Indebtedness, May 31, 2013
(In Thousands)

Type of Debt[1]	Tax Supported Debt		Revenue Supported Debt[2]	Total
	General Fund	Segregated Funds[3]		
General Obligations – State of Wisconsin	$5,011,179	$1,213,593	$1,816,162	$8,040,933

[1]Amendment of the state constitution in April 1969 permitted direct state borrowing. Previously, debt was incurred through public, nonstock, nonprofit building corporations.

[2]Revenue supported debt includes debt that is issued with initial expectation that revenues and other proceeds from the operation of the programs or facilities financed will amortize the debt without recourse to the general fund. Includes dormitories, food service, and intercollegiate athletic facilities; certain facilities on the State Fair grounds; and capital equipment.

[3]Includes the Transportation Fund and certain administrative facilities for the Wisconsin Department of Natural Resources.

Source: Wisconsin Department of Administration, Division of Executive Budget and Finance, departmental data, June 2013.

Selected Data on State Indebtedness, 1970 – 2011

Calendar Year	Outstanding State Indebtedness (Dec. 31)		As Percent of State Assessed Value	Annual Debt Limitation[1,2]	Actual Debt Incurred[1]	Debt as Percent of Limitation
	Total[1]	Per Capita				
1970	$646,414	$146.31	1.86%	$260,929	$156,810	60.1%
1975	1,078,215	235.47	1.84	439,124	217,600	49.6
1980	1,916,177	407.18	1.77	813,604	123,500	15.2
1985	2,410,628	507.93	1.96	922,661	440,955	47.8
1990	2,781,071	568.49	1.97	1,060,277	484,099	45.7
1995	3,305,471	643.46	1.64	1,511,536	368,322	24.4
1996	3,468,447	670.36	1.60	1,627,078	353,295	21.7
1997	3,604,798	693.23	1.55	1,748,057	404,310	23.1
1998	3,751,542	718.41	1.51	1,867,462	475,485	25.5
1999	3,942,659	750.92	1.48	1,999,256	482,360	24.1
2000	4,270,718	796.18	1.49	2,147,411	538,795	25.1
2001	4,452,626	824.26	1.42	2,343,628	485,645	20.7
2002	4,682,045	860.67	1.40	2,514,949	481,000	19.1
2003	4,794,398	876.17	1.33	2,705,327	499,030	18.5
2004	5,116,439	929.59	1.31	2,933,909	664,435	22.6
2005	5,445,615	983.67	1.27	3,209,502	571,990	17.8
2006	5,898,647	1,061.48	1.26	3,517,374	891,285	25.3
2007	5,893,590	1,052.05	1.18	3,734,403	483,280	12.9
2008	6,146,978	1,092.21	1.19	3,857,955	493,635	12.8
2009	6,481,078	1,146.08	1.27	3,839,340	542,765	14.1
2010	7,407,431	1,302.52	1.49	3,719,281	809,293	21.8
2011	7,878,628	1,384.16	1.62	3,651,482	816,260	22.4

[1]In thousands.

[2]An aggregate debt limit is derived for each calendar year through a formula specified in Section 18.05, Wisconsin Statutes.

Source: Wisconsin Department of Administration, Division of Executive Budget and Finance, departmental data, June 2013.

State Revenue Bond Indebtedness, May 31, 2013
(In Thousands)

Program Funded	Amount Authorized	Amount Issued	Amount Outstanding
Student loans.	$295,000	$215,000	—
Veterans mortgage loans.	280,000	90,055	—
Transportation facilities and highway projects	3,351,547	4,806,699[1]	$1,916,288
Health education loans.	92,000	129,230[2]	—
Property tax deferral loans.	10,000	—	—
Clean water	2,716,300	2,219,115[3]	822,940
Petroleum environmental cleanup	436,000	600,480[4]	188,610
TOTAL.	$7,180,847	$8,060,579	$2,927,838

Note: Revenue bonds are issued for purposes and amounts specifically authorized by the legislature. This debt is not a legal obligation of the state and is not subject to existing debt limitations.

[1]Includes $1,651,247,036 par amount of refunding bonds that do not count against the authorization.

[2]Includes $48,002,520 par amount of refunding bonds that do not count against the authorization.

[3]Includes $649,165,000 par amount of refunding bonds that do not count against the authorization.

[4]Includes $212,930,000 par amount of refunding bonds and $550,000 par amount for issuance expenses that do not count against the authorization.

Source: Wisconsin Department of Administration, Division of Executive Budget and Finance, departmental data, June 2013.

PUBLIC INDEBTEDNESS IN WISCONSIN–Continued
State Authority Indebtedness (In Thousands)

	Total Outstanding Indebtedness of State Authorities	
Wisconsin Health and Educational Facilities Authority.	$9,111,666*	(6/30/13)
Wisconsin Housing and Economic Development Authority	$1,903,820	(12/31/12)

*Preliminary amount; audit pending.
Source: Data provided by Authorities, June 2013.

Wisconsin Local Governments, 1965 – 2011 (In Millions)

	Calendar years, ending December 31							
	1965	1975	1985	1995	2000	2005	2010	2011
Counties	$192.5	$261.0	$532.5	$1,221.6	$1,449.2	$1,753.7	$2,444.8	$2,404.2
Cities	548.1	598.7	1,320.4	2,082.8	2,797.8	3,718.5	4,468.2	4,498.3
Villages	22.5	69.8	227.6	418.7	700.0	1,098.0	1,440.1	1,480.0
Towns	9.2	26.2	75.2	193.8	281.0	308.5	374.6	339.8
TOTAL[1]	$772.3	$955.7	$2,155.7	$3,916.9	$5,228.0	$6,878.8	$8,727.7	$8,722.3

Wisconsin K-12 and Technical College Districts (In Millions)

	Fiscal years, ending June 30							
	1965	1975	1985	1995	2000	2005	2010	2011
School districts.	$336.6	$798.7	$448.7	$2,104.9	$4,314.1	$5,335.5	$4,833.3	$4,670.9
Technical College districts[2] . . .	—	97.2	64.7	192.8	329.1	461.4	510.2	595.5
TOTAL[1]	$336.6	$895.9	$513.4	$2,297.7	$4,643.2	$5,796.9	$5,343.4	$5,266.4

Note: Long-term indebtedness includes issues maturing more than one year after date of issue that constitute an obligation of the taxable property in the issuing district.
[1]Detail may not add to total due to rounding.
[2]Technical College districts (previously called Vocational, Technical and Adult Education districts) were included within the municipal bonding statute provisions by Chapter 47, Laws of 1967.
Sources: Wisconsin Department of Revenue, Bureau of Local Financial Assistance, *Indebtedness 1981* and previous issues; *County and Municipal Revenues and Expenditures, 2011* and previous issues; departmental data from Wisconsin Department of Revenue, Wisconsin Department of Public Instruction, and the Wisconsin Technical College System Board (June 2013).

ANNUAL APPROPRIATION OBLIGATIONS
Outstanding, May 31, 2013
(In Thousands)

	Amount Issued	Amount Outstanding
General Fund Annual Appropriation Bonds	$3,387,740	$3,259,490
Master Lease Obligations	169,415	47,295
TOTAL.	$3,557,155	$3,306,785

Note: Appropriation obligations are not general obligations of the state, and they do not constitute "public debt" of the state as that term is used in the Wisconsin Constitution and in the Wisconsin Statutes. The payment of the principal of, and interest on appropriation obligations is subject to annual appropriation. The state is not legally obligated to appropriate any amounts for payment of debt service on the appropriation obligations, and if it does not do so, it incurs no liability to the owners of the appropriation obligations.
Source: Wisconsin Department of Administration, Division of Executive Budget and Finance, departmental data, June 2013.

WISCONSIN GENERAL PROPERTY TAX LEVIES
By Type of Property and Municipality, 2011

Type of Property	Towns	Villages	Cities	Totals
Real estate.	$3,198,390,802	$1,709,258,531	$5,213,851,572	$10,121,500,905
Residential	2,514,748,614	1,302,598,228	3,474,665,512	7,292,012,354
Commercial	182,813,329	331,910,192	1,535,676,215	2,050,399,736
Manufacturing	28,675,386	65,436,422	198,322,631	292,434,440
Forest lands	133,086,854	1,758,853	575,533	135,421,240
Agricultural	42,480,523	803,573	515,922	43,800,018
Ag forest	50,577,557	543,904	260,411	51,381,872
Undeveloped	31,037,808	1,226,150	669,362	32,933,319
Other land and improvements	214,970,732	4,981,209	3,165,986	223,117,927
Personal Property	36,853,877	40,397,446	186,067,041	263,318,364
Furniture, fixtures, equipment	9,049,074	18,084,258	93,053,080	120,186,412
Machinery, tools, patterns	17,322,333	16,108,459	60,578,956	94,009,748
Boats and other watercraft	135,050	20,149	197,248	352,447
All other personal property	10,347,386	6,184,581	32,237,757	48,769,724
Total general property taxes	$3,235,244,739	$1,749,655,971	$5,399,918,660	$10,384,819,370
Total state tax credit	274,084,951	125,691,235	347,623,844	747,400,030
TOTAL EFFECTIVE TAXES.	$2,961,159,788	$1,623,964,736	$5,052,294,816	$9,637,419,340

Note: The sums of some columns and rows may differ slightly from the reported totals because the Department of Revenue computes the tax by using the average tax rate of each town, village, and city.
Source: Wisconsin Department of Revenue, Division of State and Local Finance, Bureau of Local Government Services, *Town, Village, and City Taxes – 2011: Taxes Levied 2011 – Collected 2012*, 2012.

WISCONSIN GENERAL PROPERTY ASSESSMENTS
AND TAX LEVIES
1900 – 2011

Calendar Year	Full Value Assessment of All Property Amount (in millions)	Full Value Assessment of All Property Percent Change	Total State and Local Property Taxes Levied Amount (in millions)	Total State and Local Property Taxes Levied Percent Change	State Property Tax Relief Amount (in millions)	Average Full Value Tax Rate Per $1,000 Rate	Average Full Value Tax Rate Per $1,000 Percent Change	Average Net Rate Per $1,000 After State Relief Rate	Average Net Rate Per $1,000 After State Relief Percent Change
1900	$630	—	$19	—	—	$30.75	—	—	—
1910	2,743	—	31	—	—	11.18	—	—	—
1920	4,571	—	96	—	—	21.06	—	—	—
1930	5,896	—	121	—	—	20.49	—	—	—
1940	4,354	—	110	—	—	25.26	—	—	—
1950	9,201	—	226	—	—	24.52	—	—	—
1960	18,844	—	481	—	—	25.55	—	—	—
1970	34,790	—	1,179	—	$140	33.88	—	—	—
1980	108,480	—	2,210	—	309	20.37	—	—	—
1990	141,370	—	4,388	—	319	31.04	—	$28.78	—
1995	201,538	—	5,739	—	319	28.47	—	26.89	—
1996	216,944	7.6%	5,378	–6.3%	469	24.78	–13.0%	22.62	–15.9%
1997	233,074	7.4	5,636	4.8	469	24.18	–2.8	22.16	–2.0
1998	248,995	6.8	5,975	6.0	469	23.99	–0.8	22.11	–0.2
1999	266,568	7.1	6,191	3.6	469	23.22	–3.2	21.46	–2.9
2000	286,321	7.4	6,605	6.7	469	23.07	–0.7	21.43	–0.2
2001	312,484	9.1	7,044	6.7	469	22.54	–2.3	21.04	–1.8
2002	335,326	7.3	7,364	4.5	469	21.96	–2.6	20.56	–2.3
2003	360,710	7.6	7,687	4.4	469	21.31	–3.0	20.01	–2.7
2004	391,188	8.4	8,151	6.0	469	20.83	–2.2	19.64	–1.9
2005	427,934	9.4	8,327	2.2	469	19.46	–6.6	18.36	–6.5
2006	468,983	9.6	8,706	4.6	593	18.56	–4.6	17.30	–5.8
2007	497,920	6.2	9,251	6.3	672	18.58	0.1	17.23	–0.4
2008	514,394	3.3	9,667	4.5	747	18.79	1.2	17.34	0.6
2009	511,912	–0.5	10,106	4.5	747	19.74	5.0	18.28	5.4
2010	495,904	–3.1	10,365	2.6	747	20.90	5.9	19.39	6.1
2011	486,864	–1.8	10,385	0.2	747	21.33	2.1	19.79	2.1

Source: Wisconsin Department of Revenue, Division of State and Local Finance, Bureau of Property Tax, *Town, Village, and City Taxes – 2011: Taxes Levied 2011 – Collected 2012*, 2012, and previous issues. Percentages calculated by Wisconsin Legislative Reference Bureau.

TOTAL MUNICIPAL PROPERTY TAXES LEVIED IN WISCONSIN
1960 – 2011

Year Levied	Total Taxes (in millions)	Percentage of Taxes Levied by Property Type Residential	Commercial	Manufacturing	Agricultural	Personal[1]	Other[2]
1960	$481.4	47.5%	13.5%	10.7%	11.2%	16.5%	0.6%
1965	664.1	48.4	14.4	10.3	10.6	15.8	0.6
1970	1,179.0	47.3	15.2	10.4	9.7	16.9	0.5
1975	1,601.3	50.5	16.8	5.7	10.1	16.2	0.7
1980	2,210.0	57.7	16.2	4.8	12.5	7.5	1.3
1985	3,203.5	58.9	17.7	4.7	12.4	4.8	1.6
1990	4,388.2	60.4	20.2	4.1	8.4	5.5	1.3
1991	4,732.7	60.9	20.2	4.0	8.1	5.5	1.3
1992	5,169.5	61.7	19.8	4.0	7.9	5.4	1.2
1993	5,438.0	62.7	19.5	3.9	7.5	5.2	1.2
1994	5,572.1	63.8	19.2	3.7	7.1	5.0	1.1
1995	5,738.9	64.8	18.8	3.6	6.7	4.9	1.1
1996	5,378.0	65.7	18.9	3.6	3.6	4.6	3.7
1997	5,635.9	66.2	18.7	3.6	3.3	4.5	3.7
1998	5,975.0	66.5	18.7	3.6	2.9	4.5	3.9
1999	6,190.9	67.3	18.8	3.7	2.7	3.5	4.0
2000	6,604.5	67.9	18.9	3.7	1.7	3.4	4.3
2001	7,043.7	68.1	19.0	3.6	1.6	3.4	4.4
2002	7,363.6	69.0	18.9	3.5	0.8	3.2	4.6
2003	7,687.3	69.7	18.8	3.4	0.6	2.9	4.7
2004	8,150.8	70.3	18.8	3.2	0.5	2.7	4.5
2005	8,326.7	71.0	18.7	3.0	0.5	2.6	4.2
2006	8,706.4	71.4	18.7	2.8	0.5	2.5	4.2
2007	9,250.3	71.4	18.9	2.7	0.4	2.4	4.2
2008	9,677.1	70.9	19.2	2.7	0.4	2.6	4.2
2009	10,105.7	70.4	19.6	2.7	0.4	2.6	4.3
2010	10,364.6	70.4	19.6	2.8	0.4	2.6	4.3
2011	10,384.8	70.2	19.7	2.8	0.4	2.5	4.3

[1]An exemption for "Line A" business property was phased in beginning in 1977. "Line A" property was completely exempted by 1981.

[2]Beginning in 1996, "Other" includes agricultural property not considered agricultural land for the purposes of use value assessment.

Sources: Wisconsin Department of Revenue, Division of State and Local Finance, *Town, Village, and City Taxes – 2011: Taxes Levied 2011 – Collected 2012*, 2012 and previous issues. For 1980 and earlier, *Property Tax, 1981* and previous issues. 1960 and 1965 data are from Wisconsin Department of Taxation. Percentages calculated by Wisconsin Legislative Reference Bureau. Row totals may not add to 100.0% due to rounding.

GENERAL PROPERTY ASSESSMENTS, TAXES AND RATES
By County, 2011

County	Full Value Assessment[1]	Total Property Tax[2]	State Property Tax Credit[3]	Average Full Value Tax Rate per $1,000[4] Gross	Net
Adams	$2,562,649,600	$52,688,165	$3,847,611	$20.56	$19.06
Ashland	1,236,153,400	26,121,345	1,739,876	21.13	19.72
Barron	3,689,962,000	75,762,020	5,810,442	20.53	18.96
Bayfield	2,597,027,000	37,161,684	2,938,931	14.31	13.18
Brown	18,157,652,100	407,328,373	28,170,157	22.43	20.88
Buffalo	1,002,774,500	21,148,517	1,475,775	21.09	19.62
Burnett	2,687,878,400	38,999,625	3,510,924	14.51	13.20
Calumet	3,487,176,500	76,837,622	4,979,266	22.03	20.61
Chippewa	4,551,285,800	83,413,558	6,268,780	18.33	16.95
Clark	1,780,505,000	40,597,130	2,604,084	22.80	21.34
Columbia.	5,027,683,600	107,545,807	7,967,407	21.39	19.81
Crawford.	1,097,300,500	27,792,443	1,713,183	25.33	23.77
Dane	50,195,950,100	1,144,647,852	86,330,931	22.80	21.08
Dodge	6,040,549,400	134,042,935	9,315,435	22.19	20.65
Door	7,169,424,900	92,425,501	5,943,905	12.89	12.06
Douglas	3,406,405,900	66,373,791	4,806,923	19.48	18.07
Dunn	2,683,462,100	64,723,386	4,481,102	24.12	22.45
Eau Claire	6,727,328,500	148,648,643	10,451,231	22.10	20.54
Florence	598,773,400	10,957,346	912,520	18.30	16.78
Fond du Lac	6,965,437,800	153,295,213	10,286,351	22.01	20.53
Forest.	1,148,144,400	19,178,281	1,585,987	16.70	15.32
Grant.	2,806,187,600	62,515,827	4,442,538	22.28	20.69
Green.	2,625,141,200	64,089,227	4,739,160	24.41	22.61
Green Lake.	2,452,746,200	44,247,308	3,093,093	18.04	16.78
Iowa	1,871,063,700	45,929,803	3,211,019	24.55	22.83
Iron.	964,537,800	14,996,904	1,107,362	15.55	14.40
Jackson	1,445,753,300	30,476,526	1,944,653	21.08	19.73
Jefferson	6,583,895,500	141,099,811	10,143,223	21.43	19.89
Juneau	1,965,179,800	45,806,223	3,588,420	23.31	21.48
Kenosha	13,717,171,600	323,735,417	22,367,000	23.60	21.97
Kewaunee	1,470,715,400	31,216,674	1,974,410	21.23	19.88
La Crosse	7,879,057,100	192,264,918	13,197,648	24.40	22.73
Lafayette	1,024,432,700	25,691,102	1,761,083	25.08	23.36
Langlade	1,685,875,900	32,300,084	2,214,341	19.16	17.85
Lincoln	2,381,381,100	47,407,523	3,160,223	19.91	18.58
Manitowoc	5,374,268,200	116,554,008	7,301,142	21.69	20.33
Marathon.	9,724,225,700	224,946,769	15,019,541	23.13	21.59
Marinette.	3,647,215,600	66,440,086	5,472,219	18.22	16.72
Marquette	1,591,144,600	30,103,990	2,229,963	18.92	17.52
Menominee	318,242,300	6,559,502	465,043	20.61	19.15
Milwaukee	61,099,028,600	1,668,397,809	104,886,428	27.31	25.59
Monroe.	2,695,033,800	60,537,061	3,597,251	22.46	21.13
Oconto	3,599,182,300	66,236,509	4,949,390	18.40	17.03
Oneida	6,960,385,400	91,558,276	8,037,848	13.15	12.00
Outagamie	13,314,090,400	286,187,005	19,114,325	21.50	20.06
Ozaukee	10,706,477,500	193,486,183	16,720,288	18.07	16.51
Pepin	560,656,800	13,122,104	1,023,495	23.40	21.58
Pierce.	2,826,286,000	64,264,435	4,945,131	22.74	20.99
Polk	4,228,266,700	86,612,443	7,416,260	20.48	18.73
Portage	4,932,212,000	103,017,534	7,290,217	20.89	19.41
Price	1,466,118,800	27,680,857	2,056,010	18.88	17.48
Racine	15,041,416,400	329,272,706	22,151,874	21.89	20.42
Richland	1,084,104,900	22,865,739	1,716,743	21.09	19.51
Rock	9,861,961,100	243,540,532	14,721,572	24.69	23.20
Rusk	1,177,463,300	22,487,933	2,032,117	19.10	17.37
St. Croix	7,335,670,300	142,124,207	12,130,597	19.37	17.72
Sauk	6,713,421,100	133,251,623	9,167,459	19.85	18.48
Sawyer	3,580,824,900	41,764,203	3,875,193	11.66	10.58
Shawano	3,013,221,300	60,004,129	4,244,275	19.91	18.51
Sheboygan	8,894,480,600	195,917,124	13,657,796	22.03	20.49
Taylor	1,323,231,700	28,732,609	1,681,054	21.71	20.44
Trempealeau	1,806,682,000	40,494,287	2,744,173	22.41	20.89
Vernon	1,771,843,200	40,976,187	2,847,169	23.13	21.52
Vilas	7,344,418,900	76,611,076	7,191,310	10.43	9.45
Walworth	14,662,709,200	262,454,528	21,469,392	17.90	16.44
Washburn	2,519,185,900	40,218,133	3,456,195	15.96	14.59
Washington.	13,469,321,100	247,073,829	19,369,052	18.34	16.91
Waukesha	49,552,562,500	903,889,571	80,434,595	18.24	16.62
Waupaca	3,827,191,900	84,299,867	5,672,659	22.03	20.54
Waushara.	2,487,427,900	46,679,548	3,365,216	18.77	17.41
Winnebago.	11,969,341,000	276,147,106	16,086,022	23.07	21.73
Wood.	4,698,255,100	108,843,278	6,776,022	23.17	21.72
TOTAL.	$486,864,232,800	$10,384,819,370	$747,400,030	$21.33	$19.79

[1]Reflects actual market value of all taxable general property, as determined by the Wisconsin Department of Revenue independent of locally assessed values, which vary substantially from full value – from 75.49% in Village of Melvina, Monroe County, to 133.71% in Town of Hammond, St. Croix County. The value may reflect corrections for prior year errors, therefore understating values for the current year if prior year values were overstated, and vice-versa.

[2]Includes taxes and special charges levied by schools, counties, cities, villages, towns, special purpose districts, and the State of Wisconsin. It does not include special assessments or other charges.

[3]Total amount of general property tax credit paid by the state to taxing districts and credited to taxpayers on their tax bills.

[4]A county's average tax rate per $1,000 of assessed valuation (determined by dividing total taxes by equalized value and multiplying by 1,000) is the preferred figure for comparison purposes, rather than the general local property tax rate, because the average is based on full market value. Net tax rate per $1,000 reflects the effect of state property tax relief.

Source: Wisconsin Department of Revenue, Division of State and Local Finance, *Town, Village, and City Taxes – 2011: Taxes Levied 2011 – Collected 2012*, 2012.

HIGHLIGHTS OF TRANSPORTATION IN WISCONSIN

Roads — As of January 1, 2013, there were 115,095 miles of roads in Wisconsin. The total included 11,766 miles of state trunk highways, 19,865 miles of county trunk highways, and 81,711 miles of local roads. Seventy-nine percent (90,905 miles) of Wisconsin's road system is surfaced at bituminous grade or higher, with the remaining 21% being gravel or soil-surfaced, sealcoated, graded and drained, or unimproved.

Motor Vehicles and Drivers — Over the decades, the total number of motor vehicle registrations has increased from 819,718 in 1930 to 5,551,411 in 2012. Of 4,142,823 drivers licensed in 2011, 535,939 (12.9%) were 16-24 years old; 702,615 (17.0%) were 25-34 years old; 672,006 (16.2%) were 35-44 years old; 819,178 (19.8%) were 45-54 years old; and 707,532 (17.1%) were 55-64 years old. Of the drivers age 65 and older, 78,562 (1.9%) were 85 years and above.

In 2011, 112,516 single- or multi-vehicle traffic crashes were reported, including 515 fatal and 28,965 injury crashes. The 45-54-year-old age group had the highest percentage of drivers in crashes with 19.8%, followed by the 55-64-year-old age group with 17.1%. Of 397 drivers killed in fatal crashes, 371 were tested for blood alcohol content (BAC); 18 registered a BAC of 0.001 to 0.079 and 130 registered a BAC of 0.08 or above. Vehicle miles traveled in 2011 totaled 58.6 billion; the fatality rate for that year was 0.96 per 100 million vehicle miles, and the fatal crash rate was 0.88.

Mass Transit — As of January 2013, there were 21 urban bus systems operating in Wisconsin (15 publicly owned, 5 contracted, and 1 privately managed). There were 13 rural/intercity systems (8 publicly owned and 5 privately contracted). Shared-ride taxi service was available in 49 municipalities.

Statewide urban bus systems showed an increase in usage in 2011 with 52.3 million revenue miles traveled and 77.5 million revenue passengers.

Air Carriers — In 2012, there were 734 airports operating in Wisconsin. Of these, 98 were publicly owned and 458 privately owned, 35 of which were open to the public. The remaining specialized facilities included heliports (149) and seaplane bases (29). In 2012, certificated air carriers carried 5,371,283 passengers and transported 107,498,209 pounds of cargo.

Railroads — From 1920 to 2011, the number of railroads operating in Wisconsin decreased from 35 to 10. Over the same period, railroad road mileage declined from 7,546 to 3,402 miles. Rail freight traffic rose from 9.1 billion ton-miles in 1920 to 24.9 billion ton-miles in 2011. Freight traffic revenue was $971 million in 2011.

Harbors — In 2011, there were 10 active lake harbors on Lake Michigan and Lake Superior, which handled 40.7 million short tons of commodities. The Duluth-Superior harbor reported the greatest amount of commerce at 35.1 million short tons.

The following tables present selected data. Consult footnoted sources for more detailed information about transportation.

WISCONSIN AIRPORTS
By Type, 2006 – 2012

Type of Airport	Number of Airports						
	2006	2007	2008	2009	2010	2011	2012
Airports open to the public	129	130	130	130	131	133	133
Privately owned airports open to the public	(34)	(34)	(34)	(34)	(35)	(35)	(35)
Publicly owned airports	(95)	(96)	(96)	(96)	(96)	(98)	(98)
Private use airports.	403	415	415	414	413	419	423
Heliports	139	141	146	148	148	148	149
Seaplane bases	26	28	27	27	27	28	29
TOTAL.	697	714	718	719	719	728	734

Source: Wisconsin Department of Transportation, *Wisconsin Aviation Activity 2012*, and previous issues,
　　at: http://www.dot.wisconsin.gov/travel/air/docs/2012-aviation-activity.pdf [April 19, 2013].

WISCONSIN AIRPORT USAGE
BY CERTIFIED AIR CARRIERS, 2010 – 2012*

Airport (location)	2010		2011		2012	
	Passengers	Cargo (lbs.)	Passengers	Cargo (lbs.)	Passengers	Cargo (lbs.)
General Mitchell International						
(Milwaukee)	4,760,170	93,805,543	4,671,976	89,657,125	3,780,315	81,013,968
Dane County Regional (Madison). . .	766,953	12,998,952	741,365	13,541,051	810,953	14,159,526
Austin Straubel International						
(Green Bay)	349,733	185,186	352,157	211,115	295,028	133,999
Outagamie County Regional						
(Appleton)	272,471	10,847,630	242,346	10,739,041	228,737	10,797,313
Central Wisconsin (Mosinee)	156,251	600,198	135,965	561,085	120,637	521,788
La Crosse Municipal (La Crosse) . . .	109,962	—	102,559	—	101,925	—
Chippewa Valley Regional						
(Eau Claire)	18,369	—	19,097	—	22,335	—
Rhinelander-Oneida County						
(Rhinelander)	25,137	1,022,676	26,764	896,317	11,353	871,615
TOTAL.	6,459,046	119,460,185	6,292,229	115,605,734	5,371,283	107,498,209

Note: Data from the most recent year is preliminary.

*Wisconsin has eight scheduled air carrier airports. A certified air carrier is an airline that is registered by the Federal Aviation Administration.

Source: Wisconsin Department of Transportation, *Wisconsin Aviation Activity 2012*, at: http://www.dot.wisconsin.gov/travel/air/docs/2012-aviation-activity.pdf [April 22, 2013].

RAILROAD MILEAGE, USAGE, AND REVENUE IN WISCONSIN
1920 – 2011

Year	No. of Railroads	Mileage Operated in Wisconsin[1]		Freight Traffic (in thousands)			Passenger Traffic (in thousands)		
		Road[2]	Track[3]	Tons	Ton-Miles[4]	Revenue (in thousands)	Passengers	Miles[5]	Revenue (in thousands)
1920	35	7,546	11,615	100,991	9,052,084	$92,826	20,188	960,569	$28,646
1930	27	7,231	11,583	83,672	6,908,656	78,747	4,799	466,154	14,071
1940	22	6,646	10,484	87,980	6,910,647	69,941	3,952	445,938	8,201
1950	20	6,337	10,000	121,576	10,850,178	141,762	5,575	646,353	14,933
1960	18	6,195	9,625	93,475	9,096,855	134,065	3,127	383,457	9,800
1970	15	5,965	9,127	97,130	13,432,055	191,764	1,463	138,572	4,264
1980[6]	21	5,192	7,990	101,008	14,727,522	453,977	174	1,122	54
1990	15	4,415	6,125	116,099	14,436,776	455,541	112	783	63
2000	12	3,548	4,956	151,573	21,321,266	580,678	NA	NA	NA
2001	13	3,699	5,107	158,881	25,922,949	700,258	NA	NA	NA
2002	12	3,688	5,095	NA	21,417,016	704,167	NA	NA	NA
2003	11	3,450	4,643	118,387	26,092,960	667,736	NA	NA	NA
2004	11	3,417	4,610	106,719	27,408,816	713,951	NA	NA	NA
2005	11	3,417	4,614	109,214	27,966,142	715,206	NA	NA	NA
2006	12	3,432	4,634	114,609	28,024,633	717,421	NA	NA	NA
2007	12	3,430	4,585	109,210	22,942,906	737,119	NA	NA	NA
2008	12	3,417	4,560	109,207	22,906,152	784,264	NA	NA	NA
2009	10	3,417	4,571	107,146	20,456,847	762,649	NA	NA	NA
2010	10	3,408	4,594	108,206	21,394,264	771,203	NA	NA	NA
2011	10	3,402	4,606	106,527	24,891,634	971,369	NA	NA	NA

NA – Not available.

[1]In order to avoid duplication, mileage shown is exclusive of trackage rights.

[2]Road mileage is the measurement of stone roadbed in miles.

[3]Track mileage is the measurement of track (2 steel rails) on roadbeds in miles.

[4]A ton-mile is the movement of one ton (2,000 pounds) of cargo over the distance of one mile.

[5]Passenger miles are the combination of the number of passengers carried on Wisconsin trains and the miles traveled by the passengers while within Wisconsin boundaries.

[6]Intercity passenger service operated by Amtrak after May 1, 1971.

Source: Office of the Wisconsin Commissioner of Railroads, departmental data, June 2013.

HIGHWAY MILEAGE, BY COUNTY AND SYSTEM
January 1, 2013

	Total All Systems	State Trunk System	County Trunk System	Local Roads (City, Village, Town)	Other Roads (Parks, Forests)
Adams	1,454.38	91.45	226.80	1,136.13	—
Ashland	1,151.48	120.58	91.35	876.60	62.95
Barron	1,996.01	141.76	291.00	1,563.25	—
Bayfield	2,191.58	155.18	172.81	1,778.16	85.43
Brown	2,325.37	184.48	359.38	1,773.51	8.00
Buffalo	1,041.61	148.02	317.95	572.54	3.10
Burnett	1,573.28	106.36	220.05	1,205.01	41.86
Calumet	868.20	94.12	133.28	640.80	—
Chippewa	2,141.19	210.27	489.30	1,420.18	21.44
Clark	2,188.83	157.37	300.89	1,683.59	46.98
Columbia	1,737.98	277.96	357.28	1,102.74	—
Crawford	1,086.85	182.67	132.70	766.48	5.00
Dane	4,119.94	401.57	526.87	3,191.25	0.25
Dodge	2,065.66	237.99	540.57	1,276.93	10.17
Door	1,268.25	101.56	294.11	872.58	—
Douglas	2,092.93	161.38	337.20	1,497.12	97.23
Dunn	1,755.47	205.75	425.29	1,124.43	—
Eau Claire	1,589.83	150.40	420.71	1,000.78	17.94
Florence	527.20	66.84	49.12	378.27	32.97
Fond du Lac	1,786.48	201.58	384.41	1,200.49	—
Forest	1,079.88	152.41	109.06	776.71	41.70
Grant	2,125.95	258.85	310.87	1,556.23	—
Green	1,259.25	122.54	277.89	858.82	—
Green Lake	702.60	69.97	228.89	403.74	—
Iowa	1,317.43	169.72	364.72	782.99	—
Iron	816.99	114.00	66.89	552.33	83.77
Jackson	1,475.36	185.97	231.24	1,037.17	20.98
Jefferson	1,439.51	179.54	257.31	1,002.66	—
Juneau	1,534.80	191.87	234.20	1,092.92	15.81
Kenosha	1,091.56	116.89	257.59	717.08	—
Kewaunee	828.19	61.80	219.06	547.33	—
La Crosse	1,195.35	159.13	285.33	750.89	—
Lafayette	1,159.02	126.92	272.15	759.95	—
Langlade	1,155.02	143.36	271.11	732.88	7.67
Lincoln	1,321.60	155.55	270.01	868.79	27.25
Manitowoc	1,661.56	155.06	283.62	1,222.88	—
Marathon	3,373.16	276.99	613.52	2,476.17	6.48
Marinette	2,351.13	154.30	334.02	1,638.65	224.16
Marquette	860.00	87.11	237.27	535.55	0.07
Menominee	156.29	40.73	36.51	79.05	—
Milwaukee	3,018.22	253.69	145.34	2,617.49	1.70
Monroe	1,680.23	238.26	344.35	1,060.79	36.83
Oconto	2,042.58	149.75	314.08	1,541.29	37.46
Oneida	1,690.49	159.50	171.21	1,350.08	9.70
Outagamie	1,998.77	186.77	346.46	1,465.54	. —
Ozaukee	940.61	82.29	155.70	702.62	—
Pepin	467.47	48.52	154.72	259.23	5.00
Pierce	1,316.38	164.19	248.65	892.55	10.99
Polk	1,974.87	159.15	331.37	1,484.35	—
Portage	1,913.63	157.36	433.10	1,308.05	15.12
Price	1,424.94	155.14	220.05	1,049.75	—
Racine	1,330.56	155.92	164.08	1,010.56	—
Richland	1,130.05	150.18	296.56	683.09	0.22
Rock	2,094.88	251.77	212.95	1,609.36	20.80
Rusk	1,223.49	105.26	255.18	859.61	3.44
St. Croix	1,936.41	204.14	337.83	1,389.44	5.00
Sauk	1,861.35	220.71	307.30	1,292.74	40.60
Sawyer	1,578.81	161.33	228.94	1,096.04	92.50
Shawano	1,725.61	180.03	294.12	1,251.46	—
Sheboygan	1,578.94	166.46	450.54	944.58	17.36
Taylor	1,448.07	110.22	248.32	1,080.69	8.84
Trempealeau	1,357.59	176.31	292.08	888.20	1.00
Vernon	1,827.15	214.03	285.21	1,152.08	175.83
Vilas	1,472.58	136.27	204.17	1,132.14	—
Walworth	1,625.89	216.70	193.22	1,121.83	94.14
Washburn	1,318.36	137.10	198.72	982.54	—
Washington	1,536.18	186.86	185.93	1,163.39	—
Waukesha	3,058.01	232.77	399.55	2,425.69	—
Waupaca	1,663.18	198.40	333.79	1,130.99	—
Waushara	1,330.67	132.32	333.46	864.89	—
Winnebago	1,582.34	168.69	220.33	1,180.71	12.61
Wood	2,079.09	185.75	325.39	1,265.25	302.70
STATE	115,094.57	11,765.84	19,865.03	81,710.65	1,753.05

Source: Wisconsin Department of Transportation, Division of Transportation Investment Management, departmental data, June 2013.

WISCONSIN ROAD MILEAGE, BY SYSTEM AND SURFACE TYPE
January 1, 2013

Type of Road System	Miles	Percent	Surface Type	Miles	Percent
State trunk highways.	11,766	10.2%	Bituminous or higher	90,905	79.0%
County trunk highways	19,865	17.3	Gravel or soil-surfaced.	16,129	14.0
City streets	13,752	11.9	Sealcoat	5,363	4.7
Village streets	5,980	5.2	Graded and drained	2,577	2.2
Town roads.	61,979	53.9	Unimproved	121	0.1
Park, forest, and other roads	1,753	1.5	TOTAL.	115,095	100.0%
TOTAL.	115,095	100.0%			

Source: Wisconsin Department of Transportation, Division of Transportation Investment Management, departmental data, June 2013.

MOTOR VEHICLES IN WISCONSIN, BY TYPE
1930 – 2012

Fiscal Year (ending June 30)	Total	Autos	Trucks*	Trailers, Semitrailers	Motor Homes	Buses	Motor-cycles	Mopeds
1930	819,718	700,251	115,883	—	—	554	3,030	—
1935	722,797	597,197	116,912	5,634	—	498	2,556	—
1940	874,652	741,583	123,742	5,144	—	675	3,508	—
1945	828,425	676,978	139,591	6,484	—	1,489	3,883	—
1950	1,157,221	921,194	209,083	14,124	—	2,465	10,355	—
1955	1,369,636	1,108,084	227,367	21,643	—	3,337	9,205	—
1960	1,598,693	1,303,679	246,353	31,502	—	5,184	11,975	—
1965	1,867,223	1,517,397	269,771	44,017	—	7,218	28,820	—
1970	2,205,662	1,762,681	317,096	64,065	—	8,178	53,642	—
1975	2,737,164	2,096,694	425,854	91,609	—	11,897	111,110	—
1980	3,417,748	2,509,904	558,840	102,256	17,071	13,775	205,786	10,116
1985	3,372,029	2,310,024	765,852	72,289	17,195	10,325	176,023	20,321
1990	3,834,608	2,456,175	1,045,583	123,061	21,095	15,081	149,268	24,345
1995	4,285,753	2,464,358	1,391,374	207,042	22,554	15,593	161,762	23,070
2000	4,703,294	2,405,408	1,813,385	214,344	24,427	15,587	160,920	17,977
2005	5,226,584	2,347,042	2,216,863	342,879	22,598	12,478	249,979	34,745
2006	5,326,157	2,361,853	2,281,988	364,024	22,406	13,174	246,307	36,405
2007	5,428,629	2,357,616	2,333,538	396,229	21,147	13,516	266,036	40,547
2008	5,499,872	2,381,911	2,370,655	410,737	20,209	10,736	260,220	45,404
2009	5,532,953	2,340,991	2,396,470	417,031	20,039	12,685	291,164	54,573
2010	5,525,794	2,333,029	2,416,295	426,092	19,615	13,376	269,316	48,071
2011	5,564,794	2,300,243	2,445,056	434,782	18,792	13,745	296,808	55,368
2012	5,551,411	2,274,596	2,473,072	447,195	18,535	14,169	274,553	49,291

*"Trucks" includes minivans and sport utility vehicles.

Sources: Wisconsin Secretary of State, *Biennial Report – 1928-30;* Wisconsin Highway Commission, *Biennial Reports – 1933-35, 1938-40;* Wisconsin Motor Vehicle Department, *Wisconsin Motor Vehicle Registrations – Fiscal Years 1944-45 through 1964-65*; Wisconsin Department of Transportation, *Wisconsin Motor Vehicle Registrations – Fiscal Year 1979-80, 1980,* and previous issues, and *Wisconsin Transportation Facts* (periodical); departmental data, February 2013.

WISCONSIN MOTOR VEHICLE CRASHES
Statistical Summary, 2001 – 2011

Year	Total Licensed Drivers	Crashes[1] Total	Fatal	Injury	Persons Killed	Persons Injured	Miles Traveled (in millions)	Fatality Rate[2]	Fatal Crash Rate[3]
2001	3,835,549	125,403	684	39,358	764	58,279	57,266	1.33	1.19
2002	3,839,930	129,072	723	39,634	805	57,776	58,745	1.37	1.23
2003	3,933,924	131,191	748	39,413	836	56,882	59,617	1.40	1.25
2004	3,993,348	128,308	714	38,451	784	55,258	60,398	1.31	1.18
2005	4,049,450	125,174	700	37,515	801	53,462	60,018	1.33	1.17
2006	4,066,273	117,877	659	35,296	712	50,236	59,401	1.20	1.11
2007	4,075,764	125,123	655	36,048	737	50,676	59,493	1.24	1.10
2008	4,079,562	125,103	542	33,766	587	46,637	57,462	1.02	0.94
2009	4,085,833	109,991	488	29,907	542	41,589	58,157	0.93	0.84
2010	4,114,622	108,808	517	29,380	562	40,889	59,420	0.95	0.87
2011	4,142,823	112,516	515	28,965	565	40,144	58,554	0.96	0.88

[1]A motor vehicle crash is defined as an event caused by a single variable or chain of variables. Property damage threshold for a reportable crash was raised from $500 to $1,000, effective January 1, 1996.
[2]Per 100-million vehicle miles traveled.
[3]Per 1,000 licensed drivers.
Source: Wisconsin Department of Transportation, *2011 Wisconsin Traffic Crash Facts,* March 2013, and previous issues.

Fatal Crashes on Wisconsin Highways and Roads, 2001 – 2011

Year	Total	Interstate	State	County	Local
2001	684	35	286	167	196
2002	723	44	310	171	198
2003	748	46	317	174	211
2004	714	47	298	155	214
2005	700	42	284	163	211
2006	659	34	294	128	203
2007	655	43	259	143	210
2008	542	32	225	119	166
2009	488	27	221	93	147
2010	517	32	230	105	150
2011	515	34	236	113	132

Source: Wisconsin Department of Transportation, *2011 Wisconsin Traffic Crash Facts,* March 2013, and previous issues.

Drivers in Fatal Crashes – Age and BAC of Drivers Killed, 2011

Age of Drivers	All Drivers	Drivers Killed	Tests of Drivers Killed[1] Total	Negative	Positive	Blood Alcohol Concentration (BAC) 0.001- 0.079	Over 0.08
14 years and under . . .	2	2	2	2	0	0	0
15 years	4	1	1	1	0	0	0
16 years	10	5	5	5	0	0	0
17 years	9	4	4	3	1	0	1
18 years	18	5	5	4	1	0	1
19 years	20	9	9	6	3	0	3
20 years	18	7	7	6	1	1	0
21 years	23	12	12	6	5	0	5
22 years	21	12	12	7	5	1	4
23 years	16	5	5	1	4	0	4
24 years	25	13	13	3	9	0	9
25-34 years.	129	67	66	26	40	2	38
35-44 years.	123	60	59	28	31	6	25
45-54 years.	137	65	60	25	34	6	28
55-64 years.	107	58	52	42	10	1	9
65-74 years.	53	29	26	22	3	1	2
75-84 years.	46	31	24	23	1	0	1
85 and over.	18	12	9	9	0	0	0
TOTAL.	811[2]	397	371	219	148	18	130

Note: Drivers include motorcycle and moped drivers.
[1]Blood Alcohol Concentration (BAC) measures the level of alcohol in a person's bloodstream. The prohibited BAC for Operating While Intoxicated (OWI) is 0.08%.
[2]Includes 32 of unknown age.
Source: Wisconsin Department of Transportation, *2011 Wisconsin Traffic Crash Facts,* March 2013.

WISCONSIN MOTOR VEHICLE CRASHES–Continued
Motorcycle Crashes, 2001 – 2011

Year	Total Registered Cycles	Total	Fatal	Injury	Property Damage	Total	No Helmet or Unknown	Helmet
			Cycle Crashes				Cyclist Fatalities*	
2001	201,143	2,285	69	1,928	288	70	53	14
2002	198,495	2,184	73	1,794	317	78	59	15
2003	225,181	2,512	98	2,099	315	100	74	24
2004	221,982	2,423	81	2,015	327	80	60	18
2005	239,938	2,680	91	2,277	312	92	69	22
2006	291,534	2,441	88	2,065	288	93	69	24
2007	322,505	2,788	102	2,331	355	106	70	26
2008	327,938	2,829	86	2,318	425	87	66	19
2009	355,487	2,345	82	1,912	351	82	51	27
2010	343,878	2,426	97	1,959	370	98	72	23
2011	361,893	2,331	79	1,877	375	80	69	5

*Number of cyclists killed includes both drivers and passengers.

Source: Wisconsin Department of Transportation, *2011 Wisconsin Traffic Crash Facts,* March 2013, and previous issues.

Drivers Involved in Crashes, By Age Group, 2011

Age of Drivers	Total Licensed Drivers Number	Age Group as Percent of Total Drivers	Drivers Involved in Crashes* Number	Percent of Total Drivers in Crashes	Fatal	Injury	Property Damage
14 years and under . . .	0	0.0%	59	—	2	25	32
15 years	0	0.0	202	—	4	50	148
16 years	33,615	0.8	3,795	11.3%	10	1,046	2,739
17 years	48,923	1.2	4,592	9.4	9	1,325	3,258
18 years	56,178	1.4	5,193	9.2	18	1,527	3,648
19 years	58,656	1.4	4,930	8.4	20	1,465	3,445
20 years	63,731	1.5	4,870	7.6	18	1,452	3,400
21 years	67,167	1.6	4,944	7.4	23	1,485	3,436
22 years	68,451	1.7	4,632	6.8	21	1,384	3,227
23 years	68,849	1.7	4,461	6.5	16	1,308	3,137
24 years	70,369	1.7	4,162	5.9	25	1,177	2,960
25-34 years.	702,615	17.0	33,720	4.8	129	9,922	23,669
35-44 years.	672,006	16.2	27,336	4.1	123	7,836	19,377
45-54 years.	819,178	19.8	28,680	3.5	137	8,170	20,373
55-64 years.	707,532	17.1	20,354	2.9	107	5,821	14,426
65-74 years.	401,463	9.7	9,196	2.3	53	2,643	6,500
75-84 years.	225,528	5.4	4,791	2.1	46	1,505	3,240
85 and over.	78,562	1.9	1,373	1.7	18	438	917
Unknown.	0	0.0	15,660	—	32	2,133	13,495
TOTAL.	4,142,823	100.0%	182,950	NA	811	50,712	131,427

NA – Not applicable.

*Figure indicates the number of times a driver in this age group was involved in a crash. If a driver had more than one crash, the driver would be counted more than once.

Source: Wisconsin Department of Transportation, *2011 Wisconsin Traffic Crash Facts,* March 2013.

WISCONSIN MOTOR VEHICLE CRASHES—Continued
Possible Contributing Circumstances, 2011

Circumstance by category	All Crashes				Urban Crashes				Rural Crashes			
	Total	Fatal	Injury	Property Damage	Total	Fatal	Injury	Property Damage	Total	Fatal	Injury	Property Damage
DRIVER												
Inattentive driving	21,961	98	7,085	14,778	13,726	17	4,159	9,550	8,235	81	2,926	5,228
Failure to control	17,503	182	5,736	11,585	6,833	25	1,902	4,906	10,670	157	3,834	6,679
Failure to yield right-of-way	17,149	66	6,428	10,655	12,771	25	4,665	8,081	4,378	41	1,763	2,574
Speed too fast for conditions	13,214	78	3,594	9,542	5,236	16	1,218	4,002	7,978	62	2,376	5,540
Following too closely	9,357	10	3,117	6,230	7,050	2	2,345	4,703	2,307	8	772	1,527
Driver condition	5,722	80	2,644	2,998	2,793	17	1,118	1,658	2,929	63	1,526	1,340
Disregarded traffic control	4,379	30	1,942	2,407	3,461	9	1,504	1,948	918	21	438	459
Improper turn	2,865	5	574	2,286	2,094	1	381	1,711	771	3	193	575
Unsafe backing	2,768	1	169	2,598	1,863	1	117	1,745	905		52	853
Exceeding speed limit	2,501	84	1,076	1,341	1,406	26	551	829	1,095	58	525	512
Left of center	1,929	70	777	1,082	611	6	197	408	1,318	64	580	674
Improper overtake	1,640	8	370	1,262	999	2	183	814	641	6	187	448
Physically disabled	96	2	51	43	54	1	26	27	42	1	25	16
Other	4,578	40	1,253	3,285	3,290	17	877	2,396	1,288	23	376	889
HIGHWAY												
Snow/ice/wet	31,766	101	8,292	23,373	16,800	24	4,297	12,479	14,966	77	3,995	10,894
Visibility obscured	1,498	8	540	950	949	2	326	621	549	6	214	329
Construction zone	1,341	7	448	886	753	7	245	501	588		203	385
Loose gravel	480	6	238	236	83		45	38	397	6	193	198
Other debris	480	1	118	361	162		45	117	318	1	73	244
Narrow shoulder	261	1	102	158	81		34	47	180	1	68	111
Rough pavement	136	2	39	96	54		15	39	82	2	24	57
Low shoulder	96		36	58	12		5	7	84		31	51
Soft shoulder	95	2	38	57	7	2	2	5	88		36	52
Debris from prior crash	91	1	26	63	19		6	11	72	1	20	52
Sign obscured or missing	56	2	22	33	42		16	26	14	2	6	7
Narrow bridge	19		5	12	7		3	4	12		2	8
Other	754	3	233	518	371		98	273	383	3	135	245
VEHICLE												
Tires	1,307	11	390	906	473	2	124	347	834	9	266	559
Brakes	1,092	4	394	694	695	1	247	447	397	3	147	247
Steering	329		101	228	186		46	140	143		55	88
Other disabled	125	1	41	84	71	1	27	44	54		14	40
Head lamps	81	1	33	47	49		17	31	32	1	16	16
Suspension	76		21	55	34		9	25	42		12	30
Turn signals	69		23	45	23		8	15	46		15	30
Disabled prior to crash	54	3	23	28	35	1	14	20	19	2	9	8
Tail lamps	42	2	16	24	9		1	8	33	2	15	16
Stop lamps	36	1	12	23	18		5	13	18	1	7	10
Mirrors	33		5	28	22		3	19	11		2	9
Other	1,265	14	252	999	656	3	123	530	609	11	129	469

Note: Numbers represent the number of times a possible contributing circumstance was cited and not the number of accidents.

Source: Wisconsin Department of Transportation, *2011 Wisconsin Traffic Crash Facts*, March 2013.

MASS TRANSIT SYSTEMS IN WISCONSIN, BY TYPE
January 2013

Urban Bus	Rural/Commuter Bus	Shared-Ride Taxi[1]	
Appleton	Bay Area Rural Transit	Baraboo	Platteville
Beloit	Dunn County	Beaver Dam	Plover
Eau Claire	Kenosha County[2]	Berlin	Portage
Fond du Lac	Marshfield Shuttle[2]	Black River Falls	Prairie du Chien
Green Bay	Menominee Regional Transit	Chippewa Falls	Prairie du Sac/Sauk City
Janesville	Oneida Indian Reservation	Clark County/Neillsville	Reedsburg
Kenosha	Ozaukee County Express[2]	Clintonville	Rhinelander
La Crosse	Racine Commuter[2]	Door County	Rice Lake
Madison	Rusk County	Edgerton	Richland Center
Manitowoc	Sauk County	Fort Atkinson	Ripon
Merrill	Sawyer County	Grant County	River Falls
Milwaukee County[2]	Verona	Hartford	Shawano
Monona[2]	Washington County Express[2]	Jefferson	Stoughton
Oshkosh		La Crosse County	Sun Prairie
Racine[3]		Lake Mills	Tomah
Sheboygan		Marinette	Viroqua/Westby
Stevens Point		Marshfield	Washington County
Superior[4]		Mauston	Watertown
Waukesha (city)[2]		Medford	Waupaca
Waukesha County[2]		Monroe	Waupun
Wausau		New Richmond	West Bend
		Onalaska	Whitewater
		Ozaukee County	Wisconsin Rapids

[1]Taxi services are privately contracted except for Grant County, the City of Hartford, and Rice Lake, where they are publicly owned and operated.

[2]Privately contracted. (Note: The private service in Waukesha County is an inter-urban service. Waukesha (city) and Waukesha (county) have merged to form Waukesha Metro Transit.)

[3]Privately managed.

[4]Contracted with Duluth Transit Authority.

Source: Wisconsin Department of Transportation, Division of Transportation Investment Management, departmental data, February 2013.

WISCONSIN URBAN TRANSIT SYSTEMS
USAGE AND REVENUE, 1950 – 2011
(In Thousands)

Year	Revenue Miles	Revenue Passengers	Operating Revenue*
1950	53,362	288,996	$22,692
1955	42,807	169,129	23,134
1960	34,950	130,299	20,665
1965	32,330	110,979	20,457
1970	28,371	80,172	22,078
1975	26,119	63,587	22,454
1980	33,943	88,756	29,631
1985	31,829	79,540	39,635
1990	33,685	78,215	39,594
1991	33,820	74,764	45,489
1992	33,941	72,981	45,356
1993	33,954	71,444	46,492
1994	33,996	71,242	48,291
1995	30,734	71,875	50,171
1996	34,306	73,172	54,147
1997	38,222	74,703	55,842
1998	45,064	76,367	57,836
1999	54,585	77,169	58,101
2000	42,447	89,821	58,785
2001	46,755	87,729	60,299
2002	48,322	84,874	64,263
2003	47,753	81,650	61,868
2004	46,696	81,812	65,621
2005	52,163	83,545	67,628
2006	51,700	83,913	72,896
2007	51,748	81,229	77,236
2008	52,439	82,953	83,263
2009	52,488	77,510	82,570
2010	52,579	74,717	87,288
2011	52,316	77,533	NA

NA – Not available.

*As recognized by the Wisconsin Department of Transportation.

Sources: Wisconsin Department of Transportation, Division of Transportation Assistance, Bureau of Transit, *Wisconsin Urban Bus System Annual Report 1989,* and previous issues; departmental data, February 2013.

WISCONSIN HARBOR COMMERCE – 2011

Harbors[1]	Total Tonnage[2]	Crude Inedible Materials (except fuels)	Coal and Lignite	Primary Manufactured Goods	Food and Farm Products	Petroleum and Petroleum Products	Chemicals and Related Products	Manufactured Equipment, Machinery, and Products	Unknown
LAKE SUPERIOR									
Duluth-Superior	35,081,473	19,558,353	13,924,666	276,457	1,251,184	27,632	33,230	3,160	6,791
Ashland	15,763	—	15,743	—	—	—	—	20	—
Bayfield	7,148	280	—	—	—	514	—	6,354	—
La Pointe	6,335	—	—	—	—	514	—	5,821	—
LAKE MICHIGAN									
Milwaukee	2,901,151	1,528,917	587,433	613,852	58,361	109,757	—	2,331	500
Green Bay	2,177,628	1,048,034	713,400	317,504	—	95,927	2,763	—	—
Menominee[3]	324,192	159,608	16,525	147,095	—	—	—	964	—
Manitowoc	211,005	—	24,684	186,321	—	—	—	—	—
Detroit Harbor[4]	5,585	20	—	—	—	1,507	—	—	4,058
Racine	1,600	—	—	—	—	—	—	1,600	—
TOTAL	40,731,860	22,295,212	15,282,451	1,541,229	1,309,545	235,851	35,993	20,250	11,349

Note: Tonnage reported in short tons. One short ton equals 2,000 lbs.

[1]Harbors with reported commerce.

[2]Detail may not add due to rounding.

[3]Includes tonnage handled at Marinette, Wisconsin.

[4]Washington Island.

Source: U.S. Army Corps of Engineers, Navigation Data Center, *Waterborne Commerce Statistics Center, Waterborne Commerce of the United States, Calendar Year 2011,* Part 3, at: http://www.ndc.iwr.usace.army.mil/wcsc/webpub11/Part3_Ports_tonsbycommCY2011.HTM [April 2013].

Political Parties

9

Wisconsin political parties: state organizations and current party platforms

Wisconsin State Capitol from the 200 Block of State Street, 1939

(Wisconsin Historical Society, 1892)

POLITICAL PARTY ORGANIZATION IN WISCONSIN

What Is a Political Party?

A political party is a private, voluntary organization of people with similar political beliefs that vies with other parties for control of government. Political parties help voters select their government officials and create a consensus on the basic principles that direct governmental activities and processes.

Political parties in the United States have traditionally provided an organized framework for the orderly performance of several basic political tasks necessary to representative democracy. Parties act to:

- Provide a stable institution for building coalitions based on shared principles and priorities.
- Recruit and nominate candidates for elective and appointive offices in government.
- Promote the election of the party's slate of candidates.
- Guard the integrity of election procedures and vote canvassing.
- Educate the voters by defining issues, taking policy positions, and formulating programs.

U.S. parties offer a marked contrast to the party apparatus in other nations. In many parts of the world, political parties begin with defined ideologies and programs. Their members are recruited on the basis of these ideas, and there is not much room for disagreement within the ranks. In other cases, parties represent regional interests or ethnic groups. By contrast, parties in the United States are loosely organized groups reflecting a broad spectrum of interests. They are truly populist parties in the sense that they accommodate diversity and are instruments of party activists at the grass roots level. Political ideology, as stated in a party's national platform, is formulated first at the local level and then refined through debate and compromise at meetings representing successively larger geographic areas.

Depending on the time, place, and circumstances, political party labels in the United States may have widely different meanings, and within a single party there may be room for members whose ideologies span a wide political spectrum. Individual Republicans or Democrats, for instance, are often further identified as "liberal", "conservative", "right-wing", "left-wing", or "moderate".

Despite the diversity within a party, specific philosophies are generally associated with the various political parties. In the public's perception, the name of a particular party conjures up a surprisingly distinct set of economic, social, and political principles.

Political Parties in Wisconsin

Throughout its history, the United States has operated with a two-party political structure, rather than single-party or multiparty systems found elsewhere. Although minor parties have always been a part of American politics, few have gained the support necessary to challenge the two dominant parties at the national level. Those that did lasted only briefly, with the predominant exception of the Republican Party, which replaced the Whig Party in the 1850s. The same cannot be said of politics on the state level. In Wisconsin, for example, the Socialist Party regularly sent one or more representatives to the legislature between 1911 and 1937, and the Progressive Party was influential between 1933 and 1947, capturing a plurality of both houses of the 1937 Legislature. Third parties were relatively quiet in Wisconsin in the 1950s, but the last 30 years have seen more activity with more parties officially recognized on the ballot.

Under Wisconsin law, a "recognized political party" is a political party that qualifies for a separate ballot or column on the ballot, based on receiving at least 1% of the votes for a statewide office at the previous November election or through acquiring the required number of petition signatures (10,000 electors, including at least 1,000 electors residing in each of at least three separate congressional districts). At the beginning of 2013, Wisconsin had three recognized political parties: Constitution, Democratic, and Republican.

The Wisconsin Statutes define a political party in Section 5.02 (13) as a state committee that is legally registered with the Government Accountability Board and "all county, congressional, legislative, local and other affiliated committees authorized to operate under the same name". It must be a body "organized exclusively for political purposes under whose name candidates appear on a ballot at any election".

The delegates from the political party's local units meet in an annual state convention to draft or amend the party's state platform (a statement of its principles and objectives), select national committee members, elect state officers, consider resolutions, and conduct other party business. Every four years, party delegates from throughout the United States meet in a national convention to nominate their candidates for president and vice president and to adopt a national platform for the next four years. In Wisconsin, the slates of national convention delegates are usually based on the April presidential preference primary vote.

Statutory and Voluntary Organizations

Wisconsin law provides that each major political party must have certain local officers and committees, but over the years, these statutory organizations have been merged within the voluntary party organizations that are governed by their own constitutions and bylaws. The actual power is found in the voluntary structures.

In the case of the majority parties, voluntary organizations are composed of dues-paying members, who are affiliated with Wisconsin chapters of the national political parties. Third parties vary in the amount of regional autonomy and/or national control allowed. Given minor organizational differences, voluntary parties operate to tend to their party's interests, collect money to finance campaigns, maintain cooperation between the various county and congressional district organizations, and act as liaison with national parties. (Currently recognized parties and their voluntary organizations are discussed in the party descriptions that follow this introduction.)

The History of Wisconsin's Political Parties

In *How Wisconsin Voted,* Professor James R. Donoghue divided Wisconsin's political history into four eras. From statehood in 1848 until 1855, the Democratic Party was the dominant political party, and the Whig Party provided major opposition. This was a continuation of the party alignment that had prevailed during the state's territorial period.

The second era was one of Republican domination from 1856 to 1900. The birth of the national Republican Party is attributed to a meeting in Ripon, Wisconsin, in 1854. Its founding was based on the conditions and events that eventually led to the Civil War, and within Wisconsin these same circumstances contributed to the rapid growth of the Republican Party and the demise of the Whigs.

The second era ended at the turn of the century with the election of Governor Robert M. La Follette. The third era, from 1900 to 1945, was a time of great stress and change, encompassing the Great Depression and World Wars I and II. Until 1932, the major political battles usually occurred not between two parties, but between two factions of the Republican Party – the conservative "stalwart" Republicans and the "progressive" (La Follette) Republicans. The Democratic Party was in eclipse, and election contests tended to be decided in Republican primary elections.

The third era also saw the high point of third party influence in Wisconsin. The progressive faction formally split from the Republicans to form its own party in 1934. The new Progressive Party won gubernatorial elections in 1936 and 1942 and a plurality in both houses of the legislature in 1936. Declining popularity, however, led to its dissolution in 1946, and Progressive Party leadership urged its members and supporting voters to return to the Republican Party. The period from 1900 to 1937 was also the time of greatest strength for the Socialists.

The fourth era, from 1945 to the present, witnessed a realignment of the major parties. A resurgence of the Democratic Party ended the long Republican domination, turning the state to a more balanced, two-party, competitive system. In the late 1940s, some former Progressives, Socialists, and others began moving into a moribund Democratic Party. This influx both revitalized the party and made it more liberal. In the following decade, the Democrats worked at uniting their party and building their strength at the polls. Meanwhile, the conservative faction solidified its control of the Republican Party with the departure of more liberal-minded Progressives and addition of conservative Democrats fleeing their former party as it became more liberal.

In the years following World War II, the resurgent Democratic Party began seriously challenging the majority Republicans. Steady Democratic growth culminated in the 1957 election of William Proxmire to the U.S. Senate, the first "new" Democrat to win a major statewide election, followed by the election of Gaylord Nelson as governor in 1958. These elections marked the emergence on Wisconsin's political scene of a Democratic Party fully capable of competing successfully with the long dominant Republicans for public office. During this period, third party and independent candidates usually failed to garner any significant support on a statewide level.

The hallmark of contemporary Wisconsin politics is a highly competitive, two-party, issue-oriented system. At the beginning of the 1995 session, Republicans gained control of both houses for the first time since 1969. In 1993, 1995, and 1997, the majority party in the senate shifted during the session. Democrats controlled the senate in 1999 and 2001, while Republicans retained the control of the assembly they had won in the 1994 elections. For the first time since 1982, a Democrat was elected governor in November 2002.

Republicans controlled both the senate and assembly under a Democratic governor from 2003 to 2006. In 2006, Democrats won a majority in the senate. In 2008, they took control of the assembly for the first time since 1994. At the beginning of the 2009 session, Democrats controlled the governor's office, senate, and assembly for the first time since 1986. In 2010, a Republican governor was elected and control of the senate and assembly reverted to the Republicans.

Of the state's major elected partisan officers in January 2013, the Republicans held the positions of governor, lieutenant governor, attorney general, and state treasurer, as well as one U.S. Senate seat, five of the eight congressional seats, and majorities in the state senate and assembly. Democrats filled the position of secretary of state, and held one U.S. Senate seat and three congressional seats.

CONSTITUTION PARTY OF WISCONSIN
July 2013

Headquarters

State Headquarters: P.O. Box 070344, Milwaukee 53207-1918.

Telephone: (877) 201-2441.

State Internet Address: http://wisconsinconstitutionparty.com

State E-mail: cpowchairman@yahoo.com

National Office: P.O. Box 1782, Lancaster, PA 17608.

National Internet Address: http://www.constitutionparty.com/

State Committee – Officers

Chairman: RILEY J. HOOD, Milwaukee.

Vice Chairman: NIGEL BROWN, Janesville.

Chairman of Committees: ANDREW ZUELKE, Ripon.

Secretary: S. KENT STEFFKE, Milwaukee.

Treasurer: RALPH DENSON, Milwaukee.

State Committee – Congressional District Representatives

1st District
  Grant Gillepsie
  vacancy
2nd District
  Mike Tuttle, Newark (township)
  vacancy
3rd District
  Lorraine Decker
  Spring Raine Decker
4th District
  Janice Hood
  vacancy

5th District
  William J. Hemenway, Waukesha
  vacancy
6th District
  Dino Bohlman
  vacancy
7th District
  Larry Oftedahl, Barron
  vacancy
8th District
  Mark Gabriel, Appleton
  Brian Farmer, Appleton

Source: Constitution Party of Wisconsin

Membership. Individual membership in the Constitution Party of Wisconsin is based on statewide affiliation. Anyone who is in good standing with the state party and has paid the annual membership fee may attend the state convention and participate in lesser party committees.

Lesser Committees. Members in congressional districts, state senate and assembly districts, and county and election districts may form party committees affiliated with the state committee. The purpose of the lesser committees is to help build the party and aid its candidates seeking election.

State Committee. The Constitution Party of Wisconsin is headed by a state committee composed of 22 members: 6 state officers and 2 representatives elected by the members in each of the 8 congressional districts. The state officers are the chairman, vice chairman, chairman of committees, secretary, treasurer, and parliamentarian. The state chairman serves as the party's executive and is responsible for the day-to-day operations of the party. The officers are elected in odd-numbered years and serve 2-year terms. The congressional district representatives are elected in caucuses prior to the state convention each year.

CONSTITUTION PARTY OF WISCONSIN PLATFORM
As modified and adopted in Constitution Party National Convention, April 26, 2008
And amended in Constitution Party of Wisconsin State Convention, April 24, 2010

Preamble
The Constitution Party of Wisconsin gratefully acknowledges the blessing of the Lord God as Creator, Preserver, and Ruler of the Universe and of this Nation. It recognizes Jesus Christ as transcendent King over all nations and hereby appeals to Him for aid, comfort, guidance and the protection of His Divine Providence as we work to restore and preserve this nation as a government of the people, by the people, and for the people.

The U.S. Constitution established a republic under God, rather than a democracy.

Our republic is a nation governed by a Constitution, which is rooted in Biblical law, administered by representatives who are constitutionally elected by the citizens.

In a republic governed by Constitutional law, rooted in Biblical law, all life, liberty, and property are protected.

We affirm the principles of inherent individual rights upon which these United States of America were founded:
- That each individual is endowed by his Creator with certain unalienable rights; that among these are the rights to life, liberty, property, and the pursuit of the individual's personal interest;
- That the freedom to own, use, exchange, control, protect, and freely dispose of property is a natural, necessary, and inseparable extension of the individual's unalienable rights;
- That the legitimate function of government is to secure these rights through the preservation of domestic tranquility, the maintenance of a strong national defense, and the promotion of equal justice for all;
- That history makes clear that left unchecked, it is the nature of government to usurp the liberty of its citizens and eventually become a major violator of the people's rights; and
- That, therefore, it is essential to bind government with the chains of the Constitution and carefully divide and jealously limit government powers to those assigned by the consent of the governed.

The Constitution Party of Wisconsin calls on all who love liberty and value their inherent rights to join with us in the pursuit of these goals and in the restoration of these founding principles.

Abortion, Euthanasia, and Bio-research
The Constitution Party of Wisconsin calls upon our state officials to fulfill their obligations as lesser magistrates to uphold the U.S. Constitution and the state constitution by taking immediate action to end the practice of abortion in Wisconsin.

We further call upon our state legislators to amend the Wisconsin Constitution to recognize personhood from the moment of fertilization.

We condemn the practice of so-called "assisted suicide" and call upon our state legislators to resist any and all attempts to legalize euthanasia.

Sanctity of Life
The Declaration of Independence states: "We hold these truths to be self-evident, that all men are created equal, that they are endowed by their Creator with certain unalienable Rights, that among these are Life, Liberty and the pursuit of Happiness."

The Preamble of the Constitution states a purpose of the Constitution to be to: "Secure the Blessings of Liberty to ourselves and our Posterity."

We declare the unalienable right of Life to be secured by our Constitution "to ourselves and our Posterity." Our posterity includes children born and future generations yet unborn. Any legalization of the termination of innocent life of the born or unborn is a direct violation of our unalienable right to life.

The pre-born child, whose life begins at fertilization, is a human being created in God's image. The first duty of the law is to prevent the shedding of innocent blood. It is, therefore, the duty of all civil governments to secure and to safeguard the lives of the pre-born.

To that end, the Constitution of these United States was ordained and established for "ourselves and our posterity." Under no circumstances may the federal government fund or otherwise support any state or local government or any organization or entity, foreign or domestic, which advocates, encourages or participates in the practice of abortion. We also oppose the distribution and use of all abortifacients.

We affirm the God-given legal personhood of all unborn human beings, without exception. As to matters of rape and incest, it is unconscionable to take the life of an innocent child for the crimes of his father.

No government may legalize the taking of the unalienable right to life without justification, including the life of the pre-born; abortion may not be declared lawful by any institution of state or local government — legislative, judicial, or executive. The right to life should not be made dependent upon a vote of a majority of any legislative body.

In addition, Article IV of the Constitution guarantees to each state a republican form of government. Therefore, although a Supreme Court opinion is binding on the parties to the controversy as to the particulars of the case, it is not a political rule for the nation. Roe v. Wade is an illegitimate usurpation of authority, contrary to the law of the nation's Charter and Constitution. It must be resisted by all civil government officials, federal, state, and local, and by all branches of the government — legislative, executive, and judicial.

We affirm both the authority and duty of Congress to limit the appellate jurisdiction of the Supreme Court in all cases of abortion in accordance with the U.S. Constitution, Article III, Section 2.

In office, we shall only appoint to the federal judiciary, and to other positions of federal authority, qualified individuals who publicly acknowledge and commit themselves to the legal personhood of the pre-born child. In addition, we will do all that is within our power to encourage federal, state, and local government officials to protect the sanctity of the life of the pre-born through legislation, executive action, and judicial enforcement of the law of the land.

Further, we condemn the misuse of federal laws against pro-life demonstrators, and strongly urge the repeal of the FACE Acts as an unconstitutional expansion of federal power into areas reserved to the states or people by the Tenth Amendment.

In addition, we oppose the funding and legalization of bio-research involving human embryonic or pre-embryonic cells.

Finally, we also oppose all government "legalization" of euthanasia, infanticide and suicide.

Agricultural Freedom

Every producer of any agricultural product shall be at liberty to sell the product to any consumer, or consumers in aggregate, at any level, stage or condition of processing. We oppose government intrusion into the private and business life of farmers and farming.

Congressional Reform

"The Senators and Representatives ... shall be bound by Oath or Affirmation, to support this Constitution ..."
— U.S. Constitution, Article VI, Clause 3

With the advent of the 17th Amendment, a vital check on Congress was removed. Since then, Congress has usurped power relatively unchecked, where today, very few members of Congress make it through a single session without violating their oath of office to the Constitution.

The Congress of the United States has become an overpaid, overstaffed, self-serving institution. It confiscates taxpayer funds to finance exorbitant and unconstitutionally determined salaries, pensions, and perks. Most members of Congress have become more accountable to the Washington establishment than to the people in their home districts. Both houses of Congress are all too often unresponsive and irresponsible, arrogantly placing themselves above the very laws they enact, and beyond the control of the citizens they have sworn to represent and serve.

We seek to abolish Congressional pensions.

It is time for the American people to renew effective supervision of their public servants, to restore right standards and to take back the government. Congress must once again be accountable to the people and obedient to the Constitution, repealing all laws that delegate legislative powers to regulatory agencies, bureaucracies, private organizations, the Federal Reserve Board, international agencies, the President, and the judiciary.

The U.S. Constitution, as originally framed in Article I, Section 3, provided for U.S. Senators to be elected by state legislators. This provided the states direct representation in the legislative branch so as to deter the usurpation of powers that are Constitutionally reserved to the states or to the people.

The Seventeenth Amendment (providing for direct, popular election of U.S. Senators) took away from state governments their Constitutional role of indirect participation in the federal legislative process.

If we are to see a return to the states those powers, programs, and sources of revenue that the federal government has unconstitutionally taken away, then it is also vital that we repeal the Seventeenth Amendment and return to state legislatures the function of electing the U.S. Senate. In so doing, this would return the U.S. Senate to being a body that represents the legislatures of the several states on the federal level and, thus, a tremendously vital part of the designed checks and balances of power that our Constitution originally provided.

We support legislation to prohibit the attachment of unrelated riders to bills. Any amendments must fit within the scope and object of the original bill.

We support legislation to require that the Congressional Record contain an accurate record of proceedings. Members of Congress are not to be permitted to rewrite the speeches delivered during the course of debates, or other remarks offered from the floors of their respective houses; nor may any additional materials inserted in the Record, except those referred to in the speaker's presentation and for which space is reserved.

Cost of Big Government

James Madison said (Federalist Papers #45):

"The powers delegated by the proposed Constitution to the federal government are few and defined."

—The powers not delegated to the United States by the Constitution, nor prohibited by it to the States, are reserved to the States respectively, or to the people.l (Amendment X).

A legitimate and primary purpose of civil government is to safeguard the God-given rights of its citizens; namely, life, liberty, and property. Only those duties, functions, and programs specifically assigned to the federal government by the Constitution should be funded. We call upon Congress and the President to stop all federal expenditures which are not specifically authorized by the U. S. Constitution, and to restore to the states those powers, programs, and sources of revenue that the federal government has usurped.

Budget considerations are greatly impacted by the ever rising national debt. Interest on the debt is one of the largest expenses of government, and unless the interest is paid, the debt will continue to grow as interest is added to interest. If we are to get rid of the debt, a time needs to be set within which the debt will be funded, and then pay it off within that period. Whatever the payoff period may be, three things must happen within that time:

- The annual reductions have to be made without fail.
- All interest must be paid as it accrues; and
- The government must not spend more than it takes in during the payoff period.

One of the greatest contributors to deficit spending is war. If the country is to get rid of debt, the United States cannot become gratuitously involved in constant wars. Constitutional government, as the founders envisioned it, was not imperial. It was certainly not contemplated that America would police the world at the taxpayers' expense.

We call for the systematic reduction of the federal debt through, but not limited to, the elimination of further borrowing and the elimination of unconstitutional programs and agencies.

We call upon the President to use his Constitutional veto power to stop irresponsible and unconstitutional appropriations, and use his Constitutional authority to refuse to spend any money appropriated by Congress for unconstitutional programs or in excess of Constitutionally imposed tax revenue.

The debt could be more rapidly eliminated if certain lands and other assets currently held by the federal government were sold, and the proceeds applied to the debt. This policy should be employed, and funds from the sale of all such assets should be specifically applied to debt reduction.

We reject the misleading use of the terms "surplus" and "balanced budget" as long as we have public debt. We oppose dishonest accounting practices such as "off-budget items" used to hide unconstitutional spending practices.

We call for an end to the raiding by the federal government of the Social Security, Railroad Retirement and Medicare funds. We believe that over a protracted period the Social Security system may be privatized without disadvantage to the beneficiaries of the system. However, the program has been in place since the 1930s, and workers and their employers were taxed for the program and paid in good faith. The government promised to deliver the benefits, and must meet this commitment.

We call for the abolition of the Civil Service system, which is perceived to confer on government employees a "property right" regarding their jobs.

Crime

The amount of crime in a society is directly related to the level of moral restraint of its citizens. Government is a reflection of that moral restraint, not its legislator. Increasing the amount of moral restraint in our society is not the responsibility of government, but of those called to that mission; namely the family, and the clergy and their congregations. We call upon these to fulfill their mission, renewing the souls of our citizenry, thereby increasing the amount of moral restraint, which will result in a reduction of crime.

We assert that upon completion of his sentence, the person convicted of a crime shall be fully restored to society with full exercise of all rights of citizenship.

Defense

The very purpose of Government, as defined in the 2nd paragraph of the Declaration of Independence, is:

"... to secure these [unalienable] rights, Governments are instituted among Men ...," "that among these are Life, Liberty and the Pursuit of Happiness ...."

To fulfill this obligation, the Preamble of the Constitution states one of the duties specifically delegated to the Federal Government is to "Provide for the common defense."

U.S. Constitution, Article I, Section 8, Clauses 11-16 give Congress further direction and authority in this area, including the power "To raise and support Armies" and "To provide and maintain a Navy."

It is a primary obligation of the federal government to provide for the common defense, and to be vigilant regarding potential threats, prospective capabilities, and perceived intentions of potential enemies.

We oppose unilateral disarmament and dismemberment of America's defense infrastructure. That which is hastily torn down will not be easily rebuilt.

We condemn the presidential assumption of authority to deploy American troops into combat without a declaration of war by Congress, pursuant to Article I, Section 8, of the U.S. Constitution.

Under no circumstances would we commit U.S. forces to serve under any foreign flag or command. We are opposed to any New World Order, and we reject U.S. participation in or a relinquishing of command to any foreign authority.

The goal of U.S. security policy is to defend the national security interests of these United States. Therefore, except in time of declared war, for the purposes of state security, no state National Guard or reserve troops shall be called upon to support or conduct operations in foreign theatres.

We should be the friend of liberty everywhere, but the guarantor and provisioner of ours alone.

We call for the maintenance of a strong, state-of-the-art military on land, sea, in the air, and in space. We urge the executive and legislative branches to continue to provide for the modernization of our armed forces, in keeping with advancing technologies and a constantly changing world situation. We call for the deployment of a fully-operational strategic defense system as soon as possible.

We believe that all defense expenditures should be directly related to the protection of our nation, and that every item of expenditure must be carefully reviewed to eliminate foreign aid, waste, fraud, theft, inefficiency, and excess profits from all defense contracts and military expenditures.

We reject the policies and practices that permit women to train for or participate in combat. Because of the radical feminization of the military over the past two decades, it must be recognized that these "advances" undermine the integrity, morale, and performance of our military organizations by dual qualification standards and forced integration.

We fully support well regulated militias organized at the state level. Further, we fully support and encourage the restoration of unorganized militia at the county and community level in compliance with our patriotic and legal responsibilities as free citizens of these United States.

Under no circumstances should we have unilaterally surrendered our military base rights in Panama. The sovereign right of the United States to the United States territory of the Canal Zone has been jeopardized by treaties between the United States and Panama. Inasmuch as the United States bought both the sovereignty and the grant ownership of the ten-mile-wide Canal Zone, we propose that the government of the United States restore and protect its sovereign right and exclusive jurisdiction of the Canal Zone in perpetuity, and renegotiate the treaties with Panama by which the ownership of the canal was surrendered to Panama.

It should be a priority goal of the President and Congress to insist on enforcement of that portion of the 1978 Panama Canal Neutrality Treaty which prohibits control of the entrances to the Panama Canal by any entity not part of the Republic of Panama or these United States of America. By this standard, the award of port facilities at the entrances to the Panama Canal to Hutchison Whampoa, a Hong Kong company closely linked to the Chinese Communist People's Liberation Army, must be overturned. Similarly, Congress and the President should take advantage of Panama Canal treaty provisions to negotiate the return of a U.S. military presence at the Isthmus of Panama. At a time when the U.S. Navy is one-third its former size, it is essential that rapid transit of U.S. military vessels between the Atlantic and Pacific Oceans be assured.

Education

Education should be free from any State Government subsidy and government interference. The State Government has no legitimate role in either subsidizing or regulating education. To that end, the CPoW supports amending the Wisconsin Constitution to remove the State of Wisconsin from any role in education.

We support an orderly transition to free market education including Home Education and Private Schools (for profit and non-profit) and encourage benevolence to provide effective education for those in need.

Energy (with CPoW addendum)

James Madison said (Federalist Papers #45):

"The powers delegated by the proposed Constitution to the federal government are few and defined."

—The powers not delegated to the United States by the Constitution, nor prohibited by it to the States, are reserved to the States respectively, or to the people.l (Amendment X).

We call attention to the continuing need of these United States for a sufficient supply of energy for national security and for the immediate adoption of a policy of free market solutions to achieve energy independence for these United States. We call for abolishing the Department of Energy.

Private property rights should be respected, and the federal government should not interfere with the development of potential energy sources, including natural gas, crude oil, coal, hydroelectric power, solar energy, wind generators, and nuclear energy.

Family

The CPoW calls upon our national and state officials to oppose any action by the U.S. Courts that would establish any recognition of "same-sex marriage."

We call upon our Wisconsin legislators to uphold the recent Wisconsin Constitutional Amendment that defines marriage as the —union of one man and one womanl and prevent the establishment of any counterfeit, such as — domestic partnerships.

We call upon all state officials to outlaw all acts of sodomy.

We further call upon the Wisconsin State Legislature to repeal the provisions in the Wisconsin State Statutes that allow for "no fault divorce".

Gun Control

The 2nd Amendment strictly limits any interference with gun ownership by saying: "A well regulated Militia, being necessary to the security of a free State, the right of the people to keep and bear Arms, shall not be infringed."

The right to bear arms is inherent in the right of self defense, defense of the family, and defense against tyranny, conferred on the individual and the community by our Creator to safeguard life, liberty, and property, as well as to help preserve the independence of the nation.

The right to keep and bear arms is guaranteed by the Second Amendment to the Constitution; it may not properly be infringed upon or denied.

The Constitution Party upholds the right of the citizen to keep and bear arms. We oppose attempts to prohibit ownership of guns by law-abiding citizens, and stand against all laws which would require the registration of guns or ammunition.

We emphasize that when guns are outlawed, only outlaws will have them. In such circumstances, the peaceful citizen's protection against the criminal would be seriously jeopardized.

We call for the repeal of all federal firearms legislation, beginning with Federal Firearms Act of 1968.

We call for the rescinding of all executive orders, the prohibition of any future executive orders, and the prohibition of treaty ratification which would in any way limit the right to keep and bear arms.

Health Care and Government

James Madison said (Federalist Papers #45):

"The powers delegated by the proposed Constitution to the federal government are few and defined."

—The powers not delegated to the United States by the Constitution, nor prohibited by it to the States, are reserved to the States respectively, or to the people.l (Amendment X).

The Constitution Party opposes the governmentalization and bureaucratization of American medicine. Government regulation and subsidy constitutes a threat to both the quality and availability of patient-oriented health care and treatment.

Hospitals, doctors, and other health care providers should be accountable to patients — not to politicians, insurance bureaucrats, or HMO Administrators.

If the supply of medical care is controlled by the federal government, then officers of that government will determine which demand is satisfied. The result will be the rationing of services, higher costs, poorer results — and the power of life and death transferred from caring physicians to unaccountable political overseers.

We denounce any civil government entity using age or any other personal characteristic to: preclude people and insurance firms from freely contracting for medical coverage; conscript such people into socialized medicine, e.g., Medicare; or prohibit these people from using insurance payments and/or their own money to obtain medical services in addition to, or to augment the quality of, those services prescribed by the program.

We applaud proposals for employee-controlled "family coverage" health insurance plans based on cash value life insurance principles.

The federal government has no Constitutional provision to regulate or restrict the freedom of the people to have access to medical care, supplies or treatments. We advocate, therefore, the elimination of the federal Food and Drug Administration, as it has been the federal agency primarily responsible for prohibiting beneficial products, treatments, and technologies here in the United States that are freely available in much of the rest of the civilized world.

We affirm freedom of choice of practitioner and treatment for all citizens for their health care.

We support the right of patients to seek redress of their grievances through the courts against insurers and/or HMO's.

We condemn the misrepresentations made by the Federal Administration in securing passage of the recently enacted Medicare prescription drug bill, and the use of such legislation to secure government subsidies to special interests, such as the HMOs, and to protect the artificially high cost to consumers of prescription drugs.

Immigration

U.S. Constitution, Article V., Section 4:

The United States shall guarantee to every State in this Union a Republican Form of Government, and Shall protect each of them against Invasion: ...

James Madison:

"When we are considering the advantages that may result from an easy mode of naturalization, we ought also to consider the cautions necessary to guard against abuses. ... aliens might acquire the right of citizenship, and return to the country from which they came, and evade the laws intended to encourage the commerce and industry of the real citizens and inhabitants of America, enjoying at the same time all the advantages of citizens ... "

We affirm the integrity of the international borders of the United States and the Constitutional authority and duty of the federal government to guard and to protect those borders, including the regulation of the numbers and of the qualifications of immigrants into the country.

Each year approximately one million legal immigrants and almost as many illegal aliens enter the United States. These immigrants — including illegal aliens — have been made eligible for various kinds of public assistance, including housing, education, Social Security, and legal services. This unconstitutional drain on the federal Treasury is having a severe and adverse impact on our economy, increasing the cost of government at federal, state, and local levels, adding to the tax burden, and stressing the fabric of society. The mass importation of people with low standards of living threatens the wage structure of the American worker and the labor balance in our country.

We oppose the abuse of the H-1B and L-1 visa provisions of the immigration act which are displacing American workers with foreign.

We favor a moratorium on immigration to the United States, except in extreme hardship cases or in other individual special circumstances, until the availability of all federal subsidies and assistance be discontinued, and proper security procedures have been instituted to protect against terrorist infiltration.

We also insist that every individual group and/or private agency which requests the admission of an immigrant to the U.S., on whatever basis, be required to commit legally to provide housing and sustenance for such immigrants, bear full responsibility for the economic independence of the immigrants, and post appropriate bonds to seal such covenants.

The Constitution Party demands that the federal government restore immigration policies based on the practice that potential immigrants will be disqualified from admission to the U.S. if, on the grounds of health, criminality, morals, or financial dependence, they would impose an improper burden on the United States, any state, or any citizen of the United States.

We oppose the provision of welfare subsidies and other taxpayer-supported benefits to illegal aliens, and reject the practice of bestowing U.S. citizenship on children born to illegal alien parents while in this country.

We oppose any extension of amnesty to illegal aliens. We call for the use of U.S. troops to protect the states against invasion.

We oppose bilingual ballots. We insist that those who wish to take part in the electoral process and governance of this nation be required to read and comprehend basic English as a precondition of citizenship. We support English as the official language for all governmental business by the United States.

Money and Banking

Article I, Section 8, Clause 5 grants only to Congress the power —To coin money [and] regulate the Value thereof ...,l with no provision for such power to be delegated to any other group. Congress began immediately to fulfill this obligation with the Mint Act of 1792, establishing a U.S. Mint for producing Gold and Silver based coin, prescribing the value and content of each coin, and affixing the penalty of death to those who debase such currency.

Article I, Section 10:

—*No State shall ... coin Money; emit Bills of Credit; make any Thing but gold and silver Coin a Tender in Payment of Debts; ....*

Thus, the Constitution forbade the States from accepting or using anything other than a Gold and Silver based currency.

Money functions as both a medium of exchange and a symbol of a nation's morality.

The Founding Fathers established a system of "coin" money that was designed to prohibit the "improper and wicked" manipulation of the nation's medium of exchange while guaranteeing the power of the citizens' earnings.

The federal government has departed from the principle of "coin" money as defined by the U.S. Constitution and the Mint Act of 1792 and has granted unconstitutional control of the nation's monetary and banking system to the private Federal Reserve System.

The Constitution Party recommends a substantive reform of the system of Federal taxation. In order for such reform to be effective, it is necessary that the United States:

- Return to the money system set forth in the Constitution;
- Repeal the Federal Reserve Act, and reform the current Federal Reserve banks to become clearing houses only; and
- Prohibit fractional reserve banking.

It is our intention that no system of "debt money" shall be imposed on the people of the United States. We support a debt free, interest free money system.

DEMOCRATIC PARTY OF WISCONSIN
May 2013

Headquarters

State Headquarters: 110 King Street, Suite 203, Madison 53703.

Telephone: (608) 255-5172; Fax: (608) 255-8919.

Executive Director: MAGGIE BRICKERMAN.

Political Director: JAKE HAJDU.

Membership and Conventions Director: SEAN BERGER; CASSI FENILI, *deputy membership director.*

Compliance and Operations Director: AMANDA BRINK.

Research and Digital Director: MELISSA BALDAUFF.

Finance Director: JULIE BENKOSKE; AMBER GRANT, *deputy finance director.*

Data and Analytics Director: BRYAN POST.

Internet Address: http://www.wisdems.org

State Administrative Committee

Chair: MIKE TATE, Milwaukee.

First Vice Chair: MELISSA SCHROEDER, Merrill.

Second Vice Chair: JEF HALL, Oshkosh.

Secretary: MEG ANDRIETSCH, Racine.

Treasurer: MICHAEL CHILDERS, La Pointe.

National Committee Members: CHRISTINE BREMER MUGGLI, Wausau; ROLLIE HICKS, Eau Claire; MARTHA LOVE, Milwaukee; JASON RAE, Milwaukee.

College Democrats Representative: COLLEEN CULLEN, Milwaukee.

Milwaukee County Chair: SACHIN CHHEDA, Milwaukee.

At-Large Members: ADA DEER, Fitchburg; NIKIYA HARRIS, Milwaukee; BRYAN KENNEDY, Glendale; GRETCHEN LOWE, Madison; ARVINA MARTIN, Madison; BETHANY ORDAZ, Madison; DIAN PALMER, Brookfield; CRIS SELIN, Middleton; MARY LANG SOLLINGER, Madison; ADAM WARPINSKI, Green Bay; JOCASTA ZAMARRIPA, Milwaukee.

County Chairs Association Chair: GARY HAWLEY, Stevens Point.

Congressional District Representatives:

1st District
Melissa Lemke, chair, Racine
Mike Southers, Janesville
2nd District
Erik Paulson, chair, Madison
Laurene Bach, Waunakee
3rd District
Lisa Hermann, chair, Eau Claire
Gary Hawley, Stevens Point
4th District
Terrell Martin, chair, Milwaukee
Stephanie Findley, Milwaukee

5th District
Michael Schlotfeldt, chair, West Bend
Kristin Hansen, Waukesha
6th District
Bob Schweder, chair, Princeton
Jessica King, Oshkosh
7th District
Paul Knuth, chair, Rhinelander
Kelly Westlund, Ashland
8th District
Dottie LeClair, chair, Appleton
Thomas Marlier, Shawano

Source: Democratic Party of Wisconsin, May 2013.

County Organization. The county organization is the basic unit of the Democratic Party of Wisconsin. In each county, the membership elects the county officers. They include a chairperson, vice chairperson, secretary, and treasurer (or secretary/treasurer). Their terms of office are usually one year, but some county organizations may provide for 2-year terms.

Congressional District Organization. Congressional district organizations function mainly as a base of support for Democratic congressional candidates. They also select representatives to the state administrative committee and work with the county parties in their district. An executive committee directs each congressional district organization.

State Convention. The party holds its annual state convention in June. Each year, the convention considers resolutions, amendments to the state party constitution, and other party business. State party officers are elected in odd-numbered years, and state party platforms are adopted in even-numbered years. State convention delegates elect Democratic National Committee members every four years.

Each county unit elects delegates to the state convention, and all party members are eligible.

The number of delegates that represent each county is based on the number of party members and the percentage of the vote cast for the Democratic candidate in the most recent U.S. Senate election. In addition to the regular quota, certain Democratic officeholders are automatically delegates to the state convention.

State Officers and Administrative Committee. The Democratic Party of Wisconsin is headed by a state administrative committee, composed of party officials chosen in a variety of ways. Delegates to the state convention elect the 5 party officers and the 4 Democratic National Committee members. At each of the 8 congressional district conventions, 2 representatives are selected to serve on the state administrative committee in the spring of each odd-numbered year: the district chairperson and an additional representative of the opposite sex. The remaining voting committee members include the County Chairs Association chairperson; the Milwaukee County chairperson; a representative of the College Democrats; 2 state legislative representatives, elected by their house caucuses prior to the beginning of the new legislative term; the immediate past state chairperson and at-large administrative committee members.

The party officers are the state chairperson, first vice chairperson, second vice chairperson, treasurer, and secretary. The chairperson and first vice chairperson must be of the opposite sex.

Party officers are elected in the odd-numbered year for 2-year terms. Democratic National Committee members are elected each presidential election year and serve 4-year terms. The state chairperson and the first vice chairperson are also ex officio members of the Democratic National Committee.

Whenever a vacancy occurs, the chairperson, with the concurrence of the entire state administrative committee, appoints a successor to serve until the next annual convention, where the delegates elect an individual to fill the position for the remainder of the unexpired term.

National Committee. The Democratic National Committee is composed of the chairperson and the highest ranking officer of the opposite sex in each recognized state Democratic Party. In Wisconsin, these are the chairperson and the first vice chairperson of the state party.

An additional 200 committee memberships are apportioned to the states on the same basis as delegates to the national convention, and other specified members are appointed. Wisconsin's Democratic National Committee members are selected every 4 years at the annual state conventions held in presidential election years..

————————————

DEMOCRATIC PARTY OF WISCONSIN 2012 PLATFORM
Adopted by Convention on June 9, 2012 in Appleton, WI
Preamble

The Democratic Party of Wisconsin strives to build an open, just, and strong society where all citizens have equal opportunities to live meaningful, secure lives. We work actively for open, honest, and responsive government that is accountable to the needs and the will of the people.

Justice, Human Concerns, and Democracy

Our government must support the values of freedom, family, fairness, and responsibility to community and to all persons.

One of the primary jobs of government is to ensure that everyone can lead dignified, healthy, and fulfilling lives. We value love, commitment, stability, and nurturing of all family members. Our Constitution guarantees that we are all equal regardless of race, color, class, religion, actual or perceived gender, sexual orientation, age, occupation, national origin, physical disabilities or appearance, or political beliefs. We support marriage equality for all couples. We will work to ensure that basic civil liberties are forever preserved.

It is vital that government respect, support, and protect freedom of expression. When government attempts to limit the rights of its citizens, the fundamental philosophy on which our nation was established is destroyed. We hold sacrosanct our civil liberties, including but hardly limited to freedom of speech, the right to privacy, the presumption of innocence, the principle of habeus corpus, and due process under law. Nothing less than humane treatment of our fellow human beings is acceptable. Our government, with its checks and balances among the three branches, serves us, and protects our constitutional rights.

We must fully fund our state and local protective services. The men and women who serve us protect our lives and property and are our first line of defense, and we must provide for them.

We will work to ensure that everyone has an equal opportunity to succeed, an equal voice in government and fair, and equal treatment under the law. We recognize that minorities, senior citizens, and the poor often face formidable challenges, including obstacles to voting. Many citizens also suffer inadequate access to nutritious food, healthcare, education, and housing. We shall work to eliminate those obstacles.

We shall pursue legislation and cultural change that end racial and ethnic profiling, respect the sovereignty of our indigenous Native American host nations and ensure equality between men and women. We shall work for gender-balanced, qualified representation at all levels of government.

Empowerment of citizens in all civic affairs strengthens our nation. Government must be an open institution that people trust, complying with open meeting and public record laws and elected through transparent, publicly-funded state and national elections. We support a fair, non-partisan redistricting process.

Every citizen is guaranteed the right to vote and equal access thereto, including non-incarcerated felons. We support same-day registration and early voting. We oppose voter ID requirements as discriminatory, equivalent to a poll tax, a voter suppression tactic, and a fraudulent solution to exaggerated voter fraud. We have the right and duty to inspect and count all votes and to have a voter-verified paper ballot that guarantees accurate vote counting. The President should be elected by popular vote.

Our goal is a government and an electoral process free of the corrupting influences of money and power. We strongly oppose the decision of the US Supreme Court to allow unlimited campaign advertising by corporations, foreign and domestic. A new Amendment to the Constitution must be adopted to make clear that Corporations are not People and that money is not speech.

We expect the swift impeachment and removal from office of officials who commit high crimes and misdemeanors. Access to accurate information and a diversity of viewpoints are essential to citizen empowerment. The broadcast spectrum belongs to all citizens. Therefore we will work to ensure diverse local ownership of media outlets. We will provide strong support for public broadcasting and other community-owned media outlets. We support free and equal access to news media for all candidates for public office.

We respect the religious liberties of all people and welcome them into the Democratic Party. It is vital that we observe separation between government and religion. It is imperative to the survival of our Democratic Republic that the rights of citizens to choose their own religious and philosophical beliefs remain intact.

We require a fair immigration policy providing a reasonable legal path to residency and citizenship. The policy must include a fair opportunity for current undocumented residents to achieve legal status. All people should be afforded the same basic principles of life, liberty, justice, and fair access to economic security.

It is important to care for all generations. We need affordable, quality, licensed daycare centers and government support to pay for childcare. We cannot neglect our nation's future. We need health education and disease prevention programs concerning smoking, alcohol, drug abuse, and sexually transmitted infections.

It is essential that we preserve Social Security programs for our elderly, disabled, and eligible children. Privatizing Social Security threatens the financial security of the most vulnerable. We must enhance programs for the aging and disabled, including subsidized long-term in-home or nursing home care.

We believe access to affordable, quality health care is a right and that the best solution to our national health care crisis is a single-payer system. Such a system must provide universal access for individuals of all ages, promote preventive measures, provide medications, therapy and cover all physical and mental illnesses equally. Until that system is available, we support broader coverage and increased funding for the current health care programs on local, state and national levels, including BadgerCare and Medicaid.

Personal moral, religious, and medical decisions should be left up to the competent individual. We believe in freedom of reproductive choice, as well as the individual's right to choose death with dignity. Everyone has the right to timely obtain medications, properly and legally prescribed by their health care provider, from any licensed pharmacy. Funding for stem-cell research should not be influenced by religious beliefs but supported on its scientific merits.

Considering Wisconsin's high rate of incarceration, associated correctional costs, and long-lasting effects of incarceration, we support responsible alternatives to prison.

We oppose the death penalty as an inhumane and ineffective means of punishment. We believe in equitable sentencing standards and increasing the authority of judges to modify sentences.

The war on drugs is a colossal failure. We must discourage dangerous drug use without criminalizing the user and provide rehabilitative treatment to addicted persons. We encourage non-penal sanctions for initial minor drug violations. Marijuana should be legal and regulated like tobacco and alcohol.

We support reasonable firearms regulations to ensure the safety of citizens and law enforcement officials. We support the right to hunt, to bear arms, and a concealed carry ban.

Education, Labor, and Economics

Quality public education for all is critical to a healthy democracy and economy. Public funding for private schools diverts resources from and adversely impacts public schools. Increased governmental funding and financial aid is essential for all levels of public education. Nobody should be denied a quality education because of a personal lack of financial resources.

We believe that students have the right to receive their education in a safe, respectful, and nurturing environment, free from harassment or discrimination by teachers, staff, parents, or other students. We support fair and equitable funding for all elements of the curriculum, including the arts and physical education.

Wisconsin's current educational funding system has failed. Teacher and support staff compensation must keep pace with costs of benefits and inflation.

Revenue caps on school districts and other local governments must be eliminated. State or federal governments must fully fund their mandates.

Public investment in arts and humanities promotes healthy communities and a healthy economy. We support increased local, state, and federal funding of arts and humanities.

A strong and secure nation depends on sound economic policy that promotes and sustains full, meaningful employment. Business, labor, and the public must work together to re-establish American jobs on American soil. We support small business as a means of economic growth. We must resist outsourcing, thus reinvigorating domestic industries.

The Federal government should fund a safety net of transitional jobs for all individuals who cannot find work and have no unemployment compensation.

Public and private workers have rights to safe and equitable workplaces, living wages, pay equity for women, and secure benefits. Workers' rights to organize, bargain collectively, and strike without fear of reprisal must where lost be restored and otherwise be strengthened. Election by card check is supported to reduce employer intimidation of employees' choice of representation. Employees who benefit from union contracts should pay fair-share dues. We support public employees' rights to speedy mediation and binding arbitration of labor disputes. Businesses must be held accountable for contracts with their employees. "Right-to-work" legislation and the hiring of strikebreakers are anathema to a strong, justly-compensated workforce. Pension and other retirement funds must be strictly safeguarded and responsibly managed through regulation. In the event of bankruptcy, workers' unpaid wages must be the first claim on remaining assets.

We support a tax system that is based on ability to pay. It is immoral to overtax those less able to pay while the wealthy are taxed too little as a percentage of income. The Federal budget must reflect responsible spending and fair taxation. We call on the State Legislature to make corporate taxes on par with the national average.

Financial markets should be more effectively regulated to prevent fraud, excessive speculation, inappropriate compensation, predatory lending, and the need for taxpayer bailouts of mismanaged firms. The needs of Main Street should supercede the needs of Wall Street.

Mining authorizations should provide adequate tax revenue to support the affected communities.

America must invest in a healthy economy by supporting worker training, affordable tuition at our state supported universities and technical colleges and ample funding for research.

American companies have an obligation to our nation to be established here at home, follow our labor and environmental laws, and pay taxes for the good of the commons. Furthermore, we must protect our industries from competition by enforcing tariffs against nations that tolerate unfair worker conditions and environmental degradation.

Our wealth should be measured not only by the GDP but also by broad measures of well-being, such as the United Nations Human Development Index, that incorporate factors like health, education, literacy, employment and wages, and environmental quality.

Agriculture and Environment

We must preserve family farming by creating market systems that assure a fair return to both farmers and processors. True Cooperatives and family farm subsidies are essential to the economic viability and quality of life in rural areas. In addition we support value-added agriculture which includes farming endeavors outside traditional forms of agriculture. Regulations controlling environmental pollution from agriculture should be strengthened.

We support farming systems that are humane to animals, preserve our soil, water and forest resources, and produce wholesome, safe food for consumers. We support agricultural sustainability through growth in "buy fresh buy local" practices which insure markets for local farmers and save fuel by eliminating costly transport. We also support truth in labeling of conventional, organic, and genetically modified food.

We oppose practices by genetically modified seed producers which attempt to monopolize the seed business by requiring that all seed be purchased from them.

Protecting the ecological systems of our planet is essential to the economic and social welfare of our state and nation and to the future of humanity. Our legislators and leaders must pay heed to soil, water, and atmospheric pollution; scientific evidence of climate change; all invasive species; and decreasing biodiversity while enacting appropriate legislation to safeguard our environment. We must maintain the integrity of the vast fresh water supply in the Great Lakes. We must expand our recycling efforts.

We support retaining and expanding publicly-owned recreational and wild lands.

We must reduce greenhouse gases by developing alternative and sustainable fuels and energy sources without relaxing regulation of nuclear energy; increase production of fuel-efficient vehicles; reduce urban sprawl onto prime agricultural soils; improve and expand local, regional and national mass transportation systems; and increase recycling and waste management, all while maintaining biodiversity. We support responsible environmental regulations affecting open space, wilderness areas, soil conservation, forest management, toxic and hazardous waste disposal and cleanup, and watershed protection. We call for the use of advanced technology and environmentally-friendly practices to be implemented in industrial settings and mining natural resources and the enforcement 1 and strengthening of safety and environmental regulations. To ensure the protection of our state's valuable natural resources, we support the re-establishment of a Public Intervener's Office and an independent Department of Natural Resources.

Foreign Affairs

We stand for human rights, social and economic justice, the rule of law, and popularly adopted democratic government worldwide. Our leaders and policies must honor international law and honor and promote international agreements that provide groundwork for a just, prosperous, environmentally healthy, and peaceful world. Our United

Nations dues must be fully paid.

We call on our government to be a cooperative and effective leader, a partner in the pursuit of global accords to improve the human condition and protect the environment. We encourage international efforts to combat poverty, hunger, disease, illiteracy, discrimination, genocide, torture, genital mutilation, human slavery and trafficking, capital punishment, pollution, and climate change. We support expansion of the Peace Corps.

We oppose unfair trade and immigration policies that undermine our economy, harm working people in our country and elsewhere, and harm the environment.

We oppose unfettered international arms trade, nuclear, chemical and biological weapons, land mines, radioactive materials in conventional munitions, ballistic missile defense systems, cluster bombs, militarization of space, American-run or funded internment camps, and torture.

We support a military sufficiently strong to safeguard national security. We must provide amply for the health and well-being of members of the military during and after their service. We support efforts to eliminate the use of National Guard troops in undeclared wars.

Our military budget is disproportionately large compared to all other nations. With only 5% of the world's population we make nearly 50% of the world's total military expenditures. Our military budget should be reduced with greater emphasis placed on economic development and diplomacy to achieve global security and curtail the undue influence of the "Military Industrial Complex."

War must always be a last resort. We must address the grievances that foster terrorism rather than fight wars that perpetuate them. We must abide by the Geneva Conventions.

Preemptive war without direct threat to our country is fraudulent, illegal, and disastrous. Congressional action to stop funding for pre-emptive wars and end military assistance to nations conducting preemptive war is long overdue.

We call upon Congress to pass laws displaying visions and values that uphold our Constitution, reverse the failures and illegalities of the executive branch, and maintain the global community's respect and admiration of our country.

Conclusion

The membership of the Democratic Party of Wisconsin has crafted and adopted this platform. Our state and our country will become stronger and better by following the principles outlined herein. We expect all candidates supported by the Democratic Party to support this Platform and, when elected, to work to implement it.

REPUBLICAN PARTY OF WISCONSIN
May 2013

Headquarters and Staff

State Headquarters: 148 East Johnson Street, Madison 53703.

Telephone: (608) 257-4765; Fax: (608) 257-4141.

Internet Address: http://www.wisgop.org

Executive Director: JOE FADNESS.

Political Director: JONATHAN SCHMIEDER.

Press Secretary: JESSE DOUGHERTY.

Controller/Operations Director: ANDREW GOWDY.

Finance Director: DAN MORSE.

IT Coordinator: JOSEF LEVERATTO.

Telemarketing Manager: RICHARD DICKIE.

Executive and District Leadership

Chairman: BRAD COURTNEY, Whitefish Bay.

Vice Chairmen: 1st – BRIAN SCHIMMING, Madison; *2nd* – CRYSTAL BERG, Hartford; *3rd* – LAURIE FORCIER, Eau Claire; *4th* – KATIE McCALLUM, Middleton.

At Large Member: MARIPAT KRUEGER, Menomonie.

Finance Chairman: BILL JOHNSON, Hayward.

Secretary: DAVID ANDERSON, Wausau.

Treasurer: MIKE JONES, Milwaukee.

National Committeeman: STEVE KING, SR., Janesville.

National Committeewoman: MARY BUESTRIN, Mequon.

Immediate Past Chairman: REINCE PRIEBUS, Kenosha.

Wisconsin African American Council: GERARD RANDALL, Milwaukee.

Wisconsin Republican Labor Council: MIKE SANDVICK, Milwaukee.

Wisconsin Hispanic Heritage Council: JOE MEDINA, Waukesha.

Congressional District Chairmen and Vice Chairmen:

1st District	*5th District*
Kim Travis, Williams Bay	Kathy Kiernan, Richfield
Jan Deters, Janesville	Tom Schreibel, Hartland
2nd District	*6th District*
Kim Babler, Madison	Dan Feyen, Fond du Lac
Tim McCumber, Merrimac	Tyler Vorpagel, Fond du Lac
3rd District	*7th District*
Brian Westrate, Fall Creek	Jim Miller, Hayward
Julian Bradley, La Crosse	Jesse Garza, Hudson
4th District	*8th District*
Bob Spindell, Milwaukee	Bill Berglund, Sturgeon Bay
Michael Murphy, Milwaukee	Kevin Barthel, Lakewood

Source: Republican Party of Wisconsin at wisgop.org, May 2013.

County Organization. County party organizations are the basic building blocks of the Republican Party of Wisconsin. County party leaders are elected in county caucuses prior to April 1 of the odd-numbered year. Each committee has a chairman, first vice chairman, secretary, and treasurer.

Congressional District Organization. Each congressional district has an organization that coordinates the activities of the county organizations in the district, with special emphasis on the election of Republican congressional candidates. The district organization is directed by a committee consisting of district members of the state executive committee and, at minimum, an elected chairman, vice chairman, secretary, and treasurer. Committee officers are elected in odd-numbered years prior to the state convention.

State Officers and Executive Committee. Party leadership is vested in a 31-member state executive committee, consisting of the 10 party officers (including the chairman of the county chairmen's organization and the chairman of the Young Republicans Professionals, who are designated respectively as the third and fifth vice chairmen of the committee); the immediate past state party chairman; the chairman and vice chairman from each of the state's 8 congressional district organizations; and the Wisconsin Republican African American Council, the Wisconsin Heritage Council, the Wisconsin Labor Council, and an at-large member. State committee vacancies are filled by the committee. Five of the 10 party officers – the chairman, first and second vice chairmen, secretary, treasurer – are selected by the state executive committee at an organizational meeting within 60 days following the last general election in the even years. An at-large member of the State Executive Committee is also elected at the organizational meeting. Their 2-year terms begin upon adjournment of the organizational meeting. The persons holding those offices and the immediate past state party chairman may not vote in the selection of the new officers. The national committeeman and committeewoman are included among the 10 state executive committee officers and are elected for 4-year terms by state convention delegates in presidential election years. They serve from the adjournment of one national party convention to the end of the next and must be approved by the assembled delegates at the party's national convention. The party finance chairman is also included among the 10 party officers. The finance chairman serves at the pleasure of the newly elected state chairman and is appointed with the consent of the committee to a term that continues until a successor is named.

State Convention. The party holds its state convention in May, June, or July of each year to pass resolutions and conduct other party business. In even-numbered years, the convention adopts a state party platform and considers the endorsement of statewide candidates. A national committeeman and committeewoman are selected in those years in which a national party convention is held.

National Convention and National Committee. The Republican National Committee consists of a committeeman, committeewoman, and a chairman from each state, plus American Samoa, Washington, D.C., Guam, Puerto Rico, and the Virgin Islands. Each state and territory has its own method of electing representatives. National committee members serve from convention to convention. The national committee is led by a chairman and cochairman, who serve 2-year terms.

REPUBLICAN PARTY OF WISCONSIN PLATFORM
Adopted by Convention on May 13, 2012, Green Bay, WI
Preamble

For eight long years the state that once led the nation in meaningful reforms and innovation has floundered under a Democrat administration. Sadly, our state motto, *Forward,* has become a symbol of the past instead of the beacon that reflected our people's traditional passion and potential for the future.

We know Wisconsin deserves better. As Republicans, we will strive to ensure the Wisconsin Spirit is no longer held in check, but flourishes to lift the hearts and minds of every Wisconsin family. The soul of that spirit embodies certain principles and values that unite us; among these:

We want to strengthen and revitalize America's core values which unite a large majority of Americas.

We encourage proposals to enhance Wisconsin's job climate such as reducing the tax burden and we encourage proposals that support the free markets and minimize government interference in the marketplace.

We believe our nation's debt and spending are out of control and reforms are needed in order to curb spending and stop pushing the burden of an expanding government onto the next generation of taxpayers thereby imposing an immoral obligation on our children and grandchildren.

We support proposals to lower the rising costs of health care that can burden many families and employers.

We believe in freedom-of-choice learning environments by supporting a variety of educational options including, but not limited to, charter schools, home schooling, virtual schools, and a school choice voucher program. We believe that the academic freedom of every student must be protected.

We believe that our natural rights as embodied in the Constitution begin at conception and continue until death.

We oppose efforts to restrict the ownership, manufacture, carry, or sale of firearms and ammunition by law-abiding citizens.

We have an obligation to be good stewards of God's creation for future generations.

We believe our current dependence on foreign energy threatens our national security and economic prosperity, therefore we support the elimination of the Department of Energy and the development of free market energy resources.

We believe that federal income tax system is unfair and cumbersome.

We believe it is important for the President and Congress to fix the broken Social Security system.

We recognize the hazard created by the Federal Reserve and the eminent danger of a collapse in the value of the dollar; therefore, we can support a full audit of the Federal Reserve to support sound money.

We believe the United States should grant citizenship only to those who want to embrace and defund American values and culture.

We believe English language instruction should be available to all who need it and we support English as the official language.

We believe separation between Church and State does not mean there can be no references to God in government-sanctioned activities or public buildings.

We believe we must help defend America and Her allies and defeat our enemies.

As Republicans, we can and will make Wisconsin and our country better for future generations.

American Values and American Solutions

We want to strengthen and revitalize America's core values, life, liberty and property, which unite a large majority of Americans. Our goal is to provide long-term solutions instead of short-term fixes.

We believe government needs to reform the way it operates by bringing in ideas and systems currently employed in the private sector, to increase productivity, accountability and effectiveness, and shall utilize private solutions when appropriate.

We believe changes in government have to occur in all elected offices throughout the country and cannot be achieved by focusing only on Washington.

Wisconsin's Economy

We encourage proposals that support free markets and minimize the level of government interference in the marketplace.

We oppose policies that could penalize employment or make the state less competitive in the global marketplace.

Reducing the Federal Deficit and Spending

Our nation's debt and spending are out of control and reforms are needed in order to curb spending and stop pushing the burden of an expanding government onto the next generations of taxpayers, which is imposing an immoral obligation on our children and grandchildren.

We believe federal government spending should be transparent, earmarks should be eliminated, programs should be carefully and regularly audited, and waste should be indentified and eliminated within government agencies.

We believe our elected officials should develop a roadmap for fiscal responsibility by balancing the budget, reducing and eliminating the deficit, and building a surplus in the Treasury to provide a buffer for economic downturns.

Health Care

We support proposals to lower the rising costs of health care that can burden many families and employers.

We believe in free market solutions to bring down the cost of health care such as transparency, charity, portability, competition among insurers, tort reform, and wellness incentives should be implemented to address the underlying problems driving up the cost of health care.

We believe individuals should not be subject to government health care mandates or face penalties, and the federal government should not violate the doctor-patient relationship.

Education

We believe that every student in every educational setting should receive a quality education. We believe in freedom-of-choice learning environments by supporting a variety of educational options including, but not limited to, charter schools, home schooling, virtual schools, and a school choice voucher program.

We support reinstating state and local control of education and reducing the size and authority of the U.S. Department of Education.

We believe academic freedom of each student must be protected so that every student has the right to study without fear of reprisal. We believe public schools should develop curriculum which is content rich, fact-based and encourages critical thinking.

We believe history courses should include the study of the founding fathers, the Constitution, the Bill of Rights, the Federalist Papers and natural law.

We support the expansion of educational options that meet the needs of students and the marketplace through technical training opportunities.

We believe we should dramatically increase our emphasis on math and science education.

Constitutional Rights

We believe that our natural rights as embodied in the Constitutional begin at conception and continue until death.

We believe it is important to have references to God in the Pledge of Allegiance. As it states in the Declaration of Independence, "we are endowed by our Creator with the right to life, liberty, and the pursuit of happiness" which makes clear that certain rights can't be taken away by government.

We believe statements regarding religion and morality made by the Founding Fathers are as important today as they were over 200 years ago.

We believe the language in the Pledge of Allegiance and the Declaration of Independence are very important and must be protected. We reject the idea that because the times change so must the meaning of the language in the Pledge of Allegiance, the Declaration of Independence and the Constitution.

Right to Keep and Bear Arms

The Republican Party of Wisconsin is a vigilant supporter of the right of individuals to keep and bear arms embodied in both the Second Amendment to the Constitution of the United States and Article I, Section 25, of the Wisconsin Constitution.

We therefore oppose all efforts to restrict the ownership, manufacture, transfer, carry, or sale of firearms and ammunition by law-abiding citizens.

We believe we cannot ignore the clear lessons of history regarding the tyranny and suffering imposed upon a disarmed people.

Energy and National Security

We believe our current dependence on foreign energy threatens our national security and economic prosperity by making us vulnerable.

We support the elimination of the Department of Energy and we support the development of free market energy resources.

Environment

We support the protection of Wisconsin natural resources from any non-sovereign entity.

We have an obligation to be good stewards of God's creation for future generations and believe that no one will better care for Wisconsin's lands and natural resources than the citizens of Wisconsin.

We believe we can solve our environmental problems more quickly and cost-effectively with innovation and new technology than with more litigation and more government regulation.

We believe entrepreneurs are more likely to solve America's environmental problems than bureaucrats.

We support measures to encourage businesses to voluntarily cut pollution.

Taxes

We believe the federal income tax system is unfair and cumbersome.

We believe the tax code should be simplified and without exceptions.

We acknowledge the United States has one of the highest corporate tax rates in the industrialized world making it difficult for U.S. corporations to compete internationally and giving incentives for companies to move overseas. Therefore, we favor the option of a single simplified tax rate that closes the loopholes that some corporations use to pay less in taxes. This plan will make America the most attractive place for businesses that provide good paying jobs.

Social Security and Retirement

It is important for the President and Congress to fix the broken Social Security system.

We believe the current Social Security system is broken and if it isn't reformed, future generations will no longer have it as a retirement supplement.

We favor a Social security proposal in which personal social security savings accounts would be optional, with workers given the choice of continuing to depend on the current system with current benefits and able to pass benefits on to family members.

Supporting Sound Money

We recognize that our Founding Fathers warned of the dangers of allowing central bankers to control our currency, and because of this we believe we need transparency and stronger Congressional oversight of the Federal Reserve. We recognize that inflation is robbing Americans of their savings.

Because we recognize the hazard created by the Federal Reserve and the eminent danger of a collapse in the value of the dollar, we support a full audit of the Federal Reserve to support sound money.

Immigration and Assimilation

The United States should grant citizenship only to those who want to embrace and defend American values and culture.

We believe, along with the majority of the American people, that border control is a national security issue and current laws must be vigorously enforced.

We believe illegal immigrants who commit or have committed felonies should be deported.

We respect the efforts of legal immigrants who have gone through the legal process to make the United States of America their home. A standardized process for individuals currently with illegal status in the United States needs to be implemented in order for them to become citizens or legal residents.

We support a worker visa program, making it easier for people who work legally in the United States. When applying for a temporary worker visa, each worker should take an oath to obey American law. In a worker visa program, each worker will receive a secure identification card that will allow the government to locate him or her.

We believe there should be heavy monetary fines against employers and businesses who knowingly hire illegal immigrants, and we must make efforts to prevent abuse and exploitation of all workers.

English as Official Language

English should be the official language of government. All election ballots and other government documents should be printed in English.

We believe immigrants should be required to learn English.

We believe government should make available English language instruction to all who need it.

We believe businesses should be able to require employees to speak the English language while on the job.

Freedom of Religion

Separation between Church and State does not mean there can be no references to God in government sanctioned activities or public buildings.

We believe statements regarding religion and morality made by the Founding Fathers are as important today as they were over 200 years ago.

We believe the phrase – 'One nation under God'– in the Pledge of Allegiance is perfectly in line with the United States Constitution, protected by the First Amendment.

We believe the Founding Fathers understood that religion and morality were important to creating and building this country and talked about it regularly.

We believe the best way to ensure religious freedom is to protect all religious references and symbols; including those on public buildings, lands, or documents. This includes prayer in public schools, thanking God in a graduation speech, and religious symbols being placed on public property during their appropriate holiday season.

We reject that this violates the U.S. Constitution and discriminates against those who are of other faiths or are not religious.

Defending America

We must help defend America and Her allies and defeat our enemies. America should take the threat of terror seriously.

We believe individuals suspected of terrorist acts should be tried in a military court. There should be a death penalty for someone convicted of carrying out a terrorist attack in the United States regardless of country or origin.

We believe a foreign policy based on weakness and engagement with totalitarian regimes is dangerous to America. We should go back to the principles of the Founding Fathers and adopt a non-interventionist foreign policy that first and foremost protects Americans and American interests.

Elections

10

Elections in Wisconsin: February 2012 through May 2013 primary, spring, general, and special elections

Carvers at the Wisconsin State Historical Society

(Wisconsin Historical Society)

ELECTIONS IN WISCONSIN

I. The Wisconsin Electorate

History of the Suffrage. When Wisconsin became a state in 1848, suffrage (the right to vote) was restricted to white or Indian males who were citizens of the United States or white male immigrants in the process of being naturalized. To be eligible to vote, these men had to be at least 21 years of age and Wisconsin residents for at least one year preceding the election. Wisconsin extended suffrage to male "colored persons" in a constitutional referendum held in November 1849. In 1908, the Wisconsin Constitution was amended to require that voters had to be citizens of the United States. Women's suffrage came with the 19th Amendment to the U.S. Constitution in 1920. (Wisconsin was one of the first states in the nation to ratify this amendment, on June 10, 1919.) The most recent major suffrage change was to lower the voting age from 21 to 18 years of age. This was accomplished by the 26th Amendment to the U.S. Constitution, which was ratified by the states in July 1971.

Size of the Electorate. Based on information from the Department of Administration, it is estimated that in January 2012 there were about 4,378,741 potential voters 18 years of age and older. According to the Government Accountability Board, an estimated 70.1% of eligible voters cast 3,071,434 ballots in the 2012 presidential election.

Age and Residence Requirements. The right to vote in Wisconsin state and local elections is granted to U.S. citizens who are age 18 or older and have resided in the election district or ward for 28 days prior to the election. Residence for purposes of voting is statutorily defined as "the place where the person's habitation is fixed, without any present intent to move, and to which, when absent, the person intends to return."

Voter Registration. Beginning with the 2006 spring primary, with limited exceptions, voter registration is required for all voters prior to voting. Voters registering in Wisconsin do not have to record a political party affiliation.

State law permits registration on election day at the proper polling place, and it also provides for advance registration by mail or in person with the municipal clerk, the county clerk, or the city board of election commissioners in the case of residents of the City of Milwaukee. Municipal officials may designate other locations, such as fire stations or libraries for registration, or conduct door-to-door registration drives.

II. A Capsule View of Elections

The Wisconsin Statutes, Chapters 5 through 12, provide for four regularly scheduled elections: the spring primary, the spring election, the partisan primary, and the general election in November.

The spring primary on the third Tuesday in February of each year is followed by the spring election on the first Tuesday in April. The partisan primary is held on the second Tuesday in August in even-numbered years. It is followed by the general election on the first Tuesday after the first Monday in November.

Nonpartisan officials are chosen in the spring. These include the state superintendent of public instruction, judicial officers, county board members, county executives, and municipal and school district officers.

Partisan officials, chosen in the fall, include all other county administrative officials, members of the legislature, state constitutional officers (except for the state superintendent), and members of the U.S. Congress. Not all of these offices are filled at each election because their terms vary from two to six years.

In presidential election years, the presidential preference primary vote is held at the spring election in April, and the vote for U.S. President occurs at the general election in November. In some elections, referendum questions allow Wisconsin voters to advise the state legislature or local government on matters of public policy or to ratify a proposed law, ordinance, or amendment to the Wisconsin Constitution.

Primary Elections

Until 1905, Wisconsin candidates for public office were selected through caucuses or conventions composed of delegates, eligible voters, or members of a political party. Since then, candidates have been chosen in primary elections, but the nominating caucus remains an optional method of selecting candidates for town and village offices. Aspirants must file a declaration of candidacy to run in a primary election, and they usually are required to file nomination papers signed by a specified number of persons eligible to vote in the jurisdiction or district in which they seek office.

Nonpartisan February Spring Primary. A nonpartisan primary election must be held in February if three or more candidates run for one of the offices on the April ballot and no caucus is held to nominate candidates. The two persons receiving the highest number of votes for the specific office in the primary are nominated to run as finalists in the nonpartisan election.

Partisan Primary. The purpose of the partisan primary is to select a party's nominees for the general election in November. In a partisan primary, the voter may vote on the ballot of only one political party (unlike the general election where it is possible to select any party's candidate for a particular office). Some voters express frustration that their choices are limited because they are not permitted to vote for candidates of more than one party. It is important to remember that the primary is a nominating device for the political parties; its purpose is to nominate the candidates that one political party will support against the nominees of the other parties in the general election.

Most states have a closed primary system that requires voters to publicly declare their party affiliation before they can receive the primary ballot of that party. Wisconsin's "open primary" law does not require voters to make a public declaration of their party preference. Instead, the voter is given the primary ballots of all parties but, once inside the voting booth, may cast only one party's ballot.

Candidates must appear on the partisan primary ballot, even if unopposed, in order to be nominated by their respective parties. The candidate receiving the largest number of party votes for an office becomes the party's nominee in the November election. (In the case of a special election, which is held at a time other than the general election to fill a vacated partisan office, a primary is not held if there is no more than one candidate for a party's nomination.)

Elections

Nonpartisan April Spring Election. The officials chosen in the spring nonpartisan election are the state superintendent of public instruction; judicial officers; county executive (if the county elects one); county supervisor; town, village, and city officers; and school board members. Because the terms of office vary, not all offices are filled each year. The only nonpartisan officers elected on a statewide basis are the state superintendent of public instruction and justices of the supreme court; all others are elected from the county, circuit, district, or municipality represented.

The governor is authorized to fill vacancies that occur in nonpartisan state elective offices by appointment. Gubernatorial appointments strongly influence the composition of the Wisconsin judiciary, because many of the state's justices and judges who are appointed to the bench are later elected to office by the voters.

Partisan November General Election. In November, Wisconsin voters select their federal, state, and county partisan officials on a ballot listing the winners of the partisan primary election plus "independent" candidates who are either unaffiliated or affiliated with minor parties that are not recognized for separate ballot status. "Write-in" votes may be cast for persons whose names do not appear on the ballot.

The general election ballot includes a broad range of offices. The constitutional offices of governor, lieutenant governor, secretary of state, state treasurer, and attorney general are filled through a statewide vote. These officers are elected for 4-year terms in the even-numbered years that alternate with the U.S. presidential election.

Candidates for congressional representative and for representative to the state assembly are included on every general election ballot, because the terms for these offices are two years. Wisconsin's 33 state senators are elected for 4-year terms, with the odd-numbered senate districts electing their senators in the years when a gubernatorial election is held and even-numbered senate districts electing their senators in the presidential election years. U.S. Senators, who serve 6-year terms, are also chosen at the appropriate general election.

The state's 72 counties elect certain partisan officers for 4-year terms at each general election. Clerks of circuit court, coroners, and sheriffs are elected at the general election in which the governor is also elected, while county clerks, district attorneys, registers of deeds, surveyors, and treasurers are elected at the general election in which the president is elected. State law requires all counties either to elect a coroner or appoint a medical examiner. The post of surveyor may be filled by election or appointment at the county's option. (Milwaukee County is required by law to appoint its medical examiner and surveyor.)

Vacancies in the offices of U.S. Senator, U.S. Congressional representative, state senator, and representative to the assembly may be filled only by special election, but vacancies in state constitutional offices and most county offices are filled through appointment by the governor. The exception is that the lieutenant governor constitutionally succeeds the governor in case of a vacancy in that office.

Presidential Preference Vote

Wisconsin conducts its presidential preference vote on the first Tuesday in April of each presidential election year, in conjunction with the nonpartisan spring election. 1985 Wisconsin Act 304 gave political parties complete freedom to select delegates for their national conventions on any basis they choose, so the vote has no binding effect. It does, however, indicate voter preferences.

A committee, composed of officials of the recognized political parties, meets on the first Tuesday in January (the next day if Tuesday is a holiday) of the year prior to the presidential preference vote in April to certify to the Government Accountability Board (GAB) the list of names to be placed on the ballot. (If a party's candidate for governor received at least 10% of the vote in the previous election, the party is considered a "recognized party".) The committee lists the names of all nationally advocated or recognized candidates of the recognized parties and such other names as it chooses. The committee includes each party's state chairperson (or designee), one national committeeman and one committeewoman (designated by the party's state chairperson), the president and the minority leader of the senate (or designees), and the speaker and minority leader of the assembly (or designees). An additional member is elected by the committee to serve as chairperson.

Any person named by the committee as a potential presidential candidate may withdraw from the ballot by filing a disclaimer with the GAB. Persons not named may have their names placed on the ballot by filing a nomination petition signed by a specified number of qualified electors.

Presidential Elections

Presidential Electors. On the first Tuesday in October in each presidential election year, the five partisan constitutional state officers, all hold-over senators, and the senate and assembly candidates nominated by each political party at the partisan primary election meet at the State Capitol to select a slate of presidential electors, who will cast Wisconsin's official ballots for the offices of U.S. President and Vice President. A party selects one elector from each of the Wisconsin congressional districts and two electors at large, and then certifies its list of electors to the GAB. After the November presidential election, the party that receives a plurality of the votes statewide sends its electors to the State Capitol on the first Monday after the second Wednesday in December to perform their duties as Wisconsin's electors. They compose Wisconsin's delegation to the Electoral College – the group of 538 electors nationwide who actually cast the votes for president and vice president. Independent candidates for president list their electors on their nomination papers.

Referendum and Recall

Referendum. A "referendum" is simply a question referred to the people for determination through a vote. On the state level, Wisconsin provides for four types of referenda: 1) amendments to the state constitution, 2) measures extending the right of suffrage, 3) ratification of legislation prior to its becoming law, and 4) advisory questions.

The procedure for amending the Wisconsin Constitution requires that two consecutive legislatures must adopt an identically worded amendment proposal and a majority of the voters participating in the election must ratify the change at a subsequent election.

An advisory referendum gives the legislature a means of asking the voters their opinion on legislative policy. Advisory referenda are usually submitted to the electorate at the April or November elections. Wisconsin county boards may submit advisory or ratifying referenda to county voters. Municipalities also are permitted and sometimes required to submit referendum questions relating to village and city charter ordinances and certain other subjects.

Recall. The Wisconsin Constitution and statutes provide for the removal of elected officers through a process of petition and special election, known as "recall". Officials may be recalled after serving the first year of a term, and no reason need be given for the recall in the case of a state, congressional, legislative, state judicial, or county officer. A petition seeking recall of a city, village, town, or school district official must contain a statement of a reason for the recall. The reason must be related to the official responsibilities of the office, but the petitioners need not provide supporting evidence for the reason.

A petition for the recall of an officer must be signed by electors equal to at least 25% of the vote cast in the district or territory served by the official during the last gubernatorial election. Following the filing of a successful recall petition, an election is held to fill the office. A recall primary is required whenever two or more persons compete for a nonpartisan office or whenever more than one person competes for the nomination of a political party for a partisan office. Unless the official facing recall resigns, he or she is listed on the recall ballot along with the other candidates who have been nominated.

Prior to 1977, the recall was seldom used. In August of that year, five La Crosse school board members were recalled, and in the following month a county judge was recalled for the first time in Wisconsin history. Attempts to recall state legislators have been relatively rare. On June 4, 1996, a state senator became the first state legislator to be recalled. Subsequently, a state senator was defeated in a recall primary on October 21, 2003. On August 9, 2011, two state senators were defeated in recall elections. On June 5, 2012, an election for the recall of the governor and lieutenant governor was held for the first time in Wisconsin history. Both won their recall elections, making them the first governor and lieutenant governor to survive a recall election in U.S. history. On the same date, another state senator was defeated in a recall election.

Mechanics of the Election Process

Certifying candidates, registering voters, and recording and reporting millions of votes is a complex process governed by state law. Legislation passed in 2007 created a Government Accountability Board (GAB) that replaced both the Ethics Board and the Elections Board. The GAB is composed of 6 retired judges. The GAB, Elections Division took over responsibility for the administration of elections laws in January 2008.

The GAB, Elections Division determines the format for all federal, state, county, municipal and special district ballots, certifies to each county clerk the list of candidates for federal and state office, and performs many other duties pertaining to elections.

County clerks prepare the ballots for federal, state, and county elections and distribute them to the municipal clerks. The law requires every city, village, and town having a population of 7,500 or more to use an electronic voting system, unless otherwise permitted by the Elections Division. If an electronic voting machine is used, the equipment must generate a complete, permanent record showing all votes cast by each voter, which can be verified by the voter.

Municipal clerks supervise registration and elections in their municipalities. In cities or counties with more than 500,000 population, election duties are performed by a city board of election commissioners and a county board of election commissioners. (This provision currently applies only to the City of Milwaukee and Milwaukee County.)

Registration and Voting

The first step in casting a Wisconsin ballot usually is to register to vote. The voter must provide information including name; residence; previous residence; citizenship; date of birth; age; the voter's driver's license number or last 4 digits of the voter's social security number, if any; length of residence in the ward or election district; whether the applicant has been convicted of a felony for which he or she has not been pardoned, and if so, whether the applicant is incarcerated, on parole, probation or extended supervision; and whether the applicant is disqualified on any other ground from voting; or is currently registered to vote at any other location.

Most voter registration information is open to public inspection, but victims of domestic abuse, sexual assault, or stalking can request that their registration information be kept confidential. A voter's registration is considered permanent unless the person changes his or her residence, in which case it is necessary to transfer registration to the new residence. Municipalities, however, must cancel the registration of a person who, though eligible, does not vote during a 4-year period and does not respond to a written request to apply for continued registration.

A voter who is unable or unwilling to come to the polling place on election day may vote by absentee ballot. An absentee ballot may be cast by mail or in person at the municipal clerk's office serving the voter's residence. Every request for an absentee ballot must be made in writing.

On election day, there are usually seven inspectors (election officials) for each polling place. The number may vary, but no polling place may have fewer than three. Any member of the public may be present in any polling place for the purpose of observation and the major parties often designate official polling place observers.

Under 2011 Wisconsin Act 23, beginning with the 2012 spring primary, each voter must present one of a number of specified forms of identification when voting in an election in this state. An absentee voter who votes by mail must enclose a copy of the identification. A number of exemptions are provided. A voter who fails to present an acceptable form of identification may vote by provisional ballot. If an absentee voter who votes by mail fails to enclose a copy of an acceptable form of identification, the voter's absentee ballot is treated as provisional. A voter who casts a provisional ballot has until 4:00 p.m. on the Friday after an election to provide an acceptable form of identification in order for his or her provisional ballot to be counted. To do this, the voter may return to the polls before the closing hour or provide the identification to the municipal clerk or board of election commissioners of the municipality where he or she resides after the polls close. (As of July 1, 2013, the enforcement of Wisconsin's voter identification requirement was suspended by court order. The suspension continues while appellate courts review the matter.) With limited exceptions, Act 23 also requires a voter who votes at a polling place to enter his or her signature on the poll list (the list used by election officials which shows the names and addresses of eligible voters) when voting in an election.

III. Campaign Finance Regulation

Early Reforms. Wisconsin's first attempt to regulate election practices (Chapter 358, Laws of 1897) was passed to stymie the crudest forms of corrupt practices, such as bribery, illegal voting, election fraud, and related corruption. It also required the filing of financial statements that were open to the public.

The current ban on campaign contributions by corporations dates back to 1905 (Chapter 492). Corporations are still prohibited from donating to candidates, political parties, or committees. (Labor organizations were also banned from making such contributions by Chapter 135, Laws of 1935, but the prohibition was repealed by Chapter 429, Laws of 1959.) Under a recent U.S. Supreme Court decision, corporations may make direct expenditures supporting or opposing candidates.

The "Corrupt Practices Act" of 1911 (Chapter 650) strengthened and expanded the earlier laws. Central to the act were tightening disclosure provisions. Candidates were required to report all sources of their funding, and they were barred from trading favors, monetary or otherwise, in return for financial support.

1974 Campaign Finance Reforms. The legislature passed sweeping campaign finance reform in Chapter 334, Laws of 1973, which created the current statutory "Chapter 11 – Campaign Finance". The law regulated campaign contributions and expenditures and required central filing of financial reports. It also created the state Elections Board, with representation from the three branches of government and the major political parties, to administer and enforce both election and campaign finance laws. These duties are now performed by the GAB. Candidates, individuals, committees, and groups involved in campaigns for state offices and statewide referenda must file detailed campaign finance reports with the board, which supervises the auditing of the reports. The GAB investigates election law violations and must notify the district attorney, attorney general, or the governor of any facts or evidence that might be grounds for civil action or criminal prosecution.

Regulation of Contributions

Wisconsin regulates campaign finance according to function – contribution or expenditure – with separate dollar limits and reporting requirements.

Contributions are moneys or certain other things of value that are donated directly either to individual candidates or to political committees, with the recipients determining how the money will be spent. The state determines the contribution limits in the case of state or local offices, but candidates running for federal office are subject to the limits set by federal campaign finance laws.

Contributions by candidates from their own personal funds cannot be limited because they are considered to be free expression and are protected by the First Amendment.

Individuals. States are free to set their own limits on contributions to candidates for state or local office. Limitations usually pertain to the type of office. Wisconsin also limits the overall amount a single individual is allowed to contribute to all candidates in a calendar year.

Other than a candidate's own contributions to the campaign, no individual may contribute more than the amounts specified to the following candidates or any individuals or independent groups supporting them: constitutional officer (governor, lieutenant governor, secretary of state, state treasurer, attorney general, or superintendent of public instruction) or supreme court justice – $10,000; state senator – $1,000; representative to the assembly – $500; and all other state and local candidates – a maximum of $250 to $3,000 depending upon the office. Furthermore, no individual may make contributions to a combination of candidates or registered committees that exceed a total of $10,000 in any calendar year.

Committees. Wisconsin limits campaign contributions made by political committees. Different limits apply in terms of the amounts a particular type of committee may donate and the amounts a candidate may receive from committees. Committees subject to contribution limits include: 1) the *political action committee (PAC)*, which may be created by but operate separately from a private interest group (such as a trade association or a union) to raise and spend money to elect or defeat particular candidates; 2) the *political party committee*, organized by a formal political party; 3) the *legislative campaign committees*, organized by the respective political parties within the State Senate or the State Assembly; and 4) the candidate's *personal campaign committee*. Any committee that contributes directly to a particular candidate's campaign is subject to specific contribution limits, which vary according to the type of committee and the type of elective office. However, legislative campaign committees and political party committees are allowed to use contributions for party building activities or administrative expenses. PACs may contribute to the political parties and legislative campaign committees in which case the PAC per-candidate limitations do not apply (although other limitations remain applicable).

No committee, other than a political party or legislative campaign committee, may make contributions to a candidate for statewide constitutional office or justice of the supreme court that exceed 4% of the candidate's statutory expenditure level. (Similar limits on contributions by committees apply to candidates for other state and local offices.)

Regulation of Expenditures

Expenditures by the Candidate. Candidates may make campaign expenditures from their own personal funds and the moneys received as contributions from individuals and registered committees. There are no limits on the amount the candidates can spend on their own campaigns. There were attempts at the federal and state level in the early 1970s to limit candidates' personal expenditures, but the U.S. Supreme Court in *Buckley v. Valeo* held that this type of financing was protected by the U.S. Constitution as an exercise of free speech.

Expenditures by Independent Individuals and Committees. Individuals and committees are considered to be making independent expenditures if they do not coordinate their efforts with a candidate. Independent individuals and committees are permitted to spend unlimited amounts promoting or opposing a candidate, but in Wisconsin they are required to file a statement declaring that the expenditures will be made without consultation or coordination with any candidate. (If a candidate is knowingly involved in an expenditure, the expenditure is viewed as a contribution to the candidate, and the contributor must adhere to contribution limits.)

Expenditures by Political Party Committees. When a political party makes an expenditure to support its candidate, the expenditure is normally counted as a contribution to that candidate. Candidates are subject to aggregate limitations on the amount they may receive from parties and other committees. In *Colorado Republican Federal Campaign Committee et al. v. Federal Election Commission,* 518 U.S. 604 (1996), the U.S. Supreme Court held, however, that political party committees may make unlimited independent expenditures as long as they are not acting in consultation or coordination with a candidate.

Reporting Requirements

Registration and Reporting. Campaign finance laws are designed to track the flow of dollars received and spent by the candidates. Expenditures from the campaign depository may not be made anonymously, nor may contributions or expenditures be made in a fictitious name. Any anonymous contribution of more than $10 must be donated to a charity or the common school fund.

Generally, all candidates for state office, the four types of committees listed above, and other committees that make contributions or expenditures expressly supporting or opposing state candidates must register and file campaign finance reports with the GAB. These reports must include the name, address, and total contributions of each contributor who donates more than $20 in a calendar year and must give the occupation and principal place of employment of each contributor who makes cumulative contributions of over $100 in a calendar year. Reports must also itemize all contributions, loans, expenditures, or obligations in excess of $20. Registrants with limited financial activity may be exempted from reporting.

Each candidate must appoint one campaign treasurer and designate one campaign depository, such as a numbered bank account, before receiving any contributions or making any expenditures. The candidate and campaign treasurer are then required to file a registration statement regardless of the amount of money they expect to receive or dispense. Unless exempted from reporting, the candidate, or the treasurer acting on the candidate's behalf, must file periodic financial reports. The candidate is considered personally responsible for the accuracy of these reports.

With limited exceptions, political party committees or other committees that make or accept contributions or make expenditures amounting to more than $25 per year, and individuals (other than candidates) who accept contributions or make expenditures amounting to more than $25 per year must file registration statements. For referendum activity, the threshold is more than $750 per year. These statements include such information as the name and address of the registrant, the officers, the campaign depository, and the candidate or referendum question they support or oppose.

Since July 1, 1999, registrants with the Government Accountability Board, Ethics and Accountability Division who have accepted contributions totaling more than $20,000 within a campaign or biennial period have been required to file their reports electronically. These reports may be viewed on the GAB Web site.

Nonresident committees, groups, or individuals making contributions or expenditures in this state must also file their names and addresses and those of a designated agent in the state with the secretary of state and must also file regular reports, unless a reporting exemption applies.

Disclaimers. Candidates and political committees that are subject to state reporting requirements must identify themselves on any mass media communications, such as billboards, handbills, and radio or TV advertisements. This disclosure must contain the words "paid for" followed by the name of the candidate or organization responsible for the communication and the name of the candidate's or organization's treasurer.

IV. Public Campaign Financing

Chapter 107, Laws of 1977, and 2009 Wisconsin Act 89 provided public financing to candidates for certain state offices. Public financing was repealed by 2011 Wisconsin Act 32.

COUNTY VOTE FOR SUPREME COURT JUSTICE
February 19, 2013 Spring Primary

County	Ed Fallone	Vince Megna	Pat Roggensack*	County Total
Adams	312	82	682	1,078
Ashland	517	76	369	967
Barron	821	322	1,789	2,940
Bayfield	612	79	474	1,167
Brown	2,983	616	7,071	10,746
Buffalo	176	32	396	605
Burnett	244	48	414	706
Calumet	652	198	1,894	2,751
Chippewa	816	210	1,775	2,803
Clark	378	100	1,351	1,830
Columbia	1,243	226	1,861	3,334
Crawford	284	55	396	737
Dane	23,011	2,668	13,035	38,765
Dodge	1,111	339	4,172	5,627
Door	631	92	963	1,688
Douglas	850	170	767	1,791
Dunn	743	144	1,204	2,094
Eau Claire	2,052	280	2,783	5,130
Florence	47	17	137	201
Fond du Lac	977	233	4,217	5,427
Forest	112	30	332	474
Grant	624	135	1,160	1,922
Green	616	130	886	1,634
Green Lake	171	47	808	1,026
Iowa	604	80	645	1,329
Iron	243	138	450	835
Jackson	454	159	1,063	1,686
Jefferson	1,252	248	3,542	5,073
Juneau	243	54	713	1,010
Kenosha	2,474	628	4,923	8,045
Kewaunee	206	51	577	835
La Crosse	2,622	722	4,847	8,223
Lafayette	250	78	498	828
Langlade	387	145	873	1,408
Lincoln	627	153	1,299	2,084
Manitowoc	1,185	420	3,963	5,571
Marathon	2,199	416	4,460	7,091
Marinette	397	142	1,255	1,795
Marquette	224	82	658	965
Menominee	30	14	97	142
Milwaukee	20,251	3,599	34,814	58,988
Monroe	649	180	1,606	2,458
Oconto	424	131	1,278	1,834
Oneida	1,991	945	4,025	7,024
Outagamie	2,413	575	5,355	8,353
Ozaukee	1,432	248	7,778	9,465
Pepin	120	29	254	403
Pierce	567	153	935	1,656
Polk	565	129	1,154	1,850
Portage	1,779	205	1,875	3,866
Price	240	61	631	935
Racine	3,489	720	10,377	14,600
Richland	313	65	540	918
Rock	2,312	535	3,767	6,652
Rusk	204	77	599	884
St. Croix	973	284	2,070	3,341
Sauk	1,314	199	1,743	3,259
Sawyer	196	55	493	745
Shawano	409	169	1,466	2,044
Sheboygan	1,755	455	7,812	10,051
Taylor	193	61	630	885
Trempealeau	473	198	930	1,603
Vernon	463	87	781	1,332
Vilas	643	317	1,873	2,856
Walworth	1,050	258	4,230	5,552
Washburn	361	72	627	1,062
Washington	1,197	345	9,787	11,336
Waukesha	5,234	1,435	35,532	42,227
Waupaca	569	138	1,659	2,366
Waushara	192	62	971	1,225
Winnebago	1,826	434	4,309	6,588
Wood	1,513	311	3,122	4,954
TOTAL	108,490	22,391	231,822	363,675

*Incumbent.

Source: Official records of the Government Accountability Board, Elections Division. County totals include scattered votes.

COUNTY VOTE FOR SUPREME COURT JUSTICE
April 2, 2013 Spring Election

County	Ed Fallone	Pat Roggensack*	County Total
Adams	1,380	2,207	3,587
Ashland	1,490	964	2,462
Barron	2,581	3,509	6,093
Bayfield	1,956	1,342	3,299
Brown	12,861	17,988	30,861
Buffalo	895	1,219	2,115
Burnett	989	1,197	2,188
Calumet	2,556	4,215	6,773
Chippewa	3,388	4,437	7,832
Clark	1,878	3,577	5,458
Columbia	5,397	5,688	11,098
Crawford	1,229	1,476	2,705
Dane	61,689	29,673	91,402
Dodge	4,318	9,193	13,512
Door	3,500	3,954	7,458
Douglas	2,581	1,917	4,499
Dunn	2,804	3,009	5,816
Eau Claire	7,082	6,251	13,344
Florence	246	397	644
Fond du Lac	4,559	9,992	14,552
Forest	472	914	1,386
Grant	2,704	3,343	6,047
Green	2,776	2,965	5,743
Green Lake	1,043	2,452	3,496
Iowa	2,126	1,725	3,853
Iron	572	734	1,306
Jackson	1,511	2,173	3,684
Jefferson	5,117	8,673	13,804
Juneau	1,356	1,779	3,135
Kenosha	7,757	10,347	18,128
Kewaunee	1,218	1,874	3,094
La Crosse	7,751	7,831	15,592
Lafayette	1,291	1,695	2,987
Langlade	1,306	2,462	3,769
Lincoln	2,075	3,655	5,736
Manitowoc	6,070	10,406	16,485
Marathon	7,082	10,857	17,948
Marinette	2,828	4,302	7,132
Marquette	1,312	1,833	3,145
Menominee	153	168	321
Milwaukee	53,956	55,843	109,892
Monroe	2,614	3,761	6,381
Oconto	2,985	4,519	7,509
Oneida	2,345	3,756	6,105
Outagamie	10,476	13,646	24,127
Ozaukee	5,457	15,654	21,116
Pepin	475	588	1,063
Pierce	2,044	2,524	4,572
Polk	2,614	2,932	5,550
Portage	5,962	5,118	11,089
Price	1,288	2,119	3,408
Racine	10,658	18,720	29,393
Richland	1,192	1,294	2,486
Rock	9,436	9,610	19,060
Rusk	1,042	1,597	2,642
St. Croix	4,006	5,467	9,492
Sauk	4,619	4,809	9,433
Sawyer	977	1,252	2,231
Shawano	2,386	4,323	6,711
Sheboygan	6,347	14,766	21,126
Taylor	1,211	2,581	3,798
Trempealeau	2,132	2,543	4,678
Vernon	2,149	2,550	4,699
Vilas	1,458	3,176	4,639
Walworth	5,389	10,686	16,101
Washburn	1,203	1,371	2,574
Washington	5,076	19,432	24,518
Waukesha	16,994	59,731	76,732
Waupaca	3,015	4,522	7,539
Waushara	1,150	2,371	3,521
Winnebago	8,397	11,439	19,850
Wood	4,017	6,168	10,191
TOTAL	362,969	491,261	854,715

*Incumbent.

Source: Official records of the Government Accountability Board, Elections Division. County totals include scattered votes.

DISTRICT VOTE FOR COURT OF APPEALS
April 3, 2012 Spring Election
District I

County	Ralph Adam Fine*	County Total
Milwaukee	87,099	88,035
TOTAL.	87,099	88,035

District II

County	Richard S. Brown*	County Total
Calumet	7,459	7,487
Fond du Lac	14,492	14,496
Green Lake.	2,911	2,924
Kenosha	17,563	17,731
Manitowoc	10,811	10,857
Ozaukee	16,212	16,315
Racine	21,541	21,646
Sheboygan	16,457	16,502
Walworth.	13,342	13,444
Washington.	21,565	21,636
Waukesha	58,964	59,129
Winnebago	23,456	23,605
TOTAL.	224,773	225,772

District III

County	Mark A. Mangerson	County Total
Ashland	1,832	1,850
Barron	6,551	6,571
Bayfield	2,613	2,619
Brown	29,240	29,397
Buffalo.	2,073	2,074
Burnett	1,953	1,956
Chippewa	6,860	6,886
Door	4,766	4,779
Douglas	4,271	4,297
Dunn	4,863	4,893
Eau Claire	12,212	12,288
Florence	627	629
Forest.	1,415	1,419
Iron.	844	844
Kewaunee	2,832	2,841
Langlade	2,943	2,955
Lincoln.	4,067	4,092
Marathon.	16,899	17,005
Marinette.	6,228	6,242
Menominee	125	128
Oconto	5,763	5,775
Oneida	7,517	7,669
Outagamie	22,477	22,532
Pepin	1,147	1,157
Pierce.	4,132	4,180
Polk	5,878	5,901
Price	2,588	2,594
Rusk	2,401	2,404
St. Croix	12,767	12,849
Sawyer	2,438	2,447
Shawano	5,444	5,451
Taylor	2,415	2,422
Trempealeau	3,668	3,684
Vilas	4,129	4,152
Washburn	2,719	2,721
TOTAL.	198,697	199,703

DISTRICT VOTE FOR COURT OF APPEALS
April 3, 2012 Spring Election–Continued
District IV

County	Joanne F. Kloppenburg	County Total
Adams	2,441	2,555
Clark	4,092	4,148
Columbia.	6,814	7,280
Crawford.	2,207	2,256
Dane	67,168	69,350
Dodge	10,383	11,121
Grant	5,561	5,670
Green.	4,485	4,703
Iowa	3,891	4,048
Jackson.	2,568	2,615
Jefferson	9,499	10,449
Juneau	2,878	2,939
La Crosse	14,678	14,997
Lafayette.	2,361	2,445
Marquette	1,834	1,954
Monroe	5,846	5,998
Portage.	8,691	8,862
Richland	2,397	2,445
Rock	16,121	16,787
Sauk	7,853	8,220
Vernon	3,469	3,565
Waupaca	6,769	6,901
Waushara.	2,972	3,052
Wood	10,087	10,228
TOTAL.	205,065	212,588

*Incumbent.

Source: Official records of the Government Accountability Board, Elections Division. County totals include scattered votes.

DISTRICT VOTE FOR COURT OF APPEALS
April 2, 2013 Spring Election
District II

County	Mark Gundrum*	County Total
Calumet	4,896	4,916
Fond du Lac	10,463	10,468
Green Lake.	2,695	2,698
Kenosha	10,523	10,660
Manitowoc.	12,039	12,076
Ozaukee	14,454	14,522
Racine	19,388	19,457
Sheboygan	15,415	15,472
Walworth.	11,535	11,624
Washington.	17,605	17,679
Waukesha	51,749	51,906
Winnebago.	13,686	13,798
TOTAL.	184,448	185,276

DISTRICT VOTE FOR COURT OF APPEALS
April 2, 2013 Spring Election–Continued
District III

County	Lisa K. Stark	County Total
Ashland	1,592	1,612
Barron	4,876	4,887
Bayfield	2,453	2,459
Brown	20,717	20,821
Buffalo	1,707	1,709
Burnett	1,785	1,792
Chippewa	6,099	6,120
Door	5,357	5,371
Douglas	3,293	3,307
Dunn	4,610	4,624
Eau Claire	10,659	10,754
Florence	477	477
Forest	1,069	1,069
Iron	960	962
Kewaunee	2,269	2,274
Langlade	2,848	2,852
Lincoln	4,113	4,133
Marathon	12,939	12,992
Marinette	5,409	5,415
Menominee	210	210
Oconto	6,008	6,022
Oneida	4,486	4,495
Outagamie	16,861	16,945
Pepin	843	847
Pierce	3,570	3,584
Polk	4,577	4,588
Price	2,432	2,440
Rusk	2,042	2,044
St. Croix	7,546	7,597
Sawyer	1,743	1,750
Shawano	5,169	5,177
Taylor	2,898	2,902
Trempealeau	4,010	4,015
Vilas	3,361	3,378
Washburn	1,993	1,997
TOTAL	160,981	161,621

District IV

County	Paul Lundsten*	County Total
Adams	2,605	2,607
Clark	4,061	4,070
Columbia	7,700	7,736
Crawford	2,091	2,092
Dane	54,314	54,658
Dodge	9,455	9,487
Grant	4,605	4,615
Green	3,945	3,977
Iowa	2,810	2,821
Jackson	2,869	2,874
Jefferson	9,059	9,115
Juneau	2,383	2,396
La Crosse	10,992	11,016
Lafayette	2,193	2,197
Marquette	2,372	2,376
Monroe	5,217	5,232
Portage	6,863	6,893
Richland	1,798	1,799
Rock	12,828	12,888
Sauk	6,418	6,434
Vernon	3,565	3,578
Waupaca	5,773	5,786
Waushara	2,591	2,603
Wood	6,794	6,836
TOTAL	173,301	174,086

*Incumbent.

Source: Official records of the Government Accountability Board, Elections Division. County totals include scattered votes.

VOTE FOR CIRCUIT JUDGES
February 21, 2012 Spring Primary

Circuit Court	Vote
Dane County Circuit Court, Branch 11	
Roger A. Allen.	11,371
Ellen K. Berz.	16,388
Francis X. Sullivan.	8,919
Kenosha County Circuit Court, Branch 2	
Edward Richard Antaramian.	3,505
David R. Berman	2,412
David Ernest Celebre	1,446
William Michel	2,726
Jason A. Russell*	5,062
Menominee-Shawano County Circuit Court, Branch 2	
William F. Kussel, Jr.*.	1,445
John B. Selsing.	614
David R. Winter	1,425
Milwaukee County Circuit Court, Branch 17	
Christopher R. Lipscomb, Sr.	18,650
Nelson Wesley Phillips, III*.	19,737
Carolina Maria Stark.	20,859
Oneida County Circuit Court, Branch 2	
Michael H. Bloom	1,299
John F. O'Melia	1,322
Timothy L. Vocke	1,119
Rock County Circuit Court, Branch 7	
Tod Daniel.	1,148
Mike Haakenson.	1,560
Jack C. Hoag.	2,942
Barbara W. McCrory.	3,606
Thomas McDonald.	1,358
Harry C. O'Leary	2,005

*Incumbent

Source: Official records of the Government Accountability Board, Elections Division. Scattered votes omitted.

February 19, 2013 Spring Primary

Circuit Court	Vote
Dodge County Circuit Court, Branch 3	
Joseph F. Fischer.	1,449
Dawn N. Klockow.	910
Joseph G. Sciascia.	2,905
Manitowoc County Circuit Court, Branch 1	
Bob Dewane.	748
Steven R. Olson	2,177
Mark R. Rohrer	1,896
Steven J. Weber	901
Milwaukee County Circuit Court, Branch 45	
Rebecca Bradley*	32,997
Janet Claire Protasiewicz	16,173
Gil Urfer.	6,158

*Incumbent.

Source: Official records of the Government Accountability Board, Elections Division. Scattered votes omitted.

VOTE FOR CIRCUIT JUDGES
April 3, 2012 Spring Election

Circuit Court	Vote	Circuit Court	Vote
Ashland County		Branch 39	
Robert E. Eaton*.	2,458	Jane Carroll*.	79,488
Brown County		Branch 43	
Branch 2		Marshall B. Murray*.	78,798
Tom Walsh.	29,878	Branch 46	
Branch 6		Bonnie L. Gordon*	78,669
John P. Zakowski	33,335	Oneida County	
Buffalo-Pepin County		Branch 2	
James Judge Duvall*.	3,739	Michael H. Bloom	5,064
Calumet County		John F. O'Melia	4,465
Jeffrey S. Froehlich*.	7,810	Outagamie County	
Wayne Fulleylove-Krause.	2,097	Branch 4	
Clark County		Greg Gill, Jr.*	22,962
Jon Counsell*	4,660	Branch 6	
Dane County		Dee R. Dyer*	24,112
Branch 3		Branch 7	
John C. Albert*	58,805	John A. Des Jardins*.	24,664
Branch 8		Portage County	
Frank D. Remington	58,247	Branch 1	
Branch 11		Thomas B. Eagon	9,310
Roger A. Allen.	37,875	Michael McKenna	3,984
Ellen K. Berz.	46,947	Branch 3	
Branch 12		Thomas T. Flugaur*	10,087
David Flanagan*.	59,375	Racine County	
Door County		Branch 5	
Branch 1		Michael E. Nieskes*.	13,665
D. Todd Ehlers*	5,556	Mike Piontek.	17,283
Branch 2		Branch 10	
Peter C. Diltz*.	5,801	Timothy D. Boyle	16,054
Eau Claire County		Mark Nielsen.	16,009
Branch 1		Richland County	
Lisa K. Stark*	14,128	Andrew Sharp	2,709
Branch 3		Rock County	
William M. Gabler, Sr.*	13,129	Branch 7	
Branch 4		Jack C. Hoag.	12,958
Jon M. Theisen*	13,036	Barbara W. McCrory.	13,680
Branch 5		St. Croix County	
Paul J. Lenz*.	13,081	Branch 3	
Kenosha County		Scott R. Needham*	13,761
Branch 2		Sauk County	
Edward Richard Antaramian. . . .	12,396	Branch 1	
Jason A. Rossell*	14,243	Patrick J. Taggart*	8,749
Branch 7		Branch 3	
S. Michael Wilk*	18,671	Guy Reynolds*.	8,535
Manitowoc County		Sheboygan County	
Branch 2		Branch 5	
Gary Bendix*	8,747	James J. Bolgert*	17,173
Bob Dewane	5,710	Walworth County	
Menominee-Shawano County		Branch 1	
Branch 2		Phillip A. Koss.	13,885
William F. Kussel, Jr.*.	4,007	Washington County	
David R. Winter	3,786	Branch 4	
Milwaukee County		Andrew T. Gonring*.	22,641
Branch 4		Waukesha County	
Mel Flanagan*.	80,755	Branch 2	
Branch 8		Jennifer Dorow*	58,642
William Sosnay*.	78,327	Branch 12	
Branch 17		Kathryn W. Foster*	58,944
Nelson Wesley Phillips III*	51,864	Waupaca County	
Carolina Maria Stark.	65,825	Branch 3	
Branch 20		Raymond S. Huber*	7,795
Dennis P. Moroney*	79,249	Winnebago County	
Branch 23		Branch 1	
Hannah C. Dugan	43,093	Thomas J. Gritton*.	24,212
Lindsey Grady	65,910	Branch 4	
Branch 28		Karen L. Seifert*.	24,021
Mark A. Sanders	79,856	Wood County	
Branch 38		Branch 2	
Jeffrey A. Wagner*.	84,190	Nicholas J. Brazeau, Jr.*.	11,478

*Incumbent.

Source: Official Records of the Government Accountability Board, Elections Division. Scattered votes omitted.

VOTE FOR CIRCUIT JUDGES
April 2, 2013 Spring Election

Circuit Court	Vote	Circuit Court	Vote
Brown County		Marquette County	
Branch 3		Bernard Ben Bult	1,645
Tammy Jo Hock*	20,819	Donna Cacic Wissbaum	1,549
Branch 7		Milwaukee County	
Timothy A. Hinkfuss*	21,858	Branch 11	
Columbia County		Dave Swanson	59,989
Branch 3		Branch 26	
Alan J. White*	8,123	William S. Pocan*	60,343
Dane County		Branch 45	
Branch 16		Rebecca Bradley*	55,177
Rhonda L. Lanford.	42,976	Janet Claire Protasiewicz	48,685
Rebecca St. John*	39,080	Monroe County	
Dodge County		Branch 1	
Branch 2		Todd L. Ziegler*	5,630
John R. Storck*	10,312	Ozaukee County	
Branch 3		Branch 2	
Joseph F. Fischer.	5,215	Joe Voiland.	13,009
Joseph G. Sciascia	7,568	Tom R. Wolfgram*.	7,729
Jefferson County		Portage County	
Branch 2		Branch 2	
William F. Hue*	9,410	John V. Finn*	8,032
La Crosse County		Racine County	
Branch 1		Branch 1	
Ramona A. Gonzalez*	12,020	Gerald P. Ptacek*	20,771
Branch 2		Rock County	
Elliott M. Levine*	11,875	Branch 4	
Branch 3		Daniel T. Dillon*.	13,284
Todd W. Bjerke*	12,053	St. Croix County	
Branch 4		Branch 2	
Scott L. Horne*	12,507	Edward F. Vlack*	7,976
Lincoln County		Sheboygan County	
Branch 2		Branch 2	
Robert Russell	3,087	Timothy M. Van Akkeren*.	16,271
John Yackel*.	2,914	Trempealeau County	
Manitowoc County		John A. Damon*	4,246
Branch 1		Waukesha County	
Steven R. Olson	8,129	Branch 1	
Mark R. Rohrer	8,153	Michael O. Bohren*	48,258
Marathon County		Branch 9	
Branch 4		Donald J. Hassin, Jr.*	47,855
Greg Grau*.	14,166		
Marinette County			
Branch 2			
Allen R. Brey	3,192		
James A. Morrison*	4,175		

*Incumbent.

Source: Official Records of the Government Accountability Board, Elections Division. Scattered votes omitted.

COUNTY VOTE FOR UNITED STATES SENATOR
August 14, 2012 Primary

County	Tammy Baldwin (Dem.)	Jeff Fitzgerald (Rep.)	Eric Hovde (Rep.)	Mark W. Neumann (Rep.)	Tommy G. Thompson (Rep.)
Adams	831	172	499	532	746
Ashland	377	34	69	218	377
Barron	957	148	478	1,533	1,238
Bayfield	481	36	94	351	549
Brown	3,477	2,069	12,126	7,060	5,668
Buffalo	269	35	219	297	455
Burnett	362	56	95	373	623
Calumet	641	624	2,340	1,616	1,694
Chippewa	2,282	161	1,026	1,555	1,410
Clark	492	196	746	1,170	764
Columbia	1,527	355	1,579	1,224	2,742
Crawford	424	79	238	392	614
Dane	47,477	1,225	11,079	5,115	16,293
Dodge	1,710	3,575	2,539	2,750	3,789
Door	1,103	209	1,329	1,060	1,339
Douglas	1,492	69	198	613	836
Dunn	713	148	601	970	1,116
Eau Claire	1,923	306	1,721	2,320	2,578
Florence	114	48	98	159	226
Fond du Lac	1,336	2,065	4,745	4,156	5,261
Forest	750	59	175	225	264
Grant	1,010	290	938	1,117	2,777
Green	1,817	121	874	721	1,373
Green Lake	248	351	985	928	1,318
Iowa	1,414	78	458	362	865
Iron	225	30	55	160	382
Jackson	1,281	68	267	417	599
Jefferson	1,483	1,810	2,446	2,436	3,493
Juneau	493	186	605	677	1,915
Kenosha	5,475	1,335	2,602	2,550	3,722
Kewaunee	1,443	158	889	697	490
La Crosse	2,887	392	1,989	2,565	3,942
Lafayette	991	49	270	309	625
Langlade	539	157	683	700	520
Lincoln	683	327	1,093	935	989
Manitowoc	2,371	1,040	4,149	2,859	2,407
Marathon	3,145	1,084	4,868	3,338	3,399
Marinette	747	279	1,298	1,626	1,255
Marquette	400	133	519	462	912
Menominee	84	8	42	31	26
Milwaukee	39,289	12,341	20,991	11,183	22,810
Monroe	610	235	787	1,121	2,721
Oconto	1,039	548	2,092	1,653	1,294
Oneida	1,664	319	1,425	1,443	1,511
Outagamie	3,242	1,578	7,706	5,401	4,754
Ozaukee	1,130	3,323	6,385	2,157	5,733
Pepin	139	16	90	202	164
Pierce	1,186	80	323	563	780
Polk	598	169	212	831	1,066
Portage	4,517	388	1,635	1,286	1,275
Price	426	95	328	573	579
Racine	4,223	3,722	6,252	4,691	6,357
Richland	401	84	286	490	882
Rock	8,981	663	2,562	3,179	4,944
Rusk	582	70	358	588	557
St. Croix	961	202	498	1,499	1,991
Sauk	2,452	198	1,160	1,180	2,953
Sawyer	261	54	157	569	618
Shawano	518	452	1,828	1,589	1,361
Sheboygan	2,531	2,286	6,751	3,876	4,305
Taylor	301	142	588	721	555
Trempealeau	424	83	435	525	880
Vernon	601	175	692	765	1,543
Vilas	748	211	869	1,047	1,172
Walworth	1,355	1,819	3,028	2,862	4,127
Washburn	354	71	156	562	566
Washington	1,431	5,196	8,215	3,695	6,855
Waukesha	4,932	14,680	24,861	11,969	25,709
Waupaca	862	538	2,001	1,744	1,757
Waushara	348	356	1,112	865	1,056
Winnebago	2,319	1,615	6,528	4,878	5,490
Wood	1,366	597	2,222	2,500	1,972
TOTAL	185,265	71,871	179,557	132,786	197,928

Dem. – Democratic Party; Rep. – Republican Party.

Source: Official records of the Government Accountability Board, Elections Division. Scattered votes omitted.

COUNTY VOTE FOR UNITED STATES SENATOR
November 6, 2012 General Election

County	Riley J. Hood (Con. Write-in)	Tammy Baldwin (Dem.)	Tommy G. Thompson (Rep.)	Nimrod Y. U. Allen, III (Ind.)[1]	Joseph Kexel (Ind.)[1]	Diane E. Lorbiecki (Ind. Write-in)[1]	County Total[2]
Adams	0	5,161	4,404	52	183	0	9,810
Ashland	0	5,306	2,912	64	95	0	8,388
Barron	7	10,644	10,805	181	508	3	22,285
Bayfield	0	6,017	3,476	52	85	0	9,630
Brown	0	60,409	61,838	843	2,709	0	125,976
Buffalo	1	3,366	3,284	52	170	0	6,877
Burnett	0	3,996	4,288	36	117	0	8,438
Calumet	1	10,989	14,053	154	748	0	25,972
Chippewa	0	14,774	14,677	227	803	0	30,500
Clark	0	6,159	6,875	142	354	0	13,547
Columbia	0	16,028	13,413	100	641	0	30,203
Crawford	0	4,321	3,117	35	158	0	7,635
Dane	1	206,917	88,395	1,258	3,823	4	300,587
Dodge	0	17,867	24,646	201	1,124	0	43,899
Door	0	8,966	7,996	72	379	0	17,432
Douglas	0	14,599	7,478	159	220	0	22,464
Dunn	0	10,671	10,038	205	568	0	21,509
Eau Claire	0	29,057	23,036	361	1,291	0	53,833
Florence	0	908	1,586	12	42	0	2,550
Fond du Lac	2	21,273	29,539	321	1,114	0	52,294
Forest	0	2,288	2,028	33	104	0	4,455
Grant	0	12,027	10,902	166	520	0	23,628
Green	0	10,721	7,954	71	385	0	19,153
Green Lake	0	3,637	5,600	73	217	0	9,530
Iowa	0	7,454	4,631	60	229	0	12,382
Iron	0	1,656	1,785	13	24	0	3,478
Jackson	0	4,979	3,894	62	214	0	9,156
Jefferson	3	19,081	23,393	176	810	0	43,514
Juneau	1	5,474	5,805	59	255	1	11,609
Kenosha	0	42,825	33,273	325	2,583	0	79,111
Kewaunee	0	5,149	5,419	82	257	0	10,918
La Crosse	6	34,203	26,271	402	1,425	4	62,351
Lafayette	0	4,110	3,549	35	127	0	7,824
Langlade	0	4,580	5,255	73	256	0	10,175
Lincoln	1	7,379	6,911	188	439	0	14,935
Manitowoc	1	19,616	20,646	371	1,178	6	41,862
Marathon	0	31,751	34,688	574	1,675	3	68,787
Marinette	0	9,685	9,989	140	439	0	20,263
Marquette	0	3,744	4,032	35	181	0	8,005
Menominee	0	1,015	213	8	35	0	1,273
Milwaukee	11	312,618	155,410	2,022	7,181	3	477,884
Monroe	0	8,629	9,899	156	457	0	19,157
Oconto	0	8,792	10,032	189	502	0	19,535
Oneida	0	10,047	10,183	223	706	0	21,199
Outagamie	6	43,297	46,212	770	2,541	0	92,928
Ozaukee	2	18,285	35,463	171	1,059	2	55,050
Pepin	0	1,812	1,702	13	64	0	3,592
Pierce	0	10,254	9,850	126	364	0	20,606
Polk	0	10,192	11,310	140	483	0	22,144
Portage	0	21,469	15,710	322	709	1	38,274
Price	0	3,832	3,623	61	211	0	7,730
Racine	12	51,630	47,030	596	2,109	6	101,462
Richland	0	4,504	3,786	27	116	0	8,437
Rock	0	46,892	30,010	408	1,859	0	79,243
Rusk	0	3,298	3,393	103	242	0	7,043
St. Croix	1	20,053	24,347	149	984	0	45,572
Sauk	0	17,247	13,565	121	638	1	31,599
Sawyer	0	4,445	4,163	25	100	0	8,739
Shawano	4	8,755	10,417	155	503	1	19,852
Sheboygan	4	26,284	33,472	359	1,586	2	61,766
Taylor	0	3,859	5,049	99	270	0	9,280
Trempealeau	0	7,144	5,699	78	297	0	13,223
Vernon	0	7,543	6,051	93	327	0	14,022
Vilas	0	5,762	7,308	59	375	0	13,526
Walworth	2	21,390	28,069	237	1,588	0	51,376
Washburn	0	4,405	4,442	50	140	0	9,037
Washington	1	22,702	52,950	275	1,745	0	77,787
Waukesha	0	75,408	159,450	963	4,098	3	240,142
Waupaca	1	11,011	13,601	173	651	0	25,473
Waushara	0	5,213	6,239	77	283	0	11,822
Winnebago	2	42,782	41,545	409	2,608	2	87,541
Wood	0	18,748	18,052	333	959	0	38,132
TOTAL	**70**	**1,547,104**	**1,380,126**	**16,455**	**62,240**	**43**	**3,009,411**
Percent of Total Vote[3]	0.00%	51.41%	45.86%	0.55%	2.07%	0.00%	

Con. – Constitution Party; Dem. – Democratic Party; Rep. – Republican Party; Ind. – Independent.

[1]Independent nominations may be made for any office to be voted for at any general or partisan special election [Section 8.20 (1), Wisconsin Statutes].

[2]County totals include scattered votes.

[3]Percentages do not sum to 100%, as scattered votes are included in total vote.

Source: Official records of the Government Accountability Board, Elections Division.

DISTRICT VOTE FOR MEMBERS OF THE 113TH U.S. CONGRESS
August 14, 2012 Primary

First Congressional District

County	Rob Zerban (Dem.)	Paul Ryan* (Rep.)
Kenosha	5,132	8,841
Milwaukee (part)	1,326	10,545
Racine	3,671	17,647
Rock (part)	4,350	5,350
Walworth (part)	998	9,582
Waukesha (part)	788	13,735
TOTAL	16,265	65,700

Second Congressional District

County	Dennis Hall (Dem.)	Mark Pocan (Dem.)	Kelda Helen Roys (Dem.)	Matt Silverman (Dem.)	Chad Lee (Rep.)
Dane	730	36,188	10,380	1,601	21,508
Green	49	1,209	438	110	1,914
Iowa	43	882	407	105	1,239
Lafayette	46	569	299	134	862
Richland (part)	2	49	21	7	162
Rock (part)	241	2,434	1,028	313	3,824
Sauk	52	1,840	508	95	3,304
TOTAL	1,163	43,171	13,081	2,365	32,813

Third Congressional District

County	Ron Kind* (Dem.)	Ray Boland (Rep.)
Adams	715	1,159
Buffalo	294	599
Chippewa (part)	1,471	1,367
Crawford	436	819
Dunn	721	1,904
Eau Claire	1,918	4,311
Grant	994	3,414
Jackson (part)	1,338	683
Juneau (part)	358	1,585
La Crosse	2,951	5,810
Monroe (part)	545	3,270
Pepin	145	290
Pierce	1,235	1,303
Portage	4,444	2,405
Richland (part)	293	968
Trempealeau	456	1,142
Vernon	618	2,177
Wood (part)	823	2,462
TOTAL	19,755	35,668

DISTRICT VOTE FOR MEMBERS OF THE 113TH U.S. CONGRESS
August 14, 2012 Primary–Continued

Fourth Congressional District

County	Gwen Moore* (Dem.)	Dan Sebring (Rep.)
Milwaukee (part).	34,525	19,144
Waukesha (part)	0	0
TOTAL.	34,525	19,144

Fifth Congressional District

County	Dave Heaster (Dem.)	F. James Sensenbrenner, Jr.* (Rep.)
Dodge (part)	583	4,619
Jefferson	1,165	7,737
Milwaukee (part).	3,019	12,848
Walworth (part)	193	429
Washington.	1,150	18,342
Waukesha (part)	3,156	45,395
TOTAL.	9,266	89,370

Sixth Congressional District

County	Joe Kallas (Dem.)	Tom Petri* (Rep.)	Lauren Stephens (Rep.)
Columbia.	1,315	3,893	1,099
Dodge (part)	821	4,514	1,058
Fond du Lac	1,162	12,140	3,200
Green Lake.	232	2,747	707
Manitowoc	2,079	7,722	1,800
Marquette	334	1,448	393
Milwaukee (part).	29	232	43
Ozaukee	918	12,299	1,764
Sheboygan	2,285	13,196	2,642
Waushara.	285	2,518	572
Winnebago (part)	1,825	12,667	2,543
TOTAL.	11,285	73,376	15,821

DISTRICT VOTE FOR MEMBERS OF THE 113TH U.S. CONGRESS
August 14, 2012 Primary–Continued
Seventh Congressional District

County	Pat Kreitlow (Dem.)	Sean Duffy* (Rep.)
Ashland	350	553
Barron	935	2,782
Bayfield	454	814
Burnett	351	968
Chippewa (part)	852	1,549
Clark	575	2,172
Douglas	1,414	1,411
Florence	72	380
Forest	627	545
Iron	209	467
Jackson (part)	96	177
Juneau (part)	92	568
Langlade	475	1,498
Lincoln	695	2,492
Marathon	2,729	9,942
Monroe (part)	61	395
Oneida	1,532	3,842
Polk	562	1,863
Price	395	1,153
Rusk	606	1,276
St. Croix	909	3,170
Sawyer	254	1,154
Taylor	284	1,628
Vilas	661	2,586
Washburn	350	1,130
Wood (part)	513	2,472
TOTAL	16,053	46,987

Eighth Congressional District

County	Jamie Wall (Dem.)	Reid J. Ribble* (Rep.)
Brown	2,942	20,226
Calumet	530	5,025
Door	909	2,995
Kewaunee	1,312	1,865
Marinette	644	3,439
Menominee	70	83
Oconto	891	4,541
Outagamie	2,898	15,929
Shawano	443	4,229
Waupaca	728	4,962
Winnebago (part)	146	1,395
TOTAL	11,513	64,689

Dem. – Democratic Party; Rep. – Republican Party.
*Incumbent.
Source: Official records of the Government Accountability Board, Elections Division. Scattered votes omitted.

DISTRICT VOTE FOR MEMBERS OF THE 113TH U.S. CONGRESS
November 6, 2012 General Election

First Congressional District

County	Rob Zerban (Dem.)	Paul Ryan* (Rep.)	Keith Deschler (Ind.)
Kenosha	41,121	36,130	1,396
Milwaukee (part).	18,904	30,150	751
Racine	47,722	50,294	1,494
Rock (part).	20,928	18,888	833
Walworth (part)	16,575	27,935	856
Waukesha (part)	13,164	37,026	724
TOTAL.	158,414	200,423	6,054
Percent of Total Vote†	43.39%	54.90%	1.66%

Second Congressional District

County	Mark Pocan (Dem.)	Chad Lee (Rep.)	Joe Kopsick (Ind. Write-in)
Dane	204,185	81,979	6
Green.	10,245	8,005	0
Iowa	7,009	4,330	0
Lafayette	3,674	3,320	0
Richland (part).	825	598	0
Rock (part).	22,401	13,647	0
Sauk	17,083	12,804	0
TOTAL.	265,422	124,683	6
Percent of Total Vote†	67.90%	31.90%	0.00%

Third Congressional District

County	Ron Kind* (Dem.)	Ray Boland (Rep.)
Adams	5,183	3,799
Buffalo	4,290	2,252
Chippewa (part)	11,053	6,094
Crawford	5,203	2,158
Dunn	12,673	7,913
Eau Claire	33,641	17,720
Grant	14,529	7,117
Jackson (part)	5,365	2,345
Juneau (part)	5,238	2,995
La Crosse	41,057	19,767
Monroe (part)	9,661	6,559
Pepin	2,186	1,278
Pierce.	11,693	8,082
Portage	21,920	13,727
Richland (part).	4,064	2,285
Trempealeau	8,494	4,100
Vernon	9,224	4,418
Wood (part)	12,238	9,104
TOTAL.	217,712	121,713
Percent of Total Vote†	64.08%	35.82%

DISTRICT VOTE FOR MEMBERS OF THE 113TH U.S. CONGRESS
November 6, 2012 General Election–Continued
Fourth Congressional District

County	Gwen Moore* (Dem.)	Dan Sebring (Rep.)	Robert R. Raymond (Ind.)
Milwaukee (part).	235,257	80,787	9,277
Waukesha (part)	0	0	0
TOTAL.	235,257	80,787	9,277
Percent of Total Vote†	72.21%	24.80%	2.85%

Fifth Congressional District

County	Dave Heaster (Dem.)	F. James Sensenbrenner, Jr.* (Rep.)
Dodge (part)	5,725	13,351
Jefferson	15,310	25,237
Milwaukee (part).	31,415	39,725
Walworth (part)	3,108	2,366
Washington.	18,846	56,187
Waukesha (part)	44,074	113,469
TOTAL.	118,478	250,335
Percent of Total Vote†	32.05%	67.72%

Sixth Congressional District

County	Joe Kallas (Dem.)	Tom Petri* (Rep.)
Columbia.	14,699	13,709
Dodge (part)	9,481	13,573
Fond du Lac	16,050	33,412
Green Lake.	3,048	6,091
Manitowoc.	14,927	25,429
Marquette	2,999	4,294
Milwaukee (part).	423	660
Ozaukee	16,607	35,635
Sheboygan	21,267	37,673
Waushara.	4,009	7,160
Winnebago (part)	32,411	45,824
TOTAL.	135,921	223,460
Percent of Total Vote†	37.78%	62.12%

DISTRICT VOTE FOR MEMBERS OF THE 113TH U.S. CONGRESS
November 6, 2012 General Election–Continued
Seventh Congressional District

County	Pat Kreitlow (Dem.)	Sean Duffy* (Rep.)	Dale C. Lehner (Ind. Write-in)
Ashland	5,051	3,172	0
Barron	9,708	11,621	17
Bayfield	5,573	4,026	0
Burnett	3,587	4,526	0
Chippewa (part)	5,249	6,966	0
Clark	5,702	7,823	0
Douglas	13,381	8,936	1
Florence	868	1,506	0
Forest	1,951	2,327	0
Iron	1,465	1,908	0
Jackson (part)	375	531	0
Juneau (part)	1,101	1,451	0
Langlade	3,615	6,201	0
Lincoln	6,307	8,517	0
Marathon	27,214	40,878	0
Monroe (part)	849	1,270	0
Oneida	9,033	11,570	0
Polk	9,152	12,181	0
Price	3,277	4,045	0
Rusk	3,217	3,611	0
St. Croix	18,567	25,679	1
Sawyer	3,834	4,660	0
Taylor	3,174	6,090	0
Vilas	5,276	8,005	0
Washburn	3,939	4,788	0
Wood (part)	6,059	9,432	1
TOTAL	157,524	201,720	20
Percent of Total Vote†	43.80%	56.08%	0.01%

Eighth Congressional District

County	Jamie Wall (Dem.)	Reid J. Ribble* (Rep.)
Brown	55,730	67,021
Calumet	10,245	15,354
Door	8,544	8,636
Kewaunee	4,780	5,848
Marinette	8,807	10,617
Menominee	925	238
Oconto	7,885	10,839
Outagamie	39,288	50,666
Shawano	7,846	11,172
Waupaca	9,919	14,342
Winnebago (part)	2,318	4,141
TOTAL	156,287	198,874
Percent of Total Vote†	43.97%	55.95%

Dem. – Democratic Party; Rep. – Republican Party; Ind. – Independent.

*Incumbent.

†Percentages do not sum to 100%, as scattered votes are included in total vote.

Source: Official records of the Government Accountability Board, Elections Division.

COUNTY VOTE FOR STATE SENATORS
Primary Elections

County or Part	Senate District	Democratic	Vote	Republican	Vote
		July 12, 2011 Recall			
Adams (part)	14	Church	61	No candidate	
		Clark	232		
Brown (part)	2	Junkermann	4,018	No candidate	
		Nusbaum	7,262		
Burnett (part)	10	Moore	933	No candidate	
		Weix	800		
Columbia (part)	14	Church	914	No candidate	
		Clark	2,687		
Crawford	32	Shilling	2,346	No candidate	
		Smith	849		
Dodge (part)	18	Buckstaff	167	No candidate	
		King	571		
Dunn (part)	10	Moore	2,229	No candidate	
		Weix	1,094		
Fond du Lac (part)	14	Church	656	No candidate	
		Clark	1,088		
(part)	18	Buckstaff	4,445	No candidate	
		King	8,330		
Green Lake	14	Church	1,097	No candidate	
		Clark	1,493		
La Crosse	32	Shilling	17,688	No candidate	
		Smith	7,334		
Marquette (part)	14	Church	842	No candidate	
		Clark	1,323		
Milwaukee (part)	8	Huber	4,522	No candidate	
		Pasch	14,341		
Monroe (part)	32	Shilling	711	No candidate	
		Smith	377		
Oconto (part)	2	Junkermann	625	No candidate	
		Nusbaum	1,095		
Outagamie (part)	2	Junkermann	1,529	No candidate	
		Nusbaum	3,589		
(part)	14	Church	172	No candidate	
		Clark	316		
Ozaukee (part)	8	Huber	2,568	No candidate	
		Pasch	2,647		
Pierce (part)	10	Moore	3,857	No candidate	
		Weix	2,782		
Polk (part)	10	Moore	3,958	No candidate	
		Weix	3,405		
Richland (part)	32	Shilling	348	No candidate	
		Smith	103		
St. Croix	10	Moore	8,323	No candidate	
		Weix	7,948		
Sauk (part)	14	Church	852	No candidate	
		Clark	2,538		
Shawano (part)	2	Junkermann	1,341	No candidate	
		Nusbaum	2,188		
(part)	14	Church	0	No candidate	
		Clark	0		
Vernon	32	Shilling	4,247	No candidate	
		Smith	2,001		
Washington (part)	8	Huber	2,033	No candidate	
		Pasch	1,694		
Waukesha (part)	8	Huber	2,742	No candidate	
		Pasch	2,975		
Waupaca (part)	2	Junkermann	65	No candidate	
		Nusbaum	63		
(part)	14	Church	1,733	No candidate	
		Clark	3,689		
Waushara (part)	14	Church	1,019	No candidate	
		Clark	1,686		
Winnebago (part)	18	Buckstaff	4,383	No candidate	
		King	10,661		
		July 19, 2011 Recall			
Florence	12	No candidate		Lussow	133
				Simac	345
Forest	12	No candidate		Lussow	378
				Simac	628
Kenosha (part)	22	No candidate		Ekornaas	2,818
				Steitz	5,326
Langlade	12	No candidate		Lussow	819
				Simac	1,307
Lincoln	12	No candidate		Lussow	1,595
				Simac	1,533
Marathon (part)	12	No candidate		Lussow	119
				Simac	182
Marinette (part)	12	No candidate		Lussow	540
				Simac	1,094
Menominee	12	No candidate		Lussow	40
				Simac	66

COUNTY VOTE FOR STATE SENATORS
Primary Elections–Continued

County or Part	Senate District	Democratic	Vote	Republican	Vote
Oconto (part)	12	No candidate		Lussow	131
				Simac	315
Oneida	12	No candidate		Lussow	2,329
				Simac	3,034
Racine (part)	22	No candidate		Ekornaas	551
				Steitz	655
Shawano (part)	12	No candidate		Lussow	162
				Simac	274
Vilas	12	No candidate		Lussow	1,519
				Simac	2,522
Walworth (part)	22	No candidate		Ekornaas	0
				Steitz	0
May 8, 2012 Recall					
Barron (part)	23	Dexter	194	No candidate	
		Engel	132		
Chippewa	23	Dexter	6,337	No candidate	
		Engel	3,736		
Clark (part)	23	Dexter	2,446	No candidate	
		Engel	1,482		
Columbia (part)	13	Compas	936	No candidate	
		Ellerman	256		
Dane (part)	13	Compas	1,619	No candidate	
		Ellerman	403		
Dodge (part)	13	Compas	8,765	No candidate	
		Ellerman	3,041		
Dunn (part)	23	Dexter	1,799	No candidate	
		Engel	942		
Eau Claire (part)	23	Dexter	5,580	No candidate	
		Engel	2,630		
Jefferson (part)	13	Compas	8,449	No candidate	
		Ellerman	3,848		
Marathon (part)	23	Dexter	1,093	No candidate	
		Engel	719		
(part)	29	Buckley	7,425	No candidate	
		Seidel	12,533		
Portage (part)	29	Buckley	74	No candidate	
		Seidel	151		
Price	29	Buckley	825	No candidate	
		Seidel	1,865		
Racine (part)	21	Lehman	20,284	No candidate	
		Varebrook	9,513		
Rusk	29	Buckley	690	No candidate	
		Seidel	1,445		
Sawyer (part)	29	Buckley	36	No candidate	
		Seidel	121		
Shawano (part)	29	Buckley	132	No candidate	
		Seidel	191		
Taylor (part)	23	Dexter	33	No candidate	
		Engel	19		
(part)	29	Buckley	917	No candidate	
		Seidel	1,624		
Waukesha (part)	13	Compas	1,488	No candidate	
		Ellerman	665		
Wood (part)	23	Dexter	169	No candidate	
		Engel	76		
August 14, 2012 Primary					
Adams (part)	14	Worthington	414	Eiler	237
				Olsen*	603
(part)	24	Lassa*	339	Abrahamson	324
				Noble	424
Brown (part)	2	No candidate		Cowles*	7,134
(part)	30	Hansen*	1,799	Macco	6,895
				Suennen	2,791
Burnett (part)	10	Olson	205	Harsdorf*	619
Calumet (part)	20	Lohr	62	Grothman*	605
Columbia (part)	14	Worthington	733	Eiler	821
				Olsen*	2,688
Crawford	32	Shilling*	441	Feehan	903
Dane (part)	14	Worthington	188	Eiler	65
				Olsen*	253
(part)	16	Miller*	13,680	No candidate	
(part)	26	Risser*	19,257	No candidate	
Dodge (part)	14	Worthington	95	Eiler	292
				Olsen*	791
(part)	18	King*	261	Gudex	524
Dunn (part)	10	Olson	377	Harsdorf*	956
Fond du Lac (part)	14	Worthington	145	Eiler	441
				Olsen*	1,167
(part)	18	King*	1,033	Gudex	9,048
(part)	20	Lohr	101	Grothman*	2,071
Florence	12	Sommer	53	Tiffany*	385
		Theo	36		
Forest	12	Sommer	495	Tiffany*	575
		Theo	236		

COUNTY VOTE FOR STATE SENATORS
Primary Elections–Continued

County or Part	Senate District	Democratic	Vote	Republican	Vote
Green Lake.......	14	Worthington	221	Eiler	991
				Olsen*...........	2,504
Jackson (part)	24	Lassa*..........	66	Abrahamson	80
				Noble............	73
Juneau	14	Worthington	0	Eiler	0
				Olsen*...........	0
Kenosha (part).....	22	Wirch*..........	4,375	Stevens.........	3,372
La Crosse	32	Shilling*........	2,997	Feehan	6,024
Langlade........	12	Sommer	281	Tiffany*.........	1,632
		Theo	293		
Lincoln.........	12	Sommer	354	Tiffany*.........	2,470
		Theo	433		
Marathon (part)	12	Sommer	21	Tiffany*.........	270
		Theo	8		
Marquette	14	Worthington	354	Eiler	413
				Olsen*...........	1,496
Marinette (part)	12	Sommer	221	Tiffany*.........	1,651
		Theo	101		
(part)	30	Hansen*..........	374	Macco	836
				Suennen	923
Menominee	12	Sommer	58	Tiffany*.........	71
		Theo	45		
Milwaukee (part)....	4	Taylor*..........	11,517	No candidate	
(part)	6	Coggs*..........	4,466	Pratt (write-in)	16
		Harris............	6,388		
		Mayo............	1,351		
		Swan	767		
		Triplett	377		
(part)	8	No candidate		Darling*..........	5,561
(part)	28	Ward	2,036	Lazich*...........	10,023
Monroe (part)	24	Lassa*..........	402	Abrahamson	1,189
				Noble.............	1,543
(part)	32	Shilling*..........	159	Feehan	1,039
Oconto (part)......	2	No candidate		Cowles*..........	0
(part)	12	Sommer	406	Tiffany*.........	2,626
		Theo	189		
(part)	30	Hansen*.........	359	Macco	1,095
				Suennen	655
Oneida	12	Sommer	1,177	Tiffany*.........	3,852
		Theo	499		
Outagamie (part)....	2	No candidate		Cowles*..........	4,931
(part)	14	Worthington	17	Eiler	22
				Olsen*...........	76
Ozaukee (part).....	8	No candidate		Darling*..........	7,406
(part)	20	Lohr	525	Grothman*........	6,425
Pierce (part)	10	Olson..........	395	Harsdorf*.........	449
Polk (part)	10	Olson..........	535	Harsdorf*.........	1,910
Portage (part)	24	Lassa*..........	5,157	Abrahamson	1,409
				Noble.............	1,980
Racine (part)......	22	Wirch...........	1,200	Stevens.........	2,202
(part)	28	Ward	137	Lazich*...........	1,654
St. Croix	10	Olson..........	902	Harsdorf*.........	3,785
Sauk (part)	14	Worthington	57	Eiler	16
				Olsen*...........	114
Shawano (part).....	2	No candidate		Cowles*..........	3,502
(part)	12	Sommer	72	Tiffany*.........	523
		Theo	40		
(part)	14	Worthington	0	Eiler	0
				Olsen*...........	1
Sheboygan (part).....	20	Lohr	113	Grothman*........	1,137
Vernon (part)......	32	Shilling*........	618	Feehan	2,298
Vilas (part).......	12	Sommer	557	Tiffany*.........	2,443
		Theo	147		
Walworth (part)....	28	Ward	11	Lazich*...........	125
Washington (part) ...	8	No candidate		Darling*..........	4,961
(part)	20	Lohr	1,002	Grothman*........	13,462
Waukesha (part)....	8	No candidate		Darling*..........	8,367
(part)	28	Ward	607	Lazich*...........	8,519
Waupaca (part).....	2	No candidate		Cowles*..........	720
(part)	14	Worthington	666	Eiler	729
				Olsen*...........	3,865
Waushara (part)	14	Worthington	144	Eiler	314
				Olsen*...........	1,224
(part)	24	Lassa*..........	168	Abrahamson	718
				Noble.............	696
Winnebago (part) ...	18	King*...........	1,233	Gudex	5,617
Wood (part)	24	Lassa*..........	998	Abrahamson	2,007
				Noble.............	1,916
		November 6, 2012 Special Primary			
Waukesha (part)	33	No candidate		Farrow*.........	31,927
				Kapenga*.........	29,027

*Member of the 2011 Wisconsin Legislature.

Source: Official records of the Government Accountability Board, Elections Division. Scattered votes omitted.

COUNTY VOTE FOR STATE SENATORS
General Elections

County or Part	Senate District	Democratic	Vote	Republican	Vote
		July 19, 2011 Special Recall General Election			
Brown (part)	30	Hansen*	16,737	Vanderleest	8,281
Marinette (part)	30	Hansen*	2,929	Vanderleest	1,402
Oconto (part)	30	Hansen*	2,371	Vanderleest	1,368
Shawano (part)	30	Hansen*	14	Vanderleest	3
		August 9, 2011 Special Recall General Election			
Adams (part)	14	Clark	395	Olsen*	288
Brown (part)	2	Nusbaum	9,893	Cowles*	12,830
Burnett (part)	10	Moore	1,419	Harsdorf*	2,268
Columbia (part)	14	Clark	4,229	Olsen*	2,804
Crawford (part)	32	Shilling	2,991	Kapanke*	2,558
Dodge (part)	18	King	820	Hopper*	655
Dunn (part)	10	Moore	3,013	Harsdorf*	2,377
Fond du Lac (part) . . .	14	Clark	1,574	Olsen*	2,394
(part)	18	King	12,218	Hopper*	14,081
Green Lake	14	Clark	2,302	Olsen*	4,162
La Crosse	32	Shilling	23,114	Kapanke*	17,553
Marquette (part)	14	Clark	2,204	Olsen*	2,304
Milwaukee (part)	8	Pasch	22,241	Darling*	13,581
Monroe (part)	32	Shilling	975	Kapanke*	1,222
Oconto (part)	2	Nusbaum	1,543	Cowles*	2,334
Outagamie (part)	2	Nusbaum	5,214	Cowles*	6,742
(part)	14	Clark	567	Olsen*	748
Ozaukee (part)	8	Pasch	4,176	Darling*	8,461
Pierce (part)	10	Moore	5,210	Harsdorf*	6,015
Polk (part)	10	Moore	5,835	Harsdorf*	8,376
Richland (part)	32	Shilling	475	Kapanke*	365
St. Croix	10	Moore	11,780	Harsdorf*	18,066
Sauk (part)	14	Clark	4,210	Olsen*	2,833
Shawano (part)	2	Nusbaum	3,230	Cowles*	4,893
(part)	14	Clark	3	Olsen*	2
Vernon	32	Shilling	5,638	Kapanke*	5,026
Washington (part) . . .	8	Pasch	2,887	Darling*	7,955
Waukesha (part)	8	Pasch	4,767	Darling*	9,452
Waupaca (part)	2	Nusbaum	94	Cowles*	238
(part)	14	Clark	6,101	Olsen*	7,494
Waushara	14	Clark	2,770	Olsen*	3,524
Winnebago (part) . . .	18	King	15,153	Hopper*	12,201
		August 16, 2011 Special Recall General Election			
Florence	12	Holperin*	571	Simac	744
Forest	12	Holperin*	1,676	Simac	1,223
Kenosha (part)[1]	22	Wirch*	24,443	Steitz	16,799
Langlade	12	Holperin*	3,257	Simac	3,271
Lincoln	12	Holperin*	5,994	Simac	3,919
Marathon (part)	12	Holperin*	557	Simac	574
Marinette (part)	12	Holperin*	2,268	Simac	2,331
Menominee	12	Holperin*	331	Simac	100
Oconto (part)	12	Holperin*	665	Simac	692
Oneida	12	Holperin*	9,077	Simac	6,374
Racine (part)[1]	22	Wirch*	2,081	Steitz	2,863
Shawano (part)	12	Holperin*	814	Simac	761
Vilas	12	Holperin*	5,240	Simac	4,693
Walworth (part)[1]	22	Wirch*	0	Steitz	0
		June 5, 2012 Special Recall General Election			
Barron (part)	23	Dexter	342	Moulton*	555
Chippewa	23	Dexter	11,038	Moulton*	14,343
Clark (part)	23	Dexter	3,875	Moulton*	7,345
Columbia (part)[2]	13	Compas	1,420	Fitzgerald*	1,059
Dane (part)[2]	13	Compas	2,608	Fitzgerald*	1,738
Dodge (part)[2]	13	Compas	13,715	Fitzgerald*	21,436
Dunn (part)	23	Dexter	3,216	Moulton*	4,205
Eau Claire (part)	23	Dexter	9,733	Moulton*	8,625
Jefferson (part)[2]	13	Compas	12,888	Fitzgerald*	16,590
Marathon (part)	23	Dexter	1,964	Moulton*	4,171
(part)	29	Seidel	19,728	Petrowski*	29,927
Portage (part)	29	Seidel	285	Petrowski*	301
Price	29	Seidel	2,723	Petrowski*	3,992
Racine (part)	21	Lehman	36,358	Wanggaard*	35,539
Rusk	29	Seidel	2,323	Petrowski*	3,507
Sawyer (part)	29	Seidel	188	Petrowski*	285
Shawano (part)	29	Seidel	278	Petrowski*	572
Taylor (part)	23	Dexter	53	Moulton*	91
(part)	29	Seidel	2,219	Petrowski*	5,523
Waukesha (part)[2]	13	Compas	2,278	Fitzgerald*	6,323
Wood (part)	23	Dexter	283	Moulton*	529

COUNTY VOTE FOR STATE SENATORS
General Elections–Continued

County or Part	Senate District	Democratic	Vote	Republican	Vote
		November 6, 2012 General Election			
Adams (part)	14	Worthington	2,740	Olsen*	2,382
(part)	24	Lassa*	2,112	Noble	1,796
Brown (part)	2	No candidate		Cowles*	28,340
(part)	30	Hansen*	32,925	Macco	27,688
Burnett (part)	10	Olson	1,750	Harsdorf*	3,016
Calumet (part)	20	Lohr	1,373	Grothman*	1,758
Columbia (part)	14	Worthington	9,284	Olsen*	9,645
Crawford	32	Shilling*	4,506	Feehan	3,014
Dane (part)	14	Worthington	1,169	Olsen*	1,026
(part)	16	Miller*	72,298	No candidate	
(part)	26	Risser*	87,144	No candidate	
Dodge (part)	14	Worthington	1,905	Olsen*	2,810
(part)	18	King*	1,124	Gudex	1,152
Dunn (part)	10	Olson	5,401	Harsdorf*	5,243
Fond du Lac (part)	14	Worthington	2,137	Olsen*	3,770
(part)	18	King*	16,732	Gudex	21,352
(part)	20	Lohr	2,210	Grothman*	5,244
Florence[3]	12	Sommer	898	Tiffany	1,511
Forest[3]	12	Sommer	2,050	Tiffany	2,215
Green Lake	14	Worthington	2,989	Olsen*	6,315
Jackson	24	Lassa*	348	Noble	427
Juneau	14	Worthington	0	Olsen*	0
Kenosha (part)	22	Wirch*	31,974	Stevens	14,727
La Crosse	32	Shilling*	36,463	Feehan	24,934
Langlade[3]	12	Sommer	3,683	Tiffany	6,092
Lincoln[3]	12	Sommer	6,027	Tiffany	8,414
Marathon[3]	12	Sommer	541	Tiffany	1,210
Marquette	14	Worthington	3,444	Olsen*	4,224
Marinette (part)[3]	12	Sommer	3,798	Tiffany	5,290
(part)	30	Hansen*	5,788	Macco	4,481
Menominee[1]	12	Sommer	831	Tiffany	163
Milwaukee (part)[3]	4	Taylor*	67,064	No candidate	
(part)	6	Harris	60,543	No candidate	
(part)	8	Lueck (write-in)	323	Darling*	17,590
(part)	28	Ward	23,465	Lazich*	31,170
Monroe (part)	24	Lassa*	6,289	Noble	6,412
(part)	32	Shilling*	2,378	Feehan	2,599
Oconto (part)	2	No candidate		Cowles*	0
(part)[3]	12	Sommer	4,236	Tiffany	5,946
(part)	30	Hansen*	4,236	Macco	4,009
Oneida[3]	12	Sommer	8,838	Tiffany	11,084
Outagamie (part)	2	No candidate		Cowles*	21,359
(part)	14	Worthington	318	Olsen*	327
Ozaukee	8	Lueck (write-in)	79	Darling*	20,955
(part)	20	Lohr	8,990	Grothman*	17,520
Pierce (part)	10	Olson	3,289	Harsdorf*	3,248
Polk (part)	10	Olson	8,338	Harsdorf*	12,383
Portage (part)	24	Lassa*	22,940	Noble	14,393
Racine (part)	22	Wirch*	19,203	Stevens	7,551
(part)	28	Ward	1,973	Lazich*	4,552
St. Croix	10	Olson	16,950	Harsdorf*	28,021
Sauk (part)	14	Worthington	646	Olsen*	550
Shawano (part)	2	No candidate		Cowles*	11,743
(part)[3]	12	Sommer	1,400	Tiffany	2,051
(part)	14	Worthington	4	Olsen*	2
Sheboygan (part)	20	Lohr	1,391	Grothman*	3,041
Vilas[3]	12	Sommer	4,507	Tiffany	7,200
Vernon	32	Shilling*	7,806	Feehan	5,998
Walworth (part)	28	Ward	123	Lazich*	369
Washington (part)	8	Lueck (write-in)	20	Darling*	15,794
(part)	20	Lohr	16,540	Grothman*	39,319
Waukesha (part)	8	Lueck (write-in)	31	Darling*	22,063
(part)	28	Ward	9,492	Lazich*	24,763
Waupaca (part)	2	No candidate		Cowles*	2,750
(part)	14	Worthington	7,952	Olsen*	12,635
Waushara (part)	14	Worthington	2,154	Olsen*	3,451
(part)	24	Lassa*	2,748	Noble	3,190
Winnebago (part)	18	King*	24,623	Gudex	20,575
Wood (part)	24	Lassa*	14,240	Noble	11,041
		December 4, 2012 Special Election			
Waukesha	33	No candidate		Farrow	6,909

*Served in the 2011 Senate.

[1] Votes for Independent write-in candidate Brian Harwood: Kenosha – 23, Racine – 0, Walworth – 0.

[2] Votes for Libertarian candidate Terry Virgil: Columbia – 34, Dane – 46, Dodge – 318, Jefferson – 284, Waukesha – 81.

[3] Votes for Independent candidates: 4th SD: David D. King: Milwaukee – 10,154; 12th SD: Paul O. Ehlers: Florence – 65, Forest – 117, Langlade – 201, Lincoln – 345, Marathon – 49, Marinette – 284, Menominee – 109, Oconto – 373, Oneida – 1,081, Shawano – 94, Vilas – 246.

Source: Official records of the Government Accountatility Board, Elections Division. Scattered votes omitted.

DISTRICT VOTE FOR STATE SENATORS
Primary Elections

Senate District	Composed of Assembly Districts	Political Party	Candidates	Vote
			July 12, 2011 Recall	
2	4, 5, 6.	Dem.	Otto C. Junkermann	7,578
		Dem.	Nancy J. Nusbaum	14,197
8	22, 23, 24.	Dem.	Gladys Huber	11,865
		Dem.	Sandra K. Pasch	21,657
10	28, 29, 30.	Dem.	Shelly Moore	19,300
		Dem.	Isaac Weix	16,029
14	40, 41, 42.	Dem.	Rol Church	7,346
		Dem.	Fred Clark	15,052
18	52, 53, 54.	Dem.	John D. Buckstaff	8,995
		Dem.	Jessica King	19,562
32	94, 95, 96.	Dem.	Jennifer Shilling	25,340
		Dem.	James D. Smith	10,664
			July 19, 2011 Recall	
12	34, 35, 36.	Rep.	Robert H. Lussow	7,765
		Rep.	Kim Simac	11,300
22	64, 65, 66.	Rep.	Fred R. Ekornaas	3,369
		Rep.	Jonathan Steitz	5,981
			May 8, 2012 Recall	
13	37, 38, 39.	Dem.	Lori Compas	21,257
		Dem.	Gary Ellerman	8,213
21	61, 62, 63.	Dem.	John Lehman	20,284
		Dem.	Tamra Varebrook	9,513
23	67, 68, 69.	Dem.	Kristen Dexter	17,651
		Dem.	James Engel	9,736
29	85, 86, 87.	Dem.	Jim Buckley	10,099
		Dem.	Donna Seidel	17,930
			August 14, 2012 Primary	
2	4, 5, 6.	Rep.	Robert Cowles*	16,287
4	10, 11, 12.	Dem.	Lena C. Taylor*	11,517
6	16, 17, 18.	Dem.	Elizabeth M. Coggs	4,466
		Dem.	Nikiya Harris	6,388
		Dem.	Michael Mayo	1,351
		Dem.	Allyn Monroe Swan	767
		Dem.	Delta L. Triplett	377
		Rep.	Virginia Faye Pratt (write-in)	16
8	22, 23, 24.	Rep.	Alberta Darling*	26,295
10	28, 29, 30.	Dem.	Daniel C. Olson	2,414
		Rep.	Sheila Harsdorf*	7,719
12	34, 35, 36.	Dem.	Susan Sommer	3,695
		Dem.	Lisa Theo	2,027
		Rep.	Tom Tiffany	16,498
14	40, 41, 42.	Dem.	Margarete Worthington	3,034
		Rep.	David Wayne Eiler	4,341
		Rep.	Luther S. Olsen*	14,782
16	46, 47, 48.	Dem.	Mark Miller*	13,680
18	52, 53, 54.	Dem.	Jessica King*	2,527
		Rep.	Rick Gudex	15,189
20	58, 59, 60.	Dem.	Tanya Lohr	1,803
		Rep.	Glenn Grothman*	23,700
22	64, 65, 66.	Dem.	Robert W. Wirch*	5,575
		Rep.	Pam Stevens	5,574
24	70, 71, 72.	Dem.	Julie Lassa*	7,130
		Rep.	Steve Abrahamson	5,727
		Rep.	Scott Kenneth Noble	6,632
26	76, 77, 78.	Dem.	Fred A. Risser*	19,257
28	82, 83, 84.	Dem.	Jim Ward	2,791
		Rep.	Mary Lazich*	20,321
30	88, 89, 90.	Dem.	Dave Hansen*	2,532
		Rep.	John Macco	8,826
		Rep.	Ray Suennen	4,369
32	94, 95, 96.	Dem.	Jennifer Shilling*	4,215
		Rep.	Bill Feehan	10,264
			November 6, 2012 Primary	
33	97, 98, 99.	Rep.	Paul Farrow	31,927
		Rep.	Chris Kapenga	29,027

Dem. – Democratic Party; Rep. – Republican Party.

*Member of the 2011 Senate.

Source: Official records of the Government Accountability Board, Elections Division. Scattered votes omitted.

DISTRICT VOTE FOR STATE SENATORS
General Elections

Senate District	Composed of Assembly Districts	Political Party	Candidates	Vote	Percent of Total Vote†
			November 2, 2010 General Election		
1	1, 2, 3.	Dem.	Monk Elmer	28,800	39.83%
		Rep.	Frank Lasee	43,415	60.04
3	7, 8, 9.	Dem.	Tim Carpenter*	23,401	61.09
		Rep.	Annette Miller Krznarich	14,796	38.63
5	13, 14, 15.	Dem.	Jim Sullivan*	33,702	47.69
		Rep.	Leah Vukmir	36,852	52.15
7	19, 20, 21.	Dem.	Chris Larson	37,165	57.11
		Rep.	Jess Ripp	27,772	42.68
9	25, 26, 27.	Dem.	Jason Borden	16,775	26.86
		Rep.	Joe Leibham*	45,663	73.11
11	31, 32, 33.	Dem.	L.D. Rockwell	17,955	24.55
		Rep.	Neal Kedzie*	55,121	75.37
13	37, 38, 39.	Dem.	Dwayne Block	19,232	29.20
		Rep.	Scott Fitzgerald*	44,529	67.61
		Ind.	Vittorio Spadaro	2,071	3.14
15	43, 44, 45.	Dem.	Tim Cullen	31,918	58.98
		Rep.	Rick Richard	22,181	40.99
17	49, 50, 51.	Dem.	Carol Beals	21,580	37.38
		Rep.	Dale Schultz*	36,122	62.56
19	55, 56, 57.	Rep.	Michael Ellis*	49,179	99.04
21	61, 62, 63.	Dem.	John Lehman*	28,930	47.43
		Rep.	Van Wanggaard	32,036	52.52
23	67, 68, 69.	Dem.	Pat Kreitlow*	27,375	45.73
		Rep.	Terry Moulton	32,448	54.20
25	73, 74, 75.	Dem.	Bob Jauch*	31,437	51.27
		Rep.	Dane Deutsch	29,854	48.69
27	79, 80, 81.	Dem.	Jon Erpenbach*	51,742	61.84
		Rep.	Kurt Schlicht	31,909	38.13
29	85, 86, 87.	Dem.	Russ Decker*	29,742	47.62
		Rep.	Pam Galloway	32,640	52.26
31	91, 92, 93.	Dem.	Kathleen Vinehout*	30,314	50.27
		Rep.	Ed Thompson	29,911	49.61
33	97, 98, 99	Rep.	Rich Zipperer	62,732	99.50
			July 19, 2011 Special Recall General Election		
30	88, 89, 90.	Dem.	Dave Hansen*	22,051	65.93
		Rep.	David Vanderleest	11,054	33.05
			August 9, 2011 Special Recall General Election		
2	4, 5, 6.	Dem.	Nancy J. Nusbaum	19,974	42.43
		Rep.	Robert L. Cowles*	27,037	57.44
8	22, 23, 24.	Dem.	Sandra K. Pasch	34,071	46.31
		Rep.	Alberta Darling*	39,449	53.62
10	28, 29, 30.	Dem.	Shelly Moore	27,257	42.32
		Rep.	Sheila E. Harsdorf*	37,102	57.60
14	40, 41, 42.	Dem.	Fred Clark	24,355	47.79
		Rep.	Luther S. Olsen*	26,553	52.10
18	52, 53, 54.	Dem.	Jessica King	28,191	51.10
		Rep.	Randy Hopper*	26,937	48.83
32	94, 95, 96.	Dem.	Jennifer Shilling	33,193	55.38
		Rep.	Dan Kapanke*	26,724	44.58
			August 16, 2011 Special Recall General Election		
12	34, 35, 36.	Dem.	Jim Holperin*	30,450	55.12
		Rep.	Kim Simac	24,682	44.68
22	64, 65, 66.	Dem.	Robert W. Wirch*	26,524	57.35
		Rep.	Jonathan Steitz	19,662	42.51
		Ind.	Brian Harwood (write-in)	23	0.05
			June 5, 2012 Special Recall General Election		
13	37, 38, 39.	Dem.	Lori Compas	32,909	40.70
		Lib.	Terry Virgil	763	0.94
		Rep.	Scott Fitzgerald*	47,146	58.31
21	61, 62, 63.	Dem.	John Lehman	36,358	50.53
		Rep.	Van H. Wanggaard*	35,539	49.39
23	67, 68, 69.	Dem.	Kristen Dexter	30,504	43.29
		Rep.	Terry Moulton*	39,864	56.57
29	85, 86, 87.	Dem.	Donna Seidel	27,744	38.58
		Rep.	Jerry Petrowski*	44,107	61.34
			November 6, 2012 General Election		
2	4, 5, 6.	Rep.	Robert Cowles*	64,192	98.54
4	10, 11, 12.	Dem.	Lena C. Taylor*	67,064	86.62
		Ind.	David D. King	10,154	13.11
6	16, 17, 18.	Dem.	Nikiya Harris	60,543	98.72

DISTRICT VOTE FOR STATE SENATORS
General Elections–Continued

Senate District	Composed of Assembly Districts	Political Party	Candidates	Vote	Percent of Total Vote†
8	. . . . . 22, 23, 24.	Dem.	Beth L. Lueck (write-in)	453	0.57
		Rep.	Alberta Darling*	76,402	95.58
10.	. . . . 28, 29, 30.	Dem.	Daniel C. Olson	35,728	40.72
		Rep.	Sheila Harsdorf*	51,911	59.17
12.	. . . . 34, 35, 36.	Dem.	Susan Sommer	36,809	40.45
		Rep.	Tom Tiffany	51,176	56.24
		Ind.	Paul O. Ehlers	2,964	3.26
14.	. . . . 40, 41, 42.	Dem.	Margarete Worthington	34,742	42.40
		Rep.	Luther S. Olsen*	47,137	57.53
16.	. . . . 46, 47, 48.	Dem.	Mark Miller*	72,298	98.73
18.	. . . . 52, 53, 54.	Dem.	Jessica King*	42,479	49.60
		Rep.	Rick Gudex	43,079	50.30
20.	. . . . 58, 59, 60.	Dem.	Tanya Lohr	30,504	31.30
		Rep.	Glenn Grothman*	66,882	68.63
22.	. . . . 64, 65, 66.	Dem.	Robert W. Wirch*	51,177	69.57
		Rep.	Pam Stevens	22,278	30.29
24.	. . . . 70, 71, 72.	Dem.	Julie Lassa*	48,677	56.59
		Rep.	Scott Kenneth Noble	37,259	43.31
26.	. . . . 76, 77, 78.	Dem.	Fred A. Risser*	87,144	98.93
28.	. . . . 82, 83, 84.	Dem.	Jim Ward	35,053	36.51
		Rep.	Mary Lazich*	60,854	63.38
30.	. . . . 88, 89, 90.	Dem.	Dave Hansen*	42,949	54.23
		Rep.	John Macco	36,178	45.68
32.	. . . . 94, 95, 96.	Dem.	Jennifer Shilling*	51,153	58.28
		Rep.	Bill Feehan	36,545	41.64
		December 4, 2012 Special Election			
33.	. . . . . 97, 98, 99.	Rep.	Paul Farrow	6,909	98.07

Dem. – Democratic Party; Lib. – Libertarian Party; Rep. – Republican Party; Ind. – Independent.
*Served in preceding Senate.
†Percentages do not sum to 100%, as scattered votes have been omitted.
Source: Official records of the Government Accountability Board, Elections Division.

COUNTY VOTE FOR REPRESENTATIVES TO THE ASSEMBLY
Primary Elections

County or Part	Assembly District	Democratic	Vote	Republican	Vote
		July 12, 2011 Special Primary			
Dane (part)	48	Arnold	1,507	No candidate	
		De Felice	1,086		
		Heidt	1,190		
		Ordaz	1,149		
		Selkowe	2,452		
		Taylor	3,383		
		October 11, 2011 Special Primary			
La Crosse (part)	95	Billings	2,735	Drewes	313
		Charles	431		
		Clair	1,681		
		Krump	415		
		August 14, 2012 Primary			
Adams (part)	41	Sorenson	436	Ballweg[1]	684
(part)	72	Pluess	296	Krug[1]	727
Ashland	74	Bewley[1]	411	Sendra	468
Barron (part)	67	Bieging	0	Larson[1]	1
				Schulner[2]	0
(part)	75	Smith, S.	928	Rivard[1]	2,916
Bayfield	74	Bewley[1]	545	Sendra	690
Brown (part)	1	Johnsrud	45	Bies[1]	802
		Veeser	176		
(part)	2	Pruess	268	Jacque[1]	2,757
(part)	4	Malcheski	791	Weininger[1]	5,363
(part)	5	Ferguson	36	Steineke[1]	949
		McCabe	28		
(part)	6	Powers	60	Tauchen[1]	436
(part)	88	Bacon	643	Klenke[1]	4,240
(part)	89	Reinhard	169	Nygren[1]	1,566
(part)	90	Genrich	740	Diny	1,027
				Vanderleest	1,702
Buffalo (part)	92	Danou[1]	275	Doerr[2]	48
(part)	93	Smith, J.	5	Petryk[1]	15
Burnett (part)	28	Bever	205	Severson[1]	581
(part)	73	Milroy[1]	151	No candidate	
(part)	75	Smith, S.	9	Rivard[1]	10
Calumet (part)	3	Oswald	321	Lefeber	1,069
				Ott, A.[1]	2,905
(part)	25	Brey	9	Howe	141
		Bushman	6	Nelson	309
		Gruett	148	Sladky	36
		Starzewski	7	Tittl	407
(part)	27	Bauer	3	Kestell[1]	16
(part)	59	No candidate		LeMahieu, Daniel[1]	599
Chippewa (part)	67	Bieging	1,672	Larson[1]	2,345
				Schulner[2]	10
(part)	68	Smriga	569	Bernier[1]	881
(part)	91	Wachs	3	No candidate	
Clark (part)	68	Smriga	147	Bernier[1]	540
(part)	69	Knoff	402	Suder[1]	1,618
(part)	87	Riley	8	Williams[1]	20
Columbia (part)	37	Arnold	335	Braughler	31
		Cotting	11	Jagler	216
				Kauffeld	58
				Romlein	19
				Ruetten	39
(part)	41	Sorenson	36	Ballweg[1]	111
(part)	42	Cooper	692	Ripp[1]	2,915
(part)	81	Clark[1]	304	Frostman	886
Crawford	96	Johnson, T.	380	Nerison[1]	1,050
Dane (part)	37	Arnold	591	Braughler	65
		Cotting	138	Jagler	427
				Kauffeld	167
				Romlein	87
				Ruetten	197
(part)	38	Michalak	596	Kleefisch[1]	664
(part)	42	Cooper	182	Ripp[1]	323
(part)	43	Jorgensen[1]	510	Wynn[1]	429
(part)	46	Hebl[1]	3,323	Schaefer	2,694
(part)	47	Hall, A.	1,457	Bakk	2,491
		Kahl	3,037		
(part)	48	Sargent	5,549	Kassulke[2]	1
				Rygiewicz[2]	6
(part)	76	Taylor[1]	5,877	No candidate	
(part)	77	Berceau[1]	7,009	No candidate	
(part)	78	Fisher	497	No candidate	
		Hulsey[1]	5,215		
(part)	79	Hesselbein	3,590	No candidate	
		Lindgren	1,885		
(part)	80	Pope-Roberts[1]	2,325	Lamberson	2,226
		Uphoff	430		
		Wineke	1,874		

COUNTY VOTE FOR REPRESENTATIVES TO THE ASSEMBLY
Primary Elections–Continued

County or Part	Assembly District	Democratic	Vote	Republican	Vote
(part)	81	Clark[1]	397	Frostman	328
Dodge (part)	37	Arnold	294	Braughler	339
		Cotting	182	Jagler	1,284
				Kauffeld	536
				Romlein	217
				Ruetten	60
(part)	39	Grigg	788	Born	3,834
				Heron	1,524
				Lechner	2,282
(part)	42	Cooper	91	Ripp[1]	891
(part)	53	Flejter	184	Frassetto	86
		Schellenger	9	Schraa	383
		Staudacher	71	Schuller	110
Door	1	Johnsrud	592	Bies[1]	3,101
		Veeser	587		
Douglas (part)	73	Milroy[1]	1,794	No candidate	
(part)	74	Bewley[1]	62	Sendra	38
Dunn (part)	29	Swanson	378	Murtha[1]	908
(part)	67	Bieging	225	Larson[1]	1,094
				Schulner[2]	0
(part)	75	Smith, S.	14	Rivard[1]	38
(part)	93	Smith, J.	57	Petryk[1]	233
Eau Claire (part)	68	Smriga	401	Bernier[1]	1,196
(part)	91	Wachs	1,157	No candidate	
(part)	93	Smith, J.	342	Petryk[1]	1,398
Florence	34	Retrum	36	Swearingen	230
		Van Buren	46	Young, A.	164
Fond du Lac (part)	41	Sorenson	122	Ballweg[1]	893
(part)	42	Cooper	23	Ripp[1]	428
(part)	52	Czisny	542	Thiesfeldt[1]	6,878
(part)	53	Flejter	244	Frassetto	588
		Schellenger	24	Schraa	1,674
		Staudacher	153	Schuller	420
(part)	59	No candidate		LeMahieu, Daniel[1]	1,937
Forest (part)	34	Retrum	118	Swearingen	91
		Van Buren	118	Young, A.	52
(part)	36	Kegley	471	Mursau[1]	421
Grant	49	Beals	959	Kuhle	1,824
				Tranel[1]	3,392
Green (part)	45	De Forest	28	Rucker	307
		Ringhand[1]	429	Schmidt	451
(part)	51	Bomhack	290	Marklein[1]	869
		May-Grimm	295		
(part)	80	Pope-Roberts[1]	330	Lamberson	569
		Uphoff	37		
		Wineke	419		
Green Lake (part)	41	Sorenson	206	Ballweg[1]	2,831
(part)	42	Cooper	17	Ripp[1]	260
Iowa (part)	49	Beals	2	Kuhle	6
				Tranel[1]	14
(part)	51	Bomhack	366	Marklein[1]	1,099
		May-Grimm	683		
(part)	80	Pope-Roberts[1]	160	Lamberson	225
		Uphoff	9		
		Wineke	168		
(part)	81	Clark[1]	98	Frostman	130
Iron	74	Bewley[1]	205	Sendra	516
Jackson (part)	68	Smriga	24	Bernier[1]	71
(part)	70	Vruwink[1]	68	Vandermeer	86
				Wald	79
(part)	92	Danou[1]	1,166	Doerr[2]	9
Jefferson (part)	33	Woods	492	Nass[1]	2,752
(part)	37	Arnold	250	Braughler	329
		Cotting	279	Jagler	1,485
				Kauffeld	466
				Romlein	332
				Ruetten	179
(part)	38	Michalak	363	Kleefisch[1]	2,157
(part)	43	Jorgensen[1]	116	Wynn[1]	564
Juneau (part)	41	Sorenson	0	Ballweg[1]	0
(part)	50	Shanahan	469	Brooks[1]	2,500
Kenosha (part)	32	Peterson	33	August[1]	282
(part)	61	Steinbrink[1]	1,162	Kerkman[1]	3,913
(part)	64	Barca[1]	1,750	No candidate	
(part)	65	Hallmon	519	No candidate	
		Namath	180		
		Ohnstad	2,083		
Kewaunee	1	Johnsrud	912	Bies[1]	1,836
		Veeser	809		
La Crosse (part)	94	Doyle[1]	1,318	Evers	2,231
				Hintz, K	1,763
(part)	95	Billings[1]	1,527	No candidate	
Lafayette (part)	49	Beals	74	Kuhle	61
				Tranel[1]	87

COUNTY VOTE FOR REPRESENTATIVES TO THE ASSEMBLY
Primary Elections–Continued

County or Part	Assembly District	Democratic	Vote	Republican	Vote
(part)	51	Bomhack	315	Marklein[1]	923
		May-Grimm	632		
Langlade (part)	35	Koth	411	Czaja	1,190
(part)	36	Kegley	81	Mursau[1]	260
Lincoln	35	Koth	731	Czaja	2,200
Manitowoc (part)	1	Johnsrud	3	Bies[1]	45
		Veeser	10		
(part)	2	Pruess	382	Jacque[1]	1,868
(part)	25	Brey	894	Howe	1,221
		Bushman	238	Nelson	757
		Gruett	182	Sladky	687
		Starzewski	698	Tittl	3,182
(part)	27	Bauer	88	Kestell[1]	906
Marathon (part)	35	Czaja	25	Czaja	252
(part)	69	Knoff	129	Suder[1]	1,027
(part)	85	Johnson, J.	1,050	Snyder	3,745
		Wright	1,626		
(part)	86	Halkoski	728	Spiros	3,412
				Thorson	1,341
(part)	87	Riley	43	Williams[1]	297
Marinette (part)	36	Kegley	308	Mursau[1]	1,886
(part)	89	Reinhard	334	Nygren[1]	1,716
Marquette (part)	41	Sorenson	285	Ballweg[1]	1,287
(part)	42	Cooper	67	Ripp[1]	301
Menominee	36	Kegley	89	Mursau[1]	72
Milwaukee (part)	7	Krusick[1]	944	Koehler	27
		Riemer	1,908		
(part)	8	Manriquez	299	No candidate	
		Zamarripa[1]	599		
(part)	9	Guzman	407	No candidate	
		Zepnick[1]	781		
(part)	10	Callier	193	No candidate	
		Coby	1,974		
		Griffin	216		
		Pasch[1]	3,684		
(part)	11	Barnes	2,596	No candidate	
		Fields, Jason[1]	1,206		
(part)	12	Hall, M.	762	No candidate	
		Kessler[1]	1,937		
(part)	13	Pokrandt	680	Hutton	1,920
				Ristow	497
				Schellinger	1,267
(part)	14	Rockwood	641	Kooyenga[1]	2,728
(part)	15	Garrigues	222	Sanfelippo	2,702
		Moore	462		
(part)	16	Young, L[1]	3,054	No candidate	
(part)	17	Coleman	548	No candidate	
		Dent	1,072		
		Johnson, L.	2,054		
		Royal	1,093		
(part)	18	Brown	139	No candidate	
		Dieter	355		
		Fields, Jarett	808		
		Glabere	169		
		Goyke	1,637		
		Jackson	317		
		Parker	335		
		Vernon	639		
(part)	19	Richards[1]	1,825	No candidate	
(part)	20	Sinicki[1]	1,584	Harris	1,117
				McGartland	2,582
(part)	21	Kurtz	881	Honadel[1]	4,810
(part)	22	No candidate		Oliver	101
				Pridemore[1]	224
(part)	23	Rogers	576	Ott, J.[1]	2,739
(part)	24	Haqqi	635	Knodl[1]	1,698
(part)	82	Wied-Vincent	982	Stone[1]	6,304
(part)	83	Brownlow	164	Craig[1]	934
(part)	84	Roelke	847	Kuglitsch[1]	2,688
Monroe (part)	50	Shanahan	28	Brooks[1]	179
(part)	70	Vruwink[1]	392	Vandermeer	2,194
				Wald	919
(part)	96	Johnson, T.	134	Nerison[1]	1,107
Oconto (part)	6	Powers	0	Tauchen[1]	0
(part)	36	Kegley	558	Mursau[1]	2,719
(part)	89	Reinhard	329	Nygren[1]	1,699
Oneida (part)	34	Retrum	435	Swearingen	2,921
		Van Buren	1,005	Young, A.	944
(part)	35	Koth	176	Czaja	317
Outagamie (part)	2	Pruess	2	Jacque[1]	12
(part)	3	Oswald	348	Lefeber	544
				Ott, A.[1]	1,671

COUNTY VOTE FOR REPRESENTATIVES TO THE ASSEMBLY
Primary Elections–Continued

County or Part	Assembly District	Democratic	Vote	Republican	Vote
(part)	5	Ferguson	305	Steineke[1]	3,972
		McCabe	504		
(part)	6	Powers	111	Tauchen[1]	881
(part)	40	No candidate		Petersen[1]	93
(part)	55	Crail	192	Kaufert[1]	844
				Schroeder, J.	573
(part)	56	Lawrence	268	Murphy	2,822
		Schoenbohm	732	Pleuss	2,688
(part)	57	Bernard Schaber[1]	662	Garrow[2]	232
Ozaukee (part)	23	Rogers	311	Ott, J.[1]	5,551
(part)	24	Haqqi	56	Knodl[1]	1,627
(part)	60	Duman	498	Stroebel[1]	6,157
Pepin	93	Smith, J.	131	Petryk[1]	356
Pierce (part)	30	Odeen	399	Knudson[1]	424
(part)	93	Smith, J.	751	Petryk[1]	1,001
Polk (part)	28	Bever	539	Severson[1]	1,844
(part)	75	Smith, S.	41	Rivard[1]	146
Portage (part)	70	Vruwink[1]	512	Vandermeer	269
				Wald	310
(part)	71	Beveridge	771	Testin	1,903
		Hauser-Menting	117		
		Ladick	1,339		
		Mallison	142		
		McGinley	836		
		Schmid	101		
		Shankland	1,383		
		Steinke	118		
		Verhage	319		
(part)	72	Pluess	124	Krug[1]	193
Price	74	Bewley[1]	386	Sendra	1,080
Racine (part)	32	Peterson	24	August[1]	172
(part)	62	Bryce	522	Weatherston	5,775
		Lemke	1,202		
(part)	63	Albrecht	924	Vos[1]	6,178
(part)	64	Barca[1]	193	No candidate	
(part)	66	Mason[1]	1,039	No candidate	
(part)	83	Brownlow	141	Craig[1]	1,594
Richland (part)	49	Beals	87	Kuhle	184
				Tranel[1]	280
(part)	50	Shanahan	188	Brooks[1]	694
(part)	51	Bomhack	31	Marklein[1]	289
		May-Grimm	56		
Rock (part)	31	Schroeder, R.	986	Loudenbeck[1]	2,169
(part)	43	Jorgensen[1]	1,367	Wynn[1]	1,935
(part)	44	Kolste	1,926	Knilans[1]	3,273
		Liebert	335		
		Murray	1,610		
		Rashkin	705		
(part)	45	De Forest	1,043	Rucker	884
		Ringhand[1]	1,391	Schmidt	1,246
Rusk	87	Riley	578	Williams[1]	1,298
St. Croix (part)	28	Bever	53	Severson[1]	198
(part)	29	Swanson	338	Murtha[1]	1,316
(part)	30	Odeen	521	Knudson[1]	2,155
(part)	75	Smith, S.	6	Rivard[1]	26
(part)	93	Smith, J.	0	Petryk[1]	0
Sauk (part)	41	Sorenson	57	Ballweg[1]	116
(part)	50	Shanahan	427	Brooks[1]	1,357
(part)	51	Bomhack	158	Marklein[1]	490
		May-Grimm	172		
(part)	81	Clark[1]	1,352	Frostman	1,995
Sawyer (part)	74	Bewley[1]	20	Sendra	143
(part)	87	Riley	237	Williams[1]	976
Shawano (part)	6	Powers	346	Tauchen[1]	3,510
(part)	35	Koth	72	Czaja	296
(part)	36	Kegley	32	Mursau[1]	404
(part)	40	No candidate		Petersen[1]	1
Sheboygan (part)	26	Helmke	1,377	Endsley[1]	5,144
				LeMahieu, Devin	3,427
(part)	27	Bauer	949	Kestell[1]	5,787
(part)	59	No candidate		LeMahieu, Daniel[1]	1,115
Taylor	87	Riley	281	Williams[1]	1,640
Trempealeau (part)	68	Smriga	27	Bernier[1]	132
(part)	92	Danou[1]	413	Doerr[2]	54
Vernon (part)	50	Shanahan	9	Brooks[1]	28
(part)	96	Johnson, T.	570	Nerison[1]	2,543
Vilas (part)	34	Retrum	330	Swearingen	1,919
		Van Buren	348	Young, A.	620
(part)	74	Bewley[1]	52	Sendra	167
Walworth (part)	31	Schroeder, R.	367	Loudenbeck[1]	2,778
(part)	32	Peterson	558	August[1]	4,475
(part)	33	Woods	47	Nass[1]	887
(part)	43	Jorgensen[1]	238	Wynn[1]	690
(part)	63	Albrecht	0	Vos[1]	0

COUNTY VOTE FOR REPRESENTATIVES TO THE ASSEMBLY
Primary Elections–Continued

County or Part	Assembly District	Democratic	Vote	Republican	Vote
(part)	83	Brownlow	11	Craig[1]	120
Washburn (part)	73	Milroy[1]	193	No candidate	
(part)	75	Smith, S.	146	Rivard[1]	566
Washington (part)	22	No candidate		Oliver	331
				Pridemore[1]	1,948
(part)	24	Haqqi.	127	Knodl[1]	2,777
(part)	39	Grigg	22	Born	189
				Heron.	30
				Lechner	99
(part)	58	No candidate		Strachota[1]	7,461
(part)	59	No candidate		LeMahieu, Daniel[1]	3,421
(part)	60	Duman	80	Stroebel[1]	1,850
Waukesha (part)	13	Pokrandt	372	Hutton	3,431
				Ristow	458
				Schellinger	1,701
(part)	14	Rockwood	269	Kooyenga[1]	4,522
(part)	15	Garrigues.	138	Sanfelippo	2,581
		Moore	192		
(part)	22	No candidate		Oliver	1,243
				Pridemore[1]	6,118
(part)	24	Haqqi.	90	Knodl[1]	927
(part)	33	Woods	132	Nass[1]	2,233
(part)	38	Michalak	294	Kleefisch[1]	4,222
(part)	83	Brownlow	412	Craig[1]	5,200
(part)	84	Roelke	175	Kuglitsch[1]	2,766
(part)	97	Krumins	467	Kramer[1]	5,487
(part)	98	Prudent	527	Farrow[1]	6,971
(part)	99	Hibbard	597	Kapenga[1]	9,427
Waupaca (part)	6	Powers	67	Tauchen[1]	720
(part)	40	No candidate		Petersen[1]	4,220
Waushara (part)	40	No candidate		Petersen[1]	1,342
(part)	41	Sorenson	2	Ballweg[1]	12
(part)	72	Pluess	149	Krug[1]	1,348
Winnebago (part)	53	Flejter	114	Frassetto	1,288
		Schellenger.	136	Schraa	2,346
		Staudacher	196	Schuller	321
(part)	54	Hintz, G[1]	767	Esslinger	2,988
(part)	55	Crail	444	Kaufert[1]	3,768
				Schroeder, J.	1,914
(part)	56	Lawrence.	76	Murphy.	817
		Schoenbohm	117	Pleuss	727
(part)	57	Bernard Schaber[1].	297	Garrow[2]	117
Wood (part)	69	Knoff.	339	Suder[1]	1,332
(part)	70	Vruwink[1]	331	Vandermeer	576
				Wald	897
(part)	72	Pluess	627	Krug[1]	2,293
(part)	86	Halkoski	82	Spiros	573
				Thorson	89

February 19, 2013 Special Primary

County or Part	Assembly District	Democratic	Vote	Republican	Vote
Waukesha (part)	98	No candidate		Baumann.	1,977
				Greenwald	221
				Morzy	253
				Neylon.	2,006
				Tarantino.	774

[1]Served in the 2011 Assembly.
[2]Write-in candidate.
Source: Official records of the Government Accountability Board, Elections Division. Scattered votes omitted.

COUNTY VOTE FOR REPRESENTATIVES TO THE ASSEMBLY
Special and General Elections

County or Part	Assembly District	Democratic	Vote	Republican	Vote
Dane (part)	48	**August 9, 2011 Special Election** Taylor	5,453	No candidate	
La Crosse (part)	95	**November 8, 2011 Special Election** Billings	5,940	Drewes	2,247
		November 6, 2012 General Election			
Adams (part)	41	Sorenson	2,714	Ballweg*	2,384
(part)	72	Pluess	1,929	Krug*	2,025
Ashland	74	Bewley*	5,455	Sendra	2,630
Barron (part)[2]	67	Bieging	1	Larson*	4
(part)	75	Smith, S.	11,328	Rivard*	10,689
Bayfield	74	Bewley*	6,148	Sendra	3,252
Brown (part)	1	Veeser	2,299	Bies*	2,513
(part)	2	Pruess	6,587	Jacque*	10,700
(part)	4	Malcheski	12,770	Weininger*	16,029
(part)	5	McCabe	1,962	Steineke*	3,231
(part)[2]	6	Powers	1,134	Tauchen*	1,625
(part)	88	Bacon	13,085	Klenke*	14,445
(part)	89	Reinhard	3,544	Nygren*	5,606
(part)	90	Genrich	11,353	Vanderleest	7,432
Buffalo (part)	92	Danou*	5,198	Doerr	14
(part)	93	Smith, J.	67	Petryk*	93
Burnett (part)	28	Bever	1,958	Severson*	2,702
(part)	73	Milroy*	2,399	No candidate	
(part)	75	Smith, S.	64	Rivard*	50
Calumet (part)[1]	3	Oswald	6,574	Ott, A.*	10,861
(part)	25	Brey	1,433	Tittl	2,480
(part)	27	Bauer	57	Kestell*	85
(part)	59	No candidate		LeMahieu*	2,506
Chippewa (part)[2]	67	Bieging	9,827	Larson*	10,701
(part)	68	Smriga	4,386	Bernier*	5,078
(part)	91	Wachs	25	No candidate	
Clark (part)	68	Smriga	1,743	Bernier*	2,069
(part)	69	Knoff	3,635	Suder*	5,774
(part)	87	Riley	140	Williams*	131
Columbia (part)	37	Arnold	1,700	Jagler	912
(part)	41	Sorenson	560	Ballweg*	505
(part)	42	Cooper	8,176	Ripp*	9,960
(part)	81	Clark*	4,391	Frostman	2,714
Crawford	96	Johnson, T.	3,329	Nerison*	4,070
Dane (part)	37	Arnold	4,441	Jagler	3,112
(part)[1]	38	Michalak	3,846	Kleefisch*	2,261
(part)	42	Cooper	1,102	Ripp*	1,217
(part)	43	Jorgensen*	2,880	Wynn*	1,595
(part)	46	Hebl*	20,171	Schaeffer	10,951
(part)	47	Kahl*	22,113	Bakk	9,054
(part)[1,2]	48	Sargent	24,375	No candidate	
(part)	76	Taylor*	31,663	No candidate	
(part)	77	Berceau*	27,622	No candidate	
(part)[1]	78	Hulsey*	22,853	No candidate	
(part)	79	Hesselbein	24,683	No candidate	
(part)	80	Pope-Roberts*	15,396	Lamberson	8,581
(part)	81	Clark*	2,303	Frostman	1,245
Dodge (part)	37	Arnold	3,169	Jagler	5,147
(part)	39	Grigg	11,045	Born	16,495
(part)	42	Cooper	1,889	Ripp*	2,817
(part)	53	Flejter	1,032	Schraa	1,167
Door	1	Veeser	8,168	Bies*	9,131
Douglas (part)	73	Milroy*	17,050	No candidate	
(part)	74	Bewley*	434	Sendra	249
Dunn (part)	29	Swanson	5,710	Murtha*	4,695
(part)[2]	67	Bieging	3,497	Larson*	4,489
(part)	75	Smith, S.	147	Rivard*	171
(part)	93	Smith, J.	1,071	Petryk*	1,036
Eau Claire (part)	68	Smriga	5,444	Bernier*	5,745
(part)	91	Wachs	23,005	No candidate	
(part)	93	Smith, J.	5,477	Petryk*	5,704
Florence[1]	34	Van Buren	810	Swearingen	1,448
Fond du Lac (part)	41	Sorenson	1,650	Ballweg*	2,456
(part)	42	Cooper	457	Ripp*	1,058
(part)	52	Czisny	10,575	Thiesfeldt*	16,313
(part)	53	Flejter	3,397	Schraa	5,345
(part)	59	No candidate		LeMahieu*	5,825
Forest (part)[1]	34	Van Buren	521	Swearingen	573
(part)	36	Kegley	1,588	Mursau*	1,533
Grant	49	Beals	10,662	Tranel*	12,744
Green (part)	45	Ringhand*	2,963	Schmidt	2,301
(part)	51	May-Grimm	3,440	Marklein*	3,678

COUNTY VOTE FOR REPRESENTATIVES TO THE ASSEMBLY
Special and General Elections–Continued

County or Part	Assembly District	Democratic	Vote	Republican	Vote
(part)	80	Pope-Roberts*	3,815	Lamberson	2,324
Green Lake (part)	41	Sorenson	2,723	Ballweg*	5,631
(part)	42	Cooper	250	Ripp*	575
Iowa (part)	49	Beals	46	Tranel*	34
(part)	51	May-Grimm	4,389	Marklein*	3,806
(part)	80	Pope-Roberts*	1,653	Lamberson	866
(part)	81	Clark*	771	Frostman	411
Iron	74	Bewley*	1,378	Sendra	2,020
Jackson (part)	68	Smriga	238	Bernier*	291
(part)	70	Vruwink*	337	Vandermeer	439
(part)	92	Danou*	5,766	Doerr	3
Jefferson (part)[1]	33	Woods	6,577	Nass*	9,004
(part)	37	Arnold	3,979	Jagler	6,628
(part)[1]	38	Michalak	4,634	Kleefisch*	5,847
(part)	43	Jorgensen*	1,855	Wynn*	2,029
Juneau (part)	41	Sorenson	0	Ballweg*	0
(part)[1,2]	50	Shanahan	5,640	Brooks*	5,240
Kenosha (part)[1]	32	Peterson	654	August*	990
(part)	61	Steinbrink*	13,186	Kerkman*	16,589
(part)	64	Barca*	17,175	No candidate	
(part)	65	Ohnstad	18,373	No candidate	
Kewaunee	1	Veeser	5,560	Bies*	5,215
La Crosse (part)	94	Doyle*	18,566	Evers	12,068
(part)	95	Billings*	22,531	No candidate	
Lafayette (part)	49	Beals	406	Tranel*	411
(part)	51	May-Grimm	3,004	Marklein*	3,780
Langlade (part)[1]	35	Koth	3,173	Czaja	5,078
(part)	36	Kegley	585	Mursau*	739
Lincoln[1]	35	Koth	6,712	Czaja	7,235
Manitowoc (part)	1	Veeser	97	Bies*	134
(part)	2	Pruess	5,421	Jacque*	6,306
(part)	25	Brey	10,514	Tittl	13,807
(part)	27	Bauer	1,710	Kestell*	2,752
Marathon (part)[1]	35	Koth	603	Czaja	1,114
(part)	69	Knoff	2,435	Suder*	5,066
(part)[1]	85	Wright	13,930	Snyder	13,025
(part)	86	Halkoski	12,251	Spiros	15,142
(part)	87	Riley	916	Williams*	1,786
Marinette (part)	36	Kegley	3,349	Mursau*	6,119
(part)	89	Reinhard	4,201	Nygren*	5,837
Marquette (part)	41	Sorenson	2,596	Ballweg*	3,487
(part)	42	Cooper	693	Ripp*	767
Menominee	36	Kegley	779	Mursau*	214
Milwaukee (part)[2]	7	Riemer	16,664	No candidate	
(part)	8	Zamarripa*	7,869	No candidate	
(part)	9	Zepnick*	14,635	No candidate	
(part)	10	Pasch*	20,038	No candidate	
(part)	11	Barnes*	16,403	No candidate	
(part)	12	Kessler*	16,193	No candidate	
(part)	13	Pokrandt	8,680	Hutton	9,363
(part)	14	Rockwood	9,859	Kooyenga*	9,088
(part)	15	Moore	8,326	Sanfelippo	9,664
(part)	16	Young*	16,881	No candidate	
(part)[1,2]	17	Johnson, L.	20,288	No candidate	
(part)[1]	18	Goyke	16,276	No candidate	
(part)	19	Richards*	24,856	No candidate	
(part)	20	Sinicki*	16,995	McGartland	12,500
(part)	21	Kurtz	11,921	Honadel*	17,403
(part)	22	No candidate		Pridemore*	1,286
(part)	23	Rogers	7,547	Ott, J.*	7,879
(part)	24	Haqqi	6,593	Knodl*	5,152
(part)	82	Wied-Vincent	11,896	Stone*	18,032
(part)	83	Brownlow	1,854	Craig*	2,957
(part)	84	Roelke	7,930	Kuglitsch*	9,956
Monroe (part)[1,2]	50	Shanahan	314	Brooks*	371
(part)	70	Vruwink*	5,659	Vandermeer	7,257
(part)	96	Johnson, T.	1,695	Nerison*	3,114
Oconto (part)[2]	6	Powers	0	Tauchen*	0
(part)	36	Kegley	4,130	Mursau*	6,317
(part)	89	Reinhard	3,384	Nygren*	4,638
Oneida (part)[1]	34	Van Buren	7,121	Swearingen	10,343
(part)[2]	35	Koth	867	Czaja	1,014
Outagamie (part)	2	Pruess	25	Jacque*	76
(part)[1]	3	Oswald	4,824	Ott, A.*	6,526
(part)	5	McCabe	10,747	Steineke*	12,886
(part)[2]	6	Powers	1,832	Tauchen*	2,562
(part)	40	No candidate		Petersen*	498
(part)[1]	55	Crail	2,583	Kaufert*	4,008
(part)	56	Schoenbohm	10,572	Murphy	14,427

COUNTY VOTE FOR REPRESENTATIVES TO THE ASSEMBLY
Special and General Elections–Continued

County or Part	Assembly District	Democratic	Vote	Republican	Vote
(part)[2]	57	Bernard Schaber*	11,631	No candidate	
Ozaukee (part)	23	Rogers	6,122	Ott, J.*	14,657
(part)	24	Haqqi	1,812	Knodl*	4,232
(part)	60	Duman	8,052	Stroebel*	17,911
Pepin	93	Smith, J.	1,934	Petryk*	1,633
Pierce (part)	30	Odeen	3,539	Knudson*	2,857
(part)	93	Smith, J.	6,564	Petryk*	7,144
Polk (part)	28	Bever	9,133	Severson*	11,190
(part)	75	Smith, S.	673	Rivard*	705
Portage (part)	70	Vruwink*	2,880	Vandermeer	2,116
(part)	71	Shankland	17,619	Testin	11,279
(part)	72	Pluess	783	Krug*	824
Price	74	Bewley*	3,704	Sendra	3,725
Racine (part)[1]	32	Peterson	400	August*	531
(part)	62	Lemke	15,054	Weatherston	17,045
(part)	63	Albrecht	12,637	Vos*	17,704
(part)	64	Barca*	3,089	No candidate	
(part)	66	Mason*	16,830	No candidate	
(part)	83	Brownlow	1,903	Craig*	4,353
Richland (part)	49	Beals	863	Tranel*	1,029
(part)[1,2]	50	Shanahan	1,990	Brooks*	2,187
(part)	51	May-Grimm	826	Marklein*	1,108
Rock (part)	31	Schroeder	6,513	Loudenbeck*	7,817
(part)	43	Jorgensen*	9,203	Wynn*	6,389
(part)	44	Kolste	16,983	Knilans*	10,571
(part)	45	Ringhand*	12,790	Schmidt	6,605
Rusk	87	Riley	3,061	Williams*	3,913
St. Croix (part)	28	Bever	1,256	Severson*	1,973
(part)	29	Swanson	6,294	Murtha*	10,542
(part)	30	Odeen	10,118	Knudson*	14,404
(part)	75	Smith, S.	112	Rivard*	203
(part)	93	Smith, J.	1	Petryk*	2
Sauk (part)	41	Sorenson	655	Ballweg*	533
(part)[1,2]	50	Shanahan	3,921	Brooks*	4,943
(part)	51	May-Grimm	1,579	Marklein*	1,907
(part)	81	Clark*	10,364	Frostman	6,625
Sawyer (part)	74	Bewley*	500	Sendra	515
(part)	87	Riley	3,642	Williams*	3,859
Shawano (part)[2]	6	Powers	6,104	Tauchen*	9,215
(part)[1]	35	Koth	794	Czaja	1,040
(part)	36	Kegley	566	Mursau*	964
(part)	40	No candidate		Petersen*	5
Sheboygan (part)	26	Helmke	14,257	Endsley*	15,018
(part)	27	Bauer	11,381	Kestell*	15,264
(part)	59	No candidate		LeMahieu*	3,688
Taylor	87	Riley	3,341	Williams*	5,991
Trempealeau (part)	68	Smriga	671	Bernier*	575
(part)	92	Danou*	9,344	Doerr	33
Vernon (part)[1,2]	50	Shanahan	80	Brooks*	101
(part)	96	Johnson, T.	5,402	Nerison*	8,160
Vilas (part)[1]	34	Van Buren	3,845	Swearingen	7,078
(part)	74	Bewley*	963	Sendra	520
Walworth (part)	31	Schroeder	6,140	Loudenbeck*	8,646
(part)[1]	32	Peterson	9,774	August*	14,065
(part)[1]	33	Woods	1,057	Nass*	2,590
(part)	43	Jorgensen*	3,674	Wynn*	2,881
(part)	63	Albrecht	0	Vos*	0
(part)	83	Brownlow	125	Craig*	366
Washburn (part)	73	Milroy*	3,237	No candidate	
(part)	75	Smith, S.	2,132	Rivard*	2,023
Washington (part)	22	No candidate		Pridemore*	5,675
(part)	24	Haqqi	2,959	Knodl*	8,963
(part)	39	Grigg	401	Born	970
(part)	58	No candidate		Strachota*	26,945
(part)	59	No candidate		LeMahieu*	13,153
(part)	60	Duman	1,630	Stroebel*	5,994
Waukesha (part)	13	Pokrandt	4,578	Hutton	11,004
(part)	14	Rockwood	4,631	Kooyenga*	11,888
(part)	15	Moore	4,342	Sanfelippo	8,081
(part)	23	No candidate		Pridemore*	16,856
(part)	24	Haqqi	1,230	Knodl*	2,585
(part)[1]	33	Woods	2,595	Nass*	7,297
(part)[1]	38	Michalak	4,315	Kleefisch*	11,073
(part)	83	Brownlow	6,085	Craig*	15,358
(part)	84	Roelke	2,952	Kuglitsch*	8,423
(part)	97	Krumins	10,051	Kramer*	18,399
(part)	98	Prudent	9,503	Farrow*	22,665
(part)	99	Hibbard	8,166	Kapenga*	26,314
Waupaca (part)[2]	6	Powers	1,438	Tauchen*	2,021

COUNTY VOTE FOR REPRESENTATIVES TO THE ASSEMBLY
Special and General Elections–Continued

County or Part	Assembly District	Democratic	Vote	Republican	Vote
(part)	40	No candidate		Petersen*	16,346
Waushara (part)	40	No candidate		Petersen*	4,278
(part)	41	Sorenson	8	Ballweg*	39
(part)	72	Pluess	2,572	Krug*	3,277
Winnebago (part)	53	Flejter	5,981	Schraa	9,332
(part)	54	Hintz*	17,400	Esslinger	11,594
(part)[1]	55	Crail	7,619	Kaufert*	15,134
(part)	56	Schoenbohm	2,499	Murphy	3,879
(part)[2]	57	Bernard Schaber*	8,231	No candidate	
Wood (part)	69	Knoff	3,928	Suder*	4,945
(part)	70	Vruwink*	4,642	Vandermeer	3,562
(part)	72	Pluess	8,745	Krug*	8,012
(part)	86	Halkoski	1,393	Spiros	2,033
		April 2, 2013 Special Election			
Waukesha	98	No candidate		Neylon	6,006

*Served in 2011 Assembly.

[1]Votes for Independent candidates: 3rd AD: Josh Young: Calumet – 673, Outagamie – 516; 17th AD: Anthony R. Edwards: Milwaukee – 3,573; 18th AD: Melba Morris-Page: Milwaukee – 2,140; 32nd AD: David Stolow: Kenosha – 56, Racine – 31, Walworth – 760; 33rd AD: Terry Virgil: Jefferson – 613, Walworth – 98, Waukesha – 234; 34th AD: Todd Albano: Florence – 46, Forest – 20, Oneida – 397, Vilas – 328; Kevin M. Fitzpatrick: Florence – 106, Forest – 55, Oneida – 785, Vilas – 523; 35th AD: Patrick K. Tjugum: Langlade – 221, Lincoln – 802, Marathon – 61, Oneida – 257, Shawano – 56; 38th AD: Leroy L. Watson: Dane – 165, Jefferson – 288, Waukesha – 335; 48th AD: Terry R. Gray: Dane – 4,849; 50th AD: Ben Olson III: Juneau – 350, Monroe – 23, Richland – 66, Sauk – 279; 55th AD: Rich Martin: Outagamie – 284, Winnebago – 732; 78th AD: Jonathan Dedering: Dane – 7,323; 85th AD: Jim Maas: Marathon – 1,047.

[2]Votes for write-in candidates: 6th AD: Jon Kupsky: Brown – 0, Oconto – 0, Outagamie – 0, Shawano – 9, Waupaca – 0; 7th AD: Tiffany Lee Koehler: Milwaukee – 2; Peggy Krusick: Milwaukee – 2,499; 17th AD: Virginia Pratt: Milwaukee – 6; 48th AD: Adam Kassulke: Dane – 0; Jonathon William Rygiewicz: Dane – 13; 50th AD: Nathan Johnson: Juneau – 2, Monroe – 0, Richland – 0, Sauk – 9, Vernon – 0; 57th AD: Brian Garrow: Outagamie – 503, Winnebago – 165; 67th AD: Jayme Ryan Schulner: Barron – 0, Chippewa – 0, Dunn – 1.

Source: Official records of the Government Accountability Board, Elections Division. Scattered votes omitted.

DISTRICT VOTE FOR REPRESENTATIVES TO THE ASSEMBLY
Primary Elections

Assembly District	Political Party	Candidates	Vote
		July 12, 2011 Primary	
48.	Dem.	Fred Arnold	1,507
	Dem.	Dave De Felice.	1,086
	Dem.	Andy Heidt.	1,190
	Dem.	Bethany Ordaz	1,149
	Dem.	Vicky Selkowe.	2,452
	Dem.	Chris Taylor	3,383
		October 11, 2011 Primary	
95.	Dem.	Jill E. Billings	2,746
	Dem.	Nick Charles	431
	Dem.	Christine J. Clair.	1,681
	Dem.	David Krump	415
	Rep.	David A. Drewes.	313
		August 14, 2012 Primary	
1	Dem.	Arnie Johnsrud.	1,552
	Dem.	Patrick Veeser	1,582
	Rep.	Garey Bies*	5,784
2	Dem.	Larry Pruess	652
	Rep.	Andre Jacque*	4,637
3	Dem.	Kole Oswald	669
	Rep.	Brandi Lefeber.	1,613
	Rep.	Al Ott*	4,576
4	Dem.	Michael J. Malcheski	791
	Rep.	Chad Weininger*.	5,363
5	Dem.	Ryan Ferguson	341
	Dem.	Jeff McCabe	532
	Rep.	Jim Steineke*	4,921
6	Dem.	John Powers	584
	Rep.	Gary Tauchen*.	5,547
7	Dem.	Peggy Krusick*	944
	Dem.	Daniel Riemer	1,908
	Rep.	Tiffany Lee Koehler	27
8	Dem.	Laura Manriquez.	299
	Dem.	JoCasta Zamarripa*	599
9	Dem.	Jose Guzman.	407
	Dem.	Josh Zepnick*	781
10.	Dem.	Harriet Callier	193
	Dem.	Millie Coby	1,974
	Dem.	Ieshuh Griffin	216
	Dem.	Sandy Pasch*	3,684
11.	Dem.	Mandela Barnes	2,596
	Dem.	Jason Fields*.	1,206
12.	Dem.	Mario R. Hall	762
	Dem.	Frederick P. Kessler*	1,937
13.	Dem.	John Pokrandt	1,052
	Rep.	Rob Hutton.	5,351
	Rep.	Nate Ristow	955
	Rep.	Thomas J. Schellinger	2,968
14.	Dem.	Chris Rockwood	910
	Rep.	Dale Kooyenga*	7,250
15.	Dem.	Chuck Garrigues	360
	Dem.	Cindy Moore	654
	Rep.	Joe Sanfelippo	5,283
16.	Dem.	Leon D. Young*	3,054
17.	Dem.	Sam Coleman	548
	Dem.	Tracey Dent	1,072
	Dem.	La Tonya Johnson	2,054
	Dem.	Fred Royal	1,093
18.	Dem.	Lisa Erin Brown	139
	Dem.	James Dieter	355
	Dem.	Jarett Fields	808
	Dem.	Michael L. Glabere	169
	Dem.	Evan Goyke	1,637
	Dem.	Ty Jackson	317
	Dem.	Andrew Parker.	335
	Dem.	Lashawndra Vernon	639
19.	Dem.	Jon Richards*	1,825
20.	Dem.	Christine Sinicki*	1,584
	Rep.	Kristan T. Harris	1,117
	Rep.	Molly M. McGartland	2,582
21.	Dem.	William R. Kurtz	881
	Rep.	Mark Honadel*	4,810

DISTRICT VOTE FOR REPRESENTATIVES TO THE ASSEMBLY
Primary Elections–Continued

Assembly District	Political Party	Candidates	Vote
22.	Rep.	Nick Oliver.	1,675
	Rep.	Don Pridemore*	8,290
23.	Dem.	Cris Rogers.	887
	Rep.	Jim Ott*	8,290
24.	Dem.	Shan Haqqi.	908
	Rep.	Dan Knodl*	7,029
25.	Dem.	Jim Brey	903
	Dem.	Luke A. Bushman	244
	Dem.	Ron Gruett	330
	Dem.	Bernie Starzewski	705
	Rep.	Mike Howe.	1,362
	Rep.	Barry Nelson.	1,066
	Rep.	Jason J. Sladky	723
	Rep.	Paul Tittl	3,589
26.	Dem.	Mike Helmke	1,377
	Rep.	Michael Endsley*	5,144
	Rep.	Devin LeMahieu	3,427
27.	Dem.	Steven H. Bauer	1,040
	Rep.	Steve Kestell*	6,709
28.	Dem.	Adam T. Bever.	797
	Rep.	Erik Severson*	2,623
29.	Dem.	Jim Swanson	716
	Rep.	John Murtha*	2,224
30.	Dem.	Diane Odeen	920
	Rep.	Dean Knudson*	2,579
31.	Dem.	Ryan J. Schroeder	1,353
	Rep.	Amy Loudenbeck*.	4,947
32.	Dem.	Kim M. Peterson.	615
	Rep.	Tyler August*	4,929
33.	Dem.	Scott Allan Woods	671
	Rep.	Steve Nass*	5,872
34.	Dem.	Roberta Retrum	919
	Dem.	Merlin Van Buren	1,517
	Rep.	Rob Swearingen	5,161
	Rep.	Alex Young	1,780
35.	Dem.	Kevin Koth.	1,415
	Rep.	Mary Czaja.	4,255
36.	Dem.	Dorothy Kegley	1,539
	Rep.	Jeffrey L. Mursau*	5,762
37.	Dem.	Mary I. Arnold	1,470
	Dem.	Laura Cotting	610
	Rep.	James B. Braughler	764
	Rep.	John Jagler	3,412
	Rep.	Steve Kauffeld.	1,227
	Rep.	James W. Romlein, Sr.	655
	Rep.	Chris Ruetten	475
38.	Dem.	Scott Michalak	1,253
	Rep.	Joel Kleefisch*.	7,043
39.	Dem.	Jim Grigg	810
	Rep.	Mark L. Born	4,023
	Rep.	Tracy A. Heron.	1,554
	Rep.	Don Lechner	2,381
40.	Rep.	Kevin Petersen*	5,656
41.	Dem.	Melissa Sorenson	1,144
	Rep.	Joan Ballweg*	5,934
42.	Dem.	Paula Cooper.	1,072
	Rep.	Keith Ripp*	5,118
43.	Dem.	Andy Jorgensen*.	2,231
	Rep.	Evan Wynn*	3,618
44.	Dem.	Debra Kolste	1,926
	Dem.	Sam Liebert	335
	Dem.	Kevin M. Murray	1,610
	Dem.	Yuri Rashkin	705
	Rep.	Joe Knilans*	3,273
45.	Dem.	Sheila L. De Forest	1,071
	Dem.	Janis Ringhand*	1,820
	Rep.	Russell Rucker.	1,191
	Rep.	Beth Schmidt.	1,697
46.	Dem.	Gary Hebl*.	3,323
	Rep.	Trish Schaefer	2,694
47.	Dem.	Amanda Hall	1,457
	Dem.	Robb Kahl	3,037
	Rep.	Sandy Bakk	2,491

DISTRICT VOTE FOR REPRESENTATIVES TO THE ASSEMBLY
Primary Elections–Continued

Assembly District	Political Party	Candidates	Vote
48.	Dem.	Melissa Agard Sargent	5,549
	Rep.	Adam Kassulke (write-in)	1
	Rep.	Jonathan William Rygiewicz (write-in)	6
49.	Dem.	Carol Beals	1,122
	Rep.	Dave Kuhle	2,075
	Rep.	Travis Tranel*	3,773
50.	Dem.	Sarah Ann Shanahan	1,121
	Rep.	Ed Brooks*	4,758
51.	Dem.	Pat Bomhack	1,160
	Dem.	Maureen May-Grimm	1,838
	Rep.	Howard Marklein*	3,670
52.	Dem.	Paul G. Czisny	542
	Rep.	Jeremy Thiesfeldt*	6,878
53.	Dem.	Ryan Flejter	542
	Dem.	Koby Schellenger	169
	Dem.	Joanne Staudacher	420
	Rep.	Frank Frassetto	1,962
	Rep.	Michael Schraa	4,403
	Rep.	Kurt Schuller	851
54.	Dem.	Gordon Hintz*	767
	Rep.	Paul J. Esslinger	2,988
55.	Dem.	Jim Crail	636
	Rep.	Dean R. Kaufert*	4,612
	Rep.	Jay Schroeder	2,487
56.	Dem.	Diana Lawrence	344
	Dem.	Richard B. Schoenbohm	849
	Rep.	Dave Murphy	3,639
	Rep.	Jim Pleuss	3,415
57.	Dem.	Penny Bernard Schaber*	959
	Rep.	Brian Garrow (write-in)	349
58.	Rep.	Pat Strachota*	7,461
59.	Rep.	Daniel R. LeMahieu*	7,072
60.	Dem.	Perry Duman	578
	Rep.	Duey Stroebel*	8,007
61.	Dem.	John P. Steinbrink*	1,162
	Rep.	Samantha Kerkman*	3,913
62.	Dem.	Randy Bryce	522
	Dem.	Melissa Lemke	1,202
	Rep.	Tom Weatherston	5,775
63.	Dem.	Kelley Albrecht	924
	Rep.	Robin J. Vos*	6,178
64.	Dem.	Peter W. Barca*	1,943
65.	Dem.	Dayvin M. A. Hallmon	519
	Dem.	Albert Namath	180
	Dem.	Tod Ohnstad	2,083
66.	Dem.	Cory Mason*	1,039
67.	Dem.	Deb Bieging	1,897
	Rep.	Tom Larson*	3,440
	Rep.	Jayme Ryan Schulner (write-in)	10
68.	Dem.	Judy Smriga	1,168
	Rep.	Kathy Bernier*	2,820
69.	Dem.	Paul Knoff	870
	Rep.	Scott Suder*	3,977
70.	Dem.	Amy Sue Vruwink*	1,303
	Rep.	Nancy L. Vandermeer	3,125
	Rep.	Dan Wald	2,205
71.	Dem.	Andrew Logan Beveridge	771
	Dem.	Laura Hauser-Menting	117
	Dem.	Corey D. Ladick	1,339
	Dem.	Tom Mallison	142
	Dem.	Jeri McGinley	836
	Dem.	Hans Schmid	101
	Dem.	Katrina Shankland	1,383
	Dem.	Robert L. Steinke	118
	Dem.	David J. Verhage	319
	Rep.	Patrick Testin	1,903
72.	Dem.	Justin D. Pluess	1,196
	Rep.	Scott S. Krug*	4,561
73.	Dem.	Nick Milroy*	2,138
74.	Dem.	Janet Bewley*	1,681
	Rep.	John Sendra	3,102
75.	Dem.	Stephen Smith	1,144
	Rep.	Roger Rivard*	3,702
76.	Dem.	Chris Taylor*	5,877

DISTRICT VOTE FOR REPRESENTATIVES TO THE ASSEMBLY
Primary Elections–Continued

Assembly District	Political Party	Candidates	Vote
77.	Dem.	Terese Berceau*	7,009
78.	Dem.	Christopher Victor Fisher	497
	Dem.	Brett Hulsey*	5,215
79.	Dem.	Dianne Hesselbein	3,590
	Dem.	Ellen Lindgren	1,885
80.	Dem.	Sondy Pope-Roberts*	2,815
	Dem.	Charles Uphoff	476
	Dem.	Joseph S. Wineke	2,461
	Rep.	Tom Lamberson	3,020
81.	Dem.	Fred Clark*	2,151
	Rep.	Scott Frostman	3,339
82.	Dem.	Kathleen Wied-Vincent	982
	Rep.	Jeff Stone*	6,304
83.	Dem.	James Brownlow	728
	Rep.	Dave Craig*	7,848
84.	Dem.	Jesse J. Roelke	1,022
	Rep.	Mike Kuglitsch*	5,454
85.	Dem.	Jeff Johnson	1,050
	Dem.	Mandy Wright	1,626
	Rep.	Patrick Snyder	3,745
86.	Dem.	Dennis Halkoski	810
	Rep.	John Spiros	3,985
	Rep.	Wayne C. Thorson	1,430
87.	Dem.	Elizabeth Riley	1,147
	Rep.	Mary Williams*	4,231
88.	Dem.	Ward Bacon	643
	Rep.	John Klenke*	4,240
89.	Dem.	Joe Reinhard	832
	Rep.	John Nygren*	4,981
90.	Dem.	Eric Genrich	740
	Rep.	Joel Diny	1,027
	Rep.	David Vanderleest	1,702
91.	Dem.	Dana Wachs	1,160
92.	Dem.	Chris Danou*	1,854
	Rep.	Stephen James Doerr (write-in)	111
93.	Dem.	Jeff Smith	1,286
	Rep.	Warren Petryk*	3,003
94.	Dem.	Steve Doyle*	1,318
	Rep.	Bruce Evers	2,231
	Rep.	Kevin Hintz	1,763
95.	Dem.	Jill Billings*	1,527
96.	Dem.	Tom J. Johnson	1,084
	Rep.	Lee A. Nerison*	4,700
97.	Dem.	Marga Krumins	467
	Rep.	Bill Kramer*	5,487
98.	Dem.	Eric Prudent	527
	Rep.	Paul Farrow*	6,971
99.	Dem.	Thomas D. Hibbard	597
	Rep.	Chris Kapenga*	9,427
February 19, 2013 Special Primary			
98.	Rep.	Ed Baumann	1,977
	Rep.	Todd A. Greenwald	221
	Rep.	Matt Morzy	253
	Rep.	Adam Neylon	2,006
	Rep.	Jeanne Tarantino	774

Dem. – Democratic Party; Rep. – Republican Party.
*Served in 2011 Assembly.
Source: Official records of the Government Accountability Board, Elections Division. Scattered votes omitted.

DISTRICT VOTE FOR REPRESENTATIVES TO THE ASSEMBLY
Special and General Elections

Assembly District	Political Party	Candidates	Vote	Percent of Total Vote[1]
		August 9, 2011 Special Election		
48.	Dem.	Chris Taylor	5,453	93.50%
		November 8, 2011 Special Election		
95.	Dem.	Jill E. Billings	5,940	72.47
	Rep.	David A. Drewes.	2,247	27.42
		November 6, 2012 General Election		
1	Dem.	Patrick Veeser	16,124	48.65
	Rep.	Garey Bies*	16,993	51.27
2	Dem.	Larry Pruess	12,033	41.29
	Rep.	Andre Jacque*	17,082	58.62
3	Dem.	Kole Oswald	11,398	38.01
	Rep.	Al Ott*	17,387	57.98
	Ind.	Josh Young.	1,189	3.97
4	Dem.	Michael J. Malcheski	12,770	44.28
	Rep.	Chad Weininger*.	16,029	55.58
5	Dem.	Jeff McCabe	12,709	44.05
	Rep.	Jim Steineke*	16,117	55.86
6	Dem.	John Powers	10,508	40.48
	Rep.	Gary Tauchen*.	15,423	59.41
	Ind.	Jon Kupsky[2]	9	0.03
7	Dem.	Peggy Krusick*[2]	2,499	12.80
	Dem.	Daniel Riemer	16,664	85.35
	Ind.	Tiffany Lee Koehler[2].	2	0.01
8	Dem.	JoCasta Zamarripa*	7,869	98.26
9	Dem.	Josh Zepnick*	14,635	98.60
10.	Dem.	Sandy Pasch*	20,038	98.71
11.	Dem.	Mandela Barnes	16,403	98.79
12.	Dem.	Frederick P. Kessler*	16,193	98.59
13.	Dem.	John Pokrandt	13,258	39.38
	Rep.	Rob Hutton.	20,367	60.49
14.	Dem.	Chris Rockwood	14,490	40.81
	Rep.	Dale Kooyenga*	20,976	59.07
15.	Dem.	Cindy Moore.	12,668	41.61
	Rep.	Joe Sanfelippo	17,745	58.28
16.	Dem.	Leon D. Young*	16,881	98.78
17.	Dem.	La Tonya Johnson	20,288	84.73
	Rep.	Virginia Pratt[2]	6	0.03
	Ind.	Anthony R. Edwards.	3,573	14.92
18.	Dem.	Evan Goyke	16,276	87.93
	Ind.	Melba Morris-Page	2,140	11.56
19.	Dem.	Jon Richards*	24,856	97.65
20.	Dem.	Christine Sinicki*	16,995	57.52
	Rep.	Molly M. McGartland	12,500	42.31
21.	Dem.	William R. Kurtz.	11,921	40.61
	Rep.	Mark Honadel*	17,403	59.28
22.	Rep.	Don Pridemore*	23,817	98.56
23.	Dem.	Cris Rogers.	13,669	37.73
	Rep.	Jim Ott*	22,536	62.20
24.	Dem.	Shan Haqqi.	12,594	37.53
	Rep.	Dan Knodl*	20,932	62.37
25.	Dem.	Jim Brey	11,947	42.22
	Rep.	Paul Tittl	16,287	57.56
26.	Dem.	Mike Helmke	14,257	48.67
	Rep.	Michael Endsley*	15,018	51.27
27.	Dem.	Steven H. Bauer	13,148	42.05
	Rep.	Steve Kestell*	18,101	57.89
28.	Dem.	Adam T. Bever	12,347	43.72
	Rep.	Erik Severson*.	15,865	56.18
29.	Dem.	Jim Swanson	12,004	43.99
	Rep.	John Murtha*	15,237	55.84
30.	Dem.	Diane Odeen	13,657	44.14
	Rep.	Dean Knudson*	17,261	55.79
31.	Dem.	Ryan J. Schroeder	12,653	43.41
	Rep.	Amy Loudenbeck*.	16,463	56.47
32.	Dem.	Kim M. Peterson.	10,828	39.67
	Rep.	Tyler August*	15,586	57.10
	Ind.	David Stolow	847	3.10
33.	Dem.	Scott Allan Woods	10,229	34.00
	Rep.	Steve Nass*	18,891	62.79
	Ind.	Terry Virgil.	945	3.14
34.	Dem.	Merlin Van Buren	12,297	36.15
	Rep.	Rob Swearingen	19,442	57.16
	Ind.	Todd Albano	791	2.33
	Ind.	Kevin M. Fitzpatrick.	1,469	4.32
35.	Dem.	Kevin Koth	12,149	41.83
	Rep.	Mary Czaja.	15,481	53.30
	Ind.	Patrick K. Tjugum	1,397	4.81

DISTRICT VOTE FOR REPRESENTATIVES TO THE ASSEMBLY
Special and General Elections–Continued

Assembly District	Political Party	Candidates	Vote	Percent of Total Vote[1]
36.	Dem.	Dorothy Kegley	10,997	40.88
	Rep.	Jeffrey L. Mursau*	15,886	59.05
37.	Dem.	Mary I. Arnold	13,289	45.55
	Rep.	John Jagler	15,799	54.16
38.	Dem.	Scott Michalak	12,795	39.03
	Rep.	Joel Kleefisch*	19,181	58.51
	Ind.	Leroy L. Watson	788	2.40
39.	Dem.	Jim Grigg	11,446	39.56
	Rep.	Mark L. Born	17,465	60.36
40.	Rep.	Kevin Petersen*	21,127	98.71
41.	Dem.	Melissa Sorenson	10,906	42.01
	Rep.	Joan Ballweg*	15,035	57.92
42.	Dem.	Paula Cooper	12,567	43.37
	Rep.	Keith Ripp*	16,394	56.58
43.	Dem.	Andy Jorgensen*	17,612	57.58
	Rep.	Evan Wynn*	12,894	42.16
44.	Dem.	Debra Kolste	16,983	61.54
	Rep.	Joe Knilans*	10,571	38.30
45.	Dem.	Janis Ringhand*	15,753	63.75
	Rep.	Beth Schmidt	8,906	36.04
46.	Dem.	Gary Hebl*	20,171	64.79
	Rep.	Trish Schaefer	10,951	35.18
47.	Dem.	Robb Kahl	22,113	70.87
	Rep.	Sandy Bakk	9,054	29.02
48.	Dem.	Melissa Agard Sargent	24,375	83.20
	Rep.	Jonathon William Rygiewicz[2]	13	0.04
	Ind.	Terry R. Gray	4,849	16.55
	Ind.	Adam Kassulke[2]	0	0.00
49.	Dem.	Carol Beals	11,977	45.65
	Rep.	Travis Tranel*	14,218	54.19
50.	Dem.	Sarah Ann Shanahan	11,945	46.78
	Rep.	Ed Brooks*	12,842	50.30
	Ind.	Nathan Johnson[2]	11	0.04
	Ind.	Ben Olson III.	725	2.84
51.	Dem.	Maureen May-Grimm	13,238	48.07
	Rep.	Howard Marklein*	14,279	51.85
52.	Dem.	Paul G. Czisny	10,575	39.31
	Rep.	Jeremy Thiesfeldt*	16,313	60.65
53.	Dem.	Ryan Flejter	10,410	39.60
	Rep.	Michael Schraa	15,844	60.28
54.	Dem.	Gordon Hintz*	17,400	59.88
	Rep.	Paul J. Esslinger	11,594	39.90
55.	Dem.	Jim Crail	10,202	33.55
	Rep.	Dean R. Kaufert*	19,142	62.95
	Ind.	Rich Martin	1,016	3.34
56.	Dem.	Richard B. Schoenbohm	13,071	41.62
	Rep.	Dave Murphy	18,306	58.29
57.	Dem.	Penny Bernard Schaber*	19,862	94.03
	Rep.	Brian Garrow[2]	668	3.16
58.	Rep.	Pat Strachota*	26,945	98.89
59.	Rep.	Daniel R. LeMahieu*	25,172	99.22
60.	Dem.	Perry Duman	9,682	28.79
	Rep.	Duey Stroebel*	23,905	71.08
61.	Dem.	John P. Steinbrink*	13,186	44.25
	Rep.	Samantha Kerkman*	16,589	55.67
62.	Dem.	Melissa Lemke	15,054	46.85
	Rep.	Tom Weatherston	17,045	53.05
63.	Dem.	Kelley Albrecht	12,637	41.62
	Rep.	Robin J. Vos*	17,704	58.31
64.	Dem.	Peter W. Barca*	20,264	96.84
65.	Dem.	Tod Ohnstad	18,373	97.99
66.	Dem.	Cory Mason*	16,830	98.65
67.	Dem.	Deb Bieging	13,325	46.69
	Rep.	Tom Larson*	15,194	53.24
	Rep.	Jayme Ryan Schulner[2]	1	0.00
68.	Dem.	Judy Smriga	12,482	47.53
	Rep.	Kathy Bernier*	13,758	52.39
69.	Dem.	Paul Knoff	9,998	38.74
	Rep.	Scott Suder*	15,785	61.17
70.	Dem.	Amy Sue Vruwink*	13,518	50.19
	Rep.	Nancy L. Vandermeer	13,374	49.65
71.	Dem.	Katrina Shankland	17,619	60.82
	Rep.	Patrick Testin	11,279	38.94
72.	Dem.	Justin D. Pluess	14,029	49.77
	Rep.	Scott S. Krug*	14,138	50.16
73.	Dem.	Nick Milroy*	22,686	98.84
74.	Dem.	Janet Bewley*	18,582	58.97
	Rep.	John Sendra	12,911	40.98

DISTRICT VOTE FOR REPRESENTATIVES TO THE ASSEMBLY
Special and General Elections–Continued

Assembly District	Political Party	Candidates	Vote	Percent of Total Vote[1]
75.	Dem.	Stephen Smith	14,456	51.02
	Rep.	Roger Rivard*	13,841	48.85
76.	Dem.	Chris Taylor*.	31,663	99.11
77.	Dem.	Terese Berceau*	27,622	99.36
78.	Dem.	Brett Hulsey*	22,853	75.44
	Ind.	Jonathan Dedering	7,323	24.17
79.	Dem.	Dianne Hesselbein	24,683	98.75
80.	Dem.	Sondy Pope-Roberts*	20,864	63.85
	Rep.	Tom Lamberson	11,771	36.02
81.	Dem.	Fred Clark*	17,829	61.83
	Rep.	Scott Frostman	10,995	38.13
82.	Dem.	Kathleen Wied-Vincent	11,896	39.69
	Rep.	Jeff Stone*	18,032	60.16
83.	Dem.	James Brownlow	9,967	30.18
	Rep.	Dave Craig*	23,034	69.75
84.	Dem.	Jesse J. Roelke	10,882	37.11
	Rep.	Mike Kuglitsch*	18,379	62.67
85.	Dem.	Mandy Wright	13,930	49.70
	Rep.	Patrick Snyder	13,025	46.47
	Ind.	Jim Maas	1,047	3.74
86.	Dem.	Dennis Halkoski	13,644	44.20
	Rep.	John Spiros	17,175	55.64
87.	Dem.	Elizabeth Riley	11,100	41.43
	Rep.	Mary Williams*	15,680	58.52
88.	Dem.	Ward Bacon	13,085	47.47
	Rep.	John Klenke*	14,445	52.40
89.	Dem.	Joe Reinhard	11,129	40.87
	Rep.	John Nygren*	16,081	59.05
90.	Dem.	Eric Genrich	11,353	60.21
	Rep.	David Vanderleest	7,432	39.41
91.	Dem.	Dana Wachs	23,030	97.28
92.	Dem.	Chris Danou*	20,308	98.76
	Rep.	Stephen J. Doerr	50	0.24
93.	Dem.	Jeff Smith	15,114	49.16
	Rep.	Warren Petryk*	15,612	50.78
94.	Dem.	Steve Doyle*	18,566	60.59
	Rep.	Bruce Evers	12,068	39.38
95.	Dem.	Jill Billings*	22,531	98.89
96.	Dem.	Tom J. Johnson	10,426	40.44
	Rep	Lee A. Nerison*	15,344	59.52
97.	Dem.	Marga Krumins	10,051	35.29
	Rep.	Bill Kramer*	18,399	64.60
98.	Dem.	Eric Prudent	9,503	29.52
	Rep.	Paul Farrow*	22,665	70.42
99.	Dem.	Thomas D. Hibbard	8,166	23.67
	Rep.	Chris Kapenga*	26,314	76.28
April 2, 2013 Special Election				
98.	Rep.	Adam Neylon	6,006	99.32

Dem. – Democratic Party; Rep. – Republican Party; Ind. – Independent.

*Served in 2011 Assembly.

[1]Percentages do not equal 100%, as scattered votes have been omitted.

[2]Write-in candidate.

Source: Official records of the Government Accountability Board, Elections Division. Scattered votes omitted.

COUNTY VOTE FOR GOVERNOR
May 8, 2012 Recall Primary

County	Tom Barrett (Dem.)	Kathleen Falk (Dem.)	Gladys R. Huber (Dem.)	Doug La Follette (Dem.)	Kathleen Vinehout (Dem.)	Arthur Kohl-Riggs (Rep.)	Patrick J. O'Brien[1] (Rep.)	Scott Walker[2] (Rep.)
Adams	1,034	1,157	18	131	100	58	0	2,125
Ashland	1,451	588	19	129	78	74	0	1,319
Barron	1,696	1,376	74	136	331	148	0	5,189
Bayfield	1,855	731	24	134	125	71	0	1,668
Brown	12,105	10,803	190	759	659	1,133	0	31,966
Buffalo.	402	444	17	42	393	34	0	1,432
Burnett	697	322	36	62	94	46	0	1,799
Calumet	2,216	1,990	35	188	132	185	0	7,314
Chippewa . . .	3,426	2,338	92	205	589	149	0	6,248
Clark	949	1,145	30	121	188	90	0	4,007
Columbia. . . .	4,205	3,211	49	346	346	290	0	5,358
Crawford. . . .	823	934	28	83	154	70	0	1,314
Dane	65,078	32,244	256	2,825	5,200	4,350	2	29,035
Dodge	4,999	3,450	61	276	246	223	0	12,154
Door	2,608	1,643	27	133	196	136	0	4,561
Douglas	3,534	1,357	62	253	136	92	1	2,272
Dunn	1,992	1,405	75	141	465	106	0	3,442
Eau Claire . . .	6,663	4,184	148	378	1,806	267	0	9,234
Florence	176	151	5	8	21	21	0	639
Fond du Lac . .	5,187	3,979	91	342	318	379	0	14,435
Forest.	336	455	8	50	28	31	0	1,037
Grant	2,365	2,219	38	194	217	192	0	3,208
Green.	2,593	1,859	19	187	201	175	2	3,174
Green Lake. . .	779	670	16	69	65	76	0	2,972
Iowa	1,904	1,251	13	136	197	123	1	1,809
Iron.	453	233	10	49	22	25	0	729
Jackson.	913	737	20	71	523	64	0	1,732
Jefferson	5,330	3,451	75	294	398	299	0	11,304
Juneau	1,130	1,222	18	110	118	94	0	2,486
Kenosha	9,333	5,509	144	401	369	256	0	11,373
Kewaunee . .	954	971	26	86	86	104	0	3,095
La Crosse . . .	6,875	5,865	144	502	1,006	398	1	7,896
Lafayette	849	771	15	76	82	81	0	1,475
Langlade	829	872	20	115	64	66	0	2,567
Lincoln	1,467	1,664	26	189	144	87	0	3,213
Manitowoc . . .	3,645	3,647	69	314	267	324	0	11,853
Marathon. . . .	6,426	5,866	133	578	618	394	0	17,001
Marinette. . . .	1,654	1,757	45	149	135	158	0	4,936
Marquette . . .	843	756	11	91	75	55	0	1,931
Menominee . .	93	118	0	5	9	3	0	113
Milwaukee . . .	91,771	31,244	511	1,604	1,932	1,865	0	66,637
Monroe.	1,473	1,690	34	157	543	123	0	3,974
Oconto	1,705	1,681	31	144	131	190	0	5,720
Oneida	2,179	2,237	47	223	178	153	0	5,244
Outagamie . . .	8,573	7,416	198	559	576	748	0	23,213
Ozaukee	5,992	2,311	72	176	155	154	0	17,175
Pepin	233	205	9	23	217	22	0	781
Pierce.	1,616	761	64	95	334	95	0	2,909
Polk	1,563	801	77	149	325	83	0	3,601
Portage	5,286	3,484	48	459	326	261	0	6,770
Price	741	757	24	108	93	61	0	2,042
Racine	14,330	7,801	236	566	570	479	6	23,061
Richland	1,041	889	15	100	115	81	0	1,521
Rock	10,038	8,445	104	728	682	621	0	13,372
Rusk	641	632	22	65	117	58	1	1,714
St. Croix	3,162	1,611	156	214	412	196	1	7,582
Sauk	4,400	3,107	55	361	440	278	0	5,795
Sawyer	850	490	40	99	132	70	0	1,835
Shawano	1,550	1,524	33	135	136	172	1	5,569
Sheboygan . . .	6,540	4,402	91	308	208	278	0	17,380
Taylor	569	676	25	83	83	60	0	2,424
Trempealeau . .	1,195	986	30	94	450	80	0	2,159
Vernon	1,613	1,413	25	140	270	185	0	2,615
Vilas	1,332	1,224	20	131	97	70	0	3,911
Walworth. . . .	4,780	2,669	72	217	255	241	0	13,207
Washburn . . .	1,065	467	37	72	81	49	0	2,128
Washington. . .	6,491	2,862	73	199	238	264	0	27,723
Waukesha . . .	23,621	9,875	220	654	641	765	0	79,098
Waupaca	2,114	2,158	54	185	165	224	0	6,944
Waushara. . . .	1,096	1,057	17	90	76	130	0	3,443
Winnebago . . .	9,366	7,538	149	533	518	707	1	19,311
Wood.	3,938	3,478	71	468	270	249	0	8,689
TOTAL. . .	390,191	229,236	4,847	19,497	26,967	19,939	17	626,962

Dem. – Democratic Party; Rep. – Republican Party; Ind. – Independent.

[1]Write-in candidate.

[2]Incumbent.

Source: Official records of the Government Accountability Board, Elections Division. Scattered votes omitted.

COUNTY VOTE FOR GOVERNOR
June 5, 2012 Recall General Election

County	Tom Barrett (Dem.)	Scott Walker* (Rep.)	Hari Trivedi (Ind.)
Adams	3,658	4,497	97
Ashland	4,174	2,598	50
Barron	7,015	10,420	136
Bayfield	4,889	3,269	55
Brown	41,238	61,969	619
Buffalo	2,148	3,403	44
Burnett	2,536	3,998	40
Calumet	7,515	15,004	107
Chippewa	10,419	14,877	244
Clark	3,618	8,133	86
Columbia	13,070	12,912	161
Crawford	3,160	3,357	61
Dane	176,407	77,595	1,239
Dodge	13,958	24,851	242
Door	6,308	8,401	75
Douglas	11,711	6,374	106
Dunn	7,099	8,417	114
Eau Claire	20,595	20,740	325
Florence	717	1,338	10
Fond du Lac	16,105	29,060	309
Forest	1,485	2,180	44
Grant	8,623	9,498	137
Green	7,981	8,407	71
Green Lake	2,564	5,800	54
Iowa	5,660	4,957	77
Iron	1,267	1,613	14
Jackson	3,466	4,074	62
Jefferson	14,698	22,475	274
Juneau	4,225	5,429	83
Kenosha	29,638	28,935	349
Kewaunee	3,388	6,108	42
La Crosse	24,651	22,608	382
Lafayette	2,923	3,887	46
Langlade	2,898	5,621	71
Lincoln	5,351	7,201	106
Manitowoc	12,682	23,085	268
Marathon	21,809	36,352	398
Marinette	6,242	10,267	90
Marquette	2,764	4,102	55
Menominee	575	208	3
Milwaukee	250,476	143,455	1,935
Monroe	6,093	9,064	155
Oconto	5,782	11,049	102
Oneida	7,365	10,433	147
Outagamie	29,714	47,840	466
Ozaukee	14,095	34,303	141
Pepin	1,216	1,849	17
Pierce	6,744	8,317	59
Polk	6,593	10,133	106
Portage	15,672	14,846	242
Price	2,651	4,083	73
Racine	40,287	45,526	509
Richland	3,296	3,895	53
Rock	35,316	27,498	475
Rusk	2,167	3,722	60
St. Croix	13,177	20,894	124
Sauk	12,815	13,648	168
Sawyer	3,038	3,999	45
Shawano	5,646	11,201	88
Sheboygan	18,612	34,047	279
Taylor	2,201	5,751	76
Trempealeau	4,634	6,266	88
Vernon	5,762	6,352	100
Vilas	4,154	7,300	72
Walworth	14,346	26,221	202
Washburn	3,156	4,278	59
Washington	16,634	52,306	246
Waukesha	58,234	154,316	706
Waupaca	7,564	14,094	128
Waushara	3,754	6,463	69
Winnebago	30,885	39,881	446
Wood	13,171	18,535	281
TOTAL	1,164,480	1,335,585	14,463

Dem. – Democratic Party; Rep. – Republican Party; Ind. – Independent.

*Incumbent.

Source: Official records of the Government Accountability Board, Elections Division. Scattered votes omitted.

COUNTY VOTE FOR LIEUTENANT GOVERNOR
May 8, 2012 Recall Primary

County	Mahlon Mitchell (Dem.)	Ira Robins (Dem.)	Isaac Weix (Dem.)
Adams	1,314	679	596
Ashland	1,250	439	323
Barron	2,379	1,102	1,244
Bayfield	1,589	586	424
Brown	15,550	6,563	8,743
Buffalo	824	325	460
Burnett	760	340	435
Calumet	2,822	1,333	1,860
Chippewa	4,099	1,532	2,889
Clark	1,638	788	1,091
Columbia	4,542	1,866	1,729
Crawford	1,336	565	421
Dane	68,362	16,634	13,900
Dodge	5,302	2,617	3,132
Door	2,386	926	749
Douglas	2,929	1,266	784
Dunn	2,525	806	2,251
Eau Claire	7,787	2,640	5,450
Florence	257	113	116
Fond du Lac	5,999	3,143	4,227
Forest	523	252	271
Grant	2,969	1,181	1,085
Green	2,794	1,014	831
Green Lake	1,034	527	789
Iowa	2,192	745	752
Iron	430	181	147
Jackson	1,488	587	528
Jefferson	6,019	2,626	3,460
Juneau	1,623	679	657
Kenosha	8,668	3,781	3,646
Kewaunee	1,661	621	739
La Crosse	8,094	3,410	2,807
Lafayette	1,105	444	446
Langlade	1,091	569	799
Lincoln	1,830	833	1,326
Manitowoc	5,544	2,378	2,985
Marathon	7,851	3,563	5,093
Marinette	2,578	1,227	1,064
Marquette	1,061	559	524
Menominee	128	44	42
Milwaukee	68,226	30,096	27,973
Monroe	2,450	1,133	1,011
Oconto	2,760	1,240	1,333
Oneida	2,817	1,290	1,208
Outagamie	11,753	4,939	6,078
Ozaukee	4,071	2,586	4,414
Pepin	483	144	406
Pierce	1,650	646	1,538
Polk	1,704	742	1,470
Portage	5,437	2,105	1,879
Price	1,022	477	576
Racine	14,287	6,933	7,965
Richland	1,215	589	445
Rock	12,131	4,894	4,463
Rusk	943	402	569
St. Croix	3,020	1,230	3,212
Sauk	4,467	1,769	1,619
Sawyer	939	457	457
Shawano	2,317	1,020	1,344
Sheboygan	7,013	3,768	4,712
Taylor	833	493	703
Trempealeau	1,830	703	810
Vernon	2,259	872	649
Vilas	1,598	745	620
Walworth	4,543	2,319	3,151
Washburn	1,090	431	474
Washington	5,111	3,680	6,773
Waukesha	17,626	11,415	21,628
Waupaca	3,059	1,637	1,776
Waushara	1,565	728	831
Winnebago	10,677	4,117	5,786
Wood	5,073	2,241	2,460
TOTAL	396,302	165,325	197,148

Dem. – Democratic Party.

Source: Official records of the Government Accountability Board, Elections Division. Scattered votes omitted.

COUNTY VOTE FOR LIEUTENANT GOVERNOR
June 5, 2012 Recall General Election

County	Mahlon Mitchell (Dem.)	Rebecca Kleefisch* (Rep.)
Adams	3,672	4,357
Ashland	4,148	2,452
Barron	7,053	9,862
Bayfield	4,865	3,126
Brown	40,722	59,974
Buffalo	2,204	3,210
Burnett	2,522	3,772
Calumet	7,535	14,595
Chippewa	10,721	14,424
Clark	3,818	7,674
Columbia	13,100	12,657
Crawford	3,174	3,184
Dane	175,267	75,292
Dodge	14,148	24,392
Door	6,226	8,261
Douglas	11,503	6,303
Dunn	7,042	8,197
Eau Claire	20,599	20,291
Florence	692	1,260
Fond du Lac	15,919	28,717
Forest	1,493	2,057
Grant	8,547	9,165
Green	8,120	8,059
Green Lake	2,551	5,673
Iowa	5,799	4,722
Iron	1,242	1,516
Jackson	3,495	3,892
Jefferson	14,711	21,937
Juneau	4,227	5,250
Kenosha	29,392	28,170
Kewaunee	3,406	5,912
La Crosse	24,193	22,089
Lafayette	2,973	3,702
Langlade	2,902	5,247
Lincoln	5,430	7,015
Manitowoc	12,610	22,613
Marathon	22,148	35,204
Marinette	6,192	9,966
Marquette	2,773	3,963
Menominee	550	199
Milwaukee	244,100	141,206
Monroe	6,179	8,788
Oconto	5,802	10,744
Oneida	7,342	10,176
Outagamie	29,755	46,559
Ozaukee	14,105	33,685
Pepin	1,230	1,771
Pierce	6,612	8,063
Polk	6,558	9,759
Portage	15,577	14,378
Price	2,763	3,881
Racine	40,191	44,831
Richland	3,304	3,767
Rock	35,310	26,726
Rusk	2,271	3,503
St. Croix	13,110	20,188
Sauk	12,910	13,245
Sawyer	2,965	3,854
Shawano	5,634	10,846
Sheboygan	18,629	33,470
Taylor	2,291	5,437
Trempealeau	4,752	5,927
Vernon	5,802	6,127
Vilas	4,098	7,123
Walworth	14,483	25,590
Washburn	3,195	4,028
Washington	16,873	51,363
Waukesha	57,814	151,097
Waupaca	7,529	13,749
Waushara	3,754	6,283
Winnebago	30,553	39,237
Wood	13,345	17,987
TOTAL	1,156,520	1,301,739

Dem. – Democratic Party; Rep. – Republican Party.

*Incumbent.

Source: Official records of the Government Accountability Board, Elections Division. Scattered votes omitted.

VOTE FOR SUPERINTENDENT OF PUBLIC INSTRUCTION
BY COUNTY
April 2, 2013 Spring Election

County	Tony Evers*	Don Pridemore	County Total
Adams	2,161	1,219	3,385
Ashland	1,683	625	2,319
Barron	3,481	2,344	5,840
Bayfield	2,226	919	3,150
Brown	18,228	11,061	29,324
Buffalo	1,418	580	2,002
Burnett	1,276	842	2,121
Calumet	3,932	2,549	6,486
Chippewa	4,642	2,517	7,165
Clark	3,139	1,966	5,119
Columbia	7,045	3,396	10,457
Crawford	1,962	660	2,623
Dane	67,226	17,816	85,142
Dodge	6,487	6,215	12,714
Door	4,805	2,105	6,925
Douglas	2,774	1,508	4,287
Dunn	3,579	1,822	5,421
Eau Claire	8,398	3,889	12,312
Florence	398	212	611
Fond du Lac	7,831	5,848	13,687
Forest	874	423	1,300
Grant	4,190	1,575	5,772
Green	3,634	1,715	5,360
Green Lake	2,006	1,362	3,369
Iowa	2,723	917	3,648
Iron	860	358	1,218
Jackson	2,475	1,062	3,540
Jefferson	7,002	5,798	12,827
Juneau	2,011	1,017	3,033
Kenosha	9,939	6,582	16,576
Kewaunee	1,919	1,100	3,022
La Crosse	10,310	3,569	13,906
Lafayette	2,113	771	2,891
Langlade	2,248	1,290	3,542
Lincoln	3,509	1,809	5,324
Manitowoc	9,894	5,848	15,760
Marathon	10,015	6,558	16,606
Marinette	4,744	2,187	6,937
Marquette	1,893	1,158	3,052
Menominee	230	75	305
Milwaukee	63,459	37,950	101,710
Monroe	4,354	1,764	6,133
Oconto	4,959	2,363	7,332
Oneida	3,705	1,891	5,605
Outagamie	15,141	8,001	23,159
Ozaukee	8,569	10,305	18,918
Pepin	687	330	1,017
Pierce	2,621	1,562	4,201
Polk	3,339	2,087	5,434
Portage	5,960	3,856	9,854
Price	1,981	1,150	3,132
Racine	14,851	11,955	26,838
Richland	1,662	745	2,411
Rock	12,545	5,266	17,823
Rusk	1,562	952	2,517
St. Croix	5,181	3,446	8,672
Sauk	6,094	2,851	8,954
Sawyer	1,361	733	2,100
Shawano	4,240	2,257	6,502
Sheboygan	10,644	9,232	19,901
Taylor	2,241	1,237	3,487
Trempealeau	3,273	1,194	4,475
Vernon	3,224	1,269	4,502
Vilas	2,554	1,603	4,173
Walworth	8,124	6,346	14,534
Washburn	1,484	948	2,435
Washington	7,778	15,546	23,353
Waukesha	25,793	43,570	69,447
Waupaca	4,710	2,584	7,309
Waushara	2,035	1,335	3,375
Winnebago	11,843	6,789	18,677
Wood	5,776	3,666	9,453
TOTAL	487,030	308,050	796,511

*Incumbent.

Source: Official records of the Government Accountability Board, Elections Division. County totals include scattered votes.

DEMOCRATIC PRESIDENTIAL PREFERENCE VOTE, BY COUNTY
April 3, 2012

County	Total*	Barack Obama	Uninstructed Delegation
Adams	931	896	34
Ashland	1,234	1,201	27
Barron	2,143	2,008	121
Bayfield	1,541	1,507	32
Brown	9,103	8,904	168
Buffalo	841	794	40
Burnett	511	477	34
Calumet	2,173	2,126	39
Chippewa	2,494	2,406	82
Clark	1,363	1,308	51
Columbia	2,661	2,614	38
Crawford	961	912	46
Dane	41,662	41,113	441
Dodge	2,982	2,915	56
Door	1,653	1,619	26
Douglas	2,756	2,689	56
Dunn	1,964	1,905	55
Eau Claire	6,297	6,184	103
Florence	125	117	7
Fond du Lac	4,078	4,008	64
Forest	472	442	29
Grant	2,132	2,037	89
Green	1,821	1,779	35
Green Lake	545	512	29
Iowa	1,799	1,728	64
Iron	335	316	17
Jackson	1,196	1,143	50
Jefferson	3,205	3,128	71
Juneau	815	771	36
Kenosha	9,419	9,245	154
Kewaunee	879	863	16
La Crosse	6,596	6,494	93
Lafayette	994	950	41
Langlade	835	783	48
Lincoln	1,304	1,270	32
Manitowoc	3,473	3,394	70
Marathon	5,385	5,288	77
Marinette	1,954	1,840	103
Marquette	503	466	32
Menominee	105	103	1
Milwaukee	69,015	68,403	474
Monroe	2,048	1,977	66
Oconto	1,570	1,465	97
Oneida	2,403	2,330	66
Outagamie	8,377	8,157	197
Ozaukee	3,454	3,391	45
Pepin	553	531	21
Pierce	1,400	1,342	51
Polk	1,829	1,729	91
Portage	4,332	4,276	45
Price	1,068	1,041	26
Racine	9,601	9,391	191
Richland	1,019	977	40
Rock	9,424	9,222	176
Rusk	896	850	42
St. Croix	4,852	4,706	132
Sauk	3,367	3,308	47
Sawyer	747	719	22
Shawano	1,477	1,391	78
Sheboygan	4,295	4,144	136
Taylor	704	675	27
Trempealeau	1,449	1,393	50
Vernon	1,263	1,207	54
Vilas	914	894	13
Walworth	3,713	3,613	86
Washburn	854	794	54
Washington	3,773	3,693	66
Waukesha	9,656	9,442	178
Waupaca	1,860	1,768	90
Waushara	636	610	25
Winnebago	8,641	8,462	139
Wood	3,825	3,758	60
TOTAL	300,255	293,914	5,492

*Scattered vote included in county total.

Source: Official records of the Government Accountability Board, Elections Division.

REPUBLICAN PRESIDENTIAL PREFERENCE VOTE, BY COUNTY
April 3, 2012

County	Total*	Michele Bachmann	Newt Gingrich	Jon Huntsman	Ron Paul	Mitt Romney	Rick Santorum	Uninstructed Delegation
Adams	2,608	27	209	14	356	1,085	896	18
Ashland	1,878	20	141	19	253	549	865	23
Barron	5,653	41	420	28	534	1,922	2,665	35
Bayfield	2,433	26	208	34	300	825	1,017	18
Brown	34,086	268	2,460	185	3,514	12,530	14,858	200
Buffalo	1,856	39	223	12	217	653	695	15
Burnett	1,950	12	155	15	199	689	869	10
Calumet	8,498	66	548	45	1,081	3,109	3,596	42
Chippewa	7,643	83	658	32	799	2,493	3,509	48
Clark	4,483	55	367	27	536	1,353	2,100	36
Columbia	7,790	71	568	54	1,175	3,072	2,785	54
Crawford	1,844	15	122	18	316	667	688	15
Dane	58,302	472	3,568	888	9,774	21,882	21,133	424
Dodge	13,731	112	611	59	1,374	5,945	5,542	70
Door	5,378	52	341	38	614	2,342	1,941	34
Douglas	4,023	56	274	29	481	1,338	1,801	33
Dunn	4,530	44	344	31	599	1,438	2,043	23
Eau Claire	13,152	113	1,115	119	1,750	4,752	5,172	88
Florence	717	5	85	4	57	289	276	1
Fond du Lac	16,965	136	951	91	1,537	6,989	7,159	86
Forest	1,242	11	118	9	127	436	525	12
Grant	5,278	57	332	43	706	1,979	2,098	50
Green	4,804	39	319	38	735	1,780	1,846	41
Green Lake	3,112	20	224	14	274	1,348	1,208	19
Iowa	3,031	38	200	23	486	1,125	1,121	31
Iron	933	4	50	7	121	404	338	6
Jackson	2,102	21	242	13	302	728	780	13
Jefferson	12,729	102	626	75	1,417	5,758	4,657	76
Juneau	3,002	31	237	18	448	1,067	1,172	17
Kenosha	19,056	146	986	104	2,309	9,451	5,905	96
Kewaunee	3,128	27	177	16	296	967	1,624	16
La Crosse	14,793	146	1,483	116	2,022	5,297	5,591	102
Lafayette	2,132	29	140	17	298	803	830	9
Langlade	2,910	27	245	16	376	1,051	1,169	23
Lincoln	4,479	50	352	25	649	1,366	2,001	24
Manitowoc	12,440	122	783	86	1,274	4,643	5,450	63
Marathon	19,270	151	1,434	118	2,076	6,501	8,858	81
Marinette	5,638	53	419	24	631	2,119	2,355	28
Marquette	2,020	13	121	12	278	845	727	18
Menominee	133	2	6	2	14	60	46	3
Milwaukee	89,697	675	3,369	680	9,532	46,424	28,491	317
Monroe	5,365	67	533	38	668	1,867	2,133	46
Oconto	5,381	38	378	24	537	1,799	2,566	32
Oneida	7,056	52	585	35	1,102	2,912	2,323	36
Outagamie	26,293	183	1,811	187	3,517	9,750	10,673	129
Ozaukee	21,465	103	642	88	1,577	13,074	5,836	98
Pepin	949	11	94	6	99	307	427	3
Pierce	3,989	35	232	25	521	1,315	1,841	13
Polk	5,201	54	337	29	602	1,714	2,420	30
Portage	9,741	92	811	59	1,369	3,224	4,114	48
Price	2,675	27	206	19	361	979	1,058	20
Racine	26,065	150	1,058	123	2,237	14,065	8,253	128
Richland	2,508	22	175	13	463	882	921	23
Rock	19,202	182	1,228	139	2,713	8,233	6,493	162
Rusk	2,293	25	234	21	343	715	927	19
St. Croix	12,692	151	769	69	1,671	4,539	5,346	114
Sauk	8,391	72	600	76	1,361	3,205	2,991	58
Sawyer	2,321	28	196	20	219	926	916	9
Shawano	6,208	42	460	32	644	2,194	2,799	22
Sheboygan	18,333	90	755	79	1,684	7,906	7,706	88
Taylor	2,849	35	235	14	353	875	1,307	21
Trempealeau	3,000	32	657	17	317	891	1,061	18
Vernon	3,401	38	274	21	575	1,095	1,359	31
Vilas	4,521	28	389	22	522	2,187	1,337	24
Walworth	15,432	94	767	73	1,680	7,977	4,696	115
Washburn	2,507	21	177	13	244	909	1,126	11
Washington	28,448	118	889	84	1,831	15,540	9,852	89
Waukesha	83,628	303	2,546	232	4,985	51,355	23,888	200
Waupaca	7,569	69	602	49	836	2,720	3,234	40
Waushara	3,375	39	243	21	310	1,337	1,399	22
Winnebago	25,927	226	1,825	175	3,424	10,281	9,767	162
Wood	11,613	141	1,039	82	1,256	4,029	4,968	71
TOTAL	787,847	6,045	45,978	5,083	87,858	346,876	290,139	4,200

*Scattered vote included in county total.

Source: Official records of the Government Accountability Board, Elections Division.

2012 DEMOCRATIC NATIONAL CONVENTION DELEGATES
September 3-6, 2012 – Charlotte, North Carolina

Delegate	Address	Delegate	Address
		For Barack Obama	

Pledged Leaders and Elected Officials

Delegate	Address	Delegate	Address
Peter Barca	Kenosha	**Fourth Congressional District**	
Tom Barrett	Milwaukee	Milton Bond	Milwaukee
Jill Billings	La Crosse	Zach Bowman	Milwaukee
John Dickert	Racine	C. Michelle Bryant	Milwaukee
Jim Doyle	Verona	Sachin Chheda	Milwaukee
Kathleen Falk	Madison	Stephanie Findley	Milwaukee
Frances Huntley-Cooper	Fitchburg	Ann Jacobs	Milwaukee
Mark Miller	Monona	Vanessa Llanas	Milwaukee
Erik Paulson	Madison	Terrell Martin	Milwaukee
Erin Sievert	Waterloo	Craig Mastantuono	Milwaukee
Lena C. Taylor	Milwaukee	Joel McNally (alternate)	Milwaukee
JoCasta Zamarripa	Milwaukee	Thelma Sias	Milwaukee

At-Large

Delegate	Address	Delegate	Address
Miriam Briggs-Muhammad	Madison	**Fifth Congressional District**	
Heather Colburn	Madison	Abdulhamid Ali	Whitefish Bay
Devon Cook	Madison	Lashell Drake	Milwaukee
Colin Donovan	Green Bay	Bridget Moen	Cedarburg
Brenda Gauthier	Neopit	Larry Nelson	Waukesha
Regina Harmon (alternate)	Glendale	Martha Pincus	Fox Point
Zachary Henderson (alternate)	Sun Prarie	Frank Shansky	Milwaukee
Stacey Herzing	Milwaukee		
David Marstellar	Milwaukee	**Sixth Congressional District**	
Arvina Martin	Madison	Jacqueline Burke	Beaver Dam
Diana Miller	Madison	Jennifer Giedd	Beaver Dam
John Miller	Grafton	Jef Hall	Oshkosh
Mahlon Mitchell	Fitchburg	Gordon Hintz	Oshkosh
Victor Ouimette	Mercer	Joan Kaeding	Oshkosh
Matthew Pichler	Colgate	Thomas Kitchen	Fond du Lac
Mark Pocan	Madison	Kevin Kopplin	Watertown
Gloria Reyes	Madison		
David L. Sartori	Cudahy	**Seventh Congressional District**	
Danine Spencer	Rhinelander	Marvin Finendale	Superior
Christopher Stanley	Fond du Lac	Gary Hawley	Stevens Point
Mary Strickland	Madison	Jeff Johnson	Wausau
Teresa Thomas-Boyd	Milwaukee	Joyce Lohr	Marathon
Primitivo Torres	Milwaukee	Dorothy Miller	Mosinee
Mary Urbina-McCarthy	Milwaukee	Kaeleen Ringberg	Ashland
		Kevin Schanning	Iron River
		Kelly Westlund	Ashland

First Congressional District

Delegate	Address	Delegate	Address
Meg Andrietsch	Racine	**Eighth Congressional District**	
Leah Blough	Kenosha	Danny Cole	Abrams
Michael Goebel	Kenosha	Nelson Cox	Appleton
Ellen Holly	Elkhorn	Harold Jackson	Lac du Flambeau
Marlene Ott (alternate)	Greendale	Bill Milz (alternate)	Marinette
Beth Pramme	Racine	Patti Phillbrick-Linzmeyer	Green Bay
Andy Suchorski	Franklin	Nancy Schleis	Green Bay
Rob Zerban	Kenosha	Amy Schwaba	Marinette
		Jamie Shiner	Green Bay
		Tom Sieber	Green Bay

Second Congressional District

Delegate	Address	Delegate	Address
Laurene Bach	Madison	**Standing Committee**	
David Boetcher	Waunakee	Janan Atta-Najeeb	Mequon
Luke Fuszard	Madison	Jon Erpenbach	Middleton
Evan Giesmann (alternate)	Madison	Cassi Fenili	Madison
Jennifer Johnson	Madison	Beau Liegeois	Green Bay
Lori Kief	Madison	Gerard Maciejewski	Glendale
Barb Knutson	Madison	Candice Owley	Milwaukee
Dick Loeper	Madison	Michael Rosen	Milwaukee
Joe Lowndes	Madison	Dian Palmer	Brookfield
Bethany Ordaz	Madison	Scott Tyre	Middleton
Connie Palmer Smalley	Madison		
Jeff Pertl	Madison	**Unpledged Delegates**	
John Strasser	Madison	Tammy Baldwin	Madison
Diane Welsh (alternate)	Madison	Roland Hicks	Eau Claire
		Ron Kind	La Crosse

Third Congressional District

Delegate	Address	Delegate	Address
Veronica Burke	Onalaska	Herbert Kohl	Milwaukee
Barbara Dearth	Blanchardville	Martha Love	Milwaukee
Paul Kruse	Onalaska	Gwen Moore	Milwaukee
Robert Miller	Alma	Jason Rae	Milwaukee
Susan Van Sicklen	Dodgeville	Leila Sahar	Pewaukee
Dana Wachs	Eau Claire	Melissa Schroeder	Merrill
Bob Welsh	Wauzeka	Paula Zellner	Porterfield
Judith Willink	Augusta		
Margaret Wood (alternate)	La Crosse		

Source: Democratic Party of Wisconsin.

2012 REPUBLICAN NATIONAL CONVENTION DELEGATES
August 27-30, 2012 – Tampa, Florida

Delegate	Address	Delegate	Address

For Ron Paul

Third Congressional District
Todd Welch — Menomonie

For Mitt Romney

At-Large
Delegate	Address
Candee Arndt	Brookfield
Scott Beightol	Whitefish Bay
Crystal Berg (alternate)	Hartford
Mary Buestrin	Mequon
Gerald Couri (alternate)	Waukesha
Barbara Courtney (alternate)	Whitefish Bay
Brad Courtney	Whitefish Bay
James Crawford (alternate)	Crandon
Alberta Darling	River Hills
Russ Darrow (alternate)	West Bend
Terry Dittrich (alternate)	Hartland
Jere Fabick	Oconomowoc
Jennie Frederick (alternate)	Jackson
Keith Gilkes	Madison
Jenna Golem (alternate)	Oshkosh
Mike Grebe	Milwaukee
Diane Hendricks	Janesville
Steve King	Janesville
Rebecca Kleefisch	Oconomowoc
Scott Klug (alternate)	Madison
Linda Prehn (alternate)	Wausau
Reince Priebus	Kenosha
Gerard Randall (alternate)	Milwaukee
Robert Schuemann (alternate)	River Hills
Patricia Shabaz (alternate)	Madison
John Shiely (alternate)	Elm Grove
Tommy Thompson	Madison
Jackie Trudell	Appleton
John Van Hollen	Waunakee
Scott Walker	Wauwatosa
Tonnette Walker	Wauwatosa
Steve Ziegler	Oconomowoc

First Congressional District
Delegate	Address
Janene Deters (alternate)	Janesville
Dona Poelman	Franksville
Bryan Steil (alternate)	Janesville
Jonathan Steitz	Kenosha
Kimberly Travis	Williams Bay

Second Congressional District
Delegate	Address
Edward Grabins	Verona
Jonathan Jackson (alternate)	Prarie du Sac
Kirsten Lombard (alternate)	Madison
Andrea Lombard	Baraboo
Roger Stauter (alternate)	Monona
Jacqueline Johnson	Verona

Third Congressional District
Delegate	Address
John Danneker (alternate)	Maiden Rock
Karen Dunham (alternate)	Stevens Point
Maripat Krueger	Menomonie
Sue Lynch	West Salem
Randall Molini (alternate)	Black River Falls

Fourth Congressional District
Delegate	Address
Rick Baas	Milwaukee
Doug Haag	Milwaukee
Patricia Reiman (alternate)	Whitefish Bay
Bob Spindell	Milwaukee
Laurie Wolf (alternate)	Bayside

Fifth Congressional District
Delegate	Address
Grace Degner (alternate)	Hustisford
James Geldreich (alternate)	West Bend
David Karst (alternate)	Greenfield
Kathy Kiernan	Richfield
John Macy	Waukesha
Karen Mueller	Wales

Sixth Congressional District
Delegate	Address
Daniel Feyen	Fond du Lac
Jeff Johns (alternate)	Cedarburg
Timothy Lakin (alternate)	Fond du Lac
Lillian Nolan	Fond du Lac
Tyler Vorpagel	Fond du Lac

Seventh Congressional District
Delegate	Address
Dave Anderson	Wausau
Diane Joachim (alternate)	New Richmond
William Johnson (alternate)	Hayward
James Miller	Hayward
Charlotte Rasmussen	Stanley
Pamela Travis (alternate)	Neillsville

Eighth Congressional District
Delegate	Address
Kevin Barthel	Lakewood
Sol Grosskopf	Shawano
Rick Klatt (alternate)	Oconto Falls
Barbara Finger	Oconto
Carl Kuehne (alternate)	De Pere
Richard Resch (alternate)	De Pere

Source: Republican Party of Wisconsin.

COUNTY VOTE FOR PRESIDENT AND VICE PRESIDENT
November 6, 2012 General Election

County	Virgil Goode Jim Clymer (Con.)	Barack Obama[1] Joe Biden[1] (Dem.)	Mitt Romney Paul Ryan (Rep.)	Gary Johnson James P. Gray (Ind.)	Gloria La Riva Filberto Ramirez, Jr. (Ind.)	Jill Stein Ben Manski (Ind.)	Jerry White Phyllis Scherrer (Ind.)
Adams	16	5,542	4,644	51	3	10	5
Ashland	18	5,399	2,820	50	4	59	3
Barron	47	10,890	11,443	169	5	54	6
Bayfield	17	6,033	3,603	55	0	67	1
Brown	204	62,526	64,836	805	21	308	16
Buffalo	29	3,570	3,364	41	3	14	4
Burnett	26	3,986	4,550	64	5	24	1
Calumet	54	11,489	14,539	224	6	56	6
Chippewa	69	15,237	15,322	183	3	67	13
Clark	42	6,172	7,412	87	7	39	8
Columbia	36	17,175	13,026	180	2	69	1
Crawford	16	4,629	3,067	62	4	19	4
Dane	307	216,071	83,644	2,294	38	1,335	47
Dodge	76	18,762	25,211	267	5	83	14
Door	22	9,357	8,121	83	6	47	2
Douglas	48	14,863	7,705	151	4	104	5
Dunn	49	11,316	10,224	271	6	69	5
Eau Claire	75	30,666	23,256	494	9	176	6
Florence	6	953	1,645	12	0	1	1
Fond du Lac	115	22,379	30,355	351	5	111	8
Forest	11	2,425	2,172	23	0	6	4
Grant	62	13,594	10,255	201	9	56	5
Green	29	11,206	7,857	142	2	44	3
Green Lake	22	3,793	5,782	43	4	19	0
Iowa	13	8,105	4,287	78	0	27	2
Iron	10	1,784	1,790	27	2	9	2
Jackson	17	5,298	3,900	48	4	21	4
Jefferson	93	20,158	23,517	303	3	106	7
Juneau	22	6,242	5,411	82	2	33	3
Kenosha	97	44,867	34,977	566	20	188	11
Kewaunee	27	5,153	5,747	56	2	30	6
La Crosse	129	36,693	25,751	547	9	176	12
Lafayette	17	4,536	3,314	46	2	25	3
Langlade	26	4,573	5,816	49	2	22	3
Lincoln	37	7,563	7,455	90	1	35	3
Manitowoc	111	20,403	21,604	300	7	102	5
Marathon	126	32,363	36,617	421	6	175	15
Marinette	38	9,882	10,619	141	4	51	4
Marquette	17	4,014	3,992	43	2	13	4
Menominee	1	1,191	179	5	0	1	0
Milwaukee	594	332,438	154,924	2,623	98	1,042	78
Monroe	47	9,515	9,675	132	6	55	8
Oconto	35	8,865	10,741	138	6	43	3
Oneida	51	10,452	10,917	137	2	44	1
Outagamie	176	45,659	47,372	961	16	240	16
Ozaukee	52	19,159	36,077	317	6	127	6
Pepin	8	1,876	1,794	12	1	6	1
Pierce	58	10,235	10,397	177	5	86	7
Polk	46	10,073	12,094	226	4	79	11
Portage	73	22,075	16,615	309	7	143	5
Price	21	3,887	3,884	60	2	23	3
Racine	153	53,008	49,347	550	14	149	17
Richland	20	4,969	3,573	53	2	26	1
Rock	170	49,219	30,517	470	10	148	17
Rusk	23	3,397	3,676	52	5	25	2
St. Croix	76	19,910	25,503	455	6	112	14
Sauk	34	18,736	12,838	179	4	66	4
Sawyer	20	4,486	4,442	37	0	26	4
Shawano	40	9,000	11,022	139	6	32	4
Sheboygan	116	27,918	34,072	372	10	115	15
Taylor	31	3,763	5,601	58	7	28	6
Trempealeau	23	7,605	5,707	82	3	41	5
Vernon	42	8,044	5,942	103	8	96	2
Vilas	17	5,951	7,749	61	2	35	6
Walworth	83	22,552	29,006	441	10	102	10
Washburn	13	4,447	4,699	79	3	25	1
Washington	122	23,166	54,765	435	10	139	7
Waukesha	297	78,779	162,798	1,262	26	311	21
Waupaca	45	11,578	17,002	142	7	49	5
Waushara	29	5,335	6,562	64	4	27	7
Winnebago	136	45,449	42,122	922	14	238	24
Wood	102	18,581	19,704	286	5	136	5
TOTAL[2]	4,930	1,620,985	1,410,966	20,439	526	7,665	553
Percent of Total Vote[3]	0.16%	52.78%	45.94%	0.67%	0.02%	0.25%	0.02%

Con. – Constitution Party; Dem. – Democratic Party; Rep. – Republican Party; Ind. – Independent.

[1]Incumbent. [2]Total vote does not include votes for write-in candidates: Ross C. Rocky Anderson and Luis J. Rodriguez – 112; Roseanne Barr and Cindy Lee Sheehan – 88. [3]Percentages do not sum to 100%, as scattered votes have been omitted.

Source: Official records of the Government Accountability Board, Elections Division.

VOTE FOR PRESIDENT AND VICE PRESIDENT BY WARD
November 6, 2012 General Election

District	Obama and Biden (Dem.)	Romney and Ryan (Rep.)
ADAMS COUNTY		
Adams		
Wards 1 – 3	357	270
Adams, city		
Wards 1 – 4	497	298
Big Flats		
Wards 1 & 2	282	209
Colburn	63	58
Dell Prairie		
Wards 1 – 3	429	411
Easton		
Wards 1 & 2	270	237
Friendship, vil.	185	109
Jackson		
Wards 1 & 2	310	253
Leola	50	102
Lincoln	84	80
Monroe	135	126
New Chester		
Wards 1 – 3	266	160
New Haven	207	152
Preston		
Wards 1 & 2	392	285
Quincy		
Wards 1 – 3	497	253
Richfield	44	42
Rome		
Wards 1 – 5	826	1,025
Springville		
Wards 1 & 2	313	284
Strongs Prairie		
Wards 1 – 3	330	280
Wisconsin Dells, city		
Wards 5 & 9	5	10
TOTAL	5,542	4,644
ASHLAND COUNTY		
Agenda	101	136
Ashland	211	105
Ashland, city		
Ward 1	231	218
Ward 2	216	84
Ward 3	213	100
Ward 4	278	171
Ward 5	289	110
Ward 6	222	85
Ward 7	288	94
Ward 8	228	111
Ward 9	241	62
Ward 10	249	99
Ward 11	286	106
Butternut, vil.		
Wards 1 & 2	108	66
Chippewa	105	111
Gingles	276	143
Gordon		
Wards 1 & 2	100	82
Jacobs	216	156
La Pointe	209	51
Marengo		
Wards 1 & 2	125	82
Mellen, city	230	105
Morse		
Wards 1 – 3	183	121
Peeksville		
Wards 1 & 2	50	54
Sanborn		
Wards 1 & 2	503	68
Shanagolden	39	34
White River		
Wards 1 & 2	202	266
TOTAL	5,399	2,820
BARRON COUNTY		
Almena		
Wards 1 & 2	249	228
Almena, vil.	127	147
Arland	169	149
Barron		
Wards 1 & 2	142	257
Barron, city		
Wards 1 – 7	713	648
Bear Lake	195	164
Cameron, vil.		
Wards 1 – 3	363	388
Cedar Lake	268	376
Chetek		
Wards 1 & 2	477	552
Chetek, city		
Wards 1 – 4	482	471
Clinton	149	199

District	Obama and Biden (Dem.)	Romney and Ryan (Rep.)
Crystal Lake	195	204
Cumberland	214	230
Cumberland, city		
Wards 1 – 4	598	439
Dallas	118	168
Dallas, vil.	83	105
Dovre	185	189
Doyle		
Wards 1 & 2	106	174
Haugen, vil.	80	65
Lakeland		
Wards 1 & 2	272	297
Maple Grove		
Wards 1 & 2	163	323
Maple Plain	238	239
New Auburn, vil.		
Ward 2	1	6
Ward 3	1	1
Oak Grove		
Wards 1 & 2	255	241
Prairie Farm		
Wards 1 & 2	142	124
Prairie Farm, vil.	103	77
Prairie Lake		
Wards 1 & 2	367	481
Rice Lake		
Wards 1 – 4	779	843
Rice Lake, city		
Wards 1 – 13	2,091	1,854
Sioux Creek	122	178
Stanfold	177	194
Stanley		
Wards 1 – 4	576	734
Sumner	190	208
Turtle Lake	139	150
Turtle Lake, vil.	213	181
Vance Creek	148	159
TOTAL	10,890	11,443
BAYFIELD COUNTY		
Ashland, city		
Ward 12	0	0
Barksdale	272	198
Barnes	306	253
Bayfield	372	150
Bayfield, city		
Wards 1 – 4	260	90
Bayview	229	138
Bell	138	82
Cable	256	270
Clover	104	70
Delta	100	108
Drummond	182	139
Eileen		
Wards 1 & 2	245	170
Grand View	178	111
Hughes	168	127
Iron River		
Wards 1 & 2	418	308
Kelly	141	107
Keystone	121	87
Lincoln	101	77
Mason	94	84
Mason, vil.	32	16
Namakagon	97	123
Orienta	42	37
Oulu	177	151
Pilsen	92	52
Port Wing	173	99
Russell		
Wards 1 & 2	553	72
Tripp	67	73
Washburn	237	121
Washburn, city		
Wards 1 – 4	878	290
TOTAL	6,033	3,603
BROWN COUNTY		
Allouez, vil.		
Wards 1 & 2	1,186	856
Wards 3 & 4	940	856
Wards 5 & 6	1,037	1,295
Wards 7 – 9	907	973
Ashwaubenon, vil.		
Wards 1 & 2	690	567
Wards 3 & 4	697	654
Wards 5 & 6	764	795
Wards 7 & 8	794	996
Wards 9 & 10	796	1,203
Wards 11 & 12	754	685

VOTE FOR PRESIDENT AND VICE PRESIDENT BY WARD
November 6, 2012 General Election–Continued

District	Obama and Biden (Dem.)	Romney and Ryan (Rep.)	District	Obama and Biden (Dem.)	Romney and Ryan (Rep.)
Bellevue, vil.			New Denmark		
Wards 1 – 6	1,852	1,842	Wards 1 – 3	408	501
Wards 7 – 10	1,772	2,208	Pittsfield		
De Pere, city			Wards 1 – 3	617	996
Wards 1 – 4	1,729	1,846	Pulaski, vil.		
Ward 5	116	117	Wards 1 – 3 & 6	738	786
Wards 6 – 8	1,308	1,255	Rockland		
Wards 9 & 18	224	257	Wards 1 – 3	366	684
Wards 10 – 12	1,530	1,462	Scott		
Wards 13 – 15	1,403	1,735	Wards 1 – 4	1,019	1,213
Wards 16 & 17	5	3	Suamico, vil.		
Denmark, vil.			Wards 1 – 4	1,125	2,073
Wards 1 – 3	521	528	Wards 5 – 8	1,357	2,253
Eaton			Wrightstown		
Wards 1 & 2	409	483	Wards 1 – 3	464	731
Glenmore			Wrightstown, vil.		
Wards 1 & 2	255	377	Wards 1 – 3	557	760
Green Bay			TOTAL	62,526	64,836
Wards 1 – 3	454	704	**BUFFALO COUNTY**		
Green Bay, city			Alma	97	82
Ward 1	3	10	Alma, city		
Ward 2	550	640	Wards 1 & 2	234	210
Ward 3	1,037	748	Belvidere	118	131
Ward 4	816	919	Buffalo	207	190
Ward 5	389	404	Buffalo, city	293	261
Ward 6	750	944	Canton	76	63
Ward 7	462	456	Cross	101	106
Ward 8	797	830	Cochran, vil	119	100
Ward 9	419	232	Dover	124	111
Ward 10	452	249	Fountain City, city		
Ward 11	387	354	Wards 1 & 2	261	200
Ward 12	488	242	Gilmanton	136	89
Ward 13	504	218	Glencoe	107	128
Ward 14	455	296	Lincoln	49	61
Ward 15	725	444	Maxville	61	102
Ward 16	649	320	Milton	172	131
Ward 17	562	322	Modena	89	86
Ward 18	518	398	Mondovi	131	131
Ward 19	417	252	Mondovi, city		
Ward 20	529	257	Wards 1 – 3	631	509
Ward 21	489	193	Montana	67	79
Ward 22	223	116	Naples	154	203
Ward 23	454	283	Nelson	136	172
Ward 24	615	307	Nelson, vil.	96	62
Ward 25	553	295	Waumandee	111	157
Ward 26	557	217	TOTAL	3,570	3,364
Ward 27	303	76	**BURNETT COUNTY**		
Ward 28	617	259	Anderson	83	126
Ward 29	694	457	Blaine	58	56
Ward 30	792	264	Daniels	141	227
Ward 31	708	425	Dewey	122	136
Ward 32	605	361	Grantsburg		
Ward 33	371	252	Wards 1 – 3	226	316
Ward 34	719	509	Grantsburg, vil.		
Ward 35	434	437	Wards 1 – 3	284	372
Ward 36	386	204	Jackson	279	284
Ward 37	547	390	La Follette		
Ward 38	674	510	Wards 1 & 2	149	149
Ward 39	805	557	Lincoln	78	75
Ward 40	515	377	Meenon		
Ward 41	218	239	Wards 1 – 3	251	289
Ward 42	458	295	Oakland		
Ward 43	672	573	Wards 1 & 2	292	246
Ward 44	849	778	Roosevelt	58	62
Ward 45	707	1,173	Rusk	116	118
Ward 46	818	562	Sand Lake	167	111
Ward 47	669	843	Scott		
Hobart, vil.			Wards 1 & 2	168	241
Wards 1 – 8	1,611	2,388	Siren		
Ward 9	0	0	Wards 1 & 2	233	259
Holland			Siren, vil.		
Wards 1 & 2	331	554	Wards 1 & 2	182	170
Howard, vil.			Swiss		
Wards 1 & 12	468	579	Wards 1 & 2	255	151
Wards 2, 8 & 11	1,003	1,421	Trade Lake		
Wards 3, 4 & 6	746	631	Wards 1 & 2	197	310
Ward 5	190	198	Union	90	101
Ward 7	200	306	Webb Lake	133	145
Wards 9, 10 & 18	785	1,015	Webster, vil.		
Wards 13 & 14	446	581	Wards 1 & 2	187	136
Wards 15 & 16	492	744	West Marshland		
Humboldt			Wards 1 & 2	69	118
Wards 1 & 2	326	421	Wood River		
Lawrence			Wards 1 – 3	168	352
Wards 1 – 6	1,016	1,665	TOTAL	3,986	4,550
Ledgeview			**CALUMET COUNTY**		
Wards 1 – 3 & 8 – 10	789	1,322	Appleton, city		
Wards 4 – 7	699	1,206	Ward 12	86	68
Morrison					
Wards 1 & 2	269	624			

VOTE FOR PRESIDENT AND VICE PRESIDENT BY WARD
November 6, 2012 General Election–Continued

District	Obama and Biden (Dem.)	Romney and Ryan (Rep.)
Ward 13	599	418
Ward 14	364	405
Ward 26	636	548
Ward 44	628	502
Ward 45	595	710
Ward 46	40	58
Ward 47	0	0
Brillion		
Wards 1 & 2	287	520
Brillion, city		
Wards 1 – 4	701	835
Brothertown		
Wards 1 & 2	246	511
Charlestown	184	278
Chilton		
Wards 1 – 3	203	414
Chilton, city		
Wards 1 – 5	876	952
Harrison		
Wards 1 – 4	736	936
Wards 5 & 6	492	680
Wards 7 – 9	680	1,035
Wards 10 – 12	519	731
Hilbert, vil.		
Wards 1 & 2	207	361
Kaukauna, city		
Ward 11	0	0
Kiel, city		
Ward 7	76	75
Menasha, city		
Wards 16 – 20	627	694
New Holstein		
Wards 1 – 3	312	487
New Holstein, city		
Wards 1 – 5	853	858
Potter, vil.	47	85
Rantoul	151	276
Sherwood, vil.		
Wards 1 – 4	664	1,021
Stockbridge		
Wards 1 – 3	345	535
Stockbridge, vil.	156	214
Woodville	179	332
TOTAL	11,489	14,539
CHIPPEWA COUNTY		
Anson		
Wards 1 – 3	515	687
Ward 4	0	0
Arthur	166	216
Auburn	169	178
Birch Creek	110	192
Bloomer		
Wards 1 & 2	208	326
Bloomer, city		
Wards 1 – 4	802	942
Boyd, vil	154	127
Cadott, vil.		
Wards 1 & 2	351	273
Chippewa Falls, city		
Ward 1	530	348
Ward 2	483	451
Ward 3	599	510
Ward 4	459	334
Ward 5	477	304
Ward 6	513	345
Ward 7	469	373
Cleveland	168	241
Colburn	164	241
Cooks Valley	152	234
Cornell, city		
Wards 1 – 4	323	327
Delmar	185	257
Eagle Point		
Wards 1 – 5	798	1,032
Eau Claire, city		
Ward 16	516	351
Ward 40	0	0
Ward 41	21	13
Edson		
Wards 1 & 2	223	196
Estella	95	115
Goetz		
Wards 1 & 2	214	174
Ward 3	0	0
Hallie		
Wards 1 & 2	54	45
Howard	211	194
Lafayette		

District	Obama and Biden (Dem.)	Romney and Ryan (Rep.)
Wards 1 – 9	1,642	1,701
Lake Hallie, vil.		
Wards 1 – 8	1,718	1,547
Lake Holcombe		
Wards 1 & 2	254	310
New Auburn, vil.	95	121
Ruby	111	105
Sampson	183	281
Sigel		
Wards 1 & 2	266	225
Stanley, city		
Wards 1 – 4 & 6 – 7	477	445
Tilden		
Wards 1 – 3	370	461
Wheaton		
Wards 1 – 3	764	813
Woodmohr		
Wards 1 & 2	228	287
TOTAL	15,237	15,322
CLARK COUNTY		
Abbotsford, city		
Wards 2 – 5	278	386
Beaver	102	155
Butler	21	26
Colby		
Wards 1 – 3	104	164
Colby, city		
Wards 2 – 4	223	310
Curtiss, vil.	20	33
Dewhurst	78	103
Dorchester, vil.	112	176
Eaton		
Wards 1 & 2	81	140
Foster	35	38
Fremont		
Wards 1 & 2	165	320
Grant		
Wards 1 & 2	176	197
Granton, vil.	83	82
Green Grove		
Wards 1 & 2	104	115
Greenwood, city		
Wards 1 & 2	241	238
Hendren	98	114
Hewett		
Wards 1 & 2	88	74
Hixon		
Wards 1 & 2	114	104
Hoard		
Wards 1 & 2	89	139
Levis		
Wards 1 & 2	109	132
Longwood		
Wards 1 & 2	97	123
Loyal		
Wards 1 & 2	103	160
Loyal, city		
Wards 1 & 2	247	355
Lynn		
Wards 1 & 2	107	150
Mayville		
Wards 1 & 2	133	212
Mead	77	64
Mentor	115	124
Neillsville, city		
Ward 1	106	106
Ward 2	142	156
Ward 3	169	137
Ward 4	86	93
Ward 5	64	71
Owen, city		
Wards 1 – 3	232	185
Pine Valley		
Wards 1 & 2	284	327
Reseburg		
Wards 1 & 2	106	77
Seif	46	51
Sherman		
Wards 1 & 2	141	205
Sherwood	81	62
Stanley, city		
Ward 5	1	0
Thorp	155	131
Thorp, city		
Wards 1 – 4	388	359
Unity	120	184
Unity, vil.		
Ward 2	23	40

VOTE FOR PRESIDENT AND VICE PRESIDENT BY WARD
November 6, 2012 General Election–Continued

District	Obama and Biden (Dem.)	Romney and Ryan (Rep.)
Warner		
Wards 1 & 2	111	146
Washburn	57	84
Weston		
Wards 1 & 2	145	161
Withee.	125	169
Withee, vil.	111	107
Worden	102	136
York		
Wards 1 & 2	177	191
TOTAL	6,172	7,412
COLUMBIA COUNTY		
Arlington	276	211
Arlington, vil.	271	207
Caledonia		
Wards 1 & 2	485	389
Cambria, vil.	218	154
Columbus	174	200
Columbus, city		
Wards 1 – 8	1,648	1,045
Courtland	89	169
Dekorra		
Wards 1 – 3	769	696
Doylestown, vil.	90	49
Fall River, vil.		
Wards 1 & 2	492	337
Fort Winnebago	280	263
Fountain Prairie		
Wards 1 & 2	293	223
Friesland, vil.	54	124
Hampden	169	182
Leeds		
Wards 1 & 2	259	244
Lewiston		
Wards 1 & 2	379	307
Lodi		
Wards 1 – 5	1,044	934
Lodi, city		
Wards 1 – 6	1,065	589
Lowville		
Wards 1 & 2	350	300
Marcellon		
Wards 1 & 2	289	267
Newport.	219	175
Otsego.	213	179
Pacific		
Wards 1 – 4	867	796
Pardeeville, vil.		
Wards 1 – 3	648	448
Portage, city		
Wards 1, 9 & 10	868	539
Wards 2, 3 & 5.	929	439
Wards 4 – 8	900	519
Poynette, vil.		
Wards 1 – 4	847	448
Randolph	101	318
Randolph, vil.		
Ward 3	106	146
Rio, vil.		
Wards 1 & 2	359	175
Scott.	155	213
Springvale		
Wards 1 & 2	149	143
West Point		
Wards 1 – 3	695	560
Wisconsin Dells, city		
Wards 1 – 3 & 6	679	475
Wyocena		
Wards 1 & 2	531	422
Wyocena, vil.	215	141
TOTAL	17,175	13,026
CRAWFORD COUNTY		
Bell Center, vil.	34	17
Bridgeport.	259	280
Clayton		
Wards 1 – 3	306	163
De Soto, vil.		
Ward 2	34	20
Eastman		
Wards 1 & 2	175	181
Eastman, vil.	85	85
Ferryville, vil.	64	36
Freeman	239	134
Gays Mills, vil.	174	71
Haney	119	58
Lynxville, vil.	37	36
Marietta	144	126
Mount Sterling, vil.	61	30

District	Obama and Biden (Dem.)	Romney and Ryan (Rep.)
Prairie du Chien		
Wards 1 & 2	243	212
Prairie du Chien, city		
Ward 1	264	177
Wards 2 & 7	296	158
Ward 3	207	145
Ward 4	253	122
Ward 5	262	157
Ward 6	258	180
Scott.	159	86
Seneca.	243	182
Soldiers Grove, vil.	162	90
Steuben, vil.	38	17
Utica	223	110
Wauzeka		
Wards 1 & 2	102	101
Wauzeka, vil.	188	93
TOTAL	4,629	3,067
DANE COUNTY		
Albion		
Wards 1 & 2	732	369
Belleville, vil.		
Wards 1 & 2	759	290
Berry		
Wards 1 & 2	448	323
Black Earth	201	134
Black Earth, vil.		
Wards 1 & 2	539	230
Blooming Grove		
Wards 1 – 3	834	290
Blue Mounds	332	252
Blue Mounds, vil.	320	166
Bristol		
Wards 1 – 4	1,229	1,042
Brooklyn, vil.	338	170
Burke		
Wards 1 – 4	1,168	797
Cambridge, vil.		
Wards 2 & 3	505	334
Christiana		
Wards 1 & 2	433	313
Cottage Grove		
Wards 1, 2, 4, 5 & 7	938	615
Wards 3 & 6	531	388
Cottage Grove, vil.		
Wards 1 – 9	2,271	1,334
Cross Plains		
Wards 1 & 2	561	417
Ward 3	0	0
Cross Plains, vil.		
Wards 1 – 4	1,396	785
Dane.	273	268
Dane, vil.	323	222
Deerfield		
Wards 1 & 2	538	383
Deerfield, vil.		
Wards 1 – 3	840	434
De Forest, vil.		
Wards 1 & 3 – 6	1,305	843
Ward 2	277	126
Wards 7 – 10 & 12.	1,197	656
Ward 11	313	169
Ward 13	0	0
Dunkirk		
Wards 1, 3 & 5	523	275
Wards 2, 4 & 6	297	149
Dunn		
Wards 1 – 7	2,122	1,198
Edgerton, city		
Ward 7	33	16
Fitchburg, city		
Wards 1 – 4	2,071	529
Wards 5 – 9	2,871	1,431
Wards 10 – 13	1,759	473
Ward 14	479	216
Wards 15, 18 & 19.	1,481	822
Wards 16 & 17.	820	383
Madison		
Ward 1	323	56
Wards 2 – 9	1,877	244
Madison, city		
Ward 1	899	377
Ward 2	811	211
Ward 3	590	233
Ward 4	386	175
Ward 5	686	268
Ward 6	1,315	340
Ward 7	646	309
Ward 8	1,123	463
Ward 9	1,188	439

VOTE FOR PRESIDENT AND VICE PRESIDENT BY WARD
November 6, 2012 General Election–Continued

District	Obama and Biden (Dem.)	Romney and Ryan (Rep.)	District	Obama and Biden (Dem.)	Romney and Ryan (Rep.)
Ward 10	1,048	409	Ward 100	1,337	424
Ward 11	640	121	Ward 101	417	108
Ward 12	1,412	348	Ward 102	848	284
Ward 13	443	92	Ward 103	419	59
Ward 14	377	87	Ward 104	1,327	415
Ward 15	887	151	Ward 105	1,253	541
Ward 16	1,894	340	Ward 106	937	818
Ward 17	661	134	Ward 107	518	256
Ward 18	707	131	Ward 108	1,350	323
Ward 19	557	83	Ward 109	1,225	478
Ward 20	231	32	Ward 110	714	417
Ward 21	706	176	Ward 111	1,105	827
Ward 22	1,011	317	Ward 112	0	0
Ward 23	477	156	Ward 113	0	0
Ward 24	447	202	Ward 114	0	0
Ward 25	1,534	358	Ward 115	0	0
Ward 26	877	216	Ward 116	0	0
Ward 27	15	1	Ward 117	0	0
Ward 28	1,011	124	**Maple Bluff, vil.**		
Ward 29	2,150	124	Wards 1 & 2	576	448
Ward 30	883	94	**Marshall, vil.**		
Ward 31	937	159	Wards 1 – 5	1,202	638
Ward 32	582	114	**Mazomanie**		
Ward 33	743	108	Wards 1 & 2	432	246
Ward 34	774	127	**Mazomanie, vil.**		
Ward 35	948	146	Wards 1 – 3	679	301
Ward 36	865	275	**McFarland, vil.**		
Ward 37	1,169	225	Wards 1 – 10	3,131	1,717
Ward 38	1,727	707	**Medina**		
Ward 39	1,320	108	Wards 1 & 2	434	345
Ward 40	2,085	101	**Middleton**		
Ward 41	2,182	116	Wards 1 – 8	2,076	1,916
Ward 42	2,324	93	**Middleton, city**		
Ward 43	342	42	Wards 1 – 5, 8 & 9	3,169	1,337
Ward 44	1,527	102	Wards 6 – 7 & 14 – 18	2,701	1,037
Ward 45	2,243	178	Wards 10 – 13	2,300	881
Ward 46	2,000	244	Ward 19	0	0
Ward 47	1,215	491	**Monona, city**		
Ward 48	620	226	Wards 1 – 5	2,136	704
Ward 49	1,415	579	Wards 6 – 10	1,983	582
Ward 50	1,315	466	**Montrose**		
Ward 51	918	214	Wards 1 & 2	470	222
Ward 52	496	101	**Mount Horeb, vil.**		
Ward 53	1,981	403	Wards 1 – 4	1,265	696
Ward 54	369	251	Wards 5 – 8	1,401	717
Ward 55	1,831	786	**Oregon**		
Ward 56	1,211	742	Wards 1 – 4	1,307	813
Ward 57	665	250	**Oregon, vil.**		
Ward 58	713	216	Wards 1, 5, 6 & 11	1,287	582
Ward 59	733	347	Wards 2 – 4 & 12	1,243	604
Ward 60	503	86	Wards 7 – 10	1,218	739
Ward 61	1,677	497	Perry	321	170
Ward 62	719	86	**Pleasant Springs**		
Ward 63	1,467	291	Wards 1 – 4	1,199	896
Ward 64	1,199	161	Primrose	313	136
Ward 65	2,124	281	Rockdale, vil.	86	32
Ward 66	1,819	431	**Roxbury**		
Ward 67	786	113	Wards 1 & 2	605	444
Ward 68	876	93	**Rutland**		
Ward 69	1,513	191	Wards 1 & 2	834	462
Ward 70	961	243	**Shorewood Hills, vil.**		
Ward 71	1,236	244	Wards 1 & 2	1,040	195
Ward 72	571	46	**Springdale**		
Ward 73	645	55	Wards 1 & 2	727	534
Ward 74	466	56	**Springfield**		
Ward 75	1,005	233	Wards 1 – 3	914	765
Ward 76	818	68	**Stoughton, city**		
Ward 77	1,247	435	Wards 1 & 2	1,282	553
Ward 78	1,897	395	Wards 3 & 4	1,257	457
Ward 79	2,099	416	Wards 5 & 6	1,279	488
Ward 80	132	39	Wards 7 & 8	1,141	658
Ward 81	1,254	251	**Sun Prairie**		
Ward 82	1,128	139	Wards 1 – 3	854	541
Ward 83	1,238	241	**Sun Prairie, city**		
Ward 84	1,345	272	Wards 1 – 5	2,685	1,377
Ward 85	1,322	270	Wards 6 – 9	2,650	1,504
Ward 86	1,543	302	Wards 10 – 14	2,582	1,151
Ward 87	1,466	567	Wards 15 – 19	2,226	1,792
Ward 88	1,341	549	Vermont	386	188
Ward 89	1,422	454	**Verona**		
Ward 90	567	155	Ward 1	235	204
Ward 91	1,083	331	Wards 2 – 4	540	325
Ward 92	1,043	217	**Verona, city**		
Ward 93	264	33	Wards 1 & 5	706	468
Ward 94	635	171	Wards 2 – 4	1,394	774
Ward 95	1,339	355	Wards 6 – 9	2,178	1,248
Ward 96	1,027	394	**Vienna**		
Ward 97	1,422	559	Wards 1 & 2	460	442
Ward 98	1,660	692			
Ward 99	631	197			

VOTE FOR PRESIDENT AND VICE PRESIDENT BY WARD
November 6, 2012 General Election–Continued

District	Obama and Biden (Dem.)	Romney and Ryan (Rep.)	District	Obama and Biden (Dem.)	Romney and Ryan (Rep.)
Waunakee, vil.			Ward 2	98	292
Wards 1 – 5	2,120	1,531	Theresa, vil.		
Wards 6 – 11	1,939	1,671	Wards 1 – 3	253	454
Westport			Trenton		
Wards 1 – 5	1,566	1,221	Wards 1 & 2	275	469
Windsor			Watertown, city		
Wards 1 & 2	249	174	Wards 1 & 2	543	825
Wards 3 – 5	664	615	Wards 3 & 4	548	825
Wards 6 – 10	1,340	796	Wards 5 & 6	497	823
York	230	178	Ward 7	154	218
TOTAL	216,071	83,644	Waupun, city		
DODGE COUNTY			Wards 1 – 3 & 8	617	611
Ashippun			Wards 4 – 7	474	635
Wards 1 – 4	412	1,147	Westford		
Beaver Dam			Wards 1 & 2	343	399
Wards 1 – 4 & 7 – 11	623	608	Ward 3	2	10
Wards 5 & 6	450	458	Ward 4	0	0
Beaver Dam, city			Williamstown		
Wards 1, 3 & 5	999	583	Wards 1 – 3	118	342
Wards 2 & 6	675	430	TOTAL	18,762	25,211
Wards 4 & 10	548	320	**DOOR COUNTY**		
Wards 7, 12 & 13	928	540	Baileys Harbor		
Wards 8 & 14	577	386	Wards 1 & 2	466	341
Wards 9 & 11	794	655	Brussels		
Brownsville, vil.	104	229	Wards 1 & 2	275	303
Burnett			Clay Banks	124	127
Wards 1 & 2	232	311	Egg Harbor		
Calamus			Wards 1 & 3	348	253
Wards 1 & 2	258	273	Ward 2	161	139
Chester			Egg Harbor, vil.	117	82
Wards 1 & 2	135	244	Ephraim, vil.	131	115
Clyman	128	304	Forestville		
Clyman, vil.	101	94	Wards 1 & 2	315	258
Columbus, city			Forestville, vil.	139	107
Ward 9	0	0	Gardner		
Elba	308	298	Wards 1 & 2	359	357
Emmet			Gibraltar		
Wards 1 & 2	237	559	Wards 1 & 2	423	360
Fox Lake			Jacksonport		
Wards 1 – 4	271	423	Wards 1 & 2	257	266
Fox Lake, city			Liberty Grove		
Wards 1 – 3	393	326	Wards 1 – 3	807	616
Hartford, city			Nasewaupee		
Wards 18 – 19	0	0	Wards 1 – 3	574	649
Herman			Sevastopol		
Wards 1 & 2	129	593	Wards 1 – 5	888	960
Horicon, city			Sister Bay, vil.	344	286
Wards 1 – 6	907	932	Sturgeon Bay		
Hubbard			Wards 1 & 2	266	248
Wards 1 – 4	381	667	Sturgeon Bay, city		
Wards 5 & 6	0	0	Wards 1 – 6 & 22 – 24, 25 & 26	1,320	880
Hustisford			Wards 7 – 10, 18 – 21, 25 & 26	749	578
Wards 1 & 2	238	601	Wards 11 – 17 & 28	775	554
Hustisford, vil.			Union	251	326
Wards 1 & 2	241	356	Washington	268	316
Iron Ridge, vil.	197	309	TOTAL	9,357	8,121
Juneau, city			**DOUGLAS COUNTY**		
Wards 1 – 3	505	513	Amnicon		
Kekoskee, vil.	42	58	Wards 1 & 2	403	239
Lebanon			Bennett	177	167
Wards 1 & 2	306	670	Brule		
Leroy			Wards 1 & 2	265	136
Wards 1 & 2	158	382	Cloverland	65	65
Lomira			Dairyland	53	57
Wards 1 & 2	166	480	Gordon	238	205
Ward 3	1	2	Hawthorne		
Lomira, vil.			Wards 1 & 2	319	256
Wards 1 – 3	428	789	Highland	101	88
Lowell			Lake Nebagamon, vil.		
Wards 1 & 2	115	171	Wards 1 & 2	376	360
Wards 3 & 4	135	190	Lakeside	223	158
Lowell, vil.	77	93	Maple	284	112
Mayville, city			Oakland		
Wards 1 – 7	1,087	1,469	Wards 1 & 2	437	216
Neosho, vil.	89	237	Oliver, vil.	185	58
Oak Grove			Parkland		
Wards 1 & 2	251	328	Wards 1 & 2	483	201
Wards 3 – 6	0	0	Poplar, vil.	168	186
Portland			Solon Springs		
Wards 1 & 2	282	309	Wards 1 – 3	316	253
Randolph, vil.			Solon Springs, vil.	227	126
Wards 1 & 2	273	366	Summit		
Reeseville, vil.	173	146	Wards 1 & 2	425	167
Rubicon			Superior		
Wards 1 – 3	307	1,046	Wards 1 & 2	784	511
Shields	112	218	Superior, vil.	256	132
Theresa					
Wards 1 & 3 – 7	67	195			

VOTE FOR PRESIDENT AND VICE PRESIDENT BY WARD
November 6, 2012 General Election–Continued

District	Obama and Biden (Dem.)	Romney and Ryan (Rep.)	District	Obama and Biden (Dem.)	Romney and Ryan (Rep.)
Superior, city			Ward 20	1,277	757
Wards 1 – 3, 7 & 8	1,841	876	Ward 21	578	369
Wards 4 – 6 & 9 – 12	1,851	786	Ward 22	185	141
Wards 13 – 16 & 20 – 22	1,866	774	Ward 23	793	529
Wards 17 – 19 & 30 – 32	1,411	432	Ward 24	128	55
Wards 23 – 26 & 27 – 29	1,847	915	Ward 25	745	613
Wascott	262	229	Ward 26	297	237
TOTAL	14,863	7,705	Ward 27	85	70
DUNN COUNTY			Ward 28	198	193
Boyceville, vil.	259	214	Ward 29	852	432
Colfax			Ward 30	684	369
Wards 1 – 3	287	311	Ward 31	692	251
Colfax, vil.			Ward 32	642	306
Wards 1 & 2	289	221	Ward 33	198	192
Downing, vil.	55	45	Ward 34	263	135
Dunn			Ward 35	503	447
Wards 1 & 2	404	346	Ward 36	131	131
Eau Galle	178	259	Ward 37	350	275
Elk Mound			Ward 38	323	276
Wards 1 – 3	360	508	Ward 39	496	426
Elk Mound, vil.	201	162	Ward 42	151	161
Grant			Ward 43	187	99
Wards 1 & 2	109	128	Ward 44	29	41
Hay River			Ward 45	212	178
Wards 1 & 2	138	132	Ward 46	624	288
Knapp, vil.	86	147	Ward 47	162	157
Lucas	191	201	Ward 48	241	155
Menomonie			Ward 49	180	209
Wards 1 – 3	927	813	Ward 50	2	0
Menomonie, city			Ward 51	0	1
Wards 1 & 2	932	617	Ward 52	0	1
Wards 3 & 4	786	531	Ward 53	0	0
Wards 5 & 7	667	446	Ward 54	0	0
Ward 6	379	255	Ward 55	3	0
Wards 8 & 9	785	453	Fairchild.	65	78
Wards 10 & 11	862	651	Fairchild, vil.	129	83
New Haven	141	185	Fall Creek, vil.		
Otter Creek	135	124	Wards 1 & 2	389	343
Peru	64	61	Lincoln		
Red Cedar			Wards 1 & 2	275	321
Wards 1 – 3	538	660	Ludington	275	295
Ridgeland, vil.	61	40	Otter Creek	105	141
Rock Creek	256	256	Pleasant Valley		
Sand Creek	136	154	Wards 1 – 4	897	1,192
Sheridan.	117	123	Seymour		
Sherman.	201	291	Wards 1 – 6	958	921
Spring Brook			Union		
Wards 1 & 2	381	475	Wards 1 – 4	731	705
Stanton	171	229	Washington		
Tainter			Wards 1 – 13	2,054	2,236
Wards 1 – 3	716	677	Wilson.	84	105
Tiffany			TOTAL	30,666	23,256
Wards 1 & 2	135	190	FLORENCE COUNTY		
Weston			Aurora		
Wards 1 & 2	144	158	Wards 1 – 3	197	340
Wheeler, vil.	81	51	Commonwealth		
Wilson.	144	110	Wards 1 – 3	87	130
TOTAL	11,316	10,224	Fence	47	76
EAU CLAIRE COUNTY			Fern	38	75
Altoona, city			Florence		
Wards 1 – 11	1,977	1,555	Wards 1 – 7	438	747
Augusta, city			Homestead	88	130
Wards 1 – 5	331	294	Long Lake.	38	66
Bridge Creek			Tipler	20	81
Wards 1 & 2	276	306	TOTAL	953	1,645
Brunswick			FOND DU LAC COUNTY		
Wards 1 & 2	507	520	Alto		
Clear Creek			Wards 1 & 2	150	465
Wards 1 & 2	210	210	Ashford		
Drammen	226	210	Wards 1 – 3	288	733
Eau Claire, city			Auburn		
Ward 1	381	141	Wards 1 – 3	352	1,057
Ward 2	499	175	Brandon, vil.	172	272
Ward 3	1,292	467	Byron		
Ward 4	320	202	Wards 1 & 2	300	696
Ward 5	654	319	Calumet		
Ward 6	664	329	Ward 1	196	315
Ward 7	492	304	Ward 2	114	234
Ward 8	469	348	Campbellsport, vil.		
Ward 9	272	139	Wards 1 – 4	371	622
Ward 10	634	471	Eden		
Ward 11	545	450	Wards 1 & 2	173	467
Ward 12	1,026	653	Eden, vil.	176	238
Ward 13	249	144	Eldorado		
Ward 14	687	457	Wards 1 – 3	277	550
Ward 15	651	497	Empire		
Ward 17	693	683	Wards 1 – 4	621	1,212
Ward 18	209	276	Fairwater, vil.	70	115
Ward 19	229	192			

VOTE FOR PRESIDENT AND VICE PRESIDENT BY WARD
November 6, 2012 General Election–Continued

District	Obama and Biden (Dem.)	Romney and Ryan (Rep.)
Fond du Lac		
Wards 1 – 8	756	1,194
Ward 1A	0	0
Fond du Lac, city		
Ward 1	418	359
Ward 2	452	272
Ward 3	572	527
Ward 4	450	328
Ward 5	575	512
Ward 6	471	458
Ward 7	393	336
Ward 8	562	433
Ward 9	432	258
Ward 10	475	501
Ward 11	310	242
Ward 12	475	475
Ward 13	368	263
Ward 14	477	570
Ward 15	220	388
Ward 16	334	391
Ward 17	88	80
Ward 18	23	43
Ward 19	505	376
Ward 20	0	0
Ward 21	518	487
Ward 22	492	588
Ward 23	495	643
Ward 24	506	584
Ward 25	476	849
Ward 26	0	2
Ward 27	0	0
Forest		
Wards 1 & 2	165	474
Friendship		
Wards 1 – 3	612	801
Kewaskum, vil.		
Ward 6	0	0
Lamartine		
Wards 1 & 2	341	688
Marshfield		
Wards 1 & 2	201	456
Metomen		
Wards 1 & 2	140	258
Mount Calvary, vil.	105	188
North Fond du Lac, vil.		
Wards 1 – 7	1,273	1,095
Oakfield		
Wards 1 & 2	127	247
Oakfield, vil.		
Wards 1 & 2	242	356
Osceola		
Wards 1 & 2	296	840
Ripon		
Wards 1 & 2	309	479
Ripon, city		
Wards 1 – 3	469	495
Wards 4 – 6	509	443
Wards 7 & 8	447	382
Wards 9 – 11	507	462
Rosendale	139	276
Rosendale, vil.	216	371
Springvale	138	247
St. Cloud, vil.	96	200
Taycheedah		
Wards 1 – 5	919	1,872
Waupun		
Wards 1 & 2	280	540
Waupun, city		
Ward 9B	0	0
Wards 9, 9A & 10 – 12	745	1,050
TOTAL	22,379	30,355
FOREST COUNTY		
Alvin		
Wards 1 & 2	49	56
Argonne		
Wards 1 – 3	141	103
Armstrong Creek	111	112
Blackwell	58	39
Caswell	21	31
Crandon		
Wards 1 – 3	187	126
Crandon, city		
Wards 1 – 4	422	379
Freedom	87	135
Hiles	115	122
Laona		
Wards 1 – 3	320	300
Lincoln		
Wards 1 – 3	282	226

District	Obama and Biden (Dem.)	Romney and Ryan (Rep.)
Nashville		
Ward 1	78	120
Ward 2	151	11
Ward 3	98	138
Popple River	13	10
Ross	32	44
Wabeno		
Wards 1 – 5	260	220
TOTAL	2,425	2,172
GRANT COUNTY		
Bagley, vil.	123	47
Beetown	128	168
Bloomington	74	95
Bloomington, vil	177	160
Blue River, vil.	118	80
Boscobel		
Wards 1 & 2	110	83
Boscobel, city		
Wards 1 – 4	803	402
Cassville	101	93
Cassville, vil.		
Wards 1 & 2	226	158
Castle Rock	77	57
Clifton		
Wards 1 & 2	81	68
Cuba City, city		
Wards 1 – 4	573	338
Dickeyville, vil.		
Wards 1 & 2	291	261
Ellenboro	135	151
Fennimore		
Wards 1 & 2	126	118
Fennimore, city		
Wards 1 – 4	652	478
Glen Haven	81	98
Harrison	124	148
Hazel Green		
Wards 1 & 2	375	259
Hazel Green, vil.		
Wards 1 & 2	376	205
Hickory Grove	77	90
Jamestown		
Wards 1 – 3	501	552
Lancaster, city		
Wards 1 – 6	981	816
Liberty	119	137
Lima	198	170
Little Grant	45	65
Livingston, vil.	210	108
Marion	138	93
Millville	58	32
Montfort, vil.	169	93
Mount Hope	51	50
Mount Hope, vil.	43	23
Mount Ida	111	133
Muscoda	165	134
Muscoda, vil.		
Wards 1 & 2	372	180
North Lancaster		
Wards 1 & 2	122	141
Paris		
Wards 1 & 2	176	204
Patch Grove	82	67
Patch Grove, vil.	43	27
Platteville		
Wards 1 – 3	416	398
Platteville, city		
Wards 1 & 2	851	495
Wards 3 & 4	803	473
Wards 5 & 6	624	497
Wards 7 & 8	1,087	622
Potosi	229	181
Potosi, vil.	213	154
Smelser		
Wards 1 & 2	230	221
South Lancaster		
Wards 1 – 3	157	171
Tennyson, vil.	100	81
Waterloo	124	110
Watterstown		
Wards 1 & 2	84	67
Wingville	94	71
Woodman	36	37
Woodman, vil.	29	15
Wyalusing	105	80
TOTAL	13,594	10,255
GREEN COUNTY		
Adams	167	127

VOTE FOR PRESIDENT AND VICE PRESIDENT BY WARD
November 6, 2012 General Election–Continued

District	Obama and Biden (Dem.)	Romney and Ryan (Rep.)
Albany		
Wards 1 & 2	350	258
Albany, vil.		
Wards 1 & 2	363	139
Belleville, vil.		
Ward 3	204	88
Brodhead, city		
Wards 1 – 6	821	525
Brooklyn		
Wards 1 – 3	399	283
Brooklyn, vil.		
Ward 2	164	75
Browntown, vil..	76	62
Cadiz	214	205
Clarno		
Wards 1 & 2	301	316
Decatur		
Wards 1 – 3	524	458
Exeter		
Wards 1 – 4	740	411
Jefferson		
Wards 1 & 2	266	351
Jordan	180	168
Monroe		
Wards 1 & 2	321	347
Monroe, city		
Wards 1 – 9	3,035	2,008
Monticello, vil.		
Wards 1 & 2	438	225
Mount Pleasant		
Ward 1	82	52
Wards 2 & 3	123	86
New Glarus		
Wards 1 & 2	432	369
New Glarus, vil.		
Wards 1 – 4	888	351
Spring Grove	225	256
Sylvester		
Wards 1 & 2	266	323
Washington	282	172
York	345	202
TOTAL	11,206	7,857
GREEN LAKE COUNTY		
Berlin		
Wards 1 – 3	203	477
Berlin, city		
Wards 1 – 6	1,088	1,208
Brooklyn		
Wards 1 – 3	422	750
Green Lake		
Wards 1 & 2	198	542
Green Lake, city		
Wards 1 – 3	243	335
Kingston		
Wards 1 & 2	109	183
Kingston, vil.	77	103
Mackford	82	222
Manchester	128	270
Markesan, city		
Wards 1 – 3	270	436
Marquette	114	170
Marquette, vil.	25	44
Princeton		
Wards 1 – 4	345	500
Princeton,city		
Wards 1 – 4	328	275
St. Marie		
Wards 1 & 2	79	137
Seneca	82	130
TOTAL	3,793	5,782
IOWA COUNTY		
Arena		
Wards 1 & 2	582	288
Arena, vil..	313	120
Avoca, vil..	187	65
Barneveld, vil.		
Wards 1 & 2	426	181
Blanchardville, vil.		
Ward 2	63	31
Brigham		
Wards 1 & 2	386	228
Clyde	114	70
Cobb, vil.	165	82
Dodgeville		
Wards 1 – 4	614	397
Dodgeville, city		
Wards 1, 2 & 10	361	225
Wards 3 & 4	371	203

District	Obama and Biden (Dem.)	Romney and Ryan (Rep.)
Wards 5 & 6	373	148
Wards 7 – 9	382	213
Eden.	121	90
Highland		
Wards 1 & 2	242	149
Highland, vil.	273	138
Hollandale, vil.	107	36
Linden		
Wards 1 – 3	208	171
Linden, vil.	185	55
Livingston, vil.		
Ward 2	4	0
Mifflin		
Wards 1 & 2	161	127
Mineral Point		
Wards 1 & 2	274	241
Mineral Point, city		
Wards 1 – 6	957	393
Montfort, vil.		
Ward 2	33	21
Moscow		
Wards 1 & 2	239	129
Muscoda, vil.		
Ward 3	15	9
Pulaski	84	89
Rewey, vil.	77	26
Ridgeway		
Wards 1 & 2	254	110
Ridgeway, vil..	224	91
Waldwick		
Wards 1 & 2	166	100
Wyoming		
Wards 1 & 2	144	61
TOTAL	8,105	4,287
IRON COUNTY		
Anderson	26	20
Carey	42	58
Gurney	55	34
Hurley, city		
Ward 1	108	69
Ward 2	114	96
Ward 3	80	63
Ward 4	129	58
Kimball	156	155
Knight.	62	65
Mercer		
Wards 1 – 4	415	561
Montreal, city		
Wards 1 & 2	248	195
Oma.	92	130
Pence	58	59
Saxon	108	96
Sherman.	91	131
TOTAL	1,784	1,790
JACKSON COUNTY		
Adams		
Wards 1 – 3	417	383
Albion		
Wards 1 – 4	337	255
Alma		
Wards 1 & 4	79	83
Wards 2, 3 & 5	145	186
Alma Center, vil.	138	94
Bear Bluff	14	67
Black River Falls, city		
Wards 1 – 4	956	621
Brockway		
Wards 1 – 6	563	226
City Point	63	47
Cleveland	104	125
Curran.	94	50
Franklin	143	50
Garden Valley	103	136
Garfield	154	156
Hixton		
Wards 1 & 2	168	156
Hixton, vil.	137	88
Irving		
Wards 1 – 3	220	143
Knapp	56	100
Komensky.	122	18
Manchester	183	183
Melrose	103	116
Melrose, vil..	165	94
Merrillan, vil.	171	71
Millston	49	51
North Bend	169	90
Northfield	170	160
Springfield	134	101

VOTE FOR PRESIDENT AND VICE PRESIDENT BY WARD
November 6, 2012 General Election–Continued

District	Obama and Biden (Dem.)	Romney and Ryan (Rep.)
Taylor, vil..	141	50
TOTAL	5,298	3,900
JEFFERSON COUNTY		
Aztalan		
Wards 1 & 2	409	425
Cambridge, vil.	28	14
Cold Spring	175	286
Concord		
Wards 1 – 3	432	810
Farmington		
Wards 1 & 2	328	533
Fort Atkinson, city		
Wards 1 – 3	1,197	979
Wards 4 – 6	1,037	797
Wards 7 – 9	1,187	886
Hebron		
Wards 1 & 2	253	387
Ixonia		
Wards 1 – 6	741	1,930
Jefferson		
Wards 1 – 3	511	718
Jefferson, city		
Wards 1 – 10	1,946	1,590
Johnson Creek, vil.		
Wards 1 – 3	632	797
Koshkonong		
Wards 1 & 6	127	129
Wards 2 – 5	845	1,042
Lac La Belle, vil.		
Ward 2	0	0
Lake Mills		
Wards 1 – 3	647	633
Lake Mills, city		
Wards 1 – 8	1,841	1,448
Milford		
Wards 1 & 2	273	349
Oakland		
Wards 1 – 4	1,033	863
Palmyra		
Wards 1 & 2	262	502
Palmyra, vil.		
Wards 1 & 2	349	569
Sullivan		
Wards 1 – 3	399	909
Sullivan, vil..	116	227
Sumner	253	269
Waterloo.	228	281
Waterloo, city		
Wards 1 – 5	926	693
Watertown		
Wards 1 & 2	402	751
Watertown, city		
Ward 8	189	175
Wards 9 & 10	426	897
Wards 11 & 12	478	659
Wards 13 & 14	548	689
Wards 15 & 16	606	739
Wards 17 & 18	604	973
Whitewater, city		
Wards 10 & 11	297	228
Ward 12	433	340
TOTAL	20,158	23,517
JUNEAU COUNTY		
Armenia.	171	173
Camp Douglas, vil.	133	120
Clearfield		
Ward 1	148	152
Ward 2	38	36
Cutler	95	91
Elroy, city		
Wards 1 – 7	362	220
Finley	13	36
Fountain		
Wards 1 & 2	148	150
Germantown		
Wards 1 & 3	199	249
Ward 2	180	153
Hustler, vil.	58	32
Kildare	177	145
Kingston	5	16
Lemonweir		
Wards 1 – 4	448	335
Lindina	222	187
Lisbon		
Wards 1 & 2	235	207
Ward 3	1	0
Lyndon		
Wards 1 – 3	380	246

District	Obama and Biden (Dem.)	Romney and Ryan (Rep.)
Lyndon Station, vil..	146	61
Marion	114	135
Mauston, city		
Wards 1 – 7	978	660
Necedah		
Wards 1 – 4	455	634
Necedah, vil.	226	183
New Lisbon, city		
Wards 1 – 7	311	290
Orange	132	141
Plymouth	167	166
Seven Mile Creek		
Wards 1 & 2	94	75
Summit	157	173
Union Center, vil..	57	42
Wisconsin Dells, city		
Ward 7	0	0
Wonewoc		
Wards 1 & 2	157	171
Wonewoc, vil..	235	132
TOTAL	6,242	5,411
KENOSHA COUNTY		
Brighton		
Wards 1 – 4	313	575
Bristol, vil.		
Wards 1 – 3 & 8	581	978
Wards 4 – 7	493	776
Genoa City, vil.		
Ward 5	0	2
Kenosha, city		
Ward 1	478	161
Ward 2	329	203
Ward 3	351	197
Ward 4	552	237
Ward 5	355	131
Ward 6	294	150
Ward 7	435	66
Ward 8	627	282
Ward 9	399	169
Ward 10	407	77
Ward 11	331	100
Ward 12	392	190
Ward 13	397	349
Ward 14	392	239
Ward 15	576	286
Ward 16	297	127
Ward 17	119	59
Ward 18	481	227
Ward 19	219	70
Ward 20	357	242
Ward 21	99	87
Ward 22	748	611
Ward 23	236	136
Ward 24	457	219
Ward 25	530	255
Ward 26	273	96
Ward 27	415	130
Ward 28	325	93
Ward 29	440	96
Ward 30	395	63
Ward 31	560	224
Ward 32	257	53
Ward 33	22	6
Ward 34	304	155
Ward 35	633	280
Ward 36	257	33
Ward 37	557	238
Ward 38	630	428
Ward 39	407	262
Ward 40	215	70
Ward 41	365	169
Ward 42	312	113
Ward 43	521	292
Ward 44	282	244
Ward 45	235	135
Ward 46	359	84
Ward 47	165	73
Ward 48	279	70
Ward 49	351	86
Ward 50	414	145
Ward 51	226	106
Ward 52	497	194
Ward 53	155	114
Ward 54	508	335
Ward 55	247	158
Ward 56	316	198
Ward 57	464	366
Ward 58	26	23

VOTE FOR PRESIDENT AND VICE PRESIDENT BY WARD
November 6, 2012 General Election–Continued

District	Obama and Biden (Dem.)	Romney and Ryan (Rep.)
Ward 59	593	424
Ward 60	487	320
Ward 61	247	166
Ward 62	493	345
Ward 63	349	200
Ward 64	401	333
Ward 65	19	12
Ward 66	708	515
Ward 67	428	349
Ward 68	206	173
Ward 69	33	38
Ward 70	16	6
Ward 71	209	108
Ward 72	392	310
Ward 73	327	269
Ward 74	2	0
Ward 75	129	204
Ward 76	168	247
Ward 77	395	365
Ward 78	437	332
Ward 79	379	375
Ward 80	159	60
Ward 81	209	104
Ward 82	148	62
Ward 83	0	0
Ward 84	237	102
Ward 85	26	14
Ward 86	134	77
Ward 87	215	210
Ward 88	1	0
Paddock Lake, vil.		
Wards 1 – 6	684	811
Paris		
Wards 1 & 2	369	572
Pleasant Prairie, vil.		
Wards 1 – 3	1,306	1,399
Wards 4 & 5	684	734
Wards 6 & 7	950	832
Wards 8 – 11	1,084	1,451
Wards 12 – 14	1,217	1,203
Randall		
Wards 1 – 7	708	1,005
Salem		
Wards 1 – 5 & 10	1,341	1,896
Wards 6 – 9	1,144	1,440
Silver Lake, vil.		
Wards 1 – 3	546	643
Somers		
Wards 1 – 4	796	793
Wards 5, 6, 9 & 12	863	670
Wards 7 & 8	419	254
Wards 10 – 13	450	524
Ward 11	161	186
Twin Lakes, vil.		
Wards 1 – 8	1,233	1,433
Wheatland		
Wards 1 – 6	708	1,078
TOTAL	44,867	34,977
KEWAUNEE COUNTY		
Ahnapee	270	246
Algoma, city		
Wards 1 – 6	889	631
Carlton		
Wards 1 & 2	275	318
Casco		
Wards 1 – 3	267	377
Casco, vil.	121	159
Franklin	260	284
Kewaunee, city		
Wards 1 – 5	796	669
Lincoln	240	247
Luxemburg		
Wards 1 – 3	286	556
Luxemburg, vil.		
Wards 1 – 5	581	709
Montpelier		
Wards 1 – 3	309	471
Pierce		
Wards 1 & 2	250	219
Red River		
Wards 1 – 3	341	462
West Kewaunee		
Wards 1 & 2	268	399
TOTAL	5,153	5,747
LA CROSSE COUNTY		
Bangor	137	170
Bangor, vil.		
Wards 1 & 2	416	317

District	Obama and Biden (Dem.)	Romney and Ryan (Rep.)
Barre		
Wards 1 & 2	313	386
Burns	290	266
Campbell		
Wards 1 – 6	1,525	985
Farmington		
Wards 1 & 2	604	441
Greenfield		
Wards 1 & 2	590	579
Hamilton		
Wards 1 – 5	654	785
Holland		
Wards 1 – 6	1,069	1,138
Holmen, vil.		
Wards 1 – 11	2,596	1,934
La Crosse, city		
Ward 1	1,004	647
Ward 2	310	132
Ward 3	670	346
Ward 4	345	119
Ward 5	533	174
Ward 6	859	388
Ward 7	1,120	483
Ward 8	1,227	766
Ward 9	1,401	665
Ward 10	298	162
Ward 11	255	167
Ward 12	300	204
Ward 13	268	139
Ward 14	574	210
Ward 15	394	171
Ward 16	658	216
Ward 17	270	80
Ward 18	340	133
Ward 19	315	134
Ward 20	534	244
Ward 21	1,261	688
Ward 22	851	342
Ward 23	320	137
Ward 24	716	388
Ward 25	434	305
Ward 26	960	586
Ward 27	513	242
Ward 28	402	212
Ward 29	961	629
Medary		
Wards 1 & 2	486	480
Onalaska		
Wards 1 – 8	1,604	1,651
Onalaska, city		
Wards 1 – 4	1,613	1,597
Wards 5 – 8	1,781	1,307
Wards 9 – 12	1,648	1,794
Rockland, vil.	144	143
Shelby		
Wards 1 – 4	996	846
Wards 5 & 6	645	571
Washington	178	135
West Salem, vil.		
Wards 1 – 6	1,311	1,117
TOTAL	36,693	25,751
LAFAYETTE COUNTY		
Argyle		
Wards 1 – 3	142	102
Argyle, vil.	274	128
Belmont		
Wards 1 & 2	165	149
Belmont, vil.	249	202
Benton		
Wards 1 & 2	124	126
Benton, vil.	317	143
Blanchard	102	65
Blanchardville, vil.	230	105
Cuba City, city		
Ward 5	78	41
Darlington		
Wards 1 – 3	242	244
Darlington, city		
Wards 1 – 6	647	381
Elk Grove		
Wards 1 & 2	101	102
Fayette		
Wards 1 & 2	95	74
Gratiot	127	156
Gratiot, vil.	73	40
Hazel Green, vil.		
Ward 3	4	3
Kendall	93	86
Lamont		
Wards 1 & 2	89	68

VOTE FOR PRESIDENT AND VICE PRESIDENT BY WARD
November 6, 2012 General Election–Continued

District	Obama and Biden (Dem.)	Romney and Ryan (Rep.)	District	Obama and Biden (Dem.)	Romney and Ryan (Rep.)
Monticello.	21	37	Wilson.	108	92
New Diggings.	141	107	TOTAL	7,563	7,455
Seymour			**MANITOWOC COUNTY**		
Wards 1 & 2	77	77	Cato		
Shullsburg.	106	71	Wards 1 & 2	377	557
Shullsburg, city			Centerville	143	217
Wards 1 – 3	400	159	Cleveland, vil.		
South Wayne, vil.	103	83	Wards 1 & 2	368	394
Wayne.	88	136	Cooperstown		
White Oak Springs	28	31	Wards 1 & 2	323	435
Willow Springs	169	198	Eaton.	189	291
Wiota	251	200	Francis Creek, vil..	203	187
TOTAL	4,536	3,314	Franklin		
LANGLADE COUNTY			Wards 1 – 3	249	451
Ackley.	119	162	Gibson		
Ainsworth.	141	144	Wards 1 & 2	329	406
Antigo			Kellnersville, vil.	85	84
Wards 1 & 2	313	507	Kiel, city		
Antigo, city			Wards 1 – 6 & 8	829	1,041
Ward 1	158	194	Kossuth		
Ward 2	201	183	Wards 1 – 3	537	650
Ward 3	161	197	Liberty		
Ward 4	200	161	Wards 1 & 2	265	479
Ward 5	183	154	Manitowoc		
Ward 6	164	216	Wards 1 & 2	271	321
Ward 7	236	276	Manitowoc, city		
Ward 8	184	182	Wards 1 & 2	884	623
Ward 9	227	224	Wards 3, 4 & 22	863	730
Elcho			Wards 5 & 6	891	616
Wards 1 & 2	370	421	Wards 7 & 8	647	339
Evergreen	122	157	Wards 9 & 10	915	680
Langlade			Wards 11 & 12	952	909
Wards 1 & 2	127	151	Wards 13 & 14	824	614
Neva.	220	310	Wards 15 & 16	956	1,090
Norwood	190	331	Wards 17, 18 & 21	800	675
Parrish.	32	27	Wards 19 & 20	889	1,162
Peck	68	115	Manitowoc Rapids		
Polar			Wards 1 – 5	531	982
Wards 1 & 2	231	373	Maple Grove	130	311
Price			Maribel, vil.	84	96
Wards 1 & 2	54	68	Meeme		
Rolling			Wards 1 & 4	222	271
Wards 1 & 2	319	476	Wards 2 & 3	127	228
Summit	35	55	Mishicot		
Upham	182	308	Wards 1 & 2	290	393
Vilas.	47	85	Mishicot, vil.		
White Lake, vil..	95	77	Wards 1 – 3	381	392
Wolf River			Newton		
Wards 1 & 2	194	262	Wards 1 – 3	484	843
TOTAL	4,573	5,816	Reedsville, vil.		
LINCOLN COUNTY			Wards 1 & 2	272	306
Birch	116	126	Rockland		
Bradley			Wards 1 & 2	183	338
Wards 1 – 5	783	745	St. Nazianz, vil.	162	188
Corning			Schleswig		
Wards 1 & 2	205	237	Wards 1 & 2	495	703
Harding	110	126	Two Creeks	91	147
Harrison			Two Rivers		
Wards 1 – 3	248	291	Wards 1 & 2	500	527
King			Two Rivers, city		
Wards 1 & 2	290	300	Wards 1 & 2	703	525
Merrill			Wards 3 & 4	1,000	869
Wards 1 – 7	746	876	Wards 5 & 6	763	554
Merrill, city			Wards 7 & 8	789	470
Wards 1 & 2	305	254	Valders, vil.	219	281
Wards 3 & 4	313	266	Whitelaw, vil.	188	229
Wards 5 – 7	282	194	TOTAL	20,403	21,604
Wards 8 & 9	280	238	**MARATHON COUNTY**		
Wards 10 – 12	309	228	Abbotsford, city		
Wards 13 & 14	315	264	Ward 1	61	77
Wards 15 – 17	322	257	Ward 6	0	0
Wards 18 & 19	280	199	Athens, vil.		
Pine River			Wards 1 & 2	222	299
Wards 1 – 3	479	620	Bergen.	204	207
Rock Falls			Berlin		
Wards 1 & 2	160	214	Wards 1 & 2	164	392
Russell	167	171	Bern.	99	118
Schley			Bevent		
Wards 1 & 2	211	260	Wards 1 & 2	357	266
Scott			Birnamwood, vil.		
Wards 1 & 2	339	457	Ward 2	10	3
Skanawan	135	136	Brighton.	76	165
Somo	41	35	Brokaw, vil.	79	62
Tomahawk	129	125	Cassel	234	290
Tomahawk, city			Cleveland		
Wards 1 & 2	293	192	Wards 1 & 2	281	443
Wards 3 & 4	323	278	Colby, city.	110	109
Wards 5 & 6	274	274	Day		
			Wards 1 & 2	227	354

VOTE FOR PRESIDENT AND VICE PRESIDENT BY WARD
November 6, 2012 General Election–Continued

District	Obama and Biden (Dem.)	Romney and Ryan (Rep.)
Dorchester, vil.		
Ward 2	0	0
Ward 3	2	1
Easton		
Wards 1 & 2	238	431
Eau Pleine.	129	262
Edgar, vil.		
Wards 1 & 2	342	432
Elderon	136	197
Elderon, vil..	33	45
Emmet		
Wards 1 & 2	242	256
Fenwood, vil.	28	55
Frankfort	120	195
Franzen	108	171
Green Valley	122	199
Guenther	88	113
Halsey.	114	174
Hamburg	171	262
Harrison.	67	118
Hatley, vil.	105	168
Hewitt.	140	202
Holton.	131	245
Hull	85	214
Johnson	158	223
Knowlton		
Wards 1 – 3	462	649
Kronenwetter, vil.		
Wards 1 – 5	931	1,060
Wards 6 – 10	870	1,030
Maine		
Wards 1 – 4	553	869
Marathon		
Wards 1 & 2	212	426
Marathon City, vil.		
Wards 1 – 3	346	496
Marshfield, city		
Wards 12, 20, 21 & 24	170	188
McMillan		
Wards 1 – 3	472	691
Mosinee		
Wards 1 – 3	519	692
Mosinee, city		
Wards 1, 2, 6 & 7	507	568
Wards 3 – 5	529	579
Norrie	243	273
Plover.	150	181
Reid		
Wards 1 & 2	322	338
Rib Falls.	193	372
Rib Mountain		
Wards 1 – 10	1,845	2,557
Rietbrock	191	282
Ringle		
Wards 1 & 2	442	586
Rothschild, vil.		
Wards 1 & 2	534	390
Wards 3 & 4	560	538
Wards 5 & 6	461	533
Schofield, city		
Wards 1 – 4	604	519
Spencer		
Wards 1 & 2	329	411
Spencer, vil.		
Wards 1 – 3	382	501
Stettin		
Wards 1 & 2	430	744
Wards 3 & 4	131	198
Stratford, vil.		
Wards 1 & 2	274	484
Texas		
Wards 1 & 2	436	550
Unity, vil.	39	66
Wausau		
Wards 1 – 3	538	776
Wausau, city		
Ward 1	564	398
Ward 2	539	416
Ward 3	319	202
Ward 4	84	127
Ward 5	401	273
Ward 6	320	159
Ward 7	399	264
Ward 8	340	174
Ward 9	106	120
Ward 10	41	123
Ward 11	0	0
Ward 12	554	322
Ward 13	468	250
Ward 14	470	324
Ward 15	552	644
Ward 16	388	544
Ward 17	441	393
Ward 18	527	357
Ward 19	428	335
Ward 20	502	286
Ward 21	454	273
Ward 22	466	303
Ward 23	555	342
Ward 24	464	478
Ward 25	461	534
Ward 26	384	430
Ward 27	1	1
Ward 28	2	0
Ward 29	0	0
Ward 30	0	0
Ward 31	0	0
Ward 32	0	0
Weston	124	211
Weston, vil.		
Wards 1, 2, 4 & 5	885	1,008
Wards 3 & 8	744	676
Wards 6 & 7	533	785
Wards 9 – 13	1,340	1,325
Wien.	149	245
TOTAL	32,363	36,617
MARINETTE COUNTY		
Amberg	177	247
Athelstane		
Wards 1 & 2	158	173
Beaver		
Wards 1 & 2	217	385
Beecher	166	220
Coleman, vil.	152	192
Crivitz, vil.	237	242
Dunbar		
Wards 1 & 2	100	451
Goodman	167	152
Grover		
Wards 1 – 3	352	491
Lake		
Wards 1 & 2	269	314
Marinette, city		
Wards 1, 3 & 5	964	708
Wards 2, 4 & 6	1,048	657
Wards 7 & 8	762	559
Middle Inlet		
Wards 1 & 2	224	225
Niagara	192	309
Niagara, city		
Wards 1 – 3	368	369
Pembine		
Wards 1 & 2	210	258
Peshtigo		
Wards 1 – 6	1,055	1,154
Peshtigo, city		
Wards 1 – 7	753	718
Porterfield		
Wards 1 – 3	485	510
Pound		
Wards 1 – 3	257	430
Pound, vil..	51	107
Silver Cliff		
Wards 1 & 2	130	196
Stephenson		
Wards 1 – 3	541	537
Wards 4 & 5	317	384
Wagner	155	204
Wausaukee		
Wards 1 & 2	266	339
Wausaukee, vil..	109	88
TOTAL	9,882	10,619
MARQUETTE COUNTY		
Buffalo		
Wards 1 & 2	321	260
Crystal Lake.	157	144
Douglas	270	238
Endeavor, vil.	119	95
Harris	239	239
Mecan.	176	199
Montello		
Wards 1 – 4	285	341
Montello, city		
Wards 1 – 4	378	304
Moundville		
Wards 1 & 2	130	129
Neshkoro		
Wards 1 & 2	145	197
Neshkoro, vil.	114	100

VOTE FOR PRESIDENT AND VICE PRESIDENT BY WARD
November 6, 2012 General Election–Continued

District	Obama and Biden (Dem.)	Romney and Ryan (Rep.)
Newton		
Wards 1 & 2	118	128
Oxford		
Wards 1 & 2	221	273
Oxford, vil.	139	112
Packwaukee		
Wards 1 – 3	377	321
Shields	133	196
Springfield	197	232
Westfield		
Wards 1 & 2	195	250
Westfield, vil.		
Wards 1 & 2	300	234
TOTAL	4,014	3,992
MENOMINEE COUNTY		
Menominee		
Wards 1, 3 – 5	893	176
Ward 2	298	3
TOTAL	1,191	179
MILWAUKEE COUNTY		
Bayside, vil.		
Wards 1 & 3	602	447
Wards 2 & 4	627	497
Ward 5	333	314
Brown Deer, vil.		
Wards 1 & 2	1,723	750
Wards 3 & 4	1,436	989
Wards 5 & 6	1,496	882
Cudahy, city		
Wards 1 – 3	1,224	865
Wards 4 – 6	1,073	709
Wards 7 – 9	980	647
Ward 10	429	376
Wards 11 & 12	679	511
Wards 13 & 14	793	590
Ward 15	443	487
Fox Point, vil.		
Wards 1 – 4	998	1,084
Wards 5 – 9	1,428	1,064
Franklin, city		
Ward 1	2	1
Ward 2	465	834
Ward 3	623	818
Ward 4	301	463
Ward 5	254	410
Ward 6	278	558
Ward 7	537	829
Ward 8	510	352
Ward 9	442	474
Ward 10	177	228
Ward 11	468	600
Ward 12	288	458
Ward 13	364	656
Ward 14	351	562
Ward 15A	202	284
Ward 15B	156	218
Ward 16	429	693
Ward 17	306	381
Ward 18	146	287
Ward 19	457	776
Ward 20	272	340
Ward 21	182	134
Ward 22A	280	384
Ward 22B	259	392
Ward 23	414	717
Glendale, city		
Wards 1 & 7	815	481
Wards 2 & 8E	603	313
Wards 3 & 9	841	642
Wards 4 & 10	968	615
Wards 5 & 11	773	478
Wards 6 & 12	784	402
Ward 8	325	216
Ward 11E	247	71
Greendale, vil.		
Wards 1 & 2	599	1,079
Wards 3 & 4	1,002	1,001
Wards 5 & 6	745	938
Wards 7 & 8	813	941
Wards 9 & 10	837	1,070
Greenfield, city		
Ward 1	554	510
Ward 2	433	481
Ward 3	533	371
Ward 4	513	369
Ward 5	481	476
Ward 6	367	527
Ward 7	491	638
Ward 8	596	525
Ward 9	496	630
Ward 10	448	598
Ward 11	443	750
Ward 12	394	620
Ward 13	329	312
Ward 14	497	425
Ward 15	422	428
Ward 16	208	228
Ward 17	391	378
Ward 18	432	453
Ward 19	633	648
Ward 20	615	690
Ward 21	474	365
Hales Corners, vil.		
Wards 1 – 3	623	1,011
Wards 4 – 6	631	983
Wards 7 – 9	608	805
Milwaukee, city		
Ward 1	1,185	297
Ward 2	500	23
Ward 3	909	229
Ward 4	1,576	275
Ward 5	789	125
Ward 6	1,395	462
Ward 7	480	194
Ward 8	1,172	371
Ward 9	725	126
Ward 10	926	346
Ward 11	979	184
Ward 12	968	133
Ward 13	621	105
Ward 14	1,034	63
Ward 15	574	275
Ward 16	1,425	182
Ward 17	557	153
Ward 18	919	168
Ward 19	833	88
Ward 20	1,064	95
Ward 21	965	66
Ward 22	866	77
Ward 23	439	28
Ward 24	565	6
Ward 25	881	87
Ward 26	830	73
Ward 27	675	77
Ward 28	272	24
Ward 29	442	42
Ward 30	821	112
Ward 31	786	64
Ward 32	1,513	262
Ward 33	1,401	809
Ward 34	981	314
Ward 35	602	303
Ward 36	813	98
Ward 37	955	75
Ward 38	658	71
Ward 39	698	125
Ward 40	802	60
Ward 41	729	55
Ward 42	890	110
Ward 43	708	16
Ward 44	1,010	91
Ward 45	825	84
Ward 46	583	36
Ward 47	1,171	37
Ward 48	483	58
Ward 49	717	38
Ward 50	697	42
Ward 51	712	22
Ward 52	948	56
Ward 53	500	33
Ward 54	615	10
Ward 55	1,109	205
Ward 56	751	14
Ward 57	1,078	8
Ward 58	762	4
Ward 59	1,547	33
Ward 60	1,098	14
Ward 61	985	12
Ward 62	822	7
Ward 63	823	4
Ward 64	1,617	51
Ward 65	1,235	38
Ward 66	925	6
Ward 67	675	31
Ward 68	1,218	95
Ward 69	987	53
Ward 70	1,340	59
Ward 71	729	43

VOTE FOR PRESIDENT AND VICE PRESIDENT BY WARD
November 6, 2012 General Election–Continued

District	Obama and Biden (Dem.)	Romney and Ryan (Rep.)	District	Obama and Biden (Dem.)	Romney and Ryan (Rep.)
Ward 72	954	85	Ward 162	434	7
Ward 73	1,063	117	Ward 163	857	33
Ward 74	702	69	Ward 164	825	119
Ward 75	524	173	Ward 165	768	154
Ward 76	755	82	Ward 166	293	59
Ward 77	586	113	Ward 167	696	187
Ward 78	1,023	193	Ward 168	1,122	370
Ward 79	952	212	Ward 169	720	13
Ward 80	1,050	482	Ward 170	495	9
Ward 81	280	317	Ward 171	218	10
Ward 82	426	379	Ward 172	598	19
Ward 83	562	460	Ward 173	800	4
Ward 84	435	306	Ward 174	1,170	14
Ward 85	517	441	Ward 175	506	57
Ward 86	496	407	Ward 176	942	25
Ward 87	380	216	Ward 177	1,349	517
Ward 88	471	314	Ward 178	1,013	366
Ward 89	677	358	Ward 179	1,274	350
Ward 90	668	295	Ward 180	799	376
Ward 91	1,288	166	Ward 181	970	482
Ward 92	988	377	Ward 182	1,177	459
Ward 93	393	234	Ward 183	1,271	579
Ward 94	548	27	Ward 184	1,064	546
Ward 95	600	42	Ward 185	1,346	829
Ward 96	950	138	Ward 186	1,086	828
Ward 97	773	237	Ward 187	265	163
Ward 98	709	34	Ward 188	289	156
Ward 99	1,131	92	Ward 189	523	46
Ward 100	801	26	Ward 190	846	630
Ward 101	1,154	22	Ward 191	628	533
Ward 102	1,335	43	Ward 192	797	454
Ward 103	1,651	60	Ward 193	836	37
Ward 104	1,478	24	Ward 194	604	99
Ward 105	716	4	Ward 195	567	37
Ward 106	627	2	Ward 196	987	83
Ward 107	945	7	Ward 197	441	30
Ward 108	942	10	Ward 198	1,031	71
Ward 109	1,071	8	Ward 199	707	31
Ward 110	616	2	Ward 200	492	41
Ward 111	924	7	Ward 201	518	28
Ward 112	941	7	Ward 202	720	111
Ward 113	818	2	Ward 203	725	305
Ward 114	696	7	Ward 204	588	251
Ward 115	1,132	12	Ward 205	537	294
Ward 116	715	1	Ward 206	392	244
Ward 117	869	3	Ward 207	471	298
Ward 118	905	11	Ward 208	516	347
Ward 119	827	7	Ward 209	383	412
Ward 120	910	6	Ward 210	306	461
Ward 121	832	4	Ward 211	421	327
Ward 122	958	19	Ward 212	518	354
Ward 123	1,005	63	Ward 213	629	356
Ward 124	635	86	Ward 214	378	87
Ward 125	956	178	Ward 215	368	36
Ward 126	811	100	Ward 216	358	47
Ward 127	997	340	Ward 217	553	107
Ward 128	1,138	449	Ward 218	648	146
Ward 129	715	311	Ward 219	471	88
Ward 130	934	403	Ward 220	464	119
Ward 131	743	417	Ward 221	785	183
Ward 132	1,025	527	Ward 222	577	90
Ward 133	655	190	Ward 223	575	111
Ward 134	745	253	Ward 224	426	87
Ward 135	785	238	Ward 225	484	61
Ward 136	911	275	Ward 226	250	37
Ward 137	588	138	Ward 227	826	100
Ward 138	1,850	179	Ward 228	469	45
Ward 139	1,465	91	Ward 229	362	42
Ward 140	578	12	Ward 230	685	64
Ward 141	782	16	Ward 231	368	40
Ward 142	695	5	Ward 232	295	24
Ward 143	843	5	Ward 233	259	17
Ward 144	500	14	Ward 234	315	39
Ward 145	392	2	Ward 235	798	333
Ward 146	319	2	Ward 236	476	49
Ward 147	1,345	6	Ward 237	679	54
Ward 148	925	8	Ward 238	554	59
Ward 149	1,075	5	Ward 239	453	56
Ward 150	858	17	Ward 240	559	57
Ward 151	663	8	Ward 241	755	213
Ward 152	600	2	Ward 242	640	203
Ward 153	917	38	Ward 243	735	319
Ward 154	733	16	Ward 244	623	210
Ward 155	744	5	Ward 245	510	189
Ward 156	860	18	Ward 246	937	295
Ward 157	693	31	Ward 247	422	180
Ward 158	552	28	Ward 248	999	256
Ward 159	576	34	Ward 249	379	77
Ward 160	818	10	Ward 250	345	52
Ward 161	252	5	Ward 251	236	28

VOTE FOR PRESIDENT AND VICE PRESIDENT BY WARD
November 6, 2012 General Election–Continued

District	Obama and Biden (Dem.)	Romney and Ryan (Rep.)	District	Obama and Biden (Dem.)	Romney and Ryan (Rep.)
Ward 252	422	92	Wards 9 – 12	1,903	679
Ward 253	233	44	South Milwaukee, city		
Ward 254	215	36	Wards 1 – 4	1,471	1,186
Ward 255	313	50	Wards 5 – 8	1,368	1,112
Ward 256	311	28	Wards 9 – 12	1,516	1,479
Ward 257	594	94	Wards 13 – 16	1,465	1,185
Ward 258	587	164	Wauwatosa, city		
Ward 259	418	110	Ward 1	705	551
Ward 260	230	140	Ward 2	751	499
Ward 261	309	211	Ward 3	730	616
Ward 262	601	451	Ward 4	880	909
Ward 263	365	215	Ward 5	466	507
Ward 264	678	512	Ward 6	490	402
Ward 265	383	271	Ward 7	488	762
Ward 266	350	375	Ward 8	311	382
Ward 267	363	274	Ward 9	630	777
Ward 268	785	642	Ward 10	677	496
Ward 269	506	401	Ward 11	757	531
Ward 270	424	400	Ward 12	669	820
Ward 271	740	668	Ward 13	378	280
Ward 272	545	516	Ward 14	824	558
Ward 273	322	331	Ward 15	894	544
Ward 274	321	313	Ward 16	722	749
Ward 275	861	604	Ward 17	473	748
Ward 276	621	647	Ward 18	558	564
Ward 277	716	574	Ward 19	628	621
Ward 278	387	368	Ward 20	619	750
Ward 279	610	480	Ward 21	512	645
Ward 280	1,034	641	Ward 22	602	637
Ward 281	486	307	Ward 23	555	660
Ward 282	357	74	Ward 24	647	539
Ward 283	466	259	West Allis, city		
Ward 284	587	151	Ward 1	569	436
Ward 285	128	38	Ward 2	793	465
Ward 286	361	145	Ward 3	567	312
Ward 287	297	159	Ward 4	774	644
Ward 288	675	406	Ward 5	584	465
Ward 289	457	192	Ward 6	539	480
Ward 290	401	113	Ward 7	669	536
Ward 291	413	168	Ward 8	625	414
Ward 292	443	195	Ward 9	682	696
Ward 293	457	328	Ward 10	661	547
Ward 294	339	259	Ward 11	750	782
Ward 295	503	205	Ward 12	626	702
Ward 296	578	353	Ward 13	865	923
Ward 297	585	244	Ward 14	582	442
Ward 298	466	208	Ward 15	505	498
Ward 299	545	271	Ward 16	495	489
Ward 300	820	337	Ward 17	740	775
Ward 301	713	407	Ward 18	774	826
Ward 302	451	272	Ward 19	691	784
Ward 303	663	512	Ward 20	558	494
Ward 304	542	336	Ward 21	741	616
Ward 305	485	390	Ward 22	586	527
Ward 306	512	230	Ward 23	705	796
Ward 307	529	329	Ward 24	612	397
Ward 308	581	203	Ward 25	604	748
Ward 309	651	454	West Milwaukee, vil.		
Ward 310	256	110	Wards 1, 2 & 5	540	276
Ward 311	396	263	Wards 3, 4 & 6	564	341
Ward 312	457	477	Whitefish Bay, vil.		
Ward 313	1,039	768	Wards 1 & 2	645	869
Ward 314	365	347	Wards 3 & 4	636	657
Ward 315	744	592	Wards 5 & 6	747	753
Ward 316	422	352	Ward 7	456	323
Ward 317	497	355	Wards 8 – 10	951	787
Ward 320	35	5	Wards 9 – 11	865	589
Ward 321	213	21	Ward 12	518	423
Ward 322	118	28	TOTAL	332,438	154,924
Ward 323	240	41	MONROE COUNTY		
Ward 324	118	15	Adrian	163	244
Ward 325	302	84	Angelo		
Ward 326	0	4	Wards 1 – 3	252	326
Ward 327	0	0	Byron	281	291
Oak Creek, city			Cashton, vil.		
Wards 1 – 3	1,393	1,658	Wards 1 & 2	278	183
Wards 4 – 6	1,460	1,457	Clifton	114	106
Wards 7 – 9	1,359	1,609	Glendale	125	183
Wards 10 – 12	1,485	1,932	Grant	70	149
Wards 13 – 15	1,341	1,984	Greenfield		
Wards 16 – 19	1,404	1,393	Wards 1 & 2	157	230
River Hills, vil.			Jefferson	146	128
Wards 1 – 3	493	678	Kendall, vil.	124	65
St. Francis, city			Lafayette		
Wards 1 – 4	904	732	Wards 1 & 2	63	92
Wards 5 – 8	1,008	771	La Grange		
Wards 9 – 12	1,065	793	Wards 1A – 3A	440	527
Shorewood, vil.			Wards 1B – 3B	22	45
Wards 1 – 4	2,418	933	Leon		
Wards 5 – 8	1,999	768	Wards 1 & 2	243	342

VOTE FOR PRESIDENT AND VICE PRESIDENT BY WARD
November 6, 2012 General Election–Continued

District	Obama and Biden (Dem.)	Romney and Ryan (Rep.)
Lincoln	136	291
Little Falls		
Wards 1 & 2	367	319
Melvina, vil.	18	13
New Lyme	41	48
Norwalk, vil.	114	97
Oakdale	152	189
Oakdale, vil.	54	58
Portland	189	181
Ridgeville	130	122
Scott	13	43
Sheldon	75	147
Sparta		
Wards 1 – 6	745	814
Sparta, city		
Wards 1 – 6	724	656
Wards 7 – 12	767	560
Wards 13 – 18	605	437
Tomah		
Wards 1 & 2	286	413
Tomah, city		
Wards 1 – 6	631	489
Ward 5A	0	0
Wards 7 – 11	686	666
Wards 12 – 16	680	597
Ward 17	0	0
Warrens, vil.	71	127
Wellington		
Wards 1 & 2	145	115
Wells	138	137
Wilton		
Wards 1 – 5	120	120
Wilton, vil.	125	95
Wyeville, vil.	25	30
TOTAL	9,515	9,675
OCONTO COUNTY		
Abrams		
Wards 1 – 3	443	594
Bagley	70	91
Brazeau		
Wards 1 – 3	332	447
Breed	140	224
Chase		
Wards 1 – 5	672	893
Doty	69	128
Gillett		
Wards 1 & 2	170	381
Gillett, city		
Wards 1 – 3	282	308
How		
Wards 1 & 2	110	206
Lakewood	239	324
Lena	168	198
Lena, vil.	131	112
Little River		
Wards 1 & 2	284	271
Little Suamico		
Wards 1 – 8	1,027	1,511
Maple Valley	145	233
Morgan		
Wards 1 & 2	230	328
Mountain	261	285
Oconto		
Wards 1 – 3	355	382
Oconto, city		
Wards 1 – 7	1,130	813
Oconto Falls		
Wards 1 & 2	266	388
Oconto Falls, city		
Wards 1 – 5	585	628
Pensaukee		
Wards 1 & 2	341	403
Pulaski, vil.		
Ward 5	0	0
Riverview		
Wards 1 & 2	260	245
Spruce		
Wards 1 & 2	203	235
Stiles		
Wards 1 & 2	368	413
Suring, vil.	97	120
Townsend	297	351
Underhill	190	229
TOTAL	8,865	10,741
ONEIDA COUNTY		
Cassian		
Wards 1 & 2	324	377
Crescent		
Wards 1 – 3	696	620

District	Obama and Biden (Dem.)	Romney and Ryan (Rep.)
Enterprise	104	131
Hazelhurst		
Wards 1 & 2	370	445
Lake Tomahawk		
Wards 1 & 2	271	383
Little Rice	101	123
Lynne	42	42
Minocqua		
Wards 1 – 7	1,221	1,853
Monico	49	105
Newbold		
Ward 1	114	124
Wards 2 – 4	713	731
Nokomis		
Wards 1 & 2	480	387
Pelican		
Wards 1 – 4	782	709
Piehl	31	23
Pine Lake		
Wards 1 – 4	834	733
Rhinelander, city		
Ward 1	294	131
Wards 2 & 3	276	151
Wards 4 & 5	268	147
Wards 6 & 7	242	162
Wards 8 & 9	311	195
Ward 10	240	195
Wards 11 & 12	272	149
Wards 13 & 14	270	173
Schoepke	119	124
Stella		
Wards 1 & 2	202	162
Sugar Camp		
Wards 1 & 2	418	678
Three Lakes		
Wards 1 – 4	560	925
Woodboro	272	260
Woodruff		
Wards 1 – 3	576	679
TOTAL	10,452	10,917
OUTAGAMIE COUNTY		
Appleton, city		
Ward 1	449	267
Ward 2	851	507
Ward 3	1,082	485
Ward 4	448	375
Ward 5	0	4
Ward 6	336	213
Ward 7	579	538
Ward 8	856	226
Ward 9	474	371
Ward 10	358	285
Ward 11	269	254
Ward 15	395	437
Ward 16	384	323
Ward 17	391	389
Ward 18	261	369
Ward 19	464	954
Ward 20	314	562
Ward 21	9	20
Ward 22	3	15
Ward 23	0	0
Ward 24	253	211
Ward 25	540	364
Ward 27	567	412
Ward 28	551	407
Ward 29	719	443
Ward 30	623	390
Ward 33	595	477
Ward 34	204	91
Ward 35	535	467
Ward 36	723	570
Ward 37	429	377
Ward 38	464	712
Ward 39	207	313
Ward 40	4	11
Ward 41	19	86
Ward 42	477	411
Ward 43	444	382
Ward 48	106	50
Ward 49	53	47
Ward 50	79	59
Ward 51	538	386
Ward 52	60	54
Ward 53	16	8
Ward 54	489	469
Ward 55	255	219
Ward 56	0	1

VOTE FOR PRESIDENT AND VICE PRESIDENT BY WARD
November 6, 2012 General Election–Continued

District	Obama and Biden (Dem.)	Romney and Ryan (Rep.)
Ward 57	1	1
Ward 58	0	0
Ward 59	1	0
Bear Creek, vil.	80	57
Black Creek		
Wards 1 & 2	262	392
Black Creek, vil.		
Wards 1 & 2	289	321
Bovina		
Wards 1 & 2	284	349
Buchanan		
Wards 1 – 10	1,701	2,138
Center		
Wards 1 – 7	746	1,311
Cicero		
Wards 1 & 2	236	317
Combined Locks, vil.		
Wards 1 – 4	929	985
Dale		
Wards 1 – 3	563	974
Deer Creek	129	152
Ellington		
Wards 1 – 5	590	954
Freedom		
Wards 1 – 8	1,344	1,836
Grand Chute		
Wards 1 – 3	1,219	1,567
Wards 4 – 6	857	1,020
Ward 7	372	324
Ward 8	91	95
Wards 9 – 11	613	620
Wards 12 – 14	1,152	1,335
Wards 15 – 17	1,009	1,248
Ward 18	0	0
Greenville		
Wards 1 – 3 & 5 – 8	1,746	3,125
Wards 4 & 9	459	682
Hortonia		
Wards 1 & 2	207	409
Hortonville, vil.		
Wards 1 – 3	645	827
Howard, vil.		
Ward 17	0	0
Kaukauna		
Wards 1 – 3	276	433
Kaukauna, city		
Wards 1 – 3	1,007	724
Wards 4 & 5	1,009	831
Wards 6 & 7	1,160	802
Wards 8 – 10	1,167	893
Kimberly, vil.		
Wards 1 – 9	1,936	1,619
Liberty	170	283
Little Chute, vil.		
Wards 1, 4, 5 & 14	638	704
Wards 2, 6, 8, 12 &13	508	423
Wards 3, 9, 10 & 11	1,129	928
Ward 7	521	523
Maine	184	239
Maple Creek	135	177
New London, city		
Wards 1 & 2	354	314
Nichols, vil.	44	60
Oneida		
Wards 1 – 6	1,155	897
Osborn		
Wards 1 & 2	248	410
Seymour		
Wards 1 & 2	213	379
Seymour, city		
Wards 1 – 6	771	923
Shiocton, vil.	253	171
Vandenbroek		
Wards 1 – 3	355	511
Wrightstown, vil.		
Ward 4	28	78
TOTAL	**45,659**	**47,372**
OZAUKEE COUNTY		
Bayside, vil.		
Ward 6	46	36
Belgium		
Wards 1 – 3	264	628
Belgium, vil.		
Wards 1 – 3	412	854
Cedarburg		
Wards 1 & 2	233	671
Wards 3 & 4	274	685

District	Obama and Biden (Dem.)	Romney and Ryan (Rep.)
Wards 5, 6 & 10	266	860
Wards 7 – 9	301	795
Cedarburg, city		
Ward 1	413	685
Ward 2	332	700
Ward 3	456	624
Wards 4 & 8	348	574
Ward 5	405	535
Ward 6	388	648
Ward 7	342	723
Fredonia		
Wards 1 – 4	300	963
Fredonia, vil.		
Wards 1 – 3	357	877
Grafton		
Wards 1, 2 & 5	387	1,059
Wards 3 & 4	480	956
Grafton, vil.		
Ward 1	164	394
Ward 2	189	285
Ward 3	200	358
Ward 4	205	362
Ward 5	203	323
Ward 6	204	269
Ward 7	163	344
Ward 8	154	385
Ward 9	172	365
Ward 10	200	292
Ward 11	145	323
Ward 12	163	359
Ward 13	222	288
Ward 14	174	299
Mequon, city		
Ward 1	534	890
Ward 2	120	391
Wards 3 & 4	637	1,249
Wards 5 & 7B	205	603
Wards 6 & 7A	392	909
Wards 8 – 10	737	1,245
Wards 11 & 12	635	1,126
Wards 13 & 14	353	770
Ward 15	380	494
Ward 16	221	491
Ward 17	336	459
Ward 18	204	368
Wards 19 – 21	639	1,331
Newburg, vil.		
Ward 3	19	29
Port Washington		
Wards 1 & 2	322	670
Port Washington, city		
Ward 1	439	672
Ward 2	415	501
Ward 3	415	565
Ward 4	317	422
Ward 5	408	613
Ward 6	392	489
Ward 7	417	558
Saukville		
Wards 1 – 3	327	898
Saukville, vil.		
Wards 1 & 2	321	600
Wards 3 – 5	317	469
Wards 6 & 7	254	454
Thiensville, vil.		
Wards 1 & 2	405	778
Wards 3 & 4	436	514
TOTAL	**19,159**	**36,077**
PEPIN COUNTY		
Albany	154	149
Durand		
Wards 1 & 2	131	224
Durand, city		
Wards 1 – 3	465	426
Frankfort	116	65
Lima		
Wards 1 & 2	147	173
Pepin		
Wards 1 & 2	221	177
Pepin, vil.		
Wards 1 & 2	275	148
Stockholm	62	74
Stockholm, vil.	38	10
Waterville		
Wards 1 & 2	183	213
Waubeek	84	135
TOTAL	**1,876**	**1,794**

VOTE FOR PRESIDENT AND VICE PRESIDENT BY WARD
November 6, 2012 General Election–Continued

District	Obama and Biden (Dem.)	Romney and Ryan (Rep.)
PIERCE COUNTY		
Bay City, vil.	91	93
Clifton		
Wards 1 – 3	534	688
Diamond Bluff	125	132
Ellsworth		
Wards 1 & 2	281	364
Ellsworth, vil.		
Wards 1 – 4	722	721
Elmwood, vil.	202	196
El Paso	181	192
Gilman	260	281
Hartland	163	294
Isabelle	68	79
Maiden Rock	138	178
Maiden Rock, vil.	47	28
Martell		
Wards 1 & 2	317	362
Oak Grove		
Wards 1 – 3	484	714
Plum City, vil.	129	158
Prescott, city		
Wards 1 – 6	988	1,049
River Falls		
Wards 1 – 3	714	725
River Falls, city		
Ward 5	120	132
Wards 6 – 8	1,243	703
Wards 9 – 11	877	673
Wards 12 – 14	839	633
Rock Elm	129	106
Salem	130	132
Spring Lake		
Wards 1 & 2	157	166
Spring Valley, vil.		
Wards 1 & 2	368	328
Trenton		
Wards 1 & 2	438	532
Trimbelle		
Wards 1 & 2	407	527
Union	83	211
TOTAL	10,235	10,397
POLK COUNTY		
Alden		
Wards 1 – 4	636	897
Amery, city		
Wards 1 – 5	684	629
Apple River		
Wards 1 & 2	262	330
Balsam Lake		
Wards 1 & 2	320	428
Balsam Lake, vil.		
Wards 1 & 2	224	227
Beaver	208	215
Black Brook		
Wards 1 & 2	269	437
Bone Lake	177	203
Centuria, vil.	169	164
Clam Falls	145	137
Clayton	238	244
Clayton, vil.	102	96
Clear Lake	168	249
Clear Lake, vil.		
Wards 1 & 2	223	257
Dresser, vil.	166	259
Eureka		
Wards 1 & 2	356	526
Farmington		
Wards 1 & 2	386	602
Frederic, vil.		
Wards 1 & 2	241	250
Garfield		
Wards 1 – 3	362	527
Georgetown		
Wards 1 & 2	309	245
Johnstown	158	117
Laketown	253	286
Lincoln		
Wards 1 – 4	527	712
Lorain	71	88
Luck		
Wards 1 & 2	249	251
Luck, vil.		
Wards 1 & 2	255	260
McKinley	82	111
Milltown		
Wards 1 & 2	286	363
Milltown, vil.	208	159

District	Obama and Biden (Dem.)	Romney and Ryan (Rep.)
Osceola		
Wards 1 – 5	627	894
Osceola, vil.		
Wards 1 – 3	576	608
St. Croix Falls		
Wards 1 & 2	236	375
St. Croix Falls, city		
Wards 1 – 4	559	538
Sterling	156	190
Turtle Lake, vil.		
Ward 2A	16	15
Ward 2B	0	0
West Sweden	169	205
TOTAL	10,073	12,094
PORTAGE COUNTY		
Alban	265	209
Almond	166	211
Almond, vil.	100	91
Amherst		
Wards 1 & 2	435	400
Amherst, vil.		
Wards 1 & 2	309	245
Amherst Junction, vil.	103	93
Belmont	162	189
Buena Vista		
Wards 1 & 2	309	357
Carson		
Wards 1 & 2	396	375
Dewey	298	281
Eau Pleine	245	294
Grant		
Wards 1, 2 & 4	411	442
Ward 3	77	153
Hull		
Wards 1 – 3	626	462
Wards 4 & 5	519	481
Wards 6 – 8	577	532
Junction City, vil.	103	98
Lanark		
Wards 1 & 2	432	425
Linwood		
Wards 1 & 2	337	319
Milladore, vil.		
Ward 2	0	0
Nelsonville, vil.	58	29
New Hope	313	167
Park Ridge, vil.	186	146
Pine Grove		
Wards 1 & 2	182	193
Plover		
Wards 1 – 3	385	480
Plover, vil.		
Wards 1 – 3	1,153	1,030
Wards 4 – 6	1,330	1,231
Wards 7 – 9	1,012	734
Rosholt, vil.	128	99
Sharon		
Wards 1 – 3	652	536
Stevens Point, city		
Wards 1 – 3	921	421
Wards 4 – 6	949	495
Wards 7 – 9	825	466
Wards 10 – 12	791	353
Wards 13 – 15	888	359
Wards 16 – 18	840	686
Wards 19 – 21	788	423
Wards 22 – 24	863	592
Wards 25 – 27	744	373
Wards 28 – 30	866	539
Wards 31 – 33	837	435
Ward 34	0	0
Ward 35	1	0
Ward 36	0	0
Stockton		
Wards 1 – 5	884	820
Whiting, vil.		
Wards 1 – 4	609	351
TOTAL	22,075	16,615
PRICE COUNTY		
Catawba	77	54
Catawba, vil.	34	25
Eisenstein		
Wards 1 & 2	184	199
Elk		
Wards 1 & 2	295	334
Emery	102	84
Fifield		
Ward 1	187	197
Ward 2	73	109

VOTE FOR PRESIDENT AND VICE PRESIDENT BY WARD
November 6, 2012 General Election–Continued

District	Obama and Biden (Dem.)	Romney and Ryan (Rep.)
Flambeau	128	148
Georgetown	42	46
Hackett	49	63
Harmony	63	75
Hill	60	117
Kennan	94	80
Kennan, vil.	38	26
Knox	102	73
Lake		
Wards 1 & 2	383	297
Ogema		
Wards 1 & 2	171	208
Park Falls, city		
Wards 1 – 7	680	487
Phillips, city		
Wards 1 – 4	383	291
Prentice	100	135
Prentice, vil.	137	158
Spirit	62	112
Worcester		
Wards 1 – 3	443	566
TOTAL	3,887	3,884
RACINE COUNTY		
Burlington		
Wards 1 – 7	728	1,383
Wards 8 – 10	416	619
Ward 11	155	259
Burlington, city		
Wards 1 – 4	1,116	1,364
Wards 5 – 8	1,195	1,638
Caledonia, vil.		
Wards 1 & 2	708	1,144
Wards 3 – 5	927	1,505
Wards 6 – 8	1,039	1,130
Wards 9, 10, 12 & 13	1,561	1,550
Wards 11, 14, 15 &17	1,285	1,680
Wards 16, 18 & 19	921	1,171
Ward 20	225	348
Dover		
Wards 1 – 8	733	1,270
Elmwood Park, vil.	172	161
Mount Pleasant, vil.		
Wards 1, 2 & 16	977	842
Wards 3, 4, 6 & 7	1,265	1,096
Ward 5	397	418
Wards 8 & 9	747	1,063
Wards 10, 12 & 15	1,623	1,594
Wards 13 & 14	524	728
Wards 17 & 20	507	608
Ward 18	307	244
Wards 19 & 21 – 23	1,496	1,426
North Bay, vil.	80	90
Norway		
Wards 1 – 11	1,384	3,511
Racine, city		
Ward 1	657	169
Ward 2	812	95
Ward 3	1,090	356
Ward 4	722	29
Ward 5	567	28
Ward 6	652	114
Ward 7	533	49
Ward 8	717	71
Ward 9	904	209
Ward 10	609	351
Ward 11	647	255
Ward 12	537	312
Ward 13	712	380
Ward 14	903	383
Ward 15	748	231
Ward 16	888	520
Ward 17	493	79
Ward 18	467	18
Ward 19	466	29
Ward 20	926	584
Ward 21	768	296
Ward 22	1,005	483
Ward 23	913	345
Ward 24	766	471
Ward 25	889	246
Ward 26	69	98
Ward 27	886	732
Ward 28	829	512
Ward 29	873	457
Ward 30	783	269
Ward 31	414	226
Ward 32	691	200
Ward 33	623	277

District	Obama and Biden (Dem.)	Romney and Ryan (Rep.)
Ward 34	548	407
Ward 35	540	375
Ward 36	608	206
Raymond		
Wards 1 – 6	837	1,587
Rochester, vil.		
Wards 1 – 6	706	1,499
Sturtevant, vil.		
Wards 1 – 8	1,425	1,425
Union Grove, vil.		
Wards 1 – 7	928	1,571
Waterford		
Wards 1 – 10	1,068	2,788
Waterford, vil.		
Wards 1 – 7	1,103	1,848
Wind Point, vil.		
Wards 1 – 3	517	726
Yorkville		
Wards 1 – 5	681	1,199
TOTAL	53,008	49,347
RICHLAND COUNTY		
Akan	113	100
Bloom	115	107
Boaz, vil.	55	11
Buena Vista		
Wards 1 – 3	464	332
Ward 4	0	2
Cazenovia, vil.	114	40
Dayton	174	163
Eagle	128	128
Forest	92	79
Henrietta	175	89
Ithaca	177	137
Lone Rock, vil.	273	116
Marshall		
Wards 1 & 2	140	175
Orion	140	121
Richland		
Wards 1 – 4	343	342
Richland Center, city		
Ward 1	128	82
Ward 2	101	54
Ward 3	123	81
Ward 4	111	75
Ward 5	136	95
Ward 6	132	79
Ward 7	117	75
Ward 8	145	80
Ward 9	126	100
Ward 10	132	78
Ward 11	123	79
Ward 12	107	108
Richwood		
Wards 1 & 2	162	86
Rockbridge		
Wards 1 – 3	238	162
Sylvan		
Wards 1 & 2	124	105
Viola, vil.		
Ward 2	122	68
Westford	170	92
Willow	145	117
Yuba, vil.	24	15
TOTAL	4,969	3,573
ROCK COUNTY		
Avon	181	159
Beloit		
Wards 1 – 3	652	614
Wards 4 – 6	693	389
Wards 7 – 10	814	782
Ward 11	104	99
Beloit, city		
Ward 1	273	132
Ward 2	509	295
Ward 3	493	315
Ward 4	464	234
Ward 5	447	235
Ward 6	378	133
Ward 7	434	108
Ward 8	43	3
Ward 9	425	124
Ward 10	466	167
Ward 11	443	257
Ward 12	254	43
Ward 13	452	67
Ward 14	612	77
Ward 15	426	178
Ward 16	770	107
Ward 17	595	239

VOTE FOR PRESIDENT AND VICE PRESIDENT BY WARD
November 6, 2012 General Election–Continued

District	Obama and Biden (Dem.)	Romney and Ryan (Rep.)
Ward 18	479	166
Ward 19	325	162
Ward 20	368	164
Ward 21	460	225
Ward 22	368	327
Ward 23	579	524
Ward 24	356	257
Ward 25	0	0
Bradford		
Wards 1 & 2	217	325
Brodhead, city		
Wards 7 & 8	13	16
Center		
Wards 1 & 2	400	250
Clinton	181	339
Clinton, vil.		
Wards 1 – 3	495	492
Edgerton, city		
Wards 1 – 6	1,963	826
Evansville, city		
Wards 1 – 8	1,833	859
Footville, vil.	252	156
Fulton		
Wards 1 – 6	1,139	851
Harmony		
Ward 1	246	208
Wards 2 – 5	551	533
Ward 6	1	1
Janesville		
Wards 1 – 6	1,038	904
Wards 7 – 9	118	99
Janesville, city		
Ward 1	928	525
Ward 2	837	534
Ward 3	833	241
Ward 4	713	202
Ward 5	824	391
Ward 6	584	274
Ward 7	1,003	482
Ward 8	828	375
Ward 9	667	333
Ward 10	579	247
Ward 11	852	361
Ward 12	893	796
Ward 13	932	483
Ward 14	973	569
Ward 15	776	351
Ward 16	575	282
Ward 17	963	581
Ward 18	948	577
Ward 19	212	165
Ward 20	251	226
Ward 21	610	549
Ward 22	636	655
Ward 23	386	307
Ward 24	648	279
Ward 25	744	554
Ward 26	0	1
Ward 27	986	890
Ward 28	885	670
Ward 29	3	2
Johnstown	242	210
La Prairie		
Ward 1	177	191
Ward 2	60	70
Lima		
Wards 1 & 2	342	307
Magnolia	269	155
Milton		
Ward 1	216	221
Wards 2 – 4	733	487
Milton, city		
Wards 1 – 8	1,750	1,185
Newark		
Wards 1 – 3	417	498
Orfordville, vil.		
Wards 1 & 2	439	261
Plymouth		
Wards 1 & 2	369	307
Porter	393	230
Rock		
Wards 1 – 4 & 6	765	500
Wards 5 & 7	133	94
Spring Valley	202	206
Turtle		
Wards 1 & 4	303	329
Wards 2 & 3	325	495
Union		
Wards 1 – 4	705	428
TOTAL	49,219	30,517

District	Obama and Biden (Dem.)	Romney and Ryan (Rep.)
RUSK COUNTY		
Atlanta		
Wards 1 & 2	142	164
Big Bend		
Wards 1 & 2	132	126
Big Falls	34	47
Bruce, vil.	181	165
Cedar Rapids	8	14
Conrath, vil.	28	12
Dewey	108	193
Flambeau		
Wards 1 – 3	233	291
Glen Flora, vil.	16	16
Grant		
Wards 1 – 5	179	201
Grow	70	143
Hawkins	38	40
Hawkins, vil.	82	58
Hubbard	49	50
Ingram, vil.	28	14
Ladysmith, city		
Wards 1 – 15	745	654
Lawrence		
Wards 1 & 2	50	81
Marshall		
Wards 1 & 2	71	140
Murry	60	67
Richland		
Wards 1 & 2	60	51
Rusk	183	167
Sheldon, vil.	53	38
South Fork	29	42
Strickland		
Wards 1 & 2	69	71
Stubbs		
Wards 1 & 2	183	156
Thornapple		
Wards 1 – 5	166	253
Tony, vil.	25	23
True	69	87
Washington	90	124
Weyerhaeuser, vil.		
Wards 1 & 2	72	27
Wilkinson	10	15
Willard	109	114
Wilson	25	32
TOTAL	3,397	3,676
ST. CROIX COUNTY		
Baldwin		
Wards 1 & 2	215	350
Baldwin, vil.		
Wards 1 – 6	809	927
Cady	186	287
Cylon	133	224
Deer Park, vil.	37	73
Eau Galle		
Wards 1 & 2	271	371
Emerald	186	224
Erin Prairie	143	240
Forest	116	195
Glenwood	151	251
Glenwood City, city		
Wards 1 & 2	259	274
Hammond		
Wards 1 – 3	433	751
Hammond, vil.		
Wards 1 – 4	445	433
Hudson		
Wards 1 – 14	1,866	3,011
Hudson, city		
Wards 1 & 2	468	478
Wards 3 & 4	561	725
Wards 5 & 6	619	617
Wards 7 & 8	579	595
Wards 9 & 10	684	505
Wards 11 & 12	573	662
Kinnickinnic		
Wards 1 – 3	464	585
New Richmond, city		
Wards 1 – 6	915	909
Wards 7 – 12	990	1,083
North Hudson, vil.		
Wards 1 – 6	991	1,238
Pleasant Valley	114	163
Richmond		
Wards 1 & 2	411	545
Wards 3 – 5	308	465
River Falls, city		
Wards 1 – 4	983	860

VOTE FOR PRESIDENT AND VICE PRESIDENT BY WARD
November 6, 2012 General Election–Continued

District	Obama and Biden (Dem.)	Romney and Ryan (Rep.)
Roberts, vil.		
Wards 1 – 4	413	430
Rush River	150	159
St. Joseph		
Wards 1 – 6	939	1,361
Somerset		
Wards 1 – 6	799	1,393
Somerset, vil.		
Wards 1 – 4	509	605
Spring Valley, vil.		
Ward 3	2	2
Springfield	221	244
Stanton	216	291
Star Prairie		
Wards 1 – 6	740	1,112
Star Prairie, vil.	144	169
Troy		
Wards 1 – 7	1,166	1,729
Warren		
Wards 1 – 3	370	567
Wilson, vil.	64	52
Woodville, vil.		
Wards 1 & 2	267	348
TOTAL	19,910	25,503
SAUK COUNTY		
Baraboo		
Wards 1 – 4	610	470
Baraboo, city		
Wards 1, 2 & 11 – 14	1,318	873
Wards 3 – 6	1,076	599
Wards 7 – 10	1,227	679
Bear Creek		
Ward 2	243	122
Cazenovia, vil.		
Ward 2	6	3
Dellona		
Wards 1 & 2	469	388
Delton		
Wards 1 – 4	666	491
Excelsior		
Wards 1 – 3	498	441
Fairfield		
Wards 1 & 2	398	247
Franklin		
Wards 1 – 3	229	163
Freedom		
Wards 1 & 2	142	127
Greenfield	342	245
Honey Creek	254	173
Ironton	143	147
Ironton, vil.	69	39
Lake Delton, vil.		
Wards 1 – 3	745	462
La Valle		
Wards 1 – 3	380	362
La Valle, vil.	105	68
Lime Ridge, vil.	58	28
Loganville, vil.	82	49
Merrimac	340	307
Merrimac, vil.	129	127
North Freedom, vil.	201	101
Plain, vil.	211	245
Prairie du Sac		
Wards 1 & 2	369	289
Prairie du Sac, vil.		
Wards 1 – 4	1,486	767
Reedsburg		
Wards 1 – 3	309	348
Reedsburg, city		
Wards 1 – 3 & 13	558	366
Wards 4, 6 & 14	581	483
Wards 5 & 7 – 9	730	574
Wards 10 – 12	481	300
Rock Springs, vil.	87	80
Sauk City, vil.		
Wards 1 – 5	1,262	593
Spring Green		
Wards 1 – 4	611	363
Spring Green, vil.		
Wards 1 & 2	601	322
Sumpter		
Wards 1 – 3	248	165
Troy	246	202
Washington		
Wards 1 & 2	200	183
West Baraboo, vil.		
Wards 1 & 2	426	234
Westfield	145	169
Winfield		
Wards 1 & 2	255	236

District	Obama and Biden (Dem.)	Romney and Ryan (Rep.)
Wisconsin Dells, city		
Ward 4	26	31
Ward 8	3	1
Woodland	171	176
TOTAL	18,736	12,838
SAWYER COUNTY		
Bass Lake		
Wards 1 – 5	778	467
Couderay	101	53
Couderay, vil.	30	16
Draper	65	67
Edgewater		
Wards 1 & 2	144	197
Exeland, vil.	47	41
Hayward		
Wards 1 – 8	820	857
Hayward, city		
Wards 1 – 6	534	477
Hunter	220	184
Lenroot		
Wards 1 & 2	354	454
Meadowbrook	25	56
Meteor	35	52
Ojibwa		
Wards 1 & 2	62	75
Radisson		
Wards 1 & 2	96	116
Radisson, vil.	58	41
Round Lake		
Wards 1 & 2	298	390
Sand Lake	271	271
Spider Lake	130	147
Weirgor	73	104
Winter		
Wards 1 & 2	274	318
Winter, vil.	71	59
TOTAL	4,486	4,442
SHAWANO COUNTY		
Almon	135	143
Angelica		
Wards 1 – 3	399	571
Aniwa	92	173
Aniwa, vil.	54	63
Bartelme	296	53
Belle Plaine		
Wards 1 – 3	392	593
Birnamwood	163	189
Birnamwood, vil.	158	164
Bonduel, vil.		
Wards 1 & 2	242	429
Bowler, vil.	76	52
Cecil, vil.	116	182
Eland, vil.	83	44
Fairbanks	105	220
Germania	98	80
Grant		
Wards 1 & 2	181	328
Green Valley		
Wards 1 & 2	215	288
Gresham, vil.	146	122
Hartland	102	265
Herman		
Wards 1 & 2	164	232
Hutchins	109	190
Lessor		
Wards 1 & 2	231	393
Maple Grove	218	288
Marion, city		
Wards 4 – 6	4	3
Mattoon, vil.	78	82
Morris	98	131
Navarino	98	144
Pella	178	295
Pulaski, vil.		
Wards 4 & 7	29	39
Red Springs		
Wards 1 & 2	296	166
Richmond		
Wards 1 – 3	383	662
Seneca	128	163
Shawano, city		
Wards 1 & 2	311	321
Wards 3 & 4	306	326
Wards 5 & 6	358	274
Wards 7 & 8	310	269
Wards 9 & 10	357	337
Wards 11 & 12	345	330
Tigerton, vil.	158	174

VOTE FOR PRESIDENT AND VICE PRESIDENT BY WARD
November 6, 2012 General Election–Continued

District	Obama and Biden (Dem.)	Romney and Ryan (Rep.)
Washington		
Wards 1 – 3	414	588
Waukechon		
Wards 1 & 2	203	314
Wescott		
Wards 1 – 4	781	901
Wittenberg		
Wards 1 & 2	184	262
Wittenberg, vil.		
Wards 1 & 2	206	179
TOTAL	9,000	11,022
SHEBOYGAN COUNTY		
Adell, vil.	85	200
Cascade, vil.	137	237
Cedar Grove, vil.		
Wards 1 – 3	247	950
Elkhart Lake, vil.		
Wards 1 & 2	294	366
Glenbeulah, vil.	144	140
Greenbush		
Wards 1 – 3	357	565
Herman		
Wards 1 – 3	450	660
Holland		
Wards 1 – 3	354	1,151
Howards Grove, vil.		
Wards 1 – 4	785	1,144
Kohler, vil.		
Wards 1 – 3	502	848
Lima		
Wards 1 – 4	475	1,321
Lyndon		
Wards 1 – 3	303	639
Mitchell		
Wards 1 – 3	259	507
Mosel	206	298
Oostburg, vil.		
Wards 1 – 4	321	1,515
Plymouth		
Wards 1 – 4	753	1,212
Plymouth, city		
Wards 1 – 3	519	585
Wards 4 – 6	546	649
Wards 7 – 9	492	637
Wards 10 – 12	427	673
Random Lake, vil.		
Wards 1 & 2	280	667
Rhine		
Wards 1 – 3	577	836
Russell	61	158
Scott		
Wards 1 – 3	274	798
Sheboygan		
Wards 1 – 5	1,123	1,408
Wards 6 – 10	879	1,166
Sheboygan, city		
Ward 1	755	617
Ward 2	584	468
Ward 3	484	434
Ward 4	583	294
Ward 5	631	500
Ward 6	147	114
Ward 7	62	50
Ward 8	276	234
Ward 9	93	52
Ward 10	596	292
Ward 11	549	315
Ward 12	414	402
Ward 13	756	453
Ward 14	473	242
Ward 15	289	155
Ward 16	496	399
Ward 17	437	327
Ward 18	569	265
Ward 19	709	497
Ward 20	606	398
Ward 21	358	178
Ward 22	784	536
Ward 23	759	622
Ward 24	781	608
Ward 25	575	453
Ward 26	540	474
Sheboygan Falls		
Wards 1 – 3	380	651
Sheboygan Falls, city		
Wards 1, 2 & 9	672	1,010
Wards 3 – 5	730	766
Wards 6 – 8	692	715
Sherman		
Wards 1 & 2	257	674
Waldo, vil.	97	183
Wilson		
Wards 1 – 4	934	1,364
TOTAL	27,918	34,072
TAYLOR COUNTY		
Aurora	65	96
Browning	125	268
Chelsea	134	241
Cleveland	31	90
Deer Creek	115	224
Ford	60	70
Gilman, vil.	97	86
Goodrich	80	180
Greenwood	132	186
Grover	33	80
Hammel		
Wards 1 & 2	135	253
Holway	99	171
Jump River	55	70
Little Black		
Wards 1 & 2	230	325
Lublin, vil.	27	28
Maplehurst	67	102
McKinley	54	109
Medford		
Wards 1 – 3	434	814
Medford, city		
Wards 1 – 8	883	1,111
Molitor	76	103
Pershing	43	35
Rib Lake		
Wards 1 & 2	160	245
Rib Lake, vil.	185	202
Roosevelt	94	81
Stetsonville, vil.	108	128
Taft	73	76
Westboro	168	227
TOTAL	3,763	5,601
TREMPEALEAU COUNTY		
Albion		
Wards 1 & 2	175	137
Arcadia		
Wards 1 – 4	423	409
Arcadia, city		
Wards 1 – 3	492	350
Blair, city		
Wards 1 – 3	312	178
Burnside		
Wards 1 & 2	133	93
Caledonia		
Wards 1 & 2	262	236
Chimney Rock	74	57
Dodge	138	95
Eleva, vil.	190	96
Ettrick		
Wards 1 & 2	412	275
Ettrick, vil.	146	98
Gale		
Wards 1 & 2	479	437
Galesville, city		
Wards 1 – 3	414	332
Hale	297	235
Independence, city		
Wards 1 – 3	286	207
Lincoln		
Wards 1 & 2	192	123
Osseo, city		
Wards 1 – 3	527	345
Pigeon		
Wards 1 & 2	194	152
Pigeon Falls, vil.	110	78
Preston		
Wards 1 – 3	236	166
Strum, vil.		
Wards 1 & 2	336	174
Sumner	206	216
Trempealeau		
Wards 1 & 2	498	480
Trempealeau, vil.		
Wards 1 & 2	482	363
Unity		
Wards 1 & 2	160	114
Whitehall, city		
Wards 1 – 3	431	261
TOTAL	7,605	5,707
VERNON COUNTY		
Bergen		
Wards 1 – 3	434	345
Chaseburg, vil.	74	69

VOTE FOR PRESIDENT AND VICE PRESIDENT BY WARD
November 6, 2012 General Election–Continued

District	Obama and Biden (Dem.)	Romney and Ryan (Rep.)
Christiana		
Wards 1 & 2	260	226
Clinton		
Wards 1 & 2	121	117
Coon		
Wards 1 & 2	233	193
Coon Valley, vil.	246	172
De Soto, vil.	64	50
Forest	132	126
Franklin		
Wards 1 & 2	232	285
Genoa		
Wards 1 & 2	269	159
Genoa, vil.	86	44
Greenwood	101	84
Hamburg		
Wards 1 & 2	298	250
Harmony		
Wards 1 – 3	190	153
Hillsboro		
Wards 1 – 3	174	176
Hillsboro, city		
Wards 1 – 4	400	260
Jefferson		
Wards 1 – 4	316	247
Kickapoo	163	111
La Farge, vil.	217	108
Liberty	81	56
Ontario, vil.	97	79
Readstown, vil.	122	62
Stark		
Wards 1 & 2	112	81
Sterling	138	162
Stoddard, vil.	271	155
Union		
Wards 1 – 3	118	97
Viola, vil.	53	57
Viroqua		
Wards 1 – 4	515	447
Viroqua, city		
Wards 1 – 9	1,326	830
Webster		
Wards 1 & 2	211	120
Westby, city		
Wards 1 – 5	707	383
Wheatland	177	127
Whitestown	106	111
TOTAL	8,044	5,942
VILAS COUNTY		
Arbor Vitae		
Wards 1 – 7	880	1,192
Boulder Junction		
Wards 1 & 2	303	419
Cloverland		
Wards 1 & 2	279	428
Conover		
Wards 1 & 2	338	473
Eagle River, city		
Wards 1 – 5	314	382
Lac du Flambeau		
Wards 1 – 7	1,059	518
Land O'Lakes	229	357
Lincoln		
Wards 1 – 5	616	927
Manitowish Waters	156	370
Phelps		
Wards 1 & 2	317	467
Plum Lake		
Wards 1 & 2	164	218
Presque Isle	222	335
St. Germain		
Wards 1 & 2	523	844
Washington		
Wards 1 – 3	434	598
Winchester	117	221
TOTAL	5,951	7,749
WALWORTH COUNTY		
Bloomfield		
Wards 1 & 2	325	383
Bloomfield, vil.		
Wards 1 – 5	844	1,043
Burlington, city		
Ward 9	0	0
Darien		
Wards 1 – 3	353	517
Darien, vil.		
Wards 1 & 2	355	328

District	Obama and Biden (Dem.)	Romney and Ryan (Rep.)
Delavan		
Wards 1 – 11	1,127	1,583
Delavan, city		
Wards 1 – 14	1,842	1,671
East Troy		
Ward 1	128	383
Wards 2 & 3	261	617
Wards 4 – 6	355	807
East Troy, vil.		
Wards 1 – 5	881	1,531
Elkhorn, city		
Wards 1 – 7	2,116	2,473
Ward 8	0	0
Fontana, vil.		
Wards 1 – 3	340	603
Geneva		
Wards 1 – 8	1,021	1,523
Genoa City, vil.		
Wards 1 – 4	574	708
Lafayette		
Wards 1 – 3	426	793
La Grange		
Wards 1 – 3	483	925
Lake Geneva, city		
Wards 1 & 2	484	478
Wards 3 & 4	388	382
Wards 5, 6 & 10	431	438
Wards 7 – 9	414	369
Linn		
Wards 1 – 4 & 6	400	652
Ward 5	81	169
Lyons		
Wards 1 – 7	713	1,245
Mukwonago, vil.		
Ward 11	24	39
Richmond		
Wards 1 – 3	485	548
Sharon	189	297
Sharon, vil.		
Wards 1 & 2	352	302
Spring Prairie		
Wards 1 – 4	420	937
Sugar Creek		
Wards 1 – 5	883	1,322
Troy		
Wards 1 – 3	515	985
Walworth		
Wards 1 – 3	291	640
Walworth, vil.		
Wards 1 – 3	498	727
Whitewater		
Wards 1 & 2	359	482
Ward 3	33	32
Whitewater, city		
Wards 1 & 2	744	494
Wards 3 & 4	675	435
Wards 5 & 6	906	628
Wards 7 – 9	1,260	632
Williams Bay, vil.		
Wards 1 – 4	576	885
TOTAL	22,552	29,006
WASHBURN COUNTY		
Barronett	107	111
Bashaw		
Wards 1 – 3	246	344
Bass Lake	125	167
Beaver Brook		
Wards 1 – 3	193	224
Birchwood		
Wards 1 – 3	127	231
Birchwood, vil.	115	105
Brooklyn	81	79
Casey	139	129
Chicog		
Wards 1 & 2	110	71
Crystal		
Wards 1 & 2	65	88
Evergreen		
Wards 1 & 2	315	350
Frog Creek	40	39
Gull Lake	65	50
Long Lake	212	218
Madge		
Wards 1 – 3	187	158
Minong		
Wards 1 & 2	277	278
Minong, vil.	149	95
Sarona	83	133

VOTE FOR PRESIDENT AND VICE PRESIDENT BY WARD
November 6, 2012 General Election–Continued

District	Obama and Biden (Dem.)	Romney and Ryan (Rep.)
Shell Lake, city		
Wards 1 & 2	415	342
Spooner		
Wards 1 – 3	202	246
Spooner, city		
Wards 1 – 4	649	570
Springbrook	107	137
Stinnett	49	75
Stone Lake	121	166
Trego		
Wards 1 & 2	268	293
TOTAL	4,447	4,699
WASHINGTON COUNTY		
Addison		
Wards 1 – 6	504	1,604
Barton		
Wards 1 – 4	478	1,238
Erin		
Wards 1 – 4	654	1,916
Farmington		
Wards 1 – 5	533	1,679
Germantown	46	124
Germantown, vil.		
Wards 1, 8, 10 & 11	840	2,214
Wards 2 & 5 – 7	1,069	1,800
Wards 3, 4, 9, 16 & 17...	1,008	2,030
Wards 12 – 15 ...	922	2,394
Hartford		
Wards 1 – 5	588	1,693
Hartford, city		
Wards 1 & 2	334	759
Wards 3 – 5	425	891
Wards 6, 9, 10, 15 – 17 & 20	775	1,362
Wards 7 & 8	112	219
Wards 11 – 14	935	1,500
Jackson		
Wards 1 – 6	579	2,239
Jackson, vil.		
Wards 1 – 9	1,172	2,715
Kewaskum		
Wards 1 & 2	189	508
Kewaskum, vil.		
Wards 1 – 5	682	1,573
Milwaukee, city		
Ward 318	0	0
Newburg, vil.		
Wards 1 & 2	157	461
Polk		
Wards 1 – 6	601	1,948
Richfield, vil.		
Wards 1 & 2	422	1,372
Ward 3	186	487
Ward 4	176	678
Wards 5 & 6	519	1,661
Wards 7 – 9	573	1,580
Slinger, vil.		
Wards 1 – 8	862	2,011
Trenton		
Wards 1, 2 & 8	178	457
Wards 3 – 7	592	1,763
Wayne		
Wards 1 – 3	266	1,028
West Bend		
Wards 1 – 10	787	2,299
West Bend, city		
Wards 1 – 3	751	1,281
Wards 4 – 6	887	1,363
Wards 7 & 8	761	1,580
Wards 9 & 10	662	1,320
Wards 11 – 14	724	1,126
Wards 15 – 19	716	1,224
Wards 20 – 22	705	1,214
Wards 23, 24 & 26	795	1,451
Ward 25	1	3
TOTAL	23,166	54,765
WAUKESHA COUNTY		
Big Bend, vil.		
Wards 1 – 3	239	545
Brookfield		
Wards 1, 3 & 4	440	922
Wards 2, 6 & 8	496	731
Wards 5 & 7	264	630
Ward 9	98	192
Ward 10	122	219
Brookfield, city		
Ward 1	367	733
Ward 2	441	869
Ward 3	444	875

District	Obama and Biden (Dem.)	Romney and Ryan (Rep.)
Ward 4	252	462
Ward 5	413	968
Ward 6	206	589
Ward 7	307	635
Ward 8	466	833
Ward 9	331	719
Ward 10	359	895
Ward 11	305	685
Ward 12	387	962
Ward 13	346	851
Ward 14	222	754
Ward 15	314	737
Ward 16	110	333
Ward 17	376	804
Ward 18	285	600
Ward 19	272	576
Ward 20	300	733
Ward 21	308	595
Ward 22	459	811
Ward 23	349	643
Ward 24	466	813
Butler, vil.		
Wards 1 – 3	431	647
Chenequa, vil.	48	327
Delafield		
Wards 1, 2, 5 & 6	497	1,527
Wards 3 & 4	218	967
Wards 7 & 8	221	707
Wards 9 – 11	358	954
Delafield, city		
Wards 1 – 14	1,376	2,948
Dousman, vil.		
Wards 1 – 3	413	938
Eagle		
Wards 1 – 4	576	1,617
Eagle, vil.		
Wards 1 & 2	283	807
Elm Grove, vil.		
Wards 1 – 4	710	1,605
Wards 5 – 8	678	1,363
Genesee		
Wards 1, 3, 5 & 9	396	1,144
Wards 2, 4 & 10	447	1,153
Wards 6 – 8	522	1,286
Hartland, vil.		
Wards 1 – 6	909	1,701
Wards 7 – 12	762	1,965
Lac la Belle, vil.	44	174
Lannon, vil.		
Wards 1 & 2	249	432
Lisbon		
Wards 1 & 6	571	1,572
Ward 2	465	954
Ward 3	184	546
Wards 4 & 5	607	1,710
Menomonee Falls, vil.		
Ward 1	499	904
Ward 2	295	532
Ward 3	440	725
Ward 4	201	396
Ward 5	383	542
Ward 6	453	720
Ward 7	184	308
Ward 8	304	474
Ward 9	401	532
Ward 10	281	548
Ward 11	309	527
Ward 12	212	355
Ward 13	383	847
Ward 14	464	933
Ward 15	445	910
Ward 16	216	371
Ward 17	414	756
Ward 18	345	655
Ward 19	367	738
Ward 20	425	753
Ward 21	351	776
Ward 22	223	517
Ward 23	272	634
Merton		
Wards 1 – 3 & 7 – 9 ...	763	2,937
Wards 4 – 6 & 10	452	1,346
Merton, vil.		
Wards 1 – 4	380	1,552
Milwaukee, city		
Ward 319	0	0
Mukwonago		
Wards 1 – 3 & 7 – 11 ...	869	2,490
Wards 4 – 6	378	1,157

VOTE FOR PRESIDENT AND VICE PRESIDENT BY WARD
November 6, 2012 General Election–Continued

District	Obama and Biden (Dem.)	Romney and Ryan (Rep.)
Mukwonago, vil.		
Wards 1 – 10	1,312	2,768
Muskego, city		
Wards 1 – 3	753	1,771
Wards 4 & 5	666	1,412
Wards 6 – 8	765	1,559
Wards 9 & 10	640	1,290
Wards 11 & 12	632	1,623
Wards 13 & 14	599	1,610
Wards 15 & 16	567	1,504
Nashotah, vil.		
Wards 1 & 2	234	691
New Berlin, city		
Ward 1	451	807
Ward 2	358	624
Ward 3	459	823
Ward 4	444	735
Ward 5	706	1,047
Ward 6	190	210
Ward 7	34	93
Ward 8	589	1,056
Ward 9	556	854
Ward 10	86	209
Ward 11	160	415
Ward 12	54	125
Ward 13	54	142
Ward 14	2	5
Ward 15	375	767
Ward 16	461	1,082
Ward 17	70	116
Ward 18	665	1,163
Ward 19	49	105
Ward 20	99	253
Ward 21	464	918
Ward 22	478	829
Ward 23	319	664
Ward 24	546	1,199
Ward 25	255	533
Ward 26	310	926
Ward 27	601	1,151
North Prairie, vil.		
Wards 1 – 3	348	999
Oconomowoc		
Wards 1, 2 & 4	525	1,576
Wards 3, 6 & 7	549	1,207
Wards 5, 8 & 9	453	1,283
Ward 10	7	16
Oconomowoc, city		
Wards 1 – 3	874	1,687
Wards 4 – 6	779	1,580
Wards 7 – 9	749	1,427
Wards 10 – 12	755	1,476
Oconomowoc Lake, vil.	81	302
Ottawa		
Wards 1 – 5	722	1,771
Pewaukee, vil.		
Wards 1 – 5	877	1,834
Wards 6 – 10	789	1,286
Pewaukee, city		
Wards 1 – 4	876	2,475
Wards 5 – 7	825	2,087
Wards 8 – 10	904	2,147
Summit, vil.		
Wards 1 & 6	258	719
Wards 2 – 5	564	1,390
Sussex, vil.		
Wards 1, 3 & 8	643	1,179
Wards 2 & 4	640	1,275
Ward 5	296	650
Wards 6 & 7	362	1,115
Vernon		
Wards 1 & 8 – 11	639	1,626
Wards 2 – 7	790	2,024
Wales, vil.		
Wards 1 – 4	542	1,162
Waukesha		
Wards 1 & 8	369	589
Wards 2 – 6	744	1,939
Wards 7 – 11	592	1,555
Ward 12	2	5
Waukesha, city		
Ward 1	449	692
Ward 2	514	707
Ward 3	151	213
Ward 4	238	283
Ward 5	497	523
Ward 6	583	578
Ward 7	783	602
Ward 8	118	138
Ward 9	559	842

District	Obama and Biden (Dem.)	Romney and Ryan (Rep.)
Ward 10	335	448
Ward 11	271	326
Ward 12	596	984
Ward 13	358	691
Ward 14	501	527
Ward 15	287	306
Ward 16	324	351
Ward 17	665	1,005
Ward 18	642	527
Ward 19	531	631
Ward 20	553	939
Ward 21	430	677
Ward 22	407	572
Ward 23	358	570
Ward 24	312	363
Ward 25	387	364
Ward 26	229	177
Ward 27	16	16
Ward 28	259	217
Ward 29	234	219
Ward 30	585	974
Ward 31	431	900
Ward 32	488	868
Ward 33	457	729
Ward 34	152	188
Ward 35	405	797
Ward 36	650	1,356
Ward 37	418	523
Ward 38	631	862
TOTAL	78,779	162,798
WAUPACA COUNTY		
Bear Creek	135	250
Big Falls, vil.	17	21
Caledonia		
Wards 1 & 2	352	616
Clintonville, city		
Wards 1 – 8	915	997
Dayton		
Wards 1 – 4	665	951
Dupont		
Wards 1 & 2	116	205
Embarrass, vil.	53	97
Farmington		
Wards 1 – 6	968	1,116
Fremont		
Wards 1 & 2	146	216
Fremont, vil.	132	274
Harrison	114	135
Helvetia		
Wards 1 & 2	133	228
Iola		
Wards 1 & 2	227	319
Iola, vil.		
Wards 1 & 2	337	310
Larrabee		
Wards 1 & 2	269	419
Lebanon		
Wards 1 – 3	394	464
Lind		
Wards 1 – 3	333	471
Little Wolf		
Wards 1 – 3	250	472
Manawa, city		
Wards 1 – 3	237	297
Marion, city		
Wards 1 – 3	227	312
Matteson	191	305
Mukwa		
Wards 1 & 2	272	286
Wards 3 – 5	462	562
New London, city		
Wards 3, 4 & 8	342	361
Wards 6 & 7	334	324
Wards 9 & 10	309	247
Wards 11 & 12	305	177
Ogdensburg, vil.	47	34
Royalton		
Wards 1 & 2	276	470
St. Lawrence		
Wards 1 & 2	160	192
Scandinavia		
Wards 1 & 2	323	337
Scandinavia, vil.	99	92
Union		
Wards 1 & 2	175	224
Waupaca		
Wards 1 & 2	269	387
Waupaca, city		
Wards 1 – 12	1,409	1,238
Weyauwega	134	170

VOTE FOR PRESIDENT AND VICE PRESIDENT BY WARD
November 6, 2012 General Election–Continued

District	Obama and Biden (Dem.)	Romney and Ryan (Rep.)
Weyauwega,city		
Wards 1 – 3	371	344
Wyoming	80	82
TOTAL	11,578	14,002
WAUSHARA COUNTY		
Aurora	190	320
Berlin, city		
Ward 7	13	36
Bloomfield		
Wards 1 & 2	149	368
Coloma	177	194
Coloma, vil.	104	98
Dakota		
Wards 1 & 2	202	340
Deerfield	182	240
Hancock	108	172
Hancock, vil.	108	102
Leon		
Wards 1 – 3	381	466
Lohrville, vil.	114	79
Marion		
Wards 1 – 4	502	673
Mount Morris		
Wards 1 & 2	329	407
Oasis	85	134
Plainfield	101	156
Plainfield, vil.	188	174
Poy Sippi	171	311
Redgranite, vil.		
Wards 1 – 3	236	175
Richford		
Wards 1 & 2	82	150
Rose		
Wards 1 & 2	180	156
Saxeville	262	312
Springwater		
Wards 1 & 2	401	423
Warren	170	161
Wautoma		
Wards 1 – 3	338	402
Wautoma, city		
Wards 1 – 3	377	368
Wild Rose, vil.	185	145
TOTAL	5,335	6,562
WINNEBAGO COUNTY		
Algoma		
Wards 1, 2 & 7 – 10	931	1,256
Wards 3 – 6	888	1,301
Appleton, city		
Ward 31	63	44
Ward 32	225	149
Black Wolf		
Wards 1 – 3	658	943
Clayton		
Wards 1 – 7	879	1,478
Menasha		
Wards 1, 2, 4 & 7	1,401	1,822
Wards 3, 5 & 6	1,191	1,415
Wards 8 – 10	974	888
Wards 11 – 13	1,041	677
Menasha, city		
Ward 1B	0	0
Wards 1A, 2, 4 & 7	1,155	779
Wards 3, 14 & 15	550	388
Wards 5A, 6, 8 & 9	1,214	817
Ward 5B	0	0
Wards 10 – 13, 21 & 22	1,275	898
Neenah		
Wards 1 – 4	903	1,175
Neenah, city		
Wards 1 – 4	1,314	977
Wards 5 – 8	1,056	720
Wards 9 – 12	1,212	1,320
Wards 13 – 16	1,095	1,112
Wards 17 – 20	1,184	871
Wards 21 – 25	1,359	1,350
Nekimi		
Wards 1 & 2	359	528
Nepeuskun	160	251
Omro		
Wards 1 – 3	568	695
Omro, city		
Wards 1 – 7	855	814
Oshkosh		
Wards 1A & 2 – 5	641	913
Ward 1B	15	23
Oshkosh, city		
Ward 1	702	528
Ward 2	771	460

District	Obama and Biden (Dem.)	Romney and Ryan (Rep.)
Ward 3	792	496
Ward 4	686	499
Ward 5	639	338
Ward 6	736	373
Ward 7	776	511
Ward 8	771	392
Ward 9	551	278
Ward 10	761	460
Ward 11	684	473
Ward 12	685	352
Ward 13	690	567
Ward 14	683	596
Ward 15	704	497
Ward 16	766	656
Ward 17	752	428
Ward 18	629	609
Ward 19	479	464
Ward 20	195	279
Ward 21	576	451
Ward 22A	717	810
Ward 22B	0	0
Ward 23A	565	515
Ward 23B	55	23
Ward 24	353	347
Ward 25A	160	105
Ward 25B	589	352
Ward 26	401	323
Ward 27	775	405
Ward 28A	617	443
Ward 28B	129	89
Ward 29A	173	269
Ward 29B	0	0
Ward 30	76	73
Ward 31	218	169
Ward 32	0	0
Ward 33	0	0
Ward 34	2	0
Ward 35	0	0
Poygan		
Wards 1 & 2	323	425
Rushford		
Wards 1 & 2	371	494
Utica		
Wards 1 & 2	306	494
Vinland		
Wards 1A & 2	498	667
Ward 1B	3	0
Winchester		
Wards 1 & 2	452	656
Winneconne		
Wards 1 – 4	615	894
Ward 5	8	9
Winneconne, vil.		
Wards 1 – 4	584	773
Wolf River		
Wards 1 & 2A	167	351
Wards 2B & 2C	98	125
TOTAL	45,449	42,122
WOOD COUNTY		
Arpin		
Wards 1 – 3	182	256
Arpin, vil.	86	52
Auburndale	144	260
Auburndale, vil.	154	195
Biron, vil.	230	244
Cameron	115	181
Cary	85	142
Cranmoor	40	73
Dexter	103	83
Grand Rapids		
Wards 1 – 11	2,155	2,454
Hansen	156	248
Hewitt, vil.	191	253
Hiles	34	62
Lincoln		
Wards 1 & 2	372	549
Marshfield	195	265
Marshfield, city		
Wards 1 & 11	329	323
Ward 2	345	349
Wards 3 & 13	531	645
Wards 4 & 14	514	558
Wards 5 & 15	431	418
Wards 6 & 17	530	542
Wards 7 & 16	405	416
Wards 8, 19, 22 & 23	516	536
Wards 9 & 18	494	371
Ward 10	390	380
Milladore	181	174
Milladore, vil.	69	59

VOTE FOR PRESIDENT AND VICE PRESIDENT BY WARD
November 6, 2012 General Election–Continued

District	Obama and Biden (Dem.)	Romney and Ryan (Rep.)	District	Obama and Biden (Dem.)	Romney and Ryan (Rep.)
Nekoosa, city			Seneca		
Wards 1 – 4	570	562	Wards 1 – 3	301	325
Pittsville, city	171	266	Sherry	198	231
Port Edwards			Sigel		
Wards 1 – 4	344	371	Wards 1 – 3	277	302
Port Edwards, vil.			Vesper, vil.	117	175
Wards 1 – 3	455	514	Wisconsin Rapids, city		
Remington	55	77	Wards 1 – 5	1,244	1,007
Richfield			Wards 6 – 15 & 24	2,006	1,673
Wards 1 – 3	306	492	Wards 16 – 23 & 25	1,378	1,264
Rock	185	290	Wood	200	259
Rudolph			TOTAL	18,581	19,704
Wards 1 & 2	291	311			
Rudolph, vil.	142	109			
Saratoga					
Wards 1 – 4	569	593			
Wards 5 – 8	795	795			

Dem. – Democratic Party; Rep. – Republican Party.

Note: Other presidential and vice presidential candidates received the following votes: Virgil Goode and Jim Clymer (Constitution) – 4,930; Ross C. Rocky Anderson and Luis J. Rodriguez (write-in) (Independent) – 112; Roseanne Barr and Cindy Lee Sheehan (write-in) (Independent) – 88; Gary Johnson and James P. Gray (Independent) – 20,439; Gloria La Riva and Filberto Ramirez, Jr. (Independent) – 526; Jill Stein and Ben Manski (Independent) – 7,665; Jerry White and Phyllis Scherrer (Independent) – 553.

All municipalities are towns, unless noted as a village (vil.) or city.

Source: Official records of the Government Accountability Board, Elections Division. Scattered votes omitted.

Wisconsin State Symbols

11

Wisconsin state symbols: origin and descriptions of the official state symbols as specified by law

Raising "Wisconsin" Statue, 1914

(Wisconsin Historical Society, 9566)

WISCONSIN STATE SYMBOLS

(See front and back endpapers)

Over the years, the Wisconsin Legislature has officially recognized a wide variety of state symbols. In order of adoption, Wisconsin has designated an official seal, coat of arms, motto, flag, song, flower, bird, tree, fish, state animal, wildlife animal, domestic animal, mineral, rock, symbol of peace, insect, soil, fossil, dog, beverage, grain, dance, ballad, waltz, fruit, tartan, and pastry. (The "Badger State" nickname, however, remains unofficial.) These symbols provide a focus for expanding public awareness of Wisconsin's history and diversity. They are listed and described in Section 1.10 of the Wisconsin Statutes.

The Coat of Arms

The Great Seal

Seal and coat of arms. Article XIII, Section 4, of the Wisconsin Constitution requires the legislature to provide a "great seal" to be used by the secretary of state to authenticate all of the governor's official acts except laws. The seal consists of the coat of arms, described below, with the words "Great Seal of the State of Wisconsin" centered above and a curved line of 13 stars, representing the 13 original United States, centered below, surrounded by an ornamental border. A modified "lesser seal" serves as the seal of the secretary of state.

The coat of arms is an integral part of the state seal and also appears on the state flag. It contains a sailor with a coil of rope and a "yeoman" (usually considered a miner) with a pick, who jointly represent labor on water and land. These two figures support a quartered shield with symbols for agriculture (plow), mining (pick and shovel), manufacturing (arm and hammer), and navigation (anchor). Centered on the shield is a small U.S. coat of arms and the U.S. motto, "E pluribus unum" ("out of many, one"), referring to the union of U.S. states, to symbolize Wisconsin's loyalty to the Union. At the base, a cornucopia, or horn of plenty, stands for prosperity and abundance, while a pyramid of 13 lead ingots represents mineral wealth and the 13 original United States. Centered over the shield is a badger, the state animal, and the state motto "Forward" appears on a banner above the badger.

The history of the seal is inextricably entwined with that of the coat of arms. An official seal was created in 1836, when Wisconsin became a territory, and was revised in 1839. When Wisconsin achieved statehood in 1848, a new seal was prepared. This seal was changed in 1851 at the instigation of Governor Nelson Dewey and slightly modified to its current design in 1881 when Dewey's seal wore out and had to be recast. (See "Motto" below.) Chapter 280, Laws of 1881, provided the first precise statutory description of the great seal and coat of arms.

Motto: "Forward". The motto, "Forward", was introduced in the 1851 revision of the state seal and coat of arms. Governor Dewey had asked University of Wisconsin Chancellor John H. Lathrop to design a new seal. It is alleged the motto was selected during a chance meeting between Governor Dewey and Edward Ryan (later chief justice of the Wisconsin Supreme Court) when the governor went to New York City, carrying the Lathrop design to the engraver. Ryan objected to the Latin motto, "Excelsior", which Lathrop proposed. According to tradition,

Dewey and Ryan sat down on the steps of a Wall Street bank, designed a new seal and chose "Forward" on the spot.

Flag. An official design for Wisconsin's state flag was initially provided by the legislature in 1863. Noting that a flag had not been adopted and that Civil War regiments in the field were requesting flags, the legislature formed a 5-member joint select committee to report "a description for a proper state flag." This action resulted in the adoption of 1863 Joint Resolution 4, which provided a design for a state flag that was substantially the same as the regimental flags already in use by Wisconsin troops.

It was not until 1913, however, that language concerning flag specifications was added to the Wisconsin Statutes. Chapter 111, Laws of 1913, created a state flag provision, specifying a dark blue flag with the state coat of arms centered on each side.

The 1913 design remained unchanged until the enactment of Chapter 286, Laws of 1979, which culminated years of legislative efforts to alter or replace Wisconsin's flag so it would be more distinctive and recognizable. The most significant changes made by the 1979 act were adding the word "Wisconsin" and the statehood date "1848" in white letters, centered respectively above and below the coat of arms.

Song: "On, Wisconsin!" The music for "On, Wisconsin!" was composed in 1909 by William T. Purdy with the idea of entering it in a contest for the creation of a new University of Minnesota football song. ("Minnesota" would have replaced "On, Wisconsin" in the opening lines.) Carl Beck persuaded Purdy to dedicate the song to the University of Wisconsin football team instead, and Beck collaborated with the composer by writing the lyrics. The song was introduced at the Madison campus in November 1909. It was later acclaimed by world-famous composer and bandmaster John Philip Sousa as the best college song he had ever heard.

Lyrics more in keeping with the purposes of a state song were subsequently written in 1913 by Judge Charles D. Rosa and J. S. Hubbard, editor of the *Beloit Free Press*. Rosa and Hubbard were among the delegates from many states convened in 1913 to commemorate the centennial of the Battle of Lake Erie. Inspired by the occasion, they provided new, more solemn words to the already well-known football song.

Although "On, Wisconsin!" was widely recognized as Wisconsin's song, the state did not officially adopt it until 1959. Representative Harold W. Clemens discovered that Wisconsin was one of only 10 states without an official song. He introduced a bill to give the song the status he thought it deserved. On discovering that many different lyrics existed, an official text for the first verse was incorporated in Chapter 170, Laws of 1959:

On, Wisconsin! On, Wisconsin! Grand old badger state!
We, thy loyal sons and daughters, Hail thee, good and great.
On, Wisconsin! On, Wisconsin! Champion of the right,
'Forward', our motto — God will give thee might!

Flower: wood violet *(Viola papilionacea).* In 1908, Wisconsin school children nominated four candidates for state flower: the violet, wild rose, trailing arbutus, and white water lily. On Arbor Day 1909, the final vote was taken, and the violet won. Chapter 218, Laws of 1949, named the wood violet Wisconsin's official flower.

Bird: robin *(Turdus migratorius).* In 1926-27, Wisconsin school children voted to select a state bird. The robin received twice as many votes as those given any other bird. Chapter 218, Laws of 1949, officially made the robin the state bird.

Tree: sugar maple *(Acer saccharum).* A favorite state tree was first selected by a vote of Wisconsin school children in 1893. The maple tree won, followed by oak, pine, and elm. Another vote was conducted in 1948 among school children by the Youth Centennial Committee. In that election, the sugar maple again received the most votes, followed by white pine and birch. The 1949 Legislature, in spite of efforts by white pine advocates, named the sugar maple the official state tree by enacting Chapter 218, Laws of 1949.

Fish: muskellunge *(Esox masquinongy).* Members of the legislature attempted to adopt the muskellunge as the state fish as early as 1939. The trout was a very distant alternative suggestion. In 1955, the legislature unanimously passed legislation which became Chapter 18, Laws of 1955, to designate the muskellunge as Wisconsin's official fish.

Animals: badger *(Taxidea taxus),* **white-tailed deer** *(Odocoileus virginianus),* **dairy cow** *(Bos taurus).* Although the *badger* has been closely associated with Wisconsin since territorial days, it was not declared the official state animal until 1957. Over the years, its likeness had been incorporated in the state coat of arms, the seal, the flag, and even State Capitol architecture, as well as being immortalized in the song, "On, Wisconsin!" ("Grand old badger state!"). "Bucky Badger" has long been the mascot of the UW-Madison. In 1957, a bill to establish the badger as state animal was introduced at the request of four Jefferson County elementary school students who discovered from a historical society publication that the badger had not been given the official status most people assumed. Serious opposition developed, however, when a faction from Wisconsin's northern counties introduced a bill to make the *white-tailed deer* the official animal, citing the state's large native deer population, the animal's physical attributes, and the considerable economic benefits derived from the annual deer hunt. The legislature reached a compromise by adding two official animals. In Chapter 209, Laws of 1957, it named the badger the "state animal", and Chapter 147 designated the white-tailed deer as the state "wildlife animal".

The *dairy cow* was added as Wisconsin's official "domestic animal" by Chapter 167, Laws of 1971, in recognition of the animal's many contributions to the state. This action was termed a logical and long overdue step, consistent with the state's reputation as *America's Dairyland*, the slogan placed on state automobile license plates by Chapter 115, Laws of 1939. Governor Patrick Lucey issued 1972 Executive Order 32 recognizing the Holstein-Friesian breed as Wisconsin's official state dairy cow until May 31, 1973. He also directed the Secretary of Agriculture to designate on June 1 of each year a different breed, selected from Wisconsin's purebred dairy cows, to be the official state dairy cow. In keeping with a succession plan adopted by the Wisconsin Purebred Dairy Cattle Association whose members represent the seven major dairy breeds (Ayrshire, Brown Swiss, Guernsey, Holstein, Jersey, Milking Shorthorn, and Red & White Holstein), the Jersey is designated as the 2013 Cow of the Year, followed by the Guernsey in 2014. Members of the association also select an individual cow to represent the breed as Cow of the Year.

Badger nickname. History, rather than the law, explains Wisconsin's unofficial nickname as the "Badger State". During the lead-mining boom that began just prior to 1830 in southwestern Wisconsin, the name was first applied to miners who were too busy digging the "gray gold" to build houses. Like badgers, they moved into abandoned mine shafts and makeshift burrows for shelter. Although "badgers" had a somewhat derogatory connotation at first, it gradually gained acceptance as an apt description of the hardworking and energetic settlers of the Wisconsin Territory.

Mineral and rock: galena (lead sulphide) and **red granite.** Galena was made the official state mineral and red granite the state rock by Chapter 14, Laws of 1971. The proposal was introduced at the request of the Kenosha Gem and Mineral Society to promote geological awareness. Galena met the criteria for selection, as set by the Wisconsin Geological Society, including abundance, uniqueness, economic value, historical significance, and native nature. Red granite is an igneous rock composed of quartz and feldspar. It is mined in several sections of the state and was selected as the state rock because of its economic importance.

Symbol of peace: mourning dove *(Zenaidura macroura).* Various individuals and organizations concerned with conservation and wildlife long sought a protected status for the dove. Concluding an effort that stretched over a decade, the mourning dove was added as Wisconsin's official symbol of peace and removed from the statutory definition of game birds by Chapter 129, Laws of 1971. However, an increase in the mourning dove population led to its reinstatement as a game bird in 2001 and loss of its protected status.

Insect: honey bee *(Apis mellifera).* The honey bee was designated the official state insect by Chapter 326, Laws of 1977. The bill was introduced at the request of the third grade class of Holy Family School of Marinette and the Wisconsin Honey Producers Association. Attempts to allow all elementary school pupils in the state to decide the selection by popular ballot were unsuccessful. Other contenders for the title were the monarch butterfly, dragonfly, ladybug, and mosquito.

Soil: Antigo Silt Loam *(Typic glossoboralf).* An official state soil was created by 1983 Wisconsin Act 33 to remind Wisconsinites of their soil stewardship responsibilities. Advocates argued that soil, a natural resource that took 10,000 years to produce, is essential to Wisconsin's economy and is also the foundation of life. Selected to represent the more than 500 major soil types in Wisconsin, Antigo Silt Loam is a productive, level, silty soil of glacial origin, subsequently enriched by organic matter from prehistoric forests. The soil, named after a Wisconsin city, is found chiefly in Wisconsin and stretches in patches across the north central part of the state. It is a versatile soil that supports dairying, potato growing, and timber. The addition of the state soil was the result of a successful drive led by Professor Francis D. Hole, a UW-Madison soil scientist.

Fossil: trilobite *(Calymene celebra)*. The trilobite was designated the official state fossil by 1985 Wisconsin Act 162. Pronounced "TRY-loh-bite", the Latin term describes the 3-lobed anatomy of this small invertebrate body divided by furrows into segments. The trilobite is an extinct marine arthropod with multiple sets of paired, jointed legs. Its head and tapering body were armored in an exoskeleton that was repeatedly molted as the animal grew. Trilobites flourished in the warm, shallow saltwater sea that periodically covered Wisconsin territory hundreds of millions of years ago. Their fossil remains average 1 to 2 inches in length. The largest complete specimen is 14 inches, while incomplete parts indicate some were possibly much longer (over 30 inches). Trilobite fossils are abundant and distinctive enough to be easily recognized. Good specimens are preserved in rock formations throughout most of Wisconsin.

The Wisconsin Geological Society proposed the fossil to symbolize Wisconsin's ancient past and encourage interest in the state's rich geological heritage. A major rival for recognition as state fossil was the mastodon, a large prehistoric, elephant-like creature.

Dog: American water spaniel. The American water spaniel was named Wisconsin's official state dog by 1985 Wisconsin Act 295. Enactment of the law was the culmination of years of effort by eighth grade students of Lyle Brumm at Washington Junior High School in New London. The American water spaniel is said to be one of only five dog breeds indigenous to the United States and the only one native to Wisconsin. A New London area physician, Dr. Fred J. Pfeifer, is generally credited with developing and standardizing the breed and working to secure United Kennel Club registration for it in 1920. American Kennel Club recognition followed in 1940. The American water spaniel was developed as a practical, versatile hunting dog that combined certain physical attributes with intelligence and a good disposition. No flashy show animal, the American water spaniel is described as an unadorned, utilitarian dog that earns its keep as an outstanding hunter, watchdog, and family pet.

Beverage: milk. The Wisconsin Legislature designated milk as the official state beverage by 1987 Wisconsin Act 279. This action recognized Wisconsin's position as the nation's leading milk-producing state and the contribution of milk to the state's economy. The World Dairy Expo and various Wisconsin dairy production and dairy cattle associations supported the legislation.

Grain: corn *(Zea mays)*. Corn was designated the official state grain by 1989 Wisconsin Act 162. During legislative debate, sponsors claimed designating corn as the state grain would draw attention to its importance as a cash crop in Wisconsin and make people more aware of corn's many uses, including livestock feed, sweeteners, ethanol fuel, and biodegradable plastics.

Dance: polka. The polka was designated the state dance by 1993 Wisconsin Act 411. The legislation was introduced at the request of a second grade class from Charles Lindbergh Elementary School in Madison and supported by several groups, including the Wisconsin Polka Boosters, Inc., and the Wisconsin Folk Museum. Supporters documented the polka heritage of Wisconsin and provided evidence that the polka is deeply ingrained in Wisconsin cultural traditions.

Ballad: "Oh Wisconsin, Land of My Dreams". "Oh Wisconsin, Land of My Dreams" was designated the Wisconsin state ballad by 2001 Wisconsin Act 16. The ballad was the work of Shari Sarazin of Mauston, who set to music a poem written in the 1920s by her grandmother, Erma Barrett of Juneau County. The words to this ballad are:

> Oh Wisconsin, land of beauty, with your hillsides and your plains, with your jackpine and your birch tree, and your oak of mighty frame.
> Land of rivers, lakes and valleys, land of warmth and winter snows, land of birds and beasts and humanity, Oh Wisconsin, I love you so.
> Oh Wisconsin, land of my dreams. Oh Wisconsin, you're all I'll ever need. A little heaven here on earth could you be? Oh Wisconsin, land of my dreams.
> In the summer, golden grain fields; in the winter, drift of white snow; in the springtime, robins singing; in the autumn, flaming colors show.
> Oh I wonder who could wander, or who could want to drift for long, away from all your beauty, all your sunshine, all your sweet song?

Oh Wisconsin, land of my dreams. Oh Wisconsin, you're all I'll ever need. A little heaven here on earth could you be? Oh Wisconsin, land of my dreams.

Oh Wisconsin, land of my dreams. And when it's time, let my spirit run free in Wisconsin, land of my dreams.

Waltz: "The Wisconsin Waltz". "The Wisconsin Waltz" was designated the state waltz by 2001 Wisconsin Act 16. The music and lyrics were written by Eddie Hansen, a Waupaca native and one-time theater organist. The words to this waltz are:

Music from heaven throughout the years; the beautiful Wisconsin Waltz.

Favorite song of the pioneers; the beautiful Wisconsin Waltz.

Song of my heart on that last final day, when it is time to lay me away. One thing I ask is to let them play the beautiful Wisconsin Waltz.

My sweetheart, my complete heart, it's for you when we dance together; the beautiful Wisconsin Waltz.

I remember that September, before love turned into an ember, we danced to the Wisconsin Waltz.

Summer ended, we intended that our lives then would both be blended, but somehow our planning got lost.

Memory now sings a dream song, a faded love theme song; the beautiful Wisconsin Waltz.

Fruit: cranberry *(Vaccinium macrocarpon)*. The cranberry was designated the state fruit by 2003 Wisconsin Act 174. The legislation was the culmination of a class project by fifth grade students from Trevor Grade School in Kenosha County, who decided that the cranberry, rather than the cherry, was the best candidate for Wisconsin's state fruit. Wisconsin leads the nation in cranberry production, accounting for over half of the nation's output. Cranberries are grown in 20 of Wisconsin's 72 counties, primarily in the central part of the state.

Tartan. The state tartan was created by 2007 Wisconsin Act 217. Legislation was introduced at the request of the Saint Andrew's Society of Milwaukee, which had formed a committee to recommend an appropriate design. The design selected was chosen to reflect the diversity and uniqueness of the state. Historically, tartans served to identify Scottish highland clans and families.

Wisconsin's tartan is a hunting tartan with a blue green background and multiple stripes of various colors. The color scheme reflects the tartans of many notable Wisconsin families of Scottish ancestry and the natural resources and industries of Wisconsin. The color brown represents the fur trade; grey represents lead mining; green represents the lumber industry; blue reflects the two Great Lakes bordering Wisconsin, commercial and recreational fishing, and the resort industry; yellow signifies the dairy and brewing industries; red represents the University of Wisconsin System; and, where yellow and green stripes intersect, it represents Wisconsin's professional sports teams, exemplified by the Green Bay Packers.

Pastry: kringle. 2013 Wisconsin Act 20 designated the kringle as the state pastry. The kringle is a flaky dough pastry that can be filled with fruit, nuts, or other filling and baked with icing. The proposal was supported by the city of Racine, as they are a mass producer of the pastry.

Alphabetical
Index

12

North Central Airplane Over Madison, 1952

(Wisconsin Historical Society, 1922)

ALPHABETICAL INDEX

E

H

I

J

K

L

M

X-Y

Z

Wisconsin Symbols *continued*

Antigo Silt Loam
STATE SOIL

Honey Bee
STATE INSECT

Red Granite
STATE ROCK

Galena
STATE MINERAL

Trilobite
STATE FOSSIL

American Water Spaniel
STATE DOG

Cranberry
STATE FRUIT